2019
ALMANAC

116TH CONGRESS
1ST SESSION

VOLUME LXXV

CQ Roll Call

1201 Pennsylvania Avenue, NW
Washington, D.C. 20004

A FiscalNote business

TABLE OF CONTENTS

CONGRESS
& ITS MEMBERS

Members of the 116th Congress, First Session and

(AT THE CLOSE OF THE SESSION)

REPRESENTATIVES
D 233, R 201, I 1

— A —
Abraham, Ralph, R-La. (5)
Adams, Alma, D-N.C. (12)
Aderholt, Robert B., R-Ala. (4)
Aguilar, Pete, D-Calif. (31)
Allred, Colin, D-Texas (32)
Amash, Justin, I-Mich. (3)
Amodei, Mark, R-Nev. (2)
Armstrong, Kelly, R-N.D. AL
Arrington, Jodey C., R-Texas (19)
Axne, Cindy, D-Iowa (3)

— B —
Babin, Brian, R-Texas (36)
Bacon, Don, R-Neb. (2)
Baird, Jim, R-Ind. (4)
Balderson, Troy, R-Ohio (12)
Banks, Jim, R-Ind. (3)
Barr, Andy, R-Ky. (6)
Barragán, Nanette, D-Calif. (44)
Bass, Karen, D-Calif. (37)
Beatty, Joyce, D-Ohio (3)
Bera, Ami, D-Calif. (7)
Bergman, Jack, R-Mich. (1)
Beyer, Donald S. Jr., D-Va. (8)
Biggs, Andy, R-Ariz. (5)
Bilirakis, Gus, R-Fla. (12)
Bishop, Dan, R-N.C. (9)
Bishop, Rob, R-Utah (1)
Bishop, Sanford D. Jr., D-Ga. (2)
Blumenauer, Earl, D-Ore. (3)
Blunt Rochester, Lisa, D-Del. AL
Bonamici, Suzanne, D-Ore. (1)
Bost, Mike, R-Ill. (12)
Boyle, Brendan F., D-Pa. (2)
Brady, Kevin, R-Texas (8)
Brindisi, Anthony, D-N.Y. (22)
Brooks, Mo, R-Ala. (5)
Brooks, Susan W., R-Ind. (5)
Brown, Anthony G., D-Md. (4)
Brownley, Julia, D-Calif. (26)
Buchanan, Vern, R-Fla. (16)
Buck, Ken, R-Colo. (4)
Bucshon, Larry, R-Ind. (8)
Budd, Ted, R-N.C. (13)
Burchett, Tim R-Tenn. (2)
Burgess, Michael C., R-Texas (26)
Bustos, Cheri, D-Ill. (17)
Butterfield, G.K., D-N.C. (1)
Byrne, Bradley, R-Ala. (1)

— C —
Calvert, Ken, R-Calif. (42)
Carbajal, Salud, D-Calif. (24)
Cárdenas, Tony, D-Calif. (29)
Carson, André, D-Ind. (7)
Carter, Earl L. "Buddy", R-Ga. (1)
Carter, John, R-Texas (31)
Cartwright, Matt, D-Pa. (8)
Case, Ed, D-Hawaii (1)
Casten, Sean, D-Ill. (6)
Castor, Kathy, D-Fla. (14)
Castro, Joaquin, D-Texas (20)
Chabot, Steve, R-Ohio (1)
Cheney, Liz, R-Wyo. AL
Chu, Judy, D-Calif. (27)
Cicilline, David, D-R.I. (1)
Cisneros, Gil, D-Calif. (39)
Clark, Katherine M., D-Mass. (5)
Clarke, Yvette D., D-N.Y. (9)
Clay, William Lacy, D-Mo. (1)
Cleaver, Emanuel II, D-Mo. (5)
Cline, Ben, R-Va. (6)
Cloud, Michael, R-Texas (27)
Clyburn, James E., D-S.C. (6)
Cohen, Steve, D-Tenn. (9)
Cole, Tom, R-Okla. (4)
Collins, Doug, R-Ga. (9)
Comer, James R., R-Ky. (1)
Conaway, K. Michael, R-Texas (11)
Connolly, Gerald E., D-Va. (11)
Cook, Paul, R-Calif. (8)
Cooper, Jim, D-Tenn. (5)
Correa, Lou, D-Calif. (46)

Costa, Jim, D-Calif. (16)
Courtney, Joe, D-Conn. (2)
Cox, TJ, D-Calif. (21)
Craig, Angie, D-Minn. (2)
Crawford, Rick, R-Ark. (1)
Crenshaw, Daniel, R-Texas (2)
Crist, Charlie, D-Fla. (13)
Crow, Jason, D-Colo. (6)
Cuellar, Henry, D-Texas (28)
Cunningham, Joe, D-S.C. (1)
Curtis, John, R-Utah (3)

— D —
Davids, Sharice, D-Kan. (3)
Davidson, Warren, R-Ohio (8)
Davis, Danny K., D-Ill. (7)
Davis, Rodney, R-Ill. (13)
Davis, Susan A., D-Calif. (53)
Dean, Madeleine, D-Pa. (4)
DeFazio, Peter A., D-Ore. (4)
DeGette, Diana, D-Colo. (1)
DeLauro, Rosa, D-Conn. (3)
DelBene, Suzan, D-Wash. (1)
Delgado, Antonio, D-N.Y. (19)
Demings, Val B., D-Fla. (10)
DeSaulnier, Mark, D-Calif. (11)
DesJarlais, Scott, R-Tenn. (4)
Deutch, Ted, D-Fla. (22)
Diaz-Balart, Mario, R-Fla. (25)
Dingell, Debbie, D-Mich. (12)
Doggett, Lloyd, D-Texas (35)
Doyle, Mike, D-Pa. (18)
Duncan, Jeff, R-S.C. (3)
Dunn, Neal, R-Fla. (2)

— E, F —
Emmer, Tom, R-Minn. (6)
Engel, Eliot L., D-N.Y. (16)
Escobar, Veronica, D-Texas (16)
Eshoo, Anna G., D-Calif. (18)
Espaillat, Adriano, D-N.Y. (13)
Estes, Ron, R-Kan. (4)
Evans, Dwight, D-Pa. (3)
Ferguson, Drew, R-Ga. (3)
Finkenauer, Abby, D-Iowa (1)
Fitzpatrick, Brian, R-Pa. (1)
Fleischmann, Chuck, R-Tenn. (3)
Fletcher, Lizzie, D-Texas (7)
Flores, Bill, R-Texas (17)
Fortenberry, Jeff, R-Neb. (1)
Foster, Bill, D-Ill. (11)
Foxx, Virginia, R-N.C. (5)
Frankel, Lois, D-Fla. (21)
Fudge, Marcia L., D-Ohio (11)
Fulcher, Russ, R-Idaho (1)

— G —
Gabbard, Tulsi, D-Hawaii (2)
Gaetz, Matt, R-Fla. (1)
Gallagher, Mike, R-Wis. (8)
Gallego, Ruben, D-Ariz. (7)
Garamendi, John, D-Calif. (3)
García, Jesús "Chuy", D-Ill. (4)
Garcia, Mike, R-Calif. (25)
Garcia, Sylvia R., D-Texas (29)
Gianforte, Greg, R-Mont. AL
Gibbs, Bob, R-Ohio (7)
Gohmert, Louie, R-Texas (1)
Golden, Jared, D-Maine (2)
Gomez, Jimmy, D-Calif. (34)
Gonzalez, Anthony, R-Ohio (16)
Gonzalez, Vicente, D-Texas (15)
Gooden, Lance, R-Texas (5)
Gosar, Paul, R-Ariz. (4)
Gottheimer, Josh, D-N.J. (5)
Granger, Kay, R-Texas (12)
Graves, Garret, R-La. (6)
Graves, Sam, R-Mo. (6)
Graves, Tom, R-Ga. (14)
Green, Al, D-Texas (9)
Green, Mark E., R-Tenn. (7)
Griffith, Morgan, R-Va. (9)
Grijalva, Raúl M., D-Ariz. (3)
Grothman, Glenn, R-Wis. (6)
Guest, Michael, R-Miss. (3)
Guthrie, Brett, R-Ky. (2)

— H, I —
Haaland, Deb, D-N.M. (1)
Hagedorn, Jim, R-Minn. (1)
Harder, Josh, D-Calif. (10)

Harris, Andy, R-Md. (1)
Hartzler, Vicky, R-Mo. (4)
Hastings, Alcee L., D-Fla. (20)
Hayes, Jahana, D-Conn. (5)
Heck, Denny, D-Wash. (10)
Hern, Kevin, R-Okla. (1)
Herrera Beutler, Jaime, R-Wash. (3)
Hice, Jody B., R-Ga. (10)
Higgins, Brian, D-N.Y. (26)
Higgins, Clay, R-La. (3)
Hill, French, R-Ark. (2)
Himes, Jim, D-Conn. (4)
Holding, George, R-N.C. (2)
Hollingsworth, Trey, R-Ind. (9)
Horn, Kendra, D-Okla. (5)
Horsford, Steven, D-Nev. (4)
Houlahan, Chrissy, D-Pa. (6)
Hoyer, Steny H., D-Md. (5)
Hudson, Richard, R-N.C. (8)
Huffman, Jared, D-Calif. (2)
Huizenga, Bill, R-Mich. (2)
Hunter, Duncan, R-Calif. (50)
Hurd, Will, R-Texas (23)

— J —
Jackson Lee, Sheila, D-Texas (18)
Jacobs, Chris, R-N.Y. (27)
Jayapal, Pramila, D-Wash. (7)
Jeffries, Hakeem, D-N.Y. (8)
Johnson, Bill, R-Ohio (6)
Johnson, Dusty, R-S.D. AL
Johnson, Eddie Bernice, D-Texas (30)
Johnson, Hank, D-Ga. (4)
Johnson, Mike, R-La. (4)
Jordan, Jim, R-Ohio (4)
Joyce, David, R-Ohio (14)
Joyce, John, R-Pa. (13)

— K —
Kaptur, Marcy, D-Ohio (9)
Katko, John, R-N.Y. (24)
Keating, William, D-Mass. (9)
Keller, Fred, R-Pa. (12)
Kelly, Mike, R-Pa. (16)
Kelly, Robin, D-Ill. (2)
Kelly, Trent, R-Miss. (1)
Kennedy, Joseph P. III, D-Mass. (4)
Khanna, Ro, D-Calif. (17)
Kildee, Dan, D-Mich. (5)
Kilmer, Derek, D-Wash. (6)
Kim, Andy, D-N.J. (3)
Kind, Ron, D-Wis. (3)
King, Peter T., R-N.Y. (2)
King, Steve, R-Iowa (4)
Kinzinger, Adam, R-Ill. (16)
Kirkpatrick, Ann, D-Ariz. (2)
Krishnamoorthi, Raja, D-Ill. (8)
Kuster, Ann McLane, D-N.H. (2)
Kustoff, David, R-Tenn. (8)

— L —
LaHood, Darin, R-Ill. (18)
LaMalfa, Doug, R-Calif. (1)
Lamb, Conor, D-Pa. (17)
Lamborn, Doug, R-Colo. (5)
Langevin, Jim, D-R.I. (2)
Larsen, Rick, D-Wash. (2)
Larson, John B., D-Conn. (1)
Latta, Bob, R-Ohio (5)
Lawrence, Brenda, D-Mich. (14)
Lawson, Al, D-Fla. (5)
Lee, Barbara, D-Calif. (13)
Lee, Susie, D-Nev. (3)
Lesko, Debbie, R-Ariz. (8)
Levin, Andy, D-Mich. (9)
Levin, Mike, D-Calif. (49)
Lewis, John, D-Ga. (5)
Lieu, Ted, D-Calif. (33)
Lipinski, Daniel, D-Ill. (3)
Loebsack, Dave, D-Iowa (2)
Lofgren, Zoe, D-Calif. (19)
Long, Billy, R-Mo. (7)
Loudermilk, Barry, R-Ga. (11)
Lowenthal, Alan, D-Calif. (47)
Lowey, Nita M., D-N.Y. (17)
Lucas, Frank D., R-Okla. (3)
Luetkemeyer, Blaine, R-Mo. (3)
Luján, Ben Ray, D-N.M. (3)
Luria, Elaine, D-Va. (2)
Lynch, Stephen F., D-Mass. (8)

— M —
Malinowski, Tom, D-N.J. (7)
Maloney, Carolyn B., D-N.Y. (12)
Maloney, Sean Patrick, D-N.Y. (18)
Marchant, Kenny, R-Texas (24)
Marshall, Roger, R-Kan. (1)
Massie, Thomas, R-Ky. (4)
Mast, Brian, R-Fla. (18)
Matsui, Doris, D-Calif. (6)
McAdams, Ben, D-Utah (4)
McBath, Lucy, D-Ga. (6)
McCarthy, Kevin, R-Calif. (23)
McCaul, Michael, R-Texas (10)
McClintock, Tom, R-Calif. (4)
McCollum, Betty, D-Minn. (4)
McEachin, A. Donald, D-Va. (4)
McGovern, Jim, D-Mass. (2)
McHenry, Patrick T., R-N.C. (10)
McKinley, David B., R-W.Va. (1)
McNerney, Jerry, D-Calif. (9)
Meadows, Mark, R-N.C. (11)
Meeks, Gregory W., D-N.Y. (5)
Meng, Grace, D-N.Y. (6)
Meuser, Dan, R-Pa. (9)
Mfume, Kweisi, D-Md. (7)
Miller, Carol, R-W.Va. (3)
Mitchell, Paul, R-Mich. (10)
Moolenaar, John, R-Mich. (4)
Mooney, Alex X., R-W.Va. (2)
Moore, Gwen, D-Wis. (4)
Morelle, Joseph D., D-N.Y. (25)
Moulton, Seth, D-Mass. (6)
Mucarsel-Powell, Debbie, D-Fla. (26)
Mullin, Markwayne, R-Okla. (2)
Murphy, Greg, R-N.C. (3)
Murphy, Stephanie, D-Fla. (7)

— N, O —
Nadler, Jerrold, D-N.Y. (10)
Napolitano, Grace F., D-Calif. (32)
Neal, Richard E., D-Mass. (1)
Neguse, Joe, D-Colo. (2)
Newhouse, Dan, R-Wash. (4)
Norcross, Donald, D-N.J. (1)
Norman, Ralph, R-S.C. (5)
Nunes, Devin, R-Calif. (22)
O'Halleran, Tom, D-Ariz. (1)
Ocasio-Cortez, Alexandria, D-N.Y. (14)
Olson, Pete, R-Texas (22)
Omar, Ilhan, D-Minn. (5)

— P —
Palazzo, Steven M., R-Miss. (4)
Pallone, Frank Jr., D-N.J. (6)
Palmer, Gary, R-Ala. (6)
Panetta, Jimmy, D-Calif. (20)
Pappas, Chris, D-N.H. (1)
Pascrell, Bill Jr., D-N.J. (9)
Payne, Donald M. Jr., D-N.J. (10)
Pelosi, Nancy, D-Calif. (12)
Pence, Greg, R-Ind. (6)
Perlmutter, Ed, D-Colo. (7)
Perry, Scott, R-Pa. (10)
Peters, Scott, D-Calif. (52)
Peterson, Collin C., D-Minn. (7)
Phillips, Dean, D-Minn. (3)
Pingree, Chellie, D-Maine (1)
Pocan, Mark, D-Wis. (2)
Porter, Katie, D-Calif. (45)
Posey, Bill, R-Fla. (8)
Pressley, Ayanna S., D-Mass. (7)
Price, David E., D-N.C. (4)

— Q, R —
Quigley, Mike, D-Ill. (5)
Raskin, Jamie, D-Md. (8)
Ratcliffe, John, R-Texas (4)
Reed, Tom, R-N.Y. (23)
Reschenthaler, Guy, R-Pa. (14)
Rice, Kathleen, D-N.Y. (4)
Rice, Tom, R-S.C. (7)
Richmond, Cedric L., D-La. (2)
Riggleman, Denver, R-Va. (5)
Roby, Martha, R-Ala. (2)
Rodgers, Cathy McMorris, R-Wash. (5)
Roe, Phil, R-Tenn. (1)
Rogers, Harold, R-Ky. (5)
Rogers, Mike D., R-Ala. (3)
Rooney, Francis, R-Fla. (19)
Rose, John W., R-Tenn. (6)
Rose, Max, D-N.Y. (11)

Governors, Supreme Court and Executive Branch

Rouda, Harley, D-Calif. (48)
Rouzer, David, R-N.C. (7)
Roy, Chip, R-Texas (21)
Roybal-Allard, Lucille, D-Calif. (40)
Ruiz, Raul, D-Calif. (36)
Ruppersberger, C.A. Dutch, D-Md. (2)
Rush, Bobby L., D-Ill. (1)
Rutherford, John, R-Fla. (4)
Ryan, Tim, D-Ohio (13)

— S —

Sánchez, Linda T., D-Calif. (38)
Sarbanes, John, D-Md. (3)
Scalise, Steve, R-La. (1)
Scanlon, Mary Gay, D-Pa. (5)
Schakowsky, Jan, D-Ill. (9)
Schiff, Adam B., D-Calif. (28)
Schneider, Brad, D-Ill. (10)
Schrader, Kurt, D-Ore. (5)
Schrier, Kim, D-Wash. (8)
Schweikert, David, R-Ariz. (6)
Scott, Austin, R-Ga. (8)
Scott, David, D-Ga. (13)
Scott, Robert C., D-Va. (3)
Sensenbrenner, Jim, R-Wis. (5)
Serrano, José E., D-N.Y. (15)
Sewell, Terri A., D-Ala. (7)
Shalala, Donna E., D-Fla. (27)
Sherman, Brad, D-Calif. (30)
Sherrill, Mikie, D-N.J. (11)
Shimkus, John, R-Ill. (15)
Simpson, Mike, R-Idaho (2)
Sires, Albio, D-N.J. (8)
Slotkin, Elissa, D-Mich. (8)
Smith, Adam, D-Wash. (9)
Smith, Adrian, R-Neb. (3)
Smith, Christopher H., R-N.J. (4)
Smith, Jason, R-Mo. (8)
Smucker, Lloyd K., R-Pa. (11)
Soto, Darren, D-Fla. (9)
Spanberger, Abigail, D-Va. (7)
Spano, Ross, R-Fla. (15)
Speier, Jackie, D-Calif. (14)
Stanton, Greg, D-Ariz. (9)
Stauber, Pete, R-Minn. (8)
Stefanik, Elise, R-N.Y. (21)
Steil, Bryan, R-Wis. (1)
Steube, Greg, R-Fla. (17)
Stevens, Haley, D-Mich. (11)
Stewart, Chris, R-Utah (2)
Stivers, Steve, R-Ohio (15)
Suozzi, Tom, D-N.Y. (3)
Swalwell, Eric, D-Calif. (15)

— T —

Takano, Mark, D-Calif. (41)
Taylor, Van, R-Texas (3)
Thompson, Bennie, D-Miss. (2)
Thompson, Glenn "GT", R-Pa. (15)
Thompson, Mike, D-Calif. (5)
Thornberry, Mac, R-Texas (13)
Tiffany, Tom, R-Wis. (7)
Timmons, William R. IV, R-S.C. (4)
Tipton, Scott, R-Colo. (3)
Titus, Dina, D-Nev. (1)
Tlaib, Rashida, D-Mich. (13)
Tonko, Paul, D-N.Y. (20)
Torres, Norma J., D-Calif. (35)
Torres Small, Xochitl, D-N.M. (2)
Trahan, Lori, D-Mass. (3)
Trone, David, D-Md. (6)
Turner, Michael R., R-Ohio (10)

— U, V —

Underwood, Lauren, D-Ill. (14)
Upton, Fred, R-Mich. (6)
Van Drew, Jeff, R-N.J. (2)
Vargas, Juan C., D-Calif. (51)
Veasey, Marc, D-Texas (33)
Vela, Filemon, D-Texas (34)
Velázquez, Nydia M., D-N.Y. (7)
Visclosky, Peter J., D-Ind. (1)

— W —

Wagner, Ann, R-Mo. (2)
Walberg, Tim, R-Mich. (7)
Walden, Greg, R-Ore. (2)
Walker, Mark, R-N.C. (6)
Walorski, Jackie, R-Ind. (2)
Waltz, Michael, R-Fla. (6)
Wasserman Schultz, Debbie, D-Fla. (23)
Waters, Maxine, D-Calif. (43)

Watkins, Steve, R-Kan. (2)
Watson Coleman, Bonnie, D-N.J. (12)
Weber, Randy, R-Texas (14)
Webster, Daniel, R-Fla. (11)
Welch, Peter, D-Vt. AL
Wenstrup, Brad, R-Ohio (2)
Westerman, Bruce, R-Ark. (4)
Wexton, Jennifer, D-Va. (10)
Wild, Susan, D-Pa. (7)
Williams, Roger, R-Texas (25)
Wilson, Frederica S., D-Fla. (24)
Wilson, Joe, R-S.C. (2)
Wittman, Rob, R-Va. (1)
Womack, Steve, R-Ark. (3)
Woodall, Rob, R-Ga. (7)
Wright, Ron, R-Texas (6)

— X, Y, Z —

Yarmuth, John, D-Ky. (3)
Yoho, Ted, R-Fla. (3)
Young, Don, R-Alaska AL
Zeldin, Lee, R-N.Y. (1)

DELEGATES

D 3, R 2, I 1

González-Colón, Jenniffer, R-P.R.
Norton, Eleanor Holmes, D-D.C.
Plaskett, Stacey, D-V.I.
Radewagen, Aumua Amata Coleman, R-A.S.
Sablan, Gregorio Kilili Camacho, I-N. Marianas
San Nicolas, Michael F.Q., D-Guam

SENATORS

R 53, D 45, I 2

Alexander, Lamar, R-Tenn.
Baldwin, Tammy, D-Wis.
Barrasso, John, R-Wyo.
Bennet, Michael, D-Colo.
Blackburn, Marsha, R-Tenn.
Blumenthal, Richard, D-Conn.
Blunt, Roy, R-Mo.
Booker, Cory, D-N.J.
Boozman, John, R-Ark.
Braun, Mike, R-Ind.
Brown, Sherrod, D-Ohio
Burr, Richard M., R-N.C.
Cantwell, Maria, D-Wash.
Capito, Shelley Moore, R-W.Va.
Cardin, Benjamin L., D-Md.
Carper, Thomas R., D-Del.
Casey, Bob, D-Pa.
Cassidy, Bill, R-La.
Collins, Susan, R-Maine
Coons, Chris, D-Del.
Cornyn, John, R-Texas
Cortez Masto, Catherine, D-Nev.
Cotton, Tom, R-Ark.
Cramer, Kevin, R-N.D.
Crapo, Michael D., R-Idaho
Cruz, Ted, R-Texas
Daines, Steve, R-Mont.
Duckworth, Tammy, D-Ill.
Durbin, Richard J., D-Ill.
Enzi, Michael B., R-Wyo.
Ernst, Joni, R-Iowa
Feinstein, Dianne, D-Calif.
Fischer, Deb, R-Neb.
Gardner, Cory, R-Colo.
Gillibrand, Kirsten, D-N.Y.
Graham, Lindsey, R-S.C.
Grassley, Charles E., R-Iowa
Harris, Kamala, D-Calif.
Hassan, Maggie, D-N.H.
Hawley, Josh, R-Mo.
Heinrich, Martin, D-N.M.
Hirono, Mazie K., D-Hawaii
Hoeven, John, R-N.D.
Hyde-Smith, Cindy, R-Miss.
Inhofe, James M., R-Okla.
Johnson, Ron, R-Wis.
Jones, Doug, D-Ala.
Kaine, Tim, D-Va.
Kennedy, John, R-La.
King, Angus, I-Maine
Klobuchar, Amy, D-Minn.
Lankford, James, R-Okla.

Leahy, Patrick J., D-Vt.
Lee, Mike, R-Utah
Loeffler, Kelly, R-Ga.
Manchin, Joe III, D-W.Va.
Markey, Edward J., D-Mass.
McConnell, Mitch, R-Ky.
McSally, Martha, R-Ariz.
Menendez, Bob, D-N.J.
Merkley, Jeff, D-Ore.
Moran, Jerry, R-Kan.
Murkowski, Lisa, R-Alaska
Murphy, Christopher S., D-Conn.
Murray, Patty, D-Wash.
Paul, Rand, R-Ky.
Perdue, David, R-Ga.
Peters, Gary, D-Mich.
Portman, Rob, R-Ohio
Reed, Jack, D-R.I.
Risch, Jim, R-Idaho
Roberts, Pat, R-Kan.
Romney, Mitt, R-Utah
Rosen, Jacky, D-Nev.
Rounds, Mike, R-S.D.
Rubio, Marco, R-Fla.
Sanders, Bernie, I-Vt.
Sasse, Ben, R-Neb.
Schatz, Brian, D-Hawaii
Schumer, Charles E., D-N.Y.
Scott, Rick, R-Fla.
Scott, Tim, R-S.C.
Shaheen, Jeanne, D-N.H.
Shelby, Richard C., R-Ala.
Sinema, Kyrsten, D-Ariz.
Smith, Tina, D-Minn.
Stabenow, Debbie, D-Mich.
Sullivan, Dan, R-Alaska
Tester, Jon, D-Mont.
Thune, John, R-S.D.
Tillis, Thom, R-N.C.
Toomey, Patrick J., R-Pa.
Udall, Tom, D-N.M.
Van Hollen, Chris, D-Md.
Warner, Mark, D-Va.
Warren, Elizabeth, D-Mass.
Whitehouse, Sheldon, D-R.I.
Wicker, Roger, R-Miss.
Wyden, Ron, D-Ore.
Young, Todd, R-Ind.

GOVERNORS

R 26, D 24

Ala. — Kay Ivey, R
Alaska — Mike Dunleavy, R
Ariz. — Doug Ducey, R
Ark. — Asa Hutchinson, R
Calif. — Gavin Newsom, D
Colo. — Jared Polis, D
Conn. — Ned Lamont, D
Del. — John Carney, D
Fla. — Ron DeSantis, R
Ga. — Brian Kemp, R
Hawaii — David Ige, D
Idaho — Brad Little, R
Ill. — JB Pritzker, D
Ind. — Eric Holcomb, R
Iowa — Kim Reynolds, R
Kan. — Laura Kelly, D
Ky. — Andy Beshear, D
La. — John Bel Edwards, D
Maine — Janet Mills, D
Md. — Larry Hogan, R
Mass. — Charlie Baker, R
Mich. — Gretchen Whitmer, D
Minn. — Tim Walz, D
Miss. — Tate Reeves, R
Mo. — Michael L. Parson, R
Mont. — Steve Bullock, D
Neb. — Pete Ricketts, R
Nev. — Steve Sisolak, D
N.H. — Chris Sununu, R
N.J. — Phil Murphy, D
N.M. — Michelle Lujan Grisham, D
N.Y. — Andrew M. Cuomo, D
N.C. — Roy Cooper, D
N.D. — Doug Burgum, R
Ohio — Mike DeWine, R
Okla. — Kevin Stitt, R
Ore. — Kate Brown, D
Pa. — Tom Wolf, D

R.I. — Gina Raimondo, D
S.C. — Henry McMaster, R
S.D. — Kristi Noem, R
Tenn. — Bill Lee, R
Texas — Greg Abbott, R
Utah — Gary R. Herbert, R
Vt. — Phil Scott, R
Va. — Ralph S. Northam, D
Wash. — Jay Inslee, D
W.Va. — Jim Justice, R
Wis. — Tony Evers, D
Wyo. — Mark Gordon, R

SUPREME COURT

John G. Roberts Jr. — Md., Chief Justice
Samuel A. Alito Jr. — N.J.
Stephen G. Breyer — Mass.
Ruth Bader Ginsburg — N.Y.
Neil M. Gorsuch — Colo,
Elena Kagan — N.Y.
Brett M. Kavanaugh — Md.
Sonia Sotomayor — N.Y.
Clarence Thomas — Ga.

EXECUTIVE BRANCH

President — Donald Trump
Vice President — Mike Pence

DEPARTMENT SECRETARIES

Agriculture — Sonny Perdue
Attorney General — William Barr
Commerce — Wilbur Ross
Defense — Mark T. Esper
Education — Betsy DeVos
Energy — Dan Brouillette
Health and Human Services — Alex Azar
Homeland Security — Chad Wolf (Acting)
Housing and Urban Dev. — Ben Carson
Interior — David Bernhardt
Labor — Eugene Scalia
State — Mike Pompeo
Transportation — Elaine Chao
Treasury — Steven Mnuchin
Veterans Affairs — Robert Wilkie

OTHER EXECUTIVE BRANCH OFFICERS

CIA Director
   Gina Haspel
Director of National Intelligence
   John Ratcliffe
Joint Chiefs of Staff Chairman
   Gen. Mark Milley
OMB Director
   Russell Vought (Acting)
U.S. Trade Representative
   Robert Lighthizer
EPA Administrator
   Andrew Wheeler
U.N. Ambassador
   Kelly Craft
White House Chief of Staff
   Mark Meadows
Asst to the President for National Security
   Robert C. O'Brien
National Economic Council Director
   Larry Kudlow

Glossary of Congressional Terms

Act—The term for legislation once it has passed both chambers of Congress and has been signed by the president or passed over his veto, thus becoming law. Also used in parliamentary terminology for a bill that has been passed by one house and engrossed. (Also see engrossed bill.)

Adjournment sine die—Adjournment without a fixed day for reconvening; literally, "adjournment without a day." Usually used to connote the final adjournment of a session of Congress. A session can continue until noon Jan. 3 of the following year, when, under the 20th Amendment to the Constitution, it automatically terminates. Both chambers must agree to a concurrent resolution for either chamber to adjourn for more than three days.

Adjournment to a day certain — Adjournment under a motion or resolution that fixes the next time of meeting. Under the Constitution, neither chamber can adjourn for more than three days without the concurrence of the other. A session of Congress is not ended by adjournment to a day certain.

Amendment—A proposal by a member of Congress to alter the language, provisions or stipulations in a bill or in another amendment. An amendment usually is printed, debated and voted upon in the same manner as a bill.

Amendment in the nature of a substitute — Usually an amendment that seeks to replace the entire text of a bill by striking out everything after the enacting clause and inserting a new version of the bill. An amendment in the nature of a substitute can also refer to an amendment that replaces a large portion of the text of a bill.

Appeal — A member's challenge of a ruling or decision made by the presiding officer of the chamber. A senator can appeal to members of the Senate to override the decision. If carried by a majority vote, the appeal nullifies the presiding officer's ruling. In the House, the decision of the speaker traditionally has been final; seldom are there successful appeals to the members to reverse the speaker's stand. To appeal a ruling is considered an attack on the speaker.

Appropriations bill—A bill that gives legal authority to spend or obligate money from the Treasury. The Constitution disallows money to be drawn from the Treasury "but in Consequence of Appropriations made by Law."

By congressional custom, an appropriations bill originates in the House. It is not supposed to be considered by the full House or Senate until a related measure authorizing the spending is enacted. An appropriations bill grants the actual budget authority approved by the authorization bill, though not necessarily the full amount permissible under the authorization.

If the 12 regular appropriations bills are not enacted by the start of the fiscal year, Congress must pass a stopgap spending bill or the departments and agencies covered by the unfinished bills must shut down.

About half of all budget authority, notably that for Social Security and interest on the federal debt, does not require annual appropriations; those programs exist under permanent appropriations. (Also see authorization bill, budget authority, budget process and supplemental appropriations bill.)

Authorization bill — Basic, substantive legislation that establishes or continues the legal operation of a federal program or agency either indefinitely or for a specific period of time, or which sanctions a particular type of obligation or expenditure. Under the rules of both chambers, appropriations for a program or agency may not be considered until the program has been authorized, although this requirement is often waived. An authorization sets the maximum amount that may be appropriated to a program or agency, although sometimes it merely authorizes "such sums as may be necessary." (Also see backdoor spending authority.)

Backdoor spending authority — Budget authority provided in legislation outside the normal appropriations process. The most common forms of backdoor spending are borrowing authority, contract authority, entitlements and loan guarantees that commit the government to payments of principal and interest on loans made by banks or other private lenders. Loan guarantees result in actual outlays only when there is a default by the borrower.

In some cases, such as interest on the public debt, a permanent appropriation is provided that becomes available without further action by Congress.

Bills — Most legislative proposals before Congress are in the form of bills and are designated according to the chamber in which they originate — HR in the House of Representatives or S in the Senate — and by a number assigned in the order in which they are introduced during the two-year period of a congressional term.

"Public bills" address general questions and become public laws if they are cleared by Congress and signed by the president.

"Private bills" deal with individual matters, such as claims against the government, immigration and naturalization cases, or land titles, and become private laws if cleared and signed. (Also see private bill, resolution.)

Bills introduced—In both the House and Senate, any number of members may join in introducing a single bill or resolution. The first member listed is the sponsor of the bill, and all subsequent members listed are co-sponsors.

Many bills are committee bills and are introduced under the name of the chairman of the committee or subcommittee. All appropriations bills fall into this category. A committee frequently holds hearings on a number of related bills and may agree to one of them or to an entirely new bill. (Also see clean bill.)

Bills referred — After a bill is introduced, it is referred to the committee or committees that have jurisdiction over the subject with which the bill is concerned. Under the standing rules of the House and Senate, bills are referred by the speaker in the House and by the presiding officer in the Senate. In practice, the House and Senate parliamentarians act for these officials and refer the vast majority of bills. (Also see discharge a committee.)

Borrowing authority—Statutory authority that permits a federal agency to incur obligations and make payments for specified purposes with borrowed money.

Budget — The document sent to Congress by the president early each year estimating government revenue and expenditures for the ensuing fiscal year.

Budget Act — The common name for the Congressional Budget and Impoundment Control Act of 1974, which established the current budget process and created the Congressional Budget Office. The act also put limits on presidential authority to spend appropriated money. It has undergone several major revisions since 1974. (Also see budget process.)

Budget authority — Authority for federal agencies to enter into obligations that result in immediate or future outlays. The basic forms of budget authority are appropriations, contract authority and borrowing authority. Budget authority may be classified by (1) the period of availability (one-year, multiple-year or without a time limitation), (2) the timing of congressional action (current or permanent) or (3) the manner of determining the amount available (definite or indefinite). (Also see appropriations bill, outlays.)

Budget process — The annual budget process was created by the Congressional Budget and Impoundment Control Act of 1974, with a timetable that was modified in 1990. Under the law, the president must submit his proposed budget by the first Monday in February. Congress is supposed to complete an annual budget resolution by April 15, setting guidelines for congressional action on spending and tax measures. (Also see "pay-as-you-go" rules.)

Budget resolution — A concurrent resolution that is adopted by both chambers of Congress and sets a strict ceiling on discretionary budget authority, along with nonbinding recommendations about how the spending should be allocated. The budget resolution may also contain "reconciliation instructions" requiring authorizing and tax-writing committees to propose changes in existing law to meet deficit reduction goals. If more than one committee is involved, the Budget Committee in each chamber bundles those proposals, without change, into a reconciliation bill and sends it to the floor. The budget resolution is a congressional document and is not sent to the president. (Also see reconciliation.)

By request — A phrase used when a senator or representative introduces a bill at the request of an executive agency or private organization but does not necessarily endorse the legislation.

Calendar — An agenda or list of business awaiting possible action by each chamber. The House uses four legislative calendars. They are the Discharge, House, Private and Union calendars. (Also see individual calendar listings.)

In the Senate, all legislative matters reported from committee go on one calendar. They are listed there in the order in which committees report them or the Senate places them on the calendar, but they may be called up out of order by the majority leader, either by obtaining unanimous consent of the Senate or by a motion to call up a bill. The Senate also has one non-legislative calendar, which is used for treaties and nominations. (Also see Executive Calendar.)

Call of the calendar — Senate bills that are not brought up for debate by a motion, unanimous consent or a unanimous consent agreement are brought before the Senate for action when the calendar listing them is "called." Bills must be called in the order listed. Measures considered by this method usually are noncontroversial, and debate on the bill and any proposed amendments is limited to five minutes for each senator.

Chamber — The meeting place for the membership of either the House or the Senate; also the membership of the House or Senate meeting as such.

Chief administrative officer — An elected officer of the House who, under House rules, has operational and functional responsibility for matters assigned by the House Administration Committee. The office of the chief administrative officer was established under a 1995 change to House rules and replaced the office of director of non-legislative and financial services.

Clean bill — Frequently after a committee has finished a major revision of a bill, one of the committee members, usually the chairman, will assemble the changes and what is left of the original bill into a new measure and introduce it as a "clean bill." The revised measure, which is given a new number, is referred back to the committee, which reports it to the floor for consideration. This often is a time saver, as committee-recommended changes in a clean bill do not have to be considered and voted on by the chamber. Reporting a clean bill also protects committee amendments that could be subject to points of order concerning germaneness.

Clerk of the House — An officer of the House of Representatives who supervises its records and legislative business.

Cloture — The process by which a filibuster can be ended in the Senate other than by unanimous consent. A motion for cloture can apply to any measure before the Senate, including a proposal to change the chamber's rules. To end a filibuster, the cloture motion must obtain the votes of three-fifths of the entire Senate membership (60 if there are no vacancies), except when the filibuster is against a proposal to amend the standing rules of the Senate; then a two-thirds vote of senators present and voting is required.

Under a ruling by the president of the Senate in November 2013 that was upheld by a narrow voting majority of the chamber, the interpretation of the cloture rule was changed as applied to executive branch nominees subject to confirmation and to lower-court judges. Following the reinterpretation, cloture could be imposed on nominees (except for those named to the Supreme Court) by a simple majority vote. The rule was changed again in 2017 to include Supreme Court nominees.

The cloture request is put to a roll call vote one hour after the Senate meets on the second day following introduction of the motion. If approved, cloture limits each senator to one hour of debate. The bill or amendment in question comes to a final vote after 30 hours of consideration, including debate time and the time it takes to conduct roll calls, quorum calls and other procedural motions. (Also see filibuster.)

Committee — A division of the House or Senate that prepares legislation for action by the parent chamber or makes investigations as directed by the parent chamber.

There are several types of committees. Most standing committees are divided into subcommittees, which study legislation, hold hearings and report bills, with or without amendments, to the full committee. Only the full committee can report legislation for action by the House or Senate. (Also see standing, oversight, and select or special committees.)

Committee of the Whole — The working title of what is formally "The Committee of the Whole House [of Representatives] on the State of the Union." The membership is composed of all House members sitting as a committee. Any 100 members who are present on the floor of the chamber to consider legislation constitute a quorum of the committee.

Technically, the Committee of the Whole considers only bills directly or indirectly appropriating money, authorizing appropriations, or involving taxes or charges on the public. Because the Committee of the Whole need number only 100 representatives, a quorum is more readily attained and legislative business is expedited. Before 1971, members' positions were not individually recorded on votes taken in the Committee of the Whole. Periodically, delegates from the District of Columbia and several U.S. territories have been permitted to vote in the Committee of the Whole. A rules change adopted at the beginning of the 112th Congress, removed the permission for delegates to vote. (Also see delegate.)

When the full House resolves itself into the Committee of the Whole, it replaces the speaker with a "chairman." A measure is debated and amendments may be proposed, with votes on amendments as needed. (Also see five-minute rule.)

When the committee completes its work on the measure, it dissolves itself by "rising." The speaker returns, and the chairman of the Committee of the Whole reports to the House that the committee's work has been completed. At this time, members may demand a roll call vote on any amendment adopted in the Committee of the Whole. The final vote is on passage of the legislation.

Committee veto — A requirement added to a few statutes directing that certain policy directives by an executive department or agency be reviewed by certain congressional committees before they are implemented. Under common practice, the government department or agency and the committees involved are expected to reach a consensus before the directives are carried out.

Concurrent resolution — A concurrent resolution, designated H Con Res or S Con Res, must be adopted by both chambers to have effect, but it is not sent to the president for approval and, therefore, does not have the force of law. A concurrent resolution, for example, is used to fix the time for adjournment of a Congress. It is also used to express the sense of Congress on a foreign policy or domestic issue. The annual budget resolution is a concurrent resolution.

Conference — A meeting between designated representatives of the House and the Senate to reconcile differences between the two chambers on provisions of a bill. House conferees are appointed by the speaker; Senate conferees are appointed by the presiding officer of the Senate.

A majority of the conferees for each chamber must agree on a compromise, reflected in a "conference report," before the final bill can go back to both chambers for approval. When the conference report goes to the floor, it is difficult to amend. If it is not approved by both chambers, the bill may go back to conference under certain situations, or a new conference may be convened. Many rules and informal practices govern the conduct of conference committees.

Bills that are passed by both chambers do not have to be sent to conference. Either chamber may "concur" with the other's amendments, completing action on the legislation, or they may further amend the measure and send it back to the other chamber. Sometimes leaders of the committees of jurisdiction work out an informal compromise instead of having a formal conference. (Also see custody of the papers.)

Confirmations — (See nominations.)

Congressional Record — The daily printed account of proceedings in both the House and Senate chambers, showing substantially verbatim debate and statements and a record of floor action. Highlights of legislative and committee action are given in a Daily Digest section of the Record, and members are entitled to have their extraneous remarks printed in an appendix known as "Extension of Remarks." Members may edit and revise remarks made on the floor during debate.

The Congressional Record provides a way to distinguish remarks spoken on the floor of the House and Senate from undelivered speeches. In the Senate, all speeches, articles and other matter that members insert in the Record without actually reading them on the floor are set off by large black dots, or bullets. However, a loophole allows a member to avoid the bulleting if he or she delivers any portion of the speech in person. In the House, undelivered speeches and other material are printed in a distinctive typeface. The record is also available in electronic form. (Also see Journal.)

Congressional terms of office — Terms normally begin on Jan. 3 of the year following a general election. Terms are two years for representatives and six years for senators. Representatives elected in special elections are sworn in for the remainder of a term. Under most state laws, a person may be appointed to fill a Senate vacancy and serve until a successor is elected; the successor serves until the end of the term applying to the vacant seat.

Continuing resolution — Typically, but not always, a joint resolution, cleared by Congress and signed by the president, is used to provide new budget authority for federal agencies and programs whose regular appropriations bills have not been enacted. Also known as CRs or continuing appropriations, continuing resolutions are used to keep agencies operating when, as often happens, Congress does not finish the regular appropriations process by the Oct. 1 start of a new fiscal year.

The CR usually specifies a maximum rate at which an agency may incur obligations, based on the rate of the prior year, the president's budget request, or an appropriations bill passed by either or both chambers of Congress but not yet enacted. A CR can be a short-term measure that finances programs temporarily until the regular appropriations bill is enacted, or it can carry spending for the balance of the fiscal year in lieu of regular appropriations bills.

Contract authority — Budget authority contained in an authorization bill that permits the federal government to enter into contracts or other obligations for future payments from money not yet appropriated by Congress. The assumption is that money will be provided in a subsequent appropriations act. (Also see budget authority.)

Correcting recorded votes — Rules prohibit members from changing their votes after the result has been announced. Occasionally, however, a member may announce hours, days or months after a vote has been taken that he or she was "incorrectly recorded." In the Senate, a request to change one's vote almost always receives unanimous consent, as long as it does not change the outcome. In the House, members are prohibited from changing votes if they were tallied by the electronic voting system.

Co-sponsor — (See bills introduced.)

Current services estimates — Estimated budget authority and outlays for federal programs and operations for the forthcoming fiscal year based on continuation of existing levels of service without policy changes but with adjustments for inflation and for demographic changes that affect programs. These estimates, accompanied by the underlying economic and policy assumptions upon which they are based, are transmitted by the president to Congress when the budget is submitted.

Custody of the papers — To reconcile differences between the House and Senate versions of a bill, a conference may be arranged. The chamber with "custody of the papers" — the engrossed bill, engrossed amendments, messages of transmittal — is the only body empowered to request the conference. By custom, the chamber that asks for a conference is the last to act on the conference report.

Custody of the papers sometimes is manipulated to ensure that a particular chamber acts either first or last on the conference report. (Also see conference.)

Deferral — Executive branch action to defer, or delay, the spending of appropriated money. The 1974 Congressional Budget and Impoundment Control Act requires a special message from the president to Congress reporting a proposed deferral of spending. Deferrals may not extend beyond the end of the fiscal year in which the message is transmitted. A federal district court in 1986 struck down the president's authority to defer spending for policy reasons; the ruling was upheld by a federal appeals court in 1987. Congress can prohibit proposed deferrals by clearing a law doing so; most often, cancellations of proposed deferrals are included in appropriations bills. (Also see rescission.)

Delegate — A nonvoting official representing the District of Columbia, Guam, American Samoa, the U.S. Virgin Islands, the Northern Mariana Islands or Puerto Rico in the House. The first five serve two-year terms. Puerto Rico's nonvoting representative is known as a resident commissioner and serves a four-year term. Delegates may not vote in the full House but are permitted to vote in committees and can introduce and co-sponsor legislation. Periodically, delegates have been permitted to vote in the Committee of the Whole House, where some legislative business is conducted. That permission was eliminated by a House rules change at the beginning of the 112th Congress. (See also Committee of the Whole.)

Dilatory motion — A motion made for the purpose of killing time and preventing action on a bill or amendment. House rules outlaw dilatory motions, but enforcement is largely within the discretion of the speaker or chairman of the Committee of the Whole. The Senate does not have a rule barring dilatory motions except under cloture.

Discharge a committee — Occasionally, attempts are made to relieve a committee of jurisdiction over a bill that is before it. This is attempted more often in the House than in the Senate, and the procedure rarely is successful.

In the House, if a committee does not report a bill within 30 days after the measure is referred to it, any member may file a discharge motion. Once offered, the motion is treated as a petition needing the signatures of a majority of members (218 if there are no vacancies). After the required signatures have been obtained, there is a delay of seven days.

Afterward, on the second and fourth Mondays of each month, except during the last six days of a session, any member who has signed the petition must be recognized, if he or she so desires, to move that the committee be discharged. Debate on the motion to discharge is limited to 20 minutes. If the motion is approved, consideration of the bill becomes a matter of high privilege.

If a resolution to consider a bill is held up in the Rules Committee for more than seven legislative days, any member may enter a motion to discharge the committee. The motion is handled like any other discharge petition in the House. Occasionally, to expedite noncontroversial legislative business, a committee is discharged by unanimous consent of the House, and a petition is not required. In 1993, the signatures on pending discharge petitions — previously kept secret — were made a matter of public record. (For Senate procedure, see discharge resolution.)

Discharge Calendar — The House calendar to which motions to discharge committees are referred when they have the required number of signatures (218) and are awaiting floor action. (Also see calendar.)

Discharge petition — (See discharge a committee.)

Discharge resolution — In the Senate, a special motion that any senator may introduce to relieve a committee from consideration of a bill before it. The resolution can be called up for Senate approval or disapproval in the same manner as any other Senate business. (For House procedure, see discharge a committee.)

Discretionary spending — Budget authority provided through appropriations bills in amounts determined annually by Congress. In recent years, Congress has established caps on discretionary spending that are enforced through points of order that must be waived to permit action to exceed the cap, or by automatic spending cuts called a sequester. (Also see mandatory spending, sequester.)

Direct spending — (See mandatory spending.)

Division of a question for voting — A practice that is more common in the Senate but also used in the House whereby a member may demand a division of an amendment or a motion for purposes of voting. When the amendment or motion lends itself to such a division, the individual parts are voted on separately.

Emergency spending — Spending that the president and Congress have designated as an emergency requirement. Emergency spending is not subject to limits on discretionary spending set in the budget resolution or to pay-as-you-go rules, which require offsets. The designation is intended for unanticipated items that are not included in the budget for a fiscal year, such as spending to respond to disasters. However, most of the appropriations for the wars in Iraq and Afghanistan have been designated as emergency spending or, more recently, as overseas contingency operations not subject to discretionary spending limits.

Enacting clause — Key phrase in bills beginning, "Be it enacted by the Senate and House of Representatives." A successful motion to strike it from legislation kills the measure.

Engrossed bill — The copy of a bill as passed by one chamber, with the text as amended by floor action and certified by the clerk of the House or the secretary of the Senate.

Enrolled bill — The final copy of a bill that has been passed in identical form by both chambers. It is certified by an officer of the chamber of origin (clerk of the House or secretary of the Senate) and then sent on for the signatures of the House speaker, the Senate president pro tempore and the president of the United States. An enrolled bill is printed on parchment.

Entitlement — A program that guarantees payments to anyone who meets the eligibility criteria set in law. Examples include Social Security, Medicare, Medicaid and food stamps. (Also see mandatory spending.)

Executive Calendar — A nonlegislative calendar in the Senate that lists presidential documents such as treaties and nominations. (Also see calendar.)

Executive document — A document, usually a treaty, sent to the Senate by the president for consideration or approval. Executive documents are referred to committee in the same manner as other measures. Unlike legislative documents, treaties do not die at the end of a Congress but remain "live" proposals until acted on by the Senate or withdrawn by the president.

Executive session — A meeting of a Senate or House committee (or occasionally of either chamber) that only its members may attend. Witnesses regularly appear at committee meetings in executive session — for example, Defense Department officials during presentations of classified defense information. Other members of Congress may be invited, but the public and news media are not allowed to attend.

Filibuster — A time-delaying tactic associated with the Senate and used by a minority in an effort to prevent a vote on a bill, amendment, motion or nomination that probably would prevail if voted upon directly. The most common method is to take advantage of the Senate's rules permitting unlimited debate, but other forms of parliamentary maneuvering may be used. The chamber can vote to invoke cloture to end a filibuster, but that generally requires a majority of 60 votes, and in some cases two-thirds of the chamber. In November 2013, the Senate reinterpreted its cloture rule as it applies to executive branch nominations and lower federal court judges (other than those for the Supreme Court). A simple majority was then all that was required to cut off debate on non-Supreme Court nominations and end a filibuster. In 2017, the Senate voted to apply this rule to Supreme Court nominations as well. (Also see cloture.) The stricter rules of the House make filibusters more difficult, but delaying tactics are employed occasionally through various procedural devices allowed by House rules.

Fiscal year — Financial operations of the government are carried out in a 12-month fiscal year, beginning Oct. 1 and ending Sept. 30. The fiscal year carries the date of the calendar year in which it ends. (From fiscal 1844 to fiscal 1976, the fiscal year began July 1 and ended the following June 30.)

Five-minute rule — A debate-limiting rule of the House that is invoked when the House sits as the Committee of the Whole. Under the rule, a member offering an amendment and a member opposing it are each allowed to speak for five minutes. Debate is then closed. In practice, amendments regularly are debated for more than 10 minutes, with members gaining the floor by offering pro forma amendments or obtaining unanimous consent to speak longer than five minutes. (Also see Committee of the Whole, hour rule, strike out the last word.)

Floor manager — A member who has the task of steering legislation through floor debate and amendment to a final vote in the House or the Senate. Floor managers usually are chairmen or ranking members of the committee that reported the bill. Managers are responsible for apportioning the debate time granted to supporters of the bill. The ranking minority member of the committee normally apportions time for the minority party's participation in the debate.

Frank — A member's facsimile signature, which is used on envelopes in lieu of stamps for the member's official outgoing mail. The "franking privilege" is the right to send mail postage-free.

Germane — Pertaining to the subject matter of the measure at hand. All House amendments must be germane to the bill being considered. The Senate requires that amendments be germane when they are proposed to general appropriations bills or to bills being considered once cloture has been invoked or, frequently, when the Senate is proceeding under a unanimous consent agreement placing a time limit on consideration of a bill. The 1974 Budget Act also requires that amendments to concurrent budget resolutions be germane.

In the House, floor debate must be germane, and the first three hours of debate each day in the Senate must be germane to the pending business. (Also see cloture.)

Gramm-Rudman Deficit Reduction Act — (See sequester.)

Grandfather clause — A provision that exempts people or other entities already engaged in an activity from new rules or legislation affecting that activity.

Hearings — Committee sessions for taking testimony from witnesses. At hearings on legislation, witnesses usually include specialists, government officials, and spokesmen for individuals or entities affected by the bill or bills under study. Hearings related to special investigations bring forth a variety of witnesses. Committees sometimes use their subpoena power to summon reluctant witnesses. The public and news media may attend open hearings but are barred from closed, or "executive," hearings. The vast majority of hearings are open to the public. (Also see executive session.)

Hold-harmless clause — A provision added to legislation to ensure that recipients of federal money do not receive less in a future year than they did in the current year if a new formula for allocating money authorized in the legislation would result in a reduction to the recipients. This clause has been used most often to soften the impact of sudden reductions in federal grants.

Hopper — A box on the House clerk's desk into which members deposit bills and resolutions to introduce them.

Hour rule — A provision in the rules of the House that permits one hour of debate time for each member on amendments debated in the House of Representatives sitting as the House. Therefore, the House normally amends bills while sitting as the Committee of the Whole, where the five-minute rule on amendments operates.

House as in the Committee of the Whole — A procedure that can be used to expedite consideration of certain measures such as continuing resolutions and, when there is debate, private bills. The procedure can be invoked only with the unanimous consent of the House or a rule from the Rules Committee and has procedural elements of both the House sitting as the House of Representatives, such as the speaker presiding and the previous question motion being in order, and the House sitting as the Committee of the Whole, with the five-minute rule being in order. (Also see Committee of the Whole.)

House Calendar — A listing for action by the House of public bills and resolutions that do not directly or indirectly appropriate money or raise revenue. (Also see calendar.)

Immunity — The constitutional privilege of members of Congress to make verbal statements on the floor and in committee for which they cannot be sued or arrested for slander or libel. Also, freedom from arrest while traveling to or from sessions of Congress or on official business. Members in this status may be arrested only for treason, felonies or a breach of the peace, as defined by congressional manuals.

Joint committee — A committee composed of a specified number of members of both the House and Senate. A joint committee may be investigative or research-oriented, an example of the latter being the Joint Economic Committee. Others have housekeeping duties; examples include the joint committees on Printing and the Library of Congress. In 2011, Congress convened a Joint Select Committee on Deficit Reduction and charged it with proposing $1.2 trillion in budget savings. The committee did not agree on a plan, and it disbanded in November 2011.

Joint resolution — Like a bill, a joint resolution, designated H J Res or S J Res, requires the approval of both chambers and generally the signature of the president and has the force of law if approved. In most cases, there is no practical difference between a bill and a joint resolution. A joint resolution generally is used to address a limited matter such as a single appropriation.

Joint resolutions also are used to propose amendments to the Constitution. In that case, they require a two-thirds majority in both chambers. They do not require a presidential signature, but they must be ratified by three-fourths of the states to become a part of the Constitution. (Also see concurrent resolution, resolution.)

Journal — The official record of the proceedings of the House and Senate. The Journal records the actions taken in each chamber, but, unlike the Congressional Record, it does not include the substantially verbatim report of speeches, debates, statements and the like.

Law — An act of Congress that has been signed by the president or passed, over his veto, by Congress. Public bills, when signed, become public laws and are cited by the letters PL and a hyphenated number. The number before the hyphen corresponds to the Congress, and the one or more digits after the hyphen refer to the numerical sequence in which the president signed the bills during that Congress. Private bills, when signed, become private laws. (Also see bills, private bill.)

Legislative day — The "day" extending from the time either chamber meets after an adjournment until the time it next adjourns. Because the House normally adjourns from day to day, legislative days and calendar days usually coincide. But in the Senate, a legislative day may, and frequently does, extend over several calendar days. (Also see recess.)

Line-item veto — Presidential authority to strike individual items from appropriations bills, which presidents since Ulysses S. Grant have sought. Congress gave the president a form of the power in 1996 (PL 104-130), but this "enhanced rescission authority" was struck down by the Supreme Court in 1998 as unconstitutional because it allowed the president to change laws on his own.

Loan guarantees — Loans to third parties for which the federal government guarantees the repayment of principal or interest, in whole or in part, to the lender in the event of default.

Lobby — A group seeking to influence the passage or defeat of legislation. Originally the term referred to people frequenting the lobbies or corridors of legislative chambers to speak to lawmakers.

The definition of a lobby and the activity of lobbying is a matter of differing interpretation. By some definitions, lobbying is limited to direct attempts to influence lawmakers through personal interviews and persuasion. Under other definitions, lobbying includes attempts at indirect, or grass-roots, influence, such as persuading members of a group to write or visit their district's representative and state's senators or attempting to create a climate of opinion favorable to a desired legislative goal.

The right to attempt to influence legislation is based on the First Amendment to the Constitution, which says Congress shall make no law abridging the right of the people "to petition the government for a redress of grievances."

Majority leader — The floor leader for the majority party in each chamber. In the Senate, in consultation with the minority leader, the majority leader directs the legislative schedule for the chamber. This person is also the party's spokesman and chief strategist. In the House, the majority leader is second to the speaker in the majority party's leadership and serves as the party's legislative strategist. (Also see speaker, whip.)

Mandatory spending — Budget authority and outlays often provided under laws other than appropriations acts, although some mandatory spending is provided by annual appropriations (as is all discretionary spending). Mandatory spending, also known as direct spending, covers entitlements and payment of interest on the public debt. (Also see discretionary spending, entitlement.)

Marking up a bill — Going through the contents of a piece of legislation in committee or subcommittee to, for example, consider the provisions, act on amendments to provisions and proposed revisions to the language, and insert new sections and phraseology. If the bill is extensively amended, the committee's version may be introduced as a separate (or "clean") bill, with a new number, before being considered by the full House or Senate. (Also see clean bill.)

Minority leader — The floor leader for the minority party in each chamber.

Morning hour — The time set aside at the beginning of each legislative day for the consideration of routine business. The "hour" is of indefinite duration in the House, where it is rarely used. In the Senate, it is the first two hours of a session following an adjournment, as distinguished from a recess. Business includes such matters as messages from the president, communications from the heads of departments, messages from the House, the presentation of petitions, reports of standing and select committees, and the introduction of bills and resolutions.

During the first hour of the morning hour in the Senate, no motion to proceed to the consideration of any bill on the calendar is in order except by unanimous consent. During the second hour, motions can be made but must be decided without debate. Senate committees may meet while the Senate conducts the morning hour.

Motion — In the House or Senate chamber, a request by a member to institute any one of a wide array of parliamentary actions. He or she "moves" for a certain procedure, such as the consideration of a measure. The precedence of motions, and whether they are debatable, is set forth in the House and Senate rules.

Nominations — Presidential appointments to office subject to Senate confirmation. Although most nominations win quick Senate approval, some are controversial and become the topic of hearings and debate. Sometimes senators object to appointees for patronage reasons — for example, when a nomination to a local federal job is made without consulting the senators of the state concerned. In some situations a senator may object that the nominee is "personally obnoxious" to him. Usually other senators join in blocking such appointments out of courtesy to their colleagues. In recent years, executive branch and judicial nominations have been blocked by filibusters. As a result, the Senate in November 2013 changed its interpretation of the cloture rule used to end filibusters. (Also see cloture, filibuster, senatorial courtesy.)

One-minute speeches — Addresses by House members at the beginning of a legislative day. The speeches may cover any subject but are limited to one minute's duration.

Outlays — Actual spending that flows from the liquidation of budget authority. Outlays associated with appropriations bills and other legislation are estimates of future spending made by the Congressional Budget Office and the White House's Office of Management and Budget. The CBO's estimates govern bills for the purpose of congressional floor debate, while the OMB's numbers govern when it comes to determining whether legislation exceeds spending caps.

Outlays in a given fiscal year may result from budget authority provided in the current year or in previous years. (Also see budget authority, budget process.)

Override a veto — If the president vetoes a bill and sends it back to Congress with his objections, Congress may try to override his veto and enact the bill into law. Neither chamber is required to attempt to override a veto. The override of a veto requires a recorded vote with a two-thirds majority of those present and voting in each chamber. The question put to each chamber is: "Shall the bill pass, the objections of the president to the contrary notwithstanding?" (Also see pocket veto, veto.)

Oversight committee — A congressional committee or designated subcommittee that is charged with general oversight of one or more federal agencies' programs and activities. Usually, the oversight panel for a particular agency is also the authorizing committee for that agency's programs and operations.

Pair — A voluntary, informal arrangement that two lawmakers, usually on opposite sides of an issue, make on recorded votes. In many cases, the result is to subtract a vote from each side with no effect on the outcome.

Pairs are not authorized in the rules of either chamber, are not counted in tabulating the final result and have no official standing. However, paired members are identified in the Congressional Record, along with their positions on such votes, if known. A member who expects to be absent for a vote can pair with a member who plans to vote, with the latter agreeing to withhold his or her vote.

There are three types of pairs:

(**1**) A live pair involves a member who is present for a vote and another who is absent. The member in attendance votes and then withdraws the vote, announcing that he or she has a live pair with colleague "X" and stating how the two members would have voted, one in favor, the other opposed. A live pair may affect the outcome of a closely contested vote, since it subtracts one "yea" or one "nay" from the final tally. A live pair may cover one or several specific issues.

(**2**) A general pair, widely used in the House, does not entail any arrangement between two members and does not affect the vote. Members who expect to be absent notify the clerk that they wish to make a general pair. Each member then is paired with another desiring a pair, and their names are listed in the Congressional Record. The member may or may not be paired with another taking the opposite position, and no indication of how the members would have voted is given.

(**3**) A specific pair is similar to a general pair, except that the opposing stands of the two members are identified and printed in the Congressional Record.

"Pay as you go" — A rule making it out of order to consider legislation, including conference reports, that contain tax provisions or new or expanded entitlement spending that has the net effect of increasing the deficit or reducing the surplus.

Petition — A request or plea sent to one or both chambers from an organization or private citizens group seeking support for particular legislation or favorable consideration of a matter not yet receiving congressional attention. Petitions are referred to appropriate committees. In the House, a petition signed by a majority of members (218) can discharge a bill from a committee. (Also see discharge a committee.)

Pocket veto — The act of the president in withholding his approval of a bill after Congress has adjourned. When Congress is in session, a bill becomes law without the president's signature if he does not act upon it within 10 days, excluding Sundays, from the time he receives it. But if Congress adjourns sine die within that 10-day period, the bill, if unsigned, will die even if the president does not formally veto it.

The Supreme Court in 1986 agreed to decide whether the president could pocket veto a bill during recesses and between sessions of the same Congress or only between Congresses. The justices in 1987 declared the case moot, however, because the bill in question was invalid once the case reached the court. The House has treated pocket vetoes between sessions as regular vetoes. (Also see adjournment sine die, veto.)

Point of order — An objection raised by a member that the chamber is departing from rules governing its conduct of business. The objector cites the rule violated, with the chairman sustaining his or her objection if correctly made. The chairman restores order by suspending proceedings of the chamber until it conforms to the prescribed "order of business."

Both chambers have procedures for overcoming a point of order, either by vote or — as is most common in the House — by including language in the rule for floor consideration that waives a point of order against a given bill. (Also see rules.)

President of the Senate — Under the Constitution, the vice president of the United States presides over the Senate. In his absence, the president pro tempore, or a senator designated by the president pro tempore, presides over the chamber.

President pro tempore — The chief officer of the Senate in the absence of the vice president—literally, but loosely, the president for a time. The president pro tempore is elected by his fellow senators. Recent practice has been to elect the senator of the majority party with the longest period of continuous service. The president pro tempore is third in the line of presidential succession, after the vice president and the speaker of the House.

Previous question — A motion for the previous question, when carried, has the effect of cutting off further debate, preventing the offering of further amendments and forcing a vote on the pending matter. In the House, a motion for the previous question is not permitted in the Committee of the Whole, unless a rule governing debate provides otherwise. The motion for the previous question is not in order in the Senate.

Printed amendment — Some House rules guarantee five minutes of floor debate in support and five minutes in opposition, and no other debate time, on amendments printed in the Congressional Record at least one day prior to the amendment's consideration in the Committee of the Whole.

In the Senate, while amendments may be submitted for printing, they have no parliamentary standing or status. An amendment submitted for printing in the Senate, however, may be called up by any senator.

Private bill — A bill dealing with individual matters, such as claims against the government, immigration or land titles. If two members officially object to consideration of a private bill that is before the chamber, it is recommitted to committee. The backers still have recourse, however. The measure can be put into an omnibus claims bill — several private bills rolled into one. As with any bill, no part of an omnibus claims bill may be deleted without a vote. When the private bill goes back to the House floor in this form, it can be deleted from the omnibus bill only by majority vote.

Private Calendar — The House calendar for private bills. The Private Calendar must be called on the first Tuesday of each month, and the speaker may call it on the third Tuesday of each month, as well. (Also see calendar, private bill.)

Privileged questions — The order in which bills, motions and other legislative measures are considered on the floor of the Senate and House is governed by strict priorities. A motion to table, for instance, is more privileged than a motion to recommit. Thus, if a member moves to recommit a bill to committee for further consideration, another member can supersede the first action by moving to table it, and a vote will occur on the motion to table (or kill) before the motion to recommit. A motion to adjourn is considered "of the highest privilege" and must be considered before virtually any other motion.

Pro forma amendment — (See strike out the last word.)

Pro forma session — A meeting of the House and Senate during which no legislative business is conducted. The sessions are held to satisfy a provision of the Constitution that prohibits either chamber from adjourning for more than three days without the permission of the other chamber. When the House or Senate recesses or adjourns for more than three days, both chambers adopt concurrent resolutions providing for the recess or adjournment. Also, the Senate sometimes holds pro forma sessions during recess periods to prevent the president from making recess appointments.

Public laws — (See law.)

Questions of privilege — These are matters affecting members of Congress individually or collectively. Matters affecting the rights, safety, dignity and integrity of proceedings of the House or Senate as a whole are questions of privilege in both chambers.

Questions involving individual members are called questions of "personal privilege." A member rising to ask a question of personal privilege is given precedence over almost all other proceedings. For instance, if a member feels that he or she has been improperly impugned in comments by another member, he or she can immediately demand to be heard on the floor on a question of personal privilege. An annotation in the House rules points out that the privilege rests primarily on the Constitution, which gives members a conditional immunity from arrest and an unconditional freedom to speak in the House.

In 1993, the House changed its rules to allow the speaker to delay for two legislative days the floor consideration of a resolution raising a question of the privileges of the House unless it is offered by the majority leader or minority leader.

Quorum — The number of members whose presence is necessary for the transaction of business. In the Senate and House, it is a majority of the membership. In the Committee of the Whole, a quorum is 100. If a point of order is made that a quorum is not present, the only business that is in order is either a motion to adjourn or a motion to direct the sergeant at arms to request the attendance of absentees. In practice, however, both chambers conduct much of their business without a quorum present. (Also see Committee of the Whole.)

Quorum call — Procedures used in the House and Senate to establish that a quorum is present. In the House, quorum calls are usually conducted using the electronic voting system, and no roll call is recorded. In the Senate, quorum calls are usually conducted by calling the roll of senators. The House and Senate conduct annual quorum calls at the beginning of each session of Congress. The Senate also uses quorum calls when no senators are speaking on the floor.

Reading of bills — Traditional parliamentary procedure required bills to be read three times before they were passed. This custom is of little modern significance. Normally a bill is considered to have its first reading when it is introduced and printed, by title, in the Congressional Record. In the House, a bill's second reading comes when floor consideration begins. (The actual reading of a bill is most likely to occur at this point if at all.) The second reading in the Senate is supposed to occur on the legislative day after the measure is introduced, but before it is referred to committee. The third reading (again, usually by title) takes place when floor action has been completed on amendments.

Recess — A recess, as distinguished from adjournment, does not end a legislative day and, therefore, does not interrupt unfinished business. The House usually adjourns from day to day. The Senate often recesses, thus meeting on the same legislative day for several calendar days or even weeks at a time. The rules in each chamber set forth certain matters to be taken up and disposed of at the beginning of each legislative day.

Recognition — The power of recognition of a member is lodged in the speaker of the House and the presiding officer of the Senate. The presiding officer names the member to speak first when two or more members simultaneously request recognition. The order of recognition is governed by precedents and tradition for many situations. In the Senate, for instance, the majority leader has the right to be recognized first.

Recommit — A motion to return a bill or joint resolution to committee after the measure has been debated on the floor. In the House, the right to offer a motion to recommit is guaranteed to the minority leader or someone he or she designates, and there must be an opponent.

Under a 2009 House rules change, a motion to recommit with instructions must direct a committee to report the bill back "forthwith" — that is, immediately. Previously, the motion could include the term "promptly," which did not require that the bill be returned to the floor and instead required full committee action.

Reconciliation — The 1974 Budget Act created a reconciliation procedure for bringing existing tax and spending laws into conformity with ceilings set in the congressional budget resolution. Under the procedure, the budget resolution sets specific deficit reduction targets and instructs tax-writing and authorizing committees to propose changes in existing law to meet those targets. If more than one committee is involved, the Budget committees consolidate the recommendations, without change, into an omnibus reconciliation bill, which then must be considered and approved by both chambers of Congress.

Special rules in the Senate limit debate on a reconciliation bill to 20 hours and bar extraneous or nongermane amendments. (Also see budget resolution, sequester.)

Reconsider a vote — Until it is disposed of, a motion to reconsider the vote by which an action was taken has the effect of putting the action in abeyance. In the Senate, the motion can be made only by a member who voted on the prevailing side of the original question or by a member who did not vote at all. In the House, it can be made only by a member on the prevailing side.

A common practice in the Senate after close votes on an issue is a motion to reconsider, followed by a motion to table the motion to reconsider. On this motion to table, senators vote as they voted on the original question, which allows the motion to table to prevail, assuming there are no switches. That closes the matter, and further motions to reconsider are not entertained.

In the House, as a routine precaution, a motion to reconsider usually is made every time a measure is passed. Such a motion almost always is tabled immediately, thus shutting off the possibility of future reconsideration except by unanimous consent.

Motions to reconsider must be entered in the Senate within the next two days the Senate is in session after the original vote has been taken. In the House, they must be entered either on the same day or the next succeeding day that the House is in session. Sometimes on a close vote, a member — in the Senate, often the majority leader — will switch his or her vote to be eligible to offer a motion to reconsider.

Recorded vote — A vote upon which each member's stand is individually made known. In the Senate, this is accomplished through a roll call of the entire membership, to which each senator on the floor must answer "yea," "nay" or "present." Since January 1973, the House has used an electronic voting system for recorded votes, including "yea" and "nay" votes formerly taken by a call of the roll.

When not required by the Constitution, a recorded vote can be obtained on questions in the House on the demand of one-fifth (44 members) of a quorum or one-fourth (25) of a quorum in the Committee of the Whole. Recorded votes are required in the House for appropriations, budget and tax bills. (Also see "yeas" and "nays.")

Report — Both a verb and a noun as a congressional term. A committee that has been examining a bill referred to it by the parent chamber "reports" its findings and recommendations to the chamber when it completes consideration and returns the measure. The process is called "reporting" a bill. In some cases, a bill is reported without a written report.

A "report" is the document setting forth the committee's explanation of its action. Senate and House reports are numbered separately and are designated S Rept or H Rept. When a committee report is not unanimous, the dissenting committee members may file a statement of their views, referred to as a minority report. Members in disagreement with some provisions of a bill may file additional or supplementary views. Sometimes a bill or resolution is reported without a committee recommendation.

Legislative committees occasionally submit adverse reports. However, when a committee is opposed to a bill, it usually does not report the bill at all. Some laws require that committee reports — favorable or adverse — be filed.

Rescission — Cancellation of budget authority that was previously appropriated but has not yet been spent.

Resolution — A "simple" resolution, designated H Res or S Res, deals with matters entirely within the prerogatives of a single chamber. It requires neither adoption by the other chamber nor approval by the president, and it does not have the force of law. Most resolutions deal with the rules or procedures of one chamber. They are also used to express the sentiments of a single chamber, such as condolences to the family of a deceased member, or to comment on foreign policy or executive business. A simple resolution is the vehicle for a "rule" from the House Rules Committee. (Also see concurrent and joint resolutions, rules.)

Rider — An amendment, usually not germane, that its sponsor hopes to get through more easily by including it in other legislation. A rider becomes law if the bill to which it is attached is enacted. Amendments providing legislative directives in appropriations bills are examples of riders, although technically legislation is barred from appropriations bills.

The House, unlike the Senate, has a strict germaneness rule; thus, riders usually are Senate devices to get legislation enacted quickly or to bypass lengthy House consideration and, possibly, opposition.

Rules — Each chamber has a body of rules and precedents that govern the conduct of business. These rules deal with issues such as duties of officers, the order of business, admission to the floor, parliamentary procedures on handling amendments and voting, and jurisdictions of committees.

The House re-adopts its rules, usually with some changes, at the beginning of each Congress. Senate rules carry over from one Congress to the next.

In the House, a rule may also be a resolution reported by the Rules Committee to govern the handling of a particular bill on the floor. The committee may report a rule, also called a special order, in the form of a simple resolution. If the House adopts the resolution, the temporary rule becomes as valid as any standing rule and lapses only after action has been completed on the measure to which it pertains.

The rule sets the time limit on general debate. It also may waive points of order against provisions of the bill in question, such as non-germane language, or against certain amendments expected on the floor. It may even forbid all amendments or all amendments except those proposed by the legislative committee that handled the bill. In this instance, it is known as a "closed" rule, as opposed to an "open" rule, which puts no limitation on floor amendments, thus leaving the bill open to alteration by the adoption of germane amendments. (Also see point of order.)

Secretary of the Senate — Chief administrative officer of the Senate, responsible for overseeing the duties of Senate employees, educating Senate pages, administering oaths, overseeing the registration of lobbyists and handling other tasks necessary for the continuing operation of the Senate. (Also see Clerk of the House.)

Select or special committee — A committee set up for a special purpose and, usually, for a limited time by resolution of either the House or Senate. Most special committees are investigative and lack legislative authority: Legislation is not referred to them, and they cannot report bills to their parent chambers. Each chamber has a Select Committee on Intelligence.

Senatorial courtesy — A general practice with no written rule — sometimes referred to as "the courtesy of the Senate" — applied to consideration of executive nominations. Generally, it means nominees from a state are not to be confirmed unless they have been approved by the senators of the president's party of that state, with other senators following their colleagues' lead in the attitude they take toward consideration of such nominations. (Also see nominations.)

Sequester — Automatic percentage spending cuts for all discretionary spending and some mandatory spending, with exceptions. Under the 1985 Gramm-Rudman anti-deficit law, modified in 1987, a year-end, across-the-board sequester was triggered if the deficit exceeded a preset maximum. The Budget Control Act of 2011 required a $1.2 billion sequester, spread equally over nine years, after a joint deficit reduction committee was unable to agree on savings. For fiscal 2014 and after, the sequester resulted in lower discretionary spending caps and a second across-the-board sequester to enforce those caps. In December 2013, the caps were adjusted higher and the sequester was extended beyond fiscal 2021 for certain spending.

Sine die — (See adjournment sine die.)

Speaker — The presiding officer of the House of Representatives, selected by the majority party's caucus and formally elected by the whole House. While both parties nominate candidates, choice by the majority party is tantamount to election. The speaker is second in the line of presidential succession, after the vice president.

Special session — A session of Congress after it has adjourned sine die, completing its regular session. Special sessions are convened by the president.

Spending authority — The 1974 Budget Act defines spending authority as borrowing authority, contract authority and entitlement authority for which budget authority is not provided in advance by appropriations acts.

Sponsor — (See bills introduced.)

Standing committees — Committees that are permanently established by House and Senate rules. The standing committees are legislative committees: Legislation may be referred to them, and they may report bills and resolutions to their parent chambers.

Standing vote — A nonrecorded vote used in both the House and Senate. (A standing vote is also called a division vote.) Members in favor of a proposal stand and are counted by the presiding officer. Then members opposed stand and are counted. There is no record of how individual members voted.

Statutes at large — A chronological arrangement of the laws enacted in each session of Congress. Though indexed, the laws are not arranged by subject matter, and there is no indication of how they changed previously enacted laws.

Strike from the Record — A member of the House who is offended by remarks made on the House floor may move that the offending words be "taken down" for the speaker's cognizance and then expunged from the debate as published in the Congressional Record.

Strike out the last word — A motion whereby a House member is entitled to speak for five minutes on an amendment then being debated by the chamber. A member gains recognition from the chair by moving to "strike out the last word" of the amendment or section of the bill under consideration. The motion is pro forma, requires no vote and does not change the amendment being debated. (Also see five-minute rule.)

Substitute — A motion, amendment or entire bill introduced in place of the pending legislative business. Adoption of the substitute supplants the original text. The substitute may also be amended. (Also see amendment in the nature of a substitute.)

Supplemental appropriations bill — Legislation appropriating money after the regular annual appropriations bill for a federal department or agency has been enacted. In the past, supplemental appropriations bills often arrived about halfway through the fiscal year to pay for urgent needs, such as relief from natural disasters, that Congress and the president did not anticipate (or may not have wanted to finance).

Suspend the rules — A time-saving procedure for passing bills in the House. The wording of the motion, which may be made by any member recognized by the speaker, is "I move to suspend the rules and pass the bill." A favorable vote by two-thirds of those present is required for passage. Debate is limited to 40 minutes, and no amendments from the floor are permitted.

If a two-thirds favorable vote is not attained, the bill may be considered later under regular procedures. The suspension procedure is in order every Monday, Tuesday and Wednesday, and it is intended to be reserved for noncontroversial bills. It also may be used to concur in Senate amendments, adopt conference reports and agree to resolutions.

Table a bill — Motions to table, or to "lay on the table," are used to block or kill amendments or other parliamentary questions. When approved, a tabling motion is considered the final disposition of that issue. One of the most widely used parliamentary procedures, the motion to table is not debatable, and adoption requires a simple majority vote.

In the Senate, however, different language sometimes is used. The motion may be worded to let a bill "lie on the table," perhaps for subsequent "picking up." This motion is more flexible, keeping the bill pending for later action, if desired. Tabling motions on amendments are effective debate-ending devices in the Senate.

Treaties — Executive proposals — in the form of resolutions of ratification — that must be submitted to the Senate for approval by two-thirds of the senators present. Treaties are normally sent to the Foreign Relations Committee for scrutiny before the Senate takes action. Foreign Relations has jurisdiction over all treaties, regardless of the subject matter. After approval by the Senate, treaties are formally ratified by the president.

Trust funds — Money collected and used by the federal government for carrying out specific purposes and programs according to terms of a trust agreement or statute such as the Social Security and unemployment compensation trust funds. Such funds are administered by the government in a fiduciary capacity and are not available for the general purposes of the government.

Unanimous consent — A procedure used to expedite floor action. Proceedings of the House or Senate and action on legislation often take place upon the unanimous consent of the chamber, whether or not a rule of the chamber is being violated. It is frequently used in a routine fashion, such as by a senator requesting the unanimous consent of the Senate to have specified members of his or her staff present on the floor during debate on a specific amendment. A single member's objection blocks a unanimous consent request.

Unanimous consent agreement — A device used in the Senate to expedite legislation. Much of the Senate's legislative business, dealing with both minor and controversial issues, is conducted through unanimous consent or unanimous consent agreements. On major legislation, such agreements usually are printed and transmitted to all senators before floor debate. Once agreed to, they are binding on all members unless the Senate, by unanimous consent, agrees to modify them. An agreement may list the order in which various bills are to be considered; specify the length of time for debate on bills and contested amendments and when they are to be voted upon; and, frequently, require that all amendments introduced be germane to the bill under consideration. In this regard, unanimous consent agreements are similar to the "rules" issued by the House Rules Committee for bills pending in the House.

Union Calendar — Bills that directly or indirectly appropriate money or raise revenue are placed on this House calendar according to the date they are reported from committee. (Also see calendar.)

U.S. Code — A consolidation and codification of the general and permanent laws of the United States arranged by subject under 50 titles, the first six dealing with general or political subjects, and the other 44 alphabetically arranged from agriculture to war. The U.S. Code is updated annually, and a new set of bound volumes is published every six years. (Also see law, statutes at large.)

Veto — Disapproval by the president of a bill or joint resolution (other than one proposing an amendment to the Constitution). When Congress is in session, the president must veto a bill within 10 days, excluding Sundays, after he has received it; otherwise, it becomes law without his signature. When the president vetoes a bill, he returns it to the chamber of origin along with a message stating his objections. (Also see pocket veto, override a veto.)

Voice vote — In either the House or Senate, members answer "aye" or "no" in chorus, and the presiding officer decides the result. The term is also used loosely to indicate action by unanimous consent or without objection. (Also see "yeas" and "nays.")

Whip — In effect, the assistant majority or minority leader, in either the House or Senate. His or her job is to help marshal votes in support of party strategy and legislation.

Without objection — Used in lieu of a vote on noncontroversial motions, amendments or bills that may be passed in either chamber if no member voices an objection.

"Yeas" and "nays" — The Constitution requires that "yea" and "nay" votes be taken and recorded when requested by one-fifth of the members present. In the House, the speaker determines whether one-fifth of the members present requested a vote. In the Senate, practice requires only 11 members. The Constitution requires the yeas and nays on a veto override attempt. (Also see recorded vote.)

Yielding — When a member has been recognized to speak, no other member may speak unless he or she obtains permission from the member recognized. This permission is called yielding and usually is requested in the form, "Will the gentleman (or gentlelady) yield to me?" While this activity occasionally is seen in the Senate, the Senate has no rule or practice to parcel out time. In the House, the floor manager of a bill usually apportions debate time by yielding specific amounts of time to members who have requested it. ■

VOTE STUDIES

Votes on Judges Dominate

The Senate spends more time on nominees and less on lawmaking than ever before

When Senate Democrats in November 2013 exercised the so-called nuclear option, barring the minority party from filibustering lower court and executive branch nominees, then-Minority Leader Mitch McConnell warned that the tide would eventually turn.

"You'll regret this, and you may regret this a lot sooner than you think," he told the Democrats' leader, Harry Reid of Nevada.

McConnell, the Kentucky Republican, ascended to the top job 14 months later and since then has made Democrats rue Reid's decision by confirming judges at twice the rate Congress did when Barack Obama was president. In so doing, he's remaking the judiciary and fundamentally changing the way the Senate works.

CQ Roll Call's review of party unity voting in 2019 finds that the Senate confirmation process is, more than ever in modern history, a focus of intense partisanship. In an effort to slow McConnell, Democrats are demanding roll-call votes on routine nominations that once sailed through on a voice vote or by unanimous consent, and they're voting "no" at unprecedented rates.

All this partisan voting on nominations, meanwhile, is crowding out votes on legislation. In 2019, 82 percent of votes that split a majority of Republicans from a majority of Democrats in the Senate — party unity votes — dealt with nominations. Prior to Reid's decision, the highest figure of this millennium was 15 percent.

The polarized confirmation process tops the previous record, 2014, as Reid rushed judges through. That year 66 percent of party unity votes were on nominations.

"We're in the personnel business," McConnell said two years ago as he stood beside President Donald Trump at a Rose Garden news conference.

And in a year like 2019, when the Democrats controlled the House, the Senate was fixated on confirming the president's nominees to judgeships and executive branch jobs like never before.

This is the new, post-Armageddon Senate.

And it was easy to foresee. With the 60-vote requirement still in place to move forward with controversial bills, it's far easier to confirm more judges than to try to work out legislative compromises. Reid showed the way in 2014, but McConnell has perfected the new modus operandi. Future majority leaders will do the same, so long as there are any vacancies left to fill when McConnell is done.

Consider some figures. In 2019, the Senate took 428 votes and 315 of them, 74 percent of the total, dealt with nominations. Many were cloture votes, but McConnell and Trump pushed through all 161 nominees to the federal courts and executive branch jobs.

It was the highest percentage of Senate votes dedicated to nominations — by far — in this millennium. Before 2013, the year of Reid's fateful decision, the year with the highest percentage of nomination votes was 2011, at 22 percent.

The post-nuclear Senate has sped the confirmation process and should, with time, eliminate the vacancy problem on the federal courts. That peaked during Trump's second year in office, 2018, at 158 empty judgeships and is now down to 80 out of 890 judgeships nationwide.

It will also fundamentally alter the ideological balance on the courts. Without the need to win Democratic votes, Trump is able to nominate younger, more conservative judges. "The effect of confirming these nominees will be

The Senate McConnell has made

Majority Leader Mitch McConnell has focused to an unprecedented degree on judicial and other nominations. Those votes are also more likely to divide Republicans and Democrats than in the past.

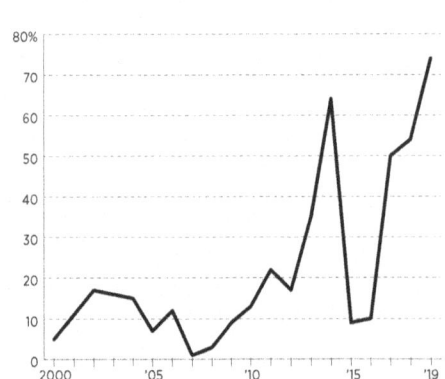

Percentage of total votes that were on nominations

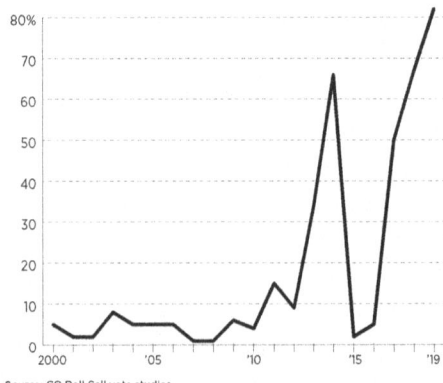

Percentage of total party unity votes that were on nominations

Source: CQ Roll Call vote studies
Jason Mann/CQ Roll Call

Two Democrats from Trump States: One on the Fence, the Other True Blue

Democrats Joe Manchin III of West Virginia and Jon Tester of Montana have a lot in common. Both senators represent conservative, rural states and know that GOP opponents will scrutinize their voting records for anything out of step with their constituents.

So the fact that Manchin sides nearly as often with Republicans on party unity votes — those that split a majority of Republicans from a majority of Democrats — and Tester is mostly loyal to his party indicates a difference in approach. Manchin in 2019 had the lowest unity score in the Senate, siding with fellow Democrats on only 50 percent of unity votes. Tester was with his party on 90 percent of those votes.

But in a Senate as fixated on confirming judges and other nominees as the current one is, the primary driver of that 40 percentage point gap was their relative support for President Donald Trump's nominees.

Manchin was far more likely to support them than Tester. In April, for example, the two split on David Bernhardt, Trump's pick to lead the Interior Department, with Manchin in favor and Tester opposed. In February, Manchin joined Republicans in voting to confirm William Barr as attorney general, while Tester was a no.

They split on many judges as well, from Matthew McFarland, who's now a district court judge in Ohio, to Robert Luck, who won a spot on the appeals court in Atlanta. Manchin voted for both, while Tester voted against. In a statement, Tester's office said he evaluated each Trump nominee and supported those who "understand and support rural states like Montana," apparently finding many lacking.

Manchin says the president deserves the benefit of the doubt. "As a former governor, I believe the president should have a fair chance to pick his team. When I'm considering nominees political party does not factor in," he said in a statement. "I look to see if the nominee is qualified for the job to which they have been appointed and cast my vote accordingly."

There were some policy differences. Of the 42 unity votes on policy matters, Manchin and Tester were on opposite sides nine times.

Manchin was in favor of seeking alternatives to paid family and medical leave for federal workers. The defense authorization law (PL 116-92) ultimately extended the paid leave. Manchin voted "yes" on moving forward with a bill (S 311) to require health care providers to care for infants born after botched abortions. Tester voted "no" and the bill failed to get cloture. Tester backed a resolution disapproving of the EPA's move to rescind President Barack Obama's plan to combat climate change by regulating greenhouse gas emissions from coal-fired power plants. Manchin, from a coal-dependent state, voted "no."

Considering the number of Senate unity votes in 2019 — 231 — only 10 percent of Manchin and Tester's differences were on policy votes, while the other 90 percent were on nominees.

Partisan voting predominates

More than 2 in 3 House votes split Republicans from Democrats, while in the Senate only a little more than half did. But the vast majority of Senate votes, and partisan Senate votes, were on nominations, a big change from prior years.

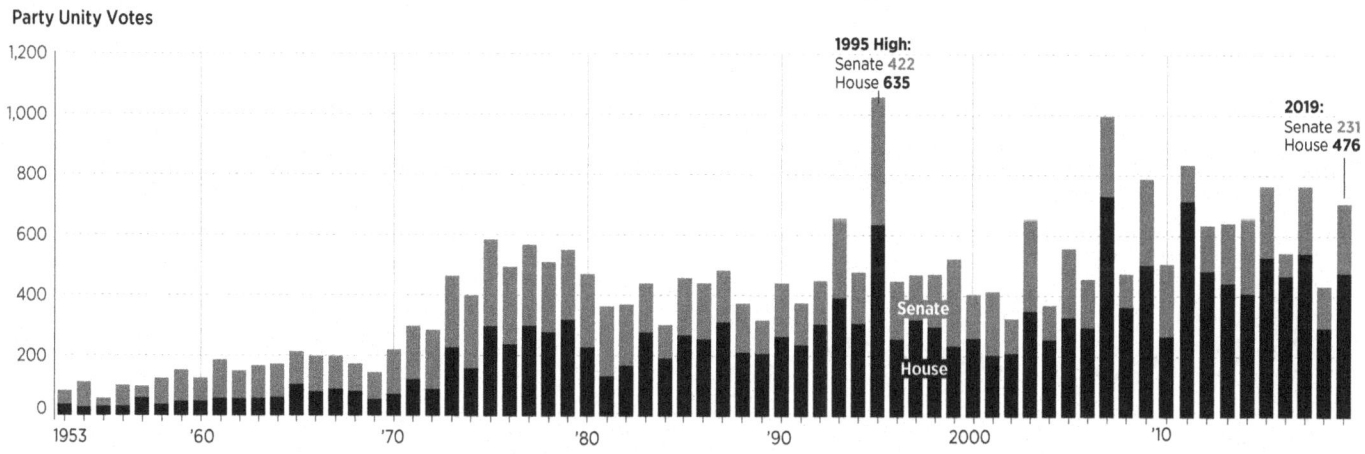

Party Unity Votes

1995 High:
Senate 422
House 635

2019:
Senate 231
House 476

Senate GOP: United But for Foreign Policy

In a year when Senate Republicans were united, with the average GOP senator voting with his or her party 94 percent of the time on votes that split the parties, foreign policy was the exception.

A number of Republicans broke with their colleagues to call out President Donald Trump for loosening sanctions on Russia, to call for Trump to pull U.S. forces out of Saudi Arabia's war with Yemen, and to block further arms sales to the Saudis.

Many Republicans are uncomfortable with Trump's friendliness with Russian dictator Vladimir Putin and in 2017 passed legislation imposing new sanctions on Russia to punish it for its interference in the 2016 presidential election, among other things. And some Republicans have grown

squeamish about the U.S. support for Saudi Arabia, given that it has helped kill thousands of Yemeni civilians and had a journalist critical of the regime, Jamal Khashoggi, murdered and dismembered.

Eleven Republicans voted with Democrats to condemn the curtailment of Russia sanctions, while seven went with the Democrats on U.S. involvement in Yemen and arms sales to the Saudis.

Still, there were only two Republicans, Susan Collins of Maine and Jerry Moran of Kansas, who voted with Democrats on all three of the votes.

Moran said he felt Russia was still a threat and that sanctions were justified. On the Yemen war and Saudi arms sales, he said he wanted to protect congressional prerogatives to

have a say in foreign policy.

Collins said easing the Russia sanctions would send the wrong message to an unrepentant Putin. On the Yemen war and Saudi arms sales, Collins cites her objections to the Saudis' "abhorrent record on human rights."

Another group of four GOP senators — Mike Lee of Utah, Lisa Murkowski of Alaska, Ron Paul of Kentucky and Todd Young of Indiana — voted with Democrats to order the pullout from Yemen and the suspension of military aid to Saudi Arabia, but did not object to Trump's move to ease the Russia sanctions.

Partisan to the max

Levels of partisan voting remained at or near record highs in 2019. The most noteworthy change is the partisan voting on judicial and executive branch nominees on which Republicans were united and Democrats often divided.

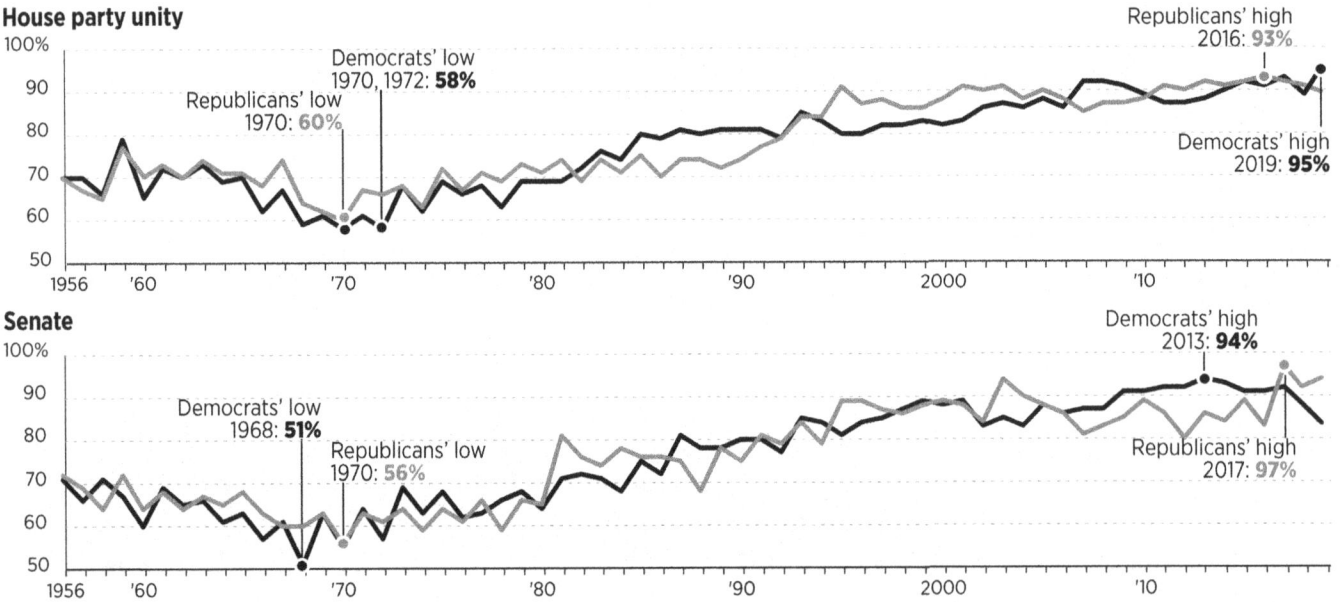

House party unity

Republicans' high 2016: **93%**

Democrats' low 1970, 1972: **58%**

Republicans' low 1970: **60%**

Democrats' high 2019: **95%**

Senate

Democrats' high 2013: **94%**

Democrats' low 1968: **51%**

Republicans' low 1970: **56%**

Republicans' high 2017: **97%**

felt long after Trump is out of the White House and McConnell is no longer majority leader," says Marty Paone, a senior adviser at the Prime Policy Group lobbying firm who spent three decades working the Senate floor for Senate Democratic leadership. "It will be felt for 30 or 40 years."

Since senators of the president's party almost always back his nominees, the growing number of confirmation votes is driving up the GOP's party unity scores. The average Republican senator's score in 2019, 94 percent, is the second-highest since CQ Roll Call began studying partisan voting in 1956.

On the Democratic side, senators more willing to give Trump his own appointees have higher scores. They are typically from electorally competitive states. But there are others, like Connecticut's Christopher S. Murphy, who still operate by an older, now dying philosophy, that presidents should usually get their picks. It's made him the Democrat in a safe seat with the lowest party unity score, at 79 percent, last year. (At the same time, Murphy voted with fellow Democrats on each of the 42 Senate policy votes that split the parties in 2019.)

"Murphy believes the Senate should give deference to the president's nominees unless the candidate is clearly unqualified or their views are outside of the conservative mainstream. Generally, he does not vote against Trump nominees because of policy differences," says his spokeswoman, Jamie Geller.

Most Democratic senators in safe seats are going the other direction. And with several senators running for the party's 2020 presidential nomination, it seemed last year there was a competition of sorts to offer Trump the least support, prompting many "no" votes on his nominees and increasing the number of partisan votes on nominees. Six of the seven senators seeking the Democratic presidential nomination — Cory Booker of New Jersey, Kamala Harris of California, Amy Klobuchar of Minnesota, Kirsten Gillibrand of New York, Bernie Sanders of Vermont and Elizabeth Warren of Massachusetts — voted with the Democrats on partisan votes 100 percent of the time in 2019. Colorado's Michael Bennet was at 94.6 percent.

Trump's combative approach to politics and the fact that he won in 2016 without a popular majority has contributed. The Democratic "resistance" calls out sena-

Majority rule

The Senate operated like the House, taking mostly votes that require only a majority. Those votes, many on nominees, resulted in GOP wins.

Frequency of party unity votes:

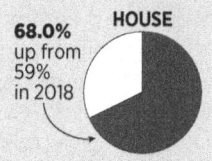

HOUSE

68.0% up from 59% in 2018

476 out of 700

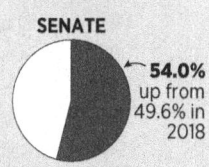

SENATE

54.0% up from 49.6% in 2018

231 out of 428

AVERAGE FOR BOTH CHAMBERS:

62.0%

How often the majority won:

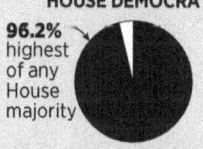

HOUSE DEMOCRATS

96.2% highest of any House majority

458 out of 476

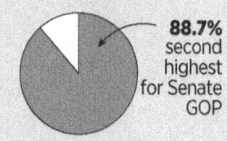

SENATE REPUBLICANS

88.7% second highest for Senate GOP

205 out of 231

AVERAGE FOR BOTH CHAMBERS:

93.8%

Average chamber party unity scores:

HOUSE

R 89% Near decade average

D 95% Highest on record

SENATE

R 94% Second-highest since 2003

D 84% Lowest since 2004

tors who vote for Trump nominees, as it did Warren when she backed Housing and Urban Development Secretary Ben Carson in a committee vote (before voting "no" on the Senate floor), or Rhode Island's Sheldon Whitehouse when he backed Mike Pompeo for CIA director.

And Democrats recall with anger McConnell's decision in 2016 to refuse a vote on Barack Obama's Supreme Court pick, Merrick Garland.

The trend is foreboding. At some point, there will be a new president who takes office with a Senate controlled by the opposition. Will that president be able to name a Cabinet, or seat a Supreme Court justice?

Consider how many Democrats voted for some of Trump's 2019 Cabinet picks. Attorney General William Barr and Interior Secretary David Bernhardt got three Democratic votes, while Labor Secretary Eugene Scalia got one. Three Democrats voted for Trump's 2017 Supreme Court pick, Neil M. Gorsuch. Just one, Joe Manchin III of West Virginia, voted for Brett M. Kavanaugh in 2018.

"It's legitimate to ask the question," says Richard Arenberg, a former aide to then-Senate Majority Leader George Mitchell of Maine who's now a senior fellow at Brown University. The confirmation process "is getting worse and worse."

In addition to transforming the judiciary, it's transformed the way the Senate operates.

For a majority leader concerned with using Senate floor time productively, policy votes stood more of a chance before the nuclear option. Getting judges confirmed was difficult since he had to work with the minority party and the president to settle on nominees who could get 60 votes. A bipartisan bill could compete for his attention.

But now, confirming nominees is easy, while votes on legislation are harder than ever, requiring compromise with minority party senators and a House controlled by the Democrats. They're also politically dangerous, opening up vulnerable senators to uncomfortable votes on amendments.

"The only legislation he is going to call up is the legislation he has to call up," says Paone. ■

Leading Scorers: Party Unity

Support shows those who, in 2019, voted most often with a majority of their party against a majority of the other party.
Opposition shows those who voted most often against their party's majority. Absences do not count. Members with identical scores are listed alphabetically.

SENATE

SUPPORT

Democrats		Republicans	
Gillibrand, Kirsten	100.0%	Barrasso, John	100.0%
Hirono, Mazie K.	100.0	Fischer, Deb	100.0
Klobuchar, Amy	100.0	Inhofe, James M.	100.0
Murray, Patty	100.0	Lankford, James	100.0
Smith, Tina	100.0	Risch, Jim	100.0
Warren, Elizabeth	100.0	Braun, Mike	99.6
Schumer, Charles E.	99.6	Crapo, Michael D.	99.6
Udall, Tom	99.6	Johnson, Ron	99.6
Markey, Edward J.	99.5	Cassidy, Bill	99.5
Blumenthal, Richard	99.1	Cruz, Ted	99.5
Schatz, Brian	99.1	9 Senators	99.1
Stabenow, Debbie	99.1		
Baldwin, Tammy	98.3		
Van Hollen, Chris	98.3		

OPPOSITION

Democrats		Republicans	
Manchin, Joe III	49.8%	Collins, Susan	21.6%
Sinema, Kyrsten	47.4	Paul, Rand	12.3
Jones, Doug	43.2	Murkowski, Lisa	10.1
Murphy, Christopher S.	21.3	Moran, Jerry	9.3
Coons, Chris	16.7	Lee, Mike	7.9
Carper, Thomas R.	16.5	Young, Todd	6.2
Shaheen, Jeanne	16.0	Alexander, Lamar	5.1
Hassan, Maggie	13.9	Graham, Lindsey	4.9
Warner, Mark	10.9	Daines, Steve	4.3
Tester, Jon	10.4	McConnell, Mitch	4.3
Kaine, Tim	10.3	Portman, Rob	4.3
Feinstein, Dianne	9.1	Gardner, Cory	3.9
Leahy, Patrick J.	8.7	Blunt, Roy	3.5
Cardin, Benjamin L.	8.7	Roberts, Pat	3.3
Rosen, Jacky	8.3	McSally, Martha	3.1

HOUSE

SUPPORT

Democrats		Republicans	
Barragan, Nanette	100.0%	Bishop, Dan	100.0%
Davis, Danny K.	100.0	Lamborn, Doug	99.6
Davis, Susan A.	100.0	Ratcliffe, John	99.5
Engel, Eliot L.	100.0	Allen, Rick W.	99.4
Eshoo, Anna G.	100.0	Byrne, Bradley	99.3
Jackson Lee, Sheila	100.0	Hice, Jody B.	99.3
Kennedy, Joseph P. III	100.0	Wright, Ron	99.2
Lewis, John	100.0	Duncan, Jeff	99.1
Neal, Richard E.	100.0	Kelly, Trent	99.1
Pingree, Chellie	100.0	Loudermilk, Barry	99.1
Roybal-Allard, Lucille	100.0	Walker, Mark	99.1
Serrano, Jose E.	100.0	Weber, Randy	99.1
Smith, Adam	100.0	Hern, Kevin	98.9
Trahan, Lori	100.0	Jordan, Jim	98.9
Welch, Peter	100.0	Norman, Ralph	98.9
		Palmer, Gary	98.9

OPPOSITION

Democrats		Republicans	
Peterson, Collin C.	21.4%	Fitzpatrick, Brian	46.2%
McAdams, Ben	18.7	Smith, Christopher H.	36.4
Van Drew, Jeff*	18.3	Katko, John	35.7
Brindisi, Anthony	15.4	Stefanik, Elise	32.6
Cunningham, Joe	15.2	Upton, Fred	28.1
Golden, Jared	13.1	King, Peter T.	27.7
Gottheimer, Josh	12.4	Reed, Tom	24.1
Spanberger, Abigail	10.8	Hurd, Will	23.5
Horn, Kendra	10.3	Rooney, Francis	23.0
Axne, Cindy	9.2	Fortenberry, Jeff	21.9
Cuellar, Henry	9.0	Hollingsworth, Trey	20.9
Torres Small, Xochitl	8.2	Stauber, Pete	19.4
Luria, Elaine	8.2	Walden, Greg	19.5
Slotkin, Elissa	8.0	Herrera Beutler, Jaime	19.1
Craig, Angie	8.0	Davis, Rodney	19.0

*Van Drew switched parties in December, becoming a Republican.

Pelosi Proves Her Mettle

She won over skeptics in her caucus and kept ideologically diverse Democrats voting in lockstep

It's easy to forget that when Democrats won the House majority in 2018, there was some question about whether Nancy Pelosi would return as speaker.

A group of veteran Democrats said it was time for generational change and attempted to recruit a challenger. Some of the incoming freshmen, many who'd won seats in conservative or moderate districts, said they would not vote for her.

The challenge ended up short-lived. Pelosi coasted to victory. Ten freshmen and five other Democrats ultimately opposed her for speaker, while 220 reelected her.

But questions remained, mainly: Could this San Francisco liberal approaching her 80th birthday hold together a caucus that now included 31 Democrats representing districts Donald Trump had won in his 2016 presidential campaign?

The 700 roll-call votes the House took in 2019 demonstrate that she did, conclusively.

House Democrats — on average — held with the party on votes that split a majority of Democrats from a majority of Republicans, party unity votes, 95 percent of the time, higher than at any time since CQ Roll Call began studying partisan voting in 1956.

This was a testament to Pelosi's skills as a party manager. Marc Sandalow, a former San Francisco Chronicle reporter who's written a Pelosi biography, explains: "Pelosi is among the most liberal members and represents a liberal district, but her leadership style is pragmatic. She understands what it takes to build a majority."

Democrats' extraordinary unity in 2019 is also the continuation of a trend in which representatives, and senators, willing to cross party lines are fewer, and the parties more clearly sorted.

It's also a statement on how electoral politics has changed. In an era when congressional races reflect the national partisan divide, fewer lawmakers in competitive states and districts are even attempting to distinguish themselves as moderates. That's a testament to their personal beliefs, to be sure, and the view that campaigns are won by energizing base voters, not by winning independent ones. It's also a calculation that partisan voting will spur campaign contributions from activist partisans across the country. To some representatives in competitive seats, it's more important to have a big campaign war chest that enables an election-year advertising blitz than a voting record that reflects a community's views.

This takes nothing away from Pelosi. House Democrats' record unity score exceeded their previous mark of 93 percent, set in 2017 at a time when the caucus was 40 members smaller and more ideologically progressive, made up mainly of liberal stalwarts in safe districts.

Pelosi lost one of her Trump-district Democrats, Jeff Van Drew of New Jersey, in January. Van Drew opposed the impeachment of Trump and switched parties. But on average the remaining 30 Democrats in Trump districts voted with their fellow partisans on 92.6 percent of unity votes last year, just 2.4 percentage points off the party average.

Take a narrower slice, the 26 Democrats in Trump districts considered endangered in this year's election by CQ Roll Call elections analyst Nathan L. Gonzales. On average, they voted with the party 92.2 percent of the time on unity votes.

And the 25 members of the Blue Dog Coalition, self-described moderates, voted with the party on average 92 percent of the time as well. Stephanie Murphy, the second term Democrat from an Orlando, Fla.-area district who is co-chairwoman of the coalition, says it's because Pelosi took moderates' views into account. She worked "with the Blue Dog Coalition to ensure that as legislation moves through committee and to the floor we have been able to make adjustments to make sure members can vote their conscience and their districts."

Murphy cites the inclusion of rules requiring the House to pay for new spending in the year's rules package, and with changes to the way the Dem-

ocrats' signature campaign finance bill (HR 1) was funded.

At the same time, Murphy acknowledges that Democrats are more united on hot-button issues from gun control to gay rights than they have been ever before. "It is because the country has moved in a more progressive way on those issues," she says.

Still, the high level of unity among moderate factions in the Democratic caucus masked differing approaches to casting ballots on the part of some individuals. It makes intuitive sense for a Democratic representative in a district that favored Trump in 2016 by 31 percentage points — Collin C. Peterson in rural western Minnesota — to buck his party. Peterson, a Blue Dog, had his caucus's lowest unity score at 79 percent.

But then there was Matt Cartwright, in a Scranton, Pa.-based district that went for Trump by 9.3 percentage points, making it the eighth-most Trump-friendly of the 30 Trump districts held by Democrats. Cartwright nonetheless voted with his fellow Democrats 99 percent of the time.

He's also a member of the Congressional Progressive Caucus and has gone on Fox News to defend Pelosi, telling its conservative viewers last year that "She doesn't stifle divergent opinions in the Democratic caucus and I think people honor that about her."

Gonzales makes the case that Democrats like Cartwright are thinking about their fundraising, which theoretically grows when they stand with the party because wealthy Democrats from inside and outside their districts come to their defense. Voting with fellow Democrats also keeps the Democratic base motivated to turn out, crucial to vulner-

able representatives' prospects.

Moderates also face pressure from Pelosi to stick with the party. Last February, after 26 in the caucus (not including Cartwright) voted with Republicans on an amendment requiring that immigration authorities be notified if an unauthorized immigrant tries to buy a gun, Pelosi called a closed-door meeting and reportedly told them to get on board: "We are either a team or we're not, and we have to make that decision," she said, according to a Washington Post report.

There is a pattern to the way endangered Democrats are voting, with those in greater peril voting more often with Republicans than those in less danger. Looking at the 30 Trump-district Democrats based on Trump's margin of victory in 2016 indicates that those in the most Trump-friendly districts, which favored the president

Two Freshman Democrats Who Broke With the Party Explain

What makes for an outlier when the average Democratic representative votes with his party on 95 percent of partisan votes?

About 40-50 votes. That's about how many times the Democrats most willing to break with the party, like Anthony Brindisi of upstate New York or Ben McAdams of Salt Lake City, parted with their colleagues.

Brindisi and McAdams have a lot in common. Brindisi voted with fellow Democrats 85 percent of the time, while McAdams voted with them 82 percent of the time when a vote split a majority of Democrats from a majority of Republicans. That made them the second- and fourth-most-likely Democrats to break with the party in 2019, behind longtime outlier Collin C. Peterson and freshman Jeff Van Drew.

Van Drew, of New Jersey, left the party in January. Peterson, through 15 terms, has a long established strategy aimed at keeping his rural Minnesota constituents satisfied with his representation. It's meant voting fairly often with Republicans.

Brindisi and McAdams, two freshmen facing tough reelection campaigns, are seeking that same balance. Brindisi won his seat over Republican Claudia Tenney by 1.8 percentage points, while Donald Trump won the district in 2016 by a whopping 15.5. Peterson's district is the only one held by a Democrat that went for Trump by a greater margin.

McAdams beat Republican Mia Love by the same 1.8 point margin, after Trump won the district in 2016 by 6.7 points. And McAdams has reason to be as worried about his reelection prospects as Brindisi. Utah, normally among the most Republican states in the country, was unusually divided on Trump. In 2012, by contrast, Mitt Romney won the presidential vote in McAdams' district by 37 points over Barack Obama. In 2008, John McCain won it by 15.

Both Brindisi and McAdams downplay their party ties. "I want to be an independent voice for my constituents," says McAdams. "I didn't come to Washington to fight for any party's agenda, but what's right for my state."

Explains Brindisi: "I will vote the way I think is in the best interest of my district. I'm not concerned with party labels."

Both were among the 26 Democrats to join Republicans last February in amending a bill (HR 8) expanding background checks for gun sales to require the FBI to inform the Homeland Security Department when an unauthorized immigrant attempts to buy a gun.

The vote prompted threats from progressives that they would seek primary challengers to the rebellious Democrats and a scolding about working together from Speaker Nancy Pelosi.

But both lawmakers stand by their vote, as they do other acts of modest rebellion. For instance, both defend their votes for a Republican amendment to a bill (HR 9) aimed at requiring Trump to comply with the Paris climate agreement that would have delayed adherence until after Trump certifies that the agreement won't result in jobs leaving the United States for China.

Brindisi says struggling factory workers in his district care about ensuring that the burden of combating climate change is shared across the globe, while McAdams says he takes each vote as it comes. "I don't think the Democrats have a monopoly on good ideas," he says.

Neither Brindisi nor McAdams voted for Pelosi for speaker. Brindisi favored former Vice President Joe Biden, while McAdams cast his ballot for Blue Dog Coalition Co-Chairwoman Stephanie Murphy, the Florida Democrat.

But after more than a year of watching Pelosi lead the Democrats, Brindisi is charitable. Party moderates, he says, "have had the ear of leadership," adding that "the legislation that has come out of the House over the last year has taken into account the needs of the more progressive wing, but also moderate members who helped deliver the majority."

McAdams is more circumspect: "I think it's been a divisive year, but also a year in which we've been able to get some good stuff done. It's mixed."

by 10 percentage points or more over Democrat Hillary Clinton, are among the most independent-minded Democrats in the House. The six in those districts — Peterson; Anthony Brindisi in upstate New York; Kendra Horn in Oklahoma City; Joe Cunningham in Charleston, S.C.; Jared Golden in rural Maine; and Xochitl Torres Small in rural southern New Mexico — voted with the party, on average, 86 percent of the time.

Peterson, who is the Agriculture Committee chairman, is in his 15th term and has a history of winning in a conservative district, had the lowest score in the group, while freshman Torres Small, whose district has had a Republican representative for all but three of the past 39 years, had the highest at 92 percent.

On the other side, those seven Democrats in districts Trump won narrowly were about as loyal to the party as the average Democrat, posting an average unity score of 95 percent. Angie Craig, a freshman representing suburbs south of Minneapolis, had the lowest score at 92 percent, while Chris Pappas, another freshman in an eastern New Hampshire district that includes the state's largest city, Manchester, had the highest score at 98 percent.

The six Democrats in districts that went for Trump by between 3 and 5 percentage points, posted an average unity score of 94.5 percent, just slightly lower than those in the districts that favored Trump more narrowly. And the seven Trump district Democrats representing places that favored Trump by between 5 and 10 percentage points had an average unity score of 92.6 percent.

However, there does not seem to be a connection between party loyalty and fundraising. Some of the most loyal endangered Democrats, such as Pappas, are lagging in fundraising. He'd raised just $854,100 for his reelection campaign as of last month. Meanwhile, Cunningham, who won a surprise victory in his conservative district, had raised $1.8 million despite one of the party's lowest unity scores, at 85 percent.

Perhaps the sample size and other factors that lead to strong fundraising, primarily the effort put in by the representative, overwhelm the importance of voting decisions.

A review of all the incumbent representatives seeking reelection that Gonzales considers endangered — 37 Democrats, 23 Republicans and one independent — finds no connection between party loyalty and fundraising. Those 21 with unity scores of 95 percent or higher had raised $1.3 million on average, while the 11 with scores below 85 percent had raised $1.2 million on average.

If the February chastising over gun control sent a message to party moderates, there were spats between Pelosi and her party's left flank too. In June, for example, the four progressives who call themselves "the squad" — Alexandria Ocasio-Cortez of New York, Ilhan Omar of Minnesota, Ayanna S. Pressley of Massachusetts and Rashida Tlaib of Michigan — voted "no" on a bill to help pay for housing and food for the flood of migrants at the southern border. They were protesting Trump's policy of separating immigrant families and his decision to use defense funding to build border fencing in defiance of Congress.

The bill (PL 116-26) passed at Pelosi's urging and she let loose to The New York Times' Maureen Dowd: "They're four people and that's how many votes they got."

In actuality, after the squad made its stand alone on a preliminary vote, 91 other Democrats joined them in voting against the funding. But it did not forebode any larger split between Pelosi and the progressives.

Members of the Progressive Caucus, on average, stuck with the party on almost every partisan vote, 99 percent, and members of the squad were nearly as loyal, at 97.5 percent.

"We have, across the caucus, a lot more in common than we don't," says Rep. Mark Pocan of Madison, Wis., the co-chairman of the Progressive Caucus. "Pelosi has been pretty masterful in listening to all elements of the caucus and making sure that everyone has felt heard."

Pocan also says Trump has driven Democrats together. It's a point on which Sandalow, the Pelosi biographer, agrees: "It's easier to keep the caucus together when you have Trump to rally against."

All this translated into a remarkably successful year for Pelosi, if success is winning passage of the bills considered on the House floor. Of 476 votes that split the parties, Democrats got their way on 458 of them, the highest victory rate for either party since CQ Roll Call started tracking it in 1960.

Her success, though, was more in messaging than in getting bills signed into law. The Democrats passed bills to raise the minimum wage, to overhaul campaign finance rules and to expand gun control regulations, but all foundered in the Senate. Pelosi's intent was not to pass laws, but to send a message to voters. The 105 new laws of 2019 were among the fewest of any Congress in modern times.

Still, even those who sought to oust her are now admitting she proved her mettle.

"She kept the party together through an incredibly contentious and difficult time," one of her longtime critics, Massachusetts Democrat Seth Moulton, told NPR in December. ∎

History: Party Unity

The table below on the left shows how frequently a majority of Democrats aligned against a majority of Republicans. The average scores in the other columns for each chamber are computed including absences.

Tallying party unity votes

In the House in 2019, the two parties aligned against each other on 476 of 700 roll call votes, or 68 percent of the time — up 9.4 percentage points from 2018. In the Senate, the parties opposed each other on 231 of 428 roll calls, or 54 percent of the time. That's up from last year's 49.6 percent. A list of roll-call votes that pitted majorities of the two parties against each other is available upon request from CQ Roll Call.

Calculations of average scores by chamber and party are based on all eligible "yea" or "nay" votes, whether or not all members participated. Under this methodology, average support and opposition scores are reduced when members do not vote. Party and chamber averages are not strictly comparable to individual member scores. (Complete member scores, pp. 47-49)

Also, in the member score tables, Sens. Angus King, I-Maine, and Bernie Sanders, I-Vt., were treated as if they were Democrats when calculating their support and opposition scores. They do not, however, qualify to be listed among the party's leaders in any category. Independent Rep. Justin Amash of Michigan was treated as a Republican for votes until he left the party in July. After, his votes are not grouped with either party's.

	Frequency of Unity Votes		House Average Scores		Senate Average Scores	
YEAR	HOUSE	SENATE	DEMOCRATS	REPUBLICANS	DEMOCRATS	REPUBLICANS
2019	68%	54%	95%	89%	84%	94%
2018	58.6	49.6	89	91	87	92
2017	76.0	68.9	93	92	92	97
2016	73.4	46.0	91	93	91	83
2015	75.1	69.3	92	92	91	89
2014	72.6	66.7	90	91	93	84
2013	68.6	69.8	88	92	94	86
2012	72.8	59.8	87	90	92	80
2011	75.8	51.1	87	91	92	86
2010	40.0	78.6	89	88	91	89
2009	50.9	72.0	91	87	91	85
2008	53.3	51.6	92	87	87	83
2007	62.0	60.2	92	85	87	81
2006	54.5	57.3	86	88	86	86
2005	49.0	62.6	88	90	88	88
2004	47.0	52.3	86	88	83	90
2003	51.7	66.7	87	91	85	94
2002	43.3	45.5	86	90	83	84
2001	40.2	55.3	83	91	89	88
2000	43.2	48.7	82	88	88	89
1999	47.3	62.8	83	86	89	88
1998	55.5	55.7	82	86	87	86
1997	50.4	50.3	82	88	85	87
1996	56.4	62.4	80	87	84	89
1995	73.2	68.8	80	91	81	89
1994	61.8	51.7	83	84	84	79
1993	65.5	67.1	85	84	85	84
1992	64.5	53.0	79	79	77	79
1991	55.1	49.3	81	77	80	81
1990	49.1	54.3	81	74	80	75
1989	56.3	35.3	81	72	78	78
1988	47.0	42.5	80	74	78	68
1987	63.7	40.7	81	74	81	75
1986	56.5	52.3	79	70	72	76
1985	61.0	49.6	80	75	75	76
1984	47.1	40.0	74	71	68	78
1983	55.6	43.7	76	74	71	74
1982	36.4	43.4	72	69	72	76
1981	37.4	47.8	69	74	71	81
1980	37.6	45.8	69	71	64	65
1979	47.3	46.7	69	73	68	66
1978	33.2	45.2	63	69	66	59
1977	42.2	42.4	68	71	63	66
1976	35.9	37.2	66	67	62	61
1975	48.4	47.8	69	72	68	64
1974	29.4	44.3	62	63	63	59
1973	41.8	39.9	68	68	69	64
1972	27.1	36.5	58	66	57	61
1971	37.8	41.6	61	67	64	63
1970	27.1	35.2	58	60	55	56
1969	31.1	36.3	61	62	63	63
1968	35.2	32.0	59	64	51	60
1967	36.3	34.6	67	74	61	60
1966	41.5	50.2	62	68	57	63
1965	52.2	41.9	70	71	63	68
1964	54.9	35.7	69	71	61	65
1963	48.7	47.2	73	74	66	67
1962	46.0	41.1	70	70	65	64
1961	50.0	62.3	72	73	69	68
1960	52.7	36.7	65	70	60	64
1959	55.2	47.9	79	77	67	72
1958	39.8	43.5	66	65	71	64
1957	59.0	35.5	70	67	66	69
1956	43.8	53.1	70	70	71	72

Background: Party Unity

Roll-call votes used for the party unity study are those on which a majority of Democrats opposed a majority of Republicans. Support indicates the percentage of time members voted in agreement with their party on such party unity votes. The tables below also show the number of party unity votes on which each party was victorious and the number of instances in which either party voted unanimously.

AVERAGE PARTY UNITY SCORE BY CHAMBER

| | | SUPPORT | |
		2018	2019
HOUSE	Democrats	89%	95%
	Republicans	91	89
SENATE	Democrats	87	84
	Republicans	92	94
CONGRESS	Democrats	89	93
	Republicans	91	90

Average scores for chamber and party are calculated based on all party unity votes for which members were eligible. A member's failure to vote lowers the score for the group.

VICTORIES IN PARTY UNITY VOTES

| | HOUSE | | SENATE | | CONGRESS | |
YEAR	Democrats	Republicans	Democrats	Republicans	Democrats	Republicans
2019	458 votes	18	26	205	484	223
2018	23	269	28	108	51	337
2017	51	488	23	201	74	689
2016	40	416	53	22	93	438
2015	68	460	93	142	161	602
2014	55	353	224	20	279	373
2013	50	389	171	32	221	421
2012	67	411	103	47	170	458
2011	82	634	87	33	169	667
2010	236	28	196	39	432	67
2009	473	29	264	22	737	51
2008	342	25	60	51	402	76
2007	658	72	179	87	837	159
2006	59	236	53	107	112	343
2005	50	278	47	182	97	460
2004	42	213	28	85	70	298
2003	39	310	56	250	95	560
2002	39	170	42	73	81	243
2001	27	177	95	115	122	292
2000	77	182	31	114	108	296
1999	58	177	77	211	135	388
1998	80	216	61	114	141	330
1997	58	261	46	104	104	365

UNANIMOUS VOTING ON UNITY VOTES

| | HOUSE | | SENATE | | CONGRESS | |
YEAR	Democrats	Republicans	Democrats	Republicans	Democrats	Republicans
2019	242 votes	162	106	158	348	320
2018	117	91	50	92	167	183
2017	242	176	125	160	367	336
2016	109	118	24	11	133	129
2015	174	177	96	77	270	254
2014	92	159	180	76	272	235
2013	97	152	106	62	203	214
2012	40	99	60	19	100	118
2011	76	209	55	31	131	240
2010	10	91	67	106	77	197
2009	29	144	79	74	108	218
2008	66	96	30	19	96	115
2007	170	177	102	35	272	212
2006	70	62	34	30	104	92
2005	82	91	69	59	151	150
2004	70	77	3	31	73	108
2003	94	109	32	130	126	239
2002	37	54	12	23	49	77
2001	1	66	37	55	38	121
2000	1	67	52	19	53	86
1999	11	59	100	63	111	122
1998	8	42	46	33	54	75
1997	11	63	35	38	46	101

Trump Fenced In

Democrats' return to the majority brought partisan opposition to the president to an all-time high

Guide to the Vote Studies

CQ Roll Call has analyzed voting patterns of members of Congress since 1945. It has conducted the three current studies — presidential support, party unity and voting participation — in a consistent manner since the 1950s.

Selecting votes CQ Roll Call bases its vote studies on all floor votes for which senators and representatives had the opportunity to vote "yea" or "nay." In 2019, there were 700 such roll-call votes in the House and 428 in the Senate. The House total excludes one quorum call in 2019.

The House total counts all votes on procedural matters, including votes to approve the journal.

The presidential support and party unity studies are based on a set of votes selected according to the criteria detailed on pages 30 and 43.

Individual scores Member scores are based only on the votes each actually cast. This makes individual support and opposition scores total 100 percent. The same method is used to identify the leading scorers on pages 27 and 38.

Overall scores To be consistent with previous years, calculations of average scores by chamber and party are based on all eligible votes, whether or not all members cast a "yea" or "nay." The lack of participation by lawmakers in a roll-call vote reduces chamber and party average support and opposition scores.

Rounding Scores In the tables that follow, scores are rounded to the nearest percentage point. Scores for the presidential and party support leaders are reported to one decimal point in order to rank them more precisely.

D onald Trump was never very good at moving his legislative agenda through Congress but last year he hit a brick wall with Democrats back in control of the House.

In CQ Roll Call's vote studies analysis for 2019, Trump set a record for futility: Among votes the president took a position on, he prevailed on only five. That mark, 8 percent of 62 votes, falls below the previous low of 13 percent set in 2016, the last year of Barack Obama's presidency.

What happened in 2019 is a mirror image of 2011, when President Barack Obama faced a Republican-led House, says Frances Lee, a congressional scholar at Princeton University. "Once Obama lost control of the House of Representatives, his success with Congress became rather similar" to Trump's, she says. Trump's overall success rate plummeted 20 percentage points; Obama's 28 points.

The president's most high-profile accomplishment last year, approval of the U.S.-Mexico-Canada trade pact (PL 116-113), came in December. The others were on the two big spending bills (PL 116-94; PL 116-93) and the annual defense policy bill (PL 116-92), all of which passed as part of a year-end rush. As an example of how thin Trump's success rate was, a failed veto override of his declaration of a national emergency along the southern border (H J Res 46) was scored a "win" only because the House needed a two-thirds majority vote, which it failed to achieve.

Overall, House Democrats opposed Trump on 93 percent of votes, another all-time record.

The relationship between the House and the president doesn't promise to improve this year either, following an impeachment process that left everyone embittered, a president hell-bent on revenge, an unsettled presidential election and increasing polarization.

"As long as we've got these rigid red-state versus blue-state voting patterns where there's not split-ticket voting, that puts presidents at a disadvantage in winning cross-party support in Congress," says Lee.

Even when Trump and Democrats came together, it wasn't for long. In January, when Trump held a signing ceremony at the White House for the USMCA, not a single Democrat attended. Speaker Nancy Pelosi said no Democrats were invited, but a White House spokesman denied that, saying some were but chose not to attend. At the ceremony, Trump took complete credit for the deal, despite overwhelming Democratic margins in the House and Senate that were needed to get it across the finish line.

The ceremony did nothing to ease the bitterness. Rep. Stephanie Murphy, a Florida Democrat, says "it was not ideal to exclude just one party from the signing ceremony." Rep. Jimmy Gomez of California, a Democrat who was deeply involved in the trade negotiations, told Politico: "It says a lot that this event is

without Democrats because he always wanted it for political purposes. I personally don't think he ever cared about the policy."

Trump has repeatedly railed against the party as the "Do Nothing Democrats," but he has largely ceded the agenda to Republicans in Congress by neglecting to offer even an outline of goals.

That failure is borne out in the data. Trump's ability to persuade Democrats, including those in competitive districts, to vote his way was minimal. In all, the 31 Democrats — including New Jersey's Jeff Van Drew, who became a Republican in January — representing districts Trump won in 2016 voted with Trump just 7 percent of the time last year compared to the 5 percent by House Democrats as a whole, according to an analysis by CQ Roll Call.

But this cuts both ways. Moderate Democrats love to say they're willing to work with the president on issues, but on many votes where the president has taken a position, Democrats in those groups barely outpaced the caucus as a whole. House members of the moderate Blue Dog Coalition supported the president on 10 percent of votes in 2019; Democratic members of the bipartisan Problem Solvers Caucus went with

What happened in 2019 is a mirror image of 2011, when Obama faced a Republican-led House.

Trump on only 5 percent of House votes.

Granted, in the current environment the opposing party has little incentive to work with the White House, says Lee, but "that was true under Obama as well."

Consider Tom O'Halleran, a two-term Democrat from Arizona, and a member of the Blue Dogs. He's been a target for Republicans since he flipped the district in 2016. Like other moderate Democrats, he stresses his desire to work with Republicans on big issues, pointing to bipartisan accomplishments like the USMCA. He also sits on the Energy and Commerce Committee and is quick to note that dozens of bills have been passed out of that committee with bipartisan support.

"This idea that we aren't working together is more of a creation of people saying we're not working versus the

reality of the fact that bills are heading over [to the Senate]," he says.

And yet O'Halleran last year sided with the president on only three votes. Murphy, who is a co-chair of the Blue Dogs and represents a swing district, likewise only voted with the president three times. She argued in an interview that there simply weren't as many opportunities to work with Trump as in the past.

"The president hasn't held consistent stances on policy issues," she says.

She has a point. One of the biggest issues facing Congress today, and one it can't agree on, is guns. Time and again, following mass shootings, Trump talks about doing something about it, but eventually backs down.

Murphy, who decided to run for Congress in 2016 following the nightclub shooting in Orlando that left 49 dead, co-sponsored and voted for multiple gun-control bills in 2019, including one that would close the so-called gun show loophole (HR 8) and extend wait times for those buying guns (HR 1112). Trump opposed both, arguing that they would "impose burdensome requirements" and delays. She also co-sponsored a bill (HR 1236) that would take guns from those deemed a threat risk and another (HR 1296) that would reinstitute the ban

Trump eschews positions on policy votes

President Donald Trump took a position on 22 percent of the votes recorded in Congress last year, and many of those were confirmation votes on his nominees. On other Senate votes, Trump took a position 10.9 percent of the time. Of those 29 votes, he won 18 and lost 11. Trump took positions on only 62 of 700 House votes, and got his way five times.

Percentage of Presidential Support Votes, for Congress as a whole

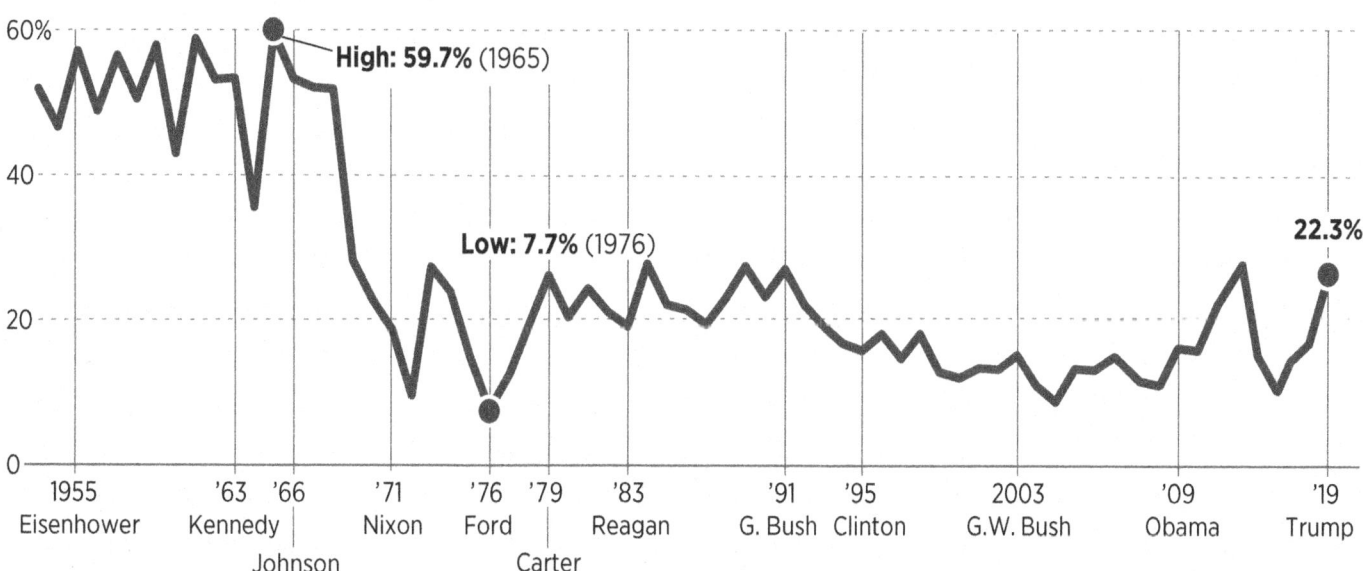

on assault weapons. Democrats eventually shelved the latter bill over concerns from moderates.

It's unlikely any of those measures will become law in the near-term; Senate Majority Leader Mitch McConnell has said he wouldn't consider any gun bill unless he was assured of Trump's support.

While there wasn't a significant difference between vulnerable Democrats and the party overall when it came to voting with Trump, the vote studies data show that those in Trump districts, in general, supported the president more than the rest of the party. Of the top 14 Democrats who backed the president's positions in 2019, six are in Trump districts.

Surprisingly, one of the most liberal members of the House, freshman Alexandria Ocasio-Cortez of New York, agreed with the president on nine votes, or 14.5 percent of the time, ranking her secon overall, tied with Utah's Ben McAdams. Eight of those votes were on bills Trump opposed, including the reauthorization of the Export-Import Bank (HR 4863), various spending bills, and a measure that would raise the cap for the state and local tax deduction (HR 5377).

Ocasio-Cortez' office did not respond to requests for comment. Another member of the self-described "Squad" of liberal women of color, Rashida Tlaib of Michigan, agreed with the president 8.1 percent of the time.

Overall, Democrats opposed Trump on 93 percent of votes, another all-time record.

Collin C. Peterson of Minnesota, who represents a district Trump won by 31 points, was the runaway winner among Democrats who backed the president. He joined with Trump on more than a quarter of votes.

Van Drew, by contrast, backed Trump on just 13 percent of votes.

House Republicans

A large swath of members who had a history of crossing the president, like Mark Sanford of South Carolina and Raul R. Labrador of Idaho, left Congress after 2018. As a result, House Republicans wound up backing the president in 2019 by a wider margin than they had the year before, when they controlled the chamber. In all, Republicans voted with Trump 91 percent of the time, up 2 points from 2018. They opposed him just 6 percent of the time.

That figure comes despite only seven Republican lawmakers posting a perfect record of joining Trump on votes, down from a whopping 72 who did so in 2018.

And yet there were still Republicans who went their own way on high-profile votes.

One of those is Elise Stefanik. Ever

since winning her upstate New York seat in 2014, the 35-year-old has cut a moderate path, one she is proud to tout, and 2019 was no different. On votes that directly confronted Trump, the Republican sided with Democrats, including terminating Trump's declaration of a national emergency on the southern border (S J Res 54) and reinstituting sanctions on Russian companies that the administration had lifted (H J Res 30). In an interview, she said neither of these was a tough vote ("I have one of the most hawkish records when it comes to combating Russian aggression," she says). She wasn't at all concerned about backlash from the president.

In all, she opposed Trump on 39 percent of votes on which he took a position in 2019. That ranks her behind only Brian Fitzpatrick of Pennsylvania, Christopher H. Smith of New Jersey and John Katko of New York. Ssince Trump became president, Stefanik has opposed him 24 percent of the time.

And yet, despite that maverick streak, Stefanik has become a darling of the right. During the impeachment inquiry in the House, she offered her full-throated defense of Trump, arguing during investigative hearings that Ukraine eventually got its aid and no investigation was announced into Joe Biden. She continues to say that Trump did nothing wrong in the Ukraine matter. "A new Republican star is born," Trump tweeted in November while sharing a post that included a video of Stefanik questioning former ambassador Marie

Support for Trump trends down

Democratic control of the House dragged down Trump's level of support from representatives and senators in 2019, but his overall support score remained high because he mostly took positions on nominees, and the Senate confirmed all 161 of them.

The year highlighted is president's third year in office

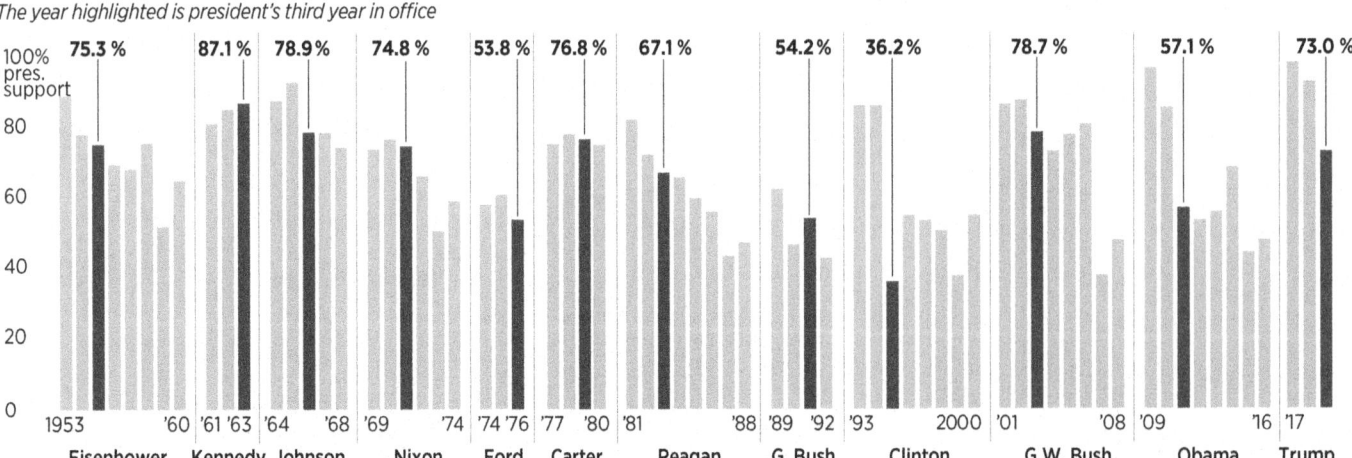

Leading Scorers: Presidential Support

Support shows those who, in 2019, voted most often for President Donald Trump's position when it was clearly known.
Opposition shows those who voted most often against his position. Absences do not count. Members with identical scores are listed alphabetically.

SENATE

SUPPORT

Democrats/Independents		Republicans	
Manchin, Joe III	71.1%	Perdue, David	99.4%
Sinema, Kyrsten	68.5	McConnell, Mitch	98.9
Jones, Doug	66.5	Hyde-Smith, Cindy	98.9
Murphy, Christopher S.	54.5	Roberts, Pat	98.8
King, Angus	51.6	Burr, Richard M.	98.8
Coons, Chris	50.6	Isakson, Johnny	98.4
Shaheen, Jeanne	50.3	Cornyn, John	98.4
Carper, Thomas R.	48.7	Hoeven, John	97.9
Hassan, Maggie	48.1	Thune, John	97.9
Warner, Mark	47.0	Cramer, Kevin	97.9
Tester, Jon	46.6	McSally, Martha	97.9
Kaine, Tim	46.3	Scott, Rick	97.9
Feinstein, Dianne	45.5	Crapo, Michael D.	97.9
Cardin, Benjamin L.	45.2	Capito, Shelley Moore	97.8
Leahy, Patrick J.	44.7	Tillis, Thom	97.8

OPPOSITION

Democrats/Independents		Republicans	
Sanders, Bernie	94.1%	Collins, Susan	14.7%
Warren, Elizabeth	93.4	Paul, Rand	13.5
Booker, Cory	89.8	Lee, Mike	12.8
Klobuchar, Amy	89.7	Moran, Jerry	7.1
Gillibrand, Kirsten	89.4	Braun, Mike	6.8
Harris, Kamala	89.1	Hawley, Josh	6.3
Markey, Edward J.	88.7	Murkowski, Lisa	6.2
Merkley, Jeff	76.7	Cruz, Ted	5.9
Hirono, Mazie K.	74.7	Rubio, Marco	5.9
Schumer, Charles E.	73.0	Young, Todd	5.9
Blumenthal, Richard	72.3	Toomey, Patrick J.	5.8
Wyden, Ron	71.3	Sasse, Ben	5.8
Schatz, Brian	70.9	Daines, Steve	5.4
Murray, Patty	69.8	Blackburn, Marsha	5.2
Stabenow, Debbie	69.7	Romney, Mitt	5.2

SUPPORT

Democrats		Republicans	
Peterson, Collin C.	26.7%	Babin, Brian	100.0%
McAdams, Ben	14.5	Bishop, Dan	100.0
Ocasio-Cortez, Alexandria	14.5	Collins, Chris	100.0
Van Drew, Jeff*	13.1	Fleischmann, Chuck	100.0
Cuellar, Henry	11.3	Miller, Carol	100.0
Golden, Jared	11.3	Murphy, Greg	100.0
Fletcher, Lizzie	9.7	Pence, Greg	100.0
Horn, Kendra	9.7	Comer, James R.	98.4
Vela, Filemon	9.7	Duncan, Jeff	98.4
Gonzalez, Vicente	8.3	Graves, Tom	98.4
Brindisi, Anthony	8.1	Kelly, Trent	98.4
Garcia, Sylvia R.	8.1	Palazzo, Steven M.	98.4
Tlaib, Rashida	8.1	Smith, Jason	98.4
Torres Small, Xochitl	8.1	Woodall, Rob	98.4
Castro, Joaquin	6.7	Estes, Ron	98.4
		Harris, Andy	98.4
		Joyce, John	98.4

OPPOSITION

Democrats		Republicans	
Barragan, Nanette	98.4%	Fitzpatrick, Brian	61.3%
Clarke, Yvette D.	98.4	Smith, Christopher H.	43.5
DeFazio, Peter A.	98.4	Katko, John	40.7
DeSaulnier, Mark	98.4	Stefanik, Elise	38.7
Engel, Eliot L.	98.4	Hurd, Will	36.7
Garcia, Jesus "Chuy"	98.4	Herrera Beutler, Jaime	34.5
Jayapal, Pramila	98.4	Upton, Fred	33.9
Kennedy, Joseph P. III	98.4	Walden, Greg	22.6
Levin, Andy	98.4	Rooney, Francis	22.2
Lowenthal, Alan	98.4	Massie, Thomas	18.6
McGovern, Jim	98.4	King, Peter T.	18.0
Meng, Grace	98.4	Zeldin, Lee	16.2
Raskin, Jamie	98.4	Kinzinger, Adam	15.3
Tonko, Paul	98.4	Gallagher, Mike	15.0
Watson Coleman, Bonnie	98.4	Hollingsworth, Trey	12.9

*Van Drew switched parties in December, becoming a Republican.

Yovanovitch. She was one of eight House Republicans named to Trump's defense team. In a post-acquittal event at the White House earlier this month Trump singled Stefanik out for praise.

Stefanik says she doesn't see any contradiction, explaining that her first consideration is "always to put the district first," whether that means defending Trump on impeachment or voting against him on the 2017 tax-cut bill (PL 115-97). When asked if the newfound attention from Trump and conservatives will change how she votes in the future, she answers simply, "No."

One member whose opposition to Trump shot up in 2019 was Smith, the dean of the New Jersey delegation who after the 2018 election became the last Republican standing in that state. In 2018, he opposed Trump on 13 percent of votes, four in all, but in 2019 that number soared to 44 percent. He joined with Democrats on raising the minimum wage to $15 an hour (HR 582), gun control bills (HR 8; HR 1112) and repealing the cap on the state and local tax deduction (HR 5377).

There were seven Republicans whose fealty to the president was 100 percent: Brian Babin of Texas, Dan Bishop of North Carolina, Chris Collins of New York (who resigned Oct. 1), Chuck Fleischmann of Tennessee, Carol Miller of West Virginia, Greg Murphy of North Carolina and Greg Pence of Indiana. ■

Nominees make for wins

Trump focused on judicial and executive branch nominees in 2019 and that's where most of his wins were.

Share of votes on which the president took a clear position:

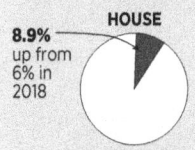

HOUSE

8.9% up from 6% in 2018

62 out of 700

SENATE

44.4% highest since 1968

190 out of 428

AVERAGE FOR BOTH CHAMBERS: **22.3%**

How often the president won:

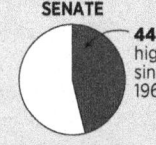

HOUSE

8.1% lowest on record

5 out of 62

SENATE

94.2% third-highest on record

179 out of 190

AVERAGE FOR BOTH CHAMBERS: **73.0%**

Average chamber presidential support scores:

HOUSE

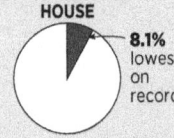

R **91%** Second-highest (high was 93% in 2017)

D **5%** Lowest on record

SENATE

R **93%** Same as in 2018

D **35%** Tied for third-lowest on record

Blue State, Purple Districts, Blue Votes

Southern California produced a remarkable wave in 2018 as seven Democrats there flipped Republican-held districts.

And yet those freshman Democrats, most of whom remain in competitive races in 2020, voted last year as if they have nothing to fear from their constituents. As a group, these freshmen opposed the president 95.7 percent of the time on votes in which he took a position. All of them voted for both articles of impeachment.

They include TJ Cox, Josh Harder, Harley Rouda, Gil Cisneros, Mike Levin and Katie Porter. The seventh, Katie Hill, resigned in November following a scandal in which nude photos of her appeared on the internet; she was also accused of having an affair with a staffer, a charge she denies.

Levin's race is not considered competitive by CQ Roll Call's elections analyst, Nathan L. Gonzales, but other forecasters have rated it as somewhat competitive.

Porter is an interesting case study. She's a protégé of Democratic Sen. Elizabeth Warren of Massachusetts, and has raised her profile in hearings questioning Trump administration officials and Wall Street titans like JPMorgan Chase CEO Jamie Dimon. All that attention landed her a spot on "Late Night with Seth Meyers" in October.

"Not everybody is as excited about financial services as I am," she told Meyers while explaining why she uses props like whiteboards and bingo cards in hearings.

In her 2018 primary she ran as a liberal in favor of "Medicare for All." She beat a more centrist candidate there, striking fears among Democratic operatives about her chances in the fall. And yet she won that race against Republican incumbent Mimi Walters by more than 12,000 votes, a fairly comfortable margin. Gonzales now considers the race "likely Democratic."

On only three votes in 2019 did she join with Trump — the defense policy bill (PL 116-92), a deal raising budget caps (PL 116-37), and the United States-Mexico-Canada trade agreement (PL 116-113). The question is whether that will be enough for voters in her Orange County district. Porter's office declined to make her available for comment.

It's true that Orange County and other parts of Southern California have changed in recent years. All seven who won their races in 2018 were in districts in which Hillary Clinton bested Trump in 2016. An influx of Asian and Latino immigrants has changed what had historically been Republican bastions. The question for these Democrats is whether the districts have changed as much as they think.

Solace in the Senate

With 100 percent support for his nominees, Trump won big in the other chamber

President Donald Trump's dismal performance in the House looks a lot better when you factor in the Senate. There, he won 94 percent of all votes, pushing his overall win percentage to 73 percent. That win rate was bolstered in large part by a perfect success rate getting his nominations confirmed in the Senate — there were only 29 legislative votes in the Senate on which he took a position.

Republicans seemed most comfortable offering rebukes to Trump on national security matters, especially those dealing with Saudi Arabia, a longtime U.S. ally. Congress has soured on the Saudi kingdom in the last few years following the murder of journalist Jamal Khashoggi. For his part, Trump has offered absolute support for Saudi Arabia and its crown prince Mohammed bin Salman, a stance that has puzzled and frustrated many Republicans.

"The pattern was set really early with the Russia sanctions in 2017," says Frances Lee, a congressional scholar at Princeton, referring to veto-proof votes that punished Russia for meddling in the 2016 election. "So it's safer for Republicans to oppose the president on foreign policy."

Of the 14 votes categorized as defense or foreign policy votes, Trump won only 57 percent of the time in 2019 (eight successes; six defeats).

Indiana's Todd Young is among Senate Republicans who have voted with Trump on nominations and most other legislation while going his own way on national security issues. But Young hasn't earned the wrath of Trump, at least not yet.

Young voted against Trump 11 times in 2019. Eight of those were on votes that would halt arms sales and exports to Saudi Arabia (S J Res 36, S J Res 37, S J Res 38), a veto override attempt on each, ending U.S. involvement in the war in Yemen (S J Res 7), and the withdrawal of troops from Afghanistan and Syria (S 1).

This month, he was at it again, joining with Democrats to curb Trump's ability to wage war on Iran (S J Res 68). Trump tweeted his opposition to the measure. In January, Rep. Matt Gaetz of Florida voted in favor of a similar measure dealing with Iran (H Con Res 83) and urged other Republicans to do the same, reportedly drawing the ire of the president. In Young's case, he took care to praise the president for the killing of Iranian Gen. Qassem Soleimani, but argued that "Congress has been AWOL on certain matters of national security" and needed to reassert its authority on war.

Young, who is chairman of a Foreign Relations subcommittee and also chairs the Senate Republican campaign arm, hasn't been very outspoken on these votes compared with his Senate colleagues. His office declined to make him available for an interview but said he has been "a leading advocate in the Senate to address the humanitarian crisis in Yemen and end the civil war." Amy Grappone, a spokeswoman, declined to say whether Young feared backlash from the president, saying only: "His votes reflect his commitment to ensuring Congress fulfills its constitutionally mandated oversight role in foreign conflicts."

Young isn't the only Indiana senator to oppose Trump more often than most. Mike Braun, who beat incumbent Democrat Joe Donnelly in 2018, was the fifth-likeliest senator to break with Trump on presidential support votes, though he did so only 7 percent of the time.

Susan Collins, the moderate from Maine who faces a potentially tough reelection campaign this year, was the Republican who opposed the president most. She voted against his position 15 percent of the time. That was a departure from the two years previous, when she opposed Trump 6 percent of the time.

Of those who supported the president most often, a few names stand out: Republican Martha McSally of Arizona, who was appointed to her seat in 2018, voted with the president 98 percent of the time. Her race in 2020 to fill the last two years of John McCain's term is considered a toss-up by CQ Roll Call elections analyst Nathan L. Gonzales, but she doesn't seem to be making many moves to the center. McSally cultivated a reputation as a centrist when she was a member of the House, though in 2018 she supported Trump 100 percent of the time there.

Thom Tillis, a Republican from North Carolina who flip-flopped on Trump's declaration of a national emergency on the southern border last year — opposing it, then supporting it — is also in a toss-up race this year. He ranked at 98 percent in fealty to Trump, which is in line with his historical voting pattern.

"What you see here is the party in lockstep mostly," says Lee. "All the Republicans on one side, all the Democrats on the other, and then even the

Background: Presidential Support

CQ Roll Call editors select presidential support votes each year based on clear statements by the president or authorized spokespersons. Success scores show how often the president prevailed. Average scores for each chamber are lowered by absences.

PRESIDENTIAL SUCCESS BY ISSUE

	Defense/Foreign Policy		Domestic		Economic Affairs		Overall	
	2019	2018	2019	2018	2019	2018	2019	2018
House	11.1%	100.0%	6.1%	91.3%	25.0%	100.0%	8.1%	93.3%
Senate	57.1	0.0	66.7	61.5	--	100.0	94.2	93.5
Congress	39.1	60.0	20.3	80.6	25	100.0	73.0	93.4

Economic affairs includes votes on taxes, trade, omnibus and some supplemental spending bills that cover both domestic and foreign policy programs.
Confirmation votes in the Senate are included only in the chamber's overall scores.

AVERAGE PRESIDENTIAL SUCCESS SCORES

	House		Senate			House		Senate	
	Democrats	Republicans	Democrats	Republicans		Democrats	Republicans	Democrats	Republicans
Eisenhower					1985	30%	67%	35%	75%
1954	44%	71%	38%	73%	1986	25	65	37	78
1955	53	60	56	72	1987	24	62	36	64
1956	52	72	39	72	1988	25	57	47	68
1957	49	54	51	69					
1958	44	67	44	67	**G. Bush**				
1959	40	68	38	72	1989	36	69	55	82
1960	44	59	43	66	1990	25	63	38	70
					1991	34	72	41	83
Kennedy					1992	25	71	32	73
1961	73	37	65	36					
1962	72	42	63	39	**Clinton**				
1963	72	32	63	44	1993	77	39	87	29
					1994	75	47	86	42
Johnson					1995	75	22	81	29
1964	74	38	61	45	1996	74	38	83	37
1965	74	41	64	48	1997	71	30	85	60
1966	63	37	57	43	1998	74	26	82	41
1967	69	46	61	53	1999	73	23	84	34
1968	64	51	48	47	2000	73	27	89	46
Nixon					**G.W. Bush**				
1969	48	57	47	66	2001	31	86	66	94
1970	53	66	45	60	2002	32	82	71	89
1971	47	72	40	64	2003	26	89	48	94
1972	47	64	44	66	2004	30	80	60	91
1973	35	62	37	61	2005	24	81	38	86
1974	46	65	39	57	2006	31	85	51	85
					2007	7	72	37	78
Ford					2008	16	64	34	70
1974	41	51	39	55					
1975	38	63	47	68	**Obama**				
1976	32	63	39	62	2009	90	26	92	50
					2010	84	29	94	41
Carter					2011	80	22	92	53
1977	63	42	70	52	2012	77	17	93	47
1978	60	36	66	41	2013	83	12	96	40
1979	64	34	68	47	2014	81	12	95	55
1980	63	40	62	45	2015	86	11	87	53
					2016	88	8	86	49
Reagan									
1981	42	68	49	80	**Trump**				
1982	39	64	43	74	2017	16	93	37	96
1983	28	70	42	73	2018	31	89	37	93
1984	34	60	41	76	2019	5	91	35	93

Democrats in array

It doesn't matter what group you look at — House Democrats sided with Trump no more than 10 percent of the time in 2019.

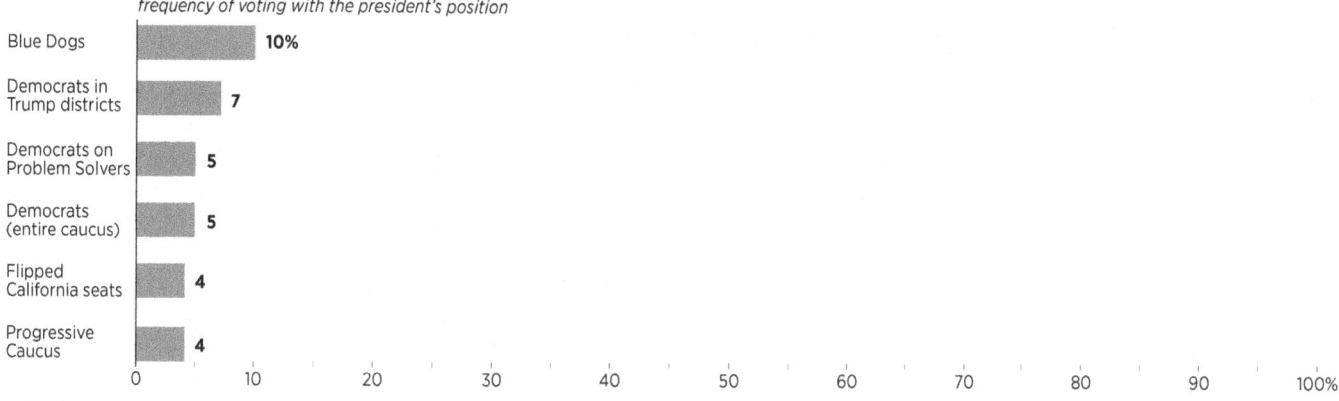

frequency of voting with the president's position

Blue Dogs	10%
Democrats in Trump districts	7
Democrats on Problem Solvers	5
Democrats (entire caucus)	5
Flipped California seats	4
Progressive Caucus	4

members who get flagged as being somewhat out of step with their party are not very out of step with their party."

Loyal Opposition

The high rate of opposition to Trump in the House extended to Senate Democrats.

In 2019, Senate Democrats supported Trump just 35 percent of the time, down 2 points from their 2018 figure. The six who opposed Trump at the highest rate were all contenders for the Democratic presidential nomination: Bernie Sanders, the Vermont independent (94 percent), Elizabeth Warren of Massachusetts (93), Cory Booker of New Jersey (90), Amy Klobuchar of Minnesota (90), Kirsten Gillibrand of New York (89) and Kamala Harris of California (89).

Klobuchar's case may be the most interesting. She has made her moderate,

sensible, Midwestern reputation a centerpiece of her presidential campaign. She has argued that her opponents' proposals, like "Medicare for All," go too far leftward.

"The way I look at it, if you want to cross a river over some troubled waters, you build a bridge," she said in a December debate while discussing the Affordable Care Act. "You don't blow one up."

But her record in 2019 belies that message. On only 10 percent of votes in the Senate last year, 11 out of 190, did she vote with Trump's position. It's a significant shift from the first two years of Trump's presidency, when she voted with him 42 and 43 percent of the time and reflects more opposition on her part to Trump nominees to executive branch jobs and federal judgeships. Klobuchar's office did not respond to a request for comment on her votes.

On the flip side, the three Democrats

who stuck with the president the most are those in states won by Trump in 2016 — Joe Manchin III in West Virginia, Kyrsten Sinema of Arizona and Doug Jones of Alabama. Jones faces a tough reelection in 2020 in a state Trump won by nearly 28 points.

The next name on the list, Christopher S. Murphy of Connecticut, may come as a surprise. He supported Trump's position 55 percent of the time, up from the low 40s the previous two years. The bulk of his votes siding with Trump have come on nominations. A liberal from a blue state, his office has argued that presidents should have wide latitude when it comes to their nominations unless that person is "clearly unqualified or their views are outside of the conservative mainstream." ■

Missing in Action

Running for president or governor, illnesses and childbirth were among the reasons
22 members of Congress had low voting rates last year

The 2020 presidential race took a toll on legislative business last year, with seven senators and three House members who were seeking the Democratic nomination each missing at least a quarter of all roll-call votes in their chambers. Four of the senators missed more than half the votes.

Even with those absences — and those of a dozen other members who missed a quarter or more of the roll calls — Congress maintained a 96.3 percent participation rate in 2019, about where it has been for the past several decades, according to CQ Roll Call's annual vote studies.

The participation rate in the House was 96.6 percent on 700 roll-call votes last year and in the Senate it was 94.1 percent on 428 roll-call votes, the latest data show. Nine senators and 23 representatives voted 100 percent of the time (see list on page 54).

Among the Democratic presidential candidates, Sen. Cory Booker of New Jersey had the most absences in Congress, making just 35 percent of the roll calls. He was closely followed by independent Sen. Bernie Sanders of Vermont, who voted 36 percent of the time; Sen. Kamala Harris of California, at 38 percent; and Sen. Elizabeth Warren of Massachusetts, at 46 percent.

Three other Democratic senators making presidential bids made more than half the votes but were below 75 percent in participation: Amy Klobuchar of Minnesota, with a 61 percent voting record; Michael Bennet of Colorado, with 72 percent; and Kirsten Gillibrand of New York, with 74 percent.

Among House Democrats who spent time on the campaign trail last year, Tulsi Gabbard of Hawaii voted 62 percent of the time, Eric Swalwell of California made 71 percent of the votes and Tim Ryan of Ohio had a 76 percent participation rate.

One senator, six representatives and five delegates had participation rates below 75 percent last year and one other House member,

Democrat A. Donald McEachin of Virginia, voted 76 percent of the time. McEachin missed votes after undergoing unspecified surgeries in August, while Democrat Alcee L. Hastings of Florida, who made 71 percent of the votes, announced in January 2019 that he needed treatment for pancreatic cancer.

GOP Rep. Jaime Herrera Beutler of Washington, who had a baby in May, had a 73 percent voting record; Republican Rep. Ralph Abraham of Louisiana, who unsuccessfully ran for governor, had a 64 percent rate; and GOP Rep. Francis Rooney of Florida, who is retiring at the end of this Congress, had a 75 percent rate. Rooney's office did not respond to a request for an explanation of his missed votes.

Republican Tom Marino of Pennsylvania, who resigned from the House in January 2019 to take a private-sector job, made just 55 percent of the roll-call votes in the first weeks of the 116th Congress. Republican Walter B. Jones of North Carolina died in February 2019 and was unable to make any of the votes early last year because of illness.

GOP Sen. Johnny Isakson of Georgia resigned at the end of 2019 and had a 67 percent voting rate during the year due to illness.

Five of the six delegates in the House, who were granted limited voting rights when Democrats took control last year, had a poor record for participation. Only Democrat Eleanor Holmes Norton of the District of Columbia took advantage of the opportunity, voting 87 percent of the time. The other five delegates were all below 75 percent in participation, with Democrat Michael F.Q. San Nicolas of Guam the lowest, at 48 percent.

Meanwhile, Speaker Nancy Pelosi maintained a long-standing tradition among House speakers of only casting votes if needed to send a message or ensure an outcome. As a result, the California Democrat had a 6 percent participation rate. ■

Triumph of Organization

Lawmakers have missed fewer votes in recent decades as congressional leaders
have gotten better at scheduling votes when most members are in town.

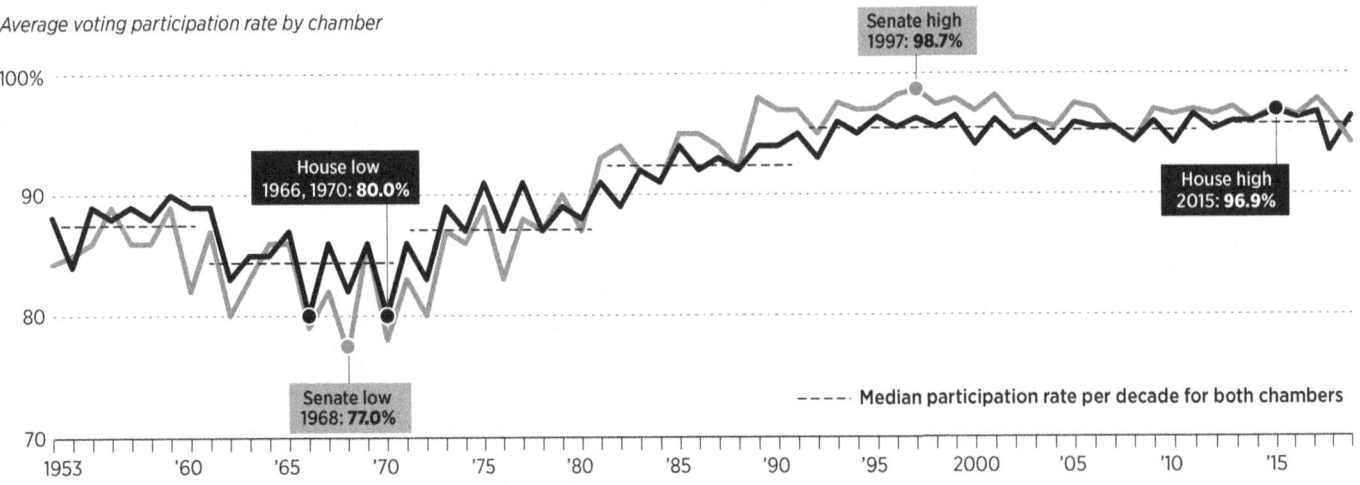

Average voting participation rate by chamber

Senate high
1997: **98.7%**

100%

House low
1966, 1970: **80.0%**

90

House high
2015: **96.9%**

80

Senate low
1968: **77.0%**

---- Median participation rate per decade for both chambers

70

1953   '60   '65   '70   '75   '80   '85   '90   '95   2000   '05   '10   '15

History: Voting Participation

These tables show the number of roll-call votes in each chamber and in Congress as a whole since 1954, as well as the frequency with which lawmakers on average cast "yea" or "nay" votes. Participation in floor votes has hovered around 96 percent over the past two decades.

YEAR	House ROLL CALL VOTES	House RATE	Senate ROLL CALL VOTES	Senate RATE	Congress as a Whole ROLL CALL VOTES	Congress as a Whole RATE
2019	700 votes	96.6%	428	94.1%	1,128	96.3%
2018	498	93.9	274	96.8	772	94.3
2017	708	96.4	325	97.9	1033	96.5
2016	621	95.3	163	95.6	784	95.4
2015	702	96.9	339	97.2	1,041	96.9
2014	562	95.6	366	95.6	928	95.6
2013	640	96.0	291	97.2	931	96.1
2012	657	95.3	251	96.6	908	95.4
2011	945	96.6	235	97.0	1,180	96.6
2010	660	94.2	299	96.6	959	94.4
2009	987	96.0	397	97.0	1,384	96.1
2008	688	94.3	215	94.3	903	94.3
2007	1,177	95.5	442	95.0	1,619	95.4
2006	541	95.5	279	97.1	820	95.7
2005	669	95.9	366	97.4	1,035	96.1
2004	543	94.1	216	95.5	759	94.2
2003	675	95.6	459	96.1	1,134	95.7
2002	483	94.6	253	96.3	736	94.8
2001	507	96.2	380	98.2	887	96.5
2000	600	94.1	298	96.9	898	94.4
1999	609	96.5	374	97.9	983	96.6
1998	533	95.5	314	97.4	847	95.7
1997	633	96.3	298	98.7	931	96.5
1996	454	95.5	306	98.2	760	95.8
1995	867	96.4	613	97.1	1,480	96.5
1994	497	95.0	329	97.0	826	95.0
1993	597	96.0	395	97.6	992	96.0
1992	473	93.0	270	95.0	743	93.4
1991	428	95.0	280	97.0	708	95.0
1990	536	94.0	326	97.0	862	95.0
1989	368	94.0	312	98.0	680	95.0
1988	451	92.0	379	92.0	830	92.0
1987	488	93.0	420	94.0	908	93.0
1986	451	92.0	354	95.0	805	93.0
1985	439	94.0	381	95.0	820	94.0
1984	408	91.0	275	91.0	683	91.0
1983	498	92.0	371	92.0	869	92.0
1982	459	89.0	465	94.0	924	90.0
1981	353	91.0	483	93.0	836	92.0
1980	604	88.0	531	87.0	1,135	87.0
1979	672	89.0	497	90.0	1,169	89.0
1978	834	87.0	516	87.0	1,350	87.0
1977	706	91.0	635	88.0	1,341	90.0
1976	661	87.0	688	83.0	1,349	86.0
1975	612	91.0	602	89.0	1,214	91.0
1974	537	87.0	544	86.0	1,081	87.0
1973	541	89.0	594	87.0	1,135	89.0
1972	329	83.0	532	80.0	861	82.0
1971*	320	86.0	423	83.0	743	85.0
1970*	266	80.0	418	78.0	684	79.0
1969*	177	86.0	245	86.0	422	86.0
1968*	233	82.0	281	77.0	514	80.0
1967*	245	86.0	315	82.0	560	85.0
1966*	193	80.0	235	79.0	428	79.0
1965*	201	87.0	258	86.0	459	87.0
1964*	113	85.0	305	86.0	418	85.0
1963*	119	85.0	229	83.0	348	84.0
1962	124	83.0	224	80.0	348	82.0
1961	116	89.0	204	87.0	320	88.0
1960	93	89.0	207	82.0	300	87.0
1959*	87	90.0	215	89.0	302	89.0
1958*	93	88.0	200	86.0	293	87.0
1957*	100	89.0	107	86.0	207	88.0
1956*	73	88.0	130	89.0	203	88.0
1955*	76	89.0	87	86.0	163	88.0
1954	76	84.0	171	85.0	247	84.0

Perfect Attendance

The number of members who did not miss any roll-call votes in 2019 dropped in the Senate but more than doubled in the House from the previous year. The number of senators with 100 percent voting records went from 14 in 2018 to nine in 2019. In the House, 11 members made all votes in 2018; the number rose to 23 last year.

SENATE
Republicans
Barrasso, John (Wyo.)
Boozman, John (Ark.)
Collins, Susan (Maine)
Grassley, Charles E. (Iowa)
Hawley, Josh (Mo.)
Lankford, James (Okla.)
McConnell, Mitch (Ky.)
Thune, John (S.D.)

Independent
King, Angus (Maine)

HOUSE
Republicans
Bacon, Don (Neb.)
Banks, Jim (Ind.)
Chabot, Steve (Ohio)
Fitzpatrick, Brian (Pa.)
Fleischmann, Chuck (Tenn.)
Guthrie, Brett (Ky.)
McKinley, David B. (W.Va.)
Moolenaar, John (Mich.)
Womack, Steve (Ark.)

Democrats
Bustos, Cheri (Ill.)
Carbajal, Salud (Calif.)
Craig, Angie (Minn.)
Cuellar, Henry (Texas)
Delgado, Antonio (N.Y.)
Garcia, Sylvia R. (Tenn.)
Heck, Denny (Wash.)
Kildee, Dan (Mich.)
Kilmer, Derek (Wash.)
Kim, Andy (N.J.)
Levin, Andy (Mich.)
Murphy, Stephanie (Fla.)
Phillips, Dean (Minn.)
Ruiz, Raul (Calif.)

*For 1955-59 and 1963-71, House and Senate percentages have been interpolated from recorded scores for each chamber's party voting participation scores.

Presidential Support (PRES)

Percentage of recorded votes cast in 2019 on which President Donald Trump took a position and on which the member voted "yea" or "nay" in agreement with the president's position. Failure to vote does not lower an individual's score.

Party Unity (UNITY)

Percentage of recorded votes cast in 2019 on which a member voted "yea" or "nay" in agreement with a majority of his or her party. (Party unity votes are those in which a majority of voting Democrats opposed a majority of voting Republicans.) Percentages are based on votes cast; this failure to vote does not lower a member's score.

Participation (VOTE)

Percentage of recorded votes cast in 2019 on which a member was eligible and present, and voted "yea" or "nay." There were a total of 700 such recorded votes in the House and 428 in the Senate. Quorum calls are not counted as votes because lawmakers are asked only to respond "present."

KEY: **Republicans** Democrats *Independents*

	PRES	UNITY	VOTE		PRES	UNITY	VOTE		PRES	UNITY	VOTE
ALABAMA				**MAINE**				**OREGON**			
Shelby	97	97	99	**Collins**	85	78	100	Wyden	29	98	97
Jones	66	57	97	*King*	52	81	100	Merkley	23	98	99
ALASKA				**MARYLAND**				**PENNSYLVANIA**			
Murkowski	94	90	92	Cardin	45	91	99	Casey	42	94	99
Sullivan	97	99	98	Van Hollen	35	98	99	**Toomey**	94	98	96
ARIZONA				**MASSACHUSETTS**				**RHODE ISLAND**			
Sinema	69	53	95	Warren	7	100	46	Reed	40	96	99
McSally	98	97	99	Markey	11	99	95	Whitehouse	42	93	94
ARKANSAS				**MICHIGAN**				**SOUTH CAROLINA**			
Boozman	97	97	100	Stabenow	30	99	98	**Graham**	97	95	97
Cotton	95	97	99	Peters	38	96	99	**Scott**	96	99	99
CALIFORNIA				**MINNESOTA**				**SOUTH DAKOTA**			
Feinstein	46	91	99	Klobuchar	10	100	61	**Thune**	98	99	100
Harris	11	100	38	Smith	31	100	99	**Rounds**	98	99	89
COLORADO				**MISSISSIPPI**				**TENNESSEE**			
Bennet	42	95	72	**Wicker**	97	97	99	**Alexander**	97	95	82
Gardner	97	96	99	**Hyde-Smith**	99	97	99	**Blackburn**	95	99	99
CONNECTICUT				**MISSOURI**				**TEXAS**			
Blumenthal	28	99	99	**Blunt**	97	97	99	**Cornyn**	98	99	99
Murphy	54	79	99	**Hawley**	94	98	100	**Cruz**	94	99	97
DELAWARE				**MONTANA**				**UTAH**			
Carper	49	83	99	Tester	47	90	99	**Lee**	87	92	99
Coons	51	83	96	**Daines**	95	96	98	**Romney**	95	97	99
FLORIDA				**NEBRASKA**				**VERMONT**			
Rubio	94	98	96	**Fischer**	97	100	99	Leahy	45	91	99
Scott	98	99	99	**Sasse**	94	99	98	*Sanders*	6	100	36
GEORGIA				**NEW HAMPSHIRE**				**VIRGINIA**			
Perdue	99	99	93	Shaheen	50	84	99	Warner	47	89	95
Isakson	98	98	67	Hassan	48	86	99	Kaine	46	90	97
HAWAII				**NEW JERSEY**				**WASHINGTON**			
Schatz	29	99	99	Menendez	32	97	99	Murray	30	100	98
Hirono	25	100	96	Booker	10	100	35	Cantwell	32	97	99
IDAHO				**NEW MEXICO**				**WEST VIRGINIA**			
Crapo	98	99	99	Udall	35	99	99	Manchin	71	50	99
Risch	96	100	98	Heinrich	36	98	97	**Capito**	98	97	97
ILLINOIS				**NEVADA**				**WISCONSIN**			
Durbin	43	94	98	Cortez Masto	40	95	99	**Johnson**	97	99	97
Duckworth	36	97	95	Rosen	44	92	99	Baldwin	35	98	99
INDIANA				**NEW YORK**				**WYOMING**			
Young	94	94	98	Schumer	27	99	99	**Enzi**	97	99	99
Braun	93	99	99	Gillibrand	11	100	74	**Barrasso**	96	100	100
IOWA				**NORTH CAROLINA**							
Grassley	97	99	100	**Burr**	99	97	90				
Ernst	97	99	99	**Tillis**	98	98	95				
KANSAS				**NORTH DAKOTA**							
Roberts	99	97	92	**Hoeven**	98	99	99				
Moran	93	91	90	**Cramer**	98	99	99				
KENTUCKY				**OHIO**							
McConnell	99	96	100	Brown	37	96	99				
Paul	86	88	90	**Portman**	97	96	99				
LOUISIANA				**OKLAHOMA**							
Cassidy	97	99	91	**Inhofe**	95	100	98				
Kennedy	96	98	97	**Lankford**	95	100	100				

District	Member	PRES	UNITY	VOTE
ALABAMA				
1	**Byrne**	98	99	97
2	**Roby**	94	90	95
3	**Rogers, M.**	98	95	96
4	**Aderholt**	98	93	96
5	**Brooks, M.**	97	98	99
6	**Palmer**	95	99	99
7	Sewell	5	98	99
ALASKA				
AL	**Young**	95	86	96
ARIZONA				
1	O'Halleran	5	96	99
2	Kirkpatrick	5	97	95
3	Grijalva	3	99	95
4	**Gosar**	97	98	95
5	**Biggs**	95	97	97
6	**Schweikert**	92	88	99
7	Gallego	5	99	97
8	**Lesko**	97	97	99
9	Stanton	6	99	99
ARKANSAS				
1	**Crawford**	95	97	94
2	**Hill, F.**	97	93	99
3	**Womack**	97	93	100
4	**Westerman**	95	98	98
CALIFORNIA				
1	**LaMalfa**	94	96	96
2	Huffman	3	99	95
3	Garamendi	5	99	98
4	**McClintock**	97	94	99
5	Thompson, M.	5	97	97
6	Matsui	5	99	99
7	Bera	5	97	99
8	**Cook**	93	89	98
9	McNerney	5	99	96
10	Harder	3	94	99
11	DeSaulnier	2	99	99
12	Pelosi	9	100	6
13	Lee B.	3	99	99
14	Speier	5	99	97
15	Swalwell	6	99	71
16	Costa	6	93	98
17	Khanna	3	99	99
18	Eshoo	5	100	97
19	Lofgren	5	99	97
20	Panetta	5	97	99
21	Cox	5	96	99
22	**Nunes**	97	96	99
23	**McCarthy**	97	92	98
24	Carbajal	5	99	100
25	Hill, K.*	2	98	96
26	Brownley	5	98	99
27	Chu	3	99	99
28	Schiff	5	99	99
29	Cárdenas	3	99	95
30	Sherman	5	99	98
31	Aguilar	5	97	99
32	Napolitano	3	99	99
33	Lieu	2	99	96
34	Gomez	3	99	99
35	Torres	5	99	98
36	Ruiz	5	98	100
37	Bass	3	99	94
38	Sánchez	5	99	97
39	Cisneros	5	96	99
40	Roybal-Allard	5	100	99
41	Takano	5	99	97
42	**Calvert**	97	89	99
43	Waters	5	98	99
44	Barragán	2	100	99
45	Porter	5	94	97
46	Correa	5	97	98
47	Lowenthal	2	99	99
48	Rouda	5	96	98
49	Levin	5	99	100
50	**Hunter**	96	97	91
51	Vargas	5	99	96
52	Peters	3	95	97
53	Davis, S.	5	100	99
COLORADO				
1	DeGette	3	99	99
2	Neguse	3	99	99
3	**Tipton**	92	91	99
4	**Buck**	90	97	86
5	**Lamborn**	95	99	97
6	Crow	5	95	99
7	Perlmutter	5	99	94
CONNECTICUT				
1	Larson	5	99	99
2	Courtney	5	99	99
3	DeLauro	5	99	96
4	Himes	5	98	98
5	Hayes	5	99	95
DELAWARE				
AL	Blunt Rochester	5	99	99
FLORIDA				
1	**Gaetz**	90	90	91
2	**Dunn**	97	95	98
3	**Yoho**	97	96	91
4	**Rutherford**	97	88	95
5	Lawson	5	97	96
6	**Waltz**	92	86	94
7	Murphy	5	95	100
8	**Posey**	92	92	97
9	Soto	5	99	99
10	Demings	5	99	99
11	**Webster**	93	94	97
12	**Bilirakis**	93	88	97
13	Crist	5	97	99
14	Castor	5	99	99
15	**Spano**	92	92	99
16	**Buchanan**	89	85	98
17	**Steube**	97	97	97
18	**Mast**	93	85	94
19	**Rooney**	78	77	75
20	Hastings	5	99	71
21	Frankel	5	99	93
22	Deutch	5	99	98
23	Wasserman Schultz	5	99	96
24	Wilson, F.	5	99	86
25	**Diaz-Balart**	89	82	99
26	Mucarsel-Powell	5	98	99
27	Shalala	5	99	99
GEORGIA				
1	**Carter, E.L.**	95	98	99
2	Bishop, S.	5	98	97
3	**Ferguson**	97	98	99
4	Johnson, H.	5	99	99
5	Lewis John	5	100	97
6	McBath	5	96	99
7	**Woodall**	98	95	98
8	**Scott, A.**	94	97	99
9	**Collins, D.**	97	97	95
10	**Hice**	97	99	95
11	**Loudermilk**	98	99	96
12	**Allen**	97	99	99
13	Scott, D.	5	99	99
14	**Graves, T.**	98	97	99
HAWAII				
1	Case	5	98	99
2	Gabbard	5	99	62
IDAHO				
1	**Fulcher**	97	99	99
2	**Simpson**	94	85	98
ILLINOIS				
1	Rush	5	99	93
2	Kelly, R.	5	99	99
3	Lipinski	5	96	97
4	García, J.	2	99	99
5	Quigley	5	99	97
6	Casten	5	99	99
7	Davis, D.	3	100	96
8	Krishnamoorthi	5	98	99
9	Schakowsky	3	99	99
10	Schneider	5	99	99
11	Foster	5	99	99
12	**Bost**	94	88	87
13	**Davis, R.**	90	81	97
14	Underwood	5	98	99
15	**Shimkus**	95	92	94
16	**Kinzinger**	85	82	95
17	Bustos	5	98	100
18	**LaHood**	95	96	98
INDIANA				
1	Visclosky	3	99	99
2	**Walorski**	95	92	97
3	**Banks**	95	96	100
4	**Baird**	97	94	99
5	**Brooks, S.**	92	86	97
6	**Pence**	100	94	99
7	Carson	6	99	99
8	**Bucshon**	93	94	97
9	**Hollingsworth**	87	79	98
IOWA				
1	Finkenauer	6	95	99
2	Loebsack	5	98	97
3	Axne	6	91	98
4	**King, S.**	97	93	97
KANSAS				
1	**Marshall**	98	96	95
2	**Watkins**	97	95	99
3	Davids	5	96	99
4	**Estes**	98	98	99
KENTUCKY				
1	**Comer**	98	97	99
2	**Guthrie**	97	95	100
3	Yarmuth	5	99	99
4	**Massie**	81	90	96
5	**Rogers, H.**	97	90	99
6	**Barr**	95	94	99
LOUISIANA				
1	**Scalise**	97	99	99
2	Richmond	5	99	93
3	**Higgins, C.**	97	95	90
4	**Johnson, M.**	96	96	93
5	**Abraham**	97	98	64
6	**Graves, G.**	93	90	98
MAINE				
1	Pingree	3	100	98
2	Golden	11	87	99
MARYLAND				
1	**Harris**	98	98	99
2	Ruppersberger	5	99	99
3	Sarbanes	5	99	99
4	Brown, A.	3	99	99
5	Hoyer	5	99	98
6	Trone	5	99	98
7	Cummings*	3	99	87
8	Raskin	2	99	99
MASSACHUSETTS				
1	Neal	5	100	98
2	McGovern	2	99	99
3	Trahan	5	100	99
4	Kennedy	2	100	98
5	Clark	5	99	99
6	Moulton	5	95	86
7	Pressley	6	98	98
8	Lynch	5	98	99
9	Keating	5	99	98
MICHIGAN				
1	**Bergman**	98	89	98
2	**Huizenga**	95	96	97
3	*Amash**	75	73	99
4	**Moolenaar**	95	93	100
5	Kildee	3	99	99
6	**Upton**	66	72	99
7	**Walberg**	97	95	99
8	Slotkin	5	92	99
9	Levin	2	99	99
10	**Mitchell**	95	93	99
11	Stevens	5	96	99
12	Dingell	3	99	95
13	Tlaib	8	98	99
14	Lawrence	5	99	96
MINNESOTA				
1	**Hagedorn**	95	95	99
2	Craig	5	92	100
3	Phillips	5	98	100
4	McCollum	5	99	99
5	Omar	5	98	94
6	**Emmer**	95	96	93
7	Peterson	27	79	99
8	**Stauber**	95	81	99
MISSISSIPPI				
1	**Kelly, T.**	98	99	99
2	Thompson, B.	5	99	95
3	**Guest**	97	96	98
4	**Palazzo**	98	98	97
MISSOURI				
1	Clay	3	99	96
2	**Wagner**	93	89	97
3	**Luetkemeyer**	97	91	99
4	**Hartzler**	95	92	97
5	Cleaver	5	99	97
6	**Graves, S.**	92	97	97
7	**Long**	95	95	98
8	**Smith, J.**	98	98	99
MONTANA				
AL	**Gianforte**	95	94	88
NEBRASKA				
1	**Fortenberry**	95	78	99
2	**Bacon**	92	83	100
3	**Smith, Adrian**	93	97	99
NEVADA				
1	Titus	5	99	96
2	**Amodei**	97	89	97
3	Lee	6	96	99
4	Horsford	5	97	99
NEW HAMPSHIRE				
1	Pappas	6	98	99
2	Kuster	7	99	98
NEW JERSEY				
1	Norcross	3	99	99
2	Van Drew*	13	82	97
3	Kim	5	95	100
4	**Smith, C.**	56	64	95
5	Gottheimer	5	88	99
6	Pallone	3	99	99
7	Malinowski	5	99	99
8	Sires	5	99	97
9	Pascrell	3	99	99
10	Payne	6	99	92
11	Sherrill	5	94	99
12	Watson Coleman	2	98	99
NEW MEXICO				
1	Haaland	5	99	99
2	Torres Small	8	92	99
3	Luján	5	99	99
NEW YORK				
1	**Zeldin**	92	87	98
2	**King, P.**	82	72	98
3	Suozzi	5	96	99
4	Rice, K.	3	96	99
5	Meeks	5	99	93
6	Meng	2	97	97
7	Velázquez	2	99	98
8	Jeffries	5	99	99
9	Clarke	2	99	99
10	Nadler	2	99	98
11	Rose	5	95	99
12	Maloney, C.	3	99	99
13	Espaillat	3	99	99
14	Ocasio-Cortez	15	96	99
15	Serrano	2	100	87
16	Engel	2	100	99
17	Lowey	5	99	98
18	Maloney, S.P.	5	96	98
19	Delgado	5	96	100
20	Tonko	2	99	97
21	**Stefanik**	61	67	99
22	Brindisi	8	85	99
23	**Reed**	89	76	98
24	**Katko**	59	64	96
25	Morelle	5	99	99
26	Higgins, B.	5	99	99
27	Collins, C.*	100	86	96
NORTH CAROLINA				
1	Butterfield	5	99	98
2	**Holding**	95	99	93
3	Jones*	--	--	0
3	**Murphy***	100	97	99
4	Price	5	99	99
5	**Foxx**	95	96	99
6	**Walker**	96	99	92
7	**Rouzer**	94	97	99
8	**Hudson**	93	94	94
9	**Bishop***	100	100	84
10	**McHenry**	95	90	98
11	**Meadows**	93	95	96
12	Adams	5	99	98
13	**Budd**	97	97	99
NORTH DAKOTA				
AL	**Armstrong**	95	91	96
OHIO				
1	**Chabot**	95	97	100
2	**Wenstrup**	95	96	96

#	Member	PRES	UNITY	VOTE
3	Beatty	5	99	94
4	Jordan	94	99	98
5	Latta	95	98	99
6	Johnson, B.	97	96	98
7	Gibbs	97	97	98
8	Davidson	95	94	98
9	Kaptur	3	99	98
10	Turner	97	85	98
11	Fudge	3	98	91
12	Balderson	95	96	99
13	Ryan	6	99	76
14	Joyce	95	82	99
15	Stivers	91	83	95
16	Gonzalez	95	83	99
OKLAHOMA				
1	Hern	97	99	99
2	Mullin	98	97	95
3	Lucas	97	91	94
4	Cole	95	85	99
5	Horn	10	90	99
OREGON				
1	Bonamici	5	99	99
2	Walden	77	81	98
3	Blumenauer	3	99	99
4	DeFazio	2	99	97
5	Schrader	5	93	97
PENNSYLVANIA				
1	Fitzpatrick	39	54	100
2	Boyle	5	99	99
3	Evans	5	99	99
4	Dean	5	99	99
5	Scanlon	5	99	99
6	Houlahan	5	95	99
7	Wild	5	95	99
8	Cartwright	5	99	95
9	Meuser	98	97	96
10	Perry	95	94	97
11	Smucker	95	94	94
12	Marino*	100	100	55
12	Keller*	94	94	96

#	Member	PRES	UNITY	VOTE
13	Joyce	98	98	94
14	Reschenthaler	97	89	97
15	Thompson, G.	98	87	97
16	Kelly, M.	95	92	97
17	Lamb	6	92	99
18	Doyle	3	99	96
RHODE ISLAND				
1	Cicilline	5	99	99
2	Langevin	5	99	99
SOUTH CAROLINA				
1	Cunningham	5	85	98
2	Wilson, J.	97	94	97
3	Duncan	98	99	99
4	Timmons	95	98	89
5	Norman	98	99	97
6	Clyburn	6	99	87
7	Rice, T.	93	96	97
SOUTH DAKOTA				
AL	Johnson	89	96	99
TENNESSEE				
1	Roe	95	93	98
2	Burchett	97	98	98
3	Fleischmann	100	91	100
4	DesJarlais	98	98	96
5	Cooper	3	96	98
6	Rose	98	98	97
7	Green	95	99	87
8	Kustoff	98	97	97
9	Cohen	3	99	99
TEXAS				
1	Gohmert	92	97	92
2	Crenshaw	93	92	98
3	Taylor	95	94	99
4	Ratcliffe	95	99	89
5	Gooden	97	99	97
6	Wright	95	99	80
7	Fletcher	10	94	99
8	Brady	98	95	95
9	Green, A.	5	99	99
10	McCaul	95	87	99

#	Member	PRES	UNITY	VOTE
11	Conaway	97	98	99
12	Granger	97	92	95
13	Thornberry	97	93	97
14	Weber	98	99	96
15	Gonzalez	8	96	94
16	Escobar	5	99	99
17	Flores	95	96	96
18	Jackson Lee	5	100	98
19	Arrington	95	96	98
20	Castro	7	99	96
21	Roy	93	95	98
22	Olson	95	98	96
23	Hurd	63	77	98
24	Marchant	93	98	90
25	Williams	97	98	97
26	Burgess	95	97	98
27	Cloud	92	97	99
28	Cuellar	11	91	100
29	Garcia, S.	8	98	100
30	Johnson, E.B.	5	99	98
31	Carter, J.	98	94	93
32	Allred	7	97	96
33	Veasey	5	99	99
34	Vela	10	97	99
35	Doggett	7	99	96
36	Babin	100	98	96
UTAH				
1	Bishop, R.	97	96	94
2	Stewart	97	97	98
3	Curtis	95	96	93
4	McAdams	15	82	99
VERMONT				
AL	Welch	3	100	98
VIRGINIA				
1	Wittman	95	97	99
2	Luria	5	92	99
3	Scott, R.	5	98	99
4	McEachin	5	98	76
5	Riggleman	95	94	99
6	Cline	95	97	99

#	Member	PRES	UNITY	VOTE
7	Spanberger	5	89	99
8	Beyer	5	99	98
9	Griffith	90	94	97
10	Wexton	5	97	99
11	Connolly	5	96	99
WASHINGTON				
1	DelBene	5	99	99
2	Larsen	5	99	99
3	Herrera Beutler	66	81	73
4	Newhouse	89	85	99
5	McMorris Rodgers	89	87	99
6	Kilmer	5	97	100
7	Jayapal	2	99	99
8	Schrier	5	97	99
9	Smith Adam	5	100	97
10	Heck	6	99	100
WEST VIRGINIA				
1	McKinley	92	89	100
2	Mooney	90	94	99
3	Miller	100	96	99
WISCONSIN				
1	Steil	95	87	99
2	Pocan	5	99	97
3	Kind	5	95	96
4	Moore	5	99	98
5	Sensenbrenner	89	96	85
6	Grothman	97	95	96
7	Duffy*	95	94	93
8	Gallagher	85	87	98
WYOMING				
AL	Cheney	97	95	97
DELEGATES				
	Radewagen (A.S.)	--	72	24
	Norton (D.C.)	--	99	87
	San Nicolas (Guam)	--	100	48
	Sablan (N. Marianas)	--	100	71
	González-Colón (P.R.)	--	65	69
	Plaskett (V.I.)	--	98	71

*Notes:

New Jersey Rep. Jeff Van Drew, now a Republican, was a Democrat for all of 2019 and is counted as such in this study.

Rep. Fred Keller, R-Fla., was sworn in on June 3, 2019. The first vote Bishop was eligible for was Vote 234.

Michigan Rep. Justin Amash, now an independent, was scored as a Republican for votes taking place before July 8, 2019.

Rep. Dan Bishop, R-NC, was sworn in on Sept. 17, 2019. The first vote Bishop was eligible for was Vote 532.

Rep. Sean P. Duffy, R-Wis., resigned on Sept. 23, 2019. The last vote Duffy was eligible for was Vote 540.

Rep. Chris Collins, R-NY, resigned on Sept. 30, 2019. The last vote Collins was eligible for was Vote 555.

Rep. Elijah E. Cummmings, D-Md., died on Oct. 17, 2019. The last vote Cummings was eligible for was Vote 560.

Rep. Katie Hill, D-Calif, resigned on Nov. 3, 2019. The last vote Hill was eligible for was Vote 609.

KEY VOTES

Key Senate and House Votes in 2019

The oldest of CQ Roll Call's annual studies, Key Votes is a selection of the major votes for both House and Senate for the past year. Editors choose the single vote on each issue that best presents a member's stance or that determined the year's legistative outcome. Charts of how each member voted on this list can be found at cq.com.

Attributes of a Key Vote

Since its 1945 founding, CQ Roll Call has selected a series of key votes in Congress on major issues of the year.

A vote is judged to be key by the extent to which it represents:
- a matter of major controversy.
- a matter of presidential or political power.
- a matter of potentially great impact on the nation and the lives of Americans.

For each group of related votes on an issue in each chamber, one key vote is usually chosen — one that, in the opinion of CQ Roll Call editors, was most important in determining the outcome of the issue for the year or best reflected the views of individual lawmakers on that issue.

SENATE VOTES

6   Russian Sanctions

Motion to invoke cloture on the joint resolution (S J Res 2) that would disapprove of President Trump's proposed action related to the application of sanctions against certain Russian companies. Motion rejected. 57-42 (R 11-42; D 45-0 ; I 1-0) on Jan. 16, 2019.

In January, Democrats launched a plan to block the Treasury Department from terminating sanctions against Oleg Deripaska, a Russian oligarch and billionaire with ties to the Kremlin.

Democrats and a number of Republicans argued that the deal Treasury struck to lift the sanctions was a sham since in some cases Deripaska could still control companies through relatives or other means. "Mr. Deripaska is a gangster," said John Kennedy of Louisiana, one of 11 Republicans who voted with Democrats to uphold the sanctions. "And I think he is stealing and has stolen a lot of money from the people of Russia." Joining Kennedy were a few vulnerable senators up for election in 2020, including Cory Gardner of Colorado and Martha McSally of Arizona.

Most other Republicans said Democrats were overturning a "highly technical" decision from "career civil servants" and were simply attempting to embarrass Trump. "Political spite for the president comes first, ahead of everything else," Majority Leader Mitch McConnell said ahead of the vote.

Treasury Secretary Steven Mnuchin made a Capitol Hill visit to sway Republicans to vote against the measure, arguing that overturning the deal could disrupt world aluminum markets. "We have been tougher on Russia with more sanctions than any other administration," he said.

In the end, Democrats came up three votes short of the 60 required to invoke cloture and the measure failed. The next day, the House passed a similar measure.

14   Troops in Syria and Afghanistan

Adoption of an amendment to express the sense of the Senate that al-Qaida, ISIS, and other terrorist groups pose a continuing threat to U.S. homeland security and the security of U.S. allies. It would call for increased international stabilization efforts and warn against "precipitous withdrawal" of U.S. military forces in Syria and Afghanistan. It would call for the administration to review military and diplomatic strategies in these nations and request that no "significant withdrawal" of U.S. forces occur until conditions have been met for the "enduring defeat" of al-Qaida and ISIS. Adopted 70-26 (R 46-4; D 23-21; I 1-1) on Jan. 31, 2019.

President Trump has made it clear he wants to pull the U.S. back from foreign entanglements, and in December 2018, when he decided it was time to withdraw troops from Syria and Afghanistan, it stunned Republicans in Washington — many of whom publicly rebuked the president. Trump's Defense secretary, James Mattis, resigned in protest.

On Jan. 31, Senate Republicans put the matter on record with a vote on a measure that condemned any "precipitous withdrawal" of troops from those two countries.

The nonbinding amendment put forward by Senate Majority Leader Mitch McConnell was considered one of the highest-profile attempts yet by the national security establishment to push back against Trump.

All of this came against a backdrop in which the president has repeatedly undermined his national security team. A day before the vote, Trump rebuffed and ridiculed America's defense, intelligence and foreign policy elites on counterterrorism and policy toward Russia, Iran, North Korea and more.

Trump tweeted that those who work in the intelligence community were "passive and naïve." The attack followed congressional testimony from his administration, led by Director of National Intelligence Dan Coats, which countered Trump's claims that Iran was pursuing nuclear weapons, that North Korea was not, and that the Islamic State and al-Qaida were all but completely defeated. The next day, Trump said the matter was all the media's fault. Six months later, Coats resigned.

John Thune of South Dakota, the second-ranking Republican in the Senate, told CNN: "I don't know how many times you can say this, but I prefer the president would stay off Twitter — particularly with regard to these important national security issues where you've got people who are experts and have the background and are professionals."

In Afghanistan, Trump is still reportedly considering bringing home as soon as possible up to half of the 14,000 U.S. troops there. In September, he withdrew troops in Syria, leading to an invasion by Turkey. The House voted to rebuke Trump.

24   William Barr Confirmation

Confirmation of President Trump's nomination of William Barr to be attorney general of the United States. Confirmed 54-45 (R 51-1; D 3-42; I 0-2) on Feb. 14, 2019.

President Trump fumed for months over the special counsel investigation into Russian interference in the 2016 election, and in November 2018 forced his first attorney general, Jeff Sessions, to resign.

Senators raised concerns that Trump's next pick to run the Justice Department, William Barr, would end Robert S. Mueller III's probe or keep that report from the public. That ultimately became a central focus of the confirmation debate.

Barr, then 68, pitched himself to senators as an end-of-career professional, ready to step into a job he previously held from 1991-93 during George Bush's administration, with the ability to bring a steady hand to the department he loves and do the right thing without caring about the political consequences.

Barr said he would resign before firing Mueller without good cause, and inform the public and Congress of as much as possible of what Mueller reports to him. The vote was mostly along party lines.

After Mueller filed his report, Barr faced criticism that he helped Trump spin the results before the public could read it.

In the meantime, Barr as expected has continued or expanded the Trump administration's conservative policies and legal arguments on immigration, civil rights enforcement and LGBT employment discrimination.

48   Withdrawing Troops from Yemen

Passage of the joint resolution (S J Res 7), as amended, that would direct the president, within 30 days of enactment, to remove U.S. armed forces from hostilities in or affecting the Republic of Yemen, including in-flight refueling of non-U.S. aircraft, unless a declaration of war or specific authorization for such use of forces has been enacted. Passed 54-46 (R 7-46 (D 45-0; I 2-0) on March 13, 2019.

Ever since the murder of journalist Jamal Khashoggi in October 2018, Congress has been reevaluating the U.S. relationship with Saudi Arabia. Back in November 2018, Sen. Bob Corker of Tennessee, a Republican who was then chairman of the Foreign Relations Committee, told the BBC that the death of the Saudi dissident and U.S. resident at the hands of Saudi captors could "tip the scales" when it came to how the U.S. dealt with the kingdom and its war in Yemen.

In March, those scales were tipped further as the Senate voted — for the second time in three months — on a measure that would end U.S. involvement in the country's civil war, which by some estimates has resulted in the deaths of as many as 60,000. The United Nations has called the war the world's worst humanitarian crisis.

The successful vote in the Senate marked a historic few weeks in Congress. In February, the House adopted its own Yemen withdrawal resolution (H J Res 37) with 18 Republicans joining them. In April, the House adopted the Senate resolution with 16 Republican votes. It was the first time that a war powers measure that passed with bipartisan support reached the president's desk.

In practical terms, however, these maneuvers by Congress had no effect. Despite Trump's long-standing desire to withdraw troops from foreign entanglements, the president vetoed the measure in April. The Senate failed to override, effectively killing the resolution.

Trump argued in a statement that the bill would "harm bilateral relationships in the region," while also objecting to language in the bill that defined "hostilities" to include mid-flight refueling. In November, the administration announced it would stop mid-flight refueling for Saudi aircraft. At the time, the U.S. was providing refueling for roughly 20 percent of Saudi aircraft.

As a message to the president, though, the vote had some impact. Congress once again rebuked him for his unstinting support for the Saudi regime and its crown prince, Mohammed bin Salman.

49   National Emergency Disapproval

Passage of the joint resolution (H J Res 46) to terminate the president's national emergency declaration concerning the security situation at the southern border. Passed 59-41 (R 12-41; D 45-0; I 2-0) on March 14, 2019.

Even as President Trump has shaken up the Republican establishment, he's enjoyed the support of the vast majority of GOP lawmakers in Congress.

But Trump's decision in February 2019 to declare a national emergency in order to redirect up to $6.7 billion in Pentagon and law enforcement funding to build fencing along the southern border was a bridge too far for some of the rank and file. It voided a congressional appropriations process that had just denied Trump the wall funding he desired.

Following the House's lead, the Senate voted on March 14 on a resolution to end the emergency and reclaim control of the money. Democrats were united in favor and were joined by 12 Republicans, who ranged from moderates like Susan Collins of Maine to institutionalists such as Roy Blunt of Missouri.

One of the 12, Tennessee's Lamar Alexander, said he was voting to preserve Congress's ability to check the president. "After a Revolutionary War against a king, our nation's founders gave to Congress the power to approve all spending so that the president would not have too much power," he said.

Even so, 41 Republicans sided with Trump. They noted that Congress had granted presidents the power to declare emergencies and divert funding in a 1976 law, and that the influx of unauthorized immigrants and asylum seekers at the border, overtaxing U.S. immigration authorities, qualified as an emergency.

The margin of 59-41, however, was not large enough to override Trump's veto, the first of his presidency, which came the next day.

52   Green New Deal

Motion to invoke cloture on the motion to proceed to the joint resolution (S J Res 8) to express the sense of the Senate that the government should adopt a Green New Deal with the goal of achieving net-zero greenhouse gas emissions, promoting job growth, building sustainable infrastructure, protecting natural resources, and promoting justice and equity. Motion rejected 0-57 (R 0-53; D 0-3; I 0-1) on March 26, 2019.

Soon after House Democrats led by New York's Alexandria Ocasio-Cortez introduced a nonbinding resolution (S J Res 8) in February dubbed the Green New Deal, an ambitious plan to tackle climate change through sweeping changes in the energy economy,

Majority Leader Mitch McConnell began looking for a way to bring it up for a Senate vote.

McConnell and his fellow Republicans lambasted the proposal as a socialistic job-killer, and wanted to force Democrats — especially those running for president — to take a stand so their votes could be used against them in the 2020 campaigns.

Even after Speaker Nancy Pelosi made clear in late February that House Democrats would focus on developing legislation to address the climate crisis that could become law rather than adopting the nonbinding resolution, McConnell pressed ahead. He offered his own resolution mirroring the Green New Deal, and labeled the agenda described in it a "far-left science fiction novel."

But Senate Democrats thwarted his bid to get them on the record by simply voting "present" on a vote to move forward with the resolution. The cloture vote failed 0-57, with three Democrats and Maine independent Angus King joining Republicans against ending debate and moving to a vote on adoption.

The vote killed the Green New Deal in the Senate, but Democrats continued pressing for action on climate change. The ranking member of the Senate Environment and Public Works Committee, Thomas R. Carper of Delaware, pushed for a resolution that would force Republicans to vote on whether they agreed with scientists who warn of calamitous changes if global carbon emissions are not reduced.

The day after the Senate cloture vote, House Democrats led by Pelosi announced they would draft legislation to direct the president to develop a plan for the U.S. to achieve the goals it agreed to in the 2015 Paris Agreement to combat climate change.

And in May, the House passed a bill (HR 9) to block funding for the Trump administration to withdraw from the Paris accord. The measure passed 231-190, with three Republicans joining Democrats in supporting the bill.

None of those measures made it to the Senate floor in 2019.

61   Altman Nomination/Ruling of the Chair

Affirmation of the ruling of the chair regarding a point of order that post-cloture time for consideration of certain judicial nominations and executive branch appointees under the provisions of Senate Rule XXII is two hours. Ruling of the chair rejected 48-51 (R 2-51; D 44-0; I 2-0) on April 3, 20198.

Senate Republicans wanted to change a long-standing rule to allow the chamber to consider presidential nominations at a much faster pace, including administration officials and lifetime appointments to the nation's federal courts.

Majority Leader Mitch McConnell and other Republicans argued the so-called "nuclear option"— where a majority could overrule the ruling of the chair to establish a new precedent for floor action — must be done to overcome Democratic obstruction. Democrats called it a short-sighted, partisan power grab.

The change reduced the time certain nominations can be considered following a cloture vote from a maximum of 30 hours to two hours. Those excepted from the new rule include the Supreme Court, circuit court, the Cabinet and 13 federal bodies, including the Securities and Exchange Commission and the Federal Reserve's Board of Governors. The move comes after the Senate made procedural changes to make it easier to confirm nominations in 2013 and 2017.

First, McConnell tried to pass the rule change (S Res 50) on April 2. Democrats voted to block the procedural motion to allow for consideration of that bill on the floor, meaning it fell short of the 60-vote threshold to break a filibuster.

The next day, following a successful cloture vote on Jeffrey Kessler, the nominee for assistant secretary of Commerce, McConnell moved to cut his nomination's post-cloture debate time from 30 hours to two hours.

The presiding officer, Arkansas Republican Tom Cotton, objected, and McConnell appealed, asking for a simple majority vote to change the rule.

The process happened a second time in the same day, after a cloture vote on Trump's nomination of Roy Kalman Altman to be a federal judge in Florida's Southern District.

177   Saudi Arabia Arms Sales

Adoption of the joint resolution (S J Res 36) that would disapprove of arms sales to the Kingdom of Saudi Arabia, United Kingdom of Great Britain and Northern Ireland, the Kingdom of Spain, and the Italian Republic. Adopted 53-45 (R 7-45; D 44-0; I 2-0) on June 20, 2019.

For a year leading up to this vote, the Trump administration had been ratcheting up pressure on Iran — first by withdrawing from a 2015 agreement that sought to curb the country's nuclear ambitions, then by imposing harsh economic sanctions, and then by moving troops and warships within striking distance of it.

On June 20, Trump reportedly considered a strike against targets in Iran before abruptly canceling it.

In May, the administration announced it would sell $8.1 billion in arms to Saudi Arabia and the United Arab Emirates, invoking a section of the Arms Export Control Act that allows the administration to bypass congressional review. Its justification for the maneuver? The situation in Iran was precipitating an emergency in the region and the arms were needed immediately. Many in Congress were not pleased.

On June 20, the Senate voted to block the sales, with seven Republicans joining all voting Democrats to advance the measure.

The Senate also voted to advance a second arms sales measure (S J Res 38) and a package of 20 other arms sales that Democrats, led by Robert Menendez of New Jersey, agreed to allow with just one "en bloc" vote. One of the seven Republicans who had joined Democrats on the first two votes, Lisa Murkowski of Alaska, voted "no."

The measures went to the House, where they were adopted easily. Trump vetoed them, as promised. The Senate failed to override the veto, marking the second time in four months that the administration prevailed on a matter dealing with the Saudis despite congressional opposition.

Sen. Todd Young, a Republican from Indiana and the head of the party's campaign operation, joined Democrats on both votes dealing with Saudi Arabia. In March, he voted to end U.S. support of Saudi Arabia in its war with Yemen. He later partnered with Menendez on a separate measure that dealt with arms sales, the war in Yemen and Saudi Arabia's human rights record.

185   Supplemental Border Appropriations

Passage of a bill (HR 3401) to authorize a total of $4.6 billion in supplemental fiscal 2019 appropriations to address humanitarian concerns for migrants at the U.S.-Mexico border. Passed 84-8 (R 50-2; D 33-6; I 1-0) on June 26, 2019.

When the Senate voted to provide the Trump administration with $4.6 billion in border security funding on June 26, the flood of unauthorized immigrants and asylum seekers at the southern border had already prompted the president to declare a national emergency.

It had also prompted Trump, reluctant to allow immigrants to go free in the country while awaiting deportation proceedings or adjudication of their asylum claims, to separate immigrant children from their parents and to house immigrants in prison-like conditions.

Immigrant advocates and many Democrats in Congress were outraged and wanted any funding to come with strings attached, aimed at improving conditions for the immigrants. But Senate Democrats, at least in offering up funding to deal with the humanitarian crisis at the border, approached the issue with pragmatism.

With the Senate in GOP hands, Democrat Patrick J. Leahy of Vermont, urged his colleagues to compromise. "Inaction is certainly not an option for those who care about alleviating the suffering of desperate children and families seeking refuge in the United States," he said. "No one Republican or Democrat is going to get everything they want."

The funding package then passed overwhelmingly, with only six Democratic liberals opposed, along with two GOP budget hawks. The bipartisan vote hurt the cause of progressives in the House who continued to push their leaders to put more restrictions on how Trump could use the money. The next day, the House cleared the bill for Trump's signature.

324   Disapproval of "Affordable Clean Energy Rule"

Adoption of the joint resolution (S J Res 53) to express disapproval of the Environmental Protection Agency's July 2019 rule that would repeal the Clean Power Plan and finalize the Affordable Clean Energy rule. Rejected 41-53 (R 1-50; D 39-3; I 1-0) on Oct. 17, 2019.

With a little over a year until the 2020 elections, Senate Minority Leader Charles E. Schumer of New York pledged in early October that Democrats would force a series of roll call votes on issues he said Republicans were ignoring. The first came a week later, on a key Obama-era program to address climate change.

In July, the Trump administration had formally repealed an EPA regulation known as the Clean Power Plan, requiring utilities to reduce greenhouse gas emissions 32 percent from 2005 levels by 2030. The EPA replaced it with a new regulation, known as the Affordable Clean Energy rule, that would only require power-sector emissions to be reduced about 1 percent by 2030.

A resolution put forward by Democratic Sen. Benjamin L. Cardin of Maryland drew upon authority under the Congressional Review Act, which allows Congress to strike down recently enacted regulations, to rescind the EPA's new regulation.

Cardin argued that eliminating the Obama administration's Clean Power Plan would cause thousands of premature deaths as greenhouse gases cause the planet to heat up. "It puts our public health at risk," he said. "It's a missed opportunity."

Republicans responded that the Clean Power Plan amounted to a federal takeover of the electricity system. "It would have crippled our economy," said Wyoming Sen. John Barrasso, chairman of the Environment and Public Works Committee.

Cardin's resolution went down 41-51, with three Democrats — Doug Jones of Alabama, Kyrsten Sinema of Arizona and Joe Manchin III of West Virginia — joining Republicans voting against rescinding the new EPA rule. Republican Sen. Susan Collins of Maine voted to rescind it.

After the vote, Democrats said Republicans would be held accountable by voters for failing to address climate change. "A day of reckoning is coming," Schumer said. "The American people are paying attention."

HOUSE VOTES

42   Russian Sanctions

Motion to agree to a joint resolution (H J Res 30) that would disapprove of President Trump's proposed action related to the application of sanctions against certain Russian companies. Motion agreed to 362-53 (D 226-0; R 136-53) on Jan. 17, 2019.

In December 2018, following intense lobbying from allies of a Russian oligarch named Oleg Deripaska, the Treasury Department announced it was terminating sanctions against three of his companies, which are involved in, among other things, aluminum mining and natural gas. Treasury said that an agreement had been reached to "undertake significant restructuring and corporate governance changes" by taking Deripaska's ownership stake below 50 percent in all three entities. Deripaska himself would continue to face sanctions in addition to any other entity in which he held a greater than 50 percent stake.

This raised alarm among many, with Democrats and some Republicans arguing that the deal was a sham, since in some cases Deripaska could still control companies through relatives or other means. Deripaska has close ties to Russian President Vladimir Putin and was at one time connected to Donald Trump's former campaign manager, Paul Manafort, who was convicted in 2018 of financial fraud following an investigation by Special Counsel Robert S. Mueller III.

It was against this backdrop that Democrats in Congress launched a plan to block the Treasury Department from terminating sanctions against Deripaska. The House passed its bill with 136 Republicans joining all voting Democrats to uphold the sanctions, one day after the Senate failed to do so on its own version of the resolution (S J Res 2).

Just days after the votes, The New York Times revealed that under a confidential arrangement with Treasury, Deripaska would retain majority ownership in one of his companies, EN+. The newspaper further reported that before sanctions had been imposed on Deripaska in April he had transferred shares of some of his companies to his children.

94   National Emergency Disapproval

Passage of the joint resolution (H J Res 46) that would terminate the president's national emergency declaration concerning the security situation at the southern border. Passed 245-182 (D 232-0; R 13-182) on Feb. 26, 2019.

House Democrats, with the support of 13 Republicans, voted on Feb. 26 to end a national emergency Trump had declared 11 days before in order to free up $6.7 billion to build fencing along the southern border with Mexico.

Trump based his decision, on Feb. 15, on the flow of migrants to the border and the administration's inability to manage the large number of families with children arriving there. He said he'd take funds from military construction projects, a counternarcotics program and a Treasury Department asset forfeiture fund to build the wall, which he had promised Mexico would pay for during his 2016 campaign.

Trump justified his decision with a 1976 law that gives presidents authority to redirect funding in emergency situations. But the fact that Congress had just denied his request for border wall funding in fiscal 2019 appropriations set up a conflict between executive and legislative power.

The 13 Republicans who voted to stop the emergency, most of them moderates in competitive seats, along with strict constitutionalists, were mostly acting in defense of congressional power, and not necessarily in opposition to the wall construction.

But that small act of defiance foreshadowed a much larger one by 12 Senate Republicans who voted to end the emergency the following month.

Both votes were symbolic, without the required two-thirds majorities to overturn a Trump veto, which he issued on March 15. It was his first as president.

Trump cited two previous examples in which presidents had used the national emergency authority to spend money without Congress' assent: one by President George Bush in advance of the Persian Gulf War, and another by his son, President George W. Bush, after the Sept. 11, 2001, terrorist attacks.

A federal district court, followed by the Ninth Circuit Court of Appeals, temporarily stopped Trump from redirecting funds, while a case on the merits was pending, only to be overruled in July by the Supreme Court. The Ninth Circuit heard arguments in the case, brought by the American Civil Liberties Union and state attorneys general on behalf of a group of states, the Sierra Club and a coalition of border towns, in November.

99   Expanding Firearm Background Checks

Passage of the bill (HR 8) to require most purchasers of firearms to undergo a background check through the National Instant Criminal Background Check System, including all sales and transfers of firearms through public and private purchases. Passed 240-190 (D 232-2; R 8-188) on Feb. 27, 2019.

The mass shootings that have plagued America entered a new phase in 2012 when Adam Lanza shot and killed 20 first graders and six staff members at Sandy Hook Elementary School in Newtown, Conn. But Republicans, who controlled the House at the time and mostly oppose new restrictions on gun ownership, refused to bring gun control measures to the floor.

When Democrats regained the majority in 2019, they pledged to act quickly and to force representatives to take a stand on gun control, one way or the other. But the vote on a bill to expand background checks to gun shows and private sales on Feb. 27 revealed that the devastating string of killings that have followed Lanza's — including the 2016 killing of 50 at an Orlando nightclub and the 2017 attack on attendees at a Las Vegas country music concert, which left 59 dead — haven't altered the politics of the gun debate at all.

The proposal to expand background checks, already required of people who purchase guns at gun shops, is widely seen as the most non-threatening of proposals for Second Amendment purists. Still, most Republican lawmakers argue that it's not practical to require private sellers to conduct checks and they argue that additional background checks will do little, if anything, to keep guns out of the hands of people who want to kill others. The National Rifle Association, the lobby for gun owners, has vehemently opposed expanding the checks.

Only eight Republicans, most of them party moderates like Will Hurd of Texas and Fred Upton of Michigan, voted for the measure. Two Democrats from rural districts where hunting is a popular pastime opposed it, Jared Golden of Maine and Collin C. Peterson of Minnesota.

President Trump has vacillated on the issue of gun control, indicating in 2018 after a former student killed 17 at Stoneman Douglas High School in Parkland, Fla., that he was open to new measures. But he issued a veto threat on the bill in advance of the vote.

118   Voter Access, Campaign Finance and Ethics

Passage of a bill (HR 1), as amended, that includes a package of provisions related to campaign finance, voter registration and access, and ethical standards for government officials. Passed 234-193 (D 234-0; R 0-193) on March 8, 2019.

House Democrats assigned the symbolically significant moniker of HR 1 to their mega overhaul measure, calling it a top priority at the outset of the 116th Congress. The tenets of the bill, including big changes to election and ethics laws, dovetailed with the anti-corruption messaging that helped propel Democrats into the majority in the House after the 2018 elections.

The proposals included in the package have continued to be a dominant theme among Democrats amid the 2020 campaigns and against the backdrop of House impeachment of President Trump stemming from concerns of foreign influence in U.S. politics.

Every House Democrat added his or her name as a co-sponsor; no Republicans supported the bill.

Despite the relatively swift passage for such a massive package — totaling more than 700 pages — the measure ran into the GOP-controlled Senate. Senate Majority Leader Mitch McConnell of Kentucky held to his pledge to deny the bill any consideration in his chamber.

He and other Republicans attack the bill for creating an optional 6-to-1 public financing system whereby every dollar raised from an individual donor would be matched six times for donations under $200, as long as candidates choose to forgo larger donations. The money for the match would come from fees imposed on companies or individuals by the government for malfeasance.

The overhaul also would smooth the process for registering to vote, and it would require additional disclosures from lobbying and other groups that spend money aimed at influencing elections.

Supporters of the bill say they're looking to this year's elections to revive its chances of enactment. "If a reform-minded president

and Congress are elected this November, we will be on the doorstep of creating a historic and new system for financing presidential and congressional elections," says Fred Wertheimer, president of Democracy 21, which lobbied in support of the bill.

184   International Emissions Reduction Plan

assage of the bill (HR 9), as amended, that would prohibit the use of federal funds for U.S. withdrawal from the Paris Agreement on climate change and would require the president to develop a plan for the United States to meet its nationally determined contribution under the accord. Passed 231-190 (D 228-0; R 3-190) on May 2, 2019.

The ambitious Green New Deal calling for a revamped energy sector to address climate change, introduced in February by House Democrats led by New York's Alexandria Ocasio-Cortez, never made it to the House floor for a vote in 2019. Speaker Nancy Pelosi said early in the year that she wanted Democrats to focus on legislation that could actually become law rather than a nonbinding resolution.

Ultimately the House approved only one such measure, seeking to block President Trump from spending money to withdraw the U.S. from the Paris Agreement on climate change negotiated in 2015 and signed by President Barack Obama in 2016.

The measure passed 231-190, with only three Republicans — Brian Fitzpatrick of Pennsylvania, Elise Stefanik of New York and Vern Buchanan of Florida — joining Democrats in support.

The bill moved on to the Senate, where it has seen no action.

Trump announced in the summer of 2017 that he would pull out of the Paris accord, in which the U.S. pledged to cut greenhouse-gas emissions as much as 28 percent from 2005 levels by 2025. However, under international law the U.S. cannot formally withdraw from the agreement until November 2020.

Pelosi made the bill to disrupt the withdrawal process a top priority and set aside two days for debate and amendments at the beginning of May.

The jockeying included an amendment offered by Arizona Republican Paul Gosar to strip the provision barring funding to pull out of the agreement. That was rejected 189-234.

New York Democrat Adriano Espaillat proposed an amendment calling the Paris deal a form of "climate justice" because it would help reduce adverse impacts on migrants, children and the most vulnerable. The amendment passed 237-185.

The House also voted 259-166 to approve an amendment by California Democrat TJ Cox that would require any federal plan to cut greenhouse-gas emissions to consider the effects on U.S. employment, technology and energy costs.

Before the final vote, Kentucky Republican Andy Barr said the U.S. should export "clean coal" to address climate change and urged votes against the bill. "One thousand more pages in the Federal Register will not change the weather," Barr said, shouting to a crowded chamber.

Although the House only passed one climate bill in 2019, Democrats continued to press forward with hearings and some provisions addressing the issue added to spending bills. Democratic Caucus Chairman Hakeem Jeffries of New York says the House Select Committee on the Climate Crisis, led by Florida Democrat Kathy Castor, has until March 31, 2020, to issue recommendations and then the party can start moving other climate bills.

217   LGBTQ Anti-Discrimination Protections

Passage of a bill (HR 5) that would prohibit discrimination or segregation based on sex, sexual orientation, and gender identity under 1964 Civil Rights Act protections, including in public facilities, public education, federal assistance programs, employment, jury service, and areas of public accommodation. Passed 236-173 (D 228-0; R 8-173) on May 17, 2019.

Social justice issues were high on the Democratic agenda in 2019, with the House passing legislation to ban discrimination based on sexual orientation or gender identity, to end gender-based pay inequity and to oppose President Trump's ban on transgender individuals serving in the military.

None of the House-approved bills saw action in the Senate.

The measure that had the most Republican support in the House was anti-discrimination protections for the LGBTQ community — and that garnered just eight GOP votes. (The bill to prohibit pay discrimination based on gender was backed by seven Republicans and legislation to oppose the transgender service ban won five Republican votes.)

The LGBTQ rights bill sponsored by Democrat David Cicilline of Rhode Island would amend the Civil Rights Act of 1964 to prohibit discrimination against lesbian, gay, bisexual, transgender and queer people in all sectors, public and private.

The chairman of the House Judiciary Committee, Democrat Jerrold Nadler of New York, said the legislation "goes straight to the heart of who we want to be as a country."

The committee's ranking Republican, Doug Collins of Georgia, countered that the bill would set back civil rights protections gained by others, including women, and would put children at risk. Transgender girls and boys, he said, would be hurt "by allowing doctors to prescribe hormones and perform major surgeries on adolescents without parental consent or involvement."

While Congress was stalled on the legislation, the Supreme Court debated the issue of LGBTQ rights in the first week of its 2019-20 term in October. The court appeared divided on the question of whether the Civil Rights Act applies to the LGBTQ community, but is expected to rule on any of three separate cases that revolve around the issue before the end of the term in the spring.

429   Supplemental Border Appropriations

Motion to concur in the Senate amendment to the Emergency Supplemental Appropriations for Humanitarian Assistance and Security at the Southern Border Act (HR 3401) that would authorize a total of $4.6 billion in supplemental fiscal 2019 appropriations to address humanitarian concerns for migrants at the U.S.-Mexico border. Agreed to 305-102 (D 129-95; R 176-7) on June 27, 2019.

Democrats' anger about President Trump's handling of border security was red hot in 2019 when they were asked to vote on legislation to provide him with $4.6 billion in supplemental funding to manage the flow of migrants. They were outraged by his policy — rescinded in 2018 — of separating immigrant children from their parents, his February 2019 decision to use defense funding to pay for border wall construction, and by his detention "in cages" of asylum seekers awaiting adjudication of their claims.

Still, the vote to provide the funding passed the House with a majority of Democrats joining a mostly united Republican caucus in favor.

Before the vote, Speaker Nancy Pelosi pressed for changes to a Senate appropriations bill as a condition of granting the funding.

Democrats proposed an amendment to increase funds for humanitarian needs and to process immigrants, to strengthen safeguards for children in government custody, and to reduce money for the Immigration and Customs Enforcement division of the Homeland Security Department, which has run controversial immigrant detention centers.

The GOP-controlled Senate refused to accept the changes and Pelosi acquiesced when it became clear to her that a standoff would only delay aid getting to the border and open her party up to blame for the conditions there.

In a letter to fellow Democrats explaining why she wanted them to pass the Senate bill, she wrote: "We have to make sure that the resources needed to protect the children are available."

It was an act of pragmatism that split her caucus, with 95 representatives, mostly progressives, voting against the funding bill.

482   Condemning President Trump's Rhetoric

Agreeing to the resolution (H Res 489) to condemn President Trump's "racist" comments suggesting that certain members of Congress should "go back" to other countries and stating that his comments have "legitimized and increased fear and hatred" toward people of color and naturalized American citizens. Adopted 240-187 (D 235-0; R 4-187; I 1-0) on July 16, 2019.

Even some Republicans said President Trump crossed a line when he tweeted on July 14 that four Democratic women of color in the House should "go back and help fix the totally broken and crime infested places from which they came."

The freshmen lawmakers known as "the Squad" — Reps. Alexandria Ocasio-Cortez of New York, Ilhan Omar of Minnesota, Ayanna S. Pressley of Massachusetts and Rashida Tlaib of Michigan — have been harsh critics of the president since taking office in January, but Trump's tweet and a subsequent rally that featured "send her back" chants against Omar left many Democrats fearing for their safety.

Speaker Nancy Pelosi moved quickly to defend the women and put forward a resolution to condemn Trump's "racist comments" about them.

Trump's response before the vote on the resolution didn't help much. "Why isn't the House voting to rebuke the filthy and hate laced things they have said? Because they are the Radical Left, and the Democrats are afraid to take them on. Sad!"

Many Republican lawmakers described Trump's words as "wrong" or "over the line." Some went further and called his comments "racist" and "xenophobic."

"He should be talking about things that unite, not divide us," said Texas Republican Rep. Will Hurd.

But others defended the president's attacks. "They're obviously not racist," GOP Rep. Andy Harris of Maryland said on a Baltimore radio show. "But again, when anyone disagrees with someone now, you call them a racist and this is no exception."

The House resolution stated, in part, that Trump's "racist comments that have legitimized and increased fear and hatred of new Americans and people of color by saying that our fellow Americans who are immigrants, and those who may look to the president like immigrants, should 'go back' to other countries, by referring to immigrants and asylum seekers as 'invaders,' and by saying that members of Congress who are immigrants (or those of our colleagues who are wrongly assumed to be immigrants) do not belong in Congress or in the United States of America."

In the end, only four Republicans and one independent (Justin Amash of Michigan) joined with all House Democrats in supporting the resolution. The four GOP members who voted for it were Hurd, Susan W. Brooks of Indiana, Brian Fitzpatrick of Pennsylvania and Fred Upton of Michigan.

560   Opposing Withdrawal from Syria

Motion to suspend the rules and pass the joint resolution (H J Res 77) that would express the sense of Congress opposing the decision to end U.S. efforts to prevent Turkish military operations against Syrian Kurdish forces in northeast Syria. Motion agreed to by a vote of 354-60 (D 225-0; R 129-60; I 0-0) on Oct. 16, 2019.

On the day the House voted on a resolution rebuking the president for his decision to pull U.S. troops from Kurdish-held parts of Syria, President Trump called the Kurds "no angels" while explaining that in the Middle East "there's a lot of sand that they can play with." Later that morning, Democratic leaders walked out of a briefing at the White House on Turkey's incursion in Syria, saying the president had a "meltdown," and had called Speaker Nancy Pelosi a "third-rate politician." Pelosi said she was praying for Trump's health.

Trump later countered that it was Pelosi who had the meltdown and tweeted out a photo of the meeting, which showed Pelosi standing and pointing at the president.

In the afternoon, a host on Fox Business tweeted out a letter from Trump to Turkish President Recep Erdogan in which the president threatened to destroy that country's economy, while adding that the world will look upon Erdogan as "the devil" if he didn't make a deal. "Don't be a fool!" Trump concluded. Erdogan reportedly threw the letter in the garbage.

Following the announcement of Trump's decision Oct. 13, Turkey invaded northern Syria, killing dozens and initially displacing over 180,000 people. The U.S. had relied on Kurds in the region in the fight against the Islamic State, or ISIS.

The House moved quickly to condemn the withdrawal. In all, 129 Republicans joined all Democrats present to vote for a nonbinding resolution (H J Res 77) opposing the withdrawal while calling on the U.S. to continue supporting the Kurds. On the House floor, many members expressed alarm at the administration's actions. "Walking away from a friend is a sad indication of policy that we don't want to support, we don't want to condone," Rep. John Shimkus, R-Ill., a retired Army veteran, said, while noting the U.S. partnership with the Kurds goes back decades. "I don't know how we get the genie back in the bottle."

Sixty Republicans voted "no," though only a few took to the floor explaining their position. Tom Reed of New York said the reason for his "no" vote had to do with a lack of an authorizing vote on the use of military force. "Make no mistake about it, by voting 'yes' on this resolution, you are authorizing the use of military force of our men and women on Syrian soil," he said.

Matt Gaetz of Florida, a reliable Trump supporter, argued that Turkey should be kicked out of NATO instead of the U.S. keeping troops in Syria. He echoed Trump's stance on the matter. "We are not the world's police force," he said. "We are not the world's piggy bank."

Senate Majority Leader Mitch McConnell, who called Trump's actions "a grave mistake," said he wanted a stronger measure in his

chamber. And yet, the matter has never come up for a vote.

69   Impeachment — Abuse of Power

Adoption of the Article I of H Res 755, which would impeach President Trump for abuse of power by using the powers of his office to solicit the interference of a foreign government in the 2020 U.S. presidential election to benefit his reelection and harm the election prospects of a political opponent. Specifically, it would state that Trump solicited the government of Ukraine to announce investigations into former Vice President Joe Biden and theories regarding foreign interference in the 2016 U.S. presidential election. It would state that Trump conditioned official actions, including the release of security assistance funds to Ukraine, on such announcements. It would state that Trump's actions were conducted "for corrupt purposes in pursuit of personal political benefit" and that such actions "compromised the national security of the United States and undermined the integrity of the United States democratic process." Adopted 230-197 (D 229-2; R 0-195; I 1-0) on Dec. 18, 2019.

Just days before Christmas, the House impeached a president for only the third time in American history.

The House leveled two articles of impeachment against President Trump, the first alleging that he abused his power. Specifically, it alleges that Trump pressured the Ukrainian government to investigate former Vice President Joe Biden and his son, Hunter, to benefit the president's 2020 reelection bid.

The House adopted that article, 230-197. No Republicans voted in favor of it and two Democrats joined Republicans in voting "no." New Jersey's Jeff Van Drew, one of those two Democrats, joined the GOP days after the vote.

Democrats built the case against Trump with weeks of public and private testimony from former administration officials and career government employees. One of the strongest pieces of evidence against Trump, though, was the White House-released readout of a phone call between Trump and Volodymyr Zelenskiy in which Trump asked the Ukrainian president for a "favor."

Democrats argued that the favor Trump requested was Zelenskiy announcing an investigation into Hunter Biden, who accepted a lucrative position on the board of a Ukrainian gas company while his father was vice president. The theory goes that an investigation into Hunter Biden — who has not been accused of any wrongdoing — would damage his father's 2020 presidential bid and thus help Trump's reelection efforts.

Democrats argued that Trump withheld congressionally appropriated military aid in exchange for the desired announcement from Zelenskiy, and further contended that the aid was released and the announcement from Zelenskiy not made because Trump's plan was foiled by an administration whistleblower. Republicans used those facts to argue for Trump's innocence.

696   Impeachment — Obstruction of Congress

Adoption of Article II of H Res 755, which would impeach President Trump for obstruction of Congress by defying, and instructing others not to comply with, subpoenas issued by the House of Representatives in relation to the House impeachment inquiry into Trump's solicitation of the government of Ukraine. Adopted 229-198 (D 228-3; R 0-195; I 1-0) on Dec. 18, 2019.

The House impeached President Trump not just for his alleged "high crime," but also for his attempts to keep Congress from investigating it. The House's second article of impeachment against the president was for Trump's obstruction of Congress.

The House leveled that second article against Trump as the president directed many of the witnesses House committees called to testify to defy congressional subpoenas.

The House adopted the second article on a 229-198 vote. No Republicans voted in favor of the second article with three Democrats joining the GOP. Maine Democrat Jared Golden was the only member of Congress to vote in favor of the first article of impeachment and against the second. Minnesota's Collin C. Peterson and New Jersey's Jeff Van Drew were the other two Democrats to vote with the GOP against the second article. Van Drew later left the Democratic party to join the GOP.

House Democrats brought the second charge after the Trump White House refused to produce documents requested by the House, in addition to compelling some witnesses to not appear before Congress. The president's defenders argued that the charge was unjust and that federal courts should have judged the dispute between the executive and legislative branches of government.

701   U.S.-Mexico-Canada Trade Agreement

Passage of the bill (HR 5430) that would implement the trade agreement reached between the United States, Mexico, and Canada that replaces the North American Free Trade Agreement. It would modify existing trade law to provide for implementation of the agreement, authorize federal agencies and other entities to implement and enforce provisions of the agreement, and authorize or appropriate more than $2 billion in funding for certain implementation activities. Passed 385-41 (D 193-38; R 192-2; I 0-1) on Dec. 19, 2019.

When U.S., Mexican and Canadian leaders signed a renegotiated North American Free Trade Agreement in November 2018, President Trump didn't seem likely to get needed Democratic support for passage.

Democrats said the agreement lacked strong enforcement of labor and environmental provisions and would reward pharmaceutical companies by giving them monopoly pricing of biologic drugs for 10 years in Canada and Mexico. The pricing language, they argued, could make it difficult for Congress to reduce the U.S. biologics monopoly pricing period from 12 years to less than 10 years.

Speaker Nancy Pelosi, D-Calif., warned the administration it would need to address her caucus' concerns.

Trade Representative Robert Lighthizer, a former trade lawyer respected by unions and considered a straight shooter among lawmakers of both parties, began negotiations with a working group appointed by Pelosi and led by Ways and Means Chairman Richard E. Neal, D-Mass.

On Dec. 10, Pelosi and Neal claimed a major victory for an agreement they said would toughen enforcement of labor rights and environmental standards. Pelosi said Democrats had turned an unacceptable trade deal into one she thought many in her caucus would support.

AFL-CIO President Richard Trumka's support improved the odds for a big Democratic endorsement.

"USMCA is not a model moving forward, but it establishes important principles we can build from," Rep. Rosa DeLauro, D-Conn., a trade skeptic and member of the working group, said in a Dec. 19 letter to colleagues. ■

TEXTS

Trump Casts Governance Against Investigation on Eve of Impeachment Vote

Following is the CQ transcript of President Donald Trump's state of the union address, delivered Feb. 5, 2019 in the chamber of the United States House of Representatives.

Madam Speaker, Mr. Vice President, Members of Congress, the First Lady of the United States, and my fellow Americans:

We meet tonight at a moment of unlimited potential. As we begin a new Congress, I stand here ready to work with you to achieve historic breakthroughs for all Americans.

Millions of our fellow citizens are watching us now, gathered in this great chamber, hoping that we will govern not as two parties but as one Nation.

The agenda I will lay out this evening is not a Republican agenda or a Democrat agenda. It is the agenda of the American people.

Many of us campaigned on the same core promises: to defend American jobs and demand fair trade for American workers; to rebuild and revitalize our Nation's infrastructure; to reduce the price of healthcare and prescription drugs; to create an immigration system that is safe, lawful, modern and secure; and to pursue a foreign policy that puts America's interests first.

There is a new opportunity in American politics, if only we have the courage to seize it. Victory is not winning for our party. Victory is winning for our country.

This year, America will recognize two important anniversaries that show us the majesty of America's mission, and the power of American pride.

In June, we mark 75 years since the start of what General Dwight D. Eisenhower called the Great Crusade — the Allied liberation of Europe in World War II. On D-Day, June 6, 1944, 15,000 young American men jumped from the sky, and 60,000 more stormed in from the sea, to save our civilization from tyranny. Here with us tonight are three of those heroes: Private First Class Joseph Reilly, Staff Sergeant Irving Locker, and Sergeant Herman Zeitchik. Gentlemen, we salute you.

In 2019, we also celebrate 50 years since brave young pilots flew a quarter of a million miles through space to plant the American flag on the face of the moon. Half a century later, we are joined by one of the Apollo 11 astronauts who planted that flag: Buzz Aldrin. This year, American astronauts will go back to space on American rockets.

In the 20th century, America saved freedom, transformed science, and redefined the middle class standard of living for the entire world to see. Now, we must step boldly and bravely into the next chapter of this great American adventure, and we must create a new standard of living for the 21st century. An amazing quality of life for all of our citizens is within our reach.

We can make our communities safer, our families stronger, our culture richer, our faith deeper, and our middle class bigger and more prosperous than ever before.

IMPEACHMENT AND INVESTIGATION

But we must reject the politics of revenge, resistance, and retribution — and embrace the boundless potential of cooperation, compromise, and the common good.

Together, we can break decades of political stalemate. We can bridge old divisions, heal old wounds, build new coalitions, forge new solutions, and unlock the extraordinary promise of America's future. The decision is ours to make.

We must choose between greatness or gridlock, results or resistance, vision or vengeance, incredible progress or pointless destruction.

Tonight, I ask you to choose greatness.

THE ECONOMY

Over the last 2 years, my Administration has moved with urgency and historic speed to confront problems neglected by leaders of both parties over many decades.

In just over 2 years since the election, we have launched an unprecedented economic boom — a boom that has rarely been seen before. We have created 5.3 million new jobs and importantly added 600,000 new manufacturing jobs — something which almost everyone said was impossible to do, but the fact is, we are just getting started.

Wages are rising at the fastest pace in decades, and growing for blue collar workers, who I promised to fight for, faster than anyone else. Nearly 5 million Americans have been lifted off food stamps. The United States economy is growing almost twice as fast today as when I took office, and we are considered far and away the hottest economy anywhere in the world. Unemployment has reached the lowest rate in half a century. African-American, Hispanic-American and Asian-American unemployment have all reached their lowest levels ever recorded. Unemployment for Americans with disabilities has also reached an all-time low. More people are working now than at any time in our history – 157 million.

We passed a massive tax cut for working families and doubled the child tax credit.

We virtually ended the estate, or death, tax on small businesses, ranches, and family farms.

We eliminated the very unpopular Obamacare individual mandate penalty — and to give critically ill patients access to life-saving cures, we passed right to try.

My Administration has cut more regulations in a short time than any other administration during its entire tenure. Companies are coming back to our country in large numbers thanks to historic reductions in taxes and regulations.

We have unleashed a revolution in American energy — the United States is now the number one producer of oil and natural gas in the world. And now, for the first time in 65 years, we are a net exporter of energy.

After 24 months of rapid progress, our economy is the envy of the world, our military is the most powerful on earth, and America is winning each and every day. Members of Congress: the State of our Union is strong. Our country is vibrant and our economy is thriving like never before.

On Friday, it was announced that we added another 304,000 jobs last month alone — almost double what was expected. An economic miracle is taking place in the United States — and the only thing that can stop it are foolish wars, politics, or ridiculous partisan investigations.

BIPARTISANSHIP

If there is going to be peace and legislation, there cannot be war and investigation. It just doesn't work that way!

We must be united at home to defeat our adversaries abroad.

This new era of cooperation can start with finally confirming the more than 300 highly qualified nominees who are still stuck in the Senate – some after years of waiting. The Senate has failed to act on these nominations, which is unfair to the nominees and to our country.

Now is the time for bipartisan action. Believe it or not, we have already proven that it is possible.

In the last Congress, both parties came together to pass unprecedented legislation to confront the opioid crisis, a sweeping new Farm Bill, historic VA reforms, and after four decades of rejection, we passed VA Accountability so we can finally terminate those who mistreat our wonderful veterans.

And just weeks ago, both parties united for ground-breaking criminal justice reform. Last year, I heard through friends the story of Alice Johnson. I was deeply moved. In 1997, Alice was sentenced to life in prison as a first-time non-violent drug offender. Over the next two decades, she became a prison minister, inspiring others to choose a better path. She had a big impact on that prison population — and far beyond.

Alice's story underscores the disparities and unfairness that can exist in criminal sentencing — and the need to remedy this injustice. She served almost 22 years and had expected to be in prison for the rest of her life.

In June, I commuted Alice's sentence — and she is here with us tonight. Alice, thank you for reminding us that we always have the power to shape our own destiny.

When I saw Alice's beautiful family greet her at the prison gates, hugging and kissing and crying and laughing, I knew I did the right thing.

Inspired by stories like Alice's, my Administration worked closely with members of both parties to sign the First Step Act into law. This legislation reformed sentencing laws that have wrongly and disproportionately harmed the African-American community. The First Step Act gives non-violent offenders the chance to re-enter society as productive, law-abiding citizens. Now, States across the country are following our lead. America is a Nation that believes in redemption.

We are also joined tonight by Matthew Charles from Tennessee. In 1996, at age 30, Matthew was sentenced to 35 years for selling drugs and related offenses. Over the next two decades, he completed more than 30 Bible studies, became a law clerk, and mentored fellow inmates. Now, Matthew is the very first person to be released from prison under the First Step Act. Matthew, on behalf of all Americans: welcome home.

IMMIGRATION

As we have seen, when we are united, we can make astonishing strides for our country. Now, Republicans and Democrats must join forces again to confront an urgent national crisis.

The Congress has 10 days left to pass a bill that will fund our Government, protect our homeland, and secure our southern border.

Now is the time for the Congress to show the world that America is committed to ending illegal immigration and putting the ruthless coyotes, cartels, drug dealers, and human traffickers out of business.

As we speak, large, organized caravans are on the march to the United States. We have just heard that Mexican cities, in order to remove the illegal immigrants from their communities, are getting trucks and buses to bring them up to our country in areas where there is little border protection. I have ordered another 3,750 troops to our southern border to prepare for the tremendous onslaught.

This is a moral issue. The lawless state of our southern border is a threat to the safety, security, and financial well-being of all Americans. We have a moral duty to create an immigration system that protects the lives and jobs of our citizens. This includes our obligation to the millions of immigrants living here today, who followed the rules and respected our laws. Legal immigrants enrich our Nation and strengthen our society in countless ways. I want people to come into our country, but they have to come in legally.

Tonight, I am asking you to defend our very dangerous southern border out of love and devotion to our fellow citizens and to our country.

No issue better illustrates the divide between America's working class and America's political class than illegal immigration. Wealthy politicians and donors push for open borders while living their lives behind walls and gates and guards.

Meanwhile, working class Americans are left to pay the price for mass illegal migration — reduced jobs, lower wages, overburdened schools and hospitals, increased crime, and a depleted social safety net.

Tolerance for illegal immigration is not compassionate — it is cruel. One in three women is sexually assaulted on the long journey north. Smugglers use migrant children as human pawns to exploit our laws and gain access to our country.

Human traffickers and sex traffickers take advantage of the wide open areas between our ports of entry to smuggle thousands of young girls and women into the United States and to sell them into prostitution and modern-day slavery.

Tens of thousands of innocent Americans are killed by lethal drugs that cross our border and flood into our cities — including meth, heroin, cocaine, and fentanyl.

The savage gang, MS-13, now operates in 20 different American States, and they almost all come through our southern border. Just yesterday, an MS-13 gang member was taken into custody for a fatal shooting on a subway platform in New York City. We are removing these gang members by the thousands, but until we secure our border they're going to keep streaming back in.

Year after year, countless Americans are murdered by criminal illegal aliens.

I've gotten to know many wonderful Angel Moms, Dads, and families – no one should ever have to suffer the horrible heartache they have endured.

Here tonight is Debra Bissell. Just three weeks ago, Debra's parents, Gerald and Sharon, were burglarized and shot to death in their Reno, Nevada, home by an illegal alien. They were in their eighties and are survived by four children, 11 grandchildren, and 20 great-grandchildren. Also here tonight are Gerald and Sharon's granddaughter, Heather, and great-granddaughter, Madison.

To Debra, Heather, Madison, please stand: few can understand your pain. But I will never forget, and I will fight for the memory of Gerald and Sharon, that it should never happen again.

Not one more American life should be lost because our Nation failed to control its very dangerous border.

In the last 2 years, our brave ICE officers made 266,000 arrests of criminal aliens, including those charged or convicted of nearly 100,000 assaults, 30,000 sex crimes, and 4,000 killings.

We are joined tonight by one of those law enforcement heroes: ICE Special Agent Elvin Hernandez. When Elvin was a boy, he and his family legally immigrated to the United States from the Dominican Republic. At the age of eight, Elvin told his dad he wanted to become a Special Agent. Today, he leads investigations into the scourge of international sex trafficking. Elvin says: "If I can make sure these young girls get their justice, I've done my job." Thanks to his work and that of his colleagues, more than 300 women and girls have been rescued from horror and more than 1,500 sadistic traffickers have been put behind bars in the last year.

Special Agent Hernandez, please stand: We will always support the brave men and women of Law Enforcement — and I pledge to you tonight that we will never abolish our heroes from ICE.

My Administration has sent to the Congress a commonsense proposal to end the crisis on our southern border.

It includes humanitarian assistance, more law enforcement, drug detection at our ports, closing loopholes that enable child smuggling, and plans for a new physical barrier, or wall, to secure the vast areas between our ports of entry. In the past, most of the people in this room voted for a wall — but the proper wall never got built. I'll get it built.

This is a smart, strategic, see-through steel barrier — not just a simple concrete wall. It will be deployed in the areas identified by border agents as having the greatest need, and as these agents will tell you, where walls go up, illegal crossings go way down.

San Diego used to have the most illegal border crossings in the country. In response, and at the request of San Diego residents and political leaders, a strong security wall was put in place. This powerful barrier almost completely ended illegal crossings.

The border city of El Paso, Texas, used to have extremely high rates of violent crime — one of the highest in the country, and considered one of our Nation's most dangerous cities. Now, with a powerful barrier in place, El Paso is one of our safest cities.

Simply put, walls work and walls save lives. So let's work together, compromise, and reach a deal that will truly make America safe.

JOBS FOR WOMEN

As we work to defend our people's safety, we must also ensure our economic resurgence continues at a rapid pace.

No one has benefitted more from our thriving economy than women, who have filled 58 percent of the new jobs created in the last year. All Americans can be proud that we have more women in the workforce than ever before — and exactly one century after the Congress passed the Constitutional amendment giving women the right to vote, we also have more women serving in the Congress than ever before.

As part of our commitment to improving opportunity for women everywhere, this Thursday we are launching the first ever Government-wide initiative focused on economic empowerment for women in developing countries.

TRADE

To build on our incredible economic success, one priority is paramount — reversing decades of calamitous trade policies.

We are now making it clear to China that after years of targeting our industries, and stealing our intellectual property, the theft of American jobs and wealth has come to an end.

Therefore, we recently imposed tariffs on $250 billion of Chinese goods — and now our Treasury is receiving billions of dollars a month from a country that never gave us a dime. But I don't blame China for taking advantage of us — I blame our leaders and representatives for allowing this travesty to happen. I have great respect for President Xi, and we are now working on a new trade deal with China. But it must include real, structural change to end unfair trade practices, reduce our chronic trade deficit, and protect American jobs.

Another historic trade blunder was the catastrophe known as NAFTA.

I have met the men and women of Michigan, Ohio, Pennsylvania, Indiana, New Hampshire, and many other States whose dreams were shattered by NAFTA. For years, politicians promised them they would negotiate for a better deal. But no one ever tried — until now.

Our new U.S.-Mexico-Canada Agreement — or USMCA — will replace NAFTA and deliver for American workers: bringing back our manufacturing jobs, expanding American agriculture, protecting intellectual property, and ensuring that more cars are proudly stamped with four beautiful words: made in the USA.

Tonight, I am also asking you to pass the United States Reciprocal Trade Act, so that if another country places an unfair tariff on an American product, we can charge them the exact same tariff on the same product that they sell to us.

Both parties should be able to unite for a great rebuilding of America's crumbling infrastructure.

I know that the Congress is eager to pass an infrastructure bill — and I am eager to work with you on legislation to deliver new and important infrastructure investment, including investments in the cutting edge industries of the future. This is not an option. This is a necessity.

HEALTH CARE

The next major priority for me, and for all of us, should be to lower the cost of healthcare and prescription drugs — and to protect patients with pre-existing conditions.

Already, as a result of my Administration's efforts, in 2018 drug prices experienced their single largest decline in 46 years.

But we must do more. It is unacceptable that Americans pay vastly more than people in other countries for the exact same drugs, often made in the exact same place. This is wrong, unfair, and together we can stop it.

I am asking the Congress to pass legislation that finally takes on the problem of global freeloading and delivers fairness and price transparency for American patients. We should also require drug companies, insurance companies, and hospitals to disclose real prices to foster competition and bring costs down.

No force in history has done more to advance the human condition than American freedom. In recent years we have made remarkable progress in the fight against HIV and AIDS. Scientific breakthroughs have brought a once-distant dream within reach. My budget will ask Democrats and Republicans to make the needed commitment to eliminate the HIV epidemic in the United States within 10 years. Together, we will defeat AIDS in America.

Tonight, I am also asking you to join me in another fight that all Americans can get behind: the fight against childhood cancer.

Joining Melania in the gallery this evening is a very brave 10-year-old girl, Grace Eline. Every birthday since she was 4, Grace asked her friends to donate to St. Jude Children's Research Hospital. She did not know that one day she might be a patient herself. Last year, Grace was diagnosed with brain cancer. Immediately, she began radiation treatment. At the same time, she rallied her community and raised more than $40,000 for the fight against cancer. When Grace completed treatment last fall, her doctors and nurses cheered with tears in their eyes as she hung up a poster that read: "Last Day of Chemo." Grace — you are an inspiration to us all.

Many childhood cancers have not seen new therapies in decades. My budget will ask the Congress for $500 million over the next 10 years to fund this critical life-saving research.

To help support working parents, the time has come to pass school choice for America's children. I am also proud to be the first President to include in my budget a plan for nationwide paid family leave — so that every new parent has the chance to bond with their newborn child.

ABORTION RESTRICTIONS

There could be no greater contrast to the beautiful image of a mother holding her infant child than the chilling displays our Nation saw in recent days. Lawmakers in New York cheered with delight upon the passage of legislation that would allow a baby to be ripped from the mother's womb moments before birth. These are living, feeling, beautiful babies who will never get the chance to share their love and dreams with the world. And then, we had the case of the governor of Virginia where he basically stated he would execute a baby after birth.

To defend the dignity of every person, I am asking the Congress to pass legislation to prohibit the late-term abortion of children who can feel pain in the mother's womb.

Let us work together to build a culture that cherishes innocent life. And let us reaffirm a fundamental truth: all children — born and unborn — are made in the holy image of God.

DEFENSE AND FOREIGN POLICY

The final part of my agenda is to protect America's National Security.

Over the last 2 years, we have begun to fully rebuild the United States Military — with $700 billion last year and $716 billion this year. We are also getting other nations to pay their fair share. For years, the United States was being treated very unfairly by NATO — but now we have secured a $100 billion increase in defense spending from NATO allies.

As part of our military build-up, the United States is developing a state-of-the-art missile defense system.

Under my Administration, we will never apologize for advancing America's interests.

For example, decades ago the United States entered into a treaty with Russia in which we agreed to limit and reduce our missile capabilities. While we followed the agreement to the letter, Russia repeatedly violated its terms. That is why I announced that the United States is officially withdrawing from the Intermediate-Range Nuclear Forces Treaty, or INF Treaty.

Perhaps we can negotiate a different agreement, adding China and others, or perhaps we can't -- in which case, we will outspend and out-innovate all others by far.

As part of a bold new diplomacy, we continue our historic push for peace on the Korean Peninsula. Our hostages have come home, nuclear testing has stopped, and there has not been a missile launch in 15 months. If I had not been elected President of the United States, we would right now, in my opinion, be in a major war with North Korea with potentially millions of people killed. Much work remains to be done, but my relationship with Kim Jong Un is a good one. And Chairman Kim and I will meet again on February 27 and 28 in Vietnam.

Two weeks ago, the United States officially recognized the legitimate government of Venezuela, and its new interim President, Juan Guaido.

We stand with the Venezuelan people in their noble quest for freedom — and we condemn the brutality of the Maduro regime, whose socialist policies have turned that nation from being the wealthiest in South America into a state of abject poverty and despair.

Here, in the United States, we are alarmed by new calls to adopt socialism in our country. America was founded on liberty and independence -- not government coercion, domination, and control. We are born free, and we will stay free. Tonight, we renew our resolve that America will never be a socialist country.

One of the most complex set of challenges we face is in the Middle East.

Our approach is based on principled realism — not discredited theories that have failed for decades to yield progress. For this reason, my Administration recognized the true capital of Israel — and proudly opened the American Embassy in Jerusalem.

Our brave troops have now been fighting in the Middle East for almost 19 years. In Afghanistan and Iraq, nearly 7,000 American heroes have given their lives. More than 52,000 Americans have been badly wounded. We have spent more than $7 trillion in the Middle East.

As a candidate for President, I pledged a new approach. Great nations do not fight endless wars.

When I took office, ISIS controlled more than 20,000 square miles in Iraq and Syria. Today, we have liberated virtually all of that territory from the grip of these bloodthirsty killers.

Now, as we work with our allies to destroy the remnants of ISIS, it is time to give our brave warriors in Syria a warm welcome home.

I have also accelerated our negotiations to reach a political settlement in Afghanistan. Our troops have fought with unmatched valor — and thanks to their bravery, we are now able to pursue a political solution to this long and bloody conflict.

In Afghanistan, my Administration is holding constructive talks with a number of Afghan groups, including the Taliban. As we make progress in these negotiations, we will be able to reduce our troop presence and focus on counter-terrorism. We do not know whether we will achieve an agreement — but we do know that after two decades of war, the hour has come to at least try for peace.

Above all, friend and foe alike must never doubt this Nation's power and will to defend our people. Eighteen years ago, terrorists attacked the USS Cole — and last month American forces killed one of the leaders of the attack.

We are honored to be joined tonight by Tom Wibberley, whose son, Navy Seaman Craig Wibberley, was one of the 17 sailors we tragically lost. Tom: we vow to always remember the heroes of the USS Cole.

My Administration has acted decisively to confront the world's leading state sponsor of terror: the radical regime in Iran.

To ensure this corrupt dictatorship never acquires nuclear weapons, I withdrew the United States from the disastrous Iran nuclear deal. And last fall, we put in place the toughest sanctions ever imposed on a country.

We will not avert our eyes from a regime that chants death to America and threatens genocide against the Jewish people. We must never ignore the vile poison of anti-Semitism, or those who spread its venomous creed. With one voice, we must confront this hatred anywhere and everywhere it occurs.

ANTISEMITISM

Just months ago, 11 Jewish-Americans were viciously murdered in an anti-Semitic attack on the Tree of Life Synagogue in Pittsburgh. SWAT Officer Timothy Matson raced into the gunfire and was shot seven times chasing down the killer. Timothy has just had his 12th surgery — but he made the trip to be here with us tonight. Officer Matson: we are forever grateful for your courage in the face of evil.

Tonight, we are also joined by Pittsburgh survivor Judah Samet. He arrived at the synagogue as the massacre began. But not only did Judah narrowly escape death last fall — more than seven decades ago, he narrowly survived the Nazi concentration camps. Today is Judah's 81st birthday. Judah says he can still remember the exact moment, nearly 75 years ago, after 10 months in a concentration camp, when he and his family were put on a train, and told they were going to another camp. Suddenly the train screeched to a halt. A soldier appeared. Judah's

family braced for the worst. Then, his father cried out with joy: "It's the Americans."

A second Holocaust survivor who is here tonight, Joshua Kaufman, was a prisoner at Dachau Concentration Camp. He remembers watching through a hole in the wall of a cattle car as American soldiers rolled in with tanks. "To me," Joshua recalls, "the American soldiers were proof that God exists, and they came down from the sky."

AMERICA FIRST

I began this evening by honoring three soldiers who fought on D-Day in the Second World War. One of them was Herman Zeitchik. But there is more to Herman's story. A year after he stormed the beaches of Normandy, Herman was one of those American soldiers who helped liberate Dachau. He was one of the Americans who helped rescue Joshua from that hell on earth. Almost 75 years later, Herman and Joshua are both together in the gallery tonight — seated side-by-side, here in the home of American freedom. Herman and Joshua: your presence this evening honors and uplifts our entire Nation.

When American soldiers set out beneath the dark skies over the English Channel in the early hours of D-Day, 1944, they were just young men of 18 and 19, hurtling on fragile landing craft toward the most momentous battle in the history of war.

They did not know if they would survive the hour. They did not know if they would grow old. But they knew that America had to prevail. Their cause was this nation, and generations yet unborn.

Why did they do it? They did it for America — they did it for us.

Everything that has come since — our triumph over communism, our giant leaps of science and discovery, our unrivaled progress toward equality and justice — all of it is possible thanks to the blood and tears and courage and vision of the Americans who came before.

Think of this Capitol — think of this very chamber, where lawmakers before you voted to end slavery, to build the railroads and the highways, to defeat fascism, to secure civil rights, to face down an evil empire.

Here tonight, we have legislators from across this magnificent republic. You have come from the rocky shores of Maine and the volcanic peaks of Hawaii; from the snowy woods of Wisconsin and the red deserts of Arizona; from the green farms of Kentucky and the golden beaches of California. Together, we represent the most extraordinary Nation in all of history.

What will we do with this moment? How will we be remembered?

I ask the men and women of this Congress: Look at the opportunities before us! Our most thrilling achievements are still ahead. Our most exciting journeys still await. Our biggest victories are still to come. We have not yet begun to dream.

We must choose whether we are defined by our differences — or whether we dare to transcend them.

We must choose whether we will squander our inheritance — or whether we will proudly declare that we are Americans. We do the incredible. We defy the impossible. We conquer the unknown.

This is the time to re-ignite the American imagination. This is the time to search for the tallest summit, and set our sights on the brightest star. This is the time to rekindle the bonds of love and loyalty and memory that link us together as citizens, as neighbors, as patriots.

This is our future — our fate — and our choice to make. I am asking you to choose greatness.

No matter the trials we face, no matter the challenges to come, we must go forward together.

We must keep America first in our hearts. We must keep freedom alive in our souls. And we must always keep faith in America's destiny — that one Nation, under God, must be the hope and the promise and the light and the glory among all the nations of the world!

Thank you. God bless you, God bless America, and good night! ∎

Former Georgia State Rep. Stacey Abrams responds

Good evening, my fellow Americans. I'm Stacey Abrams, and I am honored to join the conversation about the state of our union. Growing up, my family went back and forth between lower middle class and working poor.

Yet, even when they came home weary and bone-tired, my parents found a way to show us all who we could be. My librarian mother taught us to love learning. My father, a shipyard worker, put in overtime and extra shifts; and they made sure we volunteered to help others. Later, they both became United Methodist ministers, an expression of the faith that guides us.

These were our family values – faith, service, education and responsibility.

Now, we only had one car, so sometimes my dad had to hitchhike and walk long stretches during the 30 mile trip home from the shipyards. One rainy night, Mom got worried. We piled in the car and went out looking for him – and eventually found Dad making his way along the road, soaked and shivering in his shirtsleeves. When he got in the car, Mom asked if he'd left his coat at work. He explained he'd given it to a homeless man he'd met on the highway. When we asked why he'd given away his only jacket, Dad turned to us and said, "I knew when I left that man, he'd still be alone. But I could give him my coat, because I knew you were coming for me."

COMMUNITY

Our power and strength as Americans lives in our hard work and our belief in more. My family understood firsthand that while success is not guaranteed, we live in a nation where opportunity is possible. But we do not succeed alone – in these United States, when times are tough, we can persevere because our friends and neighbors will come for us. Our first responders will come for us.

It is this mantra – this uncommon grace of community – that has driven me to become an attorney, a small business owner, a writer, and most recently, the Democratic nominee for Governor of Georgia. My reason for running for governor was simple: I love our country and its promise of opportunity for all, and I stand here tonight because I hold fast to my father's credo – together, we are coming for America, for a better America.

Just a few weeks ago, I joined volunteers to distribute meals to furloughed federal workers. They waited in line for a box of food and a sliver of hope since they hadn't received a paycheck in weeks. Making their livelihoods a pawn for political games is a disgrace. The shutdown was a stunt engineered by the President of the United States, one that defied every tenet of fairness and abandoned not just our people – but our values.

For seven years, I led the Democratic Party in the Georgia House of Representatives. I didn't always agree with the Republican Speaker or Governor, but I understood that our constituents didn't care about our political parties – they cared about their lives. So, when we had to negotiate criminal justice reform or transportation or foster care improvements, the leaders of our state didn't shut down – we came together. And we kept our word.

It should be no different in our nation's capital. We may come from different sides of the political aisle; but, our joint commitment to the ideals of this nation cannot be negotiable.

Our most urgent work is to realize Americans' dreams of today and tomorrow. To carve a path to independence and prosperity that can last a lifetime. Children deserve an excellent education from cradle to career. We owe them safe schools and the highest standards, regardless of zip code.

REPUBLICAN LEADERSHIP

Yet this White House responds timidly while first graders practice active shooter drills and the price of higher education grows ever steeper. From now on, our leaders must be willing to tackle gun safety measures and the crippling effect of educational loans; to support educators and invest what is necessary to unleash the power of America's greatest minds.

In Georgia and around the country, people are striving for a middle class where a salary truly equals economic security. But instead, families' hopes are being crushed by Republican leadership that ignores real life or just doesn't understand it. Under the current administration, far too many hard-working Americans are falling behind, living paycheck to paycheck, most without labor unions to protect them from even worse harm.

The Republican tax bill rigged the system against working people. Rather than bringing back jobs, plants are closing, layoffs are looming and wages struggle to keep pace with the actual cost of living.

We owe more to the millions of everyday folks who keep our economy running: like truck drivers forced to buy their own rigs, farmers caught in a trade war, small business owners in search of capital, and domestic workers serving without labor protections. Women and men who could thrive if only they had the support and freedom to do so.

We know bipartisanship could craft a 21st century immigration plan, but this administration chooses to cage children and tear families apart. Compassionate treatment at the border is not the same as open borders. President Reagan understood this. President Obama understood this. Americans understand this. And Democrats stand ready to effectively secure our ports and borders. But we must all embrace that from agriculture to healthcare to entrepreneurship, America is made stronger by the presence of immigrants – not walls.

HEALTH CARE

Rather than suing to dismantle the Affordable Care Act, as Republican Attorneys General have, our leaders must protect the progress we've made and commit to expanding health care and lowering costs for everyone.

My father has battled prostate cancer for years. To help cover the costs, I found myself sinking deeper into debt – because while you can defer some payments, you can't defer cancer treatment. In this great nation, Americans are skipping blood pressure pills, forced to choose between buying medicine or paying rent. Maternal mortality rates show that mothers, especially black mothers, risk death to give birth. And in 14 states, including my home state where a majority want it, our leaders refuse to expand Medicaid, which could save rural hospitals, economies, and lives.

VOTING RIGHTS

We can do so much more: take action on climate change. Defend individual liberties with fair-minded judges. But none of these ambitions are

possible without the bedrock guarantee of our right to vote. Let's be clear: voter suppression is real. From making it harder to register and stay on the rolls to moving and closing polling places to rejecting lawful ballots, we can no longer ignore these threats to democracy.

While I acknowledged the results of the 2018 election here in Georgia – I did not and we cannot accept efforts to undermine our right to vote. That's why I started a nonpartisan organization called Fair Fight to advocate for voting rights.

This is the next battle for our democracy, one where all eligible citizens can have their say about the vision we want for our country. We must reject the cynicism that says allowing every eligible vote to be cast and counted is a "power grab." Americans understand that these are the values our brave men and women in uniform and our veterans risk their lives to defend. The foundation of our moral leadership around the globe is free and fair elections, where voters pick their leaders – not where politicians pick their voters.

JUSTICE

In this time of division and crisis, we must come together and stand for, and with, one another. America has stumbled time and again on its quest towards justice and equality; but with each generation, we have revisited our fundamental truths, and where we falter, we make amends.

We fought Jim Crow with the Civil Rights Act and the Voting Rights Act, yet we continue to confront racism from our past and in our present – which is why we must hold everyone from the very highest offices to our own families accountable for racist words and deeds – and call racism what it is. Wrong.

America achieved a measure of reproductive justice in Roe v. Wade, but we must never forget it is immoral to allow politicians to harm women and families to advance a political agenda. We affirmed marriage equality, and yet, the LGBTQ community remains under attack.

So even as I am very disappointed by the president's approach to our problems – I still don't want him to fail. But we need him to tell the truth, and to respect his duties and the extraordinary diversity that defines America.

Our progress has always found refuge in the basic instinct of the American experiment – to do right by our people. And with a renewed commitment to social and economic justice, we will create a stronger America, together. Because America wins by fighting for our shared values against all enemies: foreign and domestic. That is who we are – and when we do so, never wavering – the state of our union will always be strong.

Thank you, and may God bless the United States of America. ■

Articles of Impeachment Against Donald John Trump
House Resolution 755

**CONGRESS OF THE UNITED STATES OF AMERICA,
IN THE HOUSE OF REPRESENTATIVES,**
December 18, 2019.

Resolved, That Donald John Trump, President of the United States, is impeached for high crimes and misdemeanors and that the following articles of impeachment be exhibited to the United States Senate:

Articles of impeachment exhibited by the House of Representatives of the United States of America in the name of itself and of the people of the United States of America, against Donald John Trump, President of the United States of America, in maintenance and support of its impeachment against him for high crimes and misdemeanors.

ARTICLE I: ABUSE OF POWER

The Constitution provides that the House of Representatives "shall have the sole Power of Impeachment" and that the President "shall be removed from Office on Impeachment for, and Conviction of, Treason, Bribery, or other high Crimes and Misdemeanors." In his conduct of the office of President of the United States — and in violation of his constitutional oath faithfully to execute the office of President of the United States and, to the best of his ability, preserve, protect, and defend the Constitution of the United States, and in violation of his constitutional duty to take care that the laws be faithfully executed — Donald J. Trump has abused the powers of the Presidency, in that:

Using the powers of his high office, President Trump solicited the interference of a foreign government, Ukraine, in the 2020 United States Presidential election. He did so through a scheme or course of conduct that included soliciting the Government of Ukraine to publicly announce investigations that would benefit his reelection, harm the election prospects of a political opponent, and influence the 2020 United States Presidential election to his advantage. President Trump also sought to pressure the Government of Ukraine to take these steps by conditioning official United States Government acts of significant value to Ukraine on its public announcement of the investigations. President Trump engaged in this scheme or course of conduct for corrupt purposes in pursuit of personal political benefit. In so doing, President Trump used the powers of the Presidency in a manner that compromised the national security of the United States and undermined the integrity of the United States democratic process. He thus ignored and injured the interests of the Nation.

President Trump engaged in this scheme or course of conduct through the following means:

(1) President Trump — acting both directly and through his agents within and outside the United States Government — corruptly solicited the Government of Ukraine to publicly announce investigations into:

(A) a political opponent, former Vice President Joseph R. Biden, Jr.;

and

(B) a discredited theory promoted by Russia alleging that Ukraine — rather than Russia — interfered in the 2016 United States Presidential election.

(2) With the same corrupt motives, President Trump — acting both directly and through his agents within and outside the United States Government — conditioned two official acts on the public announcements that he had requested:

(A) the release of $391 million of United States taxpayer funds that Congress had appropriated on a bipartisan basis for the purpose of providing vital military and security assistance to Ukraine to oppose Russian aggression and which President Trump had ordered suspended; and

(B) a head of state meeting at the White House, which the President of Ukraine sought to demonstrate continued United States support for the Government of Ukraine in the face of Russian aggression.

(3) Faced with the public revelation of his actions, President Trump ultimately released the military and security assistance to the Government of Ukraine, but has persisted in openly and corruptly urging and soliciting Ukraine to undertake investigations for his personal political benefit. These actions were consistent with President Trump's previous invitations of foreign interference in United States elections.

In all of this, President Trump abused the powers of the Presidency by ignoring and injuring national security and other vital national interests to obtain an improper personal political benefit. He has also betrayed the Nation by abusing his high office to enlist a foreign power in corrupting democratic elections.

Wherefore President Trump, by such conduct, has demonstrated that he will remain a threat to national security and the Constitution if allowed to remain in office, and has acted in a manner grossly incompatible with self-governance and the rule of law. President Trump thus warrants impeachment and trial, removal from office, and disqualification to hold and enjoy any office of honor, trust, or profit under the United States.

ARTICLE II: OBSTRUCTION OF CONGRESS

The Constitution provides that the House of Representatives "shall have the sole Power of Impeachment" and that the President "shall be removed from Office on Impeachment for, and Conviction of, Treason, Bribery, or other high Crimes and Misdemeanors." In his conduct of the office of President of the United States — and in violation of his constitutional oath faithfully to execute the office of President of the United States and, to the best of his ability, preserve, protect, and defend the Constitution of the United States, and in violation of his constitutional duty to take care that the laws be faithfully executed — Donald J. Trump has directed the unprecedented, categorical, and indiscriminate defiance of subpoenas issued by the House of Representatives pursuant to its "sole Power of Impeachment." President Trump has abused the powers of the Presidency in a manner offensive to, and subversive of, the Constitution, in that:

The House of Representatives has engaged in an impeachment inquiry focused on President Trump's corrupt solicitation of the Government of Ukraine to interfere in the 2020 United States Presidential election. As part of this impeachment inquiry, the Committees undertaking the investigation served subpoenas seeking documents and testimony deemed vital to the inquiry from various Executive Branch agencies and offices, and current and former officials.

In response, without lawful cause or excuse, President Trump directed Executive Branch agencies, offices, and officials not to comply with those subpoenas. President Trump thus interposed the powers of the Presidency against the lawful subpoenas of the House of Representatives, and assumed to himself functions and judgments necessary to the exercise of the "sole Power of Impeachment" vested by the Constitution in the House of Representatives.

President Trump abused the powers of his high office through the following means:

(1) Directing the White House to defy a lawful subpoena by withholding the production of documents sought therein by the Committees.

(2) Directing other Executive Branch agencies and offices to defy lawful subpoenas and withhold the production of documents and records from the Committees — in response to which the Department of State, Office of Management and Budget, Department of Energy, and Department of Defense refused to produce a single document or record.

(3) Directing current and former Executive Branch officials not to cooperate with the Committees — in response to which nine Administration officials defied subpoenas for testimony, namely John Michael "Mick" Mulvaney, Robert B. Blair, John A. Eisenberg, Michael Ellis, Preston Wells Griffith, Russell T. Vought, Michael Duffey, Brian McCormack, and T. Ulrich Brechbuhl.

These actions were consistent with President Trump's previous efforts to undermine United States Government investigations into foreign interference in United States elections.

Through these actions, President Trump sought to arrogate to himself the right to determine the propriety, scope, and nature of an impeachment inquiry into his own conduct, as well as the unilateral prerogative to deny any and all information to the House of Representatives in the exercise of its "sole Power of Impeachment." In the history of the Republic, no President has ever ordered the complete defiance of an impeachment inquiry or sought to obstruct and impede so comprehensively the ability of the House of Representatives to investigate "high Crimes and Misdemeanors." This abuse of office served to cover up the President's own repeated misconduct and to seize and control the power of impeachment--and thus to nullify a vital constitutional safeguard vested solely in the House of Representatives.

In all of this, President Trump has acted in a manner contrary to his trust as President and subversive of constitutional government, to the great prejudice of the cause of law and justice, and to the manifest injury of the people of the United States.

Wherefore, President Trump, by such conduct, has demonstrated that he will remain a threat to the Constitution if allowed to remain in office, and has acted in a manner grossly incompatible with self-governance and the rule of law. President Trump thus warrants impeachment and trial, removal from office, and disqualification to hold and enjoy any office of honor, trust, or profit under the United States.

– Speaker of the House of Representatives.

PUBLIC LAWS

Laws Enacted in the First Session of the 116th Congress

■ **PL 116-1** (S 24) Require the federal government to provide retroactive pay to employees who are furloughed or working without compensation during the partial government shutdown. Require federal employees to be compensated at the earliest possible date once the shutdown has concluded, regardless of regularly scheduled pay dates. *Jan. 16, 2019.*

■ **PL 116-2** (HR 251) Extend for two years a Homeland Security Department program to collect information on and develop security plans for chemical facilities presenting a high security risk as potential targets for terrorist attacks. *Jan. 18, 2019.*

■ **PL 116-3** (HR 259) Extend the Medicaid Money Follows the Person Rebalancing demonstration, to extend protection for Medicaid recipients of home and community-based services against spousal impoverishment. *Jan. 24, 2019.*

■ **PL 116-4** (HR 430) Extend the program of block grants to States for temporary assistance for needy families and related programs through June 30, 2019. *Jan. 24, 2019.*

■ **PL 116-5** (HJ RES 28) Make further continuing appropriations for fiscal year 2019 that would fund the government until Feb. 28, 2019. *Jan. 25, 2019.*

■ **PL 116-6** (HJ RES 31) Provide stopgap fiscal 2019 funding for the Homeland Security Department through Feb. 28, 2019 *Feb. 15, 2019.*

■ **PL 116-7** (HR 439) Amend the charter of the Future Farmers of America. *Feb. 21, 2019.*

■ **PL 116-8** (S 483) Revise regulations on the registration and use of pesticides. *March 8, 2019.*

■ **PL 116-9** (S 47) Provide for the management of the natural resources of the United States. *March 12, 2019.*

■ **PL 116-10** (S 49) Designate the outstation of the Department of Veterans Affairs in North Ogden, Utah, as the Major Brent Taylor Vet Center Outstation. *March 21, 2019.*

■ **PL 116-11** (S 252) Authorize the honorary appointment of Robert J. Dole to the grade of colonel in the regular Army. *April 6, 2019.*

■ **PL 116-12** (S 863) Amend title 38, United States Code, to clarify the grade and pay of podiatrists of the Department of Veterans Affairs. *April 8, 2019.*

■ **PL 116-13** (HR 276) Direct the Secretary of Education to establish the Recognizing Inspiring School Employees (RISE) Award Program recognizing excellence exhibited by classified school employees providing services to students in prekindergarten through high school. *April 12, 2019.*

■ **PL 116-14** (HR 2030) Direct the Secretary of the Interior to execute and carry out agreements concerning Colorado River Drought Contingency Management and Operations. *April 16, 2019.*

■ **PL 116-15** (S 725) Change the address of the postal facility designated in honor of Captain Humayun Khan. *April 16, 2019.*

■ **PL 116-16** (HR 1839) Amend title XIX to extend protection for Medicaid recipients of home and community-based services against spousal impoverishment, establish a State Medicaid option to provide coordinated care to children with complex medical conditions through health homes, prevent the misclassification of drugs for purposes of the Medicaid drug rebate program. *April 18, 2019.*

■ **PL 116-17** (HR 1222) Amend the Pittman-Robertson Wildlife Restoration Act to facilitate the establishment of additional or expanded public target ranges in certain States. *May 10, 2019.*

■ **PL 116-18** (HR 2379) Reauthorize the Bulletproof Vest Partnership Grant Program. *May 23, 2019.*

■ **PL 116-19** (S 1693) Reauthorize the National Flood Insurance Program. *May 31, 2019.*

■ **PL 116-20** (HR 2157) Supplemental appropriations for the fiscal year ending September 30, 2019. *June 6, 2019.*

■ **PL 116-21** (S 1436) Make technical corrections to the computation of average pay under Public Law 110-279. *June 12, 2019.*

■ **PL 116-22** (S 1379) Reauthorize certain programs under the Public Health Service Act and the Federal Food, Drug, and Cosmetic Act with respect to public health security and all-hazards preparedness and response. *June 24, 2019.*

■ **PL 116-23** (HR 299) Amend title 38, United States Code, to clarify presumptions relating to the exposure of certain veterans who served in the vicinity of the Republic of Vietnam. *June 25, 2019.*

■ **PL 116-24** (HR 559) Amend section 6 of the Joint Resolution entitled " to approve the Covenant To Establish a Commonwealth of the Northern Mariana Islands in Political Union with the United States of America." *June 25, 2019.*

■ **PL 116-25** (HR 3151) Amend the Internal Revenue Code of 1986 to modernize and improve the Internal Revenue Service. *July 1, 2019.*

■ **PL 116-26** (HR 3401) Emergency supplemental appropriations for the fiscal year ending September 30, 2019. *July 1, 2019.*

■ **PL 116-27** (HR 2940) Extend the program of block grants to States for temporary assistance for needy families and related programs through September 30, 2019. *July 5, 2019.*

■ **PL 116-28** (HJ RES 60) Request the Secretary of the Interior to authorize unique and one-time arrangements for displays on the National Mall and the Washington Monument during the period beginning on July 16, 2019 and ending on July 20, 2019. *July 5, 2019.*

■ **PL 116-29** (S 2047) Provide for 2-week extension of the Medicaid community mental health services demonstration program. *July 5, 2019.*

■ **PL 116-30** (HR 866) Require that many public buildings provide lactation rooms. *July 25, 2019.*

■ **PL 116-31** (S 744) Amend section 175b of title 18, United States Code, to correct a scrivener's error. *July 25, 2019.*

■ **PL 116-32** (S 998) Amend the Omnibus Crime Control and Safe Streets Act of 1968 to expand support for police officer family services, stress reduction, and suicide prevention. *July 25, 2019.*

■ **PL 116-33** (S 1749) Clarify seasoning requirements for certain refinanced mortgage loans. *July 25, 2019.*

■ **PL 116-34** (HR 1327) Extend authorization for the September 11th Victim Compensation Fund of 2001 through fiscal year 2090. *July 29, 2019.*

■ **PL 116-35** (S 504) Amend title 36, United States Code, to authorize The American Legion to determine the requirements for membership in The American Legion. *July 30, 2019.*

■ **PL 116-36** (HR 2196) Amend title 38, United States Code, to reduce the credit hour requirement for the Edith Nourse Rogers STEM Scholarship program of the Department of Veterans Affairs. *July 31, 2019.*

■ **PL 116-37** (HR 3877) Amend the Balanced Budget and Emergency Deficit Control Act of 1985, to establish a congressional budget for fiscal years 2020 and 2021, to temporarily suspend the debt limit. *Aug. 2, 2019.*

■ **PL 116-38** (S 2249) Allow the Deputy Administrator of the Federal Aviation Administration on the date of enactment of this Act to continue to serve as such Deputy Administrator. *Aug. 2, 2019.*

■ **PL 116-39** (HR 3253) Provide for certain extensions with respect to the Medicaid program under title XIX of the Social Security Act. *Aug. 6, 2019.*

■ **PL 116-40** (HR 1569) Amend title 28, United States Code, to add Flagstaff and Yuma to the list of locations in which court shall be held in the judicial district for the State of Arizona. *Aug. 9, 2019.*

■ **PL 116-41** (HR 2695) Rename the Success Dam in Tulare County, California, as the Richard L. Schafer Dam. *Aug. 9, 2019.*

■ **PL 116-42** (HR 540) Designate the facility of the United States Postal Service located at 770 Ayrault Road in Fairport, New York, as the "Louise and Bob Slaughter Post Office." *Aug. 21, 2019.*

■ **PL 116-43** (HR 828) Designate the facility of the United States Postal Service located at 25 Route 111 in Smithtown, New York, as the "Congressman Bill Carney Post Office." *Aug. 21, 2019.*

■ **PL 116-44** (HR 829) Designate the facility of the United States Postal Service located at 1450 Montauk Highway in Mastic, New York, as the "Army Specialist Thomas J. Wilwerth Post Office Building." *Aug. 21, 2019.*

■ **PL 116-45** (HR 1198) Designate the facility of the United States Postal Service located at 404 South Boulder Highway in Henderson, Nevada, as the "Henderson Veterans Memorial Post Office Building." *Aug. 21, 2019.*

■ **PL 116-46** (HR 1449) Designate the facility of the United States Postal Service located at 3033 203rd Street in Olympia Fields, Illinois, as the "Captain Robert L. Martin Post Office." *Aug. 21, 2019.*

■ **PL 116-47** (HR 3305) Designate the facility of the United States Postal Service located at 2509 George Mason Drive in Virginia Beach, Virginia, as the "Ryan Keith Cox Post Office Building." *Aug. 21, 2019.*

■ **PL 116-48** (HR 639) Amend section 327 of the Robert T. Stafford Disaster Relief and Emergency Assistance Act to clarify that National Urban Search and Rescue Response System task forces may include Federal employees. *Aug. 22, 2019.*

■ **PL 116-49** (HR 776) Amend the Public Health Service Act to reauthorize the Emergency Medical Services for Children program. *Aug. 22, 2019.*

■ **PL 116-50** (HR 1079) Require the Director of the Office of Management and Budget to issue guidance on electronic consent forms. *Aug. 22, 2019.*

■ **PL 116-51** (HR 2336) Amend title 11, United States Code, with respect to the definition of "family farmer." *Aug. 23, 2019.*

■ **PL 116-52** (HR 2938) Exempt from the calculation of monthly income certain benefits paid by the Department of Veterans Affairs and the Department of Defense. *Aug. 23, 2019.*

■ **PL 116-53** (HR 3304) Exempt for an additional 4-year period, from the application of the means-test presumption of abuse under chapter 7, qualifying members of reserve components of the Armed Forces and members of the National Guard who, after September 11, 2001, are called to active duty or to perform a homeland defense activity for not less than 90 days. *Aug. 23, 2019.*

■ **PL 116-54** (HR 3311) Amend chapter 11 of title 11, United States Code, to address reorganization of small businesses. *Aug. 23, 2019.*

■ **PL 116-55** (HR 1250) Designate the facility of the United States Postal Service located at 11158 Highway 146 North in Hardin, Texas, as the "Lucas Lowe Post Office." *Aug. 23, 2019.*

■ **PL 116-56** (HR 3245) Transfer a bridge over the Wabash River to the New Harmony River Bridge Authority and the New Harmony and Wabash River Bridge Authority. *Aug. 23, 2019.*

■ **PL 116-57** (HR 831) Direct the Secretary of Transportation to request nominations for and make determinations regarding roads to be designated under the national scenic byways program. *Sept. 22, 2019.*

■ **PL 116-58** (HR 1200) Increase, effective as of December 1, 2019, the rates of compensation for veterans with service-connected disabilities and the rates of dependency and indemnity compensation for the survivors of certain disabled veterans. *Sept. 26, 2019.*

■ **PL 116-59** (HR 4378) Make continuing appropriations for fiscal year 2020, funding government operations at fiscal 2019 levels through Nov. 21, 2019. *Sept. 27, 2019.*

■ **PL 116-60** (HR 1058) Reauthorize certain provisions of the Public Health Service Act relating to autism. *Sept. 30, 2019.*

■ **PL 116-61** (HR 4285) Amend title 38, United States Code, to extend and modify certain authorities and requirements relating to the Department of Veterans Affairs. *Sept. 30, 2019.*

■ **PL 116-62** (S 163) Prevent catastrophic failure or shutdown of remote diesel power engines due to emission control devices. *Oct. 4, 2019.*

■ **PL 116-63** (S 1689) Permit States to transfer certain funds from the clean water revolving fund of a State to the drinking water revolving fund of the State in certain circumstances. *Oct. 4, 2019.*

■ **PL 116-64** (HR 1590) Require the Federal Emergency Management Agency to develop and conduct an exercise related to the detection and prevention of terrorist and foreign fighter travel. *Oct. 9, 2019.*

■ **PL 116-65** (S 239) Direct the Department of the Treasury to mint and issue not more than 350,000 $1 silver coins in commemoration of Christa McAuliffe, a teacher killed in the Space Shuttle Challenger Disaster. *Oct. 9, 2019.*

■ **PL 116-66** (S 1196) Designate the facility of the United States Postal Service located at 1715 Linnerud Drive in Sun Prairie, Wisconsin, as the "Fire Captain Cory Barr Post Office Building." *Oct. 31, 2019.*

■ **PL 116-67** (S 693) Amend title 36, United States Code, to require that the POW/MIA flag be displayed on all days that the flag of the United States is displayed on certain Federal property. *Nov. 7, 2019.*

■ **PL 116-68** (HR 1396) Award Congressional Gold Medals to Katherine Johnson and Dr. Christine Darden, to posthumously award Congressional Gold Medals to Dorothy Vaughan and Mary Jackson, and to award a Congressional Gold Medal to honor all of the women who contributed to the success of the National Aeronautics and Space Administration during the Space Race. *Nov. 8, 2019.*

■ **PL 116-69** (HR 3055) Appropriations for the Departments of Commerce and Justice, Science, and Related Agencies for the fiscal year ending September 30, 2020. *Nov. 21, 2019.*

■ **PL 116-70** (S 862) Repeal the sunset for collateral requirements for Small Business Administration disaster loans. *Nov. 22, 2019.*

■ **PL 116-71** (HR 2423) Require the Secretary of the Treasury to mint coins in commemoration of ratification of the 19th Amendment to the Constitution of the United States, giving women in the United States the right to vote. *Nov. 25, 2019.*

■ **PL 116-72** (HR 724) Revise section 48 of title 18, United States Code to prohibit certain acts considered to be animal cruelty. *Nov. 25, 2019.*

■ **PL 116-73** (HR 1123) Amend title 28, United States Code, to modify the composition of the eastern judicial district of Arkansas. *Nov. 26, 2019.*

■ **PL 116-74** (HR 3889) Amend the Office of National Drug Control Policy Reauthorization Act of 1998 to make technical corrections. *Nov. 27, 2019.*

■ **PL 116-75** (HR 4258) Authorize the Marshal of the Supreme Court and the Supreme Court Police to protect the Justices, employees, and official guests of the Supreme Court outside of the Supreme Court grounds. *Nov. 27, 2019.*

■ **PL 116-76** (S 1838) Amend the Hong Kong Policy Act of 1992 to direct various departments to assess whether political developments in Hong Kong justify changing Hong Kong's unique treatment under U.S. law. *Nov. 27, 2019.*

■ **PL 116-77** (S 2710) Prohibit the commercial export of covered munitions items to the Hong Kong Police Force. *Nov. 27, 2019.*

■ **PL 116-78** (HR 5277) Amend section 442 of title 18, United States Code, to exempt certain interests in mutual funds, unit investment trusts, employee benefit plans, and retirement plans from conflict of interest limitations for the Government Publishing Office. *Dec. 5, 2019.*

■ **PL 116-79** (HR 887) Designate the facility of the United States Postal Service located at 877 East 1200 South in Orem, Utah, as the "Jerry C. Washburn Post Office Building." *Dec. 12, 2019.*

■ **PL 116-80** (HR 1252) Designate the facility of the United States Postal Service located at 6531 Van Nuys Boulevard in Van Nuys, California, as the "Marilyn Monroe Post Office." *Dec. 12, 2019.*

■ **PL 116-81** (HR 1253) Designate the facility of the United States Postal Service located at 13507 Van Nuys Boulevard in Pacoima, California, as the "Ritchie Valens Post Office Building." *Dec. 12, 2019.*

■ **PL 116-82** (HR 1526) Designate the facility of the United States Postal Service located at 200 Israel Road Southeast in Tumwater, Washington, as the "Eva G. Hewitt Post Office." *Dec. 12, 2019.*

■ **PL 116-83** (HR 1844) Designate the facility of the United States Postal Service located at 66 Grove Court in Elgin, Illinois, as the "Corporal Alex Martinez Memorial Post Office Building." *Dec. 12, 2019.*

■ **PL 116-84** (HR 1972) Designate the facility of the United States Postal Service located at 1100 West Kent Avenue in Missoula, Montana, as the "Jeannette Rankin Post Office Building." *Dec. 13, 2019.*

■ **PL 116-85** (HR 2151) Designate the facility of the United States Postal Service located at 7722 South Main Street in Pine Plains, New York, as the "Senior Chief Petty Officer Shannon M. Kent Post Office." *Dec. 13, 2019.*

■ **PL 116-86** (HR 2325) Designate the facility of the United States Postal Service located at 100 Calle Alondra in San Juan, Puerto Rico, as the "65th Infantry Regiment Post Office Building." *Dec. 13, 2019.*

■ **PL 116-87** (HR 2334) Designate the Department of Veterans Affairs community-based outpatient clinic in Odessa, Texas, as the "Wilson and Young Medal of Honor VA Clinic." *Dec. 13, 2019.*

■ **PL 116-88** (HR 2451) Designate the facility of the United States Postal Service located at 575 Dexter Street in Central Falls, Rhode Island, as the "Elizabeth Buffum Chace Post Office." *Dec. 13, 2019.*

■ **PL 116-89** (HR 3144) Designate the facility of the United States Postal Service located at 8520 Michigan Avenue in Whittier, California, as the "Jose Ramos Post Office Building." *Dec. 13, 2019.*

■ **PL 116-90** (HR 3314) Designate the facility of the United States Postal Service located at 1750 McCulloch Boulevard North in Lake Havasu City, Arizona, as the "Lake Havasu City Combat Veterans Memorial Post Office Building." *Dec. 13, 2019.*

■ **PL 116-91** (HR 5363) Reauthorize mandatory funding programs for historically Black colleges and universities and other minority-serving institutions. *Dec. 19, 2019.*

■ **PL 116-92** (S 1790) Authorize FY2020 appropriations and set forth policies for Department of Defense programs and activities, including military personnel strengths. *Dec. 20, 2019.*

■ **PL 116-93** (HR 1158) Authorize cyber incident response teams at the Department of Homeland Security. *Dec. 20, 2019.*

■ **PL 116-94** (HR 1865) Require the Secretary of the Treasury to mint a coin in commemoration of the opening of the National Law Enforcement Museum in the District of Columbia. *Dec. 20, 2019.*

■ **PL 116-95** (HR 1138) Reauthorize the West Valley demonstration project. *Dec. 20, 2019.*

■ **PL 116-96** (HR 2333) Direct the Comptroller General of the United States to conduct an assessment of the responsibilities, workload, and vacancy rates of Department of Veterans Affairs suicide prevention coordinators. *Dec. 20, 2019.*

■ **PL 116-97** (HR 3196) Designate the Large Synoptic Survey Telescope as the "Vera Rubin Survey Telescope." *Dec. 20, 2019.*

■ **PL 116-98** (HR 4566) Accelerate the income tax benefits for charitable cash contributions for the relief of the families of victims of the mass shooting in Virginia Beach, Virginia on May 31, 2019. *Dec. 20, 2019.*

■ **PL 116-99** (S 50) Authorize the Secretary of the Interior to assess sanitation and safety conditions at Bureau of Indian Affairs facilities that were constructed to provide affected Columbia River Treaty tribes access to traditional fishing grounds and expend funds on construction of facilities and structures to improve those conditions. *Dec. 20, 2019.*

■ **PL 116-100** (S 216) Provide for equitable compensation to the Spokane Tribe of Indians of the Spokane Reservation for the use of tribal land for the production of hydropower by the Grand Coulee Dam. *Dec. 20, 2019.*

■ **PL 116-101** (S 256) Amend the Native American Programs Act of 1974 to provide flexibility and reauthorization to ensure the survival and continuing vitality of Native American languages. *Dec. 20, 2019.*

■ **PL 116-102** (S 737) Direct the National Science Foundation to support STEM education research focused on early childhood. *Dec. 24, 2019.*

■ **PL 116-103** (HR 150) Modernize Federal grant reporting. *Dec. 30, 2019.*

■ **PL 116-104** (HR 777) Reauthorize programs authorized under the Debbie Smith Act of 2004. *Dec. 30, 2019.*

■ **PL 116-105** (S 151) Deter criminal robocall violations and improve enforcement of section 227(b) of the Communications Act of 1934. *Dec. 30, 2019.*

HOUSE ROLL CALL VOTES

House Roll Call Index by Subject

House Roll Call Index by Bill

VOTE NUMBER

1. Quorum Call. Quorum Call - Call of the House. Quorum was present with 431 members responding (3 members did not respond). Jan. 3, 2019.

2. Election of the Speaker. Nomination of Nancy Pelosi, D-Calif., and Kevin McCarthy, R-Calif., for Speaker of House of Representatives for the 116th Congress. Pelosi elected Speaker 220-192: R 0-192; D 220-0. *Note: A "Y on the chart represents a vote for Pelosi; an "N represents a vote for McCarthy. 18 members (6 Republicans and 12 Democrats) are marked "C (usually reserved for "present to avoid a conflict of interest) because they voted for other people. 3 members (all Democrats) are marked "P for present.* Jan. 3, 2019.

3. HR21, HRES6, HJRES1. House Organizing Resolution, Fiscal 2019 Appropriations, and Homeland Security Continuing Resolution - Motion to Table the Motion to Refer. McGovern, D-Mass., motion to table the Brady, R-Texas, motion to refer the rule (H Res 5) that would provide for House floor consideration of the resolution (H Res 6) that would establish the rules of the House for the 116th Congress; consideration of the bill (HR 21) that would provide for full-year appropriations for six of the seven remaining fiscal 2019 appropriations bills; and consideration of the joint resolution (H J Res 1) that would provide short-term funding for the Homeland Security Department through Feb. 8, 2019. Motion agreed to 230-197: R 0-197; D 230-0. Jan. 3, 2019.

4. HR21, HRES6, HJRES1. House Organizing Resolution, Fiscal 2019 Appropriations, and Homeland Security Continuing Resolution - Previous Question. McGovern, D-Mass., motion to order the previous question (thus ending debate and the possibility of amendment) on the resolution (H Res 5) that would provide for House floor consideration of the resolution (H Res 6) that would establish the rules of the House for the 116th Congress; consideration of the bill (HR 21) that would provide for full-year appropriations for six of the seven remaining fiscal 2019 appropriations bills; and consideration of the joint resolution (H J Res 1) that would provide short-term funding for the Homeland Security Department through Feb. 8, 2019. Motion agreed to 233-197: R 0-197; D 233-0. Jan. 3, 2019.

5. HR21, HJRES1, HRES6. House Organizing Resolution, Fiscal 2019 Appropriations, and Homeland Security Continuing Resolution - Motion to Commit. Cole, R-Okla., motion to commit the rule to a committee composed of the majority and minority leaders, with instructions to report it back with an amendment that would provide for the consideration of the resolution H Res 11. Motion rejected 197-232: R 197-0; D 0-232. Jan. 3, 2019.

6. HRES6, HJRES1, HR21. House Organizing Resolution, Fiscal 2019 Appropriations, and Homeland Security Continuing Resolution - Rule. Adoption of the rule (H Res 5) that would provide for House floor consideration of the resolution (H Res 6) that would establish the rules of the House for the 116th Congress; consideration of the bill (HR 21) that would provide for full-year appropriations for six of the seven remaining fiscal 2019 appropriations bills; and consideration of the joint resolution (H J Res 1) that would provide short-term funding for the Homeland Security Department through Feb. 8, 2019. Adopted 234-194: R 0-194; D 234-0. Jan. 3, 2019.

		1	2	3	4	5	6
ALABAMA							
1	**Byrne**	P	N	N	N	Y	N
2	**Roby**	P	N	N	N	Y	N
3	**Rogers, M.**	P	N	N	N	Y	N
4	**Aderholt**	P	N	N	N	Y	N
5	**Brooks, M.**	P	N	N	N	Y	N
6	**Palmer**	P	N	N	N	Y	N
7	Sewell	P	Y	Y	Y	?	Y
ALASKA							
AL	Young	P	N	N	N	Y	N
ARIZONA							
1	O'Halleran	P	Y	Y	Y	N	Y
2	Kirkpatrick	P	Y	Y	Y	N	Y
3	Grijalva	P	Y	Y	Y	N	Y
4	Gosar	P	C	N	N	Y	N
5	Biggs	P	C	N	N	Y	N
6	**Schweikert**	P	N	N	N	Y	N
7	Gallego	P	Y	Y	Y	N	Y
8	**Lesko**	P	N	N	N	Y	N
9	Stanton	P	Y	Y	Y	N	Y
ARKANSAS							
1	**Crawford**	P	N	N	N	Y	N
2	**Hill, F.**	P	N	N	N	Y	N
3	**Womack**	P	N	N	N	Y	N
4	**Westerman**	P	N	N	N	Y	N
CALIFORNIA							
1	**LaMalfa**	P	N	N	N	Y	N
2	Huffman	P	Y	Y	Y	N	Y
3	Garamendi	P	Y	Y	Y	N	Y
4	**McClintock**	P	N	N	N	Y	N
5	Thompson, M.	P	Y	Y	Y	N	Y
6	Matsui	P	Y	Y	Y	N	Y
7	Bera	P	Y	Y	Y	N	Y
8	**Cook**	P	N	N	N	Y	N
9	McNerney	P	Y	Y	Y	N	Y
10	Harder	P	Y	Y	Y	N	Y
11	DeSaulnier	P	Y	Y	Y	N	Y
12	Pelosi	P	Y					
13	Lee B.	P	Y	Y	Y	N	Y
14	Speier	P	Y	Y	Y	N	Y
15	Swalwell	P	Y	Y	Y	N	Y
16	Costa	P	Y	Y	Y	N	Y
17	Khanna	P	Y	Y	Y	N	Y
18	Eshoo	P	Y	Y	Y	N	Y
19	Lofgren	P	Y	Y	Y	N	Y
20	Panetta	P	Y	Y	Y	N	Y
21	Cox	P	Y	Y	Y	N	Y
22	**Nunes**	P	N	N	N	Y	N
23	**McCarthy**	P	N	N	N	Y	N
24	Carbajal	P	Y	Y	Y	N	Y
25	Hill, K.	P	Y	Y	Y	N	Y
26	Brownley	P	Y	Y	Y	N	Y
27	Chu	P	Y	Y	Y	N	Y
28	Schiff	P	Y	Y	Y	N	Y
29	Cárdenas	P	Y	?	Y	N	Y
30	Sherman	P	Y	Y	Y	N	Y
31	Aguilar	P	Y	Y	Y	N	Y
32	Napolitano	P	Y	Y	Y	N	Y
33	Lieu	P	Y	Y	Y	N	Y
34	Gomez	P	Y	Y	Y	N	Y
35	Torres	P	Y	Y	Y	N	Y
36	Ruiz	P	Y	Y	Y	N	Y
37	Bass	P	Y	?	Y	N	Y
38	Sánchez	P	Y	Y	Y	N	Y
39	Cisneros	P	Y	Y	Y	N	Y
40	Roybal-Allard	P	Y	Y	Y	N	Y
41	Takano	P	Y	Y	Y	N	Y
42	**Calvert**	P	N	N	N	Y	N
43	Waters	P	Y	Y	Y	N	Y
44	Barragán	P	Y	Y	Y	N	Y
45	Porter	P	Y	Y	Y	N	Y
46	Correa	P	Y	Y	Y	N	Y
47	Lowenthal	P	Y	Y	Y	N	Y
48	Rouda	P	Y	Y	Y	N	Y
49	Levin	P	Y	Y	Y	N	Y
50	**Hunter**	P	N	N	N	Y	N
51	Vargas	P	Y	Y	Y	N	Y
52	Peters	P	Y	Y	Y	N	Y

		1	2	3	4	5	6
53	Davis, S.	P	Y	Y	Y	N	Y
COLORADO							
1	DeGette	P	Y	Y	Y	N	Y
2	Neguse	P	Y	Y	Y	N	Y
3	**Tipton**	P	N	N	N	Y	N
4	**Buck**	P	N	N	N	Y	N
5	**Lamborn**	P	N	N	N	Y	N
6	Crow	P	C	Y	Y	N	Y
7	Perlmutter	P	Y	Y	Y	N	Y
CONNECTICUT							
1	Larson	P	Y	Y	Y	N	Y
2	Courtney	P	Y	Y	Y	N	Y
3	DeLauro	P	Y	Y	Y	N	Y
4	Himes	P	Y	Y	Y	N	Y
5	Hayes	P	Y	Y	Y	N	Y
DELAWARE							
AL	Blunt Rochester	P	Y	Y	Y	N	Y
FLORIDA							
1	**Gaetz**	P	N	N	N	Y	N
2	**Dunn**	P	N	N	N	Y	N
3	**Yoho**	P	N	N	N	Y	N
4	**Rutherford**	P	N	N	N	Y	N
5	Lawson	P	Y	Y	Y	N	Y
6	**Waltz**	P	N	N	N	Y	N
7	Murphy	P	Y	Y	Y	N	Y
8	**Posey**	P	N	N	N	Y	N
9	Soto	P	Y	Y	Y	N	Y
10	Demings	P	Y	Y	Y	N	Y
11	**Webster**	P	N	N	N	Y	N
12	**Bilirakis**	P	N	N	N	Y	N
13	Crist	P	Y	Y	Y	N	Y
14	Castor	P	Y	Y	Y	N	Y
15	**Spano**	P	N	N	N	Y	N
16	**Buchanan**	P	N	N	N	Y	N
17	**Steube**	P	N	N	N	Y	N
18	**Mast**	P	N	N	N	Y	N
19	**Rooney**	P	N	N	N	Y	N
20	Hastings	P	Y	Y	Y	N	Y
21	Frankel	P	Y	Y	Y	N	Y
22	Deutch	P	Y	Y	Y	N	Y
23	Wasserman Schultz	P	Y	Y	Y	N	Y
24	Wilson, F.	?	Y	?	Y	N	Y
25	**Diaz-Balart**	P	N	N	N	Y	N
26	Mucarsel-Powell	P	Y	Y	Y	N	Y
27	Shalala	P	Y	Y	Y	N	Y
GEORGIA							
1	**Carter, E.L.**	P	N	N	N	Y	N
2	Bishop, S.	P	Y	Y	Y	N	Y
3	**Ferguson**	P	N	N	N	Y	N
4	Johnson, H.	P	Y	Y	Y	N	Y
5	Lewis John	P	Y	Y	Y	N	Y
6	McBath	P	Y	Y	Y	N	Y
7	**Woodall**	P	N	N	N	Y	N
8	**Scott, A.**	P	N	N	N	Y	N
9	**Collins, D.**	P	N	N	N	Y	N
10	**Hice**	P	C	N	N	Y	N
11	**Loudermilk**	P	N	N	N	Y	N
12	**Allen**	P	N	N	N	Y	N
13	Scott, D.	P	Y	Y	Y	N	Y
14	**Graves, T.**	P	N	N	N	Y	N
HAWAII							
1	Case	P	Y	Y	Y	N	Y
2	Gabbard	P	Y	Y	Y	N	Y
IDAHO							
1	**Fulcher**	P	N	N	N	Y	?
2	**Simpson**	P	N	N	N	Y	N
ILLINOIS							
1	Rush	P	Y	Y	Y	N	Y
2	Kelly, R.	P	Y	Y	Y	N	Y
3	Lipinski	P	Y	Y	Y	N	Y
4	García, J.	P	Y	Y	Y	N	Y
5	Quigley	P	Y	Y	Y	N	Y
6	Casten	P	Y	Y	Y	N	Y
7	Davis, D.	P	Y	Y	Y	N	Y
8	Krishnamoorthi	P	Y	Y	Y	N	Y
9	Schakowsky	P	Y	Y	Y	N	Y
10	Schneider	P	Y	Y	Y	N	Y
11	Foster	P	Y	Y	Y	N	Y

KEY: **Republicans**   Democrats   *Independents*

Y Voted for (yea)	**N** Voted against (nay)	**P** Voted "present"
+ Announced for	**–** Announced against	**?** Did not vote or otherwise
# Paired for	**X** Paired against	make position known

		1	2	3	4	5	6
12	**Bost**	P	N	N	N	Y	N
13	**Davis, R.**	P	N	N	N	Y	N
14	Underwood	P	Y	Y	Y	N	Y
15	**Shimkus**	P	N	N	N	Y	N
16	**Kinzinger**	P	N	N	N	Y	N
17	Bustos	P	Y	Y	Y	N	Y
18	**LaHood**	P	N	N	N	Y	N
INDIANA							
1	Visclosky	P	Y	Y	Y	N	Y
2	**Walorski**	P	N	N	N	Y	N
3	**Banks**	P	N	N	N	Y	N
4	**Baird**	P	N	N	N	Y	N
5	**Brooks, S.**	P	N	N	N	Y	N
6	**Pence**	P	N	N	N	Y	N
7	Carson	P	Y	Y	Y	N	Y
8	**Bucshon**	P	N	N	N	Y	N
9	**Hollingsworth**	P	N	N	N	Y	N
IOWA							
1	Finkenauer	P	Y	Y	Y	N	Y
2	Loebsack	P	Y	Y	Y	N	Y
3	Axne	P	Y	Y	Y	N	Y
4	**King, S.**	P	N	N	N	Y	N
KANSAS							
1	**Marshall**	P	N	N	N	Y	N
2	**Watkins**	P	N	N	N	Y	N
3	Davids	P	Y	Y	Y	N	Y
4	**Estes**	P	N	N	N	Y	N
KENTUCKY							
1	**Comer**	P	N	N	N	Y	N
2	**Guthrie**	P	N	N	N	Y	N
3	Yarmuth	P	Y	Y	Y	N	Y
4	**Massie**	P	C	N	N	Y	N
5	**Rogers, H.**	P	N	N	N	Y	N
6	**Barr**	P	N	N	N	Y	N
LOUISIANA							
1	**Scalise**	P	N	N	N	Y	N
2	Richmond	P	Y	Y	Y	N	Y
3	**Higgins, C.**	?	N	N	N	Y	N
4	**Johnson, M.**	P	N	N	N	Y	N
5	**Abraham**	P	N	N	N	Y	N
6	**Graves, G.**	P	N	N	N	Y	N
MAINE							
1	Pingree	P	Y	Y	Y	N	Y
2	Golden	P	C	Y	Y	N	Y
MARYLAND							
1	**Harris**	P	N	N	N	Y	N
2	Ruppersberger	P	Y	Y	Y	N	Y
3	Sarbanes	P	Y	Y	Y	N	Y
4	Brown, A.	P	Y	Y	Y	N	Y
5	Hoyer	P	Y	Y	Y	N	Y
6	Trone	P	Y	Y	Y	N	Y
7	Cummings	P	Y	Y	Y	N	Y
8	Raskin	P	Y	Y	Y	N	Y
MASSACHUSETTS							
1	Neal	P	Y	Y	Y	N	Y
2	McGovern	P	Y	Y	Y	N	Y
3	Trahan	P	Y	Y	Y	N	Y
4	Kennedy	P	Y	Y	Y	N	Y
5	Clark	P	Y	Y	Y	N	Y
6	Moulton	P	Y	Y	Y	N	Y
7	Pressley	P	Y	Y	Y	N	Y
8	Lynch	P	Y	Y	Y	N	Y
9	Keating	P	Y	Y	Y	N	Y
MICHIGAN							
1	**Bergman**	P	N	N	N	Y	N
2	**Huizenga**	P	N	N	N	Y	N
3	**Amash**	P	C	N	N	Y	N
4	**Moolenaar**	P	N	N	N	Y	N
5	Kildee	P	Y	Y	Y	N	Y
6	**Upton**	P	N	N	N	Y	N
7	**Walberg**	P	N	N	N	Y	N
8	Slotkin	P	P	Y	Y	N	Y
9	Levin	P	Y	Y	Y	N	Y
10	**Mitchell**	P	N	N	N	Y	N
11	Stevens	P	Y	Y	Y	N	Y
12	Dingell	P	Y	Y	Y	N	Y
13	Tlaib	P	Y	Y	Y	N	Y
14	Lawrence	P	Y	Y	Y	N	Y
MINNESOTA							
1	**Hagedorn**	P	N	N	N	Y	N
2	Craig	P	Y	Y	Y	N	Y
3	Phillips	P	Y	Y	Y	N	Y
4	McCollum	P	Y	Y	Y	N	Y
5	Omar	P	Y	Y	+	N	Y

		1	2	3	4	5	6
6	**Emmer**	P	N	N	N	Y	N
7	Peterson	P	Y	Y	Y	N	Y
8	**Stauber**	P	N	N	N	Y	N
MISSISSIPPI							
1	**Kelly, T.**	P	N	N	N	Y	N
2	Thompson, B.	P	Y	Y	Y	N	Y
3	**Guest**	P	N	N	N	Y	N
4	**Palazzo**	P	N	N	N	Y	N
MISSOURI							
1	Clay	P	Y	Y	Y	N	Y
2	**Wagner**	P	N	N	N	Y	N
3	**Luetkemeyer**	P	N	N	N	Y	N
4	**Hartzler**	P	N	N	N	Y	N
5	Cleaver	P	Y	Y	Y	N	Y
6	**Graves, S.**	P	N	N	N	Y	N
7	**Long**	P	N	N	N	Y	N
8	**Smith, J.**	P	N	N	N	Y	N
MONTANA							
AL	**Gianforte**	P	N	N	N	Y	N
NEBRASKA							
1	**Fortenberry**	P	N	N	N	Y	N
2	**Bacon**	P	N	N	N	Y	N
3	**Smith, Adrian**	P	N	N	N	Y	N
NEVADA							
1	Titus	P	Y	Y	Y	N	Y
2	**Amodei**	P	N	N	N	Y	N
3	Lee	P	Y	Y	Y	N	Y
4	Horsford	P	Y	Y	Y	N	Y
NEW HAMPSHIRE							
1	Pappas	P	Y	Y	Y	N	Y
2	Kuster	P	Y	Y	Y	N	Y
NEW JERSEY							
1	Norcross	P	Y	Y	Y	N	Y
2	Van Drew	P	P	Y	Y	N	Y
3	Kim	P	Y	Y	Y	N	Y
4	**Smith, C.**	P	N	N	N	Y	N
5	Gottheimer	P	Y	Y	Y	N	Y
6	Pallone	P	Y	Y	Y	N	Y
7	Malinowski	P	Y	Y	Y	N	Y
8	Sires	P	Y	Y	Y	N	Y
9	Pascrell	P	Y	Y	Y	N	Y
10	Payne	P	Y	Y	Y	N	Y
11	Sherrill	P	C	Y	Y	N	Y
12	Watson Coleman	P	Y	Y	Y	N	Y
NEW MEXICO							
1	Haaland	P	Y	Y	Y	N	Y
2	Torres Small	P	Y	Y	Y	N	Y
3	Luján	P	Y	Y	Y	N	Y
NEW YORK							
1	**Zeldin**	P	N	N	N	Y	N
2	**King, P.**	P	N	N	N	Y	N
3	Suozzi	P	Y	Y	Y	N	Y
4	Rice, K.	P	C	Y	Y	N	Y
5	Meeks	P	Y	Y	Y	N	Y
6	Meng	P	Y	Y	Y	N	Y
7	Velázquez	P	Y	Y	Y	N	Y
8	Jeffries	P	Y	Y	Y	N	Y
9	Clarke	P	Y	Y	Y	N	Y
10	Nadler	P	Y	Y	Y	N	Y
11	Rose	P	C	Y	Y	N	Y
12	Maloney, C.	P	Y	Y	Y	N	Y
13	Espaillat	P	Y	Y	Y	N	Y
14	Ocasio-Cortez	P	Y	Y	Y	N	Y
15	Serrano	P	Y	Y	Y	N	Y
16	Engel	P	Y	Y	Y	N	Y
17	Lowey	P	Y	Y	Y	N	Y
18	Maloney, S.P.	P	Y	Y	Y	N	Y
19	Delgado	P	Y	Y	Y	N	Y
20	Tonko	P	Y	Y	Y	N	Y
21	**Stefanik**	P	N	N	N	Y	N
22	Brindisi	P	C	Y	Y	?	Y
23	**Reed**	P	N	N	N	Y	N
24	**Katko**	P	N	N	N	Y	N
25	Morelle	P	Y	Y	Y	N	Y
26	Higgins, B.	P	Y	Y	Y	N	Y
27	**Collins, C.**	P	N	N	N	Y	N
NORTH CAROLINA							
1	Butterfield	P	Y	Y	Y	N	Y
2	**Holding**	P	N	N	N	Y	N
3	**Jones**	I	I	I	I	I	I
4	Price	P	Y	Y	Y	N	Y
5	**Foxx**	P	N	N	N	Y	N
6	**Walker**	P	N	N	N	Y	N
7	**Rouzer**	P	N	N	N	Y	N

		1	2	3	4	5	6
8	**Hudson**	P	N	N	N	Y	N
9	vacant						
10	**McHenry**	P	N	N	N	Y	N
11	**Meadows**	P	N	N	N	Y	N
12	Adams	P	Y	Y	Y	N	Y
13	**Budd**	P	N	N	N	Y	N
NORTH DAKOTA							
AL	**Armstrong**	P	N	N	N	Y	N
OHIO							
1	**Chabot**	P	N	N	N	Y	N
2	**Wenstrup**	P	N	N	N	Y	N
3	Beatty	P	Y	Y	Y	N	Y
4	**Jordan**	P	N	N	N	Y	N
5	**Latta**	P	N	N	N	Y	N
6	**Johnson, B.**	P	N	N	N	Y	N
7	**Gibbs**	P	N	N	N	Y	N
8	**Davidson**	P	N	N	N	Y	N
9	Kaptur	P	Y	Y	Y	N	Y
10	**Turner**	P	N	N	N	Y	N
11	Fudge	P	Y	Y	Y	N	Y
12	**Balderson**	P	N	N	N	Y	N
13	Ryan	P	Y	Y	Y	N	Y
14	**Joyce**	P	N	N	N	Y	N
15	**Stivers**	P	N	N	N	Y	N
16	**Gonzalez**	P	N	N	N	Y	N
OKLAHOMA							
1	**Hern**	P	N	N	N	Y	N
2	**Mullin**	P	N	N	N	Y	N
3	**Lucas**	P	N	N	N	Y	N
4	**Cole**	P	N	N	N	Y	N
5	Horn	P	Y	Y	Y	N	Y
OREGON							
1	Bonamici	P	Y	Y	Y	N	Y
2	**Walden**	P	N	N	N	Y	N
3	Blumenauer	P	Y	Y	Y	N	Y
4	DeFazio	P	Y	Y	Y	N	Y
5	Schrader	P	C	Y	Y	N	Y
PENNSYLVANIA							
1	**Fitzpatrick**	P	N	N	N	Y	N
2	Boyle	P	Y	Y	Y	N	Y
3	Evans	P	Y	Y	Y	N	Y
4	Dean	P	Y	Y	Y	N	Y
5	Scanlon	P	Y	Y	Y	N	Y
6	Houlahan	P	Y	Y	Y	N	Y
7	Wild	P	Y	?	Y	N	Y
8	Cartwright	P	Y	Y	Y	N	Y
9	**Meuser**	P	N	N	N	Y	N
10	**Perry**	P	C	N	N	Y	N
11	**Smucker**	P	N	?	?	?	?
12	**Marino**	P	N	N	N	Y	N
13	**Joyce**	P	N	N	N	Y	N
14	**Reschenthaler**	P	N	N	N	Y	N
15	**Thompson, G.**	P	N	N	N	Y	N
16	**Kelly, M.**	P	N	N	N	Y	N
17	Lamb	P	C	Y	Y	N	Y
18	Doyle	P	Y	Y	Y	N	Y
RHODE ISLAND							
1	Cicilline	P	Y	Y	Y	N	Y
2	Langevin	P	Y	Y	Y	N	Y
SOUTH CAROLINA							
1	Cunningham	P	C	Y	Y	N	Y
2	**Wilson, J.**	P	N	N	N	Y	N
3	**Duncan**	P	N	N	N	Y	N
4	**Timmons**	P	N	N	N	Y	N
5	**Norman**	P	N	N	N	Y	N
6	Clyburn	P	Y	Y	Y	N	Y
7	**Rice, T.**	P	N	N	N	Y	N
SOUTH DAKOTA							
AL	**Johnson**	P	N	N	N	Y	N
TENNESSEE							
1	**Roe**	P	N	N	N	Y	N
2	**Burchett**	P	N	N	N	Y	N
3	**Fleischmann**	P	N	N	N	Y	N
4	**DesJarlais**	P	N	N	N	Y	N
5	Cooper	P	P	Y	Y	N	Y
6	**Rose**	P	N	N	N	Y	N
7	**Green**	P	N	N	N	Y	N
8	**Kustoff**	P	N	N	N	Y	N
9	Cohen	P	Y	Y	Y	N	Y
TEXAS							
1	**Gohmert**	P	N	N	N	Y	N
2	**Crenshaw**	P	N	N	N	Y	N
3	**Taylor**	P	N	N	N	Y	N
4	**Ratcliffe**	P	N	N	N	Y	N

		1	2	3	4	5	6
5	**Gooden**	P	N	N	N	Y	N
6	**Wright**	P	N	N	N	Y	N
7	Fletcher	P	Y	Y	Y	N	Y
8	**Brady**	P	N	N	N	Y	N
9	Green, A.	P	Y	Y	Y	N	Y
10	**McCaul**	P	N	N	N	Y	N
11	**Conaway**	P	N	N	N	Y	N
12	**Granger**	P	N	N	N	Y	N
13	**Thornberry**	P	N	N	N	Y	N
14	**Weber**	P	N	N	N	Y	N
15	Gonzalez	P	Y	Y	Y	N	Y
16	Escobar	P	Y	Y	Y	N	Y
17	**Flores**	P	N	N	N	Y	N
18	Jackson Lee	P	Y	Y	Y	N	Y
19	**Arrington**	P	N	N	N	Y	N
20	Castro	P	Y	Y	Y	N	Y
21	**Roy**	P	N	N	N	Y	N
22	**Olson**	P	N	N	N	Y	N
23	**Hurd**	P	N	N	N	Y	N
24	**Marchant**	P	N	N	N	Y	?
25	**Williams**	P	N	N	N	Y	N
26	**Burgess**	P	N	N	N	Y	N
27	**Cloud**	P	N	N	N	Y	N
28	Cuellar	P	Y	Y	Y	N	Y
29	Garcia, S.	P	Y	Y	Y	N	Y
30	Johnson, E.B.	P	Y	Y	Y	N	Y
31	**Carter, J.**	P	N	N	N	Y	N
32	Allred	P	Y	Y	Y	N	Y
33	Veasey	P	Y	Y	Y	N	Y
34	Vela	P	Y	Y	Y	N	Y
35	Doggett	P	Y	Y	Y	N	Y
36	**Babin**	P	N	N	N	Y	N
UTAH							
1	**Bishop, R.**	P	N	N	N	Y	N
2	**Stewart**	P	N	N	N	Y	N
3	**Curtis**	P	N	N	N	Y	N
4	McAdams	P	C	Y	Y	N	Y
VERMONT							
AL	Welch	P	Y	Y	Y	N	Y
VIRGINIA							
1	**Wittman**	P	N	N	N	Y	?
2	Luria	P	Y	Y	Y	N	Y
3	Scott, R.	P	Y	Y	Y	N	Y
4	McEachin	P	Y	Y	Y	N	Y
5	**Riggleman**	P	N	N	N	Y	N
6	**Cline**	P	N	N	N	Y	N
7	Spanberger	P	C	Y	Y	N	Y
8	Beyer	P	Y	Y	Y	N	Y
9	**Griffith**	P	N	N	N	Y	N
10	Wexton	P	Y	Y	Y	N	Y
11	Connolly	P	Y	Y	Y	N	Y
WASHINGTON							
1	DelBene	P	Y	Y	Y	N	Y
2	Larsen	P	Y	Y	Y	N	Y
3	**Herrera Beutler**	P	N	N	N	Y	N
4	**Newhouse**	P	N	N	N	Y	N
5	**McMorris Rodgers**	P	N	N	N	Y	N
6	Kilmer	P	Y	Y	Y	N	Y
7	Jayapal	P	Y	Y	Y	N	Y
8	Schrier	P	Y	Y	Y	N	Y
9	Smith Adam	P	Y	Y	Y	N	Y
10	Heck	P	Y	Y	Y	N	Y
WEST VIRGINIA							
1	**McKinley**	P	N	N	N	Y	N
2	**Mooney**	P	N	N	N	Y	N
3	**Miller**	P	N	N	N	Y	N
WISCONSIN							
1	**Steil**	P	N	N	N	Y	N
2	Pocan	P	Y	Y	Y	N	Y
3	Kind	P	C	Y	Y	N	Y
4	Moore	P	Y	Y	Y	N	Y
5	**Sensenbrenner**	P	N	N	N	Y	N
6	**Grothman**	P	N	N	N	Y	N
7	**Duffy**						
8	**Gallagher**	P	N	N	N	Y	N
WYOMING							
AL	**Cheney**	P	N	N	N	Y	N
DELEGATES							
	Radewagen (A.S.)						
	Norton (D.C.)						
	San Nicolas (Guam)						
	Sablan (N. Marianas)						
	González-Colón (P.R.)						
	Plaskett (V.I.)						

||| HOUSE VOTES

7. HRES6. House Organizing Resolution, Title I - Passage. Agreeing to the resolution that would establish the rules of the House for the 116th Congress. Many of the rules that were in effect at the end of the 115th Congress would carry over. Among rules changed, Title I of the resolution would require that legislation with substantial bipartisan support be considered at least once a week as per a new House calendar, require that all major legislation be marked up by committee before floor consideration, and require legislative text to be publicly available 72 hours prior to floor consideration. It would restore several Democratic rules related to the budget process, including to remove the super-majority requirement for any measure that would increase federal taxes and to restore the pay-as-you-go point of order that would require new government spending to be offset with cuts or taxes. It would also modify House ethics rules, including to require annual ethics trainings for members and to require each office to adopt new anti-harassment and anti-discrimination policies. Passed 234-197: R 3-194; D 231-3. Jan. 3, 2019.

8. HJRES1. Homeland Security Continuing Resolution. Granger, R-Texas, motion to recommit the joint resolution to the House Appropriations Committee. Motion rejected 197-233: R 197-0; D 0-233.

9. HJRES1. Homeland Security Continuing Resolution. Passage of the joint resolution that would provide short-term funding for the Homeland Security Department through Feb. 8, 2019 at rates provided in the fiscal 2018 omnibus appropriations law, but with additional restrictions for use of border security funds that would prevent the appropriated dollars from being used to construct the president's proposed concrete border "wall." The bill would also provide for back-pay for all furloughed federal employees at the Homeland Security Department as compensation for pay missed during the lapse in appropriations. Passed 239-192: R 5-192; D 234-0. *Note: A "nay" was a vote in support of the president's position.* Jan. 3, 2019.

10. HR21. Homeland Security Continuing Resolution. Granger, R-Texas, motion to recommit the bill to the House Appropriations Committee with instructions to report it back immediately with an amendment that would modify aspects of the State and Foreign Operations provisions in the bill. Motion rejected 199-232: R 197-0; D 2-232. Jan. 3, 2019.

11. HR21. Fiscal 2019 Continuing Appropriations. Passage of the bill that would provide full-year continuing appropriations covering six of the seven fiscal 2019 appropriations bills that have not been enacted into law, including those that relate to Agriculture, Commerce-Justice-Science, Financial Services, Interior-Environment, State-Foreign Operations, and Transportation-HUD provisions. The bill includes provisions for a 1.9 percent pay increase for federal civilian employees and would extend the National Flood Insurance Program through fiscal 2019. It would also provide for retroactive pay for federal workers furloughed during the partial shutdown. Passed 241-190: R 7-190; D 234-0. *Note: A "nay" was a vote in support of the president's position.* Jan. 3, 2019.

12. HRES6. House Organizing Resolution, Title II - Passage. Agreeing to the resolution that would establish the rules of the House for the 116th Congress. Title II of the resolution would establish a select committee to study and make recommendations on modernizing Congress, including on matters of procedural efficiency, development of leadership, and staff recruitment and retention. It would require the committee to provide interim status reports to the House Administration and House Rules Committees and require that all policy recommendations be agreed to by at least two-thirds of the select committee's 12 members. Passed (thus cleared for the president) 418-12: R 184-12; D 234-0. Jan. 4, 2019.

		7	8	9	10	11	12
ALABAMA							
1	**Byrne**	N	Y	N	Y	N	Y
2	**Roby**	N	Y	N	Y	N	Y
3	**Rogers, M.**	N	Y	N	Y	N	Y
4	**Aderholt**	N	Y	N	Y	N	Y
5	**Brooks, M.**	N	Y	N	Y	N	Y
6	**Palmer**	N	Y	N	Y	N	Y
7	Sewell	Y	N	Y	N	Y	Y
ALASKA							
AL	**Young**	N	Y	N	Y	N	?
ARIZONA							
1	O'Halleran	Y	N	Y	N	Y	Y
2	Kirkpatrick	Y	N	Y	N	Y	Y
3	Grijalva	Y	N	Y	N	Y	Y
4	**Gosar**	N	Y	N	Y	N	Y
5	**Biggs**	N	Y	N	Y	N	N
6	**Schweikert**	N	Y	N	Y	N	Y
7	Gallego	Y	N	Y	N	Y	Y
8	**Lesko**	N	Y	N	Y	N	Y
9	Stanton	Y	N	Y	N	Y	Y
ARKANSAS							
1	**Crawford**	N	Y	N	Y	N	Y
2	**Hill, F.**	N	Y	N	Y	N	Y
3	**Womack**	N	Y	N	Y	N	Y
4	**Westerman**	N	Y	N	Y	N	Y
CALIFORNIA							
1	**LaMalfa**	N	Y	N	Y	N	Y
2	Huffman	Y	N	Y	N	Y	Y
3	Garamendi	Y	?	Y	N	Y	Y
4	**McClintock**	N	Y	N	Y	N	Y
5	Thompson, M.	Y	N	Y	N	Y	Y
6	Matsui	Y	N	Y	N	Y	Y
7	Bera	Y	N	Y	N	Y	Y
8	**Cook**	N	Y	N	Y	N	Y
9	McNerney	Y	N	Y	N	Y	Y
10	Harder	Y	N	Y	N	Y	Y
11	DeSaulnier	Y	N	Y	N	Y	Y
12	Pelosi					Y	
13	Lee B.	Y	N	Y	N	Y	Y
14	Speier	Y	N	Y	N	Y	Y
15	Swalwell	Y	N	Y	N	Y	Y
16	Costa	Y	N	Y	N	Y	Y
17	Khanna	N	N	Y	N	Y	Y
18	Eshoo	Y	N	Y	N	Y	Y
19	Lofgren	Y	N	Y	N	Y	Y
20	Panetta	Y	N	Y	N	Y	Y
21	Cox	Y	N	Y	N	Y	Y
22	**Nunes**	N	Y	N	Y	N	Y
23	**McCarthy**	N	Y	N	Y	N	Y
24	Carbajal	Y	N	Y	N	Y	Y
25	Hill, K.	Y	N	Y	N	Y	Y
26	Brownley	Y	N	Y	N	Y	Y
27	Chu	Y	N	Y	N	Y	Y
28	Schiff	Y	N	Y	N	Y	Y
29	Cárdenas	Y	N	Y	N	Y	Y
30	Sherman	Y	N	Y	N	Y	Y
31	Aguilar	Y	N	Y	N	Y	Y
32	Napolitano	Y	N	Y	N	Y	Y
33	Lieu	Y	N	Y	N	Y	Y
34	Gomez	Y	N	Y	N	Y	Y
35	Torres	Y	N	Y	N	Y	Y
36	Ruiz	Y	N	Y	N	Y	Y
37	Bass	Y	N	Y	N	Y	Y
38	Sánchez	Y	N	Y	N	Y	Y
39	Cisneros	Y	N	Y	N	Y	Y
40	Roybal-Allard	Y	N	Y	N	Y	Y
41	Takano	Y	N	Y	N	Y	Y
42	**Calvert**	N	Y	N	Y	N	Y
43	Waters	Y	N	Y	N	Y	Y
44	Barragán	Y	N	Y	N	Y	Y
45	Porter	Y	N	Y	N	Y	Y
46	Correa	Y	N	Y	N	Y	Y
47	Lowenthal	Y	N	Y	N	Y	Y
48	Rouda	Y	N	Y	N	Y	Y
49	Levin	Y	N	Y	N	Y	Y
50	**Hunter**	N	Y	N	Y	N	N
51	Vargas	Y	N	Y	N	Y	Y
52	Peters	Y	N	Y	N	Y	Y

		7	8	9	10	11	12
53	Davis, S.	Y	N	Y	N	Y	Y
COLORADO							
1	DeGette	Y	N	Y	N	Y	Y
2	Neguse	Y	N	Y	N	Y	Y
3	**Tipton**	N	Y	N	Y	N	Y
4	**Buck**	N	Y	N	Y	N	Y
5	**Lamborn**	N	Y	N	Y	N	Y
6	Crow	Y	N	Y	N	Y	Y
7	Perlmutter	Y	N	Y	N	Y	Y
CONNECTICUT							
1	Larson	Y	N	Y	N	Y	Y
2	Courtney	Y	N	Y	N	Y	Y
3	DeLauro	Y	N	Y	N	Y	Y
4	Himes	Y	N	Y	N	Y	Y
5	Hayes	Y	N	Y	N	Y	Y
DELAWARE							
AL	Blunt Rochester	Y	N	Y	N	Y	Y
FLORIDA							
1	**Gaetz**	N	Y	N	Y	N	?
2	**Dunn**	N	Y	N	Y	N	Y
3	**Yoho**	N	Y	N	Y	N	N
4	**Rutherford**	N	Y	N	Y	N	Y
5	Lawson	Y	N	Y	N	Y	Y
6	**Waltz**	N	Y	N	Y	N	Y
7	Murphy	Y	N	Y	N	Y	Y
8	**Posey**	N	Y	N	Y	N	Y
9	Soto	Y	N	Y	N	Y	Y
10	Demings	Y	N	Y	N	Y	Y
11	**Webster**	N	Y	N	Y	N	Y
12	**Bilirakis**	N	Y	N	Y	N	Y
13	Crist	Y	N	Y	N	Y	Y
14	Castor	Y	N	Y	N	Y	Y
15	**Spano**	N	Y	N	Y	N	Y
16	**Buchanan**	N	Y	N	Y	N	Y
17	**Steube**	N	Y	N	Y	N	Y
18	**Mast**	N	Y	N	Y	N	Y
19	**Rooney**	N	Y	N	Y	N	Y
20	Hastings	Y	N	Y	N	Y	Y
21	Frankel	Y	N	Y	N	Y	Y
22	Deutch	Y	N	Y	N	Y	Y
23	Wasserman Schultz	Y	N	Y	N	Y	Y
24	Wilson, F.	Y	N	Y	N	Y	Y
25	**Diaz-Balart**	N	Y	N	Y	N	Y
26	Mucarsel-Powell	Y	N	Y	N	Y	Y
27	Shalala	Y	N	Y	N	Y	Y
GEORGIA							
1	**Carter, E.L.**	N	Y	N	Y	N	Y
2	Bishop, S.	Y	N	Y	N	Y	Y
3	**Ferguson**	N	Y	N	Y	N	Y
4	Johnson, H.	Y	N	Y	N	Y	Y
5	Lewis John	Y	N	Y	N	Y	Y
6	McBath	Y	N	Y	N	Y	Y
7	**Woodall**	N	Y	N	Y	N	Y
8	**Scott, A.**	N	Y	N	Y	N	Y
9	**Collins, D.**	N	Y	N	Y	N	Y
10	**Hice**	N	Y	N	Y	N	Y
11	**Loudermilk**	N	Y	N	Y	N	Y
12	**Allen**	N	Y	N	Y	N	N
13	Scott, D.	Y	N	Y	N	Y	Y
14	**Graves, T.**	N	Y	N	Y	N	Y
HAWAII							
1	Case	Y	N	Y	N	Y	Y
2	Gabbard	N	N	Y	N	Y	Y
IDAHO							
1	**Fulcher**	N	Y	N	Y	N	Y
2	**Simpson**	N	Y	N	Y	N	Y
ILLINOIS							
1	Rush	Y	N	Y	N	Y	Y
2	Kelly, R.	Y	N	Y	N	Y	Y
3	Lipinski	Y	N	Y	N	Y	Y
4	García, J.	Y	N	Y	N	Y	Y
5	Quigley	Y	N	Y	N	Y	Y
6	Casten	Y	N	Y	N	Y	Y
7	Davis, D.	Y	N	Y	N	Y	Y
8	Krishnamoorthi	Y	N	Y	N	Y	Y
9	Schakowsky	Y	N	Y	N	Y	Y
10	Schneider	Y	N	Y	N	Y	Y
11	Foster	Y	N	Y	N	Y	Y

KEY:	**Republicans**	Democrats	*Independents*

Y	Voted for (yea)	**N**	Voted against (nay)	**P**	Voted "present"
+	Announced for	**–**	Announced against	**?**	Did not vote or otherwise
#	Paired for	**X**	Paired against		make position known

H-10 2019 CQ ALMANAC | www.cq.com

		7	8	9	10	11	12
12	**Bost**	N	Y	N	Y	N	Y
13	**Davis, R.**	N	Y	N	Y	N	Y
14	Underwood	Y	N	Y	N	Y	Y
15	**Shimkus**	N	Y	N	Y	N	Y
16	**Kinzinger**	N	Y	N	Y	N	Y
17	Bustos	Y	N	Y	N	Y	Y
18	**LaHood**	N	Y	N	Y	N	Y
INDIANA							
1	Visclosky	Y	N	Y	N	Y	Y
2	**Walorski**	N	Y	N	Y	N	Y
3	**Banks**	N	Y	N	Y	N	Y
4	**Baird**	N	Y	N	Y	N	Y
5	**Brooks, S.**	N	Y	N	Y	N	Y
6	**Pence**	N	Y	N	Y	N	Y
7	Carson	Y	N	Y	N	Y	Y
8	**Bucshon**	N	Y	N	Y	N	Y
9	**Hollingsworth**	N	Y	N	Y	N	Y
IOWA							
1	Finkenauer	Y	N	Y	N	Y	Y
2	Loebsack	Y	N	Y	N	Y	Y
3	Axne	Y	N	Y	N	Y	Y
4	**King, S.**	N	Y	N	Y	N	N
KANSAS							
1	**Marshall**	N	Y	N	Y	N	Y
2	**Watkins**	N	Y	N	Y	N	Y
3	Davids	Y	N	Y	N	Y	Y
4	**Estes**	N	Y	N	Y	N	Y
KENTUCKY							
1	**Comer**	N	Y	N	Y	N	Y
2	**Guthrie**	N	Y	N	Y	N	Y
3	Yarmuth	Y	N	Y	N	Y	Y
4	**Massie**	N	Y	N	Y	N	N
5	**Rogers, H.**	N	Y	N	Y	N	Y
6	**Barr**	N	Y	N	Y	N	Y
LOUISIANA							
1	**Scalise**	N	Y	N	Y	N	Y
2	Richmond	Y	N	Y	N	Y	Y
3	**Higgins, C.**	N	Y	N	Y	N	Y
4	**Johnson, M.**	N	Y	N	Y	N	Y
5	**Abraham**	N	Y	N	Y	N	Y
6	**Graves, G.**	N	Y	N	Y	N	Y
MAINE							
1	Pingree	Y	N	Y	N	Y	Y
2	Golden	Y	N	Y	N	Y	Y
MARYLAND							
1	**Harris**	N	Y	N	Y	N	Y
2	Ruppersberger	Y	N	Y	N	Y	Y
3	Sarbanes	Y	N	Y	N	Y	Y
4	Brown, A.	Y	N	Y	N	Y	Y
5	Hoyer	Y	N	Y	N	Y	Y
6	Trone	Y	N	Y	N	Y	Y
7	Cummings	Y	N	Y	N	Y	Y
8	Raskin	Y	N	Y	N	Y	Y
MASSACHUSETTS							
1	Neal	Y	N	Y	N	Y	Y
2	McGovern	Y	N	Y	N	Y	Y
3	Trahan	Y	N	Y	N	Y	Y
4	Kennedy	Y	N	Y	N	Y	Y
5	Clark	Y	N	Y	N	Y	Y
6	Moulton	Y	N	Y	N	Y	Y
7	Pressley	Y	N	Y	N	Y	Y
8	Lynch	Y	N	Y	N	Y	Y
9	Keating	Y	N	Y	N	Y	Y
MICHIGAN							
1	**Bergman**	N	Y	N	Y	N	Y
2	**Huizenga**	N	Y	N	Y	N	Y
3	**Amash**	N	Y	N	Y	N	Y
4	**Moolenaar**	N	Y	N	Y	N	Y
5	Kildee	Y	N	Y	N	Y	Y
6	**Upton**	N	Y	N	Y	Y	Y
7	**Walberg**	N	Y	N	Y	N	Y
8	Slotkin	Y	N	Y	N	Y	Y
9	Levin	Y	N	Y	N	Y	Y
10	**Mitchell**	N	Y	N	Y	N	Y
11	Stevens	Y	N	Y	N	Y	Y
12	Dingell	Y	N	Y	N	Y	Y
13	Tlaib	Y	N	Y	N	Y	Y
14	Lawrence	Y	N	Y	N	Y	Y
MINNESOTA							
1	**Hagedorn**	N	Y	N	Y	N	Y
2	Craig	Y	N	Y	N	Y	Y
3	Phillips	Y	N	Y	N	Y	Y
4	McCollum	Y	N	Y	N	Y	Y
5	Omar	Y	N	Y	N	Y	Y

		7	8	9	10	11	12
6	**Emmer**	N	Y	N	Y	N	Y
7	Peterson	Y	N	Y	Y	Y	Y
8	**Stauber**	N	Y	N	Y	N	Y
MISSISSIPPI							
1	**Kelly, T.**	N	Y	N	Y	N	Y
2	Thompson, B.	Y	N	Y	N	Y	Y
3	**Guest**	N	Y	N	Y	N	Y
4	**Palazzo**	N	Y	N	Y	N	Y
MISSOURI							
1	Clay	Y	N	Y	N	Y	Y
2	**Wagner**	N	Y	N	Y	N	Y
3	**Luetkemeyer**	N	Y	N	Y	N	Y
4	**Hartzler**	N	Y	N	Y	N	Y
5	Cleaver	Y	N	Y	N	Y	Y
6	**Graves, S.**	N	Y	N	Y	N	Y
7	**Long**	N	Y	N	Y	N	Y
8	**Smith, J.**	N	Y	N	Y	N	Y
MONTANA							
AL	**Gianforte**	N	Y	N	Y	N	Y
NEBRASKA							
1	**Fortenberry**	N	Y	N	Y	N	Y
2	**Bacon**	N	Y	N	Y	N	Y
3	**Smith, Adrian**	N	Y	N	Y	N	Y
NEVADA							
1	Titus	Y	N	Y	N	Y	Y
2	**Amodei**	N	Y	N	Y	N	Y
3	Lee	Y	N	Y	N	Y	Y
4	Horsford	Y	N	Y	N	Y	Y
NEW HAMPSHIRE							
1	Pappas	Y	N	Y	N	Y	Y
2	Kuster	Y	N	Y	N	Y	Y
NEW JERSEY							
1	Norcross	Y	N	Y	N	Y	Y
2	Van Drew	Y	N	Y	N	Y	Y
3	Kim	Y	N	Y	N	Y	Y
4	**Smith, C.**	N	Y	Y	Y	N	Y
5	Gottheimer	Y	N	Y	N	Y	Y
6	Pallone	Y	N	Y	N	Y	Y
7	Malinowski	Y	N	Y	N	Y	Y
8	Sires	Y	N	Y	N	Y	Y
9	Pascrell	Y	N	Y	N	Y	Y
10	Payne	Y	N	Y	N	Y	Y
11	Sherrill	Y	N	Y	N	Y	Y
12	Watson Coleman	Y	N	Y	N	Y	Y
NEW MEXICO							
1	Haaland	Y	N	Y	N	Y	Y
2	Torres Small	Y	N	Y	N	Y	Y
3	Luján	Y	N	Y	N	Y	Y
NEW YORK							
1	**Zeldin**	N	Y	N	Y	N	Y
2	**King, P.**	N	Y	N	Y	Y	Y
3	Suozzi	Y	N	Y	N	Y	Y
4	Rice, K.	Y	N	Y	N	Y	Y
5	Meeks	Y	N	Y	N	Y	Y
6	Meng	Y	N	Y	N	Y	Y
7	Velázquez	Y	N	Y	N	Y	Y
8	Jeffries	Y	N	Y	N	?	Y
9	Clarke	Y	N	Y	N	Y	Y
10	Nadler	Y	N	Y	N	Y	Y
11	Rose	Y	N	Y	N	Y	Y
12	Maloney, C.	Y	N	Y	N	Y	Y
13	Espaillat	Y	N	Y	N	Y	Y
14	Ocasio-Cortez	N	N	Y	N	Y	Y
15	Serrano	Y	N	Y	N	Y	Y
16	Engel	Y	N	Y	N	Y	Y
17	Lowey	Y	N	Y	N	Y	Y
18	Maloney, S.P.	Y	N	Y	N	Y	Y
19	Delgado	Y	N	Y	N	Y	Y
20	Tonko	Y	N	Y	N	Y	Y
21	**Stefanik**	N	Y	Y	Y	Y	Y
22	Brindisi	Y	N	Y	N	Y	Y
23	**Reed**	Y	Y	N	Y	N	Y
24	**Katko**	Y	Y	Y	Y	Y	Y
25	Morelle	Y	N	Y	N	Y	Y
26	Higgins, B.	Y	N	Y	N	Y	Y
27	**Collins, C.**	N	Y	N	Y	N	Y
NORTH CAROLINA							
1	Butterfield	Y	N	Y	N	Y	Y
2	**Holding**	N	Y	N	Y	N	Y
3	**Jones**	I	I	I	I	I	I
4	Price	Y	N	Y	N	Y	Y
5	**Foxx**	N	Y	N	Y	N	Y
6	**Walker**	N	Y	N	Y	N	Y
7	**Rouzer**	N	Y	N	Y	N	N

		7	8	9	10	11	12
8	**Hudson**	N	Y	N	Y	N	Y
9	vacant						
10	**McHenry**	N	Y	N	Y	N	Y
11	**Meadows**	N	Y	N	Y	N	N
12	Adams	Y	N	Y	N	Y	Y
13	**Budd**	N	Y	N	Y	N	Y
NORTH DAKOTA							
AL	**Armstrong**	N	Y	N	Y	N	Y
OHIO							
1	**Chabot**	N	Y	N	Y	N	Y
2	**Wenstrup**	N	Y	N	Y	N	Y
3	Beatty	Y	N	Y	N	Y	Y
4	**Jordan**	N	Y	N	Y	N	Y
5	**Latta**	N	Y	N	Y	N	Y
6	**Johnson, B.**	N	Y	N	Y	N	Y
7	**Gibbs**	N	Y	N	Y	N	Y
8	**Davidson**	N	Y	N	Y	N	Y
9	Kaptur	Y	N	Y	N	Y	Y
10	**Turner**	N	Y	N	Y	N	Y
11	Fudge	Y	N	Y	N	Y	Y
12	**Balderson**	N	Y	N	Y	N	Y
13	Ryan	Y	N	Y	N	Y	Y
14	**Joyce**	N	Y	N	Y	N	Y
15	**Stivers**	N	Y	N	Y	N	Y
16	**Gonzalez**	N	Y	N	Y	N	Y
OKLAHOMA							
1	**Hern**	N	Y	N	Y	N	Y
2	**Mullin**	N	Y	N	Y	N	Y
3	**Lucas**	N	Y	N	Y	N	Y
4	**Cole**	N	Y	N	Y	N	Y
5	Horn	Y	N	Y	N	Y	Y
OREGON							
1	Bonamici	Y	N	Y	N	Y	Y
2	**Walden**	N	Y	N	Y	Y	Y
3	Blumenauer	Y	N	Y	N	Y	Y
4	DeFazio	Y	N	Y	N	Y	Y
5	Schrader	Y	N	Y	N	Y	Y
PENNSYLVANIA							
1	**Fitzpatrick**	Y	Y	Y	Y	Y	Y
2	Boyle	Y	N	Y	N	Y	Y
3	Evans	Y	N	Y	N	Y	Y
4	Dean	Y	N	Y	N	Y	Y
5	Scanlon	Y	N	Y	N	Y	Y
6	Houlahan	Y	N	Y	N	Y	Y
7	Wild	Y	N	Y	N	Y	Y
8	Cartwright	Y	N	Y	N	Y	Y
9	**Meuser**	N	Y	N	Y	N	Y
10	**Perry**	N	Y	N	Y	N	Y
11	**Smucker**	?	?	?	?	?	Y
12	**Marino**	N	Y	N	Y	N	Y
13	**Joyce**	N	Y	N	Y	N	Y
14	**Reschenthaler**	N	Y	N	Y	N	Y
15	**Thompson, G.**	N	Y	N	Y	N	Y
16	**Kelly, M.**	N	Y	N	Y	N	Y
17	Lamb	Y	N	Y	N	Y	Y
18	Doyle	Y	N	Y	N	Y	Y
RHODE ISLAND							
1	Cicilline	Y	N	Y	N	Y	Y
2	Langevin	Y	N	Y	N	Y	Y
SOUTH CAROLINA							
1	Cunningham	Y	N	Y	N	Y	Y
2	**Wilson, J.**	N	Y	N	Y	N	Y
3	**Duncan**	N	Y	N	Y	N	Y
4	**Timmons**	N	Y	N	Y	N	Y
5	**Norman**	N	Y	N	Y	N	N
6	Clyburn	Y	N	Y	N	Y	Y
7	**Rice, T.**	N	Y	N	Y	N	Y
SOUTH DAKOTA							
AL	**Johnson**	N	Y	N	Y	N	Y
TENNESSEE							
1	**Roe**	N	Y	N	Y	N	Y
2	**Burchett**	N	Y	N	Y	N	Y
3	**Fleischmann**	N	Y	N	Y	N	Y
4	**DesJarlais**	N	Y	N	Y	N	Y
5	Cooper	Y	N	Y	N	Y	Y
6	**Rose**	N	Y	N	Y	N	Y
7	**Green**	N	Y	N	Y	N	Y
8	**Kustoff**	N	Y	N	Y	N	Y
9	Cohen	Y	N	Y	N	Y	Y
TEXAS							
1	**Gohmert**	N	Y	N	Y	N	N
2	**Crenshaw**	N	Y	N	Y	N	Y
3	**Taylor**	N	Y	N	Y	N	Y
4	**Ratcliffe**	N	Y	N	Y	N	Y

		7	8	9	10	11	12
5	**Gooden**	N	Y	N	Y	N	Y
6	**Wright**	N	Y	N	Y	N	Y
7	Fletcher	Y	N	Y	N	Y	Y
8	**Brady**	N	Y	N	Y	N	Y
9	Green, A.	Y	N	Y	N	Y	Y
10	**McCaul**	N	Y	N	Y	N	Y
11	**Conaway**	N	Y	N	Y	N	Y
12	**Granger**	N	Y	N	Y	N	Y
13	**Thornberry**	N	Y	N	Y	N	Y
14	**Weber**	N	Y	N	Y	N	Y
15	Gonzalez	Y	N	Y	N	Y	Y
16	Escobar	Y	N	Y	N	Y	Y
17	**Flores**	N	Y	N	Y	N	Y
18	Jackson Lee	Y	N	Y	N	Y	Y
19	**Arrington**	N	Y	N	Y	N	Y
20	Castro	Y	N	Y	N	Y	Y
21	**Roy**	N	Y	N	Y	N	N
22	**Olson**	N	Y	N	Y	N	Y
23	**Hurd**	N	Y	Y	Y	Y	Y
24	**Marchant**	N	Y	N	Y	N	Y
25	**Williams**	N	Y	N	Y	N	Y
26	**Burgess**	N	Y	N	Y	N	Y
27	**Cloud**	N	Y	N	Y	N	Y
28	Cuellar	Y	N	Y	N	Y	Y
29	Garcia, S.	Y	N	Y	N	Y	Y
30	Johnson, E.B.	Y	N	Y	N	Y	Y
31	**Carter, J.**	N	Y	N	Y	N	Y
32	Allred	Y	N	Y	N	Y	Y
33	Veasey	Y	N	Y	N	Y	Y
34	Vela	Y	N	Y	N	Y	Y
35	Doggett	Y	N	Y	N	Y	Y
36	**Babin**	N	Y	N	Y	N	N
UTAH							
1	**Bishop, R.**	N	Y	N	Y	N	Y
2	**Stewart**	N	Y	N	Y	N	Y
3	**Curtis**	N	Y	N	Y	N	Y
4	McAdams	Y	N	Y	N	Y	Y
VERMONT							
AL	Welch	Y	N	Y	N	Y	Y
VIRGINIA							
1	**Wittman**	N	Y	N	Y	N	Y
2	Luria	Y	N	Y	N	Y	Y
3	Scott, R.	Y	N	Y	N	Y	Y
4	McEachin	Y	N	Y	N	Y	Y
5	**Riggleman**	N	Y	N	Y	N	Y
6	**Cline**	N	Y	N	Y	N	Y
7	Spanberger	Y	N	Y	N	Y	Y
8	Beyer	Y	N	Y	N	Y	Y
9	**Griffith**	N	Y	N	Y	N	Y
10	Wexton	Y	N	Y	N	Y	Y
11	Connolly	Y	N	Y	N	Y	Y
WASHINGTON							
1	DelBene	Y	N	Y	N	Y	Y
2	Larsen	Y	N	Y	N	Y	Y
3	**Herrera Beutler**	N	Y	N	Y	N	Y
4	**Newhouse**	N	Y	N	Y	N	Y
5	**McMorris Rodgers**	N	Y	N	Y	N	Y
6	Kilmer	Y	N	Y	N	Y	Y
7	Jayapal	Y	N	Y	N	Y	Y
8	Schrier	Y	N	Y	N	Y	Y
9	Smith Adam	Y	N	Y	N	Y	Y
10	Heck	Y	N	Y	N	Y	Y
WEST VIRGINIA							
1	**McKinley**	N	Y	N	Y	N	Y
2	**Mooney**	N	Y	N	Y	N	Y
3	**Miller**	N	Y	N	Y	N	Y
WISCONSIN							
1	**Steil**	N	Y	N	Y	N	Y
2	Pocan	Y	N	Y	N	Y	Y
3	Kind	Y	N	Y	N	Y	Y
4	Moore	Y	N	Y	N	Y	Y
5	**Sensenbrenner**	N	Y	N	Y	N	Y
6	**Grothman**	N	Y	N	Y	N	Y
7	**Duffy**						
8	**Gallagher**	N	Y	N	Y	N	Y
WYOMING							
AL	**Cheney**	N	Y	N	Y	N	Y
DELEGATES							
	Radewagen (A.S.)						
	Norton (D.C.)						
	San Nicolas (Guam)						
	Sablan (N. Marianas)						
	González-Colón (P.R.)						
	Plaskett (V.I.)						

⦀ HOUSE VOTES

13. HR269. Public Health Preparedness Programs - Passage. Pallone, D-N.J., motion to suspend the rules and pass the bill that would modify and reauthorize a number of federal public health and preparedness programs and modify Food and Drug Administration regulation of non-prescription drugs. The bill would authorize $7.1 billion through fiscal 2028 for a Homeland Security and Health and Human Services program to develop medical countermeasures against weapons of mass destruction. Through fiscal 2023, it would authorize $610 million through for a Health and Human Services program to stockpile medical supplies; $685 million annually for Center for Disease Control grants to state and local public health departments to develop emergency planning; $612 million annually for the Health and Human Services biomedical research and development program to secure the U.S. from chemical, biological, radiological, and nuclear threats and prevent the spread of infectious diseases; and $250 million annually for the program's activities to prevent influenza pandemics. The bill would additionally authorize over $1 billion annually through fiscal 2023 for a number of other federal public health programs and activities. The bill would formally codify existing Food and Drug Administration regulatory systems for non-prescription drugs, including provisions related to labeling, safety determinations and approval of new drugs. It also contains provisions related to fees for facilities manufacturing non-prescription drugs. Motion agreed to 401-17: R 174-17; D 227-0. *Note: A two-thirds majority of those present and voting (279 in this case) is required for passage under suspension of the rules.* Jan. 8, 2019.

14. HR251. Chemical Facility Anti-Terrorism - Passage. Thompson, D-Miss., motion to suspend the rules and pass the bill that would extend for two years a Homeland Security Department program to collect information on and develop security plans for chemical facilities presenting a high security risk as potential targets for terrorist attacks. Motion agreed to 414-3: R 188-3; D 226-0. *Note: A two-thirds majority of those present and voting (278 in this case) is required for passage under suspension of the rules.* Jan. 8, 2019.

15. Procedural Motion - Journal. Approval of the House Journal of January 8, 2019. Motion agreed to 414-3: R 188-3; D 226-0. Jan. 8, 2019.

16. HR267, HR264, HR265, HR266. Fiscal 2019 Appropriations. Financial Services, Agriculture, Interior-Environment, and Transportation-HUD - Previous Question. McGovern, D-Mass., motion to order the previous question (thus ending debate and the possibility of amendment) on the rule (H Res 28) that would provide for House floor consideration of the bill (HR 264) that would make fiscal 2019 appropriations for financial services and general government; consideration of the bill (HR 265) that would make fiscal 2019 appropriations for the Department of Agriculture; the bill (HR 266) that would make fiscal 2019 appropriations for the departments of Interior and Environment and related agencies; and the bill (HR 267) that would make fiscal 2019 appropriations for the departments of Transportation and Housing and Urban Development. Motion agreed to 231-195: R 0-195; D 231-0. Jan. 9, 2019.

17. HR264, HR266, HR267, HR265. Fiscal 2019 Appropriations. Financial Services, Agriculture, Interior-Environment, and Transportation-HUD - Rule. Adoption of the rule (H Res 28) that would provide for House floor consideration of the bill (HR 264) that would make fiscal 2019 appropriations for financial services and general government; consideration of the bill (HR 265) that would make fiscal 2019 appropriations for the Department of Agriculture; the bill (HR 266) that would make fiscal 2019 appropriations for the departments of Interior and Environment and related agencies; and the bill (HR 267) that would make fiscal 2019 appropriations for the departments of Transportation and Housing and Urban Development. Adopted 231-195: R 0-195; D 231-0. Jan. 9, 2019.

18. HR226. Small Business Contracts - Passage. Velazquez, D-N.Y., motion to suspend the rules and pass the bill, that would require the Small Business Administration to report on government spending through "best-in-class contracts awarded to businesses classified as historically underutilized business zone, women-owned, service-disabled veteran-owned, and socially and economically disadvantaged small businesses. Motion agreed to 414-11: R 183-11; D 231-0. *Note: A two-thirds majority of those present and voting (284 in this case) is required for passage under suspension of the rules.* Jan. 9, 2019.

		13	14	15	16	17	18
ALABAMA							
1	**Byrne**	Y	Y	N	N	N	Y
2	**Roby**	Y	Y	Y	N	N	Y
3	**Rogers, M.**	Y	Y	N	N	N	Y
4	**Aderholt**	Y	Y	N	N	N	Y
5	**Brooks, M.**	N	Y	?	N	N	N
6	**Palmer**	Y	Y	N	N	N	Y
7	Sewell	Y	Y	Y	Y	Y	Y
ALASKA							
AL	**Young**	Y	Y	N	N	N	Y
ARIZONA							
1	O'Halleran	Y	Y	?	Y	Y	Y
2	Kirkpatrick	Y	Y	?	Y	Y	Y
3	Grijalva	Y	Y	Y	Y	Y	Y
4	**Gosar**	N	Y	N	N	N	N
5	**Biggs**	N	N	?	N	N	N
6	**Schweikert**	Y	Y	Y	N	N	Y
7	Gallego	Y	Y	Y	Y	Y	Y
8	**Lesko**	Y	Y	Y	N	N	Y
9	Stanton	Y	Y	Y	Y	Y	Y
ARKANSAS							
1	**Crawford**	Y	Y	N	N	N	Y
2	**Hill, F.**	Y	Y	N	N	N	Y
3	**Womack**	Y	Y	N	N	N	Y
4	**Westerman**	Y	Y	N	N	N	Y
CALIFORNIA							
1	**LaMalfa**	+	+	–	N	N	Y
2	Huffman	Y	Y	?	Y	Y	Y
3	Garamendi	Y	Y	Y	Y	Y	Y
4	**McClintock**	Y	Y	Y	N	N	Y
5	Thompson, M.	Y	Y	N	Y	Y	Y
6	Matsui	Y	Y	Y	Y	Y	Y
7	Bera	Y	Y	Y	Y	Y	Y
8	**Cook**	Y	Y	N	N	N	Y
9	McNerney	Y	Y	Y	Y	Y	Y
10	Harder	Y	Y	Y	Y	Y	Y
11	DeSaulnier	Y	Y	Y	Y	Y	Y
12	Pelosi						
13	Lee B.	Y	Y	Y	Y	Y	Y
14	Speier	Y	Y	Y	Y	Y	Y
15	Swalwell	Y	Y	Y	Y	Y	Y
16	Costa	Y	Y	N	Y	Y	Y
17	Khanna	Y	Y	Y	Y	Y	Y
18	Eshoo	Y	Y	Y	Y	Y	Y
19	Lofgren	Y	Y	Y	Y	Y	Y
20	Panetta	Y	Y	Y	Y	Y	Y
21	Cox	Y	Y	Y	Y	Y	Y
22	**Nunes**	Y	Y	?	N	N	Y
23	**McCarthy**	Y	Y	N	N	N	Y
24	Carbajal	Y	Y	Y	Y	Y	Y
25	Hill, K.	Y	Y	Y	Y	Y	Y
26	Brownley	Y	Y	N	Y	Y	Y
27	Chu	Y	Y	Y	Y	Y	Y
28	Schiff	Y	Y	Y	Y	Y	Y
29	Cárdenas	Y	Y	Y	Y	Y	Y
30	Sherman	Y	Y	Y	Y	Y	Y
31	Aguilar	Y	Y	Y	Y	Y	Y
32	Napolitano	Y	Y	Y	Y	Y	Y
33	Lieu	Y	Y	Y	Y	Y	Y
34	Gomez	Y	Y	Y	Y	Y	Y
35	Torres	Y	Y	Y	Y	Y	Y
36	Ruiz	Y	Y	N	Y	Y	Y
37	Bass	Y	Y	Y	Y	Y	Y
38	Sánchez	Y	Y	Y	Y	Y	Y
39	Cisneros	Y	Y	Y	Y	Y	Y
40	Roybal-Allard	Y	Y	Y	Y	Y	Y
41	Takano	Y	Y	Y	Y	Y	Y
42	**Calvert**	Y	Y	N	N	N	Y
43	Waters	Y	Y	N	Y	Y	Y
44	Barragán	Y	Y	Y	Y	Y	Y
45	Porter	Y	Y	Y	Y	Y	Y
46	Correa	Y	Y	Y	Y	Y	Y
47	Lowenthal	Y	Y	Y	Y	Y	Y
48	Rouda	Y	Y	Y	Y	Y	Y
49	Levin	Y	Y	Y	Y	Y	Y
50	**Hunter**	Y	Y	N	N	N	Y
51	Vargas	Y	Y	Y	Y	Y	Y
52	Peters	Y	Y	Y	Y	Y	Y

		13	14	15	16	17	18
53	Davis, S.	Y	Y	Y	Y	Y	Y
COLORADO							
1	DeGette	Y	Y	Y	Y	Y	Y
2	Neguse	Y	Y	Y	Y	Y	Y
3	**Tipton**	Y	Y	N	N	N	Y
4	**Buck**	?	?	?	?	?	?
5	**Lamborn**	Y	Y	N	N	N	Y
6	Crow	Y	Y	N	Y	Y	Y
7	Perlmutter	Y	Y	N	Y	Y	Y
CONNECTICUT							
1	Larson	Y	Y	Y	Y	Y	Y
2	Courtney	Y	Y	Y	Y	Y	Y
3	DeLauro	Y	Y	Y	Y	Y	Y
4	Himes	Y	Y	Y	Y	Y	Y
5	Hayes	Y	Y	?	Y	Y	Y
DELAWARE							
AL	Blunt Rochester	Y	Y	Y	Y	Y	Y
FLORIDA							
1	**Gaetz**	?	?	?	N	N	N
2	**Dunn**	Y	Y	N	N	N	Y
3	**Yoho**	N	Y	N	N	N	Y
4	**Rutherford**	Y	Y	N	N	N	Y
5	Lawson	Y	Y	Y	Y	Y	Y
6	**Waltz**	Y	Y	N	N	N	Y
7	Murphy	Y	Y	Y	Y	Y	Y
8	**Posey**	N	Y	N	N	N	Y
9	Soto	Y	Y	Y	Y	Y	Y
10	Demings	Y	Y	Y	Y	Y	Y
11	**Webster**	N	Y	N	N	N	Y
12	**Bilirakis**	Y	Y	N	N	N	Y
13	Crist	Y	Y	Y	Y	Y	Y
14	Castor	Y	Y	Y	Y	Y	Y
15	**Spano**	Y	Y	N	N	N	Y
16	**Buchanan**	?	?	?	N	N	Y
17	**Steube**	Y	Y	N	N	N	N
18	**Mast**	?	?	?	?	?	?
19	**Rooney**	?	?	?	N	N	Y
20	Hastings	Y	Y	?	?	?	?
21	Frankel	+	+	+	?	+	+
22	Deutch	Y	Y	Y	Y	Y	Y
23	Wasserman Schultz	Y	Y	Y	Y	Y	Y
24	Wilson, F.	?	?	?	Y	Y	Y
25	**Diaz-Balart**	Y	Y	N	N	N	Y
26	Mucarsel-Powell	Y	Y	N	Y	Y	Y
27	Shalala	Y	Y	Y	Y	Y	Y
GEORGIA							
1	**Carter, E.L.**	Y	Y	N	N	N	Y
2	Bishop, S.	Y	Y	Y	Y	Y	Y
3	**Ferguson**	Y	Y	N	N	N	Y
4	Johnson, H.	Y	Y	Y	Y	Y	Y
5	Lewis John	Y	Y	Y	Y	Y	Y
6	McBath	Y	Y	Y	Y	Y	Y
7	**Woodall**	Y	Y	N	N	N	Y
8	**Scott, A.**	Y	Y	N	N	N	Y
9	**Collins, D.**	Y	Y	N	N	N	Y
10	**Hice**	Y	Y	N	N	N	Y
11	**Loudermilk**	Y	Y	N	N	N	Y
12	**Allen**	Y	Y	N	N	N	Y
13	Scott, D.	Y	Y	Y	Y	Y	Y
14	**Graves, T.**	Y	Y	N	N	N	Y
HAWAII							
1	Case	Y	Y	Y	Y	Y	Y
2	Gabbard	Y	Y	Y	Y	Y	Y
IDAHO							
1	**Fulcher**	Y	Y	N	N	N	Y
2	**Simpson**	Y	Y	N	N	N	Y
ILLINOIS							
1	Rush	Y	?	Y	Y	Y	Y
2	Kelly, R.	Y	Y	Y	Y	Y	Y
3	Lipinski	Y	Y	Y	Y	Y	Y
4	García, J.	Y	Y	Y	Y	Y	Y
5	Quigley	Y	Y	Y	Y	Y	Y
6	Casten	Y	Y	Y	?	Y	Y
7	Davis, D.	Y	Y	Y	Y	Y	Y
8	Krishnamoorthi	Y	Y	N	Y	Y	Y
9	Schakowsky	Y	Y	Y	Y	Y	Y
10	Schneider	Y	Y	Y	Y	Y	Y
11	Foster	Y	Y	Y	Y	Y	Y

KEY: **Republicans**   Democrats   *Independents*

Y Voted for (yea)	**N** Voted against (nay)	**P** Voted "present"
+ Announced for	**–** Announced against	**?** Did not vote or otherwise
# Paired for	**X** Paired against	make position known

		13	14	15	16	17	18
12	**Bost**	Y	Y	N	N	N	Y
13	**Davis, R.**	Y	Y	N	N	N	Y
14	Underwood	Y	Y	Y	Y	Y	Y
15	**Shimkus**	Y	Y	N	N	N	Y
16	**Kinzinger**	Y	Y	Y	N	N	Y
17	Bustos	Y	Y	Y	Y	Y	Y
18	**LaHood**	Y	Y	N	N	N	Y
INDIANA							
1	Visclosky	Y	Y	Y	Y	Y	Y
2	**Walorski**	Y	Y	N	N	N	Y
3	**Banks**	Y	Y	N	N	N	Y
4	**Baird**	Y	Y	N	N	N	Y
5	**Brooks, S.**	Y	Y	?	N	N	Y
6	**Pence**	Y	Y	N	N	N	Y
7	Carson	Y	Y	Y	Y	Y	Y
8	**Bucshon**	Y	Y	N	N	N	Y
9	**Hollingsworth**	Y	Y	Y	N	N	Y
IOWA							
1	Finkenauer	Y	Y	Y	Y	Y	Y
2	Loebsack	Y	Y	Y	Y	Y	Y
3	Axne	Y	Y	N	Y	Y	Y
4	**King, S.**	N	Y	Y	N	N	N
KANSAS							
1	**Marshall**	Y	Y	N	N	N	Y
2	**Watkins**	Y	Y	N	N	N	Y
3	Davids	Y	Y	Y	Y	Y	Y
4	**Estes**	Y	Y	N	N	N	Y
KENTUCKY							
1	**Comer**	Y	Y	Y	N	N	Y
2	**Guthrie**	Y	Y	N	N	N	Y
3	Yarmuth	Y	Y	?	Y	Y	Y
4	**Massie**	N	N	N	N	N	Y
5	**Rogers, H.**	Y	Y	N	N	N	Y
6	**Barr**	Y	Y	N	N	N	Y
LOUISIANA							
1	**Scalise**	Y	Y	N	N	N	Y
2	Richmond	Y	Y	Y	Y	Y	Y
3	**Higgins, C.**	N	Y	Y	N	N	Y
4	**Johnson, M.**	Y	Y	N	N	N	Y
5	**Abraham**	Y	Y	N	N	N	Y
6	**Graves, G.**	Y	Y	N	N	N	Y
MAINE							
1	Pingree	Y	Y	Y	Y	Y	Y
2	Golden	Y	Y	N	Y	Y	Y
MARYLAND							
1	**Harris**	Y	Y	N	N	N	Y
2	Ruppersberger	Y	Y	?	Y	Y	Y
3	Sarbanes	Y	Y	Y	Y	Y	Y
4	Brown, A.	Y	Y	Y	Y	Y	Y
5	Hoyer	Y	Y	Y	Y	Y	Y
6	Trone	Y	Y	Y	Y	Y	Y
7	Cummings	Y	Y	?	Y	Y	Y
8	Raskin	Y	Y	Y	Y	Y	Y
MASSACHUSETTS							
1	Neal	Y	Y	Y	Y	Y	Y
2	McGovern	Y	Y	Y	Y	Y	Y
3	Trahan	Y	Y	Y	Y	Y	Y
4	Kennedy	Y	Y	Y	Y	Y	Y
5	Clark	Y	Y	Y	Y	Y	Y
6	Moulton	Y	Y	Y	Y	Y	Y
7	Pressley	Y	Y	Y	Y	Y	Y
8	Lynch	Y	Y	Y	Y	Y	Y
9	Keating	Y	Y	Y	Y	Y	Y
MICHIGAN							
1	**Bergman**	Y	Y	Y	N	N	Y
2	**Huizenga**	Y	Y	N	N	N	Y
3	**Amash**	N	N	N	N	N	N
4	**Moolenaar**	Y	Y	N	N	N	Y
5	Kildee	Y	Y	Y	Y	Y	Y
6	**Upton**	Y	Y	N	N	N	Y
7	**Walberg**	Y	Y	Y	N	N	Y
8	Slotkin	Y	Y	Y	Y	Y	Y
9	Levin	Y	Y	Y	Y	Y	Y
10	**Mitchell**	Y	Y	N	N	N	Y
11	Stevens	Y	Y	Y	Y	Y	Y
12	Dingell	Y	Y	Y	Y	Y	Y
13	Tlaib	Y	Y	?	Y	Y	Y
14	Lawrence	Y	Y	Y	Y	Y	Y
MINNESOTA							
1	**Hagedorn**	Y	Y	N	N	N	Y
2	Craig	Y	Y	Y	Y	Y	Y
3	Phillips	Y	Y	Y	Y	Y	Y
4	McCollum	Y	Y	Y	Y	Y	Y
5	Omar	Y	Y	Y	Y	Y	Y

		13	14	15	16	17	18
6	**Emmer**	Y	Y	N	N	N	Y
7	Peterson	Y	Y	N	Y	Y	Y
8	**Stauber**	Y	Y	N	N	N	Y
MISSISSIPPI							
1	**Kelly, T.**	Y	Y	N	N	N	Y
2	Thompson, B.	Y	Y	Y	Y	Y	Y
3	**Guest**	Y	Y	N	N	N	Y
4	**Palazzo**	Y	Y	N	N	N	Y
MISSOURI							
1	Clay	Y	Y	Y	Y	Y	Y
2	**Wagner**	Y	Y	Y	N	N	Y
3	**Luetkemeyer**	Y	Y	N	N	N	Y
4	**Hartzler**	Y	Y	N	N	N	Y
5	Cleaver	Y	Y	Y	Y	Y	Y
6	**Graves, S.**	Y	Y	N	N	N	Y
7	**Long**	Y	Y	Y	N	N	Y
8	**Smith, J.**	Y	Y	N	N	N	Y
MONTANA							
AL	**Gianforte**	Y	Y	N	N	N	Y
NEBRASKA							
1	**Fortenberry**	Y	Y	Y	N	N	Y
2	**Bacon**	Y	Y	Y	N	N	Y
3	**Smith, Adrian**	Y	Y	N	N	N	Y
NEVADA							
1	Titus	+	+	+	Y	Y	Y
2	**Amodei**	Y	Y	Y	N	N	Y
3	Lee	Y	Y	Y	Y	Y	Y
4	Horsford	Y	Y	N	Y	Y	Y
NEW HAMPSHIRE							
1	Pappas	Y	Y	Y	Y	Y	Y
2	Kuster	?	?	?	Y	Y	Y
NEW JERSEY							
1	Norcross	Y	Y	Y	Y	Y	Y
2	Van Drew	Y	Y	N	Y	Y	Y
3	Kim	Y	Y	Y	Y	Y	Y
4	**Smith, C.**	Y	Y	Y	N	N	Y
5	Gottheimer	Y	Y	N	Y	Y	Y
6	Pallone	Y	Y	Y	Y	Y	Y
7	Malinowski	Y	Y	Y	Y	Y	Y
8	Sires	Y	Y	?	Y	Y	Y
9	Pascrell	Y	Y	Y	Y	Y	Y
10	Payne	Y	Y	Y	Y	Y	Y
11	Sherrill	Y	Y	Y	Y	Y	Y
12	Watson Coleman	Y	Y	Y	Y	Y	Y
NEW MEXICO							
1	Haaland	Y	Y	Y	Y	Y	Y
2	Torres Small	Y	Y	Y	Y	Y	Y
3	Luján	Y	Y	Y	Y	Y	Y
NEW YORK							
1	**Zeldin**	Y	Y	N	N	N	Y
2	**King, P.**	Y	Y	Y	N	N	Y
3	Suozzi	Y	Y	N	Y	Y	Y
4	Rice, K.	Y	Y	N	Y	Y	Y
5	Meeks	Y	Y	Y	Y	Y	Y
6	Meng	Y	Y	N	Y	Y	Y
7	Velázquez	Y	Y	Y	Y	Y	Y
8	Jeffries	Y	Y	Y	Y	Y	Y
9	Clarke	Y	Y	Y	Y	Y	Y
10	Nadler	Y	Y	Y	Y	Y	Y
11	Rose	Y	Y	Y	Y	Y	Y
12	Maloney, C.	Y	Y	Y	Y	Y	Y
13	Espaillat	Y	Y	Y	Y	Y	Y
14	Ocasio-Cortez	Y	Y	Y	Y	Y	Y
15	Serrano	Y	Y	Y	Y	Y	Y
16	Engel	Y	Y	Y	Y	Y	Y
17	Lowey	Y	Y	Y	Y	Y	Y
18	Maloney, S.P.	Y	Y	Y	Y	Y	Y
19	Delgado	Y	Y	Y	Y	Y	Y
20	Tonko	Y	Y	P	Y	Y	Y
21	**Stefanik**	Y	Y	Y	N	N	Y
22	Brindisi	Y	Y	N	Y	Y	Y
23	**Reed**	Y	Y	N	N	N	Y
24	**Katko**	Y	Y	Y	N	N	Y
25	Morelle	Y	Y	Y	Y	Y	Y
26	Higgins, B.	Y	Y	Y	Y	Y	Y
27	**Collins, C.**	Y	Y	Y	N	N	Y
NORTH CAROLINA							
1	Butterfield	Y	Y	Y	Y	Y	Y
2	**Holding**	Y	Y	?	N	N	Y
3	**Jones**	?	?	?	?	?	?
4	Price	Y	Y	?	Y	Y	Y
5	**Foxx**	Y	Y	Y	N	N	Y
6	**Walker**	Y	Y	N	N	N	Y
7	**Rouzer**	Y	Y	N	N	N	Y

		13	14	15	16	17	18
8	**Hudson**	Y	Y	?	N	N	Y
9	vacant						
10	**McHenry**	Y	Y	N	N	N	Y
11	**Meadows**	Y	Y	?	N	N	Y
12	Adams	Y	Y	Y	Y	Y	Y
13	**Budd**	Y	Y	Y	N	N	Y
NORTH DAKOTA							
AL	**Armstrong**	Y	Y	N	N	N	Y
OHIO							
1	**Chabot**	Y	Y	N	N	N	Y
2	**Wenstrup**	Y	Y	N	N	N	Y
3	Beatty	Y	Y	Y	Y	Y	Y
4	**Jordan**	Y	Y	N	N	N	Y
5	**Latta**	Y	Y	N	N	N	Y
6	**Johnson, B.**	Y	Y	N	N	N	Y
7	**Gibbs**	Y	Y	N	N	N	Y
8	**Davidson**	Y	Y	N	N	N	Y
9	Kaptur	Y	Y	Y	Y	Y	Y
10	**Turner**	Y	Y	N	N	N	Y
11	Fudge	Y	Y	N	Y	Y	Y
12	**Balderson**	Y	Y	N	N	N	Y
13	Ryan	?	?	?	Y	Y	Y
14	**Joyce**	Y	Y	N	N	N	Y
15	**Stivers**	Y	Y	N	N	N	Y
16	**Gonzalez**	Y	Y	N	N	N	Y
OKLAHOMA							
1	**Hern**	Y	Y	N	N	N	Y
2	**Mullin**	Y	Y	N	N	N	Y
3	**Lucas**	Y	Y	N	N	N	Y
4	**Cole**	Y	Y	N	N	N	Y
5	Horn	Y	Y	Y	Y	Y	Y
OREGON							
1	Bonamici	Y	Y	Y	Y	Y	Y
2	**Walden**	Y	Y	N	N	N	Y
3	Blumenauer	Y	Y	Y	Y	Y	Y
4	DeFazio	+	+	+	+	+	+
5	Schrader	Y	Y	?	Y	Y	Y
PENNSYLVANIA							
1	**Fitzpatrick**	Y	Y	N	N	N	Y
2	Boyle	Y	Y	Y	Y	Y	Y
3	Evans	Y	Y	Y	Y	Y	Y
4	Dean	Y	Y	Y	Y	Y	Y
5	Scanlon	Y	Y	Y	Y	Y	Y
6	Houlahan	Y	Y	Y	Y	Y	Y
7	Wild	Y	Y	Y	Y	Y	Y
8	Cartwright	Y	Y	Y	Y	Y	Y
9	**Meuser**	Y	Y	N	N	N	Y
10	**Perry**	N	Y	N	N	N	Y
11	**Smucker**	Y	Y	N	N	N	Y
12	**Marino**	Y	Y	N	N	N	Y
13	**Joyce**	Y	Y	N	N	N	Y
14	**Reschenthaler**	Y	Y	N	N	N	Y
15	**Thompson, G.**	Y	Y	N	N	N	Y
16	**Kelly, M.**	?	?	?	?	?	?
17	Lamb	Y	Y	Y	Y	Y	Y
18	Doyle	Y	Y	Y	Y	Y	Y
RHODE ISLAND							
1	Cicilline	Y	Y	Y	Y	Y	Y
2	Langevin	Y	Y	Y	Y	Y	Y
SOUTH CAROLINA							
1	Cunningham	Y	Y	Y	Y	Y	Y
2	**Wilson, J.**	Y	Y	N	N	N	Y
3	**Duncan**	Y	Y	N	N	N	Y
4	**Timmons**	Y	Y	N	N	N	Y
5	**Norman**	Y	Y	Y	N	N	Y
6	Clyburn	Y	Y	Y	Y	Y	Y
7	**Rice, T.**	Y	Y	N	N	N	Y
SOUTH DAKOTA							
AL	**Johnson**	Y	Y	N	N	N	Y
TENNESSEE							
1	**Roe**	Y	Y	N	N	N	Y
2	**Burchett**	Y	Y	N	N	N	Y
3	**Fleischmann**	Y	Y	Y	N	N	Y
4	**DesJarlais**	Y	Y	N	N	N	Y
5	Cooper	Y	Y	Y	Y	Y	Y
6	**Rose**	Y	Y	N	N	N	Y
7	**Green**	N	Y	N	N	N	Y
8	**Kustoff**	Y	Y	N	N	N	Y
9	Cohen	Y	Y	?	Y	Y	Y
TEXAS							
1	**Gohmert**	N	Y	P	N	N	N
2	**Crenshaw**	Y	Y	N	N	N	Y
3	**Taylor**	Y	Y	Y	N	N	Y
4	**Ratcliffe**	N	Y	N	N	N	Y

		13	14	15	16	17	18
5	**Gooden**	Y	Y	N	N	N	Y
6	**Wright**	Y	Y	N	N	N	Y
7	Fletcher	Y	Y	Y	Y	Y	Y
8	**Brady**	Y	Y	Y	N	N	Y
9	Green, A.	Y	Y	Y	Y	Y	Y
10	**McCaul**	Y	Y	N	N	N	Y
11	**Conaway**	Y	Y	N	N	N	Y
12	**Granger**	Y	Y	Y	N	N	Y
13	**Thornberry**	Y	Y	Y	N	N	Y
14	**Weber**	N	Y	N	N	N	Y
15	Gonzalez	Y	Y	Y	Y	Y	Y
16	Escobar	Y	Y	Y	Y	Y	Y
17	**Flores**	Y	Y	N	N	N	Y
18	Jackson Lee	+	+	+	Y	Y	Y
19	**Arrington**	Y	Y	Y	N	N	Y
20	Castro	Y	Y	Y	Y	Y	Y
21	**Roy**	N	Y	N	N	N	N
22	**Olson**	Y	Y	N	N	N	Y
23	**Hurd**	Y	Y	N	N	N	Y
24	**Marchant**	Y	Y	Y	N	N	Y
25	**Williams**	Y	Y	N	N	N	Y
26	**Burgess**	Y	Y	N	N	N	Y
27	**Cloud**	Y	Y	N	N	N	Y
28	Cuellar	Y	Y	Y	Y	Y	Y
29	Garcia, S.	Y	Y	Y	Y	Y	Y
30	Johnson, E.B.	Y	Y	Y	Y	Y	Y
31	**Carter, J.**	Y	Y	Y	N	N	Y
32	Allred	Y	Y	Y	Y	Y	Y
33	Veasey	Y	Y	Y	Y	Y	Y
34	Vela	Y	Y	Y	Y	Y	Y
35	Doggett	Y	Y	Y	Y	Y	Y
36	**Babin**	N	Y	N	N	N	Y
UTAH							
1	**Bishop, R.**	Y	Y	N	N	N	Y
2	**Stewart**	Y	Y	Y	N	N	Y
3	**Curtis**	Y	Y	Y	N	N	Y
4	McAdams	Y	Y	N	Y	Y	Y
VERMONT							
AL	Welch	Y	Y	Y	Y	Y	Y
VIRGINIA							
1	**Wittman**	Y	Y	N	N	N	Y
2	Luria	Y	Y	Y	Y	Y	Y
3	Scott, R.	Y	Y	Y	Y	Y	Y
4	McEachin	Y	Y	Y	Y	Y	Y
5	**Riggleman**	Y	Y	Y	N	N	Y
6	**Cline**	Y	Y	N	N	N	N
7	Spanberger	Y	Y	Y	Y	Y	Y
8	Beyer	Y	Y	N	Y	Y	Y
9	**Griffith**	Y	Y	N	N	N	Y
10	Wexton	Y	Y	Y	Y	Y	Y
11	Connolly	Y	Y	N	Y	Y	Y
WASHINGTON							
1	DelBene	Y	Y	Y	Y	Y	Y
2	Larsen	Y	Y	Y	Y	Y	Y
3	**Herrera Beutler**	Y	Y	N	N	N	Y
4	**Newhouse**	Y	Y	N	N	N	Y
5	**McMorris Rodgers**	Y	Y	Y	N	N	Y
6	Kilmer	Y	Y	N	Y	Y	Y
7	Jayapal	Y	Y	Y	Y	Y	Y
8	Schrier	Y	Y	N	Y	Y	Y
9	Smith Adam	Y	Y	Y	Y	Y	Y
10	Heck	Y	Y	Y	Y	Y	Y
WEST VIRGINIA							
1	**McKinley**	Y	Y	N	N	N	Y
2	**Mooney**	Y	Y	N	N	N	Y
3	**Miller**	Y	Y	N	N	N	Y
WISCONSIN							
1	**Steil**	Y	Y	Y	N	N	Y
2	Pocan	Y	Y	Y	Y	Y	Y
3	Kind	Y	Y	N	Y	Y	Y
4	Moore	Y	Y	Y	Y	Y	Y
5	**Sensenbrenner**	Y	Y	N	N	N	Y
6	**Grothman**	Y	Y	Y	N	N	Y
7	**Duffy**						
8	**Gallagher**	Y	Y	N	N	N	Y
WYOMING							
AL	**Cheney**	Y	Y	N	N	N	Y
DELEGATES							
	Radewagen (A.S.)						
	Norton (D.C.)						
	San Nicolas (Guam)						
	Sablan (N. Marianas)						
	González-Colón (P.R.)						
	Plaskett (V.I.)						

19. HRES6. House Organizing Resolution, Title III - Passage. Agreeing to the resolution that would establish the rules of the House for the 116th Congress. Title III of the resolution would authorize the speaker, on behalf of the House of Representatives, to intervene in the Texas court case that found the 2010 healthcare law unconstitutional and other cases related to the law. It would also direct the Office of General Counsel to represent the House in any such litigation. Passed 235-192: R 3-192; D 232-0. Jan. 9, 2019.

20. HR264. Fiscal 2019 Financial Services Appropriations - Recommit. Graves, R-Ga., motion to recommit the bill (HR 264) to the House Appropriations Committee, with instructions to report it back immediately with an amendment to modify the amounts of certain appropriations made by the bill. The amendment would increase by $2 million the amount authorized for the Treasury Department's Office of Terrorism and Financial Intelligence; decrease by $2 million the amount authorized to the General Services Administration for activities related to federal property and buildings; and decrease by $2 million the amount authorized to the General Services Administration for space rental. Motion rejected 200-227: R 192-2; D 8-225. Jan. 9, 2019.

21. HR264. Fiscal 2019 Financial Services Appropriations - Passage. Passage of the bill that would provide $23.7 billion in discretionary funding for financial services and general government appropriations in fiscal 2019. The bill would provide $12.7 billion for the Treasury Department, of which $11.3 billion is for the Internal Revenue Service. It would provide $1.7 billion for the Securities and Exchange Commission, $7.7 billion for the operation of the federal court system, and $703 million in federal payments to the District of Columbia. The bill would also provide a 1.9 percent pay increase for civilian federal workers for 2019. Passed 240-188: R 8-188; D 232-0. *Note: A "nay" was a vote in support of the president's position.* Jan. 9, 2019.

22. HR267. Fiscal 2019 Transportation-HUD Appropriations - Recommit. Diaz-Balart, R-Fla., motion to recommit the bill to the House Appropriations Committee with instructions to report it back immediately with an amendment that would increase by a total of $142 million the amount authorized for Housing and Urban Development Department rental assistance voucher programs. The amendment required by the instructions would also reduce by a total of $71 million funds appropriated for HUD information technology maintenance and activities. Motion rejected 193-228: R 190-1; D 3-227. Jan. 10, 2019.

23. HR267. Fiscal 2019 Transportation-HUD Appropriations - Passage. Passage of the bill that would provide $71.4 billion for transportation programs for fiscal 2019 and provide for the release of $49 billion from the highway and aviation trust funds. It would provide $49.3 billion for federal highway programs; $17.7 billion for the Federal Aviation Administration; $13.5 billion for mass transit; and $2.8 billion for railroads. The bill would provide $44.5 billion for programs and activities of the Housing and Urban Development Department. From this amount, as well as offsets from payments collected by the Federal Housing Administration, the bill would provide $31.3 billion for public and Indian housing programs and $22.8 billion for the Section 8 rental assistance voucher program. Passed 244-180: R 12-180; D 232-0. *Note: A "nay" was a vote in support of the president's position.* Jan. 10, 2019.

24. HR265. Fiscal 2019 Agriculture Appropriations - Recommit. Aderholt, R-Ala., motion to recommit the bill (HR 265) to the House Appropriations Committee, with instructions to report it back immediately with amendments that would increase by $125 million the amount authorized for an Agriculture Department program related to rural utilities services. The amendments required by the instructions would also reduce by a total of $166 million the amount appropriated to several administrative offices within the Agriculture Department and funds appropriated for facility rentals by the Agriculture Department. Motion rejected 197-229: R 192-1; D 5-228. Jan. 10, 2019.

		19	20	21	22	23	24
ALABAMA							
1	**Byrne**	N	Y	N	Y	N	Y
2	**Roby**	N	Y	N	Y	N	Y
3	**Rogers, M.**	N	Y	N	Y	N	Y
4	**Aderholt**	N	Y	N	Y	N	Y
5	**Brooks, M.**	N	Y	N	Y	N	Y
6	**Palmer**	N	Y	N	Y	N	Y
7	Sewell	Y	N	Y	N	Y	N
ALASKA							
AL	**Young**	N	Y	N	Y	N	Y
ARIZONA							
1	O'Halleran	Y	N	Y	N	Y	N
2	Kirkpatrick	Y	N	Y	N	Y	N
3	Grijalva	Y	N	Y	N	Y	N
4	**Gosar**	N	Y	N	Y	N	Y
5	**Biggs**	N	Y	N	Y	N	Y
6	**Schweikert**	N	Y	N	Y	N	Y
7	Gallego	Y	N	Y	N	Y	N
8	**Lesko**	N	Y	N	Y	N	Y
9	Stanton	Y	N	Y	N	Y	N
ARKANSAS							
1	**Crawford**	N	Y	N	Y	N	Y
2	**Hill, F.**	N	Y	N	Y	N	Y
3	**Womack**	N	Y	N	Y	N	Y
4	**Westerman**	N	Y	N	Y	N	Y
CALIFORNIA							
1	**LaMalfa**	N	Y	N	?	N	Y
2	Huffman	Y	Y	Y	N	Y	N
3	Garamendi	Y	N	Y	N	Y	N
4	**McClintock**	N	Y	N	Y	N	Y
5	Thompson, M.	Y	N	Y	N	Y	N
6	Matsui	Y	N	Y	N	Y	N
7	Bera	Y	N	Y	N	Y	N
8	**Cook**	N	Y	N	Y	N	Y
9	McNerney	Y	N	Y	N	Y	N
10	Harder	Y	N	Y	N	Y	N
11	DeSaulnier	Y	N	Y	N	Y	N
12	Pelosi						
13	Lee B.	Y	N	Y	N	Y	N
14	Speier	Y	N	Y	N	Y	N
15	Swalwell	Y	N	Y	N	Y	N
16	Costa	Y	N	Y	N	Y	N
17	Khanna	Y	N	Y	N	Y	N
18	Eshoo	Y	N	Y	N	Y	N
19	Lofgren	Y	N	Y	N	Y	N
20	Panetta	Y	N	Y	N	Y	N
21	Cox	Y	N	Y	N	Y	N
22	**Nunes**	N	Y	N	Y	N	Y
23	**McCarthy**	N	Y	N	Y	N	Y
24	Carbajal	Y	N	Y	N	Y	N
25	Hill, K.	Y	N	Y	N	Y	N
26	Brownley	Y	N	Y	N	Y	N
27	Chu	Y	N	Y	N	Y	N
28	Schiff	Y	N	Y	N	Y	N
29	Cárdenas	Y	N	Y	N	Y	N
30	Sherman	Y	N	Y	N	Y	N
31	Aguilar	Y	N	Y	N	Y	N
32	Napolitano	Y	N	Y	N	Y	N
33	Lieu	Y	N	Y	N	Y	N
34	Gomez	Y	N	Y	N	Y	N
35	Torres	Y	N	Y	N	Y	N
36	Ruiz	Y	N	Y	N	Y	N
37	Bass	Y	N	Y	N	Y	N
38	Sánchez	Y	N	Y	N	Y	N
39	Cisneros	Y	N	Y	N	Y	N
40	Roybal-Allard	Y	N	Y	N	Y	N
41	Takano	Y	N	Y	N	Y	N
42	**Calvert**	N	Y	N	Y	N	Y
43	Waters	Y	N	Y	?	Y	N
44	Barragán	Y	N	Y	N	Y	N
45	Porter	Y	N	Y	N	Y	N
46	Correa	Y	N	Y	N	Y	N
47	Lowenthal	Y	N	Y	N	Y	N
48	Rouda	Y	N	Y	N	Y	N
49	Levin	Y	N	Y	N	Y	N
50	**Hunter**	N	Y	N	Y	N	Y
51	Vargas	Y	N	Y	N	Y	N
52	Peters	Y	N	Y	N	Y	N

		19	20	21	22	23	24
53	Davis, S.	Y	N	Y	N	Y	N
COLORADO							
1	DeGette	Y	N	Y	N	Y	N
2	Neguse	Y	N	Y	N	Y	N
3	**Tipton**	N	Y	N	Y	N	Y
4	**Buck**	?	?	?	Y	N	Y
5	**Lamborn**	N	Y	N	Y	N	Y
6	Crow	Y	N	Y	N	Y	N
7	Perlmutter	Y	N	Y	N	Y	N
CONNECTICUT							
1	Larson	Y	N	Y	N	Y	N
2	Courtney	Y	N	Y	N	Y	N
3	DeLauro	Y	N	Y	N	Y	N
4	Himes	Y	N	Y	N	Y	N
5	Hayes	Y	N	Y	N	Y	N
DELAWARE							
AL	Blunt Rochester	Y	N	Y	N	Y	N
FLORIDA							
1	**Gaetz**	N	Y	N	Y	N	Y
2	**Dunn**	N	Y	N	Y	N	Y
3	**Yoho**	N	Y	N	Y	N	Y
4	**Rutherford**	N	Y	N	Y	N	Y
5	Lawson	Y	N	Y	N	Y	N
6	**Waltz**	N	Y	N	Y	N	Y
7	Murphy	Y	N	Y	N	Y	N
8	**Posey**	N	Y	N	Y	N	Y
9	Soto	Y	N	Y	N	Y	N
10	Demings	Y	N	Y	N	Y	N
11	**Webster**	N	Y	N	Y	N	Y
12	**Bilirakis**	N	Y	N	Y	N	Y
13	Crist	Y	N	Y	N	Y	N
14	Castor	Y	N	Y	N	Y	N
15	**Spano**	N	Y	N	Y	N	Y
16	**Buchanan**	N	Y	N	Y	N	Y
17	**Steube**	N	Y	N	Y	N	Y
18	**Mast**	?	?	?	?	?	?
19	**Rooney**	N	Y	N	Y	N	Y
20	Hastings	Y	N	Y	N	Y	N
21	Frankel	+	-	+	-	+	-
22	Deutch	Y	N	Y	N	Y	N
23	Wasserman Schultz	Y	N	Y	N	Y	N
24	Wilson, F.	Y	N	Y	N	Y	N
25	**Diaz-Balart**	N	Y	N	Y	N	Y
26	Mucarsel-Powell	Y	N	Y	N	Y	N
27	Shalala	Y	N	Y	N	Y	N
GEORGIA							
1	**Carter, E.L.**	N	Y	N	Y	N	Y
2	Bishop, S.	Y	N	Y	N	Y	N
3	**Ferguson**	N	Y	N	Y	N	Y
4	Johnson, H.	Y	N	Y	N	Y	N
5	Lewis John	Y	N	Y	N	Y	N
6	McBath	Y	N	Y	N	Y	N
7	**Woodall**	N	Y	N	Y	N	Y
8	**Scott, A.**	N	Y	N	Y	N	Y
9	**Collins, D.**	N	Y	N	Y	N	Y
10	**Hice**	N	Y	N	Y	N	Y
11	**Loudermilk**	N	Y	N	Y	N	Y
12	**Allen**	N	Y	N	Y	N	Y
13	Scott, D.	Y	N	Y	N	?	N
14	**Graves, T.**	N	Y	N	Y	N	Y
HAWAII							
1	Case	Y	N	Y	N	Y	N
2	Gabbard	Y	N	Y	N	Y	N
IDAHO							
1	**Fulcher**	N	Y	N	Y	N	Y
2	**Simpson**	N	Y	N	Y	N	Y
ILLINOIS							
1	Rush	Y	N	Y	N	Y	N
2	Kelly, R.	Y	N	Y	N	Y	N
3	Lipinski	Y	N	Y	N	Y	N
4	García, J.	Y	N	Y	N	Y	N
5	Quigley	Y	N	Y	N	Y	N
6	Casten	Y	N	Y	N	Y	N
7	Davis, D.	Y	N	Y	N	Y	N
8	Krishnamoorthi	Y	N	Y	N	Y	N
9	Schakowsky	Y	N	Y	N	Y	N
10	Schneider	Y	N	Y	N	Y	N
11	Foster	Y	N	Y	N	Y	N

KEY:	Republicans	Democrats	*Independents*

Y Voted for (yea)	**N** Voted against (nay)	**P** Voted "present"
+ Announced for	**-** Announced against	**?** Did not vote or otherwise make position known
# Paired for	**X** Paired against	

		19	20	21	22	23	24
12	**Bost**	N	Y	N	Y	N	Y
13	**Davis, R.**	N	Y	N	Y	Y	Y
14	Underwood	Y	N	Y	N	Y	N
15	**Shimkus**	N	Y	N	Y	N	Y
16	**Kinzinger**	N	Y	Y	Y	Y	Y
17	Bustos	Y	N	Y	N	Y	N
18	**LaHood**	N	Y	N	Y	N	Y
INDIANA							
1	Visclosky	Y	N	Y	N	Y	N
2	**Walorski**	N	Y	N	Y	N	Y
3	**Banks**	N	Y	N	Y	N	Y
4	**Baird**	N	Y	N	Y	N	Y
5	**Brooks, S.**	N	Y	N	Y	N	Y
6	**Pence**	N	Y	N	Y	N	Y
7	Carson	Y	N	Y	N	Y	N
8	**Bucshon**	N	Y	N	?	?	?
9	**Hollingsworth**	N	Y	N	Y	N	Y
IOWA							
1	Finkenauer	Y	N	Y	N	Y	N
2	Loebsack	Y	N	Y	N	Y	N
3	Axne	Y	N	Y	Y	Y	N
4	**King, S.**	N	Y	N	Y	N	Y
KANSAS							
1	**Marshall**	N	Y	N	Y	N	Y
2	**Watkins**	N	Y	N	Y	N	Y
3	Davids	Y	N	Y	N	Y	N
4	**Estes**	N	Y	N	Y	N	Y
KENTUCKY							
1	**Comer**	N	Y	N	Y	N	Y
2	**Guthrie**	N	Y	N	Y	N	Y
3	Yarmuth	Y	N	Y	N	Y	N
4	**Massie**	N	N	N	Y	N	Y
5	**Rogers, H.**	N	Y	N	Y	N	Y
6	**Barr**	N	Y	N	Y	N	Y
LOUISIANA							
1	**Scalise**	N	Y	N	Y	N	Y
2	Richmond	Y	N	Y	N	Y	N
3	**Higgins, C.**	N	Y	N	Y	N	Y
4	**Johnson, M.**	N	Y	N	Y	N	Y
5	**Abraham**	N	Y	N	Y	N	Y
6	**Graves, G.**	N	Y	N	Y	N	Y
MAINE							
1	Pingree	Y	N	Y	N	Y	N
2	Golden	Y	Y	Y	N	Y	Y
MARYLAND							
1	**Harris**	N	Y	N	Y	N	Y
2	Ruppersberger	Y	N	Y	N	Y	N
3	Sarbanes	Y	N	Y	N	Y	N
4	Brown, A.	Y	N	Y	N	Y	N
5	Hoyer	Y	N	Y	N	Y	N
6	Trone	Y	N	Y	N	Y	N
7	Cummings	Y	N	Y	N	Y	N
8	Raskin	Y	N	Y	N	Y	N
MASSACHUSETTS							
1	Neal	Y	N	Y	N	Y	N
2	McGovern	Y	N	Y	N	Y	N
3	Trahan	Y	N	Y	N	Y	N
4	Kennedy	Y	N	Y	N	Y	N
5	Clark	Y	N	Y	N	Y	N
6	Moulton	Y	N	Y	N	Y	N
7	Pressley	Y	N	Y	N	Y	N
8	Lynch	?	N	Y	N	Y	N
9	Keating	Y	N	Y	N	Y	N
MICHIGAN							
1	**Bergman**	N	Y	N	Y	N	Y
2	**Huizenga**	N	Y	N	Y	N	Y
3	**Amash**	N	N	N	N	N	N
4	**Moolenaar**	N	Y	N	Y	N	Y
5	Kildee	Y	N	Y	N	Y	N
6	**Upton**	N	Y	Y	Y	Y	Y
7	**Walberg**	N	Y	N	Y	N	Y
8	Slotkin	Y	N	Y	N	Y	N
9	Levin	Y	N	Y	N	Y	N
10	**Mitchell**	N	Y	N	Y	N	Y
11	Stevens	Y	N	Y	N	Y	N
12	Dingell	Y	N	Y	N	Y	N
13	Tlaib	Y	N	Y	N	Y	N
14	Lawrence	Y	N	Y	?	Y	N
MINNESOTA							
1	**Hagedorn**	N	Y	N	Y	N	Y
2	Craig	Y	N	Y	N	Y	N
3	Phillips	Y	N	Y	N	Y	N
4	McCollum	Y	N	Y	N	Y	N
5	Omar	Y	N	Y	N	Y	N

		19	20	21	22	23	24
6	**Emmer**	N	Y	N	Y	N	Y
7	Peterson	Y	N	Y	N	Y	N
8	**Stauber**	N	Y	N	Y	N	Y
MISSISSIPPI							
1	**Kelly, T.**	N	Y	N	Y	N	Y
2	Thompson, B.	Y	N	Y	N	Y	N
3	**Guest**	?	?	N	Y	N	Y
4	**Palazzo**	N	Y	N	Y	N	Y
MISSOURI							
1	Clay	Y	N	Y	N	Y	N
2	**Wagner**	N	Y	N	Y	N	Y
3	**Luetkemeyer**	N	Y	N	Y	N	Y
4	**Hartzler**	N	Y	N	Y	N	Y
5	Cleaver	Y	N	Y	N	Y	N
6	**Graves, S.**	N	Y	N	Y	N	Y
7	**Long**	N	Y	N	Y	N	Y
8	**Smith, J.**	N	Y	N	Y	N	Y
MONTANA							
AL	**Gianforte**	N	Y	N	Y	N	Y
NEBRASKA							
1	**Fortenberry**	N	Y	N	Y	N	Y
2	**Bacon**	N	Y	N	Y	N	Y
3	**Smith, Adrian**	N	Y	N	Y	N	Y
NEVADA							
1	Titus	Y	N	Y	N	Y	N
2	**Amodei**	N	?	N	Y	N	Y
3	Lee	Y	N	Y	N	Y	N
4	Horsford	Y	N	Y	N	Y	N
NEW HAMPSHIRE							
1	Pappas	Y	N	Y	N	Y	N
2	Kuster	Y	N	Y	N	Y	N
NEW JERSEY							
1	Norcross	Y	N	Y	N	Y	N
2	Van Drew	Y	N	Y	N	Y	N
3	Kim	Y	N	Y	N	Y	N
4	**Smith, C.**	N	Y	N	Y	Y	Y
5	Gottheimer	Y	Y	Y	N	Y	N
6	Pallone	Y	N	Y	N	Y	N
7	Malinowski	Y	N	Y	N	Y	N
8	Sires	Y	N	Y	N	Y	N
9	Pascrell	Y	N	Y	N	Y	N
10	Payne	Y	N	Y	N	Y	N
11	Sherrill	Y	Y	Y	N	Y	N
12	Watson Coleman	Y	N	Y	N	Y	N
NEW MEXICO							
1	Haaland	Y	N	Y	N	Y	N
2	Torres Small	Y	N	Y	N	Y	N
3	Luján	Y	N	Y	N	Y	N
NEW YORK							
1	**Zeldin**	N	Y	N	Y	N	Y
2	**King, P.**	N	Y	N	Y	Y	Y
3	Suozzi	Y	N	Y	N	Y	N
4	Rice, K.	Y	N	Y	N	Y	N
5	Meeks	Y	N	Y	N	Y	N
6	Meng	Y	N	Y	N	Y	N
7	Velázquez	Y	N	Y	N	Y	N
8	Jeffries	Y	N	Y	N	Y	N
9	Clarke	Y	N	Y	N	Y	N
10	Nadler	Y	N	Y	N	Y	N
11	Rose	Y	Y	Y	N	Y	N
12	Maloney, C.	Y	N	+	N	Y	N
13	Espaillat	Y	N	Y	N	Y	N
14	Ocasio-Cortez	Y	N	Y	N	Y	N
15	Serrano	Y	N	Y	N	Y	N
16	Engel	Y	N	Y	N	Y	N
17	Lowey	Y	N	Y	N	Y	N
18	Maloney, S.P.	Y	N	Y	N	Y	N
19	Delgado	Y	N	Y	Y	Y	Y
20	Tonko	Y	N	Y	N	Y	N
21	**Stefanik**	N	Y	Y	Y	Y	Y
22	Brindisi	Y	Y	Y	N	Y	Y
23	**Reed**	Y	Y	N	Y	N	Y
24	**Katko**	Y	Y	Y	Y	Y	Y
25	Morelle	Y	N	Y	N	Y	N
26	Higgins, B.	Y	N	Y	N	Y	N
27	**Collins, C.**	N	Y	N	Y	N	Y
NORTH CAROLINA							
1	Butterfield	Y	N	Y	N	Y	N
2	**Holding**	N	Y	N	Y	N	Y
3	**Jones**	?	?	?	?	?	?
4	Price	Y	N	Y	N	Y	N
5	**Foxx**	N	Y	N	Y	N	Y
6	**Walker**	N	Y	N	Y	N	Y
7	**Rouzer**	N	Y	N	Y	N	Y

		19	20	21	22	23	24
8	**Hudson**	N	Y	N	Y	N	Y
9	vacant						
10	**McHenry**	N	Y	N	Y	N	Y
11	**Meadows**	N	Y	N	Y	N	Y
12	Adams	Y	N	Y	N	Y	N
13	**Budd**	N	Y	N	Y	N	Y
NORTH DAKOTA							
AL	**Armstrong**	N	Y	N	Y	N	Y
OHIO							
1	**Chabot**	N	Y	N	Y	N	Y
2	**Wenstrup**	N	Y	N	Y	N	Y
3	Beatty	Y	N	Y	N	Y	N
4	**Jordan**	N	Y	N	Y	N	Y
5	**Latta**	N	Y	N	Y	N	Y
6	**Johnson, B.**	N	Y	N	Y	N	Y
7	**Gibbs**	N	Y	N	Y	N	Y
8	**Davidson**	N	Y	N	?	?	?
9	Kaptur	Y	N	Y	N	Y	N
10	**Turner**	N	Y	N	Y	N	Y
11	Fudge	Y	N	Y	N	Y	N
12	**Balderson**	N	Y	N	Y	N	Y
13	Ryan	Y	N	Y	N	Y	N
14	**Joyce**	N	Y	N	Y	N	Y
15	**Stivers**	N	Y	N	Y	Y	Y
16	**Gonzalez**	N	Y	N	Y	N	Y
OKLAHOMA							
1	**Hern**	N	Y	N	Y	N	Y
2	**Mullin**	N	Y	N	Y	N	Y
3	**Lucas**	N	Y	N	Y	N	Y
4	**Cole**	N	Y	N	Y	N	Y
5	Horn	Y	N	Y	N	Y	N
OREGON							
1	Bonamici	Y	N	Y	N	Y	N
2	**Walden**	N	Y	Y	Y	Y	Y
3	Blumenauer	Y	N	Y	N	Y	N
4	DeFazio	Y	N	Y	N	Y	N
5	Schrader	Y	N	Y	?	Y	N
PENNSYLVANIA							
1	**Fitzpatrick**	Y	Y	Y	Y	Y	Y
2	Boyle	Y	N	Y	N	Y	N
3	Evans	Y	N	Y	N	Y	N
4	Dean	Y	N	Y	N	Y	N
5	Scanlon	Y	N	Y	N	Y	N
6	Houlahan	Y	N	Y	N	Y	N
7	Wild	Y	N	Y	N	Y	N
8	Cartwright	Y	N	Y	N	Y	N
9	**Meuser**	N	Y	N	Y	N	Y
10	**Perry**	N	Y	N	Y	N	Y
11	**Smucker**	N	Y	N	Y	N	Y
12	**Marino**	N	Y	N	Y	N	Y
13	**Joyce**	N	Y	N	Y	N	Y
14	**Reschenthaler**	N	Y	N	Y	N	Y
15	**Thompson, G.**	N	Y	N	Y	N	Y
16	**Kelly, M.**	N	Y	N	Y	N	Y
17	Lamb	Y	Y	Y	N	Y	N
18	Doyle	Y	N	Y	N	Y	N
RHODE ISLAND							
1	Cicilline	Y	N	Y	N	Y	N
2	Langevin	Y	N	Y	N	Y	N
SOUTH CAROLINA							
1	Cunningham	Y	Y	Y	Y	Y	Y
2	**Wilson, J.**	N	Y	N	Y	N	Y
3	**Duncan**	N	Y	N	Y	N	Y
4	**Timmons**	N	Y	N	Y	N	Y
5	**Norman**	N	Y	N	Y	N	Y
6	Clyburn	Y	N	Y	N	Y	N
7	**Rice, T.**	N	Y	N	Y	N	Y
SOUTH DAKOTA							
AL	**Johnson**	N	Y	N	Y	N	Y
TENNESSEE							
1	**Roe**	N	Y	N	Y	N	Y
2	**Burchett**	N	Y	N	Y	N	Y
3	**Fleischmann**	N	Y	N	Y	N	Y
4	**DesJarlais**	N	Y	N	Y	N	Y
5	Cooper	Y	N	Y	N	Y	N
6	**Rose**	N	Y	N	Y	N	Y
7	**Green**	N	Y	N	Y	N	Y
8	**Kustoff**	N	Y	N	Y	N	Y
9	Cohen	Y	N	Y	N	Y	N
TEXAS							
1	**Gohmert**	N	Y	N	Y	N	Y
2	**Crenshaw**	N	Y	N	Y	N	Y
3	**Taylor**	N	Y	N	Y	N	Y
4	**Ratcliffe**	N	Y	N	Y	N	Y

		19	20	21	22	23	24
5	**Gooden**	N	Y	N	Y	N	Y
6	**Wright**	N	Y	N	Y	N	Y
7	Fletcher	Y	N	Y	N	Y	N
8	**Brady**	N	Y	N	Y	N	Y
9	Green, A.	Y	N	Y	N	Y	N
10	**McCaul**	N	Y	N	Y	N	Y
11	**Conaway**	N	Y	N	Y	N	Y
12	**Granger**	N	Y	N	Y	N	Y
13	**Thornberry**	N	Y	N	Y	N	Y
14	**Weber**	N	Y	N	Y	N	Y
15	Gonzalez	Y	N	Y	N	Y	N
16	Escobar	Y	N	Y	N	Y	N
17	**Flores**	N	Y	N	Y	N	Y
18	Jackson Lee	Y	N	Y	N	Y	N
19	**Arrington**	N	Y	N	?	N	Y
20	Castro	Y	N	Y	N	Y	N
21	**Roy**	N	Y	N	Y	?	Y
22	**Olson**	N	Y	N	Y	N	Y
23	**Hurd**	N	Y	Y	Y	Y	Y
24	**Marchant**	N	Y	N	Y	N	Y
25	**Williams**	N	Y	N	Y	N	Y
26	**Burgess**	N	Y	N	Y	N	Y
27	**Cloud**	N	Y	N	Y	N	Y
28	Cuellar	Y	N	Y	N	Y	N
29	Garcia, S.	Y	N	Y	N	Y	N
30	Johnson, E.B.	Y	N	Y	N	Y	N
31	**Carter, J.**	N	Y	N	?	?	?
32	Allred	Y	N	Y	N	Y	N
33	Veasey	Y	N	Y	N	Y	N
34	Vela	Y	N	Y	N	Y	N
35	Doggett	Y	N	Y	N	Y	N
36	**Babin**	N	Y	N	Y	N	Y
UTAH							
1	**Bishop, R.**	N	Y	N	Y	N	Y
2	**Stewart**	N	Y	N	Y	N	Y
3	**Curtis**	N	Y	N	Y	N	Y
4	McAdams	Y	N	Y	N	Y	N
VERMONT							
AL	Welch	Y	N	Y	N	Y	N
VIRGINIA							
1	**Wittman**	N	Y	N	Y	N	Y
2	Luria	Y	N	Y	N	Y	N
3	Scott, R.	Y	N	Y	N	Y	N
4	McEachin	Y	N	Y	N	Y	N
5	**Riggleman**	N	Y	N	Y	N	Y
6	**Cline**	N	Y	N	Y	N	Y
7	Spanberger	Y	N	Y	N	Y	N
8	Beyer	Y	N	Y	N	Y	N
9	**Griffith**	N	Y	N	Y	N	Y
10	Wexton	Y	N	Y	N	Y	N
11	Connolly	Y	N	Y	N	Y	N
WASHINGTON							
1	DelBene	Y	N	Y	N	Y	N
2	Larsen	Y	N	Y	N	Y	N
3	**Herrera Beutler**	N	Y	Y	Y	Y	Y
4	**Newhouse**	N	Y	N	Y	N	Y
5	**McMorris Rodgers**	N	Y	N	Y	N	Y
6	Kilmer	Y	N	Y	N	Y	N
7	Jayapal	Y	N	Y	N	Y	N
8	Schrier	Y	N	Y	N	Y	N
9	Smith Adam	Y	N	Y	N	Y	N
10	Heck	Y	N	Y	N	Y	N
WEST VIRGINIA							
1	**McKinley**	N	Y	N	Y	N	Y
2	**Mooney**	N	Y	N	Y	N	Y
3	**Miller**	N	Y	N	Y	N	Y
WISCONSIN							
1	**Steil**	N	Y	N	Y	N	Y
2	Pocan	Y	N	Y	N	Y	N
3	Kind	Y	N	Y	N	Y	N
4	Moore	Y	N	Y	N	Y	N
5	**Sensenbrenner**	N	Y	N	+	-	+
6	**Grothman**	N	Y	N	Y	N	Y
7	**Duffy**						
8	**Gallagher**	N	Y	N	Y	N	Y
WYOMING							
AL	**Cheney**	N	Y	N	Y	N	Y
DELEGATES							
	Radewagen (A.S.)						
	Norton (D.C.)						
	San Nicolas (Guam)						
	Sablan (N. Marianas)						
	González-Colón (P.R.)						
	Plaskett (V.I.)						

||| HOUSE VOTES

25. HR265. Fiscal 2019 Agriculture Appropriations - Passage. Passage of the bill that would provide $145.4 billion in fiscal 2019 for the Agriculture Department and related agencies, including $23.2 billion in discretionary funding. The bill would provide $5.4 billion for the Food and Drug Administration, $3.8 billion for Agriculture Department rural development activities, and $2.7 billion for agricultural research programs. It would reauthorize the federal crop insurance program and authorize loan levels for federal loans related to farming and rural development. It would provide $102.6 billion for domestic food programs, including $73.2 billion for the Supplemental Nutrition Assistance Program, $23.2 billion for child nutrition programs, and $6.2 billion for the Women, Infants, and Children program. Passed 243-183: R 10-183; D 233-0. *Note: A "nay" was a vote in support of the president's position.* Jan. 10, 2019.

26. HR266. Fiscal 2019 Interior-Environment Appropriations - Recommit. Calvert, R-Calif., motion to recommit the bill (HR 266) to the House Appropriations Committee with instructions to report it back immediately with amendments that would increase by $21 million the amount authorized for Interior Department and Forest Service hazardous fuel management programs. The amendments required by the instructions would also reduce by $6 million the amount authorized for Bureau of Land Management maintenance and administration. Motion rejected 190-229: R 188-1; D 2-228. Jan. 11, 2019.

27. HR266. Fiscal 2019 Interior-Environment Appropriations - Passage. Passage of the bill that would that would provide $35.9 billion in fiscal 2019 for the Interior Department, the Environmental Protection Agency, and related agencies. The bill would provide $8.8 billion for the EPA, including $3.6 billion for state and tribal assistance grants and $1.1 billion for hazardous substance superfund activities; it would also require that $5.2 million of EPA funding be used to study algal blooms. Passed 240-179: R 10-179; D 230-0. *Note: A "nay" was a vote in support of the president's position.* Jan. 11, 2019.

28. S24. Federal Employee Compensation - Passage. Cummings, D-Md., motion to suspend the rules and pass the bill that would require the federal government to provide retroactive pay to employees who are furloughed or working without compensation during the partial government shutdown. The bill would require federal employees to be compensated at the earliest possible date once the shutdown has concluded, regardless of regularly scheduled pay dates. Motion agreed to 411-7: R 180-7; D 231-0. *Note: A two-thirds majority of those present and voting (279 in this case) is required for passage under suspension of the rules.* Jan. 11, 2019.

29. HR221. Antisemitism Special Envoy - Passage. Engel, D-N.Y., motion to suspend the rules and pass the bill that would direct the president to appoint the head of the Office to Monitor and Combat Antisemitism within the Department of State as a special envoy with the rank of ambassador, who would report directly to the secretary of State. The special envoy would coordinate U.S. efforts to monitor and combat antisemitism in foreign countries. Motion agreed to 411-1: R 185-1; D 226-0. *Note: A two-thirds majority of those present and voting (275 in this case) is required for passage under suspension of the rules.* Jan. 11, 2019.

30. HR116. Small Business Investment Company Thresholds - Passage. Velazquez, D-N.Y., motion to suspend the rules and pass the bill that would increase, from five to 15 percent, the amount of capital and surplus a federal saving association could invest in a small business investment company. Under the bill's provisions, investments in excess of five percent would be subject to approval by the appropriate federal banking regulatory agency before implementation. Motion agreed to 403-2: R 180-2; D 223-0. *Note: A two-thirds majority of those present and voting (270 in this case) is required for passage under suspension of the rules.* Jan. 14, 2019.

		25	26	27	28	29	30
ALABAMA							
1	**Byrne**	N	Y	N	Y	Y	Y
2	**Roby**	N	Y	N	Y	Y	Y
3	**Rogers, M.**	N	Y	N	Y	Y	Y
4	**Aderholt**	N	Y	N	Y	Y	Y
5	**Brooks, M.**	N	Y	N	Y	Y	Y
6	**Palmer**	N	Y	N	Y	Y	Y
7	Sewell	Y	N	Y	Y	Y	+
ALASKA							
AL	**Young**	N	Y	N	Y	Y	Y
ARIZONA							
1	O'Halleran	Y	N	Y	Y	Y	Y
2	Kirkpatrick	Y	N	Y	Y	Y	Y
3	Grijalva	Y	N	Y	Y	Y	Y
4	**Gosar**	N	Y	N	N	?	?
5	**Biggs**	N	Y	N	N	?	?
6	**Schweikert**	N	Y	N	Y	Y	Y
7	Gallego	Y	N	Y	Y	Y	Y
8	**Lesko**	N	Y	N	Y	Y	Y
9	Stanton	Y	N	Y	Y	Y	Y
ARKANSAS							
1	**Crawford**	N	Y	N	Y	Y	Y
2	**Hill, F.**	N	Y	N	Y	Y	Y
3	**Womack**	N	Y	N	Y	Y	Y
4	**Westerman**	N	Y	N	Y	Y	Y
CALIFORNIA							
1	**LaMalfa**	N	Y	N	Y	Y	Y
2	Huffman	Y	N	Y	Y	Y	Y
3	Garamendi	Y	N	Y	Y	Y	Y
4	**McClintock**	N	Y	N	Y	Y	N
5	Thompson, M.	Y	N	Y	Y	Y	Y
6	Matsui	Y	N	Y	Y	Y	Y
7	Bera	Y	N	Y	Y	Y	Y
8	**Cook**	N	Y	N	Y	Y	Y
9	McNerney	Y	N	Y	Y	Y	Y
10	Harder	Y	N	Y	Y	Y	Y
11	DeSaulnier	Y	N	Y	Y	Y	Y
12	Pelosi						
13	Lee B.	Y	N	Y	Y	Y	Y
14	Speier	Y	N	Y	Y	Y	Y
15	Swalwell	Y	N	Y	Y	Y	Y
16	Costa	Y	N	Y	Y	Y	Y
17	Khanna	Y	N	Y	Y	Y	Y
18	Eshoo	Y	N	Y	Y	Y	Y
19	Lofgren	Y	N	Y	Y	Y	Y
20	Panetta	Y	N	Y	Y	Y	Y
21	Cox	Y	N	Y	Y	Y	Y
22	**Nunes**	N	Y	N	Y	Y	Y
23	**McCarthy**	N	Y	N	Y	Y	Y
24	Carbajal	Y	N	Y	Y	Y	Y
25	Hill, K.	Y	N	Y	Y	Y	Y
26	Brownley	Y	N	Y	Y	Y	Y
27	Chu	Y	N	Y	Y	Y	Y
28	Schiff	Y	N	Y	Y	Y	Y
29	Cárdenas	Y	N	Y	Y	Y	Y
30	Sherman	Y	N	Y	Y	Y	Y
31	Aguilar	Y	N	Y	Y	Y	Y
32	Napolitano	Y	N	Y	Y	Y	Y
33	Lieu	Y	N	Y	Y	Y	Y
34	Gomez	Y	N	Y	Y	Y	Y
35	Torres	Y	N	Y	Y	Y	Y
36	Ruiz	Y	N	Y	Y	Y	Y
37	Bass	Y	N	Y	Y	Y	Y
38	Sánchez	Y	N	Y	Y	?	Y
39	Cisneros	Y	Y	Y	Y	Y	Y
40	Roybal-Allard	Y	N	Y	Y	Y	Y
41	Takano	Y	N	Y	Y	Y	Y
42	**Calvert**	N	Y	N	Y	Y	Y
43	Waters	Y	N	Y	Y	Y	Y
44	Barragán	Y	N	Y	Y	Y	Y
45	Porter	Y	N	Y	Y	Y	Y
46	Correa	Y	N	Y	Y	Y	Y
47	Lowenthal	Y	N	Y	Y	Y	Y
48	Rouda	Y	Y	Y	Y	Y	Y
49	Levin	Y	N	Y	Y	Y	Y
50	**Hunter**	N	Y	N	Y	Y	Y
51	Vargas	Y	N	Y	Y	Y	Y
52	Peters	Y	N	Y	Y	Y	Y

		25	26	27	28	29	30
53	Davis, S.	Y	N	Y	Y	Y	Y
COLORADO							
1	DeGette	Y	N	Y	Y	Y	Y
2	Neguse	Y	N	Y	Y	Y	Y
3	**Tipton**	N	Y	N	Y	Y	Y
4	**Buck**	N	Y	N	Y	Y	Y
5	**Lamborn**	N	Y	N	Y	Y	Y
6	Crow	Y	N	Y	Y	?	Y
7	Perlmutter	Y	N	Y	Y	Y	Y
CONNECTICUT							
1	Larson	Y	N	Y	Y	?	Y
2	Courtney	Y	N	Y	Y	Y	Y
3	DeLauro	Y	N	Y	Y	Y	Y
4	Himes	Y	N	Y	Y	Y	Y
5	Hayes	Y	N	Y	Y	Y	Y
DELAWARE							
AL	Blunt Rochester	Y	N	Y	Y	Y	Y
FLORIDA							
1	**Gaetz**	N	Y	N	Y	Y	Y
2	**Dunn**	N	Y	N	Y	Y	Y
3	**Yoho**	N	Y	N	N	Y	Y
4	**Rutherford**	N	Y	N	Y	Y	Y
5	Lawson	Y	?	?	?	?	Y
6	**Waltz**	N	Y	N	Y	Y	Y
7	Murphy	Y	N	Y	Y	Y	Y
8	**Posey**	N	Y	N	Y	Y	Y
9	Soto	Y	N	Y	Y	Y	Y
10	Demings	Y	N	Y	Y	Y	Y
11	**Webster**	N	Y	N	Y	Y	Y
12	**Bilirakis**	N	Y	N	Y	Y	Y
13	Crist	Y	N	Y	Y	Y	Y
14	Castor	Y	N	Y	Y	Y	Y
15	**Spano**	N	Y	N	Y	Y	Y
16	**Buchanan**	N	Y	N	Y	Y	Y
17	**Steube**	N	Y	N	Y	Y	Y
18	**Mast**	?	?	?	?	?	?
19	**Rooney**	N	Y	N	Y	Y	Y
20	Hastings	Y	N	Y	Y	Y	Y
21	Frankel	+	-	+	+	+	Y
22	Deutch	Y	N	Y	Y	Y	Y
23	Wasserman Schultz	Y	N	Y	Y	Y	Y
24	Wilson, F.	Y	N	Y	Y	?	Y
25	**Diaz-Balart**	N	Y	N	Y	Y	Y
26	Mucarsel-Powell	Y	N	Y	Y	Y	Y
27	Shalala	Y	N	Y	Y	Y	Y
GEORGIA							
1	**Carter, E.L.**	N	Y	N	Y	?	Y
2	Bishop, S.	Y	N	Y	Y	Y	?
3	**Ferguson**	N	Y	N	Y	Y	Y
4	Johnson, H.	Y	N	Y	Y	Y	Y
5	Lewis John	Y	N	Y	Y	Y	?
6	McBath	Y	N	Y	Y	Y	Y
7	**Woodall**	N	Y	N	Y	Y	Y
8	**Scott, A.**	N	Y	N	Y	Y	?
9	**Collins, D.**	N	Y	N	Y	Y	Y
10	**Hice**	N	Y	N	Y	Y	Y
11	**Loudermilk**	N	Y	N	Y	Y	?
12	**Allen**	N	Y	N	Y	Y	Y
13	Scott, D.	Y	N	Y	Y	Y	Y
14	**Graves, T.**	N	Y	N	Y	Y	Y
HAWAII							
1	Case	Y	N	Y	Y	Y	Y
2	Gabbard	Y	?	?	?	?	Y
IDAHO							
1	**Fulcher**	N	Y	N	Y	Y	Y
2	**Simpson**	N	Y	N	Y	Y	Y
ILLINOIS							
1	Rush	Y	N	Y	Y	Y	Y
2	Kelly, R.	Y	N	Y	Y	Y	Y
3	Lipinski	Y	N	Y	Y	Y	?
4	García, J.	Y	N	Y	Y	Y	Y
5	Quigley	Y	N	Y	Y	Y	?
6	Casten	Y	N	Y	Y	Y	Y
7	Davis, D.	Y	N	Y	Y	Y	?
8	Krishnamoorthi	Y	N	Y	Y	Y	Y
9	Schakowsky	Y	N	Y	Y	Y	Y
10	Schneider	Y	N	Y	Y	Y	Y
11	Foster	Y	N	Y	Y	Y	Y

KEY:	**Republicans**	Democrats	*Independents*
Y Voted for (yea)	**N** Voted against (nay)	**P** Voted "present"	
+ Announced for	**−** Announced against	**?** Did not vote or otherwise make position known	
# Paired for	**X** Paired against		

		25	26	27	28	29	30
12	**Bost**	N	Y	N	Y	Y	Y
13	**Davis, R.**	Y	Y	Y	Y	Y	Y
14	Underwood	Y	N	Y	Y	Y	Y
15	**Shimkus**	N	Y	N	Y	Y	?
16	**Kinzinger**	Y	Y	Y	Y	Y	Y
17	Bustos	Y	N	Y	Y	Y	Y
18	**LaHood**	N	Y	N	Y	Y	Y
INDIANA							
1	Visclosky	Y	N	Y	Y	Y	Y
2	**Walorski**	N	Y	N	Y	Y	Y
3	**Banks**	N	Y	N	Y	Y	Y
4	**Baird**	N	Y	N	Y	Y	+
5	**Brooks, S.**	N	Y	N	Y	Y	Y
6	**Pence**	N	Y	N	Y	Y	Y
7	Carson	Y	N	Y	Y	Y	Y
8	**Bucshon**	?	?	?	?	?	Y
9	**Hollingsworth**	N	Y	N	Y	Y	Y
IOWA							
1	Finkenauer	Y	N	Y	Y	Y	Y
2	Loebsack	Y	N	Y	Y	Y	Y
3	Axne	Y	N	Y	Y	Y	Y
4	**King, S.**	N	Y	N	Y	Y	Y
KANSAS							
1	**Marshall**	N	Y	N	Y	Y	Y
2	**Watkins**	N	Y	N	Y	Y	Y
3	Davids	Y	N	Y	Y	Y	Y
4	**Estes**	N	Y	N	Y	Y	Y
KENTUCKY							
1	**Comer**	N	Y	N	Y	Y	Y
2	**Guthrie**	N	Y	N	Y	Y	Y
3	Yarmuth	Y	N	Y	Y	Y	Y
4	**Massie**	N	Y	N	N	Y	Y
5	**Rogers, H.**	N	Y	N	Y	Y	Y
6	**Barr**	N	Y	N	Y	Y	Y
LOUISIANA							
1	**Scalise**	N	Y	N	Y	Y	Y
2	Richmond	Y	N	Y	Y	Y	Y
3	**Higgins, C.**	N	Y	N	Y	Y	Y
4	**Johnson, M.**	N	Y	N	Y	Y	Y
5	**Abraham**	N	?	?	?	?	Y
6	**Graves, G.**	N	Y	N	Y	Y	Y
MAINE							
1	Pingree	Y	N	Y	Y	Y	?
2	Golden	Y	N	Y	Y	Y	+
MARYLAND							
1	**Harris**	N	Y	N	Y	Y	Y
2	Ruppersberger	Y	N	Y	Y	Y	Y
3	Sarbanes	Y	N	Y	Y	Y	Y
4	Brown, A.	Y	N	Y	Y	Y	Y
5	Hoyer	Y	N	Y	Y	Y	Y
6	Trone	Y	N	Y	Y	Y	Y
7	Cummings	Y	N	Y	Y	Y	Y
8	Raskin	Y	N	Y	Y	Y	Y
MASSACHUSETTS							
1	Neal	Y	N	Y	Y	Y	Y
2	McGovern	Y	N	Y	Y	Y	Y
3	Trahan	Y	N	Y	Y	Y	Y
4	Kennedy	Y	N	Y	Y	Y	Y
5	Clark	Y	N	Y	Y	Y	Y
6	Moulton	Y	N	Y	Y	Y	Y
7	Pressley	Y	N	Y	Y	Y	Y
8	Lynch	Y	N	Y	Y	Y	Y
9	Keating	Y	N	Y	Y	Y	Y
MICHIGAN							
1	**Bergman**	N	Y	N	Y	Y	Y
2	**Huizenga**	N	Y	N	Y	Y	+
3	**Amash**	N	N	N	N	N	N
4	**Moolenaar**	N	Y	N	Y	Y	Y
5	Kildee	Y	N	Y	Y	Y	Y
6	**Upton**	Y	Y	Y	Y	Y	Y
7	**Walberg**	N	Y	N	Y	Y	Y
8	Slotkin	Y	N	Y	Y	Y	Y
9	Levin	Y	N	Y	Y	Y	Y
10	**Mitchell**	N	Y	N	Y	Y	Y
11	Stevens	Y	N	Y	Y	Y	Y
12	Dingell	Y	N	Y	Y	Y	Y
13	Tlaib	Y	N	Y	Y	Y	Y
14	Lawrence	Y	N	Y	Y	Y	Y
MINNESOTA							
1	**Hagedorn**	N	Y	N	Y	Y	Y
2	Craig	Y	N	Y	Y	Y	Y
3	Phillips	Y	N	Y	Y	Y	Y
4	McCollum	Y	N	Y	Y	Y	Y
5	Omar	Y	N	Y	Y	Y	Y

		25	26	27	28	29	30
6	**Emmer**	N	Y	N	Y	Y	Y
7	Peterson	Y	N	Y	Y	Y	Y
8	**Stauber**	N	Y	N	Y	Y	Y
MISSISSIPPI							
1	**Kelly, T.**	N	Y	N	Y	Y	Y
2	Thompson, B.	Y	N	Y	Y	Y	Y
3	**Guest**	N	Y	N	Y	Y	Y
4	**Palazzo**	N	Y	N	Y	Y	Y
MISSOURI							
1	Clay	Y	N	Y	Y	Y	Y
2	**Wagner**	N	?	?	?	?	Y
3	**Luetkemeyer**	N	Y	N	Y	Y	Y
4	**Hartzler**	N	Y	N	Y	Y	Y
5	Cleaver	Y	N	Y	Y	Y	Y
6	**Graves, S.**	N	Y	N	Y	Y	Y
7	**Long**	N	Y	N	Y	Y	Y
8	**Smith, J.**	N	Y	N	Y	Y	Y
MONTANA							
AL	**Gianforte**	N	Y	N	Y	Y	Y
NEBRASKA							
1	**Fortenberry**	N	Y	N	Y	Y	Y
2	**Bacon**	N	Y	N	Y	Y	Y
3	**Smith, Adrian**	N	Y	N	Y	Y	Y
NEVADA							
1	Titus	Y	N	Y	Y	Y	Y
2	**Amodei**	N	Y	N	Y	Y	?
3	Lee	Y	N	Y	Y	Y	Y
4	Horsford	Y	N	Y	Y	Y	Y
NEW HAMPSHIRE							
1	Pappas	Y	N	Y	Y	Y	Y
2	Kuster	Y	N	Y	Y	Y	Y
NEW JERSEY							
1	Norcross	Y	N	Y	Y	Y	Y
2	Van Drew	Y	N	Y	Y	Y	Y
3	Kim	Y	N	Y	Y	Y	Y
4	**Smith, C.**	Y	Y	Y	Y	Y	Y
5	Gottheimer	Y	N	Y	Y	Y	Y
6	Pallone	Y	N	Y	Y	Y	Y
7	Malinowski	Y	N	Y	Y	Y	Y
8	Sires	Y	N	Y	Y	Y	Y
9	Pascrell	Y	N	Y	Y	Y	Y
10	Payne	Y	?	?	?	?	?
11	Sherrill	Y	N	Y	Y	Y	Y
12	Watson Coleman	Y	N	Y	Y	Y	Y
NEW MEXICO							
1	Haaland	Y	N	Y	Y	Y	Y
2	Torres Small	Y	N	Y	Y	Y	Y
3	Luján	Y	N	Y	Y	Y	Y
NEW YORK							
1	**Zeldin**	N	Y	N	Y	Y	Y
2	**King, P.**	N	Y	N	Y	Y	Y
3	Suozzi	Y	N	Y	Y	Y	Y
4	Rice, K.	Y	N	Y	Y	Y	Y
5	Meeks	Y	N	Y	Y	Y	Y
6	Meng	Y	N	Y	Y	Y	Y
7	Velázquez	Y	N	Y	Y	Y	Y
8	Jeffries	Y	N	Y	Y	Y	Y
9	Clarke	Y	N	Y	Y	Y	Y
10	Nadler	Y	N	Y	Y	Y	Y
11	Rose	Y	N	Y	Y	Y	Y
12	Maloney, C.	Y	N	Y	Y	Y	Y
13	Espaillat	Y	N	Y	Y	Y	Y
14	Ocasio-Cortez	Y	N	Y	Y	Y	Y
15	Serrano	Y	N	Y	Y	Y	Y
16	Engel	Y	N	Y	Y	Y	Y
17	Lowey	Y	N	Y	Y	Y	Y
18	Maloney, S.P.	Y	N	Y	Y	Y	Y
19	Delgado	Y	N	Y	Y	Y	Y
20	Tonko	Y	N	Y	Y	Y	Y
21	**Stefanik**	Y	Y	Y	Y	Y	Y
22	Brindisi	Y	N	Y	Y	Y	Y
23	**Reed**	N	Y	N	Y	Y	Y
24	**Katko**	Y	Y	Y	Y	Y	Y
25	Morelle	Y	N	Y	Y	Y	Y
26	Higgins, B.	Y	N	Y	Y	Y	Y
27	**Collins, C.**	N	Y	N	Y	Y	Y
NORTH CAROLINA							
1	Butterfield	Y	N	Y	Y	Y	Y
2	**Holding**	N	Y	N	Y	Y	?
3	**Jones**	?	?	?	?	?	?
4	Price	Y	N	Y	Y	Y	Y
5	**Foxx**	N	Y	N	Y	Y	Y
6	**Walker**	N	Y	N	Y	Y	Y
7	**Rouzer**	N	Y	N	Y	Y	Y

		25	26	27	28	29	30
8	**Hudson**	N	Y	N	Y	Y	Y
9	vacant						
10	**McHenry**	N	Y	N	Y	Y	Y
11	**Meadows**	N	Y	N	Y	Y	Y
12	Adams	Y	N	Y	Y	Y	Y
13	**Budd**	N	Y	N	Y	Y	Y
NORTH DAKOTA							
AL	**Armstrong**	N	Y	N	Y	Y	Y
OHIO							
1	**Chabot**	N	Y	N	Y	Y	Y
2	**Wenstrup**	N	Y	N	Y	Y	Y
3	Beatty	Y	N	Y	Y	Y	Y
4	**Jordan**	N	Y	N	Y	Y	Y
5	**Latta**	N	Y	N	Y	Y	Y
6	**Johnson, B.**	N	Y	N	Y	Y	Y
7	**Gibbs**	N	Y	N	Y	Y	+
8	**Davidson**	?	?	?	?	?	Y
9	Kaptur	Y	N	Y	Y	Y	Y
10	**Turner**	N	Y	N	Y	Y	Y
11	Fudge	Y	N	Y	Y	Y	Y
12	**Balderson**	N	Y	N	Y	Y	Y
13	Ryan	Y	N	Y	Y	Y	Y
14	**Joyce**	N	Y	N	Y	Y	Y
15	**Stivers**	N	Y	N	Y	Y	Y
16	**Gonzalez**	N	Y	N	Y	Y	Y
OKLAHOMA							
1	**Hern**	N	Y	N	Y	Y	Y
2	**Mullin**	N	Y	N	Y	Y	Y
3	**Lucas**	N	Y	N	Y	Y	Y
4	**Cole**	N	Y	N	Y	Y	Y
5	Horn	Y	N	Y	Y	Y	Y
OREGON							
1	Bonamici	Y	N	Y	Y	Y	Y
2	**Walden**	Y	Y	Y	Y	Y	Y
3	Blumenauer	Y	N	Y	Y	Y	Y
4	DeFazio	Y	N	Y	Y	Y	Y
5	Schrader	Y	N	Y	Y	Y	Y
PENNSYLVANIA							
1	**Fitzpatrick**	Y	Y	Y	Y	Y	Y
2	Boyle	Y	N	Y	Y	Y	Y
3	Evans	Y	N	Y	Y	Y	Y
4	Dean	Y	N	Y	Y	Y	Y
5	Scanlon	Y	N	Y	Y	Y	Y
6	Houlahan	Y	N	Y	Y	Y	Y
7	Wild	Y	N	Y	Y	Y	Y
8	Cartwright	Y	N	Y	Y	Y	Y
9	**Meuser**	N	Y	N	Y	Y	Y
10	**Perry**	N	Y	N	Y	Y	Y
11	**Smucker**	N	Y	N	Y	Y	Y
12	**Marino**	N	?	?	?	?	?
13	**Joyce**	N	Y	N	Y	Y	Y
14	**Reschenthaler**	N	Y	N	Y	Y	Y
15	**Thompson, G.**	N	Y	N	Y	Y	Y
16	**Kelly, M.**	N	Y	N	Y	Y	Y
17	Lamb	Y	N	Y	Y	Y	Y
18	Doyle	Y	N	Y	Y	Y	Y
RHODE ISLAND							
1	Cicilline	Y	N	Y	Y	Y	Y
2	Langevin	Y	N	Y	Y	Y	Y
SOUTH CAROLINA							
1	Cunningham	Y	N	Y	Y	Y	Y
2	**Wilson, J.**	N	Y	N	Y	Y	Y
3	**Duncan**	N	Y	N	Y	Y	+
4	**Timmons**	N	Y	N	Y	Y	Y
5	**Norman**	N	Y	N	Y	Y	Y
6	Clyburn	Y	N	Y	Y	Y	Y
7	**Rice, T.**	N	Y	N	Y	Y	Y
SOUTH DAKOTA							
AL	**Johnson**	N	Y	N	Y	Y	?
TENNESSEE							
1	**Roe**	N	Y	N	Y	Y	Y
2	**Burchett**	N	Y	N	Y	Y	Y
3	**Fleischmann**	N	Y	N	Y	Y	Y
4	**DesJarlais**	N	Y	N	Y	Y	Y
5	Cooper	Y	N	Y	Y	Y	Y
6	**Rose**	N	Y	N	Y	Y	Y
7	**Green**	N	Y	N	Y	Y	Y
8	**Kustoff**	N	Y	N	Y	Y	Y
9	Cohen	Y	N	Y	Y	Y	Y
TEXAS							
1	**Gohmert**	N	Y	N	Y	Y	Y
2	**Crenshaw**	N	Y	N	Y	Y	Y
3	**Taylor**	N	Y	N	Y	Y	Y
4	**Ratcliffe**	N	Y	N	Y	?	Y

		25	26	27	28	29	30
5	**Gooden**	N	Y	N	Y	Y	Y
6	**Wright**	N	Y	N	Y	Y	Y
7	Fletcher	Y	N	Y	Y	Y	Y
8	**Brady**	N	Y	N	Y	Y	Y
9	Green, A.	Y	N	Y	Y	Y	Y
10	**McCaul**	N	Y	N	Y	Y	Y
11	**Conaway**	N	Y	N	Y	Y	Y
12	**Granger**	N	Y	N	+	Y	Y
13	**Thornberry**	N	Y	N	Y	Y	Y
14	**Weber**	N	Y	N	Y	Y	?
15	Gonzalez	Y	N	Y	Y	Y	Y
16	Escobar	Y	N	Y	Y	Y	Y
17	**Flores**	N	Y	N	?	?	Y
18	Jackson Lee	Y	N	Y	Y	Y	Y
19	**Arrington**	N	Y	N	Y	Y	Y
20	Castro	Y	N	Y	Y	Y	Y
21	**Roy**	N	Y	N	N	Y	Y
22	**Olson**	N	Y	N	Y	Y	Y
23	**Hurd**	Y	Y	Y	Y	Y	Y
24	**Marchant**	N	Y	N	Y	Y	Y
25	**Williams**	N	Y	N	Y	Y	Y
26	**Burgess**	N	Y	N	Y	Y	Y
27	**Cloud**	N	Y	N	Y	Y	Y
28	Cuellar	Y	N	Y	Y	Y	Y
29	Garcia, S.	Y	N	Y	Y	Y	Y
30	Johnson, E.B.	Y	N	Y	Y	Y	Y
31	**Carter, J.**	?	?	?	?	?	Y
32	Allred	Y	N	Y	Y	Y	Y
33	Veasey	Y	N	Y	Y	Y	Y
34	Vela	Y	N	Y	Y	Y	Y
35	Doggett	Y	N	Y	Y	Y	Y
36	**Babin**	N	Y	N	Y	Y	Y
UTAH							
1	**Bishop, R.**	N	Y	N	Y	Y	Y
2	**Stewart**	N	Y	N	Y	Y	Y
3	**Curtis**	N	Y	N	Y	Y	Y
4	McAdams	Y	N	Y	Y	Y	Y
VERMONT							
AL	Welch	Y	N	Y	Y	Y	Y
VIRGINIA							
1	**Wittman**	N	Y	N	Y	Y	Y
2	Luria	Y	N	Y	Y	Y	Y
3	Scott, R.	Y	N	Y	Y	Y	Y
4	McEachin	Y	N	Y	Y	Y	Y
5	**Riggleman**	N	Y	N	Y	Y	Y
6	**Cline**	N	Y	N	Y	Y	Y
7	Spanberger	Y	N	Y	Y	Y	Y
8	Beyer	Y	N	Y	Y	Y	Y
9	**Griffith**	N	?	?	?	?	Y
10	Wexton	Y	N	Y	Y	Y	Y
11	Connolly	Y	N	Y	Y	Y	Y
WASHINGTON							
1	DelBene	Y	N	Y	Y	Y	Y
2	Larsen	Y	N	Y	Y	Y	Y
3	**Herrera Beutler**	Y	Y	Y	Y	Y	Y
4	**Newhouse**	N	Y	N	Y	Y	Y
5	**McMorris Rodgers**	N	Y	N	Y	Y	Y
6	Kilmer	Y	N	Y	Y	Y	Y
7	Jayapal	Y	N	Y	Y	Y	Y
8	Schrier	Y	N	Y	Y	?	Y
9	Smith Adam	Y	N	Y	Y	Y	Y
10	Heck	Y	N	Y	Y	Y	Y
WEST VIRGINIA							
1	**McKinley**	N	Y	N	Y	Y	Y
2	**Mooney**	N	Y	N	Y	Y	Y
3	**Miller**	N	Y	N	Y	Y	Y
WISCONSIN							
1	**Steil**	N	Y	N	Y	Y	Y
2	Pocan	Y	N	Y	Y	Y	Y
3	Kind	Y	N	Y	Y	Y	Y
4	Moore	Y	N	Y	Y	Y	Y
5	**Sensenbrenner**	-	+	-	+	+	+
6	**Grothman**	N	Y	N	N	Y	Y
7	**Duffy**						
8	**Gallagher**	N	Y	N	Y	Y	Y
WYOMING							
AL	**Cheney**	N	Y	N	Y	Y	Y
DELEGATES							
	Radewagen (A.S.)						
	Norton (D.C.)						
	San Nicolas (Guam)						
	Sablan (N. Marianas)						
	González-Colón (P.R.)						
	Plaskett (V.I.)						

||| HOUSE VOTES

31. HJRES27. Further Continuing Fiscal 2019 Appropriations - Passage. Lowey, D-N.Y., motion to suspend the rules and pass the joint resolution that would make further continuing appropriations for fiscal 2019 through Feb. 1, 2019. Motion rejected 237-187: R 6-187; D 231-0. *Note: A two-thirds majority of those present and voting (283 in this case) is required for passage under suspension of the rules. A "nay" was a vote in support of the president's position.* Jan. 15, 2019.

32. HRES41. Rejecting White Nationalism and White Supremacy - Passage. Nadler, D-N.Y., motion to suspend the rules and agree to the resolution that would express the sense of Congress rejecting white nationalism and white supremacy as hateful expressions of intolerance that contradict the values of the House of Representatives. Motion agreed to 424-1: R 193-0; D 231-1. *Note: A two-thirds majority of those present and voting (284 in this case) is required for passage under suspension of the rules.* Jan. 15, 2019.

33. HR135. Anti-Discrimination Policies in Federal Workplaces - Passage. Cummings, D-Md., motion to suspend the rules and pass the bill that would ensure that federal agencies investigate and take necessary action into alleged instances of discrimination and/or retaliation between federal employees. It would require agencies to create a tracking system for complaints and investigations. The bill would separate the Equal Employment Opportunity Enforcement Office from Human Resources Office in an effort to minimize or eliminate interference in discrimination cases. Motion agreed to 424-0: R 193-0; D 231-0. *Note: A two-thirds majority of those present and voting (283 in this case) is required for passage under suspension of the rules.* Jan. 15, 2019.

34. HR268. Fiscal 2019 Disaster Relief Supplemental Appropriations - Previous Question. Raskin, D-Md., motion to order the previous question (thus ending debate and the possibility of amendment) on the rule (H Res 43) that would provide for House floor consideration of the bill (HR 268) that would make fiscal 2019 supplemental appropriations for disaster relief programs and services. Motion agreed to 230-194: R 0-194; D 230-0. Jan. 16, 2019.

35. HR268. Fiscal 2019 Disaster Relief Supplemental Appropriations - Rule. Adoption of the rule (H Res 43) that would provide for House floor consideration of the bill (HR 268) that would make fiscal 2019 supplemental appropriations for disaster relief programs and services. Adopted 230-193: R 0-193; D 230-0. Jan. 16, 2019.

36. HR190. Small Business Contracting - Passage. Velazquez, D-N.Y. motion to suspend the rules and pass the bill that would increase the maximum thresholds for contracts that may be awarded to so-called HUBZONE (Historically Underutilized Business Zone) small businesses, including women-owned and service disabled veteran-owned small businesses. Under existing law, five percent of all such contracts must be awarded to Women-Owned Small Businesses and three percent to Service Disabled Veteran-Owned Small Businesses. New threshold's under the bill would be set at $7 million for standard industrial manufacturing and $4 million for all other types of contracts. Adopted 230-193: R 0-193; D 230-0. *Note: A two-thirds majority of those present and voting (281 in this case) is required for passage under suspension of the rules.* Jan. 16, 2019.

		31	32	33	34	35	36
ALABAMA							
1	**Byrne**	N	Y	Y	N	N	Y
2	**Roby**	N	Y	Y	N	N	Y
3	**Rogers, M.**	N	Y	Y	N	N	Y
4	**Aderholt**	N	Y	Y	N	N	Y
5	**Brooks, M.**	N	Y	Y	N	N	Y
6	**Palmer**	N	Y	Y	N	N	Y
7	Sewell	Y	Y	Y	Y	Y	Y
ALASKA							
AL	**Young**	N	Y	Y	N	N	Y
ARIZONA							
1	O'Halleran	Y	Y	Y	Y	Y	Y
2	Kirkpatrick	Y	Y	Y	Y	Y	Y
3	Grijalva	Y	Y	Y	Y	Y	Y
4	**Gosar**	N	Y	Y	N	N	N
5	**Biggs**	N	Y	Y	N	N	N
6	**Schweikert**	N	Y	Y	N	N	Y
7	Gallego	Y	Y	Y	Y	Y	Y
8	**Lesko**	N	Y	Y	N	N	N
9	Stanton	Y	Y	Y	Y	Y	Y
ARKANSAS							
1	**Crawford**	N	Y	Y	N	N	Y
2	**Hill, F.**	N	Y	Y	N	N	Y
3	**Womack**	N	Y	Y	N	N	Y
4	**Westerman**	N	Y	Y	N	N	Y
CALIFORNIA							
1	**LaMalfa**	N	Y	Y	N	N	Y
2	Huffman	Y	Y	Y	Y	Y	Y
3	Garamendi	Y	Y	Y	Y	Y	Y
4	**McClintock**	N	Y	Y	N	N	N
5	Thompson, M.	Y	Y	Y	Y	Y	Y
6	Matsui	Y	Y	Y	+	+	+
7	Bera	Y	Y	Y	Y	Y	Y
8	**Cook**	N	Y	Y	N	N	Y
9	McNerney	Y	Y	Y	Y	Y	Y
10	Harder	Y	Y	Y	Y	Y	Y
11	DeSaulnier	Y	Y	Y	Y	Y	Y
12	Pelosi		Y				
13	Lee B.	Y	Y	Y	Y	Y	Y
14	Speier	Y	Y	Y	Y	Y	Y
15	Swalwell	Y	Y	Y	Y	Y	Y
16	Costa	Y	Y	Y	Y	Y	Y
17	Khanna	Y	Y	Y	Y	Y	Y
18	Eshoo	Y	Y	Y	Y	Y	Y
19	Lofgren	Y	Y	Y	Y	Y	Y
20	Panetta	Y	Y	Y	Y	Y	Y
21	Cox	Y	Y	Y	Y	Y	Y
22	**Nunes**	N	Y	Y	N	N	Y
23	**McCarthy**	N	Y	Y	N	N	Y
24	Carbajal	Y	Y	Y	Y	Y	Y
25	Hill, K.	Y	Y	Y	Y	Y	Y
26	Brownley	Y	Y	Y	Y	Y	Y
27	Chu	Y	Y	Y	Y	Y	Y
28	Schiff	Y	Y	Y	Y	Y	Y
29	Cárdenas	Y	Y	Y	Y	Y	Y
30	Sherman	Y	Y	Y	Y	Y	Y
31	Aguilar	Y	Y	Y	Y	Y	Y
32	Napolitano	Y	Y	Y	Y	Y	Y
33	Lieu	Y	Y	Y	Y	Y	Y
34	Gomez	Y	Y	Y	Y	Y	Y
35	Torres	Y	Y	Y	Y	Y	Y
36	Ruiz	Y	Y	Y	Y	Y	Y
37	Bass	Y	Y	Y	Y	Y	Y
38	Sánchez	Y	Y	Y	Y	Y	Y
39	Cisneros	Y	Y	Y	Y	Y	Y
40	Roybal-Allard	Y	Y	Y	Y	Y	Y
41	Takano	Y	Y	Y	Y	Y	Y
42	**Calvert**	N	Y	Y	N	N	Y
43	Waters	Y	Y	Y	Y	Y	Y
44	Barragán	Y	Y	Y	Y	Y	Y
45	Porter	Y	Y	Y	Y	Y	Y
46	Correa	Y	Y	Y	Y	Y	Y
47	Lowenthal	Y	Y	Y	Y	Y	Y
48	Rouda	Y	Y	Y	Y	Y	Y
49	Levin	Y	Y	Y	Y	Y	Y
50	**Hunter**	N	Y	Y	N	N	Y
51	Vargas	Y	Y	Y	Y	Y	Y
52	Peters	Y	Y	Y	Y	Y	Y

		31	32	33	34	35	36
53	Davis, S.	Y	Y	Y	Y	Y	Y
COLORADO							
1	DeGette	Y	Y	Y	Y	Y	Y
2	Neguse	Y	Y	Y	Y	Y	Y
3	**Tipton**	N	Y	Y	N	N	Y
4	**Buck**	N	Y	Y	N	N	Y
5	**Lamborn**	N	Y	Y	N	N	Y
6	Crow	Y	Y	Y	Y	Y	Y
7	Perlmutter	Y	Y	Y	Y	Y	Y
CONNECTICUT							
1	Larson	Y	Y	Y	Y	Y	Y
2	Courtney	Y	Y	Y	Y	Y	Y
3	DeLauro	Y	Y	Y	Y	Y	Y
4	Himes	Y	Y	Y	Y	Y	Y
5	Hayes	Y	Y	Y	Y	Y	Y
DELAWARE							
AL	Blunt Rochester	Y	Y	Y	Y	Y	Y
FLORIDA							
1	**Gaetz**	N	Y	Y	N	N	Y
2	**Dunn**	N	Y	Y	N	N	Y
3	**Yoho**	N	Y	Y	N	N	Y
4	**Rutherford**	N	Y	Y	N	N	Y
5	Lawson	Y	Y	Y	Y	Y	Y
6	**Waltz**	N	Y	Y	N	N	Y
7	Murphy	Y	Y	Y	Y	Y	Y
8	**Posey**	N	Y	Y	N	N	Y
9	Soto	Y	Y	Y	Y	Y	Y
10	Demings	Y	Y	Y	Y	Y	Y
11	**Webster**	N	Y	Y	N	N	Y
12	**Bilirakis**	N	Y	Y	N	N	Y
13	Crist	Y	Y	Y	Y	Y	Y
14	Castor	Y	Y	Y	Y	Y	Y
15	**Spano**	N	Y	Y	N	N	Y
16	**Buchanan**	N	Y	Y	N	N	Y
17	**Steube**	N	Y	Y	N	N	Y
18	**Mast**	?	?	?	?	?	?
19	**Rooney**	N	Y	Y	N	N	Y
20	Hastings	Y	Y	Y	Y	Y	?
21	Frankel	Y	Y	Y	Y	Y	?
22	Deutch	Y	Y	Y	Y	Y	Y
23	Wasserman Schultz	Y	Y	Y	Y	Y	Y
24	Wilson, F.	?	?	?	?	?	?
25	**Diaz-Balart**	N	Y	Y	N	N	Y
26	Mucarsel-Powell	Y	Y	Y	Y	Y	Y
27	Shalala	Y	Y	Y	Y	Y	Y
GEORGIA							
1	**Carter, E.L.**	N	Y	Y	N	N	Y
2	Bishop, S.	Y	Y	Y	Y	Y	Y
3	**Ferguson**	N	Y	Y	N	N	Y
4	Johnson, H.	Y	Y	Y	Y	Y	Y
5	Lewis John	Y	Y	Y	Y	Y	Y
6	McBath	Y	Y	Y	Y	Y	Y
7	**Woodall**	N	Y	Y	N	N	Y
8	**Scott, A.**	N	Y	Y	N	N	Y
9	**Collins, D.**	N	Y	Y	N	N	Y
10	**Hice**	N	Y	Y	N	N	Y
11	**Loudermilk**	N	Y	Y	N	N	Y
12	**Allen**	N	Y	Y	N	N	Y
13	Scott, D.	Y	Y	Y	Y	Y	Y
14	**Graves, T.**	N	Y	Y	N	N	Y
HAWAII							
1	Case	Y	Y	Y	Y	Y	Y
2	Gabbard	Y	Y	Y	Y	Y	Y
IDAHO							
1	**Fulcher**	N	Y	Y	N	N	Y
2	**Simpson**	N	Y	Y	N	N	Y
ILLINOIS							
1	Rush	Y	N	Y	Y	Y	Y
2	Kelly, R.	Y	Y	Y	Y	Y	Y
3	Lipinski	Y	Y	Y	Y	Y	Y
4	García, J.	Y	Y	Y	Y	Y	Y
5	Quigley	Y	Y	Y	Y	Y	Y
6	Casten	Y	Y	Y	Y	Y	Y
7	Davis, D.	Y	Y	Y	Y	Y	Y
8	Krishnamoorthi	Y	Y	Y	Y	Y	Y
9	Schakowsky	Y	Y	Y	Y	Y	Y
10	Schneider	Y	Y	Y	Y	Y	Y
11	Foster	Y	Y	Y	Y	Y	Y

KEY:	**Republicans**	Democrats	*Independents*
Y Voted for (yea)	**N** Voted against (nay)	**P** Voted "present"	
+ Announced for	**−** Announced against	**?** Did not vote or otherwise make position known	
# Paired for	**X** Paired against		

	31	32	33	34	35	36
12 **Bost**	N	Y	Y	N	N	Y
13 **Davis, R.**	N	Y	Y	N	N	Y
14 Underwood	Y	Y	Y	Y	Y	Y
15 **Shimkus**	N	Y	Y	N	N	Y
16 **Kinzinger**	N	Y	Y	N	N	Y
17 Bustos	Y	Y	Y	Y	Y	Y
18 **LaHood**	N	Y	Y	N	N	Y
INDIANA						
1 Visclosky	Y	Y	Y	Y	Y	Y
2 **Walorski**	N	Y	Y	N	N	Y
3 **Banks**	N	Y	Y	N	N	Y
4 **Baird**	N	Y	Y	N	N	Y
5 **Brooks, S.**	N	Y	Y	N	N	Y
6 **Pence**	N	Y	Y	N	N	Y
7 Carson	Y	Y	Y	Y	Y	Y
8 **Bucshon**	N	Y	Y	N	N	Y
9 **Hollingsworth**	N	Y	Y	N	N	Y
IOWA						
1 Finkenauer	Y	Y	Y	Y	Y	Y
2 Loebsack	Y	Y	Y	Y	Y	Y
3 Axne	Y	Y	Y	Y	Y	Y
4 **King, S.**	N	Y	Y	N	N	N
KANSAS						
1 **Marshall**	N	Y	Y	N	N	Y
2 **Watkins**	N	Y	Y	N	N	Y
3 Davids	Y	Y	Y	Y	Y	Y
4 **Estes**	N	Y	Y	N	N	Y
KENTUCKY						
1 **Comer**	N	Y	Y	N	N	Y
2 **Guthrie**	N	Y	Y	N	N	Y
3 Yarmuth	Y	Y	Y	Y	Y	Y
4 **Massie**	N	Y	Y	?	?	?
5 **Rogers, H.**	N	Y	Y	N	N	Y
6 **Barr**	N	Y	Y	N	N	Y
LOUISIANA						
1 **Scalise**	N	Y	Y	N	N	Y
2 Richmond	Y	Y	Y	Y	Y	Y
3 **Higgins, C.**	N	Y	Y	N	N	Y
4 **Johnson, M.**	N	Y	Y	N	N	Y
5 **Abraham**	N	Y	Y	N	N	Y
6 **Graves, G.**	N	Y	Y	N	N	Y
MAINE						
1 Pingree	Y	Y	Y	Y	Y	Y
2 Golden	Y	Y	Y	Y	Y	Y
MARYLAND						
1 **Harris**	N	Y	Y	N	N	Y
2 Ruppersberger	Y	Y	Y	Y	Y	Y
3 Sarbanes	Y	Y	Y	Y	Y	Y
4 Brown, A.	Y	Y	Y	Y	Y	Y
5 Hoyer	Y	Y	Y	Y	Y	Y
6 Trone	Y	Y	Y	Y	Y	Y
7 Cummings	Y	Y	Y	Y	Y	Y
8 Raskin	Y	Y	Y	Y	Y	Y
MASSACHUSETTS						
1 Neal	Y	Y	Y	Y	Y	Y
2 McGovern	Y	Y	Y	Y	Y	Y
3 Trahan	Y	Y	Y	Y	Y	Y
4 Kennedy	Y	Y	Y	Y	Y	Y
5 Clark	Y	Y	Y	Y	Y	Y
6 Moulton	Y	Y	Y	Y	Y	Y
7 Pressley	Y	Y	Y	Y	Y	Y
8 Lynch	Y	Y	Y	Y	Y	Y
9 Keating	Y	Y	Y	Y	Y	Y
MICHIGAN						
1 **Bergman**	N	Y	Y	N	N	Y
2 **Huizenga**	-	+	+	N	N	Y
3 **Amash**	N	Y	Y	N	N	N
4 **Moolenaar**	N	Y	Y	N	N	Y
5 Kildee	Y	Y	Y	Y	Y	Y
6 **Upton**	N	Y	Y	N	N	Y
7 **Walberg**	N	Y	Y	N	N	Y
8 Slotkin	Y	Y	Y	Y	Y	Y
9 Levin	Y	Y	Y	Y	Y	Y
10 **Mitchell**	N	Y	Y	N	N	Y
11 Stevens	Y	Y	Y	Y	Y	Y
12 Dingell	Y	Y	Y	Y	Y	Y
13 Tlaib	Y	Y	Y	Y	Y	Y
14 Lawrence	Y	Y	Y	Y	Y	Y
MINNESOTA						
1 **Hagedorn**	N	Y	Y	N	N	Y
2 Craig	Y	Y	Y	Y	Y	Y
3 Phillips	Y	Y	Y	Y	Y	Y
4 McCollum	Y	Y	Y	Y	Y	Y
5 Omar	Y	Y	Y	Y	Y	Y
6 **Emmer**	N	Y	Y	N	N	Y
7 Peterson	Y	Y	Y	Y	Y	Y
8 **Stauber**	N	Y	Y	N	N	Y
MISSISSIPPI						
1 **Kelly, T.**	N	Y	Y	N	N	Y
2 Thompson, B.	?	?	?	Y	Y	Y
3 **Guest**	N	Y	Y	N	N	Y
4 **Palazzo**	N	Y	Y	N	N	Y
MISSOURI						
1 Clay	Y	Y	Y	Y	Y	Y
2 **Wagner**	N	Y	Y	N	N	Y
3 **Luetkemeyer**	N	Y	Y	N	N	Y
4 **Hartzler**	N	Y	Y	N	N	Y
5 Cleaver	Y	Y	Y	Y	Y	Y
6 **Graves, S.**	N	Y	Y	N	N	Y
7 **Long**	N	Y	Y	N	N	Y
8 **Smith, J.**	N	Y	Y	N	N	Y
MONTANA						
AL **Gianforte**	N	Y	Y	N	N	Y
NEBRASKA						
1 **Fortenberry**	N	Y	Y	N	N	Y
2 **Bacon**	N	Y	Y	N	N	Y
3 **Smith, Adrian**	N	Y	Y	N	N	Y
NEVADA						
1 Titus	Y	Y	Y	Y	Y	Y
2 **Amodei**	N	Y	Y	N	N	Y
3 Lee	Y	Y	Y	Y	Y	Y
4 Horsford	Y	Y	Y	Y	Y	Y
NEW HAMPSHIRE						
1 Pappas	Y	Y	Y	Y	Y	Y
2 Kuster	Y	Y	Y	Y	Y	Y
NEW JERSEY						
1 Norcross	Y	Y	Y	Y	Y	Y
2 Van Drew	Y	Y	Y	Y	Y	Y
3 Kim	Y	Y	Y	Y	Y	Y
4 **Smith, C.**	Y	Y	Y	N	N	Y
5 Gottheimer	Y	Y	Y	Y	Y	Y
6 Pallone	Y	Y	Y	Y	Y	Y
7 Malinowski	Y	Y	Y	Y	Y	Y
8 Sires	Y	Y	Y	Y	Y	Y
9 Pascrell	Y	Y	Y	Y	Y	Y
10 Payne	?	?	?	?	?	?
11 Sherrill	Y	Y	Y	Y	Y	Y
12 Watson Coleman	Y	Y	Y	Y	Y	Y
NEW MEXICO						
1 Haaland	Y	Y	Y	Y	Y	Y
2 Torres Small	Y	Y	Y	Y	Y	Y
3 Luján	Y	Y	Y	Y	Y	Y
NEW YORK						
1 **Zeldin**	N	Y	Y	N	N	Y
2 **King, P.**	N	Y	Y	N	N	Y
3 Suozzi	Y	Y	Y	Y	Y	Y
4 Rice, K.	Y	Y	Y	Y	Y	Y
5 Meeks	Y	Y	Y	Y	Y	Y
6 Meng	Y	Y	Y	Y	Y	Y
7 Velázquez	Y	Y	Y	Y	Y	Y
8 Jeffries	Y	Y	Y	Y	Y	Y
9 Clarke	Y	Y	Y	Y	Y	Y
10 Nadler	Y	Y	Y	Y	Y	Y
11 Rose	Y	Y	Y	Y	Y	Y
12 Maloney, C.	Y	Y	Y	Y	Y	Y
13 Espaillat	Y	Y	Y	Y	Y	Y
14 Ocasio-Cortez	Y	Y	Y	Y	Y	Y
15 Serrano	Y	Y	Y	Y	Y	Y
16 Engel	Y	Y	Y	Y	Y	Y
17 Lowey	Y	Y	Y	Y	Y	Y
18 Maloney, S.P.	Y	Y	Y	Y	Y	Y
19 Delgado	Y	Y	Y	Y	Y	Y
20 Tonko	Y	Y	Y	Y	Y	Y
21 **Stefanik**	Y	Y	Y	N	N	Y
22 Brindisi	Y	Y	Y	Y	Y	Y
23 **Reed**	N	Y	Y	N	N	Y
24 **Katko**	Y	Y	Y	N	N	Y
25 Morelle	Y	Y	Y	Y	Y	Y
26 Higgins, B.	Y	Y	Y	Y	Y	Y
27 **Collins, C.**	N	Y	Y	N	N	Y
NORTH CAROLINA						
1 Butterfield	Y	Y	Y	Y	Y	Y
2 **Holding**	N	Y	Y	N	N	Y
3 **Jones**	?	?	?	?	?	?
4 Price	Y	Y	Y	Y	Y	Y
5 **Foxx**	N	Y	Y	N	N	Y
6 **Walker**	N	Y	Y	N	N	Y
7 **Rouzer**	N	Y	Y	N	N	Y
8 **Hudson**	N	Y	Y	N	-	Y
9 vacant						
10 **McHenry**	N	Y	Y	N	N	Y
11 **Meadows**	N	Y	Y	N	N	Y
12 Adams	Y	Y	Y	Y	Y	Y
13 **Budd**	N	Y	Y	N	N	Y
NORTH DAKOTA						
AL **Armstrong**	N	Y	Y	N	N	Y
OHIO						
1 **Chabot**	N	Y	Y	N	N	Y
2 **Wenstrup**	N	Y	Y	N	N	Y
3 Beatty	Y	Y	Y	Y	Y	Y
4 **Jordan**	N	Y	Y	N	N	Y
5 **Latta**	N	Y	Y	N	N	Y
6 **Johnson, B.**	N	Y	Y	N	N	Y
7 **Gibbs**	N	Y	Y	N	N	Y
8 **Davidson**	N	Y	Y	N	N	Y
9 Kaptur	Y	Y	Y	Y	Y	Y
10 **Turner**	N	Y	Y	N	N	Y
11 Fudge	Y	Y	Y	Y	Y	Y
12 **Balderson**	N	Y	Y	N	N	Y
13 Ryan	Y	Y	Y	Y	Y	Y
14 **Joyce**	N	Y	Y	N	N	Y
15 **Stivers**	N	Y	Y	N	N	Y
16 **Gonzalez**	N	Y	Y	N	N	Y
OKLAHOMA						
1 **Hern**	N	Y	Y	N	N	Y
2 **Mullin**	N	Y	Y	N	N	Y
3 **Lucas**	N	Y	Y	N	N	Y
4 **Cole**	N	Y	Y	N	N	Y
5 Horn	Y	Y	Y	Y	Y	Y
OREGON						
1 Bonamici	Y	Y	Y	Y	Y	Y
2 **Walden**	N	Y	Y	N	N	Y
3 Blumenauer	Y	Y	Y	Y	Y	Y
4 DeFazio	Y	Y	Y	Y	Y	Y
5 Schrader	Y	Y	Y	Y	Y	Y
PENNSYLVANIA						
1 **Fitzpatrick**	Y	Y	Y	N	N	Y
2 Boyle	Y	Y	Y	Y	Y	Y
3 Evans	Y	Y	Y	Y	Y	Y
4 Dean	Y	Y	Y	Y	Y	Y
5 Scanlon	Y	Y	Y	Y	Y	Y
6 Houlahan	Y	Y	Y	Y	Y	Y
7 Wild	Y	Y	Y	Y	Y	Y
8 Cartwright	Y	Y	Y	Y	Y	Y
9 **Meuser**	N	Y	Y	N	N	Y
10 **Perry**	N	Y	Y	N	N	Y
11 **Smucker**	N	Y	Y	N	N	Y
12 **Marino**	?	?	?	?	?	?
13 **Joyce**	N	Y	Y	N	N	Y
14 **Reschenthaler**	N	Y	Y	N	N	Y
15 **Thompson, G.**	N	Y	Y	N	N	Y
16 **Kelly, M.**	N	Y	Y	N	N	Y
17 Lamb	Y	Y	Y	Y	Y	Y
18 Doyle	Y	Y	Y	Y	Y	Y
RHODE ISLAND						
1 Cicilline	Y	Y	Y	Y	Y	Y
2 Langevin	Y	Y	Y	Y	Y	Y
SOUTH CAROLINA						
1 Cunningham	Y	Y	Y	Y	Y	Y
2 **Wilson, J.**	N	Y	Y	N	N	Y
3 **Duncan**	N	Y	Y	N	N	Y
4 **Timmons**	N	Y	Y	N	N	Y
5 **Norman**	N	Y	Y	N	N	Y
6 Clyburn	Y	Y	Y	Y	Y	Y
7 **Rice, T.**	N	Y	Y	N	N	Y
SOUTH DAKOTA						
AL **Johnson**	N	Y	Y	N	N	Y
TENNESSEE						
1 **Roe**	N	Y	Y	N	N	Y
2 **Burchett**	N	Y	Y	N	N	Y
3 **Fleischmann**	N	Y	Y	N	N	Y
4 **DesJarlais**	?	?	?	N	N	Y
5 Cooper	Y	Y	Y	Y	Y	Y
6 **Rose**	N	Y	Y	N	N	Y
7 **Green**	N	Y	Y	N	N	Y
8 **Kustoff**	N	Y	Y	N	N	Y
9 Cohen	Y	Y	Y	Y	Y	Y
TEXAS						
1 **Gohmert**	N	Y	Y	N	N	Y
2 **Crenshaw**	N	Y	Y	N	N	Y
3 **Taylor**	N	Y	Y	N	N	Y
4 **Ratcliffe**	N	Y	Y	N	N	Y
5 **Gooden**	N	Y	Y	N	N	Y
6 **Wright**	N	Y	Y	N	N	Y
7 Fletcher	Y	Y	Y	Y	Y	Y
8 **Brady**	N	Y	Y	N	N	Y
9 Green, A.	Y	Y	Y	Y	Y	+
10 **McCaul**	N	Y	Y	N	N	Y
11 **Conaway**	N	Y	Y	N	N	Y
12 **Granger**	N	Y	Y	N	N	Y
13 **Thornberry**	N	Y	Y	N	N	Y
14 **Weber**	N	Y	Y	N	N	Y
15 Gonzalez	Y	Y	Y	Y	Y	Y
16 Escobar	Y	Y	Y	Y	Y	Y
17 **Flores**	N	Y	Y	N	N	Y
18 Jackson Lee	Y	Y	Y	Y	Y	Y
19 **Arrington**	N	Y	Y	N	N	Y
20 Castro	Y	Y	Y	Y	Y	Y
21 **Roy**	N	Y	Y	N	N	N
22 **Olson**	N	Y	Y	N	N	Y
23 **Hurd**	Y	Y	Y	N	N	Y
24 **Marchant**	N	Y	Y	N	N	Y
25 **Williams**	N	Y	Y	N	N	Y
26 **Burgess**	N	Y	Y	N	N	Y
27 **Cloud**	N	Y	Y	N	N	Y
28 Cuellar	Y	Y	Y	Y	Y	Y
29 Garcia, S.	Y	Y	Y	Y	Y	Y
30 Johnson, E.B.	Y	Y	Y	Y	Y	Y
31 **Carter, J.**	N	Y	Y	N	N	Y
32 Allred	Y	Y	Y	Y	Y	Y
33 Veasey	Y	Y	Y	Y	Y	Y
34 Vela	Y	Y	Y	Y	Y	Y
35 Doggett	Y	Y	Y	Y	Y	Y
36 **Babin**	N	Y	Y	N	N	Y
UTAH						
1 **Bishop, R.**	N	Y	Y	N	N	Y
2 **Stewart**	N	Y	Y	N	N	Y
3 **Curtis**	N	Y	Y	N	N	Y
4 McAdams	Y	Y	Y	Y	Y	Y
VERMONT						
AL Welch	Y	Y	Y	Y	Y	Y
VIRGINIA						
1 **Wittman**	N	Y	Y	N	N	Y
2 Luria	Y	Y	Y	Y	Y	Y
3 Scott, R.	Y	Y	Y	Y	Y	Y
4 McEachin	Y	Y	Y	Y	Y	Y
5 **Riggleman**	N	Y	Y	N	N	Y
6 **Cline**	N	Y	Y	N	N	Y
7 Spanberger	Y	Y	Y	Y	Y	Y
8 Beyer	Y	Y	Y	?	?	?
9 **Griffith**	N	Y	Y	N	N	Y
10 Wexton	Y	Y	Y	Y	Y	Y
11 Connolly	Y	Y	Y	Y	Y	Y
WASHINGTON						
1 DelBene	Y	Y	Y	Y	Y	Y
2 Larsen	Y	Y	Y	Y	Y	Y
3 **Herrera Beutler**	Y	Y	Y	N	N	Y
4 **Newhouse**	N	Y	Y	N	N	Y
5 **McMorris Rodgers**	N	Y	Y	N	N	Y
6 Kilmer	Y	Y	Y	Y	Y	Y
7 Jayapal	Y	Y	Y	Y	Y	Y
8 Schrier	Y	Y	Y	Y	Y	Y
9 Smith Adam	Y	Y	Y	Y	Y	?
10 Heck	Y	Y	Y	Y	Y	Y
WEST VIRGINIA						
1 **McKinley**	N	Y	Y	N	N	Y
2 **Mooney**	N	Y	Y	N	N	Y
3 **Miller**	N	Y	Y	N	N	Y
WISCONSIN						
1 **Steil**	N	Y	Y	N	N	Y
2 Pocan	Y	Y	Y	Y	Y	Y
3 Kind	Y	Y	Y	Y	Y	Y
4 Moore	Y	Y	Y	Y	Y	Y
5 **Sensenbrenner**	-	+	+	-	-	+
6 **Grothman**	N	Y	Y	N	N	Y
7 **Duffy**						
8 **Gallagher**	N	Y	Y	N	N	Y
WYOMING						
AL **Cheney**	N	Y	Y	N	N	Y
DELEGATES						
Radewagen (A.S.)						
Norton (D.C.)						
San Nicolas (Guam)						
Sablan (N. Marianas)						
González-Colón (P.R.)						
Plaskett (V.I.)						

ⅠⅠⅠ HOUSE VOTES

37. HR268. Fiscal 2019 Disaster Relief Supplemental Appropriations - Physical Border Barrier Prohibition. McGovern, D-Mass., amendment that would prohibit funds provided by the bill for the Army Corps of Engineers or the Homeland Security Department from being used to construct a "new physical barrier along the southwest border of the U.S. Adopted in Committee of the Whole 230-197: R 4-189; D 225-8; I 1-0. Jan. 16, 2019.

38. HR268. Fiscal 2019 Disaster Relief Supplemental Appropriations - Recommit. Dunn, R-Fla., motion to recommit the bill to the House Appropriations Committee with instructions to report it back immediately with an amendment that would remove the language from the bill that would provide further continuing appropriations for general government operations through Feb. 8, 2019. Motion rejected 193-231: R 193-0; D 0-231. Jan. 16, 2019.

39. HR268. Fiscal 2019 Disaster Relief Supplemental Appropriations - Passage. Passage of the bill that would provide continuing appropriations for operations of the federal government at current funding levels through Feb. 8, 2019. Additionally, the bill provides $12.1 billion in supplemental disaster funds for response efforts to damage caused by hurricanes, wildfires, earthquakes and other natural disasters that occurred in 2017 and 2018. The bill includes a total of $2.7 billion for Agriculture Department disaster-related activities, including $1.1 billion for crop (including milk), tree, bush, vine, and livestock losses from 2018 hurricanes, wildfires and other declared disasters. The bill provides $1.16 billion for the Housing and Urban Development Department's Community Development Block Grants-Disaster Recovery Program, and $1.7 billion for Transportation Department programs and activities, including $1.65 billion for the cost of federal highway and bridge repairs. It provides $1.46 billion to the Defense Department to repair military facilities damaged by hurricanes Florence and Michael, primarily for repairing damage to military facilities in the Carolinas and Florida. As amended, the bill would prohibit funds provided in the bill for the Army Corps of Engineers or the Homeland Security Department from being used to construct a "new physical barrier along the southwest border of the U.S. Also as amended, the bill would permit the use of emergency funds provided to the Agriculture Department for 2018 crop losses to be used to cover harvested wine grapes that were found to have been tainted by smoke from wildfires. Passed 237-187: R 6-187; D 231-0. *Note: A "nay" was a vote in support of the president's position.* Jan. 16, 2019.

40. HJRES28. Fiscal 2019 Further Continuing Appropriations - Rule. Adoption of the rule (H Res 52) that would provide for House floor consideration of the joint resolution (H J Res 28) that would make further continuing appropriations for fiscal year 2019 that would fund the government until Feb. 28, 2019. The rule would also provide for consideration of measures under motions to suspend the rules through Jan. 25, 2019. Adopted 230-190: R 0-190; D 230-0. Jan. 17, 2019.

41. HR150. Federal Grant Recipient Data Standards - Passage. Cummings, D-Md., motion to suspend the rules and pass the bill that would direct the Office of Management and Budget to establish government-wide data standards for reports by recipients of federal grants, with the agency that issues the most federal grants within one year of enactment as the standard-setting agency. It would also direct OMB to, within four years of enactment, publicly share federal grant information as a government-wide data set. Motion agreed to 422-0: R 191-0; D 231-0. *Note: A two-thirds majority of those present and voting (282 in this case) is required for passage under suspension of the rules.* Jan. 17, 2019.

42. HJRES30. Disapproving Presidential Action On Russian Sanctions - Passage. Engel, D-N.Y., motion to suspend the rules and pass the joint resolution that would disapprove of President Trump's proposed action related to the application of sanctions against certain Russian companies. Passed 362-53: R 136-53; D 226-0. *Note: A two-thirds majority of those present and voting (277 in this case) is required for passage under suspension of the rules. A "nay" was a vote in support of the president's position.* Jan. 17, 2019.

		37	38	39	40	41	42
ALABAMA							
1	**Byrne**	N	Y	N	N	Y	N
2	**Roby**	N	Y	N	N	Y	Y
3	**Rogers, M.**	N	Y	N	N	Y	N
4	**Aderholt**	N	Y	N	N	Y	N
5	**Brooks, M.**	N	Y	N	N	Y	N
6	**Palmer**	N	Y	N	N	Y	Y
7	Sewell	Y	N	Y	Y	Y	Y
ALASKA							
AL	**Young**	N	Y	N	N	Y	N
ARIZONA							
1	O'Halleran	Y	N	Y	Y	Y	Y
2	Kirkpatrick	Y	N	Y	Y	Y	Y
3	Grijalva	Y	N	Y	Y	Y	Y
4	**Gosar**	N	Y	N	N	Y	N
5	**Biggs**	N	Y	N	N	Y	N
6	**Schweikert**	N	Y	N	N	Y	Y
7	Gallego	Y	N	Y	Y	Y	Y
8	**Lesko**	N	Y	N	N	Y	N
9	Stanton	Y	N	Y	Y	Y	Y
ARKANSAS							
1	**Crawford**	N	Y	N	N	Y	Y
2	**Hill, F.**	N	Y	N	N	Y	Y
3	**Womack**	N	Y	N	N	Y	N
4	**Westerman**	N	Y	N	N	Y	Y
CALIFORNIA							
1	**LaMalfa**	?	Y	N	N	Y	Y
2	Huffman	Y	N	Y	Y	Y	Y
3	Garamendi	Y	N	Y	Y	Y	Y
4	**McClintock**	N	Y	N	N	Y	N
5	Thompson, M.	Y	N	Y	Y	Y	Y
6	Matsui	Y	N	Y	Y	Y	Y
7	Bera	Y	N	Y	Y	Y	Y
8	**Cook**	N	Y	N	N	Y	Y
9	McNerney	Y	N	Y	Y	Y	Y
10	Harder	Y	N	Y	Y	Y	Y
11	DeSaulnier	Y	N	Y	Y	Y	Y
12	Pelosi						
13	Lee B.	Y	N	Y	Y	Y	Y
14	Speier	Y	N	Y	Y	Y	Y
15	Swalwell	Y	N	Y	Y	Y	Y
16	Costa	Y	N	Y	Y	Y	Y
17	Khanna	Y	N	Y	Y	Y	Y
18	Eshoo	Y	N	Y	Y	Y	Y
19	Lofgren	Y	N	Y	Y	Y	Y
20	Panetta	Y	N	Y	Y	Y	Y
21	Cox	Y	N	Y	Y	Y	Y
22	**Nunes**	N	Y	N	N	Y	Y
23	**McCarthy**	N	Y	N	N	Y	Y
24	Carbajal	Y	N	Y	Y	Y	Y
25	Hill, K.	Y	N	Y	Y	Y	Y
26	Brownley	Y	N	Y	Y	Y	Y
27	Chu	Y	N	?	Y	Y	Y
28	Schiff	Y	N	Y	Y	Y	Y
29	Cárdenas	Y	N	Y	Y	Y	Y
30	Sherman	Y	N	Y	Y	Y	Y
31	Aguilar	Y	N	Y	Y	Y	Y
32	Napolitano	Y	N	Y	Y	Y	Y
33	Lieu	Y	N	Y	Y	Y	Y
34	Gomez	Y	N	Y	Y	Y	Y
35	Torres	Y	N	Y	Y	Y	Y
36	Ruiz	Y	N	Y	Y	Y	Y
37	Bass	Y	N	Y	Y	Y	Y
38	Sánchez	Y	N	Y	Y	Y	Y
39	Cisneros	Y	N	Y	Y	Y	Y
40	Roybal-Allard	Y	N	Y	Y	Y	Y
41	Takano	Y	N	Y	Y	Y	Y
42	**Calvert**	N	Y	N	N	Y	Y
43	Waters	Y	N	Y	Y	Y	Y
44	Barragán	Y	N	Y	Y	Y	Y
45	Porter	Y	N	Y	Y	Y	Y
46	Correa	Y	N	Y	Y	Y	Y
47	Lowenthal	Y	N	Y	Y	Y	Y
48	Rouda	Y	N	Y	Y	Y	Y
49	Levin	Y	N	Y	Y	Y	Y
50	**Hunter**	N	Y	N	N	Y	N
51	Vargas	Y	N	Y	Y	Y	Y
52	Peters	Y	N	Y	Y	Y	Y
53	Davis, S.	Y	N	Y	Y	Y	Y
COLORADO							
1	DeGette	Y	N	Y	Y	Y	Y
2	Neguse	Y	N	Y	Y	Y	Y
3	**Tipton**	N	Y	N	N	Y	Y
4	**Buck**	N	Y	N	N	Y	Y
5	**Lamborn**	N	Y	N	N	Y	Y
6	Crow	Y	N	Y	Y	Y	Y
7	Perlmutter	Y	N	Y	Y	Y	Y
CONNECTICUT							
1	Larson	Y	N	Y	Y	Y	Y
2	Courtney	Y	N	Y	Y	Y	Y
3	DeLauro	Y	N	Y	Y	Y	Y
4	Himes	Y	N	Y	Y	Y	Y
5	Hayes	Y	N	Y	Y	Y	Y
DELAWARE							
AL	Blunt Rochester	Y	N	Y	Y	Y	Y
FLORIDA							
1	**Gaetz**	N	Y	N	?	?	?
2	**Dunn**	N	Y	N	N	Y	N
3	**Yoho**	N	Y	N	N	Y	N
4	**Rutherford**	N	Y	N	N	Y	N
5	Lawson	Y	N	Y	Y	Y	Y
6	**Waltz**	N	Y	N	N	Y	Y
7	Murphy	Y	N	Y	Y	Y	Y
8	**Posey**	N	Y	N	N	Y	N
9	Soto	Y	N	Y	Y	Y	Y
10	Demings	Y	N	Y	Y	Y	Y
11	**Webster**	N	Y	N	N	Y	Y
12	**Bilirakis**	N	Y	N	N	Y	Y
13	Crist	Y	N	Y	Y	Y	Y
14	Castor	Y	N	Y	Y	Y	Y
15	**Spano**	N	Y	N	N	Y	Y
16	**Buchanan**	N	Y	N	N	Y	Y
17	**Steube**	N	Y	N	N	Y	N
18	**Mast**	?	?	?	?	?	?
19	**Rooney**	?	?	?	N	Y	?
20	Hastings	Y	N	Y	Y	Y	Y
21	Frankel	Y	N	Y	Y	Y	Y
22	Deutch	Y	N	Y	Y	Y	Y
23	Wasserman Schultz	Y	N	Y	Y	Y	Y
24	Wilson, F.	?	?	?	?	?	?
25	**Diaz-Balart**	Y	Y	N	Y	Y	Y
26	Mucarsel-Powell	Y	N	Y	Y	Y	Y
27	Shalala	Y	N	Y	Y	Y	Y
GEORGIA							
1	**Carter, E.L.**	N	Y	N	N	Y	N
2	Bishop, S.	Y	N	Y	Y	Y	Y
3	**Ferguson**	N	Y	N	N	Y	Y
4	Johnson, H.	Y	N	Y	Y	Y	Y
5	Lewis John	Y	N	Y	Y	Y	Y
6	McBath	Y	N	Y	Y	Y	Y
7	**Woodall**	N	Y	N	N	Y	N
8	**Scott, A.**	N	Y	N	N	Y	Y
9	**Collins, D.**	N	Y	N	?	Y	Y
10	**Hice**	N	Y	N	N	Y	Y
11	**Loudermilk**	N	Y	N	N	Y	?
12	**Allen**	N	Y	N	N	Y	Y
13	Scott, D.	Y	N	Y	Y	Y	Y
14	**Graves, T.**	N	Y	N	N	Y	N
HAWAII							
1	Case	Y	N	Y	Y	Y	Y
2	Gabbard	Y	N	Y	Y	Y	?
IDAHO							
1	**Fulcher**	N	Y	N	N	Y	Y
2	**Simpson**	N	Y	N	N	Y	Y
ILLINOIS							
1	Rush	Y	N	Y	Y	Y	?
2	Kelly, R.	Y	N	Y	Y	Y	Y
3	Lipinski	Y	N	Y	Y	Y	Y
4	García, J.	Y	N	Y	Y	Y	Y
5	Quigley	Y	N	Y	Y	Y	Y
6	Casten	Y	N	Y	Y	Y	Y
7	Davis, D.	Y	N	Y	Y	Y	Y
8	Krishnamoorthi	Y	N	Y	Y	Y	Y
9	Schakowsky	Y	N	Y	Y	Y	Y
10	Schneider	Y	N	Y	Y	Y	Y
11	Foster	Y	N	Y	Y	Y	Y

KEY: **Republicans** (bold) — Democrats (roman) — *Independents* (italic)

Y Voted for (yea)	**N** Voted against (nay)	**P** Voted "present"
+ Announced for	**–** Announced against	**?** Did not vote or otherwise make position known
# Paired for	**X** Paired against	

		37	38	39	40	41	42
12	**Bost**	N	Y	N	N	Y	Y
13	**Davis, R.**	N	Y	N	N	Y	Y
14	Underwood	Y	N	Y	Y	Y	Y
15	**Shimkus**	N	Y	N	N	Y	Y
16	**Kinzinger**	N	Y	N	N	Y	Y
17	Bustos	Y	N	Y	Y	Y	Y
18	**LaHood**	N	Y	N	N	Y	Y
INDIANA							
1	Visclosky	Y	N	Y	Y	Y	Y
2	**Walorski**	N	Y	N	N	Y	Y
3	**Banks**	N	Y	N	N	Y	Y
4	**Baird**	N	Y	N	N	Y	Y
5	**Brooks, S.**	N	Y	N	N	Y	Y
6	**Pence**	N	Y	N	N	Y	N
7	Carson	Y	N	Y	Y	Y	Y
8	**Bucshon**	N	Y	N	N	Y	Y
9	**Hollingsworth**	N	Y	N	N	Y	N
IOWA							
1	Finkenauer	Y	N	Y	Y	Y	Y
2	Loebsack	Y	N	Y	Y	Y	Y
3	Axne	Y	N	Y	Y	Y	Y
4	**King, S.**	N	Y	N	N	Y	N
KANSAS							
1	**Marshall**	N	Y	N	N	Y	N
2	**Watkins**	N	Y	N	N	Y	Y
3	Davids	Y	N	Y	Y	Y	Y
4	**Estes**	N	Y	N	N	Y	N
KENTUCKY							
1	**Comer**	N	Y	N	N	Y	N
2	**Guthrie**	N	Y	N	N	Y	Y
3	Yarmuth	Y	N	Y	Y	Y	Y
4	**Massie**	?	?	-	?	?	-
5	**Rogers, H.**	N	Y	N	N	Y	Y
6	**Barr**	N	Y	N	N	Y	Y
LOUISIANA							
1	**Scalise**	N	Y	N	N	Y	Y
2	Richmond	Y	N	Y	Y	Y	Y
3	**Higgins, C.**	N	Y	N	N	Y	N
4	**Johnson, M.**	N	Y	N	N	Y	?
5	**Abraham**	N	Y	N	N	Y	N
6	**Graves, G.**	N	Y	N	N	Y	Y
MAINE							
1	Pingree	Y	N	Y	Y	Y	Y
2	Golden	Y	N	Y	Y	Y	Y
MARYLAND							
1	**Harris**	N	Y	N	N	Y	N
2	Ruppersberger	Y	N	Y	Y	Y	Y
3	Sarbanes	Y	N	Y	Y	Y	Y
4	Brown, A.	Y	N	Y	Y	Y	Y
5	Hoyer	Y	N	Y	Y	Y	Y
6	Trone	Y	N	Y	Y	Y	Y
7	Cummings	Y	N	Y	Y	Y	Y
8	Raskin	Y	N	Y	Y	Y	Y
MASSACHUSETTS							
1	Neal	Y	N	Y	Y	Y	Y
2	McGovern	Y	N	Y	Y	Y	Y
3	Trahan	Y	N	Y	Y	Y	Y
4	Kennedy	Y	N	Y	Y	Y	Y
5	Clark	Y	N	Y	Y	Y	Y
6	Moulton	Y	N	Y	Y	Y	Y
7	Pressley	Y	N	Y	Y	Y	Y
8	Lynch	Y	N	Y	Y	Y	Y
9	Keating	Y	N	Y	Y	Y	Y
MICHIGAN							
1	**Bergman**	N	Y	N	N	Y	Y
2	**Huizenga**	N	Y	N	N	Y	Y
3	**Amash**	Y	Y	N	Y	N	N
4	**Moolenaar**	N	Y	N	N	Y	Y
5	Kildee	Y	N	Y	Y	Y	Y
6	**Upton**	N	Y	N	N	Y	Y
7	**Walberg**	N	Y	N	N	Y	Y
8	Slotkin	N	N	Y	Y	Y	Y
9	Levin	Y	N	Y	Y	Y	Y
10	**Mitchell**	N	Y	N	N	Y	Y
11	Stevens	Y	N	Y	Y	Y	Y
12	Dingell	Y	N	Y	Y	Y	Y
13	Tlaib	Y	N	Y	Y	Y	Y
14	Lawrence	Y	N	Y	Y	Y	Y
MINNESOTA							
1	**Hagedorn**	N	Y	N	N	Y	Y
2	Craig	Y	N	Y	Y	Y	Y
3	Phillips	Y	N	Y	Y	Y	Y
4	McCollum	Y	N	Y	Y	Y	Y
5	Omar	Y	N	Y	Y	Y	Y

		37	38	39	40	41	42
6	**Emmer**	N	Y	N	N	Y	Y
7	Peterson	N	N	Y	Y	Y	Y
8	**Stauber**	N	Y	N	N	Y	Y
MISSISSIPPI							
1	**Kelly, T.**	N	Y	N	N	Y	N
2	Thompson, B.	Y	N	Y	Y	Y	Y
3	**Guest**	N	Y	N	N	Y	Y
4	**Palazzo**	N	Y	N	N	Y	Y
MISSOURI							
1	Clay	Y	N	Y	Y	Y	Y
2	**Wagner**	N	Y	N	N	Y	Y
3	**Luetkemeyer**	N	Y	N	N	Y	Y
4	**Hartzler**	N	Y	N	N	Y	Y
5	Cleaver	Y	N	Y	Y	Y	Y
6	**Graves, S.**	N	Y	N	N	Y	Y
7	**Long**	N	Y	N	N	Y	Y
8	**Smith, J.**	N	Y	N	N	Y	N
MONTANA							
AL	**Gianforte**	N	Y	N	N	Y	Y
NEBRASKA							
1	**Fortenberry**	N	Y	N	N	Y	N
2	**Bacon**	N	Y	N	N	Y	Y
3	**Smith, Adrian**	N	Y	N	N	Y	Y
NEVADA							
1	Titus	Y	N	Y	Y	Y	Y
2	**Amodei**	N	Y	N	N	Y	N
3	Lee	Y	N	Y	Y	Y	Y
4	Horsford	Y	N	Y	Y	Y	Y
NEW HAMPSHIRE							
1	Pappas	Y	N	Y	Y	Y	Y
2	Kuster	Y	N	Y	Y	Y	Y
NEW JERSEY							
1	Norcross	Y	N	Y	Y	Y	Y
2	Van Drew	N	N	Y	Y	Y	Y
3	Kim	N	N	Y	Y	Y	Y
4	**Smith, C.**	N	Y	Y	N	Y	Y
5	Gottheimer	Y	N	Y	Y	Y	Y
6	Pallone	Y	N	Y	Y	Y	Y
7	Malinowski	Y	N	Y	Y	Y	Y
8	Sires	Y	N	Y	Y	Y	Y
9	Pascrell	Y	N	Y	Y	Y	Y
10	Payne	?	?	?	?	?	?
11	Sherrill	Y	N	Y	Y	Y	Y
12	Watson Coleman	Y	N	Y	Y	Y	Y
NEW MEXICO							
1	Haaland	Y	N	Y	Y	Y	Y
2	Torres Small	Y	N	Y	Y	Y	Y
3	Luján	Y	N	Y	+	Y	Y
NEW YORK							
1	**Zeldin**	N	Y	N	N	Y	Y
2	**King, P.**	N	Y	N	N	Y	Y
3	Suozzi	Y	N	Y	Y	Y	Y
4	Rice, K.	Y	N	Y	Y	Y	Y
5	Meeks	Y	N	Y	Y	Y	Y
6	Meng	Y	N	Y	?	?	?
7	Velázquez	Y	N	Y	Y	Y	Y
8	Jeffries	Y	N	Y	Y	Y	Y
9	Clarke	Y	N	Y	Y	Y	Y
10	Nadler	Y	N	Y	Y	Y	Y
11	Rose	Y	N	Y	Y	Y	Y
12	Maloney, C.	Y	N	Y	Y	Y	Y
13	Espaillat	Y	N	Y	Y	Y	Y
14	Ocasio-Cortez	Y	N	Y	Y	Y	Y
15	Serrano	Y	N	Y	Y	Y	Y
16	Engel	Y	N	Y	Y	Y	Y
17	Lowey	Y	N	Y	Y	Y	Y
18	Maloney, S.P.	Y	N	Y	Y	Y	Y
19	Delgado	Y	N	Y	Y	Y	Y
20	Tonko	Y	N	Y	Y	Y	Y
21	**Stefanik**	N	Y	N	N	Y	Y
22	Brindisi	N	N	Y	Y	Y	Y
23	**Reed**	N	Y	N	N	Y	Y
24	**Katko**	N	Y	N	N	Y	Y
25	Morelle	Y	N	Y	Y	Y	Y
26	Higgins, B.	Y	N	Y	Y	Y	Y
27	**Collins, C.**	N	Y	N	N	Y	N
NORTH CAROLINA							
1	Butterfield	Y	N	Y	Y	Y	Y
2	**Holding**	N	Y	N	N	Y	Y
3	**Jones**	?	?	?	?	?	?
4	Price	Y	N	Y	Y	Y	Y
5	**Foxx**	N	Y	N	N	Y	Y
6	**Walker**	N	Y	N	?	?	?
7	**Rouzer**	N	Y	N	N	Y	Y

		37	38	39	40	41	42
8	**Hudson**	N	Y	N	N	Y	Y
9	vacant						
10	**McHenry**	N	Y	N	N	Y	Y
11	**Meadows**	N	Y	N	N	Y	Y
12	Adams	Y	N	Y	Y	Y	Y
13	**Budd**	N	Y	N	N	Y	Y
NORTH DAKOTA							
AL	**Armstrong**	N	Y	N	N	Y	Y
OHIO							
1	**Chabot**	N	Y	N	N	Y	Y
2	**Wenstrup**	N	Y	N	N	Y	Y
3	Beatty	Y	N	Y	Y	Y	Y
4	**Jordan**	N	Y	N	N	Y	Y
5	**Latta**	N	Y	N	N	Y	Y
6	**Johnson, B.**	N	Y	N	N	Y	Y
7	**Gibbs**	N	Y	N	N	Y	Y
8	**Davidson**	N	Y	N	N	Y	N
9	Kaptur	Y	N	Y	Y	Y	Y
10	**Turner**	N	Y	N	?	?	Y
11	Fudge	Y	N	Y	Y	Y	Y
12	**Balderson**	N	Y	N	N	Y	Y
13	Ryan	Y	N	Y	Y	Y	Y
14	**Joyce**	N	Y	N	N	Y	Y
15	**Stivers**	N	Y	N	N	Y	Y
16	**Gonzalez**	N	Y	N	N	Y	Y
OKLAHOMA							
1	**Hern**	N	Y	N	N	Y	N
2	**Mullin**	N	Y	N	N	Y	N
3	**Lucas**	N	Y	N	N	Y	Y
4	**Cole**	N	Y	N	N	Y	N
5	Horn	N	N	Y	Y	Y	Y
OREGON							
1	Bonamici	Y	N	Y	Y	Y	Y
2	**Walden**	N	Y	N	N	Y	Y
3	Blumenauer	Y	N	Y	Y	Y	+
4	DeFazio	Y	N	Y	Y	Y	Y
5	Schrader	Y	N	Y	Y	Y	Y
PENNSYLVANIA							
1	**Fitzpatrick**	Y	Y	N	N	Y	Y
2	Boyle	Y	N	Y	Y	Y	Y
3	Evans	Y	N	Y	Y	Y	Y
4	Dean	Y	N	Y	Y	Y	Y
5	Scanlon	Y	N	Y	Y	Y	Y
6	Houlahan	Y	N	Y	Y	Y	Y
7	Wild	Y	N	Y	Y	Y	Y
8	Cartwright	Y	N	Y	Y	Y	Y
9	**Meuser**	N	Y	N	N	Y	Y
10	**Perry**	N	Y	N	N	Y	Y
11	**Smucker**	N	Y	N	N	Y	Y
12	**Marino**	?	?	?	?	?	?
13	**Joyce**	N	Y	N	N	Y	N
14	**Reschenthaler**	N	Y	N	N	Y	Y
15	**Thompson, G.**	N	Y	N	N	Y	N
16	**Kelly, M.**	N	Y	N	N	Y	Y
17	Lamb	N	N	Y	Y	Y	Y
18	Doyle	Y	N	Y	Y	Y	?
RHODE ISLAND							
1	Cicilline	Y	N	Y	Y	Y	Y
2	Langevin	Y	N	Y	Y	Y	Y
SOUTH CAROLINA							
1	Cunningham	N	N	Y	Y	Y	Y
2	**Wilson, J.**	N	Y	N	N	Y	Y
3	**Duncan**	N	Y	N	N	Y	N
4	**Timmons**	N	Y	N	N	Y	Y
5	**Norman**	N	Y	N	N	Y	N
6	Clyburn	Y	N	Y	Y	Y	Y
7	**Rice, T.**	N	Y	N	N	Y	Y
SOUTH DAKOTA							
AL	**Johnson**	N	Y	N	N	Y	Y
TENNESSEE							
1	**Roe**	N	Y	N	N	Y	N
2	**Burchett**	N	Y	N	N	Y	Y
3	**Fleischmann**	N	Y	N	N	Y	N
4	**DesJarlais**	N	Y	N	N	Y	N
5	Cooper	Y	N	Y	Y	Y	Y
6	**Rose**	N	Y	N	N	Y	N
7	**Green**	N	Y	N	N	Y	Y
8	**Kustoff**	N	Y	N	N	Y	N
9	Cohen	Y	N	Y	Y	Y	Y
TEXAS							
1	**Gohmert**	N	Y	N	N	Y	Y
2	**Crenshaw**	N	Y	N	N	Y	Y
3	**Taylor**	N	Y	N	N	Y	Y
4	**Ratcliffe**	N	Y	N	N	Y	Y

		37	38	39	40	41	42
5	**Gooden**	N	Y	N	N	Y	Y
6	**Wright**	N	Y	N	N	Y	Y
7	Fletcher	Y	N	Y	Y	Y	Y
8	**Brady**	N	Y	N	N	Y	N
9	Green, A.	Y	N	Y	Y	Y	Y
10	**McCaul**	N	Y	N	N	Y	Y
11	**Conaway**	N	Y	N	N	Y	Y
12	**Granger**	N	Y	N	N	Y	Y
13	**Thornberry**	N	Y	N	N	Y	Y
14	**Weber**	N	Y	N	N	Y	N
15	Gonzalez	Y	N	Y	Y	Y	Y
16	Escobar	Y	N	Y	Y	Y	Y
17	**Flores**	N	Y	N	N	Y	Y
18	Jackson Lee	Y	N	Y	Y	Y	Y
19	**Arrington**	N	Y	N	N	Y	Y
20	Castro	Y	N	Y	Y	Y	Y
21	**Roy**	N	Y	N	N	Y	Y
22	**Olson**	N	Y	N	N	Y	Y
23	**Hurd**	N	Y	N	N	Y	Y
24	**Marchant**	N	Y	N	N	Y	Y
25	**Williams**	N	Y	N	N	Y	Y
26	**Burgess**	N	Y	N	N	Y	Y
27	**Cloud**	N	Y	N	N	Y	Y
28	Cuellar	Y	N	Y	Y	Y	Y
29	Garcia, S.	Y	N	Y	Y	Y	Y
30	Johnson, E.B.	Y	N	Y	Y	Y	Y
31	**Carter, J.**	N	Y	N	N	Y	Y
32	Allred	Y	N	Y	Y	Y	Y
33	Veasey	Y	N	Y	Y	Y	Y
34	Vela	Y	N	Y	Y	Y	Y
35	Doggett	Y	N	Y	Y	Y	Y
36	**Babin**	N	Y	N	N	Y	N
UTAH							
1	**Bishop, R.**	N	Y	N	N	Y	Y
2	**Stewart**	N	Y	N	N	Y	Y
3	**Curtis**	N	Y	N	N	Y	Y
4	McAdams	Y	N	Y	Y	Y	Y
VERMONT							
AL	Welch	Y	-	Y	Y	Y	Y
VIRGINIA							
1	**Wittman**	N	Y	N	N	Y	Y
2	Luria	Y	N	Y	Y	Y	Y
3	Scott, R.	Y	N	Y	Y	Y	Y
4	McEachin	+	N	Y	Y	Y	+
5	**Riggleman**	N	Y	N	N	Y	Y
6	**Cline**	N	Y	N	N	Y	Y
7	Spanberger	Y	N	Y	Y	Y	Y
8	Beyer	Y	N	Y	Y	Y	Y
9	**Griffith**	N	Y	N	N	Y	Y
10	Wexton	Y	N	Y	Y	Y	Y
11	Connolly	Y	N	Y	Y	Y	Y
WASHINGTON							
1	DelBene	Y	N	Y	Y	Y	Y
2	Larsen	Y	N	Y	Y	Y	Y
3	**Herrera Beutler**	N	Y	Y	N	Y	Y
4	**Newhouse**	N	Y	N	N	Y	Y
5	**McMorris Rodgers**	N	Y	N	N	Y	Y
6	Kilmer	Y	N	Y	Y	Y	Y
7	Jayapal	Y	N	Y	Y	Y	Y
8	Schrier	Y	N	Y	Y	Y	Y
9	Smith Adam	Y	N	Y	Y	Y	Y
10	Heck	Y	N	Y	Y	Y	Y
WEST VIRGINIA							
1	**McKinley**	N	Y	N	N	Y	Y
2	**Mooney**	N	Y	N	N	Y	N
3	**Miller**	N	Y	N	N	Y	N
WISCONSIN							
1	**Steil**	N	Y	N	N	Y	Y
2	Pocan	Y	N	Y	Y	Y	Y
3	Kind	Y	N	Y	Y	Y	Y
4	Moore	Y	N	Y	Y	Y	Y
5	**Sensenbrenner**	-	+	-	-	+	+
6	**Grothman**	N	Y	N	N	Y	N
7	**Duffy**						
8	**Gallagher**	N	Y	N	N	Y	Y
WYOMING							
AL	**Cheney**	N	Y	N	N	Y	Y
DELEGATES							
	Radewagen (A.S.)	?					
	Norton (D.C.)	Y					
	San Nicolas (Guam)	?					
	Sablan (N. Marianas)	Y					
	González-Colón (P.R.)	Y					
	Plaskett (V.I.)	Y					

43. HJRES28. Fiscal 2019 Further Continuing Appropriations - Recommit. Granger, R-Texas, motion to recommit the joint resolution to the House Appropriations Committee with instructions to report it back immediately with an amendment that would change the date through which the joint resolution would provide funds for general government operations from Feb. 28 to Jan. 15, 2019. Rejected 195-222: R 189-0; D 6-222. Jan. 17, 2019.

44. HR676. NATO Withdrawal Prohibition - Passage. Engel, D-N.Y., motion to suspend the rules and pass the bill that would prohibit the use of funds to take any action to withdraw the United States from the North Atlantic Treaty Organization, and would express the sense of Congress that the president should not withdraw the U.S. from NATO. Motion agreed to 357-22: R 149-22; D 208-0. *Note: A two-thirds majority of those present and voting (253 in this case) is required for passage under suspension of the rules.* Jan. 22, 2019.

45. HR328. State Department Cybersecurity Programs - Passage. Engel, D-N.Y., motion to suspend the rules and pass the bill that would require the State Department to develop a policy that would provide security searchers with clear guidelines for testing and reporting vulnerabilities in the department's public websites and applications. Motion agreed to 377-3: R 170-3; D 207-0. *Note: A two-thirds majority of those present and voting (254 in this case) is required for passage under suspension of the rules.* Jan. 22, 2019.

46. HJRES28. Fiscal 2019 Further Continuing Appropriations - Passage. Passage of the joint resolution that would make further continuing appropriations for fiscal 2019 through Feb. 28, 2019. Passed 229-184: R 6-183; D 223-1. *Note: A "nay" was a vote in support of the president's position.* Jan. 23, 2019.

47. HR648, HJRES31. Fiscal 2019 Further Continuing Appropriations and Homeland Security Department Continuing Appropriations - Rule. Adoption of the rule (H Res 61) that would provide for House floor consideration of a bill that is comprised of the remaining 2019 appropriations bills, except Homeland Security (HR 648), and a joint resolution that would provide stopgap funding for the Homeland Security Department through Feb. 28 (H J Res 31). The rule would also waive, through the legislative day of Jan. 30 2019, the two-thirds vote requirement to consider legislation on the same day it is reported from the House Rules Committee for appropriations legislation for the fiscal 2019, and would also provide for motions to suspend the rules through the legislative day of Feb. 1, 2019. Adopted 223-190: R 0-189; D 223-1. Jan. 23, 2019.

48. HR648. Fiscal 2019 Further Continuing Appropriations - Recommit. Granger, R-Texas, motion to recommit the bill to the House Appropriations Committee with instructions to report it back immediately with an amendment that would provide back pay for federal employees who have been furloughed or had their pay suspended during the lapse in appropriations that began Dec. 22, 2018. Motion rejected 200-215: R 190-0; D 10-215. Jan. 23, 2019.

		43	44	45	46	47	48
ALABAMA							
1	**Byrne**	Y	Y	Y	N	N	Y
2	**Roby**	Y	Y	Y	N	N	Y
3	**Rogers, M.**	Y	Y	Y	N	N	Y
4	**Aderholt**	Y	Y	Y	N	N	Y
5	**Brooks, M.**	Y	Y	Y	N	N	Y
6	**Palmer**	Y	Y	Y	N	N	Y
7	Sewell	N	Y	Y	Y	Y	N
ALASKA							
AL	**Young**	Y	Y	Y	N	N	?
ARIZONA							
1	O'Halleran	N	Y	Y	Y	Y	N
2	Kirkpatrick	N	Y	Y	Y	Y	N
3	Grijalva	N	Y	Y	Y	Y	N
4	**Gosar**	Y	N	N	N	N	Y
5	**Biggs**	Y	N	N	N	N	Y
6	**Schweikert**	Y	Y	Y	N	N	Y
7	Gallego	N	Y	Y	Y	Y	N
8	**Lesko**	Y	Y	Y	N	N	Y
9	Stanton	N	Y	Y	Y	Y	N
ARKANSAS							
1	**Crawford**	Y	Y	Y	N	N	Y
2	**Hill, F.**	Y	Y	Y	N	N	Y
3	**Womack**	Y	Y	Y	N	N	Y
4	**Westerman**	Y	Y	Y	N	N	Y
CALIFORNIA							
1	**LaMalfa**	Y	Y	Y	N	N	Y
2	Huffman	N	Y	Y	Y	Y	N
3	Garamendi	N	Y	Y	Y	Y	N
4	**McClintock**	Y	N	N	N	N	Y
5	Thompson, M.	N	Y	Y	Y	Y	N
6	Matsui	N	Y	Y	Y	Y	N
7	Bera	N	Y	Y	Y	Y	N
8	**Cook**	Y	Y	Y	N	N	Y
9	McNerney	N	?	?	?	?	?
10	Harder	N	+	+	Y	Y	N
11	DeSaulnier	N	Y	Y	Y	Y	N
12	Pelosi						
13	Lee B.	N	Y	Y	Y	Y	N
14	Speier	N	Y	Y	Y	Y	N
15	Swalwell	N	+	+	Y	Y	N
16	Costa	N	Y	Y	Y	Y	N
17	Khanna	N	Y	Y	Y	Y	N
18	Eshoo	N	Y	Y	Y	Y	N
19	Lofgren	N	Y	Y	Y	Y	N
20	Panetta	N	Y	Y	Y	Y	N
21	Cox	N	Y	Y	Y	Y	N
22	**Nunes**	Y	Y	Y	N	N	Y
23	**McCarthy**	Y	Y	Y	N	N	Y
24	Carbajal	N	Y	Y	Y	Y	N
25	Hill, K.	N	Y	Y	Y	Y	N
26	Brownley	N	Y	Y	Y	Y	N
27	Chu	N	Y	Y	Y	Y	N
28	Schiff	N	Y	Y	Y	Y	N
29	Cárdenas	N	Y	Y	Y	Y	N
30	Sherman	N	Y	Y	Y	Y	N
31	Aguilar	N	Y	Y	Y	Y	N
32	Napolitano	N	Y	Y	Y	Y	N
33	Lieu	N	Y	Y	Y	Y	N
34	Gomez	N	Y	Y	Y	Y	N
35	Torres	N	Y	Y	Y	Y	N
36	Ruiz	N	Y	Y	Y	Y	N
37	Bass	N	?	?	Y	Y	N
38	Sánchez	N	+	+	+	+	-
39	Cisneros	N	Y	Y	Y	Y	N
40	Roybal-Allard	N	Y	Y	Y	Y	N
41	Takano	N	Y	Y	Y	Y	N
42	**Calvert**	Y	Y	Y	N	N	Y
43	Waters	N	Y	Y	Y	Y	N
44	Barragán	N	Y	Y	Y	Y	N
45	Porter	N	+	+	Y	Y	N
46	Correa	N	Y	Y	Y	Y	N
47	Lowenthal	N	Y	Y	Y	Y	N
48	Rouda	N	Y	Y	Y	Y	N
49	Levin	N	Y	Y	Y	Y	N
50	**Hunter**	Y	Y	Y	N	N	Y
51	Vargas	N	?	?	Y	Y	N
52	Peters	N	Y	Y	Y	Y	N

		43	44	45	46	47	48
53	Davis, S.	N	Y	Y	Y	Y	N
COLORADO							
1	DeGette	N	Y	Y	Y	Y	N
2	Neguse	N	Y	Y	Y	Y	N
3	**Tipton**	Y	Y	Y	N	N	Y
4	**Buck**	Y	Y	Y	N	N	Y
5	**Lamborn**	Y	?	?	N	N	Y
6	Crow	N	Y	Y	Y	Y	N
7	Perlmutter	N	Y	Y	Y	Y	N
CONNECTICUT							
1	Larson	N	Y	Y	Y	Y	N
2	Courtney	N	Y	Y	Y	Y	N
3	DeLauro	N	+	+	+	+	-
4	Himes	N	Y	Y	Y	Y	-
5	Hayes	N	Y	Y	Y	Y	N
DELAWARE							
AL	Blunt Rochester	N	Y	Y	Y	Y	N
FLORIDA							
1	**Gaetz**	?	N	Y	N	N	Y
2	**Dunn**	Y	Y	Y	N	N	Y
3	**Yoho**	Y	?	?	N	N	Y
4	**Rutherford**	Y	Y	Y	N	N	Y
5	Lawson	N	Y	Y	Y	Y	N
6	**Waltz**	Y	Y	Y	N	N	Y
7	Murphy	N	Y	Y	Y	Y	N
8	**Posey**	Y	Y	Y	N	N	Y
9	Soto	N	Y	Y	Y	Y	N
10	Demings	N	Y	Y	Y	Y	N
11	**Webster**	Y	Y	Y	N	N	Y
12	**Bilirakis**	Y	Y	Y	N	N	Y
13	Crist	N	Y	Y	Y	Y	N
14	Castor	N	Y	Y	Y	Y	N
15	**Spano**	Y	Y	Y	N	N	Y
16	**Buchanan**	Y	?	?	N	N	Y
17	**Steube**	Y	N	N	N	N	Y
18	**Mast**	?	Y	Y	N	N	Y
19	**Rooney**	?	?	?	?	?	?
20	Hastings	N	Y	Y	?	?	N
21	Frankel	N	Y	Y	Y	Y	N
22	Deutch	N	Y	Y	Y	Y	N
23	Wasserman Schultz	N	Y	Y	Y	Y	N
24	Wilson, F.	?	?	?	?	?	?
25	**Diaz-Balart**	Y	Y	Y	N	N	Y
26	Mucarsel-Powell	N	Y	Y	Y	Y	N
27	Shalala	N	Y	Y	Y	Y	N
GEORGIA							
1	**Carter, E.L.**	Y	Y	Y	N	N	Y
2	Bishop, S.	N	Y	Y	Y	Y	N
3	**Ferguson**	Y	Y	Y	N	N	Y
4	Johnson, H.	N	Y	Y	Y	Y	N
5	Lewis John	N	Y	Y	Y	Y	N
6	McBath	N	Y	Y	Y	Y	N
7	**Woodall**	Y	?	?	N	N	Y
8	**Scott, A.**	Y	Y	Y	N	N	Y
9	**Collins, D.**	Y	Y	Y	N	N	Y
10	**Hice**	Y	N	N	N	N	Y
11	**Loudermilk**	?	Y	Y	N	N	Y
12	**Allen**	Y	N	N	N	N	Y
13	Scott, D.	N	Y	Y	Y	Y	N
14	**Graves, T.**	Y	Y	Y	N	N	Y
HAWAII							
1	Case	N	Y	Y	Y	Y	N
2	Gabbard	N	?	?	Y	Y	N
IDAHO							
1	**Fulcher**	Y	N	N	N	N	Y
2	**Simpson**	Y	Y	Y	N	N	Y
ILLINOIS							
1	Rush	?	?	?	Y	Y	N
2	Kelly, R.	N	Y	Y	Y	Y	N
3	Lipinski	N	?	?	Y	Y	N
4	García, J.	N	Y	Y	Y	Y	N
5	Quigley	N	Y	Y	Y	Y	N
6	Casten	N	Y	Y	Y	Y	N
7	Davis, D.	N	Y	Y	Y	Y	N
8	Krishnamoorthi	N	Y	Y	Y	Y	N
9	Schakowsky	N	+	+	Y	Y	N
10	Schneider	N	Y	Y	Y	Y	N
11	Foster	N	Y	Y	Y	Y	N

KEY:		**Republicans**		Democrats		*Independents*	
Y Voted for (yea)		**N** Voted against (nay)		**P** Voted "present"			
+ Announced for		**-** Announced against		**?** Did not vote or otherwise make position known			
# Paired for		**X** Paired against					

*NOTE: (Pennsylvania 12) Rep. Tom Marino resigned on Jan. 23. The last roll call vote he was eligible to cast was vote 45.

		43	44	45	46	47	48
12	**Bost**	Y	Y	Y	N	N	Y
13	**Davis, R.**	Y	Y	Y	N	N	Y
14	Underwood	N	Y	Y	Y	Y	N
15	**Shimkus**	Y	?	?	N	N	Y
16	**Kinzinger**	Y	Y	Y	N	N	Y
17	Bustos	N	Y	Y	Y	Y	N
18	**LaHood**	Y	Y	Y	N	N	Y
INDIANA							
1	Visclosky	N	Y	Y	Y	Y	N
2	**Walorski**	Y	Y	Y	N	N	Y
3	**Banks**	Y	Y	Y	N	N	Y
4	**Baird**	Y	+	Y	N	N	Y
5	**Brooks, S.**	Y	Y	Y	N	N	Y
6	**Pence**	Y	Y	Y	N	N	Y
7	Carson	N	Y	Y	Y	Y	N
8	**Bucshon**	Y	?	?	N	N	Y
9	**Hollingsworth**	Y	?	?	N	N	Y
IOWA							
1	Finkenauer	N	Y	Y	Y	Y	N
2	Loebsack	N	+	+	Y	Y	N
3	Axne	N	Y	Y	Y	N	N
4	**King, S.**	Y	Y	Y	N	N	Y
KANSAS							
1	**Marshall**	Y	Y	Y	N	N	Y
2	**Watkins**	Y	Y	Y	N	N	Y
3	Davids	N	Y	Y	Y	Y	Y
4	**Estes**	Y	+	+	N	N	Y
KENTUCKY							
1	**Comer**	Y	Y	Y	N	N	Y
2	**Guthrie**	Y	Y	Y	N	N	Y
3	Yarmuth	N	Y	Y	Y	Y	N
4	**Massie**	?	N	N	N	N	Y
5	**Rogers, H.**	Y	Y	Y	N	N	Y
6	**Barr**	Y	?	?	N	N	Y
LOUISIANA							
1	**Scalise**	Y	Y	Y	N	N	Y
2	Richmond	N	Y	Y	Y	Y	N
3	**Higgins, C.**	Y	Y	Y	N	N	Y
4	**Johnson, M.**	+	Y	Y	N	N	Y
5	**Abraham**	Y	?	?	?	?	?
6	**Graves, G.**	Y	Y	Y	N	N	Y
MAINE							
1	Pingree	N	Y	Y	Y	Y	N
2	Golden	N	Y	Y	Y	Y	Y
MARYLAND							
1	**Harris**	Y	N	Y	N	N	Y
2	Ruppersberger	N	Y	Y	Y	Y	N
3	Sarbanes	N	Y	Y	Y	Y	N
4	Brown, A.	N	Y	Y	Y	Y	N
5	Hoyer	N	Y	Y	Y	Y	N
6	Trone	N	Y	Y	Y	Y	N
7	Cummings	N	Y	Y	Y	Y	N
8	Raskin	N	Y	Y	Y	Y	N
MASSACHUSETTS							
1	Neal	N	?	?	?	?	?
2	McGovern	N	+	+	Y	Y	N
3	Trahan	N	Y	Y	Y	Y	N
4	Kennedy	N	Y	Y	Y	Y	N
5	Clark	N	Y	Y	Y	Y	N
6	Moulton	Y	?	?	Y	Y	N
7	Pressley	N	Y	Y	Y	Y	N
8	Lynch	N	Y	Y	Y	Y	N
9	Keating	N	Y	Y	Y	Y	N
MICHIGAN							
1	**Bergman**	Y	Y	Y	N	N	Y
2	**Huizenga**	Y	Y	Y	N	N	Y
3	**Amash**	Y	N	N	N	N	Y
4	**Moolenaar**	Y	Y	Y	N	N	Y
5	Kildee	N	Y	Y	Y	Y	N
6	**Upton**	Y	Y	Y	N	N	Y
7	**Walberg**	Y	Y	Y	N	N	Y
8	Slotkin	N	Y	Y	Y	Y	N
9	Levin	N	Y	Y	Y	Y	N
10	**Mitchell**	Y	Y	Y	N	N	Y
11	Stevens	N	Y	Y	Y	Y	N
12	Dingell	N	?	?	Y	Y	N
13	Tlaib	N	Y	Y	Y	Y	N
14	Lawrence	N	Y	Y	Y	Y	N
MINNESOTA							
1	**Hagedorn**	Y	Y	Y	N	N	Y
2	Craig	N	Y	Y	Y	Y	N
3	Phillips	N	Y	Y	Y	Y	N
4	McCollum	N	Y	Y	Y	Y	N
5	Omar	N	Y	Y	Y	Y	N

		43	44	45	46	47	48
6	**Emmer**	Y	Y	Y	N	N	Y
7	Peterson	N	Y	Y	Y	Y	N
8	**Stauber**	Y	Y	Y	N	N	Y
MISSISSIPPI							
1	**Kelly, T.**	Y	Y	Y	N	N	Y
2	Thompson, B.	N	Y	Y	Y	Y	N
3	**Guest**	Y	Y	Y	N	N	Y
4	**Palazzo**	Y	Y	Y	N	N	Y
MISSOURI							
1	Clay	N	Y	Y	Y	Y	N
2	**Wagner**	Y	Y	Y	N	N	Y
3	**Luetkemeyer**	Y	Y	Y	N	N	Y
4	**Hartzler**	Y	+	+	-	-	+
5	Cleaver	N	Y	Y	Y	Y	N
6	**Graves, S.**	Y	Y	Y	N	N	Y
7	**Long**	Y	Y	Y	N	N	Y
8	**Smith, J.**	Y	Y	Y	N	N	Y
MONTANA							
AL	**Gianforte**	Y	Y	Y	N	N	Y
NEBRASKA							
1	**Fortenberry**	Y	Y	Y	N	N	Y
2	**Bacon**	Y	Y	Y	N	N	Y
3	**Smith, Adrian**	Y	Y	Y	N	N	Y
NEVADA							
1	Titus	N	Y	Y	Y	Y	N
2	**Amodei**	Y	Y	Y	N	N	Y
3	Lee	N	Y	Y	Y	Y	N
4	Horsford	N	Y	Y	Y	Y	N
NEW HAMPSHIRE							
1	Pappas	N	Y	Y	Y	Y	N
2	Kuster	N	Y	Y	Y	Y	N
NEW JERSEY							
1	Norcross	N	Y	Y	Y	Y	N
2	Van Drew	Y	Y	Y	Y	Y	Y
3	Kim	N	Y	Y	Y	Y	N
4	**Smith, C.**	Y	Y	Y	Y	N	Y
5	Gottheimer	Y	Y	Y	Y	Y	Y
6	Pallone	N	Y	Y	Y	Y	N
7	Malinowski	N	Y	Y	Y	Y	N
8	Sires	N	Y	Y	Y	Y	N
9	Pascrell	N	Y	Y	Y	Y	N
10	Payne	?	?	?	?	?	?
11	Sherrill	N	Y	Y	Y	Y	N
12	Watson Coleman	N	Y	Y	Y	Y	N
NEW MEXICO							
1	Haaland	N	Y	Y	Y	Y	N
2	Torres Small	N	Y	Y	Y	Y	Y
3	Luján	N	Y	Y	Y	Y	N
NEW YORK							
1	**Zeldin**	Y	Y	Y	N	N	Y
2	**King, P.**	Y	?	?	N	N	Y
3	Suozzi	N	Y	Y	Y	Y	N
4	Rice, K.	N	Y	Y	Y	Y	N
5	Meeks	N	Y	Y	Y	Y	N
6	Meng	?	Y	Y	Y	Y	N
7	Velázquez	N	?	?	?	?	?
8	Jeffries	N	Y	Y	Y	Y	N
9	Clarke	N	Y	Y	Y	Y	N
10	Nadler	N	Y	Y	Y	Y	N
11	Rose	Y	Y	Y	Y	Y	Y
12	Maloney, C.	N	Y	Y	Y	Y	N
13	Espaillat	N	Y	Y	Y	Y	N
14	Ocasio-Cortez	N	Y	Y	N	Y	N
15	Serrano	N	Y	Y	Y	Y	N
16	Engel	N	Y	Y	Y	Y	N
17	Lowey	N	Y	Y	Y	Y	N
18	Maloney, S.P.	N	Y	Y	Y	Y	N
19	Delgado	N	Y	Y	Y	Y	Y
20	Tonko	N	Y	Y	Y	Y	N
21	**Stefanik**	Y	Y	Y	Y	N	Y
22	Brindisi	N	Y	Y	Y	Y	N
23	**Reed**	Y	Y	Y	N	N	Y
24	**Katko**	Y	Y	Y	Y	N	Y
25	Morelle	N	Y	Y	Y	Y	N
26	Higgins, B.	N	Y	Y	Y	Y	N
27	**Collins, C.**	Y	+	+	N	N	Y
NORTH CAROLINA							
1	Butterfield	N	Y	Y	Y	Y	N
2	**Holding**	Y	Y	Y	N	N	Y
3	**Jones**	?	?	?	?	?	?
4	Price	N	Y	Y	Y	Y	N
5	**Foxx**	Y	Y	Y	N	N	Y
6	**Walker**	?	Y	Y	N	N	Y
7	**Rouzer**	Y	Y	Y	N	N	Y

		43	44	45	46	47	48
8	**Hudson**	Y	+	+	N	N	Y
9	vacant						
10	**McHenry**	Y	Y	Y	N	N	Y
11	**Meadows**	Y	N	Y	N	N	Y
12	Adams	N	Y	Y	Y	Y	N
13	**Budd**	Y	?	?	N	N	Y
NORTH DAKOTA							
AL	**Armstrong**	Y	Y	Y	N	N	Y
OHIO							
1	**Chabot**	Y	Y	Y	N	N	Y
2	**Wenstrup**	Y	Y	Y	N	N	Y
3	Beatty	N	Y	Y	Y	Y	N
4	**Jordan**	Y	N	Y	N	N	Y
5	**Latta**	Y	Y	Y	N	N	Y
6	**Johnson, B.**	Y	Y	Y	N	N	Y
7	**Gibbs**	Y	+	+	-	-	+
8	**Davidson**	Y	Y	Y	N	N	Y
9	Kaptur	N	Y	Y	Y	Y	N
10	**Turner**	Y	Y	Y	N	N	Y
11	Fudge	N	?	?	Y	Y	N
12	**Balderson**	Y	Y	Y	N	N	Y
13	Ryan	N	Y	Y	Y	Y	N
14	**Joyce**	Y	Y	Y	N	N	Y
15	**Stivers**	Y	Y	Y	N	N	Y
16	**Gonzalez**	Y	Y	Y	N	N	Y
OKLAHOMA							
1	**Hern**	Y	Y	Y	N	N	Y
2	**Mullin**	Y	Y	Y	N	N	Y
3	**Lucas**	Y	Y	Y	N	N	Y
4	**Cole**	Y	Y	Y	N	N	Y
5	Horn	N	Y	Y	Y	Y	N
OREGON							
1	Bonamici	N	Y	Y	Y	Y	N
2	**Walden**	Y	+	+	N	N	Y
3	Blumenauer	N	Y	Y	Y	Y	N
4	DeFazio	N	?	?	Y	Y	N
5	Schrader	N	Y	Y	Y	Y	N
PENNSYLVANIA							
1	**Fitzpatrick**	Y	Y	Y	Y	N	Y
2	Boyle	N	Y	Y	Y	Y	N
3	Evans	N	Y	Y	Y	Y	N
4	Dean	N	Y	Y	Y	Y	N
5	Scanlon	N	Y	Y	Y	Y	N
6	Houlahan	N	Y	Y	Y	Y	N
7	Wild	N	Y	Y	Y	Y	N
8	Cartwright	N	?	?	?	?	?
9	**Meuser**	Y	Y	Y	N	N	Y
10	**Perry**	Y	N	Y	-	-	Y
11	**Smucker**	Y	Y	Y	N	N	Y
12	**Marino***	?	?	?			
13	**Joyce**	Y	Y	Y	N	N	Y
14	**Reschenthaler**	Y	Y	Y	N	N	Y
15	**Thompson, G.**	Y	Y	Y	N	N	Y
16	**Kelly, M.**	Y	Y	Y	N	N	Y
17	Lamb	Y	Y	Y	Y	Y	Y
18	Doyle	?	Y	Y	Y	Y	N
RHODE ISLAND							
1	Cicilline	N	Y	Y	Y	Y	N
2	Langevin	N	Y	Y	Y	Y	N
SOUTH CAROLINA							
1	Cunningham	Y	Y	Y	Y	Y	Y
2	**Wilson, J.**	Y	Y	Y	N	N	Y
3	**Duncan**	Y	Y	Y	N	N	Y
4	**Timmons**	Y	Y	Y	N	N	Y
5	**Norman**	Y	Y	Y	N	N	Y
6	Clyburn	N	Y	Y	Y	Y	N
7	**Rice, T.**	Y	Y	Y	N	N	Y
SOUTH DAKOTA							
AL	**Johnson**	Y	?	Y	N	N	Y
TENNESSEE							
1	**Roe**	Y	Y	Y	N	N	Y
2	**Burchett**	Y	N	Y	N	N	Y
3	**Fleischmann**	Y	Y	Y	N	N	Y
4	**DesJarlais**	Y	N	Y	N	N	Y
5	Cooper	N	Y	Y	Y	Y	N
6	**Rose**	Y	N	Y	N	N	Y
7	**Green**	Y	Y	Y	N	N	Y
8	**Kustoff**	Y	Y	Y	N	N	Y
9	Cohen	N	Y	Y	Y	Y	N
TEXAS							
1	**Gohmert**	Y	N	Y	N	N	Y
2	**Crenshaw**	Y	Y	Y	N	N	Y
3	**Taylor**	Y	Y	Y	N	N	Y
4	**Ratcliffe**	Y	Y	Y	N	N	Y

		43	44	45	46	47	48
5	**Gooden**	Y	Y	Y	N	N	Y
6	**Wright**	Y	?	?	?	?	?
7	Fletcher	N	Y	Y	Y	Y	N
8	**Brady**	Y	Y	Y	N	N	Y
9	Green, A.	N	Y	Y	Y	Y	N
10	**McCaul**	Y	Y	Y	N	N	Y
11	**Conaway**	Y	Y	Y	N	N	Y
12	**Granger**	Y	Y	Y	N	N	Y
13	**Thornberry**	Y	Y	Y	N	N	Y
14	**Weber**	Y	N	Y	N	N	Y
15	Gonzalez	N	+	+	Y	Y	N
16	Escobar	N	Y	Y	Y	Y	N
17	**Flores**	Y	Y	Y	N	N	Y
18	Jackson Lee	N	Y	Y	Y	Y	N
19	**Arrington**	Y	?	?	N	N	Y
20	Castro	N	Y	Y	Y	Y	N
21	**Roy**	Y	N	Y	N	N	Y
22	**Olson**	Y	Y	Y	N	N	Y
23	**Hurd**	Y	Y	Y	Y	N	Y
24	**Marchant**	Y	?	?	N	N	Y
25	**Williams**	Y	Y	Y	N	N	Y
26	**Burgess**	Y	?	?	N	N	Y
27	**Cloud**	Y	Y	Y	N	N	Y
28	Cuellar	N	Y	Y	Y	Y	N
29	Garcia, S.	N	Y	Y	Y	Y	N
30	Johnson, E.B.	N	Y	Y	Y	Y	N
31	**Carter, J.**	Y	Y	Y	N	N	Y
32	Allred	N	Y	Y	Y	Y	N
33	Veasey	N	Y	Y	Y	Y	N
34	Vela	N	Y	Y	Y	Y	N
35	Doggett	N	Y	?	Y	Y	N
36	**Babin**	Y	Y	Y	N	N	Y
UTAH							
1	**Bishop, R.**	Y	Y	Y	N	N	Y
2	**Stewart**	Y	Y	Y	N	N	Y
3	**Curtis**	Y	Y	Y	N	N	Y
4	McAdams	N	Y	Y	Y	Y	Y
VERMONT							
AL	Welch	N	Y	Y	Y	Y	N
VIRGINIA							
1	**Wittman**	Y	Y	Y	N	N	Y
2	Luria	N	Y	Y	Y	Y	N
3	Scott, R.	N	Y	Y	Y	Y	N
4	McEachin	-	Y	Y	Y	Y	N
5	**Riggleman**	Y	Y	Y	N	N	Y
6	**Cline**	Y	N	Y	N	N	Y
7	Spanberger	N	Y	Y	Y	Y	N
8	Beyer	N	Y	Y	Y	Y	N
9	**Griffith**	Y	N	Y	N	N	Y
10	Wexton	N	Y	Y	Y	Y	N
11	Connolly	N	Y	Y	Y	Y	N
WASHINGTON							
1	DelBene	N	Y	Y	Y	Y	N
2	Larsen	N	Y	Y	Y	Y	N
3	**Herrera Beutler**	Y	Y	Y	Y	N	Y
4	**Newhouse**	Y	Y	Y	N	N	Y
5	**McMorris Rodgers**	Y	Y	Y	N	N	Y
6	Kilmer	N	Y	Y	Y	Y	N
7	Jayapal	N	Y	Y	Y	Y	N
8	Schrier	N	Y	Y	Y	Y	N
9	Smith Adam	N	Y	Y	Y	Y	N
10	Heck	N	Y	Y	Y	Y	N
WEST VIRGINIA							
1	**McKinley**	Y	Y	Y	N	N	Y
2	**Mooney**	Y	Y	Y	N	N	Y
3	**Miller**	Y	Y	Y	N	N	Y
WISCONSIN							
1	**Steil**	Y	Y	Y	N	N	Y
2	Pocan	N	+	+	Y	Y	N
3	Kind	N	+	+	?	?	N
4	Moore	N	Y	Y	Y	Y	N
5	**Sensenbrenner**	+	+	+	-	-	+
6	**Grothman**	Y	Y	Y	N	N	Y
7	**Duffy**						
8	**Gallagher**	Y	Y	Y	N	N	Y
WYOMING							
AL	**Cheney**	Y	Y	Y	N	N	Y
DELEGATES							
	Radewagen (A.S.)						
	Norton (D.C.)						
	San Nicolas (Guam)						
	Sablan (N. Marianas)						
	González-Colón (P.R.)						
	Plaskett (V.I.)						

⦀ HOUSE VOTES

49. HR648. Fiscal 2019 Further Continuing Appropriations - Passage. Passage of the bill that would provide $271.8 billion for full-year fiscal 2019 funding for six of the seven spending bills that reached a conference agreement, but that lack enacted appropriations (all except Homeland Security) and would extend authorization for several expiring programs including the National Flood Insurance Program and the Temporary Assistance for Needy Families. Passed 234-180: R 10-179; D 224-1. *Note: A "nay" was a vote in support of the president's position.* Jan. 23, 2019.

50. HJRES31. Homeland Security Department Continuing Appropriations - Recommit. Granger, R-Texas, motion to recommit the joint resolution to the House Appropriations Committee with instructions to report it back immediately with an amendment that would provide stopgap fiscal 2019 funding for the Homeland Security Department through Jan. 24. Motion rejected 200-214: R 187-0; D 13-214. Jan. 24, 2019.

51. HJRES31. Homeland Security Department Continuing Appropriations - Passage. Passage of the joint resolution that would provide stopgap fiscal 2019 funding for the Homeland Security Department through Feb. 28, 2019. Passed 231-180: R 5-179; D 226-1. *Note: A "nay" was a vote in support of the president's position.* Jan. 24, 2019.

52. HR624. Executive Trading Plan Regulation - Passage. Himes, D-Conn., motion to suspend the rules and pass the bill that would require the Securities and Exchange Commission to conduct a study of Rule 10b5-1, and specifically evaluate whether the rule should be changed to limit the ability of company executives to participate in trading plans that buy or sell company stock, and to limit the time period(s) in which such executives could participate in such trading. Motion rejected 413-3: R 189-3; D 224-0. *Note: A two-thirds majority of those present and voting (278 in this case) is required for passage under suspension of the rules.* Jan. 28, 2019.

53. HR502. Virtual Currency Use In Criminal Activities - Passage. Waters, D-Calif., motion to suspend the rules and pass the bill that would require the Government Accountability Office to study how online marketplaces and virtual currencies are used to buy, sell, or facilitate sex or drug trafficking. Specifically the bill would require that the GAO report on the methods used to repatriate such funds back into the conventional banking system. Motion agreed to 412-3: R 188-3; D 224-0. *Note: A two-thirds majority of those present and voting (277 in this case) is required for passage under suspension of the rules.* Jan. 28, 2019.

54. Procedural Motion - Journal. Approval of the House Journal of Jan. 25, 2019. Approved 234-170: R 58-130; D 176-40. Jan. 28, 2019.

		49	50	51	52	53	54
ALABAMA							
1	**Byrne**	N	Y	N	Y	Y	N
2	**Roby**	N	Y	N	+	+	+
3	**Rogers, M.**	N	?	?	Y	Y	N
4	**Aderholt**	N	Y	N	Y	Y	N
5	**Brooks, M.**	N	Y	N	Y	Y	N
6	**Palmer**	N	Y	N	Y	Y	N
7	Sewell	Y	N	Y	Y	Y	Y
ALASKA							
AL	**Young**	?	?	?	Y	Y	N
ARIZONA							
1	O'Halleran	Y	N	Y	Y	Y	N
2	Kirkpatrick	Y	N	Y	Y	Y	N
3	Grijalva	Y	N	Y	Y	Y	Y
4	**Gosar**	N	Y	N	Y	Y	N
5	**Biggs**	N	Y	N	N	Y	N
6	**Schweikert**	N	Y	N	Y	Y	Y
7	Gallego	Y	N	Y	Y	Y	Y
8	**Lesko**	N	Y	N	Y	Y	Y
9	Stanton	Y	N	Y	Y	Y	Y
ARKANSAS							
1	**Crawford**	N	Y	N	Y	Y	N
2	**Hill, F.**	N	Y	N	Y	Y	N
3	**Womack**	N	Y	N	Y	Y	N
4	**Westerman**	N	Y	N	Y	Y	N
CALIFORNIA							
1	**LaMalfa**	N	Y	N	Y	Y	N
2	Huffman	Y	N	Y	Y	Y	Y
3	Garamendi	Y	N	Y	Y	Y	Y
4	**McClintock**	N	Y	N	Y	Y	Y
5	Thompson, M.	Y	N	Y	Y	Y	N
6	Matsui	Y	N	Y	Y	Y	Y
7	Bera	Y	N	Y	Y	Y	Y
8	**Cook**	N	Y	N	Y	Y	N
9	McNerney	?	?	?	Y	Y	Y
10	Harder	Y	N	Y	Y	Y	?
11	DeSaulnier	Y	N	Y	Y	Y	Y
12	Pelosi						
13	Lee B.	Y	N	Y	Y	Y	Y
14	Speier	Y	N	Y	Y	Y	Y
15	Swalwell	Y	N	Y	Y	Y	Y
16	Costa	Y	N	Y	Y	Y	N
17	Khanna	Y	N	Y	Y	Y	Y
18	Eshoo	Y	N	Y	Y	Y	Y
19	Lofgren	Y	N	Y	Y	Y	Y
20	Panetta	Y	N	Y	Y	Y	N
21	Cox	Y	N	Y	Y	Y	Y
22	**Nunes**	N	Y	N	Y	Y	Y
23	**McCarthy**	N	Y	N	Y	Y	Y
24	Carbajal	Y	N	Y	Y	Y	Y
25	Hill, K.	Y	N	Y	Y	Y	Y
26	Brownley	Y	N	Y	Y	Y	N
27	Chu	Y	N	Y	Y	Y	Y
28	Schiff	Y	N	Y	Y	Y	Y
29	Cárdenas	Y	N	Y	+	Y	Y
30	Sherman	Y	N	Y	Y	Y	Y
31	Aguilar	Y	N	Y	Y	Y	N
32	Napolitano	Y	N	Y	Y	Y	Y
33	Lieu	Y	N	Y	Y	Y	Y
34	Gomez	Y	N	Y	Y	Y	Y
35	Torres	Y	N	Y	Y	Y	Y
36	Ruiz	Y	N	Y	Y	Y	N
37	Bass	Y	N	Y	?	?	?
38	Sánchez	+	N	Y	Y	Y	Y
39	Cisneros	Y	N	Y	Y	Y	N
40	Roybal-Allard	Y	N	Y	Y	Y	Y
41	Takano	Y	N	Y	Y	Y	Y
42	**Calvert**	N	Y	N	Y	Y	N
43	Waters	Y	N	Y	Y	Y	N
44	Barragán	Y	N	Y	Y	Y	Y
45	Porter	Y	N	Y	+	+	+
46	Correa	Y	N	Y	Y	Y	Y
47	Lowenthal	Y	N	Y	Y	Y	Y
48	Rouda	Y	N	Y	Y	Y	Y
49	Levin	Y	N	Y	Y	Y	Y
50	**Hunter**	N	Y	N	Y	Y	N
51	Vargas	Y	N	Y	Y	Y	Y
52	Peters	Y	N	Y	Y	Y	Y

		49	50	51	52	53	54
53	Davis, S.	Y	N	Y	Y	Y	Y
COLORADO							
1	DeGette	Y	N	Y	Y	Y	Y
2	Neguse	Y	N	Y	Y	Y	Y
3	**Tipton**	N	Y	N	?	?	?
4	**Buck**	N	Y	N	Y	Y	Y
5	**Lamborn**	N	Y	N	Y	Y	N
6	Crow	Y	N	Y	Y	Y	N
7	Perlmutter	Y	N	Y	Y	Y	Y
CONNECTICUT							
1	Larson	Y	N	Y	Y	Y	Y
2	Courtney	Y	N	Y	Y	Y	Y
3	DeLauro	+	N	Y	Y	Y	Y
4	Himes	+	-	+	Y	Y	Y
5	Hayes	Y	N	Y	Y	Y	Y
DELAWARE							
AL	Blunt Rochester	Y	N	Y	Y	Y	Y
FLORIDA							
1	**Gaetz**	N	Y	?	Y	N	N
2	**Dunn**	N	Y	N	Y	Y	N
3	**Yoho**	N	Y	N	Y	Y	N
4	**Rutherford**	N	Y	N	Y	Y	Y
5	Lawson	Y	N	Y	Y	Y	Y
6	**Waltz**	N	Y	N	Y	Y	Y
7	Murphy	Y	N	Y	Y	Y	Y
8	**Posey**	N	Y	N	Y	Y	Y
9	Soto	Y	N	Y	Y	Y	Y
10	Demings	Y	N	Y	Y	Y	Y
11	**Webster**	N	Y	N	Y	Y	Y
12	**Bilirakis**	N	Y	N	Y	Y	Y
13	Crist	Y	N	Y	Y	Y	Y
14	Castor	Y	N	Y	Y	Y	Y
15	**Spano**	N	Y	N	Y	Y	Y
16	**Buchanan**	N	Y	N	Y	Y	Y
17	**Steube**	N	Y	N	Y	Y	N
18	**Mast**	N	Y	N	Y	Y	N
19	**Rooney**	?	?	?	Y	Y	N
20	Hastings	Y	N	Y	Y	Y	Y
21	Frankel	Y	N	Y	+	+	+
22	Deutch	Y	N	Y	Y	Y	Y
23	Wasserman Schultz	Y	N	Y	Y	Y	Y
24	Wilson, F.	?	?	?	?	?	?
25	**Diaz-Balart**	N	Y	N	Y	Y	N
26	Mucarsel-Powell	Y	N	Y	Y	Y	Y
27	Shalala	Y	N	Y	Y	Y	Y
GEORGIA							
1	**Carter, E.L.**	N	Y	N	Y	Y	N
2	Bishop, S.	Y	N	Y	Y	Y	Y
3	**Ferguson**	N	Y	N	Y	Y	N
4	Johnson, H.	Y	N	Y	Y	Y	Y
5	Lewis John	Y	N	Y	Y	Y	Y
6	McBath	Y	N	Y	Y	Y	?
7	**Woodall**	N	Y	N	Y	Y	Y
8	**Scott, A.**	N	Y	N	Y	Y	Y
9	**Collins, D.**	N	Y	N	Y	Y	Y
10	**Hice**	N	Y	N	Y	Y	N
11	**Loudermilk**	N	Y	N	Y	Y	Y
12	**Allen**	N	Y	N	Y	Y	Y
13	Scott, D.	Y	N	Y	Y	Y	Y
14	**Graves, T.**	N	Y	N	Y	Y	N
HAWAII							
1	Case	Y	N	Y	Y	?	Y
2	Gabbard	Y	N	Y	Y	Y	Y
IDAHO							
1	**Fulcher**	N	Y	N	Y	Y	N
2	**Simpson**	Y	Y	N	Y	Y	Y
ILLINOIS							
1	Rush	Y	N	Y	?	?	?
2	Kelly, R.	Y	N	Y	Y	Y	Y
3	Lipinski	Y	N	Y	Y	Y	Y
4	García, J.	Y	N	Y	Y	Y	Y
5	Quigley	Y	N	Y	Y	Y	Y
6	Casten	Y	N	Y	Y	Y	N
7	Davis, D.	Y	N	Y	?	?	?
8	Krishnamoorthi	Y	N	Y	Y	Y	Y
9	Schakowsky	Y	N	Y	Y	Y	Y
10	Schneider	Y	N	Y	Y	Y	Y
11	Foster	Y	N	Y	Y	Y	?

KEY:	**Republicans**	Democrats	*Independents*

Y	Voted for (yea)	N	Voted against (nay)	P	Voted "present"
+	Announced for	-	Announced against	?	Did not vote or otherwise make position known
#	Paired for	X	Paired against		

		49	50	51	52	53	54
12	**Bost**	N	Y	N	Y	Y	N
13	**Davis, R.**	N	Y	N	Y	Y	N
14	Underwood	Y	N	Y	Y	Y	Y
15	**Shimkus**	N	Y	N	Y	Y	N
16	**Kinzinger**	Y	Y	N	Y	Y	Y
17	Bustos	Y	N	Y	Y	Y	Y
18	**LaHood**	N	+	-	Y	Y	N
INDIANA							
1	Visclosky	Y	N	Y	Y	Y	Y
2	**Walorski**	N	Y	N	Y	Y	Y
3	**Banks**	N	Y	N	Y	Y	Y
4	**Baird**	N	Y	N	Y	Y	Y
5	**Brooks, S.**	N	Y	N	Y	Y	Y
6	**Pence**	N	Y	N	Y	Y	Y
7	Carson	Y	N	Y	Y	Y	Y
8	**Bucshon**	N	Y	N	Y	Y	N
9	**Hollingsworth**	N	Y	N	Y	Y	Y
IOWA							
1	Finkenauer	Y	N	Y	Y	Y	Y
2	Loebsack	Y	N	Y	Y	Y	Y
3	Axne	Y	N	Y	Y	Y	Y
4	**King, S.**	N	Y	N	Y	Y	N
KANSAS							
1	**Marshall**	N	?	?	Y	Y	N
2	**Watkins**	N	Y	N	Y	Y	Y
3	Davids	Y	Y	Y	Y	Y	N
4	**Estes**	N	Y	N	Y	Y	N
KENTUCKY							
1	**Comer**	N	Y	N	Y	Y	Y
2	**Guthrie**	N	Y	N	Y	Y	N
3	Yarmuth	Y	N	Y	Y	Y	Y
4	**Massie**	N	Y	N	N	N	N
5	**Rogers, H.**	N	Y	N	Y	Y	N
6	**Barr**	N	Y	N	Y	Y	Y
LOUISIANA							
1	**Scalise**	N	Y	N	Y	Y	N
2	Richmond	Y	N	Y	?	?	?
3	**Higgins, C.**	N	Y	N	Y	Y	Y
4	**Johnson, M.**	N	Y	N	Y	Y	N
5	**Abraham**	?	?	?	Y	Y	N
6	**Graves, G.**	N	Y	N	Y	Y	N
MAINE							
1	Pingree	Y	N	Y	Y	Y	Y
2	Golden	Y	Y	Y	Y	Y	N
MARYLAND							
1	**Harris**	N	Y	N	Y	Y	N
2	Ruppersberger	Y	N	Y	Y	Y	Y
3	Sarbanes	Y	N	Y	Y	Y	Y
4	Brown, A.	Y	N	Y	Y	Y	Y
5	Hoyer	Y	N	Y	Y	Y	Y
6	Trone	Y	N	Y	Y	Y	Y
7	Cummings	Y	N	Y	Y	Y	Y
8	Raskin	Y	N	Y	Y	Y	Y
MASSACHUSETTS							
1	Neal	?	N	Y	Y	Y	Y
2	McGovern	Y	N	Y	Y	Y	Y
3	Trahan	Y	N	Y	Y	Y	Y
4	Kennedy	Y	N	Y	Y	Y	Y
5	Clark	Y	N	Y	Y	Y	Y
6	Moulton	Y	N	Y	Y	Y	N
7	Pressley	Y	N	Y	Y	Y	?
8	Lynch	Y	N	Y	Y	Y	Y
9	Keating	Y	N	Y	Y	Y	N
MICHIGAN							
1	**Bergman**	N	Y	N	Y	Y	Y
2	**Huizenga**	N	Y	N	Y	Y	N
3	**Amash**	N	Y	N	N	N	N
4	**Moolenaar**	N	Y	N	Y	Y	N
5	Kildee	Y	N	Y	Y	Y	Y
6	**Upton**	Y	Y	N	Y	Y	N
7	**Walberg**	N	Y	N	Y	Y	N
8	Slotkin	Y	N	Y	Y	Y	Y
9	Levin	Y	N	Y	Y	Y	Y
10	**Mitchell**	N	Y	N	Y	Y	N
11	Stevens	Y	N	Y	Y	Y	Y
12	Dingell	Y	N	Y	Y	Y	Y
13	Tlaib	Y	N	Y	Y	Y	Y
14	Lawrence	Y	N	Y	Y	Y	Y
MINNESOTA							
1	**Hagedorn**	N	Y	N	Y	Y	N
2	Craig	Y	N	Y	Y	Y	Y
3	Phillips	Y	N	Y	Y	Y	Y
4	McCollum	Y	N	Y	Y	Y	Y
5	Omar	Y	N	Y	Y	Y	Y

		49	50	51	52	53	54
6	**Emmer**	N	Y	N	Y	Y	N
7	Peterson	Y	N	Y	Y	Y	N
8	**Stauber**	N	Y	N	Y	Y	Y
MISSISSIPPI							
1	**Kelly, T.**	N	Y	N	Y	Y	N
2	Thompson, B.	Y	N	Y	Y	Y	Y
3	**Guest**	N	Y	N	Y	Y	N
4	**Palazzo**	N	Y	N	Y	Y	N
MISSOURI							
1	Clay	Y	N	Y	Y	Y	Y
2	**Wagner**	N	Y	N	Y	Y	Y
3	**Luetkemeyer**	N	Y	N	Y	Y	Y
4	**Hartzler**	-	+	-	Y	Y	N
5	Cleaver	Y	N	Y	Y	Y	Y
6	**Graves, S.**	N	?	?	Y	Y	N
7	**Long**	N	Y	N	Y	Y	Y
8	**Smith, J.**	N	Y	N	Y	Y	N
MONTANA							
AL	**Gianforte**	N	Y	N	Y	Y	Y
NEBRASKA							
1	**Fortenberry**	N	Y	N	Y	Y	Y
2	**Bacon**	N	Y	N	Y	Y	Y
3	**Smith, Adrian**	N	Y	N	Y	Y	N
NEVADA							
1	Titus	Y	N	Y	Y	Y	Y
2	**Amodei**	N	Y	N	Y	Y	Y
3	Lee	Y	N	Y	Y	Y	Y
4	Horsford	Y	N	Y	Y	Y	N
NEW HAMPSHIRE							
1	Pappas	Y	N	Y	Y	Y	N
2	Kuster	Y	N	Y	Y	Y	Y
NEW JERSEY							
1	Norcross	Y	N	Y	Y	Y	Y
2	Van Drew	Y	Y	Y	Y	Y	N
3	Kim	Y	N	Y	Y	Y	N
4	**Smith, C.**	Y	Y	Y	Y	Y	Y
5	Gottheimer	Y	Y	Y	Y	Y	N
6	Pallone	Y	N	Y	Y	Y	Y
7	Malinowski	Y	N	Y	Y	Y	Y
8	Sires	Y	N	Y	Y	Y	Y
9	Pascrell	Y	N	Y	Y	Y	Y
10	Payne	?	?	?	?	?	?
11	Sherrill	Y	Y	Y	Y	Y	Y
12	Watson Coleman	Y	N	Y	Y	Y	Y
NEW MEXICO							
1	Haaland	Y	N	Y	Y	Y	Y
2	Torres Small	Y	Y	Y	Y	Y	N
3	Luján	Y	N	Y	Y	Y	Y
NEW YORK							
1	**Zeldin**	N	Y	N	Y	Y	N
2	**King, P.**	N	Y	N	Y	Y	N
3	Suozzi	Y	N	Y	Y	Y	N
4	Rice, K.	Y	N	Y	Y	Y	N
5	Meeks	Y	N	Y	Y	Y	Y
6	Meng	Y	N	Y	Y	Y	N
7	Velázquez	?	N	Y	Y	Y	Y
8	Jeffries	Y	N	Y	Y	Y	Y
9	Clarke	Y	N	Y	Y	Y	Y
10	Nadler	Y	N	Y	Y	Y	Y
11	Rose	Y	Y	Y	Y	Y	Y
12	Maloney, C.	Y	N	Y	Y	Y	Y
13	Espaillat	Y	N	Y	Y	Y	Y
14	Ocasio-Cortez	N	N	N	Y	Y	Y
15	Serrano	Y	N	Y	Y	Y	Y
16	Engel	Y	N	Y	Y	Y	Y
17	Lowey	Y	N	Y	?	?	?
18	Maloney, S.P.	Y	N	Y	Y	Y	N
19	Delgado	Y	N	Y	Y	Y	Y
20	Tonko	Y	N	Y	Y	Y	P
21	**Stefanik**	Y	Y	Y	Y	Y	Y
22	Brindisi	Y	Y	Y	Y	Y	N
23	**Reed**	N	Y	N	Y	Y	Y
24	**Katko**	Y	Y	Y	Y	Y	Y
25	Morelle	Y	N	Y	Y	Y	Y
26	Higgins, B.	Y	N	Y	Y	Y	Y
27	**Collins, C.**	N	Y	N	Y	Y	Y
NORTH CAROLINA							
1	Butterfield	Y	N	Y	Y	Y	Y
2	**Holding**	N	Y	N	Y	Y	N
3	**Jones**	?	?	?	?	?	?
4	Price	Y	N	Y	Y	Y	Y
5	**Foxx**	N	Y	N	Y	Y	N
6	**Walker**	N	Y	N	Y	Y	?
7	**Rouzer**	N	Y	N	Y	Y	N

		49	50	51	52	53	54
8	**Hudson**	N	Y	N	Y	Y	N
9	vacant						
10	**McHenry**	N	Y	N	Y	Y	N
11	**Meadows**	N	Y	N	Y	Y	N
12	Adams	Y	N	Y	Y	Y	Y
13	**Budd**	N	Y	-	Y	Y	Y
NORTH DAKOTA							
AL	**Armstrong**	N	Y	N	?	?	?
OHIO							
1	**Chabot**	N	Y	N	Y	Y	N
2	**Wenstrup**	N	Y	N	Y	Y	N
3	Beatty	Y	N	Y	Y	Y	Y
4	**Jordan**	N	Y	N	Y	Y	N
5	**Latta**	N	Y	N	Y	Y	N
6	**Johnson, B.**	N	Y	N	Y	Y	N
7	**Gibbs**	-	+	-	Y	Y	N
8	**Davidson**	N	Y	N	Y	Y	Y
9	Kaptur	Y	N	Y	Y	Y	Y
10	**Turner**	N	Y	N	Y	Y	N
11	Fudge	Y	N	Y	Y	Y	N
12	**Balderson**	N	Y	N	Y	Y	N
13	Ryan	Y	N	Y	Y	Y	Y
14	**Joyce**	N	Y	N	Y	Y	N
15	**Stivers**	N	Y	N	Y	Y	Y
16	**Gonzalez**	N	Y	N	Y	Y	N
OKLAHOMA							
1	**Hern**	N	Y	N	Y	Y	N
2	**Mullin**	N	Y	N	Y	Y	N
3	**Lucas**	N	Y	N	Y	Y	N
4	**Cole**	N	Y	N	Y	Y	N
5	Horn	Y	Y	Y	Y	Y	Y
OREGON							
1	Bonamici	Y	N	Y	Y	Y	Y
2	**Walden**	Y	Y	N	Y	Y	N
3	Blumenauer	Y	N	Y	Y	Y	?
4	DeFazio	Y	N	Y	Y	Y	Y
5	Schrader	Y	N	Y	Y	Y	?
PENNSYLVANIA							
1	**Fitzpatrick**	Y	Y	Y	Y	Y	N
2	Boyle	Y	N	Y	Y	Y	Y
3	Evans	Y	N	Y	Y	Y	Y
4	Dean	Y	N	Y	Y	Y	Y
5	Scanlon	Y	N	Y	Y	Y	Y
6	Houlahan	Y	N	Y	Y	Y	?
7	Wild	Y	N	Y	Y	Y	N
8	Cartwright	?	?	?	Y	Y	Y
9	**Meuser**	N	Y	N	Y	Y	?
10	**Perry**	N	Y	N	Y	Y	N
11	**Smucker**	N	Y	N	Y	Y	N
12	vacant						
13	**Joyce**	N	Y	N	Y	Y	N
14	**Reschenthaler**	N	Y	N	Y	Y	Y
15	**Thompson, G.**	N	Y	N	Y	Y	N
16	**Kelly, M.**	N	Y	N	Y	Y	Y
17	Lamb	Y	Y	Y	Y	Y	Y
18	Doyle	Y	N	Y	Y	Y	Y
RHODE ISLAND							
1	Cicilline	Y	?	?	Y	Y	Y
2	Langevin	Y	N	Y	Y	Y	Y
SOUTH CAROLINA							
1	Cunningham	Y	Y	Y	Y	Y	N
2	**Wilson, J.**	N	Y	N	Y	Y	N
3	**Duncan**	N	Y	N	Y	Y	N
4	**Timmons**	N	Y	N	Y	Y	N
5	**Norman**	N	Y	N	Y	Y	N
6	Clyburn	Y	N	Y	Y	Y	Y
7	**Rice, T.**	?	Y	N	Y	Y	Y
SOUTH DAKOTA							
AL	**Johnson**	N	Y	N	Y	Y	N
TENNESSEE							
1	**Roe**	N	Y	N	Y	Y	Y
2	**Burchett**	N	Y	N	Y	Y	N
3	**Fleischmann**	N	Y	N	Y	Y	Y
4	**DesJarlais**	N	Y	N	Y	Y	N
5	Cooper	Y	N	Y	Y	Y	Y
6	**Rose**	N	Y	N	Y	Y	N
7	**Green**	N	Y	N	Y	Y	N
8	**Kustoff**	N	Y	N	Y	Y	N
9	Cohen	Y	N	Y	Y	Y	Y
TEXAS							
1	**Gohmert**	N	Y	N	Y	Y	P
2	**Crenshaw**	N	Y	N	Y	Y	N
3	**Taylor**	N	Y	N	Y	Y	Y
4	**Ratcliffe**	N	Y	N	?	?	?

		49	50	51	52	53	54
5	**Gooden**	N	Y	N	Y	Y	Y
6	**Wright**	?	Y	N	Y	Y	N
7	Fletcher	Y	N	Y	Y	Y	Y
8	**Brady**	N	Y	N	Y	Y	Y
9	Green, A.	Y	N	Y	Y	Y	Y
10	**McCaul**	N	Y	N	Y	Y	N
11	**Conaway**	N	Y	N	Y	Y	N
12	**Granger**	N	Y	N	Y	Y	N
13	**Thornberry**	N	Y	N	Y	Y	Y
14	**Weber**	N	Y	N	Y	Y	N
15	Gonzalez	Y	N	Y	Y	Y	Y
16	Escobar	Y	N	Y	Y	Y	Y
17	**Flores**	N	Y	N	Y	Y	?
18	Jackson Lee	Y	N	Y	Y	Y	Y
19	**Arrington**	N	Y	N	Y	Y	Y
20	Castro	Y	N	Y	Y	Y	Y
21	**Roy**	N	Y	N	Y	Y	N
22	**Olson**	N	Y	N	Y	Y	N
23	**Hurd**	Y	Y	Y	Y	Y	N
24	**Marchant**	N	Y	N	Y	Y	N
25	**Williams**	N	Y	N	Y	Y	N
26	**Burgess**	N	Y	N	Y	Y	N
27	**Cloud**	N	Y	N	Y	Y	N
28	Cuellar	Y	N	Y	Y	Y	Y
29	Garcia, S.	Y	N	Y	Y	Y	Y
30	Johnson, E.B.	Y	N	Y	Y	Y	Y
31	**Carter, J.**	N	Y	?	Y	Y	N
32	Allred	Y	N	Y	Y	Y	Y
33	Veasey	Y	N	Y	Y	Y	Y
34	Vela	Y	N	Y	Y	Y	Y
35	Doggett	Y	?	?	Y	Y	Y
36	**Babin**	N	Y	N	Y	Y	N
UTAH							
1	**Bishop, R.**	N	Y	N	Y	Y	N
2	**Stewart**	N	Y	N	Y	Y	Y
3	**Curtis**	N	Y	N	Y	Y	Y
4	McAdams	Y	Y	Y	Y	Y	N
VERMONT							
AL	Welch	Y	N	Y	Y	Y	Y
VIRGINIA							
1	**Wittman**	N	Y	N	Y	Y	N
2	Luria	Y	N	Y	Y	Y	N
3	Scott, R.	Y	N	Y	Y	Y	Y
4	McEachin	Y	N	Y	Y	Y	Y
5	**Riggleman**	N	Y	N	Y	Y	Y
6	**Cline**	N	Y	N	Y	Y	N
7	Spanberger	Y	Y	Y	Y	Y	N
8	Beyer	Y	N	Y	Y	Y	Y
9	**Griffith**	N	Y	N	Y	Y	N
10	Wexton	Y	N	Y	Y	Y	Y
11	Connolly	Y	N	Y	Y	Y	N
WASHINGTON							
1	DelBene	Y	N	Y	Y	Y	Y
2	Larsen	Y	N	Y	Y	Y	Y
3	**Herrera Beutler**	Y	Y	N	Y	Y	N
4	**Newhouse**	N	Y	N	Y	Y	Y
5	**McMorris Rodgers**	N	Y	N	Y	Y	Y
6	Kilmer	Y	N	Y	Y	Y	N
7	Jayapal	Y	N	Y	Y	Y	Y
8	Schrier	Y	N	Y	Y	Y	N
9	Smith Adam	Y	N	Y	Y	Y	Y
10	Heck	Y	N	Y	Y	Y	Y
WEST VIRGINIA							
1	**McKinley**	N	Y	N	Y	Y	N
2	**Mooney**	N	Y	N	Y	Y	N
3	**Miller**	N	Y	N	Y	Y	N
WISCONSIN							
1	**Steil**	N	Y	N	Y	Y	Y
2	Pocan	Y	N	Y	Y	Y	Y
3	Kind	Y	N	Y	+	+	?
4	Moore	Y	N	Y	Y	Y	Y
5	**Sensenbrenner**	-	+	-	+	+	+
6	**Grothman**	N	Y	N	Y	Y	N
7	**Duffy**						
8	**Gallagher**	N	Y	N	Y	Y	N
WYOMING							
AL	**Cheney**	N	Y	N	Y	Y	N
DELEGATES							
	Radewagen (A.S.)						
	Norton (D.C.)						
	San Nicolas (Guam)						
	Sablan (N. Marianas)						
	González-Colón (P.R.)						
	Plaskett (V.I.)						

55. Procedural Motion - Adjournment. Gosar, R-Ariz., motion to adjourn. Motion rejected 14-395: R 14-173; D 0-222.

56. HR428. Homeland Security Threat Assessment - Passage. Rice, D-N.Y., motion to suspend the rules and pass the bill that would require the Department of Homeland Security to develop and disseminate a threat assessment regarding the use of virtual currencies by terrorist organizations to support their operations. The threat assessment would be required to be disseminated within 120 days of enactment. Motion agreed to 422-3: R 191-3; D 231-0. *Note: A two-thirds majority of those present and voting (284 in this case) is required for passage under suspension of the rules.* Jan. 29, 2019.

57. HR449. DHS Service Catalog for State and Local Agencies - Passage. Rice, D-N.Y., motion to suspend the rules and pass the bill that would require the Department of Homeland Security to continue producing the catalog that summarizes training, publications, programs, and services available to state and local law enforcement agencies. The catalog would be available through the Homeland Security Information Network. Motion agreed to 412-12: R 183-10; D 229-2. *Note: A two-thirds majority of those present and voting (283 in this case) is required for passage under suspension of the rules.* Jan. 29, 2019.

58. HR769. Counter-terrorism Advisory Board Coordination - Passage. Rice, D-N.Y., motion to suspend the rules and pass the bill that would formally establish in statute the existing counter-terrorism Advisory Board, under the Department of Homeland Security, to continue its efforts in coordinating the department's intelligence, activities, and policies related to counter-terrorism. Motion agreed to 414-12: R 186-9; D 228-3. *Note: A two-thirds majority of those present and voting (284 in this case) is required for passage under suspension of the rules.* Jan. 29, 2019.

59. HRES77. Congressional Disapproval of Government Shutdown - Motion to Table. Hoyer, D-Md., motion to table the Waters, D-Calif., motion to reconsider the vote on which the resolution was agreed to by voice vote. Motion agreed to 240-176: R 15-176; D 225-0. Jan. 29, 2019.

60. HR790. Pay Increase for Civilian Federal Employees - Previous Question. Raskin, D-Md., motion to order the previous question (thus ending debate and possibility of amendment) on the rule (H Res 87) that would provide for House floor consideration of the bill (HR 790) that would increase pay for civilian federal employees. Motion agreed to 232-190: R 0-190; D 232-0. Jan. 30, 2019.

	55	56	57	58	59	60
ALABAMA						
1 **Byrne**	N	Y	Y	Y	N	N
2 **Roby**	N	Y	Y	Y	N	N
3 **Rogers, M.**	N	Y	Y	Y	N	N
4 **Aderholt**	N	Y	Y	Y	N	N
5 **Brooks, M.**	N	Y	N	N	N	N
6 **Palmer**	N	Y	Y	Y	N	N
7 Sewell	N	Y	Y	Y	Y	Y
ALASKA						
AL **Young**	?	Y	Y	Y	N	N
ARIZONA						
1 O'Halleran	N	Y	Y	Y	Y	Y
2 Kirkpatrick	N	Y	Y	Y	Y	Y
3 Grijalva	?	Y	Y	Y	Y	Y
4 **Gosar**	Y	N	N	N	N	N
5 **Biggs**	Y	Y	N	N	N	N
6 **Schweikert**	N	Y	Y	Y	N	N
7 Gallego	N	Y	Y	Y	Y	Y
8 **Lesko**	N	Y	Y	Y	N	N
9 Stanton	N	Y	Y	Y	Y	Y
ARKANSAS						
1 **Crawford**	N	Y	Y	Y	N	N
2 **Hill, F.**	N	Y	Y	Y	N	N
3 **Womack**	N	Y	Y	N	N	N
4 **Westerman**	N	Y	Y	Y	-	N
CALIFORNIA						
1 **LaMalfa**	N	Y	Y	Y	N	N
2 Huffman	N	Y	Y	Y	Y	Y
3 Garamendi	?	Y	Y	Y	Y	Y
4 **McClintock**	N	Y	Y	Y	N	N
5 Thompson, M.	N	Y	Y	Y	Y	Y
6 Matsui	N	Y	Y	Y	Y	Y
7 Bera	N	Y	Y	Y	Y	Y
8 **Cook**	N	Y	Y	Y	N	N
9 McNerney	N	Y	Y	Y	Y	Y
10 Harder	N	Y	Y	Y	Y	Y
11 DeSaulnier	N	Y	Y	Y	Y	Y
12 Pelosi						
13 Lee B.	N	Y	Y	Y	Y	Y
14 Speier	N	Y	Y	Y	Y	Y
15 Swalwell	N	Y	Y	Y	Y	Y
16 Costa	N	Y	Y	Y	Y	Y
17 Khanna	N	Y	Y	Y	Y	Y
18 Eshoo	N	Y	Y	Y	Y	Y
19 Lofgren	N	Y	Y	Y	Y	Y
20 Panetta	N	Y	Y	Y	Y	Y
21 Cox	N	Y	Y	Y	Y	Y
22 **Nunes**	N	Y	Y	Y	N	N
23 **McCarthy**	N	Y	Y	Y	Y	N
24 Carbajal	N	Y	Y	Y	Y	Y
25 Hill, K.	N	Y	Y	Y	Y	Y
26 Brownley	N	Y	Y	Y	Y	Y
27 Chu	?	Y	Y	Y	Y	Y
28 Schiff	N	Y	Y	Y	Y	Y
29 Cárdenas	N	Y	Y	Y	Y	Y
30 Sherman	N	Y	Y	Y	Y	Y
31 Aguilar	N	Y	Y	Y	Y	Y
32 Napolitano	N	Y	Y	Y	Y	Y
33 Lieu	N	Y	Y	Y	Y	Y
34 Gomez	N	Y	Y	Y	Y	Y
35 Torres	N	Y	Y	Y	?	Y
36 Ruiz	N	Y	Y	Y	Y	Y
37 Bass	?	Y	Y	Y	Y	Y
38 Sánchez	N	Y	Y	Y	Y	Y
39 Cisneros	N	Y	Y	Y	Y	Y
40 Roybal-Allard	N	Y	Y	Y	Y	Y
41 Takano	N	Y	Y	Y	Y	Y
42 **Calvert**	N	Y	Y	Y	N	N
43 Waters	N	Y	Y	Y	Y	Y
44 Barragán	N	Y	Y	Y	?	Y
45 Porter	N	Y	Y	Y	Y	Y
46 Correa	N	Y	Y	Y	Y	Y
47 Lowenthal	N	Y	Y	Y	Y	Y
48 Rouda	N	Y	Y	Y	Y	Y
49 Levin	N	Y	Y	Y	Y	Y
50 **Hunter**	N	Y	Y	Y	N	N
51 Vargas	N	Y	Y	Y	Y	Y
52 Peters	N	Y	Y	Y	Y	Y

	55	56	57	58	59	60
53 Davis, S.	N	Y	Y	Y	Y	Y
COLORADO						
1 DeGette	N	Y	Y	Y	Y	Y
2 Neguse	N	Y	Y	Y	Y	Y
3 **Tipton**	N	Y	Y	Y	N	N
4 **Buck**	N	Y	Y	Y	?	N
5 **Lamborn**	N	Y	Y	Y	N	N
6 Crow	N	Y	Y	Y	Y	Y
7 Perlmutter	N	Y	Y	Y	Y	Y
CONNECTICUT						
1 Larson	N	Y	Y	Y	Y	Y
2 Courtney	N	Y	Y	Y	Y	Y
3 DeLauro	N	Y	Y	Y	Y	Y
4 Himes	N	Y	Y	Y	Y	Y
5 Hayes	N	Y	Y	Y	Y	Y
DELAWARE						
AL Blunt Rochester	N	Y	Y	Y	Y	Y
FLORIDA						
1 **Gaetz**	N	N	N	Y	N	N
2 **Dunn**	N	Y	Y	Y	N	N
3 **Yoho**	N	Y	Y	Y	N	N
4 **Rutherford**	N	Y	Y	Y	N	N
5 Lawson	N	Y	Y	Y	Y	Y
6 **Waltz**	N	Y	Y	Y	N	N
7 Murphy	N	Y	Y	Y	Y	Y
8 **Posey**	N	Y	Y	Y	N	N
9 Soto	N	Y	Y	Y	Y	Y
10 Demings	N	Y	Y	Y	Y	Y
11 **Webster**	N	Y	Y	Y	N	N
12 **Bilirakis**	N	Y	Y	Y	N	N
13 Crist	N	Y	Y	Y	Y	Y
14 Castor	N	Y	Y	Y	Y	Y
15 **Spano**	N	Y	Y	Y	N	N
16 **Buchanan**	N	Y	Y	Y	N	N
17 **Steube**	N	Y	Y	Y	N	N
18 **Mast**	N	Y	Y	Y	N	N
19 **Rooney**	N	Y	Y	Y	N	N
20 Hastings	-	Y	Y	Y	Y	Y
21 Frankel	-	Y	Y	Y	Y	Y
22 Deutch	N	Y	Y	Y	?	Y
23 Wasserman Schultz	N	Y	Y	Y	Y	Y
24 Wilson, F.	?	?	?	?	?	?
25 **Diaz-Balart**	N	Y	Y	Y	N	N
26 Mucarsel-Powell	N	Y	Y	Y	Y	Y
27 Shalala	N	Y	Y	Y	Y	Y
GEORGIA						
1 **Carter, E.L.**	N	Y	Y	Y	N	N
2 Bishop, S.	N	Y	Y	Y	Y	Y
3 **Ferguson**	N	Y	Y	Y	N	N
4 Johnson, H.	N	Y	Y	Y	Y	Y
5 Lewis John	N	Y	Y	Y	Y	Y
6 McBath	N	Y	Y	Y	Y	Y
7 **Woodall**	N	Y	Y	Y	N	N
8 **Scott, A.**	N	Y	Y	Y	N	N
9 **Collins, D.**	N	Y	Y	Y	N	N
10 **Hice**	Y	Y	Y	Y	N	N
11 **Loudermilk**	N	Y	Y	Y	N	N
12 **Allen**	N	Y	Y	Y	N	N
13 Scott, D.	N	Y	Y	Y	Y	Y
14 **Graves, T.**	N	Y	Y	Y	N	N
HAWAII						
1 Case	N	Y	Y	Y	Y	Y
2 Gabbard	N	Y	Y	Y	Y	Y
IDAHO						
1 **Fulcher**	N	Y	Y	Y	N	N
2 **Simpson**	N	Y	Y	Y	N	N
ILLINOIS						
1 Rush	N	Y	Y	Y	Y	Y
2 Kelly, R.	N	Y	Y	Y	Y	Y
3 Lipinski	N	Y	Y	Y	Y	Y
4 García, J.	N	Y	Y	Y	Y	Y
5 Quigley	N	Y	Y	Y	?	Y
6 Casten	N	Y	Y	Y	Y	Y
7 Davis, D.	N	Y	Y	Y	Y	Y
8 Krishnamoorthi	N	Y	Y	Y	Y	Y
9 Schakowsky	N	Y	Y	Y	Y	Y
10 Schneider	N	Y	Y	Y	Y	Y
11 Foster	N	Y	Y	Y	Y	Y

		55	56	57	58	59	60
12	**Bost**	N	Y	Y	Y	N	-
13	**Davis, R.**	N	Y	Y	Y	N	?
14	Underwood	N	Y	Y	Y	Y	Y
15	**Shimkus**	N	Y	Y	Y	N	?
16	**Kinzinger**	N	Y	Y	Y	N	N
17	Bustos	N	Y	Y	Y	Y	Y
18	**LaHood**	N	Y	Y	Y	N	-
INDIANA							
1	Visclosky	N	Y	Y	Y	Y	Y
2	**Walorski**	N	Y	Y	Y	N	N
3	**Banks**	N	Y	Y	Y	N	N
4	**Baird**	N	Y	Y	Y	N	N
5	**Brooks, S.**	N	Y	Y	Y	N	N
6	**Pence**	N	Y	Y	Y	N	N
7	Carson	N	Y	Y	Y	Y	Y
8	**Bucshon**	N	Y	Y	Y	N	N
9	**Hollingsworth**	N	Y	Y	Y	N	N
IOWA							
1	Finkenauer	N	Y	Y	Y	Y	Y
2	Loebsack	N	Y	Y	Y	Y	Y
3	Axne	N	Y	Y	Y	Y	Y
4	**King, S.**	N	Y	Y	Y	N	N
KANSAS							
1	**Marshall**	N	Y	Y	Y	N	N
2	**Watkins**	N	Y	Y	Y	N	N
3	Davids	N	Y	Y	Y	Y	Y
4	**Estes**	N	Y	Y	Y	N	N
KENTUCKY							
1	**Comer**	N	Y	Y	Y	N	?
2	**Guthrie**	N	Y	Y	Y	N	N
3	Yarmuth	N	Y	Y	Y	Y	Y
4	**Massie**	Y	N	N	N	N	N
5	**Rogers, H.**	N	Y	Y	Y	N	N
6	**Barr**	N	Y	Y	Y	N	N
LOUISIANA							
1	**Scalise**	N	Y	Y	Y	N	N
2	Richmond	N	Y	Y	Y	Y	Y
3	**Higgins, C.**	N	Y	Y	Y	N	N
4	**Johnson, M.**	N	Y	Y	Y	N	N
5	**Abraham**	N	Y	Y	Y	N	N
6	**Graves, G.**	N	Y	Y	Y	N	N
MAINE							
1	Pingree	N	Y	Y	Y	Y	Y
2	Golden	N	Y	Y	Y	Y	Y
MARYLAND							
1	**Harris**	Y	Y	N	N	N	N
2	Ruppersberger	N	Y	Y	Y	Y	Y
3	Sarbanes	N	Y	Y	Y	Y	Y
4	Brown, A.	N	Y	Y	Y	Y	Y
5	Hoyer	N	Y	Y	Y	Y	Y
6	Trone	?	?	?	?	?	Y
7	Cummings	N	Y	Y	Y	Y	Y
8	Raskin	N	Y	Y	Y	Y	Y
MASSACHUSETTS							
1	Neal	N	Y	Y	Y	Y	Y
2	McGovern	N	Y	Y	Y	Y	Y
3	Trahan	N	Y	Y	Y	Y	Y
4	Kennedy	N	Y	Y	Y	Y	Y
5	Clark	N	Y	Y	Y	Y	Y
6	Moulton	N	Y	Y	Y	Y	Y
7	Pressley	N	Y	N	Y	+	Y
8	Lynch	N	Y	Y	Y	Y	Y
9	Keating	N	Y	Y	Y	Y	Y
MICHIGAN							
1	**Bergman**	N	Y	Y	Y	N	N
2	**Huizenga**	N	Y	Y	Y	N	N
3	**Amash**	N	N	N	N	N	N
4	**Moolenaar**	N	Y	Y	Y	N	N
5	Kildee	N	Y	Y	Y	Y	Y
6	**Upton**	N	Y	Y	Y	Y	N
7	**Walberg**	N	Y	Y	Y	N	N
8	Slotkin	N	Y	Y	Y	Y	Y
9	Levin	N	Y	Y	Y	Y	Y
10	**Mitchell**	N	Y	Y	Y	N	N
11	Stevens	N	Y	Y	Y	Y	Y
12	Dingell	N	Y	Y	Y	Y	Y
13	Tlaib	N	Y	Y	N	Y	Y
14	Lawrence	N	Y	Y	Y	Y	Y
MINNESOTA							
1	**Hagedorn**	N	Y	Y	Y	N	N
2	Craig	N	Y	Y	Y	Y	Y
3	Phillips	N	Y	Y	Y	Y	Y
4	McCollum	N	Y	Y	Y	Y	Y
5	Omar	N	Y	Y	N	Y	Y

		55	56	57	58	59	60
6	**Emmer**	N	Y	Y	Y	N	N
7	Peterson	N	Y	Y	Y	Y	Y
8	**Stauber**	N	Y	+	Y	Y	N
MISSISSIPPI							
1	**Kelly, T.**	N	Y	Y	Y	N	N
2	Thompson, B.	N	Y	Y	Y	Y	Y
3	**Guest**	N	Y	Y	Y	N	N
4	**Palazzo**	N	Y	Y	Y	N	N
MISSOURI							
1	Clay	N	Y	Y	Y	Y	Y
2	**Wagner**	?	Y	Y	Y	Y	N
3	**Luetkemeyer**	N	Y	Y	Y	N	N
4	**Hartzler**	N	Y	Y	Y	N	N
5	Cleaver	N	Y	Y	Y	Y	Y
6	**Graves, S.**	N	Y	Y	Y	N	N
7	**Long**	N	Y	Y	Y	N	N
8	**Smith, J.**	N	Y	Y	Y	N	N
MONTANA							
AL	**Gianforte**	N	Y	Y	Y	N	N
NEBRASKA							
1	**Fortenberry**	N	Y	Y	Y	N	N
2	**Bacon**	N	Y	Y	Y	N	N
3	**Smith, Adrian**	N	Y	Y	Y	N	N
NEVADA							
1	Titus	N	Y	Y	Y	Y	Y
2	**Amodei**	N	Y	Y	Y	N	N
3	Lee	N	Y	Y	Y	Y	Y
4	Horsford	N	Y	Y	Y	Y	Y
NEW HAMPSHIRE							
1	Pappas	N	Y	Y	Y	Y	Y
2	Kuster	N	Y	Y	Y	Y	Y
NEW JERSEY							
1	Norcross	N	Y	Y	Y	Y	Y
2	Van Drew	N	Y	Y	Y	Y	Y
3	Kim	N	Y	Y	Y	Y	Y
4	**Smith, C.**	N	Y	Y	Y	N	N
5	Gottheimer	N	Y	Y	Y	Y	Y
6	Pallone	N	Y	Y	Y	Y	Y
7	Malinowski	N	Y	Y	Y	Y	Y
8	Sires	?	Y	Y	Y	Y	Y
9	Pascrell	N	Y	Y	Y	Y	Y
10	Payne	?	?	?	?	?	?
11	Sherrill	N	Y	Y	Y	Y	Y
12	Watson Coleman	N	Y	Y	Y	Y	Y
NEW MEXICO							
1	Haaland	N	Y	Y	Y	Y	Y
2	Torres Small	N	Y	Y	Y	Y	Y
3	Luján	N	Y	Y	Y	Y	Y
NEW YORK							
1	**Zeldin**	N	Y	Y	Y	N	N
2	**King, P.**	N	Y	Y	Y	Y	N
3	Suozzi	N	Y	Y	Y	Y	Y
4	Rice, K.	N	Y	Y	Y	Y	Y
5	Meeks	N	Y	Y	Y	Y	Y
6	Meng	?	Y	Y	Y	Y	Y
7	Velázquez	N	Y	Y	Y	Y	Y
8	Jeffries	N	Y	Y	Y	Y	Y
9	Clarke	N	Y	Y	Y	Y	Y
10	Nadler	N	Y	Y	Y	Y	Y
11	Rose	N	Y	Y	Y	?	Y
12	Maloney, C.	N	Y	Y	Y	Y	Y
13	Espaillat	N	Y	Y	Y	Y	Y
14	Ocasio-Cortez	N	Y	N	N	Y	Y
15	Serrano	N	Y	Y	Y	Y	Y
16	Engel	N	Y	Y	Y	Y	Y
17	Lowey	N	Y	Y	Y	Y	Y
18	Maloney, S.P.	N	Y	Y	Y	Y	Y
19	Delgado	N	Y	Y	Y	Y	Y
20	Tonko	N	Y	Y	Y	Y	Y
21	**Stefanik**	N	Y	Y	Y	N	N
22	Brindisi	N	Y	Y	Y	Y	Y
23	**Reed**	N	Y	Y	Y	N	N
24	**Katko**	N	Y	Y	Y	Y	N
25	Morelle	N	Y	Y	Y	Y	Y
26	Higgins, B.	N	Y	Y	Y	Y	Y
27	**Collins, C.**	N	Y	Y	Y	N	N
NORTH CAROLINA							
1	Butterfield	N	Y	Y	Y	Y	Y
2	**Holding**	N	Y	Y	Y	N	N
3	**Jones**	?	?	?	?	?	?
4	Price	N	Y	Y	Y	Y	Y
5	**Foxx**	N	Y	Y	Y	N	N
6	**Walker**	N	Y	Y	Y	N	N
7	**Rouzer**	N	Y	Y	Y	?	N

		55	56	57	58	59	60
8	**Hudson**	N	Y	Y	Y	N	N
9	vacant						
10	**McHenry**	Y	Y	Y	Y	Y	N
11	**Meadows**	Y	Y	Y	Y	N	N
12	Adams	N	Y	Y	Y	Y	Y
13	**Budd**	N	Y	Y	Y	N	N
NORTH DAKOTA							
AL	**Armstrong**	N	Y	Y	Y	N	N
OHIO							
1	**Chabot**	N	Y	Y	Y	N	N
2	**Wenstrup**	N	Y	Y	Y	N	N
3	Beatty	N	Y	Y	Y	Y	Y
4	**Jordan**	N	Y	Y	Y	N	N
5	**Latta**	N	Y	Y	Y	N	N
6	**Johnson, B.**	N	Y	Y	Y	N	N
7	**Gibbs**	N	Y	Y	Y	N	N
8	**Davidson**	N	Y	Y	Y	N	N
9	Kaptur	N	Y	Y	Y	Y	Y
10	**Turner**	N	Y	Y	Y	N	N
11	Fudge	N	Y	Y	Y	Y	Y
12	**Balderson**	N	Y	Y	Y	N	N
13	Ryan	N	Y	Y	Y	Y	Y
14	**Joyce**	N	Y	Y	Y	Y	N
15	**Stivers**	N	Y	Y	Y	Y	N
16	**Gonzalez**	N	Y	Y	Y	Y	N
OKLAHOMA							
1	**Hern**	N	Y	Y	Y	N	N
2	**Mullin**	Y	Y	Y	Y	N	?
3	**Lucas**	N	Y	Y	Y	N	N
4	**Cole**	N	Y	Y	Y	N	N
5	Horn	N	Y	Y	Y	Y	Y
OREGON							
1	Bonamici	N	Y	Y	Y	Y	Y
2	**Walden**	N	Y	Y	Y	Y	N
3	Blumenauer	N	Y	Y	Y	Y	Y
4	DeFazio	N	Y	Y	Y	Y	Y
5	Schrader	N	Y	Y	Y	Y	Y
PENNSYLVANIA							
1	**Fitzpatrick**	N	Y	Y	Y	N	N
2	Boyle	N	Y	Y	Y	Y	Y
3	Evans	N	Y	Y	Y	Y	Y
4	Dean	N	Y	Y	Y	Y	Y
5	Scanlon	N	Y	Y	Y	Y	Y
6	Houlahan	N	Y	Y	Y	Y	Y
7	Wild	N	Y	Y	Y	Y	Y
8	Cartwright	N	Y	Y	Y	Y	Y
9	**Meuser**	N	Y	Y	Y	N	N
10	**Perry**	N	Y	Y	Y	N	N
11	**Smucker**	N	Y	Y	Y	-	N
12	vacant						
13	**Joyce**	N	Y	Y	Y	N	N
14	**Reschenthaler**	?	Y	Y	Y	N	N
15	**Thompson, G.**	N	Y	Y	Y	N	N
16	**Kelly, M.**	N	Y	Y	Y	N	N
17	Lamb	N	Y	Y	Y	Y	Y
18	Doyle	N	Y	Y	Y	Y	Y
RHODE ISLAND							
1	Cicilline	N	Y	Y	Y	Y	Y
2	Langevin	N	Y	Y	Y	Y	Y
SOUTH CAROLINA							
1	Cunningham	N	Y	Y	Y	Y	Y
2	**Wilson, J.**	N	Y	Y	Y	N	N
3	**Duncan**	Y	Y	N	Y	N	N
4	**Timmons**	N	Y	Y	Y	N	N
5	**Norman**	Y	Y	Y	Y	N	N
6	Clyburn	N	Y	Y	Y	Y	Y
7	**Rice, T.**	N	Y	Y	Y	N	N
SOUTH DAKOTA							
AL	**Johnson**	N	Y	Y	Y	N	N
TENNESSEE							
1	**Roe**	N	Y	Y	Y	N	N
2	**Burchett**	N	Y	Y	Y	N	N
3	**Fleischmann**	N	Y	Y	Y	N	N
4	**DesJarlais**	?	?	?	?	?	N
5	Cooper	N	Y	Y	Y	Y	Y
6	**Rose**	N	Y	Y	Y	Y	N
7	**Green**	Y	Y	Y	Y	N	N
8	**Kustoff**	N	Y	Y	Y	N	N
9	Cohen	N	Y	Y	Y	Y	Y
TEXAS							
1	**Gohmert**	N	Y	Y	N	N	N
2	**Crenshaw**	N	Y	Y	Y	N	N
3	**Taylor**	N	Y	Y	Y	N	N
4	**Ratcliffe**	N	Y	Y	Y	N	N

		55	56	57	58	59	60
5	**Gooden**	N	Y	Y	Y	N	N
6	**Wright**	N	Y	Y	Y	N	N
7	Fletcher	N	Y	Y	Y	Y	Y
8	**Brady**	N	Y	Y	Y	N	N
9	Green, A.	N	Y	Y	Y	Y	Y
10	**McCaul**	?	Y	Y	Y	N	N
11	**Conaway**	N	Y	Y	Y	N	N
12	**Granger**	N	Y	Y	Y	N	N
13	**Thornberry**	?	Y	Y	Y	N	N
14	**Weber**	Y	Y	Y	Y	N	N
15	Gonzalez	N	Y	Y	Y	Y	Y
16	Escobar	N	Y	Y	Y	Y	Y
17	**Flores**	N	Y	Y	Y	N	N
18	Jackson Lee	N	Y	Y	Y	Y	Y
19	**Arrington**	N	Y	Y	Y	N	N
20	Castro	N	Y	Y	Y	Y	Y
21	**Roy**	N	Y	N	N	N	N
22	**Olson**	N	Y	Y	Y	N	N
23	**Hurd**	N	Y	Y	Y	N	N
24	**Marchant**	N	Y	Y	Y	N	N
25	**Williams**	N	Y	Y	Y	N	N
26	**Burgess**	Y	?	?	Y	Y	N
27	**Cloud**	N	Y	Y	Y	N	N
28	Cuellar	N	Y	Y	Y	Y	Y
29	Garcia, S.	N	Y	Y	Y	Y	Y
30	Johnson, E.B.	N	Y	Y	Y	Y	Y
31	**Carter, J.**	?	Y	Y	Y	N	N
32	Allred	N	Y	Y	Y	Y	Y
33	Veasey	N	Y	Y	Y	Y	Y
34	Vela	N	Y	Y	Y	Y	Y
35	Doggett	N	Y	Y	Y	Y	Y
36	**Babin**	Y	Y	Y	Y	N	N
UTAH							
1	**Bishop, R.**	?	Y	Y	Y	N	N
2	**Stewart**	N	Y	Y	Y	N	N
3	**Curtis**	N	Y	Y	Y	N	N
4	McAdams	N	Y	Y	Y	Y	Y
VERMONT							
AL	Welch	N	Y	Y	Y	Y	Y
VIRGINIA							
1	**Wittman**	N	Y	Y	Y	N	N
2	Luria	N	Y	Y	Y	Y	Y
3	Scott, R.	?	Y	Y	Y	Y	Y
4	McEachin	N	Y	Y	Y	Y	Y
5	**Riggleman**	N	Y	Y	Y	Y	N
6	**Cline**	N	Y	Y	Y	N	N
7	Spanberger	N	Y	Y	Y	Y	Y
8	Beyer	N	Y	Y	Y	Y	Y
9	**Griffith**	N	Y	Y	Y	N	N
10	Wexton	N	Y	Y	Y	Y	Y
11	Connolly	N	Y	Y	Y	Y	Y
WASHINGTON							
1	DelBene	N	Y	Y	Y	Y	Y
2	Larsen	?	Y	Y	Y	Y	Y
3	**Herrera Beutler**	N	Y	Y	Y	N	N
4	**Newhouse**	N	Y	Y	Y	N	N
5	**McMorris Rodgers**	N	Y	Y	Y	N	N
6	Kilmer	N	Y	Y	Y	Y	Y
7	Jayapal	N	Y	Y	Y	Y	Y
8	Schrier	N	Y	Y	Y	Y	Y
9	Smith Adam	N	Y	Y	Y	Y	Y
10	Heck	N	Y	Y	Y	Y	Y
WEST VIRGINIA							
1	**McKinley**	N	Y	Y	Y	N	N
2	**Mooney**	N	Y	Y	Y	N	N
3	**Miller**	?	Y	Y	Y	N	N
WISCONSIN							
1	**Steil**	N	Y	Y	Y	N	N
2	Pocan	N	Y	Y	Y	Y	Y
3	Kind	N	Y	Y	Y	Y	Y
4	Moore	N	Y	Y	Y	Y	Y
5	**Sensenbrenner**	-	+	+	+	-	-
6	**Grothman**	N	Y	N	N	N	N
7	**Duffy**						
8	**Gallagher**	N	Y	Y	Y	N	N
WYOMING							
AL	**Cheney**	N	Y	Y	Y	N	N
DELEGATES							
	Radewagen (A.S.)						
	Norton (D.C.)						
	San Nicolas (Guam)						
	Sablan (N. Marianas)						
	González-Colón (P.R.)						
	Plaskett (V.I.)						

||| HOUSE VOTES

61. HR790. Pay Increase for Civilian Federal Employees - Rule. Adoption of the rule (H Res 87) that would provide for House floor consideration of the bill (HR 790) that would increase pay for civilian federal employees. Adopted 231-189: R 0-189; D 231-0. Jan. 30, 2019.

62. HR790. Pay Increase for Civilian Federal Employees - IRS Employees. Trahan, D-Mass., amendment that would increase the rate of pay for eligible IRS employees for calendar year 2019 by 2.6 percent. Adopted in Committee of the Whole 243-183: R 8-183; D 234-0; I 1-0. Jan. 30, 2019.

63. HR790. Pay Increase for Civilian Federal Employees - Recommit. Brooks, R-Ind., motion to recommit the bill to the House Committee on Oversight and Reform with instructions to report it back immediately with an amendment that would prohibit the use of government funds for the purpose of providing an increase in pay for calendar year 2019 for any federal employee who has been disciplined for sexual misconduct in the workplace. Motion rejected 206-216: R 189-1; D 17-215. Jan. 30, 2019.

64. HR790. Pay Increase for Civilian Federal Employees - Passage. Passage of the bill that would increase the salaries and wages of all civilian federal employees by 2.6 percent for calendar year 2019. The pay raise would take effect immediately upon enactment, and would be backdated to apply to the first pay period that occurred after Jan. 1. Passed 259-161: R 29-161; D 230-0. Jan. 30, 2019.

65. HRES79. Congressional Disapproval of Shutdowns - Passage. Clay, D-Mo., motion to suspend the rules and agree to the resolution that would express the sense of the House of Representatives that government shutdowns cause substantial damage to federal employees, to Americans generally who benefit from government services, to the U.S. economy and to the nation's reputation and state that shutting down the U.S. government "is not an acceptable tactic or strategy" for resolving policy differences. Motion rejected 249-163: R 21-163; D 228-0. *Note: A two-thirds majority of those present and voting (275 in this case) is required for passage under suspension of the rules.* Jan. 30, 2019.

66. HR831. Reopening the National Scenic Byways Program - Passage. Norton, D-D.C., motion to suspend the rules and pass the bill that would require the Department of Transportation to reopen the reopen the National Scenic Byways Program, within 90 days of enactment, to accept new nominations of roads into the program. Motion agreed to 404-19: R 176-19; D 228-0. *Note: A two-thirds majority of those present and voting (282 in this case) is required for passage under suspension of the rules.* Feb. 6, 2019.

		61	62	63	64	65	66
ALABAMA							
1	**Byrne**	N	N	Y	N	N	Y
2	**Roby**	N	N	Y	N	N	Y
3	**Rogers, M.**	N	N	Y	N	N	Y
4	**Aderholt**	N	N	Y	N	N	Y
5	**Brooks, M.**	N	N	Y	Y	N	Y
6	**Palmer**	N	N	Y	N	N	Y
7	Sewell	Y	Y	N	Y	Y	Y
ALASKA							
AL	**Young**	N	N	Y	Y	N	Y
ARIZONA							
1	O'Halleran	Y	Y	Y	Y	Y	Y
2	Kirkpatrick	Y	Y	N	Y	Y	Y
3	Grijalva	Y	Y	N	Y	Y	Y
4	**Gosar**	N	N	Y	N	N	N
5	**Biggs**	N	N	Y	N	N	N
6	**Schweikert**	N	N	Y	N	N	Y
7	Gallego	Y	Y	N	Y	Y	Y
8	**Lesko**	N	N	Y	N	N	Y
9	Stanton	Y	Y	N	Y	Y	Y
ARKANSAS							
1	**Crawford**	N	N	Y	N	N	Y
2	**Hill, F.**	N	N	Y	N	N	Y
3	**Womack**	N	N	Y	N	N	Y
4	**Westerman**	N	N	Y	N	N	Y
CALIFORNIA							
1	**LaMalfa**	N	N	Y	N	N	Y
2	Huffman	Y	Y	N	Y	Y	Y
3	Garamendi	Y	Y	N	Y	Y	Y
4	**McClintock**	N	N	Y	N	N	N
5	Thompson, M.	Y	Y	N	Y	Y	Y
6	Matsui	Y	Y	N	Y	Y	Y
7	Bera	Y	Y	N	Y	Y	Y
8	**Cook**	N	Y	Y	Y	N	Y
9	McNerney	Y	Y	N	Y	Y	Y
10	Harder	Y	Y	N	Y	+	Y
11	DeSaulnier	Y	Y	N	Y	Y	Y
12	Pelosi						
13	Lee B.	Y	Y	N	Y	Y	Y
14	Speier	Y	Y	N	Y	Y	Y
15	Swalwell	Y	Y	N	Y	Y	Y
16	Costa	Y	Y	N	Y	Y	Y
17	Khanna	Y	Y	N	Y	Y	Y
18	Eshoo	Y	Y	N	Y	Y	Y
19	Lofgren	Y	Y	N	Y	Y	Y
20	Panetta	Y	Y	N	Y	Y	Y
21	Cox	Y	Y	N	Y	Y	Y
22	**Nunes**	N	N	Y	N	N	Y
23	**McCarthy**	N	N	Y	N	N	Y
24	Carbajal	Y	Y	N	Y	Y	Y
25	Hill, K.	Y	Y	N	+	Y	Y
26	Brownley	Y	Y	N	Y	Y	Y
27	Chu	Y	Y	N	Y	Y	Y
28	Schiff	Y	Y	N	Y	Y	Y
29	Cárdenas	Y	Y	N	Y	Y	Y
30	Sherman	Y	Y	N	Y	Y	Y
31	Aguilar	Y	Y	N	Y	Y	Y
32	Napolitano	Y	Y	N	Y	Y	Y
33	Lieu	Y	Y	N	Y	Y	Y
34	Gomez	Y	Y	N	Y	Y	Y
35	Torres	Y	Y	N	Y	Y	Y
36	Ruiz	Y	Y	N	Y	Y	Y
37	Bass	Y	Y	N	Y	Y	Y
38	Sánchez	Y	Y	N	Y	Y	Y
39	Cisneros	Y	Y	N	Y	Y	Y
40	Roybal-Allard	Y	Y	N	Y	Y	+
41	Takano	Y	Y	N	Y	Y	Y
42	**Calvert**	N	N	Y	N	N	Y
43	Waters	Y	Y	N	Y	Y	Y
44	Barragán	Y	Y	N	Y	Y	Y
45	Porter	Y	Y	Y	Y	Y	Y
46	Correa	Y	Y	N	Y	Y	Y
47	Lowenthal	Y	Y	N	Y	Y	Y
48	Rouda	Y	Y	N	Y	Y	Y
49	Levin	Y	Y	N	Y	Y	Y
50	**Hunter**	N	N	Y	N	N	Y
51	Vargas	Y	Y	N	Y	Y	Y
52	Peters	Y	Y	N	Y	Y	Y

		61	62	63	64	65	66
53	Davis, S.	Y	Y	N	Y	Y	Y
COLORADO							
1	DeGette	Y	Y	N	Y	Y	Y
2	Neguse	Y	Y	N	Y	Y	Y
3	**Tipton**	N	N	Y	N	N	Y
4	**Buck**	N	N	Y	N	N	N
5	**Lamborn**	N	N	Y	N	N	Y
6	Crow	Y	Y	N	Y	Y	Y
7	Perlmutter	Y	Y	N	Y	Y	Y
CONNECTICUT							
1	Larson	Y	Y	N	Y	Y	Y
2	Courtney	Y	Y	N	Y	Y	Y
3	DeLauro	Y	Y	N	Y	Y	Y
4	Himes	Y	Y	N	Y	Y	Y
5	Hayes	Y	Y	N	Y	Y	Y
DELAWARE							
AL	Blunt Rochester	Y	Y	N	Y	?	Y
FLORIDA							
1	**Gaetz**	N	N	Y	N	N	Y
2	**Dunn**	N	N	Y	N	N	Y
3	**Yoho**	N	N	Y	N	N	Y
4	**Rutherford**	N	N	Y	N	N	Y
5	Lawson	Y	Y	N	Y	Y	Y
6	**Waltz**	N	N	Y	N	N	Y
7	Murphy	Y	Y	N	Y	Y	Y
8	**Posey**	N	N	Y	N	Y	Y
9	Soto	Y	Y	N	Y	Y	Y
10	Demings	Y	Y	N	Y	Y	Y
11	**Webster**	N	N	Y	N	?	Y
12	**Bilirakis**	N	N	Y	N	N	Y
13	Crist	Y	Y	N	Y	Y	Y
14	Castor	Y	Y	N	Y	Y	Y
15	**Spano**	N	N	Y	N	N	Y
16	**Buchanan**	N	N	Y	N	N	Y
17	**Steube**	N	N	Y	N	N	+
18	**Mast**	N	N	Y	N	N	Y
19	**Rooney**	N	N	Y	N	N	Y
20	Hastings	Y	Y	N	Y	Y	Y
21	Frankel	Y	Y	N	Y	Y	Y
22	Deutch	Y	Y	N	Y	Y	Y
23	Wasserman Schultz	Y	Y	N	Y	Y	Y
24	Wilson, F.	?	?	?	?	?	?
25	**Diaz-Balart**	N	N	Y	N	N	Y
26	Mucarsel-Powell	Y	Y	N	Y	Y	Y
27	Shalala	Y	Y	N	Y	Y	Y
GEORGIA							
1	**Carter, E.L.**	N	N	Y	N	N	Y
2	Bishop, S.	Y	Y	N	Y	Y	Y
3	**Ferguson**	N	N	Y	N	N	Y
4	Johnson, H.	Y	Y	N	Y	Y	Y
5	Lewis John	Y	Y	N	Y	Y	Y
6	McBath	Y	Y	N	Y	Y	Y
7	**Woodall**	N	N	Y	N	N	Y
8	**Scott, A.**	N	N	Y	N	N	Y
9	**Collins, D.**	N	N	Y	N	?	Y
10	**Hice**	N	N	Y	N	N	Y
11	**Loudermilk**	N	N	Y	N	N	N
12	**Allen**	N	N	Y	N	N	Y
13	Scott, D.	Y	Y	N	Y	Y	Y
14	**Graves, T.**	N	N	Y	N	N	Y
HAWAII							
1	Case	Y	Y	N	Y	Y	Y
2	Gabbard	Y	Y	N	Y	Y	Y
IDAHO							
1	**Fulcher**	N	N	Y	N	N	Y
2	**Simpson**	N	N	Y	N	N	Y
ILLINOIS							
1	Rush	Y	Y	N	Y	Y	Y
2	Kelly, R.	Y	Y	N	Y	Y	Y
3	Lipinski	Y	Y	N	Y	Y	Y
4	García, J.	Y	Y	N	Y	Y	Y
5	Quigley	Y	Y	N	Y	Y	Y
6	Casten	Y	Y	N	Y	Y	Y
7	Davis, D.	Y	Y	N	Y	Y	Y
8	Krishnamoorthi	Y	Y	N	Y	Y	+
9	Schakowsky	Y	Y	N	Y	Y	Y
10	Schneider	Y	Y	N	Y	Y	Y
11	Foster	Y	Y	N	Y	Y	Y

		61	62	63	64	65	66
12	**Bost**	-	+	+	+	-	Y
13	**Davis, R.**	?	?	?	+	+	Y
14	Underwood	Y	Y	N	Y	Y	Y
15	**Shimkus**	?	?	?	?	?	Y
16	**Kinzinger**	N	Y	Y	Y	Y	Y
17	Bustos	Y	Y	N	Y	Y	Y
18	**LaHood**	-	-	+	-	-	Y
INDIANA							
1	Visclosky	Y	Y	N	Y	Y	Y
2	**Walorski**	N	N	Y	N	-	Y
3	**Banks**	N	N	Y	N	N	Y
4	**Baird**	N	N	Y	N	N	Y
5	**Brooks, S.**	N	N	Y	N	Y	Y
6	**Pence**	N	N	Y	N	N	Y
7	Carson	Y	Y	N	Y	Y	Y
8	**Bucshon**	N	N	Y	N	N	Y
9	**Hollingsworth**	N	N	Y	N	N	Y
IOWA							
1	Finkenauer	Y	Y	Y	Y	Y	Y
2	Loebsack	Y	Y	N	Y	Y	Y
3	Axne	Y	Y	Y	Y	Y	Y
4	**King, S.**	N	N	Y	N	N	Y
KANSAS							
1	**Marshall**	N	N	Y	N	N	Y
2	**Watkins**	N	N	Y	N	N	Y
3	Davids	Y	Y	N	Y	Y	Y
4	**Estes**	N	N	Y	N	N	Y
KENTUCKY							
1	**Comer**	?	?	?	?	?	Y
2	**Guthrie**	N	N	Y	N	N	Y
3	Yarmuth	Y	Y	N	Y	Y	Y
4	**Massie**	N	N	Y	N	N	N
5	**Rogers, H.**	N	N	Y	N	N	Y
6	**Barr**	N	N	Y	N	N	Y
LOUISIANA							
1	**Scalise**	N	N	Y	N	N	Y
2	Richmond	Y	Y	N	Y	Y	Y
3	**Higgins, C.**	N	N	Y	N	N	Y
4	**Johnson, M.**	N	N	Y	N	N	Y
5	**Abraham**	N	N	Y	N	N	Y
6	**Graves, G.**	N	N	Y	N	N	Y
MAINE							
1	Pingree	Y	Y	N	Y	Y	Y
2	Golden	Y	Y	N	Y	Y	Y
MARYLAND							
1	**Harris**	N	N	Y	N	N	N
2	Ruppersberger	Y	Y	N	Y	?	Y
3	Sarbanes	Y	Y	N	Y	Y	Y
4	Brown, A.	Y	Y	N	Y	Y	Y
5	Hoyer	Y	Y	N	Y	Y	?
6	Trone	Y	Y	N	Y	Y	Y
7	Cummings	Y	Y	N	Y	Y	Y
8	Raskin	Y	Y	N	Y	?	Y
MASSACHUSETTS							
1	Neal	Y	Y	N	Y	Y	Y
2	McGovern	Y	Y	N	Y	Y	Y
3	Trahan	Y	Y	N	Y	Y	Y
4	Kennedy	Y	Y	N	Y	Y	Y
5	Clark	Y	Y	N	Y	Y	Y
6	Moulton	Y	Y	N	Y	Y	Y
7	Pressley	Y	Y	N	Y	Y	Y
8	Lynch	Y	Y	N	Y	Y	Y
9	Keating	Y	Y	N	Y	Y	Y
MICHIGAN							
1	**Bergman**	N	N	Y	N	N	Y
2	**Huizenga**	N	N	Y	N	N	Y
3	**Amash**	N	N	N	N	N	N
4	**Moolenaar**	N	N	Y	N	N	Y
5	Kildee	Y	Y	N	Y	Y	Y
6	**Upton**	N	N	Y	N	Y	Y
7	**Walberg**	N	N	Y	N	N	Y
8	Slotkin	Y	Y	Y	Y	Y	Y
9	Levin	Y	Y	N	Y	Y	Y
10	**Mitchell**	N	N	Y	N	N	Y
11	Stevens	Y	Y	N	Y	Y	Y
12	Dingell	Y	Y	N	Y	Y	?
13	Tlaib	Y	Y	N	+	Y	Y
14	Lawrence	Y	Y	N	Y	Y	Y
MINNESOTA							
1	**Hagedorn**	N	N	Y	N	N	Y
2	Craig	Y	Y	N	Y	Y	Y
3	Phillips	Y	Y	N	Y	Y	Y
4	McCollum	Y	Y	N	Y	Y	Y
5	Omar	Y	Y	N	Y	Y	Y

		61	62	63	64	65	66
6	**Emmer**	N	N	Y	N	?	Y
7	Peterson	Y	Y	N	Y	Y	Y
8	**Stauber**	N	Y	Y	Y	Y	Y
MISSISSIPPI							
1	**Kelly, T.**	N	N	Y	N	N	Y
2	Thompson, B.	Y	Y	N	Y	Y	Y
3	**Guest**	N	N	Y	N	N	Y
4	**Palazzo**	N	N	Y	N	N	Y
MISSOURI							
1	Clay	Y	Y	N	Y	Y	Y
2	**Wagner**	N	N	Y	N	N	Y
3	**Luetkemeyer**	N	N	Y	N	N	Y
4	**Hartzler**	N	N	Y	N	N	Y
5	Cleaver	Y	Y	N	Y	Y	Y
6	**Graves, S.**	N	N	Y	N	N	Y
7	**Long**	N	N	Y	N	?	Y
8	**Smith, J.**	N	N	Y	N	N	Y
MONTANA							
AL	**Gianforte**	N	N	Y	N	N	Y
NEBRASKA							
1	**Fortenberry**	N	N	Y	Y	Y	Y
2	**Bacon**	N	N	Y	N	Y	Y
3	**Smith, Adrian**	N	N	Y	N	N	Y
NEVADA							
1	Titus	Y	Y	N	Y	Y	Y
2	**Amodei**	N	N	Y	N	N	Y
3	Lee	Y	Y	N	Y	Y	Y
4	Horsford	Y	Y	N	Y	Y	Y
NEW HAMPSHIRE							
1	Pappas	Y	Y	N	Y	Y	Y
2	Kuster	Y	Y	N	Y	Y	Y
NEW JERSEY							
1	Norcross	Y	Y	N	Y	Y	Y
2	Van Drew	Y	Y	Y	Y	Y	Y
3	Kim	Y	Y	Y	Y	Y	Y
4	**Smith, C.**	N	Y	Y	Y	Y	Y
5	Gottheimer	Y	Y	Y	Y	Y	Y
6	Pallone	Y	Y	N	Y	Y	Y
7	Malinowski	Y	Y	N	Y	Y	Y
8	Sires	Y	Y	N	Y	Y	Y
9	Pascrell	Y	Y	N	Y	Y	Y
10	Payne	?	?	?	?	?	Y
11	Sherrill	Y	Y	N	Y	Y	Y
12	Watson Coleman	Y	Y	N	Y	Y	Y
NEW MEXICO							
1	Haaland	Y	Y	N	Y	Y	Y
2	Torres Small	Y	Y	N	Y	Y	Y
3	Luján	Y	Y	N	Y	Y	Y
NEW YORK							
1	**Zeldin**	N	N	Y	Y	N	Y
2	**King, P.**	N	N	Y	Y	N	Y
3	Suozzi	Y	Y	N	Y	Y	Y
4	Rice, K.	Y	Y	N	Y	Y	Y
5	Meeks	Y	Y	N	Y	Y	Y
6	Meng	Y	Y	N	Y	Y	Y
7	Velázquez	Y	Y	N	Y	Y	Y
8	Jeffries	Y	Y	N	Y	Y	Y
9	Clarke	Y	Y	N	Y	Y	Y
10	Nadler	Y	Y	N	Y	Y	Y
11	Rose	Y	Y	N	Y	Y	Y
12	Maloney, C.	Y	Y	N	Y	Y	Y
13	Espaillat	Y	Y	N	Y	Y	Y
14	Ocasio-Cortez	Y	Y	N	Y	Y	Y
15	Serrano	Y	Y	N	Y	Y	Y
16	Engel	Y	Y	N	Y	Y	Y
17	Lowey	Y	Y	N	Y	Y	Y
18	Maloney, S.P.	Y	Y	N	Y	Y	Y
19	Delgado	Y	Y	Y	Y	Y	Y
20	Tonko	Y	Y	N	Y	Y	Y
21	**Stefanik**	N	N	Y	Y	Y	Y
22	Brindisi	Y	Y	Y	Y	Y	Y
23	**Reed**	N	N	Y	N	N	Y
24	**Katko**	N	N	Y	Y	Y	Y
25	Morelle	Y	Y	N	Y	Y	Y
26	Higgins, B.	Y	Y	N	Y	Y	Y
27	**Collins, C.**	N	N	Y	Y	N	Y
NORTH CAROLINA							
1	Butterfield	Y	Y	N	Y	Y	Y
2	**Holding**	N	N	Y	N	N	Y
3	**Jones**	?	?	?	?	?	?
4	Price	Y	Y	N	Y	Y	Y
5	**Foxx**	N	N	Y	N	N	Y
6	**Walker**	N	N	Y	N	N	Y
7	**Rouzer**	N	N	Y	N	N	Y

		61	62	63	64	65	66
8	**Hudson**	N	N	Y	N	N	Y
9	vacant						
10	**McHenry**	N	N	Y	N	N	Y
11	**Meadows**	N	N	Y	N	N	Y
12	Adams	Y	Y	N	Y	Y	Y
13	**Budd**	N	N	Y	N	N	Y
NORTH DAKOTA							
AL	**Armstrong**	N	N	Y	N	N	Y
OHIO							
1	**Chabot**	N	N	Y	N	N	Y
2	**Wenstrup**	N	N	Y	N	N	Y
3	Beatty	Y	Y	N	Y	Y	Y
4	**Jordan**	N	N	Y	N	N	N
5	**Latta**	N	N	Y	N	N	Y
6	**Johnson, B.**	N	N	Y	Y	N	Y
7	**Gibbs**	N	N	Y	N	N	Y
8	**Davidson**	N	N	Y	N	N	N
9	Kaptur	Y	Y	N	Y	Y	Y
10	**Turner**	N	N	Y	Y	N	Y
11	Fudge	Y	Y	N	Y	Y	?
12	**Balderson**	N	N	Y	N	N	Y
13	Ryan	Y	Y	N	Y	Y	Y
14	**Joyce**	N	N	Y	Y	Y	Y
15	**Stivers**	N	N	Y	N	N	Y
16	**Gonzalez**	N	N	Y	Y	Y	Y
OKLAHOMA							
1	**Hern**	N	N	Y	N	N	N
2	**Mullin**	?	?	?	?	?	Y
3	**Lucas**	N	N	Y	N	N	Y
4	**Cole**	N	Y	Y	N	Y	Y
5	Horn	Y	Y	Y	Y	N	Y
OREGON							
1	Bonamici	Y	Y	N	Y	Y	Y
2	**Walden**	N	N	Y	Y	Y	Y
3	Blumenauer	Y	Y	N	Y	Y	Y
4	DeFazio	Y	Y	N	Y	Y	Y
5	Schrader	?	Y	N	Y	Y	Y
PENNSYLVANIA							
1	**Fitzpatrick**	N	Y	Y	Y	Y	Y
2	Boyle	Y	Y	N	Y	Y	Y
3	Evans	Y	Y	N	Y	Y	Y
4	Dean	Y	Y	N	Y	Y	Y
5	Scanlon	Y	Y	N	Y	Y	Y
6	Houlahan	Y	Y	Y	Y	Y	Y
7	Wild	Y	Y	Y	Y	Y	Y
8	Cartwright	Y	Y	N	Y	Y	Y
9	**Meuser**	N	N	Y	N	N	Y
10	**Perry**	N	N	Y	N	N	N
11	**Smucker**	N	N	Y	N	N	Y
12	vacant						
13	**Joyce**	N	N	Y	N	N	Y
14	**Reschenthaler**	N	N	Y	N	N	Y
15	**Thompson, G.**	N	N	Y	N	N	Y
16	**Kelly, M.**	N	N	Y	N	N	Y
17	Lamb	Y	Y	N	Y	Y	Y
18	Doyle	Y	Y	N	Y	Y	Y
RHODE ISLAND							
1	Cicilline	Y	Y	N	Y	Y	Y
2	Langevin	Y	Y	N	Y	Y	Y
SOUTH CAROLINA							
1	Cunningham	Y	Y	Y	Y	Y	Y
2	**Wilson, J.**	N	N	Y	N	?	Y
3	**Duncan**	N	N	Y	N	N	Y
4	**Timmons**	N	N	Y	N	N	Y
5	**Norman**	N	N	Y	N	N	Y
6	Clyburn	Y	Y	N	Y	Y	Y
7	**Rice, T.**	N	N	Y	N	N	N
SOUTH DAKOTA							
AL	**Johnson**	N	N	Y	N	N	Y
TENNESSEE							
1	**Roe**	N	N	Y	N	N	Y
2	**Burchett**	N	N	Y	N	N	Y
3	**Fleischmann**	N	N	Y	N	N	Y
4	**DesJarlais**	N	N	Y	N	N	Y
5	Cooper	Y	Y	N	Y	Y	Y
6	**Rose**	N	N	Y	N	N	Y
7	**Green**	N	N	Y	N	N	Y
8	**Kustoff**	N	N	Y	N	N	Y
9	Cohen	Y	Y	N	Y	Y	Y
TEXAS							
1	**Gohmert**	N	N	Y	N	N	N
2	**Crenshaw**	N	N	Y	N	N	Y
3	**Taylor**	N	N	Y	N	N	Y
4	**Ratcliffe**	N	N	Y	N	N	Y

		61	62	63	64	65	66
5	**Gooden**	N	N	Y	N	N	Y
6	**Wright**	N	N	Y	N	N	Y
7	Fletcher	Y	Y	N	Y	Y	Y
8	**Brady**	N	N	Y	N	N	Y
9	Green, A.	Y	Y	N	Y	Y	Y
10	**McCaul**	N	N	Y	Y	Y	Y
11	**Conaway**	N	N	Y	N	N	Y
12	**Granger**	N	N	Y	N	N	Y
13	**Thornberry**	N	N	Y	N	N	Y
14	**Weber**	N	N	Y	N	N	Y
15	Gonzalez	Y	Y	N	Y	Y	Y
16	Escobar	Y	Y	N	Y	Y	Y
17	**Flores**	N	N	Y	N	Y	Y
18	Jackson Lee	Y	Y	N	Y	Y	Y
19	**Arrington**	N	N	Y	N	N	Y
20	Castro	Y	Y	N	Y	Y	Y
21	**Roy**	N	N	Y	N	N	N
22	**Olson**	N	N	Y	N	N	Y
23	**Hurd**	N	Y	Y	Y	Y	Y
24	**Marchant**	N	N	Y	N	N	Y
25	**Williams**	N	N	Y	N	N	N
26	**Burgess**	N	N	Y	N	N	N
27	**Cloud**	N	N	Y	N	N	N
28	Cuellar	Y	Y	N	Y	Y	Y
29	Garcia, S.	Y	Y	N	Y	Y	Y
30	Johnson, E.B.	Y	Y	N	Y	Y	Y
31	**Carter, J.**	N	N	Y	N	N	Y
32	Allred	Y	Y	N	Y	Y	Y
33	Veasey	Y	Y	N	Y	Y	Y
34	Vela	Y	Y	N	Y	Y	Y
35	Doggett	Y	Y	N	Y	Y	Y
36	**Babin**	?	N	Y	N	N	Y
UTAH							
1	**Bishop, R.**	N	N	Y	Y	N	?
2	**Stewart**	N	N	Y	N	N	Y
3	**Curtis**	N	N	Y	N	N	Y
4	McAdams	Y	Y	Y	Y	Y	Y
VERMONT							
AL	Welch	Y	Y	N	Y	Y	Y
VIRGINIA							
1	**Wittman**	N	Y	Y	Y	Y	Y
2	Luria	Y	Y	Y	Y	Y	Y
3	Scott, R.	Y	Y	N	Y	Y	Y
4	McEachin	Y	Y	N	Y	Y	Y
5	**Riggleman**	N	N	Y	N	Y	Y
6	**Cline**	N	N	Y	N	N	Y
7	Spanberger	Y	Y	N	Y	Y	Y
8	Beyer	Y	Y	N	Y	Y	Y
9	**Griffith**	N	N	Y	N	N	Y
10	Wexton	Y	Y	N	Y	Y	Y
11	Connolly	Y	Y	N	Y	Y	Y
WASHINGTON							
1	DelBene	Y	Y	N	Y	Y	Y
2	Larsen	Y	Y	N	Y	Y	Y
3	**Herrera Beutler**	N	N	Y	Y	N	Y
4	**Newhouse**	N	N	Y	Y	N	Y
5	**McMorris Rodgers**	N	N	Y	N	N	Y
6	Kilmer	Y	Y	N	Y	Y	Y
7	Jayapal	Y	Y	N	Y	Y	Y
8	Schrier	Y	Y	N	Y	Y	Y
9	Smith Adam	Y	Y	N	Y	Y	Y
10	Heck	Y	Y	N	Y	Y	Y
WEST VIRGINIA							
1	**McKinley**	N	N	Y	Y	N	Y
2	**Mooney**	N	N	Y	N	N	Y
3	**Miller**	N	N	Y	N	N	Y
WISCONSIN							
1	**Steil**	N	N	Y	N	Y	Y
2	Pocan	Y	Y	N	Y	Y	Y
3	Kind	Y	Y	N	Y	Y	Y
4	Moore	Y	Y	N	Y	Y	Y
5	**Sensenbrenner**	+	-	+	-	-	Y
6	**Grothman**	N	N	Y	N	N	N
7	**Duffy**						
8	**Gallagher**	N	N	Y	N	N	Y
WYOMING							
AL	**Cheney**	N	N	Y	N	N	Y
DELEGATES							
	Radewagen (A.S.)		?				
	Norton (D.C.)		Y				
	San Nicolas (Guam)		?				
	Sablan (N. Marianas)		Y				
	González-Colón (P.R.)		N				
	Plaskett (V.I.)		Y				

||| HOUSE VOTES

67. HR66. Route 66 Centennial - Passage. Norton, D-D.C., motion to suspend the rules and pass the bill that would establish the Route 66 Centennial Commission that would study and make recommendations for the federal government to honor the centennial of Route 66. Motion agreed to 399-22: R 171-22; D 228-0. *Note: A two-thirds majority of those present and voting (281 in this case) is required for passage under suspension of the rules.* Feb. 6, 2019.

68. HR840, HRES86. Veterans' Child Care and Committee Funding - Previous Question. Morelle, D-N.Y., motion to order the previous question (thus ending debate and possibility of amendment) on the rule (H Res 105) that would provide for House floor consideration of the bill that would make permanent and expand a Veterans Affairs Department program that provides child care assistance to veterans while they are receiving certain VA health care services (HR 840), and that would provide for the automatic agreement in the House to a resolution (H Res 86) that would provide $70,000 for the Select Committee on the Climate Crisis and $50,000 for the Select Committee on the Modernization of Congress to cover expenses through March 31, 2019. It would also provide for motions to suspend the rules through the legislative day of Feb. 15, 2019. Motion agreed to 227-189: R 0-189; D 227-0. Feb. 7, 2019.

69. HRES86, HR840. Veterans' Child Care and Committee Funding - Rule. Adoption of the rule (H Res 105) that would provide for House floor consideration of the bill that would make permanent and expand a Veterans Affairs Department program that provides child care assistance to veterans while they are receiving certain VA health care services (HR 840), and that would provide for the automatic agreement in the House to a resolution (H Res 86) that would provide $70,000 for the Select Committee on the Climate Crisis and $50,000 for the Select Committee on the Modernization of Congress to cover expenses through March 31, 2019. It would also provide for motions to suspend the rules through the legislative day of Feb. 15, 2019. Adopted 225-193: R 0-193; D 225-0. Feb. 7, 2019.

70. HR450. Veteran Fraud Penalties - Passage. Bass, D-Calif., motion to suspend the rules and pass the bill that would establish fines, prison sentences of up to five years, or both for individuals who engage in schemes to defraud veterans in pursuit of obtaining veterans benefits. Motion agreed to 417-0: R 191-0; D 226-0. *Note: A two-thirds majority of those present and voting (278 in this case) is required for passage under suspension of the rules.* Feb. 7, 2019.

71. HR507. Human Trafficking Data - Passage. Bass, D-Calif., motion to suspend the rules and pass the bill that would establish a working group to identify barriers to collecting data on human trafficking, recommend practices to promote better data collection and analysis, and would implement a pilot project based on the group's recommendations. It would also require the attorney general, in consultation with the Administrative Office of the United States Courts, to submit a report to Congress on efforts to increase restitution to victims of human trafficking. Motion agreed to 414-1: R 189-1; D 225-0. *Note: A two-thirds majority of those present and voting (277 in this case) is required for passage under suspension of the rules.* Feb. 7, 2019.

72. HR840. Veterans' Child Care - Prohibition on New Construction. Bergman, R-Mich., amendment that would prohibit the use of funds made available for child care assistance under the bill for the purpose of constructing any new child care facility. Rejected in Committee of the Whole 172-246: R 172-19; D 0-226; I 0-1. Feb. 8, 2019.

		67	68	69	70	71	72
ALABAMA							
1	**Byrne**	N	N	N	Y	Y	Y
2	**Roby**	Y	N	N	Y	Y	Y
3	**Rogers, M.**	Y	N	N	Y	Y	N
4	**Aderholt**	Y	N	N	Y	Y	Y
5	**Brooks, M.**	N	N	N	Y	Y	N
6	**Palmer**	N	N	N	Y	Y	Y
7	Sewell	Y	Y	Y	Y	Y	N
ALASKA							
AL	**Young**	Y	N	N	Y	Y	Y
ARIZONA							
1	O'Halleran	Y	Y	Y	Y	Y	N
2	Kirkpatrick	Y	Y	Y	Y	Y	N
3	Grijalva	Y	Y	?	Y	Y	N
4	**Gosar**	N	N	N	Y	Y	Y
5	**Biggs**	N	N	N	Y	Y	Y
6	**Schweikert**	Y	N	N	Y	Y	Y
7	Gallego	Y	Y	Y	Y	Y	N
8	**Lesko**	Y	N	N	Y	Y	Y
9	Stanton	Y	Y	Y	Y	Y	N
ARKANSAS							
1	**Crawford**	Y	N	N	Y	Y	Y
2	**Hill, F.**	Y	N	N	Y	Y	Y
3	**Womack**	Y	N	N	Y	Y	Y
4	**Westerman**	Y	N	N	Y	Y	Y
CALIFORNIA							
1	**LaMalfa**	Y	?	?	?	?	?
2	Huffman	Y	Y	Y	Y	Y	-
3	Garamendi	Y	Y	Y	Y	Y	N
4	**McClintock**	Y	N	N	Y	Y	Y
5	Thompson, M.	Y	Y	Y	Y	Y	N
6	Matsui	Y	Y	Y	Y	Y	N
7	Bera	Y	Y	Y	Y	Y	N
8	**Cook**	Y	N	N	Y	Y	Y
9	McNerney	Y	Y	Y	Y	Y	N
10	Harder	Y	Y	Y	Y	Y	N
11	DeSaulnier	Y	Y	Y	Y	Y	N
12	Pelosi						
13	Lee B.	Y	Y	Y	Y	Y	N
14	Speier	Y	Y	Y	Y	Y	N
15	Swalwell	Y	Y	Y	Y	Y	N
16	Costa	Y	Y	Y	Y	Y	N
17	Khanna	Y	Y	Y	Y	Y	N
18	Eshoo	Y	Y	Y	Y	Y	N
19	Lofgren	Y	Y	Y	Y	Y	N
20	Panetta	Y	Y	Y	Y	Y	N
21	Cox	Y	Y	Y	Y	Y	N
22	**Nunes**	Y	N	N	Y	Y	Y
23	**McCarthy**	Y	?	?	?	?	Y
24	Carbajal	Y	Y	Y	Y	Y	N
25	Hill, K.	Y	Y	Y	Y	Y	N
26	Brownley	Y	Y	Y	Y	Y	N
27	Chu	Y	Y	Y	Y	Y	N
28	Schiff	Y	Y	Y	Y	Y	N
29	Cárdenas	Y	Y	Y	Y	Y	N
30	Sherman	Y	Y	Y	Y	Y	N
31	Aguilar	Y	Y	Y	Y	Y	N
32	Napolitano	Y	Y	Y	Y	Y	N
33	Lieu	Y	Y	Y	Y	Y	N
34	Gomez	Y	Y	Y	Y	Y	N
35	Torres	Y	Y	Y	Y	Y	N
36	Ruiz	Y	Y	Y	Y	Y	N
37	Bass	Y	Y	Y	Y	Y	N
38	Sánchez	Y	Y	Y	Y	Y	N
39	Cisneros	Y	Y	Y	Y	Y	N
40	Roybal-Allard	+	Y	Y	Y	Y	N
41	Takano	Y	Y	Y	Y	Y	N
42	**Calvert**	Y	N	N	Y	Y	Y
43	Waters	Y	Y	Y	Y	Y	N
44	Barragán	Y	Y	Y	Y	Y	N
45	Porter	Y	Y	Y	Y	Y	N
46	Correa	Y	Y	Y	Y	Y	N
47	Lowenthal	Y	Y	Y	Y	Y	N
48	Rouda	Y	Y	Y	Y	Y	N
49	Levin	Y	Y	Y	Y	Y	N
50	**Hunter**	Y	N	N	Y	Y	Y
51	Vargas	Y	Y	Y	Y	Y	N
52	Peters	Y	Y	Y	Y	Y	N

		67	68	69	70	71	72
53	Davis, S.	Y	Y	Y	Y	?	N
COLORADO							
1	DeGette	Y	Y	Y	Y	Y	N
2	Neguse	Y	Y	Y	Y	Y	N
3	**Tipton**	Y	N	N	Y	Y	Y
4	**Buck**	Y	N	N	Y	Y	Y
5	**Lamborn**	Y	N	N	Y	Y	Y
6	Crow	Y	Y	Y	Y	Y	N
7	Perlmutter	Y	Y	Y	Y	Y	N
CONNECTICUT							
1	Larson	Y	Y	Y	Y	Y	N
2	Courtney	Y	Y	Y	Y	Y	N
3	DeLauro	Y	Y	Y	Y	Y	N
4	Himes	Y	Y	Y	Y	Y	N
5	Hayes	Y	Y	Y	Y	Y	N
DELAWARE							
AL	Blunt Rochester	Y	Y	Y	Y	Y	N
FLORIDA							
1	**Gaetz**	Y	N	N	Y	Y	?
2	**Dunn**	Y	N	N	Y	Y	Y
3	**Yoho**	N	N	N	Y	Y	Y
4	**Rutherford**	Y	N	N	+	Y	+
5	Lawson	Y	Y	Y	Y	Y	?
6	**Waltz**	Y	N	N	Y	Y	Y
7	Murphy	Y	Y	Y	Y	Y	N
8	**Posey**	Y	N	N	Y	Y	Y
9	Soto	Y	Y	Y	Y	Y	N
10	Demings	Y	Y	Y	Y	Y	N
11	**Webster**	Y	N	N	Y	Y	Y
12	**Bilirakis**	Y	N	N	Y	Y	Y
13	Crist	Y	Y	Y	Y	Y	N
14	Castor	Y	Y	Y	Y	Y	N
15	**Spano**	Y	N	N	Y	Y	Y
16	**Buchanan**	Y	N	N	Y	Y	Y
17	**Steube**	+	-	+	+	+	-
18	**Mast**	Y	N	N	Y	Y	Y
19	**Rooney**	Y	N	N	Y	Y	Y
20	Hastings	Y	?	?	?	?	N
21	Frankel	Y	Y	Y	Y	Y	N
22	Deutch	Y	Y	Y	Y	Y	N
23	Wasserman Schultz	Y	Y	Y	Y	Y	N
24	Wilson, F.	?	?	?	?	?	?
25	**Diaz-Balart**	Y	N	N	Y	Y	Y
26	Mucarsel-Powell	Y	Y	Y	Y	Y	N
27	Shalala	Y	Y	Y	Y	Y	N
GEORGIA							
1	**Carter, E.L.**	Y	N	N	Y	Y	Y
2	Bishop, S.	Y	Y	Y	Y	Y	N
3	**Ferguson**	Y	N	N	Y	Y	Y
4	Johnson, H.	Y	Y	Y	Y	Y	N
5	Lewis John	Y	Y	Y	Y	Y	N
6	McBath	Y	Y	Y	Y	Y	N
7	**Woodall**	Y	N	N	Y	Y	Y
8	**Scott, A.**	Y	N	N	Y	Y	Y
9	**Collins, D.**	Y	N	N	Y	Y	Y
10	**Hice**	N	N	N	Y	Y	Y
11	**Loudermilk**	Y	?	N	Y	Y	Y
12	**Allen**	N	N	N	Y	Y	Y
13	Scott, D.	Y	Y	Y	Y	Y	N
14	**Graves, T.**	N	N	N	Y	Y	N
HAWAII							
1	Case	Y	Y	Y	Y	Y	N
2	Gabbard	Y	Y	Y	Y	Y	N
IDAHO							
1	**Fulcher**	Y	N	N	Y	Y	Y
2	**Simpson**	Y	N	N	Y	Y	Y
ILLINOIS							
1	Rush	Y	Y	Y	Y	Y	N
2	Kelly, R.	Y	Y	Y	Y	Y	N
3	Lipinski	Y	Y	Y	Y	Y	N
4	García, J.	Y	Y	Y	Y	Y	N
5	Quigley	Y	Y	Y	Y	Y	N
6	Casten	Y	Y	Y	Y	Y	N
7	Davis, D.	Y	Y	Y	Y	Y	N
8	Krishnamoorthi	Y	Y	Y	Y	Y	N
9	Schakowsky	Y	Y	Y	Y	Y	N
10	Schneider	Y	Y	Y	Y	Y	N
11	Foster	Y	Y	Y	Y	Y	N

KEY:

Republicans	Democrats	*Independents*

Y	Voted for (yea)	**N**	Voted against (nay)	**P**	Voted "present"
+	Announced for	**–**	Announced against	**?**	Did not vote or otherwise make position known
#	Paired for	**X**	Paired against		

		67	68	69	70	71	72
12	**Bost**	Y	N	N	Y	Y	Y
13	**Davis, R.**	Y	N	N	Y	Y	Y
14	Underwood	Y	Y	Y	Y	Y	N
15	**Shimkus**	Y	N	N	Y	Y	Y
16	**Kinzinger**	Y	N	N	Y	Y	Y
17	Bustos	Y	Y	Y	Y	Y	N
18	**LaHood**	Y	N	N	Y	Y	Y
INDIANA							
1	Visclosky	Y	Y	Y	Y	Y	N
2	**Walorski**	Y	N	N	Y	Y	Y
3	**Banks**	Y	N	N	Y	Y	Y
4	**Baird**	Y	N	N	Y	Y	Y
5	**Brooks, S.**	Y	N	N	Y	Y	N
6	**Pence**	Y	N	N	Y	Y	Y
7	Carson	Y	Y	Y	Y	Y	N
8	**Bucshon**	Y	N	N	Y	Y	Y
9	**Hollingsworth**	Y	N	N	Y	Y	Y
IOWA							
1	Finkenauer	Y	Y	Y	Y	Y	N
2	Loebsack	Y	Y	Y	Y	Y	N
3	Axne	Y	Y	Y	Y	Y	N
4	**King, S.**	Y	N	N	Y	Y	Y
KANSAS							
1	**Marshall**	Y	N	N	Y	Y	Y
2	**Watkins**	Y	N	N	Y	Y	Y
3	Davids	Y	Y	Y	Y	Y	N
4	**Estes**	Y	N	N	Y	Y	Y
KENTUCKY							
1	**Comer**	Y	N	N	Y	Y	Y
2	**Guthrie**	Y	N	N	Y	Y	Y
3	Yarmuth	Y	Y	Y	Y	Y	N
4	**Massie**	N	N	N	Y	Y	Y
5	**Rogers, H.**	Y	N	N	Y	Y	Y
6	**Barr**	Y	N	N	Y	Y	Y
LOUISIANA							
1	**Scalise**	Y	N	N	Y	Y	Y
2	Richmond	Y	Y	Y	Y	Y	N
3	**Higgins, C.**	Y	N	N	Y	Y	Y
4	**Johnson, M.**	N	N	N	Y	?	Y
5	**Abraham**	Y	N	N	Y	Y	Y
6	**Graves, G.**	Y	N	N	Y	Y	Y
MAINE							
1	Pingree	Y	Y	Y	Y	Y	N
2	Golden	Y	Y	Y	Y	Y	N
MARYLAND							
1	**Harris**	N	N	N	Y	Y	Y
2	Ruppersberger	Y	Y	Y	Y	Y	N
3	Sarbanes	Y	Y	Y	Y	Y	N
4	Brown, A.	Y	Y	Y	Y	Y	N
5	Hoyer	?	Y	Y	Y	Y	N
6	Trone	Y	Y	Y	Y	Y	N
7	Cummings	Y	?	?	?	?	N
8	Raskin	Y	Y	Y	Y	Y	N
MASSACHUSETTS							
1	Neal	Y	Y	Y	Y	Y	N
2	McGovern	Y	Y	Y	Y	Y	N
3	Trahan	Y	Y	Y	Y	Y	N
4	Kennedy	Y	Y	Y	Y	Y	?
5	Clark	Y	Y	Y	Y	Y	N
6	Moulton	Y	Y	Y	Y	Y	N
7	Pressley	Y	Y	Y	Y	Y	N
8	Lynch	Y	Y	Y	Y	Y	N
9	Keating	Y	Y	Y	Y	Y	N
MICHIGAN							
1	**Bergman**	N	N	N	Y	Y	Y
2	**Huizenga**	Y	N	N	Y	Y	Y
3	**Amash**	N	N	N	Y	N	Y
4	**Moolenaar**	Y	N	N	Y	Y	Y
5	Kildee	Y	Y	Y	Y	Y	N
6	**Upton**	Y	N	N	Y	Y	N
7	**Walberg**	Y	N	N	Y	Y	Y
8	Slotkin	Y	Y	Y	Y	Y	N
9	Levin	Y	Y	Y	Y	Y	N
10	**Mitchell**	Y	N	N	Y	Y	N
11	Stevens	Y	Y	Y	Y	Y	N
12	Dingell	?	?	?	?	?	?
13	Tlaib	Y	Y	Y	Y	Y	N
14	Lawrence	Y	Y	Y	Y	Y	N
MINNESOTA							
1	**Hagedorn**	Y	N	N	Y	Y	Y
2	Craig	Y	Y	Y	Y	Y	N
3	Phillips	Y	Y	Y	Y	Y	N
4	McCollum	Y	Y	Y	Y	Y	N
5	Omar	Y	Y	Y	Y	Y	N

		67	68	69	70	71	72
6	**Emmer**	Y	N	N	Y	Y	Y
7	Peterson	Y	Y	Y	Y	Y	N
8	**Stauber**	Y	N	N	Y	Y	Y
MISSISSIPPI							
1	**Kelly, T.**	Y	N	N	Y	Y	Y
2	Thompson, B.	Y	Y	Y	Y	Y	N
3	**Guest**	Y	N	N	Y	Y	Y
4	**Palazzo**	Y	N	N	Y	Y	Y
MISSOURI							
1	Clay	Y	Y	Y	Y	Y	N
2	**Wagner**	Y	N	N	Y	Y	Y
3	**Luetkemeyer**	Y	N	N	Y	Y	Y
4	**Hartzler**	Y	N	N	Y	Y	Y
5	Cleaver	Y	+	+	+	+	N
6	**Graves, S.**	Y	N	N	Y	Y	Y
7	**Long**	Y	N	N	Y	Y	Y
8	**Smith, J.**	Y	N	N	Y	Y	Y
MONTANA							
AL	**Gianforte**	Y	N	N	Y	Y	Y
NEBRASKA							
1	**Fortenberry**	Y	N	N	Y	Y	Y
2	**Bacon**	Y	N	N	Y	Y	Y
3	**Smith, Adrian**	Y	N	N	Y	Y	Y
NEVADA							
1	Titus	Y	Y	Y	Y	Y	N
2	**Amodei**	Y	N	N	Y	Y	Y
3	Lee	Y	Y	Y	Y	Y	N
4	Horsford	Y	Y	Y	Y	Y	N
NEW HAMPSHIRE							
1	Pappas	Y	Y	Y	Y	Y	N
2	Kuster	Y	Y	Y	Y	Y	N
NEW JERSEY							
1	Norcross	Y	Y	Y	Y	Y	N
2	Van Drew	Y	Y	Y	Y	Y	N
3	Kim	Y	Y	Y	Y	Y	N
4	**Smith, C.**	Y	?	N	Y	Y	N
5	Gottheimer	Y	Y	Y	Y	Y	N
6	Pallone	Y	Y	Y	Y	Y	N
7	Malinowski	Y	Y	Y	Y	Y	N
8	Sires	Y	Y	?	?	?	N
9	Pascrell	Y	Y	Y	Y	Y	N
10	Payne	Y	Y	Y	Y	Y	N
11	Sherrill	Y	Y	Y	Y	Y	N
12	Watson Coleman	Y	Y	Y	Y	Y	?
NEW MEXICO							
1	Haaland	Y	Y	Y	Y	Y	N
2	Torres Small	Y	Y	Y	Y	Y	N
3	Luján	Y	Y	Y	Y	Y	N
NEW YORK							
1	**Zeldin**	Y	N	N	Y	Y	Y
2	**King, P.**	Y	N	N	Y	Y	Y
3	Suozzi	Y	Y	Y	Y	Y	N
4	Rice, K.	Y	Y	Y	Y	Y	N
5	Meeks	Y	Y	Y	Y	Y	N
6	Meng	Y	Y	Y	Y	Y	N
7	Velázquez	Y	Y	Y	Y	Y	N
8	Jeffries	Y	Y	Y	Y	Y	N
9	Clarke	Y	Y	Y	Y	Y	N
10	Nadler	Y	+	+	+	+	N
11	Rose	Y	Y	Y	Y	Y	N
12	Maloney, C.	Y	Y	Y	Y	Y	N
13	Espaillat	Y	Y	Y	Y	Y	N
14	Ocasio-Cortez	Y	Y	Y	Y	Y	N
15	Serrano	Y	Y	Y	Y	Y	N
16	Engel	Y	Y	Y	Y	Y	N
17	Lowey	Y	Y	Y	Y	Y	N
18	Maloney, S.P.	?	Y	Y	Y	Y	N
19	Delgado	Y	Y	Y	Y	Y	N
20	Tonko	Y	Y	Y	Y	Y	N
21	**Stefanik**	Y	N	N	Y	Y	N
22	Brindisi	Y	Y	Y	Y	Y	N
23	**Reed**	Y	N	N	Y	Y	Y
24	**Katko**	Y	N	N	Y	Y	N
25	Morelle	Y	Y	Y	Y	Y	N
26	Higgins, B.	Y	Y	Y	Y	Y	N
27	**Collins, C.**	Y	N	N	Y	Y	Y
NORTH CAROLINA							
1	Butterfield	Y	Y	Y	Y	Y	N
2	**Holding**	Y	N	N	Y	Y	Y
3	**Jones**	?	?	?	?	?	?
4	Price	Y	Y	Y	Y	Y	N
5	**Foxx**	Y	N	N	Y	Y	Y
6	**Walker**	?	N	N	Y	Y	Y
7	**Rouzer**	Y	N	N	Y	Y	Y

		67	68	69	70	71	72
8	**Hudson**	Y	N	N	Y	Y	N
9	vacant						
10	**McHenry**	Y	?	N	Y	Y	N
11	**Meadows**	Y	?	?	+	?	Y
12	Adams	Y	Y	Y	Y	Y	N
13	**Budd**	N	N	N	Y	Y	Y
NORTH DAKOTA							
AL	**Armstrong**	Y	N	N	Y	Y	Y
OHIO							
1	**Chabot**	Y	N	N	Y	Y	Y
2	**Wenstrup**	Y	N	N	Y	Y	+
3	Beatty	Y	Y	Y	Y	Y	N
4	**Jordan**	N	N	N	Y	Y	Y
5	**Latta**	Y	N	N	Y	Y	Y
6	**Johnson, B.**	Y	N	N	Y	Y	Y
7	**Gibbs**	Y	N	N	Y	Y	Y
8	**Davidson**	Y	N	N	Y	Y	Y
9	Kaptur	Y	Y	Y	Y	Y	N
10	**Turner**	Y	N	N	Y	Y	N
11	Fudge	?	Y	Y	Y	Y	N
12	**Balderson**	Y	N	N	Y	Y	Y
13	Ryan	Y	Y	Y	Y	Y	N
14	**Joyce**	Y	N	N	Y	Y	Y
15	**Stivers**	Y	N	N	Y	Y	N
16	**Gonzalez**	Y	N	N	Y	Y	N
OKLAHOMA							
1	**Hern**	Y	N	N	Y	Y	Y
2	**Mullin**	Y	N	N	Y	Y	Y
3	**Lucas**	Y	N	N	Y	Y	+
4	**Cole**	Y	N	N	Y	Y	Y
5	Horn	Y	Y	Y	Y	Y	N
OREGON							
1	Bonamici	Y	Y	Y	Y	Y	N
2	**Walden**	Y	N	N	Y	Y	Y
3	Blumenauer	Y	Y	Y	Y	Y	N
4	DeFazio	Y	Y	Y	Y	Y	N
5	Schrader	Y	Y	Y	Y	Y	N
PENNSYLVANIA							
1	**Fitzpatrick**	Y	N	N	Y	Y	N
2	Boyle	Y	Y	Y	Y	Y	N
3	Evans	Y	Y	Y	Y	Y	N
4	Dean	Y	Y	Y	Y	Y	N
5	Scanlon	Y	Y	Y	Y	Y	N
6	Houlahan	Y	Y	Y	Y	Y	N
7	Wild	Y	Y	Y	Y	Y	N
8	Cartwright	Y	Y	Y	Y	Y	N
9	**Meuser**	Y	N	N	Y	Y	Y
10	**Perry**	N	N	N	Y	Y	Y
11	**Smucker**	Y	N	N	Y	Y	Y
12	vacant						
13	**Joyce**	Y	N	N	Y	Y	Y
14	**Reschenthaler**	Y	N	N	Y	Y	Y
15	**Thompson, G.**	Y	N	N	Y	Y	Y
16	**Kelly, M.**	Y	N	N	Y	Y	Y
17	Lamb	Y	Y	Y	Y	Y	N
18	Doyle	Y	Y	Y	Y	Y	N
RHODE ISLAND							
1	Cicilline	Y	Y	Y	Y	Y	N
2	Langevin	Y	Y	Y	Y	Y	N
SOUTH CAROLINA							
1	Cunningham	Y	Y	Y	Y	Y	N
2	**Wilson, J.**	Y	N	N	Y	Y	Y
3	**Duncan**	Y	N	N	Y	Y	Y
4	**Timmons**	Y	N	N	Y	Y	Y
5	**Norman**	Y	N	N	Y	Y	Y
6	Clyburn	Y	Y	Y	Y	Y	?
7	**Rice, T.**	N	N	N	Y	Y	Y
SOUTH DAKOTA							
AL	**Johnson**	Y	N	N	Y	?	Y
TENNESSEE							
1	**Roe**	Y	N	N	Y	Y	Y
2	**Burchett**	Y	N	N	Y	Y	Y
3	**Fleischmann**	Y	N	N	Y	Y	Y
4	**DesJarlais**	Y	N	N	Y	Y	Y
5	Cooper	Y	Y	Y	Y	Y	N
6	**Rose**	Y	N	N	Y	Y	Y
7	**Green**	Y	N	N	Y	Y	Y
8	**Kustoff**	Y	N	N	Y	Y	Y
9	Cohen	Y	Y	Y	Y	Y	N
TEXAS							
1	**Gohmert**	?	N	N	Y	Y	?
2	**Crenshaw**	Y	N	N	Y	Y	Y
3	**Taylor**	Y	N	N	Y	Y	Y
4	**Ratcliffe**	Y	N	N	Y	Y	Y

		67	68	69	70	71	72
5	**Gooden**	Y	N	N	Y	Y	Y
6	**Wright**	Y	N	N	Y	Y	Y
7	Fletcher	Y	Y	Y	Y	Y	N
8	**Brady**	Y	N	N	Y	Y	Y
9	Green, A.	Y	Y	Y	Y	Y	N
10	**McCaul**	Y	?	N	Y	Y	Y
11	**Conaway**	Y	N	N	Y	Y	Y
12	**Granger**	Y	N	N	Y	Y	Y
13	**Thornberry**	Y	N	N	Y	Y	Y
14	**Weber**	N	N	N	Y	Y	Y
15	Gonzalez	Y	Y	Y	Y	Y	N
16	Escobar	Y	Y	Y	Y	Y	N
17	**Flores**	Y	N	N	Y	Y	Y
18	Jackson Lee	Y	Y	Y	Y	Y	N
19	**Arrington**	Y	N	N	Y	Y	Y
20	Castro	Y	Y	Y	Y	Y	N
21	**Roy**	N	N	N	Y	Y	Y
22	**Olson**	Y	N	N	Y	Y	Y
23	**Hurd**	Y	N	N	Y	Y	N
24	**Marchant**	Y	N	N	Y	?	Y
25	**Williams**	Y	N	N	Y	Y	Y
26	**Burgess**	Y	N	N	Y	Y	Y
27	**Cloud**	N	N	N	Y	Y	Y
28	Cuellar	Y	Y	Y	Y	Y	N
29	Garcia, S.	Y	Y	Y	Y	Y	N
30	Johnson, E.B.	Y	Y	Y	Y	Y	N
31	**Carter, J.**	Y	N	N	Y	Y	Y
32	Allred	Y	+	+	+	+	-
33	Veasey	Y	Y	Y	Y	Y	N
34	Vela	Y	Y	Y	Y	Y	N
35	Doggett	Y	Y	Y	Y	Y	N
36	**Babin**	Y	N	N	Y	Y	Y
UTAH							
1	**Bishop, R.**	?	N	N	?	Y	Y
2	**Stewart**	Y	N	N	Y	Y	Y
3	**Curtis**	Y	N	N	Y	Y	Y
4	McAdams	Y	Y	Y	Y	Y	N
VERMONT							
AL	Welch	Y	Y	Y	Y	Y	N
VIRGINIA							
1	**Wittman**	Y	N	N	Y	Y	Y
2	Luria	Y	Y	Y	Y	Y	N
3	Scott, R.	Y	Y	Y	Y	Y	N
4	McEachin	Y	Y	Y	Y	Y	N
5	**Riggleman**	Y	N	N	Y	Y	Y
6	**Cline**	N	N	N	Y	Y	Y
7	Spanberger	Y	Y	Y	Y	Y	N
8	Beyer	Y	Y	Y	Y	Y	N
9	**Griffith**	Y	N	N	Y	Y	Y
10	Wexton	Y	Y	Y	Y	Y	N
11	Connolly	Y	Y	Y	Y	Y	?
WASHINGTON							
1	DelBene	Y	Y	Y	Y	Y	N
2	Larsen	Y	Y	Y	Y	Y	N
3	**Herrera Beutler**	Y	N	N	Y	Y	Y
4	**Newhouse**	Y	N	N	Y	Y	Y
5	**McMorris Rodgers**	Y	N	N	Y	Y	Y
6	Kilmer	Y	Y	Y	Y	Y	N
7	Jayapal	Y	Y	Y	Y	Y	N
8	Schrier	Y	Y	Y	Y	Y	N
9	Smith Adam	Y	Y	Y	Y	Y	N
10	Heck	Y	Y	Y	Y	Y	N
WEST VIRGINIA							
1	**McKinley**	Y	N	N	Y	Y	Y
2	**Mooney**	Y	N	N	Y	Y	Y
3	**Miller**	Y	N	N	Y	Y	Y
WISCONSIN							
1	**Steil**	Y	N	N	Y	Y	Y
2	Pocan	Y	Y	Y	Y	Y	N
3	Kind	Y	Y	Y	Y	Y	N
4	Moore	Y	Y	Y	Y	Y	-
5	**Sensenbrenner**	Y	N	N	Y	Y	Y
6	**Grothman**	N	N	N	Y	Y	Y
7	**Duffy**						
8	**Gallagher**	Y	N	N	Y	Y	Y
WYOMING							
AL	**Cheney**	Y	N	N	Y	Y	Y
DELEGATES							
	Radewagen (A.S.)						?
	Norton (D.C.)						N
	San Nicolas (Guam)						?
	Sablan (N. Marianas)						N
	González-Colón (P.R.)						N
	Plaskett (V.I.)						N

⫴ HOUSE VOTES

73. HR840. Veterans' Child Care - Excluding Certain Child Care Facilities. Sherrill, D-N.J., amendment that would prohibit any child care provider that employs an individual convicted of a sex crime, a violent crime, or a drug-related felony from providing child care under the provisions of the bill. It would also stipulate that nothing in the amendment supersedes any federal or state law with more restrictive standards for child care employees. Adopted in Committee of the Whole 401-19: R 185-7; D 215-12; I 1-0. Feb. 8, 2019.

74. HR840. Veterans' Child Care - Recommit. Barr, R-Ky., motion to recommit the bill to the House Veterans' Affairs Committee with instructions to report back immediately with an amendment that would prohibit the Department of Veterans Affairs from issuing payments to any child care provider that employs an individual who has any of the following charges pending a sex crime, a violent crime, an offense involving a child victim, a drug-related felony, or any other crime that the VA secretary deems appropriate for exclusion. Motion rejected 200-214: R 189-1; D 11-213. Feb. 8, 2019.

75. HR840. Veterans' Child Care - Passage. Passage of the bill that would make permanent and expand a Veterans Affairs Department program to all VA medical facilities that provides child care assistance to veterans while they are traveling to and from, and receiving certain VA health care services. Specifically the VA would either provide child care at one of its facilities, or would pay an outside private child care provider. As amended, the bill would include substance- or drug-abuse counseling, and certain physical therapy as care that is covered under the program. Passed 400-9: R 178-9; D 222-0. Feb. 8, 2019.

76. HR1065. Social Media Assessment for Security Clearance - Passage. Hill, D-Calif., motion to suspend the rules and pass the bill that would require the Office of Management and Budget to submit a report to Congress on the examination of social media activity during security clearance investigations and the options for expansion of the practice. Specifically, the report would be required to include the current use of and legal impediments to the use of publicly available social media activity for security clearance investigations, as well as the results of any pilot programs that have done so. Motion agreed to 377-3: R 168-3; D 209-0. *Note: A two-thirds majority of those present and voting (254 in this case) is required for passage under suspension of the rules.* Feb. 11, 2019.

77. HR1079. Electronic Consent and Access Forms - Passage. Hill, D-Calif., motion to suspend the rules and pass the bill, as amended, that would direct the Office of Management and Budget to create a template for electronic consent and access forms, and issue guidance requiring each agency to accept electronic identity proofing and authentication processes for verifying electronic consent forms. Motion agreed to 379-0: R 172-0; D 207-0. *Note: A two-thirds majority of those present and voting (253 in this case) is required for passage under suspension of the rules.* Feb. 11, 2019.

78. HJRES37. Removal of Forces from Yemen - Previous Question. McGovern, D-Mass., motion to order the previous question (thus ending debate and possibility of amendment) on the rule (H Res 122) that would provide for House floor consideration of a joint resolution (H J Res 37) regarding the removal of U.S. armed forces and military support from hostilities in Yemen. The rule would also waive, through the legislative day of Feb. 17, 2019, the two-thirds vote requirement to consider legislation on the same day it is reported from the House Rules Committee, and would also provide for motions to suspend the rules through the legislative day of Feb. 17. Motion agreed to 227-195: R 0-195; D 227-0. Feb. 13, 2019.

***NOTE:**
(North Carolina 3) Rep. Walter B. Jones Jr. died on Feb. 10. The last roll call vote he was eligible to cast was vote 75.

		73	74	75	76	77	78
ALABAMA							
1	Byrne	Y	Y	Y	Y	Y	N
2	Roby	Y	Y	Y	Y	Y	N
3	Rogers, M.	Y	Y	Y	Y	Y	N
4	Aderholt	Y	Y	Y	Y	Y	N
5	Brooks, M.	Y	Y	N	?	?	N
6	Palmer	Y	Y	Y	Y	Y	N
7	Sewell	Y	N	Y	Y	Y	Y
ALASKA							
AL	Young	Y	Y	Y	Y	Y	N
ARIZONA							
1	O'Halleran	Y	N	Y	Y	Y	Y
2	Kirkpatrick	Y	N	Y	Y	Y	Y
3	Grijalva	Y	N	Y	Y	Y	Y
4	Gosar	N	Y	N	Y	Y	N
5	Biggs	N	Y	N	N	Y	N
6	Schweikert	Y	Y	Y	Y	Y	N
7	Gallego	Y	N	Y	Y	Y	Y
8	Lesko	Y	Y	Y	Y	Y	N
9	Stanton	Y	N	Y	Y	Y	Y
ARKANSAS							
1	Crawford	Y	Y	Y	Y	Y	N
2	Hill, F.	Y	Y	Y	Y	Y	N
3	Womack	Y	Y	Y	Y	Y	N
4	Westerman	Y	Y	Y	Y	Y	N
CALIFORNIA							
1	LaMalfa	?	?	?	Y	Y	N
2	Huffman	+	-	+	Y	Y	Y
3	Garamendi	Y	N	Y	Y	Y	Y
4	McClintock	Y	Y	Y	Y	Y	N
5	Thompson, M.	Y	N	Y	Y	Y	Y
6	Matsui	Y	N	Y	Y	Y	Y
7	Bera	Y	N	Y	Y	Y	Y
8	Cook	Y	Y	Y	Y	Y	N
9	McNerney	Y	N	Y	Y	Y	Y
10	Harder	Y	N	Y	Y	Y	Y
11	DeSaulnier	Y	N	Y	Y	Y	Y
12	Pelosi						
13	Lee B.	Y	N	Y	Y	Y	Y
14	Speier	Y	N	Y	Y	Y	Y
15	Swalwell	Y	N	Y	Y	Y	Y
16	Costa	Y	N	Y	?	?	Y
17	Khanna	Y	N	Y	Y	Y	Y
18	Eshoo	Y	N	Y	Y	Y	Y
19	Lofgren	Y	N	Y	?	?	Y
20	Panetta	Y	N	Y	Y	Y	Y
21	Cox	Y	N	Y	?	?	Y
22	Nunes	Y	Y	Y	Y	Y	N
23	McCarthy	Y	Y	Y	Y	Y	N
24	Carbajal	Y	N	Y	Y	Y	Y
25	Hill, K.	Y	N	Y	Y	Y	Y
26	Brownley	Y	N	Y	Y	Y	Y
27	Chu	Y	N	Y	Y	Y	Y
28	Schiff	Y	N	Y	Y	Y	Y
29	Cárdenas	Y	N	?	Y	Y	Y
30	Sherman	Y	N	Y	Y	Y	Y
31	Aguilar	Y	N	Y	Y	Y	Y
32	Napolitano	Y	N	Y	Y	Y	Y
33	Lieu	Y	N	Y	Y	Y	Y
34	Gomez	Y	N	Y	Y	Y	Y
35	Torres	Y	N	Y	Y	Y	Y
36	Ruiz	Y	N	Y	Y	Y	Y
37	Bass	N	N	Y	Y	Y	Y
38	Sánchez	Y	N	Y	Y	Y	Y
39	Cisneros	Y	N	Y	Y	Y	Y
40	Roybal-Allard	Y	N	Y	Y	Y	Y
41	Takano	Y	N	Y	Y	Y	Y
42	Calvert	Y	Y	Y	Y	Y	N
43	Waters	Y	N	Y	Y	Y	Y
44	Barragán	Y	N	Y	Y	Y	Y
45	Porter	Y	N	Y	Y	Y	Y
46	Correa	Y	N	Y	Y	Y	Y
47	Lowenthal	Y	N	Y	Y	Y	Y
48	Rouda	Y	N	Y	Y	Y	Y
49	Levin	Y	N	Y	Y	Y	Y
50	Hunter	Y	Y	Y	Y	Y	N
51	Vargas	Y	N	Y	?	?	Y
52	Peters	Y	N	Y	Y	Y	Y

		73	74	75	76	77	78
53	Davis, S.	Y	N	Y	Y	Y	Y
COLORADO							
1	DeGette	Y	N	Y	Y	Y	Y
2	Neguse	Y	N	Y	Y	Y	Y
3	Tipton	Y	Y	Y	Y	Y	N
4	Buck	Y	Y	Y	Y	Y	N
5	Lamborn	Y	Y	Y	Y	Y	N
6	Crow	Y	N	Y	+	+	Y
7	Perlmutter	Y	N	Y	Y	Y	Y
CONNECTICUT							
1	Larson	Y	N	Y	Y	Y	Y
2	Courtney	Y	N	Y	Y	Y	Y
3	DeLauro	Y	N	Y	Y	Y	Y
4	Himes	Y	N	Y	Y	Y	Y
5	Hayes	Y	N	Y	+	+	Y
DELAWARE							
AL	Blunt Rochester	Y	N	Y	Y	Y	Y
FLORIDA							
1	Gaetz	?	?	?	N	Y	N
2	Dunn	Y	Y	Y	Y	Y	N
3	Yoho	Y	Y	Y	Y	Y	N
4	Rutherford	+	+	+	Y	Y	N
5	Lawson	?	?	?	Y	Y	Y
6	Waltz	Y	Y	Y	Y	Y	N
7	Murphy	Y	N	Y	Y	Y	Y
8	Posey	Y	Y	Y	Y	Y	N
9	Soto	Y	N	Y	Y	Y	Y
10	Demings	Y	N	Y	Y	Y	Y
11	Webster	Y	Y	Y	Y	Y	N
12	Bilirakis	Y	Y	Y	Y	Y	N
13	Crist	Y	N	Y	Y	Y	Y
14	Castor	Y	N	Y	Y	Y	?
15	Spano	Y	Y	Y	Y	Y	N
16	Buchanan	Y	Y	Y	Y	Y	N
17	Steube	+	+	+	Y	Y	N
18	Mast	Y	Y	Y	Y	Y	N
19	Rooney	Y	Y	Y	Y	Y	N
20	Hastings	Y	N	Y	Y	Y	Y
21	Frankel	Y	N	Y	Y	Y	Y
22	Deutch	Y	N	Y	Y	Y	Y
23	Wasserman Schultz	Y	N	Y	Y	Y	Y
24	Wilson, F.	?	?	?	?	?	?
25	Diaz-Balart	Y	Y	Y	Y	Y	N
26	Mucarsel-Powell	Y	N	Y	Y	Y	Y
27	Shalala	Y	N	Y	Y	Y	Y
GEORGIA							
1	Carter, E.L.	Y	Y	Y	+	Y	N
2	Bishop, S.	Y	N	Y	Y	Y	Y
3	Ferguson	Y	Y	Y	Y	Y	N
4	Johnson, H.	N	N	Y	Y	?	Y
5	Lewis John	Y	N	Y	Y	Y	Y
6	McBath	Y	N	Y	Y	Y	Y
7	Woodall	Y	Y	Y	Y	Y	N
8	Scott, A.	Y	Y	Y	Y	Y	N
9	Collins, D.	Y	Y	Y	?	?	N
10	Hice	Y	Y	Y	Y	Y	N
11	Loudermilk	Y	Y	Y	?	?	N
12	Allen	Y	Y	Y	Y	Y	N
13	Scott, D.	Y	N	Y	Y	Y	Y
14	Graves, T.	Y	Y	Y	Y	Y	N
HAWAII							
1	Case	Y	N	Y	Y	Y	Y
2	Gabbard	Y	N	Y	?	?	Y
IDAHO							
1	Fulcher	Y	Y	Y	Y	Y	N
2	Simpson	Y	Y	Y	?	?	N
ILLINOIS							
1	Rush	Y	N	Y	?	?	Y
2	Kelly, R.	Y	N	Y	Y	Y	Y
3	Lipinski	Y	N	Y	?	?	Y
4	García, J.	Y	N	Y	Y	Y	Y
5	Quigley	Y	N	Y	?	?	?
6	Casten	Y	N	Y	Y	Y	Y
7	Davis, D.	N	N	Y	Y	Y	Y
8	Krishnamoorthi	Y	N	Y	Y	Y	Y
9	Schakowsky	Y	N	Y	Y	Y	Y
10	Schneider	Y	N	Y	Y	Y	Y
11	Foster	Y	-	+	Y	Y	Y

KEY:		**Republicans**		Democrats		*Independents*	
Y	Voted for (yea)	**N**	Voted against (nay)	**P**	Voted "present"		
+	Announced for	**-**	Announced against	**?**	Did not vote or otherwise		
#	Paired for	**X**	Paired against		make position known		

		73	74	75	76	77	78
12	**Bost**	Y	Y	Y	+	+	N
13	**Davis, R.**	Y	Y	Y	Y	Y	N
14	Underwood	Y	N	Y	Y	Y	Y
15	**Shimkus**	Y	Y	Y	?	?	N
16	**Kinzinger**	Y	Y	Y	+	+	-
17	Bustos	Y	N	Y	Y	Y	Y
18	**LaHood**	Y	Y	Y	Y	Y	N
INDIANA							
1	Visclosky	Y	N	Y	Y	Y	Y
2	**Walorski**	Y	Y	Y	+	+	N
3	**Banks**	Y	Y	Y	Y	Y	N
4	**Baird**	Y	Y	Y	Y	Y	N
5	**Brooks, S.**	Y	Y	Y	?	?	N
6	**Pence**	Y	Y	Y	Y	Y	N
7	Carson	Y	N	Y	Y	Y	Y
8	**Bucshon**	Y	Y	Y	Y	Y	N
9	**Hollingsworth**	Y	Y	Y	Y	Y	N
IOWA							
1	Finkenauer	Y	Y	Y	Y	Y	Y
2	Loebsack	Y	N	Y	?	?	Y
3	Axne	Y	Y	Y	Y	Y	Y
4	**King, S.**	Y	Y	Y	Y	Y	N
KANSAS							
1	**Marshall**	Y	Y	Y	Y	Y	N
2	**Watkins**	Y	Y	+	Y	Y	N
3	Davids	Y	Y	Y	Y	Y	Y
4	**Estes**	Y	Y	Y	Y	Y	N
KENTUCKY							
1	**Comer**	Y	Y	Y	Y	Y	N
2	**Guthrie**	Y	Y	Y	Y	Y	N
3	Yarmuth	Y	N	Y	Y	Y	Y
4	**Massie**	N	Y	Y	Y	Y	N
5	**Rogers, H.**	Y	Y	Y	Y	Y	N
6	**Barr**	Y	Y	Y	Y	Y	N
LOUISIANA							
1	**Scalise**	Y	Y	Y	Y	Y	N
2	Richmond	N	N	Y	?	?	Y
3	**Higgins, C.**	Y	Y	Y	Y	Y	N
4	**Johnson, M.**	Y	-	-	?	?	N
5	**Abraham**	Y	Y	Y	?	?	N
6	**Graves, G.**	Y	Y	Y	Y	Y	N
MAINE							
1	Pingree	Y	N	Y	Y	Y	?
2	Golden	Y	N	Y	Y	Y	Y
MARYLAND							
1	**Harris**	N	Y	Y	Y	Y	N
2	Ruppersberger	Y	N	Y	Y	Y	Y
3	Sarbanes	Y	N	Y	Y	Y	Y
4	Brown, A.	Y	N	Y	Y	Y	Y
5	Hoyer	Y	N	Y	Y	Y	Y
6	Trone	Y	N	Y	Y	Y	Y
7	Cummings	Y	N	Y	Y	Y	Y
8	Raskin	Y	N	Y	Y	Y	Y
MASSACHUSETTS							
1	Neal	Y	N	Y	Y	Y	Y
2	McGovern	Y	N	Y	Y	Y	Y
3	Trahan	Y	N	Y	Y	Y	Y
4	Kennedy	?	?	?	Y	Y	Y
5	Clark	Y	N	Y	Y	Y	Y
6	Moulton	Y	N	Y	Y	Y	Y
7	Pressley	N	N	Y	Y	Y	Y
8	Lynch	Y	N	Y	Y	Y	Y
9	Keating	Y	N	Y	Y	Y	Y
MICHIGAN							
1	**Bergman**	Y	Y	Y	Y	Y	N
2	**Huizenga**	Y	Y	Y	+	+	N
3	**Amash**	N	N	N	Y	Y	N
4	**Moolenaar**	Y	Y	Y	Y	Y	N
5	Kildee	Y	N	Y	Y	Y	Y
6	**Upton**	Y	Y	Y	Y	Y	N
7	**Walberg**	Y	Y	Y	Y	Y	N
8	Slotkin	Y	N	Y	Y	Y	Y
9	Levin	Y	N	Y	Y	Y	Y
10	**Mitchell**	Y	Y	Y	Y	Y	N
11	Stevens	Y	N	Y	Y	Y	Y
12	Dingell	?	?	?	?	?	?
13	Tlaib	N	N	Y	Y	Y	Y
14	Lawrence	Y	N	Y	+	+	Y
MINNESOTA							
1	**Hagedorn**	Y	Y	Y	Y	Y	N
2	Craig	Y	N	Y	Y	Y	Y
3	Phillips	Y	N	Y	Y	Y	Y
4	McCollum	Y	N	Y	Y	Y	Y
5	Omar	N	N	Y	Y	Y	Y

		73	74	75	76	77	78
6	**Emmer**	Y	Y	Y	Y	Y	N
7	Peterson	Y	Y	Y	Y	Y	Y
8	**Stauber**	Y	Y	Y	Y	Y	N
MISSISSIPPI							
1	**Kelly, T.**	Y	Y	Y	Y	Y	N
2	Thompson, B.	Y	N	Y	Y	Y	Y
3	**Guest**	Y	Y	Y	Y	Y	N
4	**Palazzo**	Y	Y	Y	Y	Y	N
MISSOURI							
1	Clay	Y	N	Y	?	?	Y
2	**Wagner**	Y	Y	Y	?	?	N
3	**Luetkemeyer**	Y	Y	Y	Y	Y	N
4	**Hartzler**	Y	Y	Y	Y	Y	N
5	Cleaver	Y	N	Y	Y	Y	Y
6	**Graves, S.**	Y	Y	Y	?	?	N
7	**Long**	Y	Y	Y	Y	Y	N
8	**Smith, J.**	Y	Y	Y	Y	Y	N
MONTANA							
AL	**Gianforte**	Y	Y	Y	Y	Y	N
NEBRASKA							
1	**Fortenberry**	Y	Y	Y	Y	Y	N
2	**Bacon**	Y	Y	Y	Y	Y	N
3	**Smith, Adrian**	Y	Y	Y	Y	Y	N
NEVADA							
1	Titus	Y	N	Y	Y	Y	Y
2	**Amodei**	Y	Y	Y	Y	Y	N
3	Lee	Y	N	Y	Y	Y	Y
4	Horsford	Y	N	Y	Y	Y	Y
NEW HAMPSHIRE							
1	Pappas	Y	N	Y	Y	Y	Y
2	Kuster	Y	N	Y	Y	Y	Y
NEW JERSEY							
1	Norcross	Y	N	Y	Y	Y	Y
2	Van Drew	Y	Y	Y	Y	Y	Y
3	Kim	Y	N	Y	Y	Y	Y
4	**Smith, C.**	Y	Y	Y	Y	Y	N
5	Gottheimer	Y	Y	Y	Y	Y	Y
6	Pallone	Y	N	Y	Y	Y	Y
7	Malinowski	Y	N	Y	Y	Y	Y
8	Sires	Y	N	Y	Y	Y	Y
9	Pascrell	Y	N	Y	Y	Y	Y
10	Payne	Y	N	Y	Y	Y	Y
11	Sherrill	Y	N	Y	Y	Y	Y
12	Watson Coleman	?	?	?	?	?	Y
NEW MEXICO							
1	Haaland	Y	N	Y	Y	Y	Y
2	Torres Small	Y	N	Y	Y	Y	Y
3	Luján	Y	N	Y	Y	Y	Y
NEW YORK							
1	**Zeldin**	Y	Y	Y	Y	Y	N
2	**King, P.**	Y	Y	Y	Y	Y	N
3	Suozzi	Y	N	Y	Y	Y	Y
4	Rice, K.	Y	N	Y	Y	Y	Y
5	Meeks	Y	N	Y	?	?	Y
6	Meng	Y	N	Y	?	?	Y
7	Velázquez	Y	N	Y	Y	Y	Y
8	Jeffries	Y	N	Y	Y	Y	Y
9	Clarke	Y	N	Y	Y	Y	Y
10	Nadler	N	N	Y	Y	Y	Y
11	Rose	Y	N	Y	Y	Y	Y
12	Maloney, C.	Y	N	Y	Y	Y	Y
13	Espaillat	Y	N	Y	Y	Y	Y
14	Ocasio-Cortez	N	N	Y	Y	Y	Y
15	Serrano	Y	N	Y	Y	Y	Y
16	Engel	Y	N	Y	Y	Y	Y
17	Lowey	Y	N	Y	Y	Y	Y
18	Maloney, S.P.	Y	N	Y	Y	Y	Y
19	Delgado	Y	Y	Y	Y	Y	Y
20	Tonko	Y	N	Y	Y	Y	Y
21	**Stefanik**	Y	Y	Y	Y	Y	N
22	Brindisi	Y	N	Y	Y	Y	Y
23	**Reed**	Y	Y	Y	Y	Y	N
24	**Katko**	Y	Y	Y	Y	Y	N
25	Morelle	Y	N	Y	Y	Y	Y
26	Higgins, B.	Y	N	Y	Y	Y	Y
27	**Collins, C.**	Y	Y	Y	?	?	N
NORTH CAROLINA							
1	Butterfield	Y	N	Y	Y	Y	Y
2	**Holding**	Y	Y	Y	Y	Y	N
3	**Jones***	?	?	?			
4	Price	Y	N	Y	Y	?	Y
5	**Foxx**	Y	Y	Y	Y	Y	N
6	**Walker**	Y	Y	N	Y	Y	N
7	**Rouzer**	Y	Y	Y	Y	Y	N

		73	74	75	76	77	78
8	**Hudson**	Y	Y	Y	Y	Y	N
9	vacant						
10	**McHenry**	Y	Y	Y	Y	Y	N
11	**Meadows**	Y	Y	Y	Y	Y	N
12	Adams	Y	N	Y	Y	Y	Y
13	**Budd**	Y	Y	N	Y	Y	N
NORTH DAKOTA							
AL	**Armstrong**	Y	Y	Y	Y	Y	N
OHIO							
1	**Chabot**	Y	Y	Y	Y	Y	N
2	**Wenstrup**	+	+	+	Y	Y	N
3	Beatty	Y	N	Y	Y	Y	Y
4	**Jordan**	Y	Y	Y	Y	Y	N
5	**Latta**	Y	Y	Y	Y	Y	N
6	**Johnson, B.**	Y	Y	Y	Y	Y	N
7	**Gibbs**	Y	Y	Y	Y	Y	N
8	**Davidson**	N	Y	N	Y	Y	N
9	Kaptur	Y	N	Y	?	?	Y
10	**Turner**	Y	Y	Y	Y	Y	N
11	Fudge	N	N	Y	Y	Y	Y
12	**Balderson**	Y	Y	Y	Y	Y	N
13	Ryan	Y	N	Y	?	?	?
14	**Joyce**	Y	Y	Y	Y	Y	N
15	**Stivers**	Y	Y	Y	Y	Y	N
16	**Gonzalez**	Y	Y	Y	Y	Y	N
OKLAHOMA							
1	**Hern**	Y	Y	Y	Y	Y	N
2	**Mullin**	Y	Y	Y	Y	Y	N
3	**Lucas**	+	+	+	Y	Y	N
4	**Cole**	Y	Y	Y	Y	Y	N
5	Horn	Y	Y	Y	Y	Y	Y
OREGON							
1	Bonamici	Y	N	Y	Y	Y	Y
2	**Walden**	Y	Y	Y	Y	Y	N
3	Blumenauer	Y	N	Y	Y	Y	Y
4	DeFazio	Y	N	Y	Y	Y	Y
5	Schrader	Y	N	Y	Y	Y	Y
PENNSYLVANIA							
1	**Fitzpatrick**	Y	Y	Y	Y	Y	N
2	Boyle	Y	N	Y	?	?	Y
3	Evans	Y	N	Y	Y	Y	Y
4	Dean	Y	N	Y	Y	Y	Y
5	Scanlon	Y	N	Y	Y	Y	Y
6	Houlahan	Y	N	Y	Y	Y	Y
7	Wild	Y	N	Y	Y	Y	Y
8	Cartwright	Y	N	Y	Y	Y	Y
9	**Meuser**	Y	Y	?	Y	Y	N
10	**Perry**	Y	Y	Y	Y	Y	N
11	**Smucker**	Y	Y	Y	Y	Y	N
12	vacant						
13	**Joyce**	Y	Y	Y	Y	Y	N
14	**Reschenthaler**	Y	Y	Y	Y	Y	N
15	**Thompson, G.**	Y	Y	Y	Y	Y	N
16	**Kelly, M.**	Y	Y	Y	Y	Y	N
17	Lamb	Y	N	Y	Y	Y	Y
18	Doyle	Y	N	Y	Y	Y	Y
RHODE ISLAND							
1	Cicilline	Y	N	Y	Y	Y	Y
2	Langevin	Y	N	Y	Y	Y	Y
SOUTH CAROLINA							
1	Cunningham	Y	Y	Y	Y	Y	Y
2	**Wilson, J.**	Y	Y	Y	Y	Y	N
3	**Duncan**	Y	Y	Y	Y	Y	N
4	**Timmons**	Y	Y	Y	Y	Y	N
5	**Norman**	Y	Y	Y	Y	Y	N
6	Clyburn	?	?	?	Y	Y	Y
7	**Rice, T.**	Y	Y	Y	Y	Y	N
SOUTH DAKOTA							
AL	**Johnson**	Y	Y	Y	Y	Y	N
TENNESSEE							
1	**Roe**	Y	Y	Y	Y	Y	N
2	**Burchett**	Y	Y	Y	Y	Y	N
3	**Fleischmann**	Y	Y	Y	Y	Y	N
4	**DesJarlais**	Y	Y	Y	Y	Y	N
5	Cooper	Y	N	Y	Y	Y	Y
6	**Rose**	Y	Y	Y	Y	Y	N
7	**Green**	Y	Y	Y	Y	Y	N
8	**Kustoff**	Y	Y	Y	Y	Y	N
9	Cohen	Y	N	Y	Y	Y	Y
TEXAS							
1	**Gohmert**	Y	Y	Y	N	Y	N
2	**Crenshaw**	Y	Y	Y	Y	Y	N
3	**Taylor**	Y	Y	Y	Y	Y	N
4	**Ratcliffe**	Y	Y	Y	?	?	N

		73	74	75	76	77	78
5	**Gooden**	Y	Y	Y	Y	Y	N
6	**Wright**	Y	Y	Y	Y	Y	N
7	Fletcher	Y	N	+	Y	Y	Y
8	**Brady**	Y	Y	Y	Y	Y	N
9	Green, A.	Y	N	Y	Y	Y	Y
10	**McCaul**	Y	Y	Y	Y	Y	N
11	**Conaway**	Y	Y	Y	Y	Y	N
12	**Granger**	Y	Y	Y	Y	Y	+
13	**Thornberry**	Y	Y	Y	Y	Y	N
14	**Weber**	Y	Y	Y	?	?	N
15	Gonzalez	Y	N	Y	Y	Y	Y
16	Escobar	Y	N	Y	?	?	Y
17	**Flores**	Y	Y	Y	Y	Y	N
18	Jackson Lee	Y	N	Y	Y	Y	Y
19	**Arrington**	Y	Y	Y	Y	Y	N
20	Castro	Y	N	Y	Y	Y	Y
21	**Roy**	N	Y	Y	Y	Y	N
22	**Olson**	Y	Y	Y	?	?	N
23	**Hurd**	Y	Y	Y	Y	Y	N
24	**Marchant**	Y	Y	?	?	?	N
25	**Williams**	Y	Y	Y	Y	Y	N
26	**Burgess**	Y	Y	Y	?	?	N
27	**Cloud**	Y	Y	Y	+	+	N
28	Cuellar	Y	N	Y	Y	Y	Y
29	Garcia, S.	Y	N	Y	Y	Y	Y
30	Johnson, E.B.	Y	N	Y	Y	Y	Y
31	**Carter, J.**	Y	Y	Y	?	?	N
32	Allred	+	-	+	+	+	+
33	Veasey	Y	N	Y	Y	Y	Y
34	Vela	Y	N	Y	Y	Y	Y
35	Doggett	Y	N	Y	Y	Y	Y
36	**Babin**	Y	Y	Y	?	?	N
UTAH							
1	**Bishop, R.**	Y	Y	Y	?	?	N
2	**Stewart**	Y	Y	Y	Y	Y	N
3	**Curtis**	Y	Y	Y	Y	Y	N
4	McAdams	Y	N	Y	Y	Y	Y
VERMONT							
AL	Welch	Y	N	Y	Y	Y	Y
VIRGINIA							
1	**Wittman**	Y	Y	Y	Y	Y	N
2	Luria	Y	Y	Y	Y	Y	Y
3	Scott, R.	N	N	Y	Y	Y	Y
4	McEachin	Y	N	Y	Y	Y	Y
5	**Riggleman**	Y	Y	Y	Y	Y	N
6	**Cline**	Y	Y	Y	Y	Y	N
7	Spanberger	Y	N	Y	Y	Y	Y
8	Beyer	Y	N	Y	Y	Y	Y
9	**Griffith**	Y	Y	Y	Y	Y	N
10	Wexton	Y	N	Y	Y	Y	Y
11	Connolly	?	?	?	Y	Y	?
WASHINGTON							
1	DelBene	Y	N	Y	Y	Y	Y
2	Larsen	Y	N	Y	Y	Y	Y
3	**Herrera Beutler**	Y	Y	Y	Y	Y	N
4	**Newhouse**	Y	Y	Y	Y	Y	N
5	**McMorris Rodgers**	Y	Y	Y	Y	Y	N
6	Kilmer	Y	N	Y	Y	Y	Y
7	Jayapal	N	N	Y	Y	Y	Y
8	Schrier	Y	Y	Y	Y	Y	Y
9	Smith Adam	Y	N	Y	Y	Y	Y
10	Heck	Y	N	Y	Y	Y	Y
WEST VIRGINIA							
1	**McKinley**	Y	Y	Y	Y	Y	N
2	**Mooney**	Y	Y	N	Y	Y	N
3	**Miller**	Y	Y	Y	Y	Y	N
WISCONSIN							
1	**Steil**	Y	Y	Y	Y	Y	N
2	Pocan	Y	N	Y	Y	Y	Y
3	Kind	Y	N	Y	+	+	Y
4	Moore	Y	N	Y	Y	Y	Y
5	**Sensenbrenner**	Y	Y	N	Y	Y	N
6	**Grothman**	Y	Y	Y	Y	Y	N
7	**Duffy**						
8	**Gallagher**	Y	Y	Y	Y	Y	N
WYOMING							
AL	**Cheney**	Y	Y	Y	Y	Y	N
DELEGATES							
	Radewagen (A.S.)	?					
	Norton (D.C.)	Y					
	San Nicolas (Guam)	?					
	Sablan (N. Marianas)	Y					
	González-Colón (P.R.)	Y					
	Plaskett (V.I.)	Y					

79. HJRES37. Removal of Forces from Yemen - Rule. Adoption of the rule (H Res 122) that would provide for House floor consideration of a joint resolution (H J Res 37) regarding the removal of U.S. armed forces and military support from hostilities in Yemen. The rule would also waive, through the legislative day of Feb. 17, 2019, the two-thirds vote requirement to consider legislation on the same day it is reported from the House Rules Committee, and would also provide for motions to suspend the rules through the legislative day of Feb. 17. Adopted 228-193: R 0-193; D 228-0. Feb. 13, 2019.

80. Procedural Motion - Journal. Approval of the House Journal of Feb. 12, 2019. Approved 215-199: R 39-151; D 176-48. Feb. 13, 2019.

81. HJRES37. Removal of Forces from Yemen - Intelligence Operations. Buck, R-Colo., amendment that would specify that nothing in the measure may be construed to influence or disrupt U.S. intelligence, counterintelligence and investigative activities. Adopted in Committee of the Whole 252-177: R 195-2; D 57-174; I 0-1. Feb. 13, 2019.

82. HJRES37. Removal of Forces from Yemen - Recommit. Kustoff, R-Tenn., motion to recommit the joint resolution to the House Foreign Affairs Committee with instructions to report back immediately with an amendment that would state that Congress finds it is in the national security interest of the U.S. to combat anti-Antisemitism around the world and to strongly support Israel. Motion agreed to 424-0: R 194-0; D 230-0. Feb. 13, 2019.

83. HJRES37. Removal of Forces from Yemen - Passage. Passage of the bill that would direct the president, within 30 days of enactment, to remove U.S. armed forces from hostilities in or affecting the Republic of Yemen, including in-flight refueling of non-U.S. aircraft, unless a declaration of war or specific authorization for such use of forces has been enacted. The bill specifies that its provisions would not apply to U.S. forces engaged in operations directed at al-Qaeda or associated forces. The measure would also require two reports regarding risks to U.S. and Saudi citizens as well as the risk of humanitarian crisis, and an assessment of the potential increased risk of terrorist attacks. Passed 248-177: R 18-177; D 230-0. *Note: A "nay" was a vote in support of the president's position.* Feb. 13, 2019.

84. HR995. Settlement Agreement Database - Passage. Hill, D-Calif., motion to suspend the rules and pass the bill that would require the Office of Management and Budget to create and maintain a database of settlement agreements entered into by federal agencies. Motion agreed to 418-0: R 195-0; D 223-0. *Note: A two-thirds majority of those present and voting (279 in this case) is required for passage under suspension of the rules.* Feb. 13, 2019.

		79	80	81	82	83	84
ALABAMA							
1	Byrne	N	N	Y	Y	N	Y
2	Roby	N	N	Y	Y	N	Y
3	Rogers, M.	N	N	Y	Y	N	Y
4	Aderholt	N	N	Y	Y	N	Y
5	Brooks, M.	N	N	Y	Y	Y	Y
6	Palmer	N	N	Y	Y	N	Y
7	Sewell	Y	Y	N	Y	Y	Y
ALASKA							
AL	Young	N	N	Y	Y	N	Y
ARIZONA							
1	O'Halleran	Y	N	Y	Y	Y	Y
2	Kirkpatrick	Y	N	N	Y	Y	Y
3	Grijalva	Y	Y	N	Y	Y	Y
4	Gosar	N	N	Y	Y	N	Y
5	Biggs	N	?	Y	Y	Y	Y
6	Schweikert	N	Y	Y	Y	Y	Y
7	Gallego	Y	Y	N	Y	Y	Y
8	Lesko	N	N	Y	Y	N	Y
9	Stanton	Y	Y	N	Y	Y	Y
ARKANSAS							
1	Crawford	N	N	Y	Y	N	Y
2	Hill, F.	N	N	Y	Y	N	Y
3	Womack	N	N	Y	Y	N	Y
4	Westerman	N	N	Y	Y	N	Y
CALIFORNIA							
1	LaMalfa	N	N	Y	Y	N	Y
2	Huffman	Y	Y	N	Y	Y	Y
3	Garamendi	Y	Y	N	Y	Y	Y
4	McClintock	N	Y	Y	Y	N	Y
5	Thompson, M.	Y	N	N	Y	Y	Y
6	Matsui	Y	N	N	Y	Y	Y
7	Bera	Y	N	N	Y	Y	Y
8	Cook	N	N	Y	Y	N	Y
9	McNerney	Y	Y	N	Y	Y	Y
10	Harder	Y	N	Y	Y	Y	Y
11	DeSaulnier	Y	Y	N	Y	Y	Y
12	Pelosi						
13	Lee B.	Y	Y	N	Y	Y	Y
14	Speier	Y	Y	N	Y	Y	Y
15	Swalwell	Y	Y	N	Y	Y	Y
16	Costa	Y	N	N	Y	Y	Y
17	Khanna	Y	Y	N	Y	Y	Y
18	Eshoo	Y	Y	N	Y	Y	Y
19	Lofgren	Y	Y	N	Y	Y	Y
20	Panetta	Y	Y	Y	Y	Y	Y
21	Cox	Y	Y	N	Y	Y	Y
22	Nunes	N	N	Y	Y	N	Y
23	McCarthy	N	Y	Y	Y	N	Y
24	Carbajal	Y	Y	N	Y	Y	Y
25	Hill, K.	Y	Y	Y	Y	Y	Y
26	Brownley	Y	N	N	Y	Y	Y
27	Chu	Y	Y	N	Y	Y	Y
28	Schiff	Y	Y	N	Y	Y	Y
29	Cárdenas	Y	Y	N	Y	Y	Y
30	Sherman	Y	Y	N	Y	Y	Y
31	Aguilar	Y	N	N	Y	Y	Y
32	Napolitano	Y	Y	N	Y	Y	Y
33	Lieu	Y	Y	N	Y	Y	Y
34	Gomez	Y	Y	N	Y	Y	Y
35	Torres	Y	Y	N	Y	Y	Y
36	Ruiz	Y	N	Y	Y	Y	Y
37	Bass	Y	Y	N	Y	Y	Y
38	Sánchez	Y	Y	?	Y	Y	Y
39	Cisneros	Y	N	Y	Y	Y	Y
40	Roybal-Allard	Y	Y	N	Y	Y	Y
41	Takano	Y	Y	N	Y	Y	Y
42	Calvert	N	N	Y	Y	N	Y
43	Waters	Y	N	Y	Y	Y	Y
44	Barragán	Y	Y	N	Y	Y	Y
45	Porter	Y	N	Y	Y	Y	Y
46	Correa	Y	N	Y	Y	Y	Y
47	Lowenthal	Y	Y	N	Y	Y	?
48	Rouda	Y	Y	N	Y	Y	Y
49	Levin	Y	Y	N	Y	Y	Y
50	Hunter	N	N	Y	Y	N	Y
51	Vargas	Y	Y	N	Y	Y	Y
52	Peters	Y	N	N	Y	Y	Y
53	Davis, S.	Y	Y	N	Y	Y	Y
COLORADO							
1	DeGette	Y	Y	N	Y	Y	Y
2	Neguse	Y	Y	N	Y	Y	Y
3	Tipton	N	N	Y	Y	N	Y
4	Buck	N	Y	Y	Y	Y	Y
5	Lamborn	N	N	Y	Y	N	Y
6	Crow	Y	N	Y	Y	Y	Y
7	Perlmutter	Y	Y	Y	Y	Y	Y
CONNECTICUT							
1	Larson	Y	Y	N	Y	Y	Y
2	Courtney	Y	Y	N	Y	Y	Y
3	DeLauro	Y	Y	N	Y	Y	Y
4	Himes	Y	N	N	Y	Y	Y
5	Hayes	Y	Y	N	Y	Y	Y
DELAWARE							
AL	Blunt Rochester	Y	Y	N	Y	Y	Y
FLORIDA							
1	Gaetz	N	N	Y	Y	Y	Y
2	Dunn	N	N	Y	Y	N	Y
3	Yoho	N	Y	Y	Y	N	Y
4	Rutherford	N	N	Y	Y	N	Y
5	Lawson	Y	N	N	Y	Y	Y
6	Waltz	N	N	Y	Y	N	Y
7	Murphy	Y	Y	N	Y	Y	Y
8	Posey	N	N	Y	Y	N	Y
9	Soto	Y	N	Y	Y	Y	Y
10	Demings	Y	Y	N	Y	Y	Y
11	Webster	N	N	Y	Y	N	Y
12	Bilirakis	N	N	Y	Y	N	Y
13	Crist	Y	N	Y	Y	Y	Y
14	Castor	Y	N	N	Y	Y	Y
15	Spano	N	N	Y	Y	N	Y
16	Buchanan	N	N	Y	Y	N	Y
17	Steube	N	N	Y	Y	N	Y
18	Mast	N	N	Y	Y	N	Y
19	Rooney	N	N	Y	Y	N	Y
20	Hastings	Y	Y	N	Y	Y	Y
21	Frankel	Y	Y	N	Y	Y	Y
22	Deutch	Y	Y	N	Y	Y	Y
23	Wasserman Schultz	Y	Y	N	Y	Y	Y
24	Wilson, F.	Y	Y	N	Y	Y	?
25	Diaz-Balart	N	N	Y	Y	N	Y
26	Mucarsel-Powell	Y	N	Y	Y	Y	Y
27	Shalala	Y	Y	N	Y	Y	Y
GEORGIA							
1	Carter, E.L.	N	N	Y	Y	N	Y
2	Bishop, S.	Y	Y	N	Y	Y	Y
3	Ferguson	N	N	Y	Y	N	Y
4	Johnson, H.	Y	Y	N	Y	Y	Y
5	Lewis John	Y	Y	N	Y	Y	Y
6	McBath	Y	Y	N	Y	Y	Y
7	Woodall	N	N	Y	Y	N	Y
8	Scott, A.	N	N	Y	Y	N	Y
9	Collins, D.	N	Y	Y	Y	N	Y
10	Hice	N	N	Y	Y	N	Y
11	Loudermilk	N	N	Y	Y	N	Y
12	Allen	N	N	Y	Y	N	Y
13	Scott, D.	Y	Y	N	Y	Y	Y
14	Graves, T.	N	N	Y	Y	N	Y
HAWAII							
1	Case	Y	Y	Y	Y	Y	Y
2	Gabbard	Y	Y	N	Y	Y	?
IDAHO							
1	Fulcher	N	N	Y	Y	N	Y
2	Simpson	N	Y	Y	Y	N	Y
ILLINOIS							
1	Rush	Y	Y	Y	Y	Y	Y
2	Kelly, R.	Y	Y	N	Y	Y	Y
3	Lipinski	Y	Y	N	Y	Y	Y
4	García, J.	Y	Y	N	Y	Y	Y
5	Quigley	?	?	?	?	?	?
6	Casten	Y	Y	N	Y	Y	Y
7	Davis, D.	Y	Y	N	Y	Y	Y
8	Krishnamoorthi	Y	N	Y	Y	Y	?
9	Schakowsky	Y	Y	N	Y	Y	?
10	Schneider	Y	Y	N	Y	Y	Y
11	Foster	Y	Y	N	Y	Y	Y

		79	80	81	82	83	84
12	**Bost**	N	N	Y	Y	N	Y
13	**Davis, R.**	N	N	Y	Y	N	Y
14	Underwood	Y	Y	N	Y	Y	Y
15	**Shimkus**	N	N	Y	Y	N	Y
16	**Kinzinger**	-	+	+	+	-	+
17	Bustos	Y	Y	Y	Y	Y	Y
18	**LaHood**	N	N	Y	Y	N	Y
INDIANA							
1	Visclosky	Y	Y	N	Y	Y	Y
2	**Walorski**	N	N	Y	Y	N	Y
3	**Banks**	N	Y	Y	Y	N	Y
4	**Baird**	N	N	Y	Y	N	Y
5	**Brooks, S.**	N	N	Y	Y	N	Y
6	**Pence**	N	N	Y	Y	N	Y
7	Carson	Y	Y	N	Y	Y	Y
8	**Bucshon**	N	Y	Y	Y	N	Y
9	**Hollingsworth**	N	Y	Y	Y	Y	Y
IOWA							
1	Finkenauer	Y	Y	Y	Y	Y	Y
2	Loebsack	Y	Y	Y	Y	Y	Y
3	Axne	Y	Y	Y	Y	Y	Y
4	**King, S.**	N	Y	Y	Y	N	Y
KANSAS							
1	**Marshall**	N	N	Y	Y	N	Y
2	**Watkins**	N	Y	Y	Y	N	Y
3	Davids	Y	N	Y	Y	Y	Y
4	**Estes**	N	N	Y	Y	N	Y
KENTUCKY							
1	**Comer**	N	N	Y	Y	N	Y
2	**Guthrie**	N	N	Y	Y	N	Y
3	Yarmuth	Y	Y	N	Y	Y	Y
4	**Massie**	N	N	N	P	Y	Y
5	**Rogers, H.**	N	N	Y	Y	N	Y
6	**Barr**	N	Y	Y	Y	N	Y
LOUISIANA							
1	**Scalise**	N	N	Y	Y	N	Y
2	Richmond	Y	Y	N	Y	Y	Y
3	**Higgins, C.**	N	Y	Y	Y	N	Y
4	**Johnson, M.**	N	N	Y	Y	N	Y
5	**Abraham**	N	N	Y	Y	N	Y
6	**Graves, G.**	N	N	Y	Y	N	Y
MAINE							
1	Pingree	?	?	N	Y	Y	Y
2	Golden	Y	N	Y	Y	Y	Y
MARYLAND							
1	**Harris**	N	N	Y	Y	N	Y
2	Ruppersberger	Y	Y	N	Y	Y	Y
3	Sarbanes	Y	Y	N	Y	Y	Y
4	Brown, A.	Y	Y	N	Y	Y	Y
5	Hoyer	Y	Y	N	Y	Y	Y
6	Trone	Y	Y	N	Y	Y	Y
7	Cummings	Y	Y	N	Y	Y	Y
8	Raskin	Y	Y	N	Y	Y	Y
MASSACHUSETTS							
1	Neal	Y	Y	N	Y	Y	Y
2	McGovern	Y	Y	N	Y	Y	Y
3	Trahan	Y	Y	N	Y	Y	Y
4	Kennedy	Y	Y	N	Y	Y	Y
5	Clark	Y	Y	N	Y	Y	Y
6	Moulton	Y	Y	Y	Y	Y	Y
7	Pressley	Y	Y	N	Y	Y	Y
8	Lynch	Y	Y	Y	Y	Y	Y
9	Keating	Y	?	N	Y	Y	Y
MICHIGAN							
1	**Bergman**	N	Y	Y	Y	N	Y
2	**Huizenga**	N	N	Y	Y	N	Y
3	**Amash**	N	N	N	P	P	Y
4	**Moolenaar**	N	N	Y	Y	N	Y
5	Kildee	Y	Y	N	Y	Y	Y
6	**Upton**	N	N	Y	Y	N	Y
7	**Walberg**	N	N	Y	Y	N	Y
8	Slotkin	Y	N	Y	Y	Y	Y
9	Levin	Y	Y	N	Y	Y	Y
10	**Mitchell**	N	N	Y	Y	N	Y
11	Stevens	Y	Y	Y	Y	Y	Y
12	Dingell	?	?	?	?	?	?
13	Tlaib	Y	Y	N	Y	Y	Y
14	Lawrence	Y	Y	N	Y	Y	Y
MINNESOTA							
1	**Hagedorn**	N	N	Y	Y	N	Y
2	Craig	Y	N	Y	Y	Y	Y
3	Phillips	Y	Y	Y	Y	Y	Y
4	McCollum	Y	Y	N	Y	Y	Y
5	Omar	Y	Y	N	Y	Y	Y

		79	80	81	82	83	84
6	**Emmer**	N	N	Y	Y	N	Y
7	Peterson	Y	N	Y	Y	Y	Y
8	**Stauber**	N	Y	Y	Y	N	Y
MISSISSIPPI							
1	**Kelly, T.**	N	N	Y	Y	N	Y
2	Thompson, B.	Y	Y	N	Y	Y	Y
3	**Guest**	N	N	Y	Y	N	Y
4	**Palazzo**	N	?	Y	Y	N	Y
MISSOURI							
1	Clay	Y	Y	N	Y	Y	Y
2	**Wagner**	?	?	Y	Y	N	Y
3	**Luetkemeyer**	N	Y	Y	Y	N	Y
4	**Hartzler**	N	N	Y	Y	N	Y
5	Cleaver	Y	Y	N	Y	Y	Y
6	**Graves, S.**	N	N	Y	Y	N	Y
7	**Long**	N	Y	Y	Y	N	Y
8	**Smith, J.**	N	N	Y	Y	N	Y
MONTANA							
AL	**Gianforte**	N	N	Y	Y	N	Y
NEBRASKA							
1	**Fortenberry**	N	Y	Y	Y	N	Y
2	**Bacon**	N	Y	Y	Y	N	Y
3	**Smith, Adrian**	N	N	Y	Y	N	Y
NEVADA							
1	Titus	Y	Y	N	Y	Y	Y
2	**Amodei**	N	N	Y	Y	N	Y
3	Lee	Y	Y	Y	Y	Y	Y
4	Horsford	Y	Y	Y	Y	Y	Y
NEW HAMPSHIRE							
1	Pappas	Y	Y	Y	Y	Y	Y
2	Kuster	Y	Y	Y	Y	Y	Y
NEW JERSEY							
1	Norcross	Y	Y	N	Y	Y	Y
2	Van Drew	Y	N	Y	Y	Y	Y
3	Kim	Y	N	Y	Y	Y	Y
4	**Smith, C.**	N	Y	Y	Y	N	Y
5	Gottheimer	Y	N	Y	Y	Y	Y
6	Pallone	Y	Y	N	Y	Y	Y
7	Malinowski	Y	Y	N	Y	Y	Y
8	Sires	Y	Y	N	Y	Y	Y
9	Pascrell	Y	Y	N	Y	Y	?
10	Payne	Y	Y	?	Y	Y	Y
11	Sherrill	Y	Y	Y	Y	Y	?
12	Watson Coleman	Y	N	N	Y	Y	Y
NEW MEXICO							
1	Haaland	Y	Y	N	Y	Y	Y
2	Torres Small	Y	N	Y	Y	Y	Y
3	Luján	Y	Y	N	Y	Y	Y
NEW YORK							
1	**Zeldin**	N	N	Y	Y	N	Y
2	**King, P.**	N	N	Y	Y	N	Y
3	Suozzi	Y	N	N	Y	Y	Y
4	Rice, K.	Y	N	N	Y	Y	Y
5	Meeks	Y	Y	N	Y	Y	Y
6	Meng	Y	N	N	Y	Y	Y
7	Velázquez	Y	Y	N	Y	Y	Y
8	Jeffries	Y	Y	N	Y	Y	Y
9	Clarke	Y	Y	N	Y	Y	Y
10	Nadler	Y	Y	N	Y	Y	Y
11	Rose	Y	N	Y	Y	Y	Y
12	Maloney, C.	Y	Y	N	Y	Y	Y
13	Espaillat	Y	Y	N	Y	Y	Y
14	Ocasio-Cortez	Y	Y	N	Y	Y	Y
15	Serrano	Y	Y	N	Y	Y	Y
16	Engel	Y	Y	N	Y	Y	Y
17	Lowey	Y	Y	N	Y	Y	Y
18	Maloney, S.P.	Y	Y	N	Y	Y	Y
19	Delgado	Y	Y	Y	Y	Y	Y
20	Tonko	Y	P	N	Y	Y	Y
21	**Stefanik**	N	Y	Y	Y	N	Y
22	Brindisi	Y	N	Y	Y	Y	Y
23	**Reed**	N	Y	Y	Y	N	Y
24	**Katko**	N	Y	Y	Y	N	Y
25	Morelle	Y	Y	Y	Y	Y	Y
26	Higgins, B.	Y	Y	N	Y	Y	Y
27	**Collins, C.**						
NORTH CAROLINA							
1	Butterfield	Y	Y	N	Y	Y	Y
2	**Holding**	N	N	Y	Y	N	Y
3	**Jones***						
4	Price	Y	?	N	Y	Y	Y
5	**Foxx**	N	N	Y	Y	N	Y
6	**Walker**	N	N	Y	Y	N	Y
7	**Rouzer**	N	N	Y	Y	N	Y

		79	80	81	82	83	84
8	**Hudson**	N	N	Y	Y	N	Y
9	vacant						
10	**McHenry**	N	N	Y	Y	N	Y
11	**Meadows**	N	N	Y	Y	Y	Y
12	Adams	Y	Y	N	Y	Y	Y
13	**Budd**	N	Y	Y	Y	N	Y
NORTH DAKOTA							
AL	**Armstrong**	N	Y	Y	Y	N	Y
OHIO							
1	**Chabot**	N	N	Y	Y	N	Y
2	**Wenstrup**	N	?	Y	Y	N	Y
3	Beatty	Y	Y	N	Y	Y	Y
4	**Jordan**	N	N	Y	Y	Y	Y
5	**Latta**	N	N	Y	Y	N	Y
6	**Johnson, B.**	N	N	Y	Y	N	Y
7	**Gibbs**	N	N	Y	Y	N	Y
8	**Davidson**	N	Y	Y	Y	Y	Y
9	Kaptur	Y	Y	Y	Y	Y	Y
10	**Turner**	N	N	Y	Y	N	Y
11	Fudge	Y	N	N	Y	Y	Y
12	**Balderson**	N	N	Y	Y	N	Y
13	Ryan	?	?	?	+	+	?
14	**Joyce**	N	N	Y	Y	N	Y
15	**Stivers**	N	Y	Y	Y	N	Y
16	**Gonzalez**	N	N	Y	Y	N	Y
OKLAHOMA							
1	**Hern**	N	N	Y	Y	N	Y
2	**Mullin**	N	N	Y	Y	N	Y
3	**Lucas**	N	N	Y	Y	N	Y
4	**Cole**	N	N	Y	Y	N	Y
5	Horn	Y	Y	Y	Y	Y	Y
OREGON							
1	Bonamici	Y	Y	N	Y	Y	Y
2	**Walden**	N	N	Y	Y	N	Y
3	Blumenauer	Y	?	N	Y	Y	Y
4	DeFazio	Y	Y	N	Y	Y	Y
5	Schrader	Y	N	Y	Y	Y	Y
PENNSYLVANIA							
1	**Fitzpatrick**	N	N	Y	Y	N	Y
2	Boyle	Y	Y	N	Y	Y	Y
3	Evans	Y	Y	N	Y	Y	Y
4	Dean	Y	Y	N	Y	Y	Y
5	Scanlon	Y	+	N	Y	Y	Y
6	Houlahan	Y	Y	Y	Y	Y	Y
7	Wild	Y	N	N	Y	Y	Y
8	Cartwright	Y	Y	N	Y	Y	Y
9	**Meuser**	N	N	Y	Y	N	Y
10	**Perry**	N	Y	Y	Y	N	Y
11	**Smucker**	N	N	Y	Y	N	Y
12	**Marino***						
13	**Joyce**	N	N	Y	Y	N	Y
14	**Reschenthaler**	N	N	Y	Y	N	Y
15	**Thompson, G.**	N	N	Y	Y	N	Y
16	**Kelly, M.**	N	N	Y	Y	N	Y
17	Lamb	Y	Y	Y	Y	Y	Y
18	Doyle	Y	Y	N	Y	Y	Y
RHODE ISLAND							
1	Cicilline	Y	N	N	Y	Y	Y
2	Langevin	Y	Y	N	Y	Y	Y
SOUTH CAROLINA							
1	Cunningham	Y	N	Y	Y	Y	Y
2	**Wilson, J.**	N	N	Y	Y	N	Y
3	**Duncan**	N	N	Y	Y	N	Y
4	**Timmons**	N	N	Y	Y	N	Y
5	**Norman**	N	N	Y	Y	N	Y
6	Clyburn	Y	N	N	Y	Y	Y
7	**Rice, T.**	N	N	Y	Y	N	Y
SOUTH DAKOTA							
AL	**Johnson**	N	N	Y	Y	N	Y
TENNESSEE							
1	**Roe**	N	N	Y	Y	N	Y
2	**Burchett**	N	N	Y	Y	N	Y
3	**Fleischmann**	N	Y	Y	Y	N	Y
4	**DesJarlais**	N	N	Y	Y	N	Y
5	Cooper	Y	Y	N	Y	Y	Y
6	**Rose**	N	N	Y	Y	N	Y
7	**Green**	N	N	Y	Y	N	Y
8	**Kustoff**	N	N	Y	Y	N	Y
9	Cohen	Y	Y	N	Y	Y	Y
TEXAS							
1	**Gohmert**	N	?	Y	Y	Y	Y
2	**Crenshaw**	N	N	Y	Y	N	Y
3	**Taylor**	?	Y	Y	Y	N	?
4	**Ratcliffe**	N	N	Y	Y	N	Y

		79	80	81	82	83	84
5	**Gooden**	N	N	Y	Y	N	Y
6	**Wright**	N	N	Y	Y	N	Y
7	Fletcher	Y	Y	N	Y	Y	Y
8	**Brady**	N	Y	Y	Y	N	Y
9	Green, A.	Y	Y	N	Y	Y	Y
10	**McCaul**	N	N	Y	Y	N	Y
11	**Conaway**	N	N	Y	Y	N	Y
12	**Granger**	-	Y	Y	Y	N	Y
13	**Thornberry**	N	Y	Y	Y	N	Y
14	**Weber**	N	N	Y	Y	N	Y
15	Gonzalez	Y	Y	N	Y	Y	Y
16	Escobar	Y	Y	N	Y	Y	Y
17	**Flores**	N	N	Y	Y	N	Y
18	Jackson Lee	Y	Y	N	Y	Y	Y
19	**Arrington**	N	Y	Y	Y	N	Y
20	Castro	Y	Y	N	Y	Y	Y
21	**Roy**	N	N	Y	Y	Y	Y
22	**Olson**	N	N	Y	Y	N	Y
23	**Hurd**	N	?	Y	Y	N	Y
24	**Marchant**	N	N	Y	Y	N	Y
25	**Williams**	N	N	Y	Y	N	Y
26	**Burgess**	N	N	Y	Y	N	Y
27	**Cloud**	N	N	Y	Y	Y	Y
28	Cuellar	Y	Y	Y	Y	Y	Y
29	Garcia, S.	Y	Y	N	Y	Y	Y
30	Johnson, E.B.	Y	Y	N	Y	Y	Y
31	**Carter, J.**	N	N	Y	Y	N	Y
32	Allred	+	+	+	+	+	+
33	Veasey	Y	Y	N	Y	Y	Y
34	Vela	Y	Y	N	Y	Y	Y
35	Doggett	Y	Y	N	Y	Y	Y
36	**Babin**	N	N	Y	Y	N	Y
UTAH							
1	**Bishop, R.**	N	N	Y	Y	N	Y
2	**Stewart**	N	N	Y	Y	N	Y
3	**Curtis**	N	N	Y	Y	N	Y
4	McAdams	Y	N	Y	Y	Y	Y
VERMONT							
AL	Welch	Y	Y	N	Y	Y	Y
VIRGINIA							
1	**Wittman**	N	N	Y	Y	N	Y
2	Luria	Y	Y	Y	Y	Y	Y
3	Scott, R.	Y	Y	Y	Y	Y	Y
4	McEachin	Y	Y	N	Y	Y	Y
5	**Riggleman**	N	N	Y	Y	N	Y
6	**Cline**	N	N	Y	Y	N	Y
7	Spanberger	Y	N	Y	Y	Y	Y
8	Beyer	Y	Y	N	Y	Y	Y
9	**Griffith**	N	N	Y	Y	Y	Y
10	Wexton	Y	Y	Y	Y	Y	Y
11	Connolly	?	N	N	Y	Y	Y
WASHINGTON							
1	DelBene	Y	Y	N	Y	Y	Y
2	Larsen	Y	Y	N	Y	Y	Y
3	**Herrera Beutler**	N	N	Y	Y	N	Y
4	**Newhouse**	N	Y	Y	Y	N	Y
5	**McMorris Rodgers**	N	Y	Y	Y	N	Y
6	Kilmer	Y	N	N	Y	Y	Y
7	Jayapal	Y	Y	N	Y	Y	Y
8	Schrier	Y	Y	Y	Y	Y	Y
9	Smith Adam	Y	Y	N	Y	Y	+
10	Heck	Y	Y	N	Y	Y	Y
WEST VIRGINIA							
1	**McKinley**	N	N	Y	Y	N	Y
2	**Mooney**	N	N	Y	Y	Y	Y
3	**Miller**	N	N	Y	Y	N	Y
WISCONSIN							
1	**Steil**	N	Y	Y	Y	N	Y
2	Pocan	Y	Y	N	Y	Y	Y
3	Kind	Y	N	N	Y	Y	Y
4	Moore	Y	Y	N	Y	Y	Y
5	**Sensenbrenner**	N	N	Y	Y	N	Y
6	**Grothman**	N	Y	Y	Y	N	Y
7	**Duffy**						
8	**Gallagher**	N	N	Y	Y	N	Y
WYOMING							
AL	**Cheney**	N	N	Y	Y	N	Y
DELEGATES							
	Radewagen (A.S.)			?			
	Norton (D.C.)			N			
	San Nicolas (Guam)			N			
	Sablan (N. Marianas)			N			
	González-Colón (P.R.)			Y			
	Plaskett (V.I.)			N			

III HOUSE VOTES

85. HJRES31. Fiscal 2019 Consolidated Appropriations - Previous Question. Perlmutter, D-Colo., motion to order the previous question (thus ending debate and the possibility of amendment) on the rule (H Res 131) that would provide for House floor consideration of the conference report to accompany the joint resolution (H J Res 31) that would provide, in total, $333 billion in full-year funding for the seven remaining fiscal 2019 appropriations bills. Agriculture; Commerce-Justice-Science; Financial Services; Homeland Security; Interior-Environment; State-Foreign Operations; and Transportation-Housing and Urban Development. Motion agreed to 229-195: R 0-195; D 229-0. Feb. 14, 2019.

86. HJRES31. Fiscal 2019 Consolidated Appropriations - Rule. Adoption of the rule (H Res 131) that would provide for House floor consideration of the conference report to accompany the joint resolution (H J Res 31) that would provide, in total, $333 billion in full-year funding for the seven remaining fiscal 2019 appropriations bills. Agriculture; Commerce-Justice-Science; Financial Services; Homeland Security; Interior-Environment; State-Foreign Operations; and Transportation-Housing and Urban Development. Adopted 230-196: R 0-196; D 230-0. Feb. 14, 2019.

87. HJRES31. Fiscal 2019 Consolidated Appropriations - Conference Report. Adoption of the conference report to accompany the joint resolution that would provide, in total, $333 billion in full-year funding for the seven remaining fiscal 2019 appropriations bills. Agriculture; Commerce-Justice-Science; Financial Services; Homeland Security; Interior-Environment; State-Foreign Operations; and Transportation-Housing and Urban Development. It would provide $49.4 billion in discretionary funds for fiscal 2019 for operations of the Homeland Security Department, as well as $12.6 billion for natural disaster response and recovery activities and $165 million for Coast Guard overseas contingency operations. Appropriations for DHS operations include $15 billion for Customs and Border Protection, including $1.38 billion for physical barriers along the U.S.-Mexico border. It would provide $7.6 billion for Immigration and Customs Enforcement, and would also require a 17 percent reduction in the number of detention beds available for individuals detained by the agency. The conference report would provide, in discretionary funding for fiscal 2019, $23 billion for the Agriculture Department and related agencies; $64.1 billion for departments of Commerce and Justice and other agencies such as NASA and the National Science Foundation; $23.4 billion in discretionary funding or financial services and general government appropriations; $35.6 billion for the Interior Department, the Environmental Protection Agency, and related agencies; $54.2 billion for for the State Department, foreign assistance and other international activities; and $71.1 billion for the departments of Transportation and Housing and Urban Development and related agencies. Adopted (thus cleared for the president) 300-128: R 87-109; D 213-19. Feb. 14, 2019.

88. HR539. Expanding Entrepreneurship Programs - Passage. Lipinski, D-Ill., motion to suspend the rules and pass the bill that would develop an Innovation Corps (I-Corps) course through the National Science Foundation to further support the commercialization of products and services through federally funded research. The bill would expand the program to include individuals who receive grants under the Small Business Innovation Research Program. Motion agreed to 385-18: R 171-18; D 214-0. *Note: A two-thirds majority of those present and voting (269 in this case) is required for passage under suspension of the rules.* Feb. 25, 2019.

89. HR276. Recognizing School Employees - Passage. Lee, D-Nev., motion to suspend the rules and pass the bill that would create the Recognizing Inspiring School Employees (RISE) Award Program to honor excellence by non-profit school employees who provide services to students enrolled in pre-kindergarten through high school. Motion agreed to 387-19: R 170-19; D 217-0. *Note: A two-thirds majority of those present and voting (271 in this case) is required for passage under suspension of the rules.* Feb. 25, 2019.

90. HR1112, HR8. Measures Expanding Background Checks - Previous Question. Raskin, D-Md., motion to order the previous question (thus ending debate and possibility of amendment) on the rule (H Res 145) that would provide for House floor consideration of the Bipartisan Background Checks Act (HR 8) and the Enhanced Background Checks Act (HR 1112). Motion agreed to 229-191: R 0-191; D 229-0. Feb. 26, 2019.

		85	86	87	88	89	90
ALABAMA							
1	**Byrne**	N	N	N	Y	Y	N
2	**Roby**	N	N	Y	Y	Y	N
3	**Rogers, M.**	N	N	N	Y	Y	N
4	**Aderholt**	?	N	N	Y	Y	N
5	**Brooks, M.**	N	N	N	N	N	N
6	**Palmer**	N	N	N	Y	Y	N
7	Sewell	Y	Y	Y	Y	Y	Y
ALASKA							
AL	**Young**	N	N	Y	Y	Y	N
ARIZONA							
1	O'Halleran	Y	Y	Y	Y	Y	Y
2	Kirkpatrick	Y	Y	Y	Y	Y	Y
3	Grijalva	Y	Y	N	Y	Y	Y
4	**Gosar**	N	N	N	N	N	N
5	**Biggs**	N	N	N	N	N	N
6	**Schweikert**	N	N	N	Y	N	N
7	Gallego	Y	Y	Y	Y	Y	Y
8	**Lesko**	N	N	N	Y	N	N
9	Stanton	Y	Y	Y	Y	Y	Y
ARKANSAS							
1	**Crawford**	N	N	N	Y	Y	N
2	**Hill, F.**	N	N	Y	Y	Y	?
3	**Womack**	N	N	Y	Y	Y	N
4	**Westerman**	N	N	N	Y	Y	N
CALIFORNIA							
1	**LaMalfa**	N	N	N	Y	Y	N
2	Huffman	Y	Y	Y	Y	Y	Y
3	Garamendi	Y	Y	Y	Y	Y	Y
4	**McClintock**	N	N	N	N	Y	N
5	Thompson, M.	Y	Y	Y	Y	Y	Y
6	Matsui	Y	Y	Y	+	+	Y
7	Bera	Y	Y	Y	Y	Y	Y
8	**Cook**	N	N	Y	Y	Y	N
9	McNerney	Y	Y	Y	Y	Y	Y
10	Harder	Y	Y	Y	Y	Y	Y
11	DeSaulnier	Y	Y	Y	Y	Y	Y
12	Pelosi						
13	Lee B.	Y	Y	Y	Y	Y	Y
14	Speier	Y	Y	Y	Y	Y	Y
15	Swalwell	Y	Y	Y	+	+	Y
16	Costa	Y	Y	Y	?	Y	Y
17	Khanna	Y	Y	Y	Y	Y	Y
18	Eshoo	Y	Y	Y	Y	Y	Y
19	Lofgren	Y	Y	Y	Y	Y	Y
20	Panetta	Y	Y	Y	Y	Y	Y
21	Cox	Y	Y	Y	Y	Y	Y
22	**Nunes**	N	N	Y	Y	Y	N
23	**McCarthy**	N	N	Y	Y	Y	N
24	Carbajal	Y	Y	Y	Y	Y	Y
25	Hill, K.	Y	Y	Y	Y	Y	Y
26	Brownley	Y	Y	Y	Y	Y	Y
27	Chu	Y	Y	Y	Y	Y	Y
28	Schiff	Y	Y	Y	Y	Y	Y
29	Cárdenas	?	Y	Y	Y	Y	Y
30	Sherman	Y	Y	Y	Y	Y	Y
31	Aguilar	Y	Y	Y	Y	Y	Y
32	Napolitano	Y	Y	Y	Y	Y	Y
33	Lieu	Y	?	Y	Y	Y	Y
34	Gomez	Y	Y	N	?	Y	Y
35	Torres	Y	Y	Y	Y	Y	Y
36	Ruiz	Y	Y	Y	Y	Y	Y
37	Bass	Y	Y	Y	Y	Y	Y
38	Sánchez	Y	Y	Y	Y	Y	Y
39	Cisneros	Y	Y	Y	Y	Y	Y
40	Roybal-Allard	Y	Y	Y	Y	Y	Y
41	Takano	Y	Y	Y	Y	Y	Y
42	**Calvert**	N	N	Y	Y	Y	N
43	Waters	Y	Y	Y	Y	Y	Y
44	Barragán	Y	Y	Y	Y	Y	Y
45	Porter	Y	Y	Y	Y	Y	Y
46	Correa	Y	Y	N	Y	Y	Y
47	Lowenthal	Y	Y	Y	Y	Y	Y
48	Rouda	Y	Y	Y	Y	Y	Y
49	Levin	Y	Y	Y	Y	Y	Y
50	**Hunter**	N	N	N	Y	N	N
51	Vargas	Y	Y	N	Y	Y	Y
52	Peters	Y	Y	Y	Y	Y	Y

		85	86	87	88	89	90
53	Davis, S.	Y	Y	Y	Y	Y	Y
COLORADO							
1	DeGette	Y	Y	Y	Y	Y	Y
2	Neguse	Y	Y	Y	Y	Y	Y
3	Tipton	N	N	N	Y	Y	N
4	**Buck**	N	N	N	N	N	N
5	**Lamborn**	N	N	N	Y	Y	N
6	Crow	Y	Y	Y	Y	Y	Y
7	Perlmutter	Y	Y	Y	Y	Y	Y
CONNECTICUT							
1	Larson	Y	Y	Y	Y	Y	Y
2	Courtney	Y	Y	Y	Y	Y	Y
3	DeLauro	Y	Y	Y	Y	Y	Y
4	Himes	Y	Y	Y	Y	Y	Y
5	Hayes	Y	Y	Y	Y	Y	Y
DELAWARE							
AL	Blunt Rochester	Y	Y	Y	Y	Y	Y
FLORIDA							
1	**Gaetz**	N	N	Y	Y	Y	N
2	**Dunn**	N	N	N	Y	Y	N
3	**Yoho**	N	N	N	N	N	N
4	**Rutherford**	N	N	N	Y	Y	N
5	Lawson	Y	Y	Y	?	?	Y
6	**Waltz**	N	N	N	Y	Y	N
7	Murphy	Y	Y	Y	Y	Y	Y
8	**Posey**	N	N	N	Y	Y	N
9	Soto	Y	Y	Y	Y	Y	Y
10	Demings	Y	Y	Y	Y	Y	Y
11	**Webster**	N	N	N	Y	Y	N
12	**Bilirakis**	N	N	N	+	+	N
13	Crist	Y	Y	Y	Y	Y	Y
14	Castor	Y	Y	Y	Y	Y	Y
15	**Spano**	N	N	N	Y	Y	N
16	**Buchanan**	N	N	Y	Y	Y	N
17	**Steube**	N	N	N	N	Y	N
18	**Mast**	N	N	N	Y	Y	N
19	**Rooney**	N	N	N	?	?	N
20	Hastings	Y	Y	Y	Y	Y	Y
21	Frankel	Y	Y	Y	+	+	+
22	Deutch	?	?	?	Y	Y	Y
23	Wasserman Schultz	Y	Y	Y	Y	Y	Y
24	Wilson, F.	Y	Y	Y	Y	Y	Y
25	**Diaz-Balart**	N	N	Y	Y	Y	N
26	Mucarsel-Powell	Y	Y	Y	Y	Y	Y
27	Shalala	Y	Y	Y	Y	Y	Y
GEORGIA							
1	**Carter, E.L.**	N	N	N	Y	Y	N
2	Bishop, S.	Y	Y	Y	Y	Y	Y
3	**Ferguson**	N	N	N	Y	Y	N
4	Johnson, H.	Y	Y	Y	Y	Y	Y
5	Lewis John	Y	Y	Y	Y	Y	Y
6	McBath	Y	Y	Y	Y	Y	Y
7	**Woodall**	N	N	N	Y	Y	N
8	**Scott, A.**	N	N	N	Y	Y	N
9	**Collins, D.**	N	N	N	Y	Y	N
10	**Hice**	N	N	N	Y	N	N
11	**Loudermilk**	N	N	N	Y	Y	N
12	**Allen**	N	N	N	Y	Y	N
13	Scott, D.	Y	Y	Y	Y	Y	Y
14	**Graves, T.**	N	N	N	Y	Y	N
HAWAII							
1	Case	Y	Y	Y	Y	Y	Y
2	Gabbard	Y	Y	Y	Y	Y	Y
IDAHO							
1	**Fulcher**	N	N	N	Y	Y	N
2	**Simpson**	N	N	Y	Y	Y	N
ILLINOIS							
1	Rush	Y	Y	Y	?	?	Y
2	Kelly, R.	Y	Y	Y	Y	Y	Y
3	Lipinski	Y	Y	Y	Y	Y	Y
4	García, J.	Y	Y	N	Y	Y	Y
5	Quigley	?	?	?	Y	Y	Y
6	Casten	Y	Y	Y	Y	Y	Y
7	Davis, D.	Y	Y	Y	+	+	Y
8	Krishnamoorthi	Y	Y	Y	Y	Y	Y
9	Schakowsky	Y	Y	Y	Y	Y	Y
10	Schneider	Y	Y	Y	Y	Y	Y
11	Foster	Y	Y	Y	Y	Y	Y

		85	86	87	88	89	90
12	**Bost**	N	N	Y	Y	Y	N
13	**Davis, R.**	N	N	Y	Y	Y	N
14	Underwood	Y	Y	Y	Y	Y	Y
15	**Shimkus**	N	N	Y	Y	Y	N
16	**Kinzinger**	-	-	+	Y	Y	N
17	Bustos	Y	Y	Y	Y	Y	Y
18	**LaHood**	N	N	N	Y	Y	N
INDIANA							
1	Visclosky	Y	Y	Y	Y	Y	Y
2	**Walorski**	N	N	Y	Y	Y	N
3	**Banks**	N	N	N	Y	Y	N
4	**Baird**	N	N	N	Y	Y	N
5	**Brooks, S.**	N	N	Y	?	?	N
6	**Pence**	N	N	Y	Y	Y	N
7	Carson	Y	Y	Y	Y	Y	Y
8	**Bucshon**	N	N	N	Y	Y	?
9	**Hollingsworth**	N	N	N	Y	Y	N
IOWA							
1	Finkenauer	Y	Y	Y	Y	Y	Y
2	Loebsack	Y	Y	Y	Y	Y	Y
3	Axne	Y	Y	Y	Y	Y	Y
4	**King, S.**	N	N	N	+	+	-
KANSAS							
1	**Marshall**	N	N	N	Y	Y	N
2	**Watkins**	N	N	N	Y	Y	N
3	Davids	Y	Y	Y	Y	Y	Y
4	**Estes**	N	N	N	Y	Y	N
KENTUCKY							
1	**Comer**	N	N	N	Y	Y	N
2	**Guthrie**	N	N	Y	Y	Y	N
3	Yarmuth	Y	Y	Y	Y	Y	Y
4	**Massie**	N	N	N	N	N	N
5	**Rogers, H.**	N	N	Y	Y	Y	N
6	**Barr**	N	N	Y	Y	Y	N
LOUISIANA							
1	**Scalise**	N	N	Y	Y	Y	N
2	Richmond	Y	Y	Y	Y	Y	Y
3	**Higgins, C.**	N	N	N	Y	Y	N
4	**Johnson, M.**	N	N	N	Y	Y	N
5	**Abraham**	N	N	N	?	?	N
6	**Graves, G.**	N	N	N	Y	Y	N
MAINE							
1	Pingree	Y	Y	Y	Y	Y	Y
2	Golden	Y	Y	Y	Y	Y	Y
MARYLAND							
1	**Harris**	N	N	N	Y	N	N
2	Ruppersberger	Y	Y	Y	Y	Y	Y
3	Sarbanes	Y	Y	Y	Y	Y	Y
4	Brown, A.	Y	Y	Y	Y	Y	Y
5	Hoyer	Y	Y	Y	Y	Y	Y
6	Trone	Y	Y	Y	?	?	Y
7	Cummings	Y	Y	Y	Y	Y	Y
8	Raskin	Y	Y	Y	Y	Y	Y
MASSACHUSETTS							
1	Neal	Y	Y	Y	Y	Y	Y
2	McGovern	Y	Y	Y	Y	Y	Y
3	Trahan	Y	Y	Y	Y	Y	Y
4	Kennedy	Y	Y	Y	Y	Y	Y
5	Clark	Y	Y	Y	Y	Y	Y
6	Moulton	Y	Y	Y	Y	Y	Y
7	Pressley	Y	Y	N	Y	Y	Y
8	Lynch	Y	Y	Y	Y	Y	Y
9	Keating	Y	Y	Y	Y	Y	Y
MICHIGAN							
1	**Bergman**	N	N	Y	Y	Y	N
2	**Huizenga**	N	N	Y	Y	Y	N
3	**Amash**	N	N	N	N	N	N
4	**Moolenaar**	N	N	Y	Y	Y	N
5	Kildee	Y	Y	Y	Y	Y	Y
6	**Upton**	N	N	Y	Y	Y	N
7	**Walberg**	N	N	N	Y	Y	N
8	Slotkin	Y	Y	Y	Y	Y	Y
9	Levin	Y	Y	Y	Y	Y	Y
10	**Mitchell**	N	N	N	Y	N	N
11	Stevens	Y	Y	Y	Y	Y	Y
12	Dingell	Y	Y	Y	Y	Y	Y
13	Tlaib	Y	Y	N	Y	Y	Y
14	Lawrence	Y	Y	Y	Y	Y	Y
MINNESOTA							
1	**Hagedorn**	N	N	Y	Y	Y	N
2	Craig	Y	Y	Y	Y	Y	Y
3	Phillips	Y	Y	Y	Y	Y	Y
4	McCollum	Y	Y	Y	Y	Y	Y
5	Omar	Y	Y	N	Y	Y	Y
6	**Emmer**	N	N	Y	Y	Y	N
7	Peterson	Y	Y	Y	Y	Y	Y
8	**Stauber**	N	N	Y	Y	Y	N
MISSISSIPPI							
1	**Kelly, T.**	N	N	N	Y	Y	N
2	Thompson, B.	Y	Y	Y	?	Y	Y
3	**Guest**	N	N	Y	Y	Y	N
4	**Palazzo**	N	N	Y	Y	Y	N
MISSOURI							
1	Clay	Y	Y	Y	Y	Y	Y
2	**Wagner**	N	N	Y	Y	Y	-
3	**Luetkemeyer**	N	N	Y	Y	Y	N
4	**Hartzler**	N	N	N	Y	Y	N
5	Cleaver	Y	Y	Y	Y	Y	Y
6	**Graves, S.**	N	N	N	Y	Y	N
7	**Long**	N	N	N	Y	Y	N
8	**Smith, J.**	N	N	N	Y	Y	N
MONTANA							
AL	**Gianforte**	N	N	Y	Y	Y	N
NEBRASKA							
1	**Fortenberry**	N	N	Y	Y	Y	N
2	**Bacon**	N	N	Y	Y	Y	N
3	**Smith, Adrian**	N	N	N	Y	Y	N
NEVADA							
1	Titus	Y	Y	Y	Y	Y	Y
2	**Amodei**	N	N	Y	Y	Y	N
3	Lee	Y	Y	Y	Y	Y	Y
4	Horsford	Y	Y	Y	Y	Y	Y
NEW HAMPSHIRE							
1	Pappas	Y	Y	Y	Y	Y	Y
2	Kuster	Y	Y	Y	Y	Y	Y
NEW JERSEY							
1	Norcross	Y	Y	Y	Y	Y	Y
2	Van Drew	Y	Y	Y	Y	Y	Y
3	Kim	Y	Y	Y	Y	Y	Y
4	**Smith, C.**	N	N	Y	Y	Y	N
5	Gottheimer	Y	Y	Y	Y	Y	Y
6	Pallone	Y	Y	Y	Y	Y	Y
7	Malinowski	Y	Y	Y	Y	Y	Y
8	Sires	Y	Y	Y	Y	Y	Y
9	Pascrell	Y	Y	Y	Y	Y	Y
10	Payne	Y	Y	Y	Y	Y	Y
11	Sherrill	Y	Y	Y	Y	Y	Y
12	Watson Coleman	Y	Y	Y	Y	Y	Y
NEW MEXICO							
1	Haaland	Y	Y	Y	Y	Y	Y
2	Torres Small	Y	Y	Y	Y	Y	Y
3	Luján	Y	Y	Y	Y	Y	Y
NEW YORK							
1	**Zeldin**	N	N	N	Y	Y	N
2	**King, P.**	N	N	Y	Y	Y	N
3	Suozzi	Y	Y	Y	Y	Y	Y
4	Rice, K.	Y	Y	Y	Y	Y	Y
5	Meeks	Y	Y	Y	Y	Y	Y
6	Meng	Y	Y	Y	Y	Y	Y
7	Velázquez	Y	Y	N	Y	Y	Y
8	Jeffries	Y	Y	Y	Y	Y	Y
9	Clarke	Y	Y	N	Y	Y	Y
10	Nadler	Y	Y	Y	Y	Y	Y
11	Rose	Y	Y	Y	Y	Y	Y
12	Maloney, C.	Y	Y	Y	Y	Y	Y
13	Espaillat	Y	Y	N	Y	Y	Y
14	Ocasio-Cortez	Y	Y	N	Y	Y	Y
15	Serrano	Y	Y	Y	Y	Y	Y
16	Engel	?	Y	Y	Y	Y	Y
17	Lowey	Y	Y	Y	?	?	?
18	Maloney, S.P.	Y	Y	Y	Y	Y	Y
19	Delgado	Y	Y	Y	Y	Y	Y
20	Tonko	Y	Y	Y	Y	Y	Y
21	**Stefanik**	N	N	Y	Y	Y	N
22	Brindisi	Y	Y	Y	+	+	Y
23	**Reed**	N	N	Y	Y	Y	N
24	**Katko**	N	N	Y	+	+	?
25	Morelle	Y	Y	Y	+	+	Y
26	Higgins, B.	Y	Y	Y	Y	Y	Y
27	**Collins, C.**						
NORTH CAROLINA							
1	Butterfield	Y	Y	Y	Y	Y	Y
2	**Holding**	N	N	N	Y	Y	N
3	**Jones***						
4	Price	Y	Y	Y	Y	Y	Y
5	**Foxx**	N	N	Y	N	Y	N
6	**Walker**	N	N	N	Y	Y	?
7	**Rouzer**	N	N	N	Y	Y	N
8	**Hudson**	N	N	N	Y	Y	N
9	vacant						
10	**McHenry**	N	N	Y	Y	Y	N
11	**Meadows**	N	N	N	Y	Y	N
12	Adams	Y	Y	Y	Y	Y	Y
13	**Budd**	N	N	N	Y	Y	N
NORTH DAKOTA							
AL	**Armstrong**	N	N	Y	Y	Y	N
OHIO							
1	**Chabot**	N	N	N	Y	Y	N
2	**Wenstrup**	N	N	Y	Y	Y	N
3	Beatty	Y	Y	Y	Y	Y	Y
4	**Jordan**	N	N	N	Y	Y	N
5	**Latta**	N	N	N	Y	Y	N
6	**Johnson, B.**	N	N	Y	Y	Y	N
7	**Gibbs**	N	N	Y	Y	Y	N
8	**Davidson**	N	N	N	Y	N	N
9	Kaptur	Y	Y	Y	Y	Y	Y
10	**Turner**	N	N	Y	Y	Y	N
11	Fudge	Y	Y	Y	Y	Y	Y
12	**Balderson**	N	N	Y	Y	Y	N
13	Ryan	Y	Y	Y	Y	Y	Y
14	**Joyce**	N	N	Y	Y	Y	N
15	**Stivers**	N	N	Y	Y	Y	N
16	**Gonzalez**	N	N	Y	Y	Y	N
OKLAHOMA							
1	**Hern**	N	N	N	N	Y	N
2	**Mullin**	N	N	N	Y	Y	N
3	**Lucas**	N	N	N	Y	Y	N
4	**Cole**	N	N	Y	Y	Y	N
5	Horn	Y	Y	Y	+	+	Y
OREGON							
1	Bonamici	Y	Y	Y	+	Y	Y
2	**Walden**	N	N	Y	Y	Y	N
3	Blumenauer	Y	Y	Y	Y	Y	Y
4	DeFazio	Y	Y	Y	+	+	?
5	Schrader	Y	Y	Y	?	?	Y
PENNSYLVANIA							
1	**Fitzpatrick**	N	N	Y	Y	Y	N
2	Boyle	Y	Y	Y	Y	Y	Y
3	Evans	Y	Y	Y	Y	Y	Y
4	Dean	Y	Y	Y	Y	Y	Y
5	Scanlon	Y	Y	Y	Y	Y	Y
6	Houlahan	Y	Y	Y	Y	Y	Y
7	Wild	Y	Y	Y	Y	Y	Y
8	Cartwright	Y	Y	Y	Y	Y	Y
9	**Meuser**	N	N	N	Y	Y	N
10	**Perry**	N	N	N	Y	N	N
11	**Smucker**	N	N	N	Y	Y	N
12	**Marino***						
13	**Joyce**	N	N	N	Y	Y	N
14	**Reschenthaler**	N	N	N	Y	Y	N
15	**Thompson, G.**	N	N	N	Y	Y	N
16	**Kelly, M.**	N	N	N	Y	Y	N
17	Lamb	Y	Y	Y	Y	Y	Y
18	Doyle	Y	Y	Y	Y	Y	Y
RHODE ISLAND							
1	Cicilline	Y	Y	Y	Y	Y	Y
2	Langevin	Y	Y	Y	Y	Y	Y
SOUTH CAROLINA							
1	Cunningham	Y	Y	Y	Y	Y	Y
2	**Wilson, J.**	N	N	N	Y	Y	N
3	**Duncan**	N	N	N	Y	Y	N
4	**Timmons**	N	N	N	Y	Y	N
5	**Norman**	N	N	N	Y	Y	N
6	Clyburn	Y	Y	Y	Y	Y	Y
7	**Rice, T.**	N	N	N	N	N	N
SOUTH DAKOTA							
AL	**Johnson**	N	N	Y	Y	Y	N
TENNESSEE							
1	**Roe**	N	N	Y	Y	Y	N
2	**Burchett**	N	N	N	Y	Y	N
3	**Fleischmann**	N	N	Y	Y	Y	N
4	**DesJarlais**	N	N	N	Y	Y	N
5	Cooper	Y	Y	Y	Y	Y	Y
6	**Rose**	N	N	N	Y	Y	N
7	**Green**	N	N	N	Y	Y	N
8	**Kustoff**	N	N	Y	Y	Y	N
9	Cohen	Y	Y	Y	+	+	+
TEXAS							
1	**Gohmert**	N	N	N	N	N	N
2	**Crenshaw**	N	N	N	Y	Y	N
3	**Taylor**	N	N	N	Y	Y	N
4	**Ratcliffe**	N	N	N	Y	Y	N
5	**Gooden**	N	N	N	Y	Y	N
6	**Wright**	N	N	N	Y	Y	N
7	Fletcher	Y	Y	Y	Y	Y	Y
8	**Brady**	N	N	N	Y	Y	N
9	Green, A.	Y	Y	Y	Y	Y	Y
10	**McCaul**	N	N	Y	Y	Y	N
11	**Conaway**	N	N	Y	Y	Y	N
12	**Granger**	N	N	Y	Y	Y	N
13	**Thornberry**	N	N	Y	Y	Y	N
14	**Weber**	N	N	N	Y	N	N
15	Gonzalez	Y	Y	N	Y	Y	Y
16	Escobar	Y	Y	N	Y	Y	Y
17	**Flores**	N	N	Y	Y	Y	N
18	Jackson Lee	Y	Y	Y	Y	Y	Y
19	**Arrington**	N	N	N	Y	Y	N
20	Castro	Y	Y	N	Y	Y	Y
21	**Roy**	N	N	N	N	N	N
22	**Olson**	N	N	Y	Y	N	N
23	**Hurd**	N	N	Y	Y	Y	N
24	**Marchant**	N	N	N	Y	Y	N
25	**Williams**	N	N	N	Y	Y	N
26	**Burgess**	N	N	N	Y	Y	N
27	**Cloud**	N	N	N	Y	Y	N
28	Cuellar	Y	Y	Y	Y	Y	Y
29	Garcia, S.	Y	Y	N	Y	Y	Y
30	Johnson, E.B.	Y	Y	Y	Y	Y	Y
31	**Carter, J.**	N	N	Y	Y	Y	N
32	Allred	+	+	+	Y	Y	Y
33	Veasey	Y	Y	Y	Y	Y	Y
34	Vela	Y	Y	N	Y	Y	Y
35	Doggett	Y	Y	N	Y	Y	Y
36	**Babin**	N	N	N	?	?	N
UTAH							
1	**Bishop, R.**	N	N	Y	Y	Y	N
2	**Stewart**	N	N	Y	Y	Y	N
3	**Curtis**	N	N	N	Y	Y	N
4	McAdams	Y	Y	Y	Y	Y	Y
VERMONT							
AL	Welch	Y	Y	Y	Y	Y	Y
VIRGINIA							
1	**Wittman**	N	N	Y	Y	Y	N
2	Luria	Y	Y	Y	Y	Y	Y
3	Scott, R.	Y	Y	Y	Y	Y	Y
4	McEachin	Y	Y	Y	Y	Y	Y
5	**Riggleman**	N	N	Y	Y	Y	N
6	**Cline**	N	N	N	N	Y	N
7	Spanberger	Y	Y	Y	Y	Y	Y
8	Beyer	Y	Y	Y	Y	?	Y
9	**Griffith**	N	N	N	N	Y	N
10	Wexton	Y	Y	Y	Y	Y	Y
11	Connolly	Y	Y	Y	Y	Y	Y
WASHINGTON							
1	DelBene	Y	Y	Y	Y	Y	Y
2	Larsen	Y	Y	Y	Y	Y	Y
3	**Herrera Beutler**	N	N	Y	+	+	N
4	**Newhouse**	N	N	Y	Y	Y	N
5	**McMorris Rodgers**	N	N	Y	Y	Y	N
6	Kilmer	Y	Y	Y	Y	Y	Y
7	Jayapal	Y	Y	N	Y	Y	Y
8	Schrier	Y	Y	Y	Y	Y	Y
9	Smith Adam	Y	Y	Y	+	+	+
10	Heck	Y	Y	Y	Y	Y	Y
WEST VIRGINIA							
1	**McKinley**	N	N	Y	Y	Y	N
2	**Mooney**	N	N	N	Y	Y	N
3	**Miller**	N	N	Y	Y	Y	N
WISCONSIN							
1	**Steil**	N	N	Y	Y	Y	N
2	Pocan	Y	Y	Y	+	+	Y
3	Kind	Y	Y	Y	Y	Y	Y
4	Moore	Y	Y	Y	Y	Y	Y
5	**Sensenbrenner**	N	N	N	Y	Y	N
6	**Grothman**	N	N	N	N	N	N
7	**Duffy**						
8	**Gallagher**	N	N	N	Y	Y	N
WYOMING							
AL	**Cheney**	N	N	Y	Y	Y	N
DELEGATES							
	Radewagen (A.S.)						
	Norton (D.C.)						
	San Nicolas (Guam)						
	Sablan (N. Marianas)						
	González-Colón (P.R.)						
	Plaskett (V.I.)						

III HOUSE VOTES

91. HR1112, HR8. Measures Expanding Background Checks - Rule. Adoption of the rule (H Res 145) that would provide for House floor consideration of the Bipartisan Background Checks Act (HR 8) and the Enhanced Background Checks Act (HR 1112). Adopted 227-194: R 0-192; D 227-2. Feb. 26, 2019.

92. HJRES46. National Emergency Disapproval Resolution - Previous Question. Torres, D-Calif., motion to order the previous question (thus ending debate and possibility of amendment) on the rule (H Res 144) that would provide for House floor consideration of the joint resolution (H J Res 46) relating to a national emergency declared by the president on February 15, 2019. Motion agreed to 228-193: R 0-193; D 228-0. Feb. 26, 2019.

93. HJRES46. National Emergency Disapproval Resolution - Rule. Adoption of the rule (H Res 144) that would provide for House floor consideration of the joint resolution (H J Res 46) relating to a national emergency declared by the president on February 15, 2019. Adopted 229-193: R 0-193; D 229-0. Feb. 26, 2019.

94. HJRES46. National Emergency Disapproval Resolution - Passage. Passage of the joint resolution that would terminate the president's national emergency declaration concerning the security situation at the southern border. Passed 245-182: R 13-182; D 232-0. *Note: A "nay" was a vote in support of the president's position.* Feb. 26, 2019.

95. S47. Public Lands Package - Passage. Grijalva, D-Ariz., motion to suspend the rules and pass the bill that would permanently reauthorize the Land and Water Conservation Fund, with at least 40 percent of the fund to be used for state projects, at least 40 percent for federal projects, and at least 3 percent toward increasing recreational access to federal lands. It would also reauthorize, through 2023, the national volcano monitoring system and the U.S. Geological Survey. Through 2022, it would reauthorize several programs related to wildlife conservation, invasive species management, and prevention of illegal poaching and trafficking. The bill also includes a number of provisions related to the designation, regulation, exchange, and management of federal public lands and forests. It would make additions and boundary adjustments to several national parks, monuments, and historic sites. It would authorize and establish procedures for the transfer of water and power facilities from the Bureau of Reclamation to state and local entities and would authorize a Reclamation water management project in south-central Washington State. It also contains provisions related to federal land access for hunting and ordering studies on federal land designation, among other provisions. Motion agreed to 363-62: R 133-62; D 230-0. *Note: A two-thirds majority of those present and voting (284 in this case) is required for passage under suspension of the rules.* Feb. 26, 2019.

96. HR8. Expanding Firearm Background Checks - TSA Pre-Check Exemption. Lesko, R-Ariz., amendment that would exempt from the bill's background check requirements any transfer of firearms to participants in Homeland Security Department-trusted traveler programs. Rejected in Committee of the Whole 182-250: R 181-15; D 1-234; I 0-1. Feb. 27, 2019.

		91	92	93	94	95	96
ALABAMA							
1	**Byrne**	N	N	N	N	Y	Y
2	**Roby**	N	N	N	N	Y	Y
3	**Rogers, M.**	N	N	N	N	Y	Y
4	**Aderholt**	N	N	N	N	Y	Y
5	**Brooks, M.**	N	N	N	N	Y	Y
6	**Palmer**	N	N	N	N	Y	Y
7	Sewell	Y	Y	Y	Y	Y	N
ALASKA							
AL	**Young**	N	N	N	N	Y	Y
ARIZONA							
1	O'Halleran	Y	Y	Y	Y	Y	N
2	Kirkpatrick	Y	Y	Y	Y	Y	N
3	Grijalva	Y	?	Y	Y	Y	N
4	**Gosar**	N	N	N	N	Y	?
5	**Biggs**	N	N	N	N	N	Y
6	**Schweikert**	N	N	N	N	Y	Y
7	Gallego	Y	Y	Y	Y	Y	N
8	**Lesko**	N	N	N	N	Y	Y
9	Stanton	Y	Y	Y	Y	Y	N
ARKANSAS							
1	**Crawford**	N	N	N	N	Y	Y
2	**Hill, F.**	N	N	N	N	Y	Y
3	**Womack**	N	N	N	N	Y	Y
4	**Westerman**	N	N	N	N	Y	Y
CALIFORNIA							
1	**LaMalfa**	N	N	N	N	N	Y
2	Huffman	Y	Y	Y	Y	Y	N
3	Garamendi	Y	Y	Y	Y	Y	N
4	**McClintock**	N	N	N	N	Y	Y
5	Thompson, M.	Y	Y	Y	Y	Y	N
6	Matsui	Y	Y	Y	Y	Y	N
7	Bera	Y	Y	Y	Y	Y	N
8	**Cook**	N	N	N	N	Y	Y
9	McNerney	Y	Y	Y	Y	Y	N
10	Harder	Y	Y	Y	Y	Y	N
11	DeSaulnier	Y	Y	Y	Y	Y	N
12	Pelosi			Y			
13	Lee B.	Y	Y	Y	Y	Y	N
14	Speier	Y	Y	Y	Y	Y	N
15	Swalwell	Y	Y	Y	Y	Y	N
16	Costa	Y	Y	Y	Y	Y	N
17	Khanna	Y	Y	Y	Y	Y	N
18	Eshoo	Y	Y	Y	Y	Y	N
19	Lofgren	Y	Y	Y	Y	Y	N
20	Panetta	Y	Y	Y	Y	Y	N
21	Cox	Y	Y	Y	Y	Y	N
22	**Nunes**	N	N	N	N	N	Y
23	**McCarthy**	N	N	N	N	N	Y
24	Carbajal	Y	Y	Y	Y	Y	N
25	Hill, K.	Y	Y	Y	Y	Y	N
26	Brownley	Y	Y	Y	Y	Y	N
27	Chu	Y	Y	Y	Y	Y	N
28	Schiff	Y	Y	Y	Y	Y	N
29	Cárdenas	Y	Y	Y	Y	Y	N
30	Sherman	Y	Y	Y	Y	Y	N
31	Aguilar	Y	Y	Y	Y	Y	N
32	Napolitano	Y	Y	Y	Y	Y	N
33	Lieu	Y	Y	Y	Y	Y	N
34	Gomez	Y	Y	Y	Y	Y	N
35	Torres	Y	Y	Y	Y	Y	N
36	Ruiz	Y	Y	Y	Y	Y	N
37	Bass	Y	Y	Y	Y	Y	N
38	Sánchez	Y	Y	Y	Y	Y	N
39	Cisneros	Y	Y	Y	Y	Y	N
40	Roybal-Allard	Y	Y	Y	Y	Y	N
41	Takano	Y	Y	Y	Y	Y	N
42	**Calvert**	N	N	N	N	Y	Y
43	Waters	Y	Y	Y	Y	Y	N
44	Barragán	Y	Y	Y	Y	Y	N
45	Porter	Y	Y	Y	Y	Y	N
46	Correa	Y	Y	Y	Y	Y	N
47	Lowenthal	Y	Y	Y	Y	Y	N
48	Rouda	Y	Y	Y	Y	Y	N
49	Levin	Y	Y	Y	Y	Y	N
50	**Hunter**	N	N	N	N	N	Y
51	Vargas	Y	Y	Y	Y	Y	N
52	Peters	Y	Y	Y	Y	Y	N

		91	92	93	94	95	96
53	Davis, S.	Y	Y	Y	Y	Y	N
COLORADO							
1	DeGette	Y	Y	Y	Y	Y	N
2	Neguse	Y	Y	Y	Y	Y	N
3	**Tipton**	N	N	N	N	Y	Y
4	**Buck**	N	N	N	N	N	Y
5	**Lamborn**	N	N	N	N	Y	Y
6	Crow	Y	Y	Y	Y	Y	N
7	Perlmutter	Y	Y	Y	Y	Y	N
CONNECTICUT							
1	Larson	Y	Y	Y	Y	Y	N
2	Courtney	Y	Y	Y	Y	Y	N
3	DeLauro	Y	Y	Y	Y	Y	N
4	Himes	Y	Y	Y	Y	Y	N
5	Hayes	Y	Y	Y	Y	Y	N
DELAWARE							
AL	Blunt Rochester	Y	Y	Y	Y	Y	N
FLORIDA							
1	**Gaetz**	N	N	N	N	Y	Y
2	**Dunn**	N	N	N	N	Y	Y
3	**Yoho**	N	N	N	N	N	Y
4	**Rutherford**	N	N	N	N	Y	Y
5	Lawson	Y	Y	Y	Y	Y	N
6	**Waltz**	N	N	N	N	Y	Y
7	Murphy	Y	Y	Y	Y	Y	N
8	**Posey**	N	N	N	N	Y	Y
9	Soto	Y	Y	Y	Y	Y	N
10	Demings	Y	Y	Y	Y	Y	N
11	**Webster**	N	N	N	N	Y	Y
12	**Bilirakis**	N	N	N	N	Y	Y
13	Crist	Y	Y	Y	Y	Y	N
14	Castor	Y	Y	Y	Y	Y	N
15	**Spano**	N	N	N	N	Y	Y
16	**Buchanan**	N	N	N	N	Y	Y
17	**Steube**	N	N	N	N	Y	Y
18	**Mast**	N	N	N	N	Y	Y
19	**Rooney**	N	N	N	N	Y	Y
20	Hastings	Y	Y	Y	Y	Y	N
21	Frankel	+	+	+	+	+	-
22	Deutch	Y	Y	Y	Y	Y	N
23	Wasserman Schultz	Y	Y	Y	Y	Y	N
24	Wilson, F.	Y	Y	Y	Y	Y	N
25	**Diaz-Balart**	N	N	N	N	Y	Y
26	Mucarsel-Powell	Y	Y	Y	Y	Y	N
27	Shalala	Y	Y	Y	Y	Y	N
GEORGIA							
1	**Carter, E.L.**	N	N	N	N	Y	Y
2	Bishop, S.	Y	Y	Y	Y	Y	N
3	**Ferguson**	N	N	N	N	Y	Y
4	Johnson, H.	Y	Y	Y	Y	Y	N
5	Lewis John	Y	Y	Y	Y	?	N
6	McBath	Y	Y	Y	Y	Y	N
7	**Woodall**	N	N	N	N	Y	Y
8	**Scott, A.**	N	N	N	N	Y	Y
9	**Collins, D.**	N	N	N	N	Y	Y
10	**Hice**	N	N	N	N	N	Y
11	**Loudermilk**	N	N	N	N	Y	Y
12	**Allen**	N	N	N	N	Y	Y
13	Scott, D.	Y	Y	Y	Y	Y	N
14	**Graves, T.**	N	N	N	N	Y	Y
HAWAII							
1	Case	Y	Y	Y	Y	Y	N
2	Gabbard	Y	Y	Y	Y	Y	N
IDAHO							
1	**Fulcher**	?	N	N	N	N	Y
2	**Simpson**	N	N	N	N	Y	Y
ILLINOIS							
1	Rush	Y	Y	Y	Y	Y	N
2	Kelly, R.	Y	Y	Y	Y	Y	N
3	Lipinski	Y	Y	Y	Y	Y	N
4	García, J.	Y	Y	Y	Y	Y	N
5	Quigley	Y	Y	Y	Y	Y	N
6	Casten	Y	Y	Y	Y	Y	N
7	Davis, D.	Y	Y	Y	Y	Y	N
8	Krishnamoorthi	Y	Y	Y	Y	Y	N
9	Schakowsky	Y	Y	Y	Y	Y	N
10	Schneider	Y	Y	Y	Y	Y	N
11	Foster	Y	Y	Y	Y	Y	N

KEY: **Republicans** (bold) Democrats *Independents*

Y Voted for (yea)	**N** Voted against (nay)	**P** Voted "present"
+ Announced for	**–** Announced against	**?** Did not vote or otherwise make position known
# Paired for	**✕** Paired against	

2019 CQ ALMANAC | www.cq.com

		91	92	93	94	95	96
12	**Bost**	N	N	N	N	Y	Y
13	**Davis, R.**	N	N	N	N	Y	Y
14	Underwood	Y	Y	Y	Y	Y	N
15	**Shimkus**	N	N	N	N	Y	Y
16	**Kinzinger**	N	N	N	N	Y	Y
17	Bustos	Y	Y	Y	Y	Y	N
18	**LaHood**	N	N	N	N	Y	Y
INDIANA							
1	Visclosky	Y	Y	Y	Y	Y	N
2	**Walorski**	N	N	N	N	Y	Y
3	**Banks**	N	N	N	N	N	Y
4	**Baird**	N	N	N	N	Y	Y
5	**Brooks, S.**	N	N	N	N	Y	Y
6	**Pence**	N	N	N	N	Y	Y
7	Carson	Y	Y	Y	Y	Y	N
8	**Bucshon**	N	N	N	N	Y	Y
9	**Hollingsworth**	N	N	N	N	Y	N
IOWA							
1	Finkenauer	Y	Y	Y	Y	Y	N
2	Loebsack	Y	Y	Y	Y	Y	N
3	Axne	Y	Y	Y	Y	Y	N
4	**King, S.**	-	-	-	N	N	Y
KANSAS							
1	**Marshall**	N	N	N	N	Y	Y
2	**Watkins**	N	N	N	N	Y	Y
3	Davids	Y	Y	Y	Y	Y	N
4	**Estes**	N	N	N	N	Y	Y
KENTUCKY							
1	**Comer**	N	N	N	N	Y	Y
2	**Guthrie**	N	N	N	N	Y	Y
3	Yarmuth	Y	Y	Y	Y	Y	N
4	**Massie**	N	N	N	Y	N	N
5	**Rogers, H.**	N	N	N	N	Y	Y
6	**Barr**	N	N	N	N	Y	Y
LOUISIANA							
1	**Scalise**	N	N	N	N	N	Y
2	Richmond	Y	Y	Y	Y	Y	N
3	**Higgins, C.**	N	N	N	N	N	Y
4	**Johnson, M.**	N	N	N	N	N	Y
5	**Abraham**	N	N	N	N	N	Y
6	**Graves, G.**	N	N	N	N	N	Y
MAINE							
1	Pingree	Y	Y	Y	Y	Y	N
2	Golden	N	Y	Y	Y	Y	N
MARYLAND							
1	**Harris**	N	N	N	N	N	Y
2	Ruppersberger	Y	Y	Y	Y	Y	N
3	Sarbanes	Y	Y	Y	Y	Y	N
4	Brown, A.	Y	Y	Y	Y	Y	N
5	Hoyer	Y	Y	Y	Y	Y	N
6	Trone	Y	Y	Y	Y	Y	N
7	Cummings	Y	Y	Y	Y	Y	N
8	Raskin	Y	Y	Y	Y	Y	N
MASSACHUSETTS							
1	Neal	Y	Y	Y	Y	Y	N
2	McGovern	Y	Y	Y	Y	Y	N
3	Trahan	Y	Y	Y	Y	Y	N
4	Kennedy	Y	Y	Y	Y	Y	N
5	Clark	Y	Y	Y	Y	Y	N
6	Moulton	Y	Y	Y	Y	Y	N
7	Pressley	Y	Y	Y	Y	Y	N
8	Lynch	Y	Y	Y	Y	Y	N
9	Keating	Y	Y	Y	Y	Y	N
MICHIGAN							
1	**Bergman**	N	N	N	N	Y	Y
2	**Huizenga**	N	N	N	N	N	Y
3	**Amash**	N	N	N	Y	N	N
4	**Moolenaar**	N	N	N	N	Y	Y
5	Kildee	Y	Y	Y	Y	Y	N
6	**Upton**	N	N	N	N	Y	Y
7	**Walberg**	N	N	N	N	Y	Y
8	Slotkin	Y	Y	Y	Y	Y	N
9	Levin	Y	Y	Y	Y	Y	N
10	**Mitchell**	N	N	N	N	Y	Y
11	Stevens	Y	Y	Y	Y	Y	N
12	Dingell	Y	Y	Y	Y	Y	N
13	Tlaib	Y	Y	Y	Y	Y	N
14	Lawrence	Y	Y	Y	Y	Y	N
MINNESOTA							
1	**Hagedorn**	?	N	N	N	N	Y
2	Craig	Y	Y	Y	Y	Y	N
3	Phillips	Y	Y	Y	Y	Y	N
4	McCollum	Y	Y	Y	Y	Y	N
5	Omar	Y	Y	Y	Y	Y	N

		91	92	93	94	95	96
6	**Emmer**	N	N	N	N	Y	Y
7	Peterson	N	Y	Y	Y	Y	N
8	**Stauber**	N	N	N	N	N	Y
MISSISSIPPI							
1	**Kelly, T.**	N	N	N	N	Y	Y
2	Thompson, B.	Y	Y	Y	Y	Y	N
3	**Guest**	N	N	N	N	Y	Y
4	**Palazzo**	N	N	N	N	Y	Y
MISSOURI							
1	Clay	Y	Y	Y	Y	Y	N
2	**Wagner**	-	-	-	-	+	Y
3	**Luetkemeyer**	N	N	N	N	Y	Y
4	**Hartzler**	N	N	N	N	Y	Y
5	Cleaver	Y	Y	Y	Y	Y	N
6	**Graves, S.**	N	N	N	N	N	Y
7	**Long**	N	N	N	N	Y	Y
8	**Smith, J.**	N	N	N	N	N	Y
MONTANA							
AL	**Gianforte**	N	N	N	N	Y	Y
NEBRASKA							
1	**Fortenberry**	N	N	N	N	Y	Y
2	**Bacon**	N	N	N	N	Y	Y
3	**Smith, Adrian**	N	N	N	N	Y	Y
NEVADA							
1	Titus	Y	Y	Y	Y	Y	N
2	**Amodei**	N	N	N	N	Y	Y
3	Lee	Y	Y	Y	Y	Y	N
4	Horsford	Y	Y	Y	Y	Y	N
NEW HAMPSHIRE							
1	Pappas	Y	Y	Y	Y	Y	N
2	Kuster	Y	Y	Y	Y	Y	N
NEW JERSEY							
1	Norcross	Y	Y	Y	Y	Y	N
2	Van Drew	Y	Y	Y	Y	Y	N
3	Kim	Y	Y	Y	Y	Y	N
4	**Smith, C.**	N	N	N	N	Y	N
5	Gottheimer	Y	Y	Y	Y	Y	N
6	Pallone	Y	Y	Y	Y	Y	N
7	Malinowski	Y	Y	Y	Y	Y	N
8	Sires	Y	Y	Y	Y	Y	N
9	Pascrell	Y	Y	Y	Y	Y	N
10	Payne	Y	Y	Y	Y	Y	N
11	Sherrill	Y	Y	Y	Y	Y	N
12	Watson Coleman	Y	Y	Y	Y	Y	N
NEW MEXICO							
1	Haaland	Y	Y	Y	Y	Y	N
2	Torres Small	Y	Y	Y	Y	Y	N
3	Luján	Y	Y	Y	Y	Y	N
NEW YORK							
1	**Zeldin**	N	N	N	N	Y	Y
2	**King, P.**	N	N	N	N	Y	N
3	Suozzi	Y	Y	Y	Y	Y	N
4	Rice, K.	Y	Y	Y	Y	Y	N
5	Meeks	Y	Y	Y	Y	Y	N
6	Meng	Y	Y	Y	Y	Y	N
7	Velázquez	Y	Y	Y	Y	Y	N
8	Jeffries	Y	Y	Y	Y	Y	N
9	Clarke	Y	Y	Y	Y	Y	N
10	Nadler	Y	Y	Y	Y	Y	N
11	Rose	Y	Y	Y	Y	Y	N
12	Maloney, C.	Y	Y	Y	Y	Y	N
13	Espaillat	Y	Y	Y	Y	Y	N
14	Ocasio-Cortez	Y	Y	Y	Y	Y	N
15	Serrano	Y	Y	Y	Y	Y	N
16	Engel	Y	Y	Y	Y	Y	N
17	Lowey	?	?	?	Y	Y	N
18	Maloney, S.P.	Y	Y	Y	Y	Y	N
19	Delgado	Y	Y	Y	Y	Y	N
20	Tonko	Y	Y	Y	Y	Y	N
21	**Stefanik**	N	N	N	Y	Y	Y
22	Brindisi	Y	Y	Y	Y	Y	N
23	**Reed**	N	N	N	N	Y	Y
24	**Katko**	?	?	?	+	+	?
25	Morelle	Y	Y	Y	Y	Y	N
26	Higgins, B.	Y	Y	Y	Y	Y	N
27	**Collins, C.**						
NORTH CAROLINA							
1	Butterfield	Y	Y	Y	Y	Y	N
2	**Holding**	N	N	N	N	N	Y
3	**Jones***						
4	Price	Y	Y	Y	Y	Y	N
5	**Foxx**	N	N	N	N	Y	Y
6	**Walker**	N	N	N	N	N	Y
7	**Rouzer**	N	N	N	N	Y	Y

		91	92	93	94	95	96
8	**Hudson**	N	N	N	N	Y	Y
9	vacant						
10	**McHenry**	N	N	-	N	Y	Y
11	**Meadows**	N	N	N	N	N	Y
12	Adams	Y	Y	Y	Y	Y	N
13	**Budd**	N	N	N	N	N	Y
NORTH DAKOTA							
AL	**Armstrong**	N	N	N	N	Y	Y
OHIO							
1	**Chabot**	N	N	N	N	N	Y
2	**Wenstrup**	N	N	N	N	N	Y
3	Beatty	Y	Y	Y	Y	Y	N
4	**Jordan**	N	N	N	N	N	Y
5	**Latta**	N	N	N	N	Y	Y
6	**Johnson, B.**	N	N	N	N	Y	Y
7	**Gibbs**	N	N	N	N	Y	Y
8	**Davidson**	N	N	N	N	N	N
9	Kaptur	Y	Y	Y	Y	Y	N
10	**Turner**	N	N	N	N	Y	Y
11	Fudge	Y	Y	Y	Y	Y	N
12	**Balderson**	N	N	N	N	Y	Y
13	Ryan	Y	Y	Y	Y	Y	N
14	**Joyce**	N	N	N	N	Y	N
15	**Stivers**	N	?	N	N	Y	N
16	**Gonzalez**	N	N	N	N	Y	Y
OKLAHOMA							
1	**Hern**	N	N	N	N	N	Y
2	**Mullin**	N	N	N	N	N	Y
3	**Lucas**	N	N	N	N	N	Y
4	**Cole**	N	N	N	N	Y	Y
5	Horn	Y	Y	Y	Y	Y	N
OREGON							
1	Bonamici	Y	Y	Y	Y	Y	N
2	**Walden**	N	N	N	Y	Y	Y
3	Blumenauer	Y	Y	Y	Y	Y	N
4	DeFazio	?	?	?	?	+	N
5	Schrader	Y	Y	Y	Y	Y	N
PENNSYLVANIA							
1	**Fitzpatrick**	N	N	N	Y	Y	N
2	Boyle	Y	Y	Y	Y	Y	N
3	Evans	Y	Y	Y	Y	Y	N
4	Dean	Y	Y	Y	Y	Y	N
5	Scanlon	Y	Y	Y	Y	Y	N
6	Houlahan	Y	Y	Y	Y	Y	N
7	Wild	Y	Y	Y	Y	Y	N
8	Cartwright	Y	Y	Y	Y	Y	N
9	**Meuser**	N	N	N	N	Y	Y
10	**Perry**	N	N	N	N	N	N
11	**Smucker**	N	N	N	N	Y	Y
12	**Marino***						
13	**Joyce**	N	N	N	N	Y	Y
14	**Reschenthaler**	N	N	N	N	Y	Y
15	**Thompson, G.**	N	N	N	N	Y	Y
16	**Kelly, M.**	N	N	N	N	Y	Y
17	Lamb	Y	Y	Y	Y	Y	N
18	Doyle	Y	Y	Y	Y	Y	N
RHODE ISLAND							
1	Cicilline	Y	Y	Y	Y	Y	N
2	Langevin	Y	Y	Y	Y	Y	N
SOUTH CAROLINA							
1	Cunningham	Y	Y	Y	Y	Y	N
2	**Wilson, J.**	N	N	N	N	Y	Y
3	**Duncan**	N	N	N	N	Y	Y
4	**Timmons**	N	N	N	N	Y	Y
5	**Norman**	N	N	N	N	N	Y
6	Clyburn	Y	Y	Y	Y	Y	N
7	**Rice, T.**	N	N	N	N	Y	Y
SOUTH DAKOTA							
AL	**Johnson**	N	N	N	Y	Y	Y
TENNESSEE							
1	**Roe**	N	N	N	N	Y	Y
2	**Burchett**	N	N	N	N	Y	Y
3	**Fleischmann**	N	N	N	N	Y	Y
4	**DesJarlais**	N	N	N	N	Y	Y
5	Cooper	Y	Y	Y	Y	Y	N
6	**Rose**	N	N	N	N	N	Y
7	**Green**	N	N	N	N	N	Y
8	**Kustoff**	N	N	N	N	Y	Y
9	Cohen	+	+	+	+	+	N
TEXAS							
1	**Gohmert**	N	N	N	N	N	Y
2	**Crenshaw**	N	N	N	N	Y	Y
3	**Taylor**	N	N	N	N	N	Y
4	**Ratcliffe**	N	N	N	N	Y	Y

		91	92	93	94	95	96
5	**Gooden**	N	N	N	N	N	Y
6	**Wright**	N	N	N	N	N	Y
7	Fletcher	Y	Y	Y	Y	Y	N
8	**Brady**	N	N	N	N	Y	Y
9	Green, A.	Y	Y	Y	Y	Y	N
10	**McCaul**	N	N	N	N	Y	Y
11	**Conaway**	N	N	N	N	Y	Y
12	**Granger**	N	N	N	N	Y	Y
13	**Thornberry**	N	N	N	N	Y	Y
14	**Weber**	N	N	N	N	N	Y
15	Gonzalez	Y	Y	Y	Y	Y	N
16	Escobar	Y	Y	Y	Y	Y	N
17	**Flores**	N	N	N	N	Y	Y
18	Jackson Lee	Y	Y	Y	Y	Y	N
19	**Arrington**	N	N	N	N	N	Y
20	Castro	Y	Y	Y	Y	Y	N
21	**Roy**	N	N	N	N	N	Y
22	**Olson**	N	N	N	N	N	Y
23	**Hurd**	N	N	N	Y	Y	Y
24	**Marchant**	N	N	N	N	N	Y
25	**Williams**	N	N	N	N	N	Y
26	**Burgess**	N	N	N	N	N	Y
27	**Cloud**	N	N	N	N	N	Y
28	Cuellar	Y	Y	Y	Y	Y	Y
29	Garcia, S.	Y	Y	Y	Y	Y	N
30	Johnson, E.B.	Y	Y	Y	Y	Y	N
31	**Carter, J.**	N	N	N	N	N	Y
32	Allred	Y	Y	Y	Y	Y	N
33	Veasey	Y	Y	Y	Y	Y	N
34	Vela	Y	Y	Y	Y	Y	N
35	Doggett	Y	Y	Y	Y	Y	N
36	**Babin**	N	N	N	N	N	Y
UTAH							
1	**Bishop, R.**	N	N	N	N	Y	Y
2	**Stewart**	N	N	N	N	Y	Y
3	**Curtis**	N	N	N	N	Y	Y
4	McAdams	Y	Y	Y	Y	Y	N
VERMONT							
AL	Welch	Y	Y	Y	Y	Y	N
VIRGINIA							
1	**Wittman**	N	N	N	N	Y	Y
2	Luria	Y	Y	Y	Y	Y	N
3	Scott, R.	Y	Y	Y	Y	Y	N
4	McEachin	Y	Y	Y	Y	Y	N
5	**Riggleman**	N	N	N	N	Y	Y
6	**Cline**	N	N	N	N	N	N
7	Spanberger	Y	Y	Y	Y	Y	N
8	Beyer	Y	Y	Y	Y	Y	N
9	**Griffith**	N	N	N	N	N	Y
10	Wexton	Y	Y	Y	Y	Y	N
11	Connolly	Y	Y	Y	Y	Y	N
WASHINGTON							
1	DelBene	Y	Y	Y	Y	Y	N
2	Larsen	Y	Y	Y	Y	Y	N
3	**Herrera Beutler**	N	N	N	Y	Y	N
4	**Newhouse**	N	N	N	N	Y	Y
5	**McMorris Rodgers**	N	N	N	Y	Y	Y
6	Kilmer	Y	Y	Y	Y	Y	N
7	Jayapal	Y	Y	Y	Y	Y	N
8	Schrier	Y	Y	Y	Y	Y	N
9	Smith Adam	+	+	+	Y	Y	N
10	Heck	Y	Y	Y	Y	Y	N
WEST VIRGINIA							
1	**McKinley**	N	N	N	N	Y	Y
2	**Mooney**	N	N	N	N	Y	Y
3	**Miller**	N	N	N	N	Y	Y
WISCONSIN							
1	**Steil**	N	N	N	N	Y	Y
2	Pocan	Y	Y	Y	Y	Y	N
3	Kind	Y	Y	Y	Y	Y	N
4	Moore	Y	Y	Y	Y	Y	N
5	**Sensenbrenner**	N	N	N	Y	N	Y
6	**Grothman**	N	N	N	N	Y	Y
7	**Duffy**						
8	**Gallagher**	N	N	N	Y	Y	N
WYOMING							
AL	**Cheney**	N	N	N	N	N	Y
DELEGATES							
	Radewagen (A.S.)						?
	Norton (D.C.)						N
	San Nicolas (Guam)						?
	Sablan (N. Marianas)						N
	González-Colón (P.R.)						Y
	Plaskett (V.I.)						N

97. HR8. Expanding Firearm Background Checks - Imminent Danger Exemption. Horn, D-Okla., amendment that would clarify that the exemption from the bill's background check requirements in the case of temporary transfer to prevent death or great bodily harm would include cases of domestic violence or abuse, sexual assault, and stalking. Adopted in the Committee of the Whole 310-119: R 79-117; D 230-2; I 1-0. Feb. 27, 2019.

98. HR8. Expanding Firearm Background Checks - Recommit. Collins, R-Ga., motion to recommit the bill to the House Judiciary Committee with instructions to report back immediately with an amendment that would require that the National Instant Criminal Background Check System (NICS) notify U.S. Immigration and Customs Enforcement when a background check for an individual seeking to purchase a firearm finds that the individual is an undocumented immigrant. Motion agreed to 220-209: R 194-1; D 26-208. Feb. 27, 2019.

99. HR8. Expanding Firearm Background Checks - Passage. Passage of the bill that would require most purchasers of firearms to undergo a background check through the National Instant Criminal Background Check System (NICS), including all sales and transfers of firearms through public and private purchases. The bill would specify instances in which a background check could be foregone at the time of a firearm's transfer, including when transferred as a loan or gift between family members, when transferred for hunting or fishing purposes, or when transferred for use in a shooting range, so long as the weapon remains in the presence of its owner. The bill's requirements for background checks would not apply to the transfer of firearms to law enforcement personnel, including any law enforcement agency, armed private security professional, or member of the armed forces, insofar as the transfer is associated with official duties. Passed 240-190: R 8-188; D 232-2. *Note: A "nay" was a vote in support of the president's position.* Feb. 27, 2019.

100. HR1112. Increased Time for Background Checks - Report on Extended Check Petitions. Schneider, D-Ill., amendment that would require the FBI to report to the public on the the number of petitions received from prospective gun purchasers in instances in which a National Instant Criminal Background Check System (NICS) determination was not made within 10 days. Adopted in Committee of the Whole 282-144: R 49-144; D 232-0; I 1-0. Feb. 28, 2019.

101. HR1112. Increased Time for Background Checks - Pick Up Time Requirement. Van Drew, D-N.J., amendment that would allow a federally licensed firearms dealer, importer, manufacturer or collector (licensee) to rely on a background check certifying that an individual meets legal requirements to purchase or receive transfer of a firearm for 25 days after the licensee is notified, if the licensee is notified more than 3 days after initial contact. The amendment would specify that the provisions of the bill would take effect 210 days after enactment. Adopted in Committee of the Whole 234-193: R 3-192; D 230-1; I 1-0. Feb. 28, 2019.

102. HR1112. Increased Time for Background Checks - Recommit. Lesko, R-Ariz., motion to recommit the bill (HR 1112) to the House Judiciary Committee with instructions to report back immediately with an amendment that would allow a victim of domestic violence to petition the Justice Department for a firearm pending transfer, if the background check submitted by a licensed firearms dealer, manufacturer, importer or collector (licensee) has not been returned following a three-day waiting period. Motion rejected 194-232: R 192-3; D 2-229. Feb. 28, 2019.

		97	98	99	100	101	102
ALABAMA							
1	**Byrne**	N	Y	N	?	N	Y
2	**Roby**	N	Y	N	N	N	Y
3	**Rogers, M.**	N	Y	N	N	N	Y
4	**Aderholt**	N	Y	N	N	N	Y
5	**Brooks, M.**	N	Y	N	N	N	Y
6	**Palmer**	N	Y	N	N	N	Y
7	Sewell	Y	N	Y	Y	Y	N
ALASKA							
AL	**Young**	Y	Y	N	N	N	Y
ARIZONA							
1	O'Halleran	Y	Y	Y	Y	Y	N
2	Kirkpatrick	Y	N	Y	Y	Y	N
3	Grijalva	?	N	Y	Y	Y	N
4	**Gosar**	?	?	N	N	N	Y
5	**Biggs**	N	Y	N	N	N	Y
6	**Schweikert**	Y	Y	N	N	N	Y
7	Gallego	Y	N	Y	Y	Y	N
8	**Lesko**	Y	Y	N	N	N	Y
9	Stanton	Y	N	Y	Y	Y	N
ARKANSAS							
1	**Crawford**	N	Y	N	N	N	Y
2	**Hill, F.**	Y	Y	N	N	N	Y
3	**Womack**	Y	Y	N	N	N	Y
4	**Westerman**	N	Y	N	N	N	Y
CALIFORNIA							
1	**LaMalfa**	N	Y	N	N	N	Y
2	Huffman	Y	N	Y	Y	Y	N
3	Garamendi	Y	N	Y	+	+	-
4	**McClintock**	Y	Y	N	Y	N	Y
5	Thompson, M.	Y	N	Y	Y	Y	N
6	Matsui	Y	N	Y	Y	Y	N
7	Bera	Y	N	Y	Y	Y	N
8	**Cook**	Y	Y	N	N	N	Y
9	McNerney	Y	N	Y	Y	Y	N
10	Harder	Y	N	Y	Y	Y	N
11	DeSaulnier	Y	N	Y	Y	Y	N
12	Pelosi		N	Y			
13	Lee B.	Y	N	Y	Y	Y	N
14	Speier	N	N	Y	Y	Y	N
15	Swalwell	Y	N	Y	Y	Y	N
16	Costa	Y	Y	Y	Y	Y	N
17	Khanna	Y	N	Y	Y	Y	N
18	Eshoo	Y	N	Y	Y	Y	N
19	Lofgren	Y	N	Y	Y	Y	N
20	Panetta	Y	N	Y	Y	Y	N
21	Cox	Y	N	Y	Y	Y	N
22	**Nunes**	N	Y	N	N	N	Y
23	**McCarthy**	N	Y	N	N	N	Y
24	Carbajal	Y	N	Y	Y	Y	N
25	Hill, K.	Y	N	Y	Y	Y	N
26	Brownley	Y	N	Y	Y	Y	N
27	Chu	Y	N	Y	Y	Y	N
28	Schiff	Y	N	Y	Y	Y	N
29	Cárdenas	Y	N	Y	Y	Y	N
30	Sherman	Y	N	Y	Y	Y	N
31	Aguilar	Y	N	Y	Y	Y	N
32	Napolitano	Y	N	Y	Y	Y	N
33	Lieu	Y	N	Y	Y	Y	N
34	Gomez	Y	N	Y	Y	Y	N
35	Torres	Y	N	Y	Y	Y	N
36	Ruiz	Y	N	Y	Y	Y	N
37	Bass	Y	N	Y	Y	Y	N
38	Sánchez	Y	N	Y	Y	Y	N
39	Cisneros	Y	N	Y	Y	Y	N
40	Roybal-Allard	Y	N	Y	Y	Y	N
41	Takano	Y	N	Y	Y	Y	N
42	**Calvert**	N	Y	N	N	N	Y
43	Waters	Y	N	Y	Y	Y	N
44	Barragán	Y	N	Y	Y	Y	N
45	Porter	Y	N	Y	Y	Y	N
46	Correa	Y	N	Y	Y	Y	N
47	Lowenthal	Y	N	Y	Y	Y	N
48	Rouda	Y	N	Y	Y	Y	N
49	Levin	Y	N	Y	Y	Y	N
50	**Hunter**	N	Y	N	N	N	Y
51	Vargas	Y	N	Y	Y	Y	N
52	Peters	Y	N	Y	Y	Y	N
53	Davis, S.	Y	N	Y	Y	Y	N
COLORADO							
1	DeGette	Y	N	Y	Y	Y	N
2	Neguse	Y	N	Y	Y	Y	N
3	**Tipton**	Y	Y	N	N	N	Y
4	**Buck**	N	Y	N	N	N	Y
5	**Lamborn**	N	Y	N	N	N	Y
6	Crow	Y	N	Y	Y	Y	N
7	Perlmutter	Y	N	Y	Y	Y	N
CONNECTICUT							
1	Larson	Y	N	Y	Y	Y	N
2	Courtney	Y	N	Y	Y	Y	N
3	DeLauro	Y	N	Y	Y	Y	N
4	Himes	Y	N	Y	Y	Y	N
5	Hayes	Y	N	Y	Y	Y	N
DELAWARE							
AL	Blunt Rochester	Y	N	Y	Y	Y	N
FLORIDA							
1	**Gaetz**	Y	Y	N	N	N	Y
2	**Dunn**	N	Y	N	N	N	Y
3	**Yoho**	N	Y	N	N	N	Y
4	**Rutherford**	N	Y	N	N	N	Y
5	Lawson	Y	N	Y	Y	Y	N
6	**Waltz**	N	Y	N	N	N	Y
7	Murphy	Y	N	Y	Y	Y	N
8	**Posey**	Y	Y	N	Y	N	Y
9	Soto	Y	N	Y	+	Y	-
10	Demings	Y	N	Y	Y	Y	N
11	**Webster**	N	Y	N	N	N	Y
12	**Bilirakis**	Y	Y	N	N	N	Y
13	Crist	Y	N	Y	Y	Y	N
14	Castor	Y	N	Y	Y	Y	N
15	**Spano**	N	Y	N	N	N	Y
16	**Buchanan**	Y	Y	N	N	N	Y
17	**Steube**	N	Y	N	N	N	Y
18	**Mast**	Y	Y	Y	Y	Y	N
19	**Rooney**	Y	Y	N	Y	N	Y
20	Hastings	Y	N	Y	Y	Y	N
21	Frankel	+	-	+	+	+	-
22	Deutch	Y	N	Y	Y	Y	N
23	Wasserman Schultz	Y	N	Y	Y	Y	N
24	Wilson, F.	Y	N	Y	Y	?	N
25	**Diaz-Balart**	Y	Y	Y	Y	Y	N
26	Mucarsel-Powell	Y	N	Y	Y	Y	N
27	Shalala	Y	N	Y	Y	Y	N
GEORGIA							
1	**Carter, E.L.**	N	Y	N	N	N	Y
2	Bishop, S.	Y	N	Y	Y	Y	N
3	**Ferguson**	N	Y	N	N	N	Y
4	Johnson, H.	Y	N	Y	Y	Y	N
5	Lewis John	Y	N	Y	Y	Y	N
6	McBath	Y	N	Y	Y	Y	N
7	**Woodall**	Y	Y	N	Y	N	Y
8	**Scott, A.**	N	Y	N	N	N	Y
9	**Collins, D.**	N	Y	N	N	N	Y
10	**Hice**	Y	N	N	N	N	Y
11	**Loudermilk**	N	Y	N	N	N	Y
12	**Allen**	N	Y	N	N	N	Y
13	Scott, D.	Y	N	Y	Y	Y	N
14	**Graves, T.**	Y	Y	N	N	N	Y
HAWAII							
1	Case	Y	N	Y	Y	Y	N
2	Gabbard	Y	N	Y	Y	Y	N
IDAHO							
1	**Fulcher**	N	Y	N	N	N	Y
2	**Simpson**	N	Y	N	N	N	Y
ILLINOIS							
1	Rush	Y	N	Y	Y	Y	N
2	Kelly, R.	Y	N	Y	Y	Y	N
3	Lipinski	Y	N	Y	Y	Y	N
4	García, J.	?	N	Y	Y	Y	N
5	Quigley	Y	N	Y	Y	Y	N
6	Casten	Y	N	Y	Y	Y	N
7	Davis, D.	Y	N	Y	Y	Y	N
8	Krishnamoorthi	Y	N	Y	Y	Y	N
9	Schakowsky	Y	N	Y	Y	Y	N
10	Schneider	Y	N	Y	Y	Y	N
11	Foster	Y	N	Y	Y	Y	N

KEY:	Republicans	Democrats	*Independents*
Y Voted for (yea)	**N** Voted against (nay)	**P** Voted "present"	
+ Announced for	**−** Announced against	**?** Did not vote or otherwise	
# Paired for	**X** Paired against	make position known	

		97	98	99	100	101	102
12	**Bost**	Y	Y	N	Y	N	Y
13	**Davis, R.**	Y	Y	N	Y	N	Y
14	Underwood	N	N	Y	Y	Y	N
15	**Shimkus**	Y	Y	N	Y	N	Y
16	**Kinzinger**	N	Y	N	Y	N	Y
17	Bustos	Y	N	Y	Y	Y	N
18	**LaHood**	N	Y	N	N	N	Y
INDIANA							
1	Visclosky	Y	N	Y	Y	Y	N
2	**Walorski**	N	Y	N	Y	N	Y
3	**Banks**	N	Y	N	N	N	Y
4	**Baird**	N	Y	N	N	N	Y
5	**Brooks, S.**	Y	Y	N	Y	N	Y
6	**Pence**	N	Y	N	N	N	Y
7	Carson	Y	N	Y	Y	Y	N
8	**Bucshon**	Y	Y	N	N	N	Y
9	**Hollingsworth**	N	Y	N	Y	N	Y
IOWA							
1	Finkenauer	Y	Y	Y	Y	Y	N
2	Loebsack	Y	N	Y	Y	Y	N
3	Axne	Y	Y	Y	Y	Y	N
4	**King, S.**	Y	Y	N	N	N	Y
KANSAS							
1	**Marshall**	N	Y	N	N	N	Y
2	**Watkins**	N	Y	N	N	N	Y
3	Davids	Y	N	Y	Y	Y	N
4	**Estes**	N	Y	N	N	N	Y
KENTUCKY							
1	**Comer**	N	Y	N	N	N	Y
2	**Guthrie**	N	Y	N	Y	N	Y
3	Yarmuth	Y	N	Y	Y	Y	N
4	**Massie**	N	Y	N	N	N	N
5	**Rogers, H.**	N	Y	N	N	N	Y
6	**Barr**	N	Y	N	N	N	Y
LOUISIANA							
1	**Scalise**	N	Y	N	N	N	Y
2	Richmond	Y	N	Y	Y	Y	N
3	**Higgins, C.**	N	Y	N	N	N	Y
4	**Johnson, M.**	Y	Y	N	N	N	Y
5	**Abraham**	N	Y	N	?	?	?
6	**Graves, G.**	Y	Y	N	Y	N	Y
MAINE							
1	Pingree	Y	N	Y	Y	Y	N
2	Golden	Y	Y	N	Y	Y	N
MARYLAND							
1	**Harris**	N	Y	N	N	N	Y
2	Ruppersberger	Y	N	Y	Y	Y	N
3	Sarbanes	Y	N	Y	Y	Y	N
4	Brown, A.	Y	N	Y	Y	Y	N
5	Hoyer	Y	N	Y	Y	Y	N
6	Trone	Y	N	Y	Y	Y	N
7	Cummings	Y	N	Y	Y	Y	N
8	Raskin	Y	N	Y	Y	Y	N
MASSACHUSETTS							
1	Neal	Y	N	Y	Y	Y	N
2	McGovern	Y	N	Y	Y	Y	N
3	Trahan	Y	N	Y	Y	Y	N
4	Kennedy	Y	N	Y	Y	Y	N
5	Clark	Y	N	Y	Y	Y	N
6	Moulton	Y	N	Y	Y	Y	N
7	Pressley	Y	N	Y	Y	Y	N
8	Lynch	Y	N	Y	Y	Y	N
9	Keating	Y	N	Y	Y	Y	N
MICHIGAN							
1	**Bergman**	N	Y	N	N	N	Y
2	**Huizenga**	Y	Y	N	Y	N	Y
3	**Amash**	N	N	N	N	Y	N
4	**Moolenaar**	N	Y	N	N	N	Y
5	Kildee	Y	N	Y	Y	Y	N
6	**Upton**	Y	Y	Y	Y	N	Y
7	**Walberg**	N	Y	N	N	N	Y
8	Slotkin	Y	Y	Y	Y	Y	N
9	Levin	Y	N	Y	Y	Y	N
10	**Mitchell**	N	Y	N	N	N	Y
11	Stevens	Y	N	Y	Y	Y	N
12	Dingell	Y	N	Y	Y	Y	N
13	Tlaib	Y	N	Y	Y	Y	N
14	Lawrence	Y	N	Y	Y	Y	N
MINNESOTA							
1	**Hagedorn**	N	Y	N	N	N	Y
2	Craig	Y	Y	Y	Y	Y	N
3	Phillips	Y	N	Y	Y	Y	N
4	McCollum	Y	N	Y	Y	Y	N
5	Omar	Y	N	Y	Y	Y	N

		97	98	99	100	101	102
6	**Emmer**	N	Y	N	N	N	Y
7	Peterson	Y	Y	N	Y	N	Y
8	**Stauber**	Y	Y	N	Y	N	Y
MISSISSIPPI							
1	**Kelly, T.**	N	Y	N	N	N	Y
2	Thompson, B.	Y	N	Y	Y	Y	N
3	**Guest**	N	Y	N	N	N	Y
4	**Palazzo**	N	Y	N	N	N	Y
MISSOURI							
1	Clay	Y	N	Y	Y	Y	N
2	**Wagner**	Y	Y	N	Y	N	Y
3	**Luetkemeyer**	N	Y	N	N	N	Y
4	**Hartzler**	Y	Y	N	N	N	Y
5	Cleaver	Y	N	Y	Y	Y	N
6	**Graves, S.**	N	Y	N	N	N	Y
7	**Long**	N	Y	N	N	N	Y
8	**Smith, J.**	N	Y	N	N	N	Y
MONTANA							
AL	**Gianforte**	Y	Y	N	N	N	Y
NEBRASKA							
1	**Fortenberry**	Y	Y	N	Y	N	Y
2	**Bacon**	Y	Y	N	Y	N	Y
3	**Smith, Adrian**	N	Y	N	N	N	Y
NEVADA							
1	Titus	Y	N	Y	Y	Y	N
2	**Amodei**	N	Y	N	N	N	Y
3	Lee	Y	Y	Y	Y	Y	N
4	Horsford	Y	N	Y	Y	Y	N
NEW HAMPSHIRE							
1	Pappas	Y	N	Y	Y	Y	N
2	Kuster	Y	N	Y	Y	Y	N
NEW JERSEY							
1	Norcross	Y	N	Y	Y	Y	N
2	Van Drew	Y	Y	Y	Y	Y	Y
3	Kim	Y	Y	Y	Y	Y	N
4	**Smith, C.**	Y	Y	Y	Y	Y	Y
5	Gottheimer	Y	Y	Y	Y	Y	N
6	Pallone	Y	N	Y	Y	Y	N
7	Malinowski	Y	N	Y	Y	Y	N
8	Sires	Y	N	Y	Y	Y	N
9	Pascrell	Y	N	Y	Y	Y	N
10	Payne	Y	N	Y	Y	Y	N
11	Sherrill	Y	Y	Y	Y	Y	N
12	Watson Coleman	Y	N	Y	Y	Y	N
NEW MEXICO							
1	Haaland	Y	N	Y	Y	Y	N
2	Torres Small	Y	Y	Y	Y	Y	N
3	Luján	Y	N	Y	Y	Y	N
NEW YORK							
1	**Zeldin**	Y	Y	N	N	N	Y
2	**King, P.**	Y	Y	Y	Y	N	Y
3	Suozzi	Y	N	Y	Y	Y	N
4	Rice, K.	Y	N	Y	Y	Y	N
5	Meeks	Y	N	Y	Y	Y	N
6	Meng	Y	N	Y	Y	Y	N
7	Velázquez	Y	N	Y	Y	Y	N
8	Jeffries	Y	N	Y	Y	Y	N
9	Clarke	Y	N	Y	Y	Y	N
10	Nadler	Y	N	Y	Y	Y	N
11	Rose	Y	Y	Y	Y	Y	N
12	Maloney, C.	Y	N	Y	Y	Y	N
13	Espaillat	Y	N	Y	Y	Y	N
14	Ocasio-Cortez	Y	N	Y	Y	Y	N
15	Serrano	Y	N	Y	Y	Y	N
16	Engel	Y	N	Y	Y	Y	N
17	Lowey	Y	N	Y	Y	Y	N
18	Maloney, S.P.	Y	N	Y	Y	Y	N
19	Delgado	Y	Y	Y	Y	Y	N
20	Tonko	Y	N	Y	Y	Y	N
21	**Stefanik**	Y	Y	N	Y	N	Y
22	Brindisi	Y	Y	Y	Y	Y	N
23	**Reed**	Y	Y	N	N	N	Y
24	**Katko**	?	?	-	?	?	?
25	Morelle	Y	N	Y	Y	Y	N
26	Higgins, B.	Y	N	Y	Y	Y	N
27	**Collins, C.**						
NORTH CAROLINA							
1	Butterfield	Y	N	Y	Y	Y	N
2	**Holding**	N	Y	N	N	N	Y
3	**Jones***						
4	Price	Y	N	Y	Y	Y	N
5	**Foxx**	N	Y	N	Y	N	Y
6	**Walker**	N	Y	N	N	N	Y
7	**Rouzer**	N	Y	N	N	N	Y

		97	98	99	100	101	102
8	**Hudson**	Y	Y	N	Y	N	Y
9	vacant						
10	**McHenry**	Y	Y	N	Y	N	Y
11	**Meadows**	Y	Y	N	N	N	Y
12	Adams	Y	N	Y	Y	Y	N
13	**Budd**	N	Y	N	Y	N	Y
NORTH DAKOTA							
AL	**Armstrong**	N	Y	N	N	N	Y
OHIO							
1	**Chabot**	Y	Y	N	N	N	Y
2	**Wenstrup**	N	Y	N	Y	N	Y
3	Beatty	Y	N	Y	Y	Y	N
4	**Jordan**	N	Y	N	N	N	Y
5	**Latta**	N	Y	N	N	N	Y
6	**Johnson, B.**	N	Y	N	N	N	Y
7	**Gibbs**	N	Y	N	N	N	Y
8	**Davidson**	Y	Y	N	N	N	Y
9	Kaptur	Y	N	Y	Y	Y	N
10	**Turner**	Y	Y	N	Y	N	Y
11	Fudge	Y	N	Y	Y	Y	N
12	**Balderson**	Y	Y	N	N	N	Y
13	Ryan	Y	N	Y	Y	Y	N
14	**Joyce**	Y	Y	N	Y	N	Y
15	**Stivers**	Y	Y	N	Y	N	Y
16	**Gonzalez**	Y	Y	N	Y	N	Y
OKLAHOMA							
1	**Hern**	N	Y	N	N	N	Y
2	**Mullin**	N	Y	N	N	N	Y
3	**Lucas**	Y	Y	N	N	N	Y
4	**Cole**	Y	Y	N	N	N	Y
5	Horn	Y	Y	Y	Y	Y	N
OREGON							
1	Bonamici	Y	N	Y	Y	Y	N
2	**Walden**	Y	Y	N	Y	N	Y
3	Blumenauer	Y	N	Y	Y	Y	N
4	DeFazio	Y	N	Y	Y	Y	N
5	Schrader	Y	Y	Y	Y	Y	N
PENNSYLVANIA							
1	**Fitzpatrick**	Y	Y	Y	Y	Y	Y
2	Boyle	Y	N	Y	Y	Y	N
3	Evans	Y	N	Y	Y	Y	N
4	Dean	Y	N	Y	Y	Y	N
5	Scanlon	Y	N	Y	Y	Y	N
6	Houlahan	Y	N	Y	Y	Y	N
7	Wild	Y	N	Y	Y	Y	N
8	Cartwright	Y	N	Y	Y	Y	N
9	**Meuser**	N	Y	N	N	N	Y
10	**Perry**	Y	Y	N	N	N	Y
11	**Smucker**	Y	Y	N	N	N	Y
12	**Marino***						
13	**Joyce**	N	Y	N	N	N	Y
14	**Reschenthaler**	N	Y	N	N	N	Y
15	**Thompson, G.**	Y	Y	N	N	N	Y
16	**Kelly, M.**	N	Y	N	N	N	Y
17	Lamb	Y	Y	Y	Y	Y	N
18	Doyle	Y	N	Y	Y	Y	N
RHODE ISLAND							
1	Cicilline	Y	N	Y	Y	Y	N
2	Langevin	Y	N	Y	Y	Y	N
SOUTH CAROLINA							
1	Cunningham	Y	Y	Y	Y	Y	N
2	**Wilson, J.**	N	Y	N	N	N	Y
3	**Duncan**	Y	Y	N	N	N	Y
4	**Timmons**	N	Y	N	N	N	Y
5	**Norman**	Y	Y	N	N	N	Y
6	Clyburn	Y	N	Y	Y	Y	N
7	**Rice, T.**	N	Y	N	Y	N	Y
SOUTH DAKOTA							
AL	**Johnson**	N	Y	N	N	N	Y
TENNESSEE							
1	**Roe**	Y	Y	N	N	N	Y
2	**Burchett**	Y	Y	N	N	N	Y
3	**Fleischmann**	N	Y	N	N	N	Y
4	**DesJarlais**	N	Y	N	N	N	Y
5	Cooper	Y	N	Y	Y	Y	N
6	**Rose**	N	Y	N	N	N	Y
7	**Green**	N	Y	N	N	N	Y
8	**Kustoff**	N	Y	N	N	N	Y
9	Cohen	Y	N	Y	Y	Y	N
TEXAS							
1	**Gohmert**	Y	Y	N	Y	N	Y
2	**Crenshaw**	Y	Y	N	N	N	Y
3	**Taylor**	N	Y	N	Y	N	Y
4	**Ratcliffe**	N	Y	N	N	N	Y

		97	98	99	100	101	102
5	**Gooden**	N	Y	N	N	N	Y
6	**Wright**	Y	Y	N	N	N	Y
7	Fletcher	Y	N	Y	Y	Y	N
8	**Brady**	N	Y	N	N	N	Y
9	Green, A.	Y	N	Y	Y	Y	N
10	**McCaul**	N	Y	N	N	N	Y
11	**Conaway**	Y	Y	N	N	N	Y
12	**Granger**	N	Y	N	N	N	Y
13	**Thornberry**	N	Y	N	N	N	Y
14	**Weber**	N	Y	N	N	N	Y
15	Gonzalez	Y	N	Y	Y	Y	N
16	Escobar	Y	N	Y	Y	Y	N
17	**Flores**	N	Y	N	Y	N	Y
18	Jackson Lee	Y	N	Y	Y	Y	N
19	**Arrington**	Y	Y	N	Y	N	Y
20	Castro	?	N	Y	Y	Y	N
21	**Roy**	N	Y	N	N	N	N
22	**Olson**	N	Y	N	N	N	Y
23	**Hurd**	Y	Y	Y	N	N	Y
24	**Marchant**	N	Y	N	?	N	Y
25	**Williams**	N	Y	N	N	N	Y
26	**Burgess**	Y	Y	N	N	N	Y
27	**Cloud**	Y	Y	N	N	N	Y
28	Cuellar	Y	N	Y	Y	Y	N
29	Garcia, S.	Y	N	Y	Y	Y	N
30	Johnson, E.B.	Y	N	Y	Y	Y	N
31	**Carter, J.**	N	Y	N	N	N	Y
32	Allred	Y	N	Y	Y	Y	N
33	Veasey	Y	N	Y	Y	Y	N
34	Vela	Y	N	Y	Y	Y	N
35	Doggett	Y	N	Y	Y	Y	N
36	**Babin**	N	Y	N	N	N	Y
UTAH							
1	**Bishop, R.**	N	Y	N	N	N	Y
2	**Stewart**	N	Y	N	N	N	Y
3	**Curtis**	N	Y	N	Y	N	Y
4	McAdams	Y	Y	Y	Y	Y	N
VERMONT							
AL	Welch	Y	N	Y	Y	Y	N
VIRGINIA							
1	**Wittman**	Y	Y	N	N	N	Y
2	Luria	Y	Y	Y	Y	Y	N
3	Scott, R.	Y	N	Y	Y	Y	N
4	McEachin	Y	N	Y	Y	Y	N
5	**Riggleman**	Y	Y	N	N	N	Y
6	**Cline**	N	Y	N	N	N	Y
7	Spanberger	Y	Y	Y	Y	Y	N
8	Beyer	Y	N	Y	Y	Y	N
9	**Griffith**	Y	Y	N	N	N	Y
10	Wexton	Y	N	Y	Y	Y	N
11	Connolly	Y	N	Y	Y	Y	N
WASHINGTON							
1	DelBene	Y	N	Y	Y	Y	N
2	Larsen	Y	N	Y	Y	Y	N
3	**Herrera Beutler**	Y	Y	N	Y	N	Y
4	**Newhouse**	Y	Y	N	Y	N	Y
5	**McMorris Rodgers**	N	Y	N	N	N	Y
6	Kilmer	Y	N	Y	Y	Y	N
7	Jayapal	Y	N	Y	Y	Y	N
8	Schrier	Y	N	Y	Y	Y	N
9	Smith Adam	Y	N	Y	Y	Y	N
10	Heck	Y	N	Y	Y	Y	N
WEST VIRGINIA							
1	**McKinley**	Y	Y	N	N	N	Y
2	**Mooney**	N	Y	N	N	N	Y
3	**Miller**	Y	Y	N	N	N	Y
WISCONSIN							
1	**Steil**	Y	Y	N	Y	N	Y
2	Pocan	Y	N	Y	Y	Y	N
3	Kind	Y	N	Y	Y	Y	N
4	Moore	Y	N	Y	Y	Y	N
5	**Sensenbrenner**	N	Y	N	N	N	Y
6	**Grothman**	N	Y	N	N	N	Y
7	**Duffy**						
8	**Gallagher**	N	Y	N	Y	N	Y
WYOMING							
AL	**Cheney**	N	Y	N	N	N	Y
DELEGATES							
	Radewagen (A.S.)	?			?	?	
	Norton (D.C.)	Y			Y	Y	
	San Nicolas (Guam)	?			?	?	
	Sablan (N. Marianas)	Y			Y	Y	
	González-Colón (P.R.)	Y			?	?	
	Plaskett (V.I.)	Y			?	?	

103. HR1112. Increased Time for Background Checks - Passage. Passage of the bill that would require a licensed gun dealer to wait up to 20 business days, as opposed to three under current law, to hear from the FBI regarding an individual's background check, in instances in which no immediate determination on the individual had been made through the NICS system, before being allowed to complete the sale or transfer of a firearm. It would allow a prospective gun purchaser to petition the Justice Department for the weapon after 10 days. The bill would also modify the language that prohibits the sale of firearms to individuals on the basis of mental illness to bar sales to individuals "adjudicated with mental illness, severe developmental disability, or severe emotional instability." Passed 228-198: R 3-191; D 225-7. *Note: A "nay" was a vote in support of the president's position.* Feb. 28, 2019.

104. HR1381. Veterans' Burn Pit Registry - Passage. Takano, D-Calif., motion to suspend the rules and pass the bill that would require the Veterans Affairs Department to allow family members of eligible veterans to report the cause of death for such veterans for inclusion in the Airborne Hazards and Open Burn Pit Registry. The registry allows veterans to document their exposure to open-air waste burning during their service and report health concerns. Motion agreed to 416-0: R 187-0; D 229-0. *Note: A two-thirds majority of those present and voting (278 in this case) is required for passage under suspension of the rules.* March 5, 2019.

105. S49. VA Facility Designation - Passage. Takano, D-Calif., motion to suspend the rules and pass the bill that would designate the U.S. Veterans Affairs Department facility located at 2357 North Washington Boulevard, North Ogden, Utah as the "Major Brent Taylor Vet Center Outstation." Motion agreed to 417-0: R 188-0; D 229-0. *Note: A two-thirds majority of those present and voting (278 in this case) is required for passage under suspension of the rules.* March 5, 2019.

106. HR1. Voter Access, Campaign Finance and Ethics Package - Previous Question. Scanlon, D-Pa., motion to order the previous question (thus ending debate and possibility of amendment) on the rule (H Res 172) that would provide for House floor consideration of the bill (HR 1) that would make a number of changes to existing law with respect to campaign finance, voter access, and the ethical conduct of politicians and elected officials. Motion agreed to 232-191: R 0-191; D 232-0. March 6, 2019.

107. HR1. Voter Access, Campaign Finance and Ethics Package - Rule. Adoption of the rule (H Res 172) that would provide for House floor consideration of the bill (HR 1) that would make a number of changes to existing law with respect to campaign finance, voter access, and the ethical conduct of politicians and elected officials. Motion agreed to 232-192: R 0-192; D 232-0. March 6, 2019.

108. HRES183. Antisemitism Resolution - Passage. Nadler, D-N.Y., motion to suspend the rules and agree to the resolution that would state that the House of Representatives condemns antisemitism, anti-Muslim discrimination, and bigotry against minorities as "hateful expressions of intolerance" contrary to the values of the United States. It would reject the perpetuation of anti-Semitic stereotypes in the U.S. and around the world, especially in the context of support for the U.S.-Israel alliance. It would also reject the justification of hatred or violence as an expression of disapproval over political events in the Middle East or elsewhere; acknowledge the harassment, discrimination, and violence suffered by Muslims and others as a result of anti-Muslim bigotry; and condemn death threats received by Jewish and Muslim members of Congress. Finally, it would encourage law enforcement and government officials to avoid "unconstitutional profiling" of individuals based on race, religion, or any other group identity and would encourage public officials to "confront the reality of antisemitism, Islamophobia, racism, and other forms of bigotry, as well as historical struggles against them." Motion agreed to 407-23: R 173-23; D 234-0. *Note: A two-thirds majority of those present and voting (287 in this case) is required for passage under suspension of the rules.* March 7, 2019.

		103	104	105	106	107	108
ALABAMA							
1	**Byrne**	N	?	?	?	?	Y
2	**Roby**	N	Y	Y	N	N	Y
3	**Rogers, M.**	N	?	?	N	N	N
4	**Aderholt**	N	Y	Y	N	N	Y
5	**Brooks, M.**	N	Y	Y	N	N	N
6	**Palmer**	N	Y	Y	N	N	Y
7	Sewell	Y	Y	Y	Y	Y	Y
ALASKA							
AL	**Young**	N	Y	Y	N	N	Y
ARIZONA							
1	O'Halleran	Y	Y	Y	Y	Y	Y
2	Kirkpatrick	Y	Y	Y	Y	Y	Y
3	Grijalva	Y	Y	Y	Y	Y	Y
4	**Gosar**	N	Y	N	N	N	N
5	**Biggs**	N	Y	Y	N	N	N
6	**Schweikert**	N	Y	Y	N	N	Y
7	Gallego	Y	Y	Y	Y	Y	Y
8	**Lesko**	N	Y	Y	N	N	Y
9	Stanton	Y	Y	Y	Y	Y	Y
ARKANSAS							
1	**Crawford**	N	Y	Y	N	N	N
2	**Hill, F.**	N	Y	Y	N	N	Y
3	**Womack**	N	Y	Y	N	N	Y
4	**Westerman**	N	Y	Y	N	N	Y
CALIFORNIA							
1	**LaMalfa**	N	Y	Y	N	N	N
2	Huffman	Y	Y	Y	Y	Y	Y
3	Garamendi	+	Y	Y	Y	Y	Y
4	**McClintock**	N	Y	Y	N	N	Y
5	Thompson, M.	Y	Y	Y	Y	Y	Y
6	Matsui	Y	Y	Y	Y	Y	Y
7	Bera	Y	Y	Y	Y	Y	Y
8	**Cook**	N	Y	Y	N	N	Y
9	McNerney	Y	Y	Y	Y	Y	Y
10	Harder	Y	Y	Y	Y	Y	Y
11	DeSaulnier	Y	Y	Y	Y	Y	Y
12	Pelosi	Y					Y
13	Lee B.	Y	Y	Y	Y	Y	Y
14	Speier	Y	Y	Y	Y	Y	Y
15	Swalwell	Y	+	+	Y	Y	Y
16	Costa	Y	Y	Y	Y	Y	Y
17	Khanna	Y	Y	Y	Y	Y	Y
18	Eshoo	Y	Y	Y	Y	Y	Y
19	Lofgren	Y	Y	Y	Y	Y	Y
20	Panetta	Y	Y	Y	Y	Y	Y
21	Cox	Y	Y	Y	Y	Y	Y
22	**Nunes**	N	Y	Y	N	N	Y
23	**McCarthy**	N	Y	Y	N	N	Y
24	Carbajal	Y	Y	Y	Y	Y	Y
25	Hill, K.	Y	Y	Y	Y	Y	Y
26	Brownley	Y	Y	Y	Y	Y	Y
27	Chu	Y	Y	Y	Y	Y	Y
28	Schiff	Y	Y	Y	Y	Y	Y
29	Cárdenas	Y	Y	Y	Y	Y	Y
30	Sherman	Y	Y	Y	Y	Y	Y
31	Aguilar	Y	Y	Y	Y	Y	Y
32	Napolitano	Y	Y	Y	Y	Y	Y
33	Lieu	Y	Y	Y	Y	Y	Y
34	Gomez	Y	Y	Y	Y	Y	Y
35	Torres	Y	Y	Y	Y	Y	Y
36	Ruiz	Y	Y	Y	Y	Y	Y
37	Bass	Y	Y	Y	Y	Y	Y
38	Sánchez	Y	Y	Y	Y	Y	Y
39	Cisneros	Y	Y	Y	Y	Y	Y
40	Roybal-Allard	Y	Y	Y	Y	Y	Y
41	Takano	Y	Y	Y	Y	Y	Y
42	**Calvert**	N	Y	Y	N	N	Y
43	Waters	Y	Y	Y	Y	Y	Y
44	Barragán	Y	Y	Y	Y	Y	Y
45	Porter	Y	Y	Y	Y	Y	Y
46	Correa	Y	Y	Y	Y	Y	Y
47	Lowenthal	Y	Y	Y	Y	Y	Y
48	Rouda	Y	Y	Y	Y	Y	Y
49	Levin	Y	Y	Y	Y	Y	Y
50	**Hunter**	N	Y	Y	N	N	Y
51	Vargas	Y	?	?	Y	Y	Y
52	Peters	Y	Y	Y	Y	Y	Y
	53 Davis, S.	Y	Y	Y	Y	Y	Y
COLORADO							
1	DeGette	Y	Y	Y	Y	Y	Y
2	Neguse	Y	Y	Y	Y	Y	Y
3	Tipton	N	Y	Y	N	N	Y
4	**Buck**	N	Y	N	N	N	N
5	**Lamborn**	N	Y	Y	N	N	Y
6	Crow	Y	Y	Y	Y	Y	Y
7	Perlmutter	Y	Y	Y	Y	Y	Y
CONNECTICUT							
1	Larson	Y	Y	Y	Y	Y	Y
2	Courtney	Y	Y	Y	Y	Y	Y
3	DeLauro	Y	Y	Y	Y	Y	Y
4	Himes	Y	Y	Y	Y	Y	Y
5	Hayes	Y	Y	Y	Y	Y	Y
DELAWARE							
AL	Blunt Rochester	Y	Y	Y	Y	Y	Y
FLORIDA							
1	**Gaetz**	N	Y	Y	N	N	Y
2	**Dunn**	N	Y	Y	N	N	Y
3	**Yoho**	N	Y	Y	N	N	N
4	**Rutherford**	N	Y	Y	-	-	Y
5	Lawson	Y	Y	Y	Y	Y	Y
6	**Waltz**	N	Y	Y	N	N	Y
7	Murphy	Y	Y	Y	Y	Y	Y
8	**Posey**	N	+	+	N	N	Y
9	Soto	+	Y	Y	Y	Y	Y
10	Demings	Y	Y	Y	Y	Y	Y
11	**Webster**	N	Y	Y	N	N	Y
12	**Bilirakis**	N	Y	N	N	N	Y
13	Crist	Y	Y	Y	Y	Y	Y
14	Castor	Y	Y	Y	Y	Y	Y
15	**Spano**	N	+	+	-	-	Y
16	**Buchanan**	N	Y	Y	N	N	Y
17	**Steube**	N	Y	N	N	N	N
18	**Mast**	N	Y	Y	N	N	Y
19	**Rooney**	N	Y	N	N	N	Y
20	Hastings	Y	Y	?	Y	Y	Y
21	Frankel	+	Y	Y	Y	Y	Y
22	Deutch	Y	Y	Y	Y	Y	Y
23	Wasserman Schultz	Y	Y	Y	Y	Y	Y
24	Wilson, F.	Y	?	?	Y	Y	Y
25	**Diaz-Balart**	N	Y	N	N	N	Y
26	Mucarsel-Powell	Y	Y	Y	Y	Y	Y
27	Shalala	Y	Y	Y	Y	Y	Y
GEORGIA							
1	**Carter, E.L.**	N	Y	N	N	N	Y
2	Bishop, S.	Y	Y	Y	Y	Y	Y
3	**Ferguson**	N	Y	N	N	N	Y
4	Johnson, H.	Y	Y	Y	Y	Y	Y
5	Lewis John	Y	Y	Y	Y	Y	Y
6	McBath	Y	Y	Y	Y	Y	Y
7	**Woodall**	N	Y	N	N	N	Y
8	**Scott, A.**	N	Y	N	N	N	Y
9	**Collins, D.**	N	Y	N	N	N	Y
10	**Hice**	N	Y	N	N	N	Y
11	**Loudermilk**	N	Y	N	N	N	Y
12	**Allen**	N	Y	N	N	N	Y
13	Scott, D.	Y	Y	Y	Y	Y	Y
14	**Graves, T.**	N	Y	N	N	N	N
HAWAII							
1	Case	Y	Y	Y	Y	Y	Y
2	Gabbard	Y	Y	Y	Y	Y	Y
IDAHO							
1	**Fulcher**	N	Y	Y	N	N	Y
2	**Simpson**	N	Y	Y	N	N	Y
ILLINOIS							
1	Rush	Y	Y	Y	Y	Y	Y
2	Kelly, R.	Y	Y	Y	Y	Y	Y
3	Lipinski	Y	Y	Y	Y	Y	Y
4	García, J.	Y	Y	Y	Y	Y	Y
5	Quigley	Y	Y	Y	Y	Y	Y
6	Casten	Y	Y	Y	Y	Y	Y
7	Davis, D.	Y	Y	Y	Y	Y	Y
8	Krishnamoorthi	Y	Y	Y	Y	Y	Y
9	Schakowsky	Y	Y	Y	Y	Y	Y
10	Schneider	Y	Y	Y	Y	Y	Y
11	Foster	Y	Y	Y	Y	Y	Y

KEY: **Republicans**   Democrats   *Independents*

Y Voted for (yea)	**N** Voted against (nay)	**P** Voted "present"	
+ Announced for	Announced against	**?** Did not vote or otherwise make position known	
# Paired for	**X** Paired against		

		103	104	105	106	107	108
12	**Bost**	N	Y	Y	N	N	Y
13	**Davis, R.**	N	Y	Y	N	N	Y
14	Underwood	Y	Y	Y	Y	Y	Y
15	**Shimkus**	N	Y	Y	N	N	Y
16	**Kinzinger**	N	Y	Y	N	N	Y
17	Bustos	Y	Y	Y	Y	Y	Y
18	**LaHood**	N	Y	Y	N	N	Y
INDIANA							
1	Visclosky	Y	Y	Y	Y	Y	Y
2	**Walorski**	N	Y	Y	N	N	Y
3	**Banks**	N	Y	Y	N	N	Y
4	**Baird**	N	Y	Y	N	N	Y
5	**Brooks, S.**	N	Y	Y	N	N	Y
6	**Pence**	N	Y	Y	N	N	Y
7	Carson	Y	Y	Y	Y	Y	Y
8	**Bucshon**	N	Y	Y	N	N	Y
9	**Hollingsworth**	N	Y	Y	N	N	Y
IOWA							
1	Finkenauer	Y	Y	Y	Y	Y	Y
2	Loebsack	Y	Y	Y	Y	Y	Y
3	Axne	Y	Y	Y	Y	Y	Y
4	**King, S.**	N	Y	Y	N	N	P
KANSAS							
1	**Marshall**	N	Y	Y	N	N	Y
2	**Watkins**	N	Y	Y	N	N	Y
3	Davids	Y	Y	Y	Y	Y	Y
4	**Estes**	N	Y	Y	N	N	Y
KENTUCKY							
1	**Comer**	N	Y	Y	N	N	Y
2	**Guthrie**	N	Y	Y	N	N	Y
3	Yarmuth	Y	Y	Y	Y	Y	Y
4	**Massie**	N	Y	Y	N	N	N
5	**Rogers, H.**	N	Y	Y	N	N	Y
6	**Barr**	N	Y	Y	N	N	Y
LOUISIANA							
1	**Scalise**	N	Y	Y	N	N	Y
2	Richmond	Y	Y	Y	Y	Y	Y
3	**Higgins, C.**	N	Y	Y	N	N	Y
4	**Johnson, M.**	N	Y	Y	N	N	Y
5	**Abraham**	?	Y	Y	N	N	Y
6	**Graves, G.**	N	Y	Y	N	N	Y
MAINE							
1	Pingree	Y	Y	Y	Y	Y	Y
2	Golden	N	Y	Y	Y	Y	Y
MARYLAND							
1	**Harris**	N	Y	Y	N	N	Y
2	Ruppersberger	Y	Y	Y	Y	Y	Y
3	Sarbanes	Y	Y	Y	Y	Y	Y
4	Brown, A.	Y	Y	Y	Y	Y	Y
5	Hoyer	Y	Y	Y	Y	Y	Y
6	Trone	Y	Y	Y	Y	?	Y
7	Cummings	Y	Y	Y	Y	Y	Y
8	Raskin	Y	Y	Y	Y	Y	Y
MASSACHUSETTS							
1	Neal	Y	Y	Y	Y	Y	Y
2	McGovern	Y	Y	Y	Y	Y	Y
3	Trahan	Y	Y	Y	Y	Y	Y
4	Kennedy	Y	Y	Y	Y	Y	Y
5	Clark	Y	?	?	?	?	Y
6	Moulton	Y	Y	Y	Y	Y	Y
7	Pressley	Y	Y	Y	Y	Y	Y
8	Lynch	Y	Y	Y	Y	Y	Y
9	Keating	Y	Y	Y	Y	Y	Y
MICHIGAN							
1	**Bergman**	N	Y	Y	N	N	Y
2	**Huizenga**	N	Y	Y	N	N	Y
3	**Amash**	N	Y	Y	N	N	Y
4	**Moolenaar**	N	Y	Y	N	N	Y
5	Kildee	Y	Y	Y	Y	Y	Y
6	**Upton**	N	Y	Y	N	N	Y
7	**Walberg**	N	Y	Y	N	N	Y
8	Slotkin	Y	Y	Y	Y	Y	Y
9	Levin	Y	Y	Y	Y	Y	Y
10	**Mitchell**	N	Y	Y	N	N	Y
11	Stevens	Y	Y	Y	Y	Y	Y
12	Dingell	Y	Y	Y	Y	Y	Y
13	Tlaib	Y	Y	Y	Y	Y	Y
14	Lawrence	Y	Y	Y	Y	Y	Y
MINNESOTA							
1	**Hagedorn**	N	Y	Y	N	N	Y
2	Craig	Y	Y	Y	Y	Y	Y
3	Phillips	Y	Y	Y	Y	Y	Y
4	McCollum	Y	Y	Y	Y	Y	Y
5	Omar	Y	Y	Y	Y	Y	Y

		103	104	105	106	107	108
6	**Emmer**	N	Y	Y	N	N	Y
7	Peterson	N	Y	Y	Y	Y	Y
8	**Stauber**	N	Y	Y	N	N	Y
MISSISSIPPI							
1	**Kelly, T.**	N	Y	Y	N	N	Y
2	Thompson, B.	Y	Y	Y	Y	Y	Y
3	**Guest**	N	Y	Y	N	N	Y
4	**Palazzo**	N	Y	Y	N	N	N
MISSOURI							
1	Clay	Y	Y	Y	Y	Y	?
2	**Wagner**	N	Y	Y	N	N	Y
3	**Luetkemeyer**	N	Y	Y	N	N	Y
4	**Hartzler**	N	Y	Y	N	N	Y
5	Cleaver	Y	Y	Y	Y	Y	Y
6	**Graves, S.**	N	Y	Y	N	N	Y
7	**Long**	N	Y	Y	N	N	Y
8	**Smith, J.**	N	Y	Y	N	N	Y
MONTANA							
AL	**Gianforte**	N	Y	Y	N	N	Y
NEBRASKA							
1	**Fortenberry**	N	Y	Y	N	N	Y
2	**Bacon**	N	Y	Y	N	N	Y
3	**Smith, Adrian**	N	Y	Y	N	N	Y
NEVADA							
1	Titus	Y	Y	Y	Y	Y	Y
2	**Amodei**	N	Y	Y	N	N	Y
3	Lee	Y	Y	Y	Y	Y	Y
4	Horsford	Y	Y	Y	?	Y	Y
NEW HAMPSHIRE							
1	Pappas	Y	Y	Y	Y	Y	Y
2	Kuster	Y	Y	Y	Y	Y	Y
NEW JERSEY							
1	Norcross	Y	Y	Y	Y	Y	Y
2	Van Drew	Y	Y	Y	Y	Y	Y
3	Kim	Y	Y	Y	Y	Y	Y
4	**Smith, C.**	Y	Y	Y	N	N	Y
5	Gottheimer	Y	Y	Y	Y	Y	Y
6	Pallone	Y	Y	Y	Y	Y	Y
7	Malinowski	Y	Y	Y	Y	Y	Y
8	Sires	Y	Y	Y	Y	Y	Y
9	Pascrell	Y	Y	Y	Y	Y	Y
10	Payne	Y	?	Y	Y	Y	Y
11	Sherrill	Y	Y	Y	Y	Y	Y
12	Watson Coleman	Y	Y	Y	Y	Y	Y
NEW MEXICO							
1	Haaland	Y	Y	Y	Y	Y	Y
2	Torres Small	N	Y	Y	Y	Y	Y
3	Luján	Y	Y	Y	Y	Y	Y
NEW YORK							
1	**Zeldin**	N	Y	Y	N	N	N
2	**King, P.**	Y	Y	Y	N	N	N
3	Suozzi	Y	Y	Y	Y	Y	Y
4	Rice, K.	Y	Y	Y	Y	Y	Y
5	Meeks	Y	Y	Y	Y	Y	Y
6	Meng	Y	Y	Y	Y	Y	Y
7	Velázquez	Y	Y	Y	Y	Y	Y
8	Jeffries	Y	Y	Y	Y	Y	Y
9	Clarke	Y	Y	Y	Y	Y	Y
10	Nadler	Y	Y	Y	Y	Y	Y
11	Rose	Y	Y	Y	Y	Y	Y
12	Maloney, C.	Y	Y	Y	Y	Y	Y
13	Espaillat	Y	Y	Y	Y	Y	Y
14	Ocasio-Cortez	Y	Y	Y	Y	Y	Y
15	Serrano	Y	Y	Y	Y	Y	Y
16	Engel	Y	Y	Y	Y	Y	Y
17	Lowey	Y	Y	Y	Y	Y	Y
18	Maloney, S.P.	Y	Y	Y	Y	Y	Y
19	Delgado	Y	Y	Y	Y	Y	Y
20	Tonko	Y	Y	Y	Y	Y	Y
21	**Stefanik**	N	Y	Y	N	N	Y
22	Brindisi	N	Y	Y	Y	Y	Y
23	**Reed**	N	Y	Y	N	N	Y
24	**Katko**	-	Y	Y	N	N	Y
25	Morelle	Y	Y	Y	Y	Y	Y
26	Higgins, B.	Y	Y	Y	Y	Y	Y
27	**Collins, C.**						
NORTH CAROLINA							
1	Butterfield	Y	Y	Y	Y	Y	Y
2	**Holding**	N	Y	Y	N	N	Y
3	**Jones***						
4	Price	Y	Y	Y	Y	Y	Y
5	**Foxx**	N	Y	Y	N	N	Y
6	**Walker**	N	Y	Y	N	N	N
7	**Rouzer**	N	Y	Y	N	N	Y

		103	104	105	106	107	108
8	**Hudson**	N	Y	Y	N	N	Y
9	vacant						
10	**McHenry**	N	+	+	N	N	Y
11	**Meadows**	N	Y	Y	N	N	Y
12	Adams	Y	Y	Y	Y	Y	Y
13	**Budd**	N	Y	Y	N	N	N
NORTH DAKOTA							
AL	**Armstrong**	N	Y	Y	N	N	Y
OHIO							
1	**Chabot**	N	Y	Y	N	N	Y
2	**Wenstrup**	N	Y	Y	N	N	Y
3	Beatty	Y	Y	Y	Y	Y	Y
4	**Jordan**	N	Y	Y	N	N	Y
5	**Latta**	N	Y	Y	N	N	Y
6	**Johnson, B.**	N	Y	Y	N	N	Y
7	**Gibbs**	N	Y	Y	N	N	Y
8	**Davidson**	N	Y	Y	N	N	Y
9	Kaptur	Y	Y	Y	Y	Y	Y
10	**Turner**	N	Y	Y	N	N	Y
11	Fudge	Y	Y	Y	Y	Y	Y
12	**Balderson**	N	Y	Y	N	N	Y
13	Ryan	Y	Y	Y	Y	Y	Y
14	**Joyce**	N	Y	Y	N	N	Y
15	**Stivers**	N	Y	Y	N	N	Y
16	**Gonzalez**	N	Y	Y	N	N	Y
OKLAHOMA							
1	**Hern**	N	Y	Y	N	N	Y
2	**Mullin**	N	Y	Y	N	N	Y
3	**Lucas**	N	Y	Y	N	N	Y
4	**Cole**	N	Y	Y	N	N	Y
5	Horn	N	Y	Y	Y	Y	Y
OREGON							
1	Bonamici	Y	Y	Y	Y	Y	Y
2	**Walden**	N	+	+	-	-	Y
3	Blumenauer	Y	Y	Y	Y	Y	Y
4	DeFazio	Y	Y	Y	Y	Y	Y
5	Schrader	Y	Y	Y	Y	Y	Y
PENNSYLVANIA							
1	**Fitzpatrick**	Y	Y	Y	N	N	Y
2	Boyle	Y	Y	Y	Y	Y	Y
3	Evans	Y	Y	Y	Y	Y	Y
4	Dean	Y	Y	Y	Y	Y	Y
5	Scanlon	Y	Y	Y	Y	Y	Y
6	Houlahan	Y	Y	Y	Y	Y	Y
7	Wild	Y	Y	Y	Y	Y	Y
8	Cartwright	Y	Y	Y	Y	Y	Y
9	**Meuser**	?	Y	Y	N	N	Y
10	**Perry**	N	Y	Y	N	N	Y
11	**Smucker**	N	Y	Y	N	N	Y
12	**Marino***						
13	**Joyce**	N	Y	Y	N	N	Y
14	**Reschenthaler**	N	Y	Y	N	N	Y
15	**Thompson, G.**	N	Y	Y	N	N	Y
16	**Kelly, M.**	N	Y	Y	N	N	Y
17	Lamb	Y	Y	Y	Y	Y	Y
18	Doyle	Y	Y	Y	Y	Y	Y
RHODE ISLAND							
1	Cicilline	Y	Y	Y	Y	Y	Y
2	Langevin	Y	Y	Y	Y	Y	Y
SOUTH CAROLINA							
1	Cunningham	Y	Y	Y	Y	Y	Y
2	**Wilson, J.**	N	?	Y	N	N	Y
3	**Duncan**	N	Y	Y	N	N	N
4	**Timmons**	N	Y	Y	N	N	Y
5	**Norman**	N	Y	Y	N	N	Y
6	Clyburn	Y	Y	Y	Y	Y	Y
7	**Rice, T.**	N	Y	Y	N	N	Y
SOUTH DAKOTA							
AL	**Johnson**	N	Y	Y	N	N	Y
TENNESSEE							
1	**Roe**	N	Y	Y	N	N	Y
2	**Burchett**	N	?	?	N	N	Y
3	**Fleischmann**	N	Y	Y	N	N	Y
4	**DesJarlais**	N	Y	Y	N	N	Y
5	Cooper	Y	Y	Y	Y	Y	Y
6	**Rose**	N	Y	Y	N	N	Y
7	**Green**	N	Y	Y	N	N	Y
8	**Kustoff**	N	Y	Y	N	N	Y
9	Cohen	Y	Y	Y	Y	Y	Y
TEXAS							
1	**Gohmert**	N	Y	Y	N	N	N
2	**Crenshaw**	N	Y	Y	N	N	Y
3	**Taylor**	N	Y	Y	N	N	Y
4	**Ratcliffe**	N	Y	Y	N	N	Y

		103	104	105	106	107	108
5	**Gooden**	N	Y	Y	N	N	Y
6	**Wright**	N	Y	Y	N	N	Y
7	Fletcher	Y	Y	Y	Y	Y	Y
8	**Brady**	N	Y	Y	N	N	Y
9	Green, A.	Y	Y	Y	Y	Y	Y
10	**McCaul**	N	Y	Y	N	N	Y
11	**Conaway**	N	Y	Y	N	N	N
12	**Granger**	N	Y	Y	N	N	Y
13	**Thornberry**	N	Y	Y	N	N	Y
14	**Weber**	N	Y	Y	N	N	Y
15	Gonzalez	Y	Y	Y	Y	Y	Y
16	Escobar	Y	Y	Y	Y	Y	Y
17	**Flores**	N	Y	Y	N	N	Y
18	Jackson Lee	Y	Y	Y	Y	Y	Y
19	**Arrington**	N	Y	Y	N	N	Y
20	Castro	Y	Y	Y	Y	Y	Y
21	**Roy**	N	Y	Y	N	N	N
22	**Olson**	N	Y	Y	N	N	Y
23	**Hurd**	N	Y	Y	N	N	Y
24	**Marchant**	N	Y	Y	N	N	Y
25	**Williams**	N	Y	Y	N	N	Y
26	**Burgess**	N	Y	Y	N	N	N
27	**Cloud**	N	Y	Y	N	N	Y
28	Cuellar	Y	Y	Y	Y	Y	Y
29	Garcia, S.	Y	Y	Y	Y	Y	Y
30	Johnson, E.B.	Y	Y	Y	Y	Y	Y
31	**Carter, J.**	N	?	?	?	?	Y
32	Allred	Y	Y	Y	Y	Y	Y
33	Veasey	Y	Y	Y	Y	Y	Y
34	Vela	Y	Y	Y	Y	Y	Y
35	Doggett	Y	Y	Y	Y	Y	Y
36	**Babin**	N	Y	Y	N	N	Y
UTAH							
1	**Bishop, R.**	N	+	+	N	N	Y
2	**Stewart**	N	Y	Y	N	N	Y
3	**Curtis**	N	Y	Y	N	N	Y
4	McAdams	N	Y	Y	Y	Y	Y
VERMONT							
AL	Welch	Y	Y	Y	Y	Y	Y
VIRGINIA							
1	**Wittman**	N	Y	Y	N	N	Y
2	Luria	Y	Y	Y	Y	Y	Y
3	Scott, R.	Y	Y	Y	Y	Y	Y
4	McEachin	Y	Y	Y	Y	Y	Y
5	**Riggleman**	N	Y	Y	N	N	Y
6	**Cline**	N	Y	Y	N	N	Y
7	Spanberger	Y	Y	Y	Y	Y	Y
8	Beyer	Y	Y	Y	Y	Y	Y
9	**Griffith**	N	Y	Y	?	N	Y
10	Wexton	Y	Y	Y	Y	Y	Y
11	Connolly	Y	Y	Y	Y	Y	Y
WASHINGTON							
1	DelBene	Y	Y	Y	Y	Y	Y
2	Larsen	Y	Y	Y	Y	Y	Y
3	**Herrera Beutler**	N	Y	Y	N	N	Y
4	**Newhouse**	N	Y	Y	N	N	Y
5	**McMorris Rodgers**	N	Y	Y	N	N	Y
6	Kilmer	Y	Y	Y	Y	Y	Y
7	Jayapal	Y	Y	Y	Y	Y	Y
8	Schrier	Y	Y	Y	Y	Y	Y
9	Smith Adam	Y	Y	Y	Y	Y	Y
10	Heck	Y	Y	Y	Y	Y	Y
WEST VIRGINIA							
1	**McKinley**	N	Y	Y	N	N	Y
2	**Mooney**	N	Y	Y	N	N	Y
3	**Miller**	N	Y	Y	N	N	Y
WISCONSIN							
1	**Steil**	N	Y	Y	N	N	Y
2	Pocan	Y	Y	Y	Y	Y	Y
3	Kind	N	Y	Y	Y	Y	Y
4	Moore	Y	Y	Y	Y	Y	Y
5	**Sensenbrenner**	N	Y	Y	N	N	Y
6	**Grothman**	N	Y	Y	N	N	Y
7	**Duffy**						
8	**Gallagher**	N	Y	Y	N	N	Y
WYOMING							
AL	**Cheney**	N	Y	Y	N	N	N
DELEGATES							
	Radewagen (A.S.)						
	Norton (D.C.)						
	San Nicolas (Guam)						
	Sablan (N. Marianas)						
	González-Colón (P.R.)						
	Plaskett (V.I.)						

‖ HOUSE VOTES

109. HR1. Voter Access, Campaign Finance and Ethics Package - Limiting Corporate Campaign Donations. Raskin, D-Md., amendment that would prevent corporate campaign expenditures unless the corporation in question has established a system by which the the political views of its shareholders could be assessed. Adopted in Committee of the Whole 219-215: R 0-198; D 218-17; I 1-0. March 7, 2019.

110. HR1. Voter Access, Campaign Finance and Ethics Package - Contractor Campaign Disclosure. Cole, R-Okla., amendment that would prohibit the government from requiring Federal contractors to disclose campaign contributions as a condition for submitting a bid on a Federal contract. Rejected in Committee of the Whole 199-235: R 198-0; D 1-234; I 0-1. March 7, 2019.

111. HR1. Voter Access, Campaign Finance and Ethics Package - Voting Age. Pressley, D-Mass., amendment that would lower the mandatory minimum voting age to 16 years of age for federal elections. Rejected in Committee of the Whole 126-305: R 2-197; D 124-108. March 7, 2019.

112. HR1. Voter Access, Campaign Finance and Ethics Package - First Amendment. Green, R-Tenn., amendment that would express the sense of Congress that free speech is a fundamental right, including with regards to protections of political speech and financial contributions to campaigns. Rejected in Committee of the Whole 200-233: R 197-0; D 3-232; I 0-1. March 7, 2019.

113. HR1. Voter Access, Campaign Finance and Ethics Package - Voter Turnout. Davidson, R-Ohio, amendment that would exempt states that have taken appropriate measures to increase voter turnout from additional federal voter registration mandates. Rejected in Committee of the Whole 194-238: R 194-0; D 0-233; I 0-1. March 7, 2019.

114. HR1. Voter Access, Campaign Finance and Ethics Package - Securities and Exchange Commission Disclosure. Davidson, R-Ohio, amendment that would effectively maintain existing law that prohibits the Securities and Exchange Commission from using agency funds to require certain financial disclosures, including political contributions; the amendment would strike language in the bill that would repeal this prohibition. Rejected in Committee of the Whole 195-237: R 195-1; D 0-235; I 0-1. March 7, 2019.

		109	110	111	112	113	114
ALABAMA							
1	**Byrne**	N	Y	N	Y	Y	Y
2	**Roby**	N	Y	N	Y	Y	Y
3	**Rogers, M.**	?	?	?	?	?	?
4	**Aderholt**	N	Y	N	Y	Y	Y
5	**Brooks, M.**	N	Y	N	Y	Y	Y
6	**Palmer**	N	Y	N	Y	Y	Y
7	Sewell	Y	N	Y	N	N	N
ALASKA							
AL	**Young**	N	Y	N	Y	Y	Y
ARIZONA							
1	O'Halleran	Y	N	N	N	?	N
2	Kirkpatrick	Y	N	Y	N	N	N
3	Grijalva	Y	N	Y	N	N	N
4	**Gosar**	N	Y	N	Y	Y	Y
5	**Biggs**	N	Y	N	Y	Y	Y
6	**Schweikert**	N	Y	N	Y	Y	Y
7	Gallego	Y	N	Y	N	N	N
8	**Lesko**	N	Y	N	Y	Y	Y
9	Stanton	Y	N	Y	N	N	N
ARKANSAS							
1	**Crawford**	N	Y	N	Y	Y	Y
2	**Hill, F.**	N	Y	N	Y	Y	Y
3	**Womack**	N	Y	N	Y	Y	Y
4	**Westerman**	N	Y	N	Y	Y	Y
CALIFORNIA							
1	**LaMalfa**	N	Y	N	Y	Y	Y
2	Huffman	Y	N	N	N	N	N
3	Garamendi	Y	N	N	N	N	N
4	**McClintock**	N	Y	N	Y	Y	Y
5	Thompson, M.	Y	N	N	N	N	N
6	Matsui	Y	N	N	N	N	N
7	Bera	Y	N	N	N	N	N
8	Cook	N	Y	N	Y	Y	Y
9	McNerney	Y	N	N	N	N	N
10	Harder	Y	N	N	N	N	N
11	DeSaulnier	Y	N	Y	N	N	N
12	Pelosi						
13	Lee B.	Y	N	Y	N	N	N
14	Speier	Y	N	Y	N	N	N
15	Swalwell	Y	N	Y	N	N	N
16	Costa	Y	N	N	N	N	N
17	Khanna	Y	N	Y	N	N	N
18	Eshoo	Y	N	Y	N	N	N
19	Lofgren	Y	N	N	N	N	N
20	Panetta	Y	N	N	N	N	N
21	Cox	Y	N	N	N	N	N
22	**Nunes**	N	Y	N	Y	Y	Y
23	**McCarthy**	N	Y	N	Y	Y	Y
24	Carbajal	Y	N	Y	N	N	N
25	Hill, K.	Y	N	Y	N	N	N
26	Brownley	Y	N	Y	N	N	N
27	Chu	Y	N	Y	N	N	N
28	Schiff	Y	N	Y	N	N	N
29	Cárdenas	Y	N	N	N	N	N
30	Sherman	Y	N	N	N	N	N
31	Aguilar	Y	N	N	N	N	N
32	Napolitano	Y	N	N	N	N	N
33	Lieu	Y	N	Y	N	N	N
34	Gomez	Y	N	?	N	N	N
35	Torres	Y	N	N	N	N	N
36	Ruiz	Y	N	Y	N	N	N
37	Bass	Y	N	Y	N	N	N
38	Sánchez	Y	N	N	N	N	N
39	Cisneros	Y	N	N	N	N	N
40	Roybal-Allard	Y	N	N	N	N	N
41	Takano	Y	N	N	N	N	N
42	**Calvert**	N	Y	N	Y	Y	Y
43	Waters	Y	N	Y	N	N	N
44	Barragán	Y	N	Y	N	N	N
45	Porter	Y	N	P	N	N	N
46	Correa	Y	N	Y	N	N	N
47	Lowenthal	Y	N	Y	N	N	N
48	Rouda	Y	N	Y	N	N	N
49	Levin	Y	N	Y	N	N	N
50	**Hunter**	N	Y	N	Y	Y	Y
51	Vargas	Y	N	Y	N	N	N
52	Peters	Y	N	Y	N	N	N

		109	110	111	112	113	114
53	Davis, S.	Y	N	N	N	N	N
COLORADO							
1	DeGette	Y	N	N	N	N	N
2	Neguse	Y	N	Y	N	N	N
3	**Tipton**	N	Y	N	Y	Y	Y
4	**Buck**	N	Y	N	Y	Y	Y
5	**Lamborn**	N	Y	N	Y	Y	Y
6	Crow	Y	N	N	N	N	N
7	Perlmutter	Y	N	N	N	N	N
CONNECTICUT							
1	Larson	Y	N	N	N	N	N
2	Courtney	Y	N	N	N	N	N
3	DeLauro	Y	N	N	N	N	N
4	Himes	Y	N	P	N	N	N
5	Hayes	Y	N	Y	N	N	N
DELAWARE							
AL	Blunt Rochester	Y	N	Y	N	N	N
FLORIDA							
1	**Gaetz**	N	Y	N	Y	Y	Y
2	**Dunn**	N	Y	N	Y	Y	Y
3	**Yoho**	N	Y	N	Y	Y	Y
4	**Rutherford**	N	Y	N	Y	Y	Y
5	Lawson	Y	N	N	N	N	N
6	**Waltz**	N	Y	N	Y	Y	Y
7	Murphy	N	N	Y	N	N	N
8	**Posey**	N	Y	N	Y	Y	Y
9	Soto	Y	N	N	N	N	N
10	Demings	Y	N	N	N	N	N
11	**Webster**	N	Y	N	Y	Y	Y
12	**Bilirakis**	N	Y	N	Y	Y	Y
13	Crist	Y	N	Y	N	N	N
14	Castor	Y	N	Y	N	N	N
15	**Spano**	N	Y	N	Y	Y	Y
16	**Buchanan**	N	Y	N	Y	Y	Y
17	**Steube**	N	Y	N	Y	Y	Y
18	**Mast**	N	Y	N	Y	N	Y
19	**Rooney**	N	Y	N	Y	Y	Y
20	Hastings	Y	N	Y	N	N	N
21	Frankel	Y	N	Y	N	N	N
22	Deutch	Y	N	Y	N	N	N
23	Wasserman Schultz	Y	N	Y	N	N	N
24	Wilson, F.	Y	N	N	N	N	N
25	**Diaz-Balart**	N	Y	N	Y	Y	Y
26	Mucarsel-Powell	Y	N	Y	N	N	N
27	Shalala	Y	N	Y	N	N	N
GEORGIA							
1	**Carter, E.L.**	N	Y	N	Y	Y	Y
2	Bishop, S.	N	N	Y	N	N	N
3	**Ferguson**	N	Y	N	Y	Y	Y
4	Johnson, H.	N	Y	Y	N	N	N
5	Lewis John	Y	N	Y	N	N	N
6	McBath	N	N	N	N	N	N
7	**Woodall**	N	Y	N	Y	Y	Y
8	**Scott, A.**	N	Y	N	Y	Y	Y
9	**Collins, D.**	N	Y	N	Y	Y	Y
10	**Hice**	N	Y	N	Y	Y	Y
11	**Loudermilk**	N	Y	N	Y	Y	Y
12	**Allen**	N	Y	N	Y	Y	Y
13	Scott, D.	Y	N	N	N	N	N
14	**Graves, T.**	N	Y	N	Y	Y	Y
HAWAII							
1	Case	Y	N	N	N	N	N
2	Gabbard	Y	N	Y	N	N	N
IDAHO							
1	**Fulcher**	N	Y	N	Y	Y	Y
2	**Simpson**	N	Y	N	Y	Y	Y
ILLINOIS							
1	Rush	Y	N	Y	N	N	N
2	Kelly, R.	Y	N	N	N	N	N
3	Lipinski	Y	N	N	N	N	N
4	García, J.	Y	N	N	N	N	N
5	Quigley	Y	N	N	N	N	N
6	Casten	N	Y	N	Y	N	N
7	Davis, D.	Y	N	N	N	N	N
8	Krishnamoorthi	Y	N	N	N	N	N
9	Schakowsky	Y	N	Y	N	N	N
10	Schneider	N	N	N	N	N	N
11	Foster	Y	N	N	N	N	N

KEY: Republicans   Democrats   *Independents*

Y Voted for (yea)	**N** Voted against (nay)	**P** Voted "present"	
+ Announced for	**−** Announced against	**?** Did not vote or otherwise	
# Paired for	**X** Paired against	make position known	

		109	110	111	112	113	114
12	**Bost**	N	Y	N	Y	Y	Y
13	**Davis, R.**	N	Y	N	Y	Y	Y
14	Underwood	Y	N	Y	N	N	N
15	**Shimkus**	N	Y	N	Y	Y	Y
16	**Kinzinger**	N	Y	N	Y	Y	Y
17	Bustos	Y	N	N	N	N	N
18	**LaHood**	N	Y	N	Y	Y	Y
INDIANA							
1	Visclosky	Y	N	N	N	N	N
2	**Walorski**	N	Y	N	Y	Y	Y
3	**Banks**	N	Y	N	Y	Y	Y
4	**Baird**	N	Y	N	Y	Y	Y
5	**Brooks, S.**	N	Y	N	Y	Y	Y
6	**Pence**	N	Y	N	Y	Y	Y
7	Carson	Y	N	Y	N	N	N
8	**Bucshon**	N	Y	N	Y	Y	Y
9	**Hollingsworth**	N	Y	N	Y	Y	Y
IOWA							
1	Finkenauer	Y	N	Y	N	N	N
2	Loebsack	Y	N	N	N	N	N
3	Axne	Y	N	N	N	N	N
4	**King, S.**	N	Y	N	Y	Y	Y
KANSAS							
1	**Marshall**	N	Y	N	Y	Y	Y
2	**Watkins**	N	Y	N	?	Y	Y
3	Davids	N	N	N	N	N	N
4	**Estes**	N	Y	N	Y	Y	Y
KENTUCKY							
1	**Comer**	N	Y	N	Y	Y	Y
2	**Guthrie**	N	Y	N	Y	Y	Y
3	Yarmuth	Y	N	Y	N	N	N
4	**Massie**	N	Y	N	Y	Y	Y
5	**Rogers, H.**	N	Y	N	Y	Y	Y
6	**Barr**	N	Y	N	Y	Y	Y
LOUISIANA							
1	**Scalise**	N	Y	N	Y	Y	Y
2	Richmond	Y	N	Y	N	N	N
3	**Higgins, C.**	N	Y	N	Y	Y	Y
4	**Johnson, M.**	N	Y	N	Y	Y	Y
5	**Abraham**	N	Y	N	Y	Y	Y
6	**Graves, G.**	N	Y	N	Y	Y	Y
MAINE							
1	Pingree	Y	N	Y	N	N	N
2	Golden	Y	N	N	N	N	N
MARYLAND							
1	**Harris**	N	Y	N	Y	Y	Y
2	Ruppersberger	Y	N	Y	N	N	N
3	Sarbanes	Y	N	N	N	N	N
4	Brown, A.	Y	N	Y	N	N	N
5	Hoyer	Y	N	N	N	N	N
6	Trone	N	N	N	N	N	N
7	Cummings	Y	N	Y	N	N	N
8	Raskin	Y	N	Y	N	N	N
MASSACHUSETTS							
1	Neal	Y	N	Y	N	N	N
2	McGovern	Y	N	Y	N	N	N
3	Trahan	Y	N	Y	N	N	N
4	Kennedy	Y	N	Y	N	N	N
5	Clark	Y	N	Y	N	N	N
6	Moulton	Y	N	Y	N	N	N
7	Pressley	Y	N	Y	N	N	N
8	Lynch	Y	N	N	N	N	N
9	Keating	Y	N	N	N	N	N
MICHIGAN							
1	**Bergman**	N	Y	N	Y	Y	Y
2	**Huizenga**	N	Y	N	Y	Y	Y
3	**Amash**	N	Y	N	Y	Y	Y
4	**Moolenaar**	N	Y	N	Y	Y	Y
5	Kildee	Y	N	Y	N	N	N
6	**Upton**	N	Y	N	Y	Y	Y
7	**Walberg**	N	Y	N	Y	Y	Y
8	Slotkin	N	N	N	N	N	N
9	Levin	Y	N	Y	N	N	N
10	**Mitchell**	N	Y	N	Y	Y	Y
11	Stevens	Y	N	N	N	N	N
12	Dingell	Y	N	N	N	N	N
13	Tlaib	Y	N	Y	N	N	N
14	Lawrence	Y	N	N	N	N	N
MINNESOTA							
1	**Hagedorn**	N	Y	N	Y	Y	Y
2	Craig	Y	N	N	N	N	N
3	Phillips	Y	N	N	N	N	N
4	McCollum	Y	N	N	N	N	N
5	Omar	Y	N	Y	N	?	N

		109	110	111	112	113	114
6	**Emmer**	N	Y	N	Y	Y	Y
7	Peterson	N	N	N	Y	N	N
8	**Stauber**	N	Y	N	Y	Y	Y
MISSISSIPPI							
1	**Kelly, T.**	N	Y	N	Y	Y	Y
2	Thompson, B.	Y	N	Y	N	N	N
3	**Guest**	N	Y	N	Y	Y	Y
4	**Palazzo**	N	Y	N	Y	Y	Y
MISSOURI							
1	Clay	?	?	?	?	?	?
2	**Wagner**	N	Y	N	Y	Y	Y
3	**Luetkemeyer**	N	Y	N	Y	Y	Y
4	**Hartzler**	N	Y	N	Y	Y	Y
5	Cleaver	Y	N	N	N	N	N
6	**Graves, S.**	N	Y	N	Y	Y	Y
7	**Long**	N	Y	N	Y	Y	Y
8	**Smith, J.**	N	Y	N	Y	Y	Y
MONTANA							
AL	**Gianforte**	N	Y	N	Y	Y	Y
NEBRASKA							
1	**Fortenberry**	N	Y	N	Y	Y	Y
2	**Bacon**	N	Y	N	Y	Y	Y
3	**Smith, Adrian**	N	Y	N	Y	Y	Y
NEVADA							
1	Titus	Y	N	N	N	N	N
2	**Amodei**	N	Y	N	Y	Y	Y
3	Lee	N	N	Y	N	N	N
4	Horsford	Y	N	Y	N	N	N
NEW HAMPSHIRE							
1	Pappas	Y	N	N	N	N	N
2	Kuster	Y	N	N	N	N	N
NEW JERSEY							
1	Norcross	Y	N	N	N	N	N
2	Van Drew	Y	N	N	N	N	N
3	Kim	Y	N	N	N	N	N
4	**Smith, C.**	N	Y	N	Y	Y	Y
5	Gottheimer	N	N	N	N	N	N
6	Pallone	Y	N	Y	N	N	N
7	Malinowski	Y	N	Y	N	N	N
8	Sires	Y	N	N	N	N	N
9	Pascrell	Y	N	N	N	N	N
10	Payne	Y	N	Y	N	N	N
11	Sherrill	Y	N	N	N	N	N
12	Watson Coleman	Y	N	N	N	N	N
NEW MEXICO							
1	Haaland	Y	N	Y	N	N	N
2	Torres Small	N	N	N	N	N	N
3	Luján	Y	N	Y	N	N	N
NEW YORK							
1	**Zeldin**	N	Y	N	Y	Y	Y
2	**King, P.**	N	Y	N	Y	Y	Y
3	Suozzi	N	N	N	N	N	N
4	Rice, K.	Y	N	N	N	N	N
5	Meeks	Y	N	N	N	N	N
6	Meng	Y	N	Y	N	N	N
7	Velázquez	Y	N	Y	N	N	N
8	Jeffries	Y	N	N	N	N	N
9	Clarke	Y	N	Y	N	N	N
10	Nadler	Y	N	N	N	N	N
11	Rose	Y	N	Y	N	N	N
12	Maloney, C.	Y	N	N	N	N	N
13	Espaillat	Y	N	Y	N	N	N
14	Ocasio-Cortez	Y	N	Y	N	N	N
15	Serrano	Y	N	Y	N	N	N
16	Engel	Y	N	N	N	N	N
17	Lowey	Y	N	Y	N	N	N
18	Maloney, S.P.	Y	N	Y	N	N	N
19	Delgado	Y	N	Y	N	N	N
20	Tonko	Y	N	Y	N	N	N
21	**Stefanik**	N	Y	N	Y	Y	Y
22	Brindisi	N	N	N	N	N	N
23	**Reed**	N	Y	N	Y	Y	Y
24	**Katko**	N	Y	N	Y	N	Y
25	Morelle	Y	N	N	N	N	N
26	Higgins, B.	Y	N	Y	N	N	N
27	**Collins, C.**						
NORTH CAROLINA							
1	Butterfield	Y	N	N	N	N	N
2	**Holding**	N	Y	N	Y	Y	Y
3	**Jones***						
4	Price	Y	N	Y	N	N	N
5	**Foxx**	N	Y	N	Y	Y	Y
6	**Walker**	N	Y	N	Y	Y	Y
7	**Rouzer**	N	Y	N	Y	Y	Y

		109	110	111	112	113	114
8	**Hudson**	N	Y	N	Y	Y	Y
9	vacant						
10	**McHenry**	N	Y	N	Y	Y	Y
11	**Meadows**	N	Y	N	Y	Y	Y
12	Adams	Y	N	Y	N	N	N
13	**Budd**	N	Y	N	Y	Y	Y
NORTH DAKOTA							
AL	**Armstrong**	N	Y	N	Y	Y	Y
OHIO							
1	**Chabot**	N	Y	N	Y	Y	Y
2	**Wenstrup**	N	Y	N	Y	Y	Y
3	Beatty	Y	N	Y	N	N	N
4	**Jordan**	N	Y	N	Y	Y	Y
5	**Latta**	N	Y	N	Y	Y	Y
6	**Johnson, B.**	N	Y	N	Y	Y	Y
7	**Gibbs**	N	Y	N	Y	Y	Y
8	**Davidson**	N	Y	N	Y	Y	Y
9	Kaptur	Y	N	N	N	N	N
10	**Turner**	N	Y	N	Y	Y	Y
11	Fudge	Y	N	Y	N	N	N
12	**Balderson**	N	Y	N	Y	Y	Y
13	Ryan	Y	N	Y	N	N	N
14	**Joyce**	N	Y	N	Y	Y	Y
15	**Stivers**	N	Y	N	Y	Y	Y
16	**Gonzalez**	N	Y	N	Y	Y	Y
OKLAHOMA							
1	**Hern**	N	Y	N	Y	Y	Y
2	**Mullin**	N	Y	N	Y	Y	Y
3	**Lucas**	N	Y	N	Y	Y	Y
4	**Cole**	N	Y	N	Y	Y	?
5	Horn	Y	N	Y	N	N	N
OREGON							
1	Bonamici	Y	N	Y	N	N	N
2	**Walden**	N	Y	N	Y	Y	Y
3	Blumenauer	Y	N	Y	N	N	N
4	DeFazio	Y	N	Y	N	N	N
5	Schrader	N	N	N	N	N	N
PENNSYLVANIA							
1	**Fitzpatrick**	N	Y	N	Y	N	N
2	Boyle	Y	N	Y	N	N	N
3	Evans	Y	N	Y	N	N	N
4	Dean	Y	N	N	N	N	N
5	Scanlon	Y	N	N	N	N	N
6	Houlahan	Y	N	N	N	N	N
7	Wild	Y	N	N	N	N	N
8	Cartwright	Y	N	N	N	N	N
9	**Meuser**	N	Y	N	Y	Y	Y
10	**Perry**	N	Y	N	Y	Y	Y
11	**Smucker**	N	Y	N	Y	Y	Y
12	**Marino***						
13	**Joyce**	N	Y	N	Y	Y	Y
14	**Reschenthaler**	N	Y	N	Y	Y	Y
15	**Thompson, G.**	N	Y	N	Y	Y	Y
16	**Kelly, M.**	N	Y	N	Y	Y	Y
17	Lamb	Y	N	N	N	N	N
18	Doyle	Y	N	N	N	N	N
RHODE ISLAND							
1	Cicilline	Y	N	Y	N	N	N
2	Langevin	Y	N	Y	N	N	N
SOUTH CAROLINA							
1	Cunningham	Y	N	N	N	N	N
2	**Wilson, J.**	N	Y	N	Y	Y	Y
3	**Duncan**	N	Y	N	Y	Y	Y
4	**Timmons**	N	Y	N	Y	Y	Y
5	**Norman**	N	Y	N	Y	Y	Y
6	Clyburn	Y	N	Y	N	N	N
7	**Rice, T.**	N	Y	N	Y	Y	Y
SOUTH DAKOTA							
AL	**Johnson**	N	Y	N	Y	Y	Y
TENNESSEE							
1	**Roe**	N	Y	N	Y	Y	Y
2	**Burchett**	N	Y	N	Y	Y	Y
3	**Fleischmann**	N	Y	N	Y	Y	Y
4	**DesJarlais**	N	Y	N	Y	Y	Y
5	Cooper	Y	N	N	N	N	N
6	**Rose**	N	Y	N	Y	Y	Y
7	**Green**	N	Y	N	Y	Y	Y
8	**Kustoff**	N	Y	N	Y	Y	Y
9	Cohen	Y	N	N	N	N	N
TEXAS							
1	**Gohmert**	N	Y	N	Y	N	Y
2	**Crenshaw**	N	Y	N	Y	Y	Y
3	**Taylor**	N	Y	N	Y	Y	Y
4	**Ratcliffe**	N	Y	N	Y	Y	Y

		109	110	111	112	113	114
5	**Gooden**	N	Y	N	Y	Y	Y
6	**Wright**	N	Y	N	Y	Y	Y
7	Fletcher	Y	N	N	N	N	N
8	**Brady**	N	Y	N	Y	Y	Y
9	Green, A.	Y	N	Y	N	N	N
10	**McCaul**	N	Y	N	Y	Y	Y
11	**Conaway**	N	Y	N	Y	Y	Y
12	**Granger**	N	Y	N	Y	Y	Y
13	**Thornberry**	N	Y	N	Y	Y	Y
14	**Weber**	N	Y	N	Y	Y	Y
15	Gonzalez	Y	N	Y	N	N	N
16	Escobar	Y	N	Y	N	N	N
17	**Flores**	N	Y	N	Y	Y	Y
18	Jackson Lee	Y	N	Y	N	N	N
19	**Arrington**	N	Y	N	Y	Y	Y
20	Castro	Y	N	Y	N	N	N
21	**Roy**	N	Y	N	Y	Y	Y
22	**Olson**	N	Y	N	Y	Y	Y
23	**Hurd**	N	Y	N	Y	Y	Y
24	**Marchant**	N	Y	N	Y	Y	Y
25	**Williams**	N	Y	N	Y	Y	Y
26	**Burgess**	N	Y	Y	Y	Y	Y
27	**Cloud**	N	Y	N	Y	Y	Y
28	Cuellar	N	N	N	N	N	N
29	Garcia, S.	Y	N	N	N	N	N
30	Johnson, E.B.	Y	N	Y	N	N	N
31	**Carter, J.**	N	Y	N	Y	Y	Y
32	Allred	Y	N	N	N	N	N
33	Veasey	Y	N	N	N	N	N
34	Vela	Y	N	N	N	N	N
35	Doggett	Y	N	Y	N	N	N
36	**Babin**	N	Y	N	Y	Y	Y
UTAH							
1	**Bishop, R.**	N	Y	N	Y	Y	Y
2	**Stewart**	N	Y	N	Y	Y	Y
3	**Curtis**	N	Y	N	Y	Y	Y
4	McAdams	N	N	N	N	N	N
VERMONT							
AL	Welch	Y	N	Y	N	N	N
VIRGINIA							
1	**Wittman**	N	Y	N	Y	Y	Y
2	Luria	Y	N	N	N	N	N
3	Scott, R.	Y	N	N	N	N	N
4	McEachin	Y	N	N	N	N	N
5	**Riggleman**	N	Y	N	Y	Y	Y
6	**Cline**	N	Y	N	Y	Y	Y
7	Spanberger	Y	N	N	N	N	N
8	Beyer	Y	N	Y	N	N	N
9	**Griffith**	N	Y	N	Y	Y	Y
10	Wexton	Y	N	N	N	N	N
11	Connolly	Y	Y	N	N	N	N
WASHINGTON							
1	DelBene	Y	N	Y	N	N	N
2	Larsen	Y	N	N	N	N	N
3	**Herrera Beutler**	N	Y	N	Y	Y	Y
4	**Newhouse**	N	Y	N	Y	Y	Y
5	**McMorris Rodgers**	N	Y	N	Y	Y	?
6	Kilmer	Y	N	Y	N	N	N
7	Jayapal	Y	N	Y	N	N	N
8	Schrier	Y	N	N	N	N	N
9	Smith Adam	Y	N	Y	N	N	N
10	Heck	Y	N	N	N	N	N
WEST VIRGINIA							
1	**McKinley**	N	Y	N	Y	Y	Y
2	**Mooney**	N	Y	N	Y	Y	Y
3	**Miller**	N	Y	N	Y	Y	Y
WISCONSIN							
1	**Steil**	N	Y	N	Y	Y	Y
2	Pocan	Y	N	Y	N	N	N
3	Kind	Y	N	N	N	N	N
4	Moore	Y	N	N	N	N	N
5	**Sensenbrenner**	N	Y	N	Y	Y	Y
6	**Grothman**	N	Y	N	Y	Y	Y
7	**Duffy**						
8	**Gallagher**	N	Y	N	Y	Y	Y
WYOMING							
AL	**Cheney**	N	Y	N	Y	Y	Y
DELEGATES							
	Radewagen (A.S.)	N	Y	N	Y	Y	Y
	Norton (D.C.)	Y	N	Y	N	N	N
	San Nicolas (Guam)	?	?	?	?	?	?
	Sablan (N. Marianas)	Y	N	Y	N	N	N
	González-Colón (P.R.)	N	Y	N	Y	Y	Y
	Plaskett (V.I.)	Y	N	Y	N	N	N

115. HR1. Voter Access, Campaign Finance and Ethics Package - Polling Place Hours. Brindisi, D-N.Y., amendment that would require all polling places in a state to be open for a total amount of time not varying by more than two hours between locations. Adopted in Committee of the Whole 237-188: R 3-188; D 234-0. March 8, 2019.

116. HR1. Voter Access, Campaign Finance and Ethics Package - Preregistering Voters. Neguse, D-Colo., amendment that would require states to accept and process voter registration documents for individuals who are at least 16 years of age. (The provision would have no effect on voting age requirements) Adopted in Committee of the Whole 239-186: R 8-186; D 231-0. March 8, 2019.

117. HR1. Voter Access, Campaign Finance and Ethics Package - Recommit. Crenshaw, R-Texas., motion to recommit the bill to the House Judiciary Committee with instructions to report it back immediately with an amendment that would express the sense of Congress that voting is "fundamental to a functioning democracy," that the United States should protect elections from foreign interference and illegal voting, and that permitting undocumented immigrants to vote "devalues" and "diminishes" the voting power of U.S. citizens. Motion rejected 197-228: R 191-1; D 6-227. March 8, 2019.

118. HR1. Voter Access, Campaign Finance and Ethics Package - Passage. Passage of the bill, as amended, that includes a package of provisions related to campaign finance, voter registration and access, and ethical standards for government officials. Among a number of provisions related to campaign finance reform, the bill would prohibit super PACs from financing political ads supporting or opposing a political candidate. It would require corporations, organizations, and political committees to disclose campaign-related expenditures of more than $1,000 and any donors contributing more than $10,000 in an election cycle. It would expand political advertising disclaimer requirements to online political ads and establish reporting requirements for online platforms selling political ads. It would prohibit foreign entities from contributing to a political campaign, super PAC, or presidential inaugural committee. The bill would also establish or modify public funding mechanisms for federal election campaigns that would match small contributions of up to $200 for congressional and presidential candidates whose campaigns do not accept contributions of more than $1,000 from any individual donor and do not use more than $50,000 of the candidate?s personal funds. The bill would establish a number of national standards related to voter registration and access. Among other provisions, it would require states to allow online registration, automatically register eligible voters, allow early voting at least 15 days before election day, and allow same-day registration and voting. It would prohibit certain practices related to voter deception or intimidation and removal of voters from voter rolls. It would require states to use independent redistricting commissions when redrawing congressional districts. It would also make election day a federal holiday, require all votes to be made via paper ballots, allow convicted felons the right to vote after serving their prison sentences, and require the Homeland Security Department to assess cyber threats to the election system. Finally, the bill would set or modify a number of federal ethics rules governing all three branches of government. It would formally prohibit members of Congress and congressional staff from using their positions to further their financial interests, and would prohibit members from serving on the board of a for-profit entity or using federal funds to settle employment discrimination cases brought against them. The bill would require the president and vice president to divest any financial interests that may create a conflict of interest, and to annually submit tax returns for the current and 9 previous years. Passed 234-193: R 0-193; D 234-0. *Note: A "nay" was a vote in support of the president's position.* March 8, 2019.

119. HR1122. Housing Voucher Program - Passage. Waters, D-Calif., motion to suspend the rules and pass the bill that would permit the secretary of Housing and Urban Development to establish a housing mobility demonstration program that would provide "mobility assistance," encouraging low-income families to move to areas with lower rates of poverty in order to provide those families with greater opportunities. Motion agreed to 387-22: R 168-22; D 219-0. *Note: A two-thirds majority of those present and voting (273 in this case) is required for passage under suspension of the rules.* March 11, 2019.

120. HR758. Financial Institution Protection - Passage. Waters, D-Calif., motion to suspend the rules and pass the bill, as amended, that would allow a financial institution to keep a customer account or transaction open, at the request of a federal or local law enforcement agency, if the customer account has been suspected of money laundering or illegal activity. The measure would make the financial institution not liable for maintaining an account or transaction in order, precluding any adverse actions against such institution. The bill would require law enforcement to provide termination dates for such requests. Motion agreed to 404-7: R 186-7; D 218-0. *Note: A two-thirds majority of those present and voting (274 in this case) is required for passage under suspension of the rules.* March 11, 2019.

		115	116	117	118	119	120
ALABAMA							
1	**Byrne**	N	N	Y	N	?	Y
2	**Roby**	N	N	Y	N	Y	Y
3	**Rogers, M.**	?	?	?	?	Y	Y
4	**Aderholt**	N	N	Y	N	Y	Y
5	**Brooks, M.**	N	N	Y	N	N	Y
6	**Palmer**	N	N	Y	N	Y	Y
7	Sewell	Y	Y	N	Y	Y	Y
ALASKA							
AL	**Young**	N	N	Y	N	N	Y
ARIZONA							
1	O'Halleran	Y	Y	N	Y	Y	Y
2	Kirkpatrick	Y	Y	N	Y	Y	Y
3	Grijalva	Y	Y	N	Y	?	?
4	**Gosar**	N	N	Y	N	N	N
5	**Biggs**	N	N	Y	N	N	Y
6	**Schweikert**	N	N	Y	N	Y	Y
7	Gallego	Y	Y	N	Y	+	+
8	**Lesko**	N	N	Y	N	Y	Y
9	Stanton	Y	Y	N	Y	Y	Y
ARKANSAS							
1	**Crawford**	?	?	?	-	Y	Y
2	**Hill, F.**	N	N	Y	N	Y	Y
3	**Womack**	N	N	Y	N	Y	Y
4	**Westerman**	N	N	Y	N	Y	Y
CALIFORNIA							
1	**LaMalfa**	N	N	Y	N	Y	Y
2	Huffman	Y	Y	N	Y	Y	Y
3	Garamendi	Y	Y	N	Y	Y	Y
4	**McClintock**	N	N	Y	N	N	Y
5	Thompson, M.	Y	Y	N	Y	Y	Y
6	Matsui	Y	Y	N	Y	Y	Y
7	Bera	Y	Y	N	Y	Y	Y
8	**Cook**	N	N	Y	N	Y	Y
9	McNerney	Y	Y	N	Y	Y	Y
10	Harder	Y	Y	N	Y	Y	Y
11	DeSaulnier	Y	Y	N	Y	Y	Y
12	Pelosi			N	Y		
13	Lee B.	Y	Y	N	Y	Y	Y
14	Speier	Y	Y	N	Y	Y	Y
15	Swalwell	Y	Y	N	Y	+	+
16	Costa	Y	Y	N	Y	Y	Y
17	Khanna	+	Y	N	Y	Y	Y
18	Eshoo	Y	Y	N	Y	Y	Y
19	Lofgren	Y	Y	N	Y	Y	Y
20	Panetta	Y	Y	N	Y	Y	Y
21	Cox	Y	Y	N	Y	Y	Y
22	**Nunes**	N	N	Y	N	Y	Y
23	**McCarthy**	N	N	Y	N	Y	Y
24	Carbajal	Y	Y	N	Y	Y	Y
25	Hill, K.	Y	Y	N	Y	Y	Y
26	Brownley	Y	Y	N	Y	Y	Y
27	Chu	Y	Y	N	Y	Y	Y
28	Schiff	Y	Y	N	Y	Y	Y
29	Cárdenas	Y	Y	N	Y	Y	Y
30	Sherman	Y	Y	N	Y	Y	Y
31	Aguilar	Y	Y	N	Y	Y	Y
32	Napolitano	Y	Y	N	Y	Y	Y
33	Lieu	Y	Y	N	Y	Y	Y
34	Gomez	Y	Y	N	Y	Y	Y
35	Torres	Y	Y	N	Y	Y	Y
36	Ruiz	Y	Y	N	Y	Y	Y
37	Bass	Y	Y	N	Y	Y	Y
38	Sánchez	Y	Y	N	Y	+	+
39	Cisneros	Y	Y	N	Y	Y	Y
40	Roybal-Allard	Y	Y	N	Y	Y	Y
41	Takano	Y	Y	N	Y	Y	Y
42	**Calvert**	N	N	Y	N	Y	Y
43	Waters	Y	Y	N	Y	Y	Y
44	Barragán	Y	Y	N	Y	Y	Y
45	Porter	Y	Y	N	Y	Y	Y
46	Correa	Y	Y	N	Y	Y	Y
47	Lowenthal	Y	Y	N	Y	Y	Y
48	Rouda	Y	Y	N	Y	Y	Y
49	Levin	Y	Y	N	Y	Y	Y
50	**Hunter**	N	N	Y	N	Y	Y
51	Vargas	Y	Y	N	Y	Y	Y
52	Peters	Y	Y	N	Y	Y	Y
53	Davis, S.	Y	Y	N	Y	Y	Y
COLORADO							
1	DeGette	Y	Y	N	Y	Y	Y
2	Neguse	Y	Y	N	Y	Y	Y
3	**Tipton**	N	N	Y	N	Y	Y
4	**Buck**	N	Y	Y	N	N	Y
5	**Lamborn**	N	N	Y	N	Y	Y
6	Crow	Y	Y	N	Y	Y	Y
7	Perlmutter	Y	Y	N	Y	Y	Y
CONNECTICUT							
1	Larson	Y	Y	N	Y	Y	Y
2	Courtney	Y	Y	N	Y	Y	Y
3	DeLauro	Y	Y	N	Y	Y	Y
4	Himes	Y	Y	N	Y	Y	Y
5	Hayes	Y	Y	N	Y	+	+
DELAWARE							
AL	Blunt Rochester	Y	Y	N	Y	Y	Y
FLORIDA							
1	**Gaetz**	N	N	Y	N	N	Y
2	**Dunn**	-	-	+	-	Y	Y
3	**Yoho**	-	N	Y	N	N	Y
4	**Rutherford**	N	N	Y	N	Y	Y
5	Lawson	Y	Y	N	Y	Y	Y
6	**Waltz**	N	N	Y	N	Y	Y
7	Murphy	Y	Y	N	Y	Y	Y
8	**Posey**	N	N	Y	N	Y	Y
9	Soto	Y	Y	N	Y	Y	Y
10	Demings	Y	Y	N	Y	Y	Y
11	**Webster**	N	N	Y	N	Y	Y
12	**Bilirakis**	?	N	Y	N	Y	Y
13	Crist	Y	Y	N	Y	Y	Y
14	Castor	Y	Y	N	Y	Y	Y
15	**Spano**	N	N	Y	N	Y	Y
16	**Buchanan**	N	N	Y	N	Y	Y
17	**Steube**	N	N	Y	N	N	Y
18	**Mast**	N	N	Y	N	Y	Y
19	**Rooney**	N	N	Y	N	Y	Y
20	Hastings	Y	Y	N	Y	Y	Y
21	Frankel	Y	Y	N	Y	Y	Y
22	Deutch	Y	Y	N	Y	Y	Y
23	Wasserman Schultz	Y	Y	N	Y	?	?
24	Wilson, F.	Y	Y	N	Y	Y	Y
25	**Diaz-Balart**	N	N	Y	N	Y	Y
26	Mucarsel-Powell	Y	Y	N	Y	Y	Y
27	Shalala	Y	Y	N	Y	Y	Y
GEORGIA							
1	**Carter, E.L.**	N	N	Y	N	Y	Y
2	Bishop, S.	Y	Y	N	Y	Y	Y
3	**Ferguson**	N	N	Y	N	Y	Y
4	Johnson, H.	Y	?	N	Y	Y	Y
5	Lewis John	Y	Y	N	Y	Y	Y
6	McBath	Y	Y	Y	Y	Y	Y
7	**Woodall**	N	N	Y	N	Y	Y
8	**Scott, A.**	N	N	Y	N	Y	Y
9	**Collins, D.**	N	N	Y	N	Y	Y
10	**Hice**	N	N	Y	N	N	Y
11	**Loudermilk**	N	N	Y	N	Y	Y
12	**Allen**	N	N	Y	N	Y	Y
13	Scott, D.	Y	Y	N	Y	Y	Y
14	**Graves, T.**	N	N	Y	N	Y	Y
HAWAII							
1	Case	Y	Y	N	Y	Y	Y
2	Gabbard	Y	Y	N	Y	?	?
IDAHO							
1	**Fulcher**	N	N	Y	N	Y	Y
2	**Simpson**	N	N	Y	N	Y	Y
ILLINOIS							
1	Rush	Y	Y	N	Y	?	?
2	Kelly, R.	Y	Y	N	Y	Y	Y
3	Lipinski	Y	Y	N	Y	Y	Y
4	García, J.	Y	Y	N	Y	Y	Y
5	Quigley	Y	Y	N	Y	Y	Y
6	Casten	Y	Y	N	Y	Y	Y
7	Davis, D.	Y	Y	N	Y	Y	Y
8	Krishnamoorthi	Y	Y	N	Y	Y	Y
9	Schakowsky	Y	Y	N	Y	Y	Y
10	Schneider	Y	Y	N	Y	Y	Y
11	Foster	Y	Y	N	Y	Y	Y

KEY: **Republicans** Democrats *Independents*

Y	Voted for (yea)	N	Voted against (nay)	P	Voted "present"
+	Announced for	-	Announced against	?	Did not vote or otherwise make position known
#	Paired for	X	Paired against		

		115	116	117	118	119	120
12	**Bost**	N	Y	Y	N	Y	Y
13	**Davis, R.**	N	N	Y	N	Y	Y
14	Underwood	Y	Y	N	Y	Y	Y
15	**Shimkus**	N	N	Y	N	Y	Y
16	**Kinzinger**	N	N	Y	N	Y	Y
17	Bustos	Y	Y	N	Y	Y	Y
18	**LaHood**	N	N	Y	N	Y	Y
INDIANA							
1	Visclosky	Y	Y	N	Y	Y	Y
2	**Walorski**	N	N	Y	N	Y	Y
3	**Banks**	N	N	Y	N	Y	Y
4	**Baird**	N	N	Y	N	Y	Y
5	**Brooks, S.**	N	N	Y	N	Y	Y
6	**Pence**	N	N	Y	N	Y	Y
7	Carson	Y	Y	N	Y	Y	Y
8	**Bucshon**	N	N	Y	N	Y	Y
9	**Hollingsworth**	N	N	Y	N	Y	Y
IOWA							
1	Finkenauer	Y	Y	N	Y	Y	Y
2	Loebsack	Y	Y	N	Y	Y	Y
3	Axne	Y	Y	N	Y	Y	Y
4	**King, S.**	N	N	Y	N	Y	Y
KANSAS							
1	**Marshall**	N	N	Y	N	Y	Y
2	**Watkins**	N	N	Y	N	Y	Y
3	Davids	Y	Y	N	Y	Y	Y
4	**Estes**	N	N	Y	N	Y	Y
KENTUCKY							
1	**Comer**	N	N	Y	N	Y	Y
2	**Guthrie**	N	N	Y	N	Y	Y
3	Yarmuth	Y	Y	N	Y	Y	Y
4	**Massie**	N	N	Y	N	N	N
5	**Rogers, H.**	N	N	Y	N	Y	Y
6	**Barr**	N	N	Y	N	Y	Y
LOUISIANA							
1	**Scalise**	N	N	Y	N	Y	Y
2	Richmond	Y	Y	N	Y	Y	Y
3	**Higgins, C.**	N	N	Y	N	N	Y
4	**Johnson, M.**	N	N	Y	N	?	?
5	**Abraham**	N	N	Y	N	?	?
6	**Graves, G.**	N	N	Y	N	Y	Y
MAINE							
1	Pingree	Y	Y	N	Y	Y	Y
2	Golden	Y	Y	N	Y	Y	Y
MARYLAND							
1	**Harris**	N	N	Y	N	N	Y
2	Ruppersberger	Y	Y	N	Y	Y	Y
3	Sarbanes	Y	Y	N	Y	Y	Y
4	Brown, A.	Y	Y	N	Y	Y	Y
5	Hoyer	Y	Y	N	Y	Y	Y
6	Trone	Y	Y	N	Y	Y	Y
7	Cummings	Y	Y	N	Y	Y	Y
8	Raskin	Y	Y	N	Y	Y	Y
MASSACHUSETTS							
1	Neal	Y	Y	N	Y	Y	Y
2	McGovern	Y	Y	N	Y	Y	Y
3	Trahan	Y	Y	N	Y	Y	Y
4	Kennedy	Y	Y	N	Y	Y	Y
5	Clark	Y	Y	N	Y	Y	Y
6	Moulton	Y	Y	N	Y	Y	Y
7	Pressley	Y	Y	N	Y	Y	Y
8	Lynch	Y	Y	N	Y	Y	Y
9	Keating	Y	Y	N	Y	Y	Y
MICHIGAN							
1	**Bergman**	N	N	Y	N	Y	Y
2	**Huizenga**	N	N	Y	N	Y	Y
3	**Amash**	N	N	N	N	N	N
4	**Moolenaar**	N	N	Y	N	Y	Y
5	Kildee	Y	Y	N	Y	Y	Y
6	**Upton**	N	Y	Y	N	?	?
7	**Walberg**	N	N	Y	N	Y	Y
8	Slotkin	Y	Y	N	Y	Y	Y
9	Levin	Y	Y	N	Y	Y	Y
10	**Mitchell**	N	N	Y	N	Y	Y
11	Stevens	Y	Y	N	Y	Y	Y
12	Dingell	Y	Y	N	Y	Y	Y
13	Tlaib	Y	Y	N	Y	+	-
14	Lawrence	Y	Y	N	Y	Y	Y
MINNESOTA							
1	**Hagedorn**	N	N	Y	N	Y	Y
2	Craig	Y	Y	N	Y	Y	Y
3	Phillips	Y	Y	N	Y	Y	Y
4	McCollum	Y	Y	N	Y	Y	Y
5	Omar	Y	Y	N	Y	Y	Y

		115	116	117	118	119	120
6	**Emmer**	N	N	Y	N	Y	Y
7	Peterson	Y	Y	N	Y	Y	Y
8	**Stauber**	N	Y	Y	N	Y	Y
MISSISSIPPI							
1	**Kelly, T.**	N	N	Y	N	Y	Y
2	Thompson, B.	Y	Y	N	Y	Y	Y
3	**Guest**	N	N	Y	N	Y	Y
4	**Palazzo**	N	N	Y	N	Y	Y
MISSOURI							
1	Clay	?	?	?	?	Y	Y
2	**Wagner**	N	N	Y	N	Y	Y
3	**Luetkemeyer**	N	N	Y	N	Y	Y
4	**Hartzler**	N	N	Y	N	+	Y
5	Cleaver	Y	Y	N	Y	Y	Y
6	**Graves, S.**	N	N	Y	N	Y	Y
7	**Long**	N	N	Y	N	Y	Y
8	**Smith, J.**	N	N	Y	N	Y	Y
MONTANA							
AL	**Gianforte**	N	N	Y	N	Y	Y
NEBRASKA							
1	**Fortenberry**	N	N	Y	N	Y	Y
2	**Bacon**	N	N	Y	N	Y	Y
3	**Smith, Adrian**	N	N	Y	N	Y	Y
NEVADA							
1	Titus	Y	Y	N	Y	Y	Y
2	**Amodei**	N	N	Y	N	Y	Y
3	Lee	Y	Y	N	Y	Y	?
4	Horsford	Y	Y	N	Y	Y	Y
NEW HAMPSHIRE							
1	Pappas	Y	Y	N	Y	Y	Y
2	Kuster	Y	Y	N	Y	Y	Y
NEW JERSEY							
1	Norcross	Y	Y	N	Y	Y	Y
2	Van Drew	Y	+	Y	Y	Y	Y
3	Kim	Y	Y	N	Y	Y	Y
4	**Smith, C.**	N	N	Y	N	Y	Y
5	Gottheimer	Y	Y	N	Y	Y	Y
6	Pallone	Y	Y	N	Y	Y	Y
7	Malinowski	Y	Y	N	Y	Y	Y
8	Sires	Y	Y	N	Y	Y	Y
9	Pascrell	Y	Y	N	Y	Y	Y
10	Payne	Y	Y	N	Y	Y	Y
11	Sherrill	Y	Y	N	Y	Y	Y
12	Watson Coleman	Y	Y	N	Y	Y	Y
NEW MEXICO							
1	Haaland	Y	Y	N	Y	Y	Y
2	Torres Small	Y	Y	N	Y	Y	Y
3	Luján	Y	Y	N	Y	Y	Y
NEW YORK							
1	**Zeldin**	N	N	Y	N	Y	Y
2	**King, P.**	N	N	Y	N	Y	Y
3	Suozzi	Y	Y	N	Y	Y	Y
4	Rice, K.	Y	Y	N	Y	Y	Y
5	Meeks	Y	Y	N	Y	?	?
6	Meng	Y	Y	N	Y	Y	Y
7	Velázquez	Y	Y	N	Y	Y	Y
8	Jeffries	Y	Y	N	Y	Y	Y
9	Clarke	Y	Y	N	Y	Y	Y
10	Nadler	Y	Y	N	Y	Y	Y
11	Rose	Y	Y	N	Y	Y	Y
12	Maloney, C.	Y	Y	N	Y	Y	Y
13	Espaillat	Y	Y	N	Y	Y	Y
14	Ocasio-Cortez	Y	Y	N	Y	Y	Y
15	Serrano	Y	Y	N	Y	Y	Y
16	Engel	Y	Y	N	Y	?	?
17	Lowey	Y	Y	N	Y	Y	Y
18	Maloney, S.P.	Y	?	?	Y	Y	Y
19	Delgado	Y	Y	N	Y	Y	Y
20	Tonko	Y	Y	N	Y	Y	Y
21	**Stefanik**	Y	N	Y	N	Y	Y
22	Brindisi	Y	Y	N	Y	Y	Y
23	**Reed**	N	N	Y	N	Y	Y
24	**Katko**	Y	N	Y	N	Y	Y
25	Morelle	Y	Y	N	Y	Y	Y
26	Higgins, B.	Y	Y	N	Y	Y	Y
27	**Collins, C.**						
NORTH CAROLINA							
1	Butterfield	Y	Y	N	Y	Y	Y
2	**Holding**	N	N	Y	N	Y	Y
3	**Jones***						
4	Price	Y	Y	N	Y	?	?
5	**Foxx**	N	N	Y	N	Y	Y
6	**Walker**	N	N	Y	N	?	Y
7	**Rouzer**	N	N	Y	N	Y	Y

		115	116	117	118	119	120
8	**Hudson**	N	N	Y	N	Y	Y
9	vacant						
10	**McHenry**	N	N	Y	N	Y	Y
11	**Meadows**	N	N	Y	N	Y	Y
12	Adams	Y	Y	N	Y	Y	Y
13	**Budd**	N	N	Y	N	Y	Y
NORTH DAKOTA							
AL	**Armstrong**	N	N	Y	N	Y	Y
OHIO							
1	**Chabot**	N	N	Y	N	Y	Y
2	**Wenstrup**	N	N	Y	N	Y	Y
3	Beatty	Y	Y	N	Y	Y	Y
4	**Jordan**	N	N	Y	N	Y	Y
5	**Latta**	N	N	Y	N	Y	Y
6	**Johnson, B.**	N	N	Y	N	Y	Y
7	**Gibbs**	N	N	Y	N	Y	Y
8	**Davidson**	N	N	Y	N	Y	Y
9	Kaptur	Y	Y	N	Y	Y	Y
10	**Turner**	N	N	Y	N	Y	Y
11	Fudge	Y	Y	N	Y	Y	Y
12	**Balderson**	N	N	Y	N	Y	Y
13	Ryan	Y	Y	N	Y	?	?
14	**Joyce**	N	N	Y	N	Y	Y
15	**Stivers**	?	?	?	?	Y	Y
16	**Gonzalez**	N	N	Y	N	Y	Y
OKLAHOMA							
1	**Hern**	N	N	Y	N	Y	Y
2	**Mullin**	N	N	Y	N	Y	Y
3	**Lucas**	N	N	Y	N	Y	Y
4	**Cole**	N	N	Y	N	Y	Y
5	Horn	Y	Y	Y	Y	Y	Y
OREGON							
1	Bonamici	Y	Y	N	Y	Y	Y
2	**Walden**	N	N	Y	N	Y	Y
3	Blumenauer	Y	Y	N	Y	Y	Y
4	DeFazio	Y	Y	N	Y	Y	Y
5	Schrader	Y	Y	Y	Y	Y	Y
PENNSYLVANIA							
1	**Fitzpatrick**	Y	Y	Y	N	Y	Y
2	Boyle	Y	Y	N	Y	Y	Y
3	Evans	Y	Y	N	Y	Y	Y
4	Dean	Y	Y	N	Y	Y	Y
5	Scanlon	Y	Y	N	Y	Y	Y
6	Houlahan	Y	Y	N	Y	Y	Y
7	Wild	Y	Y	N	Y	Y	Y
8	Cartwright	Y	Y	N	Y	Y	Y
9	**Meuser**	N	N	Y	N	Y	Y
10	**Perry**	N	N	Y	N	N	Y
11	**Smucker**	N	N	Y	N	Y	Y
12	**Marino***						
13	**Joyce**	N	N	Y	N	Y	Y
14	**Reschenthaler**	N	N	Y	N	Y	Y
15	**Thompson, G.**	N	N	Y	N	Y	Y
16	**Kelly, M.**	N	N	Y	N	Y	Y
17	Lamb	Y	Y	N	Y	Y	Y
18	Doyle	Y	Y	N	Y	Y	Y
RHODE ISLAND							
1	Cicilline	Y	?	N	Y	Y	Y
2	Langevin	Y	Y	N	Y	Y	Y
SOUTH CAROLINA							
1	Cunningham	Y	Y	Y	Y	Y	Y
2	**Wilson, J.**	N	N	Y	N	Y	Y
3	**Duncan**	N	N	Y	N	Y	Y
4	**Timmons**	N	N	Y	N	Y	Y
5	**Norman**	N	N	Y	N	Y	Y
6	Clyburn	Y	Y	N	Y	Y	Y
7	**Rice, T.**	N	N	Y	N	Y	Y
SOUTH DAKOTA							
AL	**Johnson**	N	N	Y	N	Y	Y
TENNESSEE							
1	**Roe**	N	N	Y	N	Y	Y
2	**Burchett**	N	N	Y	N	Y	Y
3	**Fleischmann**	N	N	Y	N	Y	Y
4	**DesJarlais**	N	N	Y	N	Y	Y
5	Cooper	Y	Y	N	Y	Y	Y
6	**Rose**	N	N	Y	N	Y	Y
7	**Green**	N	N	Y	N	N	Y
8	**Kustoff**	N	N	Y	N	Y	Y
9	Cohen	Y	Y	N	Y	Y	Y
TEXAS							
1	**Gohmert**	N	N	Y	N	N	Y
2	**Crenshaw**	N	N	Y	N	Y	Y
3	**Taylor**	N	N	Y	N	Y	Y
4	**Ratcliffe**	N	N	Y	N	Y	Y

		115	116	117	118	119	120
5	**Gooden**	N	N	Y	N	Y	Y
6	**Wright**	N	N	Y	N	Y	Y
7	Fletcher	Y	Y	N	Y	Y	Y
8	**Brady**	N	Y	Y	N	Y	Y
9	Green, A.	Y	Y	N	Y	Y	Y
10	**McCaul**	N	N	Y	N	Y	Y
11	**Conaway**	N	N	Y	N	Y	Y
12	**Granger**	N	N	Y	N	Y	Y
13	**Thornberry**	N	N	Y	N	Y	Y
14	**Weber**	N	N	Y	N	N	Y
15	Gonzalez	Y	Y	N	Y	Y	Y
16	Escobar	Y	Y	N	Y	Y	Y
17	**Flores**	N	N	Y	N	?	?
18	Jackson Lee	Y	Y	N	Y	Y	Y
19	**Arrington**	N	N	Y	N	Y	Y
20	Castro	Y	Y	N	Y	Y	Y
21	**Roy**	N	N	Y	N	N	N
22	**Olson**	N	N	Y	N	Y	Y
23	**Hurd**	N	N	Y	N	Y	Y
24	**Marchant**	N	N	Y	N	Y	Y
25	**Williams**	N	N	Y	N	Y	Y
26	**Burgess**	N	N	Y	N	Y	N
27	**Cloud**	N	N	Y	N	N	Y
28	Cuellar	Y	Y	N	Y	Y	Y
29	Garcia, S.	Y	Y	N	Y	Y	Y
30	Johnson, E.B.	Y	Y	N	Y	Y	Y
31	**Carter, J.**	N	N	Y	N	Y	Y
32	Allred	Y	Y	N	Y	Y	Y
33	Veasey	Y	Y	N	Y	Y	Y
34	Vela	Y	Y	N	Y	Y	Y
35	Doggett	Y	Y	N	Y	Y	Y
36	**Babin**	N	N	Y	N	Y	Y
UTAH							
1	**Bishop, R.**	N	Y	Y	N	Y	Y
2	**Stewart**	N	N	Y	N	Y	Y
3	**Curtis**	-	N	Y	N	Y	Y
4	McAdams	Y	Y	N	Y	Y	Y
VERMONT							
AL	Welch	Y	Y	N	Y	Y	Y
VIRGINIA							
1	**Wittman**	N	N	Y	N	Y	Y
2	Luria	Y	Y	N	Y	Y	Y
3	Scott, R.	Y	Y	N	Y	Y	Y
4	McEachin	Y	Y	N	Y	Y	Y
5	**Riggleman**	N	N	Y	N	Y	Y
6	**Cline**	N	N	Y	N	N	N
7	Spanberger	Y	Y	N	Y	Y	Y
8	Beyer	Y	Y	N	Y	Y	Y
9	**Griffith**	N	N	Y	N	Y	N
10	Wexton	Y	Y	N	Y	Y	Y
11	Connolly	Y	Y	N	Y	Y	Y
WASHINGTON							
1	DelBene	Y	Y	N	Y	Y	Y
2	Larsen	Y	Y	N	Y	Y	Y
3	**Herrera Beutler**	N	N	Y	N	Y	Y
4	**Newhouse**	N	N	Y	N	Y	Y
5	**McMorris Rodgers**	N	N	+	N	Y	Y
6	Kilmer	Y	Y	N	Y	Y	Y
7	Jayapal	Y	Y	N	Y	Y	Y
8	Schrier	Y	Y	N	Y	Y	Y
9	Smith Adam	Y	Y	N	Y	Y	Y
10	Heck	Y	Y	N	Y	Y	Y
WEST VIRGINIA							
1	**McKinley**	N	N	Y	N	Y	Y
2	**Mooney**	N	N	Y	N	Y	Y
3	**Miller**	N	N	Y	N	Y	Y
WISCONSIN							
1	**Steil**	N	N	Y	N	Y	Y
2	Pocan	Y	Y	N	Y	+	+
3	Kind	Y	Y	N	Y	Y	Y
4	Moore	Y	Y	N	Y	?	?
5	**Sensenbrenner**	N	N	Y	N	Y	Y
6	**Grothman**	N	N	Y	N	N	Y
7	**Duffy**						
8	**Gallagher**	N	N	Y	N	Y	Y
WYOMING							
AL	**Cheney**	N	N	Y	N	Y	Y
DELEGATES							
	Radewagen (A.S.)	?	?				
	Norton (D.C.)	Y	Y				
	San Nicolas (Guam)	?	?				
	Sablan (N. Marianas)	?	?				
	González-Colón (P.R.)	N	Y				
	Plaskett (V.I.)	Y	Y				

III HOUSE VOTES

121. HRES156. Nemtsov Investigation and Russian Cooperation - Passage. Engel, D-N.Y., motion to suspend the rules and pass the bill, as amended, that would condemn Vladimir Putin and his administration for targeting political opponents and covering up the assassination of Russian opposition leader Boris Nemtsov. It would call on the federal government to impose sanctions on individuals who organized the assassination and call on the Russian government to cooperate with an international investigation of the incident. The resolution would call for the secretary of State to submit a report to Congress detailing the circumstances of the assassination, all those involved, and whether the Russian government has taken action against them. Motion agreed to 416-1: R 187-1; D 229-0. *Note: A two-thirds majority of those present and voting (278 in this case) is required for passage under suspension of the rules.* March 12, 2019.

122. HR596. Russian Sovereignty Claim of Crimea - Passage. Engel, D-N.Y., motion to suspend the rules and pass the bill, as amended, that would state that it is U.S. policy not to recognize Russia's claim of sovereignty over Crimea. The bill would prohibit any federal agency or department from taking actions that would recognize or imply recognition of Russian control of Crimea. Motion agreed to 427-1: R 195-1; D 232-0. *Note: A two-thirds majority of those present and voting (286 in this case) is required for passage under suspension of the rules.* March 12, 2019.

123. HR1654. Federal Register Publishing Format - Passage. Norton, D-D.C., motion to suspend the rules and pass the bill, as amended, that would eliminate the requirement that the Office of the Federal Register produce printed copies of the register and eliminate the requirement that agencies provide multiple copies of documents submitted to the Federal Register. Motion agreed to 426-1: R 195-1; D 231-0. *Note: A two-thirds majority of those present and voting (285 in this case) is required for passage under suspension of the rules.* March 12, 2019.

124. HCONRES24. Publication of Special Investigator's Report - Rule. Adoption of the rule (H Res 208) that would provide for House floor consideration of the bill (H Con Res 24) that would express the sense of Congress that the report of Special Counsel Mueller should be made available to the public and to Congress. The rule would also provide for proceedings during the period from March 15 through March 22, 2019. Passed 233-195: R 0-195; D 233-0. March 13, 2019.

125. HCONRES24. Publication of Special Investigator's Report - Passage. Adoption of the resolution, as amended, that would express the sense of Congress that the report by Special Counsel Robert S. Mueller III, regarding Russian interference in the 2016 presidential election and any connections to or coordination with the Trump campaign, should be released to Congress in full and made public to the extent allowed by public disclosure laws. Adopted 420-0: R 190-0; D 230-0. March 14, 2019.

126. HR1616. European Energy Infrastructure - Passage. Sires, D-N.J., motion to suspend the rules and pass the bill, as amended, that would direct the State Department to provide diplomatic and political support to European and Eurasian countries to help improve energy sources, supply routes, security, and market integration and competition. The bill would prohibit the United States from assisting any country that engages in financial transactions with Russian military or intelligence. The bill would authorize $250 million annually through fiscal 2021 for a State Department fund to counter Russian influence in European energy, infrastructure, and elections. It would also authorize $80 million in fiscal 2020 for the U.S. Trade and Development Agency. Motion agreed to 391-24: R 167-24; D 224-0. *Note: A two-thirds majority of those present and voting (277 in this case) is required for passage under suspension of the rules.* March 25, 2019.

		121	122	123	124	125	126
ALABAMA							
1	**Byrne**	Y	Y	Y	N	Y	Y
2	**Roby**	Y	Y	Y	N	Y	Y
3	**Rogers, M.**	Y	Y	Y	N	Y	Y
4	**Aderholt**	Y	Y	Y	N	Y	Y
5	**Brooks, M.**	Y	Y	Y	N	Y	N
6	**Palmer**	Y	Y	Y	N	Y	N
7	Sewell	Y	Y	Y	Y	Y	Y
ALASKA							
AL	**Young**	?	Y	Y	N	Y	Y
ARIZONA							
1	O'Halleran	Y	Y	Y	Y	Y	Y
2	Kirkpatrick	Y	Y	Y	Y	Y	Y
3	Grijalva	Y	Y	Y	Y	Y	?
4	**Gosar**	Y	Y	Y	N	P	N
5	**Biggs**	Y	Y	Y	N	Y	N
6	**Schweikert**	Y	Y	Y	N	+	Y
7	Gallego	Y	Y	Y	Y	Y	Y
8	**Lesko**	Y	Y	Y	N	Y	Y
9	Stanton	Y	Y	Y	Y	Y	Y
ARKANSAS							
1	**Crawford**	Y	Y	Y	N	Y	Y
2	**Hill, F.**	Y	Y	Y	N	Y	Y
3	**Womack**	Y	Y	Y	N	Y	Y
4	**Westerman**	Y	Y	Y	N	Y	Y
CALIFORNIA							
1	**LaMalfa**	Y	Y	Y	N	Y	Y
2	Huffman	Y	Y	Y	Y	Y	Y
3	Garamendi	Y	Y	Y	Y	Y	Y
4	**McClintock**	Y	Y	Y	N	Y	N
5	Thompson, M.	Y	Y	Y	Y	Y	Y
6	Matsui	Y	Y	Y	Y	Y	Y
7	Bera	Y	Y	Y	Y	Y	Y
8	**Cook**	?	Y	Y	N	Y	Y
9	McNerney	Y	Y	Y	Y	Y	Y
10	Harder	Y	Y	+	Y	Y	Y
11	DeSaulnier	Y	Y	Y	Y	Y	Y
12	Pelosi						
13	Lee B.	Y	Y	Y	Y	Y	Y
14	Speier	Y	Y	Y	?	Y	?
15	Swalwell	Y	Y	Y	Y	Y	Y
16	Costa	Y	Y	Y	Y	Y	Y
17	Khanna	Y	Y	Y	Y	Y	Y
18	Eshoo	Y	Y	Y	Y	Y	Y
19	Lofgren	Y	Y	Y	?	Y	Y
20	Panetta	Y	Y	Y	Y	Y	Y
21	Cox	Y	Y	Y	Y	Y	Y
22	**Nunes**	Y	Y	Y	N	Y	Y
23	**McCarthy**	Y	Y	Y	N	Y	Y
24	Carbajal	Y	Y	Y	Y	Y	Y
25	Hill, K.	Y	Y	Y	Y	Y	Y
26	Brownley	Y	Y	Y	Y	Y	Y
27	Chu	Y	Y	Y	Y	Y	Y
28	Schiff	Y	Y	Y	Y	Y	Y
29	Cárdenas	Y	Y	Y	Y	Y	Y
30	Sherman	Y	Y	Y	Y	Y	Y
31	Aguilar	Y	Y	Y	Y	Y	Y
32	Napolitano	Y	Y	Y	Y	Y	Y
33	Lieu	Y	Y	Y	Y	Y	Y
34	Gomez	Y	Y	Y	Y	Y	Y
35	Torres	Y	Y	Y	Y	Y	Y
36	Ruiz	Y	Y	Y	Y	Y	Y
37	Bass	?	Y	Y	Y	Y	Y
38	Sánchez	Y	Y	Y	Y	Y	Y
39	Cisneros	Y	Y	Y	Y	Y	Y
40	Roybal-Allard	Y	Y	Y	Y	Y	Y
41	Takano	Y	Y	Y	Y	Y	Y
42	**Calvert**	Y	Y	Y	N	Y	Y
43	Waters	Y	Y	Y	Y	Y	Y
44	Barragán	Y	Y	Y	Y	Y	Y
45	Porter	Y	Y	Y	Y	Y	+
46	Correa	Y	Y	Y	Y	Y	Y
47	Lowenthal	Y	Y	Y	Y	Y	Y
48	Rouda	Y	Y	Y	Y	Y	Y
49	Levin	Y	Y	Y	Y	Y	Y
50	**Hunter**	Y	Y	Y	N	Y	Y
51	Vargas	Y	Y	Y	Y	Y	Y
52	Peters	Y	Y	Y	Y	Y	Y

		121	122	123	124	125	126
53	Davis, S.	Y	Y	Y	Y	Y	Y
COLORADO							
1	DeGette	Y	Y	Y	Y	Y	Y
2	Neguse	Y	Y	Y	Y	Y	Y
3	**Tipton**	Y	Y	Y	N	Y	Y
4	**Buck**	Y	Y	Y	N	Y	N
5	**Lamborn**	Y	Y	Y	N	Y	Y
6	Crow	Y	Y	Y	Y	Y	Y
7	Perlmutter	Y	Y	Y	Y	Y	Y
CONNECTICUT							
1	Larson	Y	Y	Y	Y	Y	Y
2	Courtney	Y	Y	Y	Y	Y	Y
3	DeLauro	Y	Y	Y	Y	Y	Y
4	Himes	Y	Y	Y	Y	Y	Y
5	Hayes	Y	Y	Y	Y	Y	Y
DELAWARE							
AL	Blunt Rochester	Y	Y	Y	Y	Y	Y
FLORIDA							
1	**Gaetz**	Y	Y	Y	N	P	N
2	**Dunn**	Y	Y	Y	N	Y	?
3	**Yoho**	Y	Y	Y	N	Y	Y
4	**Rutherford**	Y	Y	Y	N	Y	Y
5	Lawson	Y	Y	Y	Y	Y	Y
6	**Waltz**	Y	Y	Y	N	Y	Y
7	Murphy	Y	Y	Y	Y	Y	Y
8	**Posey**	Y	Y	N	N	Y	Y
9	Soto	Y	Y	Y	Y	Y	Y
10	Demings	Y	Y	Y	Y	Y	Y
11	**Webster**	Y	Y	Y	N	Y	Y
12	**Bilirakis**	Y	Y	Y	N	Y	+
13	Crist	Y	Y	Y	Y	Y	Y
14	Castor	Y	Y	Y	Y	Y	Y
15	**Spano**	Y	Y	Y	N	Y	Y
16	**Buchanan**	Y	Y	Y	N	Y	Y
17	**Steube**	Y	Y	Y	N	Y	N
18	**Mast**	Y	Y	Y	N	Y	Y
19	**Rooney**	Y	Y	Y	N	Y	Y
20	Hastings	Y	Y	Y	Y	?	Y
21	Frankel	Y	Y	Y	Y	Y	Y
22	Deutch	Y	Y	Y	Y	Y	Y
23	Wasserman Schultz	Y	Y	Y	Y	Y	Y
24	Wilson, F.	Y	Y	Y	Y	Y	Y
25	**Diaz-Balart**	Y	Y	Y	N	Y	Y
26	Mucarsel-Powell	Y	Y	Y	Y	Y	Y
27	Shalala	Y	Y	Y	Y	Y	Y
GEORGIA							
1	**Carter, E.L.**	Y	Y	Y	N	Y	Y
2	Bishop, S.	Y	Y	Y	Y	Y	Y
3	**Ferguson**	Y	Y	Y	N	Y	N
4	Johnson, H.	Y	Y	Y	Y	Y	Y
5	Lewis John	Y	Y	Y	Y	Y	Y
6	McBath	Y	Y	Y	Y	Y	Y
7	**Woodall**	Y	Y	Y	N	Y	Y
8	**Scott, A.**	Y	Y	Y	N	Y	Y
9	**Collins, D.**	Y	Y	Y	N	Y	Y
10	**Hice**	Y	Y	Y	N	Y	Y
11	**Loudermilk**	Y	Y	Y	N	Y	N
12	**Allen**	Y	Y	Y	N	Y	N
13	Scott, D.	Y	Y	Y	Y	Y	Y
14	**Graves, T.**	Y	Y	Y	N	Y	Y
HAWAII							
1	Case	Y	Y	Y	Y	Y	Y
2	Gabbard	?	?	?	Y	Y	Y
IDAHO							
1	**Fulcher**	Y	Y	Y	N	Y	Y
2	**Simpson**	Y	Y	Y	N	Y	Y
ILLINOIS							
1	Rush	Y	Y	Y	Y	Y	?
2	Kelly, R.	Y	Y	Y	Y	Y	Y
3	Lipinski	Y	Y	Y	Y	Y	Y
4	García, J.	Y	Y	Y	Y	Y	Y
5	Quigley	Y	Y	Y	Y	Y	Y
6	Casten	+	Y	Y	Y	Y	Y
7	Davis, D.	Y	Y	Y	Y	Y	?
8	Krishnamoorthi	Y	Y	Y	Y	Y	Y
9	Schakowsky	Y	Y	Y	Y	Y	Y
10	Schneider	Y	Y	Y	Y	Y	Y
11	Foster	Y	Y	Y	Y	Y	Y

KEY:	**Republicans**	Democrats	*Independents*

Y Voted for (yea)	**N** Voted against (nay)	**P** Voted "present"	
+ Announced for	Announced against	**?** Did not vote or otherwise	
# Paired for	**X** Paired against	make position known	

		121	122	123	124	125	126
12	**Bost**	Y	Y	Y	N	Y	Y
13	**Davis, R.**	Y	Y	Y	N	Y	Y
14	Underwood	Y	Y	Y	Y	Y	Y
15	**Shimkus**	Y	Y	Y	N	Y	Y
16	**Kinzinger**	Y	Y	Y	N	Y	Y
17	Bustos	Y	Y	Y	Y	Y	Y
18	**LaHood**	Y	Y	Y	N	Y	Y
INDIANA							
1	Visclosky	Y	Y	Y	Y	Y	Y
2	**Walorski**	Y	Y	Y	N	Y	Y
3	**Banks**	Y	Y	Y	N	Y	Y
4	**Baird**	Y	Y	Y	N	Y	Y
5	**Brooks, S.**	Y	Y	Y	N	Y	Y
6	**Pence**	Y	Y	Y	N	Y	Y
7	Carson	Y	Y	Y	Y	Y	Y
8	**Bucshon**	Y	Y	Y	N	Y	Y
9	**Hollingsworth**	Y	Y	Y	N	Y	Y
IOWA							
1	Finkenauer	Y	Y	Y	Y	Y	+
2	Loebsack	Y	Y	Y	Y	Y	Y
3	Axne	Y	Y	Y	Y	Y	Y
4	**King, S.**	Y	Y	Y	N	Y	Y
KANSAS							
1	**Marshall**	Y	Y	Y	N	?	Y
2	**Watkins**	+	Y	Y	N	Y	Y
3	Davids	Y	Y	Y	Y	Y	Y
4	**Estes**	Y	Y	Y	N	Y	Y
KENTUCKY							
1	**Comer**	Y	Y	Y	N	Y	Y
2	**Guthrie**	Y	Y	Y	N	Y	Y
3	Yarmuth	Y	Y	Y	Y	Y	Y
4	**Massie**	N	N	Y	N	P	N
5	**Rogers, H.**	?	Y	Y	N	Y	Y
6	**Barr**	Y	Y	Y	N	Y	Y
LOUISIANA							
1	**Scalise**	Y	Y	Y	N	Y	Y
2	Richmond	Y	Y	Y	Y	Y	Y
3	**Higgins, C.**	Y	Y	Y	N	Y	Y
4	**Johnson, M.**	Y	Y	Y	N	Y	?
5	**Abraham**	?	?	?	?	Y	?
6	**Graves, G.**	Y	Y	Y	N	Y	Y
MAINE							
1	Pingree	Y	Y	Y	Y	Y	Y
2	Golden	Y	Y	Y	Y	Y	Y
MARYLAND							
1	**Harris**	Y	Y	Y	N	Y	N
2	Ruppersberger	Y	Y	Y	Y	Y	Y
3	Sarbanes	Y	Y	Y	Y	Y	?
4	Brown, A.	Y	Y	Y	Y	Y	Y
5	Hoyer	Y	Y	Y	Y	Y	Y
6	Trone	Y	Y	Y	Y	Y	Y
7	Cummings	Y	Y	Y	Y	Y	Y
8	Raskin	Y	Y	Y	Y	Y	Y
MASSACHUSETTS							
1	Neal	Y	Y	Y	Y	Y	Y
2	McGovern	Y	Y	Y	Y	Y	Y
3	Trahan	Y	Y	Y	Y	Y	Y
4	Kennedy	Y	Y	Y	Y	Y	?
5	Clark	Y	Y	Y	Y	Y	Y
6	Moulton	Y	Y	Y	Y	Y	Y
7	Pressley	Y	Y	Y	Y	Y	Y
8	Lynch	Y	Y	Y	Y	Y	Y
9	Keating	Y	Y	Y	Y	Y	Y
MICHIGAN							
1	**Bergman**	Y	Y	Y	N	Y	Y
2	**Huizenga**	Y	Y	Y	N	Y	Y
3	**Amash**	Y	Y	Y	N	P	N
4	**Moolenaar**	Y	Y	Y	N	Y	Y
5	Kildee	Y	Y	Y	Y	Y	Y
6	**Upton**	Y	Y	Y	N	Y	Y
7	**Walberg**	Y	Y	Y	N	Y	Y
8	Slotkin	Y	Y	Y	Y	Y	Y
9	Levin	Y	Y	Y	Y	Y	Y
10	**Mitchell**	Y	Y	Y	N	Y	Y
11	Stevens	Y	Y	Y	Y	Y	Y
12	Dingell	?	Y	Y	Y	Y	Y
13	Tlaib	Y	Y	Y	Y	Y	Y
14	Lawrence	Y	Y	Y	Y	Y	Y
MINNESOTA							
1	**Hagedorn**	Y	Y	Y	N	Y	Y
2	Craig	Y	Y	Y	Y	Y	Y
3	Phillips	Y	Y	Y	Y	Y	Y
4	McCollum	Y	Y	Y	Y	Y	Y
5	Omar	Y	Y	Y	Y	Y	+

		121	122	123	124	125	126
6	**Emmer**	Y	Y	Y	N	Y	Y
7	Peterson	Y	Y	Y	Y	Y	Y
8	**Stauber**	Y	Y	Y	N	Y	Y
MISSISSIPPI							
1	**Kelly, T.**	Y	Y	Y	N	Y	Y
2	Thompson, B.	Y	Y	Y	Y	Y	Y
3	**Guest**	Y	Y	Y	N	Y	Y
4	**Palazzo**	Y	Y	Y	N	Y	Y
MISSOURI							
1	Clay	Y	Y	Y	Y	Y	Y
2	**Wagner**	Y	Y	Y	N	Y	Y
3	**Luetkemeyer**	Y	Y	Y	N	Y	Y
4	**Hartzler**	Y	Y	Y	N	Y	Y
5	Cleaver	Y	Y	Y	Y	+	Y
6	**Graves, S.**	Y	Y	Y	N	Y	Y
7	**Long**	Y	Y	Y	N	Y	Y
8	**Smith, J.**	Y	Y	Y	N	Y	Y
MONTANA							
AL	**Gianforte**	?	Y	Y	N	Y	Y
NEBRASKA							
1	**Fortenberry**	Y	Y	Y	N	Y	Y
2	**Bacon**	Y	Y	Y	N	Y	Y
3	**Smith, Adrian**	Y	Y	Y	N	Y	Y
NEVADA							
1	Titus	Y	Y	Y	Y	Y	Y
2	**Amodei**	Y	Y	Y	N	Y	Y
3	Lee	Y	Y	Y	Y	Y	Y
4	Horsford	Y	Y	Y	Y	Y	Y
NEW HAMPSHIRE							
1	Pappas	Y	Y	Y	Y	Y	Y
2	Kuster	Y	Y	Y	Y	Y	Y
NEW JERSEY							
1	Norcross	Y	Y	Y	Y	Y	Y
2	Van Drew	Y	Y	Y	Y	Y	Y
3	Kim	Y	Y	Y	Y	Y	Y
4	**Smith, C.**	Y	Y	Y	N	Y	Y
5	Gottheimer	Y	Y	Y	Y	Y	Y
6	Pallone	Y	Y	Y	Y	Y	Y
7	Malinowski	Y	Y	Y	Y	Y	Y
8	Sires	Y	Y	Y	Y	Y	Y
9	Pascrell	Y	Y	Y	Y	Y	Y
10	Payne	Y	Y	Y	Y	Y	Y
11	Sherrill	Y	Y	Y	Y	Y	Y
12	Watson Coleman	Y	Y	Y	Y	Y	Y
NEW MEXICO							
1	Haaland	Y	Y	Y	Y	Y	Y
2	Torres Small	Y	Y	Y	Y	Y	Y
3	Luján	Y	Y	Y	Y	Y	Y
NEW YORK							
1	**Zeldin**	Y	Y	Y	N	Y	Y
2	**King, P.**	Y	Y	Y	N	Y	Y
3	Suozzi	Y	Y	Y	Y	Y	Y
4	Rice, K.	Y	Y	Y	Y	Y	Y
5	Meeks	Y	Y	Y	Y	Y	Y
6	Meng	Y	Y	Y	Y	Y	Y
7	Velázquez	Y	Y	Y	Y	Y	?
8	Jeffries	Y	Y	Y	Y	Y	Y
9	Clarke	Y	Y	Y	Y	Y	Y
10	Nadler	Y	Y	Y	Y	Y	Y
11	Rose	Y	Y	Y	Y	Y	Y
12	Maloney, C.	Y	Y	Y	Y	Y	Y
13	Espaillat	Y	Y	Y	Y	Y	Y
14	Ocasio-Cortez	Y	Y	Y	Y	Y	Y
15	Serrano	Y	Y	Y	Y	Y	Y
16	Engel	Y	Y	Y	Y	Y	Y
17	Lowey	Y	Y	Y	Y	Y	Y
18	Maloney, S.P.	?	?	?	Y	Y	Y
19	Delgado	Y	Y	Y	Y	Y	Y
20	Tonko	Y	Y	Y	Y	Y	Y
21	**Stefanik**	Y	Y	Y	N	Y	Y
22	Brindisi	Y	Y	Y	Y	Y	Y
23	**Reed**	Y	Y	Y	N	Y	Y
24	**Katko**	Y	Y	Y	N	Y	Y
25	Morelle	Y	Y	Y	Y	Y	Y
26	Higgins, B.	Y	Y	Y	Y	Y	Y
27	**Collins, C.**						
NORTH CAROLINA							
1	Butterfield	Y	Y	Y	Y	Y	Y
2	**Holding**	Y	Y	Y	N	Y	Y
3	**Jones***						
4	Price	Y	Y	Y	Y	Y	Y
5	**Foxx**	Y	Y	Y	N	Y	Y
6	**Walker**	Y	Y	Y	N	Y	Y
7	**Rouzer**	Y	Y	Y	N	Y	Y

		121	122	123	124	125	126
8	**Hudson**	Y	Y	Y	N	Y	Y
9	vacant						
10	**McHenry**	Y	Y	Y	N	Y	Y
11	**Meadows**	Y	Y	Y	N	Y	N
12	Adams	Y	Y	Y	Y	Y	Y
13	**Budd**	Y	Y	Y	N	Y	Y
NORTH DAKOTA							
AL	**Armstrong**	Y	Y	Y	N	Y	Y
OHIO							
1	**Chabot**	Y	Y	Y	N	Y	Y
2	**Wenstrup**	Y	Y	Y	N	Y	Y
3	Beatty	Y	Y	Y	Y	Y	Y
4	**Jordan**	Y	Y	Y	N	Y	N
5	**Latta**	Y	Y	Y	N	Y	Y
6	**Johnson, B.**	Y	Y	Y	N	Y	Y
7	**Gibbs**	Y	Y	Y	N	Y	Y
8	**Davidson**	Y	Y	Y	N	Y	Y
9	Kaptur	Y	Y	Y	Y	Y	Y
10	**Turner**	Y	Y	Y	N	Y	Y
11	Fudge	Y	Y	Y	Y	Y	Y
12	**Balderson**	Y	Y	Y	N	Y	Y
13	Ryan	Y	Y	Y	Y	Y	Y
14	**Joyce**	Y	Y	Y	N	Y	Y
15	**Stivers**	Y	Y	Y	N	Y	Y
16	**Gonzalez**	Y	Y	Y	N	Y	Y
OKLAHOMA							
1	**Hern**	Y	Y	Y	N	Y	Y
2	**Mullin**	Y	Y	Y	N	Y	?
3	**Lucas**	Y	Y	Y	N	Y	Y
4	**Cole**	Y	Y	Y	N	Y	Y
5	Horn	Y	Y	Y	Y	Y	Y
OREGON							
1	Bonamici	Y	Y	Y	Y	Y	Y
2	**Walden**	+	Y	Y	N	Y	Y
3	Blumenauer	Y	Y	Y	Y	Y	Y
4	DeFazio	Y	Y	Y	Y	Y	Y
5	Schrader	Y	Y	Y	Y	Y	Y
PENNSYLVANIA							
1	**Fitzpatrick**	Y	Y	Y	N	Y	Y
2	Boyle	Y	Y	Y	Y	Y	Y
3	Evans	Y	Y	Y	Y	Y	Y
4	Dean	Y	Y	Y	Y	Y	Y
5	Scanlon	Y	Y	Y	Y	Y	Y
6	Houlahan	Y	Y	Y	Y	Y	Y
7	Wild	Y	Y	Y	Y	Y	Y
8	Cartwright	Y	Y	Y	Y	Y	Y
9	**Meuser**	Y	Y	Y	N	Y	Y
10	**Perry**	Y	Y	Y	N	Y	N
11	**Smucker**	Y	Y	Y	N	Y	Y
12	**Marino***						
13	**Joyce**	Y	Y	Y	N	Y	Y
14	**Reschenthaler**	Y	Y	Y	N	Y	Y
15	**Thompson, G.**	Y	Y	Y	N	Y	Y
16	**Kelly, M.**	Y	Y	Y	N	Y	Y
17	Lamb	Y	Y	Y	Y	Y	Y
18	Doyle	Y	Y	Y	Y	Y	Y
RHODE ISLAND							
1	Cicilline	Y	Y	Y	Y	Y	Y
2	Langevin	Y	Y	Y	Y	Y	Y
SOUTH CAROLINA							
1	Cunningham	Y	Y	Y	Y	Y	Y
2	**Wilson, J.**	Y	Y	Y	N	Y	+
3	**Duncan**	Y	Y	Y	N	Y	N
4	**Timmons**	Y	Y	Y	N	Y	Y
5	**Norman**	Y	Y	Y	N	Y	Y
6	Clyburn	Y	Y	Y	Y	Y	Y
7	**Rice, T.**	Y	Y	Y	N	Y	N
SOUTH DAKOTA							
AL	**Johnson**	Y	Y	Y	N	Y	Y
TENNESSEE							
1	**Roe**	Y	Y	Y	N	Y	Y
2	**Burchett**	Y	Y	Y	N	Y	N
3	**Fleischmann**	Y	Y	Y	N	Y	Y
4	**DesJarlais**	Y	Y	Y	N	Y	Y
5	Cooper	Y	Y	Y	Y	Y	Y
6	**Rose**	Y	Y	Y	N	Y	Y
7	**Green**	Y	Y	Y	N	Y	Y
8	**Kustoff**	Y	Y	Y	N	Y	Y
9	Cohen	Y	Y	Y	Y	Y	Y
TEXAS							
1	**Gohmert**	Y	Y	Y	N	Y	Y
2	**Crenshaw**	Y	Y	Y	N	Y	Y
3	**Taylor**	Y	Y	Y	N	Y	Y
4	**Ratcliffe**	Y	Y	Y	N	?	Y

		121	122	123	124	125	126
5	**Gooden**	Y	Y	Y	N	Y	Y
6	**Wright**	Y	Y	Y	N	Y	Y
7	Fletcher	Y	Y	Y	Y	Y	Y
8	**Brady**	Y	Y	Y	N	Y	Y
9	Green, A.	Y	Y	Y	Y	Y	Y
10	**McCaul**	Y	Y	Y	N	Y	Y
11	**Conaway**	Y	Y	Y	N	Y	Y
12	**Granger**	Y	Y	Y	N	Y	Y
13	**Thornberry**	Y	Y	Y	N	Y	Y
14	**Weber**	Y	Y	Y	N	Y	Y
15	Gonzalez	Y	Y	Y	Y	Y	Y
16	Escobar	Y	Y	Y	Y	Y	Y
17	**Flores**	Y	Y	Y	N	Y	Y
18	Jackson Lee	Y	Y	Y	Y	Y	Y
19	**Arrington**	Y	Y	Y	N	Y	Y
20	Castro	Y	Y	Y	Y	Y	Y
21	**Roy**	Y	Y	Y	N	Y	N
22	**Olson**	Y	Y	Y	N	Y	Y
23	**Hurd**	Y	Y	Y	N	Y	Y
24	**Marchant**	Y	Y	Y	N	Y	Y
25	**Williams**	Y	Y	Y	N	Y	Y
26	**Burgess**	Y	Y	Y	N	Y	Y
27	**Cloud**	Y	Y	Y	N	Y	N
28	Cuellar	Y	Y	Y	Y	Y	Y
29	Garcia, S.	Y	Y	Y	Y	Y	Y
30	Johnson, E.B.	Y	Y	Y	Y	Y	Y
31	**Carter, J.**	Y	Y	Y	N	Y	Y
32	Allred	Y	Y	Y	Y	Y	Y
33	Veasey	Y	Y	Y	Y	Y	Y
34	Vela	Y	Y	Y	Y	Y	Y
35	Doggett	Y	Y	Y	Y	Y	Y
36	**Babin**	Y	Y	Y	N	Y	Y
UTAH							
1	**Bishop, R.**	?	Y	Y	N	Y	Y
2	**Stewart**	Y	Y	Y	N	Y	Y
3	**Curtis**	+	Y	Y	N	Y	Y
4	McAdams	Y	Y	Y	Y	Y	Y
VERMONT							
AL	Welch	Y	Y	Y	Y	Y	Y
VIRGINIA							
1	**Wittman**	Y	Y	Y	N	Y	Y
2	Luria	Y	Y	Y	Y	Y	Y
3	Scott, R.	Y	Y	Y	Y	Y	Y
4	McEachin	Y	Y	Y	Y	+	Y
5	**Riggleman**	Y	Y	Y	N	Y	Y
6	**Cline**	Y	Y	Y	N	Y	N
7	Spanberger	Y	Y	Y	Y	Y	Y
8	Beyer	Y	Y	Y	Y	Y	Y
9	**Griffith**	Y	Y	Y	N	Y	N
10	Wexton	Y	Y	Y	Y	Y	Y
11	Connolly	Y	Y	Y	Y	Y	Y
WASHINGTON							
1	DelBene	Y	Y	Y	Y	Y	Y
2	Larsen	Y	Y	Y	Y	Y	Y
3	**Herrera Beutler**	Y	Y	Y	N	Y	Y
4	**Newhouse**	Y	Y	Y	N	Y	Y
5	**McMorris Rodgers**	Y	Y	Y	N	Y	Y
6	Kilmer	Y	Y	Y	Y	Y	Y
7	Jayapal	Y	Y	Y	Y	Y	Y
8	Schrier	Y	Y	Y	Y	Y	Y
9	Smith Adam	Y	Y	Y	Y	Y	Y
10	Heck	Y	Y	Y	Y	Y	Y
WEST VIRGINIA							
1	**McKinley**	Y	Y	Y	N	Y	Y
2	**Mooney**	Y	Y	Y	?	Y	Y
3	**Miller**	Y	Y	Y	N	Y	Y
WISCONSIN							
1	**Steil**	Y	Y	Y	N	Y	Y
2	Pocan	Y	Y	Y	Y	Y	Y
3	Kind	Y	Y	Y	Y	Y	Y
4	Moore	Y	Y	Y	Y	Y	Y
5	**Sensenbrenner**	Y	Y	Y	N	Y	Y
6	**Grothman**	Y	Y	Y	N	Y	Y
7	**Duffy**						
8	**Gallagher**	Y	Y	Y	N	Y	Y
WYOMING							
AL	**Cheney**	Y	Y	Y	N	Y	Y
DELEGATES							
	Radewagen (A.S.)						
	Norton (D.C.)						
	San Nicolas (Guam)						
	Sablan (N. Marianas)						
	González-Colón (P.R.)						
	Plaskett (V.I.)						

127. HJRES46. National Emergency Disapproval Resolution - Veto Override. Passage, over President Donald Trump's March 15, 2019 veto, of the joint resolution that would terminate the president's Feb. 15 national emergency declaration concerning the security situation at the southern border. Rejected 248-181: R 14-181; D 234-0. *Note: A two-thirds majority of those present and voting (286 in this case) of both chambers is required to override the president's veto. A "nay" was a vote in support of the president's veto.* March 26, 2019.

128. HR1388. Lytton Rancheria Tribe Land Trust - Passage. Grijalva, D-Ariz., motion to suspend the rules and pass the bill that would place 511 acres of land located in Sonoma County, California into a trust for the Lytton Rancheria tribe. The bill would forbid any public hunting on these lands indefinitely and forbid the Interior Department from reviewing the Memorandum of Understanding concerning the trust. Motion agreed to 404-21: R 173-21; D 231-0. *Note: A two-thirds majority of those present and voting (284 in this case) is required for passage under suspension of the rules.* March 26, 2019.

129. HR297. Federal Recognition of the Little Shell Tribe - Passage. Grijalva, D-Ariz., motion to suspend the rules and pass the bill that would federally recognize the Little Shell Tribe of Chippewa Indians of Montana. The bill would require the Department of the Interior to transfer 200 acres of land into a trust where the land would serve as the tribe's base. The bill would allow the tribe to be eligible to receive federal services and benefits, and would require the tribe to submit to the Secretary of State a membership roll consisting of the names of each individual enrolled as a member of the tribe. Motion agreed to 403-21: R 173-20; D 230-1. *Note: A two-thirds majority of those present and voting (283 in this case) is required for passage under suspension of the rules.* March 26, 2019.

130. HRES124, HR7. Gender-Based Pay Discrimination, Transgender Military Ban - Previous Question. Torres, D-Calif., motion to order the previous question (thus ending the debate and possibility of amendment) to the rule that would provide for floor consideration of the Paycheck Fairness Act (HR 7) and the resolution expressing opposition to the president's ban on transgender individuals serving in the armed forces (H Res 124). Motion agreed to 231-192: R 0-192; D 231-0. March 27, 2019.

131. HRES124, HR7. Gender-Based Pay Discrimination, Transgender Military Ban - Rule. Adoption of the rule (H Res 252) that would provide for floor consideration of the Paycheck Fairness Act (HR 7) and the resolution expressing opposition to the president's ban on transgender individuals serving in the armed forces (H Res 124). Adopted 232-190: R 0-190; D 232-0. March 27, 2019.

132. HR7. Gender-Based Pay Discrimination - Small Business Exemption. Beyer, D-Va., amendment that would exempt any employer with fewer than 100 employees from reporting requirements outlined by the bill related to demographically-disaggregated data on employee compensation. Adopted in Committee of the Whole 406-24: R 171-23; D 234-1; I 1-0. March 27, 2019.

		127	128	129	130	131	132
ALABAMA							
1	**Byrne**	N	Y	Y	N	N	Y
2	**Roby**	N	N	N	N	N	Y
3	**Rogers, M.**	N	N	Y	N	N	Y
4	**Aderholt**	N	N	Y	N	N	Y
5	**Brooks, M.**	N	N	N	N	N	Y
6	**Palmer**	N	N	N	N	N	N
7	Sewell	Y	Y	Y	Y	Y	Y
ALASKA							
AL	**Young**	N	Y	Y	N	N	Y
ARIZONA							
1	O'Halleran	Y	Y	Y	Y	Y	Y
2	Kirkpatrick	Y	Y	Y	Y	Y	Y
3	Grijalva	Y	Y	Y	Y	Y	Y
4	**Gosar**	N	Y	N	N	N	N
5	**Biggs**	N	Y	N	N	N	N
6	**Schweikert**	N	Y	N	N	N	N
7	Gallego	Y	Y	Y	Y	Y	Y
8	**Lesko**	N	N	N	N	N	Y
9	Stanton	Y	Y	Y	Y	Y	Y
ARKANSAS							
1	**Crawford**	N	Y	Y	N	N	N
2	**Hill, F.**	N	Y	Y	N	N	Y
3	**Womack**	N	Y	Y	N	N	Y
4	**Westerman**	N	Y	Y	N	N	Y
CALIFORNIA							
1	**LaMalfa**	N	Y	Y	N	N	Y
2	Huffman	Y	Y	Y	Y	Y	Y
3	Garamendi	Y	Y	Y	Y	Y	Y
4	**McClintock**	N	Y	N	N	N	Y
5	Thompson, M.	Y	Y	Y	Y	Y	Y
6	Matsui	Y	Y	Y	Y	Y	Y
7	Bera	Y	Y	Y	Y	Y	Y
8	**Cook**	N	Y	Y	N	N	Y
9	McNerney	Y	Y	Y	Y	Y	Y
10	Harder	Y	Y	Y	Y	Y	Y
11	DeSaulnier	Y	Y	Y	Y	Y	Y
12	Pelosi	Y					
13	Lee B.	Y	Y	Y	Y	Y	Y
14	Speier	?	?	?	Y	Y	Y
15	Swalwell	Y	Y	Y	Y	Y	Y
16	Costa	Y	Y	Y	Y	Y	Y
17	Khanna	Y	Y	Y	Y	Y	Y
18	Eshoo	Y	Y	Y	Y	Y	Y
19	Lofgren	Y	Y	N	Y	Y	Y
20	Panetta	Y	Y	Y	Y	Y	Y
21	Cox	Y	Y	Y	Y	Y	Y
22	**Nunes**	N	Y	Y	N	N	Y
23	**McCarthy**	N	Y	Y	N	N	Y
24	Carbajal	Y	Y	Y	Y	Y	Y
25	Hill, K.	Y	Y	Y	Y	Y	Y
26	Brownley	Y	Y	Y	Y	Y	Y
27	Chu	Y	Y	Y	Y	Y	Y
28	Schiff	Y	Y	Y	Y	Y	Y
29	Cárdenas	Y	Y	Y	Y	Y	Y
30	Sherman	Y	Y	Y	Y	Y	Y
31	Aguilar	Y	Y	Y	Y	Y	Y
32	Napolitano	Y	Y	Y	Y	Y	Y
33	Lieu	Y	Y	Y	Y	Y	Y
34	Gomez	Y	Y	Y	Y	Y	Y
35	Torres	Y	Y	Y	Y	Y	Y
36	Ruiz	Y	Y	Y	Y	Y	Y
37	Bass	Y	Y	Y	Y	Y	Y
38	Sánchez	Y	Y	Y	Y	Y	Y
39	Cisneros	Y	Y	Y	Y	Y	Y
40	Roybal-Allard	Y	Y	Y	Y	Y	Y
41	Takano	Y	Y	Y	Y	Y	Y
42	**Calvert**	N	Y	Y	N	N	Y
43	Waters	Y	Y	Y	Y	Y	N
44	Barragán	Y	Y	Y	Y	Y	Y
45	Porter	Y	Y	Y	Y	Y	Y
46	Correa	Y	Y	Y	Y	Y	Y
47	Lowenthal	Y	Y	Y	Y	Y	Y
48	Rouda	Y	Y	Y	Y	Y	Y
49	Levin	Y	Y	Y	Y	Y	Y
50	**Hunter**	N	Y	Y	N	N	Y
51	Vargas	Y	Y	Y	Y	Y	Y
52	Peters	Y	Y	Y	Y	Y	Y

		127	128	129	130	131	132
53	Davis, S.	Y	Y	Y	Y	Y	Y
COLORADO							
1	DeGette	Y	Y	Y	Y	Y	Y
2	Neguse	Y	Y	Y	Y	Y	Y
3	**Tipton**	N	Y	Y	N	N	Y
4	**Buck**	N	Y	N	N	N	Y
5	**Lamborn**	N	Y	Y	N	N	Y
6	Crow	Y	Y	Y	Y	Y	Y
7	Perlmutter	Y	Y	Y	Y	Y	Y
CONNECTICUT							
1	Larson	Y	Y	Y	Y	Y	Y
2	Courtney	Y	Y	Y	Y	Y	Y
3	DeLauro	Y	Y	Y	Y	Y	Y
4	Himes	Y	Y	Y	+	Y	Y
5	Hayes	Y	Y	Y	Y	Y	Y
DELAWARE							
AL	Blunt Rochester	Y	Y	Y	Y	Y	Y
FLORIDA							
1	**Gaetz**	N	Y	Y	N	N	Y
2	**Dunn**	N	Y	Y	N	N	Y
3	**Yoho**	N	Y	Y	N	N	Y
4	**Rutherford**	N	Y	Y	N	N	Y
5	Lawson	Y	Y	Y	Y	Y	Y
6	**Waltz**	N	Y	Y	N	N	Y
7	Murphy	Y	Y	Y	Y	Y	Y
8	**Posey**	N	Y	N	N	N	Y
9	Soto	Y	Y	Y	Y	Y	Y
10	Demings	Y	Y	Y	Y	Y	Y
11	**Webster**	N	Y	Y	N	N	Y
12	**Bilirakis**	N	Y	Y	N	N	Y
13	Crist	Y	Y	Y	Y	Y	Y
14	Castor	Y	Y	Y	Y	Y	Y
15	**Spano**	N	Y	Y	N	N	Y
16	**Buchanan**	N	Y	Y	N	N	Y
17	**Steube**	N	Y	Y	N	N	Y
18	**Mast**	N	Y	Y	N	N	Y
19	**Rooney**	Y	Y	Y	N	N	Y
20	Hastings	Y	Y	Y	Y	Y	Y
21	Frankel	Y	Y	Y	Y	Y	Y
22	Deutch	Y	?	?	Y	Y	Y
23	Wasserman Schultz	Y	Y	Y	Y	Y	Y
24	Wilson, F.	Y	Y	Y	Y	Y	Y
25	**Diaz-Balart**	N	Y	Y	N	N	Y
26	Mucarsel-Powell	Y	Y	Y	Y	Y	Y
27	Shalala	Y	Y	Y	Y	Y	Y
GEORGIA							
1	**Carter, E.L.**	N	Y	Y	N	N	Y
2	Bishop, S.	Y	Y	Y	Y	Y	Y
3	**Ferguson**	N	Y	Y	N	N	N
4	Johnson, H.	Y	Y	Y	Y	Y	Y
5	Lewis John	Y	Y	Y	Y	Y	Y
6	McBath	Y	Y	Y	Y	Y	Y
7	**Woodall**	N	Y	Y	N	N	Y
8	**Scott, A.**	N	Y	Y	N	N	Y
9	**Collins, D.**	N	Y	Y	N	N	Y
10	**Hice**	N	Y	N	N	N	Y
11	**Loudermilk**	N	Y	Y	N	N	Y
12	**Allen**	N	Y	N	N	N	N
13	Scott, D.	Y	Y	Y	Y	Y	Y
14	**Graves, T.**	N	Y	N	N	N	N
HAWAII							
1	Case	Y	Y	Y	Y	Y	Y
2	Gabbard	Y	Y	Y	Y	Y	Y
IDAHO							
1	**Fulcher**	N	Y	Y	N	N	Y
2	**Simpson**	N	Y	Y	N	N	Y
ILLINOIS							
1	Rush	Y	Y	Y	Y	Y	Y
2	Kelly, R.	Y	Y	Y	Y	Y	Y
3	Lipinski	Y	Y	Y	Y	Y	Y
4	García, J.	Y	Y	Y	Y	Y	Y
5	Quigley	Y	Y	Y	Y	Y	Y
6	Casten	Y	Y	Y	Y	Y	Y
7	Davis, D.	Y	Y	Y	Y	Y	Y
8	Krishnamoorthi	Y	Y	Y	Y	Y	Y
9	Schakowsky	Y	Y	Y	Y	Y	Y
10	Schneider	Y	Y	Y	Y	Y	Y
11	Foster	Y	Y	?	Y	Y	Y

	127	128	129	130	131	132
12 **Bost**	N	Y	Y	N	N	Y
13 **Davis, R.**	N	Y	Y	N	N	Y
14 Underwood	Y	Y	Y	Y	Y	Y
15 **Shimkus**	N	Y	Y	N	N	Y
16 **Kinzinger**	N	Y	Y	N	-	Y
17 Bustos	Y	Y	Y	Y	Y	Y
18 **LaHood**	N	Y	Y	N	N	Y
INDIANA						
1 Visclosky	Y	Y	Y	Y	Y	Y
2 **Walorski**	N	Y	Y	N	N	Y
3 **Banks**	N	Y	Y	N	N	Y
4 **Baird**	N	Y	Y	N	N	Y
5 **Brooks, S.**	N	Y	Y	N	N	Y
6 **Pence**	N	Y	Y	N	N	Y
7 Carson	Y	Y	Y	Y	Y	Y
8 **Bucshon**	N	Y	Y	N	N	Y
9 **Hollingsworth**	N	Y	Y	N	?	Y
IOWA						
1 Finkenauer	Y	Y	Y	Y	Y	Y
2 Loebsack	Y	Y	Y	Y	Y	Y
3 Axne	Y	Y	Y	Y	Y	Y
4 **King, S.**	N	Y	Y	N	N	N
KANSAS						
1 **Marshall**	N	Y	Y	N	N	Y
2 **Watkins**	N	Y	Y	N	N	Y
3 Davids	Y	Y	Y	Y	Y	Y
4 **Estes**	N	Y	Y	N	N	Y
KENTUCKY						
1 **Comer**	N	Y	Y	N	N	Y
2 **Guthrie**	N	Y	Y	N	N	Y
3 Yarmuth	Y	Y	Y	Y	Y	Y
4 **Massie**	Y	Y	Y	N	N	Y
5 **Rogers, H.**	N	Y	Y	N	N	Y
6 **Barr**	N	Y	Y	N	N	Y
LOUISIANA						
1 **Scalise**	N	Y	Y	N	N	Y
2 Richmond	Y	Y	Y	Y	Y	Y
3 **Higgins, C.**	N	Y	Y	N	N	Y
4 **Johnson, M.**	N	Y	Y	N	-	Y
5 **Abraham**	N	Y	Y	N	N	Y
6 **Graves, G.**	N	Y	Y	N	N	Y
MAINE						
1 Pingree	Y	Y	Y	Y	Y	Y
2 Golden	Y	Y	Y	Y	Y	Y
MARYLAND						
1 **Harris**	N	N	N	N	N	Y
2 Ruppersberger	Y	Y	Y	Y	Y	Y
3 Sarbanes	Y	Y	Y	Y	Y	Y
4 Brown, A.	Y	Y	Y	Y	Y	Y
5 Hoyer	Y	Y	Y	Y	Y	Y
6 Trone	Y	Y	Y	Y	Y	Y
7 Cummings	Y	Y	Y	Y	Y	Y
8 Raskin	Y	Y	Y	Y	Y	Y
MASSACHUSETTS						
1 Neal	Y	Y	Y	Y	Y	Y
2 McGovern	Y	Y	Y	Y	Y	Y
3 Trahan	Y	Y	Y	Y	Y	Y
4 Kennedy	Y	Y	Y	Y	Y	Y
5 Clark	Y	Y	Y	Y	Y	Y
6 Moulton	Y	Y	Y	Y	Y	Y
7 Pressley	Y	Y	Y	Y	Y	Y
8 Lynch	Y	Y	Y	Y	Y	Y
9 Keating	Y	Y	Y	Y	Y	Y
MICHIGAN						
1 **Bergman**	N	Y	Y	N	N	Y
2 **Huizenga**	N	Y	Y	N	N	Y
3 **Amash**	Y	N	N	N	N	Y
4 **Moolenaar**	N	Y	Y	N	N	Y
5 Kildee	Y	Y	Y	Y	Y	Y
6 **Upton**	Y	Y	Y	N	N	Y
7 **Walberg**	N	Y	Y	N	N	Y
8 Slotkin	Y	Y	Y	Y	Y	Y
9 Levin	Y	Y	Y	Y	Y	Y
10 **Mitchell**	N	Y	Y	N	N	Y
11 Stevens	Y	Y	Y	Y	Y	Y
12 Dingell	Y	Y	Y	Y	Y	Y
13 Tlaib	Y	Y	Y	Y	Y	Y
14 Lawrence	Y	Y	Y	Y	Y	Y
MINNESOTA						
1 **Hagedorn**	N	Y	Y	N	N	Y
2 Craig	Y	Y	Y	Y	Y	Y
3 Phillips	Y	Y	Y	Y	Y	Y
4 McCollum	Y	Y	Y	Y	Y	Y
5 Omar	Y	Y	Y	Y	Y	Y

	127	128	129	130	131	132
6 **Emmer**	N	Y	Y	N	N	Y
7 Peterson	Y	Y	Y	Y	Y	Y
8 **Stauber**	N	Y	Y	N	N	Y
MISSISSIPPI						
1 **Kelly, T.**	N	Y	Y	N	N	Y
2 Thompson, B.	Y	Y	Y	Y	Y	Y
3 **Guest**	N	Y	Y	N	N	Y
4 **Palazzo**	N	Y	Y	N	N	Y
MISSOURI						
1 Clay	Y	Y	Y	Y	Y	Y
2 **Wagner**	N	Y	Y	N	N	Y
3 **Luetkemeyer**	N	Y	Y	N	N	Y
4 **Hartzler**	N	Y	Y	N	N	Y
5 Cleaver	Y	Y	Y	Y	Y	Y
6 **Graves, S.**	N	Y	Y	N	N	Y
7 **Long**	N	Y	Y	N	N	Y
8 **Smith, J.**	N	Y	Y	N	N	Y
MONTANA						
AL **Gianforte**	N	Y	Y	N	N	Y
NEBRASKA						
1 **Fortenberry**	N	Y	Y	N	N	Y
2 **Bacon**	N	Y	Y	N	N	Y
3 **Smith, Adrian**	N	Y	Y	N	N	Y
NEVADA						
1 Titus	Y	Y	Y	Y	Y	Y
2 **Amodei**	N	Y	Y	?	N	N
3 Lee	Y	Y	Y	Y	Y	Y
4 Horsford	Y	Y	Y	Y	Y	Y
NEW HAMPSHIRE						
1 Pappas	Y	Y	Y	Y	Y	Y
2 Kuster	Y	Y	Y	Y	Y	Y
NEW JERSEY						
1 Norcross	Y	Y	Y	Y	Y	Y
2 Van Drew	Y	Y	Y	Y	Y	Y
3 Kim	Y	Y	Y	Y	Y	Y
4 **Smith, C.**	N	Y	Y	N	N	Y
5 Gottheimer	Y	Y	Y	Y	Y	Y
6 Pallone	Y	Y	Y	Y	Y	Y
7 Malinowski	Y	Y	Y	Y	Y	Y
8 Sires	Y	Y	Y	Y	Y	Y
9 Pascrell	Y	Y	Y	Y	Y	Y
10 Payne	Y	Y	Y	Y	Y	Y
11 Sherrill	Y	Y	Y	Y	Y	Y
12 Watson Coleman	Y	Y	Y	Y	Y	Y
NEW MEXICO						
1 Haaland	Y	Y	Y	Y	Y	Y
2 Torres Small	Y	Y	Y	?	?	Y
3 Luján	Y	Y	Y	Y	Y	Y
NEW YORK						
1 **Zeldin**	N	Y	Y	N	N	Y
2 **King, P.**	N	Y	Y	N	N	Y
3 Suozzi	Y	Y	Y	Y	Y	Y
4 Rice, K.	Y	Y	Y	Y	Y	Y
5 Meeks	Y	Y	Y	Y	Y	Y
6 Meng	Y	Y	Y	?	Y	Y
7 Velázquez	Y	Y	Y	Y	Y	Y
8 Jeffries	Y	Y	Y	Y	Y	Y
9 Clarke	Y	Y	Y	Y	Y	Y
10 Nadler	Y	Y	Y	Y	Y	Y
11 Rose	Y	Y	Y	Y	Y	Y
12 Maloney, C.	Y	Y	Y	Y	Y	Y
13 Espaillat	Y	Y	Y	Y	Y	Y
14 Ocasio-Cortez	Y	Y	Y	Y	Y	Y
15 Serrano	Y	Y	Y	?	Y	Y
16 Engel	Y	Y	Y	Y	Y	Y
17 Lowey	Y	Y	Y	Y	Y	Y
18 Maloney, S.P.	Y	Y	Y	Y	Y	Y
19 Delgado	Y	Y	Y	Y	Y	Y
20 Tonko	Y	Y	Y	Y	Y	Y
21 **Stefanik**	Y	Y	Y	N	N	Y
22 Brindisi	Y	Y	Y	Y	Y	Y
23 **Reed**	N	Y	Y	N	N	Y
24 **Katko**	Y	Y	Y	N	N	Y
25 Morelle	Y	Y	Y	Y	Y	Y
26 Higgins, B.	Y	+	Y	Y	Y	Y
27 **Collins, C.**						
NORTH CAROLINA						
1 Butterfield	Y	Y	Y	Y	Y	Y
2 **Holding**	N	Y	Y	N	N	Y
3 **Jones***						
4 Price	Y	Y	Y	Y	Y	Y
5 **Foxx**	N	Y	Y	N	N	Y
6 **Walker**	N	Y	Y	N	N	N
7 **Rouzer**	N	Y	Y	N	N	N

	127	128	129	130	131	132
8 **Hudson**	N	Y	Y	N	N	Y
9 vacant						
10 **McHenry**	N	Y	Y	N	N	Y
11 **Meadows**	N	Y	N	N	N	Y
12 Adams	Y	Y	Y	Y	Y	Y
13 **Budd**	N	Y	Y	N	N	Y
NORTH DAKOTA						
AL **Armstrong**	N	Y	Y	N	N	Y
OHIO						
1 **Chabot**	N	Y	Y	N	N	Y
2 **Wenstrup**	N	Y	Y	N	N	N
3 Beatty	Y	Y	Y	Y	Y	Y
4 **Jordan**	N	Y	N	N	N	Y
5 **Latta**	N	Y	Y	N	N	Y
6 **Johnson, B.**	N	Y	Y	N	N	Y
7 **Gibbs**	N	Y	Y	N	N	Y
8 **Davidson**	N	N	N	N	N	Y
9 Kaptur	Y	Y	Y	Y	Y	Y
10 **Turner**	N	Y	Y	N	N	Y
11 Fudge	Y	Y	Y	Y	Y	Y
12 **Balderson**	N	Y	Y	N	N	Y
13 Ryan	Y	Y	Y	Y	Y	Y
14 **Joyce**	N	Y	Y	N	N	Y
15 **Stivers**	N	Y	Y	N	N	Y
16 **Gonzalez**	N	Y	Y	N	N	Y
OKLAHOMA						
1 **Hern**	N	Y	Y	N	N	N
2 **Mullin**	N	Y	Y	N	N	Y
3 **Lucas**	N	Y	Y	N	N	Y
4 **Cole**	N	Y	Y	N	N	Y
5 Horn	Y	Y	Y	Y	Y	Y
OREGON						
1 Bonamici	Y	Y	Y	Y	Y	Y
2 **Walden**	Y	Y	Y	N	N	Y
3 Blumenauer	Y	Y	Y	Y	Y	Y
4 DeFazio	Y	Y	Y	Y	Y	Y
5 Schrader	Y	Y	Y	Y	Y	Y
PENNSYLVANIA						
1 **Fitzpatrick**	Y	Y	Y	N	N	Y
2 Boyle	Y	Y	Y	Y	Y	Y
3 Evans	Y	Y	Y	Y	Y	Y
4 Dean	Y	Y	Y	Y	Y	Y
5 Scanlon	Y	Y	Y	Y	Y	Y
6 Houlahan	Y	Y	Y	Y	Y	Y
7 Wild	Y	Y	Y	Y	Y	Y
8 Cartwright	Y	Y	Y	Y	Y	Y
9 **Meuser**	N	Y	N	N	N	Y
10 **Perry**	N	Y	Y	N	N	Y
11 **Smucker**	N	Y	Y	N	N	Y
12 **Marino***						
13 **Joyce**	N	Y	Y	N	N	Y
14 **Reschenthaler**	N	?	?	N	N	Y
15 **Thompson, G.**	N	Y	Y	N	N	Y
16 **Kelly, M.**	N	Y	Y	N	N	Y
17 Lamb	Y	Y	Y	Y	Y	Y
18 Doyle	Y	Y	Y	Y	Y	Y
RHODE ISLAND						
1 Cicilline	Y	Y	Y	Y	Y	Y
2 Langevin	Y	Y	Y	Y	Y	Y
SOUTH CAROLINA						
1 Cunningham	Y	Y	Y	Y	Y	Y
2 **Wilson, J.**	-	+	+	-	-	+
3 **Duncan**	N	Y	Y	N	N	Y
4 **Timmons**	N	Y	Y	N	N	Y
5 **Norman**	N	N	Y	N	N	N
6 Clyburn	Y	Y	Y	Y	Y	Y
7 **Rice, T.**	N	N	Y	N	N	N
SOUTH DAKOTA						
AL **Johnson**	Y	Y	Y	N	N	Y
TENNESSEE						
1 **Roe**	N	Y	Y	N	N	Y
2 **Burchett**	N	N	N	N	N	N
3 **Fleischmann**	N	Y	Y	N	N	Y
4 **DesJarlais**	N	Y	Y	?	?	?
5 Cooper	Y	Y	Y	Y	Y	Y
6 **Rose**	N	Y	Y	N	N	Y
7 **Green**	N	Y	Y	N	N	Y
8 **Kustoff**	N	Y	Y	N	N	Y
9 Cohen	Y	Y	Y	Y	Y	Y
TEXAS						
1 **Gohmert**	N	N	N	N	N	Y
2 **Crenshaw**	N	Y	Y	N	N	Y
3 **Taylor**	N	Y	Y	N	N	Y
4 **Ratcliffe**	N	Y	Y	N	N	N

	127	128	129	130	131	132
5 **Gooden**	N	Y	Y	N	N	Y
6 **Wright**	N	Y	N	N	N	Y
7 Fletcher	Y	Y	Y	Y	Y	Y
8 **Brady**	N	Y	Y	N	N	Y
9 Green, A.	Y	Y	Y	Y	Y	Y
10 **McCaul**	N	Y	Y	N	N	Y
11 **Conaway**	N	Y	Y	N	N	Y
12 **Granger**	-	+	+	-	-	+
13 **Thornberry**	N	Y	Y	N	N	Y
14 **Weber**	N	N	N	N	N	Y
15 Gonzalez	Y	Y	Y	Y	Y	Y
16 Escobar	Y	Y	Y	Y	Y	Y
17 **Flores**	N	Y	Y	N	N	Y
18 Jackson Lee	Y	Y	Y	Y	Y	Y
19 **Arrington**	N	Y	Y	N	N	Y
20 Castro	Y	Y	Y	Y	Y	Y
21 **Roy**	N	N	N	N	N	N
22 **Olson**	N	Y	Y	N	N	Y
23 **Hurd**	Y	Y	Y	N	N	Y
24 **Marchant**	N	Y	Y	N	N	Y
25 **Williams**	N	Y	Y	N	N	Y
26 **Burgess**	N	N	Y	N	N	Y
27 **Cloud**	N	N	N	N	N	Y
28 Cuellar	Y	Y	Y	Y	Y	Y
29 Garcia, S.	Y	Y	Y	Y	Y	Y
30 Johnson, E.B.	Y	Y	Y	Y	Y	Y
31 **Carter, J.**	N	Y	Y	N	N	N
32 Allred	Y	Y	Y	Y	Y	Y
33 Veasey	Y	Y	Y	Y	Y	Y
34 Vela	Y	Y	Y	Y	Y	Y
35 Doggett	Y	Y	Y	Y	Y	Y
36 **Babin**	N	N	Y	N	N	N
UTAH						
1 **Bishop, R.**	N	N	Y	N	N	Y
2 **Stewart**	N	Y	Y	N	N	Y
3 **Curtis**	N	Y	Y	N	N	Y
4 McAdams	Y	Y	Y	Y	Y	Y
VERMONT						
AL Welch	Y	Y	Y	Y	Y	Y
VIRGINIA						
1 **Wittman**	N	Y	Y	-	-	?
2 Luria	Y	Y	Y	Y	Y	Y
3 Scott, R.	Y	Y	Y	Y	Y	Y
4 McEachin	Y	Y	Y	Y	Y	Y
5 **Riggleman**	N	Y	Y	N	N	N
6 **Cline**	N	Y	N	N	N	Y
7 Spanberger	Y	Y	Y	Y	Y	Y
8 Beyer	Y	Y	Y	Y	Y	Y
9 **Griffith**	N	Y	Y	N	N	Y
10 Wexton	Y	Y	Y	Y	Y	Y
11 Connolly	Y	Y	Y	Y	Y	Y
WASHINGTON						
1 DelBene	Y	Y	Y	Y	Y	Y
2 Larsen	Y	Y	Y	Y	Y	Y
3 **Herrera Beutler**	Y	Y	Y	N	N	Y
4 **Newhouse**	N	Y	Y	N	N	Y
5 **McMorris Rodgers**	Y	Y	Y	N	N	Y
6 Kilmer	Y	Y	Y	Y	Y	Y
7 Jayapal	Y	Y	Y	Y	Y	Y
8 Schrier	Y	Y	Y	Y	Y	Y
9 Smith Adam	Y	Y	Y	Y	Y	Y
10 Heck	Y	Y	Y	Y	Y	Y
WEST VIRGINIA						
1 **McKinley**	N	Y	Y	N	N	Y
2 **Mooney**	N	N	N	N	N	N
3 **Miller**	N	Y	Y	N	N	Y
WISCONSIN						
1 **Steil**	N	Y	Y	N	N	Y
2 Pocan	Y	Y	Y	Y	Y	Y
3 Kind	Y	Y	Y	Y	Y	Y
4 Moore	Y	Y	Y	Y	Y	Y
5 **Sensenbrenner**	Y	Y	Y	N	N	Y
6 **Grothman**	N	N	Y	N	N	Y
7 **Duffy**						
8 **Gallagher**	Y	Y	Y	N	N	Y
WYOMING						
AL **Cheney**	N	Y	Y	N	N	Y
DELEGATES						
Radewagen (A.S.)						?
Norton (D.C.)						Y
San Nicolas (Guam)						?
Sablan (N. Marianas)						Y
González-Colón (P.R.)						Y
Plaskett (V.I.)						?

||| HOUSE VOTES

133. HR7. Gender-Based Pay Discrimination - Recommit. Foxx, R-N.C., motion to recommit the bill to the House Education and Labor Committee with instructions to report it back immediately with an amendment that would specify that any contingent attorney's fees should not exceed more than 49 percent of a judgment awarded to a client in any legal action brought to enforce the provisions of the bill. Motion rejected 191-236: R 191-2; D 0-234. March 27, 2019.

134. HR7. Gender-Based Pay Discrimination - Passage. Passage of the bill, as amended, that would change the language and grounds that an employer could use in a legal defense to explain a difference in pay between employees when a lawsuit is brought against the employer alleging pay discrimination on the basis of sex. The bill would narrow the defense such an employer could use by requiring employers to provide non-gender, business-based reasons for differences in pay, rather than allowing the employer to demonstrate in court that "any factor other than sex" had been the basis for the pay disparity. Under the bill, an employer would specifically need to demonstrate that the disparity is based on a bona fide factor such as education, training or experience. It would expand protections for employees against forms of retaliation and increase monetary penalties for violating the Fair Labor Standards Act. The bill would require the Department of Labor, in consultation with the Department of Education, to establish grants to implement negotiation skills training programs under the measure. The bill would require the Secretary of Labor to conduct studies regarding ways to eliminate pay discrepancies between men and women. It would require the Equal Employment Opportunity Commission to collect compensation and other employment-related data disaggregated by the sex, race, and national origin of employees, and would require the Bureau of Labor Statistics to continue to collect data on women workers. It would amend the Fair Labor Standards Act to include language that would prohibit an employer from relying on wage history for hiring purposes or pay determination, and would implement penalties for violations. The Department of Labor and the Equal Employment Opportunity Commission would be required to provide assistance material to small businesses. Additionally, certain small businesses would be exempt from certain requirements in the measure. Passed 242-187: R 7-187; D 235-0. March 27, 2019.

135. HRES124. Transgender Military Ban - Passage. Adoption of the resolution that would express that the House of Representatives opposes the president's ban on transgender individuals serving in the armed forces. The resolution would reject "the flawed scientific and medical claims upon which [the ban] is based" and would strongly urge the Defense Department not to implement the ban. Passed 238-185: R 5-185; D 233-0. March 28, 2019.

136. Procedural Motion - Journal. Approval of the House Journal of March 28, 2019. Approved 216-179: R 45-128; D 171-51. March 28, 2019.

137. HR1593. School Terrorism Threat Readiness - Passage. Thompson, D-Miss., motion to suspend the rules and pass the bill, as amended, that would require the Department of Homeland Security to create a council, known as the School Safety Coordinating Council, that would coordinate and implement activities, plans, and policies intended to enhance primary and secondary schools' responses to acts of terrorism. Motion agreed to 384-18: R 168-18; D 216-0. *Note: A two-thirds majority of those present and voting (268 in this case) is required for passage under suspension of the rules.* April 1, 2019.

138. HR1590. Foreign Fighter Threat Exercise - Passage. Thompson, D-Miss., motion to suspend the rules and pass the bill, as amended, that would require the Federal Emergency Management Agency to develop and conduct an exercise related to the detection and prevention of terrorist and foreign fighter travel. The exercise scenario would be required to involve a person traveling from the U.S. to join or provide resources to a terrorist organization, and it would be required to involve terrorist infiltration into the United States by U.S. citizens and foreign nationals. The exercise would be required to involve coordination with appropriate federal departments and agencies as well as the private sector and community stakeholders. The bill would require the Secretary of Homeland Security to submit a report to Congress detailing the initial findings of the exercise, plans for future incorporation of the findings, and any proposed legislative changes. Motion agreed to 394-7: R 183-3; D 211-4. *Note: A two-thirds majority of those present and voting (268 in this case) is required for passage under suspension of the rules.* April 1, 2019.

	133	134	135	136	137	138
ALABAMA						
1 Byrne	Y	N	N	N	Y	Y
2 Roby	Y	N	N	N	Y	Y
3 Rogers, M.	Y	N	N	N	Y	Y
4 Aderholt	Y	N	N	Y	Y	Y
5 Brooks, M.	Y	N	N	N	N	Y
6 Palmer	Y	N	N	N	Y	Y
7 Sewell	N	Y	Y	N	Y	Y
ALASKA						
AL Young	Y	N	N	N	Y	Y
ARIZONA						
1 O'Halleran	N	Y	Y	N	Y	Y
2 Kirkpatrick	N	Y	Y	N	Y	Y
3 Grijalva	N	Y	Y	Y	?	?
4 Gosar	Y	N	N	N	N	Y
5 Biggs	Y	N	N	N	N	Y
6 Schweikert	Y	N	N	Y	Y	Y
7 Gallego	N	Y	Y	Y	Y	Y
8 Lesko	Y	N	N	N	Y	Y
9 Stanton	N	Y	Y	Y	Y	Y
ARKANSAS						
1 Crawford	Y	N	N	N	Y	Y
2 Hill, F.	Y	N	N	N	Y	Y
3 Womack	Y	N	N	N	Y	Y
4 Westerman	Y	N	N	N	Y	Y
CALIFORNIA						
1 LaMalfa	Y	N	N	N	Y	Y
2 Huffman	N	Y	Y	Y	Y	Y
3 Garamendi	N	Y	Y	Y	Y	Y
4 McClintock	Y	N	N	Y	Y	Y
5 Thompson, M.	N	Y	Y	N	Y	Y
6 Matsui	N	Y	Y	N	Y	Y
7 Bera	N	Y	Y	N	Y	Y
8 Cook	Y	N	N	N	Y	Y
9 McNerney	N	Y	Y	Y	Y	Y
10 Harder	N	Y	Y	N	Y	Y
11 DeSaulnier	N	Y	Y	Y	Y	Y
12 Pelosi		Y	Y			
13 Lee B.	N	Y	Y	Y	Y	Y
14 Speier	N	Y	Y	Y	Y	Y
15 Swalwell	N	Y	Y	Y	+	+
16 Costa	N	Y	Y	N	Y	Y
17 Khanna	N	Y	Y	Y	Y	Y
18 Eshoo	N	Y	Y	Y	Y	Y
19 Lofgren	N	Y	Y	Y	Y	Y
20 Panetta	N	Y	Y	N	Y	Y
21 Cox	N	Y	Y	N	Y	Y
22 Nunes	Y	N	N	N	Y	Y
23 McCarthy	Y	N	N	Y	Y	Y
24 Carbajal	N	Y	Y	Y	Y	Y
25 Hill, K.	N	Y	Y	Y	Y	Y
26 Brownley	N	Y	Y	?	Y	Y
27 Chu	N	Y	Y	Y	Y	Y
28 Schiff	N	Y	Y	Y	Y	Y
29 Cárdenas	N	Y	Y	Y	Y	Y
30 Sherman	N	Y	Y	Y	Y	Y
31 Aguilar	N	Y	Y	N	Y	Y
32 Napolitano	N	Y	Y	Y	Y	Y
33 Lieu	N	Y	Y	Y	Y	Y
34 Gomez	N	Y	Y	Y	Y	Y
35 Torres	N	Y	Y	?	Y	Y
36 Ruiz	N	Y	Y	N	Y	Y
37 Bass	N	Y	Y	Y	Y	Y
38 Sánchez	N	Y	Y	Y	Y	Y
39 Cisneros	N	Y	Y	N	Y	Y
40 Roybal-Allard	N	Y	Y	Y	Y	Y
41 Takano	N	Y	Y	Y	Y	Y
42 Calvert	Y	N	N	N	Y	Y
43 Waters	N	Y	Y	Y	Y	Y
44 Barragán	N	Y	Y	Y	Y	Y
45 Porter	N	Y	Y	N	Y	Y
46 Correa	N	Y	Y	N	?	?
47 Lowenthal	N	Y	Y	Y	Y	Y
48 Rouda	N	Y	Y	N	Y	Y
49 Levin	N	Y	Y	Y	Y	Y
50 Hunter	Y	N	N	N	N	Y
51 Vargas	N	Y	Y	Y	Y	Y
52 Peters	N	Y	Y	?	Y	Y

	133	134	135	136	137	138
53 Davis, S.	N	Y	Y	Y	Y	Y
COLORADO						
1 DeGette	N	Y	Y	Y	Y	Y
2 Neguse	N	Y	Y	Y	Y	Y
3 Tipton	Y	N	N	Y	Y	Y
4 Buck	Y	N	N	N	Y	Y
5 Lamborn	Y	N	N	N	Y	Y
6 Crow	N	Y	Y	N	Y	Y
7 Perlmutter	N	Y	Y	Y	Y	Y
CONNECTICUT						
1 Larson	N	Y	Y	Y	Y	Y
2 Courtney	N	Y	Y	Y	Y	Y
3 DeLauro	N	Y	Y	?	Y	Y
4 Himes	N	Y	Y	Y	Y	Y
5 Hayes	N	Y	Y	Y	Y	Y
DELAWARE						
AL Blunt Rochester	N	Y	Y	Y	Y	Y
FLORIDA						
1 Gaetz	N	N	N	?	N	Y
2 Dunn	Y	N	N	N	Y	Y
3 Yoho	Y	N	N	?	?	?
4 Rutherford	Y	N	N	Y	+	+
5 Lawson	N	Y	Y	?	?	?
6 Waltz	Y	N	N	N	Y	Y
7 Murphy	N	Y	Y	Y	Y	Y
8 Posey	Y	N	N	N	+	+
9 Soto	N	Y	Y	Y	Y	Y
10 Demings	N	Y	Y	Y	Y	Y
11 Webster	Y	N	N	?	Y	Y
12 Bilirakis	Y	N	N	N	Y	Y
13 Crist	N	Y	Y	Y	Y	Y
14 Castor	N	Y	Y	Y	Y	Y
15 Spano	Y	N	N	N	Y	Y
16 Buchanan	Y	N	N	?	Y	Y
17 Steube	Y	N	N	N	N	Y
18 Mast	Y	N	N	?	?	?
19 Rooney	Y	N	N	?	?	?
20 Hastings	N	Y	Y	Y	Y	Y
21 Frankel	N	Y	Y	Y	Y	Y
22 Deutch	N	Y	Y	Y	Y	Y
23 Wasserman Schultz	N	Y	Y	Y	Y	Y
24 Wilson, F.	N	Y	Y	Y	Y	Y
25 Diaz-Balart	Y	Y	+	?	Y	Y
26 Mucarsel-Powell	N	Y	Y	N	Y	Y
27 Shalala	N	Y	Y	Y	Y	Y
GEORGIA						
1 Carter, E.L.	Y	N	N	N	Y	Y
2 Bishop, S.	N	Y	Y	Y	Y	Y
3 Ferguson	Y	N	N	N	Y	Y
4 Johnson, H.	N	Y	Y	Y	Y	Y
5 Lewis John	N	Y	Y	Y	Y	Y
6 McBath	N	Y	Y	Y	Y	Y
7 Woodall	Y	N	N	N	Y	Y
8 Scott, A.	Y	N	N	Y	Y	Y
9 Collins, D.	Y	N	N	?	?	?
10 Hice	Y	N	N	N	Y	Y
11 Loudermilk	Y	N	N	N	N	Y
12 Allen	Y	N	N	N	Y	Y
13 Scott, D.	N	Y	Y	Y	Y	Y
14 Graves, T.	Y	N	N	N	Y	Y
HAWAII						
1 Case	N	Y	Y	Y	Y	Y
2 Gabbard	N	Y	Y	?	?	?
IDAHO						
1 Fulcher	Y	N	N	N	Y	Y
2 Simpson	Y	Y	N	?	Y	Y
ILLINOIS						
1 Rush	N	Y	Y	Y	?	?
2 Kelly, R.	N	Y	Y	Y	Y	Y
3 Lipinski	N	Y	Y	Y	Y	Y
4 García, J.	N	Y	Y	Y	Y	Y
5 Quigley	N	Y	Y	Y	Y	Y
6 Casten	N	Y	Y	Y	Y	Y
7 Davis, D.	N	Y	Y	Y	?	?
8 Krishnamoorthi	N	Y	Y	Y	Y	Y
9 Schakowsky	N	Y	Y	Y	Y	Y
10 Schneider	N	Y	Y	Y	Y	Y
11 Foster	N	Y	Y	Y	Y	Y

KEY: Republicans — Democrats — *Independents*

Y	Voted for (yea)	N	Voted against (nay)	P	Voted "present"
+	Announced for	–	Announced against	?	Did not vote or otherwise make position known
#	Paired for	X	Paired against		

		133	134	135	136	137	138
12	**Bost**	Y	N	N	N	Y	Y
13	**Davis, R.**	Y	Y	N	N	Y	Y
14	Underwood	N	Y	Y	Y	Y	Y
15	**Shimkus**	Y	N	N	N	?	?
16	**Kinzinger**	Y	N	N	Y	Y	Y
17	Bustos	N	Y	Y	Y	Y	Y
18	**LaHood**	Y	N	N	N	Y	Y
INDIANA							
1	Visclosky	N	Y	Y	Y	Y	Y
2	**Walorski**	Y	N	N	?	Y	Y
3	**Banks**	Y	N	N	Y	Y	Y
4	**Baird**	Y	N	N	Y	Y	Y
5	**Brooks, S.**	Y	N	N	N	Y	Y
6	**Pence**	Y	N	N	Y	Y	Y
7	Carson	N	Y	Y	Y	Y	Y
8	**Bucshon**	Y	N	N	N	Y	Y
9	**Hollingsworth**	Y	N	Y	Y	Y	Y
IOWA							
1	Finkenauer	N	Y	Y	Y	Y	Y
2	Loebsack	N	Y	Y	Y	?	?
3	Axne	N	Y	Y	N	Y	Y
4	**King, S.**	Y	N	N	Y	Y	Y
KANSAS							
1	**Marshall**	Y	N	N	?	Y	Y
2	**Watkins**	Y	N	N	Y	Y	Y
3	Davids	N	Y	Y	N	Y	Y
4	**Estes**	Y	N	N	N	Y	Y
KENTUCKY							
1	**Comer**	Y	N	N	N	Y	Y
2	**Guthrie**	Y	N	N	N	Y	Y
3	Yarmuth	N	Y	Y	?	Y	Y
4	**Massie**	Y	N	N	N	N	N
5	**Rogers, H.**	Y	N	N	N	Y	Y
6	**Barr**	Y	N	N	Y	Y	Y
LOUISIANA							
1	**Scalise**	Y	N	N	N	Y	Y
2	Richmond	N	Y	Y	Y	Y	Y
3	**Higgins, C.**	Y	N	N	N	Y	Y
4	**Johnson, M.**	Y	N	N	N	Y	Y
5	**Abraham**	Y	N	?	?	?	?
6	**Graves, G.**	Y	N	N	N	Y	Y
MAINE							
1	Pingree	N	Y	Y	Y	Y	Y
2	Golden	N	Y	Y	N	Y	Y
MARYLAND							
1	**Harris**	Y	N	N	N	N	Y
2	Ruppersberger	N	Y	Y	Y	Y	Y
3	Sarbanes	N	Y	Y	Y	Y	Y
4	Brown, A.	N	Y	Y	Y	Y	Y
5	Hoyer	N	Y	Y	Y	Y	Y
6	Trone	N	Y	Y	Y	?	?
7	Cummings	N	Y	Y	N	Y	Y
8	Raskin	N	Y	Y	Y	Y	Y
MASSACHUSETTS							
1	Neal	N	Y	Y	Y	Y	Y
2	McGovern	N	Y	Y	Y	Y	Y
3	Trahan	N	Y	Y	Y	Y	Y
4	Kennedy	N	Y	Y	Y	Y	Y
5	Clark	N	Y	Y	Y	Y	Y
6	Moulton	N	Y	Y	Y	Y	Y
7	Pressley	N	Y	Y	Y	Y	N
8	Lynch	N	Y	Y	Y	Y	Y
9	Keating	N	Y	Y	Y	Y	Y
MICHIGAN							
1	**Bergman**	Y	N	N	Y	Y	Y
2	**Huizenga**	Y	N	N	N	Y	Y
3	**Amash**	N	N	P	N	N	N
4	**Moolenaar**	Y	N	N	N	Y	Y
5	Kildee	N	Y	Y	Y	Y	Y
6	**Upton**	Y	N	N	N	Y	Y
7	**Walberg**	Y	N	N	N	Y	Y
8	Slotkin	N	Y	Y	Y	Y	Y
9	Levin	N	Y	Y	Y	Y	Y
10	**Mitchell**	Y	N	N	N	Y	Y
11	Stevens	N	Y	Y	N	Y	Y
12	Dingell	N	Y	Y	Y	Y	Y
13	Tlaib	N	Y	Y	Y	Y	N
14	Lawrence	N	Y	Y	Y	Y	Y
MINNESOTA							
1	**Hagedorn**	Y	N	N	N	Y	Y
2	Craig	N	Y	Y	N	Y	Y
3	Phillips	N	Y	Y	Y	Y	Y
4	McCollum	N	Y	Y	Y	Y	Y
5	Omar	N	Y	Y	Y	Y	N

		133	134	135	136	137	138
6	**Emmer**	Y	N	N	N	Y	Y
7	Peterson	N	Y	Y	N	Y	Y
8	**Stauber**	Y	N	N	Y	Y	Y
MISSISSIPPI							
1	**Kelly, T.**	Y	N	N	N	Y	Y
2	Thompson, B.	N	Y	Y	Y	Y	Y
3	**Guest**	Y	N	N	N	Y	Y
4	**Palazzo**	Y	N	-	-	+	Y
MISSOURI							
1	Clay	N	Y	Y	Y	Y	Y
2	**Wagner**	Y	N	N	?	Y	Y
3	**Luetkemeyer**	Y	N	N	N	Y	Y
4	**Hartzler**	Y	N	N	N	Y	Y
5	Cleaver	N	Y	Y	Y	+	+
6	**Graves, S.**	Y	N	N	N	Y	Y
7	**Long**	Y	N	N	Y	Y	Y
8	**Smith, J.**	Y	N	N	N	Y	Y
MONTANA							
AL	**Gianforte**	Y	N	N	Y	Y	Y
NEBRASKA							
1	**Fortenberry**	Y	N	N	Y	Y	Y
2	**Bacon**	Y	N	N	Y	Y	Y
3	**Smith, Adrian**	Y	N	N	N	Y	Y
NEVADA							
1	Titus	N	Y	Y	Y	Y	Y
2	**Amodei**	Y	N	N	Y	Y	Y
3	Lee	N	Y	Y	Y	Y	Y
4	Horsford	N	Y	Y	Y	Y	Y
NEW HAMPSHIRE							
1	Pappas	N	Y	Y	N	Y	Y
2	Kuster	N	Y	Y	Y	Y	Y
NEW JERSEY							
1	Norcross	N	Y	Y	Y	Y	Y
2	Van Drew	N	Y	Y	N	Y	Y
3	Kim	N	Y	Y	N	Y	Y
4	**Smith, C.**	Y	Y	N	Y	Y	Y
5	Gottheimer	N	Y	Y	N	Y	Y
6	Pallone	N	Y	Y	Y	Y	Y
7	Malinowski	N	Y	Y	Y	Y	Y
8	Sires	N	Y	Y	Y	?	?
9	Pascrell	N	Y	Y	Y	Y	Y
10	Payne	N	Y	Y	Y	Y	Y
11	Sherrill	N	Y	Y	N	Y	Y
12	Watson Coleman	N	Y	Y	N	Y	Y
NEW MEXICO							
1	Haaland	N	Y	Y	Y	Y	Y
2	Torres Small	N	Y	Y	Y	Y	Y
3	Luján	N	Y	Y	Y	?	?
NEW YORK							
1	**Zeldin**	Y	N	N	N	Y	Y
2	**King, P.**	Y	N	N	Y	Y	Y
3	Suozzi	N	Y	Y	N	Y	Y
4	Rice, K.	N	Y	Y	N	Y	Y
5	Meeks	N	Y	Y	Y	?	?
6	Meng	N	Y	Y	N	Y	Y
7	Velázquez	N	Y	Y	Y	Y	Y
8	Jeffries	N	Y	Y	Y	?	?
9	Clarke	N	Y	Y	Y	Y	Y
10	Nadler	N	Y	Y	Y	Y	Y
11	Rose	N	Y	Y	N	Y	Y
12	Maloney, C.	N	Y	Y	Y	Y	Y
13	Espaillat	N	Y	Y	Y	Y	Y
14	Ocasio-Cortez	N	Y	Y	Y	Y	N
15	Serrano	N	Y	Y	Y	Y	Y
16	Engel	N	Y	Y	Y	Y	Y
17	Lowey	N	Y	Y	Y	Y	Y
18	Maloney, S.P.	N	Y	Y	N	Y	Y
19	Delgado	N	Y	Y	Y	Y	Y
20	Tonko	N	Y	Y	P	Y	Y
21	**Stefanik**	Y	N	N	?	Y	Y
22	Brindisi	N	Y	Y	N	Y	Y
23	**Reed**	Y	Y	Y	N	?	?
24	**Katko**	Y	N	Y	N	Y	Y
25	Morelle	N	Y	Y	Y	Y	Y
26	Higgins, B.	N	Y	Y	?	Y	Y
27	**Collins, C.**						
NORTH CAROLINA							
1	Butterfield	N	Y	Y	Y	Y	?
2	**Holding**	Y	N	N	N	Y	Y
3	**Jones***						
4	Price	N	Y	Y	Y	Y	Y
5	**Foxx**	Y	N	N	N	Y	Y
6	**Walker**	Y	N	N	?	Y	Y
7	**Rouzer**	Y	N	N	N	Y	Y

		133	134	135	136	137	138
8	**Hudson**	Y	N	N	Y	Y	Y
9	vacant						
10	**McHenry**	Y	N	N	N	Y	Y
11	**Meadows**	Y	N	N	Y	Y	Y
12	Adams	N	Y	Y	Y	Y	Y
13	**Budd**	Y	N	N	Y	Y	Y
NORTH DAKOTA							
AL	**Armstrong**	Y	N	N	Y	Y	Y
OHIO							
1	**Chabot**	Y	N	N	N	Y	Y
2	**Wenstrup**	Y	N	N	Y	Y	Y
3	Beatty	N	Y	Y	Y	Y	Y
4	**Jordan**	Y	N	N	N	Y	Y
5	**Latta**	Y	N	N	N	Y	Y
6	**Johnson, B.**	Y	N	N	N	Y	Y
7	**Gibbs**	Y	N	N	N	Y	Y
8	**Davidson**	Y	N	N	N	N	Y
9	Kaptur	N	Y	Y	Y	Y	Y
10	**Turner**	Y	N	N	N	Y	Y
11	Fudge	N	Y	Y	N	Y	Y
12	**Balderson**	Y	N	N	N	Y	Y
13	Ryan	N	Y	+	?	?	?
14	**Joyce**	Y	N	N	N	Y	Y
15	**Stivers**	Y	N	N	Y	Y	Y
16	**Gonzalez**	Y	N	N	N	Y	Y
OKLAHOMA							
1	**Hern**	Y	N	N	N	Y	Y
2	**Mullin**	Y	N	N	N	Y	Y
3	**Lucas**	Y	N	N	N	Y	Y
4	**Cole**	Y	N	N	N	Y	Y
5	Horn	N	Y	Y	Y	Y	Y
OREGON							
1	Bonamici	N	Y	Y	Y	Y	Y
2	**Walden**	Y	N	N	N	Y	Y
3	Blumenauer	N	Y	Y	Y	Y	Y
4	DeFazio	N	Y	Y	N	Y	Y
5	Schrader	N	Y	Y	N	Y	Y
PENNSYLVANIA							
1	**Fitzpatrick**	Y	Y	Y	N	Y	Y
2	Boyle	N	Y	Y	Y	?	?
3	Evans	N	Y	Y	Y	Y	Y
4	Dean	N	Y	Y	Y	Y	Y
5	Scanlon	N	Y	Y	Y	Y	Y
6	Houlahan	N	Y	Y	Y	Y	Y
7	Wild	N	Y	Y	N	Y	Y
8	Cartwright	N	Y	Y	Y	Y	Y
9	**Meuser**	Y	N	N	N	Y	Y
10	**Perry**	Y	N	N	Y	Y	Y
11	**Smucker**	Y	N	N	N	Y	?
12	**Marino***						
13	**Joyce**	Y	N	N	N	Y	Y
14	**Reschenthaler**	Y	N	N	Y	Y	Y
15	**Thompson, G.**	Y	N	N	N	Y	Y
16	**Kelly, M.**	Y	N	N	Y	Y	Y
17	Lamb	N	Y	Y	?	Y	Y
18	Doyle	N	Y	Y	Y	Y	Y
RHODE ISLAND							
1	Cicilline	N	Y	Y	Y	Y	Y
2	Langevin	N	Y	Y	Y	Y	Y
SOUTH CAROLINA							
1	Cunningham	N	Y	Y	N	Y	Y
2	**Wilson, J.**	+	-	-	+	Y	Y
3	**Duncan**	Y	N	N	N	Y	Y
4	**Timmons**	Y	N	N	N	Y	Y
5	**Norman**	Y	N	N	N	Y	Y
6	Clyburn	N	Y	Y	Y	Y	Y
7	**Rice, T.**	Y	N	N	?	Y	Y
SOUTH DAKOTA							
AL	**Johnson**	Y	N	N	N	Y	Y
TENNESSEE							
1	**Roe**	Y	N	N	N	Y	Y
2	**Burchett**	Y	N	N	N	Y	Y
3	**Fleischmann**	Y	N	N	Y	Y	Y
4	**DesJarlais**	?	?	?	?	Y	Y
5	Cooper	N	Y	Y	Y	Y	Y
6	**Rose**	Y	N	N	N	Y	Y
7	**Green**	Y	N	N	?	Y	Y
8	**Kustoff**	Y	N	N	N	Y	Y
9	Cohen	N	Y	Y	Y	Y	Y
TEXAS							
1	**Gohmert**	Y	N	N	?	N	Y
2	**Crenshaw**	Y	N	N	N	Y	Y
3	**Taylor**	Y	N	N	Y	Y	Y
4	**Ratcliffe**	Y	N	N	?	N	Y

		133	134	135	136	137	138
5	**Gooden**	Y	N	N	N	Y	Y
6	**Wright**	Y	N	N	N	Y	Y
7	Fletcher	N	Y	Y	N	Y	Y
8	**Brady**	Y	N	N	Y	Y	Y
9	Green, A.	N	Y	Y	?	Y	Y
10	**McCaul**	Y	N	N	N	Y	Y
11	**Conaway**	Y	N	N	N	N	Y
12	**Granger**	+	-	-	+	Y	Y
13	**Thornberry**	Y	N	N	Y	Y	Y
14	**Weber**	Y	N	N	N	Y	Y
15	Gonzalez	N	Y	Y	Y	+	+
16	Escobar	N	Y	Y	Y	Y	Y
17	**Flores**	Y	N	N	N	Y	Y
18	Jackson Lee	N	Y	Y	Y	Y	Y
19	**Arrington**	Y	N	N	Y	Y	Y
20	Castro	N	Y	Y	Y	Y	Y
21	**Roy**	Y	N	N	N	N	N
22	**Olson**	Y	N	N	N	Y	Y
23	**Hurd**	Y	Y	Y	N	Y	Y
24	**Marchant**	Y	N	N	?	N	Y
25	**Williams**	Y	N	N	N	Y	Y
26	**Burgess**	Y	N	N	N	N	Y
27	**Cloud**	Y	N	N	N	Y	Y
28	Cuellar	N	Y	Y	N	Y	Y
29	Garcia, S.	N	Y	Y	Y	Y	Y
30	Johnson, E.B.	N	Y	Y	Y	Y	Y
31	**Carter, J.**	Y	N	N	N	Y	Y
32	Allred	N	Y	Y	N	Y	Y
33	Veasey	N	Y	?	?	Y	Y
34	Vela	N	Y	Y	Y	Y	Y
35	Doggett	N	Y	Y	Y	Y	Y
36	**Babin**	Y	N	N	?	Y	Y
UTAH							
1	**Bishop, R.**	Y	N	N	N	Y	Y
2	**Stewart**	Y	N	N	Y	Y	Y
3	**Curtis**	Y	N	N	Y	Y	Y
4	McAdams	N	Y	Y	N	Y	Y
VERMONT							
AL	Welch	N	Y	Y	Y	Y	Y
VIRGINIA							
1	**Wittman**	Y	N	N	N	Y	Y
2	Luria	N	Y	Y	Y	Y	Y
3	Scott, R.	N	Y	Y	Y	Y	Y
4	McEachin	N	Y	Y	Y	+	+
5	**Riggleman**	Y	N	N	N	Y	Y
6	**Cline**	Y	N	N	N	Y	Y
7	Spanberger	N	Y	Y	N	Y	Y
8	Beyer	N	Y	Y	Y	Y	Y
9	**Griffith**	?	N	N	Y	N	Y
10	Wexton	N	Y	Y	N	Y	Y
11	Connolly	N	Y	Y	N	Y	Y
WASHINGTON							
1	DelBene	N	Y	Y	Y	Y	Y
2	Larsen	N	Y	Y	Y	Y	Y
3	**Herrera Beutler**	Y	N	N	?	Y	Y
4	**Newhouse**	Y	N	N	Y	Y	Y
5	**McMorris Rodgers**	Y	N	N	Y	Y	Y
6	Kilmer	N	Y	Y	N	Y	Y
7	Jayapal	N	Y	Y	Y	Y	Y
8	Schrier	N	Y	Y	Y	Y	Y
9	Smith Adam	N	Y	Y	Y	Y	Y
10	Heck	N	Y	Y	Y	Y	Y
WEST VIRGINIA							
1	**McKinley**	Y	N	N	N	Y	Y
2	**Mooney**	Y	N	N	N	Y	Y
3	**Miller**	Y	N	N	N	Y	Y
WISCONSIN							
1	**Steil**	Y	N	N	Y	Y	Y
2	Pocan	N	Y	Y	Y	Y	Y
3	Kind	N	Y	Y	N	Y	Y
4	Moore	N	Y	Y	Y	Y	Y
5	**Sensenbrenner**	Y	N	N	N	Y	Y
6	**Grothman**	Y	N	N	?	Y	Y
7	**Duffy**						
8	**Gallagher**	Y	N	N	N	Y	Y
WYOMING							
AL	**Cheney**	Y	N	N	N	Y	Y
DELEGATES							
	Radewagen (A.S.)						
	Norton (D.C.)						
	San Nicolas (Guam)						
	Sablan (N. Marianas)						
	González-Colón (P.R.)						
	Plaskett (V.I.)						

139. Procedural Motion - Journal. Passage of the House Journal April 1, 2019. Approved 207-181: R 52-126; D 155-55. April 1, 2019.

140. SJ Res 7, HRES271. Justice Department Support for Health Law, Withdrawing U.S. Forces from Yemen - Previous Question. McGovern, D-Mass., motion to order the previous question (thus ending the debate and possibility of amendment) to the rule that would provide for House floor consideration of the resolution (H Res 271) that would condemn the Trump administration's legal campaign to take away American's health care and the resolution (S J Res 7) that would direct the removal of United States armed forces from hostilities in the Republic of Yemen that have not been authorized by Congress. The rule also provides for motions to suspend the rules. Motion agreed to 231-191: R 1-191; D 230-0. April 2, 2019.

141. HRES271, SJRES7. Justice Department Support for Health Law, Withdrawing U.S. Forces from Yemen - Rule. Adoption of the rule (H Res 274) that would provide for House floor consideration of the resolution (H Res 271) that would condemn the Trump administration's legal campaign to take away American's health care and the resolution (S J Res 7) that would direct the removal of United States armed forces from hostilities in the Republic of Yemen that have not been authorized by Congress. The rule also provides for motions to suspend the rules. Adopted 230-188: R 0-188; D 230-0. April 2, 2019.

142. HR540. Post Office Name Designation - Passage. Connolly, D-Va., motion to suspend the rules and pass the bill that would designate the postal facility located at 770 Ayrault Road in Fairport, N.Y., as the "Louise and Bob Slaughter Post Office." Motion agreed to 414-7: R 183-7; D 231-0. *Note: A two-thirds majority of those present and voting (281 in this case) is required for passage under suspension of the rules.* April 2, 2019.

143. Procedural Motion - Journal. Approval of the House Journal of April 2, 2019. Approved 222-189: R 45-139; D 177-50. April 2, 2019.

144. HR1585. Violence Against Women Reauthorization - Previous Question. Scanlon, D-Penn., motion to order the previous question (thus ending the debate and possibility of amendment) to the rule that would provide for House floor consideration of the bill (HR 1585) that would reauthorize the Violence Against Women Act of 1994 and its provisions aimed at combating violent crimes against women and strengthening victim services. Motion agreed to 231-193: R 0-193; D 231-0. April 3, 2019.

		139	140	141	142	143	144
ALABAMA							
1	**Byrne**	N	N	N	Y	N	N
2	**Roby**	N	N	N	Y	N	N
3	**Rogers, M.**	N	N	N	Y	N	N
4	**Aderholt**	N	N	N	Y	N	N
5	**Brooks, M.**	N	N	N	Y	N	N
6	**Palmer**	N	N	N	Y	N	N
7	Sewell	N	Y	Y	Y	N	Y
ALASKA							
AL	**Young**	N	N	N	Y	N	N
ARIZONA							
1	O'Halleran	Y	Y	Y	Y	Y	Y
2	Kirkpatrick	N	Y	Y	Y	Y	Y
3	Grijalva	?	Y	Y	Y	Y	Y
4	**Gosar**	N	N	N	Y	N	N
5	**Biggs**	N	N	N	Y	N	N
6	**Schweikert**	Y	N	N	Y	N	Y
7	Gallego	Y	Y	Y	Y	Y	Y
8	**Lesko**	N	N	N	Y	N	N
9	Stanton	Y	Y	Y	Y	Y	Y
ARKANSAS							
1	**Crawford**	N	N	N	Y	N	N
2	**Hill, F.**	N	N	N	Y	N	N
3	**Womack**	N	N	N	Y	N	N
4	**Westerman**	N	N	N	Y	N	N
CALIFORNIA							
1	**LaMalfa**	N	N	N	Y	N	N
2	Huffman	Y	Y	Y	Y	Y	Y
3	Garamendi	Y	Y	Y	Y	N	Y
4	**McClintock**	Y	N	N	Y	Y	N
5	Thompson, M.	N	Y	Y	Y	N	Y
6	Matsui	N	Y	Y	Y	Y	Y
7	Bera	N	Y	Y	Y	Y	Y
8	**Cook**	N	N	N	Y	N	N
9	McNerney	Y	Y	Y	Y	Y	Y
10	Harder	N	Y	Y	Y	N	Y
11	DeSaulnier	Y	Y	Y	Y	Y	Y
12	Pelosi			Y			
13	Lee B.	Y	Y	Y	Y	Y	Y
14	Speier	Y	Y	Y	Y	Y	Y
15	Swalwell	+	Y	Y	Y	Y	Y
16	Costa	N	Y	Y	Y	N	Y
17	Khanna	N	Y	Y	Y	Y	Y
18	Eshoo	Y	Y	Y	Y	Y	Y
19	Lofgren	Y	Y	Y	Y	Y	Y
20	Panetta	Y	Y	Y	Y	N	Y
21	Cox	N	Y	Y	Y	Y	Y
22	**Nunes**	N	N	N	Y	N	N
23	**McCarthy**	Y	N	N	Y	N	N
24	Carbajal	Y	Y	Y	Y	Y	Y
25	Hill, K.	Y	Y	Y	Y	Y	Y
26	Brownley	N	Y	Y	Y	Y	Y
27	Chu	Y	Y	Y	Y	Y	Y
28	Schiff	Y	Y	Y	Y	Y	Y
29	Cárdenas	Y	Y	Y	Y	Y	Y
30	Sherman	Y	Y	Y	Y	Y	Y
31	Aguilar	N	Y	Y	Y	N	Y
32	Napolitano	Y	Y	Y	Y	Y	Y
33	Lieu	Y	Y	Y	Y	Y	Y
34	Gomez	Y	Y	Y	Y	Y	Y
35	Torres	?	Y	Y	Y	Y	Y
36	Ruiz	Y	Y	Y	Y	Y	Y
37	Bass	Y	Y	Y	Y	?	Y
38	Sánchez	Y	Y	Y	Y	Y	Y
39	Cisneros	N	Y	Y	Y	N	Y
40	Roybal-Allard	Y	Y	Y	Y	Y	Y
41	Takano	Y	Y	Y	Y	Y	Y
42	**Calvert**	N	N	N	Y	?	N
43	Waters	Y	Y	Y	Y	N	Y
44	Barragán	Y	Y	Y	Y	Y	Y
45	Porter	N	Y	Y	Y	N	Y
46	Correa	?	?	?	?	?	Y
47	Lowenthal	Y	Y	Y	Y	Y	Y
48	Rouda	N	Y	Y	Y	N	Y
49	Levin	Y	Y	Y	Y	Y	Y
50	**Hunter**	N	N	N	Y	N	N
51	Vargas	Y	Y	Y	Y	Y	Y
52	Peters	N	Y	Y	Y	N	Y

		139	140	141	142	143	144
53	Davis, S.	Y	Y	Y	Y	Y	Y
COLORADO							
1	DeGette	Y	Y	Y	Y	Y	Y
2	Neguse	Y	Y	Y	Y	Y	Y
3	**Tipton**	Y	N	N	Y	N	N
4	**Buck**	N	N	N	Y	N	N
5	**Lamborn**	N	N	N	Y	N	N
6	Crow	N	Y	Y	Y	N	Y
7	Perlmutter	Y	Y	Y	Y	Y	Y
CONNECTICUT							
1	Larson	Y	Y	Y	Y	Y	Y
2	Courtney	Y	Y	Y	Y	Y	Y
3	DeLauro	Y	Y	Y	Y	Y	Y
4	Himes	Y	Y	Y	Y	N	Y
5	Hayes	Y	Y	Y	Y	Y	Y
DELAWARE							
AL	Blunt Rochester	Y	Y	Y	Y	Y	Y
FLORIDA							
1	**Gaetz**	N	N	N	Y	N	N
2	**Dunn**	?	N	N	Y	N	N
3	**Yoho**	?	N	N	Y	N	N
4	**Rutherford**	?	-	-	+	?	-
5	Lawson	?	Y	Y	Y	?	Y
6	**Waltz**	Y	N	N	Y	?	N
7	Murphy	Y	Y	Y	Y	N	Y
8	**Posey**	-	N	N	Y	N	N
9	Soto	Y	Y	Y	Y	Y	Y
10	Demings	Y	Y	Y	Y	Y	Y
11	**Webster**	Y	N	N	Y	N	N
12	**Bilirakis**	Y	N	N	Y	N	N
13	Crist	Y	Y	Y	Y	N	Y
14	Castor	Y	Y	Y	Y	Y	Y
15	**Spano**	N	N	N	Y	N	N
16	**Buchanan**	?	N	N	Y	N	N
17	**Steube**	?	N	N	Y	N	N
18	**Mast**	?	?	?	Y	N	N
19	**Rooney**	?	N	?	?	?	?
20	Hastings	Y	Y	Y	Y	Y	Y
21	Frankel	?	Y	Y	Y	Y	Y
22	Deutch	Y	Y	Y	Y	Y	Y
23	Wasserman Schultz	Y	Y	Y	Y	Y	Y
24	Wilson, F.	Y	Y	Y	Y	Y	Y
25	**Diaz-Balart**	N	N	N	Y	N	N
26	Mucarsel-Powell	N	Y	Y	Y	Y	Y
27	Shalala	Y	Y	Y	Y	Y	Y
GEORGIA							
1	**Carter, E.L.**	N	N	N	Y	?	N
2	Bishop, S.	Y	Y	Y	Y	Y	Y
3	**Ferguson**	N	N	N	?	N	N
4	Johnson, H.	Y	Y	Y	Y	Y	Y
5	Lewis John	Y	Y	Y	Y	Y	Y
6	McBath	Y	Y	Y	Y	Y	Y
7	**Woodall**	N	N	?	Y	N	N
8	**Scott, A.**	N	N	N	Y	N	N
9	**Collins, D.**	?	N	N	Y	N	N
10	**Hice**	N	N	N	Y	N	N
11	**Loudermilk**	N	N	N	Y	N	N
12	**Allen**	N	N	N	Y	N	N
13	Scott, D.	Y	Y	Y	Y	Y	Y
14	**Graves, T.**	N	N	N	Y	N	N
HAWAII							
1	Case	Y	Y	Y	Y	Y	Y
2	Gabbard	?	?	?	?	?	Y
IDAHO							
1	**Fulcher**	?	N	N	Y	N	N
2	**Simpson**	Y	N	N	Y	N	N
ILLINOIS							
1	Rush	?	?	?	?	?	Y
2	Kelly, R.	N	Y	Y	Y	N	Y
3	Lipinski	Y	Y	Y	Y	Y	Y
4	García, J.	Y	Y	Y	Y	Y	Y
5	Quigley	Y	Y	Y	Y	Y	Y
6	Casten	Y	Y	Y	Y	?	Y
7	Davis, D.	?	Y	Y	Y	Y	Y
8	Krishnamoorthi	N	Y	Y	Y	N	Y
9	Schakowsky	Y	Y	Y	Y	Y	Y
10	Schneider	Y	Y	Y	Y	Y	Y
11	Foster	N	Y	Y	Y	Y	Y

KEY: **Republicans**   Democrats   *Independents*

Y Voted for (yea)	**N** Voted against (nay)	**P** Voted "present"	
+ Announced for	**−** Announced against	**?** Did not vote or otherwise	
# Paired for	**X** Paired against	make position known	

	139	140	141	142	143	144
12 **Bost**	N	N	N	Y	?	N
13 **Davis, R.**	Y	N	N	Y	N	N
14 Underwood	Y	Y	Y	Y	Y	Y
15 **Shimkus**	?	N	N	Y	N	N
16 **Kinzinger**	N	N	N	Y	Y	N
17 Bustos	Y	Y	Y	Y	Y	Y
18 **LaHood**	?	N	N	Y	N	N
INDIANA						
1 Visclosky	Y	Y	Y	Y	Y	Y
2 **Walorski**	N	N	N	Y	N	N
3 **Banks**	Y	N	N	Y	Y	N
4 **Baird**	N	N	N	Y	Y	N
5 **Brooks, S.**	N	N	N	Y	N	N
6 **Pence**	N	N	N	Y	N	N
7 Carson	Y	Y	Y	Y	N	Y
8 **Bucshon**	N	N	N	Y	N	N
9 **Hollingsworth**	Y	N	N	Y	Y	N
IOWA						
1 Finkenauer	N	Y	Y	Y	Y	Y
2 Loebsack	?	Y	Y	Y	Y	Y
3 Axne	N	Y	Y	Y	N	Y
4 **King, S.**	Y	N	N	Y	Y	N
KANSAS						
1 **Marshall**	N	N	N	Y	N	N
2 **Watkins**	Y	N	N	Y	Y	N
3 Davids	N	Y	Y	Y	N	Y
4 **Estes**	N	N	N	Y	N	-
KENTUCKY						
1 **Comer**	N	N	N	Y	N	N
2 **Guthrie**	N	N	N	Y	N	N
3 Yarmuth	Y	Y	Y	Y	Y	Y
4 **Massie**	N	N	N	N	N	N
5 **Rogers, H.**	N	N	N	Y	N	N
6 **Barr**	N	N	N	Y	Y	N
LOUISIANA						
1 **Scalise**	N	N	N	Y	N	N
2 Richmond	Y	Y	Y	Y	Y	Y
3 **Higgins, C.**	Y	N	N	Y	Y	N
4 **Johnson, M.**	N	N	N	Y	N	N
5 **Abraham**	?	?	?	?	?	N
6 **Graves, G.**	N	N	N	Y	N	N
MAINE						
1 Pingree	?	Y	Y	Y	Y	Y
2 Golden	N	Y	Y	Y	N	Y
MARYLAND						
1 **Harris**	N	N	N	N	N	N
2 Ruppersberger	Y	Y	Y	Y	Y	Y
3 Sarbanes	Y	Y	Y	Y	Y	Y
4 Brown, A.	Y	Y	Y	Y	Y	Y
5 Hoyer	Y	Y	Y	Y	Y	?
6 Trone	?	Y	Y	Y	Y	Y
7 Cummings	Y	Y	Y	Y	Y	Y
8 Raskin	Y	Y	Y	Y	Y	Y
MASSACHUSETTS						
1 Neal	Y	Y	Y	Y	Y	Y
2 McGovern	Y	Y	Y	Y	Y	Y
3 Trahan	Y	Y	Y	Y	Y	Y
4 Kennedy	Y	Y	Y	Y	Y	Y
5 Clark	Y	Y	Y	Y	Y	Y
6 Moulton	N	Y	Y	Y	N	Y
7 Pressley	Y	Y	Y	Y	Y	Y
8 Lynch	Y	Y	Y	Y	Y	Y
9 Keating	N	Y	Y	Y	Y	Y
MICHIGAN						
1 **Bergman**	Y	N	?	Y	Y	N
2 **Huizenga**	N	N	N	Y	N	N
3 **Amash**	N	N	N	Y	N	N
4 **Moolenaar**	Y	N	N	Y	Y	N
5 Kildee	Y	Y	Y	Y	Y	Y
6 **Upton**	N	N	N	Y	N	N
7 **Walberg**	N	N	N	Y	N	N
8 Slotkin	N	Y	Y	Y	N	Y
9 Levin	Y	Y	Y	Y	Y	Y
10 **Mitchell**	Y	N	N	Y	Y	N
11 Stevens	N	Y	Y	Y	Y	Y
12 Dingell	Y	Y	Y	Y	Y	Y
13 Tlaib	Y	Y	Y	Y	Y	Y
14 Lawrence	Y	Y	Y	Y	Y	Y
MINNESOTA						
1 **Hagedorn**	N	N	N	Y	N	N
2 Craig	N	Y	Y	Y	N	Y
3 Phillips	Y	Y	Y	Y	Y	Y
4 McCollum	Y	Y	Y	Y	Y	Y
5 Omar	Y	Y	Y	Y	Y	Y
6 **Emmer**	N	N	N	Y	N	N
7 Peterson	Y	Y	Y	Y	Y	Y
8 **Stauber**	Y	N	N	Y	Y	N
MISSISSIPPI						
1 **Kelly, T.**	N	N	N	Y	N	N
2 Thompson, B.	Y	Y	Y	Y	Y	Y
3 **Guest**	N	N	N	Y	N	N
4 **Palazzo**	N	N	N	Y	N	N
MISSOURI						
1 Clay	Y	Y	Y	Y	Y	Y
2 **Wagner**	Y	N	N	Y	Y	N
3 **Luetkemeyer**	Y	N	N	Y	N	N
4 **Hartzler**	N	N	N	Y	N	N
5 Cleaver	+	Y	Y	Y	Y	Y
6 **Graves, S.**	N	N	N	Y	N	N
7 **Long**	Y	N	N	Y	Y	N
8 **Smith, J.**	N	N	N	Y	N	N
MONTANA						
AL **Gianforte**	N	N	N	Y	Y	N
NEBRASKA						
1 **Fortenberry**	Y	N	N	Y	Y	N
2 **Bacon**	Y	N	N	Y	Y	N
3 **Smith, Adrian**	Y	N	N	Y	N	N
NEVADA						
1 Titus	Y	Y	Y	Y	Y	Y
2 **Amodei**	Y	N	N	?	Y	N
3 Lee	Y	Y	Y	Y	Y	Y
4 Horsford	N	Y	Y	Y	N	Y
NEW HAMPSHIRE						
1 Pappas	N	Y	Y	Y	N	Y
2 Kuster	Y	Y	Y	Y	Y	Y
NEW JERSEY						
1 Norcross	Y	Y	Y	Y	Y	Y
2 Van Drew	N	Y	Y	Y	N	Y
3 Kim	N	Y	Y	Y	N	Y
4 **Smith, C.**	Y	N	N	Y	Y	N
5 Gottheimer	N	Y	Y	Y	N	Y
6 Pallone	Y	Y	Y	Y	Y	Y
7 Malinowski	Y	Y	Y	Y	Y	Y
8 Sires	?	Y	Y	Y	Y	Y
9 Pascrell	Y	Y	Y	Y	Y	Y
10 Payne	Y	Y	Y	Y	Y	Y
11 Sherrill	N	Y	Y	Y	N	Y
12 Watson Coleman	N	Y	Y	Y	N	Y
NEW MEXICO						
1 Haaland	Y	Y	Y	Y	Y	Y
2 Torres Small	Y	Y	Y	Y	Y	Y
3 Luján	?	Y	Y	Y	Y	Y
NEW YORK						
1 **Zeldin**	N	N	N	Y	N	N
2 **King, P.**	Y	N	N	Y	N	N
3 Suozzi	Y	Y	Y	Y	N	Y
4 Rice, K.	N	Y	Y	Y	N	Y
5 Meeks	?	Y	Y	Y	N	Y
6 Meng	N	Y	Y	Y	N	Y
7 Velázquez	Y	Y	Y	Y	Y	Y
8 Jeffries	?	Y	Y	Y	Y	Y
9 Clarke	Y	Y	Y	Y	Y	Y
10 Nadler	Y	Y	Y	Y	Y	Y
11 Rose	N	Y	Y	Y	N	Y
12 Maloney, C.	Y	Y	Y	Y	Y	Y
13 Espaillat	Y	Y	Y	Y	Y	Y
14 Ocasio-Cortez	Y	Y	Y	Y	Y	Y
15 Serrano	Y	Y	Y	Y	Y	Y
16 Engel	Y	Y	Y	Y	Y	Y
17 Lowey	Y	Y	Y	Y	Y	Y
18 Maloney, S.P.	N	Y	Y	Y	N	Y
19 Delgado	Y	Y	Y	Y	Y	Y
20 Tonko	P	Y	Y	Y	P	Y
21 **Stefanik**	N	N	N	Y	N	N
22 Brindisi	N	Y	Y	Y	N	Y
23 **Reed**	?	N	N	Y	N	N
24 **Katko**	N	N	N	Y	?	N
25 Morelle	Y	Y	Y	Y	Y	Y
26 Higgins, B.	?	Y	Y	Y	Y	Y
27 **Collins, C.**						
NORTH CAROLINA						
1 Butterfield	?	Y	Y	Y	Y	Y
2 **Holding**	N	N	N	Y	N	N
3 **Jones***						
4 Price	Y	Y	Y	Y	Y	Y
5 **Foxx**	N	N	N	Y	N	N
6 **Walker**	N	N	N	Y	?	N
7 **Rouzer**	N	N	N	N	N	N
8 **Hudson**	N	N	N	Y	N	N
9 vacant						
10 **McHenry**	N	N	N	Y	N	N
11 **Meadows**	?	N	N	Y	Y	N
12 Adams	Y	Y	Y	Y	Y	Y
13 **Budd**	Y	N	N	Y	N	N
NORTH DAKOTA						
AL **Armstrong**	Y	N	N	Y	Y	N
OHIO						
1 **Chabot**	N	N	N	Y	N	N
2 **Wenstrup**	Y	N	N	Y	N	N
3 Beatty	Y	Y	Y	Y	Y	Y
4 **Jordan**	N	N	N	Y	N	N
5 **Latta**	N	N	N	Y	N	N
6 **Johnson, B.**	N	N	N	Y	N	N
7 **Gibbs**	N	N	N	Y	N	N
8 **Davidson**	Y	N	N	Y	Y	N
9 Kaptur	Y	Y	Y	Y	Y	Y
10 **Turner**	N	N	N	Y	N	N
11 Fudge	Y	Y	Y	Y	N	Y
12 **Balderson**	N	N	N	Y	N	N
13 Ryan	?	Y	Y	Y	Y	?
14 **Joyce**	Y	N	N	Y	Y	N
15 **Stivers**	Y	N	N	Y	Y	?
16 **Gonzalez**	N	N	N	Y	N	N
OKLAHOMA						
1 **Hern**	N	N	N	Y	N	N
2 **Mullin**	N	N	N	Y	N	N
3 **Lucas**	N	N	N	Y	N	N
4 **Cole**	N	N	N	Y	N	N
5 Horn	Y	Y	Y	Y	Y	Y
OREGON						
1 Bonamici	Y	Y	Y	Y	Y	Y
2 **Walden**	Y	N	N	Y	N	N
3 Blumenauer	Y	Y	Y	Y	Y	Y
4 DeFazio	Y	Y	Y	Y	Y	Y
5 Schrader	N	Y	Y	Y	N	Y
PENNSYLVANIA						
1 **Fitzpatrick**	N	N	N	Y	N	N
2 Boyle	?	Y	Y	Y	Y	Y
3 Evans	Y	Y	Y	Y	Y	Y
4 Dean	Y	Y	Y	Y	Y	Y
5 Scanlon	Y	Y	Y	Y	Y	Y
6 Houlahan	N	Y	Y	Y	N	Y
7 Wild	N	Y	Y	Y	N	Y
8 Cartwright	Y	Y	Y	Y	Y	Y
9 **Meuser**	N	N	N	Y	N	N
10 **Perry**	Y	-	-	Y	N	N
11 **Smucker**	?	N	N	Y	N	N
12 **Marino***						
13 **Joyce**	N	N	N	Y	N	N
14 **Reschenthaler**	Y	N	N	?	?	N
15 **Thompson, G.**	N	N	N	Y	N	N
16 **Kelly, M.**	N	N	N	Y	N	N
17 Lamb	Y	Y	Y	Y	Y	Y
18 Doyle	Y	Y	Y	Y	Y	Y
RHODE ISLAND						
1 Cicilline	Y	Y	Y	Y	Y	Y
2 Langevin	Y	Y	Y	Y	Y	Y
SOUTH CAROLINA						
1 Cunningham	N	Y	Y	Y	N	Y
2 **Wilson, J.**	Y	N	N	Y	N	N
3 **Duncan**	N	N	N	Y	N	N
4 **Timmons**	Y	N	N	Y	N	N
5 **Norman**	N	N	N	Y	N	N
6 Clyburn	Y	Y	Y	Y	Y	Y
7 **Rice, T.**	N	N	N	N	N	N
SOUTH DAKOTA						
AL **Johnson**	N	N	N	Y	N	N
TENNESSEE						
1 **Roe**	Y	N	N	Y	N	N
2 **Burchett**	N	N	N	Y	N	N
3 **Fleischmann**	Y	N	N	Y	Y	N
4 **DesJarlais**	Y	N	N	Y	N	N
5 Cooper	Y	Y	Y	Y	Y	Y
6 **Rose**	N	N	N	Y	N	N
7 **Green**	N	N	N	Y	N	N
8 **Kustoff**	N	N	N	Y	N	N
9 Cohen	Y	Y	Y	Y	Y	Y
TEXAS						
1 **Gohmert**	?	N	N	Y	?	N
2 **Crenshaw**	N	N	N	Y	N	N
3 **Taylor**	Y	N	N	Y	Y	N
4 **Ratcliffe**	N	N	N	Y	N	N
5 **Gooden**	N	N	N	Y	N	N
6 **Wright**	N	N	N	Y	N	N
7 Fletcher	N	Y	Y	Y	N	Y
8 **Brady**	Y	N	N	Y	Y	N
9 Green, A.	N	Y	Y	Y	Y	Y
10 **McCaul**	N	N	N	Y	Y	N
11 **Conaway**	N	N	N	Y	N	N
12 **Granger**	Y	N	N	Y	N	N
13 **Thornberry**	Y	N	N	Y	Y	N
14 **Weber**	N	N	N	Y	N	N
15 Gonzalez	+	Y	Y	Y	Y	Y
16 Escobar	Y	Y	Y	Y	Y	Y
17 **Flores**	N	N	N	N	N	N
18 Jackson Lee	Y	Y	Y	Y	Y	Y
19 **Arrington**	Y	N	N	Y	Y	N
20 Castro	Y	Y	Y	Y	Y	Y
21 **Roy**	N	Y	N	N	N	N
22 **Olson**	N	N	N	Y	N	N
23 **Hurd**	N	N	N	Y	N	N
24 **Marchant**	N	N	N	Y	N	N
25 **Williams**	N	N	N	Y	N	N
26 **Burgess**	N	N	N	Y	N	N
27 **Cloud**	N	N	N	Y	?	N
28 Cuellar	N	Y	Y	Y	N	Y
29 Garcia, S.	Y	Y	Y	Y	Y	Y
30 Johnson, E.B.	Y	Y	Y	Y	Y	Y
31 **Carter, J.**	Y	N	N	Y	N	N
32 Allred	N	Y	Y	Y	Y	Y
33 Veasey	Y	Y	Y	Y	Y	Y
34 Vela	Y	Y	Y	Y	Y	Y
35 Doggett	Y	Y	Y	Y	Y	Y
36 **Babin**	N	N	N	Y	N	N
UTAH						
1 **Bishop, R.**	?	N	N	Y	N	N
2 **Stewart**	Y	N	N	Y	N	N
3 **Curtis**	Y	N	N	Y	Y	N
4 McAdams	N	Y	Y	Y	N	Y
VERMONT						
AL Welch	Y	Y	Y	Y	Y	Y
VIRGINIA						
1 **Wittman**	N	N	N	Y	N	N
2 Luria	Y	Y	Y	Y	Y	Y
3 Scott, R.	Y	Y	Y	Y	Y	Y
4 McEachin	+	+	+	+	+	+
5 **Riggleman**	N	N	?	Y	Y	N
6 **Cline**	N	N	N	Y	N	N
7 Spanberger	N	Y	Y	Y	N	Y
8 Beyer	Y	Y	Y	Y	Y	Y
9 **Griffith**	N	N	N	Y	N	N
10 Wexton	N	Y	Y	Y	N	Y
11 Connolly	N	Y	Y	Y	N	Y
WASHINGTON						
1 DelBene	Y	Y	Y	Y	Y	Y
2 Larsen	Y	Y	Y	Y	Y	Y
3 **Herrera Beutler**	N	N	N	Y	N	N
4 **Newhouse**	Y	N	N	Y	Y	N
5 **McMorris Rodgers**	Y	N	N	Y	Y	N
6 Kilmer	N	Y	Y	Y	N	Y
7 Jayapal	Y	Y	Y	Y	Y	Y
8 Schrier	Y	Y	Y	Y	Y	Y
9 Smith Adam	Y	Y	Y	Y	Y	Y
10 Heck	Y	Y	Y	Y	Y	Y
WEST VIRGINIA						
1 **McKinley**	N	N	N	Y	N	N
2 **Mooney**	?	?	?	Y	N	N
3 **Miller**	N	N	N	Y	N	N
WISCONSIN						
1 **Steil**	Y	N	N	Y	Y	N
2 Pocan	Y	Y	Y	Y	Y	Y
3 Kind	N	Y	Y	Y	N	Y
4 Moore	Y	Y	Y	Y	Y	Y
5 **Sensenbrenner**	N	N	N	Y	N	N
6 **Grothman**	Y	N	N	N	N	N
7 **Duffy**						
8 **Gallagher**	N	N	N	Y	N	N
WYOMING						
AL **Cheney**	N	N	N	Y	N	N
DELEGATES						
Radewagen (A.S.)						
Norton (D.C.)						
San Nicolas (Guam)						
Sablan (N. Marianas)						
González-Colón (P.R.)						
Plaskett (V.I.)						

145. HR1585. Violence Against Women Reauthorization - Rule. Adoption of the rule (H Res 281) that would provide for House floor consideration of the bill (HR 1585) that would reauthorize the Violence Against Women Act of 1994 and its provisions aimed at combating violent crimes against women and strengthening victim services. Adopted 231-194: R 0-194; D 231-0. April 3, 2019.

146. HRES271. Justice Department Support for Health Law - Passage. Passage of the resolution that would express the sense of the House of Representatives that the Trump administration's stance on invalidating the 2010 health care law is "unacceptable" and that the Justice Department should protect individuals with preexisting conditions, individuals who pay high costs for prescription drugs, and individuals who "gained health insurance coverage since 2014." The resolution would recommend that the department reverse its position in the case of Texas v. United States. Passed 240-186: R 8-185; D 232-1. April 3, 2019.

147. HR1585. Violence Against Women Reauthorization - Common Languages for Resources. Jeffries, D-N.Y., amendment that would require the secretary of Labor to ensure any information or materials on resources for domestic violence survivors distributed by various federal agencies be distributed in other "commonly encountered" languages. Adopted in Committee of the Whole 363-67: R 128-67; D 234-0; I 1-0. April 3, 2019.

148. HR1585. Violence Against Women Reauthorization - Report On Grant Funding. Scanlon, D-Pa., amendment that would require the Government Accountability Office to submit a report to Congress detailing the return on investment for legal assistance grants for funding and services to victims of domestic violence. Adopted in Committee of the Whole 394-36: R 160-35; D 233-1; I 1-0. April 3, 2019.

149. HR1585. Violence Against Women Reauthorization - Victim Interview Techniques. Waters, D-Calif., amendment that would allow grant funding to be used for training campus personnel to use victim-centered, trauma-informed interview techniques, focused on the experience of the victim, and informed by evidence based research on the neurobiology of trauma in addressing victims of sexual harassment, sexual assault, domestic violence, dating violence or stalking. Adopted in Committee of the Whole 258-173: R 23-173; D 234-0; I 1-0. April 3, 2019.

150. HR1585. Violence Against Women Reauthorization - Sex Trafficking and Stalking Programs. Wagner, R-Mo., amendment that would include programs that address sex trafficking and stalking in the Creating Hope Through Outreach Options, Services and Education for Children and Youth program. Adopted in Committee of the Whole 429-0: R 196-0; D 232-0; I 1-0. April 3, 2019.

		145	146	147	148	149	150
ALABAMA							
1	**Byrne**	N	N	Y	Y	N	Y
2	**Roby**	N	N	Y	Y	N	Y
3	**Rogers, M.**	N	N	Y	Y	N	Y
4	**Aderholt**	N	N	Y	Y	N	Y
5	**Brooks, M.**	N	N	N	N	N	Y
6	**Palmer**	N	N	Y	Y	N	Y
7	Sewell	Y	Y	Y	Y	Y	Y
ALASKA							
AL	**Young**	N	N	Y	N	N	Y
ARIZONA							
1	O'Halleran	Y	Y	Y	Y	Y	Y
2	Kirkpatrick	Y	Y	Y	Y	Y	Y
3	Grijalva	Y	Y	Y	Y	Y	Y
4	**Gosar**	N	N	N	N	N	Y
5	**Biggs**	N	N	N	N	N	Y
6	**Schweikert**	N	N	Y	Y	N	Y
7	Gallego	Y	Y	Y	Y	Y	Y
8	**Lesko**	N	N	N	N	N	Y
9	Stanton	Y	Y	Y	Y	Y	Y
ARKANSAS							
1	**Crawford**	N	N	Y	Y	N	Y
2	**Hill, F.**	N	N	Y	Y	N	Y
3	**Womack**	N	N	Y	Y	N	Y
4	**Westerman**	N	N	Y	Y	N	Y
CALIFORNIA							
1	**LaMalfa**	N	N	Y	Y	N	Y
2	Huffman	Y	Y	Y	Y	Y	Y
3	Garamendi	Y	Y	Y	Y	Y	Y
4	**McClintock**	N	N	N	N	N	Y
5	Thompson, M.	Y	Y	Y	Y	Y	Y
6	Matsui	Y	Y	Y	Y	Y	Y
7	Bera	Y	Y	Y	Y	Y	Y
8	**Cook**	N	N	Y	Y	N	Y
9	McNerney	Y	Y	Y	Y	Y	Y
10	Harder	Y	Y	Y	Y	Y	Y
11	DeSaulnier	Y	Y	Y	Y	Y	Y
12	Pelosi		Y				
13	Lee B.	Y	Y	Y	Y	Y	Y
14	Speier	Y	Y	Y	Y	Y	Y
15	Swalwell	Y	Y	Y	Y	Y	Y
16	Costa	Y	Y	Y	Y	Y	Y
17	Khanna	Y	Y	Y	Y	Y	Y
18	Eshoo	Y	Y	Y	Y	Y	Y
19	Lofgren	Y	Y	Y	Y	Y	Y
20	Panetta	Y	Y	Y	Y	Y	Y
21	Cox	Y	Y	Y	Y	Y	Y
22	**Nunes**	N	N	Y	Y	N	Y
23	**McCarthy**	N	N	Y	Y	N	Y
24	Carbajal	Y	Y	Y	Y	Y	Y
25	Hill, K.	Y	Y	Y	Y	Y	Y
26	Brownley	Y	Y	Y	Y	Y	Y
27	Chu	Y	Y	Y	Y	Y	Y
28	Schiff	Y	Y	Y	Y	Y	Y
29	Cárdenas	Y	Y	Y	Y	Y	Y
30	Sherman	Y	Y	Y	Y	Y	Y
31	Aguilar	Y	Y	Y	Y	Y	Y
32	Napolitano	Y	Y	Y	Y	Y	Y
33	Lieu	Y	Y	Y	Y	Y	Y
34	Gomez	Y	Y	Y	Y	Y	Y
35	Torres	Y	Y	Y	Y	Y	Y
36	Ruiz	Y	Y	Y	Y	Y	Y
37	Bass	Y	Y	Y	Y	Y	Y
38	Sánchez	Y	Y	Y	Y	Y	Y
39	Cisneros	Y	Y	Y	Y	Y	Y
40	Roybal-Allard	Y	Y	Y	Y	Y	Y
41	Takano	Y	Y	Y	Y	Y	Y
42	**Calvert**	N	N	Y	Y	N	Y
43	Waters	Y	Y	Y	Y	Y	Y
44	Barragán	Y	Y	Y	Y	Y	Y
45	Porter	Y	Y	Y	Y	Y	Y
46	Correa	Y	Y	Y	Y	Y	Y
47	Lowenthal	Y	Y	Y	Y	Y	Y
48	Rouda	Y	Y	Y	Y	Y	Y
49	Levin	Y	Y	Y	Y	Y	Y
50	**Hunter**	N	N	N	N	N	Y
51	Vargas	Y	Y	Y	Y	Y	Y
52	Peters	Y	Y	Y	Y	Y	Y

		145	146	147	148	149	150
53	Davis, S.	Y	Y	Y	Y	Y	Y
COLORADO							
1	DeGette	Y	Y	Y	Y	Y	Y
2	Neguse	Y	Y	Y	Y	Y	Y
3	**Tipton**	N	N	Y	Y	N	Y
4	**Buck**	N	N	Y	N	N	Y
5	**Lamborn**	N	N	Y	Y	N	Y
6	Crow	Y	Y	Y	Y	Y	Y
7	Perlmutter	Y	Y	Y	Y	Y	Y
CONNECTICUT							
1	Larson	Y	Y	Y	Y	Y	?
2	Courtney	Y	Y	Y	Y	Y	?
3	DeLauro	Y	Y	Y	Y	Y	Y
4	Himes	Y	Y	Y	Y	Y	Y
5	Hayes	Y	Y	Y	Y	Y	Y
DELAWARE							
AL	Blunt Rochester	Y	Y	Y	Y	Y	Y
FLORIDA							
1	**Gaetz**	N	N	N	N	N	Y
2	**Dunn**	N	N	Y	Y	N	Y
3	**Yoho**	N	N	N	N	N	Y
4	**Rutherford**	-	-	+	+	-	+
5	Lawson	Y	Y	Y	Y	Y	Y
6	**Waltz**	N	N	Y	Y	N	Y
7	Murphy	Y	Y	Y	Y	Y	Y
8	**Posey**	N	N	N	N	N	Y
9	Soto	Y	Y	Y	Y	Y	Y
10	Demings	?	Y	Y	Y	Y	Y
11	**Webster**	N	N	N	N	N	Y
12	**Bilirakis**	N	N	Y	Y	N	Y
13	Crist	Y	Y	Y	Y	Y	Y
14	Castor	Y	Y	Y	Y	Y	Y
15	**Spano**	N	N	Y	Y	N	Y
16	**Buchanan**	N	N	Y	Y	N	Y
17	**Steube**	N	N	N	N	N	Y
18	**Mast**	N	N	Y	N	N	Y
19	**Rooney**	?	?	?	?	?	?
20	Hastings	Y	Y	Y	Y	Y	Y
21	Frankel	Y	Y	Y	Y	Y	Y
22	Deutch	Y	Y	Y	Y	Y	Y
23	Wasserman Schultz	Y	Y	Y	Y	Y	Y
24	Wilson, F.	Y	Y	Y	Y	Y	Y
25	**Diaz-Balart**	N	N	Y	N	N	Y
26	Mucarsel-Powell	Y	Y	Y	Y	Y	Y
27	Shalala	Y	Y	Y	Y	Y	Y
GEORGIA							
1	**Carter, E.L.**	N	N	Y	N	N	Y
2	Bishop, S.	Y	Y	Y	Y	Y	Y
3	**Ferguson**	N	N	N	N	N	Y
4	Johnson, H.	Y	Y	Y	Y	Y	Y
5	Lewis John	Y	Y	Y	Y	Y	Y
6	McBath	Y	Y	Y	Y	Y	Y
7	**Woodall**	N	N	Y	Y	N	Y
8	**Scott, A.**	N	N	N	N	N	Y
9	**Collins, D.**	N	N	Y	N	N	Y
10	**Hice**	N	N	N	N	N	Y
11	**Loudermilk**	N	N	N	N	N	Y
12	**Allen**	N	N	N	N	N	Y
13	Scott, D.	Y	Y	Y	Y	Y	Y
14	**Graves, T.**	N	N	N	N	N	Y
HAWAII							
1	Case	Y	Y	Y	Y	Y	Y
2	Gabbard	Y	Y	Y	Y	Y	Y
IDAHO							
1	**Fulcher**	N	N	Y	Y	N	Y
2	**Simpson**	N	N	Y	Y	Y	Y
ILLINOIS							
1	Rush	Y	Y	Y	Y	Y	Y
2	Kelly, R.	Y	Y	Y	Y	Y	Y
3	Lipinski	Y	Y	Y	Y	Y	Y
4	García, J.	Y	Y	Y	Y	Y	Y
5	Quigley	Y	Y	Y	Y	Y	Y
6	Casten	Y	Y	Y	Y	Y	Y
7	Davis, D.	Y	Y	Y	Y	Y	Y
8	Krishnamoorthi	Y	Y	Y	Y	Y	Y
9	Schakowsky	Y	Y	Y	Y	Y	Y
10	Schneider	Y	Y	Y	Y	Y	Y
11	Foster	Y	Y	Y	Y	Y	Y

KEY:	**Republicans**	Democrats	*Independents*

Y Voted for (yea)	**N** Voted against (nay)	**P** Voted "present"	
+ Announced for	**–** Announced against	**?** Did not vote or otherwise	
# Paired for	**X** Paired against	make position known	

		145	146	147	148	149	150
12	**Bost**	N	N	Y	Y	N	Y
13	**Davis, R.**	N	N	Y	Y	Y	Y
14	Underwood	Y	Y	Y	Y	Y	Y
15	**Shimkus**	N	N	Y	Y	N	Y
16	**Kinzinger**	N	N	Y	Y	N	Y
17	Bustos	Y	Y	Y	Y	Y	Y
18	**LaHood**	N	N	Y	Y	N	Y
INDIANA							
1	Visclosky	Y	Y	Y	Y	Y	Y
2	**Walorski**	N	N	Y	Y	N	Y
3	**Banks**	N	N	N	N	N	Y
4	**Baird**	N	N	N	Y	N	Y
5	**Brooks, S.**	N	N	Y	Y	N	Y
6	**Pence**	N	N	N	Y	N	Y
7	Carson	Y	Y	Y	Y	Y	Y
8	**Bucshon**	N	N	Y	Y	N	Y
9	**Hollingsworth**	N	N	Y	Y	N	Y
IOWA							
1	Finkenauer	Y	Y	Y	Y	Y	Y
2	Loebsack	Y	Y	Y	Y	Y	Y
3	Axne	Y	Y	Y	Y	Y	Y
4	**King, S.**	N	N	N	Y	N	Y
KANSAS							
1	**Marshall**	N	N	Y	Y	N	Y
2	**Watkins**	N	N	Y	Y	N	Y
3	Davids	Y	Y	Y	Y	Y	Y
4	**Estes**	N	N	N	Y	N	Y
KENTUCKY							
1	**Comer**	N	N	Y	Y	N	Y
2	**Guthrie**	N	N	Y	Y	N	Y
3	Yarmuth	Y	Y	Y	Y	Y	Y
4	**Massie**	N	N	N	N	N	Y
5	**Rogers, H.**	N	N	Y	Y	N	Y
6	**Barr**	N	N	N	Y	N	Y
LOUISIANA							
1	**Scalise**	N	N	N	Y	N	Y
2	Richmond	Y	Y	Y	Y	Y	Y
3	**Higgins, C.**	N	N	Y	N	N	Y
4	**Johnson, M.**	N	N	Y	Y	N	Y
5	**Abraham**	N	N	N	Y	N	Y
6	**Graves, G.**	N	N	N	Y	N	Y
MAINE							
1	Pingree	Y	Y	Y	Y	Y	Y
2	Golden	Y	Y	Y	N	Y	Y
MARYLAND							
1	**Harris**	N	N	N	N	N	Y
2	Ruppersberger	Y	Y	Y	Y	Y	Y
3	Sarbanes	Y	Y	Y	Y	Y	Y
4	Brown, A.	Y	Y	Y	Y	Y	Y
5	Hoyer	Y	Y	Y	Y	Y	Y
6	Trone	Y	Y	Y	Y	Y	Y
7	Cummings	Y	Y	Y	Y	Y	Y
8	Raskin	Y	Y	Y	Y	Y	Y
MASSACHUSETTS							
1	Neal	Y	Y	Y	Y	Y	Y
2	McGovern	Y	Y	Y	Y	Y	Y
3	Trahan	Y	Y	Y	Y	Y	Y
4	Kennedy	Y	Y	Y	Y	Y	Y
5	Clark	Y	Y	Y	Y	Y	Y
6	Moulton	Y	Y	Y	Y	Y	Y
7	Pressley	Y	Y	Y	Y	Y	Y
8	Lynch	Y	Y	Y	Y	Y	Y
9	Keating	Y	Y	Y	Y	Y	Y
MICHIGAN							
1	**Bergman**	N	N	Y	Y	N	Y
2	**Huizenga**	N	N	Y	Y	N	Y
3	**Amash**	N	N	N	N	N	Y
4	**Moolenaar**	N	N	Y	Y	N	Y
5	Kildee	Y	Y	Y	Y	Y	Y
6	**Upton**	N	Y	Y	Y	Y	Y
7	**Walberg**	N	N	Y	Y	N	Y
8	Slotkin	Y	Y	Y	Y	Y	Y
9	Levin	Y	Y	Y	Y	Y	Y
10	**Mitchell**	N	N	Y	N	N	Y
11	Stevens	Y	Y	Y	Y	Y	Y
12	Dingell	Y	Y	Y	Y	Y	Y
13	Tlaib	Y	Y	Y	Y	Y	Y
14	Lawrence	Y	Y	Y	Y	Y	Y
MINNESOTA							
1	**Hagedorn**	N	N	Y	Y	N	Y
2	Craig	Y	Y	Y	Y	Y	Y
3	Phillips	Y	Y	Y	Y	Y	Y
4	McCollum	Y	Y	Y	Y	Y	Y
5	Omar	Y	Y	Y	Y	Y	Y

		145	146	147	148	149	150
6	**Emmer**	N	N	Y	Y	N	Y
7	Peterson	Y	N	Y	Y	Y	Y
8	**Stauber**	N	Y	Y	Y	Y	Y
MISSISSIPPI							
1	**Kelly, T.**	N	N	N	N	N	Y
2	Thompson, B.	Y	Y	Y	Y	Y	Y
3	**Guest**	N	N	Y	Y	N	Y
4	**Palazzo**	N	N	N	N	N	Y
MISSOURI							
1	Clay	Y	Y	Y	Y	Y	Y
2	**Wagner**	N	N	Y	Y	N	Y
3	**Luetkemeyer**	N	N	Y	Y	N	Y
4	**Hartzler**	N	N	Y	Y	N	Y
5	Cleaver	Y	Y	Y	Y	Y	Y
6	**Graves, S.**	N	N	Y	Y	N	Y
7	**Long**	N	N	Y	Y	N	Y
8	**Smith, J.**	N	N	Y	Y	Y	Y
MONTANA							
AL	**Gianforte**	N	N	Y	Y	Y	Y
NEBRASKA							
1	**Fortenberry**	N	N	Y	Y	Y	Y
2	**Bacon**	N	N	Y	Y	Y	Y
3	**Smith, Adrian**	N	N	Y	Y	N	Y
NEVADA							
1	Titus	Y	Y	Y	Y	Y	Y
2	**Amodei**	N	N	Y	Y	N	Y
3	Lee	Y	Y	Y	Y	Y	Y
4	Horsford	Y	Y	Y	Y	Y	Y
NEW HAMPSHIRE							
1	Pappas	Y	Y	Y	Y	Y	Y
2	Kuster	Y	Y	Y	Y	Y	Y
NEW JERSEY							
1	Norcross	Y	Y	Y	Y	Y	Y
2	Van Drew	Y	Y	Y	Y	Y	Y
3	Kim	Y	Y	Y	Y	Y	Y
4	**Smith, C.**	N	Y	Y	Y	N	Y
5	Gottheimer	Y	Y	Y	Y	Y	Y
6	Pallone	Y	Y	Y	Y	Y	Y
7	Malinowski	Y	Y	Y	Y	Y	Y
8	Sires	Y	Y	Y	Y	Y	Y
9	Pascrell	Y	Y	Y	Y	Y	Y
10	Payne	Y	Y	?	?	?	?
11	Sherrill	Y	Y	Y	Y	Y	Y
12	Watson Coleman	Y	Y	Y	Y	Y	Y
NEW MEXICO							
1	Haaland	Y	Y	Y	Y	Y	Y
2	Torres Small	Y	Y	Y	Y	Y	Y
3	Luján	Y	Y	Y	Y	Y	Y
NEW YORK							
1	**Zeldin**	N	N	N	N	N	Y
2	**King, P.**	N	N	Y	Y	Y	Y
3	Suozzi	Y	Y	Y	Y	Y	Y
4	Rice, K.	Y	Y	Y	Y	Y	Y
5	Meeks	Y	Y	Y	Y	Y	Y
6	Meng	Y	Y	Y	Y	Y	Y
7	Velázquez	Y	Y	Y	Y	Y	Y
8	Jeffries	Y	Y	Y	Y	Y	Y
9	Clarke	Y	Y	Y	Y	Y	Y
10	Nadler	Y	Y	Y	Y	Y	Y
11	Rose	Y	Y	Y	Y	Y	Y
12	Maloney, C.	Y	Y	Y	Y	Y	Y
13	Espaillat	Y	Y	Y	Y	Y	Y
14	Ocasio-Cortez	Y	Y	Y	Y	Y	Y
15	Serrano	Y	Y	Y	Y	Y	Y
16	Engel	Y	Y	Y	Y	Y	Y
17	Lowey	Y	Y	Y	Y	Y	Y
18	Maloney, S.P.	Y	Y	Y	Y	Y	Y
19	Delgado	Y	Y	Y	Y	Y	Y
20	Tonko	Y	Y	Y	Y	Y	Y
21	**Stefanik**	N	Y	Y	Y	Y	Y
22	Brindisi	Y	Y	Y	Y	Y	Y
23	**Reed**	N	Y	Y	Y	Y	Y
24	**Katko**	N	Y	Y	Y	Y	Y
25	Morelle	Y	Y	Y	Y	Y	Y
26	Higgins, B.	Y	Y	Y	Y	Y	Y
27	**Collins, C.**						
NORTH CAROLINA							
1	Butterfield	Y	Y	Y	Y	Y	Y
2	**Holding**	N	N	+	Y	N	Y
3	**Jones***						
4	Price	Y	Y	Y	Y	Y	Y
5	**Foxx**	N	N	N	Y	N	Y
6	**Walker**	N	N	N	Y	N	Y
7	**Rouzer**	N	N	Y	Y	N	Y

		145	146	147	148	149	150
8	**Hudson**	N	N	Y	Y	N	Y
9	vacant						
10	**McHenry**	N	N	Y	Y	N	Y
11	**Meadows**	N	N	N	Y	N	Y
12	Adams	Y	Y	Y	Y	Y	Y
13	**Budd**	N	N	N	Y	N	Y
NORTH DAKOTA							
AL	**Armstrong**	N	N	Y	Y	N	Y
OHIO							
1	**Chabot**	N	N	N	Y	N	Y
2	**Wenstrup**	N	N	Y	Y	N	Y
3	Beatty	Y	Y	Y	Y	Y	Y
4	**Jordan**	N	N	N	N	N	Y
5	**Latta**	N	N	Y	Y	N	Y
6	**Johnson, B.**	N	N	Y	Y	N	Y
7	**Gibbs**	N	N	Y	N	N	Y
8	**Davidson**	N	N	Y	Y	N	Y
9	Kaptur	Y	Y	Y	Y	Y	Y
10	**Turner**	N	N	Y	Y	Y	Y
11	Fudge	Y	Y	Y	Y	Y	Y
12	**Balderson**	N	N	Y	Y	N	Y
13	Ryan	?	?	?	?	?	?
14	**Joyce**	N	N	Y	Y	Y	Y
15	**Stivers**	?	?	Y	Y	Y	Y
16	**Gonzalez**	N	P	Y	Y	Y	Y
OKLAHOMA							
1	**Hern**	N	N	N	Y	N	Y
2	**Mullin**	N	N	Y	Y	Y	Y
3	**Lucas**	N	N	Y	Y	N	Y
4	**Cole**	N	N	Y	Y	N	Y
5	Horn	Y	Y	Y	Y	Y	Y
OREGON							
1	Bonamici	Y	Y	Y	Y	Y	Y
2	**Walden**	N	N	Y	Y	Y	Y
3	Blumenauer	Y	Y	Y	Y	Y	Y
4	DeFazio	Y	Y	Y	Y	Y	Y
5	Schrader	Y	Y	Y	Y	Y	Y
PENNSYLVANIA							
1	**Fitzpatrick**	N	Y	Y	Y	Y	Y
2	Boyle	Y	Y	Y	Y	Y	Y
3	Evans	Y	Y	Y	Y	Y	Y
4	Dean	Y	Y	Y	Y	Y	Y
5	Scanlon	Y	Y	Y	Y	Y	Y
6	Houlahan	Y	Y	Y	Y	Y	Y
7	Wild	Y	Y	Y	Y	Y	Y
8	Cartwright	Y	Y	Y	Y	Y	Y
9	**Meuser**	N	N	Y	Y	N	Y
10	**Perry**	N	N	N	Y	N	Y
11	**Smucker**	N	N	Y	Y	N	Y
12	**Marino***						
13	**Joyce**	N	N	N	Y	N	Y
14	**Reschenthaler**	N	N	Y	Y	N	Y
15	**Thompson, G.**	N	N	Y	Y	N	Y
16	**Kelly, M.**	N	N	N	N	N	Y
17	Lamb	Y	Y	Y	Y	Y	Y
18	Doyle	Y	Y	Y	Y	Y	Y
RHODE ISLAND							
1	Cicilline	Y	Y	Y	Y	Y	Y
2	Langevin	Y	Y	Y	Y	Y	Y
SOUTH CAROLINA							
1	Cunningham	Y	Y	Y	Y	Y	Y
2	**Wilson, J.**	N	N	Y	Y	N	Y
3	**Duncan**	N	N	N	N	N	Y
4	**Timmons**	N	N	Y	Y	N	Y
5	**Norman**	N	N	N	Y	N	Y
6	Clyburn	Y	Y	Y	Y	Y	Y
7	**Rice, T.**	N	N	Y	Y	N	Y
SOUTH DAKOTA							
AL	**Johnson**	N	N	N	Y	N	Y
TENNESSEE							
1	**Roe**	N	N	Y	Y	N	Y
2	**Burchett**	N	N	N	Y	N	Y
3	**Fleischmann**	N	N	Y	Y	N	Y
4	**DesJarlais**	N	N	N	Y	N	Y
5	Cooper	Y	Y	Y	Y	Y	Y
6	**Rose**	N	N	N	Y	N	Y
7	**Green**	N	N	N	N	N	Y
8	**Kustoff**	N	N	Y	Y	N	Y
9	Cohen	Y	Y	Y	Y	Y	Y
TEXAS							
1	**Gohmert**	N	N	N	N	N	Y
2	**Crenshaw**	N	N	Y	Y	N	Y
3	**Taylor**	N	N	Y	Y	N	Y
4	**Ratcliffe**	N	N	N	N	N	Y

		145	146	147	148	149	150
5	**Gooden**	N	N	N	Y	N	Y
6	**Wright**	N	N	N	N	N	Y
7	Fletcher	Y	Y	Y	Y	Y	Y
8	**Brady**	N	N	Y	Y	N	Y
9	Green, A.	Y	Y	Y	Y	Y	Y
10	**McCaul**	N	N	Y	Y	N	Y
11	**Conaway**	N	N	Y	Y	N	Y
12	**Granger**	N	N	N	Y	N	Y
13	**Thornberry**	N	N	Y	Y	N	Y
14	**Weber**	N	N	N	N	N	Y
15	Gonzalez	Y	Y	Y	Y	Y	Y
16	Escobar	Y	Y	Y	Y	Y	Y
17	**Flores**	N	N	Y	Y	N	Y
18	Jackson Lee	Y	Y	Y	Y	Y	Y
19	**Arrington**	N	N	Y	Y	N	Y
20	Castro	Y	Y	Y	Y	Y	Y
21	**Roy**	N	N	N	N	N	Y
22	**Olson**	N	N	Y	Y	N	Y
23	**Hurd**	N	N	Y	Y	Y	Y
24	**Marchant**	N	N	Y	Y	N	Y
25	**Williams**	N	N	Y	Y	N	Y
26	**Burgess**	N	N	N	Y	N	Y
27	**Cloud**	N	N	N	Y	N	Y
28	Cuellar	Y	Y	Y	Y	Y	Y
29	Garcia, S.	Y	Y	Y	Y	Y	Y
30	Johnson, E.B.	Y	Y	Y	Y	Y	Y
31	**Carter, J.**	N	N	N	Y	N	Y
32	Allred	Y	Y	Y	Y	Y	Y
33	Veasey	Y	Y	Y	Y	Y	Y
34	Vela	Y	Y	Y	Y	Y	Y
35	Doggett	Y	Y	Y	Y	Y	Y
36	**Babin**	N	N	N	N	N	Y
UTAH							
1	**Bishop, R.**	N	N	N	?	N	Y
2	**Stewart**	N	N	Y	Y	N	Y
3	**Curtis**	N	N	Y	Y	N	Y
4	McAdams	Y	Y	Y	Y	Y	Y
VERMONT							
AL	Welch	Y	Y	Y	Y	Y	Y
VIRGINIA							
1	**Wittman**	N	N	Y	Y	N	Y
2	Luria	Y	Y	Y	Y	Y	Y
3	Scott, R.	Y	Y	Y	Y	Y	Y
4	McEachin	+	+	+	+	+	+
5	**Riggleman**	N	Y	Y	Y	N	Y
6	**Cline**	N	N	N	N	N	Y
7	Spanberger	Y	Y	Y	Y	Y	Y
8	Beyer	Y	Y	Y	Y	Y	Y
9	**Griffith**	N	N	Y	Y	N	Y
10	Wexton	Y	Y	Y	Y	Y	Y
11	Connolly	Y	Y	Y	Y	Y	Y
WASHINGTON							
1	DelBene	Y	Y	Y	Y	Y	Y
2	Larsen	Y	Y	Y	Y	Y	Y
3	**Herrera Beutler**	N	N	Y	Y	N	Y
4	**Newhouse**	N	N	Y	Y	N	Y
5	**McMorris Rodgers**	N	N	Y	Y	N	Y
6	Kilmer	Y	Y	Y	Y	Y	Y
7	Jayapal	Y	Y	Y	Y	Y	Y
8	Schrier	Y	Y	Y	Y	Y	Y
9	Smith Adam	Y	Y	Y	Y	Y	Y
10	Heck	Y	Y	Y	Y	Y	Y
WEST VIRGINIA							
1	**McKinley**	N	N	N	Y	N	Y
2	**Mooney**	N	N	Y	Y	N	Y
3	**Miller**	N	N	N	Y	N	Y
WISCONSIN							
1	**Steil**	N	N	Y	Y	Y	Y
2	Pocan	Y	Y	Y	Y	Y	Y
3	Kind	Y	Y	Y	Y	Y	Y
4	Moore	Y	Y	Y	Y	Y	Y
5	**Sensenbrenner**	N	N	Y	Y	N	Y
6	**Grothman**	N	N	N	Y	N	Y
7	**Duffy**						
8	**Gallagher**	N	N	Y	Y	N	Y
WYOMING							
AL	**Cheney**	N	N	N	Y	N	Y
DELEGATES							
	Radewagen (A.S.)			?	?	?	?
	Norton (D.C.)			Y	Y	Y	Y
	San Nicolas (Guam)			Y	Y	Y	Y
	Sablan (N. Marianas)			Y	Y	Y	Y
	González-Colón (P.R.)			Y	Y	N	Y
	Plaskett (V.I.)			Y	Y	Y	Y

III HOUSE VOTES

151. HR829. Wilwerth Post Office - Passage. Connolly, D-Va., motion to suspend the rules and pass the bill that would designate the postal facility located at 1450 Montauk Highway in Mastic, N.Y. as the "Army Specialist Thomas J. Wilwerth Post Office Building." Motion agreed to 423-0: R 192-0; D 231-0. *Note: A two-thirds majority of those present and voting (282 in this case) is required for passage under suspension of the rules.* April 4, 2019.

152. SJ Res 7. U.S. Military Forces in Yemen - Recommit. McCaul, R-Texas, motion to recommit the bill to the Committee on Foreign Affairs with instructions to report it back immediately with an amendment that would state that it is in the national security interest of the U.S. to oppose global efforts to place political pressure on Israel through the use of boycotts, divestment, and sanctions and to oppose all efforts to delegitimize the State of Israel. Motion rejected 194-228: R 189-2; D 5-226. April 4, 2019.

153. SJ Res 7. U.S. Military Forces in Yemen - Passage. Passage of the joint the resolution that would direct the president, within 30 days of enactment, to remove U.S. armed forces from hostilities in or affecting the Republic of Yemen, including in-flight refueling of non-U.S. aircraft, unless a declaration of war or specific authorization for such use of forces has been enacted. The bill specifies that its provisions would not apply to U.S. forces engaged in operations directed at al-Qaeda or associated forces. The measure would also require two reports regarding risks to U.S. and Saudi citizens as well as the risk of humanitarian crisis, and an assessment of the potential increased risk of terrorist attacks. Passed (thus cleared for the president) 247-175: R 16-175; D 231-0. *Note: A "nay" was a vote in support of the president's position.* April 4, 2019.

154. HR1585. Violence Against Women Reauthorization - Compliance With Immigration Laws. Torres Small, D-N.M., amendment that would state that nothing in the measure should be construed to interfere with the obligation to fully comply with applicable immigration laws. Adopted in Committee of the Whole 425-0: R 192-0; D 233-0. April 4, 2019.

155. HR1585. Violence Against Women Reauthorization - Recommit. Stefanik, R-N.Y., motion to recommit the bill to the House Judiciary Committee with instructions to report it back immediately with an amendment that would effectively extend the Violence Against Women Act through fiscal 2020, instead of through fiscal 2024. Motion rejected 185-237: R 184-7; D 1-230. April 4, 2019.

156. HR1585. Violence Against Women Reauthorization - Passage. Passage of the bill that would would reauthorize the Violence Against Women Act through fiscal 2024, including provisions aimed at protecting and assisting victims of domestic violence, dating violence, sexual violence, stalking, and sex trafficking. The measure would extend protections and assistance programs to trafficking victims. It would authorize $222 million annually for the Services and Training for Officers and Prosecutors Grant Program, which provides state and local law enforcement agencies with funds to be distributed in part to community-based victims service organizations, and would impose conditions of eligibility for the grants three years after enactment. The bill would authorize $57 million annually in grants to provide legal assistance to victims of violent crimes and their families and $50 million in rural aid to address domestic violence, stalking, and sexual assault in rural communities. It would authorize $150 million a year in grant funding for rape crisis centers, sexual assault coalitions, and additional nonprofit organizations to educate and increase awareness on the sexual assault and dating violence. The bill would establish a $16 million per year campus safety grant program that would provide prevention and education programming to college campuses in order to combat violent crimes. The bill would expand on existing prohibitions of individuals who have been convicted of various types of domestic violence (including violence toward a dating partner) and those convicted of misdemeanor stalking offenses from purchasing or possessing a firearm. It would specify that any person under a temporary court-ordered restraint related to harassing, stalking, or threatening an intimate partner or child of such intimate partner would also be prohibited from purchasing or owning a firearm. The bill would authorize $10 million annually for a pilot program where incarcerated women and their children who were born inside prison could reside together while the inmate serves her sentence. The bill would require the Federal Bureau of Investigation to classify genital mutilation, female circumcision, and female genital cutting as a part II crime. The bill would make it a crime for any law enforcement personnel to engage in sexual acts with an individual who is under arrest, detained, or in custody of federal law enforcement. Passed 263-158: R 33-157; D 230-1. April 4, 2019.

		151	152	153	154	155	156
ALABAMA							
1	**Byrne**	Y	Y	N	Y	N	N
2	**Roby**	Y	Y	N	Y	N	N
3	**Rogers, M.**	Y	Y	N	Y	N	N
4	**Aderholt**	Y	Y	N	Y	N	N
5	**Brooks, M.**	Y	Y	N	Y	N	N
6	**Palmer**	Y	Y	N	Y	Y	N
7	Sewell	Y	N	Y	Y	N	Y
ALASKA							
AL	**Young**	Y	Y	N	Y	Y	Y
ARIZONA							
1	O'Halleran	Y	N	Y	Y	N	Y
2	Kirkpatrick	Y	N	Y	Y	N	Y
3	Grijalva	Y	N	Y	Y	N	Y
4	**Gosar**	Y	Y	Y	Y	Y	N
5	**Biggs**	Y	Y	Y	Y	Y	N
6	**Schweikert**	Y	Y	Y	Y	Y	N
7	Gallego	Y	N	Y	Y	N	Y
8	**Lesko**	Y	Y	N	Y	N	N
9	Stanton	Y	N	Y	Y	N	Y
ARKANSAS							
1	**Crawford**	Y	Y	N	Y	N	N
2	**Hill, F.**	Y	Y	N	Y	N	N
3	**Womack**	Y	Y	N	Y	N	N
4	**Westerman**	Y	Y	N	Y	N	N
CALIFORNIA							
1	**LaMalfa**	Y	Y	N	Y	N	N
2	Huffman	Y	N	Y	Y	N	Y
3	Garamendi	Y	N	Y	Y	N	Y
4	**McClintock**	Y	Y	N	Y	N	N
5	Thompson, M.	Y	N	Y	Y	N	Y
6	Matsui	Y	N	Y	Y	N	Y
7	Bera	Y	N	Y	Y	N	Y
8	**Cook**	?	?	?	?	?	?
9	McNerney	Y	N	Y	Y	N	Y
10	Harder	Y	N	Y	Y	N	Y
11	DeSaulnier	Y	N	Y	Y	N	Y
12	Pelosi			Y			
13	Lee B.	Y	N	Y	Y	N	Y
14	Speier	Y	N	Y	Y	N	Y
15	Swalwell	Y	N	Y	Y	N	Y
16	Costa	Y	N	Y	Y	N	Y
17	Khanna	Y	N	Y	Y	N	Y
18	Eshoo	Y	N	Y	Y	N	Y
19	Lofgren	Y	N	Y	Y	N	Y
20	Panetta	Y	N	Y	Y	N	Y
21	Cox	Y	N	Y	Y	N	Y
22	**Nunes**	Y	Y	N	Y	Y	N
23	**McCarthy**	Y	Y	N	Y	Y	N
24	Carbajal	Y	N	Y	Y	N	Y
25	Hill, K.	Y	N	Y	Y	N	Y
26	Brownley	Y	N	Y	Y	N	Y
27	Chu	Y	N	Y	Y	N	Y
28	Schiff	Y	N	Y	Y	N	Y
29	Cárdenas	Y	N	Y	Y	N	Y
30	Sherman	Y	N	Y	Y	N	Y
31	Aguilar	Y	N	Y	Y	N	Y
32	Napolitano	Y	N	Y	Y	N	Y
33	Lieu	Y	N	Y	Y	N	Y
34	Gomez	Y	N	Y	Y	N	Y
35	Torres	Y	N	Y	Y	N	Y
36	Ruiz	Y	N	Y	Y	N	Y
37	Bass	Y	N	Y	Y	N	Y
38	Sánchez	Y	N	Y	Y	N	Y
39	Cisneros	Y	N	Y	Y	N	Y
40	Roybal-Allard	Y	N	Y	Y	N	Y
41	Takano	Y	N	Y	Y	N	Y
42	**Calvert**	Y	Y	N	Y	Y	N
43	Waters	Y	N	Y	Y	N	Y
44	Barragán	Y	N	Y	Y	N	Y
45	Porter	Y	N	Y	Y	N	Y
46	Correa	Y	N	Y	Y	N	Y
47	Lowenthal	Y	N	Y	Y	N	Y
48	Rouda	Y	N	Y	Y	N	Y
49	Levin	Y	N	Y	Y	N	Y
50	**Hunter**	Y	Y	N	Y	Y	N
51	Vargas	Y	N	Y	Y	N	Y
52	Peters	Y	N	Y	Y	N	Y

		151	152	153	154	155	156
53	Davis, S.	Y	N	Y	Y	N	Y
COLORADO							
1	DeGette	Y	N	Y	Y	N	Y
2	Neguse	Y	N	Y	Y	N	Y
3	**Tipton**	Y	Y	N	Y	N	Y
4	**Buck**	Y	Y	Y	Y	N	Y
5	**Lamborn**	Y	Y	N	Y	N	N
6	Crow	Y	N	Y	Y	N	Y
7	Perlmutter	Y	N	Y	Y	N	Y
CONNECTICUT							
1	Larson	Y	N	Y	Y	N	Y
2	Courtney	Y	N	Y	Y	N	Y
3	DeLauro	Y	N	Y	Y	N	Y
4	Himes	Y	N	Y	Y	N	Y
5	Hayes	Y	N	Y	Y	N	Y
DELAWARE							
AL	Blunt Rochester	Y	N	Y	Y	N	Y
FLORIDA							
1	**Gaetz**	Y	P	Y	Y	Y	N
2	**Dunn**	Y	Y	N	Y	Y	N
3	**Yoho**	Y	Y	N	Y	Y	N
4	**Rutherford**	+	+	-	+	+	-
5	Lawson	Y	N	Y	Y	N	Y
6	**Waltz**	Y	Y	N	Y	Y	N
7	Murphy	Y	N	Y	Y	N	Y
8	**Posey**	Y	Y	Y	Y	Y	N
9	Soto	Y	N	Y	Y	N	Y
10	Demings	Y	N	Y	Y	N	Y
11	**Webster**	Y	Y	N	Y	Y	N
12	**Bilirakis**	Y	Y	N	Y	N	N
13	Crist	Y	N	Y	Y	N	Y
14	Castor	Y	N	Y	Y	N	Y
15	**Spano**	Y	Y	N	Y	N	N
16	**Buchanan**	Y	Y	N	Y	N	N
17	**Steube**	Y	Y	N	Y	Y	N
18	**Mast**	Y	Y	Y	Y	Y	N
19	**Rooney**	?	?	?	?	?	?
20	Hastings	Y	N	Y	Y	N	Y
21	Frankel	Y	N	Y	Y	N	Y
22	Deutch	Y	N	Y	Y	N	Y
23	Wasserman Schultz	Y	N	Y	Y	N	Y
24	Wilson, F.	Y	N	Y	Y	N	Y
25	**Diaz-Balart**	Y	Y	N	Y	N	N
26	Mucarsel-Powell	Y	N	Y	Y	N	Y
27	Shalala	Y	N	Y	Y	N	Y
GEORGIA							
1	**Carter, E.L.**	Y	Y	N	Y	Y	N
2	Bishop, S.	Y	N	Y	Y	N	Y
3	**Ferguson**	Y	Y	N	Y	Y	N
4	Johnson, H.	Y	N	Y	Y	N	Y
5	Lewis John	Y	N	Y	Y	N	Y
6	McBath	Y	N	Y	Y	N	Y
7	**Woodall**	Y	Y	N	Y	Y	N
8	**Scott, A.**	Y	Y	N	Y	N	N
9	**Collins, D.**	Y	Y	N	Y	Y	N
10	**Hice**	Y	Y	N	Y	N	N
11	**Loudermilk**	Y	Y	N	Y	N	N
12	**Allen**	Y	Y	N	Y	N	N
13	Scott, D.	Y	N	Y	Y	N	Y
14	**Graves, T.**	Y	Y	N	Y	N	N
HAWAII							
1	Case	Y	N	Y	Y	N	Y
2	Gabbard	Y	N	Y	Y	N	Y
IDAHO							
1	**Fulcher**	Y	Y	N	Y	N	N
2	**Simpson**	Y	Y	N	Y	N	N
ILLINOIS							
1	Rush	Y	N	Y	Y	N	Y
2	Kelly, R.	Y	N	Y	Y	N	Y
3	Lipinski	Y	N	Y	Y	N	Y
4	García, J.	Y	N	Y	Y	N	Y
5	Quigley	Y	N	Y	Y	N	Y
6	Casten	Y	N	Y	Y	N	Y
7	Davis, D.	Y	N	Y	Y	N	Y
8	Krishnamoorthi	Y	N	Y	Y	N	Y
9	Schakowsky	Y	N	Y	Y	N	Y
10	Schneider	Y	N	Y	Y	N	Y
11	Foster	Y	N	Y	Y	N	Y

		151	152	153	154	155	156
12	**Bost**	Y	Y	N	Y	Y	Y
13	**Davis, R.**	Y	Y	N	Y	Y	Y
14	Underwood	Y	N	Y	Y	N	Y
15	**Shimkus**	Y	Y	N	Y	Y	N
16	**Kinzinger**	Y	Y	N	Y	Y	Y
17	Bustos	Y	N	Y	Y	N	Y
18	**LaHood**	Y	Y	N	Y	Y	N
INDIANA							
1	Visclosky	Y	N	+	Y	N	Y
2	**Walorski**	Y	Y	N	Y	Y	Y
3	**Banks**	Y	Y	N	Y	Y	N
4	**Baird**	Y	Y	N	Y	Y	N
5	**Brooks, S.**	Y	Y	N	Y	Y	Y
6	**Pence**	Y	Y	N	Y	Y	N
7	Carson	Y	N	Y	Y	N	Y
8	**Bucshon**	Y	Y	N	Y	Y	N
9	**Hollingsworth**	Y	Y	Y	Y	Y	N
IOWA							
1	Finkenauer	Y	N	Y	Y	N	Y
2	Loebsack	Y	N	Y	Y	N	Y
3	Axne	Y	N	Y	Y	N	Y
4	**King, S.**	Y	Y	N	Y	Y	N
KANSAS							
1	**Marshall**	Y	Y	N	Y	Y	N
2	**Watkins**	Y	Y	N	Y	Y	N
3	Davids	Y	N	Y	Y	N	Y
4	**Estes**	Y	Y	N	Y	Y	N
KENTUCKY							
1	**Comer**	Y	Y	N	Y	Y	N
2	**Guthrie**	Y	Y	N	Y	Y	N
3	Yarmuth	Y	N	Y	Y	N	Y
4	**Massie**	Y	N	Y	Y	Y	N
5	**Rogers, H.**	Y	Y	N	Y	Y	N
6	**Barr**	Y	Y	N	Y	Y	N
LOUISIANA							
1	**Scalise**	Y	Y	N	Y	Y	N
2	Richmond	Y	N	Y	Y	N	Y
3	**Higgins, C.**	Y	Y	N	Y	Y	N
4	**Johnson, M.**	Y	Y	N	Y	Y	N
5	**Abraham**	Y	Y	N	Y	Y	N
6	**Graves, G.**	Y	Y	N	Y	Y	N
MAINE							
1	Pingree	Y	N	Y	Y	N	Y
2	Golden	Y	N	Y	Y	N	Y
MARYLAND							
1	**Harris**	Y	Y	N	Y	Y	N
2	Ruppersberger	Y	N	Y	Y	N	Y
3	Sarbanes	Y	N	Y	Y	N	Y
4	Brown, A.	Y	N	Y	Y	N	Y
5	Hoyer	Y	N	Y	Y	N	Y
6	Trone	Y	N	Y	Y	N	Y
7	Cummings	Y	N	Y	Y	N	Y
8	Raskin	Y	N	Y	Y	N	Y
MASSACHUSETTS							
1	Neal	Y	N	Y	Y	N	Y
2	McGovern	Y	N	Y	Y	N	Y
3	Trahan	Y	N	Y	Y	N	Y
4	Kennedy	Y	N	Y	Y	N	Y
5	Clark	?	?	?	?	?	?
6	Moulton	Y	N	Y	Y	N	Y
7	Pressley	Y	N	Y	Y	N	Y
8	Lynch	Y	N	Y	Y	N	Y
9	Keating	Y	N	Y	Y	N	Y
MICHIGAN							
1	**Bergman**	Y	Y	N	Y	Y	N
2	**Huizenga**	Y	Y	N	Y	Y	N
3	**Amash**	Y	N	P	Y	Y	N
4	**Moolenaar**	Y	Y	N	Y	Y	N
5	Kildee	Y	N	Y	Y	N	Y
6	**Upton**	Y	Y	N	Y	Y	Y
7	**Walberg**	Y	Y	N	Y	Y	N
8	Slotkin	Y	N	Y	Y	N	Y
9	Levin	Y	N	Y	Y	N	Y
10	**Mitchell**	Y	Y	N	Y	Y	N
11	Stevens	Y	N	Y	Y	N	Y
12	Dingell	Y	N	Y	Y	N	Y
13	Tlaib	Y	N	Y	Y	N	Y
14	Lawrence	Y	N	Y	Y	N	Y
MINNESOTA							
1	**Hagedorn**	Y	Y	N	Y	Y	N
2	Craig	Y	N	Y	Y	N	Y
3	Phillips	Y	N	Y	Y	N	Y
4	McCollum	Y	N	Y	Y	N	Y
5	Omar	Y	N	Y	Y	N	Y

		151	152	153	154	155	156
6	**Emmer**	Y	Y	N	Y	Y	N
7	Peterson	Y	N	Y	Y	Y	N
8	**Stauber**	Y	Y	N	Y	Y	Y
MISSISSIPPI							
1	**Kelly, T.**	Y	Y	N	Y	Y	N
2	Thompson, B.	Y	N	Y	Y	N	Y
3	**Guest**	Y	Y	N	Y	Y	N
4	**Palazzo**	Y	Y	N	Y	Y	N
MISSOURI							
1	Clay	Y	N	Y	Y	N	Y
2	**Wagner**	Y	Y	N	Y	Y	N
3	**Luetkemeyer**	Y	Y	N	Y	Y	N
4	**Hartzler**	Y	Y	N	Y	N	N
5	Cleaver	Y	N	Y	Y	N	Y
6	**Graves, S.**	Y	Y	N	Y	Y	N
7	**Long**	Y	Y	N	Y	?	?
8	**Smith, J.**	Y	Y	N	Y	Y	N
MONTANA							
AL	**Gianforte**	Y	Y	N	Y	Y	N
NEBRASKA							
1	**Fortenberry**	Y	Y	N	Y	Y	P
2	**Bacon**	Y	Y	N	Y	Y	N
3	**Smith, Adrian**	Y	Y	N	Y	Y	N
NEVADA							
1	Titus	Y	N	Y	Y	N	Y
2	**Amodei**	Y	Y	N	Y	Y	N
3	Lee	Y	N	Y	Y	N	Y
4	Horsford	Y	N	Y	Y	N	Y
NEW HAMPSHIRE							
1	Pappas	Y	N	Y	Y	N	Y
2	Kuster	Y	N	Y	Y	N	Y
NEW JERSEY							
1	Norcross	Y	N	Y	Y	N	Y
2	Van Drew	Y	Y	Y	Y	N	Y
3	Kim	Y	N	Y	Y	N	Y
4	**Smith, C.**	Y	Y	N	Y	Y	N
5	Gottheimer	Y	Y	Y	Y	N	Y
6	Pallone	Y	N	Y	Y	N	Y
7	Malinowski	Y	N	Y	Y	N	Y
8	Sires	Y	N	Y	Y	N	Y
9	Pascrell	Y	N	Y	Y	N	Y
10	Payne	Y	N	Y	Y	N	Y
11	Sherrill	Y	N	Y	Y	N	Y
12	Watson Coleman	Y	N	Y	Y	N	Y
NEW MEXICO							
1	Haaland	Y	N	Y	Y	N	Y
2	Torres Small	Y	N	Y	Y	N	Y
3	Luján	Y	N	Y	Y	N	Y
NEW YORK							
1	**Zeldin**	Y	Y	N	Y	Y	Y
2	**King, P.**	Y	Y	N	Y	Y	Y
3	Suozzi	Y	N	Y	Y	N	Y
4	Rice, K.	Y	N	Y	Y	N	Y
5	Meeks	Y	N	Y	Y	N	Y
6	Meng	Y	N	Y	Y	N	Y
7	Velázquez	Y	N	Y	Y	N	Y
8	Jeffries	Y	N	Y	Y	N	Y
9	Clarke	Y	N	Y	Y	N	Y
10	Nadler	Y	N	Y	Y	N	Y
11	Rose	Y	N	Y	Y	N	Y
12	Maloney, C.	Y	N	Y	Y	N	Y
13	Espaillat	Y	N	Y	Y	N	Y
14	Ocasio-Cortez	Y	N	Y	Y	N	Y
15	Serrano	Y	N	Y	Y	N	Y
16	Engel	Y	N	Y	Y	N	Y
17	Lowey	Y	N	Y	Y	N	Y
18	Maloney, S.P.	Y	N	Y	Y	N	Y
19	Delgado	Y	N	Y	Y	N	Y
20	Tonko	Y	N	Y	Y	N	Y
21	**Stefanik**	Y	Y	N	Y	Y	N
22	Brindisi	Y	Y	Y	Y	N	Y
23	**Reed**	Y	Y	N	Y	Y	Y
24	**Katko**	Y	Y	N	Y	Y	Y
25	Morelle	Y	N	Y	Y	N	Y
26	Higgins, B.	Y	N	Y	Y	N	Y
27	**Collins, C.**						
NORTH CAROLINA							
1	Butterfield	Y	N	Y	Y	N	Y
2	**Holding**	Y	Y	N	Y	Y	N
3	**Jones***						
4	Price	Y	N	Y	Y	N	Y
5	**Foxx**	Y	Y	N	Y	Y	N
6	**Walker**	Y	Y	N	Y	Y	N
7	**Rouzer**	Y	Y	N	Y	Y	N

		151	152	153	154	155	156
8	**Hudson**	Y	Y	N	Y	Y	N
9	vacant						
10	**McHenry**	Y	Y	N	Y	Y	N
11	**Meadows**	Y	Y	Y	Y	Y	N
12	Adams	Y	N	Y	Y	N	Y
13	**Budd**	Y	Y	N	Y	Y	N
NORTH DAKOTA							
AL	**Armstrong**	Y	Y	N	Y	Y	N
OHIO							
1	**Chabot**	Y	Y	N	Y	Y	N
2	**Wenstrup**	Y	Y	N	Y	Y	N
3	Beatty	Y	N	Y	Y	N	Y
4	**Jordan**	Y	Y	Y	Y	Y	N
5	**Latta**	Y	Y	N	Y	Y	N
6	**Johnson, B.**	Y	Y	N	Y	Y	N
7	**Gibbs**	Y	Y	N	Y	Y	N
8	**Davidson**	Y	Y	Y	Y	Y	N
9	Kaptur	Y	N	Y	Y	N	Y
10	**Turner**	Y	Y	N	Y	Y	Y
11	Fudge	Y	N	Y	Y	N	Y
12	**Balderson**	Y	Y	N	Y	Y	Y
13	Ryan	?	?	?	?	-	+
14	**Joyce**	Y	Y	N	Y	Y	Y
15	**Stivers**	Y	Y	N	Y	Y	Y
16	**Gonzalez**	Y	Y	N	Y	Y	Y
OKLAHOMA							
1	**Hern**	Y	Y	N	Y	Y	N
2	**Mullin**	Y	Y	N	Y	Y	N
3	**Lucas**	Y	Y	N	Y	Y	N
4	**Cole**	Y	Y	N	Y	Y	Y
5	Horn	Y	N	Y	Y	N	Y
OREGON							
1	Bonamici	Y	N	Y	Y	N	Y
2	**Walden**	Y	Y	N	Y	Y	Y
3	Blumenauer	Y	N	Y	Y	N	Y
4	DeFazio	Y	N	Y	Y	N	Y
5	Schrader	Y	N	Y	Y	N	Y
PENNSYLVANIA							
1	**Fitzpatrick**	Y	Y	N	Y	N	Y
2	Boyle	Y	N	Y	Y	N	Y
3	Evans	Y	N	Y	Y	N	Y
4	Dean	Y	N	Y	Y	N	Y
5	Scanlon	Y	N	Y	Y	N	Y
6	Houlahan	Y	N	Y	Y	N	Y
7	Wild	Y	N	Y	Y	N	Y
8	Cartwright	Y	N	Y	Y	N	Y
9	**Meuser**	Y	Y	N	Y	Y	N
10	**Perry**	Y	Y	N	Y	Y	N
11	**Smucker**	Y	Y	N	Y	Y	N
12	**Marino***						
13	**Joyce**	Y	Y	N	Y	Y	N
14	**Reschenthaler**	Y	Y	N	Y	Y	N
15	**Thompson, G.**	Y	Y	N	Y	Y	N
16	**Kelly, M.**	Y	Y	N	Y	Y	N
17	Lamb	Y	N	Y	Y	N	Y
18	Doyle	Y	N	Y	Y	N	Y
RHODE ISLAND							
1	Cicilline	Y	N	Y	Y	N	Y
2	Langevin	Y	N	Y	Y	N	Y
SOUTH CAROLINA							
1	Cunningham	Y	Y	Y	Y	N	Y
2	**Wilson, J.**	Y	Y	N	Y	Y	N
3	**Duncan**	Y	Y	N	Y	Y	N
4	**Timmons**	Y	Y	N	Y	Y	N
5	**Norman**	Y	Y	N	Y	Y	N
6	Clyburn	Y	N	Y	Y	N	Y
7	**Rice, T.**	Y	Y	N	Y	Y	N
SOUTH DAKOTA							
AL	**Johnson**	Y	Y	N	Y	Y	N
TENNESSEE							
1	**Roe**	Y	Y	N	Y	Y	N
2	**Burchett**	Y	Y	N	Y	Y	Y
3	**Fleischmann**	Y	Y	N	Y	Y	N
4	**DesJarlais**	Y	Y	N	Y	Y	N
5	Cooper	Y	N	Y	Y	N	Y
6	**Rose**	Y	Y	N	Y	Y	N
7	**Green**	Y	Y	N	Y	Y	N
8	**Kustoff**	?	?	?	?	?	?
9	Cohen	Y	N	Y	Y	N	Y
TEXAS							
1	**Gohmert**	Y	Y	Y	Y	Y	N
2	**Crenshaw**	Y	Y	N	Y	Y	N
3	**Taylor**	Y	Y	N	Y	Y	N
4	**Ratcliffe**	Y	Y	N	Y	Y	N

		151	152	153	154	155	156
5	**Gooden**	Y	Y	N	Y	Y	N
6	**Wright**	Y	Y	N	Y	Y	N
7	Fletcher	Y	N	Y	Y	N	Y
8	**Brady**	Y	Y	N	Y	Y	N
9	Green, A.	Y	N	Y	Y	N	Y
10	**McCaul**	Y	Y	N	Y	Y	Y
11	**Conaway**	Y	Y	N	Y	Y	N
12	**Granger**	+	+	-	+	+	+
13	**Thornberry**	Y	Y	N	Y	Y	N
14	**Weber**	Y	Y	N	Y	Y	N
15	Gonzalez	Y	N	Y	Y	N	Y
16	Escobar	Y	N	Y	Y	N	Y
17	**Flores**	Y	Y	N	Y	Y	N
18	Jackson Lee	Y	N	Y	Y	N	Y
19	**Arrington**	Y	Y	N	Y	Y	N
20	Castro	Y	N	Y	Y	N	Y
21	**Roy**	Y	Y	Y	Y	Y	N
22	**Olson**	Y	Y	N	Y	Y	Y
23	**Hurd**	Y	Y	N	Y	Y	Y
24	**Marchant**	Y	Y	N	Y	Y	Y
25	**Williams**	Y	Y	N	Y	Y	Y
26	**Burgess**	Y	Y	N	Y	Y	N
27	**Cloud**	Y	Y	Y	Y	Y	N
28	Cuellar	Y	N	Y	Y	N	Y
29	Garcia, S.	Y	N	Y	Y	N	Y
30	Johnson, E.B.	Y	N	Y	Y	N	Y
31	**Carter, J.**	Y	Y	N	Y	Y	Y
32	Allred	Y	N	Y	Y	N	Y
33	Veasey	Y	N	Y	Y	N	Y
34	Vela	Y	N	Y	Y	N	Y
35	Doggett	Y	N	Y	Y	N	Y
36	**Babin**	Y	Y	N	Y	Y	N
UTAH							
1	**Bishop, R.**	Y	Y	N	Y	Y	N
2	**Stewart**	Y	Y	N	Y	Y	N
3	**Curtis**	Y	Y	N	Y	Y	N
4	McAdams	Y	N	Y	Y	N	Y
VERMONT							
AL	Welch	Y	N	Y	Y	N	Y
VIRGINIA							
1	**Wittman**	Y	Y	N	Y	Y	N
2	Luria	Y	Y	Y	Y	N	Y
3	Scott, R.	Y	N	Y	Y	N	Y
4	McEachin	+	-	+	+	-	+
5	**Riggleman**	Y	Y	N	Y	Y	N
6	**Cline**	Y	Y	N	Y	Y	N
7	Spanberger	Y	N	Y	Y	N	Y
8	Beyer	Y	N	Y	Y	N	Y
9	**Griffith**	Y	Y	Y	Y	Y	N
10	Wexton	Y	N	Y	Y	N	Y
11	Connolly	Y	N	Y	Y	N	Y
WASHINGTON							
1	DelBene	Y	N	Y	Y	N	Y
2	Larsen	Y	N	Y	Y	N	Y
3	**Herrera Beutler**	Y	Y	N	Y	Y	Y
4	**Newhouse**	Y	Y	N	Y	Y	N
5	**McMorris Rodgers**	Y	Y	N	Y	Y	N
6	Kilmer	Y	N	Y	Y	N	Y
7	Jayapal	Y	N	Y	Y	N	Y
8	Schrier	Y	N	Y	Y	N	Y
9	Smith Adam	Y	N	Y	Y	N	Y
10	Heck	Y	N	Y	Y	N	Y
WEST VIRGINIA							
1	**McKinley**	Y	Y	N	Y	Y	N
2	**Mooney**	Y	Y	Y	Y	Y	N
3	**Miller**	Y	Y	N	Y	Y	N
WISCONSIN							
1	**Steil**	Y	Y	N	Y	Y	Y
2	Pocan	Y	N	Y	Y	N	Y
3	Kind	Y	N	Y	Y	N	Y
4	Moore	Y	N	Y	Y	N	Y
5	**Sensenbrenner**	Y	Y	N	Y	Y	N
6	**Grothman**	Y	Y	N	Y	Y	N
7	**Duffy**						
8	**Gallagher**	Y	Y	N	Y	Y	N
WYOMING							
AL	**Cheney**	Y	Y	N	Y	Y	N
DELEGATES							
	Radewagen (A.S.)				?		
	Norton (D.C.)				Y		
	San Nicolas (Guam)				Y		
	Sablan (N. Marianas)				+		
	González-Colón (P.R.)				?		
	Plaskett (V.I.)				?		

157. HCONRES19. Congressional Soapbox Derby - Passage. Adoption of the concurrent resolution that would authorize the use of the Capitol grounds for the annual Greater Washington Soap Box Derby on June 15, 2019 and would establish terms for public access, equipment use, and commercial activity related to the event. Motion agreed to 386-0: R 173-0; D 213-0. *Note: A two-thirds majority of those present and voting (258 in this case) is required for passage under suspension of the rules.* April 8, 2019.

158. HR1331. Water Pollution Management Grants - Passage. Craig, D-Minn., motion to suspend the rules and pass the bill that would authorize $200 million annually through fiscal 2024 for an Environmental Protection Agency grant program for state and local government programs related to water pollution source management. Motion agreed to 329-56: R 117-56; D 212-0. *Note: A two-thirds majority of those present and voting (257 in this case) is required for passage under suspension of the rules.* April 8, 2019.

159. Procedural Motion - Journal. Approval of the House Journal of April 8, 2019. Approved 194-182: R 31-139; D 163-43. April 8, 2019.

160. HR1644, HRES293, HR2021. Broadband Internet Access, IRS Operations, Budget Enforcement - Previous Question. Morelle, D-N.Y., motion to order the previous question (thus ending the debate and possibility of amendment) on the rule that would provide for House floor consideration of the Save the Internet Act (HR 1644) that would repeal the Federal Communications Commission's Dec. 14, 2017 rules on broadband internet service regulation; consideration of the Investing for the People Act (HR 2021) that would set discretionary spending caps for fiscal 2020; and automatic agreement in the House to a resolution (H Res 293) providing enforcement authority for fiscal 2020 discretionary spending caps. Motion agreed to 225-192: R 0-192; D 225-0. April 9, 2019.

161. HR2021, HR1644, HRES293. Broadband Internet Access, IRS Operations, Budget Enforcement - Rule. Adoption of the the rule that would provide for House floor consideration of the Save the Internet Act (HR 1644) that would repeal the Federal Communications Commission's Dec. 14, 2017 rules on broadband internet service regulation; consideration of the Investing for the People Act (HR 2021) that would set discretionary spending caps for fiscal 2020; and automatic agreement in the House to a resolution (H Res 293) providing enforcement authority for fiscal 2020 discretionary spending caps. The resolution (H Res 293) would provide budget enforcement authority for fiscal 2020, consistent with spending caps on cap adjustments provided for in the Investing for the People Act (HR 2021). The resolution would provide discretionary budget authority of $1.3 trillion for fiscal 2020. It would authorize spending cap adjustments for overseas contingency operations, not exceeding $69 billion for security funds and not exceeding $8 billion for non-security funds. It would authorize spending cap adjustments of up to $400 million for Internal Revenue Service tax enforcement and tax compliance activities and up to $7.5 billion for the 2020 census. The resolution would prohibit any fiscal 2020 appropriations measures from providing advance appropriations, with the exception of up to $87.6 billion in new budget authority for programs related to veterans' services for fiscal 2021, and up to $28.9 billion in new budget authority for other programs funded by advanced appropriations for fiscal 2021 and 2022. Adopted 219-201: R 0-194; D 219-7. April 9, 2019.

162. HR1759. Employment Services Eligibility for Unemployed - Passage. Davis, D-Ill., motion to suspend the rules and pass the bill that would extend eligibility for reemployment services to individuals who claim unemployment compensation. Motion agreed to 393-24: R 167-24; D 226-0. *Note: A two-thirds majority of those present and voting (278 in this case) is required for passage under suspension of the rules.* April 9, 2019.

		157	158	159	160	161	162
ALABAMA							
1	**Byrne**	Y	N	N	N	N	Y
2	**Roby**	Y	Y	N	N	N	Y
3	**Rogers, M.**	Y	Y	N	N	N	Y
4	**Aderholt**	Y	N	N	N	N	Y
5	**Brooks, M.**	Y	N	N	N	N	N
6	**Palmer**	Y	N	N	N	N	Y
7	Sewell	Y	Y	N	Y	Y	Y
ALASKA							
AL	**Young**	Y	Y	N	N	N	Y
ARIZONA							
1	O'Halleran	Y	Y	N	Y	Y	Y
2	Kirkpatrick	Y	Y	N	Y	Y	Y
3	Grijalva	Y	?	?	Y	Y	Y
4	**Gosar**	?	?	?	N	N	N
5	**Biggs**	Y	N	N	N	N	N
6	**Schweikert**	Y	Y	N	N	N	Y
7	Gallego	Y	Y	Y	Y	Y	Y
8	**Lesko**	Y	Y	N	N	N	Y
9	Stanton	Y	Y	Y	Y	Y	Y
ARKANSAS							
1	**Crawford**	Y	Y	N	N	N	Y
2	**Hill, F.**	Y	Y	N	N	N	Y
3	**Womack**	Y	Y	N	N	N	Y
4	**Westerman**	Y	Y	N	N	N	Y
CALIFORNIA							
1	**LaMalfa**	Y	Y	N	N	N	Y
2	Huffman	+	+	+	Y	Y	Y
3	Garamendi	Y	Y	Y	Y	Y	Y
4	**McClintock**	Y	N	Y	N	N	N
5	Thompson, M.	Y	Y	N	Y	Y	Y
6	Matsui	Y	Y	N	Y	Y	Y
7	Bera	Y	Y	?	Y	Y	Y
8	**Cook**	?	?	?	N	N	Y
9	McNerney	Y	?	Y	Y	Y	Y
10	Harder	Y	Y	N	Y	Y	Y
11	DeSaulnier	Y	Y	Y	Y	Y	Y
12	Pelosi						
13	Lee B.	?	?	?	Y	Y	Y
14	Speier	Y	Y	Y	Y	Y	Y
15	Swalwell	+	+	+	+	+	+
16	Costa	Y	Y	N	Y	Y	Y
17	Khanna	Y	Y	Y	Y	Y	Y
18	Eshoo	+	+	+	Y	Y	Y
19	Lofgren	Y	Y	Y	Y	Y	Y
20	Panetta	Y	Y	N	Y	Y	Y
21	Cox	Y	Y	Y	Y	Y	Y
22	**Nunes**	Y	N	N	N	N	Y
23	**McCarthy**	Y	N	N	N	N	Y
24	Carbajal	Y	Y	Y	Y	Y	Y
25	Hill, K.	Y	Y	Y	Y	Y	Y
26	Brownley	Y	Y	N	Y	Y	Y
27	Chu	Y	Y	Y	Y	Y	Y
28	Schiff	Y	Y	Y	Y	Y	Y
29	Cárdenas	Y	Y	Y	Y	Y	Y
30	Sherman	Y	Y	Y	Y	Y	Y
31	Aguilar	Y	Y	N	Y	Y	Y
32	Napolitano	Y	Y	Y	Y	Y	Y
33	Lieu	Y	Y	Y	Y	Y	Y
34	Gomez	Y	Y	Y	Y	Y	Y
35	Torres	Y	Y	Y	Y	Y	Y
36	Ruiz	Y	Y	Y	Y	Y	Y
37	Bass	Y	Y	Y	Y	Y	Y
38	Sánchez	?	?	?	?	?	?
39	Cisneros	Y	Y	N	Y	Y	Y
40	Roybal-Allard	Y	Y	Y	Y	Y	Y
41	Takano	Y	Y	Y	Y	Y	Y
42	**Calvert**	Y	Y	N	N	N	Y
43	Waters	Y	Y	N	Y	Y	Y
44	Barragán	Y	Y	N	Y	Y	Y
45	Porter	Y	Y	N	Y	Y	Y
46	Correa	Y	Y	N	Y	Y	Y
47	Lowenthal	Y	Y	Y	Y	Y	Y
48	Rouda	Y	Y	N	Y	Y	Y
49	Levin	Y	Y	Y	Y	Y	Y
50	**Hunter**	Y	N	N	N	N	Y
51	Vargas	Y	Y	Y	Y	Y	Y
52	Peters	Y	Y	?	Y	Y	Y

		157	158	159	160	161	162
53	Davis, S.	Y	Y	Y	Y	Y	Y
COLORADO							
1	DeGette	Y	Y	Y	Y	Y	Y
2	Neguse	Y	Y	Y	Y	Y	Y
3	**Tipton**	Y	N	N	N	N	Y
4	**Buck**	Y	N	N	N	N	N
5	**Lamborn**	?	?	?	N	N	Y
6	Crow	Y	Y	N	Y	Y	Y
7	Perlmutter	Y	Y	Y	Y	Y	Y
CONNECTICUT							
1	Larson	Y	Y	Y	Y	Y	Y
2	Courtney	Y	Y	Y	Y	Y	Y
3	DeLauro	Y	Y	Y	Y	Y	Y
4	Himes	Y	Y	Y	Y	Y	Y
5	Hayes	Y	Y	Y	Y	Y	Y
DELAWARE							
AL	Blunt Rochester	Y	Y	Y	Y	Y	Y
FLORIDA							
1	**Gaetz**	Y	N	N	N	N	Y
2	**Dunn**	Y	N	N	N	N	Y
3	**Yoho**	Y	N	N	N	N	Y
4	**Rutherford**	Y	N	N	N	N	Y
5	Lawson	Y	Y	Y	Y	Y	Y
6	**Waltz**	Y	Y	N	N	N	Y
7	Murphy	Y	Y	N	Y	Y	Y
8	**Posey**	Y	N	N	N	N	Y
9	Soto	Y	Y	Y	Y	Y	Y
10	Demings	Y	Y	Y	Y	Y	Y
11	**Webster**	Y	Y	N	N	N	Y
12	**Bilirakis**	Y	Y	N	N	N	Y
13	Crist	Y	Y	Y	Y	Y	Y
14	Castor	Y	Y	Y	Y	Y	Y
15	**Spano**	Y	Y	N	N	N	Y
16	**Buchanan**	Y	Y	N	N	N	Y
17	**Steube**	Y	N	N	N	N	Y
18	**Mast**	Y	N	N	N	N	Y
19	**Rooney**	?	?	?	?	?	?
20	Hastings	Y	Y	Y	Y	Y	Y
21	Frankel	Y	Y	Y	Y	Y	Y
22	Deutch	Y	Y	?	Y	Y	Y
23	Wasserman Schultz	Y	Y	Y	Y	Y	Y
24	Wilson, F.	Y	Y	?	Y	Y	Y
25	**Diaz-Balart**	Y	N	N	N	N	Y
26	Mucarsel-Powell	Y	Y	Y	Y	Y	Y
27	Shalala	Y	Y	Y	Y	Y	Y
GEORGIA							
1	**Carter, E.L.**	Y	N	N	N	N	Y
2	Bishop, S.	?	?	?	Y	Y	Y
3	**Ferguson**	Y	Y	N	N	N	Y
4	Johnson, H.	Y	Y	Y	Y	Y	Y
5	Lewis John	Y	Y	Y	Y	Y	Y
6	McBath	Y	Y	Y	Y	Y	Y
7	**Woodall**	Y	Y	N	N	N	Y
8	**Scott, A.**	Y	N	N	N	N	Y
9	**Collins, D.**	Y	N	N	N	N	Y
10	**Hice**	Y	N	N	N	N	N
11	**Loudermilk**	Y	N	N	N	N	Y
12	**Allen**	Y	N	N	N	N	Y
13	Scott, D.	Y	Y	Y	Y	Y	Y
14	**Graves, T.**	Y	N	N	N	N	Y
HAWAII							
1	Case	Y	Y	Y	Y	Y	Y
2	Gabbard	?	?	?	?	?	?
IDAHO							
1	**Fulcher**	Y	Y	N	N	N	Y
2	**Simpson**	?	?	?	N	N	Y
ILLINOIS							
1	Rush	Y	Y	Y	Y	Y	Y
2	Kelly, R.	Y	Y	Y	Y	Y	Y
3	Lipinski	?	?	?	Y	Y	Y
4	García, J.	Y	Y	Y	Y	Y	Y
5	Quigley	Y	Y	Y	Y	Y	Y
6	Casten	Y	Y	Y	Y	Y	Y
7	Davis, D.	?	?	?	Y	Y	Y
8	Krishnamoorthi	Y	Y	Y	Y	Y	Y
9	Schakowsky	Y	Y	Y	Y	Y	Y
10	Schneider	Y	Y	Y	Y	Y	Y
11	Foster	Y	Y	Y	Y	Y	Y

KEY:	**Republicans**		Democrats		*Independents*	
Y	Voted for (yea)	**N**	Voted against (nay)	**P**	Voted "present"	
+	Announced for	**–**	Announced against	**?**	Did not vote or otherwise make position known	
#	Paired for	**X**	Paired against			

		157	158	159	160	161	162
12	**Bost**	Y	Y	N	N	N	Y
13	**Davis, R.**	Y	Y	N	N	N	Y
14	Underwood	Y	Y	Y	Y	Y	Y
15	**Shimkus**	Y	Y	N	N	N	Y
16	**Kinzinger**	Y	Y	Y	N	N	Y
17	Bustos	Y	Y	Y	Y	Y	Y
18	**LaHood**	Y	Y	N	N	N	Y
INDIANA							
1	Visclosky	Y	Y	Y	Y	Y	Y
2	**Walorski**	Y	Y	N	N	N	Y
3	**Banks**	Y	N	Y	N	N	Y
4	**Baird**	Y	Y	N	N	N	Y
5	**Brooks, S.**	?	?	?	N	N	Y
6	**Pence**	Y	Y	N	N	N	Y
7	Carson	Y	Y	Y	Y	Y	Y
8	**Bucshon**	Y	Y	N	N	N	Y
9	**Hollingsworth**	?	?	?	N	N	Y
IOWA							
1	Finkenauer	Y	Y	N	Y	Y	Y
2	Loebsack	Y	Y	Y	Y	Y	Y
3	Axne	Y	Y	N	Y	Y	Y
4	**King, S.**	Y	Y	Y	N	N	Y
KANSAS							
1	**Marshall**	Y	Y	N	N	N	Y
2	**Watkins**	Y	Y	Y	N	N	Y
3	Davids	Y	Y	Y	Y	Y	Y
4	**Estes**	Y	N	N	N	N	Y
KENTUCKY							
1	**Comer**	Y	Y	?	N	N	N
2	**Guthrie**	Y	Y	N	N	N	Y
3	Yarmuth	Y	Y	Y	Y	Y	Y
4	**Massie**	Y	N	N	N	N	N
5	**Rogers, H.**	+	+	+	N	N	Y
6	**Barr**	?	?	?	N	N	Y
LOUISIANA							
1	**Scalise**	Y	Y	N	N	N	Y
2	Richmond	?	Y	Y	Y	Y	Y
3	**Higgins, C.**	+	-	+	-	N	Y
4	**Johnson, M.**	Y	N	N	N	N	N
5	**Abraham**	?	?	?	?	?	?
6	**Graves, G.**	Y	Y	N	N	N	Y
MAINE							
1	Pingree	Y	Y	Y	Y	Y	Y
2	Golden	Y	Y	N	Y	Y	Y
MARYLAND							
1	**Harris**	Y	N	N	N	N	Y
2	Ruppersberger	Y	Y	Y	Y	Y	Y
3	Sarbanes	Y	Y	Y	Y	Y	Y
4	Brown, A.	Y	Y	Y	Y	Y	Y
5	Hoyer	Y	Y	Y	Y	Y	Y
6	Trone	Y	Y	?	Y	Y	Y
7	Cummings	?	?	?	Y	Y	Y
8	Raskin	Y	Y	Y	Y	Y	Y
MASSACHUSETTS							
1	Neal	Y	Y	Y	Y	Y	Y
2	McGovern	Y	Y	Y	Y	Y	Y
3	Trahan	Y	Y	Y	Y	Y	Y
4	Kennedy	Y	Y	Y	Y	Y	Y
5	Clark	?	?	?	Y	Y	Y
6	Moulton	?	?	?	Y	Y	Y
7	Pressley	Y	Y	Y	Y	Y	Y
8	Lynch	Y	Y	Y	Y	Y	Y
9	Keating	Y	Y	Y	Y	Y	Y
MICHIGAN							
1	**Bergman**	Y	Y	Y	N	N	Y
2	**Huizenga**	Y	Y	N	N	N	Y
3	**Amash**	Y	N	N	N	N	N
4	**Moolenaar**	Y	Y	N	N	N	Y
5	Kildee	Y	Y	Y	Y	Y	Y
6	**Upton**	Y	Y	N	N	N	Y
7	**Walberg**	Y	Y	N	N	N	Y
8	Slotkin	Y	Y	N	Y	Y	Y
9	Levin	Y	Y	Y	Y	Y	Y
10	**Mitchell**	Y	Y	N	N	N	Y
11	Stevens	Y	Y	N	Y	Y	Y
12	Dingell	Y	Y	Y	Y	Y	Y
13	Tlaib	Y	Y	Y	Y	Y	Y
14	Lawrence	Y	Y	Y	Y	Y	Y
MINNESOTA							
1	**Hagedorn**	Y	N	N	N	N	Y
2	Craig	Y	Y	N	Y	Y	Y
3	Phillips	Y	Y	Y	Y	N	Y
4	McCollum	Y	Y	Y	Y	Y	Y
5	Omar	Y	Y	Y	Y	Y	Y
6	**Emmer**	Y	N	N	N	N	Y
7	Peterson	Y	Y	N	Y	Y	Y
8	**Stauber**	Y	Y	N	N	N	Y
MISSISSIPPI							
1	**Kelly, T.**	?	+	+	N	N	Y
2	Thompson, B.	Y	Y	Y	Y	Y	Y
3	**Guest**	?	?	?	N	N	Y
4	**Palazzo**	?	?	?	N	N	Y
MISSOURI							
1	Clay	Y	Y	Y	Y	Y	Y
2	**Wagner**	Y	Y	Y	N	N	Y
3	**Luetkemeyer**	Y	Y	N	N	N	Y
4	**Hartzler**	Y	Y	N	N	N	Y
5	Cleaver	Y	Y	Y	Y	Y	Y
6	**Graves, S.**	Y	Y	N	N	N	Y
7	**Long**	Y	Y	Y	N	N	Y
8	**Smith, J.**	Y	N	N	N	N	Y
MONTANA							
AL	**Gianforte**	?	?	?	N	N	Y
NEBRASKA							
1	**Fortenberry**	Y	Y	Y	N	N	Y
2	**Bacon**	Y	N	Y	N	N	Y
3	**Smith, Adrian**	Y	Y	N	N	N	Y
NEVADA							
1	Titus	+	+	+	Y	Y	Y
2	**Amodei**	?	?	?	?	?	?
3	Lee	Y	Y	N	Y	Y	Y
4	Horsford	Y	Y	Y	Y	Y	Y
NEW HAMPSHIRE							
1	Pappas	Y	Y	Y	Y	Y	Y
2	Kuster	Y	Y	Y	Y	Y	Y
NEW JERSEY							
1	Norcross	Y	Y	Y	Y	Y	Y
2	Van Drew	Y	Y	N	Y	Y	Y
3	Kim	Y	Y	N	Y	Y	Y
4	**Smith, C.**	Y	Y	Y	N	N	Y
5	Gottheimer	Y	Y	N	Y	Y	Y
6	Pallone	Y	Y	Y	Y	Y	Y
7	Malinowski	Y	Y	Y	Y	Y	Y
8	Sires	Y	Y	Y	Y	Y	Y
9	Pascrell	Y	Y	Y	Y	Y	Y
10	Payne	Y	Y	Y	Y	Y	Y
11	Sherrill	Y	Y	Y	Y	Y	Y
12	Watson Coleman	Y	Y	N	Y	Y	Y
NEW MEXICO							
1	Haaland	Y	Y	Y	Y	Y	Y
2	Torres Small	Y	Y	Y	Y	N	Y
3	Luján	Y	Y	Y	Y	Y	Y
NEW YORK							
1	**Zeldin**	Y	Y	N	N	N	Y
2	**King, P.**	Y	Y	N	N	N	Y
3	Suozzi	Y	Y	N	Y	Y	Y
4	Rice, K.	Y	Y	?	?	?	?
5	Meeks	Y	Y	Y	Y	Y	Y
6	Meng	Y	Y	Y	Y	Y	Y
7	Velázquez	Y	Y	Y	Y	Y	Y
8	Jeffries	?	?	?	+	+	?
9	Clarke	Y	Y	Y	Y	Y	Y
10	Nadler	Y	Y	Y	Y	Y	Y
11	Rose	Y	Y	Y	Y	Y	Y
12	Maloney, C.	Y	Y	Y	Y	Y	Y
13	Espaillat	Y	Y	Y	Y	Y	Y
14	Ocasio-Cortez	Y	Y	Y	Y	Y	Y
15	Serrano	Y	Y	Y	Y	Y	Y
16	Engel	?	?	?	Y	Y	Y
17	Lowey	Y	Y	Y	Y	Y	Y
18	Maloney, S.P.	Y	Y	N	Y	Y	Y
19	Delgado	Y	Y	Y	Y	Y	Y
20	Tonko	Y	Y	P	Y	Y	Y
21	**Stefanik**	Y	Y	Y	N	N	Y
22	Brindisi	Y	Y	N	Y	Y	Y
23	**Reed**	Y	Y	N	N	N	Y
24	**Katko**	Y	?	N	N	N	Y
25	Morelle	Y	Y	Y	Y	Y	Y
26	Higgins, B.	Y	Y	Y	Y	Y	Y
27	**Collins, C.**						
NORTH CAROLINA							
1	Butterfield	Y	Y	Y	Y	Y	Y
2	**Holding**	Y	N	N	N	N	Y
3	**Jones***						
4	Price	Y	Y	Y	Y	Y	Y
5	**Foxx**	Y	N	N	N	N	Y
6	**Walker**	Y	Y	N	N	N	Y
7	**Rouzer**	Y	Y	N	N	N	Y
8	**Hudson**	Y	N	N	N	N	Y
9	vacant						
10	**McHenry**	Y	Y	N	N	N	Y
11	**Meadows**	Y	Y	Y	N	N	?
12	Adams	Y	Y	Y	Y	Y	Y
13	**Budd**	Y	N	N	N	N	Y
NORTH DAKOTA							
AL	**Armstrong**	Y	Y	Y	N	N	Y
OHIO							
1	**Chabot**	Y	Y	N	N	N	Y
2	**Wenstrup**	Y	Y	N	N	N	Y
3	Beatty	Y	Y	Y	Y	Y	Y
4	**Jordan**	Y	N	N	N	N	N
5	**Latta**	Y	Y	N	N	N	Y
6	**Johnson, B.**	Y	Y	N	N	N	Y
7	**Gibbs**	Y	Y	N	N	N	Y
8	**Davidson**	Y	Y	Y	N	N	Y
9	Kaptur	?	?	?	Y	Y	Y
10	**Turner**	Y	Y	N	N	N	Y
11	Fudge	Y	Y	Y	Y	Y	Y
12	**Balderson**	Y	Y	N	N	N	Y
13	Ryan	?	?	?	?	?	?
14	**Joyce**	Y	Y	N	N	N	Y
15	**Stivers**	Y	Y	Y	N	N	Y
16	**Gonzalez**	Y	Y	N	N	N	Y
OKLAHOMA							
1	**Hern**	Y	N	N	N	N	N
2	**Mullin**	?	?	?	N	N	?
3	**Lucas**	Y	Y	N	N	N	Y
4	**Cole**	Y	Y	N	N	N	Y
5	Horn	Y	Y	Y	Y	N	Y
OREGON							
1	Bonamici	Y	Y	Y	Y	Y	Y
2	**Walden**	+	+	?	N	N	Y
3	Blumenauer	Y	Y	Y	Y	Y	Y
4	DeFazio	Y	Y	Y	Y	Y	Y
5	Schrader	Y	Y	N	Y	Y	Y
PENNSYLVANIA							
1	**Fitzpatrick**	Y	Y	N	N	N	Y
2	Boyle	Y	Y	Y	Y	Y	Y
3	Evans	Y	Y	Y	Y	Y	Y
4	Dean	Y	Y	Y	Y	Y	Y
5	Scanlon	Y	Y	Y	Y	Y	Y
6	Houlahan	Y	Y	N	Y	Y	Y
7	Wild	Y	Y	Y	Y	Y	Y
8	Cartwright	Y	Y	Y	Y	Y	Y
9	**Meuser**	Y	Y	N	N	N	N
10	**Perry**	Y	Y	N	N	N	Y
11	**Smucker**	Y	Y	N	N	N	Y
12	**Marino***						
13	**Joyce**	Y	Y	N	N	N	Y
14	**Reschenthaler**	Y	Y	N	N	N	Y
15	**Thompson, G.**	Y	Y	N	N	N	Y
16	**Kelly, M.**	Y	Y	N	N	N	Y
17	Lamb	Y	Y	Y	Y	Y	Y
18	Doyle	Y	Y	?	Y	Y	Y
RHODE ISLAND							
1	Cicilline	Y	Y	Y	Y	Y	Y
2	Langevin	Y	Y	Y	Y	Y	Y
SOUTH CAROLINA							
1	Cunningham	Y	Y	N	Y	N	Y
2	**Wilson, J.**	Y	Y	N	N	N	Y
3	**Duncan**	Y	N	N	N	N	N
4	**Timmons**	Y	Y	N	N	N	Y
5	**Norman**	Y	N	N	N	N	N
6	Clyburn	Y	Y	Y	Y	Y	Y
7	**Rice, T.**	Y	N	N	N	N	Y
SOUTH DAKOTA							
AL	**Johnson**	Y	Y	N	N	N	Y
TENNESSEE							
1	**Roe**	Y	Y	N	N	N	Y
2	**Burchett**	Y	N	N	N	N	N
3	**Fleischmann**	Y	Y	Y	N	N	Y
4	**DesJarlais**	?	?	?	N	N	Y
5	Cooper	Y	Y	Y	Y	Y	Y
6	**Rose**	Y	Y	N	N	N	Y
7	**Green**	Y	N	N	N	N	N
8	**Kustoff**	Y	Y	N	N	N	Y
9	Cohen	Y	Y	Y	Y	Y	Y
TEXAS							
1	**Gohmert**	Y	N	?	N	N	Y
2	**Crenshaw**	Y	Y	N	N	N	?
3	**Taylor**	Y	N	Y	N	N	Y
4	**Ratcliffe**	Y	N	N	N	N	Y
5	**Gooden**	Y	N	N	N	N	Y
6	**Wright**	?	?	?	N	N	N
7	Fletcher	Y	Y	N	Y	Y	Y
8	**Brady**	Y	Y	Y	N	N	Y
9	Green, A.	Y	Y	N	Y	Y	Y
10	**McCaul**	Y	Y	N	N	N	Y
11	**Conaway**	Y	N	N	N	N	Y
12	**Granger**	Y	Y	N	N	N	Y
13	**Thornberry**	Y	Y	Y	N	N	Y
14	**Weber**	?	N	N	N	N	N
15	Gonzalez	+	+	+	Y	Y	Y
16	Escobar	Y	Y	Y	Y	Y	Y
17	**Flores**	Y	Y	N	N	N	Y
18	Jackson Lee	Y	Y	Y	Y	Y	Y
19	**Arrington**	?	?	?	N	N	Y
20	Castro	Y	Y	Y	Y	Y	Y
21	**Roy**	?	?	?	N	N	N
22	**Olson**	Y	N	N	N	N	N
23	**Hurd**	Y	Y	N	N	N	Y
24	**Marchant**	Y	Y	N	N	N	Y
25	**Williams**	Y	Y	N	N	N	Y
26	**Burgess**	Y	N	N	N	N	Y
27	**Cloud**	Y	N	N	N	N	Y
28	Cuellar	Y	Y	N	Y	Y	Y
29	Garcia, S.	Y	Y	Y	Y	Y	Y
30	Johnson, E.B.	Y	Y	Y	Y	Y	Y
31	**Carter, J.**	Y	Y	N	N	N	Y
32	Allred	Y	Y	Y	Y	Y	Y
33	Veasey	Y	Y	Y	Y	Y	Y
34	Vela	Y	Y	Y	Y	Y	Y
35	Doggett	Y	Y	Y	Y	Y	Y
36	**Babin**	Y	Y	N	N	N	N
UTAH							
1	**Bishop, R.**	Y	N	N	?	N	Y
2	**Stewart**	?	?	?	N	N	Y
3	**Curtis**	Y	N	N	N	N	Y
4	McAdams	Y	Y	N	Y	N	Y
VERMONT							
AL	Welch	+	+	+	+	+	+
VIRGINIA							
1	**Wittman**	Y	Y	N	N	N	Y
2	Luria	Y	Y	Y	Y	Y	Y
3	Scott, R.	Y	Y	Y	Y	Y	Y
4	McEachin	?	?	?	+	+	+
5	**Riggleman**	Y	Y	?	N	N	Y
6	**Cline**	Y	N	N	N	N	N
7	Spanberger	Y	Y	N	Y	N	Y
8	Beyer	Y	Y	Y	Y	Y	Y
9	**Griffith**	Y	Y	N	N	N	Y
10	Wexton	Y	Y	N	Y	Y	Y
11	Connolly	Y	Y	Y	Y	Y	Y
WASHINGTON							
1	DelBene	Y	Y	Y	Y	Y	Y
2	Larsen	Y	Y	Y	Y	Y	Y
3	**Herrera Beutler**	Y	Y	N	N	N	Y
4	**Newhouse**	Y	Y	Y	N	N	Y
5	**McMorris Rodgers**	Y	Y	Y	N	N	Y
6	Kilmer	Y	Y	Y	Y	Y	Y
7	Jayapal	Y	Y	Y	Y	Y	Y
8	Schrier	Y	Y	Y	Y	Y	Y
9	Smith Adam	Y	Y	Y	Y	Y	Y
10	Heck	Y	Y	Y	Y	Y	Y
WEST VIRGINIA							
1	**McKinley**	Y	Y	N	N	N	Y
2	**Mooney**	Y	Y	N	N	N	Y
3	**Miller**	Y	Y	N	N	N	Y
WISCONSIN							
1	**Steil**	Y	Y	Y	N	N	Y
2	Pocan	Y	Y	Y	Y	Y	Y
3	Kind	Y	Y	N	Y	Y	Y
4	Moore	Y	Y	Y	Y	Y	Y
5	**Sensenbrenner**	Y	N	?	N	N	Y
6	**Grothman**	Y	N	Y	N	N	Y
7	**Duffy**						
8	**Gallagher**	Y	Y	N	N	N	Y
WYOMING							
AL	**Cheney**	Y	Y	N	N	N	Y
DELEGATES							
	Radewagen (A.S.)						
	Norton (D.C.)						
	San Nicolas (Guam)						
	Sablan (N. Marianas)						
	González-Colón (P.R.)						
	Plaskett (V.I.)						

163. HR1644. Broadband Internet Access - Rural Standalone Broadband Internet Access. Delgado, D-N.Y., amendment that would require the Government Accountability Office to submit a report to Congress detailing the benefits of broadband internet access offered on a standalone basis, including recommendations to increase the availability of standalone broadband internet access service in rural areas. Adopted in Committee of the Whole 363-60: R 132-60; D 230-0, I 1-0. April 10, 2019.

164. HR1644. Broadband Internet Access - Broadband Distribution Data Collection. Wexton, D-Va., amendment that would require the Federal Communications Commission to submit a report to Congress on a plan regarding how the commission would evaluate and address problems with the collection of data through the use of Form 477, related to the deployment of broadband internet access service. Adopted in Committee of the Whole 376-46: R 146-46; D 229-0; I 1-0. April 10, 2019.

165. HR1644. Broadband Internet Access - Blocking of Unlawful Content. McAdams, D-Utah, amendment that would clarify that nothing in the bill would prohibit internet service providers from blocking content that is unlawful and clarify that the bill would not impose any legal obligation on internet service providers to determine whether content is lawful. Adopted in Committee of the Whole 423-0: R 190-0; D 232-0; I 1-0. April 10, 2019.

166. HR1644. Broadband Internet Access - Recommit. Walden, R-Ore., motion to recommit the bill to the House Energy and Commerce Committee with instructions to report it back immediately with an amendment that would clarify that nothing in the bill should be construed in such a way as to modify, impair or supersede the Internet Tax Freedom Act. Motion rejected 204-216: R 191-0; D 13-216. April 10, 2019.

167. HR1644. Broadband Internet Access - Passage. Passage of the bill that would reverse the Federal Communications Commission's Dec. 2017 decision related to regulation of broadband internet services, which classified internet service as an "information service" to be regulated under Title I FCC authorities. It would effectively restore and codify a 2015 FCC regulatory framework and any other rules repealed or amended by the 2017 decision. The restored framework would classify internet service as a "telecommunications service" to be regulated under certain Title II FCC authorities, and restored rules would include prohibitions on blocking and paid prioritization of content by internet service providers. The restored rules would be effective retroactively, and the bill would prohibit the FCC from effectively reissuing the nullified rules. It would also exempt small broadband internet providers from certain public disclosure requirements related to network management practices, performance, or commercial terms, for one year after enactment. Passed 232-190: R 1-190; D 231-0. *Note: A "nay" was a vote in support of the president's position.* April 10, 2019.

168. HR91. Columbia River Lands Maintenance - Passage. Van Drew, D-N.J., motion to suspend the rules and pass the bill that would authorize such sums as are necessary for the Interior Department and Bureau of Indian Affairs to assess and improve sanitation, safety conditions, and infrastructure on federal lands maintained for the benefit of certain Native American tribes along the Columbia River in Washington and Oregon. Motion agreed to 396-18: R 171-18; D 225-0. *Note: A two-thirds majority of those present and voting (276 in this case) is required for passage under suspension of the rules.* April 29, 2019.

		163	164	165	166	167	168
ALABAMA							
1	**Byrne**	Y	Y	Y	Y	N	N
2	**Roby**	Y	Y	Y	Y	N	Y
3	**Rogers, M.**	Y	Y	Y	Y	N	Y
4	**Aderholt**	Y	Y	Y	Y	N	Y
5	**Brooks, M.**	N	N	Y	Y	N	?
6	**Palmer**	N	Y	Y	Y	N	Y
7	Sewell	Y	Y	Y	N	Y	Y
ALASKA							
AL	**Young**	Y	Y	Y	Y	N	Y
ARIZONA							
1	O'Halleran	Y	Y	Y	N	Y	Y
2	Kirkpatrick	Y	Y	Y	N	Y	Y
3	Grijalva	Y	Y	Y	N	Y	Y
4	**Gosar**	N	N	Y	Y	N	N
5	**Biggs**	N	N	Y	Y	N	N
6	**Schweikert**	N	N	Y	Y	N	Y
7	Gallego	Y	Y	Y	N	Y	Y
8	**Lesko**	N	N	Y	Y	N	Y
9	Stanton	Y	Y	?	N	Y	Y
ARKANSAS							
1	**Crawford**	Y	Y	Y	Y	N	Y
2	**Hill, F.**	Y	Y	Y	Y	N	Y
3	**Womack**	Y	Y	Y	Y	N	Y
4	**Westerman**	Y	N	Y	Y	N	Y
CALIFORNIA							
1	**LaMalfa**	N	Y	Y	Y	N	Y
2	Huffman	Y	Y	Y	-	Y	Y
3	Garamendi	Y	Y	Y	N	Y	Y
4	**McClintock**	Y	Y	Y	Y	N	Y
5	Thompson, M.	Y	Y	Y	N	Y	Y
6	Matsui	Y	Y	Y	N	Y	Y
7	Bera	Y	Y	Y	N	Y	Y
8	**Cook**	Y	Y	Y	Y	N	Y
9	McNerney	Y	Y	Y	N	Y	Y
10	Harder	Y	Y	Y	N	Y	Y
11	DeSaulnier	Y	Y	Y	N	Y	Y
12	Pelosi					Y	
13	Lee B.	Y	Y	Y	N	Y	Y
14	Speier	Y	Y	Y	N	Y	Y
15	Swalwell	Y	Y	Y	N	Y	Y
16	Costa	Y	Y	Y	N	Y	Y
17	Khanna	Y	Y	Y	N	Y	Y
18	Eshoo	Y	Y	Y	N	Y	Y
19	Lofgren	Y	Y	Y	N	Y	Y
20	Panetta	Y	Y	Y	N	Y	Y
21	Cox	Y	Y	Y	N	Y	+
22	**Nunes**	Y	Y	Y	Y	N	Y
23	**McCarthy**	Y	Y	Y	Y	N	Y
24	Carbajal	Y	Y	Y	N	Y	Y
25	Hill, K.	Y	Y	Y	N	Y	Y
26	Brownley	Y	Y	Y	N	Y	Y
27	Chu	Y	Y	Y	N	Y	Y
28	Schiff	Y	Y	Y	N	Y	Y
29	Cárdenas	Y	Y	Y	N	Y	Y
30	Sherman	Y	Y	Y	N	Y	Y
31	Aguilar	Y	Y	Y	N	Y	Y
32	Napolitano	Y	Y	Y	N	Y	Y
33	Lieu	Y	Y	Y	N	Y	Y
34	Gomez	Y	Y	Y	N	Y	Y
35	Torres	Y	Y	Y	N	Y	?
36	Ruiz	Y	Y	Y	N	Y	Y
37	Bass	Y	Y	Y	N	Y	Y
38	Sánchez	?	?	?	?	?	Y
39	Cisneros	Y	Y	Y	N	Y	Y
40	Roybal-Allard	Y	Y	Y	N	Y	Y
41	Takano	Y	Y	Y	N	Y	Y
42	**Calvert**	Y	Y	Y	Y	N	Y
43	Waters	Y	Y	Y	N	Y	Y
44	Barragán	Y	Y	Y	N	Y	Y
45	Porter	Y	Y	Y	N	Y	Y
46	Correa	Y	Y	Y	N	Y	Y
47	Lowenthal	Y	Y	Y	N	Y	Y
48	Rouda	Y	Y	Y	N	Y	Y
49	Levin	Y	Y	Y	N	Y	Y
50	**Hunter**	N	Y	Y	Y	N	Y
51	Vargas	Y	Y	Y	N	Y	Y
52	Peters	Y	Y	Y	N	Y	Y

		163	164	165	166	167	168
53	Davis, S.	Y	Y	Y	N	Y	Y
COLORADO							
1	DeGette	Y	Y	Y	N	Y	Y
2	Neguse	Y	Y	Y	N	Y	Y
3	**Tipton**	Y	Y	Y	Y	N	Y
4	**Buck**	N	N	Y	Y	N	N
5	**Lamborn**	N	N	Y	Y	N	Y
6	Crow	Y	Y	Y	N	Y	Y
7	Perlmutter	Y	Y	Y	N	Y	Y
CONNECTICUT							
1	Larson	Y	Y	Y	N	Y	Y
2	Courtney	Y	Y	Y	N	Y	Y
3	DeLauro	Y	Y	Y	N	Y	Y
4	Himes	Y	Y	Y	N	Y	Y
5	Hayes	Y	Y	Y	N	Y	Y
DELAWARE							
AL	Blunt Rochester	Y	Y	Y	N	Y	Y
FLORIDA							
1	**Gaetz**	N	N	Y	Y	N	Y
2	**Dunn**	Y	N	Y	Y	N	?
3	**Yoho**	N	N	Y	Y	N	?
4	**Rutherford**	N	N	Y	Y	N	Y
5	Lawson	Y	Y	Y	N	Y	Y
6	**Waltz**	Y	Y	Y	Y	N	Y
7	Murphy	Y	Y	Y	N	Y	Y
8	**Posey**	N	N	Y	Y	Y	Y
9	Soto	Y	Y	Y	N	Y	Y
10	Demings	Y	Y	Y	N	Y	Y
11	**Webster**	N	N	Y	Y	N	Y
12	**Bilirakis**	Y	Y	Y	Y	N	Y
13	Crist	Y	Y	Y	N	Y	Y
14	Castor	Y	Y	Y	N	Y	Y
15	**Spano**	Y	Y	Y	Y	N	Y
16	**Buchanan**	Y	Y	Y	Y	N	Y
17	**Steube**	N	N	Y	Y	N	Y
18	**Mast**	N	Y	Y	Y	N	Y
19	**Rooney**	?	?	?	?	?	?
20	Hastings	Y	Y	Y	N	Y	?
21	Frankel	Y	Y	Y	N	Y	Y
22	Deutch	Y	Y	Y	N	Y	?
23	Wasserman Schultz	Y	Y	Y	N	Y	Y
24	Wilson, F.	Y	Y	Y	N	Y	Y
25	**Diaz-Balart**	Y	Y	Y	Y	N	Y
26	Mucarsel-Powell	Y	Y	Y	N	Y	Y
27	Shalala	Y	Y	Y	N	Y	Y
GEORGIA							
1	**Carter, E.L.**	N	Y	Y	Y	N	Y
2	Bishop, S.	Y	Y	Y	N	Y	Y
3	**Ferguson**	N	Y	Y	Y	N	Y
4	Johnson, H.	Y	Y	Y	N	Y	Y
5	Lewis John	Y	Y	Y	N	Y	Y
6	McBath	Y	Y	Y	N	Y	Y
7	**Woodall**	N	Y	Y	Y	N	Y
8	**Scott, A.**	Y	Y	Y	Y	N	Y
9	**Collins, D.**	Y	Y	Y	Y	N	Y
10	**Hice**	N	Y	Y	Y	N	Y
11	**Loudermilk**	Y	N	Y	Y	N	N
12	**Allen**	N	Y	Y	Y	N	N
13	Scott, D.	Y	Y	Y	N	Y	Y
14	**Graves, T.**	N	N	Y	Y	N	Y
HAWAII							
1	Case	Y	Y	Y	N	Y	Y
2	Gabbard	Y	Y	Y	N	Y	Y
IDAHO							
1	**Fulcher**	N	Y	Y	Y	N	Y
2	**Simpson**	Y	Y	Y	Y	N	Y
ILLINOIS							
1	Rush	Y	Y	Y	N	Y	?
2	Kelly, R.	Y	Y	Y	N	Y	Y
3	Lipinski	Y	Y	Y	N	Y	Y
4	García, J.	Y	Y	Y	N	Y	Y
5	Quigley	Y	Y	Y	N	Y	Y
6	Casten	Y	Y	Y	N	Y	Y
7	Davis, D.	Y	Y	Y	N	Y	Y
8	Krishnamoorthi	Y	Y	Y	N	Y	Y
9	Schakowsky	Y	Y	Y	N	Y	Y
10	Schneider	Y	Y	Y	N	Y	Y
11	Foster	Y	Y	Y	N	Y	Y

		163	164	165	166	167	168
12	**Bost**	Y	Y	Y	Y	N	Y
13	**Davis, R.**	N	Y	Y	Y	N	Y
14	Underwood	Y	Y	Y	N	Y	Y
15	**Shimkus**	Y	Y	Y	Y	N	Y
16	**Kinzinger**	Y	Y	Y	Y	N	Y
17	Bustos	Y	Y	Y	N	Y	Y
18	**LaHood**	Y	Y	Y	Y	N	Y
INDIANA							
1	Visclosky	Y	Y	Y	N	Y	Y
2	**Walorski**	Y	Y	Y	Y	N	Y
3	**Banks**	N	N	Y	Y	N	Y
4	**Baird**	Y	Y	Y	Y	N	Y
5	**Brooks, S.**	Y	Y	Y	Y	N	Y
6	**Pence**	Y	Y	Y	Y	N	Y
7	Carson	Y	Y	Y	N	Y	Y
8	**Bucshon**	Y	Y	Y	Y	N	Y
9	**Hollingsworth**	Y	Y	Y	Y	N	Y
IOWA							
1	Finkenauer	Y	Y	Y	N	Y	Y
2	Loebsack	Y	Y	Y	N	Y	Y
3	Axne	Y	Y	Y	Y	Y	Y
4	**King, S.**	Y	Y	Y	Y	N	Y
KANSAS							
1	**Marshall**	N	Y	Y	Y	N	Y
2	**Watkins**	Y	Y	Y	Y	N	Y
3	Davids	Y	Y	Y	N	Y	Y
4	**Estes**	Y	N	Y	Y	N	Y
KENTUCKY							
1	**Comer**	Y	Y	Y	Y	N	Y
2	**Guthrie**	Y	Y	Y	Y	N	Y
3	Yarmuth	Y	?	Y	N	Y	Y
4	**Massie**	N	N	Y	Y	N	N
5	**Rogers, H.**	Y	Y	Y	Y	N	Y
6	**Barr**	Y	N	Y	Y	N	Y
LOUISIANA							
1	**Scalise**	Y	Y	Y	Y	N	Y
2	Richmond	Y	Y	Y	N	Y	Y
3	**Higgins, C.**	Y	Y	Y	Y	N	Y
4	**Johnson, M.**	N	Y	Y	Y	N	Y
5	**Abraham**	?	?	?	?	?	?
6	**Graves, G.**	Y	Y	Y	Y	N	Y
MAINE							
1	Pingree	Y	Y	Y	N	Y	Y
2	Golden	Y	Y	Y	Y	Y	Y
MARYLAND							
1	**Harris**	N	N	Y	Y	N	Y
2	Ruppersberger	Y	Y	Y	N	Y	Y
3	Sarbanes	Y	Y	Y	N	Y	Y
4	Brown, A.	Y	Y	Y	N	Y	Y
5	Hoyer	Y	Y	Y	N	Y	Y
6	Trone	Y	Y	Y	N	Y	Y
7	Cummings	Y	Y	Y	N	Y	Y
8	Raskin	Y	Y	Y	N	Y	Y
MASSACHUSETTS							
1	Neal	Y	Y	Y	N	Y	Y
2	McGovern	Y	Y	Y	N	Y	Y
3	Trahan	Y	Y	Y	N	Y	Y
4	Kennedy	Y	Y	Y	N	Y	Y
5	Clark	Y	Y	Y	N	Y	Y
6	Moulton	Y	Y	Y	N	Y	Y
7	Pressley	Y	Y	Y	N	Y	Y
8	Lynch	Y	Y	Y	N	Y	Y
9	Keating	Y	Y	Y	N	Y	Y
MICHIGAN							
1	**Bergman**	N	Y	Y	Y	N	Y
2	**Huizenga**	Y	Y	Y	Y	N	Y
3	**Amash**	N	Y	Y	Y	N	Y
4	**Moolenaar**	Y	Y	Y	Y	N	Y
5	Kildee	Y	Y	Y	N	Y	Y
6	**Upton**	Y	Y	Y	Y	N	Y
7	**Walberg**	Y	Y	Y	Y	N	Y
8	Slotkin	Y	Y	Y	Y	Y	Y
9	Levin	Y	Y	Y	N	Y	Y
10	**Mitchell**	Y	Y	Y	Y	N	Y
11	Stevens	Y	Y	Y	N	Y	Y
12	Dingell	Y	Y	Y	N	Y	Y
13	Tlaib	Y	Y	Y	N	Y	Y
14	Lawrence	Y	Y	Y	N	Y	Y
MINNESOTA							
1	**Hagedorn**	Y	Y	Y	Y	N	Y
2	Craig	Y	Y	Y	Y	Y	Y
3	Phillips	Y	Y	Y	N	Y	Y
4	McCollum	Y	Y	Y	N	Y	Y
5	Omar	Y	Y	Y	N	Y	Y

		163	164	165	166	167	168
6	**Emmer**	N	N	Y	Y	N	Y
7	Peterson	Y	Y	Y	N	Y	Y
8	**Stauber**	Y	Y	Y	Y	N	Y
MISSISSIPPI							
1	**Kelly, T.**	N	N	Y	Y	N	Y
2	Thompson, B.	Y	Y	Y	N	Y	Y
3	**Guest**	N	Y	Y	Y	N	Y
4	**Palazzo**	Y	Y	Y	Y	N	Y
MISSOURI							
1	Clay	Y	Y	Y	N	Y	Y
2	**Wagner**	Y	Y	Y	Y	N	Y
3	**Luetkemeyer**	Y	Y	Y	Y	N	Y
4	**Hartzler**	Y	Y	Y	Y	N	Y
5	Cleaver	Y	Y	Y	N	Y	Y
6	**Graves, S.**	Y	Y	Y	Y	N	Y
7	**Long**	Y	N	Y	Y	N	Y
8	**Smith, J.**	Y	Y	Y	Y	N	Y
MONTANA							
AL	**Gianforte**	Y	Y	Y	Y	N	Y
NEBRASKA							
1	**Fortenberry**	Y	Y	Y	Y	N	?
2	**Bacon**	Y	Y	Y	Y	N	Y
3	**Smith, Adrian**	Y	Y	Y	Y	N	Y
NEVADA							
1	Titus	Y	Y	Y	N	Y	+
2	**Amodei**	?	?	?	?	?	Y
3	Lee	Y	Y	Y	N	Y	Y
4	Horsford	Y	Y	Y	N	Y	Y
NEW HAMPSHIRE							
1	Pappas	Y	Y	Y	N	Y	Y
2	Kuster	Y	Y	Y	N	Y	Y
NEW JERSEY							
1	Norcross	Y	Y	Y	N	Y	Y
2	Van Drew	Y	Y	Y	Y	Y	Y
3	Kim	Y	Y	Y	N	Y	Y
4	**Smith, C.**	Y	Y	Y	Y	N	Y
5	Gottheimer	Y	Y	Y	Y	Y	Y
6	Pallone	Y	Y	Y	N	Y	Y
7	Malinowski	Y	Y	Y	N	Y	Y
8	Sires	Y	Y	Y	N	Y	?
9	Pascrell	Y	Y	Y	N	Y	Y
10	Payne	Y	Y	Y	N	Y	Y
11	Sherrill	Y	Y	Y	Y	Y	Y
12	Watson Coleman	Y	Y	Y	N	Y	Y
NEW MEXICO							
1	Haaland	Y	Y	Y	N	Y	Y
2	Torres Small	Y	Y	Y	N	Y	Y
3	Luján	Y	Y	Y	N	Y	Y
NEW YORK							
1	**Zeldin**	N	Y	Y	Y	N	Y
2	**King, P.**	Y	Y	Y	Y	N	Y
3	Suozzi	Y	Y	Y	N	Y	Y
4	Rice, K.	?	?	?	?	+	Y
5	Meeks	Y	Y	Y	N	Y	?
6	Meng	Y	Y	Y	N	Y	Y
7	Velázquez	Y	Y	Y	N	Y	Y
8	Jeffries	Y	Y	Y	N	Y	Y
9	Clarke	Y	Y	Y	N	Y	Y
10	Nadler	Y	Y	Y	N	Y	Y
11	Rose	Y	Y	Y	N	Y	Y
12	Maloney, C.	Y	Y	Y	N	Y	Y
13	Espaillat	Y	Y	Y	N	Y	Y
14	Ocasio-Cortez	Y	Y	Y	N	Y	Y
15	Serrano	Y	Y	Y	N	Y	Y
16	Engel	Y	Y	Y	N	Y	Y
17	Lowey	Y	Y	Y	N	Y	Y
18	Maloney, S.P.	Y	Y	Y	N	Y	Y
19	Delgado	Y	Y	Y	Y	Y	Y
20	Tonko	Y	Y	Y	N	Y	Y
21	**Stefanik**	Y	Y	Y	Y	N	Y
22	Brindisi	Y	Y	Y	Y	Y	Y
23	**Reed**	Y	Y	Y	Y	N	Y
24	**Katko**	Y	Y	Y	Y	N	Y
25	Morelle	Y	Y	Y	N	Y	Y
26	Higgins, B.	Y	Y	Y	N	Y	Y
27	**Collins, C.**						
NORTH CAROLINA							
1	Butterfield	Y	Y	Y	N	Y	Y
2	**Holding**	Y	Y	Y	Y	N	?
3	**Jones***						
4	Price	Y	Y	Y	N	Y	Y
5	**Foxx**	Y	Y	Y	Y	N	N
6	**Walker**	N	N	Y	Y	N	Y
7	**Rouzer**	Y	Y	Y	Y	N	Y

		163	164	165	166	167	168
8	**Hudson**	Y	Y	Y	Y	N	Y
9	vacant						
10	**McHenry**	Y	N	Y	Y	N	Y
11	**Meadows**	Y	Y	Y	Y	N	Y
12	Adams	Y	Y	Y	N	Y	Y
13	**Budd**	N	N	Y	Y	N	N
NORTH DAKOTA							
AL	**Armstrong**	Y	Y	Y	Y	N	Y
OHIO							
1	**Chabot**	Y	N	Y	Y	N	Y
2	**Wenstrup**	Y	Y	Y	Y	N	Y
3	Beatty	Y	Y	Y	N	Y	Y
4	**Jordan**	N	N	Y	Y	N	Y
5	**Latta**	Y	Y	Y	Y	N	Y
6	**Johnson, B.**	Y	Y	Y	Y	N	Y
7	**Gibbs**	Y	Y	Y	Y	N	N
8	**Davidson**	Y	Y	Y	Y	N	N
9	Kaptur	Y	Y	Y	N	Y	Y
10	**Turner**	Y	Y	Y	Y	N	Y
11	Fudge	Y	Y	Y	N	Y	Y
12	**Balderson**	Y	Y	Y	Y	N	Y
13	Ryan	?	?	Y	N	Y	?
14	**Joyce**	Y	Y	Y	Y	N	Y
15	**Stivers**	Y	Y	Y	Y	N	Y
16	**Gonzalez**	Y	Y	Y	Y	N	Y
OKLAHOMA							
1	**Hern**	N	N	Y	Y	N	Y
2	**Mullin**	Y	Y	Y	Y	N	Y
3	**Lucas**	Y	Y	Y	Y	N	Y
4	**Cole**	Y	Y	Y	Y	N	Y
5	Horn	Y	Y	Y	Y	Y	Y
OREGON							
1	Bonamici	Y	Y	Y	N	Y	Y
2	**Walden**	Y	Y	Y	Y	N	Y
3	Blumenauer	Y	Y	Y	N	Y	Y
4	DeFazio	Y	Y	Y	N	Y	Y
5	Schrader	Y	Y	Y	Y	Y	Y
PENNSYLVANIA							
1	**Fitzpatrick**	Y	Y	Y	Y	N	Y
2	Boyle	Y	Y	Y	N	Y	Y
3	Evans	Y	Y	Y	N	Y	Y
4	Dean	Y	Y	Y	N	Y	Y
5	Scanlon	Y	Y	Y	N	Y	Y
6	Houlahan	Y	Y	Y	N	Y	Y
7	Wild	Y	Y	Y	N	Y	Y
8	Cartwright	Y	Y	Y	N	Y	Y
9	**Meuser**	N	Y	Y	Y	N	Y
10	**Perry**	Y	Y	Y	Y	N	Y
11	**Smucker**	Y	Y	Y	Y	N	Y
12	**Marino***						
13	**Joyce**	N	Y	Y	Y	N	Y
14	**Reschenthaler**	Y	Y	Y	Y	N	Y
15	**Thompson, G.**	Y	Y	Y	Y	N	Y
16	**Kelly, M.**	Y	Y	Y	Y	N	Y
17	Lamb	Y	Y	Y	N	Y	Y
18	Doyle	Y	Y	Y	N	Y	Y
RHODE ISLAND							
1	Cicilline	?	Y	Y	N	Y	Y
2	Langevin	Y	+	Y	N	Y	Y
SOUTH CAROLINA							
1	Cunningham	Y	Y	Y	Y	Y	Y
2	**Wilson, J.**	Y	Y	Y	Y	N	Y
3	**Duncan**	N	N	Y	Y	N	Y
4	**Timmons**	Y	Y	Y	Y	N	Y
5	**Norman**	N	N	Y	Y	N	N
6	Clyburn	Y	Y	Y	N	Y	Y
7	**Rice, T.**	N	N	Y	Y	N	N
SOUTH DAKOTA							
AL	**Johnson**	N	Y	Y	Y	N	Y
TENNESSEE							
1	**Roe**	Y	Y	Y	Y	N	Y
2	**Burchett**	N	N	Y	Y	N	N
3	**Fleischmann**	N	Y	Y	Y	N	Y
4	**DesJarlais**	N	N	Y	Y	N	?
5	Cooper	?	?	Y	N	Y	Y
6	**Rose**	Y	Y	Y	Y	N	Y
7	**Green**	Y	Y	Y	Y	N	N
8	**Kustoff**	Y	Y	Y	Y	N	Y
9	Cohen	Y	Y	Y	N	Y	Y
TEXAS							
1	**Gohmert**	N	N	Y	Y	N	Y
2	**Crenshaw**	N	Y	Y	Y	N	Y
3	**Taylor**	Y	Y	Y	Y	N	N
4	**Ratcliffe**	N	Y	Y	Y	N	Y

		163	164	165	166	167	168
5	**Gooden**	N	Y	Y	Y	N	Y
6	**Wright**	N	N	Y	Y	N	Y
7	Fletcher	Y	Y	Y	N	Y	Y
8	**Brady**	Y	Y	Y	Y	N	Y
9	Green, A.	Y	Y	Y	N	Y	Y
10	**McCaul**	Y	Y	Y	Y	N	Y
11	**Conaway**	N	N	Y	Y	N	Y
12	**Granger**	Y	Y	Y	Y	N	Y
13	**Thornberry**	Y	Y	Y	Y	N	Y
14	**Weber**	?	?	?	?	?	Y
15	Gonzalez	Y	Y	Y	N	Y	Y
16	Escobar	Y	Y	Y	N	Y	Y
17	**Flores**	Y	Y	Y	Y	N	Y
18	Jackson Lee	Y	Y	Y	N	Y	Y
19	**Arrington**	Y	Y	Y	Y	N	Y
20	Castro	Y	Y	Y	N	Y	Y
21	**Roy**	N	N	Y	Y	N	N
22	**Olson**	?	?	?	?	?	Y
23	**Hurd**	Y	Y	?	Y	N	Y
24	**Marchant**	N	Y	Y	Y	N	Y
25	**Williams**	N	N	Y	Y	N	Y
26	**Burgess**	Y	Y	Y	Y	N	Y
27	**Cloud**	Y	Y	Y	Y	N	Y
28	Cuellar	Y	Y	Y	N	Y	Y
29	Garcia, S.	Y	Y	Y	N	Y	Y
30	Johnson, E.B.	Y	Y	Y	N	Y	Y
31	**Carter, J.**	Y	Y	Y	Y	N	Y
32	Allred	Y	Y	Y	N	Y	Y
33	Veasey	Y	Y	Y	N	Y	Y
34	Vela	Y	Y	Y	N	Y	Y
35	Doggett	Y	Y	Y	N	Y	Y
36	**Babin**	?	?	?	?	?	Y
UTAH							
1	**Bishop, R.**	N	N	?	Y	N	Y
2	**Stewart**	Y	Y	Y	Y	N	Y
3	**Curtis**	Y	Y	Y	Y	N	Y
4	McAdams	Y	Y	Y	N	Y	Y
VERMONT							
AL	Welch	+	+	+	-	+	Y
VIRGINIA							
1	**Wittman**	Y	Y	Y	Y	N	Y
2	Luria	Y	Y	Y	N	Y	Y
3	Scott, R.	Y	Y	Y	N	Y	Y
4	McEachin	+	+	+	-	+	Y
5	**Riggleman**	Y	Y	Y	Y	N	Y
6	**Cline**	N	N	Y	Y	N	N
7	Spanberger	Y	Y	Y	Y	Y	Y
8	Beyer	Y	Y	Y	N	Y	Y
9	**Griffith**	Y	Y	Y	Y	N	Y
10	Wexton	Y	Y	Y	N	Y	Y
11	Connolly	Y	Y	Y	N	Y	Y
WASHINGTON							
1	DelBene	Y	Y	Y	N	Y	Y
2	Larsen	Y	Y	Y	N	Y	Y
3	**Herrera Beutler**	Y	Y	Y	Y	N	Y
4	**Newhouse**	Y	Y	Y	Y	N	Y
5	**McMorris Rodgers**	Y	Y	Y	Y	N	Y
6	Kilmer	Y	Y	Y	N	Y	Y
7	Jayapal	Y	Y	Y	N	Y	Y
8	Schrier	Y	Y	Y	N	Y	Y
9	Smith Adam	Y	Y	Y	N	Y	Y
10	Heck	Y	Y	Y	N	Y	Y
WEST VIRGINIA							
1	**McKinley**	Y	Y	Y	Y	N	Y
2	**Mooney**	N	N	Y	Y	N	Y
3	**Miller**	Y	Y	Y	Y	N	Y
WISCONSIN							
1	**Steil**	Y	Y	Y	Y	N	Y
2	Pocan	Y	Y	Y	N	Y	Y
3	Kind	Y	Y	Y	N	Y	Y
4	Moore	Y	Y	Y	N	Y	Y
5	**Sensenbrenner**	Y	Y	Y	Y	N	Y
6	**Grothman**	Y	N	Y	Y	N	N
7	**Duffy**						
8	**Gallagher**	Y	Y	Y	Y	N	Y
WYOMING							
AL	**Cheney**	Y	Y	Y	Y	N	Y
DELEGATES							
	Radewagen (A.S.)	?	?	?			
	Norton (D.C.)	Y	Y	Y			
	San Nicolas (Guam)	Y	Y	Y			
	Sablan (N. Marianas)	Y	Y	Y			
	González-Colón (P.R.)	Y	Y	Y			
	Plaskett (V.I.)	Y	Y	Y			

169. Procedural Motion - Journal. Approval of the House Journal of April 29, 2019. Approved 227-182: R 55-131; D 172-51. April 29, 2019.

170. HR1876. Senior Investor Task Force - Passage. Foster, D-Ill., motion to suspend the rules and pass the bill that would establish a Securities and Exchange Commission task force on investment by individuals over the age of 65. It would require the task force to submit a biennial report to Congress describing, analyzing, and making policy recommendations related to challenges faced by senior citizen investors. It would also direct the Government Accountability Office to conduct a study on the frequency and costs of financial exploitation of senior citizens, within two years of enactment. Motion agreed to 392-20: R 172-20; D 220-0. *Note: A two-thirds majority of those present and voting (275 in this case) is required for passage under suspension of the rules.* April 30, 2019.

171. HRES328. Promoting Financial Literacy - Passage. Foster, D-Ill., motion to suspend the rules and agree to the resolution, that would express the support of the House of Representatives for efforts to increase public awareness of personal finance education, including awareness of financial threats to older adults. It would urge collaboration between law enforcement, financial institutions, regulatory agencies, and private entities to report, investigate, and respond to financial exploitation of older adults. Motion agreed to 411-6: R 186-6; D 225-0. *Note: A two-thirds majority of those present and voting (278 in this case) is required for passage under suspension of the rules.* April 30, 2019.

172. HR9. International Emissions Reduction Plan - Previous Question. McGovern, D-Md., motion to order the previous question (thus ending the debate and possibility of amendment) to the rule that would provide for House floor consideration of the bill (HR 9) that would direct the president to develop a plan for the United States to meet its nationally-determined contribution under the Paris Agreement, and for other purposes. Motion agreed to 228-191: R 0-191; D 228-0. May 1, 2019.

173. HR9. International Emissions Reduction Plan - Rule. Adoption of the rule (H Res 329) that would provide for House floor consideration of the Climate Action Now Act (HR 9) that would direct the president to develop a plan for the United States to meet its nationally-determined contribution under the Paris Agreement, and for other purposes. Adopted 226-188: R 0-188; D 226-0. May 1, 2019.

174. HRES304. Cohen Testimony Transcript - Motion to Table. Hoyer, D-Md., motion to table the privileged resolution that would direct the Oversight and Reform Committee to submit a transcript of the testimony of Michael Cohen to the attorney general. Motion agreed to 226-183: R 1-183; D 225-0. May 1, 2019.

		169	170	171	172	173	174
ALABAMA							
1	**Byrne**	N	Y	Y	N	N	N
2	**Roby**	N	Y	Y	N	N	N
3	**Rogers, M.**	N	Y	Y	N	N	N
4	**Aderholt**	N	Y	Y	N	N	N
5	**Brooks, M.**	?	N	Y	N	N	N
6	**Palmer**	N	Y	Y	N	N	N
7	Sewell	Y	Y	Y	Y	Y	Y
ALASKA							
AL	**Young**	N	Y	Y	N	N	?
ARIZONA							
1	O'Halleran	N	Y	Y	Y	Y	Y
2	Kirkpatrick	N	Y	Y	Y	Y	Y
3	Grijalva	Y	Y	Y	Y	Y	Y
4	**Gosar**	N	N	N	N	N	N
5	**Biggs**	N	N	N	N	N	N
6	**Schweikert**	Y	Y	Y	N	N	N
7	Gallego	N	Y	Y	Y	Y	Y
8	**Lesko**	N	Y	Y	N	N	N
9	Stanton	Y	Y	Y	Y	Y	Y
ARKANSAS							
1	**Crawford**	N	Y	Y	N	N	N
2	**Hill, F.**	N	Y	Y	N	N	N
3	**Womack**	N	Y	Y	N	N	N
4	**Westerman**	N	Y	Y	N	N	N
CALIFORNIA							
1	**LaMalfa**	N	Y	Y	N	N	N
2	Huffman	Y	Y	Y	Y	Y	Y
3	Garamendi	Y	Y	Y	Y	Y	Y
4	**McClintock**	Y	N	N	N	N	N
5	Thompson, M.	N	Y	Y	Y	Y	Y
6	Matsui	Y	Y	Y	Y	Y	Y
7	Bera	N	Y	Y	Y	Y	Y
8	**Cook**	N	Y	Y	N	N	N
9	McNerney	Y	Y	Y	Y	Y	Y
10	Harder	N	Y	Y	Y	Y	Y
11	DeSaulnier	Y	Y	Y	Y	Y	Y
12	Pelosi						
13	Lee B.	Y	Y	Y	Y	Y	Y
14	Speier	Y	Y	Y	Y	Y	Y
15	Swalwell	N	Y	Y	Y	Y	Y
16	Costa	N	Y	Y	Y	Y	Y
17	Khanna	Y	Y	Y	Y	Y	Y
18	Eshoo	Y	Y	Y	Y	Y	Y
19	Lofgren	Y	Y	Y	Y	Y	Y
20	Panetta	Y	Y	Y	Y	Y	Y
21	Cox	+	Y	Y	Y	Y	Y
22	**Nunes**	N	Y	Y	N	N	N
23	**McCarthy**	Y	Y	Y	N	N	N
24	Carbajal	Y	Y	Y	Y	Y	Y
25	Hill, K.	Y	Y	Y	Y	Y	Y
26	Brownley	N	Y	Y	Y	Y	Y
27	Chu	Y	Y	Y	Y	Y	Y
28	Schiff	Y	Y	Y	Y	Y	Y
29	Cárdenas	Y	Y	Y	Y	Y	Y
30	Sherman	Y	Y	Y	Y	Y	Y
31	Aguilar	Y	Y	Y	Y	Y	Y
32	Napolitano	Y	Y	Y	Y	Y	Y
33	Lieu	Y	Y	Y	Y	Y	Y
34	Gomez	Y	Y	Y	Y	Y	Y
35	Torres	?	+	+	Y	Y	Y
36	Ruiz	Y	Y	Y	Y	Y	Y
37	Bass	Y	Y	Y	Y	Y	Y
38	Sánchez	Y	Y	Y	Y	Y	Y
39	Cisneros	N	Y	Y	Y	Y	Y
40	Roybal-Allard	Y	Y	Y	Y	Y	Y
41	Takano	Y	Y	Y	Y	Y	Y
42	**Calvert**	N	Y	Y	N	N	N
43	Waters	N	Y	Y	Y	Y	Y
44	Barragán	Y	Y	Y	Y	Y	Y
45	Porter	N	Y	Y	Y	Y	Y
46	Correa	N	Y	Y	Y	Y	Y
47	Lowenthal	Y	Y	Y	Y	Y	Y
48	Rouda	N	Y	Y	Y	Y	Y
49	Levin	Y	Y	Y	Y	Y	Y
50	**Hunter**	Y	Y	Y	N	N	N
51	Vargas	Y	Y	Y	?	?	?
52	Peters	N	Y	Y	Y	Y	Y

		169	170	171	172	173	174
53	Davis, S.	Y	Y	Y	Y	Y	?
COLORADO							
1	DeGette	Y	Y	Y	Y	Y	?
2	Neguse	Y	Y	Y	Y	Y	Y
3	**Tipton**	Y	Y	Y	N	N	N
4	**Buck**	N	N	Y	N	N	N
5	**Lamborn**	N	Y	Y	N	N	N
6	Crow	N	Y	Y	Y	Y	Y
7	Perlmutter	Y	Y	Y	Y	Y	Y
CONNECTICUT							
1	Larson	Y	Y	Y	Y	Y	Y
2	Courtney	Y	Y	Y	Y	Y	Y
3	DeLauro	Y	Y	Y	Y	Y	Y
4	Himes	N	Y	Y	Y	?	Y
5	Hayes	Y	Y	Y	Y	Y	Y
DELAWARE							
AL	Blunt Rochester	Y	Y	Y	Y	Y	Y
FLORIDA							
1	**Gaetz**	N	N	Y	N	N	N
2	**Dunn**	?	Y	Y	N	N	N
3	**Yoho**	?	?	?	N	N	N
4	**Rutherford**	Y	Y	Y	N	N	N
5	Lawson	Y	Y	Y	Y	Y	Y
6	**Waltz**	Y	Y	Y	N	N	N
7	Murphy	Y	Y	Y	Y	Y	Y
8	**Posey**	Y	Y	Y	N	N	N
9	Soto	Y	Y	Y	Y	Y	Y
10	Demings	Y	Y	Y	Y	Y	Y
11	**Webster**	Y	Y	Y	N	N	N
12	**Bilirakis**	Y	Y	Y	N	N	N
13	Crist	Y	Y	Y	Y	Y	Y
14	Castor	Y	Y	Y	Y	Y	Y
15	**Spano**	N	Y	Y	N	N	N
16	**Buchanan**	N	Y	Y	N	N	N
17	**Steube**	N	N	Y	N	N	N
18	**Mast**	N	Y	Y	N	N	N
19	**Rooney**	?	?	?	?	?	?
20	Hastings	?	?	?	?	?	?
21	Frankel	Y	Y	Y	Y	Y	Y
22	Deutch	?	?	?	Y	Y	Y
23	Wasserman Schultz	Y	Y	Y	Y	Y	Y
24	Wilson, F.	Y	Y	Y	Y	Y	Y
25	**Diaz-Balart**	Y	Y	Y	N	N	N
26	Mucarsel-Powell	N	Y	Y	Y	Y	Y
27	Shalala	Y	Y	Y	Y	Y	Y
GEORGIA							
1	**Carter, E.L.**	N	Y	Y	N	N	N
2	Bishop, S.	Y	Y	Y	Y	Y	Y
3	**Ferguson**	N	Y	Y	N	N	N
4	Johnson, H.	Y	Y	Y	Y	Y	?
5	Lewis John	Y	Y	Y	Y	Y	Y
6	McBath	Y	Y	Y	Y	Y	Y
7	**Woodall**	N	Y	Y	?	?	?
8	**Scott, A.**	N	Y	Y	N	N	N
9	**Collins, D.**	Y	Y	Y	N	N	N
10	**Hice**	N	Y	Y	N	N	N
11	**Loudermilk**	N	Y	Y	N	N	N
12	**Allen**	N	Y	Y	N	N	N
13	Scott, D.	Y	Y	Y	Y	Y	Y
14	**Graves, T.**	N	Y	Y	N	N	N
HAWAII							
1	Case	Y	Y	Y	Y	Y	Y
2	Gabbard	Y	Y	Y	Y	Y	Y
IDAHO							
1	**Fulcher**	N	Y	Y	N	N	N
2	**Simpson**	Y	?	?	N	N	N
ILLINOIS							
1	Rush	?	Y	Y	Y	Y	Y
2	Kelly, R.	N	Y	Y	Y	Y	Y
3	Lipinski	Y	Y	Y	Y	Y	Y
4	García, J.	Y	Y	Y	Y	Y	Y
5	Quigley	Y	Y	Y	Y	Y	Y
6	Casten	Y	Y	Y	Y	Y	Y
7	Davis, D.	Y	Y	Y	Y	Y	Y
8	Krishnamoorthi	N	Y	Y	Y	Y	Y
9	Schakowsky	Y	Y	Y	Y	Y	Y
10	Schneider	Y	Y	Y	Y	Y	Y
11	Foster	Y	Y	Y	Y	Y	Y

KEY:	Republicans	Democrats	Independents

Y	Voted for (yea)	N	Voted against (nay)	P	Voted "present"
+	Announced for	–	Announced against	?	Did not vote or otherwise make position known
#	Paired for	X	Paired against		

		169	170	171	172	173	174
12	**Bost**	N	Y	Y	N	N	N
13	**Davis, R.**	N	Y	Y	N	N	N
14	Underwood	Y	Y	Y	Y	Y	Y
15	**Shimkus**	N	Y	Y	N	N	N
16	**Kinzinger**	Y	Y	Y	N	N	N
17	Bustos	Y	Y	Y	Y	Y	Y
18	**LaHood**	N	Y	Y	N	N	N
INDIANA							
1	Visclosky	Y	Y	Y	Y	Y	Y
2	**Walorski**	N	Y	Y	N	N	N
3	**Banks**	N	Y	Y	N	N	N
4	**Baird**	N	Y	Y	N	N	N
5	**Brooks, S.**	N	Y	Y	N	N	N
6	**Pence**	N	Y	Y	N	N	N
7	Carson	Y	Y	Y	+	+	+
8	**Bucshon**	Y	Y	Y	N	N	N
9	**Hollingsworth**	Y	Y	Y	N	N	N
IOWA							
1	Finkenauer	N	Y	Y	Y	Y	Y
2	Loebsack	Y	Y	Y	Y	Y	Y
3	Axne	N	Y	Y	Y	Y	Y
4	**King, S.**	Y	Y	Y	N	N	-
KANSAS							
1	**Marshall**	N	Y	Y	N	N	N
2	**Watkins**	Y	Y	Y	N	N	N
3	Davids	N	Y	Y	Y	Y	Y
4	**Estes**	N	Y	Y	N	N	N
KENTUCKY							
1	**Comer**	N	Y	Y	N	N	N
2	**Guthrie**	N	Y	Y	N	N	N
3	Yarmuth	Y	Y	Y	Y	Y	Y
4	**Massie**	Y	N	N	N	N	N
5	**Rogers, H.**	N	Y	Y	N	N	N
6	**Barr**	N	Y	Y	N	N	N
LOUISIANA							
1	**Scalise**	N	Y	Y	N	?	?
2	Richmond	Y	Y	Y	Y	Y	Y
3	**Higgins, C.**	Y	Y	Y	N	-	N
4	**Johnson, M.**	N	Y	Y	N	N	N
5	**Abraham**	?	?	?	?	?	?
6	**Graves, G.**	Y	Y	Y	N	N	N
MAINE							
1	Pingree	Y	Y	Y	Y	Y	Y
2	Golden	N	Y	Y	Y	Y	Y
MARYLAND							
1	**Harris**	Y	N	Y	?	?	?
2	Ruppersberger	?	Y	Y	Y	Y	Y
3	Sarbanes	Y	Y	Y	Y	Y	Y
4	Brown, A.	Y	Y	Y	Y	Y	Y
5	Hoyer	Y	Y	Y	Y	Y	Y
6	Trone	Y	Y	Y	Y	Y	Y
7	Cummings	Y	Y	Y	Y	Y	Y
8	Raskin	Y	Y	Y	Y	Y	Y
MASSACHUSETTS							
1	Neal	Y	Y	Y	Y	Y	Y
2	McGovern	Y	Y	Y	Y	Y	Y
3	Trahan	Y	Y	Y	Y	Y	Y
4	Kennedy	Y	Y	Y	Y	Y	Y
5	Clark	Y	Y	Y	Y	Y	Y
6	Moulton	Y	?	?	Y	Y	Y
7	Pressley	Y	+	Y	Y	Y	Y
8	Lynch	Y	Y	Y	Y	Y	Y
9	Keating	Y	Y	Y	Y	Y	Y
MICHIGAN							
1	**Bergman**	Y	Y	Y	N	N	N
2	**Huizenga**	N	Y	Y	N	N	N
3	**Amash**	N	N	N	N	N	Y
4	**Moolenaar**	N	Y	Y	N	N	N
5	Kildee	Y	Y	Y	Y	Y	Y
6	**Upton**	N	Y	Y	N	N	N
7	**Walberg**	N	Y	Y	N	N	N
8	Slotkin	N	Y	Y	Y	Y	Y
9	Levin	Y	Y	Y	Y	Y	Y
10	**Mitchell**	N	Y	Y	N	N	N
11	Stevens	N	Y	Y	Y	Y	Y
12	Dingell	Y	Y	Y	Y	Y	Y
13	Tlaib	Y	?	Y	Y	Y	Y
14	Lawrence	Y	Y	Y	Y	Y	Y
MINNESOTA							
1	**Hagedorn**	N	Y	Y	N	N	N
2	Craig	N	Y	Y	Y	Y	Y
3	Phillips	Y	Y	Y	Y	Y	Y
4	McCollum	Y	Y	Y	Y	Y	Y
5	Omar	Y	?	Y	Y	Y	Y

		169	170	171	172	173	174
6	**Emmer**	N	Y	Y	N	N	N
7	Peterson	N	Y	Y	Y	Y	Y
8	**Stauber**	Y	Y	Y	N	N	N
MISSISSIPPI							
1	**Kelly, T.**	N	Y	Y	N	N	N
2	Thompson, B.	Y	Y	Y	Y	Y	Y
3	**Guest**	N	Y	Y	N	N	N
4	**Palazzo**	N	Y	Y	N	N	N
MISSOURI							
1	Clay	Y	Y	Y	Y	Y	Y
2	**Wagner**	Y	Y	Y	N	N	N
3	**Luetkemeyer**	N	Y	Y	N	N	N
4	**Hartzler**	N	Y	Y	N	N	N
5	Cleaver	Y	Y	Y	Y	Y	Y
6	**Graves, S.**	N	Y	Y	N	N	N
7	**Long**	Y	Y	Y	N	N	N
8	**Smith, J.**	N	Y	Y	N	N	N
MONTANA							
AL	**Gianforte**	N	Y	Y	N	N	N
NEBRASKA							
1	**Fortenberry**	?	?	?	N	N	N
2	**Bacon**	Y	Y	Y	N	N	N
3	**Smith, Adrian**	N	Y	Y	N	N	N
NEVADA							
1	Titus	+	+	+	+	+	+
2	**Amodei**	Y	Y	Y	N	N	N
3	Lee	Y	Y	Y	Y	Y	Y
4	Horsford	N	Y	Y	Y	Y	Y
NEW HAMPSHIRE							
1	Pappas	N	Y	Y	Y	Y	Y
2	Kuster	Y	Y	Y	Y	Y	Y
NEW JERSEY							
1	Norcross	Y	Y	Y	Y	Y	Y
2	Van Drew	N	Y	Y	Y	Y	Y
3	Kim	Y	Y	Y	Y	Y	Y
4	**Smith, C.**	Y	Y	Y	N	N	N
5	Gottheimer	N	Y	Y	Y	Y	Y
6	Pallone	Y	Y	Y	Y	Y	Y
7	Malinowski	Y	Y	Y	Y	Y	Y
8	Sires	?	?	?	Y	Y	Y
9	Pascrell	Y	Y	Y	Y	Y	Y
10	Payne	Y	Y	Y	Y	Y	Y
11	Sherrill	N	Y	Y	Y	Y	Y
12	Watson Coleman	N	Y	Y	Y	Y	Y
NEW MEXICO							
1	Haaland	Y	Y	Y	Y	Y	Y
2	Torres Small	Y	Y	Y	Y	Y	Y
3	Luján	Y	Y	Y	Y	Y	Y
NEW YORK							
1	**Zeldin**	N	Y	Y	N	N	N
2	**King, P.**	Y	Y	Y	N	N	N
3	Suozzi	N	Y	Y	Y	Y	Y
4	Rice, K.	N	Y	Y	Y	Y	Y
5	Meeks	?	?	?	Y	Y	Y
6	Meng	N	Y	Y	Y	Y	Y
7	Velázquez	Y	Y	Y	Y	Y	Y
8	Jeffries	Y	Y	Y	Y	Y	Y
9	Clarke	Y	Y	Y	Y	Y	Y
10	Nadler	Y	Y	Y	Y	Y	Y
11	Rose	Y	Y	Y	Y	Y	Y
12	Maloney, C.	Y	Y	Y	Y	Y	Y
13	Espaillat	Y	Y	Y	Y	Y	Y
14	Ocasio-Cortez	Y	Y	Y	Y	Y	Y
15	Serrano	Y	Y	Y	Y	Y	Y
16	Engel	Y	?	Y	Y	Y	Y
17	Lowey	Y	Y	Y	Y	Y	Y
18	Maloney, S.P.	N	Y	Y	Y	Y	Y
19	Delgado	Y	Y	Y	Y	Y	Y
20	Tonko	P	Y	Y	Y	Y	Y
21	**Stefanik**	Y	Y	Y	N	N	N
22	Brindisi	N	Y	Y	Y	Y	Y
23	**Reed**	N	Y	Y	N	N	N
24	**Katko**	Y	Y	Y	N	N	N
25	Morelle	Y	Y	Y	Y	Y	Y
26	Higgins, B.	Y	Y	Y	Y	Y	Y
27	**Collins, C.**						
NORTH CAROLINA							
1	Butterfield	Y	Y	Y	Y	Y	Y
2	**Holding**	?	Y	Y	N	N	N
3	**Jones***						
4	Price	Y	Y	Y	Y	Y	Y
5	**Foxx**	N	Y	Y	N	N	N
6	**Walker**	N	N	Y	N	N	N
7	**Rouzer**	N	Y	Y	N	N	N

		169	170	171	172	173	174
8	**Hudson**	N	Y	Y	N	N	N
9	vacant						
10	**McHenry**	N	Y	Y	N	N	N
11	**Meadows**	Y	Y	Y	N	N	N
12	Adams	Y	Y	Y	+	+	+
13	**Budd**	N	Y	Y	N	N	N
NORTH DAKOTA							
AL	**Armstrong**	Y	N	Y	N	N	-
OHIO							
1	**Chabot**	N	Y	Y	N	N	N
2	**Wenstrup**	Y	Y	Y	N	N	N
3	Beatty	Y	Y	Y	Y	Y	Y
4	**Jordan**	N	Y	Y	N	N	N
5	**Latta**	N	Y	Y	N	N	N
6	**Johnson, B.**	N	Y	Y	N	N	N
7	**Gibbs**	N	Y	Y	N	N	N
8	**Davidson**	N	Y	Y	N	N	N
9	Kaptur	Y	Y	Y	Y	Y	Y
10	**Turner**	N	Y	Y	N	N	N
11	Fudge	Y	Y	Y	Y	Y	Y
12	**Balderson**	N	Y	Y	N	N	N
13	Ryan	?	?	?	Y	Y	Y
14	**Joyce**	Y	Y	Y	N	N	N
15	**Stivers**	?	Y	Y	N	N	N
16	**Gonzalez**	N	Y	Y	N	N	N
OKLAHOMA							
1	**Hern**	Y	N	Y	N	N	-
2	**Mullin**	Y	Y	Y	N	N	N
3	**Lucas**	N	Y	Y	N	N	N
4	**Cole**	N	Y	Y	N	N	N
5	Horn	N	Y	Y	Y	Y	Y
OREGON							
1	Bonamici	Y	Y	Y	Y	Y	Y
2	**Walden**	N	Y	Y	N	N	N
3	Blumenauer	Y	Y	Y	Y	?	Y
4	DeFazio	Y	Y	Y	Y	Y	Y
5	Schrader	N	Y	Y	Y	Y	Y
PENNSYLVANIA							
1	**Fitzpatrick**	N	Y	Y	N	N	N
2	Boyle	Y	Y	Y	Y	Y	Y
3	Evans	Y	Y	Y	Y	Y	Y
4	Dean	Y	Y	Y	Y	Y	Y
5	Scanlon	Y	Y	Y	Y	Y	Y
6	Houlahan	Y	Y	Y	Y	Y	Y
7	Wild	N	Y	Y	Y	Y	Y
8	Cartwright	Y	?	?	?	?	?
9	**Meuser**	N	Y	Y	N	N	N
10	**Perry**	Y	Y	Y	-	-	-
11	**Smucker**	N	Y	Y	N	N	N
12	**Marino***						
13	**Joyce**	N	Y	Y	N	N	N
14	**Reschenthaler**	N	Y	Y	N	N	N
15	**Thompson, G.**	N	Y	Y	N	N	N
16	**Kelly, M.**	Y	Y	Y	N	N	N
17	Lamb	Y	Y	Y	Y	Y	Y
18	Doyle	Y	Y	Y	Y	Y	Y
RHODE ISLAND							
1	Cicilline	Y	Y	Y	Y	Y	Y
2	Langevin	Y	Y	Y	Y	Y	Y
SOUTH CAROLINA							
1	Cunningham	N	Y	Y	Y	Y	Y
2	**Wilson, J.**	Y	Y	Y	N	N	N
3	**Duncan**	N	Y	Y	N	N	N
4	**Timmons**	Y	Y	Y	N	N	N
5	**Norman**	N	N	Y	?	?	?
6	Clyburn	Y	Y	Y	Y	Y	Y
7	**Rice, T.**	N	Y	Y	N	N	N
SOUTH DAKOTA							
AL	**Johnson**	N	Y	Y	N	N	N
TENNESSEE							
1	**Roe**	Y	Y	Y	N	N	N
2	**Burchett**	N	N	Y	N	N	N
3	**Fleischmann**	Y	Y	Y	N	N	N
4	**DesJarlais**	N	Y	Y	N	N	N
5	Cooper	Y	Y	Y	Y	Y	Y
6	**Rose**	N	Y	Y	N	N	N
7	**Green**	N	N	Y	N	N	N
8	**Kustoff**	N	Y	Y	N	N	N
9	Cohen	Y	Y	Y	Y	Y	Y
TEXAS							
1	**Gohmert**	?	N	Y	N	N	N
2	**Crenshaw**	N	Y	Y	N	N	N
3	**Taylor**	Y	Y	Y	N	N	N
4	**Ratcliffe**	?	N	Y	N	N	N

		169	170	171	172	173	174
5	**Gooden**	N	Y	Y	N	N	N
6	**Wright**	N	Y	Y	N	N	N
7	Fletcher	Y	Y	Y	Y	Y	Y
8	**Brady**	Y	Y	Y	N	N	N
9	Green, A.	Y	Y	Y	Y	Y	Y
10	**McCaul**	N	Y	Y	N	N	N
11	**Conaway**	N	Y	Y	N	N	N
12	**Granger**	N	Y	Y	N	N	N
13	**Thornberry**	Y	Y	Y	N	N	N
14	**Weber**	N	Y	Y	N	N	N
15	Gonzalez	Y	Y	Y	Y	Y	Y
16	Escobar	Y	Y	Y	Y	Y	Y
17	**Flores**	N	Y	Y	N	N	N
18	Jackson Lee	Y	Y	Y	Y	Y	Y
19	**Arrington**	Y	Y	Y	N	N	N
20	Castro	Y	Y	Y	Y	Y	Y
21	**Roy**	N	N	N	N	N	N
22	**Olson**	?	Y	Y	N	N	N
23	**Hurd**	N	Y	Y	N	N	N
24	**Marchant**	N	Y	Y	N	?	N
25	**Williams**	N	Y	Y	N	N	N
26	**Burgess**	N	Y	Y	N	N	N
27	**Cloud**	N	Y	Y	N	N	?
28	Cuellar	N	Y	Y	Y	Y	Y
29	Garcia, S.	Y	Y	Y	Y	Y	Y
30	Johnson, E.B.	Y	Y	Y	Y	Y	Y
31	**Carter, J.**	N	Y	Y	N	N	N
32	Allred	Y	Y	Y	Y	Y	Y
33	Veasey	Y	Y	Y	Y	Y	Y
34	Vela	Y	Y	Y	Y	Y	Y
35	Doggett	Y	Y	Y	Y	Y	Y
36	**Babin**	N	Y	Y	N	N	N
UTAH							
1	**Bishop, R.**	N	Y	Y	N	N	N
2	**Stewart**	Y	Y	Y	N	N	N
3	**Curtis**	Y	Y	Y	N	N	N
4	McAdams	N	Y	Y	Y	Y	Y
VERMONT							
AL	Welch	Y	Y	Y	Y	Y	Y
VIRGINIA							
1	**Wittman**	N	Y	Y	N	N	N
2	Luria	Y	Y	Y	Y	Y	Y
3	Scott, R.	Y	Y	Y	Y	Y	Y
4	McEachin	Y	Y	Y	Y	Y	Y
5	**Riggleman**	N	Y	Y	N	N	?
6	**Cline**	N	Y	Y	N	N	N
7	Spanberger	N	Y	Y	Y	Y	Y
8	Beyer	Y	Y	Y	Y	Y	Y
9	**Griffith**	N	N	Y	N	N	N
10	Wexton	N	Y	Y	Y	Y	Y
11	Connolly	N	Y	Y	Y	Y	Y
WASHINGTON							
1	DelBene	Y	Y	Y	Y	Y	Y
2	Larsen	Y	Y	Y	Y	Y	Y
3	**Herrera Beutler**	Y	Y	Y	N	N	N
4	**Newhouse**	Y	Y	Y	N	N	N
5	**McMorris Rodgers**	Y	Y	Y	N	N	N
6	Kilmer	N	Y	Y	Y	Y	Y
7	Jayapal	Y	Y	Y	Y	Y	Y
8	Schrier	N	Y	Y	Y	Y	Y
9	Smith Adam	Y	Y	Y	Y	Y	Y
10	Heck	Y	Y	Y	Y	Y	Y
WEST VIRGINIA							
1	**McKinley**	N	Y	Y	N	N	N
2	**Mooney**	N	Y	Y	N	N	N
3	**Miller**	N	Y	Y	N	N	N
WISCONSIN							
1	**Steil**	Y	Y	Y	N	N	N
2	Pocan	Y	Y	Y	Y	Y	Y
3	Kind	N	Y	Y	Y	Y	Y
4	Moore	Y	?	Y	Y	Y	Y
5	**Sensenbrenner**	N	Y	Y	N	N	N
6	**Grothman**	N	Y	Y	N	N	N
7	**Duffy**						
8	**Gallagher**	N	Y	Y	N	N	N
WYOMING							
AL	**Cheney**	N	Y	Y	N	N	N
DELEGATES							
	Radewagen (A.S.)						
	Norton (D.C.)						
	San Nicolas (Guam)						
	Sablan (N. Marianas)						
	González-Colón (P.R.)						
	Plaskett (V.I.)						

175. HR9. International Emissions Reduction Plan - Climate Justice Finding. Espaillat, D-N.Y., amendment that would state that the Paris Agreement urges parties to consider "climate justice" and the impacts of climate change on local communities, migrants, children, and other "people in vulnerable situations." Rejected in Committee of the Whole 189-234: R 188-6; D 0-228; I 1-0. May 2, 2019.

176. HR9. International Emissions Reduction Plan - Treaty Status. Gosar, R-Ariz., amendment that would state that the Paris Agreement is a treaty and state that no further action toward its goals should occur before the Senate ratifies the agreement. Rejected in Committee of the Whole 189-233: R 189-5; D 0-227; I 0-1. May 2, 2019.

177. HR9. International Emissions Reduction Plan - Use of Federal Funds. Gosar, R-Ariz., amendment that would remove from the bill a section that would prohibit any federal funds from being used to facilitate the withdrawal of the United States from the Paris Agreement. Rejected in Committee of the Whole 189-234: R 189-6; D 0-227; I 0-1. May 2, 2019.

178. HR9. International Emissions Reduction Plan - Technology Finding. Porter, D-Calif., amendment that would state that the Paris Agreement recognizes the importance of technology in implementing actions to be taken under the agreement. Adopted in Committee of the Whole 262-163: R 31-163; D 230-0; I 1-0. May 2, 2019.

179. HR9. International Emissions Reduction Plan - Energy Technology Inclusion. Fletcher, D-Texas, amendment that would specify that nothing in the bill should be construed to require or prohibit the inclusion of any specific energy technology in the emissions reduction plan required by the bill. Adopted in Committee of the Whole 305-121: R 73-121; D 231-0; I 1-0. May 2, 2019.

180. HR9. International Emissions Reduction Plan - Voluntary Agricultural Practices. Schrier, D-Wash., amendment that would specify that nothing in the bill should be construed to require or prohibit the president from including voluntary agricultural practices that would reduce greenhouse gas emissions in the emissions reduction plan required by the bill. Adopted in Committee of the Whole 295-132: R 63-132; D 231-0; I 1-0. May 2, 2019.

		175	176	177	178	179	180
ALABAMA							
1	Byrne	N	Y	Y	N	N	N
2	Roby	N	Y	Y	N	N	N
3	Rogers, M.	N	Y	Y	N	N	N
4	Aderholt	N	Y	Y	N	N	N
5	Brooks, M.	N	Y	Y	?	N	Y
6	Palmer	N	Y	Y	N	N	N
7	Sewell	Y	N	N	Y	Y	Y
ALASKA							
AL	Young	N	Y	Y	N	N	N
ARIZONA							
1	O'Halleran	Y	N	N	Y	Y	Y
2	Kirkpatrick	Y	N	N	Y	Y	Y
3	Grijalva	Y	N	N	Y	Y	Y
4	Gosar	N	Y	Y	N	N	N
5	Biggs	N	Y	Y	N	N	N
6	Schweikert	N	Y	N	Y	Y	Y
7	Gallego	Y	N	N	Y	Y	Y
8	Lesko	N	Y	Y	N	Y	N
9	Stanton	Y	N	N	Y	Y	Y
ARKANSAS							
1	Crawford	-	+	+	-	+	-
2	Hill, F.	N	Y	Y	N	N	Y
3	Womack	N	Y	N	N	N	N
4	Westerman	N	Y	Y	N	N	N
CALIFORNIA							
1	LaMalfa	N	Y	Y	N	N	N
2	Huffman	Y	N	N	Y	Y	Y
3	Garamendi	Y	N	N	Y	Y	Y
4	McClintock	N	Y	N	N	N	N
5	Thompson, M.	Y	N	N	Y	Y	Y
6	Matsui	Y	N	N	Y	Y	Y
7	Bera	Y	N	N	Y	Y	Y
8	Cook	N	Y	Y	N	Y	N
9	McNerney	Y	N	N	Y	Y	Y
10	Harder	Y	N	N	Y	Y	Y
11	DeSaulnier	Y	N	N	Y	Y	Y
12	Pelosi						
13	Lee B.	Y	N	N	Y	Y	Y
14	Speier	Y	N	N	Y	Y	Y
15	Swalwell	Y	N	N	Y	Y	Y
16	Costa	Y	N	N	Y	Y	Y
17	Khanna	Y	N	N	Y	Y	Y
18	Eshoo	Y	N	?	Y	Y	Y
19	Lofgren	Y	N	N	Y	Y	Y
20	Panetta	Y	N	N	Y	Y	Y
21	Cox	Y	N	N	Y	Y	Y
22	Nunes	N	Y	Y	N	N	N
23	McCarthy	N	Y	Y	N	N	N
24	Carbajal	Y	N	N	Y	Y	Y
25	Hill, K.	Y	N	N	Y	Y	Y
26	Brownley	Y	N	N	Y	Y	Y
27	Chu	Y	N	N	Y	Y	Y
28	Schiff	Y	N	N	Y	Y	Y
29	Cárdenas	Y	N	N	Y	Y	Y
30	Sherman	Y	N	N	Y	Y	Y
31	Aguilar	Y	N	N	?	Y	Y
32	Napolitano	Y	N	N	Y	Y	Y
33	Lieu	Y	?	N	Y	Y	Y
34	Gomez	Y	N	N	Y	Y	Y
35	Torres	Y	N	N	Y	Y	Y
36	Ruiz	Y	N	N	Y	Y	Y
37	Bass	Y	N	N	Y	Y	Y
38	Sánchez	Y	N	N	Y	Y	Y
39	Cisneros	Y	N	N	Y	Y	Y
40	Roybal-Allard	Y	N	N	Y	Y	Y
41	Takano	Y	N	N	Y	Y	Y
42	Calvert	N	Y	Y	N	N	N
43	Waters	Y	N	N	Y	Y	Y
44	Barragán	Y	N	N	Y	Y	Y
45	Porter	Y	N	N	Y	Y	Y
46	Correa	Y	N	N	Y	Y	Y
47	Lowenthal	Y	N	N	Y	Y	Y
48	Rouda	+	-	-	+	+	+
49	Levin	Y	N	N	Y	Y	Y
50	Hunter	N	Y	Y	N	Y	N
51	Vargas	?	?	?	?	?	?
52	Peters	Y	N	?	Y	Y	Y

		175	176	177	178	179	180
53	Davis, S.	Y	N	N	Y	Y	Y
COLORADO							
1	DeGette	Y	N	N	Y	Y	Y
2	Neguse	Y	N	N	Y	Y	Y
3	Tipton	N	Y	Y	N	Y	Y
4	Buck	N	Y	Y	N	N	N
5	Lamborn	N	Y	Y	N	N	N
6	Crow	Y	N	N	Y	Y	Y
7	Perlmutter	Y	N	N	Y	Y	Y
CONNECTICUT							
1	Larson	Y	N	N	Y	Y	Y
2	Courtney	Y	N	N	Y	Y	Y
3	DeLauro	Y	N	N	Y	Y	Y
4	Himes	Y	N	N	Y	Y	Y
5	Hayes	Y	N	N	Y	Y	Y
DELAWARE							
AL	Blunt Rochester	Y	N	N	Y	Y	Y
FLORIDA							
1	Gaetz	N	Y	Y	N	Y	Y
2	Dunn	N	Y	Y	N	Y	N
3	Yoho	N	Y	Y	N	Y	Y
4	Rutherford	N	Y	Y	N	N	N
5	Lawson	Y	N	N	Y	Y	Y
6	Waltz	Y	Y	Y	Y	Y	Y
7	Murphy	Y	N	N	Y	Y	Y
8	Posey	N	Y	Y	N	Y	Y
9	Soto	Y	N	N	Y	Y	Y
10	Demings	Y	N	N	Y	Y	Y
11	Webster	N	Y	N	Y	Y	Y
12	Bilirakis	?	Y	Y	N	Y	N
13	Crist	Y	N	N	Y	Y	Y
14	Castor	Y	N	N	Y	Y	Y
15	Spano	N	Y	Y	N	Y	Y
16	Buchanan	N	N	N	Y	Y	Y
17	Steube	N	Y	Y	N	N	N
18	Mast	N	Y	Y	Y	Y	Y
19	Rooney	?	?	?	?	?	?
20	Hastings	?	?	?	?	?	?
21	Frankel	Y	N	N	Y	Y	Y
22	Deutch	Y	N	N	Y	Y	Y
23	Wasserman Schultz	Y	N	N	Y	Y	Y
24	Wilson, F.	Y	N	N	Y	Y	Y
25	Diaz-Balart	N	Y	Y	N	N	Y
26	Mucarsel-Powell	Y	N	N	Y	Y	Y
27	Shalala	Y	N	N	Y	Y	Y
GEORGIA							
1	Carter, E.L.	N	Y	Y	N	Y	Y
2	Bishop, S.	Y	N	N	Y	Y	Y
3	Ferguson	N	Y	Y	N	N	N
4	Johnson, H.	Y	N	N	Y	Y	Y
5	Lewis John	Y	N	N	Y	Y	Y
6	McBath	Y	N	N	Y	Y	Y
7	Woodall	N	Y	Y	N	Y	N
8	Scott, A.	N	Y	Y	N	N	N
9	Collins, D.	N	Y	Y	N	N	N
10	Hice	N	Y	Y	N	N	N
11	Loudermilk	?	?	?	?	?	?
12	Allen	N	Y	Y	N	N	N
13	Scott, D.	Y	N	N	Y	Y	Y
14	Graves, T.	N	Y	Y	N	N	N
HAWAII							
1	Case	Y	N	N	Y	Y	Y
2	Gabbard	Y	N	N	Y	Y	Y
IDAHO							
1	Fulcher	N	Y	Y	N	N	N
2	Simpson	N	Y	Y	N	N	N
ILLINOIS							
1	Rush	Y	N	N	Y	Y	Y
2	Kelly, R.	Y	N	N	Y	Y	Y
3	Lipinski	Y	N	N	Y	Y	Y
4	García, J.	Y	N	N	Y	Y	Y
5	Quigley	Y	N	N	Y	Y	Y
6	Casten	Y	N	N	Y	Y	Y
7	Davis, D.	Y	N	N	Y	Y	Y
8	Krishnamoorthi	Y	N	N	Y	Y	Y
9	Schakowsky	Y	N	N	Y	Y	Y
10	Schneider	Y	N	N	Y	Y	Y
11	Foster	Y	N	N	Y	Y	Y

KEY:	**Republicans**	Democrats	*Independents*

Y Voted for (yea)	**N** Voted against (nay)	**P** Voted "present"	
+ Announced for	**-** Announced against	**?** Did not vote or otherwise	
# Paired for	**X** Paired against	make position known	

		175	176	177	178	179	180
12	**Bost**	N	Y	Y	N	N	N
13	**Davis, R.**	N	Y	Y	Y	Y	Y
14	Underwood	Y	N	N	Y	Y	Y
15	**Shimkus**	N	Y	Y	N	N	N
16	**Kinzinger**	N	Y	Y	N	N	N
17	Bustos	Y	N	N	Y	Y	Y
18	**LaHood**	N	Y	Y	N	N	N
INDIANA							
1	Visclosky	Y	N	N	Y	Y	Y
2	**Walorski**	N	Y	Y	N	Y	Y
3	**Banks**	N	Y	Y	N	N	N
4	**Baird**	N	Y	Y	N	N	N
5	**Brooks, S.**	N	Y	Y	Y	Y	Y
6	**Pence**	N	Y	Y	N	N	N
7	Carson	Y	N	N	Y	Y	Y
8	**Bucshon**	N	Y	Y	N	N	N
9	**Hollingsworth**	Y	N	Y	Y	Y	Y
IOWA							
1	Finkenauer	Y	N	N	Y	Y	Y
2	Loebsack	Y	N	N	Y	Y	Y
3	Axne	Y	N	N	Y	Y	Y
4	**King, S.**	N	Y	Y	N	N	N
KANSAS							
1	**Marshall**	N	Y	Y	N	?	N
2	**Watkins**	N	Y	Y	N	N	N
3	Davids	Y	N	N	Y	Y	Y
4	**Estes**	N	Y	Y	N	N	N
KENTUCKY							
1	**Comer**	N	Y	Y	N	N	N
2	**Guthrie**	N	Y	Y	N	N	N
3	Yarmuth	Y	N	N	Y	Y	Y
4	**Massie**	N	Y	Y	N	N	N
5	**Rogers, H.**	N	Y	Y	N	N	N
6	**Barr**	N	Y	Y	N	N	N
LOUISIANA							
1	**Scalise**	N	Y	Y	N	Y	N
2	Richmond	Y	N	N	Y	Y	Y
3	**Higgins, C.**	N	Y	Y	N	Y	Y
4	**Johnson, M.**	N	Y	Y	N	N	Y
5	**Abraham**	?	?	?	?	?	?
6	**Graves, G.**	N	Y	Y	Y	Y	Y
MAINE							
1	Pingree	Y	N	N	Y	Y	Y
2	Golden	Y	N	N	Y	Y	Y
MARYLAND							
1	**Harris**	N	Y	Y	N	N	N
2	Ruppersberger	Y	N	N	Y	Y	Y
3	Sarbanes	Y	N	N	Y	Y	Y
4	Brown, A.	Y	N	N	Y	Y	Y
5	Hoyer	Y	N	N	Y	Y	Y
6	Trone	Y	N	N	Y	Y	Y
7	Cummings	Y	N	N	Y	Y	Y
8	Raskin	Y	N	?	Y	Y	Y
MASSACHUSETTS							
1	Neal	Y	N	N	Y	Y	Y
2	McGovern	Y	N	N	Y	Y	Y
3	Trahan	Y	N	N	Y	Y	Y
4	Kennedy	Y	N	N	Y	Y	Y
5	Clark	Y	N	N	Y	Y	Y
6	Moulton	Y	N	N	Y	Y	Y
7	Pressley	Y	N	N	Y	Y	Y
8	Lynch	Y	?	N	Y	Y	Y
9	Keating	Y	N	N	Y	Y	Y
MICHIGAN							
1	**Bergman**	-	Y	Y	N	N	N
2	**Huizenga**	N	Y	Y	N	Y	N
3	**Amash**	N	Y	Y	N	Y	Y
4	**Moolenaar**	N	Y	Y	N	N	N
5	Kildee	Y	N	N	Y	Y	Y
6	**Upton**	N	Y	N	Y	Y	Y
7	**Walberg**	N	Y	Y	N	Y	Y
8	Slotkin	Y	N	N	Y	Y	Y
9	Levin	Y	N	N	Y	Y	Y
10	**Mitchell**	N	Y	Y	N	N	N
11	Stevens	Y	N	N	Y	Y	Y
12	Dingell	Y	N	N	Y	Y	Y
13	Tlaib	Y	N	N	Y	Y	Y
14	Lawrence	Y	N	N	Y	Y	Y
MINNESOTA							
1	**Hagedorn**	N	Y	Y	N	N	N
2	Craig	Y	N	N	Y	Y	Y
3	Phillips	Y	N	N	Y	Y	Y
4	McCollum	Y	N	N	Y	Y	Y
5	Omar	Y	N	N	Y	Y	Y
6	**Emmer**	N	Y	Y	N	N	N
7	Peterson	Y	N	N	Y	Y	Y
8	**Stauber**	N	Y	Y	N	Y	Y
MISSISSIPPI							
1	**Kelly, T.**	N	Y	Y	N	N	N
2	Thompson, B.	Y	N	N	Y	Y	Y
3	**Guest**	N	Y	Y	N	Y	N
4	**Palazzo**	N	Y	Y	N	N	N
MISSOURI							
1	Clay	Y	N	N	Y	Y	Y
2	**Wagner**	N	Y	Y	N	Y	Y
3	**Luetkemeyer**	N	Y	Y	N	N	N
4	**Hartzler**	N	Y	Y	N	N	N
5	Cleaver	Y	N	N	Y	Y	Y
6	**Graves, S.**	N	Y	Y	N	N	N
7	**Long**	N	Y	Y	N	N	N
8	**Smith, J.**	N	Y	Y	N	N	N
MONTANA							
AL	**Gianforte**	N	Y	Y	N	N	N
NEBRASKA							
1	**Fortenberry**	N	Y	Y	Y	Y	Y
2	**Bacon**	N	Y	N	Y	Y	Y
3	**Smith, Adrian**	N	Y	Y	N	N	Y
NEVADA							
1	Titus	+	-	-	+	+	+
2	**Amodei**	N	Y	Y	N	N	N
3	Lee	Y	N	-	Y	Y	Y
4	Horsford	Y	N	N	Y	Y	Y
NEW HAMPSHIRE							
1	Pappas	Y	N	N	Y	Y	Y
2	Kuster	Y	N	N	Y	Y	Y
NEW JERSEY							
1	Norcross	Y	N	N	Y	Y	Y
2	Van Drew	Y	N	N	Y	Y	Y
3	Kim	Y	N	N	Y	Y	Y
4	**Smith, C.**	N	Y	Y	Y	Y	Y
5	Gottheimer	Y	N	N	Y	Y	Y
6	Pallone	Y	N	N	Y	Y	Y
7	Malinowski	Y	N	N	Y	Y	Y
8	Sires	Y	N	N	Y	Y	Y
9	Pascrell	Y	N	N	Y	Y	Y
10	Payne	?	?	N	Y	Y	Y
11	Sherrill	Y	N	N	Y	Y	Y
12	Watson Coleman	Y	N	N	Y	Y	Y
NEW MEXICO							
1	Haaland	Y	N	N	Y	Y	Y
2	Torres Small	Y	N	N	Y	Y	Y
3	Luján	Y	N	N	Y	Y	Y
NEW YORK							
1	**Zeldin**	N	Y	Y	Y	Y	Y
2	**King, P.**	Y	Y	Y	Y	Y	Y
3	Suozzi	Y	N	N	Y	Y	Y
4	Rice, K.	Y	N	N	Y	Y	Y
5	Meeks	Y	N	N	Y	Y	Y
6	Meng	Y	N	N	Y	Y	Y
7	Velázquez	Y	N	N	Y	Y	Y
8	Jeffries	Y	N	N	Y	Y	Y
9	Clarke	Y	N	N	Y	Y	Y
10	Nadler	Y	N	N	Y	Y	Y
11	Rose	Y	N	N	Y	Y	Y
12	Maloney, C.	Y	N	N	Y	Y	Y
13	Espaillat	Y	N	N	Y	Y	Y
14	Ocasio-Cortez	Y	N	N	Y	Y	Y
15	Serrano	Y	N	N	Y	Y	Y
16	Engel	Y	N	N	Y	Y	Y
17	Lowey	Y	N	N	Y	Y	Y
18	Maloney, S.P.	Y	N	N	Y	Y	Y
19	Delgado	Y	N	N	Y	Y	Y
20	Tonko	Y	N	N	Y	Y	Y
21	**Stefanik**	N	N	N	Y	Y	Y
22	Brindisi	Y	N	N	Y	Y	Y
23	**Reed**	N	Y	Y	Y	Y	Y
24	**Katko**	Y	N	Y	Y	Y	Y
25	Morelle	Y	N	N	Y	Y	Y
26	Higgins, B.	Y	N	N	Y	Y	Y
27	**Collins, C.**						
NORTH CAROLINA							
1	Butterfield	Y	N	N	Y	Y	Y
2	**Holding**	N	Y	Y	N	N	N
3	**Jones***						
4	Price	Y	N	N	Y	Y	Y
5	**Foxx**	N	Y	Y	Y	Y	Y
6	**Walker**	N	Y	Y	N	N	N
7	**Rouzer**	N	Y	Y	N	Y	N
8	**Hudson**	N	Y	Y	N	Y	Y
9	vacant						
10	**McHenry**	N	Y	Y	Y	Y	Y
11	**Meadows**	N	Y	Y	N	N	Y
12	Adams	+	-	-	+	+	+
13	**Budd**	N	Y	Y	N	N	Y
NORTH DAKOTA							
AL	**Armstrong**	N	?	Y	N	Y	N
OHIO							
1	**Chabot**	N	Y	Y	N	N	N
2	**Wenstrup**	N	Y	Y	N	N	N
3	Beatty	Y	N	N	Y	Y	Y
4	**Jordan**	N	Y	Y	N	N	N
5	**Latta**	N	Y	Y	N	Y	N
6	**Johnson, B.**	N	Y	Y	N	N	N
7	**Gibbs**	N	Y	Y	N	N	N
8	**Davidson**	N	Y	Y	N	N	N
9	Kaptur	Y	N	N	Y	Y	Y
10	**Turner**	N	Y	Y	Y	Y	Y
11	Fudge	Y	N	N	Y	Y	Y
12	**Balderson**	N	Y	Y	N	N	N
13	Ryan	Y	N	N	?	Y	Y
14	**Joyce**	N	Y	Y	Y	Y	Y
15	**Stivers**	N	Y	Y	N	N	N
16	**Gonzalez**	N	Y	Y	Y	Y	Y
OKLAHOMA							
1	**Hern**	N	Y	Y	N	N	N
2	**Mullin**	N	Y	Y	N	N	N
3	**Lucas**	N	Y	Y	N	N	N
4	**Cole**	N	Y	Y	N	N	N
5	Horn	Y	N	N	Y	Y	Y
OREGON							
1	Bonamici	Y	N	N	Y	Y	Y
2	**Walden**	N	Y	Y	Y	Y	Y
3	Blumenauer	Y	N	N	Y	Y	Y
4	DeFazio	Y	N	N	Y	Y	Y
5	Schrader	Y	N	N	Y	Y	Y
PENNSYLVANIA							
1	**Fitzpatrick**	Y	N	N	Y	Y	Y
2	Boyle	Y	N	N	Y	Y	Y
3	Evans	Y	N	N	Y	Y	Y
4	Dean	Y	N	N	Y	Y	Y
5	Scanlon	Y	N	N	Y	Y	Y
6	Houlahan	Y	N	N	Y	Y	Y
7	Wild	Y	N	N	Y	Y	Y
8	Cartwright	Y	N	N	Y	Y	Y
9	**Meuser**	N	Y	Y	N	N	N
10	**Perry**	N	Y	Y	N	Y	Y
11	**Smucker**	N	Y	Y	N	Y	Y
12	**Marino***						
13	**Joyce**	N	Y	Y	N	Y	N
14	**Reschenthaler**	N	Y	Y	N	N	N
15	**Thompson, G.**	N	Y	Y	N	N	N
16	**Kelly, M.**	N	Y	Y	N	N	N
17	Lamb	Y	N	N	Y	Y	Y
18	Doyle	Y	N	N	Y	Y	Y
RHODE ISLAND							
1	Cicilline	Y	N	N	Y	Y	Y
2	Langevin	Y	N	N	Y	Y	Y
SOUTH CAROLINA							
1	Cunningham	Y	N	N	Y	Y	Y
2	**Wilson, J.**	N	Y	Y	N	Y	N
3	**Duncan**	N	Y	Y	N	N	N
4	**Timmons**	N	Y	Y	N	N	N
5	**Norman**	N	Y	Y	N	N	N
6	Clyburn	Y	N	N	Y	Y	Y
7	**Rice, T.**	N	Y	Y	N	Y	Y
SOUTH DAKOTA							
AL	**Johnson**	N	Y	Y	N	N	N
TENNESSEE							
1	**Roe**	N	Y	Y	N	N	N
2	**Burchett**	N	Y	Y	N	N	Y
3	**Fleischmann**	N	Y	Y	N	N	N
4	**DesJarlais**	N	Y	Y	N	N	N
5	Cooper	Y	N	N	Y	Y	Y
6	**Rose**	?	Y	Y	N	N	N
7	**Green**	N	Y	Y	N	N	N
8	**Kustoff**	N	Y	Y	N	N	N
9	Cohen	Y	N	N	Y	Y	Y
TEXAS							
1	**Gohmert**	N	Y	Y	N	N	N
2	**Crenshaw**	N	Y	Y	N	N	N
3	**Taylor**	N	Y	Y	N	N	N
4	**Ratcliffe**	N	Y	Y	N	N	N
5	**Gooden**	N	Y	Y	N	N	N
6	**Wright**	N	Y	Y	N	N	N
7	Fletcher	Y	N	N	Y	Y	Y
8	**Brady**	N	Y	Y	N	N	N
9	Green, A.	Y	N	N	Y	Y	Y
10	**McCaul**	N	Y	Y	Y	Y	Y
11	**Conaway**	N	Y	Y	N	N	N
12	**Granger**	N	Y	Y	N	N	N
13	**Thornberry**	N	Y	Y	N	N	Y
14	**Weber**	N	Y	Y	N	N	N
15	Gonzalez	Y	N	N	Y	Y	Y
16	Escobar	Y	N	N	Y	Y	Y
17	**Flores**	N	Y	Y	N	Y	N
18	Jackson Lee	Y	N	N	Y	Y	Y
19	**Arrington**	?	Y	N	N	N	N
20	Castro	Y	N	N	Y	Y	Y
21	**Roy**	N	Y	Y	N	N	N
22	**Olson**	N	Y	Y	N	Y	N
23	**Hurd**	N	Y	Y	N	N	N
24	**Marchant**	N	Y	Y	N	N	N
25	**Williams**	N	Y	Y	N	N	N
26	**Burgess**	N	Y	Y	N	N	N
27	**Cloud**	N	Y	Y	N	N	N
28	Cuellar	Y	N	N	Y	Y	Y
29	Garcia, S.	Y	N	N	Y	Y	Y
30	Johnson, E.B.	Y	N	N	Y	Y	Y
31	**Carter, J.**	N	Y	Y	N	N	N
32	Allred	Y	N	N	Y	Y	Y
33	Veasey	Y	N	N	Y	Y	Y
34	Vela	Y	N	N	Y	Y	Y
35	Doggett	Y	N	N	Y	Y	Y
36	**Babin**	N	Y	Y	N	N	N
UTAH							
1	**Bishop, R.**	N	Y	Y	N	N	Y
2	**Stewart**	N	Y	Y	N	N	N
3	**Curtis**	N	Y	Y	N	Y	N
4	McAdams	Y	N	N	Y	Y	Y
VERMONT							
AL	Welch	Y	N	N	Y	Y	Y
VIRGINIA							
1	**Wittman**	N	Y	Y	N	N	N
2	Luria	Y	N	N	Y	Y	Y
3	Scott, R.	Y	N	N	Y	Y	Y
4	McEachin	Y	N	N	Y	Y	Y
5	**Riggleman**	N	Y	Y	N	Y	Y
6	**Cline**	N	Y	Y	N	N	Y
7	Spanberger	Y	N	N	Y	Y	Y
8	Beyer	Y	N	N	Y	Y	Y
9	**Griffith**	N	Y	Y	N	Y	Y
10	Wexton	Y	N	N	Y	Y	Y
11	Connolly	Y	N	N	Y	Y	Y
WASHINGTON							
1	DelBene	Y	N	N	Y	Y	Y
2	Larsen	Y	N	N	Y	Y	Y
3	**Herrera Beutler**	Y	Y	Y	Y	Y	Y
4	**Newhouse**	N	Y	Y	N	N	N
5	**McMorris Rodgers**	N	Y	Y	Y	Y	Y
6	Kilmer	Y	N	N	Y	Y	Y
7	Jayapal	Y	N	N	Y	Y	Y
8	Schrier	Y	N	N	Y	Y	Y
9	Smith Adam	Y	N	N	Y	Y	Y
10	Heck	Y	N	N	Y	Y	Y
WEST VIRGINIA							
1	**McKinley**	N	Y	Y	Y	Y	Y
2	**Mooney**	N	Y	Y	N	Y	N
3	**Miller**	N	Y	Y	N	Y	N
WISCONSIN							
1	**Steil**	N	Y	Y	Y	Y	Y
2	Pocan	Y	N	N	Y	Y	Y
3	Kind	Y	N	N	Y	Y	Y
4	Moore	Y	N	N	Y	Y	Y
5	**Sensenbrenner**	N	Y	Y	N	N	N
6	**Grothman**	N	Y	Y	N	Y	Y
7	**Duffy**						
8	**Gallagher**	N	Y	Y	N	Y	Y
WYOMING							
AL	**Cheney**	N	Y	Y	N	N	N
DELEGATES							
	Radewagen (A.S.)	N	Y	Y	N	Y	Y
	Norton (D.C.)	Y	N	N	Y	Y	Y
	San Nicolas (Guam)	Y	N	N	Y	Y	Y
	Sablan (N. Marianas)	Y	N	N	Y	Y	Y
	González-Colón (P.R.)	N	Y	Y	Y	N	N
	Plaskett (V.I.)	?	?	?	?	?	?

⫴ HOUSE VOTES

181. HR9. International Emissions Reduction Plan - Hurricane and Storm Finding. Van Drew, D-N.J., amendment that would state that the Paris Agreement recognizes the importance of preventing and addressing loss and damage associated with the effects of climate change, including extreme weather and slow onset events such as strong winds and flooding from hurricanes and tropical storms. Adopted in Committee of the Whole 257-167: R 28-167; D 228-0; I 1-0. May 2, 2019.

182. HR9. International Emissions Reduction Plan - U.S. Impacts. Engel, D-N.Y., for Cox, D-Calif., amendment that would require the emissions reduction plan required by the bill to describe and take into account how U.S. regions and industries would be affected by the fulfillment of the nationally determined contribution under the Paris Agreement, including potential effects on U.S. jobs, energy costs, and technology development. Adopted in Committee of the Whole 259-166: R 29-166; D 229-0; I 1-0. May 2, 2019.

183. HR9. International Emissions Reduction Plan - Recommit. Barr, R-Ky., motion to recommit the bill to the House Foreign Affairs Committee with instructions to report it back immediately with an amendment that would set the bill's effective date as the date on which the president certifies that meeting the nationally determined contribution under the Paris Agreement will not result in a "net transfer of jobs" from the U.S. to China. Motion rejected 206-214: R 192-1; D 14-213. May 2, 2019.

184. HR9. International Emissions Reduction Plan - Passage. Passage of the bill, as amended, that would prohibit the use of federal funds for U.S. withdrawal from the Paris Agreement on climate change and would require the president to develop a plan for the United States to meet its nationally determined contribution under the accord. Specifically, it would require the plan to describe how the U.S. will meet, by 2025, its proposed goal of reducing greenhouse gas emissions to 26 to 28 percent below 2005 levels. It would also require the plan to describe how the U.S. will confirm that other major parties to the accord are fulfilling their proposed contributions. The bill would require the plan to be submitted to Congress and made public no later than 120 days after enactment and to be updated annually. As amended, the bill would require the plan to describe how the U.S. can assist other parties in fulfilling contributions to the accord; require a public comment period on the plan and on subsequent updates to the plan; and order a number of reports on the impacts of the Paris Agreement on clean energy job development, the U.S. economy, and U.S. territories. Passed 231-190: R 3-190; D 228-0. *Note: A "nay" was a vote in support of the president's position.* May 2, 2019.

185. HRES273. U.S.-Taiwan Relations - Passage. Sires, D-N.J., motion to suspend the rules and agree to the resolution that would express that the House of Representatives reaffirms existing U.S. diplomatic policy toward Taiwan, including commitment to strengthening Taiwan's defense capabilities. It would encourage diplomatic relations between U.S. and Taiwan officials, reiterate that the president should conduct defense article transfers to Taiwan in accordance with existing law, and call on the secretary of State to advocate for Taiwan's "meaningful participation" in international organizations that address transnational threats and challenges, including those related to health, aviation security, and crime and terrorism. Motion agreed to 414-0: R 193-0; D 221-0. *Note: A two-thirds majority of those present and voting (276 in this case) is required for passage under suspension of the rules.* May 7, 2019.

186. HR1704. Economic Foreign Policy - Passage. Sires, D-N.J., motion to suspend the rules and pass the bill that would create the position of assistant secretary of State for economic and business matters. The assistant secretary would be responsible for foreign policy related to international economics and business, including international trade and investment policy and economic sanctions. Among other provisions related to international commercial activity, it would make the promotion of U.S. economic interests a "principal duty" of each U.S. mission to a foreign country and require the State Department to produce a report to Congress detailing such efforts, disaggregated by country and region. It would also direct the State and Commerce Departments to publish a report on business climates and commercial relations with foreign countries and regions and would direct the president to pursue negotiations with other countries to establish international standards for government-supported infrastructure investment. Motion agreed to 400-16: R 177-16; D 223-0. *Note: A two-thirds majority of those present and voting (278 in this case) is required for passage under suspension of the rules.* May 7, 2019.

	181	182	183	184	185	186
ALABAMA						
1 Byrne	N	N	Y	N	Y	Y
2 Roby	N	N	Y	N	Y	Y
3 Rogers, M.	N	N	Y	N	Y	Y
4 Aderholt	N	N	Y	N	Y	Y
5 Brooks, M.	N	N	Y	N	Y	N
6 Palmer	N	N	Y	N	Y	Y
7 Sewell	Y	Y	N	Y	Y	Y
ALASKA						
AL Young	N	N	Y	N	Y	Y
ARIZONA						
1 O'Halleran	Y	Y	N	Y	Y	Y
2 Kirkpatrick	Y	Y	N	Y	Y	Y
3 Grijalva	Y	Y	N	Y	?	?
4 Gosar	N	N	Y	N	Y	N
5 Biggs	N	N	Y	N	Y	N
6 Schweikert	Y	N	Y	N	Y	Y
7 Gallego	Y	Y	N	Y	Y	Y
8 Lesko	N	N	Y	N	Y	Y
9 Stanton	Y	Y	N	Y	Y	Y
ARKANSAS						
1 Crawford	-	-	+	-	Y	Y
2 Hill, F.	N	N	Y	N	Y	Y
3 Womack	N	N	Y	N	Y	Y
4 Westerman	N	N	Y	N	Y	Y
CALIFORNIA						
1 LaMalfa	N	N	Y	N	Y	Y
2 Huffman	Y	Y	N	Y	Y	Y
3 Garamendi	Y	Y	N	Y	Y	Y
4 McClintock	N	N	Y	N	Y	Y
5 Thompson, M.	Y	Y	N	Y	Y	Y
6 Matsui	Y	Y	N	Y	Y	Y
7 Bera	Y	Y	N	Y	Y	Y
8 Cook	N	N	Y	N	Y	Y
9 McNerney	Y	Y	N	Y	Y	Y
10 Harder	Y	Y	N	Y	Y	Y
11 DeSaulnier	Y	Y	N	Y	Y	Y
12 Pelosi		Y				
13 Lee B.	Y	Y	N	Y	?	?
14 Speier	?	Y	N	Y	Y	Y
15 Swalwell	Y	Y	N	+	+	
16 Costa	Y	Y	N	Y	?	?
17 Khanna	Y	Y	N	Y	Y	Y
18 Eshoo	Y	Y	N	Y	Y	Y
19 Lofgren	Y	Y	N	Y	Y	Y
20 Panetta	Y	Y	N	Y	Y	Y
21 Cox	Y	Y	N	Y	Y	Y
22 Nunes	N	N	Y	N	Y	Y
23 McCarthy	N	N	Y	N	Y	Y
24 Carbajal	Y	Y	N	Y	Y	Y
25 Hill, K.	Y	Y	N	Y	Y	Y
26 Brownley	Y	Y	N	Y	Y	Y
27 Chu	Y	Y	N	Y	Y	Y
28 Schiff	Y	Y	N	Y	Y	Y
29 Cárdenas	Y	Y	N	Y	Y	Y
30 Sherman	Y	Y	N	Y	Y	Y
31 Aguilar	Y	Y	N	Y	Y	Y
32 Napolitano	Y	Y	N	Y	Y	Y
33 Lieu	Y	Y	N	Y	Y	Y
34 Gomez	Y	Y	N	Y	Y	Y
35 Torres	Y	Y	N	Y	Y	Y
36 Ruiz	Y	Y	N	Y	Y	Y
37 Bass	Y	Y	N	Y	Y	Y
38 Sánchez	Y	Y	N	Y	Y	Y
39 Cisneros	Y	Y	N	Y	Y	Y
40 Roybal-Allard	Y	Y	N	Y	Y	Y
41 Takano	Y	Y	N	Y	Y	Y
42 Calvert	N	N	Y	N	Y	Y
43 Waters	Y	Y	N	Y	Y	Y
44 Barragán	Y	Y	N	Y	Y	Y
45 Porter	Y	Y	N	Y	Y	Y
46 Correa	Y	Y	N	Y	Y	Y
47 Lowenthal	Y	Y	N	Y	Y	Y
48 Rouda	+	+	-	+	Y	Y
49 Levin	Y	Y	N	Y	Y	Y
50 Hunter	N	N	Y	N	Y	Y
51 Vargas	?	?	?	?	Y	Y
52 Peters	Y	Y	N	Y	Y	Y

	181	182	183	184	185	186
53 Davis, S.	Y	Y	N	Y	Y	Y
COLORADO						
1 DeGette	Y	Y	N	Y	Y	Y
2 Neguse	Y	Y	N	Y	Y	Y
3 Tipton	N	N	Y	N	Y	Y
4 Buck	N	N	Y	N	Y	N
5 Lamborn	N	N	Y	N	Y	Y
6 Crow	Y	Y	N	Y	Y	Y
7 Perlmutter	Y	Y	N	Y	Y	Y
CONNECTICUT						
1 Larson	Y	Y	N	Y	Y	Y
2 Courtney	Y	Y	N	Y	Y	Y
3 DeLauro	Y	Y	N	Y	Y	Y
4 Himes	Y	Y	N	Y	Y	Y
5 Hayes	Y	Y	N	Y	Y	Y
DELAWARE						
AL Blunt Rochester	Y	Y	N	Y	Y	Y
FLORIDA						
1 Gaetz	N	Y	Y	N	Y	N
2 Dunn	N	N	Y	N	Y	Y
3 Yoho	N	N	Y	N	Y	Y
4 Rutherford	N	N	Y	N	Y	Y
5 Lawson	Y	Y	N	Y	Y	Y
6 Waltz	Y	Y	N	Y	Y	Y
7 Murphy	Y	Y	N	Y	Y	Y
8 Posey	N	N	Y	N	Y	Y
9 Soto	Y	Y	N	Y	Y	Y
10 Demings	Y	Y	N	Y	Y	Y
11 Webster	N	N	Y	N	Y	Y
12 Bilirakis	N	N	Y	N	Y	Y
13 Crist	Y	Y	N	Y	Y	Y
14 Castor	Y	Y	N	Y	Y	Y
15 Spano	N	N	Y	N	Y	Y
16 Buchanan	Y	Y	Y	Y	Y	Y
17 Steube	N	N	Y	N	Y	Y
18 Mast	N	N	Y	N	Y	Y
19 Rooney	?	?	?	?	?	?
20 Hastings	?	?	?	+	Y	Y
21 Frankel	Y	Y	N	Y	Y	Y
22 Deutch	Y	Y	N	Y	Y	Y
23 Wasserman Schultz	Y	Y	N	Y	Y	Y
24 Wilson, F.	Y	Y	N	Y	Y	Y
25 Diaz-Balart	N	N	Y	N	Y	Y
26 Mucarsel-Powell	Y	Y	N	Y	Y	Y
27 Shalala	Y	Y	N	Y	Y	Y
GEORGIA						
1 Carter, E.L.	Y	N	N	N	Y	Y
2 Bishop, S.	Y	Y	N	Y	Y	Y
3 Ferguson	N	N	Y	N	Y	Y
4 Johnson, H.	Y	Y	N	Y	Y	Y
5 Lewis John	Y	Y	N	Y	Y	Y
6 McBath	Y	Y	N	Y	Y	Y
7 Woodall	N	N	Y	N	Y	Y
8 Scott, A.	N	N	Y	N	Y	Y
9 Collins, D.	N	N	Y	N	Y	Y
10 Hice	N	N	Y	N	Y	Y
11 Loudermilk	?	?	?	?	Y	Y
12 Allen	N	N	Y	N	Y	Y
13 Scott, D.	Y	Y	N	Y	Y	Y
14 Graves, T.	N	N	Y	N	Y	Y
HAWAII						
1 Case	Y	Y	N	Y	Y	Y
2 Gabbard	Y	Y	N	Y	?	Y
IDAHO						
1 Fulcher	N	N	Y	N	Y	Y
2 Simpson	N	N	Y	N	Y	Y
ILLINOIS						
1 Rush	Y	Y	N	Y	Y	Y
2 Kelly, R.	Y	Y	N	Y	Y	Y
3 Lipinski	Y	Y	N	Y	Y	Y
4 García, J.	Y	Y	N	Y	Y	Y
5 Quigley	Y	Y	N	Y	Y	Y
6 Casten	Y	Y	N	Y	Y	Y
7 Davis, D.	Y	Y	N	Y	Y	Y
8 Krishnamoorthi	Y	Y	N	Y	Y	Y
9 Schakowsky	Y	Y	N	Y	Y	Y
10 Schneider	Y	Y	N	Y	Y	Y
11 Foster	Y	Y	N	Y	Y	Y

KEY:	**Republicans**	Democrats	*Independents*

Y	Voted for (yea)	N	Voted against (nay)	P	Voted "present"
+	Announced for	-	Announced against	?	Did not vote or otherwise
#	Paired for	X	Paired against		make position known

		181	182	183	184	185	186
12	**Bost**	N	N	Y	N	Y	Y
13	**Davis, R.**	Y	Y	Y	N	Y	Y
14	Underwood	Y	Y	N	Y	Y	Y
15	**Shimkus**	N	N	Y	N	Y	Y
16	**Kinzinger**	N	N	Y	N	Y	Y
17	Bustos	Y	Y	N	Y	Y	Y
18	**LaHood**	N	N	Y	N	Y	Y
INDIANA							
1	Visclosky	Y	Y	N	Y	Y	Y
2	**Walorski**	N	N	Y	N	Y	Y
3	**Banks**	N	N	Y	N	Y	Y
4	**Baird**	N	N	Y	N	Y	Y
5	**Brooks, S.**	Y	Y	Y	N	Y	Y
6	**Pence**	N	N	Y	N	Y	Y
7	Carson	Y	Y	N	Y	Y	Y
8	**Bucshon**	N	N	Y	N	Y	Y
9	**Hollingsworth**	Y	Y	Y	N	Y	Y
IOWA							
1	Finkenauer	Y	Y	N	Y	Y	Y
2	Loebsack	Y	Y	N	Y	Y	Y
3	Axne	Y	Y	N	Y	Y	Y
4	**King, S.**	N	N	Y	N	Y	N
KANSAS							
1	**Marshall**	N	N	Y	N	Y	Y
2	**Watkins**	N	N	Y	N	Y	Y
3	Davids	Y	Y	N	Y	Y	Y
4	**Estes**	N	N	Y	N	Y	Y
KENTUCKY							
1	**Comer**	N	N	Y	N	Y	N
2	**Guthrie**	N	N	Y	N	Y	Y
3	Yarmuth	Y	Y	N	Y	?	?
4	**Massie**	N	N	Y	N	Y	N
5	**Rogers, H.**	N	N	Y	N	Y	Y
6	**Barr**	N	N	Y	N	Y	Y
LOUISIANA							
1	**Scalise**	N	N	Y	N	Y	Y
2	Richmond	Y	Y	N	Y	Y	Y
3	**Higgins, C.**	N	N	Y	N	Y	Y
4	**Johnson, M.**	N	N	Y	N	Y	Y
5	**Abraham**	?	?	?	?	?	?
6	**Graves, G.**	Y	Y	Y	N	Y	Y
MAINE							
1	Pingree	Y	Y	N	Y	Y	Y
2	Golden	Y	Y	Y	Y	Y	Y
MARYLAND							
1	**Harris**	N	N	Y	N	Y	N
2	Ruppersberger	Y	Y	N	Y	Y	Y
3	Sarbanes	Y	Y	N	Y	Y	Y
4	Brown, A.	Y	Y	N	Y	Y	Y
5	Hoyer	Y	Y	N	Y	Y	Y
6	Trone	Y	Y	N	Y	Y	Y
7	Cummings	Y	Y	N	Y	Y	Y
8	Raskin	Y	Y	N	Y	Y	Y
MASSACHUSETTS							
1	Neal	Y	Y	N	Y	Y	Y
2	McGovern	Y	Y	N	Y	Y	Y
3	Trahan	Y	Y	N	Y	Y	Y
4	Kennedy	Y	Y	N	Y	Y	Y
5	Clark	Y	Y	N	Y	Y	Y
6	Moulton	Y	Y	N	Y	Y	Y
7	Pressley	Y	Y	N	Y	Y	Y
8	Lynch	Y	Y	N	Y	Y	Y
9	Keating	Y	Y	N	Y	Y	Y
MICHIGAN							
1	**Bergman**	N	N	Y	N	Y	Y
2	**Huizenga**	N	N	Y	N	Y	Y
3	**Amash**	N	N	N	N	Y	N
4	**Moolenaar**	N	N	Y	N	Y	Y
5	Kildee	Y	Y	N	Y	Y	Y
6	**Upton**	Y	Y	Y	N	Y	Y
7	**Walberg**	N	N	Y	N	Y	Y
8	Slotkin	Y	Y	Y	Y	Y	Y
9	Levin	Y	Y	N	Y	Y	Y
10	**Mitchell**	N	N	Y	N	Y	Y
11	Stevens	Y	Y	N	Y	Y	Y
12	Dingell	Y	Y	N	Y	Y	Y
13	Tlaib	Y	Y	N	Y	Y	Y
14	Lawrence	Y	Y	N	Y	Y	Y
MINNESOTA							
1	**Hagedorn**	N	N	Y	N	Y	Y
2	Craig	Y	Y	Y	Y	Y	Y
3	Phillips	Y	Y	N	Y	Y	Y
4	McCollum	Y	Y	N	Y	Y	Y
5	Omar	Y	Y	N	Y	+	+

		181	182	183	184	185	186
6	**Emmer**	N	N	Y	N	Y	Y
7	Peterson	Y	Y	Y	Y	Y	Y
8	**Stauber**	Y	N	Y	N	Y	Y
MISSISSIPPI							
1	**Kelly, T.**	N	N	Y	N	Y	Y
2	Thompson, B.	?	?	?	?	Y	Y
3	**Guest**	N	N	Y	N	Y	Y
4	**Palazzo**	N	N	Y	N	Y	Y
MISSOURI							
1	Clay	Y	Y	N	Y	Y	Y
2	**Wagner**	N	N	Y	N	Y	Y
3	**Luetkemeyer**	N	N	Y	N	Y	Y
4	**Hartzler**	N	N	Y	N	Y	Y
5	Cleaver	Y	Y	N	Y	Y	Y
6	**Graves, S.**	N	N	Y	N	Y	Y
7	**Long**	N	N	Y	N	Y	Y
8	**Smith, J.**	N	N	Y	N	Y	Y
MONTANA							
AL	**Gianforte**	N	Y	Y	N	Y	Y
NEBRASKA							
1	**Fortenberry**	Y	Y	Y	N	Y	Y
2	**Bacon**	Y	Y	Y	N	Y	Y
3	**Smith, Adrian**	N	N	Y	N	Y	Y
NEVADA							
1	Titus	+	+	-	+	Y	Y
2	**Amodei**	N	N	Y	N	Y	Y
3	Lee	Y	Y	N	Y	Y	Y
4	Horsford	Y	Y	N	Y	Y	Y
NEW HAMPSHIRE							
1	Pappas	Y	Y	N	Y	Y	Y
2	Kuster	Y	Y	N	Y	Y	Y
NEW JERSEY							
1	Norcross	Y	Y	N	Y	Y	Y
2	Van Drew	Y	Y	Y	Y	Y	Y
3	Kim	Y	Y	N	Y	Y	Y
4	**Smith, C.**	Y	Y	Y	N	Y	Y
5	Gottheimer	Y	Y	Y	Y	Y	Y
6	Pallone	Y	Y	N	Y	Y	Y
7	Malinowski	Y	Y	N	Y	Y	Y
8	Sires	Y	Y	N	Y	Y	Y
9	Pascrell	Y	Y	N	Y	Y	Y
10	Payne	Y	Y	N	Y	Y	Y
11	Sherrill	Y	Y	N	Y	Y	Y
12	Watson Coleman	Y	Y	N	Y	Y	Y
NEW MEXICO							
1	Haaland	Y	Y	N	Y	Y	Y
2	Torres Small	Y	Y	N	Y	Y	Y
3	Luján	Y	Y	N	Y	Y	Y
NEW YORK							
1	**Zeldin**	Y	Y	Y	N	Y	Y
2	**King, P.**	Y	Y	Y	N	Y	Y
3	Suozzi	Y	Y	N	Y	Y	Y
4	Rice, K.	Y	Y	N	Y	Y	Y
5	Meeks	Y	Y	N	Y	Y	Y
6	Meng	Y	Y	N	Y	?	Y
7	Velázquez	Y	Y	N	Y	Y	Y
8	Jeffries	Y	Y	N	Y	Y	Y
9	Clarke	Y	Y	N	Y	Y	Y
10	Nadler	Y	Y	N	Y	Y	Y
11	Rose	Y	Y	Y	Y	Y	Y
12	Maloney, C.	Y	Y	N	Y	Y	Y
13	Espaillat	Y	Y	N	Y	Y	Y
14	Ocasio-Cortez	Y	Y	N	Y	Y	Y
15	Serrano	Y	Y	N	Y	Y	Y
16	Engel	Y	Y	N	Y	Y	Y
17	Lowey	Y	Y	N	Y	Y	Y
18	Maloney, S.P.	Y	Y	N	Y	Y	Y
19	Delgado	Y	Y	N	Y	Y	Y
20	Tonko	Y	Y	N	Y	Y	Y
21	**Stefanik**	Y	Y	Y	Y	Y	Y
22	Brindisi	Y	Y	Y	Y	Y	Y
23	**Reed**	Y	Y	Y	N	Y	Y
24	**Katko**	Y	Y	Y	N	Y	Y
25	Morelle	Y	Y	N	Y	Y	Y
26	Higgins, B.	Y	Y	N	Y	Y	Y
27	**Collins, C.**						
NORTH CAROLINA							
1	Butterfield	Y	Y	N	Y	?	?
2	**Holding**	N	N	Y	N	Y	Y
3	**Jones***						
4	Price	Y	Y	N	Y	Y	Y
5	**Foxx**	Y	Y	Y	N	Y	Y
6	**Walker**	N	N	Y	N	Y	Y
7	**Rouzer**	N	N	Y	N	Y	Y

		181	182	183	184	185	186
8	**Hudson**	N	N	Y	N	Y	Y
9	vacant						
10	**McHenry**	N	N	Y	N	Y	Y
11	**Meadows**	N	N	Y	N	Y	Y
12	Adams	+	+	-	+	Y	Y
13	**Budd**	N	N	Y	N	Y	Y
NORTH DAKOTA							
AL	**Armstrong**	Y	N	Y	N	Y	Y
OHIO							
1	**Chabot**	N	N	Y	N	Y	Y
2	**Wenstrup**	N	N	Y	N	+	+
3	Beatty	Y	Y	N	Y	Y	Y
4	**Jordan**	N	N	Y	N	Y	N
5	**Latta**	N	N	Y	N	Y	Y
6	**Johnson, B.**	N	N	Y	N	Y	Y
7	**Gibbs**	N	N	Y	N	Y	Y
8	**Davidson**	N	N	Y	N	Y	Y
9	Kaptur	Y	Y	N	Y	Y	Y
10	**Turner**	N	Y	Y	N	Y	Y
11	Fudge	Y	?	?	?	Y	Y
12	**Balderson**	N	N	Y	N	Y	Y
13	Ryan	Y	Y	N	Y	Y	Y
14	**Joyce**	Y	Y	Y	N	Y	Y
15	**Stivers**	N	N	Y	N	Y	Y
16	**Gonzalez**	Y	Y	Y	N	Y	Y
OKLAHOMA							
1	**Hern**	N	N	Y	N	Y	N
2	**Mullin**	N	N	Y	N	Y	Y
3	**Lucas**	N	N	Y	N	Y	Y
4	**Cole**	N	N	Y	N	Y	Y
5	Horn	Y	Y	Y	Y	Y	Y
OREGON							
1	Bonamici	Y	Y	N	Y	Y	Y
2	**Walden**	Y	Y	Y	N	Y	Y
3	Blumenauer	Y	Y	N	Y	Y	Y
4	DeFazio	Y	Y	N	Y	Y	Y
5	Schrader	Y	Y	N	Y	Y	Y
PENNSYLVANIA							
1	**Fitzpatrick**	Y	Y	Y	Y	Y	Y
2	Boyle	Y	Y	N	Y	Y	Y
3	Evans	Y	Y	N	Y	Y	Y
4	Dean	Y	Y	N	Y	Y	Y
5	Scanlon	Y	Y	N	Y	Y	Y
6	Houlahan	Y	Y	Y	Y	Y	Y
7	Wild	Y	Y	N	Y	Y	Y
8	Cartwright	Y	Y	N	Y	?	?
9	**Meuser**	N	N	Y	N	Y	Y
10	**Perry**	N	N	Y	N	Y	Y
11	**Smucker**	N	N	Y	N	Y	Y
12	**Marino***						
13	**Joyce**	N	N	Y	N	Y	Y
14	**Reschenthaler**	N	N	Y	N	Y	Y
15	**Thompson, G.**	N	N	Y	N	Y	Y
16	**Kelly, M.**	N	N	Y	N	Y	Y
17	Lamb	Y	Y	Y	Y	Y	Y
18	Doyle	Y	Y	N	Y	Y	Y
RHODE ISLAND							
1	Cicilline	Y	Y	N	Y	Y	Y
2	Langevin	Y	Y	N	Y	Y	Y
SOUTH CAROLINA							
1	Cunningham	Y	Y	N	Y	Y	Y
2	**Wilson, J.**	N	N	Y	N	Y	Y
3	**Duncan**	N	N	Y	N	Y	Y
4	**Timmons**	N	N	Y	N	Y	Y
5	**Norman**	N	N	Y	N	Y	Y
6	Clyburn	Y	Y	N	Y	Y	Y
7	**Rice, T.**	N	N	Y	N	Y	N
SOUTH DAKOTA							
AL	**Johnson**	N	N	Y	N	Y	Y
TENNESSEE							
1	**Roe**	N	N	Y	N	Y	Y
2	**Burchett**	N	N	Y	N	Y	N
3	**Fleischmann**	N	N	Y	N	Y	Y
4	**DesJarlais**	N	N	Y	N	Y	Y
5	Cooper	Y	Y	N	Y	Y	Y
6	**Rose**	N	N	Y	N	Y	Y
7	**Green**	N	N	Y	N	Y	Y
8	**Kustoff**	N	N	Y	N	Y	Y
9	Cohen	Y	Y	N	Y	Y	Y
TEXAS							
1	**Gohmert**	N	N	Y	N	Y	N
2	**Crenshaw**	N	N	Y	N	Y	Y
3	**Taylor**	N	N	Y	N	Y	Y
4	**Ratcliffe**	N	N	Y	N	Y	Y

		181	182	183	184	185	186
5	**Gooden**	N	N	Y	N	Y	Y
6	**Wright**	N	N	Y	N	Y	Y
7	Fletcher	Y	Y	N	Y	+	+
8	**Brady**	N	N	Y	N	Y	Y
9	Green, A.	Y	Y	N	Y	Y	Y
10	**McCaul**	N	N	Y	N	Y	Y
11	**Conaway**	N	N	Y	N	Y	Y
12	**Granger**	N	N	Y	N	Y	Y
13	**Thornberry**	N	N	Y	N	Y	Y
14	**Weber**	N	N	Y	N	Y	Y
15	Gonzalez	Y	Y	N	Y	+	+
16	Escobar	Y	Y	N	Y	Y	Y
17	**Flores**	N	N	Y	N	Y	Y
18	Jackson Lee	?	Y	N	Y	+	+
19	**Arrington**	N	N	Y	N	Y	Y
20	Castro	Y	Y	N	Y	Y	Y
21	**Roy**	N	N	Y	N	Y	N
22	**Olson**	N	N	Y	N	Y	Y
23	**Hurd**	N	N	Y	N	Y	Y
24	**Marchant**	N	N	Y	N	Y	Y
25	**Williams**	N	N	Y	N	Y	Y
26	**Burgess**	N	N	Y	N	Y	Y
27	**Cloud**	N	N	Y	N	Y	Y
28	Cuellar	Y	Y	N	Y	Y	Y
29	Garcia, S.	Y	Y	N	Y	Y	Y
30	Johnson, E.B.	Y	Y	N	Y	Y	Y
31	**Carter, J.**	N	N	Y	N	Y	Y
32	Allred	Y	Y	N	Y	Y	Y
33	Veasey	Y	Y	N	Y	Y	Y
34	Vela	Y	Y	N	Y	Y	Y
35	Doggett	Y	Y	N	Y	Y	Y
36	**Babin**	N	N	Y	N	?	?
UTAH							
1	**Bishop, R.**	N	N	Y	N	Y	Y
2	**Stewart**	N	N	Y	N	Y	Y
3	**Curtis**	N	N	Y	N	Y	Y
4	McAdams	Y	Y	Y	Y	Y	Y
VERMONT							
AL	Welch	Y	Y	N	Y	Y	Y
VIRGINIA							
1	**Wittman**	N	N	Y	N	Y	Y
2	Luria	Y	Y	N	Y	Y	Y
3	Scott, R.	Y	Y	N	Y	Y	Y
4	McEachin	Y	Y	N	Y	Y	Y
5	**Riggleman**	N	N	Y	N	Y	Y
6	**Cline**	N	N	Y	N	Y	Y
7	Spanberger	Y	Y	N	Y	Y	Y
8	Beyer	Y	Y	N	Y	Y	Y
9	**Griffith**	N	N	Y	N	Y	Y
10	Wexton	Y	Y	N	Y	Y	Y
11	Connolly	Y	Y	N	Y	Y	Y
WASHINGTON							
1	DelBene	Y	Y	N	Y	Y	Y
2	Larsen	Y	Y	N	Y	Y	Y
3	**Herrera Beutler**	Y	Y	Y	N	Y	Y
4	**Newhouse**	N	N	Y	N	Y	Y
5	**McMorris Rodgers**	Y	Y	Y	N	Y	Y
6	Kilmer	Y	Y	N	Y	Y	Y
7	Jayapal	Y	Y	N	Y	Y	Y
8	Schrier	Y	Y	N	Y	Y	Y
9	Smith Adam	Y	Y	N	Y	Y	Y
10	Heck	Y	Y	N	Y	Y	Y
WEST VIRGINIA							
1	**McKinley**	N	N	Y	N	Y	Y
2	**Mooney**	N	N	Y	N	Y	Y
3	**Miller**	N	N	Y	N	Y	Y
WISCONSIN							
1	**Steil**	Y	Y	Y	N	Y	Y
2	Pocan	Y	Y	N	Y	Y	Y
3	Kind	Y	Y	N	Y	Y	Y
4	Moore	Y	Y	N	Y	Y	Y
5	**Sensenbrenner**	N	N	Y	N	Y	Y
6	**Grothman**	N	Y	Y	N	Y	Y
7	**Duffy**						
8	**Gallagher**	Y	Y	Y	N	Y	Y
WYOMING							
AL	**Cheney**	N	N	Y	N	Y	Y
DELEGATES							
	Radewagen (A.S.)	N	N				
	Norton (D.C.)	Y	Y				
	San Nicolas (Guam)	Y	Y				
	Sablan (N. Marianas)	Y	Y				
	González-Colón (P.R.)	N	Y				
	Plaskett (V.I.)	?	?				

||| HOUSE VOTES

187. HR1503. FDA Patent Disclosures - Passage. Eshoo, D-Calif., motion to suspend the rules and pass the bill that would require the Food and Drug Administration to include additional patent information in its list of approved drugs, including substance patents, drug product patents, and method of use patents. It would require patent holders for approved drugs to notify the FDA in writing if a patent is invalidated. It would also require the Health and Human Services secretary to solicit public comment and subsequently report to Congress on any patent information that should be added to or removed from the public listing and would require the Government Accountability Office to report to Congress on whether the inclusion or omission of patents in the listing would delay the market entry of generic drugs. Motion agreed to 422-0: R 191-0; D 231-0. *Note: A two-thirds majority of those present and voting (282 in this case) is required for passage under suspension of the rules.* May 8, 2019.

188. HR1520. FDA Biological Products Listing - Passage. Eshoo, D-Calif., motion to suspend the rules and pass the bill, as amended, that would statutorily require the Food and Drug Administration to maintain a public listing of biological products licensed by the agency, including the non-proprietary name, marketing application and licensure status, and exclusivity date of each product. It would require the FDA to publish the list in searchable, electronic format within 180 days of enactment. The bill would also require the Health and Human Services secretary to solicit public comment and subsequently report to Congress on any information that should be added to or removed from the public listing. Motion agreed to 421-0: R 192-0; D 229-0. *Note: A two-thirds majority of those present and voting (281 in this case) is required for passage under suspension of the rules.* May 8, 2019.

189. HR986, HR2157. Health Insurance Guidance, Disaster Supplemental - Previous Question. Shalala, D-Fla., motion to order the previous question (thus ending the debate and possibility of amendment) on the rule (H Res 357) that would provide for House floor consideration of the bill (HR 986) that would prohibit the Health and Human Services and Treasury departments from implementing or enforcing guidance related to Section 1332 waivers under the 2010 health care overhaul. It would also provide for floor consideration of the bill (HR 2157) that would provide $17.4 billion in supplemental disaster funds for response efforts to damage caused by hurricanes, wildfires, earthquakes, tornadoes, floods, and other natural disasters that occurred in 2017, 2018, and 2019. The rule would also provide for the automatic adoption of a Lowey, D-N.Y., manager's amendment to HR 2157 that would authorize an additional $91.2 million for "necessary expenses" to repair federal buildings and courthouses damaged as a result of Hurricane Florence and clarify the types of costs eligible for such disaster assistance. Motion agreed to 227-190: R 0-190; D 227-0. May 9, 2019.

190. HR2157, HR986. Health Insurance Guidance, Disaster Supplemental - Rule. Adoption of the rule (H Res 357) that would provide for House floor consideration of the bill (HR 986) that would prohibit the Health and Human Services and Treasury departments from implementing or enforcing guidance related to Section 1332 waivers under the 2010 health care overhaul. It would also provide for floor consideration of the bill (HR 2157) that would provide $17.4 billion in supplemental disaster funds for response efforts to damage caused by hurricanes, wildfires, earthquakes, tornadoes, floods, and other natural disasters that occurred in 2017, 2018, and 2019. The rule would also provide for the automatic adoption of a Lowey, D-N.Y., manager's amendment to HR 2157 that would authorize an additional $91.2 million for "necessary expenses" to repair federal buildings and courthouses damaged as a result of Hurricane Florence and clarify the types of costs eligible for such disaster assistance. Adopted 227-191: R 0-191; D 227-0. May 9, 2019.

191. HR986. State Health Insurance Plan Guidance - Reinsurance Program Exemption. Brown, D-Md., amendment that would specify that reinsurance programs established under section 1332 waivers that meet requirements for public notice and input be exempt from the bill's prohibition on the implementation of the Oct. 2018 guidance on the criteria for such waivers. Adopted in Committee of the Whole 351-70: R 121-70; D 229-0; I 1-0. May 9, 2019.

192. HR986. State Health Insurance Plan Guidance - Short Title. Holding, R-N.C., amendment that would change the short title of the bill to "Insert Politically Punchy Title That Doesn't Reflect the Bill Substance Act." Rejected in Committee of the Whole 184-237: R 184-7; D 0-229; I 0-1. May 9, 2019.

		187	188	189	190	191	192
ALABAMA							
1	**Byrne**	Y	Y	N	N	N	Y
2	**Roby**	Y	Y	N	N	N	Y
3	**Rogers, M.**	Y	Y	N	N	N	Y
4	**Aderholt**	Y	Y	N	N	N	Y
5	**Brooks, M.**	Y	Y	N	N	N	Y
6	**Palmer**	Y	Y	N	N	N	Y
7	Sewell	Y	Y	Y	Y	Y	N
ALASKA							
AL	**Young**	Y	Y	N	N	Y	Y
ARIZONA							
1	O'Halleran	Y	+	Y	Y	Y	N
2	Kirkpatrick	Y	Y	Y	Y	Y	N
3	Grijalva	Y	Y	Y	Y	Y	N
4	**Gosar**	Y	Y	N	N	N	Y
5	**Biggs**	Y	Y	N	N	N	Y
6	**Schweikert**	Y	Y	N	N	Y	Y
7	Gallego	Y	Y	Y	Y	Y	N
8	**Lesko**	Y	Y	N	N	Y	Y
9	Stanton	Y	Y	Y	Y	Y	N
ARKANSAS							
1	**Crawford**	Y	Y	N	N	Y	Y
2	**Hill, F.**	Y	Y	N	N	Y	Y
3	**Womack**	Y	Y	N	N	Y	Y
4	**Westerman**	Y	Y	N	N	Y	Y
CALIFORNIA							
1	**LaMalfa**	Y	Y	N	N	Y	Y
2	Huffman	Y	Y	Y	Y	Y	N
3	Garamendi	Y	Y	Y	Y	Y	N
4	**McClintock**	Y	Y	N	N	N	Y
5	Thompson, M.	Y	Y	Y	Y	Y	N
6	Matsui	Y	Y	Y	Y	Y	N
7	Bera	Y	Y	Y	Y	Y	N
8	**Cook**	Y	Y	N	N	N	Y
9	McNerney	Y	Y	Y	Y	Y	N
10	Harder	Y	Y	Y	Y	Y	N
11	DeSaulnier	Y	Y	Y	Y	Y	N
12	Pelosi						
13	Lee B.	Y	Y	Y	Y	Y	N
14	Speier	Y	Y	Y	Y	Y	N
15	Swalwell	Y	Y	+	+	+	-
16	Costa	Y	Y	Y	Y	Y	N
17	Khanna	Y	Y	Y	Y	Y	N
18	Eshoo	Y	Y	Y	Y	Y	N
19	Lofgren	Y	Y	Y	Y	Y	N
20	Panetta	Y	Y	Y	Y	Y	N
21	Cox	Y	Y	Y	Y	Y	N
22	**Nunes**	Y	Y	N	N	Y	Y
23	**McCarthy**	Y	Y	N	N	Y	Y
24	Carbajal	Y	Y	Y	Y	Y	N
25	Hill, K.	Y	Y	Y	Y	Y	N
26	Brownley	Y	Y	Y	Y	Y	N
27	Chu	Y	Y	Y	Y	Y	N
28	Schiff	Y	Y	Y	Y	Y	N
29	Cárdenas	Y	Y	?	?	?	?
30	Sherman	Y	Y	Y	Y	Y	N
31	Aguilar	Y	Y	Y	Y	Y	N
32	Napolitano	Y	Y	Y	Y	Y	N
33	Lieu	Y	Y	Y	Y	Y	N
34	Gomez	Y	Y	Y	Y	Y	N
35	Torres	Y	Y	Y	Y	Y	N
36	Ruiz	Y	Y	Y	Y	Y	N
37	Bass	Y	Y	?	?	?	?
38	Sánchez	Y	Y	Y	Y	Y	N
39	Cisneros	Y	Y	Y	Y	Y	N
40	Roybal-Allard	Y	Y	Y	Y	Y	N
41	Takano	Y	Y	Y	Y	Y	N
42	**Calvert**	Y	Y	N	N	Y	Y
43	Waters	Y	Y	Y	Y	Y	N
44	Barragán	Y	Y	Y	Y	Y	N
45	Porter	Y	Y	Y	Y	Y	N
46	Correa	Y	Y	Y	Y	Y	N
47	Lowenthal	Y	Y	Y	Y	Y	N
48	Rouda	Y	Y	Y	Y	Y	N
49	Levin	Y	Y	Y	Y	Y	N
50	**Hunter**	Y	Y	N	N	Y	Y
51	Vargas	Y	Y	Y	Y	Y	N
52	Peters	Y	Y	Y	Y	Y	N
53	Davis, S.	Y	Y	Y	Y	Y	N
COLORADO							
1	DeGette	Y	Y	Y	Y	Y	N
2	Neguse	Y	Y	Y	Y	Y	N
3	**Tipton**	Y	Y	N	N	Y	Y
4	**Buck**	Y	Y	N	N	N	Y
5	**Lamborn**	Y	Y	N	N	N	Y
6	Crow	+	+	Y	Y	Y	N
7	Perlmutter	Y	Y	Y	Y	Y	N
CONNECTICUT							
1	Larson	Y	Y	Y	Y	Y	N
2	Courtney	Y	Y	Y	Y	Y	N
3	DeLauro	Y	Y	Y	Y	Y	N
4	Himes	Y	Y	Y	Y	Y	N
5	Hayes	Y	Y	Y	Y	Y	N
DELAWARE							
AL	Blunt Rochester	Y	Y	Y	Y	Y	N
FLORIDA							
1	**Gaetz**	?	?	N	N	N	Y
2	**Dunn**	+	+	N	N	N	Y
3	**Yoho**	Y	Y	N	N	N	Y
4	**Rutherford**	Y	Y	N	N	N	Y
5	Lawson	Y	Y	Y	Y	Y	N
6	**Waltz**	Y	Y	N	N	+	Y
7	Murphy	Y	Y	Y	Y	Y	N
8	**Posey**	Y	Y	N	N	N	Y
9	Soto	Y	Y	Y	Y	Y	N
10	Demings	Y	Y	Y	Y	Y	N
11	**Webster**	Y	Y	N	N	N	Y
12	**Bilirakis**	Y	Y	N	N	N	Y
13	Crist	Y	Y	Y	Y	Y	N
14	Castor	Y	Y	Y	Y	Y	N
15	**Spano**	Y	Y	N	N	N	Y
16	**Buchanan**	Y	Y	N	N	Y	Y
17	**Steube**	Y	Y	N	N	N	Y
18	**Mast**	Y	Y	N	N	N	Y
19	**Rooney**	?	?	?	?	?	?
20	Hastings	Y	Y	Y	Y	Y	N
21	Frankel	Y	Y	Y	Y	Y	N
22	Deutch	Y	Y	Y	Y	Y	N
23	Wasserman Schultz	Y	Y	Y	Y	Y	N
24	Wilson, F.	Y	Y	Y	Y	Y	N
25	**Diaz-Balart**	Y	Y	N	N	N	Y
26	Mucarsel-Powell	Y	Y	Y	Y	Y	N
27	Shalala	Y	Y	Y	Y	Y	N
GEORGIA							
1	**Carter, E.L.**	Y	Y	N	N	N	Y
2	Bishop, S.	Y	Y	Y	Y	Y	N
3	**Ferguson**	Y	Y	N	N	N	Y
4	Johnson, H.	Y	Y	Y	Y	Y	N
5	Lewis John	Y	Y	Y	Y	Y	N
6	McBath	Y	Y	Y	Y	Y	N
7	**Woodall**	Y	Y	N	N	N	Y
8	**Scott, A.**	Y	Y	N	N	N	Y
9	**Collins, D.**	Y	Y	N	N	N	Y
10	**Hice**	Y	Y	N	N	N	Y
11	**Loudermilk**	Y	Y	N	N	N	Y
12	**Allen**	Y	Y	N	N	N	Y
13	Scott, D.	Y	Y	Y	Y	Y	N
14	**Graves, T.**	Y	Y	N	N	N	Y
HAWAII							
1	Case	Y	Y	Y	Y	Y	N
2	Gabbard	Y	Y	Y	Y	Y	?
IDAHO							
1	**Fulcher**	Y	Y	N	N	N	Y
2	**Simpson**	Y	Y	N	N	N	Y
ILLINOIS							
1	Rush	Y	Y	Y	Y	Y	N
2	Kelly, R.	Y	Y	Y	Y	Y	N
3	Lipinski	Y	Y	Y	Y	Y	N
4	García, J.	Y	Y	Y	Y	Y	N
5	Quigley	Y	Y	Y	Y	Y	N
6	Casten	Y	Y	Y	Y	Y	N
7	Davis, D.	Y	Y	Y	Y	Y	N
8	Krishnamoorthi	Y	Y	Y	Y	Y	N
9	Schakowsky	Y	Y	?	Y	Y	N
10	Schneider	Y	Y	Y	Y	Y	N
11	Foster	Y	Y	Y	Y	Y	N

KEY:	**Republicans**	Democrats	*Independents*
Y Voted for (yea)	**N** Voted against (nay)	**P** Voted "present"	
+ Announced for	**–** Announced against	**?** Did not vote or otherwise	
# Paired for	**X** Paired against	make position known	

	187	188	189	190	191	192
12 **Bost**	Y	Y	N	N	Y	Y
13 **Davis, R.**	Y	Y	N	N	Y	Y
14 Underwood	Y	Y	Y	Y	Y	N
15 **Shimkus**	Y	Y	N	N	Y	Y
16 **Kinzinger**	Y	Y	N	N	Y	Y
17 Bustos	Y	Y	Y	Y	Y	N
18 **LaHood**	Y	Y	N	N	Y	Y
INDIANA						
1 Visclosky	Y	Y	?	?	Y	N
2 **Walorski**	Y	Y	N	N	N	Y
3 **Banks**	Y	Y	N	N	N	Y
4 **Baird**	Y	Y	N	N	Y	Y
5 **Brooks, S.**	Y	Y	N	N	Y	Y
6 **Pence**	Y	Y	N	N	N	Y
7 Carson	Y	Y	Y	Y	Y	N
8 **Bucshon**	Y	Y	N	N	Y	Y
9 **Hollingsworth**	Y	Y	N	N	Y	Y
IOWA						
1 Finkenauer	Y	Y	Y	Y	Y	N
2 Loebsack	Y	Y	Y	Y	Y	N
3 Axne	Y	Y	Y	Y	Y	N
4 **King, S.**	Y	Y	N	N	Y	Y
KANSAS						
1 **Marshall**	Y	Y	N	N	Y	Y
2 **Watkins**	Y	Y	N	N	Y	Y
3 Davids	Y	Y	Y	Y	Y	N
4 **Estes**	Y	Y	N	N	N	Y
KENTUCKY						
1 **Comer**	Y	Y	N	N	N	Y
2 **Guthrie**	Y	Y	N	N	Y	Y
3 Yarmuth	Y	?	Y	Y	Y	N
4 **Massie**	Y	Y	N	N	N	Y
5 **Rogers, H.**	Y	Y	N	N	Y	Y
6 **Barr**	Y	Y	N	N	Y	Y
LOUISIANA						
1 **Scalise**	Y	Y	N	N	N	Y
2 Richmond	Y	Y	?	?	?	?
3 **Higgins, C.**	Y	Y	N	N	N	N
4 **Johnson, M.**	Y	Y	N	N	N	Y
5 **Abraham**	Y	Y	N	N	?	?
6 **Graves, G.**	Y	Y	N	N	Y	Y
MAINE						
1 Pingree	Y	Y	Y	Y	?	N
2 Golden	Y	Y	Y	Y	Y	N
MARYLAND						
1 **Harris**	Y	Y	N	N	N	Y
2 Ruppersberger	Y	Y	Y	Y	Y	N
3 Sarbanes	Y	Y	Y	Y	Y	N
4 Brown, A.	Y	Y	Y	Y	Y	N
5 Hoyer	Y	Y	Y	Y	Y	N
6 Trone	Y	Y	Y	Y	Y	N
7 Cummings	?	?	?	?	?	?
8 Raskin	Y	Y	Y	Y	Y	N
MASSACHUSETTS						
1 Neal	Y	Y	Y	Y	Y	N
2 McGovern	Y	Y	Y	Y	Y	N
3 Trahan	Y	Y	Y	Y	Y	N
4 Kennedy	Y	Y	Y	Y	Y	N
5 Clark	Y	Y	Y	Y	Y	N
6 Moulton	Y	Y	Y	Y	Y	N
7 Pressley	Y	Y	Y	Y	Y	N
8 Lynch	Y	Y	Y	Y	Y	N
9 Keating	Y	Y	Y	Y	Y	N
MICHIGAN						
1 **Bergman**	Y	Y	N	N	Y	Y
2 **Huizenga**	Y	Y	N	N	N	Y
3 **Amash**	Y	Y	N	N	N	N
4 **Moolenaar**	Y	Y	N	N	Y	Y
5 Kildee	Y	Y	Y	Y	Y	N
6 **Upton**	Y	Y	N	N	Y	Y
7 **Walberg**	Y	Y	N	N	Y	Y
8 Slotkin	Y	Y	Y	Y	Y	N
9 Levin	Y	Y	Y	Y	Y	N
10 **Mitchell**	Y	Y	N	N	N	Y
11 Stevens	Y	Y	Y	Y	Y	N
12 Dingell	Y	Y	Y	Y	Y	N
13 Tlaib	Y	Y	Y	Y	Y	N
14 Lawrence	Y	Y	Y	Y	Y	N
MINNESOTA						
1 **Hagedorn**	Y	Y	N	N	Y	Y
2 Craig	Y	Y	Y	Y	Y	N
3 Phillips	Y	Y	Y	Y	Y	N
4 McCollum	Y	Y	Y	Y	Y	N
5 Omar	+	+	Y	Y	Y	N

	187	188	189	190	191	192
6 **Emmer**	Y	Y	-	-	+	+
7 Peterson	Y	Y	Y	Y	Y	N
8 **Stauber**	Y	Y	N	N	Y	Y
MISSISSIPPI						
1 **Kelly, T.**	Y	Y	N	N	N	Y
2 Thompson, B.	Y	Y	Y	Y	Y	N
3 **Guest**	Y	Y	N	N	Y	N
4 **Palazzo**	Y	?	N	N	N	Y
MISSOURI						
1 Clay	Y	Y	Y	Y	Y	N
2 **Wagner**	Y	Y	N	N	Y	Y
3 **Luetkemeyer**	Y	Y	N	N	Y	Y
4 **Hartzler**	Y	Y	N	N	Y	Y
5 Cleaver	Y	Y	Y	Y	Y	N
6 **Graves, S.**	Y	Y	N	N	Y	Y
7 **Long**	Y	Y	N	N	Y	Y
8 **Smith, J.**	Y	Y	N	N	Y	Y
MONTANA						
AL **Gianforte**	Y	Y	N	N	Y	Y
NEBRASKA						
1 **Fortenberry**	Y	Y	N	N	Y	Y
2 **Bacon**	Y	Y	N	N	Y	Y
3 **Smith, Adrian**	Y	Y	N	N	N	Y
NEVADA						
1 Titus	Y	Y	Y	Y	Y	N
2 **Amodei**	Y	Y	N	N	Y	Y
3 Lee	Y	Y	Y	Y	Y	N
4 Horsford	Y	Y	Y	Y	Y	N
NEW HAMPSHIRE						
1 Pappas	Y	Y	Y	Y	Y	N
2 Kuster	Y	Y	Y	Y	Y	N
NEW JERSEY						
1 Norcross	Y	Y	Y	Y	Y	N
2 Van Drew	Y	Y	Y	Y	Y	N
3 Kim	Y	Y	Y	Y	Y	N
4 **Smith, C.**	Y	Y	N	N	Y	?
5 Gottheimer	Y	Y	Y	Y	Y	N
6 Pallone	Y	Y	Y	Y	Y	N
7 Malinowski	Y	Y	Y	Y	Y	N
8 Sires	Y	Y	Y	Y	Y	N
9 Pascrell	Y	Y	Y	Y	Y	N
10 Payne	Y	Y	Y	Y	Y	N
11 Sherrill	Y	Y	Y	Y	Y	N
12 Watson Coleman	Y	Y	Y	Y	Y	N
NEW MEXICO						
1 Haaland	Y	Y	Y	Y	Y	N
2 Torres Small	Y	Y	Y	Y	Y	N
3 Luján	Y	Y	Y	Y	Y	N
NEW YORK						
1 **Zeldin**	Y	Y	N	N	Y	Y
2 **King, P.**	Y	Y	N	N	Y	Y
3 Suozzi	Y	Y	Y	Y	Y	N
4 Rice, K.	Y	Y	Y	Y	Y	N
5 Meeks	Y	Y	Y	Y	Y	N
6 Meng	Y	Y	Y	Y	Y	N
7 Velázquez	Y	Y	Y	Y	Y	N
8 Jeffries	Y	Y	Y	Y	Y	N
9 Clarke	Y	Y	Y	Y	Y	N
10 Nadler	Y	Y	Y	Y	Y	N
11 Rose	Y	Y	Y	Y	Y	N
12 Maloney, C.	Y	Y	Y	Y	Y	N
13 Espaillat	Y	Y	Y	Y	Y	N
14 Ocasio-Cortez	Y	Y	Y	Y	Y	N
15 Serrano	Y	Y	Y	?	Y	N
16 Engel	Y	Y	Y	Y	Y	N
17 Lowey	Y	Y	Y	Y	Y	N
18 Maloney, S.P.	Y	Y	Y	Y	Y	N
19 Delgado	Y	Y	Y	Y	Y	N
20 Tonko	Y	Y	Y	Y	Y	N
21 **Stefanik**	Y	Y	N	N	Y	Y
22 Brindisi	Y	Y	Y	Y	Y	N
23 **Reed**	Y	Y	N	N	Y	Y
24 **Katko**	Y	Y	N	N	Y	Y
25 Morelle	Y	Y	Y	Y	Y	N
26 Higgins, B.	Y	Y	Y	Y	Y	N
27 **Collins, C.**						
NORTH CAROLINA						
1 Butterfield	Y	Y	Y	Y	Y	N
2 **Holding**	Y	Y	N	N	Y	Y
3 **Jones***						
4 Price	Y	Y	Y	Y	Y	N
5 **Foxx**	Y	Y	N	N	Y	Y
6 **Walker**	Y	Y	?	?	?	?
7 **Rouzer**	Y	Y	N	N	Y	Y

	187	188	189	190	191	192
8 **Hudson**	Y	Y	N	N	Y	Y
9 vacant						
10 **McHenry**	Y	Y	N	N	Y	Y
11 **Meadows**	Y	Y	N	N	N	Y
12 Adams	Y	Y	Y	Y	Y	N
13 **Budd**	Y	Y	N	N	N	Y
NORTH DAKOTA						
AL **Armstrong**	Y	Y	N	N	Y	Y
OHIO						
1 **Chabot**	Y	Y	N	N	Y	Y
2 **Wenstrup**	+	+	+	-	+	+
3 Beatty	Y	Y	Y	Y	Y	N
4 **Jordan**	Y	Y	N	N	N	Y
5 **Latta**	Y	Y	N	N	Y	Y
6 **Johnson, B.**	Y	Y	N	N	Y	Y
7 **Gibbs**	Y	Y	N	N	Y	Y
8 **Davidson**	Y	Y	N	N	N	Y
9 Kaptur	Y	Y	Y	Y	Y	N
10 **Turner**	Y	Y	N	N	Y	Y
11 Fudge	Y	Y	Y	Y	Y	N
12 **Balderson**	Y	Y	N	N	Y	Y
13 Ryan	Y	Y	Y	Y	?	?
14 **Joyce**	Y	Y	N	N	Y	Y
15 **Stivers**	Y	Y	N	N	Y	Y
16 **Gonzalez**	Y	Y	N	N	Y	Y
OKLAHOMA						
1 **Hern**	Y	Y	N	N	N	Y
2 **Mullin**	Y	Y	N	N	Y	Y
3 **Lucas**	Y	Y	N	N	Y	Y
4 **Cole**	Y	Y	N	N	Y	Y
5 Horn	Y	Y	Y	Y	Y	N
OREGON						
1 Bonamici	Y	Y	Y	Y	Y	N
2 **Walden**	Y	Y	N	N	Y	Y
3 Blumenauer	Y	Y	Y	Y	Y	N
4 DeFazio	Y	Y	Y	Y	Y	N
5 Schrader	Y	Y	Y	Y	Y	N
PENNSYLVANIA						
1 **Fitzpatrick**	Y	Y	N	N	Y	N
2 Boyle	Y	Y	Y	Y	Y	N
3 Evans	Y	Y	Y	Y	Y	N
4 Dean	Y	Y	Y	Y	Y	N
5 Scanlon	Y	Y	Y	Y	Y	N
6 Houlahan	Y	Y	Y	Y	Y	N
7 Wild	Y	Y	Y	Y	Y	N
8 Cartwright	Y	Y	Y	Y	Y	N
9 **Meuser**	Y	Y	N	N	Y	Y
10 **Perry**	Y	Y	N	N	N	Y
11 **Smucker**	Y	Y	N	N	Y	Y
12 **Marino***						
13 **Joyce**	Y	Y	N	N	Y	Y
14 **Reschenthaler**	Y	Y	N	N	Y	Y
15 **Thompson, G.**	Y	Y	N	N	Y	Y
16 **Kelly, M.**	Y	Y	N	N	Y	Y
17 Lamb	Y	Y	Y	Y	Y	N
18 Doyle	Y	Y	Y	Y	Y	N
RHODE ISLAND						
1 Cicilline	Y	Y	Y	Y	Y	N
2 Langevin	Y	Y	Y	Y	Y	N
SOUTH CAROLINA						
1 Cunningham	Y	Y	Y	Y	Y	N
2 **Wilson, J.**	Y	Y	N	N	Y	Y
3 **Duncan**	Y	Y	N	N	N	Y
4 **Timmons**	Y	Y	N	N	Y	Y
5 **Norman**	Y	Y	N	N	N	Y
6 Clyburn	Y	Y	Y	Y	Y	N
7 **Rice, T.**	?	Y	N	N	Y	Y
SOUTH DAKOTA						
AL **Johnson**	Y	Y	N	N	Y	Y
TENNESSEE						
1 **Roe**	Y	Y	N	N	Y	Y
2 **Burchett**	Y	Y	N	N	N	Y
3 **Fleischmann**	Y	Y	N	N	Y	Y
4 **DesJarlais**	Y	Y	N	N	N	Y
5 Cooper	Y	Y	Y	Y	Y	N
6 **Rose**	Y	Y	N	N	Y	Y
7 **Green**	Y	Y	N	N	Y	Y
8 **Kustoff**	Y	Y	N	N	Y	Y
9 Cohen	Y	Y	Y	Y	Y	N
TEXAS						
1 **Gohmert**	Y	Y	N	N	N	Y
2 **Crenshaw**	Y	Y	N	N	Y	Y
3 **Taylor**	Y	Y	N	N	Y	N
4 **Ratcliffe**	Y	Y	N	N	N	Y

	187	188	189	190	191	192
5 **Gooden**	Y	Y	N	N	N	Y
6 **Wright**	Y	Y	N	N	N	Y
7 Fletcher	Y	Y	Y	Y	Y	N
8 **Brady**	?	Y	N	N	Y	Y
9 Green, A.	Y	Y	Y	Y	Y	N
10 **McCaul**	Y	Y	N	N	Y	Y
11 **Conaway**	Y	Y	N	N	Y	Y
12 **Granger**	Y	Y	N	N	N	Y
13 **Thornberry**	Y	Y	N	N	Y	Y
14 **Weber**	Y	Y	N	N	N	Y
15 Gonzalez	Y	Y	Y	Y	Y	N
16 Escobar	Y	Y	Y	Y	Y	N
17 **Flores**	Y	Y	N	N	Y	Y
18 Jackson Lee	Y	Y	Y	Y	Y	N
19 **Arrington**	Y	Y	N	N	Y	Y
20 Castro	Y	Y	Y	Y	Y	N
21 **Roy**	Y	Y	P	N	N	N
22 **Olson**	Y	Y	?	?	?	?
23 **Hurd**	Y	Y	N	N	Y	Y
24 **Marchant**	Y	Y	N	N	Y	Y
25 **Williams**	Y	Y	N	N	N	Y
26 **Burgess**	Y	Y	N	N	Y	Y
27 **Cloud**	Y	Y	N	N	N	Y
28 Cuellar	Y	Y	Y	Y	Y	N
29 Garcia, S.	Y	Y	Y	Y	Y	N
30 Johnson, E.B.	Y	Y	Y	Y	Y	N
31 **Carter, J.**	Y	Y	N	N	N	Y
32 Allred	Y	Y	Y	Y	Y	N
33 Veasey	Y	Y	Y	Y	Y	N
34 Vela	Y	Y	Y	Y	Y	N
35 Doggett	Y	Y	Y	Y	Y	N
36 **Babin**	Y	Y	N	N	N	Y
UTAH						
1 **Bishop, R.**	Y	Y	?	?	?	?
2 **Stewart**	Y	Y	N	N	N	Y
3 **Curtis**	Y	Y	N	N	Y	Y
4 McAdams	Y	Y	Y	Y	Y	N
VERMONT						
AL Welch	Y	Y	Y	Y	Y	N
VIRGINIA						
1 **Wittman**	Y	Y	N	N	Y	Y
2 Luria	Y	Y	Y	Y	Y	N
3 Scott, R.	Y	Y	Y	Y	Y	N
4 McEachin	Y	Y	Y	Y	Y	N
5 **Riggleman**	Y	Y	N	N	N	Y
6 **Cline**	Y	Y	N	N	N	N
7 Spanberger	Y	Y	Y	Y	Y	N
8 Beyer	Y	Y	Y	Y	Y	N
9 **Griffith**	Y	Y	N	N	Y	Y
10 Wexton	Y	Y	Y	Y	Y	N
11 Connolly	Y	Y	Y	Y	Y	N
WASHINGTON						
1 DelBene	Y	Y	Y	Y	Y	N
2 Larsen	Y	Y	Y	Y	Y	N
3 **Herrera Beutler**	Y	Y	N	N	Y	Y
4 **Newhouse**	Y	Y	N	N	Y	Y
5 **McMorris Rodgers**	Y	Y	N	N	Y	Y
6 Kilmer	Y	Y	Y	Y	Y	N
7 Jayapal	Y	Y	Y	Y	Y	N
8 Schrier	Y	Y	Y	Y	Y	N
9 Smith Adam	Y	Y	Y	Y	Y	N
10 Heck	Y	Y	Y	Y	Y	N
WEST VIRGINIA						
1 **McKinley**	Y	Y	N	N	Y	Y
2 **Mooney**	Y	Y	N	N	N	Y
3 **Miller**	Y	Y	N	N	Y	Y
WISCONSIN						
1 **Steil**	Y	Y	N	N	Y	Y
2 Pocan	Y	Y	Y	Y	Y	N
3 Kind	Y	Y	Y	Y	Y	N
4 Moore	Y	Y	Y	Y	Y	N
5 **Sensenbrenner**	Y	Y	N	N	Y	Y
6 **Grothman**	Y	Y	N	N	Y	Y
7 **Duffy**						
8 **Gallagher**	Y	Y	N	N	Y	Y
WYOMING						
AL **Cheney**	Y	Y	N	N	N	Y
DELEGATES						
Radewagen (A.S.)					Y	Y
Norton (D.C.)					Y	N
San Nicolas (Guam)					?	?
Sablan (N. Marianas)					Y	N
González-Colón (P.R.)					Y	Y
Plaskett (V.I.)					Y	N

193. HR986. State Health Insurance Plan Guidance - Health Insurance Affordability. Malinowski, D-N.J., amendment that would prohibit the Health and Human Services and Treasury departments from taking any action that would reduce the affordability, for individuals with preexisting conditions, of health insurance at least as comprehensive as the "essential health benefits packages" defined under the 2010 health care law. Adopted in Committee of the Whole 302-117: R 74-117; D 227-0; I 1-0. May 9, 2019.

194. HR986. State Health Insurance Plan Guidance - Health Insurance Premiums. Wild, D-Pa., amendment that would prohibit the Health and Human Services and Treasury departments from taking any action that would result in increased health insurance premiums for individuals enrolled in health insurance at least as comprehensive as the "essential health benefits package" defined under the 2010 health care law. Adopted in Committee of the Whole 308-112: R 78-112; D 229-0; I 1-0. May 9, 2019.

195. HR986. State Health Insurance Plan Guidance - Recommit. Walden, R-Ore., motion to recommit the bill to the Energy and Commerce Committee with instructions to report it back immediately with an amendment that would include in the bill a finding that the 2018 guidance related to Section 1332 waivers does not amend Section 1332 of the 2010 health care overhaul and does not permit the Health and Human Services Department to waive protections for individuals with pre-existing conditions. It also adds a finding that the guidance stipulates that any Section 1332 waivers must ensure that access to coverage under state plans would be "at least as comprehensive and affordable" as would be provided under the Affordable Care Act. Motion rejected 182-231: R 182-4; D 0-227. May 9, 2019.

196. HR986. State Health Insurance Plan Guidance - Passage. Passage of the bill that would prohibit the Health and Human Services and Treasury departments from taking any action to implement or enforce their Oct. 2018 guidance regarding criteria for evaluating Section 1332 state health care plan waivers under the 2010 health care overhaul, and would prohibit the departments from effectively reissuing the guidance. Section 1332 waivers exempt state health care plans from certain federal requirements under the Affordable Care Act, including requirements related to qualified health plans, tax credits, and individual and employer mandates. To be eligible for such waivers, proposed state plans are required to provide care to a "comparable number" of residents that is "as comprehensive" and "as affordable" as would otherwise be provided under the ACA. The Oct. 2018 guidance modifies guidelines for considering waiver applications, emphasizing that a proposed state health care plan should be evaluated based on the number of residents that would have "access" to comparable coverage under the plan, as opposed to the number of residents that purchase such coverage. Passed 230-183: R 4-183; D 226-0. *Note: A "nay" was a vote in support of the president's position.* May 9, 2019.

197. HR2157. Fiscal 2019 Disaster Relief Supplemental Appropriations - Natural Disaster Forecasting. Perlmutter, D-Colo., amendment that would increase by $5 million funding for the National Oceanic and Atmospheric Administration for the purposes of improving hurricane, flood, and wildfire forecasting models. Adopted in Committee of the Whole 247-165: R 22-165; D 224-0; I 1-0. May 10, 2019.

198. HR2157. Fiscal 2019 Disaster Relief Supplemental Appropriations - Water Treatment Facility Repairs. Sablan, D-M.P., amendment that would increase by $8.8 million funding to repair drinking water facilities and waste water treatment plants impacted by Typhoon Yutu, which impacted the Northern Mariana Islands. dopted in Committee of the Whole 268-143: R 43-143; D 224-0; I 1-0. May 10, 2019.

	193	194	195	196	197	198
ALABAMA						
1 **Byrne**	N	N	Y	N	N	N
2 **Roby**	N	N	Y	N	N	N
3 **Rogers, M.**	N	N	Y	N	N	Y
4 **Aderholt**	N	N	Y	N	N	N
5 **Brooks, M.**	N	N	Y	N	N	N
6 **Palmer**	N	Y	Y	N	N	N
7 Sewell	Y	Y	N	Y	Y	Y
ALASKA						
AL **Young**	Y	Y	Y	N	N	Y
ARIZONA						
1 O'Halleran	Y	Y	N	Y	Y	Y
2 Kirkpatrick	Y	Y	N	Y	Y	Y
3 Grijalva	?	Y	N	Y	Y	Y
4 **Gosar**	N	N	Y	N	N	N
5 **Biggs**	N	N	Y	N	N	N
6 **Schweikert**	N	N	Y	N	N	N
7 Gallego	Y	Y	N	Y	Y	Y
8 **Lesko**	N	N	Y	N	N	N
9 Stanton	Y	Y	N	Y	Y	Y
ARKANSAS						
1 **Crawford**	N	N	Y	N	N	N
2 **Hill, F.**	N	N	Y	N	N	N
3 **Womack**	N	N	Y	N	N	N
4 **Westerman**	N	N	Y	N	N	N
CALIFORNIA						
1 **LaMalfa**	N	N	Y	N	N	N
2 Huffman	Y	Y	N	Y	Y	Y
3 Garamendi	Y	Y	N	Y	Y	Y
4 **McClintock**	N	N	Y	N	N	N
5 Thompson, M.	Y	Y	N	Y	Y	Y
6 Matsui	Y	Y	N	Y	Y	Y
7 Bera	Y	Y	N	Y	Y	Y
8 **Cook**	Y	Y	N	N	N	Y
9 McNerney	Y	Y	N	Y	Y	Y
10 Harder	Y	Y	N	Y	Y	Y
11 DeSaulnier	Y	Y	N	Y	Y	Y
12 Pelosi						
13 Lee B.	Y	Y	N	Y	Y	Y
14 Speier	Y	Y	N	Y	Y	Y
15 Swalwell	+	+	-	+	+	+
16 Costa	Y	Y	N	Y	Y	Y
17 Khanna	Y	Y	N	Y	Y	Y
18 Eshoo	Y	Y	N	Y	+	+
19 Lofgren	Y	Y	N	Y	Y	Y
20 Panetta	Y	Y	N	Y	Y	Y
21 Cox	Y	Y	N	Y	Y	Y
22 **Nunes**	N	?	?	?	N	N
23 **McCarthy**	N	N	Y	N	N	N
24 Carbajal	Y	Y	N	Y	Y	Y
25 Hill, K.	Y	Y	N	Y	Y	Y
26 Brownley	Y	Y	N	Y	Y	Y
27 Chu	Y	Y	N	Y	Y	Y
28 Schiff	Y	Y	N	Y	Y	Y
29 Cárdenas	?	?	?	?	?	?
30 Sherman	Y	Y	N	Y	Y	Y
31 Aguilar	Y	Y	N	Y	Y	Y
32 Napolitano	Y	Y	N	Y	Y	Y
33 Lieu	Y	Y	N	Y	Y	Y
34 Gomez	Y	Y	N	Y	Y	Y
35 Torres	Y	Y	N	Y	Y	Y
36 Ruiz	Y	Y	N	Y	Y	Y
37 Bass	?	?	?	?	?	?
38 Sánchez	Y	Y	N	Y	Y	Y
39 Cisneros	Y	Y	N	Y	Y	Y
40 Roybal-Allard	Y	Y	N	Y	Y	Y
41 Takano	Y	Y	N	Y	Y	Y
42 **Calvert**	Y	Y	Y	N	N	Y
43 Waters	Y	Y	N	Y	Y	Y
44 Barragán	Y	Y	N	Y	Y	Y
45 Porter	Y	Y	N	Y	Y	Y
46 Correa	Y	Y	N	Y	Y	Y
47 Lowenthal	Y	Y	N	Y	Y	Y
48 Rouda	Y	Y	N	Y	Y	Y
49 Levin	Y	Y	N	Y	Y	Y
50 **Hunter**	N	Y	Y	N	N	N
51 Vargas	Y	Y	N	Y	Y	Y
52 Peters	Y	Y	N	Y	Y	Y

	193	194	195	196	197	198
53 Davis, S.	Y	Y	N	Y	Y	Y
COLORADO						
1 DeGette	Y	Y	N	Y	Y	Y
2 Neguse	Y	Y	N	Y	Y	Y
3 **Tipton**	Y	N	Y	N	Y	N
4 **Buck**	N	N	N	Y	Y	Y
5 **Lamborn**	N	N	Y	N	N	N
6 Crow	Y	Y	N	Y	Y	Y
7 Perlmutter	Y	Y	N	Y	Y	Y
CONNECTICUT						
1 Larson	Y	Y	N	Y	Y	Y
2 Courtney	Y	Y	N	Y	Y	Y
3 DeLauro	Y	Y	N	Y	Y	Y
4 Himes	Y	Y	N	Y	Y	Y
5 Hayes	Y	Y	N	Y	Y	Y
DELAWARE						
AL Blunt Rochester	Y	Y	N	Y	Y	Y
FLORIDA						
1 **Gaetz**	N	N	Y	N	N	N
2 **Dunn**	N	N	Y	N	N	N
3 **Yoho**	N	N	Y	N	N	N
4 **Rutherford**	N	N	Y	N	N	N
5 Lawson	Y	Y	N	Y	Y	Y
6 **Waltz**	Y	Y	Y	N	Y	Y
7 Murphy	Y	Y	N	Y	Y	Y
8 **Posey**	N	N	Y	N	N	N
9 Soto	Y	Y	N	Y	Y	Y
10 Demings	Y	Y	N	Y	Y	Y
11 **Webster**	N	N	Y	N	N	N
12 **Bilirakis**	Y	Y	Y	N	Y	Y
13 Crist	Y	Y	N	Y	Y	Y
14 Castor	Y	Y	N	Y	Y	Y
15 **Spano**	Y	Y	Y	N	Y	N
16 **Buchanan**	Y	Y	Y	N	Y	N
17 **Steube**	N	N	Y	N	N	N
18 **Mast**	N	N	Y	N	N	N
19 **Rooney**	?	?	?	?	?	?
20 Hastings	Y	Y	N	Y	Y	Y
21 Frankel	Y	Y	N	Y	Y	Y
22 Deutch	Y	Y	N	Y	Y	Y
23 Wasserman Schultz	Y	Y	N	Y	Y	Y
24 Wilson, F.	Y	Y	N	Y	Y	Y
25 **Diaz-Balart**	N	N	Y	N	Y	Y
26 Mucarsel-Powell	Y	Y	N	Y	Y	Y
27 Shalala	Y	Y	N	Y	Y	Y
GEORGIA						
1 **Carter, E.L.**	N	N	Y	N	N	N
2 Bishop, S.	Y	Y	N	Y	Y	Y
3 **Ferguson**	N	N	Y	N	N	N
4 Johnson, H.	Y	Y	N	Y	Y	Y
5 Lewis John	Y	Y	N	Y	Y	Y
6 McBath	Y	Y	N	Y	Y	Y
7 **Woodall**	N	N	Y	N	N	N
8 **Scott, A.**	N	Y	N	Y	N	Y
9 **Collins, D.**	N	N	Y	N	N	N
10 **Hice**	N	N	Y	N	N	N
11 **Loudermilk**	N	N	Y	N	N	N
12 **Allen**	N	N	Y	N	N	N
13 Scott, D.	Y	Y	N	Y	Y	Y
14 **Graves, T.**	N	N	Y	N	N	N
HAWAII						
1 Case	Y	Y	N	Y	Y	Y
2 Gabbard	?	?	?	?	?	?
IDAHO						
1 **Fulcher**	N	N	Y	N	N	N
2 **Simpson**	N	N	Y	N	N	Y
ILLINOIS						
1 Rush	Y	Y	N	?	Y	Y
2 Kelly, R.	Y	Y	N	Y	Y	Y
3 Lipinski	Y	Y	N	Y	Y	Y
4 García, J.	Y	Y	N	Y	Y	Y
5 Quigley	Y	Y	N	Y	Y	Y
6 Casten	Y	Y	N	Y	Y	Y
7 Davis, D.	Y	Y	N	Y	Y	Y
8 Krishnamoorthi	Y	Y	N	Y	Y	Y
9 Schakowsky	?	Y	N	Y	Y	Y
10 Schneider	Y	Y	N	Y	Y	Y
11 Foster	Y	Y	N	Y	Y	Y

KEY: Republicans   Democrats   *Independents*

Y Voted for (yea)	**N** Voted against (nay)	**P** Voted "present"
+ Announced for	**-** Announced against	**?** Did not vote or otherwise
# Paired for	**X** Paired against	make position known

	193	194	195	196	197	198
12 **Bost**	Y	Y	Y	N	N	N
13 **Davis, R.**	Y	Y	Y	N	+	+
14 Underwood	Y	Y	N	Y	Y	Y
15 **Shimkus**	Y	Y	Y	N	N	N
16 **Kinzinger**	Y	Y	Y	N	N	Y
17 Bustos	Y	Y	N	Y	Y	Y
18 **LaHood**	N	N	Y	N	N	N
INDIANA						
1 Visclosky	Y	Y	N	Y	Y	Y
2 **Walorski**	N	N	Y	N	N	Y
3 **Banks**	N	N	Y	N	N	N
4 **Baird**	N	N	Y	N	N	N
5 **Brooks, S.**	Y	Y	Y	N	N	Y
6 **Pence**	N	N	Y	N	N	N
7 Carson	Y	Y	N	Y	Y	Y
8 **Bucshon**	Y	N	Y	N	N	N
9 **Hollingsworth**	N	N	N	N	N	N
IOWA						
1 Finkenauer	Y	Y	N	Y	Y	Y
2 Loebsack	Y	Y	N	Y	Y	Y
3 Axne	Y	Y	N	Y	Y	Y
4 **King, S.**	N	N	Y	N	N	Y
KANSAS						
1 **Marshall**	Y	Y	Y	N	?	?
2 **Watkins**	Y	Y	Y	N	N	N
3 Davids	Y	Y	N	Y	Y	Y
4 **Estes**	N	N	Y	N	N	N
KENTUCKY						
1 **Comer**	Y	Y	Y	N	N	N
2 **Guthrie**	Y	Y	Y	N	N	Y
3 Yarmuth	Y	Y	N	Y	Y	Y
4 **Massie**	N	N	N	N	N	N
5 **Rogers, H.**	N	N	Y	N	N	N
6 **Barr**	N	N	Y	N	N	N
LOUISIANA						
1 **Scalise**	N	N	Y	N	N	N
2 Richmond	?	?	-	+	+	+
3 **Higgins, C.**	N	N	Y	N	N	N
4 **Johnson, M.**	N	N	Y	N	N	N
5 **Abraham**	?	?	?	?	?	?
6 **Graves, G.**	Y	Y	Y	N	N	N
MAINE						
1 Pingree	Y	Y	N	Y	Y	Y
2 Golden	Y	Y	N	Y	Y	Y
MARYLAND						
1 **Harris**	N	N	Y	N	N	N
2 Ruppersberger	Y	Y	N	Y	Y	Y
3 Sarbanes	Y	Y	N	Y	?	Y
4 Brown, A.	Y	Y	N	Y	Y	Y
5 Hoyer	Y	Y	N	Y	Y	Y
6 Trone	Y	Y	N	Y	Y	Y
7 Cummings	?	?	?	?	?	?
8 Raskin	Y	Y	N	Y	Y	Y
MASSACHUSETTS						
1 Neal	Y	Y	N	Y	Y	Y
2 McGovern	Y	Y	N	Y	Y	Y
3 Trahan	Y	Y	N	Y	Y	Y
4 Kennedy	Y	Y	N	Y	Y	Y
5 Clark	Y	Y	N	Y	Y	Y
6 Moulton	Y	Y	N	Y	Y	Y
7 Pressley	Y	Y	N	Y	Y	Y
8 Lynch	Y	Y	N	Y	Y	Y
9 Keating	Y	Y	N	Y	?	?
MICHIGAN						
1 **Bergman**	N	N	Y	N	-	-
2 **Huizenga**	N	N	Y	N	N	N
3 **Amash**	N	N	N	N	N	N
4 **Moolenaar**	Y	Y	Y	N	N	N
5 Kildee	Y	Y	N	Y	Y	Y
6 **Upton**	Y	Y	Y	N	N	N
7 **Walberg**	N	N	Y	N	N	N
8 Slotkin	Y	Y	N	Y	Y	Y
9 Levin	Y	Y	N	Y	Y	Y
10 **Mitchell**	N	Y	Y	N	N	N
11 Stevens	Y	Y	N	Y	Y	Y
12 Dingell	Y	Y	N	Y	Y	Y
13 Tlaib	Y	Y	N	Y	Y	Y
14 Lawrence	Y	Y	N	Y	Y	Y
MINNESOTA						
1 **Hagedorn**	Y	Y	Y	N	N	N
2 Craig	Y	Y	N	Y	Y	Y
3 Phillips	Y	Y	N	Y	Y	Y
4 McCollum	Y	Y	N	Y	Y	Y
5 Omar	Y	Y	N	Y	Y	Y

	193	194	195	196	197	198
6 **Emmer**	-	-	+	-	-	-
7 Peterson	Y	Y	N	Y	Y	Y
8 **Stauber**	Y	N	Y	N	Y	Y
MISSISSIPPI						
1 **Kelly, T.**	N	N	Y	N	N	N
2 Thompson, B.	Y	Y	N	Y	Y	Y
3 **Guest**	Y	N	Y	N	N	N
4 **Palazzo**	N	N	Y	N	N	N
MISSOURI						
1 Clay	Y	Y	N	Y	Y	Y
2 **Wagner**	Y	Y	Y	N	N	N
3 **Luetkemeyer**	Y	Y	Y	N	N	N
4 **Hartzler**	Y	Y	Y	N	?	?
5 Cleaver	Y	Y	N	Y	Y	Y
6 **Graves, S.**	Y	Y	Y	N	N	N
7 **Long**	Y	Y	Y	N	N	N
8 **Smith, J.**	N	N	Y	N	N	N
MONTANA						
AL **Gianforte**	Y	Y	Y	N	N	N
NEBRASKA						
1 **Fortenberry**	Y	Y	Y	N	Y	Y
2 **Bacon**	Y	Y	Y	N	N	Y
3 **Smith, Adrian**	N	N	Y	N	N	N
NEVADA						
1 Titus	Y	Y	N	Y	Y	Y
2 **Amodei**	N	N	Y	N	N	Y
3 Lee	Y	Y	N	Y	Y	Y
4 Horsford	Y	Y	N	Y	Y	Y
NEW HAMPSHIRE						
1 Pappas	Y	Y	N	Y	Y	Y
2 Kuster	Y	Y	N	Y	Y	Y
NEW JERSEY						
1 Norcross	Y	Y	N	Y	Y	Y
2 Van Drew	Y	Y	N	Y	?	?
3 Kim	Y	Y	N	Y	Y	Y
4 **Smith, C.**	Y	Y	Y	Y	Y	Y
5 Gottheimer	Y	Y	N	Y	Y	Y
6 Pallone	Y	Y	N	Y	Y	Y
7 Malinowski	Y	Y	N	Y	Y	Y
8 Sires	Y	Y	N	Y	Y	Y
9 Pascrell	Y	Y	N	Y	Y	+
10 Payne	Y	Y	N	Y	Y	Y
11 Sherrill	Y	Y	N	Y	Y	Y
12 Watson Coleman	Y	Y	N	Y	Y	Y
NEW MEXICO						
1 Haaland	Y	Y	N	Y	Y	Y
2 Torres Small	Y	Y	N	Y	Y	Y
3 Luján	Y	Y	N	Y	Y	Y
NEW YORK						
1 **Zeldin**	Y	Y	Y	N	N	N
2 **King, P.**	Y	Y	Y	N	Y	Y
3 Suozzi	Y	Y	N	Y	Y	Y
4 Rice, K.	Y	Y	N	Y	Y	Y
5 Meeks	Y	Y	N	Y	Y	Y
6 Meng	Y	Y	N	Y	Y	Y
7 Velázquez	Y	Y	N	Y	Y	Y
8 Jeffries	Y	Y	N	Y	Y	Y
9 Clarke	Y	Y	N	Y	Y	Y
10 Nadler	Y	Y	N	Y	Y	Y
11 Rose	Y	Y	N	Y	Y	Y
12 Maloney, C.	Y	Y	N	Y	Y	Y
13 Espaillat	Y	Y	N	Y	Y	Y
14 Ocasio-Cortez	Y	Y	N	Y	Y	Y
15 Serrano	Y	Y	N	Y	Y	Y
16 Engel	Y	Y	N	Y	Y	Y
17 Lowey	Y	Y	N	Y	Y	Y
18 Maloney, S.P.	Y	Y	N	Y	Y	Y
19 Delgado	Y	Y	N	Y	Y	Y
20 Tonko	Y	Y	N	Y	Y	Y
21 **Stefanik**	Y	Y	Y	N	Y	Y
22 Brindisi	Y	Y	N	Y	Y	Y
23 **Reed**	Y	Y	Y	N	Y	Y
24 **Katko**	Y	Y	Y	Y	Y	Y
25 Morelle	Y	Y	N	Y	Y	Y
26 Higgins, B.	Y	Y	N	Y	Y	Y
27 **Collins, C.**						
NORTH CAROLINA						
1 Butterfield	Y	Y	N	Y	Y	Y
2 **Holding**	N	Y	Y	N	N	N
3 **Jones***						
4 Price	Y	Y	N	Y	Y	Y
5 **Foxx**	N	N	Y	N	N	N
6 **Walker**	?	?	?	?	?	?
7 **Rouzer**	N	Y	Y	N	N	N

	193	194	195	196	197	198
8 **Hudson**	N	Y	Y	N	N	Y
9 vacant						
10 **McHenry**	Y	Y	Y	N	N	Y
11 **Meadows**	N	N	Y	N	N	N
12 Adams	Y	Y	N	Y	Y	Y
13 **Budd**	N	N	Y	N	N	N
NORTH DAKOTA						
AL **Armstrong**	Y	Y	Y	N	N	N
OHIO						
1 **Chabot**	Y	Y	Y	N	N	N
2 **Wenstrup**	-	-	+	-	-	-
3 Beatty	Y	Y	N	Y	Y	Y
4 **Jordan**	N	N	Y	N	N	N
5 **Latta**	N	N	Y	N	N	N
6 **Johnson, B.**	Y	Y	Y	N	N	N
7 **Gibbs**	Y	N	Y	N	N	N
8 **Davidson**	N	N	Y	N	N	N
9 Kaptur	Y	Y	N	Y	Y	Y
10 **Turner**	Y	Y	Y	N	N	Y
11 Fudge	Y	Y	N	Y	Y	Y
12 **Balderson**	Y	N	Y	N	N	N
13 Ryan	?	?	?	?	?	?
14 **Joyce**	Y	Y	Y	N	N	Y
15 **Stivers**	Y	Y	Y	N	N	Y
16 **Gonzalez**	Y	Y	Y	N	N	Y
OKLAHOMA						
1 **Hern**	N	N	Y	N	N	N
2 **Mullin**	N	N	Y	N	N	N
3 **Lucas**	N	N	Y	N	Y	Y
4 **Cole**	Y	Y	Y	N	N	N
5 Horn	Y	Y	N	Y	Y	Y
OREGON						
1 Bonamici	Y	Y	N	Y	Y	Y
2 **Walden**	Y	Y	Y	N	N	N
3 Blumenauer	Y	Y	N	Y	Y	Y
4 DeFazio	Y	Y	N	Y	Y	Y
5 Schrader	Y	Y	N	Y	Y	Y
PENNSYLVANIA						
1 **Fitzpatrick**	Y	Y	Y	Y	Y	Y
2 Boyle	Y	Y	N	Y	Y	Y
3 Evans	Y	Y	N	Y	Y	Y
4 Dean	Y	Y	N	Y	Y	Y
5 Scanlon	Y	Y	N	Y	Y	Y
6 Houlahan	Y	Y	N	Y	Y	Y
7 Wild	Y	Y	N	Y	Y	Y
8 Cartwright	Y	Y	N	Y	Y	Y
9 **Meuser**	N	N	Y	N	N	N
10 **Perry**	N	N	?	N	N	N
11 **Smucker**	Y	Y	Y	N	N	N
12 **Marino***						
13 **Joyce**	Y	Y	Y	N	N	N
14 **Reschenthaler**	N	N	Y	N	N	N
15 **Thompson, G.**	Y	Y	Y	N	N	Y
16 **Kelly, M.**	N	N	Y	N	N	N
17 Lamb	Y	Y	N	Y	Y	Y
18 Doyle	Y	Y	N	Y	Y	Y
RHODE ISLAND						
1 Cicilline	Y	Y	N	Y	Y	Y
2 Langevin	Y	Y	N	Y	Y	Y
SOUTH CAROLINA						
1 Cunningham	Y	Y	N	Y	Y	Y
2 **Wilson, J.**	N	Y	Y	N	N	N
3 **Duncan**	N	N	Y	N	N	N
4 **Timmons**	N	N	Y	N	N	N
5 **Norman**	N	N	Y	N	N	N
6 Clyburn	Y	Y	N	Y	Y	Y
7 **Rice, T.**	Y	Y	Y	N	Y	N
SOUTH DAKOTA						
AL **Johnson**	N	N	Y	N	N	N
TENNESSEE						
1 **Roe**	N	N	Y	N	N	N
2 **Burchett**	N	N	Y	N	N	N
3 **Fleischmann**	N	N	Y	N	N	N
4 **DesJarlais**	N	N	Y	N	N	N
5 Cooper	Y	Y	N	Y	Y	Y
6 **Rose**	?	N	Y	N	N	N
7 **Green**	N	N	Y	N	N	N
8 **Kustoff**	N	N	Y	N	?	?
9 Cohen	Y	Y	N	Y	Y	Y
TEXAS						
1 **Gohmert**	N	N	Y	N	N	?
2 **Crenshaw**	Y	Y	Y	N	N	Y
3 **Taylor**	Y	Y	Y	N	N	N
4 **Ratcliffe**	N	?	?	?	N	N

	193	194	195	196	197	198
5 **Gooden**	N	N	Y	N	N	N
6 **Wright**	N	N	Y	N	N	N
7 Fletcher	Y	Y	N	Y	Y	Y
8 **Brady**	N	N	Y	N	N	N
9 Green, A.	Y	Y	N	Y	Y	Y
10 **McCaul**	Y	Y	Y	N	N	N
11 **Conaway**	N	N	Y	N	N	Y
12 **Granger**	N	N	Y	N	N	N
13 **Thornberry**	N	N	Y	N	Y	N
14 **Weber**	N	N	Y	N	N	N
15 Gonzalez	Y	Y	N	Y	Y	Y
16 Escobar	Y	Y	N	Y	Y	Y
17 **Flores**	Y	Y	Y	P	N	N
18 Jackson Lee	Y	Y	N	Y	Y	Y
19 **Arrington**	Y	Y	Y	N	N	N
20 Castro	Y	Y	N	Y	Y	Y
21 **Roy**	N	N	N	N	N	N
22 **Olson**	?	?	?	?	?	?
23 **Hurd**	Y	Y	Y	N	Y	Y
24 **Marchant**	N	N	Y	N	N	N
25 **Williams**	N	N	Y	N	N	N
26 **Burgess**	Y	Y	Y	N	N	N
27 **Cloud**	N	N	Y	N	N	N
28 Cuellar	Y	Y	N	Y	Y	Y
29 Garcia, S.	Y	Y	N	Y	Y	Y
30 Johnson, E.B.	Y	Y	N	Y	Y	Y
31 **Carter, J.**	Y	Y	Y	N	N	Y
32 Allred	Y	Y	N	Y	Y	Y
33 Veasey	Y	Y	N	Y	Y	Y
34 Vela	Y	Y	N	Y	Y	Y
35 Doggett	Y	Y	N	Y	Y	Y
36 **Babin**	N	N	Y	N	N	N
UTAH						
1 **Bishop, R.**	?	?	?	?	?	?
2 **Stewart**	N	N	Y	N	N	Y
3 **Curtis**	N	N	Y	N	N	N
4 McAdams	Y	Y	N	Y	Y	Y
VERMONT						
AL Welch	Y	Y	N	Y	Y	Y
VIRGINIA						
1 **Wittman**	N	N	Y	N	N	N
2 Luria	Y	Y	N	Y	Y	Y
3 Scott, R.	Y	Y	N	Y	Y	Y
4 McEachin	Y	Y	N	Y	Y	Y
5 **Riggleman**	N	N	Y	N	N	N
6 **Cline**	N	N	Y	N	N	N
7 Spanberger	Y	Y	N	Y	Y	Y
8 Beyer	Y	Y	N	Y	Y	Y
9 **Griffith**	Y	Y	Y	N	N	N
10 Wexton	Y	Y	N	Y	Y	Y
11 Connolly	Y	Y	N	Y	Y	Y
WASHINGTON						
1 DelBene	Y	Y	N	Y	Y	Y
2 Larsen	Y	Y	N	Y	Y	Y
3 **Herrera Beutler**	Y	Y	Y	N	Y	Y
4 **Newhouse**	Y	Y	Y	N	N	Y
5 **McMorris Rodgers**	Y	Y	?	N	N	N
6 Kilmer	Y	Y	N	Y	Y	Y
7 Jayapal	Y	Y	N	Y	Y	Y
8 Schrier	Y	Y	N	Y	Y	Y
9 Smith Adam	Y	Y	N	Y	Y	Y
10 Heck	Y	Y	N	Y	Y	Y
WEST VIRGINIA						
1 **McKinley**	Y	Y	Y	N	Y	N
2 **Mooney**	N	N	Y	N	N	N
3 **Miller**	N	N	Y	N	N	N
WISCONSIN						
1 **Steil**	Y	Y	Y	N	N	N
2 Pocan	Y	Y	N	Y	Y	Y
3 Kind	Y	Y	N	Y	Y	Y
4 Moore	Y	Y	N	Y	Y	Y
5 **Sensenbrenner**	N	Y	Y	Y	N	N
6 **Grothman**	Y	Y	Y	N	N	N
7 **Duffy**						
8 **Gallagher**	Y	Y	Y	N	N	N
WYOMING						
AL **Cheney**	N	N	Y	N	N	N
DELEGATES						
Radewagen (A.S.)	Y	Y			Y	Y
Norton (D.C.)	Y	Y			Y	Y
San Nicolas (Guam)	?	?			?	?
Sablan (N. Marianas)	Y	Y			Y	Y
González-Colón (P.R.)	Y	Y			Y	Y
Plaskett (V.I.)	Y	Y			?	?

III HOUSE VOTES

199. HR2157. Fiscal 2019 Disaster Relief Supplemental Appropriations - Highway Repair Regulation. Huffman, D-Calif., amendment that would clarify that no funds made available by the bill may be used to enforce a Federal Highway Administration regulation requiring certain highway construction relief projects to be completed within two fiscal years, in the case of any projects in response to disasters that occurred in fiscal 2017 or thereafter. Adopted in Committee of the Whole 241-168: R 17-168; D 223-0; I 1-0. May 10, 2019.

200. HR2157. Fiscal 2019 Disaster Relief Supplemental Appropriations - HUD Grant Publication. Fletcher, D-Texas, amendment that would require the Housing and Urban Development Department to publish, within 14 as opposed to 90 days of enactment, all mitigation activity grant allocations made by the department from funds made available by the bill. Adopted in Committee of the Whole 393-20: R 167-20; D 225-0; I 1-0. May 10, 2019.

201. HR2157. Fiscal 2019 Disaster Relief Supplemental Appropriations - Recommit. Granger, R-Texas, motion to recommit the bill to the House Appropriations Committee with instructions to report it back immediately with an amendment that would increase by $2.9 billion Health and Human Services Department funding for Head Start programs, for expenses related to the consequences of Hurricanes Florence and Michael, Typhoon Mangkhut, Super Typhoon Yutu, and other natural disasters occurring in 2018 and 2019. Motion rejected 189-215: R 175-8; D 14-207. May 10, 2019.

202. HR2157. Fiscal 2019 Disaster Relief Supplemental Appropriations - Passage. Passage of the bill, as amended, that would provide $17.4 billion in supplemental disaster funds for response efforts to damage caused by hurricanes, wildfires, earthquakes, tornadoes, floods, and other natural disasters that occurred in 2017, 2018, and 2019. It would provide $693 million in disaster nutrition and Medicaid assistance for individuals impacted by natural disasters in Puerto Rico, the Commonwealth of the Northern Mariana Islands, and American Samoa. It would extend the National Flood Insurance Program, which will expire on May 31, through Sept. 30, 2019. It would also provide funds for areas impacted by natural disasters for economic development, training and employment services, and behavioral and social health services. The bill includes a total of $4.3 billion for Agriculture Department disaster-related activities, including $3 billion for crop, tree, bush, vine, and livestock losses from hurricanes, wildfires and other declared disasters that occurred in 2018 and 2019. The bill would provide $2.2 billion for a Housing and Urban Development Department community development block grant program, and $1.7 billion for Transportation Department programs and activities, including $1.65 billion for the cost of federal highway and bridge repairs. It would provide $1.5 billion to the Defense Department to repair military facilities damaged by hurricanes Florence and Michael, $2.8 billion to the Army Corps of Engineers for civil construction projects, and $2 billion the Army Corps for facility repairs. It would also state that military construction funds provided by the bill may only be used for purposes specified in the bill. As amended, the bill would authorize an additional $1.9 billion in funding for disaster response efforts, including $955 million for Armed Services construction and repair planning, $500 million for highway and road repairs, $310 million for the Farm Service Agency emergency watershed protection program, and $91.2 million for repairs to federal buildings and courthouses damaged as a result of Hurricane Florence. Passed 257-150: R 34-150; D 223-0. *Note: A "nay" was a vote in support of the president's position.* May 10, 2019.

203. HR299. VA Health Benefit Eligibility - Passage. Takano, D-Calif., motion to suspend the rules and pass the bill, as amended, that would make certain veterans who served offshore of Vietnam between January 9, 1962 and May 7, 1975 eligible for a presumption of Agent Orange exposure for the purposes of Veterans Affairs Department disability compensation for service-connected medical conditions. It would direct the VA to conduct outreach to eligible veterans whose claims were previously denied, and it would authorize retroactive payments to such veterans. The bill would also extend dates of service constituting eligibility for certain Korea veterans to receive disability compensation related to Agent Orange exposure, and it would extend eligibility to certain veterans who served in Thailand for benefits to veterans whose children have spina bifida. Finally, it would require the VA to report to Congress on the health status of Gulf War veterans and would make several modifications to VA authority related to the department's mortgage loan program, including adjustments to loan limits and loan fees. Motion agreed to 410-0: R 185-0; D 225-0. *Note: A two-thirds majority of those present and voting (274 in this case) is required for passage under suspension of the rules.* May 14, 2019.

204. HR2379. Bulletproof Vest Grant Program - Passage. Johnson, D-Ga., motion to suspend the rules and pass the bill, as amended, that would authorize $30 million annually for a Justice Department grant program for the purchase of armor vests for state and local law enforcement and rename the program the "Patrick Leahy Bulletproof Vest Partnership Grant Program." Motion agreed to 400-9: R 175-9; D 225-0. *Note: A two-thirds majority of those present and voting (273 in this case) is required for passage under suspension of the rules.* May 14, 2019.

		199	200	201	202	203	204
ALABAMA							
1	**Byrne**	N	Y	Y	N	Y	Y
2	**Roby**	N	N	Y	Y	?	?
3	**Rogers, M.**	Y	Y	Y	N	Y	Y
4	**Aderholt**	N	N	Y	N	Y	?
5	**Brooks, M.**	N	Y	Y	N	Y	Y
6	**Palmer**	N	Y	Y	N	Y	Y
7	Sewell	Y	Y	N	Y	Y	Y
ALASKA							
AL	**Young**	N	Y	Y	N	Y	Y
ARIZONA							
1	O'Halleran	Y	Y	N	Y	Y	Y
2	Kirkpatrick	Y	Y	N	Y	Y	Y
3	Grijalva	Y	Y	N	Y	Y	Y
4	**Gosar**	N	N	N	N	Y	Y
5	**Biggs**	N	Y	N	N	Y	N
6	**Schweikert**	N	N	Y	N	Y	Y
7	Gallego	Y	Y	N	Y	Y	Y
8	**Lesko**	N	Y	Y	N	Y	Y
9	Stanton	Y	Y	N	Y	Y	Y
ARKANSAS							
1	**Crawford**	N	Y	Y	N	Y	Y
2	**Hill, F.**	N	Y	Y	N	Y	Y
3	**Womack**	N	Y	Y	N	Y	Y
4	**Westerman**	N	Y	Y	N	Y	Y
CALIFORNIA							
1	**LaMalfa**	N	Y	Y	Y	Y	Y
2	Huffman	Y	Y	N	Y	Y	Y
3	Garamendi	Y	Y	N	Y	Y	Y
4	**McClintock**	N	N	Y	N	Y	N
5	Thompson, M.	Y	Y	N	Y	Y	Y
6	Matsui	Y	Y	N	Y	Y	Y
7	Bera	Y	Y	N	Y	Y	Y
8	**Cook**	N	Y	Y	N	Y	Y
9	McNerney	Y	Y	N	Y	Y	Y
10	Harder	Y	Y	N	Y	Y	Y
11	DeSaulnier	Y	Y	N	Y	Y	Y
12	Pelosi						
13	Lee B.	Y	Y	N	Y	Y	Y
14	Speier	Y	Y	N	Y	Y	Y
15	Swalwell	+	+	-	+	+	+
16	Costa	Y	Y	N	Y	+	+
17	Khanna	Y	Y	N	Y	Y	Y
18	Eshoo	+	+	-	+	Y	Y
19	Lofgren	Y	Y	N	Y	Y	Y
20	Panetta	Y	Y	N	Y	Y	Y
21	Cox	Y	Y	N	Y	Y	Y
22	**Nunes**	N	Y	Y	N	Y	Y
23	**McCarthy**	N	Y	Y	N	Y	Y
24	Carbajal	Y	Y	N	Y	Y	Y
25	Hill, K.	Y	Y	N	Y	Y	Y
26	Brownley	Y	Y	N	Y	Y	Y
27	Chu	Y	Y	N	Y	Y	Y
28	Schiff	Y	Y	N	Y	Y	Y
29	Cárdenas	?	?	?	?	Y	Y
30	Sherman	Y	Y	N	Y	Y	Y
31	Aguilar	Y	Y	N	Y	Y	Y
32	Napolitano	Y	Y	N	Y	Y	Y
33	Lieu	Y	Y	N	Y	Y	Y
34	Gomez	Y	Y	N	Y	Y	Y
35	Torres	Y	Y	N	Y	Y	Y
36	Ruiz	Y	Y	N	Y	Y	Y
37	Bass	?	?	?	?	Y	Y
38	Sánchez	Y	Y	N	Y	Y	Y
39	Cisneros	Y	Y	N	Y	Y	Y
40	Roybal-Allard	Y	Y	N	Y	Y	Y
41	Takano	Y	Y	N	Y	Y	Y
42	**Calvert**	N	Y	Y	N	Y	Y
43	Waters	Y	Y	N	Y	Y	Y
44	Barragán	Y	Y	N	Y	Y	Y
45	Porter	Y	Y	Y	Y	Y	Y
46	Correa	Y	Y	N	Y	Y	Y
47	Lowenthal	Y	Y	N	Y	Y	Y
48	Rouda	Y	Y	N	Y	Y	Y
49	Levin	Y	Y	N	Y	Y	Y
50	**Hunter**	N	Y	Y	N	Y	Y
51	Vargas	Y	Y	N	Y	Y	Y
52	Peters	Y	Y	N	Y	Y	Y
53	Davis, S.	Y	Y	N	Y	Y	Y
COLORADO							
1	DeGette	Y	Y	N	Y	Y	Y
2	Neguse	Y	Y	N	Y	Y	Y
3	**Tipton**	N	Y	Y	N	Y	Y
4	**Buck**	N	Y	N	N	Y	Y
5	**Lamborn**	N	Y	Y	N	Y	Y
6	Crow	Y	Y	Y	Y	Y	Y
7	Perlmutter	Y	Y	N	Y	Y	Y
CONNECTICUT							
1	Larson	Y	Y	N	Y	Y	Y
2	Courtney	Y	Y	N	Y	Y	Y
3	DeLauro	Y	Y	N	Y	Y	Y
4	Himes	Y	Y	N	Y	Y	Y
5	Hayes	Y	Y	N	Y	Y	Y
DELAWARE							
AL	Blunt Rochester	Y	Y	N	Y	Y	Y
FLORIDA							
1	**Gaetz**	N	Y	N	N	Y	Y
2	**Dunn**	N	Y	Y	Y	Y	Y
3	**Yoho**	N	Y	Y	N	Y	Y
4	**Rutherford**	N	Y	Y	N	Y	Y
5	Lawson	Y	Y	N	Y	Y	Y
6	**Waltz**	Y	Y	Y	N	Y	Y
7	Murphy	Y	Y	N	Y	Y	Y
8	**Posey**	N	Y	Y	N	Y	Y
9	Soto	Y	Y	N	Y	Y	Y
10	Demings	Y	Y	N	Y	Y	Y
11	**Webster**	N	Y	Y	N	Y	Y
12	**Bilirakis**	N	Y	Y	Y	Y	Y
13	Crist	Y	Y	N	Y	Y	Y
14	Castor	Y	Y	N	Y	Y	Y
15	**Spano**	N	Y	Y	Y	Y	Y
16	**Buchanan**	N	Y	Y	N	Y	Y
17	**Steube**	N	Y	Y	N	Y	Y
18	**Mast**	N	Y	Y	N	Y	Y
19	**Rooney**	?	?	?	?	Y	Y
20	Hastings	Y	Y	N	Y	Y	Y
21	Frankel	Y	Y	N	Y	Y	Y
22	Deutch	Y	Y	N	Y	Y	Y
23	Wasserman Schultz	Y	Y	N	Y	?	?
24	Wilson, F.	Y	Y	N	Y	Y	Y
25	**Diaz-Balart**	N	Y	Y	Y	Y	Y
26	Mucarsel-Powell	Y	Y	?	Y	Y	Y
27	Shalala	Y	Y	N	Y	Y	Y
GEORGIA							
1	**Carter, E.L.**	N	Y	Y	Y	Y	Y
2	Bishop, S.	Y	Y	N	Y	Y	Y
3	**Ferguson**	N	Y	Y	N	Y	Y
4	Johnson, H.	Y	Y	N	Y	Y	Y
5	Lewis John	Y	Y	N	Y	Y	Y
6	McBath	Y	Y	N	Y	Y	Y
7	**Woodall**	N	Y	Y	N	Y	Y
8	**Scott, A.**	N	Y	Y	Y	?	?
9	**Collins, D.**	N	Y	Y	N	Y	Y
10	**Hice**	N	Y	Y	N	Y	Y
11	**Loudermilk**	N	Y	Y	N	Y	Y
12	**Allen**	N	Y	Y	Y	Y	Y
13	Scott, D.	Y	Y	N	Y	Y	Y
14	**Graves, T.**	N	Y	Y	N	Y	Y
HAWAII							
1	Case	Y	Y	N	Y	Y	Y
2	Gabbard	?	?	?	?	Y	Y
IDAHO							
1	**Fulcher**	N	Y	Y	N	Y	Y
2	**Simpson**	N	Y	Y	N	Y	Y
ILLINOIS							
1	Rush	Y	Y	N	Y	Y	Y
2	Kelly, R.	Y	Y	N	Y	Y	Y
3	Lipinski	Y	Y	N	Y	Y	Y
4	García, J.	Y	Y	N	Y	Y	Y
5	Quigley	Y	Y	N	Y	Y	Y
6	Casten	Y	Y	N	Y	Y	Y
7	Davis, D.	Y	Y	N	Y	Y	Y
8	Krishnamoorthi	Y	Y	N	Y	Y	Y
9	Schakowsky	Y	Y	N	Y	Y	Y
10	Schneider	Y	Y	N	Y	Y	Y
11	Foster	Y	Y	N	Y	Y	Y

KEY: **Republicans** Democrats *Independents*

Y	Voted for (yea)	N	Voted against (nay)	P	Voted "present"
+	Announced for	-	Announced against	?	Did not vote or otherwise make position known
#	Paired for	X	Paired against		

		199	200	201	202	203	204
12	**Bost**	N	Y	Y	Y	Y	Y
13	**Davis, R.**	-	+	+	+	Y	Y
14	Underwood	Y	Y	N	Y	Y	Y
15	**Shimkus**	Y	Y	Y	N	Y	Y
16	**Kinzinger**	Y	Y	Y	Y	Y	Y
17	Bustos	Y	Y	N	Y	Y	Y
18	**LaHood**	N	Y	Y	N	Y	Y
INDIANA							
1	Visclosky	Y	Y	N	Y	Y	Y
2	**Walorski**	N	Y	Y	N	Y	Y
3	**Banks**	N	Y	Y	N	Y	Y
4	**Baird**	N	Y	Y	N	Y	Y
5	**Brooks, S.**	N	N	Y	N	+	+
6	**Pence**	N	Y	Y	N	Y	Y
7	Carson	Y	Y	N	Y	Y	Y
8	**Bucshon**	N	Y	Y	N	Y	Y
9	**Hollingsworth**	N	Y	Y	N	Y	Y
IOWA							
1	Finkenauer	Y	Y	N	Y	Y	Y
2	Loebsack	Y	Y	N	Y	Y	Y
3	Axne	Y	Y	N	Y	Y	Y
4	**King, S.**	N	Y	Y	Y	Y	Y
KANSAS							
1	**Marshall**	?	?	?	?	Y	Y
2	**Watkins**	N	Y	Y	N	Y	Y
3	Davids	Y	Y	N	Y	Y	Y
4	**Estes**	N	Y	Y	N	Y	Y
KENTUCKY							
1	**Comer**	N	Y	Y	N	Y	Y
2	**Guthrie**	N	Y	Y	N	Y	Y
3	Yarmuth	Y	Y	N	Y	Y	Y
4	**Massie**	N	N	N	N	?	?
5	**Rogers, H.**	N	Y	Y	N	Y	Y
6	**Barr**	N	Y	Y	N	Y	Y
LOUISIANA							
1	**Scalise**	N	Y	Y	N	?	?
2	Richmond	+	+	-	+	Y	Y
3	**Higgins, C.**	N	Y	Y	N	+	+
4	**Johnson, M.**	N	Y	Y	N	?	?
5	**Abraham**	?	?	?	?	?	?
6	**Graves, G.**	Y	Y	Y	N	+	+
MAINE							
1	Pingree	Y	Y	N	Y	Y	Y
2	Golden	Y	Y	Y	Y	Y	Y
MARYLAND							
1	**Harris**	N	N	Y	N	Y	N
2	Ruppersberger	Y	Y	N	Y	Y	Y
3	Sarbanes	Y	Y	N	Y	Y	Y
4	Brown, A.	Y	Y	N	Y	Y	Y
5	Hoyer	Y	Y	N	Y	Y	Y
6	Trone	Y	Y	N	Y	Y	Y
7	Cummings	?	?	?	?	?	?
8	Raskin	Y	Y	N	Y	Y	Y
MASSACHUSETTS							
1	Neal	Y	Y	N	Y	Y	Y
2	McGovern	Y	Y	N	Y	Y	Y
3	Trahan	Y	Y	N	Y	Y	Y
4	Kennedy	Y	Y	N	Y	Y	Y
5	Clark	Y	Y	N	Y	Y	Y
6	Moulton	Y	Y	Y	Y	Y	Y
7	Pressley	Y	Y	N	Y	Y	Y
8	Lynch	Y	Y	N	Y	Y	Y
9	Keating	?	?	?	?	Y	Y
MICHIGAN							
1	**Bergman**	-	+	+	-	Y	Y
2	**Huizenga**	N	Y	+	-	Y	Y
3	**Amash**	N	N	N	N	Y	N
4	**Moolenaar**	N	Y	Y	N	Y	Y
5	Kildee	Y	Y	N	Y	Y	Y
6	**Upton**	N	Y	Y	Y	Y	Y
7	**Walberg**	N	Y	Y	N	Y	Y
8	Slotkin	Y	Y	Y	Y	Y	Y
9	Levin	Y	Y	N	Y	Y	Y
10	**Mitchell**	N	Y	Y	N	Y	Y
11	Stevens	Y	Y	N	Y	Y	Y
12	Dingell	Y	Y	N	Y	?	?
13	Tlaib	Y	Y	N	Y	Y	Y
14	Lawrence	Y	Y	N	Y	Y	Y
MINNESOTA							
1	**Hagedorn**	N	Y	Y	N	Y	Y
2	Craig	Y	Y	N	Y	Y	Y
3	Phillips	Y	Y	N	Y	Y	Y
4	McCollum	Y	Y	N	Y	Y	Y
5	Omar	Y	Y	N	Y	Y	Y

		199	200	201	202	203	204
6	**Emmer**	-	+	+	-	Y	Y
7	Peterson	Y	Y	Y	Y	Y	Y
8	**Stauber**	N	Y	Y	N	Y	Y
MISSISSIPPI							
1	**Kelly, T.**	N	Y	Y	N	Y	Y
2	Thompson, B.	Y	Y	N	Y	Y	Y
3	**Guest**	N	Y	Y	N	Y	Y
4	**Palazzo**	N	Y	Y	N	Y	Y
MISSOURI							
1	Clay	Y	Y	N	Y	Y	Y
2	**Wagner**	N	Y	Y	N	Y	Y
3	**Luetkemeyer**	N	N	Y	N	Y	Y
4	**Hartzler**	?	?	?	?	Y	Y
5	Cleaver	Y	Y	N	Y	Y	Y
6	**Graves, S.**	N	Y	Y	Y	Y	Y
7	**Long**	Y	Y	Y	N	Y	Y
8	**Smith, J.**	N	Y	Y	N	Y	Y
MONTANA							
AL	**Gianforte**	N	Y	Y	N	Y	Y
NEBRASKA							
1	**Fortenberry**	N	Y	Y	Y	Y	Y
2	**Bacon**	N	Y	Y	Y	Y	Y
3	**Smith, Adrian**	Y	Y	Y	Y	Y	Y
NEVADA							
1	Titus	Y	Y	N	Y	Y	Y
2	**Amodei**	Y	Y	Y	N	Y	Y
3	Lee	Y	Y	N	Y	Y	Y
4	Horsford	Y	Y	N	Y	Y	Y
NEW HAMPSHIRE							
1	Pappas	Y	Y	N	Y	Y	Y
2	Kuster	Y	Y	N	Y	Y	Y
NEW JERSEY							
1	Norcross	Y	Y	N	Y	Y	Y
2	Van Drew	?	?	?	?	Y	Y
3	Kim	Y	Y	N	Y	Y	Y
4	**Smith, C.**	Y	Y	Y	Y	Y	Y
5	Gottheimer	Y	Y	N	Y	Y	Y
6	Pallone	Y	Y	N	Y	Y	Y
7	Malinowski	Y	Y	N	Y	Y	Y
8	Sires	Y	Y	N	Y	?	?
9	Pascrell	+	Y	N	Y	Y	Y
10	Payne	Y	Y	N	Y	Y	Y
11	Sherrill	Y	Y	?	Y	Y	Y
12	Watson Coleman	Y	Y	N	Y	Y	Y
NEW MEXICO							
1	Haaland	Y	Y	N	Y	Y	Y
2	Torres Small	Y	Y	Y	Y	Y	Y
3	Luján	Y	Y	N	Y	Y	Y
NEW YORK							
1	**Zeldin**	N	Y	Y	N	Y	Y
2	**King, P.**	Y	Y	Y	Y	Y	Y
3	Suozzi	Y	Y	N	Y	Y	Y
4	Rice, K.	Y	Y	N	Y	Y	Y
5	Meeks	Y	Y	N	Y	Y	Y
6	Meng	Y	Y	N	Y	Y	Y
7	Velázquez	Y	Y	N	Y	Y	Y
8	Jeffries	Y	Y	N	Y	Y	Y
9	Clarke	Y	Y	N	Y	Y	Y
10	Nadler	Y	Y	N	Y	Y	Y
11	Rose	Y	Y	N	Y	Y	Y
12	Maloney, C.	Y	Y	N	Y	Y	Y
13	Espaillat	Y	Y	N	Y	Y	Y
14	Ocasio-Cortez	Y	Y	N	Y	Y	Y
15	Serrano	Y	Y	N	Y	Y	Y
16	Engel	Y	Y	N	Y	Y	Y
17	Lowey	Y	Y	N	Y	Y	Y
18	Maloney, S.P.	Y	Y	N	Y	Y	Y
19	Delgado	Y	Y	N	Y	Y	Y
20	Tonko	Y	Y	N	Y	Y	Y
21	**Stefanik**	Y	Y	Y	Y	Y	Y
22	Brindisi	Y	Y	Y	Y	Y	Y
23	**Reed**	Y	Y	Y	Y	Y	Y
24	**Katko**	Y	Y	Y	Y	Y	Y
25	Morelle	Y	Y	N	Y	Y	Y
26	Higgins, B.	Y	Y	N	Y	Y	Y
27	**Collins, C.**						
NORTH CAROLINA							
1	Butterfield	Y	Y	N	Y	Y	Y
2	**Holding**	N	Y	Y	N	Y	Y
3	**Jones***						
4	Price	Y	Y	N	Y	Y	Y
5	**Foxx**	N	Y	Y	N	Y	Y
6	**Walker**	?	?	?	?	Y	Y
7	**Rouzer**	N	Y	Y	Y	Y	Y

		199	200	201	202	203	204
8	**Hudson**	N	Y	Y	Y	Y	Y
9	vacant						
10	**McHenry**	N	Y	Y	N	Y	Y
11	**Meadows**	N	Y	Y	N	Y	Y
12	Adams	Y	Y	N	Y	Y	Y
13	**Budd**	N	Y	Y	N	?	?
NORTH DAKOTA							
AL	**Armstrong**	N	Y	Y	N	Y	Y
OHIO							
1	**Chabot**	N	Y	Y	N	Y	Y
2	**Wenstrup**	-	+	+	-	Y	Y
3	Beatty	Y	Y	N	Y	Y	Y
4	**Jordan**	N	Y	Y	N	Y	Y
5	**Latta**	N	Y	Y	N	Y	Y
6	**Johnson, B.**	N	Y	Y	N	Y	Y
7	**Gibbs**	N	Y	Y	N	Y	Y
8	**Davidson**	N	Y	Y	N	Y	Y
9	Kaptur	Y	Y	N	Y	Y	Y
10	**Turner**	N	Y	Y	N	Y	Y
11	Fudge	Y	Y	N	Y	Y	Y
12	**Balderson**	N	Y	Y	N	Y	Y
13	Ryan	?	?	?	?	Y	Y
14	**Joyce**	N	Y	Y	N	Y	Y
15	**Stivers**	N	Y	Y	Y	Y	Y
16	**Gonzalez**	N	Y	Y	N	Y	Y
OKLAHOMA							
1	**Hern**	N	Y	Y	N	Y	Y
2	**Mullin**	Y	Y	Y	N	?	?
3	**Lucas**	N	Y	Y	N	Y	Y
4	**Cole**	N	Y	Y	N	Y	Y
5	Horn	Y	Y	Y	Y	Y	Y
OREGON							
1	Bonamici	Y	Y	N	Y	Y	Y
2	**Walden**	N	Y	Y	Y	Y	Y
3	Blumenauer	Y	Y	N	Y	Y	Y
4	DeFazio	Y	Y	N	Y	Y	Y
5	Schrader	Y	Y	N	Y	Y	Y
PENNSYLVANIA							
1	**Fitzpatrick**	Y	Y	Y	Y	Y	Y
2	Boyle	Y	Y	N	Y	Y	Y
3	Evans	Y	Y	N	Y	Y	Y
4	Dean	Y	Y	N	Y	Y	Y
5	Scanlon	Y	Y	N	Y	Y	Y
6	Houlahan	Y	Y	Y	Y	Y	Y
7	Wild	Y	Y	N	Y	Y	Y
8	Cartwright	Y	Y	?	?	?	?
9	**Meuser**	N	Y	Y	N	Y	Y
10	**Perry**	N	Y	Y	N	Y	Y
11	**Smucker**	N	Y	Y	N	Y	Y
12	**Marino***						
13	**Joyce**	N	Y	Y	N	Y	Y
14	**Reschenthaler**	N	Y	Y	N	Y	Y
15	**Thompson, G.**	N	Y	Y	N	Y	Y
16	**Kelly, M.**	N	Y	Y	N	Y	Y
17	Lamb	Y	Y	Y	Y	Y	Y
18	Doyle	Y	Y	N	Y	Y	Y
RHODE ISLAND							
1	Cicilline	Y	Y	N	Y	Y	Y
2	Langevin	Y	Y	N	Y	Y	Y
SOUTH CAROLINA							
1	Cunningham	Y	Y	Y	Y	Y	Y
2	**Wilson, J.**	N	Y	Y	N	Y	Y
3	**Duncan**	N	Y	Y	N	Y	N
4	**Timmons**	N	Y	Y	N	Y	Y
5	**Norman**	N	N	Y	N	Y	Y
6	Clyburn	Y	Y	N	Y	Y	Y
7	**Rice, T.**	N	Y	Y	Y	Y	Y
SOUTH DAKOTA							
AL	**Johnson**	N	Y	Y	Y	Y	Y
TENNESSEE							
1	**Roe**	N	Y	Y	N	Y	Y
2	**Burchett**	N	Y	Y	N	Y	Y
3	**Fleischmann**	N	Y	Y	N	Y	Y
4	**DesJarlais**	N	Y	?	N	Y	Y
5	Cooper	Y	Y	N	Y	Y	Y
6	**Rose**	N	N	Y	N	Y	Y
7	**Green**	N	Y	Y	N	Y	Y
8	**Kustoff**	?	?	?	?	Y	Y
9	Cohen	Y	Y	N	Y	Y	Y
TEXAS							
1	**Gohmert**	N	N	N	N	Y	N
2	**Crenshaw**	N	Y	Y	Y	Y	Y
3	**Taylor**	N	N	Y	N	Y	Y
4	**Ratcliffe**	N	Y	Y	N	Y	Y

		199	200	201	202	203	204
5	**Gooden**	N	Y	Y	N	Y	Y
6	**Wright**	N	Y	Y	N	Y	Y
7	Fletcher	Y	Y	N	Y	Y	Y
8	**Brady**	?	Y	Y	N	Y	Y
9	Green, A.	Y	Y	N	Y	Y	Y
10	**McCaul**	N	Y	Y	Y	Y	Y
11	**Conaway**	N	Y	Y	N	Y	Y
12	**Granger**	N	Y	Y	N	Y	Y
13	**Thornberry**	N	Y	Y	N	Y	Y
14	**Weber**	N	Y	Y	N	Y	Y
15	Gonzalez	Y	Y	N	Y	Y	Y
16	Escobar	Y	Y	N	Y	Y	Y
17	**Flores**	N	Y	Y	N	Y	Y
18	Jackson Lee	Y	Y	N	Y	Y	Y
19	**Arrington**	N	Y	Y	N	Y	N
20	Castro	Y	Y	N	Y	Y	Y
21	**Roy**	N	N	N	N	Y	N
22	**Olson**	?	+	?	?	?	?
23	**Hurd**	Y	Y	Y	Y	Y	Y
24	**Marchant**	N	Y	Y	N	Y	Y
25	**Williams**	N	N	Y	N	Y	Y
26	**Burgess**	N	N	Y	N	Y	Y
27	**Cloud**	N	Y	Y	N	Y	Y
28	Cuellar	Y	Y	N	Y	Y	Y
29	Garcia, S.	Y	Y	N	Y	Y	Y
30	Johnson, E.B.	Y	Y	N	Y	Y	Y
31	**Carter, J.**	N	Y	Y	N	Y	Y
32	Allred	Y	Y	N	Y	Y	Y
33	Veasey	Y	Y	N	Y	Y	Y
34	Vela	Y	Y	N	Y	?	?
35	Doggett	?	Y	N	Y	Y	Y
36	**Babin**	N	Y	Y	N	Y	Y
UTAH							
1	**Bishop, R.**	?	?	?	?	Y	Y
2	**Stewart**	N	Y	Y	N	Y	Y
3	**Curtis**	N	Y	Y	N	Y	Y
4	McAdams	Y	Y	N	Y	Y	Y
VERMONT							
AL	Welch	Y	Y	N	Y	Y	Y
VIRGINIA							
1	**Wittman**	N	Y	Y	N	Y	Y
2	Luria	Y	Y	Y	Y	Y	Y
3	Scott, R.	Y	Y	N	Y	?	?
4	McEachin	Y	Y	N	Y	Y	Y
5	**Riggleman**	N	Y	Y	N	Y	Y
6	**Cline**	N	Y	Y	N	Y	Y
7	Spanberger	Y	Y	Y	Y	Y	Y
8	Beyer	Y	Y	N	Y	Y	Y
9	**Griffith**	N	N	Y	N	Y	N
10	Wexton	Y	Y	N	Y	Y	Y
11	Connolly	Y	Y	N	Y	Y	Y
WASHINGTON							
1	DelBene	Y	Y	N	Y	Y	Y
2	Larsen	Y	Y	N	Y	Y	Y
3	**Herrera Beutler**	Y	Y	Y	N	Y	Y
4	**Newhouse**	N	Y	Y	N	Y	Y
5	**McMorris Rodgers**	N	Y	Y	N	Y	Y
6	Kilmer	Y	Y	N	Y	Y	Y
7	Jayapal	Y	Y	N	Y	Y	Y
8	Schrier	Y	Y	N	Y	Y	Y
9	Smith Adam	Y	Y	N	Y	Y	Y
10	Heck	Y	Y	N	Y	Y	Y
WEST VIRGINIA							
1	**McKinley**	N	Y	Y	Y	Y	Y
2	**Mooney**	N	Y	Y	N	Y	Y
3	**Miller**	N	Y	Y	N	Y	Y
WISCONSIN							
1	**Steil**	N	Y	Y	N	Y	Y
2	Pocan	Y	Y	N	Y	Y	Y
3	Kind	Y	Y	N	Y	Y	Y
4	Moore	Y	Y	N	Y	Y	Y
5	**Sensenbrenner**	N	Y	Y	N	Y	Y
6	**Grothman**	N	Y	Y	N	Y	Y
7	**Duffy**						
8	**Gallagher**	N	N	Y	N	Y	Y
WYOMING							
AL	**Cheney**	N	Y	Y	N	Y	Y
DELEGATES							
	Radewagen (A.S.)	?	Y				
	Norton (D.C.)	Y	Y				
	San Nicolas (Guam)	?	?				
	Sablan (N. Marianas)	?	Y				
	González-Colón (P.R.)	N	Y				
	Plaskett (V.I.)	?	?				

205. HR312, HR5, HR987. LGBTQ Discrimination, Tribal Lands, Health Care Package - Previous Question. Scanlon, D-Pa., motion to order the previous question (thus ending the debate and possibility of amendment) on the rule (H Res 377) that would provide for floor consideration of the bill (HR 5) that would prohibit discrimination of the basis of sex, gender identity, and sexual orientation; the bill (HR 312) that would reaffirm the Mashpee Wampanoag Tribe reservation; and the bill (HR 987) consisting of a package of measures related to prescription drug costs and health insurance marketplaces. Motion agreed to 228-189: R 0-189; D 228-0. May 15, 2019.

206. HR987, HR312, HR5. LGBTQ Discrimination, Tribal Lands, Health Care Package - Rule. Adoption of the rule (H Res 377) that would provide for floor consideration of the bill (HR 5) that would prohibit discrimination of the basis of sex, gender identity, and sexual orientation; the bill (HR 312) that would reaffirm the Mashpee Wampanoag Tribe reservation; and the bill (HR 987) consisting of a package of measures related to prescription drug costs and health insurance marketplaces. Adopted 229-188: R 0-186; D 229-2. May 15, 2019.

207. HR312. Mashpee Wampanoag Lands - Passage. Passage of the bill, as amended, that would ratify 2015 Interior Department actions taking into trust approximately 321 acres of land in Massachusetts for the benefit of the Mashpee Wampanoag Tribe of Massachusetts. It would also require any pending or future legal actions related to the land to be dismissed in federal court. Passed 275-146: R 47-144; D 228-2. May 15, 2019.

208. HR375. Tribal Land Trusts - Passage. Grijalva, D-Ariz., motion to suspend the rules and pass the bill that would clarify that the 1934 Indian Reorganization Act, which authorizes the Interior Department to take land into trust for Indian tribes, applies to any federally-recognized Indian tribe regardless of date of recognition. It would also expand the definition of "Indian tribe" under the reorganization act to include any community acknowledged as a tribe by the Interior Department. Motion agreed to 323-96: R 101-88; D 222-8. *Note: A two-thirds majority of those present and voting (280 in this case) is required for passage under suspension of the rules.* May 15, 2019.

209. HR1892. Homeland Security Department Reviews - Passage. Torres Small, D-N.M., motion to suspend the rules and pass the bill that would modify requirements for the quadrennial Homeland Security Department review outlining department strategy and operations. Specifically, it would add internal advisory groups to an existing group of agency heads and department officials advising DHS on the review, require the review to base its outline of DHS mission areas on a risk assessment of threats to national security, and require DHS to provide records to Congress including information on risk assessment and incorporation of feedback in the review. Motion agreed to 415-0: R 186-0; D 229-0. *Note: A two-thirds majority of those present and voting (277 in this case) is required for passage under suspension of the rules.* May 15, 2019.

210. HR987. Generic Drug Regulations and Health Insurance Marketplaces - Removing Health Insurance Provisions. McKinley, R-W.V., for Bucshon, R-Ind. amendment that would remove from the bill Title II, which contains several provisions that would facilitate enrollment in and support Affordable Care Act health insurance marketplaces. Rejected in Committee of the Whole 189-230: R 187-2; D 2-227; I 0-1. May 16, 2019.

		205	206	207	208	209	210
ALABAMA							
1	**Byrne**	N	N	N	Y	Y	?
2	**Roby**	?	?	?	?	?	Y
3	**Rogers, M.**	N	N	N	Y	Y	Y
4	**Aderholt**	?	?	N	N	Y	Y
5	**Brooks, M.**	N	N	N	Y	Y	Y
6	**Palmer**	N	N	N	N	Y	Y
7	Sewell	Y	Y	Y	Y	Y	N
ALASKA							
AL	**Young**	N	N	Y	Y	Y	Y
ARIZONA							
1	O'Halleran	Y	Y	Y	Y	Y	N
2	Kirkpatrick	Y	Y	Y	Y	Y	N
3	Grijalva	Y	Y	Y	Y	Y	N
4	**Gosar**	N	N	N	N	Y	Y
5	**Biggs**	N	N	N	N	Y	Y
6	**Schweikert**	N	N	N	N	Y	Y
7	Gallego	Y	Y	Y	Y	Y	N
8	**Lesko**	N	N	N	N	Y	Y
9	Stanton	Y	Y	Y	Y	Y	N
ARKANSAS							
1	**Crawford**	N	N	N	Y	Y	Y
2	**Hill, F.**	N	N	N	Y	Y	Y
3	**Womack**	N	N	N	Y	Y	Y
4	**Westerman**	N	N	N	N	Y	Y
CALIFORNIA							
1	**LaMalfa**	N	N	Y	Y	Y	Y
2	Huffman	Y	Y	Y	Y	Y	N
3	Garamendi	Y	Y	Y	Y	Y	N
4	**McClintock**	N	N	Y	Y	Y	Y
5	Thompson, M.	Y	Y	Y	Y	Y	N
6	Matsui	Y	Y	Y	Y	Y	N
7	Bera	Y	Y	Y	Y	Y	N
8	**Cook**	N	N	Y	Y	Y	Y
9	McNerney	Y	Y	Y	Y	Y	N
10	Harder	Y	Y	Y	Y	Y	N
11	DeSaulnier	Y	Y	Y	Y	Y	N
12	Pelosi						
13	Lee B.	Y	Y		Y	Y	N
14	Speier	Y	Y	Y	Y	Y	N
15	Swalwell	+	+	+	+	+	-
16	Costa	Y	Y	Y	Y	Y	N
17	Khanna	Y	Y	Y	Y	Y	N
18	Eshoo	Y	Y	Y	Y	Y	N
19	Lofgren	Y	Y	Y	Y	Y	N
20	Panetta	Y	Y	Y	Y	Y	N
21	Cox	Y	Y	Y	Y	Y	N
22	**Nunes**	N	N	Y	Y	Y	Y
23	**McCarthy**	N	N	N	Y	Y	Y
24	Carbajal	Y	Y	Y	Y	Y	N
25	Hill, K.	Y	Y	Y	Y	Y	N
26	Brownley	Y	Y	Y	Y	Y	N
27	Chu	Y	Y	Y	Y	Y	N
28	Schiff	Y	Y	Y	Y	Y	N
29	Cárdenas	Y	Y	Y	Y	Y	N
30	Sherman	Y	Y	Y	Y	Y	N
31	Aguilar	Y	Y	Y	Y	Y	N
32	Napolitano	Y	Y	Y	Y	Y	N
33	Lieu	Y	Y	Y	Y	Y	N
34	Gomez	Y	Y	Y	Y	Y	N
35	Torres	Y	Y	Y	Y	Y	N
36	Ruiz	Y	Y	Y	Y	Y	N
37	Bass	Y	Y	Y	Y	Y	N
38	Sánchez	Y	Y	Y	Y	Y	N
39	Cisneros	Y	Y	Y	Y	Y	N
40	Roybal-Allard	Y	Y	Y	Y	Y	N
41	Takano	Y	Y	Y	Y	Y	N
42	**Calvert**	N	N	Y	Y	Y	Y
43	Waters	Y	Y	Y	Y	Y	N
44	Barragán	Y	Y	Y	Y	Y	N
45	Porter	Y	Y	Y	Y	Y	N
46	Correa	Y	Y	Y	Y	Y	N
47	Lowenthal	Y	Y	Y	Y	Y	N
48	Rouda	Y	Y	Y	Y	Y	N
49	Levin	Y	Y	Y	Y	Y	N
50	**Hunter**	N	N	N	N	Y	Y
51	Vargas	Y	Y	Y	Y	Y	N
52	Peters	Y	Y	Y	Y	Y	N

		205	206	207	208	209	210
53	Davis, S.	Y	Y	Y	Y	Y	N
COLORADO							
1	DeGette	Y	Y	Y	Y	Y	N
2	Neguse	Y	Y	Y	Y	Y	N
3	Tipton	N	N	N	Y	Y	Y
4	**Buck**	N	N	N	N	Y	Y
5	**Lamborn**	N	N	N	Y	Y	Y
6	Crow	Y	Y	Y	Y	Y	N
7	Perlmutter	Y	Y	Y	Y	Y	N
CONNECTICUT							
1	Larson	Y	Y	Y	Y	Y	N
2	Courtney	Y	Y	Y	N	Y	N
3	DeLauro	Y	Y	Y	N	Y	N
4	Himes	Y	Y	Y	N	Y	N
5	Hayes	Y	Y	Y	N	Y	N
DELAWARE							
AL	Blunt Rochester	Y	Y	Y	Y	Y	N
FLORIDA							
1	**Gaetz**	N	N	N	N	Y	Y
2	**Dunn**	N	N	N	Y	Y	Y
3	**Yoho**	N	N	N	N	Y	Y
4	**Rutherford**	N	N	N	+	Y	Y
5	Lawson	Y	Y	Y	Y	Y	N
6	**Waltz**	N	N	N	Y	Y	Y
7	Murphy	Y	Y	Y	Y	Y	N
8	**Posey**	N	N	N	N	Y	Y
9	Soto	Y	Y	Y	Y	Y	N
10	Demings	Y	Y	Y	Y	Y	N
11	**Webster**	N	N	N	N	Y	Y
12	**Bilirakis**	N	N	N	Y	Y	Y
13	Crist	Y	Y	Y	Y	Y	N
14	Castor	Y	Y	Y	Y	Y	N
15	**Spano**	N	N	N	Y	Y	Y
16	**Buchanan**	N	N	N	Y	Y	Y
17	**Steube**	N	N	N	N	Y	Y
18	**Mast**	N	N	N	Y	Y	Y
19	**Rooney**	N	N	Y	Y	Y	Y
20	Hastings	Y	Y	Y	Y	Y	N
21	Frankel	Y	Y	Y	Y	Y	N
22	Deutch	Y	Y	Y	Y	Y	N
23	Wasserman Schultz	Y	Y	Y	Y	Y	N
24	Wilson, F.	Y	Y	Y	Y	Y	N
25	**Diaz-Balart**	N	N	?	Y	Y	Y
26	Mucarsel-Powell	Y	Y	Y	Y	Y	N
27	Shalala	Y	Y	Y	Y	Y	N
GEORGIA							
1	**Carter, E.L.**	N	N	N	N	Y	Y
2	Bishop, S.	Y	Y	Y	Y	Y	N
3	**Ferguson**	N	N	Y	Y	?	Y
4	Johnson, H.	Y	Y	Y	Y	Y	N
5	Lewis John	Y	Y	Y	Y	Y	N
6	McBath	Y	Y	Y	Y	Y	N
7	**Woodall**	N	N	N	N	Y	Y
8	**Scott, A.**	N	N	N	Y	Y	Y
9	**Collins, D.**	N	N	N	N	Y	?
10	**Hice**	N	N	N	N	Y	Y
11	**Loudermilk**	N	N	N	N	Y	Y
12	**Allen**	N	N	N	N	Y	Y
13	Scott, D.	Y	Y	Y	Y	Y	N
14	**Graves, T.**	N	N	N	N	Y	Y
HAWAII							
1	Case	Y	Y	Y	Y	Y	N
2	Gabbard	Y	Y	Y	Y	Y	N
IDAHO							
1	**Fulcher**	N	N	N	N	Y	Y
2	**Simpson**	N	N	Y	Y	Y	Y
ILLINOIS							
1	Rush	Y	Y	Y	Y	Y	N
2	Kelly, R.	Y	Y	Y	Y	Y	N
3	Lipinski	Y	Y	Y	Y	Y	N
4	García, J.	Y	Y	Y	Y	Y	N
5	Quigley	Y	Y	Y	Y	Y	N
6	Casten	Y	Y	Y	Y	Y	N
7	Davis, D.	Y	Y	Y	Y	Y	N
8	Krishnamoorthi	Y	Y	Y	Y	Y	N
9	Schakowsky	Y	Y	Y	Y	Y	N
10	Schneider	Y	Y	Y	Y	Y	N
11	Foster	Y	Y	Y	Y	Y	N

KEY: Republicans (bold)   Democrats   *Independents*

Y Voted for (yea)	**N** Voted against (nay)	**P** Voted "present"	
+ Announced for	**–** Announced against	**?** Did not vote or otherwise make position known	
# Paired for	**X** Paired against		

		205	206	207	208	209	210
12	**Bost**	N	N	N	Y	Y	Y
13	**Davis, R.**	?	?	Y	Y	Y	Y
14	Underwood	Y	Y	Y	Y	Y	N
15	**Shimkus**	N	N	N	N	Y	Y
16	**Kinzinger**	N	N	N	Y	Y	Y
17	Bustos	Y	Y	Y	Y	Y	N
18	**LaHood**	N	N	N	N	Y	Y
INDIANA							
1	Visclosky	Y	Y	Y	Y	Y	N
2	**Walorski**	N	N	N	Y	Y	Y
3	**Banks**	N	N	N	N	Y	Y
4	**Baird**	N	N	N	Y	Y	Y
5	**Brooks, S.**	-	-	+	+	+	Y
6	**Pence**	-	-	-	-	+	Y
7	Carson	Y	Y	Y	Y	Y	N
8	**Bucshon**	N	N	N	Y	Y	+
9	**Hollingsworth**	N	N	Y	Y	Y	Y
IOWA							
1	Finkenauer	Y	Y	Y	Y	Y	N
2	Loebsack	Y	Y	Y	Y	Y	N
3	Axne	Y	Y	Y	Y	Y	N
4	**King, S.**	N	N	N	Y	Y	Y
KANSAS							
1	**Marshall**	N	N	N	Y	Y	Y
2	**Watkins**	N	N	Y	Y	Y	Y
3	Davids	Y	Y	Y	Y	Y	N
4	**Estes**	N	N	N	N	Y	Y
KENTUCKY							
1	**Comer**	N	N	N	N	Y	Y
2	**Guthrie**	N	N	N	N	Y	Y
3	Yarmuth	Y	Y	Y	Y	Y	N
4	**Massie**	N	N	Y	Y	Y	?
5	**Rogers, H.**	N	N	Y	Y	Y	Y
6	**Barr**	N	N	N	Y	Y	Y
LOUISIANA							
1	**Scalise**	N	N	N	N	Y	Y
2	Richmond	P	Y	Y	Y	Y	N
3	**Higgins, C.**	-	-	-	-	+	Y
4	**Johnson, M.**	?	?	?	?	?	?
5	**Abraham**	?	?	?	?	?	?
6	**Graves, G.**	N	N	N	N	Y	Y
MAINE							
1	Pingree	Y	Y	Y	Y	Y	N
2	Golden	Y	Y	Y	Y	Y	Y
MARYLAND							
1	**Harris**	N	N	N	Y	Y	Y
2	Ruppersberger	Y	Y	Y	Y	Y	N
3	Sarbanes	Y	Y	Y	Y	Y	N
4	Brown, A.	Y	Y	Y	Y	Y	N
5	Hoyer	Y	Y	Y	Y	Y	N
6	Trone	Y	Y	Y	Y	Y	N
7	Cummings	?	?	?	?	?	N
8	Raskin	Y	Y	Y	Y	Y	N
MASSACHUSETTS							
1	Neal	Y	Y	Y	Y	Y	N
2	McGovern	Y	Y	Y	Y	Y	N
3	Trahan	Y	Y	Y	Y	Y	N
4	Kennedy	Y	Y	Y	Y	Y	N
5	Clark	Y	Y	Y	Y	Y	N
6	Moulton	Y	Y	Y	Y	Y	?
7	Pressley	Y	Y	Y	Y	Y	N
8	Lynch	Y	Y	Y	Y	Y	N
9	Keating	?	Y	Y	Y	Y	N
MICHIGAN							
1	**Bergman**	N	N	Y	Y	Y	Y
2	**Huizenga**	N	N	N	N	Y	Y
3	**Amash**	N	N	N	Y	Y	Y
4	**Moolenaar**	N	N	Y	Y	Y	Y
5	Kildee	Y	Y	Y	Y	Y	N
6	**Upton**	N	N	Y	Y	Y	Y
7	**Walberg**	N	N	N	Y	Y	Y
8	Slotkin	Y	Y	Y	Y	Y	N
9	Levin	Y	Y	Y	Y	Y	N
10	**Mitchell**	N	N	N	Y	Y	Y
11	Stevens	Y	Y	Y	Y	Y	N
12	Dingell	Y	Y	Y	Y	Y	N
13	Tlaib	Y	Y	Y	Y	Y	N
14	Lawrence	Y	Y	Y	Y	Y	N
MINNESOTA							
1	**Hagedorn**	N	N	Y	Y	Y	Y
2	Craig	Y	Y	Y	Y	Y	N
3	Phillips	Y	Y	Y	Y	Y	N
4	McCollum	Y	Y	Y	Y	Y	N
5	Omar	Y	Y	Y	Y	Y	N

		205	206	207	208	209	210
6	**Emmer**	N	N	N	Y	Y	Y
7	Peterson	Y	Y	Y	Y	Y	N
8	**Stauber**	N	N	Y	Y	Y	Y
MISSISSIPPI							
1	**Kelly, T.**	N	N	N	N	Y	Y
2	Thompson, B.	Y	Y	Y	Y	Y	N
3	**Guest**	N	N	N	Y	Y	Y
4	**Palazzo**	N	N	N	N	Y	Y
MISSOURI							
1	Clay	Y	Y	Y	Y	Y	N
2	**Wagner**	N	N	N	Y	Y	Y
3	**Luetkemeyer**	N	N	N	Y	Y	Y
4	**Hartzler**	N	N	N	N	Y	Y
5	Cleaver	Y	Y	+	+	+	N
6	**Graves, S.**	N	N	N	N	Y	Y
7	**Long**	N	N	N	N	Y	Y
8	**Smith, J.**	N	N	N	Y	Y	Y
MONTANA							
AL	**Gianforte**	N	N	N	N	Y	Y
NEBRASKA							
1	**Fortenberry**	N	N	N	Y	Y	Y
2	**Bacon**	N	N	Y	Y	Y	Y
3	**Smith, Adrian**	N	N	N	N	Y	Y
NEVADA							
1	Titus	Y	Y	Y	N	Y	N
2	**Amodei**	N	N	Y	N	Y	Y
3	Lee	Y	Y	Y	N	Y	N
4	Horsford	Y	Y	Y	Y	Y	N
NEW HAMPSHIRE							
1	Pappas	Y	Y	Y	Y	Y	N
2	Kuster	Y	Y	Y	Y	Y	N
NEW JERSEY							
1	Norcross	?	Y	Y	Y	Y	N
2	Van Drew	Y	Y	Y	Y	Y	N
3	Kim	Y	Y	Y	Y	Y	N
4	**Smith, C.**	N	N	Y	Y	Y	N
5	Gottheimer	Y	Y	Y	Y	Y	N
6	Pallone	Y	Y	Y	Y	Y	N
7	Malinowski	Y	Y	Y	Y	Y	N
8	Sires	Y	Y	Y	Y	Y	N
9	Pascrell	Y	Y	Y	Y	Y	N
10	Payne	Y	Y	Y	Y	Y	N
11	Sherrill	Y	Y	Y	Y	Y	N
12	Watson Coleman	Y	Y	Y	Y	Y	N
NEW MEXICO							
1	Haaland	Y	Y	Y	Y	Y	N
2	Torres Small	Y	Y	Y	Y	Y	N
3	Luján	Y	Y	Y	Y	Y	N
NEW YORK							
1	**Zeldin**	N	N	N	N	Y	Y
2	**King, P.**	N	N	Y	Y	Y	Y
3	Suozzi	Y	Y	Y	Y	Y	N
4	Rice, K.	Y	Y	Y	Y	Y	N
5	Meeks	Y	Y	Y	Y	Y	?
6	Meng	Y	Y	Y	Y	Y	N
7	Velázquez	Y	Y	Y	Y	Y	N
8	Jeffries	Y	Y	Y	Y	Y	N
9	Clarke	Y	Y	Y	Y	Y	N
10	Nadler	Y	Y	Y	Y	Y	N
11	Rose	Y	Y	Y	Y	Y	-
12	Maloney, C.	Y	Y	Y	Y	Y	N
13	Espaillat	Y	Y	Y	Y	Y	N
14	Ocasio-Cortez	Y	Y	Y	Y	Y	N
15	Serrano	Y	Y	Y	Y	Y	N
16	Engel	Y	Y	Y	Y	Y	N
17	Lowey	Y	Y	Y	Y	Y	N
18	Maloney, S.P.	Y	Y	Y	Y	Y	?
19	Delgado	Y	Y	Y	Y	Y	N
20	Tonko	Y	Y	Y	Y	Y	N
21	**Stefanik**	N	N	Y	Y	Y	Y
22	Brindisi	Y	Y	Y	Y	Y	N
23	**Reed**	N	N	Y	Y	Y	Y
24	**Katko**	N	N	Y	Y	Y	Y
25	Morelle	Y	Y	Y	Y	Y	N
26	Higgins, B.	Y	Y	Y	Y	Y	N
27	**Collins, C.**						
NORTH CAROLINA							
1	Butterfield	Y	Y	Y	Y	Y	N
2	**Holding**	N	N	N	Y	Y	Y
3	**Jones***						
4	Price	Y	Y	Y	Y	Y	N
5	**Foxx**	N	N	N	N	Y	Y
6	**Walker**	N	?	N	N	Y	Y
7	**Rouzer**	N	N	Y	Y	Y	Y

		205	206	207	208	209	210
8	**Hudson**	N	N	N	N	Y	Y
9	vacant						
10	**McHenry**	N	N	Y	Y	Y	Y
11	**Meadows**	N	N	N	Y	Y	Y
12	Adams	Y	Y	Y	Y	Y	N
13	**Budd**	N	N	N	N	Y	Y
NORTH DAKOTA							
AL	**Armstrong**	N	N	Y	Y	Y	Y
OHIO							
1	**Chabot**	N	N	N	N	Y	Y
2	**Wenstrup**	N	N	N	N	Y	Y
3	Beatty	Y	Y	Y	Y	Y	N
4	**Jordan**	N	N	N	N	Y	Y
5	**Latta**	N	N	N	N	Y	Y
6	**Johnson, B.**	N	N	N	N	Y	+
7	**Gibbs**	N	N	N	N	Y	Y
8	**Davidson**	N	N	N	N	Y	Y
9	Kaptur	Y	Y	Y	Y	Y	N
10	**Turner**	N	N	N	Y	Y	Y
11	Fudge	Y	Y	Y	Y	Y	N
12	**Balderson**	N	N	N	Y	Y	Y
13	Ryan	?	?	?	?	?	?
14	**Joyce**	N	N	N	Y	Y	Y
15	**Stivers**	N	N	N	Y	Y	Y
16	**Gonzalez**	N	N	Y	Y	Y	Y
OKLAHOMA							
1	**Hern**	N	N	N	Y	Y	Y
2	**Mullin**	N	N	N	Y	Y	Y
3	**Lucas**	N	N	Y	Y	Y	Y
4	**Cole**	N	N	Y	Y	Y	Y
5	Horn	Y	Y	Y	Y	Y	N
OREGON							
1	Bonamici	Y	Y	Y	Y	Y	N
2	**Walden**	N	N	Y	Y	Y	Y
3	Blumenauer	Y	Y	Y	Y	Y	N
4	DeFazio	Y	Y	Y	Y	Y	N
5	Schrader	Y	Y	Y	Y	Y	N
PENNSYLVANIA							
1	**Fitzpatrick**	N	N	Y	Y	Y	N
2	Boyle	Y	Y	Y	Y	Y	N
3	Evans	Y	Y	Y	Y	Y	N
4	Dean	Y	Y	Y	Y	Y	N
5	Scanlon	Y	Y	Y	Y	Y	N
6	Houlahan	Y	Y	Y	Y	Y	N
7	Wild	Y	Y	Y	Y	Y	N
8	Cartwright	Y	Y	Y	Y	Y	N
9	**Meuser**	N	N	N	N	Y	Y
10	**Perry**	N	N	N	N	Y	Y
11	**Smucker**	N	N	N	Y	Y	+
12	**Marino***						
13	**Joyce**	N	N	N	N	Y	Y
14	**Reschenthaler**	N	N	N	Y	Y	Y
15	**Thompson, G.**	N	?	Y	Y	Y	Y
16	**Kelly, M.**	N	N	N	N	Y	Y
17	Lamb	Y	Y	Y	Y	Y	Y
18	Doyle	Y	Y	Y	Y	Y	N
RHODE ISLAND							
1	Cicilline	Y	Y	N	N	Y	N
2	Langevin	Y	N	N	N	Y	N
SOUTH CAROLINA							
1	Cunningham	Y	Y	Y	Y	Y	N
2	**Wilson, J.**	N	N	N	Y	Y	Y
3	**Duncan**	N	N	N	N	Y	Y
4	**Timmons**	N	N	N	N	Y	Y
5	**Norman**	N	N	N	N	Y	Y
6	Clyburn	Y	Y	Y	Y	Y	-
7	**Rice, T.**	N	N	N	Y	Y	Y
SOUTH DAKOTA							
AL	**Johnson**	N	N	N	Y	Y	Y
TENNESSEE							
1	**Roe**	N	N	N	Y	Y	Y
2	**Burchett**	N	N	N	N	Y	Y
3	**Fleischmann**	N	N	N	N	Y	Y
4	**DesJarlais**	N	N	N	N	Y	Y
5	Cooper	Y	Y	Y	Y	Y	N
6	**Rose**	N	N	N	N	Y	Y
7	**Green**	N	N	N	N	Y	Y
8	**Kustoff**	N	N	N	N	Y	Y
9	Cohen	Y	Y	Y	Y	Y	N
TEXAS							
1	**Gohmert**	N	N	N	N	?	Y
2	**Crenshaw**	N	N	N	N	Y	Y
3	**Taylor**	N	N	N	N	Y	Y
4	**Ratcliffe**	N	N	N	Y	Y	Y

		205	206	207	208	209	210
5	**Gooden**	N	N	N	N	Y	Y
6	**Wright**	N	N	N	N	Y	Y
7	Fletcher	Y	Y	Y	Y	Y	N
8	**Brady**	N	N	N	?	Y	Y
9	Green, A.	Y	Y	Y	Y	Y	N
10	**McCaul**	N	N	N	Y	?	Y
11	**Conaway**	N	N	N	Y	Y	Y
12	**Granger**	N	N	N	Y	Y	Y
13	**Thornberry**	N	N	Y	Y	Y	Y
14	**Weber**	N	?	N	N	Y	?
15	Gonzalez	Y	Y	Y	Y	Y	N
16	Escobar	Y	Y	Y	Y	Y	N
17	**Flores**	N	N	N	N	Y	Y
18	Jackson Lee	Y	Y	Y	Y	Y	N
19	**Arrington**	N	N	N	N	Y	Y
20	Castro	Y	Y	Y	Y	Y	N
21	**Roy**	N	N	N	N	Y	Y
22	**Olson**	N	N	N	N	Y	Y
23	**Hurd**	N	N	Y	Y	Y	Y
24	**Marchant**	N	N	N	N	Y	Y
25	**Williams**	N	N	N	N	Y	Y
26	**Burgess**	N	N	N	N	Y	Y
27	**Cloud**	N	N	N	N	Y	Y
28	Cuellar	Y	Y	Y	Y	Y	N
29	Garcia, S.	Y	Y	Y	Y	Y	N
30	Johnson, E.B.	Y	Y	Y	Y	Y	N
31	**Carter, J.**	N	N	N	Y	Y	Y
32	Allred	Y	Y	Y	Y	Y	N
33	Veasey	Y	Y	Y	Y	Y	N
34	Vela	Y	Y	Y	Y	Y	N
35	Doggett	Y	Y	Y	Y	?	N
36	**Babin**	N	N	Y	Y	Y	Y
UTAH							
1	**Bishop, R.**	N	N	N	Y	Y	Y
2	**Stewart**	N	N	N	N	Y	Y
3	**Curtis**	N	N	N	N	Y	Y
4	McAdams	Y	N	Y	Y	Y	N
VERMONT							
AL	Welch	Y	Y	Y	Y	Y	N
VIRGINIA							
1	**Wittman**	N	N	N	Y	Y	Y
2	Luria	Y	Y	Y	Y	Y	N
3	Scott, R.	Y	Y	Y	Y	Y	N
4	McEachin	Y	Y	Y	Y	Y	N
5	**Riggleman**	N	N	N	N	Y	Y
6	**Cline**	N	N	N	N	?	Y
7	Spanberger	Y	Y	Y	Y	Y	N
8	Beyer	Y	Y	Y	Y	Y	N
9	**Griffith**	N	N	N	Y	Y	Y
10	Wexton	Y	Y	Y	Y	Y	N
11	Connolly	Y	Y	Y	Y	Y	N
WASHINGTON							
1	DelBene	Y	Y	Y	Y	Y	N
2	Larsen	Y	Y	Y	Y	Y	N
3	**Herrera Beutler**	N	N	N	Y	Y	Y
4	**Newhouse**	N	N	N	Y	Y	Y
5	**McMorris Rodgers**	N	N	N	Y	Y	Y
6	Kilmer	Y	Y	Y	Y	Y	N
7	Jayapal	Y	Y	Y	Y	Y	N
8	Schrier	Y	Y	Y	Y	Y	N
9	Smith Adam	Y	Y	Y	Y	Y	N
10	Heck	Y	Y	Y	Y	Y	N
WEST VIRGINIA							
1	**McKinley**	N	N	N	N	Y	Y
2	**Mooney**	N	N	N	N	Y	Y
3	**Miller**	N	N	N	N	Y	Y
WISCONSIN							
1	**Steil**	N	N	N	Y	Y	Y
2	Pocan	Y	Y	Y	Y	Y	N
3	Kind	Y	Y	Y	Y	Y	N
4	Moore	Y	Y	Y	Y	Y	N
5	**Sensenbrenner**	N	N	N	N	Y	Y
6	**Grothman**	N	N	N	N	Y	Y
7	**Duffy**						
8	**Gallagher**	N	N	N	Y	Y	Y
WYOMING							
AL	**Cheney**	N	N	N	N	Y	Y
DELEGATES							
	Radewagen (A.S.)						?
	Norton (D.C.)						N
	San Nicolas (Guam)						N
	Sablan (N. Marianas)						N
	González-Colón (P.R.)						Y
	Plaskett (V.I.)						?

211. HR987. Generic Drug Regulations and Health Insurance Marketplaces - Navigator Training on Opioids. Harder, D-Calif., amendment that would require that "navigators" certified to help individuals enroll in Affordable Care Act marketplace plans receive opioid-specific training on coverage of opioid-related health care treatment under qualified plans. Adopted in Committee of the Whole 243-174: R 12-174; D 230-0; I 1-0. May 16, 2019.

212. HR987. Generic Drug Regulations and Health Insurance Marketplaces - Short-Term Health Plan Funding. Wexton, D-Va., amendment that would add to the bill findings that an Aug. 2018 Health and Human Services Department rule related to short-term, limited-duration health insurance expands the sale and marketing of such plans, which may discriminate against individuals with preexisting health conditions, may exclude essential health benefit coverage, and are not subject to Affordable Care Act financial protection requirements. Adopted in Committee of the Whole 232-185: R 1-185; D 230-0; I 1-0. May 16, 2019.

213. HR987. Generic Drug Regulations and Health Insurance Marketplaces - Recommit. Walden, R-Ore., motion to recommit the bill to the House Energy and Commerce Committee with instructions to report it back immediately with an amendment that would remove from the bill Title II, which contains several provisions that would facilitate enrollment in and support Affordable Care Act health insurance marketplaces. The amendment would replace the title with a provision that would authorize $4.96 billion annually through fiscal 2024 for the National Institutes of Health to carry out NIH Innovation Projects to conduct research on pediatric cancer. Motion rejected 188-228: R 188-0; D 0-228. May 16, 2019.

214. HR987. Generic Drug Regulations and Health Insurance Marketplaces - Passage. Passage of the bill, as amended, that comprises a package of measures related to the development and market entry of generic drugs and a package of measures related to enrollment in and federal funding to support Affordable Care Act health insurance marketplaces. Title I of the bill includes provisions intended to facilitate the development and market entry of generic and biosimilar drug products. Specifically, it would allow the Food and Drug Administration to approve a subsequent company's application to manufacture a generic drug in cases where an initial company has applied but not received final FDA approval to introduce the drug after 30 months; approval of the subsequent application would trigger a 180-day exclusivity period for sale of the generic drug by the initial applicant company, after which point other generic versions could enter the market. It would prohibit generic and brand-name drug manufacturers from entering into agreements in which brand-name manufacturers pay to delay entry of a generic drug into the market, and it would authorize the Federal Trade Commission to issue penalties and initiate civil actions to enforce the prohibition. It would allow generic drug manufacturers to bring civil action against the license holder for a brand-name drug if the license holder does not provide "sufficient quantities" of samples of the brand-name drug on "commercially reasonable, market-based terms;" it would also outline certain affirmative legal defenses for defendants and certain terms for legal remedies in the case of a successful suit. Title II of the bill includes several provisions intended to facilitate enrollment in and provide funding and support for state- and federally-operated health insurance marketplaces under the Affordable Care Act. Specifically, it would authorize $200 million in grant funding for states to establish and operate state-based ACA health insurance marketplaces. It would authorize $100 million for Health and Human Services Department consumer outreach and educational activities related to ACA marketplace plans. It would authorize $100 million for the HHS "navigator" program, which funds certified entities to help individuals enroll in qualified plans, and would make certain modifications to the duties and selection of navigators. It would prohibit the HHS, Treasury, and Labor departments from taking any action to implement or enforce an Aug. 2018 rule that effectively extends the maximum duration of coverage for short-term, limited-duration health insurance plans, which are not required to meet ACA patient protection requirements. As amended, the bill would authorize $25 million annually in grant funding for the ACA navigator program in state-based marketplaces and include a number of additional requirements related to outreach and education programs by navigators and by HHS. Passed 234-183: R 5-183; D 229-0. *Note: A "nay" was a vote in support of the president's position.* May 16, 2019.

215. Procedural Motion - Journal. Approval of the House journal of May 17, 2019. Approved 215-191: R 39-141; D 176-50. May 17, 2019.

216. HR5. LGBTQ Anti-Discrimination Protections - Recommit. Steube, R-Fla., motion to recommit the bill to the House Judiciary Committee with instructions to report it back immediately with an amendment that would clarify that nothing contained in the bill may be construed to diminish any protections under title IX of the Education Amendments of 1972, which prohibits discrimination on the basis of sex under any federally-funded education programs, stating that no person can be excluded from participation in or denied the benefits of such programs on the basis of sex. Motion rejected 181-228: R 180-1; D 1-227. May 17, 2019.

		211	212	213	214	215	216
ALABAMA							
1	**Byrne**	?	?	?	?	N	Y
2	**Roby**	N	N	Y	N	N	Y
3	**Rogers, M.**	N	N	Y	N	?	Y
4	**Aderholt**	N	N	Y	N	N	Y
5	**Brooks, M.**	N	N	Y	N	N	Y
6	**Palmer**	N	N	Y	N	N	Y
7	Sewell	Y	Y	N	Y	Y	N
ALASKA							
AL	**Young**	N	N	Y	N	?	?
ARIZONA							
1	O'Halleran	Y	Y	N	Y	Y	N
2	Kirkpatrick	Y	Y	N	Y	N	N
3	Grijalva	Y	Y	N	Y	Y	N
4	**Gosar**	N	N	Y	N	N	Y
5	**Biggs**	N	N	Y	N	N	Y
6	**Schweikert**	N	N	Y	N	Y	Y
7	Gallego	Y	Y	N	Y	Y	N
8	**Lesko**	N	N	Y	N	N	Y
9	Stanton	Y	Y	N	Y	Y	N
ARKANSAS							
1	**Crawford**	N	N	Y	N	N	Y
2	**Hill, F.**	N	N	Y	N	N	Y
3	**Womack**	N	N	Y	N	N	Y
4	**Westerman**	N	N	Y	N	?	?
CALIFORNIA							
1	**LaMalfa**	N	N	Y	N	N	Y
2	Huffman	Y	Y	N	Y	Y	N
3	Garamendi	Y	Y	N	Y	Y	N
4	**McClintock**	N	N	Y	N	Y	Y
5	Thompson, M.	Y	Y	N	Y	N	N
6	Matsui	Y	Y	N	Y	Y	N
7	Bera	Y	Y	N	Y	N	N
8	**Cook**	N	N	Y	N	N	Y
9	McNerney	Y	Y	N	Y	Y	N
10	Harder	Y	Y	N	Y	N	N
11	DeSaulnier	Y	Y	N	Y	Y	N
12	Pelosi				Y		N
13	Lee B.	Y	Y	N	Y	Y	N
14	Speier	Y	Y	N	Y	Y	N
15	Swalwell	+	+	-	+	+	-
16	Costa	Y	Y	N	Y	N	N
17	Khanna	Y	Y	N	Y	Y	N
18	Eshoo	Y	Y	N	Y	Y	N
19	Lofgren	Y	Y	N	Y	Y	N
20	Panetta	Y	Y	N	Y	N	N
21	Cox	Y	Y	N	Y	Y	N
22	**Nunes**	N	N	Y	N	N	Y
23	**McCarthy**	N	N	Y	N	Y	Y
24	Carbajal	Y	Y	N	Y	Y	N
25	Hill, K.	Y	Y	N	Y	Y	N
26	Brownley	Y	Y	N	Y	Y	N
27	Chu	Y	Y	N	Y	Y	N
28	Schiff	Y	Y	N	Y	Y	N
29	Cárdenas	Y	Y	N	Y	Y	N
30	Sherman	Y	Y	N	Y	Y	N
31	Aguilar	Y	Y	N	Y	N	N
32	Napolitano	Y	Y	N	Y	Y	N
33	Lieu	Y	Y	N	Y	Y	N
34	Gomez	Y	Y	N	Y	Y	N
35	Torres	Y	Y	N	Y	Y	N
36	Ruiz	Y	Y	N	Y	N	N
37	Bass	Y	Y	N	Y	Y	N
38	Sánchez	Y	Y	N	Y	Y	N
39	Cisneros	Y	Y	N	Y	N	N
40	Roybal-Allard	Y	Y	N	Y	Y	N
41	Takano	Y	Y	N	Y	Y	N
42	**Calvert**	N	N	Y	N	N	Y
43	Waters	Y	Y	N	Y	N	N
44	Barragán	Y	Y	N	Y	Y	N
45	Porter	Y	Y	N	Y	N	N
46	Correa	Y	Y	N	Y	N	N
47	Lowenthal	Y	Y	N	Y	Y	N
48	Rouda	Y	Y	N	Y	N	N
49	Levin	Y	Y	N	Y	Y	N
50	**Hunter**	N	N	Y	N	N	Y
51	Vargas	Y	Y	N	Y	Y	N
52	Peters	Y	Y	N	Y	N	N
53	Davis, S.	Y	Y	N	Y	Y	N
COLORADO							
1	DeGette	Y	Y	N	Y	Y	N
2	Neguse	Y	Y	N	Y	Y	N
3	**Tipton**	N	N	Y	N	Y	Y
4	**Buck**	N	N	Y	N	N	Y
5	**Lamborn**	N	N	Y	N	N	Y
6	Crow	Y	Y	N	Y	N	N
7	Perlmutter	Y	Y	N	Y	Y	N
CONNECTICUT							
1	Larson	Y	Y	N	Y	N	N
2	Courtney	Y	Y	N	Y	Y	N
3	DeLauro	Y	Y	N	Y	Y	N
4	Himes	Y	Y	N	Y	N	N
5	Hayes	Y	Y	N	Y	Y	N
DELAWARE							
AL	Blunt Rochester	Y	Y	N	Y	Y	N
FLORIDA							
1	**Gaetz**	N	N	Y	N	N	Y
2	**Dunn**	N	N	Y	N	N	Y
3	**Yoho**	N	N	Y	N	N	Y
4	**Rutherford**	N	N	Y	N	Y	Y
5	Lawson	Y	Y	N	Y	Y	N
6	**Waltz**	N	N	Y	N	Y	Y
7	Murphy	Y	Y	N	Y	Y	N
8	**Posey**	N	N	Y	N	N	Y
9	Soto	Y	Y	N	Y	Y	N
10	Demings	Y	Y	N	Y	Y	N
11	**Webster**	N	N	Y	N	Y	Y
12	**Bilirakis**	N	N	Y	N	N	Y
13	Crist	Y	Y	N	Y	Y	N
14	Castor	Y	Y	N	Y	Y	N
15	**Spano**	N	N	Y	N	N	Y
16	**Buchanan**	N	N	Y	N	N	Y
17	**Steube**	N	N	Y	N	N	Y
18	**Mast**	N	N	Y	N	N	Y
19	**Rooney**	N	N	Y	N	N	Y
20	Hastings	Y	Y	N	Y	Y	N
21	Frankel	Y	Y	N	Y	Y	N
22	Deutch	Y	Y	N	Y	Y	N
23	Wasserman Schultz	Y	Y	N	Y	Y	N
24	Wilson, F.	Y	Y	N	Y	Y	N
25	**Diaz-Balart**	N	N	Y	N	N	Y
26	Mucarsel-Powell	Y	Y	N	Y	N	N
27	Shalala	Y	Y	N	Y	Y	N
GEORGIA							
1	**Carter, E.L.**	N	N	Y	N	N	Y
2	Bishop, S.	Y	Y	N	Y	Y	N
3	**Ferguson**	N	N	Y	N	N	Y
4	Johnson, H.	Y	Y	N	Y	Y	N
5	Lewis John	Y	Y	N	Y	Y	N
6	McBath	Y	Y	N	Y	N	N
7	**Woodall**	N	N	Y	N	N	Y
8	**Scott, A.**	N	N	Y	N	N	Y
9	**Collins, D.**	?	?	?	?	Y	Y
10	**Hice**	N	N	Y	N	N	Y
11	**Loudermilk**	N	N	Y	N	N	Y
12	**Allen**	N	N	Y	N	N	Y
13	Scott, D.	Y	Y	N	Y	Y	N
14	**Graves, T.**	N	N	Y	N	N	Y
HAWAII							
1	Case	Y	Y	N	Y	Y	N
2	Gabbard	Y	Y	N	Y	Y	N
IDAHO							
1	**Fulcher**	N	N	Y	N	N	Y
2	**Simpson**	N	N	Y	N	Y	Y
ILLINOIS							
1	Rush	Y	Y	N	Y	Y	N
2	Kelly, R.	Y	Y	N	Y	Y	N
3	Lipinski	Y	Y	N	Y	Y	Y
4	García, J.	Y	Y	N	Y	Y	N
5	Quigley	Y	Y	N	Y	Y	N
6	Casten	Y	Y	N	Y	Y	N
7	Davis, D.	Y	Y	N	Y	Y	N
8	Krishnamoorthi	Y	Y	N	Y	N	N
9	Schakowsky	Y	Y	N	Y	Y	N
10	Schneider	Y	Y	N	Y	Y	N
11	Foster	Y	Y	N	Y	Y	N

KEY: **Republicans** Democrats *Independents*

Y	Voted for (yea)	N	Voted against (nay)	P	Voted "present"
+	Announced for	-	Announced against	?	Did not vote or otherwise make position known
#	Paired for	X	Paired against		

		211	212	213	214	215	216
12	**Bost**	N	N	Y	N	N	Y
13	**Davis, R.**	N	N	Y	N	N	Y
14	Underwood	Y	Y	N	Y	Y	N
15	**Shimkus**	N	N	Y	N	N	Y
16	**Kinzinger**	N	N	Y	N	N	Y
17	Bustos	Y	Y	N	Y	Y	N
18	**LaHood**	N	N	Y	N	-	+
INDIANA							
1	Visclosky	Y	Y	N	Y	Y	N
2	**Walorski**	N	N	Y	N	N	Y
3	**Banks**	N	N	Y	N	N	Y
4	**Baird**	N	N	Y	N	N	Y
5	**Brooks, S.**	N	N	Y	N	Y	Y
6	**Pence**	N	N	Y	N	N	+
7	Carson	Y	Y	N	Y	Y	N
8	**Bucshon**	-	-	+	-	+	+
9	**Hollingsworth**	Y	N	Y	N	Y	Y
IOWA							
1	Finkenauer	Y	Y	N	Y	Y	N
2	Loebsack	Y	Y	N	Y	Y	N
3	Axne	Y	Y	N	Y	N	N
4	**King, S.**	N	N	Y	N	Y	Y
KANSAS							
1	**Marshall**	N	N	Y	N	N	Y
2	**Watkins**	N	N	Y	N	Y	Y
3	Davids	Y	Y	N	Y	Y	N
4	**Estes**	N	N	Y	N	N	Y
KENTUCKY							
1	**Comer**	N	N	Y	N	N	Y
2	**Guthrie**	N	N	Y	N	N	Y
3	Yarmuth	Y	Y	N	Y	Y	N
4	**Massie**	?	?	?	?	N	N
5	**Rogers, H.**	N	N	Y	N	N	Y
6	**Barr**	N	N	Y	N	N	Y
LOUISIANA							
1	**Scalise**	N	N	Y	N	N	Y
2	Richmond	Y	Y	N	Y	Y	N
3	**Higgins, C.**	N	N	Y	N	N	Y
4	**Johnson, M.**	?	?	?	?	?	?
5	**Abraham**	?	?	?	?	N	Y
6	**Graves, G.**	N	N	Y	N	N	Y
MAINE							
1	Pingree	Y	Y	N	Y	Y	N
2	Golden	Y	Y	N	Y	N	N
MARYLAND							
1	**Harris**	N	N	Y	N	N	Y
2	Ruppersberger	Y	Y	N	Y	Y	N
3	Sarbanes	Y	Y	N	Y	Y	N
4	Brown, A.	Y	Y	N	Y	Y	N
5	Hoyer	Y	Y	N	Y	Y	N
6	Trone	Y	Y	N	Y	Y	N
7	Cummings	Y	Y	N	Y	N	N
8	Raskin	Y	Y	N	Y	Y	N
MASSACHUSETTS							
1	Neal	Y	Y	N	Y	Y	N
2	McGovern	Y	Y	N	Y	Y	N
3	Trahan	Y	Y	N	Y	Y	N
4	Kennedy	Y	Y	N	Y	Y	N
5	Clark	Y	Y	N	Y	N	N
6	Moulton	?	?	?	?	?	?
7	Pressley	Y	Y	N	Y	Y	N
8	Lynch	Y	Y	N	Y	Y	N
9	Keating	Y	Y	N	Y	Y	N
MICHIGAN							
1	**Bergman**	N	N	Y	N	N	Y
2	**Huizenga**	N	N	Y	N	N	Y
3	**Amash**	N	N	Y	N	N	Y
4	**Moolenaar**	N	N	Y	N	N	Y
5	Kildee	Y	Y	N	Y	Y	N
6	**Upton**	Y	N	N	Y	N	Y
7	**Walberg**	N	N	Y	N	N	Y
8	Slotkin	Y	Y	N	Y	N	N
9	Levin	Y	Y	N	Y	Y	N
10	**Mitchell**	N	N	Y	N	N	Y
11	Stevens	Y	Y	N	Y	Y	N
12	Dingell	Y	Y	N	Y	?	?
13	Tlaib	Y	Y	N	Y	Y	N
14	Lawrence	Y	Y	N	Y	Y	N
MINNESOTA							
1	**Hagedorn**	N	N	Y	N	N	Y
2	Craig	Y	Y	N	Y	N	N
3	Phillips	Y	Y	N	Y	Y	N
4	McCollum	Y	Y	N	Y	Y	N
5	Omar	Y	Y	N	Y	Y	N

		211	212	213	214	215	216
6	**Emmer**	N	N	Y	N	N	Y
7	Peterson	Y	Y	N	Y	?	?
8	**Stauber**	N	N	Y	N	Y	Y
MISSISSIPPI							
1	**Kelly, T.**	N	N	Y	N	N	Y
2	Thompson, B.	Y	Y	N	Y	Y	N
3	**Guest**	N	N	Y	N	N	Y
4	**Palazzo**	N	N	Y	N	N	Y
MISSOURI							
1	Clay	Y	Y	N	Y	Y	N
2	**Wagner**	N	N	Y	N	Y	Y
3	**Luetkemeyer**	N	N	Y	N	N	Y
4	**Hartzler**	N	N	Y	N	N	Y
5	Cleaver	Y	Y	N	Y	Y	N
6	**Graves, S.**	N	N	Y	N	N	Y
7	**Long**	N	N	Y	N	N	Y
8	**Smith, J.**	N	N	Y	N	N	Y
MONTANA							
AL	**Gianforte**	N	N	Y	N	N	Y
NEBRASKA							
1	**Fortenberry**	Y	N	Y	N	Y	Y
2	**Bacon**	Y	N	Y	N	Y	Y
3	**Smith, Adrian**	N	N	Y	N	N	Y
NEVADA							
1	Titus	Y	Y	N	Y	Y	N
2	**Amodei**	N	N	Y	N	Y	Y
3	Lee	Y	Y	N	Y	Y	N
4	Horsford	Y	Y	N	Y	N	N
NEW HAMPSHIRE							
1	Pappas	Y	Y	N	Y	Y	N
2	Kuster	Y	Y	N	Y	Y	N
NEW JERSEY							
1	Norcross	Y	Y	N	Y	Y	N
2	Van Drew	Y	Y	N	Y	N	N
3	Kim	Y	Y	N	Y	N	N
4	**Smith, C.**	Y	N	Y	Y	N	Y
5	Gottheimer	Y	Y	N	Y	N	N
6	Pallone	Y	Y	N	Y	Y	N
7	Malinowski	Y	Y	N	Y	Y	N
8	Sires	Y	Y	N	Y	Y	N
9	Pascrell	Y	Y	N	Y	Y	N
10	Payne	Y	Y	N	Y	Y	N
11	Sherrill	Y	Y	N	Y	N	N
12	Watson Coleman	Y	Y	N	Y	Y	N
NEW MEXICO							
1	Haaland	Y	Y	N	Y	Y	N
2	Torres Small	Y	Y	N	Y	N	N
3	Luján	Y	Y	N	Y	Y	N
NEW YORK							
1	**Zeldin**	N	N	Y	N	N	Y
2	**King, P.**	N	N	Y	N	N	Y
3	Suozzi	Y	Y	N	Y	N	N
4	Rice, K.	Y	Y	N	Y	N	N
5	Meeks	?	?	?	?	N	N
6	Meng	Y	Y	N	Y	N	N
7	Velázquez	Y	Y	N	Y	Y	N
8	Jeffries	Y	Y	N	Y	Y	N
9	Clarke	Y	Y	N	Y	Y	N
10	Nadler	Y	Y	N	Y	Y	N
11	Rose	+	+	-	+	?	-
12	Maloney, C.	Y	Y	N	Y	Y	N
13	Espaillat	Y	Y	N	Y	Y	N
14	Ocasio-Cortez	Y	Y	N	Y	Y	N
15	Serrano	Y	Y	N	Y	Y	N
16	Engel	Y	Y	N	Y	Y	N
17	Lowey	Y	Y	N	Y	Y	N
18	Maloney, S.P.	Y	Y	N	Y	N	N
19	Delgado	Y	Y	N	Y	Y	N
20	Tonko	Y	Y	N	Y	P	N
21	**Stefanik**	N	N	Y	N	Y	Y
22	Brindisi	Y	Y	N	Y	N	N
23	**Reed**	Y	N	Y	N	N	Y
24	**Katko**	Y	N	Y	Y	N	Y
25	Morelle	Y	Y	N	Y	Y	N
26	Higgins, B.	Y	Y	N	Y	Y	N
27	**Collins, C.**						
NORTH CAROLINA							
1	Butterfield	Y	Y	N	Y	Y	N
2	**Holding**	N	N	Y	N	N	Y
3	**Jones***						
4	Price	Y	Y	N	Y	Y	N
5	**Foxx**	N	N	Y	N	N	Y
6	**Walker**	N	N	Y	N	?	?
7	**Rouzer**	N	N	Y	N	N	Y

		211	212	213	214	215	216
8	**Hudson**	N	N	Y	N	N	Y
9	vacant						
10	**McHenry**	N	N	Y	N	N	Y
11	**Meadows**	N	N	Y	N	N	Y
12	Adams	Y	Y	N	Y	Y	N
13	**Budd**	N	N	Y	N	N	Y
NORTH DAKOTA							
AL	**Armstrong**	N	N	Y	N	N	Y
OHIO							
1	**Chabot**	N	N	Y	N	N	Y
2	**Wenstrup**	N	N	Y	N	Y	Y
3	Beatty	Y	Y	N	Y	Y	N
4	**Jordan**	N	N	Y	N	N	Y
5	**Latta**	N	N	Y	N	N	Y
6	**Johnson, B.**	-	-	+	-	-	#
7	**Gibbs**	N	N	Y	N	N	Y
8	**Davidson**	N	N	Y	N	Y	Y
9	Kaptur	Y	Y	N	Y	Y	N
10	**Turner**	N	N	Y	N	-	+
11	Fudge	Y	Y	N	Y	N	N
12	**Balderson**	N	N	Y	N	N	Y
13	Ryan	?	?	?	?	?	?
14	**Joyce**	N	N	Y	N	Y	Y
15	**Stivers**	N	N	Y	N	Y	Y
16	**Gonzalez**	N	N	Y	N	N	Y
OKLAHOMA							
1	**Hern**	N	N	Y	N	N	Y
2	**Mullin**	N	N	Y	N	N	Y
3	**Lucas**	N	N	Y	N	N	Y
4	**Cole**	N	N	Y	N	N	Y
5	Horn	Y	Y	N	Y	N	N
OREGON							
1	Bonamici	Y	Y	N	Y	Y	N
2	**Walden**	N	N	Y	N	Y	Y
3	Blumenauer	Y	Y	N	Y	Y	N
4	DeFazio	Y	Y	N	Y	Y	N
5	Schrader	Y	Y	N	Y	N	N
PENNSYLVANIA							
1	**Fitzpatrick**	Y	Y	Y	Y	N	Y
2	Boyle	Y	Y	N	Y	Y	N
3	Evans	Y	Y	N	Y	Y	N
4	Dean	Y	Y	N	Y	Y	N
5	Scanlon	Y	Y	N	Y	Y	N
6	Houlahan	Y	Y	N	Y	N	N
7	Wild	Y	Y	N	Y	N	N
8	Cartwright	Y	Y	N	Y	Y	N
9	**Meuser**	N	N	Y	N	N	Y
10	**Perry**	N	N	Y	N	Y	Y
11	**Smucker**	-	-	+	-	-	+
12	**Marino***						
13	**Joyce**	N	N	Y	N	N	Y
14	**Reschenthaler**	N	N	Y	N	Y	Y
15	**Thompson, G.**	N	N	Y	N	N	Y
16	**Kelly, M.**	N	N	Y	N	N	Y
17	Lamb	Y	Y	N	Y	Y	N
18	Doyle	Y	Y	N	Y	Y	N
RHODE ISLAND							
1	Cicilline	Y	Y	N	Y	Y	N
2	Langevin	Y	Y	N	Y	Y	N
SOUTH CAROLINA							
1	Cunningham	Y	Y	N	Y	N	N
2	**Wilson, J.**	N	N	Y	N	-	+
3	**Duncan**	N	N	Y	N	N	Y
4	**Timmons**	N	N	Y	N	N	Y
5	**Norman**	N	N	Y	N	N	Y
6	Clyburn	+	+	-	+	+	-
7	**Rice, T.**	N	N	Y	N	N	Y
SOUTH DAKOTA							
AL	**Johnson**	N	N	Y	N	N	Y
TENNESSEE							
1	**Roe**	N	N	Y	N	Y	Y
2	**Burchett**	N	N	Y	N	?	?
3	**Fleischmann**	N	N	Y	N	N	Y
4	**DesJarlais**	N	N	Y	N	N	Y
5	Cooper	Y	Y	N	Y	Y	N
6	**Rose**	N	N	Y	N	N	Y
7	**Green**	N	N	Y	N	N	Y
8	**Kustoff**	N	N	Y	N	N	Y
9	Cohen	Y	Y	N	Y	Y	N
TEXAS							
1	**Gohmert**	?	?	Y	N	?	Y
2	**Crenshaw**	N	N	Y	N	N	Y
3	**Taylor**	N	N	Y	N	Y	Y
4	**Ratcliffe**	N	N	Y	N	?	?

		211	212	213	214	215	216
5	**Gooden**	N	N	Y	N	N	Y
6	**Wright**	N	N	Y	N	N	Y
7	Fletcher	Y	Y	N	Y	N	N
8	**Brady**	N	?	Y	N	?	?
9	Green, A.	Y	Y	N	Y	Y	N
10	**McCaul**	N	N	Y	N	N	Y
11	**Conaway**	N	N	Y	N	N	Y
12	**Granger**	N	N	Y	N	Y	Y
13	**Thornberry**	N	N	Y	N	Y	Y
14	**Weber**	?	?	?	?	?	?
15	Gonzalez	Y	Y	N	Y	Y	N
16	Escobar	Y	Y	N	Y	Y	N
17	**Flores**	N	N	Y	N	N	Y
18	Jackson Lee	Y	Y	N	Y	Y	N
19	**Arrington**	?	N	Y	N	Y	Y
20	Castro	Y	Y	N	Y	Y	N
21	**Roy**	N	N	Y	N	N	Y
22	**Olson**	N	N	Y	N	N	Y
23	**Hurd**	Y	N	Y	N	N	Y
24	**Marchant**	N	N	Y	N	N	Y
25	**Williams**	N	N	Y	N	N	Y
26	**Burgess**	N	N	Y	N	N	Y
27	**Cloud**	N	N	Y	N	N	Y
28	Cuellar	Y	Y	N	Y	Y	N
29	Garcia, S.	Y	Y	N	Y	Y	N
30	Johnson, E.B.	Y	Y	N	Y	Y	N
31	**Carter, J.**	N	N	Y	N	Y	Y
32	Allred	Y	Y	N	Y	Y	N
33	Veasey	Y	Y	N	Y	Y	N
34	Vela	Y	Y	N	Y	Y	N
35	Doggett	Y	Y	N	Y	Y	N
36	**Babin**	N	N	Y	N	N	Y
UTAH							
1	**Bishop, R.**	N	N	Y	N	N	Y
2	**Stewart**	N	N	Y	N	N	Y
3	**Curtis**	N	N	Y	N	Y	Y
4	McAdams	Y	Y	N	Y	N	N
VERMONT							
AL	Welch	Y	Y	N	Y	Y	N
VIRGINIA							
1	**Wittman**	N	N	Y	N	N	Y
2	Luria	Y	Y	N	Y	Y	N
3	Scott, R.	Y	Y	N	Y	Y	N
4	McEachin	Y	Y	N	Y	Y	N
5	**Riggleman**	N	N	Y	N	N	Y
6	**Cline**	N	N	Y	N	N	Y
7	Spanberger	Y	Y	N	Y	N	N
8	Beyer	Y	Y	N	Y	Y	N
9	**Griffith**	N	N	Y	N	N	Y
10	Wexton	Y	Y	N	Y	Y	N
11	Connolly	Y	Y	N	Y	N	N
WASHINGTON							
1	DelBene	Y	Y	N	Y	Y	N
2	Larsen	Y	Y	N	Y	Y	N
3	**Herrera Beutler**	N	N	Y	N	N	Y
4	**Newhouse**	N	N	Y	N	Y	Y
5	**McMorris Rodgers**	N	N	Y	N	Y	Y
6	Kilmer	Y	Y	N	Y	N	N
7	Jayapal	Y	Y	N	Y	Y	N
8	Schrier	Y	Y	N	Y	N	N
9	Smith Adam	Y	Y	N	Y	Y	N
10	Heck	Y	Y	N	Y	Y	N
WEST VIRGINIA							
1	**McKinley**	N	N	Y	N	N	Y
2	**Mooney**	N	N	Y	N	N	Y
3	**Miller**	N	N	Y	N	N	Y
WISCONSIN							
1	**Steil**	Y	N	Y	N	Y	Y
2	Pocan	Y	Y	N	Y	Y	N
3	Kind	Y	Y	N	Y	N	N
4	Moore	Y	Y	N	Y	Y	N
5	**Sensenbrenner**	Y	N	Y	N	N	Y
6	**Grothman**	N	N	Y	N	N	Y
7	**Duffy**						
8	**Gallagher**	N	N	Y	N	N	Y
WYOMING							
AL	**Cheney**	N	N	Y	N	N	Y
DELEGATES							
	Radewagen (A.S.)	?	?				
	Norton (D.C.)	Y	Y				
	San Nicolas (Guam)	Y	Y				
	Sablan (N. Marianas)	Y	Y				
	González-Colón (P.R.)	Y	?				
	Plaskett (V.I.)	?	?				

⦀ HOUSE VOTES

217. HR5. LGBTQ Anti-Discrimination Protections - Passage. Passage of the bill that would prohibit discrimination or segregation based on sex, sexual orientation, and gender identity under 1964 Civil Rights Act protections, including in public facilities, public education, federal assistance programs, employment, jury service, and areas of public accommodation. It would expand the definition of "public accommodations" to include transportation services and any establishment providing a good, service, or program, including retailers, health care facilities, and legal services. The bill would define "gender identity" as "gender-related identity, appearance, mannerisms, or other gender-related characteristics of an individual," regardless of designated sex at birth. The bill would also allow the Justice Department to intervene in equal protection cases regarding sexual orientation and gender identity. Passed 236-173: R 8-173; D 228-0. *Note: A "nay" was a vote in support of the president's position.* May 17, 2019.

218. HR1952. Inter-country Adoption - Passage. Castro, D-Texas, motion to suspend the rules and pass the bill, as amended, that would require the State Department to include in its annual report to Congress on inter-country adoption a list of countries with policies prohibiting or preventing adoption involving immigration to the U.S. and to make the report publicly available. It would require the report to describe the background of such policies and any State Department efforts to help such countries reopen inter-country adoptions, and to assess the impact of adoption fees on families seeking to adopt internationally. Motion agreed to 397-0: R 182-0; D 215-0. *Note: A two-thirds majority of those present and voting (265 in this case) is required for passage under suspension of the rules.* May 20, 2019.

219. HRES106. Denouncing Female Genital Mutilation - Passage. Castro, D-Texas, motion to suspend the rules and agree to the resolution that would express the support of the House of Representatives for international efforts to end female genital mutilation/cutting, denounce such practices as a human rights violation, and urge the State Department and the U.S. Agency for International Development to include efforts to eliminate such practices within their existing gender programming. Motion agreed to 393-0: R 179-0; D 214-0. *Note: A two-thirds majority of those present and voting (262 in this case) is required for passage under suspension of the rules.* May 20, 2019.

220. HR1500, HR1994. Consumer Financial Protection, Retirement Security - Previous Question. Perlmutter, D-Colo., motion to order the previous question (thus ending debate and possibility of amendment) on the rule (H Res 389) that would provide for House floor consideration of the bill (HR 1500) that includes a number of provisions related to Consumer Financial Protection Bureau programs and operations; provide for House floor consideration of the bill (HR 1994) that would modify requirements for retirement plans and retirement accounts; and provide for proceedings during the period from May 24, 2019, through May 31, 2019. Motion agreed to 227-191: R 0-191; D 227-0. May 21, 2019.

221. HR1994, HR1500. Consumer Financial Protection, Retirement Security - Rule. Adoption of the rule (H Res 389) that would provide for House floor consideration of the bill (HR 1500) that includes a number of provisions related to Consumer Financial Protection Bureau programs and operations; provide for House floor consideration of the bill (HR 1994) that would modify requirements for retirement plans and retirement accounts; and provide for proceedings during the period from May 24, 2019, through May 31, 2019. The rule would also provide for the automatic adoption of a Neal, D-Mass., manager's amendment to HR 1994 that would make adjustments to taxes on certain military survivor benefits for children of a parent killed in action and would remove from the bill provisions that would have allowed for up to $10,000 of section 529 funding to be used toward homeschool expenses and non-tuition expenses of private or religious schools. Adopted 230-190: R 0-190; D 230-0. May 21, 2019.

222. HR1500. Consumer Financial Protection Reevaluation - CFPB Effectiveness Study. Steil, R-Wis., amendment that would require the Government Accountability Office to submit a report to Congress on the effectiveness and efficiency of the Consumer Financial Protection Bureau, the prevalence of discriminatory lending practices, and workplace rights of CFPB staff. Rejected in Committee of the Whole 190-234: R 189-1; D 1-232; I 0-1. May 22, 2019.

		217	218	219	220	221	222
ALABAMA							
1	**Byrne**	N	Y	Y	N	N	Y
2	**Roby**	N	Y	Y	N	N	Y
3	**Rogers, M.**	N	Y	Y	N	N	Y
4	**Aderholt**	N	Y	Y	N	N	Y
5	**Brooks, M.**	N	Y	Y	N	N	Y
6	**Palmer**	N	Y	Y	N	N	Y
7	Sewell	Y	Y	Y	Y	Y	N
ALASKA							
AL	Young	?	?	?	?	?	Y
ARIZONA							
1	O'Halleran	Y	Y	Y	Y	Y	N
2	Kirkpatrick	Y	Y	Y	Y	N	N
3	Grijalva	Y	?	?	Y	Y	N
4	**Gosar**	N	Y	Y	N	N	Y
5	**Biggs**	N	Y	Y	N	N	Y
6	**Schweikert**	N	Y	Y	N	N	Y
7	Gallego	Y	Y	Y	Y	Y	N
8	**Lesko**	N	Y	Y	N	N	Y
9	Stanton	Y	Y	Y	Y	Y	N
ARKANSAS							
1	**Crawford**	N	?	?	N	N	Y
2	**Hill, F.**	N	Y	Y	N	N	Y
3	**Womack**	N	Y	Y	N	N	Y
4	**Westerman**	-	Y	Y	N	N	Y
CALIFORNIA							
1	**LaMalfa**	N	Y	Y	N	N	Y
2	Huffman	Y	+	+	Y	Y	N
3	Garamendi	Y	Y	Y	Y	Y	N
4	**McClintock**	N	Y	Y	N	N	Y
5	Thompson, M.	Y	Y	Y	Y	Y	N
6	Matsui	Y	Y	Y	Y	Y	N
7	Bera	Y	Y	Y	Y	Y	N
8	**Cook**	N	Y	Y	N	N	Y
9	McNerney	Y	Y	Y	Y	Y	N
10	Harder	Y	Y	Y	Y	Y	N
11	DeSaulnier	Y	Y	Y	Y	Y	N
12	Pelosi	Y					
13	Lee B.	Y	Y	Y	Y	Y	N
14	Speier	Y	Y	Y	Y	Y	N
15	Swalwell	+	+	+	Y	Y	-
16	Costa	Y	Y	Y	Y	Y	N
17	Khanna	Y	Y	Y	Y	Y	N
18	Eshoo	Y	Y	Y	Y	Y	N
19	Lofgren	Y	Y	Y	Y	Y	N
20	Panetta	Y	Y	Y	Y	Y	N
21	Cox	Y	Y	Y	Y	Y	N
22	**Nunes**	N	Y	Y	N	N	Y
23	**McCarthy**	N	Y	Y	N	N	Y
24	Carbajal	Y	Y	Y	Y	Y	N
25	Hill, K.	Y	Y	Y	Y	Y	N
26	Brownley	Y	Y	Y	Y	Y	N
27	Chu	Y	Y	Y	Y	Y	N
28	Schiff	Y	Y	Y	Y	Y	N
29	Cárdenas	Y	Y	Y	Y	Y	N
30	Sherman	Y	Y	Y	+	Y	N
31	Aguilar	Y	Y	Y	Y	Y	N
32	Napolitano	Y	Y	Y	Y	Y	N
33	Lieu	Y	Y	Y	Y	Y	N
34	Gomez	Y	Y	Y	Y	Y	N
35	Torres	Y	Y	Y	Y	Y	N
36	Ruiz	Y	Y	Y	Y	Y	N
37	Bass	Y	Y	Y	Y	Y	N
38	Sánchez	Y	Y	Y	Y	Y	N
39	Cisneros	Y	Y	Y	Y	Y	N
40	Roybal-Allard	Y	Y	Y	Y	Y	N
41	Takano	Y	Y	Y	Y	Y	N
42	**Calvert**	N	Y	Y	N	N	Y
43	Waters	Y	Y	Y	Y	Y	N
44	Barragán	Y	Y	Y	Y	Y	N
45	Porter	Y	+	+	Y	Y	N
46	Correa	Y	Y	Y	Y	Y	N
47	Lowenthal	Y	Y	Y	Y	Y	N
48	Rouda	Y	Y	Y	Y	Y	N
49	Levin	Y	Y	Y	Y	Y	N
50	**Hunter**	N	Y	Y	N	N	Y
51	Vargas	Y	Y	Y	Y	Y	N
52	Peters	Y	Y	Y	Y	Y	N

		217	218	219	220	221	222
53	Davis, S.	Y	Y	Y	Y	Y	N
COLORADO							
1	DeGette	Y	Y	Y	Y	Y	N
2	Neguse	Y	Y	Y	Y	Y	N
3	**Tipton**	N	Y	Y	N	N	Y
4	**Buck**	N	Y	Y	N	N	Y
5	**Lamborn**	N	Y	Y	N	N	?
6	Crow	Y	Y	Y	Y	Y	N
7	Perlmutter	Y	Y	Y	Y	Y	N
CONNECTICUT							
1	Larson	Y	Y	Y	Y	Y	N
2	Courtney	Y	Y	Y	Y	Y	N
3	DeLauro	Y	+	+	Y	Y	N
4	Himes	Y	Y	Y	Y	Y	N
5	Hayes	Y	Y	Y	Y	Y	N
DELAWARE							
AL	Blunt Rochester	Y	Y	Y	Y	Y	N
FLORIDA							
1	**Gaetz**	N	Y	Y	N	N	Y
2	**Dunn**	N	Y	Y	N	N	Y
3	Yoho	N	Y	Y	N	N	Y
4	**Rutherford**	N	Y	Y	N	N	Y
5	Lawson	Y	Y	Y	Y	Y	N
6	**Waltz**	N	Y	Y	N	N	Y
7	Murphy	Y	Y	Y	Y	Y	N
8	**Posey**	N	Y	Y	N	N	Y
9	Soto	Y	Y	Y	Y	Y	N
10	Demings	Y	Y	Y	Y	Y	N
11	**Webster**	N	Y	Y	N	N	Y
12	**Bilirakis**	N	Y	Y	N	N	Y
13	Crist	Y	Y	Y	Y	Y	N
14	Castor	Y	?	?	?	?	N
15	**Spano**	N	Y	Y	N	N	Y
16	**Buchanan**	N	Y	Y	N	N	Y
17	**Steube**	-	Y	Y	N	N	Y
18	**Mast**	N	Y	Y	N	N	Y
19	**Rooney**	N	?	?	N	N	Y
20	Hastings	Y	Y	Y	Y	Y	N
21	Frankel	Y	Y	Y	Y	Y	N
22	Deutch	Y	Y	Y	Y	Y	N
23	Wasserman Schultz	Y	Y	Y	Y	Y	N
24	Wilson, F.	Y	?	?	Y	Y	N
25	**Diaz-Balart**	Y	Y	Y	N	N	Y
26	Mucarsel-Powell	Y	Y	Y	Y	Y	N
27	Shalala	Y	Y	Y	?	Y	N
GEORGIA							
1	**Carter, E.L.**	N	Y	Y	N	N	Y
2	Bishop, S.	Y	Y	Y	Y	Y	N
3	**Ferguson**	N	Y	Y	N	N	Y
4	Johnson, H.	Y	Y	Y	Y	Y	N
5	Lewis John	Y	Y	Y	Y	Y	N
6	McBath	Y	Y	Y	Y	Y	N
7	**Woodall**	N	Y	Y	N	N	Y
8	**Scott, A.**	N	Y	Y	N	N	Y
9	**Collins, D.**	N	Y	Y	N	N	Y
10	**Hice**	N	Y	Y	N	N	Y
11	**Loudermilk**	N	Y	Y	N	N	Y
12	**Allen**	N	Y	Y	N	N	Y
13	Scott, D.	Y	Y	Y	Y	Y	N
14	**Graves, T.**	N	Y	Y	N	N	Y
HAWAII							
1	Case	Y	Y	Y	Y	Y	N
2	Gabbard	Y	Y	Y	Y	Y	N
IDAHO							
1	**Fulcher**	N	Y	Y	?	?	Y
2	**Simpson**	N	Y	Y	N	N	Y
ILLINOIS							
1	Rush	Y	?	?	?	?	N
2	Kelly, R.	Y	Y	Y	Y	Y	N
3	Lipinski	Y	Y	Y	Y	Y	N
4	García, J.	Y	Y	Y	Y	Y	N
5	Quigley	Y	Y	Y	Y	Y	N
6	Casten	Y	Y	Y	Y	Y	N
7	Davis, D.	Y	Y	Y	Y	Y	N
8	Krishnamoorthi	Y	Y	Y	Y	Y	N
9	Schakowsky	Y	Y	Y	Y	Y	N
10	Schneider	Y	Y	Y	Y	Y	N
11	Foster	Y	Y	Y	Y	Y	N

KEY:	**Republicans**	Democrats	*Independents*

Y Voted for (yea)	**N** Voted against (nay)	**P** Voted "present"	
+ Announced for	**-** Announced against	**?** Did not vote or otherwise	
# Paired for	**X** Paired against	make position known	

		217	218	219	220	221	222
12	**Bost**	N	Y	Y	N	N	Y
13	**Davis, R.**	N	Y	Y	N	N	Y
14	Underwood	Y	Y	Y	Y	Y	N
15	**Shimkus**	N	?	?	N	N	Y
16	**Kinzinger**	N	Y	Y	N	N	+
17	Bustos	Y	Y	Y	Y	Y	N
18	**LaHood**	-	Y	Y	N	N	Y
INDIANA							
1	Visclosky	Y	Y	Y	Y	Y	N
2	**Walorski**	N	?	+	N	N	Y
3	**Banks**	N	Y	Y	N	N	Y
4	**Baird**	N	Y	?	N	N	Y
5	**Brooks, S.**	Y	Y	Y	N	N	Y
6	**Pence**	N	Y	Y	N	N	Y
7	Carson	Y	Y	Y	Y	Y	N
8	**Bucshon**	-	Y	Y	N	N	Y
9	**Hollingsworth**	N	Y	Y	N	N	Y
IOWA							
1	Finkenauer	Y	Y	Y	Y	Y	N
2	Loebsack	Y	Y	Y	Y	Y	N
3	Axne	Y	Y	Y	Y	Y	N
4	**King, S.**	N	Y	Y	N	N	Y
KANSAS							
1	**Marshall**	N	?	?	N	N	Y
2	**Watkins**	N	Y	Y	N	N	Y
3	Davids	Y	Y	Y	Y	Y	N
4	**Estes**	N	Y	Y	N	N	Y
KENTUCKY							
1	**Comer**	N	Y	Y	N	N	Y
2	**Guthrie**	N	Y	Y	N	N	Y
3	Yarmuth	Y	Y	Y	Y	Y	N
4	**Massie**	N	Y	Y	N	N	Y
5	**Rogers, H.**	N	Y	Y	N	N	Y
6	**Barr**	N	Y	Y	N	N	Y
LOUISIANA							
1	**Scalise**	N	Y	Y	N	N	Y
2	Richmond	Y	Y	Y	Y	Y	N
3	**Higgins, C.**	N	Y	Y	N	N	Y
4	**Johnson, M.**	-	Y	Y	N	N	Y
5	**Abraham**	N	?	?	?	?	Y
6	**Graves, G.**	N	Y	Y	N	N	Y
MAINE							
1	Pingree	Y	Y	Y	Y	Y	N
2	Golden	Y	Y	Y	Y	Y	N
MARYLAND							
1	**Harris**	N	Y	Y	N	N	Y
2	Ruppersberger	Y	Y	Y	Y	Y	N
3	Sarbanes	Y	Y	Y	Y	Y	N
4	Brown, A.	Y	Y	Y	Y	Y	N
5	Hoyer	Y	Y	Y	Y	Y	N
6	Trone	Y	Y	Y	Y	Y	N
7	Cummings	Y	Y	Y	Y	Y	N
8	Raskin	Y	Y	Y	Y	Y	N
MASSACHUSETTS							
1	Neal	Y	Y	Y	Y	Y	N
2	McGovern	Y	Y	Y	Y	Y	N
3	Trahan	Y	Y	Y	Y	Y	N
4	Kennedy	Y	Y	Y	Y	Y	N
5	Clark	Y	Y	Y	Y	Y	N
6	Moulton	?	Y	Y	Y	Y	N
7	Pressley	Y	Y	Y	Y	Y	N
8	Lynch	Y	Y	Y	Y	Y	N
9	Keating	Y	Y	Y	Y	Y	N
MICHIGAN							
1	**Bergman**	N	Y	Y	N	N	Y
2	**Huizenga**	N	+	+	+	-	Y
3	**Amash**	N	Y	Y	N	N	N
4	**Moolenaar**	N	Y	Y	N	N	Y
5	Kildee	Y	Y	Y	Y	Y	N
6	**Upton**	N	Y	Y	N	-	Y
7	**Walberg**	N	Y	Y	N	N	Y
8	Slotkin	Y	Y	Y	Y	Y	N
9	Levin	Y	Y	Y	Y	Y	N
10	**Mitchell**	N	Y	Y	N	N	Y
11	Stevens	Y	Y	Y	Y	Y	N
12	Dingell	?	Y	Y	Y	Y	N
13	Tlaib	Y	+	Y	Y	Y	N
14	Lawrence	Y	Y	Y	Y	Y	N
MINNESOTA							
1	**Hagedorn**	N	Y	Y	N	N	Y
2	Craig	Y	Y	Y	Y	Y	N
3	Phillips	Y	Y	Y	Y	Y	N
4	McCollum	Y	Y	Y	Y	Y	N
5	Omar	Y	Y	Y	Y	Y	N

		217	218	219	220	221	222
6	**Emmer**	N	Y	Y	N	N	Y
7	Peterson	?	Y	Y	Y	Y	N
8	**Stauber**	N	Y	Y	N	N	Y
MISSISSIPPI							
1	**Kelly, T.**	N	Y	Y	N	N	Y
2	Thompson, B.	Y	Y	Y	Y	Y	N
3	**Guest**	N	Y	Y	N	N	Y
4	**Palazzo**	N	Y	Y	N	N	Y
MISSOURI							
1	Clay	Y	Y	Y	Y	Y	N
2	**Wagner**	N	Y	Y	N	N	Y
3	**Luetkemeyer**	N	Y	Y	N	N	Y
4	**Hartzler**	N	Y	Y	N	N	+
5	Cleaver	Y	Y	Y	Y	Y	N
6	**Graves, S.**	N	Y	Y	N	N	Y
7	**Long**	N	Y	Y	N	N	Y
8	**Smith, J.**	N	Y	Y	N	N	Y
MONTANA							
AL	**Gianforte**	N	Y	Y	N	N	Y
NEBRASKA							
1	**Fortenberry**	N	Y	Y	N	N	Y
2	**Bacon**	N	Y	Y	N	N	Y
3	**Smith, Adrian**	N	Y	Y	N	N	Y
NEVADA							
1	Titus	Y	Y	Y	Y	Y	N
2	**Amodei**	N	Y	Y	N	N	Y
3	Lee	Y	Y	Y	Y	Y	N
4	Horsford	Y	Y	Y	Y	Y	N
NEW HAMPSHIRE							
1	Pappas	Y	Y	Y	Y	Y	N
2	Kuster	Y	Y	Y	Y	Y	N
NEW JERSEY							
1	Norcross	Y	Y	Y	Y	Y	?
2	Van Drew	Y	Y	Y	Y	Y	N
3	Kim	Y	Y	Y	Y	Y	N
4	**Smith, C.**	N	Y	Y	N	N	Y
5	Gottheimer	Y	Y	+	Y	Y	N
6	Pallone	Y	?	?	Y	Y	N
7	Malinowski	Y	Y	Y	Y	Y	N
8	Sires	Y	Y	Y	Y	Y	N
9	Pascrell	Y	Y	Y	Y	Y	N
10	Payne	Y	Y	Y	+	+	-
11	Sherrill	Y	Y	Y	Y	Y	N
12	Watson Coleman	Y	Y	Y	Y	Y	N
NEW MEXICO							
1	Haaland	Y	Y	Y	Y	Y	N
2	Torres Small	Y	Y	Y	Y	Y	N
3	Luján	Y	Y	Y	Y	Y	N
NEW YORK							
1	**Zeldin**	N	Y	Y	N	N	Y
2	**King, P.**	N	Y	Y	N	N	Y
3	Suozzi	Y	Y	Y	Y	Y	N
4	Rice, K.	Y	?	?	Y	Y	N
5	Meeks	Y	Y	Y	Y	Y	?
6	Meng	Y	?	?	Y	Y	N
7	Velázquez	Y	Y	Y	Y	Y	N
8	Jeffries	Y	Y	Y	Y	Y	N
9	Clarke	Y	Y	Y	Y	Y	N
10	Nadler	Y	Y	Y	Y	Y	N
11	Rose	+	Y	Y	Y	Y	N
12	Maloney, C.	Y	Y	Y	Y	Y	N
13	Espaillat	Y	Y	Y	Y	Y	N
14	Ocasio-Cortez	Y	Y	Y	Y	Y	N
15	Serrano	Y	Y	Y	Y	Y	N
16	Engel	Y	Y	Y	Y	Y	N
17	Lowey	Y	Y	Y	Y	Y	N
18	Maloney, S.P.	Y	Y	Y	Y	Y	N
19	Delgado	Y	Y	Y	Y	Y	N
20	Tonko	Y	Y	Y	Y	Y	N
21	**Stefanik**	Y	Y	Y	N	N	Y
22	Brindisi	Y	Y	Y	Y	Y	N
23	**Reed**	Y	Y	Y	N	N	Y
24	**Katko**	Y	Y	Y	N	N	Y
25	Morelle	Y	Y	Y	Y	Y	N
26	Higgins, B.	Y	Y	Y	Y	Y	N
27	**Collins, C.**						
NORTH CAROLINA							
1	Butterfield	Y	Y	?	Y	Y	N
2	**Holding**	N	Y	Y	N	N	Y
3	**Jones***						
4	Price	Y	Y	Y	Y	Y	N
5	**Foxx**	N	Y	Y	N	N	Y
6	**Walker**	?	Y	Y	N	N	?
7	**Rouzer**	N	?	?	N	N	Y

		217	218	219	220	221	222
8	**Hudson**	N	Y	Y	N	N	+
9	vacant						
10	**McHenry**	N	Y	Y	N	N	Y
11	**Meadows**	N	Y	?	N	N	Y
12	Adams	Y	Y	Y	Y	Y	N
13	**Budd**	N	Y	Y	N	N	Y
NORTH DAKOTA							
AL	**Armstrong**	N	Y	Y	N	N	?
OHIO							
1	**Chabot**	N	Y	Y	N	N	Y
2	**Wenstrup**	N	Y	Y	N	N	Y
3	Beatty	Y	Y	Y	Y	Y	N
4	**Jordan**	N	Y	Y	N	N	Y
5	**Latta**	N	Y	Y	N	N	Y
6	**Johnson, B.**	-	Y	Y	N	N	Y
7	**Gibbs**	N	Y	Y	N	N	Y
8	**Davidson**	N	Y	Y	N	N	Y
9	Kaptur	Y	?	?	Y	Y	N
10	**Turner**	-	Y	Y	N	N	+
11	Fudge	Y	Y	Y	Y	Y	N
12	**Balderson**	N	Y	Y	N	N	Y
13	Ryan	?	?	?	Y	Y	N
14	**Joyce**	N	Y	Y	N	N	Y
15	**Stivers**	N	Y	Y	N	N	?
16	**Gonzalez**	N	Y	Y	N	N	Y
OKLAHOMA							
1	**Hern**	N	Y	Y	N	N	Y
2	**Mullin**	N	Y	Y	N	N	Y
3	**Lucas**	N	Y	Y	N	N	Y
4	**Cole**	N	Y	Y	N	N	Y
5	Horn	Y	Y	Y	Y	Y	N
OREGON							
1	Bonamici	Y	Y	Y	Y	Y	N
2	**Walden**	Y	+	+	N	N	Y
3	Blumenauer	Y	Y	Y	Y	Y	N
4	DeFazio	Y	Y	+	Y	Y	N
5	Schrader	Y	?	?	Y	Y	N
PENNSYLVANIA							
1	**Fitzpatrick**	Y	Y	Y	N	N	Y
2	Boyle	Y	Y	Y	?	?	N
3	Evans	Y	Y	Y	Y	Y	N
4	Dean	Y	Y	Y	Y	Y	N
5	Scanlon	Y	Y	Y	Y	Y	N
6	Houlahan	Y	Y	Y	Y	Y	N
7	Wild	Y	Y	Y	Y	Y	N
8	Cartwright	Y	?	?	Y	Y	N
9	**Meuser**	N	?	?	N	N	Y
10	**Perry**	N	+	+	N	N	Y
11	**Smucker**	-	Y	Y	N	N	Y
12	**Marino***						
13	**Joyce**	N	Y	Y	N	N	Y
14	**Reschenthaler**	N	Y	Y	N	N	Y
15	**Thompson, G.**	N	?	?	N	N	Y
16	**Kelly, M.**	N	Y	Y	N	N	Y
17	Lamb	Y	Y	Y	Y	Y	N
18	Doyle	Y	Y	Y	Y	Y	N
RHODE ISLAND							
1	Cicilline	Y	Y	Y	Y	Y	N
2	Langevin	Y	Y	Y	Y	Y	N
SOUTH CAROLINA							
1	Cunningham	Y	Y	Y	Y	Y	N
2	**Wilson, J.**	-	?	?	?	?	Y
3	**Duncan**	N	Y	Y	N	N	Y
4	**Timmons**	N	Y	Y	N	N	Y
5	**Norman**	N	Y	Y	N	N	Y
6	Clyburn	+	Y	Y	Y	Y	N
7	**Rice, T.**	N	Y	Y	N	N	Y
SOUTH DAKOTA							
AL	**Johnson**	N	Y	Y	N	N	Y
TENNESSEE							
1	**Roe**	N	Y	Y	N	N	Y
2	**Burchett**	-	Y	Y	N	N	Y
3	**Fleischmann**	N	Y	Y	N	N	Y
4	**DesJarlais**	N	Y	Y	N	N	Y
5	Cooper	Y	Y	Y	Y	Y	N
6	**Rose**	N	Y	Y	N	N	Y
7	**Green**	N	Y	Y	N	N	Y
8	**Kustoff**	N	Y	Y	N	N	Y
9	Cohen	Y	Y	Y	Y	Y	N
TEXAS							
1	**Gohmert**	N	Y	Y	N	N	Y
2	**Crenshaw**	N	Y	Y	N	N	Y
3	**Taylor**	N	Y	Y	N	N	Y
4	**Ratcliffe**	?	Y	Y	N	N	Y

		217	218	219	220	221	222
5	**Gooden**	N	Y	Y	N	N	Y
6	**Wright**	N	Y	Y	N	N	Y
7	Fletcher	Y	Y	Y	Y	Y	N
8	**Brady**	-	Y	Y	N	N	Y
9	Green, A.	Y	Y	Y	Y	Y	N
10	**McCaul**	N	Y	Y	N	N	Y
11	**Conaway**	N	Y	Y	N	N	Y
12	**Granger**	N	Y	Y	N	N	Y
13	**Thornberry**	N	Y	?	N	N	Y
14	**Weber**	?	Y	Y	N	N	Y
15	Gonzalez	Y	Y	Y	Y	Y	N
16	Escobar	Y	Y	Y	Y	Y	N
17	**Flores**	N	Y	Y	N	N	Y
18	Jackson Lee	Y	Y	Y	Y	Y	N
19	**Arrington**	N	Y	Y	N	N	Y
20	Castro	Y	Y	Y	Y	Y	N
21	**Roy**	N	Y	Y	N	N	Y
22	**Olson**	N	Y	Y	N	N	Y
23	**Hurd**	Y	Y	Y	N	N	Y
24	**Marchant**	N	Y	Y	N	N	Y
25	**Williams**	N	Y	Y	N	N	Y
26	**Burgess**	N	Y	Y	N	N	Y
27	**Cloud**	N	Y	Y	N	N	Y
28	Cuellar	Y	Y	Y	Y	Y	N
29	Garcia, S.	Y	Y	Y	Y	Y	N
30	Johnson, E.B.	Y	Y	Y	Y	Y	N
31	**Carter, J.**	N	Y	Y	N	N	Y
32	Allred	Y	Y	Y	Y	Y	N
33	Veasey	Y	Y	Y	Y	Y	N
34	Vela	Y	Y	Y	Y	Y	N
35	Doggett	Y	?	Y	Y	Y	N
36	**Babin**	N	Y	Y	N	N	Y
UTAH							
1	**Bishop, R.**	N	Y	Y	N	N	Y
2	**Stewart**	N	Y	Y	N	N	Y
3	**Curtis**	N	Y	Y	N	N	Y
4	McAdams	Y	Y	Y	Y	Y	N
VERMONT							
AL	Welch	Y	Y	Y	Y	Y	N
VIRGINIA							
1	**Wittman**	N	Y	Y	N	N	Y
2	Luria	Y	Y	Y	Y	Y	N
3	Scott, R.	Y	Y	Y	Y	Y	N
4	McEachin	Y	Y	Y	Y	Y	N
5	**Riggleman**	N	Y	Y	N	N	Y
6	**Cline**	N	Y	Y	N	N	Y
7	Spanberger	Y	Y	Y	Y	Y	N
8	Beyer	Y	Y	Y	Y	Y	N
9	**Griffith**	N	Y	Y	N	N	Y
10	Wexton	Y	Y	Y	Y	Y	N
11	Connolly	Y	Y	Y	Y	Y	N
WASHINGTON							
1	DelBene	Y	Y	Y	Y	Y	N
2	Larsen	Y	Y	Y	Y	Y	N
3	**Herrera Beutler**	N	?	?	?	?	?
4	**Newhouse**	N	Y	Y	N	N	Y
5	**McMorris Rodgers**	N	Y	Y	N	N	Y
6	Kilmer	Y	Y	Y	Y	Y	N
7	Jayapal	Y	Y	Y	?	Y	N
8	Schrier	Y	Y	Y	Y	Y	N
9	Smith Adam	Y	+	+	Y	Y	N
10	Heck	Y	Y	Y	Y	Y	N
WEST VIRGINIA							
1	**McKinley**	N	Y	Y	N	N	Y
2	**Mooney**	N	Y	Y	N	N	Y
3	**Miller**	N	Y	Y	N	N	Y
WISCONSIN							
1	**Steil**	N	Y	Y	N	N	Y
2	Pocan	Y	+	+	Y	Y	N
3	Kind	Y	Y	Y	Y	Y	N
4	Moore	Y	Y	Y	Y	Y	N
5	**Sensenbrenner**	N	Y	Y	N	N	Y
6	**Grothman**	N	Y	Y	N	N	Y
7	**Duffy**						
8	**Gallagher**	N	Y	Y	N	N	Y
WYOMING							
AL	**Cheney**	N	Y	Y	N	N	Y
DELEGATES							
	Radewagen (A.S.)						Y
	Norton (D.C.)						N
	San Nicolas (Guam)						N
	Sablan (N. Marianas)						N
	González-Colón (P.R.)						Y
	Plaskett (V.I.)						N

⦀ HOUSE VOTES

223. HR1500. Consumer Financial Protection Reevaluation - Consumer Complaints. Burgess, R-Texas, amendment that would remove from the bill a section that would require all consumer complaints to be made publicly available on the Consumer Financial Protection Bureau website. Rejected in Committee of the Whole 191-236: R 191-2; D 0-233, I 0-1. May 22, 2019.

224. HR1500. Consumer Financial Protection Reevaluation - CFPB Funding. Burgess, R-Texas, amendment that would subject Consumer Financial Protection Bureau funding to congressional appropriations and authorize fiscal 2020 funding for the CFPB equal to the aggregate funds transferred to the agency by the Federal Reserve Board in fiscal 2019. Rejected in Committee of the Whole 192-235: R 192-1; D 0-233; I 0-1. May 22, 2019.

225. HR1500. Consumer Financial Protection Reevaluation - Advisory Board Appointments. Stevens, D-Mich., amendment that would require the Consumer Financial Protection Bureau to consider appointing experts in U.S. economic growth and jobs and individuals representing industries affected by the CFPB, including community banks, credit unions, and small business owners, to CFPB consumer advisory board. Adopted in Committee of the Whole 418-10: R 183-10; D 234-0; I 1-0. May 22, 2019.

226. HR1500. Consumer Financial Protection Reevaluation - Prohibiting Arbitration Agreements. Green, D-Texas, amendment that would require the Consumer Financial Protection Bureau to reissue a 2017 rule prohibiting arbitration agreements between consumers and providers of consumer financial products, such as credit card companies, that bar consumers from participating in class action lawsuits against providers. It would repeal a joint resolution that overturned the 2017 rule. It would also reduce by $10 million surplus discretionary funds that may be held by the Federal Reserve. Adopted in Committee of the Whole 235-193: R 1-192; D 233-1; I 1-0. May 22, 2019.

227. HR1500. Consumer Financial Protection Reevaluation - Recommit. Steil, R-Wis., motion to recommit the bill to the House Financial Services Committee with instructions to report it back immediately with an amendment that would clarify that no funds from civil penalties collected by the Consumer Financial Protection Bureau could be used for purposes other than compensating "actual victims" of activities for which civil penalties have been imposed under federal consumer financial laws. Under existing law, the CFPB may use such funds for the purpose of consumer education and financial literacy programs. Motion rejected 191-231: R 191-0; D 0-231. May 22, 2019.

228. HR1500. Consumer Financial Protection Reevaluation - Passage. Passage of the bill, as amended, that would statutorily clarify and establish certain objectives, authorities, and offices of the Consumer Financial Protection Bureau. Among provisions related to CFPB organization and authorities, the bill would require the CFPB director to ensure each statutorily established functional unit of the agency performs its assigned duties and functions; require the director to provide "adequate staff" to each unit to carry out these functions; and prohibit the director from reorganizing or renaming such units. It would statutorily reestablish a CFPB Office of Students and Young Consumers to inform students and young people about education-related savings, loans, and debt. It would statutorily authorize the CFPB Office of Fair Lending and Equal Opportunity to carry out any supervisory and enforcement activities regarding fair lending laws. It would statutorily designate the CFPB as the Consumer Financial Protection Bureau, replacing any references in federal laws and documents to the "Bureau of Consumer Financial Protection." Among other provisions, the bill would require the CFPB director to ensure the number and duties of political appointees on staff match those of such appointees at other federal financial regulatory agencies. It would add certain qualifications for CFPB consumer advisory board members, urging the CFPB director to appoint certain experts and representatives, including experts in consumer protection, community development, and fair lending, and representatives of communities "significantly impacted" by higher-priced mortgage loans. It would require the CFPB database of consumer complaints to remain publicly available on the CFPB website. As an offset for its provisions, the bill, as amended, would reduce by a total of $38 million the amount of discretionary surplus funds that may be held by the Federal Reserve. As amended, the bill would require the Consumer Financial Protection Bureau to reissue a 2017 rule prohibiting arbitration agreements between consumers and providers of consumer financial products, such as credit card companies, that bar consumers from participating in class action lawsuits against providers. It would reinstate memoranda of understanding between the CFPB and Education Department regarding coordination of oversight related to federal student loans. Passed 231-191: R 0-191; D 231-0. *Note: A "nay" was a vote in support of the president's position.* May 22, 2019.

		223	224	225	226	227	228
ALABAMA							
1	**Byrne**	Y	Y	Y	N	Y	N
2	**Roby**	Y	Y	Y	N	Y	N
3	**Rogers, M.**	Y	Y	Y	N	Y	N
4	**Aderholt**	Y	Y	Y	N	Y	N
5	**Brooks, M.**	Y	Y	Y	N	Y	N
6	**Palmer**	Y	Y	Y	N	Y	N
7	Sewell	N	N	Y	Y	N	Y
ALASKA							
AL	**Young**	Y	Y	Y	N	Y	N
ARIZONA							
1	O'Halleran	N	N	Y	Y	N	Y
2	Kirkpatrick	N	N	Y	Y	N	Y
3	Grijalva	N	N	Y	Y	N	Y
4	**Gosar**	Y	Y	Y	N	Y	N
5	**Biggs**	Y	N	N	N	Y	N
6	**Schweikert**	Y	Y	Y	N	Y	N
7	Gallego	N	N	Y	Y	N	Y
8	**Lesko**	Y	Y	Y	N	Y	N
9	Stanton	N	N	Y	Y	N	Y
ARKANSAS							
1	**Crawford**	Y	Y	Y	N	Y	N
2	**Hill, F.**	Y	Y	Y	N	Y	N
3	**Womack**	Y	Y	Y	N	Y	N
4	**Westerman**	Y	Y	Y	N	Y	N
CALIFORNIA							
1	**LaMalfa**	Y	Y	N	N	Y	N
2	Huffman	N	N	Y	Y	N	Y
3	Garamendi	N	N	Y	Y	N	Y
4	**McClintock**	Y	Y	N	N	Y	N
5	Thompson, M.	N	N	Y	Y	N	Y
6	Matsui	N	N	Y	Y	N	Y
7	Bera	N	N	Y	Y	N	Y
8	**Cook**	Y	Y	Y	N	Y	N
9	McNerney	N	N	Y	Y	N	Y
10	Harder	N	N	Y	Y	N	Y
11	DeSaulnier	N	N	Y	Y	N	Y
12	Pelosi						
13	Lee B.	N	N	Y	Y	N	Y
14	Speier	N	N	Y	Y	N	Y
15	Swalwell	-	-	+	+	-	+
16	Costa	N	N	Y	Y	N	Y
17	Khanna	N	N	Y	Y	N	Y
18	Eshoo	N	N	Y	Y	N	Y
19	Lofgren	N	N	Y	Y	N	Y
20	Panetta	N	N	Y	Y	N	Y
21	Cox	N	N	Y	Y	N	Y
22	**Nunes**	Y	Y	Y	N	Y	N
23	**McCarthy**	Y	Y	Y	N	Y	N
24	Carbajal	N	N	Y	Y	N	Y
25	Hill, K.	N	N	Y	Y	N	Y
26	Brownley	N	N	Y	Y	N	Y
27	Chu	N	N	Y	Y	N	Y
28	Schiff	N	N	Y	Y	N	Y
29	Cárdenas	N	N	Y	Y	N	Y
30	Sherman	N	N	Y	Y	N	Y
31	Aguilar	N	N	Y	Y	N	Y
32	Napolitano	N	N	Y	Y	N	Y
33	Lieu	N	N	Y	Y	N	Y
34	Gomez	N	N	Y	Y	N	Y
35	Torres	N	N	Y	Y	N	Y
36	Ruiz	N	N	Y	Y	N	Y
37	Bass	N	N	Y	Y	N	Y
38	Sánchez	N	N	Y	Y	N	Y
39	Cisneros	N	N	Y	Y	N	Y
40	Roybal-Allard	N	N	Y	Y	N	Y
41	Takano	N	N	Y	Y	N	Y
42	**Calvert**	Y	Y	Y	N	Y	N
43	Waters	N	N	Y	Y	N	Y
44	Barragán	N	N	Y	Y	N	Y
45	Porter	N	N	Y	Y	N	Y
46	Correa	N	N	Y	Y	N	Y
47	Lowenthal	N	N	Y	Y	N	Y
48	Rouda	N	N	Y	Y	N	Y
49	Levin	N	N	Y	Y	N	Y
50	**Hunter**	Y	Y	Y	N	Y	N
51	Vargas	N	N	Y	Y	N	Y
52	Peters	N	N	Y	Y	N	Y

		223	224	225	226	227	228
53	Davis, S.	N	N	Y	Y	N	Y
COLORADO							
1	DeGette	N	N	Y	Y	N	Y
2	Neguse	N	N	Y	Y	N	Y
3	**Tipton**	Y	Y	Y	N	Y	N
4	**Buck**	Y	Y	Y	N	Y	N
5	**Lamborn**	Y	Y	Y	N	Y	N
6	Crow	N	N	Y	Y	N	Y
7	Perlmutter	N	N	Y	Y	N	Y
CONNECTICUT							
1	Larson	N	N	Y	Y	N	Y
2	Courtney	N	N	Y	Y	N	Y
3	DeLauro	N	N	Y	Y	N	Y
4	Himes	N	N	Y	Y	N	Y
5	Hayes	N	N	Y	Y	N	Y
DELAWARE							
AL	Blunt Rochester	N	N	Y	Y	N	Y
FLORIDA							
1	**Gaetz**	N	Y	N	N	Y	N
2	**Dunn**	Y	Y	Y	N	Y	N
3	**Yoho**	Y	Y	Y	N	Y	N
4	**Rutherford**	Y	Y	Y	N	Y	N
5	Lawson	N	N	Y	Y	N	Y
6	**Waltz**	Y	Y	Y	N	Y	N
7	Murphy	N	N	Y	Y	N	Y
8	**Posey**	Y	Y	Y	N	Y	N
9	Soto	N	N	Y	Y	N	Y
10	Demings	N	N	Y	Y	N	Y
11	**Webster**	Y	Y	Y	N	Y	N
12	**Bilirakis**	Y	Y	Y	N	Y	N
13	Crist	N	N	Y	Y	N	Y
14	Castor	N	N	Y	Y	N	Y
15	**Spano**	Y	Y	Y	N	Y	N
16	**Buchanan**	Y	Y	Y	N	Y	N
17	**Steube**	Y	Y	Y	N	Y	N
18	**Mast**	Y	Y	Y	N	Y	N
19	**Rooney**	Y	Y	Y	N	Y	N
20	Hastings	N	N	Y	Y	N	Y
21	Frankel	N	N	Y	Y	N	Y
22	Deutch	N	N	Y	Y	N	Y
23	Wasserman Schultz	N	N	Y	Y	N	Y
24	Wilson, F.	N	N	Y	Y	N	Y
25	**Diaz-Balart**	Y	Y	Y	N	Y	N
26	Mucarsel-Powell	N	N	Y	Y	N	Y
27	Shalala	N	N	Y	Y	N	Y
GEORGIA							
1	**Carter, E.L.**	Y	Y	Y	N	Y	N
2	Bishop, S.	N	N	Y	Y	N	Y
3	**Ferguson**	Y	Y	N	N	Y	N
4	Johnson, H.	N	N	Y	Y	N	Y
5	Lewis John	N	N	Y	Y	N	Y
6	McBath	N	N	Y	Y	N	Y
7	**Woodall**	Y	Y	Y	N	Y	N
8	**Scott, A.**	Y	Y	Y	N	Y	N
9	**Collins, D.**	Y	Y	Y	N	Y	N
10	**Hice**	Y	Y	Y	N	Y	N
11	**Loudermilk**	Y	Y	Y	N	Y	N
12	**Allen**	Y	Y	Y	N	Y	N
13	Scott, D.	N	N	Y	Y	N	Y
14	**Graves, T.**	Y	Y	Y	N	Y	N
HAWAII							
1	Case	N	N	Y	Y	N	Y
2	Gabbard	N	N	Y	Y	N	Y
IDAHO							
1	**Fulcher**	Y	Y	Y	N	Y	N
2	**Simpson**	Y	Y	Y	N	Y	N
ILLINOIS							
1	Rush	N	N	Y	Y	N	Y
2	Kelly, R.	N	N	Y	Y	N	Y
3	Lipinski	N	N	Y	Y	N	Y
4	García, J.	N	N	Y	Y	N	Y
5	Quigley	N	N	Y	Y	N	Y
6	Casten	N	N	Y	Y	N	Y
7	Davis, D.	N	N	Y	Y	N	Y
8	Krishnamoorthi	N	N	Y	Y	N	Y
9	Schakowsky	N	N	Y	Y	N	Y
10	Schneider	N	N	Y	Y	N	Y
11	Foster	N	N	Y	Y	N	Y

		223	224	225	226	227	228
12	**Bost**	Y	Y	Y	N	Y	N
13	**Davis, R.**	Y	Y	Y	N	Y	N
14	Underwood	N	N	Y	Y	N	Y
15	**Shimkus**	Y	Y	Y	N	Y	N
16	**Kinzinger**	+	+	+	-	+	-
17	Bustos	N	N	Y	Y	N	Y
18	**LaHood**	Y	Y	Y	N	Y	N
INDIANA							
1	Visclosky	N	N	Y	Y	N	Y
2	**Walorski**	Y	Y	Y	N	Y	N
3	**Banks**	Y	Y	Y	N	Y	N
4	**Baird**	Y	Y	Y	N	Y	N
5	**Brooks, S.**	Y	Y	Y	N	Y	N
6	**Pence**	Y	Y	Y	N	Y	N
7	Carson	N	N	Y	Y	N	Y
8	**Bucshon**	Y	Y	Y	N	Y	N
9	**Hollingsworth**	Y	Y	Y	N	Y	N
IOWA							
1	Finkenauer	N	N	Y	Y	N	Y
2	Loebsack	N	N	Y	Y	N	Y
3	Axne	N	N	Y	Y	N	Y
4	**King, S.**	Y	Y	N	N	Y	N
KANSAS							
1	**Marshall**	Y	Y	Y	N	Y	N
2	**Watkins**	Y	Y	Y	N	Y	N
3	Davids	N	N	Y	Y	N	Y
4	**Estes**	Y	Y	Y	N	Y	N
KENTUCKY							
1	**Comer**	Y	Y	Y	N	Y	N
2	**Guthrie**	Y	Y	Y	N	Y	N
3	Yarmuth	N	?	Y	Y	N	Y
4	**Massie**	Y	Y	Y	N	Y	N
5	**Rogers, H.**	Y	Y	Y	N	Y	N
6	**Barr**	Y	Y	Y	N	Y	N
LOUISIANA							
1	**Scalise**	Y	Y	Y	N	Y	N
2	Richmond	N	N	Y	Y	N	Y
3	**Higgins, C.**	Y	Y	Y	N	Y	N
4	**Johnson, M.**	Y	Y	Y	N	Y	N
5	**Abraham**	Y	Y	Y	N	Y	N
6	**Graves, G.**	Y	Y	Y	N	Y	N
MAINE							
1	Pingree	N	N	Y	Y	N	Y
2	Golden	N	N	Y	Y	N	Y
MARYLAND							
1	**Harris**	Y	Y	N	N	Y	N
2	Ruppersberger	N	N	Y	Y	N	Y
3	Sarbanes	N	N	Y	Y	N	Y
4	Brown, A.	N	N	Y	Y	N	Y
5	Hoyer	N	N	Y	Y	N	Y
6	Trone	N	N	Y	Y	N	Y
7	Cummings	N	N	Y	Y	N	Y
8	Raskin	N	N	Y	Y	N	Y
MASSACHUSETTS							
1	Neal	N	N	Y	Y	N	Y
2	McGovern	N	N	Y	Y	N	Y
3	Trahan	N	N	Y	Y	N	Y
4	Kennedy	N	N	Y	Y	N	Y
5	Clark	N	N	Y	Y	N	Y
6	Moulton	N	N	Y	Y	N	Y
7	Pressley	N	N	Y	Y	N	Y
8	Lynch	N	N	Y	Y	N	Y
9	Keating	N	N	Y	Y	N	Y
MICHIGAN							
1	**Bergman**	Y	Y	Y	N	Y	N
2	**Huizenga**	Y	Y	Y	N	Y	N
3	**Amash**	Y	Y	N	N	Y	N
4	**Moolenaar**	Y	Y	Y	N	Y	N
5	Kildee	N	N	Y	Y	N	Y
6	**Upton**	Y	Y	Y	N	Y	N
7	**Walberg**	Y	Y	Y	N	Y	N
8	Slotkin	N	N	Y	Y	N	Y
9	Levin	N	N	Y	Y	N	Y
10	**Mitchell**	Y	Y	Y	N	Y	N
11	Stevens	N	N	Y	Y	N	Y
12	Dingell	N	N	Y	Y	N	Y
13	Tlaib	N	N	Y	Y	N	Y
14	Lawrence	N	N	Y	Y	N	Y
MINNESOTA							
1	**Hagedorn**	Y	Y	Y	N	Y	N
2	Craig	N	N	Y	Y	N	Y
3	Phillips	N	N	Y	Y	N	Y
4	McCollum	N	N	Y	Y	N	Y
5	Omar	N	N	Y	Y	N	Y

		223	224	225	226	227	228
6	**Emmer**	Y	Y	Y	N	Y	N
7	Peterson	N	N	Y	Y	N	Y
8	**Stauber**	Y	Y	Y	N	Y	N
MISSISSIPPI							
1	**Kelly, T.**	Y	Y	Y	N	Y	N
2	Thompson, B.	N	N	Y	Y	N	Y
3	**Guest**	Y	Y	Y	N	Y	N
4	**Palazzo**	Y	Y	Y	N	Y	N
MISSOURI							
1	Clay	N	N	Y	Y	N	Y
2	**Wagner**	Y	Y	Y	N	Y	N
3	**Luetkemeyer**	Y	Y	Y	N	Y	N
4	**Hartzler**	Y	Y	Y	N	Y	N
5	Cleaver	N	N	Y	Y	N	Y
6	**Graves, S.**	Y	Y	Y	N	Y	N
7	**Long**	Y	Y	Y	N	Y	N
8	**Smith, J.**	Y	Y	Y	N	Y	N
MONTANA							
AL	**Gianforte**	Y	Y	Y	N	Y	N
NEBRASKA							
1	**Fortenberry**	Y	Y	Y	N	Y	N
2	**Bacon**	Y	Y	Y	N	Y	N
3	**Smith, Adrian**	Y	Y	Y	N	Y	N
NEVADA							
1	Titus	N	N	Y	Y	N	Y
2	**Amodei**	Y	Y	Y	N	Y	N
3	Lee	N	N	Y	Y	N	Y
4	Horsford	N	N	Y	Y	N	Y
NEW HAMPSHIRE							
1	Pappas	N	N	Y	Y	N	Y
2	Kuster	N	N	Y	Y	N	Y
NEW JERSEY							
1	Norcross	N	N	Y	Y	N	Y
2	Van Drew	N	N	Y	Y	N	Y
3	Kim	N	N	Y	Y	N	Y
4	**Smith, C.**	Y	Y	Y	N	Y	N
5	Gottheimer	N	N	Y	Y	N	Y
6	Pallone	N	N	Y	Y	N	Y
7	Malinowski	N	N	Y	Y	N	Y
8	Sires	N	N	Y	Y	N	Y
9	Pascrell	N	N	Y	Y	N	Y
10	Payne	-	-	+	+	-	+
11	Sherrill	N	N	Y	Y	N	Y
12	Watson Coleman	N	N	Y	Y	N	Y
NEW MEXICO							
1	Haaland	N	N	Y	Y	N	Y
2	Torres Small	N	N	Y	Y	N	Y
3	Luján	N	N	Y	Y	N	Y
NEW YORK							
1	**Zeldin**	Y	Y	Y	N	Y	N
2	**King, P.**	Y	Y	Y	N	Y	N
3	Suozzi	N	N	Y	Y	N	Y
4	Rice, K.	N	N	Y	Y	N	Y
5	Meeks	?	?	?	?	?	?
6	Meng	N	N	Y	Y	N	Y
7	Velázquez	N	N	Y	Y	N	Y
8	Jeffries	N	N	Y	Y	N	Y
9	Clarke	N	N	Y	Y	N	Y
10	Nadler	N	N	Y	Y	N	Y
11	Rose	N	N	Y	Y	N	Y
12	Maloney, C.	N	N	Y	Y	N	Y
13	Espaillat	N	N	Y	Y	N	Y
14	Ocasio-Cortez	N	N	Y	Y	N	Y
15	Serrano	N	N	Y	Y	N	Y
16	Engel	N	N	Y	Y	N	Y
17	Lowey	N	N	Y	Y	N	Y
18	Maloney, S.P.	N	N	Y	Y	N	Y
19	Delgado	N	N	Y	Y	N	Y
20	Tonko	N	N	Y	Y	N	Y
21	**Stefanik**	Y	Y	Y	N	Y	N
22	Brindisi	N	N	Y	Y	N	Y
23	**Reed**	Y	Y	Y	N	Y	N
24	**Katko**	Y	Y	Y	N	Y	N
25	Morelle	N	N	Y	Y	N	Y
26	Higgins, B.	N	N	Y	Y	N	Y
27	**Collins, C.**						
NORTH CAROLINA							
1	Butterfield	N	N	Y	Y	N	Y
2	**Holding**	Y	Y	Y	N	Y	N
3	**Jones***						
4	Price	N	N	Y	Y	N	Y
5	**Foxx**	Y	Y	Y	N	Y	N
6	**Walker**	?	?	?	?	?	?
7	**Rouzer**	Y	Y	Y	N	Y	N

		223	224	225	226	227	228
8	**Hudson**	+	+	+	-	+	-
9	vacant						
10	**McHenry**	Y	Y	Y	N	Y	N
11	**Meadows**	Y	Y	Y	N	Y	N
12	Adams	N	N	Y	Y	N	Y
13	**Budd**	Y	Y	Y	N	Y	N
NORTH DAKOTA							
AL	**Armstrong**	?	?	?	?	?	?
OHIO							
1	**Chabot**	Y	Y	Y	N	Y	N
2	**Wenstrup**	Y	Y	Y	N	Y	N
3	Beatty	N	N	Y	Y	N	Y
4	**Jordan**	Y	Y	Y	N	Y	N
5	**Latta**	Y	Y	Y	N	Y	N
6	**Johnson, B.**	Y	Y	Y	N	Y	N
7	**Gibbs**	Y	Y	Y	N	Y	N
8	**Davidson**	Y	Y	Y	N	Y	N
9	Kaptur	?	N	Y	Y	N	Y
10	**Turner**	Y	Y	Y	N	Y	N
11	Fudge	N	N	Y	Y	N	Y
12	**Balderson**	Y	Y	Y	N	Y	N
13	Ryan	N	N	Y	Y	N	Y
14	**Joyce**	Y	Y	Y	N	Y	N
15	**Stivers**	?	?	?	?	?	?
16	**Gonzalez**	Y	Y	Y	N	Y	N
OKLAHOMA							
1	**Hern**	Y	Y	N	N	Y	N
2	**Mullin**	Y	Y	Y	N	Y	N
3	**Lucas**	Y	Y	Y	N	Y	N
4	**Cole**	Y	Y	Y	N	Y	N
5	Horn	N	N	Y	Y	N	Y
OREGON							
1	Bonamici	N	N	Y	Y	N	Y
2	**Walden**	Y	Y	Y	N	Y	N
3	Blumenauer	N	N	Y	Y	N	Y
4	DeFazio	N	N	Y	Y	N	Y
5	Schrader	N	N	Y	Y	N	Y
PENNSYLVANIA							
1	**Fitzpatrick**	N	Y	Y	N	Y	N
2	Boyle	N	N	Y	Y	N	Y
3	Evans	N	N	Y	Y	N	Y
4	Dean	N	N	Y	Y	N	Y
5	Scanlon	N	N	Y	Y	N	Y
6	Houlahan	N	N	Y	Y	N	Y
7	Wild	N	N	Y	Y	N	Y
8	Cartwright	N	N	Y	Y	N	Y
9	**Meuser**	Y	Y	Y	N	Y	N
10	**Perry**	Y	Y	Y	N	Y	N
11	**Smucker**	Y	Y	Y	N	Y	N
12	**Marino***						
13	**Joyce**	Y	Y	Y	N	Y	N
14	**Reschenthaler**	Y	Y	Y	N	Y	N
15	**Thompson, G.**	Y	Y	Y	N	Y	N
16	**Kelly, M.**	Y	Y	Y	N	Y	N
17	Lamb	N	N	Y	Y	N	Y
18	Doyle	N	N	Y	Y	N	Y
RHODE ISLAND							
1	Cicilline	N	N	Y	Y	N	Y
2	Langevin	N	N	Y	Y	N	Y
SOUTH CAROLINA							
1	Cunningham	N	N	Y	Y	N	Y
2	**Wilson, J.**	Y	Y	Y	N	Y	N
3	**Duncan**	Y	Y	Y	N	Y	N
4	**Timmons**	Y	Y	Y	N	Y	N
5	**Norman**	Y	Y	Y	N	Y	N
6	Clyburn	N	N	Y	Y	N	Y
7	**Rice, T.**	Y	Y	Y	N	Y	N
SOUTH DAKOTA							
AL	**Johnson**	Y	Y	Y	N	Y	N
TENNESSEE							
1	**Roe**	Y	Y	Y	N	Y	N
2	**Burchett**	Y	Y	Y	N	Y	N
3	**Fleischmann**	Y	Y	Y	N	Y	N
4	**DesJarlais**	Y	Y	Y	N	Y	N
5	Cooper	N	N	Y	Y	N	Y
6	**Rose**	Y	Y	Y	N	Y	N
7	**Green**	Y	Y	N	N	Y	N
8	**Kustoff**	Y	Y	Y	N	Y	N
9	Cohen	N	N	Y	Y	N	Y
TEXAS							
1	**Gohmert**	Y	Y	Y	N	Y	N
2	**Crenshaw**	Y	Y	Y	N	Y	N
3	**Taylor**	Y	Y	Y	N	Y	N
4	**Ratcliffe**	Y	Y	Y	N	Y	N

		223	224	225	226	227	228
5	**Gooden**	Y	Y	Y	N	Y	N
6	**Wright**	Y	Y	Y	N	Y	N
7	Fletcher	N	N	Y	Y	N	Y
8	**Brady**	Y	Y	Y	N	Y	N
9	Green, A.	N	N	Y	Y	N	Y
10	**McCaul**	Y	Y	Y	N	Y	N
11	**Conaway**	Y	Y	Y	N	Y	N
12	**Granger**	Y	Y	Y	N	Y	N
13	**Thornberry**	Y	Y	Y	N	Y	N
14	**Weber**	Y	Y	Y	N	Y	N
15	Gonzalez	N	N	Y	Y	N	Y
16	Escobar	N	N	Y	Y	N	Y
17	**Flores**	Y	Y	Y	N	Y	N
18	Jackson Lee	N	N	Y	Y	N	Y
19	**Arrington**	Y	Y	Y	N	Y	N
20	Castro	N	N	Y	Y	N	Y
21	**Roy**	Y	Y	Y	N	Y	N
22	**Olson**	Y	Y	Y	N	Y	N
23	**Hurd**	Y	Y	Y	N	Y	N
24	**Marchant**	Y	Y	Y	N	Y	N
25	**Williams**	Y	Y	Y	N	Y	N
26	**Burgess**	Y	Y	Y	N	Y	N
27	**Cloud**	Y	Y	Y	N	Y	N
28	Cuellar	N	N	Y	N	N	Y
29	Garcia, S.	N	N	Y	Y	N	Y
30	Johnson, E.B.	N	N	Y	Y	N	Y
31	**Carter, J.**	Y	Y	Y	N	Y	N
32	Allred	N	N	Y	Y	N	Y
33	Veasey	N	N	Y	Y	N	Y
34	Vela	N	N	Y	Y	N	Y
35	Doggett	N	N	Y	Y	N	Y
36	**Babin**	Y	Y	Y	N	Y	N
UTAH							
1	**Bishop, R.**	Y	Y	Y	N	Y	N
2	**Stewart**	Y	Y	Y	N	Y	N
3	**Curtis**	Y	Y	Y	N	Y	N
4	McAdams	N	N	Y	Y	N	Y
VERMONT							
AL	Welch	N	N	Y	Y	N	Y
VIRGINIA							
1	**Wittman**	Y	Y	Y	N	Y	N
2	Luria	N	N	Y	Y	N	Y
3	Scott, R.	N	N	Y	Y	N	Y
4	McEachin	N	N	Y	Y	N	Y
5	**Riggleman**	Y	Y	Y	N	Y	N
6	**Cline**	Y	Y	Y	N	Y	N
7	Spanberger	N	N	Y	Y	N	Y
8	Beyer	N	N	Y	Y	N	Y
9	**Griffith**	Y	Y	Y	N	Y	N
10	Wexton	N	N	Y	Y	N	Y
11	Connolly	N	N	Y	Y	N	Y
WASHINGTON							
1	DelBene	N	N	Y	Y	N	Y
2	Larsen	N	N	Y	Y	N	Y
3	**Herrera Beutler**	?	?	?	?	?	?
4	**Newhouse**	Y	Y	Y	N	Y	N
5	**McMorris Rodgers**	Y	Y	Y	N	Y	N
6	Kilmer	N	N	Y	Y	N	Y
7	Jayapal	N	N	Y	Y	N	Y
8	Schrier	N	N	Y	Y	N	Y
9	Smith Adam	N	N	Y	Y	N	Y
10	Heck	N	N	Y	Y	N	Y
WEST VIRGINIA							
1	**McKinley**	Y	Y	Y	N	Y	N
2	**Mooney**	Y	Y	Y	N	Y	N
3	**Miller**	Y	Y	Y	N	Y	N
WISCONSIN							
1	**Steil**	Y	Y	Y	N	Y	N
2	Pocan	N	N	Y	Y	N	Y
3	Kind	N	N	Y	Y	N	Y
4	Moore	N	N	Y	Y	N	Y
5	**Sensenbrenner**	Y	Y	Y	N	Y	N
6	**Grothman**	Y	Y	Y	N	Y	N
7	**Duffy**						
8	**Gallagher**	Y	Y	Y	N	Y	N
WYOMING							
AL	**Cheney**	Y	Y	Y	N	Y	N
DELEGATES							
	Radewagen (A.S.)	Y	Y	Y	N		
	Norton (D.C.)	N	N	Y	Y		
	San Nicolas (Guam)	N	N	Y	Y		
	Sablan (N. Marianas)	N	N	Y	Y		
	González-Colón (P.R.)	Y	Y	Y	N		
	Plaskett (V.I.)	N	N	Y	Y		

229. Procedural Motion - Journal. Approval of the House journal of May 23, 2019. Passed 223-194: R 44-144; D 179-50. May 23, 2019.

230. HR1994. Retirement Savings Plans - Recommit. McHenry, R-N.C., motion to recommit the bill to the House Ways and Means Committee with instructions to report it back immediately with an amendment that would require the Treasury Department to add to an existing list of individuals participating in an international boycott any individuals who "knowingly engage" in boycott, divestment, and sanctions activities in relation to Israel. It would define such activities as those "intended to penalize, inflict economic harm on, or otherwise limit commercial relations with Israel or persons doing business in Israel." It would also raise the international boycott factor with respect to such individuals on the list to 1, resulting in a loss of certain tax benefits. Motion rejected 200-222: R 188-2; D 12-220. May 23, 2019.

231. HR1994. Retirement Savings Plans - Passage. Passage of the bill, as amended, that would allow small businesses to offer certain retirement savings plans for their employees and make a number of modifications related to individual contributions to and use of tax-favored retirement accounts. The bill would allow small businesses to offer "pooled" retirement savings plans for their employees by combining with other unrelated businesses to offer plans with multiple employer providers. It would require each employer to register with the Labor Department to be designated as a multiple employer plan sponsor. The bill would increase certain tax credits for small businesses that establish retirement plans, including for plans including automatic enrollment. It would require employers to allow certain part-time employees to participate in defined contribution retirement plans and would make "difficulty of care" payments for home health care workers eligible for investment in such retirement plans. It would increase from 70 and one-half to 72 the age at which individuals are required to take minimum distributions from their retirement accounts and would allow individuals to continue making contributions to a regular IRA after reaching the age of 70 and one-half. It would allow individuals to withdraw up to $5,000 from retirement savings accounts to help pay for expenses related to a birth or adoption, and allow such funds to be later repaid to their accounts without penalty. It would also modify qualification requirements for safe harbor provisions exempting employers from Internal Revenue Service nondiscrimination tests related to employee participation in 401(k) plans. It would increase penalties for failure to file federal tax returns, including for retirement savings plans, and would modify distribution rules for beneficiaries of retirement savings plans. As amended, the bill would make adjustments to taxes on unearned income for child survivors of a parent killed in military action, known as Gold Star families. Passed 417-3: R 187-3; D 230-0. May 23, 2019.

232. HR2157. Fiscal 2019 Disaster Relief Supplemental Appropriations - Motion to Concur. Lowey, D-N.Y., motion to suspend the rules and concur in the Senate amendment to the Fiscal 2019 Disaster Supplemental Appropriations Act that would that would provide $19.1 billion in supplemental disaster funds for response efforts to damage caused by hurricanes, wildfires, earthquakes, tornadoes, floods, and other natural disasters that occurred in 2017, 2018, and 2019. It would provide $648 million in disaster nutrition assistance for individuals impacted by natural disasters in Puerto Rico, the Commonwealth of the Northern Mariana Islands, and American Samoa. It would extend the National Flood Insurance Program, which will expire on May 31, through Sept. 30, 2019. It would also provide funds for areas impacted by natural disasters for economic development, training and employment services, and behavioral and social health services. The bill includes a total of $4.7 billion for Agriculture Department disaster-related activities, including $3 billion for crop, tree, bush, vine, and livestock losses from hurricanes, wildfires and other declared disasters that occurred in 2018 and 2019. The bill would provide $2.4 billion for a Housing and Urban Development Department community development block grant program, and $1.7 billion for Transportation Department programs and activities, including $1.6 billion for the cost of federal highway and bridge repairs. It would provide $1.5 billion to the Defense Department to repair military facilities damaged by hurricanes Florence and Michael, $3.3 billion to the Army Corps of Engineers for civil construction projects. It would also state that military construction funds provided by the bill may only be used for purposes specified in the bill. Motion agreed to 354-58: R 132-58; D 222-0. *Note: A two-thirds majority of those present and voting (275 in this case) is required for passage under suspension of the rules.* June 3, 2019.

233. HR2940. Family Assistance Programs - Passage. Davis, D-Ill., motion to suspend the rules and pass the bill that would extend authorization and funding through Sept. 30, 2019 for the Temporary Assistance for Needy Families program and related Health and Human Services Department programs, including family assistance and child care grants, to states and territories. Motion agreed to 357-55: R 134-55; D 223-0. *Note: A two-thirds majority of those present and voting (275 in this case) is required for passage under suspension of the rules.* June 3, 2019.

234. Procedural Motion - Journal. Approval of the House journal of May 30, 2019. Approved 206-189: R 45-139; D 161-50. June 3, 2019.

		229	230	231	232	233	234
ALABAMA							
1	**Byrne**	N	Y	Y	Y	N	N
2	**Roby**	N	Y	Y	Y	Y	N
3	**Rogers, M.**	N	Y	Y	Y	Y	N
4	**Aderholt**	N	Y	Y	Y	Y	N
5	**Brooks, M.**	N	Y	Y	N	N	N
6	**Palmer**	N	Y	Y	N	N	N
7	Sewell	Y	N	Y	Y	Y	Y
ALASKA							
AL	**Young**	N	Y	Y	Y	Y	N
ARIZONA							
1	O'Halleran	N	N	Y	Y	Y	Y
2	Kirkpatrick	N	N	Y	Y	Y	N
3	Grijalva	Y	N	Y	Y	Y	?
4	**Gosar**	?	?	?	N	N	N
5	**Biggs**	N	Y	Y	N	N	N
6	**Schweikert**	Y	Y	Y	N	Y	Y
7	Gallego	Y	N	Y	Y	Y	Y
8	**Lesko**	N	Y	Y	N	N	N
9	Stanton	Y	N	Y	Y	Y	Y
ARKANSAS							
1	**Crawford**	N	Y	Y	Y	Y	N
2	**Hill, F.**	N	Y	Y	Y	Y	N
3	**Womack**	N	Y	Y	Y	Y	N
4	**Westerman**	N	Y	Y	Y	N	N
CALIFORNIA							
1	**LaMalfa**	N	Y	Y	Y	Y	N
2	Huffman	Y	N	Y	Y	Y	Y
3	Garamendi	Y	N	Y	Y	Y	Y
4	**McClintock**	Y	Y	Y	N	N	Y
5	Thompson, M.	N	N	Y	Y	Y	N
6	Matsui	Y	N	Y	?	?	?
7	Bera	N	N	Y	Y	Y	N
8	**Cook**	N	Y	Y	Y	Y	?
9	McNerney	Y	N	Y	Y	Y	?
10	Harder	N	N	Y	Y	Y	N
11	DeSaulnier	Y	N	Y	Y	Y	Y
12	Pelosi						
13	Lee B.	Y	N	Y	Y	Y	Y
14	Speier	Y	N	Y	?	?	?
15	Swalwell	Y	N	Y	?	?	?
16	Costa	N	N	Y	Y	Y	N
17	Khanna	Y	N	Y	Y	Y	Y
18	Eshoo	Y	N	Y	Y	Y	?
19	Lofgren	Y	N	Y	Y	Y	?
20	Panetta	Y	N	Y	Y	Y	Y
21	Cox	Y	N	Y	Y	Y	Y
22	**Nunes**	N	Y	Y	Y	Y	N
23	**McCarthy**	Y	Y	Y	Y	Y	Y
24	Carbajal	Y	N	Y	Y	Y	Y
25	Hill, K.	Y	N	Y	Y	Y	Y
26	Brownley	N	N	Y	Y	Y	Y
27	Chu	Y	N	?	Y	Y	Y
28	Schiff	Y	N	Y	Y	Y	Y
29	Cárdenas	N	N	Y	?	?	?
30	Sherman	Y	N	Y	+	+	+
31	Aguilar	Y	N	Y	Y	Y	Y
32	Napolitano	Y	N	Y	Y	Y	Y
33	Lieu	Y	N	Y	Y	Y	Y
34	Gomez	Y	N	Y	Y	Y	Y
35	Torres	Y	N	Y	Y	Y	?
36	Ruiz	N	N	Y	Y	Y	N
37	Bass	Y	N	Y	Y	Y	Y
38	Sánchez	Y	N	Y	Y	Y	Y
39	Cisneros	Y	N	Y	Y	Y	Y
40	Roybal-Allard	Y	N	Y	Y	Y	Y
41	Takano	Y	N	Y	Y	Y	Y
42	**Calvert**	N	Y	Y	Y	Y	?
43	Waters	N	N	Y	Y	Y	Y
44	Barragán	Y	N	Y	Y	Y	Y
45	Porter	Y	N	Y	Y	Y	N
46	Correa	N	N	Y	Y	Y	N
47	Lowenthal	Y	N	Y	Y	Y	Y
48	Rouda	N	N	Y	Y	Y	N
49	Levin	Y	N	Y	Y	Y	Y
50	**Hunter**	N	Y	Y	N	N	N
51	Vargas	Y	N	Y	Y	Y	Y
52	Peters	N	N	Y	Y	Y	N
53	Davis, S.	Y	N	Y	Y	Y	Y
COLORADO							
1	DeGette	Y	N	Y	Y	Y	Y
2	Neguse	Y	N	Y	Y	Y	Y
3	**Tipton**	N	Y	Y	Y	Y	N
4	**Buck**	N	Y	Y	N	N	N
5	**Lamborn**	N	Y	Y	N	N	N
6	Crow	N	N	Y	Y	Y	N
7	Perlmutter	Y	N	Y	Y	Y	Y
CONNECTICUT							
1	Larson	Y	N	Y	Y	Y	?
2	Courtney	Y	N	Y	Y	Y	Y
3	DeLauro	Y	N	Y	Y	Y	Y
4	Himes	N	N	Y	Y	Y	N
5	Hayes	Y	N	Y	Y	Y	N
DELAWARE							
AL	Blunt Rochester	Y	N	Y	Y	Y	Y
FLORIDA							
1	**Gaetz**	N	Y	Y	Y	N	N
2	**Dunn**	N	Y	Y	Y	Y	N
3	**Yoho**	N	Y	Y	Y	N	N
4	**Rutherford**	Y	Y	Y	Y	Y	N
5	Lawson	Y	N	Y	Y	Y	N
6	**Waltz**	Y	Y	Y	Y	Y	Y
7	Murphy	N	N	Y	Y	Y	Y
8	**Posey**	N	Y	Y	Y	Y	N
9	Soto	Y	N	Y	Y	Y	Y
10	Demings	Y	N	Y	Y	Y	Y
11	**Webster**	Y	Y	Y	Y	Y	Y
12	**Bilirakis**	Y	Y	Y	Y	Y	Y
13	Crist	Y	N	Y	Y	Y	N
14	Castor	Y	N	Y	Y	Y	Y
15	**Spano**	N	Y	Y	Y	Y	N
16	**Buchanan**	N	Y	Y	Y	Y	N
17	**Steube**	N	Y	Y	N	N	N
18	**Mast**	N	Y	Y	Y	Y	N
19	**Rooney**	N	Y	Y	N	N	N
20	Hastings	Y	N	Y	+	?	?
21	Frankel	Y	N	Y	Y	Y	Y
22	Deutch	Y	N	Y	Y	Y	Y
23	Wasserman Schultz	Y	N	Y	Y	Y	Y
24	Wilson, F.	Y	N	Y	+	+	+
25	**Diaz-Balart**	N	Y	Y	Y	Y	N
26	Mucarsel-Powell	Y	N	Y	Y	Y	N
27	Shalala	Y	N	Y	Y	Y	Y
GEORGIA							
1	**Carter, E.L.**	N	Y	Y	Y	Y	N
2	Bishop, S.	Y	N	Y	Y	Y	Y
3	**Ferguson**	N	Y	Y	Y	Y	N
4	Johnson, H.	Y	N	Y	Y	Y	Y
5	Lewis John	Y	N	Y	Y	Y	Y
6	McBath	N	N	Y	Y	Y	N
7	**Woodall**	N	Y	Y	Y	Y	N
8	**Scott, A.**	N	Y	Y	Y	Y	N
9	**Collins, D.**	?	Y	Y	Y	Y	Y
10	**Hice**	N	Y	Y	Y	N	N
11	**Loudermilk**	N	Y	Y	Y	N	N
12	**Allen**	N	Y	Y	Y	N	N
13	Scott, D.	Y	N	Y	Y	Y	Y
14	**Graves, T.**	N	Y	Y	Y	Y	N
HAWAII							
1	Case	Y	N	Y	Y	Y	Y
2	Gabbard	Y	N	Y	Y	Y	Y
IDAHO							
1	**Fulcher**	N	Y	Y	N	Y	?
2	**Simpson**	Y	Y	Y	Y	Y	Y
ILLINOIS							
1	Rush	Y	N	Y	Y	Y	Y
2	Kelly, R.	Y	N	Y	Y	Y	Y
3	Lipinski	Y	N	Y	Y	Y	Y
4	García, J.	Y	N	Y	Y	Y	Y
5	Quigley	Y	N	Y	Y	Y	Y
6	Casten	Y	N	Y	Y	Y	Y
7	Davis, D.	Y	N	Y	Y	Y	Y
8	Krishnamoorthi	N	N	Y	Y	Y	N
9	Schakowsky	Y	N	Y	Y	Y	Y
10	Schneider	Y	N	Y	+	+	?
11	Foster	Y	N	Y	Y	Y	Y

KEY: **Republicans** Democrats *Independents*

Y	Voted for (yea)	N	Voted against (nay)	P	Voted "present"
+	Announced for	-	Announced against	?	Did not vote or otherwise make position known
#	Paired for	X	Paired against		

		229	230	231	232	233	234
12	**Bost**	Y	Y	Y	Y	Y	Y
13	**Davis, R.**	N	Y	Y	Y	Y	N
14	Underwood	Y	N	Y	Y	Y	Y
15	**Shimkus**	N	Y	Y	Y	Y	N
16	**Kinzinger**	+	+	+	Y	Y	Y
17	Bustos	Y	N	Y	Y	Y	Y
18	**LaHood**	N	Y	Y	N	Y	N
INDIANA							
1	Visclosky	Y	N	Y	Y	Y	Y
2	**Walorski**	N	Y	Y	Y	Y	N
3	**Banks**	Y	Y	Y	N	N	Y
4	**Baird**	N	Y	Y	Y	Y	N
5	**Brooks, S.**	N	Y	Y	Y	Y	N
6	**Pence**	N	Y	Y	Y	Y	N
7	Carson	Y	N	Y	Y	Y	Y
8	**Bucshon**	N	Y	Y	Y	Y	Y
9	**Hollingsworth**	Y	Y	Y	N	Y	Y
IOWA							
1	Finkenauer	Y	N	Y	Y	Y	Y
2	Loebsack	Y	N	Y	Y	Y	Y
3	Axne	N	N	Y	Y	Y	N
4	**King, S.**	Y	Y	Y	Y	Y	Y
KANSAS							
1	**Marshall**	Y	Y	Y	Y	Y	Y
2	**Watkins**	Y	Y	Y	Y	Y	Y
3	Davids	Y	N	Y	Y	Y	N
4	**Estes**	N	Y	Y	N	Y	N
KENTUCKY							
1	**Comer**	N	Y	Y	N	N	N
2	**Guthrie**	N	Y	Y	Y	Y	N
3	Yarmuth	Y	N	Y	Y	Y	Y
4	**Massie**	N	N	N	N	N	N
5	**Rogers, H.**	N	Y	Y	Y	Y	N
6	**Barr**	Y	Y	Y	N	N	N
LOUISIANA							
1	**Scalise**	N	Y	Y	Y	N	N
2	Richmond	Y	N	Y	Y	Y	Y
3	**Higgins, C.**	N	Y	Y	N	Y	Y
4	**Johnson, M.**	?	?	?	N	N	N
5	**Abraham**	N	Y	Y	?	?	?
6	**Graves, G.**	N	Y	Y	Y	Y	N
MAINE							
1	Pingree	Y	N	Y	Y	Y	Y
2	Golden	N	N	Y	Y	Y	N
MARYLAND							
1	**Harris**	N	Y	Y	N	N	N
2	Ruppersberger	Y	N	Y	Y	Y	Y
3	Sarbanes	Y	N	Y	Y	Y	Y
4	Brown, A.	Y	N	Y	Y	Y	Y
5	Hoyer	Y	N	Y	Y	Y	Y
6	Trone	Y	N	Y	Y	Y	Y
7	Cummings	Y	N	Y	Y	Y	Y
8	Raskin						
MASSACHUSETTS		Y	N	Y	Y	Y	?
1	Neal						
2	McGovern	Y	N	Y	Y	Y	Y
3	Trahan	Y	N	Y	Y	Y	Y
4	Kennedy	Y	N	Y	Y	Y	Y
5	Clark	Y	N	Y	Y	Y	Y
6	Moulton	Y	N	Y	Y	Y	Y
7	Pressley	Y	Y	Y	Y	Y	Y
8	Lynch	Y	N	Y	Y	Y	Y
9	Keating	Y	N	Y	Y	Y	Y
MICHIGAN		Y	N	Y	Y	Y	Y
1	**Bergman**						
2	**Huizenga**	Y	Y	Y	N	Y	Y
3	**Amash**	N	Y	Y	N	Y	N
4	**Moolenaar**	N	N	N	N	N	N
5	Kildee	N	Y	Y	Y	Y	N
6	**Upton**	Y	N	Y	Y	Y	Y
7	**Walberg**	N	Y	Y	Y	Y	N
8	Slotkin	N	Y	Y	Y	Y	N
9	Levin	N	Y	Y	Y	Y	Y
10	**Mitchell**	Y	N	Y	Y	Y	Y
11	Stevens	N	Y	Y	Y	Y	N
12	Dingell	Y	N	Y	Y	Y	N
13	Tlaib	Y	N	+	Y	Y	Y
14	Lawrence	Y	N	Y	Y	Y	Y
MINNESOTA		Y	N	Y	Y	Y	Y
1	**Hagedorn**						
2	Craig	N	Y	Y	Y	Y	N
3	Phillips	N	N	Y	Y	Y	N
4	McCollum	Y	N	Y	Y	Y	Y
5	Omar	Y	N	Y	Y	Y	Y

		229	230	231	232	233	234
6	**Emmer**	Y	N	Y	?	?	?
7	Peterson	N	Y	Y	N	Y	N
8	**Stauber**	N	N	Y	Y	Y	N
MISSISSIPPI		+	+	+	Y	Y	Y
1	**Kelly, T.**						
2	Thompson, B.	N	Y	Y	Y	Y	N
3	**Guest**	Y	N	Y	Y	Y	Y
4	**Palazzo**	N	Y	Y	?	?	?
MISSOURI		N	Y	Y	Y	Y	N
1	Clay						
2	**Wagner**	Y	N	Y	Y	Y	Y
3	**Luetkemeyer**	Y	Y	Y	Y	Y	Y
4	**Hartzler**	N	Y	Y	Y	Y	N
5	Cleaver	N	Y	Y	Y	-	N
6	**Graves, S.**	Y	N	Y	Y	Y	Y
7	**Long**	N	Y	Y	Y	Y	N
8	**Smith, J.**	N	Y	Y	Y	Y	Y
MONTANA		N	Y	Y	Y	Y	N
AL	**Gianforte**						
NEBRASKA		N	Y	Y	N	Y	N
1	**Fortenberry**						
2	**Bacon**	Y	Y	Y	Y	Y	Y
3	**Smith, Adrian**	Y	Y	Y	Y	Y	Y
NEVADA		N	Y	Y	Y	Y	?
1	Titus						
2	**Amodei**	Y	N	Y	Y	Y	Y
3	Lee	Y	Y	Y	Y	Y	Y
4	Horsford	Y	N	Y	Y	Y	N
NEW HAMPSHIRE		N	N	Y	Y	Y	Y
1	Pappas						
2	Kuster	N	N	Y	Y	Y	Y
NEW JERSEY		N	N	Y	Y	Y	Y
1	Norcross						
2	Van Drew	Y	N	Y	Y	Y	Y
3	Kim	N	Y	Y	Y	Y	N
4	**Smith, C.**	Y	N	Y	Y	Y	Y
5	Gottheimer	Y	Y	Y	Y	Y	Y
6	Pallone	N	Y	Y	Y	Y	N
7	Malinowski	Y	N	Y	Y	Y	Y
8	Sires	Y	N	Y	Y	Y	Y
9	Pascrell	Y	N	Y	Y	Y	Y
10	Payne	Y	N	Y	Y	Y	Y
11	Sherrill	Y	N	Y	Y	Y	Y
12	Watson Coleman	N	N	Y	Y	Y	N
NEW MEXICO		Y	N	Y	Y	Y	N
1	Haaland						
2	Torres Small	Y	N	Y	Y	Y	Y
3	Luján	Y	N	Y	Y	Y	N
NEW YORK		Y	N	Y	Y	Y	Y
1	**Zeldin**						
2	**King, P.**	N	Y	Y	Y	Y	N
3	Suozzi	N	Y	Y	Y	Y	Y
4	Rice, K.	N	N	Y	Y	Y	N
5	Meeks	Y	N	Y	Y	Y	N
6	Meng	Y	N	Y	Y	Y	Y
7	Velázquez	Y	N	Y	Y	Y	N
8	Jeffries	Y	N	Y	Y	Y	Y
9	Clarke	?	?	?	Y	Y	Y
10	Nadler	Y	N	Y	Y	Y	Y
11	Rose	Y	N	Y	Y	Y	Y
12	Maloney, C.	Y	Y	Y	Y	Y	N
13	Espaillat	Y	N	Y	Y	Y	Y
14	Ocasio-Cortez	Y	N	Y	Y	Y	Y
15	Serrano	N	N	Y	Y	Y	Y
16	Engel	Y	N	Y	Y	Y	Y
17	Lowey	Y	N	Y	Y	Y	Y
18	Maloney, S.P.	Y	N	Y	Y	Y	Y
19	Delgado	N	N	Y	Y	Y	N
20	Tonko	Y	N	Y	Y	Y	Y
21	**Stefanik**	P	N	Y	Y	Y	P
22	Brindisi	Y	Y	Y	Y	Y	Y
23	**Reed**	Y	Y	Y	Y	Y	N
24	**Katko**	Y	Y	Y	Y	Y	N
25	Morelle	N	Y	Y	Y	Y	Y
26	Higgins, B.	Y	N	Y	Y	Y	Y
27	**Collins, C.**	Y	N	Y	Y	Y	Y
NORTH CAROLINA		N	Y	Y	Y	Y	N
1	Butterfield						
2	**Holding**	Y	N	Y	Y	Y	Y
3	**Jones***	N	Y	Y	Y	Y	N
4	Price						
5	**Foxx**	Y	N	Y	Y	Y	Y
6	**Walker**	N	Y	Y	N	Y	N
7	**Rouzer**	N	Y	Y	N	Y	N

		229	230	231	232	233	234
8	**Hudson**	N	Y	Y	Y	N	N
9	vacant	N	Y	Y	Y	Y	N
10	**McHenry**	N	Y	Y	Y	Y	?
11	**Meadows**	Y	Y	Y	N	N	N
12	Adams	Y	N	Y	Y	Y	Y
13	**Budd**	N	Y	Y	N	N	N
NORTH DAKOTA							
AL	**Armstrong**	?	?	?	Y	Y	N
OHIO							
1	**Chabot**	N	Y	Y	N	N	N
2	**Wenstrup**	N	Y	Y	N	Y	Y
3	Beatty	N	N	Y	+	Y	Y
4	**Jordan**	Y	Y	Y	N	N	N
5	**Latta**	N	Y	Y	Y	Y	N
6	**Johnson, B.**	N	Y	Y	?	?	?
7	**Gibbs**	N	Y	Y	Y	Y	N
8	**Davidson**	Y	Y	Y	N	N	Y
9	Kaptur	?	N	Y	Y	Y	Y
10	**Turner**	N	Y	Y	Y	Y	N
11	Fudge	N	N	Y	Y	Y	?
12	**Balderson**	N	Y	Y	Y	Y	N
13	Ryan	Y	N	Y	Y	Y	?
14	**Joyce**	Y	Y	Y	Y	Y	Y
15	**Stivers**	?	?	?	?	?	?
16	**Gonzalez**	N	Y	Y	Y	Y	N
OKLAHOMA							
1	**Hern**	N	Y	Y	Y	N	N
2	**Mullin**	N	Y	Y	Y	N	N
3	**Lucas**	N	Y	Y	Y	Y	N
4	**Cole**	N	Y	Y	Y	Y	N
5	Horn	N	Y	Y	Y	Y	N
OREGON							
1	Bonamici	Y	N	Y	Y	Y	Y
2	**Walden**	N	Y	Y	Y	Y	N
3	Blumenauer	Y	N	Y	Y	Y	Y
4	DeFazio	P	N	Y	Y	Y	+
5	Schrader	N	N	Y	Y	Y	N
PENNSYLVANIA							
1	**Fitzpatrick**	N	Y	Y	Y	Y	N
2	Boyle	Y	N	Y	Y	Y	Y
3	Evans	N	N	Y	Y	Y	Y
4	Dean	Y	N	Y	Y	Y	Y
5	Scanlon	Y	N	Y	Y	Y	Y
6	Houlahan	N	Y	Y	Y	Y	N
7	Wild	N	Y	Y	Y	Y	N
8	Cartwright	Y	N	Y	Y	Y	Y
9	**Meuser**	N	Y	Y	Y	N	N
10	**Perry**	Y	Y	Y	N	N	Y
11	**Smucker**	Y	Y	Y	Y	Y	N
12	**Marino***						
13	**Joyce**	Y	Y	Y	N	N	N
14	**Reschenthaler**	Y	Y	Y	Y	Y	N
15	**Thompson, G.**	N	Y	Y	Y	Y	N
16	**Kelly, M.**	Y	Y	Y	Y	Y	Y
17	Lamb	Y	N	Y	Y	Y	Y
18	Doyle	Y	N	Y	Y	Y	Y
RHODE ISLAND							
1	Cicilline	Y	N	Y	Y	Y	Y
2	Langevin	Y	N	Y	Y	Y	Y
SOUTH CAROLINA							
1	Cunningham	N	Y	Y	Y	Y	N
2	**Wilson, J.**	Y	Y	Y	Y	Y	Y
3	**Duncan**	N	Y	Y	N	N	N
4	**Timmons**	N	Y	Y	N	Y	N
5	**Norman**	N	Y	Y	N	N	N
6	Clyburn	Y	N	Y	Y	Y	Y
7	**Rice, T.**	N	Y	Y	Y	Y	Y
SOUTH DAKOTA							
AL	**Johnson**	N	Y	Y	Y	Y	N
TENNESSEE							
1	**Roe**	Y	Y	Y	Y	Y	Y
2	**Burchett**	N	Y	Y	N	N	N
3	**Fleischmann**	N	Y	Y	Y	Y	N
4	**DesJarlais**	N	Y	Y	N	N	N
5	Cooper	N	N	Y	Y	Y	N
6	**Rose**	N	Y	Y	Y	Y	N
7	**Green**	N	Y	Y	?	?	?
8	**Kustoff**	N	Y	Y	Y	Y	N
9	Cohen	Y	N	Y	Y	Y	Y
TEXAS							
1	**Gohmert**	?	Y	Y	Y	N	?
2	**Crenshaw**	N	Y	Y	Y	Y	N
3	**Taylor**	Y	Y	Y	N	Y	Y
4	**Ratcliffe**	N	Y	Y	N	N	N

		229	230	231	232	233	234
5	**Gooden**	N	Y	Y	N	N	N
6	**Wright**	N	Y	Y	N	N	N
7	Fletcher	N	N	Y	Y	Y	Y
8	**Brady**	Y	Y	Y	Y	Y	Y
9	Green, A.	Y	N	Y	Y	Y	N
10	**McCaul**	N	Y	Y	Y	Y	N
11	**Conaway**	N	Y	Y	Y	N	N
12	**Granger**	Y	Y	Y	Y	Y	Y
13	**Thornberry**	Y	Y	Y	Y	Y	Y
14	**Weber**	N	Y	Y	Y	N	N
15	Gonzalez	N	N	Y	Y	Y	Y
16	Escobar	Y	N	Y	Y	Y	Y
17	**Flores**	N	Y	Y	Y	Y	N
18	Jackson Lee	?	?	?	Y	Y	Y
19	**Arrington**	N	Y	Y	Y	Y	Y
20	Castro	Y	N	Y	Y	Y	Y
21	**Roy**	N	Y	N	N	N	N
22	**Olson**	N	Y	Y	Y	Y	N
23	**Hurd**	N	Y	Y	Y	Y	N
24	**Marchant**	N	Y	Y	?	?	?
25	**Williams**	N	Y	Y	Y	Y	N
26	**Burgess**	N	Y	Y	Y	N	N
27	**Cloud**	N	Y	Y	N	N	N
28	Cuellar	N	N	Y	Y	Y	N
29	Garcia, S.	Y	N	Y	Y	Y	Y
30	Johnson, E.B.	Y	N	Y	Y	Y	Y
31	**Carter, J.**	Y	Y	Y	Y	Y	N
32	Allred	Y	N	Y	Y	Y	Y
33	Veasey	Y	N	Y	Y	Y	Y
34	Vela	Y	N	Y	Y	Y	Y
35	Doggett	Y	N	Y	Y	Y	Y
36	**Babin**	N	Y	Y	Y	N	?
UTAH							
1	**Bishop, R.**	N	Y	Y	Y	Y	N
2	**Stewart**	N	Y	Y	N	Y	N
3	**Curtis**	Y	Y	Y	N	Y	N
4	McAdams	N	N	Y	Y	Y	N
VERMONT							
AL	Welch	Y	N	Y	Y	Y	Y
VIRGINIA							
1	**Wittman**	N	Y	Y	N	Y	N
2	Luria	Y	Y	Y	Y	Y	Y
3	Scott, R.	Y	N	Y	Y	Y	Y
4	McEachin	Y	N	Y	Y	Y	Y
5	**Riggleman**	N	Y	Y	Y	Y	N
6	**Cline**	N	Y	Y	N	N	N
7	Spanberger	N	Y	Y	Y	Y	N
8	Beyer	Y	N	Y	?	?	?
9	**Griffith**	N	Y	Y	Y	Y	N
10	Wexton	N	N	Y	Y	Y	N
11	Connolly	Y	N	Y	Y	Y	Y
WASHINGTON							
1	DelBene	Y	N	Y	Y	Y	Y
2	Larsen	Y	N	Y	Y	Y	Y
3	**Herrera Beutler**	?	?	?	?	?	?
4	**Newhouse**	Y	Y	Y	Y	Y	N
5	**McMorris Rodgers**	Y	Y	Y	Y	Y	Y
6	Kilmer	N	N	Y	Y	Y	N
7	Jayapal	Y	N	Y	Y	Y	Y
8	Schrier	N	N	Y	Y	Y	N
9	Smith Adam	Y	N	Y	Y	Y	?
10	Heck	Y	N	Y	Y	Y	Y
WEST VIRGINIA							
1	**McKinley**	N	Y	Y	Y	Y	N
2	**Mooney**	N	Y	Y	N	Y	N
3	**Miller**	N	Y	Y	Y	Y	N
WISCONSIN							
1	**Steil**	Y	Y	Y	N	Y	Y
2	Pocan	Y	N	Y	+	+	+
3	Kind	N	N	Y	Y	Y	N
4	Moore	Y	N	Y	Y	Y	Y
5	**Sensenbrenner**	N	Y	Y	N	N	N
6	**Grothman**	Y	Y	Y	N	N	Y
7	**Duffy**	N	Y	Y	Y	N	N
8	**Gallagher**	N	Y	Y	N	Y	N
WYOMING							
AL	**Cheney**	N	Y	Y	Y	Y	N
DELEGATES							
	Radewagen (A.S.)						
	Norton (D.C.)						
	San Nicolas (Guam)						
	Sablan (N. Marianas)						
	González-Colón (P.R.)						
	Plaskett (V.I.)						

235. HR6. Residency Status for Undocumented Immigrants - Previous Question. Shalala, D-Fla., motion to order the previous question (thus ending debate and possibility of amendment) on the rule (H Res 415) that would provide for House floor consideration of the American Dream and Promise Act bill (HR 6). Motion agreed to 228-192: R 0-192; D 228-0. June 4, 2019.

236. HR6. Residency Status for Undocumented Immigrants - Rule. Adoption of the rule (H Res 415) that would provide for floor consideration of the American Dream and Promise Act (HR 6). Adopted 219-203: R 0-194; D 219-9. June 4, 2019.

237. Procedural Motion - Journal. Approval of the House journal of June 4, 2019. Approved 212-203: R 35-155; D 177-48. June 4, 2019.

238. HRES393. Recognizing Tienanmen Square Protests - Passage. Malinowski, D-N.J., motion to suspend the rules and agree to the resolution, as amended, that would express the support of the House of Representatives for the leaders of the 1989 Tienanmen demonstrations who advocated for "political reforms" and "protections for universally recognized human rights in China." It would call on the Chinese government to support a "full, transparent, and independent accounting" of the government's role in violence during the demonstrations and to end any censorship of information related to the Tienanmen Square massacre. It would also condemn certain ongoing policies and actions of the Chinese government, including those related to internet censorship, human rights, treatment of minority groups, and "efforts to quell peaceful political dissent." Motion agreed to 423-0: R 194-0; D 229-0. *Note: Two-thirds majority of those present and voting (282 in this case) is required for passage under suspension of the rules.* June 4, 2019.

239. HR6. Residency Status for Undocumented Immigrants - Recommit. Cline, R-Va., motion to recommit the bill to the House Judiciary Committee with instructions to report it back immediately with an amendment that would disqualify an individual from legal residency status under the bill's provisions if the Homeland Security Department "knows or has reason to believe" they are or have been a member of a "criminal street gang" or participated in gang activity. It would also require DHS to make a determination on whether an undocumented immigrant whose application for residency is denied on criminal, national security, gang, or public safety grounds should be placed in removal proceedings. Motion rejected 202-221: R 192-1; D 10-220. June 4, 2019.

240. HR6. Residency Status for Undocumented Immigrants - Passage. Passage of the bill that would provide legal residency status for certain undocumented immigrants who entered the United States as children or from nations with Temporary Protected Status designation and would prohibit the Homeland Security and Justice Departments from initiating or continuing the removal of such individuals. Title I of the bill would require DHS and DOJ to grant applications for ten-year conditional permanent residency status to undocumented immigrants who entered the U.S. as minors at least four years prior to enactment, have lived continuously in the U.S. since that time, and have earned or are enrolled in a program to earn a technical, high school, or postsecondary degree. It would disqualify certain individuals from receiving such a status based on factors including criminal record, gang participation, or other threats to public safety. It would direct DHS to grant permanent resident status to conditional residents if they maintain eligibility for conditional residency and meet certain qualifications related to postsecondary education, military service, or employment. It would also require DHS to establish a streamlined residency application process for individuals enrolled in the Deferred Action for Childhood Arrivals program. Title II of the bill would require DHS and DOJ to grant applications for permanent residency status to foreign nationals from countries designated for Temporary Protected Status or Deferred Enforced Departure who have lived continuously in the U.S. for at least three years prior to enactment and are not ineligible for admission to the U.S. under current immigration law. Among other provisions related to residency status under the bill's provisions, the bill would prohibit DHS from removing eligible individuals before providing them an opportunity to apply for residency, would provide for judicial and appellate administrative review for individuals whose residency status is denied or revoked, and would require DHS to establish a grant program for nonprofit organizations to assist eligible individuals in the application process. Passed 237-187: R 7-187; D 230-0. *Note: A "nay" was a vote in support of the president's position.* June 4, 2019.

		235	236	237	238	239	240
ALABAMA							
1	Byrne	N	N	N	Y	Y	N
2	Roby	N	N	N	Y	Y	N
3	Rogers, M.	N	N	N	Y	Y	N
4	Aderholt	N	N	N	Y	Y	N
5	Brooks, M.	N	N	N	Y	Y	N
6	Palmer	N	N	N	Y	Y	N
7	Sewell	Y	Y	Y	Y	N	Y
ALASKA							
AL	Young	N	N	?	Y	Y	N
ARIZONA							
1	O'Halleran	Y	Y	Y	Y	N	Y
2	Kirkpatrick	Y	Y	N	Y	N	Y
3	Grijalva	Y	Y	P	Y	N	Y
4	Gosar	N	N	N	Y	Y	N
5	Biggs	N	N	N	N	Y	N
6	Schweikert	N	N	Y	N	Y	N
7	Gallego	Y	Y	Y	Y	N	Y
8	Lesko	N	N	N	Y	Y	N
9	Stanton	Y	Y	Y	Y	N	Y
ARKANSAS							
1	Crawford	N	N	N	Y	Y	N
2	Hill, F.	N	N	N	Y	Y	N
3	Womack	N	N	N	Y	Y	N
4	Westerman	N	N	N	Y	Y	N
CALIFORNIA							
1	LaMalfa	-	N	N	Y	Y	N
2	Huffman	Y	Y	Y	Y	N	Y
3	Garamendi	Y	Y	Y	Y	N	Y
4	McClintock	N	N	Y	Y	Y	N
5	Thompson, M.	Y	Y	N	Y	N	Y
6	Matsui	Y	Y	N	Y	N	Y
7	Bera	Y	Y	N	Y	N	Y
8	Cook	N	N	N	Y	Y	N
9	McNerney	Y	Y	Y	Y	N	Y
10	Harder	Y	Y	N	Y	N	Y
11	DeSaulnier	Y	Y	Y	Y	N	Y
12	Pelosi				Y	N	Y
13	Lee B.	Y	Y	Y	Y	N	Y
14	Speier	Y	Y	Y	Y	N	Y
15	Swalwell	?	?	?	?	?	?
16	Costa	Y	Y	N	Y	N	Y
17	Khanna	Y	Y	Y	Y	N	Y
18	Eshoo	Y	Y	Y	Y	N	Y
19	Lofgren	Y	Y	Y	Y	N	Y
20	Panetta	Y	Y	N	Y	N	Y
21	Cox	Y	Y	Y	Y	N	Y
22	Nunes	N	N	N	Y	Y	N
23	McCarthy	N	N	N	Y	Y	N
24	Carbajal	Y	Y	Y	Y	N	Y
25	Hill, K.	Y	Y	Y	Y	N	Y
26	Brownley	Y	Y	Y	Y	N	Y
27	Chu	Y	Y	Y	Y	N	Y
28	Schiff	Y	Y	Y	Y	N	Y
29	Cárdenas	Y	Y	N	Y	N	Y
30	Sherman	+	+	+	+	-	+
31	Aguilar	Y	Y	Y	Y	N	Y
32	Napolitano	Y	Y	Y	Y	N	Y
33	Lieu	Y	Y	Y	Y	N	Y
34	Gomez	Y	Y	Y	Y	N	Y
35	Torres	Y	Y	Y	Y	N	Y
36	Ruiz	Y	Y	N	Y	N	Y
37	Bass	Y	Y	Y	Y	N	Y
38	Sánchez	Y	Y	Y	Y	N	Y
39	Cisneros	Y	Y	Y	Y	N	Y
40	Roybal-Allard	Y	Y	Y	Y	N	Y
41	Takano	Y	Y	Y	Y	N	Y
42	Calvert	N	N	N	Y	Y	N
43	Waters	Y	Y	Y	Y	N	Y
44	Barragán	Y	Y	Y	Y	N	Y
45	Porter	Y	Y	Y	Y	N	Y
46	Correa	Y	Y	N	Y	N	Y
47	Lowenthal	Y	Y	Y	Y	N	Y
48	Rouda	Y	Y	N	Y	N	Y
49	Levin	Y	Y	Y	Y	N	Y
50	Hunter	N	N	N	Y	Y	N
51	Vargas	Y	Y	Y	Y	N	Y
52	Peters	Y	Y	Y	Y	N	Y

		235	236	237	238	239	240
53	Davis, S.	Y	Y	Y	Y	N	Y
COLORADO							
1	DeGette	Y	Y	Y	Y	N	Y
2	Neguse	Y	Y	Y	Y	N	Y
3	Tipton	N	N	N	Y	Y	N
4	Buck	N	N	N	Y	Y	N
5	Lamborn	N	N	N	Y	Y	N
6	Crow	Y	Y	N	Y	N	Y
7	Perlmutter	Y	Y	Y	Y	N	Y
CONNECTICUT							
1	Larson	Y	Y	Y	Y	N	Y
2	Courtney	Y	Y	Y	Y	N	Y
3	DeLauro	Y	Y	Y	Y	N	Y
4	Himes	Y	Y	N	Y	N	Y
5	Hayes	Y	Y	Y	Y	N	Y
DELAWARE							
AL	Blunt Rochester	Y	Y	Y	Y	N	Y
FLORIDA							
1	Gaetz	N	N	N	Y	Y	N
2	Dunn	N	N	N	Y	Y	N
3	Yoho	N	N	N	Y	Y	N
4	Rutherford	N	N	N	Y	Y	N
5	Lawson	Y	Y	N	Y	N	Y
6	Waltz	N	N	Y	Y	Y	N
7	Murphy	Y	Y	N	Y	N	Y
8	Posey	N	N	N	Y	Y	N
9	Soto	Y	Y	Y	Y	N	Y
10	Demings	Y	Y	Y	Y	N	Y
11	Webster	N	N	N	Y	Y	N
12	Bilirakis	N	N	N	Y	Y	N
13	Crist	Y	Y	N	Y	N	Y
14	Castor	Y	Y	Y	Y	N	Y
15	Spano	N	N	N	Y	Y	N
16	Buchanan	N	N	N	Y	Y	N
17	Steube	N	N	N	Y	Y	N
18	Mast	N	N	N	Y	Y	N
19	Rooney	N	N	N	Y	Y	N
20	Hastings	?	?	?	?	?	+
21	Frankel	Y	Y	Y	Y	N	Y
22	Deutch	Y	Y	Y	Y	N	Y
23	Wasserman Schultz	Y	Y	Y	Y	N	Y
24	Wilson, F.	+	+	+	+	-	+
25	Diaz-Balart	N	N	N	Y	Y	N
26	Mucarsel-Powell	Y	Y	Y	Y	N	Y
27	Shalala	Y	Y	Y	Y	N	Y
GEORGIA							
1	Carter, E.L.	N	N	N	Y	Y	N
2	Bishop, S.	Y	Y	Y	Y	N	Y
3	Ferguson	N	N	N	Y	Y	N
4	Johnson, H.	Y	Y	Y	Y	N	Y
5	Lewis John	Y	Y	Y	Y	N	Y
6	McBath	Y	Y	Y	Y	N	Y
7	Woodall	N	N	N	Y	Y	N
8	Scott, A.	N	N	N	Y	Y	N
9	Collins, D.	N	N	N	Y	Y	N
10	Hice	N	N	N	Y	Y	N
11	Loudermilk	N	N	N	Y	Y	N
12	Allen	N	N	N	Y	Y	N
13	Scott, D.	Y	Y	Y	Y	N	Y
14	Graves, T.	N	N	N	Y	Y	N
HAWAII							
1	Case	Y	Y	Y	Y	N	Y
2	Gabbard	Y	Y	Y	?	N	Y
IDAHO							
1	Fulcher	N	N	N	Y	Y	N
2	Simpson	N	N	Y	Y	Y	N
ILLINOIS							
1	Rush	Y	Y	Y	Y	N	Y
2	Kelly, R.	Y	Y	Y	Y	N	Y
3	Lipinski	Y	Y	Y	Y	N	Y
4	García, J.	Y	Y	Y	Y	N	Y
5	Quigley	Y	Y	Y	Y	N	Y
6	Casten	Y	Y	Y	Y	N	Y
7	Davis, D.	Y	Y	Y	Y	N	Y
8	Krishnamoorthi	Y	Y	N	Y	N	Y
9	Schakowsky	Y	Y	Y	Y	N	Y
10	Schneider	Y	Y	Y	Y	N	Y
11	Foster	Y	Y	Y	Y	N	Y

KEY: Republicans   Democrats   *Independents*

Y Voted for (yea)	**N** Voted against (nay)	**P** Voted "present"
+ Announced for	**–** Announced against	**?** Did not vote or otherwise make position known
# Paired for	**X** Paired against	

		235	236	237	238	239	240
12	**Bost**	N	N	N	Y	Y	N
13	**Davis, R.**	N	N	N	Y	Y	N
14	Underwood	Y	N	Y	Y	N	Y
15	**Shimkus**	N	N	N	Y	Y	N
16	**Kinzinger**	N	N	Y	Y	Y	N
17	Bustos	Y	Y	Y	Y	N	Y
18	**LaHood**	N	N	N	Y	Y	N
INDIANA							
1	Visclosky	Y	Y	Y	Y	N	Y
2	**Walorski**	N	N	N	Y	Y	N
3	**Banks**	N	N	Y	Y	Y	N
4	**Baird**	N	N	N	Y	Y	N
5	**Brooks, S.**	N	N	N	Y	Y	N
6	**Pence**	N	N	N	Y	Y	N
7	Carson	Y	Y	Y	Y	N	Y
8	**Bucshon**	N	N	Y	Y	Y	N
9	**Hollingsworth**	N	N	Y	Y	Y	N
IOWA							
1	Finkenauer	Y	Y	Y	Y	Y	Y
2	Loebsack	Y	Y	Y	Y	N	Y
3	Axne	Y	Y	N	Y	N	Y
4	**King, S.**	N	N	Y	Y	Y	N
KANSAS							
1	**Marshall**	N	N	N	Y	Y	N
2	**Watkins**	N	N	Y	Y	Y	N
3	Davids	Y	N	Y	Y	N	Y
4	**Estes**	N	N	N	Y	Y	N
KENTUCKY							
1	**Comer**	N	N	N	Y	Y	N
2	**Guthrie**	N	N	N	Y	Y	N
3	Yarmuth	Y	Y	Y	Y	N	Y
4	**Massie**	N	N	N	Y	Y	N
5	**Rogers, H.**	N	N	N	Y	Y	N
6	**Barr**	N	N	N	Y	Y	N
LOUISIANA							
1	**Scalise**	N	N	N	Y	Y	N
2	Richmond	Y	Y	Y	Y	N	Y
3	**Higgins, C.**	N	N	N	Y	Y	N
4	**Johnson, M.**	N	N	N	Y	Y	N
5	**Abraham**	N	N	N	Y	Y	N
6	**Graves, G.**	N	N	N	Y	Y	N
MAINE							
1	Pingree	Y	Y	Y	Y	N	Y
2	Golden	Y	N	N	Y	Y	Y
MARYLAND							
1	**Harris**	N	N	N	Y	Y	N
2	Ruppersberger	Y	Y	Y	Y	N	Y
3	Sarbanes	Y	Y	Y	Y	N	Y
4	Brown, A.	Y	Y	Y	Y	N	Y
5	Hoyer	Y	Y	Y	Y	N	Y
6	Trone	Y	Y	Y	Y	N	Y
7	Cummings	Y	Y	Y	Y	N	Y
8	Raskin						
MASSACHUSETTS		Y	Y	Y	Y	N	Y
1	Neal						
2	McGovern	Y	Y	Y	Y	N	Y
3	Trahan	Y	Y	Y	Y	N	Y
4	Kennedy	Y	Y	Y	Y	N	Y
5	Clark	Y	Y	Y	Y	N	Y
6	Moulton	Y	Y	Y	Y	N	Y
7	Pressley	Y	Y	N	Y	N	Y
8	Lynch	Y	Y	Y	Y	N	Y
9	Keating	Y	Y	Y	Y	N	Y
MICHIGAN		Y	Y	N	Y	N	Y
1	**Bergman**						
2	**Huizenga**	N	N	Y	Y	Y	N
3	**Amash**	N	N	N	Y	Y	N
4	**Moolenaar**	N	N	N	Y	N	N
5	Kildee	N	N	N	Y	Y	N
6	**Upton**	Y	Y	Y	Y	N	Y
7	**Walberg**	N	N	N	Y	Y	Y
8	Slotkin	N	N	N	Y	Y	N
9	Levin	Y	Y	Y	Y	Y	Y
10	**Mitchell**	Y	Y	Y	Y	N	Y
11	Stevens	N	N	N	Y	Y	N
12	Dingell	Y	Y	N	Y	N	Y
13	Tlaib	Y	Y	Y	Y	N	Y
14	Lawrence	Y	Y	Y	Y	N	Y
MINNESOTA		Y	Y	Y	Y	N	Y
1	**Hagedorn**						
2	Craig	N	N	N	Y	Y	N
3	Phillips	Y	Y	N	Y	Y	Y
4	McCollum	Y	Y	Y	Y	N	Y
5	Omar	Y	Y	Y	Y	N	Y

		235	236	237	238	239	240
6	**Emmer**	?	?	?	Y	N	Y
7	Peterson	N	N	N	Y	Y	N
8	**Stauber**	Y	Y	N	Y	N	Y
MISSISSIPPI		N	N	Y	Y	Y	N
1	**Kelly, T.**						
2	Thompson, B.	N	N	N	Y	Y	N
3	**Guest**	Y	Y	Y	Y	N	Y
4	**Palazzo**	N	N	N	Y	Y	N
MISSOURI		N	N	N	Y	Y	N
1	Clay						
2	**Wagner**	Y	Y	Y	Y	N	Y
3	**Luetkemeyer**	N	N	Y	Y	Y	N
4	**Hartzler**	N	N	N	Y	Y	N
5	Cleaver	N	N	N	Y	Y	N
6	**Graves, S.**	Y	Y	Y	Y	N	Y
7	**Long**	N	N	N	Y	Y	N
8	**Smith, J.**	N	N	Y	Y	Y	N
MONTANA		N	N	N	Y	Y	N
AL	**Gianforte**						
NEBRASKA		N	N	N	Y	Y	N
1	**Fortenberry**						
2	**Bacon**	N	N	Y	Y	Y	N
3	**Smith, Adrian**	N	N	Y	Y	Y	Y
NEVADA		N	N	N	Y	Y	N
1	Titus						
2	**Amodei**	Y	Y	Y	Y	N	Y
3	Lee	N	N	Y	Y	Y	N
4	Horsford	Y	Y	N	Y	N	Y
NEW HAMPSHIRE		Y	Y	N	Y	N	Y
1	Pappas						
2	Kuster	Y	Y	Y	Y	N	Y
NEW JERSEY		Y	Y	Y	Y	N	Y
1	Norcross						
2	Van Drew	Y	Y	Y	Y	N	Y
3	Kim	Y	Y	N	Y	Y	Y
4	**Smith, C.**	Y	Y	N	Y	N	Y
5	Gottheimer	N	N	N	Y	Y	Y
6	Pallone	Y	Y	Y	Y	Y	Y
7	Malinowski	Y	Y	Y	Y	N	Y
8	Sires	Y	N	Y	Y	N	Y
9	Pascrell	Y	Y	Y	Y	N	Y
10	Payne	Y	Y	Y	Y	N	Y
11	Sherrill	Y	Y	Y	Y	N	Y
12	Watson Coleman	Y	Y	N	Y	N	Y
NEW MEXICO		Y	Y	Y	Y	N	Y
1	Haaland						
2	Torres Small	Y	Y	Y	Y	N	Y
3	Luján	Y	Y	N	Y	N	Y
NEW YORK		Y	Y	Y	Y	N	Y
1	**Zeldin**						
2	**King, P.**	N	N	N	Y	?	N
3	Suozzi	N	N	Y	Y	Y	N
4	Rice, K.	Y	Y	N	Y	N	Y
5	Meeks	Y	Y	N	Y	N	Y
6	Meng	Y	Y	Y	Y	N	Y
7	Velázquez	Y	Y	N	Y	N	Y
8	Jeffries	Y	Y	Y	Y	N	Y
9	Clarke	Y	Y	Y	Y	N	Y
10	Nadler	Y	Y	Y	Y	N	Y
11	Rose	Y	Y	Y	Y	N	Y
12	Maloney, C.	Y	Y	N	Y	N	Y
13	Espaillat	Y	Y	Y	Y	N	Y
14	Ocasio-Cortez	Y	Y	Y	Y	N	Y
15	Serrano	Y	Y	Y	Y	N	Y
16	Engel	Y	Y	Y	Y	N	Y
17	Lowey	Y	Y	Y	Y	N	Y
18	Maloney, S.P.	Y	Y	Y	Y	N	Y
19	Delgado	Y	Y	Y	Y	N	Y
20	Tonko	Y	Y	Y	Y	N	Y
21	**Stefanik**	Y	Y	P	Y	N	Y
22	Brindisi	N	N	Y	Y	Y	N
23	**Reed**	Y	N	N	Y	Y	Y
24	**Katko**	?	N	N	Y	Y	N
25	Morelle	N	N	Y	Y	Y	N
26	Higgins, B.	Y	Y	Y	Y	N	Y
27	**Collins, C.**	Y	Y	Y	Y	N	Y
NORTH CAROLINA		N	N	N	Y	Y	N
1	Butterfield						
2	**Holding**	Y	Y	Y	Y	N	Y
3	**Jones***	N	N	N	Y	Y	N
4	Price						
5	**Foxx**	Y	Y	Y	Y	N	Y
6	**Walker**	N	N	N	Y	Y	N
7	**Rouzer**	N	N	N	Y	Y	N

		235	236	237	238	239	240
8	**Hudson**	N	N	N	Y	Y	N
9	vacant	N	N	N	Y	Y	N
10	**McHenry**	N	N	N	Y	Y	N
11	**Meadows**	N	N	Y	Y	Y	N
12	Adams	Y	Y	Y	Y	N	Y
13	**Budd**	N	N	N	Y	Y	N
NORTH DAKOTA							
AL	**Armstrong**	N	N	N	Y	Y	N
OHIO							
1	**Chabot**	N	N	N	Y	Y	N
2	**Wenstrup**	N	N	N	Y	Y	N
3	Beatty	Y	Y	Y	Y	N	Y
4	**Jordan**	N	N	N	Y	Y	N
5	**Latta**	N	N	N	Y	Y	N
6	**Johnson, B.**	N	N	N	Y	Y	N
7	**Gibbs**	N	N	N	Y	Y	N
8	**Davidson**	N	N	Y	Y	Y	N
9	Kaptur	Y	Y	Y	Y	N	Y
10	**Turner**	N	N	N	Y	Y	N
11	Fudge	Y	Y	Y	Y	N	Y
12	**Balderson**	N	N	N	Y	Y	N
13	Ryan	Y	Y	Y	Y	N	Y
14	**Joyce**	N	N	?	Y	Y	N
15	**Stivers**	N	N	N	Y	Y	N
16	**Gonzalez**	N	N	N	Y	Y	N
OKLAHOMA							
1	**Hern**	-	-	+	+	+	-
2	**Mullin**	?	?	?	?	?	?
3	**Lucas**	N	N	N	Y	Y	N
4	**Cole**	N	N	N	Y	Y	N
5	Horn	Y	N	N	Y	Y	Y
OREGON							
1	Bonamici	Y	Y	Y	Y	N	Y
2	**Walden**	N	N	N	Y	Y	N
3	Blumenauer	Y	Y	Y	Y	N	Y
4	DeFazio	Y	Y	Y	Y	N	Y
5	Schrader	Y	Y	N	Y	N	Y
PENNSYLVANIA							
1	**Fitzpatrick**	N	N	N	Y	Y	Y
2	Boyle	Y	Y	Y	Y	N	Y
3	Evans	Y	Y	Y	Y	N	Y
4	Dean	Y	Y	Y	Y	N	Y
5	Scanlon	Y	Y	Y	Y	N	Y
6	Houlahan	Y	Y	N	Y	N	Y
7	Wild	Y	Y	Y	Y	N	Y
8	Cartwright	Y	Y	Y	Y	N	Y
9	**Meuser**	N	N	N	Y	Y	N
10	**Perry**	N	N	Y	Y	Y	N
11	**Smucker**	N	N	N	Y	Y	N
12	**Marino***						
13	**Joyce**	N	N	N	Y	Y	N
14	**Reschenthaler**	N	N	N	Y	Y	N
15	**Thompson, G.**	N	N	N	Y	Y	N
16	**Kelly, M.**	N	N	Y	Y	Y	N
17	Lamb	Y	Y	Y	Y	N	Y
18	Doyle	Y	Y	Y	Y	N	Y
RHODE ISLAND							
1	Cicilline	Y	Y	Y	Y	N	Y
2	Langevin	Y	Y	Y	Y	N	Y
SOUTH CAROLINA							
1	Cunningham	Y	N	N	Y	Y	Y
2	**Wilson, J.**	N	N	Y	Y	Y	N
3	**Duncan**	N	N	N	Y	Y	N
4	**Timmons**	N	N	N	Y	Y	N
5	**Norman**	N	N	N	Y	Y	N
6	Clyburn	+	+	+	+	-	+
7	**Rice, T.**	N	N	Y	Y	Y	N
SOUTH DAKOTA							
AL	**Johnson**	N	N	N	Y	Y	N
TENNESSEE							
1	**Roe**	N	N	N	Y	Y	N
2	**Burchett**	N	N	N	Y	Y	N
3	**Fleischmann**	N	N	N	Y	Y	N
4	**DesJarlais**	N	N	N	Y	Y	N
5	Cooper	Y	Y	N	Y	N	Y
6	**Rose**	N	N	N	Y	Y	N
7	**Green**	?	?	?	?	?	?
8	**Kustoff**	N	N	N	Y	Y	N
9	Cohen	Y	Y	Y	Y	N	Y
TEXAS							
1	**Gohmert**	N	N	?	Y	Y	N
2	**Crenshaw**	N	N	N	Y	Y	N
3	**Taylor**	N	N	Y	Y	Y	N
4	**Ratcliffe**	N	N	N	Y	Y	N

		235	236	237	238	239	240
5	**Gooden**	N	N	N	Y	Y	N
6	**Wright**	N	N	N	Y	Y	N
7	Fletcher	Y	Y	Y	Y	N	Y
8	**Brady**	N	N	Y	Y	Y	N
9	Green, A.	Y	Y	N	Y	N	Y
10	**McCaul**	N	N	N	Y	Y	N
11	**Conaway**	N	N	N	Y	Y	N
12	**Granger**	N	N	N	Y	Y	N
13	**Thornberry**	N	N	Y	Y	Y	N
14	**Weber**	N	N	N	Y	Y	N
15	Gonzalez	Y	Y	Y	Y	N	Y
16	Escobar	Y	Y	Y	Y	N	Y
17	**Flores**	N	N	N	Y	Y	N
18	Jackson Lee	Y	Y	Y	Y	N	Y
19	**Arrington**	N	N	Y	Y	Y	N
20	Castro	Y	Y	Y	Y	N	Y
21	**Roy**	N	N	N	Y	Y	N
22	**Olson**	N	N	N	Y	Y	N
23	**Hurd**	N	N	N	Y	Y	Y
24	**Marchant**	N	N	N	Y	Y	N
25	**Williams**	N	N	N	Y	Y	N
26	**Burgess**	N	N	N	Y	Y	N
27	**Cloud**	N	N	N	Y	Y	N
28	Cuellar	Y	Y	Y	Y	N	Y
29	Garcia, S.	Y	Y	Y	Y	N	Y
30	Johnson, E.B.	Y	Y	Y	Y	N	Y
31	**Carter, J.**	N	N	N	Y	Y	N
32	Allred	Y	Y	Y	Y	N	Y
33	Veasey	Y	Y	Y	Y	N	Y
34	Vela	Y	Y	Y	Y	N	Y
35	Doggett	Y	Y	Y	Y	N	Y
36	**Babin**	N	N	N	Y	Y	N
UTAH							
1	**Bishop, R.**	N	N	?	Y	Y	N
2	**Stewart**	N	N	N	Y	Y	N
3	**Curtis**	N	N	N	Y	Y	N
4	McAdams	Y	N	N	Y	N	Y
VERMONT							
AL	Welch	Y	Y	Y	Y	N	Y
VIRGINIA							
1	**Wittman**	N	N	N	Y	Y	N
2	Luria	Y	Y	Y	Y	N	Y
3	Scott, R.	Y	Y	Y	Y	N	Y
4	McEachin	Y	Y	Y	Y	N	Y
5	**Riggleman**	N	N	N	Y	Y	N
6	**Cline**	N	N	N	Y	Y	N
7	Spanberger	Y	Y	N	Y	N	Y
8	Beyer	Y	Y	Y	Y	N	Y
9	**Griffith**	N	N	N	Y	Y	N
10	Wexton	Y	Y	N	Y	N	Y
11	Connolly	Y	Y	N	Y	N	Y
WASHINGTON							
1	DelBene	Y	Y	Y	Y	N	Y
2	Larsen	Y	Y	?	Y	N	Y
3	**Herrera Beutler**	?	?	?	?	?	?
4	**Newhouse**	N	N	Y	Y	Y	Y
5	**McMorris Rodgers**	N	N	N	Y	Y	N
6	Kilmer	Y	Y	Y	Y	N	Y
7	Jayapal	Y	Y	Y	Y	N	Y
8	Schrier	Y	Y	N	Y	N	Y
9	Smith Adam	Y	Y	Y	Y	N	Y
10	Heck	Y	Y	Y	Y	N	Y
WEST VIRGINIA							
1	**McKinley**	N	N	N	Y	Y	N
2	**Mooney**	N	N	N	Y	Y	N
3	**Miller**	N	N	N	Y	Y	N
WISCONSIN							
1	**Steil**	N	N	Y	Y	Y	N
2	Pocan	Y	Y	Y	Y	N	Y
3	Kind	Y	Y	N	Y	N	Y
4	Moore	Y	Y	Y	Y	N	Y
5	**Sensenbrenner**	N	N	N	Y	Y	N
6	**Grothman**	N	N	N	Y	Y	N
7	**Duffy**	N	N	N	Y	Y	N
8	**Gallagher**	N	N	N	Y	Y	N
WYOMING							
AL	**Cheney**	N	N	N	Y	Y	N
DELEGATES							
	Radewagen (A.S.)						
	Norton (D.C.)						
	San Nicolas (Guam)						
	Sablan (N. Marianas)						
	González-Colón (P.R.)						
	Plaskett (V.I.)						

241. HR1921. Ocean Acidification Grant Program - Passage. Johnson, D-Texas, motion to suspend the rules and pass the bill, as amended, that would authorize the establishment of a program awarding competitive prizes for the development of monitoring, management, and adaptation options in response to ocean acidification, particularly for programs to address communities, environments, or industries "in distress" due to ocean acidification. The program could be carried out by any federal agency represented on an interagency working group on ocean acidification, in coordination with the National Oceanic and Atmospheric Administration. Motion agreed to 395-22: R 168-22; D 227-0. *Note: A two-thirds majority of those present and voting (278 in this case) is required for passage under suspension of the rules.* June 5, 2019.

242. HR542. DHS Emergency Response Research - Passage. Rice, D-N.Y., motion to suspend the rules and pass the bill that would statutorily authorize a national urban security technology laboratory within the Homeland Security Department to conduct research to help emergency responders prepare for and protect against terrorist threats, including by evaluating emerging technologies, assessing the cybersecurity of such technologies, researching radiological and nuclear response and recovery, and providing technical advice to emergency responders. Motion agreed to 395-3: R 179-3; D 216-0. *Note: A two-thirds majority of those present and voting (266 in this case) is required for passage under suspension of the rules.* June 10, 2019.

243. HR2539. Surface Transportation Security - Passage. Rice, D-N.Y., motion to suspend the rules and pass the bill that includes a number of provisions related to surface transportation security. Specifically, it would require the Homeland Security Department to prioritize the assignment of Transportation Security Administration officers and intelligence analysts to locations containing high-risk surface transportation assets, such as bus terminals or rail carriers. It would require such officers and analysts to generate and disseminate intelligence products to assist state, local, and tribal law enforcement in identifying, investigating, and responding to terrorist and other security threats. It would also allow owners and operators of surface transportation assets to apply for security clearances to facilitate information sharing with DHS related to security threats and would authorize DHS to develop a training program to strengthen local law enforcement response capabilities related to surface transportation threats. Motion agreed to 384-13: R 167-13; D 217-0. *Note: A two-thirds majority of those present and voting (265 in this case) is required for passage under suspension of the rules.* June 10, 2019.

244. HR2590. DHS International Programs and Personnel - Passage. Correa, D-Calif., motion to suspend the rules and pass the bill, as amended, that would require the Homeland Security Department to provide briefings to Congress every 180 days including status updates on a three-year DHS strategy for its international programs and on DHS personnel whose primary duties take place outside of the U.S., including deployment schedule and costs, relation of placements to counter-terrorism strategy, and risk mitigation plans related to counterintelligence threats. It would also require DHS to create a plan to improve effectiveness, capacity, and collaboration of deployed personnel, including with regard to counter-terrorism and counterespionage strategy. Motion agreed to 394-2: R 179-2; D 215-0. *Note: A two-thirds majority of those present and voting (264 in this case) is required for passage under suspension of the rules.* June 10, 2019.

245. HR2740, HRES430. Fiscal 2020 Appropriations Package, Congressional Subpoenas - Previous Question. Raskin, D-Md., motion to order the previous question (thus ending debate and possibility of amendment) on the rule (H Res 431) that would provide for House floor consideration of the fiscal 2020 Labor-HHS-Education, Defense, Energy-Water, and State-Foreign Operations appropriations package (HR 2740), and a resolution (H Res 430) that would authorize the House Judiciary Committee to take civil legal actions in federal court to enforce congressional subpoenas issued to Attorney General William P. Barr and former White House Counsel Donald F. McGahn, II. Motion agreed to 227-190: R 0-190; D 227-0. June 11, 2019.

246. HRES430, HR2740. Fiscal 2020 Appropriations Package, Congressional Subpoenas - Rule. Adoption of the rule that would provide for floor consideration of the fiscal 2020 Labor-HHS-Education, Defense, Energy-Water, and State-Foreign Operations appropriations package (HR 2740), and a resolution (H Res 430) that would authorize the House Judiciary Committee to take civil legal actions in federal court to enforce congressional subpoenas issued to Attorney General William P. Barr and former White House Counsel Donald F. McGahn, II. The rule would also provide for automatic adoption of a Lowey, D-N.Y., manager's amendment to HR 2740 that would remove from the bill a section making fiscal 2020 appropriations for the legislative branch. The amendment would also rescind $11.8 million in unobligated balances available for certain foreign aid grants issued by the State Department and related agencies; and it would make a technical correction to specify that previously-appropriated funds for the Defense Department shall not be used to construct physical barriers or border security infrastructure along the U.S. southern land border. Adopted 227-190: R 0-190; D 227-0. June 11, 2019.

		241	242	243	244	245	246
ALABAMA							
1	**Byrne**	Y	Y	Y	Y	N	N
2	**Roby**	Y	Y	Y	Y	N	N
3	**Rogers, M.**	Y	Y	Y	Y	N	N
4	**Aderholt**	Y	Y	Y	Y	N	N
5	**Brooks, M.**	N	Y	N	Y	N	N
6	**Palmer**	Y	Y	Y	Y	N	N
7	Sewell	Y	Y	Y	Y	Y	Y
ALASKA							
AL	**Young**	Y	Y	Y	Y	N	N
ARIZONA							
1	O'Halleran	Y	Y	Y	Y	Y	Y
2	Kirkpatrick	Y	Y	Y	Y	Y	Y
3	Grijalva	Y	Y	Y	Y	Y	Y
4	**Gosar**	N	?	?	?	N	N
5	**Biggs**	?	Y	N	N	N	N
6	**Schweikert**	Y	Y	Y	Y	N	N
7	Gallego	Y	Y	Y	Y	Y	Y
8	**Lesko**	Y	Y	Y	Y	N	N
9	Stanton	Y	Y	Y	Y	Y	Y
ARKANSAS							
1	**Crawford**	Y	Y	Y	Y	N	N
2	**Hill, F.**	Y	Y	Y	Y	N	N
3	**Womack**	Y	Y	Y	Y	N	N
4	**Westerman**	Y	Y	Y	Y	N	N
CALIFORNIA							
1	**LaMalfa**	Y	Y	Y	Y	N	N
2	Huffman	Y	Y	Y	Y	Y	Y
3	Garamendi	Y	Y	Y	Y	Y	Y
4	**McClintock**	N	Y	Y	Y	N	N
5	Thompson, M.	Y	Y	Y	Y	Y	Y
6	Matsui	Y	Y	Y	Y	Y	Y
7	Bera	Y	Y	Y	Y	Y	Y
8	**Cook**	Y	Y	Y	Y	N	N
9	McNerney	Y	Y	Y	Y	Y	Y
10	Harder	Y	Y	Y	Y	Y	Y
11	DeSaulnier	Y	Y	Y	Y	Y	Y
12	Pelosi						
13	Lee B.	Y	Y	Y	?	Y	Y
14	Speier	Y	Y	Y	Y	Y	Y
15	Swalwell	?	Y	Y	Y	Y	Y
16	Costa	Y	Y	Y	Y	Y	Y
17	Khanna	Y	Y	Y	Y	Y	Y
18	Eshoo	Y	Y	Y	Y	Y	Y
19	Lofgren	Y	Y	Y	Y	Y	Y
20	Panetta	Y	Y	Y	Y	Y	Y
21	Cox	Y	Y	Y	Y	Y	Y
22	**Nunes**	Y	Y	Y	Y	N	N
23	**McCarthy**	Y	Y	Y	Y	N	N
24	Carbajal	Y	Y	Y	Y	Y	Y
25	Hill, K.	Y	Y	Y	Y	Y	Y
26	Brownley	Y	Y	Y	Y	Y	Y
27	Chu	Y	Y	Y	Y	Y	Y
28	Schiff	Y	Y	Y	Y	Y	Y
29	Cárdenas	Y	Y	Y	Y	Y	Y
30	Sherman	+	Y	Y	Y	Y	Y
31	Aguilar	Y	Y	Y	Y	Y	Y
32	Napolitano	Y	Y	Y	Y	Y	Y
33	Lieu	Y	Y	Y	Y	Y	Y
34	Gomez	Y	Y	Y	Y	Y	Y
35	Torres	Y	Y	Y	Y	Y	Y
36	Ruiz	Y	Y	Y	Y	Y	Y
37	Bass	Y	Y	Y	Y	Y	Y
38	Sánchez	Y	Y	Y	Y	Y	Y
39	Cisneros	Y	Y	Y	Y	Y	Y
40	Roybal-Allard	Y	Y	Y	Y	Y	Y
41	Takano	Y	Y	Y	Y	Y	Y
42	**Calvert**	Y	Y	Y	Y	N	N
43	Waters	Y	Y	Y	Y	Y	Y
44	Barragán	Y	Y	Y	Y	Y	Y
45	Porter	Y	Y	Y	Y	Y	Y
46	Correa	Y	Y	Y	Y	Y	Y
47	Lowenthal	Y	Y	Y	Y	Y	Y
48	Rouda	Y	Y	Y	Y	Y	Y
49	Levin	Y	Y	Y	Y	Y	Y
50	**Hunter**	N	Y	N	Y	N	N
51	Vargas	Y	Y	Y	Y	Y	Y
52	Peters	Y	Y	Y	Y	Y	Y

		241	242	243	244	245	246
53	Davis, S.	Y	Y	Y	Y	+	+
COLORADO							
1	DeGette	Y	Y	Y	Y	Y	Y
2	Neguse	Y	Y	Y	Y	Y	Y
3	**Tipton**	Y	Y	Y	Y	N	N
4	**Buck**	?	?	?	?	?	?
5	**Lamborn**	Y	Y	Y	Y	N	N
6	Crow	Y	Y	Y	Y	Y	Y
7	Perlmutter	Y	Y	Y	Y	Y	Y
CONNECTICUT							
1	Larson	Y	Y	Y	Y	Y	Y
2	Courtney	Y	Y	Y	Y	Y	Y
3	DeLauro	Y	Y	Y	Y	Y	Y
4	Himes	Y	Y	Y	Y	Y	Y
5	Hayes	Y	Y	Y	Y	Y	Y
DELAWARE							
AL	Blunt Rochester	Y	Y	Y	Y	Y	Y
FLORIDA							
1	**Gaetz**	Y	Y	Y	?	N	N
2	**Dunn**	Y	Y	Y	Y	N	N
3	**Yoho**	N	Y	N	Y	N	N
4	**Rutherford**	Y	Y	Y	Y	N	N
5	Lawson	Y	Y	Y	Y	Y	Y
6	**Waltz**	Y	Y	Y	Y	N	N
7	Murphy	Y	Y	Y	Y	Y	Y
8	**Posey**	Y	Y	Y	Y	N	N
9	Soto	Y	Y	Y	Y	Y	Y
10	Demings	Y	Y	Y	Y	Y	Y
11	**Webster**	Y	Y	Y	Y	N	N
12	**Bilirakis**	Y	Y	Y	Y	N	N
13	Crist	Y	+	+	+	Y	Y
14	Castor	Y	Y	Y	Y	Y	Y
15	**Spano**	Y	Y	Y	Y	N	N
16	**Buchanan**	Y	Y	Y	Y	N	N
17	**Steube**	Y	Y	Y	Y	N	N
18	**Mast**	Y	Y	Y	Y	N	N
19	**Rooney**	Y	Y	Y	Y	N	N
20	Hastings	?	?	?	?	?	?
21	Frankel	Y	Y	Y	Y	Y	Y
22	Deutch	Y	Y	Y	Y	Y	Y
23	Wasserman Schultz	Y	?	?	?	Y	Y
24	Wilson, F.	?	Y	Y	Y	Y	Y
25	**Diaz-Balart**	Y	Y	Y	Y	N	N
26	Mucarsel-Powell	Y	Y	Y	Y	Y	Y
27	Shalala	Y	Y	Y	Y	Y	Y
GEORGIA							
1	**Carter, E.L.**	Y	Y	Y	Y	N	N
2	Bishop, S.	Y	Y	Y	Y	Y	Y
3	**Ferguson**	N	Y	Y	Y	N	N
4	Johnson, H.	Y	Y	Y	Y	Y	Y
5	Lewis John	Y	Y	Y	Y	Y	Y
6	McBath	Y	Y	Y	Y	Y	Y
7	**Woodall**	Y	Y	Y	Y	N	N
8	**Scott, A.**	Y	Y	Y	Y	N	N
9	**Collins, D.**	Y	Y	Y	Y	N	N
10	**Hice**	Y	Y	Y	Y	N	N
11	**Loudermilk**	Y	Y	Y	Y	N	N
12	**Allen**	Y	Y	Y	Y	N	N
13	Scott, D.	Y	Y	Y	Y	Y	Y
14	**Graves, T.**	Y	Y	Y	Y	N	N
HAWAII							
1	Case	Y	Y	Y	Y	Y	Y
2	Gabbard	Y	Y	Y	Y	Y	Y
IDAHO							
1	**Fulcher**	Y	Y	Y	Y	N	N
2	**Simpson**	Y	Y	Y	Y	N	N
ILLINOIS							
1	Rush	Y	?	?	?	Y	Y
2	Kelly, R.	Y	Y	Y	Y	Y	Y
3	Lipinski	Y	Y	Y	Y	Y	Y
4	García, J.	Y	Y	Y	Y	Y	Y
5	Quigley	Y	Y	Y	Y	Y	Y
6	Casten	Y	Y	Y	Y	Y	Y
7	Davis, D.	Y	Y	Y	Y	Y	Y
8	Krishnamoorthi	Y	Y	Y	Y	Y	Y
9	Schakowsky	Y	Y	Y	Y	Y	Y
10	Schneider	Y	Y	Y	Y	Y	Y
11	Foster	Y	Y	Y	Y	Y	Y

KEY: **Republicans** Democrats *Independents*

Y Voted for (yea)	N Voted against (nay)	P Voted "present"
+ Announced for	- Announced against	? Did not vote or otherwise make position known
# Paired for	X Paired against	

		241	242	243	244	245	246
12	**Bost**	Y	?	?	?	-	-
13	**Davis, R.**	Y	Y	Y	Y	N	N
14	Underwood	Y	Y	Y	Y	Y	Y
15	**Shimkus**	Y	Y	Y	Y	N	N
16	**Kinzinger**	Y	Y	Y	Y	N	N
17	Bustos	Y	Y	Y	Y	Y	Y
18	**LaHood**	Y	Y	Y	Y	N	N
INDIANA							
1	Visclosky	Y	Y	Y	Y	Y	Y
2	**Walorski**	Y	Y	Y	Y	N	N
3	**Banks**	Y	Y	Y	Y	N	N
4	**Baird**	Y	Y	Y	Y	N	N
5	**Brooks, S.**	Y	Y	Y	Y	N	N
6	**Pence**	Y	Y	Y	Y	N	N
7	Carson	Y	Y	Y	Y	Y	Y
8	**Bucshon**	Y	Y	Y	Y	N	N
9	**Hollingsworth**	Y	Y	Y	Y	N	N
IOWA							
1	Finkenauer	Y	Y	Y	Y	Y	Y
2	Loebsack	Y	Y	Y	Y	Y	Y
3	Axne	Y	+	+	+	?	?
4	**King, S.**	Y	+	+	+	-	-
KANSAS							
1	**Marshall**	Y	Y	Y	Y	N	N
2	**Watkins**	Y	Y	Y	Y	N	N
3	Davids	Y	Y	Y	Y	Y	Y
4	**Estes**	Y	Y	Y	Y	N	N
KENTUCKY							
1	**Comer**	Y	Y	Y	Y	N	N
2	**Guthrie**	Y	Y	Y	Y	N	N
3	Yarmuth	Y	Y	Y	Y	Y	Y
4	**Massie**	N	N	N	Y	N	N
5	**Rogers, H.**	Y	Y	Y	Y	N	N
6	**Barr**	Y	Y	Y	Y	N	N
LOUISIANA							
1	**Scalise**	Y	Y	Y	Y	N	N
2	Richmond	Y	Y	Y	Y	Y	Y
3	**Higgins, C.**	N	Y	Y	Y	N	N
4	**Johnson, M.**	Y	Y	Y	Y	N	N
5	**Abraham**	Y	?	?	?	N	N
6	**Graves, G.**	Y	Y	Y	Y	N	N
MAINE							
1	Pingree	Y	Y	Y	Y	Y	Y
2	Golden	Y	Y	Y	Y	Y	Y
MARYLAND							
1	**Harris**	N	Y	N	Y	N	N
2	Ruppersberger	Y	Y	Y	Y	Y	Y
3	Sarbanes	Y	Y	Y	Y	Y	Y
4	Brown, A.	Y	Y	Y	Y	Y	Y
5	Hoyer	Y	Y	Y	Y	Y	Y
6	Trone	Y	?	?	?	Y	Y
7	Cummings	Y	Y	Y	Y	Y	Y
8	Raskin						
MASSACHUSETTS		Y	Y	Y	Y	Y	Y
1	Neal						
2	McGovern	Y	Y	Y	Y	Y	Y
3	Trahan	Y	Y	Y	Y	Y	Y
4	Kennedy	Y	Y	Y	Y	Y	Y
5	Clark	Y	Y	Y	Y	Y	Y
6	Moulton	Y	Y	Y	Y	Y	Y
7	Pressley	Y	?	?	?	Y	Y
8	Lynch	Y	Y	Y	Y	Y	Y
9	Keating	Y	Y	Y	Y	Y	Y
MICHIGAN		Y	Y	Y	Y	Y	Y
1	**Bergman**						
2	**Huizenga**	Y	Y	Y	Y	N	N
3	**Amash**	Y	Y	Y	Y	N	N
4	**Moolenaar**	N	N	N	Y	N	N
5	Kildee	Y	Y	Y	Y	N	N
6	**Upton**	Y	Y	Y	Y	Y	Y
7	**Walberg**	Y	Y	Y	Y	N	N
8	Slotkin	Y	Y	Y	Y	N	N
9	Levin	Y	Y	Y	Y	Y	Y
10	**Mitchell**	Y	Y	Y	Y	Y	Y
11	Stevens	Y	Y	Y	Y	N	N
12	Dingell	Y	Y	Y	Y	Y	Y
13	Tlaib	Y	Y	Y	Y	Y	Y
14	Lawrence	Y	Y	Y	Y	Y	Y
MINNESOTA		?	Y	Y	Y	Y	Y
1	**Hagedorn**						
2	Craig	Y	Y	Y	Y	N	N
3	Phillips	Y	Y	Y	Y	Y	Y
4	McCollum	Y	Y	Y	Y	Y	Y
5	Omar	Y	Y	Y	Y	Y	Y

		241	242	243	244	245	246
6	**Emmer**	Y	Y	Y	Y	Y	Y
7	Peterson	Y	Y	Y	Y	N	N
8	**Stauber**	Y	Y	Y	Y	Y	Y
MISSISSIPPI		Y	Y	Y	Y	N	N
1	**Kelly, T.**						
2	Thompson, B.	Y	Y	Y	Y	N	N
3	**Guest**	Y	Y	Y	Y	Y	Y
4	**Palazzo**	Y	Y	Y	Y	N	N
MISSOURI		Y	Y	Y	Y	N	N
1	Clay						
2	**Wagner**	Y	?	?	?	?	?
3	**Luetkemeyer**	Y	Y	Y	Y	N	N
4	**Hartzler**	Y	Y	Y	Y	N	N
5	Cleaver	Y	Y	Y	Y	N	N
6	**Graves, S.**	Y	Y	Y	Y	Y	Y
7	**Long**	?	Y	Y	Y	N	N
8	**Smith, J.**	Y	+	+	+	?	?
MONTANA		Y	Y	Y	Y	N	N
AL	**Gianforte**						
NEBRASKA		Y	Y	Y	Y	N	N
1	**Fortenberry**						
2	**Bacon**	Y	Y	Y	Y	N	N
3	**Smith, Adrian**	Y	Y	Y	Y	N	N
NEVADA		Y	Y	Y	Y	N	N
1	Titus						
2	**Amodei**	Y	Y	Y	Y	Y	Y
3	Lee	Y	Y	Y	Y	N	N
4	Horsford	Y	Y	Y	Y	Y	Y
NEW HAMPSHIRE		Y	Y	Y	Y	Y	Y
1	Pappas						
2	Kuster	Y	Y	Y	Y	Y	Y
NEW JERSEY		Y	?	?	?	?	?
1	Norcross						
2	Van Drew	Y	Y	Y	Y	Y	Y
3	Kim	Y	Y	Y	Y	Y	Y
4	**Smith, C.**	Y	Y	Y	Y	Y	Y
5	Gottheimer	Y	Y	Y	Y	N	N
6	Pallone	Y	Y	Y	Y	+	+
7	Malinowski	Y	Y	Y	Y	Y	Y
8	Sires	Y	Y	Y	Y	Y	Y
9	Pascrell	Y	Y	Y	Y	Y	Y
10	Payne	Y	Y	Y	Y	Y	Y
11	Sherrill	Y	Y	Y	Y	Y	Y
12	Watson Coleman	Y	Y	Y	Y	Y	Y
NEW MEXICO		Y	?	?	?	Y	Y
1	Haaland						
2	Torres Small	Y	Y	Y	Y	Y	Y
3	Luján	Y	Y	Y	Y	Y	Y
NEW YORK		Y	Y	Y	Y	Y	Y
1	**Zeldin**						
2	**King, P.**	Y	Y	Y	Y	N	N
3	Suozzi	Y	Y	Y	Y	N	N
4	Rice, K.	Y	Y	Y	Y	Y	Y
5	Meeks	Y	Y	Y	Y	Y	Y
6	Meng	Y	?	?	?	Y	Y
7	Velázquez	Y	Y	Y	Y	Y	Y
8	Jeffries	Y	Y	Y	Y	Y	Y
9	Clarke	Y	Y	Y	Y	Y	Y
10	Nadler	Y	Y	Y	Y	Y	Y
11	Rose	Y	Y	Y	Y	Y	Y
12	Maloney, C.	Y	Y	Y	Y	Y	Y
13	Espaillat	Y	Y	Y	Y	Y	Y
14	Ocasio-Cortez	Y	Y	Y	Y	Y	Y
15	Serrano	Y	Y	Y	Y	Y	Y
16	Engel	Y	Y	Y	Y	Y	Y
17	Lowey	Y	Y	Y	Y	Y	Y
18	Maloney, S.P.	Y	Y	Y	Y	Y	Y
19	Delgado	Y	?	Y	Y	Y	Y
20	Tonko	Y	Y	Y	Y	Y	Y
21	**Stefanik**	Y	Y	Y	Y	Y	Y
22	Brindisi	Y	Y	Y	Y	N	N
23	**Reed**	Y	Y	Y	Y	Y	Y
24	**Katko**	Y	Y	Y	Y	N	N
25	Morelle	Y	Y	Y	Y	N	N
26	Higgins, B.	Y	Y	Y	Y	Y	Y
27	**Collins, C.**	Y	?	?	?	Y	Y
NORTH CAROLINA		Y	Y	Y	Y	N	N
1	Butterfield						
2	**Holding**	Y	Y	Y	?	Y	Y
3	**Jones***	Y	Y	Y	Y	N	N
4	Price						
5	**Foxx**	Y	Y	Y	Y	Y	Y
6	**Walker**	Y	Y	Y	Y	N	N
7	**Rouzer**	Y	Y	Y	Y	N	N

		241	242	243	244	245	246
8	**Hudson**	Y	Y	Y	Y	N	N
9	vacant	Y	?	Y	Y	N	N
10	**McHenry**	Y	Y	Y	Y	N	N
11	**Meadows**	N	Y	Y	Y	N	N
12	Adams	Y	Y	Y	Y	Y	Y
13	**Budd**	Y	Y	Y	Y	N	N
NORTH DAKOTA							
AL	**Armstrong**	Y	Y	Y	Y	N	N
OHIO							
1	**Chabot**	Y	Y	Y	Y	N	N
2	**Wenstrup**	Y	Y	Y	Y	N	N
3	Beatty	Y	Y	Y	Y	Y	Y
4	**Jordan**	N	Y	N	Y	N	N
5	**Latta**	Y	Y	Y	Y	N	N
6	**Johnson, B.**	Y	Y	Y	Y	N	N
7	**Gibbs**	Y	Y	Y	Y	N	N
8	**Davidson**	Y	?	?	?	N	N
9	Kaptur	Y	Y	Y	Y	Y	Y
10	**Turner**	Y	Y	Y	Y	N	N
11	Fudge	Y	Y	Y	Y	Y	Y
12	**Balderson**	Y	Y	Y	Y	N	N
13	Ryan	Y	?	?	?	?	?
14	**Joyce**	Y	Y	Y	Y	N	N
15	**Stivers**	Y	Y	?	Y	N	N
16	**Gonzalez**	Y	Y	Y	Y	N	N
OKLAHOMA							
1	**Hern**	N	Y	Y	Y	N	N
2	**Mullin**	Y	Y	Y	Y	N	N
3	**Lucas**	Y	Y	Y	Y	N	N
4	**Cole**	Y	Y	Y	Y	N	N
5	Horn	Y	Y	Y	Y	Y	Y
OREGON							
1	Bonamici	Y	Y	Y	Y	Y	Y
2	**Walden**	Y	Y	Y	Y	N	N
3	Blumenauer	Y	Y	Y	Y	Y	Y
4	DeFazio	Y	Y	Y	Y	Y	Y
5	Schrader	Y	Y	Y	Y	Y	Y
PENNSYLVANIA							
1	**Fitzpatrick**	Y	Y	Y	Y	N	N
2	Boyle	Y	Y	Y	Y	Y	Y
3	Evans	Y	Y	Y	Y	Y	Y
4	Dean	?	?	?	?	Y	Y
5	Scanlon	Y	Y	Y	Y	Y	Y
6	Houlahan	Y	Y	Y	Y	Y	Y
7	Wild	Y	Y	Y	Y	Y	Y
8	Cartwright	Y	Y	Y	Y	Y	Y
9	**Meuser**	Y	Y	Y	Y	N	N
10	**Perry**	N	Y	Y	Y	N	N
11	**Smucker**	Y	Y	Y	Y	N	N
12	**Marino***						
13	**Joyce**	Y	Y	Y	Y	N	N
14	**Reschenthaler**	Y	Y	Y	Y	N	N
15	**Thompson, G.**	Y	Y	Y	Y	N	N
16	**Kelly, M.**	Y	?	?	?	N	N
17	Lamb	Y	Y	Y	Y	Y	Y
18	Doyle	Y	Y	Y	Y	Y	Y
RHODE ISLAND							
1	Cicilline	Y	Y	Y	Y	Y	Y
2	Langevin	Y	Y	Y	Y	Y	Y
SOUTH CAROLINA							
1	Cunningham	Y	Y	Y	Y	Y	Y
2	**Wilson, J.**	Y	Y	Y	Y	N	N
3	**Duncan**	?	Y	Y	Y	N	N
4	**Timmons**	Y	Y	Y	Y	N	N
5	**Norman**	?	Y	N	Y	N	N
6	Clyburn	?	?	?	?	Y	Y
7	**Rice, T.**	Y	Y	N	Y	N	N
SOUTH DAKOTA							
AL	**Johnson**	Y	Y	Y	Y	N	N
TENNESSEE							
1	**Roe**	Y	Y	Y	Y	N	N
2	**Burchett**	N	Y	N	Y	N	N
3	**Fleischmann**	Y	Y	Y	Y	N	N
4	**DesJarlais**	Y	Y	Y	Y	N	N
5	Cooper	Y	Y	Y	Y	Y	Y
6	**Rose**	N	Y	Y	Y	N	N
7	**Green**	?	?	?	?	?	?
8	**Kustoff**	Y	Y	Y	Y	N	N
9	Cohen	Y	Y	Y	Y	Y	Y
TEXAS							
1	**Gohmert**	N	Y	Y	?	N	N
2	**Crenshaw**	Y	Y	Y	Y	N	N
3	**Taylor**	Y	Y	Y	Y	N	N
4	**Ratcliffe**	Y	Y	Y	Y	N	N

		241	242	243	244	245	246
5	**Gooden**	Y	Y	Y	Y	N	N
6	**Wright**	Y	?	?	?	?	?
7	Fletcher	Y	Y	Y	Y	Y	Y
8	**Brady**	Y	Y	?	Y	N	N
9	Green, A.	Y	Y	Y	Y	Y	Y
10	**McCaul**	Y	Y	Y	Y	N	N
11	**Conaway**	Y	Y	Y	Y	N	N
12	**Granger**	Y	Y	Y	Y	N	N
13	**Thornberry**	Y	Y	Y	Y	N	N
14	**Weber**	Y	Y	Y	Y	N	N
15	Gonzalez	Y	?	?	?	Y	Y
16	Escobar	Y	Y	Y	Y	Y	Y
17	**Flores**	Y	Y	Y	Y	N	N
18	Jackson Lee	Y	Y	Y	Y	Y	Y
19	**Arrington**	Y	Y	Y	Y	N	N
20	Castro	Y	Y	Y	Y	Y	Y
21	**Roy**	N	N	N	N	N	N
22	**Olson**	?	Y	Y	Y	N	N
23	**Hurd**	Y	Y	Y	Y	N	N
24	**Marchant**	Y	Y	Y	Y	N	N
25	**Williams**	Y	Y	Y	Y	N	N
26	**Burgess**	Y	Y	N	Y	N	N
27	**Cloud**	Y	Y	Y	Y	N	N
28	Cuellar	Y	Y	Y	Y	Y	Y
29	Garcia, S.	Y	Y	Y	Y	Y	Y
30	Johnson, E.B.	Y	Y	Y	Y	Y	Y
31	**Carter, J.**	Y	Y	?	Y	N	N
32	Allred	Y	Y	Y	Y	Y	Y
33	Veasey	Y	Y	Y	Y	Y	Y
34	Vela	Y	Y	Y	Y	Y	Y
35	Doggett	Y	Y	Y	Y	Y	Y
36	**Babin**	Y	Y	Y	Y	N	N
UTAH							
1	**Bishop, R.**	Y	?	?	?	N	N
2	**Stewart**	Y	Y	Y	Y	N	N
3	**Curtis**	Y	Y	Y	Y	N	N
4	McAdams	Y	Y	Y	Y	Y	Y
VERMONT							
AL	Welch	Y	Y	Y	Y	Y	Y
VIRGINIA							
1	**Wittman**	Y	Y	Y	Y	N	N
2	Luria	Y	Y	Y	Y	Y	Y
3	Scott, R.	Y	Y	Y	Y	Y	Y
4	McEachin	Y	?	?	?	Y	Y
5	**Riggleman**	Y	Y	Y	Y	N	N
6	**Cline**	N	Y	Y	Y	N	N
7	Spanberger	Y	Y	Y	Y	Y	Y
8	Beyer	Y	Y	Y	Y	Y	Y
9	**Griffith**	Y	?	?	?	?	?
10	Wexton	Y	Y	Y	Y	Y	Y
11	Connolly	Y	Y	Y	Y	Y	Y
WASHINGTON							
1	DelBene	Y	Y	Y	Y	Y	Y
2	Larsen	Y	Y	Y	Y	Y	Y
3	**Herrera Beutler**	?	?	?	?	?	?
4	**Newhouse**	Y	Y	Y	Y	N	N
5	**McMorris Rodgers**	Y	Y	Y	Y	N	N
6	Kilmer	Y	Y	Y	Y	Y	Y
7	Jayapal	Y	Y	Y	Y	Y	Y
8	Schrier	Y	Y	Y	Y	Y	Y
9	Smith Adam	Y	Y	Y	Y	Y	Y
10	Heck	Y	Y	Y	Y	Y	Y
WEST VIRGINIA							
1	**McKinley**	Y	Y	Y	Y	N	N
2	**Mooney**	N	Y	Y	Y	N	N
3	**Miller**	Y	?	?	?	N	N
WISCONSIN							
1	**Steil**	Y	Y	Y	Y	N	N
2	Pocan	Y	Y	Y	Y	Y	Y
3	Kind	Y	Y	Y	Y	Y	Y
4	Moore	Y	Y	Y	Y	Y	Y
5	**Sensenbrenner**	N	+	+	+	N	N
6	**Grothman**	N	Y	Y	Y	N	N
7	**Duffy**	Y	Y	Y	Y	N	N
8	**Gallagher**	Y	Y	Y	Y	N	N
WYOMING							
AL	**Cheney**	Y	Y	Y	Y	N	N
DELEGATES							
	Radewagen (A.S.)						
	Norton (D.C.)						
	San Nicolas (Guam)						
	Sablan (N. Marianas)						
	González-Colón (P.R.)						
	Plaskett (V.I.)						

247. HRES430. Enforcing Congressional Subpoenas - Passage. Agreeing to a resolution that would authorize the House Judiciary Committee to take civil legal actions in federal court to enforce congressional subpoenas issued to Attorney General William P. Barr and former White House Counsel Donald F. McGahn, II, and to petition a federal court for the disclosure of certain redacted information regarding grand jury proceedings, as identified in the subpoenas and accompanying reports. It would affirm that other House committees may similarly pursue legal action to enforce subpoenas in federal court, with approval of the House Bipartisan Legal Advisory Group, which is composed of the speaker of the House and majority and minority leadership. It would also affirm that the Office of General Counsel of the House would represent any House committee in judicial proceedings related to the enforcement of subpoenas and would authorize the OGC to retain private counsel to assist in such proceedings. Passed 229-191: R 0-191; D 229-0. June 11, 2019.

248. HR2609. DHS Acquisition Board - Passage. Correa, D-Calif., motion to suspend the rules and pass the bill, that would require the Homeland Security Department to establish an acquisition review board chaired by the undersecretary for management to oversee, authorize, and review the progress of any DHS acquisition programs expected to cost at least $300 million at each phase of the program. It would require the under-secretary to create and approve a baseline program report for any project authorized to begin a planning phase and submit such reports to Congress. Motion agreed to 419-0: R 191-0; D 228-0. *Note: A two-thirds majority of those present and voting (280 in this case) is required for passage under suspension of the rules.* June 11, 2019.

249. Procedural Motion - Adjournment. Roy, R-Texas, motion to adjourn. Motion rejected 146-244: R 145-28; D 1-216. June 12, 2019.

250. Procedural Motion - Adjournment. Biggs, R-Ariz., motion to adjourn. Motion rejected 140-254: R 140-36; D 0-218. June 12, 2019.

251. HR2740. Fiscal 2020 Four-Bill Appropriations Package - Senior Nutrition. McGovern, D-Mass., amendment that would include "medically-tailored meals" among practices to enhance senior nutrition under certain HHS programs funded by the bill. Adopted in Committee of the Whole 338-83: R 107-83; D 231-0. June 12, 2019.

252. HR2740. Fiscal 2020 Four-Bill Appropriations Package - Immigrant Advocacy and Entrance Services. Shalala, D-Fla., amendment that would increase by $10 million the minimum amount to be used for legal services, child advocates, and post-release services within total funds authorized by the bill for Health and Human Services Department immigrant and refugee assistance activities. Adopted in Committee of the Whole 243-179: R 13-178; D 230-1. June 12, 2019.

	247	248	249	250	251	252
ALABAMA						
1 **Byrne**	N	Y	Y	Y	N	N
2 **Roby**	N	Y	?	?	N	N
3 **Rogers, M.**	N	Y	Y	Y	N	N
4 **Aderholt**	N	Y	Y	Y	N	N
5 **Brooks, M.**	N	Y	N	N	N	N
6 **Palmer**	N	Y	Y	Y	N	N
7 Sewell	Y	Y	N	?	Y	Y
ALASKA						
AL **Young**	N	Y	Y	?	Y	Y
ARIZONA						
1 O'Halleran	Y	Y	N	N	Y	Y
2 Kirkpatrick	Y	Y	N	N	Y	Y
3 Grijalva	Y	Y	N	N	Y	Y
4 **Gosar**	N	Y	?	Y	N	N
5 **Biggs**	N	Y	Y	Y	N	N
6 **Schweikert**	N	Y	Y	Y	N	N
7 Gallego	Y	Y	N	N	Y	Y
8 **Lesko**	N	Y	Y	Y	N	N
9 Stanton	Y	Y	N	N	Y	Y
ARKANSAS						
1 **Crawford**	N	Y	Y	Y	N	N
2 **Hill, F.**	N	Y	?	Y	N	N
3 **Womack**	N	Y	Y	Y	N	N
4 **Westerman**	N	Y	Y	Y	N	N
CALIFORNIA						
1 **LaMalfa**	N	Y	?	?	Y	N
2 Huffman	Y	Y	N	N	Y	Y
3 Garamendi	Y	Y	N	N	Y	Y
4 **McClintock**	N	Y	Y	Y	N	N
5 Thompson, M.	Y	Y	N	N	Y	Y
6 Matsui	Y	Y	N	N	Y	Y
7 Bera	Y	Y	N	N	Y	Y
8 **Cook**	N	Y	Y	N	Y	N
9 McNerney	Y	Y	N	N	Y	Y
10 Harder	Y	Y	N	N	Y	Y
11 DeSaulnier	Y	Y	N	N	Y	Y
12 Pelosi	Y					
13 Lee B.	Y	Y	N	N	Y	Y
14 Speier	Y	Y	Y	?	Y	Y
15 Swalwell	Y	Y	-	-	+	+
16 Costa	Y	Y	N	N	Y	Y
17 Khanna	Y	Y	N	N	Y	Y
18 Eshoo	Y	Y	N	N	Y	Y
19 Lofgren	Y	Y	N	N	Y	Y
20 Panetta	Y	Y	N	N	Y	Y
21 Cox	Y	Y	N	N	Y	Y
22 **Nunes**	N	Y	Y	N	Y	N
23 **McCarthy**	N	Y	Y	Y	N	N
24 Carbajal	Y	Y	N	N	Y	Y
25 Hill, K.	Y	Y	N	N	Y	Y
26 Brownley	Y	Y	N	?	Y	Y
27 Chu	Y	Y	N	N	Y	Y
28 Schiff	Y	Y	N	N	Y	Y
29 Cárdenas	Y	Y	N	N	Y	Y
30 Sherman	Y	Y	N	N	Y	Y
31 Aguilar	Y	Y	?	N	Y	Y
32 Napolitano	Y	Y	N	N	Y	Y
33 Lieu	Y	Y	N	N	Y	Y
34 Gomez	Y	Y	N	N	Y	Y
35 Torres	Y	Y	N	N	Y	Y
36 Ruiz	Y	Y	N	N	Y	Y
37 Bass	Y	Y	N	?	Y	Y
38 Sánchez	Y	Y	N	N	Y	?
39 Cisneros	Y	Y	N	N	Y	Y
40 Roybal-Allard	Y	Y	N	N	Y	Y
41 Takano	Y	Y	N	N	Y	Y
42 **Calvert**	N	Y	Y	Y	N	N
43 Waters	Y	Y	?	N	Y	Y
44 Barragán	Y	Y	N	N	Y	Y
45 Porter	Y	Y	N	N	Y	Y
46 Correa	Y	Y	N	N	Y	Y
47 Lowenthal	Y	Y	N	N	Y	Y
48 Rouda	Y	Y	N	N	Y	Y
49 Levin	Y	Y	N	N	Y	Y
50 **Hunter**	N	Y	Y	Y	N	N
51 Vargas	Y	Y	N	N	Y	Y
52 Peters	Y	Y	?	?	Y	Y

	247	248	249	250	251	252
53 Davis, S.	+	+	N	N	Y	Y
COLORADO						
1 DeGette	Y	Y	N	N	Y	Y
2 Neguse	Y	Y	N	N	Y	Y
3 Tipton	N	Y	N	Y	N	N
4 **Buck**	?	?	?	?	?	?
5 **Lamborn**	N	Y	Y	Y	N	N
6 Crow	Y	Y	N	N	Y	Y
7 Perlmutter	Y	Y	?	?	Y	Y
CONNECTICUT						
1 Larson	Y	Y	N	?	Y	Y
2 Courtney	Y	Y	N	N	Y	Y
3 DeLauro	Y	Y	N	N	Y	Y
4 Himes	Y	Y	N	N	Y	Y
5 Hayes	Y	Y	N	N	Y	Y
DELAWARE						
AL Blunt Rochester	Y	Y	N	N	Y	Y
FLORIDA						
1 **Gaetz**	N	Y	Y	Y	Y	N
2 **Dunn**	N	Y	Y	Y	N	N
3 **Yoho**	N	Y	Y	N	N	N
4 **Rutherford**	N	Y	N	Y	N	N
5 Lawson	Y	Y	?	N	Y	Y
6 **Waltz**	N	Y	Y	Y	Y	N
7 Murphy	Y	Y	N	N	Y	Y
8 **Posey**	N	Y	Y	Y	N	N
9 Soto	Y	Y	N	N	Y	Y
10 Demings	Y	Y	N	N	Y	Y
11 **Webster**	N	Y	Y	Y	N	N
12 **Bilirakis**	N	Y	Y	Y	N	N
13 Crist	Y	Y	N	N	Y	Y
14 Castor	Y	Y	N	N	Y	Y
15 **Spano**	N	Y	Y	Y	N	N
16 **Buchanan**	N	Y	Y	Y	N	N
17 **Steube**	N	Y	Y	Y	N	N
18 **Mast**	N	Y	Y	Y	N	N
19 **Rooney**	N	Y	?	?	N	N
20 Hastings	+	?	?	?	?	?
21 Frankel	Y	Y	-	N	Y	Y
22 Deutch	Y	Y	?	?	Y	Y
23 Wasserman Schultz	Y	Y	N	?	Y	Y
24 Wilson, F.	Y	Y	N	N	Y	Y
25 **Diaz-Balart**	N	Y	?	N	Y	Y
26 Mucarsel-Powell	Y	Y	?	N	Y	Y
27 Shalala	Y	Y	N	N	Y	Y
GEORGIA						
1 **Carter, E.L.**	N	Y	Y	Y	N	N
2 Bishop, S.	Y	Y	N	N	Y	Y
3 **Ferguson**	N	Y	Y	Y	N	N
4 Johnson, H.	Y	Y	N	N	Y	Y
5 Lewis John	Y	Y	N	N	Y	Y
6 McBath	Y	Y	N	N	Y	Y
7 **Woodall**	N	Y	N	N	Y	N
8 **Scott, A.**	N	Y	N	N	N	N
9 **Collins, D.**	N	Y	Y	Y	N	N
10 **Hice**	N	Y	Y	Y	N	N
11 **Loudermilk**	N	Y	Y	?	N	N
12 **Allen**	N	Y	Y	Y	N	N
13 Scott, D.	Y	Y	N	N	Y	Y
14 **Graves, T.**	N	Y	Y	?	N	N
HAWAII						
1 Case	Y	Y	N	N	Y	Y
2 Gabbard	?	?	N	N	Y	Y
IDAHO						
1 **Fulcher**	N	Y	Y	Y	N	N
2 **Simpson**	N	Y	?	N	Y	N
ILLINOIS						
1 Rush	Y	Y	?	N	Y	Y
2 Kelly, R.	Y	Y	N	N	Y	Y
3 Lipinski	Y	Y	N	N	Y	Y
4 García, J.	Y	Y	N	N	Y	Y
5 Quigley	Y	Y	?	N	Y	Y
6 Casten	Y	Y	N	N	Y	Y
7 Davis, D.	Y	Y	N	N	Y	Y
8 Krishnamoorthi	Y	Y	N	N	Y	Y
9 Schakowsky	Y	Y	N	N	Y	Y
10 Schneider	Y	Y	N	N	Y	Y
11 Foster	Y	Y	N	N	Y	Y

KEY:		Republicans		Democrats		*Independents*

Y Voted for (yea)	**N** Voted against (nay)	**P** Voted "present"	
+ Announced for	**−** Announced against	**?** Did not vote or otherwise	
# Paired for	**X** Paired against	make position known	

		247	248	249	250	251	252
12	**Bost**	-	+	?	?	?	?
13	**Davis, R.**	N	Y	Y	Y	Y	N
14	Underwood	Y	Y	N	N	Y	Y
15	**Shimkus**	N	Y	N	N	Y	N
16	**Kinzinger**	N	Y	N	N	Y	N
17	Bustos	Y	Y	N	N	Y	Y
18	**LaHood**	N	Y	Y	Y	N	N
INDIANA							
1	Visclosky	Y	Y	N	N	Y	Y
2	**Walorski**	N	Y	Y	Y	Y	N
3	**Banks**	N	Y	Y	N	N	N
4	**Baird**	N	Y	Y	Y	Y	N
5	**Brooks, S.**	N	Y	Y	Y	Y	N
6	**Pence**	N	Y	Y	Y	Y	N
7	Carson	Y	Y	N	N	Y	Y
8	**Bucshon**	N	Y	Y	?	N	N
9	**Hollingsworth**	N	Y	Y	Y	Y	N
IOWA							
1	Finkenauer	Y	Y	N	N	Y	Y
2	Loebsack	Y	Y	N	?	Y	Y
3	Axne	+	+	N	N	Y	Y
4	**King, S.**	-	+	Y	Y	Y	N
KANSAS							
1	**Marshall**	N	Y	Y	Y	Y	N
2	**Watkins**	N	Y	Y	Y	Y	N
3	Davids	Y	Y	N	N	Y	Y
4	**Estes**	N	Y	Y	Y	N	N
KENTUCKY							
1	**Comer**	N	Y	Y	Y	N	N
2	**Guthrie**	N	Y	Y	Y	Y	N
3	Yarmuth	Y	Y	N	N	Y	Y
4	**Massie**	N	Y	Y	Y	N	N
5	**Rogers, H.**	N	Y	Y	Y	Y	N
6	**Barr**	N	Y	Y	Y	Y	N
LOUISIANA							
1	**Scalise**	N	Y	Y	Y	N	N
2	Richmond	Y	Y	N	N	Y	Y
3	**Higgins, C.**	N	Y	Y	N	N	N
4	**Johnson, M.**	N	Y	Y	Y	N	N
5	**Abraham**	N	Y	Y	Y	N	N
6	**Graves, G.**	N	Y	N	N	Y	N
MAINE							
1	Pingree	Y	Y	N	N	Y	Y
2	Golden	Y	Y	N	N	Y	Y
MARYLAND							
1	**Harris**	N	Y	?	?	Y	N
2	Ruppersberger	Y	Y	N	N	Y	Y
3	Sarbanes	Y	Y	N	N	Y	Y
4	Brown, A.	Y	Y	N	N	Y	Y
5	Hoyer	Y	Y	?	?	?	?
6	Trone	Y	Y	N	N	Y	Y
7	Cummings	Y	Y	N	N	Y	Y
8	Raskin						
MASSACHUSETTS		Y	Y	N	N	Y	Y
1	Neal						
2	McGovern	Y	Y	N	N	Y	Y
3	Trahan	Y	Y	N	N	Y	Y
4	Kennedy	Y	Y	N	N	Y	Y
5	Clark	Y	Y	N	N	Y	Y
6	Moulton	Y	Y	?	N	Y	Y
7	Pressley	Y	Y	N	N	Y	Y
8	Lynch	Y	Y	N	N	Y	Y
9	Keating	Y	Y	N	N	Y	Y
MICHIGAN		Y	Y	N	N	Y	Y
1	**Bergman**						
2	**Huizenga**	N	Y	Y	Y	Y	N
3	**Amash**	N	Y	Y	Y	N	N
4	**Moolenaar**	N	Y	N	N	N	N
5	Kildee	N	Y	Y	Y	Y	N
6	**Upton**	Y	Y	N	N	Y	Y
7	**Walberg**	N	Y	N	N	Y	Y
8	Slotkin	N	Y	N	N	Y	N
9	Levin	Y	Y	N	N	Y	Y
10	**Mitchell**	Y	Y	N	N	Y	Y
11	Stevens	N	Y	Y	Y	Y	N
12	Dingell	Y	Y	N	N	Y	Y
13	Tlaib	Y	Y	N	N	Y	Y
14	Lawrence	Y	Y	N	N	Y	Y
MINNESOTA		Y	Y	N	N	Y	Y
1	**Hagedorn**						
2	Craig	N	Y	Y	Y	N	N
3	Phillips	Y	Y	N	N	Y	Y
4	McCollum	Y	Y	N	N	Y	Y
5	Omar	Y	Y	N	N	Y	Y
6	**Emmer**	Y	Y	?	N	Y	Y
7	Peterson	N	Y	Y	Y	N	N
8	**Stauber**	Y	Y	N	N	Y	N
MISSISSIPPI		N	Y	N	N	Y	N
1	**Kelly, T.**						
2	Thompson, B.	N	Y	Y	N	N	N
3	**Guest**	Y	Y	N	N	Y	Y
4	**Palazzo**	N	Y	Y	Y	Y	N
MISSOURI		N	Y	Y	Y	N	N
1	Clay						
2	**Wagner**	?	?	N	N	Y	Y
3	**Luetkemeyer**	N	Y	Y	Y	Y	N
4	**Hartzler**	N	Y	Y	Y	N	N
5	Cleaver	N	Y	Y	Y	Y	N
6	**Graves, S.**	Y	Y	N	N	Y	Y
7	**Long**	N	Y	N	N	Y	N
8	**Smith, J.**	N	Y	Y	N	Y	N
MONTANA		N	Y	Y	Y	Y	N
AL	**Gianforte**						
NEBRASKA		N	Y	?	?	?	?
1	**Fortenberry**						
2	**Bacon**	N	Y	N	N	Y	Y
3	**Smith, Adrian**	N	Y	N	N	N	N
NEVADA		N	Y	Y	Y	N	N
1	Titus						
2	**Amodei**	Y	Y	N	-	Y	Y
3	Lee	N	Y	Y	Y	Y	N
4	Horsford	Y	Y	N	N	Y	Y
NEW HAMPSHIRE		Y	Y	N	N	Y	Y
1	Pappas						
2	Kuster	Y	Y	N	N	Y	Y
NEW JERSEY		?	?	N	N	Y	Y
1	Norcross						
2	Van Drew	Y	Y	N	N	Y	Y
3	Kim	Y	Y	N	N	Y	Y
4	**Smith, C.**	Y	Y	N	N	Y	Y
5	Gottheimer	N	Y	N	N	Y	Y
6	Pallone	Y	Y	N	N	Y	Y
7	Malinowski	Y	Y	N	N	Y	Y
8	Sires	Y	Y	N	N	Y	Y
9	Pascrell	Y	Y	N	N	Y	Y
10	Payne	Y	Y	N	N	Y	Y
11	Sherrill	Y	Y	N	N	Y	Y
12	Watson Coleman	Y	Y	N	N	Y	Y
NEW MEXICO		Y	Y	N	N	Y	Y
1	Haaland						
2	Torres Small	Y	Y	N	N	Y	Y
3	Luján	Y	Y	N	N	Y	Y
NEW YORK		Y	Y	N	N	Y	Y
1	**Zeldin**						
2	**King, P.**	N	Y	N	N	N	N
3	Suozzi	N	Y	?	N	Y	N
4	Rice, K.	Y	Y	N	N	Y	Y
5	Meeks	Y	Y	N	N	Y	Y
6	Meng	Y	Y	N	N	Y	Y
7	Velázquez	Y	Y	N	N	Y	Y
8	Jeffries	Y	Y	N	N	Y	Y
9	Clarke	Y	Y	?	N	Y	Y
10	Nadler	Y	Y	N	N	Y	?
11	Rose	Y	Y	N	N	Y	Y
12	Maloney, C.	Y	Y	N	N	Y	Y
13	Espaillat	Y	Y	N	N	Y	Y
14	Ocasio-Cortez	Y	Y	N	N	Y	Y
15	Serrano	Y	Y	N	N	Y	Y
16	Engel	Y	Y	N	N	Y	Y
17	Lowey	Y	Y	N	N	Y	Y
18	Maloney, S.P.	Y	Y	N	N	Y	Y
19	Delgado	Y	Y	N	N	Y	Y
20	Tonko	Y	Y	N	N	Y	Y
21	**Stefanik**	Y	Y	N	N	Y	Y
22	Brindisi	N	Y	Y	Y	Y	N
23	**Reed**	Y	Y	N	N	Y	Y
24	**Katko**	N	Y	N	N	Y	Y
25	Morelle	N	Y	?	?	Y	Y
26	Higgins, B.	Y	Y	N	N	Y	Y
27	**Collins, C.**	Y	Y	N	N	Y	Y
NORTH CAROLINA		N	Y	Y	Y	Y	N
1	Butterfield						
2	**Holding**	Y	Y	N	N	Y	Y
3	**Jones***	N	Y	Y	Y	N	N
4	Price						
5	**Foxx**	Y	Y	N	N	Y	Y
6	**Walker**	N	Y	?	Y	N	N
7	**Rouzer**	N	Y	Y	Y	N	N
8	**Hudson**	N	Y	Y	Y	N	N
9	vacant	N	Y	Y	Y	Y	N
10	**McHenry**	N	Y	?	Y	Y	N
11	**Meadows**	N	Y	Y	Y	Y	N
12	Adams	Y	Y	N	N	Y	Y
13	**Budd**	N	Y	Y	Y	N	N
NORTH DAKOTA							
AL	**Armstrong**	N	Y	?	Y	Y	N
OHIO							
1	**Chabot**	N	Y	Y	Y	Y	N
2	**Wenstrup**	N	Y	Y	Y	Y	N
3	Beatty	Y	Y	N	N	Y	Y
4	**Jordan**	N	Y	Y	Y	N	N
5	**Latta**	N	Y	Y	Y	Y	N
6	**Johnson, B.**	N	Y	Y	?	Y	N
7	**Gibbs**	N	Y	Y	Y	N	N
8	**Davidson**	N	Y	Y	Y	N	N
9	Kaptur	Y	Y	N	N	Y	Y
10	**Turner**	N	Y	N	N	Y	Y
11	Fudge	Y	Y	N	N	Y	Y
12	**Balderson**	N	Y	Y	Y	Y	N
13	Ryan	Y	Y	N	N	Y	Y
14	**Joyce**	N	Y	?	N	Y	N
15	**Stivers**	N	Y	Y	Y	Y	N
16	**Gonzalez**	N	Y	Y	P	Y	Y
OKLAHOMA							
1	**Hern**	N	Y	Y	Y	N	N
2	**Mullin**	N	Y	Y	Y	N	N
3	**Lucas**	N	Y	N	N	Y	N
4	**Cole**	N	Y	N	N	Y	N
5	Horn	Y	Y	N	N	Y	Y
OREGON							
1	Bonamici	Y	Y	N	N	Y	Y
2	**Walden**	N	Y	N	N	Y	Y
3	Blumenauer	Y	Y	N	N	Y	Y
4	DeFazio	Y	Y	N	N	Y	Y
5	Schrader	Y	Y	N	?	Y	Y
PENNSYLVANIA							
1	**Fitzpatrick**	N	Y	N	N	Y	Y
2	Boyle	Y	Y	N	N	Y	Y
3	Evans	Y	Y	N	N	Y	Y
4	Dean	Y	Y	N	N	Y	Y
5	Scanlon	Y	Y	N	N	Y	Y
6	Houlahan	Y	Y	N	N	Y	Y
7	Wild	Y	Y	N	N	Y	Y
8	Cartwright	Y	Y	N	N	Y	Y
9	**Meuser**	N	Y	Y	Y	N	N
10	**Perry**	N	Y	Y	Y	Y	N
11	**Smucker**	N	Y	Y	Y	Y	N
12	**Marino***						
13	**Joyce**	N	Y	Y	Y	Y	N
14	**Reschenthaler**	N	Y	?	?	Y	N
15	**Thompson, G.**	N	Y	Y	Y	Y	N
16	**Kelly, M.**	N	Y	Y	Y	Y	N
17	Lamb	Y	Y	N	N	Y	Y
18	Doyle	Y	Y	N	N	Y	Y
RHODE ISLAND							
1	Cicilline	Y	Y	N	N	Y	Y
2	Langevin	Y	Y	N	N	Y	Y
SOUTH CAROLINA							
1	Cunningham	Y	Y	N	N	Y	Y
2	**Wilson, J.**	N	Y	Y	Y	Y	N
3	**Duncan**	N	Y	Y	Y	N	N
4	**Timmons**	N	Y	Y	Y	N	N
5	**Norman**	N	Y	Y	Y	N	N
6	Clyburn	Y	Y	N	N	Y	Y
7	**Rice, T.**	N	Y	Y	Y	Y	N
SOUTH DAKOTA							
AL	**Johnson**	N	Y	Y	Y	N	N
TENNESSEE							
1	**Roe**	N	Y	Y	Y	Y	N
2	**Burchett**	N	Y	Y	Y	N	N
3	**Fleischmann**	N	Y	Y	Y	N	N
4	**DesJarlais**	N	Y	N	Y	Y	N
5	Cooper	Y	Y	N	N	Y	Y
6	**Rose**	N	Y	Y	Y	N	N
7	**Green**	?	?	?	?	?	?
8	**Kustoff**	N	Y	Y	Y	N	N
9	Cohen	Y	Y	N	N	Y	Y
TEXAS							
1	**Gohmert**	N	Y	?	Y	N	N
2	**Crenshaw**	N	Y	Y	Y	Y	N
3	**Taylor**	N	Y	N	N	N	N
4	**Ratcliffe**	N	Y	Y	?	Y	N
5	**Gooden**	N	Y	Y	Y	N	N
6	**Wright**	?	?	?	?	?	?
7	Fletcher	Y	Y	N	N	Y	Y
8	**Brady**	N	Y	Y	Y	N	N
9	Green, A.	Y	Y	N	N	Y	Y
10	**McCaul**	N	Y	Y	Y	Y	Y
11	**Conaway**	N	Y	Y	Y	N	N
12	**Granger**	N	Y	+	+	Y	N
13	**Thornberry**	N	Y	N	N	Y	N
14	**Weber**	N	Y	Y	Y	N	N
15	Gonzalez	Y	Y	N	N	?	Y
16	Escobar	Y	Y	N	N	Y	Y
17	**Flores**	N	Y	Y	?	N	N
18	Jackson Lee	Y	Y	N	N	?	Y
19	**Arrington**	N	Y	Y	Y	Y	N
20	Castro	Y	Y	N	N	Y	Y
21	**Roy**	N	Y	Y	Y	N	N
22	**Olson**	N	Y	Y	?	N	N
23	**Hurd**	N	Y	Y	Y	Y	Y
24	**Marchant**	N	Y	Y	Y	N	N
25	**Williams**	N	Y	Y	Y	N	N
26	**Burgess**	N	Y	Y	Y	N	N
27	**Cloud**	N	Y	N	N	N	N
28	Cuellar	Y	Y	N	N	Y	Y
29	Garcia, S.	Y	Y	N	N	Y	Y
30	Johnson, E.B.	Y	Y	N	N	Y	Y
31	**Carter, J.**	N	Y	Y	Y	N	N
32	Allred	Y	Y	N	N	Y	Y
33	Veasey	Y	Y	N	N	Y	Y
34	Vela	Y	Y	N	N	Y	Y
35	Doggett	Y	Y	N	N	Y	Y
36	**Babin**	N	Y	Y	Y	N	N
UTAH							
1	**Bishop, R.**	N	Y	N	Y	N	N
2	**Stewart**	N	Y	Y	Y	Y	N
3	**Curtis**	N	Y	Y	N	Y	N
4	McAdams	Y	Y	N	N	Y	Y
VERMONT							
AL	Welch	Y	Y	N	N	Y	Y
VIRGINIA							
1	**Wittman**	N	Y	Y	Y	N	N
2	Luria	Y	Y	N	N	Y	Y
3	Scott, R.	Y	Y	N	N	Y	Y
4	McEachin	Y	Y	N	-	Y	Y
5	**Riggleman**	N	Y	Y	Y	Y	N
6	**Cline**	N	Y	Y	Y	N	N
7	Spanberger	Y	Y	N	N	Y	Y
8	Beyer	Y	Y	N	N	Y	Y
9	**Griffith**	?	?	?	Y	N	N
10	Wexton	Y	Y	N	N	Y	Y
11	Connolly	Y	Y	N	N	Y	Y
WASHINGTON							
1	DelBene	Y	Y	N	N	Y	Y
2	Larsen	Y	Y	N	N	Y	Y
3	**Herrera Beutler**	?	?	?	?	?	?
4	**Newhouse**	N	Y	Y	Y	Y	N
5	**McMorris Rodgers**	N	Y	Y	Y	Y	N
6	Kilmer	Y	Y	N	N	Y	Y
7	Jayapal	Y	Y	N	N	Y	Y
8	Schrier	Y	Y	N	N	Y	Y
9	Smith Adam	Y	Y	N	N	Y	Y
10	Heck	Y	Y	N	N	Y	Y
WEST VIRGINIA							
1	**McKinley**	N	Y	Y	Y	Y	N
2	**Mooney**	N	Y	Y	Y	Y	N
3	**Miller**	N	Y	Y	Y	Y	N
WISCONSIN							
1	**Steil**	N	Y	Y	Y	Y	N
2	Pocan	Y	Y	?	N	Y	Y
3	Kind	Y	Y	N	N	Y	Y
4	Moore	Y	Y	N	N	Y	Y
5	**Sensenbrenner**	N	Y	+	+	+	-
6	**Grothman**	N	Y	Y	Y	Y	N
7	**Duffy**	N	Y	Y	Y	Y	N
8	**Gallagher**	N	Y	N	N	Y	N
WYOMING							
AL	**Cheney**	N	Y	Y	Y	N	N
DELEGATES							
	Radewagen (A.S.)					?	?
	Norton (D.C.)					Y	Y
	San Nicolas (Guam)					?	?
	Sablan (N. Marianas)					?	?
	González-Colón (P.R.)					?	?
	Plaskett (V.I.)					Y	Y

253. HR2740. Fiscal 2020 Four-Bill Appropriations Package - Bureau of Labor Statistics. DeSaulnier, D-Calif., amendment that would increase then decrease by $1 million funding for salaries and expenses of the Bureau of Labor Statistics. Adopted in Committee of the Whole 290-134: R 57-134; D 233-0. June 12, 2019.

254. HR2740. Fiscal 2020 Four-Bill Appropriations Package - National Cancer Institute. DeSaulnier, D-Calif., amendment that would increase then decrease by $1 million funding for the National Cancer Institute. Adopted in Committee of the Whole 381-42: R 148-42; D 233-0. June 12, 2019.

255. HR2740. Fiscal 2020 Four-Bill Appropriations Package - Family Engagement Programs. DeSaulnier, D-Calif., amendment that would increase then decrease by $1 million funding for certain Education Department programs related to charter and magnet schools, family engagement, and academic enrichment. Adopted in Committee of the Whole 347-76: R 114-76; D 233-0. June 12, 2019.

256. HR2740. Fiscal 2020 Four-Bill Appropriations Package - Substance Abuse and Mental Health Programs. DeSaulnier, D-Calif., amendment that would increase then decrease by $5 million funding for Health and Human Services programs and activities related to substance abuse and mental health. Adopted in Committee of the Whole 369-55: R 136-55; D 233-0. June 12, 2019.

257. HR2740. Fiscal 2020 Four-Bill Appropriations Package - CDC Prevention Activities. Smith, R-N.J., amendment that would increase by $1 million funding for Center for Disease Control and Prevention activities related to emerging and zoonotic infectious diseases and decrease by the same amount administrative funding for the Health and Human Services Department. Adopted in Committee of the Whole 413-11: R 182-9; D 231-2. June 12, 2019.

258. HR2740. Fiscal 2020 Four-Bill Appropriations Package - Beryllium Exposure Standards. Scott, D-Va., amendment that would prohibit the Occupational Safety and Health Administration from using any funds authorized in the bill to finalize or implement a proposed rule that would change the permissible exposure standards for construction and maritime workers occupationally exposed to beryllium. Adopted in Committee of the Whole 241-181: R 10-181; D 231-0. June 12, 2019.

		253	254	255	256	257	258
ALABAMA							
1	**Byrne**	N	N	N	N	N	N
2	**Roby**	Y	Y	Y	Y	Y	N
3	**Rogers, M.**	N	N	N	N	Y	N
4	**Aderholt**	Y	Y	Y	Y	Y	N
5	**Brooks, M.**	N	N	N	N	Y	N
6	**Palmer**	N	Y	N	N	Y	N
7	Sewell	Y	Y	Y	Y	Y	Y
ALASKA							
AL	**Young**	Y	Y	Y	Y	N	Y
ARIZONA							
1	O'Halleran	Y	Y	Y	Y	Y	Y
2	Kirkpatrick	Y	Y	Y	Y	Y	Y
3	Grijalva	Y	Y	Y	Y	Y	Y
4	**Gosar**	N	N	N	N	N	N
5	**Biggs**	N	N	N	N	Y	N
6	**Schweikert**	N	Y	Y	Y	Y	Y
7	Gallego	Y	Y	Y	Y	Y	Y
8	**Lesko**	N	Y	Y	Y	Y	N
9	Stanton	Y	Y	Y	Y	Y	Y
ARKANSAS							
1	**Crawford**	Y	Y	Y	Y	Y	N
2	**Hill, F.**	N	Y	Y	Y	Y	N
3	**Womack**	Y	Y	Y	Y	Y	N
4	**Westerman**	N	Y	Y	N	Y	N
CALIFORNIA							
1	**LaMalfa**	N	Y	N	Y	Y	N
2	Huffman	Y	Y	Y	Y	Y	Y
3	Garamendi	Y	Y	Y	Y	Y	Y
4	**McClintock**	N	N	N	N	Y	N
5	Thompson, M.	Y	Y	Y	Y	Y	Y
6	Matsui	Y	Y	Y	Y	Y	Y
7	Bera	Y	Y	Y	Y	Y	Y
8	**Cook**	N	Y	Y	Y	Y	N
9	McNerney	Y	Y	Y	Y	Y	Y
10	Harder	Y	Y	Y	Y	Y	Y
11	DeSaulnier	Y	Y	Y	Y	Y	Y
12	Pelosi						
13	Lee B.	Y	Y	Y	Y	Y	Y
14	Speier	Y	Y	Y	Y	Y	Y
15	Swalwell	+	+	+	+	+	+
16	Costa	Y	Y	Y	Y	Y	Y
17	Khanna	Y	Y	Y	Y	Y	Y
18	Eshoo	Y	Y	Y	Y	Y	Y
19	Lofgren	Y	Y	Y	Y	Y	Y
20	Panetta	Y	Y	Y	Y	Y	Y
21	Cox	Y	Y	Y	Y	Y	Y
22	**Nunes**	N	Y	Y	Y	Y	N
23	**McCarthy**	N	Y	Y	Y	Y	N
24	Carbajal	Y	Y	Y	Y	Y	Y
25	Hill, K.	Y	Y	Y	Y	Y	Y
26	Brownley	Y	Y	Y	Y	Y	Y
27	Chu	Y	Y	Y	Y	Y	Y
28	Schiff	Y	Y	Y	Y	Y	Y
29	Cárdenas	Y	Y	Y	Y	Y	Y
30	Sherman	Y	Y	Y	Y	Y	+
31	Aguilar	Y	Y	Y	Y	N	Y
32	Napolitano	Y	Y	Y	Y	Y	Y
33	Lieu	Y	Y	Y	Y	Y	Y
34	Gomez	Y	Y	Y	Y	Y	Y
35	Torres	Y	Y	Y	Y	Y	Y
36	Ruiz	Y	Y	Y	Y	Y	Y
37	Bass	Y	Y	Y	Y	Y	?
38	Sánchez	Y	Y	Y	Y	Y	Y
39	Cisneros	Y	Y	Y	Y	Y	Y
40	Roybal-Allard	Y	Y	Y	Y	Y	Y
41	Takano	Y	Y	Y	Y	Y	Y
42	**Calvert**	N	Y	Y	Y	Y	N
43	Waters	Y	Y	Y	Y	Y	Y
44	Barragán	Y	Y	Y	Y	Y	Y
45	Porter	Y	Y	Y	Y	Y	Y
46	Correa	Y	Y	Y	Y	Y	Y
47	Lowenthal	Y	Y	Y	Y	Y	Y
48	Rouda	Y	Y	Y	Y	Y	Y
49	Levin	Y	Y	Y	Y	Y	Y
50	**Hunter**	N	Y	N	Y	N	N
51	Vargas	Y	Y	Y	Y	Y	Y
52	Peters	Y	Y	Y	Y	Y	Y

		253	254	255	256	257	258
53	Davis, S.	Y	Y	Y	Y	Y	Y
COLORADO							
1	DeGette	Y	Y	Y	Y	Y	Y
2	Neguse	Y	Y	Y	Y	Y	Y
3	**Tipton**	N	Y	Y	Y	Y	N
4	**Buck**	?	?	?	?	?	?
5	**Lamborn**	N	N	N	N	Y	N
6	Crow	Y	Y	Y	Y	Y	Y
7	Perlmutter	Y	Y	Y	Y	Y	Y
CONNECTICUT							
1	Larson	Y	Y	Y	Y	Y	Y
2	Courtney	Y	Y	Y	Y	Y	Y
3	DeLauro	Y	Y	Y	Y	Y	Y
4	Himes	Y	Y	Y	Y	Y	Y
5	Hayes	Y	Y	Y	Y	Y	Y
DELAWARE							
AL	Blunt Rochester	Y	Y	Y	Y	Y	Y
FLORIDA							
1	**Gaetz**	N	N	N	N	N	N
2	**Dunn**	N	N	N	N	N	N
3	**Yoho**	N	N	N	N	N	N
4	**Rutherford**	Y	Y	Y	Y	Y	N
5	Lawson	Y	Y	Y	Y	Y	Y
6	**Waltz**	N	Y	Y	Y	Y	N
7	Murphy	Y	Y	Y	Y	Y	Y
8	**Posey**	N	N	N	N	N	N
9	Soto	Y	Y	Y	Y	Y	Y
10	Demings	Y	Y	Y	Y	Y	Y
11	**Webster**	N	N	N	N	N	N
12	**Bilirakis**	N	Y	Y	Y	Y	N
13	Crist	Y	Y	Y	Y	Y	Y
14	Castor	Y	Y	Y	Y	Y	Y
15	**Spano**	N	Y	N	Y	Y	N
16	**Buchanan**	Y	Y	Y	Y	Y	N
17	**Steube**	N	Y	N	N	Y	N
18	**Mast**	N	Y	Y	Y	N	N
19	**Rooney**	N	Y	Y	N	N	N
20	Hastings	?	?	?	?	?	?
21	Frankel	Y	Y	Y	Y	Y	Y
22	Deutch	Y	Y	Y	Y	Y	Y
23	Wasserman Schultz	Y	Y	Y	Y	Y	Y
24	Wilson, F.	Y	Y	Y	Y	Y	Y
25	**Diaz-Balart**	Y	Y	Y	Y	Y	N
26	Mucarsel-Powell	Y	Y	Y	Y	Y	Y
27	Shalala	Y	Y	Y	Y	Y	Y
GEORGIA							
1	**Carter, E.L.**	N	Y	Y	Y	Y	N
2	Bishop, S.	Y	Y	Y	Y	Y	Y
3	**Ferguson**	N	N	N	N	Y	N
4	Johnson, H.	Y	Y	Y	Y	Y	Y
5	Lewis John	Y	Y	Y	Y	Y	Y
6	McBath	Y	Y	Y	Y	Y	Y
7	**Woodall**	Y	Y	N	Y	Y	N
8	**Scott, A.**	N	Y	N	Y	Y	N
9	**Collins, D.**	N	Y	Y	Y	Y	N
10	**Hice**	N	N	N	N	N	N
11	**Loudermilk**	N	Y	N	Y	Y	N
12	**Allen**	N	N	N	N	Y	N
13	Scott, D.	Y	Y	Y	Y	Y	Y
14	**Graves, T.**	N	N	N	N	N	N
HAWAII							
1	Case	Y	Y	Y	Y	Y	Y
2	Gabbard	Y	Y	Y	Y	Y	Y
IDAHO							
1	**Fulcher**	N	N	N	N	Y	N
2	**Simpson**	Y	Y	Y	Y	Y	N
ILLINOIS							
1	Rush	Y	Y	Y	Y	Y	Y
2	Kelly, R.	Y	Y	Y	Y	Y	Y
3	Lipinski	Y	Y	Y	Y	Y	Y
4	García, J.	Y	Y	Y	Y	Y	Y
5	Quigley	Y	Y	Y	Y	Y	Y
6	Casten	Y	Y	Y	Y	Y	Y
7	Davis, D.	Y	Y	Y	Y	Y	Y
8	Krishnamoorthi	Y	Y	Y	Y	Y	Y
9	Schakowsky	Y	Y	Y	Y	Y	Y
10	Schneider	Y	Y	Y	Y	Y	Y
11	Foster	Y	Y	Y	Y	Y	Y

KEY:	**Republicans**	Democrats	*Independents*

Y Voted for (yea)	**N** Voted against (nay)	**P** Voted "present"
+ Announced for	**–** Announced against	**?** Did not vote or otherwise
# Paired for	**X** Paired against	make position known

		253	254	255	256	257	258
12	**Bost**	?	?	?	?	?	?
13	**Davis, R.**	Y	?	Y	Y	Y	N
14	Underwood	Y	Y	Y	Y	Y	Y
15	**Shimkus**	Y	Y	Y	Y	Y	N
16	**Kinzinger**	Y	Y	Y	Y	Y	N
17	Bustos	Y	Y	Y	Y	Y	Y
18	**LaHood**	N	Y	Y	Y	Y	N
INDIANA							
1	Visclosky	Y	Y	Y	Y	Y	Y
2	**Walorski**	N	Y	Y	Y	Y	N
3	**Banks**	N	Y	Y	N	Y	N
4	**Baird**	N	Y	Y	Y	Y	N
5	**Brooks, S.**	Y	Y	Y	Y	Y	N
6	**Pence**	N	Y	Y	Y	Y	N
7	Carson	Y	Y	Y	Y	Y	Y
8	**Bucshon**	Y	Y	Y	Y	Y	N
9	**Hollingsworth**	Y	Y	Y	Y	Y	N
IOWA							
1	Finkenauer	Y	Y	Y	Y	Y	Y
2	Loebsack	Y	Y	Y	Y	Y	Y
3	Axne	Y	Y	Y	Y	Y	Y
4	**King, S.**	Y	Y	Y	Y	Y	N
KANSAS							
1	**Marshall**	N	N	N	N	Y	N
2	**Watkins**	N	Y	Y	Y	Y	N
3	Davids	Y	Y	Y	Y	Y	Y
4	**Estes**	N	N	Y	Y	Y	N
KENTUCKY							
1	**Comer**	N	N	N	N	Y	N
2	**Guthrie**	Y	Y	Y	Y	Y	N
3	Yarmuth	Y	Y	Y	Y	Y	Y
4	**Massie**	N	Y	N	N	Y	N
5	**Rogers, H.**	Y	Y	Y	Y	Y	N
6	**Barr**	N	Y	Y	Y	Y	N
LOUISIANA							
1	**Scalise**	N	Y	N	N	Y	N
2	Richmond	Y	Y	Y	Y	Y	Y
3	**Higgins, C.**	N	Y	N	N	Y	N
4	**Johnson, M.**	N	Y	N	Y	Y	N
5	**Abraham**	N	Y	N	N	Y	N
6	**Graves, G.**	Y	Y	Y	Y	Y	N
MAINE							
1	Pingree	Y	Y	Y	Y	Y	Y
2	Golden	Y	Y	Y	Y	Y	Y
MARYLAND							
1	**Harris**	N	N	N	N	Y	N
2	Ruppersberger	Y	Y	Y	Y	Y	Y
3	Sarbanes	Y	Y	Y	Y	Y	Y
4	Brown, A.	Y	Y	Y	Y	Y	Y
5	Hoyer	?	?	?	?	?	?
6	Trone	Y	Y	Y	Y	Y	Y
7	Cummings	Y	Y	Y	Y	Y	Y
8	Raskin						
MASSACHUSETTS		Y	Y	Y	Y	Y	Y
1	Neal						
2	McGovern	Y	Y	Y	Y	Y	Y
3	Trahan	Y	Y	Y	Y	Y	Y
4	Kennedy	Y	Y	Y	Y	Y	Y
5	Clark	Y	Y	Y	Y	Y	Y
6	Moulton	Y	Y	Y	Y	Y	Y
7	Pressley	Y	Y	Y	Y	Y	Y
8	Lynch	Y	Y	Y	Y	Y	Y
9	Keating	Y	Y	Y	Y	Y	Y
MICHIGAN		Y	Y	Y	Y	Y	Y
1	**Bergman**						
2	**Huizenga**	Y	Y	Y	Y	Y	N
3	**Amash**	N	N	N	Y	Y	N
4	**Moolenaar**	N	N	N	N	N	N
5	Kildee	Y	Y	Y	Y	Y	N
6	**Upton**	Y	Y	Y	Y	Y	Y
7	**Walberg**	Y	Y	Y	Y	Y	Y
8	Slotkin	N	Y	Y	Y	Y	N
9	Levin	Y	Y	Y	Y	Y	Y
10	**Mitchell**	Y	Y	Y	Y	Y	Y
11	Stevens	Y	Y	Y	Y	Y	N
12	Dingell	Y	Y	Y	Y	Y	Y
13	Tlaib	Y	Y	Y	Y	Y	Y
14	Lawrence	Y	Y	Y	Y	Y	Y
MINNESOTA		Y	Y	Y	Y	Y	Y
1	**Hagedorn**						
2	Craig	N	Y	N	Y	Y	N
3	Phillips	Y	Y	Y	Y	Y	Y
4	McCollum	Y	Y	Y	Y	Y	Y
5	Omar	Y	Y	Y	Y	Y	Y

		253	254	255	256	257	258
6	**Emmer**	Y	Y	Y	Y	Y	Y
7	Peterson	N	Y	Y	Y	Y	N
8	**Stauber**	Y	Y	Y	Y	Y	Y
MISSISSIPPI		Y	Y	Y	Y	Y	Y
1	**Kelly, T.**						
2	Thompson, B.	N	Y	Y	Y	Y	N
3	**Guest**	Y	Y	Y	Y	Y	Y
4	**Palazzo**	N	Y	N	N	Y	N
MISSOURI		N	Y	N	Y	Y	N
1	Clay						
2	**Wagner**	Y	Y	Y	Y	Y	Y
3	**Luetkemeyer**	N	Y	Y	Y	Y	N
4	**Hartzler**	N	Y	Y	Y	Y	Y
5	Cleaver	N	Y	Y	Y	Y	N
6	**Graves, S.**	Y	Y	Y	Y	Y	Y
7	**Long**	N	Y	N	Y	Y	N
8	**Smith, J.**	N	Y	Y	N	Y	N
MONTANA		Y	Y	Y	Y	Y	N
AL	**Gianforte**						
NEBRASKA		?	?	?	?	?	?
1	**Fortenberry**						
2	**Bacon**	Y	Y	Y	Y	Y	N
3	**Smith, Adrian**	Y	Y	Y	Y	Y	N
NEVADA		N	Y	Y	Y	Y	N
1	Titus						
2	**Amodei**	Y	Y	Y	Y	Y	Y
3	Lee	Y	Y	Y	Y	Y	N
4	Horsford	Y	Y	Y	Y	Y	Y
NEW HAMPSHIRE		Y	Y	Y	Y	N	Y
1	Pappas						
2	Kuster	Y	Y	Y	Y	Y	Y
NEW JERSEY		Y	Y	Y	Y	Y	Y
1	Norcross						
2	Van Drew	Y	Y	Y	Y	Y	Y
3	Kim	Y	Y	Y	Y	Y	Y
4	**Smith, C.**	Y	Y	Y	Y	Y	Y
5	Gottheimer	Y	Y	Y	Y	Y	Y
6	Pallone	Y	Y	Y	Y	Y	Y
7	Malinowski	Y	Y	Y	Y	Y	Y
8	Sires	Y	Y	Y	Y	Y	Y
9	Pascrell	Y	Y	Y	Y	Y	Y
10	Payne	Y	Y	Y	Y	Y	Y
11	Sherrill	Y	Y	Y	Y	Y	Y
12	Watson Coleman	Y	Y	Y	Y	Y	Y
NEW MEXICO		Y	Y	Y	Y	Y	Y
1	Haaland						
2	Torres Small	Y	Y	Y	Y	Y	Y
3	Luján	Y	Y	Y	Y	Y	Y
NEW YORK		Y	Y	Y	Y	Y	Y
1	**Zeldin**						
2	**King, P.**	N	Y	N	Y	Y	N
3	Suozzi	Y	Y	Y	Y	Y	Y
4	Rice, K.	Y	Y	Y	Y	Y	Y
5	Meeks	Y	Y	Y	Y	Y	Y
6	Meng	Y	Y	Y	Y	Y	Y
7	Velázquez	Y	Y	Y	Y	Y	Y
8	Jeffries	Y	Y	Y	Y	Y	Y
9	Clarke	Y	Y	Y	Y	Y	Y
10	Nadler	Y	Y	Y	Y	Y	Y
11	Rose	Y	Y	Y	Y	Y	Y
12	Maloney, C.	Y	Y	Y	Y	Y	Y
13	Espaillat	Y	Y	Y	Y	Y	Y
14	Ocasio-Cortez	Y	Y	Y	Y	Y	Y
15	Serrano	Y	Y	Y	Y	Y	Y
16	Engel	Y	Y	Y	Y	Y	Y
17	Lowey	Y	Y	Y	Y	Y	Y
18	Maloney, S.P.	Y	Y	Y	Y	Y	Y
19	Delgado	Y	Y	Y	Y	Y	Y
20	Tonko	Y	Y	Y	Y	Y	Y
21	**Stefanik**	Y	Y	Y	Y	Y	Y
22	Brindisi	N	Y	Y	Y	Y	Y
23	**Reed**	Y	Y	Y	Y	Y	Y
24	**Katko**	Y	Y	Y	Y	Y	N
25	Morelle	Y	Y	Y	Y	Y	Y
26	Higgins, B.	Y	Y	Y	Y	Y	Y
27	**Collins, C.**	Y	Y	Y	Y	Y	Y
NORTH CAROLINA		Y	Y	Y	Y	Y	N
1	Butterfield						
2	**Holding**	Y	Y	Y	Y	Y	Y
3	**Jones***	N	Y	N	Y	Y	N
4	Price						
5	**Foxx**	Y	Y	Y	Y	Y	Y
6	**Walker**	N	Y	Y	Y	N	N
7	**Rouzer**	N	Y	N	Y	Y	N

		253	254	255	256	257	258
8	**Hudson**	N	N	N	Y	Y	N
9	vacant	Y	Y	Y	Y	Y	N
10	**McHenry**	N	Y	Y	Y	Y	N
11	**Meadows**	N	Y	N	Y	Y	N
12	Adams	Y	Y	Y	Y	Y	Y
13	**Budd**	N	Y	N	Y	Y	N
NORTH DAKOTA							
AL	**Armstrong**	N	Y	Y	Y	Y	N
OHIO							
1	**Chabot**	Y	Y	Y	Y	Y	N
2	**Wenstrup**	Y	Y	Y	Y	Y	N
3	Beatty	Y	Y	Y	Y	Y	Y
4	**Jordan**	N	N	N	N	Y	N
5	**Latta**	N	Y	Y	Y	Y	N
6	**Johnson, B.**	Y	Y	Y	Y	Y	N
7	**Gibbs**	N	Y	Y	Y	Y	N
8	**Davidson**	N	N	?	N	Y	N
9	Kaptur	Y	Y	Y	Y	Y	Y
10	**Turner**	N	Y	Y	Y	Y	N
11	Fudge	Y	Y	Y	Y	Y	Y
12	**Balderson**	N	Y	Y	Y	Y	N
13	Ryan	Y	Y	Y	Y	Y	Y
14	**Joyce**	Y	Y	Y	Y	Y	N
15	**Stivers**	Y	Y	Y	Y	Y	N
16	**Gonzalez**	Y	Y	Y	Y	Y	N
OKLAHOMA							
1	**Hern**	N	N	N	N	Y	N
2	**Mullin**	N	Y	Y	N	Y	N
3	**Lucas**	Y	Y	Y	Y	Y	N
4	**Cole**	Y	Y	Y	Y	Y	N
5	Horn	Y	Y	Y	Y	Y	Y
OREGON							
1	Bonamici	Y	Y	Y	Y	Y	Y
2	**Walden**	Y	Y	Y	Y	Y	N
3	Blumenauer	Y	Y	Y	Y	Y	Y
4	DeFazio	Y	Y	Y	Y	Y	Y
5	Schrader	Y	Y	Y	Y	Y	Y
PENNSYLVANIA							
1	**Fitzpatrick**	Y	Y	Y	Y	Y	Y
2	Boyle	Y	Y	Y	Y	Y	Y
3	Evans	Y	Y	Y	Y	Y	Y
4	Dean	Y	Y	Y	Y	Y	Y
5	Scanlon	Y	Y	Y	Y	Y	Y
6	Houlahan	Y	Y	Y	Y	Y	Y
7	Wild	Y	Y	Y	Y	Y	Y
8	Cartwright	Y	Y	Y	Y	Y	Y
9	**Meuser**	N	Y	N	Y	Y	N
10	**Perry**	N	Y	Y	Y	Y	N
11	**Smucker**	Y	Y	Y	Y	Y	N
12	**Marino***						
13	**Joyce**	N	Y	Y	N	Y	N
14	**Reschenthaler**	Y	Y	Y	N	Y	N
15	**Thompson, G.**	Y	Y	Y	Y	Y	N
16	**Kelly, M.**	Y	Y	Y	Y	Y	N
17	Lamb	Y	Y	Y	Y	Y	Y
18	Doyle	Y	Y	Y	Y	Y	Y
RHODE ISLAND							
1	Cicilline	Y	Y	Y	Y	Y	Y
2	Langevin	Y	Y	Y	Y	Y	Y
SOUTH CAROLINA							
1	Cunningham	Y	Y	Y	Y	Y	Y
2	**Wilson, J.**	N	Y	Y	Y	Y	N
3	**Duncan**	N	N	Y	N	Y	N
4	**Timmons**	N	N	N	N	Y	N
5	**Norman**	N	N	N	N	N	N
6	Clyburn	Y	Y	Y	Y	Y	Y
7	**Rice, T.**	N	N	N	Y	Y	N
SOUTH DAKOTA							
AL	**Johnson**	N	Y	Y	Y	Y	N
TENNESSEE							
1	**Roe**	N	Y	Y	Y	Y	N
2	**Burchett**	N	N	N	Y	Y	N
3	**Fleischmann**	N	Y	Y	Y	Y	N
4	**DesJarlais**	N	Y	N	Y	Y	N
5	Cooper	Y	Y	Y	Y	Y	Y
6	**Rose**	N	Y	N	Y	Y	N
7	**Green**	?	?	?	?	?	?
8	**Kustoff**	N	Y	N	Y	Y	N
9	Cohen	Y	Y	Y	Y	Y	Y
TEXAS							
1	**Gohmert**	N	N	N	N	Y	N
2	**Crenshaw**	N	Y	Y	Y	Y	N
3	**Taylor**	N	N	N	N	Y	N
4	**Ratcliffe**	N	Y	Y	Y	Y	N

		253	254	255	256	257	258
5	**Gooden**	N	N	N	N	Y	N
6	**Wright**	?	?	?	?	?	?
7	Fletcher	Y	Y	Y	Y	Y	Y
8	**Brady**	N	Y	Y	N	Y	N
9	Green, A.	Y	Y	Y	Y	Y	Y
10	**McCaul**	Y	Y	Y	Y	Y	N
11	**Conaway**	N	Y	Y	Y	Y	N
12	**Granger**	N	Y	N	Y	Y	N
13	**Thornberry**	N	Y	Y	Y	Y	N
14	**Weber**	N	N	N	Y	Y	N
15	Gonzalez	Y	Y	Y	Y	Y	Y
16	Escobar	Y	Y	Y	Y	Y	Y
17	**Flores**	N	Y	N	Y	Y	N
18	Jackson Lee	Y	Y	Y	Y	Y	Y
19	**Arrington**	N	Y	N	Y	Y	N
20	Castro	Y	Y	Y	Y	Y	Y
21	**Roy**	N	N	N	N	N	N
22	**Olson**	N	N	N	Y	Y	N
23	**Hurd**	Y	Y	Y	Y	Y	N
24	**Marchant**	N	Y	N	Y	Y	N
25	**Williams**	N	Y	N	N	Y	N
26	**Burgess**	N	N	N	N	Y	N
27	**Cloud**	N	Y	N	N	Y	N
28	Cuellar	Y	Y	Y	Y	Y	Y
29	Garcia, S.	Y	Y	Y	Y	Y	Y
30	Johnson, E.B.	Y	Y	Y	Y	Y	Y
31	**Carter, J.**	N	Y	N	Y	Y	N
32	Allred	Y	Y	Y	Y	Y	Y
33	Veasey	Y	Y	Y	Y	Y	Y
34	Vela	Y	Y	Y	Y	Y	Y
35	Doggett	Y	Y	Y	Y	Y	Y
36	**Babin**	N	N	N	N	Y	N
UTAH							
1	**Bishop, R.**	N	N	N	N	Y	N
2	**Stewart**	N	Y	Y	Y	Y	N
3	**Curtis**	N	Y	Y	N	Y	N
4	McAdams	Y	Y	Y	Y	Y	Y
VERMONT							
AL	Welch	Y	Y	Y	Y	Y	Y
VIRGINIA							
1	**Wittman**	N	Y	N	Y	Y	N
2	Luria	Y	Y	Y	Y	Y	Y
3	Scott, R.	Y	Y	Y	Y	Y	Y
4	McEachin	Y	Y	Y	Y	Y	Y
5	**Riggleman**	N	Y	Y	Y	Y	N
6	**Cline**	N	N	N	N	Y	N
7	Spanberger	Y	Y	Y	Y	Y	Y
8	Beyer	Y	Y	Y	Y	Y	Y
9	**Griffith**	N	Y	N	N	N	Y
10	Wexton	Y	Y	Y	Y	Y	Y
11	Connolly	Y	Y	Y	Y	Y	Y
WASHINGTON							
1	DelBene	Y	Y	Y	Y	Y	Y
2	Larsen	Y	Y	Y	Y	Y	Y
3	**Herrera Beutler**	?	?	?	?	?	?
4	**Newhouse**	Y	Y	Y	Y	Y	N
5	**McMorris Rodgers**	Y	Y	Y	Y	Y	N
6	Kilmer	Y	Y	Y	Y	Y	Y
7	Jayapal	Y	Y	Y	Y	Y	Y
8	Schrier	Y	Y	Y	Y	Y	Y
9	Smith Adam	Y	Y	Y	Y	Y	Y
10	Heck	Y	Y	Y	Y	Y	Y
WEST VIRGINIA							
1	**McKinley**	Y	Y	Y	Y	Y	N
2	**Mooney**	Y	Y	N	Y	Y	N
3	**Miller**	N	Y	Y	Y	Y	N
WISCONSIN							
1	**Steil**	N	Y	Y	Y	Y	N
2	Pocan	Y	Y	Y	Y	Y	Y
3	Kind	Y	Y	Y	Y	Y	Y
4	Moore	Y	Y	Y	Y	Y	Y
5	**Sensenbrenner**	+	+	-	+	+	-
6	**Grothman**	N	Y	N	N	Y	N
7	**Duffy**	Y	Y	Y	Y	Y	N
8	**Gallagher**	Y	Y	Y	Y	Y	N
WYOMING							
AL	**Cheney**	N	N	N	N	Y	N
DELEGATES							
	Radewagen (A.S.)	?	?	?	?	?	?
	Norton (D.C.)	Y	Y	Y	Y	Y	Y
	San Nicolas (Guam)	?	?	?	?	?	?
	Sablan (N. Marianas)	?	?	?	?	?	?
	González-Colón (P.R.)	?	?	?	?	?	?
	Plaskett (V.I.)	Y	Y	Y	Y	Y	Y

III HOUSE VOTES

259. HR2740. Fiscal 2020 Four-Bill Appropriations Package - Job Corps Conservation Centers. DeFazio, D-Ore., amendment that would prohibit the use of any funds authorized by the bill to close Job Corps civilian conservation centers or to alter or terminate the interagency agreement between the Labor and Agriculture Departments governing funding and operation of such centers. Adopted in Committee of the Whole 313-109: R 81-109; D 232-0. June 12, 2019.

260. HR2740. Fiscal 2020 Four-Bill Appropriations Package - Diabetes and Digestive Aid Research. Jackson Lee, D-Texas, amendment that would increase then decrease by $10 million funding for research by the National Institute of Diabetes and Digestive Aid. Adopted in Committee of the Whole 317-105: R 86-104; D 231-1. June 12, 2019.

261. HR2740. Fiscal 2020 Four-Bill Appropriations Package - Higher Education Programs. Jackson Lee, D-Texas, amendment that would increase then decrease by $10 million funding for Education Department programs related to higher education. Adopted in Committee of the Whole 312-109: R 81-109; D 231-0. June 12, 2019.

262. HR2740. Fiscal 2020 Four-Bill Appropriations Package - Occupational Safety and Health Research. Pascrell, D-N.J., amendment that would increase by $900,000 funding for National Institute for Occupational Safety and Health research and decrease by the same amount administrative funding for the Health and Human Services Department. Adopted in Committee of the Whole 413-10: R 180-10; D 233-0. June 12, 2019.

263. HR2740. Fiscal 2020 Four-Bill Appropriations Package - Birth Defects and Developmental Disabilities Research. Davis, D-Ill., amendment that would increase by $2 million funding for Health and Human Services Department research related to birth defects and developmental disabilities and decrease by the same amount HHS administrative funding. Adopted in Committee of the Whole 410-12: R 178-12; D 232-0. June 12, 2019.

264. HR2740. Fiscal 2020 Four-Bill Appropriations Package - Previous Question. Torres, D-Calif., motion to order the previous question (thus ending debate and possibility of amendment) on the rule (H Res 436) that would provide for further House floor consideration of the fiscal 2020 Labor-HHS-Education, Defense, Energy-Water, and State-Foreign Operations appropriations package (HR 2740). Motion agreed to 230-184: R 0-184; D 230-0. June 12, 2019.

		259	260	261	262	263	264
ALABAMA							
1	**Byrne**	N	N	N	N	N	N
2	**Roby**	Y	Y	Y	Y	Y	Y
3	**Rogers, M.**	N	N	N	Y	N	N
4	**Aderholt**	Y	Y	Y	Y	Y	?
5	**Brooks, M.**	N	N	N	Y	N	N
6	**Palmer**	N	N	N	Y	Y	N
7	Sewell	Y	Y	Y	Y	Y	Y
ALASKA							
AL	**Young**	Y	N	N	Y	Y	N
ARIZONA							
1	O'Halleran	Y	Y	Y	Y	Y	Y
2	Kirkpatrick	Y	Y	Y	Y	Y	Y
3	Grijalva	Y	Y	Y	Y	Y	Y
4	**Gosar**	N	N	N	N	N	Y
5	**Biggs**	N	N	N	N	N	N
6	**Schweikert**	Y	Y	Y	Y	Y	N
7	Gallego	Y	?	Y	Y	Y	Y
8	**Lesko**	Y	N	N	Y	Y	N
9	Stanton	Y	Y	Y	Y	Y	Y
ARKANSAS							
1	**Crawford**	N	Y	Y	Y	Y	N
2	**Hill, F.**	N	Y	Y	Y	Y	N
3	**Womack**	N	Y	Y	Y	Y	N
4	**Westerman**	Y	N	N	Y	N	N
CALIFORNIA							
1	**LaMalfa**	Y	N	N	Y	Y	N
2	Huffman	Y	Y	Y	Y	Y	Y
3	Garamendi	Y	Y	Y	Y	Y	Y
4	**McClintock**	N	N	N	Y	Y	N
5	Thompson, M.	Y	Y	Y	Y	Y	Y
6	Matsui	Y	Y	Y	Y	Y	Y
7	Bera	Y	Y	Y	Y	Y	Y
8	**Cook**	Y	N	Y	Y	Y	N
9	McNerney	Y	Y	Y	Y	Y	Y
10	Harder	Y	Y	Y	Y	Y	Y
11	DeSaulnier	Y	Y	Y	Y	Y	Y
12	Pelosi						
13	Lee B.	Y	Y	Y	Y	Y	Y
14	Speier	Y	Y	Y	Y	Y	Y
15	Swalwell	?	+	+	+	+	+
16	Costa	Y	Y	Y	Y	Y	Y
17	Khanna	Y	Y	Y	Y	Y	Y
18	Eshoo	Y	Y	Y	Y	Y	Y
19	Lofgren	Y	Y	Y	Y	Y	Y
20	Panetta	Y	Y	Y	Y	Y	Y
21	Cox	Y	Y	Y	Y	Y	Y
22	**Nunes**	Y	Y	Y	Y	Y	N
23	**McCarthy**	Y	Y	N	Y	Y	N
24	Carbajal	Y	Y	Y	Y	Y	Y
25	Hill, K.	Y	Y	Y	Y	Y	Y
26	Brownley	Y	Y	Y	Y	Y	Y
27	Chu	Y	Y	Y	Y	Y	Y
28	Schiff	Y	Y	Y	Y	Y	Y
29	Cárdenas	Y	Y	Y	Y	Y	Y
30	Sherman	Y	Y	Y	Y	Y	Y
31	Aguilar	Y	Y	Y	Y	Y	Y
32	Napolitano	Y	Y	Y	Y	Y	Y
33	Lieu	Y	Y	Y	Y	Y	Y
34	Gomez	Y	Y	Y	Y	Y	Y
35	Torres	Y	Y	Y	Y	Y	Y
36	Ruiz	Y	Y	Y	Y	Y	Y
37	Bass	?	?	?	?	?	Y
38	Sánchez	Y	Y	Y	Y	Y	Y
39	Cisneros	Y	Y	Y	Y	Y	Y
40	Roybal-Allard	Y	Y	Y	Y	Y	Y
41	Takano	Y	Y	Y	Y	Y	Y
42	**Calvert**	N	Y	Y	Y	Y	N
43	Waters	Y	Y	Y	Y	Y	Y
44	Barragán	Y	Y	Y	Y	Y	Y
45	Porter	Y	Y	Y	Y	Y	Y
46	Correa	Y	Y	Y	Y	Y	Y
47	Lowenthal	Y	Y	Y	Y	Y	Y
48	Rouda	Y	Y	Y	Y	Y	Y
49	Levin	Y	Y	Y	Y	Y	Y
50	**Hunter**	Y	N	N	Y	Y	N
51	Vargas	Y	Y	Y	Y	Y	Y
52	Peters	Y	Y	Y	Y	Y	Y
53	Davis, S.	Y	Y	Y	Y	Y	Y
COLORADO							
1	DeGette	Y	Y	Y	Y	Y	Y
2	Neguse	Y	Y	Y	Y	Y	Y
3	**Tipton**	Y	N	N	Y	Y	Y
4	**Buck**	?	?	?	?	?	?
5	**Lamborn**	Y	N	N	Y	Y	N
6	Crow	Y	Y	Y	Y	Y	Y
7	Perlmutter	Y	Y	Y	Y	Y	Y
CONNECTICUT							
1	Larson	Y	Y	Y	Y	Y	Y
2	Courtney	Y	Y	Y	Y	Y	Y
3	DeLauro	Y	Y	Y	Y	Y	Y
4	Himes	Y	Y	Y	Y	Y	Y
5	Hayes	Y	Y	Y	Y	Y	Y
DELAWARE							
AL	Blunt Rochester	Y	Y	Y	Y	Y	Y
FLORIDA							
1	**Gaetz**	N	N	N	Y	Y	N
2	**Dunn**	N	N	N	Y	Y	N
3	**Yoho**	N	N	N	Y	N	N
4	**Rutherford**	Y	Y	Y	Y	Y	N
5	Lawson	Y	Y	Y	Y	Y	Y
6	**Waltz**	Y	Y	Y	Y	Y	N
7	Murphy	Y	Y	Y	Y	Y	Y
8	**Posey**	Y	N	N	Y	Y	N
9	Soto	Y	Y	Y	Y	Y	Y
10	Demings	Y	Y	Y	Y	Y	Y
11	**Webster**	Y	N	N	Y	Y	N
12	**Bilirakis**	Y	Y	Y	Y	Y	Y
13	Crist	Y	Y	Y	Y	Y	Y
14	Castor	Y	Y	Y	Y	Y	Y
15	**Spano**	Y	N	N	Y	Y	N
16	**Buchanan**	N	Y	Y	Y	Y	N
17	**Steube**	N	N	N	Y	Y	N
18	**Mast**	Y	N	N	Y	Y	N
19	**Rooney**	N	Y	N	Y	Y	N
20	Hastings	?	?	?	?	?	?
21	Frankel	Y	Y	Y	Y	Y	Y
22	Deutch	Y	Y	Y	Y	Y	Y
23	Wasserman Schultz	Y	Y	Y	Y	Y	Y
24	Wilson, F.	Y	Y	Y	Y	Y	Y
25	**Diaz-Balart**	Y	Y	Y	Y	Y	N
26	Mucarsel-Powell	Y	Y	Y	Y	Y	Y
27	Shalala	Y	Y	Y	Y	Y	Y
GEORGIA							
1	**Carter, E.L.**	N	N	N	Y	Y	N
2	Bishop, S.	Y	Y	Y	Y	Y	Y
3	**Ferguson**	N	N	N	N	Y	N
4	Johnson, H.	Y	Y	Y	Y	Y	Y
5	Lewis John	Y	Y	Y	Y	Y	Y
6	McBath	Y	Y	Y	Y	Y	Y
7	**Woodall**	N	Y	Y	Y	Y	N
8	**Scott, A.**	N	N	N	Y	Y	N
9	**Collins, D.**	N	N	N	Y	Y	N
10	**Hice**	N	N	N	N	N	N
11	**Loudermilk**	N	N	N	Y	Y	?
12	**Allen**	N	N	N	Y	Y	N
13	Scott, D.	Y	Y	Y	Y	Y	Y
14	**Graves, T.**	N	N	N	Y	Y	?
HAWAII							
1	Case	Y	Y	Y	Y	Y	Y
2	Gabbard	Y	Y	Y	Y	Y	Y
IDAHO							
1	**Fulcher**	Y	N	N	Y	Y	N
2	**Simpson**	Y	Y	Y	Y	Y	N
ILLINOIS							
1	Rush	Y	Y	?	Y	Y	Y
2	Kelly, R.	Y	Y	Y	Y	Y	Y
3	Lipinski	Y	Y	Y	Y	Y	Y
4	García, J.	Y	Y	Y	Y	Y	Y
5	Quigley	Y	Y	Y	Y	Y	Y
6	Casten	Y	Y	Y	Y	Y	Y
7	Davis, D.	Y	Y	Y	Y	Y	Y
8	Krishnamoorthi	Y	Y	Y	Y	Y	Y
9	Schakowsky	Y	Y	Y	Y	Y	Y
10	Schneider	Y	Y	Y	Y	Y	Y
11	Foster	Y	Y	Y	Y	Y	Y

KEY: Republicans   Democrats   *Independents*

Y Voted for (yea)	**N** Voted against (nay)	**P** Voted "present"
+ Announced for	**−** Announced against	**?** Did not vote or otherwise
# Paired for	**X** Paired against	make position known

		259	260	261	262	263	264
12	**Bost**	?	?	?	?	?	?
13	**Davis, R.**	Y	Y	Y	Y	Y	N
14	Underwood	Y	Y	Y	Y	Y	Y
15	**Shimkus**	N	Y	Y	Y	Y	N
16	**Kinzinger**	Y	N	N	Y	Y	N
17	Bustos	Y	Y	Y	Y	Y	Y
18	**LaHood**	N	Y	Y	Y	Y	N
INDIANA							
1	Visclosky	Y	Y	Y	Y	Y	Y
2	**Walorski**	N	Y	Y	Y	Y	N
3	**Banks**	N	N	N	Y	Y	N
4	**Baird**	N	N	N	Y	Y	N
5	**Brooks, S.**	Y	Y	Y	Y	Y	N
6	**Pence**	N	Y	Y	Y	Y	N
7	Carson	Y	Y	Y	Y	Y	Y
8	**Bucshon**	N	Y	Y	Y	Y	N
9	**Hollingsworth**	N	Y	Y	Y	Y	N
IOWA							
1	Finkenauer	Y	Y	Y	Y	Y	Y
2	Loebsack	Y	Y	Y	Y	Y	Y
3	Axne	Y	Y	Y	Y	Y	Y
4	**King, S.**	Y	N	Y	Y	Y	N
KANSAS							
1	**Marshall**	N	N	N	Y	Y	N
2	**Watkins**	N	N	N	Y	Y	N
3	Davids	Y	Y	Y	Y	Y	Y
4	**Estes**	N	N	N	Y	Y	N
KENTUCKY							
1	**Comer**	Y	N	N	Y	Y	N
2	**Guthrie**	Y	Y	Y	Y	Y	N
3	Yarmuth	Y	Y	Y	Y	Y	Y
4	**Massie**	N	N	N	Y	Y	N
5	**Rogers, H.**	Y	Y	Y	Y	Y	N
6	**Barr**	Y	Y	Y	Y	Y	N
LOUISIANA							
1	**Scalise**	N	N	N	Y	Y	N
2	Richmond	Y	Y	Y	Y	Y	Y
3	**Higgins, C.**	N	Y	Y	Y	Y	N
4	**Johnson, M.**	N	Y	Y	Y	Y	N
5	**Abraham**	N	N	N	Y	Y	N
6	**Graves, G.**	Y	Y	Y	Y	Y	N
MAINE							
1	Pingree	Y	Y	Y	Y	Y	Y
2	Golden	Y	N	Y	Y	Y	Y
MARYLAND							
1	**Harris**	Y	N	N	N	N	N
2	Ruppersberger	Y	Y	Y	Y	+	Y
3	Sarbanes	Y	Y	Y	Y	Y	Y
4	Brown, A.	Y	Y	Y	Y	Y	Y
5	Hoyer	?	Y	Y	Y	Y	Y
6	Trone	Y	Y	Y	Y	Y	Y
7	Cummings	Y	Y	Y	Y	Y	Y
8	Raskin						
MASSACHUSETTS		Y	Y	Y	Y	Y	Y
1	Neal						
2	McGovern	Y	Y	Y	Y	Y	Y
3	Trahan	Y	Y	Y	Y	Y	Y
4	Kennedy	Y	Y	Y	Y	Y	Y
5	Clark	Y	Y	Y	Y	Y	Y
6	Moulton	Y	Y	Y	Y	Y	Y
7	Pressley	Y	Y	Y	Y	Y	Y
8	Lynch	Y	Y	Y	Y	Y	Y
9	Keating	Y	Y	Y	Y	Y	Y
MICHIGAN		Y	Y	Y	Y	Y	Y
1	**Bergman**						
2	**Huizenga**	Y	Y	Y	Y	Y	N
3	**Amash**	N	N	N	Y	Y	N
4	**Moolenaar**	N	N	N	N	N	N
5	Kildee	Y	Y	Y	Y	Y	N
6	**Upton**	Y	Y	Y	Y	Y	Y
7	**Walberg**	Y	Y	Y	Y	Y	N
8	Slotkin	N	N	N	Y	Y	N
9	Levin	Y	Y	Y	Y	Y	Y
10	**Mitchell**	Y	Y	Y	Y	Y	Y
11	Stevens	N	N	Y	Y	Y	N
12	Dingell	Y	Y	Y	Y	Y	Y
13	Tlaib	Y	Y	Y	Y	Y	Y
14	Lawrence	Y	Y	Y	Y	Y	Y
MINNESOTA		Y	Y	Y	Y	Y	Y
1	**Hagedorn**						
2	Craig	Y	N	N	Y	Y	N
3	Phillips	Y	Y	Y	Y	Y	Y
4	McCollum	Y	Y	Y	Y	Y	Y
5	Omar	Y	Y	Y	Y	Y	Y

		259	260	261	262	263	264
6	**Emmer**	Y	Y	Y	Y	Y	Y
7	Peterson	Y	Y	Y	Y	Y	N
8	**Stauber**	Y	Y	Y	Y	Y	Y
MISSISSIPPI		Y	Y	Y	Y	Y	N
1	**Kelly, T.**						
2	Thompson, B.	N	N	N	Y	Y	N
3	**Guest**	Y	Y	Y	Y	Y	Y
4	**Palazzo**	Y	Y	N	Y	Y	N
MISSOURI		Y	Y	N	Y	Y	N
1	Clay						
2	**Wagner**	Y	Y	Y	Y	Y	Y
3	**Luetkemeyer**	N	Y	Y	Y	Y	N
4	**Hartzler**	Y	Y	Y	Y	Y	N
5	Cleaver	Y	N	Y	Y	Y	N
6	**Graves, S.**	Y	Y	Y	Y	Y	Y
7	**Long**	N	N	N	Y	Y	N
8	**Smith, J.**	N	N	N	Y	Y	N
MONTANA		Y	Y	Y	Y	Y	N
AL	**Gianforte**						
NEBRASKA		?	?	?	?	?	?
1	**Fortenberry**						
2	**Bacon**	Y	Y	Y	Y	Y	N
3	**Smith, Adrian**	Y	Y	N	Y	Y	N
NEVADA		Y	N	N	Y	Y	N
1	Titus						
2	**Amodei**	Y	Y	Y	Y	Y	Y
3	Lee	Y	Y	Y	Y	Y	N
4	Horsford	Y	Y	Y	Y	Y	Y
NEW HAMPSHIRE		Y	Y	Y	Y	Y	Y
1	Pappas						
2	Kuster	Y	Y	Y	Y	Y	Y
NEW JERSEY		Y	Y	Y	Y	Y	Y
1	Norcross						
2	Van Drew	Y	Y	?	Y	Y	Y
3	Kim	Y	Y	Y	Y	Y	Y
4	**Smith, C.**	Y	Y	Y	Y	Y	Y
5	Gottheimer	Y	Y	Y	Y	Y	N
6	Pallone	Y	Y	Y	Y	Y	Y
7	Malinowski	Y	Y	Y	Y	Y	Y
8	Sires	Y	Y	Y	Y	Y	Y
9	Pascrell	Y	Y	Y	Y	Y	Y
10	Payne	Y	Y	Y	Y	Y	Y
11	Sherrill	Y	Y	Y	Y	Y	Y
12	Watson Coleman	Y	Y	Y	Y	Y	Y
NEW MEXICO		Y	Y	Y	Y	Y	Y
1	Haaland						
2	Torres Small	Y	Y	Y	Y	Y	Y
3	Luján	Y	Y	Y	Y	Y	Y
NEW YORK		Y	Y	Y	Y	Y	Y
1	**Zeldin**						
2	**King, P.**	N	N	N	Y	Y	N
3	Suozzi	Y	Y	Y	Y	Y	N
4	Rice, K.	Y	Y	Y	Y	Y	Y
5	Meeks	Y	Y	Y	Y	Y	?
6	Meng	Y	Y	Y	Y	Y	Y
7	Velázquez	Y	Y	Y	Y	Y	Y
8	Jeffries	Y	Y	Y	Y	Y	Y
9	Clarke	Y	Y	Y	Y	Y	Y
10	Nadler	Y	Y	Y	Y	Y	Y
11	Rose	Y	Y	Y	Y	Y	Y
12	Maloney, C.	Y	Y	Y	Y	Y	Y
13	Espaillat	Y	Y	Y	Y	Y	Y
14	Ocasio-Cortez	Y	Y	Y	Y	Y	Y
15	Serrano	Y	Y	Y	Y	Y	Y
16	Engel	Y	Y	Y	Y	Y	Y
17	Lowey	Y	Y	Y	Y	Y	Y
18	Maloney, S.P.	Y	Y	Y	Y	Y	Y
19	Delgado	Y	Y	Y	Y	Y	Y
20	Tonko	Y	Y	Y	Y	Y	Y
21	**Stefanik**	Y	Y	Y	Y	Y	Y
22	Brindisi	Y	Y	Y	Y	Y	N
23	**Reed**	Y	Y	Y	Y	Y	Y
24	**Katko**	Y	Y	Y	Y	Y	N
25	Morelle	Y	Y	Y	Y	Y	?
26	Higgins, B.	Y	Y	Y	Y	Y	Y
27	**Collins, C.**	Y	Y	Y	Y	Y	Y
NORTH CAROLINA		Y	Y	Y	Y	Y	N
1	Butterfield						
2	**Holding**	Y	Y	Y	Y	Y	Y
3	**Jones***	N	Y	N	Y	Y	N
4	Price						
5	**Foxx**	Y	Y	Y	Y	Y	Y
6	**Walker**	N	Y	N	N	Y	N
7	**Rouzer**	N	N	N	Y	Y	N

		259	260	261	262	263	264
8	**Hudson**	N	Y	N	Y	Y	N
9	vacant	N	Y	N	Y	Y	N
10	**McHenry**	Y	Y	Y	Y	Y	N
11	**Meadows**	Y	N	N	Y	Y	N
12	Adams	Y	Y	Y	Y	Y	Y
13	**Budd**	N	Y	N	Y	Y	N
NORTH DAKOTA							
AL	**Armstrong**	N	N	Y	Y	Y	N
OHIO							
1	**Chabot**	N	Y	Y	Y	Y	N
2	**Wenstrup**	N	Y	Y	Y	Y	N
3	Beatty	Y	Y	Y	Y	Y	Y
4	**Jordan**	N	N	N	Y	Y	N
5	**Latta**	N	N	N	Y	Y	N
6	**Johnson, B.**	N	Y	Y	Y	Y	N
7	**Gibbs**	N	N	N	Y	Y	N
8	**Davidson**	N	N	N	Y	Y	N
9	Kaptur	Y	Y	Y	Y	Y	Y
10	**Turner**	N	Y	Y	Y	Y	N
11	Fudge	Y	Y	Y	Y	Y	Y
12	**Balderson**	N	N	N	Y	Y	N
13	Ryan	Y	Y	Y	Y	Y	Y
14	**Joyce**	Y	Y	Y	Y	Y	N
15	**Stivers**	N	Y	Y	Y	Y	N
16	**Gonzalez**	Y	Y	Y	Y	Y	N
OKLAHOMA							
1	**Hern**	N	N	N	Y	Y	N
2	**Mullin**	N	N	N	Y	Y	N
3	**Lucas**	Y	Y	Y	Y	Y	N
4	**Cole**	Y	Y	Y	Y	Y	N
5	Horn	Y	Y	Y	Y	Y	Y
OREGON							
1	Bonamici	Y	Y	Y	Y	Y	Y
2	**Walden**	Y	Y	Y	Y	Y	N
3	Blumenauer	Y	Y	Y	Y	Y	Y
4	DeFazio	Y	Y	Y	Y	Y	Y
5	Schrader	Y	Y	Y	Y	Y	Y
PENNSYLVANIA							
1	**Fitzpatrick**	Y	Y	Y	Y	Y	N
2	Boyle	Y	Y	Y	Y	Y	Y
3	Evans	Y	Y	Y	Y	Y	Y
4	Dean	Y	Y	Y	Y	Y	Y
5	Scanlon	Y	Y	Y	Y	Y	Y
6	Houlahan	Y	Y	Y	Y	Y	Y
7	Wild	Y	Y	Y	Y	Y	Y
8	Cartwright	Y	Y	Y	Y	Y	Y
9	**Meuser**	N	Y	N	Y	Y	N
10	**Perry**	N	N	Y	Y	Y	N
11	**Smucker**	N	Y	Y	Y	Y	N
12	**Marino***						
13	**Joyce**	N	Y	N	Y	Y	N
14	**Reschenthaler**	Y	Y	Y	Y	Y	?
15	**Thompson, G.**	N	N	N	Y	Y	N
16	**Kelly, M.**	Y	Y	Y	Y	Y	N
17	Lamb	Y	Y	Y	Y	Y	Y
18	Doyle	Y	Y	Y	Y	Y	Y
RHODE ISLAND							
1	Cicilline	Y	Y	Y	Y	Y	Y
2	Langevin	Y	Y	Y	Y	Y	Y
SOUTH CAROLINA							
1	Cunningham	Y	Y	Y	Y	Y	Y
2	**Wilson, J.**	N	N	N	Y	Y	N
3	**Duncan**	N	N	N	Y	Y	N
4	**Timmons**	N	N	N	Y	Y	N
5	**Norman**	N	N	N	Y	Y	N
6	Clyburn	Y	Y	Y	Y	Y	Y
7	**Rice, T.**	N	N	Y	Y	Y	N
SOUTH DAKOTA							
AL	**Johnson**	Y	N	N	Y	Y	N
TENNESSEE							
1	**Roe**	Y	Y	N	Y	Y	N
2	**Burchett**	N	N	N	Y	Y	N
3	**Fleischmann**	Y	Y	Y	Y	Y	N
4	**DesJarlais**	N	N	N	Y	Y	N
5	Cooper	Y	Y	Y	Y	Y	Y
6	**Rose**	N	N	N	N	Y	?
7	**Green**	?	?	?	?	?	?
8	**Kustoff**	N	Y	N	Y	Y	N
9	Cohen	Y	Y	Y	Y	Y	Y
TEXAS							
1	**Gohmert**	N	N	N	Y	Y	N
2	**Crenshaw**	N	Y	N	Y	Y	N
3	**Taylor**	N	N	N	Y	Y	N
4	**Ratcliffe**	?	?	?	?	?	-

		259	260	261	262	263	264
5	**Gooden**	N	N	N	Y	Y	N
6	**Wright**	?	?	?	?	?	?
7	Fletcher	Y	Y	Y	Y	Y	Y
8	**Brady**	N	N	Y	Y	Y	N
9	Green, A.	Y	Y	Y	Y	Y	Y
10	**McCaul**	Y	Y	Y	Y	Y	N
11	**Conaway**	N	Y	Y	Y	Y	N
12	**Granger**	Y	N	Y	Y	Y	N
13	**Thornberry**	N	N	N	Y	Y	N
14	**Weber**	N	N	N	Y	N	N
15	Gonzalez	Y	Y	Y	Y	Y	?
16	Escobar	Y	Y	Y	Y	Y	Y
17	**Flores**	N	N	N	Y	N	N
18	Jackson Lee	Y	Y	Y	Y	Y	Y
19	**Arrington**	N	N	N	Y	Y	N
20	Castro	Y	Y	Y	Y	Y	Y
21	**Roy**	N	N	N	N	N	N
22	**Olson**	N	N	N	Y	Y	N
23	**Hurd**	Y	Y	Y	Y	Y	N
24	**Marchant**	N	N	N	Y	Y	N
25	**Williams**	N	Y	Y	Y	Y	N
26	**Burgess**	N	N	N	Y	Y	N
27	**Cloud**	N	N	N	Y	Y	N
28	Cuellar	Y	Y	Y	Y	Y	Y
29	Garcia, S.	Y	Y	Y	Y	Y	Y
30	Johnson, E.B.	Y	Y	Y	Y	Y	Y
31	**Carter, J.**	N	N	N	Y	N	N
32	Allred	Y	Y	Y	Y	Y	Y
33	Veasey	Y	Y	Y	Y	Y	Y
34	Vela	Y	Y	Y	Y	Y	Y
35	Doggett	Y	Y	Y	Y	Y	Y
36	**Babin**	Y	N	N	Y	N	N
UTAH							
1	**Bishop, R.**	Y	N	N	Y	Y	N
2	**Stewart**	Y	Y	N	Y	Y	N
3	**Curtis**	Y	N	N	Y	Y	N
4	McAdams	Y	Y	Y	Y	Y	Y
VERMONT							
AL	Welch	Y	Y	Y	Y	Y	Y
VIRGINIA							
1	**Wittman**	N	N	N	Y	Y	N
2	Luria	Y	Y	Y	Y	Y	Y
3	Scott, R.	Y	Y	Y	Y	Y	Y
4	McEachin	Y	Y	Y	Y	Y	Y
5	**Riggleman**	N	Y	Y	Y	Y	N
6	**Cline**	N	N	N	Y	Y	N
7	Spanberger	Y	Y	Y	Y	Y	Y
8	Beyer	Y	Y	Y	Y	Y	Y
9	**Griffith**	Y	N	N	Y	Y	N
10	Wexton	Y	Y	Y	Y	Y	Y
11	Connolly	Y	Y	Y	Y	Y	Y
WASHINGTON							
1	DelBene	Y	Y	Y	Y	Y	Y
2	Larsen	Y	Y	Y	Y	Y	Y
3	**Herrera Beutler**	?	?	?	?	?	?
4	**Newhouse**	Y	Y	Y	Y	Y	N
5	**McMorris Rodgers**	Y	Y	Y	Y	Y	N
6	Kilmer	Y	Y	Y	Y	Y	Y
7	Jayapal	Y	Y	Y	Y	Y	Y
8	Schrier	Y	Y	Y	Y	Y	Y
9	Smith Adam	Y	Y	Y	Y	Y	Y
10	Heck	Y	Y	Y	Y	Y	Y
WEST VIRGINIA							
1	**McKinley**	Y	N	Y	Y	Y	N
2	**Mooney**	N	N	N	Y	Y	N
3	**Miller**	N	N	Y	Y	Y	N
WISCONSIN							
1	**Steil**	Y	Y	Y	Y	Y	N
2	Pocan	Y	Y	Y	Y	Y	Y
3	Kind	Y	Y	Y	Y	Y	Y
4	Moore	Y	Y	Y	Y	Y	Y
5	**Sensenbrenner**	-	+	-	+	+	-
6	**Grothman**	N	N	N	Y	Y	N
7	**Duffy**	Y	N	N	Y	Y	N
8	**Gallagher**	Y	N	N	Y	Y	N
WYOMING							
AL	**Cheney**	N	N	N	Y	Y	N
DELEGATES							
	Radewagen (A.S.)	?	?	?	?	?	
	Norton (D.C.)	Y	Y	Y	Y	Y	
	San Nicolas (Guam)	?	?	?	?	?	
	Sablan (N. Marianas)	?	?	?	?	?	
	González-Colón (P.R.)	?	?	?	?	?	
	Plaskett (V.I.)	Y	Y	Y	Y	Y	

265. HR2740. Fiscal 2020 Four-Bill Appropriations Package - Rule. Adoption of the rule that would provide for further House floor consideration of the fiscal 2020 Labor-HHS-Education, Defense, Energy-Water, and State-Foreign Operations appropriations package (HR 2740). The rule would make in order 115 additional amendments, including 57 and 51 amendments to the Defense and Energy-Water sections of the bill, respectively. Adopted 232-189: R 0-189; D 232-0. June 12, 2019.

266. HR2740. Fiscal 2020 Four-Bill Appropriations Package - Conscientious Objection Rule. Cole, R-Okla., amendment that would strike from the bill a provision prohibiting funds authorized by the bill to be used to enforce a May 2019 Health and Human Services Department rule regarding enforcement of conscientious objection protections related to abortion and other health provisions under HHS programs. Rejected in Committee of the Whole 192-230: R 189-0; D 3-230. June 12, 2019.

267. HR2740. Fiscal 2020 Four-Bill Appropriations Package - Family Planning Grant Rule. Roby, R-Ala., amendment that would strike from the bill a provision requiring the Health and Human Services Department to administer certain family planning program grants under statutory frameworks in effect as of January 18, 2017. The provision that would be struck would effectively block implementation of a March 2019 HHS rule related to grants for facilities providing abortions. Rejected in Committee of the Whole 191-231: R 188-0; D 3-231. June 12, 2019.

268. HR2740. Fiscal 2020 Four-Bill Appropriations Package - Environmental Health Sciences Research. Buchanan, R-Fla., amendment that would increase then decrease by $6.3 million funding for National Institute of Environmental Health Sciences research. Adopted in Committee of the Whole 401-23: R 169-21; D 232-2. June 12, 2019.

269. HR2740. Fiscal 2020 Four-Bill Appropriations Package - Aging and Disability Services Programs. Langevin, D-R.I., amendment that would increase by $4.5 million funding for Health and Human Services aging and disability services programs and decrease by $5 million HHS administrative funding. Adopted in Committee of the Whole 356-67: R 123-67; D 233-0. June 12, 2019.

270. HR2740. Fiscal 2020 Four-Bill Appropriations Package - Unique Health Identifier Standards. Foster, D-Ill., amendment that would strike from the bill a provision prohibiting the Health and Human Services Department from using of funds authorized by the bill to promulgate or adopt standards providing for individual unique health identifiers. Adopted in Committee of the Whole 246-178: R 41-149; D 205-29. June 12, 2019.

	265	266	267	268	269	270
ALABAMA						
1 Byrne	N	Y	Y	Y	N	N
2 Roby	N	Y	Y	Y	Y	Y
3 Rogers, M.	N	Y	Y	Y	N	N
4 Aderholt	N	Y	Y	Y	Y	Y
5 Brooks, M.	N	Y	Y	N	N	N
6 Palmer	N	Y	Y	N	N	N
7 Sewell	Y	N	N	Y	Y	Y
ALASKA						
AL Young	N	Y	Y	Y	Y	N
ARIZONA						
1 O'Halleran	Y	N	N	Y	Y	Y
2 Kirkpatrick	Y	N	N	Y	Y	Y
3 Grijalva	Y	N	N	Y	Y	Y
4 Gosar	N	Y	Y	N	N	N
5 Biggs	N	Y	Y	N	N	N
6 Schweikert	N	Y	Y	N	Y	N
7 Gallego	Y	N	N	Y	Y	Y
8 Lesko	N	Y	Y	Y	N	N
9 Stanton	Y	N	N	Y	Y	Y
ARKANSAS						
1 Crawford	N	Y	Y	Y	Y	Y
2 Hill, F.	N	Y	Y	Y	Y	N
3 Womack	N	Y	Y	Y	Y	Y
4 Westerman	N	Y	Y	Y	N	N
CALIFORNIA						
1 LaMalfa	N	Y	Y	Y	Y	N
2 Huffman	Y	N	N	Y	Y	Y
3 Garamendi	Y	N	N	Y	Y	Y
4 McClintock	N	Y	Y	Y	Y	N
5 Thompson, M.	Y	N	N	Y	Y	Y
6 Matsui	Y	N	N	Y	Y	Y
7 Bera	Y	N	N	Y	Y	Y
8 Cook	N	Y	Y	Y	Y	Y
9 McNerney	Y	N	N	Y	Y	Y
10 Harder	Y	N	N	Y	Y	Y
11 DeSaulnier	Y	N	N	Y	Y	Y
12 Pelosi						
13 Lee B.	Y	N	N	Y	Y	N
14 Speier	Y	N	N	Y	Y	Y
15 Swalwell	+	-	-	+	+	+
16 Costa	Y	N	N	Y	Y	Y
17 Khanna	Y	N	N	Y	Y	Y
18 Eshoo	Y	N	N	Y	Y	Y
19 Lofgren	Y	N	N	Y	Y	N
20 Panetta	Y	N	N	Y	Y	Y
21 Cox	Y	N	N	Y	Y	Y
22 Nunes	N	Y	Y	Y	Y	N
23 McCarthy	N	Y	Y	Y	Y	N
24 Carbajal	Y	N	N	Y	Y	Y
25 Hill, K.	Y	N	N	Y	Y	Y
26 Brownley	Y	N	N	Y	Y	Y
27 Chu	Y	N	N	Y	Y	N
28 Schiff	Y	N	N	Y	Y	Y
29 Cárdenas	Y	N	N	Y	Y	N
30 Sherman	Y	N	N	Y	Y	Y
31 Aguilar	Y	N	N	Y	Y	Y
32 Napolitano	Y	N	N	Y	Y	Y
33 Lieu	Y	N	N	Y	Y	Y
34 Gomez	Y	N	N	Y	Y	Y
35 Torres	Y	N	N	Y	Y	Y
36 Ruiz	Y	N	N	Y	Y	Y
37 Bass	Y	N	N	Y	Y	Y
38 Sánchez	Y	N	N	Y	Y	Y
39 Cisneros	Y	N	N	Y	Y	Y
40 Roybal-Allard	Y	N	N	Y	Y	Y
41 Takano	Y	N	N	Y	Y	Y
42 Calvert	N	Y	Y	Y	Y	Y
43 Waters	Y	N	N	Y	Y	Y
44 Barragán	Y	N	N	Y	Y	Y
45 Porter	Y	N	N	Y	Y	Y
46 Correa	Y	N	N	Y	Y	Y
47 Lowenthal	Y	N	N	Y	Y	Y
48 Rouda	Y	N	N	Y	Y	Y
49 Levin	Y	N	N	Y	Y	Y
50 Hunter	N	Y	Y	Y	N	N
51 Vargas	Y	N	N	Y	Y	Y
52 Peters	Y	N	N	Y	Y	Y

	265	266	267	268	269	270
53 Davis, S.	Y	N	N	Y	Y	Y
COLORADO						
1 DeGette	Y	N	N	Y	Y	Y
2 Neguse	Y	N	N	Y	Y	N
3 Tipton	N	Y	Y	Y	Y	N
4 Buck	?	?	?	?	?	?
5 Lamborn	N	Y	Y	Y	N	N
6 Crow	Y	N	N	Y	Y	Y
7 Perlmutter	Y	N	N	Y	Y	Y
CONNECTICUT						
1 Larson	Y	N	N	Y	Y	Y
2 Courtney	Y	N	N	Y	Y	Y
3 DeLauro	Y	N	N	Y	Y	Y
4 Himes	Y	N	N	Y	Y	Y
5 Hayes	Y	N	N	Y	Y	Y
DELAWARE						
AL Blunt Rochester	Y	N	N	Y	Y	Y
FLORIDA						
1 Gaetz	N	Y	Y	Y	N	N
2 Dunn	N	Y	Y	Y	N	N
3 Yoho	N	Y	Y	N	N	N
4 Rutherford	N	Y	Y	Y	N	N
5 Lawson	Y	N	N	Y	Y	Y
6 Waltz	N	Y	Y	Y	N	N
7 Murphy	Y	N	N	Y	Y	Y
8 Posey	N	Y	Y	Y	N	N
9 Soto	Y	N	N	Y	Y	Y
10 Demings	Y	N	N	Y	Y	Y
11 Webster	N	Y	Y	Y	N	N
12 Bilirakis	N	Y	Y	Y	N	N
13 Crist	Y	N	N	Y	Y	Y
14 Castor	Y	N	N	Y	Y	Y
15 Spano	N	Y	Y	Y	Y	N
16 Buchanan	N	Y	Y	Y	Y	N
17 Steube	N	Y	Y	Y	N	N
18 Mast	N	Y	Y	Y	Y	N
19 Rooney	N	Y	Y	Y	N	N
20 Hastings	?	?	?	?	?	?
21 Frankel	Y	N	N	Y	Y	Y
22 Deutch	Y	N	N	Y	Y	Y
23 Wasserman Schultz	Y	N	N	Y	Y	Y
24 Wilson, F.	Y	N	N	Y	Y	Y
25 Diaz-Balart	N	Y	Y	Y	Y	Y
26 Mucarsel-Powell	Y	N	N	Y	Y	Y
27 Shalala	Y	N	N	Y	Y	Y
GEORGIA						
1 Carter, E.L.	N	Y	Y	Y	N	N
2 Bishop, S.	Y	N	N	Y	Y	Y
3 Ferguson	N	Y	Y	Y	N	N
4 Johnson, H.	Y	N	N	Y	Y	Y
5 Lewis John	Y	N	N	Y	Y	Y
6 McBath	Y	N	N	Y	Y	Y
7 Woodall	N	Y	Y	Y	N	N
8 Scott, A.	N	Y	Y	Y	N	N
9 Collins, D.	N	Y	Y	Y	N	N
10 Hice	N	Y	Y	N	N	N
11 Loudermilk	N	Y	Y	N	N	N
12 Allen	N	Y	Y	N	N	N
13 Scott, D.	Y	N	N	Y	Y	Y
14 Graves, T.	N	Y	Y	Y	N	N
HAWAII						
1 Case	Y	N	N	Y	Y	Y
2 Gabbard	Y	?	N	Y	Y	Y
IDAHO						
1 Fulcher	N	Y	Y	Y	N	N
2 Simpson	N	Y	Y	Y	N	N
ILLINOIS						
1 Rush	Y	N	N	Y	Y	Y
2 Kelly, R.	Y	N	N	Y	Y	Y
3 Lipinski	Y	Y	Y	Y	Y	Y
4 García, J.	Y	N	N	Y	Y	Y
5 Quigley	Y	N	N	Y	Y	Y
6 Casten	Y	N	N	Y	Y	Y
7 Davis, D.	Y	N	N	Y	Y	Y
8 Krishnamoorthi	Y	N	N	Y	Y	Y
9 Schakowsky	Y	N	N	Y	Y	Y
10 Schneider	Y	N	N	Y	Y	Y
11 Foster	Y	N	N	Y	Y	Y

		265	266	267	268	269	270
12	**Bost**	?	?	?	?	?	?
13	**Davis, R.**	N	Y	Y	Y	Y	Y
14	Underwood	Y	N	N	Y	Y	Y
15	**Shimkus**	N	Y	Y	Y	Y	Y
16	**Kinzinger**	N	Y	Y	Y	Y	N
17	Bustos	Y	N	N	Y	Y	Y
18	**LaHood**	N	Y	Y	Y	Y	N
INDIANA							
1	Visclosky	Y	N	N	Y	Y	Y
2	**Walorski**	N	Y	Y	Y	Y	N
3	**Banks**	N	Y	Y	N	N	N
4	**Baird**	N	Y	Y	Y	Y	N
5	**Brooks, S.**	N	Y	Y	Y	Y	Y
6	**Pence**	N	Y	Y	Y	Y	N
7	Carson	Y	N	N	Y	Y	Y
8	**Bucshon**	N	Y	Y	Y	Y	N
9	**Hollingsworth**	?	Y	Y	Y	Y	N
IOWA							
1	Finkenauer	Y	N	N	Y	Y	Y
2	Loebsack	Y	N	N	Y	Y	Y
3	Axne	Y	N	N	Y	Y	Y
4	**King, S.**	N	Y	Y	Y	Y	Y
KANSAS							
1	**Marshall**	N	Y	Y	Y	N	N
2	**Watkins**	N	Y	Y	Y	N	N
3	Davids	Y	N	N	Y	Y	Y
4	**Estes**	N	Y	Y	Y	N	N
KENTUCKY							
1	**Comer**	N	Y	Y	Y	N	N
2	**Guthrie**	N	Y	Y	Y	Y	N
3	Yarmuth	Y	N	N	Y	Y	Y
4	**Massie**	N	Y	Y	N	Y	N
5	**Rogers, H.**	N	Y	Y	Y	Y	N
6	**Barr**	N	Y	Y	Y	N	N
LOUISIANA							
1	**Scalise**	N	Y	Y	Y	N	N
2	Richmond	Y	N	N	Y	Y	Y
3	**Higgins, C.**	N	Y	Y	Y	Y	N
4	**Johnson, M.**	N	Y	Y	Y	Y	N
5	**Abraham**	N	Y	Y	Y	N	N
6	**Graves, G.**	N	Y	Y	Y	Y	N
MAINE							
1	Pingree	Y	N	N	Y	Y	Y
2	Golden	Y	N	N	Y	Y	N
MARYLAND							
1	**Harris**	N	Y	Y	Y	N	Y
2	Ruppersberger	Y	N	N	Y	Y	Y
3	Sarbanes	Y	N	N	Y	Y	Y
4	Brown, A.	Y	N	N	Y	Y	Y
5	Hoyer	Y	N	N	Y	Y	Y
6	Trone	Y	N	N	Y	Y	N
7	Cummings	Y	N	N	Y	Y	Y
8	Raskin						
MASSACHUSETTS		Y	N	N	Y	Y	N
1	Neal						
2	McGovern	Y	N	N	Y	Y	Y
3	Trahan	Y	N	N	Y	Y	N
4	Kennedy	Y	N	N	Y	Y	Y
5	Clark	Y	N	N	Y	Y	Y
6	Moulton	Y	N	N	Y	Y	N
7	Pressley	Y	N	N	Y	Y	Y
8	Lynch	Y	N	N	Y	Y	N
9	Keating	Y	N	N	Y	Y	N
MICHIGAN		Y	N	N	Y	Y	Y
1	**Bergman**						
2	**Huizenga**	N	Y	Y	Y	Y	Y
3	**Amash**	N	Y	Y	Y	Y	N
4	**Moolenaar**	N	Y	Y	N	Y	N
5	Kildee	N	Y	Y	Y	Y	N
6	**Upton**	Y	N	N	Y	Y	N
7	**Walberg**	N	Y	Y	Y	Y	Y
8	Slotkin	N	Y	Y	Y	Y	N
9	Levin	Y	N	N	Y	Y	Y
10	**Mitchell**	Y	N	N	Y	Y	N
11	Stevens	N	Y	Y	Y	Y	N
12	Dingell	Y	N	N	Y	Y	Y
13	Tlaib	Y	N	N	Y	Y	N
14	Lawrence	Y	N	N	Y	Y	Y
MINNESOTA		Y	N	N	Y	Y	Y
1	**Hagedorn**						
2	Craig	N	Y	Y	Y	Y	N
3	Phillips	Y	N	N	Y	Y	Y
4	McCollum	Y	N	N	Y	Y	Y
5	Omar	Y	N	N	Y	Y	N

		265	266	267	268	269	270
6	**Emmer**	Y	N	N	Y	Y	N
7	Peterson	N	Y	Y	Y	Y	N
8	**Stauber**	Y	N	Y	Y	Y	Y
MISSISSIPPI		N	Y	Y	Y	Y	N
1	**Kelly, T.**						
2	Thompson, B.	N	Y	Y	Y	N	N
3	**Guest**	Y	N	N	Y	Y	Y
4	**Palazzo**	N	Y	Y	Y	Y	Y
MISSOURI		N	?	?	Y	Y	N
1	Clay						
2	**Wagner**	Y	N	N	Y	Y	Y
3	**Luetkemeyer**	Y	N	N	Y	Y	N
4	**Hartzler**	N	Y	Y	Y	Y	N
5	Cleaver	N	Y	Y	Y	Y	N
6	**Graves, S.**	Y	N	N	Y	Y	Y
7	**Long**	N	Y	Y	Y	N	N
8	**Smith, J.**	N	Y	Y	N	N	N
MONTANA		N	Y	Y	Y	Y	N
AL	**Gianforte**						
NEBRASKA		?	?	?	?	?	?
1	**Fortenberry**						
2	**Bacon**	N	Y	Y	Y	Y	N
3	**Smith, Adrian**	N	Y	Y	Y	N	N
NEVADA		N	Y	Y	Y	N	N
1	Titus						
2	**Amodei**	Y	N	N	Y	Y	Y
3	Lee	N	Y	Y	Y	Y	Y
4	Horsford	Y	N	N	Y	Y	Y
NEW HAMPSHIRE		Y	N	N	Y	Y	Y
1	Pappas						
2	Kuster	Y	N	N	Y	Y	Y
NEW JERSEY		Y	N	N	Y	Y	Y
1	Norcross						
2	Van Drew	Y	N	N	Y	Y	Y
3	Kim	Y	N	N	Y	Y	Y
4	**Smith, C.**	Y	N	N	Y	Y	Y
5	Gottheimer	N	Y	Y	Y	Y	N
6	Pallone	Y	N	N	Y	Y	Y
7	Malinowski	Y	N	N	Y	Y	Y
8	Sires	Y	N	N	Y	?	Y
9	Pascrell	Y	N	N	Y	Y	Y
10	Payne	Y	N	N	Y	Y	Y
11	Sherrill	Y	N	N	Y	Y	Y
12	Watson Coleman	Y	N	N	Y	Y	Y
NEW MEXICO		Y	N	N	Y	Y	Y
1	Haaland						
2	Torres Small	Y	N	N	Y	Y	Y
3	Luján	Y	N	N	N	Y	N
NEW YORK		Y	N	N	Y	Y	Y
1	**Zeldin**						
2	**King, P.**	N	Y	Y	Y	N	Y
3	Suozzi	N	Y	Y	Y	Y	Y
4	Rice, K.	Y	N	N	Y	Y	Y
5	Meeks	Y	N	N	Y	Y	Y
6	Meng	Y	N	N	Y	Y	Y
7	Velázquez	Y	N	N	Y	Y	Y
8	Jeffries	Y	N	N	Y	Y	Y
9	Clarke	Y	N	N	Y	Y	Y
10	Nadler	Y	N	N	Y	Y	Y
11	Rose	Y	N	N	Y	Y	N
12	Maloney, C.	Y	N	N	Y	Y	Y
13	Espaillat	Y	N	N	Y	Y	Y
14	Ocasio-Cortez	Y	N	N	Y	Y	Y
15	Serrano	Y	N	N	Y	Y	N
16	Engel	Y	N	N	Y	Y	Y
17	Lowey	Y	N	N	Y	Y	Y
18	Maloney, S.P.	Y	N	N	Y	Y	Y
19	Delgado	Y	N	N	Y	Y	Y
20	Tonko	Y	N	N	Y	Y	Y
21	**Stefanik**	Y	N	N	Y	Y	N
22	Brindisi	N	Y	Y	Y	Y	Y
23	**Reed**	Y	N	N	Y	Y	Y
24	**Katko**	N	Y	Y	Y	Y	N
25	Morelle	N	Y	Y	Y	Y	N
26	Higgins, B.	Y	N	N	Y	Y	Y
27	**Collins, C.**	Y	N	N	Y	Y	Y
NORTH CAROLINA		N	Y	Y	Y	Y	N
1	Butterfield						
2	**Holding**	Y	N	N	Y	Y	Y
3	**Jones***	N	Y	Y	Y	Y	N
4	Price						
5	**Foxx**	Y	N	N	Y	Y	Y
6	**Walker**	N	Y	Y	Y	N	N
7	**Rouzer**	N	Y	Y	N	N	N

		265	266	267	268	269	270
8	**Hudson**	N	Y	Y	Y	Y	N
9	vacant	N	Y	Y	Y	Y	N
10	**McHenry**	N	Y	Y	Y	Y	Y
11	**Meadows**	N	Y	Y	Y	Y	N
12	Adams	Y	N	N	Y	Y	Y
13	**Budd**	N	Y	Y	Y	N	N
NORTH DAKOTA							
AL	**Armstrong**	N	Y	Y	Y	N	N
OHIO							
1	**Chabot**	N	Y	Y	Y	Y	N
2	**Wenstrup**	N	Y	Y	Y	Y	N
3	Beatty	Y	N	N	Y	Y	Y
4	**Jordan**	N	Y	Y	Y	N	N
5	**Latta**	N	Y	Y	Y	Y	N
6	**Johnson, B.**	N	Y	Y	Y	Y	Y
7	**Gibbs**	N	Y	Y	Y	Y	Y
8	**Davidson**	N	Y	?	Y	Y	N
9	Kaptur	Y	N	N	Y	Y	Y
10	**Turner**	N	Y	Y	Y	Y	N
11	Fudge	Y	N	N	Y	Y	Y
12	**Balderson**	N	Y	Y	Y	Y	Y
13	Ryan	Y	N	N	Y	Y	Y
14	**Joyce**	N	Y	Y	Y	Y	N
15	**Stivers**	N	Y	Y	Y	Y	Y
16	**Gonzalez**	N	Y	Y	Y	Y	N
OKLAHOMA							
1	**Hern**	N	Y	Y	Y	N	N
2	**Mullin**	N	Y	Y	Y	Y	Y
3	**Lucas**	N	Y	Y	Y	Y	Y
4	**Cole**	N	Y	Y	Y	Y	N
5	Horn	Y	N	N	Y	Y	Y
OREGON							
1	Bonamici	Y	N	N	Y	Y	Y
2	**Walden**	N	Y	Y	Y	Y	Y
3	Blumenauer	Y	N	N	Y	Y	Y
4	DeFazio	Y	N	N	Y	Y	Y
5	Schrader	Y	N	N	Y	Y	Y
PENNSYLVANIA							
1	**Fitzpatrick**	N	Y	Y	Y	Y	Y
2	Boyle	Y	N	N	Y	Y	Y
3	Evans	Y	N	N	Y	Y	Y
4	Dean	Y	N	N	Y	Y	Y
5	Scanlon	Y	N	N	Y	Y	Y
6	Houlahan	Y	N	N	Y	Y	Y
7	Wild	Y	N	N	Y	Y	N
8	Cartwright	Y	N	N	Y	Y	N
9	**Meuser**	N	Y	Y	Y	N	N
10	**Perry**	N	Y	Y	N	Y	N
11	**Smucker**	N	Y	Y	Y	Y	N
12	**Marino***						
13	**Joyce**	N	Y	Y	Y	Y	N
14	**Reschenthaler**	N	Y	Y	Y	Y	N
15	**Thompson, G.**	N	Y	Y	Y	Y	Y
16	**Kelly, M.**	N	Y	Y	Y	Y	Y
17	Lamb	Y	N	N	Y	Y	Y
18	Doyle	Y	N	N	Y	Y	N
RHODE ISLAND							
1	Cicilline	Y	N	N	Y	Y	Y
2	Langevin	Y	N	N	Y	Y	Y
SOUTH CAROLINA							
1	Cunningham	Y	N	N	Y	Y	Y
2	**Wilson, J.**	N	Y	Y	Y	Y	N
3	**Duncan**	N	Y	Y	N	N	N
4	**Timmons**	N	Y	Y	Y	N	N
5	**Norman**	N	Y	Y	N	Y	N
6	Clyburn	Y	N	N	Y	Y	Y
7	**Rice, T.**	N	Y	Y	Y	Y	N
SOUTH DAKOTA							
AL	**Johnson**	N	Y	Y	Y	Y	N
TENNESSEE							
1	**Roe**	N	Y	Y	Y	Y	N
2	**Burchett**	N	Y	Y	N	N	N
3	**Fleischmann**	N	Y	Y	Y	Y	N
4	**DesJarlais**	N	Y	Y	Y	Y	N
5	Cooper	Y	N	N	Y	Y	Y
6	**Rose**	N	Y	Y	N	N	N
7	**Green**	?	?	?	?	?	?
8	**Kustoff**	N	Y	Y	Y	N	N
9	Cohen	Y	N	N	Y	Y	Y
TEXAS							
1	**Gohmert**	N	Y	Y	N	N	N
2	**Crenshaw**	N	Y	Y	Y	Y	Y
3	**Taylor**	N	Y	Y	Y	Y	N
4	**Ratcliffe**	-	+	+	-	+	-

		265	266	267	268	269	270
5	**Gooden**	N	Y	Y	Y	N	N
6	**Wright**	?	?	?	?	?	?
7	Fletcher	Y	N	N	Y	Y	Y
8	**Brady**	N	Y	Y	Y	Y	Y
9	Green, A.	Y	N	N	Y	Y	Y
10	**McCaul**	N	Y	Y	Y	Y	Y
11	**Conaway**	N	Y	Y	Y	N	N
12	**Granger**	N	Y	Y	Y	N	Y
13	**Thornberry**	N	Y	Y	Y	Y	N
14	**Weber**	N	Y	Y	Y	N	N
15	Gonzalez	Y	N	N	Y	Y	Y
16	Escobar	Y	N	N	Y	Y	Y
17	**Flores**	N	Y	Y	Y	N	N
18	Jackson Lee	Y	N	N	Y	Y	Y
19	**Arrington**	N	Y	Y	Y	Y	N
20	Castro	Y	N	N	Y	Y	Y
21	**Roy**	N	Y	Y	N	N	N
22	**Olson**	N	Y	Y	Y	N	Y
23	**Hurd**	N	Y	Y	Y	Y	Y
24	**Marchant**	N	Y	Y	Y	N	N
25	**Williams**	N	Y	Y	Y	Y	N
26	**Burgess**	N	Y	Y	N	N	N
27	**Cloud**	N	Y	Y	Y	Y	N
28	Cuellar	Y	Y	Y	Y	Y	Y
29	Garcia, S.	Y	N	N	Y	Y	Y
30	Johnson, E.B.	Y	N	N	Y	Y	Y
31	**Carter, J.**	N	Y	Y	Y	N	N
32	Allred	Y	N	N	Y	Y	Y
33	Veasey	Y	N	N	Y	Y	Y
34	Vela	Y	N	N	Y	Y	Y
35	Doggett	Y	N	N	Y	Y	Y
36	**Babin**	N	Y	Y	Y	N	N
UTAH							
1	**Bishop, R.**	N	Y	Y	Y	N	N
2	**Stewart**	N	Y	Y	Y	N	N
3	**Curtis**	N	Y	Y	Y	N	N
4	McAdams	Y	Y	N	Y	Y	Y
VERMONT							
AL	Welch	Y	N	N	Y	Y	Y
VIRGINIA							
1	**Wittman**	N	Y	Y	Y	N	N
2	Luria	Y	N	N	Y	Y	N
3	Scott, R.	Y	N	N	Y	Y	Y
4	McEachin	Y	N	N	Y	Y	Y
5	**Riggleman**	N	Y	Y	Y	Y	N
6	**Cline**	N	Y	Y	N	N	N
7	Spanberger	Y	N	N	Y	Y	Y
8	Beyer	Y	N	N	Y	Y	Y
9	**Griffith**	N	Y	Y	Y	Y	N
10	Wexton	Y	N	N	Y	Y	Y
11	Connolly	Y	N	N	Y	Y	N
WASHINGTON							
1	DelBene	Y	N	N	Y	Y	Y
2	Larsen	Y	N	N	Y	Y	Y
3	**Herrera Beutler**	?	?	?	?	?	?
4	**Newhouse**	N	Y	Y	Y	Y	N
5	**McMorris Rodgers**	N	Y	Y	Y	Y	N
6	Kilmer	Y	N	N	Y	Y	Y
7	Jayapal	Y	N	N	Y	Y	Y
8	Schrier	Y	N	N	Y	Y	Y
9	Smith Adam	Y	N	N	Y	Y	Y
10	Heck	Y	N	N	Y	Y	Y
WEST VIRGINIA							
1	**McKinley**	N	Y	Y	Y	Y	Y
2	**Mooney**	N	Y	Y	Y	N	N
3	**Miller**	N	Y	Y	Y	Y	Y
WISCONSIN							
1	**Steil**	N	Y	Y	Y	Y	N
2	Pocan	Y	N	N	Y	Y	N
3	Kind	Y	N	N	Y	Y	Y
4	Moore	Y	N	N	Y	Y	N
5	**Sensenbrenner**	-	+	+	-	+	-
6	**Grothman**	N	Y	Y	Y	N	N
7	**Duffy**	N	Y	Y	Y	Y	N
8	**Gallagher**	N	Y	Y	Y	Y	Y
WYOMING							
AL	**Cheney**	N	Y	Y	Y	Y	Y
DELEGATES							
	Radewagen (A.S.)		?	?	?	?	?
	Norton (D.C.)		N	N	Y	Y	Y
	San Nicolas (Guam)		?	?	?	?	?
	Sablan (N. Marianas)		?	?	?	?	?
	González-Colón (P.R.)		?	?	?	?	?
	Plaskett (V.I.)		N	N	Y	Y	Y

III HOUSE VOTES

271. HR2740. Fiscal 2020 Four-Bill Appropriations Package - Substance Abuse Programs. Foster, D-Ill., amendment that would increase then decrease by $1 funding for Health and Human Services Department substance abuse treatment and prevention programs. Adopted in Committee of the Whole 336-87: R 103-86; D 233-1. June 12, 2019.

272. HR2740. Fiscal 2020 Four-Bill Appropriations Package - Bureau of Labor Statistics. Foster, D-Ill., amendment that would increase then decrease by $1 funding for salaries and expenses of the Bureau of Labor Statistics. Adopted in Committee of the Whole 260-164: R 30-160; D 230-4. June 12, 2019.

273. HR2740. Fiscal 2020 Four-Bill Appropriations Package - Public Health Emergencies. Foster, D-Ill., amendment that would decrease by $1 million administrative funding for the Health and Human Services Department and increase by the same amount funding for HHS activities related to countering public health emergencies, including biological, nuclear, radiological, chemical, and cybersecurity threats. Adopted in Committee of the Whole 358-66: R 124-66; D 234-0. June 12, 2019.

274. HR2740. Fiscal 2020 Four-Bill Appropriations Package - HHS Administrative Funding. Schiff, D-Calif., amendment that would increase then decrease by $5 million administrative funding for the Health and Human Services Department. Adopted in Committee of the Whole 341-83: R 108-82; D 233-1. June 12, 2019.

275. HR2740. Fiscal 2020 Four-Bill Appropriations Package - Substance Abuse Prevention Programs. McKinley, R-W.Va., amendment that would increase by $10 million funding for substance abuse prevention programs within the Department of Health and Human Services and decrease by the same amount funding for program support and cross-cutting supplemental activities including national surveys on drug abuse and mental health. Adopted in Committee of the Whole 415-9: R 181-9; D 234-0. June 12, 2019.

276. HR2740. Fiscal 2020 Four-Bill Appropriations Package - Programs Assisting Children and Families. Butterfield, D-N.C. amendment that would increase by $2 million funding for various Health and Human Services Department programs and services aimed at protecting and assisting children and families and decrease by the same amount HHS administrative funding. Adopted in Committee of the Whole 356-68: R 122-68; D 234-0. June 12, 2019.

		271	272	273	274	275	276
ALABAMA							
1	**Byrne**	N	N	N	N	Y	N
2	**Roby**	N	N	Y	Y	Y	Y
3	**Rogers, M.**	N	N	Y	N	Y	Y
4	**Aderholt**	Y	N	Y	Y	Y	Y
5	**Brooks, M.**	N	N	N	N	Y	N
6	**Palmer**	N	N	Y	N	Y	N
7	Sewell	Y	Y	Y	Y	Y	Y
ALASKA							
AL	**Young**	N	Y	Y	N	N	Y
ARIZONA							
1	O'Halleran	Y	Y	Y	Y	Y	Y
2	Kirkpatrick	Y	Y	Y	Y	Y	Y
3	Grijalva	Y	Y	Y	Y	Y	Y
4	**Gosar**	N	N	N	N	Y	N
5	**Biggs**	N	N	N	N	N	N
6	**Schweikert**	Y	N	Y	Y	Y	Y
7	Gallego	Y	Y	Y	Y	Y	Y
8	**Lesko**	Y	N	Y	N	Y	N
9	Stanton	Y	Y	Y	Y	Y	Y
ARKANSAS							
1	**Crawford**	Y	N	Y	N	Y	Y
2	**Hill, F.**	Y	N	Y	Y	Y	Y
3	**Womack**	Y	N	Y	Y	Y	Y
4	**Westerman**	N	N	Y	Y	Y	Y
CALIFORNIA							
1	**LaMalfa**	Y	N	Y	N	Y	Y
2	Huffman	Y	Y	Y	Y	Y	Y
3	Garamendi	Y	Y	Y	Y	Y	Y
4	**McClintock**	Y	N	Y	N	Y	Y
5	Thompson, M.	Y	Y	Y	Y	Y	Y
6	Matsui	Y	Y	Y	Y	Y	Y
7	Bera	Y	Y	Y	Y	Y	Y
8	**Cook**	Y	N	Y	Y	Y	Y
9	McNerney	Y	Y	Y	Y	Y	Y
10	Harder	Y	Y	Y	Y	Y	Y
11	DeSaulnier	Y	Y	Y	Y	Y	Y
12	Pelosi						
13	Lee B.	Y	Y	Y	Y	Y	Y
14	Speier	Y	Y	Y	Y	Y	Y
15	Swalwell	+	+	+	+	+	+
16	Costa	Y	Y	Y	Y	Y	Y
17	Khanna	Y	Y	Y	Y	Y	Y
18	Eshoo	Y	Y	Y	Y	Y	Y
19	Lofgren	Y	Y	Y	Y	Y	Y
20	Panetta	Y	Y	Y	Y	Y	Y
21	Cox	Y	Y	Y	Y	Y	Y
22	**Nunes**	Y	N	Y	Y	Y	Y
23	**McCarthy**	Y	N	Y	Y	Y	Y
24	Carbajal	Y	Y	Y	Y	Y	Y
25	Hill, K.	Y	Y	Y	Y	Y	Y
26	Brownley	Y	Y	Y	Y	Y	Y
27	Chu	Y	Y	Y	Y	Y	Y
28	Schiff	Y	Y	Y	Y	Y	Y
29	Cárdenas	Y	Y	Y	Y	Y	Y
30	Sherman	Y	Y	Y	Y	Y	Y
31	Aguilar	Y	Y	Y	Y	Y	Y
32	Napolitano	Y	Y	Y	Y	Y	Y
33	Lieu	Y	Y	Y	Y	Y	Y
34	Gomez	Y	Y	Y	Y	Y	Y
35	Torres	Y	Y	Y	Y	Y	Y
36	Ruiz	Y	Y	Y	Y	Y	Y
37	Bass	Y	Y	Y	Y	Y	Y
38	Sánchez	Y	Y	Y	Y	Y	Y
39	Cisneros	Y	Y	Y	Y	Y	Y
40	Roybal-Allard	Y	Y	Y	Y	Y	Y
41	Takano	Y	Y	Y	Y	Y	Y
42	**Calvert**	Y	Y	Y	Y	Y	Y
43	Waters	Y	Y	Y	Y	Y	Y
44	Barragán	Y	Y	Y	Y	Y	Y
45	Porter	Y	Y	Y	Y	Y	Y
46	Correa	Y	Y	Y	Y	Y	Y
47	Lowenthal	Y	Y	Y	Y	Y	Y
48	Rouda	Y	Y	Y	Y	Y	Y
49	Levin	Y	Y	Y	Y	Y	Y
50	**Hunter**	N	N	N	N	Y	N
51	Vargas	Y	Y	Y	Y	Y	Y
52	Peters	Y	Y	Y	Y	Y	Y

		271	272	273	274	275	276
53	Davis, S.	Y	Y	Y	Y	Y	Y
COLORADO							
1	DeGette	Y	Y	Y	Y	Y	Y
2	Neguse	Y	Y	Y	Y	Y	Y
3	**Tipton**	N	N	Y	N	Y	Y
4	**Buck**	?	?	?	?	?	?
5	**Lamborn**	N	N	Y	N	Y	N
6	Crow	Y	Y	Y	Y	Y	Y
7	Perlmutter	Y	Y	Y	Y	Y	Y
CONNECTICUT							
1	Larson	Y	Y	Y	Y	Y	Y
2	Courtney	Y	Y	Y	Y	Y	Y
3	DeLauro	Y	Y	Y	Y	Y	Y
4	Himes	Y	Y	Y	Y	Y	Y
5	Hayes	Y	Y	Y	Y	Y	Y
DELAWARE							
AL	Blunt Rochester	Y	Y	Y	Y	Y	Y
FLORIDA							
1	**Gaetz**	N	N	Y	N	Y	N
2	**Dunn**	N	N	N	Y	N	N
3	**Yoho**	N	N	Y	N	Y	N
4	**Rutherford**	N	N	Y	N	Y	Y
5	Lawson	Y	Y	Y	Y	Y	Y
6	**Waltz**	Y	N	Y	Y	Y	Y
7	Murphy	Y	Y	Y	Y	Y	Y
8	**Posey**	N	N	N	N	Y	N
9	Soto	Y	Y	Y	Y	Y	Y
10	Demings	Y	Y	Y	Y	Y	Y
11	**Webster**	N	N	N	N	Y	N
12	**Bilirakis**	Y	N	Y	Y	Y	Y
13	Crist	Y	Y	Y	Y	Y	Y
14	Castor	Y	Y	Y	Y	Y	Y
15	**Spano**	N	Y	Y	Y	Y	Y
16	**Buchanan**	Y	Y	Y	Y	Y	Y
17	**Steube**	N	N	N	N	Y	N
18	**Mast**	N	N	N	N	N	N
19	**Rooney**	N	N	N	N	Y	N
20	Hastings	?	?	?	?	?	?
21	Frankel	Y	Y	Y	Y	Y	Y
22	Deutch	Y	Y	Y	Y	Y	Y
23	Wasserman Schultz	Y	Y	Y	Y	Y	Y
24	Wilson, F.	Y	Y	Y	Y	Y	Y
25	**Diaz-Balart**	Y	N	Y	Y	Y	Y
26	Mucarsel-Powell	Y	Y	Y	Y	Y	Y
27	Shalala	Y	Y	Y	Y	Y	Y
GEORGIA							
1	**Carter, E.L.**	N	N	N	N	Y	N
2	Bishop, S.	Y	Y	Y	Y	Y	Y
3	**Ferguson**	N	N	N	N	Y	N
4	Johnson, H.	Y	Y	Y	Y	Y	Y
5	Lewis John	Y	Y	Y	Y	Y	Y
6	McBath	Y	Y	Y	Y	Y	Y
7	**Woodall**	N	N	Y	N	Y	N
8	**Scott, A.**	N	N	N	Y	Y	N
9	**Collins, D.**	N	N	N	N	Y	N
10	**Hice**	N	N	N	N	Y	N
11	**Loudermilk**	N	N	Y	N	Y	N
12	**Allen**	N	N	N	N	Y	N
13	Scott, D.	Y	Y	Y	Y	Y	Y
14	**Graves, T.**	N	N	N	N	Y	N
HAWAII							
1	Case	Y	Y	Y	Y	Y	Y
2	Gabbard	Y	Y	Y	Y	Y	Y
IDAHO							
1	**Fulcher**	Y	N	N	N	Y	N
2	**Simpson**	Y	N	N	Y	Y	Y
ILLINOIS							
1	Rush	Y	Y	Y	Y	Y	Y
2	Kelly, R.	Y	Y	Y	Y	Y	Y
3	Lipinski	Y	Y	Y	Y	Y	Y
4	García, J.	Y	Y	Y	Y	Y	Y
5	Quigley	Y	Y	Y	Y	Y	Y
6	Casten	Y	Y	Y	Y	Y	Y
7	Davis, D.	Y	Y	Y	Y	Y	Y
8	Krishnamoorthi	Y	Y	Y	Y	Y	Y
9	Schakowsky	Y	Y	Y	Y	Y	Y
10	Schneider	Y	Y	Y	Y	Y	Y
11	Foster	Y	Y	Y	Y	Y	Y

KEY:	**Republicans**	Democrats	*Independents*
Y Voted for (yea)	**N** Voted against (nay)	**P** Voted "present"	
+ Announced for	**–** Announced against	**?** Did not vote or otherwise	
# Paired for	**X** Paired against	make position known	

		271	272	273	274	275	276
12	**Bost**	?	?	?	?	?	?
13	**Davis, R.**	Y	Y	Y	Y	Y	Y
14	Underwood	Y	Y	Y	Y	Y	Y
15	**Shimkus**	Y	N	Y	Y	Y	Y
16	**Kinzinger**	N	N	Y	Y	Y	Y
17	Bustos	Y	Y	Y	Y	Y	Y
18	**LaHood**	Y	N	Y	Y	Y	Y
INDIANA							
1	Visclosky	Y	Y	Y	Y	Y	Y
2	**Walorski**	Y	Y	Y	Y	Y	Y
3	**Banks**	N	N	N	Y	Y	N
4	**Baird**	Y	Y	Y	Y	Y	Y
5	**Brooks, S.**	Y	Y	Y	Y	Y	Y
6	**Pence**	Y	N	Y	Y	Y	Y
7	Carson	Y	Y	Y	Y	Y	Y
8	**Bucshon**	Y	N	N	Y	Y	Y
9	**Hollingsworth**	Y	Y	Y	Y	Y	Y
IOWA							
1	Finkenauer	Y	Y	Y	Y	Y	Y
2	Loebsack	Y	Y	Y	Y	Y	Y
3	Axne	Y	Y	Y	Y	Y	Y
4	**King, S.**	Y	Y	Y	N	N	N
KANSAS							
1	**Marshall**	N	N	Y	N	Y	N
2	**Watkins**	N	N	Y	N	Y	N
3	Davids	Y	Y	Y	Y	Y	Y
4	**Estes**	N	N	N	N	Y	N
KENTUCKY							
1	**Comer**	N	N	N	N	Y	Y
2	**Guthrie**	Y	N	Y	Y	Y	Y
3	Yarmuth	Y	Y	Y	Y	Y	Y
4	**Massie**	Y	N	Y	N	N	Y
5	**Rogers, H.**	Y	N	Y	Y	Y	Y
6	**Barr**	N	N	N	N	Y	N
LOUISIANA							
1	**Scalise**	Y	N	Y	Y	Y	Y
2	Richmond	Y	Y	Y	Y	Y	Y
3	**Higgins, C.**	N	N	N	N	N	N
4	**Johnson, M.**	Y	N	Y	Y	Y	Y
5	**Abraham**	Y	N	Y	Y	Y	Y
6	**Graves, G.**	Y	Y	Y	Y	Y	Y
MAINE							
1	Pingree	Y	Y	Y	Y	Y	Y
2	Golden	Y	N	Y	Y	Y	Y
MARYLAND							
1	**Harris**	N	N	Y	N	Y	N
2	Ruppersberger	Y	Y	Y	Y	Y	Y
3	Sarbanes	Y	Y	Y	Y	Y	Y
4	Brown, A.	Y	Y	Y	Y	Y	Y
5	Hoyer	Y	Y	Y	Y	Y	Y
6	Trone	Y	Y	Y	Y	Y	Y
7	Cummings	Y	Y	Y	Y	Y	Y
8	Raskin						
MASSACHUSETTS		Y	Y	Y	Y	Y	Y
1	Neal						
2	McGovern	Y	Y	Y	Y	Y	Y
3	Trahan	Y	Y	Y	Y	Y	Y
4	Kennedy	Y	Y	Y	Y	Y	Y
5	Clark	Y	Y	Y	Y	Y	Y
6	Moulton	Y	Y	Y	Y	Y	Y
7	Pressley	Y	Y	Y	Y	Y	Y
8	Lynch	Y	Y	Y	Y	Y	Y
9	Keating	Y	Y	Y	Y	Y	Y
MICHIGAN		Y	Y	Y	Y	Y	Y
1	**Bergman**						
2	**Huizenga**	Y	Y	Y	Y	Y	Y
3	**Amash**	N	N	Y	Y	Y	Y
4	**Moolenaar**	N	Y	N	N	N	N
5	Kildee	Y	N	Y	Y	Y	Y
6	**Upton**	Y	Y	Y	Y	Y	Y
7	**Walberg**	Y	Y	Y	Y	Y	Y
8	Slotkin	Y	N	Y	N	Y	Y
9	Levin	Y	Y	Y	Y	Y	Y
10	**Mitchell**	Y	Y	Y	Y	Y	Y
11	Stevens	Y	N	Y	Y	Y	Y
12	Dingell	Y	Y	Y	Y	Y	Y
13	Tlaib	Y	Y	Y	Y	Y	Y
14	Lawrence	Y	Y	Y	Y	Y	Y
MINNESOTA		Y	Y	Y	Y	Y	Y
1	**Hagedorn**						
2	Craig	N	N	N	N	Y	Y
3	Phillips	Y	Y	Y	Y	Y	Y
4	McCollum	Y	Y	Y	Y	Y	Y
5	Omar	Y	Y	Y	Y	Y	Y

		271	272	273	274	275	276
6	**Emmer**	Y	Y	Y	Y	Y	Y
7	Peterson	Y	N	Y	N	Y	N
8	**Stauber**	Y	N	Y	Y	Y	Y
MISSISSIPPI		Y	Y	Y	Y	Y	Y
1	**Kelly, T.**						
2	Thompson, B.	N	N	N	N	Y	N
3	**Guest**	Y	Y	Y	Y	Y	Y
4	**Palazzo**	Y	N	Y	Y	Y	Y
MISSOURI		N	N	N	N	Y	N
1	Clay						
2	**Wagner**	Y	Y	Y	Y	Y	Y
3	**Luetkemeyer**	Y	N	Y	Y	Y	Y
4	**Hartzler**	Y	N	N	Y	Y	Y
5	Cleaver	Y	Y	Y	Y	Y	Y
6	**Graves, S.**	Y	Y	Y	Y	Y	Y
7	**Long**	N	N	N	N	Y	N
8	**Smith, J.**	Y	N	Y	Y	Y	Y
MONTANA		Y	N	N	Y	Y	Y
AL	**Gianforte**						
NEBRASKA		?	?	?	?	?	?
1	**Fortenberry**						
2	**Bacon**	Y	Y	Y	N	Y	Y
3	**Smith, Adrian**	Y	N	N	Y	Y	N
NEVADA		Y	N	Y	N	Y	Y
1	Titus						
2	**Amodei**	Y	Y	Y	Y	Y	Y
3	Lee	N	N	Y	Y	Y	Y
4	Horsford	Y	Y	Y	Y	Y	Y
NEW HAMPSHIRE		Y	N	Y	Y	Y	Y
1	Pappas						
2	Kuster	Y	Y	Y	Y	Y	Y
NEW JERSEY		Y	Y	Y	Y	Y	Y
1	Norcross						
2	Van Drew	Y	Y	Y	Y	Y	Y
3	Kim	Y	Y	Y	Y	Y	Y
4	**Smith, C.**	Y	Y	Y	Y	Y	Y
5	Gottheimer	N	Y	Y	Y	Y	Y
6	Pallone	Y	Y	Y	Y	Y	Y
7	Malinowski	Y	Y	Y	Y	Y	Y
8	Sires	Y	Y	Y	Y	Y	Y
9	Pascrell	Y	Y	Y	Y	Y	Y
10	Payne	Y	Y	Y	Y	Y	Y
11	Sherrill	Y	Y	Y	Y	Y	Y
12	Watson Coleman	Y	Y	Y	Y	Y	Y
NEW MEXICO		Y	Y	Y	Y	Y	Y
1	Haaland						
2	Torres Small	Y	Y	Y	Y	Y	Y
3	Luján	Y	Y	Y	Y	Y	Y
NEW YORK		Y	Y	Y	Y	Y	Y
1	**Zeldin**						
2	**King, P.**	Y	N	N	N	Y	N
3	Suozzi	Y	Y	Y	Y	Y	Y
4	Rice, K.	Y	Y	Y	Y	Y	Y
5	Meeks	Y	Y	Y	Y	Y	Y
6	Meng	Y	Y	Y	Y	Y	Y
7	Velázquez	Y	Y	Y	Y	Y	Y
8	Jeffries	Y	Y	Y	Y	Y	Y
9	Clarke	Y	Y	Y	Y	Y	Y
10	Nadler	Y	Y	Y	Y	Y	Y
11	Rose	Y	Y	Y	Y	Y	Y
12	Maloney, C.	Y	Y	Y	Y	Y	Y
13	Espaillat	Y	Y	Y	Y	Y	Y
14	Ocasio-Cortez	Y	Y	Y	Y	Y	Y
15	Serrano	Y	Y	Y	Y	Y	Y
16	Engel	Y	Y	Y	Y	Y	Y
17	Lowey	Y	Y	Y	Y	Y	Y
18	Maloney, S.P.	Y	Y	Y	Y	Y	Y
19	Delgado	Y	Y	Y	Y	Y	Y
20	Tonko	Y	Y	Y	Y	Y	Y
21	**Stefanik**	Y	Y	Y	Y	Y	Y
22	Brindisi	Y	Y	Y	Y	Y	Y
23	**Reed**	Y	Y	Y	Y	Y	Y
24	**Katko**	Y	Y	Y	Y	Y	Y
25	Morelle	Y	Y	Y	Y	Y	Y
26	Higgins, B.	Y	Y	Y	Y	Y	Y
27	**Collins, C.**	Y	Y	Y	Y	Y	Y
NORTH CAROLINA		Y	Y	Y	Y	Y	Y
1	Butterfield						
2	**Holding**	Y	Y	Y	Y	Y	Y
3	**Jones***	Y	N	N	Y	Y	Y
4	Price						
5	**Foxx**	Y	Y	Y	Y	Y	Y
6	**Walker**	Y	N	N	Y	Y	N
7	**Rouzer**	N	N	N	N	Y	N

		271	272	273	274	275	276
8	**Hudson**	Y	N	Y	Y	Y	Y
9	vacant	Y	N	Y	Y	Y	Y
10	**McHenry**	Y	N	Y	Y	Y	Y
11	**Meadows**	Y	N	Y	N	Y	N
12	Adams	Y	Y	Y	Y	Y	Y
13	**Budd**	N	N	Y	N	Y	Y
NORTH DAKOTA							
AL	**Armstrong**	Y	N	Y	N	Y	Y
OHIO							
1	**Chabot**	Y	N	N	Y	Y	Y
2	**Wenstrup**	N	N	Y	Y	Y	Y
3	Beatty	Y	Y	Y	Y	Y	Y
4	**Jordan**	N	N	N	N	Y	N
5	**Latta**	N	N	Y	N	Y	Y
6	**Johnson, B.**	Y	N	Y	Y	Y	Y
7	**Gibbs**	Y	N	N	Y	Y	N
8	**Davidson**	N	N	Y	N	Y	N
9	Kaptur	Y	Y	Y	Y	Y	Y
10	**Turner**	Y	Y	N	N	Y	Y
11	Fudge	Y	Y	Y	Y	Y	Y
12	**Balderson**	Y	N	Y	Y	Y	Y
13	Ryan	Y	Y	Y	Y	Y	Y
14	**Joyce**	Y	Y	Y	Y	Y	Y
15	**Stivers**	Y	N	Y	Y	Y	Y
16	**Gonzalez**	Y	Y	Y	Y	Y	Y
OKLAHOMA							
1	**Hern**	N	N	Y	N	Y	Y
2	**Mullin**	N	N	Y	Y	Y	Y
3	**Lucas**	Y	N	Y	Y	Y	Y
4	**Cole**	Y	N	Y	Y	Y	Y
5	Horn	Y	Y	Y	Y	Y	Y
OREGON							
1	Bonamici	Y	Y	Y	Y	Y	Y
2	**Walden**	Y	Y	Y	Y	Y	Y
3	Blumenauer	Y	Y	Y	Y	Y	Y
4	DeFazio	N	N	Y	Y	Y	Y
5	Schrader	Y	Y	Y	Y	Y	Y
PENNSYLVANIA							
1	**Fitzpatrick**	Y	Y	Y	Y	Y	Y
2	Boyle	Y	Y	Y	Y	Y	Y
3	Evans	Y	Y	Y	Y	Y	Y
4	Dean	Y	Y	Y	Y	Y	Y
5	Scanlon	Y	Y	Y	Y	Y	Y
6	Houlahan	Y	Y	Y	Y	Y	Y
7	Wild	Y	Y	Y	Y	Y	Y
8	Cartwright	Y	Y	Y	Y	Y	Y
9	**Meuser**	N	N	Y	N	Y	Y
10	**Perry**	Y	N	Y	N	Y	Y
11	**Smucker**	Y	N	Y	Y	Y	Y
12	**Marino***						
13	**Joyce**	Y	N	Y	Y	Y	Y
14	**Reschenthaler**	Y	N	Y	Y	Y	Y
15	**Thompson, G.**	Y	N	Y	Y	Y	Y
16	**Kelly, M.**	N	N	Y	Y	Y	Y
17	Lamb	Y	Y	Y	Y	Y	Y
18	Doyle	Y	Y	Y	Y	Y	Y
RHODE ISLAND							
1	Cicilline	Y	Y	Y	Y	Y	Y
2	Langevin	Y	Y	Y	Y	Y	Y
SOUTH CAROLINA							
1	Cunningham	Y	Y	Y	Y	Y	Y
2	**Wilson, J.**	N	N	N	N	Y	Y
3	**Duncan**	Y	N	N	Y	Y	N
4	**Timmons**	N	N	N	N	Y	Y
5	**Norman**	N	N	N	N	Y	N
6	Clyburn	Y	Y	Y	Y	Y	Y
7	**Rice, T.**	N	N	N	N	Y	N
SOUTH DAKOTA							
AL	**Johnson**	Y	N	Y	Y	Y	Y
TENNESSEE							
1	**Roe**	Y	N	Y	Y	Y	Y
2	**Burchett**	N	N	N	N	Y	N
3	**Fleischmann**	Y	N	Y	Y	Y	Y
4	**DesJarlais**	N	N	Y	Y	Y	Y
5	Cooper	Y	Y	Y	Y	Y	Y
6	**Rose**	N	N	N	Y	Y	N
7	**Green**	?	?	?	?	?	?
8	**Kustoff**	Y	N	Y	Y	Y	N
9	Cohen	Y	Y	Y	Y	Y	Y
TEXAS							
1	**Gohmert**	?	N	N	N	Y	N
2	**Crenshaw**	Y	N	Y	Y	Y	N
3	**Taylor**	N	N	N	N	Y	N
4	**Ratcliffe**	-	-	-	-	+	-

		271	272	273	274	275	276
5	**Gooden**	N	N	N	N	Y	N
6	**Wright**	?	?	?	?	?	?
7	Fletcher	Y	Y	Y	Y	Y	Y
8	**Brady**	N	N	N	Y	Y	Y
9	Green, A.	Y	Y	Y	Y	Y	Y
10	**McCaul**	Y	N	Y	Y	Y	Y
11	**Conaway**	N	N	Y	N	Y	N
12	**Granger**	Y	N	Y	Y	Y	Y
13	**Thornberry**	N	N	Y	Y	Y	Y
14	**Weber**	N	N	N	N	Y	N
15	Gonzalez	Y	Y	Y	Y	Y	Y
16	Escobar	Y	Y	Y	Y	Y	Y
17	**Flores**	N	N	Y	Y	Y	Y
18	Jackson Lee	Y	Y	Y	Y	Y	Y
19	**Arrington**	N	N	Y	N	Y	N
20	Castro	Y	Y	Y	N	Y	Y
21	**Roy**	N	N	N	N	N	N
22	**Olson**	N	N	N	N	Y	N
23	**Hurd**	Y	N	Y	Y	Y	Y
24	**Marchant**	N	N	N	N	Y	N
25	**Williams**	N	N	Y	Y	Y	Y
26	**Burgess**	N	N	N	Y	Y	N
27	**Cloud**	Y	N	Y	N	Y	N
28	Cuellar	Y	Y	Y	Y	Y	Y
29	Garcia, S.	Y	Y	Y	Y	Y	Y
30	Johnson, E.B.	Y	Y	Y	Y	Y	Y
31	**Carter, J.**	N	N	N	N	Y	N
32	Allred	Y	Y	Y	Y	Y	Y
33	Veasey	Y	Y	Y	Y	Y	Y
34	Vela	Y	Y	Y	Y	Y	Y
35	Doggett	Y	Y	Y	Y	Y	Y
36	**Babin**	N	N	N	N	Y	N
UTAH							
1	**Bishop, R.**	N	N	N	N	Y	N
2	**Stewart**	Y	N	Y	Y	Y	N
3	**Curtis**	Y	N	Y	Y	Y	N
4	McAdams	Y	Y	Y	Y	Y	Y
VERMONT							
AL	Welch	Y	Y	Y	Y	Y	Y
VIRGINIA							
1	**Wittman**	N	N	N	N	Y	N
2	Luria	Y	Y	Y	Y	Y	Y
3	Scott, R.	Y	Y	Y	Y	Y	Y
4	McEachin	Y	Y	Y	Y	Y	Y
5	**Riggleman**	Y	N	Y	N	Y	Y
6	**Cline**	N	N	N	N	Y	N
7	Spanberger	Y	Y	Y	Y	Y	Y
8	Beyer	Y	Y	Y	Y	Y	Y
9	**Griffith**	Y	N	Y	N	Y	Y
10	Wexton	Y	Y	Y	Y	Y	Y
11	Connolly	Y	Y	Y	Y	Y	Y
WASHINGTON							
1	DelBene	Y	Y	Y	Y	Y	Y
2	Larsen	Y	Y	Y	Y	Y	Y
3	**Herrera Beutler**	?	?	?	?	?	?
4	**Newhouse**	Y	Y	Y	Y	Y	Y
5	**McMorris Rodgers**	Y	Y	Y	Y	Y	Y
6	Kilmer	Y	Y	Y	Y	Y	Y
7	Jayapal	Y	Y	Y	Y	Y	Y
8	Schrier	Y	Y	Y	Y	Y	Y
9	Smith Adam	Y	Y	Y	Y	Y	Y
10	Heck	Y	Y	Y	Y	Y	Y
WEST VIRGINIA							
1	**McKinley**	Y	N	Y	Y	Y	Y
2	**Mooney**	Y	N	Y	N	Y	Y
3	**Miller**	Y	N	Y	Y	Y	Y
WISCONSIN							
1	**Steil**	Y	N	Y	Y	Y	Y
2	Pocan	Y	Y	Y	Y	Y	Y
3	Kind	Y	Y	Y	Y	Y	Y
4	Moore	Y	Y	Y	Y	Y	Y
5	**Sensenbrenner**	+	+	+	+	+	+
6	**Grothman**	N	N	Y	N	Y	Y
7	**Duffy**	N	N	N	N	Y	Y
8	**Gallagher**	Y	N	N	Y	Y	Y
WYOMING							
AL	**Cheney**	N	N	N	N	Y	Y
DELEGATES							
	Radewagen (A.S.)	?	?	?	?	?	?
	Norton (D.C.)	Y	Y	Y	Y	Y	Y
	San Nicolas (Guam)	?	?	?	?	?	?
	Sablan (N. Marianas)	?	?	?	?	?	?
	González-Colón (P.R.)	?	?	?	?	?	?
	Plaskett (V.I.)	Y	Y	Y	Y	Y	Y

277. HR2740. Fiscal 2020 Four-Bill Appropriations Package - Substance Abuse Prevention Programs. Johnson, R-Ohio, amendment that would increase by $2 million funding for substance abuse prevention programs within the Health and Human Services Department and decrease by the same amount HHS administrative funding. Adopted in Committee of the Whole 408-15: R 174-15; D 234-0. June 12, 2019.

278. HR2740. Fiscal 2020 Four-Bill Appropriations Package - Chronic Disease Prevention and Health Promotion Programs. Moore, D-Wis., amendment that would increase by $500,000 funding for chronic disease prevention and health promotion programs within the Health and Human Services Department and reduce by the same amount funding for program support and cross-cutting supplemental activities within the Centers for Disease Control and Prevention. Adopted in Committee of the Whole 405-19: R 171-19; D 234-0. June 12, 2019.

279. HR2740. Fiscal 2020 Four-Bill Appropriations Package - Injury Prevention and Control Programs. Moore, D-Wis., amendment that would increase by $4.5 million funding for injury prevention and control programs within the Health and Human Services Department, and reduce by the same amount funding for various program management activities within the department. Adopted in Committee of the Whole 348-75: R 114-75; D 234-0. *Note: In the legislative day that began on Wednesday, June 12, 2019.* June 13, 2019.

280. HR2740. Fiscal 2020 Four-Bill Appropriations Package - Disability and Aging Assistance Programs. Matsui, D-Calif., amendment that would increase by $2 million funding for Health and Human Services Department-wide disability assistance, community living, aging and disability services programs, and decrease by the same amount HHS administrative funding. Adopted in Committee of the Whole 376-48: R 142-48; D 234-0. *Note: In the legislative day that began on Wednesday, June 12, 2019.* June 13, 2019.

281. HR2740. Fiscal 2020 Four-Bill Appropriations Package - Substance Abuse Prevention Programs. Barr, R-Ky., amendment that would increase by $1 million funding for substance abuse prevention programs within the Health and Human Services Department and decrease by the same amount funding for program support and cross-cutting supplemental activities including national surveys on drug abuse and mental health. Adopted in Committee of the Whole 420-4: R 186-4; D 234-0. June 13, 2019.

282. HR2740. Fiscal 2020 Four-Bill Appropriations Package - Substance Abuse and Mental Health Programs. Cleaver, D-Mo., amendment that would increase by $6.5 million funding for mental health programs within the Substance Abuse and Mental Health Services Administration and decrease by the same amount funding for program support and cross-cutting supplemental activities including national surveys on drug abuse and mental health. Adopted in Committee of the Whole 386-38: R 152-38; D 234-0. June 13, 2019.

		277	278	279	280	281	282
ALABAMA							
1	**Byrne**	Y	N	N	N	Y	N
2	**Roby**	Y	Y	Y	Y	Y	Y
3	**Rogers, M.**	Y	Y	Y	Y	Y	Y
4	**Aderholt**	Y	Y	N	Y	Y	Y
5	**Brooks, M.**	Y	N	N	N	Y	N
6	**Palmer**	Y	Y	N	N	Y	N
7	Sewell	Y	Y	Y	Y	Y	Y
ALASKA							
AL	Young	Y	Y	Y	Y	Y	Y
ARIZONA							
1	O'Halleran	Y	Y	Y	Y	Y	Y
2	Kirkpatrick	Y	Y	Y	Y	Y	Y
3	Grijalva	Y	Y	Y	Y	Y	Y
4	**Gosar**	Y	N	N	N	Y	N
5	**Biggs**	N	N	N	N	N	N
6	**Schweikert**	Y	Y	Y	Y	Y	Y
7	Gallego	Y	Y	Y	Y	Y	Y
8	**Lesko**	Y	Y	N	Y	Y	Y
9	Stanton	Y	Y	Y	Y	Y	Y
ARKANSAS							
1	**Crawford**	Y	Y	N	Y	Y	Y
2	**Hill, F.**	Y	Y	Y	N	Y	Y
3	**Womack**	Y	Y	Y	Y	Y	Y
4	**Westerman**	Y	Y	N	N	Y	Y
CALIFORNIA							
1	**LaMalfa**	Y	Y	Y	Y	Y	Y
2	Huffman	Y	Y	Y	Y	Y	Y
3	Garamendi	Y	Y	Y	Y	Y	Y
4	**McClintock**	Y	Y	N	Y	Y	Y
5	Thompson, M.	Y	Y	Y	Y	Y	Y
6	Matsui	Y	Y	Y	Y	Y	Y
7	Bera	Y	Y	Y	Y	Y	Y
8	**Cook**	Y	Y	Y	Y	Y	Y
9	McNerney	Y	Y	Y	Y	Y	Y
10	Harder	Y	Y	Y	Y	Y	Y
11	DeSaulnier	Y	Y	Y	Y	Y	Y
12	Pelosi						
13	Lee B.	Y	Y	Y	Y	Y	Y
14	Speier	Y	Y	Y	Y	Y	Y
15	Swalwell	+	+	+	+	+	+
16	Costa	Y	Y	Y	Y	Y	Y
17	Khanna	Y	Y	Y	Y	Y	Y
18	Eshoo	Y	Y	Y	Y	Y	Y
19	Lofgren	Y	Y	Y	Y	Y	Y
20	Panetta	Y	Y	Y	Y	Y	Y
21	Cox	Y	Y	Y	Y	Y	Y
22	**Nunes**	Y	Y	Y	Y	Y	Y
23	**McCarthy**	Y	Y	Y	Y	Y	Y
24	Carbajal	Y	Y	Y	Y	Y	Y
25	Hill, K.	Y	Y	Y	Y	Y	Y
26	Brownley	Y	Y	Y	Y	Y	Y
27	Chu	Y	Y	Y	Y	Y	Y
28	Schiff	Y	Y	Y	Y	Y	Y
29	Cárdenas	Y	Y	Y	Y	Y	Y
30	Sherman	Y	Y	Y	Y	Y	Y
31	Aguilar	Y	Y	Y	Y	Y	Y
32	Napolitano	Y	Y	Y	Y	Y	Y
33	Lieu	Y	Y	Y	Y	Y	Y
34	Gomez	Y	Y	Y	Y	Y	Y
35	Torres	Y	Y	Y	Y	Y	Y
36	Ruiz	Y	Y	Y	Y	Y	Y
37	Bass	Y	Y	Y	Y	Y	Y
38	Sánchez	Y	Y	Y	Y	Y	Y
39	Cisneros	Y	Y	Y	Y	Y	Y
40	Roybal-Allard	Y	Y	Y	Y	Y	Y
41	Takano	Y	Y	Y	Y	Y	Y
42	**Calvert**	Y	Y	Y	Y	Y	Y
43	Waters	Y	Y	Y	Y	Y	Y
44	Barragán	Y	Y	Y	Y	Y	Y
45	Porter	Y	Y	Y	Y	Y	Y
46	Correa	Y	Y	Y	Y	Y	Y
47	Lowenthal	Y	Y	Y	Y	Y	Y
48	Rouda	Y	Y	Y	Y	Y	Y
49	Levin	Y	Y	Y	Y	Y	Y
50	**Hunter**	N	Y	Y	N	N	N
51	Vargas	Y	Y	Y	Y	Y	Y
52	Peters	Y	Y	Y	Y	Y	Y

		277	278	279	280	281	282
53	Davis, S.	Y	Y	Y	Y	Y	Y
COLORADO							
1	DeGette	Y	Y	Y	Y	Y	Y
2	Neguse	Y	Y	Y	Y	Y	Y
3	**Tipton**	Y	Y	Y	Y	Y	Y
4	**Buck**	?	?	?	?	?	?
5	**Lamborn**	Y	Y	N	N	Y	Y
6	Crow	Y	Y	Y	Y	Y	Y
7	Perlmutter	Y	Y	Y	Y	Y	Y
CONNECTICUT							
1	Larson	Y	Y	Y	Y	Y	Y
2	Courtney	Y	Y	Y	Y	Y	Y
3	DeLauro	Y	Y	Y	Y	Y	Y
4	Himes	Y	Y	Y	Y	Y	Y
5	Hayes	Y	Y	Y	Y	Y	Y
DELAWARE							
AL	Blunt Rochester	Y	Y	Y	Y	Y	Y
FLORIDA							
1	**Gaetz**	Y	N	N	Y	Y	Y
2	**Dunn**	N	N	N	N	Y	N
3	**Yoho**	Y	N	N	N	Y	N
4	**Rutherford**	Y	Y	Y	Y	Y	Y
5	Lawson	Y	Y	Y	Y	Y	Y
6	**Waltz**	Y	Y	Y	Y	Y	Y
7	Murphy	Y	Y	Y	Y	Y	Y
8	**Posey**	Y	Y	Y	Y	Y	Y
9	Soto	Y	Y	Y	Y	Y	Y
10	Demings	Y	Y	Y	Y	Y	Y
11	**Webster**	Y	Y	Y	Y	Y	Y
12	**Bilirakis**	Y	Y	Y	Y	Y	Y
13	Crist	Y	Y	Y	Y	Y	Y
14	Castor	Y	Y	Y	Y	Y	Y
15	**Spano**	Y	Y	Y	Y	Y	Y
16	**Buchanan**	Y	Y	Y	Y	Y	Y
17	**Steube**	N	Y	N	Y	Y	Y
18	**Mast**	Y	Y	N	Y	Y	Y
19	**Rooney**	N	Y	N	N	Y	N
20	Hastings	?	?	?	?	?	?
21	Frankel	Y	Y	Y	Y	Y	Y
22	Deutch	Y	Y	Y	Y	Y	Y
23	Wasserman Schultz	Y	Y	Y	Y	Y	Y
24	Wilson, F.	Y	Y	Y	Y	Y	Y
25	**Diaz-Balart**	Y	Y	Y	Y	Y	Y
26	Mucarsel-Powell	Y	Y	Y	Y	Y	Y
27	Shalala	Y	Y	Y	Y	Y	Y
GEORGIA							
1	**Carter, E.L.**	Y	Y	N	N	Y	Y
2	Bishop, S.	Y	Y	Y	Y	Y	Y
3	**Ferguson**	Y	Y	N	N	Y	N
4	Johnson, H.	Y	Y	Y	Y	Y	Y
5	Lewis John	Y	Y	Y	Y	Y	Y
6	McBath	Y	Y	Y	Y	Y	Y
7	**Woodall**	Y	Y	N	Y	Y	Y
8	**Scott, A.**	Y	Y	N	Y	Y	Y
9	**Collins, D.**	Y	Y	N	Y	Y	Y
10	**Hice**	Y	N	N	N	N	N
11	**Loudermilk**	Y	N	N	N	Y	N
12	**Allen**	N	N	N	N	Y	N
13	Scott, D.	Y	Y	Y	Y	Y	Y
14	**Graves, T.**	Y	Y	N	N	Y	N
HAWAII							
1	Case	Y	Y	Y	Y	Y	Y
2	Gabbard	Y	Y	Y	Y	Y	Y
IDAHO							
1	**Fulcher**	Y	Y	Y	Y	Y	N
2	**Simpson**	Y	Y	Y	Y	Y	Y
ILLINOIS							
1	Rush	Y	Y	Y	Y	Y	Y
2	Kelly, R.	Y	Y	Y	Y	Y	Y
3	Lipinski	Y	Y	Y	Y	Y	Y
4	García, J.	Y	Y	Y	Y	Y	Y
5	Quigley	Y	Y	Y	Y	Y	Y
6	Casten	Y	Y	Y	Y	Y	Y
7	Davis, D.	Y	Y	Y	Y	Y	Y
8	Krishnamoorthi	Y	Y	Y	Y	Y	Y
9	Schakowsky	Y	Y	Y	Y	Y	Y
10	Schneider	Y	Y	Y	Y	Y	Y
11	Foster	Y	Y	Y	Y	Y	Y

	277	278	279	280	281	282
12 **Bost**	?	?	?	?	?	?
13 **Davis, R.**	Y	Y	Y	Y	Y	Y
14 Underwood	Y	Y	Y	Y	Y	Y
15 **Shimkus**	Y	Y	Y	Y	Y	Y
16 **Kinzinger**	Y	Y	N	Y	Y	Y
17 Bustos	Y	Y	Y	Y	Y	Y
18 **LaHood**	Y	Y	Y	Y	Y	Y
INDIANA						
1 Visclosky	Y	Y	Y	Y	Y	Y
2 **Walorski**	Y	Y	Y	Y	Y	Y
3 **Banks**	Y	Y	N	Y	Y	N
4 **Baird**	Y	Y	Y	Y	Y	Y
5 **Brooks, S.**	Y	Y	Y	Y	Y	Y
6 **Pence**	Y	Y	N	Y	Y	Y
7 Carson	Y	Y	Y	Y	Y	Y
8 **Bucshon**	Y	Y	Y	Y	Y	Y
9 **Hollingsworth**	Y	Y	Y	Y	Y	Y
IOWA						
1 Finkenauer	Y	Y	Y	Y	Y	Y
2 Loebsack	Y	Y	Y	Y	Y	Y
3 Axne	Y	Y	Y	Y	Y	Y
4 **King, S.**	Y	Y	N	Y	Y	Y
KANSAS						
1 **Marshall**	Y	Y	Y	Y	Y	Y
2 **Watkins**	Y	Y	Y	Y	Y	Y
3 Davids	Y	Y	Y	Y	Y	Y
4 **Estes**	Y	Y	N	Y	Y	N
KENTUCKY						
1 **Comer**	Y	Y	Y	N	Y	N
2 **Guthrie**	Y	Y	Y	Y	Y	Y
3 Yarmuth	Y	Y	Y	Y	Y	Y
4 **Massie**	Y	Y	N	Y	Y	N
5 **Rogers, H.**	Y	Y	Y	Y	Y	Y
6 **Barr**	Y	Y	Y	Y	Y	Y
LOUISIANA						
1 **Scalise**	Y	Y	Y	Y	Y	Y
2 Richmond	Y	Y	Y	Y	Y	Y
3 **Higgins, C.**	Y	N	N	Y	Y	Y
4 **Johnson, M.**	Y	Y	N	Y	Y	Y
5 **Abraham**	Y	Y	Y	Y	Y	Y
6 **Graves, G.**	Y	Y	Y	Y	Y	Y
MAINE						
1 Pingree	Y	Y	Y	Y	Y	Y
2 Golden	Y	Y	Y	Y	Y	Y
MARYLAND						
1 **Harris**	N	N	N	N	Y	N
2 Ruppersberger	Y	Y	Y	Y	Y	Y
3 Sarbanes	Y	Y	Y	Y	Y	Y
4 Brown, A.	Y	Y	Y	Y	Y	Y
5 Hoyer	Y	Y	Y	Y	Y	Y
6 Trone	Y	Y	Y	Y	Y	Y
7 Cummings	Y	Y	Y	Y	Y	Y
8 Raskin	Y	Y	Y	Y	Y	Y
MASSACHUSETTS	Y	Y	Y	Y	Y	Y
1 Neal						
2 McGovern	Y	Y	Y	Y	Y	Y
3 Trahan	Y	Y	Y	Y	Y	Y
4 Kennedy	Y	Y	Y	Y	Y	Y
5 Clark	Y	Y	Y	Y	Y	Y
6 Moulton	Y	Y	Y	Y	Y	Y
7 Pressley	Y	Y	Y	Y	Y	Y
8 Lynch	Y	Y	Y	Y	Y	Y
9 Keating	Y	Y	Y	Y	Y	Y
MICHIGAN	Y	Y	Y	Y	Y	Y
1 **Bergman**						
2 **Huizenga**	Y	Y	Y	Y	Y	Y
3 **Amash**	Y	Y	Y	Y	Y	Y
4 **Moolenaar**	N	N	N	N	N	N
5 Kildee	Y	Y	Y	Y	Y	Y
6 **Upton**	Y	Y	Y	Y	Y	Y
7 **Walberg**	Y	Y	Y	Y	Y	Y
8 Slotkin	Y	Y	Y	Y	Y	Y
9 Levin	Y	Y	Y	Y	Y	Y
10 **Mitchell**	Y	Y	Y	Y	Y	Y
11 Stevens	Y	Y	Y	Y	Y	Y
12 Dingell	Y	Y	Y	Y	Y	Y
13 Tlaib	Y	Y	Y	Y	Y	Y
14 Lawrence	Y	Y	Y	Y	Y	Y
MINNESOTA	Y	Y	Y	Y	Y	Y
1 **Hagedorn**						
2 Craig	Y	Y	Y	Y	Y	Y
3 Phillips	Y	Y	Y	Y	Y	Y
4 McCollum	Y	Y	Y	Y	Y	Y
5 Omar	Y	Y	Y	Y	Y	Y

	277	278	279	280	281	282
6 **Emmer**	Y	Y	Y	Y	Y	Y
7 Peterson	Y	Y	Y	Y	Y	Y
8 **Stauber**	Y	Y	Y	Y	Y	Y
MISSISSIPPI	Y	Y	Y	Y	Y	Y
1 **Kelly, T.**						
2 Thompson, B.	Y	N	N	N	Y	N
3 **Guest**	Y	Y	Y	Y	Y	Y
4 **Palazzo**	Y	Y	N	Y	Y	Y
MISSOURI	N	Y	?	N	Y	Y
1 Clay						
2 **Wagner**	Y	Y	Y	Y	Y	Y
3 **Luetkemeyer**	Y	Y	Y	Y	Y	Y
4 **Hartzler**	Y	Y	Y	Y	Y	Y
5 Cleaver	Y	Y	Y	Y	Y	Y
6 **Graves, S.**	Y	Y	Y	Y	Y	Y
7 **Long**	N	Y	N	N	Y	Y
8 **Smith, J.**	Y	Y	Y	Y	Y	Y
MONTANA	Y	Y	N	N	Y	Y
AL **Gianforte**						
NEBRASKA	?	?	?	?	?	?
1 **Fortenberry**						
2 **Bacon**	Y	Y	Y	Y	Y	Y
3 **Smith, Adrian**	Y	Y	Y	Y	Y	Y
NEVADA	Y	Y	N	N	Y	Y
1 Titus						
2 **Amodei**	Y	Y	Y	Y	Y	Y
3 Lee	Y	Y	Y	Y	Y	Y
4 Horsford	Y	Y	Y	Y	Y	Y
NEW HAMPSHIRE	Y	Y	Y	Y	Y	Y
1 Pappas						
2 Kuster	Y	Y	Y	Y	Y	Y
NEW JERSEY	Y	Y	Y	Y	Y	Y
1 Norcross						
2 Van Drew	Y	Y	Y	Y	Y	Y
3 Kim	Y	Y	Y	Y	Y	Y
4 **Smith, C.**	Y	Y	Y	Y	Y	Y
5 Gottheimer	Y	Y	Y	Y	Y	Y
6 Pallone	Y	Y	Y	Y	Y	Y
7 Malinowski	Y	Y	Y	Y	Y	Y
8 Sires	Y	Y	Y	Y	Y	Y
9 Pascrell	Y	Y	Y	Y	Y	Y
10 Payne	Y	Y	Y	Y	Y	Y
11 Sherrill	Y	Y	Y	Y	Y	Y
12 Watson Coleman	Y	Y	Y	Y	Y	Y
NEW MEXICO	Y	Y	Y	Y	Y	Y
1 Haaland						
2 Torres Small	Y	Y	Y	Y	Y	Y
3 Luján	Y	Y	Y	Y	Y	Y
NEW YORK	Y	Y	Y	Y	Y	Y
1 **Zeldin**						
2 **King, P.**	Y	Y	Y	Y	Y	N
3 Suozzi	Y	Y	Y	Y	Y	Y
4 Rice, K.	Y	Y	Y	Y	Y	Y
5 Meeks	Y	Y	Y	Y	Y	Y
6 Meng	Y	Y	Y	Y	Y	Y
7 Velázquez	Y	Y	Y	Y	Y	Y
8 Jeffries	Y	Y	Y	Y	Y	Y
9 Clarke	Y	Y	Y	Y	Y	Y
10 Nadler	Y	Y	Y	Y	Y	Y
11 Rose	Y	Y	Y	Y	Y	Y
12 Maloney, C.	Y	Y	Y	Y	Y	Y
13 Espaillat	Y	Y	Y	Y	Y	Y
14 Ocasio-Cortez	Y	Y	Y	Y	Y	Y
15 Serrano	Y	Y	Y	Y	Y	Y
16 Engel	Y	Y	Y	Y	Y	Y
17 Lowey	Y	Y	Y	Y	Y	Y
18 Maloney, S.P.	Y	Y	Y	Y	Y	Y
19 Delgado	Y	Y	Y	Y	Y	Y
20 Tonko	Y	Y	Y	Y	Y	Y
21 **Stefanik**	Y	Y	Y	Y	Y	Y
22 Brindisi	Y	Y	Y	Y	Y	Y
23 **Reed**	Y	Y	Y	Y	Y	Y
24 **Katko**	Y	Y	Y	Y	Y	Y
25 Morelle	Y	Y	Y	Y	Y	Y
26 Higgins, B.	Y	Y	Y	Y	Y	Y
27 **Collins, C.**	Y	Y	Y	Y	Y	Y
NORTH CAROLINA	Y	Y	Y	Y	Y	Y
1 Butterfield						
2 **Holding**	Y	Y	Y	Y	Y	Y
3 **Jones***	Y	Y	Y	Y	Y	Y
4 Price						
5 **Foxx**	Y	Y	Y	Y	Y	Y
6 **Walker**	Y	Y	N	Y	Y	N
7 **Rouzer**	N	Y	N	N	Y	N

	277	278	279	280	281	282
8 **Hudson**	Y	Y	Y	Y	Y	Y
9 vacant	Y	Y	Y	Y	Y	Y
10 **McHenry**	Y	Y	Y	Y	Y	Y
11 **Meadows**	Y	Y	Y	Y	Y	Y
12 Adams	Y	Y	Y	Y	Y	Y
13 **Budd**	Y	Y	N	Y	Y	N
NORTH DAKOTA						
AL **Armstrong**	Y	Y	Y	Y	Y	Y
OHIO						
1 **Chabot**	Y	Y	Y	Y	Y	Y
2 **Wenstrup**	Y	Y	N	Y	Y	Y
3 Beatty	Y	Y	Y	Y	Y	Y
4 **Jordan**	Y	Y	N	Y	Y	N
5 **Latta**	Y	Y	Y	Y	Y	Y
6 **Johnson, B.**	Y	Y	Y	Y	Y	Y
7 **Gibbs**	Y	Y	N	Y	Y	N
8 **Davidson**	Y	N	N	Y	Y	Y
9 Kaptur	Y	Y	Y	Y	Y	Y
10 **Turner**	Y	Y	Y	Y	Y	Y
11 Fudge	Y	Y	Y	Y	Y	Y
12 **Balderson**	Y	Y	Y	Y	Y	Y
13 Ryan	Y	Y	Y	Y	Y	Y
14 **Joyce**	Y	Y	Y	Y	Y	Y
15 **Stivers**	Y	Y	Y	Y	Y	Y
16 **Gonzalez**	Y	Y	Y	Y	Y	Y
OKLAHOMA						
1 **Hern**	Y	Y	N	N	Y	Y
2 **Mullin**	Y	Y	N	N	Y	Y
3 **Lucas**	Y	Y	Y	Y	Y	Y
4 **Cole**	Y	Y	Y	Y	Y	Y
5 Horn	Y	Y	Y	Y	Y	Y
OREGON						
1 Bonamici	Y	Y	Y	Y	Y	Y
2 **Walden**	Y	Y	Y	Y	Y	Y
3 Blumenauer	Y	Y	Y	Y	Y	Y
4 DeFazio	Y	Y	Y	Y	Y	Y
5 Schrader	Y	Y	Y	Y	Y	Y
PENNSYLVANIA						
1 **Fitzpatrick**	Y	Y	Y	Y	Y	Y
2 Boyle	Y	Y	Y	Y	Y	Y
3 Evans	Y	Y	Y	Y	Y	Y
4 Dean	Y	Y	Y	Y	Y	Y
5 Scanlon	Y	Y	Y	Y	Y	Y
6 Houlahan	Y	Y	Y	Y	Y	Y
7 Wild	Y	Y	Y	Y	Y	Y
8 Cartwright	Y	Y	Y	Y	Y	Y
9 **Meuser**	Y	Y	Y	Y	Y	N
10 **Perry**	Y	Y	N	Y	Y	N
11 **Smucker**	Y	Y	Y	Y	Y	Y
12 **Marino***						
13 **Joyce**	Y	Y	Y	Y	Y	Y
14 **Reschenthaler**	Y	Y	Y	Y	Y	Y
15 **Thompson, G.**	Y	Y	Y	Y	Y	Y
16 **Kelly, M.**	Y	Y	Y	Y	Y	Y
17 Lamb	Y	Y	Y	Y	Y	Y
18 Doyle	Y	Y	Y	Y	Y	Y
RHODE ISLAND						
1 Cicilline	Y	Y	Y	Y	Y	Y
2 Langevin	Y	Y	Y	Y	Y	Y
SOUTH CAROLINA						
1 Cunningham	Y	Y	Y	Y	Y	Y
2 **Wilson, J.**	Y	Y	Y	Y	Y	Y
3 **Duncan**	Y	Y	N	N	Y	N
4 **Timmons**	Y	Y	N	Y	Y	Y
5 **Norman**	Y	N	N	N	Y	Y
6 Clyburn	Y	Y	Y	Y	Y	Y
7 **Rice, T.**	Y	Y	Y	Y	Y	Y
SOUTH DAKOTA						
AL **Johnson**	Y	Y	Y	Y	Y	Y
TENNESSEE						
1 **Roe**	Y	Y	Y	Y	Y	Y
2 **Burchett**	Y	Y	N	Y	Y	N
3 **Fleischmann**	Y	Y	Y	Y	Y	Y
4 **DesJarlais**	Y	Y	Y	Y	Y	Y
5 Cooper	Y	Y	Y	Y	Y	Y
6 **Rose**	N	Y	N	N	Y	N
7 **Green**	?	?	?	?	?	?
8 **Kustoff**	Y	Y	Y	Y	Y	Y
9 Cohen	Y	Y	Y	Y	Y	Y
TEXAS						
1 **Gohmert**	?	N	N	N	Y	N
2 **Crenshaw**	Y	Y	Y	Y	Y	Y
3 **Taylor**	Y	Y	N	N	Y	Y
4 **Ratcliffe**	+	+	+	-	+	-

	277	278	279	280	281	282
5 **Gooden**	Y	Y	N	N	Y	N
6 **Wright**	?	?	?	?	?	?
7 Fletcher	Y	Y	Y	Y	Y	Y
8 **Brady**	Y	Y	N	N	Y	Y
9 Green, A.	Y	Y	Y	Y	Y	Y
10 **McCaul**	Y	Y	Y	Y	Y	Y
11 **Conaway**	Y	Y	N	N	Y	Y
12 **Granger**	Y	Y	Y	Y	Y	Y
13 **Thornberry**	Y	Y	N	Y	Y	Y
14 **Weber**	Y	N	N	N	Y	Y
15 Gonzalez	Y	Y	Y	Y	Y	Y
16 Escobar	Y	Y	Y	Y	Y	Y
17 **Flores**	Y	Y	Y	Y	Y	Y
18 Jackson Lee	Y	Y	Y	Y	Y	Y
19 **Arrington**	Y	Y	N	N	Y	N
20 Castro	Y	Y	Y	Y	Y	Y
21 **Roy**	N	N	N	N	N	N
22 **Olson**	Y	Y	N	N	Y	Y
23 **Hurd**	Y	Y	Y	Y	Y	Y
24 **Marchant**	Y	Y	N	N	Y	Y
25 **Williams**	Y	Y	Y	Y	Y	Y
26 **Burgess**	N	Y	Y	N	Y	Y
27 **Cloud**	N	Y	Y	Y	Y	N
28 Cuellar	Y	Y	Y	Y	Y	Y
29 Garcia, S.	Y	Y	Y	Y	Y	Y
30 Johnson, E.B.	Y	Y	Y	Y	Y	Y
31 **Carter, J.**	Y	Y	N	N	Y	Y
32 Allred	Y	Y	Y	Y	Y	Y
33 Veasey	Y	Y	Y	Y	Y	Y
34 Vela	Y	Y	Y	Y	Y	Y
35 Doggett	Y	Y	Y	Y	Y	Y
36 **Babin**	Y	N	N	N	Y	Y
UTAH						
1 **Bishop, R.**	Y	Y	Y	Y	Y	Y
2 **Stewart**	Y	Y	Y	Y	Y	Y
3 **Curtis**	Y	Y	Y	Y	Y	Y
4 McAdams	Y	Y	Y	Y	Y	Y
VERMONT						
AL Welch	Y	Y	Y	Y	Y	Y
VIRGINIA						
1 **Wittman**	Y	Y	N	N	Y	Y
2 Luria	Y	Y	Y	Y	Y	Y
3 Scott, R.	Y	Y	Y	Y	Y	Y
4 McEachin	Y	Y	Y	Y	Y	Y
5 **Riggleman**	Y	Y	Y	Y	Y	Y
6 **Cline**	Y	Y	N	N	Y	N
7 Spanberger	Y	Y	Y	Y	Y	Y
8 Beyer	Y	Y	Y	Y	Y	Y
9 **Griffith**	Y	Y	N	Y	Y	N
10 Wexton	Y	Y	Y	Y	Y	Y
11 Connolly	Y	Y	Y	Y	Y	Y
WASHINGTON						
1 DelBene	Y	Y	Y	Y	Y	Y
2 Larsen	Y	Y	Y	Y	Y	Y
3 **Herrera Beutler**	?	?	?	?	?	?
4 **Newhouse**	Y	Y	Y	Y	Y	Y
5 **McMorris Rodgers**	Y	Y	Y	Y	Y	Y
6 Kilmer	Y	Y	Y	Y	Y	Y
7 Jayapal	Y	Y	Y	Y	Y	Y
8 Schrier	Y	Y	Y	Y	Y	Y
9 Smith Adam	Y	Y	Y	Y	Y	Y
10 Heck	Y	Y	Y	Y	Y	Y
WEST VIRGINIA						
1 **McKinley**	Y	Y	Y	Y	Y	Y
2 **Mooney**	Y	Y	N	N	Y	Y
3 **Miller**	Y	Y	Y	Y	Y	Y
WISCONSIN						
1 **Steil**	Y	Y	Y	Y	Y	Y
2 Pocan	Y	Y	Y	Y	Y	Y
3 Kind	Y	Y	Y	Y	Y	Y
4 Moore	Y	Y	Y	Y	Y	Y
5 **Sensenbrenner**	+	+	+	+	+	+
6 **Grothman**	Y	Y	N	Y	Y	Y
7 **Duffy**	Y	Y	Y	Y	Y	Y
8 **Gallagher**	Y	Y	Y	Y	Y	Y
WYOMING						
AL **Cheney**	Y	Y	N	N	Y	Y
DELEGATES						
Radewagen (A.S.)	?	?	?	?	?	?
Norton (D.C.)	Y	Y	Y	Y	Y	Y
San Nicolas (Guam)	?	?	?	?	?	?
Sablan (N. Marianas)	?	?	?	?	?	?
González-Colón (P.R.)	?	?	?	?	?	?
Plaskett (V.I.)	Y	Y	Y	Y	Y	Y

283. HR2740. Fiscal 2020 Four-Bill Appropriations Package - Limited-Duration Insurance Plans Rule. Castor, D-Fla., amendment that would prohibit the use of funds made available under the bill for the implementation, administration or enforcement of an Aug. 2018 rule issued by the Departments of the Treasury, Labor, and Health and Human Services related to short-term limited-duration insurance plans. Adopted in Committee of the Whole 236-188: R 2-188; D 234-0. June 13, 2019.

284. HR2740. Fiscal 2020 Four-Bill Appropriations Package - Health Insurance Navigator Program. Hill, R-Ark., amendment that would strike from the bill the requirement that the Health and Human Services secretary obligate $100 million in fiscal 2020 for a health insurance marketplace navigator program, including specified obligations for advertising. Rejected in Committee of the Whole 186-237: R 186-3; D 0-234. June 13, 2019.

285. HR2740. Fiscal 2020 Four-Bill Appropriations Package - Apprenticeship Programs. Hill, R-Ark., amendment that would allow Labor Department program funding made available by the bill to be used for grants to apprenticeship programs not registered with the department under the National Apprenticeship Act. Rejected in Committee of the Whole 158-266: R 157-33; D 1-233. June 13, 2019.

286. HR2740. Fiscal 2020 Four-Bill Appropriations Package - Injury Prevention and Control Programs. Pressley, D-Mass., for Speier, D-Calif., amendment that would increase by $5.6 million funding for injury prevention and control programs within the Health and Human Services Department, and decrease by the same amount HHS administrative funding. Adopted in Committee of the Whole 401-23: R 167-23; D 234-0. June 13, 2019.

287. HR2740. Fiscal 2020 Four-Bill Appropriations Package - National Institute of Allergy and Infectious Diseases. Khanna, D-Calif., amendment that would increase by $3 million funding for the National Institute of Allergy and Infectious Diseases and decrease by the same amount funding for the Office of the Director of the National Institute of Health. Adopted in Committee of the Whole 356-68: R 122-68; D 234-0. June 13, 2019.

288. HR2740. Fiscal 2020 Four-Bill Appropriations Package - Maternal and Child Health Programs. Richmond, D-La., amendment that would increase by $7 million funding for Health and Human Services Department maternal and child health programs and decrease by the same amount funding for Health Resources and Services Administration program support. Adopted in Committee of the Whole 365-59: R 132-58; D 233-1. June 13, 2019.

Member	283	284	285	286	287	288
ALABAMA						
1 Byrne	N	Y	Y	N	N	Y
2 Roby	N	Y	Y	Y	Y	Y
3 Rogers, M.	N	Y	Y	Y	Y	Y
4 Aderholt	N	Y	Y	Y	Y	Y
5 Brooks, M.	N	Y	Y	N	N	N
6 Palmer	N	Y	Y	Y	N	N
7 Sewell	Y	N	N	Y	Y	Y
ALASKA						
AL Young	N	Y	N	Y	Y	Y
ARIZONA						
1 O'Halleran	Y	N	N	Y	Y	Y
2 Kirkpatrick	Y	N	N	Y	Y	Y
3 Grijalva	Y	N	N	Y	Y	Y
4 Gosar	N	Y	Y	N	N	N
5 Biggs	N	Y	N	N	Y	N
6 Schweikert	N	Y	Y	Y	Y	Y
7 Gallego	Y	N	N	Y	Y	Y
8 Lesko	N	Y	N	Y	N	N
9 Stanton	Y	N	N	Y	Y	Y
ARKANSAS						
1 Crawford	N	Y	Y	Y	N	Y
2 Hill, F.	N	Y	Y	Y	N	Y
3 Womack	N	Y	Y	Y	Y	Y
4 Westerman	N	Y	Y	Y	N	N
CALIFORNIA						
1 LaMalfa	N	Y	Y	Y	Y	Y
2 Huffman	Y	N	N	Y	Y	Y
3 Garamendi	Y	N	N	Y	Y	Y
4 McClintock	N	Y	Y	N	Y	Y
5 Thompson, M.	Y	N	N	Y	Y	Y
6 Matsui	Y	N	N	Y	Y	Y
7 Bera	Y	N	N	Y	Y	Y
8 Cook	N	N	N	Y	Y	Y
9 McNerney	Y	N	N	Y	Y	Y
10 Harder	Y	N	N	Y	Y	Y
11 DeSaulnier	Y	N	N	Y	Y	Y
12 Pelosi						
13 Lee B.	Y	N	N	Y	Y	Y
14 Speier	Y	N	N	Y	Y	Y
15 Swalwell	+	-	+	+	+	+
16 Costa	Y	N	N	Y	Y	Y
17 Khanna	Y	N	N	Y	Y	Y
18 Eshoo	Y	N	N	Y	Y	Y
19 Lofgren	Y	N	N	Y	Y	Y
20 Panetta	Y	N	N	Y	Y	Y
21 Cox	Y	N	N	Y	Y	Y
22 Nunes	N	Y	Y	Y	Y	Y
23 McCarthy	N	Y	Y	Y	Y	Y
24 Carbajal	Y	N	N	Y	Y	Y
25 Hill, K.	Y	N	N	Y	Y	Y
26 Brownley	Y	N	N	Y	Y	Y
27 Chu	Y	N	N	Y	Y	Y
28 Schiff	Y	N	N	Y	Y	Y
29 Cárdenas	Y	N	N	Y	Y	Y
30 Sherman	Y	N	N	Y	Y	Y
31 Aguilar	Y	N	N	Y	Y	Y
32 Napolitano	Y	N	N	Y	Y	Y
33 Lieu	Y	N	N	Y	Y	Y
34 Gomez	Y	N	N	Y	Y	Y
35 Torres	Y	N	N	Y	Y	Y
36 Ruiz	Y	N	N	Y	Y	N
37 Bass	Y	N	N	Y	Y	Y
38 Sánchez	Y	N	N	Y	Y	Y
39 Cisneros	Y	N	N	Y	Y	Y
40 Roybal-Allard	Y	N	N	Y	Y	Y
41 Takano	Y	N	N	Y	Y	Y
42 Calvert	N	Y	Y	Y	Y	Y
43 Waters	Y	N	N	Y	Y	Y
44 Barragán	Y	N	N	Y	Y	Y
45 Porter	Y	N	N	Y	Y	Y
46 Correa	Y	N	N	Y	Y	Y
47 Lowenthal	Y	N	N	Y	Y	Y
48 Rouda	Y	N	N	Y	Y	Y
49 Levin	Y	N	N	Y	Y	Y
50 Hunter	N	Y	N	Y	N	N
51 Vargas	Y	N	N	Y	Y	Y
52 Peters	Y	N	N	Y	Y	Y
53 Davis, S.	Y	N	N	Y	Y	Y
COLORADO						
1 DeGette	Y	N	N	Y	Y	Y
2 Neguse	Y	N	N	Y	Y	Y
3 Tipton	N	Y	Y	Y	Y	Y
4 Buck	?	?	?	?	?	?
5 Lamborn	N	Y	Y	Y	Y	N
6 Crow	Y	N	N	Y	Y	Y
7 Perlmutter	Y	N	N	Y	Y	Y
CONNECTICUT						
1 Larson	Y	N	N	Y	Y	Y
2 Courtney	Y	N	N	Y	Y	Y
3 DeLauro	Y	N	N	Y	Y	Y
4 Himes	Y	N	N	Y	Y	Y
5 Hayes	Y	N	N	Y	Y	Y
DELAWARE						
AL Blunt Rochester	Y	N	N	Y	Y	Y
FLORIDA						
1 Gaetz	N	Y	Y	Y	Y	N
2 Dunn	N	Y	Y	N	N	N
3 Yoho	N	Y	Y	N	N	N
4 Rutherford	N	Y	Y	Y	N	Y
5 Lawson	Y	N	N	Y	Y	Y
6 Waltz	N	Y	Y	Y	Y	Y
7 Murphy	Y	N	N	Y	Y	Y
8 Posey	N	Y	Y	Y	N	Y
9 Soto	Y	N	N	Y	Y	Y
10 Demings	Y	N	N	Y	Y	Y
11 Webster	N	Y	Y	Y	N	Y
12 Bilirakis	N	Y	Y	Y	Y	Y
13 Crist	Y	N	N	Y	Y	Y
14 Castor	Y	N	N	Y	Y	Y
15 Spano	N	Y	Y	Y	Y	Y
16 Buchanan	N	Y	Y	Y	Y	Y
17 Steube	N	Y	Y	Y	N	N
18 Mast	N	Y	N	Y	N	N
19 Rooney	N	Y	Y	Y	N	N
20 Hastings	?	?	?	?	?	?
21 Frankel	Y	N	N	Y	Y	Y
22 Deutch	Y	N	N	Y	Y	Y
23 Wasserman Schultz	Y	N	N	Y	Y	Y
24 Wilson, F.	Y	N	N	Y	Y	Y
25 Diaz-Balart	N	Y	N	Y	Y	Y
26 Mucarsel-Powell	Y	N	N	Y	Y	Y
27 Shalala	Y	N	N	Y	Y	Y
GEORGIA						
1 Carter, E.L.	N	Y	Y	Y	N	N
2 Bishop, S.	Y	N	N	Y	Y	Y
3 Ferguson	N	Y	Y	Y	Y	N
4 Johnson, H.	Y	N	N	Y	Y	Y
5 Lewis John	Y	N	N	Y	Y	Y
6 McBath	Y	N	N	Y	Y	Y
7 Woodall	N	Y	Y	N	Y	N
8 Scott, A.	N	Y	Y	N	N	N
9 Collins, D.	N	Y	Y	Y	N	N
10 Hice	N	Y	Y	N	N	N
11 Loudermilk	N	Y	Y	Y	N	Y
12 Allen	N	Y	Y	N	N	N
13 Scott, D.	Y	N	N	Y	Y	Y
14 Graves, T.	N	Y	Y	N	N	N
HAWAII						
1 Case	Y	N	N	Y	Y	Y
2 Gabbard	Y	N	N	Y	Y	Y
IDAHO						
1 Fulcher	N	Y	Y	N	N	N
2 Simpson	N	N	N	Y	Y	Y
ILLINOIS						
1 Rush	Y	N	N	Y	Y	Y
2 Kelly, R.	Y	N	N	Y	Y	Y
3 Lipinski	Y	N	N	Y	Y	Y
4 García, J.	Y	N	N	Y	Y	Y
5 Quigley	Y	N	N	Y	Y	Y
6 Casten	Y	N	N	Y	Y	Y
7 Davis, D.	Y	N	N	Y	Y	Y
8 Krishnamoorthi	Y	N	N	Y	Y	Y
9 Schakowsky	Y	N	N	Y	Y	Y
10 Schneider	Y	N	N	Y	Y	Y
11 Foster	Y	N	N	Y	Y	Y

KEY: Republicans   Democrats   *Independents*

Y Voted for (yea)	**N** Voted against (nay)	**P** Voted "present"
+ Announced for	**−** Announced against	**?** Did not vote or otherwise make position known
# Paired for	**X** Paired against	

		283	284	285	286	287	288
12	**Bost**	?	?	?	?	?	?
13	**Davis, R.**	N	Y	N	Y	Y	Y
14	Underwood	Y	N	N	Y	Y	Y
15	**Shimkus**	N	Y	N	Y	Y	Y
16	**Kinzinger**	N	Y	N	Y	Y	Y
17	Bustos	Y	N	N	Y	Y	Y
18	**LaHood**	N	Y	Y	Y	Y	Y
INDIANA							
1	Visclosky	Y	N	N	Y	Y	Y
2	**Walorski**	N	Y	Y	Y	Y	Y
3	**Banks**	N	Y	Y	Y	Y	N
4	**Baird**	N	Y	Y	Y	Y	Y
5	**Brooks, S.**	N	Y	Y	Y	Y	Y
6	**Pence**	N	Y	Y	Y	Y	Y
7	Carson	Y	N	N	Y	Y	Y
8	**Bucshon**	N	Y	Y	Y	Y	Y
9	**Hollingsworth**	N	Y	Y	Y	Y	N
IOWA							
1	Finkenauer	Y	N	N	Y	Y	Y
2	Loebsack	Y	N	N	Y	Y	Y
3	Axne	Y	N	N	Y	Y	Y
4	**King, S.**	N	Y	Y	N	Y	Y
KANSAS							
1	**Marshall**	N	Y	Y	Y	N	Y
2	**Watkins**	N	Y	Y	Y	N	Y
3	Davids	Y	N	N	Y	Y	Y
4	**Estes**	N	Y	Y	Y	N	Y
KENTUCKY							
1	**Comer**	N	Y	Y	Y	N	N
2	**Guthrie**	N	Y	Y	Y	Y	Y
3	Yarmuth	Y	N	N	Y	Y	Y
4	**Massie**	N	P	Y	N	Y	N
5	**Rogers, H.**	N	Y	Y	Y	Y	Y
6	**Barr**	N	Y	Y	Y	Y	Y
LOUISIANA							
1	**Scalise**	N	Y	Y	Y	N	Y
2	Richmond	Y	N	N	Y	Y	Y
3	**Higgins, C.**	N	Y	Y	Y	Y	Y
4	**Johnson, M.**	N	Y	Y	Y	Y	Y
5	**Abraham**	N	Y	Y	Y	N	Y
6	**Graves, G.**	N	Y	Y	Y	Y	Y
MAINE							
1	Pingree	Y	N	N	Y	Y	Y
2	Golden	Y	N	N	Y	Y	Y
MARYLAND							
1	**Harris**	N	Y	Y	N	N	N
2	Ruppersberger	Y	N	N	Y	Y	Y
3	Sarbanes	Y	N	N	Y	Y	Y
4	Brown, A.	Y	N	N	Y	Y	Y
5	Hoyer	Y	N	N	Y	Y	Y
6	Trone	Y	N	N	Y	Y	Y
7	Cummings	Y	N	N	Y	Y	Y
8	Raskin						
MASSACHUSETTS		Y	N	N	Y	Y	Y
1	Neal						
2	McGovern	Y	N	N	Y	Y	Y
3	Trahan	Y	N	N	Y	Y	Y
4	Kennedy	Y	N	N	Y	Y	Y
5	Clark	Y	N	N	Y	Y	Y
6	Moulton	Y	N	N	Y	Y	Y
7	Pressley	Y	N	N	Y	Y	Y
8	Lynch	Y	N	N	Y	Y	Y
9	Keating	Y	N	N	Y	Y	Y
MICHIGAN		Y	N	N	Y	Y	Y
1	**Bergman**						
2	**Huizenga**	N	Y	Y	Y	Y	Y
3	**Amash**	N	Y	Y	Y	Y	Y
4	**Moolenaar**	N	Y	Y	N	N	N
5	Kildee	N	Y	Y	Y	Y	Y
6	**Upton**	Y	N	N	Y	Y	Y
7	**Walberg**	N	Y	N	Y	Y	Y
8	Slotkin	N	Y	Y	Y	Y	Y
9	Levin	Y	N	N	Y	Y	Y
10	**Mitchell**	Y	N	N	Y	Y	Y
11	Stevens	N	Y	Y	Y	Y	Y
12	Dingell	Y	N	N	Y	Y	Y
13	Tlaib	Y	N	N	Y	Y	Y
14	Lawrence	Y	N	N	Y	Y	Y
MINNESOTA		Y	N	N	Y	Y	Y
1	**Hagedorn**						
2	Craig	N	Y	Y	Y	Y	Y
3	Phillips	Y	N	N	Y	Y	Y
4	McCollum	Y	N	N	Y	Y	Y
5	Omar	Y	N	N	Y	Y	Y

		283	284	285	286	287	288
6	**Emmer**	Y	N	N	Y	Y	Y
7	Peterson	N	Y	N	Y	Y	Y
8	**Stauber**	Y	N	N	Y	Y	Y
MISSISSIPPI		N	Y	N	Y	Y	Y
1	**Kelly, T.**						
2	Thompson, B.	N	Y	Y	Y	N	Y
3	**Guest**	Y	N	N	Y	Y	Y
4	**Palazzo**	N	Y	Y	Y	Y	Y
MISSOURI		N	Y	Y	Y	N	N
1	Clay						
2	**Wagner**	Y	N	N	Y	Y	Y
3	**Luetkemeyer**	N	Y	Y	Y	N	Y
4	**Hartzler**	N	Y	Y	Y	Y	Y
5	Cleaver	N	Y	Y	Y	Y	Y
6	**Graves, S.**	Y	N	N	Y	Y	Y
7	**Long**	N	Y	Y	Y	N	N
8	**Smith, J.**	N	Y	Y	Y	N	N
MONTANA		N	Y	Y	Y	N	N
AL	**Gianforte**						
NEBRASKA		?	?	?	?	?	?
1	**Fortenberry**						
2	**Bacon**	N	Y	Y	Y	Y	Y
3	**Smith, Adrian**	N	Y	N	Y	Y	N
NEVADA		N	Y	Y	Y	N	Y
1	Titus						
2	**Amodei**	Y	N	N	Y	Y	Y
3	Lee	N	Y	Y	Y	Y	Y
4	Horsford	Y	N	N	Y	Y	Y
NEW HAMPSHIRE		Y	N	N	Y	Y	Y
1	Pappas						
2	Kuster	Y	N	N	Y	Y	Y
NEW JERSEY		Y	N	N	Y	Y	Y
1	Norcross						
2	Van Drew	Y	N	N	Y	Y	Y
3	Kim	Y	N	N	Y	Y	Y
4	**Smith, C.**	Y	N	N	Y	Y	Y
5	Gottheimer	Y	Y	N	Y	Y	Y
6	Pallone	Y	N	N	Y	Y	Y
7	Malinowski	Y	N	N	Y	Y	Y
8	Sires	Y	N	N	Y	Y	Y
9	Pascrell	Y	N	N	Y	Y	Y
10	Payne	Y	N	N	Y	Y	Y
11	Sherrill	Y	N	N	Y	Y	Y
12	Watson Coleman	Y	N	N	Y	Y	Y
NEW MEXICO		Y	N	N	Y	Y	Y
1	Haaland						
2	Torres Small	Y	N	N	Y	Y	Y
3	Luján	Y	N	N	Y	Y	Y
NEW YORK		Y	N	N	Y	Y	Y
1	**Zeldin**						
2	**King, P.**	N	Y	N	Y	Y	Y
3	Suozzi	N	Y	N	Y	Y	Y
4	Rice, K.	Y	N	N	Y	Y	Y
5	Meeks	Y	N	N	Y	Y	Y
6	Meng	Y	N	N	Y	Y	Y
7	Velázquez	Y	N	N	Y	Y	Y
8	Jeffries	Y	N	N	Y	Y	Y
9	Clarke	Y	N	N	Y	Y	Y
10	Nadler	Y	N	N	Y	Y	Y
11	Rose	Y	N	N	Y	Y	Y
12	Maloney, C.	Y	N	N	Y	Y	Y
13	Espaillat	Y	N	N	Y	Y	Y
14	Ocasio-Cortez	Y	N	N	Y	Y	Y
15	Serrano	Y	N	N	Y	Y	Y
16	Engel	Y	N	N	Y	Y	Y
17	Lowey	Y	N	N	Y	Y	Y
18	Maloney, S.P.	Y	N	N	Y	Y	Y
19	Delgado	Y	N	N	Y	Y	Y
20	Tonko	Y	N	N	Y	Y	Y
21	**Stefanik**	Y	N	N	Y	Y	Y
22	Brindisi	N	Y	N	Y	Y	Y
23	**Reed**	Y	N	N	Y	Y	Y
24	**Katko**	N	Y	N	Y	Y	Y
25	Morelle	N	Y	N	Y	Y	Y
26	Higgins, B.	Y	N	N	Y	Y	Y
27	**Collins, C.**	Y	N	N	Y	Y	Y
NORTH CAROLINA		N	Y	Y	Y	Y	Y
1	Butterfield						
2	**Holding**	Y	N	N	Y	Y	Y
3	**Jones***	N	Y	Y	Y	N	Y
4	Price						
5	**Foxx**	Y	N	N	Y	Y	Y
6	**Walker**	N	Y	Y	Y	N	N
7	**Rouzer**	N	Y	Y	Y	N	N

		283	284	285	286	287	288
8	**Hudson**	N	Y	Y	Y	N	Y
9	vacant	N	Y	Y	Y	Y	Y
10	**McHenry**	N	Y	Y	Y	Y	Y
11	**Meadows**	N	Y	Y	Y	Y	N
12	Adams	Y	N	N	Y	Y	Y
13	**Budd**	N	Y	Y	Y	Y	Y
NORTH DAKOTA							
AL	**Armstrong**	N	Y	Y	Y	Y	Y
OHIO							
1	**Chabot**	N	Y	Y	Y	Y	Y
2	**Wenstrup**	N	Y	Y	Y	Y	Y
3	Beatty	Y	N	N	Y	Y	Y
4	**Jordan**	N	Y	Y	N	N	N
5	**Latta**	N	Y	Y	Y	Y	Y
6	**Johnson, B.**	N	Y	N	Y	Y	Y
7	**Gibbs**	N	Y	Y	Y	Y	N
8	**Davidson**	N	Y	Y	Y	Y	Y
9	Kaptur	Y	N	N	Y	Y	Y
10	**Turner**	N	Y	N	Y	Y	Y
11	Fudge	Y	N	N	Y	Y	Y
12	**Balderson**	N	Y	Y	Y	Y	Y
13	Ryan	Y	N	N	Y	Y	Y
14	**Joyce**	N	Y	N	Y	Y	Y
15	**Stivers**	N	Y	N	Y	Y	Y
16	**Gonzalez**	N	Y	N	Y	Y	Y
OKLAHOMA							
1	**Hern**	N	Y	Y	Y	N	N
2	**Mullin**	N	Y	Y	Y	Y	N
3	**Lucas**	N	Y	Y	Y	Y	Y
4	**Cole**	N	Y	Y	Y	Y	Y
5	Horn	Y	N	N	Y	Y	Y
OREGON							
1	Bonamici	Y	N	N	Y	Y	Y
2	**Walden**	N	Y	N	Y	Y	Y
3	Blumenauer	Y	N	N	Y	Y	Y
4	DeFazio	Y	N	N	Y	Y	Y
5	Schrader	Y	N	N	Y	Y	Y
PENNSYLVANIA							
1	**Fitzpatrick**	Y	N	N	Y	Y	Y
2	Boyle	Y	N	N	Y	Y	Y
3	Evans	Y	N	N	Y	Y	Y
4	Dean	Y	N	N	Y	Y	Y
5	Scanlon	Y	N	N	Y	Y	Y
6	Houlahan	Y	N	N	Y	Y	Y
7	Wild	Y	N	N	Y	Y	Y
8	Cartwright	Y	N	N	Y	Y	Y
9	**Meuser**	N	Y	Y	Y	N	Y
10	**Perry**	N	Y	Y	Y	Y	Y
11	**Smucker**	N	Y	Y	Y	Y	Y
12	**Marino***						
13	**Joyce**	N	Y	Y	Y	Y	Y
14	**Reschenthaler**	N	Y	N	Y	Y	Y
15	**Thompson, G.**	N	Y	Y	Y	Y	Y
16	**Kelly, M.**	N	Y	Y	Y	Y	Y
17	Lamb	Y	N	N	Y	Y	Y
18	Doyle	Y	N	N	Y	Y	Y
RHODE ISLAND							
1	Cicilline	Y	N	N	Y	Y	Y
2	Langevin	Y	N	N	Y	Y	Y
SOUTH CAROLINA							
1	Cunningham	Y	N	Y	Y	Y	Y
2	**Wilson, J.**	N	Y	Y	Y	Y	Y
3	**Duncan**	N	Y	Y	Y	N	Y
4	**Timmons**	N	Y	Y	Y	Y	N
5	**Norman**	N	Y	Y	N	N	N
6	Clyburn	Y	N	N	Y	Y	Y
7	**Rice, T.**	N	Y	Y	Y	Y	Y
SOUTH DAKOTA							
AL	**Johnson**	N	Y	Y	Y	Y	Y
TENNESSEE							
1	**Roe**	N	Y	Y	Y	Y	Y
2	**Burchett**	N	Y	Y	N	N	N
3	**Fleischmann**	N	Y	Y	Y	Y	Y
4	**DesJarlais**	N	Y	Y	Y	Y	Y
5	Cooper	Y	N	N	Y	Y	Y
6	**Rose**	N	Y	Y	N	N	N
7	**Green**	?	?	?	?	?	?
8	**Kustoff**	N	Y	Y	Y	Y	Y
9	Cohen	Y	N	N	Y	Y	Y
TEXAS							
1	**Gohmert**	N	Y	Y	Y	Y	Y
2	**Crenshaw**	N	Y	Y	Y	Y	Y
3	**Taylor**	N	Y	Y	Y	N	Y
4	**Ratcliffe**	-	+	+	+	-	-

		283	284	285	286	287	288
5	**Gooden**	N	Y	Y	Y	N	N
6	**Wright**	?	?	?	?	?	?
7	Fletcher	Y	N	N	Y	Y	Y
8	**Brady**	N	Y	Y	Y	Y	Y
9	Green, A.	Y	N	N	Y	Y	Y
10	**McCaul**	N	Y	Y	Y	N	N
11	**Conaway**	N	Y	Y	Y	Y	Y
12	**Granger**	N	Y	Y	Y	Y	Y
13	**Thornberry**	N	Y	Y	Y	Y	Y
14	**Weber**	N	Y	Y	Y	N	N
15	Gonzalez	Y	N	N	Y	Y	Y
16	Escobar	Y	N	N	Y	Y	Y
17	**Flores**	N	Y	Y	Y	Y	Y
18	Jackson Lee	Y	N	N	Y	Y	Y
19	**Arrington**	N	Y	Y	Y	Y	N
20	Castro	Y	N	N	Y	Y	Y
21	**Roy**	N	Y	Y	N	N	N
22	**Olson**	N	Y	Y	Y	N	N
23	**Hurd**	N	Y	Y	Y	Y	Y
24	**Marchant**	N	Y	Y	Y	N	N
25	**Williams**	N	Y	Y	Y	N	Y
26	**Burgess**	N	Y	Y	Y	N	Y
27	**Cloud**	N	Y	Y	Y	N	Y
28	Cuellar	Y	N	N	Y	Y	Y
29	Garcia, S.	Y	N	N	Y	Y	Y
30	Johnson, E.B.	Y	N	N	Y	Y	Y
31	**Carter, J.**	N	Y	Y	Y	N	N
32	Allred	Y	N	N	Y	Y	Y
33	Veasey	Y	N	N	Y	Y	Y
34	Vela	Y	N	N	Y	Y	Y
35	Doggett	Y	N	N	Y	Y	Y
36	**Babin**	N	Y	Y	Y	N	N
UTAH							
1	**Bishop, R.**	N	Y	N	Y	N	N
2	**Stewart**	N	Y	Y	Y	Y	N
3	**Curtis**	N	Y	Y	Y	Y	N
4	McAdams	Y	N	N	Y	Y	Y
VERMONT							
AL	Welch	Y	N	N	Y	Y	Y
VIRGINIA							
1	**Wittman**	N	Y	Y	Y	N	N
2	Luria	Y	N	N	Y	Y	Y
3	Scott, R.	Y	N	N	Y	Y	Y
4	McEachin	Y	N	N	Y	Y	Y
5	**Riggleman**	N	Y	Y	Y	Y	Y
6	**Cline**	N	Y	Y	Y	N	N
7	Spanberger	Y	N	N	Y	Y	Y
8	Beyer	Y	N	N	Y	Y	Y
9	**Griffith**	N	Y	Y	N	Y	Y
10	Wexton	Y	N	N	Y	Y	Y
11	Connolly	Y	N	N	Y	Y	Y
WASHINGTON							
1	DelBene	Y	N	N	Y	Y	Y
2	Larsen	Y	N	N	Y	Y	Y
3	**Herrera Beutler**	?	?	?	?	?	?
4	**Newhouse**	N	Y	N	Y	Y	Y
5	**McMorris Rodgers**	N	Y	Y	Y	N	Y
6	Kilmer	Y	N	N	Y	Y	Y
7	Jayapal	Y	N	N	Y	Y	Y
8	Schrier	Y	N	N	Y	Y	Y
9	Smith Adam	Y	N	N	Y	Y	Y
10	Heck	Y	N	N	Y	Y	Y
WEST VIRGINIA							
1	**McKinley**	N	Y	N	Y	N	Y
2	**Mooney**	N	Y	Y	Y	N	Y
3	**Miller**	N	Y	Y	Y	Y	Y
WISCONSIN							
1	**Steil**	N	Y	N	Y	Y	Y
2	Pocan	Y	N	N	Y	Y	Y
3	Kind	Y	N	N	Y	Y	Y
4	Moore	Y	N	N	Y	Y	Y
5	**Sensenbrenner**	-	+	+	+	-	-
6	**Grothman**	N	Y	Y	Y	N	N
7	**Duffy**	N	Y	N	Y	N	Y
8	**Gallagher**	N	Y	Y	Y	Y	Y
WYOMING							
AL	**Cheney**	N	Y	Y	Y	Y	Y
DELEGATES							
	Radewagen (A.S.)	?	?	?	?	?	?
	Norton (D.C.)	Y	N	N	Y	Y	Y
	San Nicolas (Guam)	?	?	?	?	?	?
	Sablan (N. Marianas)	?	?	?	?	?	?
	González-Colón (P.R.)	?	?	?	?	?	?
	Plaskett (V.I.)	Y	N	N	Y	Y	Y

III HOUSE VOTES

289. HR2740. Fiscal 2020 Four-Bill Appropriations Package - Reduce Labor-HHS-Education Funding. Banks, R-Ind., amendment that would decrease by 14 percent all discretionary funding made available under the Labor, Health and Human Services and Education title of the bill (Division A). Rejected in Committee of the Whole 150-273: R 150-39; D 0-234. June 13, 2019.

290. HR2740. Fiscal 2020 Four-Bill Appropriations Package - Health Resources and Services Administration. Keating, D-Mass., amendment that would increase then decrease by $1 million funding for Health Resources and Services Administration program support. Adopted in Committee of the Whole 283-141: R 53-137; D 230-4. June 13, 2019.

291. HR2740. Fiscal 2020 Four-Bill Appropriations Package - Disability and Birth Defect Programs. Miller, R-W.Va., amendment that would increase by $2 million funding for Health and Human Services Department programs targeting individuals affected by disabilities, birth defects or developmental disabilities and decrease by the same amount HHS administrative funding. Adopted in Committee of the Whole 421-3: R 187-3; D 234-0. June 13, 2019.

292. HR2740. Fiscal 2020 Four-Bill Appropriations Package - Education Department Programs. Cicilline, D-R.I. amendment that would increase by $500,000 funding for a number of programs and initiatives under the Elementary and Secondary Education Act related to national research and education enrichment programs, charter school development, assistance to magnet schools and family engagement in education programs, and would decrease by the same amount funding for Washington, D.C.-specific logistics and operations within the Department of Education. Adopted in Committee of the Whole 327-97: R 93-97; D 234-0. June 13, 2019.

293. HR2740. Fiscal 2020 Four-Bill Appropriations Package - Mental Health Programs. Bera, D-Calif., amendment that would increase then decrease by $1 funding for Health and Human Services Department programs addressing mental health. Adopted in Committee of the Whole 396-27: R 162-27; D 234-0. June 13, 2019.

294. HR2740. Fiscal 2020 Four-Bill Appropriations Package - Refugee Resettlement Death Records. Castro, D-Texas, amendment that would require the Office of Refugee Resettlement to report and record the death of unaccompanied children under its care. Adopted in Committee of the Whole 355-68: R 122-68; D 233-0. June 13, 2019.

	289	290	291	292	293	294
ALABAMA						
1 Byrne	Y	N	Y	N	Y	N
2 Roby	N	Y	Y	Y	Y	Y
3 Rogers, M.	Y	N	Y	Y	N	N
4 Aderholt	Y	Y	Y	Y	Y	Y
5 Brooks, M.	Y	N	N	N	N	N
6 Palmer	Y	N	Y	N	Y	N
7 Sewell	N	Y	Y	Y	Y	Y
ALASKA						
AL Young	Y	Y	Y	N	Y	N
ARIZONA						
1 O'Halleran	N	Y	Y	Y	Y	Y
2 Kirkpatrick	N	Y	Y	Y	Y	Y
3 Grijalva	N	Y	Y	Y	Y	Y
4 Gosar	Y	N	N	N	N	N
5 Biggs	Y	N	N	N	N	N
6 Schweikert	Y	Y	Y	Y	Y	Y
7 Gallego	N	Y	Y	Y	Y	Y
8 Lesko	Y	N	Y	Y	Y	Y
9 Stanton	N	Y	Y	Y	Y	Y
ARKANSAS						
1 Crawford	Y	Y	Y	Y	Y	N
2 Hill, F.	Y	N	Y	Y	Y	Y
3 Womack	N	Y	Y	Y	Y	Y
4 Westerman	Y	N	Y	N	Y	N
CALIFORNIA						
1 LaMalfa	Y	N	Y	N	Y	Y
2 Huffman	N	Y	Y	Y	Y	Y
3 Garamendi	N	Y	Y	Y	Y	Y
4 McClintock	Y	N	Y	N	Y	N
5 Thompson, M.	N	Y	Y	Y	Y	Y
6 Matsui	N	Y	Y	Y	Y	Y
7 Bera	N	Y	Y	Y	Y	Y
8 Cook	Y	Y	Y	Y	Y	Y
9 McNerney	N	Y	Y	Y	Y	Y
10 Harder	N	Y	Y	Y	Y	Y
11 DeSaulnier	N	Y	Y	Y	Y	Y
12 Pelosi						
13 Lee B.	N	Y	Y	Y	Y	Y
14 Speier	N	Y	Y	Y	Y	Y
15 Swalwell	–	+	+	+	+	+
16 Costa	N	Y	Y	Y	Y	Y
17 Khanna	N	Y	Y	Y	Y	Y
18 Eshoo	N	Y	Y	Y	Y	Y
19 Lofgren	N	Y	Y	Y	Y	Y
20 Panetta	N	Y	Y	Y	Y	Y
21 Cox	N	Y	Y	Y	Y	Y
22 Nunes	Y	N	Y	Y	Y	N
23 McCarthy	Y	Y	Y	Y	Y	Y
24 Carbajal	N	Y	Y	Y	Y	Y
25 Hill, K.	N	Y	Y	Y	Y	Y
26 Brownley	N	Y	Y	Y	Y	Y
27 Chu	N	Y	Y	Y	Y	Y
28 Schiff	N	Y	Y	Y	Y	Y
29 Cárdenas	N	Y	Y	Y	Y	Y
30 Sherman	N	Y	Y	Y	Y	Y
31 Aguilar	N	Y	Y	Y	Y	Y
32 Napolitano	N	Y	Y	Y	Y	Y
33 Lieu	N	Y	Y	Y	Y	Y
34 Gomez	N	Y	Y	Y	Y	Y
35 Torres	N	Y	Y	Y	Y	Y
36 Ruiz	N	Y	Y	Y	Y	Y
37 Bass	N	Y	Y	Y	Y	Y
38 Sánchez	N	Y	Y	Y	Y	Y
39 Cisneros	N	Y	Y	Y	Y	Y
40 Roybal-Allard	N	Y	Y	Y	Y	Y
41 Takano	N	Y	Y	Y	Y	Y
42 Calvert	Y	Y	Y	Y	Y	Y
43 Waters	N	Y	Y	Y	Y	Y
44 Barragán	N	Y	Y	Y	Y	Y
45 Porter	N	Y	Y	Y	Y	Y
46 Correa	N	Y	Y	Y	Y	Y
47 Lowenthal	N	Y	Y	Y	Y	Y
48 Rouda	N	Y	Y	Y	Y	Y
49 Levin	N	Y	Y	Y	Y	Y
50 Hunter	Y	N	N	N	N	N
51 Vargas	N	Y	Y	Y	Y	Y
52 Peters	N	Y	Y	Y	Y	Y
53 Davis, S.	N	Y	Y	Y	Y	Y
COLORADO						
1 DeGette	N	Y	Y	Y	Y	Y
2 Neguse	N	Y	Y	Y	Y	Y
3 Tipton	Y	N	Y	N	Y	Y
4 Buck	?	?	?	?	?	?
5 Lamborn	Y	N	Y	N	Y	N
6 Crow	N	Y	Y	Y	Y	Y
7 Perlmutter	N	Y	Y	Y	Y	Y
CONNECTICUT						
1 Larson	N	Y	Y	Y	Y	Y
2 Courtney	N	Y	Y	Y	Y	Y
3 DeLauro	N	Y	Y	Y	Y	Y
4 Himes	N	Y	Y	Y	Y	Y
5 Hayes	N	Y	Y	Y	Y	Y
DELAWARE						
AL Blunt Rochester	N	Y	Y	Y	Y	Y
FLORIDA						
1 Gaetz	Y	N	Y	N	N	N
2 Dunn	Y	N	Y	N	Y	N
3 Yoho	Y	N	Y	N	Y	N
4 Rutherford	Y	N	Y	Y	Y	Y
5 Lawson	N	Y	Y	Y	Y	Y
6 Waltz	Y	N	Y	Y	Y	Y
7 Murphy	N	Y	Y	Y	Y	Y
8 Posey	Y	N	Y	N	Y	N
9 Soto	N	Y	Y	Y	Y	Y
10 Demings	N	Y	Y	Y	Y	Y
11 Webster	N	N	Y	N	Y	N
12 Bilirakis	Y	N	Y	N	Y	Y
13 Crist	N	Y	Y	Y	Y	Y
14 Castor	N	Y	Y	Y	Y	Y
15 Spano	Y	N	Y	Y	Y	Y
16 Buchanan	N	Y	Y	Y	Y	N
17 Steube	Y	N	Y	N	Y	N
18 Mast	Y	N	Y	Y	N	N
19 Rooney	Y	N	Y	Y	N	N
20 Hastings	?	?	?	?	?	?
21 Frankel	N	Y	Y	Y	Y	Y
22 Deutch	N	Y	Y	Y	Y	Y
23 Wasserman Schultz	N	Y	Y	Y	Y	Y
24 Wilson, F.	N	Y	Y	Y	Y	Y
25 Diaz-Balart	N	Y	Y	Y	Y	Y
26 Mucarsel-Powell	N	Y	Y	Y	Y	Y
27 Shalala	N	Y	Y	Y	Y	Y
GEORGIA						
1 Carter, E.L.	Y	N	Y	N	N	N
2 Bishop, S.	N	Y	Y	Y	Y	Y
3 Ferguson	Y	N	Y	N	N	N
4 Johnson, H.	N	Y	Y	Y	Y	Y
5 Lewis John	N	Y	Y	Y	Y	Y
6 McBath	N	Y	Y	Y	Y	Y
7 Woodall	Y	N	Y	N	Y	N
8 Scott, A.	Y	N	Y	N	N	N
9 Collins, D.	Y	N	Y	N	Y	N
10 Hice	Y	N	N	N	N	N
11 Loudermilk	Y	N	Y	N	Y	N
12 Allen	Y	N	N	N	N	N
13 Scott, D.	N	Y	Y	Y	Y	Y
14 Graves, T.	N	N	N	N	N	N
HAWAII						
1 Case	N	Y	Y	Y	Y	Y
2 Gabbard	N	Y	Y	Y	Y	Y
IDAHO						
1 Fulcher	Y	N	Y	N	Y	N
2 Simpson	N	N	Y	Y	Y	Y
ILLINOIS						
1 Rush	N	Y	Y	Y	Y	Y
2 Kelly, R.	N	Y	Y	Y	Y	Y
3 Lipinski	N	Y	Y	Y	Y	Y
4 García, J.	N	Y	Y	Y	Y	Y
5 Quigley	N	Y	Y	Y	Y	Y
6 Casten	N	Y	Y	Y	Y	Y
7 Davis, D.	N	Y	Y	Y	Y	Y
8 Krishnamoorthi	N	Y	Y	Y	Y	Y
9 Schakowsky	N	Y	Y	Y	Y	Y
10 Schneider	N	Y	Y	Y	Y	Y
11 Foster	N	Y	Y	Y	Y	Y

KEY: Republicans Democrats *Independents*

Y Voted for (yea)	**N** Voted against (nay)	**P** Voted "present"
+ Announced for	**–** Announced against	**?** Did not vote or otherwise
# Paired for	**X** Paired against	make position known

		289	290	291	292	293	294
12	**Bost**	?	?	?	?	?	?
13	**Davis, R.**	N	Y	Y	Y	Y	Y
14	Underwood	N	Y	Y	Y	Y	Y
15	**Shimkus**	Y	Y	Y	Y	Y	Y
16	**Kinzinger**	N	N	Y	Y	Y	Y
17	Bustos	N	Y	Y	Y	Y	Y
18	**LaHood**	Y	N	Y	Y	Y	Y
INDIANA							
1	Visclosky	N	Y	Y	Y	Y	Y
2	**Walorski**	Y	Y	Y	Y	Y	Y
3	**Banks**	Y	N	Y	N	Y	Y
4	**Baird**	Y	Y	Y	Y	Y	Y
5	**Brooks, S.**	Y	Y	Y	Y	Y	Y
6	**Pence**	Y	N	Y	N	Y	Y
7	Carson	N	Y	Y	Y	Y	Y
8	**Bucshon**	Y	Y	Y	Y	Y	Y
9	**Hollingsworth**	N	Y	Y	Y	Y	Y
IOWA							
1	Finkenauer	N	Y	Y	Y	Y	Y
2	Loebsack	N	Y	Y	Y	Y	Y
3	Axne	N	Y	Y	Y	Y	Y
4	**King, S.**	Y	N	Y	N	Y	N
KANSAS							
1	**Marshall**	Y	N	Y	N	Y	Y
2	**Watkins**	Y	N	Y	N	Y	Y
3	Davids	N	Y	Y	Y	Y	Y
4	**Estes**	Y	N	Y	Y	N	N
KENTUCKY							
1	**Comer**	Y	N	Y	N	N	N
2	**Guthrie**	Y	Y	Y	Y	Y	Y
3	Yarmuth	N	Y	Y	Y	Y	Y
4	**Massie**	Y	N	Y	N	N	N
5	**Rogers, H.**	N	Y	Y	Y	Y	Y
6	**Barr**	Y	N	Y	Y	Y	N
LOUISIANA							
1	**Scalise**	Y	N	Y	N	Y	Y
2	Richmond	N	Y	Y	Y	Y	Y
3	**Higgins, C.**	Y	N	Y	N	Y	N
4	**Johnson, M.**	Y	Y	Y	Y	Y	Y
5	**Abraham**	Y	N	Y	N	Y	Y
6	**Graves, G.**	Y	N	Y	N	Y	Y
MAINE							
1	Pingree	N	Y	Y	Y	Y	Y
2	Golden	N	N	Y	Y	Y	Y
MARYLAND							
1	**Harris**	Y	N	N	N	N	N
2	Ruppersberger	N	Y	Y	Y	Y	Y
3	Sarbanes	N	Y	Y	Y	Y	Y
4	Brown, A.	N	Y	Y	Y	Y	Y
5	Hoyer	N	Y	Y	Y	Y	Y
6	Trone	N	Y	Y	Y	Y	Y
7	Cummings	N	Y	Y	Y	Y	Y
8	Raskin						
MASSACHUSETTS		N	Y	Y	Y	Y	Y
1	Neal						
2	McGovern	N	Y	Y	Y	Y	Y
3	Trahan	N	Y	Y	Y	Y	Y
4	Kennedy	N	Y	Y	Y	Y	Y
5	Clark	N	Y	Y	Y	Y	Y
6	Moulton	N	Y	Y	Y	Y	Y
7	Pressley	N	Y	Y	Y	Y	Y
8	Lynch	N	Y	Y	Y	Y	Y
9	Keating	N	Y	Y	Y	Y	Y
MICHIGAN		N	Y	Y	Y	Y	?
1	**Bergman**						
2	**Huizenga**	N	Y	Y	Y	Y	Y
3	**Amash**	Y	Y	Y	Y	Y	Y
4	**Moolenaar**	Y	N	N	N	N	Y
5	Kildee	Y	Y	Y	Y	Y	Y
6	**Upton**	N	Y	Y	Y	Y	Y
7	**Walberg**	N	Y	Y	Y	Y	Y
8	Slotkin	Y	N	Y	N	Y	N
9	Levin	N	Y	Y	Y	Y	Y
10	**Mitchell**	N	Y	Y	Y	Y	Y
11	Stevens	Y	N	Y	Y	Y	Y
12	Dingell	N	Y	Y	Y	Y	Y
13	Tlaib	N	Y	Y	Y	Y	Y
14	Lawrence	N	Y	Y	Y	Y	Y
MINNESOTA		N	Y	Y	Y	Y	Y
1	**Hagedorn**						
2	Craig	Y	N	Y	Y	Y	Y
3	Phillips	N	Y	Y	Y	Y	Y
4	McCollum	N	Y	Y	Y	Y	Y
5	Omar	N	Y	Y	Y	Y	Y

		289	290	291	292	293	294
6	**Emmer**	N	Y	Y	Y	Y	Y
7	Peterson	Y	N	Y	N	Y	Y
8	**Stauber**	N	Y	Y	Y	Y	Y
MISSISSIPPI		N	Y	Y	Y	Y	Y
1	**Kelly, T.**						
2	Thompson, B.	Y	N	Y	N	?	N
3	**Guest**	N	Y	Y	Y	Y	Y
4	**Palazzo**	Y	Y	Y	N	Y	Y
MISSOURI		Y	N	Y	N	N	N
1	Clay						
2	**Wagner**	N	Y	Y	Y	Y	Y
3	**Luetkemeyer**	Y	Y	Y	Y	Y	Y
4	**Hartzler**	N	N	Y	Y	Y	Y
5	Cleaver	Y	N	Y	Y	Y	Y
6	**Graves, S.**	N	Y	Y	Y	Y	Y
7	**Long**	Y	N	Y	N	Y	N
8	**Smith, J.**	Y	N	Y	N	N	Y
MONTANA		Y	N	Y	N	Y	Y
AL	**Gianforte**						
NEBRASKA		?	?	?	?	?	?
1	**Fortenberry**						
2	**Bacon**	N	N	Y	Y	Y	Y
3	**Smith, Adrian**	Y	Y	Y	N	Y	Y
NEVADA		Y	N	Y	N	Y	N
1	Titus						
2	**Amodei**	N	Y	Y	Y	Y	Y
3	Lee	Y	Y	Y	Y	Y	Y
4	Horsford	N	Y	Y	Y	Y	Y
NEW HAMPSHIRE		N	Y	Y	Y	Y	Y
1	Pappas						
2	Kuster	N	Y	Y	Y	Y	Y
NEW JERSEY		N	Y	Y	Y	Y	Y
1	Norcross						
2	Van Drew	N	Y	Y	Y	Y	Y
3	Kim	N	Y	Y	Y	Y	Y
4	**Smith, C.**	N	Y	Y	Y	Y	Y
5	Gottheimer	N	N	Y	N	Y	Y
6	Pallone	N	N	Y	Y	Y	Y
7	Malinowski	N	Y	Y	Y	Y	Y
8	Sires	N	Y	Y	Y	Y	Y
9	Pascrell	N	Y	Y	Y	Y	Y
10	Payne	N	Y	Y	Y	Y	Y
11	Sherrill	N	Y	Y	Y	Y	Y
12	Watson Coleman	N	Y	Y	Y	Y	Y
NEW MEXICO		N	Y	Y	Y	Y	Y
1	Haaland						
2	Torres Small	N	Y	Y	Y	Y	Y
3	Luján	N	Y	Y	Y	Y	Y
NEW YORK		N	Y	Y	Y	Y	Y
1	**Zeldin**						
2	**King, P.**	Y	N	Y	Y	Y	N
3	Suozzi	N	Y	Y	Y	Y	Y
4	Rice, K.	N	Y	Y	Y	Y	Y
5	Meeks	N	Y	Y	Y	Y	Y
6	Meng	N	Y	Y	Y	Y	Y
7	Velázquez	N	Y	Y	Y	Y	Y
8	Jeffries	N	Y	Y	Y	Y	Y
9	Clarke	N	Y	Y	Y	Y	Y
10	Nadler	N	Y	Y	Y	Y	Y
11	Rose	N	Y	Y	Y	Y	Y
12	Maloney, C.	N	Y	Y	Y	Y	Y
13	Espaillat	N	Y	Y	Y	Y	Y
14	Ocasio-Cortez	N	Y	Y	Y	Y	Y
15	Serrano	N	Y	Y	Y	Y	Y
16	Engel	N	Y	Y	Y	Y	Y
17	Lowey	N	Y	Y	Y	Y	Y
18	Maloney, S.P.	N	Y	Y	Y	Y	Y
19	Delgado	N	Y	Y	Y	Y	Y
20	Tonko	N	Y	Y	Y	Y	Y
21	**Stefanik**	N	Y	Y	Y	Y	Y
22	Brindisi	N	Y	Y	Y	Y	Y
23	**Reed**	N	N	Y	Y	Y	Y
24	**Katko**	N	Y	Y	Y	Y	Y
25	Morelle	N	Y	Y	Y	Y	Y
26	Higgins, B.	N	Y	Y	Y	Y	Y
27	**Collins, C.**	N	Y	Y	Y	Y	Y
NORTH CAROLINA		N	Y	Y	Y	Y	Y
1	Butterfield						
2	**Holding**	N	Y	Y	Y	Y	Y
3	**Jones***	Y	N	Y	N	Y	Y
4	Price						
5	**Foxx**	N	Y	Y	Y	Y	Y
6	**Walker**	Y	N	Y	N	Y	Y
7	**Rouzer**	Y	N	Y	N	N	N

		289	290	291	292	293	294
8	**Hudson**	Y	N	Y	N	Y	Y
9	vacant	Y	N	Y	Y	Y	Y
10	**McHenry**	Y	Y	Y	Y	Y	Y
11	**Meadows**	Y	Y	Y	N	Y	Y
12	Adams	N	Y	Y	Y	Y	Y
13	**Budd**	Y	N	Y	N	Y	N
NORTH DAKOTA							
AL	**Armstrong**	Y	N	Y	N	Y	Y
OHIO							
1	**Chabot**	Y	N	Y	N	Y	Y
2	**Wenstrup**	Y	N	Y	N	Y	N
3	Beatty	N	Y	Y	Y	Y	Y
4	**Jordan**	Y	N	Y	N	N	N
5	**Latta**	Y	N	Y	N	Y	N
6	**Johnson, B.**	Y	Y	Y	Y	Y	Y
7	**Gibbs**	Y	N	Y	Y	Y	Y
8	**Davidson**	Y	N	Y	Y	N	Y
9	Kaptur	N	Y	Y	Y	Y	Y
10	**Turner**	N	N	Y	Y	Y	Y
11	Fudge	N	Y	Y	Y	Y	Y
12	**Balderson**	Y	N	Y	Y	Y	Y
13	Ryan	N	Y	Y	Y	Y	Y
14	**Joyce**	N	Y	Y	Y	Y	Y
15	**Stivers**	N	Y	Y	Y	Y	Y
16	**Gonzalez**	N	Y	Y	Y	Y	Y
OKLAHOMA							
1	**Hern**	Y	N	Y	N	Y	N
2	**Mullin**	Y	N	Y	N	Y	Y
3	**Lucas**	N	Y	Y	Y	Y	Y
4	**Cole**	N	Y	Y	Y	Y	Y
5	Horn	N	Y	Y	Y	Y	Y
OREGON							
1	Bonamici	N	Y	Y	Y	Y	Y
2	**Walden**	N	Y	Y	Y	Y	Y
3	Blumenauer	N	Y	Y	Y	Y	Y
4	DeFazio	N	Y	Y	Y	Y	Y
5	Schrader	N	Y	Y	Y	Y	Y
PENNSYLVANIA							
1	**Fitzpatrick**	N	Y	Y	Y	Y	Y
2	Boyle	N	Y	Y	Y	Y	Y
3	Evans	N	Y	Y	Y	Y	Y
4	Dean	N	Y	Y	Y	Y	Y
5	Scanlon	N	Y	Y	Y	Y	Y
6	Houlahan	N	Y	Y	Y	Y	Y
7	Wild	N	Y	Y	Y	Y	Y
8	Cartwright	N	Y	Y	Y	Y	Y
9	**Meuser**	Y	N	Y	N	Y	N
10	**Perry**	Y	N	Y	N	Y	Y
11	**Smucker**	Y	Y	Y	Y	Y	Y
12	**Marino***						
13	**Joyce**	Y	Y	Y	Y	Y	Y
14	**Reschenthaler**	N	N	Y	Y	Y	Y
15	**Thompson, G.**	N	Y	Y	Y	Y	Y
16	**Kelly, M.**	Y	Y	Y	Y	Y	Y
17	Lamb	N	Y	Y	Y	Y	Y
18	Doyle	N	Y	Y	Y	Y	Y
RHODE ISLAND							
1	Cicilline	N	Y	Y	Y	Y	Y
2	Langevin	N	Y	Y	Y	Y	Y
SOUTH CAROLINA							
1	Cunningham	N	Y	Y	Y	Y	Y
2	**Wilson, J.**	Y	N	Y	Y	Y	Y
3	**Duncan**	Y	N	Y	N	N	N
4	**Timmons**	Y	N	Y	N	Y	Y
5	**Norman**	Y	N	Y	N	N	N
6	Clyburn	N	Y	Y	Y	Y	Y
7	**Rice, T.**	Y	N	Y	N	Y	N
SOUTH DAKOTA							
AL	**Johnson**	Y	N	Y	Y	Y	Y
TENNESSEE							
1	**Roe**	Y	Y	Y	Y	Y	Y
2	**Burchett**	Y	N	Y	N	N	N
3	**Fleischmann**	Y	N	Y	Y	Y	Y
4	**DesJarlais**	Y	N	Y	Y	Y	N
5	Cooper	N	Y	Y	Y	Y	Y
6	**Rose**	Y	N	Y	N	N	N
7	**Green**	?	?	?	?	?	?
8	**Kustoff**	Y	N	Y	N	Y	Y
9	Cohen	N	Y	Y	Y	Y	Y
TEXAS							
1	**Gohmert**	Y	N	Y	Y	N	N
2	**Crenshaw**	Y	Y	Y	N	Y	Y
3	**Taylor**	Y	N	Y	Y	Y	Y
4	**Ratcliffe**	+	-	+	-	+	-

		289	290	291	292	293	294
5	**Gooden**	Y	N	Y	N	Y	N
6	**Wright**	?	?	?	?	?	?
7	Fletcher	N	Y	Y	Y	Y	Y
8	**Brady**	?	N	Y	N	Y	Y
9	Green, A.	N	Y	Y	Y	Y	Y
10	**McCaul**	Y	N	Y	N	Y	Y
11	**Conaway**	Y	N	Y	N	Y	N
12	**Granger**	N	N	Y	Y	Y	Y
13	**Thornberry**	Y	N	Y	Y	Y	Y
14	**Weber**	Y	N	Y	N	Y	N
15	Gonzalez	N	Y	Y	Y	Y	Y
16	Escobar	N	Y	Y	Y	Y	Y
17	**Flores**	Y	N	Y	N	Y	Y
18	Jackson Lee	N	Y	Y	Y	Y	Y
19	**Arrington**	Y	N	Y	N	Y	Y
20	Castro	N	Y	Y	Y	Y	Y
21	**Roy**	Y	N	N	N	N	Y
22	**Olson**	Y	N	Y	N	Y	Y
23	**Hurd**	N	Y	Y	Y	Y	Y
24	**Marchant**	Y	N	Y	N	Y	N
25	**Williams**	Y	N	Y	N	Y	Y
26	**Burgess**	Y	N	Y	N	Y	N
27	**Cloud**	Y	N	Y	N	Y	Y
28	Cuellar	N	Y	Y	Y	Y	Y
29	Garcia, S.	N	Y	Y	Y	Y	Y
30	Johnson, E.B.	N	Y	Y	Y	Y	Y
31	**Carter, J.**	Y	N	Y	N	Y	N
32	Allred	N	Y	Y	Y	Y	Y
33	Veasey	N	Y	Y	Y	Y	Y
34	Vela	N	Y	Y	Y	Y	Y
35	Doggett	N	Y	Y	Y	Y	Y
36	**Babin**	Y	N	Y	N	Y	N
UTAH							
1	**Bishop, R.**	N	N	Y	Y	Y	N
2	**Stewart**	Y	N	Y	N	Y	N
3	**Curtis**	Y	N	Y	N	Y	Y
4	McAdams	N	Y	Y	Y	Y	Y
VERMONT							
AL	Welch	N	Y	Y	Y	Y	Y
VIRGINIA							
1	**Wittman**	Y	N	Y	N	Y	N
2	Luria	N	N	Y	Y	Y	Y
3	Scott, R.	N	Y	Y	Y	Y	Y
4	McEachin	N	Y	Y	Y	Y	Y
5	**Riggleman**	Y	N	Y	N	Y	N
6	**Cline**	Y	N	Y	N	Y	Y
7	Spanberger	N	Y	Y	Y	Y	Y
8	Beyer	N	Y	Y	Y	Y	Y
9	**Griffith**	Y	N	Y	Y	Y	Y
10	Wexton	N	Y	Y	Y	Y	Y
11	Connolly	N	Y	Y	Y	Y	Y
WASHINGTON							
1	DelBene	N	Y	Y	Y	Y	Y
2	Larsen	N	Y	Y	Y	Y	Y
3	**Herrera Beutler**	?	?	?	?	?	?
4	**Newhouse**	N	N	Y	Y	Y	Y
5	**McMorris Rodgers**	Y	Y	Y	Y	Y	Y
6	Kilmer	N	Y	Y	Y	Y	Y
7	Jayapal	N	Y	Y	Y	Y	Y
8	Schrier	N	Y	Y	Y	Y	Y
9	Smith Adam	N	Y	Y	Y	Y	Y
10	Heck	N	Y	Y	Y	Y	Y
WEST VIRGINIA							
1	**McKinley**	N	N	Y	N	Y	Y
2	**Mooney**	Y	N	Y	N	Y	Y
3	**Miller**	Y	N	Y	Y	Y	Y
WISCONSIN							
1	**Steil**	Y	N	Y	Y	Y	Y
2	Pocan	N	Y	Y	Y	Y	Y
3	Kind	N	Y	Y	Y	Y	Y
4	Moore	N	Y	Y	Y	Y	Y
5	**Sensenbrenner**	+	+	-	-	+	-
6	**Grothman**	Y	N	Y	N	N	N
7	**Duffy**	Y	N	Y	N	N	Y
8	**Gallagher**	N	N	Y	Y	Y	Y
WYOMING							
AL	**Cheney**	N	N	Y	N	Y	Y
DELEGATES							
	Radewagen (A.S.)	?	?	?	?	?	?
	Norton (D.C.)	N	Y	Y	Y	Y	Y
	San Nicolas (Guam)	?	?	?	?	?	?
	Sablan (N. Marianas)	?	?	?	?	?	?
	González-Colón (P.R.)	?	?	?	?	?	?
	Plaskett (V.I.)	N	Y	Y	Y	Y	Y

295. HR2740. Fiscal 2020 Four-Bill Appropriations Package - Education Department Office of Civil Rights. Jeffries, D-N.Y., amendment that would prohibit use of funds made available by the bill in contravention of any statutorily established authorities and functions of the Office of Civil Rights within the Department of Education. Adopted in Committee of the Whole 275-148: R 42-148; D 233-0. June 13, 2019.

296. HR2740. Fiscal 2020 Four-Bill Appropriations Package - Injury Prevention and Control Programs. Maloney, D-N.Y., amendment that would increase then decrease by $5 million funding for Centers for Disease Control and Prevention programs related to injury prevention and control. Adopted in Committee of the Whole 266-150: R 40-149; D 226-1. June 13, 2019.

297. HR2740. Fiscal 2020 Four-Bill Appropriations Package - Higher Education Programs. Adams, D-N.C., amendment that would increase by $500,000 funding for Education Department programs related to higher education and decrease by the same amount administrative funding for department. Adopted in Committee of the Whole 358-65: R 126-64; D 232-1. June 13, 2019.

298. HR2740. Fiscal 2020 Four-Bill Appropriations Package - Children and Families Services Programs. Adams, D-N.C., amendment that would increase by $3 million funding for Health and Human Services Department children and families services programs and decrease by the same amount HHS administrative funding. Adopted in Committee of the Whole 307-115: R 74-115; D 233-0. June 13, 2019.

299. HR2740. Fiscal 2020 Four-Bill Appropriations Package - Mental Health Programs. Beyer, D-Va., amendment that would decrease then increase by $500,000 funding for Health and Human Services Department programs addressing mental health. Adopted in Committee of the Whole 359-64: R 129-61; D 230-3. June 13, 2019.

300. HR2740. Fiscal 2020 Four-Bill Appropriations Package - Refugee and Immigrant Assistance Programs. Beyer, D-Va., amendment that would decrease then increase by $500,000 funding for Health and Human Services Department refugee and immigrant assistance programs. Adopted in Committee of the Whole 285-138: R 53-137; D 232-1. June 13, 2019.

		295	296	297	298	299	300
ALABAMA							
1	**Byrne**	N	N	N	N	Y	N
2	**Roby**	Y	Y	Y	Y	Y	Y
3	**Rogers, M.**	?	?	Y	N	N	N
4	**Aderholt**	N	N	N	N	Y	N
5	**Brooks, M.**	N	N	N	N	N	N
6	**Palmer**	N	N	Y	N	N	N
7	Sewell	Y	Y	Y	Y	Y	Y
ALASKA							
AL	**Young**	Y	N	Y	Y	Y	N
ARIZONA							
1	O'Halleran	Y	Y	Y	Y	Y	Y
2	Kirkpatrick	Y	Y	Y	Y	Y	Y
3	Grijalva	Y	Y	Y	Y	Y	Y
4	**Gosar**	N	N	N	N	N	N
5	**Biggs**	N	N	N	N	N	N
6	**Schweikert**	Y	N	N	Y	N	Y
7	Gallego	Y	Y	Y	Y	Y	Y
8	**Lesko**	N	N	Y	N	Y	N
9	Stanton	Y	Y	Y	Y	Y	Y
ARKANSAS							
1	**Crawford**	N	N	N	Y	N	N
2	**Hill, F.**	N	N	Y	Y	Y	Y
3	**Womack**	N	N	Y	Y	Y	Y
4	**Westerman**	N	Y	Y	Y	Y	Y
CALIFORNIA							
1	**LaMalfa**	N	N	Y	Y	Y	Y
2	Huffman	Y	Y	Y	Y	Y	Y
3	Garamendi	Y	Y	Y	Y	Y	Y
4	**McClintock**	N	N	Y	N	Y	N
5	Thompson, M.	Y	Y	Y	Y	Y	Y
6	Matsui	Y	Y	Y	Y	Y	Y
7	Bera	Y	Y	Y	Y	Y	Y
8	**Cook**	N	N	Y	Y	Y	N
9	McNerney	Y	Y	Y	Y	Y	Y
10	Harder	Y	Y	Y	Y	Y	Y
11	DeSaulnier	Y	Y	Y	Y	Y	Y
12	Pelosi						
13	Lee B.	Y	Y	Y	Y	Y	Y
14	Speier	Y	Y	Y	Y	Y	Y
15	Swalwell	+	+	+	+	+	+
16	Costa	Y	Y	Y	Y	Y	Y
17	Khanna	Y	Y	Y	Y	Y	Y
18	Eshoo	Y	Y	Y	Y	Y	Y
19	Lofgren	Y	Y	Y	Y	Y	Y
20	Panetta	Y	Y	Y	Y	Y	Y
21	Cox	Y	Y	Y	Y	Y	Y
22	**Nunes**	N	N	N	Y	Y	N
23	**McCarthy**	N	N	Y	N	Y	Y
24	Carbajal	Y	Y	Y	Y	Y	Y
25	Hill, K.	Y	Y	Y	Y	Y	Y
26	Brownley	Y	Y	Y	Y	Y	Y
27	Chu	Y	?	Y	Y	Y	Y
28	Schiff	Y	?	Y	Y	Y	Y
29	Cárdenas	Y	Y	Y	Y	Y	Y
30	Sherman	Y	Y	Y	Y	Y	Y
31	Aguilar	Y	Y	Y	Y	Y	Y
32	Napolitano	Y	Y	Y	Y	Y	Y
33	Lieu	Y	Y	Y	Y	Y	Y
34	Gomez	Y	Y	Y	Y	Y	Y
35	Torres	Y	Y	Y	Y	Y	Y
36	Ruiz	Y	Y	Y	Y	Y	Y
37	Bass	Y	Y	Y	Y	Y	Y
38	Sánchez	Y	Y	Y	Y	Y	Y
39	Cisneros	Y	Y	Y	Y	Y	Y
40	Roybal-Allard	Y	Y	Y	Y	Y	Y
41	Takano	Y	Y	Y	Y	Y	Y
42	**Calvert**	N	N	Y	Y	Y	N
43	Waters	Y	Y	Y	Y	Y	Y
44	Barragán	Y	Y	Y	Y	Y	Y
45	Porter	Y	Y	Y	Y	Y	Y
46	Correa	Y	Y	Y	Y	Y	Y
47	Lowenthal	Y	Y	Y	Y	Y	Y
48	Rouda	Y	Y	Y	Y	Y	Y
49	Levin	Y	Y	Y	Y	Y	Y
50	**Hunter**	N	N	N	N	N	N
51	Vargas	Y	Y	Y	Y	Y	Y
52	Peters	Y	Y	Y	Y	Y	Y

		295	296	297	298	299	300
53	Davis, S.	Y	Y	Y	Y	Y	Y
COLORADO							
1	DeGette	Y	Y	Y	Y	Y	Y
2	Neguse	Y	Y	Y	Y	Y	Y
3	**Tipton**	N	Y	Y	N	Y	N
4	**Buck**	?	?	?	?	?	?
5	**Lamborn**	N	N	N	N	N	N
6	Crow	Y	Y	Y	Y	Y	Y
7	Perlmutter	Y	Y	Y	Y	Y	Y
CONNECTICUT							
1	Larson	Y	Y	Y	Y	Y	Y
2	Courtney	Y	Y	Y	Y	Y	Y
3	DeLauro	Y	Y	Y	Y	Y	Y
4	Himes	Y	Y	Y	Y	Y	Y
5	Hayes	+	+	+	+	+	+
DELAWARE							
AL	Blunt Rochester	Y	Y	Y	Y	Y	Y
FLORIDA							
1	**Gaetz**	N	N	N	N	N	N
2	**Dunn**	Y	N	N	?	N	N
3	**Yoho**	N	N	N	N	N	N
4	**Rutherford**	N	N	Y	N	N	N
5	Lawson	Y	Y	Y	Y	Y	Y
6	**Waltz**	Y	N	Y	N	N	N
7	Murphy	Y	Y	Y	Y	Y	Y
8	**Posey**	N	Y	Y	Y	N	N
9	Soto	Y	Y	Y	Y	Y	Y
10	Demings	Y	Y	Y	Y	Y	Y
11	**Webster**	N	N	N	N	N	N
12	**Bilirakis**	N	Y	Y	Y	Y	N
13	Crist	Y	Y	Y	Y	Y	Y
14	Castor	Y	Y	Y	Y	Y	Y
15	**Spano**	Y	Y	Y	Y	Y	N
16	**Buchanan**	Y	N	Y	Y	Y	N
17	**Steube**	N	N	N	N	N	N
18	**Mast**	N	Y	N	N	Y	N
19	**Rooney**	N	N	N	N	N	N
20	Hastings	?	?	?	?	?	?
21	Frankel	Y	Y	Y	Y	Y	Y
22	Deutch	Y	Y	Y	Y	Y	Y
23	Wasserman Schultz	Y	Y	Y	Y	Y	Y
24	Wilson, F.	Y	Y	Y	Y	Y	Y
25	**Diaz-Balart**	N	N	N	Y	N	N
26	Mucarsel-Powell	Y	Y	Y	Y	Y	Y
27	Shalala	Y	Y	Y	Y	Y	Y
GEORGIA							
1	**Carter, E.L.**	N	N	N	Y	N	N
2	Bishop, S.	Y	?	Y	Y	Y	Y
3	**Ferguson**	N	N	N	N	N	N
4	Johnson, H.	Y	Y	Y	Y	Y	Y
5	Lewis John	Y	Y	Y	Y	Y	Y
6	McBath	Y	Y	Y	Y	Y	Y
7	**Woodall**	N	N	Y	Y	N	N
8	**Scott, A.**	N	N	N	N	N	N
9	**Collins, D.**	N	N	N	N	Y	N
10	**Hice**	N	N	N	N	N	N
11	**Loudermilk**	N	N	N	N	Y	N
12	**Allen**	N	N	N	N	N	N
13	Scott, D.	Y	Y	Y	Y	Y	Y
14	**Graves, T.**	N	N	N	N	N	N
HAWAII							
1	Case	Y	Y	Y	Y	Y	Y
2	Gabbard	Y	Y	Y	Y	Y	Y
IDAHO							
1	**Fulcher**	N	N	N	N	N	N
2	**Simpson**	N	N	N	N	Y	N
ILLINOIS							
1	Rush	Y	Y	Y	Y	Y	Y
2	Kelly, R.	Y	Y	Y	Y	Y	Y
3	Lipinski	Y	Y	Y	Y	Y	Y
4	García, J.	Y	Y	Y	Y	Y	Y
5	Quigley	Y	Y	Y	Y	Y	Y
6	Casten	Y	Y	Y	Y	Y	Y
7	Davis, D.	Y	Y	Y	Y	Y	Y
8	Krishnamoorthi	Y	Y	Y	Y	Y	Y
9	Schakowsky	Y	Y	Y	Y	Y	Y
10	Schneider	Y	Y	Y	Y	Y	Y
11	Foster	Y	Y	Y	Y	Y	Y

KEY: **Republicans**   Democrats   *Independents*

Y	Voted for (yea)	N	Voted against (nay)	P	Voted "present"
+	Announced for	–	Announced against	?	Did not vote or otherwise make position known
#	Paired for	X	Paired against		

		295	296	297	298	299	300
12	**Bost**	?	?	?	?	?	?
13	**Davis, R.**	Y	Y	Y	Y	Y	Y
14	Underwood	Y	Y	Y	Y	Y	Y
15	**Shimkus**	N	N	Y	Y	Y	N
16	**Kinzinger**	Y	Y	Y	Y	Y	N
17	Bustos	Y	Y	Y	Y	Y	Y
18	**LaHood**	Y	N	N	Y	Y	N
INDIANA							
1	Visclosky	Y	Y	Y	Y	Y	Y
2	**Walorski**	N	N	Y	Y	Y	Y
3	**Banks**	N	N	N	N	Y	N
4	**Baird**	N	N	Y	N	Y	N
5	**Brooks, S.**	N	Y	Y	Y	Y	Y
6	**Pence**	N	N	Y	N	Y	N
7	Carson	Y	Y	Y	Y	Y	Y
8	**Bucshon**	N	N	Y	Y	Y	N
9	**Hollingsworth**	N	Y	Y	Y	Y	Y
IOWA							
1	Finkenauer	Y	Y	Y	Y	Y	Y
2	Loebsack	Y	Y	Y	Y	Y	Y
3	Axne	Y	Y	Y	Y	Y	Y
4	**King, S.**	N	N	Y	Y	Y	N
KANSAS							
1	**Marshall**	N	N	N	N	N	N
2	**Watkins**	N	N	N	N	N	N
3	Davids	Y	Y	Y	Y	Y	Y
4	**Estes**	N	N	Y	N	N	N
KENTUCKY							
1	**Comer**	N	N	N	N	N	N
2	**Guthrie**	N	N	Y	N	Y	N
3	Yarmuth	Y	Y	Y	Y	Y	Y
4	**Massie**	N	N	N	Y	N	N
5	**Rogers, H.**	N	Y	Y	Y	Y	Y
6	**Barr**	N	N	Y	Y	Y	N
LOUISIANA							
1	**Scalise**	N	N	Y	N	Y	N
2	Richmond	Y	Y	Y	Y	Y	Y
3	**Higgins, C.**	N	N	Y	Y	Y	N
4	**Johnson, M.**	Y	N	Y	N	Y	N
5	**Abraham**	N	?	?	?	?	?
6	**Graves, G.**	Y	Y	Y	Y	Y	N
MAINE							
1	Pingree	Y	Y	Y	Y	Y	Y
2	Golden	Y	Y	Y	Y	N	Y
MARYLAND							
1	**Harris**	N	N	N	N	N	N
2	Ruppersberger	Y	+	Y	Y	Y	Y
3	Sarbanes	Y	Y	Y	Y	Y	Y
4	Brown, A.	Y	Y	Y	Y	Y	Y
5	Hoyer	Y	Y	Y	Y	Y	Y
6	Trone	Y	Y	Y	Y	Y	Y
7	Cummings	Y	Y	Y	Y	Y	Y
8	Raskin						
MASSACHUSETTS		Y	Y	Y	Y	Y	Y
1	Neal						
2	McGovern	Y	Y	Y	Y	Y	Y
3	Trahan	Y	Y	Y	Y	Y	Y
4	Kennedy	Y	Y	Y	Y	Y	Y
5	Clark	Y	Y	Y	Y	Y	Y
6	Moulton	Y	Y	Y	Y	Y	Y
7	Pressley	Y	Y	Y	Y	Y	Y
8	Lynch	Y	Y	Y	Y	Y	Y
9	Keating	Y	Y	Y	Y	Y	Y
MICHIGAN		Y	Y	Y	Y	Y	Y
1	**Bergman**						
2	**Huizenga**	N	N	Y	N	Y	Y
3	**Amash**	N	Y	Y	N	Y	N
4	**Moolenaar**	N	N	N	N	N	Y
5	Kildee	N	N	Y	Y	Y	N
6	**Upton**	Y	Y	Y	Y	Y	Y
7	**Walberg**	Y	Y	Y	Y	Y	Y
8	Slotkin	N	N	Y	N	Y	N
9	Levin	Y	Y	N	Y	Y	Y
10	**Mitchell**	Y	Y	Y	Y	Y	Y
11	Stevens	N	N	Y	N	Y	N
12	Dingell	Y	Y	Y	Y	Y	Y
13	Tlaib	Y	Y	Y	Y	Y	Y
14	Lawrence	Y	Y	Y	Y	Y	Y
MINNESOTA		Y	Y	Y	Y	Y	Y
1	**Hagedorn**						
2	Craig	N	N	Y	N	Y	N
3	Phillips	Y	Y	Y	Y	Y	Y
4	McCollum	Y	Y	Y	Y	Y	Y
5	Omar	Y	Y	Y	Y	Y	Y

		295	296	297	298	299	300
6	**Emmer**	Y	Y	Y	Y	Y	Y
7	Peterson	N	N	Y	N	N	N
8	**Stauber**	Y	N	Y	Y	Y	Y
MISSISSIPPI		Y	Y	Y	Y	Y	Y
1	**Kelly, T.**						
2	Thompson, B.	N	N	N	N	Y	N
3	**Guest**	Y	Y	Y	Y	Y	Y
4	**Palazzo**	N	N	Y	N	Y	N
MISSOURI		N	N	N	N	N	N
1	Clay						
2	**Wagner**	Y	Y	Y	Y	Y	Y
3	**Luetkemeyer**	N	Y	Y	Y	Y	Y
4	**Hartzler**	Y	N	Y	Y	N	Y
5	Cleaver	N	N	Y	Y	Y	Y
6	**Graves, S.**	Y	Y	Y	Y	Y	Y
7	**Long**	N	N	Y	N	Y	N
8	**Smith, J.**	N	N	Y	N	Y	N
MONTANA		N	N	Y	Y	Y	N
AL	**Gianforte**						
NEBRASKA		?	?	?	?	?	?
1	**Fortenberry**						
2	**Bacon**	Y	Y	Y	Y	Y	Y
3	**Smith, Adrian**	Y	Y	Y	N	Y	Y
NEVADA		N	N	Y	Y	Y	N
1	Titus						
2	**Amodei**	Y	Y	Y	Y	Y	Y
3	Lee	Y	Y	Y	Y	Y	Y
4	Horsford	Y	Y	Y	Y	Y	Y
NEW HAMPSHIRE		Y	Y	Y	Y	Y	Y
1	Pappas						
2	Kuster	Y	Y	Y	Y	Y	Y
NEW JERSEY		Y	Y	Y	Y	Y	Y
1	Norcross						
2	Van Drew	Y	Y	Y	Y	Y	Y
3	Kim	Y	Y	Y	Y	Y	Y
4	**Smith, C.**	Y	Y	Y	Y	Y	Y
5	Gottheimer	?	?	?	?	?	?
6	Pallone	Y	Y	Y	Y	Y	Y
7	Malinowski	Y	Y	Y	Y	Y	Y
8	Sires	Y	Y	Y	Y	Y	Y
9	Pascrell	Y	Y	Y	Y	Y	Y
10	Payne	Y	Y	Y	Y	Y	Y
11	Sherrill	Y	Y	Y	Y	Y	Y
12	Watson Coleman	Y	Y	Y	Y	Y	Y
NEW MEXICO		Y	Y	Y	Y	Y	Y
1	Haaland						
2	Torres Small	Y	Y	Y	Y	Y	Y
3	Luján	Y	Y	Y	Y	Y	Y
NEW YORK		Y	Y	Y	Y	Y	Y
1	**Zeldin**						
2	**King, P.**	Y	Y	N	Y	Y	N
3	Suozzi	Y	Y	Y	Y	Y	Y
4	Rice, K.	Y	Y	Y	Y	Y	Y
5	Meeks	Y	Y	Y	Y	Y	Y
6	Meng	Y	Y	Y	Y	Y	Y
7	Velázquez	Y	Y	Y	Y	Y	Y
8	Jeffries	Y	Y	Y	Y	Y	Y
9	Clarke	Y	Y	Y	Y	Y	Y
10	Nadler	Y	Y	Y	Y	Y	Y
11	Rose	Y	Y	Y	Y	Y	Y
12	Maloney, C.	Y	Y	Y	Y	Y	Y
13	Espaillat	Y	Y	Y	Y	Y	Y
14	Ocasio-Cortez	Y	Y	Y	Y	Y	Y
15	Serrano	Y	Y	Y	Y	Y	Y
16	Engel	Y	Y	Y	Y	Y	Y
17	Lowey	Y	Y	Y	Y	Y	Y
18	Maloney, S.P.	Y	Y	Y	Y	Y	Y
19	Delgado	Y	Y	Y	Y	Y	Y
20	Tonko	Y	Y	Y	Y	Y	Y
21	**Stefanik**	Y	Y	Y	Y	Y	Y
22	Brindisi	Y	Y	Y	Y	Y	Y
23	**Reed**	Y	Y	Y	Y	N	Y
24	**Katko**	Y	Y	Y	Y	Y	Y
25	Morelle	Y	Y	Y	Y	Y	Y
26	Higgins, B.	Y	Y	Y	Y	Y	Y
27	**Collins, C.**	Y	?	Y	Y	Y	Y
NORTH CAROLINA		N	N	Y	Y	Y	Y
1	Butterfield						
2	**Holding**	Y	Y	Y	Y	Y	Y
3	**Jones***	N	N	N	Y	N	N
4	Price						
5	**Foxx**	Y	Y	Y	Y	Y	Y
6	**Walker**	N	N	Y	N	Y	N
7	**Rouzer**	N	N	N	N	Y	N

		295	296	297	298	299	300
8	**Hudson**	N	N	Y	N	N	N
9	vacant	Y	N	N	Y	Y	N
10	**McHenry**	Y	N	Y	N	Y	Y
11	**Meadows**	N	N	N	N	Y	N
12	Adams	Y	Y	Y	Y	Y	Y
13	**Budd**	N	N	Y	N	N	N
NORTH DAKOTA							
AL	**Armstrong**	Y	N	Y	Y	Y	Y
OHIO							
1	**Chabot**	N	N	Y	Y	Y	N
2	**Wenstrup**	N	N	Y	N	N	N
3	Beatty	Y	Y	Y	Y	Y	Y
4	**Jordan**	N	N	N	N	N	N
5	**Latta**	N	N	Y	N	Y	N
6	**Johnson, B.**	N	N	Y	N	Y	N
7	**Gibbs**	N	N	Y	N	Y	N
8	**Davidson**	N	N	N	N	N	N
9	Kaptur	Y	Y	Y	Y	Y	Y
10	**Turner**	Y	Y	Y	Y	Y	Y
11	Fudge	Y	Y	Y	Y	Y	Y
12	**Balderson**	N	N	Y	N	Y	N
13	Ryan	Y	Y	Y	Y	Y	Y
14	**Joyce**	Y	Y	Y	N	Y	Y
15	**Stivers**	Y	Y	Y	N	Y	Y
16	**Gonzalez**	Y	Y	Y	Y	Y	Y
OKLAHOMA							
1	**Hern**	N	N	N	N	N	N
2	**Mullin**	N	N	N	N	N	N
3	**Lucas**	N	N	Y	Y	Y	N
4	**Cole**	Y	Y	Y	Y	Y	Y
5	Horn	Y	Y	Y	Y	Y	N
OREGON							
1	Bonamici	Y	Y	Y	Y	Y	Y
2	**Walden**	N	Y	Y	Y	Y	Y
3	Blumenauer	Y	Y	Y	Y	Y	Y
4	DeFazio	Y	Y	Y	Y	Y	Y
5	Schrader	Y	Y	Y	Y	Y	Y
PENNSYLVANIA							
1	**Fitzpatrick**	Y	Y	Y	Y	Y	Y
2	Boyle	Y	Y	Y	Y	Y	Y
3	Evans	Y	Y	Y	Y	Y	Y
4	Dean	Y	Y	Y	Y	Y	Y
5	Scanlon	Y	Y	Y	Y	Y	Y
6	Houlahan	Y	Y	Y	Y	Y	Y
7	Wild	Y	Y	Y	Y	Y	Y
8	Cartwright	Y	Y	Y	Y	Y	Y
9	**Meuser**	N	N	Y	N	N	Y
10	**Perry**	N	N	Y	Y	N	N
11	**Smucker**	N	N	Y	N	Y	N
12	**Marino***						
13	**Joyce**	-	-	+	-	+	-
14	**Reschenthaler**	N	N	Y	Y	Y	N
15	**Thompson, G.**	Y	Y	Y	Y	Y	Y
16	**Kelly, M.**	Y	Y	Y	Y	Y	Y
17	Lamb	Y	Y	Y	Y	Y	Y
18	Doyle	Y	Y	Y	Y	Y	Y
RHODE ISLAND							
1	Cicilline	Y	Y	Y	Y	Y	Y
2	Langevin	Y	Y	Y	Y	Y	Y
SOUTH CAROLINA							
1	Cunningham	Y	Y	Y	Y	N	Y
2	**Wilson, J.**	N	N	Y	Y	Y	N
3	**Duncan**	N	N	N	N	Y	N
4	**Timmons**	N	N	Y	N	Y	N
5	**Norman**	N	N	Y	N	N	N
6	Clyburn	Y	Y	Y	Y	Y	Y
7	**Rice, T.**	N	N	N	N	N	N
SOUTH DAKOTA							
AL	**Johnson**	N	N	Y	N	Y	N
TENNESSEE							
1	**Roe**	Y	N	Y	Y	Y	N
2	**Burchett**	N	N	N	N	N	N
3	**Fleischmann**	N	N	Y	N	Y	N
4	**DesJarlais**	N	N	Y	Y	Y	N
5	Cooper	Y	Y	Y	Y	Y	Y
6	**Rose**	N	N	N	N	N	N
7	**Green**	?	?	?	?	?	?
8	**Kustoff**	N	N	Y	N	N	N
9	Cohen	Y	Y	Y	Y	Y	Y
TEXAS							
1	**Gohmert**	N	N	N	N	N	N
2	**Crenshaw**	N	Y	Y	Y	Y	Y
3	**Taylor**	Y	Y	Y	N	Y	N
4	**Ratcliffe**	N	N	Y	N	N	N

		295	296	297	298	299	300
5	**Gooden**	N	N	N	N	N	N
6	**Wright**	?	?	?	?	?	?
7	Fletcher	Y	Y	Y	Y	Y	Y
8	**Brady**	N	N	N	N	N	N
9	Green, A.	Y	Y	Y	Y	Y	Y
10	**McCaul**	Y	Y	Y	Y	Y	Y
11	**Conaway**	N	N	N	N	N	N
12	**Granger**	N	N	Y	N	Y	Y
13	**Thornberry**	N	N	N	N	N	N
14	**Weber**	N	N	N	N	Y	N
15	Gonzalez	Y	Y	Y	Y	Y	Y
16	Escobar	Y	Y	Y	Y	Y	Y
17	**Flores**	N	N	Y	N	Y	Y
18	Jackson Lee	Y	Y	Y	Y	Y	Y
19	**Arrington**	N	N	N	N	N	N
20	Castro	Y	Y	Y	Y	Y	Y
21	**Roy**	N	N	N	N	N	Y
22	**Olson**	N	N	Y	N	Y	N
23	**Hurd**	Y	Y	Y	N	Y	Y
24	**Marchant**	N	N	N	N	N	N
25	**Williams**	N	N	Y	N	Y	N
26	**Burgess**	N	N	N	N	Y	N
27	**Cloud**	N	N	N	Y	N	N
28	Cuellar	Y	Y	Y	Y	Y	Y
29	Garcia, S.	Y	Y	Y	Y	Y	Y
30	Johnson, E.B.	Y	Y	Y	Y	Y	Y
31	**Carter, J.**	N	N	N	N	Y	N
32	Allred	Y	Y	Y	Y	Y	Y
33	Veasey	Y	Y	Y	Y	Y	Y
34	Vela	Y	Y	Y	Y	Y	Y
35	Doggett	Y	Y	Y	Y	Y	Y
36	**Babin**	N	N	N	N	N	N
UTAH							
1	**Bishop, R.**	N	N	N	N	N	N
2	**Stewart**	N	N	Y	N	Y	N
3	**Curtis**	N	N	Y	N	Y	N
4	McAdams	Y	Y	Y	Y	Y	Y
VERMONT							
AL	Welch	Y	Y	Y	Y	Y	Y
VIRGINIA							
1	**Wittman**	N	N	Y	N	Y	N
2	Luria	Y	Y	Y	Y	Y	Y
3	Scott, R.	Y	Y	Y	Y	Y	Y
4	McEachin	Y	Y	Y	Y	Y	Y
5	**Riggleman**	N	N	Y	Y	Y	N
6	**Cline**	N	N	N	N	N	N
7	Spanberger	Y	?	Y	Y	Y	Y
8	Beyer	Y	Y	Y	Y	Y	Y
9	**Griffith**	N	N	Y	N	Y	N
10	Wexton	Y	Y	Y	Y	Y	Y
11	Connolly	Y	Y	Y	Y	Y	Y
WASHINGTON							
1	DelBene	Y	Y	Y	Y	Y	Y
2	Larsen	Y	Y	Y	Y	Y	Y
3	**Herrera Beutler**	?	?	?	?	?	?
4	**Newhouse**	N	Y	Y	Y	Y	Y
5	**McMorris Rodgers**	Y	Y	Y	Y	Y	Y
6	Kilmer	Y	Y	Y	Y	Y	Y
7	Jayapal	Y	Y	Y	Y	Y	Y
8	Schrier	Y	Y	Y	Y	Y	Y
9	Smith Adam	Y	Y	Y	Y	Y	Y
10	Heck	Y	Y	Y	Y	Y	Y
WEST VIRGINIA							
1	**McKinley**	Y	N	Y	N	Y	N
2	**Mooney**	N	N	Y	N	Y	N
3	**Miller**	N	N	Y	N	Y	N
WISCONSIN							
1	**Steil**	Y	N	Y	Y	Y	Y
2	Pocan	Y	+	Y	Y	Y	Y
3	Kind	Y	Y	Y	Y	Y	Y
4	Moore	Y	Y	Y	Y	Y	Y
5	**Sensenbrenner**	N	N	Y	N	Y	N
6	**Grothman**	N	N	Y	N	N	N
7	**Duffy**	N	N	N	N	N	N
8	**Gallagher**	N	N	Y	Y	Y	N
WYOMING							
AL	**Cheney**	N	N	N	N	Y	Y
DELEGATES							
	Radewagen (A.S.)	?	?	?	?	?	?
	Norton (D.C.)	Y	Y	Y	Y	Y	Y
	San Nicolas (Guam)	?	?	?	?	?	?
	Sablan (N. Marianas)	?	?	?	?	?	?
	González-Colón (P.R.)	Y	N	Y	Y	Y	Y
	Plaskett (V.I.)	Y	Y	Y	Y	Y	Y

||| HOUSE VOTES

301. HR2740. Fiscal 2020 Four-Bill Appropriations Package - Health Workforce Programs. Blunt Rochester, D-Del., amendment that would decrease then increase by $1 funding for Health and Human Services Department programs related to the health workforce, including doctors, nurses, and other health care service providers. Adopted in Committee of the Whole 376-47: R 144-46; D 232-1. June 13, 2019.

302. HR2740. Fiscal 2020 Four-Bill Appropriations Package - Mental Health and Substance Abuse Programs. Murphy, D-Fla., amendment that would increase by $2 million funding for Health and Human Services Department programs addressing mental health and decrease by the same amount funding for program support and supplemental activities, including surveys and data analysis, related to HHS mental health and substance abuse programs funded by the bill. Adopted in Committee of the Whole 366-55: R 135-55; D 231-0. June 13, 2019.

303. HR2740. Fiscal 2020 Four-Bill Appropriations Package - Disease Prevention Programs. Ocasio-Cortez, D-N.Y., amendment that would increase by $15 million funding for Health and Human Services Department programs to prevent HIV/AIDS, viral hepatitis, sexually transmitted diseases, and tuberculosis and decrease by the same amount HHS administrative funding. Adopted in Committee of the Whole 264-158: R 35-155; D 229-3. June 13, 2019.

304. HR2740. Fiscal 2020 Four-Bill Appropriations Package - Schedule I Substance Legalization. Ocasio-Cortez, D-N.Y., amendment that would strike from the bill provisions prohibiting use of any funds made available in the bill for activities to promote the legalization of any Schedule I drug or substance, such as marijuana. Rejected in Committee of the Whole 91-331: R 7-183; D 84-148. June 13, 2019.

305. HR2740. Fiscal 2020 Four-Bill Appropriations Package - Injury Prevention and Control Programs. McAdams, D-Utah, amendment that would increase by $2 million funding for Health and Human Services programs related to injury prevention and control and decrease by the same amount HHS administrative funding. Adopted in Committee of the Whole 388-30: R 159-30; D 229-0. June 13, 2019.

306. HR2740. Fiscal 2020 Four-Bill Appropriations Package - Early Childhood Developmental Screenings. Schrier, D-Wash., amendment that would include early childhood developmental screenings among medical goods and services the Health and Human Services Department may accept as donations for unaccompanied children under the care of the Office of Refugee Settlement. Adopted in Committee of the Whole 371-49: R 141-49; D 230-0. June 13, 2019.

		301	302	303	304	305	306
ALABAMA							
1	**Byrne**	Y	Y	N	N	Y	N
2	**Roby**	Y	Y	Y	N	Y	Y
3	**Rogers, M.**	N	N	N	N	Y	Y
4	**Aderholt**	Y	Y	N	N	Y	Y
5	**Brooks, M.**	N	N	N	N	N	N
6	**Palmer**	Y	N	N	N	Y	N
7	Sewell	Y	Y	Y	N	Y	Y
ALASKA							
AL	**Young**	Y	Y	Y	Y	Y	Y
ARIZONA							
1	O'Halleran	Y	Y	Y	N	Y	Y
2	Kirkpatrick	Y	Y	Y	N	Y	Y
3	Grijalva	Y	Y	Y	Y	Y	Y
4	**Gosar**	N	N	N	N	N	Y
5	**Biggs**	N	N	N	N	N	Y
6	**Schweikert**	Y	Y	N	N	Y	N
7	Gallego	Y	Y	Y	Y	Y	Y
8	**Lesko**	Y	N	N	N	N	Y
9	Stanton	Y	Y	Y	Y	Y	Y
ARKANSAS							
1	**Crawford**	Y	Y	N	N	Y	Y
2	**Hill, F.**	Y	Y	Y	N	Y	Y
3	**Womack**	Y	Y	Y	N	Y	Y
4	**Westerman**	Y	Y	N	N	Y	Y
CALIFORNIA							
1	**LaMalfa**	Y	N	Y	N	Y	Y
2	Huffman	Y	Y	Y	Y	Y	Y
3	Garamendi	Y	Y	Y	Y	Y	Y
4	**McClintock**	Y	Y	Y	Y	N	N
5	Thompson, M.	Y	Y	N	N	Y	Y
6	Matsui	Y	Y	Y	N	Y	Y
7	Bera	Y	Y	Y	N	Y	Y
8	**Cook**	Y	Y	N	N	Y	Y
9	McNerney	Y	Y	Y	Y	Y	Y
10	Harder	Y	Y	Y	N	Y	Y
11	DeSaulnier	Y	Y	Y	Y	Y	Y
12	Pelosi						
13	Lee B.	Y	Y	Y	Y	Y	Y
14	Speier	Y	Y	Y	N	Y	Y
15	Swalwell	+	+	+	+	+	+
16	Costa	Y	Y	N	N	Y	Y
17	Khanna	Y	Y	Y	Y	Y	Y
18	Eshoo	Y	Y	Y	N	Y	Y
19	Lofgren	Y	Y	Y	Y	Y	Y
20	Panetta	Y	Y	Y	N	Y	Y
21	Cox	Y	Y	Y	N	Y	Y
22	**Nunes**	Y	Y	N	N	Y	Y
23	**McCarthy**	Y	Y	N	N	Y	Y
24	Carbajal	Y	Y	Y	N	Y	Y
25	Hill, K.	Y	Y	Y	N	Y	Y
26	Brownley	Y	Y	N	N	Y	Y
27	Chu	Y	Y	Y	N	Y	Y
28	Schiff	Y	Y	Y	N	Y	Y
29	Cárdenas	Y	Y	Y	N	Y	?
30	Sherman	Y	Y	Y	Y	Y	Y
31	Aguilar	Y	Y	Y	N	Y	Y
32	Napolitano	Y	Y	Y	Y	Y	Y
33	Lieu	Y	Y	Y	Y	Y	Y
34	Gomez	Y	Y	Y	Y	Y	Y
35	Torres	Y	Y	Y	N	Y	Y
36	Ruiz	Y	Y	Y	Y	Y	Y
37	Bass	Y	Y	Y	Y	Y	Y
38	Sánchez	Y	Y	Y	Y	Y	Y
39	Cisneros	Y	Y	Y	N	Y	Y
40	Roybal-Allard	Y	Y	Y	N	Y	Y
41	Takano	Y	Y	N	N	Y	Y
42	**Calvert**	Y	Y	N	N	Y	Y
43	Waters	Y	Y	Y	Y	Y	Y
44	Barragán	Y	Y	Y	Y	Y	Y
45	Porter	Y	Y	Y	N	Y	Y
46	Correa	Y	Y	Y	Y	Y	Y
47	Lowenthal	Y	Y	Y	Y	Y	Y
48	Rouda	Y	Y	Y	N	Y	Y
49	Levin	Y	Y	Y	N	Y	Y
50	**Hunter**	N	Y	N	N	Y	Y
51	Vargas	Y	Y	Y	Y	Y	Y
52	Peters	Y	Y	Y	N	Y	Y

		301	302	303	304	305	306
53	Davis, S.	Y	Y	Y	N	Y	Y
COLORADO							
1	DeGette	Y	Y	Y	Y	Y	Y
2	Neguse	Y	Y	Y	Y	Y	Y
3	**Tipton**	Y	Y	N	N	Y	Y
4	**Buck**	?	?	?	?	?	?
5	**Lamborn**	Y	Y	N	N	Y	Y
6	Crow	Y	Y	Y	N	Y	Y
7	Perlmutter	Y	Y	Y	Y	Y	Y
CONNECTICUT							
1	Larson	Y	Y	Y	N	Y	Y
2	Courtney	Y	Y	N	N	Y	Y
3	DeLauro	Y	Y	Y	N	Y	Y
4	Himes	Y	Y	Y	N	Y	Y
5	Hayes	+	+	+	-	+	+
DELAWARE							
AL	Blunt Rochester	Y	Y	Y	N	Y	Y
FLORIDA							
1	**Gaetz**	Y	Y	N	Y	N	N
2	**Dunn**	N	N	N	N	Y	Y
3	**Yoho**	N	N	N	N	N	N
4	**Rutherford**	Y	Y	Y	N	Y	Y
5	Lawson	Y	Y	Y	N	Y	Y
6	**Waltz**	Y	Y	N	N	Y	Y
7	Murphy	Y	Y	Y	N	Y	Y
8	**Posey**	Y	Y	N	N	Y	N
9	Soto	Y	Y	Y	N	Y	Y
10	Demings	Y	Y	Y	N	Y	Y
11	**Webster**	N	N	N	N	N	N
12	**Bilirakis**	Y	Y	N	N	Y	Y
13	Crist	Y	Y	Y	Y	Y	Y
14	Castor	Y	Y	Y	Y	Y	Y
15	**Spano**	Y	Y	N	N	Y	Y
16	**Buchanan**	Y	Y	N	N	Y	Y
17	**Steube**	Y	Y	N	N	Y	N
18	**Mast**	Y	Y	N	Y	Y	Y
19	**Rooney**	N	N	N	N	Y	Y
20	Hastings	?	?	?	?	?	?
21	Frankel	Y	Y	Y	N	Y	Y
22	Deutch	Y	Y	Y	N	Y	Y
23	Wasserman Schultz	Y	Y	Y	N	Y	Y
24	Wilson, F.	Y	Y	Y	N	Y	Y
25	**Diaz-Balart**	Y	Y	N	N	Y	Y
26	Mucarsel-Powell	Y	Y	Y	N	Y	Y
27	Shalala	Y	Y	Y	Y	Y	Y
GEORGIA							
1	**Carter, E.L.**	N	N	N	N	Y	N
2	Bishop, S.	Y	Y	Y	Y	Y	Y
3	**Ferguson**	Y	Y	N	N	N	N
4	Johnson, H.	Y	Y	Y	Y	Y	Y
5	Lewis John	Y	Y	Y	N	Y	Y
6	McBath	Y	Y	Y	N	Y	Y
7	**Woodall**	Y	Y	N	N	Y	Y
8	**Scott, A.**	Y	Y	N	N	Y	Y
9	**Collins, D.**	N	Y	N	N	Y	N
10	**Hice**	N	N	N	N	N	Y
11	**Loudermilk**	Y	N	N	N	Y	N
12	**Allen**	Y	Y	N	N	Y	N
13	Scott, D.	Y	Y	Y	Y	Y	Y
14	**Graves, T.**	N	N	N	N	N	N
HAWAII							
1	Case	Y	Y	N	N	Y	Y
2	Gabbard	Y	Y	Y	Y	Y	Y
IDAHO							
1	**Fulcher**	Y	Y	N	N	Y	N
2	**Simpson**	Y	Y	N	N	Y	Y
ILLINOIS							
1	Rush	Y	Y	Y	Y	Y	Y
2	Kelly, R.	Y	Y	Y	N	Y	Y
3	Lipinski	Y	Y	Y	N	Y	Y
4	García, J.	Y	Y	Y	Y	Y	Y
5	Quigley	Y	Y	Y	N	Y	Y
6	Casten	Y	Y	Y	N	Y	Y
7	Davis, D.	Y	Y	Y	Y	Y	Y
8	Krishnamoorthi	Y	Y	Y	Y	Y	Y
9	Schakowsky	Y	Y	Y	Y	Y	Y
10	Schneider	Y	Y	Y	N	Y	Y
11	Foster	Y	Y	Y	N	?	Y

		301	302	303	304	305	306
12	**Bost**	?	?	?	?	?	?
13	**Davis, R.**	Y	N	Y	N	Y	Y
14	Underwood	Y	Y	N	N	Y	Y
15	**Shimkus**	Y	Y	N	N	Y	Y
16	**Kinzinger**	Y	Y	Y	N	Y	Y
17	Bustos	Y	Y	Y	N	Y	Y
18	**LaHood**	Y	Y	Y	N	Y	Y
INDIANA							
1	Visclosky	Y	Y	Y	N	Y	Y
2	**Walorski**	Y	Y	Y	N	Y	Y
3	**Banks**	Y	Y	N	N	Y	Y
4	**Baird**	Y	Y	N	N	Y	Y
5	**Brooks, S.**	Y	Y	Y	N	Y	Y
6	**Pence**	Y	Y	N	N	Y	Y
7	Carson	Y	Y	Y	Y	Y	Y
8	**Bucshon**	Y	Y	N	N	Y	Y
9	**Hollingsworth**	Y	Y	Y	N	Y	Y
IOWA							
1	Finkenauer	Y	Y	Y	N	Y	Y
2	Loebsack	Y	Y	Y	N	Y	Y
3	Axne	Y	Y	N	N	Y	Y
4	**King, S.**	Y	Y	N	N	N	N
KANSAS							
1	**Marshall**	N	N	N	N	N	N
2	**Watkins**	Y	N	N	N	N	N
3	Davids	Y	Y	Y	N	Y	Y
4	**Estes**	Y	N	N	N	N	N
KENTUCKY							
1	**Comer**	N	N	N	N	N	N
2	**Guthrie**	Y	Y	N	N	Y	Y
3	Yarmuth	Y	Y	Y	Y	Y	Y
4	**Massie**	N	N	N	Y	N	N
5	**Rogers, H.**	Y	Y	Y	N	Y	Y
6	**Barr**	Y	Y	Y	N	Y	N
LOUISIANA							
1	**Scalise**	Y	Y	N	N	Y	Y
2	Richmond	Y	Y	Y	N	Y	Y
3	**Higgins, C.**	Y	Y	N	N	Y	Y
4	**Johnson, M.**	Y	Y	N	N	Y	Y
5	**Abraham**	?	?	?	?	?	?
6	**Graves, G.**	Y	Y	N	N	Y	Y
MAINE							
1	Pingree	Y	Y	Y	Y	Y	Y
2	Golden	Y	Y	Y	N	Y	Y
MARYLAND							
1	**Harris**	Y	N	N	N	N	Y
2	Ruppersberger	Y	Y	Y	N	Y	Y
3	Sarbanes	Y	Y	Y	N	Y	Y
4	Brown, A.	Y	Y	Y	N	Y	Y
5	Hoyer	Y	Y	Y	N	Y	Y
6	Trone	Y	Y	Y	N	Y	Y
7	Cummings	Y	Y	Y	Y	Y	Y
8	Raskin						
MASSACHUSETTS		Y	Y	Y	Y	Y	Y
1	Neal						
2	McGovern	Y	Y	Y	N	Y	Y
3	Trahan	Y	Y	Y	Y	Y	Y
4	Kennedy	Y	Y	Y	N	Y	Y
5	Clark	Y	Y	Y	N	Y	Y
6	Moulton	Y	Y	Y	N	Y	Y
7	Pressley	Y	Y	Y	Y	Y	Y
8	Lynch	Y	Y	Y	Y	Y	Y
9	Keating	Y	Y	Y	N	Y	Y
MICHIGAN		Y	Y	Y	N	Y	Y
1	**Bergman**						
2	**Huizenga**	Y	Y	N	N	Y	Y
3	**Amash**	Y	Y	N	N	Y	Y
4	**Moolenaar**	N	N	N	Y	N	Y
5	Kildee	Y	Y	N	N	Y	Y
6	**Upton**	Y	Y	Y	N	Y	Y
7	**Walberg**	Y	Y	Y	N	Y	Y
8	Slotkin	Y	Y	N	N	Y	Y
9	Levin	Y	Y	Y	N	Y	Y
10	**Mitchell**	Y	Y	Y	Y	Y	Y
11	Stevens	Y	Y	N	N	Y	Y
12	Dingell	Y	Y	Y	N	Y	Y
13	Tlaib	Y	Y	Y	N	Y	Y
14	Lawrence	Y	Y	Y	Y	Y	Y
MINNESOTA		Y	Y	Y	N	Y	Y
1	**Hagedorn**						
2	Craig	Y	Y	N	N	Y	Y
3	Phillips	Y	Y	Y	N	Y	Y
4	McCollum	Y	Y	Y	N	Y	Y
5	Omar	Y	Y	Y	N	Y	Y

		301	302	303	304	305	306
6	**Emmer**	Y	Y	Y	Y	Y	Y
7	Peterson	N	Y	N	N	Y	N
8	**Stauber**	Y	Y	Y	N	Y	Y
MISSISSIPPI		Y	Y	N	N	Y	Y
1	**Kelly, T.**						
2	Thompson, B.	Y	N	N	N	Y	N
3	**Guest**	Y	Y	Y	N	Y	Y
4	**Palazzo**	Y	Y	N	N	Y	Y
MISSOURI		Y	N	N	N	Y	N
1	Clay						
2	**Wagner**	Y	Y	Y	Y	Y	Y
3	**Luetkemeyer**	Y	Y	Y	N	Y	Y
4	**Hartzler**	Y	Y	N	N	Y	Y
5	Cleaver	Y	Y	N	N	Y	Y
6	**Graves, S.**	Y	Y	Y	Y	Y	Y
7	**Long**	Y	N	N	N	N	Y
8	**Smith, J.**	Y	N	N	N	N	Y
MONTANA		Y	N	N	N	Y	Y
AL	**Gianforte**						
NEBRASKA		?	?	?	?	?	?
1	**Fortenberry**						
2	**Bacon**	N	Y	N	N	Y	Y
3	**Smith, Adrian**	Y	Y	N	N	Y	Y
NEVADA		Y	N	N	N	Y	Y
1	Titus						
2	**Amodei**	Y	Y	Y	Y	Y	Y
3	Lee	Y	Y	Y	N	Y	Y
4	Horsford	Y	Y	Y	N	Y	Y
NEW HAMPSHIRE		Y	Y	Y	N	Y	Y
1	Pappas						
2	Kuster	Y	Y	Y	N	Y	Y
NEW JERSEY		Y	Y	Y	N	Y	Y
1	Norcross						
2	Van Drew	Y	Y	Y	N	Y	Y
3	Kim	Y	Y	Y	N	Y	Y
4	**Smith, C.**	Y	Y	Y	N	Y	Y
5	Gottheimer	?	?	?	?	?	?
6	Pallone	Y	Y	Y	N	Y	Y
7	Malinowski	Y	Y	Y	Y	Y	Y
8	Sires	Y	Y	Y	N	Y	Y
9	Pascrell	Y	Y	Y	N	Y	Y
10	Payne	Y	Y	Y	N	?	Y
11	Sherrill	Y	Y	Y	Y	Y	Y
12	Watson Coleman	Y	Y	Y	N	Y	Y
NEW MEXICO		Y	Y	Y	N	Y	Y
1	Haaland						
2	Torres Small	Y	Y	Y	Y	Y	Y
3	Luján	Y	Y	Y	N	Y	Y
NEW YORK		Y	Y	Y	N	Y	Y
1	**Zeldin**						
2	**King, P.**	Y	Y	Y	N	Y	Y
3	Suozzi	Y	Y	Y	N	Y	Y
4	Rice, K.	Y	Y	Y	N	Y	Y
5	Meeks	Y	Y	Y	Y	Y	Y
6	Meng	Y	Y	Y	N	Y	Y
7	Velázquez	Y	Y	Y	Y	Y	Y
8	Jeffries	Y	Y	Y	Y	Y	Y
9	Clarke	Y	Y	Y	N	Y	Y
10	Nadler	Y	Y	Y	Y	Y	Y
11	Rose	Y	Y	Y	Y	Y	Y
12	Maloney, C.	Y	Y	Y	N	Y	Y
13	Espaillat	Y	Y	Y	Y	Y	Y
14	Ocasio-Cortez	Y	Y	Y	Y	Y	Y
15	Serrano	Y	Y	Y	Y	Y	Y
16	Engel	Y	Y	Y	Y	Y	Y
17	Lowey	Y	Y	Y	Y	Y	Y
18	Maloney, S.P.	Y	Y	Y	N	Y	Y
19	Delgado	Y	Y	Y	N	Y	Y
20	Tonko	Y	Y	Y	N	Y	Y
21	**Stefanik**	Y	Y	Y	N	Y	Y
22	Brindisi	Y	Y	Y	N	Y	Y
23	**Reed**	Y	Y	Y	N	Y	Y
24	**Katko**	Y	Y	Y	N	Y	Y
25	Morelle	Y	Y	Y	N	Y	Y
26	Higgins, B.	Y	Y	Y	N	Y	Y
27	**Collins, C.**	Y	Y	Y	Y	Y	Y
NORTH CAROLINA		Y	Y	N	N	Y	Y
1	Butterfield						
2	**Holding**	Y	Y	Y	N	Y	Y
3	**Jones***	Y	Y	N	N	Y	Y
4	Price						
5	**Foxx**	Y	Y	Y	Y	Y	Y
6	**Walker**	Y	N	N	N	Y	Y
7	**Rouzer**	Y	N	N	N	Y	N

		301	302	303	304	305	306
8	**Hudson**	Y	Y	N	N	Y	Y
9	vacant	Y	Y	N	N	Y	Y
10	**McHenry**	Y	N	N	N	Y	Y
11	**Meadows**	Y	Y	N	N	Y	Y
12	Adams	Y	Y	Y	N	Y	Y
13	**Budd**	N	N	N	N	Y	N
NORTH DAKOTA							
AL	**Armstrong**	Y	Y	N	N	Y	Y
OHIO							
1	**Chabot**	Y	Y	N	N	Y	Y
2	**Wenstrup**	Y	Y	Y	N	Y	Y
3	Beatty	Y	Y	Y	N	Y	Y
4	**Jordan**	N	N	N	N	N	N
5	**Latta**	Y	Y	N	N	Y	Y
6	**Johnson, B.**	Y	Y	N	N	Y	Y
7	**Gibbs**	Y	Y	N	N	Y	Y
8	**Davidson**	N	N	N	N	N	N
9	Kaptur	Y	Y	Y	N	Y	Y
10	**Turner**	Y	Y	Y	N	Y	Y
11	Fudge	Y	Y	Y	N	Y	Y
12	**Balderson**	Y	Y	N	N	Y	Y
13	Ryan	Y	Y	Y	Y	Y	Y
14	**Joyce**	Y	Y	N	N	Y	Y
15	**Stivers**	Y	Y	N	N	Y	Y
16	**Gonzalez**	Y	Y	Y	N	Y	Y
OKLAHOMA							
1	**Hern**	N	N	N	N	Y	N
2	**Mullin**	Y	Y	N	N	Y	Y
3	**Lucas**	Y	Y	N	N	Y	Y
4	**Cole**	Y	Y	Y	N	Y	Y
5	Horn	N	Y	Y	N	Y	Y
OREGON							
1	Bonamici	Y	Y	Y	Y	Y	Y
2	**Walden**	Y	Y	N	N	Y	Y
3	Blumenauer	Y	Y	Y	Y	Y	Y
4	DeFazio	Y	Y	Y	Y	Y	Y
5	Schrader	Y	Y	Y	Y	Y	Y
PENNSYLVANIA							
1	**Fitzpatrick**	Y	Y	Y	N	Y	Y
2	Boyle	Y	Y	Y	N	Y	Y
3	Evans	Y	Y	Y	N	Y	Y
4	Dean	Y	Y	Y	N	Y	Y
5	Scanlon	Y	Y	Y	N	?	Y
6	Houlahan	Y	Y	Y	N	Y	Y
7	Wild	Y	Y	Y	N	Y	Y
8	Cartwright	Y	Y	Y	N	Y	Y
9	**Meuser**	Y	Y	N	N	Y	Y
10	**Perry**	Y	Y	N	N	Y	Y
11	**Smucker**	Y	Y	N	N	Y	Y
12	**Marino***						
13	**Joyce**	+	+	-	-	+	+
14	**Reschenthaler**	Y	Y	N	N	Y	Y
15	**Thompson, G.**	Y	Y	Y	N	Y	Y
16	**Kelly, M.**	Y	Y	Y	N	Y	Y
17	Lamb	Y	Y	Y	N	Y	Y
18	Doyle	Y	Y	?	?	?	?
RHODE ISLAND							
1	Cicilline	Y	Y	Y	N	Y	Y
2	Langevin	Y	Y	Y	N	Y	Y
SOUTH CAROLINA							
1	Cunningham	Y	Y	Y	N	Y	Y
2	**Wilson, J.**	Y	Y	Y	N	Y	Y
3	**Duncan**	Y	N	N	N	Y	N
4	**Timmons**	N	N	N	N	N	Y
5	**Norman**	N	N	N	N	N	N
6	Clyburn	Y	Y	Y	Y	Y	Y
7	**Rice, T.**	N	N	N	N	N	N
SOUTH DAKOTA							
AL	**Johnson**	N	Y	N	N	Y	Y
TENNESSEE							
1	**Roe**	Y	Y	N	N	Y	Y
2	**Burchett**	N	N	N	N	Y	N
3	**Fleischmann**	Y	Y	N	N	Y	Y
4	**DesJarlais**	Y	Y	N	N	Y	Y
5	Cooper	Y	Y	Y	N	Y	Y
6	**Rose**	Y	N	N	N	N	Y
7	**Green**	?	?	?	?	?	?
8	**Kustoff**	Y	Y	N	N	Y	Y
9	Cohen	Y	Y	Y	Y	Y	Y
TEXAS							
1	**Gohmert**	N	Y	N	N	Y	N
2	**Crenshaw**	Y	Y	N	N	Y	Y
3	**Taylor**	Y	Y	N	N	Y	Y
4	**Ratcliffe**	Y	N	N	N	Y	N

		301	302	303	304	305	306
5	**Gooden**	Y	N	N	N	N	N
6	**Wright**	?	?	?	?	?	?
7	Fletcher	Y	Y	Y	N	Y	Y
8	**Brady**	Y	N	N	N	Y	Y
9	Green, A.	Y	Y	Y	N	Y	Y
10	**McCaul**	Y	Y	N	N	Y	Y
11	**Conaway**	N	N	N	N	Y	Y
12	**Granger**	Y	Y	N	N	Y	Y
13	**Thornberry**	N	N	N	N	Y	Y
14	**Weber**	N	Y	N	N	Y	N
15	Gonzalez	Y	Y	Y	N	Y	Y
16	Escobar	Y	Y	Y	N	Y	Y
17	**Flores**	Y	Y	N	N	Y	Y
18	Jackson Lee	Y	Y	Y	Y	Y	Y
19	**Arrington**	N	N	N	N	N	N
20	Castro	Y	Y	Y	Y	Y	Y
21	**Roy**	N	N	N	N	N	Y
22	**Olson**	N	Y	N	N	Y	Y
23	**Hurd**	Y	Y	Y	N	Y	Y
24	**Marchant**	N	Y	N	N	Y	N
25	**Williams**	N	Y	Y	N	Y	N
26	**Burgess**	N	Y	N	N	Y	Y
27	**Cloud**	Y	N	N	N	N	Y
28	Cuellar	Y	Y	Y	N	Y	Y
29	Garcia, S.	Y	Y	Y	N	Y	Y
30	Johnson, E.B.	Y	Y	Y	Y	Y	Y
31	**Carter, J.**	N	Y	N	N	Y	N
32	Allred	Y	Y	Y	N	Y	Y
33	Veasey	Y	Y	Y	Y	Y	Y
34	Vela	Y	?	Y	Y	Y	Y
35	Doggett	Y	Y	Y	N	Y	Y
36	**Babin**	N	Y	N	N	Y	N
UTAH							
1	**Bishop, R.**	N	Y	N	N	Y	N
2	**Stewart**	N	Y	N	N	Y	Y
3	**Curtis**	N	Y	N	N	Y	Y
4	McAdams	Y	Y	Y	N	Y	Y
VERMONT							
AL	Welch	Y	Y	Y	N	Y	Y
VIRGINIA							
1	**Wittman**	Y	N	N	N	Y	Y
2	Luria	Y	Y	Y	N	Y	Y
3	Scott, R.	Y	Y	Y	N	Y	Y
4	McEachin	Y	Y	Y	N	Y	Y
5	**Riggleman**	Y	Y	N	N	Y	Y
6	**Cline**	N	N	N	N	Y	Y
7	Spanberger	Y	Y	Y	N	Y	Y
8	Beyer	Y	Y	Y	Y	Y	Y
9	**Griffith**	Y	N	N	N	Y	Y
10	Wexton	Y	Y	Y	Y	Y	Y
11	Connolly	Y	Y	Y	N	Y	Y
WASHINGTON							
1	DelBene	Y	Y	Y	N	Y	Y
2	Larsen	Y	Y	Y	N	Y	Y
3	**Herrera Beutler**	?	?	?	?	?	?
4	**Newhouse**	Y	Y	N	N	Y	Y
5	**McMorris Rodgers**	Y	Y	N	N	Y	Y
6	Kilmer	Y	Y	Y	N	Y	Y
7	Jayapal	Y	Y	Y	Y	Y	Y
8	Schrier	Y	Y	Y	N	Y	Y
9	Smith Adam	Y	Y	Y	Y	Y	Y
10	Heck	Y	Y	Y	Y	Y	Y
WEST VIRGINIA							
1	**McKinley**	Y	Y	N	N	Y	Y
2	**Mooney**	N	Y	N	N	Y	Y
3	**Miller**	Y	Y	N	N	Y	Y
WISCONSIN							
1	**Steil**	Y	Y	N	N	Y	Y
2	Pocan	Y	Y	Y	Y	Y	Y
3	Kind	Y	Y	Y	N	Y	Y
4	Moore	Y	Y	Y	Y	Y	Y
5	**Sensenbrenner**	Y	Y	N	N	Y	N
6	**Grothman**	Y	N	N	Y	?	Y
7	**Duffy**	N	Y	N	N	Y	N
8	**Gallagher**	Y	Y	N	N	Y	Y
WYOMING							
AL	**Cheney**	Y	Y	N	N	Y	N
DELEGATES							
	Radewagen (A.S.)	?	?	?	?	?	?
	Norton (D.C.)	Y	?	Y	Y	Y	Y
	San Nicolas (Guam)	?	?	?	?	?	?
	Sablan (N. Marianas)	?	?	?	?	?	?
	González-Colón (P.R.)	Y	Y	Y	N	Y	Y
	Plaskett (V.I.)	Y	Y	Y	N	Y	?

307. HR2740. Fiscal 2020 Four-Bill Appropriations Package - Health Workforce Initiatives. Lee, D-Nev., amendment that would increase by $5 million funding for health workforce initiatives under the Department of Health and Human Services, including those related to medical education and student loans. It would decrease by the same amount administrative funding for the Education Department. Adopted in Committee of the Whole 365-54: R 137-53; D 228-1. June 13, 2019.

308. HR2740. Fiscal 2020 Four-Bill Appropriations Package - Rural Health Programs. Craig, D-Minn., amendment that would increase funding by $1 million for Health and Human Services Department rural health programs and decrease funding by the same amount HHS administrative funding. Adopted in Committee of the Whole 383-36: R 154-36; D 229-0. June 13, 2019.

309. HR2740. Fiscal 2020 Four-Bill Appropriations Package - Special Education Program Grants. Craig, D-Minn., amendment that would decrease then increase by $1 million funding for Education Department state grants for special education programs. Adopted in Committee of the Whole 376-41: R 147-41; D 229-0. June 13, 2019.

310. HR2740. Fiscal 2020 Four-Bill Appropriations Package - Career, Technical, and Adult Education Programs. Craig, D-Minn., amendment that would decrease, then increase by $1 million funding for career, technical, and adult education programs. Adopted in Committee of the Whole 390-29: R 161-29; D 229-0. June 13, 2019.

311. HR2740. Fiscal 2020 Four-Bill Appropriations Package - Medicare Fraud and Abuse Prevention. Porter, D-Calif., amendment that would increase by $2 million funding allocated for a Health and Human Services program to combat fraud and abuse in the Medicare system, from funds authorized by the bill to combat health care fraud and abuse. Adopted in Committee of the Whole 316-103: R 87-103; D 229-0. June 13, 2019.

312. HR2740. Fiscal 2020 Four-Bill Appropriations Package - Health Resources and Services Administration. Porter, D-Calif., amendment that would increase by $1 million funding for Health Resources and Services Administration program management, and decrease by the same amount HHS administrative funding. Adopted in Committee of the Whole 311-110: R 80-110; D 231-0. June 13, 2019.

		307	308	309	310	311	312
ALABAMA							
1	Byrne	Y	Y	Y	Y	N	N
2	Roby	Y	Y	Y	Y	N	N
3	Rogers, M.	Y	Y	N	Y	N	N
4	Aderholt	Y	Y	Y	Y	Y	Y
5	Brooks, M.	N	N	N	N	N	N
6	Palmer	N	N	Y	Y	N	N
7	Sewell	Y	Y	Y	Y	Y	Y
ALASKA							
AL	Young	Y	Y	Y	Y	Y	N
ARIZONA							
1	O'Halleran	Y	Y	Y	Y	Y	Y
2	Kirkpatrick	Y	Y	Y	Y	Y	Y
3	Grijalva	Y	Y	Y	Y	Y	Y
4	Gosar	Y	N	N	N	N	N
5	Biggs	Y	N	N	N	N	N
6	Schweikert	Y	Y	N	N	Y	Y
7	Gallego	Y	Y	?	Y	Y	Y
8	Lesko	Y	N	Y	Y	Y	N
9	Stanton	Y	Y	Y	Y	Y	Y
ARKANSAS							
1	Crawford	Y	Y	Y	Y	Y	N
2	Hill, F.	Y	Y	Y	Y	Y	Y
3	Womack	Y	Y	Y	Y	Y	Y
4	Westerman	N	Y	Y	Y	Y	Y
CALIFORNIA							
1	LaMalfa	Y	Y	Y	N	N	N
2	Huffman	Y	Y	Y	Y	Y	Y
3	Garamendi	Y	Y	Y	Y	Y	Y
4	McClintock	N	Y	Y	Y	Y	N
5	Thompson, M.	Y	Y	Y	Y	Y	Y
6	Matsui	Y	Y	Y	Y	Y	Y
7	Bera	Y	Y	Y	Y	Y	Y
8	Cook	Y	Y	Y	Y	Y	Y
9	McNerney	Y	Y	Y	Y	Y	Y
10	Harder	?	Y	Y	Y	Y	Y
11	DeSaulnier	Y	Y	Y	Y	Y	Y
12	Pelosi						
13	Lee B.	Y	Y	Y	Y	Y	Y
14	Speier	Y	Y	Y	Y	Y	Y
15	Swalwell	+	+	+	+	+	+
16	Costa	Y	Y	Y	Y	Y	Y
17	Khanna	Y	Y	Y	Y	Y	Y
18	Eshoo	Y	Y	Y	Y	Y	Y
19	Lofgren	Y	Y	Y	Y	Y	Y
20	Panetta	Y	Y	Y	Y	Y	Y
21	Cox	Y	Y	Y	Y	Y	Y
22	Nunes	Y	Y	Y	Y	Y	Y
23	McCarthy	Y	Y	Y	Y	Y	Y
24	Carbajal	Y	Y	Y	Y	Y	Y
25	Hill, K.	Y	Y	Y	Y	Y	Y
26	Brownley	Y	Y	Y	Y	Y	Y
27	Chu	Y	Y	Y	Y	Y	Y
28	Schiff	Y	Y	Y	Y	Y	Y
29	Cárdenas	Y	Y	Y	Y	Y	Y
30	Sherman	Y	Y	Y	Y	Y	Y
31	Aguilar	Y	Y	Y	Y	Y	Y
32	Napolitano	Y	Y	Y	Y	Y	Y
33	Lieu	Y	Y	Y	Y	Y	Y
34	Gomez	Y	Y	Y	Y	Y	Y
35	Torres	Y	Y	Y	Y	Y	Y
36	Ruiz	Y	Y	Y	Y	Y	Y
37	Bass	Y	?	Y	Y	Y	Y
38	Sánchez	Y	Y	Y	Y	Y	Y
39	Cisneros	Y	Y	Y	Y	Y	Y
40	Roybal-Allard	Y	Y	Y	Y	Y	Y
41	Takano	Y	Y	Y	Y	Y	Y
42	Calvert	Y	Y	Y	Y	Y	Y
43	Waters	Y	Y	Y	Y	Y	Y
44	Barragán	Y	Y	?	Y	Y	Y
45	Porter	Y	Y	Y	Y	Y	Y
46	Correa	Y	Y	Y	Y	Y	Y
47	Lowenthal	Y	Y	Y	Y	Y	Y
48	Rouda	Y	Y	Y	Y	Y	Y
49	Levin	Y	Y	Y	Y	Y	Y
50	Hunter	Y	N	Y	Y	N	N
51	Vargas	Y	Y	Y	Y	Y	Y
52	Peters	Y	Y	Y	Y	Y	Y
53	Davis, S.	Y	Y	Y	Y	Y	Y
COLORADO							
1	DeGette	Y	Y	Y	Y	Y	Y
2	Neguse	Y	Y	Y	Y	Y	Y
3	Tipton	Y	Y	Y	Y	Y	Y
4	Buck	?	?	?	?	?	?
5	Lamborn	Y	Y	Y	Y	N	N
6	Crow	Y	Y	Y	Y	Y	Y
7	Perlmutter	Y	Y	Y	Y	Y	Y
CONNECTICUT							
1	Larson	Y	Y	Y	Y	Y	Y
2	Courtney	Y	Y	Y	Y	Y	Y
3	DeLauro	Y	Y	Y	Y	Y	Y
4	Himes	Y	Y	Y	Y	Y	Y
5	Hayes	+	+	+	+	+	+
DELAWARE							
AL	Blunt Rochester	Y	Y	Y	Y	Y	Y
FLORIDA							
1	Gaetz	N	Y	?	Y	N	N
2	Dunn	Y	Y	N	Y	Y	N
3	Yoho	Y	Y	N	Y	N	N
4	Rutherford	N	N	N	Y	Y	N
5	Lawson	Y	Y	Y	Y	Y	Y
6	Waltz	Y	Y	Y	Y	Y	Y
7	Murphy	Y	Y	Y	Y	Y	Y
8	Posey	N	N	N	Y	N	N
9	Soto	Y	Y	Y	Y	Y	Y
10	Demings	Y	Y	Y	Y	Y	Y
11	Webster	Y	Y	N	Y	N	N
12	Bilirakis	Y	Y	Y	Y	N	Y
13	Crist	Y	Y	Y	Y	Y	Y
14	Castor	Y	Y	Y	Y	Y	Y
15	Spano	Y	Y	Y	Y	N	Y
16	Buchanan	Y	Y	Y	Y	Y	Y
17	Steube	N	Y	N	N	N	N
18	Mast	Y	Y	Y	Y	Y	N
19	Rooney	N	N	N	N	N	N
20	Hastings	?	?	?	?	?	?
21	Frankel	Y	Y	Y	Y	Y	Y
22	Deutch	Y	Y	Y	Y	Y	Y
23	Wasserman Schultz	Y	Y	Y	Y	Y	Y
24	Wilson, F.	Y	Y	Y	Y	Y	Y
25	Diaz-Balart	Y	Y	Y	Y	Y	N
26	Mucarsel-Powell	Y	Y	Y	Y	Y	Y
27	Shalala	Y	Y	Y	Y	Y	Y
GEORGIA							
1	Carter, E.L.	Y	Y	Y	Y	N	N
2	Bishop, S.	Y	Y	Y	Y	Y	Y
3	Ferguson	N	N	N	N	N	N
4	Johnson, H.	Y	Y	Y	Y	?	Y
5	Lewis John	Y	Y	Y	Y	Y	Y
6	McBath	Y	Y	Y	Y	Y	Y
7	Woodall	Y	N	Y	Y	Y	N
8	Scott, A.	Y	Y	Y	Y	N	N
9	Collins, D.	Y	N	Y	N	N	N
10	Hice	N	N	N	N	N	N
11	Loudermilk	N	N	N	N	N	N
12	Allen	N	N	N	N	N	N
13	Scott, D.	Y	Y	Y	Y	Y	Y
14	Graves, T.	N	N	N	N	N	N
HAWAII							
1	Case	Y	Y	Y	Y	Y	Y
2	Gabbard	Y	Y	Y	Y	Y	Y
IDAHO							
1	Fulcher	Y	Y	Y	Y	N	N
2	Simpson	Y	Y	Y	Y	Y	N
ILLINOIS							
1	Rush	Y	Y	Y	Y	Y	Y
2	Kelly, R.	Y	Y	Y	Y	Y	Y
3	Lipinski	Y	Y	Y	Y	Y	Y
4	García, J.	Y	Y	Y	Y	Y	Y
5	Quigley	Y	Y	Y	Y	?	Y
6	Casten	Y	Y	Y	Y	Y	Y
7	Davis, D.	Y	Y	Y	Y	Y	Y
8	Krishnamoorthi	Y	Y	Y	Y	Y	Y
9	Schakowsky	Y	Y	Y	Y	Y	Y
10	Schneider	Y	Y	Y	Y	Y	Y
11	Foster	Y	Y	Y	Y	Y	Y

KEY:	Republicans	Democrats	Independents

Y	Voted for (yea)	N	Voted against (nay)	P	Voted "present"
+	Announced for	–	Announced against	?	Did not vote or otherwise make position known
#	Paired for	X	Paired against		

		307	308	309	310	311	312
12	**Bost**	?	?	?	?	?	?
13	**Davis, R.**	Y	Y	Y	Y	Y	Y
14	Underwood	N	Y	Y	Y	Y	Y
15	**Shimkus**	Y	Y	Y	Y	Y	Y
16	**Kinzinger**	Y	Y	Y	Y	N	N
17	Bustos	Y	Y	Y	Y	Y	Y
18	**LaHood**	Y	Y	Y	Y	Y	Y
INDIANA							
1	Visclosky	Y	Y	Y	Y	Y	Y
2	**Walorski**	N	Y	Y	Y	N	Y
3	**Banks**	Y	N	Y	Y	N	N
4	**Baird**	Y	Y	Y	Y	Y	N
5	**Brooks, S.**	Y	Y	Y	Y	N	Y
6	**Pence**	N	Y	Y	Y	Y	Y
7	Carson	Y	Y	Y	Y	Y	Y
8	**Bucshon**	Y	Y	Y	Y	Y	Y
9	**Hollingsworth**	Y	Y	Y	Y	N	Y
IOWA							
1	Finkenauer	Y	Y	Y	Y	Y	Y
2	Loebsack	Y	Y	Y	Y	Y	Y
3	Axne	Y	Y	Y	Y	Y	Y
4	**King, S.**	Y	Y	Y	Y	Y	N
KANSAS							
1	**Marshall**	Y	Y	N	Y	N	N
2	**Watkins**	Y	Y	N	Y	N	N
3	Davids	?	Y	Y	Y	Y	Y
4	**Estes**	N	Y	Y	N	Y	N
KENTUCKY							
1	**Comer**	N	N	N	N	N	N
2	**Guthrie**	Y	Y	Y	Y	Y	Y
3	Yarmuth	Y	Y	Y	Y	Y	Y
4	**Massie**	Y	Y	N	Y	N	N
5	**Rogers, H.**	Y	Y	Y	Y	Y	Y
6	**Barr**	Y	Y	Y	Y	N	N
LOUISIANA							
1	**Scalise**	N	N	Y	N	N	N
2	Richmond	Y	Y	Y	Y	Y	Y
3	**Higgins, C.**	Y	Y	Y	Y	Y	N
4	**Johnson, M.**	Y	Y	Y	Y	Y	Y
5	**Abraham**	?	?	?	?	?	?
6	**Graves, G.**	Y	Y	Y	Y	Y	Y
MAINE							
1	Pingree	Y	Y	Y	Y	Y	Y
2	Golden	Y	Y	Y	Y	Y	Y
MARYLAND							
1	**Harris**	N	N	N	N	N	N
2	Ruppersberger	Y	Y	Y	Y	Y	Y
3	Sarbanes	Y	Y	Y	Y	Y	Y
4	Brown, A.	Y	Y	Y	Y	Y	Y
5	Hoyer	Y	Y	Y	Y	Y	Y
6	Trone	Y	Y	Y	Y	Y	Y
7	Cummings	Y	Y	Y	Y	Y	Y
8	Raskin						
MASSACHUSETTS		Y	Y	Y	Y	Y	Y
1	Neal						
2	McGovern	Y	Y	Y	Y	Y	Y
3	Trahan	Y	Y	Y	Y	Y	Y
4	Kennedy	Y	Y	Y	Y	Y	Y
5	Clark	Y	Y	Y	Y	Y	Y
6	Moulton	Y	Y	Y	Y	Y	Y
7	Pressley	Y	Y	Y	Y	Y	Y
8	Lynch	Y	Y	Y	Y	Y	Y
9	Keating	Y	Y	Y	Y	Y	Y
MICHIGAN		Y	Y	Y	Y	Y	Y
1	**Bergman**						
2	**Huizenga**	Y	Y	Y	Y	Y	Y
3	**Amash**	N	Y	Y	Y	N	Y
4	**Moolenaar**	N	N	N	N	N	N
5	Kildee	Y	Y	Y	Y	Y	N
6	**Upton**	Y	Y	Y	Y	Y	Y
7	**Walberg**	Y	Y	Y	Y	Y	Y
8	Slotkin	Y	Y	Y	Y	Y	N
9	Levin	Y	Y	Y	Y	Y	Y
10	**Mitchell**	Y	Y	Y	Y	Y	Y
11	Stevens	Y	Y	Y	Y	Y	Y
12	Dingell	Y	Y	Y	Y	Y	Y
13	Tlaib	Y	Y	Y	Y	Y	Y
14	Lawrence	Y	Y	Y	Y	Y	Y
MINNESOTA		Y	Y	Y	Y	Y	Y
1	**Hagedorn**						
2	Craig	Y	Y	Y	Y	N	Y
3	Phillips	Y	Y	Y	Y	Y	Y
4	McCollum	Y	Y	Y	Y	Y	Y
5	Omar	Y	Y	Y	Y	Y	Y

		307	308	309	310	311	312
6	**Emmer**	Y	Y	Y	+	Y	Y
7	Peterson	N	Y	Y	Y	N	Y
8	**Stauber**	Y	Y	Y	Y	Y	Y
MISSISSIPPI		Y	Y	Y	Y	Y	Y
1	**Kelly, T.**						
2	Thompson, B.	Y	Y	N	Y	N	N
3	**Guest**	Y	Y	Y	Y	Y	Y
4	**Palazzo**	N	Y	Y	Y	Y	Y
MISSOURI		Y	Y	Y	Y	Y	N
1	Clay						
2	**Wagner**	Y	Y	Y	Y	Y	Y
3	**Luetkemeyer**	N	N	Y	Y	N	Y
4	**Hartzler**	N	Y	Y	Y	Y	Y
5	Cleaver	Y	Y	Y	Y	Y	Y
6	**Graves, S.**	Y	?	Y	Y	Y	Y
7	**Long**	Y	Y	Y	Y	N	N
8	**Smith, J.**	Y	Y	Y	Y	N	N
MONTANA		Y	Y	Y	Y	N	N
AL	**Gianforte**						
NEBRASKA		?	?	?	?	?	?
1	**Fortenberry**						
2	**Bacon**	Y	Y	Y	Y	Y	N
3	**Smith, Adrian**	Y	Y	Y	Y	Y	Y
NEVADA		Y	Y	Y	Y	N	Y
1	Titus						
2	**Amodei**	Y	Y	Y	Y	Y	Y
3	Lee	Y	Y	Y	Y	Y	Y
4	Horsford	Y	Y	Y	Y	Y	Y
NEW HAMPSHIRE		Y	Y	Y	Y	Y	Y
1	Pappas						
2	Kuster	Y	Y	Y	Y	Y	Y
NEW JERSEY		Y	Y	Y	Y	Y	Y
1	Norcross						
2	Van Drew	Y	Y	Y	Y	Y	Y
3	Kim	Y	Y	Y	Y	Y	Y
4	**Smith, C.**	Y	Y	Y	Y	Y	Y
5	Gottheimer	?	?	?	?	?	?
6	Pallone	Y	Y	Y	Y	Y	Y
7	Malinowski	Y	Y	Y	Y	Y	Y
8	Sires	Y	Y	Y	Y	Y	Y
9	Pascrell	Y	Y	Y	Y	Y	Y
10	Payne	Y	Y	Y	Y	Y	Y
11	Sherrill	Y	Y	Y	Y	Y	Y
12	Watson Coleman	Y	Y	Y	Y	Y	Y
NEW MEXICO		Y	Y	Y	Y	Y	Y
1	Haaland						
2	Torres Small	Y	Y	Y	Y	Y	Y
3	Luján	Y	Y	Y	Y	Y	Y
NEW YORK		Y	Y	Y	Y	Y	Y
1	**Zeldin**						
2	**King, P.**	N	Y	Y	Y	Y	Y
3	Suozzi	Y	Y	Y	Y	Y	Y
4	Rice, K.	Y	Y	Y	Y	Y	Y
5	Meeks	Y	Y	Y	Y	Y	Y
6	Meng	Y	Y	Y	Y	Y	Y
7	Velázquez	Y	Y	Y	Y	Y	Y
8	Jeffries	Y	Y	Y	Y	Y	Y
9	Clarke	Y	Y	Y	Y	Y	Y
10	Nadler	Y	Y	Y	Y	Y	Y
11	Rose	Y	Y	Y	Y	Y	Y
12	Maloney, C.	Y	Y	Y	Y	Y	Y
13	Espaillat	Y	Y	Y	Y	Y	Y
14	Ocasio-Cortez	Y	Y	Y	Y	Y	Y
15	Serrano	Y	Y	Y	Y	Y	Y
16	Engel	Y	Y	Y	?	Y	Y
17	Lowey	Y	Y	Y	Y	Y	Y
18	Maloney, S.P.	Y	Y	Y	Y	Y	Y
19	Delgado	Y	Y	Y	Y	Y	Y
20	Tonko	Y	Y	Y	Y	Y	Y
21	**Stefanik**	Y	Y	Y	Y	Y	Y
22	Brindisi	Y	Y	Y	Y	Y	Y
23	**Reed**	Y	Y	Y	Y	Y	Y
24	**Katko**	Y	Y	Y	Y	Y	Y
25	Morelle	Y	Y	Y	Y	Y	Y
26	Higgins, B.	Y	Y	Y	Y	Y	Y
27	**Collins, C.**	Y	Y	Y	Y	Y	Y
NORTH CAROLINA		Y	Y	Y	Y	Y	Y
1	Butterfield						
2	**Holding**	Y	Y	Y	Y	Y	Y
3	**Jones***	N	Y	Y	N	N	N
4	Price						
5	**Foxx**	Y	Y	Y	Y	Y	Y
6	**Walker**	Y	Y	Y	Y	N	Y
7	**Rouzer**	N	N	Y	Y	N	N

		307	308	309	310	311	312
8	**Hudson**	Y	Y	Y	Y	N	N
9	vacant	Y	Y	Y	Y	Y	Y
10	**McHenry**	Y	Y	Y	Y	Y	Y
11	**Meadows**	Y	Y	Y	Y	N	N
12	Adams	Y	Y	Y	Y	Y	Y
13	**Budd**	N	N	?	Y	N	N
NORTH DAKOTA							
AL	**Armstrong**	Y	Y	Y	Y	N	Y
OHIO							
1	**Chabot**	Y	Y	Y	Y	N	Y
2	**Wenstrup**	Y	Y	Y	Y	N	N
3	Beatty	Y	Y	Y	Y	Y	Y
4	**Jordan**	Y	Y	N	N	N	N
5	**Latta**	Y	Y	Y	Y	N	N
6	**Johnson, B.**	Y	Y	Y	Y	N	N
7	**Gibbs**	Y	Y	Y	Y	N	N
8	**Davidson**	N	N	N	N	N	N
9	Kaptur	Y	Y	Y	Y	Y	Y
10	**Turner**	Y	Y	Y	Y	Y	Y
11	Fudge	Y	Y	Y	Y	Y	Y
12	**Balderson**	Y	Y	Y	Y	Y	N
13	Ryan	Y	Y	Y	Y	Y	Y
14	**Joyce**	Y	Y	Y	Y	Y	N
15	**Stivers**	Y	Y	Y	Y	Y	Y
16	**Gonzalez**	Y	Y	Y	Y	Y	Y
OKLAHOMA							
1	**Hern**	N	N	Y	N	N	N
2	**Mullin**	Y	Y	Y	Y	Y	Y
3	**Lucas**	Y	Y	Y	Y	Y	Y
4	**Cole**	Y	Y	Y	Y	Y	Y
5	Horn	Y	Y	Y	Y	Y	Y
OREGON							
1	Bonamici	Y	Y	Y	Y	Y	Y
2	**Walden**	Y	Y	Y	Y	Y	Y
3	Blumenauer	Y	Y	Y	Y	Y	Y
4	DeFazio	Y	Y	Y	Y	Y	Y
5	Schrader	Y	Y	Y	Y	Y	Y
PENNSYLVANIA							
1	**Fitzpatrick**	Y	Y	Y	Y	Y	Y
2	Boyle	Y	Y	Y	Y	Y	Y
3	Evans	Y	Y	Y	Y	Y	Y
4	Dean	Y	Y	Y	Y	Y	Y
5	Scanlon	Y	Y	Y	Y	Y	Y
6	Houlahan	Y	Y	Y	Y	Y	Y
7	Wild	Y	Y	Y	Y	Y	Y
8	Cartwright	Y	Y	Y	Y	Y	Y
9	**Meuser**	N	Y	Y	Y	N	N
10	**Perry**	Y	Y	Y	Y	Y	N
11	**Smucker**	Y	Y	Y	Y	Y	Y
12	**Marino***						
13	**Joyce**	+	+	+	+	+	+
14	**Reschenthaler**	Y	Y	Y	Y	Y	Y
15	**Thompson, G.**	Y	Y	Y	Y	Y	Y
16	**Kelly, M.**	Y	Y	Y	Y	Y	Y
17	Lamb	Y	Y	Y	Y	Y	Y
18	Doyle	?	?	?	?	?	?
RHODE ISLAND							
1	Cicilline	Y	Y	Y	Y	Y	Y
2	Langevin	Y	Y	Y	Y	Y	Y
SOUTH CAROLINA							
1	Cunningham	Y	Y	Y	Y	Y	Y
2	**Wilson, J.**	N	Y	Y	Y	N	Y
3	**Duncan**	Y	Y	N	N	N	N
4	**Timmons**	Y	Y	Y	Y	N	Y
5	**Norman**	N	N	Y	N	N	N
6	Clyburn	Y	Y	Y	Y	Y	Y
7	**Rice, T.**	N	N	N	N	N	N
SOUTH DAKOTA							
AL	**Johnson**	Y	Y	Y	Y	N	Y
TENNESSEE							
1	**Roe**	Y	Y	Y	Y	Y	Y
2	**Burchett**	N	N	Y	Y	N	N
3	**Fleischmann**	Y	Y	Y	Y	N	Y
4	**DesJarlais**	Y	Y	Y	Y	Y	Y
5	Cooper	Y	Y	Y	Y	Y	Y
6	**Rose**	N	Y	N	Y	N	N
7	**Green**	?	?	?	?	?	?
8	**Kustoff**	N	Y	Y	Y	N	Y
9	Cohen	Y	Y	Y	Y	Y	Y
TEXAS							
1	**Gohmert**	N	Y	N	Y	N	N
2	**Crenshaw**	Y	Y	Y	Y	Y	Y
3	**Taylor**	Y	N	Y	Y	Y	Y
4	**Ratcliffe**	N	Y	Y	Y	N	N

		307	308	309	310	311	312
5	**Gooden**	N	N	Y	N	N	N
6	**Wright**	?	?	?	?	?	?
7	Fletcher	Y	Y	Y	Y	Y	Y
8	**Brady**	Y	N	Y	Y	N	N
9	Green, A.	Y	Y	Y	Y	Y	Y
10	**McCaul**	Y	Y	Y	Y	Y	Y
11	**Conaway**	N	Y	Y	Y	N	N
12	**Granger**	Y	Y	Y	Y	N	N
13	**Thornberry**	Y	Y	Y	Y	N	N
14	**Weber**	N	Y	N	Y	N	N
15	Gonzalez	Y	Y	Y	Y	Y	Y
16	Escobar	Y	Y	Y	Y	Y	Y
17	**Flores**	Y	Y	N	Y	Y	N
18	Jackson Lee	Y	Y	Y	Y	Y	Y
19	**Arrington**	N	N	N	N	N	N
20	Castro	Y	Y	Y	Y	Y	Y
21	**Roy**	N	N	N	N	N	N
22	**Olson**	N	Y	Y	Y	N	N
23	**Hurd**	Y	Y	Y	Y	Y	Y
24	**Marchant**	N	Y	N	Y	N	N
25	**Williams**	Y	Y	Y	Y	N	N
26	**Burgess**	Y	Y	N	Y	N	N
27	**Cloud**	Y	Y	Y	Y	N	N
28	Cuellar	Y	Y	Y	Y	Y	Y
29	Garcia, S.	Y	Y	Y	Y	Y	Y
30	Johnson, E.B.	Y	Y	Y	Y	Y	Y
31	**Carter, J.**	N	Y	N	Y	N	N
32	Allred	Y	Y	Y	Y	Y	Y
33	Veasey	Y	Y	Y	Y	Y	Y
34	Vela	Y	Y	Y	Y	Y	Y
35	Doggett	Y	Y	Y	Y	Y	Y
36	**Babin**	N	Y	N	Y	N	N
UTAH							
1	**Bishop, R.**	Y	Y	N	Y	N	N
2	**Stewart**	Y	Y	Y	Y	N	N
3	**Curtis**	Y	Y	Y	Y	N	N
4	McAdams	Y	Y	Y	Y	Y	Y
VERMONT							
AL	Welch	Y	Y	Y	Y	Y	Y
VIRGINIA							
1	**Wittman**	Y	Y	N	Y	N	N
2	Luria	Y	Y	Y	Y	Y	Y
3	Scott, R.	Y	Y	Y	Y	Y	Y
4	McEachin	Y	Y	Y	Y	Y	Y
5	**Riggleman**	Y	Y	Y	Y	N	Y
6	**Cline**	Y	Y	N	Y	N	N
7	Spanberger	Y	Y	Y	Y	Y	Y
8	Beyer	Y	Y	Y	Y	Y	Y
9	**Griffith**	Y	Y	N	Y	N	N
10	Wexton	Y	Y	Y	Y	Y	Y
11	Connolly	Y	Y	Y	Y	Y	Y
WASHINGTON							
1	DelBene	Y	Y	Y	Y	Y	Y
2	Larsen	Y	Y	Y	Y	Y	Y
3	**Herrera Beutler**	?	?	?	?	?	?
4	**Newhouse**	Y	Y	Y	Y	Y	Y
5	**McMorris Rodgers**	Y	Y	Y	Y	Y	Y
6	Kilmer	Y	Y	Y	Y	Y	Y
7	Jayapal	Y	Y	Y	Y	Y	Y
8	Schrier	Y	Y	Y	Y	Y	Y
9	Smith Adam	Y	Y	Y	Y	Y	Y
10	Heck	Y	Y	Y	Y	Y	Y
WEST VIRGINIA							
1	**McKinley**	Y	Y	Y	Y	Y	N
2	**Mooney**	N	Y	Y	Y	Y	N
3	**Miller**	Y	Y	Y	Y	Y	N
WISCONSIN							
1	**Steil**	Y	Y	Y	Y	N	Y
2	Pocan	Y	Y	Y	Y	Y	Y
3	Kind	Y	Y	Y	Y	Y	Y
4	Moore	Y	Y	Y	Y	Y	Y
5	**Sensenbrenner**	Y	N	Y	N	N	N
6	**Grothman**	N	Y	Y	Y	N	N
7	**Duffy**	Y	N	Y	Y	N	N
8	**Gallagher**	Y	Y	Y	Y	N	Y
WYOMING							
AL	**Cheney**	N	Y	Y	Y	N	N
DELEGATES							
	Radewagen (A.S.)	?	?	?	?	?	?
	Norton (D.C.)	Y	Y	?	Y	Y	Y
	San Nicolas (Guam)	?	?	?	?	?	?
	Sablan (N. Marianas)	?	?	?	?	?	?
	González-Colón (P.R.)	Y	Y	Y	Y	Y	Y
	Plaskett (V.I.)	?	?	?	?	?	?

313. HR2740. Fiscal 2020 Four-Bill Appropriations Package - ACA Enrollment Data. Porter, D-Calif., amendment that would require the Health and Human Services Department, in its report to Congress on enrollment figures for Affordable Care Act health insurance marketplaces, to detail enrollments by state, disaggregated by race, ethnicity, preferred language, age, and sex. Adopted in Committee of the Whole 235-183: R 7-183; D 228-0. June 13, 2019.

314. HR2740. Fiscal 2020 Four-Bill Appropriations Package - Minority Population HIV/AIDS Initiatives. Mucarsel-Powell, D-Fla., amendment that would increase by $5 million funding allocated for initiatives to prevent and treat HIV/AIDS in minority populations, from Health and Human Services Department administrative funding authorized by the bill. Adopted in Committee of the Whole 281-138: R 52-138; D 229-0. June 13, 2019.

315. HR2740. Fiscal 2020 Four-Bill Appropriations Package - Education Department Inspector General Office. Levin, D-Mich., amendment that would increase by $4 million funding for the Education Department Office of the Inspector General and decrease by the same amount funding for the Labor Department Office of Labor-Management Standards salaries and expenses. Adopted in Committee of the Whole 233-187: R 4-186; D 229-1. June 13, 2019.

316. HR2740. Fiscal 2020 Four-Bill Appropriations Package - Primary Health Care Programs. Pressley, D-Mass., amendment that would increase by $5 million funding for Health and Human Services Department primary health care programs and decrease by the same amount administrative funding for the Centers for Medicare and Medicaid Services. Adopted in Committee of the Whole 342-77: R 113-77; D 229-0. June 13, 2019.

317. HR2740. Fiscal 2020 Four-Bill Appropriations Package - Chronic Disease Prevention and Health Promotion. Spanberger, D-Va., amendment that would increase by $3 million funding for chronic disease prevention and health promotion, and would decrease by the same amount, funding for general department management for the Health and Human Service Department. Adopted in Committee of the Whole 364-54: R 136-54; D 228-0. June 13, 2019.

318. HR2740. Fiscal 2020 Four-Bill Appropriations Package - Emerging and Zoonotic Infectious Diseases. Delgado, D-N.Y., amendment that would increase by $1 million funding for Center for Disease Control and Prevention activities related to emerging and zoonotic infectious diseases and decrease by the same amount administrative funding for the Health and Human Services Department. Adopted in Committee of the Whole 374-44: R 146-43; D 228-1. June 13, 2019.

		313	314	315	316	317	318
ALABAMA							
1	**Byrne**	N	N	N	N	Y	N
2	**Roby**	N	Y	N	Y	Y	Y
3	**Rogers, M.**	N	N	N	Y	Y	Y
4	**Aderholt**	N	Y	N	Y	Y	Y
5	**Brooks, M.**	N	N	N	N	N	N
6	**Palmer**	N	N	N	N	Y	Y
7	Sewell	Y	Y	Y	Y	Y	Y
ALASKA							
AL	**Young**	N	Y	N	Y	Y	Y
ARIZONA							
1	O'Halleran	Y	Y	Y	Y	Y	Y
2	Kirkpatrick	Y	Y	Y	Y	Y	Y
3	Grijalva	Y	Y	Y	Y	Y	Y
4	**Gosar**	N	N	N	N	N	N
5	**Biggs**	N	N	N	N	N	N
6	**Schweikert**	N	Y	Y	N	N	N
7	Gallego	Y	Y	Y	Y	Y	Y
8	**Lesko**	N	N	N	N	N	Y
9	Stanton	Y	Y	Y	Y	Y	Y
ARKANSAS							
1	**Crawford**	N	N	N	Y	Y	Y
2	**Hill, F.**	N	N	N	Y	Y	Y
3	**Womack**	N	N	N	Y	Y	Y
4	**Westerman**	N	N	N	N	Y	Y
CALIFORNIA							
1	**LaMalfa**	N	N	N	Y	Y	Y
2	Huffman	Y	Y	Y	Y	Y	Y
3	Garamendi	Y	Y	Y	Y	Y	Y
4	**McClintock**	N	N	N	Y	Y	Y
5	Thompson, M.	Y	Y	Y	Y	Y	Y
6	Matsui	Y	Y	Y	Y	Y	Y
7	Bera	Y	Y	Y	Y	Y	Y
8	**Cook**	N	Y	N	Y	Y	Y
9	McNerney	Y	Y	Y	Y	Y	Y
10	Harder	Y	Y	Y	Y	Y	Y
11	DeSaulnier	Y	Y	Y	Y	Y	Y
12	Pelosi						
13	Lee B.	Y	Y	Y	Y	Y	Y
14	Speier	Y	Y	Y	Y	Y	Y
15	Swalwell	+	+	+	+	+	+
16	Costa	Y	Y	Y	Y	Y	Y
17	Khanna	Y	Y	Y	Y	Y	Y
18	Eshoo	Y	Y	Y	Y	Y	Y
19	Lofgren	Y	Y	Y	P	Y	Y
20	Panetta	Y	Y	Y	Y	Y	Y
21	Cox	Y	Y	Y	Y	Y	Y
22	**Nunes**	N	Y	N	Y	Y	Y
23	**McCarthy**	N	Y	N	Y	Y	Y
24	Carbajal	Y	Y	Y	Y	Y	Y
25	Hill, K.	Y	Y	Y	Y	Y	Y
26	Brownley	Y	Y	Y	Y	Y	Y
27	Chu	Y	Y	Y	Y	Y	Y
28	Schiff	Y	Y	Y	Y	Y	Y
29	Cárdenas	Y	Y	Y	Y	Y	Y
30	Sherman	Y	Y	Y	Y	Y	Y
31	Aguilar	Y	Y	Y	Y	Y	Y
32	Napolitano	Y	Y	Y	Y	Y	Y
33	Lieu	Y	Y	Y	Y	Y	Y
34	Gomez	Y	Y	Y	Y	Y	Y
35	Torres	Y	Y	Y	Y	Y	Y
36	Ruiz	Y	Y	Y	Y	Y	Y
37	Bass	Y	Y	Y	Y	Y	Y
38	Sánchez	Y	Y	Y	Y	Y	Y
39	Cisneros	Y	Y	Y	Y	Y	Y
40	Roybal-Allard	Y	Y	Y	Y	Y	Y
41	Takano	Y	Y	Y	Y	Y	Y
42	**Calvert**	N	Y	N	Y	Y	Y
43	Waters	Y	Y	Y	Y	Y	Y
44	Barragán	Y	Y	Y	Y	Y	Y
45	**Porter**	Y	Y	Y	Y	Y	Y
46	Correa	Y	Y	Y	Y	Y	Y
47	Lowenthal	Y	Y	Y	Y	Y	Y
48	Rouda	Y	Y	Y	Y	Y	Y
49	Levin	Y	Y	Y	Y	Y	Y
50	**Hunter**	N	N	N	N	N	Y
51	Vargas	Y	Y	Y	Y	Y	Y
52	Peters	Y	Y	Y	Y	Y	Y
53	Davis, S.	Y	Y	Y	Y	Y	Y
COLORADO							
1	DeGette	Y	Y	Y	Y	Y	Y
2	Neguse	Y	Y	Y	Y	Y	Y
3	**Tipton**	N	N	N	Y	Y	Y
4	**Buck**	?	?	?	?	?	?
5	**Lamborn**	N	N	N	N	Y	Y
6	Crow	Y	Y	Y	Y	Y	Y
7	Perlmutter	Y	Y	Y	Y	Y	Y
CONNECTICUT							
1	Larson	Y	Y	Y	Y	Y	Y
2	Courtney	Y	Y	Y	Y	Y	Y
3	DeLauro	Y	Y	Y	Y	Y	Y
4	Himes	Y	Y	Y	Y	Y	Y
5	Hayes	+	+	+	+	+	+
DELAWARE							
AL	Blunt Rochester	Y	Y	Y	Y	Y	Y
FLORIDA							
1	**Gaetz**	N	N	N	Y	Y	Y
2	**Dunn**	N	N	N	Y	Y	Y
3	**Yoho**	N	N	N	N	N	N
4	**Rutherford**	N	N	N	Y	Y	Y
5	Lawson	Y	Y	Y	Y	Y	Y
6	**Waltz**	N	Y	N	Y	Y	Y
7	Murphy	Y	Y	Y	Y	Y	Y
8	**Posey**	N	N	N	N	Y	Y
9	Soto	Y	Y	Y	Y	Y	Y
10	Demings	Y	Y	Y	Y	Y	Y
11	**Webster**	N	N	N	N	N	N
12	**Bilirakis**	N	Y	N	Y	Y	Y
13	Crist	Y	Y	Y	Y	Y	Y
14	Castor	Y	Y	Y	Y	Y	Y
15	**Spano**	N	N	N	Y	Y	Y
16	**Buchanan**	N	N	N	Y	Y	Y
17	**Steube**	N	N	N	Y	Y	Y
18	**Mast**	N	N	N	Y	Y	Y
19	**Rooney**	N	N	N	N	Y	N
20	Hastings	?	?	?	?	?	?
21	Frankel	Y	Y	Y	Y	Y	Y
22	Deutch	+	Y	Y	Y	Y	Y
23	Wasserman Schultz	Y	Y	Y	Y	Y	Y
24	Wilson, F.	Y	Y	Y	Y	Y	Y
25	**Diaz-Balart**	N	Y	N	Y	Y	Y
26	Mucarsel-Powell	Y	Y	Y	Y	Y	Y
27	Shalala	Y	Y	Y	Y	Y	Y
GEORGIA							
1	**Carter, E.L.**	N	N	N	N	N	N
2	Bishop, S.	Y	Y	Y	Y	Y	Y
3	**Ferguson**	N	N	N	N	N	Y
4	Johnson, H.	Y	Y	Y	Y	Y	Y
5	Lewis John	Y	Y	Y	Y	Y	Y
6	McBath	Y	Y	Y	Y	Y	Y
7	**Woodall**	N	N	N	Y	Y	Y
8	**Scott, A.**	N	N	N	N	N	Y
9	**Collins, D.**	N	N	N	N	N	N
10	**Hice**	N	N	N	N	N	N
11	**Loudermilk**	N	N	N	N	N	N
12	**Allen**	N	N	N	N	N	N
13	Scott, D.	Y	Y	Y	Y	Y	Y
14	**Graves, T.**	N	N	N	N	N	N
HAWAII							
1	Case	Y	Y	Y	Y	Y	Y
2	Gabbard	Y	Y	Y	Y	Y	Y
IDAHO							
1	**Fulcher**	N	N	N	N	Y	Y
2	**Simpson**	N	N	N	Y	Y	Y
ILLINOIS							
1	Rush	Y	Y	Y	Y	Y	Y
2	Kelly, R.	Y	Y	Y	Y	Y	Y
3	Lipinski	Y	Y	Y	Y	Y	Y
4	García, J.	Y	Y	Y	Y	Y	Y
5	Quigley	Y	Y	N	Y	Y	Y
6	Casten	Y	Y	Y	Y	Y	Y
7	Davis, D.	Y	?	Y	Y	Y	Y
8	Krishnamoorthi	Y	Y	Y	Y	Y	Y
9	Schakowsky	Y	Y	Y	Y	Y	Y
10	Schneider	Y	Y	Y	Y	Y	Y
11	Foster	Y	Y	Y	Y	Y	Y

	313	314	315	316	317	318
12 **Bost**	?	?	?	?	?	?
13 **Davis, R.**	Y	Y	Y	Y	Y	Y
14 Underwood	+	Y	Y	Y	Y	Y
15 **Shimkus**	N	Y	N	Y	Y	Y
16 **Kinzinger**	N	Y	N	Y	Y	Y
17 Bustos	Y	Y	Y	Y	Y	Y
18 **LaHood**	N	N	N	Y	Y	Y
INDIANA						
1 Visclosky	Y	Y	Y	Y	Y	Y
2 **Walorski**	N	N	N	Y	Y	Y
3 **Banks**	N	N	N	N	N	N
4 **Baird**	N	N	N	Y	Y	Y
5 **Brooks, S.**	N	Y	N	Y	Y	Y
6 **Pence**	N	N	N	Y	Y	Y
7 Carson	Y	Y	Y	Y	Y	Y
8 **Bucshon**	N	N	N	Y	Y	Y
9 **Hollingsworth**	Y	N	N	Y	Y	Y
IOWA						
1 Finkenauer	Y	Y	Y	Y	Y	Y
2 Loebsack	Y	Y	Y	Y	Y	Y
3 Axne	Y	Y	Y	Y	Y	Y
4 **King, S.**	N	N	N	Y	Y	Y
KANSAS						
1 **Marshall**	N	N	N	N	N	N
2 **Watkins**	N	N	N	N	N	N
3 Davids	Y	Y	Y	Y	Y	Y
4 **Estes**	N	N	N	Y	N	N
KENTUCKY						
1 **Comer**	N	N	N	N	N	N
2 **Guthrie**	N	Y	N	Y	Y	Y
3 Yarmuth	Y	Y	Y	Y	Y	Y
4 **Massie**	N	N	N	N	N	Y
5 **Rogers, H.**	N	N	N	Y	Y	Y
6 **Barr**	N	N	N	Y	Y	Y
LOUISIANA						
1 **Scalise**	N	N	N	N	N	Y
2 Richmond	Y	Y	Y	Y	Y	Y
3 **Higgins, C.**	N	N	N	N	Y	N
4 **Johnson, M.**	N	Y	N	Y	Y	Y
5 **Abraham**	?	?	?	?	?	?
6 **Graves, G.**	N	N	N	Y	Y	Y
MAINE						
1 Pingree	Y	Y	Y	Y	Y	Y
2 Golden	Y	Y	Y	Y	Y	Y
MARYLAND						
1 **Harris**	N	N	N	N	N	N
2 Ruppersberger	Y	Y	Y	Y	Y	Y
3 Sarbanes	Y	Y	Y	Y	Y	Y
4 Brown, A.	Y	Y	Y	Y	Y	Y
5 Hoyer	Y	Y	Y	Y	Y	Y
6 Trone	Y	Y	Y	Y	Y	Y
7 Cummings	Y	Y	Y	Y	Y	Y
8 Raskin						
MASSACHUSETTS	Y	Y	Y	Y	Y	Y
1 Neal						
2 McGovern	Y	Y	Y	Y	Y	Y
3 Trahan	Y	Y	Y	Y	Y	Y
4 Kennedy	Y	Y	Y	Y	Y	Y
5 Clark	Y	Y	Y	Y	Y	Y
6 Moulton	Y	Y	Y	Y	Y	Y
7 Pressley	Y	Y	Y	Y	Y	Y
8 Lynch	Y	Y	Y	Y	Y	Y
9 Keating	Y	Y	Y	Y	Y	Y
MICHIGAN	Y	Y	Y	Y	Y	Y
1 **Bergman**						
2 **Huizenga**	N	N	N	Y	Y	Y
3 **Amash**	N	N	N	Y	Y	Y
4 **Moolenaar**	N	N	N	N	N	N
5 Kildee	N	Y	N	Y	Y	Y
6 **Upton**	Y	Y	Y	Y	Y	Y
7 **Walberg**	N	Y	N	Y	Y	Y
8 Slotkin	N	N	N	Y	Y	Y
9 Levin	Y	Y	Y	Y	Y	N
10 **Mitchell**	Y	Y	Y	Y	Y	Y
11 Stevens	N	Y	N	Y	Y	Y
12 Dingell	Y	Y	Y	Y	Y	Y
13 Tlaib	Y	Y	Y	Y	Y	Y
14 Lawrence	Y	Y	Y	Y	Y	Y
MINNESOTA	Y	Y	Y	Y	Y	Y
1 **Hagedorn**						
2 Craig	N	N	N	Y	Y	Y
3 Phillips	Y	Y	Y	Y	Y	Y
4 McCollum	Y	Y	Y	Y	Y	Y
5 Omar	Y	Y	Y	Y	Y	Y

	313	314	315	316	317	318
6 **Emmer**	Y	Y	Y	Y	Y	Y
7 Peterson	N	N	N	N	Y	Y
8 **Stauber**	Y	Y	Y	Y	Y	Y
MISSISSIPPI	N	Y	N	Y	Y	Y
1 **Kelly, T.**						
2 Thompson, B.	N	N	N	N	N	N
3 **Guest**	Y	Y	Y	Y	Y	Y
4 **Palazzo**	N	N	N	Y	Y	Y
MISSOURI	N	N	N	N	Y	Y
1 Clay						
2 **Wagner**	Y	Y	Y	Y	Y	Y
3 **Luetkemeyer**	N	N	N	Y	Y	Y
4 **Hartzler**	N	Y	N	N	Y	Y
5 Cleaver	N	N	Y	Y	Y	Y
6 **Graves, S.**	Y	Y	Y	Y	Y	Y
7 **Long**	N	N	N	N	Y	N
8 **Smith, J.**	N	N	N	Y	Y	Y
MONTANA	N	N	N	N	Y	Y
AL **Gianforte**						
NEBRASKA	?	?	?	?	?	?
1 **Fortenberry**						
2 **Bacon**	N	N	N	Y	Y	Y
3 **Smith, Adrian**	N	Y	N	N	Y	Y
NEVADA	N	N	N	N	N	N
1 Titus						
2 **Amodei**	Y	Y	Y	Y	Y	Y
3 Lee	N	Y	N	Y	Y	Y
4 Horsford	Y	Y	Y	Y	Y	Y
NEW HAMPSHIRE	Y	Y	Y	Y	Y	Y
1 Pappas						
2 Kuster	Y	Y	Y	Y	Y	Y
NEW JERSEY	Y	Y	Y	Y	Y	Y
1 Norcross						
2 Van Drew	Y	Y	Y	Y	Y	Y
3 Kim	Y	Y	Y	Y	Y	Y
4 **Smith, C.**	Y	Y	Y	Y	Y	Y
5 Gottheimer	?	?	?	?	?	?
6 Pallone	Y	Y	Y	Y	Y	Y
7 Malinowski	Y	Y	Y	Y	Y	Y
8 Sires	Y	Y	Y	Y	Y	Y
9 Pascrell	Y	Y	Y	Y	Y	Y
10 Payne	Y	Y	Y	Y	Y	Y
11 Sherrill	Y	Y	Y	Y	Y	Y
12 Watson Coleman	Y	Y	Y	Y	Y	Y
NEW MEXICO	Y	Y	Y	Y	Y	Y
1 Haaland						
2 Torres Small	Y	Y	Y	Y	Y	Y
3 Luján	Y	Y	Y	Y	?	Y
NEW YORK	Y	Y	Y	Y	Y	Y
1 **Zeldin**						
2 **King, P.**	N	N	N	Y	Y	Y
3 Suozzi	N	Y	N	Y	Y	Y
4 Rice, K.	Y	Y	Y	Y	Y	Y
5 Meeks	Y	Y	Y	Y	Y	Y
6 Meng	Y	Y	Y	Y	Y	Y
7 Velázquez	Y	Y	Y	Y	Y	Y
8 Jeffries	Y	Y	Y	Y	?	?
9 Clarke	Y	Y	Y	Y	Y	Y
10 Nadler	Y	Y	Y	Y	Y	Y
11 Rose	Y	Y	Y	Y	Y	Y
12 Maloney, C.	Y	Y	Y	Y	Y	Y
13 Espaillat	Y	Y	Y	Y	Y	Y
14 Ocasio-Cortez	Y	Y	Y	Y	Y	Y
15 Serrano	Y	Y	Y	Y	Y	Y
16 Engel	Y	Y	Y	Y	Y	Y
17 Lowey	Y	Y	Y	Y	Y	Y
18 Maloney, S.P.	Y	Y	Y	Y	Y	Y
19 Delgado	Y	Y	Y	Y	Y	Y
20 Tonko	Y	Y	Y	Y	Y	Y
21 **Stefanik**	Y	Y	Y	Y	Y	Y
22 Brindisi	N	Y	N	Y	Y	Y
23 **Reed**	Y	Y	Y	Y	Y	Y
24 **Katko**	Y	Y	N	Y	Y	Y
25 Morelle	Y	Y	N	Y	Y	Y
26 Higgins, B.	Y	Y	Y	Y	Y	Y
27 **Collins, C.**	Y	Y	Y	Y	Y	Y
NORTH CAROLINA	N	Y	N	Y	Y	Y
1 Butterfield						
2 **Holding**	Y	Y	Y	Y	Y	Y
3 **Jones***	N	N	N	Y	Y	Y
4 Price						
5 **Foxx**	Y	Y	Y	Y	Y	Y
6 **Walker**	N	N	N	N	Y	N
7 **Rouzer**	N	N	N	N	Y	N

	313	314	315	316	317	318
8 **Hudson**	N	Y	N	Y	Y	Y
9 vacant	N	Y	N	Y	Y	Y
10 **McHenry**	N	Y	N	Y	Y	Y
11 **Meadows**	N	N	N	Y	Y	Y
12 Adams	Y	Y	Y	Y	Y	Y
13 **Budd**	N	N	N	N	N	N
NORTH DAKOTA						
AL **Armstrong**	N	N	N	Y	Y	N
OHIO						
1 **Chabot**	N	Y	N	Y	Y	Y
2 **Wenstrup**	N	N	N	N	Y	Y
3 Beatty	Y	Y	Y	Y	Y	Y
4 **Jordan**	N	N	N	N	N	N
5 **Latta**	N	N	N	Y	Y	Y
6 **Johnson, B.**	N	Y	N	Y	Y	Y
7 **Gibbs**	N	N	N	Y	Y	Y
8 **Davidson**	N	N	N	N	N	N
9 Kaptur	Y	Y	Y	Y	Y	Y
10 **Turner**	N	Y	N	Y	Y	Y
11 Fudge	Y	Y	Y	Y	Y	Y
12 **Balderson**	N	N	N	Y	Y	Y
13 Ryan	Y	Y	Y	Y	Y	Y
14 **Joyce**	N	N	N	Y	Y	Y
15 **Stivers**	N	Y	N	Y	Y	Y
16 **Gonzalez**	N	N	N	Y	Y	Y
OKLAHOMA						
1 **Hern**	N	N	N	N	N	Y
2 **Mullin**	N	N	N	Y	Y	Y
3 **Lucas**	N	Y	N	Y	Y	Y
4 **Cole**	N	Y	N	Y	Y	Y
5 Horn	Y	Y	Y	Y	Y	Y
OREGON						
1 Bonamici	Y	Y	Y	Y	Y	Y
2 **Walden**	N	Y	N	Y	Y	Y
3 Blumenauer	Y	Y	Y	Y	Y	Y
4 DeFazio	Y	Y	Y	Y	Y	Y
5 Schrader	Y	Y	Y	Y	Y	Y
PENNSYLVANIA						
1 **Fitzpatrick**	Y	Y	Y	Y	Y	Y
2 Boyle	Y	Y	Y	Y	Y	Y
3 Evans	Y	Y	Y	Y	Y	Y
4 Dean	Y	Y	Y	Y	Y	Y
5 Scanlon	Y	Y	Y	Y	Y	Y
6 Houlahan	Y	Y	Y	Y	Y	Y
7 Wild	Y	Y	Y	Y	Y	Y
8 Cartwright	Y	Y	Y	Y	Y	Y
9 **Meuser**	N	N	N	N	Y	Y
10 **Perry**	N	N	N	Y	Y	Y
11 **Smucker**	N	Y	N	Y	Y	Y
12 **Marino***						
13 **Joyce**	-	-	-	+	+	+
14 **Reschenthaler**	N	Y	N	Y	Y	Y
15 **Thompson, G.**	N	Y	N	Y	Y	Y
16 **Kelly, M.**	Y	Y	N	Y	Y	Y
17 Lamb	Y	Y	Y	Y	Y	Y
18 Doyle	?	?	?	?	?	?
RHODE ISLAND						
1 Cicilline	Y	Y	Y	Y	Y	Y
2 Langevin	Y	Y	Y	Y	Y	Y
SOUTH CAROLINA						
1 Cunningham	Y	Y	Y	Y	Y	Y
2 **Wilson, J.**	N	N	N	Y	N	Y
3 **Duncan**	N	N	N	N	Y	Y
4 **Timmons**	N	N	N	N	N	N
5 **Norman**	N	N	N	N	N	N
6 Clyburn	?	?	?	?	?	?
7 **Rice, T.**	N	N	N	N	N	N
SOUTH DAKOTA						
AL **Johnson**	N	N	N	Y	Y	Y
TENNESSEE						
1 **Roe**	N	Y	N	Y	Y	Y
2 **Burchett**	N	N	N	N	N	N
3 **Fleischmann**	N	N	N	Y	Y	Y
4 **DesJarlais**	N	N	N	Y	Y	Y
5 Cooper	Y	Y	Y	Y	Y	Y
6 **Rose**	N	N	N	N	N	N
7 **Green**	?	?	?	?	?	?
8 **Kustoff**	N	N	N	N	Y	Y
9 Cohen	Y	Y	Y	Y	Y	Y
TEXAS						
1 **Gohmert**	N	N	N	N	Y	Y
2 **Crenshaw**	N	N	N	Y	Y	Y
3 **Taylor**	N	N	N	N	Y	Y
4 **Ratcliffe**	N	N	N	Y	Y	Y

	313	314	315	316	317	318
5 **Gooden**	N	N	N	N	N	Y
6 **Wright**	?	?	?	?	?	?
7 Fletcher	Y	Y	Y	Y	Y	Y
8 **Brady**	N	N	N	N	N	Y
9 Green, A.	Y	Y	Y	Y	Y	Y
10 **McCaul**	N	Y	N	Y	Y	Y
11 **Conaway**	N	N	N	N	N	Y
12 **Granger**	N	N	N	N	Y	Y
13 **Thornberry**	N	N	N	N	Y	Y
14 **Weber**	N	N	N	Y	N	N
15 Gonzalez	Y	Y	Y	Y	Y	Y
16 Escobar	Y	Y	Y	Y	Y	Y
17 **Flores**	N	N	N	Y	Y	Y
18 Jackson Lee	Y	Y	Y	Y	Y	Y
19 **Arrington**	N	N	N	N	N	N
20 Castro	Y	Y	Y	Y	Y	Y
21 **Roy**	N	N	N	N	N	N
22 **Olson**	N	N	N	Y	Y	?
23 **Hurd**	Y	Y	N	Y	Y	Y
24 **Marchant**	N	N	N	Y	Y	Y
25 **Williams**	N	N	N	N	Y	N
26 **Burgess**	N	N	N	Y	N	Y
27 **Cloud**	N	N	N	N	N	Y
28 Cuellar	Y	Y	Y	Y	Y	Y
29 Garcia, S.	Y	Y	Y	Y	Y	Y
30 Johnson, E.B.	Y	Y	Y	Y	Y	Y
31 **Carter, J.**	N	N	N	Y	Y	Y
32 Allred	Y	Y	Y	Y	Y	Y
33 Veasey	Y	Y	Y	Y	Y	Y
34 Vela	Y	Y	Y	Y	Y	Y
35 Doggett	Y	Y	Y	Y	Y	Y
36 **Babin**	N	Y	N	Y	Y	Y
UTAH						
1 **Bishop, R.**	N	N	N	N	N	N
2 **Stewart**	N	N	N	N	Y	N
3 **Curtis**	N	N	N	N	N	N
4 McAdams	Y	Y	Y	Y	Y	Y
VERMONT						
AL Welch	Y	Y	Y	Y	Y	Y
VIRGINIA						
1 **Wittman**	N	N	N	Y	Y	Y
2 Luria	Y	Y	Y	Y	Y	Y
3 Scott, R.	Y	Y	Y	Y	Y	Y
4 McEachin	Y	Y	Y	Y	Y	Y
5 **Riggleman**	N	N	N	Y	Y	Y
6 **Cline**	N	N	N	N	N	N
7 Spanberger	Y	Y	Y	Y	Y	Y
8 Beyer	Y	Y	Y	Y	Y	Y
9 **Griffith**	N	N	N	N	N	Y
10 Wexton	Y	Y	Y	Y	Y	Y
11 Connolly	Y	Y	Y	Y	Y	Y
WASHINGTON						
1 DelBene	Y	Y	Y	Y	Y	Y
2 Larsen	Y	Y	Y	Y	Y	Y
3 **Herrera Beutler**	?	?	?	?	?	?
4 **Newhouse**	N	N	N	Y	Y	Y
5 **McMorris Rodgers**	N	Y	N	Y	Y	Y
6 Kilmer	Y	Y	Y	Y	Y	Y
7 Jayapal	Y	Y	Y	Y	Y	Y
8 Schrier	Y	Y	Y	Y	Y	Y
9 Smith Adam	Y	Y	Y	Y	Y	Y
10 Heck	Y	Y	Y	Y	Y	Y
WEST VIRGINIA						
1 **McKinley**	N	N	N	Y	Y	Y
2 **Mooney**	N	N	N	N	N	Y
3 **Miller**	N	N	N	Y	N	Y
WISCONSIN						
1 **Steil**	N	N	N	Y	Y	Y
2 Pocan	Y	Y	Y	Y	Y	Y
3 Kind	Y	Y	Y	Y	Y	Y
4 Moore	Y	Y	Y	Y	Y	Y
5 **Sensenbrenner**	N	N	N	N	Y	Y
6 **Grothman**	N	N	N	N	N	Y
7 **Duffy**	N	N	N	N	Y	Y
8 **Gallagher**	N	N	N	Y	Y	Y
WYOMING						
AL **Cheney**	N	Y	N	N	Y	Y
DELEGATES						
Radewagen (A.S.)	?	?	?	?	?	?
Norton (D.C.)	Y	Y	Y	Y	Y	Y
San Nicolas (Guam)	?	?	?	?	?	?
Sablan (N. Marianas)	?	?	?	?	?	?
González-Colón (P.R.)	N	Y	N	Y	Y	Y
Plaskett (V.I.)	?	?	?	?	?	?

319. HR2740. Fiscal 2020 Four-Bill Appropriations Package - Community School and School Safety Programs. Crow, D-Colo., amendment that would increase then decrease by $5 million funding for community school and school safety programs. Adopted in Committee of the Whole 345-73: R 117-73; D 228-0. June 13, 2019.

320. HR2740. Fiscal 2020 Four-Bill Appropriations Package - Literacy and Education Programs for Disadvantaged Populations. Houlahan, D-Pa., amendment that would increase then decrease by $1 million funding for certain literacy programs and education programs for disadvantaged populations. Adopted in Committee of the Whole 333-86: R 106-84; D 227-2. June 13, 2019.

321. HR2740. Fiscal 2020 Four-Bill Appropriations Package - Ethics Review for Human Fetal Tissue Research. Pocan, D-Wis., amendment that would prohibit use of funds made available by the bill to convene an ethics advisory board on research grants and projects that propose the use of human fetal tissue. Adopted in Committee of the Whole 225-193: R 0-190; D 225-3. June 13, 2019.

322. HR2740. Fiscal 2020 Four-Bill Appropriations Package - Opioid Alternative Programs. Pascrell, D-N.J., amendment hat would allocate $10 million for programs to implement or study opioid alternatives in emergency departments, from funds authorized by the bill for the Health and Human Services Department. Adopted in Committee of the Whole 382-32: R 156-32; D 226-0. June 13, 2019.

323. HR2740. Fiscal 2020 Four-Bill Appropriations Package - Motion to Rise. Visclosky, D-Ind., motion to rise from the Committee of the Whole. Motion agreed to 317-82: R 110-67; D 206-15; I 1-0. June 18, 2019.

324. HR2740. Fiscal 2020 Four-Bill Appropriations Package - Foreign Aid for Reproductive Health Programs. Lesko, R-Ariz., amendment that would strike from the bill a provision allocating $750 million for family planning and reproductive health programs, including in areas where population growth threatens biodiversity, from funding provided by the bill for U.S. Agency for International Development global health programs. Rejected in Committee of the Whole 188-225: R 186-0; D 2-224; I 0-1. June 18, 2019.

		319	320	321	322	323	324
ALABAMA							
1	**Byrne**	N	N	N	N	N	Y
2	**Roby**	Y	Y	N	Y	?	?
3	**Rogers, M.**	N	N	N	Y	N	Y
4	**Aderholt**	N	N	N	N	N	Y
5	**Brooks, M.**	N	N	N	N	N	Y
6	**Palmer**	N	N	N	Y	N	Y
7	Sewell	Y	Y	Y	Y	Y	N
ALASKA							
AL	**Young**	Y	Y	N	Y	?	Y
ARIZONA							
1	O'Halleran	Y	Y	Y	Y	Y	N
2	Kirkpatrick	Y	Y	Y	Y	Y	N
3	Grijalva	Y	Y	Y	Y	N	N
4	**Gosar**	N	N	N	N	N	Y
5	**Biggs**	N	N	N	N	N	Y
6	**Schweikert**	N	N	N	Y	N	Y
7	Gallego	Y	Y	Y	Y	Y	N
8	**Lesko**	N	Y	N	Y	Y	Y
9	Stanton	Y	Y	Y	Y	Y	N
ARKANSAS							
1	**Crawford**	Y	N	N	Y	Y	Y
2	**Hill, F.**	Y	Y	N	Y	Y	Y
3	**Womack**	Y	Y	N	Y	Y	Y
4	**Westerman**	Y	Y	N	Y	Y	Y
CALIFORNIA							
1	**LaMalfa**	Y	Y	N	Y	Y	Y
2	Huffman	Y	Y	Y	Y	Y	N
3	Garamendi	Y	Y	Y	Y	Y	N
4	**McClintock**	N	Y	N	Y	Y	Y
5	Thompson, M.	Y	Y	Y	Y	Y	N
6	Matsui	Y	Y	Y	Y	Y	N
7	Bera	Y	Y	Y	Y	Y	N
8	**Cook**	Y	Y	?	?	Y	Y
9	McNerney	Y	Y	Y	Y	Y	N
10	Harder	Y	Y	Y	Y	Y	N
11	DeSaulnier	Y	Y	Y	Y	Y	N
12	Pelosi						
13	Lee B.	Y	Y	Y	Y	Y	N
14	Speier	Y	Y	Y	Y	Y	N
15	Swalwell	+	+	+	+	Y	N
16	Costa	Y	Y	Y	Y	Y	N
17	Khanna	Y	Y	Y	Y	Y	N
18	Eshoo	Y	Y	Y	Y	Y	N
19	Lofgren	Y	Y	Y	Y	Y	N
20	Panetta	Y	Y	Y	Y	Y	N
21	Cox	Y	Y	Y	Y	Y	N
22	**Nunes**	Y	Y	N	Y	Y	Y
23	**McCarthy**	Y	Y	N	Y	Y	Y
24	Carbajal	Y	Y	Y	Y	Y	N
25	Hill, K.	Y	Y	Y	Y	Y	N
26	Brownley	Y	Y	Y	Y	?	N
27	Chu	Y	Y	Y	Y	Y	N
28	Schiff	Y	Y	Y	Y	Y	N
29	Cárdenas	Y	Y	Y	Y	Y	N
30	Sherman	Y	Y	Y	Y	Y	N
31	Aguilar	Y	Y	Y	Y	Y	N
32	Napolitano	Y	Y	Y	Y	Y	N
33	Lieu	Y	Y	Y	Y	Y	N
34	Gomez	Y	Y	Y	Y	Y	N
35	Torres	Y	Y	Y	Y	Y	N
36	Ruiz	Y	Y	Y	Y	Y	N
37	Bass	Y	Y	Y	Y	Y	N
38	Sánchez	Y	Y	Y	Y	Y	N
39	Cisneros	Y	Y	Y	Y	N	N
40	Roybal-Allard	Y	Y	Y	Y	Y	N
41	Takano	Y	Y	Y	Y	Y	N
42	**Calvert**	Y	Y	N	Y	Y	Y
43	Waters	Y	Y	Y	N	N	N
44	Barragán	Y	Y	Y	Y	Y	N
45	**Porter**	Y	Y	Y	Y	N	N
46	Correa	Y	Y	Y	Y	Y	N
47	Lowenthal	Y	Y	Y	Y	Y	N
48	Rouda	Y	Y	Y	Y	Y	N
49	Levin	Y	Y	Y	Y	Y	N
50	**Hunter**	N	N	N	Y	?	Y
51	Vargas	Y	Y	Y	Y	Y	N
52	Peters	Y	Y	Y	Y	Y	N

		319	320	321	322	323	324
53	Davis, S.	Y	Y	Y	Y	Y	N
COLORADO							
1	DeGette	Y	Y	Y	Y	N	N
2	Neguse	Y	Y	Y	Y	Y	N
3	**Tipton**	Y	Y	N	Y	Y	Y
4	**Buck**	?	?	?	?	N	Y
5	**Lamborn**	N	N	N	Y	N	Y
6	Crow	Y	Y	Y	Y	Y	N
7	Perlmutter	Y	Y	Y	Y	N	N
CONNECTICUT							
1	Larson	Y	Y	Y	Y	?	N
2	Courtney	Y	Y	Y	Y	Y	N
3	DeLauro	Y	Y	Y	Y	?	-
4	Himes	Y	Y	Y	Y	Y	N
5	Hayes	+	+	+	+	Y	N
DELAWARE							
AL	Blunt Rochester	Y	Y	Y	Y	Y	N
FLORIDA							
1	**Gaetz**	N	N	N	Y	?	?
2	**Dunn**	N	Y	N	Y	?	Y
3	**Yoho**	Y	N	N	N	?	?
4	**Rutherford**	N	N	N	Y	N	Y
5	Lawson	Y	Y	Y	Y	Y	N
6	**Waltz**	Y	Y	N	Y	?	-
7	Murphy	Y	Y	Y	Y	Y	N
8	**Posey**	N	Y	N	N	?	?
9	Soto	Y	Y	Y	Y	Y	N
10	Demings	Y	Y	Y	?	Y	N
11	**Webster**	N	N	N	Y	?	?
12	**Bilirakis**	Y	Y	N	Y	Y	Y
13	Crist	Y	Y	Y	Y	Y	N
14	Castor	Y	Y	Y	Y	Y	N
15	**Spano**	Y	N	N	Y	Y	N
16	**Buchanan**	Y	Y	N	Y	?	Y
17	**Steube**	N	N	N	Y	N	Y
18	**Mast**	Y	N	N	N	Y	Y
19	**Rooney**	N	N	N	N	Y	Y
20	Hastings	?	?	?	?	?	?
21	Frankel	Y	Y	Y	Y	Y	N
22	Deutch	Y	Y	Y	Y	Y	N
23	Wasserman Schultz	Y	Y	Y	Y	Y	N
24	Wilson, F.	Y	Y	Y	Y	Y	N
25	**Diaz-Balart**	Y	N	N	Y	N	Y
26	Mucarsel-Powell	Y	Y	Y	Y	Y	N
27	Shalala	Y	Y	Y	Y	Y	N
GEORGIA							
1	**Carter, E.L.**	N	N	N	Y	N	Y
2	Bishop, S.	Y	Y	Y	Y	Y	N
3	**Ferguson**	N	N	N	Y	N	Y
4	Johnson, H.	Y	Y	Y	Y	N	N
5	Lewis John	Y	Y	Y	Y	N	N
6	McBath	Y	Y	Y	Y	N	N
7	**Woodall**	N	N	N	Y	N	Y
8	**Scott, A.**	N	N	N	Y	N	Y
9	**Collins, D.**	N	N	N	Y	?	Y
10	**Hice**	N	N	N	N	N	Y
11	**Loudermilk**	N	N	N	Y	N	Y
12	**Allen**	N	N	N	Y	N	Y
13	Scott, D.	Y	Y	Y	Y	Y	N
14	**Graves, T.**	N	N	N	N	N	Y
HAWAII							
1	Case	Y	Y	Y	Y	Y	N
2	Gabbard	Y	Y	Y	Y	Y	N
IDAHO							
1	**Fulcher**	N	N	N	Y	N	Y
2	**Simpson**	Y	Y	N	Y	Y	Y
ILLINOIS							
1	Rush	Y	Y	Y	Y	Y	N
2	Kelly, R.	Y	Y	Y	Y	Y	N
3	Lipinski	Y	Y	N	Y	Y	N
4	García, J.	Y	Y	Y	Y	Y	N
5	Quigley	Y	Y	Y	Y	Y	N
6	Casten	Y	Y	Y	Y	Y	N
7	Davis, D.	Y	Y	Y	Y	Y	N
8	Krishnamoorthi	Y	Y	Y	Y	Y	N
9	Schakowsky	Y	Y	Y	Y	Y	N
10	Schneider	Y	Y	Y	Y	Y	N
11	Foster	Y	Y	Y	Y	Y	N

KEY:	Republicans	Democrats	Independents

Y	Voted for (yea)	N	Voted against (nay)	P	Voted "present"
+	Announced for	–	Announced against	?	Did not vote or otherwise
#	Paired for	X	Paired against		make position known

		319	320	321	322	323	324
12	**Bost**	?	?	?	?	Y	Y
13	**Davis, R.**	Y	Y	N	Y	Y	Y
14	Underwood	Y	Y	Y	Y	Y	N
15	**Shimkus**	Y	Y	N	Y	Y	Y
16	**Kinzinger**	Y	Y	N	Y	+	Y
17	Bustos	Y	Y	Y	Y	Y	N
18	**LaHood**	N	Y	N	Y	Y	Y
INDIANA							
1	Visclosky	Y	Y	Y	Y	Y	N
2	**Walorski**	Y	Y	N	Y	Y	Y
3	**Banks**	N	N	N	Y	Y	Y
4	**Baird**	Y	Y	N	Y	Y	Y
5	**Brooks, S.**	Y	Y	N	Y	N	Y
6	**Pence**	Y	Y	N	Y	Y	Y
7	Carson	Y	Y	Y	Y	Y	N
8	**Bucshon**	Y	Y	N	Y	Y	Y
9	**Hollingsworth**	Y	Y	N	Y	Y	Y
IOWA							
1	Finkenauer	Y	Y	Y	Y	Y	N
2	Loebsack	Y	Y	Y	Y	Y	N
3	Axne	Y	Y	Y	Y	?	?
4	**King, S.**	Y	N	N	Y	Y	Y
KANSAS							
1	**Marshall**	N	N	N	N	N	Y
2	**Watkins**	N	N	N	N	Y	Y
3	Davids	Y	Y	Y	Y	Y	N
4	**Estes**	N	N	N	N	N	Y
KENTUCKY							
1	**Comer**	N	N	N	N	N	Y
2	**Guthrie**	Y	Y	N	Y	N	Y
3	Yarmuth	Y	Y	Y	Y	Y	N
4	**Massie**	N	N	N	N	N	Y
5	**Rogers, H.**	Y	Y	N	Y	Y	Y
6	**Barr**	Y	N	N	Y	Y	Y
LOUISIANA							
1	**Scalise**	Y	N	N	Y	N	Y
2	Richmond	Y	Y	Y	Y	Y	N
3	**Higgins, C.**	Y	Y	N	N	Y	Y
4	**Johnson, M.**	Y	Y	N	Y	N	Y
5	**Abraham**	?	?	?	?	?	?
6	**Graves, G.**	Y	Y	N	Y	Y	Y
MAINE							
1	Pingree	Y	Y	Y	Y	Y	N
2	Golden	Y	Y	Y	Y	Y	N
MARYLAND							
1	**Harris**	N	N	N	Y	N	Y
2	Ruppersberger	Y	Y	Y	Y	Y	N
3	Sarbanes	Y	Y	Y	Y	Y	N
4	Brown, A.	Y	Y	Y	Y	Y	N
5	Hoyer	Y	Y	Y	Y	Y	N
6	Trone	Y	Y	Y	Y	Y	N
7	Cummings	Y	Y	Y	Y	Y	N
8	Raskin						
MASSACHUSETTS		Y	Y	Y	Y	Y	N
1	Neal						
2	McGovern	Y	Y	Y	Y	Y	N
3	Trahan	Y	Y	Y	Y	Y	N
4	Kennedy	Y	Y	Y	Y	Y	N
5	Clark	Y	Y	Y	Y	Y	N
6	Moulton	Y	Y	Y	Y	Y	N
7	Pressley	Y	Y	Y	Y	?	?
8	Lynch	Y	Y	Y	Y	Y	-
9	Keating	Y	Y	Y	Y	Y	N
MICHIGAN		Y	Y	Y	Y	Y	N
1	**Bergman**						
2	**Huizenga**	Y	Y	N	Y	Y	Y
3	**Amash**	Y	Y	N	N	N	Y
4	**Moolenaar**	N	N	N	N	N	Y
5	Kildee	Y	Y	N	Y	Y	Y
6	**Upton**	Y	Y	Y	Y	Y	N
7	**Walberg**	Y	Y	N	Y	Y	Y
8	Slotkin	Y	N	N	Y	Y	Y
9	Levin	Y	N	Y	Y	Y	N
10	**Mitchell**	Y	Y	Y	Y	Y	N
11	Stevens	Y	Y	N	Y	Y	Y
12	Dingell	Y	Y	Y	Y	Y	N
13	Tlaib	Y	Y	Y	Y	Y	N
14	Lawrence	Y	Y	Y	Y	Y	N
MINNESOTA		Y	Y	Y	Y	Y	N
1	**Hagedorn**						
2	Craig	Y	Y	N	Y	Y	Y
3	Phillips	Y	Y	Y	Y	Y	N
4	McCollum	Y	Y	Y	Y	Y	N
5	Omar	Y	Y	Y	Y	N	N

		319	320	321	322	323	324
6	**Emmer**	Y	Y	Y	Y	?	?
7	Peterson	Y	Y	N	Y	Y	Y
8	**Stauber**	Y	Y	N	Y	Y	Y
MISSISSIPPI		Y	Y	N	Y	Y	Y
1	**Kelly, T.**						
2	Thompson, B.	N	N	N	N	N	Y
3	**Guest**	Y	Y	Y	Y	Y	N
4	**Palazzo**	Y	Y	N	Y	N	Y
MISSOURI		N	N	N	Y	N	Y
1	Clay						
2	**Wagner**	Y	Y	Y	Y	?	N
3	**Luetkemeyer**	Y	Y	N	Y	Y	Y
4	**Hartzler**	Y	Y	N	?	Y	Y
5	Cleaver	Y	Y	N	Y	Y	Y
6	**Graves, S.**	Y	Y	Y	Y	N	N
7	**Long**	Y	N	N	Y	N	Y
8	**Smith, J.**	Y	N	N	Y	Y	Y
MONTANA		Y	N	N	Y	N	Y
AL	**Gianforte**						
NEBRASKA		?	?	?	?	Y	Y
1	**Fortenberry**						
2	**Bacon**	Y	Y	N	Y	Y	Y
3	**Smith, Adrian**	Y	Y	N	Y	Y	Y
NEVADA		N	N	N	Y	Y	Y
1	Titus						
2	**Amodei**	Y	Y	Y	Y	Y	N
3	Lee	Y	Y	N	Y	Y	Y
4	Horsford	Y	Y	Y	Y	Y	N
NEW HAMPSHIRE		Y	Y	Y	Y	Y	N
1	Pappas						
2	Kuster	Y	Y	Y	Y	Y	N
NEW JERSEY		Y	Y	Y	Y	Y	N
1	Norcross						
2	Van Drew	Y	Y	Y	Y	Y	-
3	Kim	Y	Y	Y	Y	Y	N
4	**Smith, C.**	Y	Y	Y	Y	Y	N
5	Gottheimer	?	?	?	?	Y	Y
6	Pallone	Y	Y	Y	Y	Y	N
7	Malinowski	Y	Y	Y	Y	Y	N
8	Sires	Y	Y	Y	Y	Y	N
9	Pascrell	Y	Y	Y	Y	Y	N
10	Payne	Y	Y	Y	Y	Y	N
11	Sherrill	Y	Y	Y	Y	Y	N
12	Watson Coleman	Y	Y	Y	Y	Y	N
NEW MEXICO		Y	Y	Y	Y	Y	N
1	Haaland						
2	Torres Small	Y	Y	Y	Y	Y	N
3	Luján	Y	Y	Y	Y	Y	N
NEW YORK		Y	Y	Y	Y	Y	N
1	**Zeldin**						
2	**King, P.**	Y	Y	N	Y	Y	Y
3	Suozzi	Y	Y	N	Y	N	Y
4	Rice, K.	Y	Y	?	?	N	N
5	Meeks	Y	Y	Y	Y	Y	N
6	Meng	Y	Y	Y	Y	?	N
7	Velázquez	Y	Y	Y	Y	Y	N
8	Jeffries	?	?	?	?	Y	N
9	Clarke	Y	Y	Y	Y	Y	N
10	Nadler	Y	Y	Y	Y	Y	N
11	Rose	Y	Y	Y	Y	Y	N
12	Maloney, C.	Y	Y	Y	Y	Y	N
13	Espaillat	Y	Y	Y	Y	Y	N
14	Ocasio-Cortez	Y	Y	Y	Y	Y	N
15	Serrano	Y	Y	Y	Y	Y	N
16	Engel	Y	Y	Y	Y	Y	N
17	Lowey	Y	Y	Y	Y	Y	N
18	Maloney, S.P.	Y	Y	Y	Y	Y	N
19	Delgado	Y	Y	Y	Y	Y	N
20	Tonko	Y	Y	Y	Y	Y	N
21	**Stefanik**	Y	Y	Y	Y	Y	N
22	Brindisi	Y	Y	N	Y	Y	Y
23	**Reed**	Y	N	Y	Y	Y	N
24	**Katko**	Y	Y	N	Y	?	?
25	Morelle	Y	Y	N	Y	Y	Y
26	Higgins, B.	Y	Y	Y	Y	Y	N
27	**Collins, C.**	Y	Y	Y	Y	Y	N
NORTH CAROLINA		Y	Y	N	Y	N	Y
1	Butterfield						
2	**Holding**	Y	Y	Y	Y	Y	N
3	**Jones***	Y	N	N	Y	?	?
4	Price						
5	**Foxx**	Y	Y	Y	Y	Y	N
6	**Walker**	Y	N	N	Y	Y	Y
7	**Rouzer**	N	N	N	Y	Y	Y

		319	320	321	322	323	324
8	**Hudson**	Y	N	N	Y	N	Y
9	vacant	Y	Y	N	Y	N	Y
10	**McHenry**	Y	Y	N	Y	Y	Y
11	**Meadows**	Y	Y	N	Y	N	Y
12	Adams	Y	Y	Y	Y	Y	N
13	**Budd**	N	N	N	Y	N	Y
NORTH DAKOTA							
AL	**Armstrong**	Y	Y	N	Y	Y	Y
OHIO							
1	**Chabot**	Y	Y	N	Y	Y	Y
2	**Wenstrup**	Y	N	N	Y	Y	Y
3	Beatty	Y	Y	Y	Y	Y	N
4	**Jordan**	N	N	N	N	N	Y
5	**Latta**	Y	N	N	Y	Y	Y
6	**Johnson, B.**	Y	Y	N	Y	Y	Y
7	**Gibbs**	Y	Y	N	Y	Y	Y
8	**Davidson**	N	N	N	Y	N	Y
9	Kaptur	Y	Y	Y	Y	Y	N
10	**Turner**	Y	Y	N	Y	Y	Y
11	Fudge	Y	Y	Y	Y	Y	N
12	**Balderson**	Y	Y	N	Y	Y	Y
13	Ryan	Y	Y	Y	?	Y	-
14	**Joyce**	Y	Y	N	Y	Y	Y
15	**Stivers**	Y	Y	N	Y	Y	Y
16	**Gonzalez**	Y	Y	N	Y	P	Y
OKLAHOMA							
1	**Hern**	N	N	N	Y	Y	Y
2	**Mullin**	Y	Y	N	Y	Y	Y
3	**Lucas**	Y	Y	N	Y	Y	Y
4	**Cole**	Y	Y	N	Y	Y	Y
5	Horn	Y	Y	Y	Y	Y	N
OREGON							
1	Bonamici	Y	Y	Y	Y	Y	N
2	**Walden**	Y	Y	N	Y	Y	Y
3	Blumenauer	Y	Y	Y	Y	Y	N
4	DeFazio	Y	Y	Y	Y	Y	N
5	Schrader	Y	Y	Y	Y	?	N
PENNSYLVANIA							
1	**Fitzpatrick**	Y	Y	N	Y	Y	Y
2	Boyle	Y	Y	Y	Y	Y	N
3	Evans	Y	Y	Y	Y	Y	N
4	Dean	Y	Y	Y	Y	Y	N
5	Scanlon	Y	Y	Y	Y	Y	N
6	Houlahan	Y	Y	Y	Y	Y	N
7	Wild	Y	Y	Y	Y	N	N
8	Cartwright	Y	Y	Y	Y	Y	N
9	**Meuser**	N	N	N	Y	N	Y
10	**Perry**	Y	Y	N	Y	N	Y
11	**Smucker**	Y	Y	N	Y	?	Y
12	**Marino***						
13	**Joyce**	+	+	N	Y	Y	Y
14	**Reschenthaler**	Y	Y	N	Y	Y	Y
15	**Thompson, G.**	Y	Y	N	Y	Y	Y
16	**Kelly, M.**	Y	Y	N	Y	Y	Y
17	Lamb	Y	Y	Y	Y	Y	N
18	Doyle	?	?	?	?	Y	N
RHODE ISLAND							
1	Cicilline	Y	Y	Y	Y	Y	N
2	Langevin	Y	Y	Y	Y	Y	N
SOUTH CAROLINA							
1	Cunningham	Y	Y	Y	Y	N	N
2	**Wilson, J.**	N	Y	N	Y	Y	Y
3	**Duncan**	N	N	N	N	N	Y
4	**Timmons**	N	N	N	Y	Y	Y
5	**Norman**	N	N	N	N	Y	Y
6	Clyburn	?	?	?	?	Y	N
7	**Rice, T.**	N	N	N	N	Y	Y
SOUTH DAKOTA							
AL	**Johnson**	Y	Y	N	Y	Y	Y
TENNESSEE							
1	**Roe**	Y	Y	N	Y	Y	Y
2	**Burchett**	N	N	N	N	N	Y
3	**Fleischmann**	Y	Y	N	Y	Y	Y
4	**DesJarlais**	Y	Y	N	Y	?	?
5	Cooper	Y	Y	Y	Y	Y	N
6	**Rose**	N	N	N	Y	N	Y
7	**Green**	?	?	?	?	N	Y
8	**Kustoff**	Y	N	N	Y	Y	Y
9	Cohen	Y	Y	Y	Y	Y	N
TEXAS							
1	**Gohmert**	N	N	N	N	N	Y
2	**Crenshaw**	Y	Y	N	Y	Y	Y
3	**Taylor**	Y	Y	N	Y	N	Y
4	**Ratcliffe**	N	N	N	Y	N	Y

		319	320	321	322	323	324
5	**Gooden**	N	N	N	N	N	Y
6	**Wright**	?	?	?	?	N	Y
7	Fletcher	Y	Y	Y	Y	Y	N
8	**Brady**	N	Y	N	Y	Y	Y
9	Green, A.	Y	Y	Y	Y	Y	N
10	**McCaul**	Y	Y	N	Y	Y	Y
11	**Conaway**	N	N	N	Y	Y	Y
12	**Granger**	N	Y	N	Y	N	Y
13	**Thornberry**	N	N	N	Y	Y	Y
14	**Weber**	Y	N	N	Y	N	Y
15	Gonzalez	Y	Y	Y	Y	?	?
16	Escobar	Y	Y	Y	Y	Y	N
17	**Flores**	Y	N	N	Y	N	Y
18	Jackson Lee	Y	Y	Y	Y	N	N
19	**Arrington**	N	N	N	N	N	Y
20	Castro	Y	Y	Y	Y	N	N
21	**Roy**	N	N	N	N	N	Y
22	**Olson**	Y	Y	N	Y	N	Y
23	**Hurd**	Y	Y	N	Y	Y	Y
24	**Marchant**	Y	N	N	Y	N	Y
25	**Williams**	Y	Y	N	Y	Y	Y
26	**Burgess**	N	N	N	?	N	Y
27	**Cloud**	N	N	N	Y	N	Y
28	Cuellar	Y	Y	Y	Y	Y	N
29	Garcia, S.	Y	Y	Y	Y	Y	N
30	Johnson, E.B.	Y	Y	Y	Y	N	N
31	**Carter, J.**	Y	Y	N	Y	Y	Y
32	Allred	Y	Y	Y	Y	Y	N
33	Veasey	Y	Y	Y	Y	Y	N
34	Vela	Y	Y	Y	Y	N	N
35	Doggett	Y	Y	Y	Y	?	?
36	**Babin**	Y	N	N	Y	N	Y
UTAH							
1	**Bishop, R.**	N	N	N	Y	?	Y
2	**Stewart**	N	Y	N	Y	N	?
3	**Curtis**	N	Y	N	Y	?	?
4	McAdams	?	Y	N	Y	Y	N
VERMONT							
AL	Welch	Y	Y	Y	Y	N	N
VIRGINIA							
1	**Wittman**	Y	N	N	Y	N	Y
2	Luria	Y	Y	Y	Y	Y	N
3	Scott, R.	Y	Y	Y	Y	Y	N
4	McEachin	Y	Y	Y	Y	Y	N
5	**Riggleman**	Y	Y	N	Y	Y	Y
6	**Cline**	N	N	N	Y	N	Y
7	Spanberger	Y	Y	Y	Y	Y	N
8	Beyer	Y	Y	Y	Y	Y	N
9	**Griffith**	N	N	N	Y	N	Y
10	Wexton	Y	Y	Y	Y	Y	N
11	Connolly	Y	Y	Y	Y	Y	N
WASHINGTON							
1	DelBene	Y	Y	Y	Y	Y	N
2	Larsen	Y	Y	Y	Y	Y	N
3	**Herrera Beutler**	?	?	?	?	?	?
4	**Newhouse**	Y	Y	N	Y	Y	Y
5	**McMorris Rodgers**	Y	Y	N	Y	Y	Y
6	Kilmer	Y	Y	Y	Y	Y	N
7	Jayapal	Y	Y	Y	Y	Y	N
8	Schrier	Y	Y	Y	Y	Y	N
9	Smith Adam	Y	Y	Y	Y	Y	N
10	Heck	Y	Y	Y	Y	Y	N
WEST VIRGINIA							
1	**McKinley**	Y	Y	N	Y	Y	Y
2	**Mooney**	N	N	N	Y	N	Y
3	**Miller**	Y	Y	N	Y	Y	Y
WISCONSIN							
1	**Steil**	Y	Y	N	Y	Y	Y
2	Pocan	Y	Y	Y	Y	Y	N
3	Kind	Y	Y	Y	Y	Y	N
4	Moore	Y	Y	Y	Y	Y	N
5	**Sensenbrenner**	N	N	N	N	Y	Y
6	**Grothman**	N	N	N	Y	Y	Y
7	**Duffy**	N	N	N	Y	?	Y
8	**Gallagher**	Y	Y	N	Y	N	Y
WYOMING							
AL	**Cheney**	N	N	N	N	N	Y
DELEGATES							
	Radewagen (A.S.)	?	?	?	?	?	?
	Norton (D.C.)	Y	Y	Y	Y	?	N
	San Nicolas (Guam)	?	?	?	?	?	?
	Sablan (N. Marianas)	?	?	?	?	Y	N
	González-Colón (P.R.)	Y	Y	N	Y	?	Y
	Plaskett (V.I.)	?	?	?	?	?	N

325. HR2740. Fiscal 2020 Four-Bill Appropriations Package - USAID Global Health Programs. Jackson Lee, D-Texas, amendment that would increase then decrease by $1 million funding for U.S. Agency for International Development global health programs. Adopted in Committee of the Whole 414-6: R 183-6; D 230-0; I 1-0. June 18, 2019.

326. HR2740. Fiscal 2020 Four-Bill Appropriations Package - Wildlife Poaching and Trafficking. Jackson Lee, D-Texas, amendment that would increase then decrease by $1 million funding allocated for State Department programs to combat wildlife poaching and trafficking. Adopted in Committee of the Whole 339-79: R 110-77; D 228-2; I 1-0. June 18, 2019.

327. HR2740. Fiscal 2020 Four-Bill Appropriations Package - International Climate Change Funds. Gosar, R-Ariz., for Luetkemeyer, R-Mo., amendment that would clarify that no funds made available by the bill may be used for contributions on behalf of the U.S. to the Intergovernmental Panel on Climate Change, the U.N. Framework Convention on Climate Change, or the Green Climate Fund. Rejected in Committee of the Whole 174-244: R 173-15; D 1-228; I 0-1. June 18, 2019.

328. HR2740. Fiscal 2020 Four-Bill Appropriations Package - U.S.-Mexico Boundary and Water Projects. Grijalva, D-Ariz., amendment that would decrease then increase by $4 million funding for planning and construction of authorized projects of the U.S.-Mexico International Boundary and Water Commission. Adopted in Committee of the Whole 310-109: R 84-104; D 225-5; I 1-0. June 18, 2019.

329. HR2740. Fiscal 2020 Four-Bill Appropriations Package - U.N. Framework Convention on Climate Change. Gosar, R-Ariz., amendment that would clarify that no funds made available by the bill may be used for the U.N. Framework Convention on Climate Change. Rejected in Committee of the Whole 170-248: R 170-17; D 0-230; I 0-1. June 18, 2019.

330. HR2740. Fiscal 2020 Four-Bill Appropriations Package - Eurasia Economic Assistance. Speier, D-Calif., amendment that would increase then decrease by $40 million funding for State Department economic assistance programs focused on Europe, Eurasia, and Central Asia. Adopted in Committee of the Whole 268-152: R 42-147; D 225-5; I 1-0. June 18, 2019.

		325	326	327	328	329	330
ALABAMA							
1	**Byrne**	Y	N	Y	N	Y	N
2	**Roby**	?	?	?	?	?	?
3	**Rogers, M.**	Y	N	Y	N	Y	N
4	**Aderholt**	Y	Y	Y	N	Y	N
5	**Brooks, M.**	Y	N	N	N	Y	N
6	**Palmer**	Y	N	Y	N	Y	N
7	Sewell	Y	Y	N	Y	N	Y
ALASKA							
AL	**Young**	Y	N	Y	Y	Y	N
ARIZONA							
1	O'Halleran	Y	Y	N	Y	N	Y
2	Kirkpatrick	Y	Y	N	Y	N	Y
3	Grijalva	Y	Y	N	Y	N	Y
4	**Gosar**	Y	N	Y	N	Y	N
5	**Biggs**	Y	N	N	N	Y	N
6	**Schweikert**	Y	Y	Y	Y	Y	Y
7	Gallego	Y	Y	N	Y	N	Y
8	**Lesko**	Y	N	Y	Y	Y	Y
9	Stanton	Y	Y	N	Y	N	Y
ARKANSAS							
1	**Crawford**	Y	Y	Y	N	Y	N
2	**Hill, F.**	Y	Y	Y	N	Y	N
3	**Womack**	Y	Y	Y	Y	Y	N
4	**Westerman**	Y	N	Y	N	Y	N
CALIFORNIA							
1	**LaMalfa**	Y	N	Y	Y	Y	Y
2	Huffman	Y	Y	N	Y	N	Y
3	Garamendi	Y	Y	N	Y	N	Y
4	**McClintock**	N	N	N	Y	N	Y
5	Thompson, M.	Y	Y	N	Y	N	Y
6	Matsui	Y	Y	N	Y	N	Y
7	Bera	Y	Y	N	Y	N	Y
8	**Cook**	Y	Y	Y	Y	Y	N
9	McNerney	Y	Y	N	Y	N	Y
10	Harder	Y	Y	N	Y	N	Y
11	DeSaulnier	Y	Y	N	Y	N	Y
12	Pelosi						
13	Lee B.	Y	Y	N	Y	N	Y
14	Speier	Y	Y	N	Y	N	Y
15	Swalwell	Y	Y	N	Y	N	Y
16	Costa	Y	Y	N	Y	N	Y
17	Khanna	Y	Y	N	Y	N	Y
18	Eshoo	Y	Y	N	Y	N	Y
19	Lofgren	Y	Y	N	Y	N	Y
20	Panetta	Y	Y	N	Y	N	Y
21	Cox	Y	Y	N	Y	N	Y
22	**Nunes**	Y	Y	Y	Y	Y	Y
23	**McCarthy**	Y	Y	Y	N	Y	N
24	Carbajal	Y	Y	N	Y	N	Y
25	Hill, K.	Y	Y	N	Y	N	Y
26	Brownley	Y	Y	N	Y	N	Y
27	Chu	Y	Y	N	Y	N	Y
28	Schiff	Y	Y	N	Y	N	Y
29	Cárdenas	Y	Y	N	Y	N	Y
30	Sherman	Y	Y	N	Y	N	Y
31	Aguilar	Y	Y	N	Y	N	Y
32	Napolitano	Y	Y	N	Y	N	Y
33	Lieu	Y	Y	N	Y	N	Y
34	Gomez	Y	Y	N	Y	N	Y
35	Torres	Y	Y	N	Y	N	Y
36	Ruiz	Y	Y	N	Y	N	Y
37	Bass	Y	Y	N	Y	N	Y
38	Sánchez	Y	Y	N	Y	N	Y
39	Cisneros	Y	Y	N	Y	N	Y
40	Roybal-Allard	Y	Y	N	Y	N	Y
41	Takano	Y	Y	N	Y	N	Y
42	**Calvert**	Y	Y	Y	Y	Y	N
43	Waters	Y	Y	N	Y	N	Y
44	Barragán	Y	Y	N	Y	N	Y
45	Porter	Y	Y	N	Y	N	Y
46	Correa	Y	Y	N	Y	N	Y
47	Lowenthal	Y	Y	N	Y	N	Y
48	Rouda	Y	Y	N	Y	N	Y
49	Levin	Y	Y	N	Y	N	Y
50	**Hunter**	Y	N	Y	N	Y	N
51	Vargas	Y	Y	N	Y	N	Y
52	Peters	Y	Y	N	Y	N	Y
53	Davis, S.	Y	Y	N	Y	N	Y
COLORADO							
1	DeGette	Y	Y	N	Y	N	Y
2	Neguse	Y	Y	N	Y	N	Y
3	**Tipton**	Y	Y	Y	Y	Y	N
4	**Buck**	Y	N	N	N	Y	N
5	**Lamborn**	Y	Y	Y	N	Y	N
6	Crow	Y	Y	N	Y	N	Y
7	Perlmutter	Y	Y	N	Y	N	Y
CONNECTICUT							
1	Larson	Y	Y	N	Y	N	Y
2	Courtney	Y	Y	N	Y	N	Y
3	DeLauro	+	+	-	+	-	+
4	Himes	Y	Y	N	Y	N	Y
5	Hayes	Y	Y	N	Y	N	Y
DELAWARE							
AL	Blunt Rochester	Y	Y	N	Y	N	Y
FLORIDA							
1	**Gaetz**	?	?	?	?	?	?
2	**Dunn**	Y	N	Y	N	Y	N
3	**Yoho**	?	?	?	?	?	?
4	**Rutherford**	Y	N	Y	N	Y	N
5	Lawson	Y	Y	N	Y	N	Y
6	**Waltz**	+	+	+	+	+	-
7	Murphy	Y	Y	N	Y	N	Y
8	**Posey**	?	?	?	?	?	?
9	Soto	Y	Y	N	Y	N	Y
10	Demings	Y	Y	N	Y	N	Y
11	**Webster**	?	?	?	?	?	?
12	**Bilirakis**	Y	Y	Y	Y	Y	Y
13	Crist	Y	Y	N	Y	N	Y
14	Castor	Y	Y	N	Y	N	Y
15	**Spano**	Y	Y	Y	Y	Y	Y
16	**Buchanan**	Y	Y	N	Y	N	N
17	**Steube**	Y	N	Y	N	Y	N
18	**Mast**	Y	N	Y	Y	Y	Y
19	**Rooney**	N	N	N	Y	N	N
20	Hastings	?	?	?	?	?	?
21	Frankel	Y	Y	N	Y	N	Y
22	Deutch	Y	Y	N	Y	N	Y
23	Wasserman Schultz	Y	Y	N	Y	N	Y
24	Wilson, F.	Y	Y	N	Y	N	Y
25	**Diaz-Balart**	Y	Y	Y	N	Y	N
26	Mucarsel-Powell	Y	Y	N	Y	N	Y
27	Shalala	Y	Y	N	Y	N	Y
GEORGIA							
1	**Carter, E.L.**	Y	N	Y	N	Y	N
2	Bishop, S.	Y	Y	?	Y	N	Y
3	**Ferguson**	Y	N	Y	N	Y	N
4	Johnson, H.	Y	Y	N	Y	N	Y
5	Lewis John	Y	Y	N	Y	N	Y
6	McBath	Y	Y	N	Y	N	Y
7	**Woodall**	Y	Y	Y	Y	Y	N
8	**Scott, A.**	Y	N	Y	N	Y	N
9	**Collins, D.**	Y	N	Y	N	Y	N
10	**Hice**	Y	N	N	N	Y	N
11	**Loudermilk**	Y	N	Y	N	Y	N
12	**Allen**	Y	N	Y	N	Y	N
13	Scott, D.	Y	Y	N	Y	N	Y
14	**Graves, T.**	Y	N	Y	N	Y	N
HAWAII							
1	Case	Y	Y	N	Y	N	Y
2	Gabbard	Y	Y	N	Y	N	Y
IDAHO							
1	**Fulcher**	Y	N	Y	Y	Y	Y
2	**Simpson**	Y	Y	Y	Y	Y	Y
ILLINOIS							
1	Rush	Y	Y	N	Y	N	Y
2	Kelly, R.	Y	Y	N	Y	N	Y
3	Lipinski	Y	Y	N	Y	N	Y
4	García, J.	Y	Y	N	Y	N	Y
5	Quigley	Y	Y	N	Y	N	Y
6	Casten	Y	Y	N	Y	N	Y
7	Davis, D.	Y	Y	N	Y	N	Y
8	Krishnamoorthi	Y	Y	N	Y	N	Y
9	Schakowsky	Y	Y	N	Y	N	Y
10	Schneider	Y	Y	N	Y	N	Y
11	Foster	Y	Y	N	Y	N	Y

KEY: Republicans   Democrats   *Independents*

Y Voted for (yea)	**N** Voted against (nay)	**P** Voted "present"
+ Announced for	**–** Announced against	**?** Did not vote or otherwise
# Paired for	**X** Paired against	make position known

		325	326	327	328	329	330
12	**Bost**	Y	Y	Y	N	Y	Y
13	**Davis, R.**	Y	?	Y	Y	N	Y
14	Underwood	Y	Y	N	Y	N	Y
15	**Shimkus**	Y	Y	Y	Y	Y	N
16	**Kinzinger**	Y	Y	N	Y	N	N
17	Bustos	Y	Y	N	Y	N	Y
18	**LaHood**	Y	Y	Y	Y	Y	N
INDIANA							
1	Visclosky	Y	Y	N	Y	N	Y
2	**Walorski**	Y	Y	Y	N	Y	N
3	**Banks**	Y	Y	Y	N	Y	N
4	**Baird**	Y	Y	Y	N	Y	N
5	**Brooks, S.**	Y	Y	N	Y	N	Y
6	**Pence**	Y	Y	Y	Y	Y	N
7	Carson	Y	Y	N	Y	N	Y
8	**Bucshon**	Y	Y	Y	Y	Y	N
9	**Hollingsworth**	Y	Y	N	Y	N	Y
IOWA							
1	Finkenauer	Y	Y	N	Y	N	Y
2	Loebsack	Y	Y	N	Y	N	Y
3	Axne	?	?	?	?	?	?
4	**King, S.**	Y	N	Y	Y	Y	N
KANSAS							
1	**Marshall**	Y	Y	Y	N	Y	N
2	**Watkins**	Y	Y	Y	Y	Y	N
3	Davids	Y	Y	N	Y	N	Y
4	**Estes**	Y	N	Y	Y	Y	N
KENTUCKY							
1	**Comer**	Y	N	Y	N	Y	N
2	**Guthrie**	Y	Y	Y	Y	Y	N
3	Yarmuth	Y	Y	N	Y	N	Y
4	**Massie**	N	N	Y	N	Y	N
5	**Rogers, H.**	Y	Y	Y	Y	Y	N
6	**Barr**	Y	Y	Y	N	Y	N
LOUISIANA							
1	**Scalise**	Y	N	Y	N	Y	N
2	Richmond	Y	Y	N	Y	N	Y
3	**Higgins, C.**	Y	N	Y	N	Y	N
4	**Johnson, M.**	Y	N	Y	N	Y	N
5	**Abraham**	?	?	?	?	?	?
6	**Graves, G.**	Y	Y	Y	Y	Y	Y
MAINE							
1	Pingree	Y	Y	N	Y	N	Y
2	Golden	Y	N	N	Y	N	Y
MARYLAND							
1	**Harris**	Y	N	Y	N	Y	N
2	Ruppersberger	Y	Y	N	Y	N	Y
3	Sarbanes	Y	Y	N	Y	N	Y
4	Brown, A.	Y	Y	N	Y	N	Y
5	Hoyer	Y	Y	N	Y	N	Y
6	Trone	Y	Y	N	Y	N	Y
7	Cummings	Y	Y	N	Y	N	Y
8	Raskin						
MASSACHUSETTS		Y	Y	N	Y	N	Y
1	Neal						
2	McGovern	Y	Y	N	Y	N	Y
3	Trahan	Y	Y	N	Y	N	Y
4	Kennedy	Y	Y	N	Y	N	Y
5	Clark	Y	Y	N	Y	N	Y
6	Moulton	Y	Y	N	Y	N	Y
7	Pressley	?	?	?	?	?	?
8	Lynch	Y	Y	N	Y	N	Y
9	Keating	Y	Y	N	Y	N	Y
MICHIGAN		Y	Y	N	Y	N	Y
1	**Bergman**						
2	**Huizenga**	Y	Y	Y	Y	Y	N
3	**Amash**	Y	Y	Y	Y	Y	N
4	**Moolenaar**	Y	N	Y	Y	Y	N
5	Kildee	Y	Y	N	Y	N	Y
6	**Upton**	Y	Y	N	Y	N	Y
7	**Walberg**	Y	Y	N	Y	N	N
8	Slotkin	Y	N	Y	Y	Y	N
9	Levin	Y	Y	N	N	N	Y
10	**Mitchell**	Y	Y	N	Y	N	Y
11	Stevens	Y	Y	Y	N	Y	N
12	Dingell	Y	Y	N	Y	N	Y
13	Tlaib	Y	Y	N	Y	N	Y
14	Lawrence	Y	Y	N	Y	N	Y
MINNESOTA		Y	Y	N	Y	N	Y
1	**Hagedorn**						
2	Craig	Y	Y	Y	Y	Y	Y
3	Phillips	Y	Y	N	Y	N	N
4	McCollum	Y	Y	N	Y	N	Y
5	Omar	Y	Y	N	Y	N	Y

		325	326	327	328	329	330
6	**Emmer**	Y	Y	N	Y	N	Y
7	Peterson	Y	N	Y	N	Y	N
8	**Stauber**	Y	N	Y	Y	N	Y
MISSISSIPPI		Y	Y	Y	Y	Y	Y
1	**Kelly, T.**						
2	Thompson, B.	Y	N	Y	N	Y	N
3	**Guest**	Y	Y	N	Y	N	Y
4	**Palazzo**	Y	Y	Y	Y	Y	N
MISSOURI		Y	N	Y	N	Y	N
1	Clay						
2	**Wagner**	Y	Y	N	Y	N	Y
3	**Luetkemeyer**	Y	Y	Y	N	Y	Y
4	**Hartzler**	Y	Y	Y	N	Y	N
5	Cleaver	Y	Y	Y	N	Y	Y
6	**Graves, S.**	Y	Y	N	Y	N	Y
7	**Long**	Y	Y	Y	Y	Y	N
8	**Smith, J.**	Y	Y	Y	N	Y	N
MONTANA		Y	N	Y	N	Y	N
AL	**Gianforte**						
NEBRASKA		Y	Y	Y	Y	Y	Y
1	**Fortenberry**						
2	**Bacon**	Y	Y	N	Y	N	Y
3	**Smith, Adrian**	Y	Y	Y	N	N	N
NEVADA		Y	N	Y	N	Y	Y
1	Titus						
2	**Amodei**	Y	Y	N	Y	N	Y
3	Lee	Y	Y	Y	Y	Y	N
4	Horsford	Y	Y	N	Y	N	Y
NEW HAMPSHIRE		Y	Y	N	Y	N	Y
1	Pappas						
2	Kuster	Y	Y	N	Y	N	Y
NEW JERSEY		Y	Y	N	Y	N	Y
1	Norcross						
2	Van Drew	Y	Y	N	Y	N	Y
3	Kim	Y	Y	N	Y	N	N
4	**Smith, C.**	Y	Y	N	Y	N	Y
5	Gottheimer	Y	Y	N	Y	N	Y
6	Pallone	Y	Y	N	Y	N	Y
7	Malinowski	Y	Y	N	Y	N	Y
8	Sires	Y	Y	N	Y	N	Y
9	Pascrell	Y	Y	N	Y	N	Y
10	Payne	Y	Y	N	Y	N	Y
11	Sherrill	Y	Y	N	Y	N	Y
12	Watson Coleman	Y	Y	N	Y	N	Y
NEW MEXICO		Y	Y	N	Y	N	Y
1	Haaland						
2	Torres Small	Y	Y	N	Y	N	Y
3	Luján	Y	Y	N	Y	N	Y
NEW YORK		Y	Y	N	Y	N	Y
1	**Zeldin**						
2	**King, P.**	Y	Y	Y	Y	N	N
3	Suozzi	Y	Y	N	Y	N	Y
4	Rice, K.	Y	Y	N	Y	N	Y
5	Meeks	Y	Y	N	Y	N	Y
6	Meng	Y	Y	N	Y	N	Y
7	Velázquez	Y	Y	N	Y	N	Y
8	Jeffries	Y	Y	N	Y	N	Y
9	Clarke	Y	Y	N	Y	N	Y
10	Nadler	Y	Y	N	Y	N	Y
11	Rose	Y	Y	N	Y	N	Y
12	Maloney, C.	Y	Y	N	Y	N	Y
13	Espaillat	Y	Y	N	Y	N	Y
14	Ocasio-Cortez	Y	Y	N	Y	N	Y
15	Serrano	Y	Y	N	Y	N	Y
16	Engel	Y	Y	N	Y	N	Y
17	Lowey	Y	Y	N	Y	N	Y
18	Maloney, S.P.	Y	Y	N	Y	N	Y
19	Delgado	Y	Y	N	Y	N	Y
20	Tonko	Y	Y	N	Y	N	Y
21	**Stefanik**	Y	Y	N	Y	N	Y
22	Brindisi	Y	Y	N	Y	N	Y
23	**Reed**	Y	Y	N	N	N	Y
24	**Katko**	Y	N	Y	Y	?	Y
25	Morelle	Y	Y	N	Y	N	Y
26	Higgins, B.	Y	Y	N	Y	N	Y
27	**Collins, C.**	Y	Y	N	Y	N	Y
NORTH CAROLINA		Y	Y	Y	Y	Y	Y
1	Butterfield						
2	**Holding**	Y	Y	N	Y	N	Y
3	**Jones***	?	?	?	?	?	?
4	Price						
5	**Foxx**	Y	Y	N	Y	N	Y
6	**Walker**	Y	Y	Y	Y	Y	Y
7	**Rouzer**	Y	N	Y	N	Y	N

		325	326	327	328	329	330
8	**Hudson**	Y	N	Y	Y	Y	N
9	vacant	Y	Y	Y	N	Y	N
10	**McHenry**	Y	Y	Y	Y	Y	N
11	**Meadows**	Y	Y	Y	Y	Y	N
12	Adams	Y	Y	N	Y	N	Y
13	**Budd**	Y	N	Y	N	Y	N
NORTH DAKOTA							
AL	**Armstrong**	Y	Y	Y	Y	Y	N
OHIO							
1	**Chabot**	Y	Y	Y	N	Y	N
2	**Wenstrup**	Y	Y	Y	Y	Y	N
3	Beatty	Y	Y	N	Y	N	Y
4	**Jordan**	Y	N	Y	N	Y	N
5	**Latta**	Y	N	Y	Y	Y	N
6	**Johnson, B.**	Y	Y	Y	N	Y	N
7	**Gibbs**	Y	N	Y	N	Y	N
8	**Davidson**	N	N	Y	N	Y	N
9	Kaptur	Y	Y	N	Y	N	Y
10	**Turner**	Y	Y	Y	Y	Y	Y
11	Fudge	Y	Y	N	Y	N	Y
12	**Balderson**	Y	N	Y	N	Y	N
13	Ryan	Y	Y	N	Y	N	Y
14	**Joyce**	Y	Y	Y	Y	Y	Y
15	**Stivers**	Y	Y	N	N	Y	N
16	**Gonzalez**	Y	Y	N	N	Y	N
OKLAHOMA							
1	**Hern**	Y	N	Y	N	Y	N
2	**Mullin**	Y	N	Y	N	Y	N
3	**Lucas**	Y	Y	Y	Y	Y	N
4	**Cole**	Y	Y	Y	Y	Y	N
5	Horn	Y	Y	N	N	N	Y
OREGON							
1	Bonamici	Y	Y	N	Y	N	Y
2	**Walden**	Y	Y	Y	Y	Y	Y
3	Blumenauer	Y	Y	N	Y	N	Y
4	DeFazio	Y	Y	N	Y	N	Y
5	Schrader	Y	Y	N	Y	N	Y
PENNSYLVANIA							
1	**Fitzpatrick**	Y	Y	N	Y	N	Y
2	Boyle	Y	Y	N	Y	N	Y
3	Evans	Y	Y	N	Y	N	Y
4	Dean	Y	Y	N	Y	N	Y
5	Scanlon	Y	Y	N	Y	N	Y
6	Houlahan	Y	Y	N	Y	N	Y
7	Wild	Y	Y	N	Y	N	Y
8	Cartwright	Y	Y	N	Y	N	Y
9	**Meuser**	Y	N	Y	N	Y	N
10	**Perry**	Y	Y	Y	N	Y	N
11	**Smucker**	Y	Y	Y	N	Y	N
12	**Marino***						
13	**Joyce**	Y	N	Y	N	Y	N
14	**Reschenthaler**	Y	Y	Y	Y	Y	N
15	**Thompson, G.**	Y	N	Y	Y	Y	N
16	**Kelly, M.**	Y	N	Y	N	Y	N
17	Lamb	Y	Y	N	Y	N	Y
18	Doyle	Y	Y	N	Y	N	Y
RHODE ISLAND							
1	Cicilline	Y	Y	N	Y	N	Y
2	Langevin	Y	Y	N	Y	N	Y
SOUTH CAROLINA							
1	Cunningham	Y	Y	N	Y	N	N
2	**Wilson, J.**	Y	Y	Y	N	Y	Y
3	**Duncan**	Y	Y	Y	N	Y	Y
4	**Timmons**	Y	N	Y	N	Y	N
5	**Norman**	Y	N	Y	N	Y	N
6	Clyburn	Y	Y	N	Y	N	Y
7	**Rice, T.**	N	N	Y	N	Y	N
SOUTH DAKOTA							
AL	**Johnson**	Y	Y	Y	N	Y	N
TENNESSEE							
1	**Roe**	Y	Y	Y	N	Y	N
2	**Burchett**	Y	N	Y	N	Y	N
3	**Fleischmann**	Y	Y	Y	Y	Y	Y
4	**DesJarlais**	Y	Y	Y	Y	Y	Y
5	Cooper	Y	Y	N	Y	N	Y
6	**Rose**	Y	N	Y	N	Y	N
7	**Green**	Y	N	Y	N	Y	N
8	**Kustoff**	Y	Y	Y	N	Y	N
9	Cohen	Y	Y	N	Y	N	Y
TEXAS							
1	**Gohmert**	Y	Y	Y	N	Y	N
2	**Crenshaw**	Y	Y	Y	N	Y	Y
3	**Taylor**	Y	Y	Y	Y	Y	N
4	**Ratcliffe**	Y	N	Y	N	Y	N

		325	326	327	328	329	330
5	**Gooden**	Y	N	Y	N	Y	N
6	**Wright**	Y	N	Y	N	Y	N
7	Fletcher	Y	Y	N	Y	N	Y
8	**Brady**	Y	N	Y	Y	Y	N
9	Green, A.	Y	Y	N	Y	N	Y
10	**McCaul**	Y	Y	Y	Y	Y	N
11	**Conaway**	Y	N	Y	N	Y	N
12	**Granger**	Y	Y	Y	Y	Y	N
13	**Thornberry**	Y	N	Y	N	Y	N
14	**Weber**	Y	Y	Y	N	Y	N
15	Gonzalez	?	?	?	?	?	?
16	Escobar	Y	Y	N	Y	N	Y
17	**Flores**	Y	Y	Y	Y	Y	N
18	Jackson Lee	Y	Y	N	Y	N	Y
19	**Arrington**	N	N	Y	N	Y	N
20	Castro	Y	Y	N	Y	N	Y
21	**Roy**	Y	N	Y	N	Y	N
22	**Olson**	Y	Y	Y	N	Y	N
23	**Hurd**	Y	Y	Y	Y	N	N
24	**Marchant**	Y	Y	Y	N	Y	N
25	**Williams**	Y	Y	Y	Y	Y	N
26	**Burgess**	Y	N	Y	N	Y	N
27	**Cloud**	Y	N	Y	N	Y	N
28	Cuellar	Y	Y	N	Y	N	N
29	Garcia, S.	Y	Y	N	Y	N	Y
30	Johnson, E.B.	Y	Y	N	Y	N	Y
31	**Carter, J.**	Y	Y	Y	N	Y	N
32	Allred	Y	Y	N	Y	N	Y
33	Veasey	Y	Y	N	Y	N	Y
34	Vela	Y	Y	N	Y	N	Y
35	Doggett	?	?	?	?	?	?
36	**Babin**	Y	Y	Y	N	Y	N
UTAH							
1	**Bishop, R.**	Y	N	Y	N	Y	N
2	**Stewart**	Y	Y	Y	N	Y	N
3	**Curtis**	?	?	?	?	?	?
4	McAdams	Y	Y	N	N	N	N
VERMONT							
AL	Welch	Y	Y	N	Y	N	Y
VIRGINIA							
1	**Wittman**	Y	Y	Y	N	Y	N
2	Luria	Y	Y	N	Y	N	Y
3	Scott, R.	Y	Y	N	Y	N	Y
4	McEachin	Y	Y	N	Y	N	Y
5	**Riggleman**	Y	Y	Y	Y	Y	N
6	**Cline**	Y	N	Y	N	Y	N
7	Spanberger	Y	Y	N	N	N	Y
8	Beyer	Y	Y	N	Y	N	Y
9	**Griffith**	Y	Y	Y	N	Y	Y
10	Wexton	Y	Y	N	Y	N	Y
11	Connolly	Y	Y	N	Y	N	Y
WASHINGTON							
1	DelBene	Y	Y	N	Y	N	Y
2	Larsen	Y	Y	N	Y	N	Y
3	**Herrera Beutler**	?	?	?	?	?	?
4	**Newhouse**	Y	Y	Y	Y	Y	Y
5	**McMorris Rodgers**	Y	Y	Y	Y	Y	Y
6	Kilmer	Y	Y	N	Y	N	Y
7	Jayapal	Y	Y	N	Y	N	Y
8	Schrier	Y	Y	N	Y	N	Y
9	Smith Adam	Y	Y	N	Y	N	Y
10	Heck	Y	Y	N	Y	N	Y
WEST VIRGINIA							
1	**McKinley**	Y	Y	Y	Y	Y	N
2	**Mooney**	Y	Y	Y	Y	Y	N
3	**Miller**	Y	Y	Y	N	Y	N
WISCONSIN							
1	**Steil**	Y	Y	Y	N	Y	N
2	Pocan	Y	Y	N	Y	N	Y
3	Kind	Y	Y	N	Y	N	Y
4	Moore	Y	Y	N	Y	N	Y
5	**Sensenbrenner**	Y	Y	Y	N	Y	Y
6	**Grothman**	Y	Y	Y	N	Y	Y
7	**Duffy**	Y	N	Y	N	Y	N
8	**Gallagher**	Y	Y	Y	Y	Y	Y
WYOMING							
AL	**Cheney**	Y	?	?	?	?	N
DELEGATES							
	Radewagen (A.S.)	?	?	?	?	?	?
	Norton (D.C.)	Y	Y	N	Y	N	Y
	San Nicolas (Guam)	?	?	?	?	?	?
	Sablan (N. Marianas)	Y	Y	N	Y	N	Y
	González-Colón (P.R.)	Y	Y	N	Y	N	N
	Plaskett (V.I.)	Y	Y	N	Y	N	Y

331. HR2740. Fiscal 2020 Four-Bill Appropriations Package - Withholding Foreign Assistance to Pakistan. Meadows, R-N.C., amendment that would increase by $33 million funds withheld from foreign assistance to Pakistan until Dr. Shakil Afridi is released from prison and acquitted from "charges relating to the assistance provided to the United States in locating Osama Bin Laden." Adopted in Committee of the Whole 387-33: R 188-1; D 198-32; I 1-0. June 18, 2019.

332. HR2740. Fiscal 2020 Four-Bill Appropriations Package - En Bloc Amendments. Lowey, D-N.Y., en bloc amendments to the Department of State, Foreign Operations, and related programs title of the bill (Division D) that would, among other provisions, prohibit the use of funds made available by the bill for a number of purposes, including to withdraw from the North Atlantic Treaty, to enter into contracts and agreements with business entities connected to President Donald Trump, or to provide military education and training to the government of Saudi Arabia. It would also make adjustments to a number of funds related to nonproliferation and anti-terrorism, international economic assistance, and foreign development. Adopted in Committee of the Whole 231-187: R 2-186; D 228-1; I 1-0. June 18, 2019.

333. HR3253. Extension of Medicaid Programs - Passage. Dingell, D-Mich., motion to suspend the rules and pass the bill that would extend through fiscal 2024 a Health and Human Services Department state grant program to help Medicaid-eligible individuals with chronic conditions transitioning out of health care institutions. It would authorize for the program $417 million for fiscal 2020, $450 million annually from fiscal 2021 through fiscal 2023, and $225 million for fiscal 2024. It would also shorten from 90 to 60 days institutional residency requirements for program eligibility and expand application requirements, requiring states to detail proposed use of funds, objectives, evaluation and sustainability. Among other Medicaid-related provisions, the bill would also extend through 2021 a demonstration program related to community mental health clinics, extend through 2024 rules protecting the financial resources of individuals with spouses in nursing homes, and increase from $6 million to $45.5 million annual funds available for the HHS Medicaid Improvement Fund. Finally, it would modify certain requirements of the Medicaid drug rebate program for prescription drug manufacturers, including to require manufacturers to pay rebates based on brand name drug prices as opposed to averaged prices including generic drugs. Motion agreed to 371-46: R 142-46; D 229-0. *Note: A two-thirds majority of those present and voting (278 in this case) is required for passage under suspension of the rules.* June 18, 2019.

334. HR2740. Fiscal 2020 Four-Bill Appropriations Package - Reduce State-Foreign Funding. Grothman, R-Wis., amendment that would reduce by 2.1 percent all discretionary funding made available by the bill for the State Department and related agencies. Rejected in Committee of the Whole 131-292: R 131-58; D 0-233; I 0-1. June 18, 2019.

335. HR2740. Fiscal 2020 Four-Bill Appropriations Package - Foreign Assistance and Economic Development. Walker, R-N.C., amendment that would decrease by a total of $24 billion funding for a number of State Department economic development and foreign assistance programs, including programs to assist migrants and refugees, fund HIV/AIDS research and prevention, and provide international disaster rehabilitation and reconstruction assistance. Rejected in Committee of the Whole 110-315: R 110-81; D 0-233; I 0-1. June 18, 2019.

336. HR2740. Fiscal 2020 Four-Bill Appropriations Package - Paris Climate Agreement Withdrawal. Palmer, R-Ala., amendment that would strike from the bill provisions allowing funds provided by the bill to be used for payments under the Paris Climate Agreement and prohibiting such funds to be used for U.S. withdrawal from the agreement. Rejected in Committee of the Whole 184-241: R 184-7; D 0-233; I 0-1. June 18, 2019.

		331	332	333	334	335	336
ALABAMA							
1	**Byrne**	Y	N	N	Y	Y	Y
2	**Roby**	?	?	N	N	N	Y
3	**Rogers, M.**	Y	N	Y	Y	Y	Y
4	**Aderholt**	Y	N	N	N	N	Y
5	**Brooks, M.**	Y	N	N	Y	Y	Y
6	**Palmer**	Y	N	N	Y	Y	Y
7	Sewell	Y	Y	Y	N	N	N
ALASKA							
AL	**Young**	Y	N	Y	N	Y	Y
ARIZONA							
1	O'Halleran	Y	Y	Y	N	N	N
2	Kirkpatrick	Y	Y	Y	N	N	N
3	Grijalva	N	Y	Y	N	N	N
4	**Gosar**	Y	N	N	Y	Y	Y
5	**Biggs**	Y	N	N	Y	Y	Y
6	**Schweikert**	Y	Y	Y	Y	Y	Y
7	Gallego	N	Y	?	N	N	N
8	**Lesko**	Y	N	N	Y	Y	Y
9	Stanton	Y	Y	Y	N	N	N
ARKANSAS							
1	**Crawford**	Y	N	Y	N	Y	Y
2	**Hill, F.**	Y	N	Y	Y	N	Y
3	**Womack**	Y	N	Y	N	N	Y
4	**Westerman**	Y	N	?	-	-	-
CALIFORNIA							
1	**LaMalfa**	Y	N	Y	N	Y	Y
2	Huffman	Y	Y	Y	N	N	N
3	Garamendi	Y	Y	Y	N	N	N
4	**McClintock**	Y	N	N	Y	Y	Y
5	Thompson, M.	Y	Y	Y	N	N	N
6	Matsui	Y	Y	Y	N	N	N
7	Bera	Y	Y	Y	N	N	N
8	**Cook**	Y	N	Y	N	Y	Y
9	McNerney	Y	Y	Y	N	N	N
10	Harder	Y	Y	Y	N	N	N
11	DeSaulnier	Y	Y	Y	N	N	N
12	Pelosi						
13	Lee B.	N	Y	Y	N	N	N
14	Speier	Y	Y	Y	N	N	N
15	Swalwell	N	Y	Y	N	N	N
16	Costa	Y	Y	Y	N	N	N
17	Khanna	Y	Y	Y	N	N	N
18	Eshoo	Y	Y	Y	N	N	N
19	Lofgren	Y	Y	Y	N	N	N
20	Panetta	Y	Y	Y	N	N	N
21	Cox	Y	Y	Y	N	N	N
22	**Nunes**	Y	N	Y	Y	Y	Y
23	**McCarthy**	Y	N	Y	N	Y	Y
24	Carbajal	Y	Y	Y	N	N	N
25	Hill, K.	Y	Y	Y	N	N	N
26	Brownley	Y	Y	Y	N	N	N
27	Chu	Y	Y	Y	N	N	N
28	Schiff	Y	Y	Y	N	N	N
29	Cárdenas	N	Y	Y	N	N	N
30	Sherman	Y	Y	Y	N	N	N
31	Aguilar	Y	Y	Y	N	N	N
32	Napolitano	Y	Y	Y	N	N	N
33	Lieu	N	Y	Y	N	N	N
34	Gomez	Y	Y	Y	N	N	N
35	Torres	Y	Y	Y	N	N	N
36	Ruiz	Y	Y	Y	N	N	N
37	Bass	Y	Y	Y	N	N	N
38	Sánchez	N	Y	Y	N	N	N
39	Cisneros	N	Y	Y	N	N	N
40	Roybal-Allard	Y	Y	Y	N	N	N
41	Takano	Y	Y	Y	N	N	N
42	**Calvert**	Y	N	Y	N	N	Y
43	Waters	Y	Y	Y	N	N	N
44	Barragán	N	Y	Y	N	N	N
45	Porter	Y	Y	Y	N	N	N
46	Correa	Y	Y	Y	N	N	N
47	Lowenthal	Y	Y	Y	N	N	N
48	Rouda	Y	Y	Y	N	N	N
49	Levin	Y	Y	Y	N	N	N
50	**Hunter**	Y	N	Y	N	Y	Y
51	Vargas	Y	Y	Y	N	N	N
52	Peters	Y	Y	Y	N	N	N
53	Davis, S.	Y	Y	Y	N	N	N
COLORADO							
1	DeGette	Y	Y	Y	N	N	N
2	Neguse	Y	Y	Y	N	N	N
3	**Tipton**	Y	N	Y	Y	N	Y
4	**Buck**	Y	N	N	Y	Y	Y
5	**Lamborn**	Y	N	Y	Y	Y	Y
6	Crow	Y	Y	Y	N	N	N
7	Perlmutter	Y	Y	Y	N	N	N
CONNECTICUT							
1	Larson	Y	Y	Y	N	N	N
2	Courtney	Y	Y	Y	N	N	N
3	DeLauro	+	+	+	-	-	-
4	Himes	Y	Y	Y	N	N	N
5	Hayes	Y	Y	Y	N	N	N
DELAWARE							
AL	Blunt Rochester	Y	Y	Y	N	N	N
FLORIDA							
1	**Gaetz**	?	?	?	?	?	?
2	**Dunn**	Y	N	Y	Y	N	Y
3	**Yoho**	?	?	?	?	?	?
4	**Rutherford**	Y	N	Y	N	N	Y
5	Lawson	Y	Y	Y	N	N	N
6	**Waltz**	+	-	-	-	-	+
7	Murphy	Y	Y	Y	N	N	N
8	**Posey**	?	?	Y	Y	Y	Y
9	Soto	Y	Y	Y	N	N	N
10	Demings	Y	Y	Y	N	N	N
11	**Webster**	?	?	Y	Y	Y	Y
12	**Bilirakis**	Y	N	Y	N	Y	Y
13	Crist	Y	Y	Y	N	N	N
14	Castor	Y	Y	Y	N	N	N
15	**Spano**	Y	N	Y	N	N	Y
16	**Buchanan**	Y	N	Y	N	N	N
17	**Steube**	Y	N	N	Y	Y	Y
18	**Mast**	Y	N	Y	Y	Y	Y
19	**Rooney**	Y	N	Y	Y	Y	Y
20	Hastings	?	?	?	?	?	?
21	Frankel	Y	Y	Y	N	N	N
22	Deutch	Y	Y	Y	N	N	N
23	Wasserman Schultz	Y	Y	Y	N	N	N
24	Wilson, F.	N	Y	Y	N	N	N
25	**Diaz-Balart**	Y	N	Y	N	N	N
26	Mucarsel-Powell	Y	Y	Y	N	N	N
27	Shalala	Y	Y	Y	N	N	N
GEORGIA							
1	**Carter, E.L.**	Y	N	Y	Y	Y	Y
2	Bishop, S.	Y	Y	Y	N	N	N
3	**Ferguson**	Y	N	Y	Y	Y	Y
4	Johnson, H.	Y	Y	Y	N	N	N
5	Lewis John	Y	Y	Y	N	N	N
6	McBath	N	Y	Y	N	N	N
7	**Woodall**	Y	N	Y	Y	Y	Y
8	**Scott, A.**	Y	N	Y	Y	Y	Y
9	**Collins, D.**	Y	N	Y	Y	Y	Y
10	**Hice**	Y	N	N	Y	Y	Y
11	**Loudermilk**	Y	N	N	Y	Y	Y
12	**Allen**	Y	N	N	Y	Y	Y
13	Scott, D.	Y	Y	Y	N	N	N
14	**Graves, T.**	Y	N	N	Y	Y	Y
HAWAII							
1	Case	Y	Y	Y	N	N	N
2	Gabbard	Y	Y	Y	N	N	N
IDAHO							
1	**Fulcher**	Y	N	Y	Y	Y	Y
2	**Simpson**	Y	N	Y	N	N	Y
ILLINOIS							
1	Rush	Y	Y	Y	N	N	N
2	Kelly, R.	Y	Y	Y	N	N	N
3	Lipinski	Y	Y	Y	N	N	N
4	García, J.	Y	Y	Y	N	N	N
5	Quigley	Y	Y	Y	N	N	N
6	Casten	N	Y	Y	N	N	?
7	Davis, D.	Y	Y	Y	N	N	N
8	Krishnamoorthi	Y	Y	Y	N	N	N
9	Schakowsky	Y	Y	Y	N	N	N
10	Schneider	Y	Y	Y	N	N	N
11	Foster	Y	Y	Y	N	N	N

KEY: Republicans Democrats *Independents*

Y Voted for (yea)	**N** Voted against (nay)	**P** Voted "present"	
+ Announced for	**−** Announced against	**?** Did not vote or otherwise make position known	
# Paired for	**X** Paired against		

		331	332	333	334	335	336
12	**Bost**	Y	N	Y	Y	N	Y
13	**Davis, R.**	Y	N	Y	N	N	Y
14	Underwood	N	Y	Y	N	N	N
15	**Shimkus**	Y	N	Y	Y	Y	Y
16	**Kinzinger**	Y	N	Y	N	N	Y
17	Bustos	Y	Y	Y	N	N	N
18	**LaHood**	Y	N	?	?	N	Y
INDIANA							
1	Visclosky	Y	Y	Y	N	N	N
2	**Walorski**	Y	N	Y	N	N	Y
3	**Banks**	Y	N	N	Y	Y	Y
4	**Baird**	Y	N	Y	N	Y	Y
5	**Brooks, S.**	Y	N	Y	N	N	Y
6	**Pence**	Y	N	Y	N	N	Y
7	Carson	N	Y	Y	N	N	N
8	**Bucshon**	Y	N	Y	Y	Y	Y
9	**Hollingsworth**	Y	N	Y	N	N	Y
IOWA							
1	Finkenauer	Y	Y	Y	N	N	N
2	Loebsack	Y	Y	Y	N	N	N
3	Axne	?	?	Y	N	N	N
4	**King, S.**	Y	N	N	Y	Y	Y
KANSAS							
1	**Marshall**	Y	N	Y	N	N	Y
2	**Watkins**	Y	N	Y	Y	Y	Y
3	Davids	N	Y	Y	N	N	N
4	**Estes**	Y	N	Y	Y	Y	Y
KENTUCKY							
1	**Comer**	Y	N	Y	Y	Y	Y
2	**Guthrie**	Y	N	Y	Y	Y	Y
3	Yarmuth	Y	Y	Y	N	N	N
4	**Massie**	Y	N	N	Y	Y	Y
5	**Rogers, H.**	Y	N	Y	N	N	Y
6	**Barr**	Y	N	Y	N	N	Y
LOUISIANA							
1	**Scalise**	Y	N	Y	Y	Y	Y
2	Richmond	Y	Y	Y	N	N	N
3	**Higgins, C.**	Y	N	Y	Y	Y	Y
4	**Johnson, M.**	Y	N	Y	Y	Y	Y
5	**Abraham**	?	?	?	?	?	?
6	**Graves, G.**	Y	N	Y	Y	N	Y
MAINE							
1	Pingree	Y	Y	Y	N	N	N
2	Golden	Y	Y	Y	N	N	N
MARYLAND							
1	**Harris**	Y	N	N	Y	Y	Y
2	Ruppersberger	Y	Y	Y	N	N	N
3	Sarbanes	Y	Y	Y	N	N	N
4	Brown, A.	Y	Y	Y	N	N	N
5	Hoyer	N	Y	Y	N	N	N
6	Trone	Y	Y	Y	N	N	N
7	Cummings	Y	Y	Y	N	N	N
8	Raskin						
MASSACHUSETTS		Y	Y	Y	N	N	N
1	Neal						
2	McGovern	Y	Y	Y	N	N	N
3	Trahan	Y	Y	Y	N	N	N
4	Kennedy	Y	Y	Y	N	N	N
5	Clark	Y	Y	Y	N	N	N
6	Moulton	Y	Y	Y	N	N	N
7	Pressley	?	?	?	?	?	?
8	Lynch	Y	Y	Y	N	N	N
9	Keating	Y	Y	Y	N	N	N
MICHIGAN		Y	Y	Y	N	N	N
1	**Bergman**						
2	**Huizenga**	Y	N	Y	Y	N	Y
3	**Amash**	Y	N	Y	Y	Y	Y
4	**Moolenaar**	Y	N	N	Y	Y	Y
5	Kildee	Y	N	Y	Y	N	Y
6	**Upton**	Y	Y	Y	N	N	N
7	**Walberg**	Y	N	Y	Y	N	N
8	Slotkin	Y	N	Y	Y	Y	Y
9	Levin	Y	Y	Y	N	N	N
10	**Mitchell**	Y	Y	Y	N	N	N
11	Stevens	Y	N	Y	Y	N	Y
12	Dingell	Y	Y	Y	N	N	N
13	Tlaib	Y	Y	Y	N	N	N
14	Lawrence	Y	Y	Y	N	N	N
MINNESOTA		Y	Y	Y	N	N	N
1	**Hagedorn**						
2	Craig	Y	N	Y	N	N	Y
3	Phillips	Y	Y	Y	N	N	N
4	McCollum	Y	Y	Y	N	N	N
5	Omar	Y	Y	Y	N	N	N

		331	332	333	334	335	336
6	**Emmer**	Y	Y	Y	N	N	N
7	Peterson	Y	N	Y	N	N	Y
8	**Stauber**	Y	Y	Y	N	N	N
MISSISSIPPI		Y	N	Y	N	N	Y
1	**Kelly, T.**						
2	Thompson, B.	Y	N	N	Y	Y	Y
3	**Guest**	Y	Y	Y	N	N	N
4	**Palazzo**	Y	N	Y	N	N	Y
MISSOURI		Y	N	Y	Y	Y	Y
1	Clay						
2	**Wagner**	N	Y	Y	N	N	N
3	**Luetkemeyer**	Y	N	Y	N	N	Y
4	**Hartzler**	Y	N	Y	N	Y	Y
5	Cleaver	Y	N	Y	Y	N	Y
6	**Graves, S.**	N	Y	Y	N	N	N
7	**Long**	Y	N	Y	Y	Y	Y
8	**Smith, J.**	Y	N	Y	Y	Y	Y
MONTANA		Y	N	Y	Y	Y	Y
AL	**Gianforte**						
NEBRASKA		Y	N	Y	Y	Y	Y
1	**Fortenberry**						
2	**Bacon**	Y	N	Y	N	N	Y
3	**Smith, Adrian**	Y	N	Y	Y	Y	Y
NEVADA		Y	N	Y	Y	Y	Y
1	Titus						
2	**Amodei**	Y	Y	Y	N	N	N
3	Lee	Y	N	Y	Y	Y	Y
4	Horsford	N	Y	Y	N	N	N
NEW HAMPSHIRE		Y	Y	Y	N	N	N
1	Pappas						
2	Kuster	Y	Y	Y	N	N	N
NEW JERSEY		Y	Y	Y	N	N	N
1	Norcross						
2	Van Drew	Y	Y	Y	N	N	N
3	Kim	Y	Y	Y	N	N	N
4	**Smith, C.**	Y	Y	Y	N	N	N
5	Gottheimer	Y	N	Y	N	N	Y
6	Pallone	Y	Y	Y	N	N	N
7	Malinowski	Y	Y	Y	N	N	N
8	Sires	Y	Y	Y	N	N	N
9	Pascrell	N	Y	Y	N	N	N
10	Payne	Y	Y	Y	N	N	N
11	Sherrill	Y	Y	Y	N	N	N
12	Watson Coleman	Y	Y	Y	N	N	N
NEW MEXICO		Y	Y	Y	N	N	N
1	Haaland						
2	Torres Small	Y	Y	Y	N	N	N
3	Luján	Y	Y	Y	N	N	N
NEW YORK		Y	Y	Y	N	N	N
1	**Zeldin**						
2	**King, P.**	Y	N	Y	Y	N	Y
3	Suozzi	Y	N	Y	N	N	Y
4	Rice, K.	N	Y	Y	N	N	N
5	Meeks	Y	Y	Y	N	N	N
6	Meng	N	Y	Y	N	N	N
7	Velázquez	Y	Y	Y	N	N	N
8	Jeffries	Y	Y	Y	N	N	N
9	Clarke	Y	Y	Y	N	N	N
10	Nadler	Y	Y	Y	N	N	N
11	Rose	Y	Y	Y	N	N	N
12	Maloney, C.	Y	Y	Y	N	N	N
13	Espaillat	Y	Y	Y	N	N	N
14	Ocasio-Cortez	Y	Y	Y	N	N	N
15	Serrano	Y	Y	Y	N	N	N
16	Engel	Y	Y	Y	N	N	N
17	Lowey	N	Y	Y	N	N	N
18	Maloney, S.P.	Y	Y	Y	N	N	N
19	Delgado	Y	Y	Y	N	N	N
20	Tonko	Y	Y	Y	N	N	N
21	**Stefanik**	Y	Y	Y	N	N	N
22	Brindisi	Y	N	Y	N	N	N
23	**Reed**	Y	Y	Y	N	N	N
24	**Katko**	Y	N	Y	N	N	Y
25	Morelle	Y	N	Y	N	N	Y
26	Higgins, B.	Y	Y	Y	N	N	N
27	**Collins, C.**	Y	Y	Y	N	N	N
NORTH CAROLINA		Y	N	Y	N	N	Y
1	Butterfield						
2	**Holding**	Y	Y	Y	N	N	N
3	**Jones***	?	?	?	?	?	?
4	Price						
5	**Foxx**	Y	Y	Y	N	N	N
6	**Walker**	Y	N	N	Y	Y	Y
7	**Rouzer**	Y	N	Y	Y	Y	Y

		331	332	333	334	335	336
8	**Hudson**	Y	N	N	Y	Y	Y
9	vacant	Y	N	Y	Y	Y	Y
10	**McHenry**	Y	N	Y	Y	N	Y
11	**Meadows**	Y	?	N	N	Y	Y
12	Adams	Y	Y	Y	N	N	N
13	**Budd**	Y	N	N	Y	Y	Y
NORTH DAKOTA							
AL	**Armstrong**	Y	N	Y	N	N	Y
OHIO							
1	**Chabot**	Y	N	Y	Y	Y	Y
2	**Wenstrup**	Y	N	Y	Y	Y	Y
3	Beatty	Y	Y	Y	N	N	N
4	**Jordan**	Y	N	N	Y	Y	Y
5	**Latta**	Y	N	Y	Y	Y	Y
6	**Johnson, B.**	Y	N	Y	Y	Y	Y
7	**Gibbs**	Y	N	Y	Y	Y	Y
8	**Davidson**	Y	N	N	Y	Y	Y
9	Kaptur	Y	Y	Y	N	N	N
10	**Turner**	Y	N	Y	N	N	Y
11	Fudge	Y	Y	Y	N	N	N
12	**Balderson**	Y	N	Y	Y	Y	Y
13	Ryan	Y	Y	Y	N	N	N
14	**Joyce**	Y	N	Y	N	N	Y
15	**Stivers**	Y	N	Y	N	N	N
16	**Gonzalez**	Y	N	Y	N	N	Y
OKLAHOMA							
1	**Hern**	Y	N	Y	Y	Y	Y
2	**Mullin**	Y	N	Y	Y	Y	Y
3	**Lucas**	Y	N	Y	Y	N	Y
4	**Cole**	Y	N	Y	N	N	Y
5	Horn	Y	Y	Y	N	N	N
OREGON							
1	Bonamici	Y	Y	Y	N	N	N
2	**Walden**	Y	N	Y	N	N	Y
3	Blumenauer	Y	?	Y	N	N	N
4	DeFazio	Y	Y	Y	N	N	N
5	Schrader	Y	Y	Y	N	N	N
PENNSYLVANIA							
1	**Fitzpatrick**	Y	Y	Y	N	N	N
2	Boyle	N	Y	Y	N	N	N
3	Evans	Y	Y	Y	N	N	N
4	Dean	N	Y	Y	N	N	N
5	Scanlon	N	Y	Y	N	N	N
6	Houlahan	Y	Y	Y	N	N	N
7	Wild	N	Y	Y	N	N	N
8	Cartwright	Y	Y	Y	N	N	N
9	**Meuser**	Y	N	Y	Y	N	Y
10	**Perry**	Y	N	Y	Y	Y	Y
11	**Smucker**	Y	N	Y	Y	N	Y
12	**Marino***						
13	**Joyce**	Y	N	Y	Y	Y	Y
14	**Reschenthaler**	Y	N	Y	N	N	Y
15	**Thompson, G.**	Y	N	Y	N	Y	Y
16	**Kelly, M.**	Y	N	Y	Y	Y	Y
17	Lamb	Y	Y	Y	N	N	N
18	Doyle	Y	Y	Y	N	N	N
RHODE ISLAND							
1	Cicilline	Y	Y	Y	N	N	N
2	Langevin	Y	Y	Y	N	N	N
SOUTH CAROLINA							
1	Cunningham	Y	Y	Y	N	N	N
2	**Wilson, J.**	Y	N	Y	Y	Y	Y
3	**Duncan**	Y	N	Y	Y	Y	Y
4	**Timmons**	Y	N	Y	Y	N	Y
5	**Norman**	Y	N	N	Y	Y	Y
6	Clyburn	Y	Y	Y	N	N	N
7	**Rice, T.**	Y	N	N	Y	Y	Y
SOUTH DAKOTA							
AL	**Johnson**	Y	N	Y	Y	Y	Y
TENNESSEE							
1	**Roe**	Y	N	Y	Y	Y	Y
2	**Burchett**	Y	N	N	N	N	Y
3	**Fleischmann**	Y	N	Y	N	N	Y
4	**DesJarlais**	Y	N	Y	Y	Y	Y
5	Cooper	Y	Y	Y	N	N	N
6	**Rose**	Y	N	N	Y	Y	Y
7	**Green**	Y	N	N	Y	Y	Y
8	**Kustoff**	Y	N	Y	Y	Y	Y
9	Cohen	N	Y	Y	N	N	N
TEXAS							
1	**Gohmert**	Y	N	N	Y	Y	Y
2	**Crenshaw**	Y	N	Y	N	N	Y
3	**Taylor**	Y	N	Y	Y	Y	Y
4	**Ratcliffe**	Y	N	N	Y	Y	Y

		331	332	333	334	335	336
5	**Gooden**	Y	N	N	Y	Y	Y
6	**Wright**	Y	N	N	N	Y	Y
7	Fletcher	Y	Y	Y	N	N	N
8	**Brady**	Y	N	Y	Y	Y	Y
9	Green, A.	Y	Y	Y	N	N	N
10	**McCaul**	Y	N	N	N	N	Y
11	**Conaway**	Y	N	Y	Y	Y	Y
12	**Granger**	Y	N	Y	N	N	Y
13	**Thornberry**	Y	N	Y	N	N	Y
14	**Weber**	Y	N	N	Y	Y	Y
15	Gonzalez	?	?	Y	N	N	N
16	Escobar	Y	Y	Y	N	N	N
17	**Flores**	Y	N	Y	Y	Y	Y
18	Jackson Lee	N	Y	Y	N	N	N
19	**Arrington**	N	N	?	Y	Y	Y
20	Castro	Y	Y	Y	N	N	N
21	**Roy**	Y	N	N	Y	Y	Y
22	**Olson**	Y	N	Y	Y	Y	Y
23	**Hurd**	Y	N	Y	N	N	Y
24	**Marchant**	Y	N	Y	?	Y	Y
25	**Williams**	Y	N	N	Y	Y	Y
26	**Burgess**	Y	N	Y	Y	Y	Y
27	**Cloud**	Y	N	N	Y	Y	Y
28	Cuellar	Y	Y	Y	N	N	N
29	Garcia, S.	Y	Y	Y	N	N	N
30	Johnson, E.B.	Y	Y	Y	N	N	N
31	**Carter, J.**	Y	N	Y	N	N	Y
32	Allred	N	Y	Y	N	N	N
33	Veasey	Y	Y	Y	N	N	N
34	Vela	Y	Y	Y	N	N	N
35	Doggett	?	?	?	?	?	?
36	**Babin**	Y	N	N	Y	Y	Y
UTAH							
1	**Bishop, R.**	Y	N	Y	Y	Y	Y
2	**Stewart**	Y	N	Y	Y	N	Y
3	**Curtis**	?	?	?	?	?	?
4	McAdams	Y	N	Y	N	N	N
VERMONT							
AL	Welch	N	Y	Y	N	N	N
VIRGINIA							
1	**Wittman**	Y	N	Y	Y	Y	Y
2	Luria	Y	Y	Y	N	N	N
3	Scott, R.	Y	Y	Y	N	N	N
4	McEachin	Y	Y	Y	N	N	N
5	**Riggleman**	Y	N	Y	Y	Y	Y
6	**Cline**	Y	N	N	Y	Y	Y
7	Spanberger	Y	Y	Y	N	N	N
8	Beyer	Y	Y	Y	N	N	N
9	**Griffith**	Y	N	Y	Y	Y	Y
10	Wexton	Y	Y	Y	N	N	N
11	Connolly	Y	Y	Y	N	N	N
WASHINGTON							
1	DelBene	Y	Y	Y	N	N	N
2	Larsen	Y	Y	Y	N	N	N
3	**Herrera Beutler**	?	?	?	?	?	?
4	**Newhouse**	Y	N	Y	N	N	Y
5	**McMorris Rodgers**	Y	N	Y	Y	N	Y
6	Kilmer	Y	Y	Y	N	N	N
7	Jayapal	Y	Y	Y	N	N	N
8	Schrier	Y	Y	Y	N	N	N
9	Smith Adam	Y	Y	Y	N	N	N
10	Heck	Y	Y	Y	N	N	N
WEST VIRGINIA							
1	**McKinley**	Y	N	Y	N	N	Y
2	**Mooney**	Y	N	Y	Y	Y	Y
3	**Miller**	Y	N	Y	Y	Y	Y
WISCONSIN							
1	**Steil**	Y	N	Y	Y	N	Y
2	Pocan	Y	Y	Y	N	N	N
3	Kind	Y	Y	Y	N	N	N
4	Moore	N	Y	Y	N	N	N
5	**Sensenbrenner**	Y	N	Y	Y	Y	Y
6	**Grothman**	Y	N	N	Y	Y	Y
7	**Duffy**	Y	N	Y	Y	N	Y
8	**Gallagher**	Y	N	Y	N	N	Y
WYOMING							
AL	**Cheney**	Y	N	Y	N	N	Y
DELEGATES							
	Radewagen (A.S.)	?	?		?	?	?
	Norton (D.C.)	Y	Y		N	N	N
	San Nicolas (Guam)	?	?		N	N	N
	Sablan (N. Marianas)	Y	Y		N	N	N
	González-Colón (P.R.)	Y	N		N	N	Y
	Plaskett (V.I.)	Y	Y		N	N	N

ⅠⅠⅠ HOUSE VOTES

337. HR2740. Fiscal 2020 Four-Bill Appropriations Package - U.N. Climate Change Convention. Arrington, R-Texas, amendment that would prohibit the use of funds made available by the bill for the U.N. Framework Convention on Climate Change. Rejected in Committee of the Whole 174-251: R 174-17; D 0-233; I 0-1. June 18, 2019.

338. HR2740. Fiscal 2020 Four-Bill Appropriations Package - Reduce State-Foreign Funding. Banks, R-Ind., amendment that would reduce by 14 percent all funding made available by the bill for the State Department and related agencies (Division D), not including amounts made available for the Defense Department. Rejected in Committee of the Whole 123-303: R 123-68; D 0-234; I 0-1. June 18, 2019.

339. HR2740. Fiscal 2020 Four-Bill Appropriations Package - En Bloc Amendments. Lowey, D-N.Y., en bloc amendments to the Department of State, Foreign Operations, and related programs title of the bill (Division D) that would increase by $500,000 funding for international broadcasting activities under the U.S. Agency for Global Media and decrease by the same amount funding for the Office of Inspector General within the Administration of Foreign Affairs; and that would increase by $500,000 funding for the International Fisheries Commission and decrease by the same amount of administrative funding for certain diplomatic and other State Department programs. Adopted in Committee of the Whole 283-144: R 51-141; D 231-1; I 1-0. June 18, 2019.

340. HR2740. Fiscal 2020 Four-Bill Appropriations Package - Reduce State-Foreign Funding. Allen, R-Ga., amendment that would reduce by one percent all discretionary funding made available under the Department of State, Foreign Operations, and related programs title of the bill (Division D). Rejected in Committee of the Whole 134-293: R 133-59; D 1-233; I 0-1. June 18, 2019.

341. HR2740. Fiscal 2020 Four-Bill Appropriations Package - En Bloc Amendments. Visclosky, D-Ind., en bloc amendments to the Defense Department title of the bill (Division C) that would, among other provisions, increase by $14 million in total funding for research, development, and evaluation for various Defense Department health programs; increase by $20 million funding for a Defense Department cooperative threat reduction program related to nuclear, chemical, and biological weapons; and increase by $5 million funding for environmental restoration activities of the Army, Navy, and Air Force, respectively. It would also reduce and redistribute a number of funds related to research and evaluation or operations and maintenance of various branches and agencies of the Defense Department. Adopted in Committee of the Whole 381-46: R 149-43; D 231-3; I 1-0. June 18, 2019.

342. HR2740. Fiscal 2020 Four-Bill Appropriations Package - Navy Research and Evaluation. Langevin, D-R.I., amendment that would increase by $10 million funding for Navy research- and evaluation-related expenses and decrease by the same amount funding for such expenses Defense-wide. Adopted in Committee of the Whole 355-73: R 134-58; D 220-15; I 1-0. June 18, 2019.

		337	338	339	340	341	342
ALABAMA							
1	**Byrne**	Y	Y	N	Y	N	Y
2	**Roby**	Y	N	N	N	Y	Y
3	**Rogers, M.**	Y	Y	Y	Y	Y	Y
4	**Aderholt**	Y	N	N	N	N	Y
5	**Brooks, M.**	Y	Y	N	Y	Y	Y
6	**Palmer**	Y	Y	N	Y	Y	Y
7	Sewell	N	N	Y	N	Y	Y
ALASKA							
AL	**Young**	Y	N	N	N	Y	Y
ARIZONA							
1	O'Halleran	N	N	Y	N	Y	Y
2	Kirkpatrick	N	N	Y	N	Y	Y
3	Grijalva	N	N	Y	N	Y	Y
4	**Gosar**	Y	Y	N	Y	N	N
5	**Biggs**	Y	Y	N	N	Y	Y
6	**Schweikert**	Y	Y	N	Y	Y	Y
7	Gallego	N	N	Y	N	Y	Y
8	**Lesko**	Y	Y	N	Y	Y	N
9	Stanton	N	N	Y	N	Y	Y
ARKANSAS							
1	**Crawford**	Y	Y	N	Y	Y	Y
2	**Hill, F.**	Y	N	Y	Y	Y	Y
3	**Womack**	Y	N	N	N	Y	Y
4	**Westerman**	-	-	N	Y	Y	Y
CALIFORNIA							
1	**LaMalfa**	Y	Y	N	Y	Y	N
2	Huffman	N	N	Y	N	Y	Y
3	Garamendi	N	N	Y	N	Y	Y
4	**McClintock**	Y	Y	N	Y	N	N
5	Thompson, M.	N	N	Y	N	Y	Y
6	Matsui	N	N	Y	N	Y	Y
7	Bera	N	N	Y	N	Y	Y
8	**Cook**	Y	Y	N	Y	Y	Y
9	McNerney	N	N	Y	N	Y	Y
10	Harder	N	N	Y	N	Y	Y
11	DeSaulnier	N	N	Y	N	Y	Y
12	Pelosi						
13	Lee B.	N	N	Y	N	Y	Y
14	Speier	N	N	Y	N	Y	Y
15	Swalwell	N	N	Y	N	Y	Y
16	Costa	N	N	Y	N	Y	Y
17	Khanna	N	N	Y	N	Y	Y
18	Eshoo	N	N	Y	N	Y	Y
19	Lofgren	N	N	Y	N	Y	N
20	Panetta	N	N	Y	N	Y	Y
21	Cox	N	N	Y	N	Y	Y
22	**Nunes**	Y	Y	N	Y	Y	Y
23	**McCarthy**	Y	N	N	Y	Y	Y
24	Carbajal	N	N	Y	N	Y	Y
25	Hill, K.	N	N	Y	N	Y	Y
26	Brownley	N	N	Y	N	Y	Y
27	Chu	N	N	Y	N	Y	Y
28	Schiff	N	N	Y	N	Y	Y
29	Cárdenas	N	N	Y	N	Y	Y
30	Sherman	N	N	Y	N	Y	Y
31	Aguilar	N	N	Y	N	Y	Y
32	Napolitano	N	N	Y	N	Y	Y
33	Lieu	N	N	Y	N	Y	Y
34	Gomez	N	N	Y	N	Y	Y
35	Torres	N	N	Y	N	Y	Y
36	Ruiz	N	N	Y	N	Y	Y
37	Bass	N	N	Y	N	Y	Y
38	Sánchez	N	N	Y	N	Y	Y
39	Cisneros	N	N	Y	N	Y	Y
40	Roybal-Allard	N	N	Y	N	Y	Y
41	Takano	N	N	Y	N	Y	Y
42	**Calvert**	Y	N	N	Y	Y	Y
43	Waters	N	N	Y	N	Y	Y
44	Barragán	N	N	Y	N	Y	Y
45	Porter	N	N	Y	N	Y	Y
46	Correa	N	N	Y	N	Y	Y
47	Lowenthal	N	N	Y	N	Y	Y
48	Rouda	N	N	Y	N	Y	Y
49	Levin	N	N	Y	N	Y	Y
50	**Hunter**	Y	Y	Y	Y	Y	Y
51	Vargas	N	N	Y	N	Y	Y
52	Peters	N	N	Y	N	Y	Y

		337	338	339	340	341	342
53	Davis, S.	N	N	Y	N	Y	Y
COLORADO							
1	DeGette	N	N	Y	N	Y	Y
2	Neguse	N	N	Y	N	Y	Y
3	**Tipton**	Y	N	N	N	Y	Y
4	**Buck**	Y	Y	N	Y	Y	N
5	**Lamborn**	Y	Y	N	Y	Y	Y
6	Crow	N	N	Y	N	Y	Y
7	Perlmutter	N	N	Y	N	Y	Y
CONNECTICUT							
1	Larson	N	N	Y	N	Y	Y
2	Courtney	N	N	Y	N	Y	Y
3	DeLauro	-	-	+	-	+	Y
4	Himes	N	N	Y	N	Y	Y
5	Hayes	N	N	Y	N	Y	Y
DELAWARE							
AL	Blunt Rochester	N	N	Y	N	Y	Y
FLORIDA							
1	**Gaetz**	?	?	?	?	?	?
2	**Dunn**	Y	N	N	Y	Y	N
3	**Yoho**	?	?	?	?	?	?
4	**Rutherford**	Y	N	N	N	Y	Y
5	Lawson	N	N	Y	N	Y	Y
6	**Waltz**	-	+	-	-	+	+
7	Murphy	N	N	Y	N	Y	Y
8	**Posey**	Y	Y	N	Y	N	Y
9	Soto	N	N	Y	N	Y	Y
10	Demings	N	N	Y	N	Y	Y
11	**Webster**	Y	Y	N	Y	N	N
12	**Bilirakis**	Y	Y	Y	Y	Y	N
13	Crist	N	N	Y	N	Y	Y
14	Castor	N	N	Y	N	Y	Y
15	**Spano**	Y	N	Y	N	Y	Y
16	**Buchanan**	Y	N	Y	N	Y	Y
17	**Steube**	Y	Y	N	Y	N	Y
18	**Mast**	Y	N	Y	N	Y	Y
19	**Rooney**	N	N	N	N	Y	Y
20	Hastings	?	?	?	?	?	?
21	Frankel	N	N	Y	N	Y	Y
22	Deutch	N	N	Y	N	Y	Y
23	Wasserman Schultz	N	N	Y	N	Y	Y
24	Wilson, F.	N	N	Y	N	Y	Y
25	**Diaz-Balart**	Y	N	N	Y	N	Y
26	Mucarsel-Powell	N	N	Y	N	Y	Y
27	Shalala	N	N	Y	N	Y	Y
GEORGIA							
1	**Carter, E.L.**	Y	Y	N	Y	Y	N
2	Bishop, S.	N	N	Y	N	Y	Y
3	**Ferguson**	Y	Y	N	Y	N	Y
4	Johnson, H.	N	N	Y	N	Y	Y
5	Lewis John	N	N	Y	N	Y	Y
6	McBath	N	N	Y	N	Y	Y
7	**Woodall**	Y	Y	N	Y	Y	N
8	**Scott, A.**	Y	Y	N	Y	Y	N
9	**Collins, D.**	Y	Y	N	Y	Y	N
10	**Hice**	Y	Y	N	Y	N	N
11	**Loudermilk**	Y	Y	N	Y	Y	N
12	**Allen**	Y	Y	N	Y	Y	N
13	Scott, D.	N	N	Y	N	Y	Y
14	**Graves, T.**	Y	Y	N	Y	Y	N
HAWAII							
1	Case	N	N	Y	N	Y	Y
2	Gabbard	N	N	Y	N	Y	Y
IDAHO							
1	**Fulcher**	Y	Y	N	Y	Y	N
2	**Simpson**	Y	N	N	N	Y	Y
ILLINOIS							
1	Rush	N	N	Y	N	Y	Y
2	Kelly, R.	N	N	Y	N	Y	Y
3	Lipinski	N	N	Y	N	Y	N
4	García, J.	N	N	Y	N	Y	Y
5	Quigley	N	N	Y	N	Y	Y
6	Casten	N	N	Y	N	Y	Y
7	Davis, D.	N	N	Y	N	Y	Y
8	Krishnamoorthi	N	N	Y	N	Y	Y
9	Schakowsky	N	N	Y	N	Y	Y
10	Schneider	N	N	Y	N	Y	Y
11	Foster	N	N	Y	N	Y	Y

KEY: **Republicans**   Democrats   *Independents*

Y Voted for (yea)	**N** Voted against (nay)	**P** Voted "present"
+ Announced for	**-** Announced against	**?** Did not vote or otherwise
# Paired for	**X** Paired against	make position known

		337	338	339	340	341	342
12	**Bost**	Y	N	Y	Y	Y	Y
13	**Davis, R.**	Y	N	N	N	Y	Y
14	Underwood	N	N	Y	N	Y	Y
15	**Shimkus**	Y	Y	Y	Y	Y	Y
16	**Kinzinger**	N	N	Y	N	Y	Y
17	Bustos	N	N	Y	N	Y	Y
18	**LaHood**	Y	N	Y	N	Y	N
INDIANA							
1	Visclosky	N	N	Y	N	Y	Y
2	**Walorski**	Y	Y	Y	Y	Y	Y
3	**Banks**	Y	Y	N	Y	Y	Y
4	**Baird**	Y	Y	Y	N	Y	Y
5	**Brooks, S.**	N	Y	Y	Y	Y	Y
6	**Pence**	Y	N	Y	N	Y	Y
7	Carson	N	N	Y	N	Y	Y
8	**Bucshon**	Y	Y	N	Y	Y	Y
9	**Hollingsworth**	N	N	N	N	Y	N
IOWA							
1	Finkenauer	N	N	Y	N	Y	Y
2	Loebsack	N	N	Y	N	Y	Y
3	Axne	N	N	Y	N	Y	Y
4	**King, S.**	Y	Y	N	Y	Y	N
KANSAS							
1	**Marshall**	Y	N	N	N	Y	Y
2	**Watkins**	Y	Y	N	Y	Y	Y
3	Davids	N	N	Y	N	Y	Y
4	**Estes**	Y	Y	Y	Y	Y	Y
KENTUCKY							
1	**Comer**	Y	Y	Y	Y	Y	N
2	**Guthrie**	Y	Y	N	Y	Y	Y
3	Yarmuth	N	N	Y	N	Y	N
4	**Massie**	Y	Y	N	Y	N	N
5	**Rogers, H.**	Y	N	N	N	Y	Y
6	**Barr**	Y	N	N	N	Y	Y
LOUISIANA							
1	**Scalise**	Y	Y	N	Y	Y	Y
2	Richmond	N	N	Y	N	Y	Y
3	**Higgins, C.**	Y	Y	N	Y	N	Y
4	**Johnson, M.**	Y	Y	N	Y	Y	Y
5	**Abraham**	?	?	?	?	?	?
6	**Graves, G.**	Y	Y	Y	Y	Y	Y
MAINE							
1	Pingree	N	N	Y	N	Y	Y
2	Golden	N	N	Y	N	Y	Y
MARYLAND							
1	**Harris**	Y	Y	N	Y	N	N
2	Ruppersberger	N	N	Y	N	Y	Y
3	Sarbanes	N	N	Y	N	Y	Y
4	Brown, A.	N	N	Y	N	Y	Y
5	Hoyer	N	N	Y	N	Y	Y
6	Trone	N	N	Y	N	Y	Y
7	Cummings	N	N	Y	N	Y	Y
8	Raskin						
MASSACHUSETTS		N	N	Y	N	Y	Y
1	Neal						
2	McGovern	N	N	Y	N	Y	Y
3	Trahan	N	N	Y	N	Y	Y
4	Kennedy	N	N	Y	N	Y	Y
5	Clark	N	N	Y	N	Y	Y
6	Moulton	N	N	Y	N	Y	Y
7	Pressley	?	?	?	?	?	?
8	Lynch	N	N	Y	N	Y	N
9	Keating	N	N	Y	N	Y	Y
MICHIGAN		N	N	Y	N	Y	Y
1	**Bergman**						
2	**Huizenga**	Y	Y	Y	Y	Y	Y
3	**Amash**	Y	Y	N	Y	Y	Y
4	**Moolenaar**	Y	Y	N	Y	N	N
5	Kildee	Y	Y	Y	Y	Y	N
6	**Upton**	N	N	Y	N	Y	Y
7	**Walberg**	N	N	Y	Y	Y	Y
8	Slotkin	Y	Y	Y	Y	Y	N
9	Levin	N	N	Y	N	Y	Y
10	**Mitchell**	N	N	Y	N	Y	Y
11	Stevens	Y	Y	Y	Y	Y	Y
12	Dingell	N	N	Y	N	Y	Y
13	Tlaib	N	N	Y	N	Y	Y
14	Lawrence	N	N	Y	N	Y	N
MINNESOTA		N	N	Y	N	Y	Y
1	**Hagedorn**						
2	Craig	Y	N	Y	N	Y	Y
3	Phillips	N	N	Y	N	Y	N
4	McCollum	N	N	Y	N	Y	Y
5	Omar	N	N	Y	N	Y	Y

		337	338	339	340	341	342
6	**Emmer**	N	N	Y	N	N	N
7	Peterson	Y	N	N	N	Y	N
8	**Stauber**	N	N	Y	N	Y	Y
MISSISSIPPI		Y	N	Y	N	Y	Y
1	**Kelly, T.**						
2	Thompson, B.	Y	Y	N	Y	Y	N
3	**Guest**	N	N	Y	N	Y	Y
4	**Palazzo**	Y	N	N	Y	Y	N
MISSOURI		Y	Y	N	Y	Y	N
1	Clay						
2	**Wagner**	N	N	Y	N	Y	Y
3	**Luetkemeyer**	Y	N	Y	Y	Y	Y
4	**Hartzler**	Y	N	N	N	Y	Y
5	Cleaver	Y	N	N	Y	Y	Y
6	**Graves, S.**	N	N	Y	N	Y	Y
7	**Long**	Y	Y	N	Y	Y	Y
8	**Smith, J.**	Y	Y	N	Y	Y	Y
MONTANA		Y	Y	N	Y	Y	Y
AL	**Gianforte**						
NEBRASKA		Y	Y	Y	N	Y	Y
1	**Fortenberry**						
2	**Bacon**	N	N	N	N	Y	N
3	**Smith, Adrian**	N	Y	N	Y	Y	N
NEVADA		Y	Y	N	Y	N	Y
1	Titus						
2	**Amodei**	N	N	Y	N	Y	Y
3	Lee	Y	Y	Y	Y	Y	Y
4	Horsford	N	N	Y	N	Y	Y
NEW HAMPSHIRE		N	N	Y	N	Y	Y
1	Pappas						
2	Kuster	N	N	Y	N	Y	Y
NEW JERSEY		N	N	Y	N	Y	Y
1	Norcross						
2	Van Drew	N	N	Y	N	Y	N
3	Kim	N	N	Y	N	Y	Y
4	**Smith, C.**	N	N	Y	N	Y	Y
5	Gottheimer	N	N	Y	N	Y	Y
6	Pallone	N	N	Y	N	Y	Y
7	Malinowski	N	N	Y	N	Y	Y
8	Sires	N	N	Y	N	Y	Y
9	Pascrell	N	N	Y	N	Y	Y
10	Payne	N	N	Y	N	Y	Y
11	Sherrill	N	N	Y	N	Y	N
12	Watson Coleman	N	N	Y	N	Y	Y
NEW MEXICO		N	N	Y	N	Y	Y
1	Haaland						
2	Torres Small	N	N	Y	N	Y	Y
3	Luján	N	N	Y	N	Y	Y
NEW YORK		N	N	Y	N	Y	Y
1	**Zeldin**						
2	**King, P.**	N	N	N	Y	Y	Y
3	Suozzi	N	N	N	N	Y	Y
4	Rice, K.	N	N	Y	N	Y	Y
5	Meeks	N	N	Y	N	Y	Y
6	Meng	N	N	Y	N	Y	Y
7	Velázquez	N	N	Y	N	Y	Y
8	Jeffries	N	N	Y	N	Y	Y
9	Clarke	N	N	Y	N	Y	Y
10	Nadler	N	N	Y	N	Y	Y
11	Rose	N	N	Y	N	Y	Y
12	Maloney, C.	N	N	N	N	N	N
13	Espaillat	N	N	Y	N	Y	Y
14	Ocasio-Cortez	N	N	Y	N	Y	Y
15	Serrano	N	N	Y	N	N	Y
16	Engel	N	N	Y	N	Y	Y
17	Lowey	N	N	Y	N	Y	Y
18	Maloney, S.P.	N	N	Y	N	Y	Y
19	Delgado	N	N	Y	N	Y	Y
20	Tonko	N	N	Y	N	Y	Y
21	**Stefanik**	N	N	Y	N	Y	Y
22	Brindisi	N	N	Y	N	Y	Y
23	**Reed**	N	N	Y	N	Y	Y
24	**Katko**	N	N	Y	N	Y	Y
25	Morelle	N	N	Y	N	Y	Y
26	Higgins, B.	N	N	Y	N	Y	Y
27	**Collins, C.**	N	N	Y	N	Y	Y
NORTH CAROLINA		Y	N	N	N	Y	Y
1	Butterfield						
2	**Holding**	N	N	Y	N	Y	Y
3	**Jones***	?	?	?	?	?	?
4	Price						
5	**Foxx**	N	N	Y	N	Y	Y
6	**Walker**	Y	N	N	Y	Y	Y
7	**Rouzer**	Y	Y	N	Y	Y	Y

		337	338	339	340	341	342
8	**Hudson**	Y	Y	N	Y	Y	Y
9	vacant	Y	Y	N	Y	Y	Y
10	**McHenry**	Y	Y	N	Y	Y	Y
11	**Meadows**	Y	Y	N	N	N	N
12	Adams	N	N	Y	N	Y	Y
13	**Budd**	Y	Y	N	Y	N	N
NORTH DAKOTA							
AL	**Armstrong**	Y	N	Y	N	Y	Y
OHIO							
1	**Chabot**	Y	Y	N	Y	Y	Y
2	**Wenstrup**	Y	Y	Y	Y	Y	Y
3	Beatty	N	N	Y	N	Y	Y
4	**Jordan**	Y	Y	N	Y	N	N
5	**Latta**	Y	Y	Y	Y	Y	Y
6	**Johnson, B.**	Y	Y	N	Y	Y	Y
7	**Gibbs**	Y	Y	N	Y	Y	N
8	**Davidson**	Y	Y	N	N	N	N
9	Kaptur	N	N	Y	N	Y	Y
10	**Turner**	Y	N	Y	N	Y	Y
11	Fudge	N	N	Y	N	Y	Y
12	**Balderson**	Y	Y	Y	Y	Y	Y
13	Ryan	N	N	Y	N	Y	Y
14	**Joyce**	Y	N	Y	N	Y	Y
15	**Stivers**	N	N	Y	N	Y	Y
16	**Gonzalez**	N	N	Y	N	Y	Y
OKLAHOMA							
1	**Hern**	Y	Y	N	Y	N	Y
2	**Mullin**	Y	Y	N	Y	Y	Y
3	**Lucas**	Y	N	N	Y	Y	Y
4	**Cole**	Y	N	N	N	Y	Y
5	Horn	N	N	Y	N	Y	Y
OREGON							
1	Bonamici	N	N	Y	N	Y	N
2	**Walden**	Y	N	N	N	Y	Y
3	Blumenauer	N	N	Y	N	Y	Y
4	DeFazio	N	N	Y	N	Y	Y
5	Schrader	N	N	Y	N	Y	Y
PENNSYLVANIA							
1	**Fitzpatrick**	N	N	Y	N	Y	Y
2	Boyle	N	N	Y	N	Y	Y
3	Evans	N	N	Y	N	Y	Y
4	Dean	N	N	Y	N	Y	Y
5	Scanlon	N	N	Y	N	Y	Y
6	Houlahan	N	N	Y	N	Y	Y
7	Wild	N	N	Y	N	Y	Y
8	Cartwright	N	N	Y	N	Y	Y
9	**Meuser**	Y	N	N	N	Y	N
10	**Perry**	Y	Y	N	Y	N	Y
11	**Smucker**	Y	Y	N	Y	Y	Y
12	**Marino***						
13	**Joyce**	Y	Y	N	Y	Y	N
14	**Reschenthaler**	Y	N	Y	N	Y	Y
15	**Thompson, G.**	Y	N	Y	N	Y	Y
16	**Kelly, M.**	Y	Y	Y	Y	Y	Y
17	Lamb	N	N	Y	N	Y	Y
18	Doyle	N	N	Y	N	Y	Y
RHODE ISLAND							
1	Cicilline	N	N	Y	N	Y	Y
2	Langevin	N	N	Y	N	Y	Y
SOUTH CAROLINA							
1	Cunningham	N	N	Y	N	Y	Y
2	**Wilson, J.**	Y	Y	N	Y	N	N
3	**Duncan**	Y	Y	N	Y	N	N
4	**Timmons**	Y	Y	N	Y	Y	Y
5	**Norman**	Y	Y	N	Y	N	N
6	Clyburn	N	N	Y	N	Y	Y
7	**Rice, T.**	Y	Y	N	Y	Y	N
SOUTH DAKOTA							
AL	**Johnson**	Y	Y	N	Y	Y	Y
TENNESSEE							
1	**Roe**	Y	Y	Y	Y	Y	Y
2	**Burchett**	Y	Y	N	Y	N	N
3	**Fleischmann**	Y	N	Y	N	Y	Y
4	**DesJarlais**	Y	Y	Y	Y	Y	Y
5	Cooper	N	N	Y	Y	Y	Y
6	**Rose**	Y	Y	N	N	N	N
7	**Green**	Y	Y	N	N	Y	N
8	**Kustoff**	Y	Y	N	Y	Y	N
9	Cohen	N	N	Y	N	Y	Y
TEXAS							
1	**Gohmert**	Y	Y	N	Y	Y	Y
2	**Crenshaw**	Y	N	N	Y	Y	Y
3	**Taylor**	Y	Y	N	Y	Y	Y
4	**Ratcliffe**	Y	Y	N	Y	N	Y

		337	338	339	340	341	342
5	**Gooden**	Y	Y	N	Y	N	N
6	**Wright**	Y	Y	N	Y	N	N
7	Fletcher	N	N	Y	N	Y	Y
8	**Brady**	Y	Y	N	Y	Y	N
9	Green, A.	N	N	Y	N	Y	Y
10	**McCaul**	Y	N	N	N	Y	Y
11	**Conaway**	Y	Y	N	Y	Y	Y
12	**Granger**	Y	N	N	N	Y	Y
13	**Thornberry**	Y	N	N	N	Y	N
14	**Weber**	Y	Y	N	Y	N	N
15	Gonzalez	N	N	Y	N	Y	Y
16	Escobar	N	N	Y	N	Y	Y
17	**Flores**	Y	Y	Y	Y	Y	Y
18	Jackson Lee	N	N	Y	N	Y	Y
19	**Arrington**	Y	Y	N	Y	N	N
20	Castro	N	N	Y	N	Y	Y
21	**Roy**	Y	Y	N	Y	N	N
22	**Olson**	Y	Y	N	Y	N	Y
23	**Hurd**	N	N	Y	N	Y	Y
24	**Marchant**	Y	N	N	Y	N	Y
25	**Williams**	Y	Y	N	Y	N	N
26	**Burgess**	Y	Y	N	Y	N	N
27	**Cloud**	Y	Y	N	Y	N	Y
28	Cuellar	N	N	Y	N	Y	Y
29	Garcia, S.	N	N	Y	N	Y	Y
30	Johnson, E.B.	N	N	Y	N	Y	Y
31	**Carter, J.**	Y	Y	N	N	Y	Y
32	Allred	N	N	Y	N	Y	Y
33	Veasey	N	N	Y	N	Y	Y
34	Vela	N	N	Y	N	Y	Y
35	Doggett	?	N	Y	N	Y	Y
36	**Babin**	Y	Y	N	Y	N	Y
UTAH							
1	**Bishop, R.**	Y	Y	N	Y	N	N
2	**Stewart**	Y	Y	N	Y	Y	Y
3	**Curtis**	?	?	?	?	?	?
4	McAdams	N	N	N	N	Y	Y
VERMONT							
AL	Welch	N	N	Y	N	Y	N
VIRGINIA							
1	**Wittman**	Y	Y	N	Y	Y	Y
2	Luria	N	N	Y	N	Y	N
3	Scott, R.	N	N	Y	N	Y	Y
4	McEachin	N	N	Y	N	Y	Y
5	**Riggleman**	Y	Y	N	Y	Y	Y
6	**Cline**	Y	Y	N	Y	N	Y
7	Spanberger	N	N	N	N	Y	N
8	Beyer	N	N	Y	N	Y	Y
9	**Griffith**	Y	Y	N	Y	N	Y
10	Wexton	N	N	Y	N	Y	Y
11	Connolly	N	N	Y	N	Y	Y
WASHINGTON							
1	DelBene	N	N	Y	N	Y	Y
2	Larsen	N	N	Y	N	Y	N
3	**Herrera Beutler**	?	?	?	?	?	?
4	**Newhouse**	Y	N	N	N	Y	Y
5	**McMorris Rodgers**	Y	N	N	Y	Y	Y
6	Kilmer	N	N	Y	N	Y	Y
7	Jayapal	N	N	Y	N	Y	Y
8	Schrier	N	N	Y	N	Y	Y
9	Smith Adam	N	N	Y	N	Y	Y
10	Heck	N	N	Y	N	Y	Y
WEST VIRGINIA							
1	**McKinley**	Y	N	N	N	Y	Y
2	**Mooney**	Y	Y	N	Y	Y	Y
3	**Miller**	Y	Y	N	Y	Y	Y
WISCONSIN							
1	**Steil**	Y	Y	Y	N	Y	Y
2	Pocan	N	N	Y	N	Y	Y
3	Kind	N	N	Y	N	Y	Y
4	Moore	N	N	Y	N	Y	Y
5	**Sensenbrenner**	Y	Y	Y	Y	N	Y
6	**Grothman**	Y	Y	Y	Y	Y	N
7	**Duffy**	Y	Y	N	Y	Y	Y
8	**Gallagher**	Y	N	Y	N	Y	Y
WYOMING							
AL	**Cheney**	Y	N	N	N	Y	Y
DELEGATES							
	Radewagen (A.S.)	?	?	?	?	?	?
	Norton (D.C.)	N	N	Y	N	Y	Y
	San Nicolas (Guam)	N	N	Y	N	Y	Y
	Sablan (N. Marianas)	N	N	Y	N	Y	Y
	González-Colón (P.R.)	Y	N	N	N	Y	Y
	Plaskett (V.I.)	N	N	Y	N	Y	Y

343. HR2740. Fiscal 2020 Four-Bill Appropriations Package - U.S. Army Medical Research. Langevin, D-R.I., amendment that would increase by $10 million funding for research, development, and evaluation for U.S. Army medical research activities under Defense Department health programs and decrease by the same amount funding for expenses related to operational testing and evaluation of weapons systems by the Defense Department. Adopted in Committee of the Whole 277-151: R 47-145; D 229-6; I 1-0. June 18, 2019.

344. HR2740. Fiscal 2020 Four-Bill Appropriations Package - Military Service of Transgender Individuals. Brown, D-Md., for Speier, D-Calif., amendment that would prohibit the use of funds made available under the Defense Department title of the bill (Division C) to implement a March 2019 department memorandum related to military service by transgender individuals and individuals with gender dysphoria. Adopted in Committee of the Whole 243-183: R 9-182; D 234-1. June 18, 2019.

345. HR2740. Fiscal 2020 Four-Bill Appropriations Package - Foreign Intelligence Searches. Amash, R-Mich., amendment that would prohibit the use of funds made available by the Defense Department title of the bill (Division C) for searches under the Foreign Intelligence Surveillance Act without explicit language in the search certification clarifying that it does not authorize the targeting of individuals outside the U.S. so as to acquire communications of an individual inside the U.S. Rejected in Committee of the Whole 175-253: R 65-127; D 110-125; I 0-1. June 18, 2019.

346. HR2740. Fiscal 2020 Four-Bill Appropriations Package - Defense Department Research and Evaluation. Kuster, D-N.H., amendment, as modified, that would increase then decrease by $5 million funding for Defense-wide research- and evaluation-related expenses. Adopted in Committee of the Whole 327-101: R 93-99; D 233-2; I 1-0. June 18, 2019.

347. HR2740. Fiscal 2020 Four-Bill Appropriations Package - Army Research and Evaluation. Visclosky, D-Ind., for Veasey, D-Texas, amendment that would increase by $9 million funding for Army research- and evaluation-related expenses and decrease by the same amount funding for Defense-wide operations and maintenance. Adopted in Committee of the Whole 389-39: R 161-31; D 227-8; I 1-0. June 18, 2019.

348. HR2740. Fiscal 2020 Four-Bill Appropriations Package - Defense Department Operations. Visclosky, D-Ind., for Jeffries, D-N.Y., amendment that would decrease then increase by $500,000 funding for Defense-wide operations and maintenance. Adopted in Committee of the Whole 254-174: R 18-174; D 235-0; I 1-0. June 18, 2019.

		343	344	345	346	347	348
ALABAMA							
1	Byrne	N	N	Y	N	Y	N
2	Roby	N	N	N	N	Y	N
3	Rogers, M.	N	N	N	Y	N	N
4	Aderholt	N	N	N	N	N	N
5	Brooks, M.	N	N	Y	N	Y	N
6	Palmer	N	N	N	N	N	N
7	Sewell	Y	Y	N	Y	Y	Y
ALASKA							
AL	Young	N	N	N	N	Y	N
ARIZONA							
1	O'Halleran	Y	Y	N	Y	Y	Y
2	Kirkpatrick	Y	Y	N	Y	Y	Y
3	Grijalva	Y	Y	N	Y	Y	Y
4	Gosar	N	N	Y	N	Y	N
5	Biggs	N	N	Y	N	Y	N
6	Schweikert	N	N	Y	Y	Y	N
7	Gallego	Y	Y	N	Y	Y	Y
8	Lesko	N	N	N	N	Y	N
9	Stanton	Y	Y	Y	Y	Y	Y
ARKANSAS							
1	Crawford	N	N	N	Y	Y	N
2	Hill, F.	N	N	Y	Y	Y	N
3	Womack	N	N	N	N	Y	N
4	Westerman	N	N	N	N	Y	N
CALIFORNIA							
1	LaMalfa	N	N	Y	Y	Y	N
2	Huffman	Y	Y	Y	Y	Y	Y
3	Garamendi	Y	Y	N	Y	Y	Y
4	McClintock	N	N	Y	N	N	N
5	Thompson, M.	Y	Y	N	Y	Y	Y
6	Matsui	Y	Y	Y	Y	Y	Y
7	Bera	Y	Y	N	Y	Y	Y
8	Cook	N	N	N	Y	Y	N
9	McNerney	Y	Y	N	Y	Y	Y
10	Harder	Y	Y	Y	Y	Y	Y
11	DeSaulnier	Y	Y	Y	Y	Y	Y
12	Pelosi						
13	Lee B.	Y	Y	Y	Y	Y	Y
14	Speier	Y	Y	Y	Y	Y	Y
15	Swalwell	Y	Y	N	Y	Y	Y
16	Costa	Y	Y	N	Y	Y	Y
17	Khanna	Y	Y	Y	Y	Y	Y
18	Eshoo	Y	Y	Y	Y	Y	Y
19	Lofgren	Y	Y	Y	Y	N	Y
20	Panetta	Y	Y	Y	Y	Y	Y
21	Cox	Y	Y	N	Y	Y	Y
22	Nunes	N	N	N	Y	Y	N
23	McCarthy	Y	N	N	Y	Y	N
24	Carbajal	Y	Y	N	Y	Y	Y
25	Hill, K.	Y	Y	N	Y	Y	Y
26	Brownley	Y	Y	N	Y	N	Y
27	Chu	Y	Y	Y	Y	Y	Y
28	Schiff	Y	Y	N	Y	Y	Y
29	Cárdenas	Y	Y	N	Y	Y	Y
30	Sherman	Y	Y	N	Y	Y	Y
31	Aguilar	Y	Y	N	Y	Y	Y
32	Napolitano	Y	Y	N	Y	Y	Y
33	Lieu	Y	Y	Y	Y	Y	Y
34	Gomez	Y	Y	Y	Y	Y	Y
35	Torres	Y	Y	N	Y	Y	Y
36	Ruiz	Y	Y	N	Y	Y	Y
37	Bass	Y	Y	Y	Y	Y	Y
38	Sánchez	Y	Y	Y	Y	Y	Y
39	Cisneros	Y	Y	N	Y	Y	Y
40	Roybal-Allard	Y	Y	Y	Y	Y	Y
41	Takano	Y	Y	Y	Y	Y	Y
42	Calvert	Y	N	N	Y	Y	N
43	Waters	Y	Y	N	Y	Y	Y
44	Barragán	Y	Y	Y	Y	Y	Y
45	Porter	Y	Y	Y	Y	Y	Y
46	Correa	Y	Y	Y	Y	Y	Y
47	Lowenthal	Y	Y	Y	Y	Y	Y
48	Rouda	Y	Y	N	Y	Y	Y
49	Levin	Y	Y	N	Y	Y	Y
50	Hunter	N	N	Y	Y	Y	N
51	Vargas	Y	Y	N	Y	Y	Y
52	Peters	Y	Y	N	Y	Y	Y
53	Davis, S.	Y	Y	Y	Y	Y	Y
COLORADO							
1	DeGette	Y	Y	Y	Y	Y	Y
2	Neguse	Y	Y	Y	Y	Y	Y
3	Tipton	N	N	N	N	Y	N
4	Buck	N	N	Y	N	N	N
5	Lamborn	N	N	Y	N	N	N
6	Crow	Y	Y	N	Y	Y	Y
7	Perlmutter	Y	Y	Y	Y	Y	Y
CONNECTICUT							
1	Larson	Y	Y	Y	Y	Y	Y
2	Courtney	Y	Y	Y	Y	Y	Y
3	DeLauro	Y	Y	Y	Y	Y	Y
4	Himes	Y	Y	N	Y	Y	Y
5	Hayes	Y	Y	Y	Y	Y	Y
DELAWARE							
AL	Blunt Rochester	Y	Y	Y	Y	Y	Y
FLORIDA							
1	Gaetz	?	?	?	?	?	?
2	Dunn	Y	N	N	N	Y	N
3	Yoho	?	?	?	?	?	?
4	Rutherford	N	N	N	N	Y	N
5	Lawson	Y	Y	N	Y	Y	Y
6	Waltz	+	-	-	+	+	-
7	Murphy	Y	Y	N	Y	Y	Y
8	Posey	N	N	Y	N	N	N
9	Soto	Y	Y	N	Y	Y	Y
10	Demings	Y	Y	N	Y	Y	Y
11	Webster	N	N	Y	N	N	N
12	Bilirakis	Y	N	N	Y	Y	N
13	Crist	Y	Y	N	Y	Y	Y
14	Castor	Y	Y	N	Y	Y	Y
15	Spano	N	N	N	Y	Y	N
16	Buchanan	Y	N	N	Y	Y	N
17	Steube	N	N	Y	N	Y	N
18	Mast	N	N	N	Y	Y	N
19	Rooney	N	N	N	N	Y	N
20	Hastings	?	?	?	?	?	?
21	Frankel	Y	Y	N	Y	Y	Y
22	Deutch	Y	Y	N	Y	Y	Y
23	Wasserman Schultz	Y	Y	N	Y	Y	Y
24	Wilson, F.	Y	Y	Y	Y	Y	Y
25	Diaz-Balart	Y	Y	N	N	Y	N
26	Mucarsel-Powell	Y	Y	N	Y	Y	Y
27	Shalala	Y	Y	N	Y	Y	Y
GEORGIA							
1	Carter, E.L.	N	N	N	Y	N	N
2	Bishop, S.	Y	Y	N	Y	Y	Y
3	Ferguson	N	N	N	N	Y	N
4	Johnson, H.	Y	Y	Y	Y	Y	Y
5	Lewis John	Y	Y	N	Y	Y	Y
6	McBath	Y	Y	N	Y	Y	Y
7	Woodall	Y	N	Y	N	Y	N
8	Scott, A.	N	N	N	N	Y	N
9	Collins, D.	N	N	N	N	Y	N
10	Hice	N	N	Y	N	Y	N
11	Loudermilk	N	N	Y	N	Y	N
12	Allen	N	N	N	N	Y	N
13	Scott, D.	Y	Y	N	Y	Y	Y
14	Graves, T.	N	N	N	Y	N	N
HAWAII							
1	Case	Y	Y	N	Y	Y	Y
2	Gabbard	Y	Y	Y	Y	Y	Y
IDAHO							
1	Fulcher	N	N	Y	N	Y	N
2	Simpson	Y	N	N	Y	Y	N
ILLINOIS							
1	Rush	Y	Y	Y	Y	Y	Y
2	Kelly, R.	Y	Y	Y	Y	Y	Y
3	Lipinski	Y	Y	N	Y	Y	Y
4	García, J.	Y	Y	N	Y	Y	Y
5	Quigley	Y	Y	N	Y	Y	Y
6	Casten	Y	Y	N	Y	Y	Y
7	Davis, D.	Y	Y	Y	Y	Y	Y
8	Krishnamoorthi	Y	Y	N	Y	Y	Y
9	Schakowsky	Y	Y	Y	Y	Y	Y
10	Schneider	Y	Y	N	Y	Y	Y
11	Foster	Y	Y	N	Y	Y	Y

		343	344	345	346	347	348
12	**Bost**	Y	N	N	Y	Y	N
13	**Davis, R.**	Y	N	Y	Y	Y	Y
14	Underwood	Y	Y	N	Y	Y	Y
15	**Shimkus**	Y	N	N	Y	Y	N
16	**Kinzinger**	Y	N	N	Y	Y	N
17	Bustos	Y	Y	N	Y	Y	Y
18	**LaHood**	N	N	N	N	Y	N
INDIANA							
1	Visclosky	Y	Y	N	Y	Y	Y
2	**Walorski**	N	N	N	Y	Y	N
3	**Banks**	N	N	N	Y	Y	N
4	**Baird**	N	N	N	Y	Y	N
5	**Brooks, S.**	N	N	N	Y	Y	N
6	**Pence**	N	N	N	Y	Y	N
7	Carson	Y	Y	N	Y	Y	Y
8	**Bucshon**	N	N	N	N	Y	N
9	**Hollingsworth**	N	Y	N	Y	Y	Y
IOWA							
1	Finkenauer	Y	Y	N	Y	Y	Y
2	Loebsack	Y	Y	N	Y	Y	Y
3	Axne	Y	Y	N	Y	Y	Y
4	**King, S.**	N	N	N	N	Y	N
KANSAS							
1	**Marshall**	N	N	N	N	N	N
2	**Watkins**	N	N	N	Y	Y	N
3	Davids	Y	Y	N	Y	Y	Y
4	**Estes**	N	N	Y	Y	Y	N
KENTUCKY							
1	**Comer**	N	N	Y	N	Y	N
2	**Guthrie**	Y	N	N	Y	Y	N
3	Yarmuth	Y	Y	Y	Y	Y	Y
4	**Massie**	N	N	Y	N	N	N
5	**Rogers, H.**	Y	N	N	N	Y	N
6	**Barr**	Y	N	N	N	Y	N
LOUISIANA							
1	**Scalise**	N	N	N	N	Y	N
2	Richmond	Y	Y	N	Y	Y	Y
3	**Higgins, C.**	N	N	N	N	Y	N
4	**Johnson, M.**	Y	N	N	Y	Y	N
5	**Abraham**	?	?	?	?	?	?
6	**Graves, G.**	Y	N	Y	Y	Y	Y
MAINE							
1	Pingree	Y	Y	Y	Y	Y	Y
2	Golden	N	Y	Y	Y	Y	Y
MARYLAND							
1	**Harris**	N	N	Y	N	N	N
2	Ruppersberger	Y	Y	N	Y	Y	Y
3	Sarbanes	Y	Y	Y	Y	Y	Y
4	Brown, A.	Y	Y	N	Y	Y	Y
5	Hoyer	Y	Y	N	Y	Y	Y
6	Trone	Y	Y	N	Y	Y	Y
7	Cummings	Y	Y	N	Y	Y	Y
8	Raskin						
MASSACHUSETTS		Y	Y	Y	Y	Y	Y
1	Neal						
2	McGovern	Y	Y	Y	Y	Y	Y
3	Trahan	Y	Y	Y	Y	Y	Y
4	Kennedy	Y	Y	N	Y	Y	Y
5	Clark	Y	Y	Y	Y	Y	Y
6	Moulton	Y	Y	Y	Y	Y	Y
7	Pressley	?	?	?	?	?	?
8	Lynch	Y	Y	Y	Y	N	Y
9	Keating	Y	Y	Y	Y	Y	Y
MICHIGAN		Y	Y	N	Y	Y	Y
1	**Bergman**						
2	**Huizenga**	Y	N	N	N	Y	N
3	**Amash**	N	N	N	N	Y	N
4	**Moolenaar**	N	Y	Y	N	N	N
5	Kildee	N	N	N	Y	Y	N
6	**Upton**	Y	Y	Y	Y	Y	Y
7	**Walberg**	N	N	N	Y	Y	Y
8	Slotkin	N	N	N	N	Y	N
9	Levin	Y	Y	N	Y	Y	Y
10	**Mitchell**	Y	Y	Y	Y	Y	Y
11	Stevens	Y	N	N	Y	Y	N
12	Dingell	Y	Y	N	Y	Y	Y
13	Tlaib	Y	Y	Y	Y	Y	Y
14	Lawrence	Y	Y	Y	Y	N	Y
MINNESOTA		Y	Y	N	Y	Y	Y
1	**Hagedorn**						
2	Craig	N	N	N	N	Y	N
3	Phillips	Y	Y	N	N	N	Y
4	McCollum	Y	Y	Y	Y	Y	Y
5	Omar	Y	Y	Y	Y	Y	Y

		343	344	345	346	347	348
6	**Emmer**	Y	Y	Y	Y	N	Y
7	Peterson	N	Y	Y	N	Y	N
8	**Stauber**	Y	N	N	Y	N	Y
MISSISSIPPI		Y	N	N	Y	Y	N
1	**Kelly, T.**						
2	Thompson, B.	N	N	Y	N	Y	N
3	**Guest**	Y	Y	N	Y	Y	Y
4	**Palazzo**	N	N	N	N	Y	N
MISSOURI		N	N	N	N	Y	N
1	Clay						
2	**Wagner**	Y	Y	Y	Y	Y	Y
3	**Luetkemeyer**	N	N	N	Y	Y	N
4	**Hartzler**	N	N	N	Y	Y	N
5	Cleaver	N	N	N	N	Y	N
6	**Graves, S.**	Y	Y	N	Y	Y	Y
7	**Long**	N	N	N	Y	Y	N
8	**Smith, J.**	Y	N	N	Y	Y	N
MONTANA		N	N	Y	Y	Y	N
AL	**Gianforte**						
NEBRASKA		N	N	Y	Y	N	N
1	**Fortenberry**						
2	**Bacon**	N	N	N	N	Y	Y
3	**Smith, Adrian**	N	N	N	N	Y	N
NEVADA		N	N	Y	N	Y	N
1	Titus						
2	**Amodei**	Y	Y	Y	Y	Y	Y
3	Lee	Y	N	N	Y	Y	N
4	Horsford	Y	Y	N	Y	Y	Y
NEW HAMPSHIRE		Y	Y	Y	Y	Y	Y
1	Pappas						
2	Kuster	Y	Y	Y	Y	Y	Y
NEW JERSEY		Y	Y	Y	Y	Y	Y
1	Norcross						
2	Van Drew	Y	Y	N	Y	Y	Y
3	Kim	N	Y	N	Y	Y	Y
4	**Smith, C.**	Y	Y	N	Y	Y	Y
5	Gottheimer	N	N	N	Y	Y	Y
6	Pallone	Y	Y	N	Y	Y	Y
7	Malinowski	Y	Y	Y	Y	Y	Y
8	Sires	Y	Y	N	Y	Y	Y
9	Pascrell	Y	Y	Y	Y	Y	Y
10	Payne	Y	Y	N	Y	Y	Y
11	Sherrill	Y	Y	Y	Y	Y	Y
12	Watson Coleman	Y	Y	N	Y	Y	Y
NEW MEXICO		Y	Y	Y	Y	Y	Y
1	Haaland						
2	Torres Small	Y	Y	Y	Y	Y	Y
3	Luján	Y	Y	N	Y	Y	Y
NEW YORK		Y	Y	Y	Y	Y	Y
1	**Zeldin**						
2	**King, P.**	Y	N	Y	N	Y	Y
3	Suozzi	Y	N	N	Y	Y	N
4	Rice, K.	Y	Y	N	Y	Y	Y
5	Meeks	Y	Y	N	Y	Y	Y
6	Meng	Y	Y	Y	Y	Y	Y
7	Velázquez	Y	Y	Y	Y	Y	Y
8	Jeffries	Y	Y	Y	Y	Y	Y
9	Clarke	Y	Y	Y	Y	Y	Y
10	Nadler	Y	Y	Y	Y	Y	Y
11	Rose	Y	Y	Y	Y	Y	Y
12	Maloney, C.	Y	Y	N	Y	Y	Y
13	Espaillat	Y	Y	Y	Y	Y	Y
14	Ocasio-Cortez	Y	Y	N	Y	Y	Y
15	Serrano	Y	Y	Y	Y	N	Y
16	Engel	Y	Y	Y	Y	Y	Y
17	Lowey	Y	Y	Y	Y	Y	Y
18	Maloney, S.P.	Y	Y	N	Y	Y	Y
19	Delgado	Y	Y	N	Y	Y	Y
20	Tonko	Y	Y	N	Y	Y	Y
21	**Stefanik**	Y	Y	Y	Y	Y	Y
22	Brindisi	Y	N	N	Y	Y	Y
23	**Reed**	N	Y	N	Y	Y	Y
24	**Katko**	Y	Y	N	Y	Y	Y
25	Morelle	Y	Y	N	Y	Y	Y
26	Higgins, B.	Y	Y	N	Y	Y	Y
27	**Collins, C.**	Y	Y	N	Y	Y	Y
NORTH CAROLINA		N	N	N	Y	Y	N
1	Butterfield						
2	**Holding**	Y	Y	N	Y	Y	Y
3	**Jones***	?	?	?	?	?	?
4	Price						
5	**Foxx**	Y	Y	Y	Y	Y	Y
6	**Walker**	N	N	N	Y	Y	N
7	**Rouzer**	N	N	Y	N	N	N

		343	344	345	346	347	348
8	**Hudson**	N	N	N	Y	Y	N
9	vacant	N	N	N	N	Y	N
10	**McHenry**	Y	N	N	Y	Y	Y
11	**Meadows**	N	N	Y	Y	N	N
12	Adams	Y	Y	Y	Y	Y	Y
13	**Budd**	N	N	Y	N	N	N
NORTH DAKOTA							
AL	**Armstrong**	N	N	N	Y	Y	N
OHIO							
1	**Chabot**	N	N	Y	Y	Y	N
2	**Wenstrup**	Y	N	N	Y	Y	N
3	Beatty	Y	Y	N	Y	Y	Y
4	**Jordan**	N	N	Y	N	N	N
5	**Latta**	N	N	N	N	Y	N
6	**Johnson, B.**	N	N	N	N	Y	N
7	**Gibbs**	N	N	N	N	Y	N
8	**Davidson**	N	N	Y	N	N	N
9	Kaptur	Y	Y	N	Y	Y	Y
10	**Turner**	Y	N	N	Y	Y	N
11	Fudge	Y	Y	N	Y	Y	Y
12	**Balderson**	N	N	N	N	Y	N
13	Ryan	Y	Y	N	Y	Y	Y
14	**Joyce**	Y	N	N	Y	Y	N
15	**Stivers**	N	N	N	Y	Y	N
16	**Gonzalez**	Y	Y	Y	Y	Y	N
OKLAHOMA							
1	**Hern**	N	N	Y	Y	Y	N
2	**Mullin**	N	N	Y	Y	Y	N
3	**Lucas**	N	N	N	Y	Y	N
4	**Cole**	Y	N	N	N	Y	N
5	Horn	Y	Y	N	Y	Y	Y
OREGON							
1	Bonamici	Y	Y	Y	Y	Y	Y
2	**Walden**	N	N	N	Y	Y	N
3	Blumenauer	Y	Y	N	Y	Y	Y
4	DeFazio	Y	Y	Y	Y	Y	Y
5	Schrader	Y	Y	Y	Y	Y	Y
PENNSYLVANIA							
1	**Fitzpatrick**	Y	Y	N	Y	Y	Y
2	Boyle	Y	Y	Y	Y	Y	Y
3	Evans	Y	Y	Y	Y	Y	Y
4	Dean	Y	Y	Y	Y	Y	Y
5	Scanlon	Y	Y	Y	Y	Y	Y
6	Houlahan	Y	Y	N	Y	Y	Y
7	Wild	Y	Y	Y	Y	Y	Y
8	Cartwright	Y	Y	N	Y	Y	Y
9	**Meuser**	N	N	N	N	N	N
10	**Perry**	N	N	Y	N	Y	N
11	**Smucker**	Y	N	N	Y	Y	N
12	**Marino***						
13	**Joyce**	N	N	N	N	Y	N
14	**Reschenthaler**	Y	N	N	Y	Y	N
15	**Thompson, G.**	Y	N	Y	Y	Y	Y
16	**Kelly, M.**	Y	N	N	Y	Y	N
17	Lamb	Y	Y	N	Y	Y	Y
18	Doyle	Y	Y	Y	Y	Y	Y
RHODE ISLAND							
1	Cicilline	Y	Y	Y	Y	Y	Y
2	Langevin	Y	Y	N	Y	Y	Y
SOUTH CAROLINA							
1	Cunningham	N	Y	N	Y	Y	Y
2	**Wilson, J.**	N	N	N	N	Y	N
3	**Duncan**	N	N	Y	N	Y	N
4	**Timmons**	N	N	N	N	Y	N
5	**Norman**	N	N	N	N	N	N
6	Clyburn	Y	Y	Y	Y	Y	Y
7	**Rice, T.**	N	N	N	N	N	N
SOUTH DAKOTA							
AL	**Johnson**	N	N	N	Y	Y	N
TENNESSEE							
1	**Roe**	N	N	Y	Y	Y	N
2	**Burchett**	N	N	Y	Y	N	N
3	**Fleischmann**	Y	N	N	Y	Y	N
4	**DesJarlais**	N	N	Y	N	Y	N
5	Cooper	Y	Y	N	Y	Y	Y
6	**Rose**	N	N	Y	N	Y	N
7	**Green**	N	N	N	N	Y	N
8	**Kustoff**	N	N	N	N	Y	N
9	Cohen	Y	Y	N	Y	Y	Y
TEXAS							
1	**Gohmert**	N	N	Y	N	N	N
2	**Crenshaw**	N	N	N	Y	Y	N
3	**Taylor**	N	N	N	Y	Y	N
4	**Ratcliffe**	N	N	N	N	N	N

		343	344	345	346	347	348
5	**Gooden**	N	N	Y	N	Y	N
6	**Wright**	N	N	Y	N	Y	N
7	Fletcher	Y	Y	N	Y	Y	Y
8	**Brady**	N	N	N	N	Y	N
9	Green, A.	Y	Y	Y	Y	Y	Y
10	**McCaul**	Y	N	N	Y	Y	Y
11	**Conaway**	N	N	N	N	Y	N
12	**Granger**	Y	N	N	N	Y	N
13	**Thornberry**	N	N	N	N	Y	N
14	**Weber**	N	N	Y	N	Y	N
15	Gonzalez	N	Y	N	Y	Y	Y
16	Escobar	Y	Y	Y	Y	Y	Y
17	**Flores**	Y	?	N	Y	Y	N
18	Jackson Lee	Y	Y	Y	Y	Y	Y
19	**Arrington**	N	N	N	N	N	N
20	Castro	Y	Y	Y	Y	Y	Y
21	**Roy**	N	N	Y	N	N	N
22	**Olson**	N	N	N	N	Y	N
23	**Hurd**	Y	Y	N	Y	Y	Y
24	**Marchant**	N	N	Y	N	Y	N
25	**Williams**	N	N	N	N	N	N
26	**Burgess**	N	N	Y	Y	Y	N
27	**Cloud**	N	N	Y	Y	Y	N
28	Cuellar	Y	Y	N	Y	Y	Y
29	Garcia, S.	Y	Y	N	Y	Y	Y
30	Johnson, E.B.	Y	Y	N	Y	Y	Y
31	**Carter, J.**	N	N	N	N	Y	N
32	Allred	Y	Y	N	Y	Y	Y
33	Veasey	Y	Y	N	Y	Y	Y
34	Vela	Y	Y	N	Y	Y	Y
35	Doggett	Y	Y	Y	Y	Y	Y
36	**Babin**	N	N	N	N	Y	N
UTAH							
1	**Bishop, R.**	N	N	Y	N	N	N
2	**Stewart**	N	N	N	Y	Y	N
3	**Curtis**	?	?	?	?	?	?
4	McAdams	N	Y	N	Y	Y	Y
VERMONT							
AL	Welch	Y	Y	Y	Y	Y	Y
VIRGINIA							
1	**Wittman**	N	N	Y	N	Y	N
2	Luria	Y	Y	N	N	Y	Y
3	Scott, R.	Y	Y	Y	Y	Y	Y
4	McEachin	Y	Y	N	Y	Y	Y
5	**Riggleman**	Y	N	N	Y	Y	N
6	**Cline**	N	N	Y	Y	Y	N
7	Spanberger	Y	Y	N	Y	Y	Y
8	Beyer	Y	Y	Y	Y	Y	Y
9	**Griffith**	N	N	Y	N	N	N
10	Wexton	Y	Y	N	Y	Y	Y
11	Connolly	Y	Y	Y	Y	Y	Y
WASHINGTON							
1	DelBene	Y	Y	Y	Y	Y	Y
2	Larsen	Y	Y	Y	Y	Y	Y
3	**Herrera Beutler**	?	?	?	?	?	?
4	**Newhouse**	Y	N	N	Y	Y	N
5	**McMorris Rodgers**	N	N	Y	Y	Y	N
6	Kilmer	Y	Y	N	Y	Y	Y
7	Jayapal	Y	Y	Y	Y	Y	Y
8	Schrier	Y	Y	N	Y	Y	Y
9	Smith Adam	Y	Y	Y	Y	Y	Y
10	Heck	Y	Y	N	Y	Y	Y
WEST VIRGINIA							
1	**McKinley**	N	N	N	Y	Y	N
2	**Mooney**	N	N	Y	N	N	N
3	**Miller**	N	N	N	Y	Y	N
WISCONSIN							
1	**Steil**	N	N	N	Y	Y	N
2	Pocan	Y	Y	Y	Y	Y	Y
3	Kind	Y	Y	N	Y	Y	Y
4	Moore	Y	Y	Y	Y	Y	Y
5	**Sensenbrenner**	N	N	Y	Y	N	N
6	**Grothman**	N	N	Y	N	N	N
7	**Duffy**	Y	N	N	N	Y	N
8	**Gallagher**	Y	N	N	Y	Y	N
WYOMING							
AL	**Cheney**	N	N	N	N	Y	N
DELEGATES							
	Radewagen (A.S.)	?	?	?	?	?	?
	Norton (D.C.)	Y	Y	N	Y	Y	Y
	San Nicolas (Guam)	Y	Y	Y	Y	Y	Y
	Sablan (N. Marianas)	Y	+	N	Y	Y	Y
	González-Colón (P.R.)	N	N	N	Y	Y	N
	Plaskett (V.I.)	Y	Y	Y	Y	Y	Y

III HOUSE VOTES

349. HR2740. Fiscal 2020 Four-Bill Appropriations Package - Defense Export Licenses. Lieu, D-Calif., amendment that would prohibit the use of funds made available by the bill to issue export licenses for certain defense articles and items as described in a number of State Department certification transmittal documents. Adopted in Committee of the Whole 237-191: R 4-188; D 232-3; I 1-0. June 18, 2019.

350. HR2740. Fiscal 2020 Four-Bill Appropriations Package - Defense and Army Research and Evaluation. Gallagher, R-Wis., amendment that would increase by $76 million funding for Defense-wide research- and evaluation-related expenses, increase by $20 million funding for Army research- and evaluation-related expenses, decrease by $96 million funding for Defense-wide operations and maintenance. Rejected in Committee of the Whole 203-225: R 190-2; D 13-222; I 0-1. June 18, 2019.

351. HR2740. Fiscal 2020 Four-Bill Appropriations Package - Navy Weapon Procurement. Gallagher, R-Wis., for Cheney, R-Wyo., amendment that would increase by $19.6 million funding for Navy procurement, production, and modification of missiles, torpedoes, and other weapons, including to acquire land for production plants, and decrease by the same amount funding for Defense-wide operations and maintenance. Rejected in Committee of the Whole 192-236: R 189-3; D 3-232; I 0-1. June 18, 2019.

352. HR2740. Fiscal 2020 Four-Bill Appropriations Package - Defense Department Operations. Blunt Rochester, D-Del., amendment that would increase then decrease by $1 million funding for Defense-wide operations and maintenance. Adopted in Committee of the Whole 424-3: R 188-3; D 235-0; I 1-0. June 18, 2019.

353. HR2740. Fiscal 2020 Four-Bill Appropriations Package - "Standoff" Missile Research. Jayapal, D-Wash., amendment that would prohibit the use of funds made available by the Defense Department title of the bill (Division C) for continued research on the "long-range standoff" air-launched missile. Rejected in Committee of the Whole 138-289: R 1-191; D 136-98; I 1-0. June 18, 2019.

354. HR2740. Fiscal 2020 Four-Bill Appropriations Package - Defense Department Operations. Crow, D-Colo., amendment that would decrease then increase by $13 million funding for Defense-wide operations and maintenance. Adopted in Committee of the Whole 277-151: R 43-149; D 233-2; I 1-0. June 18, 2019.

		349	350	351	352	353	354
ALABAMA							
1	**Byrne**	N	Y	Y	Y	N	N
2	**Roby**	N	Y	Y	Y	N	N
3	**Rogers, M.**	N	Y	Y	Y	N	N
4	**Aderholt**	N	Y	Y	Y	N	N
5	**Brooks, M.**	N	Y	Y	Y	N	N
6	**Palmer**	N	Y	Y	Y	N	N
7	Sewell	Y	N	N	Y	N	Y
ALASKA							
AL	**Young**	N	Y	Y	Y	N	N
ARIZONA							
1	O'Halleran	Y	N	N	Y	N	Y
2	Kirkpatrick	N	N	N	Y	Y	Y
3	Grijalva	Y	N	N	Y	Y	Y
4	**Gosar**	N	Y	Y	Y	N	N
5	**Biggs**	N	Y	Y	Y	N	N
6	**Schweikert**	N	Y	Y	Y	N	N
7	Gallego	Y	N	N	Y	N	Y
8	**Lesko**	N	Y	Y	Y	N	N
9	Stanton	Y	N	N	Y	N	Y
ARKANSAS							
1	**Crawford**	N	Y	Y	Y	N	N
2	**Hill, F.**	N	Y	Y	Y	N	N
3	**Womack**	N	Y	Y	Y	N	N
4	**Westerman**	N	Y	Y	Y	N	N
CALIFORNIA							
1	**LaMalfa**	N	Y	Y	?	N	N
2	Huffman	Y	N	N	Y	Y	Y
3	Garamendi	Y	N	N	Y	Y	Y
4	**McClintock**	N	N	N	Y	N	N
5	Thompson, M.	Y	N	N	Y	Y	Y
6	Matsui	Y	N	N	Y	Y	Y
7	Bera	Y	N	N	Y	Y	Y
8	**Cook**	N	Y	Y	Y	N	N
9	McNerney	Y	N	N	Y	Y	Y
10	Harder	Y	N	N	Y	N	Y
11	DeSaulnier	Y	N	N	Y	Y	Y
12	Pelosi						
13	Lee B.	Y	N	N	Y	Y	Y
14	Speier	Y	N	N	Y	Y	Y
15	Swalwell	Y	N	N	Y	Y	Y
16	Costa	Y	N	N	Y	N	Y
17	Khanna	Y	N	N	Y	Y	Y
18	Eshoo	Y	N	N	Y	Y	Y
19	Lofgren	Y	N	N	Y	Y	Y
20	Panetta	Y	Y	N	Y	N	Y
21	Cox	Y	N	N	Y	N	Y
22	**Nunes**	N	Y	Y	Y	N	N
23	**McCarthy**	N	Y	Y	Y	N	Y
24	Carbajal	Y	N	N	Y	Y	Y
25	Hill, K.	Y	N	N	Y	N	Y
26	Brownley	Y	N	N	Y	Y	Y
27	Chu	Y	N	N	Y	Y	Y
28	Schiff	Y	N	N	Y	Y	Y
29	Cárdenas	Y	N	N	Y	Y	Y
30	Sherman	Y	N	N	Y	Y	Y
31	Aguilar	Y	N	N	Y	N	Y
32	Napolitano	Y	N	N	Y	Y	Y
33	Lieu	Y	N	N	Y	Y	Y
34	Gomez	Y	N	N	Y	N	Y
35	Torres	Y	N	N	Y	N	Y
36	Ruiz	Y	N	N	Y	Y	Y
37	Bass	Y	N	N	Y	Y	Y
38	Sánchez	Y	N	N	Y	Y	Y
39	Cisneros	Y	N	N	Y	Y	Y
40	Roybal-Allard	Y	N	N	Y	Y	Y
41	Takano	Y	N	N	Y	Y	Y
42	**Calvert**	N	Y	Y	Y	N	N
43	Waters	Y	N	N	Y	Y	Y
44	Barragán	Y	N	N	Y	Y	Y
45	Porter	Y	N	N	Y	Y	Y
46	Correa	Y	N	N	Y	N	Y
47	Lowenthal	Y	N	N	Y	Y	Y
48	Rouda	Y	N	N	Y	N	Y
49	Levin	Y	N	N	Y	Y	Y
50	**Hunter**	N	Y	Y	Y	N	N
51	Vargas	Y	N	N	Y	Y	Y
52	Peters	N	N	N	Y	N	Y

		349	350	351	352	353	354
53	Davis, S.	Y	N	N	Y	Y	Y
COLORADO							
1	DeGette	Y	N	N	Y	Y	Y
2	Neguse	Y	N	N	Y	Y	Y
3	Tipton	N	Y	Y	Y	N	Y
4	**Buck**	N	Y	Y	Y	N	N
5	**Lamborn**	N	Y	Y	Y	N	N
6	Crow	Y	N	N	Y	N	Y
7	Perlmutter	Y	Y	N	Y	Y	Y
CONNECTICUT							
1	Larson	Y	N	N	Y	Y	Y
2	Courtney	Y	N	N	Y	Y	Y
3	DeLauro	Y	N	N	Y	Y	Y
4	Himes	Y	N	N	Y	Y	Y
5	Hayes	Y	N	N	Y	Y	Y
DELAWARE							
AL	Blunt Rochester	Y	N	N	Y	Y	Y
FLORIDA							
1	**Gaetz**	?	?	?	?	?	?
2	**Dunn**	N	Y	Y	Y	N	N
3	**Yoho**	?	?	?	?	?	?
4	**Rutherford**	N	Y	Y	Y	N	N
5	Lawson	Y	N	N	Y	N	Y
6	**Waltz**	–	+	+	+	–	+
7	Murphy	Y	N	N	Y	N	Y
8	**Posey**	N	Y	Y	Y	N	N
9	Soto	Y	N	N	Y	N	Y
10	Demings	Y	N	N	Y	Y	Y
11	**Webster**	N	Y	Y	Y	N	N
12	**Bilirakis**	N	Y	Y	Y	N	N
13	Crist	Y	N	N	Y	N	Y
14	Castor	Y	N	N	Y	Y	Y
15	**Spano**	N	Y	Y	Y	N	N
16	**Buchanan**	N	Y	Y	Y	N	N
17	**Steube**	N	Y	Y	Y	N	N
18	**Mast**	N	Y	Y	Y	N	Y
19	**Rooney**	N	Y	Y	Y	N	Y
20	Hastings	?	?	?	?	?	?
21	Frankel	Y	N	N	Y	Y	Y
22	Deutch	Y	N	N	Y	Y	Y
23	Wasserman Schultz	Y	N	N	Y	N	Y
24	Wilson, F.	Y	N	N	Y	Y	Y
25	**Diaz-Balart**	N	Y	Y	Y	N	Y
26	Mucarsel-Powell	Y	N	N	Y	Y	Y
27	Shalala	Y	N	N	Y	Y	Y
GEORGIA							
1	**Carter, E.L.**	N	Y	Y	Y	N	N
2	Bishop, S.	Y	N	N	Y	N	Y
3	**Ferguson**	N	Y	Y	Y	N	N
4	Johnson, H.	Y	N	N	Y	Y	Y
5	Lewis John	Y	N	N	Y	Y	Y
6	McBath	Y	N	N	Y	N	Y
7	**Woodall**	N	Y	Y	Y	N	N
8	**Scott, A.**	N	Y	Y	Y	N	N
9	**Collins, D.**	N	Y	Y	Y	N	N
10	**Hice**	N	Y	Y	Y	N	N
11	**Loudermilk**	N	Y	Y	Y	N	N
12	**Allen**	N	Y	Y	Y	N	N
13	Scott, D.	Y	N	N	Y	Y	Y
14	**Graves, T.**	N	Y	Y	Y	N	N
HAWAII							
1	Case	Y	N	N	Y	N	Y
2	Gabbard	Y	N	N	Y	Y	Y
IDAHO							
1	**Fulcher**	N	Y	Y	Y	N	N
2	**Simpson**	N	Y	Y	Y	N	N
ILLINOIS							
1	Rush	Y	N	N	Y	Y	Y
2	Kelly, R.	Y	N	N	Y	Y	Y
3	Lipinski	Y	N	N	Y	N	Y
4	García, J.	Y	N	N	Y	Y	Y
5	Quigley	Y	N	N	Y	Y	Y
6	Casten	Y	N	N	Y	N	Y
7	Davis, D.	Y	N	N	Y	Y	Y
8	Krishnamoorthi	Y	N	N	Y	Y	Y
9	Schakowsky	Y	N	N	Y	Y	Y
10	Schneider	Y	N	N	Y	N	Y
11	Foster	Y	N	N	Y	N	Y

KEY:	Republicans	Democrats	Independents

Y Voted for (yea)		**N** Voted against (nay)	**P** Voted "present"
+ Announced for		**–** Announced against	**?** Did not vote or otherwise
# Paired for		**X** Paired against	make position known

		349	350	351	352	353	354
12	**Bost**	N	Y	Y	Y	N	Y
13	**Davis, R.**	N	Y	Y	Y	N	Y
14	Underwood	Y	N	N	Y	N	Y
15	**Shimkus**	N	Y	Y	Y	N	N
16	**Kinzinger**	N	Y	Y	Y	N	Y
17	Bustos	Y	N	N	Y	N	Y
18	**LaHood**	N	Y	Y	Y	N	N
INDIANA							
1	Visclosky	Y	N	N	Y	N	Y
2	**Walorski**	N	Y	Y	Y	N	N
3	**Banks**	N	Y	Y	Y	N	N
4	**Baird**	N	Y	Y	Y	N	N
5	**Brooks, S.**	N	Y	Y	Y	N	N
6	**Pence**	N	Y	Y	Y	N	N
7	Carson	Y	N	N	Y	Y	Y
8	**Bucshon**	N	Y	Y	Y	N	N
9	**Hollingsworth**	Y	Y	Y	Y	N	Y
IOWA							
1	Finkenauer	Y	N	N	Y	N	Y
2	Loebsack	Y	N	N	Y	N	Y
3	Axne	Y	N	N	Y	N	Y
4	**King, S.**	N	Y	Y	Y	N	N
KANSAS							
1	**Marshall**	N	Y	Y	Y	N	N
2	**Watkins**	N	Y	Y	Y	N	N
3	Davids	Y	N	N	Y	Y	Y
4	**Estes**	N	Y	Y	Y	N	N
KENTUCKY							
1	**Comer**	N	Y	Y	Y	N	N
2	**Guthrie**	N	Y	Y	Y	N	Y
3	Yarmuth	Y	N	N	Y	Y	Y
4	**Massie**	Y	Y	N	Y	Y	N
5	**Rogers, H.**	N	Y	Y	Y	N	N
6	**Barr**	N	Y	Y	Y	N	N
LOUISIANA							
1	**Scalise**	N	Y	Y	Y	N	N
2	Richmond	Y	N	N	Y	N	Y
3	**Higgins, C.**	N	Y	Y	Y	N	N
4	**Johnson, M.**	N	Y	Y	Y	N	N
5	**Abraham**	?	?	?	?	?	?
6	**Graves, G.**	N	Y	Y	Y	N	N
MAINE							
1	Pingree	Y	N	N	Y	Y	Y
2	Golden	Y	N	N	Y	N	Y
MARYLAND							
1	**Harris**	N	Y	Y	N	N	N
2	Ruppersberger	Y	N	N	Y	N	Y
3	Sarbanes	Y	N	N	Y	Y	Y
4	Brown, A.	Y	N	N	Y	N	Y
5	Hoyer	Y	N	N	Y	N	Y
6	Trone	Y	N	N	Y	N	Y
7	Cummings	Y	N	N	Y	Y	Y
8	Raskin						
MASSACHUSETTS		Y	N	N	Y	Y	Y
1	Neal						
2	McGovern	Y	N	N	Y	Y	Y
3	Trahan	Y	N	N	Y	Y	Y
4	Kennedy	Y	N	N	Y	Y	Y
5	Clark	Y	N	N	Y	Y	Y
6	Moulton	Y	N	N	Y	Y	Y
7	Pressley	?	?	?	?	?	?
8	Lynch	Y	N	N	Y	Y	Y
9	Keating	Y	N	N	Y	Y	Y
MICHIGAN		Y	N	N	Y	N	Y
1	**Bergman**						
2	**Huizenga**	N	Y	Y	Y	N	N
3	**Amash**	N	Y	Y	Y	N	Y
4	**Moolenaar**	Y	Y	N	Y	N	N
5	Kildee	N	Y	Y	Y	N	N
6	**Upton**	Y	N	N	Y	Y	Y
7	**Walberg**	N	Y	Y	Y	N	Y
8	Slotkin	N	Y	Y	Y	N	N
9	Levin	Y	N	N	Y	N	Y
10	**Mitchell**	Y	N	N	Y	Y	Y
11	Stevens	N	Y	Y	Y	N	Y
12	Dingell	Y	Y	N	Y	N	Y
13	Tlaib	Y	N	N	Y	Y	Y
14	Lawrence	Y	N	N	Y	Y	Y
MINNESOTA		Y	N	N	Y	Y	Y
1	**Hagedorn**						
2	Craig	N	Y	Y	Y	N	N
3	Phillips	Y	N	N	Y	N	N
4	McCollum	Y	N	N	Y	N	Y
5	Omar	Y	N	N	Y	N	Y

		349	350	351	352	353	354
6	**Emmer**	Y	N	N	Y	Y	Y
7	Peterson	N	Y	Y	Y	N	N
8	**Stauber**	Y	N	N	Y	N	Y
MISSISSIPPI		N	Y	Y	Y	N	Y
1	**Kelly, T.**						
2	Thompson, B.	N	Y	Y	Y	N	N
3	**Guest**	Y	N	N	Y	Y	Y
4	**Palazzo**	N	Y	Y	Y	N	N
MISSOURI		N	Y	Y	Y	N	N
1	Clay						
2	**Wagner**	Y	N	N	Y	Y	Y
3	**Luetkemeyer**	N	Y	Y	Y	N	N
4	**Hartzler**	N	Y	Y	Y	N	N
5	Cleaver	N	Y	Y	Y	N	Y
6	**Graves, S.**	Y	N	N	Y	N	Y
7	**Long**	N	Y	Y	Y	N	N
8	**Smith, J.**	N	Y	Y	Y	N	N
MONTANA		N	Y	Y	Y	N	N
AL	**Gianforte**						
NEBRASKA		N	Y	Y	Y	N	N
1	**Fortenberry**						
2	**Bacon**	N	Y	Y	Y	N	Y
3	**Smith, Adrian**	N	Y	Y	Y	N	N
NEVADA		N	Y	Y	Y	N	N
1	Titus						
2	**Amodei**	Y	N	N	Y	Y	Y
3	Lee	N	Y	Y	Y	N	Y
4	Horsford	Y	N	N	Y	N	Y
NEW HAMPSHIRE		Y	N	N	Y	Y	Y
1	Pappas						
2	Kuster	Y	N	N	Y	Y	Y
NEW JERSEY		Y	N	N	Y	Y	Y
1	Norcross						
2	Van Drew	Y	N	N	Y	N	Y
3	Kim	Y	Y	Y	Y	N	Y
4	**Smith, C.**	Y	N	N	Y	N	Y
5	Gottheimer	N	Y	Y	Y	N	Y
6	Pallone	Y	Y	Y	Y	N	Y
7	Malinowski	Y	N	N	Y	Y	Y
8	Sires	Y	N	N	Y	N	Y
9	Pascrell	Y	N	N	Y	N	Y
10	Payne	Y	N	N	Y	Y	Y
11	Sherrill	Y	Y	N	Y	Y	Y
12	Watson Coleman	Y	N	N	Y	N	Y
NEW MEXICO		Y	N	N	Y	Y	Y
1	Haaland						
2	Torres Small	Y	N	N	Y	N	Y
3	Luján	Y	N	N	Y	N	Y
NEW YORK		Y	N	N	Y	N	Y
1	**Zeldin**						
2	**King, P.**	N	Y	Y	Y	N	Y
3	Suozzi	N	Y	Y	Y	N	N
4	Rice, K.	Y	Y	N	Y	N	Y
5	Meeks	Y	N	N	Y	N	Y
6	Meng	Y	N	N	Y	Y	Y
7	Velázquez	Y	N	N	Y	Y	Y
8	Jeffries	Y	N	N	Y	Y	Y
9	Clarke	Y	N	N	Y	Y	Y
10	Nadler	Y	N	N	Y	Y	Y
11	Rose	Y	N	N	Y	Y	Y
12	Maloney, C.	Y	N	N	Y	Y	Y
13	Espaillat	Y	N	N	Y	Y	Y
14	Ocasio-Cortez	Y	N	N	Y	Y	Y
15	Serrano	Y	N	N	Y	Y	Y
16	Engel	Y	N	N	Y	Y	Y
17	Lowey	Y	N	N	Y	Y	Y
18	Maloney, S.P.	Y	N	N	Y	N	Y
19	Delgado	Y	Y	N	Y	N	Y
20	Tonko	Y	N	N	Y	Y	Y
21	**Stefanik**	Y	N	N	Y	Y	Y
22	Brindisi	N	Y	Y	Y	N	Y
23	**Reed**	Y	N	N	Y	N	Y
24	**Katko**	N	Y	Y	Y	N	Y
25	Morelle	N	Y	Y	Y	N	Y
26	Higgins, B.	Y	Y	N	Y	N	Y
27	**Collins, C.**	Y	N	N	Y	N	Y
NORTH CAROLINA		N	Y	Y	Y	N	Y
1	Butterfield						
2	**Holding**	Y	N	N	Y	N	Y
3	**Jones***	?	?	?	?	?	?
4	Price						
5	**Foxx**	Y	N	N	Y	Y	Y
6	**Walker**	N	Y	Y	Y	N	N
7	**Rouzer**	N	Y	Y	Y	N	N

		349	350	351	352	353	354
8	**Hudson**	N	Y	Y	Y	N	N
9	vacant	N	Y	Y	Y	N	Y
10	**McHenry**	N	Y	Y	Y	N	N
11	**Meadows**	N	Y	Y	Y	N	N
12	Adams	Y	N	N	Y	N	Y
13	**Budd**	N	Y	Y	Y	N	N
NORTH DAKOTA							
AL	**Armstrong**	N	Y	Y	Y	N	N
OHIO							
1	**Chabot**	N	Y	Y	Y	N	N
2	**Wenstrup**	N	Y	Y	Y	N	N
3	Beatty	Y	N	N	Y	Y	Y
4	**Jordan**	N	Y	Y	Y	N	N
5	**Latta**	N	Y	Y	Y	N	N
6	**Johnson, B.**	N	Y	Y	Y	N	N
7	**Gibbs**	N	Y	Y	Y	N	N
8	**Davidson**	N	N	N	N	N	N
9	Kaptur	Y	N	N	Y	N	Y
10	**Turner**	N	Y	Y	Y	N	Y
11	Fudge	Y	N	N	Y	Y	Y
12	**Balderson**	N	Y	Y	Y	N	N
13	Ryan	Y	N	N	Y	Y	Y
14	**Joyce**	N	Y	Y	Y	N	N
15	**Stivers**	N	Y	Y	Y	N	N
16	**Gonzalez**	N	Y	Y	Y	N	Y
OKLAHOMA							
1	**Hern**	N	Y	Y	Y	N	N
2	**Mullin**	N	Y	Y	Y	N	N
3	**Lucas**	N	Y	Y	Y	N	Y
4	**Cole**	N	Y	Y	Y	N	N
5	Horn	Y	N	N	Y	N	Y
OREGON							
1	Bonamici	Y	N	N	Y	Y	Y
2	**Walden**	N	Y	Y	Y	N	N
3	Blumenauer	Y	N	N	Y	Y	Y
4	DeFazio	Y	N	N	Y	Y	Y
5	Schrader	Y	N	N	Y	N	Y
PENNSYLVANIA							
1	**Fitzpatrick**	N	Y	Y	Y	N	Y
2	Boyle	Y	N	N	Y	Y	Y
3	Evans	Y	N	N	Y	Y	Y
4	Dean	Y	N	N	Y	Y	Y
5	Scanlon	Y	N	N	Y	Y	Y
6	Houlahan	Y	N	N	Y	N	Y
7	Wild	Y	N	N	Y	N	Y
8	Cartwright	Y	N	N	Y	Y	Y
9	**Meuser**	N	Y	Y	Y	N	N
10	**Perry**	N	Y	Y	Y	N	N
11	**Smucker**	N	Y	Y	Y	N	Y
12	**Marino***						
13	**Joyce**	N	Y	Y	Y	N	N
14	**Reschenthaler**	N	Y	Y	Y	N	N
15	**Thompson, G.**	N	Y	Y	Y	N	Y
16	**Kelly, M.**	N	Y	Y	Y	N	Y
17	Lamb	Y	Y	N	Y	N	Y
18	Doyle	Y	N	N	Y	Y	Y
RHODE ISLAND							
1	Cicilline	Y	N	N	Y	Y	Y
2	Langevin	Y	N	N	Y	N	Y
SOUTH CAROLINA							
1	Cunningham	N	Y	Y	Y	N	Y
2	**Wilson, J.**	N	Y	Y	Y	N	N
3	**Duncan**	N	Y	Y	Y	N	N
4	**Timmons**	N	Y	Y	Y	N	N
5	**Norman**	N	Y	Y	Y	N	N
6	Clyburn	Y	N	N	Y	Y	Y
7	**Rice, T.**	N	Y	Y	Y	N	N
SOUTH DAKOTA							
AL	**Johnson**	N	Y	Y	Y	N	Y
TENNESSEE							
1	**Roe**	N	Y	Y	Y	N	N
2	**Burchett**	N	Y	Y	Y	N	N
3	**Fleischmann**	N	Y	Y	Y	N	Y
4	**DesJarlais**	N	Y	Y	Y	N	N
5	Cooper	Y	N	N	Y	N	Y
6	**Rose**	N	Y	Y	Y	N	N
7	**Green**	N	Y	Y	Y	N	N
8	**Kustoff**	N	Y	Y	Y	N	N
9	Cohen	Y	N	N	Y	Y	Y
TEXAS							
1	**Gohmert**	N	Y	Y	Y	N	N
2	**Crenshaw**	N	Y	Y	Y	N	N
3	**Taylor**	N	Y	Y	Y	N	N
4	**Ratcliffe**	N	Y	Y	Y	N	N

		349	350	351	352	353	354
5	**Gooden**	N	Y	Y	Y	N	N
6	**Wright**	N	Y	Y	Y	N	N
7	Fletcher	Y	Y	N	Y	N	Y
8	**Brady**	N	Y	Y	Y	N	N
9	Green, A.	Y	N	N	Y	Y	Y
10	**McCaul**	N	Y	Y	Y	N	Y
11	**Conaway**	N	Y	Y	Y	N	N
12	**Granger**	N	Y	Y	Y	N	N
13	**Thornberry**	N	Y	Y	Y	N	N
14	**Weber**	N	Y	Y	Y	N	N
15	Gonzalez	Y	N	N	Y	N	Y
16	Escobar	Y	N	N	Y	Y	Y
17	**Flores**	N	Y	Y	Y	N	N
18	Jackson Lee	Y	N	N	Y	Y	Y
19	**Arrington**	N	Y	Y	N	N	N
20	Castro	Y	N	N	Y	P	Y
21	**Roy**	N	Y	Y	Y	N	N
22	**Olson**	N	Y	Y	Y	N	N
23	**Hurd**	N	Y	Y	Y	N	Y
24	**Marchant**	N	Y	Y	Y	N	N
25	**Williams**	N	Y	Y	Y	N	N
26	**Burgess**	N	Y	Y	Y	N	N
27	**Cloud**	Y	Y	Y	Y	N	N
28	Cuellar	Y	N	N	Y	N	Y
29	Garcia, S.	Y	N	N	Y	Y	Y
30	Johnson, E.B.	Y	N	N	Y	N	Y
31	**Carter, J.**	N	Y	Y	Y	N	Y
32	Allred	Y	N	N	Y	N	Y
33	Veasey	Y	N	N	Y	N	Y
34	Vela	Y	N	N	Y	N	Y
35	Doggett	Y	N	N	Y	Y	N
36	**Babin**	N	Y	Y	Y	N	N
UTAH							
1	**Bishop, R.**	N	Y	Y	Y	N	N
2	**Stewart**	N	Y	Y	Y	N	N
3	**Curtis**	?	?	?	?	?	?
4	McAdams	Y	N	N	Y	N	Y
VERMONT							
AL	Welch	Y	N	N	Y	Y	Y
VIRGINIA							
1	**Wittman**	N	Y	Y	Y	N	N
2	Luria	Y	Y	N	Y	N	Y
3	Scott, R.	Y	N	N	Y	N	Y
4	McEachin	Y	N	N	Y	N	Y
5	**Riggleman**	N	Y	Y	Y	N	Y
6	**Cline**	N	Y	Y	Y	N	N
7	Spanberger	Y	N	N	Y	N	Y
8	Beyer	Y	N	N	Y	Y	Y
9	**Griffith**	N	Y	Y	Y	N	N
10	Wexton	Y	N	N	Y	N	Y
11	Connolly	Y	N	N	Y	N	Y
WASHINGTON							
1	DelBene	Y	N	N	Y	Y	Y
2	Larsen	Y	N	N	Y	Y	Y
3	**Herrera Beutler**	?	?	?	?	?	?
4	**Newhouse**	N	Y	Y	Y	N	Y
5	**McMorris Rodgers**	N	Y	Y	Y	N	Y
6	Kilmer	Y	N	N	Y	N	Y
7	Jayapal	Y	N	N	Y	Y	Y
8	Schrier	Y	N	N	Y	Y	Y
9	Smith Adam	Y	N	N	Y	Y	Y
10	Heck	Y	N	N	Y	Y	Y
WEST VIRGINIA							
1	**McKinley**	N	Y	Y	Y	N	N
2	**Mooney**	N	Y	Y	Y	N	N
3	**Miller**	N	Y	Y	Y	N	N
WISCONSIN							
1	**Steil**	N	Y	Y	Y	N	N
2	Pocan	Y	N	N	Y	Y	Y
3	Kind	Y	N	N	Y	N	Y
4	Moore	Y	N	N	Y	Y	Y
5	**Sensenbrenner**	N	Y	Y	Y	N	N
6	**Grothman**	N	Y	Y	Y	N	N
7	**Duffy**	N	Y	Y	Y	N	N
8	**Gallagher**	N	Y	Y	Y	N	Y
WYOMING							
AL	**Cheney**	N	Y	Y	Y	N	N
DELEGATES							
	Radewagen (A.S.)	?	?	?	?	?	?
	Norton (D.C.)	Y	N	N	Y	N	Y
	San Nicolas (Guam)	Y	N	N	Y	Y	Y
	Sablan (N. Marianas)	Y	N	N	Y	Y	Y
	González-Colón (P.R.)	N	Y	Y	Y	N	Y
	Plaskett (V.I.)	Y	N	N	Y	N	Y

355. HR2740. Fiscal 2020 Four-Bill Appropriations Package - Defense Health Program Research. Cox, D-Calif., amendment that would increase by $10 million funding for research, development, and evaluation for Defense Department health programs, and decrease by the same amount funding for Defense-wide operations and maintenance. Adopted in Committee of the Whole 404-22: R 172-20; D 231-2; I 1-0. June 18, 2019.

356. HR3055, HR2740. Fiscal 2020 Appropriations Packages - Previous Question. McGovern, D-Mass., motion to order the previous question (thus ending debate and possibility of amendment) on the rule (H Res 445) that would provide for House floor consideration of the fiscal 2020 Commerce-Justice-Science, Agriculture, Interior-Environment, Military Construction-VA, and Transportation-HUD appropriations package and provide for further House floor consideration of the fiscal 2020 Labor-HHS-Education, Defense, Energy-Water, and State-Foreign Operations appropriations package (HR 2740). Motion agreed to 232-193: R 0-193; D 232-0. June 19, 2019.

357. HR3055, HR2740. Fiscal 2020 Appropriations Packages - Rule. Adoption of the rule (H Res 445) that would provide for House floor consideration of the fiscal 2020 Commerce-Justice-Science, Agriculture, Interior-Environment, Military Construction-VA, and Transportation-HUD appropriations package and provide for further House floor consideration of the fiscal 2020 Labor-HHS-Education, Defense, Energy-Water, and State-Foreign Operations appropriations package (HR 2740). It would make in order consideration of 290 amendments to HR 3055 and provide for automatic adoption of a Lowey, D-N.Y., manager's amendment to the bill that would authorize federal employment of individuals authorized to work in the U.S. pursuant to the Deferred Action for Childhood Arrivals program. The rule would also provide for automatic adoption of a DeLauro, D-Conn., manager's amendment to HR 2740 that would increase by a total of $289.5 million funding for a number of programs under the Labor-HHS-Education title of the bill (Division A), including HHS refugee and entrant assistance activities, HHS substance abuse and mental health programs, and Education Department programs related to school safety, including emergency response to violence. Adopted 231-195: R 1-194; D 230-1. June 19, 2019.

358. HR2740. Fiscal 2020 Four-Bill Appropriations Package - Reduce Energy-Water Funding. Burgess, R-Texas, amendment that would reduce by 5 percent all funding made available by the Energy and Water Development and related agencies title of the bill (Division E). Rejected in Committee of the Whole 146-288: R 145-52; D 1-235; I 0-1. June 19, 2019.

359. HR2740. Fiscal 2020 Four-Bill Appropriations Package - Army Corps of Engineers Border Infrastructure. Burgess, R-Texas, amendment that would strike from the bill a provision prohibiting the use of funds made available by the bill for the Army Corps of Engineers to design or construct physical barriers or border security infrastructure along the U.S. southern land border. Rejected in Committee of the Whole 197-237: R 192-5; D 5-231; I 0-1. June 19, 2019.

360. HR2740. Fiscal 2020 Four-Bill Appropriations Package - En Bloc Amendments. Kaptur, D-Ohio, en bloc package of amendments to the Energy-Water title (Division E) of the bill that would, among other provisions, increase by $5 million funding for plants and capital equipment for Energy Department energy efficiency and renewable energy activities; increase by $3 million funding for the an Energy Department agency for research and development of advanced energy technologies; and increase by $2 million funding for the Office of Indian Energy programs. Adopted in Committee of the Whole 233-200: R 7-190; D 225-10; I 1-0. June 19, 2019.

		355	356	357	358	359	360
ALABAMA							
1	**Byrne**	Y	N	N	Y	Y	N
2	**Roby**	N	N	N	N	Y	N
3	**Rogers, M.**	Y	N	N	Y	Y	N
4	**Aderholt**	Y	N	N	Y	Y	N
5	**Brooks, M.**	Y	N	N	Y	Y	N
6	**Palmer**	Y	N	N	Y	Y	N
7	Sewell	Y	Y	Y	N	Y	Y
ALASKA							
AL	**Young**	Y	N	N	Y	Y	N
ARIZONA							
1	O'Halleran	Y	Y	Y	N	N	Y
2	Kirkpatrick	Y	Y	Y	N	N	Y
3	Grijalva	Y	Y	Y	N	N	Y
4	**Gosar**	Y	N	N	Y	Y	N
5	**Biggs**	Y	N	N	Y	Y	N
6	**Schweikert**	Y	N	N	Y	Y	Y
7	Gallego	Y	Y	Y	N	N	Y
8	**Lesko**	Y	N	N	Y	Y	N
9	Stanton	Y	Y	Y	N	N	Y
ARKANSAS							
1	**Crawford**	Y	N	N	Y	Y	N
2	**Hill, F.**	Y	N	N	Y	Y	N
3	**Womack**	Y	N	N	Y	Y	N
4	**Westerman**	Y	N	N	Y	Y	N
CALIFORNIA							
1	**LaMalfa**	Y	N	N	Y	Y	N
2	Huffman	Y	Y	Y	N	N	Y
3	Garamendi	Y	Y	Y	N	N	Y
4	**McClintock**	N	N	N	Y	Y	N
5	Thompson, M.	Y	Y	Y	N	N	Y
6	Matsui	Y	Y	Y	N	N	Y
7	Bera	Y	Y	Y	N	N	Y
8	**Cook**	Y	N	N	Y	Y	N
9	McNerney	Y	Y	Y	N	N	Y
10	Harder	Y	Y	Y	N	N	Y
11	DeSaulnier	Y	Y	Y	N	N	Y
12	Pelosi						
13	Lee B.	Y	Y	Y	N	N	Y
14	Speier	Y	Y	Y	N	N	Y
15	Swalwell	Y	Y	Y	N	N	Y
16	Costa	Y	Y	Y	N	N	Y
17	Khanna	Y	Y	Y	N	N	Y
18	Eshoo	Y	Y	Y	N	N	Y
19	Lofgren	Y	Y	Y	N	N	Y
20	Panetta	Y	Y	Y	N	N	Y
21	Cox	Y	Y	Y	N	N	N
22	**Nunes**	Y	N	N	Y	Y	N
23	**McCarthy**	Y	N	N	Y	Y	N
24	Carbajal	Y	Y	Y	N	N	Y
25	Hill, K.	Y	Y	Y	N	N	Y
26	Brownley	Y	Y	Y	N	N	Y
27	Chu	Y	Y	Y	N	N	Y
28	Schiff	Y	Y	Y	N	N	Y
29	Cárdenas	Y	Y	Y	N	N	Y
30	Sherman	Y	Y	Y	N	N	Y
31	Aguilar	Y	Y	Y	N	N	Y
32	Napolitano	Y	Y	Y	N	N	Y
33	Lieu	Y	Y	Y	N	N	Y
34	Gomez	N	Y	Y	N	N	Y
35	Torres	Y	Y	Y	N	N	Y
36	Ruiz	Y	Y	Y	N	N	Y
37	Bass	Y	Y	Y	N	N	Y
38	Sánchez	Y	Y	Y	N	N	Y
39	Cisneros	Y	Y	Y	N	N	Y
40	Roybal-Allard	Y	Y	Y	N	N	Y
41	Takano	Y	Y	Y	N	N	Y
42	**Calvert**	Y	N	N	N	Y	N
43	Waters	Y	Y	Y	N	N	Y
44	Barragán	Y	Y	Y	N	N	Y
45	Porter	Y	Y	Y	N	N	Y
46	Correa	Y	Y	?	N	N	Y
47	Lowenthal	Y	Y	Y	N	N	Y
48	Rouda	Y	Y	Y	N	N	Y
49	Levin	Y	Y	Y	N	N	Y
50	**Hunter**	N	N	N	Y	Y	N
51	Vargas	Y	Y	Y	N	N	Y
52	Peters	Y	Y	Y	N	N	Y

		355	356	357	358	359	360
53	Davis, S.	Y	Y	Y	N	N	Y
COLORADO							
1	DeGette	Y	Y	Y	N	N	Y
2	Neguse	Y	+	Y	N	N	Y
3	Tipton	Y	N	N	Y	Y	N
4	**Buck**	N	N	N	Y	Y	N
5	**Lamborn**	Y	N	N	Y	Y	N
6	Crow	Y	Y	Y	N	N	Y
7	Perlmutter	Y	Y	Y	N	N	Y
CONNECTICUT							
1	Larson	Y	Y	Y	N	N	Y
2	Courtney	Y	Y	Y	N	N	Y
3	DeLauro	Y	Y	Y	N	N	Y
4	Himes	Y	Y	Y	N	N	Y
5	Hayes	Y	Y	Y	N	N	Y
DELAWARE							
AL	Blunt Rochester	Y	Y	Y	N	N	Y
FLORIDA							
1	**Gaetz**	?	N	N	Y	Y	N
2	**Dunn**	Y	N	N	Y	Y	N
3	**Yoho**	?	N	Y	Y	Y	N
4	**Rutherford**	Y	N	N	Y	Y	N
5	Lawson	Y	Y	Y	N	N	Y
6	**Waltz**	+	N	N	Y	Y	N
7	Murphy	Y	Y	Y	N	N	Y
8	**Posey**	N	N	N	Y	Y	N
9	Soto	Y	Y	Y	N	N	Y
10	Demings	Y	Y	Y	N	N	Y
11	**Webster**	N	N	N	Y	Y	N
12	**Bilirakis**	Y	N	N	Y	Y	N
13	Crist	Y	Y	Y	N	N	Y
14	Castor	Y	Y	Y	N	N	Y
15	**Spano**	Y	N	N	Y	Y	N
16	**Buchanan**	Y	N	N	Y	Y	N
17	**Steube**	Y	N	N	Y	Y	N
18	**Mast**	Y	N	N	Y	Y	N
19	**Rooney**	Y	N	N	Y	Y	N
20	Hastings	?	?	?	?	?	?
21	Frankel	+	Y	Y	N	N	Y
22	Deutch	Y	Y	Y	N	N	Y
23	Wasserman Schultz	Y	Y	Y	N	N	Y
24	Wilson, F.	Y	Y	Y	N	N	Y
25	**Diaz-Balart**	Y	N	N	N	Y	N
26	Mucarsel-Powell	Y	Y	Y	N	N	Y
27	Shalala	Y	Y	Y	N	N	Y
GEORGIA							
1	**Carter, E.L.**	Y	N	N	Y	Y	N
2	Bishop, S.	Y	Y	Y	N	N	Y
3	**Ferguson**	Y	N	N	Y	Y	N
4	Johnson, H.	Y	Y	Y	N	N	Y
5	Lewis John	Y	Y	Y	N	N	Y
6	McBath	Y	Y	Y	N	N	Y
7	**Woodall**	Y	N	N	Y	Y	N
8	**Scott, A.**	N	N	N	Y	Y	N
9	**Collins, D.**	Y	?	N	Y	Y	N
10	**Hice**	Y	N	N	Y	Y	N
11	**Loudermilk**	Y	N	N	Y	Y	N
12	**Allen**	Y	N	N	Y	Y	N
13	Scott, D.	Y	Y	Y	N	N	Y
14	**Graves, T.**	Y	N	N	Y	Y	N
HAWAII							
1	Case	Y	Y	Y	N	N	Y
2	Gabbard	Y	Y	Y	N	N	Y
IDAHO							
1	**Fulcher**	Y	N	N	Y	Y	N
2	**Simpson**	Y	N	N	N	Y	N
ILLINOIS							
1	Rush	Y	Y	Y	N	N	Y
2	Kelly, R.	Y	Y	Y	N	N	Y
3	Lipinski	Y	Y	Y	N	N	Y
4	García, J.	?	Y	Y	N	N	Y
5	Quigley	Y	Y	Y	N	N	Y
6	Casten	Y	Y	Y	N	N	Y
7	Davis, D.	Y	Y	Y	N	N	Y
8	Krishnamoorthi	Y	Y	Y	N	N	Y
9	Schakowsky	Y	Y	Y	N	N	Y
10	Schneider	Y	Y	Y	N	N	Y
11	Foster	Y	Y	Y	N	N	Y

		355	356	357	358	359	360
12	**Bost**	Y	N	N	N	Y	N
13	**Davis, R.**	Y	-	N	N	Y	N
14	Underwood	Y	Y	Y	N	N	Y
15	**Shimkus**	Y	N	N	Y	Y	N
16	**Kinzinger**	Y	N	N	N	Y	N
17	Bustos	Y	Y	Y	N	N	Y
18	**LaHood**	Y	N	N	Y	Y	N
INDIANA							
1	Visclosky	Y	Y	Y	N	N	Y
2	**Walorski**	Y	N	N	Y	Y	N
3	**Banks**	Y	N	N	Y	Y	N
4	**Baird**	Y	N	N	N	Y	N
5	**Brooks, S.**	Y	N	N	Y	Y	N
6	**Pence**	Y	N	N	Y	Y	N
7	Carson	Y	Y	Y	N	N	Y
8	**Bucshon**	Y	N	N	Y	Y	N
9	**Hollingsworth**	Y	N	N	N	Y	N
IOWA							
1	Finkenauer	Y	Y	Y	N	N	Y
2	Loebsack	Y	Y	Y	N	N	Y
3	Axne	Y	Y	Y	N	N	Y
4	**King, S.**	Y	N	Y	Y	Y	N
KANSAS							
1	**Marshall**	Y	N	N	Y	Y	N
2	**Watkins**	Y	N	N	Y	Y	N
3	Davids	Y	Y	Y	N	N	Y
4	**Estes**	Y	N	N	Y	Y	N
KENTUCKY							
1	**Comer**	Y	N	N	Y	Y	N
2	**Guthrie**	Y	N	N	Y	Y	N
3	Yarmuth	Y	Y	Y	N	N	Y
4	**Massie**	N	N	N	Y	Y	N
5	**Rogers, H.**	Y	N	N	N	Y	N
6	**Barr**	Y	N	N	Y	Y	N
LOUISIANA							
1	**Scalise**	Y	N	N	Y	Y	N
2	Richmond	Y	Y	Y	N	N	Y
3	**Higgins, C.**	Y	N	N	Y	Y	N
4	**Johnson, M.**	Y	N	N	Y	Y	N
5	**Abraham**	?	N	N	Y	Y	N
6	**Graves, G.**	Y	N	N	N	Y	N
MAINE							
1	Pingree	Y	Y	Y	N	N	Y
2	Golden	Y	Y	Y	N	Y	Y
MARYLAND							
1	**Harris**	N	N	N	Y	Y	N
2	Ruppersberger	Y	Y	Y	N	N	Y
3	Sarbanes	Y	Y	Y	N	N	Y
4	Brown, A.	Y	Y	Y	N	N	Y
5	Hoyer	Y	Y	Y	N	N	Y
6	Trone	Y	Y	Y	N	N	Y
7	Cummings	Y	Y	Y	N	N	Y
8	Raskin						
MASSACHUSETTS		Y	Y	Y	N	N	Y
1	Neal						
2	McGovern	Y	Y	Y	N	N	Y
3	Trahan	Y	Y	Y	N	N	Y
4	Kennedy	Y	Y	Y	N	N	Y
5	Clark	Y	Y	Y	N	N	Y
6	Moulton	Y	Y	Y	N	N	Y
7	Pressley	?	Y	Y	N	N	Y
8	Lynch	Y	Y	Y	N	N	Y
9	Keating	Y	Y	Y	N	N	Y
MICHIGAN		Y	Y	Y	Y	N	?
1	**Bergman**						
2	**Huizenga**	Y	N	N	Y	Y	N
3	**Amash**	Y	N	N	Y	Y	N
4	**Moolenaar**	N	N	N	Y	N	N
5	Kildee	Y	N	N	Y	Y	N
6	**Upton**	Y	Y	Y	N	N	Y
7	**Walberg**	Y	N	N	N	Y	N
8	Slotkin	Y	N	N	Y	Y	N
9	Levin	Y	Y	Y	N	N	Y
10	**Mitchell**	Y	Y	Y	N	N	Y
11	Stevens	Y	N	N	Y	Y	N
12	Dingell	Y	Y	Y	N	N	Y
13	Tlaib	Y	Y	Y	N	N	Y
14	Lawrence	Y	Y	Y	N	N	Y
MINNESOTA		Y	Y	Y	N	N	Y
1	**Hagedorn**						
2	Craig	Y	N	N	Y	Y	N
3	Phillips	Y	Y	Y	N	N	Y
4	McCollum	N	Y	Y	N	N	Y
5	Omar	Y	Y	Y	N	N	Y

		355	356	357	358	359	360
6	**Emmer**	Y	Y	Y	N	N	Y
7	Peterson	N	N	N	Y	Y	N
8	**Stauber**	Y	Y	Y	N	Y	N
MISSISSIPPI		Y	N	N	N	Y	N
1	**Kelly, T.**						
2	Thompson, B.	Y	N	N	Y	Y	N
3	**Guest**	Y	Y	Y	N	N	Y
4	**Palazzo**	Y	N	N	Y	Y	N
MISSOURI		Y	N	N	Y	Y	N
1	Clay						
2	**Wagner**	Y	Y	Y	N	N	Y
3	**Luetkemeyer**	Y	N	N	Y	Y	N
4	**Hartzler**	Y	N	N	N	Y	N
5	Cleaver	Y	N	N	Y	Y	N
6	**Graves, S.**	Y	Y	Y	N	N	Y
7	**Long**	Y	N	N	Y	Y	N
8	**Smith, J.**	Y	N	N	Y	Y	N
MONTANA		Y	N	N	Y	Y	N
AL	**Gianforte**						
NEBRASKA		Y	N	N	Y	Y	N
1	**Fortenberry**						
2	**Bacon**	Y	N	N	N	Y	N
3	**Smith, Adrian**	Y	N	N	Y	Y	N
NEVADA		Y	N	N	Y	Y	N
1	Titus						
2	**Amodei**	Y	Y	Y	N	N	Y
3	Lee	Y	N	N	Y	Y	N
4	Horsford	Y	Y	Y	N	N	Y
NEW HAMPSHIRE		Y	Y	Y	N	N	Y
1	Pappas						
2	Kuster	Y	Y	Y	N	N	Y
NEW JERSEY		Y	Y	Y	N	N	Y
1	Norcross						
2	Van Drew	Y	Y	Y	N	N	Y
3	Kim	Y	Y	Y	N	Y	Y
4	**Smith, C.**	Y	Y	Y	N	N	Y
5	Gottheimer	Y	N	N	N	Y	N
6	Pallone	Y	Y	Y	N	N	Y
7	Malinowski	Y	Y	Y	N	N	Y
8	Sires	Y	Y	Y	N	N	Y
9	Pascrell	Y	Y	Y	N	N	Y
10	Payne	Y	Y	Y	N	N	Y
11	Sherrill	Y	Y	Y	N	N	Y
12	Watson Coleman	Y	Y	Y	N	N	Y
NEW MEXICO		Y	Y	Y	N	N	Y
1	Haaland						
2	Torres Small	Y	Y	Y	N	N	Y
3	Luján	Y	Y	Y	N	N	Y
NEW YORK		Y	Y	Y	N	N	Y
1	**Zeldin**						
2	**King, P.**	Y	N	N	Y	Y	N
3	Suozzi	Y	N	N	N	Y	N
4	Rice, K.	Y	Y	Y	N	N	Y
5	Meeks	Y	Y	?	N	N	Y
6	Meng	Y	Y	Y	N	N	Y
7	Velázquez	Y	Y	Y	N	N	Y
8	Jeffries	Y	Y	Y	N	N	Y
9	Clarke	Y	Y	Y	N	N	Y
10	Nadler	Y	Y	Y	N	N	Y
11	Rose	Y	Y	Y	N	N	Y
12	Maloney, C.	Y	Y	Y	N	N	Y
13	Espaillat	Y	Y	Y	N	N	Y
14	Ocasio-Cortez	Y	Y	Y	N	N	Y
15	Serrano	Y	Y	Y	N	N	Y
16	Engel	Y	Y	Y	N	N	Y
17	Lowey	Y	Y	Y	N	N	Y
18	Maloney, S.P.	Y	Y	Y	N	N	Y
19	Delgado	Y	Y	Y	N	N	Y
20	Tonko	Y	Y	Y	N	N	Y
21	**Stefanik**	Y	Y	Y	N	N	Y
22	Brindisi	Y	N	N	N	Y	N
23	**Reed**	Y	Y	Y	N	Y	Y
24	**Katko**	Y	N	N	N	Y	N
25	Morelle	Y	N	N	N	Y	Y
26	Higgins, B.	Y	Y	Y	N	N	Y
27	**Collins, C.**	Y	Y	Y	N	N	Y
NORTH CAROLINA		Y	N	N	N	Y	N
1	Butterfield						
2	**Holding**	Y	Y	Y	N	N	Y
3	**Jones***	?	N	N	Y	Y	N
4	Price						
5	**Foxx**	Y	Y	Y	N	N	Y
6	**Walker**	Y	N	N	Y	Y	N
7	**Rouzer**	Y	N	N	Y	Y	N

		355	356	357	358	359	360
8	**Hudson**	Y	N	N	Y	Y	N
9	vacant	Y	N	N	Y	Y	N
10	**McHenry**	Y	N	N	Y	Y	N
11	**Meadows**	N	N	N	Y	Y	N
12	Adams	Y	Y	Y	N	N	Y
13	**Budd**	Y	N	N	Y	Y	N
NORTH DAKOTA							
AL	**Armstrong**	Y	-	N	N	Y	N
OHIO							
1	**Chabot**	Y	N	N	Y	Y	N
2	**Wenstrup**	Y	N	N	Y	Y	N
3	Beatty	Y	Y	Y	N	N	Y
4	**Jordan**	N	N	N	Y	Y	N
5	**Latta**	Y	N	N	Y	Y	N
6	**Johnson, B.**	Y	N	N	Y	Y	N
7	**Gibbs**	Y	N	N	Y	Y	N
8	**Davidson**	N	N	N	Y	Y	N
9	Kaptur	Y	Y	Y	N	N	Y
10	**Turner**	Y	N	N	N	Y	N
11	Fudge	Y	Y	Y	N	N	Y
12	**Balderson**	Y	N	N	Y	Y	N
13	Ryan	Y	Y	Y	N	N	Y
14	**Joyce**	Y	N	N	N	N	N
15	**Stivers**	Y	N	N	N	Y	N
16	**Gonzalez**	Y	N	N	N	Y	N
OKLAHOMA							
1	**Hern**	Y	N	N	Y	Y	N
2	**Mullin**	Y	N	N	Y	Y	N
3	**Lucas**	Y	N	N	N	Y	N
4	**Cole**	Y	N	N	N	Y	N
5	Horn	Y	Y	Y	N	N	Y
OREGON							
1	Bonamici	Y	Y	Y	N	N	Y
2	**Walden**	Y	N	N	N	Y	N
3	Blumenauer	Y	Y	Y	N	N	Y
4	DeFazio	Y	Y	Y	N	N	Y
5	Schrader	Y	Y	Y	N	N	Y
PENNSYLVANIA							
1	**Fitzpatrick**	Y	N	N	N	Y	Y
2	Boyle	Y	Y	Y	N	N	Y
3	Evans	Y	Y	Y	N	N	Y
4	Dean	Y	Y	Y	N	N	Y
5	Scanlon	Y	Y	Y	N	N	Y
6	Houlahan	Y	Y	Y	N	N	Y
7	Wild	Y	Y	Y	N	Y	Y
8	Cartwright	Y	Y	Y	N	N	Y
9	**Meuser**	Y	N	N	Y	Y	N
10	**Perry**	Y	N	N	Y	Y	N
11	**Smucker**	Y	N	N	Y	Y	N
12	**Marino***						
13	**Joyce**	Y	N	N	Y	Y	N
14	**Reschenthaler**	Y	N	N	N	Y	N
15	**Thompson, G.**	Y	N	N	N	Y	N
16	**Kelly, M.**	Y	N	N	Y	Y	N
17	Lamb	Y	Y	Y	N	N	N
18	Doyle	Y	Y	Y	N	N	Y
RHODE ISLAND							
1	Cicilline	Y	Y	Y	N	N	Y
2	Langevin	Y	Y	Y	N	N	Y
SOUTH CAROLINA							
1	Cunningham	Y	Y	Y	N	N	Y
2	**Wilson, J.**	Y	N	N	N	Y	N
3	**Duncan**	Y	N	N	Y	Y	N
4	**Timmons**	Y	N	N	Y	Y	N
5	**Norman**	N	N	N	Y	Y	N
6	Clyburn	Y	Y	Y	N	N	Y
7	**Rice, T.**	Y	N	N	Y	Y	N
SOUTH DAKOTA							
AL	**Johnson**	Y	N	N	Y	Y	N
TENNESSEE							
1	**Roe**	Y	N	N	Y	Y	N
2	**Burchett**	N	N	N	Y	Y	N
3	**Fleischmann**	Y	N	N	N	Y	N
4	**DesJarlais**	Y	N	N	Y	Y	N
5	Cooper	Y	Y	N	N	N	Y
6	**Rose**	Y	N	N	Y	Y	N
7	**Green**	Y	N	N	Y	Y	N
8	**Kustoff**	Y	N	N	Y	Y	N
9	Cohen	Y	Y	Y	N	N	Y
TEXAS							
1	**Gohmert**	Y	N	N	Y	Y	N
2	**Crenshaw**	Y	N	N	Y	Y	N
3	**Taylor**	Y	N	N	Y	Y	N
4	**Ratcliffe**	N	N	N	Y	Y	N

		355	356	357	358	359	360
5	**Gooden**	Y	N	N	Y	Y	N
6	**Wright**	N	N	N	Y	Y	N
7	Fletcher	Y	Y	Y	N	N	N
8	**Brady**	Y	N	N	Y	Y	N
9	Green, A.	Y	Y	Y	N	N	Y
10	**McCaul**	Y	N	N	N	Y	N
11	**Conaway**	Y	N	N	Y	Y	N
12	**Granger**	Y	N	N	Y	N	N
13	**Thornberry**	Y	N	N	N	Y	N
14	**Weber**	Y	N	N	Y	Y	N
15	Gonzalez	Y	Y	Y	N	N	N
16	Escobar	Y	Y	Y	N	N	Y
17	**Flores**	Y	N	N	Y	Y	N
18	Jackson Lee	Y	Y	Y	N	N	Y
19	**Arrington**	N	N	N	Y	Y	N
20	Castro	Y	Y	Y	N	N	Y
21	**Roy**	Y	N	N	Y	Y	N
22	**Olson**	Y	N	N	Y	Y	N
23	**Hurd**	Y	N	N	N	N	N
24	**Marchant**	N	N	N	Y	Y	N
25	**Williams**	Y	N	N	Y	Y	N
26	**Burgess**	Y	N	N	Y	Y	N
27	**Cloud**	Y	N	N	Y	Y	N
28	Cuellar	Y	Y	Y	N	N	Y
29	Garcia, S.	Y	Y	Y	N	N	Y
30	Johnson, E.B.	Y	Y	Y	N	N	Y
31	**Carter, J.**	Y	N	N	Y	Y	N
32	Allred	Y	Y	Y	N	N	N
33	Veasey	Y	Y	Y	N	N	N
34	Vela	Y	Y	Y	N	N	N
35	Doggett	Y	Y	Y	N	N	Y
36	**Babin**	Y	N	N	Y	Y	N
UTAH							
1	**Bishop, R.**	N	N	N	Y	Y	N
2	**Stewart**	Y	N	N	Y	Y	N
3	**Curtis**	?	?	?	?	?	?
4	McAdams	Y	Y	Y	N	N	N
VERMONT							
AL	Welch	Y	Y	Y	N	N	Y
VIRGINIA							
1	**Wittman**	Y	N	N	Y	Y	N
2	Luria	Y	Y	Y	N	N	Y
3	Scott, R.	Y	Y	Y	N	N	Y
4	McEachin	Y	Y	Y	N	N	Y
5	**Riggleman**	Y	N	N	Y	Y	N
6	**Cline**	Y	N	N	Y	Y	N
7	Spanberger	Y	Y	Y	N	N	Y
8	Beyer	Y	Y	Y	N	N	Y
9	**Griffith**	Y	N	N	Y	Y	N
10	Wexton	Y	Y	Y	N	N	Y
11	Connolly	Y	Y	Y	N	N	Y
WASHINGTON							
1	DelBene	Y	Y	Y	N	N	Y
2	Larsen	Y	Y	Y	N	N	Y
3	**Herrera Beutler**	?	?	?	?	?	?
4	**Newhouse**	Y	N	?	N	Y	N
5	**McMorris Rodgers**	Y	N	N	Y	Y	N
6	Kilmer	Y	Y	Y	N	N	Y
7	Jayapal	Y	Y	Y	N	N	Y
8	Schrier	Y	Y	Y	N	N	Y
9	Smith Adam	Y	Y	Y	N	N	Y
10	Heck	Y	Y	Y	N	N	Y
WEST VIRGINIA							
1	**McKinley**	Y	N	N	N	Y	N
2	**Mooney**	Y	N	N	Y	Y	N
3	**Miller**	Y	N	N	N	Y	N
WISCONSIN							
1	**Steil**	Y	N	N	Y	Y	N
2	Pocan	Y	Y	Y	N	N	Y
3	Kind	Y	Y	Y	N	N	Y
4	Moore	Y	Y	Y	N	N	Y
5	**Sensenbrenner**	Y	N	N	Y	Y	N
6	**Grothman**	Y	N	N	Y	Y	N
7	**Duffy**	Y	N	N	Y	Y	N
8	**Gallagher**	Y	N	N	N	Y	N
WYOMING							
AL	**Cheney**	Y	N	N	N	Y	N
DELEGATES							
	Radewagen (A.S.)	?			?	?	?
	Norton (D.C.)	Y			N	N	Y
	San Nicolas (Guam)	Y			N	N	Y
	Sablan (N. Marianas)	Y			N	N	Y
	González-Colón (P.R.)	Y			N	N	Y
	Plaskett (V.I.)	Y			N	N	N

361. HR2740. Fiscal 2020 Four-Bill Appropriations Package – En Bloc Amendments. Kaptur, D-Ohio, en bloc package of amendments to the Energy-Water title (Division E) of the Fiscal 2020 Four-Bill Appropriations Package. Among others, it includes several provisions to increase funding for Army Corps of Engineers projects related to harbor, flood, and storm damage, shore protection, and aquatic ecosystem restoration; and it includes several provisions to increase or redistribute funding for Energy Department activities related to nuclear energy, fossil energy research, and energy efficiency and renewable energy. Adopted in Committee of the Whole 382-52: R 145-52; D 236-0; I 1-0. June 19, 2019.

362. HR2740. Fiscal 2020 Four-Bill Appropriations Package – Greenhouse Gas Regulations. Mullin, R-Okla., amendment that would prohibit the use of funds made available by the bill to prepare, propose, or promulgate any regulation or guidance referencing analysis contained in certain documents published by the White House council on environmental quality and by the interagency working groups on the social cost of carbon and greenhouse gases. Rejected in Committee of the Whole 186-248: R 186-11; D 0-236; I 0-1. June 19, 2019.

363. HR2740. Fiscal 2020 Four-Bill Appropriations Package – Alaska Infrastructure Impact Statement. Huffman, D-Calif., amendment that would prohibit the use of funds made available by the bill to finalize the environmental impact statement for a proposed Army Corps of Engineers infrastructure project in southwest Alaska, including a mine site, port, transportation corridor, and natural gas pipeline. Adopted 233-201: R 3-194; D 229-7; I 1-0. June 19, 2019.

364. HR2740. Fiscal 2020 Four-Bill Appropriations Package – Army Corps of Engineers Authority. Graves, R-La., amendment that would strike from the bill a section prohibiting the use of funds made available by the bill to reorganize or transfer civil works functions or authority of the Army Corps of Engineers or Army to another department or agency. Adopted in Committee of the Whole 162-269: R 150-45; D 12-223; I 0-1. June 19, 2019.

365. HR2740. Fiscal 2020 Four-Bill Appropriations Package – Reduce Energy-Water Funding. Banks, R-Ind., amendment that would reduce by 14 percent all funding made available by the Energy and Water Development and related agencies title of the bill (Division E), not including amounts made available for the Defense Department. Rejected in Committee of the Whole 132-302: R 131-66; D 1-235; I 0-1. June 19, 2019.

366. HR2740. Fiscal 2020 Four-Bill Appropriations Package – Recommit. Womack, R-Ark., motion to recommit the fiscal 2020 Labor-HHS-Education, Defense, Energy-Water, and State-Foreign Operations appropriations package to the House Appropriations Committee. Motion rejected 196-231: R 195-1; D 1-230. June 19, 2019.

		361	362	363	364	365	366
ALABAMA							
1	**Byrne**	N	Y	N	Y	Y	Y
2	**Roby**	Y	Y	N	N	N	Y
3	**Rogers, M.**	Y	Y	N	Y	Y	Y
4	**Aderholt**	Y	Y	N	N	Y	Y
5	**Brooks, M.**	N	Y	N	Y	Y	Y
6	**Palmer**	N	Y	N	Y	Y	Y
7	Sewell	Y	N	Y	N	N	N
ALASKA							
AL	**Young**	Y	Y	N	N	N	Y
ARIZONA							
1	O'Halleran	Y	N	Y	N	N	N
2	Kirkpatrick	Y	N	Y	N	N	?
3	Grijalva	Y	N	Y	N	N	N
4	**Gosar**	N	Y	N	Y	Y	Y
5	**Biggs**	N	Y	N	Y	Y	Y
6	**Schweikert**	Y	Y	N	Y	Y	Y
7	Gallego	Y	N	Y	N	N	N
8	**Lesko**	Y	Y	N	Y	Y	Y
9	Stanton	Y	N	Y	N	N	N
ARKANSAS							
1	**Crawford**	Y	Y	N	Y	Y	Y
2	**Hill, F.**	Y	Y	N	Y	N	Y
3	**Womack**	Y	Y	N	N	Y	Y
4	**Westerman**	Y	Y	N	Y	Y	Y
CALIFORNIA							
1	**LaMalfa**	Y	Y	N	Y	Y	Y
2	Huffman	Y	N	Y	Y	N	N
3	Garamendi	Y	N	Y	N	N	N
4	**McClintock**	N	Y	N	Y	Y	Y
5	Thompson, M.	Y	N	Y	N	N	N
6	Matsui	Y	N	Y	N	N	N
7	Bera	Y	N	Y	N	N	N
8	**Cook**	Y	Y	N	Y	Y	Y
9	McNerney	Y	N	Y	N	N	N
10	Harder	Y	N	Y	N	N	N
11	DeSaulnier	Y	N	Y	N	N	N
12	Pelosi						
13	Lee B.	Y	N	Y	N	N	N
14	Speier	Y	N	Y	N	N	N
15	Swalwell	Y	N	Y	N	N	N
16	Costa	Y	N	Y	Y	N	N
17	Khanna	Y	N	Y	N	N	N
18	Eshoo	Y	N	Y	N	N	N
19	Lofgren	Y	N	Y	N	N	N
20	Panetta	Y	N	Y	N	N	N
21	Cox	Y	N	Y	Y	N	N
22	**Nunes**	Y	Y	N	Y	Y	Y
23	**McCarthy**	Y	Y	N	Y	N	Y
24	Carbajal	Y	N	Y	N	N	N
25	Hill, K.	Y	N	Y	N	N	N
26	Brownley	Y	N	Y	N	N	N
27	Chu	Y	N	Y	N	N	N
28	Schiff	Y	N	Y	N	N	N
29	Cárdenas	Y	N	Y	N	N	N
30	Sherman	Y	N	Y	N	N	N
31	Aguilar	Y	N	Y	N	N	N
32	Napolitano	Y	N	Y	N	N	N
33	Lieu	Y	N	Y	N	N	N
34	Gomez	Y	N	Y	N	N	N
35	Torres	Y	N	Y	N	N	N
36	Ruiz	Y	N	Y	N	N	N
37	Bass	Y	N	Y	N	N	N
38	Sánchez	Y	N	Y	N	N	N
39	Cisneros	Y	N	Y	N	N	N
40	Roybal-Allard	Y	N	Y	N	N	N
41	Takano	Y	N	Y	N	N	N
42	**Calvert**	Y	Y	N	N	N	Y
43	Waters	Y	N	Y	N	N	N
44	Barragán	Y	N	Y	N	N	N
45	Porter	Y	N	Y	Y	N	N
46	Correa	Y	N	Y	N	N	N
47	Lowenthal	Y	N	Y	Y	N	N
48	Rouda	Y	N	Y	Y	N	N
49	Levin	Y	N	Y	N	N	N
50	**Hunter**	Y	Y	N	Y	Y	Y
51	Vargas	Y	N	Y	N	N	N
52	Peters	Y	N	Y	N	N	N
53	Davis, S.	Y	N	Y	N	N	N
COLORADO							
1	DeGette	Y	N	Y	N	N	N
2	Neguse	Y	N	Y	N	N	N
3	**Tipton**	Y	Y	N	Y	N	Y
4	**Buck**	N	Y	N	Y	Y	Y
5	**Lamborn**	Y	Y	N	Y	Y	Y
6	Crow	Y	N	Y	N	N	N
7	Perlmutter	Y	N	Y	N	N	N
CONNECTICUT							
1	Larson	Y	N	Y	N	N	N
2	Courtney	Y	N	Y	N	N	N
3	DeLauro	Y	N	Y	N	N	N
4	Himes	Y	N	Y	N	N	N
5	Hayes	Y	N	Y	N	N	N
DELAWARE							
AL	Blunt Rochester	Y	N	Y	N	N	N
FLORIDA							
1	**Gaetz**	N	N	N	Y	Y	Y
2	**Dunn**	Y	Y	Y	Y	Y	Y
3	**Yoho**	Y	Y	N	Y	Y	Y
4	**Rutherford**	Y	Y	N	N	N	Y
5	Lawson	Y	N	Y	N	N	N
6	**Waltz**	Y	Y	N	Y	N	Y
7	Murphy	Y	N	Y	N	N	N
8	**Posey**	N	Y	N	Y	N	Y
9	Soto	Y	N	Y	N	N	N
10	Demings	Y	N	Y	N	N	N
11	**Webster**	N	Y	N	Y	Y	Y
12	**Bilirakis**	Y	Y	N	Y	N	Y
13	Crist	Y	N	Y	N	N	N
14	Castor	Y	N	Y	N	N	N
15	**Spano**	Y	Y	N	Y	N	Y
16	**Buchanan**	Y	Y	N	Y	N	Y
17	**Steube**	N	Y	N	Y	N	Y
18	**Mast**	Y	Y	N	Y	N	Y
19	**Rooney**	Y	Y	N	Y	N	Y
20	Hastings	?	?	?	?	?	?
21	Frankel	Y	N	Y	N	N	N
22	Deutch	Y	N	Y	N	N	N
23	Wasserman Schultz	Y	N	Y	N	N	N
24	Wilson, F.	Y	N	Y	N	N	N
25	**Diaz-Balart**	Y	Y	N	N	N	Y
26	Mucarsel-Powell	Y	N	Y	N	N	N
27	Shalala	Y	N	Y	N	N	N
GEORGIA							
1	**Carter, E.L.**	N	Y	N	Y	Y	Y
2	Bishop, S.	Y	N	Y	N	N	N
3	**Ferguson**	N	Y	N	Y	Y	Y
4	Johnson, H.	Y	N	Y	N	N	N
5	Lewis John	Y	N	Y	N	N	N
6	McBath	Y	N	Y	N	N	N
7	**Woodall**	Y	Y	N	Y	Y	Y
8	**Scott, A.**	N	Y	N	Y	Y	Y
9	**Collins, D.**	Y	Y	N	Y	Y	Y
10	**Hice**	N	Y	N	Y	Y	Y
11	**Loudermilk**	N	Y	N	Y	Y	Y
12	**Allen**	N	Y	N	Y	Y	Y
13	Scott, D.	Y	N	Y	N	N	N
14	**Graves, T.**	N	Y	N	Y	Y	Y
HAWAII							
1	Case	Y	N	Y	N	N	N
2	Gabbard	Y	N	Y	N	N	N
IDAHO							
1	**Fulcher**	Y	Y	N	Y	Y	Y
2	**Simpson**	Y	Y	N	N	N	Y
ILLINOIS							
1	Rush	Y	N	Y	N	N	N
2	Kelly, R.	Y	N	Y	N	N	N
3	Lipinski	Y	N	Y	P	N	N
4	García, J.	Y	N	Y	N	N	N
5	Quigley	Y	N	Y	N	N	N
6	Casten	Y	N	Y	N	N	N
7	Davis, D.	Y	N	Y	N	N	N
8	Krishnamoorthi	Y	N	Y	N	N	N
9	Schakowsky	Y	N	Y	N	N	N
10	Schneider	Y	N	Y	N	N	N
11	Foster	Y	N	Y	N	N	N

KEY:		**Republicans**	Democrats	*Independents*
Y Voted for (yea)	**N** Voted against (nay)	**P** Voted "present"		
+ Announced for	**–** Announced against	**?** Did not vote or otherwise		
# Paired for	**X** Paired against	make position known		

		361	362	363	364	365	366
12	**Bost**	Y	Y	N	Y	N	Y
13	**Davis, R.**	Y	Y	N	Y	N	Y
14	Underwood	Y	N	Y	N	N	N
15	**Shimkus**	Y	Y	N	Y	Y	Y
16	**Kinzinger**	Y	Y	N	Y	N	Y
17	Bustos	Y	N	Y	N	N	N
18	**LaHood**	Y	Y	N	Y	Y	Y
INDIANA							
1	Visclosky	Y	N	Y	N	N	N
2	**Walorski**	Y	Y	N	N	Y	Y
3	**Banks**	Y	Y	N	Y	Y	Y
4	**Baird**	Y	Y	N	N	N	Y
5	**Brooks, S.**	Y	Y	N	Y	Y	Y
6	**Pence**	Y	Y	N	Y	Y	Y
7	Carson	Y	N	Y	N	N	N
8	**Bucshon**	N	Y	N	N	Y	Y
9	**Hollingsworth**	Y	Y	N	Y	N	Y
IOWA							
1	Finkenauer	Y	N	Y	N	N	N
2	Loebsack	Y	N	Y	N	N	N
3	Axne	Y	N	N	N	N	N
4	**King, S.**	N	Y	N	Y	Y	Y
KANSAS							
1	**Marshall**	Y	Y	N	Y	N	Y
2	**Watkins**	Y	Y	N	Y	Y	Y
3	Davids	Y	N	Y	N	N	N
4	**Estes**	Y	Y	N	Y	Y	Y
KENTUCKY							
1	**Comer**	Y	Y	N	Y	Y	Y
2	**Guthrie**	Y	Y	N	Y	Y	Y
3	Yarmuth	Y	N	Y	N	N	N
4	**Massie**	N	Y	N	Y	Y	Y
5	**Rogers, H.**	Y	Y	N	N	N	Y
6	**Barr**	Y	Y	N	Y	Y	Y
LOUISIANA							
1	**Scalise**	Y	Y	N	Y	Y	Y
2	Richmond	Y	N	Y	Y	N	N
3	**Higgins, C.**	Y	Y	N	Y	Y	Y
4	**Johnson, M.**	N	Y	N	Y	Y	Y
5	**Abraham**	N	Y	N	Y	Y	Y
6	**Graves, G.**	Y	Y	N	Y	N	Y
MAINE							
1	Pingree	Y	N	Y	N	N	N
2	Golden	Y	N	Y	N	N	N
MARYLAND							
1	**Harris**	N	Y	N	Y	Y	Y
2	Ruppersberger	Y	N	Y	N	N	N
3	Sarbanes	Y	N	Y	N	N	N
4	Brown, A.	Y	N	Y	N	N	N
5	Hoyer	Y	N	Y	N	N	N
6	Trone	Y	N	Y	N	N	N
7	Cummings	Y	N	Y	N	N	N
8	Raskin						
MASSACHUSETTS		Y	N	Y	N	N	N
1	Neal						
2	McGovern	Y	N	Y	N	N	N
3	Trahan	Y	N	Y	N	N	N
4	Kennedy	Y	N	Y	N	N	N
5	Clark	Y	N	Y	N	N	N
6	Moulton	Y	N	Y	N	N	N
7	Pressley	Y	N	Y	N	N	N
8	Lynch	Y	N	Y	N	N	N
9	Keating	Y	N	Y	N	N	N
MICHIGAN		Y	N	Y	N	N	N
1	**Bergman**						
2	**Huizenga**	Y	N	N	Y	Y	Y
3	**Amash**	Y	Y	N	Y	Y	Y
4	**Moolenaar**	N	Y	N	N	Y	N
5	Kildee	Y	Y	N	Y	Y	Y
6	**Upton**	Y	N	Y	N	N	N
7	**Walberg**	Y	Y	N	N	N	Y
8	Slotkin	Y	Y	N	N	N	Y
9	Levin	Y	N	Y	N	N	N
10	**Mitchell**	Y	N	Y	N	N	N
11	Stevens	Y	Y	N	Y	N	Y
12	Dingell	Y	N	Y	N	N	N
13	Tlaib	Y	N	Y	N	N	N
14	Lawrence	Y	N	Y	N	N	N
MINNESOTA		Y	N	Y	N	N	N
1	**Hagedorn**						
2	Craig	Y	Y	N	Y	Y	Y
3	Phillips	Y	N	Y	N	N	N
4	McCollum	Y	N	Y	N	N	N
5	Omar	Y	N	Y	N	N	N

		361	362	363	364	365	366
6	**Emmer**	Y	N	Y	N	N	N
7	Peterson	Y	Y	N	Y	Y	Y
8	**Stauber**	Y	N	N	Y	N	N
MISSISSIPPI		Y	Y	N	Y	N	Y
1	**Kelly, T.**						
2	Thompson, B.	Y	Y	N	Y	Y	Y
3	**Guest**	Y	N	Y	N	N	N
4	**Palazzo**	Y	Y	N	Y	Y	Y
MISSOURI		N	Y	N	Y	Y	Y
1	Clay						
2	**Wagner**	Y	N	Y	N	N	N
3	**Luetkemeyer**	Y	Y	N	Y	Y	Y
4	**Hartzler**	Y	Y	N	Y	N	Y
5	Cleaver	Y	Y	N	+	Y	Y
6	**Graves, S.**	Y	N	Y	N	N	N
7	**Long**	Y	Y	N	Y	N	Y
8	**Smith, J.**	Y	Y	N	Y	Y	Y
MONTANA		Y	Y	N	Y	Y	Y
AL	**Gianforte**						
NEBRASKA		Y	Y	N	Y	Y	Y
1	**Fortenberry**						
2	**Bacon**	Y	N	N	Y	N	Y
3	**Smith, Adrian**	Y	N	N	N	Y	Y
NEVADA		Y	Y	N	Y	Y	Y
1	Titus						
2	**Amodei**	Y	N	Y	N	N	N
3	Lee	Y	N	N	N	N	Y
4	Horsford	Y	N	Y	N	N	N
NEW HAMPSHIRE		Y	N	Y	N	N	N
1	Pappas						
2	Kuster	Y	N	Y	N	N	N
NEW JERSEY		Y	N	Y	N	N	N
1	Norcross						
2	Van Drew	Y	N	Y	N	N	N
3	Kim	Y	N	Y	N	N	N
4	**Smith, C.**	Y	N	Y	N	N	N
5	Gottheimer	Y	N	N	N	N	Y
6	Pallone	Y	N	Y	N	N	N
7	Malinowski	Y	N	Y	N	N	N
8	Sires	Y	N	Y	N	N	N
9	Pascrell	Y	N	Y	N	N	N
10	Payne	Y	N	Y	N	N	N
11	Sherrill	Y	N	Y	N	N	N
12	Watson Coleman	Y	N	Y	N	N	N
NEW MEXICO		Y	N	Y	N	N	N
1	Haaland						
2	Torres Small	Y	N	Y	N	N	N
3	Luján	Y	N	Y	N	N	N
NEW YORK		Y	N	Y	N	N	N
1	**Zeldin**						
2	**King, P.**	Y	Y	N	N	N	Y
3	Suozzi	Y	Y	N	N	N	Y
4	Rice, K.	Y	N	Y	N	N	N
5	Meeks	Y	N	Y	N	N	N
6	Meng	Y	N	Y	N	N	N
7	Velázquez	Y	N	Y	N	N	N
8	Jeffries	Y	N	Y	N	N	N
9	Clarke	Y	N	Y	N	N	N
10	Nadler	Y	N	Y	N	N	N
11	Rose	Y	N	Y	N	N	N
12	Maloney, C.	Y	N	Y	N	Y	N
13	Espaillat	Y	N	Y	N	N	N
14	Ocasio-Cortez	Y	N	Y	N	N	N
15	Serrano	Y	N	Y	N	N	N
16	Engel	Y	N	Y	N	N	N
17	Lowey	Y	N	Y	N	N	N
18	Maloney, S.P.	Y	N	Y	N	N	N
19	Delgado	Y	N	Y	Y	N	N
20	Tonko	Y	N	Y	N	N	N
21	**Stefanik**	Y	N	Y	N	N	N
22	Brindisi	Y	Y	N	Y	N	Y
23	**Reed**	Y	N	Y	N	N	N
24	**Katko**	Y	N	N	Y	N	Y
25	Morelle	Y	Y	N	Y	N	Y
26	Higgins, B.	Y	N	Y	N	N	N
27	**Collins, C.**	Y	N	Y	N	N	N
NORTH CAROLINA		Y	Y	N	Y	N	Y
1	Butterfield						
2	**Holding**	Y	N	Y	N	N	N
3	**Jones***	Y	Y	N	N	Y	Y
4	Price						
5	**Foxx**	Y	N	Y	N	N	N
6	**Walker**	Y	Y	N	Y	Y	Y
7	**Rouzer**	Y	Y	N	Y	Y	Y

		361	362	363	364	365	366
8	**Hudson**	Y	Y	N	N	Y	Y
9	vacant	Y	Y	N	Y	Y	Y
10	**McHenry**	Y	N	N	Y	Y	Y
11	**Meadows**	N	Y	N	?	Y	Y
12	Adams	Y	N	Y	N	N	N
13	**Budd**	Y	Y	N	Y	Y	Y
NORTH DAKOTA							
AL	**Armstrong**	Y	Y	N	Y	N	Y
OHIO							
1	**Chabot**	N	Y	N	Y	Y	Y
2	**Wenstrup**	Y	Y	N	Y	Y	Y
3	Beatty	Y	N	Y	N	N	N
4	**Jordan**	Y	Y	N	Y	Y	Y
5	**Latta**	Y	Y	N	Y	Y	Y
6	**Johnson, B.**	N	Y	N	Y	Y	Y
7	**Gibbs**	Y	Y	N	Y	Y	Y
8	**Davidson**	N	Y	N	Y	Y	Y
9	Kaptur	Y	N	Y	N	N	N
10	**Turner**	Y	Y	N	Y	N	Y
11	Fudge	Y	N	Y	N	N	N
12	**Balderson**	Y	Y	N	Y	Y	Y
13	Ryan	Y	N	Y	N	N	N
14	**Joyce**	Y	Y	N	N	N	Y
15	**Stivers**	Y	Y	N	Y	N	Y
16	**Gonzalez**	Y	Y	N	Y	N	Y
OKLAHOMA							
1	**Hern**	N	Y	N	Y	Y	Y
2	**Mullin**	N	Y	N	Y	Y	Y
3	**Lucas**	Y	Y	N	Y	N	Y
4	**Cole**	Y	Y	N	Y	N	Y
5	Horn	Y	N	Y	N	N	N
OREGON							
1	Bonamici	Y	N	Y	N	N	N
2	**Walden**	Y	Y	N	N	N	Y
3	Blumenauer	Y	N	Y	N	N	N
4	DeFazio	Y	N	Y	N	N	N
5	Schrader	Y	N	Y	N	N	N
PENNSYLVANIA							
1	**Fitzpatrick**	Y	N	Y	N	N	Y
2	Boyle	Y	N	Y	N	N	N
3	Evans	Y	N	Y	N	N	?
4	Dean	Y	N	Y	N	N	N
5	Scanlon	Y	N	Y	N	N	N
6	Houlahan	Y	N	Y	N	N	N
7	Wild	Y	N	Y	N	N	N
8	Cartwright	Y	N	Y	N	N	N
9	**Meuser**	N	Y	N	Y	Y	Y
10	**Perry**	Y	Y	N	Y	Y	Y
11	**Smucker**	Y	Y	N	Y	Y	Y
12	**Marino***						
13	**Joyce**	Y	Y	N	Y	Y	Y
14	**Reschenthaler**	Y	Y	N	Y	N	Y
15	**Thompson, G.**	Y	Y	N	Y	N	Y
16	**Kelly, M.**	Y	Y	N	N	Y	Y
17	Lamb	Y	N	N	N	N	N
18	Doyle	Y	N	Y	N	N	N
RHODE ISLAND							
1	Cicilline	Y	N	Y	N	N	N
2	Langevin	Y	N	Y	N	N	N
SOUTH CAROLINA							
1	Cunningham	Y	N	Y	N	N	N
2	**Wilson, J.**	Y	Y	N	Y	N	Y
3	**Duncan**	N	Y	N	Y	Y	Y
4	**Timmons**	Y	Y	N	Y	Y	Y
5	**Norman**	N	Y	N	Y	Y	Y
6	Clyburn	Y	N	Y	N	N	N
7	**Rice, T.**	N	Y	N	Y	Y	Y
SOUTH DAKOTA							
AL	**Johnson**	Y	Y	N	Y	Y	Y
TENNESSEE							
1	**Roe**	Y	Y	N	N	Y	Y
2	**Burchett**	Y	Y	N	Y	Y	Y
3	**Fleischmann**	Y	Y	N	N	N	Y
4	**DesJarlais**	Y	Y	N	Y	Y	Y
5	Cooper	Y	N	Y	N	N	N
6	**Rose**	Y	Y	N	N	Y	Y
7	**Green**	N	Y	N	Y	Y	Y
8	**Kustoff**	Y	Y	N	Y	Y	Y
9	Cohen	Y	N	Y	N	N	N
TEXAS							
1	**Gohmert**	N	Y	N	Y	Y	Y
2	**Crenshaw**	Y	Y	N	Y	N	Y
3	**Taylor**	N	Y	N	Y	Y	Y
4	**Ratcliffe**	N	Y	N	Y	Y	Y

		361	362	363	364	365	366
5	**Gooden**	N	Y	N	Y	Y	Y
6	**Wright**	N	Y	N	Y	Y	Y
7	Fletcher	Y	N	N	Y	N	N
8	**Brady**	Y	Y	N	N	Y	Y
9	Green, A.	Y	N	Y	N	N	N
10	**McCaul**	Y	Y	N	Y	N	Y
11	**Conaway**	Y	Y	N	Y	Y	Y
12	**Granger**	Y	Y	N	N	N	Y
13	**Thornberry**	Y	Y	N	Y	N	Y
14	**Weber**	Y	Y	N	Y	N	Y
15	Gonzalez	Y	N	Y	N	N	N
16	Escobar	Y	N	Y	N	N	N
17	**Flores**	Y	Y	N	Y	Y	Y
18	Jackson Lee	Y	N	Y	N	N	N
19	**Arrington**	N	Y	N	N	Y	Y
20	Castro	Y	N	Y	N	N	N
21	**Roy**	N	Y	N	N	Y	Y
22	**Olson**	Y	Y	N	Y	N	Y
23	**Hurd**	Y	Y	N	N	N	Y
24	**Marchant**	N	Y	N	N	N	Y
25	**Williams**	N	Y	N	Y	Y	Y
26	**Burgess**	N	Y	N	Y	Y	Y
27	**Cloud**	N	Y	N	Y	Y	Y
28	Cuellar	Y	N	N	N	N	N
29	Garcia, S.	Y	N	Y	N	N	N
30	Johnson, E.B.	Y	N	Y	N	N	N
31	**Carter, J.**	Y	Y	N	N	N	Y
32	Allred	Y	N	N	N	N	N
33	Veasey	Y	N	Y	N	N	N
34	Vela	Y	N	Y	Y	N	N
35	Doggett	Y	N	Y	N	N	N
36	**Babin**	Y	Y	N	Y	N	Y
UTAH							
1	**Bishop, R.**	N	Y	N	N	N	Y
2	**Stewart**	Y	Y	N	Y	Y	Y
3	**Curtis**	?	?	?	?	?	?
4	McAdams	Y	N	Y	N	N	Y
VERMONT							
AL	Welch	Y	N	Y	N	N	N
VIRGINIA							
1	**Wittman**	Y	Y	N	Y	Y	Y
2	Luria	Y	N	Y	N	N	N
3	Scott, R.	Y	N	Y	N	N	N
4	McEachin	Y	N	Y	N	N	N
5	**Riggleman**	Y	Y	N	Y	Y	Y
6	**Cline**	N	Y	N	Y	Y	Y
7	Spanberger	Y	N	Y	Y	N	N
8	Beyer	Y	N	Y	N	N	N
9	**Griffith**	Y	Y	N	Y	Y	Y
10	Wexton	Y	N	Y	N	N	N
11	Connolly	Y	N	Y	N	N	N
WASHINGTON							
1	DelBene	Y	N	Y	N	N	N
2	Larsen	Y	N	Y	N	N	N
3	**Herrera Beutler**	?	?	?	?	?	?
4	**Newhouse**	Y	Y	N	N	N	Y
5	**McMorris Rodgers**	Y	Y	N	N	Y	Y
6	Kilmer	Y	N	Y	N	N	N
7	Jayapal	Y	N	Y	N	N	N
8	Schrier	Y	N	Y	N	N	N
9	Smith Adam	Y	N	Y	N	N	N
10	Heck	Y	N	Y	N	N	N
WEST VIRGINIA							
1	**McKinley**	Y	Y	N	Y	N	Y
2	**Mooney**	Y	Y	N	Y	Y	Y
3	**Miller**	Y	Y	N	Y	Y	Y
WISCONSIN							
1	**Steil**	Y	N	N	Y	Y	Y
2	Pocan	Y	N	Y	N	N	N
3	Kind	Y	N	Y	N	N	N
4	Moore	Y	N	Y	N	N	N
5	**Sensenbrenner**	Y	Y	N	N	Y	Y
6	**Grothman**	N	Y	N	Y	Y	Y
7	**Duffy**	N	Y	N	Y	N	Y
8	**Gallagher**	Y	Y	N	N	N	Y
WYOMING							
AL	**Cheney**	Y	Y	N	Y	N	Y
DELEGATES							
	Radewagen (A.S.)	?	?	?	?	?	
	Norton (D.C.)	Y	N	Y	N	N	
	San Nicolas (Guam)	Y	N	Y	N	N	
	Sablan (N. Marianas)	Y	N	Y	N	N	
	González-Colón (P.R.)	Y	Y	N	N	N	
	Plaskett (V.I.)	Y	N	Y	Y	N	

III HOUSE VOTES

367. HR2740. Fiscal 2020 Four-Bill Appropriations Package - Passage. Passage of the fiscal 2020 Labor-HHS-Education, Defense, Energy-Water and State-Foreign Operations appropriations package, as amended, that would provide $984.7 billion in discretionary spending for four of the twelve fiscal 2020 appropriations bills, including $690.2 billion for the Defense Department, $191.7 billion for the Labor, Health and Human Services, and Education Departments, $56.4 billion for the State Department and related agencies, and $46.4 billion for the Energy Department and federal water projects. Within total funding, the bill provides $76.1 billion in overseas contingency operations funding not subject to discretionary spending caps. Among other provisions, the bill would phase out within 240 days of enactment the 2001 authorization for use of military force, which has been used to authorize military operations Iraq, Afghanistan, and Syria. It would provide $2.4 billion for HHS refugee and entrant assistance programs and establish housing requirements for unaccompanied minors in HHS custody; $11.8 billion for Energy Department weapons-related activities; and $750 million for U.S. Agency for International Development family planning and reproductive health programs abroad. It would also prohibit the use of funds made available by the bill to facilitate U.S. withdrawal from the Paris Climate Agreement or to construct physical barriers or border security infrastructure along the U.S. southern land border. As amended, the bill would provide an additional $289.5 million funding for a number of HHS and Education Department programs, including programs related to refugee and entrant assistance, substance abuse and mental health, and school safety. Passed 226-203: R 0-196; D 226-7. *Note: A "nay" was a vote in support of the president's position.* June 19, 2019.

368. HR3055. Fiscal 2020 Five-Bill Appropriations Package - NOAA Operations and Research. Rutherford, R-Fla., amendment that would increase by $3.5 million funding for National Oceanic and Atmospheric Administration operations, research, and facilities and decrease by the same amount administrative funding for the Commerce Department Telecommunications and Information Administration. Rejected in Committee of the Whole 186-245: R 153-44; D 33-200; I 0-1. June 20, 2019.

369. HR3055. Fiscal 2020 Five-Bill Appropriations Package - Census Questions. King, R-Iowa, amendment that would strike from the bill a provision prohibiting the use of funds made available by the bill for the Commerce Department to incorporate any questions not included in a 2018 census test in the 2020 decennial census. Rejected in Committee of the Whole 192-240: R 192-6; D 0-233; I 0-1. June 20, 2019.

370. HR3055. Fiscal 2020 Five-Bill Appropriations Package - Federal Marijuana Regulations. Blumenauer, D-Ore., amendment that would prohibit the use of funds made available for the Justice Department under the bill for the purpose of preventing 46 of the 50 states, the District of Columbia, the Northern Mariana Islands, Guam, Puerto Rico or the U.S. Virgin Islands, from implementing laws relating to the authorized use, distribution, possession or cultivation of marijuana. Adopted in Committee of the Whole 267-165: R 41-157; D 225-8; I 1-0. June 20, 2019.

371. HR3055. Fiscal 2020 Five-Bill Appropriations Package - Reduce Commerce-Justice-Science Funding. Banks, R-Ind., amendment that would reduce by 14 percent all discretionary funding made available under the Commerce-Justice-Science title of the bill (Division A). Rejected in Committee of the Whole 135-296: R 135-63; D 0-232; I 0-1. June 20, 2019.

372. HR3055. Fiscal 2020 Five-Bill Appropriations Package - Right Whale Protection Status. Golden, D-Maine, amendment that would prohibit the use of funds made available by the bill for the use of a certain risk reduction support tool to evaluate the protected status of right whales. Rejected in Committee of the Whole 84-345: R 71-125; D 13-219; I 0-1. June 20, 2019.

		367	368	369	370	371	372
ALABAMA							
1	**Byrne**	N	Y	Y	N	Y	Y
2	**Roby**	N	Y	Y	N	N	Y
3	**Rogers, M.**	N	Y	Y	Y	N	Y
4	**Aderholt**	N	Y	Y	N	N	Y
5	**Brooks, M.**	N	N	N	N	Y	Y
6	**Palmer**	N	Y	Y	N	Y	Y
7	Sewell	Y	N	N	Y	N	N
ALASKA							
AL	**Young**	N	Y	Y	N	Y	N
ARIZONA							
1	O'Halleran	Y	N	N	Y	N	N
2	Kirkpatrick	Y	-	-	+	-	-
3	Grijalva	Y	N	N	Y	N	N
4	**Gosar**	N	N	N	N	Y	Y
5	**Biggs**	N	Y	Y	N	Y	Y
6	**Schweikert**	N	Y	Y	Y	Y	N
7	Gallego	Y	N	N	Y	N	N
8	**Lesko**	N	N	N	N	Y	Y
9	Stanton	Y	N	N	Y	N	N
ARKANSAS							
1	**Crawford**	N	Y	Y	N	Y	N
2	**Hill, F.**	N	Y	Y	N	N	N
3	**Womack**	N	Y	Y	N	N	N
4	**Westerman**	N	Y	Y	N	Y	Y
CALIFORNIA							
1	**LaMalfa**	N	Y	Y	N	Y	N
2	Huffman	Y	N	N	Y	N	N
3	Garamendi	Y	N	N	Y	N	N
4	**McClintock**	N	N	N	Y	Y	Y
5	Thompson, M.	Y	N	N	Y	N	N
6	Matsui	Y	N	N	Y	N	N
7	Bera	Y	N	N	Y	N	N
8	**Cook**	N	Y	Y	N	N	Y
9	McNerney	Y	N	N	Y	N	N
10	Harder	Y	Y	N	Y	N	N
11	DeSaulnier	Y	N	N	Y	N	N
12	Pelosi						
13	Lee B.	Y	N	N	Y	N	N
14	Speier	Y	N	N	Y	N	N
15	Swalwell	Y	-	-	+	-	-
16	Costa	Y	Y	N	Y	N	N
17	Khanna	Y	N	N	Y	N	N
18	Eshoo	Y	N	N	Y	N	N
19	Lofgren	Y	N	N	Y	N	N
20	Panetta	Y	N	N	Y	N	N
21	Cox	Y	N	N	Y	N	N
22	**Nunes**	N	Y	Y	N	Y	Y
23	**McCarthy**	N	Y	Y	N	N	Y
24	Carbajal	Y	N	N	Y	N	N
25	Hill, K.	Y	N	N	Y	N	N
26	Brownley	Y	N	N	Y	N	N
27	Chu	Y	N	N	Y	N	N
28	Schiff	Y	N	N	Y	N	N
29	Cárdenas	Y	N	N	Y	N	N
30	Sherman	Y	N	N	Y	N	N
31	Aguilar	Y	N	N	Y	N	N
32	Napolitano	Y	N	N	Y	N	N
33	Lieu	Y	N	N	Y	N	N
34	Gomez	Y	N	N	Y	N	N
35	Torres	Y	N	N	Y	N	N
36	Ruiz	Y	N	N	Y	N	N
37	Bass	Y	N	N	Y	N	N
38	Sánchez	Y	N	N	Y	N	N
39	Cisneros	Y	N	N	Y	N	N
40	Roybal-Allard	Y	N	N	Y	N	N
41	Takano	Y	N	N	Y	N	N
42	**Calvert**	N	Y	Y	N	Y	N
43	Waters	Y	N	N	Y	N	N
44	Barragán	Y	N	N	Y	N	N
45	Porter	Y	N	N	Y	N	N
46	Correa	Y	N	N	Y	N	N
47	Lowenthal	Y	N	N	Y	N	N
48	Rouda	Y	N	N	Y	N	N
49	Levin	Y	N	N	Y	N	N
50	**Hunter**	N	N	Y	Y	Y	N
51	Vargas	Y	N	N	Y	N	N
52	Peters	Y	N	N	Y	N	N
53	Davis, S.	Y	N	N	Y	N	N
COLORADO							
1	DeGette	Y	N	N	Y	N	N
2	Neguse	Y	N	N	Y	N	N
3	**Tipton**	N	N	Y	N	N	Y
4	**Buck**	N	Y	Y	Y	Y	Y
5	**Lamborn**	N	Y	Y	N	Y	N
6	Crow	Y	N	N	Y	N	N
7	Perlmutter	Y	Y	N	Y	N	N
CONNECTICUT							
1	Larson	Y	N	N	Y	N	N
2	Courtney	Y	N	N	Y	N	Y
3	DeLauro	Y	N	N	Y	N	N
4	Himes	Y	N	N	Y	N	N
5	Hayes	Y	N	N	Y	N	N
DELAWARE							
AL	Blunt Rochester	Y	N	N	Y	N	N
FLORIDA							
1	**Gaetz**	N	Y	Y	Y	Y	Y
2	**Dunn**	N	Y	Y	N	Y	Y
3	**Yoho**	N	Y	Y	Y	N	Y
4	**Rutherford**	N	Y	Y	N	N	N
5	Lawson	Y	Y	N	Y	N	N
6	**Waltz**	N	Y	Y	N	N	N
7	Murphy	Y	Y	N	Y	N	N
8	**Posey**	N	Y	Y	N	N	N
9	Soto	Y	N	N	Y	N	N
10	Demings	Y	Y	N	Y	N	N
11	**Webster**	N	Y	Y	N	N	N
12	**Bilirakis**	N	Y	Y	N	Y	N
13	Crist	Y	N	N	Y	N	N
14	Castor	Y	N	N	Y	N	N
15	**Spano**	N	Y	Y	N	N	N
16	**Buchanan**	N	Y	Y	N	N	N
17	**Steube**	N	Y	Y	Y	Y	Y
18	**Mast**	N	Y	Y	Y	N	N
19	**Rooney**	N	Y	Y	N	Y	N
20	Hastings	?	?	?	?	?	?
21	Frankel	Y	N	N	Y	N	N
22	Deutch	Y	N	N	Y	N	N
23	Wasserman Schultz	Y	Y	N	N	N	N
24	Wilson, F.	Y	N	N	Y	N	N
25	**Diaz-Balart**	N	Y	Y	N	N	N
26	Mucarsel-Powell	Y	Y	N	Y	N	N
27	Shalala	Y	Y	N	Y	N	N
GEORGIA							
1	**Carter, E.L.**	N	Y	Y	N	N	Y
2	Bishop, S.	Y	N	N	Y	N	N
3	**Ferguson**	N	Y	Y	N	N	N
4	Johnson, H.	Y	N	N	Y	N	N
5	Lewis John	Y	N	N	Y	N	N
6	McBath	Y	N	N	Y	N	N
7	**Woodall**	N	Y	Y	N	Y	N
8	**Scott, A.**	N	Y	Y	N	Y	N
9	**Collins, D.**	N	Y	Y	N	Y	Y
10	**Hice**	N	Y	Y	N	Y	N
11	**Loudermilk**	N	Y	Y	N	Y	N
12	**Allen**	N	Y	Y	N	Y	N
13	Scott, D.	Y	N	N	Y	N	N
14	**Graves, T.**	N	Y	Y	Y	Y	N
HAWAII							
1	Case	Y	N	N	Y	N	N
2	Gabbard	Y	N	N	Y	N	N
IDAHO							
1	**Fulcher**	N	Y	Y	Y	Y	Y
2	**Simpson**	N	Y	Y	N	N	N
ILLINOIS							
1	Rush	Y	N	N	Y	N	N
2	Kelly, R.	Y	N	N	Y	N	N
3	Lipinski	Y	N	N	Y	N	N
4	García, J.	Y	N	N	Y	N	N
5	Quigley	Y	N	N	Y	N	N
6	Casten	Y	N	N	Y	N	N
7	Davis, D.	Y	N	N	Y	N	N
8	Krishnamoorthi	Y	N	N	Y	N	N
9	Schakowsky	Y	N	N	Y	N	N
10	Schneider	Y	N	N	Y	N	N
11	Foster	Y	N	N	Y	N	N

KEY:	**Republicans**	Democrats	*Independents*

Y Voted for (yea)	**N** Voted against (nay)	**P** Voted "present"
+ Announced for	**–** Announced against	**?** Did not vote or otherwise
# Paired for	**X** Paired against	make position known

		367	368	369	370	371	372
12	**Bost**	N	N	Y	N	N	Y
13	**Davis, R.**	N	Y	Y	Y	N	N
14	Underwood	Y	N	N	Y	N	N
15	**Shimkus**	N	N	Y	N	Y	N
16	**Kinzinger**	N	N	Y	N	N	N
17	Bustos	Y	N	N	Y	N	N
18	**LaHood**	N	Y	Y	N	Y	N
INDIANA							
1	Visclosky	Y	N	N	Y	N	N
2	**Walorski**	N	Y	Y	N	Y	Y
3	**Banks**	N	Y	Y	N	Y	N
4	**Baird**	N	Y	Y	N	N	Y
5	**Brooks, S.**	N	Y	Y	N	Y	N
6	**Pence**	N	Y	Y	N	N	N
7	Carson	Y	N	N	Y	N	N
8	**Bucshon**	N	Y	Y	N	Y	N
9	**Hollingsworth**	N	Y	Y	Y	N	N
IOWA							
1	Finkenauer	Y	N	N	Y	N	Y
2	Loebsack	Y	N	N	Y	N	N
3	Axne	Y	N	N	Y	N	N
4	**King, S.**	N	Y	Y	N	Y	N
KANSAS							
1	**Marshall**	N	Y	Y	N	N	N
2	**Watkins**	N	Y	Y	Y	Y	N
3	Davids	Y	N	N	N	N	N
4	**Estes**	N	Y	Y	N	Y	N
KENTUCKY							
1	**Comer**	N	Y	Y	Y	Y	Y
2	**Guthrie**	N	Y	Y	N	Y	N
3	Yarmuth	Y	Y	N	Y	N	Y
4	**Massie**	N	P	Y	Y	Y	Y
5	**Rogers, H.**	N	Y	Y	N	N	Y
6	**Barr**	N	Y	Y	N	Y	N
LOUISIANA							
1	**Scalise**	N	Y	Y	N	Y	Y
2	Richmond	Y	N	N	Y	N	N
3	**Higgins, C.**	N	Y	Y	N	Y	N
4	**Johnson, M.**	N	Y	Y	N	Y	Y
5	**Abraham**	N	Y	Y	N	Y	Y
6	**Graves, G.**	N	Y	Y	N	Y	N
MAINE							
1	Pingree	Y	N	N	Y	N	Y
2	Golden	Y	N	N	Y	N	Y
MARYLAND							
1	**Harris**	N	Y	Y	N	Y	Y
2	Ruppersberger	Y	N	N	Y	N	N
3	Sarbanes	Y	N	N	Y	N	N
4	Brown, A.	Y	N	N	Y	N	Y
5	Hoyer	Y	N	N	Y	N	N
6	Trone	Y	N	N	Y	N	N
7	Cummings	Y	N	N	Y	N	N
8	Raskin						
MASSACHUSETTS		Y	N	N	Y	N	N
1	Neal						
2	McGovern	Y	N	N	Y	N	N
3	Trahan	Y	N	N	Y	N	N
4	Kennedy	Y	N	N	Y	N	N
5	Clark	Y	N	N	Y	N	N
6	Moulton	Y	N	N	Y	N	N
7	Pressley	Y	Y	N	Y	N	N
8	Lynch	N	N	N	Y	N	N
9	Keating	Y	N	N	Y	N	N
MICHIGAN		Y	N	N	Y	N	N
1	**Bergman**						
2	**Huizenga**	N	Y	Y	N	Y	N
3	**Amash**	N	Y	Y	N	Y	Y
4	**Moolenaar**	N	N	Y	Y	Y	N
5	Kildee	N	Y	Y	N	Y	N
6	**Upton**	Y	N	N	Y	N	N
7	**Walberg**	N	Y	Y	Y	N	N
8	Slotkin	N	N	Y	N	Y	N
9	Levin	Y	N	N	Y	N	N
10	**Mitchell**	Y	N	N	Y	N	Y
11	Stevens	N	Y	Y	N	Y	Y
12	Dingell	Y	Y	N	Y	?	Y
13	Tlaib	Y	N	N	Y	N	N
14	Lawrence	N	N	N	Y	N	N
MINNESOTA		Y	N	N	Y	N	N
1	**Hagedorn**						
2	Craig	N	Y	Y	N	Y	N
3	Phillips	Y	N	N	Y	N	N
4	McCollum	Y	N	N	Y	N	N
5	Omar	Y	N	N	Y	N	N

		367	368	369	370	371	372
6	**Emmer**	N	Y	N	Y	N	N
7	Peterson	N	-	+	+	+	-
8	**Stauber**	N	Y	N	N	N	N
MISSISSIPPI		N	Y	Y	N	N	Y
1	**Kelly, T.**						
2	Thompson, B.	N	Y	Y	N	Y	N
3	**Guest**	Y	N	N	Y	N	N
4	**Palazzo**	N	Y	Y	N	Y	N
MISSOURI		N	Y	Y	N	Y	N
1	Clay						
2	**Wagner**	Y	N	N	Y	N	N
3	**Luetkemeyer**	N	Y	Y	N	Y	Y
4	**Hartzler**	N	N	Y	N	N	N
5	Cleaver	N	N	Y	N	Y	N
6	**Graves, S.**	Y	N	N	Y	N	N
7	**Long**	N	N	Y	N	Y	N
8	**Smith, J.**	N	N	Y	N	Y	N
MONTANA		N	Y	Y	N	Y	Y
AL	**Gianforte**						
NEBRASKA		N	Y	Y	Y	Y	Y
1	**Fortenberry**						
2	**Bacon**	N	Y	Y	N	N	N
3	**Smith, Adrian**	N	Y	Y	Y	Y	N
NEVADA		N	N	Y	N	Y	Y
1	Titus						
2	**Amodei**	Y	N	N	Y	N	N
3	Lee	N	Y	Y	N	Y	Y
4	Horsford	Y	N	N	Y	N	N
NEW HAMPSHIRE		Y	N	N	Y	N	N
1	Pappas						
2	Kuster	Y	N	N	Y	N	N
NEW JERSEY		Y	N	N	Y	N	N
1	Norcross						
2	Van Drew	Y	N	N	Y	N	Y
3	Kim	Y	Y	N	N	N	N
4	**Smith, C.**	Y	Y	N	Y	N	N
5	Gottheimer	N	Y	N	N	N	N
6	Pallone	Y	N	N	N	N	N
7	Malinowski	Y	N	N	Y	N	N
8	Sires	Y	N	N	Y	N	N
9	Pascrell	Y	N	N	Y	N	N
10	Payne	Y	N	N	Y	N	N
11	Sherrill	Y	N	N	Y	N	N
12	Watson Coleman	Y	N	N	Y	N	N
NEW MEXICO		Y	N	N	Y	N	N
1	Haaland						
2	Torres Small	Y	N	N	Y	N	N
3	Luján	Y	N	N	Y	N	N
NEW YORK		Y	N	N	Y	N	N
1	**Zeldin**						
2	**King, P.**	N	Y	Y	N	N	Y
3	Suozzi	N	Y	Y	N	N	N
4	Rice, K.	Y	N	N	N	N	N
5	Meeks	Y	N	N	Y	N	N
6	Meng	Y	N	N	Y	N	N
7	Velázquez	Y	N	N	Y	N	N
8	Jeffries	Y	N	N	Y	N	N
9	Clarke	Y	N	N	Y	N	N
10	Nadler	Y	N	N	Y	N	N
11	Rose	Y	N	N	Y	N	N
12	Maloney, C.	Y	N	N	Y	N	Y
13	Espaillat	Y	N	N	Y	N	N
14	Ocasio-Cortez	Y	N	N	Y	N	N
15	Serrano	N	N	N	Y	N	N
16	Engel	Y	N	N	Y	N	N
17	Lowey	Y	N	N	Y	N	N
18	Maloney, S.P.	Y	N	N	Y	N	N
19	Delgado	Y	N	N	Y	N	N
20	Tonko	Y	N	N	Y	N	N
21	**Stefanik**	Y	N	N	Y	N	N
22	Brindisi	N	Y	Y	N	N	Y
23	**Reed**	Y	Y	N	Y	N	N
24	**Katko**	N	N	Y	Y	N	N
25	Morelle	N	Y	Y	N	N	N
26	Higgins, B.	Y	N	N	Y	N	N
27	**Collins, C.**	Y	N	N	Y	N	N
NORTH CAROLINA		N	Y	Y	Y	N	N
1	Butterfield						
2	**Holding**	Y	N	N	Y	N	N
3	**Jones***	N	Y	Y	N	Y	N
4	Price						
5	**Foxx**	Y	N	N	Y	N	N
6	**Walker**	N	N	N	N	Y	N
7	**Rouzer**	N	Y	Y	N	Y	N

		367	368	369	370	371	372
8	**Hudson**	N	Y	Y	N	Y	N
9	vacant	N	N	Y	N	Y	N
10	**McHenry**	N	Y	Y	N	Y	N
11	**Meadows**	N	Y	Y	N	Y	Y
12	Adams	Y	N	N	Y	N	Y
13	**Budd**	N	Y	Y	N	Y	N
NORTH DAKOTA							
AL	**Armstrong**	N	N	Y	Y	N	N
OHIO							
1	**Chabot**	N	Y	Y	N	Y	N
2	**Wenstrup**	N	Y	Y	N	Y	Y
3	Beatty	Y	N	N	Y	N	N
4	**Jordan**	N	Y	Y	N	Y	Y
5	**Latta**	N	N	Y	N	Y	N
6	**Johnson, B.**	N	N	Y	N	Y	N
7	**Gibbs**	N	Y	Y	Y	Y	N
8	**Davidson**	N	N	Y	N	Y	Y
9	Kaptur	Y	N	N	Y	N	N
10	**Turner**	N	Y	Y	N	N	?
11	Fudge	Y	N	N	Y	N	N
12	**Balderson**	N	N	Y	Y	Y	Y
13	Ryan	Y	?	?	?	?	?
14	**Joyce**	N	Y	Y	Y	N	N
15	**Stivers**	N	Y	Y	N	N	N
16	**Gonzalez**	N	N	Y	Y	N	N
OKLAHOMA							
1	**Hern**	N	Y	Y	Y	Y	N
2	**Mullin**	N	Y	Y	N	Y	Y
3	**Lucas**	N	Y	Y	N	N	N
4	**Cole**	N	Y	Y	N	N	N
5	Horn	Y	N	N	Y	N	Y
OREGON							
1	Bonamici	Y	N	N	Y	N	N
2	**Walden**	N	N	Y	Y	N	N
3	Blumenauer	Y	N	N	Y	N	N
4	DeFazio	Y	N	N	Y	N	N
5	Schrader	Y	N	N	Y	N	N
PENNSYLVANIA							
1	**Fitzpatrick**	N	Y	Y	N	N	N
2	Boyle	Y	N	N	Y	N	N
3	Evans	Y	N	N	Y	N	N
4	Dean	Y	N	N	Y	N	N
5	Scanlon	Y	N	N	Y	N	N
6	Houlahan	Y	N	N	Y	N	N
7	Wild	Y	Y	N	Y	N	N
8	Cartwright	Y	N	N	Y	N	N
9	**Meuser**	N	Y	Y	N	Y	Y
10	**Perry**	N	Y	Y	N	Y	Y
11	**Smucker**	N	Y	Y	N	Y	Y
12	**Marino***						
13	**Joyce**	N	Y	Y	N	Y	Y
14	**Reschenthaler**	N	Y	Y	Y	N	Y
15	**Thompson, G.**	N	Y	Y	N	N	Y
16	**Kelly, M.**	N	N	Y	N	Y	Y
17	Lamb	Y	N	N	N	N	Y
18	Doyle	Y	N	N	Y	N	N
RHODE ISLAND							
1	Cicilline	Y	N	N	Y	N	N
2	Langevin	Y	N	N	Y	N	N
SOUTH CAROLINA							
1	Cunningham	Y	Y	N	Y	N	N
2	**Wilson, J.**	N	Y	Y	N	N	N
3	**Duncan**	N	Y	Y	N	Y	N
4	**Timmons**	N	Y	Y	N	Y	Y
5	**Norman**	N	Y	Y	N	Y	Y
6	Clyburn	Y	N	N	Y	N	N
7	**Rice, T.**	N	Y	Y	Y	Y	N
SOUTH DAKOTA							
AL	**Johnson**	N	N	Y	N	Y	N
TENNESSEE							
1	**Roe**	N	Y	Y	N	Y	N
2	**Burchett**	N	Y	Y	N	Y	N
3	**Fleischmann**	N	Y	Y	N	N	N
4	**DesJarlais**	N	Y	Y	N	Y	Y
5	Cooper	Y	N	N	Y	N	N
6	**Rose**	N	N	Y	N	Y	Y
7	**Green**	N	Y	Y	N	Y	Y
8	**Kustoff**	N	Y	Y	N	Y	N
9	Cohen	Y	Y	N	Y	N	N
TEXAS							
1	**Gohmert**	N	N	Y	N	N	N
2	**Crenshaw**	N	N	Y	N	N	N
3	**Taylor**	N	Y	Y	N	Y	Y
4	**Ratcliffe**	N	N	Y	N	Y	N

		367	368	369	370	371	372
5	**Gooden**	N	N	Y	N	Y	N
6	**Wright**	N	Y	Y	N	Y	N
7	Fletcher	Y	Y	N	Y	N	N
8	**Brady**	N	Y	Y	N	Y	N
9	Green, A.	Y	N	N	Y	N	N
10	**McCaul**	N	Y	N	Y	N	N
11	**Conaway**	N	Y	Y	N	Y	Y
12	**Granger**	N	Y	Y	N	N	N
13	**Thornberry**	N	Y	Y	N	N	Y
14	**Weber**	N	Y	Y	N	N	N
15	Gonzalez	Y	Y	N	Y	N	N
16	Escobar	Y	N	N	Y	N	N
17	**Flores**	N	Y	Y	N	Y	N
18	Jackson Lee	Y	N	N	Y	N	N
19	**Arrington**	N	N	Y	N	Y	N
20	Castro	Y	N	N	Y	N	N
21	**Roy**	N	N	Y	Y	Y	Y
22	**Olson**	N	Y	Y	N	Y	N
23	**Hurd**	N	N	N	N	N	N
24	**Marchant**	N	Y	Y	N	N	N
25	**Williams**	N	Y	Y	N	Y	Y
26	**Burgess**	N	Y	Y	N	Y	N
27	**Cloud**	N	Y	Y	N	Y	Y
28	Cuellar	Y	N	N	Y	N	N
29	Garcia, S.	Y	N	N	Y	N	N
30	Johnson, E.B.	Y	N	N	Y	N	N
31	**Carter, J.**	N	Y	Y	N	Y	N
32	Allred	Y	N	N	Y	N	N
33	Veasey	Y	N	N	Y	N	N
34	Vela	Y	Y	N	Y	N	Y
35	Doggett	Y	N	N	Y	N	N
36	**Babin**	N	Y	Y	N	N	N
UTAH							
1	**Bishop, R.**	N	Y	Y	N	Y	?
2	**Stewart**	N	N	Y	N	Y	Y
3	**Curtis**	?	Y	Y	N	Y	Y
4	McAdams	N	N	N	Y	N	N
VERMONT							
AL	Welch	Y	N	N	Y	N	N
VIRGINIA							
1	**Wittman**	N	N	Y	N	Y	Y
2	Luria	Y	Y	N	Y	N	N
3	Scott, R.	Y	Y	N	Y	N	N
4	McEachin	Y	N	N	Y	N	N
5	**Riggleman**	N	Y	Y	Y	Y	N
6	**Cline**	N	N	Y	N	Y	Y
7	Spanberger	Y	N	N	Y	N	N
8	Beyer	Y	Y	N	Y	N	N
9	**Griffith**	N	N	Y	Y	Y	N
10	Wexton	Y	N	N	Y	N	N
11	Connolly	Y	N	N	Y	N	N
WASHINGTON							
1	DelBene	Y	N	N	Y	N	N
2	Larsen	Y	Y	N	Y	N	Y
3	**Herrera Beutler**	?	?	?	?	?	?
4	**Newhouse**	N	Y	Y	Y	N	N
5	**McMorris Rodgers**	N	Y	Y	N	Y	N
6	Kilmer	Y	N	N	Y	N	N
7	Jayapal	Y	N	N	Y	N	N
8	Schrier	Y	N	N	Y	N	N
9	Smith Adam	Y	N	N	Y	N	N
10	Heck	N	N	N	Y	N	N
WEST VIRGINIA							
1	**McKinley**	N	N	Y	N	N	N
2	**Mooney**	N	N	Y	N	Y	Y
3	**Miller**	N	N	Y	N	Y	N
WISCONSIN							
1	**Steil**	N	Y	Y	N	Y	N
2	Pocan	Y	N	N	Y	N	N
3	Kind	Y	N	N	Y	N	N
4	Moore	Y	N	N	Y	N	N
5	**Sensenbrenner**	N	N	Y	N	Y	Y
6	**Grothman**	N	Y	Y	N	Y	N
7	**Duffy**	N	Y	Y	N	N	N
8	**Gallagher**	N	Y	Y	N	N	N
WYOMING							
AL	**Cheney**	N	Y	Y	N	N	N
DELEGATES							
	Radewagen (A.S.)		Y	N	Y	Y	N
	Norton (D.C.)		N	N	Y	N	N
	San Nicolas (Guam)		N	N	Y	N	N
	Sablan (N. Marianas)		N	N	Y	N	N
	González-Colón (P.R.)		Y	N	Y	N	N
	Plaskett (V.I.)		N	N	Y	N	?

373. HR3055. Fiscal 2020 Five-Bill Appropriations Package - Justice Department Expenses. Stevens, D-Mich., amendment that would increase then decrease by $2 million funding for Justice Department expenses for legal activities, administration of pardon and clemency petitions, and space rental in the District of Columbia. Adopted in Committee of the Whole 381-50: R 148-50; D 232-0; I 1-0. June 20, 2019.

374. HR3055. Fiscal 2020 Five-Bill Appropriations Package - Patient Protection and Affordable Care Act. Underwood, D-Ill., amendment that would prohibit the use of funds provided by the bill for the Justice Department to argue that the Patient Protection and Affordable Care Act is unconstitutional or invalid in any litigation to which the U.S. is a party. Adopted in Committee of the Whole 238-194: R 4-194; D 233-0; I 1-0. June 20, 2019.

375. HR3055. Fiscal 2020 Five-Bill Appropriations Package - Reduce Agriculture Funding. Banks, R-Ind., amendment that would reduce by 14 percent all discretionary funding made available under the Agriculture, Rural Development, Food and Drug Administration, and related agencies title of the bill (Division B). Rejected in Committee of the Whole 113-318: R 112-86; D 1-231; I 0-1. June 20, 2019.

376. HR3055. Fiscal 2020 Five-Bill Appropriations Package - Rural Services. Pence, R-Ind., amendment that would increase by $25 million funding for grants for telemedicine and distance learning services in rural areas and decrease by the same amount administrative funding for the Agriculture Department Office of the Chief Information Officer. Adopted in Committee of the Whole 425-6: R 192-5; D 232-1; I 1-0. June 20, 2019.

377. HR3055. Fiscal 2020 Five-Bill Appropriations Package - Rural Utilities Grants. Spanberger, D-Va., amendment that would increase by $55 million funding for rural utilities service grant programs, including distance learning, telemedicine, and broadband programs. It would decrease by $30 million funding for the Office of the Agriculture Department General Counsel, decrease by $12.5 million funding for the department Office of the Chief Information Officer, and decrease by $12.5 million administrative funding for the department. Adopted in Committee of the Whole 408-22: R 175-21; D 232-1; I 1-0. June 20, 2019.

378. HR3055. Fiscal 2020 Five-Bill Appropriations Package - Southern Offshore Drilling. Wasserman Schultz, D-Fla., amendment that would prohibit the use of funds made available under the bill for the purpose of conducting Interior Department offshore oil and gas leasing, pre-leasing or related activities in the Outer Continental Shelf Planning Areas for the South Atlantic, the Straits of Florida, and the central and eastern Gulf of Mexico. Adopted in Committee of the Whole 252-178: R 25-171; D 226-7; I 1-0. June 20, 2019.

		373	374	375	376	377	378
ALABAMA							
1	**Byrne**	N	N	Y	Y	Y	N
2	**Roby**	Y	N	N	Y	Y	N
3	**Rogers, M.**	Y	N	Y	N	Y	N
4	**Aderholt**	Y	N	N	Y	Y	N
5	**Brooks, M.**	N	N	Y	Y	Y	N
6	**Palmer**	N	N	Y	Y	N	N
7	Sewell	Y	Y	N	Y	Y	Y
ALASKA							
AL	**Young**	N	N	N	Y	Y	N
ARIZONA							
1	O'Halleran	Y	Y	N	Y	Y	Y
2	Kirkpatrick	+	+	–	+	+	+
3	Grijalva	Y	Y	N	Y	Y	Y
4	**Gosar**	Y	N	Y	Y	N	N
5	**Biggs**	Y	N	Y	N	N	N
6	**Schweikert**	Y	N	Y	N	N	N
7	Gallego	Y	Y	N	Y	Y	Y
8	**Lesko**	Y	N	Y	Y	Y	N
9	Stanton	Y	Y	N	Y	Y	Y
ARKANSAS							
1	**Crawford**	Y	N	N	Y	Y	N
2	**Hill, F.**	Y	N	N	Y	Y	N
3	**Womack**	Y	N	N	Y	Y	N
4	**Westerman**	N	N	Y	Y	Y	N
CALIFORNIA							
1	**LaMalfa**	Y	N	Y	Y	Y	N
2	Huffman	Y	Y	N	Y	Y	Y
3	Garamendi	Y	Y	N	Y	Y	Y
4	**McClintock**	N	N	Y	Y	Y	N
5	Thompson, M.	Y	Y	N	Y	Y	Y
6	Matsui	Y	Y	N	Y	Y	Y
7	Bera	Y	Y	N	Y	Y	Y
8	**Cook**	Y	N	N	Y	Y	N
9	McNerney	Y	Y	N	Y	Y	Y
10	Harder	Y	Y	Y	Y	Y	Y
11	DeSaulnier	Y	Y	N	Y	Y	Y
12	Pelosi						
13	Lee B.	Y	Y	N	Y	Y	Y
14	Speier	Y	Y	N	Y	Y	Y
15	Swalwell	+	+	–	+	+	+
16	Costa	Y	Y	N	Y	Y	Y
17	Khanna	Y	Y	N	Y	Y	Y
18	Eshoo	Y	Y	N	Y	Y	Y
19	Lofgren	Y	Y	N	Y	Y	Y
20	Panetta	Y	Y	N	Y	Y	Y
21	Cox	Y	Y	N	Y	Y	Y
22	**Nunes**	Y	N	Y	Y	Y	N
23	**McCarthy**	Y	N	N	Y	Y	N
24	Carbajal	Y	Y	N	Y	Y	Y
25	Hill, K.	Y	Y	N	Y	Y	Y
26	Brownley	Y	Y	N	Y	Y	Y
27	Chu	Y	Y	N	Y	Y	Y
28	Schiff	Y	Y	N	Y	Y	Y
29	Cárdenas	Y	Y	N	Y	Y	Y
30	Sherman	Y	Y	N	Y	Y	Y
31	Aguilar	Y	Y	N	Y	Y	Y
32	Napolitano	Y	Y	N	Y	Y	Y
33	Lieu	Y	Y	N	Y	Y	Y
34	Gomez	Y	Y	N	Y	Y	Y
35	Torres	Y	Y	N	Y	Y	Y
36	Ruiz	Y	Y	N	Y	Y	Y
37	Bass	Y	Y	N	Y	Y	Y
38	Sánchez	Y	Y	N	Y	Y	Y
39	Cisneros	Y	Y	N	Y	Y	Y
40	Roybal-Allard	Y	Y	N	Y	Y	Y
41	Takano	Y	Y	N	Y	Y	Y
42	**Calvert**	Y	N	N	Y	Y	N
43	Waters	Y	Y	N	Y	Y	Y
44	Barragán	Y	Y	N	Y	Y	Y
45	Porter	Y	Y	N	N	N	Y
46	Correa	Y	Y	N	Y	Y	Y
47	Lowenthal	Y	Y	N	Y	Y	Y
48	Rouda	Y	Y	N	Y	Y	Y
49	Levin	Y	Y	N	Y	Y	Y
50	**Hunter**	Y	N	Y	Y	Y	N
51	Vargas	Y	Y	N	Y	Y	Y
52	Peters	Y	Y	N	Y	Y	Y

		373	374	375	376	377	378
53	Davis, S.	Y	Y	N	Y	Y	Y
COLORADO							
1	DeGette	Y	Y	N	Y	Y	Y
2	Neguse	Y	Y	N	Y	Y	Y
3	**Tipton**	Y	N	N	Y	Y	N
4	**Buck**	Y	N	Y	Y	Y	N
5	**Lamborn**	Y	N	Y	Y	Y	N
6	Crow	Y	Y	N	Y	Y	Y
7	Perlmutter	Y	Y	N	Y	Y	Y
CONNECTICUT							
1	Larson	Y	Y	N	Y	Y	Y
2	Courtney	Y	Y	N	Y	Y	Y
3	DeLauro	Y	Y	N	Y	Y	Y
4	Himes	Y	Y	N	Y	Y	Y
5	Hayes	Y	Y	N	Y	Y	Y
DELAWARE							
AL	Blunt Rochester	Y	Y	N	Y	Y	Y
FLORIDA							
1	**Gaetz**	Y	N	Y	Y	N	Y
2	**Dunn**	Y	N	N	Y	Y	Y
3	**Yoho**	N	N	Y	Y	Y	N
4	**Rutherford**	Y	N	N	Y	Y	Y
5	Lawson	Y	Y	N	Y	Y	Y
6	**Waltz**	Y	N	Y	Y	Y	Y
7	Murphy	Y	Y	N	Y	Y	Y
8	**Posey**	Y	N	N	Y	N	Y
9	Soto	Y	Y	N	Y	Y	Y
10	Demings	Y	Y	N	Y	Y	Y
11	**Webster**	N	N	N	Y	N	Y
12	**Bilirakis**	Y	N	Y	Y	Y	Y
13	Crist	Y	Y	N	Y	Y	Y
14	Castor	Y	Y	N	Y	Y	Y
15	**Spano**	Y	N	N	Y	Y	Y
16	**Buchanan**	Y	N	N	Y	Y	Y
17	**Steube**	Y	N	Y	Y	Y	Y
18	**Mast**	N	N	N	Y	Y	Y
19	**Rooney**	Y	N	Y	N	N	Y
20	Hastings	?	?	?	?	?	?
21	Frankel	Y	Y	N	Y	Y	Y
22	Deutch	Y	Y	N	Y	Y	Y
23	Wasserman Schultz	Y	Y	N	Y	Y	Y
24	Wilson, F.	Y	Y	N	Y	Y	Y
25	**Diaz-Balart**	Y	N	N	Y	Y	Y
26	Mucarsel-Powell	Y	Y	N	Y	Y	Y
27	Shalala	Y	Y	N	Y	Y	Y
GEORGIA							
1	**Carter, E.L.**	N	N	Y	Y	Y	N
2	Bishop, S.	Y	Y	N	Y	Y	Y
3	**Ferguson**	N	N	Y	Y	Y	N
4	Johnson, H.	Y	Y	N	Y	Y	Y
5	Lewis John	Y	Y	N	Y	Y	Y
6	McBath	Y	Y	N	Y	Y	Y
7	**Woodall**	Y	N	Y	Y	Y	N
8	**Scott, A.**	Y	N	N	Y	Y	N
9	**Collins, D.**	Y	N	Y	Y	Y	N
10	**Hice**	N	N	Y	Y	N	N
11	**Loudermilk**	N	N	Y	Y	Y	N
12	**Allen**	N	N	N	Y	Y	N
13	Scott, D.	Y	Y	N	Y	Y	Y
14	**Graves, T.**	N	N	Y	Y	Y	?
HAWAII							
1	Case	Y	Y	N	Y	Y	Y
2	Gabbard	Y	Y	N	Y	Y	Y
IDAHO							
1	**Fulcher**	N	N	Y	Y	Y	N
2	**Simpson**	Y	N	N	Y	Y	Y
ILLINOIS							
1	Rush	Y	Y	N	Y	Y	Y
2	Kelly, R.	Y	Y	N	Y	Y	Y
3	Lipinski	Y	Y	N	Y	Y	Y
4	García, J.	Y	Y	N	Y	Y	Y
5	Quigley	Y	Y	N	Y	Y	Y
6	Casten	Y	Y	N	Y	Y	Y
7	Davis, D.	Y	Y	N	Y	Y	Y
8	Krishnamoorthi	Y	Y	N	Y	Y	Y
9	Schakowsky	Y	Y	N	Y	Y	Y
10	Schneider	Y	Y	N	Y	Y	Y
11	Foster	Y	Y	N	Y	Y	Y

KEY:	Republicans	Democrats	Independents

Y Voted for (yea)	N Voted against (nay)	P Voted "present"
+ Announced for	– Announced against	? Did not vote or otherwise
# Paired for	X Paired against	make position known

		373	374	375	376	377	378
12	**Bost**	Y	N	N	Y	Y	N
13	**Davis, R.**	Y	N	N	Y	Y	N
14	Underwood	Y	Y	N	Y	Y	Y
15	**Shimkus**	Y	N	N	Y	Y	N
16	**Kinzinger**	Y	N	N	Y	Y	N
17	Bustos	Y	Y	N	Y	Y	Y
18	**LaHood**	N	N	Y	Y	Y	N
INDIANA							
1	Visclosky	Y	Y	N	Y	Y	Y
2	**Walorski**	Y	N	N	Y	Y	N
3	**Banks**	N	N	Y	Y	Y	N
4	**Baird**	Y	N	N	Y	Y	N
5	**Brooks, S.**	Y	N	N	Y	Y	N
6	**Pence**	Y	N	N	Y	Y	N
7	Carson	Y	Y	N	Y	Y	Y
8	**Bucshon**	Y	N	Y	Y	Y	N
9	**Hollingsworth**	Y	N	N	Y	Y	Y
IOWA							
1	Finkenauer	Y	Y	N	Y	Y	Y
2	Loebsack	Y	Y	N	Y	Y	Y
3	Axne	Y	Y	N	Y	Y	Y
4	**King, S.**	N	N	N	Y	Y	N
KANSAS							
1	**Marshall**	Y	N	N	Y	Y	N
2	**Watkins**	Y	N	N	Y	Y	N
3	Davids	Y	Y	N	Y	Y	Y
4	**Estes**	Y	N	Y	Y	Y	N
KENTUCKY							
1	**Comer**	N	N	Y	Y	Y	N
2	**Guthrie**	Y	N	Y	Y	Y	N
3	Yarmuth	Y	Y	N	Y	Y	Y
4	**Massie**	N	N	Y	Y	N	N
5	**Rogers, H.**	Y	N	N	Y	Y	N
6	**Barr**	Y	N	Y	Y	N	N
LOUISIANA							
1	**Scalise**	Y	N	Y	Y	Y	N
2	Richmond	Y	Y	N	Y	Y	Y
3	**Higgins, C.**	Y	N	Y	Y	Y	N
4	**Johnson, M.**	Y	N	Y	Y	Y	N
5	**Abraham**	Y	N	Y	Y	Y	N
6	**Graves, G.**	Y	N	Y	Y	Y	N
MAINE							
1	Pingree	Y	Y	N	Y	Y	Y
2	Golden	Y	Y	N	Y	Y	Y
MARYLAND							
1	**Harris**	N	N	Y	Y	Y	Y
2	Ruppersberger	Y	Y	N	Y	Y	Y
3	Sarbanes	Y	Y	N	Y	Y	Y
4	Brown, A.	Y	Y	N	Y	Y	Y
5	Hoyer	Y	Y	N	Y	Y	Y
6	Trone	Y	Y	N	Y	Y	Y
7	Cummings	Y	Y	N	Y	Y	Y
8	Raskin						
MASSACHUSETTS		Y	Y	N	Y	Y	Y
1	Neal						
2	McGovern	Y	Y	N	Y	Y	Y
3	Trahan	Y	Y	N	Y	Y	Y
4	Kennedy	Y	Y	N	Y	Y	Y
5	Clark	Y	Y	N	Y	Y	Y
6	Moulton	Y	Y	N	Y	Y	Y
7	Pressley	Y	Y	N	Y	Y	Y
8	Lynch	Y	Y	N	Y	Y	Y
9	Keating	Y	Y	N	Y	Y	Y
MICHIGAN		Y	Y	N	Y	Y	Y
1	**Bergman**						
2	**Huizenga**	Y	N	N	Y	Y	N
3	**Amash**	Y	N	Y	+	Y	N
4	**Moolenaar**	N	N	Y	N	N	N
5	Kildee	Y	N	Y	Y	Y	N
6	**Upton**	Y	Y	N	Y	Y	Y
7	**Walberg**	Y	N	N	Y	Y	N
8	Slotkin	Y	N	N	Y	Y	N
9	Levin	Y	Y	N	Y	Y	Y
10	**Mitchell**	Y	Y	N	Y	Y	Y
11	Stevens	Y	N	N	Y	Y	N
12	Dingell	Y	Y	N	Y	Y	Y
13	Tlaib	Y	Y	N	Y	Y	Y
14	Lawrence	Y	Y	N	Y	Y	Y
MINNESOTA		Y	Y	N	Y	Y	Y
1	**Hagedorn**						
2	Craig	Y	N	N	Y	Y	N
3	Phillips	Y	Y	N	Y	Y	Y
4	McCollum	Y	Y	N	Y	Y	Y
5	Omar	Y	Y	N	Y	Y	Y

		373	374	375	376	377	378
6	**Emmer**	Y	Y	?	Y	Y	Y
7	Peterson	+	-	+	+	+	-
8	**Stauber**	Y	Y	N	Y	Y	N
MISSISSIPPI		Y	N	N	Y	Y	Y
1	**Kelly, T.**						
2	Thompson, B.	Y	N	Y	Y	Y	N
3	**Guest**	Y	Y	N	Y	Y	Y
4	**Palazzo**	Y	N	N	Y	Y	N
MISSOURI		N	N	Y	Y	Y	N
1	Clay						
2	**Wagner**	Y	Y	N	Y	Y	Y
3	**Luetkemeyer**	Y	N	N	Y	Y	N
4	**Hartzler**	N	N	N	Y	Y	N
5	Cleaver	N	N	N	Y	Y	N
6	**Graves, S.**	Y	Y	N	Y	Y	Y
7	**Long**	Y	N	N	Y	Y	N
8	**Smith, J.**	Y	N	N	Y	N	N
MONTANA		N	N	Y	Y	Y	N
AL	**Gianforte**						
NEBRASKA		Y	N	Y	Y	Y	N
1	**Fortenberry**						
2	**Bacon**	Y	N	N	Y	Y	N
3	**Smith, Adrian**	Y	N	N	Y	Y	N
NEVADA		N	N	N	Y	Y	N
1	Titus						
2	**Amodei**	Y	Y	N	Y	Y	Y
3	Lee	N	N	Y	Y	Y	N
4	Horsford	Y	Y	N	Y	Y	Y
NEW HAMPSHIRE		Y	Y	N	Y	Y	Y
1	Pappas						
2	Kuster	Y	Y	N	Y	Y	Y
NEW JERSEY		Y	Y	N	Y	Y	Y
1	Norcross						
2	Van Drew	Y	Y	N	Y	Y	Y
3	Kim	Y	Y	N	Y	Y	Y
4	**Smith, C.**	Y	Y	N	Y	Y	Y
5	Gottheimer	Y	N	N	Y	Y	Y
6	Pallone	Y	Y	N	Y	Y	Y
7	Malinowski	Y	Y	N	Y	Y	Y
8	Sires	Y	Y	N	Y	Y	Y
9	Pascrell	Y	Y	N	Y	Y	Y
10	Payne	Y	Y	N	Y	Y	Y
11	Sherrill	Y	Y	N	Y	Y	Y
12	Watson Coleman	Y	Y	N	Y	Y	Y
NEW MEXICO		Y	Y	N	Y	Y	Y
1	Haaland						
2	Torres Small	Y	Y	N	Y	Y	Y
3	Luján	Y	Y	N	Y	Y	Y
NEW YORK		Y	Y	N	Y	Y	Y
1	**Zeldin**						
2	**King, P.**	Y	N	N	Y	Y	Y
3	Suozzi	Y	N	N	Y	Y	Y
4	Rice, K.	Y	Y	N	Y	Y	Y
5	Meeks	Y	Y	N	Y	Y	Y
6	Meng	Y	Y	N	Y	Y	Y
7	Velázquez	Y	Y	N	Y	Y	Y
8	Jeffries	Y	Y	N	Y	Y	Y
9	Clarke	Y	Y	N	Y	Y	Y
10	Nadler	Y	Y	N	Y	Y	Y
11	Rose	Y	Y	N	Y	Y	Y
12	Maloney, C.	Y	Y	N	Y	Y	Y
13	Espaillat	Y	Y	N	Y	Y	Y
14	Ocasio-Cortez	Y	Y	N	Y	Y	Y
15	Serrano	Y	Y	N	Y	Y	Y
16	Engel	Y	Y	N	Y	Y	Y
17	Lowey	Y	Y	N	Y	Y	Y
18	Maloney, S.P.	Y	Y	N	Y	Y	Y
19	Delgado	Y	Y	N	Y	Y	Y
20	Tonko	Y	Y	N	Y	Y	Y
21	**Stefanik**	Y	Y	N	Y	Y	Y
22	Brindisi	Y	N	N	Y	Y	Y
23	**Reed**	Y	N	N	Y	Y	Y
24	**Katko**	Y	Y	N	Y	Y	N
25	Morelle	Y	Y	N	Y	Y	Y
26	Higgins, B.	Y	Y	N	Y	Y	Y
27	**Collins, C.**	?	Y	N	Y	Y	Y
NORTH CAROLINA		Y	N	N	Y	Y	N
1	Butterfield						
2	**Holding**	Y	Y	N	Y	Y	Y
3	**Jones***	Y	N	Y	Y	Y	N
4	Price						
5	**Foxx**	Y	Y	N	Y	Y	Y
6	**Walker**	Y	N	N	Y	N	N
7	**Rouzer**	N	N	Y	Y	?	N

		373	374	375	376	377	378
8	**Hudson**	Y	N	Y	Y	Y	N
9	vacant	Y	N	Y	Y	Y	N
10	**McHenry**	Y	N	Y	Y	Y	N
11	**Meadows**	Y	N	Y	Y	Y	N
12	Adams	Y	Y	N	Y	Y	Y
13	**Budd**	N	N	Y	Y	N	N
NORTH DAKOTA							
AL	**Armstrong**	Y	N	N	Y	Y	N
OHIO							
1	**Chabot**	Y	N	Y	Y	Y	N
2	**Wenstrup**	N	N	Y	Y	Y	N
3	Beatty	Y	Y	N	Y	Y	Y
4	**Jordan**	N	N	Y	Y	N	N
5	**Latta**	Y	N	Y	Y	Y	N
6	**Johnson, B.**	Y	N	Y	Y	Y	N
7	**Gibbs**	Y	N	Y	Y	Y	N
8	**Davidson**	N	N	Y	Y	Y	N
9	Kaptur	Y	Y	N	Y	Y	Y
10	**Turner**	Y	N	N	Y	Y	N
11	Fudge	Y	Y	N	Y	Y	Y
12	**Balderson**	Y	N	N	Y	Y	N
13	Ryan	?	?	?	?	?	?
14	**Joyce**	Y	N	N	Y	Y	N
15	**Stivers**	Y	N	N	Y	Y	N
16	**Gonzalez**	Y	Y	N	Y	Y	N
OKLAHOMA							
1	**Hern**	Y	N	Y	Y	Y	N
2	**Mullin**	N	N	Y	Y	Y	N
3	**Lucas**	Y	N	N	Y	+	N
4	**Cole**	Y	N	N	Y	Y	N
5	Horn	Y	Y	N	Y	Y	Y
OREGON							
1	Bonamici	Y	Y	N	Y	Y	Y
2	**Walden**	Y	N	N	Y	Y	N
3	Blumenauer	Y	Y	N	Y	Y	Y
4	DeFazio	Y	Y	N	Y	Y	Y
5	Schrader	Y	Y	N	Y	Y	Y
PENNSYLVANIA							
1	**Fitzpatrick**	Y	Y	N	Y	Y	Y
2	Boyle	Y	Y	N	Y	Y	Y
3	Evans	Y	Y	N	Y	Y	Y
4	Dean	Y	Y	N	Y	Y	Y
5	Scanlon	Y	Y	N	Y	Y	Y
6	Houlahan	Y	Y	N	Y	Y	Y
7	Wild	Y	Y	N	Y	Y	Y
8	Cartwright	Y	Y	N	Y	Y	Y
9	**Meuser**	Y	N	N	Y	Y	N
10	**Perry**	Y	N	Y	Y	Y	N
11	**Smucker**	Y	N	Y	Y	Y	N
12	**Marino***						
13	**Joyce**	Y	N	Y	Y	Y	N
14	**Reschenthaler**	Y	N	N	Y	Y	N
15	**Thompson, G.**	Y	N	N	Y	Y	N
16	**Kelly, M.**	N	N	Y	Y	Y	N
17	Lamb	Y	Y	N	Y	Y	Y
18	Doyle	Y	Y	N	Y	Y	Y
RHODE ISLAND							
1	Cicilline	Y	Y	N	Y	Y	Y
2	Langevin	Y	Y	N	Y	Y	Y
SOUTH CAROLINA							
1	Cunningham	Y	Y	N	Y	Y	Y
2	**Wilson, J.**	Y	N	N	Y	Y	N
3	**Duncan**	N	N	Y	Y	Y	N
4	**Timmons**	Y	N	Y	Y	Y	N
5	**Norman**	N	N	Y	Y	Y	N
6	Clyburn	Y	Y	N	Y	Y	Y
7	**Rice, T.**	N	N	Y	Y	Y	N
SOUTH DAKOTA							
AL	**Johnson**	Y	N	Y	Y	Y	N
TENNESSEE							
1	**Roe**	Y	N	N	Y	Y	N
2	**Burchett**	Y	N	Y	Y	Y	N
3	**Fleischmann**	Y	N	N	Y	Y	N
4	**DesJarlais**	Y	N	Y	Y	Y	N
5	Cooper	Y	Y	N	Y	Y	N
6	**Rose**	N	N	Y	Y	Y	N
7	**Green**	Y	N	Y	Y	N	N
8	**Kustoff**	Y	N	Y	Y	Y	N
9	Cohen	Y	Y	N	Y	Y	Y
TEXAS							
1	**Gohmert**	Y	N	N	Y	Y	N
2	**Crenshaw**	Y	N	N	Y	Y	N
3	**Taylor**	Y	N	Y	Y	Y	N
4	**Ratcliffe**	N	N	Y	Y	Y	N

		373	374	375	376	377	378
5	**Gooden**	Y	N	Y	Y	Y	N
6	**Wright**	Y	N	Y	Y	N	N
7	Fletcher	Y	Y	N	Y	Y	N
8	**Brady**	N	N	Y	Y	Y	N
9	Green, A.	Y	Y	N	Y	Y	Y
10	**McCaul**	Y	N	N	Y	Y	N
11	**Conaway**	Y	N	N	Y	Y	N
12	**Granger**	Y	N	N	Y	Y	N
13	**Thornberry**	Y	N	N	Y	Y	N
14	**Weber**	Y	N	Y	Y	Y	N
15	Gonzalez	Y	N	N	Y	Y	N
16	Escobar	Y	Y	N	Y	Y	Y
17	**Flores**	Y	N	Y	Y	Y	N
18	Jackson Lee	Y	Y	N	Y	Y	Y
19	**Arrington**	N	N	Y	Y	Y	N
20	Castro	Y	Y	N	Y	Y	Y
21	**Roy**	N	N	Y	Y	N	N
22	**Olson**	Y	N	Y	Y	Y	N
23	**Hurd**	Y	N	N	Y	Y	N
24	**Marchant**	Y	N	Y	Y	Y	N
25	**Williams**	Y	N	Y	Y	Y	N
26	**Burgess**	N	N	Y	Y	N	N
27	**Cloud**	N	N	Y	Y	Y	N
28	Cuellar	Y	Y	N	Y	Y	N
29	Garcia, S.	Y	Y	N	Y	Y	N
30	Johnson, E.B.	Y	Y	N	Y	Y	Y
31	**Carter, J.**	Y	N	N	Y	Y	N
32	Allred	Y	Y	N	Y	Y	Y
33	Veasey	Y	Y	N	Y	Y	Y
34	Vela	Y	Y	N	Y	Y	N
35	Doggett	Y	Y	N	Y	Y	Y
36	**Babin**	N	N	Y	Y	Y	N
UTAH							
1	**Bishop, R.**	Y	N	N	Y	Y	N
2	**Stewart**	Y	N	Y	Y	Y	N
3	**Curtis**	Y	N	Y	Y	Y	N
4	McAdams	Y	Y	N	Y	Y	Y
VERMONT							
AL	Welch	Y	Y	N	Y	Y	Y
VIRGINIA							
1	**Wittman**	Y	N	Y	Y	Y	N
2	Luria	Y	Y	N	Y	Y	Y
3	Scott, R.	Y	Y	N	Y	Y	Y
4	McEachin	Y	Y	N	Y	Y	Y
5	**Riggleman**	Y	N	Y	Y	Y	N
6	**Cline**	Y	N	Y	Y	Y	N
7	Spanberger	Y	Y	N	Y	Y	Y
8	Beyer	Y	Y	N	Y	Y	Y
9	**Griffith**	Y	N	Y	Y	Y	N
10	Wexton	Y	Y	N	Y	Y	Y
11	Connolly	Y	Y	N	Y	Y	Y
WASHINGTON							
1	DelBene	Y	Y	N	Y	Y	Y
2	Larsen	Y	Y	N	Y	Y	Y
3	**Herrera Beutler**	?	?	?	?	?	?
4	**Newhouse**	Y	N	N	Y	Y	Y
5	**McMorris Rodgers**	Y	N	Y	Y	Y	N
6	Kilmer	Y	Y	N	Y	Y	Y
7	Jayapal	Y	Y	N	Y	Y	Y
8	Schrier	Y	Y	N	Y	Y	Y
9	Smith Adam	Y	Y	N	Y	Y	Y
10	Heck	Y	Y	N	Y	Y	Y
WEST VIRGINIA							
1	**McKinley**	Y	N	N	Y	Y	N
2	**Mooney**	N	N	N	Y	Y	N
3	**Miller**	Y	N	Y	Y	Y	N
WISCONSIN							
1	**Steil**	Y	N	Y	Y	Y	N
2	Pocan	Y	Y	N	Y	Y	Y
3	Kind	Y	Y	N	Y	Y	Y
4	Moore	Y	Y	N	Y	Y	Y
5	**Sensenbrenner**	Y	N	Y	N	N	N
6	**Grothman**	Y	N	Y	Y	Y	N
7	**Duffy**	Y	N	N	Y	Y	N
8	**Gallagher**	N	N	N	Y	Y	N
WYOMING							
AL	**Cheney**	N	N	N	Y	Y	N
DELEGATES							
	Radewagen (A.S.)	Y	N	N	Y	Y	?
	Norton (D.C.)	Y	Y	N	Y	Y	Y
	San Nicolas (Guam)	Y	Y	N	Y	Y	Y
	Sablan (N. Marianas)	Y	Y	N	Y	Y	Y
	González-Colón (P.R.)	N	N	N	Y	Y	Y
	Plaskett (V.I.)	Y	Y	N	Y	Y	Y

379. HR3055. Fiscal 2020 Five-Bill Appropriations Package - Atlantic Offshore Drilling. Pallone, D-N.J., amendment that would prohibit the use of funds made available by the bill for the purpose of conducting Interior Department offshore oil and gas leasing, pre-leasing or related activities in the Outer Continental Shelf Planning Areas for the North Atlantic, Mid-Atlantic, and South Atlantic. Adopted in Committee of the Whole 247-185: R 18-180; D 228-5; I 1-0. June 20, 2019.

380. HR3055. Fiscal 2020 Five-Bill Appropriations Package - Hunting Trophy Imports. Buchanan, R-Fla., amendment that would prohibit the use of funds made available by the bill to issue permits for the importation of sport-hunted elephant or lion trophies from Zimbabwe, Zambia, or Tanzania. Adopted in Committee of the Whole 239-192: R 14-184; D 224-8; I 1-0. June 20, 2019.

381. HR3055. Fiscal 2020 Five-Bill Appropriations Package - EPA Pollution Rules. Duncan, R-S.C., amendment that would prohibit the use of funds made available by the bill to implement two Oct. 2015 Environmental Protection Agency rules regarding regulation of carbon pollution and greenhouse gas emission. Rejected in Committee of the Whole 192-240: R 192-6; D 0-233; I 0-1. June 20, 2019.

382. HR3055. Fiscal 2020 Five-Bill Appropriations Package - Alaska Timber Harvesting. Blumenauer, D-Ore., amendment that would prohibit the use of funds made available by the bill to plan or construct, for the purpose of timber harvesting by private entities, a forest development road in the Tongass National Forest in southeast Alaska. Adopted in Committee of the Whole 243-188: R 13-184; D 229-4; I 1-0. June 20, 2019.

383. HR3055. Fiscal 2020 Five-Bill Appropriations Package - EPA Greenhouse Gas Rule. Gosar, R-Ariz., amendment that would prohibit the use of funds made available by the bill to implement a Dec. 2009 Environmental Protection Agency rule making findings on greenhouse gas emissions. Rejected in Committee of the Whole 178-254: R 177-21; D 1-232; I 0-1. June 20, 2019.

384. HR3055. Fiscal 2020 Five-Bill Appropriations Package - Prohibit Oil and Gas Lease Sales. Duncan, R-S.C., amendment that would strike from the bill a prohibition on the use of funds made available under the bill for the purpose of conducting an oil or gas lease sale as required under the 2017 tax overhaul law. Rejected in Committee of the Whole 198-233: R 193-5; D 5-227; I 0-1. June 20, 2019.

	379	380	381	382	383	384
ALABAMA						
1 Byrne	N	N	Y	N	Y	Y
2 Roby	N	N	Y	N	Y	Y
3 Rogers, M.	N	N	Y	N	Y	Y
4 Aderholt	N	N	Y	N	Y	Y
5 Brooks, M.	N	N	Y	N	Y	Y
6 Palmer	N	N	Y	N	Y	Y
7 Sewell	Y	Y	N	Y	N	N
ALASKA						
AL Young	N	N	Y	N	Y	Y
ARIZONA						
1 O'Halleran	Y	Y	N	Y	N	N
2 Kirkpatrick	+	+	-	+	-	-
3 Grijalva	Y	Y	N	Y	N	N
4 Gosar	N	N	Y	N	Y	Y
5 Biggs	N	N	Y	N	Y	Y
6 Schweikert	N	Y	Y	N	Y	Y
7 Gallego	Y	Y	N	Y	N	N
8 Lesko	N	N	Y	N	Y	Y
9 Stanton	Y	Y	N	Y	N	N
ARKANSAS						
1 Crawford	N	N	Y	N	Y	Y
2 Hill, F.	N	N	Y	N	Y	Y
3 Womack	N	N	Y	N	Y	Y
4 Westerman	N	N	Y	N	Y	Y
CALIFORNIA						
1 LaMalfa	N	N	Y	N	Y	Y
2 Huffman	Y	Y	N	Y	N	N
3 Garamendi	Y	N	N	Y	N	N
4 McClintock	N	N	Y	N	Y	Y
5 Thompson, M.	Y	Y	N	Y	N	N
6 Matsui	Y	Y	N	Y	N	N
7 Bera	Y	Y	N	Y	N	N
8 Cook	N	N	Y	N	Y	Y
9 McNerney	Y	Y	N	Y	N	N
10 Harder	Y	Y	N	Y	N	N
11 DeSaulnier	Y	Y	N	Y	N	N
12 Pelosi						
13 Lee B.	Y	Y	N	Y	N	N
14 Speier	Y	?	N	Y	N	N
15 Swalwell	?	?	-	+	-	-
16 Costa	Y	Y	N	N	N	Y
17 Khanna	Y	Y	N	Y	N	N
18 Eshoo	Y	Y	N	Y	N	N
19 Lofgren	Y	Y	N	Y	N	N
20 Panetta	Y	Y	N	Y	N	N
21 Cox	Y	Y	N	Y	N	N
22 Nunes	N	N	Y	N	Y	Y
23 McCarthy	N	N	Y	N	Y	Y
24 Carbajal	Y	Y	N	Y	N	N
25 Hill, K.	Y	Y	N	Y	N	N
26 Brownley	Y	Y	N	Y	N	N
27 Chu	Y	Y	N	Y	N	N
28 Schiff	Y	Y	N	Y	N	N
29 Cárdenas	Y	Y	N	Y	N	N
30 Sherman	Y	Y	N	Y	N	N
31 Aguilar	Y	Y	N	Y	N	N
32 Napolitano	Y	N	N	Y	N	N
33 Lieu	Y	Y	N	Y	N	N
34 Gomez	Y	Y	N	Y	N	N
35 Torres	Y	Y	N	Y	N	N
36 Ruiz	Y	Y	N	Y	N	N
37 Bass	Y	Y	N	Y	N	N
38 Sánchez	Y	Y	N	Y	N	N
39 Cisneros	Y	Y	N	Y	N	N
40 Roybal-Allard	Y	Y	N	Y	N	N
41 Takano	Y	N	N	Y	N	N
42 Calvert	N	N	Y	N	Y	Y
43 Waters	Y	Y	N	Y	N	N
44 Barragán	Y	Y	N	Y	N	N
45 Porter	Y	Y	N	Y	N	N
46 Correa	Y	Y	N	Y	N	N
47 Lowenthal	Y	Y	N	Y	N	N
48 Rouda	Y	Y	N	Y	N	N
49 Levin	Y	Y	N	Y	N	N
50 Hunter	N	N	Y	N	Y	Y
51 Vargas	Y	Y	N	Y	N	N
52 Peters	Y	Y	N	Y	N	N
53 Davis, S.	Y	Y	N	Y	N	N
COLORADO						
1 DeGette	Y	Y	N	Y	N	N
2 Neguse	Y	Y	N	Y	N	N
3 Tipton	N	N	Y	N	Y	Y
4 Buck	N	N	Y	N	Y	Y
5 Lamborn	N	N	Y	N	Y	Y
6 Crow	Y	Y	N	Y	N	N
7 Perlmutter	Y	Y	N	Y	N	N
CONNECTICUT						
1 Larson	Y	Y	N	Y	N	N
2 Courtney	Y	Y	N	Y	N	N
3 DeLauro	Y	Y	N	Y	N	N
4 Himes	Y	Y	N	Y	N	N
5 Hayes	Y	Y	N	Y	N	N
DELAWARE						
AL Blunt Rochester	Y	Y	N	Y	N	N
FLORIDA						
1 Gaetz	Y	Y	Y	N	N	Y
2 Dunn	N	N	Y	N	Y	Y
3 Yoho	Y	N	Y	N	Y	Y
4 Rutherford	Y	N	Y	N	Y	Y
5 Lawson	Y	Y	N	Y	N	N
6 Waltz	Y	N	Y	N	Y	Y
7 Murphy	Y	Y	N	Y	N	N
8 Posey	N	N	Y	N	Y	Y
9 Soto	Y	Y	N	Y	N	N
10 Demings	Y	Y	N	Y	N	N
11 Webster	N	N	Y	N	Y	Y
12 Bilirakis	Y	N	Y	N	Y	Y
13 Crist	Y	Y	N	Y	N	N
14 Castor	Y	Y	N	Y	N	N
15 Spano	Y	N	Y	N	Y	Y
16 Buchanan	N	Y	Y	N	Y	Y
17 Steube	N	N	Y	N	Y	Y
18 Mast	Y	N	Y	N	N	Y
19 Rooney	Y	N	Y	N	N	Y
20 Hastings	?	?	?	?	?	?
21 Frankel	Y	Y	N	Y	N	N
22 Deutch	Y	Y	N	Y	N	N
23 Wasserman Schultz	Y	Y	N	Y	N	N
24 Wilson, F.	Y	Y	N	Y	N	N
25 Diaz-Balart	Y	N	Y	N	Y	Y
26 Mucarsel-Powell	Y	Y	N	Y	N	N
27 Shalala	Y	Y	N	Y	N	N
GEORGIA						
1 Carter, E.L.	N	N	Y	N	Y	Y
2 Bishop, S.	N	N	Y	N	N	N
3 Ferguson	N	N	Y	N	Y	Y
4 Johnson, H.	Y	Y	N	Y	N	N
5 Lewis John	Y	Y	N	Y	N	N
6 McBath	Y	Y	N	Y	N	N
7 Woodall	N	N	Y	N	Y	Y
8 Scott, A.	N	N	Y	N	Y	Y
9 Collins, D.	N	N	Y	N	Y	Y
10 Hice	N	N	Y	N	Y	Y
11 Loudermilk	N	N	Y	N	Y	Y
12 Allen	N	N	Y	N	Y	Y
13 Scott, D.	Y	Y	N	Y	N	N
14 Graves, T.	N	N	Y	N	Y	Y
HAWAII						
1 Case	Y	Y	N	Y	N	N
2 Gabbard	Y	Y	N	Y	N	N
IDAHO						
1 Fulcher	N	N	Y	N	Y	Y
2 Simpson	N	N	Y	N	Y	Y
ILLINOIS						
1 Rush	Y	Y	N	Y	N	N
2 Kelly, R.	Y	Y	N	Y	N	N
3 Lipinski	Y	Y	N	Y	N	N
4 García, J.	Y	Y	N	Y	N	N
5 Quigley	Y	Y	N	Y	N	N
6 Casten	Y	Y	N	Y	N	N
7 Davis, D.	Y	Y	N	Y	N	N
8 Krishnamoorthi	Y	Y	N	Y	N	N
9 Schakowsky	Y	Y	N	Y	N	N
10 Schneider	Y	Y	N	Y	N	N
11 Foster	Y	Y	N	Y	N	N

	379	380	381	382	383	384
12 **Bost**	N	N	Y	N	Y	Y
13 **Davis, R.**	N	N	Y	N	Y	Y
14 Underwood	Y	Y	N	Y	N	N
15 **Shimkus**	N	N	Y	N	Y	Y
16 **Kinzinger**	N	N	Y	N	Y	Y
17 Bustos	Y	Y	N	Y	N	N
18 **LaHood**	N	Y	Y	N	Y	Y
INDIANA						
1 Visclosky	Y	Y	N	Y	N	N
2 **Walorski**	N	N	Y	N	Y	Y
3 **Banks**	N	N	Y	N	Y	Y
4 **Baird**	N	N	Y	N	Y	Y
5 **Brooks, S.**	N	N	Y	N	N	Y
6 **Pence**	N	N	Y	N	Y	Y
7 Carson	Y	Y	N	Y	N	N
8 **Bucshon**	N	N	Y	N	Y	Y
9 **Hollingsworth**	Y	N	Y	N	N	Y
IOWA						
1 Finkenauer	Y	Y	N	Y	N	N
2 Loebsack	Y	Y	N	Y	N	N
3 Axne	Y	Y	N	Y	N	N
4 **King, S.**	N	N	Y	N	Y	Y
KANSAS						
1 **Marshall**	N	N	Y	N	Y	Y
2 **Watkins**	N	Y	Y	N	Y	Y
3 Davids	Y	Y	N	Y	N	N
4 **Estes**	N	N	Y	N	Y	Y
KENTUCKY						
1 **Comer**	N	N	Y	Y	Y	Y
2 **Guthrie**	N	N	Y	N	Y	Y
3 Yarmuth	Y	Y	N	Y	N	N
4 **Massie**	N	N	Y	N	Y	Y
5 **Rogers, H.**	N	N	Y	N	Y	Y
6 **Barr**	N	N	Y	N	Y	Y
LOUISIANA						
1 **Scalise**	N	N	Y	N	Y	Y
2 Richmond	Y	Y	N	Y	N	N
3 **Higgins, C.**	N	N	Y	N	Y	Y
4 **Johnson, M.**	N	N	Y	N	Y	Y
5 **Abraham**	N	N	Y	N	Y	Y
6 **Graves, G.**	N	N	Y	N	N	Y
MAINE						
1 Pingree	Y	Y	N	Y	N	N
2 Golden	Y	Y	N	Y	N	N
MARYLAND						
1 **Harris**	Y	N	Y	N	Y	Y
2 Ruppersberger	Y	Y	N	Y	N	N
3 Sarbanes	Y	Y	N	Y	N	N
4 Brown, A.	Y	Y	N	Y	N	N
5 Hoyer	Y	Y	N	Y	N	N
6 Trone	Y	Y	N	Y	N	N
7 Cummings	Y	Y	N	Y	N	N
8 Raskin						
MASSACHUSETTS	Y	Y	N	Y	N	N
1 Neal						
2 McGovern	Y	Y	N	Y	N	N
3 Trahan	Y	Y	N	Y	N	N
4 Kennedy	Y	Y	N	Y	N	N
5 Clark	Y	Y	N	Y	N	N
6 Moulton	Y	Y	N	Y	N	N
7 Pressley	Y	Y	N	Y	N	N
8 Lynch	Y	Y	N	Y	N	N
9 Keating	Y	Y	N	Y	N	N
MICHIGAN	Y	Y	N	Y	N	N
1 **Bergman**						
2 **Huizenga**	N	N	Y	N	Y	Y
3 **Amash**	N	N	Y	N	Y	Y
4 **Moolenaar**	N	N	Y	Y	Y	Y
5 Kildee	N	N	Y	N	Y	Y
6 **Upton**	Y	Y	N	Y	N	N
7 **Walberg**	N	Y	Y	Y	N	Y
8 Slotkin	N	N	Y	N	Y	Y
9 Levin	Y	Y	N	Y	N	N
10 **Mitchell**	Y	Y	N	Y	N	N
11 Stevens	N	N	Y	N	Y	Y
12 Dingell	Y	Y	N	Y	N	N
13 Tlaib	Y	Y	N	Y	N	N
14 Lawrence	Y	Y	N	Y	N	N
MINNESOTA	Y	Y	N	Y	N	N
1 **Hagedorn**						
2 Craig	N	N	Y	N	Y	Y
3 Phillips	Y	Y	N	Y	N	N
4 McCollum	Y	Y	N	Y	N	N
5 Omar	Y	Y	N	Y	N	N

	379	380	381	382	383	384
6 **Emmer**	Y	Y	N	Y	N	N
7 Peterson	-	-	+	-	+	+
8 **Stauber**	Y	N	N	Y	Y	Y
MISSISSIPPI	N	N	Y	N	Y	Y
1 **Kelly, T.**						
2 Thompson, B.	N	N	Y	N	Y	Y
3 **Guest**	Y	Y	N	Y	N	N
4 **Palazzo**	N	N	Y	N	Y	Y
MISSOURI	N	N	Y	N	Y	Y
1 Clay						
2 **Wagner**	Y	Y	N	Y	N	N
3 **Luetkemeyer**	N	N	Y	Y	Y	Y
4 **Hartzler**	N	N	Y	N	Y	Y
5 Cleaver	N	N	Y	N	Y	Y
6 **Graves, S.**	Y	Y	N	Y	N	N
7 **Long**	N	N	Y	N	Y	Y
8 **Smith, J.**	N	N	Y	N	Y	Y
MONTANA	N	N	Y	N	Y	Y
AL **Gianforte**						
NEBRASKA	N	N	Y	N	Y	Y
1 **Fortenberry**						
2 **Bacon**	N	N	Y	N	N	Y
3 **Smith, Adrian**	N	N	Y	N	N	Y
NEVADA	N	N	Y	N	Y	Y
1 Titus						
2 **Amodei**	Y	Y	N	Y	N	N
3 Lee	N	N	Y	N	Y	Y
4 Horsford	Y	Y	N	Y	N	N
NEW HAMPSHIRE	Y	Y	N	Y	N	N
1 Pappas						
2 Kuster	Y	Y	N	Y	N	N
NEW JERSEY	Y	Y	N	Y	N	N
1 Norcross						
2 Van Drew	Y	Y	N	Y	N	N
3 Kim	Y	Y	N	Y	N	N
4 **Smith, C.**	Y	Y	N	Y	N	N
5 Gottheimer	Y	Y	N	Y	N	N
6 Pallone	Y	Y	N	Y	N	N
7 Malinowski	Y	Y	N	Y	N	N
8 Sires	Y	Y	N	Y	N	N
9 Pascrell	Y	Y	N	Y	N	N
10 Payne	Y	Y	N	Y	N	N
11 Sherrill	Y	Y	N	Y	N	?
12 Watson Coleman	Y	Y	N	Y	N	N
NEW MEXICO	Y	Y	N	Y	N	N
1 Haaland						
2 Torres Small	Y	Y	N	Y	N	N
3 Luján	Y	Y	N	Y	N	N
NEW YORK	Y	Y	N	Y	N	N
1 **Zeldin**						
2 **King, P.**	Y	N	Y	Y	N	Y
3 Suozzi	Y	Y	Y	N	N	Y
4 Rice, K.	Y	Y	N	Y	N	N
5 Meeks	Y	Y	N	Y	N	N
6 Meng	Y	Y	N	Y	N	N
7 Velázquez	Y	Y	N	Y	N	N
8 Jeffries	Y	Y	N	Y	N	N
9 Clarke	Y	N	N	Y	N	N
10 Nadler	Y	Y	N	Y	N	N
11 Rose	Y	Y	N	Y	N	N
12 Maloney, C.	Y	Y	N	Y	N	N
13 Espaillat	Y	Y	N	Y	N	N
14 Ocasio-Cortez	Y	Y	N	Y	N	N
15 Serrano	Y	Y	N	Y	N	N
16 Engel	Y	Y	N	Y	N	N
17 Lowey	Y	Y	N	Y	N	N
18 Maloney, S.P.	Y	Y	N	Y	N	N
19 Delgado	Y	Y	N	Y	N	N
20 Tonko	Y	Y	N	Y	N	N
21 **Stefanik**	Y	Y	N	Y	N	N
22 Brindisi	Y	N	N	N	N	N
23 **Reed**	Y	Y	N	Y	N	N
24 **Katko**	N	N	Y	Y	N	Y
25 Morelle	Y	N	N	N	N	Y
26 Higgins, B.	Y	Y	N	Y	N	N
27 **Collins, C.**	Y	Y	N	Y	N	N
NORTH CAROLINA	N	N	Y	N	Y	Y
1 Butterfield						
2 **Holding**	Y	Y	N	Y	N	N
3 **Jones***	N	N	Y	N	Y	Y
4 Price						
5 **Foxx**	Y	Y	N	Y	N	N
6 **Walker**	N	N	Y	N	Y	Y
7 **Rouzer**	N	N	Y	N	Y	Y

	379	380	381	382	383	384
8 **Hudson**	N	N	Y	N	Y	Y
9 vacant	N	N	Y	N	Y	Y
10 **McHenry**	N	N	Y	N	N	Y
11 **Meadows**	N	N	Y	N	Y	Y
12 Adams	Y	Y	N	Y	N	N
13 **Budd**	N	N	Y	N	Y	Y
NORTH DAKOTA						
AL **Armstrong**	N	N	Y	N	Y	Y
OHIO						
1 **Chabot**	N	N	Y	Y	Y	Y
2 **Wenstrup**	N	N	N	N	Y	Y
3 Beatty	Y	Y	N	Y	N	N
4 **Jordan**	N	N	Y	N	Y	Y
5 **Latta**	N	N	Y	N	Y	Y
6 **Johnson, B.**	N	N	Y	N	Y	Y
7 **Gibbs**	N	N	Y	N	Y	Y
8 **Davidson**	N	N	Y	N	Y	Y
9 Kaptur	Y	Y	N	Y	N	N
10 **Turner**	N	Y	Y	N	Y	Y
11 Fudge	Y	Y	N	Y	N	N
12 **Balderson**	N	N	Y	N	Y	Y
13 Ryan	?	?	?	?	?	?
14 **Joyce**	N	N	Y	N	Y	Y
15 **Stivers**	N	N	Y	N	Y	Y
16 **Gonzalez**	N	N	Y	N	N	Y
OKLAHOMA						
1 **Hern**	N	N	Y	N	Y	Y
2 **Mullin**	N	N	Y	N	Y	Y
3 **Lucas**	N	N	Y	N	Y	Y
4 **Cole**	N	N	Y	N	Y	Y
5 Horn	Y	Y	N	Y	N	N
OREGON						
1 Bonamici	Y	Y	N	Y	N	N
2 **Walden**	N	N	Y	N	N	Y
3 Blumenauer	Y	Y	N	Y	N	N
4 DeFazio	Y	Y	N	Y	N	N
5 Schrader	Y	Y	N	N	N	N
PENNSYLVANIA						
1 **Fitzpatrick**	Y	Y	N	Y	N	N
2 Boyle	Y	Y	N	Y	N	N
3 Evans	Y	Y	N	Y	N	N
4 Dean	Y	Y	N	Y	N	N
5 Scanlon	Y	Y	N	Y	N	N
6 Houlahan	Y	Y	N	Y	N	N
7 Wild	Y	Y	N	Y	N	N
8 Cartwright	Y	Y	N	Y	N	N
9 **Meuser**	N	N	Y	N	Y	Y
10 **Perry**	N	N	Y	N	Y	Y
11 **Smucker**	N	N	Y	N	Y	Y
12 **Marino***						
13 **Joyce**	N	N	Y	N	Y	Y
14 **Reschenthaler**	N	N	Y	N	Y	Y
15 **Thompson, G.**	N	N	Y	N	Y	Y
16 **Kelly, M.**	N	N	Y	N	Y	Y
17 Lamb	Y	Y	N	Y	N	N
18 Doyle	Y	Y	N	Y	N	N
RHODE ISLAND						
1 Cicilline	Y	Y	N	Y	N	N
2 Langevin	Y	Y	N	Y	N	N
SOUTH CAROLINA						
1 Cunningham	Y	Y	N	N	N	N
2 **Wilson, J.**	N	N	Y	N	Y	Y
3 **Duncan**	N	N	Y	N	Y	Y
4 **Timmons**	N	N	Y	Y	Y	Y
5 **Norman**	N	N	Y	N	Y	Y
6 Clyburn	Y	Y	N	Y	N	N
7 **Rice, T.**	Y	N	Y	N	Y	Y
SOUTH DAKOTA						
AL **Johnson**	N	N	Y	N	Y	Y
TENNESSEE						
1 **Roe**	N	N	Y	N	Y	Y
2 **Burchett**	N	N	Y	N	Y	Y
3 **Fleischmann**	N	N	Y	N	Y	Y
4 **DesJarlais**	N	N	Y	N	Y	Y
5 Cooper	N	Y	Y	Y	N	N
6 **Rose**	N	N	Y	N	Y	Y
7 **Green**	N	N	Y	N	Y	Y
8 **Kustoff**	N	N	Y	N	Y	Y
9 Cohen	Y	Y	N	Y	N	N
TEXAS						
1 **Gohmert**	N	N	Y	N	Y	Y
2 **Crenshaw**	N	N	Y	N	Y	Y
3 **Taylor**	N	N	Y	N	Y	Y
4 **Ratcliffe**	N	N	Y	N	Y	Y

	379	380	381	382	383	384
5 **Gooden**	N	Y	Y	N	Y	Y
6 **Wright**	N	N	Y	N	Y	Y
7 Fletcher	N	Y	N	Y	N	Y
8 **Brady**	N	N	Y	N	Y	Y
9 Green, A.	Y	Y	N	Y	N	N
10 **McCaul**	N	N	Y	N	Y	Y
11 **Conaway**	N	N	Y	N	Y	Y
12 **Granger**	N	N	Y	N	Y	Y
13 **Thornberry**	N	N	Y	N	Y	Y
14 **Weber**	N	N	Y	N	Y	Y
15 Gonzalez	N	N	Y	N	N	Y
16 Escobar	Y	Y	N	Y	N	N
17 **Flores**	N	N	Y	N	Y	Y
18 Jackson Lee	Y	Y	N	Y	N	N
19 **Arrington**	N	N	Y	N	Y	Y
20 Castro	Y	Y	N	Y	N	N
21 **Roy**	N	N	Y	N	Y	Y
22 **Olson**	N	N	Y	N	Y	Y
23 **Hurd**	N	N	Y	N	N	Y
24 **Marchant**	N	N	Y	N	Y	Y
25 **Williams**	N	N	Y	N	Y	Y
26 **Burgess**	N	N	Y	N	Y	Y
27 **Cloud**	N	N	Y	N	Y	Y
28 Cuellar	N	Y	N	Y	N	Y
29 Garcia, S.	N	Y	N	Y	N	N
30 Johnson, E.B.	Y	Y	N	Y	N	N
31 **Carter, J.**	N	N	Y	N	Y	Y
32 Allred	Y	Y	N	Y	N	N
33 Veasey	Y	Y	N	Y	N	N
34 Vela	Y	Y	N	Y	N	N
35 Doggett	Y	Y	N	Y	N	N
36 **Babin**	N	N	Y	N	Y	Y
UTAH						
1 **Bishop, R.**	N	N	Y	N	Y	Y
2 **Stewart**	N	N	Y	N	Y	Y
3 **Curtis**	N	N	Y	N	Y	Y
4 McAdams	Y	Y	N	Y	N	N
VERMONT						
AL Welch	Y	Y	N	Y	N	N
VIRGINIA						
1 **Wittman**	N	N	Y	N	Y	Y
2 Luria	Y	Y	N	Y	N	N
3 Scott, R.	Y	Y	N	Y	N	N
4 McEachin	Y	Y	N	Y	N	N
5 **Riggleman**	N	N	Y	Y	Y	Y
6 **Cline**	N	N	Y	N	Y	Y
7 Spanberger	Y	Y	N	Y	N	N
8 Beyer	Y	Y	N	Y	N	N
9 **Griffith**	N	N	Y	N	Y	Y
10 Wexton	Y	Y	N	Y	N	N
11 Connolly	Y	Y	N	Y	N	N
WASHINGTON						
1 DelBene	Y	Y	N	Y	N	N
2 Larsen	Y	Y	N	Y	N	N
3 **Herrera Beutler**	?	?	?	?	?	?
4 **Newhouse**	N	N	Y	N	Y	Y
5 **McMorris Rodgers**	N	N	Y	N	Y	Y
6 Kilmer	Y	Y	N	Y	N	N
7 Jayapal	Y	Y	N	Y	N	N
8 Schrier	Y	Y	N	Y	N	N
9 Smith Adam	Y	Y	N	Y	N	N
10 Heck	Y	Y	N	Y	N	N
WEST VIRGINIA						
1 **McKinley**	N	N	Y	N	Y	Y
2 **Mooney**	N	N	Y	Y	Y	Y
3 **Miller**	N	N	Y	N	Y	Y
WISCONSIN						
1 **Steil**	N	N	Y	N	N	Y
2 Pocan	Y	N	N	Y	N	N
3 Kind	Y	Y	N	Y	N	N
4 Moore	Y	Y	N	Y	N	N
5 **Sensenbrenner**	N	Y	Y	N	Y	Y
6 **Grothman**	N	N	Y	N	Y	Y
7 **Duffy**	N	N	Y	N	Y	Y
8 **Gallagher**	N	N	Y	N	Y	Y
WYOMING						
AL **Cheney**	N	N	Y	N	Y	Y
DELEGATES						
Radewagen (A.S.)	N	N	Y	?	Y	Y
Norton (D.C.)	Y	Y	N	Y	N	N
San Nicolas (Guam)	Y	Y	N	Y	N	N
Sablan (N. Marianas)	Y	Y	N	Y	N	N
González-Colón (P.R.)	N	N	Y	N	Y	Y
Plaskett (V.I.)	Y	Y	N	Y	N	N

⦀ HOUSE VOTES

385. HR3055. Fiscal 2020 Five-Bill Appropriations Package - EPA Emission Standards Rule. Mullin, R-Okla., amendment that would prohibit the use of funds made available by the bill to enforce a June 2016 Environmental Protection Agency rule regarding emission standards for the oil and natural gas sector. Adopted in Committee of the Whole 191-241: R 190-8; D 1-232; I 0-1. June 20, 2019.

386. HR3055. Fiscal 2020 Five-Bill Appropriations Package - EPA Carbon and Greenhouse Gas Regulations. Mullin, R-Okla., amendment that would prohibit the use of funds made available by the bill for the Environmental Protection Agency to prepare or promulgate any regulation or guidance referencing analysis contained in certain documents published by the White House council on environmental quality and by inter-agency working groups on the social cost of carbon and greenhouse gases. Rejected in Committee of the Whole 189-243: R 188-10; D 1-232; I 0-1. June 20, 2019.

387. HR3055. Fiscal 2020 Five-Bill Appropriations Package - Outer Continental Shelf Oil and Gas Leasing. Graves, R-La., amendment that would strike from the bill a provision that would prohibit the use of funds made available by the bill for certain activities under the Outer Continental Shelf Oil and Gas Leasing Program, as proposed in a January 2018 Bureau of Ocean Energy Management notice of intent to prepare an environmental impact statement for the program. Rejected in Committee of the Whole 193-239: R 184-14; D 9-224; I 0-1. June 20, 2019.

388. HR3055. Fiscal 2020 Five-Bill Appropriations Package - Reduce Interior-Environment Funding. Hice, R-Ga., amendment that would reduce by 23.6 percent all discretionary funding made available under the Interior, Environment, and related agencies title of the bill (Division C). Rejected in Committee of the Whole 128-304: R 127-71; D 1-232; I 0-1. June 20, 2019.

389. HR3055. Fiscal 2020 Five-Bill Appropriations Package - Reduce Interior-Environment Funding. Banks, R-Ind., amendment that would reduce by 14 percent all discretionary funding made available under the Interior, Environment, and related agencies title of the bill (Division C). Rejected in Committee of the Whole 132-299: R 132-65; D 0-233; I 0-1. June 20, 2019.

390. HR3055. Fiscal 2020 Five-Bill Appropriations Package - Integrated Risk Information System. Biggs, R-Ariz., amendment that would prohibit the use of funds made available by the bill for the Environmental Protection Agency integrated risk information system, a database containing information on chemical hazards in the environment and their effects on human health. Rejected in Committee of the Whole 157-275: R 157-41; D 0-233; I 0-1. June 20, 2019.

		385	386	387	388	389	390
ALABAMA							
1	Byrne	Y	Y	Y	Y	Y	Y
2	Roby	Y	Y	Y	N	N	Y
3	Rogers, M.	Y	Y	Y	Y	Y	Y
4	Aderholt	Y	Y	Y	N	N	Y
5	Brooks, M.	Y	Y	Y	Y	Y	Y
6	Palmer	Y	Y	Y	Y	Y	Y
7	Sewell	N	N	N	N	N	N
ALASKA							
AL	Young	Y	Y	Y	N	N	N
ARIZONA							
1	O'Halleran	N	N	N	N	N	N
2	Kirkpatrick	-	-	-	-	-	-
3	Grijalva	N	N	N	N	N	N
4	Gosar	Y	Y	Y	Y	Y	Y
5	Biggs	Y	Y	Y	Y	Y	Y
6	Schweikert	Y	Y	Y	Y	Y	Y
7	Gallego	N	N	N	N	N	N
8	Lesko	Y	Y	Y	Y	Y	Y
9	Stanton	N	N	N	N	N	N
ARKANSAS							
1	Crawford	Y	Y	Y	Y	Y	Y
2	Hill, F.	Y	Y	Y	Y	N	Y
3	Womack	Y	Y	Y	N	N	Y
4	Westerman	Y	Y	Y	Y	Y	Y
CALIFORNIA							
1	LaMalfa	Y	Y	Y	N	Y	Y
2	Huffman	N	N	N	N	N	N
3	Garamendi	N	N	N	N	N	N
4	McClintock	Y	Y	Y	?	Y	Y
5	Thompson, M.	N	N	N	N	N	N
6	Matsui	N	N	N	N	N	N
7	Bera	N	N	N	N	N	N
8	Cook	Y	Y	Y	N	N	Y
9	McNerney	N	N	N	N	N	N
10	Harder	N	N	N	N	N	N
11	DeSaulnier	N	N	N	N	N	N
12	Pelosi						
13	Lee B.	N	N	N	N	N	N
14	Speier	N	N	N	N	N	N
15	Swalwell	-	-	-	-	-	-
16	Costa	Y	N	N	N	N	N
17	Khanna	N	N	N	N	N	N
18	Eshoo	N	N	N	N	N	N
19	Lofgren	N	N	N	N	N	N
20	Panetta	N	N	N	N	N	N
21	Cox	N	N	N	N	N	N
22	Nunes	Y	Y	Y	N	Y	Y
23	McCarthy	Y	Y	Y	N	N	Y
24	Carbajal	N	N	N	N	N	N
25	Hill, K.	N	N	N	N	N	N
26	Brownley	N	N	N	N	N	N
27	Chu	N	N	N	N	N	N
28	Schiff	N	N	N	N	N	N
29	Cárdenas	N	N	N	N	N	N
30	Sherman	N	N	N	N	N	N
31	Aguilar	N	N	N	N	N	N
32	Napolitano	N	N	N	N	N	N
33	Lieu	N	N	N	N	N	N
34	Gomez	N	N	N	N	N	N
35	Torres	N	N	N	N	N	N
36	Ruiz	N	N	N	N	N	N
37	Bass	N	N	N	N	N	N
38	Sánchez	N	N	N	N	N	N
39	Cisneros	N	N	N	N	N	N
40	Roybal-Allard	N	N	N	N	N	N
41	Takano	N	N	N	N	N	N
42	Calvert	Y	Y	Y	N	N	N
43	Waters	N	N	N	N	N	N
44	Barragán	N	N	N	N	N	N
45	Porter	N	N	N	N	N	N
46	Correa	N	N	N	N	N	N
47	Lowenthal	N	N	N	N	N	N
48	Rouda	N	N	N	N	N	N
49	Levin	N	N	N	N	N	N
50	Hunter	Y	Y	Y	Y	Y	Y
51	Vargas	N	N	N	N	N	N
52	Peters	N	N	N	N	N	N

		385	386	387	388	389	390
53	Davis, S.	N	N	N	N	N	N
COLORADO							
1	DeGette	N	N	N	N	N	N
2	Neguse	N	N	N	N	N	N
3	Tipton	Y	Y	Y	N	N	Y
4	Buck	Y	Y	Y	Y	Y	Y
5	Lamborn	Y	Y	Y	Y	Y	Y
6	Crow	N	N	N	N	N	N
7	Perlmutter	N	N	N	N	N	N
CONNECTICUT							
1	Larson	N	N	N	N	N	N
2	Courtney	N	N	N	N	N	N
3	DeLauro	N	N	N	N	N	N
4	Himes	N	N	N	N	N	N
5	Hayes	N	N	N	N	N	N
DELAWARE							
AL	Blunt Rochester	N	N	N	N	N	N
FLORIDA							
1	Gaetz	Y	N	N	Y	Y	Y
2	Dunn	Y	Y	Y	Y	Y	Y
3	Yoho	Y	Y	Y	Y	Y	Y
4	Rutherford	Y	Y	N	N	N	Y
5	Lawson	N	N	N	N	N	N
6	Waltz	N	N	N	N	N	N
7	Murphy	N	N	N	N	N	N
8	Posey	Y	Y	Y	N	Y	Y
9	Soto	N	N	N	N	N	N
10	Demings	N	N	N	N	N	N
11	Webster	Y	Y	Y	Y	Y	Y
12	Bilirakis	Y	Y	Y	Y	Y	Y
13	Crist	N	N	N	N	N	N
14	Castor	N	N	N	N	N	N
15	Spano	Y	Y	N	Y	Y	Y
16	Buchanan	Y	Y	Y	Y	Y	Y
17	Steube	Y	Y	Y	Y	Y	Y
18	Mast	N	Y	N	N	N	N
19	Rooney	N	N	N	N	N	N
20	Hastings	?	?	?	?	?	?
21	Frankel	N	N	N	N	N	N
22	Deutch	N	N	N	N	N	N
23	Wasserman Schultz	N	N	N	N	N	N
24	Wilson, F.	N	N	N	N	N	N
25	Diaz-Balart	Y	Y	Y	N	N	N
26	Mucarsel-Powell	N	N	N	N	N	N
27	Shalala	N	N	N	N	N	N
GEORGIA							
1	Carter, E.L.	Y	Y	Y	Y	Y	Y
2	Bishop, S.	N	N	Y	N	N	N
3	Ferguson	Y	Y	Y	Y	Y	Y
4	Johnson, H.	N	N	N	N	N	N
5	Lewis John	N	N	N	N	N	N
6	McBath	N	N	N	N	N	N
7	Woodall	Y	Y	Y	Y	Y	Y
8	Scott, A.	Y	Y	Y	Y	Y	Y
9	Collins, D.	Y	Y	Y	Y	Y	Y
10	Hice	Y	Y	Y	Y	Y	Y
11	Loudermilk	Y	Y	Y	Y	Y	Y
12	Allen	Y	Y	Y	Y	Y	Y
13	Scott, D.	N	N	N	N	N	N
14	Graves, T.	Y	Y	Y	Y	Y	Y
HAWAII							
1	Case	N	N	N	N	N	N
2	Gabbard	N	N	N	N	N	N
IDAHO							
1	Fulcher	Y	Y	Y	Y	Y	Y
2	Simpson	Y	Y	Y	N	N	N
ILLINOIS							
1	Rush	N	N	N	N	N	N
2	Kelly, R.	N	N	N	N	N	N
3	Lipinski	N	N	N	N	N	N
4	García, J.	N	N	N	N	N	N
5	Quigley	N	N	N	N	N	N
6	Casten	N	N	N	N	N	N
7	Davis, D.	N	N	N	N	N	N
8	Krishnamoorthi	N	N	N	N	N	N
9	Schakowsky	N	N	N	N	N	N
10	Schneider	N	N	N	N	N	N
11	Foster	N	N	N	N	N	N

KEY: **Republicans**   Democrats   *Independents*

Y Voted for (yea)		**N** Voted against (nay)	**P** Voted "present"
+ Announced for		**−** Announced against	**?** Did not vote or otherwise
# Paired for		**X** Paired against	make position known

		385	386	387	388	389	390
12	**Bost**	Y	Y	Y	N	N	N
13	**Davis, R.**	Y	Y	Y	N	N	N
14	Underwood	N	N	N	N	N	N
15	**Shimkus**	Y	Y	Y	Y	Y	N
16	**Kinzinger**	Y	Y	Y	N	N	N
17	Bustos	N	N	N	N	N	N
18	**LaHood**	Y	Y	Y	Y	Y	Y
INDIANA							
1	Visclosky	N	N	N	N	N	N
2	**Walorski**	Y	Y	Y	N	Y	N
3	**Banks**	Y	Y	Y	Y	Y	Y
4	**Baird**	Y	Y	Y	N	N	Y
5	**Brooks, S.**	Y	Y	Y	N	Y	N
6	**Pence**	Y	Y	Y	N	N	Y
7	Carson	N	N	N	N	N	N
8	**Bucshon**	Y	Y	Y	Y	Y	N
9	**Hollingsworth**	Y	Y	N	N	N	N
IOWA							
1	Finkenauer	N	N	N	N	N	N
2	Loebsack	N	N	N	N	N	N
3	Axne	N	N	N	N	N	N
4	**King, S.**	Y	Y	Y	Y	Y	Y
KANSAS							
1	**Marshall**	Y	Y	Y	N	N	Y
2	**Watkins**	Y	Y	Y	Y	Y	Y
3	Davids	N	N	N	N	N	N
4	**Estes**	Y	Y	Y	Y	Y	N
KENTUCKY							
1	**Comer**	Y	Y	Y	Y	Y	Y
2	**Guthrie**	Y	Y	Y	Y	Y	Y
3	Yarmuth	N	N	N	N	N	N
4	**Massie**	Y	Y	Y	Y	Y	Y
5	**Rogers, H.**	Y	Y	Y	N	N	Y
6	**Barr**	Y	Y	Y	Y	Y	Y
LOUISIANA							
1	**Scalise**	Y	Y	Y	Y	Y	Y
2	Richmond	N	N	N	N	N	N
3	**Higgins, C.**	Y	Y	Y	Y	Y	Y
4	**Johnson, M.**	Y	Y	Y	Y	Y	Y
5	**Abraham**	Y	Y	Y	N	Y	Y
6	**Graves, G.**	Y	Y	Y	Y	Y	N
MAINE							
1	Pingree	N	N	N	N	N	N
2	Golden	N	N	N	N	N	N
MARYLAND							
1	**Harris**	Y	Y	Y	Y	Y	Y
2	Ruppersberger	N	N	N	N	N	N
3	Sarbanes	N	N	N	N	N	N
4	Brown, A.	N	N	N	N	N	N
5	Hoyer	N	N	N	N	N	N
6	Trone	N	N	N	N	N	N
7	Cummings	N	N	N	N	N	N
8	Raskin						
MASSACHUSETTS		N	N	N	N	N	N
1	Neal						
2	McGovern	N	N	N	N	N	N
3	Trahan	N	N	N	N	N	N
4	Kennedy	N	N	N	N	N	N
5	Clark	N	N	N	N	N	N
6	Moulton	N	N	N	N	N	N
7	Pressley	N	N	N	N	N	N
8	Lynch	N	N	N	N	N	N
9	Keating	N	N	N	N	N	N
MICHIGAN		N	N	N	N	N	N
1	**Bergman**						
2	**Huizenga**	Y	N	Y	N	Y	N
3	**Amash**	Y	Y	Y	Y	Y	Y
4	**Moolenaar**	Y	Y	Y	Y	Y	N
5	Kildee	Y	Y	Y	N	Y	N
6	**Upton**	N	N	N	N	N	N
7	**Walberg**	N	Y	Y	N	N	N
8	Slotkin	Y	Y	Y	N	N	N
9	Levin	N	N	N	N	N	N
10	**Mitchell**	N	N	N	N	N	N
11	Stevens	Y	Y	Y	N	N	Y
12	Dingell	N	N	N	N	N	N
13	Tlaib	N	N	N	N	N	N
14	Lawrence	N	N	N	N	N	N
MINNESOTA		N	N	N	N	N	N
1	**Hagedorn**						
2	Craig	Y	Y	Y	N	N	Y
3	Phillips	N	N	N	N	N	N
4	McCollum	N	N	N	N	N	N
5	Omar	N	N	N	N	N	N
6	**Emmer**	N	N	N	N	N	N
7	Peterson	+	+	+	+	+	+
8	**Stauber**	N	N	Y	N	N	N
MISSISSIPPI		Y	Y	Y	N	N	Y
1	**Kelly, T.**						
2	Thompson, B.	Y	Y	Y	Y	Y	Y
3	**Guest**	N	N	N	N	N	N
4	**Palazzo**	Y	Y	Y	Y	Y	Y
MISSOURI		Y	Y	Y	Y	Y	Y
1	Clay						
2	**Wagner**	N	N	N	N	N	N
3	**Luetkemeyer**	Y	Y	Y	Y	Y	Y
4	**Hartzler**	Y	Y	Y	N	N	Y
5	Cleaver	Y	Y	Y	Y	Y	Y
6	**Graves, S.**	N	N	N	N	N	N
7	**Long**	Y	Y	Y	Y	Y	Y
8	**Smith, J.**	Y	Y	Y	Y	Y	Y
MONTANA		Y	Y	Y	Y	Y	Y
AL	**Gianforte**						
NEBRASKA		Y	Y	Y	N	N	Y
1	**Fortenberry**						
2	**Bacon**	Y	N	Y	N	N	N
3	**Smith, Adrian**	Y	N	Y	Y	Y	N
NEVADA		Y	Y	Y	Y	Y	Y
1	Titus						
2	**Amodei**	N	N	N	N	N	N
3	Lee	Y	N	Y	Y	Y	Y
4	Horsford	N	N	N	N	N	N
NEW HAMPSHIRE		N	N	N	N	N	N
1	Pappas						
2	Kuster	N	N	N	N	N	N
NEW JERSEY		N	N	N	N	N	N
1	Norcross						
2	Van Drew	N	N	N	N	N	N
3	Kim	N	N	N	N	N	N
4	**Smith, C.**	N	N	N	N	N	N
5	Gottheimer	N	N	N	N	N	N
6	Pallone	N	N	N	N	N	N
7	Malinowski	N	N	N	N	N	N
8	Sires	N	N	N	N	N	N
9	Pascrell	N	N	N	N	N	N
10	Payne	N	N	N	N	N	N
11	Sherrill	N	N	N	N	N	N
12	Watson Coleman	N	N	N	N	N	N
NEW MEXICO		N	N	N	N	N	N
1	Haaland						
2	Torres Small	N	N	N	N	N	N
3	Luján	N	N	N	N	N	N
NEW YORK		N	N	N	N	N	N
1	**Zeldin**						
2	**King, P.**	Y	Y	Y	N	N	N
3	Suozzi	Y	Y	N	N	N	N
4	Rice, K.	N	N	N	N	N	N
5	Meeks	N	N	N	N	N	N
6	Meng	N	N	N	N	N	N
7	Velázquez	N	N	N	N	N	N
8	Jeffries	N	N	N	N	N	N
9	Clarke	N	N	N	N	N	N
10	Nadler	N	N	N	N	N	N
11	Rose	N	N	N	N	N	N
12	Maloney, C.	N	N	N	N	N	N
13	Espaillat	N	N	N	N	N	N
14	Ocasio-Cortez	N	N	N	N	N	N
15	Serrano	N	N	N	N	N	N
16	Engel	N	N	N	N	N	N
17	Lowey	N	N	N	N	N	N
18	Maloney, S.P.	N	N	N	N	N	N
19	Delgado	N	N	N	N	N	N
20	Tonko	N	N	N	N	N	N
21	**Stefanik**	N	N	N	N	N	N
22	Brindisi	N	Y	N	N	N	N
23	**Reed**	N	N	N	N	N	N
24	**Katko**	Y	N	Y	N	N	N
25	Morelle	N	Y	N	N	N	N
26	Higgins, B.	N	N	N	N	N	N
27	**Collins, C.**	N	N	N	N	N	N
NORTH CAROLINA		Y	Y	Y	N	N	Y
1	Butterfield						
2	**Holding**	N	N	N	N	N	N
3	**Jones***	Y	Y	Y	Y	Y	Y
4	Price						
5	**Foxx**	N	N	N	N	N	N
6	**Walker**	Y	Y	Y	N	Y	Y
7	**Rouzer**	Y	Y	Y	Y	Y	Y
8	**Hudson**	Y	Y	Y	Y	Y	Y
9	vacant	Y	Y	Y	Y	Y	Y
10	**McHenry**	Y	N	N	Y	Y	N
11	**Meadows**	Y	Y	Y	Y	Y	Y
12	Adams	N	N	N	N	N	N
13	**Budd**	Y	Y	Y	Y	Y	Y
NORTH DAKOTA							
AL	**Armstrong**	Y	Y	Y	Y	N	Y
OHIO							
1	**Chabot**	Y	Y	Y	Y	Y	Y
2	**Wenstrup**	Y	Y	Y	Y	Y	Y
3	Beatty	N	N	N	N	N	N
4	**Jordan**	Y	Y	Y	Y	Y	Y
5	**Latta**	Y	Y	Y	Y	Y	Y
6	**Johnson, B.**	Y	Y	Y	Y	Y	Y
7	**Gibbs**	Y	Y	Y	Y	Y	Y
8	**Davidson**	Y	Y	Y	Y	Y	Y
9	Kaptur	N	N	N	N	N	N
10	**Turner**	Y	Y	Y	N	N	N
11	Fudge	N	N	N	N	N	N
12	**Balderson**	Y	Y	Y	Y	Y	Y
13	Ryan	?	?	?	?	?	?
14	**Joyce**	Y	Y	Y	N	N	N
15	**Stivers**	Y	Y	Y	Y	N	Y
16	**Gonzalez**	Y	Y	Y	N	N	N
OKLAHOMA							
1	**Hern**	Y	Y	Y	Y	Y	Y
2	**Mullin**	Y	Y	Y	Y	Y	Y
3	**Lucas**	Y	Y	Y	N	N	N
4	**Cole**	Y	Y	Y	N	N	Y
5	Horn	N	N	N	N	N	N
OREGON							
1	Bonamici	N	N	N	N	N	N
2	**Walden**	Y	Y	Y	N	N	N
3	Blumenauer	N	N	N	N	N	N
4	DeFazio	N	N	N	N	N	N
5	Schrader	N	N	N	N	N	N
PENNSYLVANIA							
1	**Fitzpatrick**	N	N	N	N	N	N
2	Boyle	N	N	N	N	N	N
3	Evans	N	N	N	N	N	N
4	Dean	N	N	N	N	N	N
5	Scanlon	N	N	N	N	N	N
6	Houlahan	N	N	N	N	N	N
7	Wild	N	N	N	N	N	N
8	Cartwright	N	N	N	N	N	N
9	**Meuser**	Y	Y	Y	N	Y	Y
10	**Perry**	Y	Y	Y	Y	Y	Y
11	**Smucker**	Y	Y	Y	Y	Y	Y
12	**Marino***						
13	**Joyce**	Y	Y	Y	Y	Y	Y
14	**Reschenthaler**	Y	Y	Y	N	N	Y
15	**Thompson, G.**	Y	Y	Y	N	N	Y
16	**Kelly, M.**	Y	Y	Y	Y	Y	Y
17	Lamb	N	N	N	N	N	N
18	Doyle	N	N	N	N	N	N
RHODE ISLAND							
1	Cicilline	N	N	N	N	N	N
2	Langevin	N	N	N	N	N	N
SOUTH CAROLINA							
1	Cunningham	N	N	N	N	N	N
2	**Wilson, J.**	Y	Y	Y	N	N	Y
3	**Duncan**	Y	Y	Y	Y	Y	Y
4	**Timmons**	Y	Y	Y	Y	Y	Y
5	**Norman**	Y	Y	Y	Y	Y	Y
6	Clyburn	N	N	N	N	N	N
7	**Rice, T.**	Y	Y	N	Y	Y	Y
SOUTH DAKOTA							
AL	**Johnson**	Y	Y	Y	N	Y	Y
TENNESSEE							
1	**Roe**	Y	Y	Y	Y	Y	Y
2	**Burchett**	Y	Y	Y	Y	Y	Y
3	**Fleischmann**	Y	Y	Y	N	N	Y
4	**DesJarlais**	Y	Y	Y	Y	Y	Y
5	Cooper	N	N	Y	N	N	N
6	**Rose**	Y	Y	Y	Y	Y	Y
7	**Green**	Y	Y	Y	Y	Y	Y
8	**Kustoff**	Y	Y	Y	Y	Y	Y
9	Cohen	N	N	N	N	N	N
TEXAS							
1	**Gohmert**	Y	Y	Y	Y	Y	Y
2	**Crenshaw**	Y	Y	Y	N	N	Y
3	**Taylor**	Y	Y	Y	Y	N	N
4	**Ratcliffe**	Y	Y	Y	Y	Y	Y
5	**Gooden**	Y	Y	Y	Y	Y	Y
6	**Wright**	Y	Y	Y	Y	Y	Y
7	Fletcher	N	N	Y	N	N	N
8	**Brady**	Y	Y	Y	Y	Y	Y
9	Green, A.	N	N	N	N	N	N
10	**McCaul**	Y	Y	Y	N	Y	N
11	**Conaway**	Y	Y	Y	Y	Y	Y
12	**Granger**	Y	Y	Y	N	N	Y
13	**Thornberry**	Y	Y	Y	Y	Y	Y
14	**Weber**	Y	Y	Y	Y	Y	Y
15	Gonzalez	N	N	Y	Y	N	N
16	Escobar	N	N	N	N	N	N
17	**Flores**	Y	Y	Y	Y	Y	Y
18	Jackson Lee	N	N	N	N	N	N
19	**Arrington**	Y	Y	Y	Y	Y	Y
20	Castro	N	N	N	N	N	N
21	**Roy**	Y	Y	Y	Y	Y	Y
22	**Olson**	Y	Y	Y	Y	Y	Y
23	**Hurd**	Y	Y	Y	N	N	N
24	**Marchant**	Y	Y	Y	Y	Y	Y
25	**Williams**	Y	Y	Y	Y	Y	Y
26	**Burgess**	Y	Y	Y	Y	Y	Y
27	**Cloud**	Y	Y	Y	Y	Y	Y
28	Cuellar	N	N	Y	N	N	N
29	Garcia, S.	N	Y	Y	N	N	N
30	Johnson, E.B.	N	N	N	N	N	N
31	**Carter, J.**	Y	Y	Y	N	N	Y
32	Allred	N	N	Y	N	N	N
33	Veasey	N	N	N	N	N	N
34	Vela	N	N	Y	N	N	N
35	Doggett	N	N	N	N	N	N
36	**Babin**	Y	Y	Y	Y	Y	Y
UTAH							
1	**Bishop, R.**	Y	Y	Y	Y	Y	Y
2	**Stewart**	Y	Y	Y	Y	Y	Y
3	**Curtis**	Y	Y	Y	Y	Y	Y
4	McAdams	N	N	N	N	N	N
VERMONT							
AL	Welch	N	N	N	N	N	N
VIRGINIA							
1	**Wittman**	Y	Y	Y	Y	Y	Y
2	Luria	N	N	N	N	N	N
3	Scott, R.	N	N	N	N	N	N
4	McEachin	N	N	N	N	N	N
5	**Riggleman**	Y	Y	Y	Y	Y	Y
6	**Cline**	Y	Y	Y	Y	Y	Y
7	Spanberger	N	N	N	N	N	N
8	Beyer	N	N	N	N	N	N
9	**Griffith**	Y	Y	Y	N	Y	Y
10	Wexton	N	N	N	N	N	N
11	Connolly	N	N	N	N	N	N
WASHINGTON							
1	DelBene	N	N	N	N	N	N
2	Larsen	N	N	N	N	N	N
3	**Herrera Beutler**	?	?	?	?	?	?
4	**Newhouse**	Y	Y	Y	N	N	N
5	**McMorris Rodgers**	Y	Y	Y	Y	N	Y
6	Kilmer	N	N	N	N	N	N
7	Jayapal	N	N	N	N	N	N
8	Schrier	N	N	N	N	N	N
9	Smith Adam	N	N	N	N	N	N
10	Heck	N	N	N	N	N	N
WEST VIRGINIA							
1	**McKinley**	Y	Y	Y	N	N	Y
2	**Mooney**	Y	Y	Y	Y	Y	Y
3	**Miller**	Y	Y	Y	Y	Y	Y
WISCONSIN							
1	**Steil**	Y	Y	Y	Y	Y	Y
2	Pocan	N	N	N	N	N	N
3	Kind	N	N	N	N	N	N
4	Moore	N	N	N	N	N	N
5	**Sensenbrenner**	Y	Y	Y	Y	Y	Y
6	**Grothman**	Y	Y	Y	Y	Y	Y
7	**Duffy**	Y	Y	Y	Y	N	Y
8	**Gallagher**	Y	Y	Y	N	N	Y
WYOMING							
AL	**Cheney**	Y	Y	Y	N	N	Y
DELEGATES							
	Radewagen (A.S.)	Y	Y	Y	N	N	Y
	Norton (D.C.)	N	N	N	N	N	N
	San Nicolas (Guam)	N	N	N	N	N	N
	Sablan (N. Marianas)	N	N	N	N	N	N
	González-Colón (P.R.)	Y	Y	Y	N	N	Y
	Plaskett (V.I.)	N	N	N	N	N	N

391. HR3055. Fiscal 2020 Five-Bill Appropriations Package - Prohibit Oil and Gas Exploration. Cunningham, D-S.C., amendment that would prohibit the use of funds made available by the bill to conduct or authorize any geological or geophysical oil or gas exploration in areas located in Outer Continental Shelf Planning Areas for the Atlantic Region or to prepare environmental impact statements or assessments for such explorations. Adopted in Committee of the Whole 245-187: R 19-179; D 225-8; I 1-0. June 20, 2019.

392. HR3055. Fiscal 2020 Five-Bill Appropriations Package - Land and Water Conservation Fund. Cunningham, D-S.C., amendment that would increase then decrease by $5 million funding for operations of the Land and Water Conservation Fund, including for land and water acquisition and administrative expenses. Adopted in Committee of the Whole 325-107: R 91-107; D 233-0; I 1-0. June 20, 2019.

393. HR3055. Fiscal 2020 Five-Bill Appropriations Package - Prohibit Oil and Gas Leasing. Carbajal, D-Calif., amendment that would prohibit the use of funds made available by the bill for the purpose of conducting Interior Department offshore oil and gas leasing, pre-leasing or related activities in the Outer Continental Shelf Planning Areas for Washington/Oregon, Northern California, Central California, and Southern California. Adopted in Committee of the Whole 238-192: R 11-185; D 226-7; I 1-0. June 20, 2019.

394. HR3055. Fiscal 2020 Five-Bill Appropriations Package - Fire Preparedness and Response. Hill, D-Calif., amendment that would increase by a total of $7 million funding for Interior Department and National Forest System fire preparedness, response, and research programs and hazardous fuel management activities; it would decrease by the same amount funding for financial management systems, information technology improvements, and other operational funds for the Interior Department Adopted in Committee of the Whole 377-55: R 143-55; D 233-0; I 1-0. June 20, 2019.

395. HR3055. Fiscal 2020 Five-Bill Appropriations Package - EPA Emission Standards Rule. Schrier, D-Wash., amendment that would prohibit the use of funds provided by the bill to finalize certain findings in a proposed Environmental Protection Agency rule regarding national emission standards for air pollutants from coal- and oil-fired steam-generating units. Adopted in Committee of the Whole 253-177: R 22-176; D 230-1; I 1-0. June 20, 2019.

396. HR3055. Fiscal 2020 Five-Bill Appropriations Package - American Made Products. Bost, R-Ill., amendment that would prohibit funds made available in the bill to be used in contravention of a January 2019 executive order related to the use of American made products for infrastructure projects. Adopted in Committee of the Whole 373-51: R 146-49; D 226-2; I 1-0. June 21, 2019.

Member	391	392	393	394	395	396
ALABAMA						
1 Byrne	N	N	N	N	N	Y
2 Roby	N	N	N	Y	N	Y
3 Rogers, M.	N	Y	N	Y	N	Y
4 Aderholt	N	N	N	Y	N	Y
5 Brooks, M.	N	N	N	N	N	N
6 Palmer	N	N	N	N	N	N
7 Sewell	Y	Y	Y	Y	Y	Y
ALASKA						
AL Young	N	Y	N	Y	N	Y
ARIZONA						
1 O'Halleran	Y	Y	Y	Y	Y	Y
2 Kirkpatrick	+	+	+	+	+	+
3 Grijalva	Y	Y	Y	Y	Y	Y
4 Gosar	N	N	N	Y	N	N
5 Biggs	N	N	N	N	N	N
6 Schweikert	N	N	N	Y	N	N
7 Gallego	Y	Y	Y	Y	Y	Y
8 Lesko	N	N	N	Y	N	Y
9 Stanton	Y	Y	Y	Y	Y	Y
ARKANSAS						
1 Crawford	N	N	N	N	N	Y
2 Hill, F.	N	Y	N	N	N	Y
3 Womack	N	Y	N	N	N	Y
4 Westerman	N	N	N	N	N	Y
CALIFORNIA						
1 LaMalfa	N	N	N	Y	N	Y
2 Huffman	Y	Y	Y	Y	Y	Y
3 Garamendi	N	Y	Y	Y	Y	Y
4 McClintock	N	N	N	Y	N	N
5 Thompson, M.	Y	Y	Y	Y	Y	Y
6 Matsui	Y	Y	Y	Y	Y	Y
7 Bera	Y	Y	Y	Y	Y	Y
8 Cook	N	N	N	Y	N	Y
9 McNerney	Y	Y	Y	Y	Y	Y
10 Harder	Y	Y	Y	Y	Y	Y
11 DeSaulnier	Y	Y	Y	Y	Y	Y
12 Pelosi						
13 Lee B.	Y	Y	Y	Y	Y	Y
14 Speier	Y	Y	Y	Y	Y	Y
15 Swalwell	+	+	+	+	+	+
16 Costa	Y	Y	Y	Y	Y	Y
17 Khanna	Y	Y	Y	Y	Y	Y
18 Eshoo	Y	Y	Y	Y	Y	Y
19 Lofgren	Y	Y	Y	Y	Y	Y
20 Panetta	Y	Y	Y	Y	Y	Y
21 Cox	Y	Y	Y	Y	Y	Y
22 Nunes	N	N	N	Y	N	Y
23 McCarthy	N	N	N	Y	N	N
24 Carbajal	Y	Y	Y	Y	Y	Y
25 Hill, K.	Y	Y	Y	Y	Y	Y
26 Brownley	Y	Y	Y	Y	Y	Y
27 Chu	Y	Y	Y	Y	Y	Y
28 Schiff	Y	Y	Y	Y	Y	Y
29 Cárdenas	Y	Y	Y	Y	Y	?
30 Sherman	Y	Y	Y	Y	Y	Y
31 Aguilar	Y	Y	Y	Y	Y	N
32 Napolitano	Y	Y	Y	Y	Y	Y
33 Lieu	Y	Y	Y	Y	Y	Y
34 Gomez	Y	Y	Y	Y	Y	Y
35 Torres	Y	Y	Y	Y	Y	N
36 Ruiz	Y	Y	Y	Y	Y	Y
37 Bass	Y	Y	Y	Y	Y	Y
38 Sánchez	Y	Y	Y	Y	Y	Y
39 Cisneros	Y	Y	Y	Y	Y	Y
40 Roybal-Allard	Y	Y	Y	Y	Y	Y
41 Takano	Y	Y	Y	Y	Y	Y
42 Calvert	N	N	N	N	N	N
43 Waters	Y	Y	Y	Y	Y	Y
44 Barragán	Y	Y	Y	Y	Y	Y
45 Porter	Y	Y	Y	Y	Y	Y
46 Correa	Y	Y	Y	Y	Y	Y
47 Lowenthal	Y	Y	Y	Y	Y	Y
48 Rouda	Y	Y	Y	Y	Y	Y
49 Levin	Y	Y	Y	Y	Y	Y
50 Hunter	N	N	N	Y	N	Y
51 Vargas	Y	Y	Y	Y	Y	Y
52 Peters	Y	Y	Y	Y	Y	Y
53 Davis, S.	Y	Y	Y	Y	Y	Y
COLORADO						
1 DeGette	Y	Y	Y	Y	Y	Y
2 Neguse	Y	Y	Y	Y	Y	Y
3 Tipton	N	Y	N	Y	N	Y
4 Buck	N	N	N	N	N	N
5 Lamborn	N	N	N	N	N	N
6 Crow	Y	Y	Y	Y	Y	Y
7 Perlmutter	Y	Y	Y	Y	Y	Y
CONNECTICUT						
1 Larson	Y	Y	Y	Y	Y	Y
2 Courtney	Y	Y	Y	Y	Y	Y
3 DeLauro	Y	Y	Y	Y	Y	Y
4 Himes	Y	Y	Y	Y	Y	Y
5 Hayes	Y	Y	Y	Y	Y	Y
DELAWARE						
AL Blunt Rochester	Y	Y	Y	Y	Y	Y
FLORIDA						
1 Gaetz	Y	Y	Y	Y	N	Y
2 Dunn	N	Y	N	Y	N	Y
3 Yoho	N	N	N	Y	N	Y
4 Rutherford	Y	N	Y	Y	N	Y
5 Lawson	Y	Y	Y	Y	Y	Y
6 Waltz	Y	Y	Y	Y	Y	Y
7 Murphy	Y	Y	Y	Y	Y	Y
8 Posey	Y	Y	N	Y	N	Y
9 Soto	Y	Y	Y	Y	Y	Y
10 Demings	Y	Y	Y	Y	Y	Y
11 Webster	N	N	N	N	N	Y
12 Bilirakis	Y	Y	Y	Y	Y	Y
13 Crist	Y	Y	Y	Y	Y	Y
14 Castor	Y	Y	Y	Y	Y	Y
15 Spano	N	Y	N	Y	N	Y
16 Buchanan	Y	Y	N	Y	N	Y
17 Steube	N	N	N	Y	N	Y
18 Mast	Y	Y	N	Y	N	Y
19 Rooney	Y	Y	Y	Y	Y	?
20 Hastings	?	?	?	?	?	?
21 Frankel	Y	Y	Y	Y	Y	Y
22 Deutch	Y	Y	Y	Y	Y	Y
23 Wasserman Schultz	Y	Y	Y	Y	Y	Y
24 Wilson, F.	Y	Y	Y	Y	Y	Y
25 Diaz-Balart	N	Y	N	Y	N	Y
26 Mucarsel-Powell	Y	Y	Y	Y	Y	Y
27 Shalala	Y	Y	Y	Y	Y	Y
GEORGIA						
1 Carter, E.L.	N	N	N	N	N	Y
2 Bishop, S.	N	Y	N	Y	N	Y
3 Ferguson	N	N	N	N	N	Y
4 Johnson, H.	Y	Y	Y	Y	Y	Y
5 Lewis John	Y	Y	Y	Y	Y	Y
6 McBath	Y	Y	Y	Y	Y	Y
7 Woodall	N	Y	N	N	N	Y
8 Scott, A.	N	N	N	N	N	Y
9 Collins, D.	N	N	N	N	N	N
10 Hice	N	N	N	N	N	N
11 Loudermilk	N	N	N	N	N	N
12 Allen	N	N	N	N	N	N
13 Scott, D.	Y	Y	Y	Y	Y	Y
14 Graves, T.	N	N	N	N	N	N
HAWAII						
1 Case	Y	Y	Y	Y	Y	Y
2 Gabbard	Y	Y	Y	Y	Y	Y
IDAHO						
1 Fulcher	N	N	N	N	N	Y
2 Simpson	N	Y	N	N	N	Y
ILLINOIS						
1 Rush	Y	Y	Y	Y	Y	Y
2 Kelly, R.	Y	Y	Y	Y	Y	Y
3 Lipinski	Y	Y	Y	Y	Y	Y
4 García, J.	Y	Y	Y	Y	Y	Y
5 Quigley	Y	Y	Y	Y	Y	Y
6 Casten	Y	Y	Y	Y	Y	Y
7 Davis, D.	Y	Y	Y	Y	Y	Y
8 Krishnamoorthi	Y	Y	Y	Y	Y	Y
9 Schakowsky	Y	Y	Y	Y	Y	Y
10 Schneider	Y	Y	Y	Y	Y	Y
11 Foster	Y	Y	Y	Y	Y	Y

KEY: Republicans   Democrats   *Independents*

Y Voted for (yea)	**N** Voted against (nay)	**P** Voted "present"
+ Announced for	**–** Announced against	**?** Did not vote or otherwise make position known
# Paired for	**X** Paired against	

		391	392	393	394	395	396
12	**Bost**	N	Y	N	Y	N	Y
13	**Davis, R.**	N	Y	N	Y	N	Y
14	Underwood	Y	Y	Y	Y	Y	Y
15	**Shimkus**	Y	Y	N	Y	N	Y
16	**Kinzinger**	N	Y	N	Y	N	Y
17	Bustos	Y	Y	Y	Y	Y	Y
18	**LaHood**	N	N	N	Y	N	Y
INDIANA							
1	Visclosky	Y	Y	Y	Y	Y	Y
2	**Walorski**	N	Y	N	Y	N	Y
3	**Banks**	N	N	N	N	N	N
4	**Baird**	N	Y	N	Y	N	Y
5	**Brooks, S.**	N	Y	N	Y	N	Y
6	**Pence**	N	Y	N	Y	N	Y
7	Carson	Y	Y	Y	Y	Y	Y
8	**Bucshon**	N	Y	N	Y	N	Y
9	**Hollingsworth**	N	Y	Y	Y	Y	Y
IOWA							
1	Finkenauer	Y	Y	Y	Y	Y	Y
2	Loebsack	Y	Y	Y	Y	Y	Y
3	Axne	Y	Y	Y	Y	Y	Y
4	**King, S.**	N	N	N	Y	N	Y
KANSAS							
1	**Marshall**	N	Y	N	N	N	Y
2	**Watkins**	N	N	N	Y	N	Y
3	Davids	Y	Y	Y	Y	Y	Y
4	**Estes**	N	N	N	Y	N	N
KENTUCKY							
1	**Comer**	N	Y	N	N	N	Y
2	**Guthrie**	N	N	N	Y	N	Y
3	Yarmuth	Y	Y	Y	Y	Y	Y
4	**Massie**	N	N	N	N	N	Y
5	**Rogers, H.**	N	Y	N	Y	N	Y
6	**Barr**	N	Y	N	Y	N	N
LOUISIANA							
1	**Scalise**	N	N	N	N	N	Y
2	Richmond	N	Y	Y	Y	Y	Y
3	**Higgins, C.**	N	N	N	N	N	Y
4	**Johnson, M.**	N	N	N	Y	N	Y
5	**Abraham**	N	N	N	Y	N	Y
6	**Graves, G.**	N	N	N	Y	Y	Y
MAINE							
1	Pingree	Y	Y	Y	Y	Y	Y
2	Golden	Y	Y	Y	Y	Y	Y
MARYLAND							
1	**Harris**	Y	N	N	N	N	N
2	Ruppersberger	Y	Y	Y	Y	Y	Y
3	Sarbanes	Y	Y	Y	Y	Y	Y
4	Brown, A.	Y	Y	Y	Y	Y	Y
5	Hoyer	Y	Y	Y	Y	Y	Y
6	Trone	Y	Y	Y	Y	Y	Y
7	Cummings	Y	Y	Y	Y	Y	?
8	Raskin						
MASSACHUSETTS		Y	Y	Y	Y	Y	Y
1	Neal						
2	McGovern	Y	Y	Y	Y	Y	Y
3	Trahan	Y	Y	Y	Y	Y	Y
4	Kennedy	Y	Y	Y	Y	Y	Y
5	Clark	Y	Y	Y	Y	Y	Y
6	Moulton	Y	Y	Y	Y	Y	Y
7	Pressley	Y	Y	Y	Y	Y	Y
8	Lynch	Y	Y	Y	Y	Y	Y
9	Keating	Y	Y	Y	Y	Y	Y
MICHIGAN		Y	Y	Y	Y	Y	Y
1	**Bergman**						
2	**Huizenga**	N	Y	N	Y	N	Y
3	**Amash**	N	N	N	Y	N	Y
4	**Moolenaar**	N	N	N	N	N	N
5	Kildee	N	Y	N	Y	N	Y
6	**Upton**	Y	Y	Y	Y	Y	Y
7	**Walberg**	Y	Y	N	Y	N	Y
8	Slotkin	N	N	N	Y	N	Y
9	Levin	Y	Y	Y	Y	Y	Y
10	**Mitchell**	Y	Y	Y	Y	Y	Y
11	Stevens	N	Y	N	Y	N	Y
12	Dingell	Y	Y	Y	Y	Y	Y
13	Tlaib	Y	Y	Y	Y	Y	Y
14	Lawrence	Y	Y	Y	Y	Y	Y
MINNESOTA		Y	Y	Y	Y	Y	Y
1	**Hagedorn**						
2	Craig	N	Y	N	Y	N	Y
3	Phillips	Y	Y	Y	Y	Y	Y
4	McCollum	Y	Y	Y	Y	Y	Y
5	Omar	Y	Y	Y	Y	Y	Y

		391	392	393	394	395	396
6	**Emmer**	Y	Y	Y	Y	Y	Y
7	Peterson	-	+	-	-	-	+
8	**Stauber**	N	Y	N	Y	N	Y
MISSISSIPPI		N	Y	N	Y	N	Y
1	**Kelly, T.**						
2	Thompson, B.	N	N	N	N	N	N
3	**Guest**	Y	Y	Y	Y	Y	Y
4	**Palazzo**	N	Y	N	Y	N	Y
MISSOURI		N	N	?	N	N	Y
1	Clay						
2	**Wagner**	Y	Y	Y	Y	Y	Y
3	**Luetkemeyer**	N	Y	N	Y	N	N
4	**Hartzler**	N	N	N	Y	N	Y
5	Cleaver	N	N	N	Y	N	Y
6	**Graves, S.**	Y	Y	Y	Y	Y	Y
7	**Long**	N	Y	N	Y	N	Y
8	**Smith, J.**	N	N	N	Y	N	Y
MONTANA		N	N	N	Y	N	N
AL	**Gianforte**						
NEBRASKA		N	Y	N	Y	N	Y
1	**Fortenberry**						
2	**Bacon**	N	Y	N	Y	Y	Y
3	**Smith, Adrian**	Y	Y	N	Y	Y	Y
NEVADA		N	N	N	N	N	Y
1	Titus						
2	**Amodei**	Y	Y	Y	Y	Y	Y
3	Lee	N	Y	N	N	N	Y
4	Horsford	Y	Y	Y	Y	Y	Y
NEW HAMPSHIRE		Y	Y	Y	Y	Y	Y
1	Pappas						
2	Kuster	Y	Y	Y	Y	Y	Y
NEW JERSEY		Y	Y	Y	Y	Y	Y
1	Norcross						
2	Van Drew	Y	Y	Y	Y	Y	Y
3	Kim	Y	Y	Y	Y	Y	Y
4	**Smith, C.**	Y	Y	Y	Y	Y	Y
5	Gottheimer	Y	Y	Y	Y	Y	Y
6	Pallone	Y	Y	Y	Y	Y	Y
7	Malinowski	Y	Y	Y	Y	Y	Y
8	Sires	Y	Y	Y	Y	Y	Y
9	Pascrell	Y	Y	Y	Y	Y	Y
10	Payne	Y	Y	Y	Y	Y	Y
11	Sherrill	Y	Y	Y	Y	Y	Y
12	Watson Coleman	Y	Y	Y	Y	Y	Y
NEW MEXICO		Y	Y	Y	Y	Y	Y
1	Haaland						
2	Torres Small	Y	Y	Y	Y	Y	Y
3	Luján	Y	Y	Y	Y	Y	Y
NEW YORK		Y	Y	Y	Y	Y	Y
1	**Zeldin**						
2	**King, P.**	Y	Y	Y	N	Y	Y
3	Suozzi	Y	Y	Y	Y	Y	Y
4	Rice, K.	Y	Y	Y	Y	Y	Y
5	Meeks	Y	Y	Y	Y	Y	Y
6	Meng	Y	Y	Y	Y	Y	Y
7	Velázquez	Y	Y	Y	Y	Y	Y
8	Jeffries	Y	Y	Y	Y	Y	Y
9	Clarke	Y	Y	Y	Y	Y	?
10	Nadler	Y	Y	Y	Y	Y	Y
11	Rose	Y	Y	Y	Y	Y	Y
12	Maloney, C.	Y	Y	Y	Y	Y	Y
13	Espaillat	Y	Y	Y	Y	Y	Y
14	Ocasio-Cortez	Y	Y	Y	Y	Y	Y
15	Serrano	Y	Y	Y	Y	Y	Y
16	Engel	Y	Y	Y	Y	Y	Y
17	Lowey	Y	Y	Y	Y	Y	Y
18	Maloney, S.P.	Y	Y	Y	Y	Y	Y
19	Delgado	Y	Y	Y	Y	Y	Y
20	Tonko	Y	Y	Y	Y	Y	Y
21	**Stefanik**	Y	Y	Y	Y	Y	Y
22	Brindisi	Y	Y	Y	Y	Y	Y
23	**Reed**	Y	Y	Y	Y	Y	Y
24	**Katko**	N	Y	N	Y	N	Y
25	Morelle	Y	Y	Y	Y	Y	Y
26	Higgins, B.	Y	Y	Y	Y	Y	Y
27	**Collins, C.**	Y	Y	Y	Y	Y	Y
NORTH CAROLINA		N	Y	N	Y	N	Y
1	Butterfield						
2	**Holding**	Y	Y	Y	Y	?	Y
3	**Jones***	N	N	N	Y	N	Y
4	Price						
5	**Foxx**	Y	Y	Y	Y	Y	Y
6	**Walker**	N	N	N	Y	N	N
7	**Rouzer**	N	N	N	Y	N	Y

		391	392	393	394	395	396
8	**Hudson**	N	Y	N	N	N	Y
9	vacant	N	Y	N	Y	N	N
10	**McHenry**	N	Y	N	Y	N	Y
11	**Meadows**	N	N	Y	N	N	N
12	Adams	Y	Y	Y	Y	Y	Y
13	**Budd**	N	Y	N	N	N	Y
NORTH DAKOTA							
AL	**Armstrong**	N	N	N	Y	N	N
OHIO							
1	**Chabot**	N	N	N	Y	N	Y
2	**Wenstrup**	N	Y	N	Y	N	Y
3	Beatty	Y	Y	Y	Y	Y	Y
4	**Jordan**	N	N	N	N	N	N
5	**Latta**	N	Y	N	Y	N	Y
6	**Johnson, B.**	N	N	N	Y	N	Y
7	**Gibbs**	N	Y	N	N	N	Y
8	**Davidson**	N	N	N	N	Y	N
9	Kaptur	Y	Y	Y	Y	Y	Y
10	**Turner**	N	Y	N	Y	N	Y
11	Fudge	Y	Y	Y	Y	Y	Y
12	**Balderson**	N	Y	N	N	N	Y
13	Ryan	?	?	?	?	?	Y
14	**Joyce**	N	Y	N	N	N	Y
15	**Stivers**	N	Y	?	N	N	Y
16	**Gonzalez**	N	Y	N	Y	N	Y
OKLAHOMA							
1	**Hern**	N	N	N	N	N	N
2	**Mullin**	N	N	N	Y	N	Y
3	**Lucas**	N	N	N	Y	N	Y
4	**Cole**	N	Y	N	N	N	Y
5	Horn	Y	Y	Y	Y	Y	Y
OREGON							
1	Bonamici	Y	Y	Y	Y	Y	Y
2	**Walden**	N	N	N	Y	N	Y
3	Blumenauer	Y	Y	Y	Y	?	Y
4	DeFazio	Y	Y	Y	Y	Y	Y
5	Schrader	Y	Y	Y	Y	Y	Y
PENNSYLVANIA							
1	**Fitzpatrick**	Y	Y	Y	Y	Y	Y
2	Boyle	Y	Y	Y	Y	Y	Y
3	Evans	Y	Y	Y	Y	Y	Y
4	Dean	Y	Y	Y	Y	Y	Y
5	Scanlon	Y	Y	Y	Y	Y	Y
6	Houlahan	Y	Y	Y	Y	Y	Y
7	Wild	Y	Y	Y	Y	Y	Y
8	Cartwright	Y	Y	Y	Y	Y	Y
9	**Meuser**	N	Y	N	Y	N	Y
10	**Perry**	N	N	N	Y	N	Y
11	**Smucker**	N	Y	N	Y	N	Y
12	**Marino***						
13	**Joyce**	N	Y	N	Y	N	Y
14	**Reschenthaler**	N	Y	N	Y	N	Y
15	**Thompson, G.**	N	Y	N	Y	N	Y
16	**Kelly, M.**	N	Y	N	N	N	Y
17	Lamb	Y	Y	Y	Y	Y	Y
18	Doyle	Y	Y	Y	Y	Y	Y
RHODE ISLAND							
1	Cicilline	Y	Y	Y	Y	Y	Y
2	Langevin	Y	Y	Y	Y	Y	Y
SOUTH CAROLINA							
1	Cunningham	Y	Y	Y	Y	Y	Y
2	**Wilson, J.**	N	Y	N	Y	N	Y
3	**Duncan**	N	N	N	N	N	N
4	**Timmons**	N	Y	N	Y	N	Y
5	**Norman**	N	N	N	N	N	N
6	Clyburn	Y	Y	Y	Y	Y	?
7	**Rice, T.**	Y	N	N	N	N	Y
SOUTH DAKOTA							
AL	**Johnson**	N	N	N	Y	N	Y
TENNESSEE							
1	**Roe**	N	Y	N	Y	N	Y
2	**Burchett**	N	N	N	N	N	N
3	**Fleischmann**	N	Y	N	Y	N	Y
4	**DesJarlais**	N	Y	N	Y	N	Y
5	Cooper	N	Y	N	Y	Y	Y
6	**Rose**	N	N	N	Y	N	N
7	**Green**	N	N	N	Y	N	N
8	**Kustoff**	N	N	N	Y	N	Y
9	Cohen	Y	Y	Y	Y	Y	Y
TEXAS							
1	**Gohmert**	N	N	N	Y	N	N
2	**Crenshaw**	N	Y	N	Y	N	N
3	**Taylor**	N	N	N	Y	N	N
4	**Ratcliffe**	N	N	N	N	N	Y

		391	392	393	394	395	396
5	**Gooden**	N	N	N	Y	N	N
6	**Wright**	N	N	N	Y	N	N
7	Fletcher	N	Y	N	Y	Y	Y
8	**Brady**	N	N	N	Y	N	N
9	Green, A.	Y	Y	Y	Y	Y	Y
10	**McCaul**	N	Y	N	Y	Y	Y
11	**Conaway**	N	N	N	Y	N	Y
12	**Granger**	N	N	N	Y	N	Y
13	**Thornberry**	N	N	N	Y	N	Y
14	**Weber**	N	N	N	Y	N	N
15	Gonzalez	Y	Y	N	Y	Y	Y
16	Escobar	Y	Y	Y	Y	Y	Y
17	**Flores**	N	N	N	Y	N	Y
18	Jackson Lee	Y	Y	Y	Y	Y	Y
19	**Arrington**	N	N	N	N	N	Y
20	Castro	Y	Y	Y	Y	Y	Y
21	**Roy**	N	N	N	N	N	N
22	**Olson**	N	N	N	Y	N	Y
23	**Hurd**	N	Y	N	Y	Y	Y
24	**Marchant**	N	N	N	Y	N	N
25	**Williams**	N	N	N	Y	N	Y
26	**Burgess**	N	N	N	Y	N	Y
27	**Cloud**	N	N	N	N	N	N
28	Cuellar	N	Y	N	Y	Y	Y
29	Garcia, S.	N	Y	N	Y	Y	Y
30	Johnson, E.B.	Y	Y	Y	Y	Y	Y
31	**Carter, J.**	N	N	N	Y	N	Y
32	Allred	Y	Y	Y	Y	Y	Y
33	Veasey	Y	Y	Y	Y	Y	Y
34	Vela	Y	Y	Y	Y	Y	Y
35	Doggett	Y	Y	Y	Y	Y	Y
36	**Babin**	N	N	N	Y	N	N
UTAH							
1	**Bishop, R.**	N	N	N	N	N	Y
2	**Stewart**	N	N	N	N	N	N
3	**Curtis**	N	N	N	Y	N	Y
4	McAdams	Y	Y	Y	Y	Y	Y
VERMONT							
AL	Welch	Y	Y	Y	Y	Y	Y
VIRGINIA							
1	**Wittman**	N	Y	N	Y	N	N
2	Luria	Y	Y	Y	Y	Y	Y
3	Scott, R.	Y	Y	Y	Y	Y	Y
4	McEachin	Y	Y	Y	Y	Y	Y
5	**Riggleman**	N	Y	N	Y	Y	N
6	**Cline**	N	N	N	Y	N	N
7	Spanberger	Y	Y	Y	Y	Y	Y
8	Beyer	Y	Y	Y	Y	Y	Y
9	**Griffith**	N	Y	N	Y	N	Y
10	Wexton	Y	Y	Y	Y	Y	Y
11	Connolly	Y	Y	Y	Y	Y	Y
WASHINGTON							
1	DelBene	Y	Y	Y	Y	Y	Y
2	Larsen	Y	Y	Y	Y	Y	Y
3	**Herrera Beutler**	?	?	?	?	?	?
4	**Newhouse**	N	Y	N	Y	N	Y
5	**McMorris Rodgers**	N	Y	N	Y	N	Y
6	Kilmer	Y	Y	Y	Y	Y	Y
7	Jayapal	Y	Y	Y	Y	Y	Y
8	Schrier	Y	Y	Y	Y	Y	Y
9	Smith Adam	Y	Y	Y	Y	Y	Y
10	Heck	Y	Y	Y	Y	Y	Y
WEST VIRGINIA							
1	**McKinley**	N	Y	N	Y	N	Y
2	**Mooney**	N	Y	N	Y	N	Y
3	**Miller**	N	Y	N	Y	N	Y
WISCONSIN							
1	**Steil**	N	Y	N	Y	N	Y
2	Pocan	Y	Y	Y	Y	Y	Y
3	Kind	Y	Y	Y	Y	Y	Y
4	Moore	Y	Y	Y	Y	Y	Y
5	**Sensenbrenner**	N	N	N	Y	N	Y
6	**Grothman**	N	N	N	N	N	N
7	**Duffy**	N	N	N	Y	N	Y
8	**Gallagher**	N	Y	N	Y	N	N
WYOMING							
AL	**Cheney**	N	N	N	Y	N	Y
DELEGATES							
	Radewagen (A.S.)	N	Y	N	Y	Y	?
	Norton (D.C.)	Y	Y	Y	Y	Y	?
	San Nicolas (Guam)	Y	Y	Y	Y	Y	?
	Sablan (N. Marianas)	Y	Y	Y	Y	Y	Y
	González-Colón (P.R.)	N	Y	N	Y	Y	?
	Plaskett (V.I.)	Y	Y	Y	Y	Y	Y

III HOUSE VOTES

397. HR3055. Fiscal 2020 Five-Bill Appropriations Package - VA Medical Facilities. Golden, D-Maine, amendment that would increase by $5 million funding for maintenance and operation of Veterans Health Administration medical facilities and would decrease by $5.2 million funding for VA information technology systems and telecommunications support. Adopted in Committee of the Whole 418-6: R 191-3; D 226-3; I 1-0. June 21, 2019.

398. HR3055. Fiscal 2020 Five-Bill Appropriations Package - Veterans Benefits Administration. McAdams, D-Utah, amendment that would increase then decrease by $1 administrative funding for the Veterans Benefits Administration. Adopted in Committee of the Whole 420-3: R 190-3; D 229-0; I 1-0. June 21, 2019.

399. HR3055. Fiscal 2020 Five-Bill Appropriations Package - Natural Gas Transportation. DeFazio, D-Ore., amendment that would prohibit the use of funds made available by the bill to carry out an executive order allowing for the transportation of liquefied natural gas by rail tank car or to issue special permits for such transportation. Adopted in Committee of the Whole 221-195: R 4-185; D 216-10; I 1-0. June 24, 2019.

400. HR3055. Fiscal 2020 Five-Bill Appropriations Package - Equal Access to HUD Programs. Duncan, R-S.C., amendment that would strike from the bill a provision that would prohibit the use of funds made available by the bill to change or replace two Housing and Urban Development Department rules related to equal access based on gender identity and sexual orientation for HUD community planning and development programs. Rejected in Committee of the Whole 180-236: R 180-9; D 0-226; I 0-1. June 24, 2019.

401. HR3055. Fiscal 2020 Five-Bill Appropriations Package - Transgender HUD Facility Access. Duncan, R-S.C., amendment that would strike from the bill a provision that would codify a February 2015 Housing and Urban Development rule regarding the placement of transgender persons in single-sex emergency shelters and other facilities. Rejected in Committee of the Whole 181-236: R 181-8; D 0-227; I 0-1. June 24, 2019.

402. HR3055. Fiscal 2020 Five-Bill Appropriations Package - Reduce Transportation-HUD Funding. Grothman, R-Wis., amendment that would reduce by 4.6 percent all discretionary funding made available under the Transportation, Housing and Urban Development, and related agencies title of the bill (Division E). Rejected in Committee of the Whole 145-273: R 145-44; D 0-228; I 0-1. June 24, 2019.

		397	398	399	400	401	402
ALABAMA							
1	**Byrne**	Y	Y	N	Y	Y	Y
2	**Roby**	Y	Y	N	Y	Y	N
3	**Rogers, M.**	Y	Y	N	Y	Y	Y
4	**Aderholt**	Y	Y	N	Y	Y	Y
5	**Brooks, M.**	Y	Y	N	Y	Y	Y
6	**Palmer**	Y	Y	N	Y	Y	Y
7	Sewell	Y	Y	Y	N	N	N
ALASKA							
AL	**Young**	Y	Y	N	Y	Y	N
ARIZONA							
1	O'Halleran	Y	Y	Y	N	N	N
2	Kirkpatrick	+	+	Y	N	N	N
3	Grijalva	Y	Y	Y	N	N	N
4	**Gosar**	Y	Y	N	Y	Y	Y
5	**Biggs**	Y	Y	N	Y	Y	Y
6	**Schweikert**	Y	Y	N	Y	Y	Y
7	Gallego	Y	Y	Y	N	N	N
8	**Lesko**	Y	Y	N	Y	Y	Y
9	Stanton	Y	Y	Y	N	N	N
ARKANSAS							
1	**Crawford**	Y	Y	N	Y	Y	Y
2	**Hill, F.**	Y	Y	N	Y	Y	Y
3	**Womack**	Y	Y	N	Y	Y	Y
4	**Westerman**	Y	Y	N	Y	Y	Y
CALIFORNIA							
1	**LaMalfa**	Y	Y	N	Y	Y	Y
2	Huffman	Y	Y	Y	N	N	N
3	Garamendi	Y	Y	Y	N	N	N
4	**McClintock**	Y	Y	N	Y	Y	Y
5	Thompson, M.	Y	Y	Y	N	N	N
6	Matsui	Y	Y	Y	N	N	N
7	Bera	Y	Y	Y	N	N	N
8	**Cook**	Y	Y	N	Y	Y	Y
9	McNerney	Y	Y	Y	N	N	N
10	Harder	Y	Y	Y	N	N	N
11	DeSaulnier	Y	Y	Y	N	N	N
12	Pelosi						
13	Lee B.	Y	Y	Y	?	N	N
14	Speier	Y	Y	Y	N	N	N
15	Swalwell	+	+	+	-	-	-
16	Costa	Y	Y	N	N	N	N
17	Khanna	Y	Y	Y	N	N	N
18	Eshoo	Y	Y	Y	N	N	N
19	Lofgren	Y	Y	Y	N	N	N
20	Panetta	Y	Y	Y	N	N	N
21	Cox	Y	Y	N	N	N	N
22	**Nunes**	Y	Y	N	Y	Y	Y
23	**McCarthy**	Y	Y	N	Y	Y	Y
24	Carbajal	Y	Y	Y	N	N	N
25	Hill, K.	Y	Y	Y	N	N	N
26	Brownley	N	Y	Y	N	N	N
27	Chu	Y	Y	Y	N	N	N
28	Schiff	Y	Y	Y	N	N	N
29	Cárdenas	Y	Y	Y	N	N	N
30	Sherman	Y	Y	Y	N	N	N
31	Aguilar	Y	Y	Y	N	N	N
32	Napolitano	Y	Y	Y	N	N	N
33	Lieu	Y	Y	Y	N	N	N
34	Gomez	Y	Y	Y	N	N	N
35	Torres	Y	Y	Y	N	N	N
36	Ruiz	Y	Y	Y	N	N	N
37	Bass	Y	Y	Y	N	N	N
38	Sánchez	Y	Y	Y	N	N	N
39	Cisneros	Y	Y	Y	N	N	N
40	Roybal-Allard	Y	Y	Y	N	N	N
41	Takano	Y	Y	Y	N	N	N
42	**Calvert**	Y	Y	N	Y	Y	N
43	Waters	Y	Y	Y	N	N	N
44	Barragán	Y	Y	Y	N	N	N
45	Porter	Y	Y	Y	N	N	N
46	Correa	Y	Y	N	N	N	N
47	Lowenthal	Y	Y	Y	N	N	N
48	Rouda	Y	Y	Y	N	N	N
49	Levin	Y	Y	Y	N	N	N
50	**Hunter**	Y	Y	N	Y	Y	Y
51	Vargas	Y	Y	Y	N	N	N
52	Peters	Y	Y	Y	N	N	N
53	Davis, S.	Y	Y	Y	N	N	N
COLORADO							
1	DeGette	Y	Y	Y	N	N	N
2	Neguse	Y	Y	Y	N	N	N
3	**Tipton**	Y	Y	N	Y	Y	Y
4	**Buck**	Y	Y	N	Y	Y	Y
5	**Lamborn**	Y	Y	N	Y	Y	Y
6	Crow	Y	Y	Y	N	N	N
7	Perlmutter	Y	Y	Y	N	N	N
CONNECTICUT							
1	Larson	Y	Y	Y	N	N	N
2	Courtney	Y	Y	Y	N	N	N
3	DeLauro	Y	Y	Y	N	N	N
4	Himes	Y	Y	Y	N	N	N
5	Hayes	Y	Y	Y	N	N	N
DELAWARE							
AL	Blunt Rochester	Y	Y	Y	N	N	N
FLORIDA							
1	**Gaetz**	Y	Y	N	Y	Y	Y
2	**Dunn**	Y	Y	N	Y	Y	Y
3	**Yoho**	Y	Y	N	Y	Y	Y
4	**Rutherford**	Y	Y	Y	Y	Y	N
5	Lawson	Y	Y	Y	N	N	N
6	**Waltz**	Y	Y	N	Y	Y	N
7	Murphy	Y	Y	Y	N	N	N
8	**Posey**	Y	Y	Y	Y	Y	Y
9	Soto	Y	Y	Y	N	N	N
10	Demings	Y	Y	Y	N	N	N
11	**Webster**	Y	Y	N	Y	Y	Y
12	**Bilirakis**	Y	Y	N	Y	Y	N
13	Crist	Y	Y	Y	N	N	N
14	Castor	Y	Y	Y	N	N	N
15	**Spano**	Y	Y	N	Y	Y	N
16	**Buchanan**	Y	Y	N	Y	Y	N
17	**Steube**	Y	Y	N	Y	Y	N
18	**Mast**	Y	Y	Y	Y	Y	N
19	**Rooney**	?	?	?	?	?	?
20	Hastings	?	?	Y	N	N	N
21	Frankel	Y	Y	Y	N	N	N
22	Deutch	Y	Y	Y	N	N	N
23	Wasserman Schultz	Y	Y	?	-	-	?
24	Wilson, F.	Y	Y	Y	N	N	N
25	**Diaz-Balart**	Y	Y	N	N	N	N
26	Mucarsel-Powell	Y	Y	Y	N	N	N
27	Shalala	Y	Y	Y	N	N	N
GEORGIA							
1	**Carter, E.L.**	Y	Y	N	Y	Y	Y
2	Bishop, S.	Y	Y	?	Y	?	?
3	**Ferguson**	Y	Y	N	Y	Y	Y
4	Johnson, H.	Y	Y	Y	N	N	N
5	Lewis John	Y	Y	Y	N	N	N
6	McBath	Y	Y	Y	N	N	N
7	**Woodall**	Y	Y	Y	Y	Y	Y
8	**Scott, A.**	Y	Y	Y	Y	Y	Y
9	**Collins, D.**	Y	Y	N	Y	Y	Y
10	**Hice**	Y	Y	N	Y	Y	Y
11	**Loudermilk**	Y	Y	N	Y	Y	Y
12	**Allen**	Y	Y	N	Y	Y	Y
13	Scott, D.	Y	Y	Y	N	N	N
14	**Graves, T.**	Y	Y	N	Y	Y	Y
HAWAII							
1	Case	Y	Y	Y	N	N	N
2	Gabbard	Y	Y	?	?	?	?
IDAHO							
1	**Fulcher**	Y	Y	N	Y	Y	Y
2	**Simpson**	Y	Y	N	Y	Y	N
ILLINOIS							
1	Rush	Y	Y	Y	N	N	N
2	Kelly, R.	Y	Y	Y	N	N	N
3	Lipinski	Y	Y	?	?	?	N
4	García, J.	Y	Y	Y	N	N	N
5	Quigley	Y	Y	Y	N	N	N
6	Casten	Y	Y	Y	N	N	N
7	Davis, D.	Y	Y	Y	N	N	N
8	Krishnamoorthi	Y	Y	Y	N	N	N
9	Schakowsky	Y	Y	Y	N	N	N
10	Schneider	Y	Y	Y	N	N	N
11	Foster	Y	Y	Y	N	N	N

		397	398	399	400	401	402
12	**Bost**	Y	Y	N	Y	Y	N
13	**Davis, R.**	Y	Y	N	Y	Y	N
14	Underwood	Y	Y	Y	N	N	N
15	**Shimkus**	Y	Y	N	Y	Y	Y
16	**Kinzinger**	Y	Y	N	Y	Y	N
17	Bustos	Y	Y	Y	N	N	N
18	**LaHood**	Y	Y	N	Y	Y	Y
INDIANA							
1	Visclosky	Y	Y	Y	N	N	N
2	**Walorski**	Y	Y	N	Y	Y	N
3	**Banks**	Y	Y	N	Y	Y	Y
4	**Baird**	Y	Y	N	Y	Y	Y
5	**Brooks, S.**	Y	Y	N	N	N	Y
6	**Pence**	Y	Y	N	Y	Y	Y
7	Carson	Y	Y	Y	N	N	N
8	**Bucshon**	Y	Y	N	Y	Y	Y
9	**Hollingsworth**	Y	Y	N	Y	Y	N
IOWA							
1	Finkenauer	Y	Y	Y	N	N	N
2	Loebsack	Y	Y	+	-	-	-
3	Axne	Y	Y	Y	N	N	N
4	**King, S.**	Y	Y	N	Y	Y	Y
KANSAS							
1	**Marshall**	Y	Y	N	Y	Y	N
2	**Watkins**	Y	Y	N	Y	Y	Y
3	Davids	Y	Y	Y	N	N	N
4	**Estes**	Y	Y	N	Y	Y	Y
KENTUCKY							
1	**Comer**	Y	Y	N	Y	Y	Y
2	**Guthrie**	Y	Y	N	Y	Y	Y
3	Yarmuth	Y	Y	Y	N	N	N
4	**Massie**	Y	Y	N	Y	Y	Y
5	**Rogers, H.**	Y	Y	N	Y	Y	N
6	**Barr**	Y	Y	N	Y	Y	Y
LOUISIANA							
1	**Scalise**	Y	Y	N	Y	Y	Y
2	Richmond	Y	Y	N	N	N	N
3	**Higgins, C.**	Y	Y	N	Y	Y	Y
4	**Johnson, M.**	Y	Y	N	Y	Y	Y
5	**Abraham**	Y	Y	?	?	?	?
6	**Graves, G.**	Y	Y	N	Y	Y	N
MAINE							
1	Pingree	Y	Y	Y	N	N	N
2	Golden	Y	Y	Y	N	N	N
MARYLAND							
1	**Harris**	N	Y	?	?	?	?
2	Ruppersberger	Y	Y	Y	N	N	N
3	Sarbanes	Y	Y	Y	N	N	N
4	Brown, A.	Y	Y	Y	N	N	N
5	Hoyer	Y	Y	Y	N	N	N
6	Trone	Y	Y	Y	N	N	N
7	Cummings	?	?	Y	N	N	N
8	Raskin						
MASSACHUSETTS		Y	Y	Y	N	N	N
1	Neal						
2	McGovern	Y	Y	Y	N	N	N
3	Trahan	Y	Y	Y	N	N	N
4	Kennedy	Y	Y	Y	N	N	N
5	Clark	Y	Y	Y	N	N	N
6	Moulton	Y	Y	Y	N	N	N
7	Pressley	Y	Y	?	?	?	?
8	Lynch	Y	Y	Y	N	N	N
9	Keating	Y	Y	Y	N	N	N
MICHIGAN		Y	Y	Y	N	N	N
1	**Bergman**						
2	**Huizenga**	Y	N	N	Y	Y	Y
3	**Amash**	Y	Y	N	Y	Y	Y
4	**Moolenaar**	Y	Y	N	Y	Y	Y
5	Kildee	Y	Y	N	Y	Y	Y
6	**Upton**	Y	Y	Y	N	N	N
7	**Walberg**	Y	Y	N	N	N	N
8	Slotkin	Y	Y	N	Y	Y	Y
9	Levin	Y	Y	Y	N	N	N
10	**Mitchell**	Y	Y	Y	N	N	N
11	Stevens	Y	Y	N	Y	Y	Y
12	Dingell	Y	Y	Y	N	N	N
13	Tlaib	Y	Y	Y	N	N	N
14	Lawrence	Y	Y	Y	N	N	N
MINNESOTA		Y	Y	Y	N	N	N
1	**Hagedorn**						
2	Craig	Y	Y	N	Y	Y	Y
3	Phillips	Y	Y	Y	N	N	N
4	McCollum	Y	Y	Y	N	N	N
5	Omar	Y	Y	Y	N	N	N

		397	398	399	400	401	402
6	**Emmer**	Y	Y	Y	N	N	N
7	Peterson	+	+	N	Y	Y	Y
8	**Stauber**	Y	Y	Y	N	N	N
MISSISSIPPI		Y	Y	N	Y	Y	N
1	**Kelly, T.**						
2	Thompson, B.	Y	Y	N	Y	Y	Y
3	**Guest**	Y	Y	Y	N	N	N
4	**Palazzo**	?	Y	N	Y	Y	Y
MISSOURI		Y	Y	-	+	+	+
1	Clay						
2	**Wagner**	Y	Y	Y	N	N	N
3	**Luetkemeyer**	Y	Y	N	Y	Y	Y
4	**Hartzler**	Y	Y	N	Y	Y	N
5	Cleaver	Y	Y	N	Y	Y	Y
6	**Graves, S.**	Y	Y	Y	N	N	N
7	**Long**	Y	Y	N	Y	Y	Y
8	**Smith, J.**	Y	Y	N	Y	Y	Y
MONTANA		Y	Y	N	Y	Y	Y
AL	**Gianforte**						
NEBRASKA		Y	Y	N	Y	Y	N
1	**Fortenberry**						
2	**Bacon**	Y	Y	N	Y	Y	N
3	**Smith, Adrian**	Y	Y	N	Y	Y	Y
NEVADA		Y	Y	N	Y	Y	Y
1	Titus						
2	**Amodei**	Y	Y	Y	N	N	N
3	Lee	Y	Y	N	Y	Y	N
4	Horsford	N	Y	Y	N	N	N
NEW HAMPSHIRE		Y	Y	Y	N	N	N
1	Pappas						
2	Kuster	Y	Y	Y	N	N	N
NEW JERSEY		Y	Y	Y	N	N	N
1	Norcross						
2	Van Drew	Y	Y	Y	N	N	N
3	Kim	Y	Y	Y	N	N	N
4	**Smith, C.**	Y	Y	Y	N	N	N
5	Gottheimer	Y	Y	N	Y	Y	N
6	Pallone	Y	Y	Y	N	N	N
7	Malinowski	Y	Y	Y	N	N	N
8	Sires	Y	Y	Y	N	N	N
9	Pascrell	Y	Y	Y	N	N	N
10	Payne	Y	Y	Y	N	N	N
11	Sherrill	Y	Y	Y	N	N	N
12	Watson Coleman	Y	Y	Y	N	N	N
NEW MEXICO		Y	Y	Y	N	N	N
1	Haaland						
2	Torres Small	Y	Y	Y	N	N	N
3	Luján	Y	Y	N	N	N	N
NEW YORK		Y	Y	Y	N	N	N
1	**Zeldin**						
2	**King, P.**	Y	Y	N	Y	Y	Y
3	Suozzi	Y	Y	N	Y	Y	N
4	Rice, K.	Y	Y	Y	N	N	N
5	Meeks	Y	Y	Y	N	N	N
6	Meng	Y	Y	?	?	?	?
7	Velázquez	Y	Y	Y	N	N	N
8	Jeffries	Y	Y	Y	N	N	N
9	Clarke	?	?	Y	N	N	N
10	Nadler	Y	Y	Y	N	N	N
11	Rose	Y	Y	Y	N	N	N
12	Maloney, C.	Y	Y	Y	N	N	N
13	Espaillat	Y	Y	Y	N	N	N
14	Ocasio-Cortez	Y	Y	Y	N	N	N
15	Serrano	Y	Y	Y	N	N	N
16	Engel	Y	Y	Y	N	N	N
17	Lowey	Y	Y	Y	N	N	N
18	Maloney, S.P.	Y	Y	Y	N	N	N
19	Delgado	Y	Y	Y	N	N	N
20	Tonko	Y	Y	Y	N	N	N
21	**Stefanik**	Y	Y	Y	N	N	N
22	Brindisi	Y	Y	N	N	N	N
23	**Reed**	Y	Y	Y	N	N	N
24	**Katko**	Y	Y	N	N	N	N
25	Morelle	Y	Y	N	N	N	N
26	Higgins, B.	Y	Y	Y	N	N	N
27	**Collins, C.**	Y	Y	Y	N	N	N
NORTH CAROLINA		Y	Y	N	Y	Y	N
1	Butterfield						
2	**Holding**	Y	Y	Y	N	N	N
3	**Jones***	Y	Y	N	Y	Y	Y
4	Price						
5	**Foxx**	Y	Y	Y	N	N	N
6	**Walker**	Y	Y	N	Y	Y	Y
7	**Rouzer**	Y	Y	N	Y	Y	Y

		397	398	399	400	401	402
8	**Hudson**	Y	Y	N	Y	Y	Y
9	vacant	Y	Y	N	Y	Y	Y
10	**McHenry**	Y	Y	N	Y	Y	Y
11	**Meadows**	Y	Y	N	Y	Y	Y
12	Adams	Y	Y	Y	N	N	N
13	**Budd**	Y	Y	N	Y	Y	Y
NORTH DAKOTA							
AL	**Armstrong**	Y	Y	N	Y	Y	N
OHIO							
1	**Chabot**	Y	Y	N	Y	Y	Y
2	**Wenstrup**	Y	Y	N	Y	Y	Y
3	Beatty	Y	Y	Y	N	N	N
4	**Jordan**	Y	Y	N	Y	Y	Y
5	**Latta**	Y	Y	N	Y	Y	Y
6	**Johnson, B.**	Y	Y	N	Y	Y	Y
7	**Gibbs**	Y	Y	N	Y	Y	Y
8	**Davidson**	N	N	N	Y	Y	Y
9	Kaptur	Y	Y	Y	N	N	N
10	**Turner**	Y	Y	N	Y	Y	N
11	Fudge	Y	Y	Y	N	N	N
12	**Balderson**	Y	Y	N	Y	Y	Y
13	Ryan	Y	Y	?	?	?	?
14	**Joyce**	Y	Y	N	Y	Y	N
15	**Stivers**	Y	Y	N	N	N	N
16	**Gonzalez**	Y	Y	N	Y	Y	N
OKLAHOMA							
1	**Hern**	Y	Y	N	Y	Y	Y
2	**Mullin**	Y	Y	N	Y	Y	Y
3	**Lucas**	Y	Y	?	?	?	?
4	**Cole**	Y	Y	N	Y	Y	Y
5	Horn	Y	Y	N	N	N	N
OREGON							
1	Bonamici	Y	Y	Y	N	N	N
2	**Walden**	Y	Y	N	N	N	N
3	Blumenauer	Y	Y	Y	N	N	N
4	DeFazio	Y	Y	Y	N	N	N
5	Schrader	Y	Y	Y	N	N	N
PENNSYLVANIA							
1	**Fitzpatrick**	Y	Y	Y	N	N	N
2	Boyle	Y	Y	Y	N	N	N
3	Evans	Y	Y	Y	N	N	N
4	Dean	Y	Y	Y	N	N	N
5	Scanlon	Y	Y	Y	N	N	N
6	Houlahan	Y	Y	Y	N	N	N
7	Wild	Y	Y	Y	N	N	N
8	Cartwright	Y	Y	Y	N	N	N
9	**Meuser**	Y	Y	N	Y	Y	Y
10	**Perry**	Y	Y	N	Y	Y	Y
11	**Smucker**	Y	Y	N	Y	Y	Y
12	**Marino***						
13	**Joyce**	Y	Y	N	Y	Y	Y
14	**Reschenthaler**	Y	Y	N	Y	Y	N
15	**Thompson, G.**	Y	Y	N	Y	Y	N
16	**Kelly, M.**	Y	Y	N	Y	Y	Y
17	Lamb	Y	Y	Y	N	N	N
18	Doyle	Y	Y	Y	N	N	N
RHODE ISLAND							
1	Cicilline	Y	Y	Y	N	N	N
2	Langevin	Y	Y	Y	N	N	N
SOUTH CAROLINA							
1	Cunningham	Y	Y	Y	N	N	N
2	**Wilson, J.**	Y	Y	N	Y	Y	Y
3	**Duncan**	Y	Y	N	Y	Y	Y
4	**Timmons**	Y	Y	N	Y	Y	Y
5	**Norman**	N	Y	N	Y	Y	Y
6	Clyburn	?	?	Y	N	N	N
7	**Rice, T.**	Y	Y	N	Y	Y	Y
SOUTH DAKOTA							
AL	**Johnson**	Y	Y	N	Y	Y	Y
TENNESSEE							
1	**Roe**	Y	Y	N	Y	Y	Y
2	**Burchett**	Y	Y	N	Y	Y	Y
3	**Fleischmann**	Y	Y	N	Y	Y	N
4	**DesJarlais**	Y	Y	N	Y	Y	Y
5	Cooper	Y	Y	Y	N	N	N
6	**Rose**	Y	Y	N	Y	Y	Y
7	**Green**	Y	Y	N	Y	Y	Y
8	**Kustoff**	Y	Y	N	Y	Y	Y
9	Cohen	Y	Y	Y	N	N	N
TEXAS							
1	**Gohmert**	Y	Y	?	?	?	?
2	**Crenshaw**	Y	?	N	Y	Y	Y
3	**Taylor**	Y	Y	N	Y	Y	Y
4	**Ratcliffe**	Y	Y	N	Y	Y	Y

		397	398	399	400	401	402
5	**Gooden**	Y	Y	N	Y	Y	Y
6	**Wright**	Y	Y	?	?	?	?
7	Fletcher	Y	Y	N	N	N	N
8	**Brady**	Y	Y	N	Y	Y	Y
9	Green, A.	Y	Y	+	N	N	N
10	**McCaul**	Y	Y	N	Y	Y	N
11	**Conaway**	Y	Y	N	Y	Y	Y
12	**Granger**	Y	Y	N	Y	Y	Y
13	**Thornberry**	Y	Y	N	Y	Y	Y
14	**Weber**	Y	Y	N	Y	Y	Y
15	Gonzalez	Y	Y	Y	N	N	N
16	Escobar	Y	Y	Y	N	N	N
17	**Flores**	Y	Y	N	Y	Y	Y
18	Jackson Lee	Y	Y	Y	N	N	N
19	**Arrington**	Y	N	N	Y	Y	Y
20	Castro	Y	Y	Y	N	N	N
21	**Roy**	Y	Y	N	Y	Y	Y
22	**Olson**	Y	Y	N	Y	Y	Y
23	**Hurd**	Y	Y	?	?	?	?
24	**Marchant**	Y	Y	N	Y	Y	Y
25	**Williams**	Y	Y	N	Y	Y	Y
26	**Burgess**	Y	Y	N	Y	Y	Y
27	**Cloud**	Y	Y	N	Y	Y	Y
28	Cuellar	Y	Y	N	N	N	N
29	Garcia, S.	Y	Y	Y	N	N	N
30	Johnson, E.B.	Y	Y	?	?	?	?
31	**Carter, J.**	Y	Y	N	Y	Y	Y
32	Allred	Y	Y	N	N	N	N
33	Veasey	Y	Y	Y	N	N	N
34	Vela	Y	Y	Y	N	N	N
35	Doggett	Y	Y	Y	N	N	N
36	**Babin**	Y	Y	N	Y	Y	Y
UTAH							
1	**Bishop, R.**	Y	?	N	Y	Y	Y
2	**Stewart**	Y	Y	N	Y	Y	Y
3	**Curtis**	Y	Y	N	Y	Y	Y
4	McAdams	Y	Y	N	N	N	N
VERMONT							
AL	Welch	Y	Y	Y	N	N	N
VIRGINIA							
1	**Wittman**	Y	Y	N	Y	Y	Y
2	Luria	Y	Y	Y	N	N	N
3	Scott, R.	Y	Y	Y	N	N	N
4	McEachin	Y	Y	Y	N	N	N
5	**Riggleman**	Y	Y	N	Y	Y	Y
6	**Cline**	Y	Y	N	Y	Y	Y
7	Spanberger	Y	Y	Y	N	N	N
8	Beyer	Y	Y	Y	N	N	N
9	**Griffith**	Y	Y	N	Y	Y	Y
10	Wexton	Y	Y	Y	N	N	N
11	Connolly	Y	Y	Y	N	N	N
WASHINGTON							
1	DelBene	Y	Y	Y	N	N	N
2	Larsen	Y	Y	Y	N	N	N
3	**Herrera Beutler**	?	?	N	Y	Y	N
4	**Newhouse**	Y	Y	N	Y	Y	N
5	**McMorris Rodgers**	Y	Y	-	+	+	+
6	Kilmer	Y	Y	Y	N	N	N
7	Jayapal	Y	Y	Y	N	N	N
8	Schrier	Y	Y	Y	N	N	N
9	Smith Adam	Y	Y	Y	N	N	N
10	Heck	Y	Y	Y	N	N	N
WEST VIRGINIA							
1	**McKinley**	Y	Y	N	Y	Y	N
2	**Mooney**	Y	Y	N	Y	Y	Y
3	**Miller**	Y	Y	N	Y	Y	Y
WISCONSIN							
1	**Steil**	Y	Y	N	Y	Y	Y
2	Pocan	Y	Y	Y	N	N	N
3	Kind	Y	Y	Y	N	N	N
4	Moore	Y	Y	Y	N	N	N
5	**Sensenbrenner**	Y	Y	N	Y	Y	Y
6	**Grothman**	Y	Y	N	Y	Y	Y
7	**Duffy**	Y	Y	N	Y	Y	Y
8	**Gallagher**	Y	Y	N	Y	Y	N
WYOMING							
AL	**Cheney**	Y	Y	N	Y	Y	N
DELEGATES							
	Radewagen (A.S.)	?	?	?	?	?	?
	Norton (D.C.)	+	+	Y	N	N	N
	San Nicolas (Guam)	?	?	Y	N	N	N
	Sablan (N. Marianas)	Y	Y	Y	N	N	N
	González-Colón (P.R.)	?	?	?	?	?	?
	Plaskett (V.I.)	N	Y	Y	N	N	N

403. HR3351, HR2722. Financial Service Appropriations, Election Security - Previous Question. McGovern, D-Mass., motion to order the previous question (thus limiting debate and possibility of amendment) on the rule (H Res 460) that would provide for House floor consideration of the Fiscal 2020 Financial Services Appropriations bill (HR 3351), and the Securing America's Federal Elections (SAFE) Act (HR 2722), which includes a number of provisions related to election infrastructure improvements and cybersecurity. Motion agreed to 228-188: R 0-188; D 228-0. June 25, 2019.

404. HR3351, HR2722. Financial Service Appropriations and Election Security - Rule. Adoption of the rule (H Res 460) that would provide for House floor consideration of the Fiscal 2020 Financial Services Appropriations bill (HR 3351), and the Securing America's Federal Elections (SAFE) Act (HR 2722), which includes a number of provisions related to election infrastructure improvements and cybersecurity. Adopted 225-190: R 0-188; D 225-2; I 0-0. June 25, 2019.

405. HR3055. Fiscal 2020 Five-Bill Appropriations Package - Reduce Transportation-HUD Funding. Banks, R-Ind., amendment that would reduce by 14 percent all discretionary funding made available under the Transportation, Housing and Urban Development, and related agencies title of the bill (Division E). Rejected in Committee of the Whole 131-287: R 131-58; D 0-228; I 0-1. June 25, 2019.

406. HR3055. Fiscal 2020 Five-Bill Appropriations Package - Homeless Assistance Grants. Jayapal, D-Wash., amendment that would increase by $1 million funding for Housing and Urban Development homeless assistance grant programs and decrease by the same amount administrative funding for Housing and Urban Development Department executive offices. Adopted in Committee of the Whole 294-127: R 64-127; D 229-0; I 1-0. June 25, 2019.

407. HR3055. Fiscal 2020 Five-Bill Appropriations Package - Recommit. Hurd, R-Texas, motion to recommit the bill to the House Appropriations Committee with instructions to report it back immediately with an amendment that would increase by $75 million funding for the Justice Department immigration review office and decrease by the same amount funding for Census Bureau expenses related to collecting, analyzing, and publishing statistics for periodic censuses and programs. Motion rejected 201-220: R 193-0; D 8-220. June 25, 2019.

408. HR3055. Fiscal 2020 Five-Bill Appropriations Package - Passage. Passage of the bill, as amended, that would provide $321.9 billion in discretionary spending for five of the 12 fiscal 2020 appropriations bills, including $73.9 billion for the Commerce and Justice departments and science and related agencies, $24.3 billion for the Agriculture Department and related agencies, $39.5 billion for the Interior Department, Environmental Protection Agency, and related agencies, $108.4 billion for the Veterans Affairs Department, military construction, and related agencies, and $75.8 billion for the Transportation and Housing and Urban Development departments and related agencies. It would also provide $61 billion in obligations from highway and aviation trust funds for associated Transportation Department programs. Among other provisions, the bill would provide $673 million to the Justice Department immigration review office, including to hire additional immigration judges and to provide legal resources for individuals facing deportation proceedings. It would provide $5.2 billion for Interior Department and the U.S. Forest Service wildfire preparedness and response activities and $9.5 billion for the Environmental Protection Agency, including increased funding for enforcement and compliance activities, clean air activities, and environmental restoration initiatives. It would provide $81.2 billion for VA health care programs and $2.3 billion in emergency military construction funding for bases damaged by natural disasters. It would prohibit the use of funds made available by the bill for the Census Bureau to include a question regarding citizenship on the 2020 census or for the construction of physical barriers or border security infrastructure along the U.S. southern land border. Passed 227-194: R 0-193; D 227-1. *Note: A "nay" was a vote in support of the president's position.* June 25, 2019.

	403	404	405	406	407	408
ALABAMA						
1 Byrne	N	N	Y	N	Y	N
2 Roby	N	N	Y	Y	Y	N
3 Rogers, M.	N	N	Y	Y	Y	N
4 Aderholt	N	N	N	N	Y	N
5 Brooks, M.	N	N	Y	N	Y	N
6 Palmer	N	N	N	N	Y	N
7 Sewell	Y	Y	N	Y	N	Y
ALASKA						
AL Young	N	N	N	Y	Y	N
ARIZONA						
1 O'Halleran	Y	Y	N	Y	N	Y
2 Kirkpatrick	Y	Y	N	Y	N	Y
3 Grijalva	Y	Y	N	Y	N	Y
4 Gosar	N	N	Y	N	Y	N
5 Biggs	?	?	?	?	Y	Y
6 Schweikert	N	N	Y	N	Y	N
7 Gallego	Y	Y	N	Y	N	Y
8 Lesko	N	N	Y	N	Y	N
9 Stanton	Y	Y	N	Y	N	Y
ARKANSAS						
1 Crawford	N	N	Y	N	Y	N
2 Hill, F.	N	N	Y	Y	Y	N
3 Womack	N	N	N	N	Y	N
4 Westerman	N	N	Y	N	Y	N
CALIFORNIA						
1 LaMalfa	N	N	Y	N	Y	N
2 Huffman	Y	Y	N	Y	N	Y
3 Garamendi	Y	N	N	Y	N	Y
4 McClintock	N	N	Y	N	Y	N
5 Thompson, M.	Y	Y	N	Y	N	Y
6 Matsui	Y	Y	N	Y	N	Y
7 Bera	Y	Y	N	Y	N	Y
8 Cook	N	N	Y	Y	Y	N
9 McNerney	Y	Y	N	Y	N	Y
10 Harder	Y	Y	N	Y	N	Y
11 DeSaulnier	Y	Y	N	Y	N	Y
12 Pelosi						
13 Lee B.	Y	Y	N	Y	N	Y
14 Speier	Y	Y	N	Y	N	Y
15 Swalwell	+	+	-	+	-	+
16 Costa	Y	Y	N	Y	N	Y
17 Khanna	Y	Y	N	Y	N	Y
18 Eshoo	Y	Y	N	Y	N	Y
19 Lofgren	Y	Y	N	Y	N	Y
20 Panetta	Y	Y	N	Y	N	Y
21 Cox	Y	Y	N	Y	N	Y
22 Nunes	N	N	Y	N	Y	N
23 McCarthy	N	N	N	N	Y	N
24 Carbajal	Y	Y	N	Y	N	Y
25 Hill, K.	Y	Y	N	Y	N	Y
26 Brownley	Y	Y	N	Y	N	Y
27 Chu	Y	Y	N	Y	N	Y
28 Schiff	Y	Y	N	Y	N	Y
29 Cárdenas	Y	Y	N	Y	N	Y
30 Sherman	Y	Y	N	Y	N	Y
31 Aguilar	Y	Y	N	Y	N	Y
32 Napolitano	Y	Y	N	Y	N	Y
33 Lieu	Y	Y	N	Y	N	Y
34 Gomez	Y	Y	N	Y	N	Y
35 Torres	Y	Y	N	Y	N	Y
36 Ruiz	Y	Y	N	Y	N	Y
37 Bass	Y	Y	?	Y	N	Y
38 Sánchez	Y	Y	N	Y	N	Y
39 Cisneros	Y	Y	N	Y	N	Y
40 Roybal-Allard	Y	Y	N	Y	N	Y
41 Takano	Y	Y	-	Y	N	Y
42 Calvert	N	N	N	Y	Y	N
43 Waters	Y	Y	N	Y	N	Y
44 Barragán	Y	Y	N	Y	N	Y
45 Porter	Y	Y	N	Y	Y	Y
46 Correa	Y	Y	N	Y	N	Y
47 Lowenthal	Y	Y	N	Y	N	Y
48 Rouda	Y	Y	N	Y	N	Y
49 Levin	Y	Y	N	Y	N	Y
50 Hunter	N	N	Y	N	Y	N
51 Vargas	Y	Y	N	Y	N	Y
52 Peters	Y	Y	N	Y	N	Y

	403	404	405	406	407	408
53 Davis, S.	Y	Y	N	Y	N	Y
COLORADO						
1 DeGette	Y	Y	N	Y	N	Y
2 Neguse	Y	Y	N	Y	N	Y
3 Tipton	N	N	Y	N	Y	N
4 Buck	N	N	Y	N	Y	N
5 Lamborn	N	N	Y	N	Y	N
6 Crow	Y	Y	N	Y	N	Y
7 Perlmutter	Y	Y	N	Y	N	Y
CONNECTICUT						
1 Larson	Y	Y	N	Y	N	Y
2 Courtney	Y	Y	N	Y	N	Y
3 DeLauro	Y	Y	N	Y	N	Y
4 Himes	Y	Y	N	Y	N	Y
5 Hayes	Y	Y	N	Y	N	Y
DELAWARE						
AL Blunt Rochester	Y	Y	N	Y	N	Y
FLORIDA						
1 Gaetz	N	N	Y	N	Y	N
2 Dunn	N	N	Y	N	Y	N
3 Yoho	N	N	Y	N	Y	N
4 Rutherford	N	N	N	N	Y	N
5 Lawson	Y	Y	N	Y	N	Y
6 Waltz	N	N	Y	N	Y	N
7 Murphy	Y	Y	N	Y	N	Y
8 Posey	N	N	Y	N	Y	N
9 Soto	Y	Y	N	Y	N	Y
10 Demings	Y	Y	N	Y	N	Y
11 Webster	N	N	N	N	Y	N
12 Bilirakis	N	N	N	N	Y	N
13 Crist	Y	Y	N	Y	N	Y
14 Castor	Y	Y	N	Y	N	Y
15 Spano	N	N	Y	N	Y	N
16 Buchanan	N	N	N	N	Y	N
17 Steube	N	N	Y	N	Y	N
18 Mast	N	N	N	Y	Y	N
19 Rooney	?	?	?	?	?	?
20 Hastings	Y	Y	N	Y	N	Y
21 Frankel	Y	Y	N	Y	N	Y
22 Deutch	Y	Y	N	Y	N	Y
23 Wasserman Schultz	Y	Y	N	Y	N	Y
24 Wilson, F.	Y	Y	N	Y	N	Y
25 Diaz-Balart	N	N	N	Y	Y	N
26 Mucarsel-Powell	Y	Y	N	Y	N	Y
27 Shalala	Y	Y	N	Y	N	Y
GEORGIA						
1 Carter, E.L.	N	N	Y	N	Y	N
2 Bishop, S.	Y	Y	N	Y	N	Y
3 Ferguson	N	N	Y	N	Y	N
4 Johnson, H.	Y	Y	N	Y	N	Y
5 Lewis John	Y	Y	N	Y	N	Y
6 McBath	Y	Y	N	Y	N	Y
7 Woodall	N	N	Y	N	Y	N
8 Scott, A.	N	N	Y	N	Y	N
9 Collins, D.	N	N	Y	N	Y	N
10 Hice	-	-	+	-	Y	N
11 Loudermilk	N	N	Y	N	Y	N
12 Allen	N	N	Y	N	Y	N
13 Scott, D.	Y	Y	N	Y	N	Y
14 Graves, T.	N	N	Y	N	Y	N
HAWAII						
1 Case	Y	Y	N	Y	N	Y
2 Gabbard	?	?	?	?	?	?
IDAHO						
1 Fulcher	N	N	Y	N	Y	N
2 Simpson	N	N	N	N	Y	N
ILLINOIS						
1 Rush	Y	Y	N	Y	N	Y
2 Kelly, R.	Y	Y	N	Y	N	Y
3 Lipinski	Y	Y	N	Y	N	Y
4 García, J.	Y	Y	N	Y	N	Y
5 Quigley	Y	Y	N	Y	N	Y
6 Casten	Y	Y	N	Y	N	Y
7 Davis, D.	Y	Y	N	Y	N	Y
8 Krishnamoorthi	Y	Y	N	Y	N	Y
9 Schakowsky	Y	Y	N	Y	N	Y
10 Schneider	Y	Y	N	Y	N	Y
11 Foster	Y	Y	N	Y	N	Y

KEY: **Republicans**   Democrats   *Independents*

Y Voted for (yea)	**N** Voted against (nay)	**P** Voted "present"
+ Announced for	**-** Announced against	**?** Did not vote or otherwise
# Paired for	**X** Paired against	make position known

		403	404	405	406	407	408
12	**Bost**	N	N	N	N	Y	N
13	**Davis, R.**	N	N	N	Y	Y	N
14	Underwood	Y	Y	N	Y	N	Y
15	**Shimkus**	N	N	Y	Y	Y	N
16	**Kinzinger**	N	N	N	Y	Y	N
17	Bustos	Y	Y	N	Y	N	Y
18	**LaHood**	N	N	Y	Y	Y	N
INDIANA							
1	Visclosky	Y	Y	N	Y	N	Y
2	**Walorski**	N	N	Y	Y	Y	N
3	**Banks**	N	N	Y	Y	Y	N
4	**Baird**	N	N	N	N	Y	N
5	**Brooks, S.**	N	N	Y	N	Y	N
6	**Pence**	N	N	N	N	Y	N
7	Carson	Y	Y	N	Y	N	Y
8	**Bucshon**	N	N	Y	N	Y	N
9	**Hollingsworth**	N	N	N	Y	Y	N
IOWA							
1	Finkenauer	Y	Y	N	Y	N	Y
2	Loebsack	Y	Y	N	Y	N	Y
3	Axne	Y	Y	N	Y	N	Y
4	**King, S.**	N	N	Y	N	Y	N
KANSAS							
1	**Marshall**	N	N	Y	Y	Y	N
2	**Watkins**	N	N	Y	N	Y	N
3	Davids	Y	Y	N	Y	N	Y
4	**Estes**	N	N	Y	N	Y	N
KENTUCKY							
1	**Comer**	N	N	Y	N	Y	N
2	**Guthrie**	N	N	Y	N	Y	N
3	Yarmuth	Y	Y	N	Y	N	Y
4	**Massie**	N	N	Y	N	Y	N
5	**Rogers, H.**	N	N	N	Y	Y	N
6	**Barr**	N	N	Y	N	Y	N
LOUISIANA							
1	**Scalise**	N	N	Y	N	Y	N
2	Richmond	Y	Y	N	Y	N	Y
3	**Higgins, C.**	N	N	Y	N	Y	N
4	**Johnson, M.**	N	N	Y	N	Y	N
5	**Abraham**	?	?	?	?	?	?
6	**Graves, G.**	N	N	N	N	Y	N
MAINE							
1	Pingree	Y	Y	N	Y	N	Y
2	Golden	Y	Y	N	Y	Y	Y
MARYLAND							
1	**Harris**	N	N	Y	N	Y	N
2	Ruppersberger	Y	Y	N	Y	N	Y
3	Sarbanes	Y	Y	N	Y	N	Y
4	Brown, A.	Y	Y	N	Y	N	Y
5	Hoyer	Y	Y	N	Y	N	Y
6	Trone	Y	Y	N	Y	N	Y
7	Cummings	Y	Y	N	Y	N	Y
8	Raskin						
MASSACHUSETTS		Y	Y	N	Y	N	Y
1	Neal						
2	McGovern	Y	Y	N	Y	N	Y
3	Trahan	Y	Y	N	Y	N	Y
4	Kennedy	Y	Y	N	Y	N	Y
5	Clark	Y	Y	N	Y	N	Y
6	Moulton	Y	Y	N	Y	N	Y
7	Pressley	?	?	?	?	?	?
8	Lynch	Y	Y	N	Y	N	Y
9	Keating	Y	Y	N	Y	N	Y
MICHIGAN		Y	Y	N	Y	N	Y
1	**Bergman**						
2	**Huizenga**	N	N	Y	Y	Y	N
3	**Amash**	N	N	Y	N	Y	N
4	**Moolenaar**	N	N	Y	N	Y	N
5	Kildee	N	N	Y	Y	Y	N
6	**Upton**	Y	Y	N	Y	N	Y
7	**Walberg**	N	N	N	Y	Y	N
8	Slotkin	N	N	Y	N	Y	N
9	Levin	Y	Y	N	Y	Y	Y
10	**Mitchell**	Y	Y	N	Y	N	Y
11	Stevens	N	N	Y	Y	Y	N
12	Dingell	Y	Y	N	Y	N	Y
13	Tlaib	Y	Y	N	Y	N	Y
14	Lawrence	Y	Y	N	Y	N	Y
MINNESOTA		Y	Y	N	Y	N	Y
1	**Hagedorn**						
2	Craig	N	N	N	N	Y	N
3	Phillips	Y	Y	N	Y	N	Y
4	McCollum	Y	Y	N	Y	N	Y
5	Omar	Y	Y	N	Y	N	Y
6	**Emmer**	Y	Y	N	Y	N	Y
7	Peterson	N	N	Y	N	Y	N
8	**Stauber**	Y	Y	N	Y	N	Y
MISSISSIPPI		N	N	N	Y	Y	N
1	**Kelly, T.**						
2	Thompson, B.	N	N	Y	N	Y	N
3	**Guest**	Y	Y	N	Y	N	Y
4	**Palazzo**	N	N	Y	N	Y	N
MISSOURI		N	N	Y	N	Y	N
1	Clay						
2	**Wagner**	Y	Y	N	Y	N	Y
3	**Luetkemeyer**	N	N	Y	Y	Y	N
4	**Hartzler**	N	N	N	N	Y	N
5	Cleaver	N	N	N	N	Y	N
6	**Graves, S.**	Y	Y	N	Y	N	Y
7	**Long**	N	N	N	N	Y	N
8	**Smith, J.**	N	N	Y	Y	Y	N
MONTANA		N	N	Y	N	Y	N
AL	**Gianforte**						
NEBRASKA		N	N	N	Y	Y	N
1	**Fortenberry**						
2	**Bacon**	N	N	N	Y	Y	N
3	**Smith, Adrian**	N	N	Y	Y	Y	N
NEVADA		N	N	Y	N	Y	N
1	Titus						
2	**Amodei**	Y	Y	N	Y	N	Y
3	Lee	N	N	N	Y	Y	N
4	Horsford	Y	Y	N	Y	N	Y
NEW HAMPSHIRE		Y	Y	N	Y	N	Y
1	Pappas						
2	Kuster	Y	Y	N	Y	N	Y
NEW JERSEY		Y	Y	N	Y	N	Y
1	Norcross						
2	Van Drew	Y	Y	N	Y	N	Y
3	Kim	Y	Y	N	Y	Y	Y
4	**Smith, C.**	Y	Y	N	Y	N	Y
5	Gottheimer	N	N	N	Y	Y	N
6	Pallone	Y	Y	N	Y	Y	Y
7	Malinowski	Y	Y	N	Y	N	Y
8	Sires	Y	Y	N	Y	N	Y
9	Pascrell	Y	Y	N	Y	N	Y
10	Payne	Y	Y	N	Y	N	Y
11	Sherrill	Y	Y	N	Y	N	Y
12	Watson Coleman	Y	Y	N	Y	N	Y
NEW MEXICO		Y	Y	N	Y	N	Y
1	Haaland						
2	Torres Small	Y	Y	N	Y	N	Y
3	Luján	Y	Y	N	Y	Y	Y
NEW YORK		Y	Y	N	Y	N	Y
1	**Zeldin**						
2	**King, P.**	N	N	N	Y	Y	N
3	Suozzi	N	N	N	Y	Y	N
4	Rice, K.	Y	Y	N	Y	N	Y
5	Meeks	Y	Y	N	Y	N	Y
6	Meng	?	?	?	?	?	?
7	Velázquez	Y	Y	N	Y	N	Y
8	Jeffries	Y	Y	N	Y	N	Y
9	Clarke	Y	Y	N	Y	N	Y
10	Nadler	Y	Y	N	Y	N	Y
11	Rose	Y	Y	N	Y	N	Y
12	Maloney, C.	Y	Y	N	Y	N	Y
13	Espaillat	Y	Y	N	Y	N	Y
14	Ocasio-Cortez	Y	Y	N	+	N	Y
15	Serrano	Y	Y	N	Y	N	Y
16	Engel	Y	Y	N	Y	N	Y
17	Lowey	Y	Y	N	Y	N	Y
18	Maloney, S.P.	Y	Y	N	Y	N	Y
19	Delgado	Y	Y	N	Y	N	Y
20	Tonko	Y	Y	N	Y	N	Y
21	**Stefanik**	Y	+	N	Y	N	Y
22	Brindisi	N	N	N	Y	Y	N
23	**Reed**	Y	Y	N	Y	N	Y
24	**Katko**	N	N	N	Y	Y	N
25	Morelle	N	N	N	Y	Y	N
26	Higgins, B.	Y	Y	N	Y	N	Y
27	**Collins, C.**	Y	Y	N	Y	N	Y
NORTH CAROLINA		N	N	N	Y	Y	N
1	Butterfield						
2	**Holding**	Y	Y	N	Y	N	Y
3	**Jones***	N	N	Y	N	Y	N
4	Price						
5	**Foxx**	Y	Y	N	Y	N	Y
6	**Walker**	N	N	Y	N	Y	N
7	**Rouzer**	N	N	Y	N	Y	N
8	**Hudson**	N	N	Y	N	Y	N
9	vacant	N	N	Y	Y	Y	N
10	**McHenry**	N	N	Y	Y	Y	N
11	**Meadows**	?	?	?	N	Y	N
12	Adams	Y	Y	N	Y	N	Y
13	**Budd**	N	N	Y	N	Y	N
NORTH DAKOTA							
AL	**Armstrong**	N	N	N	N	Y	N
OHIO							
1	**Chabot**	N	N	Y	N	Y	N
2	**Wenstrup**	N	N	Y	Y	Y	N
3	Beatty	Y	Y	N	Y	N	Y
4	**Jordan**	N	N	Y	N	Y	N
5	**Latta**	N	N	Y	N	Y	N
6	**Johnson, B.**	N	N	Y	N	Y	N
7	**Gibbs**	N	N	Y	Y	Y	N
8	**Davidson**	N	N	Y	N	Y	N
9	Kaptur	Y	Y	N	Y	N	Y
10	**Turner**	N	N	N	Y	Y	N
11	Fudge	Y	Y	N	Y	N	Y
12	**Balderson**	N	N	Y	Y	Y	N
13	Ryan	?	?	?	?	?	?
14	**Joyce**	N	N	N	N	Y	N
15	**Stivers**	N	N	N	Y	Y	N
16	**Gonzalez**	N	N	N	N	Y	N
OKLAHOMA							
1	**Hern**	N	N	Y	N	Y	N
2	**Mullin**	N	N	Y	N	Y	N
3	**Lucas**	?	?	?	?	?	?
4	**Cole**	N	N	N	N	Y	N
5	Horn	Y	Y	N	Y	N	Y
OREGON							
1	Bonamici	Y	Y	N	Y	N	Y
2	**Walden**	N	N	N	Y	Y	N
3	Blumenauer	Y	Y	N	Y	N	Y
4	DeFazio	Y	Y	N	Y	N	Y
5	Schrader	Y	Y	N	Y	N	Y
PENNSYLVANIA							
1	**Fitzpatrick**	N	N	N	Y	Y	N
2	Boyle	Y	Y	N	Y	N	Y
3	Evans	Y	Y	N	Y	N	Y
4	Dean	Y	Y	N	Y	N	Y
5	Scanlon	Y	Y	N	Y	N	Y
6	Houlahan	Y	Y	N	Y	N	Y
7	Wild	Y	Y	N	Y	N	Y
8	Cartwright	Y	Y	N	Y	N	Y
9	**Meuser**	N	N	Y	N	Y	N
10	**Perry**	N	N	Y	N	Y	N
11	**Smucker**	N	N	Y	Y	Y	N
12	**Marino***						
13	**Joyce**	N	N	Y	N	Y	N
14	**Reschenthaler**	N	N	N	N	Y	N
15	**Thompson, G.**	N	N	N	Y	Y	N
16	**Kelly, M.**	N	N	Y	N	Y	N
17	Lamb	Y	Y	N	Y	N	Y
18	Doyle	Y	Y	N	Y	N	Y
RHODE ISLAND							
1	Cicilline	Y	Y	N	Y	N	Y
2	Langevin	Y	Y	N	Y	N	Y
SOUTH CAROLINA							
1	Cunningham	Y	Y	N	Y	N	Y
2	**Wilson, J.**	N	N	N	Y	Y	N
3	**Duncan**	N	N	Y	N	Y	N
4	**Timmons**	N	N	Y	N	Y	N
5	**Norman**	N	N	Y	N	Y	N
6	Clyburn	+	+	-	+	-	+
7	**Rice, T.**	N	N	Y	N	Y	N
SOUTH DAKOTA							
AL	**Johnson**	N	N	Y	N	Y	N
TENNESSEE							
1	**Roe**	N	N	Y	Y	Y	N
2	**Burchett**	N	N	Y	N	Y	N
3	**Fleischmann**	N	N	N	N	Y	N
4	**DesJarlais**	N	N	Y	Y	Y	N
5	Cooper	Y	Y	N	Y	N	Y
6	**Rose**	N	N	Y	N	Y	N
7	**Green**	N	N	Y	N	Y	N
8	**Kustoff**	N	N	Y	N	Y	N
9	Cohen	Y	Y	N	Y	N	Y
TEXAS							
1	**Gohmert**	?	?	?	N	Y	N
2	**Crenshaw**	N	N	N	Y	Y	N
3	**Taylor**	N	N	Y	N	Y	N
4	**Ratcliffe**	N	N	Y	N	Y	N
5	**Gooden**	N	N	Y	N	Y	N
6	**Wright**	N	N	Y	N	Y	N
7	Fletcher	Y	Y	N	Y	N	Y
8	**Brady**	N	N	Y	N	Y	N
9	Green, A.	Y	Y	N	Y	N	Y
10	**McCaul**	N	N	Y	N	Y	N
11	**Conaway**	N	N	Y	N	Y	N
12	**Granger**	N	N	Y	N	Y	N
13	**Thornberry**	-	-	+	-	+	-
14	**Weber**	N	N	Y	N	Y	N
15	Gonzalez	Y	Y	N	Y	N	Y
16	Escobar	Y	Y	N	Y	N	Y
17	**Flores**	N	N	Y	N	Y	N
18	Jackson Lee	Y	Y	N	Y	N	Y
19	**Arrington**	N	N	Y	N	Y	N
20	Castro	Y	Y	N	Y	N	Y
21	**Roy**	-	-	+	-	Y	N
22	**Olson**	N	N	Y	N	Y	N
23	**Hurd**	N	N	N	N	Y	N
24	**Marchant**	N	N	Y	N	Y	N
25	**Williams**	N	N	Y	N	Y	N
26	**Burgess**	N	N	Y	N	Y	N
27	**Cloud**	-	-	?	-	Y	N
28	Cuellar	Y	Y	N	Y	N	Y
29	Garcia, S.	Y	Y	N	Y	N	Y
30	Johnson, E.B.	Y	Y	N	Y	N	Y
31	**Carter, J.**	N	N	Y	N	Y	N
32	Allred	Y	Y	N	Y	N	Y
33	Veasey	Y	Y	N	Y	N	Y
34	Vela	Y	Y	N	Y	N	Y
35	Doggett	Y	Y	N	Y	N	Y
36	**Babin**	N	N	Y	N	Y	N
UTAH							
1	**Bishop, R.**	N	N	Y	N	Y	N
2	**Stewart**	N	N	Y	N	Y	N
3	**Curtis**	N	N	Y	N	Y	N
4	McAdams	Y	N	N	Y	N	N
VERMONT							
AL	Welch	Y	Y	N	Y	N	Y
VIRGINIA							
1	**Wittman**	N	N	Y	N	Y	N
2	Luria	Y	Y	N	Y	Y	Y
3	Scott, R.	Y	Y	N	Y	N	Y
4	McEachin	Y	Y	N	Y	N	Y
5	**Riggleman**	N	N	Y	Y	Y	N
6	**Cline**	N	N	Y	N	Y	N
7	Spanberger	Y	Y	N	Y	Y	Y
8	Beyer	Y	Y	N	Y	N	Y
9	**Griffith**	N	N	Y	N	Y	N
10	Wexton	Y	Y	N	Y	N	Y
11	Connolly	Y	Y	N	Y	N	Y
WASHINGTON							
1	DelBene	Y	Y	N	Y	N	Y
2	Larsen	Y	Y	N	Y	N	Y
3	**Herrera Beutler**	N	N	Y	Y	Y	N
4	**Newhouse**	N	N	N	Y	Y	N
5	**McMorris Rodgers**	N	N	Y	Y	Y	N
6	Kilmer	Y	Y	N	Y	N	Y
7	Jayapal	Y	Y	N	Y	N	Y
8	Schrier	Y	Y	N	Y	N	Y
9	Smith Adam	Y	Y	N	Y	N	Y
10	Heck	Y	Y	N	Y	N	Y
WEST VIRGINIA							
1	**McKinley**	N	N	N	Y	Y	N
2	**Mooney**	N	N	Y	Y	Y	N
3	**Miller**	N	N	Y	Y	Y	N
WISCONSIN							
1	**Steil**	N	N	Y	Y	Y	N
2	Pocan	Y	Y	N	Y	N	Y
3	Kind	Y	Y	N	Y	N	Y
4	Moore	Y	Y	N	Y	N	Y
5	**Sensenbrenner**	N	N	Y	N	Y	N
6	**Grothman**	N	N	Y	N	Y	N
7	**Duffy**	N	N	N	Y	Y	N
8	**Gallagher**	N	N	N	Y	Y	N
WYOMING							
AL	**Cheney**	N	N	N	N	?	?
DELEGATES							
	Radewagen (A.S.)			N	N		
	Norton (D.C.)			N	Y		
	San Nicolas (Guam)			?	?		
	Sablan (N. Marianas)			N	Y		
	González-Colón (P.R.)			?	?		
	Plaskett (V.I.)			N	Y		

409. HR3401. Supplemental Border Appropriations - Previous Question. McGovern, D-Mass., motion to order the previous question (thus ending debate and possibility of amendment) on the rule that would provide for House floor consideration of the Emergency Supplemental Appropriations for Humanitarian Assistance and Security at the Southern Border Act (HR 3401), which would provide $4.5 billion in supplemental fiscal 2019 appropriations to address humanitarian concerns at the U.S.-Mexico border. Motion agreed to 226-188: R 0-188; D 226-0. June 25, 2019.

410. HR3401. Supplemental Border Appropriations - Rule. Adoption of the rule (H Res 462) that would provide for House floor consideration of the Emergency Supplemental Appropriations for Humanitarian Assistance and Security at the Southern Border Act (HR 3401), which would provide $4.5 billion in supplemental fiscal 2019 appropriations to address humanitarian concerns at the U.S.-Mexico border. The rule would provide for automatic adoption of a Lowey, D-N.Y., manager's amendment to HR 3401 that would increase from $15 million to $17 million funding provided by the bill for the Justice Department immigration review office and specify that at least $2 million would be used for operation of the immigration court helpdesk program. It would require the Homeland Security Department to establish final plans, standards, and protocols regarding individuals in U.S. Customs and Border Protection custody, including medical, nutrition, and sanitation standards for temporary holding facilities. It would also make a number of requirements related to standards for grantees and contractors providing services to individuals in HHS custody, translation services for DHS customs, immigration, and other services, and the maximum time an unaccompanied minor may be held at a facility not licensed by HHS. Adopted 225-189: R 0-189; D 225-0. June 25, 2019.

411. HR3351. Fiscal 2020 Financial Services Appropriations - Border Barrier Construction. King, R-Iowa, amendment that would strike from the bill a provision that would prohibit the use of funds from a Treasury Department forfeiture fund to plan or construct a wall, barrier, fence, or road along the U.S. southern border. The fund is sourced from Treasury and Homeland Security Department forfeitures and seizures and used for related law enforcement activities. Rejected in Committee of the Whole 191-226: R 186-4; D 5-222. June 25, 2019.

412. HR3351. Fiscal 2020 Financial Services Appropriations - Research Agency Relocation. Norton, D-D.C., amendment that would prohibit the use of funds made available by the bill to relocate the National Institute of Food and Agriculture or the Economic Research Service outside of the national capital region. Adopted in Committee of the Whole 226-198: R 5-189; D 221-9. June 25, 2019.

413. HR3401. Supplemental Border Appropriations - Recommit. Rutherford, R-Fla., motion to recommit the bill to the House Appropriations Committee with instructions to report it back immediately with an amendment that would increase by $64.6 million funding for Immigration and Customs Enforcement expenses related to increased immigration at the U.S. southwest border. Motion rejected 205-218: R 192-1; D 13-217. June 25, 2019.

414. HR3401. Supplemental Border Appropriations - Passage. Passage of the bill, as amended, that would provide $4.5 billion in supplemental fiscal 2019 appropriations to address humanitarian concerns for migrants at the U.S.-Mexico border. Specifically, it would provide $2.9 billion for the Health and Human Services Department office of refugee resettlement, including $866 million for the provision of care in state-licensed shelters and expansion of the number of licensed shelters and $100 million for post-release, legal, and child advocacy services. It would provide $1.2 billion for U.S. Customs and Border Protection, including $787.5 million for acquisition, construction, and operation of migrant processing facilities, $92 million for food, water, sanitary items, and other supplies for migrants, and $20 million for medical support. It would provide $128.2 million for U.S. Immigration and Customs Enforcement, including $45 million for detainee medical care and $35.9 million for the transportation of unaccompanied minors to HHS custody. It would also provide $60 million for Federal Emergency Management Agency emergency food and shelter programs providing assistance to migrants released from DHS custody, $17 million for the Justice Department immigration review office legal orientation program, and $155 million to the U.S. Marshals Service for federal prisoner detention. Among other requirements related to facilities, resources, and services provided by DHS and HHS, the bill would require DHS to establish standards and protocols related to medical, nutrition, and sanitation needs of migrants in CBP temporary holding facilities. It would establish contracting standards for unlicensed facilities used as "influx shelters" by HHS, limit the period unaccompanied minors may be held at such facilities, and require HHS to ensure that certain minors are not held at such facilities, including those with special medical needs. Passed 230-195: R 3-191; D 227-4. *Note: A "nay" was a vote in support of the president's position.* June 25, 2019.

	409	410	411	412	413	414
ALABAMA						
1 Byrne	N	N	Y	N	Y	N
2 Roby	N	N	Y	N	Y	N
3 Rogers, M.	N	N	Y	N	Y	N
4 Aderholt	N	N	Y	N	Y	N
5 Brooks, M.	N	N	Y	N	Y	N
6 Palmer	N	N	Y	N	Y	N
7 Sewell	Y	Y	N	Y	N	Y
ALASKA						
AL Young	N	N	Y	Y	Y	N
ARIZONA						
1 O'Halleran	Y	Y	N	Y	N	Y
2 Kirkpatrick	Y	Y	N	Y	N	Y
3 Grijalva	Y	Y	N	Y	N	Y
4 Gosar	N	N	Y	N	Y	N
5 Biggs	N	N	Y	N	Y	N
6 Schweikert	N	N	Y	N	Y	N
7 Gallego	Y	Y	N	Y	N	Y
8 Lesko	N	N	Y	N	Y	N
9 Stanton	Y	Y	N	Y	N	Y
ARKANSAS						
1 Crawford	N	N	Y	N	Y	N
2 Hill, F.	N	N	Y	N	Y	N
3 Womack	N	N	Y	N	Y	N
4 Westerman	N	N	Y	N	Y	N
CALIFORNIA						
1 LaMalfa	N	N	Y	N	?	N
2 Huffman	Y	Y	N	Y	N	Y
3 Garamendi	Y	Y	N	Y	N	Y
4 McClintock	N	N	Y	N	Y	N
5 Thompson, M.	Y	Y	N	Y	N	Y
6 Matsui	Y	Y	N	Y	N	Y
7 Bera	Y	Y	N	Y	N	Y
8 Cook	N	N	Y	N	Y	N
9 McNerney	Y	Y	N	Y	N	Y
10 Harder	Y	Y	N	Y	N	Y
11 DeSaulnier	Y	Y	N	Y	N	Y
12 Pelosi						Y
13 Lee B.	Y	Y	N	Y	N	Y
14 Speier	Y	Y	N	Y	N	Y
15 Swalwell	+	+	-	+	-	+
16 Costa	Y	Y	N	Y	N	Y
17 Khanna	Y	Y	N	Y	N	Y
18 Eshoo	Y	Y	N	Y	N	Y
19 Lofgren	Y	Y	N	Y	N	Y
20 Panetta	Y	Y	N	Y	N	Y
21 Cox	Y	Y	N	Y	N	Y
22 Nunes	N	N	Y	N	Y	N
23 McCarthy	N	N	Y	N	Y	N
24 Carbajal	Y	Y	N	Y	N	Y
25 Hill, K.	Y	Y	N	Y	N	Y
26 Brownley	Y	Y	N	Y	N	Y
27 Chu	Y	Y	N	Y	N	Y
28 Schiff	Y	Y	N	Y	N	Y
29 Cárdenas	Y	Y	?	?	N	Y
30 Sherman	Y	Y	N	Y	N	Y
31 Aguilar	Y	Y	N	Y	N	Y
32 Napolitano	Y	Y	N	Y	N	Y
33 Lieu	Y	?	N	Y	N	Y
34 Gomez	Y	Y	N	Y	N	Y
35 Torres	Y	Y	N	Y	N	Y
36 Ruiz	Y	Y	N	Y	N	Y
37 Bass	Y	Y	N	Y	N	Y
38 Sánchez	Y	Y	N	Y	N	Y
39 Cisneros	Y	Y	N	Y	N	Y
40 Roybal-Allard	Y	Y	N	Y	N	Y
41 Takano	Y	Y	N	Y	N	Y
42 Calvert	N	N	Y	N	Y	N
43 Waters	Y	Y	N	Y	N	Y
44 Barragán	Y	Y	N	Y	N	Y
45 Porter	Y	Y	N	Y	N	Y
46 Correa	Y	Y	N	Y	N	Y
47 Lowenthal	Y	Y	N	Y	N	Y
48 Rouda	Y	Y	N	Y	N	Y
49 Levin	Y	Y	N	Y	N	Y
50 Hunter	N	N	Y	N	Y	N
51 Vargas	Y	Y	N	Y	N	Y
52 Peters	Y	Y	?	Y	N	Y

	409	410	411	412	413	414
53 Davis, S.	Y	Y	N	Y	N	Y
COLORADO						
1 DeGette	Y	Y	N	Y	N	Y
2 Neguse	Y	Y	N	Y	N	Y
3 Tipton	N	N	Y	N	Y	N
4 Buck	N	N	Y	N	Y	N
5 Lamborn	?	?	Y	N	Y	N
6 Crow	Y	Y	N	Y	N	Y
7 Perlmutter	Y	Y	N	Y	N	Y
CONNECTICUT						
1 Larson	Y	Y	N	Y	N	Y
2 Courtney	Y	Y	N	Y	N	Y
3 DeLauro	Y	Y	N	Y	N	Y
4 Himes	Y	Y	N	N	N	Y
5 Hayes	Y	Y	N	Y	N	Y
DELAWARE						
AL Blunt Rochester	Y	Y	N	Y	N	Y
FLORIDA						
1 Gaetz	N	N	Y	N	Y	N
2 Dunn	N	N	Y	N	Y	N
3 Yoho	N	N	+	N	Y	N
4 Rutherford	N	N	Y	N	Y	N
5 Lawson	Y	Y	N	Y	N	Y
6 Waltz	N	N	Y	N	Y	N
7 Murphy	Y	Y	N	Y	N	Y
8 Posey	N	N	Y	N	Y	N
9 Soto	Y	Y	N	Y	N	Y
10 Demings	Y	Y	N	Y	N	Y
11 Webster	N	N	Y	N	Y	N
12 Bilirakis	N	N	Y	N	Y	N
13 Crist	Y	Y	N	Y	N	Y
14 Castor	Y	Y	N	Y	N	Y
15 Spano	N	N	Y	N	Y	N
16 Buchanan	N	N	Y	N	Y	N
17 Steube	N	N	Y	N	Y	N
18 Mast	N	N	Y	N	Y	N
19 Rooney	?	?	?	?	?	?
20 Hastings	Y	Y	N	Y	N	Y
21 Frankel	Y	Y	N	Y	N	Y
22 Deutch	Y	Y	N	Y	N	Y
23 Wasserman Schultz	Y	Y	N	Y	N	Y
24 Wilson, F.	Y	Y	N	Y	N	Y
25 Diaz-Balart	N	N	Y	N	Y	N
26 Mucarsel-Powell	Y	Y	N	Y	N	Y
27 Shalala	Y	Y	N	Y	N	Y
GEORGIA						
1 Carter, E.L.	N	N	Y	N	Y	N
2 Bishop, S.	Y	Y	N	Y	N	Y
3 Ferguson	N	N	Y	N	Y	N
4 Johnson, H.	Y	Y	N	Y	N	Y
5 Lewis John	Y	Y	N	Y	Y	Y
6 McBath	Y	Y	N	Y	N	Y
7 Woodall	N	N	Y	N	Y	N
8 Scott, A.	N	N	Y	N	Y	N
9 Collins, D.	N	N	Y	N	Y	N
10 Hice	N	N	Y	N	Y	N
11 Loudermilk	N	N	Y	N	Y	N
12 Allen	N	N	Y	N	Y	N
13 Scott, D.	Y	Y	N	Y	N	Y
14 Graves, T.	N	N	Y	N	Y	N
HAWAII						
1 Case	Y	Y	N	Y	N	Y
2 Gabbard	?	?	?	?	?	?
IDAHO						
1 Fulcher	N	N	Y	N	Y	N
2 Simpson	N	N	Y	N	Y	N
ILLINOIS						
1 Rush	Y	Y	N	Y	N	Y
2 Kelly, R.	Y	Y	N	Y	N	Y
3 Lipinski	Y	Y	N	Y	N	Y
4 García, J.	Y	Y	N	Y	N	Y
5 Quigley	Y	Y	N	Y	N	Y
6 Casten	Y	Y	N	Y	N	Y
7 Davis, D.	Y	Y	N	Y	N	Y
8 Krishnamoorthi	Y	Y	N	Y	N	Y
9 Schakowsky	Y	Y	N	Y	N	Y
10 Schneider	Y	Y	N	Y	N	Y
11 Foster	Y	Y	N	Y	N	Y

KEY: **Republicans** Democrats *Independents*

Y Voted for (yea)		**N** Voted against (nay)	**P** Voted "present"
+ Announced for		**–** Announced against	**?** Did not vote or otherwise
# Paired for		**X** Paired against	make position known

		409	410	411	412	413	414
12	**Bost**	N	N	Y	N	Y	N
13	**Davis, R.**	N	N	Y	N	Y	N
14	Underwood	Y	Y	N	Y	N	Y
15	**Shimkus**	N	N	Y	N	Y	N
16	**Kinzinger**	N	N	Y	N	Y	N
17	Bustos	Y	Y	N	Y	N	Y
18	**LaHood**	N	N	Y	N	Y	N
INDIANA							
1	Visclosky	Y	Y	N	Y	N	Y
2	**Walorski**	N	N	Y	N	Y	N
3	**Banks**	N	N	Y	N	Y	N
4	**Baird**	N	N	Y	N	Y	N
5	**Brooks, S.**	N	N	Y	N	Y	N
6	**Pence**	N	N	Y	N	Y	N
7	Carson	Y	Y	N	Y	N	Y
8	**Bucshon**	N	N	Y	N	Y	N
9	**Hollingsworth**	N	N	Y	N	Y	N
IOWA							
1	Finkenauer	Y	Y	N	Y	Y	Y
2	Loebsack	Y	Y	N	Y	Y	Y
3	Axne	Y	Y	N	Y	Y	Y
4	**King, S.**	N	N	Y	N	Y	N
KANSAS							
1	**Marshall**	N	N	Y	N	Y	N
2	**Watkins**	N	N	Y	N	Y	N
3	Davids	Y	Y	N	N	N	Y
4	**Estes**	N	N	Y	N	Y	N
KENTUCKY							
1	**Comer**	N	N	Y	N	Y	N
2	**Guthrie**	N	N	Y	N	Y	N
3	Yarmuth	Y	Y	N	Y	N	Y
4	**Massie**	N	N	Y	N	Y	N
5	**Rogers, H.**	N	N	Y	N	Y	N
6	**Barr**	N	N	Y	Y	Y	N
LOUISIANA							
1	**Scalise**	N	N	Y	N	Y	N
2	Richmond	?	?	?	Y	N	Y
3	**Higgins, C.**	N	N	Y	N	Y	N
4	**Johnson, M.**	N	N	Y	N	Y	N
5	**Abraham**	?	?	?	?	?	?
6	**Graves, G.**	N	N	Y	N	Y	N
MAINE							
1	Pingree	Y	Y	N	Y	N	Y
2	Golden	Y	Y	Y	Y	Y	Y
MARYLAND							
1	**Harris**	N	N	Y	N	Y	N
2	Ruppersberger	Y	Y	N	Y	N	Y
3	Sarbanes	Y	Y	N	Y	N	Y
4	Brown, A.	Y	Y	N	Y	N	Y
5	Hoyer	Y	Y	N	Y	N	Y
6	Trone	Y	Y	N	Y	N	Y
7	Cummings	Y	Y	N	Y	N	Y
8	Raskin						
MASSACHUSETTS		Y	Y	N	Y	N	Y
1	Neal						
2	McGovern	Y	Y	?	?	N	Y
3	Trahan	Y	Y	N	Y	N	Y
4	Kennedy	Y	Y	N	Y	N	Y
5	Clark	Y	Y	N	Y	N	Y
6	Moulton	Y	Y	N	Y	N	Y
7	Pressley	Y	Y	N	N	N	Y
8	Lynch	Y	Y	N	Y	N	N
9	Keating	Y	Y	N	Y	N	Y
MICHIGAN		Y	Y	N	Y	N	Y
1	**Bergman**						
2	**Huizenga**	N	N	Y	N	Y	N
3	**Amash**	N	N	Y	N	Y	N
4	**Moolenaar**	N	N	N	Y	N	N
5	Kildee	N	N	Y	N	Y	N
6	**Upton**	Y	Y	N	Y	N	Y
7	**Walberg**	N	N	Y	N	Y	N
8	Slotkin	N	N	Y	N	Y	N
9	Levin	Y	Y	N	Y	N	Y
10	**Mitchell**	+	+	N	Y	N	Y
11	Stevens	N	N	Y	N	Y	N
12	Dingell	Y	Y	N	Y	N	Y
13	Tlaib	Y	Y	N	Y	N	Y
14	Lawrence	Y	Y	N	Y	N	N
MINNESOTA		Y	Y	N	Y	N	Y
1	**Hagedorn**						
2	Craig	N	N	Y	N	Y	N
3	Phillips	Y	Y	N	Y	N	Y
4	McCollum	Y	Y	N	Y	N	Y
5	Omar	Y	Y	N	Y	N	Y

		409	410	411	412	413	414
6	**Emmer**	?	?	N	Y	N	N
7	Peterson	N	N	Y	N	Y	N
8	**Stauber**	Y	Y	Y	Y	N	Y
MISSISSIPPI		N	N	Y	N	Y	N
1	**Kelly, T.**						
2	Thompson, B.	N	N	Y	N	Y	N
3	**Guest**	Y	Y	N	Y	N	Y
4	**Palazzo**	N	N	Y	N	Y	N
MISSOURI		N	N	Y	N	Y	N
1	Clay						
2	**Wagner**	Y	Y	N	Y	N	Y
3	**Luetkemeyer**	N	N	Y	N	Y	N
4	**Hartzler**	N	N	Y	N	Y	N
5	Cleaver	N	N	Y	N	Y	N
6	**Graves, S.**	Y	Y	N	N	N	Y
7	**Long**	N	N	Y	N	Y	N
8	**Smith, J.**	?	?	Y	N	Y	N
MONTANA		N	N	Y	N	Y	N
AL	**Gianforte**						
NEBRASKA		N	N	Y	N	Y	N
1	**Fortenberry**						
2	**Bacon**	N	N	Y	N	Y	N
3	**Smith, Adrian**	N	N	Y	N	Y	N
NEVADA		N	N	Y	N	Y	N
1	Titus						
2	**Amodei**	Y	Y	N	Y	N	Y
3	Lee	?	N	Y	N	Y	N
4	Horsford	Y	Y	N	Y	N	Y
NEW HAMPSHIRE		Y	Y	N	Y	N	Y
1	Pappas						
2	Kuster	Y	Y	N	Y	N	Y
NEW JERSEY		Y	Y	N	Y	N	Y
1	Norcross						
2	Van Drew	Y	Y	N	Y	N	Y
3	Kim	Y	Y	Y	Y	Y	Y
4	**Smith, C.**	Y	Y	N	Y	N	Y
5	Gottheimer	N	N	Y	N	Y	Y
6	Pallone	Y	Y	N	N	Y	Y
7	Malinowski	Y	Y	N	Y	N	Y
8	Sires	Y	Y	N	Y	N	Y
9	Pascrell	Y	Y	N	Y	N	Y
10	Payne	Y	Y	N	Y	N	Y
11	Sherrill	Y	Y	N	Y	N	Y
12	Watson Coleman	Y	Y	N	Y	N	Y
NEW MEXICO		Y	Y	N	Y	N	Y
1	Haaland						
2	Torres Small	Y	Y	N	Y	N	Y
3	Luján	Y	Y	N	Y	N	Y
NEW YORK		Y	Y	N	Y	N	Y
1	**Zeldin**						
2	**King, P.**	N	N	Y	N	Y	N
3	Suozzi	N	N	Y	N	Y	N
4	Rice, K.	Y	Y	N	Y	N	Y
5	Meeks	Y	Y	N	Y	N	Y
6	Meng	?	?	?	?	?	?
7	Velázquez	Y	Y	N	Y	N	Y
8	Jeffries	Y	Y	N	Y	N	Y
9	Clarke	Y	Y	N	Y	N	Y
10	Nadler	Y	Y	N	Y	N	Y
11	Rose	Y	Y	N	Y	N	Y
12	Maloney, C.	Y	Y	N	Y	N	Y
13	Espaillat	Y	Y	N	Y	N	Y
14	Ocasio-Cortez	Y	Y	N	Y	N	Y
15	Serrano	Y	Y	N	Y	N	N
16	Engel	Y	Y	N	Y	N	Y
17	Lowey	Y	Y	N	Y	N	Y
18	Maloney, S.P.	Y	Y	N	Y	N	Y
19	Delgado	Y	Y	N	Y	N	Y
20	Tonko	Y	Y	N	Y	N	Y
21	**Stefanik**	Y	Y	N	Y	N	Y
22	Brindisi	N	N	Y	N	Y	N
23	**Reed**	Y	Y	Y	Y	Y	Y
24	**Katko**	N	N	Y	N	Y	N
25	Morelle	N	N	Y	N	Y	N
26	Higgins, B.	Y	Y	N	N	N	Y
27	**Collins, C.**	Y	Y	N	Y	N	Y
NORTH CAROLINA		N	N	Y	N	Y	N
1	Butterfield						
2	**Holding**	Y	Y	N	Y	N	Y
3	**Jones***	?	?	Y	N	Y	N
4	Price						
5	**Foxx**	Y	Y	N	Y	N	Y
6	**Walker**	N	N	Y	N	Y	N
7	**Rouzer**	N	N	Y	N	Y	N

		409	410	411	412	413	414
8	**Hudson**	N	N	Y	N	Y	N
9	vacant	N	N	Y	N	Y	N
10	**McHenry**	N	?	Y	N	Y	N
11	**Meadows**	?	?	Y	N	Y	N
12	Adams	Y	Y	N	Y	N	Y
13	**Budd**	N	N	Y	N	Y	N
NORTH DAKOTA							
AL	**Armstrong**	N	N	Y	N	Y	N
OHIO							
1	**Chabot**	N	N	Y	N	Y	N
2	**Wenstrup**	N	N	Y	N	Y	N
3	Beatty	Y	Y	N	Y	N	Y
4	**Jordan**	N	N	Y	N	Y	N
5	**Latta**	N	N	Y	N	Y	N
6	**Johnson, B.**	N	N	Y	N	Y	N
7	**Gibbs**	N	N	Y	N	Y	N
8	**Davidson**	N	N	N	N	Y	N
9	Kaptur	Y	Y	N	Y	N	Y
10	**Turner**	N	N	Y	N	Y	N
11	Fudge	Y	Y	N	Y	N	Y
12	**Balderson**	N	N	Y	N	Y	N
13	Ryan	?	?	?	?	?	?
14	**Joyce**	N	N	Y	N	Y	N
15	**Stivers**	N	N	Y	N	Y	N
16	**Gonzalez**	N	N	Y	N	Y	N
OKLAHOMA							
1	**Hern**	N	N	Y	N	Y	N
2	**Mullin**	N	N	Y	N	Y	N
3	**Lucas**	?	?	?	?	?	?
4	**Cole**	N	N	Y	N	Y	N
5	Horn	Y	Y	N	Y	Y	Y
OREGON							
1	Bonamici	Y	Y	N	Y	N	Y
2	**Walden**	N	N	Y	N	Y	N
3	Blumenauer	Y	Y	N	Y	N	Y
4	DeFazio	Y	Y	N	Y	N	Y
5	Schrader	Y	Y	N	Y	N	Y
PENNSYLVANIA							
1	**Fitzpatrick**	N	N	N	Y	Y	Y
2	Boyle	Y	Y	N	Y	N	Y
3	Evans	Y	Y	N	Y	N	Y
4	Dean	Y	Y	N	Y	N	Y
5	Scanlon	Y	Y	N	Y	N	Y
6	Houlahan	Y	Y	N	Y	N	Y
7	Wild	Y	Y	N	Y	N	Y
8	Cartwright	Y	Y	N	Y	N	Y
9	**Meuser**	N	N	Y	N	Y	N
10	**Perry**	N	N	Y	N	Y	N
11	**Smucker**	N	N	Y	N	Y	N
12	**Marino***						
13	**Joyce**	N	N	Y	N	Y	N
14	**Reschenthaler**	N	N	Y	N	Y	N
15	**Thompson, G.**	N	N	Y	N	Y	N
16	**Kelly, M.**	?	N	Y	N	Y	N
17	Lamb	Y	Y	Y	Y	Y	Y
18	Doyle	Y	Y	N	Y	N	Y
RHODE ISLAND							
1	Cicilline	Y	Y	N	Y	N	Y
2	Langevin	Y	Y	N	Y	N	Y
SOUTH CAROLINA							
1	Cunningham	Y	Y	N	N	Y	Y
2	**Wilson, J.**	N	N	Y	N	Y	N
3	**Duncan**	N	N	Y	N	Y	N
4	**Timmons**	N	N	Y	N	Y	N
5	**Norman**	N	N	Y	N	Y	N
6	Clyburn	+	+	-	Y	N	Y
7	**Rice, T.**	N	N	Y	N	Y	N
SOUTH DAKOTA							
AL	**Johnson**	N	N	Y	N	Y	N
TENNESSEE							
1	**Roe**	N	N	Y	N	Y	N
2	**Burchett**	N	N	Y	N	Y	N
3	**Fleischmann**	N	N	Y	N	Y	N
4	**DesJarlais**	N	N	Y	N	Y	N
5	Cooper	Y	Y	N	Y	N	Y
6	**Rose**	N	N	Y	N	Y	N
7	**Green**	N	N	Y	N	Y	N
8	**Kustoff**	N	N	Y	N	Y	N
9	Cohen	Y	Y	N	Y	N	Y
TEXAS							
1	**Gohmert**	N	N	Y	N	Y	N
2	**Crenshaw**	N	N	Y	N	Y	N
3	**Taylor**	N	N	Y	N	Y	N
4	**Ratcliffe**	N	N	Y	N	Y	N

		409	410	411	412	413	414
5	**Gooden**	N	N	Y	N	Y	N
6	**Wright**	N	N	Y	N	Y	N
7	Fletcher	Y	Y	N	Y	N	Y
8	**Brady**	N	N	Y	N	Y	N
9	Green, A.	Y	Y	N	Y	N	Y
10	**McCaul**	N	N	?	Y	Y	N
11	**Conaway**	N	N	Y	N	Y	N
12	**Granger**	N	N	Y	N	Y	N
13	**Thornberry**	-	-	+	-	+	-
14	**Weber**	N	N	Y	N	Y	N
15	Gonzalez	Y	Y	N	Y	N	Y
16	Escobar	Y	Y	N	Y	N	Y
17	**Flores**	N	N	Y	N	Y	N
18	Jackson Lee	Y	Y	N	Y	N	Y
19	**Arrington**	N	N	Y	N	Y	N
20	Castro	Y	Y	N	Y	N	Y
21	**Roy**	N	N	Y	N	Y	N
22	**Olson**	N	N	Y	N	Y	N
23	**Hurd**	N	N	N	N	Y	Y
24	**Marchant**	N	N	Y	N	Y	N
25	**Williams**	N	N	Y	N	Y	N
26	**Burgess**	N	N	Y	N	Y	N
27	**Cloud**	N	N	Y	N	Y	N
28	Cuellar	Y	Y	N	Y	N	Y
29	Garcia, S.	Y	Y	N	Y	N	Y
30	Johnson, E.B.	Y	Y	N	Y	N	Y
31	**Carter, J.**	N	N	Y	N	Y	N
32	Allred	Y	Y	N	Y	N	Y
33	Veasey	Y	Y	N	Y	N	Y
34	Vela	Y	Y	N	Y	N	Y
35	Doggett	Y	Y	N	Y	N	Y
36	**Babin**	N	N	Y	N	Y	N
UTAH							
1	**Bishop, R.**	N	N	Y	N	Y	N
2	**Stewart**	N	N	Y	N	Y	N
3	**Curtis**	N	N	Y	N	Y	N
4	McAdams	Y	Y	N	N	N	Y
VERMONT							
AL	Welch	Y	Y	N	Y	N	Y
VIRGINIA							
1	**Wittman**	N	N	Y	N	Y	N
2	Luria	Y	Y	N	Y	Y	Y
3	Scott, R.	Y	Y	N	Y	N	Y
4	McEachin	Y	Y	N	Y	N	Y
5	**Riggleman**	N	N	Y	N	Y	N
6	**Cline**	N	N	Y	N	Y	N
7	Spanberger	Y	Y	N	Y	Y	Y
8	Beyer	Y	Y	N	Y	N	Y
9	**Griffith**	N	N	Y	N	Y	N
10	Wexton	Y	Y	N	Y	N	Y
11	Connolly	Y	Y	N	Y	N	Y
WASHINGTON							
1	DelBene	Y	Y	N	Y	N	Y
2	Larsen	Y	Y	N	Y	N	Y
3	**Herrera Beutler**	N	N	Y	N	Y	N
4	**Newhouse**	N	N	Y	N	Y	N
5	**McMorris Rodgers**	N	N	+	N	Y	N
6	Kilmer	Y	Y	N	Y	N	Y
7	Jayapal	Y	Y	N	Y	N	Y
8	Schrier	Y	Y	N	Y	N	Y
9	Smith Adam	Y	Y	N	Y	N	Y
10	Heck	Y	Y	N	Y	N	Y
WEST VIRGINIA							
1	**McKinley**	N	N	Y	N	Y	N
2	**Mooney**	N	N	Y	N	Y	N
3	**Miller**	N	N	Y	N	Y	N
WISCONSIN							
1	**Steil**	N	N	Y	N	Y	N
2	Pocan	Y	Y	N	Y	N	Y
3	Kind	Y	Y	N	Y	N	Y
4	Moore	Y	Y	N	Y	N	Y
5	**Sensenbrenner**	N	N	Y	N	Y	N
6	**Grothman**	N	N	Y	N	Y	N
7	**Duffy**	N	N	?	N	Y	N
8	**Gallagher**	N	N	Y	N	Y	N
WYOMING							
AL	**Cheney**	N	N	Y	N	Y	N
DELEGATES							
	Radewagen (A.S.)			?	?		
	Norton (D.C.)			N	Y		
	San Nicolas (Guam)			?	?		
	Sablan (N. Marianas)			?	?		
	González-Colón (P.R.)			?	?		
	Plaskett (V.I.)			N	Y		

‖ HOUSE VOTES

415. HR3351. Fiscal 2020 Financial Services Appropriations - Reduce Financial Services Funding. Grothman, R-Wis., amendment that would reduce by 3.1 percent all discretionary funding made available by bill. Rejected in Committee of the Whole 151-274: R 141-52; D 0-232; I 0-1. June 26, 2019.

416. HR3351. Fiscal 2020 Financial Services Appropriations - En Bloc Amendments. Quigley, D-Ill. en bloc amendments to the Fiscal 2020 Financial Services Appropriations bill that would, among other provisions, increase by $1 million funding for a Treasury Department program providing financial assistance and training to community development financial institutions; increase by $3 million funding for the Treasury Department office of the inspector general and decrease by the same amount funding for the office of administration within the executive office of the president; and prohibit the use of funds made available by the bill to amend or revise existing laws related to Securities and Exchange Commission regulation of certain securities transactions or for the Federal Communications Commission to finalize or implement a proposed rule regarding state and local policies promoting broadband access for individuals in multiple-tenant environments, such as apartments or office buildings. Adopted in Committee of the Whole 227-200: R 0-194; D 226-6; I 1-0. June 26, 2019.

417. HR3351. Fiscal 2020 Financial Services Appropriations - Reduce Financial Services Funding. Banks, R-Ind., amendment that would reduce by 14 percent all discretionary funding made available by the bill, except for amounts made available to the Defense Department. Rejected in Committee of the Whole 141-285: R 141-52; D 0-232; I 0-1. June 26, 2019.

418. HR3351. Fiscal 2020 Financial Services Appropriations - Small Business Entrepreneurship. Suozzi, D-N.Y., amendment that would increase funding by $1 million for Small Business entrepreneurial development programs and would decrease by the same amount administrative funding for Treasury Department offices. Adopted in Committee of the Whole 406-19: R 174-19; D 231-0; I 1-0. June 26, 2019.

419. HR3351. Fiscal 2020 Financial Services Appropriations - Youth Substance Abuse Prevention. Lee, D-Nev., amendment that would increase by $1 million funding for an Office of National Drug Control Policy community-based youth substance abuse prevention program and decrease by the same amount funding for General Service Administration facility rental. Adopted in Committee of the Whole 400-27: R 168-26; D 231-1; I 1-0. June 26, 2019.

420. HR3351. Fiscal 2020 Financial Services Appropriations - Community Investment Programs. Dean, D-Pa., amendment that would increase by $2 million funding allocated for Treasury Department programs that provide financial assistance and training to community development financial institutions to incentivize investments that benefit with individuals with disabilities, from funding provided by the bill for department programs supporting such institutions. Adopted in Committee of the Whole 373-51: R 143-50; D 229-1; I 1-0. June 26, 2019.

		415	416	417	418	419	420
ALABAMA							
1	**Byrne**	Y	N	Y	N	N	N
2	**Roby**	N	N	N	Y	Y	Y
3	**Rogers, M.**	Y	N	Y	Y	Y	Y
4	**Aderholt**	N	N	Y	Y	Y	?
5	**Brooks, M.**	Y	N	Y	Y	N	Y
6	**Palmer**	Y	N	Y	Y	Y	Y
7	Sewell	N	Y	N	Y	Y	Y
ALASKA							
AL	**Young**	N	N	N	Y	Y	Y
ARIZONA							
1	O'Halleran	N	Y	N	Y	Y	Y
2	Kirkpatrick	N	Y	N	Y	Y	Y
3	Grijalva	N	Y	N	Y	Y	Y
4	**Gosar**	Y	N	Y	N	N	N
5	**Biggs**	Y	N	Y	N	N	N
6	**Schweikert**	Y	N	Y	N	N	Y
7	Gallego	N	Y	N	Y	Y	Y
8	**Lesko**	Y	N	Y	Y	Y	Y
9	Stanton	N	Y	N	Y	Y	Y
ARKANSAS							
1	**Crawford**	Y	N	Y	Y	Y	Y
2	**Hill, F.**	Y	N	Y	Y	Y	Y
3	**Womack**	Y	N	N	Y	Y	Y
4	**Westerman**	Y	N	Y	Y	Y	Y
CALIFORNIA							
1	**LaMalfa**	Y	N	Y	Y	Y	Y
2	Huffman	N	Y	N	Y	Y	Y
3	Garamendi	N	Y	N	Y	Y	Y
4	**McClintock**	Y	N	Y	N	N	Y
5	Thompson, M.	N	Y	N	Y	Y	Y
6	Matsui	N	Y	N	Y	Y	Y
7	Bera	N	Y	N	Y	Y	Y
8	**Cook**	Y	N	N	Y	Y	Y
9	McNerney	N	Y	N	Y	Y	Y
10	Harder	N	Y	N	Y	Y	Y
11	DeSaulnier	N	Y	N	Y	Y	Y
12	Pelosi						
13	Lee B.	N	Y	N	Y	Y	Y
14	Speier	N	Y	N	Y	Y	Y
15	Swalwell	-	+	-	+	+	+
16	Costa	N	Y	N	Y	Y	Y
17	Khanna	N	Y	N	Y	Y	Y
18	Eshoo	N	Y	N	Y	Y	Y
19	Lofgren	N	Y	N	Y	Y	Y
20	Panetta	N	Y	N	Y	Y	Y
21	Cox	N	Y	N	Y	Y	Y
22	**Nunes**	Y	N	Y	Y	Y	Y
23	**McCarthy**	Y	N	N	Y	Y	Y
24	Carbajal	N	Y	N	Y	Y	Y
25	Hill, K.	N	Y	N	Y	Y	Y
26	Brownley	N	Y	N	Y	Y	Y
27	Chu	N	Y	N	Y	Y	Y
28	Schiff	N	Y	N	Y	Y	Y
29	Cárdenas	N	Y	N	Y	Y	Y
30	Sherman	N	Y	N	Y	Y	Y
31	Aguilar	N	Y	N	Y	Y	Y
32	Napolitano	N	Y	N	+	Y	Y
33	Lieu	N	Y	N	Y	Y	Y
34	Gomez	N	Y	N	Y	Y	Y
35	Torres	N	Y	N	Y	Y	Y
36	Ruiz	N	Y	N	Y	Y	Y
37	Bass	N	Y	N	Y	Y	Y
38	Sánchez	?	Y	N	Y	Y	Y
39	Cisneros	N	Y	N	Y	Y	Y
40	Roybal-Allard	N	Y	N	Y	Y	Y
41	Takano	N	Y	N	Y	Y	Y
42	**Calvert**	N	N	N	Y	Y	Y
43	Waters	N	Y	N	Y	Y	Y
44	Barragán	N	Y	N	Y	Y	Y
45	Porter	N	Y	N	Y	Y	Y
46	Correa	N	Y	N	Y	Y	Y
47	Lowenthal	N	Y	N	Y	Y	Y
48	Rouda	N	Y	N	Y	Y	Y
49	Levin	N	Y	N	Y	Y	Y
50	**Hunter**	Y	N	Y	N	N	N
51	Vargas	N	Y	N	Y	Y	Y
52	Peters	N	Y	N	Y	Y	Y

		415	416	417	418	419	420
53	Davis, S.	N	Y	N	Y	Y	Y
COLORADO							
1	DeGette	N	Y	N	Y	Y	Y
2	Neguse	N	Y	N	Y	Y	Y
3	**Tipton**	N	N	N	Y	Y	Y
4	**Buck**	Y	N	Y	N	Y	N
5	**Lamborn**	Y	N	Y	Y	Y	N
6	Crow	N	Y	N	Y	Y	Y
7	Perlmutter	N	Y	N	Y	Y	Y
CONNECTICUT							
1	Larson	N	Y	N	Y	Y	Y
2	Courtney	N	Y	N	Y	Y	Y
3	DeLauro	N	Y	N	Y	Y	Y
4	Himes	N	Y	N	Y	Y	Y
5	Hayes	N	Y	N	Y	Y	Y
DELAWARE							
AL	Blunt Rochester	N	Y	N	Y	Y	Y
FLORIDA							
1	**Gaetz**	Y	N	Y	N	N	Y
2	**Dunn**	Y	N	Y	Y	N	N
3	**Yoho**	Y	N	N	N	N	N
4	**Rutherford**	N	N	Y	Y	Y	Y
5	Lawson	N	Y	N	Y	Y	Y
6	**Waltz**	N	N	Y	Y	Y	Y
7	Murphy	N	Y	N	Y	Y	Y
8	**Posey**	Y	N	Y	Y	Y	N
9	Soto	N	Y	N	Y	Y	Y
10	Demings	N	Y	N	Y	Y	Y
11	**Webster**	Y	N	Y	N	N	N
12	**Bilirakis**	Y	N	Y	Y	Y	Y
13	Crist	N	Y	N	Y	Y	Y
14	Castor	N	Y	N	Y	Y	Y
15	**Spano**	Y	N	?	Y	Y	Y
16	**Buchanan**	Y	N	N	Y	Y	Y
17	**Steube**	Y	N	Y	Y	Y	Y
18	**Mast**	Y	N	Y	Y	Y	Y
19	**Rooney**	?	?	?	?	?	?
20	Hastings	N	Y	N	Y	Y	Y
21	Frankel	N	Y	N	Y	Y	Y
22	Deutch	N	Y	N	Y	Y	Y
23	Wasserman Schultz	N	Y	N	Y	Y	Y
24	Wilson, F.	N	Y	N	Y	Y	Y
25	**Diaz-Balart**	N	N	N	Y	Y	Y
26	Mucarsel-Powell	N	Y	N	Y	Y	Y
27	Shalala	N	Y	N	Y	Y	Y
GEORGIA							
1	**Carter, E.L.**	Y	N	Y	Y	Y	Y
2	Bishop, S.	N	Y	N	Y	Y	Y
3	**Ferguson**	Y	N	Y	Y	Y	Y
4	Johnson, H.	N	Y	N	Y	Y	Y
5	Lewis John	N	Y	N	Y	Y	Y
6	McBath	N	Y	N	Y	Y	Y
7	**Woodall**	Y	N	Y	Y	Y	Y
8	**Scott, A.**	Y	N	Y	Y	Y	N
9	**Collins, D.**	Y	N	Y	Y	Y	Y
10	**Hice**	Y	N	Y	Y	N	N
11	**Loudermilk**	Y	N	Y	Y	N	N
12	**Allen**	Y	N	Y	Y	N	N
13	Scott, D.	N	Y	N	Y	Y	Y
14	**Graves, T.**	Y	N	Y	Y	Y	Y
HAWAII							
1	Case	N	Y	N	Y	Y	Y
2	Gabbard	?	?	?	?	?	?
IDAHO							
1	**Fulcher**	Y	N	Y	Y	Y	N
2	**Simpson**	N	N	N	N	N	N
ILLINOIS							
1	Rush	N	Y	N	Y	Y	Y
2	Kelly, R.	N	Y	N	Y	Y	Y
3	Lipinski	N	Y	N	Y	Y	Y
4	García, J.	N	Y	N	Y	Y	Y
5	Quigley	N	Y	N	Y	Y	Y
6	Casten	N	Y	N	Y	Y	Y
7	Davis, D.	N	Y	N	Y	Y	Y
8	Krishnamoorthi	N	Y	N	Y	Y	Y
9	Schakowsky	N	Y	N	Y	Y	Y
10	Schneider	N	Y	N	Y	Y	Y
11	Foster	N	Y	N	Y	Y	Y

KEY: **Republicans**   Democrats   *Independents*

Y Voted for (yea)	**N** Voted against (nay)	**P** Voted "present"
+ Announced for	**−** Announced against	**?** Did not vote or otherwise
# Paired for	**X** Paired against	make position known

		415	416	417	418	419	420
12	**Bost**	Y	N	N	Y	Y	Y
13	**Davis, R.**	N	N	N	Y	Y	Y
14	Underwood	N	Y	N	Y	Y	Y
15	**Shimkus**	Y	N	Y	Y	Y	Y
16	**Kinzinger**	N	N	N	Y	Y	Y
17	Bustos	N	Y	N	Y	Y	Y
18	**LaHood**	Y	N	Y	Y	Y	Y
INDIANA							
1	Visclosky	N	Y	N	Y	Y	Y
2	**Walorski**	-	-	+	+	+	+
3	**Banks**	Y	N	Y	Y	Y	Y
4	**Baird**	Y	N	N	Y	Y	Y
5	**Brooks, S.**	Y	N	Y	Y	Y	Y
6	**Pence**	Y	N	Y	Y	Y	Y
7	Carson	N	Y	N	Y	Y	Y
8	**Bucshon**	Y	N	Y	Y	Y	Y
9	**Hollingsworth**	N	N	N	Y	Y	N
IOWA							
1	Finkenauer	N	Y	N	Y	Y	Y
2	Loebsack	N	Y	N	Y	Y	Y
3	Axne	N	Y	N	Y	Y	Y
4	**King, S.**	Y	N	Y	Y	Y	Y
KANSAS							
1	**Marshall**	Y	N	Y	Y	Y	Y
2	**Watkins**	Y	N	Y	Y	Y	Y
3	Davids	N	Y	N	Y	Y	Y
4	**Estes**	Y	N	Y	Y	N	Y
KENTUCKY							
1	**Comer**	Y	N	Y	Y	Y	Y
2	**Guthrie**	Y	N	Y	Y	Y	Y
3	Yarmuth	N	Y	N	Y	Y	Y
4	**Massie**	Y	N	Y	Y	N	N
5	**Rogers, H.**	Y	N	N	Y	Y	Y
6	**Barr**	Y	N	Y	Y	Y	Y
LOUISIANA							
1	**Scalise**	Y	N	Y	Y	Y	Y
2	Richmond	N	Y	N	Y	Y	Y
3	**Higgins, C.**	Y	N	Y	Y	Y	Y
4	**Johnson, M.**	Y	N	Y	Y	Y	Y
5	**Abraham**	?	?	?	?	?	?
6	**Graves, G.**	Y	N	Y	Y	Y	Y
MAINE							
1	Pingree	N	Y	N	Y	Y	Y
2	Golden	N	Y	N	Y	Y	Y
MARYLAND							
1	**Harris**	Y	N	Y	Y	Y	N
2	Ruppersberger	N	Y	N	Y	Y	Y
3	Sarbanes	N	Y	N	Y	Y	Y
4	Brown, A.	N	Y	N	Y	Y	Y
5	Hoyer	N	Y	N	Y	Y	Y
6	Trone	N	Y	N	Y	Y	Y
7	Cummings	N	Y	N	Y	Y	Y
8	Raskin						
MASSACHUSETTS		N	Y	N	Y	Y	Y
1	Neal						
2	McGovern	N	Y	N	Y	Y	Y
3	Trahan	N	Y	N	Y	Y	Y
4	Kennedy	N	Y	N	Y	Y	Y
5	Clark	N	Y	N	Y	Y	Y
6	Moulton	N	Y	N	Y	Y	Y
7	Pressley	?	?	?	?	?	?
8	Lynch	N	Y	N	Y	Y	Y
9	Keating	N	Y	N	Y	Y	Y
MICHIGAN		N	Y	N	Y	Y	Y
1	**Bergman**						
2	**Huizenga**	Y	N	Y	Y	Y	Y
3	**Amash**	Y	N	Y	Y	Y	Y
4	**Moolenaar**	Y	N	Y	N	N	N
5	Kildee	Y	N	Y	Y	Y	Y
6	**Upton**	N	Y	N	Y	Y	Y
7	**Walberg**	Y	N	N	Y	Y	Y
8	Slotkin	Y	N	Y	Y	Y	Y
9	Levin	N	Y	N	Y	Y	Y
10	**Mitchell**	N	Y	N	Y	Y	Y
11	Stevens	Y	N	Y	Y	Y	Y
12	Dingell	N	Y	N	Y	Y	Y
13	Tlaib	N	Y	N	Y	Y	Y
14	Lawrence	N	Y	N	Y	Y	Y
MINNESOTA		N	Y	N	Y	Y	Y
1	**Hagedorn**						
2	Craig	Y	N	Y	Y	Y	Y
3	Phillips	N	Y	N	Y	Y	Y
4	McCollum	N	Y	N	Y	Y	Y
5	Omar	N	Y	N	Y	Y	Y

		415	416	417	418	419	420
6	**Emmer**	N	Y	N	Y	Y	Y
7	Peterson	Y	N	Y	Y	Y	Y
8	**Stauber**	N	N	N	Y	Y	Y
MISSISSIPPI		N	N	N	Y	Y	Y
1	**Kelly, T.**						
2	Thompson, B.	Y	N	Y	Y	N	N
3	**Guest**	N	Y	N	Y	Y	Y
4	**Palazzo**	Y	N	Y	Y	Y	Y
MISSOURI		Y	N	Y	Y	Y	Y
1	Clay						
2	**Wagner**	N	Y	N	Y	Y	Y
3	**Luetkemeyer**	Y	N	Y	Y	Y	Y
4	**Hartzler**	N	N	?	Y	Y	Y
5	Cleaver	Y	N	N	Y	Y	Y
6	**Graves, S.**	N	Y	N	Y	Y	Y
7	**Long**	Y	N	Y	Y	Y	Y
8	**Smith, J.**	Y	N	Y	Y	Y	Y
MONTANA		Y	N	Y	Y	Y	N
AL	**Gianforte**						
NEBRASKA		N	N	N	Y	Y	Y
1	**Fortenberry**						
2	**Bacon**	N	N	N	Y	Y	Y
3	**Smith, Adrian**	Y	N	Y	Y	Y	Y
NEVADA		Y	N	Y	Y	Y	Y
1	Titus						
2	**Amodei**	N	Y	N	Y	Y	Y
3	Lee	Y	N	N	Y	Y	Y
4	Horsford	N	Y	N	Y	Y	Y
NEW HAMPSHIRE		N	Y	N	Y	Y	Y
1	Pappas						
2	Kuster	N	Y	N	Y	Y	Y
NEW JERSEY		N	Y	N	Y	Y	Y
1	Norcross						
2	Van Drew	N	Y	N	Y	Y	Y
3	Kim	N	N	N	Y	Y	Y
4	**Smith, C.**	N	Y	N	Y	Y	Y
5	Gottheimer	N	N	N	Y	Y	Y
6	Pallone	N	N	N	Y	Y	Y
7	Malinowski	N	Y	N	Y	Y	Y
8	Sires	N	Y	N	Y	Y	Y
9	Pascrell	N	Y	N	Y	Y	Y
10	Payne	N	Y	N	Y	Y	Y
11	Sherrill	N	Y	N	Y	Y	N
12	Watson Coleman	N	Y	N	Y	Y	Y
NEW MEXICO		N	Y	N	Y	Y	Y
1	Haaland						
2	Torres Small	N	Y	N	Y	Y	Y
3	Luján	N	N	N	Y	Y	Y
NEW YORK		N	Y	N	Y	Y	Y
1	**Zeldin**						
2	**King, P.**	Y	N	N	Y	Y	Y
3	Suozzi	N	N	N	Y	Y	Y
4	Rice, K.	N	Y	N	Y	Y	Y
5	Meeks	N	Y	N	Y	Y	Y
6	Meng	N	Y	N	Y	Y	Y
7	Velázquez	N	Y	N	Y	Y	Y
8	Jeffries	N	Y	N	Y	Y	Y
9	Clarke	N	Y	N	Y	Y	Y
10	Nadler	N	Y	N	Y	Y	Y
11	Rose	N	Y	N	Y	Y	Y
12	Maloney, C.	N	Y	N	Y	Y	Y
13	Espaillat	N	Y	N	Y	Y	Y
14	Ocasio-Cortez	N	Y	N	Y	Y	Y
15	Serrano	N	Y	N	Y	Y	Y
16	Engel	N	Y	N	Y	Y	Y
17	Lowey	N	Y	N	Y	Y	Y
18	Maloney, S.P.	N	Y	N	Y	Y	Y
19	Delgado	N	Y	N	Y	Y	Y
20	Tonko	N	Y	N	Y	Y	Y
21	**Stefanik**	N	Y	N	Y	Y	Y
22	Brindisi	N	N	N	Y	Y	Y
23	**Reed**	N	N	N	Y	Y	Y
24	**Katko**	N	N	N	Y	Y	Y
25	Morelle	N	N	N	Y	Y	Y
26	Higgins, B.	N	Y	N	Y	Y	Y
27	**Collins, C.**	N	Y	N	Y	Y	Y
NORTH CAROLINA		-	-	-	+	+	+
1	Butterfield						
2	**Holding**	N	Y	N	Y	Y	Y
3	**Jones***	Y	N	Y	Y	Y	Y
4	Price						
5	**Foxx**	N	Y	N	Y	Y	Y
6	**Walker**	Y	N	Y	Y	Y	N
7	**Rouzer**	Y	N	Y	Y	Y	N

		415	416	417	418	419	420
8	**Hudson**	Y	N	Y	Y	Y	Y
9	vacant	Y	N	Y	Y	Y	Y
10	**McHenry**	Y	N	Y	Y	Y	Y
11	**Meadows**	N	N	Y	Y	Y	Y
12	Adams	N	Y	N	Y	Y	Y
13	**Budd**	Y	N	Y	Y	Y	N
NORTH DAKOTA							
AL	**Armstrong**	N	N	N	Y	Y	Y
OHIO							
1	**Chabot**	Y	N	Y	Y	Y	Y
2	**Wenstrup**	Y	N	Y	Y	Y	Y
3	Beatty	N	Y	N	Y	Y	Y
4	**Jordan**	Y	N	Y	Y	N	N
5	**Latta**	Y	N	Y	Y	Y	Y
6	**Johnson, B.**	Y	N	Y	Y	Y	Y
7	**Gibbs**	Y	N	Y	Y	Y	Y
8	**Davidson**	Y	N	Y	N	N	N
9	Kaptur	N	Y	N	Y	Y	Y
10	**Turner**	N	N	N	Y	Y	Y
11	Fudge	N	Y	N	Y	Y	Y
12	**Balderson**	Y	N	Y	Y	Y	Y
13	Ryan	?	?	?	?	?	?
14	**Joyce**	N	N	N	Y	Y	Y
15	**Stivers**	N	N	N	Y	Y	Y
16	**Gonzalez**	N	N	N	Y	Y	Y
OKLAHOMA							
1	**Hern**	Y	N	Y	Y	Y	Y
2	**Mullin**	?	?	?	?	?	?
3	**Lucas**	?	?	?	?	?	?
4	**Cole**	N	N	N	Y	Y	Y
5	Horn	N	Y	N	Y	Y	Y
OREGON							
1	Bonamici	N	Y	N	Y	Y	Y
2	**Walden**	N	N	N	Y	Y	Y
3	Blumenauer	N	Y	N	Y	N	Y
4	DeFazio	N	Y	N	Y	Y	Y
5	Schrader	N	Y	N	Y	Y	Y
PENNSYLVANIA							
1	**Fitzpatrick**	N	N	N	Y	Y	Y
2	Boyle	N	Y	N	Y	Y	Y
3	Evans	N	Y	N	Y	Y	Y
4	Dean	N	Y	N	Y	Y	Y
5	Scanlon	N	Y	N	Y	Y	Y
6	Houlahan	N	Y	N	Y	Y	Y
7	Wild	N	Y	N	Y	Y	Y
8	Cartwright	N	Y	N	Y	Y	Y
9	**Meuser**	Y	N	Y	Y	Y	Y
10	**Perry**	Y	N	Y	Y	Y	Y
11	**Smucker**	Y	N	Y	Y	Y	Y
12	**Marino***						
13	**Joyce**	Y	N	Y	Y	Y	Y
14	**Reschenthaler**	N	N	N	Y	Y	Y
15	**Thompson, G.**	N	N	N	Y	Y	Y
16	**Kelly, M.**	Y	N	Y	Y	Y	Y
17	Lamb	N	Y	N	Y	Y	Y
18	Doyle	N	Y	N	Y	Y	Y
RHODE ISLAND							
1	Cicilline	N	Y	N	Y	Y	Y
2	Langevin	N	Y	N	Y	Y	Y
SOUTH CAROLINA							
1	Cunningham	N	Y	N	Y	Y	Y
2	**Wilson, J.**	Y	N	Y	Y	Y	N
3	**Duncan**	Y	N	Y	N	N	N
4	**Timmons**	Y	N	Y	Y	Y	N
5	**Norman**	Y	N	Y	N	N	N
6	Clyburn	N	Y	N	Y	Y	Y
7	**Rice, T.**	Y	N	Y	N	Y	N
SOUTH DAKOTA							
AL	**Johnson**	Y	N	Y	Y	Y	Y
TENNESSEE							
1	**Roe**	Y	N	Y	Y	Y	Y
2	**Burchett**	Y	N	Y	Y	N	N
3	**Fleischmann**	N	N	N	Y	Y	Y
4	**DesJarlais**	Y	N	Y	Y	Y	Y
5	Cooper	N	Y	N	Y	Y	Y
6	**Rose**	Y	N	Y	Y	N	N
7	**Green**	Y	N	Y	Y	Y	N
8	**Kustoff**	Y	N	Y	Y	Y	Y
9	Cohen	N	Y	N	Y	Y	Y
TEXAS							
1	**Gohmert**	Y	N	Y	N	Y	N
2	**Crenshaw**	Y	N	N	Y	Y	Y
3	**Taylor**	Y	N	Y	Y	Y	Y
4	**Ratcliffe**	Y	N	Y	Y	Y	N

		415	416	417	418	419	420
5	**Gooden**	Y	N	Y	Y	N	N
6	**Wright**	Y	N	Y	N	Y	N
7	Fletcher	N	Y	N	Y	Y	Y
8	**Brady**	Y	N	Y	Y	Y	Y
9	Green, A.	N	Y	N	Y	Y	Y
10	**McCaul**	Y	N	Y	Y	Y	Y
11	**Conaway**	Y	N	Y	Y	Y	Y
12	**Granger**	Y	N	N	Y	Y	Y
13	**Thornberry**	Y	N	Y	Y	Y	Y
14	**Weber**	Y	N	Y	Y	Y	N
15	Gonzalez	N	Y	N	Y	Y	Y
16	Escobar	N	Y	N	Y	Y	Y
17	**Flores**	Y	N	Y	Y	Y	Y
18	Jackson Lee	N	Y	N	Y	Y	Y
19	**Arrington**	Y	N	Y	N	N	N
20	Castro	?	?	?	?	?	?
21	**Roy**	Y	N	Y	Y	N	N
22	**Olson**	Y	N	Y	N	Y	Y
23	**Hurd**	N	N	N	Y	Y	Y
24	**Marchant**	Y	N	Y	N	Y	N
25	**Williams**	Y	N	Y	Y	Y	Y
26	**Burgess**	Y	N	Y	Y	Y	N
27	**Cloud**	Y	N	Y	Y	Y	Y
28	Cuellar	N	Y	N	Y	Y	Y
29	Garcia, S.	N	Y	N	Y	Y	Y
30	Johnson, E.B.	N	Y	N	Y	Y	Y
31	**Carter, J.**	N	N	Y	Y	Y	Y
32	Allred	N	Y	N	Y	Y	Y
33	Veasey	N	Y	N	Y	Y	Y
34	Vela	N	Y	N	Y	Y	Y
35	Doggett	N	Y	N	Y	Y	Y
36	**Babin**	Y	N	Y	Y	Y	N
UTAH							
1	**Bishop, R.**	N	N	N	Y	Y	N
2	**Stewart**	Y	N	Y	Y	Y	Y
3	**Curtis**	Y	N	Y	Y	Y	Y
4	McAdams	N	N	N	Y	Y	Y
VERMONT							
AL	Welch	N	Y	N	Y	Y	Y
VIRGINIA							
1	**Wittman**	Y	N	Y	Y	Y	Y
2	Luria	N	Y	N	Y	Y	Y
3	Scott, R.	N	Y	N	Y	Y	Y
4	McEachin	N	Y	N	Y	Y	Y
5	**Riggleman**	Y	N	Y	Y	Y	Y
6	**Cline**	Y	N	Y	Y	Y	N
7	Spanberger	N	Y	N	Y	Y	Y
8	Beyer	N	Y	N	Y	Y	Y
9	**Griffith**	Y	N	Y	N	Y	N
10	Wexton	N	Y	N	Y	Y	Y
11	Connolly	N	Y	N	Y	Y	Y
WASHINGTON							
1	DelBene	N	Y	N	Y	Y	Y
2	Larsen	N	Y	N	Y	Y	Y
3	**Herrera Beutler**	N	N	N	Y	Y	Y
4	**Newhouse**	N	N	N	Y	Y	Y
5	**McMorris Rodgers**	Y	N	Y	Y	Y	Y
6	Kilmer	N	Y	N	Y	Y	Y
7	Jayapal	N	Y	N	Y	Y	Y
8	Schrier	N	Y	N	Y	Y	Y
9	Smith Adam	N	Y	N	Y	Y	Y
10	Heck	N	Y	N	Y	Y	Y
WEST VIRGINIA							
1	**McKinley**	N	N	N	Y	Y	Y
2	**Mooney**	Y	N	Y	Y	Y	Y
3	**Miller**	Y	N	N	Y	Y	Y
WISCONSIN							
1	**Steil**	Y	N	Y	Y	Y	Y
2	Pocan	N	Y	N	Y	Y	Y
3	Kind	N	Y	N	Y	Y	?
4	Moore	N	Y	N	Y	Y	+
5	**Sensenbrenner**	Y	N	Y	N	Y	N
6	**Grothman**	Y	N	Y	Y	Y	N
7	**Duffy**	Y	N	N	Y	Y	Y
8	**Gallagher**	N	N	N	Y	Y	Y
WYOMING							
AL	**Cheney**	N	N	N	Y	Y	Y
DELEGATES							
	Radewagen (A.S.)	N	N	Y	Y	Y	Y
	Norton (D.C.)	N	Y	N	Y	Y	Y
	San Nicolas (Guam)	N	Y	N	Y	Y	Y
	Sablan (N. Marianas)	N	Y	N	Y	Y	Y
	González-Colón (P.R.)	N	N	N	Y	Y	Y
	Plaskett (V.I.)	?	Y	N	Y	Y	Y

III HOUSE VOTES

421. HR3351. Fiscal 2020 Financial Services Appropriations - Small Business Entrepreneurship. Kim, D-N.J., amendment that would increase by $1 million funding for Small Business Administration entrepreneurial development programs and decrease by the same amount funding for salaries and expenses of the administration. Adopted in Committee of the Whole 408-17: R 177-17; D 230-0; I 1-0. June 26, 2019.

422. HR3351. Fiscal 2020 Financial Services Appropriations - Tax Counseling Program. Malinowski, D-N.J., amendment that would increase by $1 million funding allocated for an IRS program providing tax counseling for elderly individuals, from funding provided by the bill for IRS taxpayer services. Adopted in Committee of the Whole 362-65: R 129-65; D 232-0; I 1-0. June 26, 2019.

423. HR3351. Fiscal 2020 Financial Services Appropriations - Recommit. Graves, R-Ga., motion to recommit the bill to the House Appropriations Committee with instructions to report it back immediately with an amendment that would increase by $10 million funding for activities by the Treasury Department office on terrorism and financial intelligence to safeguard the U.S. financial system against national security threats and decrease by the same amount funding for General Services Administration facility rental. Motion agreed to 226-195: R 189-3; D 37-192. June 26, 2019.

424. HR3351. Fiscal 2020 Financial Services Appropriations - Passage. Passage of the bill, as amended, that would provide $24.95 billion in discretionary funding for the Treasury Department, the federal judiciary, the office of the president, a number of executive agencies such as the Federal Communications Commission, and other government operations. Among other provisions, the bill would provide $12 billion for the Internal Revenue Service, including $5.2 billion for enforcement activities and $2.6 billion for IRS taxpayer services. It would provide $7.9 billion for the federal judiciary, $1.9 billion for the Securities and Exchange Commission, $996 million for the Small Business Administration, $741 million in federal payments to the District of Columbia, and $178 million for the White House executive office of the president. It would prohibit the use of funds made available by the bill for the IRS to "target" any group for regulatory scrutiny based on ideological beliefs or for the reorganization or transfer of any function or authority of the Office of Personnel Management to another federal agency. Passed 224-196: R 0-191; D 224-5. Note: A "nay" was a vote in support of the president's position. June 26, 2019.

425. HR3401. Supplemental Border Appropriations - Question of Consideration. On the question of consideration of the resolution (H Res 466) that would provide for floor consideration of the Senate amendment to the Emergency Supplemental Appropriations for Humanitarian Assistance and Security at the Southern Border Act (HR 3401). Agreed to consider 226-188: R 0-188; D 226-0. June 27, 2019.

426. HR3401. Supplemental Border Appropriations - Rule. Adoption of the rule (H Res 466), as amended, that would provide for House floor consideration of the Senate amendment to the Emergency Supplemental Appropriations for Humanitarian Assistance and Security at the Southern Border Act (HR 3401). As amended, the rule would make in order a motion to concur in the Senate amendment to HR 3401. Adopted 322-85: R 170-14; D 152-71. June 27, 2019.

	421	422	423	424	425	426
ALABAMA						
1 Byrne	N	N	Y	N	N	Y
2 Roby	Y	Y	Y	N	N	Y
3 Rogers, M.	Y	Y	Y	N	?	?
4 Aderholt	Y	Y	Y	?	N	?
5 Brooks, M.	Y	N	Y	N	N	N
6 Palmer	Y	Y	Y	N	N	Y
7 Sewell	Y	Y	N	Y	Y	Y
ALASKA						
AL Young	Y	Y	N	N	N	Y
ARIZONA						
1 O'Halleran	Y	Y	N	Y	Y	Y
2 Kirkpatrick	Y	Y	N	Y	Y	Y
3 Grijalva	Y	Y	N	Y	Y	Y
4 Gosar	N	N	Y	N	N	N
5 Biggs	N	N	Y	N	N	N
6 Schweikert	Y	N	Y	N	N	Y
7 Gallego	Y	Y	N	Y	Y	N
8 Lesko	Y	Y	Y	N	N	Y
9 Stanton	Y	Y	N	Y	Y	Y
ARKANSAS						
1 Crawford	Y	Y	Y	N	N	Y
2 Hill, F.	Y	Y	Y	N	N	Y
3 Womack	Y	Y	Y	N	N	Y
4 Westerman	Y	Y	Y	N	N	Y
CALIFORNIA						
1 LaMalfa	Y	Y	Y	N	N	Y
2 Huffman	Y	Y	N	Y	?	Y
3 Garamendi	Y	Y	N	Y	Y	Y
4 McClintock	Y	N	Y	N	N	Y
5 Thompson, M.	Y	Y	N	Y	Y	Y
6 Matsui	Y	Y	N	Y	Y	Y
7 Bera	Y	Y	N	Y	Y	Y
8 Cook	Y	Y	N	N	N	Y
9 McNerney	Y	Y	N	Y	Y	Y
10 Harder	Y	Y	Y	Y	Y	Y
11 DeSaulnier	Y	Y	N	Y	Y	N
12 Pelosi						
13 Lee B.	Y	Y	N	Y	Y	N
14 Speier	Y	Y	N	Y	Y	Y
15 Swalwell	+	+	-	+	+	-
16 Costa	Y	Y	N	Y	Y	Y
17 Khanna	Y	Y	N	Y	Y	N
18 Eshoo	Y	Y	N	Y	Y	Y
19 Lofgren	Y	Y	N	Y	Y	N
20 Panetta	Y	Y	N	Y	Y	Y
21 Cox	Y	Y	N	Y	Y	Y
22 Nunes	Y	Y	Y	N	N	Y
23 McCarthy	Y	Y	Y	N	N	Y
24 Carbajal	Y	Y	N	Y	Y	Y
25 Hill, K.	Y	Y	N	Y	Y	Y
26 Brownley	Y	Y	N	Y	Y	N
27 Chu	Y	Y	N	Y	Y	Y
28 Schiff	Y	Y	N	Y	Y	Y
29 Cárdenas	Y	Y	N	Y	Y	Y
30 Sherman	Y	Y	N	Y	Y	Y
31 Aguilar	Y	Y	N	Y	Y	Y
32 Napolitano	Y	Y	N	Y	Y	N
33 Lieu	Y	Y	N	Y	Y	Y
34 Gomez	Y	Y	N	Y	Y	N
35 Torres	Y	Y	N	Y	Y	?
36 Ruiz	Y	Y	N	Y	Y	N
37 Bass	Y	Y	N	Y	Y	Y
38 Sánchez	Y	Y	N	Y	Y	Y
39 Cisneros	Y	Y	N	Y	Y	N
40 Roybal-Allard	Y	Y	N	Y	Y	Y
41 Takano	Y	Y	N	Y	Y	N
42 Calvert	Y	Y	Y	N	N	Y
43 Waters	Y	Y	N	Y	Y	Y
44 Barragán	Y	Y	N	Y	Y	N
45 Porter	Y	Y	N	Y	Y	N
46 Correa	Y	Y	N	Y	Y	Y
47 Lowenthal	Y	Y	N	Y	Y	N
48 Rouda	Y	Y	N	Y	Y	Y
49 Levin	Y	Y	N	Y	Y	Y
50 Hunter	Y	N	N	N	N	Y
51 Vargas	Y	Y	N	Y	Y	Y
52 Peters	Y	Y	N	Y	Y	Y

	421	422	423	424	425	426
53 Davis, S.	Y	Y	N	Y	Y	Y
COLORADO						
1 DeGette	Y	Y	N	Y	Y	N
2 Neguse	Y	Y	N	Y	Y	N
3 Tipton	Y	Y	Y	N	N	N
4 Buck	Y	N	Y	N	N	N
5 Lamborn	Y	N	Y	N	N	Y
6 Crow	Y	Y	Y	Y	Y	Y
7 Perlmutter	Y	Y	N	Y	Y	Y
CONNECTICUT						
1 Larson	Y	Y	N	Y	Y	Y
2 Courtney	Y	Y	N	Y	Y	Y
3 DeLauro	Y	Y	N	Y	Y	Y
4 Himes	Y	Y	N	Y	Y	Y
5 Hayes	Y	Y	N	Y	Y	Y
DELAWARE						
AL Blunt Rochester	Y	Y	N	Y	Y	N
FLORIDA						
1 Gaetz	Y	N	N	N	N	N
2 Dunn	Y	Y	Y	N	N	Y
3 Yoho	Y	N	N	N	N	Y
4 Rutherford	Y	Y	Y	N	N	Y
5 Lawson	Y	Y	N	Y	Y	Y
6 Waltz	Y	Y	Y	N	N	Y
7 Murphy	Y	Y	N	Y	Y	Y
8 Posey	Y	N	N	N	N	Y
9 Soto	Y	Y	N	Y	Y	N
10 Demings	Y	Y	N	Y	Y	Y
11 Webster	Y	N	N	N	N	Y
12 Bilirakis	Y	Y	Y	N	N	Y
13 Crist	Y	Y	N	Y	Y	Y
14 Castor	Y	Y	N	Y	Y	Y
15 Spano	Y	Y	N	N	N	Y
16 Buchanan	Y	Y	Y	N	N	Y
17 Steube	Y	Y	N	N	N	-
18 Mast	Y	Y	N	N	N	Y
19 Rooney	?	?	?	?	?	?
20 Hastings	Y	Y	N	Y	?	?
21 Frankel	Y	Y	N	Y	Y	Y
22 Deutch	Y	Y	N	Y	Y	Y
23 Wasserman Schultz	Y	Y	N	Y	Y	Y
24 Wilson, F.	Y	Y	N	Y	Y	+
25 Diaz-Balart	Y	Y	N	N	N	Y
26 Mucarsel-Powell	Y	Y	N	Y	N	Y
27 Shalala	Y	Y	N	Y	N	Y
GEORGIA						
1 Carter, E.L.	Y	Y	N	N	N	Y
2 Bishop, S.	Y	Y	N	Y	Y	Y
3 Ferguson	Y	N	Y	N	N	Y
4 Johnson, H.	Y	Y	Y	Y	Y	Y
5 Lewis John	Y	Y	Y	Y	N	Y
6 McBath	Y	Y	Y	Y	Y	Y
7 Woodall	Y	Y	Y	N	N	Y
8 Scott, A.	Y	N	Y	N	N	Y
9 Collins, D.	Y	Y	N	N	N	Y
10 Hice	Y	N	N	N	N	Y
11 Loudermilk	Y	N	N	N	N	Y
12 Allen	Y	N	N	N	N	Y
13 Scott, D.	Y	Y	N	Y	?	Y
14 Graves, T.	Y	Y	N	Y	N	Y
HAWAII						
1 Case	Y	Y	N	Y	Y	Y
2 Gabbard	?	?	?	?	?	?
IDAHO						
1 Fulcher	Y	N	N	N	N	Y
2 Simpson	N	N	Y	N	N	Y
ILLINOIS						
1 Rush	Y	Y	N	Y	Y	Y
2 Kelly, R.	Y	Y	N	Y	Y	N
3 Lipinski	Y	Y	N	Y	Y	N
4 García, J.	Y	Y	N	Y	Y	N
5 Quigley	Y	Y	N	Y	Y	Y
6 Casten	Y	Y	N	Y	Y	Y
7 Davis, D.	Y	Y	N	Y	Y	Y
8 Krishnamoorthi	Y	Y	N	Y	Y	Y
9 Schakowsky	Y	Y	N	Y	Y	N
10 Schneider	Y	Y	Y	Y	Y	Y
11 Foster	Y	Y	N	Y	Y	Y

KEY: **Republicans** (bold)   Democrats   *Independents*

Y Voted for (yea)	**N** Voted against (nay)	**P** Voted "present"
+ Announced for	**–** Announced against	**?** Did not vote or otherwise
# Paired for	**X** Paired against	make position known

		421	422	423	424	425	426
12	**Bost**	Y	Y	Y	N	N	Y
13	**Davis, R.**	Y	Y	Y	N	N	Y
14	Underwood	Y	Y	N	Y	Y	Y
15	**Shimkus**	Y	Y	Y	N	N	Y
16	**Kinzinger**	Y	Y	Y	N	N	+
17	Bustos	Y	Y	N	Y	Y	Y
18	**LaHood**	Y	Y	Y	N	N	Y
INDIANA							
1	Visclosky	Y	Y	N	Y	Y	Y
2	**Walorski**	+	+	+	-	-	+
3	**Banks**	Y	N	Y	N	N	Y
4	**Baird**	Y	Y	Y	N	N	Y
5	**Brooks, S.**	Y	Y	Y	N	N	Y
6	**Pence**	Y	Y	Y	N	N	Y
7	Carson	Y	Y	N	Y	Y	Y
8	**Bucshon**	Y	Y	Y	N	N	Y
9	**Hollingsworth**	Y	N	Y	N	N	Y
IOWA							
1	Finkenauer	Y	Y	Y	Y	Y	Y
2	Loebsack	Y	Y	Y	Y	Y	Y
3	Axne	Y	Y	Y	Y	Y	Y
4	**King, S.**	Y	Y	Y	N	N	Y
KANSAS							
1	**Marshall**	Y	Y	Y	N	N	Y
2	**Watkins**	Y	Y	Y	N	N	Y
3	Davids	Y	Y	N	Y	Y	Y
4	**Estes**	Y	Y	Y	N	N	Y
KENTUCKY							
1	**Comer**	Y	N	Y	N	N	Y
2	**Guthrie**	Y	Y	Y	N	N	Y
3	Yarmuth	Y	Y	N	Y	Y	Y
4	**Massie**	Y	N	N	N	N	N
5	**Rogers, H.**	Y	Y	Y	N	N	Y
6	**Barr**	Y	N	Y	N	N	Y
LOUISIANA							
1	**Scalise**	Y	Y	Y	N	N	Y
2	Richmond	Y	Y	N	Y	Y	?
3	**Higgins, C.**	Y	Y	Y	N	N	Y
4	**Johnson, M.**	Y	Y	Y	N	N	?
5	**Abraham**	?	?	?	?	?	?
6	**Graves, G.**	Y	Y	Y	N	N	Y
MAINE							
1	Pingree	Y	Y	N	Y	Y	Y
2	Golden	Y	Y	Y	Y	Y	Y
MARYLAND							
1	**Harris**	N	N	Y	N	N	Y
2	Ruppersberger	Y	Y	N	Y	Y	Y
3	Sarbanes	Y	Y	N	Y	Y	Y
4	Brown, A.	Y	Y	N	Y	Y	N
5	Hoyer	Y	Y	N	Y	Y	Y
6	Trone	Y	Y	N	Y	Y	Y
7	Cummings	Y	Y	N	Y	Y	Y
8	Raskin						
MASSACHUSETTS		Y	Y	N	Y	Y	Y
1	Neal						
2	McGovern	Y	Y	N	Y	Y	Y
3	Trahan	Y	Y	N	Y	Y	Y
4	Kennedy	Y	Y	N	Y	Y	N
5	Clark	Y	Y	N	Y	Y	N
6	Moulton	Y	Y	N	Y	Y	N
7	Pressley	?	?	?	?	?	?
8	Lynch	Y	Y	N	Y	Y	N
9	Keating	Y	Y	N	Y	Y	Y
MICHIGAN		Y	Y	N	Y	Y	N
1	**Bergman**						
2	**Huizenga**	Y	Y	Y	N	N	Y
3	**Amash**	Y	Y	Y	N	N	Y
4	**Moolenaar**	N	N	N	N	N	N
5	Kildee	Y	Y	Y	N	N	Y
6	**Upton**	Y	Y	N	Y	Y	Y
7	**Walberg**	Y	Y	Y	N	N	Y
8	Slotkin	Y	Y	Y	N	N	Y
9	Levin	Y	Y	Y	Y	Y	Y
10	**Mitchell**	Y	Y	N	Y	Y	N
11	Stevens	Y	Y	Y	N	N	Y
12	Dingell	Y	Y	N	Y	Y	Y
13	Tlaib	Y	Y	N	Y	Y	N
14	Lawrence	Y	Y	N	Y	Y	N
MINNESOTA		Y	Y	N	Y	Y	N
1	**Hagedorn**						
2	Craig	Y	Y	Y	N	N	Y
3	Phillips	Y	Y	Y	Y	Y	Y
4	McCollum	Y	Y	N	Y	Y	Y
5	Omar	Y	Y	N	Y	Y	Y

		421	422	423	424	425	426
6	**Emmer**	Y	Y	N	Y	Y	N
7	Peterson	Y	Y	Y	N	N	Y
8	**Stauber**	Y	Y	Y	N	Y	Y
MISSISSIPPI		Y	Y	Y	N	N	Y
1	**Kelly, T.**						
2	Thompson, B.	Y	N	Y	N	N	Y
3	**Guest**	Y	Y	N	Y	Y	Y
4	**Palazzo**	Y	Y	Y	N	N	Y
MISSOURI		Y	N	Y	N	N	Y
1	Clay						
2	**Wagner**	Y	Y	N	Y	Y	Y
3	**Luetkemeyer**	Y	Y	Y	N	N	Y
4	**Hartzler**	Y	Y	Y	N	N	Y
5	Cleaver	Y	Y	Y	N	N	Y
6	**Graves, S.**	Y	Y	N	Y	Y	Y
7	**Long**	Y	Y	Y	N	N	Y
8	**Smith, J.**	Y	Y	Y	N	N	Y
MONTANA		Y	N	Y	N	N	Y
AL	**Gianforte**						
NEBRASKA		Y	Y	Y	N	N	Y
1	**Fortenberry**						
2	**Bacon**	Y	Y	Y	N	N	Y
3	**Smith, Adrian**	Y	Y	Y	N	N	Y
NEVADA		Y	Y	Y	N	N	Y
1	Titus						
2	**Amodei**	Y	Y	N	Y	Y	N
3	Lee	Y	Y	Y	N	N	Y
4	Horsford	Y	Y	Y	Y	Y	Y
NEW HAMPSHIRE		Y	Y	N	Y	Y	Y
1	Pappas						
2	Kuster	Y	Y	N	Y	Y	Y
NEW JERSEY		Y	Y	N	Y	Y	Y
1	Norcross						
2	Van Drew	Y	Y	N	Y	Y	N
3	Kim	Y	Y	Y	Y	Y	Y
4	**Smith, C.**	Y	Y	Y	Y	Y	Y
5	Gottheimer	Y	Y	Y	N	N	Y
6	Pallone	Y	Y	Y	Y	Y	Y
7	Malinowski	Y	Y	N	Y	Y	Y
8	Sires	Y	Y	Y	Y	Y	N
9	Pascrell	Y	Y	N	Y	Y	Y
10	Payne	Y	Y	N	Y	Y	Y
11	Sherrill	Y	Y	N	Y	Y	Y
12	Watson Coleman	Y	Y	Y	Y	Y	Y
NEW MEXICO		Y	Y	N	Y	Y	N
1	Haaland						
2	Torres Small	Y	Y	N	Y	Y	N
3	Luján	Y	Y	Y	Y	Y	Y
NEW YORK		Y	Y	N	Y	Y	N
1	**Zeldin**						
2	**King, P.**	Y	Y	Y	N	N	Y
3	Suozzi	Y	Y	Y	N	N	Y
4	Rice, K.	Y	Y	N	Y	Y	Y
5	Meeks	?	Y	N	Y	Y	Y
6	Meng	Y	Y	N	Y	Y	N
7	Velázquez	Y	Y	N	Y	Y	N
8	Jeffries	Y	Y	N	Y	Y	N
9	Clarke	Y	Y	N	Y	Y	Y
10	Nadler	Y	Y	N	Y	Y	N
11	Rose	Y	Y	N	Y	Y	N
12	Maloney, C.	Y	Y	Y	Y	Y	Y
13	Espaillat	Y	Y	N	Y	Y	N
14	Ocasio-Cortez	Y	Y	N	Y	Y	N
15	Serrano	+	Y	N	Y	Y	N
16	Engel	Y	Y	N	Y	Y	Y
17	Lowey	Y	Y	N	Y	Y	Y
18	Maloney, S.P.	Y	Y	N	Y	Y	Y
19	Delgado	Y	Y	Y	Y	Y	Y
20	Tonko	Y	Y	Y	Y	Y	N
21	**Stefanik**	Y	Y	N	Y	Y	N
22	Brindisi	Y	Y	Y	N	N	Y
23	**Reed**	Y	Y	Y	Y	Y	Y
24	**Katko**	Y	Y	Y	N	N	Y
25	Morelle	Y	Y	Y	N	N	Y
26	Higgins, B.	Y	Y	N	Y	Y	Y
27	**Collins, C.**	Y	Y	N	Y	Y	N
NORTH CAROLINA		+	+	+	-	N	Y
1	Butterfield						
2	**Holding**	Y	Y	N	Y	Y	Y
3	**Jones***	Y	Y	Y	N	N	Y
4	Price						
5	**Foxx**	Y	Y	N	Y	Y	Y
6	**Walker**	Y	Y	Y	N	N	Y
7	**Rouzer**	Y	N	Y	N	N	Y

		421	422	423	424	425	426
8	**Hudson**	Y	N	Y	N	N	Y
9	vacant	Y	Y	Y	N	N	Y
10	**McHenry**	Y	Y	Y	N	N	Y
11	**Meadows**	Y	Y	Y	N	N	Y
12	Adams	Y	Y	N	Y	Y	Y
13	**Budd**	Y	N	Y	N	N	Y
NORTH DAKOTA							
AL	**Armstrong**	Y	N	Y	N	N	Y
OHIO							
1	**Chabot**	Y	Y	Y	N	N	Y
2	**Wenstrup**	Y	Y	Y	N	N	Y
3	Beatty	Y	Y	N	Y	Y	Y
4	**Jordan**	Y	N	Y	N	N	N
5	**Latta**	Y	Y	Y	N	N	Y
6	**Johnson, B.**	Y	Y	Y	N	N	Y
7	**Gibbs**	Y	Y	Y	N	N	Y
8	**Davidson**	N	N	Y	N	N	Y
9	Kaptur	Y	Y	N	Y	Y	?
10	**Turner**	Y	Y	Y	N	N	Y
11	Fudge	Y	Y	N	Y	Y	Y
12	**Balderson**	Y	Y	Y	N	N	Y
13	Ryan	?	?	?	?	?	?
14	**Joyce**	Y	Y	Y	N	N	Y
15	**Stivers**	Y	Y	Y	N	N	Y
16	**Gonzalez**	Y	Y	Y	N	N	Y
OKLAHOMA							
1	**Hern**	Y	Y	Y	N	N	Y
2	**Mullin**	?	?	?	?	?	?
3	**Lucas**	?	?	?	?	?	?
4	**Cole**	Y	Y	Y	N	N	Y
5	Horn	Y	Y	Y	Y	Y	Y
OREGON							
1	Bonamici	Y	Y	N	Y	Y	N
2	**Walden**	Y	Y	Y	N	N	Y
3	Blumenauer	Y	Y	N	Y	Y	N
4	DeFazio	Y	Y	N	Y	Y	N
5	Schrader	Y	Y	Y	Y	Y	?
PENNSYLVANIA							
1	**Fitzpatrick**	Y	Y	Y	N	N	Y
2	Boyle	Y	Y	N	Y	Y	Y
3	Evans	Y	Y	N	Y	Y	Y
4	Dean	Y	Y	N	Y	Y	Y
5	Scanlon	Y	Y	N	Y	Y	Y
6	Houlahan	Y	Y	Y	Y	Y	Y
7	Wild	Y	Y	Y	Y	Y	N
8	Cartwright	Y	Y	N	Y	Y	Y
9	**Meuser**	Y	N	Y	N	N	Y
10	**Perry**	Y	Y	Y	N	N	N
11	**Smucker**	Y	Y	Y	N	N	Y
12	**Marino***						
13	**Joyce**	Y	Y	Y	N	N	Y
14	**Reschenthaler**	Y	Y	Y	N	N	Y
15	**Thompson, G.**	Y	Y	Y	N	N	Y
16	**Kelly, M.**	Y	Y	Y	N	N	Y
17	Lamb	Y	Y	Y	Y	Y	Y
18	Doyle	Y	Y	N	Y	Y	Y
RHODE ISLAND							
1	Cicilline	Y	Y	N	Y	Y	N
2	Langevin	Y	Y	N	Y	Y	Y
SOUTH CAROLINA							
1	Cunningham	Y	Y	Y	Y	Y	Y
2	**Wilson, J.**	Y	N	Y	N	N	Y
3	**Duncan**	N	N	Y	N	N	Y
4	**Timmons**	Y	N	Y	N	N	Y
5	**Norman**	Y	N	Y	N	N	Y
6	Clyburn	Y	Y	N	Y	Y	Y
7	**Rice, T.**	N	N	Y	N	N	Y
SOUTH DAKOTA							
AL	**Johnson**	Y	Y	Y	N	N	Y
TENNESSEE							
1	**Roe**	Y	Y	Y	N	N	Y
2	**Burchett**	Y	N	Y	N	N	Y
3	**Fleischmann**	Y	N	Y	N	N	Y
4	**DesJarlais**	Y	Y	Y	N	?	Y
5	Cooper	Y	Y	N	Y	Y	Y
6	**Rose**	N	N	Y	N	N	Y
7	**Green**	Y	N	Y	N	N	Y
8	**Kustoff**	Y	Y	Y	N	?	?
9	Cohen	Y	Y	N	Y	Y	N
TEXAS							
1	**Gohmert**	N	N	Y	N	N	N
2	**Crenshaw**	Y	Y	Y	N	?	Y
3	**Taylor**	Y	Y	Y	N	N	?
4	**Ratcliffe**	Y	N	Y	N	N	Y

		421	422	423	424	425	426
5	**Gooden**	Y	N	Y	N	N	Y
6	**Wright**	N	N	Y	N	N	Y
7	Fletcher	Y	Y	N	Y	Y	Y
8	**Brady**	Y	Y	Y	N	N	Y
9	Green, A.	Y	Y	N	Y	Y	Y
10	**McCaul**	Y	Y	Y	N	N	Y
11	**Conaway**	Y	Y	Y	N	N	Y
12	**Granger**	Y	Y	Y	N	N	Y
13	**Thornberry**	Y	Y	Y	N	N	+
14	**Weber**	N	N	Y	N	N	Y
15	Gonzalez	Y	Y	Y	N	Y	Y
16	Escobar	Y	Y	N	Y	Y	N
17	**Flores**	Y	Y	Y	N	N	Y
18	Jackson Lee	Y	Y	N	Y	Y	N
19	**Arrington**	N	N	Y	N	N	Y
20	Castro	?	?	?	?	?	?
21	**Roy**	N	N	Y	N	N	N
22	**Olson**	Y	N	Y	N	N	Y
23	**Hurd**	Y	Y	Y	N	N	Y
24	**Marchant**	Y	N	Y	N	?	Y
25	**Williams**	Y	Y	Y	N	N	Y
26	**Burgess**	Y	Y	Y	N	N	Y
27	**Cloud**	Y	Y	Y	N	N	N
28	Cuellar	Y	Y	N	Y	Y	Y
29	Garcia, S.	Y	Y	N	Y	Y	N
30	Johnson, E.B.	Y	Y	N	Y	Y	Y
31	**Carter, J.**	Y	N	Y	N	N	Y
32	Allred	Y	Y	N	Y	Y	Y
33	Veasey	Y	Y	N	Y	Y	Y
34	Vela	Y	Y	N	N	Y	N
35	Doggett	Y	Y	N	Y	Y	N
36	**Babin**	N	N	Y	N	N	Y
UTAH							
1	**Bishop, R.**	Y	N	Y	N	N	Y
2	**Stewart**	Y	N	Y	N	N	Y
3	**Curtis**	Y	N	Y	N	N	Y
4	McAdams	Y	Y	Y	N	Y	Y
VERMONT							
AL	Welch	Y	Y	N	Y	Y	Y
VIRGINIA							
1	**Wittman**	Y	Y	Y	N	N	Y
2	Luria	Y	Y	Y	Y	Y	Y
3	Scott, R.	Y	Y	N	Y	Y	Y
4	McEachin	Y	Y	N	Y	Y	Y
5	**Riggleman**	Y	Y	Y	N	N	Y
6	**Cline**	Y	N	Y	N	N	Y
7	Spanberger	Y	Y	Y	Y	Y	Y
8	Beyer	Y	Y	N	Y	Y	N
9	**Griffith**	Y	N	Y	N	N	N
10	Wexton	Y	Y	N	Y	Y	Y
11	Connolly	Y	Y	N	Y	Y	N
WASHINGTON							
1	DelBene	Y	Y	N	Y	Y	Y
2	Larsen	Y	Y	N	Y	Y	Y
3	**Herrera Beutler**	Y	Y	Y	N	N	Y
4	**Newhouse**	Y	Y	Y	N	N	Y
5	**McMorris Rodgers**	Y	Y	Y	N	N	Y
6	Kilmer	Y	Y	N	Y	Y	Y
7	Jayapal	Y	Y	N	Y	Y	N
8	Schrier	Y	Y	Y	Y	Y	Y
9	Smith Adam	Y	Y	N	Y	Y	N
10	Heck	Y	Y	N	Y	Y	Y
WEST VIRGINIA							
1	**McKinley**	Y	Y	Y	N	N	Y
2	**Mooney**	Y	Y	Y	N	N	Y
3	**Miller**	Y	Y	Y	N	N	Y
WISCONSIN							
1	**Steil**	Y	N	Y	N	N	Y
2	Pocan	Y	Y	N	Y	Y	N
3	Kind	Y	Y	N	Y	Y	Y
4	Moore	Y	Y	N	Y	Y	N
5	**Sensenbrenner**	N	N	Y	N	N	+
6	**Grothman**	Y	N	Y	N	N	N
7	**Duffy**	Y	Y	Y	N	N	Y
8	**Gallagher**	Y	Y	Y	N	N	Y
WYOMING							
AL	**Cheney**	Y	Y	Y	N	N	Y
DELEGATES							
	Radewagen (A.S.)	Y	Y				
	Norton (D.C.)	Y	Y				
	San Nicolas (Guam)	Y	Y				
	Sablan (N. Marianas)	Y	Y				
	González-Colón (P.R.)	Y	Y				
	Plaskett (V.I.)	Y	Y				

427. HR2722. Election Security and Accessibility - Recommit. Davis, R-Ill., motion to recommit the bill to the House Administration Committee with instructions to report it back immediately with an amendment that would require state election officials to disclose to the U.S. Election Assistance Commission within 30 days the identity of any foreign national known to have handled voting equipment or have had unmonitored access to certain election-related facilities or communications technology, including voter registration databases. Motion rejected 189-220: R 183-2; D 6-218. June 27, 2019.

428. HR2722. Election Security and Accessibility - Passage. Passage of the bill, as amended, that would authorize funding for and establish a number of requirements related to voting system infrastructure, security, and audits for federal elections. Specifically, it would require each jurisdiction administering voting for a federal election to conduct votes with paper ballots that can be counted either by hand or optical scanner and to conduct manual audits for all federal elections before an election is certified. It would authorize $1.3 billion through fiscal 2026 for U.S. Election Assistance Commission grants for states to update voting systems in accordance with the bill's provisions, including for cybersecurity risk mitigation and to conduct post-election audits. Among other provisions, it would require states to use voting system hardware and software manufactured in the U.S., require that such systems are tested by the Commission at least nine months before a general federal election, and establish certain disclosure and cybersecurity incident reporting requirements for vendors of voting system equipment. It would also prohibit states from using voting systems connected to the internet or containing wireless capabilities and would require jurisdictions to ensure that each polling station has voting systems equipped for individuals with disabilities, including visual and mobility disabilities. Passed 225-184: R 1-184; D 224-0. June 27, 2019.

429. HR3401. Supplemental Border Appropriations - Motion to Concur. Lowey, D-N.Y., motion to concur in the Senate amendment to the Emergency Supplemental Appropriations for Humanitarian Assistance and Security at the Southern Border Act that would provide a total of $4.6 billion in supplemental fiscal 2019 appropriations to address humanitarian concerns for migrants at the U.S.-Mexico border. Specifically, It would provide $2.9 billion for the Health and Human Services Department office of refugee resettlement, including $866 million for the provision of care in state-licensed shelters and expansion of the number of licensed shelters and $100 million for post-release, legal, and child advocacy services. It would provide $1.1 billion for U.S. Customs and Border Protection, including $793 million for acquisition, construction, and operation of migrant processing facilities, $112 million for medical care, food, water, sanitary items, and other supplies for migrants. It would provide $209 million for U.S. Immigration and Customs Enforcement, including $45 million for detainee medical care and $35.9 million for the transportation of unaccompanied minors to HHS custody. It would provide $144.8 million to the Department of Defense for operating expenses of the Army, Marine Corps, Air Force, and National Guard for activities in response to migration at the U.S. southwest border, including medical assistance and mobile surveillance. It would also provide $30 million for Federal Emergency Management Agency emergency food and shelter programs providing assistance to migrants released from DHS custody, $15 million for the Justice Department immigration review office legal orientation program, and $155 million to the U.S. Marshals Service for federal prisoner detention. It would also establish contracting standards for unlicensed facilities used as "influx shelters" by HHS, limit the period unaccompanied minors may be held at such facilities, and require HHS to ensure that certain minors are not held at such facilities, including those with special medical needs. Motion agreed to 305-102: R 176-7; D 129-95. June 27, 2019.

430. Procedural Motion - Journal. Approval of the House Journal of June 27, 2019. Approved 159-149: R 37-94; D 122-55. June 27, 2019.

431. HR2515. Whistle-blower Protections - Passage. Waters, D-Calif., motion to suspend the rules and pass the bill, as amended, that would expand the definition of "whistle-blower" in relation to securities law to include individuals who report potential misconduct regarding securities law to their employer or another employee within their company - including individuals who do not notify the Securities and Exchange Commission of such misconduct. Motion agreed to 410-12: R 181-11; D 229-0; I 0-1. *Note: A two-thirds majority of those present and voting (282 in this case) is required for passage under suspension of the rules.* July 9, 2019.

432. HR3050. Securities Ownership Limitation - Passage. Waters, D-Calif., motion to suspend the rules and pass the bill, as amended, that would require the Securities and Exchange Commission to conduct a study on an existing threshold limitation that restricts diversified investment companies from owning more than 10 percent of the securities of a single issuer. Among other requirements, it would require the study to address the size and number of companies affected by the restriction; how investing preferences of diversified companies have changed over time; and potential impacts of altering the threshold on small companies and companies in emerging growth markets. Motion agreed to 417-2: R 189-1; D 227-1; I 1-0. *Note: A two-thirds majority of those present and voting (280 in this case) is required for passage under suspension of the rules.* July 9, 2019.

		427	428	429	430	431	432
ALABAMA							
1	**Byrne**	Y	N	Y	N	Y	Y
2	**Roby**	Y	N	Y	N	Y	Y
3	**Rogers, M.**	?	?	Y	?	Y	Y
4	**Aderholt**	Y	N	Y	N	Y	Y
5	**Brooks, M.**	Y	N	N	?	Y	Y
6	**Palmer**	Y	N	Y	N	Y	Y
7	Sewell	N	Y	Y	N	Y	Y
ALASKA							
AL	**Young**	?	?	?	?	Y	Y
ARIZONA							
1	O'Halleran	N	Y	Y	N	Y	Y
2	Kirkpatrick	N	Y	Y	N	Y	Y
3	Grijalva	N	Y	N	?	?	?
4	**Gosar**	Y	N	N	N	Y	Y
5	**Biggs**	Y	N	N	N	Y	Y
6	**Schweikert**	Y	N	Y	Y	Y	Y
7	Gallego	N	Y	N	Y	Y	Y
8	**Lesko**	Y	N	Y	Y	Y	Y
9	Stanton	N	Y	Y	Y	Y	Y
ARKANSAS							
1	**Crawford**	Y	N	Y	?	Y	Y
2	**Hill, F.**	Y	N	Y	N	Y	Y
3	**Womack**	Y	N	Y	N	Y	Y
4	**Westerman**	Y	N	Y	N	Y	Y
CALIFORNIA							
1	**LaMalfa**	Y	N	Y	?	Y	Y
2	Huffman	N	Y	N	?	Y	Y
3	Garamendi	N	Y	Y	?	Y	?
4	**McClintock**	Y	N	Y	Y	N	Y
5	Thompson, M.	N	Y	Y	N	Y	Y
6	Matsui	N	Y	Y	Y	Y	Y
7	Bera	N	Y	Y	N	Y	Y
8	**Cook**	Y	N	Y	N	Y	Y
9	McNerney	N	Y	Y	Y	Y	Y
10	Harder	N	Y	Y	N	Y	Y
11	DeSaulnier	N	Y	N	N	Y	Y
12	Pelosi						
13	Lee B.	N	Y	N	N	Y	Y
14	Speier	N	Y	N	?	Y	Y
15	Swalwell	-	+	-	+	Y	Y
16	Costa	N	Y	Y	?	Y	Y
17	Khanna	N	Y	N	Y	Y	Y
18	Eshoo	N	Y	Y	?	Y	Y
19	Lofgren	N	Y	N	?	Y	Y
20	Panetta	N	Y	Y	N	Y	Y
21	Cox	N	Y	Y	?	Y	Y
22	**Nunes**	Y	N	Y	N	Y	Y
23	**McCarthy**	Y	N	Y	Y	Y	Y
24	Carbajal	N	Y	Y	Y	Y	Y
25	Hill, K.	N	Y	N	Y	Y	Y
26	Brownley	N	Y	Y	Y	Y	Y
27	Chu	N	Y	N	Y	Y	Y
28	Schiff	N	Y	Y	N	Y	Y
29	Cárdenas	N	Y	N	Y	Y	Y
30	Sherman	N	Y	N	Y	Y	Y
31	Aguilar	N	Y	N	N	Y	Y
32	Napolitano	N	Y	N	?	Y	Y
33	Lieu	N	Y	N	Y	Y	Y
34	Gomez	N	Y	N	N	Y	Y
35	Torres	N	Y	N	N	Y	Y
36	Ruiz	N	Y	Y	Y	Y	Y
37	Bass	N	Y	N	N	Y	Y
38	Sánchez	N	Y	N	Y	Y	Y
39	Cisneros	N	Y	N	?	Y	Y
40	Roybal-Allard	N	Y	N	?	Y	Y
41	Takano	N	Y	N	Y	Y	Y
42	**Calvert**	Y	N	Y	?	Y	Y
43	Waters	N	Y	Y	N	Y	Y
44	Barragán	N	Y	N	?	Y	Y
45	Porter	N	Y	Y	N	Y	Y
46	Correa	N	Y	N	N	Y	Y
47	Lowenthal	N	Y	N	Y	Y	Y
48	Rouda	N	Y	Y	?	Y	Y
49	Levin	N	Y	Y	Y	Y	Y
50	**Hunter**	Y	N	Y	?	Y	Y
51	Vargas	N	Y	N	Y	Y	Y
52	Peters	N	Y	Y	N	Y	Y
53	Davis, S.	N	Y	Y	Y	Y	Y
COLORADO							
1	DeGette	N	Y	N	Y	Y	Y
2	Neguse	N	Y	N	Y	Y	Y
3	**Tipton**	Y	N	Y	Y	Y	Y
4	**Buck**	Y	N	?	?	Y	?
5	**Lamborn**	Y	N	Y	?	Y	Y
6	Crow	N	Y	Y	N	Y	Y
7	Perlmutter	N	Y	Y	?	Y	Y
CONNECTICUT							
1	Larson	N	Y	Y	?	Y	Y
2	Courtney	N	Y	Y	?	Y	Y
3	DeLauro	N	Y	N	Y	Y	Y
4	Himes	N	Y	Y	N	Y	Y
5	Hayes	N	Y	Y	Y	Y	Y
DELAWARE							
AL	Blunt Rochester	N	Y	Y	Y	Y	Y
FLORIDA							
1	**Gaetz**	Y	N	Y	N	Y	?
2	**Dunn**	Y	N	Y	?	Y	Y
3	**Yoho**	Y	N	Y	?	Y	Y
4	**Rutherford**	Y	N	Y	Y	Y	Y
5	Lawson	N	Y	Y	N	Y	Y
6	**Waltz**	Y	N	Y	N	Y	Y
7	Murphy	N	Y	Y	N	Y	Y
8	**Posey**	Y	N	Y	N	Y	Y
9	Soto	N	Y	N	Y	Y	Y
10	Demings	N	Y	Y	Y	Y	Y
11	**Webster**	Y	N	Y	?	Y	Y
12	**Bilirakis**	Y	N	Y	?	Y	Y
13	Crist	N	Y	Y	N	Y	Y
14	Castor	N	Y	Y	Y	Y	Y
15	**Spano**	Y	N	Y	N	Y	Y
16	**Buchanan**	Y	N	Y	?	Y	Y
17	**Steube**	+	-	+	-	Y	Y
18	**Mast**	Y	Y	Y	N	N	Y
19	**Rooney**	?	?	?	?	Y	Y
20	Hastings	?	?	?	?	Y	Y
21	Frankel	N	Y	Y	?	+	+
22	Deutch	N	Y	Y	Y	Y	Y
23	Wasserman Schultz	N	Y	Y	Y	Y	Y
24	Wilson, F.	-	+	+	+	?	?
25	**Diaz-Balart**	Y	N	Y	N	+	+
26	Mucarsel-Powell	N	Y	N	Y	Y	Y
27	Shalala	N	Y	Y	Y	Y	Y
GEORGIA							
1	**Carter, E.L.**	Y	N	+	-	Y	Y
2	Bishop, S.	N	Y	Y	Y	Y	Y
3	**Ferguson**	Y	N	Y	?	Y	Y
4	Johnson, H.	N	Y	Y	Y	Y	Y
5	Lewis John	N	Y	N	Y	Y	Y
6	McBath	N	Y	Y	N	Y	Y
7	**Woodall**	Y	N	Y	N	Y	Y
8	**Scott, A.**	Y	N	Y	?	Y	Y
9	**Collins, D.**	Y	N	Y	?	Y	Y
10	**Hice**	Y	N	Y	?	Y	Y
11	**Loudermilk**	Y	N	Y	?	Y	Y
12	**Allen**	Y	N	Y	N	Y	Y
13	Scott, D.	N	Y	Y	Y	Y	Y
14	**Graves, T.**	Y	N	Y	N	Y	Y
HAWAII							
1	Case	N	Y	Y	Y	Y	Y
2	Gabbard	?	?	?	?	Y	Y
IDAHO							
1	**Fulcher**	Y	N	Y	N	Y	Y
2	**Simpson**	Y	N	Y	?	Y	Y
ILLINOIS							
1	Rush	N	Y	Y	?	Y	Y
2	Kelly, R.	N	Y	Y	Y	Y	Y
3	Lipinski	N	Y	Y	?	Y	Y
4	García, J.	N	Y	N	Y	Y	Y
5	Quigley	N	Y	N	?	Y	Y
6	Casten	N	Y	Y	Y	Y	N
7	Davis, D.	N	Y	N	Y	Y	Y
8	Krishnamoorthi	N	Y	Y	?	Y	Y
9	Schakowsky	N	Y	N	Y	Y	Y
10	Schneider	N	Y	Y	Y	Y	Y
11	Foster	N	Y	Y	?	Y	Y

KEY: **Republicans** Democrats *Independents*

Y Voted for (yea) N Voted against (nay) P Voted "present"
\+ Announced for - Announced against ? Did not vote or otherwise make position known
\# Paired for X Paired against

***NOTE:**
(Michigan 3) Rep. Justin Amash left the Republican party on July 4. He is considered an independent starting with vote 431.

		427	428	429	430	431	432
12	**Bost**	Y	N	Y	Y	Y	Y
13	**Davis, R.**	Y	N	Y	?	Y	Y
14	Underwood	N	Y	Y	Y	Y	Y
15	**Shimkus**	Y	N	Y	?	Y	Y
16	**Kinzinger**	+	-	+	+	Y	Y
17	Bustos	N	Y	Y	Y	Y	Y
18	**LaHood**	Y	N	Y	N	Y	Y
INDIANA							
1	Visclosky	N	Y	Y	Y	Y	Y
2	**Walorski**	+	-	+	?	Y	Y
3	**Banks**	Y	N	Y	Y	Y	Y
4	**Baird**	Y	N	Y	N	Y	Y
5	**Brooks, S.**	Y	N	Y	N	+	+
6	**Pence**	Y	N	Y	N	Y	Y
7	Carson	N	Y	N	Y	Y	Y
8	**Bucshon**	Y	N	Y	Y	Y	Y
9	**Hollingsworth**	Y	N	Y	?	Y	Y
IOWA							
1	Finkenauer	Y	Y	Y	Y	Y	Y
2	Loebsack	N	Y	Y	Y	Y	Y
3	Axne	Y	Y	Y	Y	Y	Y
4	**King, S.**	Y	N	Y	-	Y	Y
KANSAS							
1	**Marshall**	Y	N	Y	?	Y	Y
2	**Watkins**	Y	N	Y	Y	Y	Y
3	Davids	N	Y	Y	Y	Y	Y
4	**Estes**	Y	N	Y	N	Y	Y
KENTUCKY							
1	**Comer**	Y	N	Y	Y	Y	Y
2	**Guthrie**	Y	N	Y	N	Y	Y
3	Yarmuth	N	Y	Y	?	Y	Y
4	**Massie**	N	N	N	?	N	N
5	**Rogers, H.**	Y	N	Y	?	Y	Y
6	**Barr**	Y	N	Y	Y	Y	Y
LOUISIANA							
1	**Scalise**	Y	N	Y	N	Y	Y
2	Richmond	?	?	?	?	Y	Y
3	**Higgins, C.**	Y	N	Y	?	N	Y
4	**Johnson, M.**	?	?	?	?	N	Y
5	**Abraham**	?	?	?	?	N	Y
6	**Graves, G.**	Y	N	Y	N	Y	Y
MAINE							
1	Pingree	N	Y	Y	Y	Y	Y
2	Golden	N	Y	Y	N	Y	Y
MARYLAND							
1	**Harris**	Y	N	Y	N	Y	Y
2	Ruppersberger	N	Y	Y	Y	Y	Y
3	Sarbanes	N	Y	Y	Y	Y	Y
4	Brown, A.	N	Y	N	Y	Y	Y
5	Hoyer	N	Y	Y	Y	Y	Y
6	Trone	N	Y	Y	Y	Y	Y
7	Cummings	N	Y	Y	Y	Y	Y
8	Raskin						
MASSACHUSETTS		N	Y	N	Y	Y	Y
1	Neal						
2	McGovern	N	Y	Y	?	Y	Y
3	Trahan	N	Y	N	Y	Y	Y
4	Kennedy	N	Y	N	Y	Y	Y
5	Clark	N	Y	N	Y	Y	Y
6	Moulton	N	Y	N	Y	Y	Y
7	Pressley	?	?	?	?	Y	Y
8	Lynch	N	Y	N	N	Y	Y
9	Keating	N	Y	Y	Y	Y	Y
MICHIGAN		N	Y	Y	?	Y	Y
1	**Bergman**						
2	**Huizenga**	Y	N	Y	Y	Y	Y
3	**Amash***	Y	N	Y	N	Y	Y
4	**Moolenaar**	N	N	N	N	N	Y
5	Kildee	N	Y	Y	Y	Y	Y
6	**Upton**	N	Y	Y	Y	Y	Y
7	**Walberg**	Y	N	Y	?	Y	Y
8	Slotkin	Y	N	Y	N	Y	Y
9	Levin	N	Y	Y	Y	Y	Y
10	**Mitchell**	N	Y	N	Y	Y	Y
11	Stevens	Y	N	Y	Y	N	Y
12	Dingell	N	Y	Y	N	Y	Y
13	Tlaib	N	Y	N	Y	Y	Y
14	Lawrence	N	Y	N	Y	Y	Y
MINNESOTA		N	Y	N	Y	Y	Y
1	**Hagedorn**						
2	Craig	Y	N	Y	N	Y	Y
3	Phillips	N	Y	Y	N	Y	Y
4	McCollum	N	Y	Y	Y	Y	Y
5	Omar	N	Y	N	Y	Y	Y

		427	428	429	430	431	432
6	**Emmer**	N	Y	N	Y	Y	Y
7	Peterson	Y	N	+	+	Y	Y
8	**Stauber**	N	Y	Y	?	Y	Y
MISSISSIPPI		Y	N	Y	Y	Y	Y
1	**Kelly, T.**						
2	Thompson, B.	Y	N	Y	N	Y	Y
3	**Guest**	N	Y	Y	N	Y	Y
4	**Palazzo**	Y	N	Y	N	?	?
MISSOURI		Y	N	Y	?	Y	Y
1	Clay						
2	**Wagner**	N	Y	N	Y	Y	Y
3	**Luetkemeyer**	Y	N	Y	?	Y	Y
4	**Hartzler**	Y	N	Y	?	Y	Y
5	Cleaver	Y	N	Y	N	Y	Y
6	**Graves, S.**	N	Y	Y	Y	Y	Y
7	**Long**	Y	N	Y	N	Y	Y
8	**Smith, J.**	Y	N	Y	?	Y	Y
MONTANA		Y	N	Y	N	Y	Y
AL	**Gianforte**						
NEBRASKA		Y	N	Y	?	?	?
1	**Fortenberry**						
2	**Bacon**	Y	N	Y	N	Y	Y
3	**Smith, Adrian**	Y	N	Y	Y	Y	Y
NEVADA		Y	N	Y	N	Y	Y
1	Titus						
2	**Amodei**	N	Y	N	Y	Y	Y
3	Lee	Y	N	Y	N	Y	Y
4	Horsford	N	Y	Y	N	Y	Y
NEW HAMPSHIRE		N	Y	N	Y	Y	Y
1	Pappas						
2	Kuster	N	Y	Y	Y	Y	Y
NEW JERSEY		N	Y	Y	Y	Y	Y
1	Norcross						
2	Van Drew	N	Y	N	Y	Y	Y
3	Kim	Y	Y	Y	N	Y	Y
4	**Smith, C.**	N	Y	Y	Y	Y	Y
5	Gottheimer	Y	N	Y	Y	Y	Y
6	Pallone	N	Y	Y	N	Y	Y
7	Malinowski	N	Y	N	Y	Y	Y
8	Sires	N	Y	Y	Y	Y	Y
9	Pascrell	N	Y	Y	?	Y	Y
10	Payne	N	Y	N	?	Y	Y
11	Sherrill	N	Y	Y	N	Y	Y
12	Watson Coleman	N	Y	Y	?	Y	Y
NEW MEXICO		N	Y	Y	N	Y	Y
1	Haaland						
2	Torres Small	N	Y	N	?	Y	Y
3	Luján	N	Y	Y	N	Y	Y
NEW YORK		N	Y	N	N	Y	Y
1	**Zeldin**						
2	**King, P.**	Y	N	Y	N	Y	Y
3	Suozzi	Y	N	Y	?	Y	Y
4	Rice, K.	N	Y	Y	?	Y	Y
5	Meeks	N	Y	Y	N	Y	Y
6	Meng	N	Y	N	Y	Y	Y
7	Velázquez	N	Y	N	N	Y	Y
8	Jeffries	N	Y	N	Y	Y	Y
9	Clarke	N	Y	N	Y	Y	Y
10	Nadler	N	Y	N	Y	Y	Y
11	Rose	N	Y	N	?	Y	Y
12	Maloney, C.	N	Y	Y	N	Y	Y
13	Espaillat	N	Y	N	Y	Y	Y
14	Ocasio-Cortez	N	Y	N	Y	Y	Y
15	Serrano	N	Y	N	Y	Y	Y
16	Engel	N	Y	Y	Y	Y	Y
17	Lowey	N	Y	N	Y	Y	Y
18	Maloney, S.P.	N	Y	N	Y	Y	Y
19	Delgado	N	Y	Y	?	Y	Y
20	Tonko	N	Y	N	Y	Y	Y
21	**Stefanik**	N	Y	N	P	Y	Y
22	Brindisi	Y	N	Y	Y	Y	Y
23	**Reed**	N	Y	Y	N	Y	Y
24	**Katko**	Y	N	Y	N	Y	Y
25	Morelle	Y	N	Y	N	Y	Y
26	Higgins, B.	N	Y	Y	Y	Y	Y
27	**Collins, C.**	N	Y	N	N	Y	Y
NORTH CAROLINA		Y	N	Y	?	Y	Y
1	Butterfield						
2	**Holding**	N	Y	N	Y	Y	Y
3	**Jones***	Y	N	Y	N	Y	Y
4	Price						
5	**Foxx**	N	Y	N	Y	Y	Y
6	**Walker**	Y	N	Y	N	Y	Y
7	**Rouzer**	Y	N	Y	Y	Y	Y

		427	428	429	430	431	432
8	**Hudson**	Y	N	Y	?	Y	Y
9	vacant	Y	N	Y	N	Y	Y
10	**McHenry**	Y	N	Y	N	Y	Y
11	**Meadows**	Y	N	Y	?	Y	Y
12	Adams	N	Y	N	Y	Y	Y
13	**Budd**	Y	N	Y	Y	Y	Y
NORTH DAKOTA							
AL	**Armstrong**	Y	N	Y	Y	Y	Y
OHIO							
1	**Chabot**	Y	N	Y	N	Y	Y
2	**Wenstrup**	Y	N	Y	?	Y	Y
3	Beatty	N	Y	Y	Y	Y	Y
4	**Jordan**	Y	N	Y	N	Y	Y
5	**Latta**	Y	N	Y	N	Y	Y
6	**Johnson, B.**	Y	N	Y	N	Y	Y
7	**Gibbs**	Y	N	Y	N	Y	Y
8	**Davidson**	Y	N	Y	Y	Y	Y
9	Kaptur	?	?	?	?	Y	Y
10	**Turner**	Y	N	Y	N	Y	Y
11	Fudge	N	Y	Y	N	Y	Y
12	**Balderson**	Y	N	Y	N	Y	Y
13	Ryan	?	?	?	?	?	?
14	**Joyce**	Y	N	Y	?	Y	Y
15	**Stivers**	Y	N	Y	Y	Y	Y
16	**Gonzalez**	Y	N	Y	?	Y	Y
OKLAHOMA							
1	**Hern**	Y	N	Y	N	N	Y
2	**Mullin**	?	?	?	?	Y	Y
3	**Lucas**	?	?	?	?	Y	Y
4	**Cole**	Y	N	Y	N	Y	Y
5	Horn	N	Y	Y	N	Y	Y
OREGON							
1	Bonamici	N	Y	N	N	Y	Y
2	**Walden**	Y	N	Y	Y	Y	Y
3	Blumenauer	N	Y	N	?	Y	Y
4	DeFazio	N	Y	N	?	Y	Y
5	Schrader	?	?	?	?	Y	Y
PENNSYLVANIA							
1	**Fitzpatrick**	Y	N	Y	N	Y	Y
2	Boyle	N	Y	N	N	Y	Y
3	Evans	N	Y	N	Y	Y	Y
4	Dean	N	Y	Y	Y	Y	Y
5	Scanlon	N	Y	N	Y	Y	Y
6	Houlahan	N	Y	Y	?	Y	Y
7	Wild	N	Y	Y	Y	?	?
8	Cartwright	N	Y	Y	?	Y	Y
9	**Meuser**	Y	N	Y	N	Y	Y
10	**Perry**	Y	N	Y	Y	Y	Y
11	**Smucker**	Y	N	Y	Y	Y	Y
12	**Marino***						
13	**Joyce**	Y	N	Y	N	Y	Y
14	**Reschenthaler**	Y	N	Y	N	Y	Y
15	**Thompson, G.**	Y	N	Y	N	Y	Y
16	**Kelly, M.**	Y	N	Y	N	Y	Y
17	Lamb	N	Y	Y	Y	Y	Y
18	Doyle	N	Y	Y	?	Y	Y
RHODE ISLAND							
1	Cicilline	N	Y	N	Y	Y	Y
2	Langevin	N	Y	Y	Y	Y	Y
SOUTH CAROLINA							
1	Cunningham	Y	Y	Y	?	Y	Y
2	**Wilson, J.**	Y	N	Y	Y	Y	Y
3	**Duncan**	Y	N	Y	N	N	Y
4	**Timmons**	Y	N	Y	N	Y	Y
5	**Norman**	Y	N	Y	Y	Y	Y
6	Clyburn	N	Y	Y	Y	Y	Y
7	**Rice, T.**	Y	N	Y	?	N	Y
SOUTH DAKOTA							
AL	**Johnson**	Y	N	Y	N	Y	Y
TENNESSEE							
1	**Roe**	Y	N	Y	?	Y	Y
2	**Burchett**	Y	N	Y	N	Y	Y
3	**Fleischmann**	Y	N	Y	N	Y	Y
4	**DesJarlais**	Y	N	Y	N	Y	Y
5	Cooper	N	Y	Y	Y	Y	Y
6	**Rose**	Y	N	Y	N	Y	Y
7	**Green**	Y	N	Y	Y	Y	Y
8	**Kustoff**	?	?	?	?	Y	Y
9	Cohen	N	Y	Y	?	Y	Y
TEXAS							
1	**Gohmert**	Y	N	N	?	Y	Y
2	**Crenshaw**	Y	N	Y	?	Y	Y
3	**Taylor**	Y	N	Y	Y	Y	Y
4	**Ratcliffe**	Y	N	Y	N	Y	Y

		427	428	429	430	431	432
5	**Gooden**	Y	N	Y	N	Y	Y
6	**Wright**	Y	N	Y	N	N	Y
7	Fletcher	N	Y	Y	?	Y	Y
8	**Brady**	Y	N	Y	Y	Y	Y
9	Green, A.	N	Y	Y	Y	Y	Y
10	**McCaul**	Y	N	Y	N	Y	Y
11	**Conaway**	Y	N	Y	N	Y	Y
12	**Granger**	Y	N	Y	?	Y	Y
13	**Thornberry**	+	-	+	+	Y	Y
14	**Weber**	Y	N	Y	N	Y	Y
15	Gonzalez	Y	N	Y	Y	Y	Y
16	Escobar	N	Y	N	Y	Y	Y
17	**Flores**	Y	N	Y	N	Y	Y
18	Jackson Lee	N	Y	N	Y	Y	Y
19	**Arrington**	Y	N	Y	Y	Y	Y
20	Castro	?	?	?	?	Y	Y
21	**Roy**	Y	N	N	N	Y	Y
22	**Olson**	Y	N	Y	N	Y	Y
23	**Hurd**	Y	N	Y	N	Y	Y
24	**Marchant**	Y	N	Y	N	Y	Y
25	**Williams**	Y	N	Y	?	Y	Y
26	**Burgess**	Y	N	Y	?	Y	Y
27	**Cloud**	Y	N	Y	?	Y	Y
28	Cuellar	N	Y	Y	Y	Y	Y
29	Garcia, S.	N	Y	N	Y	Y	Y
30	Johnson, E.B.	N	Y	Y	Y	Y	Y
31	**Carter, J.**	Y	N	Y	Y	Y	Y
32	Allred	N	Y	Y	N	Y	Y
33	Veasey	N	Y	N	Y	Y	Y
34	Vela	N	Y	N	Y	Y	Y
35	Doggett	N	Y	N	?	Y	Y
36	**Babin**	Y	N	Y	N	Y	Y
UTAH							
1	**Bishop, R.**	Y	N	Y	?	Y	Y
2	**Stewart**	Y	N	Y	?	Y	Y
3	**Curtis**	Y	N	Y	N	Y	Y
4	McAdams	Y	Y	Y	N	Y	Y
VERMONT							
AL	Welch	N	Y	N	Y	Y	Y
VIRGINIA							
1	**Wittman**	Y	N	Y	N	Y	Y
2	Luria	N	Y	Y	Y	Y	Y
3	Scott, R.	N	Y	Y	Y	Y	Y
4	McEachin	N	Y	N	Y	Y	Y
5	**Riggleman**	Y	N	Y	N	Y	Y
6	**Cline**	Y	N	Y	N	Y	Y
7	Spanberger	Y	Y	Y	N	Y	Y
8	Beyer	N	Y	N	Y	Y	Y
9	**Griffith**	Y	N	Y	?	Y	Y
10	Wexton	N	Y	Y	N	Y	Y
11	Connolly	N	Y	N	N	Y	Y
WASHINGTON							
1	DelBene	N	Y	Y	N	Y	Y
2	Larsen	N	Y	Y	?	Y	Y
3	**Herrera Beutler**	Y	N	Y	N	Y	Y
4	**Newhouse**	Y	N	Y	Y	Y	Y
5	**McMorris Rodgers**	Y	N	Y	N	Y	Y
6	Kilmer	N	Y	Y	N	Y	Y
7	Jayapal	N	Y	N	?	Y	Y
8	Schrier	N	Y	Y	N	Y	Y
9	Smith Adam	N	Y	N	?	Y	Y
10	Heck	N	Y	Y	Y	Y	Y
WEST VIRGINIA							
1	**McKinley**	Y	N	Y	N	Y	Y
2	**Mooney**	Y	N	Y	N	Y	Y
3	**Miller**	Y	N	Y	N	Y	Y
WISCONSIN							
1	**Steil**	Y	N	Y	Y	Y	Y
2	Pocan	N	Y	N	?	Y	Y
3	Kind	N	Y	Y	N	Y	Y
4	Moore	N	Y	N	Y	Y	Y
5	**Sensenbrenner**	+	-	-	+	Y	Y
6	**Grothman**	Y	N	Y	N	Y	Y
7	**Duffy**	Y	N	Y	?	+	+
8	**Gallagher**	Y	N	Y	N	Y	Y
WYOMING							
AL	**Cheney**	Y	N	Y	?	Y	Y
DELEGATES							
	Radewagen (A.S.)						
	Norton (D.C.)						
	San Nicolas (Guam)						
	Sablan (N. Marianas)						
	González-Colón (P.R.)						
	Plaskett (V.I.)						

III HOUSE VOTES

433. HR2409. Rural Small Business Capital Access - Passage. Waters, D-Calif., motion to suspend the rules and pass the bill that would require the Securities and Exchange Commission office for small business capital formation to identify and include in its annual report to Congress challenges in securing access to capital faced by rural-area small businesses. Motion agreed to 413-7: R 185-6; D 228-0; I 0-1. *Note: A two-thirds majority of those present and voting (280 in this case) is required for passage under suspension of the rules.* July 9, 2019.

434. HR2500, HR1327. Fiscal 2020 Defense Authorization - Previous Question. McGovern, D-Mass., motion to order the previous question (thus ending debate and possibility of amendment) on the rule (H Res 476) and the McGovern, D-Mass., amendment to the rule that would provide for House floor consideration of the Fiscal 2020 National Defense Authorization Act (HR 2500). It would make in order consideration of 439 amendments to the bill. It would also provide for floor consideration of the bill (HR 1327) that would permanently reauthorize the 9/11 Victim Compensation Fund, under suspension of the rules on July 11 or July 12, 2019; and it would waive rules related to the House Consensus Calendar with regards to the Military Surviving Spouses Equity Act (HR 553). It would also provide for automatic adoption of a Smith, D-Wash., amendment to HR 2500. The Smith amendment would increase by 3.1 percent basic pay for members of the uniformed services and includes provisions related to Defense Department annuity plans and benefits for surviving spouses of service members, damage claims brought against the U.S. related to the injury or death of a service member, funding for the National Defense Stockpile transaction fund, and paid family and medical leave policies for federal employees, among other provisions. Motion agreed to 232-197: R 0-196; D 232-0; I 0-1. July 10, 2019.

435. HRES476. Fiscal 2020 Defense Authorization - Additional Amendments for NDAA. McGovern, D-Mass., amendment that would modify the rule (H Res 476) to make in order two additional amendments to the Fiscal 2020 National Defense Authorization Act (HR 2500). The amendments added to the rule include a Dingell, D-Mich., amendment related to EPA designation of per- and polyfluoroalkyl substances as hazardous and a Jayapal, D-Wash., amendment related to GAO studies on nuclear security activities. Adopted 234-197: R 0-197; D 233-0; I 1-0. July 10, 2019.

436. HR1327, HR2500. Fiscal 2020 Defense Authorization - Rule. Adoption of the rule (H Res 476), as amended, that would provide for House floor consideration of the Fiscal 2020 National Defense Authorization Act (HR 2500). As amended, it would make in order consideration of 441 amendments to the bill. It would also provide for floor consideration of the bill (HR 1327) that would permanently reauthorize the 9/11 Victim Compensation Fund, under suspension of the rules on July 11 or July 12, 2019; and it would waive rules related to the House Consensus Calendar with regards to the Military Surviving Spouses Equity Act (HR 553). It would also provide for automatic adoption of a Smith, D-Wash., amendment to HR 2500. The Smith amendment would increase by 3.1 percent basic pay for members of the uniformed services and includes provisions related to Defense Department annuity plans and benefits for surviving spouses of service members, damage claims brought against the U.S. related to the injury or death of a service member, funding for the National Defense Stockpile transaction fund, and paid family and medical leave policies for federal employees, among other provisions. Adopted 234-197: R 2-195; D 232-1; I 0-1. July 10, 2019.

437. HR1044. Immigration Visa Caps - Passage. Lofgren, D-Calif., motion to suspend the rules and pass the bill, as amended, that would eliminate employment-based immigrant visas from a seven percent per-country annual cap calculation under existing law. It would establish a per-country annual cap for family-sponsored immigrant visas at 15 percent of all family visas offered each year, which may be exceeded if the other available visas are not used by citizens of other nations. It also outlines a transition period for reducing the annual percentage of employment-based visas reserved for certain categories of immigrants from countries other than the top two visa-recipient countries. Motion agreed to 365-65: R 140-57; D 224-8; I 1-0. *Note: A two-thirds majority of those present and voting (287 in this case) is required for passage under suspension of the rules.* July 10, 2019.

438. HR2500. Fiscal 2020 Defense Authorization - Military Strikes Report. Smith, D-Wash., amendment that would require an annual report on U.S. strikes against terrorist targets outside areas of active hostilities to be submitted by the Director of National Intelligence instead of the Secretary of Defense. The annual report, required under the bill's provisions, would detail the number of such strikes undertaken and assess combatant and non-combatant deaths resulting from those strikes. Adopted in Committee of the Whole 236-193: R 3-193; D 231-0; I 2-0. July 11, 2019.

		433	434	435	436	437	438
ALABAMA							
1	**Byrne**	Y	N	N	N	Y	N
2	**Roby**	Y	N	N	N	Y	N
3	**Rogers, M.**	Y	N	N	N	N	N
4	**Aderholt**	Y	N	N	N	N	N
5	**Brooks, M.**	Y	N	N	N	N	N
6	**Palmer**	Y	N	N	N	N	N
7	Sewell	Y	Y	Y	Y	Y	Y
ALASKA							
AL	**Young**	Y	N	N	N	Y	N
ARIZONA							
1	O'Halleran	Y	Y	Y	Y	Y	Y
2	Kirkpatrick	Y	Y	Y	Y	Y	Y
3	Grijalva	?	Y	Y	Y	Y	Y
4	**Gosar**	N	N	N	N	N	N
5	**Biggs**	N	N	N	N	N	N
6	**Schweikert**	Y	N	N	N	Y	N
7	Gallego	Y	Y	Y	Y	Y	Y
8	**Lesko**	Y	N	N	N	Y	N
9	Stanton	Y	Y	Y	Y	Y	Y
ARKANSAS							
1	**Crawford**	Y	N	N	N	Y	N
2	**Hill, F.**	Y	N	N	N	Y	N
3	**Womack**	Y	N	N	N	Y	N
4	**Westerman**	Y	N	N	N	Y	N
CALIFORNIA							
1	**LaMalfa**	Y	N	N	N	Y	N
2	Huffman	Y	Y	Y	Y	Y	Y
3	Garamendi	Y	Y	Y	Y	Y	Y
4	**McClintock**	Y	N	N	N	N	N
5	Thompson, M.	Y	Y	Y	Y	Y	Y
6	Matsui	Y	Y	Y	Y	Y	Y
7	Bera	Y	Y	Y	Y	Y	Y
8	**Cook**	Y	N	N	N	Y	N
9	McNerney	Y	Y	Y	Y	Y	?
10	Harder	Y	Y	Y	Y	Y	Y
11	DeSaulnier	Y	Y	Y	Y	Y	Y
12	Pelosi						
13	Lee B.	Y	Y	Y	Y	Y	Y
14	Speier	Y	Y	Y	Y	Y	Y
15	Swalwell	Y	Y	Y	Y	Y	Y
16	Costa	Y	Y	Y	Y	Y	Y
17	Khanna	Y	Y	Y	Y	Y	Y
18	Eshoo	Y	Y	Y	Y	Y	Y
19	Lofgren	Y	Y	Y	Y	Y	Y
20	Panetta	Y	Y	Y	Y	Y	Y
21	Cox	Y	Y	Y	Y	Y	Y
22	**Nunes**	Y	N	N	N	Y	N
23	**McCarthy**	Y	N	N	N	Y	N
24	Carbajal	Y	Y	Y	Y	Y	Y
25	Hill, K.	Y	Y	Y	Y	Y	Y
26	Brownley	Y	Y	Y	Y	Y	Y
27	Chu	Y	Y	Y	Y	Y	Y
28	Schiff	Y	Y	Y	Y	Y	Y
29	Cárdenas	Y	Y	Y	Y	Y	Y
30	Sherman	Y	Y	Y	Y	Y	Y
31	Aguilar	Y	Y	Y	Y	Y	Y
32	Napolitano	Y	Y	Y	Y	Y	Y
33	Lieu	Y	Y	Y	Y	Y	Y
34	Gomez	Y	Y	Y	Y	Y	Y
35	Torres	Y	Y	Y	Y	Y	Y
36	Ruiz	Y	Y	Y	Y	Y	Y
37	Bass	Y	Y	Y	Y	Y	Y
38	Sánchez	Y	Y	Y	Y	Y	Y
39	Cisneros	Y	Y	Y	Y	Y	Y
40	Roybal-Allard	Y	Y	Y	Y	Y	Y
41	Takano	Y	Y	Y	Y	Y	Y
42	**Calvert**	Y	N	N	N	Y	N
43	Waters	Y	Y	Y	Y	Y	Y
44	Barragán	Y	Y	Y	Y	Y	Y
45	Porter	Y	+	Y	Y	Y	Y
46	Correa	Y	Y	Y	Y	Y	Y
47	Lowenthal	Y	Y	Y	Y	Y	Y
48	Rouda	Y	Y	Y	Y	Y	Y
49	Levin	Y	Y	Y	Y	Y	Y
50	**Hunter**	Y	N	N	N	N	N
51	Vargas	Y	Y	Y	Y	Y	Y
52	Peters	Y	Y	Y	Y	Y	Y

		433	434	435	436	437	438
53	Davis, S.	Y	Y	Y	Y	Y	Y
COLORADO							
1	DeGette	Y	Y	Y	Y	Y	Y
2	Neguse	Y	Y	Y	Y	Y	Y
3	**Tipton**	Y	N	N	N	Y	N
4	**Buck**	Y	N	N	N	N	N
5	**Lamborn**	Y	N	N	N	Y	N
6	Crow	Y	Y	Y	Y	Y	Y
7	Perlmutter	Y	Y	Y	Y	Y	?
CONNECTICUT							
1	Larson	Y	Y	Y	Y	Y	Y
2	Courtney	Y	Y	Y	Y	Y	Y
3	DeLauro	Y	Y	Y	Y	Y	Y
4	Himes	Y	Y	Y	Y	Y	Y
5	Hayes	Y	Y	Y	Y	Y	Y
DELAWARE							
AL	Blunt Rochester	Y	Y	Y	Y	Y	Y
FLORIDA							
1	**Gaetz**	N	N	N	N	N	N
2	**Dunn**	Y	N	N	N	N	N
3	**Yoho**	Y	N	N	N	N	N
4	**Rutherford**	Y	N	N	N	Y	N
5	Lawson	Y	Y	Y	Y	Y	Y
6	**Waltz**	Y	N	N	N	Y	N
7	Murphy	Y	Y	Y	Y	Y	Y
8	**Posey**	Y	N	N	N	Y	N
9	Soto	Y	Y	Y	Y	Y	Y
10	Demings	Y	Y	Y	Y	Y	Y
11	**Webster**	Y	N	N	N	Y	N
12	**Bilirakis**	Y	N	N	N	Y	N
13	Crist	Y	Y	Y	Y	Y	Y
14	Castor	Y	Y	Y	Y	Y	Y
15	**Spano**	Y	N	N	N	Y	N
16	**Buchanan**	Y	N	N	N	Y	N
17	**Steube**	Y	N	N	N	N	N
18	**Mast**	Y	N	N	N	Y	N
19	**Rooney**	Y	N	N	N	N	N
20	Hastings	Y	Y	Y	Y	Y	Y
21	Frankel	+	Y	Y	Y	Y	Y
22	Deutch	Y	Y	Y	Y	Y	Y
23	Wasserman Schultz	Y	Y	Y	Y	Y	Y
24	Wilson, F.	?	Y	Y	Y	Y	Y
25	**Diaz-Balart**	+	N	N	N	N	N
26	Mucarsel-Powell	Y	Y	Y	Y	Y	Y
27	Shalala	Y	Y	Y	Y	Y	Y
GEORGIA							
1	**Carter, E.L.**	Y	N	N	N	N	N
2	Bishop, S.	Y	Y	Y	Y	Y	Y
3	**Ferguson**	Y	N	N	N	N	N
4	Johnson, H.	Y	Y	Y	Y	Y	Y
5	Lewis John	Y	Y	Y	Y	Y	Y
6	McBath	Y	Y	Y	Y	Y	Y
7	**Woodall**	Y	N	N	N	N	N
8	**Scott, A.**	Y	N	N	N	N	N
9	**Collins, D.**	Y	N	N	N	N	N
10	**Hice**	Y	N	N	N	N	N
11	**Loudermilk**	Y	N	N	N	N	N
12	**Allen**	Y	N	N	N	N	N
13	Scott, D.	Y	Y	Y	Y	Y	Y
14	**Graves, T.**	Y	N	N	N	N	N
HAWAII							
1	Case	Y	Y	Y	Y	Y	Y
2	Gabbard	Y	Y	Y	Y	Y	?
IDAHO							
1	**Fulcher**	Y	N	N	N	Y	N
2	**Simpson**	Y	N	N	N	Y	N
ILLINOIS							
1	Rush	Y	Y	Y	Y	Y	Y
2	Kelly, R.	Y	Y	Y	Y	Y	Y
3	Lipinski	Y	Y	Y	Y	Y	Y
4	García, J.	Y	Y	Y	Y	Y	Y
5	Quigley	Y	Y	Y	Y	Y	Y
6	Casten	Y	Y	Y	Y	Y	Y
7	Davis, D.	Y	Y	Y	Y	Y	Y
8	Krishnamoorthi	Y	Y	Y	Y	Y	Y
9	Schakowsky	Y	Y	Y	Y	Y	Y
10	Schneider	Y	Y	Y	Y	Y	Y
11	Foster	Y	Y	Y	Y	Y	Y

		433	434	435	436	437	438
12	**Bost**	Y	N	N	N	Y	N
13	**Davis, R.**	Y	N	N	N	Y	N
14	Underwood	Y	Y	Y	Y	Y	Y
15	**Shimkus**	Y	N	N	N	Y	N
16	**Kinzinger**	Y	N	N	N	Y	N
17	Bustos	Y	Y	Y	Y	Y	Y
18	**LaHood**	Y	N	N	N	Y	N
INDIANA							
1	Visclosky	Y	Y	Y	Y	Y	Y
2	**Walorski**	Y	N	N	N	Y	N
3	**Banks**	Y	N	N	N	Y	N
4	**Baird**	Y	N	N	N	Y	N
5	**Brooks, S.**	+	N	N	N	Y	N
6	**Pence**	Y	N	N	N	Y	N
7	Carson	Y	Y	Y	Y	Y	Y
8	**Bucshon**	Y	N	N	N	Y	N
9	**Hollingsworth**	Y	N	N	N	Y	N
IOWA							
1	Finkenauer	Y	Y	Y	Y	Y	Y
2	Loebsack	Y	Y	Y	Y	Y	Y
3	Axne	Y	Y	Y	Y	Y	Y
4	**King, S.**	Y	N	N	N	N	N
KANSAS							
1	**Marshall**	Y	N	N	N	Y	N
2	**Watkins**	Y	N	N	N	Y	N
3	Davids	Y	Y	Y	Y	Y	Y
4	**Estes**	Y	N	N	N	Y	N
KENTUCKY							
1	**Comer**	Y	N	N	N	Y	N
2	**Guthrie**	Y	N	N	N	Y	N
3	Yarmuth	Y	Y	Y	Y	Y	Y
4	**Massie**	N	N	N	N	Y	Y
5	**Rogers, H.**	Y	N	N	N	Y	N
6	**Barr**	Y	N	N	N	Y	N
LOUISIANA							
1	**Scalise**	Y	N	N	N	N	N
2	Richmond	Y	Y	Y	Y	N	Y
3	**Higgins, C.**	Y	N	N	N	N	-
4	**Johnson, M.**	Y	N	N	N	N	N
5	**Abraham**	Y	N	N	N	N	N
6	**Graves, G.**	Y	N	N	N	N	N
MAINE							
1	Pingree	Y	Y	Y	Y	Y	Y
2	Golden	Y	Y	Y	Y	Y	Y
MARYLAND							
1	**Harris**	Y	N	N	N	N	N
2	Ruppersberger	Y	Y	Y	Y	Y	Y
3	Sarbanes	Y	Y	Y	Y	Y	Y
4	Brown, A.	Y	Y	Y	Y	N	Y
5	Hoyer	Y	Y	Y	Y	Y	Y
6	Trone	Y	Y	Y	Y	Y	Y
7	Cummings	Y	Y	Y	Y	Y	Y
8	Raskin						
MASSACHUSETTS		Y	Y	Y	Y	Y	Y
1	Neal						
2	McGovern	Y	Y	Y	Y	?	Y
3	Trahan	Y	Y	Y	Y	Y	Y
4	Kennedy	Y	Y	Y	Y	Y	Y
5	Clark	Y	Y	Y	Y	Y	Y
6	Moulton	Y	Y	Y	Y	Y	Y
7	Pressley	Y	Y	Y	Y	Y	Y
8	Lynch	Y	Y	Y	Y	Y	Y
9	Keating	Y	Y	Y	Y	Y	Y
MICHIGAN		Y	Y	Y	Y	Y	Y
1	**Bergman**						
2	**Huizenga**	Y	N	N	N	N	N
3	*Amash*	Y	N	N	N	N	N
4	**Moolenaar**	N	N	Y	N	Y	Y
5	Kildee	Y	N	N	N	Y	N
6	**Upton**	Y	Y	Y	Y	Y	Y
7	**Walberg**	Y	N	N	N	Y	N
8	Slotkin	Y	N	N	N	Y	N
9	Levin	Y	Y	Y	Y	Y	Y
10	**Mitchell**	Y	Y	Y	Y	Y	Y
11	Stevens	Y	N	N	N	Y	N
12	Dingell	Y	Y	Y	Y	Y	Y
13	Tlaib	Y	Y	Y	Y	Y	Y
14	Lawrence	Y	Y	Y	Y	N	Y
MINNESOTA		Y	Y	Y	Y	Y	Y
1	**Hagedorn**						
2	Craig	Y	N	N	N	Y	N
3	Phillips	Y	Y	Y	Y	Y	Y
4	McCollum	Y	Y	Y	Y	Y	Y
5	Omar	Y	Y	Y	Y	Y	Y

		433	434	435	436	437	438
6	**Emmer**	Y	Y	Y	Y	N	Y
7	Peterson	Y	N	N	N	Y	N
8	**Stauber**	Y	Y	Y	Y	Y	Y
MISSISSIPPI		Y	N	N	N	Y	N
1	**Kelly, T.**						
2	Thompson, B.	Y	N	N	N	N	N
3	**Guest**	Y	Y	Y	Y	Y	Y
4	**Palazzo**	?	N	N	N	Y	N
MISSOURI		Y	N	N	N	Y	N
1	Clay						
2	**Wagner**	Y	Y	Y	Y	Y	Y
3	**Luetkemeyer**	Y	N	N	N	Y	N
4	**Hartzler**	Y	N	N	N	Y	N
5	Cleaver	Y	N	N	N	Y	N
6	**Graves, S.**	Y	Y	Y	Y	Y	Y
7	**Long**	Y	N	N	N	Y	N
8	**Smith, J.**	Y	N	N	N	Y	N
MONTANA		Y	N	N	N	Y	N
AL	**Gianforte**						
NEBRASKA		?	N	N	N	Y	N
1	**Fortenberry**						
2	**Bacon**	Y	N	N	N	N	N
3	**Smith, Adrian**	Y	N	N	N	Y	N
NEVADA		Y	N	N	N	N	N
1	Titus						
2	**Amodei**	Y	Y	Y	Y	Y	Y
3	Lee	Y	N	N	N	Y	N
4	Horsford	Y	Y	Y	Y	Y	Y
NEW HAMPSHIRE		Y	Y	Y	Y	Y	Y
1	Pappas						
2	Kuster	Y	Y	Y	Y	Y	Y
NEW JERSEY		Y	Y	Y	Y	Y	Y
1	Norcross						
2	Van Drew	Y	Y	Y	Y	Y	Y
3	Kim	Y	Y	Y	Y	Y	Y
4	**Smith, C.**	Y	Y	Y	Y	Y	Y
5	Gottheimer	Y	N	N	N	Y	N
6	Pallone	Y	Y	Y	Y	Y	Y
7	Malinowski	Y	Y	Y	Y	Y	Y
8	Sires	Y	Y	Y	Y	Y	Y
9	Pascrell	Y	Y	Y	Y	Y	Y
10	Payne	Y	Y	Y	Y	Y	Y
11	Sherrill	Y	Y	Y	Y	Y	Y
12	Watson Coleman	Y	Y	Y	Y	Y	Y
NEW MEXICO		Y	Y	Y	Y	Y	Y
1	Haaland						
2	Torres Small	Y	Y	Y	Y	Y	Y
3	Luján	Y	Y	Y	Y	Y	Y
NEW YORK		Y	Y	Y	Y	Y	Y
1	**Zeldin**						
2	**King, P.**	Y	N	N	Y	Y	N
3	Suozzi	Y	N	N	Y	Y	N
4	Rice, K.	Y	Y	Y	Y	Y	Y
5	Meeks	Y	Y	Y	Y	Y	Y
6	Meng	Y	Y	Y	Y	Y	Y
7	Velázquez	Y	Y	Y	Y	Y	Y
8	Jeffries	Y	Y	Y	Y	Y	Y
9	Clarke	Y	Y	Y	Y	Y	Y
10	Nadler	Y	Y	Y	Y	N	Y
11	Rose	Y	Y	Y	Y	Y	Y
12	Maloney, C.	Y	Y	Y	Y	Y	Y
13	Espaillat	Y	Y	Y	Y	Y	Y
14	Ocasio-Cortez	Y	Y	Y	Y	Y	Y
15	Serrano	Y	Y	Y	Y	Y	Y
16	Engel	Y	Y	Y	Y	Y	Y
17	Lowey	Y	Y	Y	Y	Y	Y
18	Maloney, S.P.	Y	Y	Y	Y	Y	Y
19	Delgado	Y	Y	Y	Y	Y	Y
20	Tonko	Y	Y	Y	Y	Y	Y
21	**Stefanik**	Y	Y	Y	Y	Y	Y
22	Brindisi	+	N	N	N	Y	N
23	**Reed**	Y	Y	Y	Y	Y	Y
24	**Katko**	Y	N	N	N	Y	N
25	Morelle	Y	N	N	N	Y	N
26	Higgins, B.	Y	Y	Y	Y	Y	Y
27	**Collins, C.**	Y	Y	Y	Y	Y	Y
NORTH CAROLINA		Y	N	N	N	Y	N
1	Butterfield						
2	**Holding**	Y	Y	Y	Y	Y	Y
3	**Jones***	Y	N	N	N	Y	N
4	Price						
5	**Foxx**	Y	Y	Y	Y	Y	Y
6	**Walker**	Y	N	N	N	N	N
7	**Rouzer**	Y	N	N	N	N	N

		433	434	435	436	437	438
8	**Hudson**	Y	N	N	N	Y	N
9	vacant	Y	N	N	N	N	N
10	**McHenry**	Y	N	N	N	Y	N
11	**Meadows**	Y	N	N	N	N	N
12	Adams	Y	Y	Y	Y	Y	Y
13	**Budd**	Y	N	N	N	Y	N
NORTH DAKOTA							
AL	**Armstrong**	Y	N	N	N	Y	N
OHIO							
1	**Chabot**	Y	N	N	N	Y	N
2	**Wenstrup**	Y	N	N	N	Y	N
3	Beatty	Y	Y	Y	Y	Y	Y
4	**Jordan**	Y	N	N	N	Y	N
5	**Latta**	Y	N	N	N	Y	N
6	**Johnson, B.**	Y	N	N	N	Y	N
7	**Gibbs**	Y	N	N	N	Y	N
8	**Davidson**	Y	N	N	N	N	N
9	Kaptur	Y	Y	Y	Y	N	Y
10	**Turner**	Y	N	N	N	Y	N
11	Fudge	Y	Y	Y	Y	N	?
12	**Balderson**	Y	N	N	N	Y	N
13	Ryan	?	Y	Y	Y	Y	Y
14	**Joyce**	Y	N	N	N	Y	N
15	**Stivers**	Y	N	N	N	Y	Y
16	**Gonzalez**	Y	N	N	N	Y	N
OKLAHOMA							
1	**Hern**	Y	N	N	N	Y	N
2	**Mullin**	Y	N	N	N	Y	N
3	**Lucas**	Y	N	N	N	Y	N
4	**Cole**	Y	N	N	N	Y	N
5	Horn	Y	Y	Y	Y	Y	Y
OREGON							
1	Bonamici	Y	Y	Y	Y	Y	Y
2	**Walden**	Y	N	N	N	Y	N
3	Blumenauer	Y	Y	Y	Y	Y	Y
4	DeFazio	Y	Y	Y	Y	Y	Y
5	Schrader	Y	Y	Y	Y	Y	Y
PENNSYLVANIA							
1	**Fitzpatrick**	Y	N	N	N	Y	Y
2	Boyle	?	Y	Y	Y	Y	Y
3	Evans	Y	Y	Y	Y	Y	Y
4	Dean	Y	Y	Y	Y	Y	Y
5	Scanlon	Y	Y	Y	Y	Y	Y
6	Houlahan	Y	Y	Y	Y	Y	Y
7	Wild	?	?	?	?	?	Y
8	Cartwright	Y	Y	Y	Y	Y	Y
9	**Meuser**	Y	N	N	N	Y	N
10	**Perry**	Y	N	N	N	Y	N
11	**Smucker**	Y	N	N	N	Y	N
12	**Marino***						
13	**Joyce**	Y	N	N	N	N	N
14	**Reschenthaler**	Y	N	N	N	Y	N
15	**Thompson, G.**	Y	N	N	N	Y	N
16	**Kelly, M.**	Y	N	N	N	Y	N
17	Lamb	Y	Y	Y	Y	Y	Y
18	Doyle	Y	Y	Y	Y	Y	Y
RHODE ISLAND							
1	Cicilline	Y	Y	Y	Y	Y	Y
2	Langevin	Y	Y	Y	Y	Y	Y
SOUTH CAROLINA							
1	Cunningham	Y	Y	Y	Y	Y	Y
2	**Wilson, J.**	Y	N	N	N	Y	N
3	**Duncan**	Y	N	N	N	N	N
4	**Timmons**	Y	N	N	N	Y	-
5	**Norman**	Y	N	N	N	N	N
6	Clyburn	Y	Y	Y	Y	N	Y
7	**Rice, T.**	Y	N	N	N	Y	N
SOUTH DAKOTA							
AL	**Johnson**	Y	N	N	N	N	N
TENNESSEE							
1	**Roe**	Y	N	N	N	Y	N
2	**Burchett**	N	N	N	N	N	N
3	**Fleischmann**	Y	N	N	N	Y	N
4	**DesJarlais**	Y	N	N	N	N	N
5	Cooper	Y	Y	Y	Y	Y	Y
6	**Rose**	Y	N	N	N	Y	N
7	**Green**	Y	N	N	N	N	N
8	**Kustoff**	Y	N	N	N	N	N
9	Cohen	Y	Y	Y	Y	Y	Y
TEXAS							
1	**Gohmert**	Y	N	N	N	N	N
2	**Crenshaw**	Y	N	N	N	Y	N
3	**Taylor**	Y	N	N	N	Y	N
4	**Ratcliffe**	Y	N	N	N	Y	N

		433	434	435	436	437	438
5	**Gooden**	Y	N	N	N	Y	N
6	**Wright**	Y	N	N	N	N	N
7	Fletcher	Y	Y	Y	Y	Y	Y
8	**Brady**	Y	N	N	N	Y	N
9	Green, A.	Y	Y	Y	Y	Y	Y
10	**McCaul**	Y	N	N	N	Y	N
11	**Conaway**	Y	N	N	N	N	N
12	**Granger**	Y	N	N	N	Y	N
13	**Thornberry**	Y	N	N	N	Y	N
14	**Weber**	Y	N	N	N	Y	N
15	Gonzalez	Y	Y	Y	Y	Y	Y
16	Escobar	Y	Y	Y	Y	Y	Y
17	**Flores**	Y	N	N	N	Y	N
18	Jackson Lee	Y	Y	Y	Y	Y	Y
19	**Arrington**	Y	N	N	N	N	N
20	Castro	Y	Y	Y	Y	Y	Y
21	**Roy**	N	N	N	N	N	N
22	**Olson**	Y	N	N	N	N	N
23	**Hurd**	Y	N	N	N	Y	N
24	**Marchant**	Y	N	N	N	N	N
25	**Williams**	Y	N	N	N	Y	N
26	**Burgess**	Y	N	N	N	N	N
27	**Cloud**	Y	N	N	N	N	N
28	Cuellar	Y	Y	Y	Y	Y	Y
29	Garcia, S.	Y	Y	Y	Y	Y	Y
30	Johnson, E.B.	Y	Y	Y	Y	Y	Y
31	**Carter, J.**	Y	N	N	N	Y	N
32	Allred	Y	Y	Y	Y	Y	Y
33	Veasey	Y	Y	Y	Y	Y	Y
34	Vela	Y	Y	Y	Y	Y	Y
35	Doggett	Y	Y	Y	Y	Y	Y
36	**Babin**	Y	N	N	N	Y	N
UTAH							
1	**Bishop, R.**	Y	N	N	N	Y	N
2	**Stewart**	Y	N	N	N	Y	N
3	**Curtis**	Y	N	N	N	Y	N
4	McAdams	Y	Y	Y	N	Y	Y
VERMONT							
AL	Welch	Y	Y	Y	Y	Y	Y
VIRGINIA							
1	**Wittman**	Y	N	N	N	Y	N
2	Luria	Y	Y	Y	Y	Y	Y
3	Scott, R.	Y	Y	Y	Y	Y	Y
4	McEachin	Y	Y	Y	Y	Y	Y
5	**Riggleman**	Y	N	N	N	Y	N
6	**Cline**	Y	N	N	N	Y	N
7	Spanberger	Y	Y	Y	Y	Y	Y
8	Beyer	Y	Y	Y	Y	Y	Y
9	**Griffith**	Y	N	N	N	Y	N
10	Wexton	Y	Y	Y	Y	Y	Y
11	Connolly	Y	Y	Y	Y	Y	Y
WASHINGTON							
1	DelBene	Y	Y	Y	Y	Y	Y
2	Larsen	Y	Y	Y	Y	Y	Y
3	**Herrera Beutler**	Y	N	N	N	Y	N
4	**Newhouse**	Y	N	N	N	Y	N
5	**McMorris Rodgers**	Y	N	N	N	Y	N
6	Kilmer	Y	Y	Y	Y	Y	Y
7	Jayapal	Y	Y	Y	Y	Y	Y
8	Schrier	Y	Y	Y	Y	Y	Y
9	Smith Adam	Y	Y	Y	Y	Y	Y
10	Heck	Y	Y	Y	Y	Y	Y
WEST VIRGINIA							
1	**McKinley**	Y	N	N	N	Y	N
2	**Mooney**	Y	N	N	N	N	N
3	**Miller**	Y	N	N	N	Y	N
WISCONSIN							
1	**Steil**	Y	N	N	N	Y	N
2	Pocan	Y	Y	Y	Y	Y	Y
3	Kind	Y	Y	Y	Y	Y	Y
4	Moore	Y	Y	Y	Y	Y	Y
5	**Sensenbrenner**	Y	N	N	N	N	N
6	**Grothman**	Y	N	N	N	N	N
7	**Duffy**	+	?	N	N	N	N
8	**Gallagher**	Y	N	N	N	Y	N
WYOMING							
AL	**Cheney**	Y	N	N	N	N	N
DELEGATES							
	Radewagen (A.S.)						?
	Norton (D.C.)						+
	San Nicolas (Guam)						Y
	Sablan (N. Marianas)						Y
	González-Colón (P.R.)						N
	Plaskett (V.I.)						?

439. HR2500. Fiscal 2020 Defense Authorization - Gender-Neutral Defense Personnel Policies. Speier, D-Calif., amendment that would require military service eligibility requirements to be based only on gender-neutral occupational standards and would require all Defense Department personnel policies to "ensure equality of treatment and opportunity" for service members without regard to race, color, national origin, religion, or sex (including gender identity or sexual orientation). It would define "gender identity" with regards to these provisions as the gender-related identity, appearance, mannerisms, or other gender-related characteristics of an individual, regardless of the individual's designated sex at birth. Adopted in Committee of the Whole 242-187: R 10-186; D 231-0; I 1-1. July 11, 2019.

440. HR2500. Fiscal 2020 Defense Authorization - Family Planning Education. Speier, D-Calif., amendment that would require the Defense Department, in consultation with the Coast Guard, to establish a uniform standard curriculum to be used in education programs on family planning for all members of the Armed Forces. Adopted in Committee of the Whole 231-199: R 1-196; D 229-2; I 1-1. July 11, 2019.

441. HR2500. Fiscal 2020 Defense Authorization - U.S. Flatware Procurement. Brindisi, D-N.Y., amendment that would require that stainless steel flatware and dinnerware procured by the Defense Department be produced in the U.S. Adopted in Committee of the Whole 243-187: R 24-173; D 218-13; I 1-1. July 11, 2019.

442. HR2500. Fiscal 2020 Defense Authorization - U.S. Munitions List. Torres, D-Calif., amendment that would prohibit the President from removing any item listed in categories I-III of the U.S. munitions list of defense-related articles. Categories I-III of the list include firearms and ammunition. Adopted in Committee of the Whole 225-205: R 4-193; D 220-11; I 1-1. July 11, 2019.

443. HR2500. Fiscal 2020 Defense Authorization - OPM Consolidation. Connolly, D-Va., amendment that would prohibit the president or a designee from transferring any functions of or consolidating any part of the Office of Personnel Management with other offices or agencies. Adopted in Committee of the Whole 247-182: R 15-181; D 230-1; I 2-0. July 11, 2019.

444. HR2500. Fiscal 2020 Defense Authorization - Tuition Assistance Program. Shalala, D-Fla., amendment that would require the Defense Department to make publicly available on the its website a list of higher education institutions that receive funding through the department's tuition assistance program and how much each institution receives. It would also require the Department to audit institutions for their continued eligibility in the program. Adopted in Committee of the Whole 251-178: R 20-177; D 230-0; I 1-1. July 11, 2019.

	439	440	441	442	443	444
ALABAMA						
1 Byrne	N	N	N	N	N	N
2 Roby	N	N	N	N	N	N
3 Rogers, M.	N	N	N	N	N	N
4 Aderholt	N	N	Y	N	N	N
5 Brooks, M.	N	N	N	N	N	N
6 Palmer	-	N	N	N	N	N
7 Sewell	Y	Y	Y	Y	Y	Y
ALASKA						
AL Young	N	N	N	N	Y	N
ARIZONA						
1 O'Halleran	Y	Y	Y	Y	Y	Y
2 Kirkpatrick	Y	Y	Y	Y	Y	Y
3 Grijalva	Y	Y	Y	Y	Y	Y
4 Gosar	N	N	N	N	N	N
5 Biggs	N	N	N	N	N	N
6 Schweikert	N	N	N	N	N	Y
7 Gallego	Y	Y	Y	Y	Y	Y
8 Lesko	N	N	N	N	N	N
9 Stanton	Y	Y	Y	Y	Y	Y
ARKANSAS						
1 Crawford	N	N	N	N	N	N
2 Hill, F.	N	N	N	N	N	N
3 Womack	N	N	N	N	N	N
4 Westerman	N	N	N	N	N	N
CALIFORNIA						
1 LaMalfa	N	N	N	N	N	N
2 Huffman	Y	Y	Y	Y	Y	Y
3 Garamendi	Y	Y	Y	Y	Y	Y
4 McClintock	N	N	N	N	N	N
5 Thompson, M.	Y	Y	Y	Y	Y	Y
6 Matsui	Y	Y	Y	Y	Y	Y
7 Bera	Y	Y	Y	Y	Y	Y
8 Cook	N	N	N	N	N	N
9 McNerney	?	+	?	?	?	?
10 Harder	Y	Y	Y	Y	Y	Y
11 DeSaulnier	Y	Y	Y	Y	Y	Y
12 Pelosi						
13 Lee B.	Y	Y	Y	Y	Y	Y
14 Speier	Y	Y	Y	Y	Y	Y
15 Swalwell	Y	Y	Y	Y	Y	Y
16 Costa	Y	Y	Y	N	Y	Y
17 Khanna	Y	Y	Y	Y	Y	Y
18 Eshoo	Y	Y	Y	Y	Y	Y
19 Lofgren	Y	Y	Y	Y	Y	Y
20 Panetta	Y	Y	Y	Y	Y	Y
21 Cox	Y	Y	Y	Y	Y	Y
22 Nunes	N	N	N	N	N	N
23 McCarthy	N	N	N	N	N	N
24 Carbajal	Y	Y	Y	Y	Y	Y
25 Hill, K.	Y	Y	Y	Y	Y	Y
26 Brownley	Y	Y	Y	Y	Y	Y
27 Chu	Y	Y	Y	Y	Y	Y
28 Schiff	Y	Y	Y	Y	Y	Y
29 Cárdenas	Y	Y	Y	Y	Y	Y
30 Sherman	Y	Y	Y	Y	Y	Y
31 Aguilar	Y	Y	Y	Y	Y	Y
32 Napolitano	Y	Y	Y	Y	Y	Y
33 Lieu	Y	Y	Y	Y	Y	Y
34 Gomez	Y	Y	Y	Y	Y	Y
35 Torres	Y	Y	Y	Y	Y	Y
36 Ruiz	Y	Y	Y	Y	Y	Y
37 Bass	Y	Y	Y	Y	Y	Y
38 Sánchez	Y	Y	Y	Y	Y	Y
39 Cisneros	Y	Y	Y	Y	Y	Y
40 Roybal-Allard	Y	Y	Y	Y	Y	Y
41 Takano	Y	Y	Y	Y	Y	Y
42 Calvert	N	N	N	N	N	N
43 Waters	Y	Y	Y	Y	Y	Y
44 Barragán	Y	Y	Y	Y	Y	Y
45 Porter	Y	Y	N	Y	Y	Y
46 Correa	Y	Y	Y	Y	Y	Y
47 Lowenthal	Y	Y	Y	Y	Y	Y
48 Rouda	Y	Y	Y	Y	Y	Y
49 Levin	Y	Y	Y	Y	Y	Y
50 Hunter	N	N	N	N	N	N
51 Vargas	Y	Y	Y	Y	Y	Y
52 Peters	Y	Y	Y	Y	Y	Y

	439	440	441	442	443	444
53 Davis, S.	Y	Y	Y	Y	Y	Y
COLORADO						
1 DeGette	Y	Y	Y	Y	Y	Y
2 Neguse	Y	Y	Y	Y	Y	Y
3 Tipton	N	N	N	N	N	N
4 Buck	N	N	N	N	N	N
5 Lamborn	N	N	N	N	N	N
6 Crow	Y	Y	Y	Y	Y	Y
7 Perlmutter	?	?	?	?	?	?
CONNECTICUT						
1 Larson	Y	Y	Y	Y	Y	Y
2 Courtney	Y	Y	Y	Y	Y	Y
3 DeLauro	Y	Y	Y	Y	Y	Y
4 Himes	Y	Y	N	Y	Y	Y
5 Hayes	Y	Y	Y	Y	Y	Y
DELAWARE						
AL Blunt Rochester	Y	Y	Y	Y	Y	Y
FLORIDA						
1 Gaetz	N	N	N	N	N	N
2 Dunn	N	N	N	N	N	N
3 Yoho	N	N	Y	N	N	N
4 Rutherford	N	N	N	N	N	N
5 Lawson	Y	Y	Y	Y	Y	Y
6 Waltz	N	N	N	N	N	N
7 Murphy	Y	Y	Y	Y	Y	Y
8 Posey	N	N	N	N	N	N
9 Soto	Y	Y	Y	Y	Y	Y
10 Demings	Y	Y	Y	Y	Y	Y
11 Webster	N	N	N	N	N	N
12 Bilirakis	N	N	N	N	?	N
13 Crist	Y	Y	Y	Y	Y	Y
14 Castor	Y	Y	Y	Y	Y	Y
15 Spano	N	N	N	N	N	N
16 Buchanan	N	N	Y	N	N	N
17 Steube	N	N	N	N	N	N
18 Mast	N	N	N	N	N	N
19 Rooney	N	N	N	N	Y	N
20 Hastings	Y	Y	Y	Y	Y	Y
21 Frankel	Y	Y	Y	Y	Y	?
22 Deutch	Y	Y	Y	Y	Y	Y
23 Wasserman Schultz	Y	Y	Y	Y	Y	Y
24 Wilson, F.	Y	Y	Y	Y	Y	Y
25 Diaz-Balart	N	N	N	N	N	N
26 Mucarsel-Powell	Y	Y	Y	Y	Y	Y
27 Shalala	Y	Y	Y	Y	Y	Y
GEORGIA						
1 Carter, E.L.	N	N	N	N	N	N
2 Bishop, S.	Y	Y	Y	N	Y	Y
3 Ferguson	N	N	N	N	N	N
4 Johnson, H.	Y	Y	Y	Y	Y	Y
5 Lewis John	Y	Y	Y	Y	Y	Y
6 McBath	Y	Y	Y	Y	Y	Y
7 Woodall	N	N	N	N	N	N
8 Scott, A.	N	N	N	N	N	N
9 Collins, D.	N	N	N	N	N	N
10 Hice	N	N	N	N	N	N
11 Loudermilk	N	N	N	N	N	N
12 Allen	N	N	N	N	N	N
13 Scott, D.	Y	Y	Y	Y	Y	Y
14 Graves, T.	N	N	N	N	N	N
HAWAII						
1 Case	Y	Y	Y	Y	Y	Y
2 Gabbard	?	?	?	?	?	?
IDAHO						
1 Fulcher	N	N	N	N	N	N
2 Simpson	N	N	N	N	N	N
ILLINOIS						
1 Rush	Y	Y	Y	Y	Y	Y
2 Kelly, R.	Y	Y	Y	Y	Y	Y
3 Lipinski	Y	N	Y	Y	Y	Y
4 García, J.	Y	Y	Y	Y	Y	Y
5 Quigley	Y	Y	Y	Y	Y	Y
6 Casten	Y	Y	Y	Y	Y	Y
7 Davis, D.	Y	Y	Y	Y	Y	Y
8 Krishnamoorthi	Y	Y	Y	Y	Y	Y
9 Schakowsky	Y	Y	Y	Y	Y	Y
10 Schneider	Y	Y	Y	Y	Y	Y
11 Foster	Y	Y	Y	Y	Y	Y

KEY: **Republicans**   Democrats   *Independents*

Y Voted for (yea)	**N** Voted against (nay)	**P** Voted "present"
+ Announced for	**–** Announced against	**?** Did not vote or otherwise
# Paired for	**X** Paired against	make position known

		439	440	441	442	443	444
12	**Bost**	N	N	Y	N	N	N
13	**Davis, R.**	N	N	Y	N	N	Y
14	Underwood	Y	Y	Y	Y	Y	Y
15	**Shimkus**	N	N	N	N	N	N
16	**Kinzinger**	N	N	N	N	N	N
17	Bustos	Y	Y	Y	Y	Y	Y
18	**LaHood**	N	N	N	N	N	N
INDIANA							
1	Visclosky	Y	Y	Y	Y	Y	Y
2	**Walorski**	N	N	N	N	N	N
3	**Banks**	N	N	N	N	N	N
4	**Baird**	N	N	N	N	N	N
5	**Brooks, S.**	Y	N	N	N	N	N
6	**Pence**	N	N	N	N	N	N
7	Carson	Y	Y	Y	Y	Y	Y
8	**Bucshon**	N	N	N	N	N	N
9	**Hollingsworth**	Y	N	N	N	N	N
IOWA							
1	Finkenauer	Y	Y	Y	Y	Y	Y
2	Loebsack	Y	Y	Y	Y	Y	Y
3	Axne	Y	Y	Y	Y	Y	Y
4	**King, S.**	N	N	N	N	N	N
KANSAS							
1	**Marshall**	N	N	N	N	N	N
2	**Watkins**	N	N	N	N	N	N
3	Davids	Y	Y	Y	Y	Y	Y
4	**Estes**	N	N	N	N	N	N
KENTUCKY							
1	**Comer**	N	N	N	N	N	N
2	**Guthrie**	N	N	N	N	N	N
3	Yarmuth	Y	Y	Y	Y	Y	Y
4	**Massie**	N	N	Y	N	N	Y
5	**Rogers, H.**	N	N	N	N	N	N
6	**Barr**	N	N	N	N	N	N
LOUISIANA							
1	**Scalise**	N	N	N	N	N	N
2	Richmond	Y	Y	Y	Y	Y	Y
3	**Higgins, C.**	-	-	-	-	-	-
4	**Johnson, M.**	N	N	N	N	N	N
5	**Abraham**	N	N	N	N	N	N
6	**Graves, G.**	N	N	Y	N	N	N
MAINE							
1	Pingree	Y	Y	Y	Y	Y	Y
2	Golden	Y	Y	Y	N	Y	Y
MARYLAND							
1	**Harris**	N	N	N	N	N	N
2	Ruppersberger	Y	Y	Y	Y	Y	Y
3	Sarbanes	Y	Y	N	Y	Y	Y
4	Brown, A.	Y	Y	Y	Y	Y	Y
5	Hoyer	Y	Y	Y	Y	Y	Y
6	Trone	Y	Y	Y	Y	Y	Y
7	Cummings	Y	Y	Y	Y	Y	Y
8	Raskin						
MASSACHUSETTS		Y	Y	Y	Y	Y	Y
1	Neal						
2	McGovern	Y	Y	Y	Y	Y	Y
3	Trahan	Y	Y	Y	Y	Y	Y
4	Kennedy	Y	Y	Y	Y	Y	Y
5	Clark	Y	Y	Y	Y	Y	Y
6	Moulton	Y	Y	Y	Y	Y	Y
7	Pressley	Y	Y	N	Y	Y	Y
8	Lynch	Y	Y	Y	Y	Y	Y
9	Keating	Y	Y	Y	Y	Y	Y
MICHIGAN		Y	Y	Y	Y	Y	Y
1	**Bergman**						
2	**Huizenga**	N	N	Y	N	N	N
3	*Amash*	N	N	N	N	N	N
4	**Moolenaar**	N	N	N	N	Y	N
5	Kildee	N	N	N	N	N	N
6	**Upton**	Y	Y	Y	Y	Y	Y
7	**Walberg**	Y	N	N	N	Y	Y
8	Slotkin	N	N	N	N	N	N
9	Levin	Y	Y	Y	Y	Y	Y
10	**Mitchell**	Y	Y	Y	Y	Y	Y
11	Stevens	N	N	N	N	N	N
12	Dingell	Y	Y	Y	Y	Y	Y
13	Tlaib	Y	Y	Y	Y	Y	Y
14	Lawrence	Y	Y	Y	Y	Y	Y
MINNESOTA		Y	Y	Y	Y	Y	Y
1	**Hagedorn**						
2	Craig	N	N	N	N	N	N
3	Phillips	Y	Y	N	Y	Y	Y
4	McCollum	Y	Y	Y	Y	Y	Y
5	Omar	Y	Y	Y	Y	Y	Y
6	**Emmer**	Y	Y	Y	Y	Y	Y
7	Peterson	N	N	N	N	N	N
8	**Stauber**	Y	N	Y	Y	Y	Y
MISSISSIPPI		N	N	Y	N	Y	N
1	**Kelly, T.**						
2	Thompson, B.	N	N	N	N	N	N
3	**Guest**	Y	Y	Y	Y	Y	Y
4	**Palazzo**	N	N	N	N	N	N
MISSOURI		N	N	N	N	N	N
1	Clay						
2	**Wagner**	Y	Y	Y	Y	Y	Y
3	**Luetkemeyer**	N	N	N	N	N	N
4	**Hartzler**	N	N	N	N	N	N
5	Cleaver	N	N	N	N	N	N
6	**Graves, S.**	Y	Y	Y	Y	Y	Y
7	**Long**	N	N	N	N	N	N
8	**Smith, J.**	N	N	N	N	N	N
MONTANA		N	N	N	N	N	N
AL	**Gianforte**						
NEBRASKA		N	N	N	N	N	N
1	**Fortenberry**						
2	**Bacon**	N	N	Y	N	Y	N
3	**Smith, Adrian**	N	N	N	N	N	Y
NEVADA		N	N	N	N	N	N
1	Titus						
2	**Amodei**	Y	Y	Y	Y	Y	Y
3	Lee	N	N	N	N	N	N
4	Horsford	Y	Y	Y	Y	Y	Y
NEW HAMPSHIRE		Y	Y	Y	Y	Y	Y
1	Pappas						
2	Kuster	Y	Y	Y	Y	Y	Y
NEW JERSEY		Y	Y	Y	Y	Y	Y
1	Norcross						
2	Van Drew	Y	Y	Y	Y	Y	Y
3	Kim	Y	Y	Y	N	Y	Y
4	**Smith, C.**	Y	Y	Y	Y	Y	Y
5	Gottheimer	N	N	Y	Y	Y	N
6	Pallone	Y	Y	Y	Y	Y	Y
7	Malinowski	Y	Y	Y	Y	Y	Y
8	Sires	Y	Y	Y	Y	Y	Y
9	Pascrell	Y	Y	Y	Y	Y	Y
10	Payne	Y	Y	Y	Y	Y	Y
11	Sherrill	Y	Y	Y	Y	Y	Y
12	Watson Coleman	Y	Y	Y	Y	Y	Y
NEW MEXICO		Y	Y	Y	Y	Y	Y
1	Haaland						
2	Torres Small	Y	Y	Y	Y	Y	Y
3	Luján	Y	Y	N	Y	Y	Y
NEW YORK		Y	Y	Y	Y	Y	Y
1	**Zeldin**						
2	**King, P.**	N	N	N	N	N	N
3	Suozzi	N	N	Y	Y	Y	N
4	Rice, K.	Y	Y	Y	Y	Y	Y
5	Meeks	Y	Y	Y	Y	Y	Y
6	Meng	Y	Y	Y	Y	Y	Y
7	Velázquez	Y	Y	Y	Y	Y	Y
8	Jeffries	Y	Y	Y	Y	Y	Y
9	Clarke	Y	Y	Y	Y	Y	Y
10	Nadler	Y	Y	Y	Y	Y	Y
11	Rose	Y	Y	Y	Y	Y	Y
12	Maloney, C.	Y	Y	Y	Y	Y	Y
13	Espaillat	Y	Y	Y	Y	Y	Y
14	Ocasio-Cortez	Y	Y	Y	Y	Y	Y
15	Serrano	Y	Y	Y	Y	Y	Y
16	Engel	Y	Y	Y	Y	Y	Y
17	Lowey	Y	Y	Y	Y	Y	Y
18	Maloney, S.P.	Y	Y	Y	Y	Y	Y
19	Delgado	Y	Y	Y	Y	Y	Y
20	Tonko	Y	Y	Y	Y	Y	Y
21	**Stefanik**	Y	Y	Y	Y	Y	Y
22	Brindisi	Y	N	Y	N	Y	N
23	**Reed**	Y	Y	Y	N	Y	Y
24	**Katko**	Y	N	Y	N	N	N
25	Morelle	Y	N	Y	N	N	Y
26	Higgins, B.	Y	Y	Y	Y	Y	Y
27	**Collins, C.**	Y	Y	Y	Y	Y	Y
NORTH CAROLINA		N	N	Y	N	N	N
1	Butterfield						
2	**Holding**	Y	Y	Y	Y	Y	Y
3	**Jones***	N	N	N	N	N	N
4	Price						
5	**Foxx**	Y	Y	Y	Y	Y	Y
6	**Walker**	N	N	N	N	N	N
7	**Rouzer**	N	N	N	N	N	N
8	**Hudson**	N	N	N	N	N	N
9	vacant	N	N	N	N	N	N
10	**McHenry**	N	N	N	N	N	N
11	**Meadows**	N	N	N	N	N	N
12	Adams	Y	Y	Y	Y	Y	Y
13	**Budd**	N	N	N	N	N	N
NORTH DAKOTA							
AL	**Armstrong**	N	N	N	N	N	N
OHIO							
1	**Chabot**	N	N	N	N	N	N
2	**Wenstrup**	N	N	N	N	N	N
3	Beatty	Y	Y	Y	Y	Y	Y
4	**Jordan**	N	N	N	N	N	N
5	**Latta**	N	N	N	N	N	N
6	**Johnson, B.**	N	N	N	N	N	N
7	**Gibbs**	N	N	N	N	N	N
8	**Davidson**	N	N	N	N	N	N
9	Kaptur	Y	Y	Y	Y	Y	Y
10	**Turner**	N	N	N	N	Y	N
11	Fudge	?	?	?	?	?	?
12	**Balderson**	N	N	N	N	N	N
13	Ryan	Y	Y	Y	Y	Y	Y
14	**Joyce**	N	N	N	N	N	N
15	**Stivers**	Y	N	N	N	N	Y
16	**Gonzalez**	N	N	N	N	N	N
OKLAHOMA							
1	**Hern**	N	N	N	N	N	N
2	**Mullin**	N	N	N	N	N	N
3	**Lucas**	N	N	N	N	N	N
4	**Cole**	N	N	N	N	Y	N
5	Horn	Y	Y	Y	N	Y	Y
OREGON							
1	Bonamici	Y	Y	Y	Y	Y	Y
2	**Walden**	Y	N	N	N	N	N
3	Blumenauer	Y	Y	Y	Y	Y	Y
4	DeFazio	Y	Y	Y	Y	Y	Y
5	Schrader	Y	Y	Y	N	Y	Y
PENNSYLVANIA							
1	**Fitzpatrick**	Y	Y	Y	Y	Y	Y
2	Boyle	Y	Y	Y	Y	Y	Y
3	Evans	Y	Y	Y	Y	Y	Y
4	Dean	Y	Y	Y	Y	Y	Y
5	Scanlon	Y	Y	Y	Y	Y	Y
6	Houlahan	Y	Y	Y	Y	Y	Y
7	Wild	Y	Y	Y	Y	Y	Y
8	Cartwright	Y	Y	Y	Y	Y	Y
9	**Meuser**	N	N	N	N	N	N
10	**Perry**	N	N	N	N	N	N
11	**Smucker**	N	N	N	N	N	N
12	**Marino***						
13	**Joyce**	N	N	N	N	N	N
14	**Reschenthaler**	N	N	N	N	N	N
15	**Thompson, G.**	N	N	N	N	Y	Y
16	**Kelly, M.**	N	N	N	N	N	N
17	Lamb	Y	Y	Y	Y	Y	Y
18	Doyle	Y	Y	Y	Y	Y	Y
RHODE ISLAND							
1	Cicilline	Y	Y	Y	Y	Y	Y
2	Langevin	Y	Y	Y	Y	Y	Y
SOUTH CAROLINA							
1	Cunningham	Y	Y	N	N	N	Y
2	**Wilson, J.**	N	N	N	N	Y	N
3	**Duncan**	N	N	N	N	N	Y
4	**Timmons**	N	N	N	N	N	N
5	**Norman**	N	N	N	N	N	N
6	Clyburn	Y	Y	Y	Y	Y	Y
7	**Rice, T.**	N	N	N	N	N	N
SOUTH DAKOTA							
AL	**Johnson**	N	N	N	N	N	N
TENNESSEE							
1	**Roe**	N	N	N	N	N	N
2	**Burchett**	N	N	N	N	N	N
3	**Fleischmann**	N	N	N	N	N	N
4	**DesJarlais**	N	N	N	N	N	N
5	Cooper	Y	Y	N	Y	Y	Y
6	**Rose**	N	N	N	N	N	N
7	**Green**	N	N	N	N	N	N
8	**Kustoff**	N	N	N	N	N	N
9	Cohen	Y	Y	Y	Y	Y	Y
TEXAS							
1	**Gohmert**	N	N	N	N	N	Y
2	**Crenshaw**	N	N	N	N	N	Y
3	**Taylor**	N	N	N	N	N	N
4	**Ratcliffe**	N	N	N	N	N	N
5	**Gooden**	N	N	N	N	N	N
6	**Wright**	N	N	N	N	N	N
7	Fletcher	Y	Y	Y	Y	Y	Y
8	**Brady**	N	N	N	N	N	N
9	Green, A.	Y	Y	Y	Y	Y	Y
10	**McCaul**	N	N	N	N	N	N
11	**Conaway**	N	N	N	N	N	N
12	**Granger**	N	N	N	N	N	N
13	**Thornberry**	N	N	N	N	N	N
14	**Weber**	N	N	N	N	N	N
15	Gonzalez	Y	Y	Y	Y	Y	Y
16	Escobar	Y	Y	Y	Y	Y	Y
17	**Flores**	N	N	N	N	N	N
18	Jackson Lee	Y	Y	Y	Y	Y	Y
19	**Arrington**	N	N	N	N	N	N
20	Castro	Y	Y	Y	Y	Y	Y
21	**Roy**	N	N	N	N	N	N
22	**Olson**	N	N	N	N	N	N
23	**Hurd**	Y	N	N	N	Y	N
24	**Marchant**	N	N	N	N	N	N
25	**Williams**	N	N	N	N	N	N
26	**Burgess**	N	N	N	N	N	N
27	**Cloud**	N	N	N	N	N	N
28	Cuellar	Y	Y	Y	N	Y	Y
29	Garcia, S.	Y	Y	Y	Y	Y	Y
30	Johnson, E.B.	Y	Y	Y	Y	Y	Y
31	**Carter, J.**	N	N	N	N	N	N
32	Allred	Y	Y	Y	Y	Y	Y
33	Veasey	Y	Y	Y	Y	Y	Y
34	Vela	Y	Y	Y	Y	Y	Y
35	Doggett	Y	Y	Y	Y	Y	Y
36	**Babin**	N	N	N	N	N	N
UTAH							
1	**Bishop, R.**	N	N	N	N	Y	N
2	**Stewart**	N	N	N	N	N	N
3	**Curtis**	N	N	N	N	N	N
4	McAdams	Y	Y	Y	N	Y	Y
VERMONT							
AL	Welch	Y	Y	Y	Y	Y	Y
VIRGINIA							
1	**Wittman**	N	N	N	N	Y	N
2	Luria	Y	Y	N	Y	Y	Y
3	Scott, R.	Y	Y	Y	Y	Y	Y
4	McEachin	Y	Y	N	Y	Y	Y
5	**Riggleman**	N	N	N	N	N	Y
6	**Cline**	N	N	N	N	N	N
7	Spanberger	Y	Y	Y	Y	Y	Y
8	Beyer	Y	Y	Y	Y	Y	Y
9	**Griffith**	N	N	Y	N	N	Y
10	Wexton	Y	Y	Y	Y	Y	Y
11	Connolly	Y	Y	Y	Y	Y	Y
WASHINGTON							
1	DelBene	Y	Y	Y	Y	Y	Y
2	Larsen	Y	Y	N	Y	Y	Y
3	**Herrera Beutler**	N	N	N	N	N	Y
4	**Newhouse**	N	N	N	N	N	N
5	**McMorris Rodgers**	N	N	N	N	N	N
6	Kilmer	Y	Y	Y	Y	Y	Y
7	Jayapal	Y	Y	Y	Y	Y	Y
8	Schrier	Y	Y	Y	Y	Y	Y
9	Smith Adam	Y	Y	Y	Y	Y	Y
10	Heck	Y	Y	Y	Y	Y	Y
WEST VIRGINIA							
1	**McKinley**	N	N	Y	N	N	N
2	**Mooney**	N	N	Y	N	N	N
3	**Miller**	N	N	N	N	N	N
WISCONSIN							
1	**Steil**	N	N	N	N	N	N
2	Pocan	Y	Y	Y	Y	Y	Y
3	Kind	Y	Y	N	N	Y	Y
4	Moore	Y	Y	N	Y	Y	Y
5	**Sensenbrenner**	N	N	Y	N	N	N
6	**Grothman**	N	N	N	N	N	Y
7	**Duffy**	N	N	Y	N	N	N
8	**Gallagher**	N	N	N	N	N	N
WYOMING							
AL	**Cheney**	N	N	N	N	N	N
DELEGATES							
	Radewagen (A.S.)	?	?	?	?	?	?
	Norton (D.C.)	+	+	+	+	+	+
	San Nicolas (Guam)	Y	Y	Y	Y	Y	Y
	Sablan (N. Marianas)	Y	Y	Y	Y	Y	Y
	González-Colón (P.R.)	N	N	Y	N	N	Y
	Plaskett (V.I.)	?	?	?	?	?	?

445. HR2500. Fiscal 2020 Defense Authorization - Overseas Operations Cost Report. Omar, D-Minn., amendment that would require the Defense Department to report to Congress on the financial costs and national security benefits of maintaining overseas military operations, including permanent military installations and bases. Adopted in Committee of the Whole 219-210: R 8-188; D 209-22; I 2-0. July 11, 2019.

446. HR2500. Fiscal 2020 Defense Authorization - Executive Branch Contract Prohibition. Smith, D-Wash., for Clark, D-Mass., amendment that would expand the prohibition on direct or indirect contracts between members of Congress and the federal government to include contracts between members and the president, vice president, or any Cabinet member. Adopted in Committee of the Whole 243-186: R 11-186; D 231-0; I 1-0. July 11, 2019.

447. HR2500. Fiscal 2020 Defense Authorization - Defense Articles to Azerbaijan. Sherman, D-Calif., amendment that would prohibit the use of funds authorized by the bill to transfer defense articles or services to Azerbaijan, unless the president certifies to Congress that such a transfer does not threaten civil aviation. Adopted in Committee of the Whole 234-195: R 9-187; D 224-7; I 1-1. July 11, 2019.

448. HR2500. Fiscal 2020 Defense Authorization - Saudi Arabia and UAE Assistance. Lieu, D-Calif., for Gabbard, D-Hawaii, amendment that would prohibit the use of funds authorized by the bill to provide any assistance to Saudi Arabia or the United Arab Emirates if such assistance could be used by either country to conduct or continue hostilities in Yemen. Adopted in Committee of the Whole 239-187: R 8-185; D 229-2; I 2-0. July 11, 2019.

449. HR2500. Fiscal 2020 Defense Authorization - Defense Articles to Saudi Arabia and UAE. Lieu, D-Calif., amendment that would prohibit the use of funds authorized by the bill to transfer or facilitate the transfer of any defense article or service to Saudi Arabia or the United Arab Emirates pursuant to any certification of emergency authority under the Arms Export Control Act. Adopted in Committee of the Whole 246-180: R 13-180; D 231-0; I 2-0. July 11, 2019.

450. HR2500. Fiscal 2020 Defense Authorization - Hostilities in Yemen. Smith, D-Wash., for Khanna, D-Calif., amendment that would prohibit the use of funds authorized by the bill for the U.S. to provide intelligence or logistical support for Saudi-led coalition strikes against the Houthis in Yemen, or for the Defense Department to provide military personnel to Saudi- and United Arab Emirates-led coalition forces engaged in such hostilities without Congressional authorization. Adopted in Committee of the Whole 240-185: R 12-180; D 226-5; I 2-0. July 11, 2019.

		445	446	447	448	449	450
ALABAMA							
1	**Byrne**	N	N	N	N	N	N
2	**Roby**	N	N	N	N	N	N
3	**Rogers, M.**	?	N	N	N	N	N
4	**Aderholt**	N	N	N	N	N	N
5	**Brooks, M.**	N	N	N	N	N	N
6	**Palmer**	N	N	N	N	N	N
7	Sewell	Y	Y	Y	Y	Y	Y
ALASKA							
AL	**Young**	N	N	N	N	N	N
ARIZONA							
1	O'Halleran	Y	Y	Y	Y	Y	Y
2	Kirkpatrick	Y	Y	Y	Y	Y	Y
3	Grijalva	Y	Y	Y	Y	Y	Y
4	**Gosar**	N	N	N	N	Y	Y
5	**Biggs**	N	N	N	N	Y	Y
6	**Schweikert**	Y	Y	Y	Y	Y	Y
7	Gallego	Y	Y	Y	Y	Y	Y
8	**Lesko**	N	N	N	N	N	N
9	Stanton	Y	Y	Y	Y	Y	Y
ARKANSAS							
1	**Crawford**	N	N	N	N	N	N
2	**Hill, F.**	N	N	N	N	N	N
3	**Womack**	N	N	N	N	N	N
4	**Westerman**	N	N	N	N	N	N
CALIFORNIA							
1	**LaMalfa**	N	N	N	N	Y	N
2	Huffman	Y	Y	Y	Y	Y	Y
3	Garamendi	Y	Y	Y	Y	Y	Y
4	**McClintock**	Y	N	N	N	N	N
5	Thompson, M.	Y	Y	Y	Y	Y	Y
6	Matsui	Y	Y	Y	Y	Y	Y
7	Bera	Y	Y	Y	Y	Y	Y
8	**Cook**	N	N	N	N	N	N
9	McNerney	?	?	?	?	?	?
10	Harder	Y	Y	Y	Y	Y	Y
11	DeSaulnier	Y	Y	Y	Y	Y	Y
12	Pelosi						
13	Lee B.	Y	Y	Y	Y	Y	Y
14	Speier	Y	Y	Y	Y	Y	Y
15	Swalwell	Y	Y	Y	Y	Y	Y
16	Costa	Y	Y	Y	Y	Y	Y
17	Khanna	Y	Y	Y	Y	Y	Y
18	Eshoo	Y	Y	Y	Y	Y	Y
19	Lofgren	Y	Y	Y	Y	Y	Y
20	Panetta	N	Y	Y	Y	Y	Y
21	Cox	Y	Y	Y	Y	Y	Y
22	**Nunes**	N	N	N	N	N	N
23	**McCarthy**	N	N	N	?	?	?
24	Carbajal	Y	Y	Y	Y	Y	Y
25	Hill, K.	Y	Y	Y	Y	Y	Y
26	Brownley	Y	Y	Y	Y	Y	Y
27	Chu	Y	Y	Y	Y	Y	Y
28	Schiff	Y	Y	Y	Y	Y	Y
29	Cárdenas	Y	Y	Y	Y	Y	Y
30	Sherman	Y	Y	Y	Y	Y	Y
31	Aguilar	Y	Y	Y	Y	Y	Y
32	Napolitano	Y	Y	Y	Y	Y	Y
33	Lieu	Y	Y	Y	Y	Y	Y
34	Gomez	Y	Y	Y	Y	Y	Y
35	Torres	Y	Y	Y	Y	Y	Y
36	Ruiz	Y	Y	Y	Y	Y	Y
37	Bass	Y	Y	Y	Y	Y	Y
38	Sánchez	Y	Y	Y	Y	Y	Y
39	Cisneros	Y	Y	Y	Y	Y	Y
40	Roybal-Allard	Y	Y	Y	Y	Y	Y
41	Takano	Y	Y	Y	Y	Y	Y
42	**Calvert**	N	N	N	N	N	N
43	Waters	Y	Y	Y	Y	Y	Y
44	Barragán	Y	Y	Y	Y	Y	Y
45	Porter	Y	Y	Y	Y	Y	Y
46	Correa	Y	Y	Y	Y	Y	Y
47	Lowenthal	Y	Y	Y	Y	Y	Y
48	Rouda	Y	Y	Y	Y	Y	Y
49	Levin	Y	Y	Y	Y	Y	Y
50	**Hunter**	N	N	N	N	N	N
51	Vargas	Y	Y	Y	Y	Y	Y
52	Peters	Y	Y	Y	Y	Y	Y

		445	446	447	448	449	450
53	Davis, S.	Y	Y	Y	Y	Y	Y
COLORADO							
1	DeGette	Y	Y	Y	Y	Y	Y
2	Neguse	Y	Y	Y	Y	Y	Y
3	**Tipton**	N	N	N	Y	N	N
4	**Buck**	N	N	N	Y	N	N
5	**Lamborn**	N	N	?	N	N	N
6	Crow	Y	Y	Y	Y	Y	N
7	Perlmutter	?	?	?	?	?	?
CONNECTICUT							
1	Larson	Y	Y	Y	Y	Y	Y
2	Courtney	Y	Y	Y	Y	Y	Y
3	DeLauro	Y	Y	Y	Y	Y	Y
4	Himes	Y	Y	Y	Y	Y	Y
5	Hayes	Y	Y	Y	Y	Y	Y
DELAWARE							
AL	Blunt Rochester	Y	Y	Y	Y	Y	Y
FLORIDA							
1	**Gaetz**	N	N	N	Y	Y	?
2	**Dunn**	N	N	N	N	N	N
3	**Yoho**	N	N	N	N	N	N
4	**Rutherford**	N	N	N	N	N	N
5	Lawson	Y	Y	Y	Y	Y	Y
6	**Waltz**	N	N	N	N	N	N
7	Murphy	Y	Y	Y	Y	Y	Y
8	**Posey**	N	N	N	N	N	N
9	Soto	Y	Y	Y	Y	Y	Y
10	Demings	Y	Y	Y	Y	Y	Y
11	**Webster**	N	N	N	N	N	N
12	**Bilirakis**	N	N	N	N	N	N
13	Crist	Y	Y	Y	Y	Y	Y
14	Castor	Y	Y	Y	Y	Y	Y
15	**Spano**	N	N	N	N	N	N
16	**Buchanan**	N	N	N	N	N	N
17	**Steube**	N	N	N	N	N	N
18	**Mast**	N	N	N	N	N	N
19	**Rooney**	N	N	N	N	N	N
20	Hastings	Y	Y	Y	Y	Y	Y
21	Frankel	Y	Y	Y	Y	Y	Y
22	Deutch	Y	Y	Y	Y	Y	Y
23	Wasserman Schultz	Y	Y	Y	Y	Y	Y
24	Wilson, F.	Y	Y	Y	Y	Y	Y
25	**Diaz-Balart**	N	N	N	N	N	N
26	Mucarsel-Powell	Y	Y	Y	Y	Y	Y
27	Shalala	Y	Y	Y	Y	Y	Y
GEORGIA							
1	**Carter, E.L.**	N	N	N	N	N	N
2	Bishop, S.	Y	Y	Y	Y	Y	Y
3	**Ferguson**	N	N	N	N	N	N
4	Johnson, H.	Y	Y	Y	Y	Y	Y
5	Lewis John	Y	Y	Y	Y	Y	Y
6	McBath	Y	Y	Y	Y	Y	Y
7	**Woodall**	N	N	N	N	N	N
8	**Scott, A.**	N	N	N	N	N	N
9	**Collins, D.**	N	N	N	N	N	N
10	**Hice**	N	N	N	N	N	N
11	**Loudermilk**	N	N	N	N	N	N
12	**Allen**	N	N	N	N	N	N
13	Scott, D.	Y	Y	Y	Y	Y	Y
14	**Graves, T.**	N	N	N	N	N	N
HAWAII							
1	Case	Y	Y	Y	Y	Y	Y
2	Gabbard	?	?	?	?	?	?
IDAHO							
1	**Fulcher**	N	N	N	N	N	N
2	**Simpson**	N	N	N	N	N	N
ILLINOIS							
1	Rush	Y	Y	Y	Y	Y	Y
2	Kelly, R.	Y	Y	Y	Y	Y	Y
3	Lipinski	Y	Y	Y	Y	Y	Y
4	García, J.	Y	Y	Y	Y	Y	Y
5	Quigley	Y	Y	Y	Y	Y	Y
6	Casten	Y	Y	Y	Y	Y	Y
7	Davis, D.	Y	Y	Y	Y	Y	Y
8	Krishnamoorthi	Y	Y	Y	Y	Y	Y
9	Schakowsky	Y	Y	Y	Y	Y	Y
10	Schneider	Y	Y	Y	Y	Y	Y
11	Foster	Y	Y	Y	Y	Y	Y

KEY: **Republicans** Democrats *Independents*

Y Voted for (yea)	N Voted against (nay)	P Voted "present"
+ Announced for	− Announced against	? Did not vote or otherwise
# Paired for	X Paired against	make position known

		445	446	447	448	449	450
12	**Bost**	N	N	N	N	N	N
13	**Davis, R.**	N	N	N	N	N	N
14	Underwood	Y	Y	Y	Y	Y	Y
15	**Shimkus**	N	N	N	N	N	N
16	**Kinzinger**	N	N	N	N	N	N
17	Bustos	Y	Y	Y	Y	Y	Y
18	**LaHood**	N	N	N	N	N	N
INDIANA							
1	Visclosky	Y	Y	Y	Y	Y	Y
2	**Walorski**	N	N	N	N	N	N
3	**Banks**	N	N	N	N	N	N
4	**Baird**	N	N	N	N	N	N
5	**Brooks, S.**	N	N	N	N	N	N
6	**Pence**	N	N	N	N	N	N
7	Carson	Y	Y	Y	Y	Y	Y
8	**Bucshon**	N	N	N	N	N	N
9	**Hollingsworth**	N	Y	N	Y	Y	N
IOWA							
1	Finkenauer	Y	Y	Y	Y	Y	Y
2	Loebsack	Y	Y	Y	Y	Y	Y
3	Axne	N	Y	Y	Y	Y	Y
4	**King, S.**	N	N	Y	N	N	N
KANSAS							
1	**Marshall**	N	N	N	N	N	N
2	**Watkins**	N	N	N	N	N	N
3	Davids	Y	Y	Y	Y	Y	Y
4	**Estes**	N	N	N	N	N	N
KENTUCKY							
1	**Comer**	N	N	N	N	N	N
2	**Guthrie**	N	N	N	N	N	N
3	Yarmuth	Y	Y	Y	Y	Y	Y
4	**Massie**	Y	Y	Y	Y	Y	Y
5	**Rogers, H.**	N	N	N	N	N	N
6	**Barr**	N	N	N	N	N	N
LOUISIANA							
1	**Scalise**	N	N	N	N	N	N
2	Richmond	Y	Y	Y	Y	Y	Y
3	**Higgins, C.**	-	-	-	-	-	-
4	**Johnson, M.**	N	N	N	?	?	?
5	**Abraham**	N	N	N	N	N	N
6	**Graves, G.**	N	N	N	N	N	N
MAINE							
1	Pingree	Y	Y	Y	Y	Y	Y
2	Golden	N	Y	Y	Y	Y	Y
MARYLAND							
1	**Harris**	N	N	N	N	N	N
2	Ruppersberger	Y	Y	Y	Y	Y	Y
3	Sarbanes	Y	Y	Y	Y	Y	Y
4	Brown, A.	Y	Y	Y	Y	Y	Y
5	Hoyer	Y	Y	Y	Y	Y	Y
6	Trone	Y	Y	Y	Y	Y	Y
7	Cummings	Y	Y	Y	Y	Y	Y
8	Raskin						
MASSACHUSETTS		Y	Y	Y	Y	Y	Y
1	Neal						
2	McGovern	Y	Y	Y	Y	Y	Y
3	Trahan	Y	Y	Y	Y	Y	Y
4	Kennedy	Y	Y	Y	Y	Y	Y
5	Clark	Y	Y	Y	Y	Y	Y
6	Moulton	Y	Y	Y	Y	Y	Y
7	Pressley	N	Y	Y	Y	Y	Y
8	Lynch	Y	Y	Y	Y	Y	Y
9	Keating	Y	Y	Y	Y	Y	Y
MICHIGAN		Y	Y	Y	Y	Y	Y
1	**Bergman**						
2	**Huizenga**	N	N	N	N	N	N
3	*Amash*	N	N	N	N	N	N
4	**Moolenaar**	Y	P	N	Y	Y	Y
5	Kildee	N	N	N	N	N	N
6	**Upton**	Y	Y	Y	Y	Y	Y
7	**Walberg**	N	N	N	N	Y	Y
8	Slotkin	N	N	N	N	N	N
9	Levin	N	Y	Y	N	Y	N
10	**Mitchell**	Y	Y	Y	Y	Y	Y
11	Stevens	N	N	N	N	N	N
12	Dingell	N	Y	Y	Y	Y	Y
13	Tlaib	Y	Y	Y	Y	Y	Y
14	Lawrence	Y	Y	Y	Y	Y	Y
MINNESOTA		Y	Y	Y	Y	Y	Y
1	**Hagedorn**						
2	Craig	N	N	N	N	N	N
3	Phillips	N	Y	N	Y	Y	Y
4	McCollum	Y	Y	Y	Y	Y	Y
5	Omar	Y	Y	Y	Y	Y	Y

		445	446	447	448	449	450
6	**Emmer**	Y	Y	Y	Y	Y	Y
7	Peterson	N	N	N	N	N	N
8	**Stauber**	N	Y	Y	Y	Y	Y
MISSISSIPPI		N	N	N	N	N	N
1	**Kelly, T.**						
2	Thompson, B.	N	N	N	N	N	N
3	**Guest**	Y	Y	Y	Y	Y	Y
4	**Palazzo**	N	N	N	N	N	N
MISSOURI		N	N	N	N	N	N
1	Clay						
2	**Wagner**	Y	Y	Y	Y	Y	Y
3	**Luetkemeyer**	N	N	N	N	N	N
4	**Hartzler**	N	N	N	N	N	N
5	Cleaver	N	N	N	N	N	N
6	**Graves, S.**	Y	Y	Y	Y	Y	Y
7	**Long**	N	N	N	N	N	N
8	**Smith, J.**	N	N	N	N	N	N
MONTANA		N	N	N	N	N	N
AL	**Gianforte**						
NEBRASKA		N	N	N	N	N	N
1	**Fortenberry**						
2	**Bacon**	N	N	N	N	N	N
3	**Smith, Adrian**	N	N	N	N	N	N
NEVADA		N	N	N	N	N	N
1	Titus						
2	**Amodei**	Y	Y	Y	Y	Y	Y
3	Lee	N	N	N	N	N	N
4	Horsford	Y	Y	Y	Y	Y	Y
NEW HAMPSHIRE		Y	Y	Y	Y	Y	Y
1	Pappas						
2	Kuster	Y	Y	Y	Y	Y	Y
NEW JERSEY		Y	Y	Y	Y	Y	Y
1	Norcross						
2	Van Drew	Y	Y	Y	Y	Y	Y
3	Kim	N	Y	Y	Y	Y	Y
4	**Smith, C.**	Y	Y	Y	Y	Y	Y
5	Gottheimer	N	N	Y	N	N	N
6	Pallone	N	Y	Y	Y	Y	Y
7	Malinowski	Y	Y	Y	Y	Y	Y
8	Sires	N	Y	Y	Y	Y	Y
9	Pascrell	Y	Y	Y	Y	Y	Y
10	Payne	Y	Y	Y	Y	Y	Y
11	Sherrill	Y	Y	Y	Y	Y	Y
12	Watson Coleman	N	Y	Y	Y	Y	N
NEW MEXICO		Y	Y	Y	Y	Y	Y
1	Haaland						
2	Torres Small	Y	Y	Y	Y	Y	Y
3	Luján	Y	Y	Y	Y	Y	Y
NEW YORK		Y	Y	Y	Y	Y	Y
1	**Zeldin**						
2	**King, P.**	N	N	N	N	N	N
3	Suozzi	N	N	Y	N	N	N
4	Rice, K.	N	Y	Y	Y	Y	Y
5	Meeks	Y	Y	Y	Y	Y	Y
6	Meng	Y	Y	Y	Y	Y	Y
7	Velázquez	Y	Y	Y	Y	Y	Y
8	Jeffries	Y	Y	Y	Y	Y	Y
9	Clarke	Y	Y	Y	Y	Y	Y
10	Nadler	Y	Y	Y	Y	Y	Y
11	Rose	Y	Y	Y	Y	Y	Y
12	Maloney, C.	Y	Y	Y	Y	Y	Y
13	Espaillat	Y	Y	Y	Y	Y	Y
14	Ocasio-Cortez	Y	Y	Y	Y	Y	Y
15	Serrano	Y	Y	Y	Y	Y	Y
16	Engel	Y	Y	Y	Y	Y	Y
17	Lowey	Y	Y	Y	Y	Y	Y
18	Maloney, S.P.	Y	Y	Y	Y	Y	Y
19	Delgado	Y	Y	Y	Y	Y	Y
20	Tonko	Y	Y	Y	Y	Y	Y
21	**Stefanik**	Y	Y	Y	Y	Y	Y
22	Brindisi	N	N	N	N	N	N
23	**Reed**	Y	Y	Y	Y	Y	Y
24	**Katko**	Y	N	N	N	N	N
25	Morelle	N	N	N	N	N	N
26	Higgins, B.	Y	Y	Y	Y	Y	Y
27	**Collins, C.**	Y	Y	Y	Y	Y	Y
NORTH CAROLINA		N	N	N	N	N	N
1	Butterfield						
2	**Holding**	Y	Y	Y	Y	Y	Y
3	**Jones***	N	N	N	N	N	N
4	Price						
5	**Foxx**	Y	Y	Y	Y	Y	Y
6	**Walker**	N	N	N	N	N	N
7	**Rouzer**	N	N	N	N	N	N

		445	446	447	448	449	450
8	**Hudson**	N	N	N	N	N	N
9	vacant	N	N	N	N	N	N
10	**McHenry**	N	N	N	N	N	N
11	**Meadows**	N	N	N	N	N	N
12	Adams	Y	Y	Y	Y	Y	Y
13	**Budd**	N	N	N	N	N	N
NORTH DAKOTA							
AL	**Armstrong**	N	N	N	N	N	N
OHIO							
1	**Chabot**	N	N	N	N	N	N
2	**Wenstrup**	N	N	N	N	N	N
3	Beatty	Y	Y	Y	Y	Y	Y
4	**Jordan**	N	N	N	N	N	N
5	**Latta**	N	N	N	N	N	N
6	**Johnson, B.**	N	N	N	N	N	N
7	**Gibbs**	N	N	N	N	N	N
8	**Davidson**	N	N	N	N	Y	Y
9	Kaptur	Y	Y	Y	Y	Y	Y
10	**Turner**	N	N	N	N	N	N
11	Fudge	?	?	?	?	?	?
12	**Balderson**	N	N	N	N	N	N
13	Ryan	Y	Y	Y	Y	Y	Y
14	**Joyce**	N	N	N	N	N	N
15	**Stivers**	N	N	N	N	N	N
16	**Gonzalez**	N	Y	N	N	N	N
OKLAHOMA							
1	**Hern**	N	N	N	N	N	N
2	**Mullin**	N	N	N	N	N	N
3	**Lucas**	N	N	N	N	N	N
4	**Cole**	N	Y	N	N	N	N
5	Horn	Y	Y	Y	Y	Y	Y
OREGON							
1	Bonamici	Y	Y	Y	Y	Y	Y
2	**Walden**	N	N	N	N	N	N
3	Blumenauer	Y	Y	Y	Y	Y	Y
4	DeFazio	Y	Y	Y	Y	Y	Y
5	Schrader	Y	Y	Y	Y	Y	Y
PENNSYLVANIA							
1	**Fitzpatrick**	Y	Y	N	N	N	N
2	Boyle	Y	Y	N	Y	Y	Y
3	Evans	Y	Y	Y	Y	Y	Y
4	Dean	Y	Y	Y	Y	Y	Y
5	Scanlon	Y	Y	Y	Y	Y	Y
6	Houlahan	N	Y	Y	Y	Y	N
7	Wild	N	Y	Y	Y	Y	Y
8	Cartwright	Y	Y	Y	Y	Y	Y
9	**Meuser**	N	N	N	N	N	N
10	**Perry**	N	N	N	N	N	N
11	**Smucker**	N	N	N	N	N	N
12	**Marino***						
13	**Joyce**	N	N	N	N	N	N
14	**Reschenthaler**	N	N	N	N	N	N
15	**Thompson, G.**	N	Y	N	N	N	N
16	**Kelly, M.**	N	N	N	N	N	N
17	Lamb	N	Y	Y	Y	Y	Y
18	Doyle	Y	Y	Y	Y	Y	Y
RHODE ISLAND							
1	Cicilline	Y	Y	Y	Y	Y	Y
2	Langevin	Y	Y	Y	Y	Y	Y
SOUTH CAROLINA							
1	Cunningham	Y	Y	N	Y	Y	Y
2	**Wilson, J.**	N	N	N	N	N	N
3	**Duncan**	N	N	N	N	N	N
4	**Timmons**	N	N	N	N	N	N
5	**Norman**	N	N	N	N	N	N
6	Clyburn	Y	Y	Y	Y	Y	Y
7	**Rice, T.**	N	N	N	N	N	N
SOUTH DAKOTA							
AL	**Johnson**	N	N	N	N	N	N
TENNESSEE							
1	**Roe**	N	N	N	N	N	N
2	**Burchett**	N	N	N	Y	N	N
3	**Fleischmann**	N	N	N	N	N	N
4	**DesJarlais**	N	N	N	N	N	N
5	Cooper	Y	Y	Y	Y	Y	Y
6	**Rose**	N	N	N	N	N	N
7	**Green**	N	N	N	N	N	N
8	**Kustoff**	N	N	N	N	N	N
9	Cohen	Y	Y	N	Y	Y	Y
TEXAS							
1	**Gohmert**	N	Y	Y	N	N	N
2	**Crenshaw**	N	N	N	?	?	?
3	**Taylor**	N	N	N	N	N	N
4	**Ratcliffe**	N	N	N	N	N	N

		445	446	447	448	449	450
5	**Gooden**	N	N	N	N	N	N
6	**Wright**	N	N	N	N	N	N
7	Fletcher	N	Y	Y	Y	Y	Y
8	**Brady**	N	N	N	N	N	N
9	Green, A.	Y	Y	Y	Y	Y	Y
10	**McCaul**	N	N	N	N	N	N
11	**Conaway**	N	N	N	N	N	N
12	**Granger**	N	N	N	N	N	N
13	**Thornberry**	N	N	N	N	N	N
14	**Weber**	N	N	N	N	N	N
15	Gonzalez	Y	Y	Y	Y	Y	Y
16	Escobar	Y	Y	Y	Y	Y	Y
17	**Flores**	N	N	N	N	N	N
18	Jackson Lee	Y	Y	Y	Y	Y	Y
19	**Arrington**	N	N	N	N	N	N
20	Castro	Y	Y	Y	Y	Y	Y
21	**Roy**	N	N	N	Y	Y	Y
22	**Olson**	N	N	N	N	N	N
23	**Hurd**	N	N	N	N	Y	N
24	**Marchant**	N	N	N	N	N	N
25	**Williams**	N	N	N	N	N	N
26	**Burgess**	N	N	N	N	N	N
27	**Cloud**	N	Y	N	N	N	Y
28	Cuellar	Y	Y	N	Y	Y	Y
29	Garcia, S.	Y	Y	Y	Y	Y	Y
30	Johnson, E.B.	Y	Y	Y	Y	Y	Y
31	**Carter, J.**	N	N	N	N	N	N
32	Allred	N	Y	Y	Y	Y	Y
33	Veasey	Y	Y	Y	Y	Y	Y
34	Vela	Y	Y	N	Y	Y	Y
35	Doggett	Y	Y	Y	Y	Y	Y
36	**Babin**	N	N	N	N	N	N
UTAH							
1	**Bishop, R.**	N	N	N	N	N	N
2	**Stewart**	N	N	N	N	N	N
3	**Curtis**	N	N	N	N	N	N
4	McAdams	N	Y	Y	Y	Y	Y
VERMONT							
AL	Welch	Y	Y	Y	Y	Y	Y
VIRGINIA							
1	**Wittman**	N	N	N	N	N	N
2	Luria	N	Y	N	Y	Y	Y
3	Scott, R.	Y	Y	Y	Y	Y	Y
4	McEachin	Y	Y	Y	Y	Y	Y
5	**Riggleman**	N	N	N	N	N	N
6	**Cline**	Y	N	Y	N	Y	N
7	Spanberger	N	Y	Y	N	Y	N
8	Beyer	Y	Y	Y	Y	Y	Y
9	**Griffith**	Y	N	Y	N	N	N
10	Wexton	Y	Y	Y	Y	Y	Y
11	Connolly	Y	Y	Y	Y	Y	Y
WASHINGTON							
1	DelBene	Y	Y	Y	Y	Y	Y
2	Larsen	Y	Y	Y	Y	Y	Y
3	**Herrera Beutler**	N	N	N	N	N	N
4	**Newhouse**	N	N	N	N	N	N
5	**McMorris Rodgers**	N	N	N	N	N	N
6	Kilmer	Y	Y	Y	Y	Y	Y
7	Jayapal	Y	Y	Y	Y	Y	Y
8	Schrier	Y	Y	Y	Y	Y	Y
9	Smith Adam	Y	Y	Y	Y	Y	Y
10	Heck	Y	Y	Y	Y	Y	Y
WEST VIRGINIA							
1	**McKinley**	N	N	N	N	N	N
2	**Mooney**	N	N	N	Y	Y	Y
3	**Miller**	N	N	N	N	N	N
WISCONSIN							
1	**Steil**	N	N	N	N	N	N
2	Pocan	Y	Y	Y	Y	Y	Y
3	Kind	Y	Y	Y	Y	Y	Y
4	Moore	Y	Y	Y	Y	Y	Y
5	**Sensenbrenner**	N	N	N	N	N	N
6	**Grothman**	Y	N	N	N	N	N
7	**Duffy**	N	N	N	N	N	N
8	**Gallagher**	N	Y	N	N	N	N
WYOMING							
AL	**Cheney**	N	N	N	?	?	?
DELEGATES							
	Radewagen (A.S.)	?	?	?	?	?	?
	Norton (D.C.)	+	+	+	+	+	+
	San Nicolas (Guam)	Y	Y	Y	Y	Y	Y
	Sablan (N. Marianas)	Y	Y	Y	Y	Y	Y
	González-Colón (P.R.)	N	N	N	N	N	N
	Plaskett (V.I.)	?	?	?	?	?	?

451. HR2500. Fiscal 2020 Defense Authorization - Cyprus Arms Sales. Cicilline, D-R.I., amendment that would require the State Department to exclude the government of Cyprus from certain existing prohibitions on defense sales and exports or transfers of arms. It would require, as a condition for such exceptions, the president to annually verify efforts by Cyprus to deny port access for Russian military vessels and to cooperate with the U.S. to implement money laundering and other financial regulations. Adopted in Committee of the Whole 252-173: R 50-141; D 201-31; I 1-1. July 11, 2019.

452. HR2500. Fiscal 2020 Defense Authorization - Civilian Casualty Report. Engel, D-N.Y., amendment that would require the Defense Department to analyze any potential disparity between U.S. government and third party estimates of civilian casualties resulting from U.S. military operations. It would impose a number of requirements related to department practices to track and report on such casualties, integrate civilian protection into operational planning, and offer "reasonable and culturally appropriate" payments to civilians injured or to the families of civilians killed. Adopted in Committee of the Whole 241-183: R 9-182; D 230-1; I 2-0. July 11, 2019.

453. HR2500. Fiscal 2020 Defense Authorization - Extend New Strategic Arms Reduction Treaty. Engel, D-N.Y., amendment that would express the sense of Congress that the U.S. should seek to extend to February 2026 the New Strategic Arms Reduction Treaty with the Russian government and would prohibit the use of funds authorized by the bill to withdraw from the treaty. It would also require the Director of National Intelligence to report to Congress on national security and intelligence implications if the treaty were to expire, including likely Russian response, and would require the State Department to report to Congress on likely reactions of North Atlantic Treaty Organization and its members to a U.S. decision to not extend or replace the treaty. Adopted in Committee of the Whole 236-189: R 4-188; D 231-0; I 1-1. July 11, 2019.

454. HR2500. Fiscal 2020 Defense Authorization - Minuteman III Missile Study. Blumenauer, D-Ore., amendment that would require the Defense Department to contract with a federally-funded research and development center to conduct a study on extending to 2050 the life of Minuteman III intercontinental ballistic missiles, including on the costs of such an extension and the benefits and risks of incorporating certain "nondestructive" testing methods and technologies to extend the life of the missiles. It would also withhold 10 percent of funds authorized by the bill for the Defense secretary's office until the study is submitted. Rejected in Committee of the Whole 164-264: R 1-196; D 161-68; I 2-0. July 11, 2019.

455. HR2500. Fiscal 2020 Defense Authorization - Nuclear Warhead Study. Blumenauer, D-Ore., amendment that would require the Energy Department Nuclear Security Administration to contract with a federally-funded research and development center to conduct a study on the department's W80-4 nuclear warhead life extension program, including an explanation for the "unexpected" increase in program costs. It would also withhold $185 million in funds authorized by the bill for the extension program until the study is submitted. Rejected in Committee of the Whole 198-229: R 2-194; D 194-35; I 2-0. July 11, 2019.

456. HR2500. Fiscal 2020 Defense Authorization - INF Treaty Withdrawal. Frankel, D-Fla., amendment that would express the sense of Congress condemning U.S. withdrawal from the Intermediate-Range Nuclear Forces Treaty with Russia and prohibit the use of funds authorized by the bill for the Defense Department to research, develop, test, or deploy intermediate-range missiles U.S. missile systems banned by the treaty, until the department submits certain materials to Congress, including a diplomatic proposal for obtaining the strategic stability benefits of the INF treaty. Adopted in Committee of the Whole 215-214: R 1-196; D 213-17; I 1-1. July 11, 2019.

	451	452	453	454	455	456
ALABAMA						
1 Byrne	N	N	N	N	N	N
2 Roby	N	N	N	N	N	N
3 Rogers, M.	N	N	N	N	N	N
4 Aderholt	N	N	N	N	N	N
5 Brooks, M.	N	N	N	N	N	N
6 Palmer	Y	N	N	N	N	N
7 Sewell	Y	Y	Y	Y	Y	Y
ALASKA						
AL Young	Y	N	N	N	N	N
ARIZONA						
1 O'Halleran	Y	Y	Y	N	Y	Y
2 Kirkpatrick	Y	Y	Y	N	Y	Y
3 Grijalva	Y	Y	Y	Y	Y	Y
4 Gosar	N	N	N	N	N	N
5 Biggs	N	N	N	N	N	N
6 Schweikert	Y	Y	Y	N	N	N
7 Gallego	Y	Y	Y	Y	Y	Y
8 Lesko	N	N	N	N	N	N
9 Stanton	Y	Y	Y	N	Y	Y
ARKANSAS						
1 Crawford	N	N	N	N	N	N
2 Hill, F.	?	N	N	N	N	N
3 Womack	N	N	N	N	N	N
4 Westerman	N	N	N	N	N	N
CALIFORNIA						
1 LaMalfa	N	N	N	N	N	N
2 Huffman	Y	Y	Y	Y	Y	Y
3 Garamendi	Y	Y	Y	Y	Y	Y
4 McClintock	Y	N	N	N	N	N
5 Thompson, M.	Y	Y	Y	Y	Y	Y
6 Matsui	Y	Y	Y	Y	Y	Y
7 Bera	Y	Y	Y	N	Y	Y
8 Cook	N	N	N	N	N	N
9 McNerney	Y	Y	Y	Y	Y	Y
10 Harder	Y	Y	Y	Y	Y	Y
11 DeSaulnier	Y	Y	Y	Y	Y	Y
12 Pelosi						
13 Lee B.	N	Y	Y	Y	Y	Y
14 Speier	Y	Y	Y	Y	Y	Y
15 Swalwell	Y	Y	Y	Y	N	Y
16 Costa	Y	Y	Y	N	Y	Y
17 Khanna	Y	Y	Y	Y	Y	Y
18 Eshoo	Y	Y	Y	Y	Y	Y
19 Lofgren	Y	Y	Y	Y	Y	Y
20 Panetta	Y	Y	Y	N	N	N
21 Cox	Y	Y	Y	N	Y	Y
22 Nunes	N	N	N	N	N	N
23 McCarthy	?	?	?	N	N	N
24 Carbajal	Y	Y	Y	Y	Y	Y
25 Hill, K.	Y	Y	Y	N	N	Y
26 Brownley	Y	Y	Y	N	Y	Y
27 Chu	Y	Y	Y	Y	Y	Y
28 Schiff	Y	Y	Y	Y	Y	Y
29 Cárdenas	Y	Y	Y	?	Y	Y
30 Sherman	Y	Y	Y	N	Y	Y
31 Aguilar	Y	Y	Y	N	N	Y
32 Napolitano	Y	Y	Y	Y	Y	Y
33 Lieu	Y	Y	Y	Y	Y	Y
34 Gomez	Y	Y	Y	Y	Y	Y
35 Torres	Y	Y	Y	Y	Y	Y
36 Ruiz	Y	Y	Y	Y	Y	Y
37 Bass	N	Y	Y	Y	Y	Y
38 Sánchez	Y	Y	Y	Y	Y	Y
39 Cisneros	Y	Y	Y	N	N	N
40 Roybal-Allard	Y	Y	Y	Y	Y	Y
41 Takano	Y	Y	Y	Y	Y	Y
42 Calvert	N	N	N	N	N	N
43 Waters	N	Y	Y	Y	Y	Y
44 Barragán	Y	Y	Y	Y	Y	Y
45 Porter	N	Y	Y	Y	Y	Y
46 Correa	Y	Y	Y	N	Y	Y
47 Lowenthal	Y	Y	Y	Y	Y	Y
48 Rouda	Y	Y	Y	N	Y	N
49 Levin	Y	Y	Y	Y	Y	Y
50 Hunter	N	N	N	N	N	N
51 Vargas	Y	Y	Y	Y	Y	Y
52 Peters	Y	Y	Y	N	N	Y

	451	452	453	454	455	456
53 Davis, S.	Y	Y	Y	Y	Y	Y
COLORADO						
1 DeGette	Y	Y	Y	Y	Y	Y
2 Neguse	N	Y	Y	Y	Y	Y
3 Tipton	N	N	N	N	N	N
4 Buck	N	N	N	N	N	N
5 Lamborn	N	N	N	N	N	N
6 Crow	Y	Y	Y	N	Y	Y
7 Perlmutter	?	?	?	?	?	?
CONNECTICUT						
1 Larson	Y	Y	Y	Y	Y	Y
2 Courtney	Y	Y	Y	Y	Y	Y
3 DeLauro	Y	Y	Y	Y	Y	Y
4 Himes	Y	Y	Y	Y	Y	Y
5 Hayes	Y	Y	Y	Y	Y	Y
DELAWARE						
AL Blunt Rochester	N	Y	Y	Y	Y	Y
FLORIDA						
1 Gaetz	?	?	?	N	N	N
2 Dunn	Y	N	N	N	N	N
3 Yoho	N	N	N	N	N	N
4 Rutherford	N	N	N	N	N	N
5 Lawson	Y	Y	Y	N	Y	N
6 Waltz	Y	N	N	N	N	N
7 Murphy	Y	Y	Y	N	Y	Y
8 Posey	N	N	Y	N	N	N
9 Soto	Y	Y	Y	Y	Y	Y
10 Demings	Y	Y	Y	N	Y	Y
11 Webster	N	N	N	N	N	N
12 Bilirakis	Y	Y	Y	N	Y	N
13 Crist	Y	Y	Y	Y	Y	Y
14 Castor	Y	Y	Y	Y	Y	Y
15 Spano	Y	N	N	N	N	N
16 Buchanan	N	N	N	N	N	N
17 Steube	Y	N	N	N	N	N
18 Mast	Y	N	N	N	N	N
19 Rooney	Y	N	N	N	N	N
20 Hastings	Y	Y	Y	Y	Y	Y
21 Frankel	Y	Y	Y	Y	Y	Y
22 Deutch	Y	Y	Y	Y	Y	Y
23 Wasserman Schultz	Y	Y	Y	Y	Y	Y
24 Wilson, F.	Y	Y	Y	Y	Y	Y
25 Diaz-Balart	Y	N	N	N	N	N
26 Mucarsel-Powell	Y	Y	Y	N	Y	Y
27 Shalala	Y	Y	Y	Y	Y	Y
GEORGIA						
1 Carter, E.L.	N	N	N	N	N	N
2 Bishop, S.	Y	Y	Y	Y	Y	Y
3 Ferguson	Y	N	N	N	N	N
4 Johnson, H.	N	Y	Y	Y	?	Y
5 Lewis John	Y	Y	Y	Y	Y	Y
6 McBath	Y	Y	Y	N	Y	Y
7 Woodall	N	N	N	N	N	N
8 Scott, A.	N	N	N	N	N	N
9 Collins, D.	N	N	N	N	N	N
10 Hice	N	N	N	N	N	N
11 Loudermilk	N	N	N	N	N	N
12 Allen	N	N	N	N	N	N
13 Scott, D.	Y	Y	Y	Y	Y	Y
14 Graves, T.	N	N	N	N	N	N
HAWAII						
1 Case	Y	Y	Y	Y	Y	Y
2 Gabbard	?	?	?	?	?	?
IDAHO						
1 Fulcher	N	N	N	N	N	N
2 Simpson	N	N	N	N	N	N
ILLINOIS						
1 Rush	N	Y	Y	Y	Y	Y
2 Kelly, R.	Y	Y	Y	Y	Y	Y
3 Lipinski	Y	Y	Y	N	Y	N
4 García, J.	Y	Y	Y	Y	Y	Y
5 Quigley	Y	Y	Y	Y	Y	Y
6 Casten	Y	Y	Y	Y	Y	Y
7 Davis, D.	Y	Y	Y	Y	Y	Y
8 Krishnamoorthi	Y	Y	Y	Y	Y	Y
9 Schakowsky	Y	Y	Y	Y	Y	Y
10 Schneider	Y	Y	Y	Y	Y	Y
11 Foster	Y	Y	Y	Y	Y	Y

KEY:	Republicans	Democrats	Independents

Y Voted for (yea)		**N** Voted against (nay)	**P** Voted "present"
+ Announced for		**–** Announced against	**?** Did not vote or otherwise
# Paired for		**X** Paired against	make position known

		451	452	453	454	455	456
12	**Bost**	N	N	N	N	N	N
13	**Davis, R.**	N	N	N	N	N	N
14	Underwood	Y	Y	Y	?	?	?
15	**Shimkus**	N	N	N	N	N	N
16	**Kinzinger**	N	N	N	N	N	N
17	Bustos	Y	Y	Y	N	N	Y
18	**LaHood**	N	N	N	N	N	N
INDIANA							
1	Visclosky	Y	Y	Y	Y	Y	Y
2	**Walorski**	N	N	N	N	N	N
3	**Banks**	N	N	N	N	N	N
4	**Baird**	N	N	N	N	N	N
5	**Brooks, S.**	N	N	N	N	N	N
6	**Pence**	N	N	N	N	N	N
7	Carson	N	Y	Y	Y	Y	Y
8	**Bucshon**	N	N	N	N	N	N
9	**Hollingsworth**	N	N	N	N	N	N
IOWA							
1	Finkenauer	Y	Y	Y	N	N	Y
2	Loebsack	Y	Y	Y	N	Y	Y
3	Axne	Y	Y	Y	N	N	N
4	**King, S.**	Y	N	N	N	N	N
KANSAS							
1	**Marshall**	Y	N	N	N	N	N
2	**Watkins**	Y	N	N	N	N	N
3	Davids	Y	Y	Y	N	Y	Y
4	**Estes**	N	N	N	N	N	N
KENTUCKY							
1	**Comer**	N	N	N	N	N	N
2	**Guthrie**	N	N	N	N	N	N
3	Yarmuth	Y	Y	Y	Y	Y	Y
4	**Massie**	N	N	N	Y	Y	N
5	**Rogers, H.**	N	N	N	N	N	N
6	**Barr**	N	N	N	N	N	N
LOUISIANA							
1	**Scalise**	Y	N	N	N	N	N
2	Richmond	Y	Y	Y	Y	Y	Y
3	**Higgins, C.**	-	-	-	-	-	-
4	**Johnson, M.**	?	?	?	N	N	N
5	**Abraham**	Y	N	N	N	N	N
6	**Graves, G.**	N	N	N	N	N	N
MAINE							
1	Pingree	Y	Y	Y	Y	Y	Y
2	Golden	Y	Y	Y	N	N	Y
MARYLAND							
1	**Harris**	N	N	N	N	N	N
2	Ruppersberger	N	Y	Y	N	N	Y
3	Sarbanes	Y	Y	Y	Y	Y	Y
4	Brown, A.	Y	Y	Y	N	N	Y
5	Hoyer	Y	Y	Y	N	Y	Y
6	Trone	Y	Y	Y	Y	Y	Y
7	Cummings	N	Y	Y	Y	Y	Y
8	Raskin						
MASSACHUSETTS		Y	Y	Y	Y	Y	Y
1	Neal						
2	McGovern	Y	Y	Y	Y	Y	Y
3	Trahan	Y	Y	Y	Y	Y	Y
4	Kennedy	Y	Y	Y	Y	Y	Y
5	Clark	Y	Y	Y	Y	Y	Y
6	Moulton	Y	Y	Y	Y	Y	Y
7	Pressley	Y	Y	Y	N	N	N
8	Lynch	N	Y	Y	Y	Y	Y
9	Keating	N	Y	Y	N	Y	Y
MICHIGAN		Y	Y	Y	Y	Y	Y
1	**Bergman**						
2	**Huizenga**	N	N	N	N	N	N
3	*Amash*	N	N	N	N	N	N
4	**Moolenaar**	N	Y	N	Y	Y	N
5	Kildee	N	N	N	N	N	N
6	**Upton**	Y	Y	Y	Y	Y	Y
7	**Walberg**	Y	N	N	N	N	N
8	Slotkin	N	N	N	N	N	N
9	Levin	Y	Y	Y	Y	Y	Y
10	**Mitchell**	Y	Y	Y	Y	Y	Y
11	Stevens	N	N	N	N	N	N
12	Dingell	Y	Y	Y	N	Y	Y
13	Tlaib	Y	Y	Y	Y	Y	Y
14	Lawrence	N	Y	Y	Y	Y	Y
MINNESOTA		Y	Y	Y	Y	Y	Y
1	**Hagedorn**						
2	Craig	N	N	N	N	N	N
3	Phillips	Y	Y	Y	N	N	Y
4	McCollum	Y	Y	Y	N	Y	Y
5	Omar	Y	Y	Y	Y	Y	Y

		451	452	453	454	455	456
6	**Emmer**	N	Y	Y	Y	Y	Y
7	Peterson	N	N	N	N	N	N
8	**Stauber**	Y	Y	Y	N	N	N
MISSISSIPPI		N	N	N	N	N	N
1	**Kelly, T.**						
2	Thompson, B.	N	N	N	N	N	N
3	**Guest**	N	Y	Y	Y	Y	Y
4	**Palazzo**	N	N	N	N	N	N
MISSOURI		Y	N	N	N	N	N
1	Clay						
2	**Wagner**	Y	Y	Y	Y	Y	Y
3	**Luetkemeyer**	N	Y	N	N	N	N
4	**Hartzler**	N	N	N	N	N	N
5	Cleaver	N	N	N	N	N	N
6	**Graves, S.**	N	Y	Y	Y	Y	Y
7	**Long**	N	N	N	N	N	N
8	**Smith, J.**	N	N	N	N	N	N
MONTANA		Y	N	N	N	N	N
AL	**Gianforte**						
NEBRASKA		Y	N	N	N	N	N
1	**Fortenberry**						
2	**Bacon**	Y	Y	N	N	N	N
3	**Smith, Adrian**	N	N	N	N	N	N
NEVADA		Y	N	N	N	N	N
1	Titus						
2	**Amodei**	Y	Y	Y	Y	Y	Y
3	Lee	N	N	N	N	N	N
4	Horsford	Y	Y	Y	N	Y	Y
NEW HAMPSHIRE		Y	Y	Y	Y	Y	Y
1	Pappas						
2	Kuster	Y	Y	Y	Y	Y	Y
NEW JERSEY		Y	Y	Y	Y	Y	Y
1	Norcross						
2	Van Drew	Y	Y	Y	Y	Y	Y
3	Kim	Y	Y	Y	N	N	N
4	**Smith, C.**	Y	Y	Y	N	Y	Y
5	Gottheimer	Y	Y	Y	N	N	N
6	Pallone	Y	Y	Y	N	N	N
7	Malinowski	Y	Y	Y	Y	Y	Y
8	Sires	Y	Y	Y	Y	Y	Y
9	Pascrell	Y	Y	Y	Y	Y	Y
10	Payne	Y	Y	Y	Y	Y	Y
11	Sherrill	Y	Y	Y	Y	Y	Y
12	Watson Coleman	Y	Y	Y	N	Y	N
NEW MEXICO		N	Y	Y	Y	Y	Y
1	Haaland						
2	Torres Small	Y	Y	Y	N	N	Y
3	Luján	Y	Y	Y	N	N	Y
NEW YORK		Y	Y	Y	N	N	Y
1	**Zeldin**						
2	**King, P.**	Y	N	N	N	N	N
3	Suozzi	Y	N	N	N	N	N
4	Rice, K.	Y	Y	Y	N	Y	Y
5	Meeks	Y	Y	Y	Y	Y	Y
6	Meng	Y	Y	Y	Y	Y	Y
7	Velázquez	Y	Y	Y	Y	Y	Y
8	Jeffries	Y	Y	Y	Y	Y	Y
9	Clarke	Y	Y	Y	Y	Y	Y
10	Nadler	N	Y	Y	Y	Y	Y
11	Rose	Y	Y	Y	Y	Y	Y
12	Maloney, C.	Y	Y	Y	Y	Y	Y
13	Espaillat	Y	Y	Y	Y	Y	Y
14	Ocasio-Cortez	Y	Y	Y	Y	Y	Y
15	Serrano	N	Y	Y	Y	Y	Y
16	Engel	Y	Y	Y	Y	Y	Y
17	Lowey	Y	Y	Y	Y	Y	Y
18	Maloney, S.P.	Y	Y	Y	Y	Y	Y
19	Delgado	Y	Y	Y	N	N	Y
20	Tonko	Y	Y	Y	N	N	Y
21	**Stefanik**	Y	Y	Y	Y	Y	Y
22	Brindisi	N	N	N	N	N	N
23	**Reed**	Y	Y	Y	N	N	N
24	**Katko**	Y	N	N	N	N	N
25	Morelle	N	N	N	N	N	N
26	Higgins, B.	Y	Y	Y	Y	Y	Y
27	**Collins, C.**	Y	Y	Y	N	Y	Y
NORTH CAROLINA		Y	N	N	N	N	N
1	Butterfield						
2	**Holding**	N	Y	Y	Y	Y	Y
3	**Jones***	N	N	N	N	N	N
4	Price						
5	**Foxx**	N	Y	Y	Y	Y	Y
6	**Walker**	N	N	N	N	N	N
7	**Rouzer**	N	N	N	N	N	N

		451	452	453	454	455	456
8	**Hudson**	N	N	N	N	N	N
9	vacant	N	N	N	N	N	N
10	**McHenry**	N	N	N	N	N	N
11	**Meadows**	N	N	N	N	N	N
12	Adams	N	Y	Y	Y	Y	Y
13	**Budd**	N	N	N	N	N	N
NORTH DAKOTA							
AL	**Armstrong**	N	N	N	N	N	N
OHIO							
1	**Chabot**	N	N	N	N	N	N
2	**Wenstrup**	N	N	N	N	N	N
3	Beatty	Y	Y	Y	Y	Y	Y
4	**Jordan**	N	N	N	N	N	N
5	**Latta**	N	N	N	N	N	N
6	**Johnson, B.**	N	N	N	N	N	N
7	**Gibbs**	Y	N	N	N	N	N
8	**Davidson**	Y	N	N	N	N	N
9	Kaptur	Y	Y	Y	Y	Y	Y
10	**Turner**	N	N	N	N	N	N
11	Fudge	?	?	?	?	?	?
12	**Balderson**	N	N	N	N	N	N
13	Ryan	Y	?	Y	Y	Y	Y
14	**Joyce**	N	N	N	N	N	N
15	**Stivers**	Y	N	N	N	N	N
16	**Gonzalez**	Y	N	N	N	N	N
OKLAHOMA							
1	**Hern**	N	N	N	N	N	N
2	**Mullin**	N	N	N	N	N	N
3	**Lucas**	N	N	N	N	N	N
4	**Cole**	N	Y	N	N	N	N
5	Horn	Y	Y	Y	N	Y	Y
OREGON							
1	Bonamici	Y	Y	Y	Y	Y	Y
2	**Walden**	Y	N	N	N	N	N
3	Blumenauer	Y	Y	Y	Y	Y	Y
4	DeFazio	Y	Y	Y	Y	Y	Y
5	Schrader	Y	Y	Y	Y	Y	Y
PENNSYLVANIA							
1	**Fitzpatrick**	Y	Y	N	N	N	N
2	Boyle	N	Y	Y	Y	Y	Y
3	Evans	Y	Y	Y	Y	Y	Y
4	Dean	Y	Y	Y	Y	Y	Y
5	Scanlon	Y	Y	Y	Y	Y	Y
6	Houlahan	Y	Y	Y	Y	Y	Y
7	Wild	Y	Y	Y	Y	Y	Y
8	Cartwright	Y	Y	Y	Y	Y	Y
9	**Meuser**	N	N	N	N	N	N
10	**Perry**	Y	N	N	N	N	N
11	**Smucker**	N	?	N	N	-	N
12	**Marino***						
13	**Joyce**	N	N	N	N	N	N
14	**Reschenthaler**	N	Y	N	N	N	N
15	**Thompson, G.**	Y	N	N	N	N	N
16	**Kelly, M.**	Y	N	N	N	N	N
17	Lamb	Y	Y	Y	N	Y	N
18	Doyle	Y	Y	Y	Y	Y	Y
RHODE ISLAND							
1	Cicilline	Y	Y	Y	Y	Y	Y
2	Langevin	Y	Y	Y	N	Y	Y
SOUTH CAROLINA							
1	Cunningham	N	Y	Y	N	N	N
2	**Wilson, J.**	N	N	N	N	N	N
3	**Duncan**	N	N	N	N	N	N
4	**Timmons**	N	N	N	N	N	N
5	**Norman**	N	N	N	N	N	N
6	Clyburn	Y	Y	Y	N	N	Y
7	**Rice, T.**	N	N	N	N	N	N
SOUTH DAKOTA							
AL	**Johnson**	N	N	N	N	N	N
TENNESSEE							
1	**Roe**	N	N	N	N	N	N
2	**Burchett**	N	N	N	N	N	N
3	**Fleischmann**	Y	N	N	N	N	N
4	**DesJarlais**	N	N	N	N	N	N
5	Cooper	N	Y	Y	N	N	N
6	**Rose**	N	N	N	N	N	N
7	**Green**	Y	N	N	N	N	N
8	**Kustoff**	N	N	N	N	N	N
9	Cohen	N	Y	Y	Y	Y	Y
TEXAS							
1	**Gohmert**	Y	N	N	N	N	N
2	**Crenshaw**	?	?	?	N	N	N
3	**Taylor**	N	N	N	N	N	N
4	**Ratcliffe**	N	N	N	N	N	N

		451	452	453	454	455	456
5	**Gooden**	N	N	N	N	N	N
6	**Wright**	N	N	N	N	N	N
7	Fletcher	Y	Y	Y	N	N	Y
8	**Brady**	N	N	N	N	N	N
9	Green, A.	Y	Y	Y	Y	Y	Y
10	**McCaul**	N	Y	N	N	N	N
11	**Conaway**	N	N	N	N	N	N
12	**Granger**	N	N	N	N	N	N
13	**Thornberry**	N	N	N	N	N	N
14	**Weber**	Y	N	N	N	N	N
15	Gonzalez	Y	Y	Y	Y	Y	Y
16	Escobar	Y	Y	Y	Y	Y	Y
17	**Flores**	Y	N	N	N	N	N
18	Jackson Lee	Y	Y	Y	Y	Y	Y
19	**Arrington**	N	N	N	N	N	N
20	Castro	Y	Y	Y	Y	Y	Y
21	**Roy**	Y	N	N	N	Y	N
22	**Olson**	N	N	N	N	N	N
23	**Hurd**	N	N	N	N	N	N
24	**Marchant**	N	N	N	N	N	N
25	**Williams**	N	N	N	N	N	N
26	**Burgess**	N	N	N	N	N	N
27	**Cloud**	N	N	N	N	N	N
28	Cuellar	Y	Y	Y	N	Y	Y
29	Garcia, S.	Y	Y	Y	Y	Y	Y
30	Johnson, E.B.	Y	Y	Y	N	Y	Y
31	**Carter, J.**	N	N	N	N	N	N
32	Allred	Y	Y	Y	N	Y	Y
33	Veasey	Y	Y	Y	N	N	Y
34	Vela	Y	Y	?	Y	Y	Y
35	Doggett	Y	Y	Y	Y	Y	Y
36	**Babin**	N	N	N	N	N	N
UTAH							
1	**Bishop, R.**	N	N	N	N	N	N
2	**Stewart**	N	N	N	N	N	N
3	**Curtis**	N	N	N	N	N	N
4	McAdams	Y	Y	Y	N	Y	Y
VERMONT							
AL	Welch	Y	Y	Y	Y	Y	Y
VIRGINIA							
1	**Wittman**	N	N	N	N	N	N
2	Luria	Y	N	Y	N	N	N
3	Scott, R.	Y	Y	Y	N	N	N
4	McEachin	N	Y	Y	N	N	Y
5	**Riggleman**	Y	N	N	N	N	N
6	**Cline**	Y	N	N	N	N	N
7	Spanberger	Y	Y	Y	N	N	Y
8	Beyer	Y	Y	Y	Y	Y	Y
9	**Griffith**	Y	N	N	N	N	N
10	Wexton	Y	Y	Y	N	Y	Y
11	Connolly	N	Y	Y	N	N	Y
WASHINGTON							
1	DelBene	Y	Y	Y	Y	Y	Y
2	Larsen	Y	Y	Y	Y	Y	Y
3	**Herrera Beutler**	N	N	N	N	N	N
4	**Newhouse**	N	N	N	N	N	N
5	**McMorris Rodgers**	N	N	N	N	N	N
6	Kilmer	Y	Y	Y	Y	Y	Y
7	Jayapal	Y	Y	Y	Y	Y	Y
8	Schrier	Y	Y	Y	Y	Y	Y
9	Smith Adam	Y	Y	Y	Y	Y	Y
10	Heck	Y	Y	Y	Y	Y	Y
WEST VIRGINIA							
1	**McKinley**	N	N	N	N	N	N
2	**Mooney**	N	N	N	N	N	N
3	**Miller**	Y	N	N	N	N	N
WISCONSIN							
1	**Steil**	N	N	N	N	N	N
2	Pocan	Y	Y	Y	Y	Y	Y
3	Kind	N	Y	Y	Y	Y	Y
4	Moore	N	Y	Y	Y	Y	Y
5	**Sensenbrenner**	Y	N	N	N	N	N
6	**Grothman**	N	N	N	N	N	N
7	**Duffy**	N	N	N	N	N	N
8	**Gallagher**	N	N	N	N	N	N
WYOMING							
AL	**Cheney**	?	?	?	N	N	N
DELEGATES							
	Radewagen (A.S.)	?	?	?	?	?	?
	Norton (D.C.)	+	+	+	+	+	+
	San Nicolas (Guam)	Y	Y	Y	?	?	?
	Sablan (N. Marianas)	Y	Y	Y	Y	Y	Y
	González-Colón (P.R.)	Y	N	N	N	N	N
	Plaskett (V.I.)	?	?	?	?	?	?

457. HR2500. Fiscal 2020 Defense Authorization – Trump Property Reimbursements. Lieu, D-Calif., amendment that would prohibit the use of funds authorized by the bill for the Defense Department to reimburse certain expenses at properties owned by or connected to President Donald Trump or his businesses. It would allow the president to waive the limitation if he reimburses the Treasury Department for the associated expenses. Adopted in Committee of the Whole 223-205: R 0-197; D 222-8; I 1-0. July 11, 2019.

458. HR2500. Fiscal 2020 Defense Authorization – Restricting Military Parade Funding. Raskin, D-Md., amendment that would prohibit the use of funds authorized by the bill for the Defense Department to fund any military exhibition or parade for review by the president outside of authorized military activities, with the exception of customary ceremonial honors and duties. Adopted in Committee of the Whole 221-207: R 0-196; D 219-11; I 2-0. July 11, 2019.

459. HR2500. Fiscal 2020 Defense Authorization – Overseas Contingency Funding. Lee, D-Calif., for Khanna, D-Calif., amendment that would decrease by $16.8 billion funding for operations and maintenance for overseas contingency operations. Rejected in Committee of the Whole 115-307: R 2-187; D 111-120; I 2-0. July 12, 2019.

460. HR2500. Fiscal 2020 Defense Authorization – Military Detainees. Amash, I-Mich., amendment that would require that any individual detained by the U.S. under authorized use of military force or the provisions of the bill be immediately transferred from military custody for court proceedings. It would repeal existing law authorizing military custody disposition procedures under law of war for any individual detained under AUMF and would prohibit the transfer of any individual detained or arrested in the U.S. into military custody. Rejected in Committee of the Whole 187-236: R 4-186; D 181-50; I 2-0. July 12, 2019.

461. HR2500. Fiscal 2020 Defense Authorization – High-Altitude Aviation Training. Tipton, R-Colo., amendment that would express the sense of Congress that the high-altitude Army National Guard aviation training site in Gypsum, Colo., is the only Defense Department school teaching aviators how to safely fly rotary-wing aircraft in mountainous, high-altitude environments and that this training is critical to U.S. national security. Adopted in Committee of the Whole 417-6: R 190-0; D 226-5; I 1-1. July 12, 2019.

462. HR2500. Fiscal 2020 Defense Authorization – Low-Yield Warheads. Turner, R-Ohio, amendment that would strike from the bill a provision prohibiting the deployment of certain low-yield warheads and replace it with a provision requiring the Defense Department to certify to Congress whether the deployment of such missile warheads is in the best interests of U.S. national security and whether alternatives to such missile warheads have similar capabilities. Rejected in Committee of the Whole 201-221: R 190-0; D 10-220; I 1-1. July 12, 2019.

		457	458	459	460	461	462
ALABAMA							
1	Byrne	N	N	N	N	Y	Y
2	Roby	N	N	N	N	Y	Y
3	Rogers, M.	N	N	N	N	Y	Y
4	Aderholt	N	N	N	N	Y	Y
5	Brooks, M.	N	N	N	N	Y	Y
6	Palmer	N	N	N	N	Y	Y
7	Sewell	Y	Y	N	Y	Y	N
ALASKA							
AL	Young	N	N	N	N	Y	Y
ARIZONA							
1	O'Halleran	Y	Y	N	N	Y	N
2	Kirkpatrick	Y	Y	N	N	Y	N
3	Grijalva	Y	Y	Y	Y	N	N
4	Gosar	N	N	N	N	Y	N
5	Biggs	N	N	N	N	Y	Y
6	Schweikert	N	N	N	N	Y	Y
7	Gallego	Y	Y	N	Y	Y	N
8	Lesko	N	N	N	N	Y	Y
9	Stanton	Y	Y	N	Y	Y	N
ARKANSAS							
1	Crawford	N	N	N	N	Y	Y
2	Hill, F.	N	N	N	N	Y	Y
3	Womack	N	N	N	N	Y	Y
4	Westerman	N	N	N	N	Y	Y
CALIFORNIA							
1	LaMalfa	N	N	N	N	Y	Y
2	Huffman	Y	Y	Y	Y	Y	N
3	Garamendi	Y	Y	N	Y	N	N
4	McClintock	N	N	N	N	Y	Y
5	Thompson, M.	Y	Y	Y	Y	Y	N
6	Matsui	Y	Y	Y	Y	Y	N
7	Bera	Y	Y	N	Y	Y	N
8	Cook	N	N	N	N	Y	Y
9	McNerney	Y	Y	Y	Y	Y	N
10	Harder	Y	Y	N	N	Y	Y
11	DeSaulnier	Y	Y	Y	Y	Y	N
12	Pelosi						
13	Lee B.	Y	Y	Y	Y	N	N
14	Speier	Y	Y	Y	Y	Y	N
15	Swalwell	Y	Y	Y	Y	Y	N
16	Costa	Y	Y	N	N	Y	N
17	Khanna	Y	Y	Y	Y	Y	N
18	Eshoo	Y	Y	Y	Y	Y	N
19	Lofgren	Y	Y	Y	Y	Y	N
20	Panetta	Y	Y	Y	Y	Y	N
21	Cox	Y	Y	N	N	Y	N
22	Nunes	N	N	N	N	Y	Y
23	McCarthy	N	N	N	N	Y	Y
24	Carbajal	Y	Y	N	Y	Y	N
25	Hill, K.	Y	Y	N	N	Y	N
26	Brownley	Y	Y	N	Y	Y	N
27	Chu	Y	Y	Y	Y	Y	N
28	Schiff	Y	Y	Y	Y	Y	N
29	Cárdenas	Y	Y	Y	Y	Y	N
30	Sherman	Y	Y	N	Y	Y	N
31	Aguilar	Y	Y	Y	Y	Y	N
32	Napolitano	Y	Y	Y	Y	Y	N
33	Lieu	Y	Y	Y	Y	Y	N
34	Gomez	Y	Y	Y	Y	Y	N
35	Torres	Y	Y	Y	Y	Y	N
36	Ruiz	Y	Y	N	Y	Y	N
37	Bass	Y	Y	Y	Y	Y	N
38	Sánchez	Y	Y	Y	Y	Y	N
39	Cisneros	Y	Y	N	Y	Y	N
40	Roybal-Allard	Y	Y	Y	Y	Y	N
41	Takano	Y	Y	Y	Y	Y	N
42	Calvert	N	N	N	N	Y	Y
43	Waters	Y	Y	Y	Y	Y	N
44	Barragán	Y	Y	Y	Y	Y	N
45	Porter	Y	Y	N	Y	Y	N
46	Correa	Y	Y	N	Y	Y	N
47	Lowenthal	Y	Y	Y	Y	Y	N
48	Rouda	Y	Y	N	Y	Y	N
49	Levin	Y	Y	N	Y	Y	N
50	Hunter	N	N	N	N	Y	Y
51	Vargas	Y	Y	Y	Y	Y	N
52	Peters	Y	Y	N	N	Y	N
53	Davis, S.	Y	Y	N	Y	Y	N
COLORADO							
1	DeGette	Y	Y	N	Y	Y	N
2	Neguse	Y	Y	Y	Y	Y	N
3	Tipton	N	N	N	N	Y	Y
4	Buck	N	N	N	N	Y	Y
5	Lamborn	N	N	N	N	Y	Y
6	Crow	N	Y	N	Y	Y	N
7	Perlmutter	?	?	?	?	?	?
CONNECTICUT							
1	Larson	Y	Y	N	Y	Y	N
2	Courtney	Y	Y	N	Y	Y	N
3	DeLauro	Y	Y	N	Y	Y	N
4	Himes	Y	Y	N	Y	Y	N
5	Hayes	Y	Y	N	Y	Y	N
DELAWARE							
AL	Blunt Rochester	Y	Y	Y	Y	Y	N
FLORIDA							
1	Gaetz	N	N	N	Y	N	Y
2	Dunn	N	N	N	Y	Y	Y
3	Yoho	N	N	Y	Y	Y	Y
4	Rutherford	N	N	N	N	Y	Y
5	Lawson	Y	Y	N	Y	Y	N
6	Waltz	N	N	N	N	Y	Y
7	Murphy	Y	Y	N	Y	Y	N
8	Posey	N	N	N	N	Y	Y
9	Soto	Y	Y	N	Y	Y	N
10	Demings	Y	Y	N	Y	Y	N
11	Webster	N	N	N	N	Y	Y
12	Bilirakis	N	N	N	N	Y	Y
13	Crist	Y	Y	N	Y	Y	N
14	Castor	Y	Y	Y	Y	Y	N
15	Spano	N	N	N	N	Y	Y
16	Buchanan	N	N	N	N	Y	Y
17	Steube	N	N	N	N	Y	Y
18	Mast	N	N	N	N	Y	Y
19	Rooney	N	N	N	N	Y	Y
20	Hastings	Y	Y	Y	Y	Y	N
21	Frankel	Y	Y	N	Y	Y	N
22	Deutch	Y	Y	Y	Y	Y	N
23	Wasserman Schultz	Y	Y	N	Y	Y	N
24	Wilson, F.	Y	Y	Y	Y	Y	N
25	Diaz-Balart	N	N	N	N	Y	Y
26	Mucarsel-Powell	Y	Y	N	Y	Y	N
27	Shalala	Y	Y	N	Y	Y	N
GEORGIA							
1	Carter, E.L.	N	N	N	Y	N	Y
2	Bishop, S.	Y	Y	N	Y	Y	N
3	Ferguson	N	N	N	N	Y	Y
4	Johnson, H.	Y	Y	Y	Y	N	N
5	Lewis John	Y	Y	Y	Y	Y	N
6	McBath	Y	Y	N	N	Y	N
7	Woodall	N	N	N	N	Y	Y
8	Scott, A.	N	N	N	N	Y	Y
9	Collins, D.	N	N	N	N	Y	Y
10	Hice	N	N	N	N	Y	Y
11	Loudermilk	N	N	N	N	Y	Y
12	Allen	N	N	N	N	Y	Y
13	Scott, D.	Y	Y	N	Y	Y	N
14	Graves, T.	N	N	N	N	Y	Y
HAWAII							
1	Case	Y	Y	N	N	Y	N
2	Gabbard	?	?	?	?	?	?
IDAHO							
1	Fulcher	N	N	N	N	Y	Y
2	Simpson	N	N	N	N	Y	Y
ILLINOIS							
1	Rush	Y	Y	Y	Y	Y	N
2	Kelly, R.	Y	Y	N	Y	Y	N
3	Lipinski	Y	Y	N	N	Y	Y
4	García, J.	Y	Y	Y	Y	Y	N
5	Quigley	Y	Y	N	Y	Y	N
6	Casten	Y	Y	N	Y	Y	N
7	Davis, D.	Y	Y	Y	Y	Y	N
8	Krishnamoorthi	Y	Y	N	Y	Y	N
9	Schakowsky	Y	Y	Y	Y	Y	N
10	Schneider	Y	Y	N	Y	Y	N
11	Foster	Y	Y	N	Y	Y	N

KEY:		**Republicans**		Democrats		*Independents*	
Y	Voted for (yea)		**N**	Voted against (nay)		**P**	Voted "present"
+	Announced for		**–**	Announced against		**?**	Did not vote or otherwise
#	Paired for		**X**	Paired against			make position known

		457	458	459	460	461	462
12	**Bost**	N	N	N	N	Y	Y
13	**Davis, R.**	N	N	N	N	Y	Y
14	Underwood	?	?	N	N	Y	N
15	**Shimkus**	N	N	N	N	Y	Y
16	**Kinzinger**	N	N	N	N	Y	Y
17	Bustos	Y	Y	N	N	Y	N
18	**LaHood**	N	N	N	N	Y	Y
INDIANA							
1	Visclosky	Y	Y	N	Y	Y	N
2	**Walorski**	N	N	N	N	Y	Y
3	**Banks**	N	N	N	N	Y	Y
4	**Baird**	N	N	N	N	Y	Y
5	**Brooks, S.**	N	N	N	N	Y	Y
6	**Pence**	N	N	N	N	Y	Y
7	Carson	Y	Y	N	N	Y	Y
8	**Bucshon**	N	N	N	N	Y	Y
9	**Hollingsworth**	N	N	N	N	Y	Y
IOWA							
1	Finkenauer	Y	Y	N	N	Y	N
2	Loebsack	Y	Y	N	Y	Y	N
3	Axne	Y	Y	N	N	Y	Y
4	**King, S.**	N	N	N	N	Y	Y
KANSAS							
1	**Marshall**	N	N	N	N	Y	Y
2	**Watkins**	N	N	N	N	Y	Y
3	Davids	Y	Y	N	N	Y	N
4	**Estes**	N	N	N	N	Y	Y
KENTUCKY							
1	**Comer**	N	N	N	N	Y	Y
2	**Guthrie**	N	N	N	N	Y	Y
3	Yarmuth	Y	Y	Y	Y	Y	N
4	**Massie**	N	N	Y	Y	Y	Y
5	**Rogers, H.**	N	N	N	N	Y	Y
6	**Barr**	N	N	N	N	Y	Y
LOUISIANA							
1	**Scalise**	N	N	N	N	Y	Y
2	Richmond	Y	Y	Y	Y	Y	N
3	**Higgins, C.**	-	-	-	-	+	-
4	**Johnson, M.**	N	N	N	N	Y	Y
5	**Abraham**	N	N	N	N	Y	Y
6	**Graves, G.**	N	N	N	N	Y	Y
MAINE							
1	Pingree	Y	Y	Y	Y	Y	N
2	Golden	Y	Y	N	N	Y	N
MARYLAND							
1	**Harris**	N	N	N	N	Y	Y
2	Ruppersberger	Y	Y	N	Y	Y	N
3	Sarbanes	Y	Y	Y	Y	Y	N
4	Brown, A.	Y	Y	N	Y	Y	N
5	Hoyer	Y	Y	N	Y	Y	N
6	Trone	Y	Y	N	Y	Y	N
7	Cummings	Y	Y	Y	Y	Y	N
8	Raskin						
MASSACHUSETTS		Y	Y	Y	Y	Y	N
1	Neal						
2	McGovern	Y	Y	Y	Y	Y	N
3	Trahan	Y	Y	Y	Y	Y	N
4	Kennedy	Y	Y	Y	Y	Y	N
5	Clark	Y	Y	Y	Y	Y	N
6	Moulton	Y	Y	Y	Y	Y	N
7	Pressley	Y	Y	N	Y	Y	N
8	Lynch	Y	Y	Y	Y	Y	N
9	Keating	Y	Y	N	Y	Y	N
MICHIGAN		Y	Y	N	Y	N	N
1	**Bergman**						
2	**Huizenga**	N	N	N	N	Y	Y
3	*Amash*	N	N	N	N	Y	Y
4	**Moolenaar**	P	Y	Y	Y	N	Y
5	Kildee	N	N	N	N	Y	Y
6	**Upton**	Y	Y	Y	Y	Y	N
7	**Walberg**	N	N	N	N	Y	Y
8	Slotkin	N	N	N	N	Y	Y
9	Levin	Y	N	N	Y	Y	N
10	**Mitchell**	Y	Y	Y	Y	Y	N
11	Stevens	N	N	N	N	Y	Y
12	Dingell	Y	Y	N	Y	Y	N
13	Tlaib	Y	Y	N	Y	Y	N
14	Lawrence	Y	Y	Y	Y	Y	N
MINNESOTA		Y	Y	?	?	?	?
1	**Hagedorn**						
2	Craig	N	N	N	N	Y	Y
3	Phillips	Y	Y	N	N	Y	N
4	McCollum	Y	Y	N	Y	Y	N
5	Omar	Y	Y	Y	N	Y	N

		457	458	459	460	461	462
6	**Emmer**	Y	Y	Y	Y	Y	N
7	Peterson	N	N	N	N	Y	Y
8	**Stauber**	N	N	N	N	Y	Y
MISSISSIPPI		N	N	N	N	Y	Y
1	**Kelly, T.**						
2	Thompson, B.	N	N	N	N	Y	Y
3	**Guest**	Y	Y	Y	N	Y	N
4	**Palazzo**	N	N	N	N	Y	Y
MISSOURI		N	N	N	N	Y	Y
1	Clay						
2	**Wagner**	Y	Y	Y	Y	Y	N
3	**Luetkemeyer**	N	N	N	N	Y	Y
4	**Hartzler**	N	N	N	N	Y	Y
5	Cleaver	N	N	N	N	Y	Y
6	**Graves, S.**	Y	Y	Y	Y	Y	N
7	**Long**	N	N	+	+	-	-
8	**Smith, J.**	N	N	N	N	Y	Y
MONTANA		N	N	N	N	Y	Y
AL	**Gianforte**						
NEBRASKA		N	N	N	N	Y	Y
1	**Fortenberry**						
2	**Bacon**	N	N	N	N	Y	Y
3	**Smith, Adrian**	N	N	N	N	Y	Y
NEVADA		N	N	N	N	Y	Y
1	Titus						
2	**Amodei**	Y	Y	Y	Y	Y	N
3	Lee	N	N	N	N	Y	Y
4	Horsford	Y	Y	N	N	Y	N
NEW HAMPSHIRE		Y	Y	N	Y	Y	N
1	Pappas						
2	Kuster	Y	Y	Y	Y	Y	N
NEW JERSEY		Y	Y	Y	Y	Y	N
1	Norcross						
2	Van Drew	Y	Y	N	Y	Y	N
3	Kim	Y	Y	N	N	Y	Y
4	**Smith, C.**	N	N	N	N	Y	N
5	Gottheimer	N	N	N	N	Y	Y
6	Pallone	Y	Y	N	N	Y	Y
7	Malinowski	Y	Y	Y	Y	Y	N
8	Sires	Y	Y	N	Y	Y	N
9	Pascrell	Y	Y	N	Y	Y	N
10	Payne	Y	Y	N	Y	Y	N
11	Sherrill	Y	Y	Y	Y	Y	N
12	Watson Coleman	N	N	N	Y	Y	N
NEW MEXICO		Y	Y	Y	Y	Y	N
1	Haaland						
2	Torres Small	Y	Y	Y	Y	Y	N
3	Luján	Y	N	N	N	Y	N
NEW YORK		Y	Y	Y	Y	Y	N
1	**Zeldin**						
2	**King, P.**	N	N	N	N	Y	Y
3	Suozzi	N	N	?	N	Y	Y
4	Rice, K.	Y	Y	N	Y	Y	N
5	Meeks	Y	Y	N	N	Y	N
6	Meng	Y	Y	Y	Y	Y	N
7	Velázquez	Y	Y	Y	Y	Y	N
8	Jeffries	Y	Y	Y	Y	Y	N
9	Clarke	Y	Y	Y	Y	Y	N
10	Nadler	Y	Y	Y	Y	Y	N
11	Rose	Y	Y	Y	Y	Y	N
12	Maloney, C.	Y	N	N	Y	Y	N
13	Espaillat	Y	Y	Y	Y	Y	N
14	Ocasio-Cortez	Y	Y	Y	Y	Y	N
15	Serrano	Y	Y	Y	Y	Y	N
16	Engel	Y	Y	Y	Y	Y	N
17	Lowey	Y	Y	Y	Y	Y	N
18	Maloney, S.P.	Y	Y	N	Y	Y	N
19	Delgado	Y	Y	N	N	Y	N
20	Tonko	Y	Y	N	N	Y	N
21	**Stefanik**	Y	Y	N	Y	Y	N
22	Brindisi	N	N	N	N	Y	Y
23	**Reed**	Y	N	N	N	Y	N
24	**Katko**	N	N	N	N	Y	Y
25	Morelle	N	N	N	N	Y	Y
26	Higgins, B.	Y	Y	N	Y	Y	N
27	**Collins, C.**	Y	Y	N	Y	Y	N
NORTH CAROLINA		N	N	N	N	Y	Y
1	Butterfield						
2	**Holding**	Y	Y	Y	Y	Y	N
3	**Jones***	N	N	N	N	Y	Y
4	Price						
5	**Foxx**	Y	Y	Y	Y	Y	N
6	**Walker**	N	N	N	N	Y	Y
7	**Rouzer**	N	N	N	N	Y	Y

		457	458	459	460	461	462
8	**Hudson**	N	N	N	N	Y	Y
9	vacant	N	N	N	N	Y	Y
10	**McHenry**	N	N	N	N	Y	Y
11	**Meadows**	N	N	N	N	Y	Y
12	Adams	Y	Y	Y	Y	Y	N
13	**Budd**	N	N	N	N	Y	Y
NORTH DAKOTA							
AL	**Armstrong**	N	N	N	N	Y	Y
OHIO							
1	**Chabot**	N	N	N	N	Y	Y
2	**Wenstrup**	N	N	N	N	Y	Y
3	Beatty	Y	Y	Y	Y	Y	N
4	**Jordan**	N	?	N	N	Y	Y
5	**Latta**	N	N	N	N	Y	Y
6	**Johnson, B.**	N	N	N	N	Y	Y
7	**Gibbs**	N	N	N	N	Y	Y
8	**Davidson**	N	N	N	N	Y	Y
9	Kaptur	Y	Y	N	Y	Y	N
10	**Turner**	N	N	N	N	Y	Y
11	Fudge	?	?	?	?	?	?
12	**Balderson**	N	N	N	N	Y	Y
13	Ryan	Y	Y	Y	Y	Y	N
14	**Joyce**	N	N	N	N	Y	Y
15	**Stivers**	N	N	N	N	Y	Y
16	**Gonzalez**	N	N	N	N	Y	Y
OKLAHOMA							
1	**Hern**	N	N	N	N	Y	Y
2	**Mullin**	N	N	N	N	Y	Y
3	**Lucas**	N	N	N	N	Y	Y
4	**Cole**	N	N	N	N	Y	Y
5	Horn	N	Y	N	N	Y	N
OREGON							
1	Bonamici	Y	Y	Y	Y	Y	N
2	**Walden**	N	N	N	N	Y	Y
3	Blumenauer	Y	Y	Y	Y	N	N
4	DeFazio	Y	Y	Y	Y	Y	N
5	Schrader	Y	Y	Y	Y	Y	N
PENNSYLVANIA							
1	**Fitzpatrick**	N	N	N	N	Y	Y
2	Boyle	Y	Y	N	Y	Y	N
3	Evans	Y	Y	Y	Y	Y	N
4	Dean	Y	Y	Y	Y	Y	N
5	Scanlon	Y	Y	Y	Y	Y	N
6	Houlahan	Y	Y	N	N	Y	N
7	Wild	Y	Y	N	N	Y	N
8	Cartwright	Y	Y	Y	Y	Y	N
9	**Meuser**	N	N	N	N	Y	Y
10	**Perry**	N	N	N	N	Y	Y
11	**Smucker**	N	N	N	N	Y	Y
12	**Marino***						
13	**Joyce**	N	N	N	N	Y	Y
14	**Reschenthaler**	N	N	N	N	Y	Y
15	**Thompson, G.**	N	N	N	N	Y	Y
16	**Kelly, M.**	N	N	N	N	Y	Y
17	Lamb	N	Y	N	N	Y	N
18	Doyle	Y	Y	Y	Y	Y	N
RHODE ISLAND							
1	Cicilline	Y	Y	Y	Y	Y	N
2	Langevin	Y	Y	N	Y	Y	N
SOUTH CAROLINA							
1	Cunningham	Y	N	N	N	Y	N
2	**Wilson, J.**	N	N	N	N	Y	Y
3	**Duncan**	N	N	N	N	Y	Y
4	**Timmons**	N	N	N	N	Y	Y
5	**Norman**	N	N	N	N	Y	Y
6	Clyburn	Y	Y	N	Y	Y	N
7	**Rice, T.**	N	N	?	?	?	?
SOUTH DAKOTA							
AL	**Johnson**	N	N	N	N	Y	Y
TENNESSEE							
1	**Roe**	N	N	N	N	Y	Y
2	**Burchett**	N	N	N	N	Y	Y
3	**Fleischmann**	N	N	N	N	Y	Y
4	**DesJarlais**	N	N	N	N	Y	Y
5	Cooper	Y	Y	N	Y	Y	N
6	**Rose**	N	N	N	N	Y	Y
7	**Green**	N	N	N	N	Y	Y
8	**Kustoff**	N	N	N	N	Y	Y
9	Cohen	Y	Y	Y	Y	Y	N
TEXAS							
1	**Gohmert**	N	N	N	N	Y	Y
2	**Crenshaw**	N	N	N	N	Y	Y
3	**Taylor**	N	N	N	N	Y	Y
4	**Ratcliffe**	N	N	N	N	Y	Y

		457	458	459	460	461	462
5	**Gooden**	N	N	N	N	Y	Y
6	**Wright**	N	N	?	?	?	?
7	Fletcher	Y	Y	N	N	Y	N
8	**Brady**	N	N	?	?	?	?
9	Green, A.	Y	Y	Y	Y	Y	N
10	**McCaul**	N	N	N	N	Y	Y
11	**Conaway**	N	N	N	N	Y	Y
12	**Granger**	N	N	N	N	Y	Y
13	**Thornberry**	N	N	N	N	Y	Y
14	**Weber**	N	N	N	N	Y	Y
15	Gonzalez	Y	Y	N	Y	Y	N
16	Escobar	Y	Y	Y	Y	Y	N
17	**Flores**	N	N	N	N	Y	Y
18	Jackson Lee	Y	Y	Y	Y	Y	N
19	**Arrington**	N	N	N	N	Y	Y
20	Castro	Y	Y	Y	Y	Y	N
21	**Roy**	N	N	N	N	Y	Y
22	**Olson**	N	N	N	N	Y	Y
23	**Hurd**	N	N	N	N	Y	Y
24	**Marchant**	N	N	N	N	Y	Y
25	**Williams**	N	N	N	N	Y	Y
26	**Burgess**	N	N	N	N	Y	Y
27	**Cloud**	N	N	N	N	Y	Y
28	Cuellar	Y	Y	N	N	Y	Y
29	Garcia, S.	Y	Y	Y	Y	Y	N
30	Johnson, E.B.	Y	Y	N	Y	Y	N
31	**Carter, J.**	N	N	N	N	Y	Y
32	Allred	Y	Y	N	N	Y	N
33	Veasey	Y	Y	N	N	Y	N
34	Vela	Y	Y	N	Y	Y	N
35	Doggett	Y	Y	Y	Y	Y	N
36	**Babin**	N	N	N	N	Y	Y
UTAH							
1	**Bishop, R.**	N	N	N	N	Y	Y
2	**Stewart**	N	N	N	N	Y	Y
3	**Curtis**	N	N	N	N	Y	Y
4	McAdams	N	N	N	N	Y	N
VERMONT							
AL	Welch	Y	Y	Y	Y	Y	N
VIRGINIA							
1	**Wittman**	N	N	N	N	Y	Y
2	Luria	N	N	N	N	Y	N
3	Scott, R.	Y	Y	N	Y	Y	N
4	McEachin	Y	Y	N	Y	Y	N
5	**Riggleman**	N	N	N	N	Y	Y
6	**Cline**	N	N	N	N	Y	Y
7	Spanberger	Y	N	N	N	Y	N
8	Beyer	Y	Y	Y	Y	Y	N
9	**Griffith**	N	N	N	Y	Y	Y
10	Wexton	Y	Y	N	Y	Y	N
11	Connolly	Y	Y	N	Y	Y	N
WASHINGTON							
1	DelBene	Y	Y	N	Y	Y	N
2	Larsen	Y	Y	Y	Y	Y	N
3	**Herrera Beutler**	N	N	N	N	Y	Y
4	**Newhouse**	N	N	N	N	Y	Y
5	**McMorris Rodgers**	N	N	N	N	Y	Y
6	Kilmer	Y	Y	N	Y	Y	N
7	Jayapal	Y	Y	Y	Y	Y	N
8	Schrier	Y	Y	N	N	Y	N
9	Smith Adam	Y	Y	N	Y	Y	N
10	Heck	Y	Y	N	Y	Y	N
WEST VIRGINIA							
1	**McKinley**	N	N	N	N	Y	Y
2	**Mooney**	N	N	N	N	Y	Y
3	**Miller**	N	N	N	N	Y	Y
WISCONSIN							
1	**Steil**	N	N	N	N	Y	Y
2	Pocan	Y	Y	Y	Y	Y	N
3	Kind	Y	Y	Y	Y	Y	N
4	Moore	Y	Y	Y	Y	Y	N
5	**Sensenbrenner**	N	N	N	N	Y	Y
6	**Grothman**	N	N	?	?	?	?
7	**Duffy**	N	N	-	-	+	+
8	**Gallagher**	N	N	N	N	Y	Y
WYOMING							
AL	**Cheney**	N	N	N	N	Y	Y
DELEGATES							
	Radewagen (A.S.)	?	?	?	?	?	?
	Norton (D.C.)	+	+	N	N	Y	-
	San Nicolas (Guam)	?	?	?	?	?	?
	Sablan (N. Marianas)	Y	Y	Y	Y	Y	N
	González-Colón (P.R.)	N	N	?	?	?	?
	Plaskett (V.I.)	?	?	?	?	?	?

463. HR2500. Fiscal 2020 Defense Authorization - Military Force Against Iran. Khanna, D-Calif., amendment that would clarify that no previous authorization for use of military force or other existing law authorizes the use of military force against Iran and would prohibit the use of federal funds for such purposes without congressional authorization or declaration of war. Adopted in Committee of the Whole 251-170: R 27-163; D 222-7; I 2-0. July 12, 2019.

464. HR2500. Fiscal 2020 Defense Authorization - Repeal 2002 AUMF. Lee, D-Calif., amendment that would repeal the 2002 authorization for use of military force against Iraq. Adopted in Committee of the Whole 242-180: R 14-176; D 226-4; I 2-0. July 12, 2019.

465. HR2500. Fiscal 2020 Defense Authorization - Sense of Congress on 2001 AUMF. Lee, D-Calif., amendment that would express the sense of Congress that the use of the 2001 authorization for use of military force as a legal basis for use of force in 19 countries has surpassed the scope intended by Congress and served as a "blank check for any president to wage war at any time and at any place." It would also express the sense of Congress that any new authorization replacing the 2001 AUMF should include a sunset clause and "clear and specific" objectives, targets, and geographic scope. Adopted in Committee of the Whole 237-183: R 21-167; D 214-16; I 2-0. July 12, 2019.

466. HR2500. Fiscal 2020 Defense Authorization - DoD Housing for Unaccompanied Children. Garcia, D-Texas, amendment that would prohibit the use of Defense Department facilities to house or detain unaccompanied children who are undocumented immigrants. Rejected in Committee of the Whole 198-223: R 1-188; D 196-34; I 1-1. July 12, 2019.

467. HR2500. Fiscal 2020 Defense Authorization - Military Enforcement of Immigration Policies. Ocasio-Cortez, D-N.Y., amendment that would prohibit the use of any fiscal 2020 funds authorized for the Defense Department to provide military support for local law enforcement to enforce any part of the Immigration and Nationality Act. Rejected in Committee of the Whole 179-241: R 0-189; D 177-52; I 2-0. July 12, 2019.

468. HR2500. Fiscal 2020 Defense Authorization - DoD Housing for Undocumented Immigrants. Ocasio-Cortez, D-N.Y., amendment that would prohibit the use of funds authorized by the bill for the Defense Department to provide housing in department facility for any detained undocumented immigrant. Rejected in Committee of the Whole 173-245: R 1-187; D 170-58; I 2-0. July 12, 2019.

		463	464	465	466	467	468
ALABAMA							
1	Byrne	N	N	N	N	N	N
2	Roby	N	N	N	N	N	N
3	Rogers, M.	N	N	N	N	N	N
4	Aderholt	N	N	N	N	N	N
5	Brooks, M.	N	N	N	N	N	N
6	Palmer	N	N	N	N	N	N
7	Sewell	Y	Y	Y	Y	N	N
ALASKA							
AL	Young	N	N	N	N	N	N
ARIZONA							
1	O'Halleran	N	Y	Y	Y	N	N
2	Kirkpatrick	Y	Y	Y	Y	Y	Y
3	Grijalva	Y	Y	Y	Y	Y	Y
4	Gosar	Y	Y	Y	N	N	N
5	Biggs	Y	Y	N	N	N	N
6	Schweikert	Y	Y	N	N	N	N
7	Gallego	Y	Y	Y	Y	Y	Y
8	Lesko	N	N	N	N	N	N
9	Stanton	Y	Y	Y	Y	Y	Y
ARKANSAS							
1	Crawford	N	N	N	N	N	N
2	Hill, F.	N	N	N	N	N	N
3	Womack	N	N	N	N	N	N
4	Westerman	N	N	N	N	N	N
CALIFORNIA							
1	LaMalfa	N	N	N	N	N	N
2	Huffman	Y	Y	Y	Y	Y	Y
3	Garamendi	Y	Y	Y	Y	Y	Y
4	McClintock	N	N	N	N	N	N
5	Thompson, M.	Y	Y	Y	Y	Y	Y
6	Matsui	Y	Y	Y	Y	Y	Y
7	Bera	Y	Y	Y	Y	Y	Y
8	Cook	N	N	N	N	N	N
9	McNerney	Y	Y	Y	Y	Y	Y
10	Harder	Y	Y	Y	Y	N	Y
11	DeSaulnier	Y	Y	Y	Y	Y	Y
12	Pelosi						
13	Lee B.	Y	Y	Y	Y	Y	Y
14	Speier	Y	Y	Y	Y	Y	N
15	Swalwell	Y	Y	Y	Y	Y	Y
16	Costa	Y	Y	Y	Y	Y	Y
17	Khanna	Y	Y	Y	Y	Y	Y
18	Eshoo	Y	Y	Y	Y	Y	Y
19	Lofgren	Y	Y	Y	Y	Y	Y
20	Panetta	Y	Y	Y	Y	Y	Y
21	Cox	Y	Y	Y	N	N	N
22	Nunes	N	N	N	N	N	N
23	McCarthy	N	N	N	N	N	N
24	Carbajal	Y	Y	Y	Y	Y	N
25	Hill, K.	Y	Y	Y	N	N	N
26	Brownley	Y	Y	Y	Y	Y	Y
27	Chu	Y	Y	Y	Y	Y	Y
28	Schiff	Y	Y	Y	Y	Y	Y
29	Cárdenas	Y	Y	Y	Y	Y	Y
30	Sherman	Y	Y	Y	Y	Y	Y
31	Aguilar	Y	Y	Y	Y	Y	Y
32	Napolitano	Y	Y	Y	Y	Y	Y
33	Lieu	Y	Y	Y	Y	Y	Y
34	Gomez	Y	Y	Y	Y	Y	Y
35	Torres	Y	Y	Y	Y	Y	Y
36	Ruiz	Y	Y	Y	Y	Y	Y
37	Bass	Y	Y	Y	Y	Y	Y
38	Sánchez	Y	Y	Y	Y	Y	Y
39	Cisneros	Y	Y	Y	Y	N	N
40	Roybal-Allard	Y	Y	Y	Y	Y	?
41	Takano	Y	Y	Y	Y	Y	Y
42	Calvert	N	N	N	N	N	N
43	Waters	Y	Y	Y	Y	Y	Y
44	Barragán	Y	Y	Y	Y	Y	Y
45	Porter	Y	Y	Y	N	Y	N
46	Correa	Y	Y	Y	Y	Y	Y
47	Lowenthal	Y	Y	Y	Y	N	N
48	Rouda	Y	Y	Y	Y	Y	Y
49	Levin	Y	Y	Y	N	N	Y
50	Hunter	N	N	N	N	N	N
51	Vargas	Y	Y	Y	Y	Y	Y
52	Peters	Y	Y	Y	Y	Y	N
53	Davis, S.	Y	Y	Y	Y	Y	Y
COLORADO							
1	DeGette	Y	Y	Y	Y	Y	Y
2	Neguse	Y	Y	Y	Y	Y	Y
3	Tipton	N	N	N	N	N	N
4	Buck	N	Y	Y	N	N	N
5	Lamborn	N	N	N	N	N	N
6	Crow	Y	Y	Y	Y	N	Y
7	Perlmutter	?	?	?	?	?	?
CONNECTICUT							
1	Larson	Y	Y	Y	Y	Y	Y
2	Courtney	Y	Y	Y	Y	Y	Y
3	DeLauro	Y	Y	Y	Y	Y	Y
4	Himes	Y	Y	Y	Y	Y	Y
5	Hayes	Y	Y	Y	Y	Y	N
DELAWARE							
AL	Blunt Rochester	Y	Y	Y	Y	Y	Y
FLORIDA							
1	Gaetz	Y	N	Y	N	N	N
2	Dunn	N	N	N	N	N	N
3	Yoho	Y	Y	Y	N	N	N
4	Rutherford	N	N	-	N	N	N
5	Lawson	Y	Y	Y	Y	N	N
6	Waltz	N	N	N	N	N	N
7	Murphy	N	Y	N	N	N	N
8	Posey	N	N	N	N	N	N
9	Soto	Y	Y	Y	Y	Y	Y
10	Demings	Y	Y	Y	Y	Y	Y
11	Webster	N	N	N	N	N	N
12	Bilirakis	N	N	N	N	N	N
13	Crist	Y	Y	Y	Y	N	N
14	Castor	Y	Y	Y	Y	Y	Y
15	Spano	N	N	N	N	N	N
16	Buchanan	N	N	N	N	N	N
17	Steube	N	N	N	N	N	N
18	Mast	N	N	N	N	N	N
19	Rooney	Y	N	N	N	N	N
20	Hastings	Y	Y	Y	Y	Y	Y
21	Frankel	Y	Y	Y	Y	Y	Y
22	Deutch	Y	Y	Y	Y	Y	Y
23	Wasserman Schultz	Y	Y	Y	Y	Y	N
24	Wilson, F.	Y	Y	Y	Y	Y	Y
25	Diaz-Balart	N	N	N	N	N	N
26	Mucarsel-Powell	Y	Y	Y	Y	N	Y
27	Shalala	Y	Y	Y	Y	Y	Y
GEORGIA							
1	Carter, E.L.	N	N	N	N	N	N
2	Bishop, S.	Y	Y	Y	Y	Y	Y
3	Ferguson	N	N	N	N	N	N
4	Johnson, H.	Y	Y	Y	Y	Y	Y
5	Lewis John	Y	Y	Y	Y	Y	Y
6	McBath	Y	Y	Y	Y	N	Y
7	Woodall	N	N	Y	N	N	N
8	Scott, A.	N	N	N	N	N	N
9	Collins, D.	N	N	N	N	N	N
10	Hice	N	N	N	N	N	N
11	Loudermilk	N	N	N	N	N	N
12	Allen	N	N	N	N	N	N
13	Scott, D.	Y	Y	Y	Y	N	Y
14	Graves, T.	N	N	N	N	N	N
HAWAII							
1	Case	Y	Y	N	N	Y	N
2	Gabbard	?	?	?	?	?	?
IDAHO							
1	Fulcher	N	N	N	N	N	N
2	Simpson	N	N	N	N	N	N
ILLINOIS							
1	Rush	Y	Y	Y	Y	Y	Y
2	Kelly, R.	Y	Y	Y	Y	Y	Y
3	Lipinski	Y	Y	Y	Y	P	Y
4	García, J.	Y	Y	Y	Y	Y	Y
5	Quigley	Y	Y	Y	Y	Y	Y
6	Casten	Y	Y	Y	N	Y	N
7	Davis, D.	Y	Y	Y	Y	Y	Y
8	Krishnamoorthi	Y	Y	Y	Y	Y	Y
9	Schakowsky	Y	Y	Y	Y	Y	Y
10	Schneider	Y	Y	Y	Y	Y	Y
11	Foster	Y	Y	Y	Y	Y	Y

KEY:	Republicans	*Democrats*	*Independents*

Y Voted for (yea)	**N** Voted against (nay)	**P** Voted "present"	
+ Announced for	**-** Announced against	**?** Did not vote or otherwise	
# Paired for	**X** Paired against	make position known	

		463	464	465	466	467	468
12	**Bost**	N	N	N	N	N	N
13	**Davis, R.**	N	N	N	N	N	N
14	Underwood	Y	Y	Y	N	N	Y
15	**Shimkus**	N	N	N	N	N	N
16	**Kinzinger**	N	N	N	N	N	N
17	Bustos	Y	Y	Y	Y	N	N
18	**LaHood**	N	N	N	N	N	N
INDIANA							
1	Visclosky	Y	Y	Y	N	Y	Y
2	**Walorski**	N	N	N	N	N	N
3	**Banks**	N	N	N	N	N	N
4	**Baird**	N	N	N	N	N	N
5	**Brooks, S.**	N	N	N	N	N	N
6	**Pence**	N	N	N	N	N	N
7	Carson	Y	Y	Y	Y	Y	Y
8	**Bucshon**	N	N	N	N	N	N
9	**Hollingsworth**	Y	N	Y	N	N	N
IOWA							
1	Finkenauer	Y	Y	N	Y	N	N
2	Loebsack	Y	Y	Y	Y	N	N
3	Axne	Y	Y	N	N	N	N
4	**King, S.**	N	N	N	N	N	N
KANSAS							
1	**Marshall**	N	N	N	N	N	N
2	**Watkins**	N	N	N	N	N	N
3	Davids	Y	Y	Y	Y	Y	Y
4	**Estes**	N	N	N	N	N	N
KENTUCKY							
1	**Comer**	Y	Y	N	N	N	N
2	**Guthrie**	N	N	N	N	N	N
3	Yarmuth	Y	Y	Y	Y	Y	Y
4	**Massie**	Y	Y	Y	N	N	N
5	**Rogers, H.**	N	N	N	N	N	N
6	**Barr**	N	N	N	N	N	N
LOUISIANA							
1	**Scalise**	N	N	N	N	N	N
2	Richmond	Y	Y	Y	N	Y	Y
3	**Higgins, C.**	-	-	-	-	-	-
4	**Johnson, M.**	N	N	N	N	N	N
5	**Abraham**	N	N	N	N	N	N
6	**Graves, G.**	N	N	N	N	N	-
MAINE							
1	Pingree	Y	Y	Y	Y	Y	Y
2	Golden	Y	Y	N	N	N	N
MARYLAND							
1	**Harris**	N	N	N	N	N	N
2	Ruppersberger	Y	Y	Y	Y	Y	Y
3	Sarbanes	Y	Y	Y	Y	Y	Y
4	Brown, A.	Y	Y	Y	Y	Y	Y
5	Hoyer	Y	Y	Y	Y	Y	Y
6	Trone	Y	Y	Y	Y	Y	Y
7	Cummings	Y	Y	Y	Y	Y	Y
8	Raskin						
MASSACHUSETTS		Y	Y	Y	Y	Y	Y
1	Neal						
2	McGovern	Y	Y	Y	Y	Y	Y
3	Trahan	Y	Y	Y	Y	Y	Y
4	Kennedy	Y	Y	Y	Y	Y	Y
5	Clark	Y	Y	Y	Y	Y	Y
6	Moulton	Y	Y	Y	Y	Y	Y
7	Pressley	Y	Y	Y	N	N	N
8	Lynch	Y	Y	Y	Y	Y	Y
9	Keating	N	Y	Y	Y	N	Y
MICHIGAN		Y	Y	Y	Y	Y	Y
1	**Bergman**						
2	**Huizenga**	N	N	N	N	N	N
3	*Amash*	N	N	N	N	N	N
4	**Moolenaar**	Y	Y	Y	N	Y	Y
5	Kildee	N	N	N	N	N	N
6	**Upton**	Y	Y	Y	Y	Y	Y
7	**Walberg**	Y	Y	N	N	N	N
8	Slotkin	N	N	N	N	N	N
9	Levin	Y	Y	Y	N	N	N
10	**Mitchell**	Y	Y	Y	Y	Y	Y
11	Stevens	N	N	N	N	N	N
12	Dingell	Y	Y	Y	N	N	N
13	Tlaib	Y	Y	Y	Y	Y	Y
14	Lawrence	Y	Y	Y	Y	Y	Y
MINNESOTA		?	?	?	?	?	?
1	**Hagedorn**						
2	Craig	N	N	N	N	N	N
3	Phillips	Y	Y	N	N	N	N
4	McCollum	Y	Y	Y	Y	N	Y
5	Omar	Y	Y	Y	Y	Y	Y

		463	464	465	466	467	468
6	**Emmer**	Y	Y	Y	Y	Y	Y
7	Peterson	N	N	N	N	N	N
8	**Stauber**	Y	Y	N	N	N	N
MISSISSIPPI		N	N	N	N	N	N
1	**Kelly, T.**						
2	Thompson, B.	N	N	N	N	N	N
3	**Guest**	Y	Y	Y	Y	Y	Y
4	**Palazzo**	N	N	N	N	N	N
MISSOURI		N	N	N	N	N	N
1	Clay						
2	**Wagner**	Y	Y	Y	Y	N	Y
3	**Luetkemeyer**	N	N	N	N	N	N
4	**Hartzler**	N	N	N	N	N	N
5	Cleaver	N	N	N	N	N	N
6	**Graves, S.**	Y	Y	Y	Y	N	+
7	**Long**	+	+	+	+	+	+
8	**Smith, J.**	N	N	N	N	N	N
MONTANA		N	N	N	N	N	N
AL	**Gianforte**						
NEBRASKA		N	N	N	N	N	N
1	**Fortenberry**						
2	**Bacon**	N	N	N	N	N	N
3	**Smith, Adrian**	N	N	N	N	N	N
NEVADA		N	N	N	N	N	N
1	Titus						
2	**Amodei**	Y	Y	Y	Y	Y	Y
3	Lee	N	N	N	N	N	N
4	Horsford	Y	Y	N	Y	N	N
NEW HAMPSHIRE		Y	Y	Y	Y	N	Y
1	Pappas						
2	Kuster	Y	Y	Y	N	Y	N
NEW JERSEY		Y	Y	Y	N	Y	N
1	Norcross						
2	Van Drew	Y	Y	Y	Y	Y	Y
3	Kim	N	N	N	N	N	N
4	**Smith, C.**	Y	Y	Y	Y	N	N
5	Gottheimer	N	N	N	N	N	N
6	Pallone	N	Y	N	Y	N	N
7	Malinowski	Y	Y	Y	Y	Y	Y
8	Sires	Y	Y	Y	N	Y	N
9	Pascrell	Y	Y	Y	Y	Y	Y
10	Payne	Y	Y	Y	Y	Y	Y
11	Sherrill	Y	Y	Y	Y	Y	Y
12	Watson Coleman	Y	Y	Y	Y	N	Y
NEW MEXICO		Y	Y	Y	Y	Y	Y
1	Haaland						
2	Torres Small	Y	Y	Y	Y	Y	Y
3	Luján	Y	Y	Y	N	N	N
NEW YORK		Y	Y	Y	Y	Y	Y
1	**Zeldin**						
2	**King, P.**	N	N	N	N	N	N
3	Suozzi	N	N	N	N	N	N
4	Rice, K.	Y	Y	Y	Y	Y	Y
5	Meeks	N	Y	N	N	N	N
6	Meng	?	Y	Y	Y	Y	Y
7	Velázquez	Y	Y	Y	Y	Y	Y
8	Jeffries	Y	Y	Y	Y	Y	Y
9	Clarke	Y	Y	Y	Y	Y	Y
10	Nadler	Y	Y	Y	Y	Y	Y
11	Rose	Y	Y	Y	Y	Y	Y
12	Maloney, C.	Y	Y	Y	Y	N	Y
13	Espaillat	Y	Y	Y	Y	Y	Y
14	Ocasio-Cortez	Y	Y	Y	Y	Y	Y
15	Serrano	Y	Y	Y	Y	Y	Y
16	Engel	Y	Y	Y	Y	Y	Y
17	Lowey	Y	Y	Y	Y	Y	Y
18	Maloney, S.P.	Y	Y	Y	Y	Y	Y
19	Delgado	Y	Y	Y	Y	Y	Y
20	Tonko	Y	Y	Y	Y	N	Y
21	**Stefanik**	Y	Y	Y	Y	Y	Y
22	Brindisi	N	N	N	N	N	N
23	**Reed**	Y	Y	N	N	N	N
24	**Katko**	Y	N	N	N	N	N
25	Morelle	N	N	N	N	N	N
26	Higgins, B.	Y	Y	Y	Y	N	N
27	**Collins, C.**	Y	Y	Y	Y	Y	Y
NORTH CAROLINA		N	N	N	N	N	N
1	Butterfield						
2	**Holding**	Y	Y	Y	Y	Y	Y
3	**Jones***	N	N	N	N	N	N
4	Price						
5	**Foxx**	Y	Y	Y	Y	Y	Y
6	**Walker**	N	N	N	N	N	N
7	**Rouzer**	N	N	N	N	N	N

		463	464	465	466	467	468
8	**Hudson**	N	N	N	N	N	N
9	vacant	N	N	N	N	N	N
10	**McHenry**	N	N	N	N	N	N
11	**Meadows**	Y	N	Y	N	N	N
12	Adams	Y	Y	Y	Y	Y	Y
13	**Budd**	N	N	N	N	N	N
NORTH DAKOTA							
AL	**Armstrong**	N	N	N	N	N	N
OHIO							
1	**Chabot**	N	N	N	N	N	N
2	**Wenstrup**	N	N	N	N	N	N
3	Beatty	Y	Y	Y	Y	Y	Y
4	**Jordan**	Y	N	Y	N	N	N
5	**Latta**	N	N	N	N	N	N
6	**Johnson, B.**	N	N	N	N	N	N
7	**Gibbs**	N	N	N	N	N	N
8	**Davidson**	Y	Y	N	N	N	N
9	Kaptur	Y	Y	Y	N	N	N
10	**Turner**	N	N	N	N	N	N
11	Fudge	?	?	?	?	?	?
12	**Balderson**	N	N	N	N	N	N
13	Ryan	Y	Y	Y	Y	Y	Y
14	**Joyce**	N	N	N	N	N	N
15	**Stivers**	N	N	N	N	N	N
16	**Gonzalez**	Y	N	N	N	N	N
OKLAHOMA							
1	**Hern**	N	N	N	N	N	N
2	**Mullin**	N	N	N	N	N	N
3	**Lucas**	N	N	N	N	N	N
4	**Cole**	Y	N	Y	N	N	N
5	Horn	Y	Y	Y	N	N	N
OREGON							
1	Bonamici	Y	Y	Y	Y	Y	Y
2	**Walden**	N	N	N	N	N	N
3	Blumenauer	Y	Y	Y	Y	Y	Y
4	DeFazio	Y	Y	Y	Y	Y	Y
5	Schrader	Y	Y	Y	Y	Y	N
PENNSYLVANIA							
1	**Fitzpatrick**	Y	Y	Y	N	N	N
2	Boyle	Y	Y	Y	Y	Y	Y
3	Evans	Y	Y	Y	Y	Y	Y
4	Dean	Y	Y	Y	Y	Y	Y
5	Scanlon	Y	Y	Y	Y	N	Y
6	Houlahan	Y	Y	Y	Y	N	N
7	Wild	Y	Y	Y	Y	N	N
8	Cartwright	Y	Y	Y	Y	Y	N
9	**Meuser**	N	N	N	N	N	N
10	**Perry**	N	N	N	N	N	N
11	**Smucker**	N	N	N	N	N	N
12	**Marino***						
13	**Joyce**	N	N	N	N	N	N
14	**Reschenthaler**	N	N	N	N	N	N
15	**Thompson, G.**	N	N	N	N	N	N
16	**Kelly, M.**	N	N	N	N	N	N
17	Lamb	Y	N	N	N	N	N
18	Doyle	Y	Y	Y	Y	Y	Y
RHODE ISLAND							
1	Cicilline	Y	Y	Y	Y	Y	Y
2	Langevin	Y	Y	Y	Y	Y	N
SOUTH CAROLINA							
1	Cunningham	Y	Y	Y	N	N	N
2	**Wilson, J.**	N	N	N	N	N	N
3	**Duncan**	N	N	N	N	N	N
4	**Timmons**	N	N	N	N	N	N
5	**Norman**	N	N	N	N	N	N
6	Clyburn	Y	Y	Y	Y	Y	Y
7	**Rice, T.**	?	?	?	?	?	?
SOUTH DAKOTA							
AL	**Johnson**	N	N	N	N	N	N
TENNESSEE							
1	**Roe**	N	N	?	?	?	?
2	**Burchett**	Y	N	N	N	N	N
3	**Fleischmann**	N	N	N	N	N	N
4	**DesJarlais**	N	N	N	N	N	N
5	Cooper	Y	N	Y	Y	Y	Y
6	**Rose**	N	N	N	N	N	N
7	**Green**	N	N	N	N	N	N
8	**Kustoff**	N	N	N	N	N	N
9	Cohen	Y	Y	Y	Y	Y	Y
TEXAS							
1	**Gohmert**	N	N	Y	N	N	N
2	**Crenshaw**	N	N	N	N	N	N
3	**Taylor**	N	N	N	N	N	N
4	**Ratcliffe**	N	N	N	N	N	N

		463	464	465	466	467	468
5	**Gooden**	N	N	N	N	N	N
6	**Wright**	?	?	?	?	?	?
7	Fletcher	Y	Y	Y	N	Y	N
8	**Brady**	?	?	?	?	?	?
9	Green, A.	Y	Y	Y	Y	Y	Y
10	**McCaul**	N	N	N	N	N	N
11	**Conaway**	N	N	N	N	N	N
12	**Granger**	N	N	N	N	N	N
13	**Thornberry**	N	N	N	N	N	N
14	**Weber**	N	N	N	N	N	N
15	Gonzalez	Y	Y	Y	Y	Y	N
16	Escobar	Y	Y	Y	Y	Y	Y
17	**Flores**	N	N	N	N	N	N
18	Jackson Lee	Y	Y	Y	Y	Y	Y
19	**Arrington**	N	N	N	N	N	N
20	Castro	Y	Y	Y	Y	Y	Y
21	**Roy**	Y	Y	Y	N	N	N
22	**Olson**	N	N	N	N	N	N
23	**Hurd**	N	N	N	N	N	N
24	**Marchant**	N	N	N	N	N	N
25	**Williams**	Y	Y	N	N	N	N
26	**Burgess**	Y	N	Y	N	N	N
27	**Cloud**	Y	Y	Y	N	N	N
28	Cuellar	N	Y	N	N	Y	N
29	Garcia, S.	Y	Y	Y	Y	Y	Y
30	Johnson, E.B.	Y	Y	Y	N	Y	Y
31	**Carter, J.**	N	N	N	Y	N	Y
32	Allred	Y	Y	Y	N	Y	N
33	Veasey	Y	Y	Y	Y	Y	Y
34	Vela	Y	Y	Y	Y	Y	Y
35	Doggett	Y	Y	Y	Y	Y	Y
36	**Babin**	N	N	N	N	N	N
UTAH							
1	**Bishop, R.**	N	N	N	N	N	N
2	**Stewart**	N	N	N	N	N	N
3	**Curtis**	N	N	N	N	N	N
4	McAdams	Y	Y	N	Y	N	N
VERMONT							
AL	Welch	Y	Y	Y	Y	Y	Y
VIRGINIA							
1	**Wittman**	N	N	N	N	N	N
2	Luria	Y	N	N	Y	N	N
3	Scott, R.	Y	Y	Y	Y	Y	Y
4	McEachin	Y	Y	Y	Y	Y	Y
5	**Riggleman**	N	N	N	N	N	N
6	**Cline**	Y	N	Y	N	N	N
7	Spanberger	Y	Y	Y	N	N	N
8	Beyer	Y	Y	Y	Y	Y	Y
9	**Griffith**	Y	N	Y	N	N	N
10	Wexton	Y	Y	Y	Y	N	N
11	Connolly	Y	Y	Y	Y	Y	Y
WASHINGTON							
1	DelBene	Y	Y	Y	Y	Y	Y
2	Larsen	Y	Y	Y	Y	Y	Y
3	**Herrera Beutler**	N	N	Y	N	N	N
4	**Newhouse**	N	N	N	N	N	N
5	**McMorris Rodgers**	N	N	N	N	N	N
6	Kilmer	Y	Y	Y	Y	Y	Y
7	Jayapal	Y	Y	Y	Y	Y	Y
8	Schrier	Y	Y	Y	Y	Y	N
9	Smith Adam	Y	Y	Y	Y	Y	Y
10	Heck	Y	Y	Y	Y	Y	Y
WEST VIRGINIA							
1	**McKinley**	N	N	N	N	N	N
2	**Mooney**	Y	Y	Y	N	N	N
3	**Miller**	N	N	N	N	N	N
WISCONSIN							
1	**Steil**	N	N	N	N	N	N
2	Pocan	Y	Y	Y	Y	Y	Y
3	Kind	Y	Y	Y	Y	Y	Y
4	Moore	Y	Y	Y	Y	Y	Y
5	**Sensenbrenner**	N	N	N	N	N	N
6	**Grothman**	?	?	?	?	?	?
7	**Duffy**	-	-	-	-	-	-
8	**Gallagher**	N	N	N	N	N	N
WYOMING							
AL	**Cheney**	N	N	N	N	N	N
DELEGATES							
	Radewagen (A.S.)	?	?	?	?	?	?
	Norton (D.C.)	+	+	+	+	+	+
	San Nicolas (Guam)	?	?	?	?	?	?
	Sablan (N. Marianas)	Y	Y	Y	Y	Y	Y
	González-Colón (P.R.)	?	?	?	?	?	?
	Plaskett (V.I.)	?	?	?	?	?	?

469. HR2500. Fiscal 2020 Defense Authorization - DoD Housing for ICE Detainees. Thompson, D-Miss., amendment that would prohibit the use of Defense Department facilities, equipment, or personnel to house or construct housing for any foreign nationals detained by Immigration and Customs Enforcement. Adopted in Committee of the Whole 213-204: R 0-188; D 211-16; I 2-0. July 12, 2019.

470. HR2500. Fiscal 2020 Defense Authorization - Saudi Arabia and UAE Arms Exports. Malinowski, D-N.J, amendment that would prohibit the president from issuing any license allowing for the export of air-to-ground munitions or related items to Saudi Arabia or the United Arab Emirates. It would require the president to suspend any such licenses previously issued. Adopted in Committee of the Whole 236-182: R 5-182; D 229-0; I 2-0. July 12, 2019.

471. HR2500. Fiscal 2020 Defense Authorization - Nuclear Security Activity Studies. Jayapal, D-Wash., amendment that would require the Government Accountability Office to report to Congress on cost analyses for nuclear security activities and require the Defense Department to contract with federally-funded research and development centers to conduct studies on cost savings associated with alternatives to current U.S. nuclear deterrence policy and force structures. Adopted in Committee of the Whole 230-189: R 5-183; D 223-6; I 2-0. July 12, 2019.

472. HR2500. Fiscal 2020 Defense Authorization - Recommit. Thornberry, R-Texas, motion to recommit the bill to the Armed Services Committee with instructions to report it back immediately with an amendment that would increase funds authorized by the bill for military department operations and maintenance by a total of more than $1.6 billion, including $606.5 million for the Army, $361.3 million for the Navy, $250.1 million for the Air Force, $155.4 million for the Army National Guard, and $125.3 million for the Air National Guard, and $83.3 million for the Marine Corps. It would increase by four percent monthly basic pay rates for members of the uniformed services, and increase by a total of more than $959 million funds authorized by the bill for military personnel. Motion rejected 204-212: R 188-0; D 16-211; I 0-1. July 12, 2019.

473. HR2500. Fiscal 2020 Defense Authorization - Passage. Passage of the bill that would authorize $724.9 billion in discretionary defense spending, including $256 billion for Defense Department operations and maintenance, including operations in Afghanistan and Syria, $140.5 billion for weapons and other procurement, and $187.6 billion for personnel-related expenses. Within the total, the bill would authorize $69 billion for overseas contingency operations not subject to discretionary spending caps. The bill would authorize $22.7 billion for Energy Department defense-related activities, including for nuclear weapon programs programs and environmental restoration activities; $33 billion for the Defense health program; $11.5 billion for military construction, family housing, and base realignment and closure activities; and approximately $11 billion for missile defense programs. Among other provisions, the bill would authorize a 3.1 percent pay increase for members of the armed forces; authorize the creation of a Space Corps within the Air Force; require the Defense Department to submit a number of reports on the effects of climate change and develop a climate vulnerability and risk-assessment tool; expand protections for victims of sexual assault involving members of the armed forces; and prohibit the transfer of F-35 aircraft to Turkey unless the Turkish government certifies that it will not purchase S-400 air defense technology from Russia. It would prohibit the use of funds authorized by the bill for the department to construct any physical barriers or border security infrastructure along the U.S-Mexico border. It would also prohibit the use of funds authorized to detain additional individuals at the U.S. naval station in Guantanamo Bay, Cuba, and modify limitations on the transfer or release of current detainees to certain countries. As amended, the bill would prohibit the use of federal funds for the use of military force against Iran absent congressional authorization or declaration of war, repeal the 2002 authorization for use of military force against Iraq, and prohibit the transfer of certain defense articles and services to Saudi Arabia or the United Arab Emirates, with regards to hostilities in Yemen. It would require Defense Department personnel policies to ensure equal treatment and opportunity for service members without regard to race, color, national origin, religion or sex, including gender-related identity regardless of designated sex at birth. Passed 220-197: R 0-188; D 220-8; I 0-1. *Note: A "nay" was a vote in support of the president's position.* July 12, 2019.

474. HR1327. 9/11 Victim Compensation Fund - Passage. Nadler, D-N.Y., motion to suspend the rules and pass the bill that would reauthorize through fiscal 2090 the 9/11 Victim Compensation Fund to compensate first responders and other individuals with health conditions caused by toxin exposure due to the attacks on Sept. 11, 2001. It would authorize such sums as may be necessary for the fund and allow claims to be filed through Oct. 1, 2089. It would also require the reimbursement of any claims previously reduced due to insufficient funds and includes a number of modifications to fund management, including to provide exceptions to a cap for reimbursement of noneconomic damages. Motion agreed to 402-12: R 176-11; D 226-0; I 0-1. *Note: A two-thirds majority of those present and voting (276 in this case) is required for passage under suspension of the rules.* July 12, 2019.

		469	470	471	472	473	474
ALABAMA							
1	**Byrne**	N	N	N	Y	N	Y
2	**Roby**	N	N	N	Y	N	Y
3	**Rogers, M.**	N	N	N	Y	N	?
4	**Aderholt**	N	N	N	Y	N	Y
5	**Brooks, M.**	N	N	N	Y	N	N
6	**Palmer**	N	N	N	Y	N	Y
7	Sewell	Y	Y	Y	N	Y	Y
ALASKA							
AL	**Young**	N	N	N	Y	N	Y
ARIZONA							
1	O'Halleran	Y	Y	Y	N	Y	Y
2	Kirkpatrick	Y	Y	Y	N	Y	Y
3	Grijalva	Y	Y	Y	N	Y	Y
4	**Gosar**	N	N	N	Y	N	N
5	**Biggs**	N	N	N	Y	N	N
6	**Schweikert**	N	N	N	Y	N	Y
7	Gallego	Y	Y	Y	N	Y	Y
8	**Lesko**	N	N	N	Y	N	Y
9	Stanton	Y	Y	Y	N	Y	Y
ARKANSAS							
1	**Crawford**	N	N	N	Y	N	Y
2	**Hill, F.**	N	N	N	Y	N	Y
3	**Womack**	N	N	N	Y	N	Y
4	**Westerman**	N	N	N	Y	N	Y
CALIFORNIA							
1	**LaMalfa**	N	N	N	Y	N	Y
2	Huffman	Y	Y	Y	N	Y	Y
3	Garamendi	Y	Y	Y	N	Y	Y
4	**McClintock**	N	N	Y	Y	N	Y
5	Thompson, M.	Y	Y	Y	N	Y	Y
6	Matsui	Y	Y	Y	N	Y	Y
7	Bera	Y	Y	Y	N	Y	Y
8	**Cook**	N	N	N	Y	N	Y
9	McNerney	Y	Y	Y	N	Y	Y
10	Harder	Y	Y	Y	Y	Y	Y
11	DeSaulnier	Y	Y	Y	N	Y	Y
12	Pelosi					Y	Y
13	Lee B.	Y	Y	Y	N	N	Y
14	Speier	N	Y	Y	N	Y	Y
15	Swalwell	Y	Y	Y	N	Y	Y
16	Costa	Y	Y	Y	N	Y	Y
17	Khanna	Y	Y	Y	N	Y	?
18	Eshoo	Y	Y	Y	N	Y	Y
19	Lofgren	Y	Y	Y	N	Y	Y
20	Panetta	Y	Y	Y	N	Y	Y
21	Cox	Y	Y	Y	N	Y	Y
22	**Nunes**	N	N	N	Y	N	Y
23	**McCarthy**	N	N	N	Y	N	Y
24	Carbajal	Y	Y	Y	N	Y	Y
25	Hill, K.	Y	Y	Y	N	Y	Y
26	Brownley	Y	Y	Y	N	Y	Y
27	Chu	Y	Y	Y	N	Y	Y
28	Schiff	Y	Y	Y	N	Y	Y
29	Cárdenas	?	Y	Y	N	Y	Y
30	Sherman	Y	Y	Y	N	Y	Y
31	Aguilar	Y	Y	Y	N	Y	Y
32	Napolitano	Y	Y	Y	N	Y	Y
33	Lieu	Y	Y	Y	N	Y	Y
34	Gomez	Y	Y	Y	N	Y	Y
35	Torres	Y	Y	Y	N	Y	Y
36	Ruiz	Y	Y	Y	N	Y	Y
37	Bass	Y	Y	Y	N	Y	Y
38	Sánchez	Y	Y	Y	N	Y	Y
39	Cisneros	Y	Y	Y	N	Y	Y
40	Roybal-Allard	Y	Y	Y	N	Y	Y
41	Takano	Y	Y	Y	N	Y	Y
42	**Calvert**	N	N	N	Y	N	Y
43	Waters	Y	Y	Y	N	Y	Y
44	Barragán	Y	Y	Y	N	Y	Y
45	Porter	Y	Y	Y	N	Y	Y
46	Correa	Y	Y	Y	N	Y	Y
47	Lowenthal	Y	Y	Y	N	Y	Y
48	Rouda	Y	Y	Y	N	Y	Y
49	Levin	Y	Y	Y	N	Y	Y
50	**Hunter**	N	N	N	Y	N	Y
51	Vargas	Y	Y	Y	N	Y	Y
52	Peters	Y	Y	Y	N	Y	Y
53	Davis, S.	Y	Y	Y	N	Y	Y
COLORADO							
1	DeGette	Y	Y	Y	N	Y	Y
2	Neguse	Y	Y	Y	N	Y	Y
3	**Tipton**	N	N	N	Y	N	Y
4	**Buck**	N	N	N	Y	N	N
5	**Lamborn**	N	N	N	Y	N	Y
6	Crow	Y	Y	Y	N	Y	Y
7	Perlmutter	?	?	?	?	+	+
CONNECTICUT							
1	Larson	Y	Y	Y	N	Y	Y
2	Courtney	Y	Y	Y	N	Y	Y
3	DeLauro	Y	Y	Y	N	Y	Y
4	Himes	Y	Y	Y	N	Y	Y
5	Hayes	Y	Y	Y	N	Y	Y
DELAWARE							
AL	Blunt Rochester	Y	Y	Y	N	Y	Y
FLORIDA							
1	**Gaetz**	N	Y	N	Y	N	Y
2	**Dunn**	N	N	N	Y	N	Y
3	**Yoho**	N	N	N	Y	N	Y
4	**Rutherford**	N	N	N	Y	N	Y
5	Lawson	N	Y	Y	N	Y	Y
6	**Waltz**	N	N	N	Y	N	Y
7	Murphy	N	Y	N	Y	Y	Y
8	**Posey**	N	N	N	Y	N	Y
9	Soto	Y	Y	Y	N	Y	Y
10	Demings	Y	Y	Y	N	Y	Y
11	**Webster**	N	N	N	Y	N	Y
12	**Bilirakis**	N	N	N	Y	N	Y
13	Crist	Y	Y	Y	N	Y	Y
14	Castor	Y	Y	Y	N	Y	Y
15	**Spano**	N	N	N	Y	N	Y
16	**Buchanan**	N	N	N	Y	N	Y
17	**Steube**	N	N	N	Y	N	Y
18	**Mast**	N	N	N	Y	N	Y
19	**Rooney**	N	N	N	Y	N	Y
20	Hastings	Y	Y	Y	N	Y	Y
21	Frankel	Y	Y	Y	N	Y	Y
22	Deutch	Y	Y	Y	N	Y	Y
23	Wasserman Schultz	Y	Y	Y	N	Y	Y
24	Wilson, F.	Y	Y	Y	N	Y	Y
25	**Diaz-Balart**	N	N	N	Y	N	Y
26	Mucarsel-Powell	Y	Y	Y	N	Y	Y
27	Shalala	Y	Y	Y	N	Y	Y
GEORGIA							
1	**Carter, E.L.**	N	N	N	Y	N	Y
2	Bishop, S.	Y	Y	Y	N	Y	Y
3	**Ferguson**	N	N	N	Y	N	Y
4	Johnson, H.	Y	Y	Y	N	Y	Y
5	Lewis John	Y	Y	Y	N	Y	Y
6	McBath	Y	Y	Y	N	Y	Y
7	**Woodall**	N	N	N	Y	N	Y
8	**Scott, A.**	N	N	N	Y	N	Y
9	**Collins, D.**	N	N	N	Y	N	Y
10	**Hice**	N	N	N	Y	N	N
11	**Loudermilk**	N	N	N	Y	N	Y
12	**Allen**	N	N	N	Y	N	Y
13	Scott, D.	Y	Y	Y	N	Y	Y
14	**Graves, T.**	N	N	N	Y	N	Y
HAWAII							
1	Case	N	Y	Y	N	Y	Y
2	Gabbard	?	?	?	?	?	?
IDAHO							
1	**Fulcher**	N	N	N	Y	N	Y
2	**Simpson**	N	N	N	Y	N	Y
ILLINOIS							
1	Rush	Y	Y	Y	N	Y	Y
2	Kelly, R.	Y	Y	Y	N	Y	Y
3	Lipinski	Y	Y	Y	N	Y	Y
4	García, J.	Y	Y	Y	N	Y	Y
5	Quigley	Y	Y	Y	N	Y	Y
6	Casten	Y	Y	Y	N	Y	Y
7	Davis, D.	Y	Y	Y	N	Y	Y
8	Krishnamoorthi	Y	Y	Y	N	Y	Y
9	Schakowsky	Y	Y	Y	N	Y	Y
10	Schneider	Y	Y	Y	N	Y	Y
11	Foster	Y	Y	Y	N	Y	Y

KEY: **Republicans** Democrats *Independents*

- **Y** Voted for (yea)
- **+** Announced for
- **#** Paired for
- **N** Voted against (nay)
- **-** Announced against
- **X** Paired against
- **P** Voted "present"
- **?** Did not vote or otherwise make position known

		469	470	471	472	473	474
12	Bost	N	N	N	Y	N	Y
13	Davis, R.	N	N	N	Y	N	Y
14	Underwood	Y	Y	Y	N	Y	Y
15	Shimkus	N	N	N	Y	N	Y
16	Kinzinger	N	N	N	Y	N	Y
17	Bustos	Y	Y	Y	N	Y	Y
18	LaHood	N	N	N	Y	N	Y
INDIANA							
1	Visclosky	Y	Y	Y	N	Y	Y
2	Walorski	N	N	N	Y	N	Y
3	Banks	N	N	N	Y	N	Y
4	Baird	N	N	N	Y	N	Y
5	Brooks, S.	N	N	N	Y	N	Y
6	Pence	N	N	N	Y	N	Y
7	Carson	Y	Y	Y	N	Y	Y
8	Bucshon	N	N	N	Y	N	Y
9	Hollingsworth	N	Y	N	Y	N	Y
IOWA							
1	Finkenauer	Y	Y	Y	Y	Y	Y
2	Loebsack	Y	Y	Y	N	Y	Y
3	Axne	N	Y	Y	Y	Y	Y
4	King, S.	N	N	N	Y	N	Y
KANSAS							
1	Marshall	N	N	N	Y	N	Y
2	Watkins	N	N	N	Y	N	Y
3	Davids	Y	Y	Y	N	Y	Y
4	Estes	N	N	N	Y	N	Y
KENTUCKY							
1	Comer	N	N	N	Y	N	Y
2	Guthrie	N	N	N	Y	N	Y
3	Yarmuth	Y	Y	Y	N	Y	Y
4	Massie	N	N	N	Y	N	N
5	Rogers, H.	N	N	N	Y	N	Y
6	Barr	N	N	N	Y	N	Y
LOUISIANA							
1	Scalise	N	N	N	Y	N	Y
2	Richmond	Y	Y	Y	?	?	?
3	Higgins, C.	-	-	-	+	-	+
4	Johnson, M.	N	N	N	Y	N	Y
5	Abraham	N	N	N	Y	N	Y
6	Graves, G.	-	-	-	+	-	+
MAINE							
1	Pingree	Y	Y	Y	N	Y	Y
2	Golden	N	Y	Y	N	Y	Y
MARYLAND							
1	Harris	N	N	N	Y	N	N
2	Ruppersberger	Y	Y	N	N	Y	Y
3	Sarbanes	Y	Y	Y	N	Y	Y
4	Brown, A.	Y	Y	Y	N	Y	Y
5	Hoyer	Y	Y	Y	N	Y	Y
6	Trone	Y	Y	Y	N	Y	Y
7	Cummings	Y	Y	Y	N	Y	Y
8	Raskin	Y	Y	Y	N	Y	Y
MASSACHUSETTS							
1	Neal	Y	Y	Y	N	Y	Y
2	McGovern	Y	Y	Y	N	Y	Y
3	Trahan	Y	Y	Y	N	Y	Y
4	Kennedy	Y	Y	Y	N	Y	Y
5	Clark	Y	Y	Y	N	Y	Y
6	Moulton	Y	Y	Y	N	Y	Y
7	Pressley	Y	Y	N	N	Y	Y
8	Lynch	Y	Y	Y	N	Y	Y
9	Keating	N	Y	Y	N	Y	Y
MICHIGAN							
1	Bergman	N	N	N	Y	N	Y
2	Huizenga	N	N	N	Y	N	Y
3	*Amash*	N	N	N	Y	N	Y
4	Moolenaar	Y	Y	Y	N	N	N
5	Kildee	N	N	N	Y	N	Y
6	Upton	Y	Y	N	Y	N	Y
7	Walberg	N	N	N	Y	N	Y
8	Slotkin	N	N	N	Y	N	Y
9	Levin	Y	Y	Y	N	Y	Y
10	Mitchell	Y	Y	Y	N	N	Y
11	Stevens	N	N	N	Y	N	Y
12	Dingell	Y	Y	Y	N	Y	Y
13	Tlaib	Y	Y	Y	N	Y	Y
14	Lawrence	Y	Y	Y	N	Y	Y
MINNESOTA		?	?	?	?	?	?
1	Hagedorn						
2	Craig	N	N	N	Y	N	Y
3	Phillips	N	Y	Y	Y	N	Y
4	McCollum	Y	Y	Y	N	Y	Y
5	Omar	Y	Y	Y	N	Y	Y

		469	470	471	472	473	474
6	Emmer	Y	Y	N	Y	N	Y
7	Peterson	N	N	N	Y	N	Y
8	Stauber	N	Y	N	Y	N	Y
MISSISSIPPI							
1	Kelly, T.	N	N	N	Y	N	Y
2	Thompson, B.	Y	Y	Y	N	Y	Y
3	Guest	N	N	N	Y	N	Y
4	Palazzo	N	N	N	Y	N	Y
MISSOURI							
1	Clay	Y	Y	Y	N	Y	Y
2	Wagner	N	N	N	Y	N	Y
3	Luetkemeyer	N	N	N	Y	N	Y
4	Hartzler	N	N	N	Y	N	Y
5	Cleaver	Y	Y	Y	N	Y	Y
6	Graves, S.	+	+	+	-	+	+
7	Long	+	+	+	-	+	-
8	Smith, J.	N	N	N	Y	N	Y
MONTANA							
AL	Gianforte	N	N	N	Y	N	Y
NEBRASKA							
1	Fortenberry	N	N	N	Y	N	Y
2	Bacon	N	N	N	Y	N	Y
3	Smith, Adrian	N	N	N	Y	N	Y
NEVADA							
1	Titus	Y	Y	Y	N	Y	Y
2	Amodei	Y	Y	Y	N	Y	Y
3	Lee	Y	Y	Y	N	Y	Y
4	Horsford	Y	Y	Y	N	Y	Y
NEW HAMPSHIRE							
1	Pappas	Y	Y	Y	N	Y	Y
2	Kuster	Y	Y	Y	N	Y	Y
NEW JERSEY							
1	Norcross	Y	Y	Y	N	Y	Y
2	Van Drew	Y	Y	Y	N	Y	Y
3	Kim	N	Y	Y	N	Y	Y
4	Smith, C.	N	N	N	Y	N	Y
5	Gottheimer	N	N	N	Y	N	Y
6	Pallone	Y	Y	Y	N	Y	Y
7	Malinowski	Y	Y	Y	N	Y	Y
8	Sires	Y	Y	Y	N	Y	Y
9	Pascrell	Y	Y	Y	N	Y	Y
10	Payne	Y	Y	Y	N	Y	Y
11	Sherrill	Y	Y	Y	N	Y	Y
12	Watson Coleman	Y	Y	Y	N	Y	Y
NEW MEXICO							
1	Haaland	Y	Y	Y	N	Y	Y
2	Torres Small	Y	Y	Y	N	Y	Y
3	Luján	Y	Y	Y	N	Y	Y
NEW YORK							
1	Zeldin	N	N	N	Y	N	Y
2	King, P.	N	N	N	Y	N	Y
3	Suozzi	Y	Y	Y	N	Y	Y
4	Rice, K.	Y	Y	Y	N	Y	Y
5	Meeks	N	N	N	Y	N	Y
6	Meng	Y	Y	Y	N	Y	Y
7	Velázquez	Y	Y	Y	N	Y	Y
8	Jeffries	Y	Y	Y	N	Y	Y
9	Clarke	Y	Y	Y	N	Y	Y
10	Nadler	Y	Y	Y	N	Y	Y
11	Rose	Y	Y	Y	N	Y	Y
12	Maloney, C.	Y	Y	Y	N	Y	Y
13	Espaillat	Y	Y	Y	N	Y	Y
14	Ocasio-Cortez	Y	Y	Y	N	Y	Y
15	Serrano	Y	Y	Y	N	Y	Y
16	Engel	Y	Y	Y	N	Y	Y
17	Lowey	Y	Y	Y	N	Y	Y
18	Maloney, S.P.	Y	Y	Y	N	Y	+
19	Delgado	N	Y	Y	N	Y	Y
20	Tonko	Y	Y	Y	N	Y	Y
21	Stefanik	N	N	N	Y	N	Y
22	Brindisi	N	N	N	Y	N	Y
23	Reed	N	Y	Y	Y	N	Y
24	Katko	N	N	N	Y	N	Y
25	Morelle	Y	Y	Y	N	Y	Y
26	Higgins, B.	Y	Y	Y	N	Y	Y
27	Collins, C.	Y	Y	N	Y	N	Y
NORTH CAROLINA							
1	Butterfield	Y	Y	Y	N	Y	Y
2	Holding	N	N	N	Y	N	Y
3	Jones*	N	N	N	Y	N	Y
4	Price	Y	Y	Y	N	Y	Y
5	Foxx	N	N	N	Y	N	Y
6	Walker	N	N	N	Y	N	Y
7	Rouzer	N	N	N	Y	N	Y

		469	470	471	472	473	474
8	Hudson	N	N	N	Y	N	Y
9	vacant						
10	McHenry	N	N	N	Y	N	Y
11	Meadows	N	N	N	Y	N	Y
12	Adams	Y	Y	Y	N	Y	Y
13	Budd	N	N	N	Y	N	Y
NORTH DAKOTA							
AL	Armstrong	N	N	N	Y	N	Y
OHIO							
1	Chabot	N	N	N	Y	N	Y
2	Wenstrup	N	N	N	Y	N	Y
3	Beatty	?	Y	Y	N	Y	Y
4	Jordan	N	N	N	Y	N	Y
5	Latta	N	N	N	Y	N	Y
6	Johnson, B.	N	N	N	Y	N	Y
7	Gibbs	N	N	N	Y	N	Y
8	Davidson	N	N	N	Y	N	Y
9	Kaptur	Y	Y	Y	N	Y	Y
10	Turner	N	N	N	Y	N	Y
11	Fudge	?	?	?	?	?	?
12	Balderson	N	N	N	Y	N	Y
13	Ryan	Y	Y	Y	N	Y	Y
14	Joyce	N	N	N	Y	N	Y
15	Stivers	N	N	N	Y	N	Y
16	Gonzalez	N	N	N	Y	N	Y
OKLAHOMA							
1	Hern	N	N	N	Y	N	Y
2	Mullin	N	N	N	Y	N	Y
3	Lucas	N	N	N	Y	N	Y
4	Cole	N	N	N	Y	N	Y
5	Horn	Y	Y	Y	Y	Y	Y
OREGON							
1	Bonamici	Y	Y	Y	N	Y	Y
2	Walden	N	N	N	Y	N	Y
3	Blumenauer	Y	Y	Y	N	Y	Y
4	DeFazio	Y	Y	Y	N	Y	Y
5	Schrader	Y	Y	Y	N	Y	Y
PENNSYLVANIA							
1	Fitzpatrick	N	N	N	Y	N	Y
2	Boyle	Y	Y	Y	N	Y	Y
3	Evans	Y	Y	Y	N	Y	Y
4	Dean	Y	Y	Y	N	Y	Y
5	Scanlon	Y	Y	Y	N	Y	Y
6	Houlahan	Y	Y	Y	N	Y	Y
7	Wild	Y	Y	Y	N	Y	Y
8	Cartwright	Y	Y	Y	N	Y	Y
9	Meuser	N	N	N	Y	N	Y
10	Perry	N	N	N	Y	N	Y
11	Smucker	N	N	N	Y	N	Y
12	Marino*						
13	Joyce	N	N	N	Y	N	Y
14	Reschenthaler	N	N	N	Y	N	Y
15	Thompson, G.	N	N	N	Y	N	Y
16	Kelly, M.	N	N	N	Y	N	Y
17	Lamb	N	Y	N	Y	N	Y
18	Doyle	Y	Y	Y	N	Y	Y
RHODE ISLAND							
1	Cicilline	Y	Y	Y	N	Y	Y
2	Langevin	Y	Y	Y	N	Y	Y
SOUTH CAROLINA							
1	Cunningham	N	Y	Y	N	Y	Y
2	Wilson, J.	N	N	N	Y	N	Y
3	Duncan	N	?	N	Y	N	Y
4	Timmons	N	N	N	Y	N	Y
5	Norman	N	N	N	Y	N	Y
6	Clyburn	Y	Y	Y	?	?	?
7	Rice, T.	?	?	?	?	?	?
SOUTH DAKOTA							
AL	Johnson	N	N	N	Y	N	Y
TENNESSEE							
1	Roe	?	?	?	?	?	?
2	Burchett	N	N	N	Y	N	Y
3	Fleischmann	N	N	N	Y	N	Y
4	DesJarlais	N	N	N	Y	N	Y
5	Cooper	Y	Y	Y	N	Y	Y
6	Rose	N	N	N	Y	N	Y
7	Green	N	N	N	Y	N	Y
8	Kustoff	N	N	N	Y	N	Y
9	Cohen	Y	Y	Y	N	Y	Y
TEXAS							
1	Gohmert	N	N	N	Y	N	Y
2	Crenshaw	N	N	N	Y	N	Y
3	Taylor	N	N	N	Y	N	Y
4	Ratcliffe	N	N	N	Y	N	Y

		469	470	471	472	473	474
5	Gooden	N	N	N	Y	N	Y
6	Wright	?	?	?	?	?	?
7	Fletcher	Y	Y	Y	N	Y	Y
8	Brady	?	?	?	+	-	+
9	Green, A.	Y	Y	Y	N	Y	Y
10	McCaul	N	N	N	Y	N	Y
11	Conaway	N	N	N	Y	N	Y
12	Granger	N	N	N	Y	N	Y
13	Thornberry	N	N	N	Y	N	Y
14	Weber	N	N	N	Y	N	Y
15	Gonzalez	Y	Y	Y	N	Y	Y
16	Escobar	Y	Y	Y	N	Y	Y
17	Flores	N	N	N	Y	N	Y
18	Jackson Lee	Y	Y	Y	N	Y	Y
19	Arrington	N	N	N	Y	N	N
20	Castro	Y	Y	Y	N	Y	Y
21	Roy	N	Y	N	Y	N	Y
22	Olson	N	N	N	Y	N	Y
23	Hurd	N	N	N	Y	N	Y
24	Marchant	N	N	N	Y	N	Y
25	Williams	N	N	N	Y	N	Y
26	Burgess	N	Y	N	Y	N	Y
27	Cloud	N	N	N	Y	N	N
28	Cuellar	Y	Y	Y	N	Y	Y
29	Garcia, S.	Y	Y	Y	N	Y	Y
30	Johnson, E.B.	Y	Y	Y	N	Y	Y
31	Carter, J.	N	N	N	Y	N	Y
32	Allred	Y	Y	Y	N	Y	Y
33	Veasey	Y	Y	Y	N	Y	Y
34	Vela	Y	Y	Y	N	Y	Y
35	Doggett	Y	Y	Y	N	Y	+
36	Babin	N	N	N	Y	N	Y
UTAH							
1	Bishop, R.	N	N	N	Y	N	Y
2	Stewart	N	N	N	Y	N	Y
3	Curtis	N	N	N	Y	N	Y
4	McAdams	Y	Y	Y	Y	Y	Y
VERMONT							
AL	Welch	Y	Y	Y	N	Y	Y
VIRGINIA							
1	Wittman	N	N	N	Y	N	Y
2	Luria	N	Y	N	Y	N	Y
3	Scott, R.	Y	Y	Y	N	Y	Y
4	McEachin	Y	Y	Y	N	Y	Y
5	Riggleman	N	N	N	Y	N	Y
6	Cline	N	N	N	Y	N	Y
7	Spanberger	Y	Y	Y	N	Y	Y
8	Beyer	Y	Y	Y	N	Y	Y
9	Griffith	N	N	N	Y	N	Y
10	Wexton	Y	Y	Y	N	Y	Y
11	Connolly	Y	Y	Y	N	Y	Y
WASHINGTON							
1	DelBene	Y	Y	Y	N	Y	Y
2	Larsen	Y	Y	Y	N	Y	Y
3	Herrera Beutler	N	N	N	Y	N	Y
4	Newhouse	N	N	N	Y	N	Y
5	McMorris Rodgers	N	N	N	Y	N	Y
6	Kilmer	Y	Y	Y	N	Y	Y
7	Jayapal	Y	Y	Y	N	Y	Y
8	Schrier	Y	Y	Y	N	Y	Y
9	Smith Adam	Y	Y	Y	N	Y	Y
10	Heck	Y	Y	Y	N	Y	Y
WEST VIRGINIA							
1	McKinley	N	N	N	Y	N	Y
2	Mooney	N	N	N	Y	N	Y
3	Miller	N	N	N	Y	N	Y
WISCONSIN							
1	Steil	N	N	N	Y	N	Y
2	Pocan	Y	Y	Y	N	Y	Y
3	Kind	Y	Y	Y	N	Y	Y
4	Moore	Y	Y	Y	N	Y	Y
5	Sensenbrenner	N	N	N	Y	N	Y
6	Grothman	?	?	?	?	-	?
7	Duffy	-	-	-	+	-	+
8	Gallagher	N	N	N	Y	N	Y
WYOMING							
AL	Cheney	N	N	N	Y	N	Y
DELEGATES							
	Radewagen (A.S.)	?	?	?			
	Norton (D.C.)	+	+	+			
	San Nicolas (Guam)	?	?	?			
	Sablan (N. Marianas)	Y	Y	Y			
	González-Colón (P.R.)	?	?	?			
	Plaskett (V.I.)	?	?	?			

III HOUSE VOTES

475. HR2744. USAID Logo Usage - Passage. Engel, D-N.Y., motion to suspend the rules and pass the bill that would authorize the U.S. Agency for International Development to use the USAID logo and other markings, including the U.S. flag, to identify products provided through foreign assistance programs. Motion agreed to 414-1: R 186-1; D 227-0; I 1-0. *Note: A two-thirds majority of those present and voting (277 in this case) is required for passage under suspension of the rules.* July 15, 2019.

476. HRES432. Sudanese Political Reform - Passage. Engel, D-N.Y., motion to suspend the rules and agree to the resolution, as amended, that would express the sense of the of the House of Representatives condemning and calling for an immediate end to Sudanese government's use of violence against and detention and intimidation of peaceful protesters, journalists, medical professionals and human rights defenders. It would express support for the transfer of power in Sudan from the military to an inclusive, civilian-led government and for the right of the Sudanese people to express their demands for political change and democratic government. It would encourage the U.S. government and African Union to support such political reforms. Motion agreed to 414-1: R 186-1; D 227-0; I 1-0. *Note: A two-thirds majority of those present and voting (277 in this case) is required for passage under suspension of the rules.* July 15, 2019.

477. HR2037. Saudi Arabia Sanctions - Passage. Engel, D-N.Y., motion to suspend the rules and pass the bill, as amended, that would require the National Intelligence director to report to Congress identifying any Saudi Arabian government officials responsible for directing, ordering, or tampering with evidence related to the murder of journalist Jamal Khashoggi and listing foreign individuals involved in the murder. It would require the president to impose visa sanctions against such individuals, denying them permission to enter or remain in the United States. It would also require the State Department to report to Congress on human rights violations in Saudi Arabia and U.S. actions to address such violations. Motion agreed to 405-7: R 178-7; D 226-0; I 1-0. *Note: A two-thirds majority of those present and voting (275 in this case) is required for passage under suspension of the rules.* July 15, 2019.

478. SJ Res 38, SJRES37, HRES497, SJRES36, HR3494, HRES489. Intelligence Authorization, Condemning Resolution, Contempt of Congress, Arms Exports - Previous Question. Raskin, D-Md., motion to order the previous question (thus ending debate and the possibility of amendment) on the rule (H Res 491) that would provide for House floor consideration of the Fiscal 2018, 2019, and 2020 Intelligence Authorization (HR 3494); the resolution (H Res 489) titled, "A resolution condemning President Trump's racist comments directed at Members of Congress"; the resolution (H Res 497) that would hold Attorney General Barr and Commerce Secretary Wilbur Ross in contempt for failure to comply with congressional subpoenas; and certain joint resolutions related to sales and exports under the Arms Export Control Act. It would also provide for automatic adoption of a Schiff, D-Calif., manager's amendment to the Fiscal 2018, 2019, and 2020 Intelligence Authorization (HR 3494) that would express the sense of Congress that any CIA officer killed during an assignment in a foreign country should receive death benefits and would formally authorize the CIA to pay death benefits equal to an officer's annual salary to any survivor designated by the officer. Among other provisions, it would require the CIA to brief Congress on the benefits and challenges of providing CIA officers Defense Department and VA with health care services, and to make recommendations to facilitate the provision of such services. Motion agreed to 230-189: R 0-188; D 230-0; I 0-1. July 16, 2019.

479. SJ Res 37, HRES497, SJRES36, HR3494, HRES489, SJRES38. Intelligence Authorization, Condemning Resolution, Contempt of Congress, Arms Exports - Rule. Adoption of the rule (H Res 491) that would provide for House floor consideration of the Fiscal 2018, 2019, and 2020 Intelligence Authorization (HR 3494); the resolution (H Res 489) titled, "A resolution condemning President Trump's racist comments directed at Members of Congress"; the resolution (H Res 497) that would hold Attorney General Barr and Commerce Secretary Wilbur Ross in contempt for failure to comply with congressional subpoenas; and certain joint resolutions related to sales and exports under the Arms Export Control Act. It would also provide for automatic adoption of a Schiff, D-Calif., manager's amendment to the Fiscal 2018, 2019, and 2020 Intelligence Authorization (HR 3494) that would express the sense of Congress that any CIA officer killed during an assignment in a foreign country should receive death benefits and would formally authorize the CIA to pay death benefits equal to an officer's annual salary to any survivor designated by the officer. Among other provisions, it would require the CIA to brief Congress on the benefits and challenges of providing CIA officers Defense Department and VA with health care services, and to make recommendations to facilitate the provision of such services. Adopted 233-190: R 0-189; D 233-0; I 0-1. July 16, 2019.

480. HRES489. Condemning President Trump's Rhetoric - Motion to Strike. Collins, R-Ga., motion to strike from the record comments by Rep. Nancy Pelosi, D-Calif. Motion rejected 190-232: R 190-0; D 0-231; I 0-1. July 16, 2019.

		475	476	477	478	479	480
ALABAMA							
1	**Byrne**	Y	Y	Y	N	N	Y
2	**Roby**	Y	Y	Y	N	N	Y
3	**Rogers, M.**	Y	Y	Y	N	N	Y
4	**Aderholt**	Y	Y	Y	N	N	Y
5	**Brooks, M.**	Y	Y	Y	N	N	Y
6	**Palmer**	Y	Y	Y	N	N	Y
7	Sewell	Y	Y	Y	Y	Y	N
ALASKA							
AL	**Young**	?	?	?	N	N	Y
ARIZONA							
1	O'Halleran	Y	Y	Y	Y	Y	N
2	Kirkpatrick	Y	Y	Y	Y	Y	N
3	Grijalva	Y	Y	?	Y	Y	N
4	**Gosar**	Y	Y	Y	N	N	Y
5	**Biggs**	?	?	?	?	?	?
6	**Schweikert**	Y	Y	Y	N	N	Y
7	Gallego	Y	Y	Y	Y	Y	N
8	**Lesko**	Y	Y	Y	N	N	Y
9	Stanton	Y	Y	Y	Y	Y	N
ARKANSAS							
1	**Crawford**	Y	Y	Y	N	N	Y
2	**Hill, F.**	Y	Y	Y	N	N	Y
3	**Womack**	Y	Y	Y	N	N	Y
4	**Westerman**	Y	Y	Y	N	N	Y
CALIFORNIA							
1	**LaMalfa**	Y	Y	N	N	N	Y
2	Huffman	Y	Y	Y	Y	Y	N
3	Garamendi	Y	Y	Y	Y	Y	N
4	**McClintock**	Y	Y	N	N	N	Y
5	Thompson, M.	Y	Y	Y	Y	Y	N
6	Matsui	Y	Y	Y	Y	Y	N
7	Bera	Y	Y	Y	Y	Y	N
8	**Cook**	Y	Y	Y	N	N	Y
9	McNerney	Y	Y	Y	Y	Y	N
10	Harder	Y	Y	Y	Y	Y	N
11	DeSaulnier	Y	Y	Y	Y	Y	N
12	Pelosi						
13	Lee B.	Y	Y	Y	Y	Y	N
14	Speier	Y	Y	Y	Y	Y	N
15	Swalwell	Y	Y	Y	Y	Y	N
16	Costa	Y	Y	Y	Y	Y	N
17	Khanna	Y	Y	Y	Y	Y	N
18	Eshoo	Y	Y	Y	Y	Y	N
19	Lofgren	Y	Y	Y	Y	Y	N
20	Panetta	Y	Y	Y	Y	Y	N
21	Cox	Y	Y	Y	Y	Y	N
22	**Nunes**	Y	Y	Y	N	N	Y
23	**McCarthy**	Y	Y	Y	N	N	Y
24	Carbajal	Y	Y	Y	Y	Y	N
25	Hill, K.	Y	Y	Y	Y	Y	N
26	Brownley	Y	Y	Y	Y	Y	N
27	Chu	Y	Y	Y	Y	Y	N
28	Schiff	Y	Y	Y	Y	Y	N
29	Cárdenas	Y	Y	Y	?	Y	N
30	Sherman	Y	Y	Y	Y	Y	N
31	Aguilar	Y	Y	Y	Y	Y	N
32	Napolitano	Y	Y	Y	Y	Y	N
33	Lieu	Y	Y	Y	Y	Y	N
34	Gomez	Y	Y	Y	Y	Y	N
35	Torres	Y	Y	Y	Y	Y	N
36	Ruiz	Y	Y	Y	Y	Y	N
37	Bass	Y	Y	Y	Y	Y	N
38	Sánchez	Y	Y	Y	Y	Y	N
39	Cisneros	Y	Y	Y	Y	Y	N
40	Roybal-Allard	Y	Y	Y	Y	Y	N
41	Takano	Y	Y	Y	Y	Y	N
42	**Calvert**	Y	Y	Y	N	N	Y
43	Waters	Y	Y	Y	Y	Y	N
44	Barragán	Y	Y	Y	Y	Y	N
45	Porter	Y	Y	Y	Y	Y	N
46	Correa	Y	Y	Y	Y	Y	N
47	Lowenthal	Y	Y	Y	Y	Y	N
48	Rouda	Y	Y	Y	Y	Y	N
49	Levin	Y	Y	Y	Y	Y	N
50	**Hunter**	Y	Y	Y	N	N	Y
51	Vargas	Y	Y	Y	Y	Y	N
52	Peters	Y	Y	Y	Y	Y	N

		475	476	477	478	479	480
53	Davis, S.	Y	Y	Y	Y	Y	N
COLORADO							
1	DeGette	Y	Y	Y	Y	Y	N
2	Neguse	Y	Y	Y	Y	Y	N
3	**Tipton**	Y	Y	Y	N	N	Y
4	**Buck**	Y	Y	Y	N	N	Y
5	**Lamborn**	?	?	?	N	N	Y
6	Crow	Y	Y	Y	Y	Y	N
7	Perlmutter	Y	Y	Y	Y	Y	N
CONNECTICUT							
1	Larson	Y	Y	Y	Y	Y	N
2	Courtney	Y	Y	Y	Y	Y	N
3	DeLauro	Y	Y	Y	Y	Y	N
4	Himes	Y	Y	Y	Y	Y	N
5	Hayes	Y	Y	Y	Y	Y	N
DELAWARE							
AL	Blunt Rochester	?	?	?	Y	Y	N
FLORIDA							
1	**Gaetz**	Y	Y	N	N	N	Y
2	**Dunn**	Y	Y	?	N	N	Y
3	**Yoho**	Y	Y	N	N	N	Y
4	**Rutherford**	Y	Y	Y	N	N	Y
5	Lawson	Y	Y	Y	Y	Y	N
6	**Waltz**	Y	Y	Y	N	N	Y
7	Murphy	Y	Y	Y	Y	Y	N
8	**Posey**	Y	Y	Y	N	N	Y
9	Soto	Y	Y	Y	Y	Y	?
10	Demings	Y	Y	Y	Y	Y	N
11	**Webster**	Y	Y	Y	N	N	Y
12	**Bilirakis**	Y	Y	Y	N	N	Y
13	Crist	Y	Y	Y	Y	Y	N
14	Castor	Y	Y	Y	Y	Y	N
15	**Spano**	Y	Y	Y	N	N	Y
16	**Buchanan**	Y	Y	Y	N	N	Y
17	**Steube**	Y	Y	Y	N	N	Y
18	**Mast**	Y	Y	Y	N	N	Y
19	**Rooney**	Y	Y	Y	N	N	Y
20	Hastings	Y	Y	Y	Y	Y	N
21	Frankel	Y	Y	Y	Y	Y	N
22	Deutch	Y	Y	Y	Y	Y	N
23	Wasserman Schultz	Y	Y	Y	Y	Y	N
24	Wilson, F.	Y	Y	Y	Y	Y	N
25	**Diaz-Balart**	Y	Y	Y	N	N	Y
26	Mucarsel-Powell	Y	Y	Y	Y	Y	N
27	Shalala	Y	Y	Y	Y	Y	N
GEORGIA							
1	**Carter, E.L.**	Y	Y	Y	N	N	Y
2	Bishop, S.	?	?	?	Y	Y	N
3	**Ferguson**	Y	Y	Y	N	N	Y
4	Johnson, H.	Y	Y	Y	Y	Y	N
5	Lewis John	Y	Y	Y	Y	Y	N
6	McBath	Y	Y	Y	Y	Y	N
7	**Woodall**	Y	Y	Y	N	N	Y
8	**Scott, A.**	Y	Y	Y	N	N	Y
9	**Collins, D.**	Y	Y	Y	N	N	Y
10	**Hice**	Y	Y	Y	N	N	Y
11	**Loudermilk**	Y	Y	Y	N	N	Y
12	**Allen**	Y	Y	Y	N	N	Y
13	Scott, D.	Y	Y	Y	Y	Y	N
14	**Graves, T.**	Y	Y	Y	N	N	Y
HAWAII							
1	Case	Y	Y	Y	Y	Y	N
2	Gabbard	Y	Y	Y	Y	Y	N
IDAHO							
1	**Fulcher**	Y	Y	Y	N	N	Y
2	**Simpson**	+	+	+	N	N	Y
ILLINOIS							
1	Rush	Y	Y	Y	Y	Y	N
2	Kelly, R.	Y	Y	Y	Y	Y	N
3	Lipinski	?	?	?	?	?	N
4	García, J.	Y	Y	Y	Y	Y	N
5	Quigley	Y	Y	Y	Y	Y	N
6	Casten	Y	Y	Y	Y	Y	N
7	Davis, D.	Y	Y	Y	Y	Y	N
8	Krishnamoorthi	Y	Y	Y	Y	Y	N
9	Schakowsky	Y	Y	Y	Y	Y	N
10	Schneider	Y	Y	Y	Y	Y	N
11	Foster	Y	Y	Y	Y	Y	N

KEY: **Republicans** Democrats *Independents*

Y	Voted for (yea)	N	Voted against (nay)	P	Voted "present"
+	Announced for	-	Announced against	?	Did not vote or otherwise make position known
#	Paired for	X	Paired against		

		475	476	477	478	479	480
12	**Bost**	Y	Y	Y	N	N	Y
13	**Davis, R.**	Y	Y	+	N	N	Y
14	Underwood	Y	Y	Y	Y	Y	N
15	**Shimkus**	Y	Y	Y	N	N	Y
16	**Kinzinger**	Y	Y	Y	N	N	Y
17	Bustos	Y	Y	Y	Y	Y	N
18	**LaHood**	Y	Y	Y	N	N	Y
INDIANA							
1	Visclosky	Y	Y	Y	Y	Y	N
2	**Walorski**	Y	Y	Y	N	N	Y
3	**Banks**	Y	Y	Y	N	N	Y
4	**Baird**	Y	Y	Y	N	N	Y
5	**Brooks, S.**	Y	Y	Y	N	N	Y
6	**Pence**	Y	Y	Y	N	N	Y
7	Carson	Y	Y	Y	Y	Y	N
8	**Bucshon**	Y	Y	Y	N	N	Y
9	**Hollingsworth**	Y	Y	Y	N	N	Y
IOWA							
1	Finkenauer	Y	Y	Y	Y	Y	N
2	Loebsack	Y	Y	Y	Y	Y	N
3	Axne	Y	Y	Y	Y	Y	N
4	**King, S.**	Y	Y	Y	N	N	Y
KANSAS							
1	**Marshall**	Y	Y	Y	N	N	Y
2	**Watkins**	Y	Y	Y	N	N	Y
3	Davids	Y	Y	Y	Y	Y	N
4	**Estes**	Y	Y	Y	N	N	Y
KENTUCKY							
1	**Comer**	Y	Y	Y	N	N	Y
2	**Guthrie**	Y	Y	Y	N	N	Y
3	Yarmuth	Y	Y	Y	Y	Y	N
4	**Massie**	Y	N	N	N	N	Y
5	**Rogers, H.**	Y	Y	Y	N	N	Y
6	**Barr**	Y	Y	Y	N	N	Y
LOUISIANA							
1	**Scalise**	Y	Y	Y	N	N	Y
2	Richmond	Y	Y	Y	Y	Y	N
3	**Higgins, C.**	+	+	+	?	?	Y
4	**Johnson, M.**	Y	Y	Y	N	N	Y
5	**Abraham**	?	?	?	?	?	Y
6	**Graves, G.**	Y	Y	Y	N	N	Y
MAINE							
1	Pingree	Y	Y	Y	Y	Y	N
2	Golden	Y	Y	Y	Y	Y	N
MARYLAND							
1	**Harris**	Y	Y	Y	N	N	Y
2	Ruppersberger	Y	Y	Y	Y	Y	N
3	Sarbanes	Y	Y	Y	Y	Y	N
4	Brown, A.	Y	Y	Y	Y	Y	N
5	Hoyer	Y	Y	Y	Y	Y	N
6	Trone	Y	Y	Y	Y	Y	N
7	Cummings	Y	Y	Y	Y	Y	N
8	Raskin						
MASSACHUSETTS		Y	Y	Y	Y	Y	N
1	Neal						
2	McGovern	Y	Y	Y	Y	Y	N
3	Trahan	Y	Y	Y	Y	Y	N
4	Kennedy	Y	Y	Y	Y	Y	N
5	Clark	Y	Y	Y	Y	Y	N
6	Moulton	Y	Y	Y	Y	Y	N
7	Pressley	?	?	?	Y	Y	N
8	Lynch	Y	Y	Y	Y	Y	N
9	Keating	Y	Y	Y	Y	Y	?
MICHIGAN		Y	Y	Y	Y	Y	N
1	**Bergman**						
2	**Huizenga**	Y	Y	Y	N	N	Y
3	*Amash*	Y	Y	Y	N	N	Y
4	**Moolenaar**	Y	Y	Y	N	N	N
5	Kildee	Y	Y	Y	N	N	Y
6	**Upton**	Y	Y	Y	Y	Y	N
7	**Walberg**	Y	Y	Y	N	N	Y
8	Slotkin	Y	Y	Y	N	N	Y
9	Levin	Y	Y	Y	Y	Y	N
10	**Mitchell**	Y	Y	Y	Y	Y	N
11	Stevens	Y	Y	Y	N	N	Y
12	Dingell	Y	Y	Y	Y	Y	N
13	Tlaib	Y	Y	Y	Y	Y	N
14	Lawrence	Y	Y	Y	Y	Y	N
MINNESOTA		Y	Y	Y	Y	Y	N
1	**Hagedorn**						
2	Craig	Y	Y	Y	N	N	Y
3	Phillips	Y	Y	Y	Y	Y	N
4	McCollum	Y	Y	Y	Y	Y	N
5	Omar	Y	Y	Y	Y	Y	N

		475	476	477	478	479	480
6	**Emmer**	Y	Y	Y	Y	Y	N
7	Peterson	Y	Y	Y	N	N	Y
8	**Stauber**	Y	Y	Y	Y	Y	?
MISSISSIPPI		Y	Y	Y	N	N	Y
1	**Kelly, T.**						
2	Thompson, B.	Y	Y	Y	N	N	Y
3	**Guest**	Y	Y	Y	Y	Y	N
4	**Palazzo**	Y	Y	Y	N	N	Y
MISSOURI		Y	Y	Y	N	N	Y
1	Clay						
2	**Wagner**	Y	Y	Y	Y	Y	N
3	**Luetkemeyer**	Y	Y	Y	N	N	Y
4	**Hartzler**	Y	Y	Y	N	N	Y
5	Cleaver	Y	Y	Y	N	N	Y
6	**Graves, S.**	Y	Y	Y	Y	Y	N
7	**Long**	Y	Y	Y	N	N	Y
8	**Smith, J.**	Y	Y	Y	N	N	Y
MONTANA		Y	Y	Y	N	N	Y
AL	**Gianforte**						
NEBRASKA		Y	Y	Y	N	N	Y
1	**Fortenberry**						
2	**Bacon**	Y	Y	Y	N	N	Y
3	**Smith, Adrian**	Y	Y	Y	N	N	Y
NEVADA		Y	Y	Y	N	N	Y
1	Titus						
2	**Amodei**	Y	Y	Y	Y	Y	N
3	Lee	Y	Y	Y	N	N	Y
4	Horsford	Y	Y	Y	Y	Y	N
NEW HAMPSHIRE		Y	Y	Y	Y	Y	N
1	Pappas						
2	Kuster	Y	Y	Y	Y	Y	N
NEW JERSEY		Y	Y	Y	Y	Y	N
1	Norcross						
2	Van Drew	Y	Y	Y	Y	Y	N
3	Kim	Y	Y	Y	Y	Y	N
4	**Smith, C.**	Y	Y	Y	Y	Y	N
5	Gottheimer	Y	Y	Y	N	N	Y
6	Pallone	Y	Y	Y	Y	Y	N
7	Malinowski	Y	Y	Y	Y	Y	N
8	Sires	Y	Y	Y	Y	Y	N
9	Pascrell	Y	Y	Y	Y	Y	N
10	Payne	Y	Y	Y	Y	Y	N
11	Sherrill	Y	Y	Y	Y	Y	N
12	Watson Coleman	Y	Y	Y	Y	Y	N
NEW MEXICO		Y	Y	Y	Y	Y	N
1	Haaland						
2	Torres Small	Y	Y	Y	Y	Y	N
3	Luján	Y	Y	Y	Y	Y	N
NEW YORK		Y	Y	Y	Y	Y	N
1	**Zeldin**						
2	**King, P.**	Y	Y	Y	N	N	Y
3	Suozzi	Y	Y	Y	N	N	Y
4	Rice, K.	Y	Y	Y	Y	Y	N
5	Meeks	Y	Y	Y	Y	Y	N
6	Meng	Y	Y	Y	Y	Y	N
7	Velázquez	Y	Y	Y	Y	Y	N
8	Jeffries	Y	Y	Y	Y	Y	N
9	Clarke	?	?	?	Y	Y	N
10	Nadler	Y	Y	Y	Y	Y	N
11	Rose	Y	Y	Y	Y	Y	N
12	Maloney, C.	Y	Y	Y	Y	Y	N
13	Espaillat	Y	Y	Y	Y	Y	N
14	Ocasio-Cortez	Y	Y	Y	Y	Y	N
15	Serrano	Y	Y	Y	Y	Y	N
16	Engel	Y	Y	Y	Y	Y	N
17	Lowey	Y	Y	Y	Y	Y	N
18	Maloney, S.P.	Y	Y	Y	Y	Y	N
19	Delgado	Y	Y	Y	Y	Y	N
20	Tonko	Y	Y	Y	Y	Y	N
21	**Stefanik**	Y	Y	Y	Y	Y	N
22	Brindisi	Y	Y	Y	N	N	Y
23	**Reed**	Y	Y	Y	Y	Y	N
24	**Katko**	Y	Y	Y	N	N	Y
25	Morelle	Y	Y	Y	N	N	Y
26	Higgins, B.	Y	Y	Y	Y	Y	N
27	**Collins, C.**	Y	Y	Y	?	Y	N
NORTH CAROLINA		Y	Y	Y	N	N	?
1	Butterfield						
2	**Holding**	Y	Y	Y	Y	Y	N
3	**Jones***	Y	Y	N	N	N	Y
4	Price						
5	**Foxx**	Y	Y	Y	Y	Y	N
6	**Walker**	Y	Y	Y	N	N	Y
7	**Rouzer**	Y	Y	Y	N	N	Y

		475	476	477	478	479	480
8	**Hudson**	Y	Y	Y	N	N	Y
9	vacant	Y	Y	Y	N	N	Y
10	**McHenry**	Y	Y	Y	N	N	Y
11	**Meadows**	Y	Y	Y	N	N	Y
12	Adams	Y	Y	Y	Y	Y	N
13	**Budd**	Y	Y	Y	N	N	Y
NORTH DAKOTA							
AL	**Armstrong**	Y	Y	Y	N	N	Y
OHIO							
1	**Chabot**	Y	Y	Y	N	N	Y
2	**Wenstrup**	Y	Y	Y	N	N	Y
3	Beatty	Y	Y	Y	Y	Y	N
4	**Jordan**	Y	Y	Y	N	N	Y
5	**Latta**	Y	Y	Y	-	N	Y
6	**Johnson, B.**	Y	Y	Y	N	N	Y
7	**Gibbs**	Y	Y	Y	N	N	Y
8	**Davidson**	Y	Y	Y	N	N	Y
9	Kaptur	Y	Y	Y	Y	Y	N
10	**Turner**	Y	Y	Y	N	N	Y
11	Fudge	Y	Y	Y	Y	Y	N
12	**Balderson**	Y	Y	Y	N	N	Y
13	Ryan	Y	Y	Y	Y	Y	N
14	**Joyce**	Y	Y	Y	N	N	Y
15	**Stivers**	Y	Y	Y	N	N	Y
16	**Gonzalez**	Y	Y	Y	N	N	Y
OKLAHOMA							
1	**Hern**	Y	Y	Y	N	N	Y
2	**Mullin**	Y	Y	Y	N	N	Y
3	**Lucas**	Y	Y	Y	N	N	Y
4	**Cole**	Y	Y	Y	N	N	Y
5	Horn	Y	Y	Y	Y	Y	N
OREGON							
1	Bonamici	Y	Y	Y	Y	Y	N
2	**Walden**	Y	Y	Y	N	N	Y
3	Blumenauer	Y	Y	Y	Y	Y	N
4	DeFazio	Y	Y	Y	Y	Y	N
5	Schrader	Y	Y	Y	Y	Y	N
PENNSYLVANIA							
1	**Fitzpatrick**	Y	Y	Y	N	N	Y
2	Boyle	Y	Y	Y	Y	Y	N
3	Evans	Y	Y	Y	Y	Y	N
4	Dean	Y	Y	Y	Y	Y	N
5	Scanlon	Y	Y	Y	Y	Y	N
6	Houlahan	Y	Y	Y	Y	Y	N
7	Wild	Y	Y	Y	Y	Y	N
8	Cartwright	Y	Y	Y	Y	Y	N
9	**Meuser**	Y	Y	Y	N	N	Y
10	**Perry**	Y	Y	Y	N	N	Y
11	**Smucker**	Y	Y	Y	N	N	Y
12	**Marino***						
13	**Joyce**	Y	Y	Y	N	N	Y
14	**Reschenthaler**	Y	Y	Y	N	N	Y
15	**Thompson, G.**	Y	Y	Y	N	N	Y
16	**Kelly, M.**	Y	Y	Y	N	N	Y
17	Lamb	Y	Y	Y	Y	Y	N
18	Doyle	Y	Y	Y	?	Y	N
RHODE ISLAND							
1	Cicilline	Y	Y	Y	Y	Y	N
2	Langevin	Y	Y	Y	Y	Y	N
SOUTH CAROLINA							
1	Cunningham	Y	Y	Y	Y	Y	N
2	**Wilson, J.**	Y	Y	Y	N	N	Y
3	**Duncan**	Y	Y	Y	N	N	Y
4	**Timmons**	Y	Y	Y	N	N	Y
5	**Norman**	Y	Y	Y	N	N	Y
6	Clyburn	?	?	?	Y	Y	N
7	**Rice, T.**	Y	Y	Y	N	N	Y
SOUTH DAKOTA							
AL	**Johnson**	Y	Y	Y	N	N	Y
TENNESSEE							
1	**Roe**	Y	Y	Y	N	N	Y
2	**Burchett**	Y	Y	Y	N	N	Y
3	**Fleischmann**	Y	Y	Y	N	N	Y
4	**DesJarlais**	Y	Y	Y	N	N	Y
5	Cooper	Y	Y	Y	Y	Y	N
6	**Rose**	Y	Y	Y	N	N	Y
7	**Green**	Y	Y	Y	N	N	Y
8	**Kustoff**	Y	Y	Y	N	N	Y
9	Cohen	Y	Y	Y	Y	Y	N
TEXAS							
1	**Gohmert**	Y	Y	N	?	?	?
2	**Crenshaw**	Y	Y	Y	N	N	Y
3	**Taylor**	Y	Y	Y	N	N	Y
4	**Ratcliffe**	Y	Y	Y	N	N	Y

		475	476	477	478	479	480
5	**Gooden**	Y	Y	Y	N	N	Y
6	**Wright**	Y	Y	Y	N	N	Y
7	Fletcher	Y	Y	Y	Y	Y	N
8	**Brady**	?	?	?	N	N	Y
9	Green, A.	Y	Y	Y	Y	Y	N
10	**McCaul**	Y	Y	Y	N	N	Y
11	**Conaway**	Y	Y	Y	N	N	Y
12	**Granger**	+	+	+	-	-	+
13	**Thornberry**	Y	Y	Y	N	N	Y
14	**Weber**	Y	Y	Y	N	N	Y
15	Gonzalez	+	+	+	Y	Y	N
16	Escobar	Y	Y	Y	Y	Y	N
17	**Flores**	Y	Y	Y	N	N	Y
18	Jackson Lee	Y	Y	Y	Y	Y	N
19	**Arrington**	Y	Y	Y	N	N	Y
20	Castro	Y	Y	Y	Y	Y	N
21	**Roy**	Y	Y	Y	N	N	Y
22	**Olson**	Y	Y	Y	N	N	Y
23	**Hurd**	Y	Y	Y	N	N	Y
24	**Marchant**	?	?	?	?	?	?
25	**Williams**	?	?	?	?	?	?
26	**Burgess**	Y	Y	Y	?	?	?
27	**Cloud**	Y	Y	Y	N	N	Y
28	Cuellar	Y	Y	Y	Y	Y	N
29	Garcia, S.	Y	Y	Y	Y	Y	N
30	Johnson, E.B.	Y	Y	Y	Y	Y	N
31	**Carter, J.**	Y	Y	Y	N	N	Y
32	Allred	Y	Y	Y	Y	Y	N
33	Veasey	Y	Y	Y	Y	Y	N
34	Vela	Y	Y	Y	Y	Y	N
35	Doggett	Y	Y	Y	Y	Y	N
36	**Babin**	Y	Y	Y	N	N	Y
UTAH							
1	**Bishop, R.**	Y	Y	Y	N	N	Y
2	**Stewart**	Y	Y	Y	N	N	Y
3	**Curtis**	Y	Y	Y	N	N	Y
4	McAdams	Y	Y	Y	Y	Y	N
VERMONT							
AL	Welch	Y	Y	Y	Y	Y	N
VIRGINIA							
1	**Wittman**	Y	Y	Y	N	N	Y
2	Luria	Y	Y	Y	Y	Y	N
3	Scott, R.	Y	Y	Y	Y	Y	N
4	McEachin	Y	Y	Y	Y	Y	N
5	**Riggleman**	Y	Y	Y	N	N	Y
6	**Cline**	Y	Y	Y	N	N	Y
7	Spanberger	Y	Y	Y	Y	Y	N
8	Beyer	Y	Y	Y	Y	Y	N
9	**Griffith**	N	Y	Y	N	N	Y
10	Wexton	Y	Y	Y	Y	Y	N
11	Connolly	Y	Y	Y	Y	Y	N
WASHINGTON							
1	DelBene	Y	Y	Y	Y	Y	N
2	Larsen	Y	Y	Y	Y	Y	N
3	**Herrera Beutler**	Y	Y	Y	N	N	Y
4	**Newhouse**	Y	Y	Y	N	N	Y
5	**McMorris Rodgers**	Y	Y	Y	N	N	Y
6	Kilmer	Y	Y	Y	Y	Y	N
7	Jayapal	Y	Y	Y	Y	Y	N
8	Schrier	Y	Y	Y	Y	Y	N
9	Smith Adam	Y	Y	Y	Y	Y	N
10	Heck	Y	Y	Y	Y	Y	N
WEST VIRGINIA							
1	**McKinley**	Y	Y	Y	N	N	Y
2	**Mooney**	Y	Y	Y	N	N	Y
3	**Miller**	Y	Y	Y	N	N	Y
WISCONSIN							
1	**Steil**	Y	Y	Y	N	N	Y
2	Pocan	Y	Y	Y	Y	Y	N
3	Kind	Y	Y	Y	Y	Y	N
4	Moore	Y	Y	Y	Y	Y	N
5	**Sensenbrenner**	Y	Y	Y	N	N	Y
6	**Grothman**	Y	Y	Y	N	N	Y
7	**Duffy**	Y	Y	Y	N	N	Y
8	**Gallagher**	Y	Y	Y	N	N	Y
WYOMING							
AL	**Cheney**	Y	Y	Y	N	N	Y
DELEGATES							
	Radewagen (A.S.)						
	Norton (D.C.)						
	San Nicolas (Guam)						
	Sablan (N. Marianas)						
	González-Colón (P.R.)						
	Plaskett (V.I.)						

481. HRES489. Condemning President Trump's Rhetoric – Motion to Proceed in Order. Nadler, D-N.Y., motion to proceed in order that would allow Rep. Nancy Pelosi, D-Calif., to retain speaking privileges for the legislative day. Motion agreed to 231-190: R 0-189; D 231-0; I 0-1. July 16, 2019.

482. HRES489. Condemning President Trump's Rhetoric – Passage. Agreeing to the resolution that would express the sense of the House of Representatives condemning President Trump's recent "racist" comments suggesting that certain members of Congress should "go back" to other countries and stating that his comments have "legitimized and increased fear and hatred" toward people of color and naturalized American citizens. It would express support for policies "keeping America open" to individuals lawfully seeking refuge and asylum and affirm that immigrants and their descendants have made America stronger. Adopted 240-187: R 4-187; D 235-0; I 1-0. *Note: A "nay" was a vote in support of the president's position.* July 16, 2019.

483. HRES498. Impeachment Resolution – Motion to Table. McCarthy, R-Calif., motion to table a resolution related to the impeaching of President Donald Trump. Motion agreed to 332-95: R 194-0; D 137-95; I 1-0. July 17, 2019.

484. HR582. Minimum Wage Increase – Previous Question. Morelle, D-N.Y., motion to order the previous question (thus ending debate and the possibility of amendment) on the rule (H Res 492) that would provide House floor consideration of the Raise the Wage Act (HR 582) that would incrementally increase the federal minimum wage to $15 per hour over five years. It would provide for automatic adoption of a manager's amendment to the bill and for floor consideration of one additional amendment to the bill. The Scott, D-Va., manager's amendment to the bill (HR 582) would extend the period over which the minimum wage would be incrementally increased, such that it would reach $15/hour by Oct. 1, 2025, instead of by Oct. 1, 2024. Motion agreed to 231-194: R 0-193; D 231-0; I 0-1. July 17, 2019.

485. HR582. Minimum Wage Increase – Rule. Adoption of the rule (H Res 492) that would provide for House floor consideration of the Raise the Wage Act (HR 582) that would incrementally increase the federal minimum wage to $15 per hour over five years. It would provide for automatic adoption of a manager's amendment to the bill and for floor consideration of one additional amendment to the bill. The Scott, D-Va., manager's amendment to the bill (HR 582) would extend the period over which the minimum wage would be incrementally increased, such that it would reach $15/hour by Oct. 1, 2025, instead of by Oct. 1, 2024. Adopted 231-197: R 0-194; D 231-2; I 0-1. July 17, 2019.

486. SJ Res 36. Saudi Arabia Arms Sales – Passage. Passage of the joint resolution that would disapprove of the issuance of manufacturing, technical assistance, or export licenses related to certain defense articles and services to Saudi Arabia, the United Kingdom, Spain, and Italy, including for the transfer of guidance kits for Paveway laser-guided bomb systems and services related to the manufacture of Paveway system components. Passed (thus cleared for the president) 238-190: R 4-190; D 233-0; I 1-0. *Note: A "nay" was a vote in support of the president's position.* July 17, 2019.

		481	482	483	484	485	486
ALABAMA							
1	**Byrne**	N	N	Y	N	N	N
2	**Roby**	N	N	Y	N	N	N
3	**Rogers, M.**	N	N	Y	N	N	N
4	**Aderholt**	N	N	Y	N	N	N
5	**Brooks, M.**	N	N	Y	N	N	N
6	**Palmer**	N	N	Y	N	N	N
7	Sewell	Y	Y	Y	Y	Y	Y
ALASKA							
AL	**Young**	N	N	Y	N	N	N
ARIZONA							
1	O'Halleran	Y	Y	Y	Y	Y	Y
2	Kirkpatrick	Y	Y	N	Y	Y	Y
3	Grijalva	Y	Y	N	Y	Y	Y
4	**Gosar**	N	N	Y	N	N	N
5	**Biggs**	?	-	Y	N	N	N
6	**Schweikert**	N	N	Y	N	N	N
7	Gallego	Y	Y	Y	Y	Y	Y
8	**Lesko**	N	N	Y	N	N	N
9	Stanton	Y	Y	Y	Y	Y	Y
ARKANSAS							
1	**Crawford**	N	N	Y	N	N	N
2	**Hill, F.**	N	N	Y	N	N	N
3	**Womack**	N	N	Y	N	N	N
4	**Westerman**	N	N	Y	N	N	N
CALIFORNIA							
1	**LaMalfa**	N	N	Y	N	N	N
2	Huffman	Y	Y	N	Y	Y	Y
3	Garamendi	Y	Y	Y	Y	Y	Y
4	**McClintock**	N	N	Y	N	N	N
5	Thompson, M.	Y	Y	N	Y	Y	Y
6	Matsui	Y	Y	N	Y	Y	Y
7	Bera	Y	Y	Y	Y	Y	Y
8	**Cook**	N	N	Y	N	N	N
9	McNerney	Y	Y	N	Y	Y	Y
10	Harder	Y	Y	Y	Y	Y	Y
11	DeSaulnier	Y	Y	N	Y	Y	Y
12	Pelosi		Y				
13	Lee B.	Y	Y	N	Y	Y	Y
14	Speier	Y	Y	N	Y	Y	Y
15	Swalwell	Y	Y	N	Y	Y	Y
16	Costa	Y	Y	Y	Y	Y	Y
17	Khanna	Y	Y	Y	Y	Y	Y
18	Eshoo	Y	Y	Y	Y	Y	Y
19	Lofgren	Y	Y	N	Y	Y	Y
20	Panetta	Y	Y	Y	Y	Y	Y
21	Cox	Y	Y	Y	Y	Y	Y
22	**Nunes**	N	N	Y	N	N	N
23	**McCarthy**	N	N	Y	N	N	N
24	Carbajal	Y	Y	Y	Y	Y	Y
25	Hill, K.	Y	Y	Y	Y	Y	Y
26	Brownley	Y	Y	Y	Y	Y	Y
27	Chu	Y	Y	Y	Y	Y	Y
28	Schiff	Y	Y	Y	Y	Y	Y
29	Cárdenas	Y	Y	N	Y	Y	Y
30	Sherman	Y	Y	N	Y	Y	Y
31	Aguilar	Y	Y	Y	Y	Y	Y
32	Napolitano	Y	Y	N	Y	Y	Y
33	Lieu	Y	Y	N	Y	Y	Y
34	Gomez	Y	Y	N	Y	Y	Y
35	Torres	Y	Y	N	Y	Y	Y
36	Ruiz	Y	Y	Y	Y	Y	Y
37	Bass	Y	Y	N	Y	Y	Y
38	Sánchez	Y	Y	Y	Y	Y	Y
39	Cisneros	Y	Y	Y	Y	Y	Y
40	Roybal-Allard	Y	Y	N	?	Y	Y
41	Takano	Y	Y	Y	Y	Y	Y
42	**Calvert**	N	N	Y	N	N	N
43	Waters	Y	Y	N	Y	Y	Y
44	Barragán	Y	Y	N	Y	Y	Y
45	Porter	Y	Y	Y	Y	Y	Y
46	Correa	Y	Y	Y	Y	Y	Y
47	Lowenthal	Y	Y	N	Y	Y	Y
48	Rouda	Y	Y	Y	Y	Y	Y
49	Levin	Y	Y	N	Y	Y	Y
50	**Hunter**	N	N	Y	N	N	N
51	Vargas	Y	Y	N	Y	Y	Y
52	Peters	Y	Y	Y	Y	Y	Y

		481	482	483	484	485	486
53	Davis, S.	Y	Y	Y	Y	Y	Y
COLORADO							
1	DeGette	Y	Y	N	Y	Y	Y
2	Neguse	Y	Y	N	Y	Y	Y
3	**Tipton**	N	N	Y	N	N	N
4	**Buck**	N	N	Y	N	N	N
5	**Lamborn**	N	N	Y	N	N	N
6	Crow	Y	Y	Y	Y	Y	Y
7	Perlmutter	Y	Y	Y	Y	Y	Y
CONNECTICUT							
1	Larson	Y	Y	Y	Y	Y	Y
2	Courtney	Y	Y	Y	Y	Y	Y
3	DeLauro	Y	Y	Y	Y	Y	Y
4	Himes	Y	Y	Y	Y	Y	Y
5	Hayes	Y	Y	Y	Y	Y	Y
DELAWARE							
AL	Blunt Rochester	Y	Y	Y	Y	Y	Y
FLORIDA							
1	**Gaetz**	N	N	Y	N	N	N
2	**Dunn**	N	N	Y	N	N	N
3	**Yoho**	N	N	Y	N	N	N
4	**Rutherford**	N	N	Y	N	N	N
5	Lawson	Y	Y	Y	Y	Y	Y
6	**Waltz**	N	N	Y	N	N	N
7	Murphy	Y	Y	Y	Y	Y	Y
8	**Posey**	N	N	Y	N	N	N
9	Soto	?	Y	Y	Y	Y	Y
10	Demings	Y	Y	Y	Y	Y	Y
11	**Webster**	N	N	Y	N	N	N
12	**Bilirakis**	N	N	Y	N	N	N
13	Crist	Y	Y	Y	Y	Y	Y
14	Castor	Y	Y	Y	Y	Y	Y
15	**Spano**	N	N	Y	N	N	N
16	**Buchanan**	N	N	Y	N	N	N
17	**Steube**	N	N	Y	N	N	N
18	**Mast**	N	N	Y	N	N	N
19	**Rooney**	N	N	Y	N	N	N
20	Hastings	Y	Y	Y	Y	Y	Y
21	Frankel	Y	Y	Y	Y	Y	Y
22	Deutch	Y	Y	Y	Y	Y	Y
23	Wasserman Schultz	Y	Y	Y	Y	Y	Y
24	Wilson, F.	Y	Y	N	Y	Y	Y
25	**Diaz-Balart**	N	N	Y	N	N	N
26	Mucarsel-Powell	Y	Y	Y	Y	Y	Y
27	Shalala	Y	Y	Y	Y	Y	Y
GEORGIA							
1	**Carter, E.L.**	N	N	Y	N	N	N
2	Bishop, S.	Y	Y	Y	Y	Y	Y
3	**Ferguson**	N	N	Y	N	N	N
4	Johnson, H.	Y	Y	Y	Y	Y	Y
5	Lewis John	Y	Y	Y	Y	Y	Y
6	McBath	Y	Y	Y	Y	Y	Y
7	**Woodall**	N	N	Y	N	N	N
8	**Scott, A.**	N	N	Y	N	N	N
9	**Collins, D.**	N	N	Y	N	N	N
10	**Hice**	N	N	Y	N	N	N
11	**Loudermilk**	N	N	Y	N	N	N
12	**Allen**	N	N	Y	N	N	N
13	Scott, D.	Y	Y	N	Y	Y	Y
14	**Graves, T.**	N	N	Y	N	N	N
HAWAII							
1	Case	Y	Y	Y	Y	Y	Y
2	Gabbard	Y	Y	?	?	?	?
IDAHO							
1	**Fulcher**	N	N	Y	N	N	N
2	**Simpson**	N	N	Y	N	N	N
ILLINOIS							
1	Rush	Y	Y	Y	Y	Y	Y
2	Kelly, R.	Y	Y	N	Y	Y	Y
3	Lipinski	Y	Y	Y	Y	Y	Y
4	García, J.	Y	Y	N	Y	Y	Y
5	Quigley	Y	Y	Y	Y	Y	Y
6	Casten	Y	Y	Y	Y	Y	Y
7	Davis, D.	?	Y	N	Y	Y	Y
8	Krishnamoorthi	Y	Y	Y	Y	Y	Y
9	Schakowsky	Y	Y	N	Y	Y	Y
10	Schneider	Y	Y	Y	Y	Y	Y
11	Foster	Y	Y	Y	Y	Y	Y

KEY:	Republicans	Democrats	*Independents*
Y Voted for (yea)	**N** Voted against (nay)		**P** Voted "present"
+ Announced for	**–** Announced against		**?** Did not vote or otherwise
# Paired for	**X** Paired against		make position known

		481	482	483	484	485	486
12	**Bost**	N	N	Y	N	N	N
13	**Davis, R.**	N	N	Y	N	N	N
14	Underwood	Y	Y	Y	Y	Y	Y
15	**Shimkus**	N	N	Y	N	N	N
16	**Kinzinger**	N	N	Y	N	N	N
17	Bustos	Y	Y	Y	Y	Y	Y
18	**LaHood**	N	N	Y	N	N	N
INDIANA							
1	Visclosky	Y	Y	Y	Y	Y	Y
2	**Walorski**	N	N	Y	N	N	N
3	**Banks**	N	N	Y	N	N	N
4	**Baird**	N	N	Y	N	N	N
5	**Brooks, S.**	N	Y	Y	N	N	N
6	**Pence**	N	N	Y	N	N	N
7	Carson	Y	Y	N	Y	Y	Y
8	**Bucshon**	N	N	Y	N	N	N
9	**Hollingsworth**	N	N	Y	N	N	Y
IOWA							
1	Finkenauer	Y	Y	Y	Y	Y	Y
2	Loebsack	Y	Y	Y	Y	Y	Y
3	Axne	Y	Y	Y	Y	Y	Y
4	**King, S.**	N	N	Y	N	N	N
KANSAS							
1	**Marshall**	N	N	Y	N	N	N
2	**Watkins**	N	N	Y	N	N	N
3	Davids	Y	Y	Y	Y	Y	Y
4	**Estes**	N	N	Y	N	N	N
KENTUCKY							
1	**Comer**	N	N	Y	N	N	N
2	**Guthrie**	N	N	Y	N	N	N
3	Yarmuth	Y	Y	Y	Y	Y	Y
4	**Massie**	N	N	Y	N	N	Y
5	**Rogers, H.**	N	N	Y	N	N	N
6	**Barr**	N	N	Y	N	N	N
LOUISIANA							
1	**Scalise**	N	N	Y	N	N	N
2	Richmond	Y	Y	N	Y	Y	Y
3	**Higgins, C.**	N	N	Y	N	N	N
4	**Johnson, M.**	N	N	Y	N	N	N
5	**Abraham**	N	N	?	?	?	?
6	**Graves, G.**	N	N	Y	N	N	N
MAINE							
1	Pingree	Y	Y	N	Y	Y	Y
2	Golden	Y	Y	Y	Y	Y	Y
MARYLAND							
1	**Harris**	N	N	Y	N	N	N
2	Ruppersberger	Y	Y	Y	Y	Y	Y
3	Sarbanes	Y	Y	Y	Y	Y	Y
4	Brown, A.	Y	Y	N	Y	Y	Y
5	Hoyer	Y	Y	Y	Y	Y	Y
6	Trone	Y	Y	Y	Y	Y	Y
7	Cummings	Y	Y	Y	Y	Y	Y
8	Raskin						
MASSACHUSETTS		Y	Y	N	Y	Y	Y
1	Neal						
2	McGovern	Y	Y	Y	Y	Y	Y
3	Trahan	Y	Y	N	Y	Y	Y
4	Kennedy	Y	Y	N	Y	Y	Y
5	Clark	Y	Y	N	Y	Y	Y
6	Moulton	Y	Y	N	Y	Y	Y
7	Pressley	Y	Y	N	Y	Y	Y
8	Lynch	Y	Y	N	Y	Y	Y
9	Keating	Y	Y	Y	Y	Y	Y
MICHIGAN		Y	Y	Y	Y	Y	Y
1	**Bergman**						
2	**Huizenga**	N	N	Y	N	N	N
3	*Amash*	N	N	Y	N	N	N
4	**Moolenaar**	N	Y	Y	N	N	Y
5	Kildee	N	N	Y	N	N	N
6	**Upton**	Y	Y	N	Y	Y	Y
7	**Walberg**	N	Y	Y	N	N	N
8	Slotkin	N	N	Y	N	N	N
9	Levin	Y	Y	Y	Y	Y	Y
10	**Mitchell**	Y	Y	N	Y	Y	Y
11	Stevens	N	N	Y	N	N	N
12	Dingell	Y	Y	Y	Y	Y	Y
13	Tlaib	Y	Y	N	Y	Y	Y
14	Lawrence	Y	Y	N	Y	Y	Y
MINNESOTA		Y	Y	N	Y	Y	Y
1	**Hagedorn**						
2	Craig	N	N	Y	N	N	N
3	Phillips	Y	Y	Y	Y	Y	Y
4	McCollum	Y	Y	Y	Y	Y	Y
5	Omar	Y	Y	N	Y	Y	Y

		481	482	483	484	485	486
6	**Emmer**	Y	Y	N	Y	Y	Y
7	Peterson	N	N	Y	N	N	N
8	**Stauber**	?	Y	Y	Y	Y	Y
MISSISSIPPI		N	N	Y	N	N	N
1	**Kelly, T.**						
2	Thompson, B.	N	N	Y	N	N	N
3	**Guest**	Y	Y	N	Y	Y	Y
4	**Palazzo**	N	N	Y	N	N	N
MISSOURI		N	N	Y	N	N	N
1	Clay						
2	**Wagner**	Y	Y	N	Y	Y	Y
3	**Luetkemeyer**	N	N	Y	N	N	N
4	**Hartzler**	N	N	Y	N	N	N
5	Cleaver	N	N	Y	N	N	N
6	**Graves, S.**	Y	Y	Y	Y	Y	Y
7	**Long**	N	N	Y	N	N	N
8	**Smith, J.**	N	N	Y	N	N	N
MONTANA		N	N	Y	N	N	N
AL	**Gianforte**						
NEBRASKA		N	N	Y	N	N	N
1	**Fortenberry**						
2	**Bacon**	N	N	Y	N	N	N
3	**Smith, Adrian**	N	N	Y	N	N	N
NEVADA		N	N	Y	N	N	N
1	Titus						
2	**Amodei**	Y	Y	N	Y	Y	Y
3	Lee	N	N	Y	N	N	N
4	Horsford	Y	Y	Y	Y	Y	Y
NEW HAMPSHIRE		Y	Y	Y	Y	Y	Y
1	Pappas						
2	Kuster	Y	Y	Y	Y	Y	Y
NEW JERSEY		Y	Y	Y	Y	Y	Y
1	Norcross						
2	Van Drew	Y	Y	N	Y	Y	Y
3	Kim	Y	Y	Y	Y	Y	Y
4	**Smith, C.**	Y	Y	Y	Y	Y	Y
5	Gottheimer	N	N	Y	N	N	N
6	Pallone	Y	Y	Y	Y	Y	Y
7	Malinowski	Y	Y	N	Y	Y	Y
8	Sires	Y	Y	Y	Y	Y	Y
9	Pascrell	Y	Y	Y	Y	Y	Y
10	Payne	Y	Y	N	Y	Y	Y
11	Sherrill	Y	Y	N	Y	Y	Y
12	Watson Coleman	Y	Y	Y	Y	Y	Y
NEW MEXICO		Y	Y	N	Y	Y	Y
1	Haaland						
2	Torres Small	Y	Y	Y	Y	Y	Y
3	Luján	Y	Y	Y	Y	Y	Y
NEW YORK		Y	Y	Y	Y	Y	Y
1	**Zeldin**						
2	**King, P.**	N	N	Y	N	N	N
3	Suozzi	N	N	Y	N	N	N
4	Rice, K.	Y	Y	Y	Y	Y	Y
5	Meeks	Y	Y	Y	Y	Y	Y
6	Meng	Y	Y	Y	Y	Y	Y
7	Velázquez	Y	Y	N	Y	Y	Y
8	Jeffries	Y	Y	N	Y	Y	Y
9	Clarke	Y	Y	Y	Y	Y	Y
10	Nadler	Y	Y	N	Y	Y	Y
11	Rose	Y	Y	N	Y	Y	Y
12	Maloney, C.	Y	Y	Y	Y	Y	Y
13	Espaillat	Y	Y	N	Y	Y	Y
14	Ocasio-Cortez	Y	Y	N	Y	Y	Y
15	Serrano	Y	Y	N	Y	Y	Y
16	Engel	Y	Y	Y	Y	Y	Y
17	Lowey	Y	Y	N	Y	Y	Y
18	Maloney, S.P.	Y	Y	N	Y	Y	Y
19	Delgado	Y	Y	Y	Y	Y	Y
20	Tonko	Y	Y	Y	Y	Y	Y
21	**Stefanik**	Y	Y	N	Y	Y	Y
22	Brindisi	N	N	Y	N	N	N
23	**Reed**	Y	Y	Y	Y	Y	Y
24	**Katko**	N	N	Y	N	N	N
25	Morelle	N	N	Y	N	N	N
26	Higgins, B.	Y	Y	Y	Y	Y	Y
27	**Collins, C.**	Y	Y	N	Y	Y	Y
NORTH CAROLINA		?	N	Y	N	N	N
1	Butterfield						
2	**Holding**	Y	Y	N	Y	Y	Y
3	**Jones***	N	N	Y	N	N	N
4	Price						
5	**Foxx**	Y	Y	Y	Y	Y	Y
6	**Walker**	N	N	Y	N	N	N
7	**Rouzer**	N	N	?	?	?	?

		481	482	483	484	485	486
8	**Hudson**	N	N	Y	N	N	N
9	vacant	?	N	?	?	?	?
10	**McHenry**	N	N	Y	N	N	N
11	**Meadows**	N	N	Y	N	N	N
12	Adams	Y	Y	N	Y	Y	Y
13	**Budd**	N	N	Y	N	N	N
NORTH DAKOTA							
AL	**Armstrong**	N	N	Y	N	N	N
OHIO							
1	**Chabot**	N	N	Y	N	N	N
2	**Wenstrup**	N	N	Y	N	N	N
3	Beatty	Y	Y	N	?	Y	Y
4	**Jordan**	N	N	Y	N	N	N
5	**Latta**	N	N	Y	N	N	N
6	**Johnson, B.**	N	N	Y	N	N	N
7	**Gibbs**	N	N	Y	N	N	N
8	**Davidson**	N	N	Y	N	N	N
9	Kaptur	Y	Y	Y	Y	Y	Y
10	**Turner**	N	N	Y	N	N	N
11	Fudge	Y	Y	N	Y	Y	Y
12	**Balderson**	N	N	Y	N	N	N
13	Ryan	Y	Y	Y	Y	Y	Y
14	**Joyce**	N	N	Y	N	N	N
15	**Stivers**	N	N	Y	N	N	N
16	**Gonzalez**	N	N	Y	N	N	N
OKLAHOMA							
1	**Hern**	N	N	Y	N	N	N
2	**Mullin**	N	N	Y	N	N	N
3	**Lucas**	N	N	Y	N	N	N
4	**Cole**	N	N	Y	N	N	N
5	Horn	Y	Y	Y	Y	Y	Y
OREGON							
1	Bonamici	Y	Y	N	Y	Y	Y
2	**Walden**	N	N	Y	N	N	N
3	Blumenauer	Y	Y	N	Y	Y	Y
4	DeFazio	Y	Y	P	Y	Y	Y
5	Schrader	Y	Y	Y	Y	Y	Y
PENNSYLVANIA							
1	**Fitzpatrick**	N	Y	Y	N	N	N
2	Boyle	Y	Y	N	Y	Y	Y
3	Evans	Y	Y	N	Y	Y	Y
4	Dean	Y	Y	N	Y	Y	Y
5	Scanlon	Y	Y	N	Y	Y	Y
6	Houlahan	Y	Y	Y	Y	Y	Y
7	Wild	Y	Y	Y	Y	Y	Y
8	Cartwright	Y	Y	Y	Y	Y	Y
9	**Meuser**	N	N	Y	N	N	N
10	**Perry**	N	N	Y	N	N	N
11	**Smucker**	N	N	Y	N	N	N
12	**Marino***						
13	**Joyce**	N	N	Y	N	N	N
14	**Reschenthaler**	N	N	Y	N	N	N
15	**Thompson, G.**	N	N	Y	N	N	N
16	**Kelly, M.**	N	N	Y	N	N	N
17	Lamb	Y	Y	Y	Y	Y	Y
18	Doyle	Y	Y	N	Y	Y	Y
RHODE ISLAND							
1	Cicilline	Y	Y	N	Y	Y	Y
2	Langevin	Y	Y	Y	Y	Y	Y
SOUTH CAROLINA							
1	Cunningham	Y	Y	Y	Y	N	Y
2	**Wilson, J.**	N	N	Y	N	N	N
3	**Duncan**	N	N	Y	N	N	N
4	**Timmons**	N	N	Y	N	N	N
5	**Norman**	N	N	Y	N	N	N
6	Clyburn	Y	Y	Y	Y	Y	Y
7	**Rice, T.**	N	N	Y	N	N	N
SOUTH DAKOTA							
AL	**Johnson**	N	N	Y	N	N	N
TENNESSEE							
1	**Roe**	N	N	Y	N	N	N
2	**Burchett**	N	N	Y	N	N	N
3	**Fleischmann**	N	N	Y	N	N	N
4	**DesJarlais**	N	N	Y	N	N	N
5	Cooper	Y	Y	Y	Y	Y	Y
6	**Rose**	N	N	Y	N	N	N
7	**Green**	N	N	Y	N	N	N
8	**Kustoff**	N	N	Y	N	N	N
9	Cohen	Y	Y	N	Y	Y	Y
TEXAS							
1	**Gohmert**	?	?	Y	N	N	N
2	**Crenshaw**	N	N	Y	N	N	N
3	**Taylor**	N	N	Y	N	N	N
4	**Ratcliffe**	N	N	Y	N	N	N

		481	482	483	484	485	486
5	**Gooden**	N	N	Y	N	N	N
6	**Wright**	N	N	Y	N	N	N
7	Fletcher	Y	Y	Y	Y	Y	Y
8	**Brady**	N	N	Y	N	N	N
9	Green, A.	Y	Y	N	Y	Y	Y
10	**McCaul**	N	N	Y	N	N	N
11	**Conaway**	N	N	Y	N	N	N
12	**Granger**	-	-	Y	N	N	N
13	**Thornberry**	N	N	Y	N	N	N
14	**Weber**	N	N	Y	N	N	N
15	Gonzalez	Y	Y	Y	Y	Y	Y
16	Escobar	Y	Y	N	Y	Y	Y
17	**Flores**	N	N	Y	N	N	N
18	Jackson Lee	Y	Y	N	Y	Y	Y
19	**Arrington**	N	N	Y	N	N	N
20	Castro	Y	Y	N	Y	Y	Y
21	**Roy**	N	N	Y	N	N	N
22	**Olson**	N	N	Y	N	N	N
23	**Hurd**	N	Y	Y	N	N	N
24	**Marchant**	?	?	Y	N	N	N
25	**Williams**	?	?	Y	N	N	N
26	**Burgess**	?	?	Y	N	N	N
27	**Cloud**	N	N	Y	N	N	N
28	Cuellar	Y	Y	Y	Y	Y	Y
29	Garcia, S.	Y	Y	N	Y	Y	Y
30	Johnson, E.B.	Y	Y	N	Y	Y	Y
31	**Carter, J.**	N	N	Y	N	N	N
32	Allred	Y	Y	Y	Y	Y	Y
33	Veasey	Y	Y	Y	Y	Y	Y
34	Vela	Y	Y	N	Y	Y	Y
35	Doggett	Y	Y	N	Y	Y	Y
36	**Babin**	N	N	Y	N	N	N
UTAH							
1	**Bishop, R.**	N	N	Y	N	N	N
2	**Stewart**	N	N	Y	N	N	N
3	**Curtis**	N	N	Y	N	N	N
4	McAdams	Y	Y	Y	Y	N	Y
VERMONT							
AL	Welch	Y	Y	N	Y	Y	Y
VIRGINIA							
1	**Wittman**	N	N	Y	N	N	N
2	Luria	Y	Y	Y	Y	Y	Y
3	Scott, R.	Y	Y	Y	Y	Y	Y
4	McEachin	Y	Y	Y	Y	Y	Y
5	**Riggleman**	N	N	Y	N	N	N
6	**Cline**	N	N	Y	N	N	N
7	Spanberger	Y	Y	Y	Y	Y	Y
8	Beyer	Y	Y	Y	Y	Y	Y
9	**Griffith**	N	N	Y	N	N	N
10	Wexton	Y	Y	Y	Y	Y	Y
11	Connolly	Y	Y	Y	Y	Y	Y
WASHINGTON							
1	DelBene	Y	Y	Y	Y	Y	Y
2	Larsen	Y	Y	N	Y	Y	Y
3	**Herrera Beutler**	N	N	Y	?	N	N
4	**Newhouse**	N	N	Y	N	N	N
5	**McMorris Rodgers**	N	N	Y	N	N	N
6	Kilmer	Y	Y	Y	Y	Y	Y
7	Jayapal	Y	Y	N	Y	Y	Y
8	Schrier	Y	Y	Y	Y	Y	Y
9	Smith Adam	Y	Y	Y	Y	Y	Y
10	Heck	Y	Y	Y	Y	Y	Y
WEST VIRGINIA							
1	**McKinley**	N	N	Y	N	N	N
2	**Mooney**	N	N	Y	N	N	Y
3	**Miller**	N	N	Y	N	N	N
WISCONSIN							
1	**Steil**	N	N	Y	N	N	N
2	Pocan	Y	Y	N	Y	Y	Y
3	Kind	Y	Y	Y	Y	Y	Y
4	Moore	Y	Y	N	Y	Y	Y
5	**Sensenbrenner**	N	N	Y	N	N	N
6	**Grothman**	N	N	Y	N	N	N
7	**Duffy**	N	N	Y	N	N	N
8	**Gallagher**	N	N	Y	N	N	Y
WYOMING							
AL	**Cheney**	N	N	Y	N	N	N
DELEGATES							
	Radewagen (A.S.)						
	Norton (D.C.)						
	San Nicolas (Guam)						
	Sablan (N. Marianas)						
	González-Colón (P.R.)						
	Plaskett (V.I.)						

487. SJ Res 37. United Arab Emirates Arms Export - Passage. Passage of the joint resolution that would disapprove of the issuance of export licenses related to the transfer of guidance kits for the Paveway II laser-guided bomb system to the United Arab Emirates, United Kingdom, and France. Passed (thus cleared for the president) 238-190: R 4-190; D 233-0; I 1-0. Note: A "nay" was a vote in support of the president's position. July 17, 2019.

488. SJ Res 38. Saudi Arabia Arms Export - Passage. Passage of the joint resolution that would disapprove of the issuance of export licenses related to the transfer of certain defense articles and services to Saudi Arabia and the United Kingdom, specifically for articles and services to support the manufacture of the Aurora fuzing system used by the Paveway IV laser-guided bomb system. Passed (thus cleared for the president) 237-190: R 4-190; D 232-0; I 1-0. Note: A "nay" was a vote in support of the president's position. July 17, 2019.

489. HRES497. Barr and Ross Contempt - Passage. Agreeing to the resolution that would find Attorney General William P. Barr and Commerce Secretary Wilbur Ross in contempt of Congress for failing to comply with subpoenas issued by the House Oversight and Reform Committee requiring Barr and Ross to provide documents related to efforts to add a citizenship question the 2020 census. It would direct the speaker of the House and the Oversight and Reform Committee to take actions to enforce the subpoenas, including actions to initiate or intervene in civil legal actions in federal court. Passed 230-198: R 0-194; D 229-4; I 1-0. Note: A "nay" was a vote in support of the president's position. July 17, 2019.

490. HR3494. Fiscal 2018, 2019, 2020 Intelligence Authorization - Climate Security Council. Chabot, R-Ohio, amendment that would strike from the bill a provision that would establish a climate security advisory council under the Office of the Director of National Intelligence. Rejected in Committee of the Whole 178-255: R 177-19; D 0-235; I 1-1. July 17, 2019.

491. HR3494. Fiscal 2018, 2019, 2020 Intelligence Authorization - Foreign Threat Response Center. Kennedy, D-Mass., amendment that would establish a foreign threat response center under the Office of the Director of National Intelligence that would analyze and integrate U.S. intelligence related to foreign threats and coordinate federal efforts to deter such threats to the national security or political and economic systems of the U.S. and its allies. Adopted in Committee of the Whole 237-196: R 1-195; D 235-0; I 1-1. July 17, 2019.

492. HR3494. Fiscal 2018, 2019, 2020 Intelligence Authorization - Passage. Passage of the bill, as amended, that would authorize a classified amount of funding for fiscal 2018, 2019, and 2020 for 16 federal intelligence agencies and U.S. intelligence-related activities, including foreign intelligence activities of the FBI and the Defense, State, and Homeland Security departments. Among other provisions, it would direct the Office of the Director of National Intelligence to submit a number of reports to Congress including intelligence assessments and strategies related to foreign interference in U.S. elections, particularly by Russia; Russian influence on, threats to, and interference in foreign elections, economies, and security; Chinese efforts to exert influence in the U.S. and other nations; security threats posed by domestic terrorism; and security threats posed by new technologies, including facial recognition technology and virtual currencies. It would require the ODNI to establish a climate security advisory council to facilitate coordination between the intelligence community and federal entities on activities related to climate change. It includes a number of provisions related to intelligence personnel policies, including those that would require reviews of workplace environment and diversity in the intelligence community workforce. The bill includes a number of defense-related provisions also included in the Fiscal 2020 National Defense Authorization (HR 2500), including those that would require the Defense Department to report to Congress on foreign entities that pose a threat to critical U.S. technologies, research, and intellectual property, including Russian and Chinese academic institutions. Passed 397-31: R 171-23; D 226-7; I 0-1. July 17, 2019.

		487	488	489	490	491	492
ALABAMA							
1	**Byrne**	N	N	N	Y	N	Y
2	**Roby**	N	N	N	Y	N	Y
3	**Rogers, M.**	N	N	N	Y	N	Y
4	**Aderholt**	N	N	N	Y	N	Y
5	**Brooks, M.**	N	N	N	Y	N	N
6	**Palmer**	N	N	N	Y	N	Y
7	Sewell	Y	Y	Y	N	Y	Y
ALASKA							
AL	**Young**	N	N	N	Y	N	Y
ARIZONA							
1	O'Halleran	Y	Y	Y	N	Y	Y
2	Kirkpatrick	Y	Y	Y	N	Y	Y
3	Grijalva	Y	Y	Y	N	Y	Y
4	**Gosar**	N	N	N	Y	N	N
5	**Biggs**	N	N	N	Y	N	N
6	**Schweikert**	N	N	N	Y	N	Y
7	Gallego	Y	Y	Y	N	Y	Y
8	**Lesko**	N	N	N	Y	N	Y
9	Stanton	Y	Y	Y	N	Y	Y
ARKANSAS							
1	**Crawford**	N	N	N	Y	N	Y
2	**Hill, F.**	N	N	N	Y	N	Y
3	**Womack**	N	N	N	Y	N	Y
4	**Westerman**	N	N	N	Y	N	Y
CALIFORNIA							
1	**LaMalfa**	N	N	N	Y	N	Y
2	Huffman	Y	Y	Y	N	Y	N
3	Garamendi	Y	Y	Y	N	Y	Y
4	**McClintock**	N	N	N	Y	N	N
5	Thompson, M.	Y	Y	Y	N	Y	Y
6	Matsui	Y	Y	Y	N	Y	Y
7	Bera	Y	Y	Y	N	Y	Y
8	**Cook**	N	N	N	Y	N	Y
9	McNerney	Y	Y	Y	N	Y	Y
10	Harder	Y	Y	Y	N	Y	Y
11	DeSaulnier	Y	Y	Y	N	Y	Y
12	Pelosi						
13	Lee B.	Y	Y	Y	N	Y	N
14	Speier	Y	?	Y	N	Y	Y
15	Swalwell	Y	Y	Y	N	Y	Y
16	Costa	Y	Y	Y	N	Y	Y
17	Khanna	Y	Y	Y	N	Y	Y
18	Eshoo	Y	Y	Y	N	Y	Y
19	Lofgren	Y	Y	Y	N	Y	N
20	Panetta	Y	Y	Y	N	Y	Y
21	Cox	Y	Y	Y	N	Y	Y
22	**Nunes**	N	N	N	Y	N	Y
23	**McCarthy**	N	N	N	Y	N	Y
24	Carbajal	Y	Y	Y	N	Y	Y
25	Hill, K.	Y	Y	Y	N	Y	Y
26	Brownley	Y	Y	Y	N	Y	Y
27	Chu	Y	Y	Y	N	Y	Y
28	Schiff	Y	Y	Y	N	Y	Y
29	Cárdenas	Y	Y	Y	N	Y	Y
30	Sherman	Y	Y	Y	N	Y	Y
31	Aguilar	Y	Y	Y	N	Y	Y
32	Napolitano	Y	Y	Y	N	Y	Y
33	Lieu	Y	Y	Y	N	Y	Y
34	Gomez	Y	Y	Y	N	Y	Y
35	Torres	Y	Y	Y	N	Y	Y
36	Ruiz	Y	Y	Y	N	Y	Y
37	Bass	Y	Y	Y	N	Y	Y
38	Sánchez	Y	Y	Y	N	Y	Y
39	Cisneros	Y	Y	Y	N	Y	Y
40	Roybal-Allard	Y	Y	Y	N	Y	Y
41	Takano	Y	Y	Y	N	Y	Y
42	**Calvert**	N	N	N	Y	N	Y
43	Waters	Y	Y	Y	N	Y	Y
44	Barragán	Y	Y	Y	N	Y	Y
45	Porter	Y	Y	Y	N	Y	Y
46	Correa	Y	Y	Y	N	Y	Y
47	Lowenthal	Y	Y	Y	N	Y	Y
48	Rouda	Y	Y	Y	N	Y	Y
49	Levin	Y	Y	Y	N	Y	Y
50	**Hunter**	N	N	N	Y	N	Y
51	Vargas	Y	Y	Y	N	Y	Y
52	Peters	Y	Y	Y	N	Y	Y

		487	488	489	490	491	492
53	Davis, S.	Y	Y	Y	N	Y	Y
COLORADO							
1	DeGette	Y	Y	Y	N	Y	Y
2	Neguse	Y	Y	Y	N	Y	Y
3	**Tipton**	N	N	N	Y	N	Y
4	**Buck**	N	N	N	Y	N	Y
5	**Lamborn**	N	N	N	Y	N	Y
6	Crow	Y	Y	Y	N	Y	Y
7	Perlmutter	Y	Y	Y	N	Y	Y
CONNECTICUT							
1	Larson	Y	Y	Y	N	Y	Y
2	Courtney	Y	Y	Y	N	Y	Y
3	DeLauro	Y	Y	Y	N	Y	Y
4	Himes	Y	Y	Y	N	Y	Y
5	Hayes	Y	Y	Y	N	Y	Y
DELAWARE							
AL	Blunt Rochester	Y	Y	Y	N	Y	Y
FLORIDA							
1	**Gaetz**	N	N	N	N	N	N
2	**Dunn**	N	N	N	Y	N	Y
3	**Yoho**	N	N	N	Y	N	Y
4	**Rutherford**	N	N	N	Y	N	Y
5	Lawson	Y	Y	Y	N	Y	Y
6	**Waltz**	N	N	N	Y	N	Y
7	Murphy	Y	Y	Y	N	Y	Y
8	**Posey**	N	N	N	Y	N	N
9	Soto	Y	Y	Y	N	Y	Y
10	Demings	Y	Y	Y	N	Y	Y
11	**Webster**	N	N	N	Y	N	Y
12	**Bilirakis**	N	N	N	Y	N	Y
13	Crist	Y	Y	Y	N	Y	Y
14	Castor	Y	Y	Y	N	Y	Y
15	**Spano**	N	N	N	Y	N	Y
16	**Buchanan**	N	N	N	Y	N	Y
17	**Steube**	N	N	N	Y	N	Y
18	**Mast**	N	N	N	Y	N	Y
19	**Rooney**	N	N	N	Y	N	Y
20	Hastings	Y	Y	Y	N	Y	Y
21	Frankel	Y	Y	Y	N	Y	Y
22	Deutch	Y	Y	Y	N	Y	Y
23	Wasserman Schultz	Y	Y	Y	N	Y	Y
24	Wilson, F.	Y	Y	Y	N	Y	Y
25	**Diaz-Balart**	N	N	N	Y	N	Y
26	Mucarsel-Powell	Y	Y	Y	N	Y	Y
27	Shalala	Y	Y	Y	N	Y	Y
GEORGIA							
1	**Carter, E.L.**	N	N	N	Y	N	Y
2	Bishop, S.	Y	Y	Y	N	Y	Y
3	**Ferguson**	N	N	N	Y	N	Y
4	Johnson, H.	Y	Y	Y	N	Y	Y
5	Lewis John	Y	Y	Y	N	Y	Y
6	McBath	Y	Y	Y	N	Y	Y
7	**Woodall**	N	N	N	Y	N	Y
8	**Scott, A.**	N	N	N	Y	N	Y
9	**Collins, D.**	N	N	N	Y	N	Y
10	**Hice**	N	N	N	Y	N	Y
11	**Loudermilk**	N	N	N	Y	N	Y
12	**Allen**	N	N	N	Y	N	Y
13	Scott, D.	Y	Y	Y	N	Y	Y
14	**Graves, T.**	N	N	N	Y	N	Y
HAWAII							
1	Case	Y	Y	Y	N	Y	Y
2	Gabbard	?	?	?	?	?	?
IDAHO							
1	**Fulcher**	N	N	N	Y	N	Y
2	**Simpson**	N	N	N	Y	N	Y
ILLINOIS							
1	Rush	Y	Y	Y	N	Y	Y
2	Kelly, R.	Y	Y	Y	N	Y	Y
3	Lipinski	Y	Y	Y	N	Y	Y
4	García, J.	Y	Y	Y	N	Y	Y
5	Quigley	Y	Y	Y	N	Y	Y
6	Casten	Y	Y	Y	N	Y	Y
7	Davis, D.	Y	Y	Y	N	Y	Y
8	Krishnamoorthi	Y	Y	Y	N	Y	Y
9	Schakowsky	Y	Y	Y	N	Y	Y
10	Schneider	Y	Y	Y	N	Y	Y
11	Foster	Y	Y	Y	N	Y	Y

KEY: Republicans   Democrats   *Independents*

Y Voted for (yea)	**N** Voted against (nay)	**P** Voted "present"	
+ Announced for	**−** Announced against	**?** Did not vote or otherwise	
# Paired for	**X** Paired against	make position known	

		487	488	489	490	491	492
12	**Bost**	N	N	N	Y	N	Y
13	**Davis, R.**	N	N	N	Y	N	Y
14	Underwood	Y	Y	Y	N	Y	Y
15	**Shimkus**	N	N	N	Y	N	Y
16	**Kinzinger**	N	N	N	Y	N	Y
17	Bustos	Y	Y	Y	N	Y	Y
18	**LaHood**	N	N	N	Y	N	Y
INDIANA							
1	Visclosky	Y	Y	Y	N	Y	Y
2	**Walorski**	N	N	N	Y	N	Y
3	**Banks**	N	N	N	Y	N	Y
4	**Baird**	N	N	N	Y	N	Y
5	**Brooks, S.**	N	N	N	Y	N	Y
6	**Pence**	N	N	N	Y	N	Y
7	Carson	Y	Y	Y	N	Y	Y
8	**Bucshon**	N	N	N	Y	N	Y
9	**Hollingsworth**	Y	Y	N	N	N	Y
IOWA							
1	Finkenauer	Y	Y	Y	N	Y	Y
2	Loebsack	Y	Y	Y	N	Y	Y
3	Axne	Y	Y	Y	N	Y	Y
4	**King, S.**	N	N	N	Y	N	Y
KANSAS							
1	**Marshall**	N	N	N	Y	N	Y
2	**Watkins**	N	N	N	Y	N	Y
3	Davids	Y	Y	Y	N	Y	Y
4	**Estes**	N	N	N	Y	N	Y
KENTUCKY							
1	**Comer**	N	N	N	Y	N	N
2	**Guthrie**	N	N	N	Y	N	Y
3	Yarmuth	Y	Y	Y	N	Y	Y
4	**Massie**	Y	Y	N	Y	N	N
5	**Rogers, H.**	N	N	N	Y	N	Y
6	**Barr**	N	N	N	Y	N	Y
LOUISIANA							
1	**Scalise**	N	N	N	Y	N	Y
2	Richmond	Y	Y	Y	N	Y	Y
3	**Higgins, C.**	N	N	N	Y	N	Y
4	**Johnson, M.**	N	N	N	Y	N	Y
5	**Abraham**	?	?	?	?	?	?
6	**Graves, G.**	N	N	N	N	N	Y
MAINE							
1	Pingree	Y	Y	Y	N	Y	Y
2	Golden	Y	Y	N	N	Y	Y
MARYLAND							
1	**Harris**	N	N	N	Y	N	N
2	Ruppersberger	Y	Y	Y	N	Y	Y
3	Sarbanes	Y	Y	Y	N	Y	Y
4	Brown, A.	Y	Y	Y	N	Y	Y
5	Hoyer	Y	Y	Y	N	Y	Y
6	Trone	Y	Y	Y	N	Y	Y
7	Cummings	Y	Y	Y	N	Y	Y
8	Raskin						
MASSACHUSETTS		Y	Y	Y	N	Y	Y
1	Neal						
2	McGovern	Y	Y	Y	N	Y	Y
3	Trahan	Y	Y	Y	N	Y	Y
4	Kennedy	Y	Y	Y	N	Y	Y
5	Clark	Y	Y	Y	N	Y	Y
6	Moulton	Y	Y	Y	N	Y	Y
7	Pressley	Y	Y	Y	N	Y	Y
8	Lynch	Y	Y	Y	N	Y	Y
9	Keating	Y	Y	Y	N	Y	Y
MICHIGAN		Y	Y	Y	N	Y	Y
1	**Bergman**						
2	**Huizenga**	N	N	N	Y	N	Y
3	*Amash*	N	N	N	Y	N	Y
4	**Moolenaar**	Y	Y	Y	Y	N	N
5	Kildee	N	N	N	Y	N	Y
6	**Upton**	Y	Y	Y	N	Y	Y
7	**Walberg**	N	N	N	N	N	Y
8	Slotkin	N	N	N	Y	N	Y
9	Levin	Y	Y	Y	N	Y	Y
10	**Mitchell**	Y	Y	Y	N	Y	Y
11	Stevens	N	N	N	Y	N	Y
12	Dingell	Y	Y	Y	N	Y	Y
13	Tlaib	Y	Y	Y	N	Y	Y
14	Lawrence	Y	Y	Y	N	Y	N
MINNESOTA		Y	Y	Y	N	Y	Y
1	**Hagedorn**						
2	Craig	N	N	N	Y	N	Y
3	Phillips	Y	Y	Y	N	Y	Y
4	McCollum	Y	Y	Y	N	Y	Y
5	Omar	Y	Y	Y	N	Y	Y

		487	488	489	490	491	492
6	**Emmer**	Y	Y	Y	N	Y	Y
7	Peterson	N	N	N	Y	N	Y
8	**Stauber**	Y	Y	Y	N	Y	Y
MISSISSIPPI		N	N	N	Y	N	Y
1	**Kelly, T.**						
2	Thompson, B.	N	N	N	Y	N	Y
3	**Guest**	Y	Y	Y	N	Y	Y
4	**Palazzo**	N	N	N	Y	N	Y
MISSOURI		N	N	N	Y	N	Y
1	Clay						
2	**Wagner**	Y	Y	Y	N	Y	Y
3	**Luetkemeyer**	N	N	N	Y	N	Y
4	**Hartzler**	N	N	N	Y	N	Y
5	Cleaver	N	N	N	Y	N	Y
6	**Graves, S.**	Y	Y	Y	N	Y	Y
7	**Long**	N	N	N	Y	N	Y
8	**Smith, J.**	N	N	N	Y	N	Y
MONTANA		N	N	N	Y	N	Y
AL	**Gianforte**						
NEBRASKA		N	N	N	Y	N	Y
1	**Fortenberry**						
2	**Bacon**	N	N	N	N	N	Y
3	**Smith, Adrian**	N	N	N	Y	N	Y
NEVADA		N	N	N	Y	N	Y
1	Titus						
2	**Amodei**	Y	Y	Y	N	Y	Y
3	Lee	N	N	N	Y	N	Y
4	Horsford	Y	Y	Y	N	Y	Y
NEW HAMPSHIRE		Y	Y	Y	N	Y	Y
1	Pappas						
2	Kuster	Y	Y	Y	N	Y	Y
NEW JERSEY		Y	Y	Y	N	Y	Y
1	Norcross						
2	Van Drew	Y	Y	Y	N	Y	Y
3	Kim	Y	Y	N	N	Y	Y
4	**Smith, C.**	Y	Y	Y	N	Y	Y
5	Gottheimer	N	N	N	N	N	Y
6	Pallone	Y	Y	Y	N	Y	Y
7	Malinowski	Y	Y	Y	N	Y	Y
8	Sires	Y	Y	Y	N	Y	Y
9	Pascrell	Y	Y	Y	N	Y	Y
10	Payne	Y	Y	Y	N	Y	Y
11	Sherrill	Y	Y	Y	N	Y	Y
12	Watson Coleman	Y	Y	Y	N	Y	Y
NEW MEXICO		Y	Y	Y	N	Y	Y
1	Haaland						
2	Torres Small	Y	Y	Y	N	Y	Y
3	Luján	Y	Y	Y	N	Y	Y
NEW YORK		Y	Y	Y	N	Y	Y
1	**Zeldin**						
2	**King, P.**	N	N	N	Y	N	Y
3	Suozzi	N	N	N	Y	N	Y
4	Rice, K.	Y	Y	Y	N	Y	Y
5	Meeks	Y	Y	Y	N	Y	Y
6	Meng	Y	Y	Y	N	Y	Y
7	Velázquez	Y	Y	Y	N	Y	Y
8	Jeffries	Y	Y	Y	N	Y	Y
9	Clarke	Y	Y	Y	N	Y	Y
10	Nadler	Y	Y	Y	N	Y	Y
11	Rose	Y	Y	Y	N	Y	Y
12	Maloney, C.	Y	Y	Y	N	Y	Y
13	Espaillat	Y	Y	Y	N	Y	Y
14	Ocasio-Cortez	Y	Y	Y	N	Y	Y
15	Serrano	Y	Y	Y	N	Y	Y
16	Engel	Y	Y	Y	N	Y	Y
17	Lowey	Y	Y	Y	N	Y	Y
18	Maloney, S.P.	Y	Y	Y	N	Y	Y
19	Delgado	Y	Y	Y	N	Y	Y
20	Tonko	Y	Y	Y	N	Y	Y
21	**Stefanik**	Y	Y	Y	N	Y	Y
22	Brindisi	N	N	N	N	N	Y
23	**Reed**	Y	Y	N	N	Y	Y
24	**Katko**	N	N	N	N	N	Y
25	Morelle	N	N	N	N	N	Y
26	Higgins, B.	Y	Y	Y	N	Y	Y
27	**Collins, C.**	Y	Y	Y	N	Y	Y
NORTH CAROLINA		N	N	N	Y	N	Y
1	Butterfield						
2	**Holding**	Y	Y	Y	N	Y	Y
3	**Jones***	N	N	N	Y	N	Y
4	Price						
5	**Foxx**	Y	Y	Y	N	Y	Y
6	**Walker**	N	N	N	Y	N	Y
7	**Rouzer**	?	?	?	?	?	?

		487	488	489	490	491	492
8	**Hudson**	N	N	N	Y	N	Y
9	vacant	?	?	?	?	?	?
10	**McHenry**	N	N	N	N	N	Y
11	**Meadows**	N	N	N	Y	N	N
12	Adams	Y	Y	Y	N	Y	Y
13	**Budd**	N	N	N	Y	N	N
NORTH DAKOTA							
AL	**Armstrong**	N	N	N	Y	N	Y
OHIO							
1	**Chabot**	N	N	N	Y	N	Y
2	**Wenstrup**	N	N	N	Y	N	Y
3	Beatty	Y	Y	Y	N	Y	Y
4	**Jordan**	N	N	N	Y	N	N
5	**Latta**	N	N	N	Y	N	Y
6	**Johnson, B.**	N	N	N	Y	N	Y
7	**Gibbs**	N	N	N	Y	N	Y
8	**Davidson**	N	N	N	Y	N	Y
9	Kaptur	Y	Y	Y	N	Y	Y
10	**Turner**	N	N	N	Y	N	Y
11	Fudge	Y	Y	Y	N	Y	Y
12	**Balderson**	N	N	N	Y	N	Y
13	Ryan	Y	Y	Y	N	Y	Y
14	**Joyce**	N	N	N	Y	N	Y
15	**Stivers**	N	N	N	Y	N	Y
16	**Gonzalez**	N	N	N	Y	N	Y
OKLAHOMA							
1	**Hern**	N	N	N	Y	N	Y
2	**Mullin**	N	N	N	Y	N	Y
3	**Lucas**	N	N	N	Y	N	Y
4	**Cole**	N	N	N	Y	N	Y
5	Horn	Y	Y	Y	N	Y	Y
OREGON							
1	Bonamici	Y	Y	Y	N	Y	Y
2	**Walden**	N	N	N	Y	N	Y
3	Blumenauer	Y	Y	Y	N	Y	N
4	DeFazio	Y	Y	Y	N	Y	N
5	Schrader	Y	Y	Y	N	Y	Y
PENNSYLVANIA							
1	**Fitzpatrick**	N	N	N	N	N	Y
2	Boyle	Y	Y	Y	N	Y	Y
3	Evans	Y	Y	Y	N	Y	Y
4	Dean	Y	Y	Y	N	Y	Y
5	Scanlon	Y	Y	Y	N	Y	Y
6	Houlahan	Y	Y	Y	N	Y	Y
7	Wild	Y	Y	Y	N	Y	Y
8	Cartwright	Y	Y	Y	N	Y	Y
9	**Meuser**	N	N	N	Y	N	Y
10	**Perry**	N	N	N	Y	N	N
11	**Smucker**	N	N	N	Y	N	Y
12	**Marino***						
13	**Joyce**	N	N	N	Y	N	Y
14	**Reschenthaler**	N	N	N	Y	N	Y
15	**Thompson, G.**	N	N	N	N	N	Y
16	**Kelly, M.**	N	N	N	Y	N	Y
17	Lamb	Y	Y	N	N	Y	Y
18	Doyle	Y	Y	Y	N	Y	Y
RHODE ISLAND							
1	Cicilline	Y	Y	Y	N	Y	Y
2	Langevin	Y	Y	Y	N	Y	Y
SOUTH CAROLINA							
1	Cunningham	Y	Y	Y	N	Y	Y
2	**Wilson, J.**	N	N	N	Y	N	Y
3	**Duncan**	N	N	N	Y	N	N
4	**Timmons**	N	N	N	Y	N	Y
5	**Norman**	N	N	N	Y	N	N
6	Clyburn	Y	Y	Y	N	Y	Y
7	**Rice, T.**	N	N	N	Y	N	Y
SOUTH DAKOTA							
AL	**Johnson**	N	N	N	Y	N	Y
TENNESSEE							
1	**Roe**	N	N	N	Y	N	N
2	**Burchett**	N	N	N	Y	N	N
3	**Fleischmann**	N	N	N	Y	N	Y
4	**DesJarlais**	N	N	N	Y	N	Y
5	Cooper	Y	Y	Y	N	Y	Y
6	**Rose**	N	N	N	Y	N	Y
7	**Green**	N	N	N	Y	N	Y
8	**Kustoff**	N	N	N	Y	N	Y
9	Cohen	Y	Y	Y	N	Y	Y
TEXAS							
1	**Gohmert**	N	N	N	Y	N	N
2	**Crenshaw**	N	N	N	Y	N	Y
3	**Taylor**	N	N	N	Y	N	Y
4	**Ratcliffe**	N	N	N	Y	N	Y

		487	488	489	490	491	492
5	**Gooden**	N	N	N	Y	N	Y
6	**Wright**	N	N	N	Y	N	Y
7	Fletcher	Y	Y	Y	N	Y	Y
8	**Brady**	N	N	N	Y	N	Y
9	Green, A.	Y	Y	Y	N	Y	Y
10	**McCaul**	N	N	N	N	N	Y
11	**Conaway**	N	N	N	Y	N	Y
12	**Granger**	N	N	N	Y	N	Y
13	**Thornberry**	N	N	N	Y	N	Y
14	**Weber**	N	N	N	Y	N	Y
15	Gonzalez	Y	Y	Y	N	Y	Y
16	Escobar	Y	Y	Y	N	Y	Y
17	**Flores**	N	N	N	Y	N	Y
18	Jackson Lee	Y	Y	Y	N	Y	Y
19	**Arrington**	N	N	N	Y	N	Y
20	Castro	Y	Y	Y	N	Y	Y
21	**Roy**	N	N	N	Y	N	N
22	**Olson**	N	N	N	Y	N	Y
23	**Hurd**	N	N	N	N	N	Y
24	**Marchant**	N	N	N	Y	N	Y
25	**Williams**	N	N	N	Y	N	Y
26	**Burgess**	N	N	N	Y	N	N
27	**Cloud**	N	N	N	Y	N	Y
28	Cuellar	Y	Y	Y	N	Y	Y
29	Garcia, S.	Y	Y	Y	N	Y	Y
30	Johnson, E.B.	Y	Y	Y	N	Y	Y
31	**Carter, J.**	N	N	N	Y	N	Y
32	Allred	Y	Y	Y	N	Y	Y
33	Veasey	Y	Y	Y	N	Y	Y
34	Vela	Y	Y	Y	N	Y	Y
35	Doggett	Y	Y	Y	N	Y	Y
36	**Babin**	N	N	N	Y	N	Y
UTAH							
1	**Bishop, R.**	N	N	N	Y	N	Y
2	**Stewart**	N	N	N	Y	N	Y
3	**Curtis**	N	N	N	Y	N	Y
4	McAdams	Y	Y	Y	N	Y	Y
VERMONT							
AL	Welch	Y	Y	Y	N	Y	Y
VIRGINIA							
1	**Wittman**	N	N	N	Y	N	Y
2	Luria	Y	Y	Y	N	Y	Y
3	Scott, R.	Y	Y	Y	N	Y	Y
4	McEachin	Y	Y	Y	N	Y	Y
5	**Riggleman**	N	N	N	Y	N	Y
6	**Cline**	N	N	N	Y	N	N
7	Spanberger	Y	Y	Y	N	Y	Y
8	Beyer	Y	Y	Y	N	Y	Y
9	**Griffith**	N	N	N	Y	N	Y
10	Wexton	Y	Y	Y	N	Y	Y
11	Connolly	Y	Y	Y	N	Y	Y
WASHINGTON							
1	DelBene	Y	Y	Y	N	Y	N
2	Larsen	Y	Y	Y	N	Y	Y
3	**Herrera Beutler**	N	N	N	N	N	Y
4	**Newhouse**	N	N	N	Y	N	Y
5	**McMorris Rodgers**	N	N	N	Y	N	Y
6	Kilmer	Y	Y	Y	N	Y	Y
7	Jayapal	Y	Y	Y	N	Y	Y
8	Schrier	Y	Y	Y	N	Y	Y
9	Smith Adam	Y	Y	Y	N	Y	Y
10	Heck	Y	Y	Y	N	Y	Y
WEST VIRGINIA							
1	**McKinley**	N	N	N	Y	N	Y
2	**Mooney**	Y	Y	N	Y	N	N
3	**Miller**	N	N	N	Y	N	Y
WISCONSIN							
1	**Steil**	N	N	N	Y	N	Y
2	Pocan	Y	Y	Y	N	Y	Y
3	Kind	Y	Y	Y	N	Y	Y
4	Moore	Y	Y	Y	N	Y	Y
5	**Sensenbrenner**	N	N	N	Y	N	Y
6	**Grothman**	N	N	N	Y	N	N
7	**Duffy**	N	N	N	Y	N	Y
8	**Gallagher**	Y	Y	N	N	N	Y
WYOMING							
AL	**Cheney**	N	N	N	Y	N	Y
DELEGATES							
	Radewagen (A.S.)				Y	N	
	Norton (D.C.)				N	Y	
	San Nicolas (Guam)				?	?	
	Sablan (N. Marianas)				N	Y	
	González-Colón (P.R.)				Y	N	
	Plaskett (V.I.)				N	Y	

493. HR748. Health Plan Tax Repeal - Passage. Neal, D-Mass., motion to suspend the rules and pass the bill, that would repeal the 40 percent excise tax, known as the "Cadillac tax" on the incremental costs of employer-sponsored health care plans above certain thresholds. The tax was imposed by the 2010 health care overhaul and set to take effect at the beginning of 2022. Passed 419-6: R 189-2; D 230-3; I 0-1. *Note: A two-thirds majority of those present and voting (284 in this case) is required for passage under suspension of the rules.* July 17, 2019.

494. HR582. Minimum Wage Increase - GAO Report. O'Halleran, D-Ariz., amendment that would require the Government Accountability Office to submit a report to Congress, prior to the effective date of the third annual wage increase, that identifies and analyzes the effects of the first two wage increases on the economy and workforce, nationally and regionally. It would require Congress to assess and make recommendations to address the findings of the report, including with regard to the implementation of subsequent wage increases. Adopted in Committee of the Whole 248-181: R 15-180; D 233-0; I 0-1. July 18, 2019.

495. HR582. Minimum Wage Increase - Recommit. Meuser, R-Pa., motion to recommit the bill to the House Education and Labor Committee with instructions to report it back immediately with an amendment that would exempt from the bill's requirements businesses that employ fewer than 10 individuals or that have an annual gross volume of sales and business of less than $1 million. Motion rejected 210-218: R 195-0; D 14-218; I 1-0. July 18, 2019.

496. HR582. Minimum Wage Increase - Passage. Passage of the bill, as amended, that would increase the federal minimum wage to $8.40 per hour on the first day of the third month after enactment and would incrementally increase it annually to reach $15 per hour six years after the effective date. On the seventh year, the bill would require the Labor Department to determine the minimum wage based on increases in the median hourly wage of all employees. The bill would also increase the minimum wage for tipped employees, teens, and individuals with disabilities, with incremental increases over five years until each of these rates reaches $15 per hour, at which point the separate minimum wages would be repealed. Passed 231-199: R 3-192; D 228-6; I 0-1. *Note: A "nay" was a vote in support of the president's position.* July 18, 2019.

497. HRES246. Opposing BDS Movement - Passage. Agreeing to the resolution that would state that the House of Representatives opposes all efforts to "delegitimize" Israel, including the global boycott, divestment, and sanctions movement targeting Israel. It would express support for a negotiated solution to the Israeli-Palestinian conflict, state that the BDS movement undermines the possibility for such a solution, and encourage ongoing U.S.-Israel cooperation on civilian science and technology initiatives to counter the effects of the movement. Motion agreed to 398-17: R 189-1; D 209-16. *Note: A two-thirds majority of those present and voting (277 in this case) is required for passage under suspension of the rules.* July 23, 2019.

498. HR549. Venezuela TPS - Passage. Mucarsel-Powell, D-Fla., motion to suspend the rules and pass the bill, as amended, that would grant temporary protected status to Venezuelans in the U.S. for an initial 18-month period. To receive TPS status, qualifying individuals must be continuously present in the U.S. after enactment, be legally admissible to the U.S. as immigrants, and register with the Homeland Security Department. It would require DHS to give prior consent for individuals covered under TPS to travel abroad in emergencies or extenuating circumstances. Motion rejected 268-154: R 37-154; D 230-0; I 1-0. *Note: A two-thirds majority of those present and voting (282 in this case) is required for passage under suspension of the rules.* July 23, 2019.

		493	494	495	496	497	498
ALABAMA							
1	**Byrne**	Y	N	Y	N	Y	N
2	**Roby**	Y	N	Y	N	?	?
3	**Rogers, M.**	Y	N	Y	N	Y	N
4	**Aderholt**	Y	N	Y	N	Y	N
5	**Brooks, M.**	Y	N	Y	N	Y	N
6	**Palmer**	Y	N	Y	N	Y	N
7	Sewell	Y	Y	N	Y	Y	Y
ALASKA							
AL	**Young**	Y	N	Y	N	Y	Y
ARIZONA							
1	O'Halleran	Y	Y	N	Y	Y	Y
2	Kirkpatrick	Y	Y	N	Y	Y	Y
3	Grijalva	Y	Y	N	Y	N	Y
4	Gosar	Y	N	Y	N	Y	N
5	Biggs	Y	N	Y	N	Y	N
6	Schweikert	Y	N	Y	N	Y	N
7	Gallego	Y	Y	N	Y	Y	Y
8	Lesko	Y	N	Y	N	Y	N
9	Stanton	Y	Y	N	Y	Y	Y
ARKANSAS							
1	**Crawford**	Y	N	Y	N	Y	N
2	**Hill, F.**	Y	N	Y	N	Y	N
3	**Womack**	Y	N	Y	N	Y	N
4	**Westerman**	Y	N	Y	N	Y	N
CALIFORNIA							
1	**LaMalfa**	Y	N	Y	N	Y	N
2	Huffman	Y	Y	N	Y	P	Y
3	Garamendi	Y	Y	N	Y	Y	Y
4	**McClintock**	Y	N	Y	N	Y	N
5	Thompson, M.	Y	Y	N	Y	Y	Y
6	Matsui	Y	Y	N	Y	Y	Y
7	Bera	Y	Y	N	Y	Y	Y
8	**Cook**	Y	N	Y	N	Y	N
9	McNerney	Y	Y	N	Y	Y	Y
10	Harder	Y	Y	N	Y	Y	Y
11	DeSaulnier	Y	Y	N	Y	Y	Y
12	Pelosi	Y				Y	
13	Lee B.	Y	Y	N	Y	N	Y
14	Speier	Y	Y	N	Y	Y	Y
15	Swalwell	Y	Y	N	Y	Y	Y
16	Costa	Y	Y	N	Y	Y	Y
17	Khanna	Y	Y	N	Y	Y	Y
18	Eshoo	Y	Y	N	Y	Y	Y
19	Lofgren	Y	Y	N	Y	Y	Y
20	Panetta	Y	Y	N	Y	Y	Y
21	Cox	Y	Y	N	Y	Y	Y
22	**Nunes**	Y	N	Y	N	Y	N
23	**McCarthy**	Y	N	Y	N	Y	N
24	Carbajal	Y	Y	N	Y	Y	Y
25	Hill, K.	Y	Y	N	Y	Y	Y
26	Brownley	Y	Y	N	Y	Y	Y
27	Chu	Y	Y	N	Y	Y	Y
28	Schiff	Y	Y	N	Y	Y	Y
29	Cárdenas	Y	Y	N	Y	Y	Y
30	Sherman	Y	Y	N	Y	Y	Y
31	Aguilar	Y	Y	N	Y	Y	Y
32	Napolitano	Y	Y	N	Y	Y	Y
33	Lieu	Y	Y	N	Y	Y	Y
34	Gomez	Y	Y	N	Y	Y	Y
35	Torres	Y	Y	N	Y	Y	Y
36	Ruiz	Y	Y	N	Y	Y	Y
37	Bass	Y	Y	N	Y	P	Y
38	Sánchez	Y	Y	N	Y	Y	Y
39	Cisneros	Y	Y	N	Y	Y	Y
40	Roybal-Allard	Y	Y	N	Y	Y	Y
41	Takano	Y	Y	N	Y	Y	Y
42	**Calvert**	Y	N	Y	N	Y	N
43	Waters	Y	Y	N	Y	Y	Y
44	Barragán	Y	Y	N	Y	Y	Y
45	Porter	Y	Y	N	Y	Y	Y
46	Correa	Y	Y	N	Y	Y	Y
47	Lowenthal	Y	Y	N	Y	Y	Y
48	Rouda	Y	Y	N	Y	Y	Y
49	Levin	Y	Y	N	Y	Y	Y
50	**Hunter**	Y	N	Y	N	Y	N
51	Vargas	Y	Y	N	Y	Y	Y
52	Peters	N	Y	N	Y	Y	Y
53	Davis, S.	Y	Y	N	Y	Y	Y
COLORADO							
1	DeGette	Y	Y	N	Y	Y	Y
2	Neguse	Y	Y	N	Y	Y	Y
3	**Tipton**	Y	N	Y	N	Y	N
4	**Buck**	Y	N	Y	N	Y	N
5	**Lamborn**	Y	N	Y	N	Y	N
6	Crow	Y	Y	N	Y	Y	Y
7	Perlmutter	Y	Y	N	Y	Y	Y
CONNECTICUT							
1	Larson	Y	Y	N	Y	Y	Y
2	Courtney	Y	Y	N	Y	Y	Y
3	DeLauro	Y	Y	N	Y	Y	Y
4	Himes	Y	Y	N	Y	Y	Y
5	Hayes	Y	Y	N	Y	Y	Y
DELAWARE							
AL	Blunt Rochester	Y	Y	N	Y	Y	Y
FLORIDA							
1	**Gaetz**	Y	N	Y	N	Y	N
2	**Dunn**	Y	N	Y	N	Y	N
3	**Yoho**	Y	N	Y	N	Y	N
4	**Rutherford**	Y	N	Y	N	Y	N
5	Lawson	Y	Y	N	Y	Y	Y
6	**Waltz**	Y	N	Y	N	Y	Y
7	Murphy	Y	Y	N	Y	Y	Y
8	**Posey**	Y	N	Y	N	Y	N
9	Soto	Y	Y	N	Y	Y	Y
10	Demings	Y	Y	N	Y	Y	Y
11	**Webster**	Y	N	Y	N	Y	N
12	**Bilirakis**	?	N	Y	N	Y	Y
13	Crist	Y	Y	N	Y	Y	Y
14	Castor	Y	Y	N	Y	Y	Y
15	**Spano**	Y	N	Y	N	Y	N
16	**Buchanan**	Y	N	Y	N	Y	N
17	**Steube**	Y	N	Y	N	Y	N
18	**Mast**	Y	Y	Y	Y	Y	Y
19	**Rooney**	Y	Y	Y	Y	Y	Y
20	Hastings	Y	Y	Y	Y	Y	Y
21	Frankel	Y	Y	N	Y	Y	Y
22	Deutch	Y	Y	N	Y	Y	Y
23	Wasserman Schultz	Y	Y	N	Y	Y	Y
24	Wilson, F.	Y	Y	N	Y	?	?
25	**Diaz-Balart**	Y	Y	Y	N	Y	Y
26	Mucarsel-Powell	Y	Y	N	Y	Y	Y
27	Shalala	Y	Y	N	Y	Y	Y
GEORGIA							
1	**Carter, E.L.**	Y	N	Y	N	Y	N
2	Bishop, S.	Y	Y	N	Y	Y	Y
3	**Ferguson**	Y	N	Y	N	Y	N
4	Johnson, H.	Y	Y	N	Y	P	Y
5	Lewis John	Y	Y	N	Y	Y	Y
6	McBath	Y	Y	N	Y	Y	Y
7	**Woodall**	Y	N	Y	N	Y	N
8	**Scott, A.**	Y	N	Y	N	Y	N
9	**Collins, D.**	Y	N	Y	N	Y	N
10	**Hice**	Y	N	Y	N	Y	N
11	**Loudermilk**	Y	N	Y	N	Y	N
12	**Allen**	Y	N	Y	N	Y	N
13	Scott, D.	Y	Y	N	Y	Y	Y
14	**Graves, T.**	Y	N	Y	N	Y	N
HAWAII							
1	Case	Y	Y	N	Y	Y	Y
2	Gabbard	?	?	?	?	?	Y
IDAHO							
1	**Fulcher**	Y	N	Y	N	Y	N
2	**Simpson**	Y	N	Y	N	Y	N
ILLINOIS							
1	Rush	Y	Y	N	Y	N	Y
2	Kelly, R.	Y	Y	N	Y	Y	Y
3	Lipinski	Y	Y	N	Y	N	Y
4	García, J.	Y	Y	N	Y	N	Y
5	Quigley	Y	Y	N	Y	Y	Y
6	Casten	Y	Y	N	Y	Y	Y
7	Davis, D.	Y	Y	N	Y	P	Y
8	Krishnamoorthi	Y	Y	N	Y	Y	Y
9	Schakowsky	Y	Y	N	Y	Y	Y
10	Schneider	Y	Y	N	Y	Y	Y
11	Foster	Y	Y	N	Y	Y	Y

KEY:	**Republicans**	Democrats	*Independents*

Y Voted for (yea)	**N** Voted against (nay)	**P** Voted "present"
+ Announced for	**−** Announced against	**?** Did not vote or otherwise make position known
# Paired for	**X** Paired against	

	493	494	495	496	497	498
12 **Bost**	Y	Y	Y	N	Y	Y
13 **Davis, R.**	Y	Y	Y	N	Y	Y
14 Underwood	Y	Y	N	Y	Y	Y
15 **Shimkus**	Y	N	Y	N	Y	N
16 **Kinzinger**	Y	Y	Y	N	Y	Y
17 Bustos	Y	Y	N	Y	Y	Y
18 **LaHood**	Y	N	Y	N	Y	N
INDIANA						
1 Visclosky	Y	Y	N	Y	Y	Y
2 **Walorski**	Y	N	Y	N	Y	N
3 **Banks**	Y	N	Y	N	Y	N
4 **Baird**	Y	N	Y	N	Y	N
5 **Brooks, S.**	Y	N	Y	N	Y	N
6 **Pence**	Y	N	Y	N	Y	Y
7 Carson	Y	Y	N	Y	N	Y
8 **Bucshon**	Y	N	Y	N	Y	N
9 **Hollingsworth**	Y	N	Y	N	Y	N
IOWA						
1 Finkenauer	Y	Y	N	Y	Y	Y
2 Loebsack	Y	Y	N	Y	Y	Y
3 Axne	Y	Y	N	Y	Y	Y
4 **King, S.**	Y	N	Y	N	Y	N
KANSAS						
1 **Marshall**	Y	N	Y	N	Y	N
2 **Watkins**	Y	N	Y	N	Y	N
3 Davids	Y	Y	Y	Y	Y	Y
4 **Estes**	Y	N	Y	N	Y	N
KENTUCKY						
1 **Comer**	Y	N	Y	N	Y	N
2 **Guthrie**	Y	N	Y	N	Y	N
3 Yarmuth	Y	Y	N	Y	Y	Y
4 **Massie**	Y	N	Y	N	N	N
5 **Rogers, H.**	Y	N	Y	N	Y	N
6 **Barr**	Y	N	Y	N	Y	N
LOUISIANA						
1 **Scalise**	Y	N	Y	N	Y	N
2 Richmond	Y	Y	N	Y	+	+
3 **Higgins, C.**	Y	N	Y	N	Y	Y
4 **Johnson, M.**	Y	N	Y	N	Y	N
5 **Abraham**	?	?	?	?	?	?
6 **Graves, G.**	Y	N	Y	N	Y	N
MAINE						
1 Pingree	Y	Y	N	Y	N	Y
2 Golden	Y	Y	N	Y	Y	Y
MARYLAND						
1 **Harris**	N	N	Y	N	Y	N
2 Ruppersberger	Y	Y	N	Y	Y	Y
3 Sarbanes	Y	Y	N	Y	Y	Y
4 Brown, A.	Y	Y	N	Y	Y	Y
5 Hoyer	Y	Y	N	Y	Y	Y
6 Trone	Y	Y	N	Y	Y	Y
7 Cummings	Y	Y	N	Y	Y	Y
8 Raskin						
MASSACHUSETTS	Y	Y	N	Y	Y	Y
1 Neal						
2 McGovern	Y	Y	N	Y	Y	Y
3 Trahan	Y	Y	N	Y	Y	Y
4 Kennedy	Y	Y	N	Y	Y	Y
5 Clark	Y	Y	N	Y	Y	Y
6 Moulton	Y	Y	N	Y	Y	Y
7 Pressley	Y	Y	N	Y	?	?
8 Lynch	Y	Y	N	Y	Y	Y
9 Keating	Y	Y	N	Y	Y	Y
MICHIGAN	Y	Y	N	Y	Y	Y
1 **Bergman**						
2 **Huizenga**	Y	N	Y	N	Y	N
3 *Amash*	Y	N	Y	N	Y	N
4 **Moolenaar**	N	N	Y	N	P	Y
5 Kildee	Y	N	Y	N	Y	N
6 **Upton**	Y	Y	N	Y	Y	Y
7 **Walberg**	Y	Y	Y	N	Y	N
8 Slotkin	Y	N	Y	N	Y	N
9 Levin	Y	Y	Y	Y	Y	Y
10 **Mitchell**	Y	Y	N	Y	Y	Y
11 Stevens	Y	N	Y	N	Y	N
12 Dingell	Y	Y	N	Y	Y	Y
13 Tlaib	Y	Y	N	Y	N	Y
14 Lawrence	Y	Y	N	Y	N	Y
MINNESOTA	Y	Y	N	Y	Y	Y
1 **Hagedorn**						
2 Craig	Y	N	Y	N	Y	N
3 Phillips	Y	Y	N	Y	Y	Y
4 McCollum	Y	Y	N	Y	Y	Y
5 Omar	Y	Y	N	Y	N	Y

	493	494	495	496	497	498
6 **Emmer**	Y	Y	N	Y	N	Y
7 Peterson	Y	N	Y	N	Y	N
8 Stauber	Y	Y	Y	Y	Y	Y
MISSISSIPPI	Y	N	Y	N	Y	N
1 **Kelly, T.**						
2 Thompson, B.	Y	N	Y	N	Y	N
3 **Guest**	Y	Y	N	Y	Y	Y
4 **Palazzo**	Y	N	Y	N	Y	N
MISSOURI	Y	N	Y	N	Y	N
1 Clay						
2 **Wagner**	Y	Y	N	Y	Y	Y
3 **Luetkemeyer**	Y	N	Y	N	Y	N
4 **Hartzler**	Y	N	Y	N	Y	N
5 Cleaver	Y	Y	Y	N	Y	Y
6 **Graves, S.**	Y	Y	N	Y	Y	Y
7 **Long**	Y	N	Y	N	?	?
8 **Smith, J.**	Y	N	Y	N	Y	N
MONTANA	Y	N	Y	N	Y	N
AL **Gianforte**						
NEBRASKA	Y	N	Y	N	?	?
1 **Fortenberry**						
2 **Bacon**	Y	?	?	?	Y	Y
3 **Smith, Adrian**	Y	N	Y	N	Y	Y
NEVADA	Y	N	Y	N	Y	N
1 Titus						
2 **Amodei**	Y	Y	N	Y	Y	Y
3 Lee	Y	N	Y	N	Y	N
4 Horsford	Y	Y	N	Y	Y	Y
NEW HAMPSHIRE	Y	Y	N	Y	Y	Y
1 Pappas						
2 Kuster	Y	Y	N	Y	Y	Y
NEW JERSEY	Y	Y	N	Y	Y	Y
1 Norcross						
2 Van Drew	Y	Y	N	Y	Y	Y
3 Kim	Y	Y	Y	Y	Y	Y
4 **Smith, C.**	Y	Y	N	Y	Y	Y
5 Gottheimer	Y	Y	Y	Y	Y	Y
6 Pallone	Y	Y	Y	Y	Y	Y
7 Malinowski	Y	Y	N	Y	Y	Y
8 Sires	Y	Y	N	Y	Y	Y
9 Pascrell	Y	Y	N	Y	Y	Y
10 Payne	Y	Y	N	Y	Y	Y
11 Sherrill	Y	Y	N	Y	Y	Y
12 Watson Coleman	Y	Y	N	Y	Y	Y
NEW MEXICO	Y	Y	N	Y	N	Y
1 Haaland						
2 Torres Small	+	Y	N	Y	Y	Y
3 Luján	Y	Y	N	N	Y	Y
NEW YORK	Y	Y	N	Y	Y	Y
1 **Zeldin**						
2 **King, P.**	Y	N	Y	N	Y	N
3 Suozzi	Y	Y	Y	N	Y	Y
4 Rice, K.	Y	Y	N	Y	Y	Y
5 Meeks	Y	Y	N	Y	Y	Y
6 Meng	Y	Y	N	Y	Y	Y
7 Velázquez	Y	Y	N	Y	Y	Y
8 Jeffries	Y	Y	N	Y	Y	Y
9 Clarke	Y	Y	N	Y	Y	Y
10 Nadler	Y	Y	N	Y	Y	Y
11 Rose	Y	Y	N	Y	Y	Y
12 Maloney, C.	Y	Y	N	Y	Y	Y
13 Espaillat	Y	Y	N	Y	Y	Y
14 Ocasio-Cortez	Y	Y	N	Y	Y	Y
15 Serrano	Y	Y	N	Y	N	Y
16 Engel	Y	Y	N	Y	Y	Y
17 Lowey	Y	Y	N	Y	Y	Y
18 Maloney, S.P.	Y	Y	N	Y	Y	Y
19 Delgado	Y	Y	N	Y	Y	Y
20 Tonko	Y	Y	N	Y	Y	Y
21 **Stefanik**	Y	Y	N	Y	Y	Y
22 Brindisi	Y	Y	Y	N	Y	Y
23 **Reed**	Y	Y	Y	N	Y	Y
24 **Katko**	Y	N	Y	N	Y	Y
25 Morelle	Y	Y	Y	N	Y	Y
26 Higgins, B.	Y	Y	N	Y	Y	Y
27 **Collins, C.**	Y	Y	N	Y	Y	Y
NORTH CAROLINA	Y	N	Y	N	Y	N
1 Butterfield						
2 **Holding**	Y	Y	N	Y	Y	Y
3 **Jones***	Y	N	Y	N	Y	N
4 Price						
5 **Foxx**	Y	Y	N	Y	Y	Y
6 **Walker**	Y	N	Y	N	Y	N
7 **Rouzer**	?	N	Y	N	Y	N

	493	494	495	496	497	498
8 **Hudson**	Y	N	Y	N	Y	N
9 vacant	?	N	Y	N	Y	N
10 **McHenry**	Y	N	Y	N	Y	N
11 **Meadows**	?	N	Y	N	Y	N
12 Adams	Y	Y	N	Y	Y	Y
13 **Budd**	Y	N	Y	N	Y	N
NORTH DAKOTA						
AL **Armstrong**	?	N	Y	N	+	N
OHIO						
1 **Chabot**	Y	N	Y	N	Y	N
2 **Wenstrup**	Y	N	Y	N	Y	N
3 Beatty	Y	Y	N	Y	Y	Y
4 **Jordan**	Y	N	Y	N	Y	N
5 **Latta**	Y	N	Y	N	Y	N
6 **Johnson, B.**	Y	N	Y	N	Y	N
7 **Gibbs**	Y	N	Y	N	Y	N
8 **Davidson**	Y	N	Y	N	Y	N
9 Kaptur	Y	Y	N	Y	Y	Y
10 **Turner**	Y	N	Y	N	Y	N
11 Fudge	Y	Y	N	Y	Y	Y
12 **Balderson**	Y	N	Y	N	Y	N
13 Ryan	Y	Y	N	Y	?	?
14 **Joyce**	Y	N	Y	N	Y	N
15 **Stivers**	Y	N	Y	N	Y	Y
16 **Gonzalez**	Y	N	Y	N	Y	Y
OKLAHOMA						
1 **Hern**	Y	N	Y	N	Y	N
2 **Mullin**	Y	N	Y	N	Y	N
3 **Lucas**	Y	N	Y	N	Y	N
4 **Cole**	Y	N	Y	N	Y	Y
5 Horn	Y	Y	Y	N	Y	Y
OREGON						
1 Bonamici	Y	Y	N	Y	Y	Y
2 **Walden**	Y	N	Y	N	Y	N
3 Blumenauer	Y	Y	N	Y	N	Y
4 DeFazio	Y	Y	N	Y	Y	Y
5 Schrader	Y	Y	Y	N	Y	Y
PENNSYLVANIA						
1 **Fitzpatrick**	Y	Y	Y	Y	Y	Y
2 Boyle	Y	Y	N	Y	Y	Y
3 Evans	Y	Y	N	Y	Y	Y
4 Dean	Y	Y	N	Y	Y	Y
5 Scanlon	Y	Y	N	Y	Y	Y
6 Houlahan	Y	Y	N	Y	Y	Y
7 Wild	Y	Y	Y	Y	Y	Y
8 Cartwright	Y	Y	N	Y	Y	Y
9 **Meuser**	Y	N	Y	N	Y	N
10 **Perry**	Y	N	Y	N	Y	N
11 **Smucker**	Y	N	Y	N	Y	N
12 **Marino***						
13 **Joyce**	Y	N	Y	N	Y	N
14 **Reschenthaler**	Y	N	Y	N	Y	N
15 **Thompson, G.**	Y	N	Y	N	Y	Y
16 **Kelly, M.**	Y	N	Y	N	Y	N
17 Lamb	Y	Y	N	Y	Y	Y
18 Doyle	Y	Y	N	Y	Y	Y
RHODE ISLAND						
1 Cicilline	Y	Y	N	Y	Y	Y
2 Langevin	Y	Y	N	Y	Y	Y
SOUTH CAROLINA						
1 Cunningham	Y	Y	Y	N	Y	Y
2 **Wilson, J.**	Y	N	Y	N	Y	N
3 **Duncan**	Y	N	Y	N	Y	N
4 **Timmons**	Y	N	Y	N	Y	N
5 **Norman**	Y	N	Y	N	Y	N
6 Clyburn	Y	Y	N	Y	Y	Y
7 **Rice, T.**	Y	N	Y	N	Y	N
SOUTH DAKOTA						
AL **Johnson**	Y	N	Y	N	Y	N
TENNESSEE						
1 **Roe**	Y	N	Y	N	Y	N
2 **Burchett**	Y	N	Y	N	Y	N
3 **Fleischmann**	Y	N	Y	N	Y	N
4 **DesJarlais**	Y	N	Y	N	Y	N
5 Cooper	N	Y	N	Y	Y	Y
6 **Rose**	Y	N	Y	N	Y	N
7 **Green**	Y	N	Y	N	Y	N
8 **Kustoff**	Y	N	Y	N	Y	N
9 Cohen	Y	Y	N	Y	Y	Y
TEXAS						
1 **Gohmert**	Y	N	Y	N	?	?
2 **Crenshaw**	Y	N	Y	N	Y	Y
3 **Taylor**	Y	N	Y	N	Y	N
4 **Ratcliffe**	Y	N	Y	N	Y	N

	493	494	495	496	497	498
5 **Gooden**	Y	N	Y	N	Y	N
6 **Wright**	Y	N	Y	N	Y	N
7 Fletcher	Y	Y	N	Y	Y	Y
8 **Brady**	Y	N	Y	N	Y	N
9 Green, A.	Y	Y	-	Y	Y	Y
10 **McCaul**	Y	N	Y	N	Y	Y
11 **Conaway**	Y	N	Y	N	Y	N
12 **Granger**	Y	N	Y	N	Y	N
13 **Thornberry**	Y	N	Y	N	Y	N
14 **Weber**	Y	N	Y	N	Y	N
15 Gonzalez	Y	Y	N	Y	?	Y
16 Escobar	Y	Y	N	Y	Y	Y
17 **Flores**	Y	N	Y	N	Y	N
18 Jackson Lee	Y	Y	N	Y	Y	Y
19 **Arrington**	Y	N	Y	N	Y	N
20 Castro	Y	Y	N	Y	Y	Y
21 **Roy**	N	N	Y	N	Y	N
22 **Olson**	Y	N	Y	N	Y	N
23 **Hurd**	Y	N	Y	N	Y	Y
24 **Marchant**	Y	N	Y	N	Y	N
25 **Williams**	Y	N	Y	N	Y	N
26 **Burgess**	Y	N	Y	N	Y	N
27 **Cloud**	Y	N	Y	N	Y	N
28 Cuellar	Y	Y	Y	Y	Y	Y
29 Garcia, S.	Y	Y	N	Y	Y	Y
30 Johnson, E.B.	Y	Y	N	Y	Y	Y
31 **Carter, J.**	Y	N	Y	N	Y	N
32 Allred	Y	Y	N	Y	Y	Y
33 Veasey	Y	Y	N	Y	Y	Y
34 Vela	Y	Y	N	Y	Y	Y
35 Doggett	Y	Y	N	Y	Y	Y
36 **Babin**	Y	N	Y	N	Y	N
UTAH						
1 **Bishop, R.**	Y	N	Y	N	Y	N
2 **Stewart**	Y	N	Y	N	?	?
3 **Curtis**	Y	N	Y	N	Y	Y
4 McAdams	Y	Y	Y	N	Y	Y
VERMONT						
AL Welch	Y	Y	N	Y	Y	Y
VIRGINIA						
1 **Wittman**	Y	N	Y	N	Y	N
2 Luria	Y	Y	N	Y	Y	Y
3 Scott, R.	Y	Y	N	Y	Y	Y
4 McEachin	Y	Y	N	Y	Y	Y
5 **Riggleman**	Y	N	Y	N	Y	N
6 **Cline**	Y	N	Y	N	Y	N
7 Spanberger	Y	Y	Y	Y	Y	Y
8 Beyer	Y	Y	N	Y	Y	Y
9 **Griffith**	Y	N	Y	N	Y	N
10 Wexton	Y	Y	N	Y	Y	Y
11 Connolly	Y	Y	N	Y	Y	Y
WASHINGTON						
1 DelBene	Y	Y	N	Y	Y	Y
2 Larsen	Y	Y	N	Y	Y	Y
3 **Herrera Beutler**	Y	Y	Y	N	Y	Y
4 **Newhouse**	Y	N	Y	N	Y	N
5 **McMorris Rodgers**	Y	N	Y	N	Y	Y
6 Kilmer	Y	Y	N	Y	Y	Y
7 Jayapal	Y	Y	N	Y	N	Y
8 Schrier	Y	Y	N	Y	Y	Y
9 Smith Adam	Y	Y	N	Y	Y	Y
10 Heck	Y	Y	N	Y	Y	Y
WEST VIRGINIA						
1 **McKinley**	Y	N	Y	N	Y	N
2 **Mooney**	Y	N	Y	N	Y	N
3 **Miller**	Y	N	Y	N	Y	N
WISCONSIN						
1 **Steil**	Y	Y	Y	N	Y	Y
2 Pocan	Y	Y	N	Y	N	Y
3 Kind	N	Y	N	Y	Y	Y
4 Moore	Y	Y	N	Y	N	Y
5 **Sensenbrenner**	Y	N	Y	N	Y	N
6 **Grothman**	Y	Y	Y	N	Y	N
7 **Duffy**	Y	N	Y	N	Y	Y
8 **Gallagher**	Y	N	Y	N	Y	Y
WYOMING						
AL **Cheney**	Y	N	Y	N	Y	N
DELEGATES						
Radewagen (A.S.)						
Norton (D.C.)						
San Nicolas (Guam)						
Sablan (N. Marianas)						
González-Colón (P.R.)						
Plaskett (V.I.)						

499. HR3304. Military Bankruptcy Test Exemption - Passage. Cicilline, D-R.I., motion to suspend the rules and pass the bill, as amended, that would extend through 2023 a statutory exemption from Chapter 7 bankruptcy means testing for qualifying reservists and National Guard members who have served on active duty for at least 90 days after Sept. 11, 2001. Motion agreed to 417-1: R 190-0; D 227-0; I 0-1. *Note: A two-thirds majority of those present and voting (279 in this case) is required for passage under suspension of the rules.* July 23, 2019.

500. HRES507, HR397, HR3239. Pensions, Border Facility Standards, Congressional Subpoenas - Previous Question. Adoption of the rule (H Res 509) that would provide for House floor consideration of the Rehabilitation for Multiemployer Pensions Act (HR 397), making in order consideration of one amendment to the bill, and would provide for House floor consideration of the Humanitarian Standards for Individuals in Customs and Border Protection Custody Act (HR 3239), providing for automatic adoption of a manager's amendment to the bill and making in order consideration of two additional amendments to the bill. It would provide for automatic agreement in the House to a resolution (H Res 507) that would ratify and affirm all current and future investigations and subpoenas issued by House committees related or issued to President Donald Trump, his family and businesses, the White House, former and current White House officials, and any entities seeking information related to such individuals and entities. It would also provide for standard floor proceedings from July 29 through Sept. 6, 2019, during the planned Aug. recess. Motion agreed to 234-198: R 0-197; D 234-0; I 0-1. July 24, 2019.

501. HR3239, HR397, HRES507. Pensions, Border Facility Standards, Congressional Subpoenas - Rule. Adoption of the rule (H Res 509) that would provide for House floor consideration of the Rehabilitation for Multiemployer Pensions Act (HR 397), making in order consideration of one amendment to the bill, and would provide for House floor consideration of the Humanitarian Standards for Individuals in Customs and Border Protection Custody Act (HR 3239), providing for automatic adoption of a manager's amendment to the bill and making in order consideration of two additional amendments to the bill. It would provide for automatic agreement in the House to a resolution (H Res 507) that would ratify and affirm all current and future investigations and subpoenas issued by House committees related or issued to President Donald Trump, his family and businesses, the White House, former and current White House officials, and any entities seeking information related to such individuals and entities. It would also provide for standard floor proceedings from July 29 through Sept. 6, 2019, during the planned Aug. recess. The Nadler, D-N.Y., manager's amendment to the Humanitarian Standards for Individuals in Customs and Border Protection Custody Act (HR 3239) would state that nothing in the bill may be construed to authorize U.S. Customs and Border Protection to detain individuals for longer than 72 hours; to contradict a March 2017 Homeland Security Department rule establishing standards to prevent, detect, and respond to sexual assault and abuse of individuals in CBP custody; or to contradict existing DHS practices related to hiring, background checks, and termination of employment for individuals convicted of crimes involving a child victim. Adopted 234-195: R 0-194; D 234-0; I 0-1. July 24, 2019.

502. HR3375. Robocall Enforcement and Deterrence - Passage. Pallone, D-N.J., motion to suspend the rules and pass the bill that would require the Federal Communications Commission to implement certain consumer regulations related to robocalls, or mass telephone calls placed by an automatic dialer, including regulations that would require phone companies to offer call authentication technology at no cost to consumers. It would extend, from two years to four years, the time period during which the FCC and law enforcement agencies could prosecute illegal robocallers following the commission of such a crime. It would require the FCC to submit evidence of certain robocall violations to the Justice Department for potential criminal prosecution. It would require the FCC to work with federal and state law enforcement agencies and with foreign governments to address one-ring scams and incentivize phone companies to stop calls made to perpetrate one-ring scams. Motion agreed to 429-3: R 195-2; D 234-0; I 0-1. *Note: A two-thirds majority of those present and voting (288 in this case) is required for passage under suspension of the rules.* July 24, 2019.

503. HR397. Pension Plan Loans - Loan Interest Rates. Roe, R-Tenn., amendment that would require loans issued by the Treasury Department Pension Rehabilitation Administration established by the bill to have an interest rate of 5 percent for five years after being made and an interest of rate 9 percent thereafter. Rejected in Committee of the Whole 186-245: R 186-11; D 0-233; I 0-1. July 24, 2019.

504. HR397. Pension Plan Loans - Recommit. Mast, R-Fla., motion to recommit the bill to the Education and Labor Committee with instructions to report it back immediately with an amendment that would require, as a condition of receiving a Pension Rehabilitation Administration loan, that multiemployer defined benefit pension plans do not knowingly engage in commerce- or investment-related boycotts, divestments, or sanctions intended to penalize, inflict economic harm on, or coerce political action by Israel. Motion rejected 200-232: R 197-0; D 3-231; I 0-1. July 24, 2019.

		499	500	501	502	503	504
ALABAMA							
1	**Byrne**	Y	N	N	Y	Y	Y
2	**Roby**	?	N	N	Y	Y	Y
3	**Rogers, M.**	Y	N	N	Y	Y	Y
4	**Aderholt**	Y	N	N	Y	Y	Y
5	**Brooks, M.**	Y	N	N	Y	Y	Y
6	**Palmer**	Y	N	N	Y	Y	Y
7	Sewell	Y	Y	Y	Y	N	N
ALASKA							
AL	**Young**	Y	N	N	Y	Y	Y
ARIZONA							
1	O'Halleran	Y	Y	Y	Y	N	N
2	Kirkpatrick	Y	Y	Y	Y	N	N
3	Grijalva	Y	Y	Y	Y	N	N
4	**Gosar**	Y	N	N	Y	Y	Y
5	**Biggs**	Y	N	N	N	Y	Y
6	**Schweikert**	Y	N	N	Y	Y	Y
7	Gallego	Y	Y	Y	Y	N	N
8	**Lesko**	Y	N	N	Y	Y	Y
9	Stanton	Y	Y	Y	Y	N	N
ARKANSAS							
1	**Crawford**	Y	N	N	Y	Y	Y
2	**Hill, F.**	Y	N	N	Y	Y	Y
3	**Womack**	Y	N	N	Y	Y	Y
4	**Westerman**	Y	N	-	Y	Y	Y
CALIFORNIA							
1	**LaMalfa**	Y	N	N	Y	Y	Y
2	Huffman	Y	Y	Y	Y	N	N
3	Garamendi	Y	Y	Y	Y	N	N
4	**McClintock**	Y	N	N	Y	Y	Y
5	Thompson, M.	Y	Y	Y	Y	N	N
6	Matsui	Y	Y	Y	Y	N	N
7	Bera	Y	Y	Y	Y	N	N
8	**Cook**	Y	N	N	Y	Y	Y
9	McNerney	?	Y	Y	Y	N	N
10	Harder	Y	Y	Y	Y	N	N
11	DeSaulnier	Y	Y	Y	Y	N	N
12	Pelosi						
13	Lee B.	Y	Y	Y	Y	N	N
14	Speier	Y	Y	Y	Y	N	N
15	Swalwell	Y	Y	Y	Y	N	N
16	Costa	Y	Y	Y	Y	N	N
17	Khanna	?	Y	Y	Y	N	N
18	Eshoo	Y	Y	Y	Y	N	N
19	Lofgren	Y	Y	Y	Y	N	N
20	Panetta	Y	Y	Y	Y	N	N
21	Cox	Y	Y	Y	Y	N	N
22	**Nunes**	Y	N	N	Y	Y	Y
23	**McCarthy**	Y	N	N	Y	Y	Y
24	Carbajal	Y	Y	Y	Y	N	N
25	Hill, K.	Y	Y	Y	Y	N	N
26	Brownley	Y	Y	Y	Y	N	N
27	Chu	Y	Y	Y	Y	N	N
28	Schiff	Y	Y	Y	Y	N	N
29	Cárdenas	Y	Y	Y	Y	N	N
30	Sherman	Y	Y	Y	Y	N	N
31	Aguilar	Y	Y	Y	Y	N	N
32	Napolitano	Y	Y	Y	Y	N	N
33	Lieu	Y	Y	Y	Y	N	N
34	Gomez	Y	Y	Y	Y	N	N
35	Torres	Y	Y	Y	Y	N	N
36	Ruiz	Y	Y	Y	Y	N	N
37	Bass	Y	Y	Y	Y	N	N
38	Sánchez	Y	Y	Y	Y	N	N
39	Cisneros	Y	Y	Y	Y	N	N
40	Roybal-Allard	Y	Y	Y	Y	N	N
41	Takano	Y	Y	Y	Y	N	N
42	**Calvert**	Y	N	N	Y	Y	Y
43	Waters	Y	Y	Y	Y	N	N
44	Barragán	Y	Y	Y	Y	N	N
45	Porter	Y	Y	Y	Y	N	N
46	Correa	Y	Y	Y	Y	N	N
47	Lowenthal	Y	Y	Y	Y	N	N
48	Rouda	Y	Y	Y	Y	N	N
49	Levin	Y	Y	Y	Y	N	N
50	**Hunter**	Y	N	N	Y	Y	Y
51	Vargas	Y	Y	Y	Y	N	N
52	Peters	Y	Y	Y	Y	N	N
53	Davis, S.	Y	Y	Y	Y	N	N
COLORADO							
1	DeGette	Y	Y	Y	Y	N	N
2	Neguse	Y	Y	Y	Y	N	N
3	**Tipton**	Y	N	N	Y	Y	Y
4	**Buck**	Y	N	N	Y	Y	Y
5	**Lamborn**	Y	N	N	Y	Y	Y
6	Crow	Y	Y	Y	Y	N	N
7	Perlmutter	Y	Y	Y	Y	N	N
CONNECTICUT							
1	Larson	Y	Y	Y	Y	N	N
2	Courtney	Y	Y	Y	Y	N	N
3	DeLauro	Y	Y	Y	Y	N	N
4	Himes	Y	Y	Y	Y	N	N
5	Hayes	Y	Y	Y	Y	N	N
DELAWARE							
AL	Blunt Rochester	Y	Y	Y	Y	N	N
FLORIDA							
1	**Gaetz**	Y	N	N	Y	Y	Y
2	**Dunn**	Y	N	N	Y	Y	Y
3	**Yoho**	Y	N	N	Y	Y	Y
4	**Rutherford**	Y	N	N	Y	Y	Y
5	Lawson	Y	Y	Y	Y	N	N
6	**Waltz**	Y	N	N	Y	Y	Y
7	Murphy	Y	Y	Y	Y	N	N
8	**Posey**	Y	N	N	Y	Y	Y
9	Soto	Y	Y	Y	Y	N	N
10	Demings	Y	Y	Y	Y	N	N
11	**Webster**	Y	N	N	Y	Y	Y
12	**Bilirakis**	Y	N	N	Y	Y	Y
13	Crist	Y	Y	Y	Y	N	N
14	Castor	Y	Y	Y	Y	N	N
15	**Spano**	Y	N	N	Y	Y	Y
16	**Buchanan**	Y	N	N	Y	Y	Y
17	**Steube**	Y	N	N	Y	Y	Y
18	**Mast**	Y	N	N	Y	Y	Y
19	**Rooney**	Y	N	N	Y	Y	Y
20	Hastings	Y	Y	Y	Y	N	N
21	Frankel	Y	Y	Y	Y	N	N
22	Deutch	Y	Y	Y	Y	N	N
23	Wasserman Schultz	Y	Y	Y	Y	N	N
24	Wilson, F.	?	Y	Y	Y	N	N
25	**Diaz-Balart**	Y	N	N	Y	Y	Y
26	Mucarsel-Powell	Y	Y	Y	Y	N	N
27	Shalala	Y	Y	Y	Y	N	N
GEORGIA							
1	**Carter, E.L.**	Y	N	N	Y	Y	Y
2	Bishop, S.	Y	Y	Y	Y	N	N
3	**Ferguson**	Y	N	N	Y	Y	Y
4	Johnson, H.	Y	Y	Y	Y	N	N
5	Lewis John	Y	Y	Y	Y	N	N
6	McBath	Y	Y	Y	Y	N	Y
7	**Woodall**	Y	N	N	Y	Y	Y
8	**Scott, A.**	Y	N	N	Y	Y	Y
9	**Collins, D.**	Y	N	N	Y	Y	Y
10	**Hice**	Y	N	N	Y	Y	Y
11	**Loudermilk**	Y	N	N	Y	Y	Y
12	**Allen**	Y	N	N	Y	Y	Y
13	Scott, D.	Y	Y	Y	Y	N	N
14	**Graves, T.**	Y	N	N	Y	Y	Y
HAWAII							
1	Case	Y	Y	Y	Y	N	N
2	Gabbard	Y	Y	Y	Y	N	N
IDAHO							
1	**Fulcher**	Y	N	N	Y	Y	Y
2	**Simpson**	Y	N	N	Y	Y	Y
ILLINOIS							
1	Rush	Y	Y	Y	Y	N	N
2	Kelly, R.	Y	Y	Y	Y	N	N
3	Lipinski	Y	Y	Y	Y	N	N
4	García, J.	Y	Y	Y	Y	N	N
5	Quigley	Y	Y	Y	Y	N	N
6	Casten	Y	Y	Y	Y	N	N
7	Davis, D.	Y	Y	Y	Y	N	N
8	Krishnamoorthi	Y	Y	Y	Y	N	N
9	Schakowsky	Y	Y	Y	Y	N	N
10	Schneider	Y	Y	Y	Y	N	N
11	Foster	Y	Y	Y	Y	N	N

KEY: **Republicans** Democrats *Independents*

Y Voted for (yea)	N Voted against (nay)	P Voted "present"
+ Announced for	- Announced against	? Did not vote or otherwise make position known
# Paired for	X Paired against	

		499	500	501	502	503	504
12	**Bost**	Y	N	N	Y	Y	Y
13	**Davis, R.**	Y	N	N	Y	Y	Y
14	Underwood	Y	Y	Y	Y	N	N
15	**Shimkus**	Y	N	N	Y	Y	Y
16	**Kinzinger**	Y	N	N	Y	Y	Y
17	Bustos	Y	Y	Y	Y	N	N
18	**LaHood**	Y	N	N	Y	Y	Y
INDIANA							
1	Visclosky	Y	Y	Y	Y	N	N
2	**Walorski**	Y	N	N	Y	Y	Y
3	**Banks**	Y	N	N	Y	Y	Y
4	**Baird**	Y	N	N	Y	Y	Y
5	**Brooks, S.**	Y	N	N	Y	Y	Y
6	**Pence**	Y	N	N	Y	Y	Y
7	Carson	?	Y	Y	Y	N	N
8	**Bucshon**	Y	N	N	Y	Y	Y
9	**Hollingsworth**	Y	N	N	Y	Y	Y
IOWA							
1	Finkenauer	Y	Y	Y	Y	N	N
2	Loebsack	Y	Y	Y	Y	N	N
3	Axne	Y	Y	Y	Y	N	N
4	**King, S.**	Y	N	N	Y	Y	Y
KANSAS							
1	**Marshall**	Y	N	N	Y	Y	Y
2	**Watkins**	Y	N	N	Y	Y	Y
3	Davids	Y	Y	Y	Y	N	N
4	**Estes**	Y	N	N	Y	Y	Y
KENTUCKY							
1	**Comer**	Y	N	N	Y	Y	Y
2	**Guthrie**	Y	N	N	Y	Y	Y
3	Yarmuth	Y	Y	Y	Y	N	N
4	**Massie**	Y	N	N	N	Y	Y
5	**Rogers, H.**	Y	N	N	Y	Y	Y
6	**Barr**	Y	N	N	Y	Y	Y
LOUISIANA							
1	**Scalise**	Y	N	N	Y	Y	Y
2	Richmond	+	Y	Y	Y	N	N
3	**Higgins, C.**	Y	N	N	Y	Y	Y
4	**Johnson, M.**	Y	N	N	Y	Y	Y
5	**Abraham**	?	N	N	Y	Y	Y
6	**Graves, G.**	Y	N	N	Y	Y	Y
MAINE							
1	Pingree	Y	Y	Y	Y	N	N
2	Golden	Y	Y	Y	Y	N	N
MARYLAND							
1	**Harris**	Y	N	N	Y	Y	Y
2	Ruppersberger	Y	Y	Y	Y	N	N
3	Sarbanes	Y	Y	Y	Y	N	N
4	Brown, A.	Y	Y	Y	Y	N	N
5	Hoyer	Y	Y	Y	Y	N	N
6	Trone	Y	Y	Y	Y	N	N
7	Cummings	Y	Y	Y	Y	N	N
8	Raskin						
MASSACHUSETTS		Y	Y	Y	Y	N	N
1	Neal						
2	McGovern	Y	Y	Y	Y	N	N
3	Trahan	Y	Y	Y	Y	N	N
4	Kennedy	Y	Y	Y	Y	N	N
5	Clark	Y	Y	Y	Y	N	N
6	Moulton	Y	Y	Y	Y	N	N
7	Pressley	?	Y	Y	Y	?	N
8	Lynch	Y	Y	Y	Y	N	N
9	Keating	Y	Y	Y	Y	N	N
MICHIGAN		Y	Y	Y	Y	N	N
1	**Bergman**						
2	**Huizenga**	Y	N	N	Y	Y	Y
3	*Amash*	Y	N	N	Y	Y	Y
4	**Moolenaar**	N	N	N	N	N	N
5	Kildee	Y	N	N	Y	Y	Y
6	**Upton**	Y	Y	Y	Y	N	N
7	**Walberg**	Y	N	N	Y	Y	Y
8	Slotkin	Y	N	N	Y	Y	Y
9	Levin	Y	Y	Y	Y	N	N
10	**Mitchell**	Y	Y	Y	Y	N	N
11	Stevens	Y	N	N	Y	Y	Y
12	Dingell	Y	Y	Y	Y	N	N
13	Tlaib	Y	Y	Y	Y	N	N
14	Lawrence	Y	Y	Y	Y	N	N
MINNESOTA		Y	Y	Y	Y	N	N
1	**Hagedorn**						
2	Craig	Y	N	N	Y	Y	Y
3	Phillips	Y	Y	Y	Y	N	N
4	McCollum	Y	Y	Y	Y	N	N
5	Omar	Y	Y	Y	Y	N	N

		499	500	501	502	503	504
6	**Emmer**	Y	Y	Y	Y	N	N
7	Peterson	Y	N	N	Y	Y	Y
8	**Stauber**	Y	Y	Y	Y	N	N
MISSISSIPPI		Y	N	N	Y	N	Y
1	**Kelly, T.**						
2	Thompson, B.	Y	N	N	Y	Y	Y
3	**Guest**	Y	Y	Y	Y	N	N
4	**Palazzo**	Y	N	N	Y	Y	Y
MISSOURI		Y	N	N	Y	Y	Y
1	Clay						
2	**Wagner**	Y	Y	Y	Y	N	N
3	**Luetkemeyer**	Y	N	N	Y	Y	Y
4	**Hartzler**	Y	N	N	Y	Y	Y
5	Cleaver	Y	N	N	Y	N	Y
6	**Graves, S.**	Y	Y	Y	Y	N	N
7	**Long**	?	N	N	Y	Y	Y
8	**Smith, J.**	Y	N	N	Y	Y	Y
MONTANA		Y	N	N	Y	Y	Y
AL	**Gianforte**						
NEBRASKA		?	N	N	Y	Y	Y
1	**Fortenberry**						
2	**Bacon**	Y	N	N	Y	N	Y
3	**Smith, Adrian**	Y	N	N	Y	Y	Y
NEVADA		Y	N	N	Y	Y	Y
1	Titus						
2	**Amodei**	Y	Y	Y	Y	N	N
3	Lee	Y	N	N	Y	Y	Y
4	Horsford	Y	Y	Y	Y	N	N
NEW HAMPSHIRE		Y	Y	Y	Y	N	N
1	Pappas						
2	Kuster	Y	Y	Y	Y	N	N
NEW JERSEY		Y	Y	Y	Y	N	N
1	Norcross						
2	Van Drew	Y	Y	Y	Y	N	N
3	Kim	Y	Y	Y	Y	N	Y
4	**Smith, C.**	Y	Y	Y	Y	N	N
5	Gottheimer	Y	N	N	Y	N	Y
6	Pallone	Y	Y	Y	Y	N	N
7	Malinowski	Y	Y	Y	Y	N	N
8	Sires	Y	Y	Y	Y	N	N
9	Pascrell	Y	Y	Y	Y	N	N
10	Payne	Y	Y	Y	Y	N	N
11	Sherrill	Y	Y	Y	Y	N	N
12	Watson Coleman	Y	Y	Y	Y	N	N
NEW MEXICO		Y	Y	Y	Y	N	N
1	Haaland						
2	Torres Small	Y	Y	Y	Y	N	N
3	Luján	Y	Y	Y	Y	N	N
NEW YORK		Y	Y	Y	Y	N	N
1	**Zeldin**						
2	**King, P.**	Y	N	N	Y	Y	Y
3	Suozzi	+	N	N	Y	N	Y
4	Rice, K.	Y	Y	Y	Y	N	N
5	Meeks	Y	Y	Y	Y	N	N
6	Meng	Y	Y	Y	Y	N	N
7	Velázquez	Y	Y	Y	Y	N	N
8	Jeffries	Y	Y	Y	Y	N	N
9	Clarke	Y	Y	Y	Y	N	N
10	Nadler	Y	Y	Y	Y	N	N
11	Rose	Y	Y	Y	Y	N	N
12	Maloney, C.	Y	Y	Y	Y	N	N
13	Espaillat	Y	Y	Y	Y	N	N
14	Ocasio-Cortez	Y	Y	Y	Y	N	N
15	Serrano	Y	Y	Y	Y	N	N
16	Engel	Y	Y	Y	Y	N	N
17	Lowey	Y	Y	Y	Y	N	N
18	Maloney, S.P.	Y	Y	Y	Y	N	N
19	Delgado	Y	Y	Y	Y	N	N
20	Tonko	Y	Y	Y	Y	N	N
21	**Stefanik**	Y	Y	Y	Y	N	N
22	Brindisi	Y	N	N	Y	N	Y
23	**Reed**	Y	Y	Y	Y	N	N
24	**Katko**	Y	N	N	Y	Y	Y
25	Morelle	Y	N	N	Y	N	Y
26	Higgins, B.	Y	Y	Y	Y	N	N
27	**Collins, C.**	Y	Y	Y	Y	N	N
NORTH CAROLINA		Y	N	N	Y	Y	Y
1	Butterfield						
2	**Holding**	Y	Y	Y	Y	N	N
3	**Jones***	Y	N	N	Y	Y	Y
4	Price						
5	**Foxx**	Y	Y	Y	Y	N	N
6	**Walker**	Y	N	N	Y	Y	Y
7	**Rouzer**	Y	N	N	Y	Y	Y

		499	500	501	502	503	504
8	**Hudson**	Y	N	N	Y	Y	Y
9	vacant	Y	N	N	Y	Y	Y
10	**McHenry**	Y	N	N	Y	Y	Y
11	**Meadows**	Y	N	N	Y	Y	Y
12	Adams	Y	Y	Y	Y	N	N
13	**Budd**	Y	N	N	Y	Y	Y
NORTH DAKOTA							
AL	**Armstrong**	Y	N	N	Y	Y	Y
OHIO							
1	**Chabot**	Y	N	N	Y	Y	Y
2	**Wenstrup**	Y	N	N	Y	Y	Y
3	Beatty	Y	Y	Y	Y	N	N
4	**Jordan**	Y	N	N	Y	Y	Y
5	**Latta**	Y	N	N	Y	Y	Y
6	**Johnson, B.**	Y	N	N	Y	Y	Y
7	**Gibbs**	Y	N	?	Y	Y	Y
8	**Davidson**	Y	N	N	Y	Y	Y
9	Kaptur	Y	Y	Y	Y	N	N
10	**Turner**	Y	N	-	Y	Y	Y
11	Fudge	Y	Y	Y	Y	N	N
12	**Balderson**	Y	N	N	Y	Y	Y
13	Ryan	?	Y	Y	Y	N	N
14	**Joyce**	Y	N	N	Y	Y	Y
15	**Stivers**	Y	N	N	Y	Y	Y
16	**Gonzalez**	Y	N	N	Y	Y	Y
OKLAHOMA							
1	**Hern**	Y	N	N	Y	Y	Y
2	**Mullin**	Y	N	N	Y	Y	Y
3	**Lucas**	Y	N	N	Y	Y	Y
4	**Cole**	Y	N	N	Y	Y	Y
5	Horn	Y	Y	Y	Y	N	N
OREGON							
1	Bonamici	Y	Y	Y	Y	N	N
2	**Walden**	Y	N	N	Y	Y	Y
3	Blumenauer	Y	Y	Y	Y	N	N
4	DeFazio	Y	Y	Y	Y	N	N
5	Schrader	Y	Y	Y	Y	N	N
PENNSYLVANIA							
1	**Fitzpatrick**	Y	N	N	Y	N	Y
2	Boyle	Y	Y	Y	Y	N	N
3	Evans	Y	Y	Y	Y	N	N
4	Dean	Y	Y	Y	Y	N	N
5	Scanlon	Y	Y	Y	Y	N	N
6	Houlahan	Y	Y	Y	Y	N	N
7	Wild	Y	Y	Y	Y	N	N
8	Cartwright	Y	Y	Y	Y	N	N
9	**Meuser**	Y	N	N	Y	Y	Y
10	**Perry**	Y	N	N	Y	Y	Y
11	**Smucker**	Y	N	N	Y	Y	Y
12	**Marino***						
13	**Joyce**	Y	N	N	Y	Y	Y
14	**Reschenthaler**	Y	N	N	Y	Y	Y
15	**Thompson, G.**	Y	N	N	Y	Y	Y
16	**Kelly, M.**	Y	N	N	Y	Y	Y
17	Lamb	Y	Y	Y	Y	N	N
18	Doyle	Y	Y	Y	Y	N	N
RHODE ISLAND							
1	Cicilline	Y	Y	Y	Y	N	N
2	Langevin	Y	Y	Y	Y	N	N
SOUTH CAROLINA							
1	Cunningham	Y	Y	Y	Y	N	N
2	**Wilson, J.**	Y	N	N	Y	Y	Y
3	**Duncan**	Y	N	N	Y	Y	Y
4	**Timmons**	Y	N	N	Y	Y	Y
5	**Norman**	Y	N	N	Y	Y	Y
6	Clyburn	Y	Y	Y	Y	N	N
7	**Rice, T.**	Y	N	N	Y	Y	Y
SOUTH DAKOTA							
AL	**Johnson**	Y	N	N	Y	Y	Y
TENNESSEE							
1	**Roe**	Y	N	N	Y	Y	Y
2	**Burchett**	Y	N	N	Y	Y	Y
3	**Fleischmann**	Y	N	N	Y	Y	Y
4	**DesJarlais**	Y	N	N	Y	Y	Y
5	Cooper	Y	Y	Y	Y	N	N
6	**Rose**	Y	N	N	Y	Y	Y
7	**Green**	Y	N	N	Y	Y	Y
8	**Kustoff**	Y	N	N	Y	Y	Y
9	Cohen	Y	Y	Y	Y	N	N
TEXAS							
1	**Gohmert**	?	N	N	Y	Y	Y
2	**Crenshaw**	Y	N	N	Y	Y	Y
3	**Taylor**	Y	N	N	Y	Y	Y
4	**Ratcliffe**	Y	N	N	Y	Y	Y

		499	500	501	502	503	504
5	**Gooden**	Y	N	N	Y	Y	Y
6	**Wright**	Y	N	N	Y	Y	Y
7	Fletcher	Y	Y	Y	Y	N	N
8	**Brady**	Y	N	N	Y	Y	Y
9	Green, A.	Y	Y	Y	Y	N	N
10	**McCaul**	Y	N	N	Y	Y	Y
11	**Conaway**	Y	N	N	Y	Y	Y
12	**Granger**	Y	N	N	Y	Y	Y
13	**Thornberry**	Y	N	N	Y	Y	Y
14	**Weber**	Y	N	N	Y	Y	Y
15	Gonzalez	Y	Y	Y	Y	N	N
16	Escobar	Y	Y	Y	Y	N	N
17	**Flores**	Y	N	N	Y	Y	Y
18	Jackson Lee	Y	Y	Y	Y	N	N
19	**Arrington**	Y	N	N	Y	Y	Y
20	Castro	Y	Y	Y	Y	N	N
21	**Roy**	Y	N	N	Y	Y	Y
22	**Olson**	Y	N	N	Y	Y	Y
23	**Hurd**	Y	N	N	Y	Y	Y
24	**Marchant**	Y	N	N	Y	Y	Y
25	**Williams**	Y	N	N	Y	Y	Y
26	**Burgess**	Y	N	N	Y	Y	Y
27	**Cloud**	Y	N	N	Y	Y	Y
28	Cuellar	Y	Y	Y	Y	N	N
29	Garcia, S.	Y	Y	Y	Y	N	N
30	Johnson, E.B.	Y	Y	Y	Y	N	N
31	**Carter, J.**	Y	N	N	Y	Y	Y
32	Allred	Y	Y	Y	Y	N	N
33	Veasey	Y	Y	Y	Y	N	N
34	Vela	Y	Y	Y	Y	N	N
35	Doggett	Y	Y	Y	Y	N	N
36	**Babin**	Y	N	N	Y	Y	Y
UTAH							
1	**Bishop, R.**	Y	N	N	Y	Y	Y
2	**Stewart**	?	N	N	Y	Y	Y
3	**Curtis**	Y	N	N	Y	Y	Y
4	McAdams	Y	Y	Y	Y	N	N
VERMONT							
AL	Welch	Y	Y	Y	Y	N	N
VIRGINIA							
1	**Wittman**	Y	N	N	Y	Y	Y
2	Luria	Y	Y	Y	Y	N	Y
3	Scott, R.	Y	Y	Y	Y	N	N
4	McEachin	Y	Y	Y	Y	N	N
5	**Riggleman**	Y	N	N	Y	Y	Y
6	**Cline**	Y	N	N	Y	Y	Y
7	Spanberger	Y	Y	Y	Y	N	N
8	Beyer	Y	Y	Y	Y	N	N
9	**Griffith**	Y	N	N	Y	Y	Y
10	Wexton	Y	Y	Y	Y	N	N
11	Connolly	Y	Y	Y	Y	N	N
WASHINGTON							
1	DelBene	Y	Y	Y	Y	N	N
2	Larsen	Y	Y	Y	Y	N	N
3	**Herrera Beutler**	Y	N	N	Y	N	Y
4	**Newhouse**	Y	N	N	Y	Y	Y
5	**McMorris Rodgers**	Y	N	N	Y	Y	Y
6	Kilmer	Y	Y	Y	Y	N	N
7	Jayapal	Y	Y	Y	Y	N	N
8	Schrier	Y	Y	Y	Y	N	N
9	Smith Adam	Y	Y	Y	Y	N	N
10	Heck	Y	Y	Y	Y	N	N
WEST VIRGINIA							
1	**McKinley**	Y	N	N	Y	N	Y
2	**Mooney**	Y	N	N	Y	Y	Y
3	**Miller**	Y	N	N	Y	Y	Y
WISCONSIN							
1	**Steil**	Y	N	N	Y	Y	Y
2	Pocan	Y	Y	Y	Y	N	N
3	Kind	Y	Y	Y	Y	N	N
4	Moore	Y	Y	Y	Y	N	N
5	**Sensenbrenner**	Y	N	N	Y	Y	Y
6	**Grothman**	Y	N	N	Y	N	Y
7	**Duffy**	Y	N	N	Y	Y	Y
8	**Gallagher**	Y	N	N	Y	Y	Y
WYOMING							
AL	**Cheney**	Y	N	N	Y	Y	Y
DELEGATES							
	Radewagen (A.S.)						
	Norton (D.C.)						
	San Nicolas (Guam)						
	Sablan (N. Marianas)						
	González-Colón (P.R.)						
	Plaskett (V.I.)						

505. HR397. Pension Plan Loans - Passage. Passage of the bill, as amended, that would establish the Pension Rehabilitation Administration within the Treasury Department to provide 30-year loans to multiemployer defined benefit pension plans in critical or declining financial status, to allow such plans to meet pension obligations to current retirees. It would also authorize the Pension Benefit Guaranty Corporation to provide financial assistance to qualifying pension plans and would appropriate such sums as may be necessary for such assistance. It would establish a dedicated Treasury trust fund for expenses of the new administration, with funding generated through Treasury Department bond sales. It would require the administration to establish the loan program by Sept. 30, 2019 and issue rules regarding the program, in consultation with the PBGC and the Treasury and Labor departments, by Dec. 31, 2019. It would require loans issued under the program to have "as low an interest rate as is feasible" and would require loan recipients to provide annual status reports to the Treasury Department. Among other provisions, it would increase a number of penalties related to failure to file tax returns and retirement plan returns. It would modify certain distribution rules for funds distributed upon an employee's death to designated beneficiaries under multiemployer defined contribution pension plans. Passed 264-169: R 29-168; D 235-0; I 0-1. July 24, 2019.

506. HR3239. Border Facility Humanitarian Standards - Recommit. Kinzinger, R-Ill., motion to recommit the bill to the House Judiciary Committee with instructions to report it back immediately with an amendment that would express the sense of Congress that members of the U.S. Border Patrol should be commended for continuing to carry out their duties in a "professional" manner, including caring for the large number of families, unaccompanied migrant children, and single adults being processed in U.S. Customs and Border Protection facilities. Motion agreed to 239-192: R 197-0; D 41-192; I 1-0. July 24, 2019.

507. HR3239. Border Facility Humanitarian Standards - Passage. Passage of the bill, as amended, that would require U.S. Customs and Border Protection to establish and implement standards of care for migrants in CBP custody. It would require CBP, in coordination with the Health and Human Services Department, to develop guidelines and protocols for the provision of health screenings and appropriate medical care. Among other requirements, it would require that all detainees receive initial in-person screenings by a licensed medical professional and require that such screenings occur within 6 hours of arrival at a facility for children, elderly individuals, and individuals who are pregnant or have severe disabilities or illnesses. It would require CBP to provide over-the-counter medications; private, safe, and clean restrooms, diaper changing facilities, and personal hygiene products; interpretation services for all detainees; facilities maintained at a reasonable temperature; and at least one gallon of water and three meals per day for each detainee. It would require CBP personnel to receive humanitarian response training, including with regard to reporting and identifying sexual abuse and exploitation. It would also require the Homeland Security Department inspector general to inspect CBP facilities and ports of entry, including to assess compliance with the bill's provisions. Passed 233-195: R 1-194; D 232-0; I 0-1. *Note: A "nay" was a vote in support of the president's position.* July 24, 2019.

508. HR549, HR3877. Budget Caps, Venezuela TPS - Previous Question. Perlmutter, D-Colo., motion to order the previous question (thus ending debate and the possibility of amendment) on the rule (H Res 519) that would provide for House floor consideration of the Bipartisan Budget Act (HR 3877) and the Venezuela TPS Act (HR 549), as amended. It would also waive clause 6(a) of Rule XIII to allow any resolution reported from the Rules Committee through July 26, 2019, to be considered on the same day without a two-thirds vote. Motion agreed to 234-195: R 0-194; D 234-0; I 0-1. July 25, 2019.

509. HR549, HR3877. Budget Caps, Venezuela TPS - Passage. Adoption of the rule (H Res 519) that would provide for House floor consideration of the Bipartisan Budget Act (HR 3877) and the Venezuela TPS Act (HR 549), as amended. It would also waive clause 6(a) of Rule XIII to allow any resolution reported from the Rules Committee through July 26, 2019, to be considered on the same day without a two-thirds vote. Adopted 232-197: R 0-195; D 232-1; I 0-1. July 25, 2019.

510. HR693. Horse Soring Protections - Passage. Schrader, D-Ore., motion to suspend the rules and pass the bill, that would require the Department of Agriculture to create a new licensing process under which the department's Animal and Plant Health Inspection Service would appoint inspectors to ensure that chemicals, pressure, and devices that cause pain to horses' front legs or hooves are not being used to harm horses, pursuant to the 1970 Horse Protection Act. The bill would increase from $3,000 to $5,000 the maximum fine and increase from one year to three years the maximum prison sentence for violations of the Horse Protection Act. Motion agreed to 333-96: R 100-95; D 233-0; I 0-1. *Note: A two-thirds majority of those present and voting (286 in this case) is required for passage under suspension of the rules.* July 25, 2019.

		505	506	507	508	509	510
ALABAMA							
1	**Byrne**	N	Y	N	N	N	N
2	**Roby**	N	Y	N	N	N	N
3	**Rogers, M.**	N	Y	N	N	N	N
4	**Aderholt**	N	Y	N	N	N	N
5	**Brooks, M.**	N	Y	N	N	N	N
6	**Palmer**	N	Y	N	N	N	N
7	Sewell	Y	N	Y	Y	Y	Y
ALASKA							
AL	**Young**	Y	Y	Y	N	N	N
ARIZONA							
1	O'Halleran	Y	N	Y	Y	Y	Y
2	Kirkpatrick	Y	N	Y	Y	Y	Y
3	Grijalva	Y	N	Y	Y	Y	Y
4	**Gosar**	N	Y	N	N	N	N
5	**Biggs**	N	Y	N	N	N	N
6	**Schweikert**	N	Y	N	N	N	Y
7	Gallego	Y	N	Y	Y	Y	Y
8	**Lesko**	N	Y	N	N	N	N
9	Stanton	Y	N	Y	Y	Y	Y
ARKANSAS							
1	**Crawford**	N	Y	N	N	N	Y
2	**Hill, F.**	N	Y	N	N	N	Y
3	**Womack**	N	Y	N	N	N	N
4	**Westerman**	N	Y	N	N	N	N
CALIFORNIA							
1	**LaMalfa**	N	Y	N	N	N	N
2	Huffman	Y	N	Y	Y	Y	Y
3	Garamendi	Y	N	Y	Y	Y	Y
4	**McClintock**	N	Y	N	?	?	?
5	Thompson, M.	Y	N	Y	Y	Y	Y
6	Matsui	Y	N	Y	Y	Y	Y
7	Bera	Y	N	Y	Y	Y	Y
8	**Cook**	Y	Y	N	N	N	Y
9	McNerney	Y	N	Y	Y	Y	Y
10	Harder	Y	Y	Y	Y	N	Y
11	DeSaulnier	Y	N	Y	Y	Y	Y
12	Pelosi	Y					
13	Lee B.	Y	N	Y	Y	Y	Y
14	Speier	Y	N	Y	Y	Y	Y
15	Swalwell	Y	N	Y	Y	Y	Y
16	Costa	Y	Y	Y	Y	Y	Y
17	Khanna	Y	N	Y	Y	Y	Y
18	Eshoo	Y	N	Y	Y	Y	Y
19	Lofgren	Y	N	Y	Y	Y	Y
20	Panetta	Y	N	Y	Y	Y	Y
21	Cox	Y	Y	Y	Y	Y	Y
22	**Nunes**	N	Y	N	N	N	N
23	**McCarthy**	N	Y	N	N	N	N
24	Carbajal	Y	N	Y	Y	Y	Y
25	Hill, K.	Y	N	Y	Y	Y	Y
26	Brownley	Y	N	Y	Y	Y	Y
27	Chu	Y	N	Y	Y	Y	Y
28	Schiff	Y	N	Y	Y	Y	Y
29	Cárdenas	Y	N	Y	Y	Y	Y
30	Sherman	Y	N	Y	Y	Y	Y
31	Aguilar	Y	N	Y	Y	Y	Y
32	Napolitano	Y	N	Y	Y	Y	Y
33	Lieu	Y	N	Y	Y	Y	Y
34	Gomez	Y	N	Y	Y	Y	Y
35	Torres	Y	N	Y	Y	Y	Y
36	Ruiz	Y	N	Y	Y	Y	Y
37	Bass	Y	N	+	Y	Y	Y
38	Sánchez	Y	N	Y	Y	Y	Y
39	Cisneros	Y	Y	Y	Y	Y	Y
40	Roybal-Allard	Y	N	Y	Y	Y	Y
41	Takano	Y	N	Y	Y	Y	Y
42	**Calvert**	N	Y	N	N	N	Y
43	Waters	Y	N	Y	Y	Y	Y
44	Barragán	Y	N	Y	Y	Y	Y
45	Porter	Y	Y	Y	Y	Y	Y
46	Correa	Y	N	Y	Y	?	Y
47	Lowenthal	Y	N	Y	Y	Y	Y
48	Rouda	Y	N	Y	Y	Y	Y
49	Levin	Y	Y	Y	Y	Y	Y
50	**Hunter**	N	Y	N	N	N	N
51	Vargas	Y	N	Y	Y	Y	Y
52	Peters	Y	Y	Y	Y	Y	Y
53	Davis, S.	Y	N	Y	Y	Y	Y
COLORADO							
1	DeGette	Y	N	Y	Y	Y	Y
2	Neguse	Y	N	Y	Y	Y	Y
3	**Tipton**	N	Y	N	N	N	Y
4	**Buck**	N	Y	N	N	N	Y
5	**Lamborn**	N	Y	N	N	N	N
6	Crow	Y	N	Y	Y	Y	Y
7	Perlmutter	Y	N	Y	Y	Y	Y
CONNECTICUT							
1	Larson	Y	N	Y	Y	Y	Y
2	Courtney	Y	N	Y	Y	Y	Y
3	DeLauro	Y	N	Y	Y	Y	Y
4	Himes	Y	N	Y	Y	Y	Y
5	Hayes	Y	N	Y	Y	Y	Y
DELAWARE							
AL	Blunt Rochester	Y	N	Y	Y	Y	Y
FLORIDA							
1	**Gaetz**	N	Y	N	N	N	?
2	**Dunn**	N	Y	N	N	N	N
3	**Yoho**	Y	Y	N	N	N	Y
4	**Rutherford**	N	Y	N	N	N	N
5	Lawson	Y	N	Y	Y	Y	Y
6	**Waltz**	N	Y	N	N	N	Y
7	Murphy	Y	Y	Y	Y	Y	Y
8	**Posey**	N	Y	N	N	N	Y
9	Soto	Y	N	Y	Y	Y	Y
10	Demings	Y	N	Y	Y	Y	Y
11	**Webster**	N	Y	N	N	N	N
12	**Bilirakis**	N	Y	N	N	N	Y
13	Crist	Y	N	Y	Y	Y	Y
14	Castor	Y	N	Y	Y	Y	Y
15	**Spano**	N	Y	N	N	N	N
16	**Buchanan**	N	Y	N	N	N	Y
17	**Steube**	N	Y	N	N	N	N
18	**Mast**	N	Y	N	N	N	Y
19	**Rooney**	N	Y	N	N	N	Y
20	Hastings	Y	N	Y	Y	Y	Y
21	Frankel	Y	N	Y	Y	Y	Y
22	Deutch	Y	N	Y	Y	Y	Y
23	Wasserman Schultz	Y	N	Y	Y	Y	Y
24	Wilson, F.	Y	N	Y	Y	Y	Y
25	**Diaz-Balart**	N	Y	N	N	N	Y
26	Mucarsel-Powell	Y	N	Y	Y	Y	Y
27	Shalala	Y	N	Y	Y	Y	Y
GEORGIA							
1	**Carter, E.L.**	N	Y	N	N	N	Y
2	Bishop, S.	Y	N	Y	Y	Y	Y
3	**Ferguson**	N	Y	N	N	N	N
4	Johnson, H.	Y	N	Y	Y	Y	Y
5	Lewis John	Y	N	Y	Y	Y	Y
6	McBath	Y	Y	Y	Y	Y	Y
7	**Woodall**	N	Y	N	N	N	N
8	**Scott, A.**	N	Y	N	N	N	N
9	**Collins, D.**	N	Y	N	N	N	N
10	**Hice**	N	Y	N	N	N	N
11	**Loudermilk**	N	Y	N	N	N	N
12	**Allen**	N	Y	N	N	N	N
13	Scott, D.	Y	N	Y	Y	Y	Y
14	**Graves, T.**	N	Y	N	N	N	N
HAWAII							
1	Case	Y	Y	Y	Y	Y	Y
2	Gabbard	Y	?	Y	Y	Y	Y
IDAHO							
1	**Fulcher**	N	Y	N	N	N	Y
2	**Simpson**	N	Y	N	N	N	N
ILLINOIS							
1	Rush	Y	N	Y	Y	Y	Y
2	Kelly, R.	Y	N	Y	Y	Y	Y
3	Lipinski	Y	Y	Y	Y	Y	Y
4	García, J.	Y	N	Y	Y	Y	Y
5	Quigley	Y	N	Y	Y	Y	Y
6	Casten	Y	N	Y	Y	Y	Y
7	Davis, D.	Y	N	Y	Y	Y	Y
8	Krishnamoorthi	Y	N	Y	Y	Y	Y
9	Schakowsky	Y	N	Y	Y	Y	Y
10	Schneider	Y	N	Y	Y	Y	Y
11	Foster	Y	N	Y	Y	Y	Y

KEY: **Republicans** Democrats *Independents*

Y Voted for (yea) N Voted against (nay) P Voted "present"
+ Announced for - Announced against ? Did not vote or otherwise make position known
# Paired for X Paired against

		505	506	507	508	509	510
12	**Bost**	Y	Y	N	N	N	Y
13	**Davis, R.**	Y	Y	N	N	N	Y
14	Underwood	Y	Y	Y	Y	Y	Y
15	**Shimkus**	N	Y	N	N	N	Y
16	**Kinzinger**	Y	Y	N	N	N	Y
17	Bustos	Y	N	Y	Y	Y	Y
18	**LaHood**	N	Y	N	N	N	Y
INDIANA							
1	Visclosky	Y	N	Y	Y	Y	?
2	**Walorski**	N	Y	N	N	N	Y
3	**Banks**	N	Y	N	N	N	Y
4	**Baird**	N	Y	N	N	N	N
5	**Brooks, S.**	Y	Y	N	N	N	Y
6	**Pence**	N	Y	N	N	N	Y
7	Carson	Y	N	Y	Y	Y	Y
8	**Bucshon**	N	Y	N	N	N	N
9	**Hollingsworth**	N	Y	N	N	N	N
IOWA							
1	Finkenauer	Y	N	Y	Y	Y	Y
2	Loebsack	Y	N	Y	Y	Y	Y
3	Axne	Y	Y	Y	Y	Y	Y
4	**King, S.**	N	Y	N	N	N	N
KANSAS							
1	**Marshall**	N	Y	N	N	N	Y
2	**Watkins**	N	Y	N	N	N	Y
3	Davids	Y	N	Y	Y	Y	Y
4	**Estes**	N	Y	N	N	N	Y
KENTUCKY							
1	**Comer**	N	Y	N	N	N	N
2	**Guthrie**	N	Y	N	N	N	N
3	Yarmuth	Y	N	Y	Y	Y	Y
4	**Massie**	N	Y	N	N	N	N
5	**Rogers, H.**	N	Y	N	N	N	N
6	**Barr**	N	Y	N	N	N	N
LOUISIANA							
1	**Scalise**	N	Y	N	N	N	N
2	Richmond	Y	N	Y	Y	Y	Y
3	**Higgins, C.**	N	Y	N	N	N	N
4	**Johnson, M.**	N	Y	N	N	N	Y
5	**Abraham**	N	Y	N	N	N	N
6	**Graves, G.**	N	Y	N	N	N	N
MAINE							
1	Pingree	Y	N	Y	Y	Y	Y
2	Golden	Y	Y	Y	Y	Y	Y
MARYLAND							
1	**Harris**	N	Y	?	N	N	N
2	Ruppersberger	Y	N	Y	Y	Y	Y
3	Sarbanes	Y	N	Y	Y	Y	Y
4	Brown, A.	Y	N	Y	Y	Y	Y
5	Hoyer	Y	N	Y	Y	Y	Y
6	Trone	Y	N	Y	Y	Y	Y
7	Cummings	Y	N	Y	Y	Y	Y
8	Raskin						
MASSACHUSETTS		Y	N	Y	Y	Y	Y
1	Neal						
2	McGovern	Y	N	Y	Y	Y	Y
3	Trahan	Y	N	Y	Y	Y	Y
4	Kennedy	Y	N	Y	Y	Y	Y
5	Clark	Y	N	Y	Y	Y	Y
6	Moulton	Y	N	Y	Y	Y	Y
7	Pressley	Y	Y	Y	Y	Y	Y
8	Lynch	Y	N	Y	Y	Y	Y
9	Keating	Y	N	Y	Y	Y	Y
MICHIGAN		Y	N	Y	Y	Y	Y
1	**Bergman**						
2	**Huizenga**	Y	Y	N	N	N	N
3	*Amash*	Y	Y	N	N	N	Y
4	**Moolenaar**	N	Y	N	N	N	N
5	Kildee	N	Y	N	N	N	Y
6	**Upton**	Y	N	Y	Y	Y	Y
7	**Walberg**	N	Y	N	N	N	Y
8	Slotkin	Y	Y	N	N	N	Y
9	Levin	Y	Y	Y	Y	Y	Y
10	**Mitchell**	Y	N	Y	Y	Y	Y
11	Stevens	N	Y	N	N	N	Y
12	Dingell	Y	N	Y	Y	Y	Y
13	Tlaib	Y	N	Y	Y	Y	Y
14	Lawrence	Y	N	Y	Y	Y	Y
MINNESOTA		Y	N	Y	Y	Y	Y
1	**Hagedorn**						
2	Craig	N	Y	N	N	N	Y
3	Phillips	Y	Y	Y	Y	Y	Y
4	McCollum	Y	Y	Y	Y	Y	Y
5	Omar	Y	N	Y	Y	Y	Y

		505	506	507	508	509	510
6	**Emmer**	Y	N	Y	Y	Y	Y
7	Peterson	N	Y	N	N	N	N
8	**Stauber**	Y	Y	Y	Y	Y	Y
MISSISSIPPI		Y	Y	N	N	N	Y
1	**Kelly, T.**						
2	Thompson, B.	N	Y	N	N	N	N
3	**Guest**	Y	N	Y	Y	Y	Y
4	**Palazzo**	N	Y	N	N	N	Y
MISSOURI		N	Y	N	N	N	N
1	Clay						
2	**Wagner**	Y	N	Y	Y	Y	Y
3	**Luetkemeyer**	N	Y	N	N	N	Y
4	**Hartzler**	N	Y	N	N	N	Y
5	Cleaver	Y	Y	N	N	N	N
6	**Graves, S.**	Y	N	Y	Y	Y	Y
7	**Long**	N	Y	N	N	N	N
8	**Smith, J.**	N	Y	N	N	N	Y
MONTANA		N	Y	N	N	N	N
AL	**Gianforte**						
NEBRASKA		N	Y	N	N	N	Y
1	**Fortenberry**						
2	**Bacon**	Y	Y	N	N	N	Y
3	**Smith, Adrian**	Y	Y	N	N	N	Y
NEVADA		N	Y	?	N	N	N
1	Titus						
2	**Amodei**	Y	N	Y	Y	Y	Y
3	Lee	N	Y	N	N	N	Y
4	Horsford	Y	Y	Y	Y	Y	Y
NEW HAMPSHIRE		Y	Y	Y	Y	Y	Y
1	Pappas						
2	Kuster	Y	N	Y	Y	Y	Y
NEW JERSEY		Y	N	Y	Y	Y	Y
1	Norcross						
2	Van Drew	Y	N	Y	Y	Y	Y
3	Kim	Y	Y	Y	Y	Y	Y
4	**Smith, C.**	Y	N	Y	Y	Y	Y
5	Gottheimer	Y	Y	N	N	N	Y
6	Pallone	Y	Y	Y	Y	Y	Y
7	Malinowski	Y	N	Y	Y	Y	Y
8	Sires	Y	Y	Y	Y	Y	Y
9	Pascrell	Y	Y	Y	Y	Y	Y
10	Payne	Y	N	Y	Y	Y	Y
11	Sherrill	Y	N	Y	Y	Y	Y
12	Watson Coleman	Y	Y	Y	Y	Y	Y
NEW MEXICO		Y	N	Y	Y	Y	Y
1	Haaland						
2	Torres Small	Y	N	Y	Y	Y	Y
3	Luján	Y	Y	Y	Y	Y	Y
NEW YORK		Y	N	Y	Y	Y	Y
1	**Zeldin**						
2	**King, P.**	Y	Y	N	N	N	Y
3	Suozzi	Y	Y	N	N	N	Y
4	Rice, K.	Y	N	Y	Y	Y	Y
5	Meeks	Y	N	Y	Y	Y	Y
6	Meng	Y	N	Y	Y	Y	Y
7	Velázquez	Y	N	Y	Y	Y	Y
8	Jeffries	Y	N	Y	Y	Y	Y
9	Clarke	Y	N	Y	Y	Y	Y
10	Nadler	Y	N	Y	Y	Y	Y
11	Rose	Y	N	Y	Y	Y	Y
12	Maloney, C.	Y	N	Y	Y	Y	Y
13	Espaillat	Y	N	Y	Y	Y	Y
14	Ocasio-Cortez	Y	N	Y	Y	Y	Y
15	Serrano	Y	N	Y	Y	Y	Y
16	Engel	Y	N	Y	Y	Y	Y
17	Lowey	Y	N	Y	Y	Y	Y
18	Maloney, S.P.	Y	N	Y	Y	Y	Y
19	Delgado	Y	N	Y	Y	Y	Y
20	Tonko	Y	Y	Y	Y	Y	Y
21	**Stefanik**	Y	N	Y	Y	Y	Y
22	Brindisi	N	Y	N	N	N	Y
23	**Reed**	Y	Y	Y	Y	Y	Y
24	**Katko**	N	Y	N	N	N	Y
25	Morelle	Y	Y	N	N	N	Y
26	Higgins, B.	Y	N	Y	Y	Y	Y
27	**Collins, C.**	Y	N	Y	Y	Y	Y
NORTH CAROLINA		Y	Y	N	N	N	Y
1	Butterfield						
2	**Holding**	Y	N	Y	Y	Y	Y
3	**Jones***	N	Y	N	N	N	N
4	Price						
5	**Foxx**	Y	N	Y	Y	Y	Y
6	**Walker**	N	Y	N	N	N	N
7	**Rouzer**	N	Y	N	N	N	Y

		505	506	507	508	509	510
8	**Hudson**	N	Y	N	N	N	N
9	vacant	N	Y	N	N	N	Y
10	**McHenry**	N	Y	N	N	N	Y
11	**Meadows**	N	Y	N	N	N	N
12	Adams	Y	N	Y	Y	Y	Y
13	**Budd**	N	Y	N	N	N	Y
NORTH DAKOTA							
AL	**Armstrong**	N	Y	N	N	?	N
OHIO							
1	**Chabot**	N	Y	N	N	N	Y
2	**Wenstrup**	N	Y	N	N	N	Y
3	Beatty	Y	N	Y	Y	Y	Y
4	**Jordan**	N	Y	N	N	N	N
5	**Latta**	N	Y	N	N	N	Y
6	**Johnson, B.**	N	Y	N	N	N	Y
7	**Gibbs**	Y	Y	N	N	N	Y
8	**Davidson**	N	Y	N	N	N	N
9	Kaptur	Y	N	Y	Y	Y	Y
10	**Turner**	Y	Y	N	N	N	Y
11	Fudge	Y	N	Y	Y	Y	Y
12	**Balderson**	N	Y	N	N	N	N
13	Ryan	Y	Y	Y	Y	Y	Y
14	**Joyce**	Y	Y	N	N	N	Y
15	**Stivers**	Y	Y	N	N	N	Y
16	**Gonzalez**	N	Y	N	N	N	Y
OKLAHOMA							
1	**Hern**	N	Y	N	N	N	N
2	**Mullin**	N	Y	N	N	N	N
3	**Lucas**	N	Y	N	N	N	N
4	**Cole**	N	Y	N	N	N	N
5	Horn	Y	Y	Y	Y	Y	Y
OREGON							
1	Bonamici	Y	N	Y	Y	Y	Y
2	**Walden**	N	Y	N	N	N	Y
3	Blumenauer	Y	N	Y	Y	Y	Y
4	DeFazio	Y	N	Y	Y	Y	Y
5	Schrader	Y	Y	Y	Y	Y	Y
PENNSYLVANIA							
1	**Fitzpatrick**	Y	Y	N	N	N	Y
2	Boyle	Y	N	Y	Y	Y	Y
3	Evans	Y	N	Y	Y	Y	Y
4	Dean	Y	N	Y	Y	Y	Y
5	Scanlon	Y	N	Y	Y	Y	Y
6	Houlahan	Y	Y	Y	Y	Y	Y
7	Wild	Y	N	Y	Y	Y	Y
8	Cartwright	Y	N	Y	Y	Y	Y
9	**Meuser**	N	Y	N	N	N	Y
10	**Perry**	N	Y	N	N	N	Y
11	**Smucker**	N	Y	N	N	N	Y
12	**Marino***						
13	**Joyce**	N	Y	N	N	N	Y
14	**Reschenthaler**	N	Y	N	N	N	Y
15	**Thompson, G.**	N	Y	N	?	N	Y
16	**Kelly, M.**	N	Y	N	N	N	Y
17	Lamb	Y	N	Y	Y	Y	Y
18	Doyle	Y	N	Y	Y	Y	Y
RHODE ISLAND							
1	Cicilline	Y	N	Y	Y	Y	Y
2	Langevin	Y	N	Y	Y	Y	Y
SOUTH CAROLINA							
1	Cunningham	Y	Y	Y	Y	Y	Y
2	**Wilson, J.**	N	Y	N	N	N	Y
3	**Duncan**	N	Y	N	N	N	N
4	**Timmons**	N	Y	N	N	N	N
5	**Norman**	N	Y	N	N	N	N
6	Clyburn	Y	N	Y	Y	Y	Y
7	**Rice, T.**	N	Y	N	N	N	Y
SOUTH DAKOTA							
AL	**Johnson**	N	Y	N	N	N	N
TENNESSEE							
1	**Roe**	N	Y	N	N	N	N
2	**Burchett**	Y	Y	N	N	N	Y
3	**Fleischmann**	N	Y	N	N	N	N
4	**DesJarlais**	N	Y	N	N	N	N
5	Cooper	Y	N	Y	Y	Y	Y
6	**Rose**	N	Y	N	N	N	N
7	**Green**	N	Y	N	N	N	N
8	**Kustoff**	N	Y	N	N	N	N
9	Cohen	Y	N	Y	Y	Y	Y
TEXAS							
1	**Gohmert**	N	Y	N	N	N	N
2	**Crenshaw**	N	Y	N	N	N	N
3	**Taylor**	N	Y	N	N	N	Y
4	**Ratcliffe**	N	Y	N	N	N	N

		505	506	507	508	509	510
5	**Gooden**	N	Y	N	N	N	Y
6	**Wright**	N	Y	N	N	N	N
7	Fletcher	Y	N	Y	Y	Y	Y
8	**Brady**	N	Y	N	?	N	N
9	Green, A.	Y	N	Y	Y	Y	Y
10	**McCaul**	N	Y	N	N	N	Y
11	**Conaway**	N	Y	N	N	N	N
12	**Granger**	N	Y	N	N	N	Y
13	**Thornberry**	N	Y	N	N	N	N
14	**Weber**	N	Y	N	N	N	Y
15	Gonzalez	Y	Y	?	Y	Y	Y
16	Escobar	Y	N	Y	Y	Y	Y
17	**Flores**	N	Y	N	N	N	Y
18	Jackson Lee	Y	N	Y	Y	Y	Y
19	**Arrington**	N	Y	N	N	N	Y
20	Castro	Y	N	Y	Y	Y	Y
21	**Roy**	N	Y	N	N	N	N
22	**Olson**	N	Y	N	N	N	N
23	**Hurd**	Y	Y	N	N	N	Y
24	**Marchant**	N	Y	N	N	N	N
25	**Williams**	N	Y	N	N	N	Y
26	**Burgess**	N	Y	N	N	N	Y
27	**Cloud**	N	Y	N	N	N	N
28	Cuellar	Y	Y	Y	Y	Y	Y
29	Garcia, S.	Y	N	Y	Y	Y	Y
30	Johnson, E.B.	Y	N	Y	Y	Y	Y
31	**Carter, J.**	N	Y	N	N	N	N
32	Allred	Y	N	Y	Y	Y	Y
33	Veasey	Y	N	Y	Y	Y	Y
34	Vela	Y	Y	Y	Y	Y	Y
35	Doggett	Y	N	Y	Y	Y	Y
36	**Babin**	N	Y	N	N	N	Y
UTAH							
1	**Bishop, R.**	N	Y	N	N	N	N
2	**Stewart**	N	Y	N	N	N	Y
3	**Curtis**	N	Y	N	N	N	Y
4	McAdams	Y	Y	Y	Y	Y	Y
VERMONT							
AL	Welch	Y	N	Y	Y	Y	Y
VIRGINIA							
1	**Wittman**	N	Y	N	N	N	Y
2	Luria	Y	Y	Y	Y	Y	Y
3	Scott, R.	Y	N	Y	Y	Y	Y
4	McEachin	Y	N	Y	Y	Y	Y
5	**Riggleman**	N	Y	N	N	N	Y
6	**Cline**	N	Y	N	N	N	N
7	Spanberger	Y	Y	Y	Y	Y	Y
8	Beyer	Y	N	Y	Y	Y	Y
9	**Griffith**	Y	Y	N	N	N	Y
10	Wexton	Y	N	Y	Y	Y	Y
11	Connolly	Y	N	Y	Y	Y	Y
WASHINGTON							
1	DelBene	Y	N	Y	Y	Y	Y
2	Larsen	Y	N	Y	Y	Y	Y
3	**Herrera Beutler**	N	Y	N	N	N	Y
4	**Newhouse**	N	Y	N	N	N	N
5	**McMorris Rodgers**	N	Y	N	N	N	Y
6	Kilmer	Y	N	Y	Y	Y	Y
7	Jayapal	Y	N	Y	Y	Y	Y
8	Schrier	Y	N	Y	Y	Y	Y
9	Smith Adam	Y	N	Y	Y	Y	Y
10	Heck	Y	N	Y	Y	Y	Y
WEST VIRGINIA							
1	**McKinley**	Y	Y	N	N	N	Y
2	**Mooney**	N	Y	N	N	N	N
3	**Miller**	N	Y	N	N	N	N
WISCONSIN							
1	**Steil**	N	Y	N	N	N	Y
2	Pocan	Y	N	Y	Y	Y	Y
3	Kind	Y	Y	Y	Y	Y	Y
4	Moore	Y	N	Y	Y	Y	Y
5	**Sensenbrenner**	N	Y	N	N	N	Y
6	**Grothman**	N	Y	N	N	N	Y
7	**Duffy**	Y	Y	N	N	N	N
8	**Gallagher**	N	Y	N	N	N	Y
WYOMING							
AL	**Cheney**	N	Y	N	N	N	N
DELEGATES							
	Radewagen (A.S.)						
	Norton (D.C.)						
	San Nicolas (Guam)						
	Sablan (N. Marianas)						
	González-Colón (P.R.)						
	Plaskett (V.I.)						

511. HR3877. Budget Cap Adjustment - Passage. Passage of the bill that would establish enforceable budget levels in the House and Senate for fiscal 2020 and 2021 and suspend the public debt limit through July 31, 2021. It would increase discretionary budget caps for defense and non-defense spending, and would provide a total of $1.37 trillion for fiscal 2020 and $1.38 trillion for fiscal 2021 in discretionary budget authority, including for overseas contingency operations. Spending cap adjustments in the bill would increase discretionary budget authority by a total of $324 billion over those two years. For fiscal 2020, it would provide $738 billion in budget authority for defense spending, including $71.5 billion for OCO funding not subject to discretionary spending caps, and $629.5 billion in budget authority for non-defense spending, including $8 billion for OCO funding. It would provide budget authority in similar amounts for fiscal 2021. It would additionally authorize up to $2.5 million in fiscal 2020 spending for the 2020 census. The bill would restrict adjustments to spending limits for mandatory programs in the Senate and limit advance funding that may be included in appropriations bills in either chamber. It would require that the budgetary effects of the bill not be entered on pay-as-you-go scorecards in either chamber. It would provide for $77.3 billion in offsets over 10 years, including by extending sequestration requirements under the Budget Control Act for certain mandatory spending through fiscal 2029. It would also extend through fiscal 2029 authorization for processing fees on certain customs services. Passed 284-149: R 65-132; D 219-16; I 0-1. *Note: A "yea" was a vote in support of the president's position.* July 25, 2019.

512. HR3877. Budget Cap Adjustment - Title Change. Massie, R-Ky., amendment to the bill that would change the bill's title to read, "A bill to kick the can down the road, and for other purposes." Rejected in Committee of the Whole 47-384: R 41-156; D 5-228; I 1-0. July 25, 2019.

513. HR549. Venezuela TPS - Recommit. Reschenthaler, R-Pa., motion to recommit the bill to the House Judiciary Committee with instructions to report it back immediately with an amendment that would state that Venezuela would be designated for temporary protected status under the bill's provisions "because of the economic, humanitarian, security, and refugee crisis that is a direct result of years of socialist policies implemented by the regimes of Huge Chavez and Nicolas Maduro." Motion rejected 215-217: R 197-0; D 17-217; I 1-0. July 25, 2019.

514. HR549. Venezuela TPS - Passage. Passage of the bill, as amended, that would grant temporary protected status to Venezuelans in the U.S. for an initial 18-month period. To receive TPS status, qualifying individuals must be continuously present in the U.S. after enactment, be legally admissible to the U.S. as immigrants, and register with the Homeland Security Department. It would require DHS to give prior consent for individuals covered under TPS to travel abroad in emergencies or extenuating circumstances. Passed 272-158: R 39-158; D 232-0; I 1-0. July 25, 2019.

515. HR1420. Federal IT System Energy Efficiency - Passage. Rush, D-Ill., motion to suspend the rules and pass the bill, as amended, that would require each federal agency to work with the Office of Management and Budget, the Energy Department, and the Environmental Protection Agency to develop an implementation plan for the maintenance, purchase, and use of energy-efficient and energy-saving information technologies at federally owned and operated facilities. It would set requirements for these plans and require the OMB to establish performance goals for their implementation. It would also require the Energy Department, EPA, and OMB to take a number of actions assessing and promoting data sharing related to energy usage by federal data centers. Motion agreed to 384-23: R 164-22; D 220-0; I 0-1. *Note: A two-thirds majority of those present and voting (272 in this case) is required for passage under suspension of the rules.* Sept. 9, 2019.

516. HR1768. Diesel Emissions Reduction - Passage. Rush, D-Ill., motion to suspend the rules and pass the bill that would reauthorize $100 million annually through fiscal 2024 for EPA programs under the Diesel Emissions Reduction Act that provide grants and loans to retrofit diesel vehicles to meet emission standards. Motion agreed to 295-114: R 76-112; D 219-1; I 0-1. *Note: A two-thirds majority of those present and voting (273 in this case) is required for passage under suspension of the rules.* Sept. 9, 2019.

	511	512	513	514	515	516
ALABAMA						
1 **Byrne**	N	N	Y	N	?	?
2 **Roby**	Y	N	Y	N	Y	Y
3 **Rogers, M.**	Y	N	Y	N	Y	Y
4 **Aderholt**	Y	N	Y	N	Y	Y
5 **Brooks, M.**	N	Y	Y	N	N	N
6 **Palmer**	N	N	Y	N	Y	N
7 Sewell	Y	N	N	Y	Y	Y
ALASKA						
AL **Young**	Y	N	Y	Y	Y	Y
ARIZONA						
1 O'Halleran	Y	N	N	Y	Y	Y
2 Kirkpatrick	Y	N	N	Y	Y	Y
3 Grijalva	Y	N	N	Y	Y	Y
4 **Gosar**	N	Y	Y	N	N	N
5 **Biggs**	N	Y	Y	N	N	N
6 **Schweikert**	N	N	Y	N	Y	N
7 Gallego	Y	N	N	Y	Y	Y
8 **Lesko**	N	Y	Y	N	N	N
9 Stanton	Y	N	N	Y	Y	Y
ARKANSAS						
1 **Crawford**	N	N	Y	N	Y	N
2 **Hill, F.**	Y	N	Y	Y	Y	N
3 **Womack**	Y	N	Y	Y	Y	N
4 **Westerman**	N	N	Y	N	Y	N
CALIFORNIA						
1 **LaMalfa**	N	N	Y	N	Y	Y
2 Huffman	Y	N	N	Y	Y	Y
3 Garamendi	Y	N	N	Y	Y	Y
4 **McClintock**	N	Y	Y	N	Y	N
5 Thompson, M.	Y	N	N	Y	Y	Y
6 Matsui	Y	N	N	Y	Y	Y
7 Bera	Y	N	N	Y	Y	Y
8 **Cook**	Y	N	Y	N	Y	Y
9 McNerney	Y	N	N	Y	Y	Y
10 Harder	N	N	N	Y	Y	Y
11 DeSaulnier	Y	N	N	Y	Y	Y
12 Pelosi	Y					
13 Lee B.	Y	N	N	Y	Y	Y
14 Speier	Y	N	N	?	?	
15 Swalwell	Y	N	N	Y	Y	Y
16 Costa	Y	N	N	+	+	
17 Khanna	Y	N	N	Y	Y	Y
18 Eshoo	Y	N	N	Y	Y	Y
19 Lofgren	Y	N	N	Y	Y	Y
20 Panetta	Y	N	N	Y	Y	Y
21 Cox	Y	N	N	Y	Y	Y
22 **Nunes**	Y	N	Y	N	Y	Y
23 **McCarthy**	Y	N	Y	N	?	?
24 Carbajal	Y	N	N	Y	Y	Y
25 Hill, K.	Y	N	N	Y	Y	Y
26 Brownley	Y	N	N	Y	Y	Y
27 Chu	Y	N	N	Y	Y	Y
28 Schiff	Y	N	N	Y	Y	Y
29 Cárdenas	Y	?	N	Y	Y	Y
30 Sherman	Y	N	N	Y	Y	Y
31 Aguilar	Y	N	N	Y	Y	Y
32 Napolitano	Y	N	N	Y	Y	Y
33 Lieu	Y	N	N	Y	Y	Y
34 Gomez	Y	N	N	Y	Y	Y
35 Torres	Y	N	N	Y	Y	Y
36 Ruiz	Y	N	N	Y	Y	Y
37 Bass	Y	N	N	Y	Y	Y
38 Sánchez	Y	N	N	Y	Y	Y
39 Cisneros	Y	N	N	Y	Y	Y
40 Roybal-Allard	Y	N	N	Y	Y	Y
41 Takano	Y	N	N	Y	Y	Y
42 **Calvert**	Y	N	Y	N	Y	Y
43 Waters	Y	N	?	Y	Y	Y
44 Barragán	Y	N	N	Y	Y	Y
45 Porter	Y	N	Y	Y	Y	Y
46 Correa	Y	N	N	Y	Y	Y
47 Lowenthal	Y	N	N	Y	Y	Y
48 Rouda	Y	N	N	Y	Y	Y
49 Levin	Y	N	N	Y	Y	Y
50 **Hunter**	N	Y	Y	N	Y	N
51 Vargas	Y	N	N	Y	Y	Y
52 Peters	N	N	N	Y	Y	Y

	511	512	513	514	515	516
53 Davis, S.	Y	N	N	Y	Y	Y
COLORADO						
1 DeGette	Y	N	N	Y	Y	Y
2 Neguse	Y	N	N	Y	Y	Y
3 Tipton	N	N	Y	N	Y	N
4 **Buck**	N	Y	Y	N	Y	N
5 **Lamborn**	N	N	Y	N	?	?
6 Crow	Y	N	N	Y	Y	Y
7 Perlmutter	Y	N	N	Y	Y	Y
CONNECTICUT						
1 Larson	Y	N	N	Y	Y	Y
2 Courtney	Y	N	N	Y	Y	Y
3 DeLauro	Y	N	N	Y	Y	Y
4 Himes	Y	N	N	Y	Y	Y
5 Hayes	Y	N	N	Y	Y	Y
DELAWARE						
AL Blunt Rochester	Y	N	N	Y	Y	Y
FLORIDA						
1 **Gaetz**	N	Y	Y	N	Y	Y
2 **Dunn**	Y	N	Y	N	Y	Y
3 **Yoho**	N	Y	Y	N	N	N
4 **Rutherford**	Y	N	Y	N	Y	N
5 Lawson	Y	N	N	Y	Y	Y
6 **Waltz**	N	N	Y	N	Y	Y
7 Murphy	N	Y	Y	N	Y	Y
8 **Posey**	N	Y	Y	N	-	-
9 Soto	Y	N	N	Y	Y	Y
10 Demings	Y	N	N	Y	Y	Y
11 **Webster**	N	Y	Y	N	?	N
12 **Bilirakis**	Y	N	Y	N	Y	Y
13 Crist	Y	N	N	Y	Y	Y
14 Castor	Y	N	N	Y	Y	Y
15 **Spano**	N	N	Y	N	Y	Y
16 **Buchanan**	N	N	Y	N	Y	Y
17 **Steube**	N	N	N	N	N	N
18 **Mast**	Y	N	Y	N	Y	Y
19 **Rooney**	N	N	Y	Y	Y	Y
20 Hastings	Y	N	N	Y	Y	Y
21 Frankel	Y	N	N	Y	Y	Y
22 Deutch	Y	N	N	Y	?	?
23 Wasserman Schultz	Y	N	N	Y	Y	Y
24 Wilson, F.	Y	N	N	Y	?	Y
25 **Diaz-Balart**	Y	N	Y	N	Y	Y
26 Mucarsel-Powell	Y	N	N	Y	Y	Y
27 Shalala	Y	N	N	Y	Y	Y
GEORGIA						
1 **Carter, E.L.**	N	N	Y	N	Y	N
2 Bishop, S.	Y	N	N	Y	Y	Y
3 **Ferguson**	N	N	Y	N	Y	N
4 Johnson, H.	Y	N	N	Y	Y	Y
5 Lewis John	Y	N	N	Y	Y	Y
6 McBath	Y	N	N	Y	Y	Y
7 **Woodall**	Y	N	Y	Y	Y	Y
8 **Scott, A.**	N	N	Y	N	Y	N
9 **Collins, D.**	Y	N	Y	N	+	+
10 **Hice**	N	Y	Y	N	Y	N
11 **Loudermilk**	N	N	Y	N	Y	N
12 **Allen**	N	N	Y	N	Y	N
13 Scott, D.	Y	N	N	Y	Y	Y
14 **Graves, T.**	N	N	Y	Y	Y	N
HAWAII						
1 Case	Y	N	N	Y	Y	Y
2 Gabbard	Y	N	N	Y	Y	Y
IDAHO						
1 **Fulcher**	N	Y	Y	N	?	N
2 **Simpson**	Y	N	Y	N	Y	Y
ILLINOIS						
1 Rush	Y	N	N	Y	Y	Y
2 Kelly, R.	Y	N	N	Y	Y	Y
3 Lipinski	N	N	N	Y	Y	Y
4 García, J.	Y	N	N	Y	Y	Y
5 Quigley	Y	N	N	Y	Y	Y
6 Casten	Y	N	N	Y	Y	Y
7 Davis, D.	Y	N	N	Y	Y	Y
8 Krishnamoorthi	Y	N	N	Y	Y	Y
9 Schakowsky	Y	N	N	Y	Y	Y
10 Schneider	Y	N	N	Y	Y	Y
11 Foster	Y	N	N	Y	Y	Y

KEY:		Republicans		Democrats		*Independents*
Y Voted for (yea)		**N** Voted against (nay)		**P** Voted "present"		
+ Announced for		**−** Announced against		**?** Did not vote or otherwise make position known		
# Paired for		**X** Paired against				

		511	512	513	514	515	516
12	**Bost**	Y	N	Y	Y	Y	Y
13	**Davis, R.**	Y	N	Y	N	Y	Y
14	Underwood	Y	N	N	Y	Y	Y
15	**Shimkus**	N	N	Y	N	Y	Y
16	**Kinzinger**	Y	N	Y	Y	Y	Y
17	Bustos	Y	N	N	Y	Y	Y
18	**LaHood**	N	N	Y	N	Y	Y
INDIANA							
1	Visclosky	Y	N	N	Y	Y	Y
2	**Walorski**	N	N	Y	N	Y	Y
3	**Banks**	N	N	Y	N	Y	N
4	**Baird**	N	N	Y	N	Y	Y
5	**Brooks, S.**	Y	N	Y	N	Y	Y
6	**Pence**	Y	N	Y	N	Y	Y
7	Carson	Y	N	N	Y	Y	Y
8	**Bucshon**	N	N	Y	N	Y	Y
9	**Hollingsworth**	N	Y	Y	N	Y	Y
IOWA							
1	Finkenauer	Y	N	Y	Y	Y	Y
2	Loebsack	Y	N	N	Y	?	?
3	Axne	Y	N	Y	Y	Y	Y
4	**King, S.**	N	Y	Y	N	Y	Y
KANSAS							
1	**Marshall**	N	N	Y	N	Y	N
2	**Watkins**	N	N	Y	N	Y	N
3	Davids	Y	N	N	Y	Y	Y
4	**Estes**	N	N	Y	N	Y	N
KENTUCKY							
1	**Comer**	N	Y	Y	N	N	N
2	**Guthrie**	Y	N	Y	N	Y	Y
3	Yarmuth	Y	N	N	Y	Y	Y
4	**Massie**	N	Y	Y	N	N	N
5	**Rogers, H.**	Y	N	Y	N	Y	Y
6	**Barr**	N	N	Y	N	Y	N
LOUISIANA							
1	**Scalise**	Y	N	Y	N	Y	N
2	Richmond	Y	N	N	Y	Y	Y
3	**Higgins, C.**	N	N	Y	Y	N	Y
4	**Johnson, M.**	N	N	Y	N	N	N
5	**Abraham**	N	N	Y	N	?	?
6	**Graves, G.**	N	N	Y	N	Y	Y
MAINE							
1	Pingree	Y	N	N	Y	?	?
2	Golden	Y	N	Y	Y	Y	Y
MARYLAND							
1	**Harris**	N	Y	Y	N	N	N
2	Ruppersberger	Y	N	N	Y	Y	Y
3	Sarbanes	Y	N	N	Y	Y	Y
4	Brown, A.	Y	N	N	Y	Y	Y
5	Hoyer	Y	N	N	Y	Y	Y
6	Trone	Y	N	N	Y	Y	Y
7	Cummings	Y	N	N	Y	?	?
8	Raskin						
MASSACHUSETTS		Y	N	N	Y	Y	Y
1	Neal						
2	McGovern	Y	N	N	Y	Y	Y
3	Trahan	Y	N	N	Y	Y	Y
4	Kennedy	Y	N	N	Y	Y	Y
5	Clark	Y	N	N	Y	Y	Y
6	Moulton	Y	N	N	Y	Y	Y
7	Pressley	Y	N	N	Y	Y	Y
8	Lynch	N	N	N	Y	Y	Y
9	Keating	Y	N	N	Y	Y	Y
MICHIGAN		Y	N	N	Y	Y	Y
1	**Bergman**						
2	**Huizenga**	Y	N	Y	N	Y	N
3	*Amash*	N	Y	Y	N	Y	N
4	**Moolenaar**	N	Y	Y	Y	N	N
5	Kildee	N	N	Y	N	Y	N
6	**Upton**	Y	N	N	Y	Y	Y
7	**Walberg**	Y	N	Y	N	Y	Y
8	Slotkin	N	N	Y	N	Y	N
9	Levin	Y	N	Y	Y	Y	Y
10	**Mitchell**	Y	N	N	Y	Y	Y
11	Stevens	N	N	Y	N	Y	N
12	Dingell	Y	N	N	Y	Y	Y
13	Tlaib	Y	N	N	Y	Y	Y
14	Lawrence	Y	N	N	Y	Y	Y
MINNESOTA		Y	N	N	Y	Y	Y
1	**Hagedorn**						
2	Craig	N	N	Y	N	Y	N
3	Phillips	Y	N	N	Y	Y	Y
4	McCollum	Y	Y	N	Y	Y	Y
5	Omar	Y	N	N	Y	Y	Y

		511	512	513	514	515	516
6	**Emmer**	N	N	N	Y	Y	Y
7	Peterson	N	N	Y	N	Y	N
8	**Stauber**	N	N	Y	Y	Y	N
MISSISSIPPI		Y	N	Y	N	Y	Y
1	**Kelly, T.**						
2	Thompson, B.	N	N	Y	N	Y	Y
3	**Guest**	Y	N	N	Y	Y	Y
4	**Palazzo**	N	N	Y	N	Y	N
MISSOURI		Y	N	Y	N	Y	N
1	Clay						
2	**Wagner**	Y	N	N	Y	Y	Y
3	**Luetkemeyer**	N	N	Y	N	Y	N
4	**Hartzler**	Y	N	Y	N	Y	Y
5	Cleaver	Y	N	Y	Y	Y	N
6	**Graves, S.**	Y	N	N	Y	Y	Y
7	**Long**	N	N	Y	N	Y	N
8	**Smith, J.**	N	N	Y	N	Y	Y
MONTANA		N	N	Y	N	Y	N
AL	**Gianforte**						
NEBRASKA		N	N	Y	N	Y	Y
1	**Fortenberry**						
2	**Bacon**	Y	N	Y	Y	Y	Y
3	**Smith, Adrian**	Y	N	Y	Y	Y	Y
NEVADA		N	N	Y	N	Y	Y
1	Titus						
2	**Amodei**	Y	N	N	Y	Y	Y
3	Lee	N	N	Y	N	Y	Y
4	Horsford	Y	N	N	Y	Y	Y
NEW HAMPSHIRE		Y	N	N	Y	Y	Y
1	Pappas						
2	Kuster	Y	N	N	Y	Y	Y
NEW JERSEY		Y	N	N	Y	Y	Y
1	Norcross						
2	Van Drew	Y	N	N	Y	Y	Y
3	Kim	Y	N	Y	Y	Y	Y
4	**Smith, C.**	Y	N	Y	Y	Y	Y
5	Gottheimer	Y	N	Y	Y	Y	Y
6	Pallone	Y	N	Y	Y	Y	Y
7	Malinowski	Y	N	N	Y	Y	Y
8	Sires	Y	N	N	Y	Y	Y
9	Pascrell	Y	N	N	Y	Y	Y
10	Payne	Y	N	N	Y	Y	Y
11	Sherrill	Y	N	N	Y	Y	Y
12	Watson Coleman	Y	N	Y	Y	Y	Y
NEW MEXICO		Y	N	N	Y	Y	Y
1	Haaland						
2	Torres Small	Y	N	N	Y	Y	Y
3	Luján	Y	N	N	Y	Y	Y
NEW YORK		Y	N	N	Y	Y	Y
1	**Zeldin**						
2	**King, P.**	N	N	Y	N	Y	Y
3	Suozzi	Y	N	Y	Y	Y	Y
4	Rice, K.	Y	N	N	Y	Y	Y
5	Meeks	N	N	N	Y	Y	Y
6	Meng	Y	N	N	Y	Y	Y
7	Velázquez	Y	N	N	Y	?	?
8	Jeffries	Y	N	N	Y	Y	Y
9	Clarke	Y	N	N	Y	Y	Y
10	Nadler	Y	N	N	Y	Y	Y
11	Rose	Y	N	N	Y	Y	Y
12	Maloney, C.	Y	N	Y	Y	Y	Y
13	Espaillat	Y	N	N	Y	Y	Y
14	Ocasio-Cortez	Y	N	N	Y	Y	Y
15	Serrano	Y	N	N	Y	Y	Y
16	Engel	Y	N	N	Y	Y	Y
17	Lowey	Y	N	N	Y	Y	Y
18	Maloney, S.P.	Y	N	N	Y	Y	Y
19	Delgado	Y	N	N	Y	Y	Y
20	Tonko	Y	N	N	Y	Y	Y
21	**Stefanik**	Y	N	N	Y	Y	Y
22	Brindisi	Y	N	Y	Y	Y	Y
23	**Reed**	N	Y	Y	Y	Y	Y
24	**Katko**	N	N	Y	Y	Y	Y
25	Morelle	Y	N	Y	Y	Y	Y
26	Higgins, B.	Y	N	N	Y	Y	Y
27	**Collins, C.**	Y	N	N	Y	Y	Y
NORTH CAROLINA		Y	N	Y	N	Y	Y
1	Butterfield						
2	**Holding**	Y	N	N	Y	Y	Y
3	**Jones***	N	N	Y	N	Y	N
4	Price						
5	**Foxx**	Y	N	N	Y	Y	Y
6	**Walker**	N	N	Y	N	Y	N
7	**Rouzer**	N	N	Y	N	Y	N

		511	512	513	514	515	516
8	**Hudson**	N	Y	Y	N	+	-
9	vacant	N	Y	Y	N	+	-
10	**McHenry**	Y	N	Y	N	Y	Y
11	**Meadows**	N	Y	Y	N	?	?
12	Adams	Y	N	N	Y	Y	Y
13	**Budd**	N	Y	Y	N	Y	N
NORTH DAKOTA							
AL	**Armstrong**	N	N	Y	N	Y	Y
OHIO							
1	**Chabot**	N	N	Y	N	Y	N
2	**Wenstrup**	N	N	Y	N	Y	N
3	Beatty	Y	N	N	Y	Y	Y
4	**Jordan**	N	Y	Y	N	N	N
5	**Latta**	N	N	Y	N	Y	N
6	**Johnson, B.**	Y	N	Y	N	Y	Y
7	**Gibbs**	N	N	Y	N	Y	N
8	**Davidson**	N	Y	Y	N	N	N
9	Kaptur	Y	N	N	Y	Y	Y
10	**Turner**	Y	N	Y	N	Y	N
11	Fudge	Y	N	N	Y	Y	Y
12	**Balderson**	N	N	Y	N	Y	N
13	Ryan	Y	N	N	?	?	?
14	**Joyce**	Y	N	Y	Y	Y	Y
15	**Stivers**	N	N	Y	Y	Y	Y
16	**Gonzalez**	N	N	Y	Y	Y	Y
OKLAHOMA							
1	**Hern**	N	N	Y	N	N	N
2	**Mullin**	N	N	Y	N	Y	N
3	**Lucas**	Y	N	Y	N	Y	Y
4	**Cole**	Y	N	Y	Y	Y	Y
5	Horn	Y	N	Y	Y	Y	Y
OREGON							
1	Bonamici	Y	N	N	Y	Y	Y
2	**Walden**	Y	N	Y	N	Y	Y
3	Blumenauer	N	N	N	Y	+	+
4	DeFazio	Y	N	N	Y	Y	Y
5	Schrader	N	N	N	Y	Y	Y
PENNSYLVANIA							
1	**Fitzpatrick**	Y	N	Y	Y	Y	Y
2	Boyle	Y	N	N	Y	Y	Y
3	Evans	Y	N	N	Y	Y	Y
4	Dean	Y	N	N	Y	Y	Y
5	Scanlon	Y	N	N	Y	Y	Y
6	Houlahan	Y	N	N	Y	Y	Y
7	Wild	Y	N	N	Y	Y	Y
8	Cartwright	Y	N	N	Y	Y	Y
9	**Meuser**	Y	N	Y	N	Y	N
10	**Perry**	N	Y	Y	N	N	N
11	**Smucker**	N	N	Y	N	Y	Y
12	**Marino***						
13	**Joyce**	N	N	Y	N	Y	Y
14	**Reschenthaler**	Y	N	Y	N	Y	Y
15	**Thompson, G.**	Y	N	Y	Y	Y	N
16	**Kelly, M.**	N	N	Y	N	Y	Y
17	Lamb	Y	N	N	Y	Y	Y
18	Doyle	Y	N	N	Y	Y	Y
RHODE ISLAND							
1	Cicilline	Y	N	N	Y	Y	Y
2	Langevin	Y	N	N	Y	Y	Y
SOUTH CAROLINA							
1	Cunningham	N	N	Y	Y	Y	Y
2	**Wilson, J.**	Y	N	Y	N	Y	N
3	**Duncan**	N	N	Y	N	Y	N
4	**Timmons**	N	N	Y	N	Y	N
5	**Norman**	N	Y	Y	N	Y	N
6	Clyburn	Y	N	N	Y	+	+
7	**Rice, T.**	N	N	Y	N	Y	N
SOUTH DAKOTA							
AL	**Johnson**	N	N	Y	N	Y	N
TENNESSEE							
1	**Roe**	N	N	Y	N	Y	Y
2	**Burchett**	N	Y	Y	N	N	N
3	**Fleischmann**	Y	N	Y	N	Y	N
4	**DesJarlais**	N	Y	Y	N	Y	N
5	Cooper	N	Y	N	Y	Y	Y
6	**Rose**	N	N	Y	N	Y	N
7	**Green**	N	Y	Y	N	Y	N
8	**Kustoff**	Y	N	Y	N	Y	N
9	Cohen	Y	N	N	Y	Y	Y
TEXAS							
1	**Gohmert**	N	Y	Y	N	N	N
2	**Crenshaw**	N	N	Y	Y	Y	Y
3	**Taylor**	N	N	Y	N	N	N
4	**Ratcliffe**	N	N	Y	N	Y	N

		511	512	513	514	515	516
5	**Gooden**	N	N	Y	N	N	N
6	**Wright**	N	Y	Y	N	N	N
7	Fletcher	Y	N	N	Y	Y	Y
8	**Brady**	Y	N	Y	N	Y	N
9	Green, A.	Y	N	N	Y	Y	Y
10	**McCaul**	Y	N	Y	Y	Y	Y
11	**Conaway**	Y	N	Y	N	Y	N
12	**Granger**	Y	N	Y	N	Y	N
13	**Thornberry**	Y	N	Y	N	Y	N
14	**Weber**	N	Y	Y	N	N	N
15	Gonzalez	Y	N	N	Y	Y	Y
16	Escobar	Y	N	N	Y	Y	Y
17	**Flores**	N	N	Y	N	Y	Y
18	Jackson Lee	Y	N	N	Y	Y	Y
19	**Arrington**	N	N	Y	N	Y	N
20	Castro	Y	N	N	Y	Y	Y
21	**Roy**	N	Y	Y	N	N	N
22	**Olson**	N	N	Y	N	Y	N
23	**Hurd**	Y	N	Y	Y	Y	Y
24	**Marchant**	N	N	Y	N	Y	N
25	**Williams**	N	N	Y	N	Y	N
26	**Burgess**	N	Y	Y	N	Y	Y
27	**Cloud**	N	Y	Y	N	Y	N
28	Cuellar	Y	N	N	Y	Y	Y
29	Garcia, S.	Y	N	N	Y	Y	Y
30	Johnson, E.B.	Y	N	N	Y	Y	Y
31	**Carter, J.**	Y	N	Y	N	Y	N
32	Allred	Y	N	N	Y	Y	Y
33	Veasey	Y	N	N	Y	Y	Y
34	Vela	Y	N	N	Y	Y	Y
35	Doggett	Y	N	N	Y	Y	Y
36	**Babin**	Y	N	Y	N	Y	N
UTAH							
1	**Bishop, R.**	Y	N	Y	N	Y	N
2	**Stewart**	Y	N	Y	N	Y	N
3	**Curtis**	N	N	Y	Y	Y	N
4	McAdams	N	Y	N	Y	Y	Y
VERMONT							
AL	Welch	Y	N	N	Y	?	?
VIRGINIA							
1	**Wittman**	N	N	Y	N	Y	Y
2	Luria	Y	N	N	Y	Y	Y
3	Scott, R.	Y	N	N	Y	Y	Y
4	McEachin	Y	N	N	Y	+	+
5	**Riggleman**	N	N	Y	N	Y	N
6	**Cline**	N	N	Y	N	N	N
7	Spanberger	N	N	Y	Y	Y	Y
8	Beyer	Y	N	N	Y	Y	Y
9	**Griffith**	N	Y	Y	N	Y	N
10	Wexton	Y	N	N	Y	Y	Y
11	Connolly	Y	N	N	Y	Y	Y
WASHINGTON							
1	DelBene	Y	N	N	Y	Y	Y
2	Larsen	Y	N	N	Y	Y	Y
3	**Herrera Beutler**	N	N	Y	Y	Y	Y
4	**Newhouse**	N	N	Y	N	Y	N
5	**McMorris Rodgers**	N	N	Y	Y	Y	Y
6	Kilmer	Y	N	N	Y	Y	Y
7	Jayapal	Y	N	N	Y	Y	Y
8	Schrier	Y	N	N	Y	Y	Y
9	Smith Adam	Y	N	N	Y	Y	Y
10	Heck	Y	N	N	Y	Y	Y
WEST VIRGINIA							
1	**McKinley**	N	Y	Y	N	Y	N
2	**Mooney**	N	Y	Y	N	Y	N
3	**Miller**	Y	N	Y	N	Y	N
WISCONSIN							
1	**Steil**	N	N	Y	Y	Y	Y
2	Pocan	Y	N	N	Y	Y	Y
3	Kind	N	N	N	Y	+	+
4	Moore	Y	N	N	Y	Y	Y
5	**Sensenbrenner**	N	N	Y	N	Y	N
6	**Grothman**	N	N	Y	N	Y	N
7	**Duffy**	N	N	Y	Y	Y	N
8	**Gallagher**	N	Y	Y	Y	Y	Y
WYOMING							
AL	**Cheney**	Y	N	Y	N	Y	N
DELEGATES							
	Radewagen (A.S.)						
	Norton (D.C.)						
	San Nicolas (Guam)						
	Sablan (N. Marianas)						
	González-Colón (P.R.)						
	Plaskett (V.I.)						

III HOUSE VOTES

517. HR1146, HR1941, HR205. Oil and Gas Leasing - Previous Question. Hastings, D-Fla., motion to order the previous question on the rule (H Res 548) that would provide for House floor consideration of the Protecting and Securing Florida's Coastline Act (HR 205) that would permanently extend the moratorium on leasing in certain areas of the Gulf of Mexico; provide for consideration of the Arctic Cultural and Coastal Plain Protection Act (HR 1146) that would repeal the Arctic National Wildlife Refuge oil and gas program; and provide for consideration of the Coastal and Marine Economies Protection Act (HR 1941) that would prohibit the Interior Department from including certain planning areas in any leasing programs. The rule would provide for automatic adoption of three Grijalva, D-Ariz., manager's amendments, one to each bill. Each manager's amendment would make technical corrections to its respective bill to conform language related to non-rig unit operation fees. The Grijalva, D-Ariz., manager's amendment to the Arctic Cultural and Coastal Plain Protection Act (HR 1146) would also slightly increase annual inspection fees for certain facilities, drilling rigs, and non-rig units. Motion agreed to 232-196: R 1-195; D 231-0; I 0-1. Sept. 10, 2019.

518. HR1146, HR1941, HR205. Oil and Gas Leasing - Rule. Adoption of the rule (H Res 548) that would provide for House floor consideration of the Protecting and Securing Florida's Coastline Act (HR 205) that would permanently extend the moratorium on leasing in certain areas of the Gulf of Mexico; provide for consideration of the Arctic Cultural and Coastal Plain Protection Act (HR 1146) that would repeal the Arctic National Wildlife Refuge oil and gas program; and provide for consideration of the Coastal and Marine Economies Protection Act (HR 1941) that would prohibit the Interior Department from including certain planning areas in any leasing programs. The rule would provide for automatic adoption of three Grijalva, D-Ariz., manager's amendments, one to each bill. Each manager's amendment would make technical corrections to its respective bill to conform language related to non-rig unit operation fees. The Grijalva, D-Ariz., manager's amendment to the Arctic Cultural and Coastal Plain Protection Act (HR 1146) would also slightly increase annual inspection fees for certain facilities, drilling rigs, and non-rig units. Adopted 231-196: R 1-195; D 230-0; I 0-1. Sept. 10, 2019.

519. HR2852. Housing Mortgage Appraisal - Passage. San Nicolas, D-Guam, motion to suspend the rules and pass the bill, as amended, that would authorize state-licensed appraisers to conduct appraisals for single-family homes purchased by Federal Housing Administration-insured mortgages. (Under current law, such appraisers must be state-certified) It would require state-licensed appraisers for single-family housing mortgages to complete a course consisting of at least 7 hours of training related to FHA appraisal requirements. It would require HUD to issue guidance to mortgage lenders outlining how to implement these provisions. Motion agreed to 419-5: R 192-4; D 227-0; I 0-1. *Note: A two-thirds majority of those present and voting (283 in this case) is required for passage under suspension of the rules.* Sept. 10, 2019.

520. HR205. Gulf of Mexico Oil and Gas Leasing - Job Availability. Gosar, R-Ariz., amendment no. 3 that would delay enactment of Sec. 2 of the bill until the Interior and Labor departments determine that its provisions would not adversely affect jobs available to minorities and women. The section would permanently extend a moratorium on oil and gas leasing by the Interior Department in certain areas of the Gulf of Mexico. Rejected in Committee of the Whole 182-251: R 182-15; D 0-234; I 0-2. Sept. 11, 2019.

521. HR205. Gulf of Mexico Oil and Gas Leasing - Passage. Passage of the bill, as amended, that would permanently extend an existing moratorium on oil and gas leasing by the Interior Department in certain areas of the Gulf of Mexico, which is currently set to expire in June 2022. It would also require the Interior Department to collect inspection fees from certain oil and gas facilities operating on the outer Continental Shelf and set annual levels and schedules for fees collected from facilities above the waterline, drilling rigs, and non-rig units. Such fees would be deposited into a Treasury Department ocean energy safety fund established under the bill's provisions, with funds to be made available through annual appropriations acts to carry out inspections of outer Continental Shelf facilities. Passed 248-180: R 22-174; D 226-5; I 0-1. *Note: A "nay" was a vote in support of the president's position.* Sept. 11, 2019.

522. HR1941. Atlantic and Pacific Oil and Gas Leasing - Short Title. Gosar, R-Ariz., amendment no. 2 that would change the short title of the bill to the "Russian Energy Reliance and United States Poverty Act." Rejected in Committee of the Whole 161-272: R 161-36; D 0-234; I 0-2. Sept. 11, 2019.

	517	518	519	520	521	522
ALABAMA						
1 **Byrne**	N	N	Y	Y	N	Y
2 **Roby**	N	N	Y	Y	N	N
3 **Rogers, M.**	N	N	Y	Y	N	Y
4 **Aderholt**	N	N	Y	Y	N	Y
5 **Brooks, M.**	N	N	Y	Y	N	Y
6 **Palmer**	N	N	Y	Y	N	N
7 Sewell	Y	Y	Y	N	Y	N
ALASKA						
AL **Young**	N	N	Y	Y	N	Y
ARIZONA						
1 O'Halleran	Y	Y	Y	N	Y	N
2 Kirkpatrick	Y	Y	Y	N	Y	N
3 Grijalva	Y	Y	Y	N	Y	N
4 **Gosar**	N	N	Y	Y	N	Y
5 **Biggs**	N	N	N	Y	N	Y
6 **Schweikert**	N	N	Y	Y	N	Y
7 Gallego	Y	Y	?	N	Y	N
8 **Lesko**	N	N	Y	Y	N	Y
9 Stanton	Y	Y	Y	N	Y	N
ARKANSAS						
1 **Crawford**	N	N	Y	Y	N	Y
2 **Hill, F.**	N	N	Y	Y	N	N
3 **Womack**	N	N	Y	Y	N	Y
4 **Westerman**	N	N	Y	Y	N	Y
CALIFORNIA						
1 **LaMalfa**	N	N	Y	Y	N	Y
2 Huffman	Y	Y	Y	N	Y	N
3 Garamendi	Y	?	?	N	Y	N
4 **McClintock**	N	N	Y	Y	N	Y
5 Thompson, M.	Y	Y	Y	N	Y	N
6 Matsui	Y	Y	Y	N	Y	N
7 Bera	Y	Y	Y	N	Y	N
8 **Cook**	N	N	Y	Y	N	Y
9 McNerney	Y	Y	Y	N	Y	N
10 Harder	Y	Y	Y	N	Y	N
11 DeSaulnier	Y	Y	Y	N	Y	N
12 Pelosi						
13 Lee B.	Y	Y	Y	N	Y	N
14 Speier	Y	Y	Y	N	Y	N
15 Swalwell	Y	Y	Y	N	Y	N
16 Costa	Y	Y	Y	N	Y	N
17 Khanna	Y	Y	Y	N	Y	N
18 Eshoo	Y	Y	Y	N	Y	N
19 Lofgren	Y	Y	Y	N	Y	N
20 Panetta	Y	Y	Y	N	Y	N
21 Cox	Y	Y	Y	N	Y	N
22 **Nunes**	N	N	Y	Y	N	Y
23 **McCarthy**	N	N	Y	Y	N	Y
24 Carbajal	Y	Y	Y	N	Y	N
25 Hill, K.	Y	Y	Y	N	Y	N
26 Brownley	Y	Y	Y	N	Y	N
27 Chu	Y	Y	Y	N	Y	N
28 Schiff	Y	Y	Y	N	Y	N
29 Cárdenas	Y	Y	Y	N	Y	N
30 Sherman	Y	Y	Y	N	Y	N
31 Aguilar	Y	Y	Y	N	Y	N
32 Napolitano	Y	Y	Y	N	Y	N
33 Lieu	Y	Y	Y	N	Y	N
34 Gomez	Y	Y	Y	N	Y	N
35 Torres	Y	Y	Y	N	Y	N
36 Ruiz	Y	Y	Y	N	Y	N
37 Bass	Y	Y	?	N	Y	N
38 Sánchez	Y	Y	Y	N	Y	N
39 Cisneros	Y	Y	Y	N	Y	N
40 Roybal-Allard	Y	Y	Y	N	Y	N
41 Takano	Y	Y	Y	N	Y	N
42 **Calvert**	N	N	Y	Y	N	Y
43 Waters	Y	Y	Y	N	Y	N
44 Barragán	Y	Y	Y	N	Y	N
45 Porter	Y	Y	Y	N	Y	N
46 Correa	Y	Y	Y	N	Y	N
47 Lowenthal	Y	Y	Y	N	Y	N
48 Rouda	Y	Y	Y	N	Y	N
49 Levin	Y	Y	Y	N	Y	N
50 **Hunter**	N	N	Y	Y	N	Y
51 Vargas	Y	Y	Y	N	Y	N
52 Peters	Y	Y	?	N	Y	N

	517	518	519	520	521	522
53 Davis, S.	Y	Y	Y	N	Y	N
COLORADO						
1 DeGette	Y	Y	Y	N	Y	N
2 Neguse	Y	Y	Y	N	Y	N
3 **Tipton**	N	N	Y	Y	N	Y
4 **Buck**	N	N	N	Y	N	Y
5 **Lamborn**	N	N	Y	Y	N	Y
6 Crow	Y	Y	Y	N	Y	N
7 Perlmutter	Y	Y	Y	N	Y	N
CONNECTICUT						
1 Larson	Y	Y	Y	N	Y	N
2 Courtney	Y	Y	Y	N	Y	N
3 DeLauro	Y	Y	Y	N	Y	N
4 Himes	Y	Y	Y	N	Y	N
5 Hayes	Y	Y	Y	N	Y	N
DELAWARE						
AL Blunt Rochester	Y	Y	Y	N	Y	N
FLORIDA						
1 **Gaetz**	N	N	Y	Y	Y	Y
2 **Dunn**	N	N	Y	Y	Y	Y
3 **Yoho**	N	N	N	Y	N	Y
4 **Rutherford**	N	N	Y	Y	N	Y
5 Lawson	Y	Y	Y	N	Y	N
6 **Waltz**	N	N	Y	Y	N	Y
7 Murphy	Y	Y	Y	N	Y	N
8 **Posey**	N	N	Y	Y	Y	Y
9 Soto	Y	Y	Y	N	Y	N
10 Demings	Y	Y	Y	N	Y	N
11 **Webster**	N	N	Y	Y	N	Y
12 **Bilirakis**	N	N	Y	Y	N	Y
13 Crist	Y	Y	Y	N	Y	N
14 Castor	Y	Y	Y	N	Y	N
15 **Spano**	N	N	Y	Y	N	Y
16 **Buchanan**	N	N	Y	Y	N	Y
17 **Steube**	N	N	Y	Y	N	Y
18 **Mast**	N	N	Y	Y	N	Y
19 **Rooney**	Y	Y	Y	N	Y	N
20 Hastings	Y	Y	Y	N	Y	N
21 Frankel	Y	Y	Y	N	Y	N
22 Deutch	Y	Y	Y	N	Y	N
23 Wasserman Schultz	?	Y	Y	N	Y	N
24 Wilson, F.	Y	Y	Y	N	Y	N
25 **Diaz-Balart**	N	N	Y	Y	N	Y
26 Mucarsel-Powell	Y	Y	Y	N	Y	N
27 Shalala	Y	Y	Y	N	Y	N
GEORGIA						
1 **Carter, E.L.**	N	N	Y	Y	N	Y
2 Bishop, S.	Y	Y	Y	N	Y	N
3 **Ferguson**	N	N	Y	Y	N	N
4 Johnson, H.	Y	Y	Y	N	Y	N
5 Lewis John	Y	Y	Y	N	Y	N
6 McBath	Y	Y	Y	N	Y	N
7 **Woodall**	N	N	Y	Y	N	Y
8 **Scott, A.**	N	N	Y	Y	N	Y
9 **Collins, D.**	N	N	Y	Y	N	Y
10 **Hice**	N	N	Y	Y	N	Y
11 **Loudermilk**	N	N	Y	Y	N	Y
12 **Allen**	N	N	Y	Y	N	Y
13 Scott, D.	Y	Y	Y	N	Y	N
14 **Graves, T.**	N	N	Y	Y	N	Y
HAWAII						
1 Case	Y	Y	Y	N	Y	N
2 Gabbard	Y	Y	Y	N	Y	N
IDAHO						
1 **Fulcher**	N	N	Y	Y	N	Y
2 **Simpson**	N	N	Y	Y	N	Y
ILLINOIS						
1 Rush	Y	Y	Y	N	Y	N
2 Kelly, R.	Y	Y	Y	N	Y	N
3 Lipinski	Y	Y	Y	N	Y	N
4 García, J.	Y	Y	Y	N	Y	N
5 Quigley	Y	Y	Y	N	Y	N
6 Casten	Y	Y	Y	N	Y	N
7 Davis, D.	Y	Y	Y	N	Y	N
8 Krishnamoorthi	Y	Y	Y	N	Y	N
9 Schakowsky	Y	Y	Y	N	Y	N
10 Schneider	Y	Y	Y	N	Y	N
11 Foster	Y	Y	Y	N	Y	N

KEY: **Republicans**   Democrats   *Independents*

Y Voted for (yea)	**N** Voted against (nay)	**P** Voted "present"	
+ Announced for	**-** Announced against	**?** Did not vote or otherwise make position known	
# Paired for	**X** Paired against		

		517	518	519	520	521	522
12	**Bost**	N	N	Y	Y	N	Y
13	**Davis, R.**	N	N	Y	Y	N	Y
14	Underwood	Y	Y	Y	N	Y	N
15	**Shimkus**	N	N	Y	Y	N	Y
16	**Kinzinger**	N	N	Y	N	N	Y
17	Bustos	Y	Y	Y	N	Y	N
18	**LaHood**	N	N	Y	Y	N	Y
INDIANA							
1	Visclosky	Y	Y	Y	N	Y	N
2	**Walorski**	N	N	Y	Y	N	Y
3	**Banks**	N	N	Y	Y	N	Y
4	**Baird**	N	N	Y	Y	N	Y
5	**Brooks, S.**	N	N	Y	Y	N	Y
6	**Pence**	N	N	Y	Y	N	Y
7	Carson	Y	Y	Y	N	Y	N
8	**Bucshon**	N	N	Y	Y	N	Y
9	**Hollingsworth**	N	N	Y	Y	Y	N
IOWA							
1	Finkenauer	Y	Y	Y	N	Y	N
2	Loebsack	Y	Y	Y	N	Y	N
3	Axne	Y	Y	Y	N	Y	N
4	**King, S.**	N	N	Y	Y	N	Y
KANSAS							
1	**Marshall**	N	N	Y	Y	N	Y
2	**Watkins**	N	N	Y	Y	N	Y
3	Davids	Y	Y	Y	N	Y	N
4	**Estes**	N	N	Y	Y	N	Y
KENTUCKY							
1	**Comer**	N	N	Y	Y	N	Y
2	**Guthrie**	N	N	Y	Y	N	Y
3	Yarmuth	Y	Y	Y	N	Y	N
4	**Massie**	N	N	N	Y	N	Y
5	**Rogers, H.**	N	N	Y	Y	N	Y
6	**Barr**	N	N	Y	Y	N	N
LOUISIANA							
1	**Scalise**	N	N	Y	Y	N	Y
2	Richmond	Y	Y	Y	N	Y	N
3	**Higgins, C.**	N	N	Y	Y	N	N
4	**Johnson, M.**	N	N	Y	Y	N	Y
5	**Abraham**	?	?	?	?	?	?
6	**Graves, G.**	N	N	Y	Y	N	Y
MAINE							
1	Pingree	Y	Y	Y	N	Y	N
2	Golden	Y	Y	Y	N	Y	N
MARYLAND							
1	**Harris**	N	N	Y	Y	N	Y
2	Ruppersberger	Y	Y	Y	N	Y	N
3	Sarbanes	Y	Y	Y	N	Y	N
4	Brown, A.	Y	Y	Y	N	Y	N
5	Hoyer	Y	Y	Y	N	Y	N
6	Trone	Y	Y	Y	N	Y	N
7	Cummings	Y	Y	Y	N	Y	N
8	Raskin						
MASSACHUSETTS		Y	Y	Y	N	Y	N
1	Neal						
2	McGovern	Y	Y	Y	N	Y	N
3	Trahan	Y	Y	Y	N	Y	N
4	Kennedy	Y	Y	Y	N	Y	N
5	Clark	Y	Y	Y	N	Y	N
6	Moulton	Y	Y	Y	N	Y	N
7	Pressley	Y	Y	Y	N	Y	N
8	Lynch	Y	Y	Y	N	Y	N
9	Keating	Y	Y	Y	N	Y	N
MICHIGAN		Y	Y	Y	N	Y	N
1	**Bergman**						
2	**Huizenga**	N	N	Y	Y	N	Y
3	*Amash*	N	N	Y	Y	N	Y
4	**Moolenaar**	N	N	N	N	N	N
5	Kildee	N	N	Y	Y	N	Y
6	**Upton**	Y	Y	Y	N	Y	N
7	**Walberg**	N	N	Y	Y	N	N
8	Slotkin	N	N	Y	Y	N	Y
9	Levin	Y	Y	Y	N	Y	N
10	**Mitchell**	Y	Y	Y	N	Y	N
11	Stevens	N	N	Y	Y	N	Y
12	Dingell	Y	Y	Y	N	Y	N
13	Tlaib	Y	Y	Y	N	Y	N
14	Lawrence	Y	Y	Y	N	Y	N
MINNESOTA		Y	Y	Y	?	?	?
1	**Hagedorn**						
2	Craig	N	N	Y	Y	N	Y
3	Phillips	Y	Y	Y	N	Y	N
4	McCollum	Y	Y	Y	N	Y	N
5	Omar	Y	Y	Y	N	Y	N

		517	518	519	520	521	522
6	**Emmer**	Y	Y	Y	N	Y	N
7	Peterson	N	N	Y	Y	N	Y
8	**Stauber**	Y	Y	Y	N	N	N
MISSISSIPPI		N	N	Y	Y	N	Y
1	**Kelly, T.**						
2	Thompson, B.	N	N	Y	Y	N	Y
3	**Guest**	Y	Y	Y	N	Y	N
4	**Palazzo**	N	N	Y	Y	N	N
MISSOURI		N	N	Y	Y	N	Y
1	Clay						
2	**Wagner**	Y	Y	Y	N	Y	N
3	**Luetkemeyer**	N	N	Y	Y	N	Y
4	**Hartzler**	N	N	Y	Y	N	Y
5	Cleaver	N	N	Y	Y	N	Y
6	**Graves, S.**	Y	Y	Y	N	Y	N
7	**Long**	N	N	Y	Y	N	Y
8	**Smith, J.**	N	N	Y	Y	N	Y
MONTANA		N	N	Y	Y	N	Y
AL	**Gianforte**						
NEBRASKA		N	N	Y	Y	N	Y
1	**Fortenberry**						
2	**Bacon**	N	N	Y	Y	N	Y
3	**Smith, Adrian**	N	N	Y	Y	N	N
NEVADA		N	N	Y	Y	N	Y
1	Titus						
2	**Amodei**	Y	Y	Y	N	Y	N
3	Lee	N	N	Y	Y	N	Y
4	Horsford	Y	Y	Y	N	Y	N
NEW HAMPSHIRE		Y	Y	Y	N	Y	N
1	Pappas						
2	Kuster	Y	Y	Y	N	Y	N
NEW JERSEY		Y	Y	Y	N	Y	N
1	Norcross						
2	Van Drew	Y	Y	Y	N	Y	N
3	Kim	Y	Y	Y	N	Y	N
4	**Smith, C.**	Y	Y	Y	N	Y	N
5	Gottheimer	N	N	Y	N	Y	N
6	Pallone	Y	Y	Y	N	Y	N
7	Malinowski	Y	Y	Y	N	Y	N
8	Sires	Y	Y	Y	N	Y	N
9	Pascrell	Y	Y	Y	N	Y	N
10	Payne	Y	Y	Y	N	Y	N
11	Sherrill	Y	Y	Y	N	Y	N
12	Watson Coleman	Y	Y	Y	N	Y	N
NEW MEXICO		Y	Y	Y	N	Y	N
1	Haaland						
2	Torres Small	Y	Y	Y	N	Y	N
3	Luján	Y	Y	Y	N	Y	N
NEW YORK		Y	Y	Y	N	Y	N
1	**Zeldin**						
2	**King, P.**	N	N	Y	Y	N	Y
3	Suozzi	N	N	Y	N	Y	N
4	Rice, K.	Y	Y	Y	N	Y	N
5	Meeks	Y	Y	Y	N	Y	N
6	Meng	Y	Y	Y	N	Y	N
7	Velázquez	Y	Y	Y	N	Y	N
8	Jeffries	Y	Y	Y	N	Y	N
9	Clarke	Y	Y	Y	N	Y	N
10	Nadler	Y	Y	Y	N	Y	N
11	Rose	Y	Y	Y	N	Y	N
12	Maloney, C.	Y	Y	Y	N	Y	N
13	Espaillat	Y	Y	Y	N	Y	N
14	Ocasio-Cortez	Y	Y	Y	N	Y	N
15	Serrano	Y	Y	Y	N	Y	N
16	Engel	Y	Y	Y	N	Y	N
17	Lowey	Y	Y	Y	N	Y	N
18	Maloney, S.P.	Y	Y	Y	N	Y	N
19	Delgado	Y	Y	Y	N	Y	N
20	Tonko	Y	Y	Y	N	Y	N
21	**Stefanik**	Y	Y	Y	N	Y	N
22	Brindisi	N	N	Y	N	Y	N
23	**Reed**	Y	Y	Y	N	Y	N
24	**Katko**	N	N	Y	Y	N	Y
25	Morelle	N	N	Y	N	Y	N
26	Higgins, B.	Y	Y	Y	N	Y	N
27	**Collins, C.**	Y	Y	Y	N	Y	N
NORTH CAROLINA		N	N	Y	Y	N	Y
1	Butterfield						
2	**Holding**	Y	Y	Y	N	Y	N
3	**Jones***	N	N	Y	Y	N	Y
4	Price						
5	**Foxx**	Y	Y	Y	N	Y	N
6	**Walker**	N	N	Y	Y	N	Y
7	**Rouzer**	N	N	Y	Y	N	Y

		517	518	519	520	521	522
8	**Hudson**	N	N	Y	Y	N	N
9	vacant	N	N	Y	Y	N	Y
10	**McHenry**	N	N	Y	Y	Y	N
11	**Meadows**	N	N	Y	Y	N	Y
12	Adams	Y	Y	Y	N	Y	N
13	**Budd**	N	N	Y	Y	N	Y
NORTH DAKOTA							
AL	**Armstrong**	N	N	Y	Y	N	N
OHIO							
1	**Chabot**	N	N	Y	Y	N	Y
2	**Wenstrup**	N	N	Y	Y	N	Y
3	Beatty	Y	Y	Y	N	Y	N
4	**Jordan**	N	N	Y	Y	N	Y
5	**Latta**	N	N	Y	Y	N	Y
6	**Johnson, B.**	N	N	Y	Y	N	Y
7	**Gibbs**	N	N	Y	Y	N	Y
8	**Davidson**	N	N	Y	Y	N	Y
9	Kaptur	Y	Y	Y	N	Y	N
10	**Turner**	N	N	Y	Y	N	Y
11	Fudge	Y	Y	Y	N	Y	N
12	**Balderson**	N	N	Y	Y	N	Y
13	Ryan	Y	Y	Y	N	Y	N
14	**Joyce**	N	N	Y	Y	N	Y
15	**Stivers**	N	N	Y	Y	N	Y
16	**Gonzalez**	N	N	Y	Y	N	Y
OKLAHOMA							
1	**Hern**	N	N	Y	Y	N	Y
2	**Mullin**	N	N	Y	Y	N	Y
3	**Lucas**	N	N	Y	Y	N	Y
4	**Cole**	N	N	Y	Y	N	Y
5	Horn	Y	Y	Y	N	Y	N
OREGON							
1	Bonamici	Y	Y	Y	N	Y	N
2	**Walden**	N	N	Y	Y	N	N
3	Blumenauer	Y	Y	Y	N	Y	N
4	DeFazio	Y	?	Y	N	Y	N
5	Schrader	Y	Y	Y	N	Y	N
PENNSYLVANIA							
1	**Fitzpatrick**	N	N	Y	N	Y	N
2	Boyle	Y	Y	Y	N	Y	N
3	Evans	Y	Y	Y	N	Y	N
4	Dean	Y	Y	Y	N	Y	N
5	Scanlon	Y	Y	Y	N	Y	N
6	Houlahan	Y	Y	Y	N	Y	N
7	Wild	Y	Y	Y	N	Y	N
8	Cartwright	Y	Y	Y	N	Y	N
9	**Meuser**	N	N	Y	Y	N	Y
10	**Perry**	N	N	Y	Y	N	Y
11	**Smucker**	N	N	Y	Y	N	Y
12	**Marino***						
13	**Joyce**	N	N	Y	Y	N	Y
14	**Reschenthaler**	N	N	Y	Y	N	Y
15	**Thompson, G.**	N	N	Y	Y	N	Y
16	**Kelly, M.**	N	N	Y	Y	N	Y
17	Lamb	Y	Y	Y	N	Y	N
18	Doyle	Y	Y	Y	N	Y	N
RHODE ISLAND							
1	Cicilline	Y	Y	?	N	Y	N
2	Langevin	Y	Y	Y	N	Y	N
SOUTH CAROLINA							
1	Cunningham	Y	Y	Y	N	Y	N
2	**Wilson, J.**	N	N	Y	Y	N	Y
3	**Duncan**	N	N	Y	Y	N	Y
4	**Timmons**	N	N	Y	Y	N	N
5	**Norman**	N	N	Y	Y	N	Y
6	Clyburn	+	+	+	-	+	-
7	**Rice, T.**	N	N	Y	Y	N	N
SOUTH DAKOTA							
AL	**Johnson**	N	N	Y	N	N	N
TENNESSEE							
1	**Roe**	N	N	Y	Y	N	Y
2	**Burchett**	N	N	Y	Y	N	Y
3	**Fleischmann**	N	N	Y	Y	N	Y
4	**DesJarlais**	N	N	Y	Y	N	Y
5	Cooper	Y	Y	Y	N	Y	N
6	**Rose**	N	N	Y	Y	N	Y
7	**Green**	N	N	Y	Y	N	Y
8	**Kustoff**	N	N	Y	Y	N	Y
9	Cohen	Y	Y	Y	N	Y	N
TEXAS							
1	**Gohmert**	N	N	Y	Y	N	Y
2	**Crenshaw**	N	N	Y	Y	N	Y
3	**Taylor**	N	N	Y	Y	N	Y
4	**Ratcliffe**	N	N	Y	Y	N	Y

		517	518	519	520	521	522
5	**Gooden**	N	N	Y	Y	N	Y
6	**Wright**	N	N	Y	Y	N	Y
7	Fletcher	Y	Y	Y	N	N	N
8	**Brady**	N	N	Y	Y	N	Y
9	Green, A.	Y	Y	Y	N	Y	N
10	**McCaul**	N	N	Y	Y	N	Y
11	**Conaway**	N	N	Y	Y	N	Y
12	**Granger**	N	N	Y	Y	N	Y
13	**Thornberry**	N	N	Y	Y	N	Y
14	**Weber**	N	N	Y	Y	N	Y
15	Gonzalez	Y	Y	Y	N	Y	N
16	Escobar	Y	Y	Y	N	Y	N
17	**Flores**	N	N	Y	Y	N	Y
18	Jackson Lee	Y	Y	Y	N	Y	N
19	**Arrington**	N	N	Y	Y	N	Y
20	Castro	Y	Y	Y	N	Y	N
21	**Roy**	N	N	Y	Y	N	Y
22	**Olson**	N	N	Y	Y	N	Y
23	**Hurd**	N	N	Y	Y	N	Y
24	**Marchant**	N	N	Y	Y	N	Y
25	**Williams**	N	N	Y	Y	N	N
26	**Burgess**	N	N	Y	Y	N	Y
27	**Cloud**	N	N	Y	Y	N	Y
28	Cuellar	Y	Y	Y	N	N	N
29	Garcia, S.	Y	Y	Y	N	N	N
30	Johnson, E.B.	Y	Y	Y	N	Y	N
31	**Carter, J.**	N	N	Y	Y	N	Y
32	Allred	Y	Y	Y	N	Y	N
33	Veasey	Y	Y	Y	N	Y	N
34	Vela	Y	Y	Y	N	N	N
35	Doggett	Y	Y	Y	N	Y	N
36	**Babin**	N	N	Y	Y	N	Y
UTAH							
1	**Bishop, R.**	N	N	Y	Y	N	Y
2	**Stewart**	N	N	Y	Y	N	Y
3	**Curtis**	N	N	Y	Y	N	Y
4	McAdams	Y	Y	Y	N	Y	N
VERMONT							
AL	Welch	Y	Y	Y	N	Y	N
VIRGINIA							
1	**Wittman**	N	N	Y	Y	N	Y
2	Luria	Y	Y	Y	N	Y	N
3	Scott, R.	Y	Y	Y	N	Y	N
4	McEachin	+	+	+	-	+	-
5	**Riggleman**	N	N	Y	Y	N	Y
6	**Cline**	N	N	Y	Y	N	Y
7	Spanberger	Y	Y	Y	N	Y	N
8	Beyer	Y	Y	Y	N	Y	N
9	**Griffith**	N	N	Y	Y	N	Y
10	Wexton	Y	Y	Y	N	Y	N
11	Connolly	Y	Y	Y	N	Y	N
WASHINGTON							
1	DelBene	Y	Y	Y	N	Y	N
2	Larsen	Y	Y	Y	N	Y	N
3	**Herrera Beutler**	N	N	Y	Y	Y	Y
4	**Newhouse**	N	N	Y	Y	N	Y
5	**McMorris Rodgers**	N	N	Y	Y	N	N
6	Kilmer	Y	Y	Y	N	Y	N
7	Jayapal	Y	Y	Y	N	Y	N
8	Schrier	Y	Y	Y	N	Y	N
9	Smith Adam	Y	Y	Y	N	Y	N
10	**Heck**	Y	Y	Y	N	Y	N
WEST VIRGINIA							
1	**McKinley**	N	N	Y	Y	N	Y
2	**Mooney**	N	N	Y	Y	N	Y
3	**Miller**	N	N	Y	Y	N	Y
WISCONSIN							
1	**Steil**	N	N	Y	Y	N	N
2	Pocan	Y	Y	Y	N	Y	N
3	Kind	Y	Y	Y	N	Y	N
4	Moore	Y	Y	Y	N	Y	N
5	**Sensenbrenner**	N	N	Y	Y	N	N
6	**Grothman**	N	N	Y	Y	N	Y
7	**Duffy**	N	N	Y	Y	N	N
8	**Gallagher**	N	N	Y	Y	Y	N
WYOMING							
AL	**Cheney**	N	N	Y	Y	N	Y
DELEGATES							
	Radewagen (A.S.)				?		?
	Norton (D.C.)				N		N
	San Nicolas (Guam)				N		N
	Sablan (N. Marianas)				N		N
	González-Colón (P.R.)				Y		Y
	Plaskett (V.I.)				N		N

III HOUSE VOTES

523. HR1941. Atlantic and Pacific Oil and Gas Leasing - Job Availability. Gosar, R-Ariz., amendment no. 7 that would postpone the effective date of Sec. 2 of the bill until the Interior and Labor departments determine that its provisions would not adversely affect jobs available to minorities and women. Sec. 2 would prohibit the Interior Department from any further oil and gas leasing within the Atlantic Region or Pacific Region outer Continental Shelf planning areas. Rejected in Committee of the Whole 179-252: R 179-18; D 0-232; I 0-2. Sept. 11, 2019.

524. HR1941. Atlantic and Pacific Oil and Gas Leasing - Recommit. Graves, R-La., motion to recommit the bill to the House Natural Resources Committee with instructions to report it back immediately with an amendment that would postpone the effective date of Sec. 2 of the bill until the president certifies that enactment of the bill would not increase the national average price of gasoline. Sec. 2 would prohibit the Interior Department from any further oil and gas leasing within the Atlantic Region or Pacific Region outer Continental Shelf planning areas. Motion rejected 194-233: R 193-2; D 1-230; I 0-1. Sept. 11, 2019.

525. HR1941. Atlantic and Pacific Oil and Gas Leasing - Passage. Passage of the bill, as amended, that would prohibit the Interior Department from any further oil and gas leasing within the Atlantic Region or Pacific Region outer Continental Shelf planning areas. It would also require the Interior Department to collect inspection fees from certain oil and gas facilities operating on the outer Continental Shelf and set annual levels and schedules for fees collected from facilities above the waterline, drilling rigs, and non-rig units. Such fees would be deposited into a Treasury Department ocean energy safety fund established under the bill's provisions, with funds to be made available through annual appropriations acts to carry out inspections of outer Continental Shelf facilities. Passed 238-189: R 12-183; D 226-5; I 0-1. *Note: A "nay" was a vote in support of the president's position.* Sept. 11, 2019.

526. HR1146. Alaska Oil and Gas Leasing - Local Community Consultation. Young, R-Alaska, amendment no. 1 that would postpone the effective date of the bill's repeal of the Arctic National Wildlife Refuge oil and gas program until the village of Kaktovic, Alaska, formally approves the repeal and the Interior Department consults with the Inupiat people regarding the effects of the bill on their quality of life, human rights, and future. Rejected in Committee of the Whole 193-230: R 189-3; D 4-225; I 0-2. Sept. 12, 2019.

527. HR1146. Alaska Oil and Gas Leasing - Job Availability. Gosar, R-Ariz., amendment no. 2 that would postpone the effective date of the bill's repeal of the Arctic National Wildlife Refuge oil and gas program until the Interior and Labor departments determine that the repeal would not adversely affect jobs available to Native Americans, minorities, and women. Rejected in Committee of the Whole 184-237: R 183-8; D 1-227; I 0-2. Sept. 12, 2019.

528. HR1146. Alaska Oil and Gas Leasing - Impact on Caribou. Gosar, R-Ariz., amendment no. 3, as modified, that would postpone the effective date of the bill's repeal of the Arctic National Wildlife Refuge oil and gas program until the Interior Department and Fish and Wildlife Service determine that the repeal would not adversely affect caribou herd populations. Rejected in Committee of the Whole 187-237: R 185-8; D 2-227; I 0-2. Sept. 12, 2019.

	523	524	525	526	527	528
ALABAMA						
1 **Byrne**	Y	Y	N	Y	Y	Y
2 **Roby**	Y	Y	N	Y	Y	Y
3 **Rogers, M.**	Y	Y	N	Y	Y	Y
4 **Aderholt**	Y	Y	N	Y	Y	Y
5 **Brooks, M.**	Y	Y	N	Y	Y	Y
6 **Palmer**	Y	Y	N	Y	Y	Y
7 Sewell	N	N	Y	N	N	N
ALASKA						
AL **Young**	Y	Y	N	Y	Y	Y
ARIZONA						
1 O'Halleran	N	N	Y	N	N	N
2 Kirkpatrick	N	N	Y	N	N	N
3 Grijalva	N	N	Y	N	N	N
4 **Gosar**	Y	Y	N	Y	Y	Y
5 **Biggs**	Y	Y	N	Y	Y	Y
6 **Schweikert**	Y	Y	N	Y	Y	Y
7 Gallego	N	N	Y	N	N	N
8 **Lesko**	Y	Y	N	Y	Y	Y
9 Stanton	N	N	Y	N	N	N
ARKANSAS						
1 **Crawford**	Y	Y	N	Y	Y	Y
2 **Hill, F.**	Y	Y	N	Y	Y	Y
3 **Womack**	Y	Y	N	Y	Y	Y
4 **Westerman**	Y	Y	N	Y	Y	Y
CALIFORNIA						
1 **LaMalfa**	Y	Y	N	Y	Y	Y
2 Huffman	N	N	Y	N	N	N
3 Garamendi	N	N	Y	N	N	N
4 **McClintock**	Y	Y	N	Y	Y	Y
5 Thompson, M.	N	N	Y	N	N	N
6 Matsui	N	N	Y	N	N	N
7 Bera	N	N	Y	N	N	N
8 **Cook**	Y	Y	N	Y	Y	Y
9 McNerney	N	N	Y	N	N	N
10 Harder	N	Y	Y	N	N	-
11 DeSaulnier	N	N	Y	N	N	N
12 Pelosi						
13 Lee B.	N	N	Y	N	N	N
14 Speier	N	N	Y	N	N	N
15 Swalwell	N	N	Y	N	N	N
16 Costa	N	N	Y	Y	Y	Y
17 Khanna	N	N	Y	N	N	N
18 Eshoo	N	N	Y	N	N	N
19 Lofgren	N	N	Y	N	N	N
20 Panetta	N	N	Y	N	N	N
21 Cox	N	N	Y	N	N	N
22 **Nunes**	Y	Y	N	Y	Y	Y
23 **McCarthy**	Y	Y	N	Y	Y	Y
24 Carbajal	N	N	Y	N	N	N
25 Hill, K.	N	N	Y	N	N	N
26 Brownley	N	N	Y	N	N	N
27 Chu	N	N	Y	N	N	N
28 Schiff	N	N	Y	N	N	N
29 Cárdenas	N	N	Y	N	N	N
30 Sherman	N	N	Y	N	N	N
31 Aguilar	N	N	Y	N	N	N
32 Napolitano	N	N	Y	N	N	N
33 Lieu	N	N	Y	N	N	N
34 Gomez	N	N	Y	N	N	N
35 Torres	N	N	Y	N	N	N
36 Ruiz	N	N	Y	N	N	N
37 Bass	N	N	Y	N	N	N
38 Sánchez	N	N	Y	N	N	N
39 Cisneros	N	N	Y	N	N	N
40 Roybal-Allard	N	N	Y	N	N	N
41 Takano	N	N	Y	N	N	N
42 **Calvert**	Y	Y	N	Y	Y	Y
43 Waters	N	N	Y	N	N	N
44 Barragán	N	N	Y	N	N	N
45 Porter	N	N	Y	N	N	N
46 Correa	N	N	Y	?	?	?
47 Lowenthal	N	N	Y	N	N	N
48 Rouda	N	N	Y	N	N	N
49 Levin	N	N	Y	N	N	N
50 **Hunter**	Y	Y	N	Y	Y	Y
51 Vargas	N	N	Y	N	N	N
52 Peters	N	N	Y	N	N	N

	523	524	525	526	527	528
53 Davis, S.	N	N	Y	N	N	N
COLORADO						
1 DeGette	N	N	Y	N	N	N
2 Neguse	N	N	Y	N	N	N
3 **Tipton**	Y	Y	N	Y	Y	Y
4 **Buck**	Y	Y	N	Y	Y	Y
5 **Lamborn**	Y	Y	N	Y	Y	Y
6 Crow	N	N	Y	N	N	N
7 Perlmutter	N	N	Y	N	N	N
CONNECTICUT						
1 Larson	N	N	Y	N	N	N
2 Courtney	N	N	Y	N	N	N
3 DeLauro	N	N	Y	N	N	N
4 Himes	N	N	Y	N	N	N
5 Hayes	N	N	Y	N	N	N
DELAWARE						
AL Blunt Rochester	N	N	Y	N	N	N
FLORIDA						
1 **Gaetz**	N	N	Y	Y	Y	Y
2 **Dunn**	Y	Y	N	Y	Y	Y
3 **Yoho**	Y	Y	N	?	?	?
4 **Rutherford**	N	Y	Y	Y	Y	Y
5 Lawson	N	N	Y	N	N	N
6 **Waltz**	Y	Y	Y	Y	Y	Y
7 Murphy	N	N	Y	N	N	N
8 **Posey**	Y	Y	N	Y	Y	Y
9 Soto	N	N	Y	N	N	N
10 Demings	N	N	Y	N	N	N
11 **Webster**	N	Y	N	Y	N	Y
12 **Bilirakis**	N	Y	Y	Y	Y	Y
13 Crist	N	N	Y	N	N	N
14 Castor	N	N	Y	N	N	N
15 **Spano**	Y	Y	N	Y	Y	Y
16 **Buchanan**	N	Y	Y	Y	Y	Y
17 **Steube**	N	Y	N	Y	Y	Y
18 **Mast**	N	Y	Y	Y	Y	Y
19 **Rooney**	N	Y	N	Y	Y	Y
20 Hastings	N	N	Y	N	N	N
21 Frankel	N	N	Y	N	N	N
22 Deutch	N	N	Y	N	N	N
23 Wasserman Schultz	N	N	Y	N	N	N
24 Wilson, F.	N	N	Y	?	?	N
25 **Diaz-Balart**	N	Y	N	Y	N	N
26 Mucarsel-Powell	N	N	Y	N	N	N
27 Shalala	N	N	Y	N	N	N
GEORGIA						
1 **Carter, E.L.**	Y	Y	N	Y	Y	Y
2 Bishop, S.	N	N	Y	N	N	N
3 **Ferguson**	Y	Y	N	Y	Y	Y
4 Johnson, H.	N	N	Y	N	N	N
5 Lewis John	N	N	Y	N	N	N
6 McBath	N	N	Y	N	N	N
7 **Woodall**	Y	Y	N	Y	Y	Y
8 **Scott, A.**	Y	Y	N	Y	Y	Y
9 **Collins, D.**	Y	Y	N	Y	Y	Y
10 **Hice**	Y	Y	N	Y	Y	Y
11 **Loudermilk**	Y	Y	N	Y	Y	Y
12 **Allen**	Y	Y	N	Y	Y	Y
13 Scott, D.	N	N	Y	N	N	N
14 **Graves, T.**	Y	Y	N	Y	Y	Y
HAWAII						
1 Case	N	N	Y	N	N	N
2 Gabbard	N	N	Y	?	?	?
IDAHO						
1 **Fulcher**	Y	Y	N	Y	Y	Y
2 **Simpson**	Y	Y	N	Y	Y	Y
ILLINOIS						
1 Rush	N	N	Y	N	N	N
2 Kelly, R.	N	N	Y	N	N	N
3 Lipinski	N	N	Y	N	N	N
4 García, J.	N	N	Y	N	N	N
5 Quigley	N	N	Y	N	N	N
6 Casten	N	N	Y	N	N	N
7 Davis, D.	N	N	Y	N	N	N
8 Krishnamoorthi	N	N	Y	N	N	N
9 Schakowsky	N	N	Y	N	N	N
10 Schneider	N	N	Y	N	N	N
11 Foster	?	N	Y	N	N	N

KEY:	**Republicans**	Democrats	*Independents*

Y Voted for (yea)   **N** Voted against (nay)   **P** Voted "present"
+ Announced for   **-** Announced against   **?** Did not vote or otherwise make position known
# Paired for   **X** Paired against

		523	524	525	526	527	528
12	**Bost**	Y	Y	N	Y	Y	Y
13	**Davis, R.**	Y	Y	N	Y	Y	Y
14	Underwood	N	N	Y	N	N	N
15	**Shimkus**	Y	Y	N	Y	Y	Y
16	**Kinzinger**	N	Y	N	Y	Y	Y
17	Bustos	N	N	Y	N	N	N
18	**LaHood**	Y	Y	N	Y	Y	Y
INDIANA							
1	Visclosky	N	N	Y	N	N	N
2	**Walorski**	Y	Y	N	Y	Y	Y
3	**Banks**	Y	Y	N	Y	Y	Y
4	**Baird**	Y	Y	N	Y	Y	Y
5	**Brooks, S.**	Y	Y	N	Y	Y	Y
6	**Pence**	Y	Y	N	Y	Y	Y
7	Carson	N	N	Y	N	N	N
8	**Bucshon**	Y	Y	N	Y	Y	Y
9	**Hollingsworth**	Y	Y	Y	Y	Y	Y
IOWA							
1	Finkenauer	N	N	Y	N	N	N
2	Loebsack	N	N	Y	N	N	N
3	Axne	N	N	Y	N	N	N
4	**King, S.**	Y	Y	N	Y	Y	Y
KANSAS							
1	**Marshall**	Y	Y	N	Y	Y	Y
2	**Watkins**	Y	Y	N	Y	Y	Y
3	Davids	N	N	Y	N	N	N
4	**Estes**	Y	Y	N	Y	Y	Y
KENTUCKY							
1	**Comer**	Y	Y	N	Y	Y	Y
2	**Guthrie**	Y	Y	N	Y	Y	Y
3	Yarmuth	N	N	Y	N	N	N
4	**Massie**	Y	Y	N	Y	Y	Y
5	**Rogers, H.**	Y	Y	N	Y	Y	Y
6	**Barr**	Y	Y	N	Y	Y	Y
LOUISIANA							
1	**Scalise**	Y	Y	N	Y	Y	Y
2	Richmond	N	N	Y	N	N	N
3	**Higgins, C.**	Y	Y	N	Y	Y	Y
4	**Johnson, M.**	N	Y	N	Y	Y	Y
5	**Abraham**	?	?	?	?	?	?
6	**Graves, G.**	Y	Y	N	Y	Y	Y
MAINE							
1	Pingree	N	N	Y	N	N	N
2	Golden	N	N	Y	N	N	N
MARYLAND							
1	**Harris**	Y	Y	N	Y	Y	Y
2	Ruppersberger	N	N	Y	N	N	N
3	Sarbanes	N	N	Y	N	N	N
4	Brown, A.	N	N	Y	N	N	N
5	Hoyer	N	N	Y	N	N	N
6	Trone	N	N	Y	N	N	N
7	Cummings	N	N	Y	?	?	?
8	Raskin						
MASSACHUSETTS		N	N	Y	N	N	N
1	Neal						
2	McGovern	N	N	Y	N	N	N
3	Trahan	N	N	Y	N	N	N
4	Kennedy	N	N	Y	N	N	N
5	Clark	N	N	Y	N	N	N
6	Moulton	N	N	Y	N	N	N
7	Pressley	N	N	Y	N	N	N
8	Lynch	N	N	Y	N	N	N
9	Keating	N	N	Y	N	N	N
MICHIGAN		N	N	Y	N	N	N
1	**Bergman**						
2	**Huizenga**	Y	Y	N	Y	Y	Y
3	*Amash*	Y	Y	N	Y	+	+
4	**Moolenaar**	N	N	N	N	N	N
5	Kildee	Y	Y	N	Y	Y	Y
6	**Upton**	N	N	Y	N	N	N
7	**Walberg**	Y	Y	N	Y	Y	Y
8	Slotkin	Y	Y	N	Y	Y	Y
9	Levin	N	N	Y	N	N	N
10	**Mitchell**	N	N	Y	N	N	N
11	Stevens	Y	Y	N	Y	Y	Y
12	Dingell	N	N	Y	N	N	N
13	Tlaib	N	N	Y	N	N	N
14	Lawrence	N	N	Y	N	N	N
MINNESOTA		?	?	?	N	N	N
1	**Hagedorn**						
2	Craig	Y	Y	N	Y	Y	Y
3	Phillips	N	N	Y	N	N	N
4	McCollum	N	N	Y	N	N	N
5	Omar	N	N	Y	N	N	N

		523	524	525	526	527	528
6	**Emmer**	N	N	Y	N	N	N
7	Peterson	Y	Y	N	Y	Y	Y
8	**Stauber**	N	N	N	Y	N	Y
MISSISSIPPI		Y	Y	N	Y	Y	Y
1	**Kelly, T.**						
2	Thompson, B.	Y	Y	N	Y	Y	Y
3	**Guest**	N	N	Y	N	N	N
4	**Palazzo**	Y	Y	N	Y	Y	Y
MISSOURI		Y	Y	N	Y	Y	Y
1	Clay						
2	**Wagner**	N	N	Y	N	N	N
3	**Luetkemeyer**	Y	Y	N	Y	Y	Y
4	**Hartzler**	Y	Y	N	Y	Y	Y
5	Cleaver	Y	Y	N	Y	Y	Y
6	**Graves, S.**	N	N	Y	N	N	N
7	**Long**	Y	Y	N	Y	Y	Y
8	**Smith, J.**	Y	Y	N	Y	Y	Y
MONTANA		Y	Y	N	Y	Y	Y
AL	**Gianforte**						
NEBRASKA		Y	Y	N	Y	Y	Y
1	**Fortenberry**						
2	**Bacon**	Y	Y	N	Y	Y	Y
3	**Smith, Adrian**	Y	Y	N	Y	Y	Y
NEVADA		Y	Y	-	Y	Y	Y
1	Titus						
2	**Amodei**	N	N	Y	N	N	N
3	Lee	Y	Y	N	Y	Y	Y
4	Horsford	N	N	Y	N	N	N
NEW HAMPSHIRE		N	N	Y	N	N	N
1	Pappas						
2	Kuster	N	N	Y	N	N	N
NEW JERSEY		N	N	Y	N	N	N
1	Norcross						
2	Van Drew	N	N	Y	N	N	N
3	Kim	N	N	Y	N	N	N
4	**Smith, C.**	N	N	Y	N	N	N
5	Gottheimer	N	?	Y	N	N	N
6	Pallone	N	N	Y	N	N	N
7	Malinowski	N	N	Y	N	N	N
8	Sires	N	N	Y	N	N	N
9	Pascrell	N	N	Y	N	N	N
10	Payne	N	N	Y	N	N	N
11	Sherrill	N	N	Y	N	N	N
12	Watson Coleman	N	N	Y	N	N	N
NEW MEXICO		N	N	Y	N	N	N
1	Haaland						
2	Torres Small	N	N	Y	N	N	N
3	Luján	N	N	Y	N	N	N
NEW YORK		N	N	Y	N	N	N
1	**Zeldin**						
2	**King, P.**	Y	Y	Y	Y	Y	Y
3	Suozzi	N	Y	Y	Y	Y	Y
4	Rice, K.	N	N	Y	N	N	N
5	Meeks	N	N	Y	-	-	-
6	Meng	N	N	Y	N	N	N
7	Velázquez	N	N	Y	N	N	N
8	Jeffries	N	N	Y	N	N	N
9	Clarke	N	N	Y	N	N	N
10	Nadler	N	N	Y	N	N	N
11	Rose	N	N	Y	N	N	N
12	Maloney, C.	N	N	Y	N	N	N
13	Espaillat	N	N	Y	N	N	N
14	Ocasio-Cortez	N	N	Y	N	N	N
15	Serrano	N	N	Y	N	N	N
16	Engel	N	N	Y	N	N	N
17	Lowey	N	N	Y	N	N	N
18	Maloney, S.P.	N	N	Y	N	N	N
19	Delgado	N	N	Y	N	N	N
20	Tonko	N	N	Y	N	N	N
21	**Stefanik**	N	N	Y	N	N	N
22	Brindisi	N	Y	N	Y	N	N
23	**Reed**	N	N	Y	N	N	N
24	**Katko**	Y	Y	N	?	Y	Y
25	Morelle	N	Y	N	Y	N	N
26	Higgins, B.	N	N	Y	N	N	N
27	**Collins, C.**	N	N	Y	N	N	N
NORTH CAROLINA		Y	Y	N	?	?	?
1	Butterfield						
2	**Holding**	N	N	Y	N	N	N
3	**Jones***	Y	Y	N	Y	Y	Y
4	Price						
5	**Foxx**	N	N	Y	N	N	N
6	**Walker**	Y	Y	N	Y	Y	Y
7	**Rouzer**	Y	Y	N	Y	Y	Y

		523	524	525	526	527	528
8	**Hudson**	Y	Y	N	Y	Y	Y
9	vacant	Y	Y	N	Y	Y	Y
10	**McHenry**	Y	Y	N	Y	Y	Y
11	**Meadows**	Y	Y	N	Y	Y	Y
12	Adams	N	N	Y	N	N	N
13	**Budd**	Y	Y	N	Y	Y	Y
NORTH DAKOTA							
AL	**Armstrong**	Y	Y	N	Y	Y	Y
OHIO							
1	**Chabot**	Y	Y	N	Y	Y	Y
2	**Wenstrup**	Y	Y	N	Y	Y	Y
3	Beatty	N	N	Y	N	N	N
4	**Jordan**	Y	Y	N	Y	Y	Y
5	**Latta**	Y	Y	N	Y	Y	Y
6	**Johnson, B.**	Y	Y	N	Y	Y	Y
7	**Gibbs**	Y	Y	N	Y	Y	Y
8	**Davidson**	Y	Y	N	Y	Y	Y
9	Kaptur	N	N	Y	N	N	N
10	**Turner**	Y	Y	N	Y	?	Y
11	Fudge	N	N	Y	N	N	N
12	**Balderson**	Y	Y	N	Y	Y	Y
13	Ryan	N	N	Y	N	N	N
14	**Joyce**	Y	Y	N	Y	Y	Y
15	**Stivers**	Y	Y	N	Y	Y	Y
16	**Gonzalez**	Y	Y	N	Y	Y	Y
OKLAHOMA							
1	**Hern**	Y	Y	N	Y	Y	Y
2	**Mullin**	Y	Y	N	Y	Y	Y
3	**Lucas**	Y	Y	N	Y	Y	Y
4	**Cole**	Y	Y	N	Y	Y	Y
5	Horn	N	N	Y	N	N	N
OREGON							
1	Bonamici	N	N	Y	N	N	N
2	**Walden**	Y	Y	N	Y	Y	Y
3	Blumenauer	N	N	Y	N	N	N
4	DeFazio	N	N	Y	N	N	N
5	Schrader	N	N	Y	N	N	N
PENNSYLVANIA							
1	**Fitzpatrick**	N	Y	Y	N	N	N
2	Boyle	N	N	Y	N	N	N
3	Evans	N	N	Y	N	N	N
4	Dean	N	N	Y	N	N	N
5	Scanlon	N	N	Y	N	N	N
6	Houlahan	N	N	Y	N	N	N
7	Wild	N	N	Y	N	N	N
8	Cartwright	N	N	Y	N	N	N
9	**Meuser**	Y	Y	N	Y	Y	Y
10	**Perry**	Y	Y	N	Y	Y	Y
11	**Smucker**	Y	Y	N	Y	Y	Y
12	**Marino***						
13	**Joyce**	Y	Y	N	Y	Y	Y
14	**Reschenthaler**	Y	Y	N	Y	Y	Y
15	**Thompson, G.**	Y	Y	N	Y	Y	Y
16	**Kelly, M.**	Y	Y	N	Y	Y	Y
17	Lamb	N	N	Y	N	N	N
18	Doyle	N	N	Y	N	N	N
RHODE ISLAND							
1	Cicilline	N	N	Y	N	N	N
2	Langevin	N	N	Y	N	N	N
SOUTH CAROLINA							
1	Cunningham	N	N	Y	N	N	N
2	**Wilson, J.**	Y	Y	N	Y	Y	Y
3	**Duncan**	Y	Y	N	Y	Y	Y
4	**Timmons**	Y	Y	N	Y	Y	Y
5	**Norman**	Y	Y	N	Y	Y	Y
6	Clyburn	-	-	+	-	-	-
7	**Rice, T.**	Y	Y	N	Y	Y	Y
SOUTH DAKOTA							
AL	**Johnson**	N	Y	N	Y	N	Y
TENNESSEE							
1	**Roe**	Y	Y	N	Y	Y	Y
2	**Burchett**	Y	Y	N	Y	Y	Y
3	**Fleischmann**	Y	Y	N	Y	Y	Y
4	**DesJarlais**	Y	Y	N	Y	Y	Y
5	Cooper	N	N	Y	N	N	N
6	**Rose**	Y	Y	N	Y	Y	Y
7	**Green**	Y	Y	N	Y	Y	Y
8	**Kustoff**	Y	Y	N	Y	Y	Y
9	Cohen	N	N	Y	N	N	N
TEXAS							
1	**Gohmert**	Y	Y	N	Y	Y	Y
2	**Crenshaw**	Y	Y	N	Y	Y	Y
3	**Taylor**	Y	Y	N	Y	Y	Y
4	**Ratcliffe**	Y	Y	N	Y	Y	Y

		523	524	525	526	527	528
5	**Gooden**	Y	Y	N	Y	Y	Y
6	**Wright**	Y	Y	N	Y	Y	Y
7	Fletcher	N	N	N	N	N	N
8	**Brady**	Y	Y	N	Y	Y	Y
9	Green, A.	N	N	Y	N	N	N
10	**McCaul**	Y	Y	N	Y	Y	Y
11	**Conaway**	Y	Y	N	Y	Y	Y
12	**Granger**	Y	Y	N	Y	Y	Y
13	**Thornberry**	Y	Y	N	Y	Y	Y
14	**Weber**	Y	Y	N	Y	Y	Y
15	Gonzalez	N	N	N	Y	N	N
16	Escobar	N	N	Y	N	N	N
17	**Flores**	Y	Y	N	Y	Y	Y
18	Jackson Lee	N	N	Y	N	N	N
19	**Arrington**	Y	Y	N	Y	Y	Y
20	Castro	N	N	Y	?	?	?
21	**Roy**	Y	Y	N	Y	Y	Y
22	**Olson**	Y	Y	N	Y	Y	Y
23	**Hurd**	Y	Y	N	Y	Y	Y
24	**Marchant**	Y	Y	N	?	?	?
25	**Williams**	Y	Y	N	Y	Y	Y
26	**Burgess**	Y	Y	N	Y	Y	Y
27	**Cloud**	Y	Y	N	Y	Y	Y
28	Cuellar	N	N	N	N	N	N
29	Garcia, S.	N	N	N	N	N	N
30	Johnson, E.B.	N	N	Y	N	N	N
31	**Carter, J.**	Y	Y	N	Y	Y	Y
32	Allred	N	N	Y	N	N	N
33	Veasey	N	N	Y	N	N	N
34	Vela	N	N	Y	N	N	N
35	Doggett	N	N	Y	N	N	N
36	**Babin**	Y	Y	N	Y	Y	Y
UTAH							
1	**Bishop, R.**	Y	Y	N	Y	Y	Y
2	**Stewart**	Y	Y	N	Y	Y	Y
3	**Curtis**	Y	Y	N	Y	Y	Y
4	McAdams	N	N	Y	N	N	N
VERMONT							
AL	Welch	N	N	Y	N	N	N
VIRGINIA							
1	**Wittman**	Y	Y	N	Y	Y	Y
2	Luria	N	N	Y	N	N	N
3	Scott, R.	N	N	Y	N	N	N
4	McEachin	-	-	+	-	-	-
5	**Riggleman**	Y	Y	N	Y	Y	Y
6	**Cline**	Y	Y	N	Y	Y	Y
7	Spanberger	N	N	Y	N	N	N
8	Beyer	N	N	Y	N	?	N
9	**Griffith**	Y	Y	N	Y	Y	Y
10	Wexton	N	N	Y	N	N	N
11	Connolly	N	N	Y	N	N	N
WASHINGTON							
1	DelBene	N	N	Y	N	N	N
2	Larsen	N	N	Y	Y	N	N
3	**Herrera Beutler**	N	Y	Y	Y	N	Y
4	**Newhouse**	Y	Y	N	Y	Y	Y
5	**McMorris Rodgers**	N	Y	N	Y	Y	Y
6	Kilmer	N	N	Y	N	N	N
7	Jayapal	N	N	Y	N	N	N
8	Schrier	N	N	Y	N	N	N
9	Smith Adam	N	N	Y	N	N	N
10	Heck	N	N	Y	N	N	N
WEST VIRGINIA							
1	**McKinley**	Y	Y	N	Y	Y	Y
2	**Mooney**	Y	Y	N	Y	Y	Y
3	**Miller**	Y	Y	N	Y	Y	Y
WISCONSIN							
1	**Steil**	Y	Y	N	Y	Y	Y
2	Pocan	N	N	Y	N	N	N
3	Kind	N	N	Y	N	N	N
4	Moore	N	N	Y	N	N	N
5	**Sensenbrenner**	Y	Y	N	Y	Y	N
6	**Grothman**	Y	Y	N	Y	Y	Y
7	**Duffy**	Y	Y	N	?	?	Y
8	**Gallagher**	Y	Y	N	Y	Y	Y
WYOMING							
AL	**Cheney**	Y	Y	N	Y	Y	Y
DELEGATES							
	Radewagen (A.S.)	?			?	?	?
	Norton (D.C.)	-			N	N	N
	San Nicolas (Guam)	N			N	N	N
	Sablan (N. Marianas)	N			N	N	N
	González-Colón (P.R.)	Y			Y	Y	Y
	Plaskett (V.I.)	N			N	N	N

529. HR1146. Alaska Oil and Gas Leasing - Recommit. Curtis, R-Utah, motion to recommit the bill to the House Natural Resources Committee with instructions to report it back immediately with an amendment that would postpone the effective date of Sec. 2 of the bill until the president certifies that enactment of the bill would not result in a net increase of Russian oil and gas imports into the United States. Sec. 2 would repeal existing law authorizing an Interior Department program for the leasing, development, and transportation of oil and gas in and from the coastal plane of the Arctic National Wildlife Refuge. Motion rejected 189-229: R 189-2; D 0-226; I 0-1. Sept. 12, 2019.

530. HR1146. Alaska Oil and Gas Leasing - Passage. Passage of the bill that would that would repeal existing law authorizing an Interior Department program for the leasing, development, and transportation of oil and gas in and from the coastal plane of the Arctic National Wildlife Refuge. It would also require the Interior Department to collect inspection fees from certain oil and gas facilities operating on the outer Continental Shelf and set annual levels and schedules for fees collected from facilities above the waterline, drilling rigs, and non-rig units. Such fees would be deposited into a Treasury Department ocean energy safety fund established under the bill's provisions, with funds to be made available through annual appropriations acts to carry out inspections of outer Continental Shelf facilities. Passed 225-193: R 4-187; D 221-5; I 0-1. *Note: A "nay" was a vote in support of the president's position.* Sept. 12, 2019.

531. S1790. Fiscal 2020 Defense Authorization - Motion to Instruct. Thornberry, R-Texas, motion to instruct conferees on the part of the House to agree to a section of the Senate bill that would provide for the replenishment of funds authorized for military construction projects prior to fiscal 2020 that were instead used for military construction projects in connection with the national emergency along the southern U.S. border, with amendments that would specify such projects and funding amounts. Motion rejected 198-219: R 191-0; D 7-218; I 0-1. Sept. 17, 2019.

532. S1790. Fiscal 2020 Defense Authorization - Motion to Close Conference. Smith, D-Wash., motion that certain portions of the conference between the House and Senate on the bill be closed to the public at such times as classified national security information may be discussed. Motion agreed to 407-4: R 191-1; D 216-2; I 0-1. Sept. 17, 2019.

533. HR1423. Forced Arbitration - Previous Question. Torres, D-Calif., motion to order the previous question (thus ending debate and possibility of amendment) on the rule (H Res 588) that would provide for consideration of the Forced Arbitration Injustice Repeal (FAIR) Act (HR 1423) that would prohibit the enforcement of pre-dispute arbitration agreements for the resolution of employment, consumer, antitrust, or civil rights disputes. The rule would provide for automatic adoption of a manager's amendment to HR 1423 making technical corrections to the bill, and provide for floor consideration of two additional amendments to the bill. The rule would also waive, through the legislative day of Friday, Sept. 20, 2019, the two-thirds vote requirement to consider legislation related to continuing appropriations on the same day it is reported from the House Rules Committee, and it would provide for motions to suspend the rules on the legislative days of Sept. 19 and Sept. 20. Motion agreed to 228-195: R 1-194; D 227-0; I 0-1. Sept. 18, 2019.

534. HR1423. Forced Arbitration - Rule. Adoption of the rule (H Res 558) that would provide for consideration of the Forced Arbitration Injustice Repeal (FAIR) Act (HR 1423) that would prohibit the enforcement of pre-dispute arbitration agreements for the resolution of employment, consumer, antitrust, or civil rights disputes. The rule would provide for automatic adoption of a manager's amendment to HR 1423 making technical corrections to the bill, and provide for floor consideration of two additional amendments to the bill. The rule would also waive, through the legislative day of Friday, Sept. 20, 2019, the two-thirds vote requirement to consider legislation related to continuing appropriations on the same day it is reported from the House Rules Committee, and it would provide for motions to suspend the rules on the legislative days of Sept. 19 and Sept. 20. Adopted 228-196: R 0-195; D 228-0; I 0-1. Sept. 18, 2019.

*NOTES:

(North Carolina 3) Rep. Greg Murphy was sworn-in Sept. 10. The first roll call vote he was eligible to cast was vote 532.

(North Carolina 9) Rep. Dan Bishop was sworn-in Sept. 10. The first roll call vote he was eligible to cast was vote 532.

(Pennsylvania 12) Rep. Fred Keller was sworn-in Sept. 10. The first roll call vote he was eligible to cast was vote 532.

		529	530	531	532	533	534
ALABAMA							
1	**Byrne**	Y	N	Y	Y	N	N
2	**Roby**	Y	N	?	?	N	N
3	**Rogers, M.**	Y	N	Y	Y	N	N
4	**Aderholt**	Y	N	Y	Y	N	N
5	**Brooks, M.**	Y	N	Y	N	N	N
6	**Palmer**	Y	N	Y	Y	N	N
7	Sewell	N	Y	N	?	Y	Y
ALASKA							
AL	**Young**	Y	N	Y	Y	N	N
ARIZONA							
1	O'Halleran	N	Y	N	Y	Y	Y
2	Kirkpatrick	N	Y	N	Y	Y	Y
3	Grijalva	N	Y	N	Y	Y	Y
4	**Gosar**	Y	N	Y	N	N	N
5	**Biggs**	Y	N	Y	Y	N	N
6	**Schweikert**	Y	N	Y	N	N	N
7	Gallego	N	Y	N	Y	Y	Y
8	**Lesko**	Y	N	Y	N	N	N
9	Stanton	N	Y	N	Y	Y	Y
ARKANSAS							
1	**Crawford**	Y	N	Y	Y	?	?
2	**Hill, F.**	Y	N	Y	Y	N	N
3	**Womack**	Y	N	Y	N	N	N
4	**Westerman**	Y	N	Y	N	N	N
CALIFORNIA							
1	**LaMalfa**	Y	N	?	?	N	N
2	Huffman	N	Y	N	Y	Y	Y
3	Garamendi	N	Y	N	Y	?	?
4	**McClintock**	Y	N	Y	N	N	N
5	Thompson, M.	N	Y	N	Y	Y	Y
6	Matsui	N	Y	N	Y	Y	Y
7	Bera	N	Y	N	Y	Y	Y
8	**Cook**	Y	N	Y	Y	N	N
9	McNerney	N	Y	N	Y	Y	Y
10	Harder	N	Y	N	Y	Y	Y
11	DeSaulnier	N	Y	-	+	Y	Y
12	Pelosi	N	Y	N	Y	Y	Y
13	Lee B.	N	Y	N	Y	Y	Y
14	Speier	N	Y	N	Y	Y	Y
15	Swalwell	N	Y	N	Y	Y	Y
16	Costa	N	N	N	Y	Y	Y
17	Khanna	N	Y	N	Y	Y	Y
18	Eshoo	N	Y	N	Y	Y	Y
19	Lofgren	N	Y	N	Y	Y	Y
20	Panetta	N	Y	N	Y	Y	Y
21	Cox	N	Y	N	Y	Y	Y
22	**Nunes**	Y	N	Y	Y	N	N
23	**McCarthy**	Y	N	Y	Y	N	N
24	Carbajal	N	Y	N	Y	Y	Y
25	Hill, K.	N	Y	N	Y	Y	Y
26	Brownley	N	Y	N	Y	Y	Y
27	Chu	N	Y	N	Y	Y	Y
28	Schiff	N	Y	N	Y	Y	Y
29	Cárdenas	N	Y	N	Y	Y	Y
30	Sherman	N	Y	N	Y	Y	Y
31	Aguilar	N	Y	N	Y	Y	Y
32	Napolitano	N	Y	N	Y	Y	Y
33	Lieu	N	Y	N	Y	Y	Y
34	Gomez	N	Y	N	Y	Y	Y
35	Torres	N	Y	N	Y	Y	Y
36	Ruiz	N	Y	N	Y	Y	Y
37	Bass	N	Y	N	?	Y	Y
38	Sánchez	N	Y	N	Y	Y	Y
39	Cisneros	N	Y	N	Y	Y	Y
40	Roybal-Allard	N	Y	N	Y	Y	Y
41	Takano	N	Y	N	Y	Y	Y
42	**Calvert**	Y	N	Y	Y	N	N
43	Waters	N	Y	N	Y	Y	Y
44	Barragán	N	Y	N	Y	Y	Y
45	Porter	N	Y	N	Y	Y	Y
46	Correa	?	?	N	Y	Y	Y
47	Lowenthal	N	Y	N	Y	Y	Y
48	Rouda	N	Y	N	Y	Y	Y
49	Levin	N	Y	N	Y	Y	Y
50	**Hunter**	Y	N	Y	Y	N	N
51	Vargas	N	Y	N	Y	Y	Y
52	Peters	N	Y	N	Y	Y	Y

		529	530	531	532	533	534
53	Davis, S.	N	Y	N	Y	Y	Y
COLORADO							
1	DeGette	N	Y	N	Y	Y	Y
2	Neguse	N	Y	N	Y	Y	Y
3	**Tipton**	Y	N	Y	Y	N	N
4	**Buck**	Y	N	Y	N	N	N
5	**Lamborn**	Y	N	Y	N	N	N
6	Crow	N	Y	N	Y	Y	Y
7	Perlmutter	N	Y	N	Y	Y	Y
CONNECTICUT							
1	Larson	N	Y	N	Y	Y	Y
2	Courtney	N	Y	N	Y	Y	Y
3	DeLauro	N	Y	N	Y	Y	Y
4	Himes	N	Y	N	Y	Y	Y
5	Hayes	N	Y	N	Y	Y	Y
DELAWARE							
AL	Blunt Rochester	N	Y	N	Y	Y	Y
FLORIDA							
1	**Gaetz**	Y	N	Y	Y	N	N
2	**Dunn**	Y	N	Y	Y	N	N
3	Yoho	?	?	Y	Y	N	N
4	**Rutherford**	Y	N	Y	N	N	N
5	Lawson	N	Y	N	Y	Y	Y
6	**Waltz**	Y	N	Y	N	N	N
7	Murphy	N	Y	N	Y	Y	Y
8	**Posey**	Y	N	Y	N	N	N
9	Soto	N	Y	N	Y	Y	Y
10	Demings	N	Y	N	Y	Y	Y
11	**Webster**	Y	N	?	?	?	?
12	**Bilirakis**	Y	N	Y	N	N	N
13	Crist	N	Y	N	Y	Y	Y
14	Castor	N	Y	N	Y	Y	Y
15	**Spano**	Y	N	Y	N	N	N
16	**Buchanan**	Y	N	Y	N	N	N
17	**Steube**	Y	N	Y	N	N	N
18	**Mast**	Y	N	?	?	?	?
19	**Rooney**	N	Y	Y	Y	N	N
20	Hastings	N	Y	N	Y	Y	Y
21	Frankel	N	Y	N	Y	Y	Y
22	Deutch	N	Y	N	Y	Y	Y
23	Wasserman Schultz	N	Y	N	Y	Y	Y
24	Wilson, F.	N	Y	?	?	Y	Y
25	**Diaz-Balart**	Y	N	Y	N	N	N
26	Mucarsel-Powell	N	Y	N	Y	Y	Y
27	Shalala	N	Y	N	Y	Y	Y
GEORGIA							
1	**Carter, E.L.**	Y	N	Y	N	N	N
2	Bishop, S.	N	Y	N	Y	Y	Y
3	**Ferguson**	Y	N	Y	N	N	N
4	Johnson, H.	N	Y	N	Y	Y	Y
5	Lewis John	N	Y	N	Y	Y	Y
6	McBath	N	Y	N	Y	Y	Y
7	**Woodall**	Y	N	Y	Y	N	N
8	**Scott, A.**	Y	N	Y	N	N	N
9	**Collins, D.**	Y	N	Y	Y	N	N
10	**Hice**	Y	N	Y	Y	N	N
11	**Loudermilk**	Y	N	Y	N	N	N
12	**Allen**	Y	N	Y	Y	N	N
13	Scott, D.	N	Y	N	?	Y	Y
14	**Graves, T.**	Y	N	Y	N	N	N
HAWAII							
1	Case	N	Y	N	Y	Y	Y
2	Gabbard	?	?	?	?	Y	Y
IDAHO							
1	**Fulcher**	Y	N	Y	N	N	N
2	**Simpson**	Y	N	Y	N	N	N
ILLINOIS							
1	Rush	N	Y	N	Y	Y	Y
2	Kelly, R.	N	Y	N	Y	Y	Y
3	Lipinski	N	Y	N	Y	Y	Y
4	García, J.	N	Y	N	Y	Y	Y
5	Quigley	N	Y	N	?	Y	Y
6	Casten	N	Y	N	Y	Y	Y
7	Davis, D.	N	Y	N	Y	Y	Y
8	Krishnamoorthi	N	Y	N	Y	Y	Y
9	Schakowsky	N	Y	N	Y	Y	Y
10	Schneider	N	Y	N	Y	Y	Y
11	Foster	N	Y	N	Y	Y	Y

KEY:	Republicans		Democrats		*Independents*	
Y Voted for (yea)		**N** Voted against (nay)		**P** Voted "present"	
+ Announced for		**−** Announced against		Did not vote or otherwise	
# Paired for		**X** Paired against		make position known	

		529	530	531	532	533	534
12	**Bost**	Y	N	Y	Y	N	N
13	**Davis, R.**	Y	N	Y	Y	N	N
14	Underwood	N	Y	N	Y	Y	Y
15	**Shimkus**	Y	N	Y	Y	N	N
16	**Kinzinger**	Y	N	Y	Y	N	N
17	Bustos	N	Y	N	Y	Y	Y
18	**LaHood**	Y	N	Y	Y	N	N
INDIANA							
1	Visclosky	N	Y	N	Y	Y	Y
2	**Walorski**	Y	N	Y	Y	N	N
3	**Banks**	Y	N	Y	Y	N	N
4	**Baird**	Y	?	Y	Y	N	N
5	**Brooks, S.**	Y	N	Y	Y	N	N
6	**Pence**	Y	N	Y	Y	N	N
7	Carson	N	Y	N	Y	Y	Y
8	**Bucshon**	Y	N	Y	Y	N	N
9	**Hollingsworth**	Y	N	Y	Y	N	N
IOWA							
1	Finkenauer	N	Y	N	Y	Y	Y
2	Loebsack	N	Y	N	?	Y	Y
3	Axne	N	Y	N	Y	Y	Y
4	**King, S.**	Y	N	Y	Y	N	N
KANSAS							
1	**Marshall**	Y	N	Y	Y	N	N
2	**Watkins**	Y	N	Y	Y	N	N
3	Davids	N	Y	N	Y	Y	Y
4	**Estes**	Y	N	Y	Y	N	N
KENTUCKY							
1	**Comer**	Y	N	Y	Y	N	N
2	**Guthrie**	Y	N	Y	Y	N	N
3	Yarmuth	N	Y	N	Y	Y	Y
4	**Massie**	Y	N	Y	N	N	N
5	**Rogers, H.**	Y	N	Y	Y	N	N
6	**Barr**	Y	N	Y	Y	N	N
LOUISIANA							
1	**Scalise**	Y	N	Y	Y	N	N
2	Richmond	N	Y	N	Y	Y	Y
3	**Higgins, C.**	Y	N	Y	Y	N	N
4	**Johnson, M.**	Y	N	Y	Y	N	N
5	**Abraham**	?	?	?	?	?	?
6	**Graves, G.**	Y	N	Y	Y	N	N
MAINE							
1	Pingree	N	Y	N	Y	Y	Y
2	Golden	N	Y	N	Y	Y	Y
MARYLAND							
1	**Harris**	Y	N	Y	Y	N	N
2	Ruppersberger	N	Y	N	Y	Y	Y
3	Sarbanes	N	Y	N	Y	Y	Y
4	Brown, A.	N	Y	N	Y	Y	Y
5	Hoyer	N	Y	N	?	Y	Y
6	Trone	N	Y	N	?	Y	Y
7	Cummings	?	?	?	?	?	?
8	Raskin	N	Y	N	Y	Y	Y
MASSACHUSETTS							
1	Neal	N	Y	N	Y	Y	Y
2	McGovern	N	Y	N	Y	Y	Y
3	Trahan	N	Y	N	Y	Y	Y
4	Kennedy	N	Y	N	Y	Y	Y
5	Clark	N	Y	N	Y	Y	Y
6	Moulton	N	Y	N	Y	Y	Y
7	Pressley	N	Y	N	Y	Y	Y
8	Lynch	N	Y	N	Y	Y	Y
9	Keating	N	Y	N	Y	Y	Y
MICHIGAN							
1	**Bergman**	Y	N	Y	Y	N	N
2	**Huizenga**	+	-	Y	Y	N	N
3	*Amash*	N	N	N	N	N	N
4	**Moolenaar**	Y	N	Y	Y	N	N
5	Kildee	N	Y	N	Y	Y	Y
6	**Upton**	Y	N	Y	Y	N	N
7	**Walberg**	Y	N	Y	Y	N	N
8	Slotkin	N	Y	N	Y	Y	Y
9	Levin	N	Y	N	Y	Y	Y
10	**Mitchell**	Y	N	Y	Y	N	N
11	Stevens	N	Y	N	Y	Y	Y
12	Dingell	N	Y	N	Y	Y	Y
13	Tlaib	N	Y	N	N	Y	Y
14	Lawrence	N	Y	N	Y	Y	Y
MINNESOTA							
1	**Hagedorn**	Y	N	Y	Y	N	N
2	Craig	N	Y	N	Y	Y	Y
3	Phillips	N	Y	N	Y	Y	Y
4	McCollum	N	Y	N	Y	Y	Y
5	Omar	N	Y	N	Y	Y	Y
6	**Emmer**	Y	N	Y	Y	N	N
7	Peterson	N	N	Y	Y	Y	Y
8	**Stauber**	Y	N	Y	Y	N	N
MISSISSIPPI							
1	**Kelly, T.**	Y	N	Y	Y	N	N
2	Thompson, B.	N	Y	?	?	?	?
3	**Guest**	Y	N	Y	Y	N	N
4	**Palazzo**	Y	N	Y	Y	N	N
MISSOURI							
1	Clay	N	Y	N	?	Y	Y
2	**Wagner**	Y	N	Y	Y	N	N
3	**Luetkemeyer**	Y	N	Y	Y	N	N
4	**Hartzler**	Y	N	Y	Y	N	N
5	Cleaver	N	Y	N	Y	Y	Y
6	**Graves, S.**	Y	N	Y	Y	N	N
7	**Long**	Y	N	Y	Y	N	N
8	**Smith, J.**	Y	N	Y	Y	N	N
MONTANA							
AL	**Gianforte**	Y	N	Y	Y	N	N
NEBRASKA							
1	**Fortenberry**	Y	N	Y	Y	N	N
2	**Bacon**	Y	N	Y	Y	N	N
3	**Smith, Adrian**	Y	N	Y	Y	N	N
NEVADA							
1	Titus	N	Y	N	Y	Y	Y
2	**Amodei**	Y	N	Y	Y	N	N
3	Lee	N	Y	N	Y	Y	Y
4	Horsford	N	Y	N	Y	Y	Y
NEW HAMPSHIRE							
1	Pappas	N	Y	N	Y	Y	Y
2	Kuster	N	Y	N	Y	Y	Y
NEW JERSEY							
1	Norcross	N	Y	N	Y	Y	Y
2	Van Drew	N	Y	Y	Y	Y	Y
3	Kim	N	Y	N	Y	Y	Y
4	**Smith, C.**	N	Y	Y	?	N	N
5	Gottheimer	N	Y	N	Y	Y	Y
6	Pallone	N	Y	N	Y	Y	Y
7	Malinowski	N	Y	N	Y	Y	Y
8	Sires	N	Y	N	Y	Y	Y
9	Pascrell	N	Y	N	Y	Y	Y
10	Payne	N	Y	N	Y	Y	Y
11	Sherrill	N	Y	N	Y	Y	Y
12	Watson Coleman	N	Y	N	Y	Y	Y
NEW MEXICO							
1	Haaland	N	Y	N	Y	Y	Y
2	Torres Small	N	Y	Y	Y	Y	Y
3	Luján	N	Y	N	Y	Y	Y
NEW YORK							
1	**Zeldin**	Y	N	Y	Y	N	N
2	**King, P.**	Y	N	Y	Y	N	N
3	Suozzi	N	Y	N	Y	Y	Y
4	Rice, K.	-	+	N	Y	Y	Y
5	Meeks	N	Y	N	Y	Y	Y
6	Meng	N	Y	N	Y	Y	Y
7	Velázquez	N	Y	N	Y	Y	Y
8	Jeffries	N	Y	N	Y	Y	Y
9	Clarke	N	Y	N	Y	Y	Y
10	Nadler	N	Y	N	Y	Y	Y
11	Rose	N	Y	N	Y	Y	Y
12	Maloney, C.	N	Y	N	Y	Y	Y
13	Espaillat	N	Y	N	Y	Y	Y
14	Ocasio-Cortez	N	Y	N	Y	Y	Y
15	Serrano	N	Y	N	Y	Y	Y
16	Engel	N	Y	N	Y	Y	Y
17	Lowey	N	Y	N	Y	Y	Y
18	Maloney, S.P.	N	Y	Y	Y	Y	Y
19	Delgado	N	Y	N	Y	Y	Y
20	Tonko	N	Y	N	Y	Y	Y
21	**Stefanik**	Y	Y	Y	Y	N	N
22	Brindisi	N	Y	N	Y	Y	Y
23	**Reed**	Y	N	Y	Y	N	N
24	**Katko**	Y	N	Y	Y	N	N
25	Morelle	N	Y	N	Y	Y	Y
26	Higgins, B.	N	Y	N	Y	Y	Y
27	**Collins, C.**	?	?	Y	Y	N	N
NORTH CAROLINA							
1	Butterfield	N	Y	N	Y	Y	Y
2	**Holding**	Y	N	Y	Y	N	N
3	**Murphy***				Y	N	N
4	Price	N	Y	N	Y	Y	Y
5	**Foxx**	Y	N	Y	Y	N	N
6	**Walker**	Y	N	Y	?	N	N
7	**Rouzer**	Y	N	Y	Y	N	N
8	**Hudson**	Y	N	Y	Y	N	N
9	**Bishop***				Y	N	N
10	**McHenry**	Y	N	Y	Y	N	N
11	**Meadows**	Y	N	Y	Y	N	N
12	Adams	N	Y	N	Y	Y	Y
13	**Budd**	Y	N	Y	Y	N	N
NORTH DAKOTA							
AL	**Armstrong**	Y	N	Y	Y	N	N
OHIO							
1	**Chabot**	Y	N	Y	Y	N	N
2	**Wenstrup**	Y	N	Y	Y	N	N
3	Beatty	N	Y	N	Y	Y	Y
4	**Jordan**	Y	N	Y	Y	N	N
5	**Latta**	Y	N	Y	Y	N	N
6	**Johnson, B.**	Y	N	Y	Y	N	N
7	**Gibbs**	Y	N	Y	Y	N	N
8	**Davidson**	Y	N	Y	Y	N	N
9	Kaptur	N	Y	N	Y	Y	Y
10	**Turner**	Y	N	Y	Y	N	N
11	Fudge	N	Y	N	Y	Y	Y
12	**Balderson**	Y	N	Y	Y	N	N
13	Ryan	N	Y	?	?	?	?
14	**Joyce**	Y	N	Y	Y	N	N
15	**Stivers**	Y	N	Y	Y	N	N
16	**Gonzalez**	Y	N	Y	Y	N	N
OKLAHOMA							
1	**Hern**	Y	N	Y	Y	N	N
2	**Mullin**	Y	N	Y	Y	N	N
3	**Lucas**	Y	N	Y	Y	N	N
4	**Cole**	Y	N	Y	Y	N	N
5	Horn	N	Y	N	Y	Y	Y
OREGON							
1	Bonamici	N	Y	N	Y	Y	Y
2	**Walden**	Y	N	Y	Y	N	N
3	Blumenauer	N	Y	N	N	Y	Y
4	DeFazio	N	Y	N	-	Y	Y
5	Schrader	N	Y	N	Y	Y	Y
PENNSYLVANIA							
1	**Fitzpatrick**	Y	Y	Y	Y	N	N
2	Boyle	N	Y	N	Y	Y	Y
3	Evans	N	Y	N	Y	Y	Y
4	Dean	N	Y	N	Y	Y	Y
5	Scanlon	N	Y	N	Y	Y	Y
6	Houlahan	N	Y	N	Y	Y	Y
7	Wild	N	Y	N	Y	Y	Y
8	Cartwright	N	Y	N	Y	Y	Y
9	**Meuser**	Y	N	Y	Y	N	N
10	**Perry**	Y	N	Y	Y	N	N
11	**Smucker**	Y	N	Y	Y	N	N
12	**Keller***				Y	N	N
13	**Joyce**	Y	N	Y	Y	N	N
14	**Reschenthaler**	Y	N	Y	Y	N	N
15	**Thompson, G.**	Y	N	Y	Y	N	N
16	**Kelly, M.**	Y	N	Y	Y	N	N
17	Lamb	Y	N	Y	Y	Y	Y
18	Doyle	N	Y	N	Y	Y	Y
RHODE ISLAND		N	Y	N			
1	Cicilline	N	Y	N	Y	Y	Y
2	Langevin	N	Y	N	Y	Y	Y
SOUTH CAROLINA							
1	Cunningham	N	Y	Y	Y	Y	Y
2	**Wilson, J.**	Y	N	Y	Y	N	N
3	**Duncan**	Y	N	Y	Y	N	N
4	**Timmons**	Y	N	Y	Y	N	N
5	**Norman**	Y	N	Y	Y	N	N
6	Clyburn	-	+	?	+	+	+
7	**Rice, T.**	Y	N	Y	Y	N	N
SOUTH DAKOTA							
AL	**Johnson**	Y	N	Y	Y	N	N
TENNESSEE							
1	**Roe**	Y	N	Y	Y	N	N
2	**Burchett**	Y	N	Y	Y	N	N
3	**Fleischmann**	Y	N	Y	Y	N	N
4	**DesJarlais**	Y	N	Y	Y	N	N
5	Cooper	N	Y	N	Y	Y	Y
6	**Rose**	Y	N	Y	Y	N	N
7	**Green**	Y	N	Y	Y	N	N
8	**Kustoff**	Y	N	Y	Y	N	N
9	Cohen	N	Y	N	Y	Y	Y
TEXAS							
1	**Gohmert**	Y	N	Y	Y	N	N
2	**Crenshaw**	Y	N	Y	Y	N	N
3	**Taylor**	Y	N	Y	Y	N	N
4	**Ratcliffe**	Y	N	Y	Y	N	N
5	**Gooden**	Y	N	Y	Y	N	N
6	**Wright**	Y	N	Y	Y	N	N
7	Fletcher	N	N	N	Y	Y	Y
8	**Brady**	Y	N	Y	Y	N	N
9	Green, A.	N	Y	N	Y	Y	Y
10	**McCaul**	+	N	Y	Y	N	N
11	**Conaway**	Y	N	Y	Y	N	N
12	**Granger**	Y	N	Y	Y	N	N
13	**Thornberry**	Y	N	Y	Y	N	N
14	**Weber**	Y	N	Y	Y	N	N
15	Gonzalez	-	-	-	Y	Y	Y
16	Escobar	N	Y	N	Y	Y	Y
17	**Flores**	Y	N	Y	Y	N	N
18	Jackson Lee	N	Y	N	Y	Y	Y
19	**Arrington**	Y	N	?	Y	N	N
20	Castro	?	?	N	Y	Y	Y
21	**Roy**	Y	N	Y	Y	N	N
22	**Olson**	Y	N	Y	Y	N	N
23	**Hurd**	Y	N	Y	Y	N	N
24	**Marchant**	?	?	Y	Y	N	N
25	**Williams**	Y	N	Y	Y	N	N
26	**Burgess**	Y	N	Y	Y	N	N
27	**Cloud**	Y	N	Y	Y	N	N
28	Cuellar	N	N	N	Y	Y	Y
29	Garcia, S.	N	Y	N	Y	Y	Y
30	Johnson, E.B.	N	Y	N	Y	Y	Y
31	**Carter, J.**	Y	N	Y	Y	N	N
32	Allred	N	Y	N	Y	Y	Y
33	Veasey	N	Y	N	Y	Y	Y
34	Vela	N	N	N	Y	Y	Y
35	Doggett	N	Y	N	Y	Y	Y
36	**Babin**	Y	N	Y	Y	N	N
UTAH							
1	**Bishop, R.**	Y	N	Y	Y	N	N
2	**Stewart**	Y	N	Y	Y	N	N
3	**Curtis**	Y	N	Y	Y	N	N
4	McAdams	N	Y	Y	Y	Y	Y
VERMONT							
AL	Welch	N	Y	N	Y	Y	Y
VIRGINIA							
1	**Wittman**	Y	N	Y	Y	N	N
2	Luria	N	Y	Y	Y	Y	Y
3	Scott, R.	N	Y	N	Y	Y	Y
4	McEachin	-	+	-	+	+	+
5	**Riggleman**	Y	N	Y	Y	N	N
6	**Cline**	Y	N	Y	Y	N	N
7	Spanberger	N	Y	N	Y	Y	Y
8	Beyer	N	Y	N	Y	Y	Y
9	**Griffith**	Y	N	Y	Y	N	N
10	Wexton	N	Y	N	Y	Y	Y
11	Connolly	N	Y	N	Y	Y	Y
WASHINGTON							
1	DelBene	N	Y	N	Y	Y	Y
2	Larsen	N	Y	N	Y	Y	Y
3	**Herrera Beutler**	Y	N	Y	Y	N	N
4	**Newhouse**	Y	N	Y	Y	N	N
5	**McMorris Rodgers**	Y	N	Y	Y	N	N
6	Kilmer	N	Y	N	Y	Y	Y
7	Jayapal	N	Y	N	Y	Y	Y
8	Schrier	N	Y	N	Y	Y	Y
9	Smith Adam	N	Y	N	Y	Y	Y
10	Heck	N	Y	N	Y	Y	Y
WEST VIRGINIA							
1	**McKinley**	Y	N	Y	Y	N	N
2	**Mooney**	Y	N	Y	Y	N	N
3	**Miller**	Y	N	Y	Y	N	N
WISCONSIN							
1	**Steil**	Y	N	Y	Y	N	N
2	Pocan	N	Y	N	Y	Y	Y
3	Kind	N	Y	N	Y	Y	Y
4	Moore	N	Y	N	Y	Y	Y
5	**Sensenbrenner**	Y	N	Y	Y	N	N
6	**Grothman**	Y	N	Y	Y	N	N
7	**Duffy**						
8	**Gallagher**	Y	N	Y	Y	N	N
WYOMING							
AL	**Cheney**	Y	N	Y	Y	N	N
DELEGATES							
	Radewagen (A.S.)						
	Norton (D.C.)						
	San Nicolas (Guam)						
	Sablan (N. Marianas)						
	González-Colón (P.R.)						
	Plaskett (V.I.)						

535. HR4285. Veterans' Program Extensions - Passage. Takano, D-Calif., motion to suspend the rules and pass the bill that would extend a number of Veterans Affairs Department authorities and programs. Specifically, it would extend through Sept. 30, 2020, VA authorities related to operation of a VA regional office in Manila, Philippines, travel assistance for veterans receiving care at VA centers, and provision of vendee loans. It would extend through fiscal 2021 VA authority related to provision of financial assistance and support services for low-income veteran families in permanent housing. Motion agreed to 417-1: R 190-1; D 226-0; I 1-0. *Note: A two-thirds majority of those present and voting (279 in this case) is required for passage under suspension of the rules.* Sept. 18, 2019.

536. HR4378. Fiscal 2020 Short-Term Appropriations - Previous Question. McGovern, D-Mass., motion to order the previous question (thus ending debate and possibility of amendment) on the rule (H Res 564) providing for House floor consideration of the Fiscal 2020 Short-Term Appropriations bill (HR 4378) that would make continuing appropriations for fiscal year 2020, funding government operations at fiscal 2019 levels through Nov. 21, 2019. Motion agreed to 228-197: R 0-196; D 228-0; I 0-1. Sept. 19, 2019.

537. HR4378. Fiscal 2020 Short-Term Appropriations - Rule. Adoption of the rule (H Res 564) that would provide for House floor consideration of the Fiscal 2020 Short-Term Appropriations bill (HR 4378) that would make continuing appropriations for fiscal year 2020, funding government operations at fiscal 2019 levels through Nov. 21, 2019. Adopted 227-196: R 0-195; D 227-0; I 0-1. Sept. 19, 2019.

538. HR4378. Fiscal 2020 Short-Term Appropriations - Passage. Passage of the bill that would provide funding for federal government operations and services through Nov. 21, 2019, at fiscal 2019 levels. Among other provisions, it would extend through Nov. 21 authorizations for certain expiring programs and entities, including the National Flood Insurance Program, the Export-Import Bank, certain Medicare and Medicaid programs, and other health-related HHS programs; it would allow for increased funding rates for certain activities, including the 2020 census and FEMA disaster relief; and it would provide for reimbursements to the Agriculture Department Commodity Credit Corporation for payments made to farmers impacted by retaliatory tariffs and other export barriers. Passed 301-123: R 76-119; D 225-3; I 0-1. Sept. 19, 2019.

539. HR1423. Forced Arbitration - Labor Organization Arbitration. Jordan, R-Ohio, amendment no. 1 that would strike from the bill a provision that would restrict the applicability of the bill's provisions on any arbitration agreement between an employer and a labor organization, or between labor organizations. Rejected in Committee of the Whole 161-253: R 160-25; D 0-227; I 1-1. Sept. 20, 2019.

540. HR1423. Forced Arbitration - Passage. Passage of the bill, as amended, that would prohibit the enforcement of pre-dispute arbitration agreements that require employment, consumer, antitrust, or civil rights disputes to be resolved through arbitration. It would also prohibit the enforcement of pre-dispute joint-action waivers with respect to such disputes. It would require issues regarding the applicability of the bill's provisions to a contract to be determined through federal courts, not arbitration. It would clarify that nothing in the bill would contradict any arbitration provision in a contract between an employer and a labor organization, or between labor organizations, unless the provision would waive the rights of workers to seek judicial enforcement of their rights under federal or state law. Passed 225-186: R 2-183; D 223-2; I 0-1. *Note: A "nay" was a vote in support of the president's position.* Sept. 20, 2019.

		535	536	537	538	539	540
ALABAMA							
1	**Byrne**	Y	N	N	N	Y	N
2	**Roby**	Y	N	Y	Y	Y	N
3	**Rogers, M.**	Y	N	N	Y	Y	N
4	**Aderholt**	Y	N	N	Y	Y	N
5	**Brooks, M.**	Y	N	N	N	Y	N
6	**Palmer**	Y	N	N	N	Y	N
7	Sewell	Y	Y	Y	Y	N	Y
ALASKA							
AL	**Young**	Y	N	N	Y	N	N
ARIZONA							
1	O'Halleran	Y	Y	Y	Y	N	Y
2	Kirkpatrick	Y	Y	Y	Y	N	Y
3	Grijalva	Y	Y	Y	Y	N	Y
4	**Gosar**	Y	N	N	N	Y	N
5	**Biggs**	Y	N	N	N	Y	N
6	**Schweikert**	Y	N	N	N	Y	N
7	Gallego	Y	Y	Y	Y	N	Y
8	**Lesko**	Y	N	N	N	Y	N
9	Stanton	Y	Y	Y	Y	N	Y
ARKANSAS							
1	**Crawford**	?	?	?	+	?	-
2	**Hill, F.**	Y	N	N	Y	Y	N
3	**Womack**	Y	N	N	Y	Y	N
4	**Westerman**	Y	N	N	N	Y	N
CALIFORNIA							
1	**LaMalfa**	Y	N	N	N	Y	N
2	Huffman	Y	Y	Y	Y	-	+
3	Garamendi	?	?	Y	Y	N	Y
4	**McClintock**	Y	N	N	N	Y	N
5	Thompson, M.	Y	Y	Y	Y	N	Y
6	Matsui	Y	Y	Y	Y	N	Y
7	Bera	Y	Y	Y	Y	N	Y
8	**Cook**	Y	N	N	Y	N	N
9	McNerney	Y	Y	Y	Y	N	Y
10	Harder	Y	Y	Y	Y	N	Y
11	DeSaulnier	Y	Y	Y	Y	N	Y
12	Pelosi						
13	Lee B.	Y	Y	Y	Y	N	Y
14	Speier	Y	Y	Y	Y	N	Y
15	Swalwell	Y	Y	Y	Y	N	Y
16	Costa	Y	Y	Y	Y	N	Y
17	Khanna	Y	Y	Y	Y	N	Y
18	Eshoo	Y	Y	Y	Y	N	Y
19	Lofgren	Y	Y	Y	Y	N	Y
20	Panetta	Y	Y	Y	Y	N	Y
21	Cox	Y	Y	Y	Y	N	Y
22	**Nunes**	Y	N	N	Y	N	N
23	**McCarthy**	Y	N	N	Y	Y	N
24	Carbajal	Y	Y	Y	Y	N	Y
25	Hill, K.	Y	Y	Y	Y	N	Y
26	Brownley	Y	Y	Y	Y	N	Y
27	Chu	Y	Y	Y	Y	N	Y
28	Schiff	Y	Y	Y	Y	N	Y
29	Cárdenas	Y	Y	Y	Y	N	Y
30	Sherman	Y	Y	Y	Y	N	Y
31	Aguilar	Y	Y	Y	Y	N	Y
32	Napolitano	Y	Y	Y	Y	N	Y
33	Lieu	Y	Y	Y	Y	N	Y
34	Gomez	Y	Y	Y	Y	N	Y
35	Torres	Y	Y	Y	Y	N	Y
36	Ruiz	Y	Y	Y	Y	N	Y
37	Bass	Y	Y	Y	Y	N	Y
38	Sánchez	Y	Y	Y	Y	N	Y
39	Cisneros	Y	Y	Y	Y	N	Y
40	Roybal-Allard	Y	Y	Y	Y	N	Y
41	Takano	Y	Y	Y	Y	N	Y
42	**Calvert**	Y	N	N	Y	N	N
43	Waters	Y	Y	Y	Y	N	Y
44	Barragán	Y	Y	Y	Y	N	Y
45	Porter	Y	Y	Y	Y	N	Y
46	Correa	Y	Y	Y	Y	N	Y
47	Lowenthal	Y	Y	Y	Y	N	Y
48	Rouda	Y	Y	Y	Y	N	Y
49	Levin	Y	Y	Y	Y	N	Y
50	**Hunter**	Y	N	N	N	Y	N
51	Vargas	Y	Y	Y	N	N	Y
52	Peters	Y	Y	Y	Y	N	Y

		535	536	537	538	539	540
53	Davis, S.	Y	Y	Y	Y	N	Y
COLORADO							
1	DeGette	Y	Y	Y	Y	N	Y
2	Neguse	Y	Y	Y	Y	N	Y
3	**Tipton**	Y	N	N	N	Y	N
4	**Buck**	Y	N	N	N	?	?
5	**Lamborn**	Y	N	N	N	Y	N
6	Crow	Y	Y	Y	Y	N	Y
7	Perlmutter	Y	Y	Y	Y	N	Y
CONNECTICUT							
1	Larson	Y	Y	Y	Y	N	Y
2	Courtney	Y	Y	Y	Y	N	Y
3	DeLauro	Y	Y	Y	Y	N	Y
4	Himes	Y	Y	Y	Y	N	Y
5	Hayes	Y	Y	Y	Y	N	Y
DELAWARE							
AL	Blunt Rochester	Y	Y	Y	Y	N	Y
FLORIDA							
1	**Gaetz**	Y	N	N	Y	Y	N
2	**Dunn**	Y	N	N	Y	Y	N
3	**Yoho**	Y	N	N	N	Y	N
4	**Rutherford**	Y	N	N	Y	Y	N
5	Lawson	Y	Y	Y	Y	N	Y
6	**Waltz**	Y	N	N	N	Y	N
7	Murphy	Y	Y	Y	Y	N	Y
8	**Posey**	Y	N	N	N	Y	N
9	Soto	Y	Y	Y	Y	N	Y
10	Demings	Y	Y	Y	Y	N	Y
11	**Webster**	?	N	N	N	Y	N
12	**Bilirakis**	Y	N	N	Y	Y	N
13	Crist	Y	Y	Y	Y	N	Y
14	Castor	Y	Y	Y	Y	N	Y
15	**Spano**	Y	N	N	N	Y	N
16	**Buchanan**	Y	N	N	Y	N	N
17	**Steube**	Y	N	N	N	Y	N
18	**Mast**	?	N	N	N	N	N
19	**Rooney**	?	N	N	N	Y	N
20	Hastings	Y	Y	Y	Y	N	Y
21	Frankel	Y	Y	Y	Y	N	Y
22	Deutch	Y	Y	Y	Y	N	Y
23	Wasserman Schultz	Y	Y	Y	Y	N	Y
24	Wilson, F.	Y	Y	Y	Y	N	Y
25	**Diaz-Balart**	Y	N	N	N	N	N
26	Mucarsel-Powell	Y	Y	Y	Y	N	Y
27	Shalala	Y	Y	Y	Y	N	Y
GEORGIA							
1	**Carter, E.L.**	Y	N	N	Y	N	N
2	Bishop, S.	Y	Y	Y	Y	N	Y
3	**Ferguson**	Y	N	N	N	Y	N
4	Johnson, H.	Y	Y	Y	Y	N	Y
5	Lewis John	Y	Y	Y	Y	N	Y
6	McBath	Y	Y	Y	Y	N	Y
7	**Woodall**	Y	N	N	Y	Y	N
8	**Scott, A.**	Y	N	N	N	N	N
9	**Collins, D.**	Y	N	N	Y	Y	N
10	**Hice**	Y	N	N	N	Y	N
11	**Loudermilk**	Y	N	N	Y	Y	N
12	**Allen**	Y	N	N	N	Y	N
13	Scott, D.	Y	Y	Y	Y	N	Y
14	**Graves, T.**	Y	N	N	N	N	N
HAWAII							
1	Case	Y	Y	Y	Y	N	Y
2	Gabbard	Y	Y	Y	Y	N	Y
IDAHO							
1	**Fulcher**	Y	N	N	N	Y	N
2	**Simpson**	Y	N	N	Y	Y	N
ILLINOIS							
1	Rush	Y	Y	Y	Y	N	Y
2	Kelly, R.	Y	Y	Y	Y	N	Y
3	Lipinski	Y	Y	Y	Y	N	Y
4	García, J.	Y	Y	Y	Y	N	Y
5	Quigley	Y	Y	Y	Y	N	Y
6	Casten	Y	Y	Y	Y	N	Y
7	Davis, D.	Y	Y	Y	Y	-	+
8	Krishnamoorthi	Y	Y	Y	Y	N	Y
9	Schakowsky	Y	Y	Y	Y	N	Y
10	Schneider	Y	Y	Y	Y	N	Y
11	Foster	Y	Y	Y	Y	N	Y

KEY:	**Republicans**	*Democrats*	*Independents*

Y Voted for (yea)	**N** Voted against (nay)	**P** Voted "present"	
+ Announced for	**–** Announced against	**?** Did not vote or otherwise	
# Paired for	**X** Paired against	make position known	

		535	536	537	538	539	540
12	**Bost**	Y	N	N	Y	N	N
13	**Davis, R.**	Y	N	N	Y	N	N
14	Underwood	Y	Y	Y	Y	N	Y
15	**Shimkus**	Y	N	N	?	?	?
16	**Kinzinger**	Y	N	N	N	N	N
17	Bustos	Y	Y	Y	Y	N	Y
18	**LaHood**	Y	N	N	N	Y	N
INDIANA							
1	Visclosky	Y	Y	Y	Y	N	Y
2	**Walorski**	Y	N	N	Y	Y	N
3	**Banks**	Y	N	N	N	Y	N
4	**Baird**	Y	N	N	N	Y	N
5	**Brooks, S.**	Y	N	N	Y	Y	N
6	**Pence**	Y	N	N	Y	Y	N
7	Carson	Y	Y	Y	Y	N	Y
8	**Bucshon**	Y	N	N	N	Y	N
9	**Hollingsworth**	Y	N	N	N	Y	N
IOWA							
1	Finkenauer	Y	Y	Y	Y	N	Y
2	Loebsack	Y	Y	Y	Y	N	Y
3	Axne	Y	Y	Y	Y	N	Y
4	**King, S.**	Y	N	N	N	Y	N
KANSAS							
1	**Marshall**	Y	N	N	N	Y	N
2	**Watkins**	Y	N	N	N	Y	N
3	Davids	Y	Y	Y	Y	N	Y
4	**Estes**	Y	N	N	N	Y	N
KENTUCKY							
1	**Comer**	Y	N	N	N	Y	N
2	**Guthrie**	Y	N	N	N	Y	N
3	Yarmuth	Y	Y	Y	Y	N	Y
4	**Massie**	Y	N	N	N	Y	N
5	**Rogers, H.**	Y	N	N	Y	Y	N
6	**Barr**	Y	N	N	N	Y	N
LOUISIANA							
1	**Scalise**	Y	N	N	Y	Y	N
2	Richmond	Y	Y	Y	Y	N	Y
3	**Higgins, C.**	Y	N	N	N	N	N
4	**Johnson, M.**	Y	N	N	N	Y	N
5	**Abraham**	?	?	?	?	?	?
6	**Graves, G.**	Y	N	N	N	Y	N
MAINE							
1	Pingree	Y	Y	Y	Y	N	Y
2	Golden	Y	Y	Y	Y	N	Y
MARYLAND							
1	**Harris**	Y	N	N	N	Y	N
2	Ruppersberger	Y	Y	Y	Y	N	Y
3	Sarbanes	Y	Y	Y	Y	N	Y
4	Brown, A.	Y	Y	Y	Y	N	Y
5	Hoyer	Y	Y	Y	Y	N	Y
6	Trone	Y	Y	Y	Y	N	Y
7	Cummings	?	?	?	?	?	?
8	Raskin	Y	Y	Y	Y	N	Y
MASSACHUSETTS							
1	Neal	Y	Y	Y	Y	N	Y
2	McGovern	Y	Y	Y	Y	N	Y
3	Trahan	Y	Y	Y	Y	N	Y
4	Kennedy	Y	Y	Y	Y	N	Y
5	Clark	Y	Y	Y	Y	N	Y
6	Moulton	Y	Y	Y	Y	N	Y
7	Pressley	Y	Y	Y	Y	N	Y
8	Lynch	Y	Y	Y	Y	N	Y
9	Keating	Y	Y	Y	Y	N	Y
MICHIGAN							
1	**Bergman**	Y	N	N	N	-	-
2	**Huizenga**	Y	N	N	N	Y	N
3	*Amash*	Y	N	N	N	Y	N
4	**Moolenaar**	Y	N	N	Y	Y	N
5	Kildee	Y	Y	Y	Y	N	Y
6	**Upton**	Y	N	N	Y	Y	N
7	**Walberg**	Y	N	N	N	Y	N
8	Slotkin	Y	Y	Y	Y	N	Y
9	Levin	Y	Y	Y	Y	N	Y
10	**Mitchell**	Y	N	N	N	Y	N
11	Stevens	Y	Y	Y	Y	N	Y
12	Dingell	Y	Y	Y	Y	N	Y
13	Tlaib	Y	Y	Y	Y	N	Y
14	Lawrence	Y	Y	Y	Y	N	Y
MINNESOTA							
1	**Hagedorn**	Y	N	N	N	?	?
2	Craig	Y	Y	Y	Y	N	Y
3	Phillips	Y	Y	Y	Y	N	Y
4	McCollum	Y	Y	Y	Y	N	Y
5	Omar	Y	Y	Y	Y	N	Y
6	**Emmer**	Y	N	N	N	N	N
7	Peterson	Y	Y	?	Y	N	N
8	**Stauber**	Y	N	N	N	N	N
MISSISSIPPI							
1	**Kelly, T.**	Y	N	N	N	Y	N
2	Thompson, B.	?	?	?	?	?	?
3	**Guest**	Y	N	N	Y	N	N
4	**Palazzo**	Y	N	N	Y	Y	N
MISSOURI							
1	Clay	Y	Y	Y	Y	N	Y
2	**Wagner**	Y	N	N	Y	Y	N
3	**Luetkemeyer**	Y	N	N	Y	Y	N
4	**Hartzler**	Y	N	N	Y	Y	N
5	Cleaver	Y	Y	Y	Y	N	Y
6	**Graves, S.**	Y	N	N	N	Y	N
7	**Long**	Y	N	N	Y	Y	N
8	**Smith, J.**	Y	N	N	N	Y	N
MONTANA							
AL	**Gianforte**	Y	N	N	Y	Y	N
NEBRASKA							
1	**Fortenberry**	Y	N	N	Y	Y	N
2	**Bacon**	Y	N	N	Y	N	N
3	**Smith, Adrian**	Y	N	N	N	Y	N
NEVADA							
1	Titus	Y	Y	Y	Y	N	Y
2	**Amodei**	Y	N	N	Y	Y	N
3	Lee	Y	Y	Y	Y	N	Y
4	Horsford	Y	Y	Y	Y	N	Y
NEW HAMPSHIRE							
1	Pappas	Y	Y	Y	Y	N	Y
2	Kuster	Y	Y	Y	Y	N	Y
NEW JERSEY							
1	Norcross	Y	Y	Y	Y	N	Y
2	Van Drew	Y	Y	Y	Y	N	Y
3	Kim	Y	Y	Y	Y	N	Y
4	**Smith, C.**	Y	N	N	Y	N	Y
5	Gottheimer	Y	Y	Y	Y	N	Y
6	Pallone	Y	Y	Y	Y	N	Y
7	Malinowski	Y	Y	Y	Y	N	Y
8	Sires	Y	Y	Y	Y	N	Y
9	Pascrell	Y	Y	Y	Y	N	Y
10	Payne	Y	Y	Y	Y	N	Y
11	Sherrill	Y	Y	Y	Y	N	Y
12	Watson Coleman	Y	Y	Y	Y	N	Y
NEW MEXICO							
1	Haaland	Y	Y	Y	Y	N	Y
2	Torres Small	Y	Y	Y	Y	N	Y
3	Luján	Y	Y	Y	Y	N	Y
NEW YORK							
1	**Zeldin**	Y	N	N	N	N	N
2	**King, P.**	Y	N	N	Y	?	?
3	Suozzi	Y	Y	Y	Y	N	Y
4	Rice, K.	Y	Y	Y	Y	N	Y
5	Meeks	Y	Y	Y	Y	N	Y
6	Meng	Y	Y	Y	Y	N	Y
7	Velázquez	Y	Y	Y	Y	N	Y
8	Jeffries	Y	Y	Y	Y	N	Y
9	Clarke	Y	Y	Y	Y	N	Y
10	Nadler	Y	Y	Y	Y	N	Y
11	Rose	Y	Y	Y	Y	N	Y
12	Maloney, C.	?	Y	Y	Y	N	Y
13	Espaillat	Y	Y	Y	Y	N	Y
14	Ocasio-Cortez	Y	Y	Y	Y	N	Y
15	Serrano	Y	Y	Y	Y	N	Y
16	Engel	Y	Y	Y	Y	N	Y
17	Lowey	Y	Y	Y	Y	N	Y
18	Maloney, S.P.	Y	Y	Y	Y	N	Y
19	Delgado	Y	Y	Y	Y	N	Y
20	Tonko	Y	Y	Y	Y	N	Y
21	**Stefanik**	Y	N	N	Y	N	N
22	Brindisi	Y	Y	Y	Y	N	Y
23	**Reed**	Y	?	?	+	?	-
24	**Katko**	Y	N	N	Y	N	N
25	Morelle	Y	Y	Y	Y	N	Y
26	Higgins, B.	Y	Y	Y	Y	N	Y
27	**Collins, C.**	Y	N	N	Y	Y	N
NORTH CAROLINA							
1	Butterfield	Y	Y	Y	Y	N	Y
2	**Holding**	Y	N	N	N	Y	N
3	**Murphy**	Y	N	N	N	Y	N
4	Price	Y	Y	Y	Y	N	Y
5	**Foxx**	Y	N	N	N	Y	N
6	**Walker**	Y	N	N	N	Y	N
7	**Rouzer**	Y	N	N	N	Y	N
8	**Hudson**	Y	N	N	N	Y	N
9	**Bishop**	Y	N	N	N	Y	N
10	**McHenry**	Y	N	N	Y	Y	N
11	**Meadows**	Y	N	N	N	Y	N
12	Adams	Y	Y	Y	Y	N	Y
13	**Budd**	Y	N	N	N	Y	N
NORTH DAKOTA							
AL	**Armstrong**	Y	N	?	N	Y	N
OHIO							
1	**Chabot**	Y	N	N	N	Y	N
2	**Wenstrup**	Y	N	N	N	Y	N
3	Beatty	Y	Y	+	+	-	+
4	**Jordan**	Y	N	N	N	Y	N
5	**Latta**	Y	N	N	N	Y	N
6	**Johnson, B.**	Y	N	N	Y	Y	N
7	**Gibbs**	Y	N	N	N	Y	N
8	**Davidson**	Y	N	N	N	Y	N
9	Kaptur	Y	Y	Y	Y	N	Y
10	**Turner**	?	N	N	Y	N	N
11	Fudge	Y	Y	Y	Y	N	Y
12	**Balderson**	Y	N	N	N	Y	N
13	Ryan	?	Y	Y	Y	N	Y
14	**Joyce**	Y	N	N	Y	N	N
15	**Stivers**	?	N	N	Y	Y	N
16	**Gonzalez**	Y	N	N	Y	N	N
OKLAHOMA							
1	**Hern**	Y	N	N	N	Y	N
2	**Mullin**	Y	N	N	N	Y	N
3	**Lucas**	Y	N	N	Y	Y	N
4	**Cole**	Y	N	N	Y	Y	N
5	Horn	Y	Y	Y	Y	N	Y
OREGON							
1	Bonamici	Y	Y	Y	Y	N	Y
2	**Walden**	Y	N	N	Y	Y	N
3	Blumenauer	Y	Y	Y	Y	N	Y
4	DeFazio	Y	Y	Y	Y	N	Y
5	Schrader	Y	Y	Y	Y	N	Y
PENNSYLVANIA							
1	**Fitzpatrick**	Y	N	N	Y	N	N
2	Boyle	Y	Y	Y	Y	N	Y
3	Evans	Y	Y	Y	Y	N	Y
4	Dean	Y	Y	Y	Y	N	Y
5	Scanlon	Y	Y	Y	Y	N	Y
6	Houlahan	Y	Y	Y	Y	N	Y
7	Wild	Y	Y	Y	Y	N	Y
8	Cartwright	Y	Y	Y	Y	N	Y
9	**Meuser**	Y	N	N	Y	Y	N
10	**Perry**	Y	N	N	N	Y	N
11	**Smucker**	Y	N	N	N	Y	N
12	**Keller**	Y	N	N	N	+	-
13	**Joyce**	Y	N	N	N	Y	N
14	**Reschenthaler**	Y	N	N	Y	N	N
15	**Thompson, G.**	Y	N	N	Y	Y	N
16	**Kelly, M.**	Y	N	N	N	Y	N
17	Lamb	Y	Y	Y	Y	N	Y
18	Doyle	Y	Y	Y	Y	N	Y
RHODE ISLAND							
1	Cicilline	Y	Y	Y	Y	N	Y
2	Langevin	Y	Y	Y	Y	N	Y
SOUTH CAROLINA							
1	Cunningham	Y	+	+	+	-	+
2	**Wilson, J.**	Y	N	N	N	Y	N
3	**Duncan**	Y	N	N	N	Y	N
4	**Timmons**	Y	N	N	N	Y	N
5	**Norman**	Y	N	N	N	Y	N
6	Clyburn	+	+	+	+	-	+
7	**Rice, T.**	Y	N	N	N	Y	N
SOUTH DAKOTA							
AL	**Johnson**	Y	N	N	N	Y	N
TENNESSEE							
1	**Roe**	Y	N	N	Y	Y	N
2	**Burchett**	Y	N	N	N	Y	N
3	**Fleischmann**	Y	N	N	Y	Y	N
4	**DesJarlais**	Y	N	N	N	Y	N
5	Cooper	Y	Y	Y	Y	N	Y
6	**Rose**	Y	N	N	Y	Y	N
7	**Green**	Y	N	N	N	Y	N
8	**Kustoff**	Y	N	N	Y	Y	N
9	Cohen	Y	Y	Y	Y	N	Y
TEXAS							
1	**Gohmert**	Y	N	N	N	Y	N
2	**Crenshaw**	Y	N	N	N	Y	N
3	**Taylor**	Y	N	N	N	Y	N
4	**Ratcliffe**	?	N	N	N	Y	N
5	**Gooden**	Y	N	N	N	Y	N
6	**Wright**	Y	N	N	N	Y	N
7	Fletcher	Y	Y	Y	Y	N	Y
8	**Brady**	Y	N	N	Y	Y	N
9	Green, A.	Y	Y	Y	Y	N	Y
10	**McCaul**	Y	N	N	Y	Y	N
11	**Conaway**	Y	N	N	Y	Y	N
12	**Granger**	Y	N	N	Y	Y	N
13	**Thornberry**	Y	N	N	N	Y	N
14	**Weber**	Y	N	N	N	?	?
15	Gonzalez	Y	Y	Y	N	N	Y
16	Escobar	Y	Y	Y	Y	N	Y
17	**Flores**	Y	N	N	Y	Y	N
18	Jackson Lee	Y	Y	Y	Y	?	?
19	**Arrington**	Y	N	N	N	Y	N
20	Castro	Y	Y	Y	Y	N	Y
21	**Roy**	Y	N	N	N	Y	N
22	**Olson**	Y	N	N	N	Y	N
23	**Hurd**	Y	N	N	Y	Y	N
24	**Marchant**	Y	N	N	N	?	?
25	**Williams**	Y	N	N	N	Y	N
26	**Burgess**	Y	N	N	N	Y	N
27	**Cloud**	Y	N	N	N	Y	N
28	Cuellar	Y	Y	Y	Y	N	N
29	Garcia, S.	Y	Y	Y	Y	N	Y
30	Johnson, E.B.	Y	Y	Y	Y	N	Y
31	**Carter, J.**	Y	N	N	Y	Y	N
32	Allred	Y	Y	Y	Y	N	Y
33	Veasey	Y	Y	Y	Y	N	Y
34	Vela	Y	Y	Y	N	N	Y
35	Doggett	Y	Y	Y	Y	N	Y
36	**Babin**	Y	N	N	N	?	?
UTAH							
1	**Bishop, R.**	Y	N	N	Y	Y	N
2	**Stewart**	Y	N	N	N	Y	N
3	**Curtis**	Y	N	N	N	Y	N
4	McAdams	Y	Y	Y	Y	N	Y
VERMONT							
AL	Welch	Y	Y	Y	Y	N	Y
VIRGINIA							
1	**Wittman**	Y	N	N	N	Y	N
2	Luria	Y	Y	Y	Y	N	Y
3	Scott, R.	Y	Y	Y	Y	N	Y
4	McEachin	+	+	+	+	-	+
5	**Riggleman**	Y	N	N	N	Y	N
6	**Cline**	Y	N	N	N	Y	N
7	Spanberger	Y	Y	Y	Y	N	Y
8	Beyer	Y	Y	Y	Y	N	Y
9	**Griffith**	Y	N	N	N	N	N
10	Wexton	?	Y	Y	Y	N	Y
11	Connolly	Y	Y	Y	Y	N	Y
WASHINGTON							
1	DelBene	Y	Y	Y	Y	N	Y
2	Larsen	Y	Y	Y	Y	N	Y
3	**Herrera Beutler**	Y	N	N	Y	Y	N
4	**Newhouse**	Y	N	N	Y	Y	N
5	**McMorris Rodgers**	Y	N	N	N	Y	N
6	Kilmer	Y	Y	Y	Y	N	Y
7	Jayapal	Y	Y	Y	Y	N	Y
8	Schrier	Y	Y	Y	Y	N	Y
9	Smith Adam	Y	Y	Y	Y	N	Y
10	Heck	Y	Y	Y	Y	N	Y
WEST VIRGINIA							
1	**McKinley**	Y	N	N	Y	N	N
2	**Mooney**	N	N	N	N	Y	N
3	**Miller**	Y	N	N	Y	N	N
WISCONSIN							
1	**Steil**	Y	N	N	Y	N	N
2	Pocan	Y	Y	Y	Y	N	Y
3	Kind	Y	Y	Y	Y	N	Y
4	Moore	Y	Y	Y	Y	N	Y
5	**Sensenbrenner**	Y	N	N	N	Y	N
6	**Grothman**	Y	N	N	Y	Y	N
7	**Duffy**						
8	**Gallagher**	Y	N	N	N	Y	N
WYOMING							
AL	**Cheney**	Y	N	N	N	+	-
DELEGATES							
	Radewagen (A.S.)					?	
	Norton (D.C.)					N	
	San Nicolas (Guam)					?	
	Sablan (N. Marianas)					N	
	González-Colón (P.R.)					?	
	Plaskett (V.I.)					N	

III HOUSE VOTES

541. HR3190. Rohingya Humanitarian Assistance - Passage. Levin, D-Mich., motion to suspend the rules and pass the bill, as amended, that would authorize $221 million in humanitarian assistance for use in Burma and Bangladesh and other areas where the Rohingya people have taken refuge. Among other provisions, the measure would require the president to impose sanctions on individuals or entities that knowingly participated in serious human rights abuses in Burma or impeded investigations or prosecutions of alleged abuses, and it would require the State Department to develop guidance, reports, and strategies related to the mining industry, human rights violations, and economic development in the region. Motion agreed to 394-21: R 170-20; D 224-0; I 0-1. *Note: A two-thirds majority of those present and voting (277 in this case) is required for passage under suspension of the rules.* Sept. 24, 2019.

542. HR2203, HR3525, HRES576. Border Security; Whistle-blower Claim - Previous Question. Scanlon, D-Pa., motion to order the previous question (thus ending debate on and possibility of amendment) on the rule (H Res 577), as amended, that would provide for consideration of the bill (HR 2203) related to border security activities and procedures of the Homeland Security Department; provide for consideration of the bill (HR 3525) that would establish medical screening practices for individuals apprehended at U.S. ports of entry; provide for consideration of the resolution (H Res 576) that would express the sense of the House regarding the Aug. 12 whistle-blower complaint related to Ukraine; and provide for motions to suspend the rules through the legislative day of Thursday, Sept. 26, 2019. Motion agreed to 227-191: R 0-190; D 227-0; I 0-1. Sept. 25, 2019.

543. HR2203, HR3525, HRES576. Border Security; Whistle-blower Claim - Rule. Adoption of the rule (H Res 577), as amended, that would provide for consideration of the bill (HR 2203) related to border security activities and procedures of the Homeland Security Department; provide for consideration of the bill (HR 3525) that would establish medical screening practices for individuals apprehended at U.S. ports of entry; provide for consideration of the resolution (H Res 576) that would express the sense of the House regarding the Aug. 12 whistle-blower complaint related to Ukraine; and provide for motions to suspend the rules through the legislative day of Sept. 26, 2019. The rule would provide for the automatic adoption of a Thompson, D-Miss., manager's amendment to HR 2203 that would strike a number of provisions in the bill, including provisions that would establish a DHS commission to investigate the treatment of migrant families and children, provisions that would require a number of Government Accountability Office reports on DHS activities, and a provision that would prohibit the separation of families near U.S. ports of entry. As amended, the rule would also provide for the automatic adoption of an amendment to H Res 576 that would replace the resolving text of the resolution with the text of a whistle-blower complaint transmittal resolution (S Res 325) agreed to in the Senate. Adopted 228-191: R 0-189; D 228-1; I 0-1. Sept. 25, 2019.

544. HR1595. Marijuana Banking Protection - Passage. Perlmutter, D-Colo., motion to suspend the rules and pass the bill, as amended, that would prohibit federal banking regulators from penalizing financial service institutions for providing services to marijuana-related businesses and service providers operating in accordance with state law. It would protect all ancillary businesses that provide services to marijuana-related businesses from criminal liability. Motion agreed to 321-103: R 91-102; D 229-1; I 1-0. *Note: A two-thirds majority of those present and voting (283 in this case) is required for passage under suspension of the rules.* Sept. 25, 2019.

545. HR2203. DHS Oversight - Recommit. Green, R-Tenn., motion to recommit the bill to the Committee on Homeland Security with instructions to report it back immediately with an amendment that would instruct the ombudsman's office established under the bill's provisions to receive complaints from victims of crimes committed in "sanctuary jurisdictions" by aliens unlawfully present in the United States. It would require the ombudsman to include information on such complaints in an annual report to Congress, including the names of sanctuary jurisdictions and relevant actions by Immigration and Customs Enforcement. Motion rejected 207-216: R 191-0; D 16-215; I 0-1. Sept. 25, 2019.

546. HR2203. DHS Oversight - Passage. Passage of the bill, as amended, that would establish an independent ombudsman for within the Homeland Security Department to process, investigate, and resolve complaints against DHS border and immigration agencies and personnel and to review the compliance of Customs and Border Protection and Immigration and Customs Enforcement personnel with departmental policies and standards of care for undocumented immigrants in custody. It would require the ombudsman to make a number of policy recommendations for DHS border security operations, including to foster cooperation between CBP, ICE, and border communities. Passed 230-194: R 0-192; D 230-1; I 0-1. *Note: A "nay" was a vote in support of the president's position.* Sept. 25, 2019.

		541	542	543	544	545	546
ALABAMA							
1	**Byrne**	N	N	N	N	Y	N
2	**Roby**	Y	N	N	N	Y	N
3	**Rogers, M.**	Y	N	N	Y	Y	N
4	**Aderholt**	Y	N	N	N	Y	N
5	**Brooks, M.**	N	N	N	Y	Y	N
6	**Palmer**	Y	N	N	N	Y	N
7	Sewell	Y	Y	Y	N	N	Y
ALASKA							
AL	Young	Y	N	N	Y	Y	N
ARIZONA							
1	O'Halleran	Y	Y	Y	Y	N	Y
2	Kirkpatrick	Y	Y	Y	Y	N	Y
3	Grijalva	?	Y	Y	Y	N	Y
4	**Gosar**	N	N	N	N	Y	N
5	**Biggs**	N	N	N	N	Y	N
6	**Schweikert**	Y	N	-	Y	Y	N
7	Gallego	Y	Y	Y	Y	N	Y
8	**Lesko**	N	N	N	N	Y	N
9	Stanton	Y	Y	Y	Y	N	Y
ARKANSAS							
1	**Crawford**	?	?	?	?	?	-
2	**Hill, F.**	Y	N	N	Y	Y	N
3	**Womack**	Y	N	N	Y	Y	N
4	**Westerman**	Y	N	N	N	Y	N
CALIFORNIA							
1	**LaMalfa**	Y	N	N	N	Y	N
2	Huffman	Y	Y	Y	Y	N	Y
3	Garamendi	Y	Y	Y	N	N	Y
4	**McClintock**	Y	N	N	Y	Y	N
5	Thompson, M.	Y	Y	Y	Y	N	Y
6	Matsui	Y	Y	Y	Y	N	Y
7	Bera	Y	Y	Y	Y	N	Y
8	**Cook**	Y	N	N	N	Y	N
9	McNerney	Y	Y	Y	Y	N	Y
10	Harder	Y	Y	Y	Y	Y	Y
11	DeSaulnier	Y	Y	Y	Y	N	Y
12	Pelosi						
13	Lee B.	?	Y	Y	Y	N	Y
14	Speier	Y	Y	Y	Y	N	Y
15	Swalwell	Y	Y	Y	Y	N	Y
16	Costa	Y	Y	Y	Y	N	Y
17	Khanna	Y	Y	Y	Y	N	Y
18	Eshoo	Y	Y	Y	Y	N	Y
19	Lofgren	Y	Y	Y	Y	N	Y
20	Panetta	Y	Y	Y	Y	N	Y
21	Cox	Y	Y	Y	Y	N	Y
22	**Nunes**	Y	N	N	Y	Y	N
23	**McCarthy**	Y	N	N	Y	Y	N
24	Carbajal	Y	Y	Y	Y	N	Y
25	Hill, K.	Y	Y	Y	Y	N	Y
26	Brownley	Y	Y	Y	Y	N	Y
27	Chu	Y	Y	Y	Y	N	Y
28	Schiff	Y	Y	Y	Y	N	Y
29	Cárdenas	Y	Y	Y	Y	N	Y
30	Sherman	Y	Y	Y	Y	N	Y
31	Aguilar	Y	Y	Y	Y	N	Y
32	Napolitano	Y	Y	Y	Y	N	Y
33	Lieu	Y	Y	Y	Y	N	Y
34	Gomez	Y	Y	Y	Y	N	Y
35	Torres	Y	Y	+	N	Y	Y
36	Ruiz	Y	Y	Y	Y	N	Y
37	Bass	Y	Y	Y	Y	N	Y
38	Sánchez	Y	Y	Y	Y	N	Y
39	Cisneros	Y	Y	Y	Y	N	Y
40	Roybal-Allard	Y	Y	Y	Y	N	Y
41	Takano	Y	Y	Y	Y	N	Y
42	**Calvert**	Y	N	N	N	Y	N
43	Waters	Y	Y	Y	Y	N	Y
44	Barragán	Y	Y	Y	Y	N	Y
45	Porter	Y	Y	Y	Y	N	Y
46	Correa	Y	Y	Y	N	N	Y
47	Lowenthal	Y	Y	Y	Y	N	Y
48	Rouda	Y	Y	Y	Y	N	Y
49	Levin	Y	Y	Y	Y	N	Y
50	**Hunter**	Y	N	N	Y	Y	N
51	Vargas	Y	Y	Y	Y	N	Y
52	Peters	Y	Y	Y	Y	N	Y
53	Davis, S.	?	Y	Y	Y	N	Y
COLORADO							
1	DeGette	Y	Y	Y	Y	N	Y
2	Neguse	Y	Y	Y	Y	N	Y
3	**Tipton**	N	N	N	N	Y	N
4	**Buck**	N	N	N	N	Y	N
5	**Lamborn**	Y	N	N	N	Y	N
6	Crow	Y	Y	Y	Y	N	Y
7	Perlmutter	Y	Y	Y	Y	N	Y
CONNECTICUT							
1	Larson	Y	Y	Y	Y	N	Y
2	Courtney	Y	Y	Y	Y	N	Y
3	DeLauro	Y	Y	Y	Y	N	Y
4	Himes	Y	Y	Y	Y	N	Y
5	Hayes	Y	Y	Y	Y	N	Y
DELAWARE							
AL	Blunt Rochester	Y	Y	Y	Y	N	Y
FLORIDA							
1	**Gaetz**	Y	N	N	Y	Y	N
2	**Dunn**	Y	N	N	N	Y	N
3	**Yoho**	Y	N	N	Y	Y	N
4	**Rutherford**	Y	N	N	N	Y	N
5	Lawson	Y	Y	Y	Y	N	Y
6	**Waltz**	Y	N	N	N	Y	N
7	Murphy	Y	Y	Y	Y	N	Y
8	**Posey**	Y	N	N	N	Y	N
9	Soto	Y	Y	Y	Y	N	Y
10	Demings	Y	Y	Y	Y	N	Y
11	**Webster**	Y	N	N	N	Y	N
12	**Bilirakis**	Y	N	N	N	Y	N
13	Crist	Y	Y	Y	Y	N	Y
14	Castor	Y	Y	Y	Y	N	Y
15	**Spano**	N	N	N	Y	Y	N
16	**Buchanan**	Y	N	N	N	Y	N
17	**Steube**	N	N	N	Y	Y	N
18	**Mast**	Y	N	N	N	Y	N
19	**Rooney**	Y	N	N	Y	Y	N
20	Hastings	Y	Y	Y	Y	N	Y
21	Frankel	Y	Y	Y	Y	N	Y
22	Deutch	Y	Y	Y	Y	N	Y
23	Wasserman Schultz	Y	Y	Y	Y	N	Y
24	Wilson, F.	Y	Y	Y	Y	N	Y
25	**Diaz-Balart**	Y	N	N	N	Y	N
26	Mucarsel-Powell	Y	Y	Y	Y	N	Y
27	Shalala	Y	Y	Y	N	N	Y
GEORGIA							
1	**Carter, E.L.**	Y	N	N	Y	Y	N
2	Bishop, S.	Y	Y	Y	Y	N	Y
3	**Ferguson**	Y	N	N	N	Y	N
4	Johnson, H.	Y	Y	Y	Y	N	Y
5	Lewis John	Y	Y	Y	Y	N	Y
6	McBath	Y	Y	Y	Y	N	Y
7	**Woodall**	Y	N	N	N	Y	N
8	**Scott, A.**	Y	N	N	N	Y	N
9	**Collins, D.**	Y	N	N	Y	Y	N
10	**Hice**	N	N	N	N	Y	N
11	**Loudermilk**	Y	N	N	Y	Y	N
12	**Allen**	Y	N	N	N	Y	N
13	Scott, D.	Y	Y	Y	Y	N	Y
14	**Graves, T.**	Y	N	N	Y	Y	N
HAWAII							
1	Case	Y	Y	Y	Y	N	Y
2	Gabbard	?	Y	Y	Y	N	Y
IDAHO							
1	**Fulcher**	N	N	N	N	Y	N
2	**Simpson**	Y	N	N	Y	Y	N
ILLINOIS							
1	Rush	Y	Y	Y	Y	N	Y
2	Kelly, R.	Y	Y	Y	Y	N	Y
3	Lipinski	Y	Y	Y	Y	N	Y
4	García, J.	Y	Y	Y	Y	N	Y
5	Quigley	Y	Y	Y	Y	N	Y
6	Casten	Y	Y	Y	Y	N	Y
7	Davis, D.	Y	Y	Y	Y	N	Y
8	Krishnamoorthi	Y	Y	?	Y	N	Y
9	Schakowsky	Y	Y	Y	Y	N	Y
10	Schneider	Y	Y	Y	Y	N	Y
11	Foster	Y	Y	Y	Y	N	Y

	541	542	543	544	545	546
12 **Bost**	Y	N	N	Y	Y	N
13 **Davis, R.**	Y	N	N	Y	Y	N
14 Underwood	Y	Y	Y	Y	N	Y
15 **Shimkus**	Y	N	N	N	Y	N
16 **Kinzinger**	Y	N	N	Y	Y	N
17 Bustos	Y	Y	Y	Y	N	Y
18 **LaHood**	Y	N	N	N	Y	N
INDIANA						
1 Visclosky	Y	Y	Y	Y	N	Y
2 **Walorski**	Y	N	N	N	Y	N
3 **Banks**	Y	N	N	Y	Y	N
4 **Baird**	Y	N	N	Y	Y	N
5 **Brooks, S.**	Y	N	N	N	Y	N
6 **Pence**	Y	N	N	N	Y	N
7 Carson	Y	Y	Y	Y	N	Y
8 **Bucshon**	Y	N	N	N	Y	N
9 **Hollingsworth**	Y	N	N	Y	Y	N
IOWA						
1 Finkenauer	Y	Y	Y	Y	Y	Y
2 Loebsack	Y	Y	Y	Y	N	Y
3 Axne	Y	Y	Y	Y	Y	Y
4 **King, S.**	N	N	N	N	Y	N
KANSAS						
1 **Marshall**	Y	?	?	?	?	?
2 **Watkins**	Y	N	N	Y	Y	N
3 Davids	Y	Y	Y	Y	N	Y
4 **Estes**	Y	N	N	Y	Y	N
KENTUCKY						
1 **Comer**	Y	N	N	Y	Y	N
2 **Guthrie**	Y	N	N	N	Y	N
3 Yarmuth	Y	Y	Y	Y	N	Y
4 **Massie**	N	N	N	Y	Y	N
5 **Rogers, H.**	Y	N	N	N	Y	N
6 **Barr**	Y	N	N	Y	Y	N
LOUISIANA						
1 **Scalise**	Y	N	N	N	Y	N
2 Richmond	Y	Y	Y	Y	N	Y
3 **Higgins, C.**	+	-	-	+	+	-
4 **Johnson, M.**	N	N	N	N	Y	N
5 **Abraham**	?	?	?	?	?	?
6 **Graves, G.**	Y	-	-	N	Y	N
MAINE						
1 Pingree	Y	Y	Y	Y	N	Y
2 Golden	Y	Y	Y	Y	Y	Y
MARYLAND						
1 **Harris**	Y	N	N	N	Y	N
2 Ruppersberger	?	Y	Y	Y	N	Y
3 Sarbanes	Y	Y	Y	Y	N	Y
4 Brown, A.	Y	Y	Y	Y	N	Y
5 Hoyer	Y	Y	Y	Y	N	Y
6 Trone	Y	Y	Y	Y	N	Y
7 Cummings	?	?	?	?	?	?
8 Raskin	Y	Y	Y	Y	N	Y
MASSACHUSETTS						
1 Neal	Y	Y	Y	Y	N	Y
2 McGovern	Y	Y	Y	Y	N	Y
3 Trahan	Y	Y	Y	Y	N	Y
4 Kennedy	Y	Y	Y	Y	N	Y
5 Clark	Y	Y	Y	Y	N	Y
6 Moulton	Y	Y	Y	Y	N	Y
7 Pressley	Y	Y	Y	Y	N	Y
8 Lynch	Y	Y	Y	Y	N	Y
9 Keating	Y	Y	Y	Y	N	Y
MICHIGAN						
1 **Bergman**	Y	N	N	N	Y	N
2 **Huizenga**	Y	N	N	N	?	?
3 *Amash*	N	N	N	Y	N	N
4 **Moolenaar**	Y	N	N	N	Y	N
5 Kildee	Y	Y	Y	Y	N	Y
6 **Upton**	Y	N	N	Y	Y	N
7 **Walberg**	?	N	N	N	Y	N
8 Slotkin	Y	Y	Y	Y	Y	Y
9 Levin	Y	Y	Y	Y	N	Y
10 **Mitchell**	Y	N	N	Y	Y	N
11 Stevens	Y	Y	Y	Y	N	Y
12 Dingell	Y	Y	Y	Y	N	Y
13 Tlaib	Y	Y	Y	Y	N	Y
14 Lawrence	Y	Y	Y	Y	N	Y
MINNESOTA						
1 **Hagedorn**	Y	N	N	Y	Y	N
2 Craig	Y	Y	Y	Y	N	Y
3 Phillips	Y	Y	Y	Y	N	Y
4 McCollum	Y	Y	Y	Y	N	Y
5 Omar	Y	Y	Y	Y	N	Y

	541	542	543	544	545	546
6 **Emmer**	Y	N	N	Y	Y	N
7 Peterson	Y	Y	Y	Y	Y	N
8 **Stauber**	Y	N	N	Y	Y	N
MISSISSIPPI						
1 **Kelly, T.**	Y	N	N	N	Y	N
2 Thompson, B.	Y	Y	Y	Y	N	Y
3 **Guest**	Y	N	N	N	Y	N
4 **Palazzo**	Y	N	N	N	Y	N
MISSOURI						
1 Clay	Y	Y	Y	Y	N	Y
2 **Wagner**	Y	N	N	Y	Y	N
3 **Luetkemeyer**	Y	N	N	Y	Y	N
4 **Hartzler**	Y	N	N	N	Y	N
5 Cleaver	Y	Y	Y	Y	N	Y
6 **Graves, S.**	Y	N	N	N	Y	N
7 **Long**	Y	N	N	Y	Y	N
8 **Smith, J.**	Y	N	N	N	Y	N
MONTANA						
AL **Gianforte**	Y	N	N	N	Y	N
NEBRASKA						
1 **Fortenberry**	Y	N	N	N	Y	N
2 **Bacon**	Y	N	N	Y	Y	N
3 **Smith, Adrian**	Y	N	N	N	Y	N
NEVADA						
1 Titus	Y	Y	Y	Y	N	Y
2 **Amodei**	Y	N	N	Y	Y	N
3 Lee	Y	Y	Y	Y	N	Y
4 Horsford	Y	Y	Y	Y	N	Y
NEW HAMPSHIRE						
1 Pappas	Y	Y	Y	Y	N	Y
2 Kuster	Y	+	Y	Y	N	Y
NEW JERSEY						
1 Norcross	Y	Y	Y	Y	N	Y
2 Van Drew	Y	+	Y	Y	Y	Y
3 Kim	Y	Y	Y	Y	N	Y
4 **Smith, C.**	Y	N	N	N	Y	N
5 Gottheimer	Y	Y	Y	Y	Y	Y
6 Pallone	Y	Y	Y	Y	N	Y
7 Malinowski	Y	Y	Y	Y	N	Y
8 Sires	Y	Y	Y	Y	N	Y
9 Pascrell	Y	Y	Y	Y	N	Y
10 Payne	Y	Y	Y	Y	N	Y
11 Sherrill	Y	Y	Y	Y	Y	Y
12 Watson Coleman	Y	Y	Y	Y	N	Y
NEW MEXICO						
1 Haaland	Y	Y	Y	Y	N	Y
2 Torres Small	Y	Y	Y	Y	N	Y
3 Luján	Y	Y	Y	Y	N	Y
NEW YORK						
1 **Zeldin**	Y	N	N	Y	Y	N
2 **King, P.**	Y	N	N	Y	Y	N
3 Suozzi	Y	Y	Y	Y	N	Y
4 Rice, K.	Y	Y	Y	Y	N	Y
5 Meeks	Y	Y	?	Y	N	Y
6 Meng	Y	Y	Y	Y	N	Y
7 Velázquez	Y	Y	Y	Y	N	Y
8 Jeffries	Y	Y	Y	Y	N	Y
9 Clarke	Y	Y	Y	Y	N	Y
10 Nadler	Y	Y	Y	Y	N	Y
11 Rose	Y	Y	Y	Y	N	Y
12 Maloney, C.	Y	Y	Y	Y	N	Y
13 Espaillat	Y	Y	Y	Y	N	Y
14 Ocasio-Cortez	Y	Y	Y	Y	N	Y
15 Serrano	Y	Y	Y	Y	N	Y
16 Engel	Y	Y	Y	Y	N	Y
17 Lowey	Y	Y	Y	Y	N	Y
18 Maloney, S.P.	Y	Y	Y	Y	N	Y
19 Delgado	Y	Y	Y	Y	N	Y
20 Tonko	Y	Y	Y	Y	N	Y
21 **Stefanik**	+	N	N	Y	Y	N
22 Brindisi	Y	Y	Y	Y	Y	Y
23 **Reed**	Y	N	N	Y	Y	N
24 **Katko**	Y	N	N	Y	Y	N
25 Morelle	Y	Y	Y	Y	N	Y
26 Higgins, B.	Y	Y	Y	Y	N	Y
27 **Collins, C.**	Y	N	N	Y	Y	N
NORTH CAROLINA						
1 Butterfield	?	Y	Y	Y	N	Y
2 **Holding**	Y	N	N	N	Y	N
3 **Murphy**	?	N	N	N	Y	N
4 Price	Y	Y	Y	Y	N	Y
5 **Foxx**	Y	N	N	N	Y	N
6 **Walker**	Y	N	N	N	Y	N
7 **Rouzer**	Y	N	N	N	Y	N

	541	542	543	544	545	546
8 **Hudson**	Y	N	N	N	Y	N
9 **Bishop**	N	N	N	N	Y	N
10 **McHenry**	Y	N	N	N	Y	N
11 **Meadows**	Y	N	N	N	Y	N
12 Adams	Y	Y	Y	Y	N	Y
13 **Budd**	Y	N	N	N	Y	N
NORTH DAKOTA						
AL **Armstrong**	Y	N	N	Y	Y	N
OHIO						
1 **Chabot**	Y	N	N	N	Y	N
2 **Wenstrup**	Y	N	N	N	Y	N
3 Beatty	Y	Y	Y	Y	N	Y
4 **Jordan**	Y	?	?	N	Y	N
5 **Latta**	Y	N	N	N	Y	N
6 **Johnson, B.**	Y	N	N	Y	Y	N
7 **Gibbs**	Y	N	N	Y	Y	N
8 **Davidson**	Y	N	N	Y	Y	N
9 Kaptur	Y	Y	Y	Y	N	Y
10 **Turner**	Y	N	N	N	Y	N
11 Fudge	Y	Y	Y	Y	N	Y
12 **Balderson**	Y	N	N	Y	Y	N
13 Ryan	?	Y	Y	Y	N	Y
14 **Joyce**	Y	N	N	Y	Y	N
15 **Stivers**	Y	N	N	Y	Y	N
16 **Gonzalez**	Y	N	N	Y	Y	N
OKLAHOMA						
1 **Hern**	Y	N	N	Y	Y	N
2 **Mullin**	Y	N	N	N	Y	N
3 **Lucas**	Y	N	N	N	Y	N
4 **Cole**	Y	N	N	Y	Y	N
5 Horn	Y	Y	Y	Y	Y	Y
OREGON						
1 Bonamici	Y	Y	Y	Y	N	Y
2 **Walden**	Y	N	N	Y	Y	N
3 Blumenauer	Y	Y	Y	Y	N	Y
4 DeFazio	Y	Y	Y	Y	N	Y
5 Schrader	Y	Y	Y	Y	N	Y
PENNSYLVANIA						
1 **Fitzpatrick**	Y	N	N	Y	Y	N
2 Boyle	Y	Y	Y	Y	N	Y
3 Evans	Y	Y	Y	Y	N	Y
4 Dean	Y	+	Y	Y	N	Y
5 Scanlon	Y	Y	Y	Y	N	Y
6 Houlahan	Y	Y	Y	Y	N	Y
7 Wild	Y	Y	Y	Y	N	Y
8 Cartwright	Y	Y	Y	Y	N	Y
9 **Meuser**	Y	N	N	Y	Y	N
10 **Perry**	Y	N	N	Y	Y	N
11 **Smucker**	Y	N	N	Y	Y	N
12 **Keller**	Y	N	N	Y	Y	N
13 **Joyce**	Y	-	-	N	Y	N
14 **Reschenthaler**	Y	N	N	Y	Y	N
15 **Thompson, G.**	Y	N	N	Y	Y	N
16 **Kelly, M.**	Y	N	N	Y	Y	N
17 Lamb	Y	Y	Y	Y	Y	Y
18 Doyle	Y	Y	Y	Y	N	Y
RHODE ISLAND						
1 Cicilline	Y	Y	Y	Y	N	Y
2 Langevin	Y	Y	Y	Y	N	Y
SOUTH CAROLINA						
1 Cunningham	Y	Y	Y	Y	Y	Y
2 **Wilson, J.**	Y	N	N	N	Y	N
3 **Duncan**	Y	N	N	N	Y	N
4 **Timmons**	Y	N	N	Y	Y	N
5 **Norman**	N	N	N	Y	Y	N
6 Clyburn	+	+	+	+	-	+
7 **Rice, T.**	Y	N	N	Y	Y	N
SOUTH DAKOTA						
AL **Johnson**	Y	N	N	N	Y	N
TENNESSEE						
1 **Roe**	Y	N	N	Y	Y	N
2 **Burchett**	N	N	N	N	Y	N
3 **Fleischmann**	Y	N	N	Y	Y	N
4 **DesJarlais**	Y	N	N	N	Y	N
5 Cooper	Y	Y	Y	Y	N	Y
6 **Rose**	Y	N	N	N	Y	N
7 **Green**	Y	N	N	Y	Y	N
8 **Kustoff**	Y	N	N	N	Y	N
9 Cohen	Y	Y	Y	Y	N	Y
TEXAS						
1 **Gohmert**	N	N	N	N	Y	N
2 **Crenshaw**	Y	N	N	Y	Y	N
3 **Taylor**	Y	N	N	Y	Y	N
4 **Ratcliffe**	Y	N	N	N	Y	N

	541	542	543	544	545	546
5 **Gooden**	Y	N	N	Y	Y	N
6 **Wright**	?	?	?	?	?	?
7 Fletcher	Y	Y	Y	Y	N	Y
8 **Brady**	Y	N	N	N	Y	N
9 Green, A.	Y	Y	Y	Y	N	Y
10 **McCaul**	Y	N	N	N	Y	N
11 **Conaway**	Y	N	N	N	Y	N
12 **Granger**	Y	N	N	N	Y	N
13 **Thornberry**	Y	N	N	N	Y	N
14 **Weber**	Y	N	N	N	Y	N
15 Gonzalez	Y	Y	Y	Y	N	Y
16 Escobar	Y	Y	Y	Y	N	Y
17 **Flores**	Y	N	N	Y	Y	N
18 Jackson Lee	Y	+	Y	Y	N	Y
19 **Arrington**	Y	N	N	N	Y	N
20 Castro	Y	Y	Y	Y	N	Y
21 **Roy**	N	N	N	N	Y	N
22 **Olson**	Y	N	N	Y	Y	N
23 **Hurd**	Y	N	N	N	Y	N
24 **Marchant**	Y	N	N	N	Y	N
25 **Williams**	Y	N	N	N	Y	N
26 **Burgess**	Y	N	N	N	Y	N
27 **Cloud**	N	N	N	N	Y	N
28 Cuellar	Y	Y	Y	Y	N	Y
29 Garcia, S.	Y	Y	Y	Y	N	Y
30 Johnson, E.B.	Y	Y	Y	Y	N	Y
31 **Carter, J.**	Y	N	N	N	Y	N
32 Allred	Y	Y	Y	Y	N	Y
33 Veasey	Y	Y	Y	Y	N	Y
34 Vela	Y	Y	Y	Y	N	Y
35 Doggett	Y	Y	Y	Y	N	Y
36 **Babin**	Y	N	N	N	Y	N
UTAH						
1 **Bishop, R.**	Y	N	N	Y	Y	N
2 **Stewart**	Y	N	N	N	Y	N
3 **Curtis**	Y	N	N	Y	Y	N
4 McAdams	Y	Y	N	Y	Y	Y
VERMONT						
AL Welch	Y	Y	Y	Y	N	Y
VIRGINIA						
1 **Wittman**	Y	N	N	N	Y	N
2 Luria	Y	Y	Y	Y	N	Y
3 Scott, R.	Y	Y	Y	Y	N	Y
4 McEachin	+	+	+	+	-	+
5 **Riggleman**	N	N	N	Y	Y	N
6 **Cline**	N	N	N	N	Y	N
7 Spanberger	Y	Y	Y	Y	Y	Y
8 Beyer	Y	Y	Y	Y	N	Y
9 **Griffith**	Y	N	N	Y	Y	N
10 Wexton	Y	Y	Y	Y	N	Y
11 Connolly	Y	Y	Y	Y	N	Y
WASHINGTON						
1 DelBene	Y	Y	Y	Y	N	Y
2 Larsen	Y	Y	Y	Y	N	Y
3 **Herrera Beutler**	Y	N	N	Y	Y	N
4 **Newhouse**	Y	N	N	Y	Y	N
5 **McMorris Rodgers**	Y	N	N	Y	Y	N
6 Kilmer	Y	Y	Y	Y	N	Y
7 Jayapal	Y	Y	Y	Y	N	Y
8 Schrier	Y	Y	Y	Y	N	Y
9 Smith Adam	Y	Y	Y	Y	N	Y
10 Heck	Y	Y	Y	Y	N	Y
WEST VIRGINIA						
1 **McKinley**	Y	N	N	Y	Y	N
2 **Mooney**	N	N	N	Y	Y	N
3 **Miller**	Y	N	N	Y	Y	N
WISCONSIN						
1 **Steil**	Y	N	N	Y	Y	N
2 Pocan	Y	Y	Y	Y	N	Y
3 Kind	Y	Y	Y	Y	N	Y
4 Moore	Y	Y	Y	Y	N	Y
5 **Sensenbrenner**	Y	N	N	N	Y	N
6 **Grothman**	Y	N	N	Y	?	N
7 **Duffy**						
8 **Gallagher**	Y	N	N	N	Y	N
WYOMING						
AL **Cheney**	?	N	N	N	Y	N
DELEGATES						
Radewagen (A.S.)						
Norton (D.C.)						
San Nicolas (Guam)						
Sablan (N. Marianas)						
González-Colón (P.R.)						
Plaskett (V.I.)						

547. HRES590. Impeachment Inquiry Disapproval - Motion to Table. Hoyer, D-Md., motion to table (kill) a privileged resolution that would express disapproval of actions of Speaker Nancy Pelosi, D-Calif., on Sept. 24, 2019, to initiate an impeachment inquiry against President Donald Trump. Motion agreed to 232-193: R 0-193; D 231-0; I 1-0. Sept. 25, 2019.

548. HRES576. Whistle-blower Complaint - Passage. Agreeing to the resolution, as amended, that would express the sense of the House that the inspector general of the intelligence community should transmit to the Senate and House Intelligence Committees the Aug. 12, 2019 whistle-blower complaint alleging that President Trump pressured Ukrainian President Volodymyr Zelensky to investigate former Vice President Joe Biden and his family. Passed 421-0: R 189-0; D 231-0; I 1-0. Sept. 25, 2019.

549. SJ Res 54. National Emergency Termination - Previous Question. Morelle, D-N.Y., motion to order the previous question (thus ending debate and possibility of amendment) on the rule (H Res 591) that would provide for House floor consideration of the bill (S J Res 54) that would terminate the national emergency declared by the President Donald Trump on Feb. 15, 2019, related to the construction of a physical barrier along the U.S.-Mexico border. Motion agreed to 230-187: R 0-187; D 229-0; I 1-0. Sept. 26, 2019.

550. SJ Res 54. National Emergency Termination - Rule. Adoption of the rule (H Res 591) that would provide for House floor consideration of the Border National Emergency Termination Resolution (S J Res 54) that would terminate the national emergency declared by the President Donald Trump on Feb. 15, 2019, related to the construction of a physical barrier along the U.S.-Mexico border. Adopted 229-186: R 0-186; D 228-0; I 1-0. Sept. 26, 2019.

551. HR3525. Border Patrol Medical Screenings - Recommit. Green, R-Tenn., motion to recommit the bill to the House Homeland Security Committee with instructions to report it back immediately with an amendment that would postpone the effective date of the bill until Sept. 30, 2027. Motion rejected 202-213: R 186-0; D 16-212; I 0-1. Sept. 26, 2019.

552. HR3525. Border Patrol Medical Screenings - Passage. Passage of the bill, as amended, that would that would require the Homeland Security Department to establish uniform procedures for medical screening of individuals taken into custody by U.S. Border Patrol between U.S. ports of entry. It would require that such screenings be conducted by a medical professional within 12 hours for adults and within 6 hours for minors. It would also require DHS to assess capability gaps in the provision of medical screenings, particularly for vulnerable populations. Passed 230-184: R 2-182; D 227-2; I 1-0. *Note: A "nay" was a vote in support of the president's position.* Sept. 26, 2019.

		547	548	549	550	551	552
ALABAMA							
1	**Byrne**	N	Y	N	N	Y	N
2	**Roby**	N	Y	N	N	Y	N
3	**Rogers, M.**	N	Y	N	N	Y	N
4	**Aderholt**	N	Y	N	N	Y	?
5	**Brooks, M.**	N	Y	N	N	Y	N
6	**Palmer**	N	Y	N	N	Y	N
7	Sewell	Y	Y	Y	Y	N	Y
ALASKA							
AL	**Young**	N	Y	N	N	Y	N
ARIZONA							
1	O'Halleran	Y	Y	Y	Y	N	Y
2	Kirkpatrick	Y	Y	Y	Y	N	Y
3	Grijalva	Y	Y	Y	Y	N	Y
4	**Gosar**	N	Y	N	N	Y	N
5	**Biggs**	N	Y	N	N	Y	N
6	**Schweikert**	N	Y	N	N	Y	N
7	Gallego	Y	Y	Y	Y	N	Y
8	**Lesko**	N	Y	N	N	Y	N
9	Stanton	Y	Y	Y	Y	N	Y
ARKANSAS							
1	**Crawford**	-	+	?	?	?	+
2	**Hill, F.**	N	Y	N	N	Y	N
3	**Womack**	N	Y	N	N	Y	N
4	**Westerman**	N	Y	N	N	Y	N
CALIFORNIA							
1	**LaMalfa**	N	Y	N	N	Y	N
2	Huffman	Y	Y	Y	Y	N	Y
3	Garamendi	Y	Y	Y	?	N	Y
4	**McClintock**	N	Y	N	N	Y	N
5	Thompson, M.	Y	Y	Y	Y	N	Y
6	Matsui	Y	Y	Y	Y	N	Y
7	Bera	Y	Y	Y	Y	N	Y
8	**Cook**	N	Y	N	N	Y	N
9	McNerney	Y	Y	Y	Y	N	Y
10	Harder	Y	Y	Y	Y	N	Y
11	DeSaulnier	Y	Y	Y	Y	N	Y
12	Pelosi						
13	Lee B.	Y	Y	Y	Y	N	Y
14	Speier	Y	Y	Y	Y	N	Y
15	Swalwell	Y	Y	Y	Y	N	Y
16	Costa	Y	Y	Y	Y	N	Y
17	Khanna	Y	Y	Y	Y	N	Y
18	Eshoo	Y	Y	Y	Y	N	Y
19	Lofgren	Y	Y	Y	Y	N	Y
20	Panetta	Y	Y	Y	Y	N	Y
21	Cox	Y	Y	Y	Y	N	Y
22	**Nunes**	N	?	N	N	Y	N
23	**McCarthy**	N	Y	N	N	Y	N
24	Carbajal	Y	Y	Y	Y	N	Y
25	Hill, K.	Y	Y	Y	Y	N	Y
26	Brownley	Y	Y	Y	Y	N	Y
27	Chu	Y	Y	Y	Y	N	Y
28	Schiff	Y	Y	Y	Y	N	Y
29	Cárdenas	Y	Y	Y	Y	N	Y
30	Sherman	Y	Y	Y	Y	N	Y
31	Aguilar	Y	Y	Y	Y	N	Y
32	Napolitano	Y	Y	Y	Y	N	Y
33	Lieu	Y	Y	Y	Y	N	Y
34	Gomez	Y	Y	Y	Y	N	Y
35	Torres	Y	Y	Y	Y	N	Y
36	Ruiz	Y	Y	Y	Y	N	Y
37	Bass	Y	Y	Y	Y	N	Y
38	Sánchez	Y	Y	Y	Y	N	Y
39	Cisneros	Y	Y	Y	Y	N	Y
40	Roybal-Allard	Y	Y	Y	Y	N	Y
41	Takano	Y	Y	Y	Y	N	Y
42	**Calvert**	N	Y	N	N	Y	N
43	Waters	Y	Y	Y	Y	N	Y
44	Barragán	Y	Y	Y	Y	N	Y
45	Porter	Y	Y	Y	Y	N	Y
46	Correa	Y	Y	Y	Y	N	Y
47	Lowenthal	Y	Y	Y	Y	N	Y
48	Rouda	Y	Y	Y	Y	N	Y
49	Levin	Y	Y	Y	Y	N	Y
50	**Hunter**	N	Y	N	N	Y	N
51	Vargas	Y	Y	Y	Y	N	Y
52	Peters	Y	Y	Y	Y	N	Y

		547	548	549	550	551	552
53	Davis, S.	Y	Y	Y	Y	N	Y
COLORADO							
1	DeGette	Y	Y	Y	Y	N	Y
2	Neguse	Y	Y	Y	Y	N	Y
3	**Tipton**	N	Y	N	N	Y	N
4	**Buck**	N	Y	N	N	Y	N
5	**Lamborn**	N	Y	N	N	Y	N
6	Crow	Y	Y	Y	Y	N	Y
7	Perlmutter	Y	Y	Y	Y	N	Y
CONNECTICUT							
1	Larson	Y	Y	Y	Y	N	Y
2	Courtney	Y	Y	Y	Y	N	Y
3	DeLauro	Y	Y	Y	Y	N	Y
4	Himes	Y	Y	?	?	?	?
5	Hayes	Y	Y	Y	Y	N	Y
DELAWARE							
AL	Blunt Rochester	Y	Y	Y	Y	N	Y
FLORIDA							
1	**Gaetz**	N	Y	N	N	Y	N
2	**Dunn**	N	Y	N	N	Y	N
3	**Yoho**	N	Y	N	N	Y	N
4	**Rutherford**	N	Y	N	N	Y	N
5	Lawson	Y	Y	Y	Y	N	Y
6	**Waltz**	N	Y	N	N	Y	N
7	Murphy	Y	Y	Y	Y	N	Y
8	**Posey**	N	Y	N	N	Y	N
9	Soto	Y	Y	Y	Y	N	Y
10	Demings	Y	Y	Y	Y	N	Y
11	**Webster**	N	Y	N	N	Y	N
12	**Bilirakis**	N	Y	N	N	Y	N
13	Crist	Y	Y	Y	Y	N	Y
14	Castor	Y	Y	Y	Y	N	Y
15	**Spano**	N	Y	N	N	Y	N
16	**Buchanan**	N	Y	N	N	Y	N
17	**Steube**	N	Y	N	N	Y	N
18	**Mast**	N	Y	N	N	Y	N
19	**Rooney**	N	Y	?	?	?	?
20	Hastings	Y	Y	Y	Y	N	Y
21	Frankel	Y	Y	Y	Y	N	Y
22	Deutch	Y	Y	Y	Y	N	Y
23	Wasserman Schultz	Y	Y	Y	Y	N	Y
24	Wilson, F.	Y	Y	Y	Y	N	Y
25	**Diaz-Balart**	N	Y	N	N	Y	N
26	Mucarsel-Powell	Y	Y	Y	Y	N	Y
27	Shalala	Y	Y	Y	Y	N	Y
GEORGIA							
1	**Carter, E.L.**	N	Y	N	N	Y	N
2	Bishop, S.	Y	Y	Y	Y	N	Y
3	**Ferguson**	N	Y	N	N	Y	N
4	Johnson, H.	Y	Y	Y	Y	N	Y
5	Lewis John	Y	Y	Y	Y	N	Y
6	McBath	Y	Y	Y	Y	N	Y
7	**Woodall**	N	Y	N	N	Y	N
8	**Scott, A.**	N	Y	N	N	Y	N
9	**Collins, D.**	N	Y	N	N	Y	N
10	**Hice**	N	Y	N	N	Y	N
11	**Loudermilk**	N	Y	N	N	Y	N
12	**Allen**	N	Y	N	N	Y	N
13	Scott, D.	Y	Y	Y	Y	N	Y
14	**Graves, T.**	N	Y	N	N	Y	N
HAWAII							
1	Case	Y	Y	Y	Y	N	Y
2	Gabbard	Y	Y	Y	Y	N	Y
IDAHO							
1	**Fulcher**	N	Y	N	N	Y	N
2	**Simpson**	N	Y	N	N	Y	N
ILLINOIS							
1	Rush	Y	Y	Y	Y	N	Y
2	Kelly, R.	Y	Y	Y	Y	N	Y
3	Lipinski	Y	Y	Y	Y	N	Y
4	García, J.	Y	Y	Y	Y	N	Y
5	Quigley	Y	Y	Y	Y	N	Y
6	Casten	Y	Y	Y	Y	N	Y
7	Davis, D.	Y	Y	Y	Y	N	Y
8	Krishnamoorthi	Y	Y	Y	Y	N	Y
9	Schakowsky	Y	Y	Y	Y	N	Y
10	Schneider	Y	Y	Y	Y	N	Y
11	Foster	Y	Y	Y	Y	N	Y

KEY:		Republicans		Democrats		*Independents*	
Y	Voted for (yea)	**N**	Voted against (nay)	**P**	Voted "present"		
+	Announced for	**-**	Announced against	**?**	Did not vote or otherwise		
#	Paired for	**X**	Paired against		make position known		

	547	548	549	550	551	552
12 **Bost**	N	Y	N	N	Y	N
13 **Davis, R.**	N	Y	N	N	Y	N
14 Underwood	Y	Y	Y	Y	N	Y
15 **Shimkus**	N	Y	N	N	Y	N
16 **Kinzinger**	N	Y	N	N	Y	N
17 Bustos	Y	Y	Y	Y	N	Y
18 **LaHood**	N	Y	N	N	Y	N
INDIANA						
1 Visclosky	Y	Y	Y	Y	N	Y
2 **Walorski**	N	Y	N	N	Y	N
3 **Banks**	N	Y	N	N	Y	N
4 **Baird**	N	Y	N	N	Y	N
5 **Brooks, S.**	N	Y	N	N	Y	N
6 **Pence**	N	Y	N	N	Y	N
7 Carson	Y	Y	Y	Y	N	Y
8 **Bucshon**	N	Y	N	N	Y	N
9 **Hollingsworth**	N	Y	N	N	Y	N
IOWA						
1 Finkenauer	Y	Y	Y	Y	Y	Y
2 Loebsack	Y	Y	Y	Y	N	Y
3 Axne	Y	Y	Y	Y	Y	Y
4 **King, S.**	N	Y	N	N	Y	N
KANSAS						
1 **Marshall**	?	?	N	N	Y	N
2 **Watkins**	N	Y	N	N	Y	N
3 Davids	Y	Y	Y	Y	N	Y
4 **Estes**	N	Y	N	N	Y	N
KENTUCKY						
1 **Comer**	N	Y	N	N	Y	N
2 **Guthrie**	N	Y	N	N	Y	N
3 Yarmuth	Y	Y	Y	Y	N	Y
4 **Massie**	N	P	N	N	Y	N
5 **Rogers, H.**	N	Y	N	N	Y	N
6 **Barr**	N	Y	N	N	Y	N
LOUISIANA						
1 **Scalise**	N	Y	N	N	Y	N
2 Richmond	Y	Y	Y	Y	N	Y
3 **Higgins, C.**	-	+	-	-	+	-
4 **Johnson, M.**	N	Y	?	?	?	?
5 **Abraham**	?	?	?	?	?	?
6 **Graves, G.**	N	Y	N	N	Y	N
MAINE						
1 Pingree	Y	Y	Y	Y	N	Y
2 Golden	Y	Y	Y	Y	Y	Y
MARYLAND						
1 **Harris**	N	Y	N	N	Y	N
2 Ruppersberger	Y	Y	Y	Y	N	Y
3 Sarbanes	Y	Y	Y	Y	N	Y
4 Brown, A.	Y	Y	Y	Y	N	Y
5 Hoyer	Y	Y	Y	Y	N	Y
6 Trone	Y	Y	Y	Y	N	Y
7 Cummings	?	?	?	?	?	?
8 Raskin	Y	Y	Y	Y	N	Y
MASSACHUSETTS						
1 Neal	Y	Y	Y	Y	N	Y
2 McGovern	Y	Y	Y	Y	N	Y
3 Trahan	Y	Y	Y	Y	N	Y
4 Kennedy	Y	Y	Y	Y	N	Y
5 Clark	Y	Y	Y	Y	N	Y
6 Moulton	Y	Y	Y	Y	N	Y
7 Pressley	Y	Y	Y	Y	N	Y
8 Lynch	Y	Y	Y	Y	N	Y
9 Keating	Y	Y	Y	Y	N	Y
MICHIGAN						
1 **Bergman**	N	Y	N	N	Y	N
2 **Huizenga**	N	Y	N	N	Y	N
3 *Amash*	Y	Y	Y	Y	N	Y
4 **Moolenaar**	N	Y	N	N	Y	N
5 Kildee	Y	Y	Y	Y	N	Y
6 **Upton**	N	Y	N	N	Y	N
7 **Walberg**	N	Y	N	N	Y	N
8 Slotkin	Y	Y	Y	Y	N	Y
9 Levin	Y	Y	Y	Y	N	Y
10 **Mitchell**	N	Y	N	N	Y	N
11 Stevens	Y	Y	Y	Y	N	Y
12 Dingell	Y	Y	Y	Y	N	Y
13 Tlaib	Y	Y	Y	Y	N	Y
14 Lawrence	Y	Y	Y	Y	N	Y
MINNESOTA						
1 **Hagedorn**	N	Y	N	N	Y	N
2 Craig	Y	Y	Y	Y	N	Y
3 Phillips	Y	Y	Y	Y	N	Y
4 McCollum	Y	Y	Y	Y	N	Y
5 Omar	Y	Y	Y	Y	N	Y

	547	548	549	550	551	552
6 **Emmer**	N	Y	N	N	Y	N
7 Peterson	Y	Y	Y	Y	Y	N
8 **Stauber**	N	Y	N	N	Y	N
MISSISSIPPI						
1 **Kelly, T.**	N	Y	N	N	Y	N
2 Thompson, B.	Y	Y	Y	Y	N	Y
3 **Guest**	N	Y	N	N	Y	N
4 **Palazzo**	N	Y	N	N	Y	N
MISSOURI						
1 Clay	Y	Y	Y	Y	N	Y
2 **Wagner**	N	Y	N	N	Y	N
3 **Luetkemeyer**	N	Y	N	N	Y	N
4 **Hartzler**	N	Y	N	N	Y	N
5 Cleaver	Y	Y	Y	Y	N	Y
6 **Graves, S.**	N	Y	N	N	Y	N
7 **Long**	N	Y	N	N	Y	N
8 **Smith, J.**	N	Y	N	N	Y	N
MONTANA						
AL **Gianforte**	N	Y	N	N	Y	N
NEBRASKA						
1 **Fortenberry**	N	Y	N	N	Y	N
2 **Bacon**	N	Y	N	N	Y	N
3 **Smith, Adrian**	N	Y	N	N	Y	N
NEVADA						
1 Titus	Y	Y	Y	Y	N	Y
2 **Amodei**	N	Y	N	N	Y	N
3 Lee	Y	Y	Y	Y	N	Y
4 Horsford	Y	Y	Y	Y	N	Y
NEW HAMPSHIRE						
1 Pappas	Y	Y	Y	Y	N	Y
2 Kuster	Y	Y	Y	Y	N	Y
NEW JERSEY						
1 Norcross	Y	Y	Y	Y	N	Y
2 Van Drew	Y	Y	Y	Y	Y	N
3 Kim	Y	Y	Y	Y	Y	Y
4 **Smith, C.**	N	Y	N	N	Y	N
5 Gottheimer	Y	Y	Y	Y	Y	Y
6 Pallone	Y	Y	Y	Y	N	Y
7 Malinowski	Y	Y	Y	Y	N	Y
8 Sires	Y	Y	Y	Y	N	Y
9 Pascrell	Y	Y	Y	Y	N	Y
10 Payne	Y	Y	Y	Y	N	Y
11 Sherrill	Y	Y	Y	Y	Y	Y
12 Watson Coleman	Y	Y	Y	Y	N	Y
NEW MEXICO						
1 Haaland	Y	Y	Y	Y	N	Y
2 Torres Small	Y	Y	Y	Y	Y	Y
3 Luján	Y	Y	Y	Y	N	Y
NEW YORK						
1 **Zeldin**	N	Y	N	N	Y	N
2 **King, P.**	N	Y	N	N	Y	N
3 Suozzi	Y	Y	Y	Y	N	Y
4 Rice, K.	Y	Y	Y	Y	N	Y
5 Meeks	Y	Y	Y	Y	N	Y
6 Meng	Y	Y	Y	Y	N	Y
7 Velázquez	Y	Y	Y	Y	N	Y
8 Jeffries	Y	Y	Y	Y	N	Y
9 Clarke	Y	Y	Y	Y	N	Y
10 Nadler	Y	Y	Y	Y	N	Y
11 Rose	Y	Y	Y	Y	N	Y
12 Maloney, C.	Y	Y	Y	Y	N	Y
13 Espaillat	Y	Y	Y	Y	N	Y
14 Ocasio-Cortez	Y	Y	Y	Y	N	Y
15 Serrano	Y	Y	Y	Y	N	Y
16 Engel	Y	Y	Y	Y	N	Y
17 Lowey	Y	Y	Y	Y	N	Y
18 Maloney, S.P.	Y	Y	Y	Y	N	Y
19 Delgado	Y	Y	Y	Y	Y	Y
20 Tonko	Y	Y	Y	Y	N	Y
21 **Stefanik**	N	Y	N	N	Y	N
22 Brindisi	Y	Y	Y	Y	Y	Y
23 **Reed**	N	Y	N	N	Y	N
24 **Katko**	N	Y	N	N	Y	N
25 Morelle	Y	Y	Y	Y	N	Y
26 Higgins, B.	Y	Y	Y	Y	N	Y
27 **Collins, C.**	N	Y	N	N	Y	N
NORTH CAROLINA						
1 Butterfield	Y	Y	Y	Y	N	Y
2 **Holding**	N	Y	N	N	Y	N
3 **Murphy**	N	Y	N	N	Y	N
4 Price	Y	Y	Y	Y	N	Y
5 **Foxx**	N	Y	N	N	Y	N
6 **Walker**	N	Y	?	?	?	?
7 **Rouzer**	N	Y	N	N	Y	N

	547	548	549	550	551	552
8 **Hudson**	N	Y	N	N	Y	N
9 **Bishop**	N	Y	N	N	Y	N
10 **McHenry**	N	Y	-	-	+	-
11 **Meadows**	N	Y	N	N	Y	Y
12 Adams	Y	Y	Y	Y	N	Y
13 **Budd**	N	Y	N	N	Y	N
NORTH DAKOTA						
AL **Armstrong**	N	Y	N	N	Y	N
OHIO						
1 **Chabot**	N	Y	N	N	Y	N
2 **Wenstrup**	N	Y	N	N	Y	N
3 Beatty	Y	Y	Y	Y	N	Y
4 **Jordan**	N	Y	N	N	Y	N
5 **Latta**	N	Y	N	N	Y	N
6 **Johnson, B.**	N	Y	N	N	Y	N
7 **Gibbs**	N	Y	N	N	Y	N
8 **Davidson**	N	Y	N	N	Y	N
9 Kaptur	Y	Y	Y	Y	N	Y
10 **Turner**	N	Y	N	N	Y	N
11 Fudge	Y	Y	Y	Y	N	Y
12 **Balderson**	N	Y	N	N	Y	N
13 Ryan	Y	Y	Y	Y	N	Y
14 **Joyce**	N	+	N	N	Y	N
15 **Stivers**	N	Y	N	N	Y	N
16 **Gonzalez**	N	Y	N	N	Y	N
OKLAHOMA						
1 **Hern**	N	Y	N	N	Y	N
2 **Mullin**	N	Y	N	N	Y	N
3 **Lucas**	N	Y	N	N	Y	N
4 **Cole**	N	Y	N	N	Y	N
5 Horn	Y	Y	Y	Y	Y	Y
OREGON						
1 Bonamici	Y	Y	Y	Y	N	Y
2 **Walden**	N	Y	N	N	Y	N
3 Blumenauer	Y	Y	Y	Y	N	Y
4 DeFazio	Y	Y	Y	Y	N	Y
5 Schrader	Y	Y	Y	Y	Y	Y
PENNSYLVANIA						
1 **Fitzpatrick**	N	Y	N	N	Y	Y
2 Boyle	Y	Y	Y	Y	?	Y
3 Evans	Y	Y	Y	Y	N	Y
4 Dean	Y	Y	Y	Y	N	Y
5 Scanlon	Y	Y	Y	Y	N	Y
6 Houlahan	Y	Y	Y	Y	N	Y
7 Wild	Y	Y	Y	Y	N	Y
8 Cartwright	Y	Y	Y	Y	N	Y
9 **Meuser**	N	Y	N	N	Y	N
10 **Perry**	N	Y	N	N	Y	N
11 **Smucker**	N	Y	N	N	Y	N
12 **Keller**	N	Y	N	N	Y	N
13 **Joyce**	N	Y	N	N	Y	N
14 **Reschenthaler**	N	Y	N	N	Y	N
15 **Thompson, G.**	N	Y	N	N	Y	N
16 **Kelly, M.**	N	Y	N	N	Y	N
17 Lamb	Y	Y	Y	Y	N	Y
18 Doyle	Y	Y	Y	Y	N	Y
RHODE ISLAND						
1 Cicilline	Y	Y	Y	Y	N	Y
2 Langevin	Y	Y	Y	Y	N	Y
SOUTH CAROLINA						
1 Cunningham	Y	Y	Y	Y	Y	Y
2 **Wilson, J.**	N	Y	N	N	Y	N
3 **Duncan**	N	Y	N	N	Y	N
4 **Timmons**	N	Y	N	N	Y	N
5 **Norman**	N	Y	-	-	+	-
6 Clyburn	+	+	Y	Y	N	Y
7 **Rice, T.**	N	Y	N	N	Y	N
SOUTH DAKOTA						
AL **Johnson**	N	Y	N	N	Y	N
TENNESSEE						
1 **Roe**	N	Y	N	N	Y	N
2 **Burchett**	N	Y	N	N	Y	N
3 **Fleischmann**	N	Y	N	N	Y	N
4 **DesJarlais**	N	Y	N	N	Y	N
5 Cooper	Y	Y	Y	Y	N	Y
6 **Rose**	N	Y	N	N	Y	N
7 **Green**	N	Y	N	N	Y	N
8 **Kustoff**	N	Y	N	N	Y	N
9 Cohen	Y	Y	Y	Y	N	Y
TEXAS						
1 **Gohmert**	N	P	N	N	Y	N
2 **Crenshaw**	N	Y	N	N	Y	N
3 **Taylor**	N	Y	N	N	Y	N
4 **Ratcliffe**	N	Y	?	?	?	?

	547	548	549	550	551	552
5 **Gooden**	N	Y	N	N	Y	N
6 **Wright**	?	?	N	N	Y	N
7 Fletcher	Y	Y	Y	Y	N	Y
8 **Brady**	N	Y	N	N	Y	?
9 Green, A.	Y	Y	Y	Y	N	Y
10 **McCaul**	N	Y	N	N	Y	N
11 **Conaway**	N	Y	N	N	Y	N
12 **Granger**	N	Y	N	N	Y	N
13 **Thornberry**	N	Y	N	N	Y	N
14 **Weber**	N	Y	N	N	Y	N
15 Gonzalez	Y	Y	Y	Y	N	Y
16 Escobar	Y	Y	+	+	-	+
17 **Flores**	N	Y	N	N	Y	N
18 Jackson Lee	Y	Y	Y	Y	N	Y
19 **Arrington**	N	Y	N	N	Y	N
20 Castro	Y	Y	Y	Y	N	Y
21 **Roy**	N	Y	N	N	Y	N
22 **Olson**	N	Y	N	N	Y	N
23 **Hurd**	N	Y	-	-	+	-
24 **Marchant**	N	Y	N	N	Y	N
25 **Williams**	N	Y	N	N	Y	N
26 **Burgess**	N	Y	N	N	Y	N
27 **Cloud**	N	Y	N	N	Y	N
28 Cuellar	Y	Y	Y	Y	N	Y
29 Garcia, S.	Y	Y	Y	Y	N	Y
30 Johnson, E.B.	Y	Y	Y	Y	N	Y
31 **Carter, J.**	N	Y	N	N	Y	N
32 Allred	Y	Y	Y	Y	N	Y
33 Veasey	Y	Y	Y	Y	N	Y
34 Vela	Y	Y	Y	Y	N	Y
35 Doggett	Y	Y	Y	Y	N	Y
36 **Babin**	N	Y	N	-	Y	N
UTAH						
1 **Bishop, R.**	N	Y	N	N	Y	N
2 **Stewart**	N	Y	N	N	Y	N
3 **Curtis**	N	Y	N	N	Y	N
4 McAdams	Y	Y	Y	Y	Y	Y
VERMONT						
AL Welch	Y	Y	Y	Y	N	Y
VIRGINIA						
1 **Wittman**	N	Y	N	N	Y	N
2 Luria	Y	Y	Y	Y	N	Y
3 Scott, R.	Y	Y	Y	Y	N	Y
4 McEachin	+	+	+	+	-	+
5 **Riggleman**	N	Y	N	N	Y	N
6 **Cline**	N	Y	N	N	Y	N
7 Spanberger	Y	Y	Y	Y	Y	Y
8 Beyer	Y	Y	Y	Y	N	Y
9 **Griffith**	N	Y	N	N	Y	N
10 Wexton	Y	Y	Y	Y	N	Y
11 Connolly	Y	Y	Y	Y	N	Y
WASHINGTON						
1 DelBene	Y	Y	Y	Y	N	Y
2 Larsen	Y	Y	Y	Y	N	Y
3 **Herrera Beutler**	N	Y	N	N	Y	N
4 **Newhouse**	N	Y	N	N	Y	N
5 **McMorris Rodgers**	N	Y	N	N	Y	N
6 Kilmer	Y	Y	Y	Y	N	Y
7 Jayapal	Y	Y	Y	Y	N	Y
8 Schrier	Y	Y	Y	Y	N	Y
9 Smith Adam	Y	Y	Y	Y	N	Y
10 Heck	Y	Y	Y	Y	N	Y
WEST VIRGINIA						
1 **McKinley**	N	Y	N	N	Y	N
2 **Mooney**	N	Y	N	N	Y	N
3 **Miller**	N	Y	N	N	Y	N
WISCONSIN						
1 **Steil**	N	Y	N	N	Y	N
2 Pocan	Y	Y	Y	Y	N	Y
3 Kind	Y	Y	?	?	?	+
4 Moore	Y	Y	Y	Y	N	Y
5 **Sensenbrenner**	N	Y	N	N	Y	N
6 **Grothman**	N	Y	N	N	Y	N
7 **Duffy**						
8 **Gallagher**	N	Y	N	N	+	-
WYOMING						
AL **Cheney**	N	Y	?	?	?	?
DELEGATES						
Radewagen (A.S.)						
Norton (D.C.)						
San Nicolas (Guam)						
Sablan (N. Marianas)						
González-Colón (P.R.)						
Plaskett (V.I.)						

553. SJ Res 54. National Emergency Termination - Passage. Passage of the joint resolution that would terminate the national emergency declared by the President Donald Trump on Feb. 15, 2019, related to the construction of a physical barrier along the U.S.-Mexico border. Passed (thus cleared for the president) 236-174: R 11-174; D 224-0; I 1-0. *Note: A "nay" was a vote in support of the president's position.* Sept. 27, 2019.

554. HR3722. Opioid Trafficking Task Force - Passage. Correa, D-Calif., motion to suspend the rules and pass the bill that would authorize the Homeland Security Department to establish a joint task force to enhance border security operations to prevent narcotics such as fentanyl and other synthetic opioids from entering the U.S. Additionally, the bill would expand the authority of DHS joint task forces to collaborate with other federal agencies and private sector organizations. Motion agreed to 403-1: R 184-0; D 219-0; I 0-1. *Note: A two-thirds majority of those present and voting (270 in this case) is required for passage under suspension of the rules.* Sept. 27, 2019.

555. HRES603. Impeachment Inquiry Disapproval - Motion to Table. Hoyer, D-Md., motion to table (kill) a privileged resolution that would express disapproval of actions of Speaker Nancy Pelosi, D-Calif., on Sept. 24, 2019, to initiate an impeachment inquiry against President Donald Trump. Motion agreed to 222-184: R 0-184; D 221-0; I 1-0. Sept. 27, 2019.

556. HR2385. Veterans' Cemeteries Education Programs - Passage. Takano, D-Calif., motion to suspend the rules and pass the bill that would authorize the Veterans Affairs Department to establish a grant program under the National Cemetery Administration Veterans Legacy Program, which supports education programs related to veterans' cemeteries. Specifically, it would authorize grants of up to $500,000 to educational institutions, local education agencies, and nonprofits to fund research, production of education materials, and community engagement related to veterans' cemeteries and the history of veterans interred in veterans' cemeteries. Motion agreed to 409-1: R 192-0; D 217-0; I 0-1. *Note: A two-thirds majority of those present and voting (274 in this case) is required for passage under suspension of the rules.* Oct. 15, 2019.

557. HR95. Homeless Veterans Dependent Housing - Passage. Takano, D-Calif., motion to suspend the rules and pass the bill that would authorize the Veterans Affairs Department to reimburse 50 percent of the costs of housing services provided for minor dependents of homeless veterans under the Homeless Providers Grant and Per Diem program. The VA program provides funding to community housing agencies that serve homeless veterans. Motion agreed to 408-0: R 192-0; D 215-0; I 1-0. *Note: A two-thirds majority of those present and voting (272 in this case) is required for passage under suspension of the rules.* Oct. 15, 2019.

558. HR1815, HR3624. SEC Disclosure Rules; SEC Outsourcing Disclosures - Previous Question. DeSaulnier, D-Calif., motion to order the previous question (thus ending debate and possibility of amendment) on the rule (H Res 629) that would provide for House floor consideration of the SEC Disclosure Effectiveness Testing Act (HR 1815) and the Outsourcing Accountability Act (HR 3624). The rule would provide for automatic adoption of a manager's amendment to HR 1815 that would make technical corrections to the bill; provide for floor consideration of four additional amendments to HR 1815; and provide for floor consideration of two amendments to HR 3624. Motion agreed to 228-191: R 1-190; D 227-0; I 0-1. Oct. 16, 2019.

		553	554	555	556	557	558
ALABAMA							
1	**Byrne**	N	Y	N	Y	Y	N
2	**Roby**	N	Y	N	?	?	?
3	**Rogers, M.**	N	Y	N	Y	Y	N
4	**Aderholt**	N	Y	N	Y	Y	N
5	**Brooks, M.**	N	Y	N	Y	Y	N
6	**Palmer**	N	Y	N	Y	Y	N
7	Sewell	Y	Y	Y	Y	Y	Y
ALASKA							
AL	**Young**	N	Y	N	Y	Y	N
ARIZONA							
1	O'Halleran	Y	Y	Y	Y	Y	Y
2	Kirkpatrick	Y	Y	Y	Y	Y	Y
3	Grijalva	Y	Y	Y	?	?	Y
4	**Gosar**	N	Y	N	Y	Y	N
5	**Biggs**	N	Y	N	Y	Y	N
6	**Schweikert**	N	Y	N	Y	Y	N
7	Gallego	Y	Y	Y	+	+	Y
8	**Lesko**	N	Y	N	Y	Y	N
9	Stanton	Y	Y	Y	Y	Y	Y
ARKANSAS							
1	**Crawford**	-	?	-	Y	Y	N
2	**Hill, F.**	N	Y	N	Y	Y	N
3	**Womack**	N	Y	N	Y	Y	N
4	**Westerman**	N	Y	N	Y	Y	N
CALIFORNIA							
1	**LaMalfa**	N	Y	N	Y	Y	N
2	Huffman	Y	Y	+	Y	Y	Y
3	Garamendi	Y	Y	Y	Y	Y	Y
4	**McClintock**	N	Y	N	Y	Y	N
5	Thompson, M.	Y	Y	Y	Y	Y	Y
6	Matsui	Y	Y	Y	Y	Y	Y
7	Bera	Y	Y	Y	Y	Y	Y
8	**Cook**	N	Y	N	Y	Y	N
9	McNerney	Y	Y	Y	Y	Y	Y
10	Harder	Y	Y	Y	Y	Y	Y
11	DeSaulnier	Y	Y	Y	Y	Y	Y
12	Pelosi						
13	Lee B.	Y	Y	Y	Y	Y	Y
14	Speier	Y	Y	Y	Y	Y	Y
15	Swalwell	Y	Y	Y	Y	Y	Y
16	Costa	Y	Y	Y	Y	Y	Y
17	Khanna	Y	Y	Y	Y	Y	Y
18	Eshoo	Y	Y	Y	Y	Y	Y
19	Lofgren	Y	?	?	Y	Y	Y
20	Panetta	Y	Y	Y	Y	Y	Y
21	Cox	Y	Y	Y	Y	Y	Y
22	**Nunes**	N	Y	N	Y	Y	N
23	**McCarthy**	N	Y	N	Y	Y	N
24	Carbajal	Y	Y	Y	Y	Y	Y
25	Hill, K.	?	?	?	Y	Y	Y
26	Brownley	Y	Y	Y	Y	Y	Y
27	Chu	Y	Y	Y	Y	Y	Y
28	Schiff	Y	Y	Y	Y	+	Y
29	Cárdenas	Y	Y	Y	Y	Y	?
30	Sherman	Y	Y	Y	Y	Y	Y
31	Aguilar	Y	Y	Y	Y	Y	Y
32	Napolitano	Y	Y	Y	Y	Y	Y
33	Lieu	Y	Y	Y	Y	Y	Y
34	Gomez	Y	Y	Y	Y	Y	Y
35	Torres	Y	Y	Y	Y	Y	Y
36	Ruiz	Y	Y	Y	Y	Y	Y
37	Bass	Y	Y	Y	Y	Y	Y
38	Sánchez	Y	Y	Y	Y	Y	Y
39	Cisneros	Y	Y	Y	Y	Y	Y
40	Roybal-Allard	Y	Y	Y	+	+	Y
41	Takano	Y	Y	Y	Y	Y	Y
42	**Calvert**	N	Y	N	Y	Y	N
43	Waters	Y	Y	Y	Y	Y	Y
44	Barragán	Y	Y	Y	Y	Y	Y
45	Porter	Y	Y	Y	Y	Y	Y
46	Correa	Y	Y	Y	Y	Y	Y
47	Lowenthal	Y	Y	Y	Y	Y	Y
48	Rouda	Y	Y	Y	Y	Y	Y
49	Levin	Y	Y	Y	Y	Y	Y
50	**Hunter**	N	Y	N	Y	Y	N
51	Vargas	Y	Y	Y	Y	Y	Y
52	Peters	Y	Y	Y	Y	Y	Y

		553	554	555	556	557	558
53	Davis, S.	Y	Y	Y	Y	Y	Y
COLORADO							
1	DeGette	Y	Y	Y	Y	Y	Y
2	Neguse	Y	Y	Y	Y	Y	Y
3	**Tipton**	N	Y	N	Y	Y	N
4	**Buck**	N	Y	N	Y	Y	N
5	**Lamborn**	N	Y	N	Y	Y	N
6	Crow	Y	Y	Y	Y	Y	Y
7	Perlmutter	Y	Y	Y	Y	Y	Y
CONNECTICUT							
1	Larson	Y	Y	Y	Y	Y	Y
2	Courtney	Y	Y	Y	Y	Y	Y
3	DeLauro	Y	Y	Y	Y	Y	Y
4	Himes	Y	Y	Y	Y	Y	Y
5	Hayes	Y	Y	Y	Y	Y	Y
DELAWARE							
AL	Blunt Rochester	Y	Y	Y	Y	Y	Y
FLORIDA							
1	**Gaetz**	N	Y	N	Y	Y	N
2	**Dunn**	N	Y	N	Y	Y	N
3	**Yoho**	N	Y	N	Y	Y	?
4	**Rutherford**	N	Y	N	Y	Y	N
5	Lawson	Y	Y	Y	?	?	?
6	**Waltz**	N	Y	N	Y	Y	N
7	Murphy	Y	Y	Y	Y	Y	Y
8	**Posey**	N	Y	N	Y	Y	N
9	Soto	Y	Y	Y	Y	Y	Y
10	Demings	Y	Y	Y	Y	Y	Y
11	**Webster**	N	Y	N	Y	Y	N
12	**Bilirakis**	N	Y	N	Y	Y	N
13	Crist	Y	Y	Y	Y	Y	Y
14	Castor	Y	Y	Y	Y	Y	Y
15	**Spano**	N	Y	N	Y	Y	N
16	**Buchanan**	N	Y	N	Y	Y	N
17	**Steube**	N	Y	N	Y	Y	N
18	**Mast**	N	Y	N	Y	Y	N
19	**Rooney**	Y	Y	N	?	?	?
20	Hastings	Y	Y	Y	Y	Y	Y
21	Frankel	Y	Y	Y	Y	Y	Y
22	Deutch	Y	Y	Y	Y	Y	Y
23	Wasserman Schultz	Y	Y	Y	Y	Y	Y
24	Wilson, F.	Y	Y	Y	Y	Y	Y
25	**Diaz-Balart**	N	Y	N	Y	Y	N
26	Mucarsel-Powell	Y	Y	Y	Y	Y	Y
27	Shalala	Y	Y	Y	Y	Y	Y
GEORGIA							
1	**Carter, E.L.**	N	Y	N	Y	Y	N
2	Bishop, S.	Y	Y	Y	Y	Y	Y
3	**Ferguson**	N	Y	N	Y	Y	N
4	Johnson, H.	Y	Y	Y	Y	Y	Y
5	Lewis John	Y	Y	Y	Y	Y	Y
6	McBath	Y	Y	Y	Y	Y	Y
7	**Woodall**	N	Y	N	Y	Y	N
8	**Scott, A.**	N	Y	N	Y	Y	N
9	**Collins, D.**	N	Y	N	Y	Y	N
10	**Hice**	N	Y	N	Y	Y	N
11	**Loudermilk**	N	Y	N	Y	Y	N
12	**Allen**	N	Y	N	Y	Y	N
13	Scott, D.	Y	Y	Y	Y	Y	Y
14	**Graves, T.**	N	Y	N	Y	Y	N
HAWAII							
1	Case	Y	Y	Y	Y	Y	Y
2	Gabbard	?	?	?	?	?	?
IDAHO							
1	**Fulcher**	N	Y	N	Y	Y	N
2	**Simpson**	N	Y	N	Y	Y	N
ILLINOIS							
1	Rush	Y	Y	Y	Y	Y	Y
2	Kelly, R.	Y	Y	Y	Y	Y	Y
3	Lipinski	Y	Y	Y	Y	Y	Y
4	García, J.	Y	Y	Y	Y	Y	Y
5	Quigley	Y	Y	Y	Y	Y	Y
6	Casten	Y	Y	Y	Y	Y	Y
7	Davis, D.	Y	Y	Y	Y	Y	Y
8	Krishnamoorthi	Y	Y	Y	?	Y	Y
9	Schakowsky	Y	Y	Y	Y	Y	Y
10	Schneider	Y	Y	Y	Y	Y	Y
11	Foster	Y	Y	Y	Y	Y	Y

***NOTE:**
(New York 27) Rep. Chris Collins resigned September 30. The last roll call vote he was eligible to cast was vote 555.

		553	554	555	556	557	558
12	**Bost**	N	Y	N	Y	Y	N
13	**Davis, R.**	N	Y	N	Y	Y	N
14	Underwood	Y	Y	Y	Y	Y	Y
15	**Shimkus**	N	Y	N	Y	Y	N
16	**Kinzinger**	N	Y	N	Y	Y	N
17	Bustos	Y	Y	Y	Y	Y	Y
18	**LaHood**	N	Y	N	Y	Y	N
INDIANA							
1	Visclosky	Y	Y	Y	Y	Y	Y
2	**Walorski**	N	Y	N	Y	Y	N
3	**Banks**	N	Y	N	Y	Y	N
4	**Baird**	N	Y	N	Y	Y	N
5	**Brooks, S.**	N	Y	N	Y	Y	N
6	**Pence**	N	Y	N	Y	Y	N
7	Carson	Y	Y	Y	Y	Y	Y
8	**Bucshon**	N	Y	N	Y	Y	N
9	**Hollingsworth**	N	Y	N	Y	Y	N
IOWA							
1	Finkenauer	Y	Y	Y	Y	Y	Y
2	Loebsack	Y	Y	Y	Y	Y	Y
3	Axne	Y	Y	Y	Y	Y	Y
4	**King, S.**	N	Y	N	Y	Y	N
KANSAS							
1	**Marshall**	N	Y	N	Y	Y	?
2	**Watkins**	N	Y	N	Y	Y	N
3	Davids	Y	Y	Y	Y	Y	Y
4	**Estes**	N	Y	N	Y	Y	N
KENTUCKY							
1	**Comer**	N	Y	N	Y	Y	N
2	**Guthrie**	N	Y	N	Y	Y	N
3	Yarmuth	Y	Y	Y	Y	Y	Y
4	**Massie**	Y	Y	N	Y	Y	N
5	**Rogers, H.**	N	Y	N	Y	Y	N
6	**Barr**	N	Y	N	Y	Y	N
LOUISIANA							
1	**Scalise**	N	Y	N	Y	Y	N
2	Richmond	Y	Y	Y	Y	Y	Y
3	**Higgins, C.**	-	+	-	+	+	N
4	**Johnson, M.**	?	?	-	Y	Y	N
5	**Abraham**	?	?	?	Y	Y	N
6	**Graves, G.**	N	Y	N	Y	Y	N
MAINE							
1	Pingree	Y	Y	Y	?	?	Y
2	Golden	Y	Y	Y	Y	Y	Y
MARYLAND							
1	**Harris**	N	Y	N	Y	Y	N
2	Ruppersberger	Y	Y	Y	Y	Y	Y
3	Sarbanes	Y	Y	Y	Y	Y	Y
4	Brown, A.	Y	Y	Y	Y	Y	Y
5	Hoyer	Y	Y	Y	Y	Y	Y
6	Trone	Y	Y	Y	Y	Y	Y
7	Cummings	?	?	?	?	?	?
8	Raskin	Y	Y	Y	Y	Y	Y
MASSACHUSETTS							
1	Neal	Y	Y	Y	Y	Y	Y
2	McGovern	Y	Y	Y	Y	Y	Y
3	Trahan	Y	Y	Y	+	+	Y
4	Kennedy	Y	Y	Y	Y	Y	Y
5	Clark	Y	Y	Y	Y	Y	Y
6	Moulton	Y	Y	Y	Y	Y	Y
7	Pressley	Y	Y	Y	Y	Y	Y
8	Lynch	Y	Y	Y	Y	Y	Y
9	Keating	Y	Y	Y	Y	Y	Y
MICHIGAN							
1	**Bergman**	N	Y	N	Y	Y	N
2	**Huizenga**	N	Y	N	Y	Y	N
3	*Amash*	Y	N	Y	N	Y	N
4	**Moolenaar**	N	Y	N	Y	Y	N
5	Kildee	Y	Y	Y	Y	Y	Y
6	**Upton**	Y	Y	N	Y	Y	N
7	**Walberg**	N	Y	N	Y	Y	N
8	Slotkin	Y	Y	Y	Y	Y	Y
9	Levin	Y	Y	Y	Y	Y	Y
10	**Mitchell**	N	Y	N	Y	Y	N
11	Stevens	Y	Y	Y	Y	Y	Y
12	Dingell	Y	Y	Y	Y	Y	Y
13	Tlaib	Y	Y	Y	Y	Y	Y
14	Lawrence	+	+	+	Y	Y	Y
MINNESOTA							
1	**Hagedorn**	N	Y	N	Y	Y	N
2	Craig	Y	Y	Y	Y	Y	Y
3	Phillips	Y	Y	Y	Y	Y	Y
4	McCollum	Y	Y	Y	Y	Y	Y
5	Omar	Y	Y	Y	+	Y	+

		553	554	555	556	557	558
6	**Emmer**	N	Y	N	Y	Y	N
7	Peterson	Y	Y	Y	Y	Y	Y
8	**Stauber**	N	Y	N	Y	Y	N
MISSISSIPPI							
1	**Kelly, T.**	N	+	N	Y	Y	N
2	Thompson, B.	Y	Y	Y	?	?	Y
3	**Guest**	N	Y	N	Y	Y	N
4	**Palazzo**	N	Y	N	Y	Y	N
MISSOURI							
1	Clay	Y	Y	Y	Y	Y	Y
2	**Wagner**	N	Y	N	Y	Y	N
3	**Luetkemeyer**	N	Y	N	Y	Y	N
4	**Hartzler**	N	Y	N	Y	Y	N
5	Cleaver	Y	Y	Y	Y	Y	Y
6	**Graves, S.**	N	Y	N	Y	Y	N
7	**Long**	N	Y	N	Y	Y	N
8	**Smith, J.**	N	Y	N	Y	Y	N
MONTANA							
AL	**Gianforte**	N	Y	N	Y	Y	N
NEBRASKA							
1	**Fortenberry**	N	Y	N	Y	Y	N
2	**Bacon**	N	Y	N	Y	Y	N
3	**Smith, Adrian**	N	Y	N	Y	Y	N
NEVADA							
1	Titus	Y	Y	Y	Y	Y	Y
2	**Amodei**	N	Y	N	Y	Y	N
3	Lee	Y	Y	Y	Y	Y	Y
4	Horsford	Y	Y	Y	Y	Y	Y
NEW HAMPSHIRE							
1	Pappas	Y	Y	Y	Y	Y	Y
2	Kuster	+	+	+	Y	Y	Y
NEW JERSEY							
1	Norcross	Y	Y	Y	Y	Y	Y
2	Van Drew	Y	Y	Y	Y	Y	Y
3	Kim	Y	Y	Y	Y	Y	Y
4	**Smith, C.**	N	Y	N	Y	Y	N
5	Gottheimer	Y	Y	Y	Y	Y	Y
6	Pallone	Y	Y	Y	Y	Y	Y
7	Malinowski	Y	Y	Y	Y	Y	Y
8	Sires	Y	Y	Y	Y	Y	Y
9	Pascrell	Y	Y	Y	Y	+	Y
10	Payne	Y	Y	Y	Y	Y	Y
11	Sherrill	Y	Y	Y	Y	Y	Y
12	Watson Coleman	Y	Y	Y	Y	Y	Y
NEW MEXICO							
1	Haaland	Y	Y	Y	+	+	Y
2	Torres Small	Y	Y	Y	Y	Y	Y
3	Luján	Y	Y	Y	Y	Y	Y
NEW YORK							
1	**Zeldin**	N	Y	N	Y	Y	N
2	**King, P.**	N	Y	N	Y	Y	N
3	Suozzi	Y	Y	Y	Y	Y	Y
4	Rice, K.	Y	Y	Y	Y	Y	Y
5	Meeks	Y	Y	Y	?	?	Y
6	Meng	Y	Y	Y	Y	Y	Y
7	Velázquez	Y	Y	Y	Y	Y	Y
8	Jeffries	Y	Y	Y	Y	Y	Y
9	Clarke	Y	Y	Y	Y	Y	Y
10	Nadler	Y	Y	Y	Y	Y	Y
11	Rose	Y	Y	Y	Y	Y	Y
12	Maloney, C.	Y	Y	Y	Y	Y	Y
13	Espaillat	Y	Y	Y	Y	Y	Y
14	Ocasio-Cortez	Y	Y	Y	Y	Y	Y
15	Serrano	Y	Y	Y	Y	Y	Y
16	Engel	Y	Y	Y	Y	Y	Y
17	Lowey	Y	Y	Y	Y	Y	Y
18	Maloney, S.P.	Y	?	Y	Y	Y	Y
19	Delgado	Y	Y	Y	Y	Y	Y
20	Tonko	Y	Y	Y	Y	Y	Y
21	**Stefanik**	Y	Y	N	Y	Y	N
22	Brindisi	Y	Y	Y	Y	Y	Y
23	**Reed**	N	Y	N	Y	Y	N
24	**Katko**	Y	Y	N	Y	Y	N
25	Morelle	Y	Y	Y	Y	Y	Y
26	Higgins, B.	Y	Y	Y	Y	Y	Y
27	**Collins, C.***	N	Y	N			
NORTH CAROLINA							
1	Butterfield	Y	Y	Y	Y	Y	Y
2	**Holding**	N	Y	N	Y	Y	N
3	**Murphy**	N	Y	N	Y	Y	N
4	Price	Y	Y	Y	Y	Y	Y
5	**Foxx**	N	Y	N	Y	Y	N
6	**Walker**	N	Y	N	Y	Y	N
7	**Rouzer**	N	Y	N	Y	Y	N

		553	554	555	556	557	558
8	**Hudson**	N	Y	N	Y	Y	Y
9	**Bishop**	N	Y	N	+	+	-
10	**McHenry**	-	+	-	Y	Y	N
11	**Meadows**	N	Y	N	Y	Y	N
12	Adams	Y	Y	Y	Y	Y	Y
13	**Budd**	N	Y	N	Y	Y	-
NORTH DAKOTA							
AL	**Armstrong**	N	Y	N	Y	Y	N
OHIO							
1	**Chabot**	N	Y	N	Y	Y	N
2	**Wenstrup**	N	Y	N	Y	Y	N
3	Beatty	+	+	+	+	+	Y
4	**Jordan**	N	Y	N	Y	Y	N
5	**Latta**	N	Y	N	Y	Y	N
6	**Johnson, B.**	N	Y	N	Y	Y	N
7	**Gibbs**	N	Y	N	Y	Y	N
8	**Davidson**	N	Y	N	Y	Y	N
9	Kaptur	Y	Y	Y	Y	Y	Y
10	**Turner**	?	?	?	Y	Y	N
11	Fudge	Y	Y	Y	Y	Y	Y
12	**Balderson**	N	Y	?	Y	Y	N
13	Ryan	Y	Y	Y	?	?	?
14	**Joyce**	N	Y	N	Y	Y	N
15	**Stivers**	N	Y	N	Y	Y	N
16	**Gonzalez**	N	Y	N	Y	Y	N
OKLAHOMA							
1	**Hern**	N	Y	N	Y	Y	N
2	**Mullin**	N	Y	N	Y	Y	N
3	**Lucas**	N	Y	N	Y	Y	N
4	**Cole**	N	Y	N	Y	Y	N
5	Horn	Y	Y	Y	Y	Y	Y
OREGON							
1	Bonamici	Y	Y	Y	Y	Y	Y
2	**Walden**	Y	Y	N	Y	Y	N
3	Blumenauer	Y	Y	Y	Y	Y	Y
4	DeFazio	Y	Y	Y	Y	Y	Y
5	Schrader	Y	Y	Y	Y	Y	Y
PENNSYLVANIA							
1	**Fitzpatrick**	Y	Y	N	Y	Y	N
2	Boyle	Y	Y	Y	Y	Y	Y
3	Evans	Y	Y	Y	Y	Y	Y
4	Dean	Y	Y	Y	Y	Y	Y
5	Scanlon	Y	?	Y	Y	Y	Y
6	Houlahan	Y	Y	Y	Y	Y	Y
7	Wild	Y	Y	Y	Y	Y	Y
8	Cartwright	Y	Y	Y	Y	Y	Y
9	**Meuser**	N	Y	N	Y	Y	N
10	**Perry**	N	Y	N	Y	Y	N
11	**Smucker**	N	Y	N	Y	Y	N
12	**Keller**	N	Y	N	Y	Y	N
13	**Joyce**	N	Y	N	Y	Y	N
14	**Reschenthaler**	N	Y	N	Y	Y	N
15	**Thompson, G.**	N	Y	N	Y	Y	N
16	**Kelly, M.**	N	Y	N	Y	Y	N
17	Lamb	Y	Y	Y	Y	Y	Y
18	Doyle	Y	Y	Y	Y	Y	Y
RHODE ISLAND							
1	Cicilline	Y	Y	Y	Y	Y	Y
2	Langevin	Y	Y	Y	Y	Y	Y
SOUTH CAROLINA							
1	Cunningham	Y	Y	Y	Y	Y	Y
2	**Wilson, J.**	N	Y	N	Y	Y	N
3	**Duncan**	N	Y	N	Y	Y	N
4	**Timmons**	N	Y	N	Y	Y	N
5	**Norman**	-	+	-	Y	Y	N
6	Clyburn	+	+	+	Y	Y	Y
7	**Rice, T.**	N	Y	N	Y	Y	N
SOUTH DAKOTA							
AL	**Johnson**	Y	Y	N	Y	Y	N
TENNESSEE							
1	**Roe**	N	Y	N	Y	Y	N
2	**Burchett**	N	Y	N	Y	Y	N
3	**Fleischmann**	N	Y	N	Y	Y	N
4	**DesJarlais**	N	?	?	Y	Y	N
5	Cooper	Y	Y	Y	Y	Y	Y
6	**Rose**	N	Y	N	Y	Y	N
7	**Green**	N	Y	N	Y	Y	N
8	**Kustoff**	N	Y	N	Y	Y	N
9	Cohen	Y	Y	Y	Y	Y	Y
TEXAS							
1	**Gohmert**	N	Y	N	Y	Y	N
2	**Crenshaw**	N	Y	N	Y	Y	N
3	**Taylor**	N	Y	N	Y	Y	N
4	**Ratcliffe**	?	?	?	Y	Y	N

		553	554	555	556	557	558
5	**Gooden**	N	Y	N	Y	Y	N
6	**Wright**	N	Y	N	Y	Y	N
7	Fletcher	Y	Y	Y	Y	Y	Y
8	**Brady**	N	Y	N	Y	Y	N
9	Green, A.	Y	Y	Y	Y	Y	Y
10	**McCaul**	N	Y	N	Y	Y	N
11	**Conaway**	N	Y	N	Y	Y	N
12	**Granger**	N	Y	N	Y	Y	N
13	**Thornberry**	N	Y	N	Y	Y	N
14	**Weber**	N	Y	N	Y	Y	N
15	Gonzalez	Y	Y	Y	?	?	Y
16	Escobar	+	+	+	Y	Y	Y
17	**Flores**	N	Y	N	Y	Y	N
18	Jackson Lee	Y	Y	Y	Y	Y	Y
19	**Arrington**	?	Y	N	Y	Y	N
20	Castro	Y	Y	Y	?	?	Y
21	**Roy**	N	Y	N	Y	Y	N
22	**Olson**	N	Y	N	Y	Y	N
23	**Hurd**	+	+	-	Y	Y	N
24	**Marchant**	?	?	?	?	?	N
25	**Williams**	N	Y	N	Y	Y	N
26	**Burgess**	N	Y	N	Y	Y	N
27	**Cloud**	N	Y	N	Y	Y	N
28	Cuellar	Y	Y	Y	Y	Y	Y
29	Garcia, S.	Y	Y	Y	Y	Y	Y
30	Johnson, E.B.	Y	Y	Y	Y	Y	Y
31	**Carter, J.**	N	Y	N	Y	Y	N
32	Allred	Y	Y	Y	Y	Y	Y
33	Veasey	Y	Y	Y	Y	Y	Y
34	Vela	Y	Y	Y	Y	Y	Y
35	Doggett	Y	Y	Y	Y	Y	Y
36	**Babin**	N	Y	N	Y	Y	N
UTAH							
1	**Bishop, R.**	N	Y	N	Y	Y	N
2	**Stewart**	N	Y	N	Y	Y	N
3	**Curtis**	N	Y	N	Y	Y	N
4	McAdams	Y	Y	Y	Y	Y	Y
VERMONT							
AL	Welch	Y	Y	Y	Y	Y	Y
VIRGINIA							
1	**Wittman**	N	Y	N	Y	Y	N
2	Luria	Y	Y	Y	Y	Y	Y
3	Scott, R.	Y	Y	Y	Y	Y	Y
4	McEachin	+	+	+	+	+	+
5	**Riggleman**	N	Y	N	Y	Y	N
6	**Cline**	N	Y	N	Y	Y	N
7	Spanberger	Y	Y	Y	Y	Y	Y
8	Beyer	Y	?	Y	Y	Y	Y
9	**Griffith**	N	Y	N	Y	Y	N
10	Wexton	Y	Y	Y	Y	Y	Y
11	Connolly	Y	Y	Y	Y	Y	Y
WASHINGTON							
1	DelBene	Y	Y	Y	Y	Y	Y
2	Larsen	Y	Y	Y	Y	?	Y
3	**Herrera Beutler**	Y	Y	N	Y	Y	N
4	**Newhouse**	N	Y	N	Y	Y	N
5	**McMorris Rodgers**	Y	Y	N	Y	Y	N
6	Kilmer	Y	Y	Y	Y	Y	Y
7	Jayapal	Y	Y	Y	Y	Y	Y
8	Schrier	Y	Y	Y	Y	Y	Y
9	Smith Adam	Y	?	?	Y	Y	Y
10	Heck	Y	Y	Y	Y	Y	Y
WEST VIRGINIA							
1	**McKinley**	N	Y	N	Y	Y	N
2	**Mooney**	N	Y	N	Y	Y	N
3	**Miller**	N	Y	N	Y	Y	N
WISCONSIN							
1	**Steil**	N	Y	N	Y	Y	N
2	Pocan	Y	Y	Y	Y	Y	Y
3	Kind	+	+	?	Y	Y	Y
4	Moore	Y	Y	Y	Y	Y	Y
5	**Sensenbrenner**	Y	Y	N	Y	Y	N
6	**Grothman**	N	Y	N	Y	Y	N
7	**Duffy**						
8	**Gallagher**	?	?	?	Y	Y	N
WYOMING							
AL	**Cheney**	?	?	?	Y	Y	N
DELEGATES							
	Radewagen (A.S.)						
	Norton (D.C.)						
	San Nicolas (Guam)						
	Sablan (N. Marianas)						
	González-Colón (P.R.)						
	Plaskett (V.I.)						

559. HR1815, HR3624. SEC Disclosure Rules; SEC Outsourcing Disclosures - Rule. Adoption of the rule (H Res 629) that would provide for House floor consideration of the SEC Disclosure Effectiveness Testing Act (HR 1815) and the Outsourcing Accountability Act (HR 3624). The rule would provide for automatic adoption of a manager's amendment to HR 1815 that would make technical corrections to the bill; provide for floor consideration of four additional amendments to HR 1815; and provide for floor consideration of two amendments to HR 3624. Adopted 228-190: R 0-189; D 228-0; I 0-1. Oct. 16, 2019.

560. HJRES77. Opposing U.S. Withdrawal from Syria - Passage. Engel, D-N.Y., motion to suspend the rules and pass the joint resolution that would express the sense of Congress opposing the decision to end U.S. efforts to prevent Turkish military operations against Syrian Kurdish forces in northeast Syria. It would call on Turkish President Erdogan to immediately cease military action in northeast Syria; call on the U.S. to continue its support of Syrian Kurdish communities and to ensure the Turkish military acts with restraint in Syria; and call on the Trump administration to present a "clear and specific" plan for the defeat of ISIS. Motion agreed to 354-60: R 129-60; D 225-0. *Note: A two-thirds majority of those present and voting (276 in this case) is required for passage under suspension of the rules. A "nay" was a vote in support of the president's position.* Oct. 16, 2019.

561. HR1815. SEC Disclosure Rules - Exempt Disclosures. Huizenga, R-Mich., amendment no. 1 that would add Form CRS to a list of certain disclosures exempt from the bill's investor testing requirements. Form CRS is a client relationship disclosure document for investment bankers and broker-dealers adopted by the SEC in June 2019. Rejected in Committee of the Whole 188-229: R 186-0; D 2-227; I 0-2. Oct. 17, 2019.

562. HR1815. SEC Disclosure Rules - Senior Investment Challenges. Gottheimer, D-N.J., amendment no. 2 that would require the SEC investor testing required by the bill to take into account challenges faced by investors age 65 or older. Adopted in Committee of the Whole 240-178: R 11-176; D 228-1; I 1-1. Oct. 17, 2019.

563. HR1815. SEC Disclosure Rules - Strike Retroactive Testing Requirement. Wagner, R-Mo., amendment no. 3 that would stipulate that the SEC investor testing required by the bill would apply for any regulation issued after Jan. 21, 2021. It would strike from the bill provisions outlining requirements related to investor testing for regulations issued prior to this date. Rejected in Committee of the Whole 188-230: R 187-0; D 1-228; I 0-2. Oct. 17, 2019.

564. HR1815. SEC Disclosure Rules - Passage. Passage of the bill, as amended, that would require the Securities and Exchange Commission to conduct investor testing prior to issuing any rule or regulation requiring the disclosure of information or documents that are intended to or likely to be relied upon by retail investors to inform investment decisions, to evaluate the effectiveness of such disclosures. It would also require the SEC to conduct such testing for existing regulations. The bill would require investor testing to include one-on-one interviews of retail investors related to their use of SEC-disclosed documents or information. Among other provisions, it would exempt certain disclosures from the testing requirement, require the SEC to conduct additional investor testing if the agency makes substantive changes to a rule, and require the SEC to report to Congress annually on the implementation and results of testing. Passed 229-186: R 0-185; D 229-0; I 0-1. *Note: A "nay" was a vote in support of the president's position.* Oct. 17, 2019.

		559	560	561	562	563	564
ALABAMA							
1	Byrne	N	N	Y	N	Y	N
2	Roby	N	Y	Y	N	Y	N
3	Rogers, M.	N	Y	Y	N	Y	N
4	Aderholt	N	Y	Y	N	Y	N
5	Brooks, M.	N	N	Y	N	Y	N
6	Palmer	N	Y	Y	N	Y	N
7	Sewell	Y	Y	N	Y	N	Y
ALASKA							
AL	Young	N	Y	Y	Y	Y	N
ARIZONA							
1	O'Halleran	Y	Y	N	Y	N	Y
2	Kirkpatrick	Y	Y	N	Y	N	Y
3	Grijalva	Y	Y	N	N	?	Y
4	Gosar	N	N	Y	N	Y	N
5	Biggs	N	N	Y	N	Y	N
6	Schweikert	N	Y	Y	N	Y	N
7	Gallego	Y	Y	N	Y	N	Y
8	Lesko	N	N	?	N	Y	N
9	Stanton	Y	Y	N	Y	N	Y
ARKANSAS							
1	Crawford	N	Y	Y	N	Y	N
2	Hill, F.	N	Y	Y	N	Y	N
3	Womack	N	Y	Y	N	Y	N
4	Westerman	N	Y	Y	N	Y	N
CALIFORNIA							
1	LaMalfa	N	Y	Y	N	Y	N
2	Huffman	Y	Y	N	Y	N	Y
3	Garamendi	Y	Y	N	Y	N	Y
4	McClintock	N	N	Y	N	Y	N
5	Thompson, M.	Y	Y	N	Y	N	Y
6	Matsui	Y	Y	N	Y	N	Y
7	Bera	Y	Y	N	Y	N	Y
8	Cook	N	Y	Y	N	Y	N
9	McNerney	Y	Y	N	Y	N	Y
10	Harder	Y	Y	N	Y	N	Y
11	DeSaulnier	Y	Y	N	Y	N	Y
12	Pelosi						
13	Lee B.	Y	Y	N	Y	N	Y
14	Speier	Y	+	N	Y	N	Y
15	Swalwell	Y	Y	N	Y	N	Y
16	Costa	Y	Y	N	Y	N	Y
17	Khanna	Y	Y	N	Y	N	Y
18	Eshoo	Y	Y	N	Y	N	Y
19	Lofgren	Y	Y	N	Y	N	Y
20	Panetta	Y	Y	N	Y	N	Y
21	Cox	Y	Y	N	Y	N	Y
22	Nunes	N	Y	Y	N	Y	N
23	McCarthy	N	Y	Y	N	Y	N
24	Carbajal	Y	Y	N	Y	N	Y
25	Hill, K.	Y	Y	N	Y	N	Y
26	Brownley	Y	Y	N	Y	N	Y
27	Chu	Y	Y	N	Y	N	Y
28	Schiff	Y	Y	N	Y	N	Y
29	Cárdenas	Y	Y	N	?	?	Y
30	Sherman	Y	Y	N	Y	N	Y
31	Aguilar	Y	Y	N	Y	N	Y
32	Napolitano	Y	Y	N	Y	N	Y
33	Lieu	Y	Y	N	Y	N	Y
34	Gomez	Y	Y	N	Y	N	Y
35	Torres	Y	Y	N	Y	N	Y
36	Ruiz	Y	Y	N	Y	N	Y
37	Bass	Y	Y	N	Y	N	Y
38	Sánchez	Y	Y	N	Y	N	Y
39	Cisneros	Y	Y	N	Y	N	Y
40	Roybal-Allard	Y	Y	N	Y	N	Y
41	Takano	Y	Y	N	Y	N	Y
42	Calvert	N	Y	Y	N	Y	N
43	Waters	Y	Y	N	Y	N	Y
44	Barragán	Y	Y	N	Y	N	Y
45	Porter	Y	Y	N	Y	N	Y
46	Correa	Y	Y	N	Y	N	Y
47	Lowenthal	Y	Y	N	Y	N	Y
48	Rouda	Y	Y	N	Y	N	Y
49	Levin	Y	Y	N	Y	N	Y
50	Hunter	N	N	Y	N	Y	N
51	Vargas	Y	Y	N	Y	N	Y
52	Peters	Y	Y	N	Y	N	Y
53	Davis, S.	Y	Y	N	Y	N	Y
COLORADO							
1	DeGette	Y	Y	N	Y	N	Y
2	Neguse	Y	Y	N	Y	N	Y
3	Tipton	N	Y	Y	N	Y	N
4	Buck	N	Y	Y	N	Y	N
5	Lamborn	N	Y	Y	N	Y	N
6	Crow	Y	Y	N	Y	N	Y
7	Perlmutter	Y	Y	N	Y	N	Y
CONNECTICUT							
1	Larson	Y	Y	N	Y	N	Y
2	Courtney	Y	Y	N	Y	N	Y
3	DeLauro	Y	Y	N	Y	N	+
4	Himes	Y	Y	N	Y	N	Y
5	Hayes	Y	Y	N	Y	N	Y
DELAWARE							
AL	Blunt Rochester	Y	Y	N	Y	N	Y
FLORIDA							
1	Gaetz	N	N	Y	N	Y	N
2	Dunn	N	N	Y	N	Y	N
3	Yoho	?	?	?	?	?	?
4	Rutherford	N	N	Y	N	Y	N
5	Lawson	?	?	?	?	?	?
6	Waltz	N	Y	Y	N	Y	N
7	Murphy	Y	Y	N	Y	N	Y
8	Posey	N	N	Y	N	Y	N
9	Soto	Y	Y	N	Y	N	Y
10	Demings	Y	Y	N	Y	N	Y
11	Webster	N	?	Y	Y	Y	N
12	Bilirakis	N	Y	Y	N	Y	N
13	Crist	Y	Y	N	Y	N	Y
14	Castor	Y	Y	N	Y	N	Y
15	Spano	N	Y	Y	N	Y	N
16	Buchanan	N	Y	Y	N	Y	N
17	Steube	N	N	Y	N	Y	N
18	Mast	N	N	Y	Y	Y	N
19	Rooney	?	?	Y	Y	Y	N
20	Hastings	Y	Y	N	Y	N	Y
21	Frankel	Y	Y	N	Y	N	Y
22	Deutch	Y	Y	N	Y	N	Y
23	Wasserman Schultz	Y	Y	N	Y	N	Y
24	Wilson, F.	Y	Y	?	Y	N	Y
25	Diaz-Balart	N	Y	Y	N	Y	N
26	Mucarsel-Powell	Y	Y	N	Y	N	Y
27	Shalala	Y	Y	N	Y	N	Y
GEORGIA							
1	Carter, E.L.	N	Y	Y	N	Y	N
2	Bishop, S.	Y	Y	N	Y	N	Y
3	Ferguson	N	Y	Y	N	Y	N
4	Johnson, H.	Y	Y	N	Y	N	Y
5	Lewis John	Y	Y	N	Y	N	Y
6	McBath	Y	Y	N	Y	N	Y
7	Woodall	N	Y	Y	N	Y	N
8	Scott, A.	N	Y	Y	N	Y	N
9	Collins, D.	N	Y	Y	N	Y	N
10	Hice	N	P	Y	N	Y	N
11	Loudermilk	N	N	?	?	?	?
12	Allen	N	N	Y	N	Y	N
13	Scott, D.	Y	Y	N	Y	N	Y
14	Graves, T.	N	N	Y	N	Y	N
HAWAII							
1	Case	Y	Y	N	Y	N	Y
2	Gabbard	?	?	N	?	?	Y
IDAHO							
1	Fulcher	?	N	Y	N	Y	N
2	Simpson	N	Y	Y	N	Y	N
ILLINOIS							
1	Rush	Y	?	?	?	N	Y
2	Kelly, R.	Y	Y	N	Y	N	Y
3	Lipinski	Y	Y	N	Y	N	Y
4	García, J.	Y	Y	N	Y	N	Y
5	Quigley	Y	Y	N	Y	N	Y
6	Casten	Y	Y	N	Y	N	Y
7	Davis, D.	Y	Y	N	Y	N	Y
8	Krishnamoorthi	Y	Y	N	Y	N	Y
9	Schakowsky	Y	Y	N	Y	N	Y
10	Schneider	Y	Y	N	Y	N	Y
11	Foster	Y	Y	N	Y	N	Y

KEY:	**Republicans**	Democrats	*Independents*
Y Voted for (yea)	**N** Voted against (nay)	**P** Voted "present"	
+ Announced for	**−** Announced against	**?** Did not vote or otherwise	
# Paired for	**X** Paired against	make position known	

*NOTE:
(Maryland 7) Rep. Elijah Cummings died Oct. 17. The last roll call vote he was eligible to cast was vote 560.

	559	560	561	562	563	564
12 **Bost**	N	Y	Y	N	Y	N
13 **Davis, R.**	N	Y	Y	N	Y	N
14 Underwood	Y	Y	N	Y	N	Y
15 **Shimkus**	N	Y	Y	N	Y	N
16 **Kinzinger**	N	Y	Y	N	Y	N
17 Bustos	Y	Y	N	Y	N	Y
18 **LaHood**	N	Y	Y	N	Y	N
INDIANA						
1 Visclosky	Y	Y	N	Y	N	Y
2 **Walorski**	N	Y	Y	N	Y	N
3 **Banks**	N	Y	Y	N	Y	N
4 **Baird**	N	N	Y	N	Y	N
5 **Brooks, S.**	N	Y	Y	N	Y	N
6 **Pence**	N	N	Y	N	Y	N
7 Carson	Y	Y	N	Y	N	Y
8 **Bucshon**	N	Y	Y	N	Y	N
9 **Hollingsworth**	?	N	Y	N	Y	N
IOWA						
1 Finkenauer	Y	Y	N	Y	N	Y
2 Loebsack	Y	Y	N	Y	N	Y
3 Axne	Y	Y	N	Y	N	Y
4 **King, S.**	N	N	Y	N	Y	N
KANSAS						
1 **Marshall**	?	N	Y	N	Y	N
2 **Watkins**	N	N	Y	N	Y	N
3 Davids	Y	Y	N	Y	N	Y
4 **Estes**	N	N	Y	N	Y	N
KENTUCKY						
1 **Comer**	N	N	Y	N	Y	N
2 **Guthrie**	N	Y	Y	N	Y	N
3 Yarmuth	Y	Y	N	Y	N	Y
4 **Massie**	N	N	Y	N	Y	N
5 **Rogers, H.**	N	Y	Y	N	Y	N
6 **Barr**	N	Y	Y	N	Y	N
LOUISIANA						
1 **Scalise**	N	Y	Y	N	Y	N
2 Richmond	Y	Y	N	Y	N	Y
3 **Higgins, C.**	N	Y	Y	N	Y	N
4 **Johnson, M.**	N	Y	Y	N	Y	N
5 **Abraham**	N	N	Y	N	Y	N
6 **Graves, G.**	N	Y	Y	N	Y	N
MAINE						
1 Pingree	Y	Y	N	Y	N	Y
2 Golden	Y	Y	N	Y	N	Y
MARYLAND						
1 **Harris**	N	N	Y	N	Y	N
2 Ruppersberger	Y	Y	N	Y	N	Y
3 Sarbanes	Y	Y	N	Y	N	Y
4 Brown, A.	Y	Y	N	Y	N	Y
5 Hoyer	Y	Y	N	Y	N	Y
6 Trone	Y	Y	N	Y	N	Y
7 Cummings*	?	?				
8 Raskin	Y	Y	N	Y	N	Y
MASSACHUSETTS						
1 Neal	Y	Y	N	Y	N	Y
2 McGovern	Y	Y	N	Y	N	Y
3 Trahan	Y	Y	N	Y	N	Y
4 Kennedy	Y	Y	N	Y	N	Y
5 Clark	Y	Y	N	Y	N	Y
6 Moulton	Y	Y	N	Y	N	Y
7 Pressley	Y	Y	N	Y	N	Y
8 Lynch	Y	Y	N	Y	N	Y
9 Keating	Y	Y	N	Y	N	Y
MICHIGAN						
1 **Bergman**	N	N	Y	N	Y	N
2 **Huizenga**	N	Y	Y	N	Y	N
3 *Amash*	N	P	N	N	N	N
4 **Moolenaar**	N	Y	Y	N	Y	N
5 Kildee	Y	Y	N	Y	N	Y
6 **Upton**	N	Y	Y	N	Y	N
7 **Walberg**	N	N	Y	N	Y	N
8 Slotkin	Y	Y	Y	Y	N	Y
9 Levin	Y	Y	N	Y	N	Y
10 **Mitchell**	N	Y	Y	N	Y	N
11 Stevens	Y	Y	N	Y	N	Y
12 Dingell	Y	Y	N	Y	N	Y
13 Tlaib	Y	Y	N	Y	N	Y
14 Lawrence	Y	Y	N	Y	N	Y
MINNESOTA						
1 **Hagedorn**	N	Y	Y	N	Y	N
2 Craig	Y	Y	N	Y	N	Y
3 Phillips	Y	Y	N	Y	N	Y
4 McCollum	Y	Y	N	Y	N	Y
5 Omar	+	+	N	Y	N	Y

	559	560	561	562	563	564
6 **Emmer**	N	Y	Y	N	Y	N
7 Peterson	Y	?	N	Y	N	Y
8 **Stauber**	N	Y	Y	N	Y	N
MISSISSIPPI						
1 **Kelly, T.**	N	N	Y	N	Y	N
2 Thompson, B.	Y	Y	N	Y	N	Y
3 **Guest**	N	N	Y	N	Y	N
4 **Palazzo**	N	N	Y	N	Y	N
MISSOURI						
1 Clay	Y	Y	N	Y	N	Y
2 **Wagner**	N	Y	Y	N	Y	N
3 **Luetkemeyer**	N	N	Y	N	Y	N
4 **Hartzler**	N	Y	Y	N	Y	N
5 Cleaver	Y	Y	N	Y	N	Y
6 **Graves, S.**	N	Y	Y	N	Y	N
7 **Long**	N	N	Y	N	Y	N
8 **Smith, J.**	N	N	Y	N	Y	N
MONTANA						
AL **Gianforte**	N	Y	Y	N	Y	N
NEBRASKA						
1 **Fortenberry**	N	Y	Y	N	Y	N
2 **Bacon**	N	Y	Y	Y	Y	N
3 **Smith, Adrian**	N	Y	Y	N	Y	N
NEVADA						
1 Titus	Y	Y	N	Y	N	Y
2 **Amodei**	N	Y	Y	N	Y	N
3 Lee	Y	Y	N	Y	N	Y
4 Horsford	Y	Y	N	Y	N	Y
NEW HAMPSHIRE						
1 Pappas	Y	Y	N	Y	N	Y
2 Kuster	Y	Y	N	Y	N	Y
NEW JERSEY						
1 Norcross	Y	Y	N	Y	N	Y
2 Van Drew	Y	Y	N	Y	N	Y
3 Kim	Y	Y	N	Y	N	Y
4 **Smith, C.**	N	Y	Y	Y	Y	N
5 Gottheimer	Y	Y	N	Y	N	Y
6 Pallone	Y	Y	N	Y	N	Y
7 Malinowski	Y	Y	N	Y	N	Y
8 Sires	Y	Y	N	Y	N	Y
9 Pascrell	Y	Y	N	Y	N	Y
10 Payne	Y	Y	N	Y	N	Y
11 Sherrill	Y	Y	N	Y	N	Y
12 Watson Coleman	Y	Y	N	Y	N	Y
NEW MEXICO						
1 Haaland	Y	Y	N	Y	N	Y
2 Torres Small	Y	Y	N	Y	N	Y
3 Luján	Y	Y	N	Y	N	Y
NEW YORK						
1 **Zeldin**	N	Y	Y	N	Y	N
2 **King, P.**	N	Y	Y	N	Y	N
3 Suozzi	Y	Y	N	Y	N	Y
4 Rice, K.	Y	Y	N	Y	N	Y
5 Meeks	Y	Y	N	Y	N	Y
6 Meng	Y	Y	N	Y	N	Y
7 Velázquez	Y	Y	N	Y	N	Y
8 Jeffries	Y	Y	N	Y	N	Y
9 Clarke	Y	Y	N	Y	N	Y
10 Nadler	Y	Y	N	Y	N	Y
11 Rose	Y	Y	N	Y	N	Y
12 Maloney, C.	Y	Y	N	Y	N	Y
13 Espaillat	Y	Y	N	Y	N	Y
14 Ocasio-Cortez	Y	Y	?	Y	N	Y
15 Serrano	Y	Y	N	Y	N	Y
16 Engel	Y	Y	N	Y	N	Y
17 Lowey	Y	Y	N	Y	N	Y
18 Maloney, S.P.	Y	Y	N	Y	N	Y
19 Delgado	Y	Y	N	Y	N	Y
20 Tonko	Y	Y	N	Y	N	Y
21 **Stefanik**	N	Y	Y	Y	Y	N
22 Brindisi	Y	Y	N	Y	N	Y
23 **Reed**	N	N	Y	Y	Y	N
24 **Katko**	N	Y	Y	Y	Y	N
25 Morelle	Y	Y	N	Y	N	Y
26 Higgins, B.	Y	Y	N	Y	N	Y
27 vacant						
NORTH CAROLINA						
1 Butterfield	Y	Y	N	Y	N	Y
2 **Holding**	N	Y	Y	N	Y	N
3 **Murphy**	N	N	Y	N	Y	N
4 Price	Y	Y	N	Y	N	Y
5 **Foxx**	N	N	Y	N	Y	N
6 **Walker**	N	Y	Y	N	Y	N
7 **Rouzer**	N	Y	Y	N	Y	N

	559	560	561	562	563	564
8 **Hudson**	N	Y	Y	N	Y	N
9 **Bishop**	-	-	+	-	+	-
10 **McHenry**	N	Y	Y	N	Y	N
11 **Meadows**	N	N	Y	N	Y	N
12 Adams	Y	Y	N	Y	N	Y
13 **Budd**	-	-	Y	N	Y	N
NORTH DAKOTA						
AL **Armstrong**	N	Y	Y	N	Y	N
OHIO						
1 **Chabot**	N	Y	Y	N	Y	N
2 **Wenstrup**	N	Y	Y	N	Y	N
3 Beatty	Y	Y	N	Y	N	Y
4 **Jordan**	N	N	Y	N	Y	N
5 **Latta**	N	Y	Y	N	Y	N
6 **Johnson, B.**	N	Y	Y	N	Y	N
7 **Gibbs**	N	P	Y	N	Y	N
8 **Davidson**	N	N	Y	N	Y	N
9 Kaptur	Y	Y	N	Y	N	Y
10 **Turner**	N	Y	Y	N	Y	N
11 Fudge	Y	Y	N	Y	N	Y
12 **Balderson**	N	Y	Y	N	Y	N
13 Ryan	?	?	?	?	?	?
14 **Joyce**	N	Y	Y	N	Y	N
15 **Stivers**	N	Y	Y	N	Y	N
16 **Gonzalez**	N	Y	Y	N	Y	N
OKLAHOMA						
1 **Hern**	N	Y	Y	N	Y	N
2 **Mullin**	N	N	Y	N	Y	N
3 **Lucas**	N	Y	Y	N	Y	N
4 **Cole**	N	Y	Y	N	Y	N
5 Horn	Y	Y	Y	Y	N	Y
OREGON						
1 Bonamici	Y	Y	N	Y	N	Y
2 **Walden**	N	Y	Y	N	Y	N
3 Blumenauer	Y	Y	N	Y	N	Y
4 DeFazio	Y	Y	N	Y	N	Y
5 Schrader	Y	Y	N	Y	N	Y
PENNSYLVANIA						
1 **Fitzpatrick**	N	Y	Y	Y	Y	N
2 Boyle	Y	Y	N	Y	N	Y
3 Evans	Y	Y	N	Y	N	Y
4 Dean	Y	Y	N	Y	N	Y
5 Scanlon	Y	Y	N	Y	N	Y
6 Houlahan	Y	Y	N	Y	N	Y
7 Wild	Y	Y	N	Y	N	Y
8 Cartwright	Y	Y	N	Y	N	Y
9 **Meuser**	N	N	Y	N	Y	N
10 **Perry**	N	Y	Y	N	Y	N
11 **Smucker**	N	Y	Y	N	Y	N
12 **Keller**	N	Y	Y	N	Y	N
13 **Joyce**	N	N	Y	N	Y	N
14 **Reschenthaler**	N	Y	Y	N	Y	N
15 **Thompson, G.**	N	Y	Y	N	Y	N
16 **Kelly, M.**	N	Y	Y	N	Y	N
17 Lamb	Y	Y	N	Y	N	Y
18 Doyle	Y	Y	N	Y	N	Y
RHODE ISLAND						
1 Cicilline	Y	Y	N	Y	N	Y
2 Langevin	Y	Y	N	Y	N	Y
SOUTH CAROLINA						
1 Cunningham	Y	Y	N	Y	N	Y
2 **Wilson, J.**	N	Y	Y	N	Y	N
3 **Duncan**	N	N	Y	N	Y	N
4 **Timmons**	N	Y	Y	N	Y	N
5 **Norman**	N	N	Y	N	Y	N
6 Clyburn	Y	Y	N	Y	N	Y
7 **Rice, T.**	N	N	Y	N	Y	N
SOUTH DAKOTA						
AL **Johnson**	N	Y	Y	N	Y	N
TENNESSEE						
1 **Roe**	N	Y	Y	N	Y	N
2 **Burchett**	N	N	Y	N	Y	N
3 **Fleischmann**	N	N	Y	N	Y	N
4 **DesJarlais**	N	N	Y	N	Y	N
5 Cooper	Y	Y	N	Y	N	Y
6 **Rose**	N	N	Y	N	Y	N
7 **Green**	N	Y	Y	N	Y	N
8 **Kustoff**	N	Y	Y	N	Y	N
9 Cohen	Y	Y	N	Y	N	Y
TEXAS						
1 **Gohmert**	N	N	?	?	?	?
2 **Crenshaw**	N	Y	Y	N	Y	N
3 **Taylor**	N	Y	Y	N	Y	N
4 **Ratcliffe**	N	Y	?	?	?	?

	559	560	561	562	563	564
5 **Gooden**	N	N	?	?	?	?
6 **Wright**	N	Y	?	?	?	?
7 Fletcher	Y	Y	N	Y	N	Y
8 **Brady**	N	Y	Y	N	Y	N
9 Green, A.	Y	Y	N	Y	N	Y
10 **McCaul**	N	Y	Y	N	Y	N
11 **Conaway**	N	Y	Y	N	Y	N
12 **Granger**	N	Y	+	-	+	-
13 **Thornberry**	N	Y	Y	N	Y	N
14 **Weber**	N	N	?	?	?	?
15 Gonzalez	Y	Y	N	Y	N	Y
16 Escobar	Y	Y	N	Y	N	Y
17 **Flores**	N	Y	Y	N	Y	N
18 Jackson Lee	Y	Y	N	Y	N	Y
19 **Arrington**	N	Y	Y	N	Y	N
20 Castro	Y	Y	N	Y	N	Y
21 **Roy**	N	P	Y	N	Y	N
22 **Olson**	N	Y	Y	N	Y	N
23 **Hurd**	N	Y	Y	Y	Y	N
24 **Marchant**	N	Y	Y	N	Y	?
25 **Williams**	N	N	?	?	?	?
26 **Burgess**	N	N	Y	N	Y	N
27 **Cloud**	N	Y	Y	N	Y	N
28 Cuellar	Y	Y	N	Y	N	Y
29 Garcia, S.	Y	Y	N	Y	N	Y
30 Johnson, E.B.	Y	Y	N	Y	N	Y
31 **Carter, J.**	N	N	Y	N	Y	N
32 Allred	Y	Y	N	Y	N	Y
33 Veasey	Y	Y	N	Y	N	Y
34 Vela	Y	Y	N	Y	N	Y
35 Doggett	Y	Y	N	Y	N	Y
36 **Babin**	-	N	?	?	?	?
UTAH						
1 **Bishop, R.**	N	Y	Y	N	Y	N
2 **Stewart**	N	Y	Y	N	Y	N
3 **Curtis**	N	Y	Y	N	Y	N
4 McAdams	Y	Y	N	Y	N	Y
VERMONT						
AL Welch	Y	Y	N	Y	N	Y
VIRGINIA						
1 **Wittman**	N	Y	Y	N	Y	N
2 Luria	Y	Y	N	Y	N	Y
3 Scott, R.	Y	Y	N	Y	N	Y
4 McEachin	+	+	-	+	-	+
5 **Riggleman**	N	Y	Y	N	Y	N
6 **Cline**	N	Y	Y	N	Y	N
7 Spanberger	Y	Y	N	Y	N	Y
8 Beyer	Y	Y	N	Y	N	Y
9 **Griffith**	N	Y	Y	N	Y	N
10 Wexton	Y	Y	N	Y	N	Y
11 Connolly	Y	Y	N	Y	N	Y
WASHINGTON						
1 DelBene	Y	Y	N	Y	N	Y
2 Larsen	Y	Y	N	Y	N	Y
3 **Herrera Beutler**	N	Y	Y	N	Y	N
4 **Newhouse**	N	Y	Y	N	Y	N
5 **McMorris Rodgers**	N	Y	Y	N	Y	N
6 Kilmer	Y	Y	N	Y	N	Y
7 Jayapal	Y	Y	N	Y	N	Y
8 Schrier	Y	Y	N	Y	N	Y
9 Smith Adam	Y	Y	N	Y	N	Y
10 Heck	Y	Y	N	Y	N	Y
WEST VIRGINIA						
1 **McKinley**	N	Y	Y	N	Y	N
2 **Mooney**	N	N	Y	N	Y	N
3 **Miller**	N	N	Y	N	Y	N
WISCONSIN						
1 **Steil**	N	Y	Y	N	Y	N
2 Pocan	Y	Y	N	Y	N	Y
3 Kind	Y	Y	N	Y	N	Y
4 Moore	Y	Y	N	Y	N	Y
5 **Sensenbrenner**	N	Y	Y	N	Y	N
6 **Grothman**	N	Y	Y	N	Y	N
7 **Duffy**						
8 **Gallagher**	N	Y	Y	N	Y	N
WYOMING						
AL **Cheney**	N	Y	Y	N	Y	N
DELEGATES						
Radewagen (A.S.)			?	?	?	
Norton (D.C.)			N	Y	N	
San Nicolas (Guam)			?	?	?	
Sablan (N. Marianas)			N	Y	N	
González-Colón (P.R.)			Y	N	Y	
Plaskett (V.I.)			N	Y	N	

565. HR3624. SEC Outsourcing Disclosures - Disclosure Exemptions. Huizenga, R-Mich., amendment no. 1 that would exempt from the bill's disclosure requirements publicly traded companies that are required to make disclosures under existing law related to "conflict minerals" from the Democratic Republic of the Congo or related to CEO pay ratios. Rejected in Committee of the Whole 184-229: R 184-3; D 0-225; I 0-1. Oct. 18, 2019.

566. HR3624. SEC Outsourcing Disclosures - Non-Material Disclosures. Hill, R-Ark., amendment no. 2 that would state that publicly traded companies would not be required to make disclosures under the bill's provisions if the information to be disclosed is "not material." Rejected in Committee of the Whole 187-224: R 186-0; D 0-224; I 1-0. Oct. 18, 2019.

567. HR3624. SEC Outsourcing Disclosures - Passage. Passage of the bill that would require publicly traded companies to disclose the total number and percentage of their employees who are based in each state, U.S. territory, and foreign country. It would require such information disclosed to be disaggregated by state, territory, or country and to include percentage changes from the company's last annual report. It would exempt small and new "emerging growth" companies from the bill's disclosure requirements. It would authorize SEC rule-making authority to implement the bill's provisions. Passed 226-184: R 2-183; D 224-0; I 0-1. Oct. 18, 2019.

568. HRES630. Censuring Rep. Adam Schiff - Motion to Table. Hoyer, D-Md., motion to table (kill) the Biggs, R-Ariz., privileged resolution that would censure and condemn Rep. Adam Schiff, D-Calif. for his actions as chairman of the House Intelligence Committee related to the Aug. 12, 2019, whistle-blower complaint and other accusations against President Trump. Motion agreed to 218-185: R 0-185; D 217-0; I 1-0. Oct. 21, 2019.

569. HR4406. Small Business Development Centers - Passage. Velazquez, D-N.Y., motion to suspend the rules and pass the bill, as amended, that would reauthorize through fiscal 2023, a Small Business Administration Small Business Development Center program, a grant program for centers that provide financial, technical, and other assistance to small businesses. It would authorize $175 million annually for program administration, including up to $2 million annually for SBDC programs in certain economically challenged communities. Among other provisions, it would require the SBA to create a working group to determine best methods for data collection, and it would require the agency to submit an annual report to Congress detailing all entrepreneurial development activities undertaken that year. Additionally, it would increase from $500,000 to $600,000 the amount authorized for SBA expenses related to the SBDC advisory board and accreditation program. Motion agreed to 375-25: R 157-24; D 218-0; I 0-1. *Note: A two-thirds majority of those present and voting (267 in this case) is required for passage under suspension of the rules.* Oct. 21, 2019.

570. HR4407. Small Business Mentoring Program - Passage. Velazquez, D-N.Y., motion to suspend the rules and pass the bill that would reauthorize through fiscal 2022 the Small Business Administration Service Corps of Retired Executives Association program, which provides mentoring and workshops for prospective and existing small business owners. It would authorize $11.7 million annually for program operations, modify certain program requirements, and formally rename the program as the SCORE program. Among other provisions, it would require SCORE program chapters to develop and implement plans to better provide services to under-served communities, including rural areas and economically disadvantaged communities, and it would require the program to include online training and training related to whistle-blower protections. Motion agreed to 389-8: R 171-7; D 218-0; I 0-1. *Note: A two-thirds majority of those present and voting (265 in this case) is required for passage under suspension of the rules.* Oct. 21, 2019.

		565	566	567	568	569	570
ALABAMA							
1	Byrne	Y	Y	N	N	Y	Y
2	Roby	Y	Y	N	N	Y	Y
3	Rogers, M.	Y	Y	N	N	Y	Y
4	Aderholt	Y	Y	N	N	Y	Y
5	Brooks, M.	Y	Y	N	N	Y	N
6	Palmer	Y	Y	N	N	Y	Y
7	Sewell	N	N	Y	Y	Y	Y
ALASKA							
AL	Young	Y	Y	N	N	Y	Y
ARIZONA							
1	O'Halleran	N	N	Y	Y	Y	Y
2	Kirkpatrick	N	N	Y	Y	Y	Y
3	Grijalva	N	?	Y	Y	?	Y
4	Gosar	Y	?	?	N	N	N
5	Biggs	Y	Y	N	N	N	N
6	Schweikert	Y	Y	N	N	Y	Y
7	Gallego	N	N	Y	Y	Y	Y
8	Lesko	Y	Y	N	N	N	Y
9	Stanton	N	N	Y	Y	Y	Y
ARKANSAS							
1	Crawford	Y	Y	N	N	N	Y
2	Hill, F.	Y	Y	N	N	Y	Y
3	Womack	Y	Y	N	N	Y	Y
4	Westerman	Y	Y	N	N	Y	Y
CALIFORNIA							
1	LaMalfa	Y	Y	N	N	N	Y
2	Huffman	N	N	Y	Y	Y	Y
3	Garamendi	N	N	Y	Y	Y	Y
4	McClintock	Y	Y	N	N	N	Y
5	Thompson, M.	N	N	Y	Y	Y	Y
6	Matsui	N	N	Y	Y	Y	Y
7	Bera	N	N	Y	Y	Y	Y
8	Cook	Y	Y	N	N	Y	Y
9	McNerney	N	N	Y	Y	Y	Y
10	Harder	N	N	Y	Y	Y	Y
11	DeSaulnier	N	N	Y	Y	Y	Y
12	Pelosi						
13	Lee B.	N	N	Y	Y	Y	Y
14	Speier	N	N	Y	Y	Y	Y
15	Swalwell	N	N	Y	Y	Y	Y
16	Costa	N	N	Y	Y	Y	Y
17	Khanna	N	N	Y	Y	Y	Y
18	Eshoo	-	-	+	Y	Y	Y
19	Lofgren	N	N	Y	Y	Y	Y
20	Panetta	N	N	Y	Y	Y	Y
21	Cox	N	N	Y	Y	Y	Y
22	Nunes	Y	Y	N	N	Y	Y
23	McCarthy	Y	Y	N	N	Y	Y
24	Carbajal	N	N	Y	Y	Y	Y
25	Hill, K.	N	N	Y	Y	Y	Y
26	Brownley	N	N	Y	Y	Y	Y
27	Chu	N	N	Y	Y	Y	Y
28	Schiff	N	N	Y	Y	Y	Y
29	Cárdenas	N	N	Y	Y	Y	Y
30	Sherman	N	N	Y	Y	Y	Y
31	Aguilar	N	N	Y	Y	Y	Y
32	Napolitano	N	N	Y	Y	Y	Y
33	Lieu	N	N	Y	Y	Y	Y
34	Gomez	-	N	Y	Y	Y	Y
35	Torres	N	N	Y	Y	Y	Y
36	Ruiz	N	N	Y	Y	Y	Y
37	Bass	N	N	Y	Y	Y	Y
38	Sánchez	N	N	Y	Y	Y	Y
39	Cisneros	N	N	Y	Y	Y	Y
40	Roybal-Allard	N	N	Y	?	Y	Y
41	Takano	N	N	Y	+	+	+
42	Calvert	Y	Y	N	N	Y	Y
43	Waters	N	N	Y	Y	Y	Y
44	Barragán	N	N	Y	Y	Y	Y
45	Porter	N	N	Y	Y	Y	Y
46	Correa	N	N	Y	Y	Y	Y
47	Lowenthal	N	N	Y	Y	Y	Y
48	Rouda	N	N	Y	Y	Y	Y
49	Levin	N	N	Y	Y	Y	Y
50	Hunter	Y	Y	N	N	Y	Y
51	Vargas	N	N	Y	Y	Y	Y
52	Peters	N	N	Y	+	+	+
53	Davis, S.	N	N	Y	Y	Y	Y
COLORADO							
1	DeGette	N	N	Y	Y	Y	Y
2	Neguse	N	N	Y	Y	Y	Y
3	Tipton	Y	Y	N	N	Y	Y
4	Buck	Y	Y	N	N	N	N
5	Lamborn	Y	Y	N	N	Y	Y
6	Crow	N	N	Y	Y	Y	Y
7	Perlmutter	N	N	Y	Y	Y	Y
CONNECTICUT							
1	Larson	N	N	Y	Y	Y	Y
2	Courtney	N	N	Y	Y	Y	Y
3	DeLauro	N	N	Y	Y	Y	Y
4	Himes	N	N	Y	Y	Y	Y
5	Hayes	N	N	Y	Y	Y	Y
DELAWARE							
AL	Blunt Rochester	N	N	Y	Y	Y	Y
FLORIDA							
1	Gaetz	Y	Y	N	?	?	?
2	Dunn	Y	Y	N	N	Y	Y
3	Yoho	?	?	?	N	N	Y
4	Rutherford	Y	Y	N	N	Y	+
5	Lawson	?	?	?	Y	Y	Y
6	Waltz	Y	Y	N	N	Y	Y
7	Murphy	N	N	Y	Y	Y	Y
8	Posey	Y	Y	N	N	Y	Y
9	Soto	N	N	Y	Y	Y	Y
10	Demings	N	N	Y	Y	Y	Y
11	Webster	Y	Y	N	N	N	Y
12	Bilirakis	Y	Y	N	N	Y	Y
13	Crist	N	N	Y	Y	Y	Y
14	Castor	N	N	Y	Y	Y	Y
15	Spano	Y	Y	N	N	Y	Y
16	Buchanan	Y	Y	N	N	Y	Y
17	Steube	Y	Y	N	N	Y	Y
18	Mast	Y	Y	N	N	Y	Y
19	Rooney	Y	Y	N	?	?	?
20	Hastings	N	N	Y	Y	Y	Y
21	Frankel	N	N	Y	Y	Y	Y
22	Deutch	N	N	Y	Y	Y	Y
23	Wasserman Schultz	N	N	Y	Y	Y	Y
24	Wilson, F.	N	N	Y	Y	Y	Y
25	Diaz-Balart	Y	Y	N	N	Y	Y
26	Mucarsel-Powell	N	N	Y	Y	Y	Y
27	Shalala	N	N	Y	Y	Y	Y
GEORGIA							
1	Carter, E.L.	Y	Y	N	N	Y	Y
2	Bishop, S.	N	N	Y	Y	Y	Y
3	Ferguson	Y	Y	N	N	N	Y
4	Johnson, H.	N	N	Y	Y	Y	Y
5	Lewis John	N	N	Y	Y	Y	Y
6	McBath	N	N	Y	Y	Y	Y
7	Woodall	Y	Y	N	N	Y	Y
8	Scott, A.	Y	Y	N	N	Y	Y
9	Collins, D.	Y	Y	N	-	+	+
10	Hice	Y	Y	N	N	Y	Y
11	Loudermilk	?	?	?	N	N	Y
12	Allen	Y	Y	N	N	Y	Y
13	Scott, D.	N	N	Y	Y	Y	Y
14	Graves, T.	Y	Y	N	N	Y	Y
HAWAII							
1	Case	N	N	Y	Y	Y	Y
2	Gabbard	?	?	?	?	?	?
IDAHO							
1	Fulcher	Y	Y	N	N	Y	Y
2	Simpson	Y	Y	N	N	Y	Y
ILLINOIS							
1	Rush	N	N	?	Y	Y	Y
2	Kelly, R.	N	N	Y	Y	Y	Y
3	Lipinski	N	N	Y	?	?	?
4	García, J.	N	N	Y	Y	Y	Y
5	Quigley	N	N	Y	Y	Y	Y
6	Casten	N	N	Y	Y	Y	Y
7	Davis, D.	N	N	Y	?	?	?
8	Krishnamoorthi	N	N	Y	Y	Y	Y
9	Schakowsky	-	N	Y	Y	Y	Y
10	Schneider	N	N	Y	Y	Y	Y
11	Foster	N	N	Y	Y	Y	Y

KEY:	**Republicans**	Democrats	*Independents*
Y Voted for (yea)	**N** Voted against (nay)	**P** Voted "present"	
+ Announced for	**-** Announced against	**?** Did not vote or otherwise	
# Paired for	**X** Paired against	make position known	

		565	566	567	568	569	570
12	**Bost**	Y	Y	N	N	Y	Y
13	**Davis, R.**	Y	Y	N	N	Y	Y
14	Underwood	N	N	Y	Y	Y	Y
15	**Shimkus**	Y	Y	N	N	Y	Y
16	**Kinzinger**	Y	Y	N	N	Y	Y
17	Bustos	N	N	Y	Y	Y	Y
18	**LaHood**	Y	Y	N	N	Y	Y
INDIANA							
1	Visclosky	N	N	Y	Y	Y	Y
2	**Walorski**	Y	Y	N	N	Y	Y
3	**Banks**	Y	Y	N	N	Y	Y
4	**Baird**	Y	Y	N	N	Y	Y
5	**Brooks, S.**	Y	Y	N	N	Y	Y
6	**Pence**	Y	Y	N	N	Y	Y
7	Carson	N	N	Y	Y	Y	Y
8	**Bucshon**	Y	Y	N	N	Y	Y
9	**Hollingsworth**	Y	Y	N	N	Y	Y
IOWA							
1	Finkenauer	N	N	Y	Y	Y	Y
2	Loebsack	N	N	Y	?	?	?
3	Axne	N	N	Y	Y	Y	Y
4	**King, S.**	Y	Y	N	N	N	Y
KANSAS							
1	**Marshall**	Y	Y	N	N	Y	Y
2	**Watkins**	Y	Y	N	N	Y	Y
3	Davids	N	N	Y	Y	Y	Y
4	**Estes**	Y	Y	N	N	Y	Y
KENTUCKY							
1	**Comer**	Y	Y	N	N	Y	Y
2	**Guthrie**	Y	Y	N	N	Y	Y
3	Yarmuth	N	N	Y	Y	Y	Y
4	**Massie**	Y	Y	?	N	N	N
5	**Rogers, H.**	Y	Y	N	N	Y	Y
6	**Barr**	Y	Y	N	N	Y	Y
LOUISIANA							
1	**Scalise**	Y	Y	N	-	?	?
2	Richmond	?	?	?	?	Y	Y
3	**Higgins, C.**	Y	Y	N	N	Y	Y
4	**Johnson, M.**	Y	Y	N	N	N	Y
5	**Abraham**	Y	Y	N	N	Y	Y
6	**Graves, G.**	Y	Y	N	N	Y	Y
MAINE							
1	Pingree	N	N	Y	+	?	?
2	Golden	N	N	Y	Y	Y	Y
MARYLAND							
1	**Harris**	Y	Y	N	N	N	Y
2	Ruppersberger	N	N	Y	Y	Y	Y
3	Sarbanes	N	N	Y	Y	Y	Y
4	Brown, A.	N	N	Y	Y	Y	Y
5	Hoyer	N	N	Y	Y	Y	Y
6	Trone	N	N	Y	Y	Y	Y
7	vacant						
8	Raskin	N	N	Y	Y	Y	Y
MASSACHUSETTS							
1	Neal	N	N	Y	Y	Y	Y
2	McGovern	N	N	Y	Y	Y	Y
3	Trahan	N	N	Y	Y	Y	Y
4	Kennedy	N	N	Y	?	?	?
5	Clark	N	N	Y	Y	Y	Y
6	Moulton	N	N	Y	Y	Y	Y
7	Pressley	N	N	Y	Y	Y	Y
8	Lynch	N	N	Y	Y	Y	Y
9	Keating	N	N	Y	Y	Y	Y
MICHIGAN							
1	**Bergman**	Y	Y	N	N	Y	Y
2	**Huizenga**	Y	Y	N	N	Y	Y
3	*Amash*	N	Y	N	Y	N	N
4	**Moolenaar**	Y	Y	N	N	Y	Y
5	Kildee	N	N	Y	Y	Y	Y
6	**Upton**	Y	Y	N	-	+	+
7	**Walberg**	Y	Y	N	N	Y	?
8	Slotkin	N	N	Y	Y	Y	Y
9	Levin	N	N	Y	Y	Y	Y
10	**Mitchell**	Y	Y	N	N	Y	Y
11	Stevens	N	N	Y	Y	Y	Y
12	Dingell	N	N	Y	?	?	?
13	Tlaib	N	N	Y	Y	Y	Y
14	Lawrence	N	N	Y	Y	Y	Y
MINNESOTA							
1	**Hagedorn**	Y	Y	N	N	Y	Y
2	Craig	N	N	Y	Y	Y	Y
3	Phillips	N	N	Y	Y	Y	Y
4	McCollum	N	N	Y	Y	Y	Y
5	Omar	N	N	Y	Y	Y	Y

		565	566	567	568	569	570
6	**Emmer**	Y	Y	N	N	Y	Y
7	Peterson	N	N	Y	Y	Y	Y
8	**Stauber**	Y	Y	N	N	Y	Y
MISSISSIPPI							
1	**Kelly, T.**	Y	Y	N	N	Y	Y
2	Thompson, B.	N	N	Y	Y	Y	Y
3	**Guest**	Y	Y	N	N	Y	Y
4	**Palazzo**	Y	Y	N	N	Y	Y
MISSOURI							
1	Clay	N	N	Y	Y	Y	Y
2	**Wagner**	Y	Y	N	N	Y	?
3	**Luetkemeyer**	Y	Y	N	N	Y	Y
4	**Hartzler**	Y	Y	N	N	Y	Y
5	Cleaver	N	N	Y	Y	Y	Y
6	**Graves, S.**	Y	Y	N	N	Y	Y
7	**Long**	Y	Y	N	N	Y	Y
8	**Smith, J.**	Y	Y	N	N	Y	Y
MONTANA							
AL	**Gianforte**	Y	Y	N	N	Y	Y
NEBRASKA							
1	**Fortenberry**	N	Y	N	N	Y	Y
2	**Bacon**	Y	Y	N	N	Y	Y
3	**Smith, Adrian**	Y	Y	N	N	Y	Y
NEVADA							
1	Titus	N	N	Y	Y	Y	Y
2	**Amodei**	Y	Y	N	N	Y	Y
3	Lee	N	N	Y	Y	Y	Y
4	Horsford	N	N	Y	Y	Y	Y
NEW HAMPSHIRE							
1	Pappas	N	N	Y	Y	Y	Y
2	Kuster	N	N	Y	Y	Y	Y
NEW JERSEY							
1	Norcross	N	N	Y	Y	Y	Y
2	Van Drew	N	N	Y	Y	Y	Y
3	Kim	N	N	Y	Y	Y	Y
4	**Smith, C.**	N	Y	Y	N	Y	Y
5	Gottheimer	N	N	Y	Y	Y	Y
6	Pallone	N	N	Y	Y	Y	Y
7	Malinowski	N	N	Y	Y	Y	Y
8	Sires	N	N	Y	?	?	?
9	Pascrell	N	N	Y	Y	Y	Y
10	Payne	N	N	Y	Y	Y	Y
11	Sherrill	N	N	Y	Y	Y	Y
12	Watson Coleman	N	N	Y	Y	Y	Y
NEW MEXICO							
1	Haaland	N	N	Y	?	?	?
2	Torres Small	N	N	Y	Y	Y	Y
3	Luján	N	N	Y	Y	Y	Y
NEW YORK							
1	**Zeldin**	Y	Y	N	N	Y	Y
2	**King, P.**	Y	Y	N	N	Y	Y
3	Suozzi	N	N	Y	Y	Y	Y
4	Rice, K.	N	N	Y	Y	Y	Y
5	Meeks	N	N	Y	Y	Y	Y
6	Meng	N	N	Y	?	?	?
7	Velázquez	N	N	Y	Y	Y	Y
8	Jeffries	N	N	Y	Y	Y	Y
9	Clarke	N	N	Y	Y	Y	Y
10	Nadler	N	N	Y	Y	Y	Y
11	Rose	N	N	Y	Y	Y	Y
12	Maloney, C.	N	N	Y	Y	Y	Y
13	Espaillat	N	N	Y	Y	Y	Y
14	Ocasio-Cortez	N	N	Y	Y	Y	Y
15	Serrano	N	N	Y	Y	Y	Y
16	Engel	N	N	Y	Y	Y	Y
17	Lowey	N	N	Y	Y	Y	Y
18	Maloney, S.P.	N	N	Y	Y	Y	Y
19	Delgado	N	N	Y	Y	Y	Y
20	Tonko	N	N	Y	Y	Y	Y
21	**Stefanik**	Y	Y	N	N	Y	Y
22	Brindisi	N	N	Y	Y	Y	Y
23	**Reed**	Y	Y	N	N	Y	Y
24	**Katko**	Y	Y	N	N	Y	Y
25	Morelle	N	N	Y	Y	Y	Y
26	Higgins, B.	N	N	Y	Y	Y	Y
27	vacant						
NORTH CAROLINA							
1	Butterfield	N	N	Y	Y	Y	Y
2	**Holding**	Y	Y	N	N	Y	Y
3	**Murphy**	Y	Y	N	N	Y	Y
4	Price	N	N	Y	Y	Y	Y
5	**Foxx**	Y	Y	N	N	Y	Y
6	**Walker**	Y	Y	N	N	Y	Y
7	**Rouzer**	Y	Y	N	N	Y	Y

		565	566	567	568	569	570
8	**Hudson**	Y	Y	N	N	Y	Y
9	**Bishop**	+	+	-	-	+	+
10	**McHenry**	Y	Y	N	N	Y	Y
11	**Meadows**	Y	Y	N	N	?	?
12	Adams	N	N	Y	Y	Y	Y
13	**Budd**	Y	Y	N	N	Y	Y
NORTH DAKOTA							
AL	**Armstrong**	Y	Y	N	N	Y	Y
OHIO							
1	**Chabot**	Y	Y	N	N	Y	Y
2	**Wenstrup**	Y	Y	N	N	Y	?
3	Beatty	-	-	+	Y	Y	Y
4	**Jordan**	Y	Y	N	N	Y	Y
5	**Latta**	Y	Y	N	N	Y	Y
6	**Johnson, B.**	Y	Y	N	N	Y	Y
7	**Gibbs**	Y	Y	N	N	Y	Y
8	**Davidson**	Y	Y	N	N	N	Y
9	Kaptur	N	?	Y	Y	Y	Y
10	**Turner**	Y	Y	N	N	Y	Y
11	Fudge	?	?	?	Y	Y	Y
12	**Balderson**	Y	Y	N	N	Y	Y
13	Ryan	N	N	Y	Y	Y	Y
14	**Joyce**	Y	Y	N	N	Y	Y
15	**Stivers**	Y	Y	N	N	Y	Y
16	**Gonzalez**	Y	Y	N	N	Y	Y
OKLAHOMA							
1	**Hern**	Y	Y	N	N	Y	Y
2	**Mullin**	Y	Y	N	N	Y	Y
3	**Lucas**	Y	Y	N	N	Y	Y
4	**Cole**	Y	Y	N	N	Y	+
5	Horn	N	N	Y	Y	Y	Y
OREGON							
1	Bonamici	N	N	Y	Y	Y	Y
2	**Walden**	Y	Y	N	N	Y	Y
3	Blumenauer	N	?	Y	Y	Y	Y
4	DeFazio	N	N	Y	Y	Y	Y
5	Schrader	N	N	Y	Y	Y	Y
PENNSYLVANIA							
1	**Fitzpatrick**	Y	Y	N	N	Y	Y
2	Boyle	N	N	Y	Y	Y	Y
3	Evans	N	N	Y	Y	Y	Y
4	Dean	N	N	Y	Y	Y	Y
5	Scanlon	N	N	Y	Y	Y	Y
6	Houlahan	N	N	Y	Y	Y	Y
7	Wild	N	N	Y	Y	Y	Y
8	Cartwright	N	N	Y	Y	Y	Y
9	**Meuser**	Y	Y	N	?	?	?
10	**Perry**	Y	Y	N	N	N	Y
11	**Smucker**	Y	Y	N	N	Y	Y
12	**Keller**	Y	Y	N	-	+	+
13	**Joyce**	Y	Y	N	N	Y	Y
14	**Reschenthaler**	Y	Y	N	N	Y	Y
15	**Thompson, G.**	Y	Y	N	N	Y	Y
16	**Kelly, M.**	Y	Y	N	N	Y	Y
17	Lamb	N	N	Y	Y	Y	Y
18	Doyle	N	N	Y	Y	Y	Y
RHODE ISLAND							
1	Cicilline	N	N	Y	Y	Y	Y
2	Langevin	N	N	Y	Y	Y	Y
SOUTH CAROLINA							
1	Cunningham	N	N	Y	Y	Y	Y
2	**Wilson, J.**	Y	Y	N	N	?	?
3	**Duncan**	Y	Y	N	N	Y	Y
4	**Timmons**	Y	Y	N	-	+	+
5	**Norman**	Y	Y	N	N	Y	Y
6	Clyburn	?	?	?	Y	Y	Y
7	**Rice, T.**	N	Y	N	N	Y	Y
SOUTH DAKOTA							
AL	**Johnson**	Y	Y	N	N	Y	Y
TENNESSEE							
1	**Roe**	Y	Y	N	N	Y	Y
2	**Burchett**	Y	Y	N	N	Y	Y
3	**Fleischmann**	Y	Y	N	N	Y	Y
4	**DesJarlais**	Y	Y	N	N	Y	Y
5	Cooper	N	N	Y	Y	Y	Y
6	**Rose**	Y	Y	N	N	Y	Y
7	**Green**	Y	Y	N	N	Y	Y
8	**Kustoff**	Y	Y	N	N	Y	Y
9	Cohen	N	N	Y	Y	Y	Y
TEXAS							
1	**Gohmert**	Y	Y	N	N	N	Y
2	**Crenshaw**	Y	Y	N	N	Y	Y
3	**Taylor**	Y	Y	N	N	-	Y
4	**Ratcliffe**	Y	Y	N	N	Y	Y

		565	566	567	568	569	570
5	**Gooden**	Y	Y	N	?	?	?
6	**Wright**	?	?	?	N	N	Y
7	Fletcher	N	N	Y	Y	Y	Y
8	**Brady**	Y	Y	N	N	Y	Y
9	Green, A.	N	N	Y	Y	Y	Y
10	**McCaul**	Y	Y	N	N	Y	Y
11	**Conaway**	Y	Y	N	N	Y	Y
12	**Granger**	+	+	-	N	Y	Y
13	**Thornberry**	Y	Y	N	N	Y	Y
14	**Weber**	?	?	?	N	N	Y
15	Gonzalez	N	N	Y	Y	Y	Y
16	Escobar	N	N	Y	Y	Y	Y
17	**Flores**	Y	Y	N	N	Y	Y
18	Jackson Lee	N	N	Y	Y	Y	Y
19	**Arrington**	Y	Y	N	N	Y	Y
20	Castro	N	N	Y	Y	Y	Y
21	**Roy**	Y	Y	N	N	N	N
22	**Olson**	Y	Y	N	N	Y	Y
23	**Hurd**	Y	Y	N	N	Y	Y
24	**Marchant**	?	?	?	N	Y	Y
25	**Williams**	?	?	?	N	Y	Y
26	**Burgess**	Y	Y	N	N	N	Y
27	**Cloud**	Y	Y	N	N	Y	Y
28	Cuellar	N	N	Y	Y	Y	Y
29	Garcia, S.	N	N	Y	Y	Y	Y
30	Johnson, E.B.	N	N	Y	Y	Y	Y
31	**Carter, J.**	?	?	?	N	Y	Y
32	Allred	N	N	Y	+	+	+
33	Veasey	N	N	Y	Y	Y	Y
34	Vela	N	N	Y	Y	Y	Y
35	Doggett	N	N	Y	Y	Y	Y
36	**Babin**	?	?	?	N	+	Y
UTAH							
1	**Bishop, R.**	Y	Y	N	N	Y	Y
2	**Stewart**	Y	Y	N	?	?	?
3	**Curtis**	Y	Y	N	?	?	?
4	McAdams	N	N	Y	Y	Y	Y
VERMONT							
AL	Welch	N	N	Y	Y	Y	Y
VIRGINIA							
1	**Wittman**	Y	Y	N	N	Y	Y
2	Luria	N	N	Y	Y	Y	Y
3	Scott, R.	N	N	Y	Y	Y	Y
4	McEachin	-	-	+	+	+	+
5	**Riggleman**	Y	Y	N	N	Y	Y
6	**Cline**	Y	Y	N	N	N	Y
7	Spanberger	N	N	Y	Y	Y	Y
8	Beyer	N	N	Y	Y	Y	Y
9	**Griffith**	Y	Y	N	N	Y	N
10	Wexton	N	N	Y	Y	Y	Y
11	Connolly	N	N	Y	Y	Y	Y
WASHINGTON							
1	DelBene	N	N	Y	Y	Y	Y
2	Larsen	N	N	Y	Y	Y	Y
3	**Herrera Beutler**	Y	Y	N	N	Y	Y
4	**Newhouse**	Y	Y	N	N	Y	Y
5	**McMorris Rodgers**	Y	Y	N	N	Y	Y
6	Kilmer	N	N	Y	Y	Y	Y
7	Jayapal	N	N	Y	Y	Y	Y
8	Schrier	N	N	Y	Y	Y	Y
9	Smith Adam	N	N	Y	Y	Y	Y
10	Heck	N	N	Y	Y	Y	Y
WEST VIRGINIA							
1	**McKinley**	Y	Y	Y	N	Y	Y
2	**Mooney**	Y	Y	N	N	Y	Y
3	**Miller**	Y	Y	N	N	Y	Y
WISCONSIN							
1	**Steil**	Y	Y	N	N	Y	Y
2	Pocan	N	N	Y	Y	Y	Y
3	Kind	N	N	Y	Y	Y	Y
4	Moore	N	N	Y	Y	Y	Y
5	**Sensenbrenner**	Y	Y	N	N	Y	Y
6	**Grothman**	Y	Y	N	N	N	Y
7	**Duffy**						
8	**Gallagher**	Y	Y	N	N	Y	Y
WYOMING							
AL	**Cheney**	Y	Y	N	N	Y	Y
DELEGATES							
	Radewagen (A.S.)	?	?				
	Norton (D.C.)	N	N				
	San Nicolas (Guam)	?	?				
	Sablan (N. Marianas)	?	?				
	González-Colón (P.R.)	?	?				
	Plaskett (V.I.)	N	N				

III HOUSE VOTES

571. HR2513. Financial Crime Enforcement and Disclosures – Previous Question. Woodall, R-Ga., motion to order the previous question (thus ending debate and possibility of amendment) on the rule (H Res 646) that would provide for House floor consideration of the Corporate Transparency Act (HR 2513). The rule would provide for automatic adoption of a Waters, D-Calif., manager's amendment to HR 2513 that would add to the bill the text of a measure related to activities and practices of the Financial Crimes Enforcement Network to detect and prevent money laundering. The rule would also provide for floor consideration of five additional amendments to HR 2513. Motion agreed to 228-194: R 0-193; D 228-0; I 0-1. Oct. 22, 2019.

572. HR2513. Financial Crime Enforcement and Disclosures – Rule. Adoption of the rule (H Res 646) that would provide for House floor consideration of the Corporate Transparency Act (HR 2513). The rule would provide for automatic adoption of a Waters, D-Calif., manager's amendment to HR 2513 that would add to the bill the text of a measure related to activities and practices of the Financial Crimes Enforcement Network to detect and prevent money laundering. The rule would also provide for floor consideration of five additional amendments to HR 2513. Adopted 227-195: R 0-194; D 227-0; I 0-1. Oct. 22, 2019.

573. HR2513. Financial Crime Enforcement and Disclosures – Annual Report. Burgess, R-Texas, amendment no. 1 that would require the Treasury Department to submit an annual report to Congress detailing certain beneficial ownership information collected under existing financial disclosure law, including aggregate data on the industry types and the location and number of owners for each reporting corporation or company. Adopted in Committee of the Whole 395-23: R 168-22; D 226-0; I 1-1. Oct. 22, 2019.

574. HR2513. Financial Crime Enforcement and Disclosures – Public Information. Maloney, D-N.Y., for Levin, D-Mich., amendment no. 4 that would permit the Financial Crimes Enforcement Network to publicize guidance and other materials relating to the beneficial ownership information collected under the bill's provisions, provided that personally identifiable information has been removed. Adopted in Committee of the Whole 235-188: R 6-184; D 228-3; I 1-1. Oct. 22, 2019.

575. HR2513. Financial Crime Enforcement and Disclosures – Ownership Verification Rule Repeal. Davidson, R-Ohio, amendment no. 5 that would replace the text of the bill with provisions that would repeal a May 2016 Treasury Department rule establishing requirements for financial service institutions to verify the identity of their beneficial owners of their customers. It would also require the Financial Crimes Enforcement Network to conduct a study and submit a report to Congress reviewing existing federal information databases available to law enforcement to discern the beneficial ownership of companies and estimating the costs of compliance for the 2016 rule. Rejected in Committee of the Whole 166-258: R 164-28; D 1-229; I 1-1. Oct. 22, 2019.

576. HR2513. Financial Crime Enforcement and Disclosures – Recommit. Davidson, R-Ohio, motion to recommit the bill to the House Financial Services Committee with instructions to report it back immediately with an amendment that would require the Financial Crimes Enforcement Network to disclose beneficial ownership information pursuant to a request by U.S. law enforcement agencies or federal agencies on behalf of foreign law enforcement agencies, only if the request is accompanied by a court-issued subpoena. Motion rejected 197-224: R 192-0; D 4-224; I 1-0. Oct. 22, 2019.

Member	571	572	573	574	575	576
ALABAMA						
1 Byrne	N	N	Y	N	Y	Y
2 Roby	N	N	Y	N	Y	Y
3 Rogers, M.	N	N	Y	N	N	Y
4 Aderholt	N	N	Y	N	Y	Y
5 Brooks, M.	N	N	N	N	Y	Y
6 Palmer	N	N	Y	N	Y	Y
7 Sewell	Y	Y	Y	Y	N	N
ALASKA						
AL Young	N	N	Y	N	Y	Y
ARIZONA						
1 O'Halleran	Y	Y	Y	Y	N	N
2 Kirkpatrick	Y	Y	Y	Y	N	N
3 Grijalva	Y	Y	Y	Y	N	N
4 Gosar	N	N	N	N	Y	Y
5 Biggs	N	N	N	N	Y	Y
6 Schweikert	N	N	N	Y	N	Y
7 Gallego	Y	Y	Y	Y	N	N
8 Lesko	N	N	Y	N	Y	Y
9 Stanton	Y	Y	Y	Y	N	N
ARKANSAS						
1 Crawford	N	N	Y	N	Y	Y
2 Hill, F.	N	N	Y	N	N	Y
3 Womack	N	N	Y	N	Y	Y
4 Westerman	N	N	Y	N	Y	Y
CALIFORNIA						
1 LaMalfa	N	N	Y	N	Y	Y
2 Huffman	Y	Y	Y	Y	N	N
3 Garamendi	Y	Y	Y	Y	N	N
4 McClintock	N	N	Y	N	Y	Y
5 Thompson, M.	Y	Y	Y	Y	N	N
6 Matsui	Y	Y	Y	Y	N	N
7 Bera	Y	Y	Y	Y	N	N
8 Cook	N	N	Y	N	Y	Y
9 McNerney	Y	Y	Y	Y	N	N
10 Harder	Y	Y	Y	Y	N	N
11 DeSaulnier	Y	Y	Y	Y	N	N
12 Pelosi						
13 Lee B.	Y	Y	Y	Y	N	N
14 Speier	Y	Y	Y	Y	N	N
15 Swalwell	Y	Y	Y	Y	N	-
16 Costa	Y	Y	Y	Y	N	N
17 Khanna	Y	Y	Y	Y	N	N
18 Eshoo	Y	Y	Y	Y	N	N
19 Lofgren	Y	Y	Y	Y	N	N
20 Panetta	Y	Y	Y	Y	N	N
21 Cox	Y	Y	Y	Y	N	N
22 Nunes	N	N	Y	N	Y	Y
23 McCarthy	N	N	Y	N	Y	Y
24 Carbajal	Y	Y	Y	Y	N	N
25 Hill, K.	Y	Y	Y	Y	N	N
26 Brownley	Y	Y	Y	Y	N	N
27 Chu	Y	Y	Y	Y	N	N
28 Schiff	Y	Y	Y	Y	N	N
29 Cárdenas	Y	Y	Y	Y	N	N
30 Sherman	Y	Y	Y	Y	N	N
31 Aguilar	Y	Y	Y	Y	N	N
32 Napolitano	Y	Y	Y	Y	N	N
33 Lieu	Y	Y	Y	Y	N	N
34 Gomez	Y	Y	Y	Y	N	N
35 Torres	Y	Y	Y	Y	N	N
36 Ruiz	Y	Y	Y	Y	N	N
37 Bass	Y	Y	Y	Y	N	N
38 Sánchez	Y	Y	Y	Y	N	N
39 Cisneros	Y	Y	Y	Y	N	N
40 Roybal-Allard	Y	Y	Y	Y	N	N
41 Takano	+	+	+	+	-	-
42 Calvert	N	N	Y	N	Y	Y
43 Waters	Y	Y	Y	Y	N	N
44 Barragán	Y	Y	Y	Y	N	N
45 Porter	Y	Y	Y	Y	N	N
46 Correa	Y	Y	Y	Y	N	N
47 Lowenthal	Y	Y	Y	Y	N	N
48 Rouda	Y	Y	Y	Y	N	N
49 Levin	Y	Y	Y	Y	N	N
50 Hunter	N	N	?	?	Y	Y
51 Vargas	Y	Y	Y	Y	N	N
52 Peters	?	?	?	?	?	?
53 Davis, S.	Y	Y	Y	Y	N	N
COLORADO						
1 DeGette	Y	Y	Y	Y	N	N
2 Neguse	Y	Y	Y	Y	N	N
3 Tipton	N	N	Y	N	Y	Y
4 Buck	N	N	N	N	Y	Y
5 Lamborn	N	N	Y	N	Y	Y
6 Crow	Y	Y	Y	Y	N	N
7 Perlmutter	Y	Y	Y	Y	N	N
CONNECTICUT						
1 Larson	Y	Y	Y	Y	N	N
2 Courtney	Y	Y	Y	Y	N	N
3 DeLauro	Y	Y	Y	Y	N	N
4 Himes	Y	Y	Y	Y	N	N
5 Hayes	Y	Y	Y	Y	N	N
DELAWARE						
AL Blunt Rochester	Y	Y	Y	Y	N	N
FLORIDA						
1 Gaetz	N	N	N	N	Y	Y
2 Dunn	N	N	Y	N	Y	Y
3 Yoho	N	N	Y	N	Y	Y
4 Rutherford	N	N	Y	N	Y	Y
5 Lawson	Y	Y	Y	Y	N	N
6 Waltz	N	N	Y	N	Y	Y
7 Murphy	Y	Y	Y	Y	N	N
8 Posey	N	N	Y	N	Y	Y
9 Soto	Y	Y	Y	Y	N	N
10 Demings	Y	Y	Y	Y	N	N
11 Webster	N	N	Y	N	Y	Y
12 Bilirakis	N	N	Y	N	Y	?
13 Crist	Y	Y	Y	Y	N	N
14 Castor	Y	Y	Y	Y	N	N
15 Spano	N	N	Y	N	Y	Y
16 Buchanan	N	N	Y	N	Y	Y
17 Steube	N	N	Y	N	Y	Y
18 Mast	N	N	Y	N	Y	Y
19 Rooney	N	N	Y	Y	Y	Y
20 Hastings	Y	Y	Y	Y	N	N
21 Frankel	Y	Y	Y	Y	N	N
22 Deutch	Y	Y	Y	Y	N	N
23 Wasserman Schultz	Y	Y	Y	Y	N	N
24 Wilson, F.	Y	Y	?	Y	N	N
25 Diaz-Balart	N	N	Y	N	Y	Y
26 Mucarsel-Powell	Y	Y	Y	Y	N	N
27 Shalala	Y	Y	Y	Y	N	N
GEORGIA						
1 Carter, E.L.	N	N	Y	N	Y	Y
2 Bishop, S.	Y	Y	Y	Y	N	N
3 Ferguson	N	N	Y	N	Y	Y
4 Johnson, H.	Y	Y	Y	Y	N	N
5 Lewis John	Y	Y	Y	Y	N	N
6 McBath	Y	Y	Y	Y	N	N
7 Woodall	N	N	Y	N	Y	Y
8 Scott, A.	N	N	Y	N	Y	Y
9 Collins, D.	-	-	+	-	+	+
10 Hice	N	N	Y	N	Y	Y
11 Loudermilk	N	N	Y	N	?	Y
12 Allen	N	N	Y	N	Y	Y
13 Scott, D.	Y	Y	Y	Y	N	N
14 Graves, T.	N	N	N	N	N	Y
HAWAII						
1 Case	Y	Y	Y	Y	N	N
2 Gabbard	?	?	?	?	?	?
IDAHO						
1 Fulcher	N	N	Y	N	Y	Y
2 Simpson	N	N	Y	N	Y	Y
ILLINOIS						
1 Rush	Y	Y	Y	Y	N	N
2 Kelly, R.	Y	Y	Y	Y	N	N
3 Lipinski	Y	Y	Y	Y	N	N
4 García, J.	Y	Y	Y	Y	N	N
5 Quigley	Y	Y	Y	Y	N	N
6 Casten	Y	Y	Y	Y	N	N
7 Davis, D.	Y	Y	Y	Y	N	N
8 Krishnamoorthi	Y	Y	Y	Y	N	N
9 Schakowsky	Y	Y	Y	Y	N	N
10 Schneider	Y	Y	Y	Y	N	N
11 Foster	Y	Y	?	Y	N	N

KEY: Republicans   Democrats   *Independents*

Y Voted for (yea)	**N** Voted against (nay)	**P** Voted "present"
+ Announced for	**–** Announced against	**?** Did not vote or otherwise
# Paired for	**X** Paired against	make position known

		571	572	573	574	575	576
12	**Bost**	N	N	Y	N	N	Y
13	**Davis, R.**	N	N	Y	?	N	Y
14	Underwood	Y	Y	Y	Y	N	N
15	**Shimkus**	N	N	Y	N	Y	Y
16	**Kinzinger**	N	N	Y	N	N	Y
17	Bustos	Y	Y	Y	Y	N	N
18	**LaHood**	N	N	Y	N	N	Y
INDIANA							
1	Visclosky	Y	Y	Y	Y	N	N
2	**Walorski**	N	N	+	N	Y	Y
3	**Banks**	N	N	N	N	Y	Y
4	**Baird**	N	N	Y	N	Y	Y
5	**Brooks, S.**	N	N	Y	N	Y	Y
6	**Pence**	N	N	Y	N	Y	Y
7	Carson	Y	Y	Y	Y	?	N
8	**Bucshon**	N	N	Y	N	Y	Y
9	**Hollingsworth**	N	N	Y	N	N	Y
IOWA							
1	Finkenauer	Y	Y	Y	Y	N	N
2	Loebsack	Y	Y	Y	Y	N	N
3	Axne	Y	Y	Y	Y	N	N
4	**King, S.**	N	N	Y	N	Y	Y
KANSAS							
1	**Marshall**	N	N	Y	N	Y	Y
2	**Watkins**	N	N	Y	N	Y	Y
3	Davids	Y	Y	Y	Y	N	N
4	**Estes**	N	N	Y	N	Y	Y
KENTUCKY							
1	**Comer**	N	N	Y	N	Y	Y
2	**Guthrie**	N	N	Y	N	Y	Y
3	Yarmuth	Y	Y	Y	Y	N	N
4	**Massie**	N	N	N	N	Y	Y
5	**Rogers, H.**	N	N	Y	N	Y	Y
6	**Barr**	N	N	Y	N	N	Y
LOUISIANA							
1	**Scalise**	N	N	Y	N	Y	Y
2	Richmond	Y	Y	Y	Y	N	N
3	**Higgins, C.**	N	N	N	N	Y	Y
4	**Johnson, M.**	N	N	Y	N	Y	Y
5	**Abraham**	N	N	Y	N	Y	Y
6	**Graves, G.**	N	N	Y	N	Y	Y
MAINE							
1	Pingree	Y	Y	Y	Y	N	N
2	Golden	Y	Y	Y	Y	N	N
MARYLAND							
1	**Harris**	N	N	Y	N	Y	Y
2	Ruppersberger	Y	Y	Y	Y	N	N
3	Sarbanes	Y	Y	Y	Y	N	N
4	Brown, A.	Y	Y	Y	Y	N	N
5	Hoyer	Y	Y	Y	Y	N	N
6	Trone	Y	Y	Y	Y	N	N
7	vacant						
8	Raskin	Y	Y	Y	Y	N	N
MASSACHUSETTS							
1	Neal	Y	Y	Y	Y	N	N
2	McGovern	Y	Y	Y	Y	N	N
3	Trahan	Y	Y	Y	Y	N	N
4	Kennedy	Y	Y	Y	Y	N	N
5	Clark	Y	Y	Y	Y	N	N
6	Moulton	Y	Y	?	Y	N	N
7	Pressley	Y	Y	Y	Y	N	N
8	Lynch	Y	Y	Y	Y	N	N
9	Keating	Y	Y	Y	Y	N	N
MICHIGAN							
1	**Bergman**	N	N	Y	N	Y	Y
2	**Huizenga**	N	N	Y	N	Y	Y
3	*Amash*	N	N	N	N	Y	Y
4	**Moolenaar**	N	N	Y	N	Y	Y
5	Kildee	Y	Y	Y	Y	N	N
6	**Upton**	N	N	Y	N	Y	Y
7	**Walberg**	N	N	Y	N	Y	Y
8	Slotkin	Y	Y	Y	N	N	N
9	Levin	Y	Y	Y	Y	N	N
10	**Mitchell**	N	N	Y	Y	Y	Y
11	Stevens	Y	Y	Y	Y	N	N
12	Dingell	Y	Y	Y	Y	N	N
13	Tlaib	Y	Y	Y	Y	N	N
14	Lawrence	Y	Y	Y	Y	N	N
MINNESOTA							
1	**Hagedorn**	N	N	Y	N	Y	Y
2	Craig	Y	Y	Y	Y	N	N
3	Phillips	Y	Y	Y	Y	N	N
4	McCollum	Y	Y	Y	Y	N	N
5	Omar	Y	Y	+	Y	N	N

		571	572	573	574	575	576
6	**Emmer**	N	N	Y	N	N	Y
7	Peterson	Y	Y	Y	Y	N	N
8	**Stauber**	N	N	Y	N	Y	Y
MISSISSIPPI							
1	**Kelly, T.**	N	N	Y	N	Y	Y
2	Thompson, B.	Y	Y	Y	Y	N	N
3	**Guest**	N	N	Y	N	Y	Y
4	**Palazzo**	N	N	Y	N	Y	Y
MISSOURI							
1	Clay	Y	Y	Y	Y	N	N
2	**Wagner**	N	N	Y	N	N	Y
3	**Luetkemeyer**	N	N	Y	N	N	Y
4	**Hartzler**	N	N	Y	N	Y	Y
5	Cleaver	Y	Y	Y	Y	N	N
6	**Graves, S.**	N	N	Y	N	Y	Y
7	**Long**	N	N	Y	N	Y	Y
8	**Smith, J.**	N	N	?	N	Y	Y
MONTANA							
AL	**Gianforte**	N	N	Y	N	Y	Y
NEBRASKA							
1	**Fortenberry**	N	N	Y	N	Y	Y
2	**Bacon**	N	N	Y	N	Y	Y
3	**Smith, Adrian**	N	N	+	N	Y	Y
NEVADA							
1	Titus	Y	Y	Y	Y	N	N
2	**Amodei**	N	N	Y	N	Y	Y
3	Lee	Y	Y	Y	Y	N	N
4	Horsford	Y	Y	Y	Y	N	N
NEW HAMPSHIRE							
1	Pappas	Y	Y	Y	Y	N	N
2	Kuster	Y	Y	Y	Y	N	N
NEW JERSEY							
1	Norcross	Y	Y	Y	Y	N	N
2	Van Drew	Y	Y	Y	N	N	Y
3	Kim	Y	Y	Y	Y	N	N
4	**Smith, C.**	N	N	Y	Y	N	Y
5	Gottheimer	Y	Y	Y	Y	N	N
6	Pallone	Y	Y	Y	Y	N	N
7	Malinowski	Y	Y	Y	Y	N	N
8	Sires	Y	Y	Y	Y	N	N
9	Pascrell	Y	Y	Y	Y	N	N
10	Payne	Y	Y	Y	?	N	N
11	Sherrill	Y	Y	Y	Y	N	N
12	Watson Coleman	Y	Y	Y	Y	N	N
NEW MEXICO							
1	Haaland	Y	Y	Y	Y	N	N
2	Torres Small	Y	Y	Y	Y	N	N
3	Luján	Y	Y	Y	Y	N	N
NEW YORK							
1	**Zeldin**	N	N	Y	?	?	?
2	**King, P.**	N	N	Y	Y	N	Y
3	Suozzi	Y	Y	Y	Y	N	N
4	Rice, K.	Y	Y	Y	Y	N	N
5	Meeks	Y	Y	Y	Y	N	N
6	Meng	Y	Y	Y	Y	N	N
7	Velázquez	Y	Y	Y	Y	N	N
8	Jeffries	Y	Y	Y	Y	N	N
9	Clarke	Y	Y	Y	Y	N	N
10	Nadler	Y	Y	Y	Y	N	N
11	Rose	Y	Y	Y	Y	N	N
12	Maloney, C.	Y	Y	Y	Y	N	N
13	Espaillat	Y	Y	Y	Y	N	N
14	Ocasio-Cortez	Y	Y	Y	Y	N	N
15	Serrano	Y	?	Y	Y	N	N
16	Engel	Y	Y	Y	Y	N	N
17	Lowey	Y	Y	Y	Y	N	N
18	Maloney, S.P.	Y	Y	Y	Y	N	N
19	Delgado	Y	Y	Y	Y	N	N
20	Tonko	Y	Y	Y	Y	N	N
21	**Stefanik**	N	N	Y	N	N	Y
22	Brindisi	Y	Y	Y	N	N	Y
23	**Reed**	N	N	Y	N	Y	Y
24	**Katko**	N	N	Y	Y	N	Y
25	Morelle	Y	Y	Y	Y	N	N
26	Higgins, B.	Y	Y	Y	Y	N	N
27	vacant						
NORTH CAROLINA							
1	Butterfield	Y	Y	Y	Y	N	N
2	**Holding**	N	N	Y	N	Y	Y
3	**Murphy**	N	N	Y	N	Y	Y
4	Price	Y	Y	Y	Y	N	N
5	**Foxx**	N	N	Y	N	Y	Y
6	**Walker**	N	N	Y	N	Y	Y
7	**Rouzer**	N	N	Y	N	Y	Y

		571	572	573	574	575	576
8	**Hudson**	N	N	Y	N	Y	Y
9	**Bishop**	-	-	+	-	+	+
10	**McHenry**	N	N	Y	N	Y	Y
11	**Meadows**	N	N	Y	N	Y	Y
12	Adams	Y	Y	Y	Y	N	N
13	**Budd**	N	N	Y	N	Y	Y
NORTH DAKOTA							
AL	**Armstrong**	N	N	Y	N	Y	Y
OHIO							
1	**Chabot**	N	N	Y	N	Y	Y
2	**Wenstrup**	N	N	Y	N	Y	Y
3	Beatty	Y	Y	Y	Y	N	N
4	**Jordan**	N	N	?	?	?	Y
5	**Latta**	N	N	Y	N	Y	Y
6	**Johnson, B.**	N	N	Y	N	Y	Y
7	**Gibbs**	N	N	Y	N	Y	Y
8	**Davidson**	N	N	N	N	Y	Y
9	Kaptur	Y	Y	Y	Y	N	N
10	**Turner**	N	N	Y	N	Y	Y
11	Fudge	Y	Y	Y	Y	N	N
12	**Balderson**	N	N	Y	N	N	Y
13	Ryan	Y	Y	Y	Y	N	N
14	**Joyce**	N	N	Y	N	Y	Y
15	**Stivers**	N	N	Y	N	N	Y
16	**Gonzalez**	N	N	Y	N	Y	Y
OKLAHOMA							
1	**Hern**	N	N	Y	N	Y	Y
2	**Mullin**	N	N	Y	N	Y	Y
3	**Lucas**	N	N	Y	N	N	Y
4	**Cole**	-	N	Y	N	N	Y
5	Horn	Y	Y	Y	Y	N	Y
OREGON							
1	Bonamici	Y	Y	Y	Y	N	N
2	**Walden**	N	N	Y	N	Y	Y
3	Blumenauer	Y	Y	Y	Y	N	N
4	DeFazio	Y	Y	Y	Y	N	N
5	Schrader	Y	Y	Y	Y	N	N
PENNSYLVANIA							
1	**Fitzpatrick**	N	N	Y	Y	N	Y
2	Boyle	Y	Y	Y	Y	N	N
3	Evans	Y	Y	Y	Y	N	N
4	Dean	Y	Y	Y	Y	N	N
5	Scanlon	Y	Y	Y	Y	N	N
6	Houlahan	Y	Y	Y	Y	N	N
7	Wild	Y	Y	Y	Y	N	N
8	Cartwright	Y	Y	Y	Y	N	N
9	**Meuser**	N	N	Y	N	Y	Y
10	**Perry**	N	N	Y	N	Y	Y
11	**Smucker**	N	N	Y	?	Y	Y
12	**Keller**	N	N	Y	N	Y	Y
13	**Joyce**	N	N	Y	N	Y	Y
14	**Reschenthaler**	N	N	Y	N	Y	Y
15	**Thompson, G.**	N	N	Y	N	Y	Y
16	**Kelly, M.**	N	N	Y	N	Y	Y
17	Lamb	Y	Y	Y	Y	N	N
18	Doyle	Y	Y	Y	Y	N	N
RHODE ISLAND							
1	Cicilline	Y	Y	Y	Y	N	N
2	Langevin	Y	Y	Y	Y	N	N
SOUTH CAROLINA							
1	Cunningham	Y	Y	Y	Y	N	Y
2	**Wilson, J.**	N	N	Y	N	Y	Y
3	**Duncan**	N	N	N	N	Y	Y
4	**Timmons**	-	-	+	-	+	+
5	**Norman**	N	N	N	N	Y	Y
6	Clyburn	Y	Y	Y	Y	N	N
7	**Rice, T.**	N	N	N	N	Y	Y
SOUTH DAKOTA							
AL	**Johnson**	N	N	Y	N	Y	Y
TENNESSEE							
1	**Roe**	N	N	Y	N	Y	Y
2	**Burchett**	N	N	N	N	Y	Y
3	**Fleischmann**	N	N	Y	N	Y	Y
4	**DesJarlais**	N	N	Y	N	Y	Y
5	Cooper	Y	Y	Y	Y	N	N
6	**Rose**	N	N	Y	N	Y	Y
7	**Green**	N	N	Y	N	Y	Y
8	**Kustoff**	N	N	Y	N	N	Y
9	Cohen	Y	Y	Y	Y	N	N
TEXAS							
1	**Gohmert**	N	N	N	N	Y	Y
2	**Crenshaw**	N	N	Y	N	N	Y
3	**Taylor**	N	N	Y	N	Y	Y
4	**Ratcliffe**	N	N	Y	N	Y	Y

		571	572	573	574	575	576
5	**Gooden**	N	N	N	N	Y	Y
6	**Wright**	N	N	Y	N	Y	Y
7	Fletcher	Y	Y	Y	Y	N	N
8	**Brady**	N	N	Y	N	Y	Y
9	Green, A.	Y	Y	Y	Y	N	N
10	**McCaul**	N	N	Y	N	N	Y
11	**Conaway**	N	N	Y	N	Y	Y
12	**Granger**	N	N	Y	N	Y	Y
13	**Thornberry**	N	N	Y	N	Y	Y
14	**Weber**	N	N	Y	N	Y	Y
15	Gonzalez	Y	Y	?	Y	N	N
16	Escobar	Y	Y	Y	Y	N	N
17	**Flores**	N	N	Y	N	Y	Y
18	Jackson Lee	Y	Y	Y	Y	N	N
19	**Arrington**	N	N	Y	N	Y	Y
20	Castro	Y	Y	Y	Y	N	N
21	**Roy**	N	N	N	N	Y	Y
22	**Olson**	N	N	Y	N	Y	Y
23	**Hurd**	N	N	Y	N	Y	Y
24	**Marchant**	N	N	Y	N	Y	Y
25	**Williams**	N	N	Y	N	Y	Y
26	**Burgess**	N	N	Y	N	Y	Y
27	**Cloud**	N	N	N	N	Y	Y
28	Cuellar	Y	Y	Y	Y	Y	N
29	Garcia, S.	Y	Y	Y	Y	N	N
30	Johnson, E.B.	Y	Y	Y	Y	N	N
31	**Carter, J.**	N	N	Y	N	Y	Y
32	Allred	+	+	Y	Y	N	N
33	Veasey	Y	Y	Y	Y	N	N
34	Vela	Y	Y	Y	Y	N	N
35	Doggett	Y	Y	Y	Y	N	N
36	**Babin**	N	N	Y	N	Y	Y
UTAH							
1	**Bishop, R.**	N	N	Y	N	Y	Y
2	**Stewart**	N	N	Y	N	Y	Y
3	**Curtis**	N	N	Y	N	Y	Y
4	McAdams	Y	Y	Y	Y	N	N
VERMONT							
AL	Welch	Y	Y	Y	Y	N	N
VIRGINIA							
1	**Wittman**	N	N	Y	N	Y	Y
2	Luria	Y	Y	Y	Y	N	N
3	Scott, R.	Y	Y	Y	Y	N	N
4	McEachin	+	+	+	+	-	-
5	**Riggleman**	N	N	N	N	Y	Y
6	**Cline**	N	N	N	N	Y	Y
7	Spanberger	Y	Y	Y	Y	N	N
8	Beyer	Y	Y	Y	Y	N	N
9	**Griffith**	N	N	Y	N	Y	Y
10	Wexton	Y	Y	Y	Y	N	N
11	Connolly	Y	Y	Y	Y	N	N
WASHINGTON							
1	DelBene	Y	Y	Y	Y	N	N
2	Larsen	Y	Y	Y	Y	N	N
3	**Herrera Beutler**	N	N	Y	N	Y	Y
4	**Newhouse**	N	N	Y	N	Y	Y
5	**McMorris Rodgers**	N	N	Y	N	Y	Y
6	Kilmer	Y	Y	Y	Y	N	N
7	Jayapal	Y	Y	Y	Y	N	N
8	Schrier	Y	Y	Y	Y	N	N
9	Smith Adam	Y	Y	Y	Y	N	N
10	Heck	Y	Y	Y	Y	N	N
WEST VIRGINIA							
1	**McKinley**	N	N	Y	N	Y	Y
2	**Mooney**	N	N	N	N	Y	Y
3	**Miller**	N	N	Y	N	Y	Y
WISCONSIN							
1	**Steil**	N	N	Y	N	N	Y
2	Pocan	Y	Y	Y	Y	N	N
3	Kind	Y	Y	Y	Y	N	N
4	Moore	Y	Y	?	Y	N	N
5	**Sensenbrenner**	N	N	Y	N	Y	Y
6	**Grothman**	N	N	Y	N	Y	Y
7	**Duffy**						
8	**Gallagher**	N	N	Y	N	N	Y
WYOMING							
AL	**Cheney**	N	N	Y	N	Y	Y
DELEGATES							
	Radewagen (A.S.)			?	?	?	
	Norton (D.C.)			Y	Y	N	
	San Nicolas (Guam)			Y	Y	N	
	Sablan (N. Marianas)			Y	Y	N	
	González-Colón (P.R.)			Y	N	Y	
	Plaskett (V.I.)			Y	Y	?	

577. HR2513. Financial Crime Enforcement and Disclosures - Passage. Passage of the bill that would require each corporation and limited liability company to file a report with the Financial Crimes Enforcement Network detailing identifiable information on its beneficial owners and require that such reports be updated annually. It would exempt from such reporting requirements certain corporate entities subject to existing disclosure laws or any company with more than 20 employees or over $5 million in annual revenue. Among other provisions, it would establish procedures for the disclosure of ownership information by FinCEN to law enforcement agencies and establish civil and criminal penalties for violations of the bill's reporting requirement. As amended, the bill would authorize $20 million annually for fiscal 2020 and 2021 for FinCEN to carry out bill's provisions. It would also include a number of provisions related to FinCEN activities and practices to detect and prevent money laundering. Passed 249-173: R 25-167; D 224-5; I 0-1. Oct. 22, 2019.

578. HR2426. Copyright Claims Court - Passage. Jeffries, D-N.Y., motion to suspend the rules and pass the bill, as amended, that would establish the Copyright Claims Board within the U.S. Copyright Office to serve as a forum for the resolution of certain claims, counterclaims, and defenses in copyright infringement cases, on a voluntary basis. Among other provisions, it would establish maximum damages of $7,500 for each work and $15,000 total per claim. It would require the board to be composed of three copyright officers, appointed by the Copyright Office for renewable six year terms, and it would require the office to hire at least two copyright claims attorneys and additional support staff to assist with administration of the board. Motion agreed to 410-6: R 185-5; D 225-0; I 0-1. *Note: A two-thirds majority of those present and voting (278 in this case) is required for passage under suspension of the rules.* Oct. 22, 2019.

579. HR4617. Election Security - Previous Question. Hastings, D-Fla., motion to order the previous question (thus ending debate and possibility of amendment) on the rule (H Res 650) that would provide for House floor consideration of the Stopping Harmful Interference in Elections for a Lasting Democracy (SHIELD) Act (HR 4617). The rule would provide for automatic adoption of a Lofgren, D-Calif, manager's amendment to HR 4617 and floor consideration of 14 additional amendments to the bill. The Lofgren manager's amendment to HR 4617 would except from the bill's foreign contact disclosure requirements communications with foreign entities for the purposes of enabling observation of U.S. elections, provided that such communications do not involve discussion of an exchange of money for a campaign. It would also prohibit entry to the U.S. and allow for the deportation of foreign nationals who interfere in U.S. elections. Motion agreed to 223-180: R 0-179; D 223-0; I 0-1. Oct. 23, 2019.

580. HR4617. Election Security - Rule. Adoption of the rule (H Res 650) that would provide for House floor consideration of the Stopping Harmful Interference in Elections for a Lasting Democracy (SHIELD) Act (HR 4617). The rule would provide for automatic adoption of a Lofgren, D-Calif, manager's amendment to HR 4617 and floor consideration of 14 additional amendments to the bill. The Lofgren manager's amendment to HR 4617 would except from the bill's foreign contact disclosure requirements communications with foreign entities for the purposes of enabling observation of U.S. elections, provided that such communications do not involve discussion of an exchange of money for a campaign. It would also prohibit entry to the U.S. and allow for the deportation of foreign nationals who interfere in U.S. elections. Adopted 226-180: R 0-179; D 226-0; I 0-1. Oct. 23, 2019.

581. HR4617. Election Security - Correcting False Election Information. Lesko, R-Ariz., amendment no. 2 that would strike from the bill a section that would require the Justice Department to correct false information related to elections by communicating corrected information to the public, if state or local election officials have not already done so. Rejected in Committee of the Whole 180-231: R 179-1; D 0-229; I 1-1. Oct. 23, 2019.

582. HR4617. Election Security - Recommit. Davis, R-Ill., motion to recommit the bill (HR 4617) to the House Administration Committee with instructions to report it back immediately with an amendment that would replace the text of the bill with a number of provisions regarding activities and foreign interference related to federal elections. Among other provisions, it would clarify the definition of foreign propagandists to include individuals engaged in communications activities within the U.S., with the exception of journalistic activities, for the purposes of registration with the Justice Department. It would expand certain existing Federal Election Commission regulations to require paid advertisement disclaimers for political advertising to include internet communications. It would also prohibit the distribution of federal election assistance to states that allow the transmission of a ballots by certain third parties, and it would classify improper interference in elections by foreign nationals as an inadmissible and deportable offense. Motion rejected 182-225: R 178-0; D 3-225; I 1-0. Oct. 23, 2019.

		577	578	579	580	581	582
ALABAMA							
1	**Byrne**	N	Y	N	N	Y	Y
2	**Roby**	N	Y	N	N	Y	Y
3	**Rogers, M.**	Y	Y	N	N	Y	Y
4	**Aderholt**	Y	Y	N	N	Y	Y
5	**Brooks, M.**	N	Y	N	N	Y	Y
6	**Palmer**	N	Y	N	N	Y	Y
7	Sewell	Y	Y	Y	Y	N	N
ALASKA							
AL	**Young**	N	Y	N	N	Y	Y
ARIZONA							
1	O'Halleran	Y	Y	Y	Y	N	N
2	Kirkpatrick	Y	Y	Y	Y	N	N
3	Grijalva	Y	Y	Y	Y	N	N
4	**Gosar**	N	Y	N	N	Y	Y
5	**Biggs**	N	Y	N	N	Y	Y
6	**Schweikert**	N	Y	N	N	Y	Y
7	Gallego	Y	Y	Y	Y	N	N
8	**Lesko**	N	Y	N	N	Y	Y
9	Stanton	Y	Y	Y	Y	N	N
ARKANSAS							
1	**Crawford**	N	Y	N	N	Y	Y
2	**Hill, F.**	N	Y	N	N	Y	Y
3	**Womack**	N	Y	N	N	Y	Y
4	**Westerman**	N	Y	N	N	Y	Y
CALIFORNIA							
1	**LaMalfa**	N	Y	N	N	Y	Y
2	Huffman	Y	Y	Y	Y	N	N
3	Garamendi	Y	Y	Y	Y	N	N
4	**McClintock**	N	Y	N	N	Y	Y
5	Thompson, M.	Y	Y	Y	Y	N	N
6	Matsui	Y	Y	Y	Y	N	N
7	Bera	Y	Y	Y	Y	N	N
8	**Cook**	N	Y	N	N	Y	Y
9	McNerney	Y	Y	Y	Y	N	N
10	Harder	Y	Y	Y	Y	N	N
11	DeSaulnier	Y	Y	Y	Y	N	N
12	Pelosi						
13	Lee B.	Y	Y	Y	Y	N	N
14	Speier	Y	Y	Y	Y	N	N
15	Swalwell	Y	Y	Y	Y	N	N
16	Costa	Y	Y	Y	Y	N	N
17	Khanna	Y	Y	Y	Y	N	N
18	Eshoo	Y	Y	+	+	-	N
19	Lofgren	Y	Y	Y	Y	N	N
20	Panetta	Y	+	Y	Y	N	N
21	Cox	Y	Y	Y	Y	N	N
22	**Nunes**	N	Y	N	N	Y	Y
23	**McCarthy**	N	Y	N	N	Y	Y
24	Carbajal	Y	Y	Y	Y	N	N
25	Hill, K.	Y	Y	Y	Y	N	N
26	Brownley	Y	Y	Y	Y	N	N
27	Chu	Y	Y	Y	Y	N	N
28	Schiff	Y	Y	Y	Y	N	N
29	Cárdenas	Y	Y	Y	Y	N	N
30	Sherman	Y	Y	Y	Y	N	N
31	Aguilar	Y	Y	Y	Y	N	N
32	Napolitano	Y	Y	Y	Y	N	N
33	Lieu	Y	Y	Y	Y	N	N
34	Gomez	Y	Y	Y	Y	N	N
35	Torres	Y	Y	Y	Y	N	N
36	Ruiz	Y	Y	Y	Y	N	N
37	Bass	Y	Y	Y	Y	N	N
38	Sánchez	Y	Y	Y	Y	N	N
39	Cisneros	Y	Y	Y	Y	N	N
40	Roybal-Allard	Y	Y	Y	Y	N	N
41	Takano	+	-	+	+	-	-
42	**Calvert**	N	Y	N	N	Y	Y
43	Waters	Y	Y	Y	Y	N	N
44	Barragán	Y	Y	Y	Y	N	N
45	Porter	Y	Y	Y	Y	N	N
46	Correa	Y	Y	Y	Y	N	N
47	Lowenthal	Y	Y	Y	Y	N	N
48	Rouda	Y	Y	Y	Y	N	N
49	Levin	Y	Y	Y	Y	N	N
50	**Hunter**	N	Y	N	N	Y	Y
51	Vargas	Y	Y	Y	Y	N	N
52	Peters	+	+	?	?	?	?
53	Davis, S.	Y	Y	Y	Y	N	N
COLORADO							
1	DeGette	Y	Y	Y	Y	N	N
2	Neguse	Y	Y	Y	Y	N	N
3	**Tipton**	N	Y	N	N	Y	Y
4	**Buck**	N	Y	N	N	Y	Y
5	**Lamborn**	N	Y	N	N	Y	Y
6	Crow	Y	Y	Y	Y	N	N
7	Perlmutter	Y	Y	Y	Y	N	N
CONNECTICUT							
1	Larson	Y	Y	Y	Y	N	N
2	Courtney	Y	Y	Y	Y	N	N
3	DeLauro	Y	Y	Y	Y	N	N
4	Himes	Y	Y	Y	Y	N	N
5	Hayes	Y	Y	Y	Y	N	N
DELAWARE							
AL	Blunt Rochester	Y	Y	Y	Y	N	N
FLORIDA							
1	**Gaetz**	N	Y	N	N	Y	Y
2	**Dunn**	N	Y	N	N	Y	Y
3	**Yoho**	N	Y	N	N	Y	Y
4	**Rutherford**	Y	Y	N	N	Y	Y
5	Lawson	Y	Y	Y	Y	N	N
6	**Waltz**	Y	Y	N	N	Y	Y
7	Murphy	Y	Y	Y	Y	N	N
8	**Posey**	N	Y	N	N	Y	Y
9	Soto	Y	Y	Y	Y	N	N
10	Demings	Y	Y	Y	Y	N	N
11	**Webster**	N	Y	N	N	Y	Y
12	**Bilirakis**	?	?	?	?	?	?
13	Crist	Y	Y	Y	Y	N	N
14	Castor	Y	Y	Y	Y	N	N
15	**Spano**	N	Y	N	N	Y	Y
16	**Buchanan**	N	Y	N	N	Y	Y
17	**Steube**	N	Y	N	N	Y	?
18	**Mast**	N	Y	N	N	Y	Y
19	**Rooney**	Y	?	N	N	Y	Y
20	Hastings	Y	?	Y	Y	N	N
21	Frankel	Y	Y	Y	Y	N	N
22	Deutch	Y	Y	Y	Y	N	N
23	Wasserman Schultz	Y	Y	Y	Y	N	N
24	Wilson, F.	Y	Y	Y	Y	N	N
25	**Diaz-Balart**	N	Y	N	N	Y	Y
26	Mucarsel-Powell	Y	Y	Y	Y	N	N
27	Shalala	Y	Y	Y	Y	N	N
GEORGIA							
1	**Carter, E.L.**	N	Y	N	N	Y	Y
2	Bishop, S.	Y	Y	Y	Y	N	N
3	**Ferguson**	N	Y	N	N	Y	Y
4	Johnson, H.	Y	Y	Y	Y	N	N
5	Lewis John	Y	Y	Y	Y	N	N
6	McBath	Y	Y	Y	Y	N	N
7	**Woodall**	N	Y	N	?	Y	Y
8	**Scott, A.**	Y	Y	N	N	Y	Y
9	**Collins, D.**	-	+	?	?	+	+
10	**Hice**	N	Y	N	N	Y	Y
11	**Loudermilk**	Y	Y	N	N	Y	Y
12	**Allen**	N	Y	N	N	Y	Y
13	Scott, D.	Y	Y	Y	Y	N	N
14	**Graves, T.**	Y	Y	N	N	Y	Y
HAWAII							
1	Case	Y	Y	Y	Y	N	N
2	Gabbard	?	?	?	?	?	?
IDAHO							
1	**Fulcher**	N	Y	N	N	Y	Y
2	**Simpson**	N	Y	N	N	Y	Y
ILLINOIS							
1	Rush	Y	Y	Y	Y	N	N
2	Kelly, R.	Y	Y	Y	Y	N	N
3	Lipinski	Y	Y	Y	Y	N	N
4	García, J.	Y	Y	Y	Y	N	N
5	Quigley	Y	Y	Y	Y	N	N
6	Casten	Y	Y	Y	Y	N	N
7	Davis, D.	Y	Y	?	Y	N	N
8	Krishnamoorthi	Y	Y	Y	Y	N	N
9	Schakowsky	Y	Y	Y	Y	N	N
10	Schneider	Y	Y	Y	Y	N	N
11	Foster	Y	Y	Y	Y	N	N

KEY: **Republicans** Democrats *Independents*

Y	Voted for (yea)	N	Voted against (nay)	P	Voted "present"
+	Announced for	-	Announced against	?	Did not vote or otherwise make position known
#	Paired for	X	Paired against		

		577	578	579	580	581	582
12	**Bost**	N	Y	N	N	Y	Y
13	**Davis, R.**	N	Y	N	N	Y	Y
14	Underwood	Y	Y	Y	Y	N	N
15	**Shimkus**	N	Y	N	N	Y	Y
16	**Kinzinger**	N	Y	N	N	Y	Y
17	Bustos	Y	Y	Y	Y	N	N
18	**LaHood**	N	Y	N	N	Y	Y
INDIANA							
1	Visclosky	Y	Y	Y	Y	N	N
2	**Walorski**	N	Y	N	N	Y	Y
3	**Banks**	N	Y	N	N	Y	Y
4	**Baird**	N	Y	N	N	Y	Y
5	**Brooks, S.**	N	Y	N	N	Y	Y
6	**Pence**	N	Y	N	N	Y	Y
7	Carson	Y	Y	Y	Y	N	N
8	**Bucshon**	N	Y	N	N	Y	Y
9	**Hollingsworth**	N	Y	N	N	Y	Y
IOWA							
1	Finkenauer	Y	Y	Y	Y	N	N
2	Loebsack	Y	Y	Y	Y	N	N
3	Axne	Y	Y	Y	Y	N	N
4	**King, S.**	N	Y	N	N	Y	Y
KANSAS							
1	**Marshall**	N	Y	N	N	Y	Y
2	**Watkins**	N	Y	N	N	Y	Y
3	Davids	Y	Y	Y	Y	N	N
4	**Estes**	N	Y	-	N	+	+
KENTUCKY							
1	**Comer**	N	Y	N	N	Y	Y
2	**Guthrie**	N	Y	N	N	Y	Y
3	Yarmuth	Y	Y	Y	Y	N	N
4	**Massie**	N	N	N	N	Y	Y
5	**Rogers, H.**	N	Y	N	N	Y	Y
6	**Barr**	N	Y	N	N	Y	Y
LOUISIANA							
1	**Scalise**	N	Y	N	N	Y	Y
2	Richmond	Y	Y	Y	Y	N	N
3	**Higgins, C.**	N	Y	N	N	Y	Y
4	**Johnson, M.**	N	Y	N	N	Y	Y
5	**Abraham**	N	Y	N	N	Y	Y
6	**Graves, G.**	Y	Y	N	N	Y	Y
MAINE							
1	Pingree	Y	Y	Y	Y	N	N
2	Golden	Y	Y	Y	Y	N	N
MARYLAND							
1	**Harris**	N	Y	N	N	Y	Y
2	Ruppersberger	Y	Y	Y	Y	N	N
3	Sarbanes	Y	Y	Y	Y	N	N
4	Brown, A.	Y	Y	Y	Y	N	N
5	Hoyer	Y	Y	Y	Y	N	N
6	Trone	Y	Y	Y	Y	N	N
7	vacant						
8	Raskin	Y	Y	Y	Y	N	N
MASSACHUSETTS							
1	Neal	Y	Y	Y	Y	N	N
2	McGovern	Y	Y	Y	Y	N	N
3	Trahan	Y	Y	Y	Y	N	N
4	Kennedy	Y	Y	Y	Y	N	N
5	Clark	Y	Y	Y	Y	N	N
6	Moulton	Y	Y	Y	Y	N	N
7	Pressley	Y	Y	Y	Y	N	N
8	Lynch	Y	Y	Y	Y	N	N
9	Keating	Y	Y	Y	Y	N	N
MICHIGAN							
1	**Bergman**	N	Y	-	-	Y	Y
2	**Huizenga**	Y	Y	N	N	Y	Y
3	*Amash*	N	N	N	N	Y	Y
4	**Moolenaar**	N	Y	N	N	Y	Y
5	Kildee	Y	Y	Y	Y	N	N
6	**Upton**	Y	Y	N	N	Y	Y
7	**Walberg**	N	Y	N	N	Y	Y
8	Slotkin	Y	Y	Y	Y	N	N
9	Levin	Y	Y	Y	Y	N	N
10	**Mitchell**	N	Y	N	N	?	?
11	Stevens	Y	Y	Y	Y	N	N
12	Dingell	Y	Y	Y	Y	N	N
13	Tlaib	Y	Y	Y	Y	N	N
14	Lawrence	Y	Y	Y	Y	N	N
MINNESOTA							
1	**Hagedorn**	N	Y	N	N	Y	Y
2	Craig	Y	Y	Y	Y	N	N
3	Phillips	Y	Y	Y	Y	N	N
4	McCollum	Y	Y	Y	Y	N	N
5	Omar	Y	Y	Y	Y	N	N

		577	578	579	580	581	582
6	**Emmer**	N	Y	N	N	Y	Y
7	Peterson	N	Y	Y	Y	N	N
8	**Stauber**	N	Y	N	N	Y	Y
MISSISSIPPI							
1	**Kelly, T.**	N	N	N	N	Y	Y
2	Thompson, B.	Y	Y	Y	Y	N	N
3	**Guest**	N	Y	N	N	Y	Y
4	**Palazzo**	N	Y	N	N	Y	Y
MISSOURI							
1	Clay	Y	Y	Y	Y	N	N
2	**Wagner**	Y	Y	N	N	Y	Y
3	**Luetkemeyer**	Y	Y	N	N	Y	Y
4	**Hartzler**	N	Y	N	N	Y	Y
5	Cleaver	Y	Y	Y	Y	N	N
6	**Graves, S.**	N	Y	N	N	Y	Y
7	**Long**	N	Y	N	N	Y	Y
8	**Smith, J.**	N	Y	N	N	Y	Y
MONTANA							
AL	**Gianforte**	N	N	N	N	Y	Y
NEBRASKA							
1	**Fortenberry**	N	Y	N	N	Y	Y
2	**Bacon**	N	Y	N	N	Y	Y
3	**Smith, Adrian**	N	Y	N	N	Y	Y
NEVADA							
1	Titus	Y	Y	Y	Y	N	N
2	**Amodei**	N	Y	?	?	?	?
3	Lee	Y	Y	Y	Y	N	N
4	Horsford	Y	Y	Y	Y	N	N
NEW HAMPSHIRE							
1	Pappas	Y	Y	Y	Y	N	N
2	Kuster	Y	Y	Y	Y	N	N
NEW JERSEY							
1	Norcross	Y	Y	Y	Y	N	N
2	Van Drew	N	Y	Y	Y	N	N
3	Kim	Y	Y	Y	Y	N	N
4	**Smith, C.**	Y	Y	N	N	Y	Y
5	Gottheimer	Y	Y	Y	Y	N	Y
6	Pallone	Y	Y	Y	Y	N	N
7	Malinowski	Y	Y	Y	Y	N	N
8	Sires	Y	Y	Y	Y	N	N
9	Pascrell	Y	Y	Y	Y	N	N
10	Payne	Y	Y	Y	Y	N	N
11	Sherrill	Y	Y	Y	Y	N	N
12	Watson Coleman	Y	Y	Y	Y	N	N
NEW MEXICO							
1	Haaland	Y	Y	Y	Y	N	N
2	Torres Small	Y	Y	Y	Y	N	N
3	Luján	Y	Y	Y	Y	N	N
NEW YORK							
1	**Zeldin**	?	Y	N	N	Y	Y
2	**King, P.**	Y	Y	N	N	Y	Y
3	Suozzi	Y	Y	Y	Y	N	N
4	Rice, K.	Y	Y	Y	Y	N	N
5	Meeks	Y	Y	Y	Y	N	N
6	Meng	Y	Y	Y	Y	N	N
7	Velázquez	Y	Y	Y	Y	N	N
8	Jeffries	Y	Y	Y	Y	N	N
9	Clarke	Y	Y	Y	Y	N	N
10	Nadler	Y	Y	Y	Y	N	N
11	Rose	Y	Y	Y	Y	N	N
12	Maloney, C.	Y	Y	Y	Y	N	N
13	Espaillat	Y	Y	Y	Y	N	N
14	Ocasio-Cortez	Y	Y	Y	Y	N	N
15	Serrano	Y	Y	Y	Y	N	N
16	Engel	Y	Y	Y	Y	N	N
17	Lowey	Y	Y	?	?	N	N
18	Maloney, S.P.	Y	Y	Y	Y	N	N
19	Delgado	Y	Y	Y	Y	N	N
20	Tonko	Y	Y	Y	Y	N	N
21	**Stefanik**	Y	Y	N	N	Y	Y
22	Brindisi	N	Y	Y	Y	N	Y
23	**Reed**	N	Y	N	N	Y	Y
24	**Katko**	Y	Y	N	N	Y	Y
25	Morelle	Y	Y	?	Y	N	N
26	Higgins, B.	Y	Y	Y	Y	N	N
27	vacant						
NORTH CAROLINA							
1	Butterfield	Y	?	Y	Y	N	N
2	**Holding**	N	Y	N	N	Y	Y
3	**Murphy**	N	Y	N	N	Y	Y
4	Price	Y	?	Y	Y	N	N
5	**Foxx**	N	Y	N	N	Y	Y
6	**Walker**	N	Y	N	N	Y	Y
7	**Rouzer**	N	Y	N	N	Y	Y

		577	578	579	580	581	582
8	**Hudson**	N	Y	N	N	Y	Y
9	**Bishop**	-	+	?	?	Y	Y
10	**McHenry**	N	Y	N	N	Y	Y
11	**Meadows**	N	Y	N	N	Y	Y
12	Adams	Y	Y	Y	Y	N	N
13	**Budd**	N	Y	N	N	Y	Y
NORTH DAKOTA							
AL	**Armstrong**	N	Y	N	N	?	?
OHIO							
1	**Chabot**	N	Y	N	N	Y	Y
2	**Wenstrup**	N	Y	N	N	Y	Y
3	Beatty	Y	Y	Y	Y	N	N
4	**Jordan**	N	Y	N	N	Y	Y
5	**Latta**	N	Y	N	N	Y	Y
6	**Johnson, B.**	N	Y	N	N	Y	Y
7	**Gibbs**	N	Y	N	N	Y	Y
8	**Davidson**	N	N	N	N	Y	Y
9	Kaptur	Y	Y	Y	Y	N	N
10	**Turner**	N	?	N	N	Y	Y
11	Fudge	Y	Y	?	?	N	N
12	**Balderson**	N	Y	N	N	Y	Y
13	Ryan	Y	Y	Y	Y	N	N
14	**Joyce**	N	Y	N	N	Y	Y
15	**Stivers**	N	Y	?	?	?	?
16	**Gonzalez**	N	Y	N	N	Y	Y
OKLAHOMA							
1	**Hern**	N	Y	N	N	Y	Y
2	**Mullin**	N	Y	N	N	Y	Y
3	**Lucas**	N	Y	N	N	Y	Y
4	**Cole**	N	Y	N	N	Y	Y
5	Horn	Y	Y	Y	Y	N	N
OREGON							
1	Bonamici	Y	Y	Y	Y	N	N
2	**Walden**	N	Y	N	N	Y	Y
3	Blumenauer	Y	Y	Y	Y	N	N
4	DeFazio	Y	Y	Y	Y	N	N
5	Schrader	Y	Y	Y	Y	N	N
PENNSYLVANIA							
1	**Fitzpatrick**	Y	Y	N	N	N	Y
2	Boyle	Y	Y	Y	Y	N	N
3	Evans	Y	Y	+	Y	N	N
4	Dean	Y	Y	Y	Y	N	N
5	Scanlon	Y	Y	Y	Y	N	N
6	Houlahan	Y	Y	Y	Y	N	N
7	Wild	Y	Y	Y	Y	N	N
8	Cartwright	Y	Y	Y	Y	N	N
9	**Meuser**	N	Y	?	?	?	?
10	**Perry**	N	Y	N	N	Y	Y
11	**Smucker**	N	Y	-	-	+	+
12	**Keller**	N	Y	-	-	+	+
13	**Joyce**	N	Y	?	?	?	?
14	**Reschenthaler**	N	Y	?	?	?	?
15	**Thompson, G.**	N	Y	-	-	+	+
16	**Kelly, M.**	N	Y	?	?	?	?
17	Lamb	Y	Y	Y	Y	N	N
18	Doyle	Y	Y	Y	Y	N	N
RHODE ISLAND							
1	Cicilline	Y	Y	Y	Y	N	N
2	Langevin	Y	Y	Y	Y	N	N
SOUTH CAROLINA							
1	Cunningham	Y	Y	Y	Y	N	N
2	**Wilson, J.**	N	Y	N	N	Y	Y
3	**Duncan**	N	Y	N	N	Y	Y
4	**Timmons**	-	+	-	-	+	+
5	**Norman**	N	N	N	N	Y	Y
6	Clyburn	Y	Y	Y	Y	N	N
7	**Rice, T.**	N	Y	N	N	Y	Y
SOUTH DAKOTA							
AL	**Johnson**	N	Y	N	N	Y	Y
TENNESSEE							
1	**Roe**	N	Y	-	-	Y	Y
2	**Burchett**	N	Y	N	N	Y	Y
3	**Fleischmann**	N	Y	N	N	Y	Y
4	**DesJarlais**	N	Y	N	N	Y	Y
5	Cooper	Y	Y	Y	Y	N	N
6	**Rose**	N	Y	N	N	Y	Y
7	**Green**	N	Y	N	N	Y	Y
8	**Kustoff**	Y	Y	N	N	Y	Y
9	Cohen	Y	Y	Y	Y	N	N
TEXAS							
1	**Gohmert**	N	Y	N	N	Y	Y
2	**Crenshaw**	N	Y	N	N	Y	Y
3	**Taylor**	N	Y	N	N	Y	Y
4	**Ratcliffe**	N	Y	N	N	Y	Y

		577	578	579	580	581	582
5	**Gooden**	N	Y	N	N	Y	Y
6	**Wright**	N	Y	N	N	Y	Y
7	Fletcher	Y	Y	Y	Y	N	N
8	**Brady**	N	Y	N	N	Y	Y
9	Green, A.	Y	Y	Y	Y	N	N
10	**McCaul**	Y	Y	N	N	Y	Y
11	**Conaway**	N	Y	N	N	Y	Y
12	**Granger**	Y	Y	N	N	Y	Y
13	**Thornberry**	N	Y	N	N	Y	Y
14	**Weber**	N	Y	N	N	Y	Y
15	Gonzalez	N	Y	Y	Y	N	N
16	Escobar	Y	Y	Y	Y	N	N
17	**Flores**	N	Y	N	N	Y	Y
18	Jackson Lee	Y	Y	Y	Y	N	N
19	**Arrington**	N	Y	N	N	Y	Y
20	Castro	Y	Y	Y	Y	N	N
21	**Roy**	N	Y	N	N	Y	Y
22	**Olson**	Y	Y	N	N	Y	Y
23	**Hurd**	N	Y	N	N	Y	Y
24	**Marchant**	N	Y	N	N	Y	Y
25	**Williams**	Y	Y	N	N	Y	Y
26	**Burgess**	N	Y	N	N	Y	Y
27	**Cloud**	N	Y	N	N	Y	Y
28	Cuellar	N	Y	Y	Y	N	N
29	Garcia, S.	Y	Y	Y	Y	N	N
30	Johnson, E.B.	Y	Y	Y	Y	N	N
31	**Carter, J.**	N	Y	N	N	Y	Y
32	Allred	Y	Y	Y	Y	N	N
33	Veasey	Y	Y	Y	Y	N	N
34	Vela	Y	Y	Y	Y	N	N
35	Doggett	Y	Y	Y	Y	N	N
36	**Babin**	N	Y	N	N	Y	Y
UTAH							
1	**Bishop, R.**	N	Y	N	N	Y	Y
2	**Stewart**	N	Y	N	N	Y	Y
3	**Curtis**	N	Y	N	N	Y	Y
4	McAdams	Y	Y	Y	Y	N	N
VERMONT							
AL	Welch	Y	Y	Y	Y	N	N
VIRGINIA							
1	**Wittman**	N	Y	N	N	Y	Y
2	Luria	Y	Y	Y	Y	?	N
3	Scott, R.	Y	Y	Y	Y	N	N
4	McEachin	+	+	+	+	-	-
5	**Riggleman**	N	Y	N	N	Y	Y
6	**Cline**	N	Y	N	N	Y	Y
7	Spanberger	Y	Y	Y	Y	N	N
8	Beyer	Y	Y	Y	Y	N	N
9	**Griffith**	N	Y	N	N	Y	Y
10	Wexton	Y	Y	Y	Y	N	N
11	Connolly	Y	Y	Y	Y	N	N
WASHINGTON							
1	DelBene	Y	Y	Y	Y	N	N
2	Larsen	Y	Y	Y	Y	N	N
3	**Herrera Beutler**	N	Y	N	N	Y	Y
4	**Newhouse**	N	Y	N	N	Y	?
5	**McMorris Rodgers**	N	Y	N	N	Y	Y
6	Kilmer	Y	Y	Y	Y	N	N
7	Jayapal	Y	Y	Y	Y	N	N
8	Schrier	Y	Y	Y	Y	N	N
9	Smith Adam	Y	Y	Y	Y	N	N
10	Heck	Y	Y	Y	Y	N	N
WEST VIRGINIA							
1	**McKinley**	N	Y	N	N	Y	Y
2	**Mooney**	N	Y	N	N	Y	Y
3	**Miller**	N	Y	N	N	Y	Y
WISCONSIN							
1	**Steil**	N	Y	-	-	+	+
2	Pocan	Y	Y	Y	Y	N	N
3	Kind	Y	Y	Y	Y	?	?
4	Moore	Y	Y	Y	Y	N	N
5	**Sensenbrenner**	N	?	N	N	Y	Y
6	**Grothman**	N	Y	?	?	?	?
7	**Duffy**						
8	**Gallagher**	Y	Y	N	N	Y	Y
WYOMING							
AL	**Cheney**	Y	Y	N	N	Y	Y
DELEGATES							
	Radewagen (A.S.)					?	
	Norton (D.C.)					N	
	San Nicolas (Guam)					N	
	Sablan (N. Marianas)					N	
	González-Colón (P.R.)					?	
	Plaskett (V.I.)					N	

583. HR4617. Election Security - Passage. Passage of the bill that would expand disclosure requirements for political advertisements and prohibit certain activities related to political campaigns, particularly with regards to foreign influence. Specifically, the bill would require political campaign committees to report foreign contacts by the campaign to the Federal Election Commission and Federal Bureau of Investigation, within one week of the contact. It would require such disclosures in the case of any direct or indirect foreign communication between the candidate or campaign officials and foreign nationals that involves any offer or proposal for a contribution or provision of services between the two entities. It would require candidates and campaign officials to notify their campaign committees within three days of such contact. It would establish criminal penalties for violations of these disclosure requirements, including fines of up to $500,000 or a prison term of up to five years. The bill would expand certain existing FEC regulations for political advertising to include internet communications, including to require paid advertisement disclaimers and prohibit spending by foreign nationals for online and digital political ads. Among other provisions, it would also establish criminal penalties for any attempts to hinder, interfere with, or prevent a person from voting or registering to vote, and it would require reports to Congress within 180 days of each federal election detailing reports of deceptive practices and evaluating the influence of foreign financing in U.S. elections. Passed 227-181: R 0-179; D 227-1; I 0-1. *Note: A "nay" was a vote in support of the president's position.* Oct. 23, 2019.

584. HR777. DNA Evidence Backlog - Passage. Nadler, D-N.Y., motion to suspend the rules and pass the bill that would reauthorize the Debbie Smith DNA Backlog Grant Program through fiscal 2024, at the current funding level of $151 million annually. It would modify language describing eligible grant activities to prioritize the analysis of DNA samples from sexual assault and other violent crime cases, and samples from cases without a suspect. It would require state and local DNA testing laboratories that receive grant funding to prioritize samples from homicides and sexual assaults. It would also reauthorize through fiscal 2024 two associated Justice Department grant programs regarding training and education on the collection and analysis of DNA samples and evidence related to sexual assault. Motion agreed to 402-1: R 178-0; D 224-0; I 0-1. *Note: A two-thirds majority of those present and voting (269 in this case) is required for passage under suspension of the rules.* Oct. 23, 2019.

585. HR2440. Harbor Maintenance Fund Caps - Passage. DeFazio, D-Ore., motion to suspend the rules and pass the bill that would adjust discretionary caps for expenditures from the Harbor Maintenance Trust Fund, establishing annual cap adjustments based on the balance of the fund at the end of the fiscal year two years prior. Under the bill's provisions, amounts appropriated from the fund to be used for harbor maintenance and operations would not be subject to regular discretionary spending caps. It would also require the annual Treasury Department report on the fund to include a description of expected expenditures to meet the navigation needs for the next fiscal year. Motion agreed to 296-109: R 79-107; D 217-1; I 0-1. *Note: A two-thirds majority of those present and voting (270 in this case) is required for passage under suspension of the rules.* Oct. 28, 2019.

586. HR2115. Drug Price Disclosures - Passage. Schakowsky, D-Ill., motion to suspend the rules and pass the bill that would require the Health and Human Services Department to make publicly available information disclosed by pharmacy benefit managers related to the negotiation of rebates and discounts for prescription drugs. It would require prescription drug plan sponsors to implement real-time benefit tools, integrated with electronic prescribing or health record systems, that would transmit information to patients related to the price and availability of alternative prescription drugs. Motion agreed to 403-0: R 184-0; D 218-0; I 1-0. *Note: A two-thirds majority of those present and voting (269 in this case) is required for passage under suspension of the rules.* Oct. 28, 2019.

587. HRES296. Armenian Genocide Recognition - Previous Question. McGovern, D-Mass., motion to order the previous question (thus ending debate and possibility of amendment) on the rule (H Res 655) that would provide for House floor consideration of a resolution (H Res 296) titled, "A resolution affirming the United States record on the Armenian Genocide." Motion agreed to 224-189: R 0-189; D 223-0; I 1-0. Oct. 29, 2019.

588. HRES296. Armenian Genocide Recognition - Rule. Adoption of the rule (H Res 655) that would provide for House floor consideration of a resolution (H Res 296) titled, "A resolution affirming the United States record on the Armenian Genocide." Adopted 223-191: R 0-190; D 222-1; I 1-0. Oct. 29, 2019.

		583	584	585	586	587	588
ALABAMA							
1	**Byrne**	N	Y	Y	Y	N	N
2	**Roby**	N	Y	?	?	N	N
3	**Rogers, M.**	N	Y	N	Y	N	N
4	**Aderholt**	N	Y	N	Y	N	N
5	**Brooks, M.**	N	Y	N	Y	N	N
6	**Palmer**	N	Y	N	Y	N	N
7	Sewell	Y	Y	Y	Y	Y	Y
ALASKA							
AL	**Young**	N	Y	Y	Y	N	N
ARIZONA							
1	O'Halleran	Y	Y	Y	Y	Y	Y
2	Kirkpatrick	Y	Y	Y	Y	Y	Y
3	Grijalva	Y	Y	Y	Y	Y	Y
4	**Gosar**	N	Y	?	?	N	N
5	**Biggs**	N	Y	N	Y	N	N
6	**Schweikert**	N	Y	N	Y	N	N
7	Gallego	Y	Y	Y	Y	Y	Y
8	**Lesko**	N	Y	N	Y	N	N
9	Stanton	Y	Y	Y	Y	Y	Y
ARKANSAS							
1	**Crawford**	N	Y	N	Y	N	N
2	**Hill, F.**	N	Y	N	Y	N	N
3	**Womack**	N	Y	N	Y	N	N
4	**Westerman**	N	Y	Y	Y	N	N
CALIFORNIA							
1	**LaMalfa**	N	Y	Y	Y	N	N
2	Huffman	Y	Y	+	+	+	+
3	Garamendi	Y	Y	Y	Y	Y	Y
4	**McClintock**	N	Y	N	Y	N	N
5	Thompson, M.	Y	Y	+	+	+	+
6	Matsui	Y	Y	Y	Y	Y	Y
7	Bera	Y	Y	Y	Y	Y	Y
8	**Cook**	N	Y	Y	Y	N	N
9	McNerney	Y	Y	Y	Y	Y	Y
10	Harder	Y	Y	Y	Y	Y	Y
11	DeSaulnier	Y	Y	Y	Y	Y	Y
12	Pelosi						
13	Lee B.	Y	Y	Y	Y	Y	Y
14	Speier	Y	Y	Y	Y	Y	Y
15	Swalwell	Y	Y	Y	Y	Y	Y
16	Costa	Y	Y	+	+	Y	Y
17	Khanna	Y	Y	Y	Y	Y	Y
18	Eshoo	Y	Y	Y	Y	Y	Y
19	Lofgren	Y	Y	Y	Y	Y	Y
20	Panetta	Y	Y	Y	Y	Y	Y
21	Cox	Y	Y	?	?	Y	Y
22	**Nunes**	N	Y	N	Y	N	N
23	**McCarthy**	N	Y	N	Y	N	N
24	Carbajal	Y	Y	Y	Y	Y	Y
25	Hill, K.	Y	Y	?	?	?	?
26	Brownley	Y	Y	Y	Y	Y	Y
27	Chu	Y	Y	Y	Y	Y	Y
28	Schiff	Y	Y	Y	Y	Y	Y
29	Cárdenas	Y	Y	Y	Y	Y	Y
30	Sherman	Y	Y	Y	Y	Y	Y
31	Aguilar	Y	Y	Y	Y	Y	Y
32	Napolitano	Y	Y	Y	Y	Y	Y
33	Lieu	Y	Y	Y	Y	Y	Y
34	Gomez	Y	Y	Y	Y	Y	Y
35	Torres	Y	Y	Y	Y	Y	Y
36	Ruiz	Y	Y	Y	Y	Y	Y
37	Bass	Y	?	Y	Y	?	?
38	Sánchez	Y	Y	Y	Y	Y	Y
39	Cisneros	Y	Y	Y	Y	Y	Y
40	Roybal-Allard	Y	Y	Y	Y	Y	Y
41	Takano	+	+	Y	Y	Y	Y
42	**Calvert**	N	Y	Y	Y	N	N
43	Waters	Y	Y	Y	Y	Y	Y
44	Barragán	Y	Y	Y	Y	Y	Y
45	Porter	Y	Y	Y	Y	Y	Y
46	Correa	Y	Y	Y	Y	Y	Y
47	Lowenthal	Y	Y	Y	Y	Y	Y
48	Rouda	Y	Y	Y	Y	Y	Y
49	Levin	Y	Y	Y	Y	Y	Y
50	**Hunter**	N	Y	Y	Y	N	N
51	Vargas	Y	Y	Y	Y	Y	Y
52	Peters	+	+	Y	Y	Y	Y
53	Davis, S.	Y	Y	Y	Y	Y	Y
COLORADO							
1	DeGette	Y	Y	Y	Y	Y	Y
2	Neguse	Y	Y	Y	Y	Y	Y
3	**Tipton**	N	Y	N	Y	N	N
4	**Buck**	N	Y	N	Y	N	N
5	**Lamborn**	N	Y	?	?	N	N
6	Crow	Y	Y	Y	Y	Y	Y
7	Perlmutter	Y	Y	Y	Y	Y	Y
CONNECTICUT							
1	Larson	Y	Y	Y	Y	Y	Y
2	Courtney	Y	Y	Y	Y	Y	Y
3	DeLauro	Y	Y	Y	Y	Y	Y
4	Himes	Y	Y	Y	Y	Y	Y
5	Hayes	Y	Y	Y	Y	Y	Y
DELAWARE							
AL	Blunt Rochester	Y	Y	Y	Y	Y	Y
FLORIDA							
1	**Gaetz**	N	Y	N	Y	N	N
2	**Dunn**	N	Y	Y	Y	N	N
3	**Yoho**	N	Y	Y	Y	N	N
4	**Rutherford**	N	Y	Y	Y	N	N
5	Lawson	Y	Y	Y	Y	Y	Y
6	**Waltz**	N	Y	Y	Y	N	N
7	Murphy	Y	Y	Y	Y	Y	Y
8	**Posey**	N	Y	Y	Y	N	N
9	Soto	Y	Y	Y	Y	Y	Y
10	Demings	Y	Y	Y	Y	Y	Y
11	**Webster**	N	Y	Y	Y	N	N
12	**Bilirakis**	?	?	Y	Y	N	N
13	Crist	Y	Y	Y	Y	Y	Y
14	Castor	Y	Y	Y	Y	Y	Y
15	**Spano**	N	Y	Y	Y	N	N
16	**Buchanan**	N	Y	Y	Y	N	N
17	**Steube**	?	?	N	Y	N	N
18	**Mast**	N	Y	Y	Y	N	N
19	**Rooney**	N	Y	?	?	N	N
20	Hastings	Y	Y	Y	Y	Y	Y
21	Frankel	Y	Y	Y	Y	Y	Y
22	Deutch	Y	Y	Y	Y	Y	Y
23	Wasserman Schultz	Y	Y	Y	Y	Y	Y
24	Wilson, F.	Y	Y	Y	Y	Y	Y
25	**Diaz-Balart**	N	Y	N	Y	N	N
26	Mucarsel-Powell	Y	Y	Y	Y	Y	Y
27	Shalala	Y	Y	Y	Y	Y	Y
GEORGIA							
1	**Carter, E.L.**	N	Y	N	Y	N	N
2	Bishop, S.	Y	Y	Y	Y	Y	Y
3	**Ferguson**	N	Y	N	Y	N	N
4	Johnson, H.	Y	Y	Y	Y	Y	Y
5	Lewis John	Y	Y	Y	Y	Y	Y
6	McBath	Y	Y	Y	Y	Y	Y
7	**Woodall**	N	Y	N	Y	N	N
8	**Scott, A.**	N	Y	N	Y	N	N
9	**Collins, D.**	-	+	N	Y	N	N
10	**Hice**	N	Y	-	+	-	-
11	**Loudermilk**	N	Y	N	Y	N	N
12	**Allen**	N	Y	N	Y	N	N
13	Scott, D.	Y	Y	Y	Y	Y	Y
14	**Graves, T.**	N	Y	N	Y	N	N
HAWAII							
1	Case	Y	Y	Y	Y	Y	Y
2	Gabbard	?	?	Y	Y	?	?
IDAHO							
1	**Fulcher**	N	Y	N	Y	N	N
2	**Simpson**	N	Y	Y	Y	N	N
ILLINOIS							
1	Rush	Y	Y	Y	Y	Y	Y
2	Kelly, R.	Y	Y	Y	Y	Y	Y
3	Lipinski	Y	Y	Y	Y	Y	Y
4	García, J.	Y	Y	Y	Y	Y	Y
5	Quigley	Y	Y	Y	Y	Y	Y
6	Casten	Y	Y	Y	Y	Y	Y
7	Davis, D.	Y	Y	Y	Y	Y	Y
8	Krishnamoorthi	Y	Y	Y	Y	Y	Y
9	Schakowsky	Y	Y	Y	Y	Y	Y
10	Schneider	Y	Y	Y	Y	Y	Y
11	Foster	Y	Y	Y	Y	Y	Y

KEY: **Republicans** Democrats *Independents*

Y	Voted for (yea)	N	Voted against (nay)	P	Voted "present"
+	Announced for	-	Announced against	?	Did not vote or otherwise make position known
#	Paired for	X	Paired against		

	583	584	585	586	587	588
12 **Bost**	N	Y	Y	Y	N	N
13 **Davis, R.**	N	Y	Y	Y	-	-
14 Underwood	Y	Y	Y	Y	Y	Y
15 **Shimkus**	N	Y	Y	Y	N	N
16 **Kinzinger**	N	Y	Y	Y	N	N
17 Bustos	Y	Y	Y	Y	Y	Y
18 **LaHood**	N	Y	N	Y	N	N
INDIANA						
1 Visclosky	Y	Y	Y	Y	Y	Y
2 **Walorski**	N	Y	Y	Y	N	N
3 **Banks**	N	Y	N	Y	N	N
4 **Baird**	N	Y	Y	Y	N	N
5 **Brooks, S.**	N	Y	Y	Y	N	N
6 **Pence**	N	Y	Y	Y	N	N
7 Carson	Y	Y	Y	Y	Y	Y
8 **Bucshon**	N	Y	Y	Y	N	N
9 **Hollingsworth**	N	Y	Y	Y	N	N
IOWA						
1 Finkenauer	Y	Y	Y	Y	Y	Y
2 Loebsack	Y	Y	Y	Y	Y	Y
3 Axne	Y	Y	Y	Y	Y	Y
4 **King, S.**	N	Y	N	Y	N	N
KANSAS						
1 **Marshall**	N	Y	N	Y	N	N
2 **Watkins**	N	Y	N	Y	N	N
3 Davids	Y	?	Y	Y	Y	Y
4 **Estes**	-	+	N	Y	N	N
KENTUCKY						
1 **Comer**	N	Y	N	Y	N	N
2 **Guthrie**	N	Y	N	Y	N	N
3 Yarmuth	Y	Y	Y	Y	Y	Y
4 **Massie**	N	Y	N	Y	N	N
5 **Rogers, H.**	N	Y	N	Y	N	N
6 **Barr**	N	Y	N	Y	N	N
LOUISIANA						
1 **Scalise**	N	Y	Y	Y	N	N
2 Richmond	Y	Y	Y	Y	Y	Y
3 **Higgins, C.**	N	Y	Y	Y	N	N
4 **Johnson, M.**	N	Y	Y	Y	N	N
5 **Abraham**	N	Y	Y	Y	N	N
6 **Graves, G.**	N	Y	Y	Y	N	N
MAINE						
1 Pingree	Y	Y	Y	Y	Y	Y
2 Golden	Y	Y	Y	Y	Y	Y
MARYLAND						
1 **Harris**	N	Y	N	Y	N	N
2 Ruppersberger	Y	Y	Y	Y	Y	Y
3 Sarbanes	Y	Y	Y	Y	Y	Y
4 Brown, A.	Y	Y	Y	Y	Y	Y
5 Hoyer	Y	Y	Y	Y	Y	Y
6 Trone	Y	Y	Y	Y	Y	Y
7 vacant						
8 Raskin	Y	?	Y	Y	Y	Y
MASSACHUSETTS						
1 Neal	Y	Y	Y	Y	Y	Y
2 McGovern	Y	Y	Y	Y	Y	Y
3 Trahan	Y	Y	Y	Y	Y	Y
4 Kennedy	Y	Y	?	?	Y	Y
5 Clark	Y	Y	Y	Y	Y	Y
6 Moulton	Y	Y	Y	Y	+	+
7 Pressley	Y	Y	Y	Y	Y	Y
8 Lynch	Y	Y	Y	Y	Y	Y
9 Keating	Y	Y	Y	Y	Y	Y
MICHIGAN						
1 **Bergman**	N	Y	Y	Y	N	N
2 **Huizenga**	N	Y	Y	Y	N	N
3 *Amash*	N	N	N	Y	Y	Y
4 **Moolenaar**	N	Y	N	Y	N	N
5 Kildee	Y	Y	Y	Y	Y	Y
6 **Upton**	N	Y	Y	Y	N	N
7 **Walberg**	N	Y	Y	Y	N	N
8 Slotkin	Y	Y	Y	Y	Y	Y
9 Levin	Y	Y	Y	Y	Y	Y
10 **Mitchell**	?	?	Y	Y	N	N
11 Stevens	Y	Y	Y	Y	Y	Y
12 Dingell	Y	Y	Y	Y	Y	Y
13 Tlaib	Y	Y	Y	Y	Y	Y
14 Lawrence	Y	Y	Y	Y	Y	Y
MINNESOTA						
1 **Hagedorn**	N	Y	Y	Y	N	N
2 Craig	Y	Y	Y	Y	Y	Y
3 Phillips	Y	Y	Y	Y	Y	Y
4 McCollum	Y	Y	Y	Y	Y	Y
5 Omar	Y	Y	+	Y	Y	Y

	583	584	585	586	587	588
6 **Emmer**	N	Y	Y	Y	N	N
7 Peterson	N	Y	Y	Y	Y	Y
8 **Stauber**	N	Y	Y	Y	N	N
MISSISSIPPI						
1 **Kelly, T.**	N	Y	N	Y	N	N
2 Thompson, B.	Y	Y	Y	Y	Y	Y
3 **Guest**	N	Y	N	Y	N	N
4 **Palazzo**	N	Y	Y	Y	N	N
MISSOURI						
1 Clay	Y	Y	Y	Y	Y	Y
2 **Wagner**	N	Y	Y	Y	N	N
3 **Luetkemeyer**	N	Y	N	?	N	N
4 **Hartzler**	N	Y	Y	Y	N	N
5 Cleaver	Y	+	Y	Y	Y	Y
6 **Graves, S.**	N	Y	Y	Y	N	N
7 **Long**	N	Y	N	Y	?	N
8 **Smith, J.**	N	Y	N	Y	N	N
MONTANA						
AL **Gianforte**	N	Y	N	Y	N	N
NEBRASKA						
1 **Fortenberry**	N	Y	N	Y	N	N
2 **Bacon**	N	Y	Y	Y	N	N
3 **Smith, Adrian**	N	Y	N	Y	N	N
NEVADA						
1 Titus	Y	Y	Y	Y	Y	Y
2 **Amodei**	?	?	Y	Y	N	N
3 Lee	Y	Y	Y	Y	Y	Y
4 Horsford	Y	Y	Y	Y	Y	Y
NEW HAMPSHIRE						
1 Pappas	Y	Y	Y	Y	Y	Y
2 Kuster	Y	Y	Y	Y	Y	Y
NEW JERSEY						
1 Norcross	Y	Y	Y	Y	Y	Y
2 Van Drew	Y	Y	Y	Y	Y	Y
3 Kim	Y	Y	Y	Y	Y	Y
4 **Smith, C.**	N	Y	Y	Y	N	N
5 Gottheimer	Y	Y	Y	Y	Y	Y
6 Pallone	Y	Y	Y	Y	Y	Y
7 Malinowski	Y	Y	Y	Y	Y	Y
8 Sires	Y	Y	Y	Y	Y	Y
9 Pascrell	Y	Y	Y	Y	Y	N
10 Payne	Y	Y	Y	Y	Y	Y
11 Sherrill	Y	Y	Y	Y	Y	Y
12 Watson Coleman	Y	Y	Y	Y	Y	Y
NEW MEXICO						
1 Haaland	Y	Y	Y	Y	Y	Y
2 Torres Small	Y	Y	Y	Y	Y	Y
3 Luján	Y	Y	Y	Y	Y	Y
NEW YORK						
1 **Zeldin**	N	Y	Y	Y	N	N
2 **King, P.**	N	Y	Y	Y	N	N
3 Suozzi	Y	Y	Y	Y	Y	Y
4 Rice, K.	Y	Y	Y	Y	Y	Y
5 Meeks	Y	Y	?	?	Y	Y
6 Meng	Y	Y	?	?	Y	Y
7 Velázquez	Y	Y	Y	Y	Y	Y
8 Jeffries	Y	Y	Y	Y	Y	Y
9 Clarke	Y	Y	Y	Y	Y	Y
10 Nadler	Y	Y	Y	Y	Y	Y
11 Rose	Y	Y	Y	Y	Y	Y
12 Maloney, C.	Y	Y	Y	Y	Y	Y
13 Espaillat	Y	Y	Y	Y	Y	Y
14 Ocasio-Cortez	Y	Y	Y	Y	Y	Y
15 Serrano	Y	Y	Y	Y	Y	Y
16 Engel	Y	Y	Y	Y	Y	Y
17 Lowey	Y	Y	Y	Y	Y	Y
18 Maloney, S.P.	Y	Y	Y	Y	Y	Y
19 Delgado	Y	Y	Y	Y	Y	Y
20 Tonko	Y	Y	Y	Y	Y	Y
21 **Stefanik**	N	Y	Y	Y	N	N
22 Brindisi	Y	Y	Y	Y	Y	Y
23 **Reed**	N	Y	N	Y	N	N
24 **Katko**	N	Y	Y	Y	N	N
25 Morelle	Y	Y	Y	Y	Y	Y
26 Higgins, B.	Y	Y	Y	Y	Y	Y
27 vacant						
NORTH CAROLINA						
1 Butterfield	Y	Y	Y	Y	Y	Y
2 **Holding**	N	Y	N	Y	N	N
3 **Murphy**	N	Y	Y	Y	N	N
4 Price	Y	Y	Y	Y	Y	Y
5 **Foxx**	N	Y	N	Y	N	N
6 **Walker**	N	Y	N	Y	N	N
7 **Rouzer**	N	Y	Y	Y	N	N

	583	584	585	586	587	588
8 **Hudson**	N	Y	N	Y	N	N
9 **Bishop**	N	Y	N	Y	N	N
10 **McHenry**	N	Y	N	Y	N	N
11 **Meadows**	N	Y	N	Y	N	N
12 Adams	Y	Y	Y	Y	Y	Y
13 **Budd**	N	Y	N	Y	N	N
NORTH DAKOTA						
AL **Armstrong**	?	?	N	Y	N	N
OHIO						
1 **Chabot**	N	Y	N	Y	N	N
2 **Wenstrup**	N	Y	N	Y	N	N
3 Beatty	Y	Y	+	+	+	+
4 **Jordan**	N	Y	N	Y	N	N
5 **Latta**	N	Y	N	Y	N	N
6 **Johnson, B.**	N	Y	N	Y	N	N
7 **Gibbs**	N	Y	Y	Y	N	N
8 **Davidson**	N	Y	N	Y	N	N
9 Kaptur	Y	Y	Y	Y	Y	Y
10 **Turner**	N	Y	N	Y	N	N
11 Fudge	Y	Y	Y	Y	Y	Y
12 **Balderson**	N	Y	Y	Y	N	N
13 Ryan	Y	Y	?	?	?	?
14 **Joyce**	N	Y	Y	Y	N	N
15 **Stivers**	?	?	N	Y	N	N
16 **Gonzalez**	N	Y	Y	Y	N	N
OKLAHOMA						
1 **Hern**	N	Y	N	Y	N	N
2 **Mullin**	N	Y	Y	Y	N	N
3 **Lucas**	N	Y	Y	Y	N	N
4 **Cole**	N	Y	N	Y	N	N
5 Horn	Y	Y	Y	Y	Y	Y
OREGON						
1 Bonamici	Y	Y	Y	Y	Y	Y
2 **Walden**	N	Y	Y	Y	N	N
3 Blumenauer	Y	Y	Y	Y	Y	Y
4 DeFazio	Y	Y	Y	Y	Y	Y
5 Schrader	Y	Y	Y	Y	Y	Y
PENNSYLVANIA						
1 **Fitzpatrick**	N	Y	Y	Y	N	N
2 Boyle	Y	Y	Y	Y	Y	Y
3 Evans	Y	Y	Y	Y	Y	Y
4 Dean	Y	Y	Y	Y	Y	Y
5 Scanlon	Y	Y	Y	Y	Y	Y
6 Houlahan	Y	Y	Y	Y	Y	Y
7 Wild	Y	Y	Y	?	Y	Y
8 Cartwright	Y	Y	?	?	?	?
9 **Meuser**	?	?	N	Y	N	N
10 **Perry**	N	Y	N	Y	N	N
11 **Smucker**	-	+	N	Y	N	N
12 **Keller**	-	?	N	Y	N	N
13 **Joyce**	?	?	N	Y	N	N
14 **Reschenthaler**	?	?	Y	Y	N	N
15 **Thompson, G.**	+	+	Y	Y	N	N
16 **Kelly, M.**	?	+	Y	Y	N	N
17 Lamb	Y	Y	Y	Y	Y	Y
18 Doyle	Y	Y	?	?	Y	Y
RHODE ISLAND						
1 Cicilline	Y	Y	Y	Y	Y	Y
2 Langevin	Y	Y	Y	Y	Y	Y
SOUTH CAROLINA						
1 Cunningham	Y	Y	Y	Y	Y	Y
2 **Wilson, J.**	N	Y	Y	Y	N	N
3 **Duncan**	N	Y	N	Y	N	N
4 **Timmons**	-	+	-	+	-	-
5 **Norman**	N	?	N	Y	N	N
6 Clyburn	Y	Y	Y	Y	Y	Y
7 **Rice, T.**	N	Y	N	Y	N	N
SOUTH DAKOTA						
AL **Johnson**	N	Y	N	Y	N	N
TENNESSEE						
1 **Roe**	N	Y	N	Y	N	N
2 **Burchett**	N	Y	N	Y	N	N
3 **Fleischmann**	N	Y	N	Y	N	N
4 **DesJarlais**	N	Y	N	Y	N	N
5 Cooper	Y	Y	Y	Y	Y	Y
6 **Rose**	N	Y	N	Y	N	N
7 **Green**	N	Y	N	Y	N	N
8 **Kustoff**	N	Y	N	Y	N	N
9 Cohen	Y	Y	Y	Y	Y	Y
TEXAS						
1 **Gohmert**	N	Y	?	?	N	N
2 **Crenshaw**	N	Y	N	Y	N	N
3 **Taylor**	N	Y	N	Y	N	N
4 **Ratcliffe**	N	Y	N	Y	N	N

	583	584	585	586	587	588
5 **Gooden**	N	Y	N	Y	N	N
6 **Wright**	N	Y	?	?	?	?
7 Fletcher	Y	Y	Y	Y	Y	Y
8 **Brady**	N	Y	N	Y	N	N
9 Green, A.	Y	Y	Y	Y	Y	Y
10 **McCaul**	N	Y	Y	Y	N	N
11 **Conaway**	N	Y	N	Y	N	N
12 **Granger**	N	Y	N	Y	N	N
13 **Thornberry**	N	Y	N	Y	N	N
14 **Weber**	N	Y	Y	Y	N	N
15 Gonzalez	Y	Y	Y	Y	Y	Y
16 Escobar	Y	Y	Y	Y	Y	Y
17 **Flores**	N	Y	N	Y	N	N
18 Jackson Lee	Y	Y	Y	Y	Y	Y
19 **Arrington**	N	Y	N	Y	N	N
20 Castro	Y	Y	Y	Y	Y	Y
21 **Roy**	N	Y	N	Y	N	N
22 **Olson**	N	Y	Y	Y	N	N
23 **Hurd**	N	Y	Y	Y	N	N
24 **Marchant**	N	Y	?	?	?	?
25 **Williams**	N	Y	?	?	?	?
26 **Burgess**	N	Y	N	Y	N	N
27 **Cloud**	N	Y	Y	Y	N	N
28 Cuellar	Y	Y	Y	Y	Y	Y
29 Garcia, S.	Y	Y	Y	Y	Y	Y
30 Johnson, E.B.	Y	Y	Y	Y	Y	Y
31 **Carter, J.**	N	Y	?	?	?	?
32 Allred	Y	Y	Y	Y	Y	Y
33 Veasey	Y	Y	Y	Y	Y	Y
34 Vela	Y	Y	Y	Y	Y	Y
35 Doggett	Y	Y	Y	Y	Y	Y
36 **Babin**	N	Y	Y	Y	N	N
UTAH						
1 **Bishop, R.**	N	Y	N	Y	N	N
2 **Stewart**	N	Y	N	Y	N	N
3 **Curtis**	N	Y	N	Y	N	N
4 McAdams	Y	Y	N	Y	Y	Y
VERMONT						
AL Welch	Y	Y	Y	Y	Y	Y
VIRGINIA						
1 **Wittman**	N	Y	Y	Y	N	N
2 Luria	Y	Y	Y	Y	Y	Y
3 Scott, R.	Y	Y	Y	Y	Y	Y
4 McEachin	+	+	+	+	+	+
5 **Riggleman**	N	Y	N	Y	N	N
6 **Cline**	N	Y	N	Y	N	N
7 Spanberger	Y	Y	Y	Y	Y	Y
8 Beyer	Y	Y	Y	Y	Y	Y
9 **Griffith**	N	Y	N	?	N	N
10 Wexton	Y	Y	Y	Y	Y	Y
11 Connolly	Y	Y	Y	Y	Y	Y
WASHINGTON						
1 DelBene	Y	Y	Y	Y	Y	Y
2 Larsen	Y	Y	Y	Y	Y	Y
3 **Herrera Beutler**	N	Y	Y	Y	N	N
4 **Newhouse**	N	Y	Y	Y	N	N
5 **McMorris Rodgers**	N	Y	Y	Y	N	N
6 Kilmer	Y	Y	Y	Y	Y	Y
7 Jayapal	Y	Y	Y	Y	Y	Y
8 Schrier	Y	Y	Y	Y	Y	Y
9 Smith Adam	Y	Y	Y	Y	Y	Y
10 Heck	Y	Y	Y	Y	Y	Y
WEST VIRGINIA						
1 **McKinley**	N	Y	Y	Y	N	N
2 **Mooney**	N	Y	N	Y	N	N
3 **Miller**	N	Y	Y	Y	N	N
WISCONSIN						
1 **Steil**	-	+	N	Y	N	N
2 Pocan	Y	Y	+	+	Y	Y
3 Kind	+	+	Y	Y	Y	Y
4 Moore	Y	Y	Y	Y	Y	Y
5 **Sensenbrenner**	N	Y	N	Y	N	N
6 **Grothman**	?	?	N	Y	N	N
7 **Duffy**						
8 **Gallagher**	N	Y	Y	Y	N	N
WYOMING						
AL **Cheney**	N	Y	N	Y	N	N
DELEGATES						
Radewagen (A.S.)						
Norton (D.C.)						
San Nicolas (Guam)						
Sablan (N. Marianas)						
González-Colón (P.R.)						
Plaskett (V.I.)						

ⅠⅠⅠ HOUSE VOTES

589. HR2181, HR823, HR1373. Colorado Federal Lands; Grand Canyon Leasing Ban; Chaco Lands Leasing Ban - Previous Question. Shalala, D-Fla., motion to order the previous question (thus ending debate and possibility of amendment) on the rule (H Res 656) that would provide for House floor consideration of the Colorado Outdoor Recreation and Economy Act (HR 823), the Grand Canyon Centennial Protection Act (HR 1373), and the Chaco Cultural Heritage Area Protection Act (HR 2181). The rule would provide for automatic adoption of a Grijalva, D-Ariz., manager's amendment to HR 823 and a Grijalva manager's amendment to HR 2181. Both manager's amendments would add standard language to their respective bills related to the determination of budgetary effects under statutory pay-as-you-go rules. The amendment to HR 823 would also designate a site along U.S. Route 24 in Colorado as the "Sandy Treat Overlook." The rule would also provide for floor consideration of six additional amendments to HR 823, three amendments to HR 1373, and four additional amendments to HR 2181. Motion agreed to 222-191: R 1-188; D 221-2; I 0-1. Oct. 29, 2019.

590. HR1373, HR823, HR2181. Colorado Federal Lands; Grand Canyon Leasing Ban; Chaco Lands Leasing Ban - Rule. Adoption of the rule (H Res 656) that would provide for House floor consideration of the Colorado Outdoor Recreation and Economy Act (HR 823), the Grand Canyon Centennial Protection Act (HR 1373), and the Chaco Cultural Heritage Area Protection Act (HR 2181). The rule would provide for automatic adoption of a Grijalva, D-Ariz., manager's amendment to HR 823 and a Grijalva manager's amendment to HR 2181. Both manager's amendments would add standard language to their respective bills related to the determination of budgetary effects under statutory pay-as-you-go rules. The amendment to HR 823 would also designate a site along U.S. Route 24 in Colorado as the "Sandy Treat Overlook." The rule would also provide for floor consideration of six additional amendments to HR 823, three amendments to HR 1373, and four additional amendments to HR 2181. Adopted 221-187: R 0-186; D 221-0; I 0-1. Oct. 29, 2019.

591. HRES296. Armenian Genocide Recognition - Passage. Agreeing to the resolution that would express the sense of the House that it is U.S. policy to officially recognize and commemorate the Armenian Genocide; reject efforts to associate the U.S. government with denial of the Armenian Genocide or any other genocide; and encourage public education on the Armenian Genocide, the role of the U.S. in the humanitarian relief effort, and the relevance of the genocide to modern crimes against humanity. Passed 405-11: R 178-11; D 226-0; I 1-0. Oct. 29, 2019.

592. HR4695. Turkey Sanctions - Passage. Engel, D-N.Y., motion to suspend the rules and pass the bill that would require the president to impose a number of sanctions related to the Turkish invasion of northern Syria. Specifically, it would require the president to impose asset-blocking and visa sanctions on senior Turkish officials involved in planning, facilitating, or leading the invasion, and on Turkish and other foreign financial institutions that have facilitated transactions for the Turkish defense industry related to the invasion. It would prohibit the export of any defense articles, services, or technology that could be used for Turkish military operations in northern Syria, and it would impose sanctions on any foreign persons who have provided such articles. The bill would also require the State and Defense Department to submit to Congress a number of plans and reports related to military conflict and Turkish activity in Syria, including a plan for U.S. assistance to the Syrian Democratic Forces and to minority communities affected by the Turkish invasion, and a strategy to prevent the resurgence of ISIS and its affiliates. Motion agreed to 403-16: R 176-15; D 226-1; I 1-0. *Note: A two-thirds majority of those present and voting (280 in this case) is required for passage under suspension of the rules.* Oct. 29, 2019.

593. HR2181. Chaco Lands Leasing Ban - Federal-State Land Transfers. Gosar, R-Ariz., amendment no. 2 that would allow the Interior Department to convey or exchange federal lands that would be withdrawn under the bill's provisions to or with state trust land entities. Rejected in Committee of the Whole 191-233: R 189-3; D 1-229; I 1-1. Oct. 30, 2019.

594. HR2181. Chaco Lands Leasing Ban - Impact on Native American Mineral Rights. Gosar, R-Ariz., amendment no. 3 that would postpone the effective date of the bill until the Interior Department determines that the withdrawal of lands from eligibility for mining and mineral leasing under the bill's provisions would not impact the developmental potential or economic value of mineral rights held by Native Americans in the greater Chaco region. Rejected in Committee of the Whole 181-243: R 180-13; D 1-228; I 0-2. Oct. 30, 2019.

	589	590	591	592	593	594
ALABAMA						
1 **Byrne**	N	N	Y	Y	Y	Y
2 **Roby**	N	N	Y	Y	Y	Y
3 **Rogers, M.**	N	N	N	Y	Y	Y
4 **Aderholt**	N	N	Y	Y	Y	Y
5 **Brooks, M.**	N	N	Y	Y	Y	Y
6 **Palmer**	N	N	Y	Y	Y	Y
7 Sewell	Y	Y	Y	N	N	N
ALASKA						
AL **Young**	N	N	Y	Y	Y	Y
ARIZONA						
1 O'Halleran	Y	Y	Y	Y	N	N
2 Kirkpatrick	Y	Y	Y	Y	N	N
3 Grijalva	Y	Y	Y	Y	N	N
4 **Gosar**	N	N	P	N	Y	Y
5 **Biggs**	N	N	Y	N	Y	Y
6 **Schweikert**	N	N	Y	Y	Y	Y
7 Gallego	Y	Y	Y	N	N	N
8 **Lesko**	N	N	Y	Y	Y	Y
9 Stanton	Y	Y	Y	Y	N	N
ARKANSAS						
1 **Crawford**	N	N	Y	Y	Y	Y
2 **Hill, F.**	N	N	Y	Y	Y	Y
3 **Womack**	N	N	Y	Y	Y	Y
4 **Westerman**	N	N	Y	Y	Y	Y
CALIFORNIA						
1 **LaMalfa**	N	N	Y	N	Y	Y
2 Huffman	+	+	+	+	N	N
3 Garamendi	Y	Y	Y	Y	N	N
4 **McClintock**	N	N	Y	Y	Y	Y
5 Thompson, M.	+	+	+	+	–	–
6 Matsui	Y	Y	Y	Y	N	N
7 Bera	Y	Y	Y	Y	N	N
8 **Cook**	N	N	Y	Y	Y	Y
9 McNerney	Y	Y	Y	Y	N	N
10 Harder	Y	Y	Y	Y	N	N
11 DeSaulnier	Y	Y	Y	Y	N	N
12 Pelosi			Y			
13 Lee B.	Y	Y	Y	Y	N	N
14 Speier	Y	Y	Y	Y	N	N
15 Swalwell	Y	Y	Y	Y	N	N
16 Costa	Y	Y	Y	Y	N	N
17 Khanna	Y	Y	Y	Y	N	N
18 Eshoo	Y	Y	Y	Y	N	N
19 Lofgren	Y	Y	Y	Y	N	N
20 Panetta	Y	Y	Y	Y	N	N
21 Cox	Y	Y	Y	Y	N	N
22 **Nunes**	N	N	Y	Y	Y	Y
23 **McCarthy**	N	N	Y	Y	Y	Y
24 Carbajal	Y	Y	Y	Y	N	N
25 Hill, K.	?	?	?	?	?	?
26 Brownley	Y	Y	Y	Y	N	N
27 Chu	Y	Y	Y	Y	N	N
28 Schiff	Y	Y	Y	Y	N	N
29 Cárdenas	Y	Y	Y	Y	N	N
30 Sherman	Y	Y	Y	Y	N	N
31 Aguilar	Y	Y	Y	Y	N	N
32 Napolitano	Y	Y	Y	Y	N	N
33 Lieu	Y	Y	Y	Y	N	N
34 Gomez	Y	Y	Y	Y	N	N
35 Torres	Y	Y	Y	N	N	N
36 Ruiz	Y	Y	Y	Y	N	N
37 Bass	?	?	Y	Y	N	N
38 Sánchez	Y	Y	Y	Y	N	N
39 Cisneros	Y	Y	Y	Y	N	N
40 Roybal-Allard	Y	Y	Y	Y	N	N
41 Takano	Y	Y	Y	Y	N	N
42 **Calvert**	N	N	Y	Y	Y	N
43 Waters	Y	Y	Y	Y	N	N
44 Barragán	Y	Y	Y	Y	N	N
45 Porter	Y	Y	Y	N	N	N
46 Correa	Y	Y	Y	N	N	N
47 Lowenthal	Y	Y	Y	N	N	N
48 Rouda	Y	Y	Y	Y	N	N
49 Levin	Y	Y	Y	Y	N	N
50 **Hunter**	N	N	Y	Y	Y	Y
51 Vargas	Y	Y	Y	Y	N	N
52 Peters	Y	Y	Y	N	N	N

	589	590	591	592	593	594
53 Davis, S.	Y	Y	Y	N	N	N
COLORADO						
1 DeGette	Y	Y	Y	Y	N	N
2 Neguse	Y	Y	Y	Y	N	N
3 **Tipton**	N	N	Y	Y	Y	Y
4 **Buck**	N	N	Y	Y	Y	Y
5 **Lamborn**	N	N	Y	Y	Y	Y
6 Crow	Y	Y	Y	Y	N	N
7 Perlmutter	Y	Y	Y	Y	N	N
CONNECTICUT						
1 Larson	Y	Y	Y	Y	N	N
2 Courtney	Y	Y	Y	Y	N	N
3 DeLauro	Y	Y	Y	Y	N	N
4 Himes	Y	Y	Y	Y	N	N
5 Hayes	Y	Y	Y	Y	N	N
DELAWARE						
AL Blunt Rochester	Y	Y	Y	Y	N	N
FLORIDA						
1 **Gaetz**	Y	N	Y	Y	Y	Y
2 **Dunn**	N	N	Y	Y	Y	Y
3 **Yoho**	N	N	Y	Y	Y	Y
4 **Rutherford**	N	N	Y	Y	Y	Y
5 Lawson	Y	Y	Y	Y	N	N
6 **Waltz**	N	N	Y	Y	Y	Y
7 Murphy	Y	Y	Y	Y	N	N
8 **Posey**	N	N	Y	Y	Y	Y
9 Soto	Y	Y	Y	Y	N	N
10 Demings	Y	Y	Y	Y	N	N
11 **Webster**	N	N	Y	Y	Y	Y
12 **Bilirakis**	N	N	Y	Y	Y	Y
13 Crist	Y	Y	Y	Y	N	N
14 Castor	Y	Y	Y	Y	N	N
15 **Spano**	N	N	Y	Y	Y	Y
16 **Buchanan**	N	N	Y	Y	Y	Y
17 **Steube**	N	N	Y	Y	Y	Y
18 **Mast**	N	N	Y	Y	Y	Y
19 **Rooney**	N	N	Y	Y	?	N
20 Hastings	Y	Y	Y	Y	N	N
21 Frankel	Y	?	Y	Y	N	N
22 Deutch	Y	Y	Y	Y	N	N
23 Wasserman Schultz	Y	?	Y	Y	N	N
24 Wilson, F.	Y	Y	Y	Y	N	N
25 **Diaz-Balart**	N	N	Y	Y	Y	Y
26 Mucarsel-Powell	Y	Y	Y	Y	N	N
27 Shalala	Y	Y	Y	Y	N	N
GEORGIA						
1 **Carter, E.L.**	N	N	Y	Y	Y	Y
2 Bishop, S.	Y	Y	Y	Y	N	N
3 **Ferguson**	N	N	Y	N	Y	Y
4 Johnson, H.	Y	Y	Y	Y	N	N
5 Lewis John	Y	Y	Y	Y	N	N
6 McBath	Y	Y	Y	Y	N	N
7 **Woodall**	N	N	Y	Y	Y	Y
8 **Scott, A.**	N	N	Y	Y	Y	Y
9 **Collins, D.**	N	N	Y	Y	Y	Y
10 **Hice**	–	–	+	+	+	+
11 **Loudermilk**	N	N	Y	N	Y	Y
12 **Allen**	N	N	Y	N	Y	Y
13 Scott, D.	Y	Y	Y	Y	N	N
14 **Graves, T.**	N	N	Y	Y	N	N
HAWAII						
1 Case	Y	Y	Y	Y	N	?
2 Gabbard	?	?	Y	?	?	?
IDAHO						
1 **Fulcher**	N	N	Y	Y	Y	Y
2 **Simpson**	N	N	Y	Y	Y	N
ILLINOIS						
1 Rush	Y	Y	Y	Y	N	N
2 Kelly, R.	Y	Y	Y	Y	?	N
3 Lipinski	Y	Y	Y	Y	N	N
4 García, J.	Y	Y	Y	Y	N	N
5 Quigley	Y	Y	Y	Y	N	N
6 Casten	Y	Y	Y	Y	N	N
7 Davis, D.	Y	Y	Y	Y	N	N
8 Krishnamoorthi	Y	Y	Y	Y	N	N
9 Schakowsky	Y	Y	Y	Y	N	N
10 Schneider	Y	Y	Y	Y	N	N
11 Foster	Y	Y	Y	Y	N	N

KEY:	**Republicans**	Democrats	*Independents*

Y Voted for (yea)	**N** Voted against (nay)	**P** Voted "present"
+ Announced for	**–** Announced against	**?** Did not vote or otherwise
# Paired for	**X** Paired against	make position known

		589	590	591	592	593	594
12	**Bost**	N	N	Y	Y	Y	Y
13	**Davis, R.**	N	N	Y	Y	Y	Y
14	Underwood	Y	Y	Y	Y	N	N
15	**Shimkus**	N	N	Y	Y	Y	Y
16	**Kinzinger**	N	N	Y	Y	Y	Y
17	Bustos	Y	Y	Y	Y	N	N
18	**LaHood**	N	N	Y	Y	Y	Y
INDIANA							
1	Visclosky	Y	Y	Y	Y	N	N
2	**Walorski**	N	N	Y	Y	Y	Y
3	**Banks**	N	N	Y	Y	Y	Y
4	**Baird**	N	N	N	N	Y	Y
5	**Brooks, S.**	N	N	N	Y	Y	Y
6	**Pence**	N	N	N	N	Y	Y
7	Carson	Y	Y	Y	Y	N	N
8	**Bucshon**	N	N	N	Y	Y	Y
9	**Hollingsworth**	N	N	Y	Y	Y	Y
IOWA							
1	Finkenauer	Y	Y	Y	Y	N	N
2	Loebsack	Y	Y	Y	Y	N	N
3	Axne	Y	Y	Y	Y	N	N
4	**King, S.**	N	N	Y	Y	Y	Y
KANSAS							
1	**Marshall**	N	N	Y	Y	Y	Y
2	**Watkins**	N	N	Y	Y	Y	Y
3	Davids	Y	Y	Y	Y	N	N
4	**Estes**	N	N	Y	Y	Y	Y
KENTUCKY							
1	**Comer**	N	N	Y	Y	Y	Y
2	**Guthrie**	N	N	Y	Y	Y	Y
3	Yarmuth	Y	Y	Y	Y	N	N
4	**Massie**	N	N	Y	N	Y	Y
5	**Rogers, H.**	N	N	Y	Y	Y	Y
6	**Barr**	N	N	Y	Y	Y	Y
LOUISIANA							
1	**Scalise**	N	N	Y	Y	Y	Y
2	Richmond	Y	Y	Y	Y	N	N
3	**Higgins, C.**	N	N	Y	Y	Y	Y
4	**Johnson, M.**	N	N	Y	Y	Y	Y
5	**Abraham**	N	N	Y	N	Y	Y
6	**Graves, G.**	N	N	Y	Y	Y	Y
MAINE							
1	Pingree	Y	Y	Y	Y	N	N
2	Golden	Y	Y	Y	Y	N	N
MARYLAND							
1	**Harris**	N	N	N	Y	Y	Y
2	Ruppersberger	Y	Y	Y	Y	N	N
3	Sarbanes	Y	Y	Y	Y	N	N
4	Brown, A.	Y	Y	Y	Y	N	N
5	Hoyer	Y	Y	Y	Y	N	N
6	Trone	Y	Y	Y	Y	N	N
7	vacant						
8	Raskin	Y	Y	Y	Y	N	N
MASSACHUSETTS							
1	Neal	Y	Y	Y	Y	N	N
2	McGovern	Y	Y	Y	Y	N	N
3	Trahan	Y	Y	Y	Y	N	N
4	Kennedy	Y	Y	Y	Y	N	N
5	Clark	Y	Y	Y	Y	N	N
6	Moulton	+	Y	Y	Y	N	N
7	Pressley	Y	Y	Y	Y	N	N
8	Lynch	Y	Y	Y	Y	N	N
9	Keating	Y	Y	Y	Y	N	N
MICHIGAN							
1	**Bergman**	N	N	Y	Y	Y	Y
2	**Huizenga**	N	N	Y	Y	Y	Y
3	*Amash*	N	N	Y	Y	Y	N
4	**Moolenaar**	N	N	Y	Y	Y	Y
5	Kildee	Y	Y	Y	Y	N	N
6	**Upton**	N	N	Y	Y	Y	N
7	**Walberg**	N	N	Y	Y	Y	Y
8	Slotkin	Y	Y	Y	Y	N	N
9	Levin	Y	Y	Y	Y	N	N
10	**Mitchell**	N	N	Y	Y	Y	Y
11	Stevens	Y	Y	Y	Y	N	N
12	Dingell	Y	Y	Y	Y	N	N
13	Tlaib	Y	Y	Y	Y	N	N
14	Lawrence	Y	Y	Y	Y	N	?
MINNESOTA							
1	**Hagedorn**	N	N	Y	Y	Y	Y
2	Craig	Y	Y	Y	Y	N	N
3	Phillips	Y	Y	Y	Y	N	N
4	McCollum	Y	Y	Y	Y	N	N
5	Omar	Y	Y	P	N	N	N
6	**Emmer**	N	N	Y	Y	Y	Y
7	Peterson	Y	Y	Y	Y	N	N
8	**Stauber**	N	N	Y	Y	Y	Y
MISSISSIPPI							
1	**Kelly, T.**	N	N	Y	N	Y	Y
2	Thompson, B.	Y	Y	Y	Y	N	N
3	**Guest**	N	N	Y	N	Y	Y
4	**Palazzo**	N	N	Y	Y	Y	Y
MISSOURI							
1	Clay	Y	Y	Y	Y	N	N
2	**Wagner**	N	N	Y	Y	Y	Y
3	**Luetkemeyer**	N	N	Y	Y	Y	Y
4	**Hartzler**	N	N	Y	Y	Y	Y
5	Cleaver	Y	Y	Y	Y	N	N
6	**Graves, S.**	N	N	Y	Y	Y	Y
7	**Long**	N	N	Y	Y	Y	Y
8	**Smith, J.**	N	N	Y	Y	Y	Y
MONTANA							
AL	**Gianforte**	N	N	Y	Y	Y	Y
NEBRASKA							
1	**Fortenberry**	N	N	Y	Y	Y	N
2	**Bacon**	N	N	Y	Y	Y	Y
3	**Smith, Adrian**	N	N	Y	Y	Y	Y
NEVADA							
1	Titus	Y	Y	Y	Y	N	N
2	**Amodei**	N	N	Y	Y	Y	Y
3	Lee	Y	Y	Y	Y	N	N
4	Horsford	Y	Y	Y	Y	N	N
NEW HAMPSHIRE							
1	Pappas	Y	Y	Y	Y	N	N
2	Kuster	Y	Y	Y	Y	N	N
NEW JERSEY							
1	Norcross	Y	Y	Y	Y	N	N
2	Van Drew	Y	Y	Y	Y	N	N
3	Kim	Y	Y	Y	Y	N	N
4	**Smith, C.**	N	N	Y	Y	Y	N
5	Gottheimer	Y	Y	Y	Y	N	N
6	Pallone	Y	Y	Y	Y	N	N
7	Malinowski	Y	Y	Y	Y	N	N
8	Sires	Y	Y	Y	Y	N	N
9	Pascrell	Y	Y	Y	Y	N	N
10	Payne	Y	Y	Y	Y	N	N
11	Sherrill	Y	Y	Y	Y	N	N
12	Watson Coleman	Y	Y	Y	Y	N	N
NEW MEXICO							
1	Haaland	Y	Y	Y	Y	N	N
2	Torres Small	N	Y	Y	Y	N	N
3	Luján	Y	Y	Y	Y	N	N
NEW YORK							
1	**Zeldin**	N	N	?	?	Y	Y
2	**King, P.**	N	N	Y	Y	Y	N
3	Suozzi	Y	Y	Y	Y	N	N
4	Rice, K.	Y	Y	Y	Y	N	N
5	Meeks	Y	Y	Y	Y	N	N
6	Meng	Y	Y	Y	Y	N	N
7	Velázquez	Y	Y	Y	Y	N	N
8	Jeffries	Y	Y	Y	Y	N	N
9	Clarke	Y	Y	Y	Y	N	N
10	Nadler	Y	Y	Y	Y	N	N
11	Rose	Y	Y	Y	Y	N	N
12	Maloney, C.	Y	Y	Y	Y	N	N
13	Espaillat	Y	Y	Y	Y	N	N
14	Ocasio-Cortez	Y	Y	Y	Y	N	N
15	Serrano	Y	Y	Y	Y	N	N
16	Engel	Y	Y	Y	Y	N	N
17	Lowey	Y	Y	Y	Y	N	N
18	Maloney, S.P.	Y	Y	Y	Y	N	N
19	Delgado	Y	Y	Y	Y	N	N
20	Tonko	Y	Y	Y	Y	N	N
21	**Stefanik**	N	N	Y	Y	N	N
22	Brindisi	Y	Y	Y	Y	N	N
23	**Reed**	N	N	Y	Y	Y	Y
24	**Katko**	N	N	Y	Y	N	N
25	Morelle	Y	Y	Y	Y	N	N
26	Higgins, B.	Y	Y	Y	Y	N	N
27	vacant						
NORTH CAROLINA							
1	Butterfield	Y	Y	Y	Y	N	N
2	**Holding**	N	N	Y	Y	Y	Y
3	**Murphy**	N	N	Y	Y	Y	Y
4	Price	Y	Y	Y	Y	N	N
5	**Foxx**	N	N	N	Y	Y	Y
6	**Walker**	N	N	Y	Y	Y	Y
7	**Rouzer**	N	N	Y	Y	Y	Y
8	**Hudson**	N	N	Y	Y	+	+
9	**Bishop**	N	N	Y	Y	Y	Y
10	**McHenry**	N	N	Y	Y	Y	Y
11	**Meadows**	N	N	N	Y	Y	Y
12	Adams	Y	Y	Y	Y	N	N
13	**Budd**	N	N	Y	Y	Y	Y
NORTH DAKOTA							
AL	**Armstrong**	N	N	Y	Y	Y	Y
OHIO							
1	**Chabot**	N	N	Y	Y	Y	Y
2	**Wenstrup**	N	N	Y	Y	Y	Y
3	Beatty	+	?	?	?	?	?
4	**Jordan**	?	?	Y	Y	Y	Y
5	**Latta**	N	N	Y	Y	Y	Y
6	**Johnson, B.**	N	N	Y	Y	Y	Y
7	**Gibbs**	N	N	Y	Y	Y	Y
8	**Davidson**	N	N	Y	Y	Y	Y
9	Kaptur	Y	Y	Y	Y	N	N
10	**Turner**	N	N	Y	Y	Y	Y
11	Fudge	Y	Y	Y	Y	N	N
12	**Balderson**	N	N	Y	Y	Y	Y
13	Ryan	?	?	Y	Y	N	N
14	**Joyce**	N	N	Y	Y	Y	Y
15	**Stivers**	N	?	Y	Y	Y	Y
16	**Gonzalez**	N	N	Y	Y	Y	Y
OKLAHOMA							
1	**Hern**	N	N	Y	Y	Y	Y
2	**Mullin**	N	N	Y	Y	Y	Y
3	**Lucas**	N	N	Y	Y	Y	Y
4	**Cole**	N	N	N	N	Y	N
5	Horn	N	Y	Y	Y	N	N
OREGON							
1	Bonamici	Y	Y	Y	Y	N	N
2	**Walden**	N	N	Y	Y	Y	Y
3	Blumenauer	Y	Y	Y	Y	N	N
4	DeFazio	Y	Y	Y	Y	N	N
5	Schrader	Y	Y	Y	Y	N	N
PENNSYLVANIA							
1	**Fitzpatrick**	N	N	Y	Y	N	N
2	Boyle	Y	Y	Y	Y	N	N
3	Evans	Y	Y	Y	Y	N	N
4	Dean	Y	Y	Y	Y	N	N
5	Scanlon	Y	?	Y	Y	N	N
6	Houlahan	Y	Y	Y	Y	N	N
7	Wild	Y	Y	Y	Y	N	N
8	Cartwright	?	?	Y	Y	N	N
9	**Meuser**	N	N	Y	Y	Y	Y
10	**Perry**	N	N	Y	Y	Y	Y
11	**Smucker**	N	N	Y	Y	Y	Y
12	**Keller**	N	N	Y	Y	Y	Y
13	**Joyce**	N	N	Y	Y	Y	Y
14	**Reschenthaler**	N	N	Y	Y	Y	Y
15	**Thompson, G.**	N	N	Y	Y	Y	Y
16	**Kelly, M.**	N	N	Y	Y	Y	Y
17	Lamb	Y	Y	Y	Y	N	N
18	Doyle	Y	Y	Y	Y	N	N
RHODE ISLAND							
1	Cicilline	Y	Y	Y	Y	N	N
2	Langevin	Y	Y	Y	Y	N	N
SOUTH CAROLINA							
1	Cunningham	Y	Y	Y	Y	N	N
2	**Wilson, J.**	N	N	Y	Y	Y	Y
3	**Duncan**	N	N	Y	N	Y	Y
4	**Timmons**	-	-	+	+	+	+
5	**Norman**	N	N	Y	N	Y	Y
6	Clyburn	Y	Y	Y	Y	N	N
7	**Rice, T.**	N	N	Y	Y	Y	Y
SOUTH DAKOTA							
AL	**Johnson**	N	N	Y	Y	Y	Y
TENNESSEE							
1	**Roe**	N	N	Y	Y	Y	Y
2	**Burchett**	N	N	Y	Y	Y	Y
3	**Fleischmann**	N	N	Y	Y	Y	Y
4	**DesJarlais**	N	N	Y	Y	Y	Y
5	Cooper	Y	Y	Y	Y	N	N
6	**Rose**	N	N	Y	Y	?	?
7	**Green**	N	N	Y	Y	Y	Y
8	**Kustoff**	N	N	Y	Y	Y	Y
9	Cohen	Y	Y	Y	Y	N	N
TEXAS							
1	**Gohmert**	N	N	Y	Y	Y	Y
2	**Crenshaw**	N	N	Y	Y	Y	Y
3	**Taylor**	N	N	Y	Y	Y	Y
4	**Ratcliffe**	?	?	?	Y	Y	Y
5	**Gooden**	N	N	Y	Y	Y	Y
6	**Wright**	?	?	?	?	Y	Y
7	Fletcher	Y	Y	Y	Y	N	N
8	**Brady**	N	N	N	Y	Y	Y
9	Green, A.	Y	Y	Y	Y	N	N
10	**McCaul**	N	N	Y	Y	Y	Y
11	**Conaway**	N	N	Y	Y	Y	Y
12	**Granger**	N	N	Y	Y	Y	Y
13	**Thornberry**	N	N	N	Y	Y	Y
14	**Weber**	N	N	Y	Y	Y	Y
15	Gonzalez	Y	Y	Y	Y	N	N
16	Escobar	Y	Y	Y	Y	N	N
17	**Flores**	N	N	Y	Y	Y	Y
18	Jackson Lee	Y	Y	Y	Y	N	N
19	**Arrington**	N	N	Y	Y	Y	Y
20	Castro	Y	Y	Y	Y	N	N
21	**Roy**	N	N	Y	Y	Y	Y
22	**Olson**	N	N	Y	Y	Y	Y
23	**Hurd**	N	N	Y	Y	Y	Y
24	**Marchant**	?	?	Y	Y	Y	Y
25	**Williams**	?	?	?	?	Y	Y
26	**Burgess**	N	?	Y	Y	Y	Y
27	**Cloud**	N	N	Y	Y	Y	Y
28	Cuellar	Y	Y	Y	Y	N	N
29	Garcia, S.	Y	Y	Y	Y	N	N
30	Johnson, E.B.	Y	Y	P	Y	N	N
31	**Carter, J.**	?	?	?	?	Y	Y
32	Allred	Y	Y	Y	Y	N	N
33	Veasey	Y	Y	Y	Y	N	N
34	Vela	Y	Y	Y	Y	N	N
35	Doggett	Y	Y	Y	Y	N	N
36	**Babin**	N	N	Y	Y	Y	Y
UTAH							
1	**Bishop, R.**	N	N	Y	Y	Y	Y
2	**Stewart**	N	N	Y	Y	Y	Y
3	**Curtis**	N	N	Y	Y	Y	Y
4	McAdams	Y	Y	Y	Y	Y	Y
VERMONT							
AL	Welch	Y	Y	Y	Y	N	N
VIRGINIA							
1	**Wittman**	N	N	Y	Y	Y	Y
2	Luria	Y	Y	Y	Y	N	N
3	Scott, R.	Y	Y	Y	Y	N	N
4	McEachin	+	+	+	+	-	-
5	**Riggleman**	N	N	Y	Y	Y	Y
6	**Cline**	N	N	Y	Y	Y	Y
7	Spanberger	Y	Y	Y	Y	N	N
8	Beyer	Y	Y	Y	Y	N	N
9	**Griffith**	N	N	Y	Y	Y	Y
10	Wexton	Y	Y	Y	Y	N	N
11	Connolly	Y	Y	Y	Y	N	N
WASHINGTON							
1	DelBene	Y	Y	Y	Y	N	N
2	Larsen	Y	Y	Y	Y	N	N
3	**Herrera Beutler**	N	N	Y	Y	Y	N
4	**Newhouse**	N	N	Y	Y	Y	Y
5	**McMorris Rodgers**	N	N	Y	Y	Y	Y
6	Kilmer	Y	Y	Y	Y	N	N
7	Jayapal	Y	Y	Y	Y	N	N
8	Schrier	Y	Y	Y	Y	N	N
9	Smith Adam	Y	Y	Y	Y	N	N
10	Heck	Y	Y	Y	Y	N	N
WEST VIRGINIA							
1	**McKinley**	N	N	Y	Y	Y	Y
2	**Mooney**	N	N	Y	Y	Y	Y
3	**Miller**	N	?	Y	Y	Y	Y
WISCONSIN							
1	**Steil**	N	N	Y	Y	Y	Y
2	Pocan	Y	Y	Y	Y	N	N
3	Kind	Y	Y	Y	Y	N	N
4	Moore	Y	Y	Y	Y	N	N
5	**Sensenbrenner**	N	N	Y	Y	Y	Y
6	**Grothman**	N	N	Y	Y	Y	Y
7	**Duffy**						
8	**Gallagher**	N	N	Y	Y	Y	Y
WYOMING							
AL	**Cheney**	N	N	Y	Y	Y	Y
DELEGATES							
	Radewagen (A.S.)					?	?
	Norton (D.C.)					N	N
	San Nicolas (Guam)					N	N
	Sablan (N. Marianas)					N	N
	González-Colón (P.R.)					?	?
	Plaskett (V.I.)					N	N

595. HR2181. Chaco Lands Leasing Ban - Continuing Oil and Gas Developments. Arrington, R-Texas, amendment no. 4 that would allow operators to continue new oil and gas developments on the federal lands that would be withdrawn under the bill's provisions, provided that those operators have complied with existing law and regulations related to archaeological sites and historic preservation in the Chaco Culture National Historical Park. Rejected in Committee of the Whole 181-245: R 180-13; D 0-231; I 1-1. Oct. 30, 2019.

596. HR2181. Chaco Lands Leasing Ban - Recommit. Arrington, R-Texas, motion to recommit the bill to the House Natural Resources Committee with instructions to report it back immediately with an amendment that would indefinitely postpone the effective date of the bill if the Interior Department and the governor of New Mexico determine that the withdrawal of lands from eligibility for mining and mineral leasing under its provisions would result in a loss of revenue for the state, including revenues used to fund schools, roads, fire and police protection, and other public services. Motion rejected 199-222: R 193-0; D 6-221; I 0-1. Oct. 30, 2019.

597. HR2181. Chaco Lands Leasing Ban - Passage. Passage of the bill that would effectively prohibit any new mining or mineral production activities on federal lands within 10 miles of the Chaco Culture National Historical Park in New Mexico. Specifically, it would withdraw the lands from eligibility for activities permitted under federal laws governing public lands, mining, and mineral and geothermal leasing. The withdrawal would not prohibit the conveyance or exchange of such federal lands to or with Indian tribes. The bill would also require the termination of existing oil and gas leases on federal lands where extraction has not begun by the end of the initial lease. Passed 245-174: R 17-173; D 228-0; I 0-1. Oct. 30, 2019.

598. HR1373. Grand Canyon Leasing Ban - Impact on Job Availability. Gosar, R-Ariz., for Lesko, R-Ariz., amendment no. 1 that would postpone the effective date of the bill until the Interior and Labor departments determine that its provisions would not adversely affect jobs available to Native Americans, other minorities, and women. Rejected in Committee of the Whole 185-240: R 185-7; D 0-231; I 0-2. Oct. 30, 2019.

599. HR1373. Grand Canyon Leasing Ban - Exempt Arizona's Fourth District. Gosar, R-Ariz., amendment no. 2 that would exempt any federal lands in Arizona's 4th Congressional District from the bill's provisions that would withdraw certain lands from eligibility for mining and mineral leasing. Rejected in Committee of the Whole 178-243: R 178-13; D 0-228; I 0-2. Oct. 30, 2019.

600. HR1373. Grand Canyon Leasing Ban - Mineral Survey Requirement. Gosar, R-Ariz., amendment no. 3 that would postpone the effective date of the withdrawal of lands from eligibility for mining and mineral leasing under the bill's provisions until the Interior Department conducts a mineral survey of the area proposed for withdrawal and determines that there are no mineral or geothermal resources present, other than uranium. Rejected in Committee of the Whole 186-237: R 183-9; D 2-227; I 1-1. Oct. 30, 2019.

		595	596	597	598	599	600
ALABAMA							
1	**Byrne**	Y	Y	N	Y	Y	Y
2	**Roby**	Y	Y	N	Y	Y	Y
3	**Rogers, M.**	Y	Y	N	Y	Y	Y
4	**Aderholt**	Y	Y	N	Y	Y	Y
5	**Brooks, M.**	Y	Y	N	Y	Y	Y
6	**Palmer**	Y	Y	N	Y	Y	Y
7	Sewell	N	N	Y	N	N	N
ALASKA							
AL	**Young**	Y	Y	Y	Y	Y	Y
ARIZONA							
1	O'Halleran	N	N	Y	N	N	N
2	Kirkpatrick	N	N	Y	N	N	N
3	Grijalva	N	N	Y	N	N	N
4	**Gosar**	Y	Y	N	Y	Y	Y
5	**Biggs**	Y	Y	N	Y	Y	Y
6	**Schweikert**	Y	Y	N	Y	Y	Y
7	Gallego	N	N	Y	N	N	N
8	**Lesko**	Y	Y	N	Y	Y	Y
9	Stanton	N	N	Y	N	N	N
ARKANSAS							
1	**Crawford**	Y	Y	N	Y	Y	Y
2	**Hill, F.**	Y	Y	Y	Y	Y	Y
3	**Womack**	Y	Y	N	Y	Y	Y
4	**Westerman**	Y	Y	N	Y	Y	Y
CALIFORNIA							
1	**LaMalfa**	Y	Y	N	Y	Y	Y
2	Huffman	N	N	Y	N	N	N
3	Garamendi	N	N	Y	N	N	N
4	**McClintock**	Y	Y	N	Y	Y	Y
5	Thompson, M.	-	-	+	-	-	-
6	Matsui	N	N	Y	N	N	N
7	Bera	N	N	Y	N	N	N
8	**Cook**	N	Y	Y	N	Y	N
9	McNerney	N	N	Y	N	N	N
10	Harder	N	N	Y	N	N	N
11	DeSaulnier	N	N	Y	N	N	N
12	Pelosi						
13	Lee B.	N	N	Y	N	N	N
14	Speier	N	N	Y	N	N	N
15	Swalwell	N	N	Y	N	N	N
16	Costa	N	N	Y	N	N	N
17	Khanna	N	N	Y	N	N	N
18	Eshoo	N	-	Y	N	N	N
19	Lofgren	N	N	Y	N	N	N
20	Panetta	N	N	Y	N	N	N
21	Cox	N	N	Y	N	N	N
22	**Nunes**	Y	Y	N	Y	Y	Y
23	**McCarthy**	Y	Y	N	Y	Y	Y
24	Carbajal	N	N	Y	N	N	N
25	Hill, K.	?	?	?	?	?	?
26	Brownley	N	N	Y	N	N	N
27	Chu	N	N	Y	N	N	N
28	Schiff	N	N	Y	N	N	N
29	Cárdenas	N	N	Y	N	N	N
30	Sherman	N	N	Y	N	N	N
31	Aguilar	N	N	Y	N	N	N
32	Napolitano	N	N	Y	N	N	N
33	Lieu	N	N	Y	N	N	N
34	Gomez	N	N	Y	N	N	N
35	Torres	N	N	Y	N	N	N
36	Ruiz	N	N	Y	N	N	N
37	Bass	N	N	Y	N	N	N
38	Sánchez	N	N	Y	N	N	N
39	Cisneros	N	N	Y	N	N	N
40	Roybal-Allard	N	N	Y	N	N	N
41	Takano	N	N	Y	N	N	N
42	**Calvert**	N	Y	Y	Y	Y	Y
43	Waters	N	N	Y	N	N	N
44	Barragán	N	N	Y	N	N	N
45	Porter	N	N	Y	N	N	N
46	Correa	N	N	Y	N	N	N
47	Lowenthal	N	N	Y	N	N	N
48	Rouda	N	N	Y	N	N	N
49	Levin	N	N	Y	N	N	N
50	**Hunter**	Y	Y	N	Y	Y	Y
51	Vargas	N	N	Y	N	N	N
52	Peters	N	N	Y	N	N	N

		595	596	597	598	599	600
53	Davis, S.	N	N	Y	N	N	N
COLORADO							
1	DeGette	N	N	Y	N	N	N
2	Neguse	N	N	Y	N	N	N
3	**Tipton**	N	Y	N	Y	Y	Y
4	**Buck**	Y	Y	N	Y	Y	Y
5	**Lamborn**	Y	Y	N	Y	Y	Y
6	Crow	N	N	Y	N	N	N
7	Perlmutter	N	N	Y	N	N	N
CONNECTICUT							
1	Larson	N	N	Y	N	N	N
2	Courtney	N	N	Y	N	N	N
3	DeLauro	N	N	Y	N	N	N
4	Himes	N	N	Y	N	N	N
5	Hayes	N	N	Y	N	N	N
DELAWARE							
AL	Blunt Rochester	N	N	Y	N	N	N
FLORIDA							
1	**Gaetz**	Y	Y	N	Y	Y	Y
2	**Dunn**	Y	Y	N	Y	Y	Y
3	**Yoho**	Y	Y	N	Y	Y	Y
4	**Rutherford**	Y	Y	N	Y	Y	Y
5	Lawson	N	N	Y	N	N	N
6	**Waltz**	Y	Y	N	Y	Y	Y
7	Murphy	N	N	Y	N	N	N
8	**Posey**	Y	Y	N	Y	Y	Y
9	Soto	N	N	Y	N	N	N
10	Demings	N	N	Y	N	N	N
11	**Webster**	Y	Y	N	Y	Y	Y
12	**Bilirakis**	Y	Y	N	Y	Y	Y
13	Crist	N	N	Y	N	N	N
14	Castor	N	N	Y	N	N	N
15	**Spano**	Y	Y	N	Y	Y	Y
16	**Buchanan**	Y	Y	N	Y	Y	Y
17	**Steube**	Y	Y	N	Y	Y	Y
18	**Mast**	Y	Y	Y	Y	Y	Y
19	**Rooney**	N	Y	?	N	N	N
20	Hastings	N	N	Y	N	N	N
21	Frankel	N	N	Y	N	N	N
22	Deutch	N	N	Y	N	N	N
23	Wasserman Schultz	N	N	Y	N	N	N
24	Wilson, F.	N	N	Y	N	N	N
25	**Diaz-Balart**	Y	Y	N	Y	Y	Y
26	Mucarsel-Powell	N	N	Y	N	N	N
27	Shalala	N	N	Y	N	N	N
GEORGIA							
1	**Carter, E.L.**	Y	Y	N	Y	Y	Y
2	Bishop, S.	N	N	Y	N	N	N
3	**Ferguson**	Y	Y	N	Y	Y	Y
4	Johnson, H.	N	N	Y	N	N	N
5	Lewis John	N	N	Y	N	N	N
6	McBath	N	N	Y	N	N	N
7	**Woodall**	Y	Y	N	Y	Y	Y
8	**Scott, A.**	Y	Y	N	Y	Y	Y
9	**Collins, D.**	Y	Y	N	Y	Y	Y
10	**Hice**	+	+	-	+	+	+
11	**Loudermilk**	Y	Y	N	Y	Y	Y
12	**Allen**	Y	Y	N	Y	Y	Y
13	Scott, D.	N	N	Y	N	N	N
14	**Graves, T.**	Y	Y	N	Y	Y	Y
HAWAII							
1	Case	N	N	Y	N	N	N
2	Gabbard	?	?	?	?	?	?
IDAHO							
1	**Fulcher**	Y	Y	N	Y	Y	Y
2	**Simpson**	N	Y	Y	N	N	N
ILLINOIS							
1	Rush	N	N	Y	N	-	-
2	Kelly, R.	N	N	Y	N	N	N
3	Lipinski	N	N	Y	N	N	N
4	García, J.	N	N	Y	N	N	N
5	Quigley	N	N	Y	N	N	N
6	Casten	N	N	Y	N	N	N
7	Davis, D.	N	N	Y	N	N	N
8	Krishnamoorthi	N	N	Y	N	N	N
9	Schakowsky	N	N	Y	N	N	N
10	Schneider	N	N	Y	N	N	N
11	Foster	N	N	Y	N	N	N

KEY:	Republicans	Democrats	*Independents*

Y Voted for (yea)	**N** Voted against (nay)	**P** Voted "present"	
+ Announced for	**−** Announced against	**?** Did not vote or otherwise	
# Paired for	**X** Paired against	make position known	

		595	596	597	598	599	600
12	**Bost**	Y	Y	N	Y	Y	Y
13	**Davis, R.**	Y	Y	N	Y	Y	Y
14	Underwood	N	N	Y	N	N	N
15	**Shimkus**	Y	Y	N	Y	Y	Y
16	**Kinzinger**	Y	Y	N	N	Y	Y
17	Bustos	N	N	Y	N	N	N
18	**LaHood**	Y	Y	N	Y	Y	Y
INDIANA							
1	Visclosky	N	N	Y	N	N	N
2	**Walorski**	Y	Y	N	Y	Y	Y
3	**Banks**	Y	Y	N	Y	Y	Y
4	**Baird**	Y	Y	N	Y	Y	Y
5	**Brooks, S.**	Y	Y	N	Y	Y	Y
6	**Pence**	Y	Y	N	Y	Y	Y
7	Carson	N	N	Y	N	N	N
8	**Bucshon**	Y	Y	N	Y	Y	Y
9	**Hollingsworth**	Y	Y	N	Y	Y	Y
IOWA							
1	Finkenauer	N	N	Y	N	N	N
2	Loebsack	N	N	Y	N	N	N
3	Axne	N	N	Y	N	N	N
4	**King, S.**	Y	Y	N	?	Y	Y
KANSAS							
1	**Marshall**	Y	Y	N	Y	Y	Y
2	**Watkins**	Y	Y	N	Y	Y	Y
3	Davids	N	N	Y	N	N	N
4	**Estes**	Y	Y	N	Y	Y	Y
KENTUCKY							
1	**Comer**	Y	Y	N	Y	Y	Y
2	**Guthrie**	Y	Y	N	Y	Y	Y
3	Yarmuth	N	N	Y	N	N	N
4	**Massie**	Y	Y	N	Y	Y	Y
5	**Rogers, H.**	Y	Y	N	Y	Y	Y
6	**Barr**	Y	Y	N	Y	Y	Y
LOUISIANA							
1	**Scalise**	Y	Y	N	Y	Y	Y
2	Richmond	N	N	Y	N	N	N
3	**Higgins, C.**	Y	Y	N	Y	Y	Y
4	**Johnson, M.**	Y	Y	N	Y	Y	Y
5	**Abraham**	Y	Y	N	Y	Y	Y
6	**Graves, G.**	Y	Y	N	Y	Y	Y
MAINE							
1	Pingree	N	N	Y	N	N	N
2	Golden	N	Y	Y	N	N	N
MARYLAND							
1	**Harris**	Y	Y	N	Y	Y	Y
2	Ruppersberger	N	N	Y	N	N	N
3	Sarbanes	N	N	Y	N	N	N
4	Brown, A.	N	N	Y	N	N	N
5	Hoyer	N	N	Y	N	N	N
6	Trone	N	N	Y	N	N	N
7	vacant						
8	Raskin	N	N	Y	N	N	N
MASSACHUSETTS							
1	Neal	N	N	Y	N	N	N
2	McGovern	N	N	Y	N	N	N
3	Trahan	N	N	Y	N	N	N
4	Kennedy	N	N	Y	N	N	N
5	Clark	N	N	Y	N	N	N
6	Moulton	N	N	Y	N	N	N
7	Pressley	N	N	Y	N	N	N
8	Lynch	N	N	Y	N	N	N
9	Keating	N	N	Y	N	N	N
MICHIGAN							
1	**Bergman**	Y	Y	N	Y	Y	Y
2	**Huizenga**	Y	Y	N	Y	Y	Y
3	*Amash*	Y	N	N	N	N	Y
4	**Moolenaar**	Y	Y	N	Y	Y	Y
5	Kildee	N	N	Y	N	N	N
6	**Upton**	N	Y	Y	Y	N	N
7	**Walberg**	Y	Y	N	Y	Y	Y
8	Slotkin	N	N	Y	N	N	N
9	Levin	N	N	Y	N	N	N
10	**Mitchell**	Y	Y	N	Y	Y	Y
11	Stevens	N	N	Y	N	N	N
12	Dingell	N	N	Y	N	N	N
13	Tlaib	N	N	Y	N	N	N
14	Lawrence	N	N	Y	N	N	N
MINNESOTA							
1	**Hagedorn**	Y	Y	N	Y	Y	Y
2	Craig	N	N	Y	N	N	N
3	Phillips	N	N	Y	N	N	N
4	McCollum	N	N	Y	N	N	N
5	Omar	N	N	Y	N	N	N
6	**Emmer**	Y	Y	N	Y	Y	Y
7	Peterson	N	N	Y	N	N	N
8	**Stauber**	Y	Y	N	Y	Y	Y
MISSISSIPPI							
1	**Kelly, T.**	Y	Y	N	Y	Y	Y
2	Thompson, B.	N	N	Y	N	N	N
3	**Guest**	Y	Y	N	Y	Y	Y
4	**Palazzo**	Y	Y	-	Y	Y	Y
MISSOURI							
1	Clay	N	N	Y	N	N	N
2	**Wagner**	Y	Y	N	Y	Y	Y
3	**Luetkemeyer**	Y	Y	N	Y	Y	Y
4	**Hartzler**	Y	Y	N	Y	Y	Y
5	Cleaver	N	N	Y	N	N	N
6	**Graves, S.**	Y	Y	N	Y	Y	Y
7	**Long**	Y	Y	N	Y	Y	Y
8	**Smith, J.**	Y	Y	N	Y	Y	Y
MONTANA							
AL	**Gianforte**	Y	Y	N	Y	Y	Y
NEBRASKA							
1	**Fortenberry**	Y	Y	Y	Y	N	N
2	**Bacon**	Y	Y	N	Y	Y	Y
3	**Smith, Adrian**	Y	Y	N	Y	Y	Y
NEVADA							
1	Titus	N	N	Y	N	N	N
2	**Amodei**	Y	Y	N	Y	Y	Y
3	Lee	N	N	Y	N	N	N
4	Horsford	N	N	Y	N	N	N
NEW HAMPSHIRE							
1	Pappas	N	N	Y	N	N	N
2	Kuster	N	N	Y	N	N	N
NEW JERSEY							
1	Norcross	N	N	Y	N	N	N
2	Van Drew	N	N	Y	N	N	N
3	Kim	N	N	Y	N	N	N
4	**Smith, C.**	N	Y	Y	N	N	N
5	Gottheimer	N	N	Y	N	N	N
6	Pallone	N	N	Y	N	N	N
7	Malinowski	N	N	Y	N	?	N
8	Sires	N	N	Y	N	N	N
9	Pascrell	N	N	Y	N	N	N
10	Payne	N	N	Y	N	N	N
11	Sherrill	N	N	Y	N	N	N
12	Watson Coleman	N	N	Y	N	N	N
NEW MEXICO							
1	Haaland	N	N	Y	N	N	N
2	Torres Small	N	Y	Y	N	N	N
3	Luján	N	N	Y	N	N	N
NEW YORK							
1	**Zeldin**	Y	Y	N	Y	Y	Y
2	**King, P.**	N	Y	Y	N	N	N
3	Suozzi	N	N	Y	N	N	N
4	Rice, K.	N	N	Y	N	N	N
5	Meeks	N	N	Y	N	N	N
6	Meng	N	N	Y	N	N	N
7	Velázquez	N	N	Y	N	N	N
8	Jeffries	N	N	Y	N	N	N
9	Clarke	N	N	Y	N	N	N
10	Nadler	N	N	Y	N	N	N
11	Rose	N	N	Y	N	N	N
12	Maloney, C.	N	N	Y	N	N	N
13	Espaillat	N	N	Y	N	N	N
14	Ocasio-Cortez	N	N	Y	N	N	N
15	Serrano	N	N	Y	N	N	N
16	Engel	N	N	Y	N	N	N
17	Lowey	N	N	Y	N	N	N
18	Maloney, S.P.	N	N	Y	N	N	N
19	Delgado	N	N	Y	N	N	N
20	Tonko	N	N	Y	N	N	N
21	**Stefanik**	N	Y	Y	Y	N	Y
22	Brindisi	N	Y	Y	N	N	Y
23	**Reed**	Y	Y	Y	Y	Y	Y
24	**Katko**	N	Y	Y	Y	N	Y
25	Morelle	N	N	Y	N	N	N
26	Higgins, B.	N	N	Y	N	N	N
27	vacant						
NORTH CAROLINA							
1	Butterfield	N	N	Y	N	N	N
2	**Holding**	Y	Y	N	Y	Y	Y
3	**Murphy**	Y	Y	N	Y	Y	Y
4	Price	N	N	Y	N	N	N
5	**Foxx**	Y	Y	N	Y	Y	Y
6	**Walker**	Y	Y	N	Y	Y	Y
7	**Rouzer**	Y	Y	N	Y	Y	Y
8	**Hudson**	+	+	-	+	+	+
9	**Bishop**	Y	Y	N	Y	Y	Y
10	**McHenry**	Y	Y	N	Y	Y	Y
11	**Meadows**	Y	Y	N	Y	Y	?
12	Adams	N	N	Y	N	N	N
13	**Budd**	Y	Y	N	Y	Y	Y
NORTH DAKOTA							
AL	**Armstrong**	Y	Y	N	Y	Y	Y
OHIO							
1	**Chabot**	Y	Y	N	Y	Y	Y
2	**Wenstrup**	Y	Y	N	Y	Y	Y
3	Beatty	?	?	+	-	-	-
4	**Jordan**	Y	Y	N	Y	Y	Y
5	**Latta**	Y	Y	N	Y	Y	Y
6	**Johnson, B.**	Y	Y	N	Y	Y	Y
7	**Gibbs**	Y	Y	N	Y	Y	Y
8	**Davidson**	Y	Y	N	Y	Y	Y
9	Kaptur	N	N	Y	N	N	N
10	**Turner**	Y	Y	N	Y	Y	Y
11	Fudge	N	N	Y	N	N	N
12	**Balderson**	Y	Y	N	Y	Y	Y
13	Ryan	N	N	Y	N	N	N
14	**Joyce**	Y	Y	N	Y	Y	Y
15	**Stivers**	Y	Y	N	Y	Y	Y
16	**Gonzalez**	Y	Y	N	Y	Y	Y
OKLAHOMA							
1	**Hern**	Y	Y	N	Y	Y	Y
2	**Mullin**	Y	Y	N	Y	Y	Y
3	**Lucas**	Y	Y	N	Y	Y	Y
4	**Cole**	N	Y	Y	Y	N	N
5	Horn	N	N	Y	N	N	N
OREGON							
1	Bonamici	N	N	Y	N	N	N
2	**Walden**	Y	Y	N	Y	Y	Y
3	Blumenauer	N	N	Y	N	N	N
4	DeFazio	N	N	Y	N	N	N
5	Schrader	N	N	Y	N	N	N
PENNSYLVANIA							
1	**Fitzpatrick**	N	Y	Y	N	N	N
2	Boyle	N	N	Y	N	N	N
3	Evans	N	N	Y	N	N	N
4	Dean	N	N	Y	N	N	N
5	Scanlon	N	N	Y	N	N	N
6	Houlahan	N	N	Y	N	N	N
7	Wild	N	N	Y	N	N	N
8	Cartwright	N	N	Y	N	N	N
9	**Meuser**	Y	Y	N	Y	Y	Y
10	**Perry**	Y	Y	N	Y	Y	Y
11	**Smucker**	Y	Y	N	Y	Y	Y
12	**Keller**	Y	Y	N	Y	Y	Y
13	**Joyce**	Y	Y	N	Y	Y	Y
14	**Reschenthaler**	Y	Y	N	Y	Y	Y
15	**Thompson, G.**	Y	Y	N	Y	Y	Y
16	**Kelly, M.**	Y	Y	N	Y	Y	Y
17	Lamb	N	N	Y	N	N	N
18	Doyle	N	N	Y	N	N	N
RHODE ISLAND							
1	Cicilline	N	N	Y	N	N	N
2	Langevin	N	N	Y	N	N	N
SOUTH CAROLINA							
1	Cunningham	N	N	Y	N	N	N
2	**Wilson, J.**	Y	Y	N	Y	Y	Y
3	**Duncan**	Y	Y	N	Y	Y	Y
4	**Timmons**	+	+	-	+	+	+
5	**Norman**	Y	Y	N	Y	Y	Y
6	Clyburn	N	N	Y	N	N	N
7	**Rice, T.**	Y	Y	N	Y	Y	Y
SOUTH DAKOTA							
AL	**Johnson**	Y	Y	N	Y	Y	Y
TENNESSEE							
1	**Roe**	Y	Y	N	Y	Y	Y
2	**Burchett**	Y	Y	N	Y	Y	Y
3	**Fleischmann**	Y	Y	N	Y	Y	Y
4	**DesJarlais**	Y	Y	N	Y	Y	Y
5	Cooper	N	Y	Y	N	N	N
6	**Rose**	?	?	?	?	?	?
7	**Green**	Y	Y	N	Y	Y	Y
8	**Kustoff**	Y	Y	N	Y	Y	Y
9	Cohen	N	N	Y	N	N	N
TEXAS							
1	**Gohmert**	Y	Y	N	Y	Y	Y
2	**Crenshaw**	Y	Y	N	Y	Y	Y
3	**Taylor**	Y	Y	N	Y	Y	Y
4	**Ratcliffe**	Y	Y	N	Y	Y	Y
5	**Gooden**	Y	Y	N	Y	Y	Y
6	**Wright**	Y	Y	N	Y	?	Y
7	Fletcher	N	N	Y	N	N	N
8	**Brady**	Y	Y	N	Y	?	Y
9	Green, A.	N	N	Y	N	N	N
10	**McCaul**	Y	Y	N	Y	Y	Y
11	**Conaway**	Y	Y	N	Y	Y	Y
12	**Granger**	Y	Y	N	Y	Y	Y
13	**Thornberry**	Y	Y	N	Y	Y	Y
14	**Weber**	Y	Y	N	Y	Y	Y
15	Gonzalez	N	N	Y	N	N	N
16	Escobar	N	N	Y	N	N	N
17	**Flores**	Y	Y	N	Y	Y	Y
18	Jackson Lee	N	N	Y	N	N	N
19	**Arrington**	Y	Y	N	Y	Y	Y
20	Castro	N	N	Y	N	N	N
21	**Roy**	Y	Y	N	Y	N	Y
22	**Olson**	Y	Y	N	Y	Y	Y
23	**Hurd**	Y	Y	N	Y	Y	Y
24	**Marchant**	Y	Y	N	Y	Y	Y
25	**Williams**	Y	Y	N	Y	Y	Y
26	**Burgess**	Y	Y	Y	Y	Y	Y
27	**Cloud**	Y	Y	N	Y	Y	Y
28	Cuellar	N	N	Y	N	N	N
29	Garcia, S.	N	N	Y	N	N	N
30	Johnson, E.B.	N	N	Y	N	N	N
31	**Carter, J.**	Y	Y	N	Y	Y	Y
32	Allred	N	N	Y	N	N	N
33	Veasey	N	N	Y	N	N	N
34	Vela	N	N	Y	N	?	N
35	Doggett	N	N	Y	N	N	N
36	**Babin**	Y	Y	N	Y	Y	Y
UTAH							
1	**Bishop, R.**	Y	Y	N	Y	Y	Y
2	**Stewart**	Y	Y	N	Y	Y	Y
3	**Curtis**	Y	Y	?	Y	Y	Y
4	McAdams	N	Y	Y	N	N	Y
VERMONT							
AL	Welch	N	N	Y	N	N	N
VIRGINIA							
1	**Wittman**	Y	Y	N	Y	Y	Y
2	Luria	N	N	Y	N	N	N
3	Scott, R.	N	N	Y	N	N	N
4	McEachin	-	-	+	-	-	-
5	**Riggleman**	Y	Y	N	Y	Y	Y
6	**Cline**	Y	Y	N	Y	Y	Y
7	Spanberger	N	Y	Y	N	N	N
8	Beyer	N	N	Y	N	N	N
9	**Griffith**	Y	Y	N	Y	Y	Y
10	Wexton	N	N	Y	N	N	N
11	Connolly	N	N	Y	N	N	N
WASHINGTON							
1	DelBene	N	N	Y	N	N	N
2	Larsen	N	N	Y	N	N	N
3	**Herrera Beutler**	N	Y	Y	N	N	Y
4	**Newhouse**	Y	Y	N	Y	Y	Y
5	**McMorris Rodgers**	Y	Y	N	Y	Y	Y
6	Kilmer	N	N	Y	N	N	N
7	Jayapal	N	N	Y	N	N	N
8	Schrier	N	N	Y	N	N	N
9	Smith Adam	N	N	Y	N	N	N
10	Heck	N	N	Y	N	N	N
WEST VIRGINIA							
1	**McKinley**	Y	Y	N	Y	Y	Y
2	**Mooney**	Y	Y	N	Y	Y	Y
3	**Miller**	Y	Y	N	Y	Y	Y
WISCONSIN							
1	**Steil**	Y	Y	N	Y	Y	Y
2	Pocan	N	N	Y	N	N	N
3	Kind	N	N	Y	N	N	N
4	Moore	N	N	Y	N	N	N
5	**Sensenbrenner**	Y	Y	N	Y	Y	Y
6	**Grothman**	Y	Y	N	Y	Y	Y
7	**Duffy**						
8	**Gallagher**	Y	Y	N	Y	Y	Y
WYOMING							
AL	**Cheney**	Y	Y	N	Y	Y	Y
DELEGATES							
	Radewagen (A.S.)	?			?	?	?
	Norton (D.C.)	N			N	N	N
	San Nicolas (Guam)	N			N	N	?
	Sablan (N. Marianas)	N			N	N	N
	González-Colón (P.R.)	?			?	?	?
	Plaskett (V.I.)	N			N	N	N

601. HR1373. Grand Canyon Leasing Ban - Recommit. Wittman, R-Va., motion to recommit the bill to the House Natural Resources Committee with instructions to report it back immediately with an amendment that would postpone the effective date of the bill until the Interior Department determines that its provisions would not result in increased mineral imports from Russia, Kazakhstan, Uzbekistan, and Namibia. Motion rejected 196-226: R 193-0; D 3-225; I 0-1. Oct. 30, 2019.

602. HR1373. Grand Canyon Leasing Ban - Passage. Passage of the bill that would effectively prohibit any new mining or mineral production activities on approximately one million acres of federal lands in the Grand Canyon region of Arizona. Specifically, it would withdraw the lands from eligibility for activities permitted under federal laws governing public lands, mining, and mineral and geothermal leasing. Passed 236-185: R 9-183; D 227-1; I 0-1. *Note: A "nay" was a vote in support of the president's position.* Oct. 30, 2019.

603. HRES660. Impeachment Procedures - Previous Question. McGovern, D-Mass., motion to order the previous question (thus ending debate and possibility of amendment) on the resolution that would outline procedures and authorize the ongoing investigation by House committees related to the impeachment inquiry into President Donald Trump. Among other provisions, it would direct the House Select Intelligence Committee to conduct open hearings related to the investigation; grant subpoena and interrogatory authority for such hearings to the committee chair and ranking member; authorize the public disclosure of witness depositions conducted by the committee; and direct the committee to issue a publicly available report on its findings and recommendations. It would also require the Judiciary Committee to conduct proceedings according to certain procedures, including those allowing for the participation of the president and his legal counsel, and it would authorize the transfer of records and materials related to the inquiry from House committees to the Judiciary Committee. Motion agreed to 231-196: R 0-194; D 230-2; I 1-0. Oct. 31, 2019.

604. HRES660. Impeachment Procedures - Passage. Agreeing to the resolution that would outline procedures and authorize the ongoing investigation by House committees related to the impeachment inquiry into President Donald Trump. Among other provisions, it would direct the House Select Intelligence Committee to conduct open hearings related to the investigation; grant subpoena and interrogatory authority for such hearings to the committee chair and ranking member; authorize the public disclosure of witness depositions conducted by the committee; and direct the committee to issue a publicly available report on its findings and recommendations. It would also require the Judiciary Committee to conduct proceedings according to certain procedures, including those allowing for the participation of the president and his legal counsel, and it would authorize the transfer of records and materials related to the inquiry from House committees to the Judiciary Committee. Passed 232-196: R 0-194; D 231-2; I 1-0. *Note: A "nay" was a vote in support of the president's position.* Oct. 31, 2019.

605. HR823. Colorado Federal Lands - Exempt Colorado's Third District. Curtis, R-Utah, amendment no. 1 that would exempt any lands or waters in Colorado's 3rd Congressional District from the bill's provisions. Rejected in Committee of the Whole 180-240: R 180-9; D 0-229; I 0-2. Oct. 31, 2019.

606. HR823. Colorado Federal Lands - Reduce Land Transfer Acreage. Tipton, R-Colo., amendment no. 5 that would reduce, from 2,560 to 915 acres, the acreage of land that the bill would transfer from the U.S. Forest Service to the National Park Service, for inclusion in the Curecanti National Recreation Area in Colorado. Rejected in Committee of the Whole 185-231: R 184-2; D 0-228; I 1-1. Oct. 31, 2019.

		601	602	603	604	605	606
ALABAMA							
1	Byrne	Y	N	N	N	Y	Y
2	Roby	Y	N	N	N	Y	Y
3	Rogers, M.	Y	N	N	N	?	?
4	Aderholt	Y	N	N	N	Y	Y
5	Brooks, M.	Y	N	N	N	Y	Y
6	Palmer	Y	N	N	N	Y	Y
7	Sewell	N	Y	Y	Y	N	N
ALASKA							
AL	Young	Y	N	N	N	Y	Y
ARIZONA							
1	O'Halleran	N	Y	Y	Y	N	N
2	Kirkpatrick	N	Y	Y	Y	N	N
3	Grijalva	N	Y	Y	Y	N	N
4	Gosar	Y	N	N	N	Y	Y
5	Biggs	Y	N	N	N	Y	Y
6	Schweikert	Y	N	N	N	Y	Y
7	Gallego	N	Y	Y	Y	N	N
8	Lesko	Y	N	N	N	Y	Y
9	Stanton	N	Y	Y	Y	N	N
ARKANSAS							
1	Crawford	Y	N	N	N	Y	Y
2	Hill, F.	Y	N	N	N	Y	Y
3	Womack	Y	N	N	N	Y	Y
4	Westerman	Y	N	N	N	Y	Y
CALIFORNIA							
1	LaMalfa	Y	N	N	N	Y	Y
2	Huffman	N	Y	Y	Y	N	N
3	Garamendi	N	Y	Y	Y	N	N
4	McClintock	Y	N	N	N	Y	Y
5	Thompson, M.	-	+	Y	Y	N	N
6	Matsui	N	Y	Y	Y	N	N
7	Bera	N	Y	Y	Y	N	N
8	Cook	Y	Y	N	N	Y	Y
9	McNerney	N	Y	Y	Y	N	N
10	Harder	N	Y	Y	Y	N	N
11	DeSaulnier	N	Y	Y	Y	N	N
12	Pelosi		Y				
13	Lee B.	N	Y	Y	Y	N	N
14	Speier	N	Y	Y	Y	N	N
15	Swalwell	N	Y	Y	Y	N	N
16	Costa	N	Y	Y	Y	N	N
17	Khanna	N	Y	Y	Y	N	N
18	Eshoo	N	Y	Y	Y	N	N
19	Lofgren	N	Y	Y	?	?	
20	Panetta	N	Y	Y	Y	N	N
21	Cox	N	Y	Y	Y	N	N
22	Nunes	Y	N	N	N	Y	Y
23	McCarthy	Y	N	N	N	Y	Y
24	Carbajal	N	Y	Y	Y	N	N
25	Hill, K.	?	?	Y	Y	N	N
26	Brownley	N	Y	Y	Y	N	N
27	Chu	N	Y	Y	Y	N	N
28	Schiff	N	Y	Y	Y	N	N
29	Cárdenas	N	Y	Y	Y	N	N
30	Sherman	N	Y	Y	Y	N	N
31	Aguilar	N	Y	Y	Y	N	N
32	Napolitano	N	Y	Y	Y	N	N
33	Lieu	N	Y	Y	Y	N	N
34	Gomez	N	Y	Y	Y	N	N
35	Torres	N	Y	Y	Y	N	N
36	Ruiz	N	Y	Y	Y	N	N
37	Bass	N	Y	Y	Y	N	N
38	Sánchez	N	Y	Y	Y	N	N
39	Cisneros	N	Y	Y	Y	N	N
40	Roybal-Allard	N	Y	Y	Y	N	N
41	Takano	N	Y	Y	Y	N	N
42	Calvert	Y	N	N	N	Y	Y
43	Waters	N	Y	Y	Y	N	N
44	Barragán	N	Y	Y	Y	N	N
45	Porter	N	Y	Y	Y	N	N
46	Correa	N	Y	Y	Y	N	N
47	Lowenthal	N	Y	Y	Y	N	N
48	Rouda	N	Y	Y	Y	N	N
49	Levin	N	Y	Y	Y	N	N
50	Hunter	Y	N	N	N	Y	Y
51	Vargas	N	Y	Y	Y	N	N
52	Peters	N	Y	Y	Y	N	N

		601	602	603	604	605	606
53	Davis, S.	N	Y	Y	Y	?	?
COLORADO							
1	DeGette	N	Y	Y	Y	N	N
2	Neguse	N	Y	Y	Y	N	N
3	Tipton	Y	N	N	N	Y	Y
4	Buck	Y	N	N	N	Y	Y
5	Lamborn	Y	N	N	N	Y	Y
6	Crow	N	Y	Y	Y	N	N
7	Perlmutter	N	Y	Y	Y	N	N
CONNECTICUT							
1	Larson	N	Y	Y	Y	N	N
2	Courtney	N	Y	Y	Y	N	N
3	DeLauro	N	Y	Y	Y	N	N
4	Himes	N	Y	Y	Y	N	N
5	Hayes	N	Y	Y	Y	N	N
DELAWARE							
AL	Blunt Rochester	N	Y	Y	Y	N	N
FLORIDA							
1	Gaetz	Y	N	N	N	Y	Y
2	Dunn	Y	N	N	N	Y	Y
3	Yoho	Y	N	N	N	Y	Y
4	Rutherford	Y	N	N	N	Y	Y
5	Lawson	N	Y	Y	Y	N	N
6	Waltz	Y	N	N	N	Y	Y
7	Murphy	N	Y	Y	Y	N	N
8	Posey	Y	N	N	N	Y	Y
9	Soto	N	Y	Y	Y	N	N
10	Demings	N	Y	Y	Y	N	N
11	Webster	Y	N	N	N	Y	Y
12	Bilirakis	Y	N	N	N	Y	Y
13	Crist	N	Y	Y	Y	N	N
14	Castor	N	Y	Y	Y	N	N
15	Spano	Y	N	N	N	Y	Y
16	Buchanan	Y	N	N	N	Y	Y
17	Steube	Y	N	N	N	Y	Y
18	Mast	Y	N	N	N	Y	Y
19	Rooney	Y	Y	N	N	Y	Y
20	Hastings	N	Y	Y	Y	N	N
21	Frankel	N	Y	Y	Y	N	N
22	Deutch	N	Y	Y	Y	N	N
23	Wasserman Schultz	N	Y	Y	Y	N	N
24	Wilson, F.	N	Y	Y	Y	N	N
25	Diaz-Balart	Y	N	N	N	Y	Y
26	Mucarsel-Powell	N	Y	Y	Y	N	N
27	Shalala	N	Y	Y	Y	N	N
GEORGIA							
1	Carter, E.L.	Y	N	N	N	Y	Y
2	Bishop, S.	N	Y	Y	Y	N	N
3	Ferguson	Y	N	N	N	Y	Y
4	Johnson, H.	N	Y	Y	Y	N	N
5	Lewis John	N	Y	Y	Y	N	N
6	McBath	N	Y	Y	Y	N	N
7	Woodall	Y	N	N	N	Y	Y
8	Scott, A.	Y	N	N	N	Y	Y
9	Collins, D.	Y	N	N	N	Y	Y
10	Hice	+	-	-	-	+	+
11	Loudermilk	Y	N	N	N	Y	Y
12	Allen	Y	N	N	N	Y	Y
13	Scott, D.	N	Y	Y	Y	N	N
14	Graves, T.	Y	N	N	N	Y	Y
HAWAII							
1	Case	N	Y	Y	Y	N	N
2	Gabbard	?	?	Y	Y	N	N
IDAHO							
1	Fulcher	Y	N	N	N	Y	Y
2	Simpson	Y	N	N	N	Y	Y
ILLINOIS							
1	Rush	N	Y	Y	Y	N	N
2	Kelly, R.	N	Y	Y	Y	N	N
3	Lipinski	N	Y	Y	Y	N	N
4	García, J.	N	Y	Y	Y	N	N
5	Quigley	N	Y	Y	Y	N	N
6	Casten	N	Y	Y	Y	N	N
7	Davis, D.	N	Y	Y	Y	N	N
8	Krishnamoorthi	N	Y	Y	Y	N	N
9	Schakowsky	N	Y	Y	Y	N	N
10	Schneider	N	Y	Y	Y	N	N
11	Foster	N	Y	Y	Y	N	N

KEY:	Republicans	Democrats	Independents

Y	Voted for (yea)	N	Voted against (nay)	P	Voted "present"
+	Announced for		Announced against	?	Did not vote or otherwise
#	Paired for	X	Paired against		make position known

		601	602	603	604	605	606
12	**Bost**	Y	N	N	N	Y	Y
13	**Davis, R.**	Y	N	N	N	Y	Y
14	Underwood	N	Y	Y	Y	N	N
15	**Shimkus**	Y	N	N	N	Y	Y
16	**Kinzinger**	Y	N	N	N	Y	Y
17	Bustos	N	Y	Y	Y	N	N
18	**LaHood**	Y	N	N	N	Y	Y
INDIANA							
1	Visclosky	N	Y	Y	Y	N	N
2	**Walorski**	Y	N	N	N	Y	Y
3	**Banks**	Y	N	N	N	Y	Y
4	**Baird**	Y	N	N	N	Y	Y
5	**Brooks, S.**	Y	N	N	N	Y	Y
6	**Pence**	Y	N	N	N	Y	Y
7	Carson	N	N	Y	Y	N	N
8	**Bucshon**	Y	N	N	N	Y	Y
9	**Hollingsworth**	Y	N	N	N	Y	Y
IOWA							
1	Finkenauer	N	Y	Y	Y	N	N
2	Loebsack	N	Y	Y	Y	N	N
3	Axne	N	Y	Y	Y	N	N
4	**King, S.**	Y	N	N	N	Y	Y
KANSAS							
1	**Marshall**	Y	N	N	N	Y	Y
2	**Watkins**	Y	N	N	N	Y	Y
3	Davids	N	Y	Y	Y	N	N
4	**Estes**	Y	N	N	N	Y	Y
KENTUCKY							
1	**Comer**	Y	N	N	N	Y	Y
2	**Guthrie**	Y	N	N	N	Y	Y
3	Yarmuth	N	Y	Y	Y	N	N
4	**Massie**	Y	N	N	N	Y	Y
5	**Rogers, H.**	Y	N	N	N	N	Y
6	**Barr**	Y	N	N	N	Y	Y
LOUISIANA							
1	**Scalise**	Y	N	N	N	Y	Y
2	Richmond	N	Y	Y	Y	N	N
3	**Higgins, C.**	Y	N	N	N	Y	Y
4	**Johnson, M.**	Y	N	N	N	Y	Y
5	**Abraham**	Y	N	N	N	Y	Y
6	**Graves, G.**	Y	N	N	N	Y	Y
MAINE							
1	Pingree	N	Y	Y	Y	N	N
2	Golden	N	Y	Y	Y	N	N
MARYLAND							
1	**Harris**	Y	N	N	N	Y	Y
2	Ruppersberger	N	Y	Y	Y	N	N
3	Sarbanes	N	Y	Y	Y	N	N
4	Brown, A.	N	Y	Y	Y	N	N
5	Hoyer	N	Y	Y	Y	N	N
6	Trone	N	Y	Y	Y	N	N
7	vacant						
8	Raskin	N	Y	Y	Y	N	N
MASSACHUSETTS							
1	Neal	N	Y	Y	Y	N	N
2	McGovern	N	Y	Y	Y	N	N
3	Trahan	N	Y	Y	Y	N	N
4	Kennedy	N	Y	Y	Y	N	N
5	Clark	N	Y	Y	Y	N	N
6	Moulton	N	Y	Y	Y	N	N
7	Pressley	N	Y	Y	Y	N	N
8	Lynch	N	Y	Y	Y	N	N
9	Keating	N	Y	Y	Y	N	N
MICHIGAN							
1	**Bergman**	Y	N	N	N	Y	Y
2	**Huizenga**	Y	N	N	N	Y	Y
3	*Amash*	N	N	Y	Y	N	Y
4	**Moolenaar**	Y	N	N	N	Y	Y
5	Kildee	N	Y	Y	Y	N	N
6	**Upton**	Y	Y	N	N	N	Y
7	**Walberg**	Y	N	N	N	Y	?
8	Slotkin	N	Y	Y	Y	N	N
9	Levin	N	Y	Y	Y	N	N
10	**Mitchell**	Y	N	N	N	Y	?
11	Stevens	N	Y	Y	Y	N	N
12	Dingell	N	Y	Y	Y	N	N
13	Tlaib	N	Y	Y	Y	N	N
14	Lawrence	N	Y	Y	Y	N	N
MINNESOTA							
1	**Hagedorn**	Y	N	N	N	Y	Y
2	Craig	N	Y	Y	Y	N	N
3	Phillips	N	Y	Y	Y	N	N
4	McCollum	N	Y	Y	Y	N	N
5	Omar	N	Y	Y	Y	N	N

		601	602	603	604	605	606
6	**Emmer**	Y	N	N	N	Y	Y
7	Peterson	N	Y	N	N	N	N
8	**Stauber**	Y	N	N	N	Y	Y
MISSISSIPPI							
1	**Kelly, T.**	Y	N	N	N	Y	Y
2	Thompson, B.	N	Y	Y	Y	?	?
3	**Guest**	Y	N	N	N	Y	Y
4	**Palazzo**	Y	N	N	N	Y	Y
MISSOURI							
1	Clay	N	Y	Y	Y	N	N
2	**Wagner**	Y	N	N	N	?	?
3	**Luetkemeyer**	Y	N	N	N	Y	Y
4	**Hartzler**	Y	N	N	N	Y	Y
5	Cleaver	N	Y	Y	Y	N	N
6	**Graves, S.**	Y	N	N	N	Y	Y
7	**Long**	Y	N	N	N	Y	Y
8	**Smith, J.**	Y	N	N	N	Y	Y
MONTANA							
AL	**Gianforte**	Y	N	N	N	Y	Y
NEBRASKA							
1	**Fortenberry**	Y	N	N	N	Y	Y
2	**Bacon**	Y	N	N	N	Y	Y
3	**Smith, Adrian**	Y	N	N	N	Y	Y
NEVADA							
1	Titus	N	Y	Y	Y	N	N
2	**Amodei**	Y	N	N	N	Y	Y
3	Lee	N	Y	Y	Y	N	N
4	Horsford	N	Y	Y	Y	N	N
NEW HAMPSHIRE							
1	Pappas	N	Y	Y	Y	N	N
2	Kuster	N	Y	Y	Y	N	N
NEW JERSEY							
1	Norcross	N	Y	Y	Y	N	N
2	Van Drew	N	Y	N	N	N	N
3	Kim	N	Y	Y	Y	N	N
4	**Smith, C.**	Y	Y	N	N	N	Y
5	Gottheimer	N	Y	Y	Y	N	N
6	Pallone	N	Y	Y	Y	N	N
7	Malinowski	N	Y	Y	Y	N	N
8	Sires	N	Y	Y	Y	N	?
9	Pascrell	N	Y	Y	Y	N	N
10	Payne	N	Y	Y	Y	N	N
11	Sherrill	N	Y	Y	Y	N	N
12	Watson Coleman	N	Y	Y	Y	N	N
NEW MEXICO							
1	Haaland	N	Y	Y	Y	N	N
2	Torres Small	N	Y	Y	Y	N	N
3	Luján	N	Y	Y	Y	N	N
NEW YORK							
1	**Zeldin**	Y	N	N	N	Y	Y
2	**King, P.**	Y	N	N	N	N	Y
3	Suozzi	N	Y	Y	Y	N	N
4	Rice, K.	N	Y	Y	Y	N	N
5	Meeks	N	Y	Y	Y	N	N
6	Meng	N	Y	Y	Y	N	N
7	Velázquez	N	Y	Y	Y	N	N
8	Jeffries	N	Y	Y	Y	N	N
9	Clarke	N	Y	Y	Y	N	N
10	Nadler	N	Y	Y	Y	N	N
11	Rose	N	Y	Y	Y	N	N
12	Maloney, C.	N	Y	Y	Y	N	N
13	Espaillat	N	Y	Y	Y	N	N
14	Ocasio-Cortez	N	Y	Y	Y	N	N
15	Serrano	N	Y	Y	Y	N	N
16	Engel	N	Y	Y	Y	N	N
17	Lowey	N	Y	Y	Y	?	?
18	Maloney, S.P.	N	Y	Y	Y	N	N
19	Delgado	N	Y	Y	Y	N	N
20	Tonko	N	Y	Y	Y	N	N
21	**Stefanik**	Y	Y	N	N	N	Y
22	Brindisi	Y	Y	Y	Y	N	N
23	**Reed**	Y	N	N	N	Y	Y
24	**Katko**	Y	Y	N	N	N	Y
25	Morelle	N	Y	Y	Y	N	N
26	Higgins, B.	N	Y	Y	Y	N	N
27	vacant						
NORTH CAROLINA							
1	Butterfield	N	Y	Y	Y	N	N
2	**Holding**	Y	N	N	N	Y	Y
3	**Murphy**	Y	N	N	N	Y	Y
4	Price	N	Y	Y	Y	N	N
5	**Foxx**	Y	N	N	N	Y	Y
6	**Walker**	Y	N	N	N	Y	Y
7	**Rouzer**	Y	N	N	N	Y	Y

		601	602	603	604	605	606
8	**Hudson**	+	-	N	N	+	+
9	**Bishop**	Y	N	N	N	Y	+
10	**McHenry**	Y	N	N	N	Y	Y
11	**Meadows**	Y	N	N	N	Y	Y
12	Adams	N	Y	Y	Y	N	N
13	**Budd**	Y	N	N	N	Y	Y
NORTH DAKOTA							
AL	**Armstrong**	Y	N	N	N	Y	Y
OHIO							
1	**Chabot**	Y	N	N	N	Y	Y
2	**Wenstrup**	Y	N	N	N	Y	Y
3	Beatty	-	+	Y	Y	-	-
4	**Jordan**	Y	N	N	N	Y	Y
5	**Latta**	Y	N	N	N	Y	Y
6	**Johnson, B.**	Y	N	N	N	Y	Y
7	**Gibbs**	Y	N	N	N	Y	Y
8	**Davidson**	Y	N	N	N	Y	Y
9	Kaptur	N	Y	Y	Y	N	N
10	**Turner**	Y	N	N	N	Y	Y
11	Fudge	N	Y	Y	Y	N	N
12	**Balderson**	Y	N	N	N	Y	Y
13	Ryan	N	Y	Y	Y	N	N
14	**Joyce**	Y	N	N	N	Y	Y
15	**Stivers**	Y	N	N	N	Y	Y
16	**Gonzalez**	Y	N	N	N	Y	Y
OKLAHOMA							
1	**Hern**	Y	N	N	N	Y	Y
2	**Mullin**	Y	N	N	N	Y	Y
3	**Lucas**	Y	N	N	N	Y	Y
4	**Cole**	Y	Y	N	N	Y	Y
5	Horn	Y	Y	Y	Y	N	N
OREGON							
1	Bonamici	N	Y	Y	Y	N	N
2	**Walden**	Y	N	N	N	Y	Y
3	Blumenauer	N	Y	Y	Y	N	N
4	DeFazio	N	Y	Y	Y	N	N
5	Schrader	N	Y	Y	Y	N	N
PENNSYLVANIA							
1	**Fitzpatrick**	Y	Y	N	N	N	N
2	Boyle	N	Y	Y	Y	N	N
3	Evans	N	Y	Y	Y	N	N
4	Dean	N	Y	Y	Y	N	N
5	Scanlon	N	Y	Y	Y	N	N
6	Houlahan	N	Y	Y	Y	N	N
7	Wild	N	Y	Y	Y	N	N
8	Cartwright	N	Y	Y	Y	N	N
9	**Meuser**	Y	N	N	N	Y	Y
10	**Perry**	Y	N	N	N	Y	Y
11	**Smucker**	Y	N	N	N	Y	?
12	**Keller**	Y	N	N	N	Y	Y
13	**Joyce**	Y	N	N	N	Y	Y
14	**Reschenthaler**	Y	N	N	N	Y	Y
15	**Thompson, G.**	Y	N	N	N	Y	Y
16	**Kelly, M.**	Y	N	N	N	Y	Y
17	Lamb	N	Y	Y	Y	N	N
18	Doyle	N	Y	Y	Y	N	N
RHODE ISLAND							
1	Cicilline	N	Y	Y	Y	N	N
2	Langevin	N	Y	Y	Y	N	N
SOUTH CAROLINA							
1	Cunningham	N	Y	Y	Y	N	N
2	**Wilson, J.**	Y	N	N	N	Y	Y
3	**Duncan**	Y	N	N	N	Y	Y
4	**Timmons**	+	-	-	-	+	+
5	**Norman**	Y	N	N	N	Y	Y
6	Clyburn	N	Y	Y	Y	N	N
7	**Rice, T.**	Y	N	N	N	Y	Y
SOUTH DAKOTA							
AL	**Johnson**	Y	N	N	N	Y	Y
TENNESSEE							
1	**Roe**	Y	N	N	N	Y	Y
2	**Burchett**	Y	N	N	N	Y	Y
3	**Fleischmann**	Y	N	N	N	Y	Y
4	**DesJarlais**	Y	N	N	N	Y	Y
5	Cooper	N	Y	Y	Y	N	N
6	**Rose**	?	?	?	-	?	?
7	**Green**	Y	N	N	N	Y	Y
8	**Kustoff**	Y	N	N	N	Y	Y
9	Cohen	N	Y	Y	Y	N	N
TEXAS							
1	**Gohmert**	Y	N	N	N	?	Y
2	**Crenshaw**	Y	N	N	N	Y	Y
3	**Taylor**	Y	N	N	N	Y	Y
4	**Ratcliffe**	Y	N	N	N	Y	Y

		601	602	603	604	605	606
5	**Gooden**	Y	N	N	N	Y	Y
6	**Wright**	Y	N	N	N	Y	Y
7	Fletcher	N	Y	Y	Y	N	N
8	**Brady**	Y	N	N	N	Y	?
9	Green, A.	N	Y	Y	Y	N	N
10	**McCaul**	Y	N	N	N	Y	Y
11	**Conaway**	Y	N	N	N	Y	Y
12	**Granger**	Y	N	N	N	Y	Y
13	**Thornberry**	Y	N	N	N	Y	Y
14	**Weber**	Y	N	N	N	Y	Y
15	Gonzalez	N	Y	Y	Y	N	N
16	Escobar	N	Y	Y	Y	N	N
17	**Flores**	Y	N	N	N	Y	Y
18	Jackson Lee	N	Y	Y	Y	N	N
19	**Arrington**	Y	N	N	N	Y	Y
20	Castro	N	Y	Y	Y	N	N
21	**Roy**	Y	N	N	N	Y	Y
22	**Olson**	Y	N	N	N	Y	Y
23	**Hurd**	Y	N	N	N	Y	Y
24	**Marchant**	Y	N	N	N	Y	Y
25	**Williams**	Y	N	N	N	Y	Y
26	**Burgess**	Y	N	N	N	Y	Y
27	**Cloud**	Y	N	N	N	Y	Y
28	Cuellar	N	Y	Y	Y	N	N
29	Garcia, S.	N	Y	Y	Y	N	N
30	Johnson, E.B.	N	Y	Y	Y	N	N
31	**Carter, J.**	Y	N	N	N	?	Y
32	Allred	N	Y	Y	Y	N	N
33	Veasey	N	Y	Y	Y	N	N
34	Vela	N	Y	Y	Y	N	N
35	Doggett	N	Y	Y	Y	N	N
36	**Babin**	Y	N	N	N	Y	Y
UTAH							
1	**Bishop, R.**	Y	N	N	N	Y	Y
2	**Stewart**	Y	N	N	N	Y	Y
3	**Curtis**	Y	N	N	N	Y	Y
4	McAdams	Y	Y	Y	Y	N	N
VERMONT							
AL	Welch	N	Y	Y	Y	N	N
VIRGINIA							
1	**Wittman**	Y	N	N	N	Y	Y
2	Luria	N	Y	Y	Y	N	N
3	Scott, R.	N	Y	Y	Y	N	N
4	McEachin	-	+	+	+	-	-
5	**Riggleman**	Y	N	N	N	Y	Y
6	**Cline**	Y	N	N	N	Y	Y
7	Spanberger	N	Y	Y	Y	N	N
8	Beyer	N	Y	Y	Y	N	N
9	**Griffith**	Y	N	N	N	Y	Y
10	Wexton	N	Y	Y	Y	N	N
11	Connolly	N	Y	Y	Y	N	N
WASHINGTON							
1	DelBene	N	Y	Y	Y	N	N
2	Larsen	N	Y	Y	Y	N	N
3	**Herrera Beutler**	Y	Y	N	N	Y	Y
4	**Newhouse**	Y	N	N	N	Y	Y
5	**McMorris Rodgers**	Y	?	N	N	Y	Y
6	Kilmer	N	Y	Y	Y	N	N
7	Jayapal	N	Y	Y	Y	N	N
8	Schrier	N	Y	Y	Y	N	N
9	Smith Adam	N	Y	Y	Y	N	N
10	Heck	N	Y	Y	Y	N	N
WEST VIRGINIA							
1	**McKinley**	Y	N	N	N	Y	Y
2	**Mooney**	Y	N	N	N	Y	Y
3	**Miller**	Y	N	N	N	Y	Y
WISCONSIN							
1	**Steil**	Y	N	N	N	Y	Y
2	Pocan	N	Y	Y	Y	N	N
3	Kind	N	Y	Y	Y	N	N
4	Moore	N	Y	Y	Y	N	N
5	**Sensenbrenner**	Y	N	N	N	Y	Y
6	**Grothman**	Y	N	N	N	Y	Y
7	**Duffy**						
8	**Gallagher**	Y	N	N	N	Y	Y
WYOMING							
AL	**Cheney**	Y	N	N	N	Y	Y
DELEGATES							
	Radewagen (A.S.)					?	?
	Norton (D.C.)					N	N
	San Nicolas (Guam)					N	N
	Sablan (N. Marianas)					N	N
	González-Colón (P.R.)					?	?
	Plaskett (V.I.)					?	?

607. HR823. Colorado Federal Lands - National Guard Aviation Training Site. Crow, D-Colo., amendment no. 6 that would express the sense of Congress that military aviation training on federal lands in Colorado, including at the Army National Guard high-altitude aviation training site in Gypsum, Colo., is critical to U.S. national security and the readiness of the armed forces. Adopted in Committee of the Whole 410-6: R 183-5; D 226-0; I 1-1. Oct. 31, 2019.

608. HR823. Colorado Federal Lands - Recommit. Tipton, R-Colo., motion to recommit the bill to the House Natural Resources Committee with instructions to report it back immediately with an amendment that would state that nothing in the bill would restrict or preclude military flights over any area subject to the bill's provisions, including for flight testing, training, and transportation. Motion rejected 199-210: R 184-1; D 14-209; I 1-0. Oct. 31, 2019.

609. HR823. Colorado Federal Lands - Passage. Passage of the bill that would modify land use authorities for over 400,000 acres of land in Colorado, particularly in areas in or along the Continental Divide, San Juan Mountains, Thompson Divide, and Curecanti National Recreation Area. The bill would effectively prohibit any new mining or mineral production activities on approximately 61,000 acres of federal lands in the San Juan Mountains and approximately 200,000 acres of federal lands within the Thompson Divide. Specifically, it would withdraw the lands from eligibility for activities permitted under federal laws governing public lands, mining, and mineral and geothermal leasing. Additionally, the bill would designate the Camp Hale National Historic Landscape and authorize $10 million for its administration by the U.S. Forest Service. Passed 227-182: R 5-180; D 222-1; I 0-1. *Note: A "nay" was a vote in support of the president's position.* Oct. 31, 2019.

610. HR4162. VA Education Benefit Election - Passage. Takano, D-Calif., motion to suspend the rules and pass the bill that would extend the period during which service members may elect to accept or decline eligibility for certain Veterans Affairs Department educational assistance benefits under a 1984 GI Bill. It would also end new enrollment in the program after fiscal 2029. Motion agreed to 408-0: R 187-0; D 220-0; I 1-0. *Note: A two-thirds majority of those present and voting (272 in this case) is required for passage under suspension of the rules.* Nov. 12, 2019.

611. HR3224. Female Veterans Health Care Programs - Passage. Takano, D-Calif., motion to suspend the rules and pass the bill that would expand a number of medical and other services under the Veterans Affairs Department, particularly for female veterans. Among other provisions, it would require all VA medical centers and clinics to offer women's health primary care services during regular business hours, expand a VA program that provides retreat-based counseling for female veterans, and authorize $1 million annually for a VA residency program for primary and emergency care clinicians focused on women's health. It would establish a women's health office within the Veterans Health Administration to oversee women's health care services and promote the expansion of clinical, research, and educational activities related to women's health care. The bill would also authorize $20 million for fiscal 2020 for the VA to support organizations providing assistance to female veterans and their families; extend to 14 days the period that newborn children of veterans are eligible for newborn care; and require a number of reports to Congress related to VA services provided to female veterans. Finally, the bill would establish a program to assist veterans who have experienced intimate partner violence or sexual assault and require the VA to establish policies to address harassment and sexual assault within the department, including reporting procedures and mandatory training for employees. Motion agreed to 399-11: R 177-10; D 222-0; I 0-1. *Note: A two-thirds majority of those present and voting (274 in this case) is required for passage under suspension of the rules.* Nov. 12, 2019.

612. HR3537. Veteran Entrepreneurship Program - Passage. Schneider, D-Ill., motion to suspend the rules and pass the bill that would codify the Boots to Business Program under the Small Business Administration, which provides entrepreneurship training to veterans, recently discharged service members, and military spouses interested in business ownership. It would authorize the program for five fiscal years, beginning on the first Oct. 1 after enactment. Among other provisions, it would allow the SBA to collaborate with public and private entities to develop courses and to issue grants to veteran business outreach centers and other entities to carry out the program. The bill would require the SBA to submit an annual report to Congress on the program, including program costs, demographic information of participants, and an evaluation of program effectiveness. Motion agreed to 424-1: R 196-0; D 228-0; I 0-1. *Note: A two-thirds majority of those present and voting (284 in this case) is required for passage under suspension of the rules.* Nov. 13, 2019.

		607	608	609	610	611	612
ALABAMA							
1	**Byrne**	Y	Y	N	Y	Y	Y
2	**Roby**	Y	Y	N	Y	Y	Y
3	**Rogers, M.**	?	?	?	Y	Y	Y
4	**Aderholt**	Y	Y	N	Y	Y	Y
5	**Brooks, M.**	Y	Y	N	Y	Y	Y
6	**Palmer**	Y	Y	N	Y	Y	Y
7	Sewell	Y	N	Y	Y	Y	Y
ALASKA							
AL	**Young**	Y	Y	N	Y	Y	Y
ARIZONA							
1	O'Halleran	Y	N	Y	Y	Y	Y
2	Kirkpatrick	Y	N	Y	Y	Y	Y
3	Grijalva	Y	N	Y	Y	Y	Y
4	**Gosar**	N	Y	N	Y	N	Y
5	**Biggs**	N	Y	N	Y	N	Y
6	**Schweikert**	Y	Y	N	Y	Y	Y
7	Gallego	Y	N	Y	Y	Y	Y
8	**Lesko**	Y	Y	N	Y	Y	Y
9	Stanton	Y	N	Y	Y	Y	Y
ARKANSAS							
1	**Crawford**	Y	Y	N	Y	Y	Y
2	**Hill, F.**	Y	Y	N	Y	Y	Y
3	**Womack**	Y	Y	N	Y	Y	Y
4	**Westerman**	Y	Y	N	Y	Y	Y
CALIFORNIA							
1	**LaMalfa**	Y	?	N	Y	Y	Y
2	Huffman	Y	N	Y	Y	Y	Y
3	Garamendi	Y	N	Y	Y	Y	Y
4	**McClintock**	Y	Y	N	Y	Y	Y
5	Thompson, M.	Y	N	Y	Y	Y	Y
6	Matsui	Y	N	Y	Y	Y	Y
7	Bera	Y	N	Y	Y	Y	Y
8	**Cook**	Y	Y	N	Y	Y	Y
9	McNerney	Y	N	Y	Y	Y	Y
10	Harder	Y	N	Y	Y	Y	Y
11	DeSaulnier	Y	N	Y	Y	Y	Y
12	Pelosi						
13	Lee B.	Y	N	Y	Y	Y	Y
14	Speier	Y	N	Y	Y	Y	Y
15	Swalwell	Y	N	Y	Y	Y	Y
16	Costa	Y	N	Y	Y	Y	Y
17	Khanna	Y	N	Y	Y	Y	Y
18	Eshoo	Y	N	?	Y	Y	Y
19	Lofgren	?	?	?	Y	Y	Y
20	Panetta	Y	N	Y	Y	Y	Y
21	Cox	Y	Y	Y	Y	Y	Y
22	**Nunes**	Y	Y	N	Y	Y	Y
23	**McCarthy**	Y	Y	N	Y	Y	Y
24	Carbajal	Y	N	Y	Y	Y	Y
25	Hill, K.*	Y	N	Y			
26	Brownley	Y	N	Y	Y	Y	Y
27	Chu	Y	N	Y	Y	Y	Y
28	Schiff	Y	N	Y	Y	Y	Y
29	Cárdenas	Y	N	Y	Y	Y	Y
30	Sherman	Y	N	Y	?	?	Y
31	Aguilar	Y	N	?	Y	Y	Y
32	Napolitano	Y	N	Y	Y	Y	Y
33	Lieu	Y	N	Y	Y	Y	Y
34	Gomez	Y	N	Y	Y	Y	Y
35	Torres	Y	N	Y	Y	Y	Y
36	Ruiz	Y	N	Y	Y	Y	Y
37	Bass	Y	N	Y	Y	Y	Y
38	Sánchez	Y	N	Y	Y	Y	Y
39	Cisneros	Y	N	Y	Y	Y	Y
40	Roybal-Allard	Y	N	Y	Y	Y	Y
41	Takano	Y	N	Y	Y	Y	Y
42	**Calvert**	Y	Y	N	Y	Y	Y
43	Waters	Y	N	Y	?	Y	Y
44	Barragán	Y	N	Y	Y	Y	Y
45	Porter	Y	Y	Y	Y	Y	Y
46	Correa	Y	N	Y	Y	Y	Y
47	Lowenthal	Y	N	Y	Y	Y	Y
48	Rouda	Y	N	Y	Y	Y	Y
49	Levin	Y	N	Y	Y	Y	Y
50	**Hunter**	Y	Y	N	Y	N	Y
51	Vargas	Y	N	Y	Y	Y	Y
52	Peters	Y	N	Y	Y	Y	Y
53	Davis, S.	?	?	?	Y	Y	Y
COLORADO							
1	DeGette	Y	N	Y	Y	Y	Y
2	Neguse	Y	N	Y	Y	Y	Y
3	**Tipton**	Y	Y	N	Y	Y	Y
4	**Buck**	Y	Y	N	Y	N	Y
5	**Lamborn**	Y	Y	N	Y	Y	Y
6	Crow	Y	N	Y	Y	Y	Y
7	Perlmutter	Y	N	Y	Y	Y	Y
CONNECTICUT							
1	Larson	Y	N	Y	Y	Y	Y
2	Courtney	Y	N	Y	Y	Y	Y
3	DeLauro	Y	N	Y	Y	Y	Y
4	Himes	?	N	Y	Y	Y	Y
5	Hayes	Y	N	Y	Y	Y	Y
DELAWARE							
AL	Blunt Rochester	Y	N	Y	Y	Y	Y
FLORIDA							
1	**Gaetz**	Y	Y	N	Y	Y	Y
2	**Dunn**	Y	Y	N	Y	Y	Y
3	**Yoho**	Y	Y	N	Y	Y	Y
4	**Rutherford**	Y	Y	N	Y	Y	Y
5	Lawson	Y	N	Y	Y	Y	Y
6	**Waltz**	Y	Y	N	Y	Y	Y
7	Murphy	Y	N	Y	Y	Y	Y
8	**Posey**	Y	Y	N	Y	Y	Y
9	Soto	Y	N	Y	Y	Y	Y
10	Demings	Y	N	Y	Y	Y	Y
11	**Webster**	Y	Y	N	Y	Y	Y
12	**Bilirakis**	Y	Y	N	Y	Y	Y
13	Crist	Y	N	Y	Y	Y	Y
14	Castor	Y	N	Y	Y	Y	Y
15	**Spano**	Y	Y	N	Y	Y	Y
16	**Buchanan**	Y	Y	N	Y	Y	Y
17	**Steube**	Y	Y	N	Y	Y	Y
18	**Mast**	Y	Y	N	Y	Y	Y
19	**Rooney**	Y	Y	Y	?	?	Y
20	Hastings	Y	N	Y	Y	Y	Y
21	Frankel	Y	N	Y	Y	Y	Y
22	Deutch	Y	N	Y	Y	Y	Y
23	Wasserman Schultz	Y	N	Y	Y	Y	Y
24	Wilson, F.	Y	N	Y	?	?	Y
25	**Diaz-Balart**	Y	Y	N	Y	Y	Y
26	Mucarsel-Powell	Y	N	Y	Y	Y	Y
27	Shalala	Y	N	Y	Y	Y	Y
GEORGIA							
1	**Carter, E.L.**	Y	Y	N	Y	Y	Y
2	Bishop, S.	Y	N	Y	Y	Y	Y
3	**Ferguson**	Y	Y	N	Y	Y	Y
4	Johnson, H.	Y	N	Y	Y	Y	Y
5	Lewis John	Y	N	Y	Y	Y	Y
6	McBath	Y	N	Y	Y	Y	Y
7	**Woodall**	Y	Y	N	Y	Y	Y
8	**Scott, A.**	Y	Y	N	Y	Y	Y
9	**Collins, D.**	Y	Y	N	Y	Y	Y
10	**Hice**	+	+	-	Y	N	Y
11	**Loudermilk**	Y	?	?	?	?	Y
12	**Allen**	Y	Y	N	Y	Y	Y
13	Scott, D.	Y	N	Y	Y	Y	Y
14	**Graves, T.**	Y	Y	N	Y	Y	Y
HAWAII							
1	Case	Y	N	Y	Y	Y	Y
2	Gabbard	Y	N	Y	?	?	?
IDAHO							
1	**Fulcher**	Y	Y	N	Y	Y	Y
2	**Simpson**	Y	Y	Y	Y	Y	Y
ILLINOIS							
1	Rush	Y	N	Y	?	?	Y
2	Kelly, R.	Y	N	Y	?	?	Y
3	Lipinski	Y	N	Y	Y	Y	Y
4	García, J.	Y	N	Y	Y	Y	Y
5	Quigley	Y	N	Y	Y	Y	Y
6	Casten	Y	N	Y	Y	Y	Y
7	Davis, D.	Y	N	Y	?	?	Y
8	Krishnamoorthi	Y	N	Y	Y	Y	Y
9	Schakowsky	Y	N	Y	Y	Y	Y
10	Schneider	Y	N	Y	Y	Y	Y
11	Foster	Y	N	Y	Y	Y	Y

KEY: **Republicans** Democrats *Independents*

Y	Voted for (yea)	N	Voted against (nay)	P	Voted "present"
+	Announced for	-	Announced against	?	Did not vote or otherwise make position known
#	Paired for	X	Paired against		

***NOTE:**
(California 25) Rep. Katie Hill resigned on Nov. 3. The last roll call vote she was eligible to cast was vote 609.

	607	608	609	610	611	612
12 **Bost**	Y	Y	N	Y	Y	Y
13 **Davis, R.**	Y	Y	N	Y	Y	Y
14 Underwood	Y	N	Y	Y	Y	Y
15 **Shimkus**	Y	Y	N	Y	Y	Y
16 **Kinzinger**	Y	Y	N	Y	Y	Y
17 Bustos	Y	N	Y	Y	Y	Y
18 **LaHood**	Y	Y	N	Y	Y	Y
INDIANA						
1 Visclosky	Y	N	Y	+	+	Y
2 **Walorski**	Y	Y	N	Y	Y	Y
3 **Banks**	Y	Y	N	Y	Y	Y
4 **Baird**	Y	Y	N	Y	Y	Y
5 **Brooks, S.**	Y	Y	N	Y	Y	Y
6 **Pence**	Y	Y	N	Y	Y	Y
7 Carson	Y	N	Y	Y	Y	Y
8 **Bucshon**	Y	Y	N	Y	Y	Y
9 **Hollingsworth**	Y	Y	N	Y	Y	Y
IOWA						
1 Finkenauer	Y	Y	Y	Y	Y	Y
2 Loebsack	Y	N	Y	Y	Y	Y
3 Axne	Y	Y	Y	Y	Y	Y
4 **King, S.**	Y	Y	N	Y	Y	Y
KANSAS						
1 **Marshall**	Y	Y	N	Y	Y	Y
2 **Watkins**	Y	Y	N	Y	Y	Y
3 Davids	Y	N	Y	Y	Y	Y
4 **Estes**	Y	Y	N	Y	Y	Y
KENTUCKY						
1 **Comer**	Y	Y	N	Y	Y	Y
2 **Guthrie**	Y	Y	N	Y	Y	Y
3 Yarmuth	Y	N	Y	Y	Y	Y
4 **Massie**	Y	Y	N	Y	N	Y
5 **Rogers, H.**	Y	Y	N	Y	Y	Y
6 **Barr**	Y	Y	N	Y	Y	Y
LOUISIANA						
1 **Scalise**	Y	Y	N	Y	Y	Y
2 Richmond	Y	N	Y	Y	Y	Y
3 **Higgins, C.**	Y	Y	N	Y	Y	Y
4 **Johnson, M.**	Y	Y	N	Y	Y	Y
5 **Abraham**	Y	Y	N	Y	Y	Y
6 **Graves, G.**	Y	Y	N	Y	Y	Y
MAINE						
1 Pingree	Y	N	Y	Y	Y	Y
2 Golden	Y	Y	Y	Y	Y	Y
MARYLAND						
1 **Harris**	Y	Y	N	Y	N	Y
2 Ruppersberger	Y	N	Y	Y	Y	Y
3 Sarbanes	Y	N	Y	Y	Y	Y
4 Brown, A.	Y	N	Y	Y	Y	Y
5 Hoyer	Y	N	Y	Y	Y	Y
6 Trone	Y	N	Y	Y	Y	Y
7 vacant						
8 Raskin	Y	N	Y	Y	Y	Y
MASSACHUSETTS						
1 Neal	Y	N	Y	Y	Y	Y
2 McGovern	Y	N	Y	Y	Y	Y
3 Trahan	Y	N	Y	Y	Y	Y
4 Kennedy	Y	N	Y	Y	Y	Y
5 Clark	Y	N	Y	Y	Y	Y
6 Moulton	Y	N	Y	Y	Y	Y
7 Pressley	Y	N	Y	Y	Y	Y
8 Lynch	Y	N	Y	Y	Y	Y
9 Keating	Y	N	Y	Y	Y	Y
MICHIGAN						
1 **Bergman**	Y	Y	N	Y	Y	Y
2 **Huizenga**	Y	Y	N	Y	Y	Y
3 *Amash*	N	Y	N	Y	N	N
4 **Moolenaar**	Y	Y	N	Y	Y	Y
5 Kildee	Y	N	Y	Y	Y	Y
6 **Upton**	Y	Y	N	Y	Y	Y
7 **Walberg**	?	?	?	Y	Y	Y
8 Slotkin	Y	Y	Y	Y	Y	Y
9 Levin	Y	N	Y	Y	Y	Y
10 **Mitchell**	?	?	?	Y	Y	Y
11 Stevens	Y	N	Y	Y	Y	Y
12 Dingell	Y	N	Y	Y	Y	Y
13 Tlaib	Y	N	Y	Y	Y	Y
14 Lawrence	Y	N	Y	Y	Y	Y
MINNESOTA						
1 **Hagedorn**	Y	Y	N	Y	Y	Y
2 Craig	Y	N	Y	Y	Y	Y
3 Phillips	Y	N	Y	Y	Y	Y
4 McCollum	Y	N	Y	Y	Y	Y
5 Omar	Y	N	Y	Y	Y	Y

	607	608	609	610	611	612
6 **Emmer**	Y	Y	N	Y	Y	Y
7 Peterson	Y	N	Y	Y	Y	Y
8 **Stauber**	Y	Y	N	Y	Y	Y
MISSISSIPPI						
1 **Kelly, T.**	Y	Y	N	Y	Y	Y
2 Thompson, B.	?	?	?	Y	Y	Y
3 **Guest**	Y	Y	N	Y	Y	Y
4 **Palazzo**	Y	Y	N	Y	Y	Y
MISSOURI						
1 Clay	Y	N	Y	Y	Y	Y
2 **Wagner**	?	?	?	Y	Y	Y
3 **Luetkemeyer**	Y	Y	N	Y	Y	Y
4 **Hartzler**	Y	Y	N	Y	Y	Y
5 Cleaver	Y	N	Y	Y	Y	Y
6 **Graves, S.**	Y	Y	N	Y	Y	Y
7 **Long**	Y	Y	N	Y	Y	Y
8 **Smith, J.**	Y	Y	N	Y	Y	Y
MONTANA						
AL **Gianforte**	Y	Y	N	Y	Y	Y
NEBRASKA						
1 **Fortenberry**	Y	Y	N	Y	Y	Y
2 **Bacon**	Y	Y	N	Y	Y	Y
3 **Smith, Adrian**	Y	Y	N	Y	Y	Y
NEVADA						
1 Titus	Y	N	Y	Y	Y	Y
2 **Amodei**	Y	Y	N	Y	Y	Y
3 Lee	Y	N	Y	Y	Y	Y
4 Horsford	Y	N	Y	Y	Y	Y
NEW HAMPSHIRE						
1 Pappas	Y	N	Y	Y	Y	Y
2 Kuster	Y	N	Y	Y	Y	Y
NEW JERSEY						
1 Norcross	Y	N	Y	Y	Y	Y
2 Van Drew	Y	Y	Y	Y	Y	Y
3 Kim	Y	N	Y	Y	Y	Y
4 **Smith, C.**	Y	Y	Y	Y	Y	Y
5 Gottheimer	Y	Y	Y	Y	Y	Y
6 Pallone	Y	N	Y	Y	Y	Y
7 Malinowski	Y	N	Y	Y	Y	Y
8 Sires	?	?	?	Y	Y	Y
9 Pascrell	Y	N	Y	Y	Y	Y
10 Payne	Y	N	Y	Y	Y	Y
11 Sherrill	?	?	?	Y	Y	Y
12 Watson Coleman	Y	N	Y	Y	Y	Y
NEW MEXICO						
1 Haaland	Y	N	Y	Y	Y	Y
2 Torres Small	Y	N	Y	Y	Y	Y
3 Luján	Y	N	Y	Y	Y	Y
NEW YORK						
1 **Zeldin**	Y	Y	N	Y	Y	Y
2 **King, P.**	Y	Y	N	Y	Y	Y
3 Suozzi	Y	N	Y	Y	Y	Y
4 Rice, K.	Y	N	Y	Y	Y	Y
5 Meeks	Y	N	Y	Y	Y	Y
6 Meng	Y	N	Y	Y	Y	Y
7 Velázquez	Y	N	Y	Y	Y	Y
8 Jeffries	Y	N	Y	Y	Y	Y
9 Clarke	Y	N	Y	Y	Y	Y
10 Nadler	Y	N	Y	Y	Y	Y
11 Rose	Y	Y	Y	Y	Y	Y
12 Maloney, C.	Y	N	Y	Y	Y	Y
13 Espaillat	Y	N	Y	Y	Y	Y
14 Ocasio-Cortez	Y	N	Y	Y	Y	Y
15 Serrano	Y	N	Y	Y	Y	?
16 Engel	Y	N	Y	Y	Y	Y
17 Lowey	?	?	?	Y	Y	Y
18 Maloney, S.P.	Y	N	Y	Y	Y	Y
19 Delgado	Y	N	Y	Y	Y	Y
20 Tonko	Y	N	Y	Y	Y	Y
21 **Stefanik**	Y	Y	N	Y	Y	Y
22 Brindisi	Y	N	Y	Y	Y	Y
23 **Reed**	Y	Y	N	Y	Y	Y
24 **Katko**	Y	Y	N	Y	Y	Y
25 Morelle	Y	N	Y	Y	Y	Y
26 Higgins, B.	Y	N	Y	Y	Y	Y
27 vacant						
NORTH CAROLINA						
1 Butterfield	Y	N	Y	Y	Y	Y
2 **Holding**	Y	Y	N	Y	Y	Y
3 **Murphy**	Y	Y	N	Y	Y	Y
4 Price	Y	N	Y	Y	Y	Y
5 **Foxx**	Y	Y	N	Y	Y	Y
6 **Walker**	Y	Y	N	Y	Y	Y
7 **Rouzer**	Y	Y	N	Y	Y	Y

	607	608	609	610	611	612
8 **Hudson**	+	+	-	Y	Y	Y
9 **Bishop**	Y	Y	N	Y	+	Y
10 **McHenry**	Y	Y	N	Y	Y	Y
11 **Meadows**	Y	Y	N	Y	Y	Y
12 Adams	Y	N	Y	Y	Y	Y
13 **Budd**	Y	Y	N	Y	Y	Y
NORTH DAKOTA						
AL **Armstrong**	Y	Y	N	Y	Y	Y
OHIO						
1 **Chabot**	Y	Y	N	Y	Y	Y
2 **Wenstrup**	Y	Y	N	Y	Y	Y
3 Beatty	+	-	+	Y	Y	Y
4 **Jordan**	Y	Y	N	Y	Y	Y
5 **Latta**	Y	Y	N	Y	Y	Y
6 **Johnson, B.**	Y	Y	N	Y	Y	Y
7 **Gibbs**	Y	Y	N	Y	Y	Y
8 **Davidson**	Y	Y	N	Y	N	Y
9 Kaptur	Y	N	Y	Y	Y	Y
10 **Turner**	Y	Y	N	?	?	Y
11 Fudge	Y	N	Y	Y	Y	Y
12 **Balderson**	Y	Y	N	Y	Y	Y
13 Ryan	Y	N	Y	Y	Y	Y
14 **Joyce**	Y	Y	N	Y	Y	Y
15 **Stivers**	Y	Y	N	Y	Y	Y
16 **Gonzalez**	Y	Y	N	Y	Y	Y
OKLAHOMA						
1 **Hern**	Y	Y	N	Y	Y	Y
2 **Mullin**	Y	Y	N	Y	Y	Y
3 **Lucas**	Y	Y	N	Y	Y	Y
4 **Cole**	Y	Y	N	Y	Y	Y
5 Horn	Y	Y	Y	Y	Y	Y
OREGON						
1 Bonamici	Y	N	Y	Y	Y	Y
2 **Walden**	Y	Y	N	Y	Y	Y
3 Blumenauer	Y	N	Y	Y	Y	Y
4 DeFazio	Y	N	Y	Y	Y	Y
5 Schrader	Y	N	Y	Y	Y	Y
PENNSYLVANIA						
1 **Fitzpatrick**	Y	Y	Y	Y	Y	Y
2 Boyle	Y	N	Y	Y	Y	Y
3 Evans	Y	N	Y	Y	Y	Y
4 Dean	Y	N	Y	?	Y	Y
5 Scanlon	Y	N	Y	Y	Y	Y
6 Houlahan	Y	Y	Y	Y	Y	Y
7 Wild	Y	N	Y	Y	Y	Y
8 Cartwright	Y	N	Y	Y	Y	Y
9 **Meuser**	Y	Y	N	Y	Y	Y
10 **Perry**	Y	Y	N	Y	Y	Y
11 **Smucker**	Y	Y	N	+	+	Y
12 **Keller**	Y	Y	N	Y	Y	Y
13 **Joyce**	Y	Y	N	Y	Y	Y
14 **Reschenthaler**	Y	Y	N	Y	Y	Y
15 **Thompson, G.**	Y	Y	N	Y	Y	Y
16 **Kelly, M.**	Y	Y	N	Y	Y	Y
17 Lamb	Y	Y	Y	Y	Y	Y
18 Doyle	Y	?	Y	Y	Y	Y
RHODE ISLAND						
1 Cicilline	Y	N	Y	Y	Y	Y
2 Langevin	Y	N	Y	Y	Y	Y
SOUTH CAROLINA						
1 Cunningham	Y	N	Y	Y	Y	Y
2 **Wilson, J.**	Y	Y	N	Y	Y	Y
3 **Duncan**	N	Y	N	Y	Y	Y
4 **Timmons**	+	+	-	+	+	+
5 **Norman**	Y	?	?	Y	N	Y
6 Clyburn	Y	N	Y	Y	Y	Y
7 **Rice, T.**	N	Y	N	Y	Y	Y
SOUTH DAKOTA						
AL **Johnson**	Y	Y	N	Y	Y	Y
TENNESSEE						
1 **Roe**	Y	Y	N	Y	Y	Y
2 **Burchett**	Y	Y	N	Y	Y	Y
3 **Fleischmann**	Y	Y	N	Y	Y	Y
4 **DesJarlais**	Y	Y	?	Y	Y	Y
5 Cooper	Y	N	Y	Y	Y	Y
6 **Rose**	?	?	?	Y	Y	Y
7 **Green**	Y	Y	N	Y	Y	Y
8 **Kustoff**	Y	Y	N	Y	Y	Y
9 Cohen	Y	N	Y	Y	Y	Y
TEXAS						
1 **Gohmert**	Y	Y	N	Y	Y	Y
2 **Crenshaw**	Y	Y	N	Y	Y	Y
3 **Taylor**	Y	Y	N	Y	N	Y
4 **Ratcliffe**	Y	Y	N	Y	Y	Y

	607	608	609	610	611	612
5 **Gooden**	Y	Y	N	Y	Y	Y
6 **Wright**	Y	Y	N	Y	Y	Y
7 Fletcher	Y	N	Y	Y	Y	Y
8 **Brady**	?	?	?	Y	Y	Y
9 Green, A.	Y	N	Y	Y	Y	Y
10 **McCaul**	Y	Y	N	Y	Y	Y
11 **Conaway**	Y	Y	N	Y	Y	Y
12 **Granger**	Y	Y	N	Y	Y	Y
13 **Thornberry**	Y	Y	N	+	+	Y
14 **Weber**	Y	Y	N	Y	Y	Y
15 Gonzalez	Y	N	Y	+	+	Y
16 Escobar	Y	N	Y	Y	Y	Y
17 **Flores**	Y	N	N	Y	Y	Y
18 Jackson Lee	Y	N	Y	Y	Y	Y
19 **Arrington**	Y	Y	N	Y	Y	Y
20 Castro	Y	N	Y	Y	Y	Y
21 **Roy**	N	Y	N	Y	Y	Y
22 **Olson**	Y	Y	N	?	Y	Y
23 **Hurd**	Y	Y	N	+	+	Y
24 **Marchant**	Y	Y	N	?	?	Y
25 **Williams**	Y	Y	N	Y	Y	Y
26 **Burgess**	Y	Y	N	Y	Y	Y
27 **Cloud**	Y	Y	N	Y	Y	Y
28 Cuellar	Y	N	Y	Y	Y	Y
29 Garcia, S.	Y	N	Y	Y	Y	Y
30 Johnson, E.B.	Y	N	Y	Y	Y	Y
31 **Carter, J.**	Y	Y	N	Y	Y	Y
32 Allred	Y	N	Y	Y	Y	Y
33 Veasey	Y	N	Y	Y	Y	Y
34 Vela	Y	N	Y	Y	Y	Y
35 Doggett	Y	N	Y	Y	Y	Y
36 **Babin**	Y	Y	N	Y	Y	Y
UTAH						
1 **Bishop, R.**	Y	Y	N	Y	Y	Y
2 **Stewart**	Y	Y	N	Y	Y	Y
3 **Curtis**	Y	Y	N	Y	Y	Y
4 McAdams	Y	Y	N	Y	Y	Y
VERMONT						
AL Welch	Y	?	Y	Y	Y	Y
VIRGINIA						
1 **Wittman**	Y	Y	N	?	?	Y
2 Luria	Y	N	Y	Y	Y	Y
3 Scott, R.	Y	N	Y	Y	Y	Y
4 McEachin	+	-	+	+	+	+
5 **Riggleman**	Y	Y	N	Y	Y	Y
6 **Cline**	Y	Y	N	Y	Y	Y
7 Spanberger	Y	Y	Y	Y	Y	Y
8 Beyer	Y	N	Y	Y	Y	?
9 **Griffith**	Y	Y	N	Y	Y	Y
10 Wexton	Y	N	Y	Y	Y	Y
11 Connolly	Y	N	Y	Y	Y	Y
WASHINGTON						
1 DelBene	Y	N	Y	Y	Y	Y
2 Larsen	Y	N	Y	Y	Y	Y
3 **Herrera Beutler**	Y	Y	N	Y	Y	Y
4 **Newhouse**	Y	Y	N	Y	Y	Y
5 **McMorris Rodgers**	Y	Y	N	Y	Y	Y
6 Kilmer	Y	N	Y	Y	Y	Y
7 Jayapal	Y	N	Y	Y	Y	Y
8 Schrier	Y	N	Y	Y	Y	Y
9 Smith Adam	Y	N	Y	Y	Y	Y
10 Heck	Y	N	Y	Y	Y	Y
WEST VIRGINIA						
1 **McKinley**	Y	Y	N	Y	Y	Y
2 **Mooney**	Y	Y	N	Y	Y	Y
3 **Miller**	Y	Y	N	Y	Y	Y
WISCONSIN						
1 **Steil**	Y	Y	N	Y	Y	Y
2 Pocan	Y	N	Y	+	+	Y
3 Kind	Y	N	Y	Y	Y	Y
4 Moore	Y	N	Y	Y	Y	Y
5 **Sensenbrenner**	Y	Y	N	Y	Y	Y
6 **Grothman**	Y	Y	N	Y	Y	Y
7 **Duffy**						
8 **Gallagher**	Y	Y	N	Y	Y	Y
WYOMING						
AL **Cheney**	Y	Y	N	Y	Y	Y
DELEGATES						
Radewagen (A.S.)	?					
Norton (D.C.)	Y					
San Nicolas (Guam)	Y					
Sablan (N. Marianas)	Y					
González-Colón (P.R.)	?					
Plaskett (V.I.)	?					

613. HR499. Disabled Veteran-Owned Business Classification - Passage. Schneider, D-Ill., motion to suspend the rules and pass the bill that would allow the spouse of a deceased veteran with a service-connected disability to continue to classify their small business as a service-disabled veteran-owned small business for up to three years after the veteran's death, in the case of a veteran who had less than a 100 percent disability rating. Motion agreed to 423-0: R 194-0; D 228-0; I 1-0. *Note: A two-thirds majority of those present and voting (282 in this case) is required for passage under suspension of the rules.* Nov. 13, 2019.

614. HR3734. Veterans Small Business Task Force - Passage. Schneider, D-Ill., motion to suspend the rules and pass the bill that would require an inter-agency task force on the development of veteran-owned small businesses to report annually to Congress on its appointments, activities, outreach to veterans, and plans for promoting services available to veterans. Additionally, it would require the Government Accountability Office to submit a report to Congress on the accessibility of credit used by small businesses owned and controlled by veterans, service-disabled veterans, reservists, or their spouses. Motion agreed to 421-3: R 193-2; D 228-0; I 0-1. *Note: A two-thirds majority of those present and voting (283 in this case) is required for passage under suspension of the rules.* Nov. 13, 2019.

615. HRES661, HRES693, HR4863. Export-Import Bank Reauthorization - Previous Question. DeSaulnier, D-Calif., motion to order the previous question (thus ending debate and possibility of amendment) on the rule (H Res 695) that would provide for House floor consideration of the United States Export Finance Agency Act (HR 4863), including floor consideration of 21 amendments to the bill. The rule would also provide for automatic agreement to a resolution (H Res 661) that would allow the House general counsel to retain private counsel in support of the ongoing impeachment inquiry into President Donald Trump and automatic agreement to a resolution (H Res 693) that would authorize the directors of the House Diversity and Inclusion Office and the House Whistle-blower Ombudsman Office, respectively, to appoint and fix the pay of their employees. It would modify the House Rules for the 116th Congress to extend authorities and operations of the House Select Committee on the Modernization of Congress through the end of the 116th Congress. Additionally, the rule would provide for a motion to discharge a concurrent resolution (H Con Res 70) from the House Foreign Affairs Committee to be offered on Thursday, Nov. 21, 2019, and it would waive section 7 of the War Powers Resolution related to the concurrent resolution. The concurrent resolution (H Con Res 70) would direct the president to withdraw U.S. military forces from hostilities in Syria, unless a specific use of force is authorized by Congress. Motion agreed to 226-198: R 0-195; D 226-2; I 0-1. Nov. 14, 2019.

616. HR4863, HRES661, HRES693. Export-Import Bank Reauthorization - Rule. Adoption of the rule (H Res 695) that would provide for House floor consideration of the United States Export Finance Agency Act (HR 4863), including floor consideration of 21 amendments to the bill. The rule would also provide for automatic agreement to a resolution (H Res 661) that would allow the House general counsel to retain private counsel in support of the ongoing impeachment inquiry into President Donald Trump and automatic agreement to a resolution (H Res 693) that would authorize the directors of the House Diversity and Inclusion Office and the House Whistle-blower Ombudsman Office, respectively, to appoint and fix the pay of their employees.
It would modify the House Rules for the 116th Congress to extend authorities and operations of the House Select Committee on the Modernization of Congress through the end of the 116th Congress. Additionally, the rule would provide for a motion to discharge a concurrent resolution (H Con Res 70) from the House Foreign Affairs Committee to be offered on Thursday, Nov. 21, 2019, and it would waive section 7 of the War Powers Resolution related to the concurrent resolution. The concurrent resolution (H Con Res 70) would direct the president to withdraw U.S. military forces from hostilities in Syria, unless a specific use of force is authorized by Congress. Adopted 228-198: R 0-196; D 228-1; I 0-1. Nov. 14, 2019.

617. HR4863. Export-Import Bank Reauthorization - Human Rights and Free Speech Sanctions. Torres, D-Calif., amendment no. 2 that would prohibit the Export-Import Bank from approving transactions by any individual subject to certain sanctions related to human rights or free speech violations, including sanctions related to demonstrations in Hong Kong and political repression of religious and ethnic minorities in China and Myanmar. Adopted in Committee of the Whole 419-2: R 192-1; D 226-0; I 1-1. Nov. 15, 2019.

618. HR4863. Export-Import Bank Reauthorization - Energy Efficiency Office. Flores, R-Texas, for Burgess, R-Texas, amendment no. 3 that would require the Export-Import Bank to establish an office focusing on energy efficiency and clean energy exports. It would also require the Ex-Im Bank to consider potential energy price increases resulting from agency-supported exports, and it would allow the agency to withhold financing from a project for energy affordability reasons. It would require the agency to report annually to Congress on increased energy affordability or emissions reductions resulting from agency-financed exports. Rejected in Committee of the Whole 188-232: R 182-11; D 6-219; I 0-2. Nov. 15, 2019.

		613	614	615	616	617	618
ALABAMA							
1	**Byrne**	Y	Y	N	N	Y	Y
2	**Roby**	Y	Y	N	N	Y	Y
3	**Rogers, M.**	Y	Y	N	N	Y	Y
4	**Aderholt**	Y	Y	N	N	Y	Y
5	**Brooks, M.**	Y	Y	N	N	Y	Y
6	**Palmer**	Y	Y	N	N	Y	Y
7	Sewell	Y	Y	Y	Y	Y	N
ALASKA							
AL	**Young**	Y	Y	N	N	Y	Y
ARIZONA							
1	O'Halleran	Y	Y	Y	Y	Y	N
2	Kirkpatrick	Y	Y	Y	Y	Y	N
3	Grijalva	Y	Y	Y	Y	Y	N
4	**Gosar**	Y	Y	N	N	N	N
5	**Biggs**	Y	N	N	N	Y	N
6	**Schweikert**	Y	Y	N	N	Y	Y
7	Gallego	Y	Y	Y	Y	?	?
8	**Lesko**	Y	Y	N	N	Y	Y
9	Stanton	Y	Y	Y	Y	Y	N
ARKANSAS							
1	**Crawford**	Y	Y	N	N	Y	Y
2	**Hill, F.**	Y	Y	N	N	Y	Y
3	**Womack**	Y	Y	N	N	Y	Y
4	**Westerman**	Y	Y	N	N	Y	Y
CALIFORNIA							
1	**LaMalfa**	Y	Y	N	N	Y	Y
2	Huffman	Y	Y	Y	Y	Y	N
3	Garamendi	Y	Y	Y	Y	Y	N
4	**McClintock**	Y	?	N	N	Y	Y
5	Thompson, M.	Y	Y	Y	Y	Y	N
6	Matsui	Y	Y	Y	Y	Y	N
7	Bera	Y	Y	Y	Y	Y	N
8	**Cook**	Y	Y	N	N	Y	Y
9	McNerney	Y	Y	Y	Y	Y	N
10	Harder	Y	Y	Y	Y	Y	N
11	DeSaulnier	Y	Y	Y	Y	Y	N
12	Pelosi						
13	Lee B.	Y	Y	Y	Y	Y	N
14	Speier	Y	Y	Y	Y	Y	N
15	Swalwell	Y	Y	Y	Y	Y	N
16	Costa	Y	Y	Y	Y	Y	N
17	Khanna	Y	Y	Y	Y	Y	N
18	Eshoo	Y	Y	Y	Y	Y	N
19	Lofgren	Y	Y	Y	Y	?	?
20	Panetta	Y	Y	Y	Y	Y	N
21	Cox	Y	Y	Y	Y	Y	N
22	**Nunes**	Y	Y	N	N	Y	Y
23	**McCarthy**	Y	Y	N	N	Y	Y
24	Carbajal	Y	Y	Y	Y	Y	N
25	vacant						
26	Brownley	Y	Y	Y	Y	Y	N
27	Chu	Y	Y	Y	Y	Y	N
28	Schiff	Y	Y	+	Y	Y	N
29	Cárdenas	Y	Y	Y	Y	Y	N
30	Sherman	Y	Y	Y	Y	Y	N
31	Aguilar	Y	Y	Y	Y	Y	N
32	Napolitano	Y	Y	Y	Y	Y	N
33	Lieu	Y	Y	Y	Y	Y	N
34	Gomez	Y	Y	Y	Y	Y	N
35	Torres	Y	Y	Y	Y	Y	N
36	Ruiz	Y	Y	Y	Y	Y	N
37	Bass	Y	Y	Y	Y	Y	N
38	Sánchez	Y	Y	Y	Y	Y	N
39	Cisneros	Y	Y	Y	Y	Y	N
40	Roybal-Allard	Y	Y	Y	Y	Y	N
41	Takano	Y	Y	Y	Y	Y	N
42	**Calvert**	Y	Y	N	N	Y	Y
43	Waters	Y	Y	Y	Y	Y	N
44	Barragán	Y	Y	Y	Y	Y	N
45	Porter	Y	Y	Y	N	Y	N
46	Correa	Y	Y	Y	Y	Y	N
47	Lowenthal	Y	Y	Y	Y	Y	N
48	Rouda	Y	Y	Y	Y	Y	N
49	Levin	Y	Y	Y	Y	Y	N
50	**Hunter**	Y	Y	N	N	Y	Y
51	Vargas	Y	Y	Y	Y	Y	N
52	Peters	Y	Y	Y	Y	Y	N
53	Davis, S.	Y	Y	Y	Y	Y	N
COLORADO							
1	DeGette	Y	Y	Y	Y	Y	N
2	Neguse	Y	Y	Y	Y	Y	N
3	**Tipton**	Y	Y	N	N	Y	Y
4	**Buck**	Y	Y	N	N	Y	Y
5	**Lamborn**	Y	Y	N	N	Y	Y
6	Crow	Y	Y	Y	Y	Y	N
7	Perlmutter	Y	Y	Y	Y	Y	N
CONNECTICUT							
1	Larson	Y	Y	Y	Y	Y	N
2	Courtney	Y	Y	Y	Y	Y	N
3	DeLauro	Y	Y	Y	Y	Y	N
4	Himes	Y	Y	Y	Y	Y	N
5	Hayes	Y	Y	Y	Y	Y	N
DELAWARE							
AL	Blunt Rochester	Y	Y	Y	Y	Y	N
FLORIDA							
1	**Gaetz**	Y	Y	N	N	Y	Y
2	**Dunn**	Y	Y	N	N	Y	Y
3	**Yoho**	Y	Y	-	N	Y	Y
4	**Rutherford**	Y	Y	N	N	Y	Y
5	Lawson	Y	Y	Y	Y	Y	N
6	**Waltz**	+	Y	N	N	Y	Y
7	Murphy	Y	Y	Y	Y	Y	N
8	**Posey**	Y	Y	N	N	Y	Y
9	Soto	Y	Y	Y	Y	Y	N
10	Demings	Y	Y	Y	Y	Y	N
11	**Webster**	Y	Y	N	N	Y	Y
12	**Bilirakis**	Y	Y	N	N	Y	Y
13	Crist	Y	Y	Y	Y	Y	N
14	Castor	Y	Y	Y	Y	Y	N
15	**Spano**	Y	Y	N	N	Y	Y
16	**Buchanan**	Y	Y	N	N	Y	Y
17	**Steube**	Y	Y	N	N	Y	Y
18	**Mast**	Y	Y	N	N	Y	Y
19	**Rooney**	Y	Y	N	N	Y	N
20	Hastings	Y	Y	Y	Y	Y	N
21	Frankel	Y	Y	Y	Y	Y	N
22	Deutch	Y	Y	Y	Y	Y	N
23	Wasserman Schultz	Y	Y	Y	Y	Y	N
24	Wilson, F.	Y	Y	Y	Y	Y	N
25	**Diaz-Balart**	Y	Y	N	N	Y	Y
26	Mucarsel-Powell	Y	Y	Y	Y	Y	N
27	Shalala	Y	Y	Y	Y	Y	N
GEORGIA							
1	**Carter, E.L.**	Y	Y	N	N	Y	Y
2	Bishop, S.	Y	Y	Y	Y	Y	N
3	**Ferguson**	Y	Y	N	N	Y	Y
4	Johnson, H.	Y	Y	Y	Y	Y	N
5	Lewis John	Y	Y	Y	Y	Y	N
6	McBath	Y	Y	Y	Y	Y	N
7	**Woodall**	Y	Y	N	N	Y	Y
8	**Scott, A.**	Y	Y	N	N	Y	Y
9	**Collins, D.**	Y	Y	N	N	Y	Y
10	**Hice**	Y	Y	N	N	Y	N
11	**Loudermilk**	Y	Y	N	N	Y	Y
12	**Allen**	Y	Y	N	N	Y	Y
13	Scott, D.	Y	Y	Y	Y	Y	N
14	**Graves, T.**	Y	Y	N	N	Y	Y
HAWAII							
1	Case	Y	Y	Y	Y	Y	N
2	Gabbard	?	?	?	?	?	?
IDAHO							
1	**Fulcher**	Y	Y	N	N	Y	Y
2	**Simpson**	Y	Y	N	N	Y	Y
ILLINOIS							
1	Rush	Y	Y	Y	Y	Y	N
2	Kelly, R.	Y	Y	Y	Y	Y	N
3	Lipinski	Y	Y	Y	Y	Y	N
4	García, J.	Y	Y	Y	Y	Y	N
5	Quigley	Y	Y	Y	Y	Y	N
6	Casten	Y	Y	Y	Y	Y	N
7	Davis, D.	Y	Y	Y	Y	Y	N
8	Krishnamoorthi	Y	Y	Y	Y	Y	N
9	Schakowsky	Y	Y	Y	Y	Y	N
10	Schneider	Y	Y	Y	Y	Y	N
11	Foster	Y	Y	Y	Y	Y	N

KEY: **Republicans** Democrats *Independents*

Y	Voted for (yea)	N	Voted against (nay)	P	Voted "present"
+	Announced for	-	Announced against	?	Did not vote or otherwise make position known
#	Paired for	X	Paired against		

		613	614	615	616	617	618
12	**Bost**	Y	Y	N	N	Y	Y
13	**Davis, R.**	Y	Y	N	N	Y	Y
14	Underwood	Y	Y	Y	Y	+	N
15	**Shimkus**	Y	Y	N	N	Y	Y
16	**Kinzinger**	Y	Y	N	N	Y	Y
17	Bustos	Y	Y	Y	Y	Y	N
18	**LaHood**	Y	Y	N	N	Y	Y
INDIANA							
1	Visclosky	Y	Y	Y	Y	Y	N
2	**Walorski**	Y	Y	N	N	Y	Y
3	**Banks**	Y	Y	N	N	Y	Y
4	**Baird**	Y	Y	N	N	Y	Y
5	**Brooks, S.**	Y	Y	N	N	Y	Y
6	**Pence**	Y	Y	N	N	Y	Y
7	Carson	Y	Y	Y	Y	Y	N
8	**Bucshon**	Y	Y	N	N	Y	Y
9	**Hollingsworth**	Y	Y	N	N	Y	Y
IOWA							
1	Finkenauer	Y	Y	Y	Y	Y	N
2	Loebsack	Y	Y	Y	Y	Y	N
3	Axne	Y	Y	Y	Y	Y	N
4	**King, S.**	Y	Y	N	N	Y	N
KANSAS							
1	**Marshall**	Y	Y	N	N	?	?
2	**Watkins**	Y	Y	N	N	Y	Y
3	Davids	Y	Y	Y	Y	Y	N
4	**Estes**	Y	Y	N	N	Y	Y
KENTUCKY							
1	**Comer**	Y	Y	N	N	Y	Y
2	**Guthrie**	Y	Y	N	N	Y	Y
3	Yarmuth	Y	Y	Y	Y	Y	N
4	**Massie**	Y	N	N	N	Y	Y
5	**Rogers, H.**	Y	Y	N	N	Y	Y
6	**Barr**	Y	Y	N	N	Y	Y
LOUISIANA							
1	**Scalise**	Y	Y	N	N	Y	Y
2	Richmond	Y	Y	Y	Y	Y	N
3	**Higgins, C.**	Y	Y	N	N	Y	Y
4	**Johnson, M.**	Y	Y	N	N	Y	N
5	**Abraham**	Y	Y	N	N	Y	Y
6	**Graves, G.**	Y	Y	N	N	Y	Y
MAINE							
1	Pingree	Y	Y	Y	Y	Y	N
2	Golden	Y	Y	Y	Y	Y	N
MARYLAND							
1	**Harris**	Y	Y	N	N	Y	Y
2	Ruppersberger	Y	Y	Y	Y	Y	N
3	Sarbanes	Y	Y	Y	Y	Y	N
4	Brown, A.	Y	Y	Y	Y	Y	N
5	Hoyer	Y	Y	Y	Y	Y	N
6	Trone	Y	Y	Y	Y	Y	N
7	vacant	I	I	I	I	I	I
8	Raskin	Y	Y	Y	Y	Y	N
MASSACHUSETTS							
1	Neal	Y	Y	Y	Y	Y	N
2	McGovern	Y	Y	Y	Y	Y	N
3	Trahan	Y	Y	Y	Y	Y	N
4	Kennedy	Y	Y	Y	Y	Y	N
5	Clark	Y	Y	Y	Y	Y	N
6	Moulton	Y	Y	Y	Y	Y	N
7	Pressley	Y	Y	Y	Y	Y	N
8	Lynch	Y	Y	Y	Y	Y	?
9	Keating	Y	Y	Y	Y	Y	N
MICHIGAN							
1	**Bergman**	Y	Y	N	N	Y	Y
2	**Huizenga**	Y	Y	N	N	Y	Y
3	*Amash*	Y	N	N	N	N	N
4	**Moolenaar**	Y	Y	N	N	Y	Y
5	Kildee	Y	Y	Y	Y	Y	N
6	**Upton**	Y	Y	N	N	Y	Y
7	**Walberg**	Y	Y	N	N	Y	Y
8	Slotkin	Y	Y	Y	Y	Y	N
9	Levin	Y	Y	Y	Y	Y	N
10	**Mitchell**	Y	Y	N	N	Y	Y
11	Stevens	Y	Y	Y	Y	Y	N
12	Dingell	Y	Y	Y	Y	Y	N
13	Tlaib	Y	Y	Y	Y	Y	N
14	Lawrence	Y	Y	Y	Y	Y	N
MINNESOTA							
1	**Hagedorn**	Y	Y	N	N	Y	Y
2	Craig	Y	Y	N	Y	Y	N
3	Phillips	Y	Y	N	Y	Y	N
4	McCollum	Y	Y	Y	Y	Y	N
5	Omar	Y	Y	+	+	+	-
6	**Emmer**	Y	Y	N	N	Y	Y
7	Peterson	Y	Y	Y	Y	Y	N
8	**Stauber**	Y	Y	N	N	Y	Y
MISSISSIPPI							
1	**Kelly, T.**	Y	Y	N	N	Y	Y
2	Thompson, B.	Y	Y	Y	Y	Y	N
3	**Guest**	Y	Y	N	N	Y	Y
4	**Palazzo**	Y	Y	N	N	Y	Y
MISSOURI							
1	Clay	Y	Y	Y	Y	Y	N
2	**Wagner**	Y	Y	N	N	Y	Y
3	**Luetkemeyer**	Y	Y	N	N	Y	Y
4	**Hartzler**	Y	Y	N	N	Y	Y
5	Cleaver	Y	Y	Y	Y	Y	N
6	**Graves, S.**	Y	Y	N	N	Y	Y
7	**Long**	Y	Y	N	N	Y	Y
8	**Smith, J.**	Y	Y	N	N	Y	Y
MONTANA							
AL	**Gianforte**	Y	Y	N	N	Y	Y
NEBRASKA							
1	**Fortenberry**	Y	Y	N	N	Y	Y
2	**Bacon**	Y	Y	N	N	Y	Y
3	**Smith, Adrian**	Y	Y	N	N	Y	Y
NEVADA							
1	Titus	Y	Y	Y	Y	Y	N
2	**Amodei**	Y	Y	N	N	Y	Y
3	Lee	Y	Y	Y	Y	Y	N
4	Horsford	Y	Y	Y	Y	Y	?
NEW HAMPSHIRE							
1	Pappas	Y	Y	Y	Y	Y	N
2	Kuster	Y	Y	Y	Y	Y	N
NEW JERSEY							
1	Norcross	Y	Y	Y	Y	Y	N
2	Van Drew	Y	Y	Y	Y	Y	N
3	Kim	Y	Y	Y	Y	Y	N
4	**Smith, C.**	Y	Y	N	N	Y	N
5	Gottheimer	Y	Y	Y	Y	Y	N
6	Pallone	Y	Y	Y	Y	Y	N
7	Malinowski	Y	Y	Y	Y	Y	N
8	Sires	Y	Y	Y	Y	Y	N
9	Pascrell	Y	Y	Y	Y	Y	N
10	Payne	Y	Y	Y	Y	Y	N
11	Sherrill	Y	Y	Y	Y	Y	N
12	Watson Coleman	Y	Y	Y	Y	Y	N
NEW MEXICO							
1	Haaland	Y	Y	Y	Y	Y	N
2	Torres Small	Y	Y	Y	Y	Y	N
3	Luján	Y	Y	Y	Y	Y	N
NEW YORK							
1	**Zeldin**	Y	Y	N	N	Y	Y
2	**King, P.**	Y	Y	N	N	Y	Y
3	Suozzi	Y	Y	Y	Y	Y	N
4	Rice, K.	Y	Y	Y	Y	Y	N
5	Meeks	Y	Y	Y	Y	Y	N
6	Meng	Y	Y	Y	Y	Y	N
7	Velázquez	Y	Y	Y	Y	Y	N
8	Jeffries	Y	Y	Y	Y	Y	N
9	Clarke	Y	Y	Y	Y	Y	N
10	Nadler	Y	Y	Y	Y	Y	N
11	Rose	Y	Y	Y	Y	Y	N
12	Maloney, C.	Y	Y	Y	Y	Y	N
13	Espaillat	Y	Y	Y	Y	Y	N
14	Ocasio-Cortez	Y	Y	Y	Y	Y	N
15	Serrano	?	?	?	?	?	?
16	Engel	Y	Y	Y	Y	Y	N
17	Lowey	Y	Y	Y	Y	Y	N
18	Maloney, S.P.	Y	Y	Y	Y	Y	N
19	Delgado	Y	Y	Y	Y	Y	N
20	Tonko	Y	Y	Y	Y	Y	N
21	**Stefanik**	Y	Y	N	N	Y	Y
22	Brindisi	Y	Y	Y	Y	Y	N
23	**Reed**	Y	Y	N	N	Y	Y
24	**Katko**	Y	Y	N	N	Y	Y
25	Morelle	Y	Y	Y	Y	Y	N
26	Higgins, B.	Y	Y	Y	Y	Y	N
27	**Collins, C.**						
NORTH CAROLINA							
1	Butterfield	Y	Y	Y	Y	Y	N
2	**Holding**	Y	Y	N	N	Y	Y
3	**Murphy**	Y	Y	N	N	Y	Y
4	Price	Y	Y	Y	Y	Y	N
5	**Foxx**	Y	Y	N	N	Y	Y
6	**Walker**	Y	Y	N	N	Y	Y
7	**Rouzer**	Y	Y	N	N	Y	Y
8	**Hudson**	Y	Y	N	N	Y	Y
9	**Bishop**	Y	Y	N	N	Y	Y
10	**McHenry**	Y	Y	N	N	Y	Y
11	**Meadows**	Y	Y	N	N	Y	N
12	Adams	Y	Y	Y	Y	Y	N
13	**Budd**	Y	Y	N	N	Y	Y
NORTH DAKOTA							
AL	**Armstrong**	Y	Y	N	N	Y	Y
OHIO							
1	**Chabot**	Y	Y	N	N	Y	Y
2	**Wenstrup**	Y	Y	N	N	Y	Y
3	Beatty	Y	Y	Y	Y	Y	N
4	**Jordan**	Y	Y	N	N	Y	Y
5	**Latta**	Y	Y	N	N	Y	Y
6	**Johnson, B.**	Y	Y	N	N	Y	Y
7	**Gibbs**	Y	Y	N	N	Y	Y
8	**Davidson**	Y	Y	N	N	Y	Y
9	Kaptur	Y	Y	Y	Y	Y	N
10	**Turner**	Y	Y	N	N	Y	Y
11	Fudge	Y	Y	Y	Y	Y	N
12	**Balderson**	Y	Y	N	N	Y	Y
13	Ryan	Y	Y	Y	Y	Y	N
14	**Joyce**	Y	Y	N	N	Y	?
15	**Stivers**	Y	Y	N	N	Y	Y
16	**Gonzalez**	Y	Y	N	N	Y	Y
OKLAHOMA							
1	**Hern**	Y	Y	N	N	Y	Y
2	**Mullin**	Y	Y	N	N	Y	Y
3	**Lucas**	Y	Y	N	N	Y	Y
4	**Cole**	Y	Y	N	N	Y	Y
5	Horn	Y	Y	Y	Y	Y	N
OREGON							
1	Bonamici	Y	Y	Y	Y	Y	N
2	**Walden**	Y	Y	N	N	Y	Y
3	Blumenauer	Y	Y	Y	Y	Y	N
4	DeFazio	Y	Y	Y	Y	Y	N
5	Schrader	Y	Y	Y	Y	Y	Y
PENNSYLVANIA							
1	**Fitzpatrick**	Y	Y	N	N	Y	Y
2	Boyle	Y	Y	Y	Y	Y	N
3	Evans	Y	Y	Y	Y	Y	N
4	Dean	Y	Y	Y	Y	Y	N
5	Scanlon	Y	Y	Y	Y	Y	N
6	Houlahan	Y	Y	Y	Y	Y	N
7	Wild	Y	Y	Y	Y	Y	Y
8	Cartwright	Y	Y	Y	Y	Y	N
9	**Meuser**	Y	Y	N	N	Y	Y
10	**Perry**	Y	Y	N	N	Y	N
11	**Smucker**	Y	Y	N	N	Y	Y
12	**Keller**	Y	Y	N	N	Y	Y
13	**Joyce**	Y	Y	N	N	Y	Y
14	**Reschenthaler**	Y	Y	N	N	Y	Y
15	**Thompson, G.**	Y	Y	N	N	Y	Y
16	**Kelly, M.**	Y	Y	N	N	Y	Y
17	Lamb	Y	Y	Y	Y	Y	Y
18	Doyle	Y	Y	Y	Y	Y	N
RHODE ISLAND							
1	Cicilline	Y	Y	Y	Y	Y	N
2	Langevin	Y	Y	Y	Y	Y	N
SOUTH CAROLINA							
1	Cunningham	Y	Y	Y	Y	Y	N
2	**Wilson, J.**	Y	Y	N	N	Y	Y
3	**Duncan**	Y	Y	N	N	Y	N
4	**Timmons**	+	+	-	-	+	+
5	**Norman**	Y	Y	N	N	Y	Y
6	Clyburn	Y	Y	Y	Y	Y	N
7	**Rice, T.**	Y	Y	N	N	Y	Y
SOUTH DAKOTA							
AL	**Johnson**	Y	Y	N	N	Y	Y
TENNESSEE							
1	**Roe**	Y	Y	N	N	Y	Y
2	**Burchett**	Y	Y	N	N	Y	Y
3	**Fleischmann**	Y	Y	N	N	Y	Y
4	**DesJarlais**	Y	Y	N	N	Y	Y
5	Cooper	Y	Y	Y	Y	Y	N
6	**Rose**	Y	Y	N	N	Y	Y
7	**Green**	Y	Y	N	N	Y	Y
8	**Kustoff**	Y	Y	N	N	Y	Y
9	Cohen	Y	Y	Y	Y	Y	N
TEXAS							
1	**Gohmert**	Y	Y	N	N	Y	Y
2	**Crenshaw**	Y	Y	N	N	Y	Y
3	**Taylor**	Y	Y	N	N	Y	Y
4	**Ratcliffe**	Y	Y	N	N	?	Y
5	**Gooden**	Y	Y	N	N	Y	Y
6	**Wright**	Y	Y	N	N	Y	Y
7	Fletcher	Y	Y	Y	Y	Y	Y
8	**Brady**	Y	Y	N	N	Y	Y
9	Green, A.	Y	Y	Y	Y	Y	N
10	**McCaul**	Y	Y	N	N	Y	Y
11	**Conaway**	Y	Y	N	N	Y	Y
12	**Granger**	Y	Y	N	N	Y	Y
13	**Thornberry**	Y	Y	N	N	Y	Y
14	**Weber**	Y	Y	N	N	Y	Y
15	Gonzalez	Y	Y	Y	Y	Y	N
16	Escobar	Y	Y	Y	Y	Y	N
17	**Flores**	Y	Y	N	N	Y	Y
18	Jackson Lee	Y	Y	Y	Y	Y	N
19	**Arrington**	+	Y	N	N	Y	Y
20	Castro	Y	Y	Y	Y	Y	N
21	**Roy**	Y	Y	N	N	Y	N
22	**Olson**	Y	Y	N	N	Y	Y
23	**Hurd**	Y	Y	N	N	Y	Y
24	**Marchant**	Y	Y	N	N	?	?
25	**Williams**	Y	Y	N	N	Y	Y
26	**Burgess**	Y	Y	N	N	Y	Y
27	**Cloud**	Y	Y	N	N	Y	Y
28	Cuellar	Y	Y	Y	Y	Y	N
29	Garcia, S.	Y	Y	Y	Y	Y	N
30	Johnson, E.B.	Y	Y	Y	Y	Y	N
31	**Carter, J.**	Y	Y	N	N	Y	Y
32	Allred	Y	Y	Y	Y	Y	N
33	Veasey	Y	Y	Y	Y	Y	N
34	Vela	Y	Y	Y	Y	Y	Y
35	Doggett	Y	Y	Y	Y	Y	N
36	**Babin**	Y	Y	N	N	Y	Y
UTAH							
1	**Bishop, R.**	Y	Y	N	N	Y	Y
2	**Stewart**	Y	Y	N	N	Y	Y
3	**Curtis**	Y	Y	N	N	Y	Y
4	McAdams	Y	Y	Y	Y	Y	N
VERMONT							
AL	Welch	Y	Y	Y	Y	Y	N
VIRGINIA							
1	**Wittman**	Y	Y	N	N	Y	Y
2	Luria	Y	Y	Y	Y	Y	N
3	Scott, R.	Y	Y	Y	Y	Y	N
4	McEachin	+	+	Y	Y	+	-
5	**Riggleman**	Y	Y	N	N	Y	Y
6	**Cline**	Y	Y	N	N	Y	Y
7	Spanberger	Y	Y	Y	Y	Y	N
8	Beyer	?	?	Y	Y	Y	N
9	**Griffith**	Y	Y	N	N	Y	Y
10	Wexton	Y	Y	Y	Y	Y	N
11	Connolly	Y	Y	Y	Y	?	Y
WASHINGTON							
1	DelBene	Y	Y	Y	Y	Y	N
2	Larsen	Y	Y	Y	Y	Y	N
3	**Herrera Beutler**	Y	Y	N	N	Y	Y
4	**Newhouse**	Y	Y	N	N	Y	Y
5	**McMorris Rodgers**	Y	Y	N	N	Y	Y
6	Kilmer	Y	Y	Y	Y	Y	N
7	Jayapal	Y	Y	Y	Y	Y	N
8	Schrier	Y	Y	Y	Y	Y	N
9	Smith Adam	Y	Y	Y	Y	Y	N
10	Heck	Y	Y	Y	Y	Y	N
WEST VIRGINIA							
1	**McKinley**	Y	Y	N	N	Y	Y
2	**Mooney**	Y	Y	N	N	Y	Y
3	**Miller**	Y	Y	N	N	Y	Y
WISCONSIN							
1	**Steil**	Y	Y	N	N	Y	Y
2	Pocan	Y	Y	Y	Y	Y	N
3	Kind	Y	Y	Y	Y	Y	?
4	Moore	Y	Y	Y	Y	Y	N
5	**Sensenbrenner**	Y	Y	N	N	Y	Y
6	**Grothman**	Y	Y	N	N	Y	Y
7	**Duffy**						
8	**Gallagher**	Y	Y	N	N	Y	Y
WYOMING							
AL	**Cheney**	Y	Y	N	N	Y	Y
DELEGATES							
	Radewagen (A.S.)					?	?
	Norton (D.C.)					Y	N
	San Nicolas (Guam)					Y	N
	Sablan (N. Marianas)					Y	N
	González-Colón (P.R.)					?	?
	Plaskett (V.I.)					?	?

619. HR4863. Export-Import Bank Reauthorization - Opioid Trafficking Sanctions. McAdams, D-Utah, amendment no. 4 that would prohibit the Export-Import Bank from approving transactions by any individual subject to sanctions related to the illegal trafficking of synthetic opioids. Adopted in Committee of the Whole 414-1: R 191-0; D 222-0; I 1-1. Nov. 15, 2019.

620. HR4863. Export-Import Bank Reauthorization - China and Mexico Opioid Trafficking. Davidson, R-Ohio, amendment no. 5 that would prohibit the Export-Import Bank from authorizing financial assistance to certain foreign governments, including China and Mexico, if they do not "closely cooperate" with the United States to prevent opioid trafficking, including by sharing intelligence, prosecuting traffickers, or implementing regulations related to the production and export of illicit opioids. Rejected in Committee of the Whole 210-214: R 194-0; D 16-212; I 0-2. Nov. 15, 2019.

621. HR4863. Export-Import Bank Reauthorization - Businesses Affected by Tariffs. Stevens, D-Mich., amendment no. 18 that would require the Export-Import Bank outreach plan required by the bill to include an emphasis on small businesses impacted by retaliatory tariffs. Adopted in Committee of the Whole 396-27: R 168-26; D 227-0; I 1-1. Nov. 15, 2019.

622. HR4863. Export-Import Bank Reauthorization - Human Rights and Criminal Organization Sanctions. Torres Small, D-N.M., amendment no. 21 that would prohibit the Export-Import Bank from approving transactions by any individual subject to sanctions related to human rights abuses, including human trafficking or sex trafficking, or subject to sanctions based on involvement with transnational criminal organizations. Adopted in Committee of the Whole 417-2: R 190-1; D 226-0; I 1-1. Nov. 15, 2019.

623. HR4863. Export-Import Bank Reauthorization - Recommit. Riggleman, R-Va., motion to recommit the bill to the House Financial Services Committee with instructions to report it back immediately with an amendment that would prohibit the Export-Import Bank from issuing a loan, guarantee, or insurance that would benefit the government of China with respect to supporting the People's Liberation Army, Chinese intelligence agency, or policies related to Chinese international development activities, human rights violations, or illicit transfer of technologies or intellectual property from the U.S. It would exempt transactions that would create export opportunities for U.S. small businesses or that are required for exporting humanitarian goods or services. Motion rejected 203-218: R 194-0; D 9-217; I 0-1. Nov. 15, 2019.

624. HR4863. Export-Import Bank Reauthorization - Passage. Passage of the bill that would reauthorize the charter of the Export-Import Bank through fiscal 2029 and would increase the amount of loans, guarantees, and insurance the bank may have outstanding at any one time from $135 million to $175 million, increasing the amount annually through fiscal 2026. It would re-designate the agency as the "United States Export Finance Agency." Among other provisions, it would establish a number of offices within the agency, including an office focused on promoting the inclusion of minorities and women in the agency's workforce and activities and an office focused on financing for exports related to renewable energy, energy efficiency, and energy storage. It would increase from 25% to 30% the amount of Ex-Im Bank lending activity that must be directed to small businesses by fiscal 2029 and require the agency to prepare an outreach plan to inform small businesses about agency services. It would prohibit the agency from approving any transactions involving individuals subject to certain trade and economic sanctions or involving the People's Liberation Army or Chinese intelligence agency. It would establish alternative procedures for agency operations in the event of a quorum lapse on the board of directors, authorizing a temporary board that would include the U.S. trade representative and Trade and Commerce secretaries and could approve agency transactions. Passed 235-184: R 13-179; D 222-4; I 0-1. *Note: A "nay" was a vote in support of the president's position.* Nov. 15, 2019.

	619	620	621	622	623	624
ALABAMA						
1 **Byrne**	Y	Y	Y	Y	Y	N
2 **Roby**	Y	Y	Y	Y	Y	Y
3 **Rogers, M.**	Y	Y	Y	Y	Y	N
4 **Aderholt**	Y	Y	Y	Y	Y	N
5 **Brooks, M.**	Y	Y	Y	Y	Y	N
6 **Palmer**	Y	Y	N	Y	Y	N
7 Sewell	Y	N	Y	Y	N	Y
ALASKA						
AL **Young**	Y	Y	N	Y	Y	N
ARIZONA						
1 O'Halleran	Y	N	Y	Y	N	Y
2 Kirkpatrick	Y	N	Y	Y	N	Y
3 Grijalva	Y	N	Y	Y	N	Y
4 **Gosar**	Y	Y	N	Y	Y	N
5 **Biggs**	Y	Y	N	Y	Y	N
6 **Schweikert**	Y	Y	Y	Y	Y	N
7 Gallego	?	?	?	?	?	?
8 **Lesko**	Y	Y	N	Y	Y	N
9 Stanton	Y	N	Y	Y	N	Y
ARKANSAS						
1 **Crawford**	Y	Y	Y	Y	Y	N
2 **Hill, F.**	Y	Y	Y	Y	Y	N
3 **Womack**	Y	Y	Y	Y	Y	N
4 **Westerman**	Y	Y	Y	Y	Y	N
CALIFORNIA						
1 **LaMalfa**	?	Y	N	Y	Y	N
2 Huffman	Y	N	Y	Y	N	N
3 Garamendi	Y	N	Y	Y	N	Y
4 **McClintock**	Y	Y	N	Y	Y	N
5 Thompson, M.	Y	N	Y	Y	N	Y
6 Matsui	Y	N	Y	Y	N	Y
7 Bera	Y	N	Y	Y	N	Y
8 **Cook**	Y	Y	Y	Y	Y	N
9 McNerney	Y	N	Y	Y	N	Y
10 Harder	Y	N	Y	Y	N	Y
11 DeSaulnier	Y	N	Y	Y	N	Y
12 Pelosi						
13 Lee B.	Y	N	Y	Y	N	Y
14 Speier	Y	Y	Y	Y	N	Y
15 Swalwell	Y	N	Y	Y	N	Y
16 Costa	Y	N	Y	Y	N	Y
17 Khanna	Y	N	Y	Y	N	Y
18 Eshoo	Y	N	Y	Y	N	Y
19 Lofgren	?	?	?	?	?	?
20 Panetta	Y	N	Y	Y	N	Y
21 Cox	Y	Y	Y	Y	N	Y
22 **Nunes**	Y	Y	Y	Y	Y	N
23 **McCarthy**	Y	Y	Y	Y	Y	N
24 Carbajal	Y	N	Y	Y	N	Y
25 vacant						
26 Brownley	Y	N	Y	Y	N	Y
27 Chu	Y	N	Y	Y	N	Y
28 Schiff	Y	N	Y	Y	N	Y
29 Cárdenas	Y	N	Y	Y	N	Y
30 Sherman	Y	N	Y	Y	N	Y
31 Aguilar	Y	N	Y	Y	N	Y
32 Napolitano	Y	N	Y	Y	N	Y
33 Lieu	Y	N	Y	Y	N	Y
34 Gomez	Y	N	Y	Y	N	Y
35 Torres	?	N	Y	Y	N	Y
36 Ruiz	Y	N	Y	Y	N	Y
37 Bass	Y	N	Y	Y	N	Y
38 Sánchez	Y	N	Y	Y	N	Y
39 Cisneros	Y	N	Y	Y	N	Y
40 Roybal-Allard	Y	N	Y	Y	N	Y
41 Takano	Y	N	Y	Y	N	Y
42 **Calvert**	Y	Y	Y	Y	Y	N
43 Waters	Y	N	Y	Y	N	Y
44 Barragán	Y	N	Y	Y	N	Y
45 Porter	Y	N	Y	Y	Y	Y
46 Correa	Y	N	Y	Y	N	Y
47 Lowenthal	Y	N	Y	Y	N	Y
48 Rouda	Y	N	Y	Y	N	Y
49 Levin	Y	N	Y	Y	N	Y
50 **Hunter**	Y	Y	Y	Y	Y	Y
51 Vargas	Y	N	Y	Y	N	Y
52 Peters	Y	N	Y	Y	N	Y
53 Davis, S.	Y	N	Y	Y	N	Y
COLORADO						
1 DeGette	Y	N	Y	Y	N	Y
2 Neguse	Y	N	Y	Y	N	Y
3 **Tipton**	Y	Y	Y	Y	Y	N
4 **Buck**	Y	Y	Y	Y	Y	N
5 **Lamborn**	Y	Y	Y	Y	Y	N
6 Crow	Y	N	Y	Y	N	Y
7 Perlmutter	Y	N	Y	Y	N	Y
CONNECTICUT						
1 Larson	Y	N	Y	Y	N	Y
2 Courtney	Y	N	Y	Y	N	Y
3 DeLauro	Y	N	Y	Y	N	Y
4 Himes	Y	N	Y	Y	N	Y
5 Hayes	Y	N	Y	Y	N	Y
DELAWARE						
AL Blunt Rochester	Y	N	Y	Y	N	Y
FLORIDA						
1 **Gaetz**	Y	Y	N	Y	Y	N
2 **Dunn**	Y	Y	Y	Y	Y	N
3 **Yoho**	Y	Y	Y	Y	Y	N
4 **Rutherford**	Y	Y	Y	Y	Y	N
5 Lawson	Y	N	Y	Y	N	Y
6 **Waltz**	Y	Y	Y	Y	Y	N
7 Murphy	Y	N	Y	Y	N	Y
8 **Posey**	Y	Y	Y	Y	Y	N
9 Soto	Y	N	Y	Y	N	Y
10 Demings	Y	N	Y	Y	N	Y
11 **Webster**	Y	Y	Y	Y	Y	N
12 **Bilirakis**	Y	Y	Y	Y	Y	N
13 Crist	Y	N	Y	Y	N	Y
14 Castor	Y	N	Y	Y	N	Y
15 **Spano**	Y	Y	Y	Y	Y	N
16 **Buchanan**	Y	Y	Y	Y	Y	N
17 **Steube**	Y	Y	N	Y	Y	N
18 **Mast**	Y	Y	N	Y	Y	N
19 **Rooney**	Y	Y	Y	Y	Y	N
20 Hastings	Y	N	Y	Y	N	Y
21 Frankel	Y	N	Y	Y	N	Y
22 Deutch	Y	N	Y	Y	N	Y
23 Wasserman Schultz	Y	N	Y	Y	N	Y
24 Wilson, F.	Y	N	Y	Y	N	Y
25 **Diaz-Balart**	Y	Y	Y	Y	Y	N
26 Mucarsel-Powell	Y	N	Y	Y	N	Y
27 Shalala	Y	N	Y	Y	N	Y
GEORGIA						
1 **Carter, E.L.**	Y	Y	Y	Y	Y	N
2 Bishop, S.	Y	N	Y	Y	N	Y
3 **Ferguson**	Y	Y	N	Y	Y	N
4 Johnson, H.	Y	N	Y	Y	N	Y
5 Lewis John	Y	N	Y	Y	N	Y
6 McBath	Y	N	Y	Y	N	Y
7 **Woodall**	Y	Y	Y	?	Y	N
8 **Scott, A.**	Y	Y	Y	Y	Y	N
9 **Collins, D.**	Y	Y	Y	Y	Y	N
10 **Hice**	Y	Y	N	Y	Y	N
11 **Loudermilk**	Y	Y	Y	Y	Y	N
12 **Allen**	Y	Y	N	Y	Y	N
13 Scott, D.	Y	N	Y	Y	N	Y
14 **Graves, T.**	Y	Y	Y	Y	Y	N
HAWAII						
1 Case	Y	N	Y	Y	N	Y
2 Gabbard	?	?	?	?	?	?
IDAHO						
1 **Fulcher**	Y	Y	Y	Y	Y	N
2 **Simpson**	Y	Y	Y	Y	Y	N
ILLINOIS						
1 Rush	Y	N	Y	+	N	Y
2 Kelly, R.	Y	N	Y	Y	N	Y
3 Lipinski	Y	N	Y	Y	N	Y
4 García, J.	Y	N	Y	Y	N	Y
5 Quigley	Y	N	Y	Y	N	Y
6 Casten	Y	N	Y	Y	N	Y
7 Davis, D.	Y	N	Y	Y	N	Y
8 Krishnamoorthi	Y	N	Y	Y	N	Y
9 Schakowsky	Y	N	Y	Y	N	Y
10 Schneider	Y	N	Y	Y	N	Y
11 Foster	Y	N	Y	Y	N	Y

KEY:	Republicans	Democrats	*Independents*

Y Voted for (yea)	**N** Voted against (nay)	**P** Voted "present"	
+ Announced for	**–** Announced against	**?** Did not vote or otherwise	
# Paired for	**X** Paired against	make position known	

		619	620	621	622	623	624
12	**Bost**	Y	Y	Y	Y	Y	N
13	**Davis, R.**	Y	Y	Y	Y	Y	N
14	Underwood	Y	N	Y	Y	N	Y
15	**Shimkus**	Y	Y	Y	Y	Y	N
16	**Kinzinger**	Y	Y	Y	Y	Y	Y
17	Bustos	Y	N	Y	Y	N	Y
18	**LaHood**	Y	Y	Y	Y	Y	N
INDIANA							
1	Visclosky	Y	N	Y	Y	N	Y
2	**Walorski**	Y	Y	Y	Y	Y	N
3	**Banks**	Y	Y	Y	Y	Y	N
4	**Baird**	Y	Y	Y	+	Y	N
5	**Brooks, S.**	Y	Y	Y	Y	Y	N
6	**Pence**	Y	Y	Y	Y	Y	N
7	Carson	Y	N	Y	Y	N	Y
8	**Bucshon**	Y	Y	Y	Y	Y	N
9	**Hollingsworth**	Y	Y	Y	Y	Y	N
IOWA							
1	Finkenauer	Y	N	Y	Y	Y	Y
2	Loebsack	Y	N	Y	Y	N	Y
3	Axne	Y	N	Y	Y	N	Y
4	**King, S.**	Y	Y	Y	Y	Y	N
KANSAS							
1	**Marshall**	?	?	?	?	?	?
2	**Watkins**	Y	Y	Y	Y	Y	N
3	Davids	Y	N	Y	Y	N	Y
4	**Estes**	Y	Y	Y	Y	Y	N
KENTUCKY							
1	**Comer**	Y	Y	Y	Y	Y	N
2	**Guthrie**	Y	Y	Y	Y	Y	N
3	Yarmuth	Y	N	Y	Y	N	Y
4	**Massie**	Y	Y	N	N	Y	N
5	**Rogers, H.**	Y	Y	Y	Y	Y	N
6	**Barr**	Y	Y	Y	Y	Y	N
LOUISIANA							
1	**Scalise**	Y	Y	Y	Y	Y	N
2	Richmond	Y	N	Y	Y	N	Y
3	**Higgins, C.**	Y	Y	Y	Y	Y	N
4	**Johnson, M.**	Y	Y	Y	Y	Y	N
5	**Abraham**	Y	Y	Y	Y	Y	N
6	**Graves, G.**	Y	Y	Y	Y	Y	N
MAINE							
1	Pingree	Y	N	Y	Y	N	Y
2	Golden	Y	Y	Y	Y	N	Y
MARYLAND							
1	**Harris**	Y	Y	N	Y	Y	N
2	Ruppersberger	Y	N	Y	Y	N	Y
3	Sarbanes	Y	N	Y	Y	N	Y
4	Brown, A.	Y	N	Y	Y	N	Y
5	Hoyer	Y	N	Y	Y	N	Y
6	Trone	Y	N	Y	Y	N	Y
7	vacant	I	I	I	I	I	I
8	Raskin	Y	N	Y	Y	N	Y
MASSACHUSETTS							
1	Neal	Y	N	Y	Y	N	Y
2	McGovern	Y	N	Y	Y	N	Y
3	Trahan	+	N	Y	Y	N	Y
4	Kennedy	Y	N	Y	Y	N	Y
5	Clark	Y	N	Y	Y	N	Y
6	Moulton	Y	Y	Y	Y	N	Y
7	Pressley	+	N	Y	Y	N	N
8	Lynch	Y	N	Y	Y	N	Y
9	Keating	Y	N	Y	Y	N	Y
MICHIGAN							
1	**Bergman**	Y	Y	Y	Y	Y	N
2	**Huizenga**	Y	Y	Y	Y	Y	N
3	*Amash*	N	N	N	N	N	N
4	**Moolenaar**	Y	Y	Y	Y	Y	N
5	Kildee	Y	N	Y	Y	N	Y
6	**Upton**	Y	Y	Y	Y	Y	Y
7	**Walberg**	Y	Y	Y	Y	Y	N
8	Slotkin	Y	Y	Y	Y	N	Y
9	Levin	Y	N	Y	Y	N	Y
10	**Mitchell**	Y	Y	Y	Y	Y	N
11	Stevens	Y	N	Y	Y	N	Y
12	Dingell	Y	N	Y	Y	N	Y
13	Tlaib	Y	N	Y	Y	N	N
14	Lawrence	Y	N	Y	Y	N	Y
MINNESOTA							
1	**Hagedorn**	Y	Y	Y	Y	Y	N
2	Craig	Y	N	Y	Y	N	Y
3	Phillips	Y	N	Y	Y	N	Y
4	McCollum	Y	N	Y	Y	N	Y
5	Omar	+	-	+	+	-	-

		619	620	621	622	623	624
6	**Emmer**	Y	Y	Y	Y	Y	N
7	Peterson	Y	Y	Y	Y	N	Y
8	**Stauber**	Y	Y	Y	Y	Y	N
MISSISSIPPI							
1	**Kelly, T.**	Y	Y	N	Y	Y	N
2	Thompson, B.	Y	N	Y	Y	N	Y
3	**Guest**	Y	Y	Y	Y	Y	N
4	**Palazzo**	Y	Y	Y	Y	Y	N
MISSOURI							
1	Clay	Y	N	Y	Y	N	Y
2	**Wagner**	Y	Y	Y	Y	Y	Y
3	**Luetkemeyer**	Y	Y	Y	Y	Y	Y
4	**Hartzler**	Y	Y	Y	Y	Y	N
5	Cleaver	Y	N	Y	Y	N	Y
6	**Graves, S.**	Y	Y	Y	Y	Y	Y
7	**Long**	Y	Y	Y	Y	Y	Y
8	**Smith, J.**	Y	Y	Y	Y	Y	N
MONTANA							
AL	**Gianforte**	Y	Y	Y	Y	Y	N
NEBRASKA							
1	**Fortenberry**	Y	Y	Y	Y	Y	N
2	**Bacon**	Y	Y	Y	Y	Y	N
3	**Smith, Adrian**	Y	Y	N	Y	Y	N
NEVADA							
1	Titus	Y	N	Y	Y	N	Y
2	**Amodei**	Y	Y	Y	Y	Y	N
3	Lee	+	N	Y	Y	Y	Y
4	Horsford	Y	N	Y	Y	N	Y
NEW HAMPSHIRE							
1	Pappas	Y	N	Y	Y	N	Y
2	Kuster	Y	N	Y	Y	N	Y
NEW JERSEY							
1	Norcross	Y	N	Y	Y	N	Y
2	Van Drew	Y	Y	Y	Y	Y	Y
3	Kim	Y	N	Y	Y	N	Y
4	**Smith, C.**	Y	Y	Y	Y	Y	N
5	Gottheimer	Y	N	Y	Y	N	Y
6	Pallone	Y	N	Y	Y	N	Y
7	Malinowski	Y	N	Y	Y	N	Y
8	Sires	Y	N	Y	Y	N	Y
9	Pascrell	Y	N	Y	Y	N	Y
10	Payne	Y	N	Y	Y	N	Y
11	Sherrill	Y	N	Y	Y	N	Y
12	Watson Coleman	Y	N	Y	Y	N	Y
NEW MEXICO							
1	Haaland	Y	N	Y	Y	N	Y
2	Torres Small	Y	N	Y	Y	N	Y
3	Luján	Y	N	Y	Y	N	Y
NEW YORK							
1	**Zeldin**	Y	Y	Y	Y	Y	N
2	**King, P.**	Y	Y	Y	Y	Y	N
3	Suozzi	Y	N	Y	Y	N	Y
4	Rice, K.	Y	N	Y	Y	N	Y
5	Meeks	Y	N	Y	Y	N	Y
6	Meng	Y	N	Y	Y	N	Y
7	Velázquez	Y	N	Y	Y	N	Y
8	Jeffries	Y	N	Y	Y	N	Y
9	Clarke	Y	N	Y	Y	N	Y
10	Nadler	Y	N	Y	Y	N	Y
11	Rose	Y	Y	Y	Y	Y	Y
12	Maloney, C.	Y	N	Y	Y	N	Y
13	Espaillat	Y	N	Y	Y	N	Y
14	Ocasio-Cortez	Y	N	Y	Y	N	N
15	Serrano	?	?	?	?	?	?
16	Engel	Y	N	Y	Y	N	Y
17	Lowey	Y	N	Y	Y	N	Y
18	Maloney, S.P.	Y	N	Y	Y	N	Y
19	Delgado	Y	N	Y	Y	N	Y
20	Tonko	Y	N	Y	Y	N	Y
21	**Stefanik**	Y	Y	Y	Y	Y	Y
22	Brindisi	Y	Y	Y	Y	N	Y
23	**Reed**	Y	Y	Y	Y	Y	Y
24	**Katko**	Y	Y	Y	Y	Y	Y
25	Morelle	Y	N	Y	Y	N	Y
26	Higgins, B.	Y	N	Y	Y	N	Y
27	**Collins, C.**						
NORTH CAROLINA							
1	Butterfield	Y	N	Y	Y	N	Y
2	**Holding**	?	Y	Y	Y	Y	N
3	**Murphy**	Y	Y	Y	Y	Y	N
4	Price	Y	N	Y	Y	N	Y
5	**Foxx**	Y	Y	Y	Y	Y	N
6	**Walker**	Y	Y	Y	Y	Y	N
7	**Rouzer**	Y	Y	Y	Y	Y	N

		619	620	621	622	623	624
8	**Hudson**	Y	Y	Y	Y	Y	N
9	**Bishop**	Y	Y	Y	Y	Y	N
10	**McHenry**	Y	Y	Y	Y	Y	N
11	**Meadows**	Y	Y	Y	Y	Y	N
12	Adams	Y	N	Y	Y	N	Y
13	**Budd**	?	Y	Y	Y	Y	N
NORTH DAKOTA							
AL	**Armstrong**	Y	Y	Y	Y	Y	N
OHIO							
1	**Chabot**	Y	Y	Y	Y	Y	N
2	**Wenstrup**	Y	Y	Y	Y	Y	N
3	Beatty	Y	N	Y	Y	N	Y
4	**Jordan**	Y	Y	N	Y	Y	N
5	**Latta**	Y	Y	Y	Y	Y	N
6	**Johnson, B.**	Y	Y	Y	Y	Y	N
7	**Gibbs**	Y	Y	Y	Y	Y	N
8	**Davidson**	Y	Y	Y	Y	Y	N
9	Kaptur	Y	N	Y	?	N	Y
10	**Turner**	Y	Y	Y	Y	Y	N
11	Fudge	Y	N	Y	Y	N	Y
12	**Balderson**	Y	Y	Y	Y	Y	N
13	Ryan	Y	Y	Y	Y	N	Y
14	**Joyce**	Y	Y	Y	Y	Y	N
15	**Stivers**	Y	Y	Y	Y	Y	N
16	**Gonzalez**	Y	Y	Y	Y	Y	N
OKLAHOMA							
1	**Hern**	Y	Y	Y	Y	Y	N
2	**Mullin**	Y	Y	Y	Y	Y	N
3	**Lucas**	Y	Y	Y	Y	Y	N
4	**Cole**	Y	Y	Y	Y	Y	N
5	Horn	Y	N	Y	Y	N	Y
OREGON							
1	Bonamici	Y	N	Y	Y	N	Y
2	**Walden**	Y	Y	Y	Y	Y	N
3	Blumenauer	Y	N	Y	Y	N	Y
4	DeFazio	Y	N	Y	Y	N	Y
5	Schrader	Y	Y	Y	Y	Y	Y
PENNSYLVANIA							
1	**Fitzpatrick**	Y	Y	Y	Y	Y	Y
2	Boyle	Y	N	Y	Y	N	Y
3	Evans	Y	N	Y	Y	N	Y
4	Dean	Y	N	Y	Y	N	Y
5	Scanlon	Y	N	Y	Y	N	Y
6	Houlahan	Y	N	Y	Y	N	Y
7	Wild	Y	Y	Y	Y	N	Y
8	Cartwright	Y	N	Y	Y	N	Y
9	**Meuser**	Y	Y	Y	Y	Y	N
10	**Perry**	Y	Y	Y	Y	Y	N
11	**Smucker**	Y	Y	Y	Y	Y	N
12	**Keller**	Y	Y	Y	Y	Y	N
13	**Joyce**	Y	Y	Y	Y	Y	N
14	**Reschenthaler**	Y	Y	Y	Y	Y	N
15	**Thompson, G.**	Y	Y	Y	Y	Y	N
16	**Kelly, M.**	Y	Y	Y	Y	Y	N
17	Lamb	Y	Y	Y	Y	N	Y
18	Doyle	Y	N	Y	Y	N	Y
RHODE ISLAND							
1	Cicilline	Y	N	Y	Y	N	Y
2	Langevin	Y	N	Y	Y	N	Y
SOUTH CAROLINA							
1	Cunningham	Y	N	Y	Y	N	Y
2	**Wilson, J.**	Y	Y	Y	Y	Y	N
3	**Duncan**	Y	Y	N	?	Y	N
4	**Timmons**	+	+	+	+	+	-
5	**Norman**	Y	Y	Y	Y	Y	N
6	Clyburn	Y	N	Y	Y	N	Y
7	**Rice, T.**	Y	Y	Y	Y	Y	N
SOUTH DAKOTA							
AL	**Johnson**	Y	Y	Y	Y	Y	N
TENNESSEE							
1	**Roe**	Y	Y	Y	Y	Y	N
2	**Burchett**	Y	Y	N	Y	Y	N
3	**Fleischmann**	Y	Y	Y	Y	Y	N
4	**DesJarlais**	Y	Y	Y	Y	Y	N
5	Cooper	Y	N	Y	Y	N	Y
6	**Rose**	Y	Y	Y	Y	Y	N
7	**Green**	Y	Y	N	Y	Y	N
8	**Kustoff**	Y	Y	Y	Y	Y	N
9	Cohen	Y	N	Y	Y	N	Y
TEXAS							
1	**Gohmert**	Y	Y	Y	Y	Y	N
2	**Crenshaw**	Y	Y	Y	Y	Y	N
3	**Taylor**	Y	Y	Y	Y	Y	N
4	**Ratcliffe**	Y	Y	Y	Y	Y	N

		619	620	621	622	623	624
5	**Gooden**	Y	Y	Y	Y	Y	N
6	**Wright**	Y	Y	N	Y	Y	N
7	Fletcher	Y	N	Y	Y	N	Y
8	**Brady**	Y	Y	Y	Y	Y	N
9	Green, A.	Y	N	Y	Y	N	Y
10	**McCaul**	Y	Y	Y	Y	Y	N
11	**Conaway**	Y	Y	Y	Y	Y	N
12	**Granger**	Y	Y	Y	Y	Y	N
13	**Thornberry**	Y	Y	Y	Y	Y	N
14	**Weber**	Y	Y	N	Y	Y	N
15	Gonzalez	Y	N	Y	Y	N	Y
16	Escobar	Y	N	Y	Y	N	Y
17	**Flores**	Y	Y	Y	Y	Y	?
18	Jackson Lee	+	N	Y	Y	N	Y
19	**Arrington**	Y	Y	Y	Y	Y	N
20	Castro	Y	N	Y	Y	N	Y
21	**Roy**	Y	Y	N	Y	Y	N
22	**Olson**	Y	Y	Y	Y	Y	N
23	**Hurd**	Y	Y	Y	Y	Y	N
24	**Marchant**	?	?	?	?	?	?
25	**Williams**	Y	Y	Y	Y	Y	N
26	**Burgess**	Y	Y	Y	Y	Y	N
27	**Cloud**	Y	Y	Y	Y	Y	N
28	Cuellar	Y	N	Y	Y	N	Y
29	Garcia, S.	Y	N	Y	Y	N	Y
30	Johnson, E.B.	Y	N	Y	Y	N	Y
31	**Carter, J.**	Y	Y	Y	Y	Y	N
32	Allred	Y	N	Y	Y	N	Y
33	Veasey	Y	N	Y	Y	N	Y
34	Vela	Y	N	Y	Y	N	Y
35	Doggett	Y	N	Y	Y	N	Y
36	**Babin**	Y	Y	N	Y	Y	N
UTAH							
1	**Bishop, R.**	Y	Y	Y	Y	Y	N
2	**Stewart**	Y	Y	Y	Y	Y	N
3	**Curtis**	Y	Y	Y	Y	Y	N
4	McAdams	Y	N	Y	Y	N	Y
VERMONT							
AL	Welch	Y	N	Y	Y	N	Y
VIRGINIA							
1	**Wittman**	Y	Y	Y	Y	Y	N
2	Luria	Y	Y	Y	Y	N	Y
3	Scott, R.	Y	N	Y	Y	N	Y
4	McEachin	+	-	+	+	-	+
5	**Riggleman**	Y	Y	Y	Y	Y	N
6	**Cline**	Y	Y	Y	Y	Y	N
7	Spanberger	Y	Y	Y	Y	Y	Y
8	Beyer	Y	N	Y	Y	N	Y
9	**Griffith**	Y	Y	Y	Y	Y	N
10	Wexton	Y	N	Y	Y	N	Y
11	Connolly	Y	N	Y	Y	N	Y
WASHINGTON							
1	DelBene	Y	N	Y	Y	N	Y
2	Larsen	Y	N	Y	Y	N	Y
3	**Herrera Beutler**	Y	Y	Y	Y	Y	+
4	**Newhouse**	Y	Y	Y	Y	Y	Y
5	**McMorris Rodgers**	Y	Y	Y	Y	Y	N
6	Kilmer	Y	N	Y	Y	N	Y
7	Jayapal	Y	N	Y	Y	N	Y
8	Schrier	Y	N	Y	Y	N	Y
9	Smith Adam	Y	N	?	Y	N	Y
10	Heck	Y	N	Y	Y	N	Y
WEST VIRGINIA							
1	**McKinley**	Y	Y	Y	Y	Y	N
2	**Mooney**	Y	Y	N	Y	Y	N
3	**Miller**	Y	Y	Y	Y	Y	N
WISCONSIN							
1	**Steil**	Y	Y	Y	Y	Y	N
2	Pocan	Y	N	Y	Y	N	Y
3	Kind	?	N	Y	Y	N	Y
4	Moore	Y	N	Y	Y	N	Y
5	**Sensenbrenner**	Y	Y	Y	Y	Y	N
6	**Grothman**	Y	Y	Y	Y	Y	N
7	**Duffy**						
8	**Gallagher**	Y	Y	Y	Y	Y	N
WYOMING							
AL	**Cheney**	Y	Y	Y	Y	Y	N
DELEGATES							
	Radewagen (A.S.)	?	?	?	?		
	Norton (D.C.)	Y	N	Y	Y		
	San Nicolas (Guam)	Y	N	Y	Y		
	Sablan (N. Marianas)	Y	N	Y	Y		
	González-Colón (P.R.)	?	?	?	?		
	Plaskett (V.I.)	?	?	?	?		

III HOUSE VOTES

625. HR3702. Disaster Assistance Block Grants - Passage. Green, D-Texas, motion to suspend the rules and pass the bill, as amended, that would permanently authorize the Housing and Urban Development Department community development block grant disaster recovery program to allow state and local governments to use CDBG funds for disaster assistance activities. It would codify certain HUD practices and establish requirements related to program administration, and it would require HUD to issue a final rule for program implementation within one year of enactment. It would also establish a Treasury Department reserve fund to provide technical assistance and capacity-building to program grantees following a disaster. Among other provisions, the bill would require HUD to coordinate with the Federal Emergency Management Agency and the Small Business Administration to share information on disaster recovery needs to avoid duplication of benefits. It would require grantees to prioritize households with the lowest incomes in allocating assistance; comply with HUD-approved procurement processes; and consult with affected residents and local stakeholders in developing a grant proposal. It would require grantees to use between 7% and 10% of funds awarded for administrative costs and at least 15% of funds awarded for expenses related to disaster mitigation planning. Motion agreed to 290-118: R 71-117; D 219-0; I 0-1. *Note: A two-thirds majority of those present and voting (272 in this case) is required for passage under suspension of the rules.* Nov. 18, 2019.

626. HR4634. Terrorism Risk Insurance - Passage. Waters, D-Calif., motion to suspend the rules and pass the bill, as amended, that would reauthorize, through fiscal 2027, the Treasury Department Terrorism Risk Insurance Program, which offers federal compensation to insurers for losses above specified values resulting from acts of terrorism. It would modify payment deadlines for recoupment surcharges paid by policyholders to the SEC under the program. It would also require the president's working group on financial markets to evaluate the availability and affordability of terrorism risk insurance for places of worship and others, and it would require the Government Accountability Office to conduct a study on the potential costs of cyberterrorism and its impacts on the private insurance market. Motion agreed to 385-22: R 167-21; D 218-0; I 0-1. *Note: A two-thirds majority of those present and voting (272 in this case) is required for passage under suspension of the rules.* Nov. 18, 2019.

627. HR4344. SEC Recovery of Illicit Funds - Passage. Green, D-Texas, motion to suspend the rules and pass the bill, as amended, that would modify the statute of limitations applied to Securities and Exchange Commission disgorgement cases seeking the return of illicit funds gained in violation of securities law. Specifically, it would establish a 14-year statute of limitations for such cases, as well as for relief sought by the SEC through injunctions. The bill would also require the SEC to submit a report to Congress on enforcement actions brought by the SEC in the ten years after enactment. Motion agreed to 314-95: R 93-94; D 221-0; I 0-1. *Note: A two-thirds majority of those present and voting (273 in this case) is required for passage under suspension of the rules.* Nov. 18, 2019.

628. HR3055. Further Fiscal 2020 Short-Term Appropriations - Previous Question. McGovern, D-Mass., motion to order the previous question (thus ending debate and possibility of amendment) on the rule (H Res 708) that would provide for House floor consideration of the Senate amendment to the bill (HR 3055). The rule would make in order a motion to concur in the Senate amendment to the bill, with a further House amendment that would make continuing appropriations for federal government operations and services through Dec. 20, 2019. Motion agreed to 228-192: R 0-191; D 228-0; I 0-1. Nov. 19, 2019.

629. HR3055. Further Fiscal 2020 Short-Term Appropriations - Rule. Adoption of the rule (H Res 708) that would provide for House floor consideration of the Senate amendment to the bill (HR 3055). The rule would make in order a motion to concur in the Senate amendment to the bill, with a further House amendment that would make continuing appropriations for federal government operations and services through Dec. 20, 2019. Adopted 230-194: R 0-193; D 230-0; I 0-1. Nov. 19, 2019.

630. HR5084. Corporate Board Diversity - Passage. Green, D-Texas, motion to suspend the rules and pass the bill that would require any publicly traded company, in its annual disclosure to the Securities and Exchange Commission, to include voluntarily self-reported data on racial, ethnic, and gender composition and veteran status of its board members and executive officers. It would also require the company to disclose whether it has adopted any policy, plan, or strategy to promote racial, ethnic, and gender diversity on its board or executive leadership, and it would require the SEC to establish an advisory group to identify strategies to increase diversity on the boards of public companies. Motion agreed to 281-135: R 55-134; D 226-0; I 0-1. *Note: A two-thirds majority of those present and voting (278 in this case) is required for passage under suspension of the rules.* Nov. 19, 2019.

		625	626	627	628	629	630
ALABAMA							
1	**Byrne**	N	Y	N	N	N	N
2	**Roby**	Y	Y	N	N	N	N
3	**Rogers, M.**	Y	Y	Y	N	N	N
4	**Aderholt**	Y	Y	Y	N	N	N
5	**Brooks, M.**	N	Y	N	N	N	N
6	**Palmer**	N	N	N	N	N	N
7	Sewell	Y	Y	Y	Y	Y	+
ALASKA							
AL	**Young**	N	Y	Y	N	N	N
ARIZONA							
1	O'Halleran	Y	Y	Y	Y	Y	?
2	Kirkpatrick	Y	Y	Y	Y	Y	Y
3	Grijalva	?	?	?	Y	Y	Y
4	**Gosar**	N	N	N	N	N	N
5	**Biggs**	N	N	N	N	N	N
6	**Schweikert**	N	Y	N	N	N	N
7	Gallego	Y	Y	Y	Y	Y	Y
8	**Lesko**	N	Y	N	N	N	N
9	Stanton	Y	Y	Y	Y	Y	Y
ARKANSAS							
1	**Crawford**	N	Y	Y	N	N	N
2	**Hill, F.**	Y	Y	Y	N	N	Y
3	**Womack**	N	Y	Y	N	N	N
4	**Westerman**	N	Y	N	N	N	N
CALIFORNIA							
1	**LaMalfa**	Y	Y	Y	N	N	?
2	Huffman	Y	Y	Y	Y	Y	Y
3	Garamendi	Y	Y	Y	Y	Y	Y
4	**McClintock**	N	N	N	N	?	?
5	Thompson, M.	Y	Y	Y	Y	Y	Y
6	Matsui	Y	Y	Y	Y	Y	Y
7	Bera	Y	Y	Y	Y	Y	Y
8	**Cook**	Y	Y	Y	N	N	?
9	McNerney	Y	Y	Y	Y	Y	Y
10	Harder	Y	Y	Y	Y	Y	Y
11	DeSaulnier	Y	Y	Y	Y	Y	Y
12	Pelosi						
13	Lee B.	Y	Y	Y	Y	Y	Y
14	Speier	Y	Y	Y	?	Y	Y
15	Swalwell	Y	Y	Y	Y	Y	Y
16	Costa	Y	Y	Y	Y	Y	Y
17	Khanna	Y	Y	Y	Y	Y	Y
18	Eshoo	Y	Y	Y	Y	Y	+
19	Lofgren	Y	Y	Y	Y	Y	Y
20	Panetta	Y	Y	Y	Y	Y	Y
21	Cox	?	?	Y	Y	Y	Y
22	**Nunes**	N	Y	Y	N	N	N
23	**McCarthy**	N	Y	N	N	N	N
24	Carbajal	Y	Y	Y	Y	Y	Y
25	vacant						
26	Brownley	Y	Y	Y	Y	Y	Y
27	Chu	Y	Y	Y	Y	Y	Y
28	Schiff	Y	Y	Y	Y	Y	Y
29	Cárdenas	Y	Y	Y	Y	Y	Y
30	Sherman	Y	Y	Y	Y	Y	Y
31	Aguilar	Y	Y	Y	Y	Y	Y
32	Napolitano	Y	Y	Y	Y	Y	Y
33	Lieu	Y	Y	Y	Y	Y	Y
34	Gomez	Y	Y	Y	Y	Y	Y
35	Torres	Y	Y	Y	Y	Y	Y
36	Ruiz	Y	Y	Y	Y	Y	Y
37	Bass	Y	Y	Y	Y	Y	Y
38	Sánchez	Y	Y	Y	Y	Y	Y
39	Cisneros	Y	Y	Y	Y	Y	Y
40	Roybal-Allard	Y	Y	Y	Y	Y	Y
41	Takano	Y	Y	Y	Y	Y	Y
42	**Calvert**	Y	Y	Y	N	N	Y
43	Waters	Y	Y	Y	Y	Y	Y
44	Barragán	Y	Y	Y	Y	Y	Y
45	Porter	Y	Y	Y	Y	Y	Y
46	Correa	Y	Y	Y	Y	Y	Y
47	Lowenthal	Y	Y	Y	Y	Y	Y
48	Rouda	Y	Y	Y	Y	Y	Y
49	Levin	Y	Y	Y	Y	Y	Y
50	**Hunter**	N	Y	N	N	N	N
51	Vargas	Y	Y	Y	Y	Y	Y
52	Peters	Y	Y	Y	Y	Y	Y

		625	626	627	628	629	630
53	Davis, S.	Y	Y	Y	Y	Y	Y
COLORADO							
1	DeGette	Y	Y	Y	Y	Y	Y
2	Neguse	Y	Y	Y	Y	Y	Y
3	**Tipton**	Y	Y	N	N	N	Y
4	**Buck**	N	N	N	N	N	N
5	**Lamborn**	N	Y	N	N	N	N
6	Crow	Y	Y	Y	Y	Y	Y
7	Perlmutter	Y	Y	Y	Y	Y	Y
CONNECTICUT							
1	Larson	Y	Y	Y	Y	Y	Y
2	Courtney	Y	Y	Y	Y	Y	Y
3	DeLauro	Y	Y	Y	Y	Y	Y
4	Himes	Y	Y	Y	Y	Y	Y
5	Hayes	Y	Y	Y	Y	Y	Y
DELAWARE							
AL	Blunt Rochester	Y	Y	Y	Y	Y	Y
FLORIDA							
1	**Gaetz**	N	N	N	N	N	N
2	**Dunn**	N	Y	N	N	N	N
3	**Yoho**	N	Y	N	N	N	N
4	**Rutherford**	Y	Y	Y	N	N	N
5	Lawson	Y	Y	Y	Y	Y	Y
6	**Waltz**	N	Y	Y	N	N	Y
7	Murphy	Y	Y	Y	Y	Y	Y
8	**Posey**	Y	Y	Y	N	N	Y
9	Soto	Y	Y	Y	Y	Y	Y
10	Demings	Y	Y	Y	Y	Y	Y
11	**Webster**	N	Y	Y	N	N	N
12	**Bilirakis**	?	?	?	?	?	?
13	Crist	Y	Y	Y	Y	Y	Y
14	Castor	Y	Y	Y	Y	Y	Y
15	**Spano**	Y	Y	Y	N	N	N
16	**Buchanan**	Y	Y	Y	N	N	Y
17	**Steube**	N	N	N	N	N	N
18	**Mast**	N	N	N	N	N	N
19	**Rooney**	?	?	?	N	N	N
20	Hastings	Y	Y	Y	Y	Y	Y
21	Frankel	Y	Y	Y	Y	Y	Y
22	Deutch	Y	Y	Y	Y	Y	Y
23	Wasserman Schultz	Y	Y	Y	Y	Y	Y
24	Wilson, F.	Y	Y	Y	Y	Y	Y
25	**Diaz-Balart**	Y	Y	Y	N	N	Y
26	Mucarsel-Powell	Y	Y	Y	Y	Y	Y
27	Shalala	Y	Y	Y	Y	Y	Y
GEORGIA							
1	**Carter, E.L.**	N	Y	Y	N	N	N
2	Bishop, S.	Y	Y	Y	Y	Y	Y
3	**Ferguson**	?	?	?	N	N	N
4	Johnson, H.	Y	Y	Y	Y	Y	Y
5	Lewis John	Y	Y	Y	Y	Y	Y
6	McBath	Y	+	Y	Y	Y	Y
7	**Woodall**	N	Y	N	N	N	N
8	**Scott, A.**	N	Y	Y	N	N	N
9	**Collins, D.**	N	Y	Y	N	N	N
10	**Hice**	N	N	N	N	N	N
11	**Loudermilk**	Y	Y	N	N	N	N
12	**Allen**	N	Y	N	N	N	N
13	Scott, D.	Y	Y	Y	Y	Y	Y
14	**Graves, T.**	N	Y	Y	N	N	N
HAWAII							
1	Case	Y	Y	Y	Y	Y	Y
2	Gabbard	?	?	?	?	?	?
IDAHO							
1	**Fulcher**	N	Y	N	N	N	N
2	**Simpson**	Y	Y	N	N	N	N
ILLINOIS							
1	Rush	Y	Y	Y	Y	Y	Y
2	Kelly, R.	Y	Y	Y	Y	Y	Y
3	Lipinski	Y	Y	Y	Y	Y	Y
4	García, J.	Y	Y	Y	Y	Y	Y
5	Quigley	Y	Y	Y	Y	Y	Y
6	Casten	Y	Y	Y	Y	Y	Y
7	Davis, D.	Y	Y	Y	Y	Y	Y
8	Krishnamoorthi	Y	Y	Y	Y	Y	Y
9	Schakowsky	Y	Y	Y	Y	Y	Y
10	Schneider	Y	Y	Y	Y	Y	Y
11	Foster	Y	Y	Y	Y	Y	Y

KEY: **Republicans** Democrats *Independents*

Y	Voted for (yea)	N	Voted against (nay)	P	Voted "present"
+	Announced for	-	Announced against	?	Did not vote or otherwise make position known
#	Paired for	X	Paired against		

		625	626	627	628	629	630
12	**Bost**	Y	Y	Y	N	N	Y
13	**Davis, R.**	N	Y	Y	N	N	Y
14	Underwood	Y	Y	Y	Y	Y	Y
15	**Shimkus**	Y	Y	Y	N	N	N
16	**Kinzinger**	Y	Y	Y	N	N	N
17	Bustos	Y	Y	Y	Y	Y	Y
18	**LaHood**	N	Y	Y	N	N	N
INDIANA							
1	Visclosky	Y	Y	Y	Y	Y	Y
2	**Walorski**	Y	Y	Y	N	N	N
3	**Banks**	Y	Y	Y	N	N	N
4	**Baird**	Y	Y	Y	N	N	N
5	**Brooks, S.**	+	+	+	N	N	Y
6	**Pence**	Y	Y	N	N	N	N
7	Carson	Y	Y	Y	Y	Y	Y
8	**Bucshon**	Y	Y	Y	N	N	N
9	**Hollingsworth**	Y	Y	Y	N	N	N
IOWA							
1	Finkenauer	Y	Y	Y	Y	Y	Y
2	Loebsack	Y	Y	Y	Y	Y	Y
3	Axne	Y	Y	Y	Y	Y	Y
4	**King, S.**	Y	Y	N	N	N	N
KANSAS							
1	**Marshall**	N	Y	N	N	N	N
2	**Watkins**	N	Y	N	N	N	N
3	Davids	Y	Y	Y	Y	Y	Y
4	**Estes**	N	Y	N	N	N	N
KENTUCKY							
1	**Comer**	N	Y	Y	N	N	N
2	**Guthrie**	N	Y	Y	N	N	Y
3	Yarmuth	Y	Y	Y	Y	Y	Y
4	**Massie**	N	N	N	N	N	N
5	**Rogers, H.**	Y	Y	Y	N	N	Y
6	**Barr**	Y	Y	N	N	N	Y
LOUISIANA							
1	**Scalise**	N	Y	N	N	N	N
2	Richmond	Y	Y	Y	Y	Y	Y
3	**Higgins, C.**	N	Y	Y	N	N	N
4	**Johnson, M.**	N	Y	N	N	N	N
5	**Abraham**	N	Y	Y	N	N	N
6	**Graves, G.**	N	Y	N	N	N	Y
MAINE							
1	Pingree	Y	Y	Y	Y	Y	Y
2	Golden	Y	Y	Y	Y	Y	Y
MARYLAND							
1	**Harris**	N	N	N	N	N	N
2	Ruppersberger	?	?	?	Y	Y	Y
3	Sarbanes	Y	Y	Y	Y	Y	Y
4	Brown, A.	Y	Y	Y	Y	Y	Y
5	Hoyer	Y	Y	Y	Y	Y	Y
6	Trone	Y	Y	Y	Y	Y	Y
7	vacant	|	|	|	|	|	|
8	Raskin	Y	Y	Y	Y	Y	Y
MASSACHUSETTS							
1	Neal	Y	Y	Y	Y	Y	Y
2	McGovern	Y	Y	Y	Y	Y	Y
3	Trahan	Y	Y	Y	Y	Y	Y
4	Kennedy	Y	Y	Y	Y	Y	Y
5	Clark	Y	Y	Y	Y	Y	Y
6	Moulton	+	+	+	Y	Y	Y
7	Pressley	+	+	+	Y	Y	Y
8	Lynch	Y	Y	Y	Y	Y	Y
9	Keating	Y	Y	Y	Y	Y	Y
MICHIGAN							
1	**Bergman**	N	Y	Y	N	N	Y
2	**Huizenga**	Y	Y	Y	N	N	Y
3	*Amash*	N	N	N	N	N	N
4	**Moolenaar**	Y	Y	Y	N	N	N
5	Kildee	Y	Y	Y	Y	Y	Y
6	**Upton**	Y	Y	Y	N	N	Y
7	**Walberg**	Y	Y	Y	N	N	Y
8	Slotkin	Y	Y	Y	Y	Y	Y
9	Levin	Y	Y	Y	Y	Y	Y
10	**Mitchell**	N	Y	N	N	N	N
11	Stevens	Y	Y	Y	Y	Y	Y
12	Dingell	Y	Y	Y	Y	Y	Y
13	Tlaib	Y	Y	Y	Y	Y	Y
14	Lawrence	Y	Y	Y	Y	Y	Y
MINNESOTA							
1	**Hagedorn**	Y	Y	N	N	N	N
2	Craig	Y	Y	Y	Y	Y	Y
3	Phillips	Y	Y	Y	Y	Y	Y
4	McCollum	Y	Y	Y	Y	Y	Y
5	Omar	Y	Y	Y	Y	Y	Y

		625	626	627	628	629	630
6	**Emmer**	N	Y	N	N	N	N
7	Peterson	Y	Y	Y	Y	Y	Y
8	**Stauber**	Y	Y	Y	N	N	Y
MISSISSIPPI							
1	**Kelly, T.**	N	Y	Y	N	N	N
2	Thompson, B.	Y	Y	Y	Y	Y	Y
3	**Guest**	N	Y	N	N	N	N
4	**Palazzo**	N	Y	N	N	N	N
MISSOURI							
1	Clay	Y	Y	Y	Y	Y	Y
2	**Wagner**	Y	Y	Y	N	N	Y
3	**Luetkemeyer**	Y	Y	Y	N	N	Y
4	**Hartzler**	Y	Y	Y	N	N	N
5	Cleaver	Y	Y	Y	Y	Y	Y
6	**Graves, S.**	N	Y	Y	N	N	Y
7	**Long**	N	Y	Y	N	N	N
8	**Smith, J.**	N	Y	N	N	N	N
MONTANA							
AL	**Gianforte**	Y	Y	Y	N	N	N
NEBRASKA							
1	**Fortenberry**	N	Y	Y	N	N	Y
2	**Bacon**	Y	Y	Y	N	N	Y
3	**Smith, Adrian**	Y	Y	Y	N	N	N
NEVADA							
1	Titus	Y	Y	Y	Y	Y	Y
2	**Amodei**	Y	Y	N	N	N	N
3	Lee	Y	Y	Y	Y	Y	Y
4	Horsford	?	?	?	?	Y	Y
NEW HAMPSHIRE							
1	Pappas	Y	Y	Y	Y	Y	Y
2	Kuster	+	Y	Y	Y	Y	Y
NEW JERSEY							
1	Norcross	Y	Y	Y	Y	Y	Y
2	Van Drew	Y	Y	Y	Y	Y	Y
3	Kim	Y	Y	Y	Y	Y	Y
4	**Smith, C.**	N	Y	Y	N	N	Y
5	Gottheimer	Y	Y	Y	Y	Y	Y
6	Pallone	Y	Y	Y	Y	Y	Y
7	Malinowski	Y	Y	Y	Y	Y	Y
8	Sires	Y	Y	Y	Y	Y	Y
9	Pascrell	Y	Y	Y	Y	Y	Y
10	Payne	Y	Y	Y	Y	Y	Y
11	Sherrill	Y	Y	Y	Y	Y	Y
12	Watson Coleman	Y	Y	Y	Y	Y	Y
NEW MEXICO							
1	Haaland	Y	Y	Y	Y	Y	Y
2	Torres Small	Y	Y	Y	Y	Y	Y
3	Luján	Y	Y	Y	Y	Y	Y
NEW YORK							
1	**Zeldin**	Y	Y	Y	N	N	N
2	**King, P.**	Y	Y	Y	N	N	Y
3	Suozzi	Y	Y	Y	Y	Y	Y
4	Rice, K.	Y	Y	Y	Y	Y	Y
5	Meeks	Y	Y	Y	Y	Y	Y
6	Meng	?	?	?	Y	Y	Y
7	Velázquez	Y	Y	Y	Y	Y	Y
8	Jeffries	Y	Y	Y	Y	Y	Y
9	Clarke	Y	Y	Y	Y	Y	Y
10	Nadler	Y	Y	Y	Y	Y	Y
11	Rose	Y	Y	Y	Y	Y	Y
12	Maloney, C.	Y	Y	Y	Y	Y	Y
13	Espaillat	Y	Y	Y	Y	Y	Y
14	Ocasio-Cortez	Y	Y	Y	Y	Y	Y
15	Serrano	?	?	?	?	?	?
16	Engel	Y	Y	Y	Y	Y	Y
17	Lowey	Y	Y	Y	Y	Y	Y
18	Maloney, S.P.	Y	Y	Y	Y	Y	Y
19	Delgado	Y	Y	Y	Y	Y	Y
20	Tonko	Y	Y	Y	Y	Y	Y
21	**Stefanik**	Y	Y	Y	N	N	Y
22	Brindisi	Y	Y	Y	Y	Y	Y
23	**Reed**	Y	Y	Y	N	N	Y
24	**Katko**	Y	Y	Y	N	N	Y
25	Morelle	Y	+	Y	Y	Y	+
26	Higgins, B.	Y	Y	Y	Y	Y	Y
27	**Collins, C.**						
NORTH CAROLINA							
1	Butterfield	?	?	?	Y	Y	Y
2	**Holding**	N	Y	N	N	N	Y
3	**Murphy**	N	N	N	N	N	N
4	Price	Y	Y	Y	Y	Y	Y
5	**Foxx**	N	N	Y	N	N	N
6	**Walker**	N	Y	Y	N	N	N
7	**Rouzer**	N	Y	N	N	N	N

		625	626	627	628	629	630
8	**Hudson**	N	Y	Y	N	N	Y
9	**Bishop**	N	Y	N	N	N	-
10	**McHenry**	Y	Y	Y	N	N	Y
11	**Meadows**	N	N	Y	?	N	N
12	Adams	Y	Y	Y	Y	Y	Y
13	**Budd**	Y	Y	N	N	N	N
NORTH DAKOTA							
AL	**Armstrong**	N	Y	N	N	N	N
OHIO							
1	**Chabot**	N	Y	N	N	N	N
2	**Wenstrup**	N	Y	N	N	N	N
3	Beatty	Y	Y	Y	Y	Y	Y
4	**Jordan**	N	N	N	?	N	N
5	**Latta**	N	Y	Y	N	N	N
6	**Johnson, B.**	N	Y	Y	N	N	N
7	**Gibbs**	N	Y	Y	N	N	N
8	**Davidson**	N	Y	N	N	N	N
9	Kaptur	Y	Y	Y	Y	Y	Y
10	**Turner**	Y	Y	Y	N	N	Y
11	Fudge	Y	Y	Y	Y	Y	Y
12	**Balderson**	N	Y	N	N	N	N
13	Ryan	Y	Y	Y	Y	Y	Y
14	**Joyce**	Y	Y	Y	N	N	Y
15	**Stivers**	Y	Y	N	N	N	Y
16	**Gonzalez**	Y	Y	Y	N	N	Y
OKLAHOMA							
1	**Hern**	N	Y	N	N	N	N
2	**Mullin**	N	Y	N	N	N	N
3	**Lucas**	Y	Y	Y	N	N	Y
4	**Cole**	Y	Y	Y	N	N	Y
5	Horn	Y	Y	Y	Y	Y	Y
OREGON							
1	Bonamici	Y	Y	Y	Y	Y	Y
2	**Walden**	Y	Y	Y	N	N	Y
3	Blumenauer	Y	Y	Y	Y	Y	Y
4	DeFazio	Y	Y	Y	Y	Y	Y
5	Schrader	Y	Y	Y	Y	Y	Y
PENNSYLVANIA							
1	**Fitzpatrick**	Y	Y	Y	N	N	Y
2	Boyle	Y	Y	Y	Y	Y	Y
3	Evans	Y	Y	Y	Y	Y	Y
4	Dean	Y	Y	Y	Y	Y	Y
5	Scanlon	Y	Y	Y	Y	Y	Y
6	Houlahan	Y	Y	Y	Y	Y	Y
7	Wild	Y	Y	Y	Y	Y	Y
8	Cartwright	Y	Y	Y	Y	Y	Y
9	**Meuser**	Y	Y	N	N	N	N
10	**Perry**	N	Y	N	N	N	N
11	**Smucker**	N	Y	N	N	N	N
12	**Keller**	Y	Y	Y	N	N	N
13	**Joyce**	N	Y	N	N	N	N
14	**Reschenthaler**	N	Y	N	N	N	N
15	**Thompson, G.**	N	Y	Y	N	N	N
16	**Kelly, M.**	Y	Y	N	N	N	N
17	Lamb	Y	Y	Y	Y	Y	Y
18	Doyle	Y	Y	Y	Y	Y	Y
RHODE ISLAND							
1	Cicilline	Y	Y	Y	Y	Y	Y
2	Langevin	Y	Y	Y	Y	Y	Y
SOUTH CAROLINA							
1	Cunningham	Y	Y	Y	Y	Y	Y
2	**Wilson, J.**	N	Y	N	N	N	N
3	**Duncan**	N	Y	N	N	N	N
4	**Timmons**	+	+	-	-	-	-
5	**Norman**	N	Y	N	N	N	N
6	Clyburn	Y	Y	Y	Y	Y	Y
7	**Rice, T.**	Y	Y	N	N	N	N
SOUTH DAKOTA							
AL	**Johnson**	N	Y	N	N	N	N
TENNESSEE							
1	**Roe**	Y	Y	Y	N	N	N
2	**Burchett**	N	N	N	N	N	N
3	**Fleischmann**	N	Y	N	N	N	N
4	**DesJarlais**	N	Y	N	N	N	N
5	Cooper	Y	Y	Y	Y	Y	Y
6	**Rose**	Y	Y	N	N	N	N
7	**Green**	N	Y	N	N	N	N
8	**Kustoff**	Y	Y	Y	N	N	N
9	Cohen	Y	Y	Y	Y	Y	Y
TEXAS							
1	**Gohmert**	?	?	?	?	?	?
2	**Crenshaw**	N	Y	Y	N	N	Y
3	**Taylor**	N	Y	N	N	N	N
4	**Ratcliffe**	N	Y	N	N	N	Y

		625	626	627	628	629	630
5	**Gooden**	N	Y	Y	N	N	N
6	**Wright**	?	?	?	N	N	N
7	Fletcher	Y	Y	Y	Y	Y	Y
8	**Brady**	N	N	Y	N	N	N
9	Green, A.	Y	Y	Y	Y	Y	Y
10	**McCaul**	N	Y	Y	N	N	Y
11	**Conaway**	N	Y	N	N	N	N
12	**Granger**	N	Y	Y	N	N	Y
13	**Thornberry**	N	Y	N	N	N	Y
14	**Weber**	N	N	N	N	N	N
15	Gonzalez	+	+	+	Y	Y	Y
16	Escobar	Y	Y	Y	Y	Y	Y
17	**Flores**	N	Y	Y	N	N	N
18	Jackson Lee	Y	Y	Y	Y	Y	Y
19	**Arrington**	N	Y	N	N	N	N
20	Castro	Y	Y	Y	Y	Y	Y
21	**Roy**	N	N	N	N	N	N
22	**Olson**	N	Y	Y	N	N	N
23	**Hurd**	N	Y	Y	-	N	Y
24	**Marchant**	?	?	?	N	N	Y
25	**Williams**	N	Y	Y	N	N	Y
26	**Burgess**	N	Y	N	N	N	N
27	**Cloud**	N	Y	N	N	N	N
28	Cuellar	Y	Y	Y	Y	Y	Y
29	Garcia, S.	Y	Y	Y	Y	Y	Y
30	Johnson, E.B.	Y	Y	Y	Y	Y	Y
31	**Carter, J.**	?	?	?	N	N	N
32	Allred	Y	Y	Y	Y	Y	Y
33	Veasey	Y	Y	Y	Y	Y	Y
34	Vela	Y	Y	Y	Y	Y	Y
35	Doggett	Y	Y	Y	Y	Y	Y
36	**Babin**	N	N	N	N	N	N
UTAH							
1	**Bishop, R.**	N	Y	?	N	N	N
2	**Stewart**	N	Y	Y	N	N	Y
3	**Curtis**	N	Y	Y	N	N	N
4	McAdams	Y	Y	Y	Y	Y	Y
VERMONT							
AL	Welch	Y	Y	Y	Y	Y	Y
VIRGINIA							
1	**Wittman**	N	Y	N	N	N	N
2	Luria	Y	Y	Y	Y	Y	Y
3	Scott, R.	Y	Y	Y	Y	Y	Y
4	McEachin	?	?	?	Y	Y	Y
5	**Riggleman**	Y	Y	N	N	N	N
6	**Cline**	N	Y	N	N	N	N
7	Spanberger	Y	Y	Y	Y	Y	Y
8	Beyer	Y	Y	Y	Y	Y	Y
9	**Griffith**	N	Y	N	N	N	N
10	Wexton	Y	Y	Y	Y	Y	Y
11	Connolly	Y	Y	Y	Y	Y	Y
WASHINGTON							
1	DelBene	Y	Y	Y	Y	Y	Y
2	Larsen	Y	Y	Y	Y	Y	Y
3	**Herrera Beutler**	Y	Y	Y	N	N	Y
4	**Newhouse**	Y	Y	Y	N	N	?
5	**McMorris Rodgers**	Y	Y	Y	N	N	Y
6	Kilmer	Y	Y	Y	Y	Y	Y
7	Jayapal	Y	Y	Y	Y	Y	Y
8	Schrier	Y	Y	Y	Y	Y	Y
9	Smith Adam	Y	Y	Y	Y	Y	Y
10	Heck	Y	Y	Y	Y	Y	Y
WEST VIRGINIA							
1	**McKinley**	Y	Y	N	N	N	N
2	**Mooney**	Y	Y	N	N	N	N
3	**Miller**	N	Y	N	N	N	Y
WISCONSIN							
1	**Steil**	Y	Y	Y	N	N	Y
2	Pocan	Y	Y	Y	Y	Y	Y
3	Kind	Y	Y	Y	Y	Y	Y
4	Moore	Y	Y	Y	Y	Y	Y
5	**Sensenbrenner**	N	N	Y	N	N	N
6	**Grothman**	N	Y	N	N	N	N
7	**Duffy**						
8	**Gallagher**	Y	Y	Y	N	N	N
WYOMING							
AL	**Cheney**	N	Y	N	N	N	N
DELEGATES							
	Radewagen (A.S.)						
	Norton (D.C.)						
	San Nicolas (Guam)						
	Sablan (N. Marianas)						
	González-Colón (P.R.)						
	Plaskett (V.I.)						

III HOUSE VOTES

631. HR3055. Further Fiscal 2020 Short-Term Appropriations - Motion to Concur.
Lowey, D-N.Y., motion to concur in the Senate amendment to the short-term continuing resolution (HR 3055), with a further House amendment that would provide funding for federal government operations and services through Dec. 20, 2019, at fiscal 2019 levels. Among other provisions, it would extend through Dec. 20 authorizations for certain expiring programs and entities, including certain Medicaid and Medicare programs and other health-related HHS programs. It would increase or modify funding rates for certain activities, including to provide for a 3.1 percent pay increase for the members of the armed forces and to provide $7.3 billion for activities related to the 2020 decennial census. It would repeal a $7.6 billion rescission of federal highway funding set to take effect in July 2020; extend certain federal surveillance authorities under the Patriot Act and other existing law through March 15, 2020; and modify provisions related to the Justice Department fund for victims of state-sponsored terrorism, including to designate 50 percent of funds for victims of the Sept. 11 terrorist attacks. Motion agreed to 231-192: R 12-181; D 219-10; I 0-1. Nov. 19, 2019.

632. HR1309. Workplace Violence Prevention - Previous Question. DeSaulnier, D-Calif., motion to order the previous question (thus ending debate and possibility of amendment) on the rule (H Res 713) that would provide for House floor consideration of the Workplace Violence Prevention for Health Care and Social Service Workers Act (HR 1309). The rule would provide for automatic adoption of a Scott, D-Va., manager's amendment to HR 1309 and provide for floor consideration of 10 additional amendments to the bill. The Scott manager's amendment to HR 1309 would specify that the Occupational Safety and Health Administration workplace violence standards to be issued under the bill's provisions would not apply to entities providing child day care services or to health practitioner offices not located in health care facilities. Motion agreed to 223-194: R 0-193; D 223-0; I 0-1. Nov. 20, 2019.

633. HR1309. Workplace Violence Prevention - Rule. Adoption of the rule that would provide for House floor consideration of the Workplace Violence Prevention for Health Care and Social Service Workers Act (HR 1309). The rule would provide for automatic adoption of a Scott, D-Va., manager's amendment to HR 1309 and provide for floor consideration of 10 additional amendments to the bill. The manager's amendment to HR 1309 would specify that the Occupational Safety and Health Administration workplace violence standards to be issued under the bill's provisions would not apply to entities providing child day care services or to health practitioner offices not located in health care facilities. Adopted 209-205: R 0-192; D 209-12; I 0-1. Nov. 20, 2019.

634. HR737. Shark Fin Import Ban - Passage. Huffman, D-Calif., motion to suspend the rules and pass the bill (HR 737), as amended, that would prohibit any individual from possessing, selling, or purchasing shark fins or products containing shark fins and impose a fine of up to $100,000 for violations. It would provide an exemption for shark fins lawfully acquired with a government permit for research or noncommercial purposes. It would clarify that the prohibition would not apply to dogfish fins or tails. It would require the Commerce Department to add rays and skates to a list of species for which it tracks import data on fish and fish products. Motion agreed to 310-107: R 89-104; D 221-2; I 0-1. *Note: A two-thirds majority of those present and voting (278 in this case) is required for passage under suspension of the rules.* Nov. 20, 2019.

635. S1838. Hong Kong Autonomy and Human Rights - Passage. Engel, D-N.Y., motion to suspend the rules and pass the bill that would state U.S. policy and require a number of actions and reports related to human rights in Hong Kong and the autonomy of Hong Kong from mainland China. Specifically, it would require the State Department to submit an annual certification to Congress related to the autonomy of Hong Kong from China, as a condition for treatment of Hong Kong as a separate entity from China under U.S. commercial and other law. It would require the president to report to Congress on Hong Kong's compliance with U.S. export control laws, including related to the transfer of certain technologies and services to China. It would require the president to submit an annual report to Congress identifying individuals responsible for actions in contravention of international agreements related to the autonomy of Hong Kong or for human rights violations in Hong Kong, and would require the president to impose economic, visa, and travel sanctions against such individuals. It would also prohibit the State Department from denying visas to Hong Kong residents based on politically-motivated arrest or other adverse action by the Hong Kong government against the applicant. Motion agreed to 417-1: R 192-1; D 224-0; I 1-0. *Note: A two-thirds majority of those present and voting (279 in this case) is required for passage under suspension of the rules.* Nov. 20, 2019.

636. S2710. Hong Kong Munitions Export Prohibition - Passage. Sherman, D-Calif., motion to suspend the rules and pass the bill (S 2710) that would require the president to prohibit the issuance of licenses to export certain munitions items, including tear gas, pepper spray, rubber bullets, and handcuffs, to the Hong Kong police force. It would sunset the prohibition one year after enactment. Motion agreed to 417-0: R 192-0; D 224-0; I 1-0. *Note: A two-thirds majority of those present and voting (278 in this case) is required for passage under suspension of the rules.* Nov. 20, 2019.

	631	632	633	634	635	636
ALABAMA						
1 Byrne	N	N	N	N	Y	Y
2 Roby	N	N	N	N	Y	Y
3 Rogers, M.	N	N	N	N	Y	Y
4 Aderholt	N	N	N	N	Y	Y
5 Brooks, M.	N	N	N	N	Y	Y
6 Palmer	N	N	N	N	Y	Y
7 Sewell	Y	Y	Y	Y	Y	Y
ALASKA						
AL Young	Y	N	N	N	Y	Y
ARIZONA						
1 O'Halleran	Y	Y	Y	Y	Y	Y
2 Kirkpatrick	Y	Y	Y	Y	Y	Y
3 Grijalva	Y	Y	Y	Y	Y	Y
4 Gosar	N	N	N	N	Y	Y
5 Biggs	N	N	N	N	Y	Y
6 Schweikert	N	N	N	Y	Y	Y
7 Gallego	Y	Y	Y	Y	Y	Y
8 Lesko	N	N	N	N	Y	Y
9 Stanton	Y	Y	Y	Y	Y	Y
ARKANSAS						
1 Crawford	N	N	N	N	Y	Y
2 Hill, F.	N	N	N	N	Y	Y
3 Womack	N	N	N	N	Y	Y
4 Westerman	N	N	N	N	Y	Y
CALIFORNIA						
1 LaMalfa	N	N	N	Y	Y	Y
2 Huffman	Y	Y	Y	Y	Y	Y
3 Garamendi	Y	Y	Y	Y	Y	Y
4 McClintock	N	N	N	N	Y	Y
5 Thompson, M.	Y	Y	Y	Y	Y	Y
6 Matsui	Y	Y	Y	Y	Y	Y
7 Bera	Y	Y	Y	Y	Y	Y
8 Cook	N	N	N	Y	Y	Y
9 McNerney	Y	Y	Y	Y	Y	Y
10 Harder	Y	Y	Y	Y	Y	Y
11 DeSaulnier	Y	Y	Y	Y	Y	Y
12 Pelosi					Y	Y
13 Lee B.	Y	Y	Y	Y	Y	Y
14 Speier	Y	Y	Y	Y	Y	Y
15 Swalwell	Y	Y	Y	Y	Y	Y
16 Costa	Y	Y	Y	Y	Y	Y
17 Khanna	Y	Y	Y	Y	Y	Y
18 Eshoo	Y	Y	Y	Y	Y	Y
19 Lofgren	Y	Y	Y	Y	Y	Y
20 Panetta	Y	Y	Y	Y	Y	Y
21 Cox	Y	Y	Y	Y	Y	Y
22 Nunes	N	N	N	N	Y	Y
23 McCarthy	N	N	N	Y	Y	Y
24 Carbajal	Y	Y	Y	Y	Y	Y
25 vacant						
26 Brownley	Y	Y	Y	Y	Y	Y
27 Chu	Y	Y	Y	Y	Y	Y
28 Schiff	Y	Y	Y	Y	Y	Y
29 Cárdenas	Y	Y	Y	Y	Y	Y
30 Sherman	Y	Y	Y	Y	Y	Y
31 Aguilar	Y	Y	Y	Y	Y	Y
32 Napolitano	Y	Y	Y	Y	Y	Y
33 Lieu	Y	Y	Y	N	Y	Y
34 Gomez	Y	Y	Y	Y	Y	Y
35 Torres	Y	Y	Y	Y	Y	Y
36 Ruiz	Y	Y	Y	Y	Y	Y
37 Bass	Y	Y	Y	Y	Y	Y
38 Sánchez	Y	Y	Y	Y	Y	Y
39 Cisneros	Y	Y	Y	Y	Y	Y
40 Roybal-Allard	Y	Y	Y	Y	Y	Y
41 Takano	Y	Y	Y	Y	Y	Y
42 Calvert	N	N	N	Y	Y	Y
43 Waters	Y	Y	Y	Y	Y	Y
44 Barragán	Y	Y	Y	Y	Y	Y
45 Porter	Y	+	+	+	+	+
46 Correa	Y	Y	N	Y	Y	Y
47 Lowenthal	Y	Y	Y	Y	Y	Y
48 Rouda	Y	Y	Y	Y	Y	Y
49 Levin	Y	Y	Y	Y	Y	Y
50 Hunter	N	N	N	Y	Y	Y
51 Vargas	N	Y	Y	Y	Y	Y
52 Peters	Y	Y	Y	Y	Y	Y

	631	632	633	634	635	636
53 Davis, S.	Y	Y	Y	Y	Y	Y
COLORADO						
1 DeGette	+	Y	Y	Y	Y	Y
2 Neguse	Y	Y	Y	Y	Y	Y
3 Tipton	N	N	N	N	Y	Y
4 Buck	N	N	N	N	Y	Y
5 Lamborn	N	N	N	N	Y	Y
6 Crow	Y	Y	Y	Y	Y	Y
7 Perlmutter	Y	Y	Y	Y	Y	Y
CONNECTICUT						
1 Larson	Y	Y	Y	Y	Y	Y
2 Courtney	Y	Y	Y	Y	Y	Y
3 DeLauro	Y	Y	Y	Y	Y	Y
4 Himes	Y	Y	Y	Y	Y	Y
5 Hayes	Y	Y	Y	Y	Y	Y
DELAWARE						
AL Blunt Rochester	Y	Y	Y	Y	Y	Y
FLORIDA						
1 Gaetz	N	N	N	N	Y	Y
2 Dunn	N	N	N	N	Y	Y
3 Yoho	N	N	N	N	Y	Y
4 Rutherford	N	N	N	N	Y	Y
5 Lawson	Y	Y	Y	Y	Y	Y
6 Waltz	N	N	N	Y	Y	Y
7 Murphy	Y	Y	Y	Y	Y	Y
8 Posey	N	N	N	N	Y	Y
9 Soto	Y	Y	Y	Y	Y	Y
10 Demings	Y	Y	Y	Y	Y	Y
11 Webster	N	N	N	Y	Y	?
12 Bilirakis	?	N	N	Y	Y	?
13 Crist	Y	Y	Y	Y	Y	Y
14 Castor	Y	Y	Y	Y	Y	Y
15 Spano	N	N	N	N	Y	Y
16 Buchanan	N	N	N	N	Y	Y
17 Steube	N	N	N	N	Y	Y
18 Mast	N	N	N	Y	Y	Y
19 Rooney	N	N	N	Y	Y	Y
20 Hastings	Y	Y	Y	Y	Y	Y
21 Frankel	Y	Y	Y	Y	Y	Y
22 Deutch	Y	Y	Y	Y	Y	Y
23 Wasserman Schultz	Y	Y	Y	Y	Y	Y
24 Wilson, F.	Y	Y	Y	Y	Y	Y
25 Diaz-Balart	N	N	N	N	Y	Y
26 Mucarsel-Powell	Y	Y	Y	Y	Y	Y
27 Shalala	Y	Y	Y	Y	Y	Y
GEORGIA						
1 Carter, E.L.	N	N	N	N	Y	Y
2 Bishop, S.	Y	?	?	?	?	?
3 Ferguson	N	N	N	N	Y	Y
4 Johnson, H.	Y	Y	Y	Y	Y	Y
5 Lewis John	Y	+	+	+	+	+
6 McBath	Y	Y	Y	Y	Y	Y
7 Woodall	N	N	N	N	Y	Y
8 Scott, A.	N	N	N	N	Y	Y
9 Collins, D.	N	N	N	N	Y	Y
10 Hice	N	N	N	N	Y	Y
11 Loudermilk	N	N	N	N	Y	Y
12 Allen	N	N	N	N	Y	Y
13 Scott, D.	Y	Y	Y	Y	Y	Y
14 Graves, T.	N	N	N	N	Y	Y
HAWAII						
1 Case	Y	Y	Y	Y	Y	Y
2 Gabbard	?	?	?	?	?	?
IDAHO						
1 Fulcher	N	N	N	N	Y	Y
2 Simpson	Y	N	N	Y	Y	Y
ILLINOIS						
1 Rush	Y	Y	Y	Y	Y	Y
2 Kelly, R.	Y	Y	Y	Y	Y	Y
3 Lipinski	Y	Y	Y	Y	Y	Y
4 García, J.	Y	Y	Y	Y	Y	Y
5 Quigley	Y	Y	Y	Y	Y	Y
6 Casten	Y	Y	Y	Y	Y	Y
7 Davis, D.	Y	Y	Y	Y	Y	Y
8 Krishnamoorthi	Y	Y	Y	Y	Y	Y
9 Schakowsky	Y	Y	+	Y	Y	Y
10 Schneider	Y	Y	Y	Y	Y	Y
11 Foster	Y	Y	Y	Y	Y	Y

		631	632	633	634	635	636
12	**Bost**	N	N	N	Y	Y	Y
13	**Davis, R.**	Y	N	N	Y	Y	Y
14	Underwood	Y	Y	Y	Y	Y	Y
15	**Shimkus**	N	N	N	N	Y	Y
16	**Kinzinger**	N	N	N	Y	Y	Y
17	Bustos	Y	Y	Y	Y	Y	Y
18	**LaHood**	N	N	N	N	Y	Y
INDIANA							
1	Visclosky	Y	Y	Y	Y	Y	Y
2	**Walorski**	N	N	N	Y	Y	Y
3	**Banks**	N	N	N	N	Y	Y
4	**Baird**	N	N	N	N	Y	Y
5	**Brooks, S.**	N	N	N	Y	Y	Y
6	**Pence**	N	N	N	Y	Y	Y
7	Carson	Y	Y	Y	Y	Y	Y
8	**Bucshon**	N	N	N	N	Y	Y
9	**Hollingsworth**	N	N	N	Y	Y	Y
IOWA							
1	Finkenauer	Y	Y	Y	Y	Y	Y
2	Loebsack	Y	Y	Y	Y	Y	Y
3	Axne	Y	Y	Y	Y	Y	Y
4	**King, S.**	N	N	N	N	Y	Y
KANSAS							
1	**Marshall**	N	N	N	Y	Y	Y
2	**Watkins**	N	N	N	Y	Y	Y
3	Davids	Y	Y	Y	Y	Y	Y
4	**Estes**	N	N	N	Y	Y	Y
KENTUCKY							
1	**Comer**	N	N	N	N	Y	Y
2	**Guthrie**	N	N	N	Y	Y	Y
3	Yarmuth	Y	Y	Y	Y	Y	Y
4	**Massie**	N	N	N	N	N	Y
5	**Rogers, H.**	N	N	N	Y	Y	Y
6	**Barr**	N	N	N	Y	Y	Y
LOUISIANA							
1	**Scalise**	N	N	N	N	Y	Y
2	Richmond	Y	?	?	?	?	?
3	**Higgins, C.**	N	N	N	N	Y	Y
4	**Johnson, M.**	N	N	N	N	Y	Y
5	**Abraham**	N	N	N	N	Y	Y
6	**Graves, G.**	N	N	N	N	Y	Y
MAINE							
1	Pingree	Y	Y	Y	Y	Y	Y
2	Golden	Y	Y	Y	Y	Y	Y
MARYLAND							
1	**Harris**	N	N	N	N	Y	Y
2	Ruppersberger	Y	Y	Y	Y	Y	Y
3	Sarbanes	Y	Y	Y	Y	Y	Y
4	Brown, A.	Y	Y	Y	Y	Y	Y
5	Hoyer	Y	Y	Y	Y	Y	Y
6	Trone	Y	Y	Y	Y	Y	Y
7	vacant	I	I	I	I	I	I
8	Raskin	Y	Y	Y	Y	Y	Y
MASSACHUSETTS							
1	Neal	Y	Y	Y	Y	Y	Y
2	McGovern	Y	Y	Y	Y	Y	Y
3	Trahan	Y	Y	Y	Y	Y	Y
4	Kennedy	Y	Y	Y	Y	Y	Y
5	Clark	Y	Y	Y	Y	Y	Y
6	Moulton	Y	Y	Y	Y	Y	Y
7	Pressley	N	Y	Y	Y	Y	Y
8	Lynch	Y	Y	Y	Y	Y	Y
9	Keating	Y	Y	Y	Y	Y	Y
MICHIGAN							
1	**Bergman**	N	N	N	Y	Y	Y
2	**Huizenga**	N	N	N	N	Y	Y
3	*Amash*	N	N	N	N	Y	Y
4	**Moolenaar**	N	N	N	Y	Y	Y
5	Kildee	Y	Y	Y	Y	Y	Y
6	**Upton**	N	N	N	Y	Y	Y
7	**Walberg**	N	N	N	N	Y	Y
8	Slotkin	Y	Y	Y	Y	Y	Y
9	Levin	Y	Y	Y	Y	Y	Y
10	**Mitchell**	N	N	N	Y	Y	Y
11	Stevens	Y	Y	Y	Y	Y	Y
12	Dingell	Y	Y	Y	Y	Y	Y
13	Tlaib	N	Y	Y	Y	Y	Y
14	Lawrence	Y	Y	Y	Y	Y	Y
MINNESOTA							
1	**Hagedorn**	N	N	N	Y	Y	Y
2	Craig	Y	Y	Y	Y	Y	Y
3	Phillips	Y	Y	Y	Y	Y	Y
4	McCollum	Y	Y	Y	Y	Y	Y
5	Omar	N	Y	Y	Y	Y	Y

		631	632	633	634	635	636
6	**Emmer**	N	N	N	Y	Y	Y
7	Peterson	Y	Y	N	Y	Y	Y
8	**Stauber**	N	N	N	Y	Y	Y
MISSISSIPPI							
1	**Kelly, T.**	N	N	N	N	Y	Y
2	Thompson, B.	Y	Y	Y	Y	Y	Y
3	**Guest**	N	N	N	Y	Y	Y
4	**Palazzo**	N	N	N	N	Y	Y
MISSOURI							
1	Clay	Y	Y	Y	Y	Y	Y
2	**Wagner**	N	N	N	Y	Y	Y
3	**Luetkemeyer**	N	N	N	N	Y	Y
4	**Hartzler**	N	N	N	N	Y	Y
5	Cleaver	Y	Y	Y	Y	Y	Y
6	**Graves, S.**	N	N	N	N	Y	Y
7	**Long**	N	N	N	N	Y	Y
8	**Smith, J.**	N	N	N	N	Y	Y
MONTANA							
AL	**Gianforte**	N	N	N	N	Y	Y
NEBRASKA							
1	**Fortenberry**	N	N	N	Y	Y	Y
2	**Bacon**	N	N	N	Y	Y	Y
3	**Smith, Adrian**	N	N	N	N	Y	Y
NEVADA							
1	Titus	Y	Y	Y	Y	Y	Y
2	**Amodei**	N	N	N	Y	Y	Y
3	Lee	Y	Y	Y	Y	Y	Y
4	Horsford	Y	Y	Y	Y	Y	Y
NEW HAMPSHIRE							
1	Pappas	Y	Y	Y	Y	Y	Y
2	Kuster	Y	Y	Y	Y	Y	Y
NEW JERSEY							
1	Norcross	Y	Y	Y	Y	Y	Y
2	Van Drew	Y	Y	N	N	Y	Y
3	Kim	Y	Y	Y	Y	Y	Y
4	**Smith, C.**	Y	N	N	Y	Y	Y
5	Gottheimer	Y	Y	N	Y	Y	Y
6	Pallone	Y	Y	Y	Y	Y	Y
7	Malinowski	Y	Y	Y	Y	Y	Y
8	Sires	Y	Y	Y	Y	Y	Y
9	Pascrell	Y	Y	Y	Y	Y	Y
10	Payne	Y	Y	Y	Y	Y	Y
11	Sherrill	Y	Y	N	Y	Y	Y
12	Watson Coleman	Y	Y	Y	Y	Y	Y
NEW MEXICO							
1	Haaland	Y	Y	Y	Y	Y	Y
2	Torres Small	Y	Y	Y	Y	Y	Y
3	Luján	Y	Y	Y	Y	Y	Y
NEW YORK							
1	**Zeldin**	N	N	N	Y	Y	Y
2	**King, P.**	N	N	N	Y	Y	Y
3	Suozzi	Y	Y	Y	Y	Y	Y
4	Rice, K.	Y	Y	Y	Y	Y	Y
5	Meeks	Y	Y	Y	Y	Y	Y
6	Meng	N	Y	Y	Y	Y	Y
7	Velázquez	Y	Y	Y	Y	Y	Y
8	Jeffries	Y	Y	Y	Y	Y	Y
9	Clarke	N	Y	Y	Y	Y	Y
10	Nadler	Y	Y	Y	Y	Y	Y
11	Rose	Y	Y	Y	Y	Y	Y
12	Maloney, C.	Y	Y	Y	Y	Y	Y
13	Espaillat	Y	Y	Y	Y	Y	Y
14	Ocasio-Cortez	N	Y	Y	Y	Y	Y
15	Serrano	?	?	?	?	?	?
16	Engel	Y	Y	Y	Y	Y	Y
17	Lowey	Y	Y	Y	Y	Y	Y
18	Maloney, S.P.	Y	Y	Y	Y	Y	Y
19	Delgado	Y	Y	Y	Y	Y	Y
20	Tonko	Y	Y	Y	Y	Y	Y
21	**Stefanik**	Y	N	N	Y	Y	Y
22	Brindisi	Y	Y	N	Y	Y	Y
23	**Reed**	N	N	N	Y	Y	Y
24	**Katko**	Y	N	N	Y	Y	Y
25	Morelle	Y	Y	Y	Y	Y	Y
26	Higgins, B.	Y	Y	Y	Y	Y	Y
27	**Collins, C.**						
NORTH CAROLINA							
1	Butterfield	Y	Y	Y	Y	Y	Y
2	**Holding**	N	N	N	N	Y	Y
3	**Murphy**	N	N	N	N	Y	Y
4	Price	Y	Y	Y	Y	Y	Y
5	**Foxx**	N	N	N	N	Y	Y
6	**Walker**	N	N	N	N	Y	Y
7	**Rouzer**	N	N	N	N	Y	Y

		631	632	633	634	635	636
8	**Hudson**	N	N	?	Y	Y	Y
9	**Bishop**	N	N	N	N	Y	Y
10	**McHenry**	N	N	N	Y	Y	Y
11	**Meadows**	N	N	N	N	Y	Y
12	Adams	Y	Y	Y	Y	Y	Y
13	**Budd**	N	N	N	Y	Y	Y
NORTH DAKOTA							
AL	**Armstrong**	Y	N	N	N	Y	Y
OHIO							
1	**Chabot**	N	N	N	Y	Y	Y
2	**Wenstrup**	N	N	N	N	Y	Y
3	Beatty	Y	Y	Y	Y	Y	Y
4	**Jordan**	N	N	N	N	Y	Y
5	**Latta**	N	N	N	N	Y	Y
6	**Johnson, B.**	N	N	N	N	Y	Y
7	**Gibbs**	N	N	N	N	Y	Y
8	**Davidson**	N	N	N	Y	Y	Y
9	Kaptur	Y	Y	Y	Y	Y	Y
10	**Turner**	N	N	N	Y	Y	Y
11	Fudge	Y	?	?	?	?	?
12	**Balderson**	N	N	N	N	Y	Y
13	Ryan	Y	Y	Y	Y	Y	Y
14	**Joyce**	N	N	N	Y	Y	Y
15	**Stivers**	N	N	N	Y	Y	Y
16	**Gonzalez**	N	N	N	Y	Y	Y
OKLAHOMA							
1	**Hern**	N	N	N	N	Y	Y
2	**Mullin**	N	N	N	N	Y	Y
3	**Lucas**	N	N	N	N	Y	Y
4	**Cole**	Y	N	N	Y	Y	Y
5	Horn	Y	Y	N	Y	Y	Y
OREGON							
1	Bonamici	Y	Y	Y	Y	Y	Y
2	**Walden**	N	N	N	Y	Y	Y
3	Blumenauer	N	Y	Y	Y	Y	Y
4	DeFazio	N	Y	Y	Y	Y	Y
5	Schrader	Y	Y	N	Y	Y	Y
PENNSYLVANIA							
1	**Fitzpatrick**	Y	N	N	Y	Y	Y
2	Boyle	Y	Y	Y	Y	Y	Y
3	Evans	Y	Y	Y	Y	Y	Y
4	Dean	Y	Y	Y	Y	Y	Y
5	Scanlon	Y	Y	Y	Y	Y	Y
6	Houlahan	Y	Y	Y	Y	Y	Y
7	Wild	Y	Y	Y	Y	Y	Y
8	Cartwright	Y	Y	Y	Y	Y	Y
9	**Meuser**	N	N	N	Y	Y	Y
10	**Perry**	N	N	N	Y	Y	Y
11	**Smucker**	N	N	N	Y	Y	Y
12	**Keller**	N	N	N	Y	Y	Y
13	**Joyce**	N	N	N	N	Y	Y
14	**Reschenthaler**	N	N	N	Y	Y	Y
15	**Thompson, G.**	N	N	N	Y	Y	Y
16	**Kelly, M.**	N	N	N	Y	Y	Y
17	Lamb	Y	Y	Y	Y	Y	Y
18	Doyle	Y	Y	Y	Y	Y	Y
RHODE ISLAND							
1	Cicilline	Y	Y	Y	Y	Y	Y
2	Langevin	Y	Y	Y	Y	Y	Y
SOUTH CAROLINA							
1	Cunningham	Y	Y	N	Y	Y	Y
2	**Wilson, J.**	N	N	N	N	Y	Y
3	**Duncan**	N	N	N	N	Y	Y
4	**Timmons**	-	-	-	+	+	+
5	**Norman**	N	N	N	N	Y	Y
6	Clyburn	Y	Y	Y	Y	Y	Y
7	**Rice, T.**	N	N	N	Y	Y	Y
SOUTH DAKOTA							
AL	**Johnson**	N	N	N	N	Y	Y
TENNESSEE							
1	**Roe**	N	N	N	Y	Y	Y
2	**Burchett**	N	N	N	Y	Y	Y
3	**Fleischmann**	N	N	N	N	Y	Y
4	**DesJarlais**	N	N	N	N	Y	Y
5	Cooper	Y	?	?	?	?	?
6	**Rose**	N	N	N	N	Y	Y
7	**Green**	N	N	N	N	Y	Y
8	**Kustoff**	N	N	N	Y	Y	Y
9	Cohen	Y	Y	Y	Y	Y	Y
TEXAS							
1	**Gohmert**	?	N	N	N	Y	Y
2	**Crenshaw**	N	N	N	Y	Y	Y
3	**Taylor**	N	N	N	N	Y	Y
4	**Ratcliffe**	?	N	N	N	Y	Y

		631	632	633	634	635	636
5	**Gooden**	N	N	N	Y	Y	Y
6	**Wright**	N	N	N	Y	Y	Y
7	Fletcher	Y	Y	Y	Y	Y	Y
8	**Brady**	N	N	N	N	Y	Y
9	Green, A.	Y	Y	Y	Y	Y	Y
10	**McCaul**	Y	N	N	Y	Y	Y
11	**Conaway**	N	N	N	Y	Y	Y
12	**Granger**	N	N	N	Y	Y	Y
13	**Thornberry**	N	N	N	N	Y	Y
14	**Weber**	N	N	N	N	Y	Y
15	Gonzalez	Y	Y	Y	Y	Y	Y
16	Escobar	Y	Y	Y	Y	Y	Y
17	**Flores**	N	?	?	?	?	?
18	Jackson Lee	Y	Y	Y	Y	Y	Y
19	**Arrington**	N	N	N	Y	Y	Y
20	Castro	Y	Y	Y	Y	Y	Y
21	**Roy**	N	N	N	N	Y	Y
22	**Olson**	N	N	N	Y	Y	Y
23	**Hurd**	Y	N	N	Y	Y	Y
24	**Marchant**	N	N	N	N	Y	Y
25	**Williams**	N	N	N	N	Y	Y
26	**Burgess**	N	N	N	Y	Y	Y
27	**Cloud**	N	N	N	N	Y	Y
28	Cuellar	Y	Y	Y	Y	Y	Y
29	Garcia, S.	Y	Y	Y	Y	Y	Y
30	Johnson, E.B.	Y	Y	Y	Y	Y	Y
31	**Carter, J.**	N	?	?	?	?	?
32	Allred	Y	Y	Y	Y	Y	Y
33	Veasey	Y	Y	Y	Y	Y	Y
34	Vela	N	Y	?	Y	Y	Y
35	Doggett	Y	Y	Y	Y	Y	Y
36	**Babin**	N	N	N	Y	Y	Y
UTAH							
1	**Bishop, R.**	N	N	N	N	Y	Y
2	**Stewart**	N	N	N	N	Y	Y
3	**Curtis**	N	N	N	N	Y	Y
4	McAdams	Y	Y	N	Y	Y	Y
VERMONT							
AL	Welch	Y	Y	Y	Y	Y	Y
VIRGINIA							
1	**Wittman**	N	N	N	N	Y	Y
2	Luria	Y	Y	Y	Y	Y	Y
3	Scott, R.	Y	Y	Y	Y	Y	Y
4	McEachin	Y	?	?	?	?	?
5	**Riggleman**	N	N	N	Y	Y	Y
6	**Cline**	N	N	N	N	Y	Y
7	Spanberger	Y	Y	N	Y	Y	Y
8	Beyer	Y	Y	Y	Y	Y	Y
9	**Griffith**	N	N	N	Y	Y	Y
10	Wexton	Y	Y	Y	Y	Y	Y
11	Connolly	Y	Y	Y	Y	Y	Y
WASHINGTON							
1	DelBene	Y	Y	Y	Y	Y	Y
2	Larsen	Y	Y	Y	Y	Y	Y
3	**Herrera Beutler**	Y	N	N	N	Y	Y
4	**Newhouse**	N	N	N	N	Y	Y
5	**McMorris Rodgers**	N	N	N	N	Y	Y
6	Kilmer	Y	Y	Y	Y	Y	Y
7	Jayapal	Y	Y	Y	Y	Y	Y
8	Schrier	Y	Y	Y	Y	Y	Y
9	Smith Adam	Y	Y	Y	Y	Y	Y
10	Heck	Y	Y	Y	Y	Y	Y
WEST VIRGINIA							
1	**McKinley**	N	N	N	N	Y	Y
2	**Mooney**	N	N	N	Y	Y	Y
3	**Miller**	N	N	N	N	Y	Y
WISCONSIN							
1	**Steil**	N	N	N	Y	Y	Y
2	Pocan	Y	Y	Y	Y	Y	Y
3	Kind	Y	Y	Y	Y	Y	Y
4	Moore	Y	Y	Y	Y	Y	Y
5	**Sensenbrenner**	N	N	N	N	Y	Y
6	**Grothman**	N	N	N	Y	Y	Y
7	**Duffy**						
8	**Gallagher**	N	?	?	?	?	?
WYOMING							
AL	**Cheney**	N	N	N	N	Y	Y
DELEGATES							
	Radewagen (A.S.)						
	Norton (D.C.)						
	San Nicolas (Guam)						
	Sablan (N. Marianas)						
	González-Colón (P.R.)						
	Plaskett (V.I.)						

||| HOUSE VOTES

637. HR1309. Workplace Violence Prevention - Remove Deadline and Other Requirements. Byrne, R-Ala., substitute amendment no. 3 that would modify language in the bill to remove a requirement that the Occupational Safety and Health Administration workplace violence prevention standard required by the bill be based on existing 2015 OSHA guidelines. It would add findings to the bill describing recent studies and rule-making related to workplace violence in the health care and social service industries, including to express that the 2015 OSHA guidelines are "not enforceable." Among other provisions, it would remove requirements in the bill establishing a deadline for OSHA promulgation of a final standard, and it would remove or reduce requirements related to types of violence addressed, mandatory employee training, and anti-retaliation policies under workplace violence prevention plans. It would require the Labor Department to conduct an education campaign for affected employers and employees regarding existing OSHA materials on workplace violence, during the rule-making process for the new OSHA standard. Rejected in Committee of the Whole 177-238: R 175-17; D 1-220; I 1-1. Nov. 21, 2019.

638. HR1309. Workplace Violence Prevention - Violent Incident Reporting. Harder, D-Calif., amendment no. 4 that would clarify that nothing in the bill should be understood to limit or prevent health care workers, social service workers, or other personnel from reporting violent incidents to the appropriate law enforcement agencies. Adopted in Committee of the Whole 414-1: R 193-1; D 219-0; I 2-0. Nov. 21, 2019.

639. HR1309. Workplace Violence Prevention - Existing Legal Protections. Wexton, D-Va., amendment no. 9 that would clarify that nothing in the bill should be understood to limit or diminish any protections in federal, state, or local law related to domestic violence, stalking, dating violence, or sexual assault. Adopted in Committee of the Whole 415-1: R 192-1; D 221-0; I 2-0. Nov. 21, 2019.

640. HR1309. Workplace Violence Prevention - OSHA Technical Assistance for Employers. Delgado, D-N.Y., amendment no. 10 that would require that the Occupational Safety and Health Administration standard on workplace violence prevention required by the bill provide for a period, of up to a year, during which the agency would prioritize providing technical assistance and advice to employers subject to the standard. Adopted in Committee of the Whole 242-176: R 19-175; D 222-0; I 1-1. Nov. 21, 2019.

641. HR1309. Workplace Violence Prevention - Motion to Table. Hoyer, D-Md., motion to table the Kelly, R-Pa., motion to appeal of the ruling of the chair, effectively ruling a Kelly motion to recommit the bill not germane. The motion to table would sustain a ruling of the chair regarding a Courtney, D-Conn., point of order that the amendment contained in the Kelly motion to recommit the bill was not germane. The Kelly motion to recommit would have moved to recommit the bill to the House Education and Labor Committee with instructions to report it back immediately with an amendment that would express the sense of Congress that the House majority in the 116th Congress has "failed to deliver results" by prioritizing the impeachment of President Trump over working with the Trump administration and Republicans in Congress to enact legislation related to "critical issues," including implementation of the United States-Mexico-Canada trade agreement, annual Defense authorizations and appropriations for fiscal 2020, prescription drug pricing, and "secure operational control" of the U.S.-Mexico border. Motion agreed to 222-188: R 2-188; D 219-0; I 1-0. Nov. 21, 2019.

642. HR1309. Workplace Violence Prevention - Passage. Passage of the bill, as amended, that would require the Occupational Safety and Health Administration to issue a final workplace violence prevention standard that would require employers in the health care and social service industries to develop and implement comprehensive plans to prevent and protect employees from violent incidents at work. It would require OSHA to issue an interim final standard, based on 2015 OSHA guidelines, within one year of enactment and a final standard within 42 months of enactment. Among other provisions, it would require employers to develop and implement workplace violence prevention plans within six months of issuance of the interim final standard. It would require employers to develop plans with the participation of employees or employee representatives and to provide annual employee training related to the plans. It would require that the plans include certain procedures for reporting, responding to, and mitigating risks of incidents of workplace violence, including for employers to investigate and take corrective actions in response to violent incidents. It would require employers to maintain a record of all such incidents and incident response. The bill's provisions would apply to employers of any individuals who work in certain health care facilities -- including hospitals, nursing homes, or drug abuse treatment centers -- or individuals who provide certain services -- including home-based health care or social work and emergency services. Passed 251-158: R 32-157; D 219-0; I 0-1. *Note: A "nay" was a vote in support of the president's position.* Nov. 21, 2019.

		637	638	639	640	641	642
ALABAMA							
1	**Byrne**	Y	Y	Y	N	?	?
2	**Roby**	Y	Y	Y	N	N	N
3	**Rogers, M.**	Y	Y	Y	N	N	N
4	**Aderholt**	Y	Y	Y	N	N	N
5	**Brooks, M.**	Y	Y	Y	N	N	N
6	**Palmer**	Y	Y	Y	N	N	N
7	Sewell	N	Y	Y	Y	Y	Y
ALASKA							
AL	**Young**	N	Y	Y	N	N	Y
ARIZONA							
1	O'Halleran	N	Y	Y	Y	Y	Y
2	Kirkpatrick	N	Y	Y	Y	Y	Y
3	Grijalva	N	Y	Y	Y	Y	Y
4	**Gosar**	N	Y	Y	N	N	?
5	**Biggs**	N	Y	Y	N	N	N
6	**Schweikert**	Y	Y	Y	N	N	N
7	Gallego	N	Y	Y	Y	Y	Y
8	**Lesko**	Y	Y	Y	N	N	Y
9	Stanton	N	Y	Y	Y	Y	Y
ARKANSAS							
1	**Crawford**	Y	Y	Y	N	N	N
2	**Hill, F.**	Y	Y	Y	N	N	N
3	**Womack**	Y	Y	Y	N	N	N
4	**Westerman**	Y	Y	Y	N	N	N
CALIFORNIA							
1	**LaMalfa**	Y	Y	Y	N	N	N
2	Huffman	-	+	+	+	+	+
3	Garamendi	N	Y	Y	Y	Y	Y
4	**McClintock**	Y	Y	Y	N	N	N
5	Thompson, M.	N	Y	Y	Y	Y	Y
6	Matsui	N	Y	Y	Y	Y	Y
7	Bera	N	Y	Y	Y	Y	Y
8	**Cook**	Y	Y	Y	N	N	Y
9	McNerney	N	Y	Y	Y	Y	Y
10	Harder	N	Y	Y	Y	Y	Y
11	DeSaulnier	N	Y	Y	Y	Y	Y
12	Pelosi						
13	Lee B.	N	Y	Y	Y	Y	Y
14	Speier	N	Y	Y	Y	Y	Y
15	Swalwell	N	Y	Y	Y	Y	Y
16	Costa	N	Y	Y	Y	Y	Y
17	Khanna	N	Y	Y	Y	Y	Y
18	Eshoo	N	Y	Y	Y	Y	Y
19	Lofgren	N	Y	Y	Y	Y	Y
20	Panetta	N	Y	Y	Y	Y	Y
21	Cox	N	Y	Y	Y	Y	Y
22	**Nunes**	Y	Y	Y	N	N	N
23	**McCarthy**	Y	Y	Y	N	N	N
24	Carbajal	N	Y	Y	Y	Y	Y
25	vacant						
26	Brownley	N	Y	Y	Y	Y	Y
27	Chu	N	Y	Y	Y	Y	Y
28	Schiff	N	Y	Y	Y	Y	Y
29	Cárdenas	?	Y	Y	Y	Y	Y
30	Sherman	N	Y	Y	Y	Y	Y
31	Aguilar	?	?	?	?	?	?
32	Napolitano	N	Y	Y	Y	Y	Y
33	Lieu	N	Y	Y	Y	Y	Y
34	Gomez	N	Y	Y	Y	Y	Y
35	Torres	N	Y	Y	Y	Y	Y
36	Ruiz	N	Y	Y	Y	Y	Y
37	Bass	N	Y	Y	Y	Y	Y
38	Sánchez	N	Y	Y	Y	Y	Y
39	Cisneros	N	Y	Y	Y	Y	Y
40	Roybal-Allard	N	Y	Y	Y	Y	Y
41	Takano	N	Y	Y	Y	Y	Y
42	**Calvert**	Y	Y	Y	N	N	N
43	Waters	N	Y	Y	Y	Y	Y
44	Barragán	N	Y	Y	Y	Y	Y
45	Porter	N	Y	Y	Y	Y	Y
46	Correa	N	Y	Y	Y	Y	Y
47	Lowenthal	N	Y	Y	Y	Y	Y
48	Rouda	N	Y	Y	Y	Y	Y
49	Levin	N	Y	Y	Y	Y	Y
50	**Hunter**	Y	Y	Y	N	N	N
51	Vargas	N	Y	Y	Y	Y	Y
52	Peters	N	Y	Y	Y	Y	Y
53	Davis, S.	N	Y	Y	Y	Y	Y
COLORADO							
1	DeGette	N	Y	Y	Y	Y	Y
2	Neguse	N	Y	Y	Y	Y	Y
3	**Tipton**	Y	Y	Y	N	N	Y
4	**Buck**	Y	Y	Y	N	N	N
5	**Lamborn**	Y	Y	Y	N	N	N
6	Crow	N	Y	Y	Y	Y	Y
7	Perlmutter	N	Y	Y	Y	Y	Y
CONNECTICUT							
1	Larson	N	Y	Y	Y	Y	Y
2	Courtney	N	Y	Y	Y	Y	Y
3	DeLauro	N	Y	Y	Y	Y	Y
4	Himes	N	Y	Y	Y	Y	Y
5	Hayes	N	Y	Y	Y	Y	Y
DELAWARE							
AL	Blunt Rochester	N	Y	Y	Y	Y	Y
FLORIDA							
1	**Gaetz**	Y	Y	Y	N	N	N
2	**Dunn**	Y	Y	Y	N	N	N
3	**Yoho**	Y	Y	Y	N	N	N
4	**Rutherford**	Y	Y	Y	N	N	N
5	Lawson	N	Y	Y	Y	Y	Y
6	**Waltz**	Y	Y	Y	N	N	N
7	Murphy	N	Y	Y	Y	Y	Y
8	**Posey**	Y	Y	Y	N	N	N
9	Soto	N	Y	Y	Y	Y	Y
10	Demings	N	Y	Y	Y	Y	Y
11	**Webster**	Y	Y	Y	N	N	N
12	**Bilirakis**	Y	Y	Y	N	N	N
13	Crist	N	Y	Y	Y	Y	Y
14	Castor	N	Y	Y	Y	Y	Y
15	**Spano**	Y	Y	Y	N	N	N
16	**Buchanan**	Y	Y	Y	N	N	N
17	**Steube**	Y	Y	Y	N	N	N
18	**Mast**	Y	Y	Y	N	N	N
19	**Rooney**	Y	Y	Y	N	N	N
20	Hastings	N	Y	Y	Y	Y	Y
21	Frankel	N	Y	Y	Y	Y	Y
22	Deutch	N	Y	Y	Y	Y	Y
23	Wasserman Schultz	N	Y	Y	Y	Y	Y
24	Wilson, F.	N	Y	Y	Y	Y	Y
25	**Diaz-Balart**	Y	Y	Y	N	N	N
26	Mucarsel-Powell	N	Y	Y	Y	Y	Y
27	Shalala	N	Y	Y	Y	Y	Y
GEORGIA							
1	**Carter, E.L.**	Y	Y	Y	N	N	N
2	Bishop, S.	?	?	?	?	?	?
3	**Ferguson**	Y	Y	Y	N	N	N
4	Johnson, H.	N	Y	Y	Y	Y	Y
5	Lewis John	-	+	+	+	+	+
6	McBath	N	Y	Y	Y	Y	Y
7	**Woodall**	Y	Y	Y	N	N	N
8	**Scott, A.**	Y	Y	Y	N	N	N
9	**Collins, D.**	Y	Y	Y	N	N	N
10	**Hice**	Y	Y	Y	N	N	N
11	**Loudermilk**	Y	Y	Y	N	N	N
12	**Allen**	Y	Y	Y	N	N	N
13	Scott, D.	N	Y	Y	Y	Y	Y
14	**Graves, T.**	Y	Y	Y	N	N	N
HAWAII							
1	Case	N	Y	?	Y	Y	Y
2	Gabbard	?	?	?	?	?	?
IDAHO							
1	**Fulcher**	Y	Y	Y	N	N	N
2	**Simpson**	Y	Y	Y	N	N	N
ILLINOIS							
1	Rush	N	Y	Y	Y	Y	Y
2	Kelly, R.	N	Y	Y	Y	Y	Y
3	Lipinski	N	Y	Y	Y	Y	Y
4	García, J.	N	Y	Y	Y	Y	Y
5	Quigley	N	Y	Y	Y	Y	Y
6	Casten	N	Y	Y	Y	Y	Y
7	Davis, D.	N	Y	Y	Y	Y	Y
8	Krishnamoorthi	N	Y	Y	Y	Y	Y
9	Schakowsky	N	Y	Y	Y	Y	Y
10	Schneider	N	Y	Y	Y	Y	Y
11	Foster	N	Y	Y	Y	Y	Y

KEY: **Republicans** Democrats *Independents*

Y	Voted for (yea)	N	Voted against (nay)	P	Voted "present"
+	Announced for	-	Announced against	?	Did not vote or otherwise make position known
#	Paired for	X	Paired against		

		637	638	639	640	641	642
12	**Bost**	Y	Y	Y	Y	N	Y
13	**Davis, R.**	Y	Y	Y	Y	N	Y
14	Underwood	N	Y	Y	Y	Y	Y
15	**Shimkus**	Y	Y	Y	N	N	N
16	**Kinzinger**	Y	Y	Y	N	N	N
17	Bustos	N	Y	Y	Y	Y	Y
18	**LaHood**	Y	Y	Y	N	N	N
INDIANA							
1	Visclosky	N	Y	Y	Y	Y	Y
2	**Walorski**	Y	Y	Y	N	N	N
3	**Banks**	Y	Y	Y	N	N	N
4	**Baird**	Y	Y	Y	N	N	N
5	**Brooks, S.**	Y	Y	Y	N	N	Y
6	**Pence**	Y	Y	Y	N	N	N
7	Carson	N	Y	Y	Y	Y	Y
8	**Bucshon**	Y	Y	Y	N	N	Y
9	**Hollingsworth**	Y	Y	Y	Y	N	N
IOWA							
1	Finkenauer	N	Y	Y	Y	Y	Y
2	Loebsack	N	Y	Y	Y	Y	Y
3	Axne	N	Y	Y	Y	Y	Y
4	**King, S.**	N	Y	Y	N	N	N
KANSAS							
1	**Marshall**	Y	Y	Y	N	N	N
2	**Watkins**	Y	Y	Y	N	N	?
3	Davids	N	Y	Y	Y	Y	Y
4	**Estes**	Y	Y	Y	N	N	N
KENTUCKY							
1	**Comer**	Y	Y	Y	N	N	N
2	**Guthrie**	Y	Y	Y	N	N	N
3	Yarmuth	N	Y	Y	Y	Y	Y
4	**Massie**	N	N	N	N	Y	N
5	**Rogers, H.**	Y	Y	Y	N	N	N
6	**Barr**	Y	Y	Y	N	N	N
LOUISIANA							
1	**Scalise**	Y	Y	Y	N	N	N
2	Richmond	?	?	?	?	?	?
3	**Higgins, C.**	Y	Y	Y	N	N	N
4	**Johnson, M.**	Y	Y	Y	N	N	N
5	**Abraham**	Y	Y	Y	N	N	N
6	**Graves, G.**	Y	Y	Y	Y	N	Y
MAINE							
1	Pingree	N	Y	Y	Y	Y	Y
2	Golden	N	Y	Y	Y	Y	Y
MARYLAND							
1	**Harris**	Y	Y	Y	N	N	N
2	Ruppersberger	N	Y	Y	Y	Y	Y
3	Sarbanes	N	Y	Y	Y	Y	Y
4	Brown, A.	N	Y	Y	Y	Y	Y
5	Hoyer	N	Y	Y	Y	Y	Y
6	Trone	N	Y	Y	Y	Y	Y
7	vacant	I	I	I	I	I	I
8	Raskin	N	Y	Y	Y	Y	Y
MASSACHUSETTS							
1	Neal	N	Y	Y	Y	Y	Y
2	McGovern	N	Y	Y	Y	Y	Y
3	Trahan	N	Y	Y	Y	Y	Y
4	Kennedy	N	Y	Y	Y	Y	Y
5	Clark	N	Y	Y	Y	Y	Y
6	Moulton	-	+	+	+	+	+
7	Pressley	N	Y	Y	Y	Y	Y
8	Lynch	N	Y	Y	Y	Y	Y
9	Keating	N	Y	Y	Y	Y	Y
MICHIGAN							
1	**Bergman**	Y	Y	Y	N	N	N
2	**Huizenga**	Y	Y	Y	N	N	N
3	*Amash*	Y	Y	Y	N	Y	N
4	**Moolenaar**	Y	Y	Y	N	N	N
5	Kildee	N	Y	Y	Y	Y	Y
6	**Upton**	N	Y	Y	Y	N	Y
7	**Walberg**	Y	Y	Y	N	N	N
8	Slotkin	N	Y	Y	Y	Y	Y
9	Levin	N	Y	Y	Y	Y	Y
10	**Mitchell**	Y	Y	Y	N	N	N
11	Stevens	N	Y	Y	Y	Y	Y
12	Dingell	N	Y	Y	Y	Y	Y
13	Tlaib	?	Y	Y	Y	Y	Y
14	Lawrence	N	Y	Y	Y	Y	Y
MINNESOTA							
1	**Hagedorn**	Y	Y	Y	N	N	N
2	Craig	N	Y	Y	Y	Y	Y
3	Phillips	N	Y	Y	Y	Y	Y
4	McCollum	N	Y	Y	Y	Y	Y
5	Omar	N	?	Y	Y	Y	Y

		637	638	639	640	641	642
6	**Emmer**	Y	Y	Y	N	N	N
7	Peterson	N	Y	Y	Y	Y	Y
8	**Stauber**	N	Y	Y	Y	N	Y
MISSISSIPPI							
1	**Kelly, T.**	Y	Y	Y	N	N	N
2	Thompson, B.	N	Y	Y	Y	Y	Y
3	**Guest**	Y	Y	Y	N	N	N
4	**Palazzo**	Y	Y	Y	N	N	N
MISSOURI							
1	Clay	N	Y	Y	Y	Y	Y
2	**Wagner**	Y	Y	Y	N	N	N
3	**Luetkemeyer**	Y	Y	Y	N	N	N
4	**Hartzler**	N	Y	Y	Y	N	Y
5	Cleaver	N	Y	Y	Y	Y	Y
6	**Graves, S.**	Y	Y	Y	N	N	N
7	**Long**	Y	Y	Y	N	N	N
8	**Smith, J.**	Y	Y	Y	N	N	N
MONTANA							
AL	**Gianforte**	Y	Y	Y	N	N	N
NEBRASKA							
1	**Fortenberry**	N	Y	Y	Y	N	Y
2	**Bacon**	Y	Y	Y	Y	N	Y
3	**Smith, Adrian**	Y	Y	Y	N	N	N
NEVADA							
1	Titus	N	Y	Y	Y	Y	Y
2	**Amodei**	Y	Y	Y	N	N	N
3	Lee	N	Y	Y	Y	Y	Y
4	Horsford	N	Y	Y	Y	Y	Y
NEW HAMPSHIRE							
1	Pappas	N	Y	Y	Y	Y	Y
2	Kuster	N	Y	Y	Y	Y	Y
NEW JERSEY							
1	Norcross	N	Y	Y	Y	Y	Y
2	Van Drew	N	Y	Y	Y	Y	Y
3	Kim	N	Y	Y	Y	Y	Y
4	**Smith, C.**	N	Y	Y	Y	N	Y
5	Gottheimer	N	Y	Y	Y	Y	Y
6	Pallone	N	Y	Y	Y	Y	Y
7	Malinowski	N	Y	Y	Y	Y	Y
8	Sires	N	Y	Y	Y	Y	Y
9	Pascrell	N	Y	Y	Y	Y	Y
10	Payne	N	Y	Y	Y	Y	Y
11	Sherrill	N	Y	Y	Y	Y	Y
12	Watson Coleman	N	Y	Y	Y	Y	Y
NEW MEXICO							
1	Haaland	N	Y	Y	Y	Y	Y
2	Torres Small	N	Y	Y	Y	Y	Y
3	Luján	N	Y	Y	Y	Y	Y
NEW YORK							
1	**Zeldin**	Y	Y	Y	N	N	Y
2	**King, P.**	Y	Y	Y	N	N	Y
3	Suozzi	N	Y	Y	Y	Y	Y
4	Rice, K.	N	Y	Y	Y	Y	Y
5	Meeks	N	Y	Y	Y	Y	Y
6	Meng	N	Y	Y	Y	Y	Y
7	Velázquez	N	Y	Y	Y	Y	Y
8	Jeffries	N	Y	Y	Y	Y	Y
9	Clarke	N	Y	Y	Y	Y	Y
10	Nadler	N	Y	Y	Y	Y	Y
11	Rose	N	Y	Y	Y	Y	Y
12	Maloney, C.	N	Y	Y	Y	Y	Y
13	Espaillat	N	Y	Y	Y	Y	Y
14	Ocasio-Cortez	N	Y	Y	Y	Y	Y
15	Serrano	?	?	?	?	?	?
16	Engel	N	Y	Y	Y	Y	Y
17	Lowey	N	Y	Y	Y	Y	Y
18	Maloney, S.P.	N	Y	Y	Y	Y	Y
19	Delgado	N	Y	Y	Y	Y	Y
20	Tonko	N	Y	Y	Y	Y	Y
21	**Stefanik**	N	Y	Y	Y	N	Y
22	Brindisi	N	Y	Y	Y	Y	Y
23	**Reed**	N	Y	Y	Y	N	Y
24	**Katko**	N	Y	Y	Y	?	Y
25	Morelle	N	Y	Y	Y	Y	Y
26	Higgins, B.	N	Y	Y	Y	Y	Y
27	**Collins, C.**						
NORTH CAROLINA							
1	Butterfield	N	Y	Y	Y	Y	Y
2	**Holding**	Y	Y	Y	N	N	N
3	**Murphy**	Y	Y	Y	N	N	N
4	Price	N	Y	Y	Y	Y	Y
5	**Foxx**	Y	Y	Y	N	N	N
6	**Walker**	Y	Y	Y	N	N	N
7	**Rouzer**	Y	Y	Y	N	N	N

		637	638	639	640	641	642
8	**Hudson**	Y	Y	?	N	N	N
9	**Bishop**	Y	Y	Y	N	N	N
10	**McHenry**	Y	Y	Y	N	N	N
11	**Meadows**	Y	Y	Y	N	N	N
12	Adams	N	Y	Y	Y	Y	Y
13	**Budd**	Y	Y	Y	N	N	N
NORTH DAKOTA							
AL	**Armstrong**	Y	Y	Y	N	N	N
OHIO							
1	**Chabot**	Y	Y	Y	N	N	N
2	**Wenstrup**	Y	Y	Y	N	N	N
3	Beatty	N	?	Y	Y	Y	Y
4	**Jordan**	Y	Y	Y	N	N	N
5	**Latta**	Y	Y	Y	N	N	N
6	**Johnson, B.**	Y	Y	Y	N	N	N
7	**Gibbs**	Y	Y	Y	N	N	N
8	**Davidson**	Y	Y	Y	Y	N	N
9	Kaptur	N	Y	Y	Y	Y	Y
10	**Turner**	Y	Y	Y	N	N	N
11	Fudge	?	?	?	?	?	?
12	**Balderson**	Y	Y	Y	N	N	N
13	Ryan	N	Y	Y	Y	Y	Y
14	**Joyce**	Y	Y	Y	Y	N	Y
15	**Stivers**	?	?	?	?	?	?
16	**Gonzalez**	Y	Y	Y	N	N	N
OKLAHOMA							
1	**Hern**	Y	Y	Y	N	N	N
2	**Mullin**	Y	Y	Y	N	N	N
3	**Lucas**	Y	Y	Y	N	N	N
4	**Cole**	Y	Y	Y	N	N	Y
5	Horn	N	Y	Y	Y	Y	Y
OREGON							
1	Bonamici	N	Y	Y	Y	Y	Y
2	**Walden**	Y	Y	Y	N	N	Y
3	Blumenauer	N	Y	Y	Y	Y	Y
4	DeFazio	N	Y	Y	Y	Y	Y
5	Schrader	N	Y	Y	Y	Y	Y
PENNSYLVANIA							
1	**Fitzpatrick**	N	Y	Y	Y	N	Y
2	Boyle	N	Y	Y	Y	Y	Y
3	Evans	-	+	+	+	+	+
4	Dean	N	Y	Y	Y	Y	Y
5	Scanlon	N	Y	Y	Y	Y	Y
6	Houlahan	N	Y	Y	Y	Y	Y
7	Wild	N	Y	Y	Y	Y	Y
8	Cartwright	N	Y	Y	Y	Y	Y
9	**Meuser**	Y	Y	Y	N	N	N
10	**Perry**	Y	Y	Y	N	N	N
11	**Smucker**	Y	Y	Y	N	N	N
12	**Keller**	Y	Y	Y	N	N	N
13	**Joyce**	Y	Y	Y	N	N	N
14	**Reschenthaler**	?	?	?	?	?	?
15	**Thompson, G.**	Y	Y	Y	N	N	N
16	**Kelly, M.**	Y	Y	Y	N	N	N
17	Lamb	N	Y	Y	Y	Y	Y
18	Doyle	N	Y	Y	Y	Y	Y
RHODE ISLAND							
1	Cicilline	N	Y	Y	Y	Y	Y
2	Langevin	N	Y	Y	Y	Y	Y
SOUTH CAROLINA							
1	Cunningham	N	Y	Y	Y	Y	Y
2	**Wilson, J.**	Y	Y	Y	N	N	N
3	**Duncan**	Y	Y	Y	N	N	N
4	**Timmons**	+	+	+	-	-	-
5	**Norman**	Y	Y	Y	N	N	N
6	Clyburn	N	Y	Y	Y	Y	Y
7	**Rice, T.**	Y	Y	Y	N	N	N
SOUTH DAKOTA							
AL	**Johnson**	Y	Y	Y	N	N	N
TENNESSEE							
1	**Roe**	Y	Y	Y	N	N	Y
2	**Burchett**	Y	Y	Y	N	N	N
3	**Fleischmann**	Y	Y	Y	N	N	N
4	**DesJarlais**	Y	Y	Y	N	N	N
5	Cooper	?	?	?	?	?	?
6	**Rose**	Y	Y	Y	N	N	N
7	**Green**	N	Y	Y	N	N	N
8	**Kustoff**	Y	Y	Y	N	N	N
9	Cohen	N	Y	Y	Y	Y	Y
TEXAS							
1	**Gohmert**	Y	Y	Y	N	N	N
2	**Crenshaw**	Y	Y	Y	N	N	?
3	**Taylor**	Y	Y	Y	N	N	N
4	**Ratcliffe**	Y	Y	Y	N	N	N

		637	638	639	640	641	642
5	**Gooden**	Y	Y	Y	N	N	N
6	**Wright**	Y	Y	Y	N	N	N
7	Fletcher	N	Y	Y	Y	Y	Y
8	**Brady**	Y	Y	Y	N	N	N
9	Green, A.	N	Y	Y	Y	Y	Y
10	**McCaul**	Y	Y	Y	N	N	N
11	**Conaway**	Y	Y	Y	N	N	N
12	**Granger**	Y	Y	Y	N	N	N
13	**Thornberry**	Y	Y	Y	N	N	N
14	**Weber**	Y	Y	Y	N	N	N
15	Gonzalez	N	?	Y	Y	Y	Y
16	Escobar	N	Y	Y	Y	Y	Y
17	**Flores**	?	?	?	?	?	?
18	Jackson Lee	N	Y	Y	Y	Y	Y
19	**Arrington**	Y	Y	Y	N	N	N
20	Castro	N	Y	Y	Y	Y	Y
21	**Roy**	Y	Y	Y	N	Y	N
22	**Olson**	Y	Y	Y	N	N	N
23	**Hurd**	Y	Y	Y	Y	N	Y
24	**Marchant**	Y	Y	Y	N	N	Y
25	**Williams**	Y	Y	Y	N	N	N
26	**Burgess**	Y	Y	Y	N	N	Y
27	**Cloud**	N	Y	Y	N	N	N
28	Cuellar	N	Y	Y	Y	Y	Y
29	Garcia, S.	N	Y	Y	Y	Y	Y
30	Johnson, E.B.	N	Y	Y	Y	Y	Y
31	**Carter, J.**	?	Y	Y	N	N	N
32	Allred	N	Y	Y	Y	Y	Y
33	Veasey	N	Y	Y	Y	Y	Y
34	Vela	N	Y	Y	Y	Y	Y
35	Doggett	N	Y	Y	Y	Y	Y
36	**Babin**	Y	Y	Y	N	N	N
UTAH							
1	**Bishop, R.**	Y	Y	Y	N	N	N
2	**Stewart**	Y	Y	Y	N	N	N
3	**Curtis**	Y	Y	Y	N	N	N
4	McAdams	Y	Y	Y	Y	Y	Y
VERMONT							
AL	Welch	N	Y	Y	Y	Y	Y
VIRGINIA							
1	**Wittman**	Y	Y	Y	N	N	N
2	Luria	N	Y	Y	Y	Y	Y
3	Scott, R.	N	Y	Y	Y	Y	Y
4	McEachin	?	?	?	?	?	?
5	**Riggleman**	Y	Y	Y	N	?	N
6	**Cline**	Y	Y	Y	N	N	N
7	Spanberger	N	Y	Y	Y	Y	Y
8	Beyer	N	Y	Y	Y	Y	Y
9	**Griffith**	?	Y	Y	N	N	N
10	Wexton	N	Y	Y	Y	Y	Y
11	Connolly	N	Y	Y	Y	Y	Y
WASHINGTON							
1	DelBene	N	Y	Y	Y	Y	Y
2	Larsen	N	Y	Y	Y	Y	Y
3	**Herrera Beutler**	Y	Y	Y	Y	N	Y
4	**Newhouse**	Y	Y	Y	N	N	Y
5	**McMorris Rodgers**	Y	Y	Y	N	N	Y
6	Kilmer	N	Y	Y	Y	Y	Y
7	Jayapal	N	Y	Y	Y	Y	Y
8	Schrier	N	Y	Y	Y	Y	Y
9	Smith Adam	N	Y	Y	Y	Y	Y
10	Heck	N	Y	Y	Y	Y	Y
WEST VIRGINIA							
1	**McKinley**	Y	Y	Y	N	N	Y
2	**Mooney**	Y	Y	Y	N	N	N
3	**Miller**	Y	Y	Y	N	N	N
WISCONSIN							
1	**Steil**	Y	Y	Y	N	N	N
2	Pocan	N	Y	Y	Y	Y	Y
3	Kind	N	Y	Y	Y	Y	Y
4	Moore	N	?	?	?	?	?
5	**Sensenbrenner**	Y	Y	Y	N	N	N
6	**Grothman**	Y	Y	Y	Y	N	N
7	**Duffy**						
8	**Gallagher**	Y	Y	Y	N	N	N
WYOMING							
AL	**Cheney**	Y	Y	Y	N	N	N
DELEGATES							
	Radewagen (A.S.)	?	?	?	?		
	Norton (D.C.)	N	Y	Y	Y		
	San Nicolas (Guam)	N	Y	Y	Y		
	Sablan (N. Marianas)	N	Y	Y	Y		
	González-Colón (P.R.)	Y	Y	Y	N		
	Plaskett (V.I.)	N	Y	Y	Y		

||| HOUSE VOTES

643. HRES546. Russian G-7 Readmission - Passage. Sires, D-N.J., motion to suspend the rules and agree to the resolution that would express the sense of the House of Representatives reiterating its support for the sovereignty and territorial integrity of Ukraine. It would condemn Russia's "aggressive" actions in Ukraine, including its occupation of Crimea, and its "assaults on democratic societies worldwide." It would call on leaders of G-7 countries to oppose Russia's readmission into the group unless and until it ends its occupation of Ukrainian territory and halts anti-democratic efforts worldwide. Motion agreed to 339-71: R 116-71; D 222-0; I 1-0. *Note: A two-thirds majority of those present and voting (274 in this case) is required for passage under suspension of the rules.* Dec. 3, 2019.

644. S178. Chinese Human Rights Violations - Passage. Sires, D-N.J., motion to suspend the rules and pass the bill, as amended, that would state U.S. policy and require a number of U.S. actions to address Chinese actions related to Uighurs and other ethnic minorities in the Xinjiang autonomous region. Specifically, it would require the president to identify items that allow the Chinese government to suppress individual privacy, freedom of movement, and other basic human rights; it would require the president to add such items to a federal list of controlled export items, requiring licenses for the export or transfer of such items to or within China. It would require the president to submit to Congress a list of senior Chinese officials responsible for or knowingly engaged in serious human rights abuses against Turkic Muslims in the region and to impose sanctions against such individuals. Motion agreed to 407-1: R 185-1; D 221-0; I 1-0. *Note: A two-thirds majority of those present and voting (272 in this case) is required for passage under suspension of the rules.* Dec. 3, 2019.

645. HR2534, HCONRES77. Insider Trading Prohibition - Previous Question. Perlmutter, D-Colo., motion to order the previous question (thus ending debate and possibility of amendment) on the rule (H Res 739) that would provide for House floor consideration of the Insider Trading Prohibition Act (HR 2534), including consideration of two amendments to the bill. It would also provide for a motion to discharge a concurrent resolution (H Con Res 77) from the House Foreign Affairs Committee to be offered on Wednesday, Dec. 11, 2019, and it would waive section 7 of the War Powers Resolution related to the concurrent resolution. The concurrent resolution (H Con Res 77) would direct the president to withdraw U.S. military forces from hostilities in Syria, unless a specific use of force is authorized by Congress. Motion agreed to 226-193: R 0-192; D 226-0; I 0-1. Dec. 4, 2019.

646. HCONRES77, HR2534. Insider Trading Prohibition - Rule. Adoption of the rule (H Res 739) that would provide for House floor consideration of the Insider Trading Prohibition Act (HR 2534), including consideration of two amendments to the bill. It would also provide for a motion to discharge a concurrent resolution (H Con Res 77) from the House Foreign Affairs Committee to be offered on Wednesday, Dec. 11, 2019, and it would waive section 7 of the War Powers Resolution related to the concurrent resolution. The concurrent resolution (H Con Res 77) would direct the president to withdraw U.S. military forces from hostilities in Syria, unless a specific use of force is authorized by Congress. Adopted 225-196: R 0-195; D 225-0; I 0-1. Dec. 4, 2019.

647. S151. Robocall Enforcement and Deterrence - Passage. Pallone, D-N.J., motion to suspend the rules and pass the bill, as amended, that would require the Federal Communications Commission to take certain actions and implement regulations related to robocalls -- mass telephone calls placed by an automatic dialer -- including regulations that would require phone companies to offer call authentication technology at no cost to consumers. It would allow the FCC to issue civil penalties of up to $10,000 for intentional violation of robocalling laws. It would extend, from two years to four years after a violation, the time period during which the FCC and law enforcement agencies can prosecute illegal robocallers, and it would require the FCC to submit evidence of certain violations to the Justice Department for potential criminal prosecution. It would also require the Justice Department and the FCC to convene an inter-agency task force to study enforcement of robocalling law. Among other provisions, it would require the FCC to take actions to address "one-ring" phone call scams and to evaluate the effectiveness of its policies to reduce access to number resources by potential violators of robocalling laws, and update such policies if appropriate. It would require the FCC to submit a number of reports to Congress related to robocalls, including on the transmission of misleading or inaccurate caller identification information, enforcement of related laws and regulations, and effectiveness of the regulations required by the bill. Motion agreed to 417-3: R 193-2; D 224-0; I 0-1. *Note: A two-thirds majority of those present and voting (280 in this case) is required for passage under suspension of the rules.* Dec. 4, 2019.

648. HR2534. Insider Trading Prohibition - Use of Insider Information. Huizenga, R-Mich., amendment no. 2 that would replace language in the bill to prohibit any individual from trading securities while "using" as opposed to being "aware of" material, nonpublic information related to such securities. Rejected in Committee of the Whole 196-231: R 195-0; D 0-230; I 1-1. Dec. 5, 2019.

	643	644	645	646	647	648
ALABAMA						
1 Byrne	?	?	N	N	Y	Y
2 Roby	Y	Y	N	N	Y	Y
3 Rogers, M.	Y	Y	N	N	Y	Y
4 Aderholt	N	Y	N	N	Y	Y
5 Brooks, M.	N	Y	N	N	Y	Y
6 Palmer	N	Y	N	N	Y	Y
7 Sewell	Y	Y	Y	Y	Y	N
ALASKA						
AL Young	Y	Y	?	N	Y	Y
ARIZONA						
1 O'Halleran	Y	Y	Y	Y	Y	N
2 Kirkpatrick	Y	Y	Y	Y	Y	N
3 Grijalva	Y	?	Y	Y	Y	N
4 Gosar	N	Y	N	N	Y	?
5 Biggs	N	?	N	N	N	Y
6 Schweikert	Y	Y	N	N	Y	Y
7 Gallego	Y	Y	Y	Y	Y	N
8 Lesko	N	Y	N	N	Y	Y
9 Stanton	Y	Y	Y	Y	Y	N
ARKANSAS						
1 Crawford	N	Y	N	N	Y	Y
2 Hill, F.	Y	Y	N	N	Y	Y
3 Womack	Y	Y	N	N	Y	Y
4 Westerman	Y	Y	N	N	Y	Y
CALIFORNIA						
1 LaMalfa	N	Y	N	N	Y	Y
2 Huffman	Y	Y	Y	Y	Y	N
3 Garamendi	Y	Y	Y	Y	Y	N
4 McClintock	Y	Y	N	N	Y	Y
5 Thompson, M.	Y	Y	Y	Y	Y	N
6 Matsui	Y	Y	Y	Y	Y	N
7 Bera	Y	Y	Y	Y	+	N
8 Cook	Y	Y	N	N	Y	Y
9 McNerney	Y	Y	Y	+	Y	N
10 Harder	Y	Y	Y	Y	Y	N
11 DeSaulnier	Y	Y	Y	Y	Y	N
12 Pelosi		Y				
13 Lee B.	Y	Y	Y	Y	Y	N
14 Speier	Y	Y	Y	Y	Y	N
15 Swalwell	Y	Y	Y	Y	Y	N
16 Costa	Y	Y	Y	Y	Y	N
17 Khanna	Y	Y	Y	Y	Y	N
18 Eshoo	Y	Y	Y	Y	Y	N
19 Lofgren	Y	Y	Y	Y	Y	N
20 Panetta	Y	Y	Y	Y	Y	N
21 Cox	Y	Y	Y	Y	Y	N
22 Nunes	Y	Y	N	N	Y	Y
23 McCarthy	Y	Y	N	N	Y	Y
24 Carbajal	Y	Y	Y	Y	Y	N
25 vacant						
26 Brownley	Y	Y	Y	Y	Y	N
27 Chu	Y	Y	Y	Y	Y	N
28 Schiff	Y	Y	Y	Y	Y	N
29 Cárdenas	Y	Y	Y	Y	Y	N
30 Sherman	Y	Y	Y	Y	Y	N
31 Aguilar	Y	Y	Y	Y	Y	N
32 Napolitano	Y	Y	Y	Y	Y	N
33 Lieu	Y	Y	Y	Y	Y	N
34 Gomez	Y	Y	Y	Y	Y	N
35 Torres	Y	Y	Y	Y	Y	N
36 Ruiz	Y	Y	Y	Y	Y	N
37 Bass	Y	Y	Y	Y	Y	N
38 Sánchez	Y	Y	Y	Y	Y	N
39 Cisneros	Y	Y	Y	Y	Y	N
40 Roybal-Allard	Y	Y	Y	Y	Y	N
41 Takano	Y	Y	Y	Y	Y	N
42 Calvert	Y	Y	N	N	Y	Y
43 Waters	Y	Y	Y	Y	Y	N
44 Barragán	Y	Y	Y	Y	Y	N
45 Porter	Y	Y	Y	Y	Y	N
46 Correa	Y	Y	Y	Y	Y	N
47 Lowenthal	Y	Y	Y	Y	Y	N
48 Rouda	Y	Y	Y	Y	Y	N
49 Levin	Y	Y	Y	Y	Y	N
50 Hunter	?	?	N	N	Y	?
51 Vargas	Y	Y	Y	Y	Y	N
52 Peters	Y	Y	Y	Y	Y	N
53 Davis, S.	Y	Y	Y	Y	Y	N
COLORADO						
1 DeGette	Y	Y	Y	Y	?	N
2 Neguse	Y	Y	Y	Y	Y	N
3 Tipton	Y	Y	N	N	Y	Y
4 Buck	N	Y	N	N	Y	Y
5 Lamborn	?	Y	N	N	Y	Y
6 Crow	Y	Y	Y	Y	Y	N
7 Perlmutter	Y	Y	Y	Y	Y	N
CONNECTICUT						
1 Larson	Y	Y	Y	Y	Y	N
2 Courtney	Y	Y	Y	Y	Y	N
3 DeLauro	Y	Y	Y	Y	Y	N
4 Himes	Y	Y	Y	Y	Y	N
5 Hayes	Y	Y	Y	Y	Y	N
DELAWARE						
AL Blunt Rochester	Y	Y	Y	Y	Y	N
FLORIDA						
1 Gaetz	N	Y	N	N	Y	Y
2 Dunn	N	Y	N	N	Y	Y
3 Yoho	N	Y	N	N	Y	Y
4 Rutherford	Y	Y	N	N	Y	Y
5 Lawson	Y	Y	Y	Y	Y	N
6 Waltz	Y	Y	N	?	?	Y
7 Murphy	Y	Y	Y	Y	Y	N
8 Posey	N	Y	N	N	Y	Y
9 Soto	Y	Y	Y	Y	Y	N
10 Demings	Y	Y	Y	Y	Y	N
11 Webster	N	Y	N	N	Y	Y
12 Bilirakis	N	Y	N	N	Y	Y
13 Crist	Y	Y	Y	Y	Y	N
14 Castor	Y	Y	Y	Y	Y	N
15 Spano	Y	Y	N	N	Y	Y
16 Buchanan	?	?	N	N	Y	Y
17 Steube	N	Y	N	N	Y	Y
18 Mast	N	Y	N	N	Y	Y
19 Rooney	?	?	N	N	Y	Y
20 Hastings	Y	Y	Y	Y	Y	N
21 Frankel	Y	Y	Y	Y	Y	N
22 Deutch	Y	Y	Y	Y	Y	N
23 Wasserman Schultz	Y	Y	Y	Y	Y	N
24 Wilson, F.	Y	Y	Y	Y	Y	?
25 Diaz-Balart	Y	Y	N	N	Y	Y
26 Mucarsel-Powell	Y	Y	Y	Y	Y	N
27 Shalala	Y	Y	Y	Y	Y	N
GEORGIA						
1 Carter, E.L.	N	Y	N	N	Y	Y
2 Bishop, S.	Y	Y	Y	Y	Y	N
3 Ferguson	N	Y	N	N	Y	Y
4 Johnson, H.	Y	Y	Y	Y	Y	N
5 Lewis John	Y	Y	Y	Y	Y	N
6 McBath	Y	Y	Y	Y	Y	N
7 Woodall	N	Y	N	N	Y	Y
8 Scott, A.	N	Y	N	N	Y	Y
9 Collins, D.	N	Y	N	N	Y	Y
10 Hice	N	Y	N	N	Y	Y
11 Loudermilk	N	Y	N	N	Y	Y
12 Allen	N	Y	N	N	Y	Y
13 Scott, D.	Y	Y	Y	Y	Y	N
14 Graves, T.	N	Y	N	N	Y	Y
HAWAII						
1 Case	Y	Y	Y	Y	Y	N
2 Gabbard	?	?	?	?	?	?
IDAHO						
1 Fulcher	Y	Y	N	N	Y	Y
2 Simpson	Y	Y	N	N	Y	Y
ILLINOIS						
1 Rush	Y	Y	Y	Y	Y	N
2 Kelly, R.	Y	?	Y	Y	Y	N
3 Lipinski	Y	Y	Y	Y	Y	N
4 García, J.	Y	Y	Y	Y	Y	N
5 Quigley	Y	Y	Y	Y	Y	N
6 Casten	Y	Y	Y	Y	Y	N
7 Davis, D.	Y	Y	Y	Y	Y	N
8 Krishnamoorthi	Y	Y	Y	Y	Y	N
9 Schakowsky	Y	Y	Y	Y	Y	N
10 Schneider	Y	Y	Y	Y	Y	N
11 Foster	Y	Y	Y	Y	Y	N

KEY: Republicans   Democrats   *Independents*

Y Voted for (yea)	**N** Voted against (nay)	**P** Voted "present"
+ Announced for	**-** Announced against	**?** Did not vote or otherwise
# Paired for	**X** Paired against	make position known

		643	644	645	646	647	648
12	**Bost**	Y	Y	N	N	Y	Y
13	**Davis, R.**	Y	Y	N	N	Y	Y
14	Underwood	Y	Y	Y	Y	Y	N
15	**Shimkus**	Y	Y	N	N	Y	Y
16	**Kinzinger**	Y	Y	N	N	Y	Y
17	Bustos	Y	Y	Y	Y	Y	N
18	**LaHood**	Y	Y	N	N	Y	Y
INDIANA							
1	Visclosky	Y	Y	Y	Y	Y	N
2	**Walorski**	Y	Y	N	N	Y	Y
3	**Banks**	Y	Y	N	N	Y	Y
4	**Baird**	Y	Y	N	N	Y	Y
5	**Brooks, S.**	Y	Y	N	N	Y	Y
6	**Pence**	N	Y	N	N	Y	Y
7	Carson	Y	Y	Y	Y	Y	N
8	**Bucshon**	Y	Y	N	N	Y	Y
9	**Hollingsworth**	Y	Y	N	N	Y	Y
IOWA							
1	Finkenauer	Y	Y	Y	Y	Y	N
2	Loebsack	Y	Y	Y	Y	Y	N
3	Axne	Y	Y	Y	Y	Y	N
4	**King, S.**	N	Y	N	N	Y	Y
KANSAS							
1	**Marshall**	?	?	N	N	Y	Y
2	**Watkins**	Y	Y	N	N	Y	Y
3	Davids	Y	Y	Y	Y	Y	N
4	**Estes**	Y	Y	N	N	Y	Y
KENTUCKY							
1	**Comer**	N	Y	N	N	Y	Y
2	**Guthrie**	Y	Y	N	N	Y	Y
3	Yarmuth	?	?	Y	Y	Y	N
4	**Massie**	N	N	N	N	N	Y
5	**Rogers, H.**	Y	Y	N	N	Y	Y
6	**Barr**	Y	Y	N	N	Y	Y
LOUISIANA							
1	**Scalise**	Y	Y	N	N	Y	Y
2	Richmond	Y	Y	Y	Y	Y	N
3	**Higgins, C.**	N	Y	N	N	Y	Y
4	**Johnson, M.**	Y	Y	N	N	Y	Y
5	**Abraham**	N	Y	N	N	Y	Y
6	**Graves, G.**	Y	Y	N	N	Y	Y
MAINE							
1	Pingree	Y	Y	Y	Y	Y	N
2	Golden	Y	Y	Y	Y	Y	N
MARYLAND							
1	**Harris**	N	Y	N	N	Y	Y
2	Ruppersberger	Y	Y	Y	Y	Y	N
3	Sarbanes	Y	Y	Y	Y	Y	N
4	Brown, A.	Y	Y	Y	Y	Y	N
5	Hoyer	Y	Y	Y	Y	Y	N
6	Trone	Y	Y	Y	Y	Y	N
7	vacant	|	|	|	|	|	|
8	Raskin	Y	Y	Y	Y	Y	N
MASSACHUSETTS							
1	Neal	Y	Y	Y	Y	Y	N
2	McGovern	+	+	+	+	+	N
3	Trahan	Y	Y	Y	Y	Y	N
4	Kennedy	?	?	Y	Y	Y	N
5	Clark	Y	Y	Y	Y	Y	N
6	Moulton	+	+	Y	Y	Y	N
7	Pressley	Y	Y	Y	Y	Y	N
8	Lynch	Y	Y	Y	Y	Y	N
9	Keating	?	?	Y	Y	Y	N
MICHIGAN							
1	**Bergman**	N	Y	N	N	Y	Y
2	**Huizenga**	Y	Y	N	N	Y	Y
3	*Amash*	Y	Y	N	N	N	Y
4	**Moolenaar**	Y	Y	N	N	Y	Y
5	Kildee	Y	Y	Y	Y	Y	N
6	**Upton**	Y	Y	N	N	Y	Y
7	**Walberg**	Y	Y	N	N	Y	Y
8	Slotkin	Y	Y	Y	Y	Y	N
9	Levin	Y	Y	Y	Y	Y	N
10	**Mitchell**	N	Y	N	N	Y	Y
11	Stevens	Y	Y	Y	Y	Y	N
12	Dingell	Y	Y	?	?	+	N
13	Tlaib	Y	Y	Y	Y	Y	N
14	Lawrence	Y	Y	Y	Y	Y	N
MINNESOTA							
1	**Hagedorn**	Y	Y	N	N	Y	Y
2	Craig	Y	Y	Y	Y	Y	N
3	Phillips	Y	Y	Y	Y	Y	N
4	McCollum	Y	Y	Y	Y	Y	N
5	Omar	Y	Y	Y	Y	Y	N

		643	644	645	646	647	648
6	**Emmer**	Y	Y	N	N	Y	Y
7	Peterson	Y	Y	Y	Y	Y	N
8	**Stauber**	Y	Y	N	N	Y	Y
MISSISSIPPI							
1	**Kelly, T.**	N	Y	N	N	Y	Y
2	Thompson, B.	Y	Y	Y	Y	Y	N
3	**Guest**	N	Y	N	N	Y	Y
4	**Palazzo**	N	Y	N	N	Y	Y
MISSOURI							
1	Clay	Y	Y	Y	Y	Y	N
2	**Wagner**	Y	Y	N	N	Y	Y
3	**Luetkemeyer**	Y	Y	N	N	Y	Y
4	**Hartzler**	Y	Y	N	N	Y	Y
5	Cleaver	Y	Y	Y	Y	Y	N
6	**Graves, S.**	Y	Y	N	N	Y	Y
7	**Long**	N	Y	N	N	Y	Y
8	**Smith, J.**	N	Y	N	N	Y	Y
MONTANA							
AL	**Gianforte**	N	Y	N	N	Y	Y
NEBRASKA							
1	**Fortenberry**	N	Y	N	N	Y	Y
2	**Bacon**	Y	Y	N	N	Y	Y
3	**Smith, Adrian**	Y	Y	-	N	Y	Y
NEVADA							
1	Titus	Y	Y	Y	Y	Y	N
2	**Amodei**	Y	Y	N	N	Y	Y
3	Lee	Y	Y	Y	Y	Y	N
4	Horsford	Y	Y	Y	Y	Y	N
NEW HAMPSHIRE							
1	Pappas	Y	Y	Y	Y	Y	N
2	Kuster	Y	Y	Y	Y	Y	N
NEW JERSEY							
1	Norcross	Y	Y	Y	Y	Y	N
2	Van Drew	Y	Y	Y	Y	Y	N
3	Kim	Y	Y	Y	Y	Y	N
4	**Smith, C.**	Y	Y	N	N	Y	Y
5	Gottheimer	Y	Y	Y	Y	Y	N
6	Pallone	Y	Y	Y	Y	Y	N
7	Malinowski	Y	Y	Y	Y	Y	N
8	Sires	Y	Y	Y	Y	Y	N
9	Pascrell	Y	Y	Y	Y	Y	N
10	Payne	Y	Y	Y	Y	Y	N
11	Sherrill	Y	Y	Y	Y	Y	N
12	Watson Coleman	Y	Y	Y	Y	Y	N
NEW MEXICO							
1	Haaland	Y	Y	Y	Y	Y	N
2	Torres Small	Y	Y	Y	Y	Y	N
3	Luján	Y	Y	Y	Y	Y	N
NEW YORK							
1	**Zeldin**	N	Y	N	N	Y	Y
2	**King, P.**	Y	Y	N	N	Y	Y
3	Suozzi	Y	Y	Y	Y	Y	N
4	Rice, K.	Y	Y	Y	Y	Y	N
5	Meeks	Y	Y	Y	Y	Y	N
6	Meng	Y	Y	Y	Y	Y	N
7	Velázquez	Y	Y	Y	Y	Y	N
8	Jeffries	Y	Y	Y	Y	Y	N
9	Clarke	Y	Y	Y	Y	Y	N
10	Nadler	Y	Y	Y	Y	Y	N
11	Rose	Y	Y	Y	Y	Y	N
12	Maloney, C.	Y	Y	Y	Y	Y	N
13	Espaillat	Y	Y	Y	Y	Y	N
14	Ocasio-Cortez	Y	Y	Y	Y	Y	N
15	Serrano	?	?	?	?	?	?
16	Engel	Y	Y	Y	Y	Y	N
17	Lowey	Y	Y	Y	Y	Y	N
18	Maloney, S.P.	Y	Y	Y	Y	Y	N
19	Delgado	Y	Y	Y	Y	Y	N
20	Tonko	Y	Y	Y	Y	Y	N
21	**Stefanik**	Y	Y	N	N	Y	Y
22	Brindisi	Y	Y	Y	Y	Y	N
23	**Reed**	Y	Y	N	N	Y	Y
24	**Katko**	Y	Y	N	N	Y	Y
25	Morelle	Y	Y	Y	Y	Y	N
26	Higgins, B.	Y	Y	Y	Y	Y	N
27	**Collins, C.**						
NORTH CAROLINA							
1	Butterfield	Y	Y	Y	Y	Y	N
2	**Holding**	?	?	N	N	Y	Y
3	**Murphy**	N	Y	N	N	Y	Y
4	Price	Y	Y	Y	Y	Y	N
5	**Foxx**	Y	Y	N	N	Y	Y
6	**Walker**	Y	Y	N	N	Y	Y
7	**Rouzer**	Y	Y	N	N	Y	Y

		643	644	645	646	647	648
8	**Hudson**	N	Y	N	N	Y	Y
9	**Bishop**	N	Y	N	N	Y	Y
10	**McHenry**	Y	Y	N	N	Y	Y
11	**Meadows**	N	Y	N	N	Y	Y
12	Adams	Y	Y	Y	Y	Y	N
13	**Budd**	N	Y	N	N	Y	Y
NORTH DAKOTA							
AL	**Armstrong**	Y	Y	N	N	Y	Y
OHIO							
1	**Chabot**	Y	Y	N	N	Y	Y
2	**Wenstrup**	Y	Y	N	N	Y	Y
3	Beatty	Y	Y	Y	Y	Y	N
4	**Jordan**	N	Y	N	N	Y	Y
5	**Latta**	Y	Y	N	N	Y	Y
6	**Johnson, B.**	Y	Y	N	N	Y	Y
7	**Gibbs**	N	Y	N	N	Y	Y
8	**Davidson**	N	Y	N	N	Y	Y
9	Kaptur	Y	Y	Y	Y	Y	N
10	**Turner**	Y	Y	N	N	Y	Y
11	Fudge	Y	Y	Y	Y	Y	N
12	**Balderson**	Y	Y	N	N	Y	Y
13	Ryan	Y	Y	Y	Y	Y	N
14	**Joyce**	Y	Y	N	N	Y	Y
15	**Stivers**	Y	Y	N	N	Y	Y
16	**Gonzalez**	Y	Y	N	N	Y	Y
OKLAHOMA							
1	**Hern**	N	Y	N	N	Y	Y
2	**Mullin**	N	Y	N	N	Y	Y
3	**Lucas**	Y	Y	N	N	Y	Y
4	**Cole**	Y	Y	N	N	Y	Y
5	Horn	Y	Y	Y	Y	Y	N
OREGON							
1	Bonamici	Y	Y	Y	Y	Y	N
2	**Walden**	Y	Y	N	N	Y	Y
3	Blumenauer	Y	Y	Y	Y	Y	N
4	DeFazio	Y	Y	Y	Y	Y	N
5	Schrader	Y	Y	Y	Y	Y	N
PENNSYLVANIA							
1	**Fitzpatrick**	Y	Y	N	N	Y	Y
2	Boyle	Y	Y	Y	Y	Y	N
3	Evans	Y	Y	Y	Y	Y	N
4	Dean	Y	Y	Y	Y	Y	N
5	Scanlon	Y	Y	Y	Y	Y	N
6	Houlahan	Y	Y	Y	Y	Y	N
7	Wild	Y	Y	Y	Y	Y	N
8	Cartwright	Y	Y	?	?	?	?
9	**Meuser**	N	Y	N	N	Y	Y
10	**Perry**	N	Y	N	N	Y	Y
11	**Smucker**	Y	Y	N	N	Y	Y
12	**Keller**	Y	Y	N	N	Y	Y
13	**Joyce**	N	Y	N	N	Y	Y
14	**Reschenthaler**	Y	Y	N	N	Y	Y
15	**Thompson, G.**	Y	Y	N	N	Y	Y
16	**Kelly, M.**	Y	Y	N	N	Y	Y
17	Lamb	+	+	Y	Y	Y	N
18	Doyle	Y	Y	Y	Y	Y	N
RHODE ISLAND							
1	Cicilline	Y	Y	Y	Y	Y	N
2	Langevin	Y	Y	Y	Y	Y	N
SOUTH CAROLINA							
1	Cunningham	+	+	+	+	+	N
2	**Wilson, J.**	Y	Y	N	N	Y	Y
3	**Duncan**	N	Y	N	N	Y	Y
4	**Timmons**	N	Y	N	N	Y	Y
5	**Norman**	N	Y	N	N	Y	Y
6	Clyburn	Y	Y	Y	Y	Y	N
7	**Rice, T.**	Y	Y	N	N	Y	Y
SOUTH DAKOTA							
AL	**Johnson**	Y	Y	N	N	Y	Y
TENNESSEE							
1	**Roe**	Y	Y	N	N	Y	Y
2	**Burchett**	Y	Y	N	N	Y	Y
3	**Fleischmann**	N	Y	N	N	Y	Y
4	**DesJarlais**	N	Y	N	N	Y	Y
5	Cooper	Y	Y	Y	Y	Y	N
6	**Rose**	N	Y	N	N	Y	Y
7	**Green**	Y	Y	N	N	Y	Y
8	**Kustoff**	Y	Y	N	N	Y	Y
9	Cohen	Y	Y	Y	Y	Y	N
TEXAS							
1	**Gohmert**	Y	Y	N	N	Y	Y
2	**Crenshaw**	Y	Y	N	N	Y	Y
3	**Taylor**	Y	Y	N	N	Y	Y
4	**Ratcliffe**	Y	Y	?	N	Y	Y

		643	644	645	646	647	648
5	**Gooden**	N	Y	N	N	Y	Y
6	**Wright**	Y	Y	N	N	Y	Y
7	Fletcher	Y	Y	Y	Y	Y	N
8	**Brady**	N	Y	N	N	Y	Y
9	Green, A.	Y	Y	Y	Y	Y	N
10	**McCaul**	Y	Y	N	N	Y	Y
11	**Conaway**	N	Y	N	N	Y	Y
12	**Granger**	Y	Y	N	N	Y	Y
13	**Thornberry**	Y	Y	N	N	Y	Y
14	**Weber**	N	Y	N	N	Y	Y
15	Gonzalez	Y	Y	Y	Y	Y	N
16	Escobar	Y	Y	Y	Y	Y	N
17	**Flores**	?	?	N	N	Y	Y
18	Jackson Lee	Y	Y	Y	Y	Y	N
19	**Arrington**	Y	Y	N	N	Y	Y
20	Castro	Y	Y	Y	Y	Y	N
21	**Roy**	Y	Y	N	N	Y	Y
22	**Olson**	Y	Y	N	N	Y	Y
23	**Hurd**	Y	Y	N	N	Y	Y
24	**Marchant**	Y	Y	N	N	Y	Y
25	**Williams**	Y	Y	N	N	Y	Y
26	**Burgess**	N	Y	N	N	Y	Y
27	**Cloud**	N	Y	N	N	Y	Y
28	Cuellar	Y	Y	Y	Y	Y	N
29	Garcia, S.	Y	Y	Y	Y	Y	N
30	Johnson, E.B.	Y	Y	Y	Y	Y	N
31	**Carter, J.**	?	?	?	?	?	Y
32	Allred	Y	Y	Y	Y	Y	N
33	Veasey	Y	Y	Y	Y	Y	N
34	Vela	Y	Y	Y	Y	Y	N
35	Doggett	Y	Y	Y	Y	Y	N
36	**Babin**	N	Y	N	N	Y	Y
UTAH							
1	**Bishop, R.**	N	Y	N	N	Y	Y
2	**Stewart**	N	Y	N	N	Y	Y
3	**Curtis**	Y	?	N	N	Y	Y
4	McAdams	Y	Y	Y	Y	Y	N
VERMONT							
AL	Welch	Y	Y	Y	Y	Y	N
VIRGINIA							
1	**Wittman**	Y	Y	N	N	Y	Y
2	Luria	Y	Y	Y	Y	Y	N
3	Scott, R.	Y	Y	Y	Y	Y	N
4	McEachin	Y	Y	Y	Y	Y	N
5	**Riggleman**	Y	Y	N	N	Y	Y
6	**Cline**	Y	Y	N	N	Y	Y
7	Spanberger	Y	Y	Y	Y	Y	N
8	Beyer	Y	Y	Y	Y	Y	N
9	**Griffith**	?	?	N	N	Y	Y
10	Wexton	Y	Y	Y	Y	Y	N
11	Connolly	Y	Y	Y	Y	Y	N
WASHINGTON							
1	DelBene	Y	Y	Y	Y	Y	N
2	Larsen	Y	Y	Y	Y	Y	N
3	**Herrera Beutler**	Y	Y	N	N	Y	Y
4	**Newhouse**	Y	Y	?	N	Y	Y
5	**McMorris Rodgers**	Y	Y	N	N	Y	Y
6	Kilmer	Y	Y	Y	Y	Y	N
7	Jayapal	Y	Y	Y	Y	Y	N
8	Schrier	Y	Y	Y	Y	Y	N
9	Smith Adam	Y	Y	Y	Y	Y	N
10	Heck	Y	Y	Y	Y	Y	N
WEST VIRGINIA							
1	**McKinley**	Y	Y	N	N	Y	Y
2	**Mooney**	Y	Y	N	N	Y	Y
3	**Miller**	N	Y	N	N	Y	Y
WISCONSIN							
1	**Steil**	Y	Y	N	N	Y	Y
2	Pocan	Y	Y	Y	Y	Y	N
3	Kind	Y	Y	Y	Y	Y	N
4	Moore	+	+	Y	Y	Y	N
5	**Sensenbrenner**	Y	Y	N	N	Y	Y
6	**Grothman**	N	Y	N	N	Y	Y
7	**Duffy**						
8	**Gallagher**	Y	Y	N	N	Y	Y
WYOMING							
AL	**Cheney**	Y	Y	N	N	Y	Y
DELEGATES							
	Radewagen (A.S.)						?
	Norton (D.C.)						N
	San Nicolas (Guam)						?
	Sablan (N. Marianas)						N
	González-Colón (P.R.)						Y
	Plaskett (V.I.)						N

649. HR2534. Insider Trading Prohibition - Passage. Passage of the bill, as amended, that would statutorily prohibit and codify a standard definition of insider trading under securities law. Specifically, it would prohibit any individual from buying, selling, or causing the purchase or sale of any security using material, nonpublic information, if the individual is aware that the information was wrongfully obtained or that its use would be deemed wrongful. The bill would prohibit the communication of such information to another individual if it is reasonably foreseeable that such individual would use the information in securities trading or communicate the information to another individual who may do so. It would define securities trading activity as wrongful under the bill's provisions if it is based on information obtained by or the use of which would constitute theft, bribery, misrepresentation, or espionage; a violation of federal computer data and privacy laws; misappropriation or deception; or a breach of fiduciary duty, contract, or other relationship of trust and confidence. Passed 410-13: R 182-12; D 228-0; I 0-1. Dec. 5, 2019.

650. HR4, HRES326. Voting Rights Enforcement; Israeli-Palestinian Conflict - Previous Question. Raskin, D-Md., motion to order the previous question (thus ending debate and possibility of amendment) on the rule (H Res 741) for the Voting Rights Advancement Act (HR 4) and a resolution (H Res 326) that would express the sense of the House of Representatives that a U.S. proposal for a solution to the Israeli-Palestinian conflict should expressly endorse a two-state solution. Motion agreed to 228-196: R 0-195; D 228-0; I 0-1. Dec. 5, 2019.

651. HRES326, HR4. Voting Rights Enforcement; Israeli-Palestinian Conflict - Rule. Adoption of the rule (H Res 741) for the Voting Rights Advancement Act (HR 4) and a resolution (H Res 326) that would express the sense of the House of Representatives that a U.S. proposal for a solution to the Israeli-Palestinian conflict should expressly endorse a two-state solution. The rule would provide for automatic adoption of a Nadler, D-N.Y., manager's amendment to HR 4 that would require state and local governments to obtain approval from the Justice Department before implementing any change that would reduce Sunday early voting times or that would make certain changes to voter registration list maintenance in jurisdictions where two or more racial or language minority groups represent at least 20% of the voting-age population. The rule would also provide for automatic adoption of the Engel, D-N.Y., manager's amendment no. 1 to H Res 326 that would express that it is in the interest of the U.S. to honor its commitments outlined in a 2016 U.S.-Israel memorandum of understanding related to military and security assistance to Israel and to resume the provision of foreign assistance to Palestinians, and it would provide for automatic adoption of the Engel manager's amendment no. 2 to the preamble. Adopted 226-196: R 0-194; D 226-1; I 0-1. Dec. 5, 2019.

652. HRES326. Israeli-Palestinian Conflict - Passage. Agreeing to the resolution, as amended, that would express the sense of the House of Representatives that only a two-state solution can ensure Israel's survival as a Jewish and democratic state and fulfill the "legitimate aspirations" for a Palestinian state. It would express that a U.S. proposal to achieve a solution to the Israeli-Palestinian conflict should expressly endorse a two-state solution and that the U.S. remains "indispensable" to any effort to achieve this goal. It would express that it is in the interest of the U.S. to honor its commitments outlined in a 2016 U.S.-Israel memorandum of understanding related to military and security assistance to Israel and to resume the provision of foreign assistance to Palestinians. It would discourage actions by Israel or Palestinians that would delay a peaceful end to the conflict, including unilateral annexation of territory or efforts to achieve Palestinian statehood status outside of negotiations with Israel. Passed 226-188: R 5-183; D 221-4; I 0-1. Dec. 6, 2019.

653. HR4. Voting Rights Enforcement - Recommit. Davis, R-Ill., motion to recommit the bill to the House Judiciary Committee with instructions to report it back immediately with an amendment that would clarify that nothing contained in the bill may be construed to allow fines paid to the federal government in relation to voting rights violations, including fines required by a settlement agreement, to be used to make a payment in support of a federal congressional campaign. Motion rejected 200-215: R 188-0; D 11-215; I 1-0. Dec. 6, 2019.

654. HR4. Voting Rights Enforcement - Passage. Passage of the bill, as amended, that would effectively restore pre-clearance requirements under the Voting Rights Act for any changes to voting procedures in states and localities with a history of voting rights violations within the previous 25 years. It would establish formulas to identify such jurisdictions, which would be required to submit proposed changes to the Justice Department for review and approval before they may be implemented. It would also require states and localities to review any newly enacted or adopted election practices to identify whether it includes certain practices that could impact the ability to vote based on race or language, including changes to voter identification requirements and changes to jurisdictional boundaries or voting locations in jurisdictions with large minority populations. It would require jurisdictions that adopt such practices to submit them for federal pre-clearance. Passed 228-187: R 1-186; D 227-0; I 0-1. *Note: A "nay" was a vote in support of the president's position.* Dec. 6, 2019.

		649	650	651	652	653	654
ALABAMA							
1	**Byrne**	Y	N	N	?	?	?
2	**Roby**	Y	N	N	N	Y	N
3	**Rogers, M.**	Y	N	N	N	Y	N
4	**Aderholt**	Y	N	N	N	Y	N
5	**Brooks, M.**	Y	N	N	N	Y	N
6	**Palmer**	Y	N	N	N	Y	N
7	Sewell	Y	Y	Y	Y	N	Y
ALASKA							
AL	**Young**	Y	N	N	N	Y	N
ARIZONA							
1	O'Halleran	Y	Y	Y	Y	N	Y
2	Kirkpatrick	Y	Y	Y	Y	N	Y
3	Grijalva	Y	Y	Y	Y	N	Y
4	**Gosar**	?	?	?	?	?	?
5	**Biggs**	N	N	N	N	Y	N
6	**Schweikert**	Y	N	N	N	Y	N
7	Gallego	Y	Y	Y	Y	N	Y
8	**Lesko**	Y	N	N	N	Y	N
9	Stanton	Y	Y	Y	Y	N	Y
ARKANSAS							
1	**Crawford**	Y	N	N	N	Y	N
2	**Hill, F.**	N	N	N	N	Y	N
3	**Womack**	Y	N	N	N	Y	N
4	**Westerman**	Y	N	N	N	Y	N
CALIFORNIA							
1	**LaMalfa**	Y	N	N	N	Y	N
2	Huffman	Y	Y	Y	Y	N	Y
3	Garamendi	Y	Y	Y	Y	N	Y
4	**McClintock**	Y	N	N	N	Y	N
5	Thompson, M.	Y	Y	Y	Y	N	Y
6	Matsui	Y	Y	Y	Y	N	Y
7	Bera	Y	Y	Y	Y	N	Y
8	**Cook**	Y	N	N	N	Y	N
9	McNerney	Y	Y	Y	Y	N	Y
10	Harder	Y	Y	Y	Y	N	Y
11	DeSaulnier	Y	Y	Y	Y	N	Y
12	Pelosi						Y
13	Lee B.	Y	Y	Y	Y	N	Y
14	Speier	Y	Y	Y	Y	N	Y
15	Swalwell	Y	Y	Y	Y	N	Y
16	Costa	Y	Y	Y	Y	N	Y
17	Khanna	Y	Y	Y	Y	N	Y
18	Eshoo	?	Y	Y	Y	N	Y
19	Lofgren	Y	Y	Y	Y	N	Y
20	Panetta	Y	Y	Y	Y	N	Y
21	Cox	Y	Y	Y	Y	N	Y
22	**Nunes**	Y	N	N	N	Y	N
23	**McCarthy**	Y	N	N	N	Y	N
24	Carbajal	Y	Y	Y	Y	N	Y
25	vacant						
26	Brownley	Y	Y	Y	Y	N	Y
27	Chu	Y	Y	Y	Y	N	Y
28	Schiff	Y	Y	Y	Y	N	Y
29	Cárdenas	Y	Y	Y	Y	N	Y
30	Sherman	Y	Y	Y	Y	N	Y
31	Aguilar	Y	Y	Y	Y	N	Y
32	Napolitano	Y	Y	Y	Y	N	Y
33	Lieu	Y	Y	Y	Y	N	Y
34	Gomez	Y	Y	Y	Y	N	Y
35	Torres	Y	Y	Y	Y	N	Y
36	Ruiz	Y	Y	Y	Y	N	Y
37	Bass	Y	Y	Y	?	?	?
38	Sánchez	Y	Y	Y	Y	N	Y
39	Cisneros	Y	Y	Y	Y	N	Y
40	Roybal-Allard	Y	Y	Y	Y	N	Y
41	Takano	Y	Y	Y	Y	N	Y
42	**Calvert**	Y	N	N	N	Y	N
43	Waters	Y	Y	Y	Y	N	Y
44	Barragán	Y	Y	Y	Y	N	Y
45	Porter	Y	Y	Y	+	-	+
46	Correa	Y	Y	Y	Y	N	Y
47	Lowenthal	Y	Y	Y	Y	N	Y
48	Rouda	Y	Y	Y	Y	N	Y
49	Levin	Y	Y	Y	Y	N	Y
50	**Hunter**	?	?	?	?	?	?
51	Vargas	Y	Y	Y	Y	N	Y
52	Peters	Y	Y	Y	Y	N	Y
53	Davis, S.	Y	Y	Y	Y	N	Y
COLORADO							
1	DeGette	Y	Y	Y	Y	N	Y
2	Neguse	Y	Y	Y	Y	N	Y
3	**Tipton**	Y	N	N	N	Y	N
4	**Buck**	Y	N	N	N	Y	N
5	**Lamborn**	Y	N	N	N	Y	N
6	Crow	Y	Y	Y	Y	N	Y
7	Perlmutter	Y	Y	Y	Y	N	Y
CONNECTICUT							
1	Larson	Y	Y	Y	Y	-	+
2	Courtney	Y	Y	Y	Y	N	Y
3	DeLauro	Y	Y	Y	Y	N	Y
4	Himes	Y	Y	Y	Y	N	Y
5	Hayes	Y	Y	Y	Y	N	Y
DELAWARE							
AL	Blunt Rochester	Y	Y	Y	Y	N	Y
FLORIDA							
1	**Gaetz**	Y	N	N	N	Y	N
2	**Dunn**	Y	N	N	N	Y	N
3	**Yoho**	N	N	N	N	Y	N
4	**Rutherford**	Y	N	N	N	Y	N
5	Lawson	Y	Y	Y	Y	N	Y
6	**Waltz**	Y	N	N	N	Y	N
7	Murphy	Y	Y	Y	Y	N	Y
8	**Posey**	Y	N	N	Y	Y	N
9	Soto	Y	Y	Y	Y	N	Y
10	Demings	Y	Y	Y	Y	N	Y
11	**Webster**	Y	N	N	N	Y	N
12	**Bilirakis**	Y	N	N	N	Y	N
13	Crist	Y	Y	Y	Y	N	Y
14	Castor	Y	Y	Y	Y	N	Y
15	**Spano**	Y	N	N	N	Y	N
16	**Buchanan**	Y	N	N	N	Y	N
17	**Steube**	Y	N	N	N	Y	N
18	**Mast**	Y	N	N	N	Y	N
19	**Rooney**	Y	N	N	Y	Y	N
20	Hastings	Y	Y	Y	Y	N	Y
21	Frankel	Y	Y	Y	Y	N	Y
22	Deutch	Y	Y	Y	Y	N	Y
23	Wasserman Schultz	Y	Y	Y	Y	N	Y
24	Wilson, F.	Y	Y	Y	Y	N	Y
25	**Diaz-Balart**	Y	N	N	N	Y	N
26	Mucarsel-Powell	Y	Y	Y	Y	N	Y
27	Shalala	Y	Y	Y	Y	N	Y
GEORGIA							
1	**Carter, E.L.**	Y	N	N	N	Y	N
2	Bishop, S.	Y	Y	Y	Y	N	Y
3	**Ferguson**	Y	N	N	N	Y	N
4	Johnson, H.	Y	Y	Y	Y	N	Y
5	Lewis John	Y	Y	Y	Y	N	Y
6	McBath	Y	Y	Y	Y	N	Y
7	**Woodall**	Y	N	N	N	Y	N
8	**Scott, A.**	Y	N	N	N	Y	N
9	**Collins, D.**	Y	N	N	N	Y	N
10	**Hice**	Y	N	N	N	Y	N
11	**Loudermilk**	Y	N	N	N	Y	N
12	**Allen**	Y	N	N	N	Y	N
13	Scott, D.	Y	Y	Y	Y	N	Y
14	**Graves, T.**	Y	N	N	N	Y	N
HAWAII							
1	Case	Y	Y	Y	Y	N	Y
2	Gabbard	?	?	?	?	?	?
IDAHO							
1	**Fulcher**	Y	N	N	N	Y	N
2	**Simpson**	Y	N	N	N	Y	N
ILLINOIS							
1	Rush	Y	Y	Y	Y	N	Y
2	Kelly, R.	Y	Y	Y	Y	N	Y
3	Lipinski	Y	Y	Y	Y	N	Y
4	García, J.	Y	Y	Y	P	N	Y
5	Quigley	Y	Y	Y	Y	N	Y
6	Casten	Y	Y	Y	Y	N	Y
7	Davis, D.	Y	Y	Y	Y	N	Y
8	Krishnamoorthi	Y	Y	Y	Y	N	Y
9	Schakowsky	Y	Y	Y	Y	N	Y
10	Schneider	Y	Y	Y	Y	N	Y
11	Foster	Y	Y	Y	Y	N	Y

KEY: **Republicans** Democrats *Independents*

Y	Voted for (yea)	N	Voted against (nay)	P	Voted "present"
+	Announced for	-	Announced against	?	Did not vote or otherwise make position known
#	Paired for	X	Paired against		

H-224 2019 CQ ALMANAC | www.cq.com

	649	650	651	652	653	654
12 **Bost**	Y	N	N	N	Y	N
13 **Davis, R.**	Y	N	N	N	Y	N
14 Underwood	Y	Y	Y	Y	N	Y
15 **Shimkus**	Y	N	N	?	?	?
16 **Kinzinger**	Y	N	N	-	+	-
17 Bustos	Y	Y	Y	Y	N	Y
18 **LaHood**	Y	N	N	N	Y	N
INDIANA						
1 Visclosky	Y	Y	Y	Y	N	Y
2 **Walorski**	Y	N	N	N	Y	N
3 **Banks**	Y	N	N	N	Y	N
4 **Baird**	Y	N	N	N	Y	N
5 **Brooks, S.**	Y	N	N	N	Y	N
6 **Pence**	Y	N	N	N	Y	N
7 Carson	Y	Y	Y	Y	N	Y
8 **Bucshon**	Y	N	N	N	Y	N
9 **Hollingsworth**	Y	N	N	N	Y	N
IOWA						
1 Finkenauer	Y	Y	Y	Y	Y	Y
2 Loebsack	Y	Y	Y	Y	N	Y
3 Axne	Y	Y	Y	Y	Y	Y
4 **King, S.**	N	N	N	N	Y	N
KANSAS						
1 **Marshall**	Y	N	N	N	Y	N
2 **Watkins**	Y	N	N	Y	Y	N
3 Davids	Y	Y	Y	Y	N	Y
4 **Estes**	Y	N	N	N	Y	N
KENTUCKY						
1 **Comer**	Y	N	N	N	Y	N
2 **Guthrie**	Y	N	N	N	Y	N
3 Yarmuth	Y	Y	Y	Y	N	Y
4 **Massie**	N	N	N	N	Y	N
5 **Rogers, H.**	Y	N	N	N	Y	N
6 **Barr**	Y	N	N	?	?	?
LOUISIANA						
1 **Scalise**	Y	N	N	N	Y	N
2 Richmond	Y	Y	Y	Y	N	Y
3 **Higgins, C.**	Y	N	N	N	Y	N
4 **Johnson, M.**	Y	N	N	N	Y	N
5 **Abraham**	Y	N	N	N	Y	N
6 **Graves, G.**	Y	N	N	N	Y	N
MAINE						
1 Pingree	Y	Y	Y	Y	N	Y
2 Golden	Y	Y	Y	Y	N	Y
MARYLAND						
1 **Harris**	N	N	N	N	Y	N
2 Ruppersberger	Y	Y	Y	Y	N	Y
3 Sarbanes	Y	Y	Y	Y	N	Y
4 Brown, A.	Y	Y	Y	Y	N	Y
5 Hoyer	Y	Y	Y	Y	N	Y
6 Trone	Y	Y	Y	Y	N	Y
7 vacant						
8 Raskin	Y	Y	Y	Y	N	Y
MASSACHUSETTS						
1 Neal	Y	Y	Y	Y	N	Y
2 McGovern	Y	Y	Y	Y	N	Y
3 Trahan	Y	Y	Y	Y	N	Y
4 Kennedy	Y	Y	Y	Y	N	Y
5 Clark	Y	Y	Y	Y	N	Y
6 Moulton	Y	Y	Y	Y	N	Y
7 Pressley	Y	Y	Y	N	N	Y
8 Lynch	Y	Y	Y	Y	N	Y
9 Keating	Y	Y	Y	Y	N	Y
MICHIGAN						
1 **Bergman**	Y	N	N	N	Y	N
2 **Huizenga**	N	N	N	N	Y	N
3 *Amash*	N	N	N	N	Y	N
4 **Moolenaar**	Y	N	N	N	Y	N
5 Kildee	Y	Y	Y	Y	N	Y
6 **Upton**	Y	N	N	Y	Y	N
7 **Walberg**	Y	N	N	N	Y	N
8 Slotkin	Y	Y	Y	Y	Y	Y
9 Levin	Y	Y	Y	Y	N	Y
10 **Mitchell**	Y	N	N	N	Y	N
11 Stevens	Y	Y	Y	Y	N	Y
12 Dingell	Y	Y	Y	Y	N	Y
13 Tlaib	Y	Y	N	N	N	Y
14 Lawrence	Y	Y	Y	Y	N	Y
MINNESOTA						
1 **Hagedorn**	Y	N	N	N	Y	N
2 Craig	Y	Y	Y	Y	N	Y
3 Phillips	Y	Y	Y	Y	N	Y
4 McCollum	Y	Y	Y	P	N	Y
5 Omar	Y	Y	Y	N	N	Y

	649	650	651	652	653	654
6 **Emmer**	Y	N	N	-	+	-
7 Peterson	Y	Y	Y	Y	N	Y
8 **Stauber**	Y	N	N	N	Y	N
MISSISSIPPI						
1 **Kelly, T.**	Y	N	N	N	Y	N
2 Thompson, B.	Y	Y	Y	Y	N	Y
3 **Guest**	Y	N	N	N	Y	N
4 **Palazzo**	Y	N	N	N	Y	N
MISSOURI						
1 Clay	Y	Y	Y	Y	N	Y
2 **Wagner**	Y	N	N	N	Y	N
3 **Luetkemeyer**	Y	N	N	N	Y	N
4 **Hartzler**	Y	N	N	N	Y	N
5 Cleaver	Y	Y	Y	Y	N	Y
6 **Graves, S.**	Y	N	N	N	Y	N
7 **Long**	Y	N	N	N	Y	N
8 **Smith, J.**	Y	N	N	N	Y	N
MONTANA						
AL **Gianforte**	Y	N	N	N	Y	N
NEBRASKA						
1 **Fortenberry**	Y	N	N	N	Y	N
2 **Bacon**	Y	N	N	N	Y	N
3 **Smith, Adrian**	Y	N	N	N	Y	N
NEVADA						
1 Titus	Y	Y	Y	Y	N	Y
2 **Amodei**	Y	N	N	N	Y	N
3 Lee	Y	Y	Y	Y	N	Y
4 Horsford	Y	Y	Y	Y	N	Y
NEW HAMPSHIRE						
1 Pappas	Y	Y	Y	Y	N	Y
2 Kuster	Y	Y	Y	Y	N	Y
NEW JERSEY						
1 Norcross	Y	Y	Y	Y	N	Y
2 Van Drew	Y	Y	Y	Y	Y	Y
3 Kim	Y	Y	Y	Y	Y	Y
4 **Smith, C.**	Y	N	N	N	Y	N
5 Gottheimer	Y	Y	Y	Y	Y	Y
6 Pallone	Y	Y	Y	Y	N	Y
7 Malinowski	Y	Y	Y	Y	N	Y
8 Sires	Y	Y	Y	Y	N	Y
9 Pascrell	Y	Y	Y	Y	N	Y
10 Payne	Y	Y	Y	Y	N	Y
11 Sherrill	Y	Y	Y	Y	N	Y
12 Watson Coleman	Y	Y	Y	Y	N	Y
NEW MEXICO						
1 Haaland	Y	Y	Y	Y	N	Y
2 Torres Small	Y	Y	Y	Y	Y	Y
3 Luján	Y	Y	Y	Y	N	Y
NEW YORK						
1 **Zeldin**	Y	N	N	N	Y	N
2 **King, P.**	Y	N	N	N	Y	N
3 Suozzi	Y	Y	Y	Y	N	Y
4 Rice, K.	Y	Y	Y	Y	N	Y
5 Meeks	Y	Y	Y	Y	N	Y
6 Meng	Y	Y	Y	Y	N	Y
7 Velázquez	Y	Y	Y	Y	N	Y
8 Jeffries	Y	Y	Y	Y	N	Y
9 Clarke	Y	Y	Y	Y	N	Y
10 Nadler	Y	Y	Y	Y	N	Y
11 Rose	Y	Y	Y	Y	N	Y
12 Maloney, C.	Y	Y	Y	Y	N	Y
13 Espaillat	Y	Y	Y	Y	N	Y
14 Ocasio-Cortez	Y	Y	Y	N	N	Y
15 Serrano	?	?	?	?	?	?
16 Engel	Y	Y	Y	Y	N	Y
17 Lowey	Y	Y	Y	Y	N	Y
18 Maloney, S.P.	Y	Y	Y	Y	N	Y
19 Delgado	Y	Y	Y	Y	N	Y
20 Tonko	Y	Y	Y	Y	N	Y
21 **Stefanik**	Y	N	N	N	Y	N
22 Brindisi	Y	Y	Y	Y	Y	Y
23 **Reed**	?	N	N	Y	Y	N
24 **Katko**	Y	N	N	N	Y	N
25 Morelle	Y	Y	Y	Y	N	Y
26 Higgins, B.	Y	Y	Y	Y	N	Y
27 **Collins, C.**						
NORTH CAROLINA						
1 Butterfield	Y	Y	Y	Y	N	Y
2 **Holding**	Y	N	N	N	Y	N
3 **Murphy**	Y	N	N	N	Y	N
4 Price	Y	Y	Y	Y	N	Y
5 **Foxx**	Y	N	N	N	Y	N
6 **Walker**	Y	N	N	N	Y	N
7 **Rouzer**	Y	N	N	N	Y	N

	649	650	651	652	653	654
8 **Hudson**	Y	N	N	N	Y	N
9 **Bishop**	N	N	N	N	Y	N
10 **McHenry**	Y	N	N	N	Y	?
11 **Meadows**	Y	N	N	N	Y	N
12 Adams	Y	Y	Y	Y	N	Y
13 **Budd**	Y	N	N	N	Y	N
NORTH DAKOTA						
AL **Armstrong**	N	N	N	N	Y	N
OHIO						
1 **Chabot**	Y	N	N	N	Y	N
2 **Wenstrup**	Y	N	N	N	Y	N
3 Beatty	Y	Y	Y	Y	N	Y
4 **Jordan**	Y	N	N	N	Y	N
5 **Latta**	Y	N	N	N	Y	N
6 **Johnson, B.**	Y	N	N	N	Y	N
7 **Gibbs**	Y	N	N	N	Y	N
8 **Davidson**	N	N	N	N	Y	N
9 Kaptur	Y	Y	Y	Y	N	Y
10 **Turner**	Y	N	N	N	Y	N
11 Fudge	Y	Y	Y	Y	N	Y
12 **Balderson**	Y	N	N	N	Y	N
13 Ryan	Y	Y	Y	Y	N	Y
14 **Joyce**	Y	N	N	N	Y	N
15 **Stivers**	Y	N	N	N	Y	N
16 **Gonzalez**	Y	N	N	N	Y	N
OKLAHOMA						
1 **Hern**	Y	N	N	N	Y	N
2 **Mullin**	Y	N	N	N	Y	N
3 **Lucas**	Y	N	N	N	Y	N
4 **Cole**	Y	N	N	N	Y	N
5 Horn	Y	Y	Y	Y	Y	Y
OREGON						
1 Bonamici	Y	Y	Y	Y	N	Y
2 **Walden**	Y	N	N	N	Y	N
3 Blumenauer	Y	Y	Y	Y	N	Y
4 DeFazio	Y	Y	Y	Y	N	Y
5 Schrader	Y	Y	?	Y	N	Y
PENNSYLVANIA						
1 **Fitzpatrick**	Y	N	N	N	Y	Y
2 Boyle	Y	Y	Y	Y	N	Y
3 Evans	Y	Y	Y	Y	N	Y
4 Dean	Y	Y	Y	Y	N	Y
5 Scanlon	Y	Y	Y	Y	N	Y
6 Houlahan	Y	Y	Y	Y	N	Y
7 Wild	Y	Y	Y	Y	N	Y
8 Cartwright	?	?	?	?	?	?
9 **Meuser**	Y	N	N	N	Y	N
10 **Perry**	Y	N	N	N	Y	N
11 **Smucker**	Y	N	N	N	Y	N
12 **Keller**	Y	N	N	N	Y	N
13 **Joyce**	Y	N	N	N	Y	N
14 **Reschenthaler**	Y	N	N	N	Y	N
15 **Thompson, G.**	Y	N	N	N	Y	N
16 **Kelly, M.**	Y	N	N	N	Y	N
17 Lamb	Y	Y	Y	Y	N	Y
18 Doyle	Y	Y	Y	Y	N	Y
RHODE ISLAND						
1 Cicilline	Y	Y	Y	Y	N	Y
2 Langevin	Y	Y	Y	Y	N	Y
SOUTH CAROLINA						
1 Cunningham	Y	Y	+	Y	Y	Y
2 **Wilson, J.**	Y	N	N	N	Y	N
3 **Duncan**	Y	N	N	N	Y	N
4 **Timmons**	Y	N	N	N	Y	N
5 **Norman**	Y	N	N	-	+	-
6 Clyburn	Y	Y	Y	Y	N	Y
7 **Rice, T.**	Y	N	N	N	Y	N
SOUTH DAKOTA						
AL **Johnson**	Y	N	N	N	Y	N
TENNESSEE						
1 **Roe**	Y	N	N	N	Y	N
2 **Burchett**	Y	N	N	N	Y	N
3 **Fleischmann**	Y	N	N	N	Y	N
4 **DesJarlais**	Y	N	N	N	Y	N
5 Cooper	Y	Y	Y	Y	N	Y
6 **Rose**	Y	N	N	N	Y	N
7 **Green**	Y	N	N	N	Y	N
8 **Kustoff**	Y	N	N	N	Y	N
9 Cohen	Y	Y	Y	Y	N	Y
TEXAS						
1 **Gohmert**	Y	N	N	N	Y	N
2 **Crenshaw**	Y	N	N	N	Y	N
3 **Taylor**	Y	N	N	N	Y	N
4 **Ratcliffe**	Y	N	?	N	Y	N

	649	650	651	652	653	654
5 **Gooden**	Y	N	N	N	Y	N
6 **Wright**	Y	N	N	N	Y	N
7 Fletcher	Y	Y	Y	Y	N	Y
8 **Brady**	Y	N	N	N	Y	N
9 Green, A.	Y	Y	Y	Y	N	Y
10 **McCaul**	Y	N	N	N	Y	N
11 **Conaway**	Y	N	N	N	Y	N
12 **Granger**	Y	N	N	N	Y	N
13 **Thornberry**	Y	N	N	N	Y	N
14 **Weber**	Y	N	N	N	Y	N
15 Gonzalez	Y	Y	Y	Y	N	Y
16 Escobar	Y	Y	Y	Y	N	Y
17 **Flores**	Y	N	N	N	Y	N
18 Jackson Lee	Y	Y	Y	Y	N	Y
19 **Arrington**	Y	N	N	N	Y	N
20 Castro	Y	Y	Y	Y	N	Y
21 **Roy**	N	N	N	N	Y	N
22 **Olson**	Y	N	N	N	Y	N
23 **Hurd**	Y	N	N	N	Y	N
24 **Marchant**	Y	N	N	?	?	?
25 **Williams**	Y	N	N	N	Y	N
26 **Burgess**	Y	N	N	N	Y	N
27 **Cloud**	Y	N	N	N	Y	N
28 Cuellar	Y	Y	Y	Y	N	Y
29 Garcia, S.	Y	Y	Y	Y	N	Y
30 Johnson, E.B.	Y	Y	Y	Y	N	Y
31 **Carter, J.**	Y	N	N	N	Y	N
32 Allred	Y	Y	Y	Y	N	Y
33 Veasey	Y	Y	Y	Y	N	Y
34 Vela	Y	Y	Y	Y	N	Y
35 Doggett	Y	Y	Y	Y	N	Y
36 **Babin**	Y	N	N	N	Y	N
UTAH						
1 **Bishop, R.**	Y	N	N	N	Y	N
2 **Stewart**	Y	N	N	N	Y	N
3 **Curtis**	Y	N	N	N	Y	N
4 McAdams	Y	Y	Y	Y	Y	Y
VERMONT						
AL Welch	Y	Y	Y	Y	N	Y
VIRGINIA						
1 **Wittman**	Y	N	N	N	Y	N
2 Luria	Y	Y	Y	Y	N	Y
3 Scott, R.	Y	Y	Y	Y	N	Y
4 McEachin	Y	Y	Y	Y	N	Y
5 **Riggleman**	Y	N	N	N	Y	N
6 **Cline**	Y	N	N	N	Y	N
7 Spanberger	Y	Y	Y	Y	Y	Y
8 Beyer	Y	Y	Y	Y	N	Y
9 **Griffith**	N	N	N	N	Y	N
10 Wexton	Y	Y	Y	Y	N	Y
11 Connolly	Y	Y	Y	Y	N	Y
WASHINGTON						
1 DelBene	Y	Y	Y	Y	N	Y
2 Larsen	Y	Y	Y	Y	N	Y
3 **Herrera Beutler**	Y	N	N	N	Y	N
4 **Newhouse**	Y	N	N	N	Y	N
5 **McMorris Rodgers**	Y	N	N	N	Y	N
6 Kilmer	Y	Y	Y	Y	N	Y
7 Jayapal	Y	?	Y	Y	N	Y
8 Schrier	Y	Y	Y	Y	N	Y
9 Smith Adam	Y	Y	Y	Y	N	Y
10 Heck	Y	Y	Y	Y	N	Y
WEST VIRGINIA						
1 **McKinley**	Y	N	N	N	Y	N
2 **Mooney**	Y	N	N	N	Y	N
3 **Miller**	Y	N	N	N	Y	N
WISCONSIN						
1 **Steil**	Y	N	N	N	Y	N
2 Pocan	Y	Y	Y	Y	N	Y
3 Kind	Y	Y	Y	Y	N	Y
4 Moore	Y	Y	Y	Y	N	Y
5 **Sensenbrenner**	Y	N	N	N	Y	N
6 **Grothman**	Y	N	N	N	Y	N
7 **Duffy**						
8 **Gallagher**	Y	N	N	N	Y	N
WYOMING						
AL **Cheney**	Y	N	N	N	Y	N
DELEGATES						
Radewagen (A.S.)						
Norton (D.C.)						
San Nicolas (Guam)						
Sablan (N. Marianas)						
González-Colón (P.R.)						
Plaskett (V.I.)						

655. HR4761. DHS Narcotics Detection - Passage. Clarke, D-N.Y., motion to suspend the rules and pass the bill that would require Customs and Border Protection to implement a strategy to ensure that chemical screening devices used by the department are able to identify narcotics in an operational environment at purity levels less than or equal to 10%, or to provide ports of entry with an alternate method for identifying narcotics at lower purity levels, within 180 days of enactment. It would also require CBP to test new chemical screening devices for effectiveness at identifying narcotics at various purity levels, before purchasing them. Additionally, it would require the Department of Homeland Security to implement a plan to develop a centralized spectral database for chemical screening devices. Motion agreed to 393-1: R 179-0; D 214-0; I 0-1. Dec. 9, 2019.

656. HR4739. DHS Opioid Exposure Procedures - Passage. Clarke, D-N.Y., motion to suspend the rules and pass the bill that would require Customs and Border Protection to issue a policy that would specify effective procedures for the safe handling of potential synthetic opioids, including fentanyl, by CBP personnel and canines, and to reduce the health risks associated with accidental exposure to synthetic opioids. It would require CBP to develop mandatory and recurrent training related to such policies; ensure that protective equipment is available to personnel who are at risk of exposure; and regularly monitor the effectiveness of implementation of the policy. It would also require the Homeland Security Department inspector general to conduct annual audits of policy implementation. Motion agreed to 393-0: R 179-0; D 213-0; I 1-0. *Note: A two-thirds majority of those present and voting (262 in this case) is required for passage under suspension of the rules.* Dec. 9, 2019.

657. HR729. Coastal Communities and Habitats - Previous Question. Agreeing to the Morelle, D-N.Y., motion to order the previous question (thus ending debate and possibility of amendment) on the rule (H Res 748) that would provide for House floor consideration of the Coastal and Great Lakes Communities Enhancement Act (HR 729). It would provide for floor consideration, including en bloc consideration, of 29 amendments to the bill. Motion agreed to 226-188: R 0-187; D 226-0; I 0-1. Dec. 10, 2019.

658. HR729. Coastal Communities and Habitats - Rule. Adoption of the rule (H Res 748) that would provide for House floor consideration of the Coastal and Great Lakes Communities Enhancement Act (HR 729). It would provide for floor consideration, including en bloc consideration, of 29 amendments to the bill. Adopted 226-189: R 0-187; D 226-1; I 0-1. Dec. 10, 2019.

659. HR5363. Higher Education Funding - Passage. Adams, D-N.C., motion to suspend the rules and pass the bill, as amended, that would indefinitely extend funding, at the current funding level of $225 million annually, for Education Department grants to support historically black colleges and universities and other minority serving institutions. It would increase annual funding levels for Pell grants, authorizing $1.5 billion for fiscal 2020 and $1.2 billion annually for fiscal 2021 and succeeding fiscal years. The bill would also require the Education Department to establish procedures to use certain tax return information obtained directly from the Internal Revenue Service in determining students' eligibility for federal financial aid and income-based student loan repayment plans, as opposed to requiring students to submit such information. It would require the IRS to disclose such information to the Education Department, upon request by the department and with the consent of the student. Motion agreed to 319-96: R 93-95; D 226-0; I 0-1. *Note: A two-thirds majority of those present and voting (277 in this case) is required for passage under suspension of the rules.* Dec. 10, 2019.

660. HR729. Coastal Communities and Habitats - En Bloc Amendments. Adoption of the Case, D-Hawaii, en bloc amendments to the bill. Adopted in Committee of the Whole 249-166: R 22-164; D 226-1; I 1-1. Dec. 10, 2019.

ALABAMA	655	656	657	658	659	660
1 Byrne	Y	Y	N	N	N	N
2 Roby	Y	Y	N	N	N	N
3 Rogers, M.	Y	Y	N	N	?	?
4 Aderholt	?	?	?	?	?	?
5 Brooks, M.	Y	Y	N	N	N	N
6 Palmer	Y	Y	N	N	N	N
7 Sewell	Y	Y	Y	Y	Y	Y
ALASKA						
AL Young	Y	Y	N	N	Y	N
ARIZONA						
1 O'Halleran	Y	Y	Y	Y	Y	Y
2 Kirkpatrick	Y	Y	Y	Y	Y	Y
3 Grijalva	Y	Y	Y	Y	Y	Y
4 Gosar	Y	Y	N	N	N	N
5 Biggs	Y	Y	N	N	N	N
6 Schweikert	Y	Y	N	N	N	N
7 Gallego	Y	Y	Y	Y	Y	Y
8 Lesko	Y	Y	?	N	N	N
9 Stanton	Y	Y	Y	Y	Y	Y
ARKANSAS						
1 Crawford	+	+	N	N	N	N
2 Hill, F.	Y	Y	N	N	Y	N
3 Womack	Y	Y	N	N	N	N
4 Westerman	Y	Y	N	N	Y	N
CALIFORNIA						
1 LaMalfa	?	?	N	N	N	N
2 Huffman	Y	Y	Y	Y	Y	Y
3 Garamendi	Y	Y	Y	Y	Y	Y
4 McClintock	Y	Y	N	N	N	N
5 Thompson, M.	Y	Y	Y	Y	Y	Y
6 Matsui	Y	Y	Y	Y	Y	Y
7 Bera	Y	Y	Y	Y	Y	Y
8 Cook	Y	Y	N	N	Y	N
9 McNerney	?	?	Y	Y	Y	Y
10 Harder	Y	Y	Y	Y	Y	Y
11 DeSaulnier	Y	Y	Y	Y	Y	Y
12 Pelosi						
13 Lee B.	Y	Y	Y	Y	Y	Y
14 Speier	Y	Y	Y	Y	Y	Y
15 Swalwell	Y	Y	Y	Y	Y	Y
16 Costa	Y	Y	Y	Y	Y	Y
17 Khanna	Y	Y	Y	Y	Y	Y
18 Eshoo	Y	Y	Y	Y	Y	Y
19 Lofgren	Y	Y	Y	Y	Y	Y
20 Panetta	Y	Y	Y	Y	Y	Y
21 Cox	Y	Y	Y	Y	Y	Y
22 Nunes	Y	Y	N	N	N	N
23 McCarthy	Y	Y	N	N	N	N
24 Carbajal	Y	Y	Y	Y	Y	Y
25 vacant						
26 Brownley	Y	Y	Y	Y	Y	Y
27 Chu	Y	Y	Y	Y	Y	Y
28 Schiff	Y	Y	Y	Y	Y	Y
29 Cárdenas	Y	Y	Y	Y	Y	Y
30 Sherman	Y	Y	Y	Y	Y	Y
31 Aguilar	Y	Y	Y	Y	Y	Y
32 Napolitano	Y	Y	Y	Y	Y	Y
33 Lieu	?	?	?	?	?	?
34 Gomez	Y	Y	Y	Y	Y	Y
35 Torres	Y	?	Y	Y	Y	Y
36 Ruiz	Y	Y	Y	Y	Y	Y
37 Bass	Y	Y	Y	Y	Y	Y
38 Sánchez	Y	Y	Y	Y	Y	Y
39 Cisneros	Y	Y	Y	Y	Y	Y
40 Roybal-Allard	Y	Y	Y	Y	Y	Y
41 Takano	Y	Y	Y	Y	Y	Y
42 Calvert	Y	Y	N	N	N	N
43 Waters	Y	Y	Y	Y	Y	Y
44 Barragán	Y	Y	Y	Y	Y	Y
45 Porter	Y	Y	Y	N	Y	Y
46 Correa	Y	Y	Y	Y	Y	Y
47 Lowenthal	Y	Y	Y	Y	Y	Y
48 Rouda	Y	Y	Y	Y	Y	Y
49 Levin	Y	Y	Y	Y	Y	Y
50 Hunter	?	?	?	?	?	?
51 Vargas	Y	Y	Y	Y	Y	Y
52 Peters	Y	Y	Y	Y	Y	Y

	655	656	657	658	659	660
53 Davis, S.	Y	Y	Y	Y	Y	Y
COLORADO						
1 DeGette	Y	Y	Y	Y	Y	Y
2 Neguse	Y	Y	Y	Y	Y	Y
3 Tipton	Y	Y	N	N	N	N
4 Buck	Y	N	N	N	N	N
5 Lamborn	?	?	N	N	N	N
6 Crow	Y	Y	Y	Y	Y	Y
7 Perlmutter	Y	Y	Y	Y	Y	Y
CONNECTICUT						
1 Larson	Y	Y	Y	Y	Y	Y
2 Courtney	Y	Y	Y	Y	Y	Y
3 DeLauro	Y	Y	Y	Y	Y	Y
4 Himes	Y	Y	Y	Y	Y	Y
5 Hayes	Y	Y	Y	Y	Y	Y
DELAWARE						
AL Blunt Rochester	Y	Y	Y	Y	Y	Y
FLORIDA						
1 Gaetz	Y	Y	N	N	N	N
2 Dunn	Y	Y	N	N	N	N
3 Yoho	?	?	N	N	N	N
4 Rutherford	+	+	N	N	N	N
5 Lawson	?	?	Y	Y	Y	Y
6 Waltz	Y	Y	N	N	Y	N
7 Murphy	Y	Y	Y	Y	Y	Y
8 Posey	Y	Y	N	N	N	N
9 Soto	+	+	Y	Y	Y	Y
10 Demings	Y	Y	Y	Y	Y	Y
11 Webster	Y	Y	N	N	N	N
12 Bilirakis	Y	Y	N	N	N	N
13 Crist	Y	Y	Y	Y	Y	Y
14 Castor	Y	Y	Y	Y	Y	Y
15 Spano	Y	Y	N	N	Y	N
16 Buchanan	Y	Y	N	N	Y	N
17 Steube	Y	Y	N	N	N	N
18 Mast	Y	Y	N	N	N	Y
19 Rooney	?	?	?	?	?	?
20 Hastings	Y	Y	Y	Y	Y	Y
21 Frankel	Y	Y	Y	Y	Y	Y
22 Deutch	Y	Y	Y	Y	Y	Y
23 Wasserman Schultz	Y	Y	?	?	?	?
24 Wilson, F.	?	?	Y	Y	Y	Y
25 Diaz-Balart	Y	Y	N	N	Y	N
26 Mucarsel-Powell	Y	Y	Y	Y	Y	Y
27 Shalala	Y	Y	Y	Y	Y	Y
GEORGIA						
1 Carter, E.L.	Y	Y	N	N	N	N
2 Bishop, S.	Y	Y	Y	Y	Y	Y
3 Ferguson	Y	Y	N	N	N	N
4 Johnson, H.	Y	Y	Y	Y	Y	Y
5 Lewis John	Y	Y	Y	Y	Y	Y
6 McBath	Y	Y	Y	Y	Y	Y
7 Woodall	Y	Y	N	N	?	N
8 Scott, A.	Y	Y	N	N	N	N
9 Collins, D.	Y	Y	N	N	N	N
10 Hice	Y	Y	N	N	N	N
11 Loudermilk	Y	Y	N	N	N	N
12 Allen	Y	Y	N	N	N	N
13 Scott, D.	Y	Y	Y	Y	Y	Y
14 Graves, T.	Y	Y	N	N	N	N
HAWAII						
1 Case	Y	Y	Y	Y	Y	Y
2 Gabbard	?	?	?	?	?	?
IDAHO						
1 Fulcher	Y	Y	N	N	N	N
2 Simpson	Y	Y	-	-	+	N
ILLINOIS						
1 Rush	?	?	Y	Y	Y	Y
2 Kelly, R.	Y	Y	Y	Y	Y	Y
3 Lipinski	Y	Y	Y	Y	Y	Y
4 García, J.	Y	Y	Y	Y	Y	Y
5 Quigley	Y	Y	Y	Y	Y	Y
6 Casten	Y	Y	Y	Y	Y	Y
7 Davis, D.	+	+	Y	Y	Y	Y
8 Krishnamoorthi	Y	Y	Y	Y	Y	Y
9 Schakowsky	Y	Y	Y	Y	Y	Y
10 Schneider	Y	Y	Y	Y	Y	Y
11 Foster	Y	Y	Y	Y	Y	Y

KEY:	**Republicans**	*Democrats*	*Independents*
Y Voted for (yea)	**N** Voted against (nay)	**P** Voted "present"	
+ Announced for	**-** Announced against	**?** Did not vote or otherwise make position known	
# Paired for	**X** Paired against		

	655	656	657	658	659	660
12 **Bost**	Y	Y	N	N	Y	N
13 **Davis, R.**	Y	Y	N	N	Y	N
14 Underwood	Y	Y	Y	Y	Y	Y
15 **Shimkus**	Y	Y	N	N	N	N
16 **Kinzinger**	Y	Y	N	N	Y	N
17 Bustos	Y	Y	Y	Y	Y	Y
18 **LaHood**	Y	Y	N	N	N	N
INDIANA						
1 Visclosky	Y	Y	Y	Y	Y	Y
2 **Walorski**	Y	Y	N	N	N	N
3 **Banks**	Y	Y	N	N	N	N
4 **Baird**	Y	Y	N	N	N	N
5 **Brooks, S.**	+	+	N	N	Y	N
6 **Pence**	Y	Y	N	N	Y	N
7 Carson	Y	Y	Y	Y	Y	Y
8 **Bucshon**	Y	Y	N	N	Y	N
9 **Hollingsworth**	Y	Y	N	N	Y	N
IOWA						
1 Finkenauer	Y	Y	Y	Y	Y	Y
2 Loebsack	?	?	Y	Y	Y	Y
3 Axne	Y	Y	Y	Y	Y	Y
4 **King, S.**	Y	Y	N	N	N	N
KANSAS						
1 **Marshall**	Y	Y	N	N	N	N
2 **Watkins**	Y	Y	N	N	N	N
3 Davids	Y	Y	Y	Y	Y	Y
4 **Estes**	Y	Y	N	N	N	N
KENTUCKY						
1 **Comer**	Y	Y	N	N	Y	N
2 **Guthrie**	Y	Y	N	N	Y	N
3 Yarmuth	Y	Y	Y	Y	Y	Y
4 **Massie**	Y	Y	N	N	N	N
5 **Rogers, H.**	Y	Y	N	N	Y	N
6 **Barr**	Y	Y	N	N	Y	N
LOUISIANA						
1 **Scalise**	Y	Y	N	N	Y	N
2 Richmond	Y	Y	Y	Y	Y	Y
3 **Higgins, C.**	Y	Y	N	N	N	N
4 **Johnson, M.**	Y	Y	N	N	Y	N
5 **Abraham**	Y	Y	N	N	Y	N
6 **Graves, G.**	Y	Y	N	N	Y	Y
MAINE						
1 Pingree	Y	Y	Y	Y	Y	Y
2 Golden	Y	Y	Y	Y	Y	Y
MARYLAND						
1 **Harris**	Y	Y	N	N	N	N
2 Ruppersberger	Y	Y	Y	Y	Y	Y
3 Sarbanes	Y	Y	Y	Y	Y	Y
4 Brown, A.	Y	Y	?	?	+	Y
5 Hoyer	Y	Y	Y	Y	Y	Y
6 Trone	Y	Y	Y	Y	Y	Y
7 vacant	|	|	|	|	|	|
8 Raskin	Y	Y	Y	Y	Y	Y
MASSACHUSETTS						
1 Neal	Y	Y	Y	Y	Y	Y
2 McGovern	Y	Y	Y	Y	Y	Y
3 Trahan	Y	Y	Y	Y	Y	Y
4 Kennedy	?	?	Y	Y	Y	Y
5 Clark	Y	Y	Y	Y	Y	Y
6 Moulton	Y	Y	Y	Y	Y	Y
7 Pressley	Y	Y	Y	Y	Y	Y
8 Lynch	?	?	Y	Y	Y	Y
9 Keating	+	+	Y	Y	Y	Y
MICHIGAN						
1 **Bergman**	Y	Y	N	N	Y	N
2 **Huizenga**	Y	Y	N	N	Y	Y
3 *Amash*	N	Y	N	N	N	N
4 **Moolenaar**	Y	Y	N	N	Y	Y
5 Kildee	Y	Y	Y	Y	Y	Y
6 **Upton**	Y	Y	N	N	Y	Y
7 **Walberg**	Y	Y	N	N	Y	N
8 Slotkin	Y	Y	Y	Y	Y	Y
9 Levin	Y	Y	Y	Y	Y	Y
10 **Mitchell**	Y	Y	N	N	Y	Y
11 Stevens	Y	Y	Y	Y	Y	Y
12 Dingell	Y	Y	Y	Y	Y	Y
13 Tlaib	Y	Y	Y	Y	Y	Y
14 Lawrence	Y	Y	Y	Y	Y	?
MINNESOTA						
1 **Hagedorn**	Y	Y	N	N	N	N
2 Craig	Y	Y	Y	Y	Y	Y
3 Phillips	Y	Y	Y	Y	Y	Y
4 McCollum	Y	Y	Y	Y	Y	Y
5 Omar	Y	Y	Y	Y	Y	Y

	655	656	657	658	659	660
6 **Emmer**	?	Y	N	N	N	N
7 Peterson	Y	Y	Y	Y	Y	Y
8 **Stauber**	Y	Y	N	N	Y	Y
MISSISSIPPI						
1 **Kelly, T.**	Y	Y	N	N	Y	N
2 Thompson, B.	Y	Y	Y	Y	Y	Y
3 **Guest**	Y	Y	N	N	Y	N
4 **Palazzo**	+	+	N	N	N	N
MISSOURI						
1 Clay	Y	Y	Y	Y	Y	Y
2 **Wagner**	Y	Y	N	N	Y	N
3 **Luetkemeyer**	+	+	N	N	Y	N
4 **Hartzler**	+	+	N	N	Y	N
5 Cleaver	Y	Y	Y	Y	Y	Y
6 **Graves, S.**	Y	Y	N	N	N	N
7 **Long**	Y	Y	N	N	N	N
8 **Smith, J.**	Y	Y	N	N	N	N
MONTANA						
AL **Gianforte**	Y	Y	N	N	N	N
NEBRASKA						
1 **Fortenberry**	Y	Y	N	N	Y	Y
2 **Bacon**	Y	Y	N	N	N	N
3 **Smith, Adrian**	Y	Y	N	N	N	N
NEVADA						
1 Titus	Y	Y	Y	Y	Y	Y
2 **Amodei**	Y	Y	N	N	Y	N
3 Lee	Y	Y	Y	Y	Y	Y
4 Horsford	Y	Y	Y	Y	Y	Y
NEW HAMPSHIRE						
1 Pappas	Y	Y	Y	Y	Y	Y
2 Kuster	Y	Y	Y	Y	Y	Y
NEW JERSEY						
1 Norcross	Y	Y	Y	Y	Y	Y
2 Van Drew	Y	Y	Y	Y	Y	Y
3 Kim	Y	Y	Y	Y	Y	Y
4 **Smith, C.**	Y	Y	N	N	Y	Y
5 Gottheimer	Y	Y	Y	Y	Y	Y
6 Pallone	Y	Y	Y	Y	Y	Y
7 Malinowski	Y	Y	Y	Y	Y	Y
8 Sires	Y	Y	Y	Y	Y	Y
9 Pascrell	Y	Y	Y	Y	Y	Y
10 Payne	Y	Y	Y	Y	Y	Y
11 Sherrill	Y	Y	Y	Y	Y	Y
12 Watson Coleman	Y	Y	Y	Y	Y	Y
NEW MEXICO						
1 Haaland	Y	Y	Y	Y	Y	Y
2 Torres Small	Y	Y	Y	Y	Y	Y
3 Luján	Y	Y	Y	Y	Y	Y
NEW YORK						
1 **Zeldin**	Y	Y	N	N	Y	N
2 **King, P.**	?	?	N	N	Y	Y
3 Suozzi	Y	Y	Y	Y	Y	Y
4 Rice, K.	Y	Y	Y	Y	Y	Y
5 Meeks	?	?	Y	Y	Y	Y
6 Meng	?	?	Y	Y	Y	Y
7 Velázquez	Y	Y	Y	Y	Y	Y
8 Jeffries	Y	Y	Y	Y	Y	Y
9 Clarke	Y	Y	+	Y	Y	+
10 Nadler	Y	Y	Y	Y	Y	Y
11 Rose	Y	Y	Y	Y	Y	Y
12 Maloney, C.	Y	Y	Y	Y	Y	Y
13 Espaillat	Y	Y	Y	Y	Y	Y
14 Ocasio-Cortez	Y	Y	Y	Y	Y	Y
15 Serrano	?	?	?	?	?	?
16 Engel	Y	Y	Y	Y	Y	Y
17 Lowey	Y	Y	Y	Y	Y	Y
18 Maloney, S.P.	Y	Y	Y	Y	Y	Y
19 Delgado	Y	Y	Y	Y	Y	Y
20 Tonko	Y	Y	Y	Y	Y	Y
21 **Stefanik**	Y	Y	N	N	Y	Y
22 Brindisi	Y	Y	Y	Y	Y	Y
23 **Reed**	Y	Y	N	N	Y	Y
24 **Katko**	Y	Y	N	N	Y	Y
25 Morelle	Y	Y	Y	Y	Y	Y
26 Higgins, B.	Y	Y	Y	Y	Y	Y
27 **Collins, C.**						
NORTH CAROLINA						
1 Butterfield	Y	Y	Y	Y	Y	Y
2 **Holding**	Y	Y	N	N	N	N
3 **Murphy**	Y	Y	N	N	Y	N
4 Price	Y	Y	Y	Y	Y	Y
5 **Foxx**	Y	Y	N	N	Y	N
6 **Walker**	Y	Y	N	N	Y	N
7 **Rouzer**	Y	Y	N	N	N	-

	655	656	657	658	659	660
8 **Hudson**	Y	Y	N	N	Y	N
9 **Bishop**	Y	Y	N	N	N	N
10 **McHenry**	Y	Y	N	N	Y	N
11 **Meadows**	Y	?	N	N	N	N
12 Adams	Y	Y	Y	Y	Y	Y
13 **Budd**	Y	Y	N	N	N	N
NORTH DAKOTA						
AL **Armstrong**	Y	Y	N	N	Y	N
OHIO						
1 **Chabot**	Y	Y	N	N	Y	N
2 **Wenstrup**	Y	Y	N	N	N	N
3 Beatty	Y	Y	Y	Y	Y	Y
4 **Jordan**	Y	Y	N	N	N	N
5 **Latta**	Y	Y	N	N	Y	N
6 **Johnson, B.**	Y	Y	N	N	N	N
7 **Gibbs**	Y	Y	N	N	N	N
8 **Davidson**	Y	Y	N	N	N	N
9 Kaptur	Y	Y	Y	Y	Y	Y
10 **Turner**	Y	Y	N	N	Y	N
11 Fudge	Y	Y	Y	Y	Y	Y
12 **Balderson**	Y	Y	N	N	Y	N
13 Ryan	Y	Y	Y	Y	Y	Y
14 **Joyce**	Y	Y	N	N	Y	Y
15 **Stivers**	Y	Y	N	N	Y	N
16 **Gonzalez**	Y	Y	N	N	Y	N
OKLAHOMA						
1 **Hern**	Y	Y	N	N	N	N
2 **Mullin**	Y	Y	N	N	N	N
3 **Lucas**	Y	Y	N	N	Y	N
4 **Cole**	Y	Y	N	N	Y	N
5 Horn	Y	Y	Y	Y	Y	Y
OREGON						
1 Bonamici	Y	Y	Y	Y	Y	Y
2 **Walden**	Y	Y	N	N	Y	N
3 Blumenauer	Y	Y	Y	Y	Y	Y
4 DeFazio	Y	Y	Y	Y	Y	Y
5 Schrader	Y	Y	Y	Y	Y	Y
PENNSYLVANIA						
1 **Fitzpatrick**	Y	Y	N	N	Y	Y
2 Boyle	Y	Y	Y	Y	Y	Y
3 Evans	Y	Y	Y	Y	Y	Y
4 Dean	Y	Y	Y	Y	Y	Y
5 Scanlon	Y	Y	Y	Y	Y	Y
6 Houlahan	Y	Y	Y	Y	Y	Y
7 Wild	Y	Y	Y	Y	Y	Y
8 Cartwright	Y	Y	Y	Y	Y	Y
9 **Meuser**	Y	Y	?	?	?	?
10 **Perry**	Y	Y	N	N	Y	-
11 **Smucker**	Y	Y	N	N	Y	-
12 **Keller**	Y	Y	N	N	Y	?
13 **Joyce**	Y	Y	N	N	N	?
14 **Reschenthaler**	Y	Y	N	N	Y	N
15 **Thompson, G.**	Y	Y	N	N	Y	-
16 **Kelly, M.**	Y	Y	N	N	Y	?
17 Lamb	Y	Y	Y	Y	Y	Y
18 Doyle	Y	Y	Y	Y	Y	Y
RHODE ISLAND						
1 Cicilline	Y	Y	Y	Y	Y	Y
2 Langevin	Y	Y	Y	Y	Y	Y
SOUTH CAROLINA						
1 Cunningham	Y	Y	Y	Y	Y	Y
2 **Wilson, J.**	Y	Y	N	N	Y	N
3 **Duncan**	Y	Y	N	N	N	N
4 **Timmons**	Y	Y	N	N	N	N
5 **Norman**	Y	Y	N	N	N	N
6 Clyburn	?	?	Y	Y	Y	Y
7 **Rice, T.**	Y	Y	N	N	N	N
SOUTH DAKOTA						
AL **Johnson**	Y	Y	N	N	Y	N
TENNESSEE						
1 **Roe**	Y	Y	N	N	Y	N
2 **Burchett**	Y	Y	N	N	N	N
3 **Fleischmann**	Y	Y	N	N	N	N
4 **DesJarlais**	Y	Y	N	N	N	N
5 Cooper	Y	Y	Y	Y	Y	Y
6 **Rose**	Y	Y	N	N	N	N
7 **Green**	Y	Y	N	N	N	N
8 **Kustoff**	Y	Y	N	N	Y	N
9 Cohen	Y	Y	Y	Y	Y	Y
TEXAS						
1 **Gohmert**	Y	Y	N	N	N	N
2 **Crenshaw**	Y	Y	N	N	N	N
3 **Taylor**	Y	Y	N	N	N	N
4 **Ratcliffe**	Y	Y	N	N	N	N

	655	656	657	658	659	660
5 **Gooden**	?	?	?	?	?	?
6 **Wright**	Y	Y	N	N	N	N
7 Fletcher	Y	Y	Y	Y	Y	Y
8 **Brady**	Y	Y	N	N	N	N
9 Green, A.	Y	Y	Y	Y	Y	Y
10 **McCaul**	Y	Y	N	N	Y	N
11 **Conaway**	Y	Y	N	N	N	N
12 **Granger**	Y	Y	N	N	Y	N
13 **Thornberry**	Y	Y	N	N	N	N
14 **Weber**	Y	Y	N	N	N	N
15 Gonzalez	Y	Y	Y	Y	Y	Y
16 Escobar	Y	Y	Y	Y	Y	Y
17 **Flores**	Y	Y	N	N	N	N
18 Jackson Lee	Y	Y	Y	Y	Y	Y
19 **Arrington**	Y	Y	N	N	N	N
20 Castro	Y	Y	Y	Y	Y	Y
21 **Roy**	Y	Y	N	N	N	N
22 **Olson**	Y	Y	N	N	N	N
23 **Hurd**	Y	Y	N	N	Y	Y
24 **Marchant**	?	?	?	?	?	N
25 **Williams**	Y	Y	N	N	N	N
26 **Burgess**	Y	Y	N	N	N	N
27 **Cloud**	Y	Y	N	N	N	N
28 Cuellar	Y	Y	Y	Y	Y	Y
29 Garcia, S.	Y	Y	Y	Y	Y	Y
30 Johnson, E.B.	Y	Y	Y	Y	Y	Y
31 **Carter, J.**	?	?	?	?	Y	N
32 Allred	Y	Y	Y	Y	Y	Y
33 Veasey	Y	Y	Y	Y	Y	Y
34 Vela	Y	Y	Y	Y	Y	Y
35 Doggett	Y	Y	Y	Y	Y	Y
36 **Babin**	Y	Y	N	N	N	N
UTAH						
1 **Bishop, R.**	Y	Y	N	?	Y	N
2 **Stewart**	?	?	N	N	N	N
3 **Curtis**	Y	Y	N	N	N	N
4 McAdams	Y	Y	Y	Y	Y	N
VERMONT						
AL Welch	Y	Y	Y	Y	Y	Y
VIRGINIA						
1 **Wittman**	Y	Y	N	N	Y	N
2 Luria	Y	Y	Y	Y	Y	Y
3 Scott, R.	Y	Y	Y	Y	Y	Y
4 McEachin	+	+	Y	Y	Y	Y
5 **Riggleman**	Y	Y	N	N	N	N
6 **Cline**	Y	Y	N	N	N	N
7 Spanberger	Y	Y	Y	Y	Y	Y
8 Beyer	Y	Y	Y	Y	Y	Y
9 **Griffith**	Y	Y	N	N	N	N
10 Wexton	Y	Y	Y	Y	Y	Y
11 Connolly	Y	Y	Y	Y	Y	Y
WASHINGTON						
1 DelBene	Y	Y	Y	Y	Y	Y
2 Larsen	Y	Y	Y	Y	Y	Y
3 **Herrera Beutler**	Y	Y	N	N	Y	Y
4 **Newhouse**	Y	Y	N	N	N	N
5 **McMorris Rodgers**	Y	Y	N	N	Y	N
6 Kilmer	Y	Y	Y	Y	Y	Y
7 Jayapal	Y	Y	Y	Y	Y	Y
8 Schrier	Y	Y	Y	Y	Y	Y
9 Smith Adam	Y	Y	Y	Y	?	Y
10 Heck	Y	Y	Y	Y	Y	Y
WEST VIRGINIA						
1 **McKinley**	Y	Y	N	N	Y	N
2 **Mooney**	Y	Y	N	N	N	N
3 **Miller**	Y	Y	N	N	N	N
WISCONSIN						
1 **Steil**	Y	Y	N	N	Y	N
2 Pocan	Y	Y	Y	Y	Y	Y
3 Kind	+	+	Y	Y	Y	Y
4 Moore	Y	Y	Y	Y	Y	?
5 **Sensenbrenner**	Y	Y	-	-	-	N
6 **Grothman**	Y	Y	N	N	N	N
7 **Duffy**						
8 **Gallagher**	Y	Y	N	N	Y	N
WYOMING						
AL **Cheney**	Y	Y	N	N	N	N
DELEGATES						
Radewagen (A.S.)						?
Norton (D.C.)						Y
San Nicolas (Guam)						?
Sablan (N. Marianas)						Y
González-Colón (P.R.)						Y
Plaskett (V.I.)						Y

661. HR729. Coastal Communities and Habitats - Chesapeake Bay Oyster Research. Brown, D-Md., amendment no. 4 that would authorize $2 million annually through fiscal 2025 for the National Oceanic and Atmospheric Administration to award grants to certain entities, including academic researchers and members of the seafood industry, to conduct research on the conservation, restoration, or management of oysters in the Chesapeake Bay. Adopted in Committee of the Whole 235-179: R 13-174; D 221-4; I 1-1. Dec. 10, 2019.

662. HR729. Coastal Communities and Habitats - Algal Bloom Projects. Crist, D-Fla., amendment no. 12 that would add harmful algal blooms to a list of factors negatively impacting coastal waters that may be addressed by projects eligible for Commerce Department grants to states related to coastal climate change adaptation. Adopted in Committee of the Whole 297-121: R 66-120; D 230-0; I 1-1. Dec. 10, 2019.

663. HR729. Coastal Communities and Habitats - Digital Data for Coastal Management. Panetta, D-Calif., amendment no. 14 that would add to the bill a finding stating that partnerships between institutions of higher education and federal agencies help ensure effective communication of digital data focused on coastal management issues. Adopted in Committee of the Whole 389-29: R 159-28; D 229-0; I 1-1. Dec. 10, 2019.

664. HR729. Coastal Communities and Habitats - Coral Shoreline Projects. Mucarsel-Powell, D-Fla., amendment no. 23 that would add corals to a list of natural elements that may be incorporated in projects eligible for a grant program established by the bill to support climate-resilient living shoreline projects. Adopted in Committee of the Whole 285-134: R 57-130; D 227-3; I 1-1. Dec. 10, 2019.

665. HR729. Coastal Communities and Habitats - Military Installation Climate Resiliency. Luria, D-Va., amendment no. 26 that would require the National Oceanic and Atmospheric Administration to consider the potential of a project to support the resiliency or community infrastructure supportive of a military installation, when evaluating projects for a grant program established by the bill to support climate-resilient living shoreline projects. Adopted in Committee of the Whole 368-51: R 137-50; D 230-0; I 1-1. Dec. 10, 2019.

666. HR729. Coastal Communities and Habitats - Modify Marine Mammal Protections. Johnson, R-La., amendment no. 29 that would modify provisions related to National Oceanic and Atmospheric Administration authorization of activities that may result in the incidental "taking," including killing or harassment, of marine mammals under an exemption from an existing moratorium prohibiting the taking and importing of marine mammals. It would require that conditions imposed under such NOAA authorizations would not result in more than minor changes to or alter the location or design of the authorized activity. It would modify requirements related to applications, approval, and extension for such authorizations. Rejected in Committee of the Whole 160-259: R 160-27; D 0-230; I 0-2. Dec. 10, 2019.

		661	662	663	664	665	666
ALABAMA							
1	**Byrne**	N	N	Y	N	Y	Y
2	**Roby**	N	Y	Y	Y	Y	Y
3	**Rogers, M.**	N	Y	Y	N	N	Y
4	**Aderholt**	?	?	?	?	?	?
5	**Brooks, M.**	N	N	N	N	N	Y
6	**Palmer**	N	Y	Y	N	Y	Y
7	Sewell	Y	Y	Y	Y	Y	N
ALASKA							
AL	**Young**	N	N	Y	N	Y	Y
ARIZONA							
1	O'Halleran	Y	Y	Y	Y	Y	N
2	Kirkpatrick	Y	Y	Y	Y	Y	N
3	Grijalva	Y	Y	Y	Y	Y	N
4	**Gosar**	N	N	N	N	N	Y
5	**Biggs**	N	N	N	N	N	Y
6	**Schweikert**	N	Y	Y	Y	Y	Y
7	Gallego	Y	Y	Y	Y	Y	N
8	**Lesko**	N	N	Y	N	Y	Y
9	Stanton	Y	Y	Y	Y	Y	N
ARKANSAS							
1	**Crawford**	N	N	Y	N	N	Y
2	**Hill, F.**	N	N	Y	N	Y	Y
3	**Womack**	N	N	Y	N	N	Y
4	**Westerman**	N	N	Y	N	Y	Y
CALIFORNIA							
1	**LaMalfa**	N	N	Y	N	Y	Y
2	Huffman	Y	Y	Y	Y	Y	N
3	Garamendi	Y	Y	Y	Y	Y	N
4	**McClintock**	N	N	Y	N	Y	Y
5	Thompson, M.	Y	Y	Y	Y	Y	N
6	Matsui	Y	Y	Y	Y	Y	N
7	Bera	Y	Y	Y	Y	Y	N
8	**Cook**	N	Y	Y	N	Y	Y
9	McNerney	Y	Y	Y	Y	Y	N
10	Harder	Y	Y	Y	Y	Y	N
11	DeSaulnier	Y	Y	Y	Y	Y	N
12	Pelosi						
13	Lee B.	Y	Y	Y	Y	Y	N
14	Speier	Y	Y	Y	Y	Y	N
15	Swalwell	Y	Y	Y	Y	Y	N
16	Costa	Y	Y	Y	Y	Y	N
17	Khanna	Y	Y	Y	Y	Y	N
18	Eshoo	Y	Y	Y	Y	Y	N
19	Lofgren	Y	Y	Y	Y	Y	N
20	Panetta	Y	Y	Y	Y	Y	N
21	Cox	N	Y	Y	N	Y	N
22	**Nunes**	N	N	Y	N	Y	Y
23	**McCarthy**	N	N	Y	N	Y	Y
24	Carbajal	Y	Y	Y	Y	Y	N
25	vacant						
26	Brownley	Y	Y	Y	Y	Y	N
27	Chu	Y	Y	Y	Y	Y	N
28	Schiff	Y	Y	Y	Y	Y	N
29	Cárdenas	Y	Y	Y	Y	Y	N
30	Sherman	Y	Y	Y	Y	Y	N
31	Aguilar	Y	Y	Y	Y	Y	N
32	Napolitano	Y	Y	Y	Y	Y	N
33	Lieu	?	?	?	?	?	?
34	Gomez	Y	Y	Y	Y	Y	N
35	Torres	Y	Y	Y	Y	Y	N
36	Ruiz	Y	Y	Y	Y	Y	N
37	Bass	Y	Y	Y	Y	Y	N
38	Sánchez	Y	Y	Y	Y	Y	N
39	Cisneros	Y	Y	Y	Y	Y	N
40	Roybal-Allard	Y	Y	Y	Y	Y	N
41	Takano	Y	Y	Y	Y	Y	N
42	**Calvert**	N	Y	Y	N	Y	Y
43	Waters	Y	Y	Y	Y	Y	N
44	Barragán	Y	Y	Y	Y	Y	N
45	Porter	N	Y	Y	Y	Y	N
46	Correa	Y	Y	Y	Y	Y	N
47	Lowenthal	Y	Y	Y	Y	Y	N
48	Rouda	Y	Y	Y	Y	Y	N
49	Levin	Y	Y	Y	Y	Y	N
50	**Hunter**	?	?	?	?	?	?
51	Vargas	Y	Y	Y	Y	Y	N
52	Peters	Y	Y	Y	Y	Y	N
53	Davis, S.	Y	Y	Y	Y	Y	N
COLORADO							
1	DeGette	Y	Y	Y	Y	Y	N
2	Neguse	Y	Y	Y	Y	Y	N
3	**Tipton**	N	N	Y	N	Y	Y
4	**Buck**	N	N	N	N	N	Y
5	**Lamborn**	N	N	Y	N	Y	Y
6	Crow	Y	Y	Y	Y	Y	N
7	Perlmutter	Y	Y	Y	Y	Y	N
CONNECTICUT							
1	Larson	Y	Y	Y	Y	Y	N
2	Courtney	Y	Y	Y	Y	Y	N
3	DeLauro	Y	Y	Y	Y	Y	N
4	Himes	Y	Y	Y	Y	Y	N
5	Hayes	Y	Y	Y	Y	Y	N
DELAWARE							
AL	Blunt Rochester	Y	Y	Y	Y	Y	N
FLORIDA							
1	**Gaetz**	N	N	Y	N	N	Y
2	**Dunn**	N	Y	Y	Y	Y	Y
3	**Yoho**	N	N	Y	Y	N	Y
4	**Rutherford**	N	Y	Y	Y	Y	Y
5	Lawson	?	Y	Y	Y	Y	N
6	**Waltz**	N	Y	Y	Y	Y	Y
7	Murphy	Y	Y	Y	Y	Y	N
8	**Posey**	N	Y	Y	Y	Y	Y
9	Soto	Y	Y	Y	Y	Y	N
10	Demings	Y	Y	Y	Y	Y	N
11	**Webster**	N	N	Y	Y	Y	Y
12	**Bilirakis**	N	Y	Y	Y	Y	Y
13	Crist	Y	Y	Y	Y	Y	N
14	Castor	Y	Y	Y	Y	Y	N
15	**Spano**	N	Y	Y	Y	Y	Y
16	**Buchanan**	N	Y	Y	Y	Y	N
17	**Steube**	N	Y	Y	Y	Y	N
18	**Mast**	N	Y	Y	Y	Y	N
19	**Rooney**	?	?	?	?	?	?
20	Hastings	Y	Y	Y	Y	Y	N
21	Frankel	Y	Y	Y	Y	Y	N
22	Deutch	Y	Y	Y	Y	Y	N
23	Wasserman Schultz	?	?	?	?	?	?
24	Wilson, F.	Y	Y	Y	Y	Y	N
25	**Diaz-Balart**	N	Y	Y	Y	Y	N
26	Mucarsel-Powell	Y	Y	Y	Y	Y	N
27	Shalala	Y	Y	?	Y	Y	N
GEORGIA							
1	**Carter, E.L.**	N	N	Y	N	N	N
2	Bishop, S.	Y	Y	Y	Y	Y	N
3	**Ferguson**	N	N	N	N	N	Y
4	Johnson, H.	?	Y	Y	Y	Y	N
5	Lewis John	Y	Y	Y	Y	Y	N
6	McBath	Y	Y	Y	Y	Y	N
7	**Woodall**	N	N	Y	N	Y	N
8	**Scott, A.**	N	N	Y	N	Y	N
9	**Collins, D.**	N	N	N	N	N	Y
10	**Hice**	N	N	N	N	N	Y
11	**Loudermilk**	N	N	N	N	N	Y
12	**Allen**	N	N	N	N	N	Y
13	Scott, D.	Y	Y	Y	Y	Y	N
14	**Graves, T.**	N	N	N	N	N	N
HAWAII							
1	Case	Y	Y	Y	Y	Y	N
2	Gabbard	?	?	?	?	?	?
IDAHO							
1	**Fulcher**	N	N	Y	N	N	N
2	**Simpson**	N	N	Y	Y	Y	Y
ILLINOIS							
1	Rush	+	Y	Y	Y	Y	N
2	Kelly, R.	Y	Y	Y	Y	Y	N
3	Lipinski	Y	Y	Y	Y	Y	N
4	García, J.	Y	Y	Y	Y	Y	N
5	Quigley	Y	Y	Y	Y	Y	N
6	Casten	Y	Y	Y	Y	Y	N
7	Davis, D.	Y	Y	Y	Y	Y	N
8	Krishnamoorthi	Y	Y	Y	Y	Y	N
9	Schakowsky	Y	Y	Y	Y	Y	N
10	Schneider	Y	Y	Y	Y	Y	N
11	Foster	Y	Y	Y	Y	Y	N

		661	662	663	664	665	666
12	**Bost**	N	N	Y	N	Y	Y
13	**Davis, R.**	N	Y	Y	Y	Y	Y
14	Underwood	Y	Y	Y	Y	Y	N
15	**Shimkus**	N	N	Y	N	Y	Y
16	**Kinzinger**	N	N	Y	Y	Y	Y
17	Bustos	Y	Y	Y	Y	Y	N
18	**LaHood**	N	Y	Y	N	N	Y
INDIANA							
1	Visclosky	Y	Y	Y	Y	Y	N
2	**Walorski**	N	Y	Y	N	Y	Y
3	**Banks**	N	N	Y	N	Y	Y
4	**Baird**	N	Y	Y	N	Y	Y
5	**Brooks, S.**	N	Y	Y	Y	Y	N
6	**Pence**	N	N	Y	N	Y	Y
7	Carson	Y	Y	Y	Y	Y	N
8	**Bucshon**	N	N	Y	N	Y	Y
9	**Hollingsworth**	N	Y	Y	Y	Y	Y
IOWA							
1	Finkenauer	Y	Y	Y	Y	Y	N
2	Loebsack	Y	Y	Y	Y	Y	N
3	Axne	Y	Y	Y	Y	Y	N
4	**King, S.**	Y	N	N	N	N	Y
KANSAS							
1	**Marshall**	N	N	Y	N	Y	N
2	**Watkins**	N	N	Y	N	Y	Y
3	Davids	Y	Y	Y	Y	Y	N
4	**Estes**	N	N	Y	N	N	Y
KENTUCKY							
1	**Comer**	N	N	Y	N	N	Y
2	**Guthrie**	N	N	Y	N	Y	Y
3	Yarmuth	Y	Y	Y	Y	Y	N
4	**Massie**	N	N	N	N	N	Y
5	**Rogers, H.**	N	Y	Y	Y	Y	Y
6	**Barr**	N	N	Y	N	Y	Y
LOUISIANA							
1	**Scalise**	N	N	Y	N	Y	Y
2	Richmond	Y	Y	Y	Y	Y	N
3	**Higgins, C.**	N	Y	Y	N	N	Y
4	**Johnson, M.**	N	N	Y	N	Y	Y
5	**Abraham**	N	N	N	N	N	Y
6	**Graves, G.**	Y	Y	Y	N	Y	Y
MAINE							
1	Pingree	Y	Y	Y	Y	Y	N
2	Golden	Y	Y	Y	Y	Y	N
MARYLAND							
1	**Harris**	Y	Y	N	N	N	Y
2	Ruppersberger	Y	Y	Y	Y	Y	N
3	Sarbanes	Y	Y	Y	Y	Y	N
4	Brown, A.	Y	Y	Y	Y	Y	N
5	Hoyer	Y	Y	Y	Y	Y	N
6	Trone	Y	Y	Y	Y	Y	N
7	vacant	|	|	|	|	|	|
8	Raskin	Y	Y	Y	Y	Y	N
MASSACHUSETTS							
1	Neal	Y	Y	Y	Y	Y	N
2	McGovern	Y	Y	Y	Y	Y	N
3	Trahan	Y	Y	Y	Y	Y	N
4	Kennedy	Y	Y	Y	Y	Y	N
5	Clark	Y	Y	Y	Y	Y	N
6	Moulton	Y	Y	Y	Y	Y	N
7	Pressley	Y	Y	Y	Y	Y	N
8	Lynch	Y	Y	Y	Y	Y	N
9	Keating	Y	Y	Y	Y	Y	N
MICHIGAN							
1	**Bergman**	N	Y	Y	Y	Y	Y
2	**Huizenga**	N	Y	Y	Y	Y	Y
3	*Amash*	N	N	N	N	N	N
4	**Moolenaar**	N	Y	Y	N	Y	Y
5	Kildee	Y	Y	Y	Y	Y	N
6	**Upton**	Y	Y	Y	Y	Y	N
7	**Walberg**	N	Y	Y	Y	Y	Y
8	Slotkin	Y	Y	Y	Y	Y	N
9	Levin	Y	Y	Y	Y	Y	N
10	**Mitchell**	N	Y	Y	Y	Y	Y
11	Stevens	Y	Y	Y	Y	Y	N
12	Dingell	Y	Y	Y	Y	Y	N
13	Tlaib	Y	Y	Y	Y	Y	N
14	Lawrence	Y	Y	Y	Y	Y	N
MINNESOTA							
1	**Hagedorn**	N	N	Y	N	Y	Y
2	Craig	Y	Y	Y	Y	Y	N
3	Phillips	Y	Y	Y	Y	Y	N
4	McCollum	Y	Y	Y	Y	Y	N
5	Omar	Y	Y	Y	Y	Y	N

		661	662	663	664	665	666
6	**Emmer**	N	N	Y	N	Y	Y
7	Peterson	N	Y	Y	N	Y	N
8	**Stauber**	N	Y	Y	Y	Y	Y
MISSISSIPPI							
1	**Kelly, T.**	N	N	Y	N	Y	Y
2	Thompson, B.	Y	Y	Y	Y	Y	N
3	**Guest**	N	N	Y	N	Y	Y
4	**Palazzo**	N	N	Y	N	Y	Y
MISSOURI							
1	Clay	Y	Y	Y	Y	Y	N
2	**Wagner**	N	Y	Y	Y	Y	Y
3	**Luetkemeyer**	N	N	Y	N	Y	Y
4	**Hartzler**	N	N	Y	N	Y	Y
5	Cleaver	Y	Y	Y	Y	Y	N
6	**Graves, S.**	N	N	Y	N	Y	Y
7	**Long**	N	N	N	N	N	Y
8	**Smith, J.**	N	N	N	N	N	Y
MONTANA							
AL	**Gianforte**	N	N	Y	N	Y	Y
NEBRASKA							
1	**Fortenberry**	N	Y	Y	Y	Y	N
2	**Bacon**	N	Y	Y	Y	Y	N
3	**Smith, Adrian**	N	N	Y	N	Y	Y
NEVADA							
1	Titus	Y	Y	Y	Y	Y	N
2	**Amodei**	N	Y	Y	N	Y	Y
3	Lee	Y	Y	Y	Y	Y	N
4	Horsford	Y	Y	Y	Y	Y	N
NEW HAMPSHIRE							
1	Pappas	Y	Y	Y	Y	Y	N
2	Kuster	Y	Y	Y	Y	Y	N
NEW JERSEY							
1	Norcross	Y	Y	Y	Y	Y	N
2	Van Drew	Y	Y	Y	Y	Y	N
3	Kim	Y	Y	Y	Y	Y	N
4	**Smith, C.**	Y	Y	Y	Y	Y	N
5	Gottheimer	Y	Y	Y	Y	Y	N
6	Pallone	Y	Y	Y	Y	Y	N
7	Malinowski	Y	Y	Y	Y	Y	N
8	Sires	Y	Y	Y	Y	Y	N
9	Pascrell	Y	Y	Y	Y	Y	N
10	Payne	Y	Y	Y	Y	Y	N
11	Sherrill	Y	Y	Y	Y	Y	N
12	Watson Coleman	Y	Y	Y	Y	Y	N
NEW MEXICO							
1	Haaland	Y	Y	Y	Y	Y	N
2	Torres Small	Y	Y	Y	Y	Y	N
3	Luján	Y	Y	Y	Y	Y	N
NEW YORK							
1	**Zeldin**	N	Y	Y	N	Y	Y
2	**King, P.**	Y	Y	Y	Y	Y	N
3	Suozzi	Y	Y	Y	Y	Y	N
4	Rice, K.	Y	Y	Y	Y	Y	N
5	Meeks	Y	Y	Y	Y	Y	N
6	Meng	Y	Y	Y	Y	Y	N
7	Velázquez	Y	Y	Y	Y	Y	N
8	Jeffries	Y	Y	Y	Y	Y	N
9	Clarke	?	Y	Y	Y	Y	N
10	Nadler	Y	Y	Y	Y	Y	N
11	Rose	Y	Y	Y	Y	Y	N
12	Maloney, C.	Y	Y	Y	Y	Y	N
13	Espaillat	Y	Y	Y	Y	Y	N
14	Ocasio-Cortez	Y	Y	Y	Y	Y	N
15	Serrano	?	?	?	?	?	?
16	Engel	Y	Y	Y	Y	Y	N
17	Lowey	Y	Y	Y	Y	Y	N
18	Maloney, S.P.	Y	Y	Y	Y	Y	N
19	Delgado	Y	Y	Y	Y	Y	N
20	Tonko	Y	Y	Y	Y	Y	N
21	**Stefanik**	Y	Y	Y	Y	Y	N
22	Brindisi	Y	Y	Y	Y	Y	N
23	**Reed**	N	Y	Y	Y	Y	Y
24	**Katko**	Y	Y	Y	Y	Y	N
25	Morelle	Y	Y	Y	Y	Y	N
26	Higgins, B.	Y	Y	Y	Y	Y	N
27	**Collins, C.**						
NORTH CAROLINA							
1	Butterfield	Y	Y	Y	Y	Y	N
2	**Holding**	N	N	Y	Y	Y	Y
3	**Murphy**	N	N	Y	Y	Y	N
4	Price	Y	Y	Y	Y	Y	N
5	**Foxx**	N	N	Y	N	Y	Y
6	**Walker**	N	N	Y	N	N	Y
7	**Rouzer**	N	N	Y	Y	Y	Y

		661	662	663	664	665	666
8	**Hudson**	N	N	Y	N	N	Y
9	**Bishop**	N	N	N	N	N	Y
10	**McHenry**	N	N	Y	Y	Y	Y
11	**Meadows**	N	N	Y	N	N	Y
12	Adams	Y	Y	Y	Y	Y	N
13	**Budd**	N	N	Y	N	Y	Y
NORTH DAKOTA							
AL	**Armstrong**	N	N	Y	N	Y	Y
OHIO							
1	**Chabot**	N	N	Y	Y	Y	Y
2	**Wenstrup**	N	N	Y	N	Y	Y
3	Beatty	Y	Y	Y	Y	Y	N
4	**Jordan**	N	N	Y	N	N	Y
5	**Latta**	N	Y	Y	N	Y	Y
6	**Johnson, B.**	N	Y	Y	N	Y	Y
7	**Gibbs**	N	N	Y	N	Y	Y
8	**Davidson**	N	N	Y	N	N	Y
9	Kaptur	Y	Y	Y	Y	Y	N
10	**Turner**	N	Y	Y	Y	Y	N
11	Fudge	Y	Y	Y	Y	Y	N
12	**Balderson**	N	Y	Y	N	Y	Y
13	Ryan	Y	Y	Y	Y	Y	N
14	**Joyce**	N	Y	Y	Y	Y	N
15	**Stivers**	N	Y	Y	N	Y	Y
16	**Gonzalez**	N	Y	Y	N	Y	Y
OKLAHOMA							
1	**Hern**	N	Y	Y	N	Y	Y
2	**Mullin**	Y	Y	Y	Y	Y	Y
3	**Lucas**	N	Y	Y	Y	Y	Y
4	**Cole**	N	Y	Y	Y	Y	Y
5	Horn	Y	Y	Y	Y	Y	N
OREGON							
1	Bonamici	Y	Y	Y	Y	Y	N
2	**Walden**	N	Y	Y	N	Y	Y
3	Blumenauer	Y	Y	Y	Y	Y	N
4	DeFazio	Y	Y	Y	Y	Y	N
5	Schrader	Y	Y	Y	Y	Y	N
PENNSYLVANIA							
1	**Fitzpatrick**	Y	Y	Y	Y	Y	N
2	Boyle	Y	Y	Y	Y	Y	N
3	Evans	Y	Y	Y	Y	Y	N
4	Dean	Y	Y	Y	Y	Y	N
5	Scanlon	Y	Y	Y	Y	Y	N
6	Houlahan	Y	Y	Y	Y	Y	N
7	Wild	Y	Y	Y	Y	Y	N
8	Cartwright	Y	Y	Y	Y	Y	N
9	**Meuser**	?	?	?	?	?	?
10	**Perry**	-	-	-	-	-	+
11	**Smucker**	-	-	+	-	+	+
12	**Keller**	?	?	?	?	?	?
13	**Joyce**	?	?	?	?	?	?
14	**Reschenthaler**	N	N	Y	N	Y	Y
15	**Thompson, G.**	-	-	+	-	+	+
16	**Kelly, M.**	?	?	?	?	?	?
17	Lamb	Y	Y	Y	Y	Y	N
18	Doyle	Y	Y	Y	Y	Y	N
RHODE ISLAND							
1	Cicilline	Y	Y	Y	Y	Y	N
2	Langevin	Y	Y	Y	Y	Y	N
SOUTH CAROLINA							
1	Cunningham	Y	Y	Y	Y	Y	N
2	**Wilson, J.**	N	N	Y	N	N	Y
3	**Duncan**	N	N	N	N	N	Y
4	**Timmons**	N	N	Y	N	Y	N
5	**Norman**	N	N	N	N	N	N
6	Clyburn	Y	Y	Y	Y	Y	N
7	**Rice, T.**	N	N	Y	N	N	Y
SOUTH DAKOTA							
AL	**Johnson**	N	N	Y	Y	Y	Y
TENNESSEE							
1	**Roe**	N	N	Y	N	Y	Y
2	**Burchett**	N	N	Y	N	N	Y
3	**Fleischmann**	N	N	Y	N	Y	Y
4	**DesJarlais**	N	N	Y	N	Y	Y
5	Cooper	Y	Y	Y	Y	Y	N
6	**Rose**	N	N	Y	N	Y	Y
7	**Green**	N	N	Y	N	Y	Y
8	**Kustoff**	N	N	Y	N	Y	Y
9	Cohen	Y	Y	Y	Y	Y	N
TEXAS							
1	**Gohmert**	N	N	N	N	N	Y
2	**Crenshaw**	N	N	Y	N	Y	Y
3	**Taylor**	N	N	Y	N	Y	Y
4	**Ratcliffe**	N	N	Y	N	Y	Y

		661	662	663	664	665	666
5	**Gooden**	?	?	?	?	?	?
6	**Wright**	N	N	N	N	N	Y
7	Fletcher	Y	Y	Y	Y	Y	N
8	**Brady**	N	N	N	N	N	Y
9	Green, A.	Y	Y	Y	Y	Y	N
10	**McCaul**	N	Y	Y	Y	Y	N
11	**Conaway**	N	N	Y	N	Y	Y
12	**Granger**	N	N	Y	Y	Y	Y
13	**Thornberry**	N	N	Y	N	Y	Y
14	**Weber**	N	N	N	N	N	Y
15	Gonzalez	Y	Y	Y	Y	Y	N
16	Escobar	Y	Y	Y	Y	Y	N
17	**Flores**	N	N	N	N	N	Y
18	Jackson Lee	Y	Y	Y	Y	Y	N
19	**Arrington**	N	N	Y	N	Y	Y
20	Castro	Y	Y	Y	Y	Y	N
21	**Roy**	N	N	N	N	N	Y
22	**Olson**	N	N	Y	N	N	Y
23	**Hurd**	N	Y	Y	Y	Y	Y
24	**Marchant**	N	N	Y	N	Y	Y
25	**Williams**	N	N	Y	N	Y	Y
26	**Burgess**	N	N	N	N	Y	Y
27	**Cloud**	N	N	Y	N	N	Y
28	Cuellar	Y	Y	Y	Y	Y	N
29	Garcia, S.	Y	Y	Y	Y	Y	N
30	Johnson, E.B.	Y	Y	Y	Y	Y	N
31	**Carter, J.**	N	N	N	N	Y	Y
32	Allred	Y	Y	Y	Y	Y	N
33	Veasey	Y	Y	Y	Y	Y	N
34	Vela	Y	Y	Y	Y	Y	N
35	Doggett	Y	Y	Y	Y	Y	N
36	**Babin**	N	N	N	N	N	Y
UTAH							
1	**Bishop, R.**	N	N	Y	N	Y	Y
2	**Stewart**	N	N	Y	N	Y	Y
3	**Curtis**	N	N	Y	N	Y	Y
4	McAdams	N	Y	Y	N	Y	N
VERMONT							
AL	Welch	Y	Y	Y	Y	Y	N
VIRGINIA							
1	**Wittman**	Y	N	Y	Y	Y	Y
2	Luria	Y	Y	Y	Y	Y	N
3	Scott, R.	Y	Y	Y	Y	Y	N
4	McEachin	Y	Y	Y	Y	Y	N
5	**Riggleman**	N	Y	Y	Y	Y	Y
6	**Cline**	N	N	N	N	N	Y
7	Spanberger	Y	Y	Y	Y	Y	N
8	Beyer	Y	Y	Y	Y	Y	N
9	**Griffith**	N	N	N	N	N	Y
10	Wexton	Y	Y	Y	Y	Y	N
11	Connolly	Y	Y	Y	Y	Y	N
WASHINGTON							
1	DelBene	Y	Y	Y	Y	Y	N
2	Larsen	Y	Y	Y	Y	Y	N
3	**Herrera Beutler**	N	Y	Y	Y	Y	Y
4	**Newhouse**	N	Y	Y	Y	Y	Y
5	**McMorris Rodgers**	N	?	Y	Y	Y	Y
6	Kilmer	Y	Y	Y	Y	Y	N
7	Jayapal	Y	Y	Y	Y	Y	N
8	Schrier	Y	Y	Y	Y	Y	N
9	Smith Adam	Y	Y	Y	Y	Y	N
10	Heck	Y	Y	Y	Y	Y	N
WEST VIRGINIA							
1	**McKinley**	N	N	Y	N	Y	Y
2	**Mooney**	N	N	Y	N	N	Y
3	**Miller**	N	N	Y	N	Y	Y
WISCONSIN							
1	**Steil**	N	Y	Y	Y	Y	Y
2	Pocan	Y	Y	Y	Y	Y	N
3	Kind	Y	Y	Y	Y	Y	N
4	Moore	Y	Y	Y	Y	Y	N
5	**Sensenbrenner**	N	N	Y	N	Y	Y
6	**Grothman**	N	N	Y	N	N	Y
7	**Duffy**						
8	**Gallagher**	N	Y	Y	N	Y	Y
WYOMING							
AL	**Cheney**	N	N	Y	N	Y	Y
DELEGATES							
	Radewagen (A.S.)	?	?	?	?	?	?
	Norton (D.C.)	Y	Y	Y	Y	Y	N
	San Nicolas (Guam)	?	?	?	?	?	?
	Sablan (N. Marianas)	Y	Y	Y	Y	Y	N
	González-Colón (P.R.)	Y	Y	Y	Y	Y	Y
	Plaskett (V.I.)	Y	Y	Y	Y	Y	N

667. HR729. Coastal Communities and Habitats - Passage. Passage of the bill, as amended, that would authorize or reauthorize a number of Commerce and Interior department programs and activities related to coastal community development and climate change adaptation. Specifically, it would authorize, in new Commerce Department grant funding, grants to states to implement coastal climate change preparedness and response plans; $50 million annually through fiscal 2025 for climate-resilient "living shoreline" projects using natural materials and systems to protect coastal communities and habitats; $12 million annually through fiscal 2024 for "working waterfronts" projects to improve public access to coastal waters for business and recreation; and $5 million annually for preservation and restoration of Native American tribal coastal lands. It would reauthorize a National Oceanic and Atmospheric Administration grant program for colleges and other institutions to conduct research related to coastal and Great Lake science, conservation, and management; it would authorize $87.5 million for the program in fiscal 2020 and amounts increasing annually through fiscal 2025, and authorize an additional $6 million annually through fiscal 2025 for university research on certain issues related to coastal habitats, including control of aquatic nonnative species and harmful algal bloom prevention. It would reauthorize $47.5 million annually through fiscal 2024 for operations of the Integrated Ocean Observing System, through which NOAA disseminates data on marine areas. It would reauthorize the NOAA digital coast partnership program, a collection of web-based visualization and predictive tools and resources to assist with management of coastal communities. Passed 262-151: R 34-150; D 228-0; I 0-1. Dec. 10, 2019.

668. HR3, HR5038, S1790. Agricultural Workers; Fiscal 2020 Defense Authorization; Drug Price Negotiation - Previous Question. Shalala, D-Fla., motion to order the previous question (thus ending debate and possibility of amendment) on the rule (H Res 758) that would provide for consideration of the Farm Workforce Modernization Act (HR 5038); the conference report to accompany the fiscal 2020 National Defense Authorization Act (S 1790); and the Elijah E. Cummings Lower Drug Costs Now Act (HR 3). Motion agreed to 227-189: R 1-188; D 226-0; I 0-1. Dec. 11, 2019.

669. HR3, S1790, HR5038. Agricultural Workers; Fiscal 2020 Defense Authorization; Drug Price Negotiation - Rule. Adoption of the rule (H Res 758) that would provide for consideration of the Farm Workforce Modernization Act (HR 5038); the conference report to accompany the fiscal 2020 National Defense Authorization Act (S 1790); and the Elijah E. Cummings Lower Drug Costs Now Act (HR 3). The rule would provide for automatic adoption of a Nadler, D-N.Y., manager's amendment to HR 5038 that would decrease from 2,500 to 500 the number of H-2A non-immigrant visas available for sheep and goat herding per fiscal year. The rule would also provide for floor consideration of 12 amendments to HR 3 and provide for automatic adoption of the Pallone, D-N.J., manager's amendment to the bill. The Pallone manager's amendment to HR 3 would require the Labor Department, in consultation with the Health and Human Services and Treasury departments, to issue regulations to implement models related to agreement processes and enforcement mechanisms for inflation rebates by prescription drug manufacturers, if the department determines that a sufficient number of prescription drug prices have increased and that such models are feasible, not later than Dec. 31, 2022. The amendment would also make technical corrections and adjust effective dates for several provisions in the bill. Adopted 222-190: R 1-184; D 221-5; I 0-1. Dec. 11, 2019.

670. HR729. Coastal Communities and Habitats - Motion to Table. McCollum, D-Minn., motion to table (kill) the Himes, D-Conn., motion to reconsider the vote by which the House passed, 262-151, the Coastal and Great Lakes Communities Enhancement Act (HR 729) on Tuesday, Dec. 10, 2019. Motion agreed to 229-192: R 1-192; D 227-0; I 1-0. Dec. 11, 2019.

671. S1790, HRES758, HR3, HR5038. Agricultural Workers; Fiscal 2020 Defense Authorization; Drug Price Negotiation - Motion to Table. Nadler, D-N.Y., motion to table (kill) the McGovern, D-Mass., motion to reconsider the vote by which the House adopted, 222-190, the rule (H Res 758) on Wednesday, Dec. 11, 2019. Motion agreed to 196-170: R 0-170; D 195-0; I 1-0. Dec. 11, 2019.

672. S1790. Fiscal 2020 Defense Authorization - Conference Report. Adoption of the conference report to accompany the bill that would authorize, in total, $738 billion in discretionary defense spending, including $256.7 billion for Defense Department operations and maintenance, including operations in Afghanistan and Syria, $143 billion for weapons and other procurement, and $188 billion for personnel-related expenses. Within the total, the bill would authorize $71.5 billion for overseas contingency operations not subject to discretionary spending caps. The bill would authorize $23.1 billion for Energy Department defense-related activities, including for nuclear weapon programs and environmental restoration activities; $33 billion for the Defense health program; $11.8 billion for military construction, family housing, and base realignment and closure activities; and approximately $11 billion for missile defense programs. Adopted (thus sent to the Senate) 377-48: R 189-6; D 188-41; I 0-1. *Note: A "yea" was a vote in support of the president's position.* Dec. 11, 2019.

	667	668	669	670	671	672
ALABAMA						
1 Byrne	N	N	N	N	N	Y
2 Roby	N	N	N	N	N	Y
3 Rogers, M.	N	N	N	N	N	Y
4 Aderholt	?	?	?	?	?	Y
5 Brooks, M.	N	N	N	N	N	Y
6 Palmer	N	N	N	N	N	Y
7 Sewell	Y	Y	Y	Y	?	Y
ALASKA						
AL Young	Y	N	N	N	N	Y
ARIZONA						
1 O'Halleran	Y	Y	Y	?	?	Y
2 Kirkpatrick	Y	Y	Y	Y	Y	Y
3 Grijalva	Y	Y	Y	Y	Y	N
4 Gosar	N	?	N	N	N	Y
5 Biggs	N	N	N	N	N	Y
6 Schweikert	N	N	N	N	N	Y
7 Gallego	Y	Y	Y	Y	Y	Y
8 Lesko	N	N	N	N	?	Y
9 Stanton	Y	Y	Y	Y	?	Y
ARKANSAS						
1 Crawford	N	N	N	N	N	Y
2 Hill, F.	N	N	?	N	N	Y
3 Womack	N	N	N	N	N	Y
4 Westerman	N	N	N	N	N	Y
CALIFORNIA						
1 LaMalfa	N	?	?	N	N	Y
2 Huffman	Y	Y	Y	Y	?	N
3 Garamendi	Y	Y	Y	Y	Y	Y
4 McClintock	N	N	N	N	N	N
5 Thompson, M.	Y	Y	Y	Y	Y	Y
6 Matsui	Y	Y	Y	Y	Y	Y
7 Bera	Y	Y	Y	Y	Y	Y
8 Cook	N	N	N	N	N	Y
9 McNerney	Y	Y	Y	Y	Y	Y
10 Harder	Y	Y	Y	Y	?	Y
11 DeSaulnier	Y	Y	Y	Y	Y	N
12 Pelosi						
13 Lee B.	Y	Y	Y	Y	Y	N
14 Speier	Y	Y	Y	Y	Y	Y
15 Swalwell	Y	Y	Y	Y	Y	Y
16 Costa	Y	Y	Y	Y	Y	Y
17 Khanna	Y	Y	N	Y	N	N
18 Eshoo	Y	Y	Y	Y	Y	Y
19 Lofgren	Y	Y	Y	Y	Y	Y
20 Panetta	Y	Y	Y	Y	Y	Y
21 Cox	Y	Y	Y	Y	Y	Y
22 Nunes	N	N	N	N	?	Y
23 McCarthy	N	N	N	N	N	Y
24 Carbajal	Y	Y	Y	Y	Y	Y
25 vacant						
26 Brownley	Y	Y	Y	Y	?	Y
27 Chu	Y	Y	Y	Y	Y	N
28 Schiff	Y	Y	Y	Y	Y	Y
29 Cárdenas	Y	Y	Y	Y	Y	Y
30 Sherman	Y	Y	Y	Y	Y	Y
31 Aguilar	Y	Y	Y	Y	Y	Y
32 Napolitano	Y	Y	Y	Y	Y	N
33 Lieu	?	?	?	?	?	?
34 Gomez	Y	Y	Y	Y	+	Y
35 Torres	Y	Y	Y	Y	Y	Y
36 Ruiz	Y	Y	Y	Y	Y	Y
37 Bass	Y	Y	Y	Y	?	N
38 Sánchez	Y	Y	Y	Y	Y	Y
39 Cisneros	Y	Y	Y	Y	Y	Y
40 Roybal-Allard	Y	Y	Y	Y	Y	Y
41 Takano	Y	Y	Y	Y	Y	Y
42 Calvert	N	N	N	N	N	Y
43 Waters	Y	Y	Y	Y	Y	Y
44 Barragán	Y	+	+	+	+	+
45 Porter	Y	?	Y	Y	Y	Y
46 Correa	Y	Y	Y	Y	?	Y
47 Lowenthal	Y	Y	Y	Y	?	N
48 Rouda	Y	Y	Y	Y	Y	Y
49 Levin	Y	Y	Y	Y	Y	Y
50 Hunter	?	?	?	?	?	?
51 Vargas	Y	Y	Y	Y	Y	Y
52 Peters	Y	N	Y	Y	Y	Y

	667	668	669	670	671	672
53 Davis, S.	Y	Y	Y	Y	Y	Y
COLORADO						
1 DeGette	Y	Y	Y	Y	Y	N
2 Neguse	Y	Y	Y	Y	Y	N
3 Tipton	N	N	N	N	?	Y
4 Buck	N	N	N	N	N	N
5 Lamborn	N	N	N	N	N	Y
6 Crow	Y	Y	Y	Y	?	Y
7 Perlmutter	Y	Y	Y	Y	Y	Y
CONNECTICUT						
1 Larson	Y	Y	Y	Y	Y	Y
2 Courtney	Y	Y	Y	Y	Y	Y
3 DeLauro	Y	Y	Y	Y	Y	Y
4 Himes	Y	Y	Y	Y	Y	Y
5 Hayes	Y	Y	Y	Y	Y	Y
DELAWARE						
AL Blunt Rochester	Y	Y	Y	Y	Y	Y
FLORIDA						
1 Gaetz	Y	N	N	N	?	Y
2 Dunn	N	N	N	N	N	Y
3 Yoho	N	N	N	N	N	Y
4 Rutherford	N	?	N	N	N	Y
5 Lawson	Y	Y	Y	Y	Y	Y
6 Waltz	Y	N	N	N	N	Y
7 Murphy	Y	Y	Y	Y	Y	Y
8 Posey	N	N	N	N	N	Y
9 Soto	Y	Y	Y	Y	Y	Y
10 Demings	Y	Y	Y	Y	Y	Y
11 Webster	N	N	N	N	N	Y
12 Bilirakis	N	N	N	N	N	Y
13 Crist	Y	Y	Y	Y	Y	Y
14 Castor	Y	Y	Y	Y	Y	Y
15 Spano	N	N	N	N	N	Y
16 Buchanan	Y	N	N	N	N	Y
17 Steube	Y	N	N	N	?	Y
18 Mast	N	N	N	N	N	Y
19 Rooney	?	?	?	?	?	?
20 Hastings	Y	Y	Y	Y	Y	Y
21 Frankel	Y	Y	Y	Y	Y	Y
22 Deutch	Y	Y	Y	Y	Y	Y
23 Wasserman Schultz	?	Y	Y	Y	Y	Y
24 Wilson, F.	Y	Y	Y	Y	Y	Y
25 Diaz-Balart	Y	N	N	N	N	Y
26 Mucarsel-Powell	Y	Y	Y	Y	?	Y
27 Shalala	Y	Y	Y	Y	Y	Y
GEORGIA						
1 Carter, E.L.	N	N	N	N	N	Y
2 Bishop, S.	Y	Y	Y	Y	Y	Y
3 Ferguson	N	N	N	N	N	Y
4 Johnson, H.	Y	Y	Y	Y	Y	Y
5 Lewis John	Y	Y	Y	Y	Y	Y
6 McBath	Y	Y	Y	Y	Y	Y
7 Woodall	N	N	N	N	?	Y
8 Scott, A.	N	N	N	N	N	Y
9 Collins, D.	N	N	N	N	?	Y
10 Hice	N	N	N	N	N	Y
11 Loudermilk	N	N	N	N	N	Y
12 Allen	?	N	N	N	N	Y
13 Scott, D.	Y	Y	Y	Y	?	Y
14 Graves, T.	N	N	N	N	N	Y
HAWAII						
1 Case	Y	Y	Y	Y	?	Y
2 Gabbard	?	?	?	?	?	N
IDAHO						
1 Fulcher	N	N	N	N	N	Y
2 Simpson	N	Y	N	N	N	Y
ILLINOIS						
1 Rush	Y	Y	Y	Y	Y	Y
2 Kelly, R.	Y	Y	Y	Y	?	Y
3 Lipinski	Y	Y	Y	Y	Y	Y
4 García, J.	Y	Y	Y	Y	Y	N
5 Quigley	Y	Y	Y	Y	Y	Y
6 Casten	Y	Y	Y	Y	Y	Y
7 Davis, D.	Y	Y	Y	Y	Y	N
8 Krishnamoorthi	Y	Y	Y	Y	Y	Y
9 Schakowsky	Y	Y	Y	Y	Y	N
10 Schneider	Y	Y	Y	Y	Y	Y
11 Foster	Y	Y	Y	Y	Y	Y

	667	668	669	670	671	672
12 **Bost**	N	N	N	N	?	Y
13 **Davis, R.**	N	N	N	N	N	Y
14 Underwood	Y	Y	Y	Y	Y	Y
15 **Shimkus**	N	N	N	N	N	Y
16 **Kinzinger**	N	N	N	N	N	Y
17 Bustos	Y	Y	Y	Y	Y	Y
18 **LaHood**	N	N	N	N	N	Y
INDIANA						
1 Visclosky	Y	Y	Y	Y	Y	Y
2 **Walorski**	Y	N	N	N	N	Y
3 **Banks**	N	N	N	N	N	Y
4 **Baird**	N	N	N	N	N	Y
5 **Brooks, S.**	Y	N	N	N	N	Y
6 **Pence**	N	N	N	N	N	Y
7 Carson	Y	Y	?	Y	Y	Y
8 **Bucshon**	N	N	N	N	N	Y
9 **Hollingsworth**	N	N	N	N	N	Y
IOWA						
1 Finkenauer	Y	Y	Y	Y	Y	Y
2 Loebsack	Y	Y	Y	Y	Y	Y
3 Axne	Y	Y	Y	Y	Y	Y
4 **King, S.**	N	N	?	N	N	Y
KANSAS						
1 **Marshall**	N	N	N	N	N	Y
2 **Watkins**	N	N	N	N	N	Y
3 Davids	Y	Y	Y	Y	Y	Y
4 **Estes**	N	N	N	N	-	Y
KENTUCKY						
1 **Comer**	N	N	N	N	N	Y
2 **Guthrie**	N	N	N	N	N	Y
3 Yarmuth	Y	Y	Y	Y	Y	Y
4 **Massie**	N	N	N	N	N	N
5 **Rogers, H.**	N	N	N	N	N	Y
6 **Barr**	N	N	N	N	N	Y
LOUISIANA						
1 **Scalise**	N	N	N	N	N	Y
2 Richmond	Y	Y	Y	Y	Y	Y
3 **Higgins, C.**	N	N	N	N	N	Y
4 **Johnson, M.**	N	N	N	N	N	Y
5 **Abraham**	N	N	N	N	N	Y
6 **Graves, G.**	N	N	N	N	N	Y
MAINE						
1 Pingree	Y	Y	Y	Y	Y	Y
2 Golden	Y	Y	Y	Y	Y	Y
MARYLAND						
1 **Harris**	Y	N	N	N	N	Y
2 Ruppersberger	Y	Y	?	Y	Y	Y
3 Sarbanes	Y	Y	Y	Y	?	Y
4 Brown, A.	Y	Y	Y	Y	Y	Y
5 Hoyer	Y	Y	Y	Y	Y	Y
6 Trone	Y	Y	Y	Y	Y	Y
7 vacant	|	|	|	|	|	|
8 Raskin	Y	Y	Y	Y	?	N
MASSACHUSETTS						
1 Neal	Y	Y	Y	Y	?	Y
2 McGovern	Y	Y	Y	Y	Y	N
3 Trahan	Y	Y	Y	Y	Y	Y
4 Kennedy	Y	Y	Y	Y	Y	N
5 Clark	Y	Y	Y	Y	Y	Y
6 Moulton	Y	Y	Y	Y	Y	Y
7 Pressley	Y	Y	Y	Y	Y	N
8 Lynch	Y	Y	Y	Y	Y	Y
9 Keating	Y	Y	Y	Y	Y	Y
MICHIGAN						
1 **Bergman**	Y	N	N	N	N	Y
2 **Huizenga**	Y	N	N	N	N	Y
3 *Amash*	N	N	N	Y	Y	N
4 **Moolenaar**	Y	N	N	N	N	Y
5 Kildee	Y	Y	Y	Y	Y	N
6 **Upton**	Y	N	N	N	N	Y
7 **Walberg**	Y	N	N	N	N	Y
8 Slotkin	Y	Y	Y	Y	Y	Y
9 Levin	Y	Y	Y	Y	Y	N
10 **Mitchell**	Y	N	N	N	N	Y
11 Stevens	Y	Y	Y	Y	Y	Y
12 Dingell	Y	Y	Y	Y	Y	N
13 Tlaib	Y	Y	Y	Y	Y	N
14 Lawrence	Y	Y	Y	Y	Y	Y
MINNESOTA						
1 **Hagedorn**	N	N	N	N	?	Y
2 Craig	Y	Y	Y	Y	Y	Y
3 Phillips	Y	Y	Y	Y	Y	Y
4 McCollum	Y	Y	Y	Y	Y	Y
5 Omar	Y	Y	Y	Y	Y	N

	667	668	669	670	671	672
6 **Emmer**	N	N	N	N	N	Y
7 Peterson	Y	Y	Y	Y	Y	Y
8 **Stauber**	Y	N	N	N	N	Y
MISSISSIPPI						
1 **Kelly, T.**	N	N	N	N	N	Y
2 Thompson, B.	Y	Y	Y	Y	Y	Y
3 **Guest**	N	N	N	N	N	Y
4 **Palazzo**	N	N	N	N	N	Y
MISSOURI						
1 Clay	Y	Y	Y	Y	Y	Y
2 **Wagner**	N	N	N	N	N	Y
3 **Luetkemeyer**	N	N	N	N	N	Y
4 **Hartzler**	N	N	N	N	N	Y
5 Cleaver	Y	Y	Y	Y	Y	Y
6 **Graves, S.**	N	N	N	N	N	Y
7 **Long**	N	N	N	N	N	Y
8 **Smith, J.**	N	N	N	N	N	Y
MONTANA						
AL **Gianforte**	N	N	N	N	N	Y
NEBRASKA						
1 **Fortenberry**	Y	N	N	N	?	Y
2 **Bacon**	N	N	N	N	N	Y
3 **Smith, Adrian**	N	N	N	N	N	Y
NEVADA						
1 Titus	Y	Y	Y	Y	Y	Y
2 **Amodei**	N	N	N	N	N	Y
3 Lee	Y	Y	Y	Y	Y	Y
4 Horsford	Y	Y	Y	Y	Y	Y
NEW HAMPSHIRE						
1 Pappas	Y	Y	Y	Y	?	Y
2 Kuster	Y	Y	Y	Y	Y	Y
NEW JERSEY						
1 Norcross	Y	Y	Y	Y	Y	Y
2 Van Drew	Y	Y	Y	Y	Y	Y
3 Kim	Y	Y	Y	Y	Y	Y
4 **Smith, C.**	Y	N	N	N	N	Y
5 Gottheimer	Y	Y	Y	Y	Y	Y
6 Pallone	Y	Y	Y	Y	Y	Y
7 Malinowski	Y	Y	Y	Y	Y	Y
8 Sires	Y	Y	Y	Y	Y	Y
9 Pascrell	Y	Y	Y	Y	+	Y
10 Payne	Y	Y	Y	Y	Y	Y
11 Sherrill	Y	Y	Y	Y	Y	Y
12 Watson Coleman	Y	Y	Y	Y	Y	N
NEW MEXICO						
1 Haaland	Y	Y	Y	Y	?	Y
2 Torres Small	Y	Y	Y	Y	Y	Y
3 Luján	Y	Y	Y	Y	Y	Y
NEW YORK						
1 **Zeldin**	Y	N	N	N	N	Y
2 **King, P.**	Y	N	N	N	?	Y
3 Suozzi	Y	Y	Y	Y	Y	Y
4 Rice, K.	Y	Y	Y	Y	?	Y
5 Meeks	Y	Y	Y	Y	Y	Y
6 Meng	Y	Y	Y	Y	Y	N
7 Velázquez	Y	Y	Y	Y	Y	N
8 Jeffries	Y	Y	Y	Y	Y	Y
9 Clarke	Y	Y	Y	Y	Y	N
10 Nadler	Y	Y	Y	Y	Y	N
11 Rose	Y	Y	Y	Y	Y	Y
12 Maloney, C.	Y	Y	Y	Y	Y	Y
13 Espaillat	Y	Y	Y	Y	?	N
14 Ocasio-Cortez	Y	Y	N	Y	Y	N
15 Serrano	?	?	?	?	?	?
16 Engel	Y	Y	Y	Y	Y	N
17 Lowey	Y	Y	Y	Y	Y	Y
18 Maloney, S.P.	Y	Y	Y	Y	?	Y
19 Delgado	Y	Y	Y	Y	Y	Y
20 Tonko	Y	Y	Y	Y	Y	N
21 **Stefanik**	Y	N	N	N	N	Y
22 Brindisi	Y	Y	Y	Y	Y	Y
23 **Reed**	Y	N	N	N	N	Y
24 **Katko**	Y	N	N	N	N	Y
25 Morelle	Y	Y	Y	Y	Y	Y
26 Higgins, B.	Y	Y	Y	Y	Y	Y
27 **Collins, C.**						
NORTH CAROLINA						
1 Butterfield	Y	Y	Y	Y	Y	Y
2 **Holding**	N	N	N	N	N	Y
3 **Murphy**	N	N	N	N	N	Y
4 Price	Y	Y	Y	Y	Y	Y
5 **Foxx**	N	N	N	N	N	Y
6 **Walker**	N	?	N	N	N	Y
7 **Rouzer**	N	N	N	N	N	Y

	667	668	669	670	671	672
8 **Hudson**	N	N	N	N	N	Y
9 **Bishop**	N	N	N	N	N	Y
10 **McHenry**	N	N	N	N	N	Y
11 **Meadows**	N	N	N	N	N	Y
12 Adams	Y	Y	Y	Y	Y	Y
13 **Budd**	N	N	N	N	N	Y
NORTH DAKOTA						
AL **Armstrong**	N	N	N	N	N	Y
OHIO						
1 **Chabot**	N	N	N	N	N	Y
2 **Wenstrup**	N	N	N	N	-	Y
3 Beatty	Y	Y	Y	Y	Y	Y
4 **Jordan**	N	N	N	N	N	Y
5 **Latta**	N	N	N	N	N	Y
6 **Johnson, B.**	N	N	N	N	N	Y
7 **Gibbs**	N	N	?	N	N	Y
8 **Davidson**	N	N	N	N	N	Y
9 Kaptur	Y	Y	Y	Y	Y	Y
10 **Turner**	Y	N	N	N	?	Y
11 Fudge	Y	Y	Y	Y	Y	Y
12 **Balderson**	N	N	N	N	N	Y
13 Ryan	Y	Y	Y	Y	Y	Y
14 **Joyce**	Y	N	N	N	N	Y
15 **Stivers**	Y	N	N	N	N	Y
16 **Gonzalez**	Y	N	N	N	?	Y
OKLAHOMA						
1 **Hern**	N	N	N	N	N	Y
2 **Mullin**	N	N	N	N	N	Y
3 **Lucas**	N	N	N	N	N	Y
4 **Cole**	Y	N	N	N	N	Y
5 Horn	Y	Y	Y	Y	Y	Y
OREGON						
1 Bonamici	Y	Y	Y	Y	Y	Y
2 **Walden**	N	N	N	N	N	Y
3 Blumenauer	Y	Y	Y	Y	Y	N
4 DeFazio	Y	Y	Y	Y	Y	N
5 Schrader	Y	Y	Y	Y	?	Y
PENNSYLVANIA						
1 **Fitzpatrick**	Y	N	N	N	N	Y
2 Boyle	Y	Y	Y	Y	Y	Y
3 Evans	Y	Y	Y	Y	Y	Y
4 Dean	Y	Y	Y	Y	Y	Y
5 Scanlon	Y	Y	Y	Y	Y	Y
6 Houlahan	Y	Y	Y	Y	Y	Y
7 Wild	Y	Y	Y	Y	Y	Y
8 Cartwright	Y	Y	Y	Y	Y	Y
9 **Meuser**	?	N	N	N	N	Y
10 **Perry**	-	N	N	N	N	Y
11 **Smucker**	-	N	N	N	N	Y
12 **Keller**	?	N	N	N	N	Y
13 **Joyce**	?	N	-	N	N	Y
14 **Reschenthaler**	N	N	N	N	?	Y
15 **Thompson, G.**	-	N	N	N	N	Y
16 **Kelly, M.**	?	N	N	N	N	Y
17 Lamb	Y	Y	Y	Y	Y	Y
18 Doyle	Y	Y	Y	Y	Y	N
RHODE ISLAND						
1 Cicilline	Y	Y	Y	Y	Y	Y
2 Langevin	Y	Y	Y	Y	?	Y
SOUTH CAROLINA						
1 Cunningham	Y	Y	Y	Y	Y	Y
2 **Wilson, J.**	N	N	N	N	N	Y
3 **Duncan**	N	N	N	N	N	Y
4 **Timmons**	N	N	N	N	N	Y
5 **Norman**	N	-	-	-	-	Y
6 Clyburn	Y	Y	Y	Y	Y	Y
7 **Rice, T.**	N	N	N	N	N	N
SOUTH DAKOTA						
AL **Johnson**	N	N	N	N	N	Y
TENNESSEE						
1 **Roe**	N	N	N	N	N	Y
2 **Burchett**	N	N	N	N	N	Y
3 **Fleischmann**	N	N	N	N	N	Y
4 **DesJarlais**	N	N	N	N	N	Y
5 Cooper	Y	Y	Y	Y	?	Y
6 **Rose**	N	N	N	N	N	Y
7 **Green**	N	N	N	N	?	Y
8 **Kustoff**	N	N	N	N	N	Y
9 Cohen	Y	Y	Y	Y	Y	N
TEXAS						
1 **Gohmert**	N	N	N	N	N	N
2 **Crenshaw**	N	N	N	N	N	Y
3 **Taylor**	N	N	N	N	N	Y
4 **Ratcliffe**	N	N	N	N	N	Y

	667	668	669	670	671	672
5 **Gooden**	?	N	N	N	N	Y
6 **Wright**	N	N	N	N	?	Y
7 Fletcher	Y	Y	Y	Y	Y	Y
8 **Brady**	N	N	N	N	?	Y
9 Green, A.	Y	Y	Y	Y	Y	Y
10 **McCaul**	N	N	N	N	N	Y
11 **Conaway**	N	N	N	N	+	Y
12 **Granger**	N	N	N	N	N	Y
13 **Thornberry**	N	N	N	N	N	Y
14 **Weber**	N	N	N	N	N	Y
15 Gonzalez	Y	Y	Y	Y	Y	Y
16 Escobar	Y	Y	Y	Y	Y	Y
17 **Flores**	N	N	N	N	N	Y
18 Jackson Lee	Y	Y	Y	Y	Y	Y
19 **Arrington**	N	N	N	N	N	Y
20 Castro	Y	Y	Y	Y	Y	Y
21 **Roy**	?	N	N	N	N	Y
22 **Olson**	N	N	N	N	?	Y
23 **Hurd**	Y	N	N	N	N	Y
24 **Marchant**	N	N	N	N	?	Y
25 **Williams**	N	N	N	N	N	Y
26 **Burgess**	N	N	N	N	N	Y
27 **Cloud**	N	N	N	N	N	Y
28 Cuellar	Y	Y	Y	Y	Y	Y
29 Garcia, S.	Y	Y	Y	Y	Y	Y
30 Johnson, E.B.	Y	Y	Y	Y	Y	Y
31 **Carter, J.**	N	N	N	N	N	Y
32 Allred	Y	Y	Y	Y	Y	Y
33 Veasey	Y	Y	Y	Y	Y	Y
34 Vela	Y	Y	Y	Y	Y	Y
35 Doggett	Y	Y	N	Y	?	Y
36 **Babin**	N	N	N	N	N	Y
UTAH						
1 **Bishop, R.**	N	N	N	N	N	Y
2 **Stewart**	N	N	N	N	N	Y
3 **Curtis**	N	N	N	N	N	Y
4 McAdams	Y	Y	N	Y	?	Y
VERMONT						
AL Welch	Y	Y	Y	Y	Y	N
VIRGINIA						
1 **Wittman**	Y	N	N	N	N	Y
2 Luria	Y	Y	Y	Y	Y	Y
3 Scott, R.	Y	Y	Y	Y	Y	Y
4 McEachin	Y	Y	Y	Y	Y	Y
5 **Riggleman**	N	N	N	N	N	Y
6 **Cline**	N	N	N	N	N	Y
7 Spanberger	Y	Y	Y	Y	?	Y
8 Beyer	Y	Y	Y	Y	?	Y
9 **Griffith**	N	N	N	N	N	N
10 Wexton	Y	?	Y	Y	Y	Y
11 Connolly	Y	Y	Y	Y	Y	Y
WASHINGTON						
1 DelBene	Y	Y	Y	Y	?	Y
2 Larsen	Y	Y	Y	Y	Y	Y
3 **Herrera Beutler**	Y	N	N	N	N	Y
4 **Newhouse**	N	?	?	N	N	Y
5 **McMorris Rodgers**	N	N	N	N	N	Y
6 Kilmer	Y	Y	Y	Y	Y	Y
7 Jayapal	Y	Y	Y	Y	Y	N
8 Schrier	Y	Y	Y	Y	Y	Y
9 Smith Adam	Y	Y	Y	Y	?	Y
10 Heck	Y	Y	Y	Y	Y	Y
WEST VIRGINIA						
1 **McKinley**	N	N	N	N	N	Y
2 **Mooney**	N	N	N	N	N	Y
3 **Miller**	N	N	N	N	N	Y
WISCONSIN						
1 **Steil**	N	N	N	N	N	Y
2 Pocan	Y	Y	Y	Y	Y	N
3 Kind	Y	Y	Y	Y	Y	Y
4 Moore	Y	Y	Y	Y	Y	Y
5 **Sensenbrenner**	N	N	N	N	N	Y
6 **Grothman**	N	N	N	N	?	Y
7 **Duffy**						
8 **Gallagher**	N	N	N	N	N	Y
WYOMING						
AL **Cheney**	N	N	-	N	N	Y
DELEGATES						
Radewagen (A.S.)						
Norton (D.C.)						
San Nicolas (Guam)						
Sablan (N. Marianas)						
González-Colón (P.R.)						
Plaskett (V.I.)						

673. HR5038. Undocumented Agricultural Workers - Recommit. Biggs, R-Ariz., motion to recommit the Farm Workforce Modernization Act to the House Judiciary Committee with instructions to report it back immediately with an amendment that would strike from the bill provisions related to the applicability of law to agricultural workers under the H-2A visa program, including a provision requiring that such workers not be denied any right or remedy applicable to U.S. agricultural workers under federal or state labor law, and a provision that would grant such workers access to free federal mediation and conciliation services to assist in resolving disputes between workers and employers. Motion rejected 193-230: R 191-2; D 1-228; I 1-0. Dec. 11, 2019.

674. HR5038. Undocumented Agricultural Workers - Passage. Passage of the bill that would allow certain undocumented agricultural workers in the United States to apply for permanent residency status. It would also overhaul the H-2A non-immigrant visa program and replace the E-verify employment status verification system with a similar system for use by the agricultural sector. It would allow undocumented agricultural workers who have worked for at least 180 work days in the two years before enactment and lived continuously in the U.S. since that time status to apply for certified agricultural worker status, which would authorize such individuals to continue working in the U.S. for five and a half years. It would also allow such individuals to eventually apply for a green card, or legal permanent resident status, if they have worked in agriculture for at least 10 years prior to enactment and at least 4 years as a certified agricultural worker, or for at least 8 years as a certified agricultural worker. It would authorize such sums as may be necessary for Homeland Security Department for related activities, including for a grant program for nonprofits to assist eligible individuals with applications. The bill would overhaul the H-2A visa program, which grants non-immigrant visas for temporary or seasonal agricultural workers. Passed 260-165: R 34-161; D 226-3; I 0-1. Dec. 11, 2019.

675. HR5038. Undocumented Agricultural Workers - Motion to Table. McGovern, D-Mass., motion to table (kill) the Lofgren, D-Calif., motion to reconsider the vote by which the House passed, 260-165, the Farm Workforce Modernization Act (HR 5038) on Wednesday, Dec. 11, 2019. Motion agreed to 216-164: R 7-164; D 208-0; I 1-0. Dec. 11, 2019.

676. HR3. Drug Price Negotiation - Drug Price and Manufacturing Substitute. Walden, R-Ore., substitute amendment no. 1 that consists of the provisions of the Lower Costs, More Cures Act (HR 19). The substitute amendment would make a number of modifications to payments and pricing structures under Medicare Parts B and D and Medicaid, including to place a $3,100 annual out-of-pocket cap on costs for Medicare Part D beneficiaries and to require insurance companies to establish a monthly post-deductible cap of $50 on insulin for Part D beneficiaries, starting in 2022. It would establish or modify a number of requirements related to availability of drug pricing information, payment systems, and availability of refunds from drug manufacturers. It would make a number of modifications to FDA regulations related to biosimilar drug products and generic drug exclusivity. It would expedite or simplify certain procedures for the approval and market entry of generic drugs, and it would prohibit generic and brand-name drug manufacturers from entering into agreements in which brand-name manufacturers pay to delay entry of a generic drug into the market. It would require Health and Human Services Department to establish a requirement that direct-to-consumer television advertisements for Medicare- or Medicaid-eligible prescription drugs or biological products include truthful information indicating the list price of the drug or product advertised. It would also reduce from 10% to 7.5% the threshold for medical expense tax deductions to allow taxpayers to deduct medical expenses exceeding 7.5% of their adjusted gross income. Rejected in Committee of the Whole 201-223: R 192-2; D 8-221; I 1-0. Dec. 12, 2019.

677. HR3. Drug Price Negotiation - Rural Hospital Residency Program Grants. O'Halleran, D-Ariz., amendment no. 5 that would require the Health and Human Services Department to establish grant programs to award grants of no more than $250,000 to encourage hospitals in rural and medically under-served areas, including critical access hospitals, to establish medical residency training programs or to establish partnerships with other hospitals to host residents under such a program. It would authorize such sums as may be necessary for such grants through fiscal 2029. Adopted in Committee of the Whole 351-73: R 123-72; D 228-0; I 0-1. Dec. 12, 2019.

678. HR3. Drug Price Negotiation - New Medical Treatments Study. Gottheimer, D-N.J., amendment no. 7 that would require the Health and Human Services Department to conduct a study to identify diseases or conditions that lack treatments approved by the Food and Drug Administration and instances in which development of such treatments could fill unmet medical needs for serious, life-threatening, or rare diseases and conditions. The amendment would also require the study to identify incentives that would lead to the development, approval, and marketing of such treatments. Adopted in Committee of the Whole 380-45: R 156-39; D 224-5; I 0-1. Dec. 12, 2019.

		673	674	675	676	677	678
ALABAMA							
1	**Byrne**	Y	N	N	Y	N	N
2	**Roby**	Y	N	N	Y	Y	Y
3	**Rogers, M.**	Y	N	N	Y	Y	Y
4	**Aderholt**	Y	N	N	Y	N	N
5	**Brooks, M.**	Y	N	N	Y	N	Y
6	**Palmer**	Y	N	N	Y	N	Y
7	Sewell	N	Y	Y	N	Y	Y
ALASKA							
AL	**Young**	Y	Y	?	Y	N	Y
ARIZONA							
1	O'Halleran	N	Y	?	N	Y	Y
2	Kirkpatrick	N	Y	Y	N	Y	Y
3	Grijalva	N	Y	Y	N	Y	Y
4	**Gosar**	Y	N	N	?	?	?
5	**Biggs**	Y	N	N	Y	N	N
6	**Schweikert**	Y	N	N	Y	N	Y
7	Gallego	N	Y	?	N	Y	Y
8	**Lesko**	Y	N	N	Y	Y	Y
9	Stanton	N	Y	Y	N	Y	Y
ARKANSAS							
1	**Crawford**	Y	N	?	Y	N	N
2	**Hill, F.**	Y	N	N	Y	N	Y
3	**Womack**	Y	N	N	Y	N	Y
4	**Westerman**	Y	N	N	Y	N	Y
CALIFORNIA							
1	**LaMalfa**	Y	Y	Y	Y	Y	N
2	Huffman	N	Y	Y	N	Y	Y
3	Garamendi	N	Y	Y	N	Y	Y
4	**McClintock**	Y	N	?	Y	N	N
5	Thompson, M.	N	Y	Y	N	Y	Y
6	Matsui	N	Y	Y	N	Y	Y
7	Bera	N	Y	Y	N	Y	Y
8	**Cook**	Y	Y	?	Y	Y	Y
9	McNerney	N	Y	Y	?	Y	Y
10	Harder	N	Y	Y	N	Y	Y
11	DeSaulnier	N	Y	Y	N	?	Y
12	Pelosi		Y				
13	Lee B.	N	Y	Y	N	Y	Y
14	Speier	N	Y	Y	N	?	Y
15	Swalwell	N	Y	Y	N	Y	Y
16	Costa	N	Y	Y	N	Y	Y
17	Khanna	N	Y	Y	N	Y	Y
18	Eshoo	N	Y	Y	N	Y	Y
19	Lofgren	N	Y	Y	N	Y	Y
20	Panetta	N	Y	Y	N	Y	Y
21	Cox	N	Y	Y	N	Y	Y
22	**Nunes**	Y	Y	N	Y	N	Y
23	**McCarthy**	Y	N	N	Y	N	Y
24	Carbajal	N	Y	Y	N	Y	Y
25	vacant						
26	Brownley	N	Y	Y	N	Y	Y
27	Chu	N	Y	Y	N	Y	Y
28	Schiff	N	Y	Y	N	Y	Y
29	Cárdenas	N	Y	Y	N	Y	?
30	Sherman	N	Y	Y	N	Y	Y
31	Aguilar	N	Y	Y	N	Y	Y
32	Napolitano	N	Y	Y	N	Y	Y
33	Lieu	?	?	?	?	?	?
34	Gomez	N	Y	Y	N	Y	Y
35	Torres	N	Y	Y	N	Y	Y
36	Ruiz	N	Y	Y	N	Y	Y
37	Bass	N	Y	Y	N	Y	Y
38	Sánchez	N	Y	?	N	Y	Y
39	Cisneros	N	Y	Y	N	Y	Y
40	Roybal-Allard	N	Y	Y	N	Y	Y
41	Takano	N	Y	Y	N	Y	Y
42	**Calvert**	Y	N	?	Y	Y	Y
43	Waters	N	Y	Y	N	Y	Y
44	Barragán	-	+	?	N	Y	Y
45	Porter	N	Y	Y	N	Y	Y
46	Correa	N	Y	Y	N	Y	Y
47	Lowenthal	N	Y	Y	N	Y	Y
48	Rouda	N	Y	Y	Y	Y	Y
49	Levin	N	Y	Y	N	Y	Y
50	**Hunter**	?	?	?	?	?	?
51	Vargas	N	Y	Y	N	Y	Y
52	Peters	N	Y	Y	Y	Y	Y
53	Davis, S.	N	Y	Y	N	Y	Y
COLORADO							
1	DeGette	N	Y	Y	N	Y	Y
2	Neguse	N	Y	Y	N	Y	Y
3	**Tipton**	Y	Y	N	Y	Y	Y
4	**Buck**	Y	N	N	Y	N	Y
5	**Lamborn**	Y	N	?	Y	N	N
6	Crow	N	Y	Y	N	Y	Y
7	Perlmutter	N	Y	Y	N	Y	Y
CONNECTICUT							
1	Larson	N	Y	Y	N	Y	Y
2	Courtney	N	Y	Y	N	Y	Y
3	DeLauro	N	Y	Y	N	Y	Y
4	Himes	N	Y	Y	N	Y	Y
5	Hayes	N	Y	Y	N	Y	Y
DELAWARE							
AL	Blunt Rochester	N	Y	Y	N	Y	Y
FLORIDA							
1	**Gaetz**	Y	N	N	Y	N	Y
2	**Dunn**	Y	N	N	Y	Y	Y
3	**Yoho**	Y	N	N	Y	Y	Y
4	**Rutherford**	Y	N	N	Y	N	N
5	Lawson	N	Y	Y	N	Y	Y
6	**Waltz**	Y	N	?	Y	Y	Y
7	Murphy	N	Y	Y	N	Y	Y
8	**Posey**	Y	N	?	Y	Y	Y
9	Soto	N	Y	Y	N	Y	Y
10	Demings	N	Y	?	N	Y	Y
11	**Webster**	Y	N	N	Y	Y	Y
12	**Bilirakis**	Y	N	N	Y	Y	Y
13	Crist	N	Y	Y	N	Y	Y
14	Castor	N	Y	Y	N	Y	Y
15	**Spano**	Y	N	N	Y	Y	Y
16	**Buchanan**	Y	N	N	Y	Y	Y
17	**Steube**	Y	N	N	Y	N	N
18	**Mast**	Y	N	N	Y	N	Y
19	**Rooney**	?	?	?	?	?	?
20	Hastings	N	Y	Y	N	Y	Y
21	Frankel	N	Y	Y	N	Y	Y
22	Deutch	N	Y	?	N	Y	Y
23	Wasserman Schultz	N	Y	?	N	Y	Y
24	Wilson, F.	N	Y	Y	N	Y	Y
25	**Diaz-Balart**	Y	Y	N	Y	Y	Y
26	Mucarsel-Powell	N	Y	Y	N	Y	Y
27	Shalala	N	Y	Y	N	Y	Y
GEORGIA							
1	**Carter, E.L.**	Y	N	N	Y	Y	Y
2	Bishop, S.	N	Y	Y	N	Y	Y
3	**Ferguson**	Y	N	N	Y	Y	N
4	Johnson, H.	N	Y	?	N	Y	Y
5	Lewis John	N	Y	Y	-	+	+
6	McBath	N	Y	Y	N	Y	Y
7	**Woodall**	Y	N	N	Y	Y	Y
8	**Scott, A.**	Y	N	N	Y	Y	Y
9	**Collins, D.**	Y	N	?	Y	Y	Y
10	**Hice**	Y	N	N	Y	N	N
11	**Loudermilk**	Y	N	N	Y	Y	Y
12	**Allen**	Y	N	N	Y	Y	Y
13	Scott, D.	N	Y	Y	N	Y	Y
14	**Graves, T.**	Y	N	N	Y	N	Y
HAWAII							
1	Case	N	Y	Y	N	Y	Y
2	Gabbard	N	Y	?	?	?	?
IDAHO							
1	**Fulcher**	Y	Y	N	Y	N	Y
2	**Simpson**	N	Y	Y	Y	Y	Y
ILLINOIS							
1	Rush	N	Y	Y	N	Y	Y
2	Kelly, R.	N	Y	Y	N	Y	Y
3	Lipinski	N	Y	Y	N	Y	Y
4	García, J.	N	Y	?	N	Y	N
5	Quigley	N	Y	Y	N	Y	Y
6	Casten	N	Y	Y	N	Y	Y
7	Davis, D.	N	Y	Y	N	Y	Y
8	Krishnamoorthi	N	Y	Y	N	Y	Y
9	Schakowsky	N	Y	Y	N	Y	N
10	Schneider	N	Y	Y	N	Y	Y
11	Foster	N	Y	Y	N	Y	Y

KEY: **Republicans** Democrats *Independents*

Y	Voted for (yea)	N	Voted against (nay)	P	Voted "present"
+	Announced for	-	Announced against	?	Did not vote or otherwise make position known
#	Paired for	X	Paired against		

	673	674	675	676	677	678
12 **Bost**	Y	Y	N	Y	Y	Y
13 **Davis, R.**	+	Y	N	Y	Y	Y
14 Underwood	N	Y	Y	N	Y	Y
15 **Shimkus**	Y	Y	Y	Y	N	N
16 **Kinzinger**	Y	Y	?	Y	Y	Y
17 Bustos	N	Y	Y	N	Y	Y
18 **LaHood**	Y	N	N	Y	N	N
INDIANA						
1 Visclosky	N	Y	Y	N	Y	Y
2 **Walorski**	Y	N	N	Y	Y	Y
3 **Banks**	Y	N	N	Y	Y	Y
4 **Baird**	Y	Y	N	Y	Y	Y
5 **Brooks, S.**	Y	Y	Y	Y	Y	Y
6 **Pence**	Y	N	N	Y	Y	N
7 Carson	N	Y	Y	N	Y	Y
8 **Bucshon**	Y	N	N	Y	Y	Y
9 **Hollingsworth**	Y	N	N	Y	Y	Y
IOWA						
1 Finkenauer	N	Y	Y	N	Y	Y
2 Loebsack	N	Y	Y	N	Y	Y
3 Axne	N	Y	Y	N	Y	Y
4 **King, S.**	Y	N	N	Y	Y	Y
KANSAS						
1 **Marshall**	Y	N	N	Y	Y	Y
2 **Watkins**	Y	N	N	Y	Y	Y
3 Davids	N	Y	Y	N	Y	Y
4 **Estes**	Y	N	?	Y	N	Y
KENTUCKY						
1 **Comer**	Y	N	N	Y	N	Y
2 **Guthrie**	Y	N	N	Y	Y	Y
3 Yarmuth	N	Y	Y	N	Y	Y
4 **Massie**	Y	N	N	N	N	N
5 **Rogers, H.**	Y	N	N	Y	Y	Y
6 **Barr**	Y	N	N	Y	Y	Y
LOUISIANA						
1 **Scalise**	Y	N	N	Y	N	Y
2 Richmond	N	Y	Y	N	Y	Y
3 **Higgins, C.**	Y	N	?	Y	Y	Y
4 **Johnson, M.**	Y	N	N	Y	N	Y
5 **Abraham**	Y	N	N	Y	N	Y
6 **Graves, G.**	Y	N	N	Y	Y	Y
MAINE						
1 Pingree	N	Y	Y	N	Y	Y
2 Golden	N	N	Y	N	Y	Y
MARYLAND						
1 **Harris**	Y	N	N	Y	N	N
2 Ruppersberger	N	Y	Y	N	Y	Y
3 Sarbanes	N	Y	Y	N	Y	Y
4 Brown, A.	N	Y	Y	N	Y	Y
5 Hoyer	N	Y	Y	N	Y	Y
6 Trone	N	Y	Y	N	Y	Y
7 vacant						
8 Raskin	N	Y	Y	N	Y	Y
MASSACHUSETTS						
1 Neal	N	Y	?	N	Y	Y
2 McGovern	N	Y	Y	N	Y	Y
3 Trahan	N	Y	Y	N	Y	Y
4 Kennedy	N	Y	Y	N	Y	Y
5 Clark	N	Y	Y	N	Y	Y
6 Moulton	N	Y	Y	N	Y	Y
7 Pressley	N	Y	Y	N	Y	Y
8 Lynch	N	Y	Y	N	Y	Y
9 Keating	N	Y	Y	N	Y	Y
MICHIGAN						
1 **Bergman**	Y	N	N	Y	Y	Y
2 **Huizenga**	Y	N	N	Y	Y	Y
3 *Amash*	Y	N	Y	Y	N	N
4 **Moolenaar**	Y	N	N	Y	Y	Y
5 Kildee	N	Y	Y	N	Y	Y
6 **Upton**	Y	Y	N	Y	Y	Y
7 **Walberg**	Y	N	N	Y	Y	Y
8 Slotkin	N	Y	Y	N	Y	Y
9 Levin	N	Y	Y	N	Y	Y
10 **Mitchell**	N	Y	N	Y	N	Y
11 Stevens	N	Y	Y	N	Y	Y
12 Dingell	N	Y	Y	N	Y	Y
13 Tlaib	N	P	Y	N	Y	Y
14 Lawrence	N	Y	Y	N	Y	Y
MINNESOTA						
1 **Hagedorn**	Y	N	N	Y	Y	Y
2 Craig	N	Y	Y	N	Y	Y
3 Phillips	N	Y	Y	N	Y	Y
4 McCollum	N	Y	Y	N	Y	Y
5 Omar	N	Y	Y	N	Y	Y

	673	674	675	676	677	678
6 **Emmer**	Y	N	N	Y	Y	Y
7 Peterson	N	Y	Y	N	Y	Y
8 **Stauber**	Y	N	N	Y	Y	Y
MISSISSIPPI						
1 **Kelly, T.**	Y	N	N	Y	Y	Y
2 Thompson, B.	N	Y	Y	N	Y	Y
3 **Guest**	Y	N	N	Y	Y	Y
4 **Palazzo**	Y	N	N	Y	Y	Y
MISSOURI						
1 Clay	N	Y	Y	N	Y	Y
2 **Wagner**	Y	N	N	Y	Y	Y
3 **Luetkemeyer**	Y	N	?	Y	Y	Y
4 **Hartzler**	Y	N	N	Y	Y	Y
5 Cleaver	N	Y	Y	N	Y	Y
6 **Graves, S.**	Y	N	N	Y	Y	Y
7 **Long**	Y	N	N	Y	Y	Y
8 **Smith, J.**	Y	N	N	Y	Y	Y
MONTANA						
AL **Gianforte**	Y	N	N	Y	Y	Y
NEBRASKA						
1 **Fortenberry**	Y	N	N	Y	Y	Y
2 **Bacon**	Y	N	N	Y	N	Y
3 **Smith, Adrian**	Y	N	N	Y	Y	N
NEVADA						
1 Titus	N	Y	?	N	Y	Y
2 **Amodei**	Y	Y	N	Y	Y	Y
3 Lee	N	Y	Y	N	Y	Y
4 Horsford	N	Y	Y	N	Y	Y
NEW HAMPSHIRE						
1 Pappas	N	Y	Y	N	Y	Y
2 Kuster	N	Y	Y	N	Y	Y
NEW JERSEY						
1 Norcross	N	Y	Y	N	Y	Y
2 Van Drew	N	Y	?	Y	Y	Y
3 Kim	N	Y	Y	N	Y	Y
4 **Smith, C.**	Y	Y	?	Y	Y	Y
5 Gottheimer	N	Y	Y	Y	Y	Y
6 Pallone	N	Y	Y	N	Y	Y
7 Malinowski	N	Y	Y	N	Y	Y
8 Sires	N	Y	?	N	Y	Y
9 Pascrell	N	Y	Y	N	Y	Y
10 Payne	N	Y	Y	N	Y	Y
11 Sherrill	N	Y	Y	N	Y	Y
12 Watson Coleman	N	Y	Y	N	Y	Y
NEW MEXICO						
1 Haaland	N	Y	Y	N	Y	Y
2 Torres Small	N	Y	Y	N	Y	Y
3 Luján	N	Y	Y	N	Y	Y
NEW YORK						
1 **Zeldin**	Y	N	N	?	Y	Y
2 **King, P.**	Y	Y	N	Y	Y	Y
3 Suozzi	N	Y	?	Y	Y	Y
4 Rice, K.	N	Y	Y	N	Y	Y
5 Meeks	N	Y	Y	N	Y	Y
6 Meng	N	Y	Y	N	Y	Y
7 Velázquez	N	Y	Y	N	Y	Y
8 Jeffries	N	Y	?	N	Y	Y
9 Clarke	N	Y	Y	N	Y	Y
10 Nadler	N	Y	?	N	Y	Y
11 Rose	N	Y	Y	N	Y	Y
12 Maloney, C.	N	Y	Y	N	Y	Y
13 Espaillat	N	Y	Y	N	Y	Y
14 Ocasio-Cortez	N	Y	Y	N	Y	Y
15 Serrano	?	?	?	?	?	?
16 Engel	N	Y	Y	N	Y	Y
17 Lowey	N	Y	Y	N	Y	Y
18 Maloney, S.P.	N	Y	Y	N	Y	Y
19 Delgado	N	Y	Y	N	Y	Y
20 Tonko	N	Y	Y	N	Y	Y
21 **Stefanik**	Y	Y	N	Y	Y	Y
22 Brindisi	N	Y	Y	Y	Y	Y
23 **Reed**	Y	Y	?	Y	Y	Y
24 **Katko**	Y	Y	N	Y	Y	Y
25 Morelle	N	Y	Y	N	Y	Y
26 Higgins, B.	N	Y	?	N	Y	Y
27 **Collins, C.**						
NORTH CAROLINA						
1 Butterfield	N	Y	Y	N	Y	Y
2 **Holding**	?	N	N	Y	N	N
3 **Murphy**	Y	N	N	Y	Y	N
4 Price	N	Y	Y	N	Y	Y
5 **Foxx**	Y	N	N	Y	N	Y
6 **Walker**	Y	N	N	Y	N	N
7 **Rouzer**	Y	N	N	Y	Y	Y

	673	674	675	676	677	678
8 **Hudson**	Y	N	N	Y	N	Y
9 **Bishop**	Y	N	N	Y	N	N
10 **McHenry**	Y	N	N	Y	N	Y
11 **Meadows**	Y	N	N	Y	N	N
12 Adams	N	Y	Y	N	Y	Y
13 **Budd**	Y	N	N	Y	N	Y
NORTH DAKOTA						
AL **Armstrong**	Y	N	?	Y	Y	N
OHIO						
1 **Chabot**	Y	N	N	Y	Y	Y
2 **Wenstrup**	Y	N	N	Y	Y	Y
3 Beatty	N	Y	Y	N	Y	Y
4 **Jordan**	Y	N	N	Y	N	N
5 **Latta**	Y	N	N	Y	Y	Y
6 **Johnson, B.**	Y	N	N	Y	Y	Y
7 **Gibbs**	Y	N	N	Y	Y	Y
8 **Davidson**	Y	N	N	Y	N	Y
9 Kaptur	N	Y	Y	N	Y	Y
10 **Turner**	Y	N	N	Y	Y	Y
11 Fudge	N	Y	Y	N	Y	Y
12 **Balderson**	Y	N	N	Y	Y	Y
13 Ryan	N	Y	Y	N	Y	Y
14 **Joyce**	Y	Y	N	Y	Y	Y
15 **Stivers**	Y	Y	N	Y	Y	Y
16 **Gonzalez**	Y	N	N	Y	N	Y
OKLAHOMA						
1 **Hern**	Y	N	N	Y	N	Y
2 **Mullin**	Y	N	N	Y	Y	Y
3 **Lucas**	Y	N	N	Y	Y	Y
4 **Cole**	Y	Y	N	Y	Y	Y
5 Horn	N	Y	Y	N	Y	Y
OREGON						
1 Bonamici	N	Y	Y	N	Y	Y
2 **Walden**	Y	Y	Y	Y	Y	Y
3 Blumenauer	N	Y	Y	N	Y	Y
4 DeFazio	N	Y	?	N	Y	Y
5 Schrader	N	Y	Y	Y	Y	Y
PENNSYLVANIA						
1 **Fitzpatrick**	Y	Y	N	Y	Y	Y
2 Boyle	N	Y	Y	N	Y	Y
3 Evans	N	Y	?	N	Y	Y
4 Dean	N	Y	Y	N	Y	Y
5 Scanlon	N	Y	Y	N	Y	Y
6 Houlahan	N	Y	Y	N	Y	Y
7 Wild	N	Y	Y	N	Y	Y
8 Cartwright	N	Y	Y	N	Y	Y
9 **Meuser**	Y	N	N	Y	Y	Y
10 **Perry**	Y	N	N	Y	N	N
11 **Smucker**	Y	Y	N	Y	Y	Y
12 **Keller**	Y	N	N	Y	Y	Y
13 **Joyce**	Y	N	N	Y	N	Y
14 **Reschenthaler**	Y	N	N	Y	Y	Y
15 **Thompson, G.**	Y	Y	N	Y	Y	Y
16 **Kelly, M.**	Y	N	N	Y	N	Y
17 Lamb	N	Y	Y	N	Y	Y
18 Doyle	N	Y	Y	N	Y	Y
RHODE ISLAND						
1 Cicilline	N	Y	Y	N	Y	Y
2 Langevin	N	Y	Y	N	Y	Y
SOUTH CAROLINA						
1 Cunningham	N	Y	Y	N	Y	Y
2 **Wilson, J.**	Y	N	N	Y	Y	Y
3 **Duncan**	Y	N	N	Y	Y	Y
4 **Timmons**	Y	N	?	Y	N	Y
5 **Norman**	Y	N	N	Y	N	Y
6 Clyburn	N	Y	Y	N	Y	Y
7 **Rice, T.**	Y	N	N	Y	Y	Y
SOUTH DAKOTA						
AL **Johnson**	Y	N	N	Y	Y	Y
TENNESSEE						
1 **Roe**	Y	N	N	Y	Y	Y
2 **Burchett**	Y	N	N	+	-	-
3 **Fleischmann**	Y	N	N	Y	Y	Y
4 **DesJarlais**	Y	N	N	Y	Y	Y
5 Cooper	N	Y	Y	N	Y	Y
6 **Rose**	Y	N	N	Y	Y	Y
7 **Green**	Y	N	?	Y	Y	N
8 **Kustoff**	Y	N	N	Y	Y	N
9 Cohen	N	Y	Y	N	Y	Y
TEXAS						
1 **Gohmert**	Y	N	N	Y	Y	N
2 **Crenshaw**	Y	N	N	Y	N	Y
3 **Taylor**	Y	N	N	Y	N	Y
4 **Ratcliffe**	Y	N	N	Y	N	N

	673	674	675	676	677	678
5 **Gooden**	Y	N	N	Y	N	Y
6 **Wright**	Y	N	?	Y	N	Y
7 Fletcher	N	Y	Y	N	Y	Y
8 **Brady**	Y	N	N	Y	N	Y
9 Green, A.	N	Y	Y	N	Y	Y
10 **McCaul**	Y	N	N	Y	Y	Y
11 **Conaway**	Y	N	N	Y	N	N
12 **Granger**	Y	N	N	Y	N	N
13 **Thornberry**	Y	N	N	Y	Y	Y
14 **Weber**	Y	N	?	Y	N	N
15 Gonzalez	N	Y	Y	N	Y	Y
16 Escobar	N	Y	Y	N	Y	Y
17 **Flores**	Y	N	N	Y	N	N
18 Jackson Lee	N	Y	Y	N	Y	Y
19 **Arrington**	Y	N	N	Y	N	Y
20 Castro	N	Y	Y	N	Y	Y
21 **Roy**	Y	N	N	Y	N	N
22 **Olson**	Y	N	N	Y	N	N
23 **Hurd**	Y	Y	N	Y	Y	Y
24 **Marchant**	Y	N	?	Y	N	N
25 **Williams**	Y	N	N	Y	N	Y
26 **Burgess**	Y	N	N	Y	Y	Y
27 **Cloud**	Y	N	N	Y	N	N
28 Cuellar	N	Y	Y	N	Y	Y
29 Garcia, S.	N	Y	Y	N	Y	Y
30 Johnson, E.B.	N	Y	Y	N	Y	Y
31 **Carter, J.**	Y	N	?	Y	N	N
32 Allred	N	Y	Y	N	Y	Y
33 Veasey	N	Y	Y	N	Y	Y
34 Vela	N	Y	Y	N	Y	Y
35 Doggett	N	Y	?	N	Y	N
36 **Babin**	Y	N	?	Y	N	N
UTAH						
1 **Bishop, R.**	Y	N	N	Y	Y	N
2 **Stewart**	Y	N	N	Y	Y	Y
3 **Curtis**	Y	N	N	Y	Y	Y
4 McAdams	Y	N	Y	Y	Y	Y
VERMONT						
AL Welch	N	Y	Y	N	Y	Y
VIRGINIA						
1 **Wittman**	Y	N	N	Y	Y	Y
2 Luria	N	Y	Y	N	Y	Y
3 Scott, R.	N	N	Y	N	Y	Y
4 McEachin	N	Y	Y	N	Y	Y
5 **Riggleman**	Y	N	N	Y	Y	Y
6 **Cline**	Y	N	N	Y	Y	Y
7 Spanberger	N	Y	Y	N	Y	Y
8 Beyer	N	Y	Y	N	Y	Y
9 **Griffith**	Y	N	N	Y	Y	Y
10 Wexton	N	Y	Y	N	Y	Y
11 Connolly	N	Y	Y	N	Y	Y
WASHINGTON						
1 DelBene	N	Y	Y	N	Y	Y
2 Larsen	N	Y	Y	N	Y	Y
3 **Herrera Beutler**	Y	Y	N	Y	Y	Y
4 **Newhouse**	Y	Y	Y	Y	Y	Y
5 **McMorris Rodgers**	Y	Y	Y	Y	Y	Y
6 Kilmer	N	Y	Y	N	Y	Y
7 Jayapal	N	Y	Y	N	Y	N
8 Schrier	N	Y	Y	N	Y	Y
9 Smith Adam	N	Y	?	N	Y	Y
10 Heck	N	Y	Y	N	Y	Y
WEST VIRGINIA						
1 **McKinley**	Y	Y	N	Y	Y	Y
2 **Mooney**	Y	N	N	Y	Y	Y
3 **Miller**	Y	N	N	Y	N	Y
WISCONSIN						
1 **Steil**	Y	N	N	Y	Y	Y
2 Pocan	N	Y	Y	N	Y	N
3 Kind	N	Y	Y	N	Y	Y
4 Moore	N	Y	Y	N	Y	Y
5 **Sensenbrenner**	Y	N	N	Y	N	Y
6 **Grothman**	Y	N	N	Y	N	Y
7 **Duffy**						
8 **Gallagher**	Y	N	?	Y	Y	Y
WYOMING						
AL **Cheney**	Y	N	N	Y	Y	Y
DELEGATES						
Radewagen (A.S.)				Y	Y	Y
Norton (D.C.)				N	Y	Y
San Nicolas (Guam)				?	?	?
Sablan (N. Marianas)				?	?	?
González-Colón (P.R.)				N	Y	Y
Plaskett (V.I.)				N	Y	Y

679. HR3. Drug Price Negotiation - Federal Health Plan Contracts. Luria, D-Va., amendment no. 10 that would prohibit the federal office of personnel management from contracting with a health benefits plan if the plan carrier has elected not to participate in the fair price negotiation program established by the bill. Adopted in Committee of the Whole 231-192: R 3-191; D 228-0; I 0-1. Dec. 12, 2019.

680. HR3. Drug Price Negotiation - VA Drug Procurement. Cunningham, D-S.C., amendment no. 11 that would require drug manufacturers contracting with the Veterans Affairs Department to comply with maximum prices set for any drug under the bill's provisions, if the VA determines that such maximum prices are less than those determined under existing law regarding VA drug procurement. Adopted in Committee of the Whole 234-192: R 4-191; D 230-0; I 0-1. Dec. 12, 2019.

681. HR3. Drug Price Negotiation - Recommit. Upton, R-Mich., motion to recommit the Elijah E. Cummings Lower Drug Costs Now Act (HR 3) to the House Energy and Commerce Committee with instructions to report it back immediately with an amendment that would prohibit the provisions of the bill from going into effect unless the Health and Human Services Department certifies that the implementation of such provisions is not projected to result in fewer new drug applications in relation to unmet medical needs and potential cures. Motion rejected 196-226: R 193-0; D 3-225; I 0-1. Dec. 12, 2019.

682. HR3. Drug Price Negotiation - Passage. Passage of the bill, as amended, that would allow the Health and Human Services Department to negotiate prices for certain drugs under Medicare programs and would make a number of modifications to Medicare programs related to drug costs and plan benefits. Specifically, the bill would establish a fair price negotiation program in which HHS would enter into agreements with drug manufacturers to negotiate maximum fair prices for certain drugs. It would allow the department to negotiate a "maximum fair price" for insulin and up to 250 other Medicare-eligible, brand-name drugs that do not have generic competition, including 125 drugs that account for the greatest national spending and 125 drugs that account for the greatest spending under Medicare parts C and D. The bill would require the department to negotiate the maximum price of at least 25 drugs for 2023 and at least 50 drugs in each subsequent year. It would require that such maximum prices would not exceed 120% of a drug's average international price or 85% of the average manufacturer price for drugs for a year. The bill would subject drug manufacturers who do not reach a negotiated agreement for a drug to excise taxes based on gross sales of that drug. It would require manufacturers to offer negotiated prices to private health insurers. The bill would also make adjustments to payments, pricing structures, and programs related to Medicare parts B and D. Among other provisions, it would place a $2,000 annual out-of-pocket cap on costs for Medicare Part D beneficiaries, expand eligibility for a Part D low-income subsidy program, and add comprehensive vision, dental, and hearing coverage under Medicare Part B. Finally, it would authorize funding for HHS programs to address opioid and substance use disorders and authorize funding for National Institutes of Health and Food and Drug Administration activities related to the development of new drugs and medical treatments. Passed 230-192: R 2-191; D 228-0; I 0-1. Note: A "nay" was a vote in support of the president's position. Dec. 12, 2019.

683. HRES761, HR1865, HR1158. Fiscal 2020 Consolidated Appropriations Acts - Previous Question. Morelle, D-N.Y., motion to order the previous question on the rule (H Res 765) that would provide for House floor consideration of the Senate amendment to the Fiscal 2020 Consolidated Appropriations Act (HR 1158), with a further House amendment, and provide for House floor consideration of Senate amendment to the Fiscal 2020 Further Consolidated Appropriations Act (HR 1865), with a further House amendment, as modified. The rule would also provide for automatic adoption of the resolution (H Res 761) that would allow designated individuals to be admitted to the Hall of the House in order to obtain footage of the House in session for inclusion in the Capitol Visitor Center visitor orientation film. The rule would provide for automatic adoption of a Lowey, D-N.Y., manager's amendment modifying the House amendment to the Senate amendment to the Fiscal 2020 Further Consolidated Appropriations Act (HR 1865). Motion agreed to 220-192: R 0-191; D 220-0; I 0-1. Dec. 17, 2019.

684. HR1865, HR1158, HRES761. Fiscal 2020 Consolidated Appropriations Acts - Rule. Adoption of the rule (H Res 765) that would provide for House floor consideration of the Senate amendment to the Fiscal 2020 Consolidated Appropriations Act (HR 1158), with a further House amendment, and provide for House floor consideration of Senate amendment to the Fiscal 2020 Further Consolidated Appropriations Act (HR 1865), with a further House amendment, as modified. The rule would also provide for automatic adoption of the resolution (H Res 761) that would allow designated individuals to be admitted to the Hall of the House in order to obtain footage of the House in session for inclusion in the Capitol Visitor Center visitor orientation film. The rule would provide for automatic adoption of a Lowey, D-N.Y., manager's amendment modifying the House amendment to the Senate amendment to the Fiscal 2020 Further Consolidated Appropriations Act (HR 1865).. Adopted 219-189: R 0-186; D 219-2; I 0-1. Dec. 17, 2019.

	679	680	681	682	683	684
ALABAMA						
1 Byrne	N	N	Y	N	N	N
2 Roby	N	N	Y	N	N	N
3 Rogers, M.	N	N	Y	N	N	N
4 Aderholt	N	N	Y	N	N	N
5 Brooks, M.	N	N	Y	N	N	N
6 Palmer	N	N	Y	N	N	N
7 Sewell	Y	Y	N	Y	Y	Y
ALASKA						
AL Young	N	N	Y	N	N	N
ARIZONA						
1 O'Halleran	Y	Y	N	Y	Y	Y
2 Kirkpatrick	Y	Y	N	Y	Y	Y
3 Grijalva	Y	Y	N	Y	Y	Y
4 Gosar	?	?	?	?	N	N
5 Biggs	N	N	Y	N	N	N
6 Schweikert	N	N	Y	N	N	?
7 Gallego	Y	Y	N	Y	Y	Y
8 Lesko	N	N	Y	N	N	N
9 Stanton	Y	Y	N	Y	Y	Y
ARKANSAS						
1 Crawford	N	N	Y	N	N	N
2 Hill, F.	N	N	Y	N	N	N
3 Womack	N	N	Y	N	N	N
4 Westerman	N	N	Y	N	N	N
CALIFORNIA						
1 LaMalfa	N	N	Y	N	N	N
2 Huffman	Y	Y	N	Y	Y	Y
3 Garamendi	Y	Y	N	Y	Y	Y
4 McClintock	N	N	Y	N	N	N
5 Thompson, M.	Y	Y	N	Y	Y	Y
6 Matsui	Y	Y	N	Y	Y	Y
7 Bera	Y	Y	N	Y	Y	Y
8 Cook	N	N	Y	N	N	N
9 McNerney	Y	Y	N	Y	Y	Y
10 Harder	Y	Y	N	Y	Y	Y
11 DeSaulnier	Y	Y	N	Y	Y	Y
12 Pelosi						
13 Lee B.	Y	Y	N	Y	Y	Y
14 Speier	Y	Y	N	Y	Y	Y
15 Swalwell	Y	Y	N	Y	Y	Y
16 Costa	Y	Y	N	Y	Y	Y
17 Khanna	Y	Y	N	Y	Y	Y
18 Eshoo	Y	Y	N	Y	Y	Y
19 Lofgren	Y	Y	N	Y	Y	Y
20 Panetta	Y	Y	N	Y	Y	Y
21 Cox	Y	Y	N	Y	Y	Y
22 Nunes	N	N	Y	N	N	N
23 McCarthy	N	N	Y	N	N	N
24 Carbajal	Y	Y	N	Y	Y	Y
25 vacant						
26 Brownley	Y	Y	N	Y	Y	Y
27 Chu	Y	Y	N	Y	Y	Y
28 Schiff	Y	Y	N	Y	Y	Y
29 Cárdenas	Y	Y	N	Y	Y	Y
30 Sherman	Y	Y	N	Y	Y	Y
31 Aguilar	Y	Y	N	Y	Y	Y
32 Napolitano	Y	Y	N	Y	Y	Y
33 Lieu	?	?	?	?	Y	Y
34 Gomez	Y	Y	N	Y	Y	Y
35 Torres	Y	Y	N	Y	Y	Y
36 Ruiz	Y	Y	N	Y	Y	Y
37 Bass	Y	Y	N	Y	Y	Y
38 Sánchez	Y	Y	N	Y	Y	Y
39 Cisneros	Y	Y	N	Y	Y	Y
40 Roybal-Allard	Y	Y	N	Y	Y	Y
41 Takano	Y	Y	N	Y	Y	Y
42 Calvert	N	N	Y	N	N	N
43 Waters	Y	Y	N	Y	Y	Y
44 Barragán	Y	Y	N	Y	Y	Y
45 Porter	Y	Y	N	Y	Y	Y
46 Correa	Y	Y	N	Y	Y	Y
47 Lowenthal	Y	Y	N	Y	Y	Y
48 Rouda	Y	Y	N	Y	Y	Y
49 Levin	Y	Y	N	Y	Y	Y
50 Hunter	?	?	?	?	?	?
51 Vargas	Y	Y	N	Y	?	?
52 Peters	Y	Y	N	Y	Y	Y
53 Davis, S.	Y	Y	N	Y	Y	Y
COLORADO						
1 DeGette	Y	Y	N	Y	Y	Y
2 Neguse	Y	Y	N	Y	Y	Y
3 Tipton	N	N	Y	N	N	N
4 Buck	N	N	Y	N	N	N
5 Lamborn	N	N	Y	N	N	N
6 Crow	Y	Y	N	Y	Y	Y
7 Perlmutter	Y	Y	N	Y	Y	Y
CONNECTICUT						
1 Larson	Y	Y	N	Y	Y	Y
2 Courtney	Y	Y	N	Y	Y	Y
3 DeLauro	Y	Y	N	Y	Y	Y
4 Himes	Y	Y	N	Y	Y	Y
5 Hayes	Y	Y	N	Y	Y	Y
DELAWARE						
AL Blunt Rochester	Y	Y	N	Y	Y	Y
FLORIDA						
1 Gaetz	N	N	Y	N	N	N
2 Dunn	N	N	Y	N	N	N
3 Yoho	N	N	Y	N	N	N
4 Rutherford	N	N	Y	N	N	N
5 Lawson	Y	Y	N	Y	Y	Y
6 Waltz	N	N	Y	N	N	N
7 Murphy	Y	Y	N	Y	Y	Y
8 Posey	N	N	Y	N	N	N
9 Soto	Y	Y	N	Y	Y	Y
10 Demings	Y	Y	N	Y	Y	Y
11 Webster	N	N	Y	N	N	N
12 Bilirakis	N	N	Y	N	N	N
13 Crist	Y	Y	N	Y	Y	Y
14 Castor	Y	Y	N	Y	Y	Y
15 Spano	N	N	Y	N	N	N
16 Buchanan	N	N	Y	N	N	N
17 Steube	N	N	Y	N	N	N
18 Mast	N	N	Y	N	N	N
19 Rooney	?	?	?	N	N	N
20 Hastings	Y	Y	N	Y	Y	Y
21 Frankel	Y	Y	N	Y	Y	Y
22 Deutch	Y	Y	N	Y	Y	Y
23 Wasserman Schultz	Y	Y	N	Y	Y	Y
24 Wilson, F.	Y	Y	N	Y	?	?
25 Diaz-Balart	N	N	Y	N	N	N
26 Mucarsel-Powell	Y	Y	N	Y	Y	Y
27 Shalala	Y	Y	N	Y	Y	Y
GEORGIA						
1 Carter, E.L.	N	N	Y	N	N	N
2 Bishop, S.	Y	Y	N	Y	Y	Y
3 Ferguson	N	N	Y	N	N	N
4 Johnson, H.	Y	Y	N	Y	Y	Y
5 Lewis John	+	+	N	+	Y	Y
6 McBath	Y	Y	N	Y	Y	Y
7 Woodall	N	N	Y	N	N	N
8 Scott, A.	N	N	Y	N	N	N
9 Collins, D.	N	N	Y	N	N	N
10 Hice	N	N	Y	N	N	N
11 Loudermilk	N	N	Y	N	N	N
12 Allen	N	N	Y	N	N	N
13 Scott, D.	Y	Y	N	Y	Y	Y
14 Graves, T.	N	N	Y	N	N	N
HAWAII						
1 Case	Y	Y	N	Y	Y	Y
2 Gabbard	?	?	?	?	?	?
IDAHO						
1 Fulcher	N	N	Y	N	N	N
2 Simpson	N	N	Y	N	N	N
ILLINOIS						
1 Rush	Y	Y	N	Y	Y	Y
2 Kelly, R.	Y	Y	N	Y	Y	Y
3 Lipinski	Y	Y	N	Y	Y	N
4 García, J.	Y	Y	N	Y	Y	Y
5 Quigley	Y	Y	N	Y	Y	Y
6 Casten	Y	Y	N	Y	Y	Y
7 Davis, D.	Y	Y	N	Y	Y	Y
8 Krishnamoorthi	Y	Y	N	Y	Y	Y
9 Schakowsky	Y	Y	N	Y	Y	Y
10 Schneider	Y	Y	N	Y	Y	Y
11 Foster	Y	Y	N	Y	Y	Y

		679	680	681	682	683	684
12	**Bost**	N	N	Y	N	N	N
13	**Davis, R.**	N	Y	Y	N	N	N
14	Underwood	Y	Y	N	Y	Y	Y
15	**Shimkus**	N	N	Y	N	?	?
16	**Kinzinger**	N	N	Y	N	N	N
17	Bustos	Y	Y	N	Y	Y	Y
18	**LaHood**	N	N	Y	N	N	N
INDIANA							
1	Visclosky	Y	Y	N	Y	Y	Y
2	**Walorski**	N	N	Y	N	N	N
3	**Banks**	N	N	Y	N	N	N
4	**Baird**	N	N	Y	N	N	N
5	**Brooks, S.**	N	N	Y	N	N	N
6	**Pence**	N	N	Y	N	N	N
7	Carson	Y	Y	N	Y	Y	Y
8	**Bucshon**	N	N	Y	N	N	N
9	**Hollingsworth**	N	N	Y	N	?	?
IOWA							
1	Finkenauer	Y	Y	N	Y	Y	Y
2	Loebsack	Y	Y	N	Y	Y	Y
3	Axne	Y	Y	N	Y	Y	Y
4	**King, S.**	N	N	Y	N	N	N
KANSAS							
1	**Marshall**	N	N	Y	N	N	N
2	**Watkins**	N	N	Y	N	N	N
3	Davids	Y	Y	N	Y	Y	Y
4	**Estes**	N	N	Y	N	N	N
KENTUCKY							
1	**Comer**	N	N	Y	N	N	N
2	**Guthrie**	N	N	Y	N	N	N
3	Yarmuth	Y	Y	N	Y	Y	Y
4	**Massie**	N	N	Y	N	N	N
5	**Rogers, H.**	N	N	Y	N	N	N
6	**Barr**	N	N	Y	N	N	N
LOUISIANA							
1	**Scalise**	N	N	Y	N	N	N
2	Richmond	Y	Y	N	Y	Y	Y
3	**Higgins, C.**	N	N	Y	N	N	N
4	**Johnson, M.**	N	N	Y	N	N	?
5	**Abraham**	N	N	Y	N	N	N
6	**Graves, G.**	N	N	Y	N	N	N
MAINE							
1	Pingree	Y	Y	N	Y	Y	Y
2	Golden	Y	Y	N	Y	Y	Y
MARYLAND							
1	**Harris**	N	N	Y	N	N	N
2	Ruppersberger	Y	Y	N	Y	Y	Y
3	Sarbanes	Y	Y	N	Y	Y	Y
4	Brown, A.	Y	Y	N	Y	Y	Y
5	Hoyer	Y	Y	N	Y	Y	Y
6	Trone	Y	Y	N	Y	Y	Y
7	vacant						
8	Raskin	Y	Y	N	Y	Y	Y
MASSACHUSETTS							
1	Neal	Y	Y	N	Y	Y	Y
2	McGovern	Y	Y	N	Y	Y	Y
3	Trahan	Y	Y	N	Y	Y	Y
4	Kennedy	Y	Y	N	Y	Y	Y
5	Clark	Y	Y	N	Y	Y	Y
6	Moulton	Y	Y	N	Y	Y	Y
7	Pressley	Y	Y	N	Y	+	+
8	Lynch	Y	Y	N	Y	Y	Y
9	Keating	Y	Y	N	Y	Y	Y
MICHIGAN							
1	**Bergman**	N	N	Y	N	N	N
2	**Huizenga**	N	N	Y	N	N	N
3	*Amash*	N	N	N	N	N	N
4	**Moolenaar**	N	N	Y	N	N	N
5	Kildee	Y	Y	N	Y	Y	Y
6	**Upton**	N	N	Y	N	N	N
7	**Walberg**	N	N	Y	N	N	N
8	Slotkin	Y	Y	N	Y	Y	Y
9	Levin	Y	Y	N	Y	Y	Y
10	**Mitchell**	N	N	Y	N	N	N
11	Stevens	Y	Y	N	Y	Y	Y
12	Dingell	Y	Y	N	Y	Y	Y
13	Tlaib	Y	Y	N	Y	Y	Y
14	Lawrence	Y	Y	N	Y	Y	Y
MINNESOTA							
1	**Hagedorn**	N	N	Y	N	N	N
2	Craig	Y	Y	N	Y	Y	Y
3	Phillips	Y	Y	N	Y	Y	Y
4	McCollum	Y	Y	N	Y	Y	Y
5	Omar	Y	Y	N	Y	Y	Y

		679	680	681	682	683	684
6	**Emmer**	N	N	Y	N	N	N
7	Peterson	Y	Y	N	Y	Y	Y
8	**Stauber**	N	N	Y	N	N	N
MISSISSIPPI							
1	**Kelly, T.**	N	N	Y	N	N	N
2	Thompson, B.	Y	Y	N	Y	?	?
3	**Guest**	N	N	Y	N	N	N
4	**Palazzo**	N	N	Y	N	N	N
MISSOURI							
1	Clay	Y	Y	N	Y	?	?
2	**Wagner**	N	N	Y	N	N	N
3	**Luetkemeyer**	N	N	Y	N	N	N
4	**Hartzler**	N	N	Y	N	N	N
5	Cleaver	Y	Y	N	Y	Y	Y
6	**Graves, S.**	N	N	Y	N	N	N
7	**Long**	N	N	Y	N	N	N
8	**Smith, J.**	N	N	Y	N	N	N
MONTANA							
AL	**Gianforte**	N	N	Y	N	N	N
NEBRASKA							
1	**Fortenberry**	Y	Y	Y	N	N	N
2	**Bacon**	N	N	Y	N	N	N
3	**Smith, Adrian**	N	N	Y	N	N	N
NEVADA							
1	Titus	Y	Y	N	Y	Y	Y
2	**Amodei**	N	N	Y	N	N	N
3	Lee	Y	Y	N	Y	Y	Y
4	Horsford	Y	Y	N	Y	?	Y
NEW HAMPSHIRE							
1	Pappas	Y	Y	N	Y	Y	Y
2	Kuster	Y	Y	N	Y	Y	Y
NEW JERSEY							
1	Norcross	Y	Y	N	Y	Y	Y
2	Van Drew	Y	Y	N	Y	?	?
3	Kim	Y	Y	N	Y	Y	Y
4	**Smith, C.**	N	N	Y	N	N	N
5	Gottheimer	Y	Y	Y	Y	Y	Y
6	Pallone	Y	Y	N	Y	Y	Y
7	Malinowski	?	Y	N	Y	Y	Y
8	Sires	Y	Y	N	Y	Y	Y
9	Pascrell	Y	Y	N	Y	Y	Y
10	Payne	Y	Y	N	Y	Y	Y
11	Sherrill	Y	Y	Y	Y	Y	Y
12	Watson Coleman	Y	Y	N	Y	Y	Y
NEW MEXICO							
1	Haaland	Y	Y	N	Y	Y	Y
2	Torres Small	Y	Y	N	Y	Y	Y
3	Luján	Y	Y	N	Y	Y	Y
NEW YORK							
1	**Zeldin**	N	N	Y	N	N	N
2	**King, P.**	?	N	Y	N	N	N
3	Suozzi	Y	Y	N	Y	Y	Y
4	Rice, K.	Y	Y	N	Y	Y	Y
5	Meeks	?	Y	N	Y	Y	Y
6	Meng	Y	Y	N	Y	Y	Y
7	Velázquez	Y	Y	N	Y	Y	Y
8	Jeffries	Y	Y	N	Y	Y	Y
9	Clarke	Y	Y	N	Y	Y	Y
10	Nadler	Y	Y	N	Y	+	+
11	Rose	Y	Y	N	Y	Y	Y
12	Maloney, C.	Y	Y	N	Y	Y	Y
13	Espaillat	Y	Y	N	Y	Y	Y
14	Ocasio-Cortez	Y	Y	N	Y	Y	Y
15	Serrano	?	?	?	?	?	?
16	Engel	Y	Y	N	Y	Y	Y
17	Lowey	Y	Y	N	Y	Y	Y
18	Maloney, S.P.	Y	Y	N	Y	Y	Y
19	Delgado	Y	Y	N	Y	Y	Y
20	Tonko	Y	Y	N	Y	?	?
21	**Stefanik**	N	N	Y	N	N	N
22	Brindisi	Y	Y	N	Y	Y	Y
23	**Reed**	N	N	Y	N	N	N
24	**Katko**	N	Y	Y	N	-	-
25	Morelle	Y	Y	N	Y	Y	Y
26	Higgins, B.	Y	Y	N	Y	Y	Y
27	**Collins, C.**						
NORTH CAROLINA							
1	Butterfield	Y	Y	N	Y	Y	Y
2	**Holding**	N	N	Y	N	N	N
3	**Murphy**	N	N	Y	N	N	N
4	Price	Y	Y	N	Y	Y	Y
5	**Foxx**	N	N	Y	N	N	N
6	**Walker**	N	N	Y	N	N	N
7	**Rouzer**	N	N	Y	N	N	N

		679	680	681	682	683	684
8	**Hudson**	N	N	Y	N	N	N
9	**Bishop**	N	N	Y	N	N	N
10	**McHenry**	N	N	Y	N	N	N
11	**Meadows**	N	N	Y	N	N	N
12	Adams	Y	Y	N	Y	Y	Y
13	**Budd**	N	N	Y	N	N	N
NORTH DAKOTA							
AL	**Armstrong**	N	N	Y	N	N	N
OHIO							
1	**Chabot**	N	N	Y	N	N	N
2	**Wenstrup**	N	N	Y	N	N	N
3	Beatty	Y	Y	N	Y	Y	Y
4	**Jordan**	N	N	Y	N	N	?
5	**Latta**	N	N	Y	N	N	N
6	**Johnson, B.**	N	N	Y	N	N	N
7	**Gibbs**	N	N	Y	N	N	N
8	**Davidson**	N	N	Y	N	N	N
9	Kaptur	Y	Y	N	Y	Y	Y
10	**Turner**	N	N	Y	N	N	N
11	Fudge	Y	Y	N	Y	Y	Y
12	**Balderson**	N	N	Y	N	N	N
13	Ryan	Y	Y	N	Y	Y	Y
14	**Joyce**	N	N	Y	N	N	N
15	**Stivers**	N	N	Y	N	N	N
16	**Gonzalez**	N	N	Y	N	N	N
OKLAHOMA							
1	**Hern**	N	N	Y	N	N	N
2	**Mullin**	N	N	Y	N	N	N
3	**Lucas**	N	N	Y	N	?	?
4	**Cole**	N	N	Y	N	N	N
5	Horn	Y	Y	N	Y	Y	Y
OREGON							
1	Bonamici	Y	Y	N	Y	Y	Y
2	**Walden**	N	N	Y	N	N	N
3	Blumenauer	Y	Y	N	Y	Y	Y
4	DeFazio	Y	Y	N	Y	Y	Y
5	Schrader	Y	Y	N	Y	Y	Y
PENNSYLVANIA							
1	**Fitzpatrick**	Y	Y	Y	Y	N	N
2	Boyle	Y	Y	N	Y	Y	Y
3	Evans	Y	Y	N	Y	Y	Y
4	Dean	Y	Y	N	Y	Y	Y
5	Scanlon	Y	Y	N	Y	Y	Y
6	Houlahan	Y	Y	N	Y	Y	Y
7	Wild	Y	Y	N	Y	Y	Y
8	Cartwright	Y	Y	N	Y	Y	Y
9	**Meuser**	N	N	Y	N	N	N
10	**Perry**	Y	N	Y	N	N	N
11	**Smucker**	N	N	Y	N	N	N
12	**Keller**	N	N	Y	N	N	N
13	**Joyce**	N	N	Y	N	N	N
14	**Reschenthaler**	N	N	Y	N	N	N
15	**Thompson, G.**	N	N	Y	N	N	N
16	**Kelly, M.**	N	N	Y	N	N	N
17	Lamb	Y	Y	N	Y	Y	Y
18	Doyle	Y	Y	N	Y	Y	Y
RHODE ISLAND							
1	Cicilline	Y	Y	N	Y	Y	Y
2	Langevin	Y	Y	N	Y	Y	Y
SOUTH CAROLINA							
1	Cunningham	Y	Y	N	Y	Y	Y
2	**Wilson, J.**	N	N	Y	N	N	N
3	**Duncan**	N	N	Y	N	N	N
4	**Timmons**	N	N	Y	N	N	N
5	**Norman**	N	N	Y	N	N	-
6	Clyburn	Y	Y	N	Y	Y	Y
7	**Rice, T.**	N	N	Y	N	N	N
SOUTH DAKOTA							
AL	**Johnson**	N	N	Y	N	N	N
TENNESSEE							
1	**Roe**	N	N	Y	N	N	N
2	**Burchett**	-	-	+	-	N	N
3	**Fleischmann**	N	N	Y	N	N	N
4	**DesJarlais**	N	N	Y	N	N	N
5	Cooper	Y	Y	N	Y	Y	Y
6	**Rose**	N	N	Y	N	N	N
7	**Green**	N	N	Y	N	N	N
8	**Kustoff**	N	N	Y	N	N	N
9	Cohen	Y	Y	N	Y	Y	Y
TEXAS							
1	**Gohmert**	N	N	Y	N	N	N
2	**Crenshaw**	N	N	Y	N	N	N
3	**Taylor**	N	N	Y	N	N	N
4	**Ratcliffe**	N	N	Y	N	N	?

		679	680	681	682	683	684
5	**Gooden**	N	N	Y	N	N	N
6	**Wright**	N	N	Y	N	N	N
7	Fletcher	Y	Y	N	Y	Y	Y
8	**Brady**	N	N	Y	N	N	N
9	Green, A.	Y	Y	N	Y	Y	Y
10	**McCaul**	N	N	Y	N	N	N
11	**Conaway**	N	N	Y	N	N	N
12	**Granger**	N	N	Y	N	N	N
13	**Thornberry**	N	N	Y	N	N	N
14	**Weber**	N	N	Y	N	N	N
15	Gonzalez	Y	Y	N	Y	Y	Y
16	Escobar	Y	Y	N	Y	Y	Y
17	**Flores**	N	N	Y	N	?	?
18	Jackson Lee	Y	Y	N	Y	Y	Y
19	**Arrington**	N	N	Y	N	N	N
20	Castro	Y	Y	N	Y	Y	Y
21	**Roy**	N	N	Y	N	N	N
22	**Olson**	N	N	Y	N	N	N
23	**Hurd**	N	N	Y	N	N	N
24	**Marchant**	N	N	Y	N	N	N
25	**Williams**	N	N	Y	N	N	N
26	**Burgess**	N	N	Y	N	N	N
27	**Cloud**	N	N	Y	N	N	N
28	Cuellar	Y	Y	N	Y	Y	Y
29	Garcia, S.	Y	Y	N	Y	Y	Y
30	Johnson, E.B.	Y	Y	N	Y	?	?
31	**Carter, J.**	N	N	Y	N	N	N
32	Allred	Y	Y	N	Y	Y	Y
33	Veasey	Y	Y	N	Y	Y	Y
34	Vela	Y	Y	N	Y	Y	Y
35	Doggett	Y	Y	N	Y	Y	Y
36	**Babin**	N	N	Y	N	N	N
UTAH							
1	**Bishop, R.**	N	N	Y	N	N	N
2	**Stewart**	N	N	Y	N	N	N
3	**Curtis**	N	N	Y	N	N	N
4	McAdams	Y	Y	Y	Y	Y	N
VERMONT							
AL	Welch	Y	Y	N	Y	Y	Y
VIRGINIA							
1	**Wittman**	N	N	Y	N	N	N
2	Luria	Y	Y	N	Y	Y	Y
3	Scott, R.	Y	Y	N	Y	Y	Y
4	McEachin	Y	Y	N	Y	Y	Y
5	**Riggleman**	N	N	Y	N	N	N
6	**Cline**	N	N	Y	N	N	N
7	Spanberger	Y	Y	N	Y	Y	Y
8	Beyer	Y	Y	N	Y	Y	Y
9	**Griffith**	N	N	Y	N	N	N
10	Wexton	Y	Y	N	Y	Y	Y
11	Connolly	Y	Y	N	Y	Y	Y
WASHINGTON							
1	DelBene	Y	Y	N	Y	Y	Y
2	Larsen	Y	Y	N	Y	Y	Y
3	**Herrera Beutler**	N	N	Y	N	N	N
4	**Newhouse**	N	N	Y	N	N	N
5	**McMorris Rodgers**	N	N	Y	N	N	N
6	Kilmer	Y	Y	N	Y	Y	Y
7	Jayapal	Y	Y	N	Y	Y	Y
8	Schrier	Y	Y	N	Y	Y	Y
9	Smith Adam	Y	Y	N	Y	Y	Y
10	Heck	Y	Y	N	Y	Y	Y
WEST VIRGINIA							
1	**McKinley**	N	N	Y	N	N	N
2	**Mooney**	N	N	Y	N	N	N
3	**Miller**	N	N	Y	N	N	N
WISCONSIN							
1	**Steil**	N	N	Y	N	N	N
2	Pocan	Y	Y	N	Y	Y	Y
3	Kind	Y	Y	N	Y	Y	Y
4	Moore	Y	Y	N	Y	Y	Y
5	**Sensenbrenner**	N	N	Y	N	N	N
6	**Grothman**	N	N	Y	N	N	N
7	**Duffy**						
8	**Gallagher**	N	N	Y	N	N	N
WYOMING							
AL	**Cheney**	N	N	Y	N	N	N
DELEGATES							
	Radewagen (A.S.)	N	N				
	Norton (D.C.)	Y	Y				
	San Nicolas (Guam)	?	?				
	Sablan (N. Marianas)	?	?				
	González-Colón (P.R.)	N	N				
	Plaskett (V.I.)	Y	Y				

||| HOUSE VOTES

685. HR4183. VA Benefits Study - Passage. Takano, D-Calif., motion to suspend the rules and pass the bill, as amended, that would require the Government Accountability Office to conduct a study on disability and pension benefits provided by the Veterans Affairs Department to members of the National Guard and U.S. military reserve. Among other requirements, it would require the study to examine the number of service-connected disability compensation and pension claims submitted, approved, and disapproved for such veterans in the period between Jan. 1, 2008 and Dec. 31, 2018; compare such information with regard to benefits received by veterans who served in the regular military; and identify common barriers for National Guard members and reservists in obtaining VA benefits, including barriers relating to documentation of injuries incurred while serving. Motion agreed to 408-1: R 187-1; D 220-0; I 1-0. *Note: A two-thirds majority of those present and voting (273 in this case) is required for passage under suspension of the rules.* Dec. 17, 2019.

686. HR3530. VA Health Professional Credentials - Passage. Takano, D-Calif., motion to suspend the rules and pass the bill, as amended, that would require the Veterans Affairs Department to ensure that its medical centers compile, verify and continuously monitor documentation related to professional certification and credentials for department health care professionals, including documentation of professional licensure, training and education, malpractice history, and any restrictions related to malpractice. It would also require the department to ensure that all personnel who work with controlled substances hold an active registration with the Drug Enforcement Administration. Motion agreed to 409-1: R 187-1; D 221-0; I 1-0. *Note: A two-thirds majority of those present and voting (274 in this case) is required for passage under suspension of the rules.* Dec. 17, 2019.

687. HR722. Utah Mountain Designation - Passage. Haaland, D-N.M., motion to suspend the rules and pass the bill that would designate a mountain located south of Elk Ridge City, Utah, as "Miracle Mountain," to acknowledge the significance of the mountain to the city's residents and surrounding communities in relation to halting the progress of the Sept. 2018 Bald Mountain Fire. Motion agreed to 410-0: R 188-0; D 221-0; I 1-0. *Note: A two-thirds majority of those present and voting (274 in this case) is required for passage under suspension of the rules.* Dec. 17, 2019.

688. HR2548. FEMA Hazard Mitigation Grants - Passage. Fletcher, D-Texas, motion to suspend the rules and pass the bill, as amended, that would make acquisition or relocation projects that have already been initiated eligible for certain Federal Emergency Management Agency hazard mitigation assistance grants to state and local agencies, provided that the project complies with all other grant eligibility requirements and federal project requirements. Motion agreed to 409-7: R 186-6; D 223-0; I 0-1. *Note: A two-thirds majority of those present and voting (278 in this case) is required for passage under suspension of the rules.* Dec. 17, 2019.

689. HR1865. Fiscal 2020 Further Consolidated Appropriation Act - Motion to Concur. Lowey, D-N.Y. motion to concur in the Senate amendment to the Fiscal 2020 Further Consolidated Appropriations Act, with a further House amendment, as modified, that would provide approximately $540 billion in discretionary funding for eight of the twelve fiscal 2020 appropriations. Labor-HHS-Education, Agriculture, Energy-Water, Interior-Environment, Legislative Branch, Military Construction-VA, State-Foreign Operations, and Transportation-HUD. It would provide $184.9 billion for the Labor, Health and Human Services, and Education departments and related agencies; $23.5 billion for the Agriculture Department and related agencies; $48.3 billion for the Energy Department and federal water projects; $36 billion for the Interior Department, Environmental Protection Agency, and related agencies; $5 billion for legislative branch entities; $110.4 billion for the Veterans Affairs Department, military construction, and related agencies; $54.7 billion for the State Department and related agencies; and $74.3 billion for the Transportation and Housing and Urban Development departments and related agencies. Motion agreed to 297-120: R 79-112; D 218-7; I 0-1. Dec. 17, 2019.

690. HR1158. Fiscal 2020 Consolidated Appropriations Act - Motion to Concur. Lowey, D-N.Y., motion to concur in the Senate amendment to the Fiscal 2020 Consolidated Appropriations Act, with a further House amendment, that would provide $860.3 billion in discretionary spending for four of the twelve fiscal 2020 appropriations bills. Defense, Homeland Security, Commerce-Justice-Science, and Financial Services. It would provide $695.1 for the Defense Department, $68 billion for the Homeland Security Department, $73.2 billion for the Commerce and Justice departments and science and related agencies, and $23.8 billion for the Treasury Department, Internal Revenue Service, and other agencies. Motion agreed to 280-138: R 130-62; D 150-75; I 0-1. Dec. 17, 2019.

		685	686	687	688	689	690
ALABAMA							
1	**Byrne**	Y	Y	Y	Y	N	N
2	**Roby**	Y	Y	Y	Y	Y	Y
3	**Rogers, M.**	Y	Y	Y	Y	N	Y
4	**Aderholt**	Y	Y	Y	Y	Y	Y
5	**Brooks, M.**	Y	Y	Y	Y	N	Y
6	**Palmer**	Y	Y	Y	Y	N	N
7	Sewell	Y	Y	Y	Y	Y	Y
ALASKA							
AL	**Young**	Y	Y	Y	Y	Y	Y
ARIZONA							
1	O'Halleran	Y	Y	Y	Y	Y	Y
2	Kirkpatrick	Y	Y	Y	Y	Y	Y
3	Grijalva	Y	Y	Y	Y	Y	N
4	**Gosar**	Y	Y	Y	Y	N	N
5	**Biggs**	Y	Y	Y	N	N	N
6	**Schweikert**	Y	Y	Y	Y	N	N
7	Gallego	Y	Y	Y	Y	Y	N
8	**Lesko**	Y	Y	Y	Y	N	Y
9	Stanton	Y	Y	Y	Y	Y	Y
ARKANSAS							
1	**Crawford**	Y	Y	Y	Y	N	Y
2	**Hill, F.**	Y	Y	Y	Y	Y	Y
3	**Womack**	Y	Y	Y	Y	Y	Y
4	**Westerman**	Y	Y	Y	Y	N	Y
CALIFORNIA							
1	**LaMalfa**	Y	Y	Y	Y	Y	Y
2	Huffman	Y	Y	Y	Y	Y	N
3	Garamendi	Y	Y	Y	Y	Y	Y
4	**McClintock**	Y	Y	Y	Y	N	N
5	Thompson, M.	Y	Y	Y	Y	Y	Y
6	Matsui	Y	Y	Y	Y	Y	Y
7	Bera	Y	Y	Y	Y	Y	Y
8	**Cook**	Y	Y	Y	Y	Y	Y
9	McNerney	Y	Y	Y	Y	Y	Y
10	Harder	Y	Y	Y	Y	Y	Y
11	DeSaulnier	Y	Y	Y	Y	Y	N
12	Pelosi						
13	Lee B.	Y	Y	Y	Y	Y	N
14	Speier	Y	Y	Y	Y	Y	N
15	Swalwell	Y	Y	Y	Y	Y	Y
16	Costa	Y	Y	Y	Y	Y	Y
17	Khanna	Y	Y	Y	Y	Y	N
18	Eshoo	Y	Y	Y	Y	Y	N
19	Lofgren	Y	Y	Y	Y	Y	N
20	Panetta	Y	Y	Y	Y	Y	N
21	Cox	Y	Y	Y	Y	Y	Y
22	**Nunes**	Y	Y	Y	Y	N	Y
23	**McCarthy**	Y	Y	Y	Y	Y	Y
24	Carbajal	Y	Y	Y	Y	Y	Y
25	vacant						
26	Brownley	Y	Y	Y	Y	Y	Y
27	Chu	Y	Y	Y	Y	Y	N
28	Schiff	Y	Y	Y	Y	Y	Y
29	Cárdenas	Y	Y	Y	Y	Y	N
30	Sherman	Y	Y	Y	Y	Y	Y
31	Aguilar	Y	Y	Y	Y	Y	N
32	Napolitano	Y	Y	Y	Y	Y	N
33	Lieu	Y	Y	Y	Y	Y	N
34	Gomez	Y	Y	Y	Y	Y	N
35	Torres	Y	Y	Y	Y	Y	N
36	Ruiz	Y	Y	Y	Y	Y	Y
37	Bass	Y	Y	Y	Y	Y	N
38	Sánchez	Y	Y	Y	Y	Y	N
39	Cisneros	Y	Y	Y	Y	Y	Y
40	Roybal-Allard	Y	Y	Y	Y	Y	N
41	Takano	Y	Y	Y	Y	Y	N
42	**Calvert**	Y	Y	Y	Y	Y	Y
43	Waters	Y	Y	Y	Y	Y	N
44	Barragán	Y	Y	Y	Y	Y	N
45	Porter	Y	Y	Y	Y	Y	Y
46	Correa	Y	Y	Y	Y	Y	N
47	Lowenthal	Y	Y	Y	Y	Y	N
48	Rouda	Y	Y	Y	Y	Y	Y
49	Levin	Y	Y	Y	Y	Y	Y
50	**Hunter**	?	?	?	?	?	?
51	Vargas	?	?	?	?	?	?
52	Peters	Y	Y	Y	Y	N	Y

		685	686	687	688	689	690
53	Davis, S.	Y	Y	Y	Y	Y	Y
COLORADO							
1	DeGette	Y	Y	Y	Y	Y	N
2	Neguse	Y	Y	Y	Y	Y	N
3	**Tipton**	Y	Y	Y	Y	N	Y
4	**Buck**	Y	Y	Y	Y	N	N
5	**Lamborn**	Y	Y	Y	Y	N	Y
6	Crow	Y	Y	Y	Y	Y	Y
7	Perlmutter	Y	Y	Y	Y	Y	Y
CONNECTICUT							
1	Larson	Y	Y	Y	Y	Y	Y
2	Courtney	Y	Y	Y	Y	Y	Y
3	DeLauro	Y	Y	Y	Y	Y	Y
4	Himes	Y	Y	Y	Y	Y	Y
5	Hayes	Y	Y	Y	Y	Y	Y
DELAWARE							
AL	Blunt Rochester	Y	Y	Y	Y	Y	Y
FLORIDA							
1	**Gaetz**	Y	Y	Y	Y	N	N
2	**Dunn**	Y	Y	Y	Y	Y	Y
3	**Yoho**	Y	Y	Y	N	N	N
4	**Rutherford**	Y	Y	Y	Y	Y	Y
5	Lawson	Y	Y	Y	Y	Y	Y
6	**Waltz**	Y	Y	Y	Y	N	Y
7	Murphy	Y	Y	Y	Y	Y	Y
8	**Posey**	Y	Y	Y	Y	N	Y
9	Soto	Y	Y	Y	Y	Y	Y
10	Demings	Y	Y	Y	Y	Y	Y
11	**Webster**	Y	Y	Y	Y	N	Y
12	**Bilirakis**	Y	Y	Y	Y	Y	Y
13	Crist	Y	Y	Y	Y	Y	Y
14	Castor	Y	Y	Y	Y	Y	Y
15	**Spano**	Y	Y	Y	Y	N	N
16	**Buchanan**	Y	Y	Y	Y	Y	Y
17	**Steube**	Y	Y	Y	Y	N	N
18	**Mast**	Y	Y	Y	Y	Y	Y
19	**Rooney**	Y	Y	Y	Y	N	N
20	Hastings	Y	Y	Y	Y	Y	Y
21	Frankel	Y	Y	Y	Y	Y	Y
22	Deutch	Y	Y	Y	Y	Y	Y
23	Wasserman Schultz	Y	Y	Y	Y	Y	Y
24	Wilson, F.	?	?	?	?	Y	Y
25	**Diaz-Balart**	Y	Y	Y	Y	Y	Y
26	Mucarsel-Powell	Y	Y	Y	Y	Y	Y
27	Shalala	Y	Y	Y	Y	Y	Y
GEORGIA							
1	**Carter, E.L.**	Y	Y	Y	Y	N	Y
2	Bishop, S.	Y	Y	Y	Y	Y	Y
3	**Ferguson**	Y	Y	Y	Y	N	Y
4	Johnson, H.	Y	Y	Y	Y	Y	Y
5	Lewis John	Y	Y	Y	+	+	?
6	McBath	Y	Y	Y	Y	Y	Y
7	**Woodall**	Y	Y	Y	Y	Y	Y
8	**Scott, A.**	Y	Y	Y	Y	N	Y
9	**Collins, D.**	Y	Y	Y	Y	N	Y
10	**Hice**	Y	Y	Y	Y	N	N
11	**Loudermilk**	Y	Y	Y	Y	N	Y
12	**Allen**	Y	Y	Y	Y	N	Y
13	Scott, D.	Y	Y	Y	Y	Y	Y
14	**Graves, T.**	Y	Y	Y	Y	Y	Y
HAWAII							
1	Case	Y	Y	Y	Y	Y	Y
2	Gabbard	?	?	?	?	?	?
IDAHO							
1	**Fulcher**	Y	Y	Y	Y	N	N
2	**Simpson**	Y	Y	Y	Y	Y	Y
ILLINOIS							
1	Rush	Y	Y	Y	Y	Y	Y
2	Kelly, R.	Y	Y	Y	Y	Y	Y
3	Lipinski	Y	Y	Y	Y	Y	Y
4	García, J.	Y	Y	Y	Y	Y	N
5	Quigley	Y	Y	Y	Y	Y	Y
6	Casten	Y	Y	Y	Y	Y	Y
7	Davis, D.	Y	Y	Y	Y	Y	Y
8	Krishnamoorthi	Y	Y	Y	Y	Y	Y
9	Schakowsky	Y	Y	Y	Y	Y	N
10	Schneider	Y	Y	Y	Y	Y	Y
11	Foster	Y	Y	Y	Y	Y	Y

KEY: **Republicans** Democrats *Independents*

Y	Voted for (yea)	N	Voted against (nay)	P	Voted "present"
+	Announced for	-	Announced against	?	Did not vote or otherwise make position known
#	Paired for	X	Paired against		

H-236 2019 CQ ALMANAC | www.cq.com

	685	686	687	688	689	690
12 **Bost**	Y	Y	Y	Y	Y	Y
13 **Davis, R.**	Y	Y	Y	Y	Y	Y
14 Underwood	Y	Y	Y	Y	Y	Y
15 **Shimkus**	?	?	?	?	?	?
16 **Kinzinger**	Y	Y	Y	Y	Y	Y
17 Bustos	Y	Y	Y	Y	Y	Y
18 **LaHood**	Y	Y	Y	Y	N	N
INDIANA						
1 Visclosky	Y	Y	Y	Y	Y	Y
2 **Walorski**	Y	Y	Y	Y	Y	Y
3 **Banks**	Y	Y	Y	Y	N	Y
4 **Baird**	Y	Y	Y	Y	Y	Y
5 **Brooks, S.**	Y	Y	Y	Y	Y	Y
6 **Pence**	Y	Y	Y	Y	Y	Y
7 Carson	Y	Y	Y	Y	Y	Y
8 **Bucshon**	Y	Y	Y	Y	Y	Y
9 **Hollingsworth**	?	?	?	?	?	?
IOWA						
1 Finkenauer	Y	Y	Y	Y	Y	Y
2 Loebsack	Y	Y	Y	Y	Y	Y
3 Axne	Y	Y	Y	Y	Y	Y
4 **King, S.**	Y	Y	Y	Y	N	N
KANSAS						
1 **Marshall**	Y	Y	Y	Y	N	Y
2 **Watkins**	Y	Y	Y	Y	N	Y
3 Davids	Y	Y	Y	Y	Y	Y
4 **Estes**	Y	Y	Y	Y	N	Y
KENTUCKY						
1 **Comer**	Y	Y	Y	Y	Y	N
2 **Guthrie**	Y	Y	Y	Y	Y	Y
3 Yarmuth	Y	Y	Y	Y	Y	Y
4 **Massie**	Y	Y	Y	N	N	N
5 **Rogers, H.**	Y	Y	Y	Y	Y	Y
6 **Barr**	Y	Y	Y	Y	Y	Y
LOUISIANA						
1 **Scalise**	Y	Y	Y	Y	N	Y
2 Richmond	Y	Y	Y	Y	Y	N
3 **Higgins, C.**	Y	Y	Y	Y	N	N
4 **Johnson, M.**	?	?	?	Y	N	N
5 **Abraham**	Y	Y	Y	Y	N	Y
6 **Graves, G.**	Y	Y	Y	Y	N	Y
MAINE						
1 Pingree	Y	Y	Y	Y	Y	Y
2 Golden	Y	Y	Y	Y	Y	Y
MARYLAND						
1 **Harris**	Y	Y	Y	Y	N	Y
2 Ruppersberger	Y	Y	Y	Y	Y	Y
3 Sarbanes	Y	Y	Y	Y	Y	Y
4 Brown, A.	Y	Y	Y	Y	Y	Y
5 Hoyer	Y	Y	Y	Y	Y	Y
6 Trone	Y	Y	Y	Y	Y	Y
7 vacant						
8 Raskin	Y	Y	Y	Y	Y	N
MASSACHUSETTS						
1 Neal	Y	Y	Y	Y	Y	Y
2 McGovern	Y	Y	Y	Y	Y	N
3 Trahan	Y	Y	Y	Y	Y	N
4 Kennedy	Y	Y	Y	Y	Y	N
5 Clark	Y	Y	Y	Y	Y	Y
6 Moulton	Y	Y	Y	Y	Y	Y
7 Pressley	+	+	+	Y	Y	N
8 Lynch	Y	Y	Y	Y	Y	Y
9 Keating	Y	Y	Y	Y	Y	Y
MICHIGAN						
1 **Bergman**	Y	Y	Y	Y	Y	Y
2 **Huizenga**	Y	Y	Y	Y	N	N
3 *Amash*	Y	Y	Y	N	N	N
4 **Moolenaar**	Y	Y	Y	Y	Y	Y
5 Kildee	Y	Y	Y	Y	Y	Y
6 **Upton**	Y	Y	Y	Y	Y	Y
7 **Walberg**	Y	Y	Y	Y	Y	Y
8 Slotkin	Y	Y	Y	Y	Y	Y
9 Levin	Y	Y	Y	Y	Y	N
10 **Mitchell**	Y	Y	Y	Y	Y	Y
11 Stevens	Y	Y	Y	Y	Y	Y
12 Dingell	Y	Y	Y	Y	Y	Y
13 Tlaib	Y	Y	Y	Y	Y	N
14 Lawrence	Y	Y	Y	Y	Y	Y
MINNESOTA						
1 **Hagedorn**	Y	Y	Y	Y	Y	Y
2 Craig	Y	Y	Y	Y	Y	Y
3 Phillips	Y	Y	Y	Y	Y	Y
4 McCollum	Y	Y	Y	Y	Y	Y
5 Omar	Y	Y	Y	Y	N	N

	685	686	687	688	689	690
6 **Emmer**	Y	Y	Y	Y	N	N
7 Peterson	Y	Y	Y	Y	Y	Y
8 **Stauber**	Y	Y	Y	Y	Y	Y
MISSISSIPPI						
1 **Kelly, T.**	Y	Y	Y	Y	N	Y
2 Thompson, B.	?	?	?	?	?	?
3 **Guest**	Y	Y	Y	Y	N	Y
4 **Palazzo**	Y	Y	Y	Y	Y	Y
MISSOURI						
1 Clay	?	?	?	Y	Y	Y
2 **Wagner**	Y	Y	Y	Y	Y	Y
3 **Luetkemeyer**	Y	Y	Y	Y	Y	Y
4 **Hartzler**	Y	Y	Y	Y	Y	Y
5 Cleaver	Y	Y	Y	Y	Y	Y
6 **Graves, S.**	Y	Y	Y	Y	N	Y
7 **Long**	Y	Y	Y	Y	N	Y
8 **Smith, J.**	Y	Y	Y	Y	N	N
MONTANA						
AL **Gianforte**	Y	Y	Y	Y	N	Y
NEBRASKA						
1 **Fortenberry**	Y	Y	Y	Y	Y	Y
2 **Bacon**	Y	Y	Y	Y	Y	Y
3 **Smith, Adrian**	Y	Y	Y	Y	Y	Y
NEVADA						
1 Titus	Y	Y	Y	Y	Y	N
2 **Amodei**	Y	Y	Y	Y	Y	Y
3 Lee	Y	Y	Y	Y	Y	Y
4 Horsford	Y	Y	Y	Y	Y	Y
NEW HAMPSHIRE						
1 Pappas	Y	Y	Y	Y	Y	Y
2 Kuster	Y	Y	Y	Y	Y	Y
NEW JERSEY						
1 Norcross	Y	Y	Y	Y	Y	N
2 Van Drew	?	?	?	?	Y	Y
3 Kim	Y	Y	Y	Y	Y	Y
4 **Smith, C.**	Y	Y	Y	Y	Y	Y
5 Gottheimer	Y	Y	Y	Y	Y	Y
6 Pallone	Y	Y	Y	Y	N	N
7 Malinowski	Y	Y	Y	Y	Y	Y
8 Sires	Y	Y	Y	Y	Y	Y
9 Pascrell	?	Y	Y	Y	Y	N
10 Payne	Y	Y	Y	Y	Y	Y
11 Sherrill	Y	Y	Y	Y	Y	Y
12 Watson Coleman	Y	Y	Y	Y	Y	N
NEW MEXICO						
1 Haaland	Y	Y	Y	Y	Y	N
2 Torres Small	Y	Y	Y	Y	Y	Y
3 Luján	Y	Y	Y	Y	Y	N
NEW YORK						
1 **Zeldin**	Y	Y	Y	Y	N	N
2 **King, P.**	Y	Y	Y	Y	Y	Y
3 Suozzi	Y	Y	Y	Y	Y	N
4 Rice, K.	Y	Y	Y	Y	Y	Y
5 Meeks	Y	Y	Y	Y	Y	Y
6 Meng	Y	Y	Y	Y	Y	N
7 Velázquez	Y	Y	Y	Y	Y	N
8 Jeffries	Y	Y	Y	Y	Y	Y
9 Clarke	Y	Y	Y	Y	Y	N
10 Nadler	+	+	+	+	+	-
11 Rose	Y	Y	Y	Y	Y	Y
12 Maloney, C.	Y	Y	Y	Y	Y	N
13 Espaillat	Y	Y	Y	Y	Y	N
14 Ocasio-Cortez	Y	Y	Y	Y	N	N
15 Serrano	?	?	?	?	?	?
16 Engel	Y	Y	Y	Y	Y	N
17 Lowey	Y	Y	Y	Y	Y	Y
18 Maloney, S.P.	Y	Y	Y	Y	Y	Y
19 Delgado	Y	Y	Y	Y	Y	Y
20 Tonko	?	?	?	Y	Y	N
21 **Stefanik**	Y	Y	Y	Y	Y	Y
22 Brindisi	Y	Y	Y	Y	Y	Y
23 **Reed**	Y	Y	Y	Y	Y	Y
24 **Katko**	+	+	+	Y	Y	Y
25 Morelle	Y	Y	Y	Y	Y	Y
26 Higgins, B.	Y	Y	Y	Y	Y	Y
27 **Collins, C.**	Y	Y	Y	Y	Y	Y
NORTH CAROLINA						
1 Butterfield	Y	Y	Y	Y	Y	Y
2 **Holding**	Y	Y	Y	Y	N	N
3 **Murphy**	Y	Y	Y	Y	N	Y
4 Price	Y	Y	Y	Y	Y	Y
5 **Foxx**	Y	Y	Y	Y	N	Y
6 **Walker**	Y	Y	Y	?	?	?
7 **Rouzer**	Y	Y	Y	Y	N	N

	685	686	687	688	689	690
8 **Hudson**	Y	Y	Y	Y	N	Y
9 **Bishop**	Y	Y	Y	Y	N	N
10 **McHenry**	Y	Y	Y	Y	Y	Y
11 **Meadows**	Y	Y	Y	Y	N	N
12 Adams	Y	Y	Y	Y	Y	Y
13 **Budd**	Y	Y	Y	Y	N	N
NORTH DAKOTA						
AL **Armstrong**	Y	Y	Y	Y	N	N
OHIO						
1 **Chabot**	Y	Y	Y	Y	N	Y
2 **Wenstrup**	Y	Y	Y	Y	N	Y
3 Beatty	Y	Y	Y	Y	Y	Y
4 **Jordan**	?	?	?	Y	N	N
5 **Latta**	Y	Y	Y	Y	N	N
6 **Johnson, B.**	Y	Y	Y	Y	Y	Y
7 **Gibbs**	Y	Y	Y	Y	Y	Y
8 **Davidson**	Y	Y	Y	Y	N	N
9 Kaptur	Y	Y	Y	Y	Y	Y
10 **Turner**	Y	Y	Y	Y	Y	Y
11 Fudge	Y	Y	Y	Y	Y	Y
12 **Balderson**	Y	Y	Y	Y	Y	Y
13 Ryan	Y	Y	Y	Y	Y	Y
14 **Joyce**	Y	Y	Y	Y	Y	Y
15 **Stivers**	Y	Y	Y	Y	Y	Y
16 **Gonzalez**	Y	Y	Y	Y	N	Y
OKLAHOMA						
1 **Hern**	Y	Y	Y	Y	N	N
2 **Mullin**	Y	Y	Y	Y	N	N
3 **Lucas**	?	?	?	?	?	?
4 **Cole**	Y	Y	Y	Y	Y	Y
5 Horn	Y	Y	Y	Y	Y	Y
OREGON						
1 Bonamici	Y	Y	Y	Y	Y	N
2 **Walden**	Y	Y	Y	Y	Y	Y
3 Blumenauer	Y	Y	Y	Y	Y	N
4 DeFazio	Y	Y	Y	Y	Y	N
5 Schrader	Y	Y	Y	Y	Y	Y
PENNSYLVANIA						
1 **Fitzpatrick**	Y	Y	Y	Y	Y	Y
2 Boyle	Y	Y	Y	Y	Y	N
3 Evans	Y	Y	Y	Y	Y	Y
4 Dean	Y	Y	Y	Y	Y	Y
5 Scanlon	Y	Y	Y	Y	Y	Y
6 Houlahan	Y	Y	Y	Y	Y	Y
7 Wild	Y	Y	Y	Y	Y	Y
8 Cartwright	Y	Y	Y	Y	Y	Y
9 **Meuser**	Y	Y	Y	Y	N	Y
10 **Perry**	Y	Y	Y	Y	N	N
11 **Smucker**	Y	Y	Y	Y	N	N
12 **Keller**	Y	Y	Y	Y	N	N
13 **Joyce**	Y	Y	Y	Y	N	N
14 **Reschenthaler**	Y	Y	Y	Y	Y	Y
15 **Thompson, G.**	Y	Y	Y	Y	Y	Y
16 **Kelly, M.**	Y	Y	Y	Y	N	N
17 Lamb	Y	Y	Y	Y	Y	Y
18 Doyle	Y	Y	Y	Y	Y	N
RHODE ISLAND						
1 Cicilline	Y	Y	Y	Y	Y	Y
2 Langevin	Y	Y	Y	Y	Y	Y
SOUTH CAROLINA						
1 Cunningham	Y	Y	Y	Y	Y	Y
2 **Wilson, J.**	Y	Y	Y	Y	Y	Y
3 **Duncan**	Y	Y	Y	N	N	N
4 **Timmons**	Y	Y	Y	Y	N	N
5 **Norman**	N	N	Y	N	N	N
6 Clyburn	Y	Y	Y	Y	Y	Y
7 **Rice, T.**	Y	Y	Y	Y	N	N
SOUTH DAKOTA						
AL **Johnson**	Y	Y	Y	Y	N	N
TENNESSEE						
1 **Roe**	Y	Y	Y	Y	Y	Y
2 **Burchett**	Y	Y	Y	Y	N	N
3 **Fleischmann**	Y	Y	Y	Y	Y	Y
4 **DesJarlais**	Y	Y	Y	Y	N	Y
5 Cooper	Y	Y	Y	Y	Y	Y
6 **Rose**	Y	Y	Y	Y	N	Y
7 **Green**	Y	Y	Y	Y	N	Y
8 **Kustoff**	Y	Y	Y	Y	Y	Y
9 Cohen	Y	Y	Y	Y	Y	N
TEXAS						
1 **Gohmert**	Y	Y	Y	Y	N	N
2 **Crenshaw**	Y	Y	Y	Y	N	Y
3 **Taylor**	Y	Y	Y	Y	N	N
4 **Ratcliffe**	?	?	?	Y	N	N

	685	686	687	688	689	690
5 **Gooden**	Y	Y	Y	Y	N	Y
6 **Wright**	Y	Y	Y	Y	N	N
7 Fletcher	Y	Y	Y	Y	Y	Y
8 **Brady**	Y	Y	Y	Y	Y	Y
9 Green, A.	Y	Y	Y	Y	Y	N
10 **McCaul**	Y	Y	Y	Y	Y	Y
11 **Conaway**	Y	Y	Y	Y	Y	Y
12 **Granger**	Y	Y	Y	Y	Y	Y
13 **Thornberry**	Y	Y	Y	Y	Y	Y
14 **Weber**	Y	Y	Y	Y	N	Y
15 Gonzalez	Y	Y	Y	Y	Y	N
16 Escobar	Y	Y	Y	Y	Y	N
17 **Flores**	?	?	?	Y	N	Y
18 Jackson Lee	Y	Y	Y	Y	Y	N
19 **Arrington**	Y	Y	Y	Y	N	N
20 Castro	Y	Y	Y	Y	Y	N
21 **Roy**	Y	Y	Y	Y	N	N
22 **Olson**	Y	Y	Y	Y	N	Y
23 **Hurd**	Y	Y	Y	Y	Y	Y
24 **Marchant**	Y	Y	Y	Y	N	Y
25 **Williams**	Y	Y	Y	Y	N	Y
26 **Burgess**	Y	Y	Y	Y	N	Y
27 **Cloud**	Y	Y	Y	Y	N	N
28 Cuellar	Y	Y	Y	Y	Y	N
29 Garcia, S.	Y	Y	Y	Y	Y	N
30 Johnson, E.B.	?	?	?	?	?	?
31 **Carter, J.**	Y	Y	Y	Y	Y	Y
32 Allred	Y	Y	Y	Y	Y	Y
33 Veasey	Y	Y	Y	Y	Y	Y
34 Vela	Y	Y	Y	Y	Y	N
35 Doggett	Y	Y	Y	Y	N	N
36 **Babin**	Y	Y	Y	Y	N	Y
UTAH						
1 **Bishop, R.**	Y	Y	Y	Y	-	Y
2 **Stewart**	Y	Y	Y	Y	N	Y
3 **Curtis**	Y	Y	Y	Y	N	N
4 McAdams	Y	Y	Y	Y	N	N
VERMONT						
AL Welch	Y	Y	Y	Y	Y	N
VIRGINIA						
1 **Wittman**	Y	Y	Y	Y	N	Y
2 Luria	Y	Y	Y	Y	Y	Y
3 Scott, R.	Y	Y	Y	Y	Y	Y
4 McEachin	Y	Y	Y	Y	Y	Y
5 **Riggleman**	Y	Y	Y	Y	N	Y
6 **Cline**	Y	Y	Y	Y	N	N
7 Spanberger	Y	Y	Y	Y	Y	Y
8 Beyer	Y	Y	Y	Y	Y	Y
9 **Griffith**	Y	Y	Y	Y	N	N
10 Wexton	Y	Y	Y	Y	Y	Y
11 Connolly	Y	Y	Y	Y	Y	Y
WASHINGTON						
1 DelBene	Y	Y	Y	Y	Y	Y
2 Larsen	Y	Y	Y	Y	Y	Y
3 **Herrera Beutler**	Y	Y	Y	Y	Y	Y
4 **Newhouse**	Y	Y	Y	Y	Y	Y
5 **McMorris Rodgers**	Y	Y	Y	Y	N	N
6 Kilmer	Y	Y	Y	Y	Y	Y
7 Jayapal	Y	Y	Y	Y	Y	N
8 Schrier	Y	Y	Y	Y	Y	Y
9 Smith Adam	Y	Y	Y	Y	Y	N
10 Heck	Y	Y	Y	Y	Y	Y
WEST VIRGINIA						
1 **McKinley**	Y	Y	Y	Y	Y	Y
2 **Mooney**	Y	Y	Y	Y	Y	N
3 **Miller**	Y	Y	Y	Y	Y	Y
WISCONSIN						
1 **Steil**	Y	Y	Y	Y	N	N
2 Pocan	Y	Y	Y	Y	Y	N
3 Kind	Y	Y	Y	Y	N	Y
4 Moore	Y	Y	Y	Y	Y	N
5 **Sensenbrenner**	Y	Y	Y	Y	N	N
6 **Grothman**	Y	Y	Y	N	N	N
7 **Duffy**						
8 **Gallagher**	Y	Y	Y	Y	N	N
WYOMING						
AL **Cheney**	Y	Y	Y	Y	N	Y
DELEGATES						
Radewagen (A.S.)						
Norton (D.C.)						
San Nicolas (Guam)						
Sablan (N. Marianas)						
González-Colón (P.R.)						
Plaskett (V.I.)						

691. Procedural Motion - Adjournment. Biggs, R-Ariz., motion to adjourn. Motion rejected 188-226: R 188-0; D 0-225; I 0-1. Dec. 18, 2019.

692. HRES770. Condemning Reps. Nadler and Schiff - Motion to Table. Hoyer, D-Md., motion to table (kill) the privileged resolution that would that would express disapproval of actions by House Judiciary Committee Chairman Jerrold Nadler, D-N.Y., and House Intelligence Committee Chairman Adam Schiff, D-Calif., in relation to the impeachment inquiry into President Donald Trump. Motion agreed to 226-191: R 0-190; D 225-1; I 1-0. Dec. 18, 2019.

693. HRES755. Impeachment of President Trump - Previous Question. McGovern, D-Mass., motion to order the previous question (thus ending debate and possibility of amendment) on the rule (H Res 767) for the resolution (H Res 755) containing two articles of impeachment against President Trump for abuse of power and obstruction of Congress, respectively. The rule would provide for six hours of debate on the Articles of Impeachment, equally divided between the chair and ranking member of the House Judiciary Committee or their designees. Motion agreed to 229-197: R 0-195; D 228-2; I 1-0. Dec. 18, 2019.

694. HRES755. Impeachment of President Trump - Rule. Adoption of the rule (H Res 767) for the resolution (H Res 755) containing two articles of impeachment against President Trump for abuse of power and obstruction of Congress, respectively. The rule would provide for six hours of debate on the Articles of Impeachment, equally divided between the chair and ranking member of the House Judiciary Committee or their designees. Adopted 228-197: R 0-195; D 227-2; I 1-0. Dec. 18, 2019.

695. HRES755. Impeachment of President Trump - Article I - Abuse of Power. Adoption of Article I of the resolution, which would impeach President Donald Trump for abuse of power by using the powers of his office to solicit the interference of a foreign government in the 2020 U.S. presidential election to benefit his reelection and harm the election prospects of a political opponent. Specifically, it would state that Trump solicited the government of Ukraine to announce investigations into former vice president Joe Biden and theories regarding foreign interference in the 2016 U.S. presidential election. It would state that Trump conditioned official actions, including the release of security assistance funds to Ukraine, on such announcements. It would state that Trump's actions were conducted "for corrupt purposes in pursuit of personal political benefit" and that such actions "compromised the national security of the United States and undermined the integrity of the United States democratic process." Adopted 230-197: R 0-195; D 229-2; I 1-0. *Note: A "nay" was a vote in support of the president's position.* Dec. 18, 2019.

696. HRES755. Impeachment of President Trump - Article II - Obstruction of Congress. Adoption of Article II of the resolution, which would impeach President Donald Trump for obstruction of Congress by defying, and instructing others not to comply with, subpoenas issued by the House of Representatives in relation to the House impeachment inquiry into Trump's solicitation of the government of Ukraine. Adopted 229-198: R 0-195; D 228-3; I 1-0. *Note: A "nay" was a vote in support of the president's position.* Dec. 18, 2019.

		691	692	693	694	695	696
ALABAMA							
1	**Byrne**	Y	N	N	N	N	N
2	**Roby**	Y	N	N	N	N	N
3	**Rogers, M.**	Y	N	N	N	N	N
4	**Aderholt**	Y	N	N	N	N	N
5	**Brooks, M.**	Y	N	N	N	N	N
6	**Palmer**	Y	N	N	N	N	N
7	Sewell	N	Y	Y	Y	Y	Y
ALASKA							
AL	**Young**	?	?	N	N	N	N
ARIZONA							
1	O'Halleran	N	Y	Y	Y	Y	Y
2	Kirkpatrick	N	Y	Y	Y	Y	Y
3	Grijalva	N	Y	Y	Y	Y	Y
4	**Gosar**	Y	N	N	N	N	N
5	**Biggs**	Y	N	N	N	N	N
6	**Schweikert**	Y	N	N	N	N	N
7	Gallego	N	Y	Y	?	Y	Y
8	**Lesko**	Y	N	N	N	N	N
9	Stanton	N	Y	Y	Y	Y	Y
ARKANSAS							
1	**Crawford**	Y	N	N	N	N	N
2	**Hill, F.**	Y	N	N	N	N	N
3	**Womack**	Y	N	N	N	N	N
4	**Westerman**	Y	N	N	N	N	N
CALIFORNIA							
1	**LaMalfa**	Y	N	N	N	N	N
2	Huffman	N	Y	Y	Y	Y	Y
3	Garamendi	N	Y	Y	Y	Y	Y
4	**McClintock**	Y	N	N	N	N	N
5	Thompson, M.	N	Y	Y	Y	Y	Y
6	Matsui	N	Y	Y	Y	Y	Y
7	Bera	N	Y	Y	Y	Y	Y
8	**Cook**	Y	N	N	N	N	N
9	McNerney	N	Y	Y	Y	Y	Y
10	Harder	N	Y	Y	Y	Y	Y
11	DeSaulnier	N	Y	Y	Y	Y	Y
12	Pelosi					Y	Y
13	Lee B.	N	Y	Y	Y	Y	Y
14	Speier	N	Y	Y	Y	Y	Y
15	Swalwell	N	Y	Y	Y	Y	Y
16	Costa	N	Y	Y	Y	Y	Y
17	Khanna	N	Y	Y	Y	Y	Y
18	Eshoo	N	Y	Y	Y	Y	Y
19	Lofgren	N	Y	Y	Y	Y	Y
20	Panetta	N	Y	Y	Y	Y	Y
21	Cox	N	Y	Y	Y	Y	Y
22	**Nunes**	Y	N	N	N	N	N
23	**McCarthy**	Y	N	N	N	N	N
24	Carbajal	N	Y	Y	Y	Y	Y
25	vacant						
26	Brownley	N	Y	Y	Y	Y	Y
27	Chu	N	Y	Y	Y	Y	Y
28	Schiff	N	Y	Y	Y	Y	Y
29	Cárdenas	N	Y	Y	Y	Y	Y
30	Sherman	N	Y	Y	Y	Y	Y
31	Aguilar	N	Y	Y	Y	Y	Y
32	Napolitano	N	Y	Y	Y	Y	Y
33	Lieu	N	Y	Y	Y	Y	Y
34	Gomez	N	Y	Y	Y	Y	Y
35	Torres	N	Y	Y	Y	Y	Y
36	Ruiz	N	Y	Y	Y	Y	Y
37	Bass	N	Y	Y	Y	Y	Y
38	Sánchez	N	Y	Y	Y	Y	Y
39	Cisneros	N	Y	Y	Y	Y	Y
40	Roybal-Allard	N	Y	Y	Y	Y	Y
41	Takano	N	Y	Y	Y	Y	Y
42	**Calvert**	Y	N	N	N	N	N
43	Waters	N	Y	Y	Y	Y	Y
44	Barragán	N	Y	Y	Y	Y	Y
45	Porter	N	Y	Y	Y	Y	Y
46	Correa	N	Y	Y	Y	Y	Y
47	Lowenthal	N	Y	Y	Y	Y	Y
48	Rouda	N	Y	Y	Y	Y	Y
49	Levin	N	Y	Y	Y	Y	Y
50	**Hunter**	?	?	?	?	?	?
51	Vargas	N	Y	Y	Y	Y	Y
52	Peters	N	Y	Y	Y	Y	Y

		691	692	693	694	695	696
53	Davis, S.	N	Y	Y	Y	Y	Y
COLORADO							
1	DeGette	N	Y	Y	Y	Y	Y
2	Neguse	N	Y	Y	Y	Y	Y
3	**Tipton**	Y	N	N	N	N	N
4	**Buck**	Y	N	N	N	N	N
5	**Lamborn**	Y	N	N	N	N	N
6	Crow	N	Y	Y	Y	Y	Y
7	Perlmutter	N	Y	Y	Y	Y	Y
CONNECTICUT							
1	Larson	N	Y	Y	Y	Y	Y
2	Courtney	N	Y	Y	Y	Y	Y
3	DeLauro	N	Y	Y	Y	Y	Y
4	Himes	N	Y	Y	Y	Y	Y
5	Hayes	N	Y	Y	Y	Y	Y
DELAWARE							
AL	Blunt Rochester	N	Y	Y	Y	Y	Y
FLORIDA							
1	**Gaetz**	Y	N	N	N	N	N
2	**Dunn**	Y	N	N	N	N	N
3	**Yoho**	Y	N	N	N	N	N
4	**Rutherford**	Y	N	N	N	N	N
5	Lawson	?	Y	Y	Y	Y	Y
6	**Waltz**	Y	N	N	N	N	N
7	Murphy	N	Y	Y	Y	Y	Y
8	**Posey**	?	N	N	N	N	N
9	Soto	N	Y	Y	Y	Y	Y
10	Demings	N	Y	Y	Y	Y	Y
11	**Webster**	Y	N	N	N	N	N
12	**Bilirakis**	Y	N	N	N	N	N
13	Crist	N	Y	Y	Y	Y	Y
14	Castor	N	Y	Y	Y	Y	Y
15	**Spano**	Y	N	N	N	N	N
16	**Buchanan**	Y	N	N	N	N	N
17	**Steube**	Y	N	N	N	N	N
18	**Mast**	Y	N	N	N	N	N
19	**Rooney**	?	?	N	N	N	N
20	Hastings	N	Y	Y	Y	Y	Y
21	Frankel	N	Y	Y	Y	Y	Y
22	Deutch	N	Y	Y	Y	Y	Y
23	Wasserman Schultz	N	Y	Y	Y	Y	Y
24	Wilson, F.	N	Y	Y	Y	Y	Y
25	**Diaz-Balart**	Y	N	N	N	N	N
26	Mucarsel-Powell	N	Y	Y	Y	Y	Y
27	Shalala	N	Y	Y	Y	Y	Y
GEORGIA							
1	**Carter, E.L.**	Y	N	N	N	N	N
2	Bishop, S.	N	Y	Y	Y	Y	Y
3	**Ferguson**	Y	N	N	N	N	N
4	Johnson, H.	N	Y	Y	Y	Y	Y
5	Lewis John	N	Y	Y	Y	Y	Y
6	McBath	N	Y	Y	Y	Y	Y
7	**Woodall**	?	?	N	N	N	N
8	**Scott, A.**	Y	N	N	N	N	N
9	**Collins, D.**	Y	N	N	N	N	N
10	**Hice**	Y	N	N	N	N	N
11	**Loudermilk**	Y	N	N	N	N	N
12	**Allen**	Y	N	N	N	N	N
13	Scott, D.	N	Y	Y	Y	Y	Y
14	**Graves, T.**	Y	N	N	N	N	N
HAWAII							
1	Case	N	Y	Y	Y	Y	Y
2	Gabbard	?	?	?	?	P	P
IDAHO							
1	**Fulcher**	Y	N	N	N	N	N
2	**Simpson**	Y	N	N	N	N	N
ILLINOIS							
1	Rush	N	Y	Y	Y	Y	Y
2	Kelly, R.	N	Y	Y	Y	Y	Y
3	Lipinski	N	Y	Y	Y	Y	Y
4	García, J.	N	Y	Y	Y	Y	Y
5	Quigley	N	Y	Y	Y	Y	Y
6	Casten	N	Y	Y	Y	Y	Y
7	Davis, D.	N	Y	Y	Y	Y	Y
8	Krishnamoorthi	N	Y	Y	Y	Y	Y
9	Schakowsky	N	Y	Y	Y	Y	Y
10	Schneider	N	Y	Y	Y	Y	Y
11	Foster	N	Y	Y	Y	Y	Y

KEY:	Republicans	Democrats	Independents
Y Voted for (yea)	**N** Voted against (nay)	**P** Voted "present"	
+ Announced for	**–** Announced against	**?** Did not vote or otherwise	
# Paired for	**X** Paired against	make position known	

		691	692	693	694	695	696
12	**Bost**	Y	N	N	N	N	N
13	**Davis, R.**	Y	N	N	N	N	N
14	Underwood	N	Y	Y	Y	Y	Y
15	**Shimkus**	?	?	?	?	?	?
16	**Kinzinger**	Y	N	N	N	N	N
17	Bustos	N	Y	Y	Y	Y	Y
18	**LaHood**	Y	N	N	N	N	N
INDIANA							
1	Visclosky	N	Y	Y	Y	Y	Y
2	**Walorski**	Y	N	N	N	N	N
3	**Banks**	Y	N	N	N	N	N
4	**Baird**	Y	N	N	N	N	N
5	**Brooks, S.**	Y	N	N	N	N	N
6	**Pence**	Y	N	N	N	N	N
7	Carson	N	Y	Y	Y	Y	Y
8	**Bucshon**	Y	N	N	N	N	N
9	**Hollingsworth**	Y	N	N	N	N	N
IOWA							
1	Finkenauer	N	Y	Y	Y	Y	Y
2	Loebsack	N	Y	Y	Y	Y	Y
3	Axne	N	Y	Y	Y	Y	Y
4	**King, S.**	Y	N	N	N	N	N
KANSAS							
1	**Marshall**	Y	N	N	N	N	N
2	**Watkins**	Y	N	N	N	N	N
3	Davids	N	Y	Y	Y	Y	Y
4	**Estes**	Y	N	N	N	N	N
KENTUCKY							
1	**Comer**	Y	N	N	N	N	N
2	**Guthrie**	Y	N	N	N	N	N
3	Yarmuth	N	Y	Y	Y	Y	Y
4	**Massie**	Y	N	N	N	N	N
5	**Rogers, H.**	?	N	N	N	N	N
6	**Barr**	Y	N	N	N	N	N
LOUISIANA							
1	**Scalise**	Y	N	N	N	N	N
2	Richmond	N	Y	Y	Y	Y	Y
3	**Higgins, C.**	Y	N	N	N	N	N
4	**Johnson, M.**	Y	N	N	N	N	N
5	**Abraham**	Y	N	N	N	N	N
6	**Graves, G.**	Y	N	N	N	N	N
MAINE							
1	Pingree	N	Y	Y	Y	Y	Y
2	Golden	N	Y	Y	Y	Y	N
MARYLAND							
1	**Harris**	Y	N	N	N	N	N
2	Ruppersberger	N	Y	Y	Y	Y	Y
3	Sarbanes	N	Y	Y	Y	Y	Y
4	Brown, A.	N	Y	Y	Y	Y	Y
5	Hoyer	N	Y	Y	Y	Y	Y
6	Trone	N	Y	Y	Y	Y	Y
7	vacant						
8	Raskin	N	Y	Y	Y	Y	Y
MASSACHUSETTS							
1	Neal	N	Y	Y	Y	Y	Y
2	McGovern	N	Y	Y	Y	Y	Y
3	Trahan	N	Y	Y	Y	Y	Y
4	Kennedy	N	Y	Y	Y	Y	Y
5	Clark	N	Y	Y	Y	Y	Y
6	Moulton	N	Y	Y	Y	Y	Y
7	Pressley	N	Y	Y	Y	Y	Y
8	Lynch	N	Y	Y	Y	Y	Y
9	Keating	N	Y	Y	Y	Y	Y
MICHIGAN							
1	**Bergman**	Y	N	N	N	N	N
2	**Huizenga**	Y	N	N	N	N	N
3	*Amash*	N	Y	Y	Y	Y	Y
4	**Moolenaar**	Y	N	N	N	N	N
5	Kildee	N	Y	Y	Y	Y	Y
6	**Upton**	Y	N	N	N	N	N
7	**Walberg**	Y	N	N	N	N	N
8	Slotkin	N	Y	Y	Y	Y	Y
9	Levin	N	Y	Y	Y	Y	Y
10	**Mitchell**	Y	N	N	N	N	N
11	Stevens	N	Y	Y	Y	Y	Y
12	Dingell	N	Y	Y	Y	Y	Y
13	Tlaib	N	Y	Y	Y	Y	Y
14	Lawrence	N	Y	Y	Y	Y	Y
MINNESOTA							
1	**Hagedorn**	Y	N	N	N	N	N
2	Craig	N	Y	Y	Y	Y	Y
3	Phillips	N	Y	Y	Y	Y	Y
4	McCollum	N	Y	Y	Y	Y	Y
5	Omar	-	+	Y	Y	Y	Y

		691	692	693	694	695	696
6	**Emmer**	Y	N	N	N	N	N
7	Peterson	N	N	N	N	N	N
8	**Stauber**	Y	N	N	N	N	N
MISSISSIPPI							
1	**Kelly, T.**	Y	N	N	N	N	N
2	Thompson, B.	N	Y	Y	Y	Y	Y
3	**Guest**	Y	N	N	N	N	N
4	**Palazzo**	Y	N	N	N	N	N
MISSOURI							
1	Clay	?	?	Y	Y	Y	Y
2	**Wagner**	Y	N	N	N	N	N
3	**Luetkemeyer**	Y	N	N	N	N	N
4	**Hartzler**	Y	N	N	N	N	N
5	Cleaver	N	Y	Y	Y	Y	Y
6	**Graves, S.**	Y	N	N	N	N	N
7	**Long**	Y	N	N	N	N	N
8	**Smith, J.**	Y	N	N	N	N	N
MONTANA							
AL	**Gianforte**	Y	N	N	N	N	N
NEBRASKA							
1	**Fortenberry**	Y	N	N	N	N	N
2	**Bacon**	Y	N	N	N	N	N
3	**Smith, Adrian**	Y	N	N	N	N	N
NEVADA							
1	Titus	N	Y	Y	Y	Y	Y
2	**Amodei**	Y	N	N	N	N	N
3	Lee	N	Y	Y	Y	Y	Y
4	Horsford	N	Y	Y	Y	Y	Y
NEW HAMPSHIRE							
1	Pappas	N	Y	Y	Y	Y	Y
2	Kuster	N	Y	Y	Y	Y	Y
NEW JERSEY							
1	Norcross	N	Y	Y	Y	Y	Y
2	Van Drew	?	?	N	N	N	N
3	Kim	N	Y	Y	Y	Y	Y
4	**Smith, C.**	Y	N	N	N	N	N
5	Gottheimer	N	Y	Y	Y	Y	Y
6	Pallone	N	Y	Y	Y	Y	Y
7	Malinowski	N	Y	Y	Y	Y	Y
8	Sires	N	Y	Y	Y	Y	Y
9	Pascrell	N	Y	Y	Y	Y	Y
10	Payne	N	Y	Y	Y	Y	Y
11	Sherrill	N	Y	Y	Y	Y	Y
12	Watson Coleman	N	Y	Y	Y	Y	Y
NEW MEXICO							
1	Haaland	N	Y	Y	Y	Y	Y
2	Torres Small	N	Y	Y	Y	Y	Y
3	Luján	N	Y	Y	Y	Y	Y
NEW YORK							
1	**Zeldin**	Y	N	N	N	N	N
2	**King, P.**	Y	N	N	N	N	N
3	Suozzi	N	Y	Y	Y	Y	Y
4	Rice, K.	N	Y	Y	Y	Y	Y
5	Meeks	N	Y	Y	Y	Y	Y
6	Meng	N	Y	Y	Y	Y	Y
7	Velázquez	N	Y	Y	Y	Y	Y
8	Jeffries	N	Y	Y	Y	Y	Y
9	Clarke	N	Y	Y	Y	Y	Y
10	Nadler	N	Y	Y	Y	Y	Y
11	Rose	N	Y	Y	Y	Y	Y
12	Maloney, C.	N	Y	Y	Y	Y	Y
13	Espaillat	N	Y	Y	Y	Y	Y
14	Ocasio-Cortez	N	Y	Y	Y	Y	Y
15	Serrano	?	?	?	?	+	+
16	Engel	N	Y	Y	Y	Y	Y
17	Lowey	N	Y	Y	Y	Y	Y
18	Maloney, S.P.	N	Y	Y	Y	Y	Y
19	Delgado	N	Y	Y	Y	Y	Y
20	Tonko	N	Y	Y	Y	Y	Y
21	**Stefanik**	Y	N	N	N	N	N
22	Brindisi	N	Y	Y	Y	Y	Y
23	**Reed**	Y	N	N	N	N	N
24	**Katko**	Y	N	N	N	N	N
25	Morelle	N	Y	Y	Y	Y	Y
26	Higgins, B.	N	Y	Y	Y	Y	Y
27	**Collins, C.**						
NORTH CAROLINA							
1	Butterfield	N	Y	Y	Y	Y	Y
2	**Holding**	?	?	N	N	N	N
3	**Murphy**	Y	N	N	N	N	N
4	Price	N	Y	Y	Y	Y	Y
5	**Foxx**	Y	N	N	N	N	N
6	**Walker**	Y	N	N	N	N	N
7	**Rouzer**	Y	N	N	N	N	N

		691	692	693	694	695	696
8	**Hudson**	Y	N	N	N	N	N
9	**Bishop**	Y	N	N	N	N	N
10	**McHenry**	Y	N	N	N	N	N
11	**Meadows**	Y	N	N	N	N	N
12	Adams	N	Y	Y	Y	Y	Y
13	**Budd**	Y	N	N	N	N	N
NORTH DAKOTA							
AL	**Armstrong**	Y	N	N	N	N	N
OHIO							
1	**Chabot**	Y	N	N	N	N	N
2	**Wenstrup**	Y	N	N	N	N	N
3	Beatty	N	Y	Y	Y	Y	Y
4	**Jordan**	Y	N	N	N	N	N
5	**Latta**	Y	N	N	N	N	N
6	**Johnson, B.**	Y	N	N	N	N	N
7	**Gibbs**	Y	N	N	N	N	N
8	**Davidson**	Y	N	N	N	N	N
9	Kaptur	N	Y	Y	Y	Y	Y
10	**Turner**	Y	N	N	N	N	N
11	Fudge	N	Y	Y	Y	Y	Y
12	**Balderson**	Y	N	N	N	N	N
13	Ryan	N	Y	Y	Y	Y	Y
14	**Joyce**	Y	N	N	N	N	N
15	**Stivers**	Y	N	N	N	N	N
16	**Gonzalez**	Y	N	N	N	N	N
OKLAHOMA							
1	**Hern**	Y	N	N	N	N	N
2	**Mullin**	Y	N	N	N	N	N
3	**Lucas**	Y	N	N	N	N	N
4	**Cole**	Y	N	N	N	N	N
5	Horn	N	Y	Y	Y	Y	Y
OREGON							
1	Bonamici	N	Y	Y	Y	Y	Y
2	**Walden**	Y	N	N	N	N	N
3	Blumenauer	N	Y	Y	Y	Y	Y
4	DeFazio	N	Y	Y	Y	Y	Y
5	Schrader	N	Y	Y	Y	Y	Y
PENNSYLVANIA							
1	**Fitzpatrick**	Y	N	N	N	N	N
2	Boyle	N	Y	Y	Y	Y	Y
3	Evans	N	Y	Y	Y	Y	Y
4	Dean	N	Y	Y	Y	Y	Y
5	Scanlon	N	Y	Y	Y	Y	Y
6	Houlahan	N	Y	Y	Y	Y	Y
7	Wild	N	Y	Y	Y	Y	Y
8	Cartwright	N	Y	Y	Y	Y	Y
9	**Meuser**	Y	N	N	N	N	N
10	**Perry**	Y	N	N	N	N	N
11	**Smucker**	Y	N	N	N	N	N
12	**Keller**	Y	N	N	N	N	N
13	**Joyce**	Y	N	N	N	N	N
14	**Reschenthaler**	Y	N	N	N	N	N
15	**Thompson, G.**	Y	N	N	N	N	N
16	**Kelly, M.**	Y	N	N	N	N	N
17	Lamb	N	Y	Y	Y	Y	Y
18	Doyle	N	Y	Y	Y	Y	Y
RHODE ISLAND							
1	Cicilline	N	Y	Y	Y	Y	Y
2	Langevin	?	?	Y	Y	Y	Y
SOUTH CAROLINA							
1	Cunningham	N	Y	Y	Y	Y	Y
2	**Wilson, J.**	Y	N	N	N	N	N
3	**Duncan**	Y	N	N	N	N	N
4	**Timmons**	Y	N	N	N	N	N
5	**Norman**	Y	N	N	N	N	N
6	Clyburn	N	Y	Y	Y	Y	Y
7	**Rice, T.**	Y	N	N	N	N	N
SOUTH DAKOTA							
AL	**Johnson**	Y	N	N	N	N	N
TENNESSEE							
1	**Roe**	Y	N	N	N	N	N
2	**Burchett**	Y	N	N	N	N	N
3	**Fleischmann**	Y	N	N	N	N	N
4	**DesJarlais**	Y	N	N	N	N	N
5	Cooper	N	Y	Y	Y	Y	Y
6	**Rose**	Y	N	N	N	N	N
7	**Green**	Y	N	N	N	N	N
8	**Kustoff**	Y	N	N	N	N	N
9	Cohen	N	Y	Y	Y	Y	Y
TEXAS							
1	**Gohmert**	Y	N	N	N	N	N
2	**Crenshaw**	Y	N	N	N	N	N
3	**Taylor**	Y	N	N	N	N	N
4	**Ratcliffe**	Y	N	N	N	N	N

		691	692	693	694	695	696
5	**Gooden**	Y	N	N	N	N	N
6	**Wright**	Y	N	N	N	N	N
7	Fletcher	N	Y	Y	Y	Y	Y
8	**Brady**	Y	N	N	N	N	N
9	Green, A.	N	Y	Y	Y	Y	Y
10	**McCaul**	Y	N	N	N	N	N
11	**Conaway**	Y	N	N	N	N	N
12	**Granger**	Y	N	N	N	N	N
13	**Thornberry**	Y	N	N	N	N	N
14	**Weber**	Y	N	N	N	N	N
15	Gonzalez	N	Y	Y	Y	Y	Y
16	Escobar	N	Y	Y	Y	Y	Y
17	**Flores**	Y	N	N	N	N	N
18	Jackson Lee	N	Y	Y	Y	Y	Y
19	**Arrington**	Y	N	N	N	N	N
20	Castro	N	Y	Y	Y	Y	Y
21	**Roy**	Y	N	N	N	N	N
22	**Olson**	Y	N	N	N	N	N
23	**Hurd**	Y	N	N	N	N	N
24	**Marchant**	Y	N	N	N	N	N
25	**Williams**	Y	N	N	N	N	N
26	**Burgess**	Y	N	N	N	N	N
27	**Cloud**	Y	N	N	N	N	N
28	Cuellar	N	Y	Y	Y	Y	Y
29	Garcia, S.	N	Y	Y	Y	Y	Y
30	Johnson, E.B.	N	Y	Y	Y	Y	Y
31	**Carter, J.**	Y	N	N	N	N	N
32	Allred	N	Y	Y	Y	Y	Y
33	Veasey	N	Y	Y	Y	Y	Y
34	Vela	N	Y	Y	Y	Y	Y
35	Doggett	N	Y	Y	Y	Y	Y
36	**Babin**	Y	N	N	N	N	N
UTAH							
1	**Bishop, R.**	?	?	N	N	N	N
2	**Stewart**	Y	N	N	N	N	N
3	**Curtis**	Y	N	N	N	N	N
4	McAdams	N	Y	Y	Y	Y	Y
VERMONT							
AL	Welch	N	Y	Y	Y	Y	Y
VIRGINIA							
1	**Wittman**	Y	N	N	N	N	N
2	Luria	N	Y	Y	Y	Y	Y
3	Scott, R.	N	Y	Y	Y	Y	Y
4	McEachin	N	Y	Y	Y	Y	Y
5	**Riggleman**	Y	N	N	N	N	N
6	**Cline**	Y	N	N	N	N	N
7	Spanberger	N	Y	Y	Y	Y	Y
8	Beyer	N	Y	Y	Y	Y	Y
9	**Griffith**	Y	N	N	N	N	N
10	Wexton	N	Y	Y	Y	Y	Y
11	Connolly	N	Y	Y	Y	Y	Y
WASHINGTON							
1	DelBene	N	Y	Y	Y	Y	Y
2	Larsen	N	Y	Y	Y	Y	Y
3	**Herrera Beutler**	Y	N	N	N	N	N
4	**Newhouse**	Y	N	N	N	N	N
5	**McMorris Rodgers**	Y	N	N	N	N	N
6	Kilmer	N	Y	Y	Y	Y	Y
7	Jayapal	N	Y	Y	Y	Y	Y
8	Schrier	N	Y	Y	Y	Y	Y
9	Smith Adam	N	Y	Y	Y	Y	Y
10	Heck	N	Y	Y	Y	Y	Y
WEST VIRGINIA							
1	**McKinley**	Y	N	N	N	N	N
2	**Mooney**	Y	N	N	N	N	N
3	**Miller**	Y	N	N	N	N	N
WISCONSIN							
1	**Steil**	Y	N	N	N	N	N
2	Pocan	N	Y	Y	Y	Y	Y
3	Kind	N	Y	Y	Y	Y	Y
4	Moore	N	Y	Y	Y	Y	Y
5	**Sensenbrenner**	Y	N	N	N	N	N
6	**Grothman**	Y	N	N	N	N	N
7	**Duffy**						
8	**Gallagher**	Y	N	N	N	N	N
WYOMING							
AL	**Cheney**	Y	N	N	N	N	N
DELEGATES							
	Radewagen (A.S.)						
	Norton (D.C.)						
	San Nicolas (Guam)						
	Sablan (N. Marianas)						
	González-Colón (P.R.)						
	Plaskett (V.I.)						

697. HR5377. State and Local Tax Deductions - Previous Question. Torres, D-Calif., motion to order the previous question on the rule (H Res 772) that would provide for House floor consideration of the Restoring Tax Fairness for States and Localities Act (HR 5377). It would provide for up to one hour of debate on the bill. Motion agreed to 227-195: R 0-194; D 227-0; I 0-1. Dec. 19, 2019.

698. HR5377. State and Local Tax Deductions - Rule. Adoption of the rule (H Res 772) that would provide for House floor consideration of the Restoring Tax Fairness for States and Localities Act (HR 5377). It would provide for up to one hour of debate on the bill. Adopted 227-196: R 0-193; D 227-2; I 0-1. Dec. 19, 2019.

699. HR5377. State and Local Tax Deductions - Recommit. Rice, R-S.C., motion to recommit the Restoring Tax Fairness for States and Localities Act to the House Ways and Means Committee with instructions to report it back immediately with an amendment that would make an exception to the bill's elimination of the $10,000 cap on federal tax deductions for state and local taxes, such that the cap would still apply for taxpayers whose adjusted gross incomes exceed $100 million in a taxable year. It would double to $1,000 the tax deductions established by the bill for professional development costs for teachers and first responders. Motion agreed to 388-36: R 192-2; D 195-34; I 1-0. Dec. 19, 2019.

700. HR5377. State and Local Tax Deductions - Passage. Passage of the bill, as amended, that would reduce or eliminate the existing $10,000 cap on federal tax deductions for state and local taxes, which was established under the 2017 tax law, for tax years 2019 through 2021. Specifically, it would double the cap to $20,000 for married couples filing a joint tax return for tax year 2019, and it would eliminate the cap for tax years 2020 and 2021. As amended, the bill would retain the cap for taxpayers whose adjusted gross incomes exceed $100 million in a taxable year. As an offset, the bill would increase the top individual income tax rate from 37% to 39.6% and it would reduce the corresponding income thresholds at which the top tax bracket applies. The bill would also permanently increase from $250 to $1,000 a tax deduction for professional development costs for elementary and secondary school teachers, and it would establish a new tax deduction of up to $1,000 for first responders, including for costs associated with related professional development courses. Passed 218-206: R 5-189; D 213-16; I 0-1. *Note: A "nay" was a vote in support of the president's position.* Dec. 19, 2019.

701. HR5430. United States-Mexico-Canada Trade Agreement - Passage. Passage of the bill that would implement the trade agreement reached between the United States, Mexico, and Canada that replaces the North American Free-Trade Agreement. It would modify existing trade law to provide for implementation of the agreement, authorize federal agencies and other entities to implement and enforce provisions of the agreement, and authorize or appropriate more than $2 billion in funding for certain implementation activities. Among other provisions, the bill would require the Treasury and Labor departments to issue regulations to implement trade provisions in the USMCA and outline classification standards for the origin of goods under such provisions. It would require the establishment of inter-agency committees related to implementation and enforcement of the agreement's provisions related to automobiles, environmental obligations, and labor obligations. It would provide for additional enforcement and monitoring mechanisms related to forced labor, labor reforms in Mexico, and remedies for labor rights violations. It would require the EPA to construct and maintain facilities to treat wastewater and pollution sources resulting from trans-boundary water flows originating in Mexico. It would provide for transition procedures in the case of withdrawal of any country from the agreement. The bill would authorize $1.5 billion for the North American Development Bank, a binational institution that funds environmental infrastructure projects in the U.S.-Mexico border region, and it would require the bank to prioritize the financing of projects related to water pollution. It would make supplemental fiscal 2020 appropriations to provide $300 million for Environmental Protection Agency grants for construction of wastewater facilities in the U.S.-Mexico border region; $210 million for Labor Department international grant programs, including $180 million for grants to support labor justice system reforms in Mexico; $40 million for enforcement of environmental obligations under the USMCA; and $16 million for National Oceanic and Atmospheric Administration activities related to addressing marine debris and combating illegal and unregulated fishing in coordination with Mexico. The USMCA, which would be implemented by the bill, would increase from 60%-62.5% to 75% the North American content threshold for automobiles to qualify for duty-free access, and it would establish additional thresholds for steel and aluminum content and content made by workers earning at least $16 per hour. It would establish trade regulations for products created using agricultural biotechnology. It would require signatories to implement and maintain certain multilateral environmental agreements to which they are already signatories, and to adopt and maintain certain internationally recognized labor rights, including to prohibit the importation of goods produced by forced labor. Passed 385-41: R 192-2; D 193-38; I 0-1. *Note: A "yea" was a vote in support of the president's position.* Dec. 19, 2019.

		697	698	699	700	701
ALABAMA						
1	**Byrne**	N	N	Y	N	Y
2	**Roby**	N	N	Y	N	Y
3	**Rogers, M.**	N	N	Y	N	Y
4	**Aderholt**	N	N	Y	N	Y
5	**Brooks, M.**	N	N	Y	N	Y
6	**Palmer**	N	N	Y	N	Y
7	Sewell	Y	Y	Y	Y	Y
ALASKA						
AL	**Young**	N	N	Y	N	Y
ARIZONA						
1	O'Halleran	Y	Y	Y	Y	Y
2	Kirkpatrick	Y	Y	Y	Y	Y
3	Grijalva	Y	Y	Y	Y	Y
4	**Gosar**	N	N	N	N	Y
5	**Biggs**	N	N	N	N	Y
6	**Schweikert**	N	N	Y	N	Y
7	Gallego	Y	Y	Y	Y	Y
8	**Lesko**	N	N	Y	N	Y
9	Stanton	Y	+	Y	N	Y
ARKANSAS						
1	**Crawford**	N	N	Y	N	Y
2	**Hill, F.**	N	N	Y	N	Y
3	**Womack**	N	N	Y	N	Y
4	**Westerman**	N	N	Y	N	Y
CALIFORNIA						
1	**LaMalfa**	N	N	Y	N	Y
2	Huffman	Y	Y	Y	Y	N
3	Garamendi	Y	Y	Y	Y	Y
4	**McClintock**	N	N	Y	N	Y
5	Thompson, M.	Y	Y	Y	Y	Y
6	Matsui	Y	Y	Y	Y	Y
7	Bera	Y	Y	Y	Y	Y
8	**Cook**	N	N	Y	N	Y
9	McNerney	Y	Y	Y	Y	Y
10	Harder	Y	Y	Y	Y	Y
11	DeSaulnier	Y	Y	Y	Y	N
12	Pelosi					Y
13	Lee B.	Y	Y	N	Y	N
14	Speier	Y	Y	Y	Y	Y
15	Swalwell	Y	Y	N	Y	Y
16	Costa	Y	Y	Y	Y	Y
17	Khanna	Y	Y	Y	Y	Y
18	Eshoo	Y	Y	Y	Y	Y
19	Lofgren	Y	Y	Y	Y	Y
20	Panetta	Y	Y	Y	Y	Y
21	Cox	Y	Y	Y	Y	Y
22	**Nunes**	N	N	Y	N	Y
23	**McCarthy**	N	N	Y	N	Y
24	Carbajal	Y	Y	Y	Y	Y
25	vacant					
26	Brownley	Y	Y	Y	Y	Y
27	Chu	Y	Y	Y	Y	Y
28	Schiff	Y	Y	Y	Y	Y
29	Cárdenas	Y	Y	Y	Y	N
30	Sherman	Y	Y	Y	Y	Y
31	Aguilar	Y	Y	N	Y	Y
32	Napolitano	Y	Y	N	Y	Y
33	Lieu	Y	Y	N	Y	N
34	Gomez	Y	Y	Y	Y	Y
35	Torres	Y	Y	Y	Y	Y
36	Ruiz	Y	Y	Y	Y	Y
37	Bass	Y	Y	N	Y	Y
38	Sánchez	Y	Y	Y	Y	Y
39	Cisneros	Y	Y	Y	Y	Y
40	Roybal-Allard	Y	Y	Y	Y	Y
41	Takano	Y	Y	Y	Y	Y
42	**Calvert**	N	N	Y	N	Y
43	Waters	Y	Y	N	Y	Y
44	Barragán	Y	Y	N	Y	N
45	Porter	Y	Y	Y	Y	Y
46	Correa	Y	Y	N	Y	Y
47	Lowenthal	Y	Y	Y	Y	N
48	Rouda	Y	Y	Y	Y	Y
49	Levin	Y	Y	Y	Y	Y
50	**Hunter**	?	?	?	?	?
51	Vargas	Y	Y	Y	Y	Y
52	Peters	Y	Y	Y	Y	Y

		697	698	699	700	701
53	Davis, S.	Y	Y	Y	Y	Y
COLORADO						
1	DeGette	Y	Y	Y	Y	Y
2	Neguse	Y	Y	N	Y	Y
3	**Tipton**	N	N	Y	N	Y
4	**Buck**	N	N	Y	N	Y
5	**Lamborn**	N	N	Y	N	Y
6	Crow	Y	Y	Y	Y	Y
7	Perlmutter	Y	Y	Y	Y	Y
CONNECTICUT						
1	Larson	Y	Y	Y	Y	Y
2	Courtney	Y	Y	Y	Y	Y
3	DeLauro	Y	Y	Y	Y	Y
4	Himes	Y	Y	Y	Y	Y
5	Hayes	Y	Y	?	Y	Y
DELAWARE						
AL	Blunt Rochester	Y	Y	Y	Y	Y
FLORIDA						
1	**Gaetz**	N	N	Y	N	Y
2	**Dunn**	N	N	Y	N	Y
3	**Yoho**	N	N	Y	N	N
4	**Rutherford**	N	N	Y	N	Y
5	Lawson	Y	Y	Y	Y	Y
6	**Waltz**	N	N	Y	N	Y
7	Murphy	Y	Y	Y	N	Y
8	**Posey**	N	N	Y	N	Y
9	Soto	Y	Y	Y	Y	Y
10	Demings	Y	Y	Y	Y	Y
11	**Webster**	N	N	Y	N	Y
12	**Bilirakis**	N	N	Y	N	Y
13	Crist	Y	Y	Y	Y	Y
14	Castor	Y	Y	Y	Y	Y
15	**Spano**	N	N	Y	N	Y
16	**Buchanan**	N	N	Y	N	Y
17	**Steube**	N	N	Y	N	Y
18	**Mast**	N	N	Y	N	Y
19	**Rooney**	N	N	Y	N	Y
20	Hastings	Y	Y	Y	Y	Y
21	Frankel	Y	Y	Y	Y	Y
22	Deutch	Y	Y	Y	Y	Y
23	Wasserman Schultz	Y	Y	Y	Y	Y
24	Wilson, F.	Y	Y	Y	Y	Y
25	**Diaz-Balart**	N	N	Y	N	Y
26	Mucarsel-Powell	Y	Y	Y	Y	Y
27	Shalala	Y	Y	Y	Y	Y
GEORGIA						
1	**Carter, E.L.**	N	N	Y	N	Y
2	Bishop, S.	Y	Y	Y	Y	Y
3	**Ferguson**	N	N	Y	N	Y
4	Johnson, H.	Y	Y	Y	Y	Y
5	Lewis John	Y	Y	Y	Y	Y
6	McBath	Y	Y	Y	Y	Y
7	**Woodall**	N	N	Y	N	Y
8	**Scott, A.**	N	N	Y	N	Y
9	**Collins, D.**	N	N	Y	N	Y
10	**Hice**	N	N	Y	N	Y
11	**Loudermilk**	N	N	Y	N	Y
12	**Allen**	N	N	Y	N	Y
13	Scott, D.	Y	Y	Y	Y	Y
14	**Graves, T.**	N	N	Y	N	Y
HAWAII						
1	Case	Y	Y	Y	Y	Y
2	Gabbard	Y	Y	Y	Y	Y
IDAHO						
1	**Fulcher**	N	N	Y	N	Y
2	**Simpson**	N	N	Y	N	Y
ILLINOIS						
1	Rush	Y	Y	Y	Y	Y
2	Kelly, R.	Y	Y	Y	Y	Y
3	Lipinski	Y	Y	Y	Y	Y
4	García, J.	Y	Y	Y	Y	N
5	Quigley	Y	Y	Y	Y	Y
6	Casten	Y	Y	N	Y	Y
7	Davis, D.	Y	Y	Y	Y	Y
8	Krishnamoorthi	Y	Y	Y	Y	Y
9	Schakowsky	Y	Y	Y	Y	Y
10	Schneider	Y	Y	Y	Y	Y
11	Foster	Y	Y	Y	Y	Y

KEY: **Republicans** Democrats *Independents*

Y	Voted for (yea)	N	Voted against (nay)	P	Voted "present"
+	Announced for	–	Announced against	?	Did not vote or otherwise make position known
#	Paired for	X	Paired against		

	697	698	699	700	701
12 **Bost**	N	N	Y	N	Y
13 **Davis, R.**	N	N	Y	N	Y
14 Underwood	Y	Y	N	Y	Y
15 **Shimkus**	?	?	?	?	?
16 **Kinzinger**	N	N	Y	N	Y
17 Bustos	Y	Y	Y	Y	Y
18 **LaHood**	N	N	Y	N	Y
INDIANA					
1 Visclosky	Y	Y	N	Y	N
2 **Walorski**	N	N	Y	N	Y
3 **Banks**	N	N	Y	N	Y
4 **Baird**	N	N	Y	N	Y
5 **Brooks, S.**	N	N	Y	N	Y
6 **Pence**	N	N	Y	N	Y
7 Carson	Y	Y	Y	Y	Y
8 **Bucshon**	N	N	Y	N	Y
9 **Hollingsworth**	N	N	Y	N	Y
IOWA					
1 Finkenauer	Y	Y	Y	N	Y
2 Loebsack	Y	Y	Y	Y	Y
3 Axne	Y	Y	Y	N	Y
4 **King, S.**	N	N	Y	N	Y
KANSAS					
1 **Marshall**	N	N	Y	N	Y
2 **Watkins**	N	N	Y	N	Y
3 Davids	Y	Y	Y	Y	Y
4 **Estes**	N	N	Y	N	Y
KENTUCKY					
1 **Comer**	N	N	Y	N	Y
2 **Guthrie**	N	N	Y	N	Y
3 Yarmuth	Y	Y	Y	Y	Y
4 **Massie**	N	N	Y	N	N
5 **Rogers, H.**	N	N	Y	N	Y
6 **Barr**	N	N	Y	N	Y
LOUISIANA					
1 **Scalise**	N	N	Y	N	Y
2 Richmond	Y	Y	N	Y	Y
3 **Higgins, C.**	N	N	Y	N	Y
4 **Johnson, M.**	N	N	Y	N	Y
5 **Abraham**	N	N	Y	N	Y
6 **Graves, G.**	N	N	Y	N	Y
MAINE					
1 Pingree	Y	Y	Y	Y	N
2 Golden	Y	N	Y	N	N
MARYLAND					
1 **Harris**	N	N	Y	N	Y
2 Ruppersberger	Y	Y	Y	Y	Y
3 Sarbanes	Y	Y	Y	Y	Y
4 Brown, A.	Y	Y	Y	Y	N
5 Hoyer	Y	Y	Y	Y	Y
6 Trone	Y	Y	Y	Y	Y
7 vacant					
8 Raskin	Y	Y	Y	Y	N
MASSACHUSETTS					
1 Neal	Y	Y	Y	Y	Y
2 McGovern	Y	Y	Y	Y	N
3 Trahan	Y	Y	Y	Y	Y
4 Kennedy	Y	Y	Y	Y	N
5 Clark	Y	Y	Y	Y	Y
6 Moulton	Y	Y	Y	Y	Y
7 Pressley	+	Y	Y	Y	N
8 Lynch	Y	Y	Y	Y	Y
9 Keating	Y	Y	Y	Y	Y
MICHIGAN					
1 **Bergman**	N	N	Y	N	Y
2 **Huizenga**	N	N	Y	N	Y
3 *Amash*	N	N	Y	N	N
4 **Moolenaar**	N	N	Y	N	Y
5 Kildee	Y	Y	Y	Y	Y
6 **Upton**	N	N	Y	N	Y
7 **Walberg**	N	N	Y	N	Y
8 Slotkin	Y	Y	Y	Y	Y
9 Levin	Y	Y	N	Y	N
10 **Mitchell**	N	N	Y	N	Y
11 Stevens	Y	Y	N	Y	Y
12 Dingell	Y	Y	Y	Y	Y
13 Tlaib	Y	Y	Y	Y	N
14 Lawrence	Y	Y	Y	Y	Y
MINNESOTA					
1 **Hagedorn**	N	N	Y	N	Y
2 Craig	Y	Y	Y	Y	Y
3 Phillips	Y	Y	Y	Y	Y
4 McCollum	Y	Y	Y	Y	Y
5 Omar	Y	Y	N	Y	N

	697	698	699	700	701
6 **Emmer**	N	N	Y	N	Y
7 Peterson	Y	Y	Y	Y	Y
8 **Stauber**	N	N	Y	N	Y
MISSISSIPPI					
1 **Kelly, T.**	N	N	Y	N	Y
2 Thompson, B.	Y	Y	N	Y	Y
3 **Guest**	N	N	Y	N	Y
4 **Palazzo**	N	N	Y	N	Y
MISSOURI					
1 Clay	Y	Y	N	Y	N
2 **Wagner**	N	N	Y	N	Y
3 **Luetkemeyer**	N	N	Y	N	Y
4 **Hartzler**	N	N	Y	N	Y
5 Cleaver	Y	Y	N	Y	Y
6 **Graves, S.**	N	N	Y	N	Y
7 **Long**	N	N	Y	N	Y
8 **Smith, J.**	N	N	Y	N	Y
MONTANA					
AL **Gianforte**	N	N	Y	N	Y
NEBRASKA					
1 **Fortenberry**	N	N	Y	N	Y
2 **Bacon**	N	N	Y	N	Y
3 **Smith, Adrian**	N	N	Y	N	Y
NEVADA					
1 Titus	Y	Y	Y	Y	Y
2 **Amodei**	N	N	Y	N	Y
3 Lee	Y	Y	Y	N	Y
4 Horsford	Y	Y	Y	Y	Y
NEW HAMPSHIRE					
1 Pappas	Y	Y	Y	N	Y
2 Kuster	Y	Y	Y	N	Y
NEW JERSEY					
1 Norcross	Y	Y	Y	Y	N
2 Van Drew	Y	Y	Y	Y	Y
3 Kim	Y	Y	Y	Y	Y
4 **Smith, C.**	N	N	Y	Y	Y
5 Gottheimer	Y	Y	Y	Y	Y
6 Pallone	Y	Y	Y	Y	N
7 Malinowski	Y	Y	Y	Y	Y
8 Sires	Y	Y	Y	Y	Y
9 Pascrell	Y	Y	Y	Y	N
10 Payne	Y	Y	N	Y	Y
11 Sherrill	Y	Y	Y	Y	Y
12 Watson Coleman	Y	Y	N	Y	N
NEW MEXICO					
1 Haaland	Y	Y	Y	Y	Y
2 Torres Small	Y	Y	Y	Y	Y
3 Luján	Y	Y	Y	Y	Y
NEW YORK					
1 **Zeldin**	N	N	Y	N	Y
2 **King, P.**	N	N	Y	Y	Y
3 Suozzi	Y	Y	Y	Y	Y
4 Rice, K.	Y	Y	Y	Y	Y
5 Meeks	Y	Y	Y	Y	Y
6 Meng	Y	Y	Y	Y	N
7 Velázquez	Y	Y	Y	Y	N
8 Jeffries	Y	Y	N	Y	Y
9 Clarke	Y	Y	Y	Y	N
10 Nadler	Y	Y	?	?	?
11 Rose	Y	Y	Y	Y	Y
12 Maloney, C.	Y	Y	Y	Y	N
13 Espaillat	Y	Y	N	Y	N
14 Ocasio-Cortez	Y	Y	Y	N	N
15 Serrano	?	?	-	+	-
16 Engel	Y	Y	Y	Y	Y
17 Lowey	Y	Y	Y	Y	Y
18 Maloney, S.P.	Y	Y	Y	Y	Y
19 Delgado	Y	Y	Y	Y	Y
20 Tonko	Y	Y	Y	Y	N
21 **Stefanik**	N	N	Y	N	Y
22 Brindisi	Y	Y	Y	Y	Y
23 **Reed**	N	N	Y	Y	Y
24 **Katko**	N	N	Y	Y	Y
25 Morelle	Y	Y	Y	Y	Y
26 Higgins, B.	Y	Y	Y	Y	Y
27 **Collins, C.**					
NORTH CAROLINA					
1 Butterfield	Y	Y	Y	+	Y
2 **Holding**	N	N	Y	N	Y
3 **Murphy**	N	N	Y	N	Y
4 Price	Y	Y	Y	Y	Y
5 **Foxx**	N	N	Y	N	Y
6 **Walker**	N	N	Y	N	Y
7 **Rouzer**	N	N	Y	N	Y

	697	698	699	700	701
8 **Hudson**	N	?	Y	N	Y
9 **Bishop**	N	N	Y	N	Y
10 **McHenry**	N	N	Y	N	Y
11 **Meadows**	N	N	?	?	?
12 Adams	Y	Y	Y	Y	Y
13 **Budd**	N	N	Y	N	Y
NORTH DAKOTA					
AL **Armstrong**	N	N	Y	N	Y
OHIO					
1 **Chabot**	N	N	Y	N	Y
2 **Wenstrup**	N	N	Y	N	Y
3 Beatty	?	Y	Y	Y	Y
4 **Jordan**	N	N	Y	N	Y
5 **Latta**	N	N	Y	N	Y
6 **Johnson, B.**	N	N	Y	N	Y
7 **Gibbs**	N	N	Y	N	Y
8 **Davidson**	N	N	Y	N	Y
9 Kaptur	?	Y	Y	Y	N
10 **Turner**	N	N	Y	N	Y
11 Fudge	Y	Y	N	Y	N
12 **Balderson**	N	N	Y	N	Y
13 Ryan	Y	Y	Y	Y	Y
14 **Joyce**	N	N	Y	N	Y
15 **Stivers**	N	N	Y	N	Y
16 **Gonzalez**	N	N	Y	N	Y
OKLAHOMA					
1 **Hern**	N	N	Y	N	Y
2 **Mullin**	N	N	Y	N	Y
3 **Lucas**	N	N	Y	N	Y
4 **Cole**	N	N	Y	N	Y
5 Horn	Y	Y	Y	N	Y
OREGON					
1 Bonamici	Y	Y	Y	Y	Y
2 **Walden**	N	N	Y	N	Y
3 Blumenauer	Y	Y	Y	Y	Y
4 DeFazio	Y	Y	Y	Y	N
5 Schrader	Y	Y	Y	Y	Y
PENNSYLVANIA					
1 **Fitzpatrick**	N	N	Y	Y	Y
2 Boyle	Y	Y	Y	Y	Y
3 Evans	Y	Y	Y	Y	Y
4 Dean	Y	Y	Y	Y	Y
5 Scanlon	Y	Y	Y	Y	Y
6 Houlahan	Y	Y	Y	Y	Y
7 Wild	Y	Y	Y	Y	Y
8 Cartwright	Y	Y	Y	Y	Y
9 **Meuser**	N	N	Y	N	Y
10 **Perry**	N	N	Y	N	Y
11 **Smucker**	N	N	Y	N	Y
12 **Keller**	N	N	Y	N	Y
13 **Joyce**	N	N	Y	N	Y
14 **Reschenthaler**	N	N	Y	N	Y
15 **Thompson, G.**	N	N	Y	N	Y
16 **Kelly, M.**	N	N	Y	N	Y
17 Lamb	Y	Y	Y	Y	Y
18 Doyle	Y	Y	Y	Y	Y
RHODE ISLAND					
1 Cicilline	Y	Y	Y	Y	Y
2 Langevin	Y	Y	Y	Y	Y
SOUTH CAROLINA					
1 Cunningham	Y	Y	Y	Y	Y
2 **Wilson, J.**	N	N	Y	N	Y
3 **Duncan**	N	N	Y	N	Y
4 **Timmons**	N	N	Y	N	Y
5 **Norman**	N	N	Y	N	Y
6 Clyburn	Y	Y	N	Y	Y
7 **Rice, T.**	N	N	Y	N	Y
SOUTH DAKOTA					
AL **Johnson**	N	N	Y	N	Y
TENNESSEE					
1 **Roe**	N	N	Y	N	Y
2 **Burchett**	N	N	Y	N	Y
3 **Fleischmann**	N	N	Y	N	Y
4 **DesJarlais**	N	N	Y	N	Y
5 Cooper	Y	Y	Y	Y	Y
6 **Rose**	N	N	Y	N	Y
7 **Green**	N	N	Y	N	Y
8 **Kustoff**	N	N	Y	N	Y
9 Cohen	Y	Y	Y	Y	Y
TEXAS					
1 **Gohmert**	N	N	Y	N	Y
2 **Crenshaw**	N	N	Y	N	Y
3 **Taylor**	N	N	Y	N	Y
4 **Ratcliffe**	N	N	Y	N	Y

	697	698	699	700	701
5 **Gooden**	N	N	Y	N	Y
6 **Wright**	N	N	Y	N	Y
7 Fletcher	Y	Y	N	Y	Y
8 **Brady**	N	N	Y	N	Y
9 Green, A.	Y	Y	Y	Y	Y
10 **McCaul**	N	N	Y	N	Y
11 **Conaway**	N	N	Y	N	Y
12 **Granger**	N	N	Y	N	Y
13 **Thornberry**	N	N	Y	N	Y
14 **Weber**	N	N	Y	N	Y
15 Gonzalez	Y	Y	Y	Y	Y
16 Escobar	Y	Y	Y	Y	Y
17 **Flores**	N	N	Y	N	Y
18 Jackson Lee	Y	Y	Y	Y	Y
19 **Arrington**	N	N	Y	N	Y
20 Castro	Y	Y	N	N	Y
21 **Roy**	N	N	Y	N	Y
22 **Olson**	N	N	Y	N	Y
23 **Hurd**	N	N	Y	N	Y
24 **Marchant**	?	?	Y	N	Y
25 **Williams**	N	N	Y	N	Y
26 **Burgess**	N	N	Y	N	Y
27 **Cloud**	N	N	Y	N	Y
28 Cuellar	Y	Y	Y	Y	Y
29 Garcia, S.	Y	Y	N	Y	Y
30 Johnson, E.B.	Y	Y	Y	Y	Y
31 **Carter, J.**	N	N	Y	N	Y
32 Allred	Y	Y	N	N	Y
33 Veasey	Y	Y	Y	Y	Y
34 Vela	Y	Y	Y	Y	Y
35 Doggett	Y	Y	Y	N	Y
36 **Babin**	N	N	Y	N	Y
UTAH					
1 **Bishop, R.**	N	N	Y	N	Y
2 **Stewart**	N	N	Y	N	Y
3 **Curtis**	N	N	Y	N	Y
4 McAdams	Y	N	Y	N	Y
VERMONT					
AL Welch	Y	Y	Y	Y	Y
VIRGINIA					
1 **Wittman**	N	N	Y	N	Y
2 Luria	Y	Y	Y	Y	Y
3 Scott, R.	Y	Y	Y	Y	Y
4 McEachin	?	?	N	Y	N
5 **Riggleman**	N	N	Y	N	Y
6 **Cline**	N	N	Y	N	Y
7 Spanberger	Y	Y	Y	N	Y
8 Beyer	Y	Y	Y	Y	Y
9 **Griffith**	N	N	Y	N	Y
10 Wexton	Y	Y	Y	Y	Y
11 Connolly	Y	Y	Y	Y	Y
WASHINGTON					
1 DelBene	Y	Y	Y	Y	Y
2 Larsen	Y	Y	Y	Y	Y
3 **Herrera Beutler**	N	N	Y	N	Y
4 **Newhouse**	N	N	Y	N	Y
5 **McMorris Rodgers**	N	N	Y	N	Y
6 Kilmer	Y	Y	Y	Y	Y
7 Jayapal	Y	Y	N	Y	N
8 Schrier	Y	Y	Y	Y	Y
9 Smith Adam	Y	Y	Y	Y	Y
10 Heck	Y	Y	Y	Y	Y
WEST VIRGINIA					
1 **McKinley**	N	N	Y	N	Y
2 **Mooney**	N	N	Y	N	Y
3 **Miller**	N	N	Y	N	Y
WISCONSIN					
1 **Steil**	N	N	Y	N	Y
2 Pocan	Y	Y	N	N	N
3 Kind	Y	Y	Y	Y	Y
4 Moore	Y	Y	N	Y	Y
5 **Sensenbrenner**	N	N	Y	N	Y
6 **Grothman**	N	N	Y	N	Y
7 **Duffy**					
8 **Gallagher**	N	N	Y	N	Y
WYOMING					
AL **Cheney**	N	N	Y	N	Y
DELEGATES					
Radewagen (A.S.)					
Norton (D.C.)					
San Nicolas (Guam)					
Sablan (N. Marianas)					
González-Colón (P.R.)					
Plaskett (V.I.)					

Senate
Roll Call
Votes

Senate Roll Call Index by Subject

Senate Roll Call Index by Bill Number

VOTE NUMBER

1. S1. Middle East Security Package - Cloture. McConnell, R-Ky., motion to invoke cloture (thus limiting debate) on the motion to proceed to the measure that is comprised of a number of bills related to security policies in the Middle East. Motion rejected 56-44: R 52-1; D 4-41; I 0-1. *Note: Three-fifths of the total Senate (60) is required to invoke cloture.* Jan. 08, 2019.

2. S1. Middle East Security Package - Cloture. McConnell, R-Ky., motion to invoke cloture (thus limiting debate) on the motion to proceed to the measure that is comprised of a number of bills related to security policies in the Middle East. Motion rejected 53-43: R 49-0; D 4-41; I 0-2. *Note: Three-fifths of the total Senate (60) is required to invoke cloture.* Jan. 10, 2019.

3. S1. Middle East Security Package - Cloture. McConnell, R-Ky., motion to invoke cloture (thus limiting debate) on the motion to proceed to the measure that is comprised of a number of bills related to security policies in the Middle East. Motion rejected 50-43: R 47-1; D 3-40; I 0-2. *Note: Three-fifths of the total Senate (60) is required to invoke cloture.* Jan. 14, 2019.

4. SJRES2. Russia Sanctions - Motion to Table. McConnell, R-Ky., motion to table the Schumer, D-N.Y., motion to proceed to the joint resolution that would disapprove of President Trump's proposed action related to the application of sanctions against certain Russian companies. Motion rejected 42-57: R 42-11; D 0-44; I 0-2. Jan. 15, 2019.

5. SJRES2. Russia Sanctions - Motion to Proceed. Schumer, D-N.Y., motion to proceed to the joint resolution that would disapprove of President Trump's proposed action related to the application of sanctions against certain Russian companies. Motion agreed to 57-42: R 11-42; D 44-0; I 2-0. Jan. 15, 2019.

6. SJRES2. Russia Sanctions - Cloture. McConnell, R-Ky., motion to invoke cloture (thus limiting debate) on the joint resolution that would disapprove of President Trump's proposed action related to the application of sanctions against certain Russian companies. Motion rejected 57-42: R 11-42; D 45-0; I 1-0. *Note: Three-fifths of the total Senate (60) is required to invoke cloture. A "nay" was a vote in support of the president's position.* Jan. 16, 2019.

	1	2	3	4	5	6		1	2	3	4	5	6
ALABAMA							**MONTANA**						
Shelby	Y	Y	Y	Y	N	N	Tester	N	N	N	N	Y	Y
Jones	Y	Y	Y	N	Y	Y	**Daines**	Y	Y	Y	N	Y	Y
ALASKA							**NEBRASKA**						
Murkowski	Y	Y	Y	Y	N	N	**Fischer**	Y	Y	Y	Y	N	N
Sullivan	Y	Y	Y	Y	N	N	**Sasse**	Y	Y	Y	N	Y	Y
ARIZONA							**NEVADA**						
Sinema	Y	Y	Y	N	Y	Y	Cortez Masto	N	N	N	N	Y	Y
McSally	Y	Y	Y	N	Y	Y	Rosen	N	N	N	N	Y	Y
ARKANSAS							**NEW HAMPSHIRE**						
Boozman	Y	Y	Y	N	Y	Y	Shaheen	N	N	N	N	Y	Y
Cotton	Y	Y	Y	N	Y	Y	Hassan	N	N	N	N	Y	Y
CALIFORNIA							**NEW JERSEY**						
Feinstein	N	N	N	N	Y	Y	Menendez	Y	N	N	Y	Y	Y
Harris	N	N	N	N	Y	Y	Booker	N	N	N	N	Y	Y
COLORADO							**NEW MEXICO**						
Bennet	N	N	N	N	Y	Y	Udall	N	N	N	N	Y	Y
Gardner	Y	Y	Y	Y	Y	Y	Heinrich	N	N	N	N	Y	Y
CONNECTICUT							**NEW YORK**						
Blumenthal	N	N	N	N	Y	Y	Schumer	N	N	N	N	Y	Y
Murphy	N	N	N	N	Y	Y	Gillibrand	N	N	N	?	?	Y
DELAWARE							**NORTH CAROLINA**						
Carper	N	N	N	N	Y	Y	**Burr**	Y	Y	?	Y	N	N
Coons	N	N	N	N	Y	Y	**Tillis**	Y	Y	Y	Y	N	N
FLORIDA							**NORTH DAKOTA**						
Rubio	Y	Y	Y	N	Y	Y	**Hoeven**	Y	Y	Y	Y	N	N
Scott	Y	Y	Y	Y	N	N	**Cramer**	Y	Y	Y	Y	N	N
GEORGIA							**OHIO**						
Isakson	Y	Y	?	Y	N	N	Brown	N	N	N	N	Y	Y
Perdue	Y	?	?	Y	N	N	Portman	Y	Y	Y	Y	N	N
HAWAII							**OKLAHOMA**						
Schatz	N	N	N	N	Y	Y	**Inhofe**	Y	Y	Y	Y	N	N
Hirono	N	N	N	N	Y	Y	**Lankford**	Y	Y	Y	Y	N	N
IDAHO							**OREGON**						
Crapo	Y	Y	?	Y	N	N	Wyden	N	N	N	N	Y	Y
Risch	Y	Y	Y	Y	N	N	Merkley	N	N	N	N	Y	Y
ILLINOIS							**PENNSYLVANIA**						
Durbin	N	N	-	N	Y	Y	Casey	N	N	N	N	Y	Y
Duckworth	N	N	?	N	Y	Y	**Toomey**	Y	Y	Y	Y	N	N
INDIANA							**RHODE ISLAND**						
Young	Y	Y	Y	Y	N	N	Reed	N	N	N	N	Y	Y
Braun	Y	Y	Y	Y	N	N	Whitehouse	N	N	N	N	Y	Y
IOWA							**SOUTH CAROLINA**						
Grassley	Y	Y	Y	Y	N	N	**Graham**	Y	Y	Y	Y	N	N
Ernst	Y	Y	Y	Y	N	N	**Scott**	Y	Y	Y	Y	N	N
KANSAS							**SOUTH DAKOTA**						
Roberts	Y	Y	Y	Y	N	N	**Thune**	Y	Y	Y	Y	N	N
Moran	Y	?	?	N	Y	Y	**Rounds**	Y	Y	Y	Y	N	N
KENTUCKY							**TENNESSEE**						
McConnell	N	Y	N	Y	N	N	**Alexander**	Y	Y	Y	Y	N	N
Paul	Y	Y	Y	Y	N	N	**Blackburn**	Y	Y	Y	Y	N	N
LOUISIANA							**TEXAS**						
Cassidy	Y	Y	Y	Y	N	N	**Cornyn**	Y	?	Y	Y	N	N
Kennedy	Y	Y	Y	N	Y	Y	**Cruz**	Y	?	Y	Y	N	N
MAINE							**UTAH**						
Collins	Y	Y	Y	N	Y	Y	**Lee**	Y	Y	Y	Y	N	N
King	N	N	N	N	Y	Y	**Romney**	Y	Y	Y	Y	N	N
MARYLAND							**VERMONT**						
Cardin	N	N	N	N	Y	Y	Leahy	N	N	N	N	Y	Y
Van Hollen	N	N	N	N	Y	Y	*Sanders*	N	N	N	N	Y	?
MASSACHUSETTS							**VIRGINIA**						
Warren	N	N	N	N	Y	Y	Warner	N	N	N	N	Y	Y
Markey	N	N	N	N	Y	Y	Kaine	N	N	N	N	Y	Y
MICHIGAN							**WASHINGTON**						
Stabenow	N	N	N	N	Y	Y	Murray	N	N	N	N	Y	Y
Peters	N	N	N	N	Y	Y	Cantwell	N	N	N	N	Y	Y
MINNESOTA							**WEST VIRGINIA**						
Klobuchar	N	N	N	N	Y	Y	Manchin	Y	Y	Y	N	Y	Y
Smith	N	N	N	N	Y	Y	**Capito**	Y	Y	Y	Y	N	N
MISSISSIPPI							**WISCONSIN**						
Wicker	Y	Y	Y	Y	N	N	**Johnson**	Y	Y	Y	Y	N	N
Hyde-Smith	Y	Y	Y	Y	N	N	Baldwin	N	N	N	N	Y	Y
MISSOURI							**WYOMING**						
Blunt	Y	Y	Y	Y	N	N	**Enzi**	Y	Y	Y	Y	N	N
Hawley	Y	Y	Y	Y	N	N	**Barrasso**	Y	Y	Y	Y	N	N

KEY:	**Republicans**	Democrats	*Independents*

Y Voted for (yea)	**N** Voted against (nay)	**P** Voted "present"	
+ Announced for	**-** Announced against	**?** Did not vote or otherwise make position known	
# Paired for	**X** Paired against		

7. S109. Abortion Funding - Cloture. McConnell, R-Ky., motion to invoke cloture (thus limiting debate) on his motion to proceed to the bill that would prohibit federal funds from being used to fund abortions or to fund health benefits covering abortions. Motion rejected 48-47: R 46-2; D 2-43; I 0-2. *Note: Three-fifths of the total Senate (60) is required to invoke cloture. A "yea" was a vote in support of the president's position.* Jan. 17, 2019.

8. Procedural Motion - Require Attendance. McConnell, R-Ky., motion to instruct the sergeant at arms to request the attendance of absent senators. Motion agreed to 88-8: R 43-7; D 43-1; I 2-0. Jan. 24, 2019.

9. HR268. Fiscal 2019 Disaster Relief Supplemental Appropriations - Cloture. McConnell, R-Ky., motion to invoke cloture (thus limiting debate) on the substitute amendment to the Disaster Supplemental Appropriations Act. The substitute amendment would provide full-year funding for the seven remaining fiscal 2019 appropriations bills: Agriculture; Commerce-Justice-Science; Financial Services; Homeland Security; Interior-Environment; State-Foreign; and Transportation-Housing and Urban Development. It would also provide $12.7 billion for natural disaster relief programs and would reauthorize a number of policies with lapsed authorities, including Violence Against Women Act programs and Temporary Assistance for Needy Families. Motion rejected 50-47: R 49-2; D 1-43; I 0-2. *Note: Three-fifths of the total Senate (60) is required to invoke cloture. A "yea" was a vote in support of the president's position.* Jan. 24, 2019.

10. HR268. Fiscal 2019 Disaster Relief Supplemental Appropriations - Cloture. McConnell, R-Ky., motion to invoke cloture (thus limiting debate) on the Schumer, D-N.Y., amendment to the Disaster Supplemental Appropriations Act. The amendment would provide for a short-term continuing resolution for federal government operations through Feb. 8, 2019 and provide $14.2 billion in supplemental funds for response efforts to damage caused by hurricanes, wildfires, earthquakes and other natural disasters in 2017 and 2018. The bill would also prohibit funds provided in the bill for the Army Corps of Engineers or the Homeland Security Department from being used to construct a "new physical barrier" along the southwest border of the U.S. Motion rejected 52-44: R 6-44; D 44-0; I 2-0. *Note: Three-fifths of the total Senate (60) is required to invoke cloture.* Jan. 24, 2019.

11. S1. Middle East Security Package - Cloture. McConnell, R-Ky., motion to invoke cloture (thus limiting debate) on the motion to proceed to the measure that is comprised of a number of bills related to security policies in the Middle East. Motion agreed to 74-19: R 49-0; D 24-18; I 1-1. *Note: Three-fifths of the total Senate (60) is required to invoke cloture.* Jan. 28, 2019.

12. S1. Middle East Security Package - Motion to Proceed. McConnell, R-Ky., motion to proceed to the measure that is comprised of a number of bills related to security policies in the Middle East. Motion agreed to 76-22: R 51-0; D 24-21; I 1-1. Jan. 29, 2019.

	7	8	9	10	11	12
ALABAMA						
Shelby	Y	Y	Y	N	Y	Y
Jones	N	Y	N	Y	Y	Y
ALASKA						
Murkowski	N	Y	Y	Y	Y	Y
Sullivan	Y	Y	Y	N	Y	Y
ARIZONA						
Sinema	N	Y	N	Y	Y	Y
McSally	Y	Y	Y	N	Y	Y
ARKANSAS						
Boozman	Y	Y	Y	N	Y	Y
Cotton	Y	N	N	N	Y	Y
CALIFORNIA						
Feinstein	N	Y	N	Y	N	N
Harris	N	Y	N	Y	?	N
COLORADO						
Bennet	N	Y	N	Y	Y	Y
Gardner	Y	Y	Y	Y	Y	Y
CONNECTICUT						
Blumenthal	N	Y	N	Y	Y	Y
Murphy	N	Y	N	Y	N	N
DELAWARE						
Carper	N	Y	N	Y	N	N
Coons	N	Y	N	Y	Y	Y
FLORIDA						
Rubio	Y	Y	Y	N	N	Y
Scott	Y	Y	Y	N	Y	Y
GEORGIA						
Isakson	Y	Y	Y	N	Y	Y
Perdue	Y	Y	Y	N	Y	Y
HAWAII						
Schatz	N	Y	N	Y	?	N
Hirono	N	Y	N	Y	N	N
IDAHO						
Crapo	?	Y	Y	N	Y	Y
Risch	Y	?	?	?	Y	Y
ILLINOIS						
Durbin	N	Y	N	Y	N	N
Duckworth	N	Y	N	Y	Y	Y
INDIANA						
Young	Y	Y	Y	N	Y	Y
Braun	Y	Y	Y	N	Y	Y
IOWA						
Grassley	Y	Y	Y	N	Y	Y
Ernst	Y	Y	Y	N	Y	Y
KANSAS						
Roberts	Y	Y	Y	N	Y	Y
Moran	Y	Y	Y	N	Y	?
KENTUCKY						
McConnell	Y	Y	Y	N	Y	Y
Paul	?	?	?	?	?	?
LOUISIANA						
Cassidy	Y	Y	Y	N	Y	Y
Kennedy	Y	N	N	N	Y	Y
MAINE						
Collins	N	Y	Y	Y	Y	Y
King	N	Y	N	Y	Y	Y
MARYLAND						
Cardin	N	Y	N	Y	Y	Y
Van Hollen	N	Y	N	Y	N	N
MASSACHUSETTS						
Warren	N	Y	N	Y	N	N
Markey	N	Y	N	Y	Y	Y
MICHIGAN						
Stabenow	N	Y	N	Y	Y	Y
Peters	N	Y	N	Y	N	N
MINNESOTA						
Klobuchar	N	Y	N	Y	N	Y
Smith	N	Y	N	Y	Y	Y
MISSISSIPPI						
Wicker	Y	Y	Y	N	Y	Y
Hyde-Smith	Y	Y	Y	N	Y	Y
MISSOURI						
Blunt	Y	Y	Y	N	Y	Y
Hawley	Y	Y	Y	N	Y	Y

	7	8	9	10	11	12
MONTANA						
Tester	N	Y	N	Y	Y	Y
Daines	Y	Y	Y	N	Y	Y
NEBRASKA						
Fischer	Y	Y	Y	N	Y	Y
Sasse	Y	Y	Y	N	Y	Y
NEVADA						
Cortez Masto	N	Y	N	Y	Y	Y
Rosen	N	?	?	?	Y	Y
NEW HAMPSHIRE						
Shaheen	N	Y	N	Y	N	N
Hassan	N	Y	N	Y	Y	N
NEW JERSEY						
Menendez	N	Y	N	Y	Y	Y
Booker	N	N	N	Y	?	N
NEW MEXICO						
Udall	N	Y	N	Y	N	N
Heinrich	N	Y	N	Y	N	N
NEW YORK						
Schumer	N	Y	N	Y	Y	Y
Gillibrand	N	Y	N	Y	N	N
NORTH CAROLINA						
Burr	?	Y	Y	?	?	Y
Tillis	Y	Y	Y	N	?	Y
NORTH DAKOTA						
Hoeven	Y	N	Y	N	?	Y
Cramer	Y	Y	Y	N	?	Y
OHIO						
Brown	N	Y	N	Y	N	N
Portman	Y	Y	Y	N	Y	Y
OKLAHOMA						
Inhofe	Y	?	Y	N	Y	Y
Lankford	Y	Y	Y	N	Y	Y
OREGON						
Wyden	N	Y	N	Y	Y	Y
Merkley	N	Y	N	Y	N	N
PENNSYLVANIA						
Casey	Y	Y	N	Y	Y	Y
Toomey	Y	N	Y	N	Y	Y
RHODE ISLAND						
Reed	N	Y	N	Y	N	N
Whitehouse	N	Y	N	Y	Y	Y
SOUTH CAROLINA						
Graham	?	Y	Y	N	Y	Y
Scott	Y	Y	Y	N	Y	Y
SOUTH DAKOTA						
Thune	Y	Y	Y	N	Y	Y
Rounds	Y	Y	Y	N	Y	Y
TENNESSEE						
Alexander	?	N	Y	Y	Y	Y
Blackburn	Y	Y	Y	N	Y	Y
TEXAS						
Cornyn	Y	Y	Y	N	Y	Y
Cruz	Y	Y	Y	N	Y	Y
UTAH						
Lee	Y	N	N	N	Y	Y
Romney	Y	Y	Y	Y	Y	Y
VERMONT						
Leahy	N	Y	N	Y	N	N
Sanders	N	Y	N	Y	N	N
VIRGINIA						
Warner	N	Y	N	Y	Y	Y
Kaine	N	Y	N	Y	N	N
WASHINGTON						
Murray	N	Y	N	Y	Y	Y
Cantwell	N	Y	N	Y	Y	Y
WEST VIRGINIA						
Manchin	Y	Y	Y	Y	Y	Y
Capito	Y	Y	Y	N	Y	Y
WISCONSIN						
Johnson	Y	Y	Y	N	Y	Y
Baldwin	N	Y	N	Y	N	N
WYOMING						
Enzi	Y	N	Y	N	Y	Y
Barrasso	Y	Y	Y	N	Y	Y

KEY: **Republicans**   Democrats   *Independents*

Y Voted for (yea)	N Voted against (nay)	P Voted "present"
+ Announced for	– Announced against	? Did not vote or otherwise
# Paired for	X Paired against	make position known

13. S1. Middle East Security Package - Cloture. McConnell, R-Ky., motion to invoke cloture (thus limiting debate) on his amendment no. 65 to the bill. The amendment would express the sense of the Senate that al Qaeda, ISIS, and other terrorist groups pose a continuing threat to U.S. homeland security and the security of U.S. allies. It would call for increased international stabilization efforts and warn against "precipitous withdrawal" of U.S. military forces in Syria and Afghanistan. Motion agreed to 68-23: R 43-3; D 24-19; I 1-1. *Note: Three-fifths of the total Senate (60) is required to invoke cloture.* Jan. 31, 2019.

14. S1. Middle East Security Package - Military Withdrawal. McConnell, R-Ky., amendment no. 65, as amended, that would express the sense of the Senate that al Qaeda, ISIS, and other terrorist groups pose a continuing threat to the U.S. homeland security and the security of U.S. allies. It would call for increased international stabilization efforts and warn against "precipitous withdrawal" of U.S. military forces in Syria and Afghanistan. Adopted 70-26: R 46-4; D 23-21; I 1-1. *Note: A "nay" was a vote in support of the president's position.* Feb. 04, 2019.

15. S1. Middle East Security Package - Cloture. McConnell, R-Ky., motion to invoke cloture (thus limiting debate) on the bill that would authorize $3.3 billion annually in foreign military financing to Israel through fiscal year 2028, codify the 2016 Memorandum of Understanding with Israel related to security assistance, extend war reserve stockpile access and loan guarantees for Israel through fiscal year 2023, and authorize a U.S.-Israel joint project to counter unmanned aerial vehicles. Motion agreed to 72-24: R 49-1; D 22-22; I 1-1. *Note: Three-fifths of the total Senate (60) is required to invoke cloture.* Feb. 04, 2019.

16. S1. Middle East Security Package - Passage. Passage of a bill that would authorize $3.3 billion annually in foreign military financing to Israel through fiscal year 2028, codify the 2016 Memorandum of Understanding with Israel related to security assistance, extend war reserve stockpile access and loan guarantees for Israel through fiscal year 2023, and authorize a U.S.-Israel joint project to counter unmanned aerial vehicles. It would allow state and local governments to restrict contracts with entities whose commercial activity is intended to economically harm or limit commercial relations with Israel for purposes of coercing political action or policy of the Israeli government. Passed 77-23: R 52-1; D 24-21; I 1-1. Feb. 05, 2019.

17. S47. Public Lands Package - Cloture. McConnell, R-Ky., motion to invoke cloture (thus limiting debate) on his motion to proceed to the bill that includes a number of provisions related to the designation, regulation, exchange, and management of federal public lands and forests. It would make additions and boundary adjustments to several national parks, monuments, and historic sites. The bill would permanently reauthorize the Land and Water Conservation Fund, with at least 40 percent of the fund to be used for state projects, at least 40 percent for federal projects, and at least 3 percent toward increasing recreational access to federal lands. Motion agreed to 99-1: R 52-1; D 45-0; I 2-0. *Note: Three-fifths of the total Senate (60) is required to invoke cloture.* Feb. 05, 2019.

18. S47. Public Lands Package - Motion to Table. Murkowski, R-Alaska, motion to table the Lankford, R-Okla., second-degree amendment no. 158 to Murkowski substitute amendment no. 111 to S 47. The Lankford amendment would require at least 5 percent of funds authorized for the Land and Water Conservation Fund to be used for deferred maintenance needs on federal lands. It would also require that funds appropriated for federal land acquisition include any funds necessary to address maintenance needs on the acquired land, and would authorize agencies to accept donations to address maintenance needs. Motion agreed to 66-33: R 20-33; D 44-0; I 2-0. *Note: Sen. Johnson, R-Wis., received unanimous consent after the vote concluded to change his vote position from "yea" to "nay." This change is reflected in the tally.* Feb. 07, 2019.

	13	14	15	16	17	18
ALABAMA						
Shelby	Y	Y	Y	Y	Y	Y
Jones	Y	Y	Y	Y	Y	Y
ALASKA						
Murkowski	Y	?	?	Y	Y	Y
Sullivan	?	Y	Y	Y	Y	Y
ARIZONA						
Sinema	Y	Y	Y	Y	Y	Y
McSally	Y	Y	Y	Y	Y	N
ARKANSAS						
Boozman	Y	Y	Y	Y	Y	Y
Cotton	Y	Y	Y	Y	Y	N
CALIFORNIA						
Feinstein	Y	Y	N	N	Y	Y
Harris	N	N	N	N	Y	Y
COLORADO						
Bennet	Y	Y	Y	Y	Y	Y
Gardner	Y	?	?	Y	Y	Y
CONNECTICUT						
Blumenthal	Y	Y	Y	Y	Y	Y
Murphy	N	N	N	N	Y	Y
DELAWARE						
Carper	Y	Y	N	N	Y	Y
Coons	Y	Y	Y	Y	Y	Y
FLORIDA						
Rubio	Y	Y	Y	Y	Y	N
Scott	Y	Y	Y	Y	Y	N
GEORGIA						
Isakson	?	Y	Y	Y	Y	Y
Perdue	?	?	?	Y	Y	Y
HAWAII						
Schatz	N	N	N	N	Y	Y
Hirono	N	N	N	N	Y	Y
IDAHO						
Crapo	Y	Y	Y	Y	Y	N
Risch	Y	Y	Y	Y	Y	N
ILLINOIS						
Durbin	-	N	N	N	Y	Y
Duckworth	Y	Y	Y	Y	Y	Y
INDIANA						
Young	Y	Y	Y	Y	Y	N
Braun	Y	Y	Y	Y	Y	N
IOWA						
Grassley	Y	Y	Y	Y	Y	N
Ernst	Y	Y	Y	Y	Y	N
KANSAS						
Roberts	Y	Y	Y	Y	Y	Y
Moran	?	Y	Y	Y	Y	N
KENTUCKY						
McConnell	Y	Y	Y	Y	Y	N
Paul	?	N	N	N	N	N
LOUISIANA						
Cassidy	Y	Y	Y	Y	Y	N
Kennedy	N	N	N	N	Y	N
MAINE						
Collins	Y	Y	Y	Y	Y	Y
King	Y	Y	Y	Y	Y	Y
MARYLAND						
Cardin	N	N	Y	Y	Y	Y
Van Hollen	N	N	N	N	Y	Y
MASSACHUSETTS						
Warren	N	N	N	N	Y	Y
Markey	N	N	N	N	Y	Y
MICHIGAN						
Stabenow	Y	Y	Y	Y	Y	Y
Peters	Y	Y	N	Y	Y	Y
MINNESOTA						
Klobuchar	N	N	Y	Y	Y	Y
Smith	N	N	Y	Y	Y	Y
MISSISSIPPI						
Wicker	Y	Y	Y	Y	Y	Y
Hyde-Smith	Y	Y	Y	Y	Y	Y
MISSOURI						
Blunt	?	Y	Y	Y	Y	Y
Hawley	Y	Y	Y	Y	Y	N
MONTANA						
Tester	Y	Y	Y	Y	Y	Y
Daines	Y	Y	Y	Y	Y	Y
NEBRASKA						
Fischer	Y	Y	Y	Y	Y	N
Sasse	Y	Y	Y	Y	Y	N
NEVADA						
Cortez Masto	Y	Y	Y	Y	Y	Y
Rosen	Y	Y	Y	Y	Y	Y
NEW HAMPSHIRE						
Shaheen	Y	Y	N	Y	Y	Y
Hassan	Y	Y	Y	Y	Y	Y
NEW JERSEY						
Menendez	Y	Y	Y	Y	Y	Y
Booker	N	N	N	N	Y	+
NEW MEXICO						
Udall	N	N	N	N	Y	Y
Heinrich	N	N	N	N	Y	Y
NEW YORK						
Schumer	N	N	Y	N	Y	Y
Gillibrand	N	N	N	N	Y	Y
NORTH CAROLINA						
Burr	Y	Y	Y	Y	Y	Y
Tillis	Y	Y	Y	Y	Y	Y
NORTH DAKOTA						
Hoeven	Y	Y	Y	Y	Y	N
Cramer	Y	Y	Y	Y	Y	N
OHIO						
Brown	?	N	N	N	Y	Y
Portman	Y	Y	Y	Y	Y	N
OKLAHOMA						
Inhofe	Y	Y	Y	Y	Y	N
Lankford	Y	Y	Y	Y	Y	N
OREGON						
Wyden	N	N	Y	Y	Y	Y
Merkley	N	N	N	N	Y	Y
PENNSYLVANIA						
Casey	Y	Y	Y	Y	Y	Y
Toomey	Y	Y	Y	Y	Y	N
RHODE ISLAND						
Reed	Y	Y	N	N	Y	Y
Whitehouse	Y	Y	Y	Y	Y	Y
SOUTH CAROLINA						
Graham	Y	Y	Y	Y	Y	Y
Scott	Y	Y	Y	Y	Y	Y
SOUTH DAKOTA						
Thune	Y	Y	Y	Y	Y	N
Rounds	Y	Y	Y	Y	Y	N
TENNESSEE						
Alexander	?	Y	Y	Y	Y	Y
Blackburn	Y	Y	Y	Y	Y	Y
TEXAS						
Cornyn	Y	Y	Y	Y	Y	N
Cruz	N	N	Y	Y	Y	N
UTAH						
Lee	N	N	Y	Y	Y	N
Romney	Y	Y	Y	Y	Y	N
VERMONT						
Leahy	N	N	N	N	Y	Y
Sanders	N	N	N	N	Y	Y
VIRGINIA						
Warner	Y	Y	Y	Y	Y	Y
Kaine	Y	Y	N	N	Y	Y
WASHINGTON						
Murray	Y	Y	Y	Y	Y	Y
Cantwell	Y	?	?	Y	Y	Y
WEST VIRGINIA						
Manchin	Y	Y	Y	Y	Y	Y
Capito	Y	Y	Y	Y	Y	Y
WISCONSIN						
Johnson	Y	Y	Y	Y	Y	N
Baldwin	N	N	N	N	Y	Y
WYOMING						
Enzi	Y	Y	Y	Y	Y	N
Barrasso	Y	Y	Y	Y	Y	N

KEY: **Republicans**   Democrats   *Independents*

Y	Voted for (yea)	**N**	Voted against (nay)	**P** Voted "present"
+	Announced for	**-**	Announced against	**?** Did not vote or otherwise
#	Paired for	**X**	Paired against	make position known

19. S47. Public Lands Package - Motion to Table. Murkowski, R-Alaska, motion to table the Lee, R-Utah, second-degree amendment no. 158 to Murkowski substitute amendment no. 111 to S 47. The Lee, R-Utah, amendment would authorize the Land and Water Conservation Fund through fiscal 2023, instead of authorizing the fund permanently. Motion agreed to 68-30: R 23-29; D 43-1; I 2-0. Feb. 07, 2019.

20. S47. Public Lands Package - Motion to Table. Murkowski, R-Alaska, motion to table the Lee, R-Utah, amendment no. 187 to the Murkowski amendment no. 112 to the bill. The Lee amendment would state that the establishment of national monuments in Utah may only be undertaken by express authorization of Congress. Motion agreed to 60-33: R 16-33; D 42-0; I 2-0. Feb. 11, 2019.

21. S47. Public Lands Package - Cloture. McConnell, R-Ky, motion to invoke cloture (thus limiting debate) on the bill that would permanently reauthorize the Land and Water Conservation Fund, with at least 40 percent of the fund to be used for state projects, at least 40 percent for federal projects, and at least 3 percent toward increasing recreational access to federal lands. It would also reauthorize, through 2023, the national volcano monitoring system and the U.S. Geological Survey. Through 2022, it would reauthorize several programs related to wildlife conservation, invasive species management, and prevention of illegal poaching and trafficking. The bill also includes a number of provisions related to the designation, regulation, exchange, and management of federal public lands and forests. It would make additions and boundary adjustments to several national parks, monuments, and historic sites. It would authorize and establish procedures for the transfer of water and power facilities from the Bureau of Reclamation to state and local entities and would authorize a Reclamation water management project in south-central Washington State. It also contains provisions related to federal land access for hunting and ordering studies on federal land designation. Motion agreed to 87-7: R 42-7; D 43-0; I 2-0. *Note: Three-fifths of the total Senate (60) is required to invoke cloture.* Feb. 11, 2019.

22. S47. Public Lands Package - Passage. Passage of the bill, as amended, that would permanently reauthorize the Land and Water Conservation Fund, with at least 40 percent of the fund to be used for state projects, at least 40 percent for federal projects, and at least 3 percent toward increasing recreational access to federal lands. It would also reauthorize, through 2023, the national volcano monitoring system and the U.S. Geological Survey. Through 2022, it would reauthorize several programs related to wildlife conservation, invasive species management, and prevention of illegal poaching and trafficking. The bill also includes a number of provisions related to the designation, regulation, exchange, and management of federal public lands and forests. Passed 92-8: R 45-8; D 45-0; I 2-0. Feb. 12, 2019.

23. Barr Nomination - Cloture. Motion to invoke cloture (thus limiting debate) on the nomination of William Pelham Barr of Virginia to be attorney general of the United States. Motion agreed to 55-44: R 52-1; D 3-41; I 0-2. *Note: A majority of senators voting (50 in this case), a quorum being present, is required to invoke cloture on all nominations.* Feb. 12, 2019.

24. Barr Nomination - Confirmation. Confirmation of President Trump's nomination of William Pelham Barr of Virginia to be attorney general of the United States. Confirmed 54-45: R 51-1; D 3-42; I 0-2. *Note: A "yea" was a vote in support of the president's position.* Feb. 14, 2019.

	19	20	21	22	23	24
ALABAMA						
Shelby	Y	Y	Y	Y	Y	Y
Jones	Y	Y	Y	Y	Y	Y
ALASKA						
Murkowski	Y	Y	Y	Y	Y	Y
Sullivan	Y	N	Y	Y	Y	Y
ARIZONA						
Sinema	Y	Y	Y	Y	Y	Y
McSally	N	N	Y	Y	Y	Y
ARKANSAS						
Boozman	Y	N	Y	Y	Y	Y
Cotton	N	N	Y	Y	Y	Y
CALIFORNIA						
Feinstein	Y	Y	Y	Y	N	N
Harris	Y	Y	Y	Y	N	N
COLORADO						
Bennet	Y	Y	Y	Y	N	N
Gardner	Y	Y	Y	Y	Y	Y
CONNECTICUT						
Blumenthal	Y	Y	Y	Y	N	N
Murphy	Y	Y	Y	Y	N	N
DELAWARE						
Carper	Y	Y	Y	Y	N	N
Coons	Y	Y	Y	Y	N	N
FLORIDA						
Rubio	N	N	Y	Y	Y	Y
Scott	N	N	Y	Y	Y	Y
GEORGIA						
Isakson	Y	Y	Y	Y	Y	Y
Perdue	N	N	Y	Y	Y	Y
HAWAII						
Schatz	Y	Y	Y	Y	N	N
Hirono	Y	Y	Y	Y	N	N
IDAHO						
Crapo	N	N	Y	Y	Y	Y
Risch	N	N	Y	Y	Y	Y
ILLINOIS						
Durbin	Y	Y	Y	Y	N	N
Duckworth	Y	Y	Y	Y	N	N
INDIANA						
Young	Y	Y	Y	Y	Y	Y
Braun	N	N	Y	Y	Y	Y
IOWA						
Grassley	N	N	Y	Y	Y	Y
Ernst	Y	N	Y	Y	Y	Y
KANSAS						
Roberts	Y	Y	Y	Y	Y	Y
Moran	Y	N	Y	Y	Y	Y
KENTUCKY						
McConnell	N	N	Y	Y	Y	Y
Paul	N	N	N	N	N	N
LOUISIANA						
Cassidy	?	N	Y	Y	Y	Y
Kennedy	N	N	N	Y	Y	Y
MAINE						
Collins	Y	Y	Y	Y	Y	Y
King	Y	Y	Y	Y	N	N
MARYLAND						
Cardin	Y	Y	Y	Y	N	N
Van Hollen	Y	Y	Y	Y	N	N
MASSACHUSETTS						
Warren	Y	Y	Y	Y	N	N
Markey	Y	Y	Y	Y	N	N
MICHIGAN						
Stabenow	Y	?	?	Y	N	N
Peters	Y	Y	Y	Y	N	N
MINNESOTA						
Klobuchar	Y	?	?	Y	Y	N
Smith	Y	Y	Y	Y	N	N
MISSISSIPPI						
Wicker	N	N	Y	Y	Y	Y
Hyde-Smith	Y	Y	Y	Y	Y	Y
MISSOURI						
Blunt	Y	N	Y	Y	Y	Y
Hawley	N	N	Y	Y	Y	Y
MONTANA						
Tester	Y	Y	Y	Y	N	N
Daines	Y	Y	Y	Y	Y	Y
NEBRASKA						
Fischer	N	N	Y	Y	Y	Y
Sasse	N	?	+	N	Y	Y
NEVADA						
Cortez Masto	Y	Y	Y	Y	N	N
Rosen	Y	Y	Y	Y	N	N
NEW HAMPSHIRE						
Shaheen	Y	Y	Y	Y	N	N
Hassan	Y	Y	Y	Y	N	N
NEW JERSEY						
Menendez	Y	Y	Y	Y	N	N
Booker	-	Y	Y	Y	?	N
NEW MEXICO						
Udall	Y	Y	Y	Y	N	N
Heinrich	Y	Y	Y	Y	N	N
NEW YORK						
Schumer	Y	Y	Y	Y	N	N
Gillibrand	Y	?	Y	Y	N	N
NORTH CAROLINA						
Burr	Y	Y	Y	Y	Y	?
Tillis	Y	Y	Y	Y	Y	Y
NORTH DAKOTA						
Hoeven	N	?	?	Y	Y	Y
Cramer	N	N	Y	Y	Y	Y
OHIO						
Brown	Y	Y	Y	Y	N	N
Portman	Y	Y	Y	Y	Y	Y
OKLAHOMA						
Inhofe	N	N	N	N	Y	Y
Lankford	N	N	N	N	Y	Y
OREGON						
Wyden	Y	Y	Y	Y	N	N
Merkley	Y	Y	Y	Y	N	N
PENNSYLVANIA						
Casey	Y	Y	Y	Y	N	N
Toomey	N	N	N	N	Y	Y
RHODE ISLAND						
Reed	Y	Y	Y	Y	N	N
Whitehouse	N	Y	Y	Y	N	N
SOUTH CAROLINA						
Graham	Y	Y	Y	Y	Y	Y
Scott	N	N	Y	Y	Y	Y
SOUTH DAKOTA						
Thune	Y	Y	Y	Y	Y	Y
Rounds	Y	Y	Y	Y	Y	Y
TENNESSEE						
Alexander	Y	Y	Y	Y	Y	Y
Blackburn	Y	N	Y	Y	Y	Y
TEXAS						
Cornyn	N	-	+	Y	Y	Y
Cruz	N	?	?	Y	Y	Y
UTAH						
Lee	N	N	N	N	Y	Y
Romney	N	N	Y	Y	Y	Y
VERMONT						
Leahy	Y	Y	Y	Y	N	N
Sanders	Y	Y	Y	Y	N	N
VIRGINIA						
Warner	Y	Y	Y	Y	N	N
Kaine	Y	Y	Y	Y	N	N
WASHINGTON						
Murray	Y	Y	Y	Y	N	N
Cantwell	Y	Y	Y	Y	N	N
WEST VIRGINIA						
Manchin	Y	Y	Y	Y	Y	Y
Capito	Y	Y	Y	Y	Y	Y
WISCONSIN						
Johnson	N	N	N	N	Y	Y
Baldwin	Y	Y	Y	Y	N	N
WYOMING						
Enzi	N	N	Y	Y	Y	Y
Barrasso	N	N	Y	Y	Y	Y

KEY:

	Republicans	Democrats	*Independents*
Y Voted for (yea)	N Voted against (nay)		P Voted "present"
+ Announced for	− Announced against		? Did not vote or otherwise make position known
# Paired for	X Paired against		

25. HJRES31. Fiscal 2019 Consolidated Appropriations - Cloture. McConnell, R-Ky., motion to invoke cloture (thus limiting debate) on the conference report to accompany the joint resolution that would provide, in total, $333 billion in full-year funding for the seven remaining fiscal 2019 appropriations bills: Agriculture; Commerce-Justice-Science; Financial Services; Homeland Security; Interior-Environment; State-For-eign Operations; and Transportation-Housing and Urban Development. It would provide $49.4 billion in discretionary funds for fiscal 2019 for operations of the Homeland Security Department, as well as $12.6 billion for natural disaster response and recovery activities and $165 million for Coast Guard overseas contingency operations. Motion agreed to 84-15: R 42-10; D 40-5; I 2-0. *Note: Three-fifths of the total Senate (60) is required to invoke cloture.* Feb. 14, 2019.

26. HJRES31. Fiscal 2019 Consolidated Appropriations - Conference Report. Adoption of the conference report to accompany the joint resolution that would provide, in total, $333 billion in full-year funding for the seven remaining fiscal 2019 appropriations bills: Agriculture; Commerce-Justice-Science; Financial Services; Homeland Security; Interior-Environment; State-Foreign Operations; and Trans-portation-Housing and Urban Development. Adopted (thus sent to the Senate) 83-16: R 41-11; D 40-5; I 2-0. *Note: A "yea" was a vote in support of the president's position.* Feb. 14, 2019.

27. S311. Abortion Medical Care - Cloture. McConnell, R-Ky., motion to invoke cloture (thus limiting debate) on his motion to proceed to the bill that would require health care practitioners to provide medical care to any infant that survives an abortion procedure, to the extent legally required for any infant born at the same gestational age. Motion reject-ed 53-44: R 50-0; D 3-42; I 0-2. *Note: Three-fifths of the total Senate (60) is required to invoke cloture. A "yea" was a vote in support of the president's position.* Feb. 25, 2019.

28. Miller Nomination - Cloture. Motion to invoke cloture (thus limiting debate) on the nomination of Eric D. Miller of Washington to be a U.S. circuit judge for the 9th Circuit. Motion agreed to 51-46: R 51-0; D 0-45; I 0-1. *Note: A majority of senators voting (49 in this case), a quorum being present, is required to invoke cloture on all nominations.* Feb. 25, 2019.

29. Miller Nomination - Confirmation. Confirmation of President Trump's nomination of Eric D. Miller of Washington to be United States circuit judge for the 9th Circuit. Confirmed 53-46: R 53-0; D 0-44; I 0-2. *Note: A "yea" was a vote in support of the president's position.* Feb. 26, 2019.

30. Desmond Nomination - Cloture. Motion to invoke cloture (thus limiting debate) on the nomination of Michael J. Desmond of California to be chief counsel for the Internal Revenue Service and an assistant general counsel in the Department of the Treasury. Motion agreed to 84-15: R 53-0; D 30-14; I 1-1. *Note: A majority of senators voting (50 in this case), a quorum being present, is required to invoke cloture on all nominations.* Feb. 26, 2019.

	25	26	27	28	29	30
ALABAMA						
Shelby	Y	Y	Y	Y	Y	Y
Jones	Y	Y	Y	N	N	Y
ALASKA						
Murkowski	Y	Y	?	?	Y	Y
Sullivan	Y	Y	Y	Y	Y	Y
ARIZONA						
Sinema	Y	Y	N	N	–	–
McSally	Y	Y	Y	Y	Y	Y
ARKANSAS						
Boozman	Y	Y	Y	Y	Y	Y
Cotton	N	N	Y	Y	Y	Y
CALIFORNIA						
Feinstein	Y	Y	N	N	N	Y
Harris	N	N	N	N	N	N
COLORADO						
Bennet	Y	Y	N	N	N	Y
Gardner	Y	Y	Y	Y	Y	Y
CONNECTICUT						
Blumenthal	Y	Y	N	N	N	Y
Murphy	Y	Y	N	N	N	Y
DELAWARE						
Carper	Y	Y	N	N	N	Y
Coons	Y	Y	N	N	N	Y
FLORIDA						
Rubio	N	N	Y	Y	Y	Y
Scott	Y	Y	Y	Y	Y	Y
GEORGIA						
Isakson	Y	Y	Y	Y	Y	Y
Perdue	Y	Y	Y	Y	Y	Y
HAWAII						
Schatz	Y	Y	N	N	N	N
Hirono	Y	Y	N	N	N	N
IDAHO						
Crapo	Y	Y	Y	Y	Y	Y
Risch	Y	Y	Y	Y	Y	Y
ILLINOIS						
Durbin	Y	Y	N	N	N	Y
Duckworth	Y	Y	N	N	N	N
INDIANA						
Young	Y	Y	Y	Y	Y	Y
Braun	Y	N	Y	Y	Y	Y
IOWA						
Grassley	Y	Y	Y	Y	Y	Y
Ernst	Y	Y	Y	Y	Y	Y
KANSAS						
Roberts	Y	Y	Y	Y	Y	Y
Moran	Y	Y	Y	Y	Y	Y
KENTUCKY						
McConnell	Y	Y	Y	Y	Y	Y
Paul	N	N	Y	Y	Y	Y
LOUISIANA						
Cassidy	Y	Y	Y	Y	Y	Y
Kennedy	Y	Y	Y	Y	Y	Y
MAINE						
Collins	Y	Y	Y	Y	Y	Y
King	Y	Y	N	N	N	Y
MARYLAND						
Cardin	Y	Y	N	N	N	Y
Van Hollen	Y	Y	N	N	N	Y
MASSACHUSETTS						
Warren	N	N	N	N	N	N
Markey	N	N	N	N	N	N
MICHIGAN						
Stabenow	Y	Y	N	N	N	Y
Peters	Y	Y	N	N	N	Y
MINNESOTA						
Klobuchar	Y	Y	N	N	N	N
Smith	Y	Y	N	N	N	Y
MISSISSIPPI						
Wicker	Y	Y	Y	Y	Y	Y
Hyde-Smith	Y	Y	Y	Y	Y	Y
MISSOURI						
Blunt	Y	Y	Y	Y	Y	Y
Hawley	N	N	Y	Y	Y	Y

	25	26	27	28	29	30
MONTANA						
Tester	Y	Y	N	N	N	Y
Daines	Y	Y	Y	Y	Y	Y
NEBRASKA						
Fischer	Y	Y	Y	Y	Y	Y
Sasse	N	N	Y	Y	Y	Y
NEVADA						
Cortez Masto	Y	Y	N	N	N	Y
Rosen	Y	Y	N	N	N	Y
NEW HAMPSHIRE						
Shaheen	Y	Y	N	N	N	Y
Hassan	Y	Y	N	N	N	Y
NEW JERSEY						
Menendez	Y	Y	N	N	N	N
Booker	N	N	N	N	N	N
NEW MEXICO						
Udall	Y	Y	N	N	N	Y
Heinrich	Y	Y	N	N	N	Y
NEW YORK						
Schumer	Y	Y	N	N	N	N
Gillibrand	N	N	N	N	N	N
NORTH CAROLINA						
Burr	?	?	Y	Y	Y	Y
Tillis	Y	Y	Y	Y	Y	Y
NORTH DAKOTA						
Hoeven	Y	Y	Y	Y	Y	Y
Cramer	Y	Y	?	?	Y	Y
OHIO						
Brown	Y	Y	N	N	N	Y
Portman	Y	Y	Y	Y	Y	Y
OKLAHOMA						
Inhofe	N	N	Y	Y	Y	Y
Lankford	Y	Y	Y	Y	Y	Y
OREGON						
Wyden	Y	Y	N	N	N	Y
Merkley	Y	Y	N	N	N	N
PENNSYLVANIA						
Casey	Y	Y	N	N	N	Y
Toomey	N	N	Y	Y	Y	Y
RHODE ISLAND						
Reed	Y	Y	N	N	N	N
Whitehouse	Y	Y	N	N	N	N
SOUTH CAROLINA						
Graham	Y	Y	Y	Y	Y	Y
Scott	N	N	?	Y	Y	Y
SOUTH DAKOTA						
Thune	Y	Y	Y	Y	Y	Y
Rounds	Y	Y	Y	Y	Y	Y
TENNESSEE						
Alexander	Y	Y	Y	Y	Y	Y
Blackburn	Y	Y	Y	Y	Y	Y
TEXAS						
Cornyn	Y	Y	Y	Y	Y	Y
Cruz	N	N	Y	Y	Y	Y
UTAH						
Lee	N	N	Y	Y	Y	Y
Romney	Y	Y	Y	Y	Y	Y
VERMONT						
Leahy	Y	Y	N	N	N	Y
Sanders	Y	Y	N	?	N	N
VIRGINIA						
Warner	Y	Y	N	N	N	Y
Kaine	Y	Y	N	N	N	Y
WASHINGTON						
Murray	Y	Y	N	N	N	Y
Cantwell	Y	Y	N	N	N	Y
WEST VIRGINIA						
Manchin	Y	Y	Y	N	N	Y
Capito	Y	Y	Y	Y	Y	Y
WISCONSIN						
Johnson	Y	Y	Y	Y	Y	Y
Baldwin	Y	Y	N	N	N	Y
WYOMING						
Enzi	Y	Y	Y	Y	Y	Y
Barrasso	Y	Y	Y	Y	Y	Y

KEY:

	Republicans		Democrats		*Independents*	
Y	Voted for (yea)	N	Voted against (nay)	P	Voted "present"	
+	Announced for	–	Announced against	?	Did not vote or otherwise	
#	Paired for	X	Paired against		make position known	

31. Desmond Nomination - Confirmation. Confirmation of President Trump's nomination of Michael J. Desmond of California to be chief counsel for the Internal Revenue Service and an assistant general counsel in the Department of the Treasury. Confirmed 83-15: R 52-0; D 30-14; I 1-1. *Note: A "yea" was a vote in support of the president's position.* Feb. 27, 2019.

32. Wheeler Nomination - Cloture. Motion to invoke cloture (thus limiting debate) on the nomination of Andrew Wheeler of Virginia to be administrator of the Environmental Protection Agency. Motion agreed to 52-46: R 52-0; D 0-44; I 0-2. *Note: A majority of senators voting (49 in this case), a quorum being present, is required to invoke cloture on all nominations.* Feb. 27, 2019.

33. Wheeler Nomination - Confirmation. Confirmation of President Trump's nomination of Andrew Wheeler of Virginia to be administrator of the Environmental Protection Agency. Confirmed 52-47: R 52-1; D 0-44; I 0-2. *Note: A "yea" was a vote in support of the president's position.* Feb. 28, 2019.

34. Rushing Nomination - Cloture. Motion to invoke cloture (thus limiting debate) on the nomination of Allison Jones Rushing of North Carolina to be a U.S. circuit judge for the 4th Circuit. Motion agreed to 52-43: R 52-0; D 0-42; I 0-1. *Note: A majority of senators voting (48 in this case), a quorum being present, is required to invoke cloture on all nominations.* March 04, 2019.

35. Rushing Nomination - Confirmation. Confirmation of President Trump's nomination of Allison Jones Rushing of North Carolina to be United States circuit judge for the 4th Circuit. Confirmed 53-44: R 53-0; D 0-43; I 0-1. *Note: A "yea" was a vote in support of the president's position.* March 05, 2019.

36. Readler Nomination - Cloture. Motion to invoke cloture (thus limiting debate) on the nomination of Chad A. Readler of Ohio to be a U.S. circuit judge for the 6th Circuit. Motion agreed to 53-45: R 53-0; D 0-44; I 0-1. *Note: A majority of senators voting (49 in this case), a quorum being present, is required to invoke cloture on all nominations.* March 05, 2019.

	31	32	33	34	35	36
ALABAMA						
Shelby	Y	Y	Y	Y	Y	Y
Jones	Y	N	N	N	N	N
ALASKA						
Murkowski	Y	Y	Y	?	Y	Y
Sullivan	Y	Y	Y	Y	Y	Y
ARIZONA						
Sinema	?	?	?	-	-	-
McSally	Y	Y	Y	Y	Y	Y
ARKANSAS						
Boozman	Y	Y	Y	Y	Y	Y
Cotton	Y	Y	Y	Y	Y	Y
CALIFORNIA						
Feinstein	Y	N	N	N	N	N
Harris	N	N	N	N	N	N
COLORADO						
Bennet	Y	N	N	N	N	N
Gardner	Y	Y	Y	Y	Y	Y
CONNECTICUT						
Blumenthal	Y	N	N	N	N	N
Murphy	Y	N	N	N	N	N
DELAWARE						
Carper	Y	N	N	N	N	N
Coons	Y	N	N	N	N	N
FLORIDA						
Rubio	Y	Y	Y	Y	Y	Y
Scott	+	+	Y	Y	Y	Y
GEORGIA						
Isakson	Y	Y	Y	Y	Y	Y
Perdue	Y	Y	Y	Y	Y	Y
HAWAII						
Schatz	N	N	N	N	N	N
Hirono	N	N	N	N	N	N
IDAHO						
Crapo	Y	Y	Y	Y	Y	Y
Risch	Y	Y	Y	Y	Y	Y
ILLINOIS						
Durbin	Y	N	N	N	N	N
Duckworth	N	N	N	N	N	N
INDIANA						
Young	Y	Y	Y	Y	Y	Y
Braun	Y	Y	Y	Y	Y	Y
IOWA						
Grassley	Y	Y	Y	Y	Y	Y
Ernst	Y	Y	Y	Y	Y	Y
KANSAS						
Roberts	Y	Y	Y	Y	Y	Y
Moran	Y	Y	Y	Y	Y	Y
KENTUCKY						
McConnell	Y	Y	Y	Y	Y	Y
Paul	Y	Y	Y	Y	Y	Y
LOUISIANA						
Cassidy	Y	Y	Y	Y	Y	Y
Kennedy	Y	Y	Y	Y	Y	Y
MAINE						
Collins	Y	Y	N	Y	Y	Y
King	Y	N	N	N	N	N
MARYLAND						
Cardin	Y	N	N	N	N	N
Van Hollen	Y	N	N	N	N	N
MASSACHUSETTS						
Warren	N	N	N	N	N	N
Markey	N	N	N	N	N	N
MICHIGAN						
Stabenow	Y	N	N	N	N	N
Peters	Y	N	N	N	N	N
MINNESOTA						
Klobuchar	N	N	N	N	N	N
Smith	Y	N	N	N	N	N
MISSISSIPPI						
Wicker	Y	Y	Y	Y	Y	Y
Hyde-Smith	Y	Y	Y	Y	Y	Y
MISSOURI						
Blunt	Y	Y	Y	Y	Y	Y
Hawley	Y	Y	Y	Y	Y	Y

	31	32	33	34	35	36
MONTANA						
Tester	Y	N	N	N	N	N
Daines	Y	Y	Y	Y	Y	Y
NEBRASKA						
Fischer	Y	Y	Y	Y	Y	Y
Sasse	Y	Y	Y	Y	Y	Y
NEVADA						
Cortez Masto	Y	N	N	N	N	N
Rosen	Y	N	N	N	N	N
NEW HAMPSHIRE						
Shaheen	Y	N	N	N	N	N
Hassan	Y	N	N	N	N	N
NEW JERSEY						
Menendez	N	N	N	N	N	N
Booker	N	N	N	N	N	N
NEW MEXICO						
Udall	Y	N	N	N	N	N
Heinrich	Y	N	N	-	-	N
NEW YORK						
Schumer	N	N	N	N	N	N
Gillibrand	N	N	N	N	N	N
NORTH CAROLINA						
Burr	Y	Y	Y	Y	Y	Y
Tillis	Y	Y	Y	Y	Y	Y
NORTH DAKOTA						
Hoeven	Y	Y	Y	Y	Y	Y
Cramer	Y	Y	Y	Y	Y	Y
OHIO						
Brown	Y	N	N	?	N	N
Portman	Y	Y	Y	Y	Y	Y
OKLAHOMA						
Inhofe	Y	Y	Y	Y	Y	Y
Lankford	Y	Y	Y	Y	Y	Y
OREGON						
Wyden	Y	N	N	N	N	N
Merkley	N	N	N	N	N	N
PENNSYLVANIA						
Casey	Y	N	N	N	N	N
Toomey	Y	Y	Y	Y	Y	Y
RHODE ISLAND						
Reed	N	N	N	N	N	N
Whitehouse	N	N	N	N	N	N
SOUTH CAROLINA						
Graham	Y	Y	Y	Y	Y	Y
Scott	Y	Y	Y	Y	Y	Y
SOUTH DAKOTA						
Thune	Y	Y	Y	Y	Y	Y
Rounds	Y	Y	Y	Y	Y	Y
TENNESSEE						
Alexander	Y	Y	Y	Y	Y	Y
Blackburn	Y	Y	Y	Y	Y	Y
TEXAS						
Cornyn	Y	Y	Y	Y	Y	Y
Cruz	Y	Y	Y	Y	Y	Y
UTAH						
Lee	Y	Y	Y	Y	Y	Y
Romney	Y	Y	Y	Y	Y	Y
VERMONT						
Leahy	Y	N	N	N	N	N
Sanders	N	N	N	?	?	?
VIRGINIA						
Warner	Y	N	N	N	N	N
Kaine	Y	N	N	N	N	N
WASHINGTON						
Murray	Y	N	N	N	N	N
Cantwell	Y	N	N	N	N	N
WEST VIRGINIA						
Manchin	Y	N	N	N	N	N
Capito	Y	Y	Y	Y	Y	Y
WISCONSIN						
Johnson	Y	Y	Y	Y	Y	Y
Baldwin	Y	N	N	N	N	N
WYOMING						
Enzi	Y	Y	Y	Y	Y	Y
Barrasso	Y	Y	Y	Y	Y	Y

KEY:	**Republicans**	Democrats	*Independents*
Y Voted for (yea)	N Voted against (nay)	P Voted "present"	
+ Announced for	- Announced against	? Did not vote or otherwise make position known	
# Paired for	X Paired against		

37. Readler Nomination - Confirmation. Confirmation of President Trump's nomination of Chad A. Readler of Ohio to be a United States circuit judge for the 6th Circuit. Confirmed 52-47: R 52-1; D 0-44; I 0-2. *Note: A "yea" was a vote in support of the president's position.* March 06, 2019.

38. Murphy Nomination - Cloture. Motion to invoke cloture (thus limiting debate) on the nomination of Eric E. Murphy of Ohio to be a U.S. circuit judge for the 6th Circuit. Motion agreed to 53-46: R 53-0; D 0-44; I 0-2. *Note: A majority of senators voting (50 in this case), a quorum being present, is required to invoke cloture on all nominations.* March 06, 2019.

39. Murphy Nomination - Confirmation. Confirmation of President Trump's nomination of Eric Murphy of Ohio to be United States circuit judge for the 6th Circuit. Confirmed 52-46: R 52-0; D 0-44; I 0-2. *Note: A "yea" was a vote in support of the president's position.* March 07, 2019.

40. Fleming Nomination - Confirmation. Confirmation of President Trump's nomination of John Fleming of Louisiana to be assistant secretary of Commerce for Economic Development. Confirmed 67-30: R 51-0; D 15-29; I 1-1. *Note: A "yea" was a vote in support of the president's position.* March 07, 2019.

41. Matey Nomination - Cloture. McConnell, R-Ky., motion to invoke cloture (thus limiting debate) on the nomination of Paul Matey of New Jersey to be a U.S. circuit judge for the 3rd Circuit. Motion agreed to 50-44: R 50-0; D 0-43; I 0-1. *Note: A majority of senators voting (48 in this case), a quorum being present, is required to invoke cloture on all nominations.* March 11, 2019.

42. Matey Nomination - Confirmation. Confirmation of President Trump's nomination of Paul Matey of New Jersey to be U.S. circuit judge for the 3rd Circuit. Confirmed 54-45: R 53-0; D 1-43; I 0-2. *Note: A "yea" was a vote is support of the president's position.* March 12, 2019.

	37	38	39	40	41	42
ALABAMA						
Shelby	Y	Y	Y	Y	Y	Y
Jones	N	N	?	?	N	N
ALASKA						
Murkowski	Y	Y	Y	Y	?	Y
Sullivan	Y	Y	Y	Y	Y	Y
ARIZONA						
Sinema	N	N	N	N	N	N
McSally	Y	Y	Y	Y	Y	Y
ARKANSAS						
Boozman	Y	Y	Y	Y	Y	Y
Cotton	Y	Y	Y	Y	Y	Y
CALIFORNIA						
Feinstein	N	N	N	Y	N	N
Harris	N	N	N	N	N	N
COLORADO						
Bennet	N	N	N	N	N	N
Gardner	Y	Y	Y	Y	Y	Y
CONNECTICUT						
Blumenthal	N	N	N	N	N	N
Murphy	N	N	N	Y	N	N
DELAWARE						
Carper	N	N	N	Y	N	N
Coons	N	N	N	Y	N	N
FLORIDA						
Rubio	Y	Y	Y	Y	Y	Y
Scott	Y	Y	Y	Y	Y	Y
GEORGIA						
Isakson	Y	Y	Y	Y	Y	Y
Perdue	Y	Y	?	?	+	Y
HAWAII						
Schatz	N	N	N	N	N	N
Hirono	N	N	N	N	N	N
IDAHO						
Crapo	Y	Y	Y	Y	Y	Y
Risch	Y	Y	Y	Y	Y	Y
ILLINOIS						
Durbin	N	N	N	N	N	N
Duckworth	N	N	N	Y	N	N
INDIANA						
Young	Y	Y	Y	Y	Y	Y
Braun	Y	Y	Y	Y	Y	Y
IOWA						
Grassley	Y	Y	Y	Y	Y	Y
Ernst	Y	Y	Y	Y	Y	Y
KANSAS						
Roberts	Y	Y	Y	Y	Y	Y
Moran	Y	Y	Y	+	Y	Y
KENTUCKY						
McConnell	Y	Y	Y	Y	Y	Y
Paul	Y	Y	Y	Y	Y	Y
LOUISIANA						
Cassidy	Y	Y	Y	Y	Y	Y
Kennedy	Y	Y	Y	Y	Y	Y
MAINE						
Collins	N	Y	Y	Y	Y	Y
King	N	N	N	Y	N	N
MARYLAND						
Cardin	N	N	N	Y	N	N
Van Hollen	N	N	N	N	N	N
MASSACHUSETTS						
Warren	N	N	N	N	N	N
Markey	N	N	N	N	N	N
MICHIGAN						
Stabenow	N	N	N	N	N	N
Peters	N	N	N	N	N	N
MINNESOTA						
Klobuchar	N	N	N	N	N	N
Smith	N	N	N	N	N	N
MISSISSIPPI						
Wicker	Y	Y	Y	Y	Y	Y
Hyde-Smith	Y	Y	Y	Y	Y	Y
MISSOURI						
Blunt	Y	Y	Y	Y	Y	Y
Hawley	Y	Y	Y	Y	Y	Y

	37	38	39	40	41	42
MONTANA						
Tester	N	N	N	N	N	N
Daines	Y	Y	Y	Y	Y	Y
NEBRASKA						
Fischer	Y	Y	Y	Y	Y	Y
Sasse	Y	Y	Y	Y	Y	Y
NEVADA						
Cortez Masto	N	N	N	Y	N	N
Rosen	N	N	N	N	N	N
NEW HAMPSHIRE						
Shaheen	N	N	N	N	N	N
Hassan	N	N	N	N	N	N
NEW JERSEY						
Menendez	N	N	N	N	N	N
Booker	N	N	N	N	N	N
NEW MEXICO						
Udall	N	N	N	N	N	N
Heinrich	N	N	N	N	N	N
NEW YORK						
Schumer	N	N	N	N	N	N
Gillibrand	N	N	N	N	N	N
NORTH CAROLINA						
Burr	Y	Y	Y	Y	Y	Y
Tillis	Y	Y	Y	Y	Y	Y
NORTH DAKOTA						
Hoeven	Y	Y	Y	Y	Y	Y
Cramer	Y	Y	Y	Y	Y	Y
OHIO						
Brown	N	N	N	N	N	N
Portman	Y	Y	Y	Y	Y	Y
OKLAHOMA						
Inhofe	Y	Y	Y	Y	Y	Y
Lankford	Y	Y	Y	Y	Y	Y
OREGON						
Wyden	N	N	N	N	N	N
Merkley	N	N	N	N	N	N
PENNSYLVANIA						
Casey	N	N	N	N	N	N
Toomey	Y	Y	Y	Y	Y	Y
RHODE ISLAND						
Reed	N	N	N	N	N	N
Whitehouse	N	N	N	Y	N	N
SOUTH CAROLINA						
Graham	Y	Y	Y	Y	?	Y
Scott	Y	Y	Y	Y	Y	Y
SOUTH DAKOTA						
Thune	Y	Y	Y	Y	Y	Y
Rounds	Y	Y	Y	Y	Y	Y
TENNESSEE						
Alexander	Y	Y	Y	Y	Y	Y
Blackburn	Y	Y	Y	Y	Y	Y
TEXAS						
Cornyn	Y	Y	Y	Y	Y	Y
Cruz	Y	Y	Y	Y	Y	Y
UTAH						
Lee	Y	Y	Y	Y	Y	Y
Romney	Y	Y	Y	Y	Y	Y
VERMONT						
Leahy	N	N	N	N	N	N
Sanders	N	N	N	N	?	N
VIRGINIA						
Warner	N	N	N	N	N	N
Kaine	N	N	N	N	N	N
WASHINGTON						
Murray	N	N	N	N	?	?
Cantwell	N	N	N	N	N	N
WEST VIRGINIA						
Manchin	?	?	N	Y	?	Y
Capito	Y	Y	Y	Y	Y	Y
WISCONSIN						
Johnson	Y	Y	Y	Y	Y	Y
Baldwin	N	N	N	N	N	N
WYOMING						
Enzi	Y	Y	Y	Y	Y	Y
Barrasso	Y	Y	Y	Y	Y	Y

KEY:	Republicans	Democrats	Independents

Y Voted for (yea)	N Voted against (nay)	P Voted "present"
+ Announced for	– Announced against	? Did not vote or otherwise
# Paired for	X Paired against	make position known

43. Rao Nomination - Cloture. Motion to invoke cloture (thus limiting debate) on the nomination of Neomi Rao of the District of Columbia to be a U.S. circuit judge for the District of Columbia Circuit. Motion agreed to 53-46: R 53-0; D 0-44; I 0-2. *Note: A majority of senators voting (50 in this case), a quorum being present, is required to invoke cloture on all nominations.* March 12, 2019.

44. Rao Nomination - Confirmation. Confirmation of President Trump's nomination of Neomi Rao of the District of Columbia to be U.S. circuit judge for the District of Columbia Circuit. Confirmed 53-46: R 53-0; D 0-44; I 0-2. *Note: A "yea" was a vote in support of the president's position.* March 13, 2019.

45. Beach Nomination - Cloture. Motion to invoke cloture (thus limiting debate) on the nomination of William Beach of Kansas to be commissioner of Labor Statistics, Department of Labor. Motion agreed to 55-43: R 53-0; D 2-41; I 0-2. *Note: A majority of senators voting (50 in this case), a quorum being present, is required to invoke cloture on all nominations.* March 13, 2019.

46. Beach Nomination - Confirmation. Confirmation of President Trump's nomination of William Beach of Kansas to be commissioner of Labor Statistics, Department of Labor. Confirmed 55-44: R 53-0; D 2-42; I 0-2. *Note: A "yea" was a vote in support of the president's position.* March 13, 2019.

47. SJRES7. U.S. Military Forces in Yemen - Motion to Table. Sanders, I-Vt., motion to table the Inhofe, R-Okla, amendment no. 194 to the bill that would expand the exemption in the measure for U.S. armed forces "engaged in operations directed at al Qaeda or associated forces" to allow ongoing operations that defend civilian population centers in coalition countries from ballistic and cruise missiles, and drone threats. Motion agreed to 52-48: R 5-48; D 45-0; I 2-0. March 13, 2019.

48. SJRES7. U.S. Military Forces in Yemen - Passage. Passage of the joint resolution, as amended, that would direct the president, within 30 days of enactment, to remove U.S. armed forces from hostilities in or affecting the Republic of Yemen, including in-flight refueling of non-U.S. aircraft, unless a declaration of war or specific authorization for such use of forces has been enacted. Passed 54-46: R 7-46; D 45-0; I 2-0. *Note: A "nay" was a vote in support of the president's position.* March 13, 2019.

	43	44	45	46	47	48
ALABAMA						
Shelby	Y	Y	Y	Y	N	N
Jones	N	N	N	N	Y	Y
ALASKA						
Murkowski	Y	Y	Y	Y	N	Y
Sullivan	Y	Y	Y	Y	N	N
ARIZONA						
Sinema	N	N	Y	Y	Y	Y
McSally	Y	Y	Y	Y	N	N
ARKANSAS						
Boozman	Y	Y	Y	Y	N	N
Cotton	Y	Y	Y	Y	N	N
CALIFORNIA						
Feinstein	N	N	N	N	Y	Y
Harris	N	N	N	N	Y	Y
COLORADO						
Bennet	N	N	N	N	Y	Y
Gardner	Y	Y	Y	Y	N	N
CONNECTICUT						
Blumenthal	N	N	N	N	Y	Y
Murphy	N	N	N	N	Y	Y
DELAWARE						
Carper	N	N	N	N	Y	Y
Coons	N	N	N	N	Y	Y
FLORIDA						
Rubio	Y	Y	Y	Y	N	N
Scott	Y	Y	Y	Y	N	N
GEORGIA						
Isakson	Y	Y	Y	Y	N	N
Perdue	Y	Y	Y	Y	N	N
HAWAII						
Schatz	N	N	N	N	Y	Y
Hirono	N	N	N	N	Y	Y
IDAHO						
Crapo	Y	Y	Y	Y	N	N
Risch	Y	Y	Y	Y	N	N
ILLINOIS						
Durbin	N	N	N	N	Y	Y
Duckworth	N	N	?	N	Y	Y
INDIANA						
Young	Y	Y	Y	Y	Y	Y
Braun	Y	Y	Y	Y	N	N
IOWA						
Grassley	Y	Y	Y	Y	N	N
Ernst	Y	Y	Y	Y	N	N
KANSAS						
Roberts	Y	Y	Y	Y	N	N
Moran	Y	Y	Y	Y	Y	Y
KENTUCKY						
McConnell	Y	Y	Y	Y	N	N
Paul	Y	Y	Y	Y	Y	Y
LOUISIANA						
Cassidy	Y	Y	Y	Y	N	N
Kennedy	Y	Y	Y	Y	N	N
MAINE						
Collins	Y	Y	Y	Y	N	Y
King	N	N	N	N	Y	Y
MARYLAND						
Cardin	N	N	N	N	Y	Y
Van Hollen	N	N	N	N	Y	Y
MASSACHUSETTS						
Warren	N	N	N	N	Y	Y
Markey	N	N	N	N	Y	Y
MICHIGAN						
Stabenow	N	N	N	N	Y	Y
Peters	N	N	N	N	Y	Y
MINNESOTA						
Klobuchar	N	N	N	N	Y	Y
Smith	N	N	N	N	Y	Y
MISSISSIPPI						
Wicker	Y	Y	Y	Y	N	N
Hyde-Smith	Y	Y	Y	Y	N	N
MISSOURI						
Blunt	Y	Y	Y	Y	N	N
Hawley	Y	Y	Y	Y	N	N

	43	44	45	46	47	48
MONTANA						
Tester	N	N	N	N	Y	Y
Daines	Y	Y	Y	Y	Y	Y
NEBRASKA						
Fischer	Y	Y	Y	Y	N	N
Sasse	Y	Y	Y	N	N	N
NEVADA						
Cortez Masto	N	N	N	N	Y	Y
Rosen	N	N	N	N	Y	Y
NEW HAMPSHIRE						
Shaheen	N	N	N	N	Y	Y
Hassan	N	N	N	N	Y	Y
NEW JERSEY						
Menendez	N	N	N	N	Y	Y
Booker	N	N	N	N	Y	Y
NEW MEXICO						
Udall	N	N	N	N	Y	Y
Heinrich	N	N	N	N	Y	Y
NEW YORK						
Schumer	N	N	N	N	Y	Y
Gillibrand	N	N	N	N	Y	Y
NORTH CAROLINA						
Burr	Y	Y	Y	Y	N	N
Tillis	Y	Y	Y	Y	N	N
NORTH DAKOTA						
Hoeven	Y	Y	Y	Y	N	N
Cramer	Y	Y	Y	Y	N	N
OHIO						
Brown	N	N	N	N	Y	Y
Portman	Y	Y	Y	Y	N	N
OKLAHOMA						
Inhofe	Y	Y	Y	Y	N	N
Lankford	Y	Y	Y	Y	N	N
OREGON						
Wyden	N	N	N	N	Y	Y
Merkley	N	N	N	N	Y	Y
PENNSYLVANIA						
Casey	N	N	N	N	Y	Y
Toomey	Y	Y	Y	Y	N	N
RHODE ISLAND						
Reed	N	N	N	N	Y	Y
Whitehouse	N	N	N	N	Y	Y
SOUTH CAROLINA						
Graham	Y	Y	Y	Y	N	N
Scott	Y	Y	Y	Y	N	N
SOUTH DAKOTA						
Thune	Y	Y	Y	Y	N	N
Rounds	Y	Y	Y	Y	N	N
TENNESSEE						
Alexander	Y	Y	Y	Y	N	N
Blackburn	Y	Y	Y	Y	N	N
TEXAS						
Cornyn	Y	Y	Y	Y	N	N
Cruz	Y	Y	Y	Y	N	N
UTAH						
Lee	Y	Y	Y	Y	Y	Y
Romney	Y	Y	Y	Y	N	N
VERMONT						
Leahy	N	N	N	N	Y	Y
Sanders	N	N	N	N	Y	Y
VIRGINIA						
Warner	N	N	N	N	Y	Y
Kaine	N	N	N	N	Y	Y
WASHINGTON						
Murray	?	?	?	?	Y	Y
Cantwell	N	N	N	N	Y	Y
WEST VIRGINIA						
Manchin	N	N	Y	Y	Y	Y
Capito	Y	Y	Y	Y	N	N
WISCONSIN						
Johnson	Y	Y	Y	Y	N	N
Baldwin	N	N	N	N	Y	Y
WYOMING						
Enzi	Y	Y	Y	Y	N	N
Barrasso	Y	Y	Y	Y	N	N

KEY: **Republicans** | Democrats | *Independents*

Y Voted for (yea)	N Voted against (nay)	P Voted "present"
+ Announced for	– Announced against	? Did not vote or otherwise make position known
# Paired for	X Paired against	

49. HJRES46. National Emergency Disapproval Resolution - Passage. Passage of the joint resolution that would terminate the president's national emergency declaration concerning the security situation at the southern border. Passed (thus cleared for the president) 59-41: R 12-41; D 45-0; I 2-0. *Note: A "nay" was a vote in support of the president's position.* March 14, 2019.

50. Bade Nomination - Cloture. Motion to invoke cloture (thus limiting debate) on the nomination of Bridget Bade of Arizona to be a U.S. circuit judge for the 9th Circuit. Motion agreed to 77-20: R 52-0; D 24-19; I 1-1. *Note: A majority of senators voting (49 in this case), a quorum being present, is required to invoke cloture on all nominations.* March 25, 2019.

51. Bade Nomination - Confirmation. Confirmation of President Trump's nomination of Bridget Bade of Arizona to be a U.S. circuit judge for the 9th Circuit. Confirmed 78-21: R 53-0; D 24-20; I 1-1. *Note: A "yea" was a vote in support of the president's position.* March 26, 2019.

52. SJRES8. Green New Deal - Cloture. McConnell, R-Ky., motion to invoke cloture (thus limiting debate) on his motion to proceed to the joint resolution that would express the sense of the Senate that the government should adopt a "Green New Deal" with the goal of achieving net-zero greenhouse gas emissions, promoting job growth, building sustainable infrastructure, protecting natural resources, and promoting justice and equity. Motion rejected 0-57: R 0-53; D 0-3; I 0-1. *Note: Three-fifths of the total Senate (60) is required to invoke cloture. A "nay" was a vote in support of the president's position.* March 26, 2019.

53. HR268. Fiscal 2019 Disaster Relief Supplemental Appropriations - Cloture. McConnell, R-Ky., motion to invoke cloture (thus limiting debate) on his motion to proceed to the bill that would make fiscal 2019 supplemental appropriations for response efforts to damage caused by hurricanes, wildfires, earthquakes and other natural disasters that occurred in 2017 and 2018. Motion agreed to 90-10: R 43-10; D 45-0; I 2-0. *Note: Three-fifths of the total Senate (60) is required to invoke cloture.* March 26, 2019.

54. Nason Nomination - Confirmation. Confirmation of President Trump's nomination of Nicole R. Nason of New York to be administrator of the Federal Highway Administration. Motion agreed to 95-1: R 51-0; D 43-0; I 1-1. *Note: A "yea" was a vote in support of the president's position.* March 28, 2019.

	49	50	51	52	53	54
ALABAMA						
Shelby	N	Y	Y	N	Y	Y
Jones	Y	Y	Y	N	Y	Y
ALASKA						
Murkowski	Y	Y	Y	N	Y	Y
Sullivan	N	Y	Y	N	Y	?
ARIZONA						
Sinema	Y	Y	Y	N	Y	Y
McSally	N	Y	Y	N	Y	Y
ARKANSAS						
Boozman	N	Y	Y	N	Y	Y
Cotton	N	Y	Y	N	Y	Y
CALIFORNIA						
Feinstein	Y	Y	Y	P	Y	Y
Harris	Y	N	N	P	Y	Y
COLORADO						
Bennet	Y	Y	Y	P	Y	Y
Gardner	N	Y	Y	N	Y	Y
CONNECTICUT						
Blumenthal	Y	N	N	P	Y	Y
Murphy	Y	Y	Y	P	Y	Y
DELAWARE						
Carper	Y	Y	Y	P	Y	Y
Coons	Y	Y	Y	P	Y	Y
FLORIDA						
Rubio	Y	Y	Y	N	Y	Y
Scott	N	Y	Y	N	Y	Y
GEORGIA						
Isakson	N	Y	Y	N	Y	Y
Perdue	N	Y	Y	N	Y	Y
HAWAII						
Schatz	Y	Y	Y	P	Y	Y
Hirono	Y	N	N	P	Y	Y
IDAHO						
Crapo	N	Y	Y	N	N	Y
Risch	N	Y	Y	N	N	Y
ILLINOIS						
Durbin	Y	Y	Y	P	Y	Y
Duckworth	Y	Y	Y	P	Y	Y
INDIANA						
Young	N	Y	Y	N	Y	Y
Braun	N	Y	Y	N	N	Y
IOWA						
Grassley	N	Y	Y	N	Y	Y
Ernst	N	Y	Y	N	Y	Y
KANSAS						
Roberts	N	Y	Y	N	Y	Y
Moran	Y	Y	Y	N	Y	+
KENTUCKY						
McConnell	N	Y	Y	N	Y	Y
Paul	Y	Y	Y	N	N	Y
LOUISIANA						
Cassidy	N	Y	Y	N	Y	Y
Kennedy	N	Y	Y	N	Y	Y
MAINE						
Collins	Y	Y	Y	N	Y	Y
King	Y	Y	Y	N	Y	Y
MARYLAND						
Cardin	Y	Y	Y	P	Y	Y
Van Hollen	Y	Y	Y	P	Y	Y
MASSACHUSETTS						
Warren	Y	?	N	P	Y	Y
Markey	Y	N	N	P	Y	Y
MICHIGAN						
Stabenow	Y	N	N	P	Y	?
Peters	Y	N	N	P	Y	Y
MINNESOTA						
Klobuchar	Y	N	N	P	Y	Y
Smith	Y	N	N	P	Y	Y
MISSISSIPPI						
Wicker	Y	Y	Y	N	Y	Y
Hyde-Smith	N	Y	Y	N	Y	Y
MISSOURI						
Blunt	Y	Y	Y	N	Y	Y
Hawley	N	Y	Y	N	Y	Y
MONTANA						
Tester	Y	Y	Y	P	Y	Y
Daines	N	Y	Y	N	Y	Y
NEBRASKA						
Fischer	N	Y	Y	N	Y	Y
Sasse	N	Y	Y	N	Y	Y
NEVADA						
Cortez Masto	Y	N	N	P	Y	Y
Rosen	Y	Y	Y	P	Y	Y
NEW HAMPSHIRE						
Shaheen	Y	Y	Y	P	Y	Y
Hassan	Y	Y	Y	P	Y	Y
NEW JERSEY						
Menendez	Y	N	N	P	Y	Y
Booker	Y	N	N	P	Y	?
NEW MEXICO						
Udall	Y	?	?	P	Y	Y
Heinrich	Y	Y	Y	P	Y	Y
NEW YORK						
Schumer	Y	N	N	P	Y	Y
Gillibrand	Y	N	N	P	Y	Y
NORTH CAROLINA						
Burr	N	Y	Y	N	Y	Y
Tillis	N	Y	Y	N	Y	Y
NORTH DAKOTA						
Hoeven	N	Y	Y	N	Y	Y
Cramer	N	Y	Y	N	Y	Y
OHIO						
Brown	Y	Y	Y	P	Y	Y
Portman	Y	Y	Y	N	Y	Y
OKLAHOMA						
Inhofe	N	+	Y	N	N	Y
Lankford	N	Y	Y	N	N	Y
OREGON						
Wyden	Y	N	N	P	Y	Y
Merkley	Y	N	N	P	Y	Y
PENNSYLVANIA						
Casey	Y	N	N	P	Y	Y
Toomey	Y	Y	Y	N	Y	Y
RHODE ISLAND						
Reed	Y	Y	Y	P	Y	Y
Whitehouse	Y	Y	Y	P	Y	Y
SOUTH CAROLINA						
Graham	N	Y	Y	N	Y	Y
Scott	N	Y	Y	N	Y	Y
SOUTH DAKOTA						
Thune	N	Y	Y	N	Y	Y
Rounds	N	Y	Y	N	Y	Y
TENNESSEE						
Alexander	Y	Y	Y	N	Y	Y
Blackburn	N	Y	Y	N	Y	Y
TEXAS						
Cornyn	N	Y	Y	N	Y	Y
Cruz	N	Y	Y	N	Y	Y
UTAH						
Lee	Y	Y	Y	N	N	Y
Romney	Y	Y	Y	N	Y	Y
VERMONT						
Leahy	Y	Y	Y	P	Y	Y
Sanders	Y	N	N	P	Y	N
VIRGINIA						
Warner	Y	Y	Y	P	Y	Y
Kaine	Y	Y	Y	P	Y	Y
WASHINGTON						
Murray	Y	N	N	P	Y	Y
Cantwell	Y	N	N	P	Y	Y
WEST VIRGINIA						
Manchin	Y	Y	Y	N	Y	Y
Capito	N	Y	Y	N	Y	Y
WISCONSIN						
Johnson	N	Y	Y	N	N	Y
Baldwin	Y	N	N	P	Y	Y
WYOMING						
Enzi	N	Y	Y	N	N	Y
Barrasso	N	Y	Y	N	N	Y

KEY:

	Republicans	Democrats	*Independents*
Y	Voted for (yea)	N Voted against (nay)	P Voted "present"
+	Announced for	– Announced against	? Did not vote or otherwise
#	Paired for	X Paired against	make position known

55. HR268. Fiscal 2019 Disaster Relief Supplemental Appropriations - Cloture. McConnell, R-Ky., motion to invoke cloture (thus limiting debate) on the Shelby, R-Ala. substitute amendment to the bill. The amendment would provide $13.5 billion in supplemental fiscal 2019 appropriations for response efforts to damage caused by hurricanes, wildfires, earthquakes and other natural disasters in 2017 and 2018. It would also reauthorize Violence Against Women Act programs through fiscal 2019 and state that funds used by the Army Corps of Engineers from the Harbor Maintenance Trust Fund would not count against statutory appropriations caps and could be used for water infrastructure projects. Motion rejected 44-49: R 43-4; D 1-43; I 0-2. *Note: Three-fifths of the total Senate (60) is required to invoke cloture.* April 01, 2019.

56. HR268. Fiscal 2019 Disaster Relief Supplemental Appropriations - Cloture. McConnell, R-Ky., motion to invoke cloture (thus limiting debate) on the bill that would provide $14.2 billion in supplemental fiscal 2019 appropriations for response efforts to damage caused by hurricanes, wildfires, earthquakes and other natural disasters in 2017 and 2018. The bill would also prohibit funds provided in the bill for the Army Corps of Engineers or the Homeland Security Department from being used to construct a "new physical barrier" along the southwest border of the U.S. Motion rejected 46-48: R 0-48; D 44-0; I 2-0. *Note: Three-fifths of the total Senate (60) is required to invoke cloture.* April 01, 2019.

57. SRES50. Senate Nomination Post-Cloture Debate Rule - Cloture. McConnell, R-Ky., motion to invoke cloture (thus limiting debate) on his motion to proceed to the resolution that would reduce post-cloture time for consideration of certain nominations from 30 to two hours. The change in Senate rules would apply to floor consideration of nominations for district court judgeships and for lower-level executive branch positions. It would not apply to consideration of nominations to cabinet- and other high-level executive positions nor to membership on certain regulatory boards and commissions, including the Securities and Exchange Commission, the Federal Election Commission, and the Federal Trade Commission. Motion rejected 51-48: R 51-2; D 0-44; I 0-2. *Note: Three-fifths of the total Senate (60) is required to invoke cloture.* April 02, 2019.

58. Kessler Nomination - Cloture. Motion to invoke cloture (thus limiting debate) on the nomination of Jeffrey Kessler of Virginia to be an assistant secretary of Commerce. Motion agreed to 95-3: R 52-0; D 42-2; I 1-1. *Note: A majority of senators voting (50 in this case), a quorum being present, is required to invoke cloture on all nominations.* April 03, 2019.

59. Kessler Nomination - Ruling of the Chair. Judgment of the Senate to affirm the ruling of the chair regarding the McConnell, R-Ky., point of order that post-cloture time for consideration of certain executive nominations under the provisions of Rule XXII is two hours. The change in Senate rules would apply to floor consideration of nominations for some lower-level executive branch positions, reducing the time for consideration of such nominations from 30 to two hours. It would not apply to consideration of certain nominations to cabinet- and other high-level executive positions. Ruling of the chair rejected 48-51: R 2-51; D 44-0; I 2-0. *Note: The ruling of the chair did not stand and the point of order was sustained.* April 03, 2019.

60. Altman Nomination - Cloture. Motion to invoke cloture (thus limiting debate) on the nomination of Roy Kalman Altman of Florida to be a U.S. district judge for the Southern District of Florida. Motion agreed to 66-33: R 52-1; D 14-30; I 0-2. *Note: A majority of senators voting (50 in this case), a quorum being present, is required to invoke cloture on all nominations.* April 03, 2019.

	55	56	57	58	59	60
ALABAMA						
Shelby	Y	N	Y	Y	N	Y
Jones	Y	Y	N	Y	Y	Y
ALASKA						
Murkowski	Y	N	Y	Y	N	Y
Sullivan	?	?	Y	Y	N	Y
ARIZONA						
Sinema	N	Y	N	Y	Y	Y
McSally	?	?	Y	Y	N	Y
ARKANSAS						
Boozman	Y	N	Y	Y	N	Y
Cotton	Y	N	Y	Y	N	Y
CALIFORNIA						
Feinstein	N	Y	N	Y	Y	Y
Harris	?	?	?	?	?	?
COLORADO						
Bennet	N	Y	N	Y	Y	N
Gardner	Y	N	Y	Y	N	Y
CONNECTICUT						
Blumenthal	N	Y	N	Y	Y	N
Murphy	N	Y	N	Y	Y	N
DELAWARE						
Carper	N	Y	N	Y	Y	N
Coons	N	Y	N	Y	Y	N
FLORIDA						
Rubio	Y	N	Y	Y	N	Y
Scott	Y	N	Y	Y	N	Y
GEORGIA						
Isakson	Y	N	Y	Y	N	Y
Perdue	Y	N	Y	Y	N	Y
HAWAII						
Schatz	N	Y	N	Y	Y	N
Hirono	N	Y	N	Y	Y	N
IDAHO						
Crapo	Y	N	Y	Y	N	Y
Risch	Y	N	Y	Y	N	Y
ILLINOIS						
Durbin	N	Y	N	Y	Y	N
Duckworth	N	Y	N	Y	Y	Y
INDIANA						
Young	Y	N	Y	Y	N	Y
Braun	N	N	Y	Y	N	Y
IOWA						
Grassley	Y	N	Y	Y	N	Y
Ernst	Y	N	Y	Y	N	Y
KANSAS						
Roberts	Y	N	Y	Y	N	Y
Moran	Y	N	Y	Y	N	Y
KENTUCKY						
McConnell	N	Y	N	Y	N	Y
Paul	N	N	Y	Y	N	N
LOUISIANA						
Cassidy	+	N	Y	Y	N	Y
Kennedy	Y	N	Y	Y	N	Y
MAINE						
Collins	Y	N	Y	Y	Y	Y
King	N	Y	N	Y	Y	N
MARYLAND						
Cardin	N	Y	N	Y	Y	N
Van Hollen	N	Y	N	Y	Y	N
MASSACHUSETTS						
Warren	N	Y	N	N	Y	N
Markey	N	Y	N	Y	Y	N
MICHIGAN						
Stabenow	N	Y	N	Y	Y	N
Peters	N	Y	N	Y	Y	N
MINNESOTA						
Klobuchar	N	Y	N	Y	Y	N
Smith	N	Y	N	Y	Y	N
MISSISSIPPI						
Wicker	Y	N	Y	Y	N	Y
Hyde-Smith	Y	N	Y	?	N	Y
MISSOURI						
Blunt	Y	N	Y	Y	N	Y
Hawley	Y	N	Y	Y	N	Y

	55	56	57	58	59	60
MONTANA						
Tester	N	Y	N	Y	Y	Y
Daines	Y	N	Y	Y	N	Y
NEBRASKA						
Fischer	Y	N	Y	Y	N	Y
Sasse	Y	N	Y	Y	N	Y
NEVADA						
Cortez Masto	N	Y	N	Y	Y	Y
Rosen	N	Y	N	Y	Y	Y
NEW HAMPSHIRE						
Shaheen	N	Y	N	Y	Y	Y
Hassan	N	Y	N	Y	Y	Y
NEW JERSEY						
Menendez	N	Y	N	Y	Y	N
Booker	N	Y	N	Y	Y	N
NEW MEXICO						
Udall	N	Y	N	Y	Y	N
Heinrich	N	Y	N	Y	Y	N
NEW YORK						
Schumer	N	Y	N	Y	Y	N
Gillibrand	N	Y	N	N	Y	N
NORTH CAROLINA						
Burr	?	?	Y	Y	N	Y
Tillis	Y	N	Y	Y	N	Y
NORTH DAKOTA						
Hoeven	Y	N	Y	Y	N	Y
Cramer	Y	N	Y	Y	N	Y
OHIO						
Brown	N	Y	N	Y	Y	N
Portman	Y	N	Y	Y	N	Y
OKLAHOMA						
Inhofe	N	Y	N	Y	Y	N
Lankford	Y	N	Y	Y	N	Y
OREGON						
Wyden	N	Y	N	Y	Y	N
Merkley	N	Y	N	Y	Y	N
PENNSYLVANIA						
Casey	N	Y	N	Y	Y	N
Toomey	?	?	Y	Y	N	Y
RHODE ISLAND						
Reed	N	Y	N	Y	Y	N
Whitehouse	N	Y	N	Y	Y	N
SOUTH CAROLINA						
Graham	Y	N	Y	Y	N	Y
Scott	Y	N	Y	Y	N	Y
SOUTH DAKOTA						
Thune	Y	N	Y	Y	N	Y
Rounds	Y	N	Y	Y	N	Y
TENNESSEE						
Alexander	Y	N	Y	Y	N	Y
Blackburn	Y	N	Y	Y	N	Y
TEXAS						
Cornyn	Y	N	Y	Y	N	Y
Cruz	Y	N	Y	Y	N	Y
UTAH						
Lee	-	-	N	Y	Y	Y
Romney	Y	N	Y	Y	N	Y
VERMONT						
Leahy	N	Y	N	Y	Y	N
Sanders	N	Y	N	N	Y	N
VIRGINIA						
Warner	N	Y	N	Y	Y	N
Kaine	N	Y	N	Y	Y	N
WASHINGTON						
Murray	N	Y	N	Y	Y	N
Cantwell	N	Y	N	Y	Y	N
WEST VIRGINIA						
Manchin	N	Y	N	Y	Y	Y
Capito	Y	N	Y	Y	N	Y
WISCONSIN						
Johnson	Y	N	Y	Y	N	Y
Baldwin	N	Y	N	Y	Y	N
WYOMING						
Enzi	N	N	Y	Y	N	Y
Barrasso	Y	N	Y	Y	N	Y

KEY:	Republicans	Democrats	*Independents*

Y Voted for (yea)	N Voted against (nay)	P Voted "present"	
+ Announced for	− Announced against	? Did not vote or otherwise	
# Paired for	X Paired against	make position known	

61. Altman Nomination - Ruling of the Chair. Judgment of the Senate to affirm the ruling of the chair regarding the McConnell, R-Ky., point of order that post-cloture time for consideration of certain judicial nominations under the provisions of Rule XXII is two hours. The change in Senate rules would apply to floor consideration of all judicial nominations with the exception of nominations for Circuit Court or Supreme Court judgeships. It would reduce the time for consideration of such nominations from 30 to two hours. Ruling of the chair rejected 48-51: R 2-51; D 44-0; I 2-0. *Note: The ruling of the chair did not stand and the point of order was sustained.* April 03, 2019.

62. Altman Nomination - Confirmation. Confirmation of President Trump's nomination of Roy Kalman Altman of Florida to be a U.S. district judge for the Southern District of Florida. Confirmed 66-33: R 52-1; D 14-30; I 0-2. *Note: A "yea" was a vote in support of the president's position.* April 04, 2019.

63. Calabria Nomination - Cloture. Motion to invoke cloture (thus limiting debate) on the nomination of Mark Anthony Calabria of Virginia to be director of the Federal Housing Finance Agency. Motion agreed to 53-46: R 53-0; D 0-44; I 0-2. *Note: A majority of senators voting (50 in this case), a quorum being present, is required to invoke cloture on all nominations.* April 04, 2019.

64. Calabria Nomination - Confirmation. Confirmation of President Trump's nomination of Mark Anthony Calabria of Virginia to be director of the Federal Housing Finance Agency. Confirmed 52-44: R 52-0; D 0-43; I 0-1. *Note: A "yea" was a vote in support of the president's position.* April 04, 2019.

65. Domenico Nomination - Cloture. Motion to invoke cloture (thus limiting debate) on the nomination of Daniel Desmond Domenico of Colorado to be a U.S. district judge for the District of Colorado. Motion agreed to 55-42: R 51-0; D 4-40; I 0-2. *Note: A majority of senators voting (49 in this case), a quorum being present, is required to invoke cloture on all nominations.* April 09, 2019.

66. Domenico Nomination - Confirmation. Confirmation of President Trump's nomination of Daniel Desmond Domenico of Colorado to be a U.S. district judge for the District of Colorado. Confirmed 57-42: R 53-0; D 4-40; I 0-2. *Note: A "yea" was a vote in support of the president's position.* April 09, 2019.

	61	62	63	64	65	66
ALABAMA						
Shelby	N	Y	Y	Y	Y	Y
Jones	Y	Y	N	N	Y	Y
ALASKA						
Murkowski	N	Y	Y	Y	Y	Y
Sullivan	N	Y	Y	Y	Y	Y
ARIZONA						
Sinema	Y	Y	N	N	Y	Y
McSally	N	Y	Y	Y	Y	Y
ARKANSAS						
Boozman	N	Y	Y	Y	Y	Y
Cotton	N	Y	Y	Y	Y	Y
CALIFORNIA						
Feinstein	Y	Y	N	N	N	N
Harris	?	?	?	?	N	N
COLORADO						
Bennet	Y	N	N	N	Y	Y
Gardner	N	Y	Y	Y	Y	Y
CONNECTICUT						
Blumenthal	Y	N	N	N	N	N
Murphy	Y	Y	N	N	N	N
DELAWARE						
Carper	Y	N	N	N	N	N
Coons	Y	N	N	N	N	N
FLORIDA						
Rubio	N	Y	Y	Y	Y	Y
Scott	N	Y	Y	Y	Y	Y
GEORGIA						
Isakson	N	Y	Y	Y	Y	Y
Perdue	N	Y	Y	Y	Y	Y
HAWAII						
Schatz	Y	N	N	N	N	N
Hirono	Y	N	N	N	N	N
IDAHO						
Crapo	N	Y	Y	Y	Y	Y
Risch	N	Y	Y	Y	Y	Y
ILLINOIS						
Durbin	Y	N	N	N	N	N
Duckworth	Y	N	N	N	?	N
INDIANA						
Young	N	Y	Y	Y	Y	Y
Braun	N	Y	Y	Y	Y	Y
IOWA						
Grassley	N	Y	Y	Y	Y	Y
Ernst	N	Y	Y	Y	Y	Y
KANSAS						
Roberts	N	Y	Y	Y	Y	Y
Moran	N	Y	Y	Y	Y	Y
KENTUCKY						
McConnell	N	Y	Y	Y	Y	Y
Paul	N	N	Y	Y	Y	Y
LOUISIANA						
Cassidy	N	Y	Y	Y	Y	Y
Kennedy	N	Y	Y	Y	Y	Y
MAINE						
Collins	Y	Y	Y	Y	Y	Y
King	Y	N	N	N	N	N
MARYLAND						
Cardin	Y	Y	N	N	N	N
Van Hollen	Y	N	N	N	N	N
MASSACHUSETTS						
Warren	Y	N	N	N	N	N
Markey	Y	N	N	N	N	N
MICHIGAN						
Stabenow	Y	N	N	N	N	N
Peters	Y	N	N	N	N	N
MINNESOTA						
Klobuchar	Y	N	N	N	N	N
Smith	Y	N	N	N	N	N
MISSISSIPPI						
Wicker	N	Y	Y	Y	Y	Y
Hyde-Smith	N	Y	Y	Y	Y	Y
MISSOURI						
Blunt	N	Y	Y	Y	Y	Y
Hawley	N	Y	Y	Y	Y	Y
MONTANA						
Tester	Y	Y	N	N	N	N
Daines	N	Y	Y	Y	Y	Y
NEBRASKA						
Fischer	N	Y	Y	Y	Y	Y
Sasse	N	Y	Y	Y	Y	Y
NEVADA						
Cortez Masto	Y	Y	N	N	N	N
Rosen	Y	Y	N	N	N	N
NEW HAMPSHIRE						
Shaheen	Y	Y	N	N	N	N
Hassan	Y	Y	N	N	N	N
NEW JERSEY						
Menendez	Y	N	N	N	N	N
Booker	Y	N	N	?	N	?
NEW MEXICO						
Udall	Y	N	N	N	N	N
Heinrich	Y	N	N	N	N	N
NEW YORK						
Schumer	Y	N	N	N	N	N
Gillibrand	Y	N	N	N	N	N
NORTH CAROLINA						
Burr	N	Y	Y	Y	Y	Y
Tillis	N	Y	Y	Y	Y	Y
NORTH DAKOTA						
Hoeven	N	Y	Y	Y	Y	Y
Cramer	N	Y	Y	Y	Y	Y
OHIO						
Brown	Y	N	N	N	N	N
Portman	N	Y	Y	Y	Y	Y
OKLAHOMA						
Inhofe	N	Y	Y	Y	Y	Y
Lankford	N	Y	Y	Y	Y	Y
OREGON						
Wyden	Y	N	N	N	N	N
Merkley	Y	N	N	N	N	N
PENNSYLVANIA						
Casey	Y	N	N	N	N	N
Toomey	N	Y	Y	Y	Y	Y
RHODE ISLAND						
Reed	Y	N	N	N	N	N
Whitehouse	Y	N	N	N	N	N
SOUTH CAROLINA						
Graham	N	Y	Y	Y	Y	Y
Scott	N	Y	Y	Y	Y	Y
SOUTH DAKOTA						
Thune	N	Y	Y	Y	Y	Y
Rounds	N	Y	Y	Y	Y	Y
TENNESSEE						
Alexander	N	Y	Y	Y	Y	Y
Blackburn	N	Y	Y	Y	Y	Y
TEXAS						
Cornyn	N	Y	Y	Y	Y	Y
Cruz	N	Y	Y	Y	?	Y
UTAH						
Lee	Y	Y	Y	?	Y	Y
Romney	N	Y	Y	Y	Y	Y
VERMONT						
Leahy	Y	N	N	N	N	N
Sanders	Y	N	N	?	N	N
VIRGINIA						
Warner	Y	Y	N	N	N	N
Kaine	Y	Y	N	N	N	N
WASHINGTON						
Murray	Y	N	N	N	N	N
Cantwell	Y	N	N	N	N	N
WEST VIRGINIA						
Manchin	Y	Y	N	N	Y	Y
Capito	N	Y	Y	Y	Y	Y
WISCONSIN						
Johnson	N	Y	Y	Y	?	Y
Baldwin	Y	N	N	N	N	N
WYOMING						
Enzi	N	Y	Y	Y	Y	Y
Barrasso	N	Y	Y	Y	Y	Y

KEY:		Republicans		Democrats		*Independents*

Y	Voted for (yea)	N	Voted against (nay)	P	Voted "present"
+	Announced for	–	Announced against	?	Did not vote or otherwise
#	Paired for	X	Paired against		make position known

||| SENATE VOTES

67. Wyrick Nomination - Cloture. Motion to invoke cloture (thus limiting debate) on the nomination of Patrick R. Wyrick of Oklahoma to be a U.S. district judge for the Western District of Oklahoma. Motion agreed to 53-46: R 53-0; D 0-44; I 0-2. *Note: A majority of senators voting (50 in this case), a quorum being present, is required to invoke cloture on all nominations.* April 09, 2019.

68. Wyrick Nomination - Confirmation. Confirmation of President Trump's nomination of Patrick R. Wyrick of Oklahoma to be a U.S. district judge for the Western District of Oklahoma. Confirmed 53-47: R 53-0; D 0-45; I 0-2. *Note: A "yea" was a vote in support of the president's position.* April 09, 2019.

69. Stanton Nomination - Cloture. Motion to invoke cloture (thus limiting debate) on the nomination of Cheryl Marie Stanton of South Carolina to be administrator of the Wage and Hour Division, Department of Labor. Motion agreed to 53-47: R 53-0; D 0-45; I 0-2. *Note: A majority of senators voting (51 in this case), a quorum being present, is required to invoke cloture on all nominations.* April 09, 2019.

70. Stanton Nomination - Confirmation. Confirmation of President Trump's nomination of Cheryl Marie Stanton of South Carolina to be administrator of the Wage and Hour Division, Department of Labor. Confirmed 53-45: R 53-0; D 0-43; I 0-2. *Note: A "yea" was a vote in support of the president's position.* April 10, 2019.

71. Abizaid Nomination - Confirmation. Confirmation of President Trump's nomination of John P. Abizaid of Nevada to be ambassador extraordinary and plenipotentiary of the U.S. to the Kingdom of Saudi Arabia. Confirmed 92-7: R 53-0; D 38-6; I 1-1. *Note: A "yea" was a vote in support of the president's postion.* April 10, 2019.

72. Brady Nomination - Cloture. Motion to invoke cloture on the nomination of Holly A. Brady of Indiana to be a U.S. district judge for the Northern District of Indiana. Motion agreed to 56-43: R 53-0; D 3-41; I 0-2. *Note: A majority of senators voting (50 in this case), a quorum being present, is required to invoke cloture on all nominations.* April 10, 2019.

	67	68	69	70	71	72
ALABAMA						
Shelby	Y	Y	Y	Y	Y	Y
Jones	N	N	N	N	Y	Y
ALASKA						
Murkowski	Y	Y	Y	Y	Y	Y
Sullivan	Y	Y	Y	Y	Y	Y
ARIZONA						
Sinema	N	N	N	N	Y	Y
McSally	Y	Y	Y	Y	Y	Y
ARKANSAS						
Boozman	Y	Y	Y	Y	Y	Y
Cotton	Y	Y	Y	Y	Y	Y
CALIFORNIA						
Feinstein	N	N	N	N	Y	N
Harris	N	N	N	N	N	N
COLORADO						
Bennet	N	N	N	N	Y	N
Gardner	Y	Y	Y	Y	Y	Y
CONNECTICUT						
Blumenthal	N	N	N	N	Y	N
Murphy	N	N	N	N	Y	N
DELAWARE						
Carper	N	N	N	N	Y	N
Coons	N	N	N	N	Y	N
FLORIDA						
Rubio	Y	Y	Y	Y	Y	Y
Scott	Y	Y	Y	Y	Y	Y
GEORGIA						
Isakson	Y	Y	Y	Y	Y	Y
Perdue	Y	Y	Y	Y	Y	Y
HAWAII						
Schatz	N	N	N	N	Y	N
Hirono	N	N	N	N	Y	N
IDAHO						
Crapo	Y	Y	Y	Y	Y	Y
Risch	Y	Y	Y	Y	Y	Y
ILLINOIS						
Durbin	N	N	N	N	Y	N
Duckworth	N	N	N	N	Y	N
INDIANA						
Young	Y	Y	Y	Y	Y	Y
Braun	Y	Y	Y	Y	Y	Y
IOWA						
Grassley	Y	Y	Y	Y	Y	Y
Ernst	Y	Y	Y	Y	Y	Y
KANSAS						
Roberts	Y	Y	Y	Y	Y	Y
Moran	Y	Y	Y	Y	Y	Y
KENTUCKY						
McConnell	Y	Y	Y	Y	Y	Y
Paul	Y	Y	Y	Y	Y	Y
LOUISIANA						
Cassidy	Y	Y	Y	Y	Y	Y
Kennedy	Y	Y	Y	Y	Y	Y
MAINE						
Collins	Y	Y	Y	Y	Y	Y
King	N	N	N	N	Y	N
MARYLAND						
Cardin	N	N	N	N	Y	N
Van Hollen	N	N	N	N	Y	N
MASSACHUSETTS						
Warren	N	N	N	N	N	N
Markey	N	N	N	N	N	N
MICHIGAN						
Stabenow	N	N	N	N	Y	N
Peters	N	N	N	N	Y	N
MINNESOTA						
Klobuchar	N	N	N	?	Y	N
Smith	N	N	N	N	Y	N
MISSISSIPPI						
Wicker	Y	Y	Y	Y	Y	Y
Hyde-Smith	Y	Y	Y	Y	Y	Y
MISSOURI						
Blunt	Y	Y	Y	Y	Y	Y
Hawley	Y	Y	Y	Y	Y	Y
MONTANA						
Tester	N	N	N	N	Y	N
Daines	Y	Y	Y	Y	Y	Y
NEBRASKA						
Fischer	Y	Y	Y	Y	Y	Y
Sasse	Y	Y	Y	Y	Y	Y
NEVADA						
Cortez Masto	N	N	N	N	Y	N
Rosen	N	N	N	N	Y	N
NEW HAMPSHIRE						
Shaheen	N	N	N	N	Y	N
Hassan	N	N	N	N	Y	N
NEW JERSEY						
Menendez	N	N	N	N	Y	N
Booker	?	N	N	?	?	?
NEW MEXICO						
Udall	N	N	N	N	N	N
Heinrich	N	N	N	N	Y	N
NEW YORK						
Schumer	N	N	N	N	Y	N
Gillibrand	N	N	N	N	N	N
NORTH CAROLINA						
Burr	Y	Y	Y	Y	Y	Y
Tillis	Y	Y	Y	Y	Y	Y
NORTH DAKOTA						
Hoeven	Y	Y	Y	Y	Y	Y
Cramer	Y	Y	Y	Y	Y	Y
OHIO						
Brown	N	N	N	N	Y	N
Portman	Y	Y	Y	Y	Y	Y
OKLAHOMA						
Inhofe	Y	Y	Y	Y	Y	Y
Lankford	Y	Y	Y	Y	Y	Y
OREGON						
Wyden	N	N	N	N	N	N
Merkley	N	N	N	N	N	N
PENNSYLVANIA						
Casey	N	N	N	N	Y	N
Toomey	Y	Y	Y	Y	Y	Y
RHODE ISLAND						
Reed	N	N	N	N	Y	N
Whitehouse	N	N	N	N	Y	N
SOUTH CAROLINA						
Graham	Y	Y	Y	Y	Y	Y
Scott	Y	Y	Y	Y	Y	Y
SOUTH DAKOTA						
Thune	Y	Y	Y	Y	Y	Y
Rounds	Y	Y	Y	Y	Y	Y
TENNESSEE						
Alexander	Y	Y	Y	Y	Y	Y
Blackburn	Y	Y	Y	Y	Y	Y
TEXAS						
Cornyn	Y	Y	Y	Y	Y	Y
Cruz	Y	Y	Y	Y	Y	Y
UTAH						
Lee	Y	Y	Y	Y	Y	Y
Romney	Y	Y	Y	Y	Y	Y
VERMONT						
Leahy	N	N	N	N	Y	N
Sanders	N	N	N	N	N	N
VIRGINIA						
Warner	N	N	N	N	Y	N
Kaine	N	N	N	N	Y	N
WASHINGTON						
Murray	N	N	N	N	Y	N
Cantwell	N	N	N	N	Y	N
WEST VIRGINIA						
Manchin	N	N	N	N	Y	Y
Capito	Y	Y	Y	Y	Y	Y
WISCONSIN						
Johnson	Y	Y	Y	Y	Y	Y
Baldwin	N	N	N	N	Y	N
WYOMING						
Enzi	Y	Y	Y	Y	Y	Y
Barrasso	Y	Y	Y	Y	Y	Y

KEY: Republicans Democrats *Independents*

Y Voted for (yea)	N Voted against (nay)	P Voted "present"
+ Announced for	– Announced against	? Did not vote or otherwise make position known
# Paired for	X Paired against	

73. Brady Nomination - Confirmation. Confirmation of President Trump's nomination of Holly A. Brady of Indiana to be a U.S. district judge for the Northern District of Indiana. Confirmed 56-42: R 53-0; D 3-40; I 0-2. *Note: A "yea" was a vote in support of the president's position.* April 10, 2019.

74. Morales Nomination - Cloture. Motion to invoke cloture (thus limiting debate) on the nomination of David Steven Morales of Texas to be a U.S. district judge for the Southern District of Texas. Motion agreed to 57-41: R 53-0; D 4-39; I 0-2. *Note: A majority of senators voting (50 in this case), a quorum being present, is required to invoke cloture on all nominations.* April 10, 2019.

75. Morales Nomination - Confirmation. Confirmation of President Trump's nomination of David Steven Morales of Texas to be a U.S district judge for the Southern District of Texas. Confirmed 56-41: R 52-0; D 4-39; I 0-2. *Note: A "yea" was a vote in support of the president's position.* April 10, 2019.

76. Bernhardt Nomination - Cloture. Motion to invoke cloture (thus limiting debate) on the nomination of David Bernhardt of Virginia to be secretary of Interior. Motion agreed to 56-41: R 52-0; D 3-40; I 1-1. *Note: A majority of senators voting (49 in this case), a quorum being present, is required to invoke cloture on all nominations.* April 10, 2019.

77. Bernhardt Nomination - Confirmation. Confirmation of President Trump's nomination of David Bernhardt of Virginia to be secretary of Interior. Confirmed 56-41: R 52-0; D 3-40; I 1-1. *Note: A "yea" was a vote in support of the president's position.* April 11, 2019.

78. Cooper Nomination - Cloture. Motion to invoke cloture (thus limiting debate) on the nomination of William Cooper of Maryland to be general counsel of the Department of Energy. Motion agreed to 63-32: R 49-0; D 13-31; I 1-1. *Note: A majority of senators voting (48 in this case), a quorum being present, is required to invoke cloture on all nominations.* April 29, 2019.

	73	74	75	76	77	78
ALABAMA						
Shelby	Y	Y	Y	Y	Y	Y
Jones	Y	Y	Y	N	N	Y
ALASKA						
Murkowski	Y	Y	Y	Y	Y	Y
Sullivan	Y	Y	Y	Y	Y	Y
ARIZONA						
Sinema	Y	Y	Y	Y	Y	Y
McSally	Y	Y	Y	Y	Y	Y
ARKANSAS						
Boozman	Y	Y	Y	Y	Y	Y
Cotton	Y	Y	Y	Y	Y	Y
CALIFORNIA						
Feinstein	N	N	N	N	N	Y
Harris	?	?	?	-	-	N
COLORADO						
Bennet	N	N	N	N	N	N
Gardner	Y	Y	Y	Y	Y	Y
CONNECTICUT						
Blumenthal	N	N	N	N	N	N
Murphy	N	N	N	N	N	Y
DELAWARE						
Carper	N	N	N	N	N	Y
Coons	N	N	N	N	N	Y
FLORIDA						
Rubio	Y	Y	Y	Y	Y	?
Scott	Y	Y	Y	Y	Y	Y
GEORGIA						
Isakson	Y	Y	Y	Y	Y	Y
Perdue	Y	Y	?	?	?	?
HAWAII						
Schatz	N	N	N	N	N	N
Hirono	N	N	N	N	N	N
IDAHO						
Crapo	Y	Y	Y	Y	Y	Y
Risch	Y	Y	Y	Y	Y	Y
ILLINOIS						
Durbin	N	N	N	N	N	N
Duckworth	N	N	N	N	N	N
INDIANA						
Young	Y	Y	Y	Y	Y	Y
Braun	Y	Y	Y	Y	Y	Y
IOWA						
Grassley	Y	Y	Y	Y	Y	Y
Ernst	Y	Y	Y	Y	Y	Y
KANSAS						
Roberts	Y	Y	Y	Y	Y	Y
Moran	Y	Y	Y	Y	Y	Y
KENTUCKY						
McConnell	Y	Y	Y	Y	Y	Y
Paul	Y	Y	Y	Y	Y	Y
LOUISIANA						
Cassidy	Y	Y	Y	Y	Y	Y
Kennedy	Y	Y	Y	Y	Y	?
MAINE						
Collins	Y	Y	Y	Y	Y	Y
King	N	N	N	Y	Y	Y
MARYLAND						
Cardin	N	N	N	N	N	N
Van Hollen	N	N	N	N	N	N
MASSACHUSETTS						
Warren	N	N	N	N	N	N
Markey	N	N	N	N	N	N
MICHIGAN						
Stabenow	N	N	N	N	N	N
Peters	N	N	N	N	N	N
MINNESOTA						
Klobuchar	N	N	N	N	N	N
Smith	N	N	N	N	N	N
MISSISSIPPI						
Wicker	Y	Y	Y	Y	Y	Y
Hyde-Smith	Y	Y	Y	Y	Y	Y
MISSOURI						
Blunt	Y	Y	Y	Y	Y	Y
Hawley	Y	Y	Y	Y	Y	Y
MONTANA						
Tester	N	N	N	N	N	Y
Daines	Y	Y	Y	Y	Y	Y
NEBRASKA						
Fischer	Y	Y	Y	Y	Y	Y
Sasse	Y	Y	Y	Y	Y	Y
NEVADA						
Cortez Masto	N	N	N	N	N	N
Rosen	N	N	N	N	N	N
NEW HAMPSHIRE						
Shaheen	N	N	N	N	N	Y
Hassan	N	N	N	N	N	Y
NEW JERSEY						
Menendez	N	N	N	N	N	N
Booker	?	?	?	?	-	N
NEW MEXICO						
Udall	N	N	N	N	N	N
Heinrich	N	N	N	N	N	Y
NEW YORK						
Schumer	N	N	N	N	N	N
Gillibrand	N	N	N	N	N	N
NORTH CAROLINA						
Burr	Y	Y	Y	Y	Y	?
Tillis	Y	Y	Y	Y	Y	Y
NORTH DAKOTA						
Hoeven	Y	Y	Y	Y	Y	Y
Cramer	Y	Y	Y	Y	Y	Y
OHIO						
Brown	N	N	N	N	N	N
Portman	Y	Y	Y	Y	Y	Y
OKLAHOMA						
Inhofe	Y	Y	Y	Y	Y	Y
Lankford	Y	Y	Y	Y	Y	Y
OREGON						
Wyden	N	N	N	N	N	N
Merkley	N	N	N	N	N	N
PENNSYLVANIA						
Casey	N	N	N	N	N	N
Toomey	Y	Y	Y	Y	Y	Y
RHODE ISLAND						
Reed	N	N	N	N	N	N
Whitehouse	N	N	N	N	N	N
SOUTH CAROLINA						
Graham	Y	Y	Y	Y	Y	Y
Scott	Y	Y	Y	Y	Y	Y
SOUTH DAKOTA						
Thune	Y	Y	Y	Y	Y	Y
Rounds	Y	Y	Y	Y	Y	Y
TENNESSEE						
Alexander	Y	Y	Y	Y	Y	Y
Blackburn	Y	Y	Y	Y	Y	Y
TEXAS						
Cornyn	Y	Y	Y	Y	Y	Y
Cruz	Y	Y	Y	Y	Y	Y
UTAH						
Lee	Y	Y	Y	Y	Y	Y
Romney	Y	Y	Y	Y	Y	Y
VERMONT						
Leahy	N	N	N	N	N	?
Sanders	N	N	N	N	N	N
VIRGINIA						
Warner	N	N	N	N	N	Y
Kaine	N	Y	Y	N	N	Y
WASHINGTON						
Murray	N	N	N	N	N	N
Cantwell	N	N	N	N	N	Y
WEST VIRGINIA						
Manchin	Y	Y	Y	Y	Y	Y
Capito	Y	Y	Y	Y	Y	Y
WISCONSIN						
Johnson	Y	Y	Y	Y	Y	Y
Baldwin	N	N	N	N	N	N
WYOMING						
Enzi	Y	Y	Y	Y	Y	Y
Barrasso	Y	Y	Y	Y	Y	Y

KEY: Republicans Democrats *Independents*

Y	Voted for (yea)	N	Voted against (nay)	P	Voted "present"
+	Announced for	-	Announced against	?	Did not vote or otherwise make position known
#	Paired for	X	Paired against		

||| SENATE VOTES

79. Cooper Nomination - Confirmation. Confirmation of President Trump's nomination of William Cooper of Maryland to be general counsel of the Department of Energy. Confirmed 68-31: R 53-0; D 14-30; I 1-1. *Note: A "yea" was a vote in support of the president's position.* April 30, 2019.

80. Cooper Nomination - Cloture. Motion to invoke cloture (thus limiting debate) on the nomination of R. Clarke Cooper of Florida to be an assistant secretary of State. Motion agreed to 91-8: R 53-0; D 37-7; I 1-1. *Note: A majority of senators voting (50 in this case), a quorum being present, is required to invoke cloture on all nominations.* April 30, 2019.

81. Cooper Nomination - Confirmation. Confirmation of President Trump's nomination of R. Clarke Cooper of Florida to be an assistant secretary of State. Confirmed 90-8: R 52-0; D 37-7; I 1-1. *Note: A "yea" was a vote in support of the president's position.* April 30, 2019.

82. Hartogensis Nomination - Cloture. Motion to invoke cloture (thus limiting debate) on the nomination of Gordon Hartogensis of Connecticut to be director of the Pension Benefit Guaranty Corporation Motion agreed to 72-27: R 53-0; D 18-26; I 1-1. *Note: A majority of senators voting (50 in this case), a quorum being present, is required to invoke cloture on all nominations.* April 30, 2019.

83. Hartogensis Nomination - Confirmation. Confirmation of President Trump's nomination of Gordon Hartogensis of Connecticut to be director of the Pension Benefit Guaranty Corporation. Confirmed 72-27: R 53-0; D 18-26; I 1-1. *Note: A "yea" was a vote in support of the president's position.* April 30, 2019.

84. Barker Nomination - Cloture. Motion to invoke cloture (thus limiting debate) on the nomination of J. Campbell Barker to be a U.S. district judge for the Eastern District of Texas. Motion agreed to 52-46: R 52-0; D 0-44; I 0-2. *Note: A majority of senators voting (49 in this case), a quorum being present, is required to invoke cloture on all nominations.* April 30, 2019.

	79	80	81	82	83	84
ALABAMA						
Shelby	Y	Y	Y	Y	Y	Y
Jones	Y	Y	Y	Y	Y	N
ALASKA						
Murkowski	Y	Y	Y	Y	Y	Y
Sullivan	Y	Y	Y	Y	Y	Y
ARIZONA						
Sinema	Y	Y	Y	Y	Y	Y
McSally	Y	Y	Y	Y	Y	Y
ARKANSAS						
Boozman	Y	Y	Y	Y	Y	Y
Cotton	Y	Y	Y	Y	Y	Y
CALIFORNIA						
Feinstein	Y	Y	Y	Y	Y	N
Harris	?	?	?	?	?	?
COLORADO						
Bennet	N	N	Y	Y	Y	N
Gardner	Y	Y	Y	Y	Y	Y
CONNECTICUT						
Blumenthal	N	Y	Y	Y	Y	N
Murphy	Y	Y	Y	Y	Y	N
DELAWARE						
Carper	Y	Y	Y	Y	Y	Y
Coons	Y	Y	Y	N	N	N
FLORIDA						
Rubio	Y	Y	Y	Y	Y	Y
Scott	Y	Y	Y	Y	Y	Y
GEORGIA						
Isakson	Y	Y	Y	Y	Y	Y
Perdue	Y	Y	Y	Y	Y	Y
HAWAII						
Schatz	N	Y	Y	N	N	N
Hirono	N	N	N	N	N	N
IDAHO						
Crapo	Y	Y	Y	Y	Y	Y
Risch	Y	Y	Y	Y	Y	Y
ILLINOIS						
Durbin	N	Y	Y	Y	Y	N
Duckworth	N	Y	Y	N	N	N
INDIANA						
Young	Y	Y	Y	Y	Y	Y
Braun	Y	Y	Y	Y	Y	Y
IOWA						
Grassley	Y	Y	Y	Y	Y	Y
Ernst	Y	Y	Y	Y	Y	Y
KANSAS						
Roberts	Y	Y	Y	Y	Y	Y
Moran	Y	Y	Y	Y	Y	Y
KENTUCKY						
McConnell	Y	Y	Y	Y	Y	Y
Paul	Y	Y	Y	Y	Y	Y
LOUISIANA						
Cassidy	Y	Y	Y	Y	Y	Y
Kennedy	Y	Y	Y	Y	Y	Y
MAINE						
Collins	Y	Y	Y	Y	Y	Y
King	Y	Y	Y	Y	Y	N
MARYLAND						
Cardin	N	Y	Y	N	N	N
Van Hollen	Y	Y	Y	N	N	N
MASSACHUSETTS						
Warren	N	N	N	N	N	N
Markey	N	N	N	N	N	N
MICHIGAN						
Stabenow	N	N	N	N	N	N
Peters	N	N	N	N	N	N
MINNESOTA						
Klobuchar	N	Y	Y	N	N	N
Smith	N	Y	Y	N	N	N
MISSISSIPPI						
Wicker	Y	Y	Y	Y	Y	Y
Hyde-Smith	Y	Y	Y	Y	Y	Y
MISSOURI						
Blunt	Y	Y	Y	Y	Y	Y
Hawley	Y	Y	Y	Y	Y	Y

	79	80	81	82	83	84
MONTANA						
Tester	Y	Y	Y	N	N	N
Daines	Y	Y	Y	Y	Y	Y
NEBRASKA						
Fischer	Y	Y	Y	Y	Y	Y
Sasse	Y	Y	Y	Y	Y	Y
NEVADA						
Cortez Masto	N	Y	Y	Y	Y	N
Rosen	N	Y	Y	Y	Y	N
NEW HAMPSHIRE						
Shaheen	Y	Y	Y	Y	Y	N
Hassan	Y	Y	Y	Y	Y	N
NEW JERSEY						
Menendez	N	Y	Y	N	N	N
Booker	N	N	N	N	N	N
NEW MEXICO						
Udall	N	Y	Y	N	N	N
Heinrich	N	Y	Y	N	N	N
NEW YORK						
Schumer	N	Y	Y	N	N	N
Gillibrand	N	N	N	N	N	N
NORTH CAROLINA						
Burr	Y	Y	Y	Y	Y	Y
Tillis	Y	Y	Y	Y	Y	Y
NORTH DAKOTA						
Hoeven	Y	Y	Y	Y	Y	Y
Cramer	Y	Y	Y	Y	Y	Y
OHIO						
Brown	N	N	Y	Y	Y	N
Portman	Y	Y	Y	Y	Y	Y
OKLAHOMA						
Inhofe	Y	Y	Y	Y	Y	Y
Lankford	Y	Y	Y	Y	Y	Y
OREGON						
Wyden	N	Y	Y	Y	Y	N
Merkley	N	Y	Y	N	N	N
PENNSYLVANIA						
Casey	N	Y	Y	Y	Y	N
Toomey	Y	Y	Y	Y	Y	Y
RHODE ISLAND						
Reed	N	Y	Y	N	N	N
Whitehouse	N	Y	Y	N	N	N
SOUTH CAROLINA						
Graham	Y	Y	Y	Y	Y	Y
Scott	Y	Y	Y	Y	Y	Y
SOUTH DAKOTA						
Thune	Y	Y	Y	Y	Y	Y
Rounds	Y	Y	Y	Y	Y	Y
TENNESSEE						
Alexander	Y	Y	Y	Y	Y	Y
Blackburn	Y	Y	Y	Y	Y	Y
TEXAS						
Cornyn	Y	Y	Y	Y	Y	Y
Cruz	Y	Y	Y	Y	Y	Y
UTAH						
Lee	Y	Y	#	Y	Y	Y
Romney	Y	Y	Y	Y	Y	Y
VERMONT						
Leahy	N	Y	Y	N	N	N
Sanders	N	N	N	N	N	N
VIRGINIA						
Warner	Y	Y	Y	Y	Y	Y
Kaine	Y	Y	Y	N	N	N
WASHINGTON						
Murray	N	Y	Y	N	N	N
Cantwell	Y	Y	Y	Y	Y	N
WEST VIRGINIA						
Manchin	Y	Y	Y	Y	Y	N
Capito	Y	Y	Y	Y	Y	+
WISCONSIN						
Johnson	Y	Y	Y	Y	Y	Y
Baldwin	N	Y	Y	N	N	N
WYOMING						
Enzi	Y	Y	Y	Y	Y	Y
Barrasso	Y	Y	Y	Y	Y	Y

KEY: **Republicans**   Democrats   *Independents*

Y	Voted for (yea)	N	Voted against (nay)	P	Voted "present"
+	Announced for	–	Announced against	?	Did not vote or otherwise make position known
#	Paired for	X	Paired against		

85. Barker Nomination - Confirmation. Confirmation of President Trump's nomination of J. Campbell Barker to be U.S. district judge for the Eastern District of Texas. Confirmed 51-47: R 51-0; D 0-45; I 0-2. *Note: A "yea" was a vote in support of the president's position.* May 01, 2019.

86. Brasher Nomination - Cloture. Motion to invoke cloture (thus limiting debate) on the nomination of Andrew Brasher of Alabama to be a U.S. district judge for the Middle District of Alabama. Motion agreed to 52-47: R 52-0; D 0-45; I 0-2. *Note: A majority of senators voting (50 in this case), a quorum being present, is required to invoke cloture on all nominations.* May 01, 2019.

87. Brasher Nomination - Confirmation. President Trump's nomination of Andrew Brasher of Alabama to be U.S. district judge for the Middle District of Alabama. Confirmed 52-47: R 52-0; D 0-45; I 0-2. *Note: A "yea" was a vote in support of the president's position.* May 01, 2019.

88. Ruiz Nomination - Cloture. Motion to invoke cloture (thus limiting debate) on the nomination of Rodolfo Armando Ruiz II of Florida to be a U.S. district judge for the Southern District of Florida. Motion agreed to 89-10: R 52-0; D 36-9; I 1-1. *Note: A majority of senators voting (50 in this case), a quorum being present, is required to invoke cloture on all nominations.* May 01, 2019.

89. Arias-Marxuach Nomination - Cloture. Motion to invoke cloture (thus limiting debate) on the nomination of Raul M. Arias-Marxuach of Puerto Rico to be a U.S. district judge for the District of Puerto Rico. Motion agreed to 94-5: R 52-0; D 41-4; I 1-1. *Note: A majority of senators voting (50 in this case), a quorum being present, is required to invoke cloture on all nominations.* May 01, 2019.

90. Wolson Nomiation - Cloture. Motion to invoke cloture (thus limiting debate) on the nomination of Joshua Wolson of Pennsylvania to be a U.S. district judge for the Eastern District of Pennsylvania. Motion agreed to 64-35: R 52-0; D 11-34; I 1-1. *Note: A majority of senators voting (50 in this case), a quorum being present, is required to invoke cloture on all nominations.* May 01, 2019.

	85	86	87	88	89	90		85	86	87	88	89	90
ALABAMA							**MONTANA**						
Shelby	Y	Y	Y	Y	Y	Y	Tester	N	N	N	Y	Y	Y
Jones	N	N	N	Y	Y	Y	**Daines**	Y	Y	Y	Y	Y	Y
ALASKA							**NEBRASKA**						
Murkowski	Y	Y	Y	Y	Y	Y	**Fischer**	Y	Y	Y	Y	Y	Y
Sullivan	Y	Y	Y	Y	Y	Y	**Sasse**	Y	Y	Y	Y	Y	Y
ARIZONA							**NEVADA**						
Sinema	N	N	N	Y	Y	Y	Cortez Masto	N	N	N	Y	Y	N
McSally	Y	Y	Y	Y	Y	Y	Rosen	N	N	N	Y	Y	Y
ARKANSAS							**NEW HAMPSHIRE**						
Boozman	Y	Y	Y	Y	Y	Y	Shaheen	N	N	N	Y	Y	Y
Cotton	Y	Y	Y	Y	Y	Y	Hassan	N	N	N	Y	Y	N
CALIFORNIA							**NEW JERSEY**						
Feinstein	N	N	N	Y	Y	N	Menendez	N	N	N	Y	Y	N
Harris	N	N	N	Y	Y	N	Booker	N	N	N	Y	Y	N
COLORADO							**NEW MEXICO**						
Bennet	N	N	N	Y	Y	N	Udall	N	N	N	Y	Y	N
Gardner	Y	Y	Y	Y	Y	Y	Heinrich	N	N	N	Y	Y	N
CONNECTICUT							**NEW YORK**						
Blumenthal	N	N	N	Y	Y	N	Schumer	N	N	N	Y	Y	N
Murphy	N	N	N	Y	Y	Y	Gillibrand	N	N	N	N	N	N
DELAWARE							**NORTH CAROLINA**						
Carper	N	N	N	Y	Y	Y	**Burr**	Y	Y	Y	Y	Y	Y
Coons	N	N	N	Y	Y	Y	**Tillis**	Y	Y	Y	Y	Y	Y
FLORIDA							**NORTH DAKOTA**						
Rubio	Y	Y	Y	Y	Y	Y	**Hoeven**	Y	Y	Y	Y	Y	Y
Scott	Y	Y	Y	Y	Y	Y	**Cramer**	Y	Y	Y	Y	Y	Y
GEORGIA							**OHIO**						
Isakson	Y	Y	Y	Y	Y	Y	Brown	N	N	N	Y	Y	N
Perdue	Y	Y	Y	Y	Y	Y	**Portman**	Y	Y	Y	Y	Y	Y
HAWAII							**OKLAHOMA**						
Schatz	N	N	N	Y	Y	N	**Inhofe**	+	Y	Y	Y	Y	Y
Hirono	N	N	N	N	N	N	**Lankford**	Y	Y	Y	Y	Y	Y
IDAHO							**OREGON**						
Crapo	Y	Y	Y	Y	Y	Y	Wyden	N	N	N	Y	Y	N
Risch	Y	Y	Y	Y	Y	Y	Merkley	N	N	N	Y	Y	N
ILLINOIS							**PENNSYLVANIA**						
Durbin	N	N	N	Y	Y	N	Casey	N	N	N	Y	Y	N
Duckworth	N	N	N	Y	Y	N	**Toomey**	Y	Y	Y	Y	Y	Y
INDIANA							**RHODE ISLAND**						
Young	?	?	?	?	?	?	Reed	N	N	N	Y	Y	N
Braun	Y	Y	Y	Y	Y	Y	Whitehouse	N	N	N	Y	Y	N
IOWA							**SOUTH CAROLINA**						
Grassley	Y	Y	Y	Y	Y	Y	**Graham**	Y	Y	Y	Y	Y	Y
Ernst	Y	Y	Y	Y	Y	Y	**Scott**	Y	Y	Y	Y	Y	Y
KANSAS							**SOUTH DAKOTA**						
Roberts	Y	Y	Y	Y	Y	Y	**Thune**	Y	Y	Y	Y	Y	Y
Moran	Y	Y	Y	Y	Y	Y	**Rounds**	Y	Y	Y	Y	Y	Y
KENTUCKY							**TENNESSEE**						
McConnell	Y	Y	Y	Y	Y	Y	**Alexander**	Y	Y	Y	Y	Y	Y
Paul	Y	Y	Y	Y	Y	Y	**Blackburn**	Y	Y	Y	Y	Y	Y
LOUISIANA							**TEXAS**						
Cassidy	Y	Y	Y	Y	Y	Y	**Cornyn**	Y	Y	Y	Y	Y	Y
Kennedy	Y	Y	Y	Y	Y	Y	**Cruz**	Y	Y	Y	Y	Y	Y
MAINE							**UTAH**						
Collins	Y	Y	Y	Y	Y	Y	**Lee**	Y	Y	Y	Y	Y	Y
King	N	N	N	Y	Y	Y	**Romney**	Y	Y	Y	Y	Y	Y
MARYLAND							**VERMONT**						
Cardin	N	N	N	N	Y	N	Leahy	N	N	N	Y	Y	N
Van Hollen	N	N	N	N	Y	N	*Sanders*	N	N	N	N	N	N
MASSACHUSETTS							**VIRGINIA**						
Warren	N	N	N	N	N	N	Warner	N	N	N	Y	Y	N
Markey	N	N	N	N	N	N	Kaine	N	N	N	Y	Y	N
MICHIGAN							**WASHINGTON**						
Stabenow	N	N	N	Y	Y	N	Murray	N	N	N	Y	Y	N
Peters	N	N	N	N	Y	N	Cantwell	N	N	N	Y	Y	N
MINNESOTA							**WEST VIRGINIA**						
Klobuchar	N	N	N	N	Y	N	Manchin	N	N	N	Y	Y	Y
Smith	N	N	N	Y	Y	N	**Capito**	Y	Y	Y	Y	Y	Y
MISSISSIPPI							**WISCONSIN**						
Wicker	Y	Y	Y	Y	Y	Y	**Johnson**	Y	Y	Y	Y	Y	Y
Hyde-Smith	Y	Y	Y	Y	Y	Y	Baldwin	N	N	N	Y	Y	N
MISSOURI							**WYOMING**						
Blunt	Y	Y	Y	Y	Y	Y	**Enzi**	Y	Y	Y	Y	Y	Y
Hawley	Y	Y	Y	Y	Y	Y	**Barrasso**	Y	Y	Y	Y	Y	Y

KEY:	**Republicans**	Democrats	*Independents*
Y Voted for (yea)	N Voted against (nay)	P Voted "present"	
+ Announced for	– Announced against	? Did not vote or otherwise	
# Paired for	X Paired against	make position known	

III SENATE VOTES

91. Ruiz Nomination - Confirmation. Confirmation of President Trump's nomination of Rodolfo Armando Ruiz II of Florida to be U.S. district judge for the Southern District of Florida. Confirmed 90-8: R 53-0; D 36-7; I 1-1. *Note: A "yea" was a vote in support of the president's position.* May 02, 2019.

92. Arias-Marxuach Nomination - Confirmation. Confirmation of President Trump's nomination of Raul M. Arias-Marxuach of Puerto Rico to be U.S. district judge for the District of Puerto Rico. Confirmed 95-3: R 53-0; D 41-2; I 1-1. *Note: A "yea" was a vote in support of the president's position.* May 02, 2019.

93. Wolson Nomination - Confirmation. Confirmation of President Trump's nomination of Joshua Wolson of Pennsylvania to be U.S. district judge for the Eastern District of Pennsylvania. Confirmed 65-33: R 53-0; D 11-32; I 1-1. *Note: A "yea" was a vote in support of the president's position.* May 02, 2019.

94. SJRES7. U.S. Military Forces in Yemen - Veto Override. Passage over President Trump's April 17, 2019, veto of the joint resolution that would direct the president, within 30 days of enactment, to remove U.S. armed forces from hostilities in or affecting the Republic of Yemen, including in-flight refueling of non-U.S. aircraft, unless a declaration of war or specific authorization for such use of forces has been enacted. The bill specifies that its provisions would not apply to U.S. forces engaged in operations directed at al-Qaeda or associated forces. Rejected 53-45: R 7-45; D 44-0; I 2-0. *Note: A two-thirds majority of those present and voting (66 in this case) of both chambers is required to override the president's veto. A "nay" was a vote in support of the president's veto.* May 02, 2019.

95. Bianco Nomination - Cloture. Motion to invoke cloture (thus limiting debate) on the nomination of Joseph Bianco of New York to be a U.S. circuit judge for the 2nd Circuit. Motion agreed to 51-40: R 48-0; D 3-38; I 0-2. *Note: A majority of senators voting (46 in this case), a quorum being present, is required to invoke cloture on all nominations.* May 06, 2019.

96. Reed Nomination - Cloture. Motion to invoke cloture (thus limiting debate) on the nomination of Kimberly Reed of West Virginia to be president of the Export-Import Bank of the U.S. Motion agreed to 82-17: R 36-16; D 45-0; I 1-1. *Note: A majority of senators voting (50 in this case), a quorum being present, is required to invoke cloture on all nominations.* May 07, 2019.

	91	92	93	94	95	96
ALABAMA						
Shelby	Y	Y	Y	N	Y	N
Jones	Y	Y	Y	Y	Y	Y
ALASKA						
Murkowski	Y	Y	Y	Y	?	?
Sullivan	Y	Y	Y	N	Y	Y
ARIZONA						
Sinema	Y	Y	Y	Y	Y	Y
McSally	Y	Y	Y	N	Y	Y
ARKANSAS						
Boozman	Y	Y	Y	N	Y	Y
Cotton	Y	Y	Y	N	Y	Y
CALIFORNIA						
Feinstein	Y	Y	N	Y	N	Y
Harris	Y	Y	N	Y	?	Y
COLORADO						
Bennet	?	?	?	?	N	Y
Gardner	Y	Y	Y	N	Y	Y
CONNECTICUT						
Blumenthal	Y	Y	N	Y	N	Y
Murphy	Y	Y	Y	Y	N	Y
DELAWARE						
Carper	Y	Y	Y	Y	N	Y
Coons	Y	Y	Y	Y	N	Y
FLORIDA						
Rubio	Y	Y	Y	-	?	N
Scott	Y	Y	Y	N	Y	Y
GEORGIA						
Isakson	Y	Y	Y	N	?	Y
Perdue	Y	Y	Y	N	Y	Y
HAWAII						
Schatz	Y	Y	N	Y	N	Y
Hirono	Y	Y	N	Y	N	Y
IDAHO						
Crapo	Y	Y	Y	N	Y	Y
Risch	Y	Y	Y	N	Y	Y
ILLINOIS						
Durbin	Y	Y	N	Y	N	Y
Duckworth	Y	Y	N	Y	N	Y
INDIANA						
Young	Y	Y	Y	Y	Y	N
Braun	Y	Y	Y	N	Y	N
IOWA						
Grassley	Y	Y	Y	N	Y	Y
Ernst	Y	Y	Y	N	Y	Y
KANSAS						
Roberts	Y	Y	Y	N	Y	Y
Moran	Y	Y	Y	Y	?	Y
KENTUCKY						
McConnell	Y	Y	Y	N	Y	Y
Paul	Y	Y	Y	Y	Y	Y
LOUISIANA						
Cassidy	Y	Y	Y	N	Y	Y
Kennedy	Y	Y	Y	N	Y	N
MAINE						
Collins	Y	Y	Y	Y	Y	Y
King	Y	Y	Y	Y	N	Y
MARYLAND						
Cardin	Y	Y	N	Y	N	Y
Van Hollen	Y	Y	N	Y	N	Y
MASSACHUSETTS						
Warren	N	N	N	Y	N	Y
Markey	N	Y	N	Y	N	Y
MICHIGAN						
Stabenow	N	Y	N	Y	N	Y
Peters	N	Y	N	Y	N	Y
MINNESOTA						
Klobuchar	N	Y	N	Y	?	Y
Smith	Y	Y	N	Y	N	Y
MISSISSIPPI						
Wicker	Y	Y	Y	N	Y	Y
Hyde-Smith	Y	Y	Y	N	Y	Y
MISSOURI						
Blunt	Y	Y	Y	N	Y	Y
Hawley	Y	Y	Y	N	Y	N

	91	92	93	94	95	96
MONTANA						
Tester	Y	Y	Y	Y	N	Y
Daines	Y	Y	Y	Y	Y	N
NEBRASKA						
Fischer	Y	Y	Y	N	Y	Y
Sasse	Y	Y	Y	N	Y	N
NEVADA						
Cortez Masto	Y	Y	Y	Y	N	Y
Rosen	Y	Y	Y	Y	N	Y
NEW HAMPSHIRE						
Shaheen	Y	Y	Y	Y	N	Y
Hassan	Y	Y	Y	Y	N	Y
NEW JERSEY						
Menendez	Y	Y	N	Y	N	Y
Booker	?	?	?	Y	?	Y
NEW MEXICO						
Udall	Y	Y	N	Y	N	Y
Heinrich	Y	Y	N	Y	N	Y
NEW YORK						
Schumer	N	Y	N	Y	N	Y
Gillibrand	N	N	N	Y	?	Y
NORTH CAROLINA						
Burr	Y	Y	Y	N	Y	Y
Tillis	Y	Y	Y	N	Y	Y
NORTH DAKOTA						
Hoeven	Y	Y	Y	N	Y	Y
Cramer	Y	Y	Y	N	Y	Y
OHIO						
Brown	Y	Y	N	Y	N	Y
Portman	Y	Y	Y	N	Y	Y
OKLAHOMA						
Inhofe	Y	Y	Y	N	Y	N
Lankford	Y	Y	Y	N	Y	N
OREGON						
Wyden	Y	Y	N	Y	N	Y
Merkley	Y	Y	N	Y	N	Y
PENNSYLVANIA						
Casey	Y	Y	Y	Y	N	Y
Toomey	Y	Y	Y	N	?	N
RHODE ISLAND						
Reed	Y	Y	N	Y	N	Y
Whitehouse	Y	Y	N	Y	N	Y
SOUTH CAROLINA						
Graham	Y	Y	Y	N	Y	Y
Scott	Y	Y	Y	N	Y	Y
SOUTH DAKOTA						
Thune	Y	Y	Y	N	Y	Y
Rounds	Y	Y	Y	N	Y	Y
TENNESSEE						
Alexander	Y	Y	Y	N	Y	Y
Blackburn	Y	Y	Y	N	Y	N
TEXAS						
Cornyn	Y	Y	Y	N	Y	Y
Cruz	Y	Y	Y	N	Y	N
UTAH						
Lee	Y	Y	Y	Y	Y	N
Romney	Y	Y	Y	N	Y	Y
VERMONT						
Leahy	Y	Y	Y	Y	N	Y
Sanders	N	N	N	Y	N	N
VIRGINIA						
Warner	Y	Y	N	Y	N	Y
Kaine	Y	Y	N	Y	N	Y
WASHINGTON						
Murray	Y	Y	N	Y	N	Y
Cantwell	Y	Y	N	Y	N	Y
WEST VIRGINIA						
Manchin	Y	Y	Y	Y	Y	Y
Capito	Y	Y	Y	N	Y	Y
WISCONSIN						
Johnson	Y	Y	Y	N	Y	Y
Baldwin	Y	Y	N	Y	N	Y
WYOMING						
Enzi	Y	Y	Y	N	Y	Y
Barrasso	Y	Y	Y	N	Y	N

KEY:	**Republicans**	Democrats	*Independents*

Y	Voted for (yea)	N	Voted against (nay)	P	Voted "present"
+	Announced for	-	Announced against	?	Did not vote or otherwise make position known
#	Paired for	X	Paired against		

97. Bachus Nomination - Cloture. Motion to invoke cloture (thus limiting debate) on the nomination of former Rep. Spencer Bachus III of Alabama to be a member of the Board of Directors of the Export-Import Bank of the U.S. Motion agreed to 74-24: R 35-17; D 38-6; I 1-1. *Note: A majority of senators voting (50 in this case), a quorum being present, is required to invoke cloture on all nominations.* May 07, 2019.

98. Pryor Nomination - Cloture. Motion to invoke cloture (thus limiting debate) on the nomination of Judith Pryor to be a member of the Board of Directors of the Export-Import Bank of the U.S. Motion agreed to 79-19: R 34-18; D 44-0; I 1-1. *Note: A majority of senators voting (50 in this case), a quorum being present, is required to invoke cloture on all nominations.* May 07, 2019.

99. Bianco Nomination - Confirmation. Confirmation of President Trump's nomination of Joseph Bianco of New York to be a U.S. circuit judge for the 2nd Circuit. Confirmed 54-42: R 52-0; D 2-40; I 0-2. *Note: A "yea" was a vote in support of the president's position.* May 08, 2019.

100. Reed Nomination - Confirmation. Confirmation of President Trump's nomination of Kimberly Reed of West Virginia to be president of the Export-Import Bank of the U.S. Confirmed 79-17: R 36-16; D 42-0; I 1-1. *Note: A "yea" was a vote in support of the president's position.* May 08, 2019.

101. Bachus Nomination - Confirmation. Confirmation of President Trump's nomination of former Rep. Spencer Bachus III of Alabama to be a member of the Board of Directors of the Export-Import Bank of the U.S. Confirmed 72-22: R 35-17; D 36-5; I 1-0. *Note: A "yea" was a vote in support of the president's position.* May 08, 2019.

102. Pryor Nomination - Confirmation. Confirmation of President Trump's nomination of Judith Pryor of Ohio to be a member of the Board of Directors of the Export-Import Bank of the U.S. Confirmed 77-19: R 34-18; D 42-0; I 1-1. *Note: A "yea" was a vote in support of the president's position.* May 08, 2019.

	97	98	99	100	101	102
ALABAMA						
Shelby	N	N	Y	N	N	N
Jones	Y	Y	Y	Y	Y	Y
ALASKA						
Murkowski	?	?	?	?	?	?
Sullivan	Y	N	Y	Y	Y	N
ARIZONA						
Sinema	Y	Y	+	+	+	+
McSally	Y	Y	Y	Y	Y	Y
ARKANSAS						
Boozman	Y	Y	Y	Y	Y	Y
Cotton	Y	Y	Y	Y	Y	Y
CALIFORNIA						
Feinstein	Y	Y	N	Y	Y	Y
Harris	N	Y	N	Y	N	Y
COLORADO						
Bennet	Y	Y	N	Y	Y	Y
Gardner	Y	Y	Y	Y	Y	Y
CONNECTICUT						
Blumenthal	Y	Y	N	Y	Y	Y
Murphy	Y	Y	N	Y	Y	Y
DELAWARE						
Carper	Y	Y	N	Y	Y	Y
Coons	Y	Y	N	Y	Y	Y
FLORIDA						
Rubio	N	N	Y	N	N	N
Scott	Y	Y	Y	Y	Y	Y
GEORGIA						
Isakson	Y	Y	Y	Y	Y	Y
Perdue	Y	Y	Y	Y	Y	Y
HAWAII						
Schatz	Y	Y	N	Y	Y	Y
Hirono	Y	Y	N	Y	Y	Y
IDAHO						
Crapo	Y	Y	Y	Y	Y	Y
Risch	Y	Y	Y	Y	Y	Y
ILLINOIS						
Durbin	Y	Y	N	Y	Y	Y
Duckworth	Y	Y	N	Y	Y	Y
INDIANA						
Young	N	N	Y	N	N	N
Braun	N	N	Y	N	N	N
IOWA						
Grassley	N	N	Y	N	N	N
Ernst	Y	Y	Y	Y	Y	Y
KANSAS						
Roberts	Y	Y	Y	Y	Y	Y
Moran	Y	Y	Y	Y	Y	Y
KENTUCKY						
McConnell	Y	Y	Y	Y	Y	Y
Paul	N	N	Y	Y	N	N
LOUISIANA						
Cassidy	Y	Y	Y	Y	Y	Y
Kennedy	N	N	Y	N	N	N
MAINE						
Collins	Y	Y	Y	Y	Y	Y
King	Y	Y	N	Y	Y	Y
MARYLAND						
Cardin	Y	Y	N	Y	Y	Y
Van Hollen	Y	Y	N	Y	Y	Y
MASSACHUSETTS						
Warren	N	Y	N	Y	N	Y
Markey	N	Y	N	Y	N	Y
MICHIGAN						
Stabenow	Y	Y	N	Y	Y	Y
Peters	Y	Y	N	Y	Y	Y
MINNESOTA						
Klobuchar	N	Y	?	?	?	?
Smith	Y	Y	N	Y	Y	Y
MISSISSIPPI						
Wicker	Y	Y	Y	Y	Y	Y
Hyde-Smith	Y	Y	Y	Y	Y	Y
MISSOURI						
Blunt	Y	Y	Y	Y	Y	Y
Hawley	N	N	Y	N	N	N

	97	98	99	100	101	102
MONTANA						
Tester	Y	Y	N	Y	Y	Y
Daines	N	N	Y	N	N	N
NEBRASKA						
Fischer	Y	Y	Y	Y	Y	Y
Sasse	N	N	Y	N	N	N
NEVADA						
Cortez Masto	Y	Y	N	Y	Y	Y
Rosen	Y	Y	N	Y	Y	Y
NEW HAMPSHIRE						
Shaheen	Y	Y	N	Y	Y	Y
Hassan	Y	Y	N	Y	Y	Y
NEW JERSEY						
Menendez	Y	Y	N	Y	Y	Y
Booker	?	?	?	?	?	?
NEW MEXICO						
Udall	Y	Y	N	Y	Y	Y
Heinrich	Y	Y	N	Y	Y	Y
NEW YORK						
Schumer	Y	Y	N	Y	Y	Y
Gillibrand	N	Y	N	Y	N	Y
NORTH CAROLINA						
Burr	Y	Y	Y	Y	Y	Y
Tillis	Y	Y	Y	Y	Y	Y
NORTH DAKOTA						
Hoeven	Y	Y	Y	Y	Y	Y
Cramer	Y	Y	Y	Y	Y	Y
OHIO						
Brown	Y	Y	N	Y	Y	Y
Portman	Y	Y	Y	Y	Y	Y
OKLAHOMA						
Inhofe	N	N	Y	N	N	N
Lankford	N	N	Y	N	N	N
OREGON						
Wyden	Y	Y	N	Y	Y	Y
Merkley	N	Y	N	Y	N	Y
PENNSYLVANIA						
Casey	Y	Y	N	Y	Y	Y
Toomey	N	N	Y	N	N	N
RHODE ISLAND						
Reed	Y	Y	N	Y	Y	Y
Whitehouse	Y	Y	N	Y	?	Y
SOUTH CAROLINA						
Graham	Y	Y	Y	Y	Y	Y
Scott	Y	Y	Y	Y	Y	Y
SOUTH DAKOTA						
Thune	Y	Y	Y	Y	Y	Y
Rounds	Y	Y	Y	Y	Y	Y
TENNESSEE						
Alexander	Y	Y	Y	Y	Y	Y
Blackburn	N	N	Y	N	N	N
TEXAS						
Cornyn	Y	Y	Y	Y	Y	Y
Cruz	N	N	Y	N	N	N
UTAH						
Lee	N	N	Y	N	N	N
Romney	Y	Y	Y	Y	Y	Y
VERMONT						
Leahy	Y	Y	N	Y	Y	Y
Sanders	N	N	N	Y	?	N
VIRGINIA						
Warner	Y	Y	N	Y	Y	Y
Kaine	Y	Y	N	Y	Y	Y
WASHINGTON						
Murray	Y	Y	N	Y	Y	Y
Cantwell	Y	Y	N	Y	Y	Y
WEST VIRGINIA						
Manchin	Y	Y	Y	Y	Y	Y
Capito	Y	Y	Y	Y	Y	Y
WISCONSIN						
Johnson	Y	Y	Y	Y	Y	Y
Baldwin	Y	Y	N	Y	Y	Y
WYOMING						
Enzi	Y	Y	Y	N	Y	Y
Barrasso	N	N	Y	N	N	N

KEY:	Republicans		Democrats		Independents	
Y	Voted for (yea)	N	Voted against (nay)	P	Voted "present"	
+	Announced for	–	Announced against	?	Did not vote or otherwise make position known	
#	Paired for	X	Paired against			

103. Dhillon Nomination - Cloture. Motion to invoke cloture (thus limiting debate) on the nomination of Janet Dhillon of Pennsylvania to to be a member of the Equal Employment Opportunity Commission. Motion agreed to 52-44: R 52-0; D 0-42; I 0-2. *Note: A majority of senators voting (48 in this case), a quorum being present, is required to invoke cloture on all nominations.* May 08, 2019.

104. Dhillon Nomination - Confirmation. Confirmation of President Trump's nomination of Janet Dhillon of Pennsylvania to be a member of the Equal Employment Opportunity Commission. Confirmed 50-43: R 50-0; D 0-41; I 0-2. *Note: A "yea" was a vote in support of the president's position.* May 08, 2019.

105. Park Nomination - Cloture. Motion to invoke cloture (thus limiting debate) on the nomination of Michael Park of New York to be a U.S. circuit judge for the 2nd Circuit Motion agreed to 51-43: R 51-0; D 0-41; I 0-2. *Note: A majority of senators voting (47 in this case), a quorum being present, is required to invoke cloture on all nominations.* May 08, 2019.

106. Park Nomination - Confirmation. Confirmation of President Trump's nomination of Michael Park of New York to be a U.S. circuit judge for the 2nd Circuit. Confirmed 52-41: R 52-0; D 0-39; I 0-2. *Note: A "yea" was a vote in support of the president's position.* May 09, 2019.

107. Truncale Nomination - Cloture. Motion to invoke cloture (thus limiting debate) on the nomination of Michael J. Truncale of Texas to be a U.S. district judge for the Eastern District of Texas. Motion agreed to 49-43: R 49-1; D 0-40; I 0-2. *Note: A majority of senators voting (47 in this case), a quorum being present, is required to invoke cloture on all nominations.* May 13, 2019.

108. Truncale Nomination - Confirmation. Confirmation of President Trump's nomination of Michael J. Truncale of Texas to be a U.S. district judge for the Eastern District of Texas. Confirmed 49-46: R 49-1; D 0-43; I 0-2. *Note: A "yea" was a vote in support of the president's position.* May 14, 2019.

	103	104	105	106	107	108
ALABAMA						
Shelby	Y	Y	Y	Y	Y	Y
Jones	N	N	N	N	N	N
ALASKA						
Murkowski	?	?	Y	Y	Y	Y
Sullivan	Y	Y	Y	Y	Y	Y
ARIZONA						
Sinema	-	-	-	-	N	N
McSally	Y	Y	Y	Y	Y	Y
ARKANSAS						
Boozman	Y	Y	Y	Y	Y	Y
Cotton	Y	Y	Y	Y	Y	Y
CALIFORNIA						
Feinstein	N	N	N	N	N	N
Harris	N	N	N	-	N	N
COLORADO						
Bennet	N	?	?	?	N	N
Gardner	Y	Y	Y	Y	Y	Y
CONNECTICUT						
Blumenthal	N	N	N	N	N	N
Murphy	N	N	N	N	N	N
DELAWARE						
Carper	N	N	N	N	N	N
Coons	N	N	N	N	N	N
FLORIDA						
Rubio	Y	+	+	Y	Y	Y
Scott	Y	?	?	Y	+	Y
GEORGIA						
Isakson	Y	Y	Y	Y	Y	Y
Perdue	Y	Y	Y	Y	Y	Y
HAWAII						
Schatz	N	N	N	N	N	N
Hirono	N	N	N	N	-	-
IDAHO						
Crapo	Y	Y	Y	Y	Y	Y
Risch	Y	Y	Y	Y	Y	Y
ILLINOIS						
Durbin	N	N	N	N	N	N
Duckworth	N	N	N	N	N	N
INDIANA						
Young	Y	Y	Y	Y	Y	Y
Braun	Y	Y	Y	Y	Y	Y
IOWA						
Grassley	Y	Y	Y	Y	Y	Y
Ernst	Y	Y	Y	Y	Y	Y
KANSAS						
Roberts	Y	Y	Y	Y	Y	Y
Moran	Y	Y	Y	?	Y	Y
KENTUCKY						
McConnell	Y	Y	Y	Y	Y	Y
Paul	Y	Y	Y	Y	Y	Y
LOUISIANA						
Cassidy	Y	Y	Y	Y	Y	?
Kennedy	Y	Y	Y	Y	Y	?
MAINE						
Collins	Y	Y	Y	Y	Y	Y
King	N	N	N	N	N	N
MARYLAND						
Cardin	N	N	N	?	N	N
Van Hollen	N	N	N	N	N	N
MASSACHUSETTS						
Warren	N	N	N	N	?	N
Markey	N	N	N	N	N	N
MICHIGAN						
Stabenow	N	N	N	N	N	N
Peters	N	N	N	N	N	N
MINNESOTA						
Klobuchar	?	?	?	N	N	N
Smith	N	N	N	N	N	N
MISSISSIPPI						
Wicker	Y	Y	Y	Y	Y	Y
Hyde-Smith	Y	Y	Y	Y	Y	Y
MISSOURI						
Blunt	Y	Y	Y	Y	Y	Y
Hawley	Y	Y	Y	Y	Y	Y

	103	104	105	106	107	108
MONTANA						
Tester	N	N	N	N	N	N
Daines	Y	Y	Y	Y	Y	Y
NEBRASKA						
Fischer	Y	Y	Y	Y	Y	Y
Sasse	Y	Y	Y	Y	Y	Y
NEVADA						
Cortez Masto	N	N	N	N	N	N
Rosen	N	N	N	N	N	N
NEW HAMPSHIRE						
Shaheen	N	N	N	N	N	N
Hassan	N	N	N	N	N	N
NEW JERSEY						
Menendez	N	N	N	N	N	N
Booker	?	?	?	?	?	N
NEW MEXICO						
Udall	N	N	N	?	N	N
Heinrich	N	N	N	N	N	N
NEW YORK						
Schumer	N	N	N	N	N	N
Gillibrand	N	N	N	N	?	?
NORTH CAROLINA						
Burr	Y	Y	Y	Y	?	Y
Tillis	Y	Y	Y	Y	Y	Y
NORTH DAKOTA						
Hoeven	Y	Y	Y	Y	Y	Y
Cramer	Y	Y	Y	Y	Y	Y
OHIO						
Brown	N	N	N	N	?	N
Portman	Y	Y	Y	Y	Y	Y
OKLAHOMA						
Inhofe	Y	Y	Y	Y	Y	Y
Lankford	Y	Y	Y	Y	Y	Y
OREGON						
Wyden	N	N	N	N	N	N
Merkley	N	N	N	N	N	N
PENNSYLVANIA						
Casey	N	N	N	N	N	N
Toomey	Y	Y	Y	Y	?	Y
RHODE ISLAND						
Reed	N	N	N	N	N	N
Whitehouse	N	N	N	N	N	N
SOUTH CAROLINA						
Graham	Y	Y	Y	Y	Y	Y
Scott	Y	Y	Y	Y	Y	Y
SOUTH DAKOTA						
Thune	Y	Y	Y	Y	Y	Y
Rounds	Y	Y	Y	Y	Y	?
TENNESSEE						
Alexander	Y	Y	Y	Y	Y	Y
Blackburn	Y	Y	Y	Y	Y	Y
TEXAS						
Cornyn	Y	Y	Y	Y	Y	Y
Cruz	Y	Y	Y	Y	Y	Y
UTAH						
Lee	Y	Y	Y	Y	Y	Y
Romney	Y	Y	Y	Y	N	N
VERMONT						
Leahy	N	N	N	N	N	N
Sanders	N	N	N	N	N	N
VIRGINIA						
Warner	N	N	N	N	N	N
Kaine	N	N	N	N	N	N
WASHINGTON						
Murray	N	N	N	N	N	N
Cantwell	N	N	N	N	N	N
WEST VIRGINIA						
Manchin	N	N	N	N	N	N
Capito	Y	Y	Y	Y	Y	Y
WISCONSIN						
Johnson	Y	Y	Y	Y	Y	Y
Baldwin	N	N	N	N	N	N
WYOMING						
Enzi	Y	Y	Y	Y	Y	Y
Barrasso	Y	Y	Y	Y	Y	Y

KEY: **Republicans**   Democrats   *Independents*

Y Voted for (yea)	N Voted against (nay)	P Voted "present"
+ Announced for	- Announced against	? Did not vote or otherwise make position known
# Paired for	X Paired against	

109. Lee Nomination - Cloture. Motion to invoke cloture (thus limiting debate) on the nomination of Kenneth Kiyul Lee of California to be a U.S. circuit judge for the 9th Circuit. Motion agreed to 50-45: R 50-0; D 0-43; I 0-2. *Note: A majority of senators voting (48 in this case), a quorum being present, is required to invoke cloture on all nominations.* May 14, 2019.

110. Lee Nomination - Confirmation. Confirmation of President Trump's nomination of Kenneth Kiyul Lee of California to be a U.S. circuit judge for the 9th Circuit. Confirmed 52-45: R 52-0; D 0-43; I 0-2. *Note: A "yea" was a vote in support of the president's position.* May 15, 2019.

111. Vitter Nomination - Cloture. Motion to invoke cloture (thus limiting debate) on the nomination of Wendy Vitter of Louisiana to be a U.S. district judge for the Eastern District of Louisiana. Motion agreed to 51-45: R 51-0; D 0-42; I 0-2. *Note: A majority of senators voting (49 in this case), a quorum being present, is required to invoke cloture on all nominations.* May 15, 2019.

112. Bulatao Nomination - Cloture. Motion to invoke cloture (thus limiting debate) on the nomination of Brian J. Bulatao of Texas to be an Under Secretary of State (Management). Motion agreed to 90-5: R 52-0; D 37-4; I 1-1. *Note: A majority of senators voting (48 in this case), a quorum being present, is required to invoke cloture on all nominations.* May 15, 2019.

113. Rosen Nomination - Cloture. Motion to invoke cloture (thus limiting debate) on the nomination of Jeffrey A. Rosen of Virginia to be deputy attorney general. Motion agreed to 52-44: R 52-0; D 0-42; I 0-2. *Note: A majority of senators voting (49 in this case), a quorum being present, is required to invoke cloture on all nominations.* May 15, 2019.

114. Vitter Nomination - Confirmation. Confirmation of President Trump's nomination of Wendy Vitter of Louisiana to be a U.S. district judge for the Eastern District of Louisiana. Confirmed 52-45: R 52-1; D 0-42; I 0-2. *Note: A "yea" was a vote in support of the president's position.* May 16, 2019.

	109	110	111	112	113	114
ALABAMA						
Shelby	Y	Y	Y	Y	Y	Y
Jones	N	N	N	Y	N	N
ALASKA						
Murkowski	Y	Y	Y	Y	Y	Y
Sullivan	Y	Y	Y	Y	Y	Y
ARIZONA						
Sinema	N	N	N	Y	N	N
McSally	Y	Y	Y	Y	Y	Y
ARKANSAS						
Boozman	Y	Y	Y	Y	Y	Y
Cotton	Y	Y	Y	Y	Y	Y
CALIFORNIA						
Feinstein	N	N	N	Y	N	N
Harris	N	N	N	N	N	-
COLORADO						
Bennet	N	N	N	Y	N	N
Gardner	Y	Y	Y	Y	Y	Y
CONNECTICUT						
Blumenthal	N	N	N	Y	N	N
Murphy	N	N	N	Y	N	N
DELAWARE						
Carper	N	N	N	Y	N	N
Coons	N	N	N	Y	N	N
FLORIDA						
Rubio	Y	Y	Y	Y	Y	Y
Scott	Y	Y	Y	Y	Y	Y
GEORGIA						
Isakson	Y	Y	Y	Y	Y	Y
Perdue	Y	Y	Y	Y	Y	Y
HAWAII						
Schatz	N	N	N	N	N	N
Hirono	-	-	-	-	-	N
IDAHO						
Crapo	Y	Y	Y	Y	Y	Y
Risch	Y	Y	Y	Y	Y	Y
ILLINOIS						
Durbin	N	N	N	Y	N	N
Duckworth	N	N	N	Y	N	N
INDIANA						
Young	Y	Y	Y	Y	Y	Y
Braun	Y	Y	Y	Y	Y	Y
IOWA						
Grassley	Y	Y	Y	Y	Y	Y
Ernst	Y	Y	Y	Y	Y	Y
KANSAS						
Roberts	Y	Y	Y	Y	Y	Y
Moran	Y	Y	Y	Y	Y	Y
KENTUCKY						
McConnell	Y	Y	Y	Y	Y	Y
Paul	Y	Y	Y	Y	Y	Y
LOUISIANA						
Cassidy	?	Y	Y	Y	Y	Y
Kennedy	?	Y	Y	Y	Y	Y
MAINE						
Collins	Y	Y	N	Y	Y	N
King	N	N	N	Y	N	N
MARYLAND						
Cardin	N	N	N	Y	N	N
Van Hollen	N	N	N	Y	N	N
MASSACHUSETTS						
Warren	N	N	?	?	?	N
Markey	N	N	N	Y	N	N
MICHIGAN						
Stabenow	N	N	N	Y	N	N
Peters	N	N	N	Y	N	N
MINNESOTA						
Klobuchar	N	N	N	?	N	N
Smith	N	N	N	Y	N	N
MISSISSIPPI						
Wicker	Y	Y	Y	Y	Y	Y
Hyde-Smith	Y	Y	Y	Y	Y	Y
MISSOURI						
Blunt	Y	Y	Y	Y	Y	Y
Hawley	Y	Y	Y	Y	Y	Y
MONTANA						
Tester	N	N	N	Y	N	N
Daines	Y	Y	Y	Y	Y	Y
NEBRASKA						
Fischer	Y	Y	Y	Y	Y	Y
Sasse	Y	Y	Y	Y	Y	Y
NEVADA						
Cortez Masto	N	N	N	Y	N	N
Rosen	N	N	N	Y	N	N
NEW HAMPSHIRE						
Shaheen	N	N	N	Y	N	N
Hassan	N	N	N	Y	N	N
NEW JERSEY						
Menendez	N	N	N	Y	N	N
Booker	N	?	?	?	?	?
NEW MEXICO						
Udall	N	N	N	N	N	N
Heinrich	N	N	N	Y	N	N
NEW YORK						
Schumer	N	N	N	Y	N	N
Gillibrand	?	N	N	N	N	?
NORTH CAROLINA						
Burr	Y	Y	Y	Y	Y	Y
Tillis	Y	Y	Y	Y	Y	Y
NORTH DAKOTA						
Hoeven	Y	Y	Y	Y	Y	Y
Cramer	Y	Y	Y	Y	Y	Y
OHIO						
Brown	N	N	N	Y	N	N
Portman	Y	Y	Y	Y	Y	Y
OKLAHOMA						
Inhofe	Y	Y	Y	Y	Y	Y
Lankford	Y	Y	Y	Y	Y	Y
OREGON						
Wyden	N	N	N	Y	N	N
Merkley	N	N	N	Y	N	N
PENNSYLVANIA						
Casey	N	N	N	Y	N	N
Toomey	Y	Y	Y	Y	Y	Y
RHODE ISLAND						
Reed	N	N	N	Y	N	N
Whitehouse	N	N	N	Y	N	N
SOUTH CAROLINA						
Graham	Y	Y	Y	Y	Y	Y
Scott	Y	Y	Y	Y	Y	Y
SOUTH DAKOTA						
Thune	Y	Y	Y	Y	Y	Y
Rounds	?	Y	Y	Y	Y	Y
TENNESSEE						
Alexander	Y	Y	Y	Y	Y	Y
Blackburn	Y	Y	Y	Y	Y	Y
TEXAS						
Cornyn	Y	Y	Y	Y	Y	Y
Cruz	Y	?	?	?	?	Y
UTAH						
Lee	Y	Y	Y	Y	Y	Y
Romney	Y	Y	Y	Y	Y	Y
VERMONT						
Leahy	N	N	N	Y	N	N
Sanders	N	N	N	N	N	N
VIRGINIA						
Warner	N	N	N	Y	N	N
Kaine	N	N	N	Y	N	N
WASHINGTON						
Murray	N	N	N	Y	N	N
Cantwell	N	N	N	Y	N	N
WEST VIRGINIA						
Manchin	N	N	N	Y	N	N
Capito	Y	Y	Y	Y	Y	Y
WISCONSIN						
Johnson	Y	Y	Y	Y	Y	Y
Baldwin	N	N	N	Y	N	N
WYOMING						
Enzi	Y	Y	Y	Y	Y	Y
Barrasso	Y	Y	Y	Y	Y	Y

KEY: Republicans   Democrats   *Independents*

Y Voted for (yea)	**N** Voted against (nay)	**P** Voted "present"
+ Announced for	**-** Announced against	**?** Did not vote or otherwise make position known
# Paired for	**X** Paired against	

115. Bulatao Nomination - Confirmation. Confirmation of President Trump's nomination of Brian J. Bulatao of Texas to be an Under Secretary of State (Management). Confirmed 92-5: R 53-0; D 38-4; I 1-1. *Note: A "yea" was a vote in support of the president's position.* May 16, 2019.

116. Rosen Nomination - Confirmation. Confirmation of President Trump's nomination of Jeffrey A. Rosen of Virginia to be deputy attorney general. Confirmed 52-45: R 52-0; D 0-43; I 0-2. *Note: A "yea" was a vote in support of the president's position.* May 16, 2019.

117. Collins Nomination - Cloture. Motion to invoke cloture (thus limiting debate) on the nomination of Daniel Collins of California to be a U.S. circuit judge for the 9th Circuit. Motion agreed to 51-43: R 51-0; D 0-42; I 0-1. *Note: A majority of senators voting (48 in this case), a quorum being present, is required to invoke cloture on all nominations.* May 20, 2019.

118. Collins Nomination - Confirmation. Confirmation of President Trump's nomination of Daniel Collins of California to be a U.S. circuit judge for the 9th Circuit. Confirmed 53-46: R 53-0; D 0-44; I 0-2. *Note: A "yea" was a vote in support of the president's position.* May 21, 2019.

119. Nielson Nomination - Cloture. Motion to invoke cloture (thus limiting debate) on the nomination of Howard Nielson, Jr. of Utah to be a U.S. district judge for the District of Utah. Motion agreed to 52-47: R 52-1; D 0-44; I 0-2. *Note: A majority of senators voting (50 in this case), a quorum being present, is required to invoke cloture on all nominations.* May 21, 2019.

120. Clark Nomination - Cloture. Motion to invoke cloture (thus limiting debate) on the nomination of Stephen Clark, Sr. of Missouri to be a U.S. district judge for the Eastern District of Missouri. Motion agreed to 53-45: R 52-0; D 1-43; I 0-2. *Note: A majority of senators voting (50 in this case), a quorum being present, is required to invoke cloture on all nominations.* May 21, 2019.

	115	116	117	118	119	120		115	116	117	118	119	120
ALABAMA							**MONTANA**						
Shelby	Y	Y	Y	Y	Y	Y	Tester	Y	N	N	N	N	N
Jones	Y	N	N	N	N	N	Daines	Y	Y	Y	Y	Y	Y
ALASKA							**NEBRASKA**						
Murkowski	Y	Y	Y	Y	Y	Y	Fischer	Y	Y	Y	Y	Y	Y
Sullivan	Y	Y	Y	Y	Y	Y	Sasse	Y	Y	Y	Y	Y	Y
ARIZONA							**NEVADA**						
Sinema	Y	N	N	N	N	N	Cortez Masto	Y	N	N	N	N	N
McSally	Y	Y	Y	Y	Y	Y	Rosen	Y	N	N	N	N	N
ARKANSAS							**NEW HAMPSHIRE**						
Boozman	Y	Y	Y	Y	Y	Y	Shaheen	Y	N	N	N	N	N
Cotton	Y	Y	Y	Y	Y	Y	Hassan	Y	N	N	N	N	N
CALIFORNIA							**NEW JERSEY**						
Feinstein	Y	N	N	N	N	N	Menendez	Y	N	N	N	N	N
Harris	?	-	N	N	N	N	Booker	?	N	?	N	N	N
COLORADO							**NEW MEXICO**						
Bennet	Y	N	N	?	?	?	Udall	Y	N	N	N	N	N
Gardner	Y	Y	Y	Y	Y	Y	Heinrich	Y	N	N	N	N	N
CONNECTICUT							**NEW YORK**						
Blumenthal	N	N	N	N	N	N	Schumer	Y	N	N	N	N	N
Murphy	Y	N	N	N	N	N	Gillibrand	?	?	?	N	N	N
DELAWARE							**NORTH CAROLINA**						
Carper	Y	N	N	N	N	N	Burr	Y	Y	Y	Y	Y	?
Coons	Y	N	N	N	N	N	Tillis	Y	Y	Y	Y	Y	Y
FLORIDA							**NORTH DAKOTA**						
Rubio	Y	Y	Y	Y	Y	Y	Hoeven	Y	Y	Y	Y	Y	Y
Scott	Y	Y	Y	Y	Y	Y	Cramer	Y	Y	Y	Y	Y	Y
GEORGIA							**OHIO**						
Isakson	Y	Y	Y	Y	Y	Y	Brown	Y	N	N	N	N	N
Perdue	Y	Y	Y	Y	Y	Y	Portman	Y	Y	Y	Y	Y	Y
HAWAII							**OKLAHOMA**						
Schatz	Y	N	N	N	N	N	Inhofe	Y	Y	+	Y	Y	Y
Hirono	N	N	N	N	N	N	Lankford	Y	Y	Y	Y	Y	Y
IDAHO							**OREGON**						
Crapo	Y	Y	Y	Y	Y	Y	Wyden	Y	N	N	N	N	N
Risch	Y	Y	Y	Y	Y	Y	Merkley	Y	N	N	N	N	N
ILLINOIS							**PENNSYLVANIA**						
Durbin	Y	N	N	N	N	N	Casey	Y	N	N	N	N	N
Duckworth	Y	N	N	N	N	N	Toomey	Y	Y	Y	Y	Y	Y
INDIANA							**RHODE ISLAND**						
Young	Y	Y	Y	Y	Y	Y	Reed	Y	N	N	N	N	N
Braun	Y	Y	Y	Y	Y	Y	Whitehouse	Y	N	N	N	N	N
IOWA							**SOUTH CAROLINA**						
Grassley	Y	Y	Y	Y	Y	Y	Graham	Y	Y	Y	Y	Y	Y
Ernst	Y	Y	Y	Y	Y	Y	Scott	Y	Y	Y	Y	Y	Y
KANSAS							**SOUTH DAKOTA**						
Roberts	Y	Y	Y	Y	Y	Y	Thune	Y	Y	Y	Y	Y	Y
Moran	Y	Y	Y	Y	Y	Y	Rounds	Y	Y	Y	Y	Y	Y
KENTUCKY							**TENNESSEE**						
McConnell	Y	Y	Y	Y	Y	Y	Alexander	Y	?	Y	Y	Y	Y
Paul	Y	Y	Y	Y	Y	Y	Blackburn	Y	Y	Y	Y	Y	Y
LOUISIANA							**TEXAS**						
Cassidy	Y	Y	Y	Y	Y	Y	Cornyn	Y	Y	Y	Y	Y	Y
Kennedy	Y	Y	Y	Y	Y	Y	Cruz	Y	Y	Y	Y	Y	Y
MAINE							**UTAH**						
Collins	Y	Y	Y	Y	N	Y	Lee	Y	Y	Y	Y	Y	Y
King	Y	N	N	N	N	N	Romney	Y	Y	Y	Y	Y	Y
MARYLAND							**VERMONT**						
Cardin	Y	N	N	N	N	N	Leahy	Y	N	N	N	N	N
Van Hollen	Y	N	N	N	N	N	*Sanders*	N	N	?	N	N	N
MASSACHUSETTS							**VIRGINIA**						
Warren	N	N	N	N	N	N	Warner	Y	N	N	N	N	N
Markey	N	N	N	N	N	N	Kaine	Y	N	N	N	N	N
MICHIGAN							**WASHINGTON**						
Stabenow	Y	N	N	N	N	N	Murray	Y	N	N	N	N	N
Peters	Y	N	N	N	N	N	Cantwell	Y	N	N	N	N	N
MINNESOTA							**WEST VIRGINIA**						
Klobuchar	Y	N	N	N	N	N	Manchin	Y	N	N	N	N	Y
Smith	Y	N	N	N	N	N	Capito	Y	Y	Y	Y	Y	Y
MISSISSIPPI							**WISCONSIN**						
Wicker	Y	Y	Y	Y	Y	Y	Johnson	Y	Y	+	Y	Y	Y
Hyde-Smith	Y	Y	Y	Y	Y	Y	Baldwin	Y	N	-	N	N	N
MISSOURI							**WYOMING**						
Blunt	Y	Y	Y	Y	Y	Y	Enzi	Y	Y	Y	Y	Y	Y
Hawley	Y	Y	Y	Y	Y	Y	Barrasso	Y	Y	Y	Y	Y	Y

KEY:	Republicans	Democrats	*Independents*

Y Voted for (yea)	N Voted against (nay)	P Voted "present"	
+ Announced for	- Announced against	? Did not vote or otherwise	
# Paired for	X Paired against	make position known	

121. Nichols Nomination - Cloture. Motion to invoke cloture (thus limiting debate) on the nomination of Carl J. Nichols of the District of Columbia to be a U.S. district judge for the District of Columbia. Motion agreed to 55-42: R 52-0; D 3-40; I 0-2. *Note: A majority of senators voting (49 in this case), a quorum being present, is required to invoke cloture on all nominations.* May 21, 2019.

122. Bell Nomination - Cloture. Motion to invoke cloture (thus limiting debate) on the nomination of Kenneth Bell of North Carolina to be a U.S. district judge for the Western District of North Carolina. Motion agreed to 56-42: R 53-0; D 3-40; I 0-2. *Note: A majority of senators voting (50 in this case), a quorum being present, is required to invoke cloture on all nominations.* May 21, 2019.

123. Nielson Nomination - Confirmation. Confirmation of President Trump's nomination of Howard Nielson, Jr. of Utah to be a U.S. district judge for the District of Utah. Confirmed 51-47: R 51-1; D 0-44; I 0-2. *Note: A "yea" was a vote in support of the president's position.* May 22, 2019.

124. Clark Nomination - Confirmation. Confirmation of President Trump's nomination of Stephen Clark, Sr. of Missouri to be a U.S. district judge for the Eastern District of Missouri. Confirmed 53-45: R 52-0; D 1-43; I 0-2. *Note: A "yea" was a vote in support of the president's position.* May 22, 2019.

125. Nichols Nomination - Confirmation. Confirmation of President Trump's nomination of Carl J. Nichols of the District of Columbia to be a U.S. district judge for the District of Columbia. Confirmed 55-43: R 52-0; D 3-41; I 0-2. *Note: A "yea" was a vote in support of the president's position.* May 22, 2019.

126. Bell Nomination - Confirmation. Confirmation of President Trump's nomination of Kenneth Bell of North Carolina to be a U.S. district judge for the Western District of North Carolina. Confirmed 55-43: R 52-0; D 3-41; I 0-2. *Note: A "yea" was a vote in support of the president's position.* May 22, 2019.

	121	122	123	124	125	126
ALABAMA						
Shelby	Y	Y	Y	Y	Y	Y
Jones	Y	Y	N	N	Y	Y
ALASKA						
Murkowski	Y	Y	Y	Y	Y	Y
Sullivan	Y	Y	Y	Y	Y	Y
ARIZONA						
Sinema	Y	Y	N	N	Y	Y
McSally	Y	Y	Y	Y	Y	Y
ARKANSAS						
Boozman	Y	Y	Y	Y	Y	Y
Cotton	Y	Y	Y	Y	Y	Y
CALIFORNIA						
Feinstein	N	N	N	N	N	N
Harris	N	N	-	-	-	-
COLORADO						
Bennet	?	?	N	N	N	N
Gardner	Y	Y	Y	Y	Y	Y
CONNECTICUT						
Blumenthal	N	N	N	N	N	N
Murphy	N	N	N	N	N	N
DELAWARE						
Carper	N	N	N	N	N	N
Coons	N	N	N	N	N	N
FLORIDA						
Rubio	Y	Y	Y	Y	Y	Y
Scott	Y	Y	Y	Y	Y	Y
GEORGIA						
Isakson	Y	Y	Y	Y	Y	Y
Perdue	Y	Y	Y	Y	Y	Y
HAWAII						
Schatz	N	N	N	N	N	N
Hirono	N	N	N	N	N	N
IDAHO						
Crapo	Y	Y	Y	Y	Y	Y
Risch	Y	Y	Y	Y	Y	Y
ILLINOIS						
Durbin	N	N	N	N	N	N
Duckworth	N	N	N	N	N	N
INDIANA						
Young	Y	Y	Y	Y	Y	Y
Braun	Y	Y	Y	Y	Y	Y
IOWA						
Grassley	Y	Y	Y	Y	Y	Y
Ernst	Y	Y	Y	Y	Y	Y
KANSAS						
Roberts	Y	Y	Y	Y	Y	Y
Moran	Y	Y	Y	Y	Y	Y
KENTUCKY						
McConnell	Y	Y	Y	Y	Y	Y
Paul	Y	Y	Y	Y	Y	Y
LOUISIANA						
Cassidy	Y	Y	Y	Y	Y	Y
Kennedy	Y	Y	Y	Y	Y	Y
MAINE						
Collins	Y	Y	N	Y	Y	Y
King	N	N	N	N	N	N
MARYLAND						
Cardin	N	N	N	N	N	N
Van Hollen	N	N	N	N	N	N
MASSACHUSETTS						
Warren	N	N	N	N	N	N
Markey	N	N	N	N	N	N
MICHIGAN						
Stabenow	N	N	N	N	N	N
Peters	N	N	N	N	N	N
MINNESOTA						
Klobuchar	N	N	N	N	N	N
Smith	N	N	N	N	N	N
MISSISSIPPI						
Wicker	Y	Y	Y	Y	Y	Y
Hyde-Smith	Y	Y	Y	Y	Y	Y
MISSOURI						
Blunt	Y	Y	Y	Y	Y	Y
Hawley	Y	Y	Y	Y	Y	Y
MONTANA						
Tester	N	N	N	N	N	N
Daines	Y	Y	Y	Y	Y	Y
NEBRASKA						
Fischer	Y	Y	Y	Y	Y	Y
Sasse	Y	Y	Y	Y	Y	Y
NEVADA						
Cortez Masto	N	N	N	N	N	N
Rosen	N	N	N	N	N	N
NEW HAMPSHIRE						
Shaheen	N	N	N	N	N	N
Hassan	N	N	N	N	N	N
NEW JERSEY						
Menendez	N	N	N	N	N	N
Booker	?	?	N	N	N	N
NEW MEXICO						
Udall	N	N	N	N	N	N
Heinrich	N	N	N	N	N	N
NEW YORK						
Schumer	N	N	N	N	N	N
Gillibrand	N	N	N	N	N	N
NORTH CAROLINA						
Burr	?	Y	Y	Y	Y	Y
Tillis	Y	Y	+	+	+	+
NORTH DAKOTA						
Hoeven	Y	Y	Y	Y	Y	Y
Cramer	Y	Y	Y	Y	Y	Y
OHIO						
Brown	N	N	N	N	N	N
Portman	Y	Y	Y	Y	Y	Y
OKLAHOMA						
Inhofe	Y	Y	Y	Y	Y	Y
Lankford	Y	Y	Y	Y	Y	Y
OREGON						
Wyden	N	N	N	N	N	N
Merkley	N	N	N	N	N	N
PENNSYLVANIA						
Casey	N	N	N	N	N	N
Toomey	Y	Y	Y	Y	Y	Y
RHODE ISLAND						
Reed	N	N	N	N	N	N
Whitehouse	N	N	N	N	N	N
SOUTH CAROLINA						
Graham	Y	Y	Y	Y	Y	Y
Scott	Y	Y	Y	Y	Y	Y
SOUTH DAKOTA						
Thune	Y	Y	Y	Y	Y	Y
Rounds	Y	Y	Y	Y	Y	Y
TENNESSEE						
Alexander	Y	Y	Y	Y	Y	Y
Blackburn	Y	Y	Y	Y	Y	Y
TEXAS						
Cornyn	Y	Y	Y	Y	Y	Y
Cruz	Y	Y	Y	Y	Y	Y
UTAH						
Lee	Y	Y	Y	Y	Y	Y
Romney	Y	Y	Y	Y	Y	Y
VERMONT						
Leahy	N	N	N	N	N	N
Sanders	N	N	N	N	N	N
VIRGINIA						
Warner	N	N	N	N	N	N
Kaine	N	N	N	N	N	N
WASHINGTON						
Murray	N	N	N	N	N	N
Cantwell	N	N	N	N	N	N
WEST VIRGINIA						
Manchin	Y	Y	N	Y	Y	Y
Capito	Y	Y	Y	Y	Y	Y
WISCONSIN						
Johnson	Y	Y	Y	Y	Y	Y
Baldwin	N	N	N	N	N	N
WYOMING						
Enzi	Y	Y	Y	Y	Y	Y
Barrasso	Y	Y	Y	Y	Y	Y

KEY:	Republicans	Democrats	Independents

Y	Voted for (yea)	N	Voted against (nay)	P	Voted "present"
+	Announced for	-	Announced against	?	Did not vote or otherwise
#	Paired for	X	Paired against		make position known

127. S151. Robocall Enforcement and Deterrence - Passage. Passage of the bill, as amended, that would allow the Federal Communications Commission to issue civil penalties of up to $10,000 per call for individuals who intentionally violate telemarketing laws. It would require the FCC to submit an annual report to Congress detailing the enforcement of the laws, regulations, and policies related to robocalls and "spoofed" calls, including the number of complaints received by the FCC, the number of citations and notices of liability issued, and the amount of the proposed forfeiture penalty for each notice. The bill would require the FCC, within 18 months of enactment, to require voice communication providers to adopt a certain framework for call authentication standards to digitally certify caller identifications. It would require the FCC to submit a report to Congress on the extent of implementation and the effectiveness of the framework within one year of enactment, and to review and revise the framework every three years. Passed 97-1: R 50-1; D 45-0; I 2-0. *Note: In the legislative day that began on May 22, 2019.* May 23, 2019.

128. HR2157. Fiscal 2019 Disaster Supplemental Appropriations - Motion to Waive. Cornyn, R-Texas, motion to waive all applicable sections of the Congressional Budget Act with respect to the Fiscal 2019 Supplemental Disaster Appropriations Act, as amended (HR 2157). Motion agreed to 84-9: R 38-9; D 44-0; I 2-0. *Note: In the legislative day that began on May 22, 2019. A three-fifths majority vote (60) of the total Senate is required to waive the Budget Act.* May 23, 2019.

129. HR2157. Fiscal 2019 Disaster Supplemental Appropriations - Passage. Passage of the bill, as amended, that would provide $19.1 billion in supplemental disaster funds for response efforts to damage caused by hurricanes, wildfires, earthquakes, tornadoes, floods, and other natural disasters that occurred in 2017, 2018, and 2019. It would provide $648 million in disaster nutrition assistance for individuals impacted by natural disasters in Puerto Rico, the Commonwealth of the Northern Mariana Islands, and American Samoa. It would extend the National Flood Insurance Program, which will expire on May 31, through Sept. 30, 2019. It would also provide funds for areas impacted by natural disasters for economic development, training and employment services, and behavioral and social health services. Passed 85-8: R 39-8; D 44-0; I 2-0. *Note: In the legislative day that began on May 22, 2019. A "yea" was a vote in support of the president's position.* May 23, 2019.

130. S1332. Fiscal 2020 Budget Levels - Cloture. McConnell, R-Ky., motion to invoke cloture on the motion to proceed to the bill that would provide for $4.58 trillion in new budget authority in fiscal 2020, not including off-budget accounts. It would assume $3.44 trillion in discretionary spending in fiscal 2020. It would provide in new budget authority for fiscal 2020 $6.3 billion for social security administrative expenses and $33 million for the U.S. postal service. It would also recommend federal revenue levels, new budget authorities, outlays, deficits, and debt for fiscal 2020 through 2029. The bill would prohibit in the Senate motions to waive or suspend points of order under the Congressional Budget Act (or other budgetary concurrent resolution), unless the point of order had previously been raised by a Senator. Motion rejected 22-69: R 22-26; D 0-42; I 0-1. *Note: Three-fifths of the total Senate (60) is required to invoke cloture.* June 03, 2019.

131. Saul Nomination - Cloture. Motion to invoke cloture (thus limiting debate) on the nomination of Andrew Saul of New York to be commissioner of Social Security. Motion agreed to 74-17: R 48-0; D 25-17; I 1-0. *Note: A majority of senators voting (46 in this case), a quorum being present, is required to invoke cloture on all nominations.* June 03, 2019.

132. SRES212. 19th Amendment Centennial - Passage. Passage of the resolution that would state that the Senate celebrates the 100th anniversary of the passage and ratification of the 19th Amendment to the United States Constitution. The resolution would commemorate the women's suffrage movement and the role of women in democracy. Passed 93-0: R 51-0; D 41-0; I 1-0. June 04, 2019.

	127	128	129	130	131	132
ALABAMA						
Shelby	Y	Y	Y	Y	Y	Y
Jones	Y	Y	Y	N	Y	Y
ALASKA						
Murkowski	Y	Y	Y	N	Y	Y
Sullivan	Y	Y	Y	N	Y	Y
ARIZONA						
Sinema	Y	Y	Y	N	Y	Y
McSally	Y	N	N	N	Y	Y
ARKANSAS						
Boozman	Y	Y	Y	N	Y	Y
Cotton	Y	Y	Y	N	Y	Y
CALIFORNIA						
Feinstein	Y	Y	Y	N	N	Y
Harris	Y	Y	Y	?	?	?
COLORADO						
Bennet	Y	Y	Y	N	Y	Y
Gardner	Y	Y	Y	N	Y	Y
CONNECTICUT						
Blumenthal	Y	Y	Y	N	N	?
Murphy	Y	Y	Y	N	Y	Y
DELAWARE						
Carper	Y	Y	Y	N	Y	Y
Coons	Y	Y	Y	N	Y	Y
FLORIDA						
Rubio	Y	Y	Y	N	Y	Y
Scott	Y	Y	Y	N	Y	Y
GEORGIA						
Isakson	Y	Y	Y	Y	Y	Y
Perdue	Y	Y	Y	?	?	Y
HAWAII						
Schatz	Y	Y	Y	N	N	Y
Hirono	Y	Y	Y	N	N	Y
IDAHO						
Crapo	Y	N	N	Y	Y	Y
Risch	Y	N	N	Y	Y	Y
ILLINOIS						
Durbin	Y	+	+	N	Y	Y
Duckworth	Y	Y	Y	N	N	Y
INDIANA						
Young	Y	Y	Y	N	Y	Y
Braun	Y	N	N	N	Y	Y
IOWA						
Grassley	Y	Y	Y	Y	Y	Y
Ernst	Y	Y	Y	Y	Y	Y
KANSAS						
Roberts	Y	Y	Y	N	Y	Y
Moran	Y	?	?	?	?	+
KENTUCKY						
McConnell	Y	Y	Y	N	Y	Y
Paul	N	N	N	Y	Y	Y
LOUISIANA						
Cassidy	Y	Y	Y	N	Y	Y
Kennedy	Y	Y	Y	Y	Y	Y
MAINE						
Collins	Y	Y	Y	N	Y	Y
King	Y	Y	Y	N	Y	Y
MARYLAND						
Cardin	Y	Y	Y	N	Y	Y
Van Hollen	Y	Y	Y	N	N	Y
MASSACHUSETTS						
Warren	Y	Y	Y	?	?	?
Markey	Y	Y	Y	N	N	Y
MICHIGAN						
Stabenow	Y	Y	Y	N	Y	Y
Peters	Y	Y	Y	N	Y	Y
MINNESOTA						
Klobuchar	Y	Y	Y	N	N	Y
Smith	Y	Y	Y	N	N	Y
MISSISSIPPI						
Wicker	Y	Y	Y	N	Y	Y
Hyde-Smith	Y	Y	Y	?	?	Y
MISSOURI						
Blunt	Y	Y	Y	N	Y	Y
Hawley	Y	Y	Y	N	Y	Y

	127	128	129	130	131	132
MONTANA						
Tester	Y	Y	Y	N	N	Y
Daines	Y	Y	Y	Y	Y	Y
NEBRASKA						
Fischer	Y	Y	Y	Y	Y	Y
Sasse	Y	Y	Y	Y	Y	Y
NEVADA						
Cortez Masto	Y	Y	Y	N	N	Y
Rosen	Y	Y	Y	N	N	Y
NEW HAMPSHIRE						
Shaheen	Y	Y	Y	N	N	Y
Hassan	Y	Y	Y	N	N	Y
NEW JERSEY						
Menendez	Y	Y	Y	N	N	Y
Booker	Y	Y	Y	?	?	Y
NEW MEXICO						
Udall	Y	Y	Y	N	N	Y
Heinrich	Y	Y	Y	N	N	Y
NEW YORK						
Schumer	Y	Y	Y	N	N	Y
Gillibrand	Y	Y	Y	N	N	?
NORTH CAROLINA						
Burr	Y	Y	Y	N	N	Y
Tillis	Y	Y	Y	Y	Y	Y
NORTH DAKOTA						
Hoeven	Y	Y	Y	N	Y	Y
Cramer	Y	Y	Y	N	Y	Y
OHIO						
Brown	Y	Y	Y	N	N	Y
Portman	Y	Y	Y	N	Y	Y
OKLAHOMA						
Inhofe	?	Y	Y	Y	Y	Y
Lankford	Y	Y	Y	Y	Y	Y
OREGON						
Wyden	Y	Y	Y	N	N	Y
Merkley	Y	Y	Y	N	N	Y
PENNSYLVANIA						
Casey	Y	Y	Y	N	N	Y
Toomey	Y	?	?	Y	Y	Y
RHODE ISLAND						
Reed	Y	Y	Y	N	N	Y
Whitehouse	Y	Y	Y	N	N	Y
SOUTH CAROLINA						
Graham	Y	Y	Y	N	N	Y
Scott	Y	Y	Y	Y	Y	Y
SOUTH DAKOTA						
Thune	Y	Y	Y	N	N	Y
Rounds	?	?	?	N	Y	Y
TENNESSEE						
Alexander	Y	+	+	-	+	+
Blackburn	Y	N	N	Y	Y	Y
TEXAS						
Cornyn	Y	Y	Y	Y	Y	Y
Cruz	Y	Y	Y	Y	Y	Y
UTAH						
Lee	Y	N	N	Y	Y	Y
Romney	Y	N	N	Y	Y	Y
VERMONT						
Leahy	Y	Y	Y	N	Y	Y
Sanders	Y	Y	Y	?	?	?
VIRGINIA						
Warner	Y	Y	Y	N	Y	Y
Kaine	Y	Y	Y	N	Y	Y
WASHINGTON						
Murray	Y	Y	Y	N	N	Y
Cantwell	Y	Y	Y	N	Y	Y
WEST VIRGINIA						
Manchin	Y	Y	Y	N	Y	Y
Capito	Y	+	+	+	Y	Y
WISCONSIN						
Johnson	Y	Y	Y	N	Y	Y
Baldwin	Y	Y	Y	N	N	Y
WYOMING						
Enzi	Y	?	?	N	Y	Y
Barrasso	Y	N	Y	Y	Y	Y

KEY: **Republicans**   Democrats   *Independents*

Y Voted for (yea)	N Voted against (nay)	P Voted "present"
+ Announced for	– Announced against	? Did not vote or otherwise
# Paired for	X Paired against	make position known

133. Saul Nomination - Confirmation. Confirmation of President Trump's nomination of Andrew Saul of New York to be a commissioner of Social Security. Confirmed 77-16: R 51-0; D 25-16; I 1-0. *Note: A "yea" was a vote in support of the president's position.* June 04, 2019.

134. Schenker Nomination - Cloture. Motion to invoke cloture (thus limiting debate) on the nomination of David Schenker of New Jersey to be an assistant secretary of State (Near Eastern Affairs). Motion agreed to 83-10: R 51-0; D 31-10; I 1-0. *Note: A majority of senators voting (47 in this case), a quorum being present, is required to invoke cloture on all nominations.* June 04, 2019.

135. Tarbert Nomination - Cloture. Motion to invoke cloture (thus limiting debate) on the nomination of Heath Tarbert of Maryland to be chairman of the Commodity Futures Trading Commission. Motion agreed to 82-9: R 51-0; D 30-9; I 1-0. *Note: A majority of senators voting (46 in this case), a quorum being present, is required to invoke cloture on all nominations.* June 04, 2019.

136. Tarbert Nomination - Cloture. Motion to invoke cloture (thus limiting debate) on the nomination of Heath Tarbert of Maryland to be a commissioner of the Commodity Futures Trading Commission. Motion agreed to 83-10: R 51-0; D 31-10; I 1-0. *Note: A majority of senators voting (47 in this case), a quorum being present, is required to invoke cloture on all nominations.* June 04, 2019.

137. Schenker Nomination - Confirmation. Confirmation of President Trump's nomination of David Schenker of New Jersey to be an assistant secretary of State (Near Eastern Affairs). Confirmed 83-11: R 51-0; D 31-11; I 1-0. *Note: A "yea" was a vote in support of the president's position.* June 05, 2019.

138. Tarbert Nomination - Confirmation. Confirmation of President Trump's nomination of Heath Tarbert of Maryland to be a chairman of the Commodity Futures Trading Commission. Confirmed 84-9: R 50-0; D 33-9; I 1-0. *Note: A "yea" was a vote in support of the president's position.* June 05, 2019.

	133	134	135	136	137	138
ALABAMA						
Shelby	Y	Y	Y	Y	Y	Y
Jones	Y	Y	Y	Y	Y	Y
ALASKA						
Murkowski	Y	Y	Y	Y	Y	Y
Sullivan	Y	Y	Y	Y	Y	Y
ARIZONA						
Sinema	Y	Y	Y	Y	Y	Y
McSally	Y	Y	Y	Y	Y	Y
ARKANSAS						
Boozman	Y	Y	Y	Y	Y	Y
Cotton	Y	Y	Y	Y	Y	Y
CALIFORNIA						
Feinstein	N	Y	Y	Y	Y	Y
Harris	?	?	?	?	N	N
COLORADO						
Bennet	Y	Y	Y	Y	Y	Y
Gardner	Y	Y	Y	Y	Y	Y
CONNECTICUT						
Blumenthal	?	?	?	N	Y	N
Murphy	Y	Y	Y	Y	Y	Y
DELAWARE						
Carper	Y	Y	?	?	Y	Y
Coons	Y	Y	Y	Y	Y	Y
FLORIDA						
Rubio	Y	Y	Y	Y	Y	Y
Scott	Y	Y	Y	Y	Y	Y
GEORGIA						
Isakson	Y	Y	Y	Y	Y	Y
Perdue	Y	Y	Y	Y	Y	Y
HAWAII						
Schatz	N	Y	N	N	Y	N
Hirono	N	N	N	N	N	N
IDAHO						
Crapo	Y	Y	Y	Y	Y	Y
Risch	Y	Y	Y	Y	Y	Y
ILLINOIS						
Durbin	Y	Y	Y	Y	Y	Y
Duckworth	N	Y	Y	Y	+	+
INDIANA						
Young	Y	Y	Y	Y	Y	Y
Braun	Y	Y	Y	Y	Y	Y
IOWA						
Grassley	Y	Y	Y	Y	Y	Y
Ernst	Y	Y	Y	Y	Y	Y
KANSAS						
Roberts	Y	Y	Y	Y	Y	Y
Moran	+	+	+	+	+	+
KENTUCKY						
McConnell	Y	Y	Y	Y	Y	Y
Paul	Y	Y	Y	Y	Y	Y
LOUISIANA						
Cassidy	Y	Y	Y	Y	Y	Y
Kennedy	Y	Y	Y	Y	Y	Y
MAINE						
Collins	Y	Y	Y	Y	Y	Y
King	Y	Y	Y	Y	Y	Y
MARYLAND						
Cardin	Y	Y	Y	Y	Y	Y
Van Hollen	N	Y	?	Y	Y	Y
MASSACHUSETTS						
Warren	?	?	?	?	?	?
Markey	N	N	N	N	N	N
MICHIGAN						
Stabenow	Y	N	Y	Y	N	Y
Peters	Y	Y	Y	Y	Y	Y
MINNESOTA						
Klobuchar	N	N	N	N	N	N
Smith	N	N	Y	Y	N	Y
MISSISSIPPI						
Wicker	Y	Y	Y	Y	Y	Y
Hyde-Smith	Y	Y	Y	Y	Y	Y
MISSOURI						
Blunt	Y	Y	Y	Y	Y	Y
Hawley	Y	Y	Y	Y	Y	Y

	133	134	135	136	137	138
MONTANA						
Tester	Y	Y	Y	Y	Y	Y
Daines	Y	Y	Y	Y	Y	Y
NEBRASKA						
Fischer	Y	Y	Y	Y	Y	Y
Sasse	Y	Y	Y	Y	Y	Y
NEVADA						
Cortez Masto	Y	Y	Y	Y	Y	Y
Rosen	Y	Y	Y	Y	Y	Y
NEW HAMPSHIRE						
Shaheen	Y	Y	Y	Y	Y	Y
Hassan	Y	Y	Y	Y	Y	Y
NEW JERSEY						
Menendez	Y	Y	Y	Y	Y	Y
Booker	N	N	N	N	N	N
NEW MEXICO						
Udall	N	N	N	N	N	Y
Heinrich	N	Y	Y	Y	Y	Y
NEW YORK						
Schumer	Y	Y	N	N	Y	N
Gillibrand	?	?	?	?	?	?
NORTH CAROLINA						
Burr	Y	Y	Y	Y	Y	Y
Tillis	Y	Y	Y	Y	Y	Y
NORTH DAKOTA						
Hoeven	Y	Y	Y	Y	Y	Y
Cramer	Y	Y	Y	Y	Y	Y
OHIO						
Brown	Y	N	Y	Y	N	Y
Portman	Y	Y	Y	Y	Y	Y
OKLAHOMA						
Inhofe	Y	Y	Y	Y	Y	Y
Lankford	Y	Y	Y	Y	Y	Y
OREGON						
Wyden	Y	Y	Y	Y	Y	Y
Merkley	N	Y	N	N	Y	N
PENNSYLVANIA						
Casey	Y	Y	Y	Y	Y	Y
Toomey	Y	Y	Y	Y	Y	Y
RHODE ISLAND						
Reed	N	Y	N	N	Y	Y
Whitehouse	N	Y	Y	Y	Y	Y
SOUTH CAROLINA						
Graham	Y	Y	Y	Y	Y	Y
Scott	Y	Y	Y	Y	Y	Y
SOUTH DAKOTA						
Thune	Y	Y	Y	Y	Y	Y
Rounds	Y	Y	Y	Y	Y	Y
TENNESSEE						
Alexander	+	+	+	+	+	+
Blackburn	Y	Y	Y	Y	Y	Y
TEXAS						
Cornyn	Y	Y	Y	Y	Y	Y
Cruz	Y	Y	Y	Y	Y	+
UTAH						
Lee	Y	Y	Y	Y	Y	Y
Romney	Y	Y	Y	Y	Y	Y
VERMONT						
Leahy	Y	Y	Y	Y	Y	Y
Sanders	?	?	?	?	?	?
VIRGINIA						
Warner	Y	Y	Y	Y	Y	Y
Kaine	Y	N	Y	Y	N	Y
WASHINGTON						
Murray	N	Y	Y	Y	Y	Y
Cantwell	Y	Y	Y	Y	Y	Y
WEST VIRGINIA						
Manchin	Y	Y	Y	Y	Y	Y
Capito	Y	Y	Y	Y	Y	Y
WISCONSIN						
Johnson	Y	Y	Y	Y	Y	Y
Baldwin	N	N	Y	Y	N	Y
WYOMING						
Enzi	Y	Y	Y	Y	Y	Y
Barrasso	Y	Y	Y	Y	Y	Y

KEY: **Republicans**   Democrats   *Independents*

Y Voted for (yea)	**N** Voted against (nay)	**P** Voted "present"
+ Announced for	**−** Announced against	**?** Did not vote or otherwise make position known
# Paired for	**X** Paired against	

139. Tarbert Nomination - Confirmation. Confirmation of President Trump's nomination of Heath Tarbert of Maryland to be a commissioner of the Commodity Futures Trading Commission. Confirmed 85-9: R 51-0; D 33-9; I 1-0. *Note: A "yea" was a vote in support of the president's position.* June 05, 2019.

140. Combs Nomination - Cloture. Motion to invoke cloture (thus limiting debate) on the nomination of Susan Combs of Texas to be an assistant secretary of the Interior. Motion agreed to 56-37: R 50-0; D 5-37; I 1-0. *Note: A majority of senators voting (47 in this case), a quorum being present, is required to invoke cloture on all nominations.* June 05, 2019.

141. Combs Nomination - Confirmation. Confirmation of President Trump's nomination of Susan Combs of Texas to be an assistant secretary of the Interior. Confirmed 57-36: R 51-0; D 5-36; I 1-0. *Note: A "yea" was a vote in support of the president's position.* June 05, 2019.

142. Holte Nomination - Cloture. Motion to invoke cloture (thus limiting debate) on the nomination of Ryan Holte to be a judge of the U.S. Court of Federal Claims. Motion agreed to 60-33: R 51-0; D 8-33; I 1-0. *Note: A majority of senators voting (47 in this case), a quorum being present, is required to invoke cloture on all nominations.* June 05, 2019.

143. Alston Nomination - Cloture. Motion to invoke cloture (thus limiting debate) on the nomination of Rossie Alston, Jr. of Virginia to be a U.S. district judge for the Eastern District of Virginia. Motion agreed to 74-19: R 51-0; D 22-19; I 1-0. *Note: A majority of senators voting (47 in this case), a quorum being present, is required to invoke cloture on all nominations.* June 05, 2019.

144. Hertling Nomination - Cloture. Motion to invoke cloture (thus limiting debate) on the nomination of Richard Hertling of Maryland to be a judge of the U.S. Court of Federal Claims. Motion agreed to 66-23: R 48-0; D 17-23; I 1-0. *Note: A majority of senators voting (47 in this case), a quorum being present, is required to invoke cloture on all nominations.* June 05, 2019.

	139	140	141	142	143	144
ALABAMA						
Shelby	Y	Y	Y	Y	Y	Y
Jones	Y	Y	Y	Y	Y	Y
ALASKA						
Murkowski	Y	Y	Y	Y	Y	Y
Sullivan	Y	Y	Y	Y	Y	Y
ARIZONA						
Sinema	Y	Y	Y	Y	Y	Y
McSally	Y	Y	Y	Y	Y	Y
ARKANSAS						
Boozman	Y	Y	Y	Y	Y	Y
Cotton	Y	Y	Y	Y	Y	Y
CALIFORNIA						
Feinstein	Y	N	N	N	Y	Y
Harris	N	N	N	N	N	N
COLORADO						
Bennet	Y	N	N	N	Y	N
Gardner	Y	Y	Y	Y	Y	Y
CONNECTICUT						
Blumenthal	N	N	N	N	N	N
Murphy	Y	Y	Y	N	Y	Y
DELAWARE						
Carper	Y	N	N	Y	Y	Y
Coons	Y	N	N	Y	Y	Y
FLORIDA						
Rubio	Y	Y	Y	Y	Y	+
Scott	Y	Y	Y	Y	Y	Y
GEORGIA						
Isakson	Y	Y	Y	Y	Y	Y
Perdue	Y	Y	Y	Y	Y	Y
HAWAII						
Schatz	N	N	N	N	N	N
Hirono	N	N	N	N	N	N
IDAHO						
Crapo	Y	Y	Y	Y	Y	Y
Risch	Y	Y	Y	Y	Y	Y
ILLINOIS						
Durbin	Y	N	N	Y	Y	Y
Duckworth	?	–	N	N	N	N
INDIANA						
Young	Y	Y	Y	Y	Y	Y
Braun	Y	Y	Y	Y	Y	Y
IOWA						
Grassley	Y	Y	Y	Y	Y	Y
Ernst	Y	Y	Y	Y	Y	Y
KANSAS						
Roberts	Y	Y	Y	Y	Y	Y
Moran	+	+	+	+	+	+
KENTUCKY						
McConnell	Y	Y	Y	Y	Y	Y
Paul	Y	Y	Y	Y	Y	Y
LOUISIANA						
Cassidy	Y	+	Y	Y	Y	Y
Kennedy	Y	Y	Y	Y	Y	Y
MAINE						
Collins	Y	Y	Y	Y	Y	Y
King	Y	Y	Y	Y	Y	Y
MARYLAND						
Cardin	Y	N	N	N	Y	Y
Van Hollen	Y	N	N	N	Y	N
MASSACHUSETTS						
Warren	?	?	?	?	?	?
Markey	N	N	–	–	–	–
MICHIGAN						
Stabenow	Y	N	N	N	Y	N
Peters	Y	N	N	N	N	N
MINNESOTA						
Klobuchar	N	N	N	N	N	?
Smith	Y	N	N	N	Y	N
MISSISSIPPI						
Wicker	Y	Y	Y	Y	Y	Y
Hyde-Smith	Y	Y	Y	Y	Y	Y
MISSOURI						
Blunt	Y	Y	Y	Y	Y	Y
Hawley	Y	Y	Y	Y	Y	Y

	139	140	141	142	143	144
MONTANA						
Tester	Y	N	N	Y	Y	Y
Daines	Y	Y	Y	Y	Y	Y
NEBRASKA						
Fischer	Y	Y	Y	Y	Y	Y
Sasse	Y	Y	Y	Y	Y	Y
NEVADA						
Cortez Masto	Y	N	N	N	N	N
Rosen	Y	N	N	N	Y	N
NEW HAMPSHIRE						
Shaheen	Y	N	N	N	Y	N
Hassan	Y	N	N	N	Y	N
NEW JERSEY						
Menendez	Y	N	N	N	N	N
Booker	N	N	?	?	?	?
NEW MEXICO						
Udall	Y	N	N	N	N	N
Heinrich	Y	N	N	N	N	Y
NEW YORK						
Schumer	N	N	N	N	N	N
Gillibrand	?	?	?	?	?	?
NORTH CAROLINA						
Burr	Y	Y	Y	Y	Y	Y
Tillis	Y	Y	Y	Y	Y	Y
NORTH DAKOTA						
Hoeven	Y	Y	Y	Y	Y	Y
Cramer	Y	Y	Y	Y	Y	Y
OHIO						
Brown	Y	N	N	Y	N	N
Portman	Y	Y	Y	Y	Y	Y
OKLAHOMA						
Inhofe	Y	Y	Y	Y	Y	?
Lankford	Y	Y	Y	Y	Y	Y
OREGON						
Wyden	Y	N	N	N	N	N
Merkley	N	N	N	N	N	N
PENNSYLVANIA						
Casey	Y	N	N	Y	Y	N
Toomey	Y	Y	Y	Y	Y	?
RHODE ISLAND						
Reed	Y	N	N	N	Y	Y
Whitehouse	Y	N	N	N	Y	Y
SOUTH CAROLINA						
Graham	Y	Y	Y	Y	Y	Y
Scott	Y	Y	Y	Y	Y	Y
SOUTH DAKOTA						
Thune	Y	Y	Y	Y	Y	Y
Rounds	Y	Y	Y	Y	Y	Y
TENNESSEE						
Alexander	+	+	+	+	+	+
Blackburn	Y	Y	Y	Y	Y	Y
TEXAS						
Cornyn	Y	Y	Y	Y	Y	Y
Cruz	Y	Y	Y	Y	Y	Y
UTAH						
Lee	Y	Y	Y	Y	Y	Y
Romney	Y	Y	Y	Y	Y	Y
VERMONT						
Leahy	Y	N	N	N	Y	Y
Sanders	?	?	?	?	?	?
VIRGINIA						
Warner	Y	N	N	N	Y	Y
Kaine	Y	N	N	N	Y	Y
WASHINGTON						
Murray	Y	N	N	N	N	N
Cantwell	Y	Y	Y	N	N	N
WEST VIRGINIA						
Manchin	Y	Y	Y	Y	Y	Y
Capito	Y	Y	Y	Y	Y	Y
WISCONSIN						
Johnson	Y	Y	Y	Y	Y	Y
Baldwin	Y	N	N	N	N	Y
WYOMING						
Enzi	Y	Y	Y	Y	Y	Y
Barrasso	Y	Y	Y	Y	Y	Y

KEY:	**Republicans**	Democrats	*Independents*
Y Voted for (yea)	N Voted against (nay)	P Voted "present"	
+ Announced for	– Announced against	? Did not vote or otherwise	
# Paired for	X Paired against	make position known	

145. Holte Nomination - Confirmation. Confirmation of President Trump's nomination of Ryan Holte of Ohio to be a judge of the U.S. Court of Federal Claims. Confirmed 60-35: R 51-0; D 8-34; I 1-1. *Note: A "yea" was a vote in support of the president's position.* June 10, 2019.

146. Alston Nomination - Confirmation. Confirmation of President Trump's nomination of Rossie Alston, Jr. of Virginia to be a U.S. district judge for the Eastern District of Virginia. Confirmed 75-20: R 51-0; D 23-19; I 1-1. *Note: A "yea" was a vote in support of the president's position.* June 10, 2019.

147. Hertling Nomination - Confirmation. Confirmation of President Trump's nomination of Richard Hertling of Maryland to be a judge of the U.S. Court of Federal Claims. Confirmed 69-27: R 51-0; D 17-26; I 1-1. *Note: A "yea" was a vote in support of the president's position.* June 10, 2019.

148. Morrison Nomination - Cloture. Motion to invoke cloture (thus limiting debate) on the nomination of Sarah Morrison of Ohio to be a U.S. district judge for the Southern District of Ohio. Motion agreed to 89-7: R 51-0; D 37-6; I 1-1. *Note: A majority of senators voting (49 in this case), a quorum being present, is required to invoke cloture on all nominations.* June 10, 2019.

149. Morrison Nomination - Confirmation. Confirmation of President Trump's nomination of Sarah Morrison of Ohio to be a U.S. district judge for the Southern District of Ohio. Confirmed 89-7: R 50-0; D 38-6; I 1-1. *Note: A "yea" was a vote in support of the president's position.* June 11, 2019.

150. Barker Nomination - Cloture. Motion to invoke cloture (thus limiting debate) on the nomination of Pamela Barker of Ohio to be a U.S. district judge for the Northern District of Ohio. Motion agreed to 89-7: R 50-0; D 38-6; I 1-1. *Note: A majority of senators voting (49 in this case), a quorum being present, is required to invoke cloture on all nominations.* June 11, 2019.

	145	146	147	148	149	150		145	146	147	148	149	150
ALABAMA							**MONTANA**						
Shelby	Y	Y	Y	Y	Y	Y	Tester	Y	Y	Y	Y	Y	Y
Jones	Y	Y	Y	Y	Y	Y	Daines	Y	Y	Y	Y	Y	Y
ALASKA							**NEBRASKA**						
Murkowski	Y	Y	Y	Y	Y	Y	Fischer	Y	Y	Y	Y	?	?
Sullivan	Y	Y	Y	Y	Y	Y	Sasse	Y	Y	Y	Y	Y	Y
ARIZONA							**NEVADA**						
Sinema	Y	Y	Y	Y	Y	Y	Cortez Masto	N	N	N	Y	Y	Y
McSally	Y	Y	Y	Y	Y	Y	Rosen	N	Y	N	Y	Y	Y
ARKANSAS							**NEW HAMPSHIRE**						
Boozman	Y	Y	Y	Y	Y	Y	Shaheen	N	Y	N	Y	Y	Y
Cotton	Y	Y	Y	Y	Y	Y	Hassan	N	Y	N	Y	Y	Y
CALIFORNIA							**NEW JERSEY**						
Feinstein	N	Y	Y	Y	Y	Y	Menendez	N	N	N	Y	Y	Y
Harris	-	-	-	?	N	N	Booker	N	Y	N	N	?	?
COLORADO							**NEW MEXICO**						
Bennet	N	Y	N	Y	Y	Y	Udall	N	N	N	Y	Y	Y
Gardner	Y	Y	Y	Y	Y	Y	Heinrich	N	N	Y	Y	Y	Y
CONNECTICUT							**NEW YORK**						
Blumenthal	N	N	N	N	N	Y	Schumer	N	N	N	Y	Y	Y
Murphy	N	Y	Y	Y	Y	Y	Gillibrand	N	N	N	N	N	N
DELAWARE							**NORTH CAROLINA**						
Carper	Y	Y	Y	Y	Y	Y	Burr	Y	Y	Y	Y	Y	Y
Coons	Y	Y	Y	Y	Y	Y	Tillis	Y	Y	Y	Y	Y	Y
FLORIDA							**NORTH DAKOTA**						
Rubio	Y	Y	Y	Y	Y	Y	Hoeven	Y	Y	Y	Y	Y	Y
Scott	Y	Y	Y	Y	Y	Y	Cramer	Y	Y	Y	Y	Y	Y
GEORGIA							**OHIO**						
Isakson	Y	Y	Y	Y	Y	Y	Brown	Y	N	N	Y	Y	Y
Perdue	Y	Y	Y	Y	Y	Y	Portman	Y	Y	Y	Y	Y	Y
HAWAII							**OKLAHOMA**						
Schatz	N	N	N	Y	Y	Y	Inhofe	Y	Y	Y	Y	Y	Y
Hirono	N	N	N	N	Y	N	Lankford	Y	Y	Y	Y	Y	Y
IDAHO							**OREGON**						
Crapo	Y	Y	Y	Y	Y	Y	Wyden	N	N	N	Y	Y	Y
Risch	Y	Y	Y	Y	Y	Y	Merkley	N	N	N	Y	Y	Y
ILLINOIS							**PENNSYLVANIA**						
Durbin	Y	Y	Y	Y	Y	Y	Casey	N	Y	N	Y	Y	Y
Duckworth	N	N	N	Y	Y	Y	Toomey	Y	Y	Y	Y	Y	Y
INDIANA							**RHODE ISLAND**						
Young	Y	Y	Y	Y	Y	Y	Reed	N	Y	Y	Y	Y	Y
Braun	Y	Y	Y	Y	Y	Y	Whitehouse	N	Y	Y	Y	Y	Y
IOWA							**SOUTH CAROLINA**						
Grassley	Y	Y	Y	Y	Y	Y	Graham	Y	Y	Y	Y	Y	Y
Ernst	Y	Y	Y	Y	?	?	Scott	Y	Y	Y	Y	Y	Y
KANSAS							**SOUTH DAKOTA**						
Roberts	Y	Y	Y	Y	Y	Y	Thune	Y	Y	Y	Y	Y	Y
Moran	Y	Y	Y	Y	Y	Y	Rounds	Y	Y	Y	Y	Y	Y
KENTUCKY							**TENNESSEE**						
McConnell	Y	Y	Y	Y	Y	Y	Alexander	?	+	+	+	+	+
Paul	Y	Y	Y	Y	Y	Y	Blackburn	Y	Y	Y	Y	Y	Y
LOUISIANA							**TEXAS**						
Cassidy	Y	Y	Y	Y	Y	Y	Cornyn	Y	Y	Y	Y	Y	Y
Kennedy	Y	Y	Y	Y	Y	Y	Cruz	Y	Y	Y	Y	Y	Y
MAINE							**UTAH**						
Collins	Y	Y	Y	Y	Y	Y	Lee	Y	Y	Y	Y	Y	Y
King	Y	Y	Y	Y	Y	Y	Romney	Y	Y	Y	Y	Y	Y
MARYLAND							**VERMONT**						
Cardin	N	Y	Y	Y	Y	Y	Leahy	N	Y	Y	Y	Y	Y
Van Hollen	N	Y	N	Y	Y	Y	*Sanders*	N	N	N	N	N	N
MASSACHUSETTS							**VIRGINIA**						
Warren	?	?	N	N	N	N	Warner	N	N	Y	Y	Y	Y
Markey	N	N	N	N	N	N	Kaine	N	Y	Y	Y	Y	Y
MICHIGAN							**WASHINGTON**						
Stabenow	N	Y	N	Y	Y	Y	Murray	N	N	N	Y	Y	Y
Peters	N	N	N	Y	Y	Y	Cantwell	N	N	N	Y	Y	Y
MINNESOTA							**WEST VIRGINIA**						
Klobuchar	?	?	?	?	N	N	Manchin	Y	Y	Y	Y	Y	Y
Smith	N	N	N	Y	Y	Y	Capito	?	?	?	?	Y	Y
MISSISSIPPI							**WISCONSIN**						
Wicker	Y	Y	Y	Y	Y	Y	Johnson	Y	Y	Y	Y	Y	Y
Hyde-Smith	Y	Y	Y	Y	Y	Y	Baldwin	N	N	Y	Y	Y	Y
MISSOURI							**WYOMING**						
Blunt	Y	Y	Y	Y	Y	Y	Enzi	Y	Y	Y	Y	Y	Y
Hawley	Y	Y	Y	Y	Y	Y	Barrasso	Y	Y	Y	Y	Y	Y

KEY: Republicans   Democrats   *Independents*

Y Voted for (yea)	**N** Voted against (nay)	**P** Voted "present"
+ Announced for	**-** Announced against	**?** Did not vote or otherwise
# Paired for	**X** Paired against	make position known

151. Maze Nomination - Cloture. Motion to invoke cloture (thus limiting debate) on the nomination of Corey Maze of Alabama to be a U.S. district judge for the Northern District of Alabama. Motion agreed to 62-34: R 50-0; D 12-32; I 0-2. *Note: A majority of senators voting (49 in this case), a quorum being present, is required to invoke cloture on all nominations.* June 11, 2019.

152. Smith Nomination - Cloture. Motion to invoke cloture (thus limiting debate) on the nomination of Rodney Smith of Florida to be a U.S. district judge for the Southern District of Florida. Motion agreed to 77-19: R 50-0; D 26-18; I 1-1. *Note: A majority of senators voting (49 in this case), a quorum being present, is required to invoke cloture on all nominations.* June 11, 2019.

153. Barber Nomination - Cloture. Motion to invoke cloture (thus limiting debate) on the nomination of Thomas Barber of Florida to be a U.S. district judge for the Middle District of Florida. Motion agreed to 75-21: R 50-0; D 24-20; I 1-1. *Note: A majority of senators voting (49 in this case), a quorum being present, is required to invoke cloture on all nominations.* June 11, 2019.

154. Boulee Nomination - Cloture. Motion to invoke cloture (thus limiting debate) on the nomination of Jean-Paul Boulee of Georgia to be a U.S. district judge for the Northern District of Georgia. Motion agreed to 84-12: R 50-0; D 33-11; I 1-1. *Note: A majority of senators voting (49 in this case), a quorum being present, is required to invoke cloture on all nominations.* June 11, 2019.

155. Barker Nomination - Confirmation. Confirmation of President Trump's nomination of Pamela Barker of Ohio to be a U.S. district judge for the Northern District of Ohio. Confirmed 91-5: R 51-0; D 39-5; I 1-0. *Note: A "yea" was a vote in support of the president's position.* June 12, 2019.

156. Maze Nomination - Confirmation. Confirmation of President Trump's nomination of Corey Maze of Alabama to be a U.S. district judge for the Northern District of Alabama. Confirmed 62-34: R 51-0; D 11-33; I 0-1. *Note: A "yea" was a vote in support of the president's position.* June 12, 2019.

	151	152	153	154	155	156
ALABAMA						
Shelby	Y	Y	Y	Y	Y	Y
Jones	Y	Y	Y	Y	Y	Y
ALASKA						
Murkowski	Y	Y	Y	Y	Y	Y
Sullivan	Y	Y	Y	Y	Y	Y
ARIZONA						
Sinema	Y	Y	Y		Y	Y
McSally	Y	Y	Y	Y	Y	Y
ARKANSAS						
Boozman	Y	Y	Y	Y	Y	Y
Cotton	Y	Y	Y	Y	Y	Y
CALIFORNIA						
Feinstein	N	Y	Y	Y	Y	N
Harris	N	N	N	N	N	N
COLORADO						
Bennet	N	Y	Y	Y	Y	N
Gardner	Y	Y	Y	Y	Y	Y
CONNECTICUT						
Blumenthal	N	N	N	Y	Y	N
Murphy	N	Y	Y	Y	Y	N
DELAWARE						
Carper	Y	Y	Y		Y	Y
Coons	N	Y	Y	Y	Y	N
FLORIDA						
Rubio	Y	Y	Y	Y	Y	Y
Scott	Y	Y	Y	Y	Y	Y
GEORGIA						
Isakson	Y	Y	Y	Y	Y	Y
Perdue	Y	Y	Y	Y	Y	Y
HAWAII						
Schatz	Y	N	N	N	Y	Y
Hirono	N	N	N	N	Y	N
IDAHO						
Crapo	Y	Y	Y	Y	Y	Y
Risch	Y	Y	Y	Y	Y	Y
ILLINOIS						
Durbin	N	Y	Y	N	Y	N
Duckworth	N	Y	Y	Y	Y	N
INDIANA						
Young	Y	Y	Y	Y	Y	Y
Braun	Y	Y	Y	Y	Y	Y
IOWA						
Grassley	Y	Y	Y	Y	Y	Y
Ernst	?	?	?	?	Y	Y
KANSAS						
Roberts	Y	Y	Y	Y	Y	Y
Moran	Y	Y	Y	Y	Y	Y
KENTUCKY						
McConnell	Y	Y	Y	Y	Y	Y
Paul	Y	Y	Y	Y	Y	Y
LOUISIANA						
Cassidy	Y	Y	Y	Y	Y	Y
Kennedy	Y	Y	Y	Y	Y	Y
MAINE						
Collins	Y	Y	Y	Y	Y	Y
King	N	Y	Y	Y	Y	N
MARYLAND						
Cardin	Y	Y	Y	Y	Y	Y
Van Hollen	N	N	N	N	Y	N
MASSACHUSETTS						
Warren	N	N	N	N	N	N
Markey	N	N	N	N	N	N
MICHIGAN						
Stabenow	N	N	N	Y	Y	N
Peters	N	N	N	Y	Y	N
MINNESOTA						
Klobuchar	N	N	N	N	N	N
Smith	N	N	N	Y	N	N
MISSISSIPPI						
Wicker	Y	Y	Y	Y	Y	Y
Hyde-Smith	Y	Y	Y	Y	Y	Y
MISSOURI						
Blunt	Y	Y	Y	Y	Y	Y
Hawley	Y	Y	Y	Y	Y	Y

	151	152	153	154	155	156
MONTANA						
Tester	N	Y	Y	Y	Y	N
Daines	Y	Y	Y	Y	?	?
NEBRASKA						
Fischer	?	?	?	?	Y	Y
Sasse	Y	Y	Y	Y	Y	Y
NEVADA						
Cortez Masto	Y	Y	Y	Y	Y	Y
Rosen	Y	Y	Y	Y	Y	Y
NEW HAMPSHIRE						
Shaheen	Y	Y	Y	Y	Y	N
Hassan	Y	N	Y	Y	Y	Y
NEW JERSEY						
Menendez	N	N	N	N	Y	N
Booker	?	?	?	?	?	?
NEW MEXICO						
Udall	N	Y	Y	Y	Y	N
Heinrich	N	Y	Y	Y	Y	N
NEW YORK						
Schumer	N	N	N	N	N	N
Gillibrand	N	N	N	N	N	N
NORTH CAROLINA						
Burr	Y	Y	Y	Y	Y	Y
Tillis	Y	Y	Y	Y	Y	Y
NORTH DAKOTA						
Hoeven	Y	Y	Y	Y	Y	Y
Cramer	Y	Y	Y	Y	Y	Y
OHIO						
Brown	Y	Y	N	Y	Y	Y
Portman	Y	Y	Y	Y	Y	Y
OKLAHOMA						
Inhofe	Y	Y	Y	Y	Y	Y
Lankford	Y	Y	Y	Y	Y	Y
OREGON						
Wyden	N	N	N	Y	Y	N
Merkley	N	N	N	Y	Y	N
PENNSYLVANIA						
Casey	N	N	N	Y	Y	N
Toomey	Y	Y	Y	Y	Y	Y
RHODE ISLAND						
Reed	N	Y	Y	Y	Y	N
Whitehouse	N	Y	Y	Y	Y	N
SOUTH CAROLINA						
Graham	Y	Y	Y	Y	Y	Y
Scott	Y	Y	Y	Y	Y	Y
SOUTH DAKOTA						
Thune	Y	Y	Y	Y	Y	Y
Rounds	Y	Y	Y	Y	Y	Y
TENNESSEE						
Alexander	+	+	+	+	?	?
Blackburn	Y	Y	Y	Y	Y	Y
TEXAS						
Cornyn	Y	Y	Y	Y	Y	Y
Cruz	Y	Y	Y	Y	Y	Y
UTAH						
Lee	Y	Y	Y	Y	Y	Y
Romney	Y	Y	Y	Y	Y	Y
VERMONT						
Leahy	Y	Y	Y	Y	Y	Y
Sanders	N	N	N	N	?	?
VIRGINIA						
Warner	N	Y	Y	Y	Y	N
Kaine	N	Y	Y	Y	Y	N
WASHINGTON						
Murray	N	Y	N	Y	Y	N
Cantwell	N	Y	N	Y	Y	N
WEST VIRGINIA						
Manchin	Y	Y	Y	Y	Y	Y
Capito	Y	Y	Y	Y	Y	Y
WISCONSIN						
Johnson	Y	Y	Y	Y	Y	Y
Baldwin	N	Y	N	Y	Y	N
WYOMING						
Enzi	Y	Y	Y	Y	Y	Y
Barrasso	Y	Y	Y	Y	Y	Y

KEY:	**Republicans**	Democrats	*Independents*
Y Voted for (yea)	N Voted against (nay)	P Voted "present"	
+ Announced for	– Announced against	? Did not vote or otherwise	
# Paired for	X Paired against	make position known	

157. Smith Nomination - Confirmation. Confirmation of President Trump's nomination of Rodney Smith of Florida to be a U.S. district judge for the Southern District of Florida. Confirmed 78-18: R 51-0; D 26-18; I 1-0. *Note: A "yea" was a vote in support of the president's position.* June 12, 2019.

158. Barber Nomination - Confirmation. Confirmation of President Trump's nomination of Thomas Barber of Florida to be a U.S. district judge for the Middle District of Florida. Confirmed 77-19: R 51-0; D 25-19; I 1-0. *Note: A "yea" was a vote in support of the president's position.* June 12, 2019.

159. Boulee Nomination - Confirmation. Confirmation of President Trump's nomination of Jean-Paul Boulee of Georgia to be a U.S. district judge for the Northern District of Georgia. Confirmed 85-11: R 51-0; D 33-11; I 1-0. *Note: A "yea" was a vote in support of the president's position.* June 12, 2019.

160. Stilwell Nomination - Cloture. Motion to invoke cloture (thus limiting debate) on the nomination of David Stilwell of Hawaii to be an assistant secretary of State (East Asian and Pacific Affairs). Motion agreed to 93-4: R 51-0; D 41-3; I 1-1. *Note: A majority of senators voting (49 in this case), a quorum being present, is required to invoke cloture on all nominations.* June 12, 2019.

161. SJRES20. Bahrain Arm Sales - Motion to Discharge. Paul, R-Ky., motion to discharge the Senate Foreign Relations Committee from further consideration of a joint resolution that would disapprove of the proposed export to the government of the Kingdom of Bahrain of certain defense articles and services. Motion rejected 43-56: R 3-49; D 39-6; I 1-1. *Note: A "nay" was a vote in support of the president's position.* June 13, 2019.

162. SJRES26. Qatar Arm Sales - Motion to Discharge. Paul, R-Ky., motion to discharge the Senate Foreign Relations Committee from further consideration of a joint resolution that would disapprove of the proposed export to the government of Qatar of certain defense articles and services. Motion rejected 42-57: R 3-49; D 38-7; I 1-1. *Note: A "nay" was a vote in support of the president's position.* June 13, 2019.

State/Senator	157	158	159	160	161	162
ALABAMA						
Shelby	Y	Y	Y	Y	N	N
Jones	Y	Y	Y	Y	N	N
ALASKA						
Murkowski	Y	Y	Y	Y	N	N
Sullivan	Y	Y	Y	Y	N	N
ARIZONA						
Sinema	Y	Y	Y	Y	N	N
McSally	Y	Y	Y	Y	N	N
ARKANSAS						
Boozman	Y	Y	Y	Y	N	N
Cotton	Y	Y	Y	Y	N	N
CALIFORNIA						
Feinstein	Y	Y	Y	Y	Y	Y
Harris	N	N	N	N	Y	Y
COLORADO						
Bennet	Y	Y	Y	Y	Y	Y
Gardner	Y	Y	Y	Y	N	N
CONNECTICUT						
Blumenthal	N	N	N	Y	Y	Y
Murphy	Y	Y	Y	Y	Y	Y
DELAWARE						
Carper	Y	Y	Y	Y	Y	Y
Coons	Y	Y	Y	Y	Y	Y
FLORIDA						
Rubio	Y	Y	Y	Y	N	N
Scott	Y	Y	Y	Y	N	N
GEORGIA						
Isakson	Y	Y	Y	Y	N	N
Perdue	Y	Y	Y	Y	N	N
HAWAII						
Schatz	N	N	N	Y	Y	Y
Hirono	N	N	N	Y	Y	Y
IDAHO						
Crapo	Y	Y	Y	Y	N	N
Risch	Y	Y	Y	Y	N	N
ILLINOIS						
Durbin	Y	Y	Y	Y	Y	Y
Duckworth	Y	Y	Y	Y	Y	Y
INDIANA						
Young	Y	Y	Y	Y	N	N
Braun	Y	Y	Y	Y	N	N
IOWA						
Grassley	Y	Y	Y	Y	N	N
Ernst	Y	Y	Y	Y	N	N
KANSAS						
Roberts	Y	Y	Y	Y	N	N
Moran	Y	Y	Y	Y	Y	N
KENTUCKY						
McConnell	Y	Y	Y	Y	N	N
Paul	Y	Y	Y	Y	Y	Y
LOUISIANA						
Cassidy	Y	Y	Y	Y	N	N
Kennedy	Y	Y	Y	Y	N	N
MAINE						
Collins	Y	Y	Y	Y	N	N
King	Y	Y	Y	Y	N	N
MARYLAND						
Cardin	Y	Y	Y	Y	Y	Y
Van Hollen	N	N	Y	Y	Y	Y
MASSACHUSETTS						
Warren	N	N	N	N	Y	Y
Markey	N	N	N	Y	Y	Y
MICHIGAN						
Stabenow	N	N	Y	Y	Y	Y
Peters	N	N	Y	Y	Y	Y
MINNESOTA						
Klobuchar	N	N	N	Y	Y	Y
Smith	N	N	Y	Y	Y	Y
MISSISSIPPI						
Wicker	Y	Y	Y	Y	N	N
Hyde-Smith	Y	Y	Y	Y	N	N
MISSOURI						
Blunt	Y	Y	Y	Y	N	N
Hawley	Y	Y	Y	Y	N	N
MONTANA						
Tester	Y	Y	Y	Y	N	N
Daines	?	?	?	?	N	N
NEBRASKA						
Fischer	Y	Y	Y	Y	N	N
Sasse	Y	Y	Y	Y	N	N
NEVADA						
Cortez Masto	Y	Y	Y	Y	Y	Y
Rosen	Y	Y	Y	Y	Y	Y
NEW HAMPSHIRE						
Shaheen	Y	Y	Y	Y	N	N
Hassan	N	Y	Y	Y	Y	Y
NEW JERSEY						
Menendez	N	N	N	Y	Y	Y
Booker	?	?	?	?	Y	Y
NEW MEXICO						
Udall	Y	Y	Y	Y	Y	Y
Heinrich	Y	Y	Y	Y	Y	Y
NEW YORK						
Schumer	N	N	N	Y	Y	Y
Gillibrand	N	N	N	N	Y	Y
NORTH CAROLINA						
Burr	Y	Y	Y	Y	N	N
Tillis	Y	Y	Y	Y	N	N
NORTH DAKOTA						
Hoeven	Y	Y	Y	Y	N	N
Cramer	Y	Y	Y	Y	N	N
OHIO						
Brown	N	Y	N	N	Y	Y
Portman	Y	Y	Y	Y	N	N
OKLAHOMA						
Inhofe	Y	Y	Y	Y	N	N
Lankford	Y	Y	Y	Y	N	N
OREGON						
Wyden	N	N	Y	Y	Y	Y
Merkley	N	N	Y	Y	Y	Y
PENNSYLVANIA						
Casey	N	Y	N	Y	Y	Y
Toomey	Y	Y	Y	Y	N	N
RHODE ISLAND						
Reed	Y	Y	Y	Y	Y	Y
Whitehouse	Y	Y	Y	Y	Y	Y
SOUTH CAROLINA						
Graham	Y	Y	Y	Y	N	N
Scott	Y	Y	Y	Y	N	N
SOUTH DAKOTA						
Thune	Y	Y	Y	Y	N	N
Rounds	Y	Y	Y	Y	N	N
TENNESSEE						
Alexander	+	+	+	+	-	-
Blackburn	Y	Y	Y	Y	N	N
TEXAS						
Cornyn	Y	Y	?	Y	N	N
Cruz	Y	Y	Y	Y	N	Y
UTAH						
Lee	Y	Y	Y	Y	Y	Y
Romney	Y	Y	Y	Y	N	N
VERMONT						
Leahy	Y	Y	Y	Y	Y	Y
Sanders	?	?	?	N	Y	Y
VIRGINIA						
Warner	Y	Y	Y	Y	N	N
Kaine	Y	Y	Y	Y	Y	Y
WASHINGTON						
Murray	Y	N	Y	Y	Y	Y
Cantwell	Y	N	Y	Y	Y	Y
WEST VIRGINIA						
Manchin	Y	Y	Y	Y	N	N
Capito	Y	Y	Y	Y	N	N
WISCONSIN						
Johnson	Y	Y	Y	Y	N	N
Baldwin	Y	N	Y	Y	Y	Y
WYOMING						
Enzi	Y	Y	Y	Y	N	N
Barrasso	Y	Y	Y	Y	N	N

KEY: Republicans   Democrats   *Independents*

Y Voted for (yea) — N Voted against (nay) — P Voted "present"
+ Announced for — − Announced against — ? Did not vote or otherwise make position known
# Paired for — X Paired against

163. Crawford Nomination - Cloture. Motion to invoke cloture (thus limiting debate) on the nomination of Edward Crawford of Ohio to be ambassador to Ireland. Motion agreed to 92-7: R 52-0; D 39-6; I 1-1. *Note: A majority of senators voting (50 in this case), a quorum being present, is required to invoke cloture on all nominations.* June 13, 2019.

164. Stilwell Nomination - Confirmation. Confirmation of President Trump's nomination of David Stilwell of Hawaii to be an assistant secretary of State (East Asian and Pacific Affairs). Confirmed 94-3: R 52-0; D 41-2; I 1-1. *Note: A "yea" was a vote in support of the president's position.* June 13, 2019.

165. Crawford Nomination - Confirmation. Confirmation of President Trump's nomination of Edward Crawford of Ohio to be ambassador to Ireland. Confirmed 90-4: R 51-0; D 38-4; I 1-0. *Note: A "yea" was a vote in support of the president's position.* June 13, 2019.

166. Cairncross Nomination - Cloture. Motion to invoke cloture (thus limiting debate) on the nomination of Sean Cairncross of Minnesota to be chief executive officer of the Millennium Challenge Corporation. Motion agreed to 59-37: R 53-0; D 5-36; I 1-1. *Note: A majority of senators voting (49 in this case), a quorum being present, is required to invoke cloture on all nominations.* June 18, 2019.

167. Cairncross Nomination - Confirmation. Confirmation of President Trump's nomination of Sean Cairncross of Minnesota to be chief executive officer of the Millennium Challenge Corporation. Confirmed 59-37: R 53-0; D 5-36; I 1-1. *Note: A "yea" was a vote in support of the president's position.* June 18, 2019.

168. Kacsmaryk Nomination - Cloture. Motion to invoke cloture (thus limiting debate) on the nomination of Matthew Kacsmaryk of Texas to be a U.S. district judge for the Northern District of Texas. Motion agreed to 52-44: R 52-1; D 0-41; I 0-2. *Note: A majority of senators voting (49 in this case), a quorum being present, is required to invoke cloture on all nominations.* June 18, 2019.

	163	164	165	166	167	168
ALABAMA						
Shelby	Y	Y	Y	Y	Y	Y
Jones	Y	Y	Y	Y	Y	N
ALASKA						
Murkowski	Y	Y	Y	Y	Y	Y
Sullivan	Y	Y	Y	Y	Y	Y
ARIZONA						
Sinema	Y	Y	Y	Y	Y	N
McSally	Y	Y	Y	Y	Y	Y
ARKANSAS						
Boozman	Y	Y	Y	Y	Y	Y
Cotton	Y	Y	Y	Y	Y	Y
CALIFORNIA						
Feinstein	N	Y	Y	N	N	N
Harris	N	N	N	?	?	?
COLORADO						
Bennet	Y	Y	Y	N	N	N
Gardner	Y	Y	Y	Y	Y	Y
CONNECTICUT						
Blumenthal	Y	Y	Y	N	N	N
Murphy	Y	Y	Y	N	N	N
DELAWARE						
Carper	Y	Y	Y	Y	Y	N
Coons	Y	Y	Y	Y	Y	N
FLORIDA						
Rubio	Y	Y	Y	Y	Y	Y
Scott	Y	Y	Y	Y	Y	Y
GEORGIA						
Isakson	Y	Y	Y	Y	Y	Y
Perdue	Y	Y	Y	Y	Y	Y
HAWAII						
Schatz	Y	Y	Y	N	N	N
Hirono	N	Y	N	-	-	-
IDAHO						
Crapo	Y	Y	Y	Y	Y	Y
Risch	Y	Y	Y	Y	Y	Y
ILLINOIS						
Durbin	Y	Y	Y	N	N	N
Duckworth	N	Y	N	N	N	N
INDIANA						
Young	Y	Y	Y	Y	Y	Y
Braun	Y	Y	Y	Y	Y	Y
IOWA						
Grassley	Y	Y	Y	Y	Y	Y
Ernst	Y	Y	Y	Y	Y	Y
KANSAS						
Roberts	Y	Y	Y	Y	Y	Y
Moran	Y	Y	Y	Y	Y	Y
KENTUCKY						
McConnell	Y	Y	Y	Y	Y	Y
Paul	Y	Y	?	Y	Y	Y
LOUISIANA						
Cassidy	Y	Y	Y	Y	Y	Y
Kennedy	Y	Y	Y	Y	Y	Y
MAINE						
Collins	Y	Y	Y	Y	Y	N
King	Y	Y	Y	Y	Y	N
MARYLAND						
Cardin	Y	Y	Y	N	N	N
Van Hollen	Y	Y	Y	N	N	N
MASSACHUSETTS						
Warren	N	N	N	N	N	N
Markey	Y	Y	Y	N	N	N
MICHIGAN						
Stabenow	Y	Y	Y	N	N	N
Peters	Y	Y	Y	N	N	N
MINNESOTA						
Klobuchar	Y	?	?	N	N	N
Smith	Y	Y	Y	N	N	N
MISSISSIPPI						
Wicker	Y	Y	Y	Y	Y	Y
Hyde-Smith	Y	Y	Y	Y	Y	Y
MISSOURI						
Blunt	Y	Y	Y	Y	Y	Y
Hawley	Y	Y	Y	Y	Y	Y

	163	164	165	166	167	168
MONTANA						
Tester	Y	Y	Y	N	N	N
Daines	Y	Y	Y	Y	Y	Y
NEBRASKA						
Fischer	Y	Y	Y	Y	Y	Y
Sasse	Y	Y	Y	Y	Y	Y
NEVADA						
Cortez Masto	Y	Y	Y	N	N	N
Rosen	Y	Y	Y	N	N	N
NEW HAMPSHIRE						
Shaheen	Y	Y	Y	N	N	N
Hassan	Y	Y	Y	N	N	N
NEW JERSEY						
Menendez	Y	Y	Y	N	N	N
Booker	Y	Y	Y	N	N	N
NEW MEXICO						
Udall	Y	Y	Y	?	N	N
Heinrich	Y	Y	Y	N	N	N
NEW YORK						
Schumer	Y	Y	Y	N	N	N
Gillibrand	N	?	?	?	?	?
NORTH CAROLINA						
Burr	Y	Y	Y	Y	Y	Y
Tillis	Y	Y	Y	Y	Y	Y
NORTH DAKOTA						
Hoeven	Y	Y	Y	Y	Y	Y
Cramer	Y	Y	Y	Y	Y	Y
OHIO						
Brown	Y	Y	Y	N	N	N
Portman	Y	Y	Y	Y	Y	Y
OKLAHOMA						
Inhofe	Y	Y	Y	Y	Y	Y
Lankford	Y	Y	Y	Y	Y	Y
OREGON						
Wyden	Y	Y	Y	N	?	?
Merkley	Y	Y	Y	N	N	N
PENNSYLVANIA						
Casey	Y	Y	Y	N	N	N
Toomey	Y	Y	Y	Y	Y	Y
RHODE ISLAND						
Reed	Y	Y	Y	N	N	N
Whitehouse	Y	Y	?	N	N	N
SOUTH CAROLINA						
Graham	Y	Y	Y	Y	Y	Y
Scott	Y	Y	Y	Y	Y	Y
SOUTH DAKOTA						
Thune	Y	Y	Y	Y	Y	Y
Rounds	Y	Y	Y	Y	Y	Y
TENNESSEE						
Alexander	+	+	+	Y	Y	Y
Blackburn	Y	Y	Y	Y	Y	Y
TEXAS						
Cornyn	Y	Y	Y	Y	Y	Y
Cruz	Y	Y	Y	Y	Y	Y
UTAH						
Lee	Y	Y	Y	Y	Y	Y
Romney	Y	Y	Y	Y	Y	Y
VERMONT						
Leahy	Y	Y	Y	N	N	N
Sanders	N	N	?	N	N	N
VIRGINIA						
Warner	Y	Y	Y	N	N	N
Kaine	Y	Y	Y	N	N	N
WASHINGTON						
Murray	Y	Y	Y	N	N	N
Cantwell	Y	Y	Y	N	N	N
WEST VIRGINIA						
Manchin	Y	Y	Y	Y	Y	N
Capito	Y	Y	Y	Y	Y	Y
WISCONSIN						
Johnson	Y	Y	Y	Y	Y	Y
Baldwin	Y	Y	Y	N	N	N
WYOMING						
Enzi	Y	Y	Y	Y	Y	Y
Barrasso	Y	Y	Y	Y	Y	Y

KEY: **Republicans**   Democrats   *Independents*

Y	Voted for (yea)	N	Voted against (nay)	P	Voted "present"
+	Announced for	–	Announced against	?	Did not vote or otherwise make position known
#	Paired for	X	Paired against		

169. Winsor Nomination - Cloture. Motion to invoke cloture (thus limiting debate) on the nomination of Allen Winsor of Florida to be a U.S. district judge for the Northern District of Florida. Motion agreed to 54-42: R 53-0; D 1-40; I 0-2. *Note: A majority of senators voting (49 in this case), a quorum being present, is required to invoke cloture on all nominations.* June 18, 2019.

170. Cain Nomination - Cloture. Motion to invoke cloture (thus limiting debate) on the nomination of James Cain, Jr. of Louisiana to be a U.S. district judge for the Western District of Louisiana. Motion agreed to 76-20: R 53-0; D 22-19; I 1-1. *Note: A majority of senators voting (49 in this case), a quorum being present, is required to invoke cloture on all nominations.* June 18, 2019.

171. Guidry Nomination - Cloture. Motion to invoke cloture (thus limiting debate) on the nomination of Greg Guidry of Louisiana to be a U.S. district judge for the Eastern District of Louisiana. Motion agreed to 53-43: R 53-0; D 0-41; I 0-2. *Note: A majority of senators voting (49 in this case), a quorum being present, is required to invoke cloture on all nominations.* June 18, 2019.

172. Kacsmaryk Nomination - Confirmation. Confirmation of President Trump's nomination of Matthew Kacsmaryk of Texas to be a U.S. district judge for the Northern District of Texas. Confirmed 52-46: R 52-1; D 0-43; I 0-2. *Note: A "yea" was a vote in support of the president's position.* June 19, 2019.

173. Winsor Nomination - Confirmation. Confirmation of President Trump's nomination of Allen Winsor of Florida to be a U.S. district judge for the Northern District of Florida. Confirmed 54-44: R 53-0; D 1-42; I 0-2. *Note: A "yea" was a vote in support of the president's position.* June 19, 2019.

174. Cain Nomination - Confirmation. Confirmation of President Trump's nomination of James Cain, Jr. of Louisiana to be a U.S. district judge for the Western District of Louisiana. Confirmed 77-21: R 53-0; D 23-20; I 1-1. *Note: A "yea" was a vote in support of the president's position.* June 19, 2019.

	169	170	171	172	173	174
ALABAMA						
Shelby	Y	Y	Y	Y	Y	Y
Jones	N	Y	N	N	N	Y
ALASKA						
Murkowski	Y	Y	Y	Y	Y	Y
Sullivan	Y	Y	Y	Y	Y	Y
ARIZONA						
Sinema	N	Y	N	N	N	Y
McSally	Y	Y	Y	Y	Y	Y
ARKANSAS						
Boozman	Y	Y	Y	Y	Y	Y
Cotton	Y	Y	Y	Y	Y	Y
CALIFORNIA						
Feinstein	N	Y	N	N	N	Y
Harris	?	?	?	N	N	N
COLORADO						
Bennet	N	Y	N	N	N	Y
Gardner	Y	Y	Y	Y	Y	Y
CONNECTICUT						
Blumenthal	N	N	N	N	N	N
Murphy	N	Y	N	N	N	Y
DELAWARE						
Carper	N	Y	N	N	N	Y
Coons	N	Y	N	N	N	Y
FLORIDA						
Rubio	Y	Y	Y	Y	Y	Y
Scott	Y	Y	Y	Y	Y	Y
GEORGIA						
Isakson	Y	Y	Y	Y	Y	Y
Perdue	Y	Y	Y	Y	Y	Y
HAWAII						
Schatz	N	N	N	N	N	N
Hirono	-	-	-	N	N	Y
IDAHO						
Crapo	Y	Y	Y	Y	Y	Y
Risch	Y	Y	Y	Y	Y	Y
ILLINOIS						
Durbin	N	Y	N	N	N	Y
Duckworth	N	N	N	N	N	N
INDIANA						
Young	Y	Y	Y	Y	Y	Y
Braun	Y	Y	Y	Y	Y	Y
IOWA						
Grassley	Y	Y	Y	Y	Y	Y
Ernst	Y	Y	Y	Y	Y	Y
KANSAS						
Roberts	Y	Y	Y	Y	Y	Y
Moran	Y	Y	Y	Y	Y	Y
KENTUCKY						
McConnell	Y	Y	Y	Y	Y	Y
Paul	Y	Y	Y	Y	Y	Y
LOUISIANA						
Cassidy	Y	Y	Y	Y	Y	Y
Kennedy	Y	Y	Y	Y	Y	Y
MAINE						
Collins	Y	Y	Y	N	Y	Y
King	N	Y	N	N	N	Y
MARYLAND						
Cardin	N	Y	N	N	N	Y
Van Hollen	N	N	N	N	N	N
MASSACHUSETTS						
Warren	N	N	N	N	N	N
Markey	N	N	N	N	N	N
MICHIGAN						
Stabenow	N	N	N	N	N	N
Peters	N	N	N	N	N	N
MINNESOTA						
Klobuchar	N	N	N	N	N	N
Smith	N	N	N	N	N	N
MISSISSIPPI						
Wicker	Y	Y	Y	Y	Y	Y
Hyde-Smith	Y	Y	Y	Y	Y	Y
MISSOURI						
Blunt	Y	Y	Y	Y	Y	Y
Hawley	Y	Y	Y	Y	Y	Y

	169	170	171	172	173	174
MONTANA						
Tester	N	Y	N	N	N	Y
Daines	Y	Y	Y	Y	Y	Y
NEBRASKA						
Fischer	Y	Y	Y	Y	Y	Y
Sasse	Y	Y	Y	Y	Y	Y
NEVADA						
Cortez Masto	N	Y	N	N	N	Y
Rosen	N	Y	N	N	N	Y
NEW HAMPSHIRE						
Shaheen	N	Y	N	N	N	Y
Hassan	N	Y	N	N	N	Y
NEW JERSEY						
Menendez	N	N	N	N	N	N
Booker	N	N	N	?	?	?
NEW MEXICO						
Udall	N	Y	N	N	N	Y
Heinrich	N	Y	N	N	N	Y
NEW YORK						
Schumer	N	N	N	N	N	N
Gillibrand	?	?	?	?	?	?
NORTH CAROLINA						
Burr	Y	Y	Y	Y	Y	Y
Tillis	Y	Y	Y	Y	Y	Y
NORTH DAKOTA						
Hoeven	Y	Y	Y	Y	Y	Y
Cramer	Y	Y	Y	Y	Y	Y
OHIO						
Brown	N	N	N	N	N	N
Portman	Y	Y	Y	Y	Y	Y
OKLAHOMA						
Inhofe	Y	Y	Y	Y	Y	Y
Lankford	Y	Y	Y	Y	Y	Y
OREGON						
Wyden	?	?	?	N	N	N
Merkley	N	N	N	N	N	N
PENNSYLVANIA						
Casey	N	N	N	N	N	N
Toomey	Y	Y	Y	Y	Y	Y
RHODE ISLAND						
Reed	N	Y	N	N	N	Y
Whitehouse	N	Y	N	N	N	Y
SOUTH CAROLINA						
Graham	Y	Y	Y	Y	Y	Y
Scott	Y	Y	Y	Y	Y	Y
SOUTH DAKOTA						
Thune	Y	Y	Y	Y	Y	Y
Rounds	Y	Y	Y	Y	Y	Y
TENNESSEE						
Alexander	Y	Y	Y	Y	Y	Y
Blackburn	Y	Y	Y	Y	Y	Y
TEXAS						
Cornyn	Y	Y	Y	Y	Y	Y
Cruz	Y	Y	Y	Y	Y	Y
UTAH						
Lee	Y	Y	Y	Y	Y	Y
Romney	Y	Y	Y	Y	Y	Y
VERMONT						
Leahy	N	Y	N	N	N	Y
Sanders	N	N	N	N	N	N
VIRGINIA						
Warner	N	Y	N	N	N	Y
Kaine	N	Y	N	N	N	Y
WASHINGTON						
Murray	N	N	N	N	N	N
Cantwell	N	N	N	N	N	N
WEST VIRGINIA						
Manchin	Y	Y	N	N	Y	Y
Capito	Y	Y	Y	Y	Y	Y
WISCONSIN						
Johnson	Y	Y	Y	Y	Y	Y
Baldwin	N	N	N	N	N	N
WYOMING						
Enzi	Y	Y	Y	Y	Y	Y
Barrasso	Y	Y	Y	Y	Y	Y

KEY: Republicans   Democrats   *Independents*

Y Voted for (yea)	**N** Voted against (nay)	**P** Voted "present"
+ Announced for	**–** Announced against	**?** Did not vote or otherwise
# Paired for	**X** Paired against	make position known

175. Guidry Nomination - Confirmation. Confirmation of President Trump's nomination of Greg Guidry of Louisiana to be a U.S. district judge for the Eastern District of Louisiana. Confirmed 53-46: R 53-0; D 0-44; I 0-2. *Note: A "yea" was a vote in support of the president's position.* June 19, 2019.

176. S1790. Fiscal 2020 Defense Authorization - Cloture. McConnell, R-Ky., motion to invoke cloture on the motion to proceed to the bill that would authorize $642.5 billion for the Defense Department's base budget, $23.2 billion for national security programs within the Energy Department and $75.9 billion to support overseas contingency operations. Among other provisions, the bill would authorize a 3.1 percent pay increase for members of the armed forces as well as authorizing $155.8 billion for costs of pay, allowances, bonuses, death benefits, and permanent change of station moves for military personnel. The bill would authorize $33 billion for the Defense Health Program and $3.31 billion in disaster recovery funding at Navy, Air Force, and Army National Guard bases located in Nebraska, North Carolina, and Florida. The bill would authorize the creation of the Space Force and establish a Space Acquisition Council. Motion agreed to 89-10: R 53-0; D 35-9; I 1-1. *Note: Three-fifths of the total Senate (60) is required to invoke cloture.* June 19, 2019.

177. SJRES36. Saudi Arabia Arms Sales - Passage. Passage of the joint resolution that would disapprove of arm sales to the Kingdom of Saudi Arabia, United Kingdom of Great Britain and Northern Ireland, the Kingdom of Spain, and the Italian Republic. Passed 53-45: R 7-45; D 44-0; I 2-0. *Note: A "nay" was a vote in support of the president's position.* June 20, 2019.

178. SJRES38. Saudi Arabia Arms Export - Passage. Passage of the joint resolution that would disapprove of the proposed export of defense articles to the Kingdom of Saudi Arabia and the United Kingdom of Great Britain and Northern Ireland. Passed 53-45: R 7-45; D 44-0; I 2-0. *Note: A "nay" was a vote in support of the president's position.* June 20, 2019.

179. SJRES40, SJRES48, SJRES47, SJRES46, SJRES45, SJRES44, SJRES43, SJRES42, SJRES41, SJRES39, SJRES37, SJRES35, SJRES34, SJRES33, SJRES32, SJRES31, SJRES30, SJRES29, SJRES28, SJRES27. Foreign Arms Sales - Passage. Passage of the joint resolutions that would disapprove of arm sales and defense weapons to Saudi Arabia, the United Arab Emirates, India, Israel, Republic of Korea, United Kingdom of Great Britain and Northern Ireland, Australia, Republic of France, and the Hashemite Kingdom of Jordan. Passed 51-45: R 5-45; D 44-0; I 2-0. *Note: A "nay" was a vote in support of the president's position.* June 20, 2019.

180. Baranwal Nomination - Confirmation. Confirmation of President Trump's nomination of Rita Baranwal of Pennsylvania to be an assistant secretary of Energy (Nuclear Energy). Confirmed 86-5: R 49-0; D 36-5; I 1-0. *Note: A "yea" was a vote in support of the president's position.* June 20, 2019.

	175	176	177	178	179	180
ALABAMA						
Shelby	Y	Y	N	N	N	Y
Jones	N	Y	Y	Y	Y	Y
ALASKA						
Murkowski	Y	Y	Y	Y	N	Y
Sullivan	Y	Y	N	N	N	Y
ARIZONA						
Sinema	N	Y	Y	Y	Y	Y
McSally	Y	Y	N	N	N	Y
ARKANSAS						
Boozman	Y	Y	N	N	N	Y
Cotton	Y	Y	N	N	N	Y
CALIFORNIA						
Feinstein	N	Y	Y	Y	Y	Y
Harris	N	N	Y	Y	Y	?
COLORADO						
Bennet	N	Y	Y	Y	Y	Y
Gardner	Y	Y	N	N	N	Y
CONNECTICUT						
Blumenthal	N	Y	Y	Y	Y	Y
Murphy	N	Y	Y	Y	Y	Y
DELAWARE						
Carper	N	N	Y	Y	Y	Y
Coons	N	Y	Y	Y	Y	Y
FLORIDA						
Rubio	Y	Y	N	N	N	Y
Scott	Y	Y	N	N	N	Y
GEORGIA						
Isakson	Y	Y	N	N	N	Y
Perdue	Y	Y	N	N	N	Y
HAWAII						
Schatz	N	Y	Y	Y	Y	N
Hirono	N	Y	Y	Y	Y	Y
IDAHO						
Crapo	Y	Y	N	N	N	Y
Risch	Y	Y	N	N	N	Y
ILLINOIS						
Durbin	N	Y	Y	Y	Y	Y
Duckworth	N	Y	Y	Y	Y	Y
INDIANA						
Young	Y	Y	Y	Y	Y	Y
Braun	Y	Y	N	N	N	Y
IOWA						
Grassley	Y	Y	N	N	N	Y
Ernst	Y	Y	N	N	N	Y
KANSAS						
Roberts	Y	Y	N	N	N	Y
Moran	Y	Y	Y	Y	Y	?
KENTUCKY						
McConnell	Y	Y	N	N	N	Y
Paul	Y	Y	Y	Y	Y	Y
LOUISIANA						
Cassidy	Y	Y	N	N	N	?
Kennedy	Y	Y	N	N	N	Y
MAINE						
Collins	Y	Y	Y	Y	Y	Y
King	N	Y	Y	Y	Y	Y
MARYLAND						
Cardin	N	Y	Y	Y	Y	Y
Van Hollen	N	Y	Y	Y	Y	Y
MASSACHUSETTS						
Warren	N	N	Y	Y	Y	N
Markey	N	N	Y	Y	Y	N
MICHIGAN						
Stabenow	N	Y	Y	Y	Y	Y
Peters	N	Y	Y	Y	Y	Y
MINNESOTA						
Klobuchar	N	N	Y	Y	Y	?
Smith	N	Y	Y	Y	Y	Y
MISSISSIPPI						
Wicker	Y	Y	N	N	N	Y
Hyde-Smith	Y	Y	N	N	N	Y
MISSOURI						
Blunt	Y	Y	N	N	N	Y
Hawley	Y	Y	N	N	N	Y

	175	176	177	178	179	180
MONTANA						
Tester	N	Y	Y	Y	Y	Y
Daines	Y	Y	N	N	N	Y
NEBRASKA						
Fischer	Y	Y	N	N	N	Y
Sasse	Y	Y	N	N	N	Y
NEVADA						
Cortez Masto	N	Y	Y	Y	Y	N
Rosen	N	Y	Y	Y	Y	N
NEW HAMPSHIRE						
Shaheen	N	Y	Y	Y	Y	Y
Hassan	N	Y	Y	Y	Y	Y
NEW JERSEY						
Menendez	N	Y	Y	Y	Y	Y
Booker	?	?	Y	Y	Y	?
NEW MEXICO						
Udall	N	N	Y	Y	Y	Y
Heinrich	N	Y	Y	Y	Y	Y
NEW YORK						
Schumer	N	Y	Y	Y	Y	Y
Gillibrand	N	N	?	?	?	?
NORTH CAROLINA						
Burr	Y	Y	N	N	N	Y
Tillis	Y	Y	N	N	N	Y
NORTH DAKOTA						
Hoeven	Y	Y	N	N	N	Y
Cramer	Y	Y	N	N	N	Y
OHIO						
Brown	N	Y	Y	Y	Y	Y
Portman	Y	Y	N	N	N	Y
OKLAHOMA						
Inhofe	Y	Y	N	N	N	Y
Lankford	Y	Y	N	N	N	Y
OREGON						
Wyden	N	N	Y	Y	Y	Y
Merkley	N	N	Y	Y	Y	Y
PENNSYLVANIA						
Casey	N	Y	Y	Y	Y	Y
Toomey	Y	Y	N	N	N	?
RHODE ISLAND						
Reed	N	Y	Y	Y	Y	Y
Whitehouse	N	Y	Y	Y	Y	Y
SOUTH CAROLINA						
Graham	Y	Y	Y	Y	Y	Y
Scott	Y	Y	N	N	N	Y
SOUTH DAKOTA						
Thune	Y	Y	N	N	N	Y
Rounds	Y	Y	?	?	?	?
TENNESSEE						
Alexander	Y	Y	N	N	N	Y
Blackburn	Y	Y	N	N	?	Y
TEXAS						
Cornyn	Y	Y	N	N	N	Y
Cruz	Y	Y	N	N	N	Y
UTAH						
Lee	Y	Y	Y	Y	+	Y
Romney	Y	Y	N	N	N	Y
VERMONT						
Leahy	N	Y	Y	Y	Y	Y
Sanders	N	N	Y	Y	Y	?
VIRGINIA						
Warner	N	Y	Y	Y	Y	Y
Kaine	N	Y	Y	Y	Y	Y
WASHINGTON						
Murray	N	Y	Y	Y	Y	Y
Cantwell	N	Y	Y	Y	Y	Y
WEST VIRGINIA						
Manchin	N	Y	Y	Y	Y	Y
Capito	Y	Y	N	N	N	Y
WISCONSIN						
Johnson	Y	Y	N	N	N	Y
Baldwin	N	Y	Y	Y	Y	Y
WYOMING						
Enzi	Y	Y	N	N	N	Y
Barrasso	Y	Y	N	N	N	Y

KEY:

	Republicans	Democrats	*Independents*
Y Voted for (yea)	**N** Voted against (nay)		**P** Voted "present"
+ Announced for	**−** Announced against		**?** Did not vote or otherwise make position known
# Paired for	**X** Paired against		

181. S1790. Fiscal 2020 Defense Authorization - Motion to Proceed. McConnell, R-Ky., motion to proceed to the National Defense Authorization Act for fiscal year 2020 that would authorize $642.5 billion for the Defense Department's base budget, $23.2 billion for national security programs within the Energy Department and $75.9 billion to support overseas contingency operations. Motion agreed to 86-6: R 49-0; D 36-6; I 1-0. June 24, 2019.

182. HR3401. Supplemental Border Appropriations - Passage. Passage of the bill that would provide a total of $4.6 billion in supplemental fiscal 2019 appropriations to address humanitarian concerns for migrants at the U.S.-Mexico border. It would also establish contracting standards for unlicensed facilities used as "influx shelters" by HHS, limit the period unaccompanied minors may be held at such facilities, and require HHS to ensure that certain minors are not held at such facilities, including those with special medical needs. Rejected 37-55: R 0-52; D 36-3; I 1-0. *Note: Per a unanimous consent agreement, 60 votes are required for passage.* June 26, 2019.

183. HR3401. Supplemental Border Appropriations - Motion to Table. Graham, R-S.C., motion to table (kill) the Paul, R-Ky., amendment no. 902 to amendment no. 901 to the bill that would rescind all funding for the East-West Center and the Inter-America Foundation, and funding previously appropriated for global health programs within the fiscal 2019 State and Foreign Operations appropriations measure. Motion agreed to 77-15: R 37-15; D 39-0; I 1-0. June 26, 2019.

184. HR3401. Supplemental Border Appropriations - Immigration Aid Package. Adoption of the Shelby, R-Ala., amendment no. 901 to the bill that would provide a total of $4.6 billion in supplemental fiscal 2019 appropriations to address humanitarian concerns for migrants at the U.S.-Mexico border. Adopted 84-8: R 50-2; D 33-6; I 1-0. *Note: Per a unanimous consent agreement, 60 votes were required for adoption of the amendment.* June 26, 2019.

185. HR3401. Supplemental Border Appropriations - Passage. Passage of the bill, as amended, that would provide a total of $4.6 billion in supplemental fiscal 2019 appropriations to address humanitarian concerns for migrants at the U.S.-Mexico border. Passed 84-8: R 50-2; D 33-6; I 1-0. *Note: Per a unanimous consent agreement, 60 votes were required for passage.* June 26, 2019.

186. S1790. Fiscal 2020 Defense Authorization - Cloture. McConnell, R-Ky., motion to invoke cloture on the Inhofe, R-Okla., substitute amendment no. 764, as modified, to the bill that would authorize $642.5 billion for the Defense Department's base budget, $23.2 billion for national security programs within the Energy Department, $75.9 billion to support overseas contingency operations, and $33 billion for the Defense Health Program. The substitute amendment contains a number of modifications including provisions that would set stricter standards for drinking water with regards to perfluoroalkyl and polyfluoroalkyl chemicals release, disclosure, and detection; establish a lead Inspector General for the Overseas Contingency Operations, impose sanctions on foreign synthetic opioid traffickers; limit the procurement quantity of Littoral Combat Ships to 35; and would require a number of reports including one on the military activities of China and Russia in the Arctic. Motion agreed to 87-7: R 50-2; D 36-5; I 1-0. June 27, 2019.

	181	182	183	184	185	186		181	182	183	184	185	186
ALABAMA							**MONTANA**						
Shelby	Y	N	Y	Y	Y	Y	Tester	Y	Y	Y	Y	Y	Y
Jones	Y	Y	Y	Y	Y	Y	**Daines**	Y	N	Y	Y	Y	Y
ALASKA							**NEBRASKA**						
Murkowski	Y	N	Y	Y	Y	Y	**Fischer**	Y	N	Y	Y	Y	Y
Sullivan	Y	N	Y	Y	Y	Y	**Sasse**	?	N	Y	Y	Y	Y
ARIZONA							**NEVADA**						
Sinema	Y	Y	Y	Y	Y	Y	Cortez Masto	Y	Y	Y	Y	Y	Y
McSally	Y	N	Y	Y	Y	Y	Rosen	Y	Y	Y	Y	Y	Y
ARKANSAS							**NEW HAMPSHIRE**						
Boozman	Y	N	Y	Y	Y	Y	Shaheen	Y	Y	Y	Y	Y	Y
Cotton	Y	N	Y	Y	Y	Y	Hassan	Y	Y	Y	Y	Y	Y
CALIFORNIA							**NEW JERSEY**						
Feinstein	Y	Y	Y	Y	Y	Y	Menendez	Y	Y	Y	N	N	Y
Harris	?	?	?	?	?	?	Booker	Y	?	?	?	?	N
COLORADO							**NEW MEXICO**						
Bennet	Y	?	?	?	?	?	Udall	N	Y	Y	Y	Y	Y
Gardner	Y	N	Y	Y	Y	Y	Heinrich	Y	Y	Y	Y	Y	Y
CONNECTICUT							**NEW YORK**						
Blumenthal	Y	Y	Y	Y	Y	Y	Schumer	Y	Y	Y	Y	Y	Y
Murphy	Y	Y	Y	Y	Y	Y	Gillibrand	?	?	?	?	?	?
DELAWARE							**NORTH CAROLINA**						
Carper	N	Y	Y	Y	Y	Y	**Burr**	Y	N	Y	Y	Y	Y
Coons	Y	Y	Y	Y	Y	Y	**Tillis**	Y	N	N	Y	Y	Y
FLORIDA							**NORTH DAKOTA**						
Rubio	Y	N	Y	Y	Y	Y	**Hoeven**	Y	N	Y	Y	Y	Y
Scott	Y	N	Y	Y	Y	Y	**Cramer**	Y	N	Y	Y	Y	Y
GEORGIA							**OHIO**						
Isakson	Y	N	Y	Y	Y	Y	Brown	Y	Y	Y	Y	Y	Y
Perdue	Y	N	N	Y	Y	Y	**Portman**	Y	N	Y	Y	Y	Y
HAWAII							**OKLAHOMA**						
Schatz	Y	Y	Y	Y	Y	Y	**Inhofe**	Y	N	Y	Y	Y	Y
Hirono	Y	Y	Y	N	N	Y	**Lankford**	Y	N	N	Y	Y	Y
IDAHO							**OREGON**						
Crapo	Y	N	Y	Y	Y	Y	Wyden	N	Y	Y	N	N	N
Risch	Y	N	Y	Y	Y	Y	Merkley	N	N	Y	N	N	N
ILLINOIS							**PENNSYLVANIA**						
Durbin	Y	Y	Y	Y	Y	Y	Casey	Y	Y	Y	Y	Y	Y
Duckworth	Y	Y	Y	Y	Y	Y	**Toomey**	?	N	N	Y	Y	Y
INDIANA							**RHODE ISLAND**						
Young	Y	N	Y	Y	Y	Y	Reed	Y	Y	Y	Y	Y	Y
Braun	Y	N	N	Y	Y	Y	Whitehouse	Y	Y	Y	Y	Y	Y
IOWA							**SOUTH CAROLINA**						
Grassley	Y	N	N	Y	Y	Y	**Graham**	Y	N	Y	Y	Y	Y
Ernst	Y	N	N	Y	Y	Y	**Scott**	Y	N	N	Y	Y	Y
KANSAS							**SOUTH DAKOTA**						
Roberts	Y	N	Y	Y	Y	Y	**Thune**	Y	N	Y	Y	Y	Y
Moran	Y	N	Y	Y	Y	Y	**Rounds**	?	?	?	?	?	?
KENTUCKY							**TENNESSEE**						
McConnell	Y	N	Y	Y	Y	Y	**Alexander**	Y	N	Y	Y	Y	Y
Paul	Y	N	N	N	N	N	**Blackburn**	Y	N	N	Y	Y	Y
LOUISIANA							**TEXAS**						
Cassidy	Y	N	Y	Y	Y	Y	**Cornyn**	Y	N	Y	Y	Y	Y
Kennedy	?	N	N	Y	Y	Y	**Cruz**	Y	N	N	Y	Y	Y
MAINE							**UTAH**						
Collins	Y	N	Y	Y	Y	Y	**Lee**	Y	N	N	N	N	N
King	Y	Y	Y	Y	Y	Y	**Romney**	Y	N	Y	Y	Y	Y
MARYLAND							**VERMONT**						
Cardin	Y	Y	Y	Y	Y	Y	Leahy	Y	Y	Y	Y	Y	Y
Van Hollen	Y	Y	Y	N	N	Y	*Sanders*	?	?	?	?	?	?
MASSACHUSETTS							**VIRGINIA**						
Warren	?	?	?	?	?	?	Warner	Y	Y	Y	Y	Y	Y
Markey	N	N	Y	N	N	N	Kaine	Y	Y	Y	Y	Y	Y
MICHIGAN							**WASHINGTON**						
Stabenow	Y	Y	Y	Y	Y	Y	Murray	Y	Y	Y	Y	Y	Y
Peters	Y	Y	Y	Y	Y	Y	Cantwell	Y	Y	Y	Y	Y	Y
MINNESOTA							**WEST VIRGINIA**						
Klobuchar	N	?	?	?	?	N	Manchin	Y	N	Y	Y	Y	Y
Smith	Y	Y	Y	Y	Y	Y	**Capito**	Y	N	Y	Y	Y	Y
MISSISSIPPI							**WISCONSIN**						
Wicker	Y	N	Y	Y	Y	Y	**Johnson**	Y	N	Y	Y	Y	Y
Hyde-Smith	Y	N	Y	Y	Y	Y	Baldwin	Y	Y	Y	Y	Y	Y
MISSOURI							**WYOMING**						
Blunt	Y	N	Y	Y	Y	Y	**Enzi**	Y	N	N	N	Y	Y
Hawley	Y	N	Y	Y	Y	Y	**Barrasso**	Y	N	Y	Y	Y	Y

KEY:		**Republicans**		Democrats		*Independents*	
Y	Voted for (yea)	**N**	Voted against (nay)	**P**	Voted "present"		
+	Announced for	**–**	Announced against	**?**	Did not vote or otherwise		
#	Paired for	**X**	Paired against		make position known		

187. S1790. Fiscal 2020 Defense Authorization - Military Authorization to Oppose Hostile Forces. McConnell, R-Ky., for Romney, R-Utah, amendment no. 861 to the bill that would ensure that funds authorized in the bill may be used by U.S. armed forces to defend themselves and U.S. citizens against attack by the government, military forces, or proxies of a foreign nation or by other hostile forces. Adopted 90-4: R 52-0; D 37-4; I 1-0. June 27, 2019.

188. S1790. Fiscal 2020 Defense Authorization - Passage. Passage of the bill, as amended, that would authorize $642.5 billion for the Defense Department's base budget, $23.2 billion for national security programs within the Energy Department and $75.9 billion to support overseas contingency operations. Passed 86-8: R 49-3; D 36-5; I 1-0. *Note: Per a unanimous consent agreement, 60 votes are required for passage.* June 27, 2019.

189. S1790. Fiscal 2020 Defense Authorization - Prohibit Military Operations in Iran. Adoption of the Udall, D-N.M., amendment no. 883 to the bill that would prohibit any funds authorized by the bill be used to conduct hostilities against the Government of Iran or in the territory of Iran. Rejected 50-40: R 4-40; D 44-0; I 2-0. *Note: In the legislative day that began on June 27, 2019. If adopted, the amendment would be retroactively incorporated into the bill (S 1790), which was passed earlier in the same legislative day. Per a unanimous consent agreement, 60 votes were required for adoption of the amendment.* June 28, 2019.

190. Bress Nomination - Cloture. Motion to invoke cloture (thus limiting debate) on the nomination of Daniel Bress of California to be a U.S. circuit judge for the 9th Circuit. Motion agreed to 50-42: R 50-0; D 0-41; I 0-1. *Note: A majority of senators voting (47 in this case), a quorum being present, is required to invoke cloture on all nominations.* July 08, 2019.

191. Bress Nomination - Confirmation. Confirmation of President Trump's nomination of Daniel Bress of California to be U.S. circuit judge for the 9th Circuit. Confirmed 53-45: R 53-0; D 0-44; I 0-1. *Note: A "yea" was a vote in support of the president's position.* July 09, 2019.

192. Wetherell Nomination - Cloture. Motion to invoke cloture (thus limiting debate) on the nomination of T. Kent Wetherell, II of Florida to be a U.S. district judge for the Northern District of Florida. Motion agreed to 82-16: R 53-0; D 28-16; I 1-0. *Note: A majority of senators voting (50 in this case), a quorum being present, is required to invoke cloture on all nominations.* July 09, 2019.

	187	188	189	190	191	192
ALABAMA						
Shelby	Y	Y	N	Y	Y	Y
Jones	Y	Y	Y	N	N	Y
ALASKA						
Murkowski	Y	Y	N	Y	Y	Y
Sullivan	Y	Y	N	Y	Y	Y
ARIZONA						
Sinema	Y	Y	Y	N	N	Y
McSally	Y	Y	N	Y	Y	Y
ARKANSAS						
Boozman	Y	Y	N	Y	Y	Y
Cotton	Y	Y	N	Y	Y	Y
CALIFORNIA						
Feinstein	Y	Y	Y	N	N	Y
Harris	?	?	Y	–	N	N
COLORADO						
Bennet	?	?	Y	N	N	Y
Gardner	Y	Y	N	Y	Y	Y
CONNECTICUT						
Blumenthal	Y	Y	Y	N	N	N
Murphy	Y	Y	Y	N	N	Y
DELAWARE						
Carper	Y	Y	Y	N	N	Y
Coons	Y	Y	?	N	N	Y
FLORIDA						
Rubio	Y	Y	N	+	Y	Y
Scott	Y	Y	–	Y	Y	Y
GEORGIA						
Isakson	Y	Y	N	Y	Y	Y
Perdue	Y	Y	N	Y	Y	Y
HAWAII						
Schatz	Y	Y	Y	N	N	N
Hirono	N	Y	Y	N	N	N
IDAHO						
Crapo	Y	Y	N	Y	Y	Y
Risch	Y	Y	N	Y	Y	Y
ILLINOIS						
Durbin	Y	Y	Y	N	N	Y
Duckworth	N	Y	Y	N	N	Y
INDIANA						
Young	Y	Y	N	Y	Y	Y
Braun	Y	N	?	Y	Y	Y
IOWA						
Grassley	Y	Y	N	Y	Y	Y
Ernst	Y	Y	N	Y	Y	Y
KANSAS						
Roberts	Y	Y	?	Y	Y	Y
Moran	Y	Y	Y	Y	Y	Y
KENTUCKY						
McConnell	Y	Y	N	Y	Y	Y
Paul	Y	N	Y	Y	Y	Y
LOUISIANA						
Cassidy	Y	Y	N	?	Y	Y
Kennedy	Y	Y	N	Y	Y	Y
MAINE						
Collins	Y	Y	Y	Y	Y	Y
King	Y	Y	Y	N	N	Y
MARYLAND						
Cardin	Y	Y	Y	N	N	Y
Van Hollen	Y	Y	Y	N	N	N
MASSACHUSETTS						
Warren	?	?	Y	?	N	N
Markey	Y	N	Y	N	N	N
MICHIGAN						
Stabenow	Y	Y	Y	N	N	N
Peters	Y	Y	Y	N	N	Y
MINNESOTA						
Klobuchar	Y	N	Y	N	N	N
Smith	Y	Y	Y	N	N	N
MISSISSIPPI						
Wicker	Y	Y	N	Y	Y	Y
Hyde-Smith	Y	Y	N	Y	Y	Y
MISSOURI						
Blunt	Y	Y	?	Y	Y	Y
Hawley	Y	Y	N	Y	Y	Y

	187	188	189	190	191	192
MONTANA						
Tester	Y	Y	Y	N	N	Y
Daines	Y	Y	N	Y	Y	Y
NEBRASKA						
Fischer	Y	Y	N	Y	Y	Y
Sasse	Y	Y	N	Y	Y	Y
NEVADA						
Cortez Masto	Y	Y	Y	N	N	Y
Rosen	Y	Y	Y	N	N	Y
NEW HAMPSHIRE						
Shaheen	Y	Y	Y	N	N	Y
Hassan	Y	Y	Y	N	N	Y
NEW JERSEY						
Menendez	Y	Y	Y	N	N	N
Booker	N	N	Y	N	N	N
NEW MEXICO						
Udall	Y	Y	Y	N	N	Y
Heinrich	Y	Y	Y	N	N	Y
NEW YORK						
Schumer	Y	Y	Y	N	N	N
Gillibrand	?	?	Y	?	?	?
NORTH CAROLINA						
Burr	Y	Y	?	Y	Y	Y
Tillis	Y	Y	N	+	Y	Y
NORTH DAKOTA						
Hoeven	Y	Y	N	Y	Y	Y
Cramer	Y	Y	?	Y	Y	Y
OHIO						
Brown	Y	Y	Y	N	N	Y
Portman	Y	Y	N	Y	Y	Y
OKLAHOMA						
Inhofe	Y	Y	–	Y	Y	Y
Lankford	Y	Y	N	Y	Y	Y
OREGON						
Wyden	Y	N	Y	N	N	N
Merkley	Y	N	Y	N	N	N
PENNSYLVANIA						
Casey	Y	Y	Y	N	N	Y
Toomey	Y	Y	N	Y	Y	Y
RHODE ISLAND						
Reed	Y	Y	Y	N	N	Y
Whitehouse	Y	Y	Y	N	N	Y
SOUTH CAROLINA						
Graham	Y	Y	N	Y	Y	Y
Scott	Y	Y	N	Y	Y	Y
SOUTH DAKOTA						
Thune	Y	Y	N	Y	Y	Y
Rounds	?	?	?	Y	Y	Y
TENNESSEE						
Alexander	Y	Y	N	Y	Y	Y
Blackburn	Y	Y	?	Y	Y	Y
TEXAS						
Cornyn	Y	Y	N	Y	Y	Y
Cruz	Y	Y	N	Y	Y	Y
UTAH						
Lee	Y	N	Y	Y	Y	Y
Romney	Y	Y	N	Y	Y	Y
VERMONT						
Leahy	N	Y	Y	?	N	Y
Sanders	?	?	Y	?	?	?
VIRGINIA						
Warner	Y	Y	Y	N	N	Y
Kaine	Y	Y	Y	N	N	Y
WASHINGTON						
Murray	Y	Y	Y	N	N	Y
Cantwell	Y	Y	Y	N	N	Y
WEST VIRGINIA						
Manchin	Y	Y	Y	N	N	Y
Capito	Y	Y	N	Y	Y	Y
WISCONSIN						
Johnson	Y	Y	N	Y	Y	Y
Baldwin	Y	Y	Y	N	N	N
WYOMING						
Enzi	Y	Y	N	Y	Y	Y
Barrasso	Y	Y	N	Y	Y	Y

KEY:	**Republicans**	Democrats	*Independents*

Y Voted for (yea)	**N** Voted against (nay)	**P** Voted "present"
+ Announced for	**–** Announced against	**?** Did not vote or otherwise make position known
# Paired for	**X** Paired against	

193. Leichty Nomination - Cloture. Motion to invoke cloture (thus limiting debate) on the nomination of Damon Leichty of Indiana to be a U.S. district judge for the Northern District of Indiana. Motion agreed to 87-11: R 53-0; D 33-11; I 1-0. *Note: A majority of senators voting (50 in this case), a quorum being present, is required to invoke cloture on all nominations.* July 09, 2019.

194. Ranjan Nomination - Cloture. Motion to invoke cloture (thus limiting debate) on the nomination of J. Nicholas Ranjan of Pennsylvania to be a U.S. district judge for the Western District of Pennsylvania. Motion agreed to 83-15: R 53-0; D 29-15; I 1-0. *Note: A majority of senators voting (50 in this case), a quorum being present, is required to invoke cloture on all nominations.* July 09, 2019.

195. Wetherell Nomination - Confirmation. Confirmation of President Trump's nomination of T. Kent Wetherell, II of Florida to be U.S. district judge for the Northern District of Florida. Confirmed 78-15: R 52-0; D 25-15; I 1-0. *Note: A "yea" was a vote in support of the president's position.* July 10, 2019.

196. Ranjan Nomination - Confirmation. Confirmation of President Trump's nomination of J. Nicholas Ranjan of Pennsylvania to be U.S. district judge for the Western District of Pennsylvania. Confirmed 80-14: R 52-0; D 27-14; I 1-0. *Note: A "yea" was a vote in support of the president's position.* July 10, 2019.

197. Leichty Nomination - Confirmation. Confirmation of President Trump's nomination of Damon Leichty of Indiana to be U.S. district judge for the Northern District of Indiana. Confirmed 85-10: R 53-0; D 31-10; I 1-0. *Note: A "yea" was a vote in support of the president's position.* July 10, 2019.

198. King Nomination - Cloture. Motion to invoke cloture (thus limiting debate) on the nomination of Robert King of Kentucky to be assistant secretary for Postsecondary Education, Department of Education. Motion agreed to 56-39: R 53-0; D 3-38; I 0-1. *Note: A majority of senators voting (48 in this case), a quorum being present, is required to invoke cloture on all nominations.* July 10, 2019.

	193	194	195	196	197	198		193	194	195	196	197	198
ALABAMA							**MONTANA**						
Shelby	Y	Y	Y	Y	Y	Y	Tester	Y	Y	Y	Y	Y	N
Jones	Y	Y	Y	Y	Y	Y	Daines	Y	Y	Y	Y	Y	Y
ALASKA							**NEBRASKA**						
Murkowski	Y	Y	Y	Y	Y	Y	**Fischer**	Y	Y	Y	Y	Y	Y
Sullivan	Y	Y	Y	Y	Y	Y	**Sasse**	Y	Y	Y	Y	Y	Y
ARIZONA							**NEVADA**						
Sinema	Y	Y	Y	Y	Y	Y	Cortez Masto	Y	Y	Y	Y	Y	N
McSally	Y	Y	Y	Y	Y	Y	Rosen	Y	Y	Y	Y	Y	N
ARKANSAS							**NEW HAMPSHIRE**						
Boozman	Y	Y	Y	Y	Y	Y	Shaheen	Y	Y	Y	Y	Y	N
Cotton	Y	Y	Y	Y	Y	Y	Hassan	Y	Y	Y	Y	Y	N
CALIFORNIA							**NEW JERSEY**						
Feinstein	Y	Y	Y	Y	Y	N	Menendez	Y	Y	N	Y	Y	N
Harris	N	N	N	N	N	?	Booker	N	Y	?	?	?	?
COLORADO							**NEW MEXICO**						
Bennet	Y	N	Y	N	Y	N	Udall	Y	N	Y	N	Y	N
Gardner	Y	Y	Y	Y	Y	Y	Heinrich	Y	N	?	?	?	?
CONNECTICUT							**NEW YORK**						
Blumenthal	N	N	N	N	N	N	Schumer	Y	Y	N	Y	Y	N
Murphy	Y	Y	Y	Y	Y	N	Gillibrand	?	?	?	?	?	?
DELAWARE							**NORTH CAROLINA**						
Carper	Y	Y	Y	Y	Y	N	**Burr**	Y	Y	Y	Y	Y	Y
Coons	Y	Y	Y	Y	Y	N	**Tillis**	Y	Y	Y	Y	Y	Y
FLORIDA							**NORTH DAKOTA**						
Rubio	Y	Y	Y	Y	Y	Y	**Hoeven**	Y	Y	Y	Y	Y	Y
Scott	Y	Y	Y	Y	Y	Y	**Cramer**	Y	Y	Y	Y	Y	Y
GEORGIA							**OHIO**						
Isakson	Y	Y	Y	Y	Y	Y	Brown	Y	Y	Y	Y	Y	N
Perdue	Y	Y	Y	Y	Y	Y	**Portman**	Y	Y	Y	Y	Y	Y
HAWAII							**OKLAHOMA**						
Schatz	N	Y	N	Y	N	N	**Inhofe**	Y	Y	Y	Y	Y	Y
Hirono	N	N	N	N	Y	N	**Lankford**	Y	Y	Y	Y	Y	Y
IDAHO							**OREGON**						
Crapo	Y	Y	Y	Y	Y	Y	Wyden	Y	N	N	N	Y	N
Risch	Y	Y	Y	Y	Y	Y	Merkley	Y	N	N	N	Y	N
ILLINOIS							**PENNSYLVANIA**						
Durbin	Y	Y	Y	Y	N	N	Casey	Y	Y	Y	Y	Y	N
Duckworth	Y	Y	?	?	?	N	**Toomey**	Y	Y	Y	Y	Y	Y
INDIANA							**RHODE ISLAND**						
Young	Y	Y	+	+	Y	Y	Reed	Y	Y	Y	Y	Y	N
Braun	Y	Y	Y	Y	Y	Y	Whitehouse	Y	Y	Y	Y	Y	N
IOWA							**SOUTH CAROLINA**						
Grassley	Y	Y	Y	Y	Y	Y	**Graham**	Y	Y	Y	Y	Y	Y
Ernst	Y	Y	Y	Y	Y	Y	**Scott**	Y	Y	Y	Y	Y	Y
KANSAS							**SOUTH DAKOTA**						
Roberts	Y	Y	Y	Y	Y	Y	**Thune**	Y	Y	Y	Y	Y	Y
Moran	Y	Y	Y	Y	Y	Y	**Rounds**	Y	Y	Y	Y	Y	Y
KENTUCKY							**TENNESSEE**						
McConnell	Y	Y	Y	Y	Y	Y	**Alexander**	Y	Y	Y	Y	Y	Y
Paul	Y	Y	Y	Y	Y	Y	**Blackburn**	Y	Y	Y	Y	Y	Y
LOUISIANA							**TEXAS**						
Cassidy	Y	Y	Y	Y	Y	Y	**Cornyn**	Y	Y	Y	Y	Y	Y
Kennedy	Y	Y	Y	Y	Y	Y	**Cruz**	Y	Y	Y	Y	Y	Y
MAINE							**UTAH**						
Collins	Y	Y	Y	Y	Y	Y	**Lee**	Y	Y	Y	Y	Y	Y
King	Y	Y	Y	Y	Y	N	**Romney**	Y	Y	Y	Y	Y	Y
MARYLAND							**VERMONT**						
Cardin	Y	Y	Y	Y	Y	N	Leahy	Y	Y	Y	Y	Y	N
Van Hollen	Y	Y	N	Y	Y	N	*Sanders*	?	?	?	?	?	?
MASSACHUSETTS							**VIRGINIA**						
Warren	N	N	N	N	N	N	Warner	Y	Y	?	Y	Y	N
Markey	N	N	N	N	N	N	Kaine	Y	Y	Y	Y	Y	N
MICHIGAN							**WASHINGTON**						
Stabenow	N	N	N	N	N	N	Murray	N	N	Y	N	N	N
Peters	Y	Y	Y	Y	Y	N	Cantwell	N	N	Y	N	Y	N
MINNESOTA							**WEST VIRGINIA**						
Klobuchar	N	N	N	N	N	N	Manchin	Y	Y	Y	Y	Y	Y
Smith	N	N	N	N	N	N	**Capito**	Y	Y	Y	Y	Y	Y
MISSISSIPPI							**WISCONSIN**						
Wicker	Y	Y	Y	Y	Y	Y	**Johnson**	Y	Y	Y	Y	Y	Y
Hyde-Smith	Y	Y	Y	Y	Y	Y	Baldwin	Y	Y	N	Y	Y	N
MISSOURI							**WYOMING**						
Blunt	Y	Y	Y	Y	Y	Y	**Enzi**	Y	Y	Y	Y	Y	Y
Hawley	Y	Y	Y	Y	Y	Y	**Barrasso**	Y	Y	Y	Y	Y	Y

KEY:

	Republicans	Democrats	Independents

Y	Voted for (yea)	N	Voted against (nay)	P	Voted "present"
+	Announced for	–	Announced against	?	Did not vote or otherwise
#	Paired for	X	Paired against		make position known

199. Pallasch Nomination - Cloture. Motion to invoke cloture (thus limiting debate) on the nomination of John Pallasch of Kentucky to be assistant secretary of Labor. Motion agreed to 54-41: R 53-0; D 1-40; I 0-1. *Note: A majority of senators voting (48 in this case), a quorum being present, is required to invoke cloture on all nominations.* July 10, 2019.

200. King Nomination - Confirmation. Confirmation of President Trump's nomination of Robert King of Kentucky to be assistant secretary for Postsecondary Education, Department of Education. Confirmed 56-37: R 53-0; D 3-36; I 0-1. *Note: A "yea" was a vote in support of the president's position.* July 11, 2019.

201. Pallasch Nomination - Confirmation. Confirmation of President Trump's nomination of John Pallasch of Kentucky to be an assistant secretary of Labor. Confirmed 54-39: R 53-0; D 1-38; I 0-1. *Note: A "yea" was a vote in support of the president's position.* July 11, 2019.

202. Wright Nomination - Cloture. Motion to invoke cloture (thus limiting debate) on the nomination of Peter Wright of Michigan to be assistant administrator, Office of Solid Waste, Environmental Protection Agency. Motion agreed to 53-39: R 53-0; D 0-38; I 0-1. *Note: A majority of senators voting (47 in this case), a quorum being present, is required to invoke cloture on all nominations.* July 11, 2019.

203. Wright Nomination - Confirmation. Confirmation of President Trump's nomination of Peter Wright of Michigan to be assistant administrator, Office of Solid Waste, Environmental Protection Agency. Confirmed 52-38: R 52-0; D 0-37; I 0-1. *Note: A "yea" was a vote in support of the president's position.* July 11, 2019.

204. Phipps Nomination - Cloture. Motion to invoke cloture (thus limiting debate) on the nomination of Peter Joseph Phipps of Pennsylvania to be a U.S. Circuit judge for the 3rd Circuit. Motion agreed to 53-40: R 50-0; D 3-38; I 0-2. *Note: A majority of senators voting (47 in this case), a quorum being present, is required to invoke cloture on all nominations.* July 15, 2019.

	199	200	201	202	203	204
ALABAMA						
Shelby	Y	Y	Y	Y	Y	Y
Jones	N	Y	N	N	N	Y
ALASKA						
Murkowski	Y	Y	Y	Y	Y	Y
Sullivan	Y	Y	Y	Y	Y	Y
ARIZONA						
Sinema	N	Y	N	N	N	Y
McSally	Y	Y	Y	Y	Y	Y
ARKANSAS						
Boozman	Y	Y	Y	Y	Y	Y
Cotton	Y	Y	Y	Y	Y	Y
CALIFORNIA						
Feinstein	N	N	N	N	N	N
Harris	?	?	?	?	?	N
COLORADO						
Bennet	N	?	?	?	?	?
Gardner	Y	Y	Y	Y	Y	Y
CONNECTICUT						
Blumenthal	N	N	N	N	N	N
Murphy	N	N	N	N	N	N
DELAWARE						
Carper	N	N	N	N	N	N
Coons	N	N	N	N	N	N
FLORIDA						
Rubio	Y	Y	Y	Y	Y	Y
Scott	Y	Y	Y	Y	Y	Y
GEORGIA						
Isakson	Y	Y	Y	Y	Y	Y
Perdue	Y	Y	Y	Y	Y	Y
HAWAII						
Schatz	N	N	N	N	N	N
Hirono	N	N	N	N	N	N
IDAHO						
Crapo	Y	Y	Y	Y	Y	Y
Risch	Y	Y	Y	Y	Y	Y
ILLINOIS						
Durbin	N	N	N	-	-	N
Duckworth	N	N	N	N	N	N
INDIANA						
Young	Y	Y	Y	Y	Y	Y
Braun	Y	Y	Y	Y	Y	Y
IOWA						
Grassley	Y	Y	Y	Y	Y	Y
Ernst	Y	Y	Y	Y	Y	Y
KANSAS						
Roberts	Y	Y	Y	Y	Y	Y
Moran	Y	Y	Y	Y	?	+
KENTUCKY						
McConnell	Y	Y	Y	Y	Y	Y
Paul	Y	Y	Y	Y	Y	?
LOUISIANA						
Cassidy	Y	Y	Y	Y	Y	Y
Kennedy	Y	Y	Y	Y	Y	Y
MAINE						
Collins	Y	Y	Y	Y	Y	Y
King	N	N	N	N	N	N
MARYLAND						
Cardin	N	N	N	N	N	N
Van Hollen	N	N	N	N	N	N
MASSACHUSETTS						
Warren	N	?	?	?	?	N
Markey	N	N	N	N	N	N
MICHIGAN						
Stabenow	N	N	N	N	N	N
Peters	N	N	N	N	N	N
MINNESOTA						
Klobuchar	N	N	N	N	N	?
Smith	N	N	N	N	N	N
MISSISSIPPI						
Wicker	Y	Y	Y	Y	Y	Y
Hyde-Smith	Y	Y	Y	Y	Y	Y
MISSOURI						
Blunt	Y	Y	Y	Y	Y	Y
Hawley	Y	Y	Y	Y	Y	Y

	199	200	201	202	203	204
MONTANA						
Tester	N	N	N	N	N	N
Daines	Y	Y	Y	Y	Y	Y
NEBRASKA						
Fischer	Y	Y	Y	Y	Y	Y
Sasse	Y	Y	Y	Y	Y	?
NEVADA						
Cortez Masto	N	N	N	N	N	N
Rosen	N	N	N	N	N	N
NEW HAMPSHIRE						
Shaheen	N	N	N	N	N	N
Hassan	N	N	N	N	N	N
NEW JERSEY						
Menendez	N	N	N	N	N	N
Booker	?	?	?	?	?	?
NEW MEXICO						
Udall	N	N	N	N	N	N
Heinrich	?	?	?	?	?	N
NEW YORK						
Schumer	N	N	N	N	N	N
Gillibrand	?	?	?	?	?	?
NORTH CAROLINA						
Burr	Y	Y	Y	Y	Y	Y
Tillis	Y	Y	Y	Y	Y	Y
NORTH DAKOTA						
Hoeven	Y	Y	Y	Y	Y	Y
Cramer	Y	Y	Y	Y	Y	Y
OHIO						
Brown	N	N	N	N	N	N
Portman	Y	Y	Y	Y	Y	Y
OKLAHOMA						
Inhofe	Y	Y	Y	Y	Y	Y
Lankford	Y	Y	Y	Y	Y	Y
OREGON						
Wyden	N	N	N	N	N	N
Merkley	N	N	N	N	N	N
PENNSYLVANIA						
Casey	N	N	N	N	N	N
Toomey	Y	Y	Y	Y	Y	Y
RHODE ISLAND						
Reed	N	N	N	N	N	N
Whitehouse	N	N	N	N	N	N
SOUTH CAROLINA						
Graham	Y	Y	Y	Y	Y	Y
Scott	Y	Y	Y	Y	Y	Y
SOUTH DAKOTA						
Thune	Y	Y	Y	Y	Y	Y
Rounds	Y	Y	Y	Y	Y	Y
TENNESSEE						
Alexander	Y	Y	Y	Y	Y	Y
Blackburn	Y	Y	Y	Y	Y	Y
TEXAS						
Cornyn	Y	Y	Y	Y	Y	Y
Cruz	Y	Y	Y	Y	Y	Y
UTAH						
Lee	Y	Y	Y	Y	Y	Y
Romney	Y	Y	Y	Y	Y	Y
VERMONT						
Leahy	N	N	N	N	N	N
Sanders	?	?	?	?	?	N
VIRGINIA						
Warner	N	N	N	N	N	N
Kaine	N	N	N	N	N	N
WASHINGTON						
Murray	N	N	N	N	N	N
Cantwell	N	N	N	N	N	N
WEST VIRGINIA						
Manchin	Y	Y	Y	N	?	Y
Capito	Y	Y	Y	Y	Y	Y
WISCONSIN						
Johnson	Y	Y	Y	Y	Y	Y
Baldwin	N	N	N	N	N	N
WYOMING						
Enzi	Y	Y	Y	Y	Y	Y
Barrasso	Y	Y	Y	Y	Y	Y

KEY: **Republicans**   Democrats   *Independents*

Y Voted for (yea)	**N** Voted against (nay)	**P** Voted "present"
+ Announced for	**−** Announced against	**?** Did not vote or otherwise
# Paired for	**X** Paired against	make position known

205. Phipps Nomination - Confirmation. Confirmation of President Trump's nomination of Peter Joseph Phipps of Pennsylvania to be a U.S. circuit judge for the 3rd Circuit. Confirmed 56-40: R 53-0; D 3-38; I 0-2. *Note: A "yea" was a vote in support of the president's position.* July 16, 2019.

206. Treaty. Spain Tax Treaty - Cloture. McConnell, R-Ky., motion to invoke cloture (thus limiting debate) on the resolution of ratification of the Protocol Amending the Tax Convention with Spain. Motion agreed to 94-1: R 52-1; D 41-0; I 1-0. *Note: Three-fifths of the total Senate (60) is required to invoke cloture.* July 16, 2019.

207. Treaty. Spain Tax Treaty - Enforcment Date Adjustment. Adoption of the Paul, R-Ky., amendment to the resolution of ratification on the Protocol Amending the Tax Convention with Spain that would enforce the protocol as if it had been agreed to on Jan. 1, 2019 instead of in accordance with the original three-month waiting period to follow ratification. Rejected 4-92: R 4-49; D 0-42; I 0-1. July 16, 2019.

208. Treaty. Spain Tax Treaty - Information Sharing Limitation. Adoption of the Paul, R-Ky., amendment to the Protocol Amending the Tax Convention with Spain that would strike "such information as individualized relevant to an individual investigation" in reference to the authorities of contracting states when exchanging information in order to carry out or enforce tax laws and provisions of the treaty. Rejected 4-92: R 4-49; D 0-42; I 0-1. July 16, 2019.

209. Treaty. Spain Tax Treaty - Adoption. Adoption of the resolution of ratification of the Protocol Amending the Tax Convention with Spain that would amend the U.S. bilateral tax agreement with Spain for the purposes of the avoidance of double taxation. Adopted (thus consenting to ratification) 94-2: R 51-2; D 42-0; I 1-0. *Note: A two-thirds majority of those present and voting (64 in this case) is required for adoption of resolutions of ratification.* July 16, 2019.

210. Treaty. Swiss Tax Treaty - Adoption. Adoption of the resolution of ratification for the Protocol Amending Tax Convention with Swiss Confederation. Adopted (thus consenting to ratification) 95-2: R 50-2; D 43-0; I 2-0. *Note: A two-thirds majority of those present and voting (65 in this case) is required for adoption of resolutions of ratification.* July 17, 2019.

	205	206	207	208	209	210
ALABAMA						
Shelby	Y	Y	N	N	Y	Y
Jones	Y	Y	N	N	Y	Y
ALASKA						
Murkowski	Y	Y	N	N	Y	Y
Sullivan	Y	Y	Y	Y	Y	Y
ARIZONA						
Sinema	Y	Y	N	N	Y	Y
McSally	Y	Y	N	N	Y	Y
ARKANSAS						
Boozman	Y	Y	N	N	Y	Y
Cotton	Y	Y	N	N	Y	Y
CALIFORNIA						
Feinstein	N	Y	N	N	Y	Y
Harris	-	?	?	?	?	?
COLORADO						
Bennet	?	?	?	?	?	?
Gardner	Y	Y	N	N	Y	Y
CONNECTICUT						
Blumenthal	N	Y	N	N	Y	Y
Murphy	N	Y	N	N	Y	Y
DELAWARE						
Carper	N	Y	N	N	Y	Y
Coons	N	Y	N	N	Y	Y
FLORIDA						
Rubio	Y	Y	N	N	Y	Y
Scott	Y	Y	N	N	Y	Y
GEORGIA						
Isakson	Y	Y	N	N	Y	?
Perdue	Y	Y	N	N	Y	Y
HAWAII						
Schatz	N	Y	N	N	Y	Y
Hirono	N	Y	N	N	Y	Y
IDAHO						
Crapo	Y	Y	N	N	Y	Y
Risch	Y	Y	N	N	Y	Y
ILLINOIS						
Durbin	N	Y	N	N	Y	Y
Duckworth	N	Y	N	N	Y	Y
INDIANA						
Young	Y	Y	N	N	Y	Y
Braun	Y	Y	N	N	Y	Y
IOWA						
Grassley	Y	Y	N	N	Y	Y
Ernst	Y	Y	N	N	Y	Y
KANSAS						
Roberts	Y	Y	N	N	Y	Y
Moran	Y	Y	N	N	Y	Y
KENTUCKY						
McConnell	Y	Y	N	N	Y	Y
Paul	Y	N	Y	Y	N	N
LOUISIANA						
Cassidy	Y	Y	N	N	Y	Y
Kennedy	Y	Y	N	N	Y	Y
MAINE						
Collins	Y	Y	N	N	Y	Y
King	N	Y	N	N	Y	Y
MARYLAND						
Cardin	N	Y	N	N	Y	Y
Van Hollen	N	Y	N	N	Y	Y
MASSACHUSETTS						
Warren	N	Y	N	N	Y	Y
Markey	N	Y	N	N	Y	Y
MICHIGAN						
Stabenow	N	Y	N	N	Y	Y
Peters	N	Y	N	N	Y	Y
MINNESOTA						
Klobuchar	N	Y	N	N	Y	Y
Smith	N	Y	N	N	Y	Y
MISSISSIPPI						
Wicker	Y	Y	N	N	Y	Y
Hyde-Smith	Y	Y	N	N	Y	Y
MISSOURI						
Blunt	Y	Y	N	N	Y	Y
Hawley	Y	Y	N	N	Y	Y

	205	206	207	208	209	210
MONTANA						
Tester	N	Y	N	N	Y	Y
Daines	Y	Y	N	N	Y	Y
NEBRASKA						
Fischer	Y	Y	N	N	Y	Y
Sasse	Y	Y	N	N	Y	Y
NEVADA						
Cortez Masto	N	Y	N	N	Y	Y
Rosen	N	Y	N	N	Y	Y
NEW HAMPSHIRE						
Shaheen	N	Y	N	N	Y	Y
Hassan	N	Y	N	N	Y	Y
NEW JERSEY						
Menendez	N	Y	N	N	Y	Y
Booker	?	?	N	N	Y	Y
NEW MEXICO						
Udall	N	Y	N	N	Y	Y
Heinrich	N	Y	N	N	Y	Y
NEW YORK						
Schumer	N	Y	N	N	Y	Y
Gillibrand	?	?	?	?	?	Y
NORTH CAROLINA						
Burr	Y	Y	N	N	Y	Y
Tillis	Y	Y	N	N	Y	Y
NORTH DAKOTA						
Hoeven	Y	Y	N	N	Y	Y
Cramer	Y	Y	N	N	Y	Y
OHIO						
Brown	N	Y	N	N	Y	Y
Portman	Y	Y	N	N	Y	Y
OKLAHOMA						
Inhofe	Y	Y	N	N	Y	Y
Lankford	Y	Y	N	N	Y	Y
OREGON						
Wyden	N	Y	N	N	Y	Y
Merkley	N	Y	N	N	Y	Y
PENNSYLVANIA						
Casey	N	Y	N	N	Y	Y
Toomey	Y	Y	N	N	Y	Y
RHODE ISLAND						
Reed	N	Y	N	N	Y	Y
Whitehouse	N	Y	N	N	Y	Y
SOUTH CAROLINA						
Graham	Y	Y	N	N	Y	Y
Scott	Y	Y	N	N	Y	Y
SOUTH DAKOTA						
Thune	Y	Y	N	N	Y	Y
Rounds	Y	Y	N	N	Y	Y
TENNESSEE						
Alexander	Y	Y	N	N	Y	Y
Blackburn	Y	Y	N	N	Y	Y
TEXAS						
Cornyn	Y	Y	N	N	Y	Y
Cruz	Y	Y	Y	Y	Y	Y
UTAH						
Lee	Y	Y	Y	Y	N	N
Romney	Y	Y	N	N	Y	Y
VERMONT						
Leahy	N	Y	N	N	Y	Y
Sanders	N	?	?	?	?	Y
VIRGINIA						
Warner	N	Y	N	N	Y	Y
Kaine	N	Y	N	N	Y	Y
WASHINGTON						
Murray	N	Y	N	N	Y	Y
Cantwell	N	Y	N	N	Y	Y
WEST VIRGINIA						
Manchin	Y	Y	N	N	Y	Y
Capito	Y	Y	N	N	Y	Y
WISCONSIN						
Johnson	Y	Y	N	N	Y	Y
Baldwin	N	Y	N	N	Y	Y
WYOMING						
Enzi	Y	Y	N	N	Y	Y
Barrasso	Y	N	Y	N	Y	Y

KEY:	Republicans	Democrats	Independents

Y	Voted for (yea)	**N**	Voted against (nay)	**P**	Voted "present"
+	Announced for	**-**	Announced against	**?**	Did not vote or otherwise
#	Paired for	**X**	Paired against		make position known

211. Treaty. Japan Tax Treaty - Adoption. Adoption of the resolution of ratification for the Protocol Amending the Tax Convention with Japan. Adopted (thus consenting to ratification) 95-2: R 50-2; D 43-0; I 2-0. *Note: A two-thirds majority of those present and voting (65 in this case) is required for adoption of resolutions of ratification.* July 17, 2019.

212. Treaty. Luxembourg Tax Treaty - Adoption. Adoption of the resolution of ratification for the Protocol Amending Tax Convention with Luxembourg. Adopted (thus consenting to ratification) 93-3: R 50-2; D 42-1; I 1-0. *Note: A two-thirds majority of those present and voting (64 in this case) is required for adoption of resolutions of ratification.* July 17, 2019.

213. Corker Nomination - Cloture. Motion to invoke cloture (thus limiting debate) on the nomination of Clifton L. Corker or Tennessee to be a U.S. district judge for the Eastern District of Tennessee. Motion agreed to 55-41: R 52-0; D 3-40; I 0-1. *Note: A majority of senators voting (49 in this case), a quorum being present, is required to invoke cloture on all nominations.* July 17, 2019.

214. Blanchard Nomination - Cloture. Motion to invoke cloture (thus limiting debate) on the nomination of Lynda Blanchard of Alabama to be ambassador to the Republic of Slovenia. Motion agreed to 55-41: R 52-0; D 3-40; I 0-1. *Note: A majority of senators voting (49 in this case), a quorum being present, is required to invoke cloture on all nominations.* July 17, 2019.

215. Tapia Nomination - Cloture. Motion to invoke cloture (thus limiting debate) on the nomination of Donald R. Tapia of Arizona to be ambassador to Jamaica. Motion agreed to 67-28: R 51-0; D 15-28; I 1-0. *Note: A majority of senators voting (48 in this case), a quorum being present, is required to invoke cloture on all nominations.* July 17, 2019.

216. Corker Nomination - Confirmation. Confirmation of President Trump's nomination of Clifton L. Corker or Tennessee to be a U.S. district judge for the Eastern District of Tennessee. Confirmed 55-39: R 52-0; D 3-38; I 0-1. *Note: A "yea" was a vote in support of the president's position.* July 18, 2019.

	211	212	213	214	215	216
ALABAMA						
Shelby	Y	Y	Y	Y	Y	Y
Jones	Y	Y	Y	Y	Y	Y
ALASKA						
Murkowski	Y	Y	Y	Y	Y	Y
Sullivan	Y	Y	Y	Y	Y	Y
ARIZONA						
Sinema	Y	Y	Y	Y	Y	Y
McSally	Y	Y	Y	Y	Y	Y
ARKANSAS						
Boozman	Y	Y	Y	Y	Y	Y
Cotton	Y	Y	Y	Y	Y	Y
CALIFORNIA						
Feinstein	Y	Y	N	N	N	N
Harris	?	?	?	?	?	?
COLORADO						
Bennet	?	?	?	?	?	N
Gardner	Y	Y	Y	Y	Y	Y
CONNECTICUT						
Blumenthal	Y	Y	N	N	N	N
Murphy	Y	Y	N	Y	Y	N
DELAWARE						
Carper	Y	Y	N	N	Y	N
Coons	Y	Y	N	N	Y	N
FLORIDA						
Rubio	Y	Y	Y	Y	Y	Y
Scott	Y	Y	Y	Y	Y	Y
GEORGIA						
Isakson	?	?	?	?	?	?
Perdue	Y	Y	Y	Y	Y	Y
HAWAII						
Schatz	Y	Y	N	N	N	N
Hirono	Y	Y	N	N	N	N
IDAHO						
Crapo	Y	Y	Y	Y	Y	Y
Risch	Y	Y	Y	Y	Y	Y
ILLINOIS						
Durbin	Y	N	N	N	N	N
Duckworth	Y	Y	N	N	Y	N
INDIANA						
Young	Y	Y	Y	Y	Y	Y
Braun	Y	Y	Y	Y	Y	Y
IOWA						
Grassley	Y	Y	Y	Y	Y	Y
Ernst	Y	Y	Y	Y	Y	Y
KANSAS						
Roberts	Y	Y	Y	Y	Y	Y
Moran	Y	Y	Y	Y	Y	Y
KENTUCKY						
McConnell	Y	Y	Y	Y	Y	Y
Paul	N	N	Y	Y	Y	Y
LOUISIANA						
Cassidy	Y	Y	Y	Y	Y	Y
Kennedy	Y	Y	Y	Y	Y	Y
MAINE						
Collins	Y	Y	Y	Y	Y	Y
King	Y	Y	N	N	Y	N
MARYLAND						
Cardin	Y	Y	N	N	Y	N
Van Hollen	Y	Y	N	N	N	N
MASSACHUSETTS						
Warren	Y	Y	N	N	N	N
Markey	Y	Y	N	N	N	N
MICHIGAN						
Stabenow	Y	Y	N	N	N	?
Peters	Y	Y	N	N	N	N
MINNESOTA						
Klobuchar	Y	Y	N	N	N	N
Smith	Y	Y	N	N	N	N
MISSISSIPPI						
Wicker	Y	Y	Y	Y	Y	Y
Hyde-Smith	Y	Y	Y	Y	Y	Y
MISSOURI						
Blunt	Y	Y	Y	Y	Y	Y
Hawley	Y	Y	Y	Y	Y	Y

	211	212	213	214	215	216
MONTANA						
Tester	Y	Y	N	N	N	N
Daines	Y	Y	Y	Y	Y	Y
NEBRASKA						
Fischer	Y	Y	Y	Y	Y	Y
Sasse	Y	Y	Y	Y	Y	Y
NEVADA						
Cortez Masto	Y	Y	N	N	Y	-
Rosen	Y	Y	N	N	Y	N
NEW HAMPSHIRE						
Shaheen	Y	Y	N	N	Y	N
Hassan	Y	Y	N	N	Y	N
NEW JERSEY						
Menendez	Y	Y	N	N	Y	N
Booker	Y	Y	N	N	N	?
NEW MEXICO						
Udall	Y	Y	N	N	N	N
Heinrich	Y	Y	N	N	N	N
NEW YORK						
Schumer	Y	Y	N	N	N	N
Gillibrand	Y	Y	N	N	N	N
NORTH CAROLINA						
Burr	Y	Y	Y	Y	Y	Y
Tillis	Y	Y	Y	Y	?	Y
NORTH DAKOTA						
Hoeven	Y	Y	Y	Y	Y	Y
Cramer	Y	Y	Y	Y	Y	Y
OHIO						
Brown	Y	Y	N	N	N	N
Portman	Y	Y	Y	Y	Y	Y
OKLAHOMA						
Inhofe	Y	Y	Y	Y	Y	Y
Lankford	Y	Y	Y	Y	Y	Y
OREGON						
Wyden	Y	Y	N	N	N	N
Merkley	Y	Y	N	N	N	N
PENNSYLVANIA						
Casey	Y	Y	N	N	N	N
Toomey	Y	Y	Y	Y	Y	Y
RHODE ISLAND						
Reed	Y	Y	N	N	N	N
Whitehouse	Y	Y	N	N	N	N
SOUTH CAROLINA						
Graham	Y	Y	Y	Y	Y	Y
Scott	Y	Y	Y	Y	Y	Y
SOUTH DAKOTA						
Thune	Y	Y	Y	Y	Y	Y
Rounds	Y	Y	Y	Y	Y	Y
TENNESSEE						
Alexander	Y	Y	Y	Y	Y	Y
Blackburn	Y	Y	Y	Y	Y	Y
TEXAS						
Cornyn	Y	Y	Y	Y	Y	Y
Cruz	Y	Y	Y	Y	Y	Y
UTAH						
Lee	N	N	Y	Y	Y	Y
Romney	Y	Y	Y	Y	Y	Y
VERMONT						
Leahy	Y	Y	N	N	Y	N
Sanders	Y	?	?	?	?	?
VIRGINIA						
Warner	Y	Y	N	N	N	N
Kaine	Y	Y	N	N	N	N
WASHINGTON						
Murray	Y	Y	N	N	N	N
Cantwell	Y	Y	N	N	N	N
WEST VIRGINIA						
Manchin	Y	Y	Y	N	Y	Y
Capito	Y	Y	Y	Y	Y	Y
WISCONSIN						
Johnson	Y	Y	Y	Y	Y	Y
Baldwin	Y	Y	N	N	N	N
WYOMING						
Enzi	Y	Y	Y	Y	Y	Y
Barrasso	Y	Y	Y	Y	Y	Y

KEY:		Republicans	Democrats	*Independents*
Y	Voted for (yea)	N Voted against (nay)	P Voted "present"
+	Announced for	– Announced against	? Did not vote or otherwise
#	Paired for	X Paired against	make position known

217. Blanchard Nomination - Confirmation. Confirmation of President Trump's nomination of Lynda Blanchard of Alabama to be ambassador to the Republic of Slovenia. Confirmed 54-40: R 51-1; D 3-38; I 0-1. *Note: A "yea" was a vote in support of the president's position.* July 18, 2019.

218. Tapia Nomination - Confirmation. Confirmation of President Trump's nomination of Donald R. Tapia of Arizona to be ambassador to Jamaica. Confirmed 66-26: R 51-0; D 14-26; I 1-0. *Note: A "yea" was a vote in support of the president's position.* July 18, 2019.

219. Esper Nomination - Cloture. Motion to invoke cloture (thus limiting debate) on the nomination of Mark T. Esper of Virginia to be secretary of Defense. Motion agreed to 85-6: R 48-0; D 36-6; I 1-0. *Note: A majority of senators voting (46 in this case), a quorum being present, is required to invoke cloture on all nominations.* July 22, 2019.

220. Esper Nomination - Confirmation. Confirmation of President Trump's nomination of Mark T. Esper of Virginia to be secretary of Defense. Confirmed 90-8: R 52-0; D 37-8; I 1-0. *Note: A "yea" was a vote in support of the president's position.* July 23, 2019.

221. Dickson Nomination - Cloture. Motion to invoke cloture (thus limiting debate) on the nomination of Stephen M. Dickson of Georgia to be administrator of the Federal Aviation Administration. Motion agreed to 52-45: R 52-0; D 0-44; I 0-1. *Note: A majority of senators voting (49 in this case), a quorum being present, is required to invoke cloture on all nominations.* July 23, 2019.

222. HR1327. 9/11 Victim Compensation Fund - Funding Limitations. Lee, R-Utah, amendment no. 928 that would limit the funds authorized in the bill to $10.2 billion through fiscal 2029, and to an additional $10 billion from fiscal 2030 through fiscal 2092 for the September 11th Victim Compensation Fund. Rejected 32-66: R 32-19; D 0-45; I 0-2. *Note: Per a unanimous consent agreement, 60 votes were required for adoption of the amendment.* July 23, 2019.

	217	218	219	220	221	222
ALABAMA						
Shelby	Y	Y	Y	Y	Y	Y
Jones	Y	Y	Y	Y	N	N
ALASKA						
Murkowski	Y	Y	?	Y	Y	N
Sullivan	Y	Y	Y	Y	Y	Y
ARIZONA						
Sinema	Y	Y	Y	Y	N	N
McSally	Y	Y	Y	Y	Y	N
ARKANSAS						
Boozman	Y	Y	Y	Y	Y	N
Cotton	Y	Y	Y	Y	Y	N
CALIFORNIA						
Feinstein	N	N	Y	Y	N	N
Harris	?	?	N	N	N	N
COLORADO						
Bennet	N	N	?	Y	N	N
Gardner	Y	Y	Y	Y	Y	N
CONNECTICUT						
Blumenthal	N	N	Y	Y	N	N
Murphy	Y	Y	Y	Y	N	N
DELAWARE						
Carper	N	Y	Y	Y	N	N
Coons	N	Y	Y	Y	N	N
FLORIDA						
Rubio	Y	Y	Y	Y	Y	Y
Scott	Y	Y	Y	Y	Y	Y
GEORGIA						
Isakson	?	?	?	+	+	?
Perdue	Y	Y	Y	Y	Y	Y
HAWAII						
Schatz	N	N	Y	Y	N	N
Hirono	N	N	Y	Y	N	N
IDAHO						
Crapo	Y	Y	Y	Y	Y	Y
Risch	Y	Y	Y	Y	Y	Y
ILLINOIS						
Durbin	N	N	Y	Y	N	N
Duckworth	N	Y	Y	Y	N	N
INDIANA						
Young	Y	Y	Y	Y	Y	Y
Braun	Y	Y	Y	Y	Y	Y
IOWA						
Grassley	Y	Y	Y	Y	Y	Y
Ernst	Y	Y	Y	Y	Y	N
KANSAS						
Roberts	Y	Y	Y	Y	Y	N
Moran	Y	?	+	Y	Y	N
KENTUCKY						
McConnell	Y	Y	Y	Y		N
Paul	Y	Y	Y	Y	Y	Y
LOUISIANA						
Cassidy	Y	Y	Y	Y	Y	Y
Kennedy	Y	Y	?	Y	Y	Y
MAINE						
Collins	N	Y	Y	Y	Y	N
King	N	Y	Y	Y	N	N
MARYLAND						
Cardin	N	Y	Y	Y	N	N
Van Hollen	N	N	Y	Y	N	N
MASSACHUSETTS						
Warren	N	?	N	N	N	N
Markey	N	N	N	N	N	N
MICHIGAN						
Stabenow	?	?	Y	Y	N	N
Peters	N	N	Y	Y	N	N
MINNESOTA						
Klobuchar	N	N	N	N	N	N
Smith	N	N	Y	Y	N	N
MISSISSIPPI						
Wicker	Y	Y	Y	Y	Y	Y
Hyde-Smith	Y	Y	Y	Y	Y	Y
MISSOURI						
Blunt	Y	Y	Y	Y	Y	N
Hawley	Y	Y	Y	Y	Y	N

	217	218	219	220	221	222
MONTANA						
Tester	N	N	Y	Y	N	N
Daines	Y	Y	Y	Y	Y	Y
NEBRASKA						
Fischer	Y	Y	Y	Y	Y	Y
Sasse	Y	Y	Y	Y	Y	Y
NEVADA						
Cortez Masto	-	+	Y	Y	N	N
Rosen	N	Y	Y	Y	N	N
NEW HAMPSHIRE						
Shaheen	N	Y	Y	Y	N	N
Hassan	N	Y	Y	Y	N	N
NEW JERSEY						
Menendez	N	Y	Y	Y	N	N
Booker	?	?	?	N	N	N
NEW MEXICO						
Udall	N	N	Y	Y	N	N
Heinrich	N	N	Y	Y	N	N
NEW YORK						
Schumer	N	N	Y	Y	N	N
Gillibrand	N	N	?	N	N	N
NORTH CAROLINA						
Burr	Y	Y	Y	Y	Y	?
Tillis	Y	Y	Y	Y	Y	Y
NORTH DAKOTA						
Hoeven	Y	Y	Y	Y	Y	N
Cramer	Y	Y	Y	Y	Y	N
OHIO						
Brown	N	N	Y	Y	N	N
Portman	Y	Y	Y	Y	Y	N
OKLAHOMA						
Inhofe	Y	Y	Y	Y	Y	Y
Lankford	Y	Y	Y	Y	Y	Y
OREGON						
Wyden	N	N	N	N	N	N
Merkley	N	N	N	N	N	N
PENNSYLVANIA						
Casey	N	N	Y	Y	N	N
Toomey	Y	Y	?	Y	Y	Y
RHODE ISLAND						
Reed	N	N	Y	Y	N	N
Whitehouse	N	Y	Y	Y	?	N
SOUTH CAROLINA						
Graham	Y	Y	Y	Y	Y	N
Scott	Y	Y	Y	Y	Y	Y
SOUTH DAKOTA						
Thune	Y	Y	Y	Y	Y	N
Rounds	Y	Y	Y	Y	Y	Y
TENNESSEE						
Alexander	Y	Y	Y	Y	Y	N
Blackburn	Y	Y	Y	Y	Y	Y
TEXAS						
Cornyn	Y	Y	Y	Y	Y	N
Cruz	Y	Y	Y	Y	Y	Y
UTAH						
Lee	Y	Y	Y	Y	Y	Y
Romney	Y	Y	Y	Y	Y	Y
VERMONT						
Leahy	N	Y	Y	Y	N	N
Sanders	?	?	?	?	?	N
VIRGINIA						
Warner	N	N	Y	Y	N	N
Kaine	N	N	Y	Y	N	N
WASHINGTON						
Murray	N	N	Y	Y	N	N
Cantwell	N	N	Y	Y	N	N
WEST VIRGINIA						
Manchin	N	Y	Y	Y	N	N
Capito	Y	Y	Y	Y	Y	N
WISCONSIN						
Johnson	Y	Y	Y	Y	Y	Y
Baldwin	N	N	Y	Y	N	N
WYOMING						
Enzi	Y	Y	Y	Y	Y	Y
Barrasso	Y	Y	Y	Y	Y	Y

KEY: **Republicans**   Democrats   *Independents*

Y Voted for (yea)	**N** Voted against (nay)	**P** Voted "present"
+ Announced for	**–** Announced against	**?** Did not vote or otherwise make position known
# Paired for	**X** Paired against	

223. HR1327. 9/11 Victim Compensation Fund - Sequestration Requirement. Paul, R-Ky., amendment no. 929 that would require the president to issue a sequestration order to reduce all direct spending except for certain welfare and veterans programs for fiscal 2020 through 2025 by a uniform percentage that would reduce total direct spending by $2 billion for each fiscal year. Rejected 22-77: R 22-30; D 0-45; I 0-2. *Note: Per a unanimous consent agreement, 60 votes were required for adoption of the amendment.* July 23, 2019.

224. HR1327. 9/11 Victim Compensation Fund - Passage. Passage of the bill that would reauthorize through fiscal 2090 the September 11th Victim Compensation Fund to compensate first responders and other individuals with health conditions caused by toxin exposure due to the attacks on September 11, 2001. It would authorize such sums as may be necessary for the fund and allow claims to be filed through Oct. 1, 2089. Passed (thus cleared for the president) 97-2: R 50-2; D 45-0; I 2-0. July 23, 2019.

225. Dickson Nomination - Confirmation. Confirmation of President Trump's nomination of Stephen M. Dickson of Georgia to be administrator of the Federal Aviation Administration. Confirmed 52-40: R 52-0; D 0-39; I 0-1. *Note: A "yea" was a vote in support of the president's position.* July 24, 2019.

226. Berger Nomination - Cloture. Motion to invoke cloture (thus limiting debate) on the nomination of Wendy Williams Berger of Florida to be a U.S. district judge for the Middle District of Florida. Motion agreed to 55-37: R 52-0; D 3-36; I 0-1. *Note: A majority of senators voting (47 in this case), a quorum being present, is required to invoke cloture on all nominations.* July 24, 2019.

227. Buescher Nomination - Cloture. Motion to invoke cloture (thus limiting debate) on the nomination of Brian C. Buescher of Nebraska to be a U.S. district judge for the District of Nebraska. Motion agreed to 52-39: R 52-0; D 0-38; I 0-1. *Note: A majority of senators voting (46 in this case), a quorum being present, is required to invoke cloture on all nominations.* July 24, 2019.

228. Berger Nomination - Confirmation. Confirmation of President Trump's nomination of Wendy Williams Berger of Florida to be U.S. District Judge for the Middle District of Florida. Confirmed 54-37: R 51-0; D 3-36; I 0-1. *Note: A "yea" was a vote in support of the president's position.* July 24, 2019.

	223	224	225	226	227	228
ALABAMA						
Shelby	N	Y	Y	Y	Y	Y
Jones	N	Y	N	Y	N	Y
ALASKA						
Murkowski	N	Y	Y	Y	Y	Y
Sullivan	N	Y	Y	Y	Y	Y
ARIZONA						
Sinema	N	Y	N	Y	N	Y
McSally	N	Y	Y	Y	Y	Y
ARKANSAS						
Boozman	N	Y	Y	Y	Y	Y
Cotton	Y	Y	Y	Y	Y	Y
CALIFORNIA						
Feinstein	N	Y	N	N	N	N
Harris	N	Y	?	-	-	-
COLORADO						
Bennet	N	Y	?	?	?	?
Gardner	N	Y	Y	Y	Y	Y
CONNECTICUT						
Blumenthal	N	Y	N	N	N	N
Murphy	N	Y	N	N	N	N
DELAWARE						
Carper	N	Y	N	N	N	N
Coons	N	Y	N	N	N	N
FLORIDA						
Rubio	N	Y	Y	Y	Y	Y
Scott	N	Y	Y	Y	Y	Y
GEORGIA						
Isakson	?	?	+	?	?	?
Perdue	N	Y	Y	Y	Y	Y
HAWAII						
Schatz	N	Y	N	N	N	N
Hirono	N	Y	N	N	N	N
IDAHO						
Crapo	Y	Y	Y	Y	Y	Y
Risch	Y	Y	Y	Y	Y	Y
ILLINOIS						
Durbin	N	Y	N	N	N	N
Duckworth	N	Y	N	N	N	N
INDIANA						
Young	N	Y	Y	Y	Y	Y
Braun	Y	Y	Y	Y	Y	Y
IOWA						
Grassley	Y	Y	Y	Y	Y	Y
Ernst	N	Y	Y	Y	Y	Y
KANSAS						
Roberts	N	Y	Y	Y	Y	Y
Moran	N	Y	Y	Y	Y	Y
KENTUCKY						
McConnell	N	Y	Y	Y	Y	Y
Paul	Y	N	Y	Y	Y	Y
LOUISIANA						
Cassidy	Y	Y	Y	Y	Y	Y
Kennedy	Y	Y	Y	Y	Y	Y
MAINE						
Collins	N	Y	Y	Y	Y	Y
King	N	Y	N	N	N	N
MARYLAND						
Cardin	N	Y	N	N	N	N
Van Hollen	N	Y	N	N	N	N
MASSACHUSETTS						
Warren	N	Y	?	?	?	?
Markey	N	Y	N	N	N	N
MICHIGAN						
Stabenow	N	Y	N	N	N	N
Peters	N	Y	N	N	N	N
MINNESOTA						
Klobuchar	N	Y	?	?	?	?
Smith	N	Y	N	N	N	N
MISSISSIPPI						
Wicker	Y	Y	Y	Y	Y	Y
Hyde-Smith	Y	Y	Y	Y	Y	Y
MISSOURI						
Blunt	N	Y	Y	Y	Y	Y
Hawley	N	Y	Y	Y	Y	Y

	223	224	225	226	227	228
MONTANA						
Tester	N	Y	N	N	N	N
Daines	Y	Y	Y	Y	Y	Y
NEBRASKA						
Fischer	N	Y	Y	Y	Y	Y
Sasse	Y	Y	Y	Y	Y	Y
NEVADA						
Cortez Masto	N	Y	N	N	N	N
Rosen	N	Y	N	N	N	N
NEW HAMPSHIRE						
Shaheen	N	Y	N	N	N	N
Hassan	N	Y	N	N	N	N
NEW JERSEY						
Menendez	N	Y	N	N	N	N
Booker	N	Y	?	?	?	?
NEW MEXICO						
Udall	N	Y	N	N	N	N
Heinrich	N	Y	N	N	N	N
NEW YORK						
Schumer	N	Y	N	N	N	N
Gillibrand	N	Y	?	?	?	?
NORTH CAROLINA						
Burr	N	Y	Y	Y	Y	Y
Tillis	N	Y	Y	Y	Y	Y
NORTH DAKOTA						
Hoeven	N	Y	Y	Y	Y	Y
Cramer	N	Y	Y	Y	Y	Y
OHIO						
Brown	N	Y	N	N	N	N
Portman	N	Y	Y	Y	Y	Y
OKLAHOMA						
Inhofe	Y	Y	Y	Y	Y	Y
Lankford	Y	Y	Y	Y	Y	Y
OREGON						
Wyden	N	Y	N	N	N	N
Merkley	N	Y	N	N	N	N
PENNSYLVANIA						
Casey	N	Y	N	N	N	N
Toomey	Y	Y	Y	Y	Y	Y
RHODE ISLAND						
Reed	N	Y	N	N	N	N
Whitehouse	N	Y	N	N	?	N
SOUTH CAROLINA						
Graham	N	Y	Y	Y	Y	Y
Scott	Y	Y	Y	Y	Y	Y
SOUTH DAKOTA						
Thune	Y	Y	Y	Y	Y	Y
Rounds	N	Y	Y	Y	Y	Y
TENNESSEE						
Alexander	N	Y	Y	Y	Y	Y
Blackburn	Y	Y	Y	Y	Y	Y
TEXAS						
Cornyn	N	Y	Y	Y	Y	Y
Cruz	Y	Y	Y	Y	Y	Y
UTAH						
Lee	Y	N	Y	Y	Y	Y
Romney	Y	Y	Y	Y	Y	Y
VERMONT						
Leahy	N	Y	N	N	N	N
Sanders	N	Y	?	?	?	?
VIRGINIA						
Warner	N	Y	N	N	N	N
Kaine	N	Y	N	N	N	N
WASHINGTON						
Murray	N	Y	N	N	N	N
Cantwell	N	Y	N	N	N	N
WEST VIRGINIA						
Manchin	N	Y	N	Y	*Y*	Y
Capito	N	Y	Y	Y	Y	?
WISCONSIN						
Johnson	N	Y	Y	Y	Y	Y
Baldwin	N	Y	N	N	N	N
WYOMING						
Enzi	Y	Y	Y	Y	Y	Y
Barrasso	Y	Y	Y	Y	Y	Y

KEY:

	Republicans	Democrats	*Independents*
Y Voted for (yea)	**N** Voted against (nay)	**P** Voted "present"	
+ Announced for	**–** Announced against	**?** Did not vote or otherwise make position known	
# Paired for	**X** Paired against		

229. Buescher Nomination - Confirmation. Confirmation of President Trump's nomination of Brian C. Buescher of Nebraska to be U.S. district judge for the District of Nebraska. Confirmed 51-40: R 51-0; D 0-39; I 0-1. *Note: A "yea" was a vote in support of the president's position.* July 24, 2019.

230. Milley Nomination - Confirmation. Confirmation of President Trump's nomination of General Mark A. Milley to be general and chairman of the Joint Chiefs of Staff. Confirmed 89-1: R 50-0; D 38-1; I 1-0. *Note: A "yea" was a vote in support of the president's position.* July 25, 2019.

231. SJRES36. Saudi Arabia Arms Sales - Veto Override. Passage over President Trump's July 24, 2019, veto of the joint resolution that would disapprove of the issuance of manufacturing, technical assistance, or export licenses related to certain defense articles and services to Saudi Arabia, the United Kingdom, Spain, and Italy, including for the transfer of guidance kits for Paveway laser-guided bomb systems and services related to the manufacture of Paveway system components. Rejected 45-40: R 5-40; D 39-0; I 1-0. *Note: A two-thirds majority of those present and voting (57 in this case) of both chambers is required to override the president's veto. A "nay" was a vote in support of the president's veto.* July 29, 2019.

232. SJRES37. United Arab Emirates Arms Export - Veto Override. Passage over President Trump's July 24, 2019 veto of the joint resolution that would disapprove of the issuance of export licenses related to the transfer of guidance kits for the Paveway II laser-guided bomb system to the United Arab Emirates, United Kingdom, and France. Rejected 45-39: R 5-39; D 39-0; I 1-0. *Note: A two-thirds majority of those present and voting (56 in this case) of both chambers is required to override the president's veto. A "nay" was a vote in support of the president's veto.* July 29, 2019.

233. SJRES38. Saudi Arabia Arms Export - Veto Override. Passage over President Trump's veto on July 24, 2019, of the joint resolution that would disapprove of the issuance of export licenses related to the transfer of certain defense articles and services to Saudi Arabia and the United Kingdom, specifically for articles and services to support the manufacture of the Aurora fuzing system used by the Paveway IV laser-guided bomb system. Rejected 46-41: R 6-41; D 39-0; I 1-0. *Note: A two-thirds majority of those present and voting (58 in this case) of both chambers is required to override the president's veto. A "nay" was a vote in support of the president's veto.* July 29, 2019.

234. Liburdi Nomination - Cloture. Motion to invoke cloture (thus limiting debate) on the nomination of Michael T. Liburdi of Arizona to be a U.S. district judge for the District of Arizona. Motion agreed to 51-37: R 48-0; D 3-36; I 0-1. *Note: A majority of senators voting (45 in this case), a quorum being present, is required to invoke cloture on all nominations.* July 29, 2019.

	229	230	231	232	233	234
ALABAMA						
Shelby	Y	Y	N	N	N	Y
Jones	N	Y	Y	Y	Y	Y
ALASKA						
Murkowski	Y	Y	Y	Y	Y	Y
Sullivan	Y	Y	?	?	?	?
ARIZONA						
Sinema	N	Y	Y	Y	Y	Y
McSally	Y	Y	N	N	N	Y
ARKANSAS						
Boozman	Y	Y	N	N	N	Y
Cotton	Y	Y	N	N	N	Y
CALIFORNIA						
Feinstein	N	Y	Y	Y	Y	N
Harris	-	?	?	?	?	-
COLORADO						
Bennet	?	Y	?	?	?	?
Gardner	Y	Y	?	-	N	Y
CONNECTICUT						
Blumenthal	N	Y	Y	Y	Y	N
Murphy	N	Y	Y	Y	Y	N
DELAWARE						
Carper	N	Y	Y	Y	Y	N
Coons	N	Y	Y	Y	Y	N
FLORIDA						
Rubio	Y	Y	N	N	N	Y
Scott	Y	Y	N	N	N	Y
GEORGIA						
Isakson	?	?	?	?	?	?
Perdue	Y	?	?	?	?	?
HAWAII						
Schatz	N	Y	Y	Y	Y	N
Hirono	N	Y	Y	Y	Y	N
IDAHO						
Crapo	Y	Y	N	?	?	Y
Risch	Y	Y	N	N	N	Y
ILLINOIS						
Durbin	N	Y	Y	Y	Y	N
Duckworth	N	Y	+	+	+	-
INDIANA						
Young	Y	Y	Y	Y	Y	Y
Braun	Y	Y	N	N	N	Y
IOWA						
Grassley	Y	Y	N	N	N	Y
Ernst	Y	Y	N	N	N	Y
KANSAS						
Roberts	Y	Y	N	N	N	Y
Moran	Y	+	Y	Y	Y	Y
KENTUCKY						
McConnell	Y	Y	N	N	N	Y
Paul	Y	Y	?	?	?	?
LOUISIANA						
Cassidy	Y	Y	N	N	?	?
Kennedy	Y	Y	N	N	N	Y
MAINE						
Collins	Y	Y	Y	Y	Y	Y
King	N	Y	Y	Y	Y	N
MARYLAND						
Cardin	N	Y	Y	Y	Y	N
Van Hollen	N	Y	Y	Y	Y	N
MASSACHUSETTS						
Warren	?	?	?	?	?	?
Markey	N	Y	Y	Y	Y	N
MICHIGAN						
Stabenow	N	Y	Y	Y	Y	N
Peters	N	Y	Y	Y	Y	N
MINNESOTA						
Klobuchar	?	?	?	?	?	?
Smith	N	Y	Y	Y	Y	N
MISSISSIPPI						
Wicker	Y	Y	N	N	N	Y
Hyde-Smith	Y	Y	N	N	N	Y
MISSOURI						
Blunt	Y	Y	N	N	N	Y
Hawley	Y	Y	N	N	N	Y

	229	230	231	232	233	234
MONTANA						
Tester	N	Y	Y	Y	Y	N
Daines	Y	Y	N	N	N	Y
NEBRASKA						
Fischer	Y	Y	N	N	N	Y
Sasse	Y	Y	?	-	N	Y
NEVADA						
Cortez Masto	N	Y	Y	Y	Y	N
Rosen	N	Y	Y	Y	Y	N
NEW HAMPSHIRE						
Shaheen	N	Y	Y	Y	Y	N
Hassan	N	Y	Y	Y	Y	N
NEW JERSEY						
Menendez	N	Y	Y	Y	Y	N
Booker	?	?	Y	Y	Y	N
NEW MEXICO						
Udall	N	Y	Y	Y	Y	N
Heinrich	N	Y	Y	Y	Y	N
NEW YORK						
Schumer	N	Y	Y	Y	Y	N
Gillibrand	?	?	?	?	?	?
NORTH CAROLINA						
Burr	Y	Y	N	N	N	Y
Tillis	Y	Y	N	N	N	Y
NORTH DAKOTA						
Hoeven	Y	Y	N	N	N	Y
Cramer	Y	Y	N	N	N	Y
OHIO						
Brown	N	Y	Y	Y	Y	N
Portman	Y	Y	N	N	N	Y
OKLAHOMA						
Inhofe	Y	Y	N	N	N	Y
Lankford	Y	Y	N	N	N	Y
OREGON						
Wyden	N	Y	Y	Y	Y	N
Merkley	N	N	Y	Y	Y	N
PENNSYLVANIA						
Casey	N	Y	Y	Y	Y	N
Toomey	Y	Y	N	N	N	Y
RHODE ISLAND						
Reed	N	Y	Y	Y	Y	N
Whitehouse	N	Y	Y	Y	Y	N
SOUTH CAROLINA						
Graham	Y	Y	?	+	N	Y
Scott	Y	Y	N	N	N	Y
SOUTH DAKOTA						
Thune	Y	Y	N	N	N	Y
Rounds	Y	Y	N	N	N	Y
TENNESSEE						
Alexander	Y	Y	N	N	N	Y
Blackburn	Y	Y	N	N	N	Y
TEXAS						
Cornyn	Y	Y	N	N	N	Y
Cruz	Y	Y	-	-	N	Y
UTAH						
Lee	Y	Y	Y	Y	Y	Y
Romney	Y	Y	N	N	N	Y
VERMONT						
Leahy	N	?	Y	Y	Y	N
Sanders	?	?	?	?	?	?
VIRGINIA						
Warner	N	Y	Y	Y	Y	N
Kaine	N	Y	Y	Y	Y	N
WASHINGTON						
Murray	N	Y	Y	Y	Y	N
Cantwell	N	Y	Y	Y	Y	N
WEST VIRGINIA						
Manchin	N	Y	Y	Y	Y	Y
Capito	?	Y	N	N	N	Y
WISCONSIN						
Johnson	Y	Y	N	N	N	Y
Baldwin	N	Y	Y	Y	Y	N
WYOMING						
Enzi	Y	Y	N	N	N	Y
Barrasso	Y	Y	N	N	N	Y

KEY:

Republicans	Democrats	*Independents*

Y Voted for (yea)	**N** Voted against (nay)	**P** Voted "present"
+ Announced for	**-** Announced against	**?** Did not vote or otherwise make position known
# Paired for	**X** Paired against	

235. Welte Nomination - Cloture. Motion to invoke cloture (thus limiting debate) on the nomination of Peter D. Welte of North Dakota to be a U.S. district judge for the District of North Dakota. Motion agreed to 66-21: R 48-0; D 17-21; I 1-0. *Note: A majority of senators voting (44 in this case), a quorum being present, is required to invoke cloture on all nominations.* July 29, 2019.

236. Liburdi Nomination - Confirmation. Confirmation of President Trump's nomination of Michael T. Liburdi of Arizona to be a U.S. district judge for the District of Arizona. Confirmed 53-37: R 50-0; D 3-36; I 0-1. *Note: A "yea" was a vote in support of the president's position.* July 30, 2019.

237. Welte Nomination - Confirmation. Confirmation of President Trump's nomination of Peter D. Welte of North Dakota to be a U.S. district judge for the District of North Dakota. Confirmed 68-22: R 50-0; D 17-22; I 1-0. *Note: A "yea" was a vote in support of the president's position.* July 30, 2019.

238. Hendrix Nomination - Cloture. Motion to invoke cloture (thus limiting debate) on the nomination of James Westley Hendrix of Texas to be a U.S. district judge for the Northern District of Texas. Motion agreed to 85-5: R 50-0; D 34-5; I 1-0. *Note: A majority of senators voting (46 in this case), a quorum being present, is required to invoke cloture on all nominations.* July 30, 2019.

239. Hendrix Nomination - Confirmation. Confirmation of President Trump's nomination of James Westley Hendrix of Texas to be a U.S. district judge for the Northern District of Texas. Confirmed 89-1: R 51-0; D 37-1; I 1-0. *Note: A "yea" was a vote in support of the president's position.* July 30, 2019.

240. Jordan Nomination - Cloture. Motion to invoke cloture (thus limiting debate) on the nomination of Sean D. Jordan of Texas to be a U.S. district judge for the Eastern District of Texas. Motion agreed to 54-36: R 51-0; D 3-35; I 0-1. *Note: A majority of senators voting (46 in this case), a quorum being present, is required to invoke cloture on all nominations.* July 30, 2019.

	235	236	237	238	239	240
ALABAMA						
Shelby	Y	Y	Y	Y	Y	Y
Jones	Y	Y	Y	Y	Y	Y
ALASKA						
Murkowski	Y	Y	Y	Y	Y	Y
Sullivan	?	Y	Y	Y	Y	Y
ARIZONA						
Sinema	Y	Y	Y	Y	Y	Y
McSally	Y	Y	Y	Y	Y	Y
ARKANSAS						
Boozman	Y	Y	Y	Y	Y	Y
Cotton	Y	Y	Y	Y	Y	Y
CALIFORNIA						
Feinstein	Y	N	Y	Y	Y	N
Harris	-	-	-	-	-	-
COLORADO						
Bennet	?	?	?	?	?	?
Gardner	Y	Y	Y	Y	Y	Y
CONNECTICUT						
Blumenthal	N	N	N	N	N	N
Murphy	Y	N	Y	Y	Y	N
DELAWARE						
Carper	Y	N	Y	Y	Y	N
Coons	Y	N	Y	Y	Y	N
FLORIDA						
Rubio	Y	Y	Y	Y	Y	Y
Scott	Y	Y	Y	Y	Y	Y
GEORGIA						
Isakson	?	?	?	?	?	?
Perdue	?	Y	Y	Y	Y	Y
HAWAII						
Schatz	N	N	N	Y	Y	N
Hirono	N	N	N	N	Y	N
IDAHO						
Crapo	Y	Y	Y	Y	Y	Y
Risch	Y	Y	Y	Y	Y	Y
ILLINOIS						
Durbin	Y	N	Y	Y	Y	N
Duckworth	-	N	N	Y	Y	N
INDIANA						
Young	Y	Y	Y	Y	Y	Y
Braun	Y	Y	Y	Y	Y	Y
IOWA						
Grassley	Y	Y	Y	Y	Y	Y
Ernst	Y	Y	Y	Y	Y	Y
KANSAS						
Roberts	Y	Y	Y	Y	Y	Y
Moran	Y	Y	Y	Y	Y	Y
KENTUCKY						
McConnell	Y	Y	Y	Y	Y	Y
Paul	?	?	?	?	Y	Y
LOUISIANA						
Cassidy	?	?	?	?	?	?
Kennedy	Y	Y	Y	Y	Y	Y
MAINE						
Collins	Y	Y	Y	Y	Y	Y
King	Y	N	Y	Y	Y	N
MARYLAND						
Cardin	N	N	N	Y	Y	N
Van Hollen	N	N	N	Y	Y	N
MASSACHUSETTS						
Warren	?	?	?	?	?	?
Markey	N	N	N	N	+	-
MICHIGAN						
Stabenow	N	N	N	Y	Y	N
Peters	Y	N	Y	Y	Y	N
MINNESOTA						
Klobuchar	?	?	?	?	?	?
Smith	N	N	N	Y	Y	N
MISSISSIPPI						
Wicker	Y	Y	Y	Y	Y	Y
Hyde-Smith	Y	Y	Y	Y	Y	Y
MISSOURI						
Blunt	Y	Y	Y	Y	Y	Y
Hawley	Y	Y	Y	Y	Y	Y

	235	236	237	238	239	240
MONTANA						
Tester	Y	N	Y	Y	Y	N
Daines	Y	Y	Y	Y	Y	Y
NEBRASKA						
Fischer	Y	Y	Y	Y	Y	Y
Sasse	Y	Y	Y	Y	Y	Y
NEVADA						
Cortez Masto	Y	N	Y	Y	Y	N
Rosen	Y	N	Y	Y	Y	N
NEW HAMPSHIRE						
Shaheen	Y	N	Y	Y	Y	N
Hassan	Y	N	Y	Y	Y	N
NEW JERSEY						
Menendez	N	N	N	Y	Y	N
Booker	?	?	?	?	?	?
NEW MEXICO						
Udall	N	N	N	Y	Y	N
Heinrich	N	N	N	Y	Y	N
NEW YORK						
Schumer	N	N	N	Y	Y	N
Gillibrand	?	?	?	?	?	?
NORTH CAROLINA						
Burr	Y	Y	Y	Y	Y	Y
Tillis	Y	Y	Y	Y	Y	Y
NORTH DAKOTA						
Hoeven	Y	Y	Y	Y	Y	Y
Cramer	Y	Y	Y	Y	Y	Y
OHIO						
Brown	N	N	N	N	Y	N
Portman	Y	Y	Y	Y	Y	Y
OKLAHOMA						
Inhofe	Y	Y	Y	Y	Y	Y
Lankford	Y	Y	Y	Y	Y	Y
OREGON						
Wyden	N	N	N	N	Y	N
Merkley	N	N	N	Y	Y	N
PENNSYLVANIA						
Casey	N	N	N	Y	Y	N
Toomey	Y	Y	Y	Y	Y	Y
RHODE ISLAND						
Reed	N	N	N	Y	Y	N
Whitehouse	N	N	N	Y	Y	N
SOUTH CAROLINA						
Graham	Y	Y	Y	Y	Y	Y
Scott	Y	Y	Y	Y	Y	Y
SOUTH DAKOTA						
Thune	Y	Y	Y	Y	Y	Y
Rounds	Y	Y	Y	Y	Y	Y
TENNESSEE						
Alexander	Y	Y	Y	Y	Y	Y
Blackburn	Y	Y	Y	Y	Y	Y
TEXAS						
Cornyn	Y	Y	Y	Y	Y	Y
Cruz	Y	Y	Y	Y	Y	Y
UTAH						
Lee	Y	Y	Y	Y	Y	Y
Romney	Y	Y	Y	Y	Y	Y
VERMONT						
Leahy	Y	N	Y	Y	Y	N
Sanders	?	?	?	?	?	?
VIRGINIA						
Warner	Y	N	Y	Y	Y	N
Kaine	Y	N	Y	Y	Y	N
WASHINGTON						
Murray	N	N	N	Y	Y	N
Cantwell	N	N	N	Y	Y	N
WEST VIRGINIA						
Manchin	Y	Y	Y	Y	Y	Y
Capito	Y	Y	Y	Y	Y	Y
WISCONSIN						
Johnson	Y	Y	Y	Y	Y	Y
Baldwin	N	N	N	Y	Y	N
WYOMING						
Enzi	Y	Y	Y	Y	Y	Y
Barrasso	Y	Y	Y	Y	Y	Y

KEY:	Republicans	Democrats	*Independents*
Y Voted for (yea)	N Voted against (nay)		P Voted "present"
+ Announced for	- Announced against		? Did not vote or otherwise
# Paired for	X Paired against		make position known

241. Jordan Nomination - Confirmation. Confirmation of President Trump's nomination of Sean D. Jordan of Texas to be a U.S. district judge for the Eastern District of Texas. Confirmed 54-34: R 51-0; D 3-33; I 0-1. *Note: A "yea" was a vote in support of the president's position.* July 30, 2019.

242. Pittman Nomination - Cloture. Motion to invoke cloture (thus limiting debate) on the nomination of Mark T. Pittman of Texas to be a U.S. district judge for for the Northern District of Texas. Motion agreed to 54-34: R 51-0; D 3-33; I 0-1. *Note: A majority of senators voting (45 in this case), a quorum being present, is required to invoke cloture on all nominations.* July 30, 2019.

243. Brown Nomination - Cloture. Motion to invoke cloture (thus limiting debate) on the nomination of Jeffrey Vincent Brown of Texas to be a U.S. district judge for the Southern District of Texas. Motion agreed to 51-37: R 51-0; D 0-36; I 0-1. *Note: A majority of senators voting (45 in this case), a quorum being present, is required to invoke cloture on all nominations.* July 30, 2019.

244. Starr Nomination - Cloture. Motion to invoke cloture (thus limiting debate) on the nomination of Brantley Starr of Texas to be a U.S. district judge for the Northern District of Texas. Motion agreed to 51-37: R 51-0; D 0-36; I 0-1. *Note: A majority of senators voting (45 in this case), a quorum being present, is required to invoke cloture on all nominations.* July 30, 2019.

245. Haines Nomination - Cloture. Motion to invoke cloture (thus limiting debate) on the nomination of Stephanie L. Haines of Pennsylvania to be a U.S. district judge for the Western District of Pennsylvania. Motion agreed to 87-1: R 51-0; D 35-1; I 1-0. *Note: A majority of senators voting (45 in this case), a quorum being present, is required to invoke cloture on all nominations.* July 30, 2019.

246. Brown Nomination - Cloture. Motion to invoke cloture (thus limiting debate) on the nomination of Ada E. Brown of Texas to be a U.S. district judge for the Northern District of Texas. Motion agreed to 79-9: R 51-0; D 27-9; I 1-0. *Note: A majority of senators voting (45 in this case), a quorum being present, is required to invoke cloture on all nominations.* July 30, 2019.

	241	242	243	244	245	246
ALABAMA						
Shelby	Y	Y	Y	Y	Y	Y
Jones	Y	Y	N	N	Y	Y
ALASKA						
Murkowski	Y	Y	Y	Y	Y	Y
Sullivan	Y	Y	Y	Y	Y	Y
ARIZONA						
Sinema	Y	Y	N	N	Y	Y
McSally	Y	Y	Y	Y	Y	Y
ARKANSAS						
Boozman	Y	Y	Y	Y	Y	Y
Cotton	Y	Y	Y	Y	Y	Y
CALIFORNIA						
Feinstein	N	N	N	N	Y	Y
Harris	-	-	-	-	-	?
COLORADO						
Bennet	?	?	?	?	?	?
Gardner	Y	Y	Y	Y	Y	Y
CONNECTICUT						
Blumenthal	N	N	N	N	Y	N
Murphy	N	N	N	N	Y	Y
DELAWARE						
Carper	N	N	N	N	Y	Y
Coons	N	N	N	N	Y	Y
FLORIDA						
Rubio	Y	Y	Y	Y	Y	Y
Scott	Y	Y	Y	Y	Y	Y
GEORGIA						
Isakson	?	?	?	?	?	?
Perdue	Y	Y	Y	Y	Y	Y
HAWAII						
Schatz	N	N	N	N	Y	N
Hirono	N	N	N	N	N	N
IDAHO						
Crapo	Y	Y	Y	Y	Y	Y
Risch	Y	Y	Y	Y	Y	Y
ILLINOIS						
Durbin	N	N	N	N	Y	Y
Duckworth	N	N	N	N	Y	Y
INDIANA						
Young	Y	Y	Y	Y	Y	-Y
Braun	Y	Y	Y	Y	Y	Y
IOWA						
Grassley	Y	Y	Y	Y	Y	Y
Ernst	Y	Y	Y	Y	Y	Y
KANSAS						
Roberts	Y	Y	Y	Y	Y	Y
Moran	Y	Y	Y	Y	Y	Y
KENTUCKY						
McConnell	Y	Y	Y	Y	Y	Y
Paul	Y	Y	Y	Y	Y	Y
LOUISIANA						
Cassidy	?	?	?	?	?	?
Kennedy	Y	Y	Y	Y	Y	Y
MAINE						
Collins	Y	Y	Y	Y	Y	Y
King	N	N	N	N	Y	Y
MARYLAND						
Cardin	N	N	N	N	Y	Y
Van Hollen	N	N	N	N	Y	Y
MASSACHUSETTS						
Warren	?	?	?	?	?	?
Markey	-	-	-	-	+	-
MICHIGAN						
Stabenow	N	N	N	N	Y	N
Peters	N	N	N	N	Y	Y
MINNESOTA						
Klobuchar	?	?	?	?	?	?
Smith	N	N	N	N	Y	Y
MISSISSIPPI						
Wicker	Y	Y	Y	Y	Y	Y
Hyde-Smith	Y	Y	Y	Y	Y	Y
MISSOURI						
Blunt	Y	Y	Y	Y	Y	Y
Hawley	Y	Y	Y	Y	Y	Y

	241	242	243	244	245	246
MONTANA						
Tester	N	N	N	N	Y	Y
Daines	Y	Y	Y	Y	Y	Y
NEBRASKA						
Fischer	Y	Y	Y	Y	Y	Y
Sasse	Y	Y	Y	Y	Y	Y
NEVADA						
Cortez Masto	N	N	N	N	Y	Y
Rosen	N	N	N	N	Y	Y
NEW HAMPSHIRE						
Shaheen	N	N	N	N	Y	Y
Hassan	N	N	N	N	Y	Y
NEW JERSEY						
Menendez	N	N	N	N	Y	Y
Booker	?	?	?	?	?	?
NEW MEXICO						
Udall	N	N	N	N	Y	Y
Heinrich	N	N	N	N	Y	Y
NEW YORK						
Schumer	N	N	N	N	Y	N
Gillibrand	?	?	?	?	?	?
NORTH CAROLINA						
Burr	Y	Y	Y	Y	Y	Y
Tillis	Y	Y	Y	Y	Y	Y
NORTH DAKOTA						
Hoeven	Y	Y	Y	Y	Y	Y
Cramer	Y	Y	Y	Y	Y	Y
OHIO						
Brown	N	N	N	N	Y	N
Portman	Y	Y	Y	Y	Y	Y
OKLAHOMA						
Inhofe	Y	Y	Y	Y	Y	Y
Lankford	Y	Y	Y	Y	Y	Y
OREGON						
Wyden	N	N	N	N	Y	N
Merkley	N	N	N	N	Y	Y
PENNSYLVANIA						
Casey	N	N	N	N	Y	Y
Toomey	Y	Y	Y	Y	Y	Y
RHODE ISLAND						
Reed	N	N	N	N	Y	Y
Whitehouse	N	N	N	N	Y	Y
SOUTH CAROLINA						
Graham	Y	Y	Y	Y	Y	Y
Scott	Y	Y	Y	Y	Y	Y
SOUTH DAKOTA						
Thune	Y	Y	Y	Y	Y	Y
Rounds	Y	Y	Y	Y	Y	Y
TENNESSEE						
Alexander	Y	Y	Y	Y	Y	Y
Blackburn	Y	Y	Y	Y	Y	Y
TEXAS						
Cornyn	Y	Y	Y	Y	Y	Y
Cruz	Y	Y	Y	Y	Y	Y
UTAH						
Lee	Y	Y	Y	Y	Y	Y
Romney	Y	Y	Y	Y	Y	Y
VERMONT						
Leahy	N	N	N	N	Y	Y
Sanders	?	?	?	?	?	?
VIRGINIA						
Warner	-	-	-	-	+	+
Kaine	-	-	-	-	+	+
WASHINGTON						
Murray	N	N	N	N	Y	N
Cantwell	N	N	N	N	Y	N
WEST VIRGINIA						
Manchin	Y	Y	N	N	Y	Y
Capito	Y	Y	Y	Y	Y	Y
WISCONSIN						
Johnson	Y	Y	Y	Y	Y	Y
Baldwin	N	N	N	N	Y	Y
WYOMING						
Enzi	Y	Y	Y	Y	Y	Y
Barrasso	Y	Y	Y	Y	Y	Y

KEY: Republicans | Democrats | *Independents*

Y Voted for (yea)	N Voted against (nay)	P Voted "present"
+ Announced for	- Announced against	? Did not vote or otherwise
# Paired for	X Paired against	make position known

||| SENATE VOTES

247. Grimberg Nomination - Cloture. Motion to invoke cloture (thus limiting debate) on the nomination of Steven D. Grimberg of Georgia to be a U.S. district judge for the Northern District of Georgia. Motion agreed to 72-16: R 51-0; D 20-16; I 1-0. *Note: A majority of senators voting (45 in this case), a quorum being present, is required to invoke cloture on all nominations.* July 30, 2019.

248. Pulliam Nomination - Cloture. Motion to invoke cloture (thus limiting debate) on the nomination of Jason K. Pulliam of Texas to be a U.S. district judge for the Western District of Texas. Motion agreed to 54-34: R 51-0; D 3-33; I 0-1. *Note: A majority of senators voting (45 in this case), a quorum being present, is required to invoke cloture on all nominations.* July 30, 2019.

249. Pacold Nomination - Cloture. Motion to invoke cloture (thus limiting debate) on the nomination of Martha Maria Pacold of Illinois to be a U.S. district judge for the Northern District of Illinois. Motion agreed to 86-2: R 51-0; D 34-2; I 1-0. *Note: A majority of senators voting (45 in this case), a quorum being present, is required to invoke cloture on all nominations.* July 30, 2019.

250. Seeger Nomination - Cloture. Motion to invoke cloture (thus limiting debate) on the nomination of Steven C. Seeger of Illinois to be a U.S. district judge for the Northern District of Illinois. Motion agreed to 87-1: R 51-0; D 35-1; I 1-0. *Note: A majority of senators voting (45 in this case), a quorum being present, is required to invoke cloture on all nominations.* July 30, 2019.

251. Stickman Nomination - Cloture. Motion to invoke cloture (thus limiting debate) on the nomination of William Shaw Stickman IV of Pennsylvania to be a U.S. district judge for the Western District of Pennsylvania. Motion agreed to 57-31: R 51-0; D 6-30; I 0-1. *Note: A majority of senators voting (45 in this case), a quorum being present, is required to invoke cloture on all nominations.* July 30, 2019.

252. Craft Nomination - Cloture. Motion to invoke cloture (thus limiting debate) on the nomination of Kelly Craft of Kentucky to be U.S. representative to the United Nations and U.S. representative to the Security Council of the United States. Motion agreed to 57-33: R 51-0; D 6-32; I 0-1. *Note: A majority of senators voting (46 in this case), a quorum being present, is required to invoke cloture on all nominations.* July 30, 2019.

	247	248	249	250	251	252
ALABAMA						
Shelby	Y	Y	Y	Y	Y	Y
Jones	Y	Y	Y	Y	Y	N
ALASKA						
Murkowski	Y	Y	Y	Y	Y	Y
Sullivan	Y	Y	Y	Y	Y	Y
ARIZONA						
Sinema	Y	Y	Y	Y	Y	Y
McSally	Y	Y	Y	Y	Y	Y
ARKANSAS						
Boozman	Y	Y	Y	Y	Y	Y
Cotton	Y	Y	Y	Y	Y	Y
CALIFORNIA						
Feinstein	Y	N	Y	Y	N	N
Harris	-	-	-	-	-	?
COLORADO						
Bennet	?	?	?	?	?	?
Gardner	Y	Y	Y	Y	Y	Y
CONNECTICUT						
Blumenthal	N	N	Y	Y	N	N
Murphy	Y	N	Y	Y	N	Y
DELAWARE						
Carper	Y	N	Y	Y	N	N
Coons	Y	N	Y	Y	N	Y
FLORIDA						
Rubio	Y	Y	Y	Y	Y	Y
Scott	Y	Y	Y	Y	Y	Y
GEORGIA						
Isakson	+	?	?	?	?	+
Perdue	Y	Y	Y	Y	Y	Y
HAWAII						
Schatz	N	N	Y	Y	N	N
Hirono	N	N	N	N	N	N
IDAHO						
Crapo	Y	Y	Y	Y	Y	Y
Risch	Y	Y	Y	Y	Y	Y
ILLINOIS						
Durbin	Y	N	Y	Y	N	N
Duckworth	Y	N	Y	Y	N	N
INDIANA						
Young	Y	Y	Y	Y	Y	Y
Braun	Y	Y	Y	Y	Y	Y
IOWA						
Grassley	Y	Y	Y	Y	Y	Y
Ernst	Y	Y	Y	Y	Y	Y
KANSAS						
Roberts	Y	Y	Y	Y	Y	Y
Moran	Y	Y	Y	Y	Y	Y
KENTUCKY						
McConnell	Y	Y	Y	Y	Y	Y
Paul	Y	Y	Y	Y	Y	Y
LOUISIANA						
Cassidy	?	?	?	?	?	?
Kennedy	Y	Y	Y	Y	Y	Y
MAINE						
Collins	Y	Y	Y	Y	Y	Y
King	Y	N	Y	Y	N	N
MARYLAND						
Cardin	Y	N	Y	Y	N	N
Van Hollen	N	N	Y	Y	N	N
MASSACHUSETTS						
Warren	?	?	?	?	?	?
Markey	-	-	-	+	-	-
MICHIGAN						
Stabenow	N	N	Y	Y	N	N
Peters	Y	N	Y	Y	N	N
MINNESOTA						
Klobuchar	?	?	?	?	?	?
Smith	N	N	Y	Y	N	N
MISSISSIPPI						
Wicker	Y	Y	Y	Y	Y	Y
Hyde-Smith	Y	Y	Y	Y	Y	Y
MISSOURI						
Blunt	Y	Y	Y	Y	Y	Y
Hawley	Y	Y	Y	Y	Y	Y

	247	248	249	250	251	252
MONTANA						
Tester	Y	N	Y	Y	N	N
Daines	Y	Y	Y	Y	Y	Y
NEBRASKA						
Fischer	Y	Y	Y	Y	Y	Y
Sasse	Y	Y	Y	Y	Y	Y
NEVADA						
Cortez Masto	Y	N	Y	Y	N	N
Rosen	Y	N	Y	Y	N	N
NEW HAMPSHIRE						
Shaheen	Y	N	Y	Y	Y	Y
Hassan	Y	N	Y	Y	N	Y
NEW JERSEY						
Menendez	N	N	N	Y	N	N
Booker	?	?	?	?	?	?
NEW MEXICO						
Udall	N	N	Y	Y	N	N
Heinrich	N	N	Y	Y	N	N
NEW YORK						
Schumer	N	N	Y	Y	N	N
Gillibrand	?	?	?	?	?	?
NORTH CAROLINA						
Burr	Y	Y	Y	Y	Y	Y
Tillis	Y	Y	Y	Y	Y	Y
NORTH DAKOTA						
Hoeven	Y	Y	Y	Y	Y	Y
Cramer	Y	Y	Y	Y	Y	Y
OHIO						
Brown	N	N	Y	Y	N	N
Portman	Y	Y	Y	Y	Y	Y
OKLAHOMA						
Inhofe	Y	Y	Y	Y	Y	Y
Lankford	Y	Y	Y	Y	Y	Y
OREGON						
Wyden	N	N	Y	Y	N	N
Merkley	N	N	Y	Y	N	N
PENNSYLVANIA						
Casey	Y	N	Y	Y	N	N
Toomey	Y	Y	Y	Y	Y	Y
RHODE ISLAND						
Reed	Y	N	Y	Y	N	N
Whitehouse	Y	N	Y	Y	N	N
SOUTH CAROLINA						
Graham	Y	Y	Y	Y	Y	Y
Scott	Y	Y	Y	Y	Y	Y
SOUTH DAKOTA						
Thune	Y	Y	Y	Y	Y	Y
Rounds	Y	Y	Y	Y	Y	Y
TENNESSEE						
Alexander	Y	Y	Y	Y	Y	Y
Blackburn	Y	Y	Y	Y	Y	Y
TEXAS						
Cornyn	Y	Y	Y	Y	Y	Y
Cruz	Y	Y	Y	Y	Y	Y
UTAH						
Lee	Y	Y	Y	Y	Y	Y
Romney	Y	Y	Y	Y	Y	Y
VERMONT						
Leahy	Y	N	Y	Y	N	N
Sanders	?	?	?	?	?	?
VIRGINIA						
Warner	+	-	+	+	-	N
Kaine	+	-	+	+	-	N
WASHINGTON						
Murray	N	N	Y	Y	N	N
Cantwell	N	N	Y	Y	N	N
WEST VIRGINIA						
Manchin	Y	Y	Y	Y	Y	Y
Capito	Y	Y	Y	Y	Y	Y
WISCONSIN						
Johnson	Y	Y	Y	Y	Y	Y
Baldwin	N	N	Y	Y	N	N
WYOMING						
Enzi	Y	Y	Y	Y	Y	Y
Barrasso	Y	Y	Y	Y	Y	Y

KEY: Republicans | Democrats | *Independents*

Y Voted for (yea)	**N** Voted against (nay)	**P** Voted "present"
+ Announced for	**–** Announced against	**?** Did not vote or otherwise make position known
# Paired for	**X** Paired against	

253. Pittman Nomination - Confirmation. Confirmation of President Trump's nomination of Mark T. Pittman of Texas to be a U.S. district judge for the Northern District of Texas. Confirmed 54-36: R 51-0; D 3-35; I 0-1. *Note: A "yea" was a vote in support of the president's position.* July 31, 2019.

254. Brown Nomination - Confirmation. Confirmation of President Trump's nomination of Jeffrey Vincent Brown of Texas to be a U.S. district judge for the Southern District of Texas. Confirmed 50-40: R 50-1; D 0-38; I 0-1. *Note: A "yea" was a vote in support of the president's position.* July 31, 2019.

255. Starr Nomination - Confirmation. Confirmation of President Trump's nomination of Brantley Starr of Texas to be a U.S. district judge for the Northern District of Texas. Confirmed 51-39: R 51-0; D 0-38; I 0-1. *Note: A "yea" was a vote in support of the president's position.* July 31, 2019.

256. Pulliam Nomination - Confirmation. Confirmation of President Trump's nomination of Jason K. Pulliam of Texas to be a U.S. district judge for the Western District of Texas. Confirmed 54-36: R 51-0; D 3-35; I 0-1. *Note: A "yea" was a vote in support of the president's position.* July 31, 2019.

257. Pacold Nomination - Confirmation. Confirmation of President Trump's nomination of Martha Maria Pacold of Illinois to be a U.S. district judge for the Northern District of Illinois. Confirmed 87-3: R 51-0; D 35-3; I 1-0. *Note: A "yea" was a vote in support of the president's position.* July 31, 2019.

258. Stickman Nomination - Confirmation. Confirmation of President Trump's nomination of William Shaw Stickman IV of Pennsylvania to be a U.S. district judge for the Western District of Pennsylvania. Confirmed 56-34: R 51-0; D 5-33; I 0-1. *Note: A "yea" was a vote in support of the president's position.* July 31, 2019.

	253	254	255	256	257	258
ALABAMA						
Shelby	Y	Y	Y	Y	Y	Y
Jones	Y	N	N	Y	Y	Y
ALASKA						
Murkowski	Y	Y	Y	Y	Y	Y
Sullivan	Y	Y	Y	Y	Y	Y
ARIZONA						
Sinema	Y	N	N	Y	Y	Y
McSally	Y	Y	Y	Y	Y	Y
ARKANSAS						
Boozman	Y	Y	Y	Y	Y	Y
Cotton	Y	Y	Y	Y	Y	Y
CALIFORNIA						
Feinstein	N	N	N	N	Y	N
Harris	-	-	-	-	-	-
COLORADO						
Bennet	?	?	?	?	?	?
Gardner	Y	Y	Y	Y	Y	Y
CONNECTICUT						
Blumenthal	N	N	N	N	Y	N
Murphy	N	N	N	N	Y	N
DELAWARE						
Carper	N	N	N	N	Y	N
Coons	?	?	?	?	?	?
FLORIDA						
Rubio	Y	Y	Y	Y	Y	Y
Scott	Y	Y	Y	Y	Y	Y
GEORGIA						
Isakson	?	?	?	?	?	?
Perdue	Y	Y	Y	Y	Y	Y
HAWAII						
Schatz	N	N	N	N	Y	N
Hirono	N	N	N	N	N	N
IDAHO						
Crapo	Y	Y	Y	Y	Y	Y
Risch	Y	Y	Y	Y	Y	Y
ILLINOIS						
Durbin	N	N	N	N	Y	N
Duckworth	N	N	N	N	Y	N
INDIANA						
Young	Y	Y	Y	Y	Y	Y
Braun	Y	Y	Y	Y	Y	Y
IOWA						
Grassley	Y	Y	Y	Y	Y	Y
Ernst	Y	Y	Y	Y	Y	Y
KANSAS						
Roberts	Y	Y	Y	Y	Y	Y
Moran	Y	Y	Y	Y	Y	Y
KENTUCKY						
McConnell	Y	Y	Y	Y	Y	Y
Paul	Y	Y	Y	Y	Y	Y
LOUISIANA						
Cassidy	Y	Y	Y	Y	Y	Y
Kennedy	Y	Y	Y	Y	Y	Y
MAINE						
Collins	Y	N	Y	Y	Y	Y
King	N	N	N	N	Y	N
MARYLAND						
Cardin	N	N	N	N	Y	N
Van Hollen	N	N	N	N	Y	N
MASSACHUSETTS						
Warren	?	?	?	?	?	?
Markey	N	N	N	N	N	N
MICHIGAN						
Stabenow	N	N	N	N	Y	N
Peters	N	N	N	N	Y	N
MINNESOTA						
Klobuchar	?	?	?	?	?	?
Smith	N	N	N	N	Y	N
MISSISSIPPI						
Wicker	Y	Y	Y	Y	Y	Y
Hyde-Smith	Y	Y	Y	Y	Y	Y
MISSOURI						
Blunt	Y	Y	Y	Y	Y	Y
Hawley	Y	Y	Y	Y	Y	Y

	253	254	255	256	257	258
MONTANA						
Tester	N	N	N	N	N	N
Daines	Y	Y	Y	Y	Y	Y
NEBRASKA						
Fischer	Y	Y	Y	Y	Y	Y
Sasse	Y	Y	Y	Y	Y	Y
NEVADA						
Cortez Masto	N	N	N	N	Y	N
Rosen	N	N	N	N	Y	N
NEW HAMPSHIRE						
Shaheen	N	N	N	N	Y	N
Hassan	N	N	N	N	Y	N
NEW JERSEY						
Menendez	N	N	N	N	N	N
Booker	?	?	?	?	?	?
NEW MEXICO						
Udall	N	N	N	N	N	N
Heinrich	N	N	N	N	N	N
NEW YORK						
Schumer	N	N	N	N	Y	N
Gillibrand	?	?	?	?	?	?
NORTH CAROLINA						
Burr	?	?	?	?	?	?
Tillis	Y	Y	Y	Y	Y	Y
NORTH DAKOTA						
Hoeven	Y	Y	Y	Y	Y	Y
Cramer	Y	Y	Y	Y	Y	Y
OHIO						
Brown	N	N	N	N	Y	N
Portman	Y	Y	Y	Y	Y	Y
OKLAHOMA						
Inhofe	Y	Y	Y	Y	Y	Y
Lankford	Y	Y	Y	Y	Y	Y
OREGON						
Wyden	N	N	N	N	Y	N
Merkley	N	N	N	N	Y	N
PENNSYLVANIA						
Casey	N	N	N	N	Y	Y
Toomey	Y	Y	Y	Y	Y	Y
RHODE ISLAND						
Reed	N	N	N	N	Y	N
Whitehouse	N	N	N	N	Y	N
SOUTH CAROLINA						
Graham	Y	Y	Y	Y	Y	Y
Scott	Y	Y	Y	Y	Y	Y
SOUTH DAKOTA						
Thune	Y	Y	Y	Y	Y	Y
Rounds	Y	Y	Y	Y	Y	Y
TENNESSEE						
Alexander	Y	Y	Y	Y	Y	Y
Blackburn	Y	Y	Y	Y	Y	Y
TEXAS						
Cornyn	Y	Y	Y	Y	Y	Y
Cruz	Y	Y	Y	Y	Y	Y
UTAH						
Lee	Y	Y	Y	Y	Y	Y
Romney	Y	Y	Y	Y	Y	Y
VERMONT						
Leahy	N	N	N	N	Y	N
Sanders	?	?	?	?	?	?
VIRGINIA						
Warner	N	N	N	N	Y	N
Kaine	N	N	N	N	Y	Y
WASHINGTON						
Murray	N	N	N	N	Y	N
Cantwell	N	N	N	N	Y	N
WEST VIRGINIA						
Manchin	Y	N	N	Y	Y	Y
Capito	Y	Y	Y	Y	Y	Y
WISCONSIN						
Johnson	Y	Y	Y	Y	Y	Y
Baldwin	N	N	N	N	Y	N
WYOMING						
Enzi	Y	Y	Y	Y	Y	Y
Barrasso	Y	Y	Y	Y	Y	Y

KEY: **Republicans** Democrats *Independents*

Y Voted for (yea)	**N** Voted against (nay)	**P** Voted "present"	
+ Announced for	**-** Announced against	**?** Did not vote or otherwise	
# Paired for	**X** Paired against	make position known	

259. Craft Nomination - Confirmation. Confirmation of President Trump's nomination of Kelly Craft of Kentucky to be U.S. representative to the United Nations and U.S. representative to the Security Council of the United States. Confirmed 56-34: R 51-0; D 5-33; I 0-1. *Note: A "yea" was a vote in support of the president's position.* July 31, 2019.

260. HR3877. Budget Cap Adjustment - Decrease Budget Cap. Paul, R-Ky., substitute amendment to the Bipartisan Budget Act that would establish enforceable budget levels in the House and Senate for fiscal 2020 through 2029. Specifically, it would establish a budget cap of $3.44 trillion for mandatory and discretionary spending in fiscal 2020, and establish annual budget caps through fiscal 2029 at similar amounts, none of which would exceed $3.5 trillion. It would also increase the public debt limit by $500 billion if Congress refers to the states for ratification a "balanced budget" amendment to the Constitution that would require that federal outlays not exceed revenue, include a spending limitation as a percentage of gross domestic product, and require tax increases to be approved by a two-thirds vote in both houses. Rejected 23-70: R 23-29; D 0-40; I 0-1. *Note: Per a unanimous consent agreement, 60 votes were required for adoption of the amendment.* Aug. 01, 2019.

261. HR3877. Budget Cap Adjustment - Cloture. McConnell, R-Ky., motion to invoke cloture on the bill that would establish enforceable budget levels in the House and Senate for fiscal 2020 and 2021 and suspend the public debt limit through July 31, 2021. Motion agreed to 67-27: R 30-22; D 36-5; I 1-0. *Note: Three-fifths of the total Senate (60) is required to invoke cloture.* Aug. 01, 2019.

262. HR3877. Budget Cap Adjustment - Passage. Passage of the bill that would establish enforceable budget levels in the House and Senate for fiscal 2020 and 2021 and suspend the public debt limit through July 31, 2021. It would increase discretionary budget caps for defense and non-defense spending, and would provide a total of $1.37 trillion for fiscal 2020 and $1.38 trillion for fiscal 2021 in discretionary budget authority, including for overseas contingency operations. Spending cap adjustments in the bill would increase discretionary budget authority by a total of $324 billion over those two years. It would require that the budgetary effects of the bill not be entered on pay-as-you-go scorecards in either chamber. It would provide for $77.3 billion in offsets over 10 years, including by extending sequestration requirements under the Budget Control Act for certain mandatory spending through fiscal 2029. It would also extend through fiscal 2029 authorization for processing fees on certain customs services. Passed (thus cleared for the president) 67-28: R 29-23; D 37-5; I 1-0. *Note: A "yea" was a vote in support of the president's position.* Aug. 01, 2019.

263. Craft Nomination - Cloture. Motion to invoke cloture (thus limiting debate) on the nomination of Kelly Craft of Kentucky to be United Nations ambassador and U.S. representative to the sessions of the General Assembly of the United Nations. Motion agreed to 54-38: R 49-0; D 5-37; I 0-1. *Note: A majority of senators voting (47 in this case), a quorum being present, is required to invoke cloture on all nominations.* Sept. 09, 2019.

264. Craft Nomination - Confirmation. Confirmation of President Trump's nomination of Kelly Craft of Kentucky to be United Nations ambassador and U.S. representative to the sessions of the General Assembly of the United Nations. Confirmed 56-38: R 51-0; D 5-37; I 0-1. *Note: A "yea" was a vote in support of the president's postion.* Sept. 10, 2019.

	259	260	261	262	263	264		259	260	261	262	263	264
ALABAMA							**MONTANA**						
Shelby	Y	N	Y	Y	Y	Y	Tester	N	N	N	N	N	N
Jones	N	N	Y	Y	N	N	Daines	Y	Y	N	N	Y	Y
ALASKA							**NEBRASKA**						
Murkowski	Y	N	Y	Y	Y	Y	Fischer	Y	Y	N	N	Y	Y
Sullivan	Y	N	Y	Y	Y	Y	Sasse	Y	Y	N	N	Y	Y
ARIZONA							**NEVADA**						
Sinema	Y	N	Y	Y	+	+	Cortez Masto	N	N	Y	Y	N	N
McSally	Y	N	Y	Y	Y	Y	Rosen	N	N	Y	Y	N	N
ARKANSAS							**NEW HAMPSHIRE**						
Boozman	Y	N	Y	Y	Y	Y	Shaheen	Y	N	Y	Y	Y	Y
Cotton	Y	N	N	N	Y	Y	Hassan	Y	N	Y	Y	Y	Y
CALIFORNIA							**NEW JERSEY**						
Feinstein	N	N	Y	Y	N	N	Menendez	N	N	Y	Y	N	N
Harris	?	?	?	?	?	?	Booker	?	?	?	?	?	N
COLORADO							**NEW MEXICO**						
Bennet	?	?	N	N	N	N	Udall	N	N	Y	Y	N	N
Gardner	Y	N	N	N	Y	Y	Heinrich	N	N	Y	Y	N	N
CONNECTICUT							**NEW YORK**						
Blumenthal	N	N	Y	Y	N	N	Schumer	N	N	Y	Y	N	N
Murphy	Y	N	Y	Y	Y	Y	Gillibrand	?	?	?	Y	N	N
DELAWARE							**NORTH CAROLINA**						
Carper	N	N	N	N	N	N	Burr	?	N	Y	Y	Y	Y
Coons	?	N	Y	Y	Y	Y	Tillis	Y	N	N	N	?	Y
FLORIDA							**NORTH DAKOTA**						
Rubio	Y	Y	N	N	Y	Y	Hoeven	Y	N	Y	Y	Y	Y
Scott	Y	N	N	N	Y	Y	Cramer	Y	N	Y	Y	Y	Y
GEORGIA							**OHIO**						
Isakson	+	?	?	?	Y	Y	Brown	N	N	Y	Y	N	N
Perdue	Y	N	Y	Y	Y	Y	Portman	Y	N	Y	Y	Y	Y
HAWAII							**OKLAHOMA**						
Schatz	N	N	Y	Y	N	N	Inhofe	Y	N	Y	Y	Y	Y
Hirono	N	N	Y	Y	N	N	Lankford	Y	Y	N	N	Y	Y
IDAHO							**OREGON**						
Crapo	Y	Y	Y	Y	Y	Y	Wyden	N	N	Y	Y	N	N
Risch	Y	Y	N	N	Y	Y	Merkley	N	N	Y	Y	N	N
ILLINOIS							**PENNSYLVANIA**						
Durbin	N	N	Y	Y	N	N	Casey	N	N	Y	Y	N	N
Duckworth	N	N	Y	Y	N	N	Toomey	Y	Y	N	N	Y	Y
INDIANA							**RHODE ISLAND**						
Young	Y	Y	Y	Y	Y	Y	Reed	N	N	Y	Y	N	N
Braun	Y	Y	N	N	Y	Y	Whitehouse	N	N	Y	Y	N	N
IOWA							**SOUTH CAROLINA**						
Grassley	Y	N	Y	Y	Y	Y	Graham	Y	N	Y	Y	?	Y
Ernst	Y	Y	Y	Y	Y	Y	Scott	Y	N	N	N	Y	Y
KANSAS							**SOUTH DAKOTA**						
Roberts	Y	N	Y	Y	?	?	Thune	Y	N	Y	Y	Y	Y
Moran	Y	Y	Y	Y	Y	Y	Rounds	Y	N	Y	Y	Y	Y
KENTUCKY							**TENNESSEE**						
McConnell	Y	N	Y	Y	Y	Y	Alexander	Y	N	Y	Y	+	+
Paul	Y	Y	N	N	Y	Y	Blackburn	Y	Y	N	N	Y	Y
LOUISIANA							**TEXAS**						
Cassidy	Y	N	Y	N	Y	Y	Cornyn	Y	Y	Y	Y	Y	Y
Kennedy	Y	Y	N	N	Y	Y	Cruz	Y	Y	N	N	Y	Y
MAINE							**UTAH**						
Collins	Y	N	Y	Y	Y	Y	Lee	Y	Y	N	N	Y	Y
King	N	N	Y	Y	N	N	Romney	Y	Y	N	N	Y	Y
MARYLAND							**VERMONT**						
Cardin	N	N	Y	Y	N	N	Leahy	N	N	Y	Y	N	N
Van Hollen	N	N	Y	Y	N	N	*Sanders*	?	?	?	?	?	?
MASSACHUSETTS							**VIRGINIA**						
Warren	?	?	?	?	N	?	Warner	N	N	Y	Y	N	N
Markey	N	N	Y	Y	N	N	Kaine	N	N	Y	Y	N	N
MICHIGAN							**WASHINGTON**						
Stabenow	N	N	Y	Y	N	N	Murray	N	N	Y	Y	N	N
Peters	N	N	Y	Y	N	N	Cantwell	N	N	Y	Y	N	N
MINNESOTA							**WEST VIRGINIA**						
Klobuchar	?	N	N	N	N	N	Manchin	Y	N	N	N	Y	Y
Smith	N	N	Y	Y	N	N	Capito	Y	N	Y	Y	Y	Y
MISSISSIPPI							**WISCONSIN**						
Wicker	Y	N	Y	Y	Y	Y	Johnson	Y	Y	N	N	Y	Y
Hyde-Smith	Y	N	Y	Y	Y	Y	Baldwin	N	N	Y	Y	N	N
MISSOURI							**WYOMING**						
Blunt	Y	N	Y	Y	Y	Y	Enzi	Y	Y	N	N	Y	Y
Hawley	Y	N	N	N	Y	Y	Barrasso	Y	Y	Y	Y	Y	Y

KEY: **Republicans** Democrats *Independents*

Y Voted for (yea)		**N** Voted against (nay)		**P** Voted "present"
+ Announced for		**–** Announced against		**?** Did not vote or otherwise make position known
# Paired for		**X** Paired against		

265. Darling Nomination - Cloture. Motion to invoke cloture (thus limiting debate) on the nomination of Elizabeth Darling of Texas to be commissioner of the Administration on Children, Youth, and Families. Motion agreed to 57-37: R 51-0; D 5-37; I 1-0. *Note: A majority of senators voting (48 in this case), a quorum being present, is required to invoke cloture on all nominations.* Sept. 10, 2019.

266. Darling Nomination - Confirmation. Confirmation of President Trump's nomination of Elizabeth Darling of Texas to be commissioner of the Administration on Children, Youth, and Families. Confirmed 57-37: R 51-0; D 5-37; I 1-0. *Note: A "yea" was a vote in support of the presidents position.* Sept. 10, 2019.

267. Akard Nomination - Cloture. Motion to invoke cloture (thus limiting debate) on the nomination of Stephen Akard of Indiana to be director of the Office of Foreign Missions. Motion agreed to 91-3: R 51-0; D 39-3; I 1-0. *Note: A majority of senators voting (48 in this case), a quorum being present, is required to invoke cloture on all nominations.* Sept. 10, 2019.

268. Cabaniss Nomination - Cloture. Motion to invoke cloture (thus limiting debate) on the nomination of Dale Cabaniss of Virginia to be director of the Office of Personnel Management. Motion agreed to 53-41: R 51-0; D 2-40; I 0-1. *Note: A majority of senators voting (48 in this case), a quorum being present, is required to invoke cloture on all nominations.* Sept. 10, 2019.

269. Byrne Nomination - Cloture. Motion to invoke cloture (thus limiting debate) on the nomination of James Byrne of Texas to be deputy secretary of the Veterans Affairs Department. Motion agreed to 81-13: R 51-0; D 29-13; I 1-0. *Note: A majority of senators voting (48 in this case), a quorum being present, is required to invoke cloture on all nominations.* Sept. 10, 2019.

270. Akard Nomination - Confirmation. Confirmation of President Trump's nomination of Stephen Akard of Indiana to be director of the Office of Foreign Missions. Confirmed 90-2: R 51-0; D 38-2; I 1-0. *Note: A "yea" was a vote in support of the presidents position.* Sept. 11, 2019.

	265	266	267	268	269	270
ALABAMA						
Shelby	Y	Y	Y	Y	Y	Y
Jones	Y	Y	Y	Y	Y	Y
ALASKA						
Murkowski	Y	Y	Y	Y	Y	Y
Sullivan	Y	Y	Y	Y	Y	Y
ARIZONA						
Sinema	+	+	+	+	+	Y
McSally	Y	Y	Y	Y	Y	Y
ARKANSAS						
Boozman	Y	Y	Y	Y	Y	Y
Cotton	Y	Y	Y	Y	Y	Y
CALIFORNIA						
Feinstein	N	N	Y	N	Y	Y
Harris	?	?	?	?	?	?
COLORADO						
Bennet	N	N	Y	N	Y	?
Gardner	Y	Y	Y	Y	Y	Y
CONNECTICUT						
Blumenthal	N	N	Y	N	Y	Y
Murphy	Y	Y	Y	Y	Y	Y
DELAWARE						
Carper	N	N	Y	N	Y	Y
Coons	N	N	Y	N	Y	Y
FLORIDA						
Rubio	Y	Y	Y	Y	Y	Y
Scott	Y	Y	Y	Y	Y	Y
GEORGIA						
Isakson	Y	Y	Y	Y	Y	Y
Perdue	Y	Y	Y	Y	Y	Y
HAWAII						
Schatz	N	N	Y	N	Y	Y
Hirono	N	N	Y	N	N	Y
IDAHO						
Crapo	Y	Y	Y	Y	Y	Y
Risch	Y	Y	Y	Y	Y	Y
ILLINOIS						
Durbin	N	N	Y	N	Y	Y
Duckworth	N	N	Y	N	Y	Y
INDIANA						
Young	Y	Y	Y	Y	Y	Y
Braun	Y	Y	Y	Y	Y	Y
IOWA						
Grassley	Y	Y	Y	Y	Y	Y
Ernst	Y	Y	Y	Y	Y	Y
KANSAS						
Roberts	?	?	?	?	?	?
Moran	Y	Y	Y	Y	Y	Y
KENTUCKY						
McConnell	Y	Y	Y	Y	Y	Y
Paul	Y	Y	Y	Y	Y	Y
LOUISIANA						
Cassidy	Y	Y	Y	Y	Y	Y
Kennedy	Y	Y	Y	Y	Y	Y
MAINE						
Collins	Y	Y	Y	Y	Y	Y
King	Y	Y	Y	N	Y	Y
MARYLAND						
Cardin	N	N	Y	N	Y	Y
Van Hollen	N	N	Y	N	Y	Y
MASSACHUSETTS						
Warren	?	?	?	?	?	?
Markey	N	N	N	N	N	N
MICHIGAN						
Stabenow	N	N	Y	N	N	Y
Peters	N	N	Y	N	Y	Y
MINNESOTA						
Klobuchar	N	N	Y	N	N	?
Smith	N	N	Y	N	Y	Y
MISSISSIPPI						
Wicker	Y	Y	Y	Y	Y	Y
Hyde-Smith	Y	Y	Y	Y	Y	Y
MISSOURI						
Blunt	Y	Y	Y	Y	Y	Y
Hawley	Y	Y	Y	Y	Y	Y
MONTANA						
Tester	Y	Y	Y	N	Y	Y
Daines	Y	Y	Y	Y	Y	Y
NEBRASKA						
Fischer	Y	Y	Y	Y	Y	Y
Sasse	Y	Y	Y	Y	Y	Y
NEVADA						
Cortez Masto	N	N	Y	N	Y	Y
Rosen	N	N	Y	N	Y	Y
NEW HAMPSHIRE						
Shaheen	N	N	Y	N	Y	Y
Hassan	N	N	Y	N	Y	Y
NEW JERSEY						
Menendez	N	N	Y	N	Y	Y
Booker	N	N	N	N	N	?
NEW MEXICO						
Udall	N	N	Y	N	Y	Y
Heinrich	N	N	Y	N	Y	Y
NEW YORK						
Schumer	N	N	Y	N	N	Y
Gillibrand	N	N	N	N	N	N
NORTH CAROLINA						
Burr	Y	Y	Y	Y	Y	Y
Tillis	Y	Y	Y	Y	Y	Y
NORTH DAKOTA						
Hoeven	Y	Y	Y	Y	Y	Y
Cramer	Y	Y	Y	Y	Y	Y
OHIO						
Brown	N	N	Y	N	N	Y
Portman	Y	Y	Y	Y	Y	Y
OKLAHOMA						
Inhofe	Y	Y	Y	Y	Y	Y
Lankford	Y	Y	Y	Y	Y	Y
OREGON						
Wyden	N	N	Y	N	N	Y
Merkley	N	N	Y	N	N	Y
PENNSYLVANIA						
Casey	N	N	Y	N	Y	Y
Toomey	Y	Y	Y	Y	Y	Y
RHODE ISLAND						
Reed	N	N	Y	N	N	Y
Whitehouse	Y	Y	Y	N	Y	Y
SOUTH CAROLINA						
Graham	Y	Y	Y	Y	Y	Y
Scott	Y	Y	Y	Y	Y	Y
SOUTH DAKOTA						
Thune	Y	Y	Y	Y	Y	Y
Rounds	Y	Y	Y	Y	Y	Y
TENNESSEE						
Alexander	+	+	+	+	?	+
Blackburn	Y	Y	Y	Y	Y	Y
TEXAS						
Cornyn	Y	Y	Y	Y	Y	Y
Cruz	Y	Y	Y	Y	Y	Y
UTAH						
Lee	Y	Y	Y	Y	Y	Y
Romney	Y	Y	Y	Y	Y	Y
VERMONT						
Leahy	N	N	Y	N	Y	Y
Sanders	?	?	?	?	?	?
VIRGINIA						
Warner	N	N	Y	N	Y	Y
Kaine	N	N	Y	N	Y	Y
WASHINGTON						
Murray	N	N	Y	N	N	Y
Cantwell	N	N	Y	N	N	Y
WEST VIRGINIA						
Manchin	Y	Y	Y	N	Y	Y
Capito	Y	Y	Y	Y	Y	Y
WISCONSIN						
Johnson	Y	Y	Y	Y	Y	Y
Baldwin	N	N	Y	N	Y	Y
WYOMING						
Enzi	Y	Y	Y	Y	Y	Y
Barrasso	Y	Y	Y	Y	Y	Y

KEY:	Republicans	Democrats	Independents
Y Voted for (yea)	N Voted against (nay)		P Voted "present"
+ Announced for	− Announced against		? Did not vote or otherwise
# Paired for	X Paired against		make position known

271. Cabaniss Nomination - Confirmation. Confirmation of President Trump's nomination of Dale Cabaniss of Virginia to be director of the Office of Personnel Management. Confirmed 54-38: R 51-0; D 3-37; I 0-1. *Note: A "yea" was a vote in support of the president's position.* Sept. 11, 2019.

272. Byrne Nomination - Confirmation. Confirmation of President Trump's nomination of James Byrne of Virginia to be deputy secretary of the Veterans Affairs Department. Confirmed 81-11: R 51-0; D 29-11; I 1-0. *Note: A "yea" was a vote in support of the president's position.* Sept. 11, 2019.

273. Bowman Nomination - Cloture. Motion to invoke cloture (thus limiting debate) on the nomination of Michelle Bowman of Kansas to be a member of the Board of Governors of the Federal Reserve System. Motion agreed to 62-31: R 50-1; D 12-29; I 0-1. *Note: A majority of senators voting (47 in this case), a quorum being present, is required to invoke cloture on all nominations.* Sept. 11, 2019.

274. Feddo Nomination - Cloture. Motion to invoke cloture (thus limiting debate) on the nomination of Thomas Peter Feddo of Virginia to be assistant secretary of the Treasury Department. Motion agreed to 92-1: R 50-0; D 41-0; I 1-0. *Note: A majority of senators voting (47 in this case), a quorum being present, is required to invoke cloture on all nominations.* Sept. 11, 2019.

275. Nordquist Nomination - Cloture. Motion to invoke cloture (thus limiting debate) on the nomination of Jennifer D. Nordquist of Virginia to be the U.S. executive director for the International Bank for Reconstruction and Development. Motion agreed to 94-0: R 52-0; D 41-0; I 1-0. *Note: A majority of senators voting (47 in this case), a quorum being present, is required to invoke cloture on all nominations.* Sept. 11, 2019.

276. Haines Nomination - Confirmation. Confirmation of President Trump's nomination of Stephanie L. Haines of Pennsylvanis to be a U.S. district judge for the Western District of Pennsylvania. Confirmed 94-0: R 52-0; D 41-0; I 1-0. *Note: A "yea" was a vote in support of the president's position.* Sept. 11, 2019.

	271	272	273	274	275	276
ALABAMA						
Shelby	Y	Y	Y	Y	Y	Y
Jones	Y	Y	Y	Y	Y	Y
ALASKA						
Murkowski	Y	Y	Y	Y	Y	Y
Sullivan	Y	Y	Y	Y	Y	Y
ARIZONA						
Sinema	Y	Y	Y		Y	Y
McSally	Y	Y	Y	Y	Y	Y
ARKANSAS						
Boozman	Y	Y	Y	Y	Y	Y
Cotton	Y	Y	Y	Y	Y	Y
CALIFORNIA						
Feinstein	N	Y	N	Y	Y	Y
Harris	?	?	?	?	?	–
COLORADO						
Bennet	?	?	Y	Y	Y	Y
Gardner	Y	Y	Y	Y	Y	Y
CONNECTICUT						
Blumenthal	N	Y	N	Y	Y	Y
Murphy	Y	Y	N	Y	Y	Y
DELAWARE						
Carper	N	Y	Y	Y	Y	Y
Coons	N	Y	Y	Y	Y	Y
FLORIDA						
Rubio	Y	Y	Y	Y	Y	Y
Scott	Y	Y	Y	Y	Y	Y
GEORGIA						
Isakson	Y	Y	Y	?	Y	Y
Perdue	Y	Y	Y	Y	Y	Y
HAWAII						
Schatz	N	Y	N	Y	Y	Y
Hirono	N	N	N	Y	Y	Y
IDAHO						
Crapo	Y	Y	Y	Y	Y	Y
Risch	Y	Y	Y	Y	Y	Y
ILLINOIS						
Durbin	N	Y	N	Y	Y	Y
Duckworth	N	Y	N	Y	Y	Y
INDIANA						
Young	Y	Y	Y	Y	Y	Y
Braun	Y	Y	Y	Y	Y	Y
IOWA						
Grassley	Y	Y	Y	Y	Y	Y
Ernst	Y	Y	Y	Y	Y	Y
KANSAS						
Roberts	?	?	?	?	?	?
Moran	Y	Y	Y	Y	Y	Y
KENTUCKY						
McConnell	Y	Y	Y	Y	Y	Y
Paul	Y	Y	N	N	Y	Y
LOUISIANA						
Cassidy	Y	Y	Y	Y	Y	Y
Kennedy	Y	Y	Y	Y	Y	Y
MAINE						
Collins	Y	Y	Y	Y	Y	Y
King	N	Y	N	Y	Y	Y
MARYLAND						
Cardin	N	Y	N	Y	Y	Y
Van Hollen	N	Y	N	Y	Y	Y
MASSACHUSETTS						
Warren	?	?	?	?	?	?
Markey	N	N	N	Y	Y	Y
MICHIGAN						
Stabenow	N	N	N	Y	Y	Y
Peters	N	Y	Y	Y	Y	Y
MINNESOTA						
Klobuchar	?	?	?	?	?	?
Smith	N	Y	N	Y	Y	Y
MISSISSIPPI						
Wicker	Y	Y	Y	Y	Y	Y
Hyde-Smith	Y	Y	Y	Y	Y	Y
MISSOURI						
Blunt	Y	Y	Y	Y	Y	Y
Hawley	Y	Y	Y	Y	Y	Y

	271	272	273	274	275	276
MONTANA						
Tester	N	Y	Y	Y	Y	Y
Daines	Y	Y	Y	Y	Y	Y
NEBRASKA						
Fischer	Y	Y	Y	Y	Y	Y
Sasse	Y	Y	Y	Y	Y	Y
NEVADA						
Cortez Masto	N	Y	N	Y	Y	Y
Rosen	N	Y	N	Y	Y	Y
NEW HAMPSHIRE						
Shaheen	N	Y	Y	Y	Y	Y
Hassan	N	Y	Y	Y	Y	Y
NEW JERSEY						
Menendez	N	Y	N	Y	Y	Y
Booker	?	?	?	?	?	?
NEW MEXICO						
Udall	N	Y	N	Y	Y	Y
Heinrich	N	Y	N	Y	Y	Y
NEW YORK						
Schumer	N	N	N	Y	Y	Y
Gillibrand	N	N	N	Y	Y	Y
NORTH CAROLINA						
Burr	Y	Y	Y	Y	Y	Y
Tillis	Y	Y	+	Y	Y	Y
NORTH DAKOTA						
Hoeven	Y	Y	Y	Y	Y	Y
Cramer	Y	Y	Y	Y	Y	Y
OHIO						
Brown	N	N	N	Y	Y	Y
Portman	Y	Y	Y	Y	Y	Y
OKLAHOMA						
Inhofe	Y	Y	Y	Y	Y	Y
Lankford	Y	Y	Y	Y	Y	Y
OREGON						
Wyden	N	N	N	Y	Y	Y
Merkley	N	N	N	Y	Y	Y
PENNSYLVANIA						
Casey	N	Y	N	Y	Y	Y
Toomey	Y	Y	Y	Y	Y	Y
RHODE ISLAND						
Reed	N	N	N	Y	Y	Y
Whitehouse	N	Y	N	Y	Y	Y
SOUTH CAROLINA						
Graham	Y	Y	Y	Y	Y	Y
Scott	Y	Y	Y	Y	Y	Y
SOUTH DAKOTA						
Thune	Y	Y	Y	Y	Y	Y
Rounds	Y	Y	Y	Y	Y	Y
TENNESSEE						
Alexander	+	+	Y	Y	Y	Y
Blackburn	Y	Y	Y	Y	Y	Y
TEXAS						
Cornyn	Y	Y	Y	Y	Y	Y
Cruz	Y	Y	Y	Y	Y	Y
UTAH						
Lee	Y	Y	Y	Y	Y	Y
Romney	Y	Y	Y	Y	Y	Y
VERMONT						
Leahy	N	Y	N	Y	Y	Y
Sanders	?	?	?	?	?	?
VIRGINIA						
Warner	N	Y	Y	Y	Y	Y
Kaine	N	Y	Y	Y	Y	Y
WASHINGTON						
Murray	N	N	N	Y	Y	Y
Cantwell	N	N	N	Y	Y	Y
WEST VIRGINIA						
Manchin	N	Y	Y	Y	Y	Y
Capito	Y	Y	Y	Y	Y	Y
WISCONSIN						
Johnson	Y	Y	Y	Y	Y	Y
Baldwin	N	Y	N	Y	Y	Y
WYOMING						
Enzi	Y	Y	Y	Y	Y	Y
Barrasso	Y	Y	Y	Y	Y	Y

KEY:

Republicans	Democrats	*Independents*

Y Voted for (yea)	**N** Voted against (nay)	**P** Voted "present"
+ Announced for	**–** Announced against	**?** Did not vote or otherwise make position known
# Paired for	**X** Paired against	

277. Brown Nomination - Confirmation. Confirmation of President Trump's nomination of nomination of Ada E. Brown of Texas to be a U.S. district judge for the Northern District of Texas. Confirmed 80-13: R 52-0; D 27-13; I 1-0. *Note: A "yea" was a vote in support of the president's position.* Sept. 11, 2019.

278. Grimberg Nomination - Confirmation. Confirmation of President Trump's nomination of nomination of Steven D. Grimberg of Georgia to be U.S. District Judge for the Northern District of Georgia. Confirmed 75-18: R 52-0; D 22-18; I 1-0. *Note: A "yea" was a vote in support of the president's position.* Sept. 11, 2019.

279. Seeger Nomination - Confirmation. Confirmation of President Trump's nomination of nomination of Steven C. Seeger of Illinois to be a U.S. district judge for the Northern District of Illinois. Confirmed 90-1: R 51-0; D 38-1; I 1-0. *Note: A "yea" was a vote in support of the president's position.* Sept. 11, 2019.

280. Bowman Nomination - Confirmation. Confirmation of President Trump's nomination of Michelle Bowman of Kansas to be a member of the Board of Governors of the Federal Reserve System. Confirmed 60-31: R 49-1; D 11-29; I 0-1. *Note: A "yea" was vote in support of the president's position.* Sept. 12, 2019.

281. Feddo Nomination - Confirmation. Confirmation of President Trump's nomination of Thomas Peter Feddo of Virginia to be assistant secretary of the Treasury Department. Confirmed 85-1: R 44-1; D 40-0; I 1-0. *Note: A "yea" was a vote in support of the president's position.* Sept. 12, 2019.

282. Rakolta Nomination - Cloture. Motion to invoke cloture (thus limiting debate) on the nomination of John Rakolta, Jr. of Michigan to be ambassador to the United Arab Emirates. Motion agreed to 55-27: R 44-0; D 10-27; I 1-0. *Note: A majority of senators voting (42 in this case), a quorum being present, is required to invoke cloture on all nominations.* Sept. 16, 2019.

	277	278	279	280	281	282
ALABAMA						
Shelby	Y	Y	Y	Y	Y	Y
Jones	Y	Y	Y	Y	Y	Y
ALASKA						
Murkowski	Y	Y	Y	Y	Y	Y
Sullivan	Y	Y	Y	Y	Y	Y
ARIZONA						
Sinema	Y	N	Y	Y	Y	Y
McSally	Y	Y	Y	Y	?	Y
ARKANSAS						
Boozman	Y	Y	Y	Y	Y	Y
Cotton	Y	Y	Y	Y	Y	Y
CALIFORNIA						
Feinstein	Y	Y	Y	N	Y	N
Harris	?	-	-	?	?	?
COLORADO						
Bennet	Y	Y	Y	Y	Y	?
Gardner	Y	Y	Y	Y	Y	Y
CONNECTICUT						
Blumenthal	N	N	Y	N	Y	N
Murphy	Y	Y	Y	N	Y	Y
DELAWARE						
Carper	Y	Y	Y	Y	Y	N
Coons	?	?	?	?	?	Y
FLORIDA						
Rubio	Y	Y	Y	+	+	Y
Scott	Y	Y	Y	Y	Y	Y
GEORGIA						
Isakson	Y	Y	Y	Y	?	Y
Perdue	Y	Y	Y	Y	?	Y
HAWAII						
Schatz	N	N	Y	N	Y	?
Hirono	N	N	Y	N	Y	N
IDAHO						
Crapo	Y	Y	Y	Y	Y	Y
Risch	Y	Y	Y	Y	Y	?
ILLINOIS						
Durbin	Y	Y	Y	N	Y	N
Duckworth	Y	Y	Y	N	Y	N
INDIANA						
Young	Y	Y	Y	Y	Y	Y
Braun	Y	Y	Y	Y	Y	Y
IOWA						
Grassley	Y	Y	Y	Y	Y	Y
Ernst	Y	Y	Y	Y	Y	Y
KANSAS						
Roberts	?	?	?	?	?	?
Moran	Y	Y	Y	Y	+	Y
KENTUCKY						
McConnell	Y	Y	Y	Y	Y	Y
Paul	Y	Y	Y	N	N	Y
LOUISIANA						
Cassidy	Y	Y	Y	Y	Y	Y
Kennedy	Y	Y	Y	Y	Y	?
MAINE						
Collins	Y	Y	Y	Y	Y	Y
King	Y	Y	Y	N	Y	Y
MARYLAND						
Cardin	Y	Y	Y	N	Y	N
Van Hollen	Y	Y	Y	N	Y	N
MASSACHUSETTS						
Warren	?	?	?	?	?	?
Markey	N	N	Y	N	Y	N
MICHIGAN						
Stabenow	N	Y	Y	N	Y	Y
Peters	Y	Y	Y	Y	Y	Y
MINNESOTA						
Klobuchar	?	?	?	?	?	?
Smith	Y	N	Y	N	Y	N
MISSISSIPPI						
Wicker	Y	Y	Y	Y	Y	?
Hyde-Smith	Y	Y	Y	Y	Y	?
MISSOURI						
Blunt	Y	Y	Y	Y	Y	Y
Hawley	Y	Y	Y	Y	Y	Y

	277	278	279	280	281	282
MONTANA						
Tester	Y	Y	Y	Y	Y	Y
Daines	Y	Y	Y	Y	Y	Y
NEBRASKA						
Fischer	Y	Y	Y	Y	Y	Y
Sasse	Y	Y	Y	Y	Y	Y
NEVADA						
Cortez Masto	N	N	Y	N	Y	N
Rosen	Y	Y	Y	N	Y	N
NEW HAMPSHIRE						
Shaheen	Y	Y	Y	Y	Y	Y
Hassan	Y	Y	Y	Y	Y	Y
NEW JERSEY						
Menendez	Y	N	Y	N	Y	N
Booker	?	?	?	?	?	?
NEW MEXICO						
Udall	Y	N	Y	N	Y	N
Heinrich	Y	N	Y	N	Y	N
NEW YORK						
Schumer	N	N	Y	N	Y	N
Gillibrand	N	N	N	N	Y	?
NORTH CAROLINA						
Burr	Y	Y	Y	Y	Y	Y
Tillis	Y	Y	Y	Y	Y	Y
NORTH DAKOTA						
Hoeven	Y	Y	Y	Y	Y	Y
Cramer	Y	Y	Y	Y	Y	Y
OHIO						
Brown	N	N	Y	N	Y	N
Portman	Y	Y	Y	Y	Y	Y
OKLAHOMA						
Inhofe	Y	Y	Y	Y	?	Y
Lankford	Y	Y	Y	Y	Y	Y
OREGON						
Wyden	N	N	Y	N	Y	N
Merkley	Y	N	Y	N	Y	N
PENNSYLVANIA						
Casey	Y	Y	Y	N	Y	N
Toomey	Y	Y	Y	Y	Y	?
RHODE ISLAND						
Reed	Y	Y	Y	N	Y	N
Whitehouse	Y	Y	Y	N	Y	N
SOUTH CAROLINA						
Graham	Y	Y	?	Y	Y	Y
Scott	Y	Y	Y	Y	Y	Y
SOUTH DAKOTA						
Thune	Y	Y	Y	Y	Y	Y
Rounds	Y	Y	Y	Y	Y	Y
TENNESSEE						
Alexander	Y	Y	Y	+	+	+
Blackburn	Y	Y	Y	Y	Y	Y
TEXAS						
Cornyn	Y	Y	Y	Y	Y	Y
Cruz	Y	Y	Y	Y	Y	?
UTAH						
Lee	Y	Y	Y	Y	Y	Y
Romney	Y	Y	Y	Y	Y	?
VERMONT						
Leahy	Y	Y	Y	N	Y	N
Sanders	?	?	?	?	?	?
VIRGINIA						
Warner	Y	Y	Y	Y	Y	N
Kaine	Y	Y	Y	Y	Y	N
WASHINGTON						
Murray	N	N	Y	N	Y	?
Cantwell	N	N	Y	N	Y	N
WEST VIRGINIA						
Manchin	Y	Y	?	Y	Y	Y
Capito	Y	Y	Y	Y	Y	Y
WISCONSIN						
Johnson	Y	Y	Y	Y	Y	Y
Baldwin	N	N	Y	N	Y	N
WYOMING						
Enzi	Y	Y	Y	Y	Y	Y
Barrasso	Y	Y	Y	Y	Y	Y

KEY:	**Republicans**	Democrats	*Independents*
Y Voted for (yea)	N Voted against (nay)	P Voted "present"	
+ Announced for	- Announced against	? Did not vote or otherwise make position known	
# Paired for	X Paired against		

283. Rakolta Nomination – Confirmation. Confirmation of President Trump's nomination of John Rakolta, Jr. of Michigan to be ambassador to the United Arab Emirates. Confirmed 63-30: R 51-0; D 11-30; I 1-0. *Note: A "yea" was a vote in support of the president's position.* Sept. 17, 2019.

284. Howery Nomination – Cloture. Motion to invoke cloture (thus limiting debate) on the nomination of Kenneth A. Howery of Texas to be ambassador to the Kingdom of Sweden. Motion agreed to 63-29: R 51-0; D 11-29; I 1-0. *Note: A majority of senators voting (47 in this case), a quorum being present, is required to invoke cloture on all nominations.* Sept. 17, 2019.

285. Howery Nomination – Confirmation. Confirmation of President Trump's nomination of Kenneth A. Howery of Texas to be ambassador to the Kingdom of Sweden. Confirmed 62-32: R 51-0; D 10-32; I 1-0. *Note: A "yea" was a vote in support of the president's position.* Sept. 17, 2019.

286. Destro Nomination – Cloture. Motion to invoke cloture (thus limiting debate) on the nomination of Robert A. Destro of Virginia to be assistant secretary of State. Motion agreed to 49-44: R 49-1; D 0-42; I 0-1. *Note: A majority of senators voting (47 in this case), a quorum being present, is required to invoke cloture on all nominations.* Sept. 17, 2019.

287. McIntosh Nomination – Cloture. Motion to invoke cloture (thus limiting debate) on the nomination Brent James McIntosh of Michigan to be an under secretary of the Treasury. Motion agreed to 54-40: R 50-1; D 4-38; I 0-1. *Note: A majority of senators voting (48 in this case), a quorum being present, is required to invoke cloture on all nominations.* Sept. 17, 2019.

288. Callanan Nomination – Cloture. Motion to invoke cloture (thus limiting debate) on the nomination of Brian Callanan of New Jersey to be general counsel for the Department of the Treasury. Motion agreed to 55-37: R 49-1; D 6-35; I 0-1. *Note: A majority of senators voting (47 in this case), a quorum being present, is required to invoke cloture on all nominations.* Sept. 17, 2019.

	283	284	285	286	287	288
ALABAMA						
Shelby	Y	Y	Y	Y	Y	Y
Jones	Y	Y	Y	N	Y	Y
ALASKA						
Murkowski	Y	Y	Y	Y	Y	Y
Sullivan	Y	Y	Y	Y	Y	Y
ARIZONA						
Sinema	Y	Y	Y	N	Y	Y
McSally	Y	Y	Y	Y	Y	Y
ARKANSAS						
Boozman	Y	Y	Y	Y	Y	Y
Cotton	Y	Y	Y	Y	Y	Y
CALIFORNIA						
Feinstein	N	N	N	N	N	N
Harris	?	?	?	?	?	?
COLORADO						
Bennet	?	?	N	N	N	N
Gardner	Y	Y	Y	Y	Y	Y
CONNECTICUT						
Blumenthal	N	N	N	N	N	N
Murphy	Y	Y	Y	N	Y	Y
DELAWARE						
Carper	N	Y	N	N	Y	Y
Coons	Y	Y	Y	N	N	N
FLORIDA						
Rubio	Y	Y	Y	Y	Y	Y
Scott	Y	Y	Y	Y	Y	Y
GEORGIA						
Isakson	Y	Y	Y	Y	Y	Y
Perdue	Y	Y	Y	Y	Y	Y
HAWAII						
Schatz	N	N	N	N	N	N
Hirono	N	N	N	N	N	N
IDAHO						
Crapo	Y	Y	Y	Y	Y	Y
Risch	Y	Y	Y	Y	Y	Y
ILLINOIS						
Durbin	N	N	N	N	N	N
Duckworth	N	N	N	N	N	N
INDIANA						
Young	Y	Y	Y	Y	Y	Y
Braun	Y	Y	Y	Y	Y	Y
IOWA						
Grassley	Y	Y	Y	Y	Y	Y
Ernst	Y	Y	Y	Y	Y	Y
KANSAS						
Roberts	?	?	?	?	?	?
Moran	Y	Y	Y	Y	Y	Y
KENTUCKY						
McConnell	Y	Y	Y	Y	Y	Y
Paul	Y	Y	Y	Y	N	N
LOUISIANA						
Cassidy	Y	Y	Y	Y	Y	Y
Kennedy	Y	Y	Y	Y	Y	Y
MAINE						
Collins	Y	Y	Y	N	Y	Y
King	Y	Y	Y	N	N	N
MARYLAND						
Cardin	N	N	N	N	N	Y
Van Hollen	Y	N	N	N	N	N
MASSACHUSETTS						
Warren	?	?	?	?	?	?
Markey	N	N	N	N	N	N
MICHIGAN						
Stabenow	Y	N	N	N	N	N
Peters	Y	N	N	N	N	N
MINNESOTA						
Klobuchar	N	N	N	N	N	?
Smith	N	N	N	N	N	N
MISSISSIPPI						
Wicker	Y	Y	Y	Y	Y	Y
Hyde-Smith	Y	Y	Y	Y	Y	Y
MISSOURI						
Blunt	Y	Y	Y	Y	Y	Y
Hawley	Y	Y	Y	Y	Y	Y

	283	284	285	286	287	288
MONTANA						
Tester	Y	N	N	N	N	N
Daines	Y	Y	Y	Y	Y	Y
NEBRASKA						
Fischer	Y	Y	Y	Y	Y	Y
Sasse	Y	Y	Y	Y	Y	Y
NEVADA						
Cortez Masto	N	N	N	N	N	N
Rosen	N	N	N	N	N	N
NEW HAMPSHIRE						
Shaheen	Y	Y	Y	N	N	N
Hassan	Y	Y	Y	N	N	N
NEW JERSEY						
Menendez	N	N	N	N	N	N
Booker	?	?	?	?	?	?
NEW MEXICO						
Udall	N	N	N	N	N	N
Heinrich	N	N	N	N	N	N
NEW YORK						
Schumer	N	N	N	N	N	N
Gillibrand	N	N	N	N	N	N
NORTH CAROLINA						
Burr	Y	Y	Y	Y	Y	Y
Tillis	Y	Y	Y	Y	Y	Y
NORTH DAKOTA						
Hoeven	Y	Y	Y	Y	Y	Y
Cramer	Y	Y	Y	Y	Y	Y
OHIO						
Brown	N	N	N	N	N	N
Portman	Y	Y	Y	Y	Y	Y
OKLAHOMA						
Inhofe	Y	Y	Y	Y	Y	Y
Lankford	Y	Y	Y	Y	Y	Y
OREGON						
Wyden	N	?	N	N	N	N
Merkley	N	Y	Y	N	N	N
PENNSYLVANIA						
Casey	N	N	N	N	N	N
Toomey	Y	Y	Y	Y	Y	Y
RHODE ISLAND						
Reed	N	N	N	N	N	N
Whitehouse	N	N	N	N	N	N
SOUTH CAROLINA						
Graham	Y	Y	Y	Y	Y	Y
Scott	Y	Y	Y	Y	Y	Y
SOUTH DAKOTA						
Thune	Y	Y	Y	Y	Y	Y
Rounds	Y	Y	Y	Y	Y	Y
TENNESSEE						
Alexander	+	+	+	+	+	+
Blackburn	Y	Y	Y	Y	Y	Y
TEXAS						
Cornyn	Y	Y	Y	Y	Y	Y
Cruz	Y	Y	Y	?	Y	Y
UTAH						
Lee	Y	Y	Y	Y	Y	Y
Romney	Y	Y	Y	Y	Y	Y
VERMONT						
Leahy	N	N	N	N	N	N
Sanders	?	?	?	?	?	?
VIRGINIA						
Warner	N	Y	Y	N	N	N
Kaine	N	Y	N	N	N	N
WASHINGTON						
Murray	N	N	N	N	N	N
Cantwell	N	N	N	N	N	N
WEST VIRGINIA						
Manchin	Y	Y	Y	N	Y	Y
Capito	Y	Y	Y	Y	Y	Y
WISCONSIN						
Johnson	Y	Y	Y	Y	Y	?
Baldwin	N	N	N	N	N	N
WYOMING						
Enzi	Y	Y	Y	Y	Y	Y
Barrasso	Y	Y	Y	Y	Y	Y

KEY:

	Republicans	Democrats	Independents

Y	Voted for (yea)	N	Voted against (nay)	P	Voted "present"
+	Announced for	–	Announced against	?	Did not vote or otherwise make position known
#	Paired for	X	Paired against		

289. Destro Nomination - Confirmation. Confirmation of President Trump's nomination of Robert A. Destro of Virginia to be assistant secretary of State. Confirmed 49-44: R 49-1; D 0-42; I 0-1. *Note: A "yea" was a vote in support of the president's position.* Sept. 18, 2019.

290. McIntosh Nomination - Confirmation. Confirmation of President Trump's nomination of Brent James McIntosh of Michigan to be an under secretary of the Treasury. Confirmed 54-38: R 50-0; D 4-37; I 0-1. *Note: A "yea" was a vote in support of the president's position.* Sept. 18, 2019.

291. Callanan Nomination - Confirmation. Confirmation of President Trump's nomination of Brian Callanan of New Jersey to be general counsel for the Department of the Treasury. Confirmed 55-39: R 49-1; D 6-37; I 0-1. *Note: A "yea" was a vote in support of the president's position.* Sept. 18, 2019.

292. HR2740. Fiscal 2020 Four-Bill Appropriations Package - Cloture. McConnell, R-Ky., motion to invoke cloture (thus limiting debate) on the McConnell, R-Ky., motion to proceed to the fiscal 2020 Labor-HHS-Education, Defense, Energy-Water, and State-Foreign Operations appropriations package. The bill would provide $984.7 billion in discretionary spending for four of the twelve fiscal 2020 appropriations bills, including $690.2 billion for the Defense Department, $191.7 billion for the Labor, Health and Human Services, and Education Departments, $56.4 billion for the State Department and related agencies, and $46.4 billion for the Energy Department and federal water projects. Motion rejected 51-44: R 49-2; D 2-41; I 0-1. *Note: Three-fifths of the total Senate (60) is required to invoke cloture.* Sept. 18, 2019.

293. S1790. Fiscal 2020 Defense Authorization - Cloture. McConnell, R-Ky., motion to invoke cloture (thus limiting debate) on the McConnell, R-Ky., motion that the Senate disagree to the House amendment to the fiscal 2020 NDAA, agree to the request of the House to go to conference, and that the chair be authorized to appoint conferees on behalf of the Senate on the bill that would authorize $642.5 billion for the Defense Department's base budget, $23.2 billion for national security programs within the Energy Department and $75.9 billion to support overseas contingency operations. Motion agreed to 87-7: R 50-1; D 36-6; I 1-0. *Note: Three-fifths of the total Senate (60) is required to invoke cloture.* Sept. 18, 2019.

294. McGuire Nomination - Cloture. Motion to invoke cloture (thus limiting debate) on the nomination of Brian McGuire of New York to be a deputy under secretary of the Treasury. Motion agreed to 82-6: R 46-1; D 35-5; I 1-0. *Note: A majority of senators voting (45 in this case), a quorum being present, is required to invoke cloture on all nominations.* Sept. 23, 2019.

	289	290	291	292	293	294
ALABAMA						
Shelby	Y	Y	Y	Y	Y	Y
Jones	N	Y	Y	Y	Y	Y
ALASKA						
Murkowski	Y	Y	Y	Y	Y	Y
Sullivan	Y	Y	Y	Y	Y	Y
ARIZONA						
Sinema	N	Y	Y	N	Y	Y
McSally	Y	Y	Y	Y	Y	Y
ARKANSAS						
Boozman	Y	Y	Y	Y	Y	Y
Cotton	Y	Y	Y	Y	Y	Y
CALIFORNIA						
Feinstein	N	N	N	N	Y	Y
Harris	N	N	N	N	N	?
COLORADO						
Bennet	N	?	N	N	?	?
Gardner	Y	Y	Y	Y	Y	Y
CONNECTICUT						
Blumenthal	N	N	N	N	Y	Y
Murphy	N	Y	Y	N	Y	Y
DELAWARE						
Carper	N	N	Y	N	Y	Y
Coons	N	N	N	N	Y	Y
FLORIDA						
Rubio	Y	Y	Y	Y	Y	Y
Scott	Y	Y	Y	Y	Y	Y
GEORGIA						
Isakson	Y	Y	Y	Y	Y	?
Perdue	Y	Y	Y	Y	Y	Y
HAWAII						
Schatz	N	N	N	N	Y	Y
Hirono	N	N	N	N	N	Y
IDAHO						
Crapo	Y	Y	Y	Y	Y	Y
Risch	Y	Y	Y	Y	Y	?
ILLINOIS						
Durbin	N	N	N	N	Y	Y
Duckworth	N	N	N	N	Y	Y
INDIANA						
Young	Y	Y	Y	Y	Y	Y
Braun	Y	Y	Y	Y	Y	Y
IOWA						
Grassley	Y	Y	Y	Y	Y	Y
Ernst	Y	Y	Y	Y	Y	Y
KANSAS						
Roberts	?	?	?	?	?	?
Moran	Y	Y	Y	Y	Y	Y
KENTUCKY						
McConnell	Y	Y	Y	N	Y	Y
Paul	Y	Y	N	N	N	N
LOUISIANA						
Cassidy	Y	Y	Y	Y	Y	Y
Kennedy	Y	Y	Y	Y	Y	Y
MAINE						
Collins	N	Y	Y	Y	Y	Y
King	N	N	N	N	Y	Y
MARYLAND						
Cardin	N	N	N	N	Y	Y
Van Hollen	N	N	N	N	N	Y
MASSACHUSETTS						
Warren	?	?	N	N	N	?
Markey	N	N	N	N	N	N
MICHIGAN						
Stabenow	N	N	N	N	Y	Y
Peters	N	N	N	Y	Y	Y
MINNESOTA						
Klobuchar	?	?	?	?	?	Y
Smith	N	N	N	N	Y	Y
MISSISSIPPI						
Wicker	Y	Y	Y	Y	Y	Y
Hyde-Smith	Y	Y	Y	Y	Y	Y
MISSOURI						
Blunt	Y	Y	Y	Y	Y	Y
Hawley	Y	Y	Y	Y	Y	Y

	289	290	291	292	293	294
MONTANA						
Tester	N	N	N	N	Y	Y
Daines	Y	Y	Y	Y	Y	Y
NEBRASKA						
Fischer	Y	Y	Y	Y	Y	Y
Sasse	Y	Y	Y	Y	Y	Y
NEVADA						
Cortez Masto	N	N	N	N	Y	Y
Rosen	N	N	N	N	Y	Y
NEW HAMPSHIRE						
Shaheen	N	N	N	N	Y	Y
Hassan	N	N	N	N	Y	Y
NEW JERSEY						
Menendez	N	N	N	N	Y	Y
Booker	?	?	?	?	?	?
NEW MEXICO						
Udall	N	N	N	N	Y	Y
Heinrich	N	N	N	N	Y	Y
NEW YORK						
Schumer	N	N	N	N	Y	Y
Gillibrand	N	N	N	N	N	N
NORTH CAROLINA						
Burr	Y	Y	Y	Y	Y	Y
Tillis	Y	Y	Y	Y	Y	?
NORTH DAKOTA						
Hoeven	Y	Y	Y	Y	Y	Y
Cramer	Y	Y	Y	Y	Y	Y
OHIO						
Brown	N	N	N	N	Y	N
Portman	Y	Y	Y	Y	Y	Y
OKLAHOMA						
Inhofe	Y	Y	Y	Y	Y	Y
Lankford	Y	Y	Y	Y	Y	Y
OREGON						
Wyden	N	N	N	N	N	Y
Merkley	N	N	N	N	N	N
PENNSYLVANIA						
Casey	N	N	N	N	Y	N
Toomey	Y	Y	Y	Y	Y	?
RHODE ISLAND						
Reed	N	N	N	N	Y	Y
Whitehouse	N	N	N	N	Y	?
SOUTH CAROLINA						
Graham	Y	Y	Y	Y	Y	?
Scott	Y	Y	Y	Y	Y	Y
SOUTH DAKOTA						
Thune	Y	Y	Y	Y	Y	Y
Rounds	?	?	?	?	?	Y
TENNESSEE						
Alexander	+	+	+	Y	Y	Y
Blackburn	Y	Y	Y	Y	Y	Y
TEXAS						
Cornyn	Y	Y	Y	Y	Y	Y
Cruz	Y	Y	Y	Y	Y	Y
UTAH						
Lee	Y	Y	Y	Y	Y	Y
Romney	Y	Y	Y	Y	Y	Y
VERMONT						
Leahy	N	N	N	N	Y	Y
Sanders	?	?	?	?	?	?
VIRGINIA						
Warner	N	N	N	N	N	Y
Kaine	N	N	N	N	N	Y
WASHINGTON						
Murray	N	N	N	N	Y	Y
Cantwell	N	N	N	N	Y	Y
WEST VIRGINIA						
Manchin	N	Y	Y	N	Y	Y
Capito	Y	Y	Y	Y	Y	Y
WISCONSIN						
Johnson	Y	Y	Y	Y	Y	Y
Baldwin	N	N	N	N	Y	Y
WYOMING						
Enzi	Y	Y	Y	Y	Y	Y
Barrasso	Y	Y	Y	Y	Y	Y

KEY: **Republicans**   Democrats   *Independents*

Y	Voted for (yea)	N Voted against (nay)	P Voted "present"
+	Announced for	− Announced against	? Did not vote or otherwise make position known
#	Paired for	X Paired against	

295. Cella Nomination - Cloture. Motion to invoke cloture (thus limiting debate) on the nomination of Joseph Cella of Michigan to be ambassador to the Republic of Fiji; concurrently to serve as ambassador to the Kingdom of Kiribati, the Republic of Nauru, the Kingdom of Tonga, and Tuvalu. Motion agreed to 55-37: R 51-0; D 3-37; I 1-0. *Note: A majority of senators voting (47 in this case), a quorum being present, is required to invoke cloture on all nominations.* Sept. 24, 2019.

296. Jorjani Nomination - Cloture. Motion to invoke cloture (thus limiting debate) on Daniel Jorjani of Kentucky to be solicitor for the Interior Department. Motion agreed to 50-41: R 50-1; D 0-39; I 0-1. *Note: A majority of senators voting (46 in this case), a quorum being present, is required to invoke cloture on all nominations.* Sept. 24, 2019.

297. Black Nomination - Cloture. Motion to invoke cloture (thus limiting debate) on the nomination of David Black of North Dakota to be deputy commissioner of the Social Security Administration. Motion agreed to 66-25: R 50-0; D 15-25; I 1-0. *Note: A majority of senators (46 in this case), a quorum being present, is required to invoke cloture on all nominations.* Sept. 24, 2019.

298. McGuire Nomination - Confirmation. Confirmation of President Trump's nomination of Brian McGuire of New York to be a deputy under secretary of the Treasury. Confirmed 88-6: R 52-0; D 35-6; I 1-0. *Note: A "yea" was a vote in support of the president's position.* Sept. 24, 2019.

299. Cella Nomination - Confirmation. Confirmation of President Trump's nomination of Joseph Cella of Michigan to be ambassador to the Republic of Fiji; concurrently to serve as ambassador to the Kingdom of Kiribati, the Republic of Nauru, the Kingdom of Tonga, and Tuvalu. Confirmed 56-38: R 52-0; D 3-38; I 1-0. *Note: A "yea" was a vote in support of the president's position.* Sept. 24, 2019.

300. Jorjani Nomination - Confirmation. Confirmation of President Trump's nomination of Daniel Jorjani of Kentucky to be solicitor for the Interior Department. Confirmed 51-43: R 51-1; D 0-41; I 0-1. *Note: A "yea" was a vote in support of the president's position.* Sept. 24, 2019.

	295	296	297	298	299	300
ALABAMA						
Shelby	Y	Y	Y	Y	Y	Y
Jones	?	?	?	?	?	?
ALASKA						
Murkowski	Y	Y	Y	Y	Y	Y
Sullivan	Y	Y	Y	Y	Y	Y
ARIZONA						
Sinema	Y	N	Y	Y	Y	N
McSally	Y	Y	Y	Y	Y	Y
ARKANSAS						
Boozman	Y	Y	Y	Y	Y	Y
Cotton	Y	Y	Y	Y	Y	Y
CALIFORNIA						
Feinstein	N	N	Y	Y	N	N
Harris	?	?	?	?	?	-
COLORADO						
Bennet	N	N	Y	Y	N	N
Gardner	Y	Y	Y	Y	Y	Y
CONNECTICUT						
Blumenthal	N	N	N	Y	N	N
Murphy	Y	N	Y	Y	Y	N
DELAWARE						
Carper	N	N	Y	Y	N	N
Coons	N	N	Y	Y	N	N
FLORIDA						
Rubio	Y	Y	Y	Y	Y	Y
Scott	Y	Y	Y	Y	Y	Y
GEORGIA						
Isakson	Y	Y	Y	Y	Y	Y
Perdue	Y	Y	Y	Y	Y	Y
HAWAII						
Schatz	N	N	N	Y	N	N
Hirono	N	N	N	Y	N	N
IDAHO						
Crapo	Y	Y	Y	Y	Y	Y
Risch	Y	Y	Y	Y	Y	Y
ILLINOIS						
Durbin	N	N	N	Y	N	N
Duckworth	N	N	N	Y	N	N
INDIANA						
Young	Y	Y	Y	Y	Y	Y
Braun	Y	Y	Y	Y	Y	Y
IOWA						
Grassley	Y	Y	Y	Y	Y	Y
Ernst	Y	Y	Y	Y	Y	Y
KANSAS						
Roberts	Y	Y	Y	Y	Y	Y
Moran	Y	Y	Y	Y	Y	Y
KENTUCKY						
McConnell	Y	Y	Y	Y	Y	Y
Paul	Y	Y	Y	Y	Y	Y
LOUISIANA						
Cassidy	Y	Y	Y	Y	Y	Y
Kennedy	Y	Y	Y	Y	Y	Y
MAINE						
Collins	Y	N	Y	Y	Y	N
King	Y	N	Y	Y	Y	N
MARYLAND						
Cardin	N	N	Y	Y	N	N
Van Hollen	N	N	N	Y	N	N
MASSACHUSETTS						
Warren	?	?	?	N	N	N
Markey	N	N	N	N	N	N
MICHIGAN						
Stabenow	N	N	N	Y	N	N
Peters	N	N	N	Y	N	N
MINNESOTA						
Klobuchar	N	N	N	Y	N	N
Smith	N	N	N	Y	N	N
MISSISSIPPI						
Wicker	Y	Y	Y	Y	Y	Y
Hyde-Smith	Y	Y	Y	Y	Y	Y
MISSOURI						
Blunt	Y	Y	Y	Y	Y	Y
Hawley	Y	Y	Y	Y	Y	Y

	295	296	297	298	299	300
MONTANA						
Tester	N	N	N	Y	N	N
Daines	Y	Y	Y	Y	Y	Y
NEBRASKA						
Fischer	Y	Y	Y	Y	Y	Y
Sasse	Y	Y	Y	Y	Y	Y
NEVADA						
Cortez Masto	N	N	N	Y	N	N
Rosen	N	N	N	Y	N	N
NEW HAMPSHIRE						
Shaheen	N	N	Y	Y	N	N
Hassan	N	N	Y	Y	N	N
NEW JERSEY						
Menendez	N	N	N	Y	N	N
Booker	?	?	?	?	?	-
NEW MEXICO						
Udall	N	N	N	Y	N	N
Heinrich	N	N	N	Y	N	N
NEW YORK						
Schumer	N	N	N	Y	N	N
Gillibrand	N	N	N	N	N	N
NORTH CAROLINA						
Burr	Y	Y	Y	Y	Y	Y
Tillis	?	?	?	?	?	?
NORTH DAKOTA						
Hoeven	Y	Y	Y	Y	Y	Y
Cramer	Y	Y	Y	Y	Y	Y
OHIO						
Brown	N	N	N	Y	N	N
Portman	Y	Y	Y	Y	Y	Y
OKLAHOMA						
Inhofe	Y	Y	Y	Y	Y	Y
Lankford	Y	Y	Y	Y	Y	Y
OREGON						
Wyden	N	N	Y	Y	N	N
Merkley	N	N	N	N	N	N
PENNSYLVANIA						
Casey	N	N	Y	N	N	N
Toomey	Y	Y	Y	Y	Y	Y
RHODE ISLAND						
Reed	N	N	N	Y	N	N
Whitehouse	?	?	?	?	?	?
SOUTH CAROLINA						
Graham	?	?	?	Y	Y	Y
Scott	Y	Y	Y	Y	Y	Y
SOUTH DAKOTA						
Thune	Y	Y	Y	Y	Y	Y
Rounds	Y	Y	Y	Y	Y	Y
TENNESSEE						
Alexander	Y	Y	Y	Y	Y	Y
Blackburn	Y	Y	?	Y	Y	Y
TEXAS						
Cornyn	Y	Y	Y	Y	Y	Y
Cruz	Y	Y	Y	Y	Y	Y
UTAH						
Lee	Y	Y	Y	Y	Y	Y
Romney	Y	Y	Y	Y	Y	Y
VERMONT						
Leahy	N	N	Y	Y	N	N
Sanders	?	?	?	?	?	?
VIRGINIA						
Warner	N	?	Y	Y	N	N
Kaine	N	N	Y	Y	N	N
WASHINGTON						
Murray	N	N	N	Y	N	N
Cantwell	N	N	N	Y	N	N
WEST VIRGINIA						
Manchin	Y	Y	Y	Y	Y	N
Capito	Y	Y	Y	Y	Y	Y
WISCONSIN						
Johnson	Y	Y	Y	Y	Y	Y
Baldwin	N	N	N	Y	N	N
WYOMING						
Enzi	Y	Y	Y	Y	Y	Y
Barrasso	Y	Y	Y	Y	Y	Y

KEY:		**Republicans**		Democrats		*Independents*

Y Voted for (yea)	**N** Voted against (nay)	**P** Voted "present"
+ Announced for	**–** Announced against	**?** Did not vote or otherwise make position known
# Paired for	**X** Paired against	

301. Black Nomination - Confirmation. Confirmation of President Trump's nomination of David Black of North Dakota to be deputy commissioner of the Social Security Administration. Confirmed 68-26: R 52-0; D 15-26; I 1-0. *Note: A "yea" was a vote in support of the president's position.* Sept. 24, 2019.

302. SJRES54. Border National Emergency Termination - Passage. Passage of the joint resolution that would terminate President Trump's national emergency declaration regarding the construction of a wall along the U.S.-Mexico border. Passed 54-41: R 11-41; D 42-0; I 1-0. *Note: A "nay" was a vote in support of the president's position.* Sept. 25, 2019.

303. SRES331. Fiscal 2020 Defense Authorization - Foreign Technology Sources. Agreeing to the resolution that would instruct Senate conferees for the fiscal 2020 NDAA to insist on the inclusion of provisions that would limit transactions for acquisition, importation, transfer or use of information or communications technology from foreign sources, and would require the secretary of Commerce to receive congressional approval to lift export controls regarding Chinese technology manufacturer Huawei Technologies Co. Ltd. Passed 91-4: R 48-4; D 42-0; I 1-0. Sept. 25, 2019.

304. SRES332. Fiscal 2020 Defense Authorization - Survivor Benefit Plans. Agreeing to the resolution that would instruct Senate conferees for the fiscal 2020 NDAA to insist upon a provision contained in the House amendment that would repeal a requirement that survivor annuities in survivor benefit plans be reduced by the amount of dependency and indemnity compensation benefits a survivor receives from the Veterans Affairs Department. Passed 94-0: R 51-0; D 42-0; I 1-0. Sept. 25, 2019.

305. SRES333. Fiscal 2020 Defense Authorization - Family Leave for Federal Employees. Agreeing to the resolution that would instruct Senate conferees for the fiscal 2020 NDAA (S 1790) to insist upon the provisions contained in the House amendment relating to paid family leave for federal employees, including authorizing the Office of Personnel Management to promulgate regulations that would increase the amount of leave available to such employees. Rejected 47-48: R 4-48; D 42-0; I 1-0. Sept. 25, 2019.

306. SRES335. Fiscal 2020 Defense Authorization - Military Construction Funds. Agreeing to the resolution that would instruct Senate conferees for the fiscal 2020 NDAA to insist upon including a provision in the Senate bill that would authorize $3.6 billion for the Defense Department to replenish certain military constructions funds previously authorized for previous fiscal years. Passed 52-42: R 50-1; D 2-40; I 0-1. Sept. 25, 2019.

	301	302	303	304	305	306
ALABAMA						
Shelby	Y	N	Y	Y	N	Y
Jones	?	Y	Y	Y	Y	Y
ALASKA						
Murkowski	Y	Y	Y	Y	Y	Y
Sullivan	Y	N	Y	Y	N	Y
ARIZONA						
Sinema	Y	Y	Y	Y	Y	Y
McSally	Y	N	Y	Y	N	Y
ARKANSAS						
Boozman	Y	N	Y	Y	N	Y
Cotton	Y	N	Y	Y	N	Y
CALIFORNIA						
Feinstein	Y	Y	Y	Y	Y	N
Harris	?	?	?	?	+	?
COLORADO						
Bennet	Y	Y	Y	Y	Y	N
Gardner	Y	N	Y	Y	N	Y
CONNECTICUT						
Blumenthal	N	Y	Y	Y	Y	N
Murphy	Y	Y	Y	Y	Y	N
DELAWARE						
Carper	Y	Y	Y	Y	Y	N
Coons	Y	Y	Y	Y	Y	N
FLORIDA						
Rubio	Y	+	+	+	-	+
Scott	Y	N	Y	Y	N	Y
GEORGIA						
Isakson	Y	N	Y	Y	N	Y
Perdue	Y	N	Y	Y	N	Y
HAWAII						
Schatz	N	Y	Y	Y	Y	N
Hirono	N	Y	Y	Y	Y	N
IDAHO						
Crapo	Y	N	N	Y	N	Y
Risch	Y	N	N	Y	N	Y
ILLINOIS						
Durbin	N	Y	Y	Y	Y	N
Duckworth	N	Y	Y	Y	Y	N
INDIANA						
Young	Y	N	Y	Y	N	Y
Braun	Y	N	Y	Y	N	Y
IOWA						
Grassley	Y	N	Y	Y	N	Y
Ernst	Y	N	Y	Y	N	Y
KANSAS						
Roberts	Y	N	Y	Y	N	Y
Moran	Y	Y	Y	Y	N	Y
KENTUCKY						
McConnell	Y	N	Y	Y	N	Y
Paul	Y	Y	N	Y	N	N
LOUISIANA						
Cassidy	Y	N	Y	Y	N	Y
Kennedy	Y	N	Y	Y	N	Y
MAINE						
Collins	Y	Y	Y	Y	Y	Y
King	Y	Y	Y	Y	Y	N
MARYLAND						
Cardin	Y	Y	Y	Y	Y	N
Van Hollen	N	Y	Y	Y	Y	N
MASSACHUSETTS						
Warren	N	?	?	?	?	?
Markey	N	Y	Y	Y	Y	N
MICHIGAN						
Stabenow	N	Y	Y	Y	Y	N
Peters	N	Y	Y	Y	Y	N
MINNESOTA						
Klobuchar	N	Y	Y	Y	Y	N
Smith	N	Y	Y	Y	Y	N
MISSISSIPPI						
Wicker	Y	Y	Y	Y	N	Y
Hyde-Smith	Y	N	Y	Y	N	Y
MISSOURI						
Blunt	Y	N	Y	Y	N	Y
Hawley	Y	N	Y	Y	N	Y

	301	302	303	304	305	306
MONTANA						
Tester	N	Y	Y	Y	Y	N
Daines	Y	N	Y	Y	N	Y
NEBRASKA						
Fischer	Y	N	Y	Y	N	Y
Sasse	Y	N	Y	Y	N	Y
NEVADA						
Cortez Masto	N	Y	Y	Y	Y	N
Rosen	N	Y	Y	Y	Y	N
NEW HAMPSHIRE						
Shaheen	Y	Y	Y	Y	Y	N
Hassan	Y	Y	Y	Y	Y	N
NEW JERSEY						
Menendez	N	Y	Y	Y	Y	N
Booker	?	?	?	?	?	?
NEW MEXICO						
Udall	N	Y	Y	Y	Y	N
Heinrich	N	Y	Y	Y	Y	N
NEW YORK						
Schumer	N	Y	Y	Y	Y	N
Gillibrand	N	Y	Y	Y	Y	N
NORTH CAROLINA						
Burr	Y	N	Y	?	N	?
Tillis	?	N	Y	Y	N	Y
NORTH DAKOTA						
Hoeven	Y	N	Y	Y	N	Y
Cramer	Y	N	Y	Y	N	Y
OHIO						
Brown	N	Y	Y	Y	Y	N
Portman	Y	Y	Y	Y	Y	Y
OKLAHOMA						
Inhofe	Y	N	Y	Y	N	Y
Lankford	Y	N	Y	Y	N	Y
OREGON						
Wyden	Y	Y	Y	Y	Y	N
Merkley	N	Y	Y	Y	Y	N
PENNSYLVANIA						
Casey	Y	Y	Y	Y	Y	N
Toomey	Y	Y	Y	Y	N	Y
RHODE ISLAND						
Reed	N	Y	Y	Y	Y	N
Whitehouse	?	Y	Y	Y	Y	N
SOUTH CAROLINA						
Graham	Y	N	Y	Y	N	Y
Scott	Y	N	Y	Y	N	Y
SOUTH DAKOTA						
Thune	Y	N	Y	Y	N	Y
Rounds	Y	N	Y	Y	N	Y
TENNESSEE						
Alexander	Y	Y	Y	Y	N	Y
Blackburn	Y	N	Y	Y	N	Y
TEXAS						
Cornyn	Y	N	Y	Y	N	Y
Cruz	Y	N	Y	Y	N	Y
UTAH						
Lee	Y	Y	Y	Y	N	Y
Romney	Y	Y	Y	Y	Y	Y
VERMONT						
Leahy	Y	Y	Y	Y	Y	N
Sanders	?	?	?	?	?	?
VIRGINIA						
Warner	Y	Y	Y	Y	Y	N
Kaine	Y	Y	Y	Y	Y	N
WASHINGTON						
Murray	N	Y	Y	Y	Y	N
Cantwell	N	Y	Y	Y	Y	N
WEST VIRGINIA						
Manchin	Y	Y	Y	Y	Y	N
Capito	Y	N	Y	Y	N	Y
WISCONSIN						
Johnson	Y	N	Y	Y	N	Y
Baldwin	N	Y	Y	Y	Y	N
WYOMING						
Enzi	Y	N	N	Y	N	Y
Barrasso	Y	N	Y	Y	N	Y

KEY:	Republicans	Democrats	*Independents*

Y	Voted for (yea)	N	Voted against (nay)	P	Voted "present"
+	Announced for	-	Announced against	?	Did not vote or otherwise make position known
#	Paired for	X	Paired against		

307. SRES336. Fiscal 2020 Defense Authorization - Family and Medical Leave. Agreeing to the resolution that would instruct Senate conferees for the fiscal 2020 NDAA to insist that members of the conference consider potential "commonsense" solutions regarding family and medical leave, including voluntary compensatory time programs and incentives through the tax code. Passed 55-39: R 51-0; D 3-39; I 1-0. Sept. 25, 2019.

308. Hyten Nomination - Cloture. Motion to invoke cloture (thus limiting debate) on the nomination of Air Force General John E. Hyten to be Vice Chairman of the Joint Chiefs of Staff. Motion agreed to 73-21: R 51-1; D 21-20; I 1-0. *Note: A majority of senators voting (48 in this case), a quorum being present, is required to invoke cloture on all nominations.* Sept. 25, 2019.

309. Scalia Nomination - Cloture. Motion to invoke cloture (thus limiting debate) on the nomination of Eugene Scalia of Virginia to be secretary of the Labor Department. Motion agreed to 52-42: R 52-0; D 0-41; I 0-1. *Note: A majority of senators voting (48 in this case), a quorum being present, is required to invoke cloture on all nominations.* Sept. 25, 2019.

310. HR4378. Fiscal 2020 Short-Term Appropriations - Mandatory Funding Reduction. Paul, R-Ky., amendment to the Fiscal 2020 Short-Term Appropriations Act that would reduce by two percent all funding for federal government operations and services provided by the bill through Nov. 21, 2019. Rejected 24-73: R 24-29; D 0-43; I 0-1. Sept. 26, 2019.

311. HR4378. Fiscal 2020 Short-Term Appropriations - Passage. Passage of the bill that would provide funding for federal government operations and services through Nov. 21, 2019, at fiscal 2019 levels. Among other provisions, it would extend through Nov. 21 authorizations for certain expiring programs and entities, including the National Flood Insurance Program, the Export-Import Bank, certain Medicare and Medicaid programs, and other health-related HHS programs; it would allow for increased funding rates for certain activities, including the 2020 census and FEMA disaster relief; and it would provide for reimbursements to the Agriculture Department Commodity Credit Corporation for payments made to farmers impacted by retaliatory tariffs and other export barriers. Passed (thus cleared for the president) 81-16: R 37-16; D 43-0; I 1-0. *Note: Per a unanimous consent agreement, 60 votes were required for passage.* Sept. 26, 2019.

312. Hyten Nomination - Confirmation. Confirmation of President Trump's nomination of Air Force General John E. Hyten to be vice chairman of the Joint Chiefs of Staff. Confirmed 75-22: R 52-1; D 22-21; I 1-0. *Note: A "yea" was a vote in support of the president's position.* Sept. 26, 2019.

	307	308	309	310	311	312
ALABAMA						
Shelby	Y	Y	Y	N	Y	Y
Jones	Y	Y	N	N	Y	Y
ALASKA						
Murkowski	Y	Y	Y	N	Y	Y
Sullivan	Y	Y	Y	Y	Y	Y
ARIZONA						
Sinema	Y	Y	N	N	Y	Y
McSally	Y	Y	Y	N	Y	Y
ARKANSAS						
Boozman	Y	Y	Y	N	Y	Y
Cotton	Y	Y	Y	N	Y	Y
CALIFORNIA						
Feinstein	N	Y	N	N	Y	Y
Harris	?	?	?	N	Y	N
COLORADO						
Bennet	N	?	?	N	Y	Y
Gardner	Y	Y	Y	N	Y	Y
CONNECTICUT						
Blumenthal	N	N	N	N	Y	N
Murphy	N	Y	N	N	Y	Y
DELAWARE						
Carper	N	Y	N	N	Y	Y
Coons	N	Y	N	N	Y	Y
FLORIDA						
Rubio	+	+	+	Y	Y	Y
Scott	Y	Y	Y	N	N	Y
GEORGIA						
Isakson	Y	Y	Y	N	Y	Y
Perdue	Y	Y	Y	N	N	Y
HAWAII						
Schatz	N	Y	N	N	Y	Y
Hirono	N	N	N	N	Y	N
IDAHO						
Crapo	Y	Y	Y	Y	Y	Y
Risch	Y	Y	Y	Y	N	Y
ILLINOIS						
Durbin	N	Y	N	N	Y	Y
Duckworth	N	N	N	N	Y	N
INDIANA						
Young	Y	Y	Y	Y	Y	Y
Braun	Y	Y	Y	Y	N	Y
IOWA						
Grassley	Y	Y	Y	Y	Y	Y
Ernst	Y	N	Y	Y	N	N
KANSAS						
Roberts	Y	Y	Y	N	Y	Y
Moran	Y	Y	Y	N	Y	Y
KENTUCKY						
McConnell	Y	Y	Y	N	Y	Y
Paul	Y	Y	Y	Y	N	Y
LOUISIANA						
Cassidy	Y	Y	Y	N	Y	Y
Kennedy	Y	Y	Y	Y	Y	Y
MAINE						
Collins	Y	Y	Y	N	Y	Y
King	Y	Y	N	N	Y	Y
MARYLAND						
Cardin	N	N	N	N	Y	N
Van Hollen	N	N	N	N	Y	N
MASSACHUSETTS						
Warren	?	?	?	?	?	?
Markey	N	N	N	N	Y	N
MICHIGAN						
Stabenow	N	N	N	N	Y	N
Peters	N	N	N	N	Y	N
MINNESOTA						
Klobuchar	N	N	N	N	Y	N
Smith	N	Y	N	N	Y	Y
MISSISSIPPI						
Wicker	Y	Y	Y	N	Y	Y
Hyde-Smith	Y	Y	Y	N	Y	Y
MISSOURI						
Blunt	Y	Y	Y	N	Y	Y
Hawley	Y	Y	Y	N	N	Y

	307	308	309	310	311	312
MONTANA						
Tester	N	Y	N	N	Y	Y
Daines	Y	Y	Y	Y	N	Y
NEBRASKA						
Fischer	Y	Y	Y	Y	Y	Y
Sasse	Y	Y	Y	Y	N	Y
NEVADA						
Cortez Masto	N	Y	N	N	Y	Y
Rosen	N	Y	N	N	Y	Y
NEW HAMPSHIRE						
Shaheen	N	Y	N	N	Y	Y
Hassan	N	Y	N	N	Y	Y
NEW JERSEY						
Menendez	N	N	N	N	Y	N
Booker	?	?	?	-	+	?
NEW MEXICO						
Udall	N	N	N	N	Y	Y
Heinrich	N	Y	N	N	Y	Y
NEW YORK						
Schumer	N	N	N	N	Y	N
Gillibrand	N	N	N	N	Y	N
NORTH CAROLINA						
Burr	?	Y	Y	Y	Y	Y
Tillis	Y	Y	Y	Y	Y	Y
NORTH DAKOTA						
Hoeven	Y	Y	Y	N	Y	Y
Cramer	Y	Y	Y	N	Y	Y
OHIO						
Brown	N	N	N	N	Y	N
Portman	Y	Y	Y	N	Y	Y
OKLAHOMA						
Inhofe	Y	Y	Y	N	N	Y
Lankford	Y	Y	Y	Y	Y	Y
OREGON						
Wyden	N	N	N	N	Y	N
Merkley	N	N	N	N	Y	N
PENNSYLVANIA						
Casey	N	N	N	N	Y	N
Toomey	Y	Y	Y	N	N	Y
RHODE ISLAND						
Reed	N	N	N	N	Y	Y
Whitehouse	N	Y	N	N	Y	Y
SOUTH CAROLINA						
Graham	Y	Y	Y	N	Y	Y
Scott	Y	Y	Y	N	N	Y
SOUTH DAKOTA						
Thune	Y	Y	Y	N	Y	Y
Rounds	Y	Y	Y	N	N	Y
TENNESSEE						
Alexander	Y	Y	Y	N	Y	Y
Blackburn	Y	Y	Y	Y	N	Y
TEXAS						
Cornyn	Y	Y	Y	Y	Y	Y
Cruz	Y	Y	Y	Y	N	Y
UTAH						
Lee	Y	Y	Y	Y	N	Y
Romney	Y	Y	Y	N	Y	Y
VERMONT						
Leahy	N	Y	N	N	Y	Y
Sanders	?	?	?	?	?	?
VIRGINIA						
Warner	N	Y	N	N	Y	Y
Kaine	N	Y	N	N	Y	Y
WASHINGTON						
Murray	N	N	N	N	Y	N
Cantwell	N	N	N	N	Y	N
WEST VIRGINIA						
Manchin	Y	Y	N	N	Y	Y
Capito	Y	Y	Y	N	Y	Y
WISCONSIN						
Johnson	Y	Y	Y	Y	Y	Y
Baldwin	N	N	N	N	Y	N
WYOMING						
Enzi	Y	Y	Y	N	Y	Y
Barrasso	Y	Y	Y	Y	Y	Y

KEY: **Republicans**   Democrats   *Independents*

Y Voted for (yea)	**N** Voted against (nay)	**P** Voted "present"
+ Announced for	**–** Announced against	**?** Did not vote or otherwise make position known
# Paired for	**X** Paired against	

313. Scalia Nomination - Confirmation. Confirmation of President Trump's nomination of Eugene Scalia of Virginia to be secretary of the Labor Department. Confirmed 53-44: R 53-0; D 0-43; I 0-1. *Note: A "yea" was a vote in support of the president's position.* Sept. 26, 2019.

314. Barrett Nomination - Cloture. Motion to invoke cloture (thus limiting debate) on the nomination of Barbara McConnell Barrett of Arizona to be secretary of the Air Force. Motion agreed to 84-7: R 52-0; D 31-7; I 1-0. *Note: A majority of senators voting (46 in this case), a quorum being present, is required to invoke cloture on all nominations.* Oct. 15, 2019.

315. Volk Nomination - Cloture. Motion to invoke cloture (thus limiting debate) on the nomination of Frank William Volk of West Virginia to be a U.S. district judge for the Southern District of West Virginia. Motion agreed to 90-0: R 50-0; D 39-0; I 1-0. *Note: A majority of senators voting (46 in this case), a quorum being present, is required to invoke cloture on all nominations.* Oct. 16, 2019.

316. Eskridge Nomination - Cloture. Motion to invoke cloture (thus limiting debate) on the nomination of Charles R. Eskridge III of Texas to be a U.S. district judge for the Southern District of Texas. Motion agreed to 61-29: R 50-0; D 10-29; I 1-0. *Note: A majority of senators voting (46 in this case), a quorum being present, is required to invoke cloture on all nominations.* Oct. 16, 2019.

317. Novak Nomination - Cloture. Motion to invoke cloture (thus limiting debate) on the nomination of David John Novak of Virginia to be a U.S. district judge for the Eastern District of Virginia. Motion agreed to 86-4: R 50-0; D 35-4; I 1-0. *Note: A majority of senators voting (46 in this case), a quorum being present, is required to invoke cloture on all nominations.* Oct. 16, 2019.

318. Kovner Nomination - Cloture. Motion to invoke cloture (thus limiting debate) on the nomination of Rachel P. Kovner of New York to be a U.S. district judge for the Eastern District of New York. Motion agreed to 85-3: R 49-0; D 35-3; I 1-0. *Note: A majority of senators voting (45 in this case), a quorum being present, is required to invoke cloture on all nominations.* Oct. 16, 2019.

	313	314	315	316	317	318		313	314	315	316	317	318
ALABAMA							**MONTANA**						
Shelby	Y	Y	Y	Y	Y	Y	Tester	N	Y	Y	N	Y	Y
Jones	N	Y	Y	N	Y	Y	**Daines**	Y	Y	Y	Y	Y	Y
ALASKA							**NEBRASKA**						
Murkowski	Y	Y	Y	Y	Y	Y	**Fischer**	Y	Y	Y	Y	Y	Y
Sullivan	Y	Y	Y	Y	Y	Y	**Sasse**	Y	Y	Y	Y	Y	Y
ARIZONA							**NEVADA**						
Sinema	N	Y	Y	Y	Y	Y	Cortez Masto	N	Y	Y	N	Y	Y
McSally	Y	Y	Y	Y	Y	Y	Rosen	N	Y	Y	N	Y	Y
ARKANSAS							**NEW HAMPSHIRE**						
Boozman	Y	Y	Y	Y	Y	Y	Shaheen	N	Y	Y	N	Y	Y
Cotton	Y	Y	Y	Y	Y	Y	Hassan	N	Y	Y	N	Y	Y
CALIFORNIA							**NEW JERSEY**						
Feinstein	N	Y	Y	Y	Y	Y	Menendez	N	Y	Y	N	Y	Y
Harris	N	?	-	-	-	-	Booker	?	?	?	?	?	?
COLORADO							**NEW MEXICO**						
Bennet	N	?	?	?	?	?	Udall	N	Y	Y	N	Y	Y
Gardner	Y	Y	Y	Y	Y	Y	Heinrich	N	Y	Y	N	N	N
CONNECTICUT							**NEW YORK**						
Blumenthal	N	N	Y	N	Y	Y	Schumer	N	Y	Y	N	Y	Y
Murphy	N	Y	Y	Y	Y	Y	Gillibrand	N	N	Y	N	N	N
DELAWARE							**NORTH CAROLINA**						
Carper	N	Y	Y	Y	Y	Y	**Burr**	Y	Y	Y	Y	Y	Y
Coons	N	?	Y	Y	Y	Y	**Tillis**	Y	Y	Y	Y	Y	Y
FLORIDA							**NORTH DAKOTA**						
Rubio	Y	Y	Y	Y	Y	Y	**Hoeven**	Y	Y	Y	Y	Y	Y
Scott	Y	Y	Y	Y	Y	Y	**Cramer**	Y	Y	Y	Y	Y	Y
GEORGIA							**OHIO**						
Isakson	Y	Y	?	?	?	?	Brown	N	Y	Y	N	Y	Y
Perdue	Y	Y	Y	Y	Y	Y	**Portman**	Y	Y	Y	Y	Y	Y
HAWAII							**OKLAHOMA**						
Schatz	N	Y	Y	N	Y	Y	**Inhofe**	Y	Y	Y	Y	Y	?
Hirono	N	?	?	?	?	?	**Lankford**	Y	Y	Y	Y	Y	Y
IDAHO							**OREGON**						
Crapo	Y	Y	Y	Y	Y	Y	Wyden	N	N	Y	N	N	N
Risch	Y	Y	Y	Y	Y	Y	Merkley	N	N	Y	N	Y	Y
ILLINOIS							**PENNSYLVANIA**						
Durbin	N	Y	Y	N	Y	Y	Casey	N	Y	Y	N	Y	Y
Duckworth	N	N	Y	N	Y	Y	**Toomey**	Y	Y	Y	Y	Y	Y
INDIANA							**RHODE ISLAND**						
Young	Y	Y	Y	Y	Y	Y	Reed	N	Y	Y	N	Y	Y
Braun	Y	Y	Y	Y	Y	Y	Whitehouse	N	Y	Y	Y	Y	Y
IOWA							**SOUTH CAROLINA**						
Grassley	Y	Y	Y	Y	Y	Y	**Graham**	Y	Y	Y	Y	Y	Y
Ernst	Y	Y	Y	Y	Y	Y	**Scott**	Y	Y	Y	Y	Y	Y
KANSAS							**SOUTH DAKOTA**						
Roberts	Y	Y	Y	Y	Y	Y	**Thune**	Y	Y	Y	Y	Y	Y
Moran	Y	Y	Y	Y	Y	Y	**Rounds**	Y	Y	Y	Y	Y	Y
KENTUCKY							**TENNESSEE**						
McConnell	Y	Y	Y	Y	Y	Y	**Alexander**	Y	+	+	+	+	+
Paul	Y	Y	Y	Y	Y	Y	**Blackburn**	Y	Y	Y	Y	Y	Y
LOUISIANA							**TEXAS**						
Cassidy	Y	Y	Y	Y	Y	Y	**Cornyn**	Y	Y	Y	Y	Y	Y
Kennedy	Y	Y	Y	Y	Y	Y	**Cruz**	Y	Y	Y	Y	Y	Y
MAINE							**UTAH**						
Collins	Y	Y	Y	Y	Y	Y	**Lee**	Y	Y	Y	Y	Y	Y
King	N	Y	Y	Y	Y	Y	**Romney**	Y	Y	Y	Y	Y	Y
MARYLAND							**VERMONT**						
Cardin	N	Y	Y	Y	Y	Y	Leahy	N	Y	Y	N	Y	Y
Van Hollen	N	Y	Y	N	Y	Y	*Sanders*	?	?	?	?	?	?
MASSACHUSETTS							**VIRGINIA**						
Warren	?	?	?	?	?	?	Warner	N	Y	Y	Y	Y	Y
Markey	N	N	Y	N	N	Y	Kaine	N	Y	Y	Y	Y	Y
MICHIGAN							**WASHINGTON**						
Stabenow	N	Y	Y	N	Y	?	Murray	N	Y	Y	N	Y	Y
Peters	N	Y	Y	N	Y	Y	Cantwell	N	Y	Y	N	Y	Y
MINNESOTA							**WEST VIRGINIA**						
Klobuchar	N	?	?	?	?	?	Manchin	N	Y	Y	N	Y	Y
Smith	N	N	Y	N	Y	Y	**Capito**	Y	Y	Y	Y	Y	Y
MISSISSIPPI							**WISCONSIN**						
Wicker	Y	Y	Y	Y	Y	Y	**Johnson**	Y	Y	+	+	+	+
Hyde-Smith	Y	Y	Y	Y	Y	Y	Baldwin	N	Y	Y	N	Y	Y
MISSOURI							**WYOMING**						
Blunt	Y	Y	Y	Y	Y	Y	**Enzi**	Y	Y	Y	Y	Y	Y
Hawley	Y	Y	Y	Y	Y	Y	**Barrasso**	Y	Y	Y	Y	Y	Y

KEY:		**Republicans**		Democrats		*Independents*

Y	Voted for (yea)	N	Voted against (nay)	P	Voted "present"
+	Announced for	−	Announced against	?	Did not vote or otherwise make position known
#	Paired for	X	Paired against		

319. Barrett Nomination - Confirmation. Confirmation of President Trump's nomination of Barbara McConnell Barrett of Arizona to be secretary of the Air Force. Confirmed 85-7: R 51-0; D 33-7; I 1-0. *Note: A "yea" was a vote in support of the president's position.* Oct. 16, 2019.

320. Volk Nomination - Confirmation. Confirmation of President Trump's nomination of Frank William Volk of West Virginia to be a U.S. district judge for the Southern District of West Virginia. Confirmed 92-0: R 51-0; D 40-0; I 1-0. *Note: A "yea" was a vote in support of the president's position.* Oct. 16, 2019.

321. Eskridge Nomination - Confirmation. Confirmation of President Trump's nomination of Charles R. Eskridge III of Texas to be a U.S. district judge for the Southern District of Texas. Confirmed 61-31: R 51-0; D 10-30; I 0-1. *Note: A "yea" was a vote in support of the president's position.* Oct. 16, 2019.

322. Novak Nomination - Confirmation. Confirmation of President Trump's nomination of David John Novak of Virginia to be a U.S. district judge for the Eastern District of Virginia. Confirmed 89-3: R 51-0; D 37-3; I 1-0. *Note: A "yea" was a vote in support of the president's position.* Oct. 16, 2019.

323. Kovner Nomination - Confirmation. Confirmation of President Trump's nomination of Rachel P. Kovner to be a U.S. district judge for the Eastern District of New York. Confirmed 88-3: R 50-0; D 37-3; I 1-0. *Note: A "yea" was a vote in support of the president's postion.* Oct. 16, 2019.

324. SJRES53. Disapproval of Affordable Clean Energy Rule - Passage. Passage of the joint resolution that would express disapproval of the Environmental Protection Agency's July 2019 rule that would repeal the Clean Power Plan and finalize the Affordable Clean Energy rule. Under the measure, the July rule would have no force or effect. Rejected 41-53: R 1-50; D 39-3; I 1-0. *Note: A "nay" was a vote in support of the president's position.* Oct. 17, 2019.

	319	320	321	322	323	324
ALABAMA						
Shelby	Y	Y	Y	Y	Y	N
Jones	Y	Y	N	Y	Y	N
ALASKA						
Murkowski	Y	Y	Y	Y	Y	N
Sullivan	Y	Y	Y	Y	Y	N
ARIZONA						
Sinema	Y	Y	Y	Y	Y	N
McSally	Y	Y	Y	Y	Y	N
ARKANSAS						
Boozman	Y	Y	Y	Y	Y	N
Cotton	Y	Y	Y	Y	Y	N
CALIFORNIA						
Feinstein	Y	Y	Y	Y	Y	Y
Harris	?	-	-	-	-	+
COLORADO						
Bennet	?	?	?	?	?	Y
Gardner	Y	Y	Y	Y	Y	N
CONNECTICUT						
Blumenthal	N	Y	N	Y	Y	Y
Murphy	Y	Y	Y	Y	Y	Y
DELAWARE						
Carper	Y	Y	Y	Y	Y	Y
Coons	Y	Y	Y	Y	Y	Y
FLORIDA						
Rubio	Y	Y	Y	Y	Y	N
Scott	Y	Y	Y	Y	Y	N
GEORGIA						
Isakson	?	?	?	?	?	-
Perdue	Y	Y	Y	Y	Y	N
HAWAII						
Schatz	Y	Y	N	Y	Y	Y
Hirono	Y	Y	N	Y	Y	Y
IDAHO						
Crapo	Y	Y	Y	Y	Y	N
Risch	Y	Y	Y	Y	Y	N
ILLINOIS						
Durbin	Y	Y	N	Y	Y	Y
Duckworth	N	Y	N	Y	Y	Y
INDIANA						
Young	Y	Y	Y	Y	Y	N
Braun	Y	Y	Y	Y	Y	N
IOWA						
Grassley	Y	Y	Y	Y	Y	N
Ernst	Y	Y	Y	Y	Y	N
KANSAS						
Roberts	Y	Y	Y	Y	Y	N
Moran	Y	Y	Y	Y	Y	N
KENTUCKY						
McConnell	Y	Y	Y	Y	Y	N
Paul	Y	Y	Y	Y	?	N
LOUISIANA						
Cassidy	Y	Y	Y	Y	Y	N
Kennedy	Y	Y	Y	Y	Y	N
MAINE						
Collins	Y	Y	Y	Y	Y	Y
King	Y	Y	N	Y	Y	Y
MARYLAND						
Cardin	Y	Y	Y	Y	Y	Y
Van Hollen	Y	Y	N	Y	Y	Y
MASSACHUSETTS						
Warren	?	?	?	?	?	Y
Markey	N	Y	N	N	N	Y
MICHIGAN						
Stabenow	Y	Y	N	Y	Y	Y
Peters	Y	Y	N	Y	Y	Y
MINNESOTA						
Klobuchar	?	?	?	?	?	?
Smith	N	Y	N	Y	Y	Y
MISSISSIPPI						
Wicker	Y	Y	Y	Y	Y	N
Hyde-Smith	Y	Y	Y	Y	Y	N
MISSOURI						
Blunt	Y	Y	Y	Y	Y	N
Hawley	Y	Y	Y	Y	Y	N

	319	320	321	322	323	324
MONTANA						
Tester	Y	Y	N	Y	Y	Y
Daines	Y	Y	Y	Y	Y	N
NEBRASKA						
Fischer	Y	Y	Y	Y	Y	N
Sasse	Y	Y	Y	Y	Y	N
NEVADA						
Cortez Masto	Y	Y	N	Y	Y	Y
Rosen	Y	Y	N	Y	Y	Y
NEW HAMPSHIRE						
Shaheen	Y	Y	Y	Y	Y	Y
Hassan	Y	Y	N	Y	Y	Y
NEW JERSEY						
Menendez	Y	Y	N	Y	Y	Y
Booker	?	?	?	?	?	+
NEW MEXICO						
Udall	Y	Y	N	Y	Y	Y
Heinrich	Y	Y	N	Y	N	Y
NEW YORK						
Schumer	Y	Y	N	Y	Y	Y
Gillibrand	N	Y	N	N	N	Y
NORTH CAROLINA						
Burr	Y	Y	Y	Y	Y	N
Tillis	Y	Y	Y	Y	Y	N
NORTH DAKOTA						
Hoeven	Y	Y	Y	Y	Y	N
Cramer	Y	Y	Y	Y	Y	N
OHIO						
Brown	Y	Y	N	Y	Y	Y
Portman	Y	Y	Y	Y	Y	N
OKLAHOMA						
Inhofe	Y	Y	Y	Y	Y	N
Lankford	Y	Y	Y	Y	Y	N
OREGON						
Wyden	N	Y	N	N	Y	Y
Merkley	N	Y	N	Y	Y	Y
PENNSYLVANIA						
Casey	Y	Y	N	Y	Y	Y
Toomey	Y	Y	Y	Y	Y	N
RHODE ISLAND						
Reed	Y	Y	N	Y	Y	Y
Whitehouse	Y	Y	N	Y	Y	Y
SOUTH CAROLINA						
Graham	Y	Y	Y	Y	Y	N
Scott	Y	Y	Y	Y	Y	N
SOUTH DAKOTA						
Thune	Y	Y	Y	Y	Y	N
Rounds	Y	Y	Y	Y	Y	N
TENNESSEE						
Alexander	+	+	+	+	+	-
Blackburn	Y	Y	Y	Y	Y	N
TEXAS						
Cornyn	Y	Y	Y	Y	Y	N
Cruz	Y	Y	Y	Y	Y	N
UTAH						
Lee	Y	Y	Y	Y	Y	N
Romney	Y	Y	Y	Y	Y	N
VERMONT						
Leahy	Y	Y	N	Y	Y	Y
Sanders	?	?	?	?	?	?
VIRGINIA						
Warner	Y	Y	Y	Y	Y	Y
Kaine	Y	Y	Y	Y	Y	Y
WASHINGTON						
Murray	Y	Y	N	Y	Y	Y
Cantwell	Y	Y	N	Y	Y	Y
WEST VIRGINIA						
Manchin	Y	Y	N	Y	Y	N
Capito	Y	Y	Y	Y	Y	N
WISCONSIN						
Johnson	Y	Y	Y	Y	Y	N
Baldwin	Y	Y	N	Y	Y	Y
WYOMING						
Enzi	Y	Y	Y	Y	Y	N
Barrasso	Y	Y	Y	Y	Y	N

KEY:

	Republicans	Democrats	*Independents*

Y	Voted for (yea)	N	Voted against (nay)	P	Voted "present"
+	Announced for	-	Announced against	?	Did not vote or otherwise
#	Paired for	X	Paired against		make position known

325. SJRES54. Border National Emergency Termination - Veto Override. Passage over President Trump's veto of the Border National Emergency Termination Resolution that would terminate the national emergency declared by the President Trump on Feb. 15, 2019, related to the construction of a physical barrier along the U.S.-Mexico border. Rejected 53-36: R 10-36; D 42-0; I 1-0. *Note: A two-thirds majority of those present and voting (60 in this case) of both chambers is required to override the president's veto. A "nay" was a vote in support of the president's veto. Oct. 17, 2019.*

326 - Treaty. North Macedonia NATO Membership Treaty - Cloture. McConnell, R-Ky., motion to invoke cloture (thus limiting debate) on the North Atlantic Treaty of 1949 on the Accession of the Republic of North Macedonia. Motion agreed to 84-2: R 47-2; D 36-0; I 1-0. *Note: Three-fifths of the total Senate (60) is required to invoke cloture. Oct. 21, 2019.*

327 - Treaty. North Macedonia NATO Membership Treaty - Adoption. Adoption of the resolution of ratification of the Protocol to the North Atlantic Treaty of 1949 on the Accession of the Republic of North Macedonia. Adopted (thus consenting to ratification) 91-2: R 50-2; D 40-0; I 1-0. *Note: A two-thirds majority of those present and voting (62 in this case) is required for adoption of resolutions of ratification. A "yea" was a vote in support of the president's position. Oct. 22, 2019.*

328. Bremberg Nomination - Cloture. Motion to invoke cloture (thus limiting debate) on the nomination of Andrew P. Bremberg of Virginia to be representative to the Office of the United Nations and other international organizations in Geneva, Switzerland. Motion agreed to 50-43: R 50-2; D 0-40; I 0-1. *Note: A majority of senators voting (47 in this case), a quorum being present, is required to invoke cloture on all nominations. Oct. 22, 2019.*

329. Bremberg Nomination - Confirmation. Confirmation of President Trump's nomination of Andrew P. Bremberg of Virginia to be representative to the Office of the United Nations and other international organizations in Geneva, Switzerland. Confirmed 50-44: R 50-2; D 0-41; I 0-1. *Note: A "yea" was a vote in support of the president's position. Oct. 22, 2019.*

330. HR3055. Fiscal 2020 Appropriations. Package Two - Cloture. McConnell, R-Ky., motion to invoke cloture (thus limiting debate) on the McConnell, R-Ky., motion to proceed to the Commerce-Justice-Science, Agriculture, Interior-Environment, and Transportation-HUD appropriations package. Motion agreed to 92-2: R 50-2; D 41-0; I 1-0. *Note: Three-fifths of the total Senate (60) is required to invoke cloture. Oct. 22, 2019.*

	325	326	327	328	329	330		325	326	327	328	329	330
ALABAMA							**MONTANA**						
Shelby	N	Y	Y	Y	Y	Y	Tester	Y	Y	Y	N	N	Y
Jones	Y	Y	Y	N	N	Y	Daines	N	Y	Y	Y	Y	Y
ALASKA							**NEBRASKA**						
Murkowski	Y	?	Y	N	N	Y	Fischer	N	Y	Y	Y	Y	Y
Sullivan	N	Y	Y	Y	Y	Y	Sasse	N	Y	Y	Y	Y	Y
ARIZONA							**NEVADA**						
Sinema	Y	Y	Y	N	N	Y	Cortez Masto	Y	Y	Y	N	N	Y
McSally	N	Y	Y	Y	Y	Y	Rosen	Y	Y	Y	N	N	Y
ARKANSAS							**NEW HAMPSHIRE**						
Boozman	N	Y	Y	Y	Y	Y	Shaheen	Y	Y	Y	N	N	Y
Cotton	N	Y	Y	Y	Y	Y	Hassan	Y	?	Y	N	N	Y
CALIFORNIA							**NEW JERSEY**						
Feinstein	Y	Y	Y	N	N	Y	Menendez	Y	Y	Y	N	N	Y
Harris	?	?	?	?	?	?	Booker	?	?	?	?	?	?
COLORADO							**NEW MEXICO**						
Bennet	Y	?	?	?	N	Y	Udall	Y	Y	Y	N	N	Y
Gardner	N	Y	Y	Y	Y	Y	Heinrich	Y	Y	Y	N	N	Y
CONNECTICUT							**NEW YORK**						
Blumenthal	Y	Y	Y	N	N	Y	Schumer	Y	Y	Y	N	N	Y
Murphy	Y	Y	Y	N	N	Y	Gillibrand	Y	Y	Y	N	N	Y
DELAWARE							**NORTH CAROLINA**						
Carper	Y	Y	Y	N	N	Y	Burr	N	Y	Y	Y	Y	Y
Coons	Y	Y	Y	N	N	Y	Tillis	N	Y	Y	Y	Y	Y
FLORIDA							**NORTH DAKOTA**						
Rubio	Y	Y	Y	Y	Y	Y	Hoeven	N	Y	Y	Y	Y	Y
Scott	N	Y	Y	Y	Y	Y	Cramer	N	Y	Y	Y	Y	Y
GEORGIA							**OHIO**						
Isakson	?	?	?	?	?	?	Brown	Y	Y	Y	N	N	Y
Perdue	?	Y	Y	Y	Y	Y	Portman	Y	Y	Y	Y	Y	Y
HAWAII							**OKLAHOMA**						
Schatz	Y	?	Y	N	N	Y	Inhofe	N	Y	Y	Y	Y	Y
Hirono	Y	Y	Y	N	N	Y	Lankford	N	Y	Y	Y	Y	Y
IDAHO							**OREGON**						
Crapo	N	Y	Y	Y	Y	Y	Wyden	Y	Y	Y	N	N	Y
Risch	N	Y	Y	Y	Y	Y	Merkley	Y	Y	Y	N	N	Y
ILLINOIS							**PENNSYLVANIA**						
Durbin	Y	Y	Y	N	N	Y	Casey	Y	Y	Y	N	N	Y
Duckworth	Y	Y	Y	N	N	Y	Toomey	Y	?	Y	Y	Y	Y
INDIANA							**RHODE ISLAND**						
Young	N	Y	Y	Y	Y	Y	Reed	Y	Y	Y	N	N	Y
Braun	N	Y	Y	Y	Y	Y	Whitehouse	Y	?	?	?	?	?
IOWA							**SOUTH CAROLINA**						
Grassley	N	Y	Y	Y	Y	Y	Graham	N	Y	Y	Y	Y	Y
Ernst	N	Y	Y	Y	Y	Y	Scott	N	Y	Y	Y	Y	Y
KANSAS							**SOUTH DAKOTA**						
Roberts	N	Y	Y	Y	Y	Y	Thune	N	Y	Y	Y	Y	Y
Moran	?	Y	Y	Y	Y	Y	Rounds	N	Y	Y	Y	Y	Y
KENTUCKY							**TENNESSEE**						
McConnell	N	Y	Y	Y	Y	Y	Alexander	+	Y	Y	Y	Y	Y
Paul	Y	N	N	Y	Y	N	Blackburn	N	Y	Y	Y	Y	N
LOUISIANA							**TEXAS**						
Cassidy	-	Y	Y	Y	Y	Y	Cornyn	-	Y	Y	Y	Y	Y
Kennedy	N	?	Y	Y	Y	Y	Cruz	-	Y	Y	Y	Y	Y
MAINE							**UTAH**						
Collins	Y	Y	Y	N	N	Y	Lee	Y	N	N	Y	Y	Y
King	Y	Y	Y	N	N	Y	Romney	Y	Y	Y	Y	Y	Y
MARYLAND							**VERMONT**						
Cardin	Y	Y	Y	N	N	Y	Leahy	Y	Y	Y	N	N	Y
Van Hollen	Y	Y	Y	N	N	Y	*Sanders*	?	?	?	?	?	?
MASSACHUSETTS							**VIRGINIA**						
Warren	Y	?	?	?	?	?	Warner	Y	Y	Y	N	N	Y
Markey	Y	Y	Y	N	N	Y	Kaine	Y	Y	Y	N	N	Y
MICHIGAN							**WASHINGTON**						
Stabenow	Y	+	Y	N	N	Y	Murray	Y	Y	Y	N	N	Y
Peters	Y	Y	Y	N	N	Y	Cantwell	Y	Y	Y	N	N	Y
MINNESOTA							**WEST VIRGINIA**						
Klobuchar	?	?	Y	N	N	Y	Manchin	Y	Y	Y	N	N	Y
Smith	Y	Y	Y	N	N	Y	Capito	N	Y	Y	Y	Y	Y
MISSISSIPPI							**WISCONSIN**						
Wicker	Y	Y	Y	Y	Y	Y	Johnson	N	Y	Y	Y	Y	Y
Hyde-Smith	N	Y	Y	Y	Y	Y	Baldwin	Y	Y	Y	N	N	Y
MISSOURI							**WYOMING**						
Blunt	Y	Y	Y	Y	Y	Y	Enzi	N	Y	Y	Y	Y	Y
Hawley	N	Y	Y	Y	Y	Y	Barrasso	N	Y	Y	Y	Y	Y

KEY:	Republicans	Democrats	*Independents*
Y Voted for (yea)	N Voted against (nay)	P Voted "present"	
+ Announced for	– Announced against	? Did not vote or otherwise	
# Paired for	X Paired against	make position known	

331. SJRES50. Disapproval of IRS State, Local Tax Rule - Passage. Passage of the joint resolution that would provide for congressional disapproval of the Internal Revenue Service's June 2019 rule that would provide rules regarding the availability of allowable charitable contribution deductions, applicable to situations in which a taxpayer receives or expects to receive a corresponding state or local tax credit. Under the measure, the June rule would have no force or effect. Rejected 43-52: R 1-51; D 41-1; I 1-0. *Note: A "nay" was a vote in support of the president's position.* Oct. 23, 2019.

332. Walker Nomination - Cloture. Motion to invoke cloture (thus limiting debate) on the nomination of Justin Walker of Kentucky to be a U.S. district judge for the Western District of Kentucky. Motion agreed to 50-39: R 50-0; D 0-38; I 0-1. *Note: A majority of senators voting (45 in this case), a quorum being present, is required to invoke cloture on all nominations.* Oct. 24, 2019.

333. Walker Nomination - Confirmation. Confirmation of President Trump's nomination of Justin Walker of Kentucky to be a U.S. district judge for the Western District of Kentucky. Confirmed 50-41: R 50-0; D 0-40; I 0-1. *Note: A "yea" was a vote in support of the president's position.* Oct. 24, 2019.

334. HR3055. Fiscal 2020 Appropriations. Package Two - Food Distribution Program Study. Adoption of the Cortez Masto, D-Nev., amendment no. 961 to the Shelby, R-Ala., amendment no. 948 to the bill that would require the Agriculture Department to conduct a study examining challenges encountered by federal food distribution programs on Native American reservations when serving populations unable to physically travel to a distribution location for food. Adopted 90-1: R 48-1; D 41-0; I 1-0. Oct. 28, 2019.

335. HR3055. Fiscal 2020 Appropriations. Package Two - Federal Spending Reduction. Adoption of the Paul, R-Ky., amendment no. 1019 to the Shelby, R-Ala., amendment no. 948 to the bill that would reduce all funding in the bill to an amount equal to 2 percent less than the amount of funding made available for fiscal 2019. Rejected 24-67: R 24-25; D 0-41; I 0-1. Oct. 28, 2019.

336. HR3055. Fiscal 2020 Appropriations. Package Two - Land Ownership Disputes. Adoption of the Jones, D-Ala., amendment no. 1067 to the Shelby, amendment no. 948 to the bill that would that would require $5 million of funds appropriated to the Farm Service Agency to be used for an Agriculture Department relending program that helps "socially disadvantaged" farmers and ranchers resolve disputes regarding property inheritance and land ownership. Adopted 91-1: R 48-1; D 42-0; I 1-0. Oct. 28, 2019.

	331	332	333	334	335	336
ALABAMA						
Shelby	N	Y	Y	Y	N	Y
Jones	Y	N	N	Y	N	Y
ALASKA						
Murkowski	N	Y	Y	Y	N	Y
Sullivan	N	Y	Y	Y	Y	Y
ARIZONA						
Sinema	Y	N	N	Y	N	Y
McSally	N	Y	Y	Y	N	Y
ARKANSAS						
Boozman	N	Y	Y	Y	N	Y
Cotton	N	Y	Y	Y	N	Y
CALIFORNIA						
Feinstein	Y	N	N	Y	N	Y
Harris	?	?	?	?	?	?
COLORADO						
Bennet	N	N	N	Y	N	Y
Gardner	N	Y	Y	Y	N	Y
CONNECTICUT						
Blumenthal	Y	N	N	Y	N	Y
Murphy	Y	N	N	Y	N	Y
DELAWARE						
Carper	Y	?	N	Y	N	Y
Coons	Y	?	?	Y	N	Y
FLORIDA						
Rubio	N	Y	Y	Y	Y	Y
Scott	N	Y	Y	Y	N	Y
GEORGIA						
Isakson	?	?	?	?	?	?
Perdue	N	Y	Y	Y	Y	Y
HAWAII						
Schatz	Y	N	N	Y	N	Y
Hirono	Y	N	N	Y	N	Y
IDAHO						
Crapo	N	Y	Y	Y	Y	Y
Risch	N	Y	Y	Y	Y	Y
ILLINOIS						
Durbin	Y	N	N	Y	N	Y
Duckworth	Y	N	N	Y	N	Y
INDIANA						
Young	N	Y	Y	Y	N	Y
Braun	N	Y	Y	Y	Y	Y
IOWA						
Grassley	N	Y	Y	Y	Y	Y
Ernst	N	Y	Y	Y	Y	Y
KANSAS						
Roberts	N	Y	Y	Y	N	Y
Moran	N	?	?	Y	N	Y
KENTUCKY						
McConnell	N	Y	Y	Y	N	Y
Paul	Y	Y	Y	Y	Y	Y
LOUISIANA						
Cassidy	N	Y	Y	?	?	?
Kennedy	N	Y	Y	Y	Y	Y
MAINE						
Collins	N	Y	Y	Y	N	Y
King	Y	N	N	Y	N	Y
MARYLAND						
Cardin	Y	N	N	Y	N	Y
Van Hollen	Y	N	N	Y	N	Y
MASSACHUSETTS						
Warren	?	?	?	?	?	?
Markey	Y	N	N	Y	N	Y
MICHIGAN						
Stabenow	Y	N	N	Y	N	Y
Peters	Y	N	N	Y	N	Y
MINNESOTA						
Klobuchar	Y	N	N	Y	N	Y
Smith	Y	N	N	Y	N	Y
MISSISSIPPI						
Wicker	N	Y	Y	Y	N	Y
Hyde-Smith	N	?	?	Y	N	Y
MISSOURI						
Blunt	N	Y	Y	Y	N	Y
Hawley	N	Y	Y	Y	N	Y

	331	332	333	334	335	336
MONTANA						
Tester	Y	N	N	Y	N	Y
Daines	N	Y	Y	Y	Y	Y
NEBRASKA						
Fischer	N	Y	Y	Y	Y	Y
Sasse	N	Y	Y	Y	Y	Y
NEVADA						
Cortez Masto	Y	N	N	Y	N	Y
Rosen	Y	N	N	Y	N	Y
NEW HAMPSHIRE						
Shaheen	Y	N	N	Y	N	Y
Hassan	Y	N	N	Y	N	Y
NEW JERSEY						
Menendez	Y	N	N	Y	N	Y
Booker	Y	?	?	?	?	?
NEW MEXICO						
Udall	N	N	N	Y	N	Y
Heinrich	Y	N	N	Y	N	Y
NEW YORK						
Schumer	Y	N	N	Y	N	Y
Gillibrand	Y	N	N	Y	N	Y
NORTH CAROLINA						
Burr	N	Y	Y	Y	N	Y
Tillis	N	Y	Y	?	?	?
NORTH DAKOTA						
Hoeven	N	Y	Y	Y	N	Y
Cramer	N	Y	Y	Y	N	Y
OHIO						
Brown	Y	N	N	Y	N	Y
Portman	N	Y	Y	Y	N	Y
OKLAHOMA						
Inhofe	N	Y	Y	Y	Y	Y
Lankford	N	Y	Y	Y	Y	Y
OREGON						
Wyden	Y	N	N	Y	N	Y
Merkley	Y	N	N	Y	N	Y
PENNSYLVANIA						
Casey	Y	N	N	Y	N	Y
Toomey	N	Y	Y	?	?	?
RHODE ISLAND						
Reed	Y	N	N	+	-	Y
Whitehouse	?	?	?	Y	N	Y
SOUTH CAROLINA						
Graham	N	Y	Y	Y	N	Y
Scott	N	Y	Y	Y	Y	Y
SOUTH DAKOTA						
Thune	N	Y	Y	Y	N	Y
Rounds	N	Y	Y	Y	N	Y
TENNESSEE						
Alexander	N	Y	Y	Y	N	Y
Blackburn	N	Y	Y	N	Y	N
TEXAS						
Cornyn	N	Y	Y	Y	Y	Y
Cruz	N	Y	Y	Y	Y	Y
UTAH						
Lee	N	Y	Y	Y	Y	Y
Romney	N	Y	Y	Y	Y	Y
VERMONT						
Leahy	Y	N	N	Y	N	Y
Sanders	?	?	?	?	?	?
VIRGINIA						
Warner	Y	N	N	Y	N	Y
Kaine	Y	?	N	Y	N	Y
WASHINGTON						
Murray	Y	N	N	Y	N	Y
Cantwell	Y	N	N	Y	N	Y
WEST VIRGINIA						
Manchin	Y	N	N	Y	N	Y
Capito	N	Y	Y	Y	N	Y
WISCONSIN						
Johnson	N	Y	Y	Y	Y	Y
Baldwin	Y	N	N	Y	N	Y
WYOMING						
Enzi	N	Y	Y	Y	Y	Y
Barrasso	N	Y	Y	Y	Y	Y

337. SJRES52. Disapproval of Health Insurance Coverage Rule - Passage. Passage of the joint resolution that would provide for congressional disapproval of the Oct. 2018 guidance released by the Health and Human Services and Treasury departments regarding criteria for evaluating Section 1332 state health care plan waivers under the 2010 health care overhaul. Under the measure, the guidance would have no force or effect. Rejected 43-52: R 1-52; D 41-0; I 1-0. *Note: A "nay" was a vote in support of the president's position.* Oct. 30, 2019.

338. HR3055. Fiscal 2020 Appropriations. Package Two - Cloture. Agreeing to the McConnell, R-Ky., motion to invoke cloture (thus limiting debate) on the Shelby, R-Ala., amendment no. 948 to the bill that would provide approximately $214 billion in discretionary spending for four of the 12 fiscal 2020 appropriations bills, including $70.8 billion for the Commerce and Justice departments and science and related agencies, $23.1 billion for the Agriculture Department and related agencies, $35.8 billion for the Interior Department, Environmental Protection Agency, and related agencies, and $74.3 billion for the Transportation and Housing and Urban Development departments and related agencies. Motion agreed to 88-5: R 47-5; D 40-0; I 1-0. *Note: Three-fifths of the total Senate (60) is required to invoke cloture.* Oct. 30, 2019.

339. HR3055. Fiscal 2020 Appropriations. Package Two - Land Acquisition Funding Restrictions. Adoption of the Lee, R-Utah, amendment no. 1209 to the Shelby, R-Ala., amendment no. 948 to the Fiscal 2020 Appropriations: Package Two that would prohibit the use of certain funding from the Land and Water Conservation Fund for land acquisitions. Rejected 29-64: R 29-23; D 0-40; I 0-1. Oct. 31, 2019.

340. HR3055. Fiscal 2020 Appropriations. Package Two - Mass Transit Account. Adoption of the Jones, D-Ala., amendment no. 1141, as modified, to the Shelby, R-Ala., amendment no. 948 to the bill that would prohibit the use of any of the funds made available by the bill, or any other law, to adjust apportionments or withhold funds from apportionments for the Mass Transit Account within the Highway Trust Fund. Adopted 82-11: R 41-11; D 40-0; I 1-0. Oct. 31, 2019.

341. HR3055. Fiscal 2020 Appropriations. Package Two - Passage. Passage of the bill that would authorize approximately $214 billion in spending for four of the 12 fiscal 2020 appropriations bills. It would prohibit the use of funds made available by the bill for any coordinated activities between NASA, the Office of Science and Technology Policy, or the National Space Council and China or any Chinese-owned company; for any activities that would support or justify the use of torture by any U.S. government employee; or for the Justice Department to prevent states from implementing laws to authorize the use or distribution of medical marijuana. Passed (thus cleared for the president) 84-9: R 43-9; D 40-0; I 1-0. *Note: Per a unanimous consent agreement, 60 votes were required for passage.* Oct. 31, 2019.

342. HR2740. Fiscal 2020 Appropriations. Package One - Cloture. Agreeing to the McConnell, R-Ky., motion to invoke cloture (thus limiting debate) on the McConnell, R-Ky., motion to proceed to the Fiscal 2020 Appropriations: Package One consisting of the Labor-HHS-Education, Defense, Energy-Water, and State-Foreign Operations spending bills. Motion rejected 51-41: R 49-2; D 2-38; I 0-1. *Note: Three-fifths of the total Senate (60) is required to invoke cloture.* Oct. 31, 2019.

	337	338	339	340	341	342
ALABAMA						
Shelby	N	Y	N	Y	Y	Y
Jones	Y	Y	N	Y	Y	Y
ALASKA						
Murkowski	N	Y	N	Y	Y	Y
Sullivan	N	Y	Y	Y	Y	Y
ARIZONA						
Sinema	Y	Y	N	Y	Y	N
McSally	N	Y	N	Y	Y	Y
ARKANSAS						
Boozman	N	Y	N	Y	Y	Y
Cotton	N	Y	N	Y	Y	Y
CALIFORNIA						
Feinstein	Y	Y	N	Y	Y	N
Harris	+	?	–	?	?	?
COLORADO						
Bennet	?	?	?	?	?	?
Gardner	N	Y	N	Y	Y	Y
CONNECTICUT						
Blumenthal	Y	Y	N	Y	Y	N
Murphy	Y	Y	N	Y	Y	N
DELAWARE						
Carper	Y	Y	N	Y	Y	N
Coons	Y	Y	N	Y	Y	N
FLORIDA						
Rubio	N	Y	Y	Y	Y	Y
Scott	N	N	Y	N	N	Y
GEORGIA						
Isakson	N	Y	?	?	?	?
Perdue	N	Y	N	N	Y	Y
HAWAII						
Schatz	Y	Y	N	Y	Y	N
Hirono	Y	Y	N	Y	Y	N
IDAHO						
Crapo	N	Y	Y	Y	Y	Y
Risch	N	Y	Y	Y	Y	Y
ILLINOIS						
Durbin	Y	Y	N	Y	Y	N
Duckworth	Y	Y	N	Y	Y	N
INDIANA						
Young	N	Y	N	Y	Y	Y
Braun	N	Y	Y	N	N	Y
IOWA						
Grassley	N	Y	Y	Y	Y	Y
Ernst	N	Y	Y	Y	Y	Y
KANSAS						
Roberts	N	Y	N	Y	Y	Y
Moran	N	Y	Y	Y	Y	+
KENTUCKY						
McConnell	N	Y	N	Y	Y	N
Paul	N	N	Y	N	N	N
LOUISIANA						
Cassidy	N	?	Y	Y	Y	Y
Kennedy	N	Y	Y	Y	Y	Y
MAINE						
Collins	Y	Y	N	Y	Y	Y
King	Y	Y	N	Y	Y	N
MARYLAND						
Cardin	Y	Y	N	Y	Y	N
Van Hollen	Y	Y	N	Y	Y	N
MASSACHUSETTS						
Warren	?	?	?	?	?	?
Markey	Y	Y	N	Y	Y	N
MICHIGAN						
Stabenow	Y	Y	N	Y	Y	N
Peters	Y	Y	N	Y	Y	Y
MINNESOTA						
Klobuchar	Y	?	?	?	?	?
Smith	Y	Y	N	Y	Y	N
MISSISSIPPI						
Wicker	N	Y	Y	Y	Y	Y
Hyde-Smith	N	Y	N	Y	Y	Y
MISSOURI						
Blunt	N	Y	N	Y	Y	Y
Hawley	N	Y	Y	Y	Y	Y

	337	338	339	340	341	342
MONTANA						
Tester	Y	Y	N	Y	Y	N
Daines	N	Y	N	Y	Y	Y
NEBRASKA						
Fischer	N	Y	Y	Y	Y	Y
Sasse	N	Y	Y	N	N	Y
NEVADA						
Cortez Masto	Y	Y	N	Y	Y	N
Rosen	Y	Y	N	Y	Y	N
NEW HAMPSHIRE						
Shaheen	Y	Y	N	Y	Y	N
Hassan	Y	Y	N	Y	Y	N
NEW JERSEY						
Menendez	Y	Y	N	Y	Y	N
Booker	?	?	–	+	+	?
NEW MEXICO						
Udall	Y	Y	N	Y	Y	N
Heinrich	Y	Y	N	Y	Y	N
NEW YORK						
Schumer	Y	Y	N	Y	Y	N
Gillibrand	Y	Y	N	Y	Y	N
NORTH CAROLINA						
Burr	N	Y	N	Y	Y	Y
Tillis	N	Y	Y	Y	Y	Y
NORTH DAKOTA						
Hoeven	N	Y	N	Y	Y	Y
Cramer	N	Y	N	Y	Y	Y
OHIO						
Brown	Y	Y	N	Y	Y	N
Portman	N	Y	N	Y	Y	Y
OKLAHOMA						
Inhofe	N	Y	Y	Y	Y	Y
Lankford	N	Y	Y	N	Y	Y
OREGON						
Wyden	Y	Y	N	Y	Y	N
Merkley	Y	Y	N	Y	Y	N
PENNSYLVANIA						
Casey	Y	Y	N	Y	Y	N
Toomey	N	Y	Y	N	N	Y
RHODE ISLAND						
Reed	Y	Y	N	Y	Y	N
Whitehouse	Y	Y	N	Y	Y	N
SOUTH CAROLINA						
Graham	N	Y	N	Y	Y	Y
Scott	N	Y	N	Y	Y	Y
SOUTH DAKOTA						
Thune	N	Y	Y	Y	Y	Y
Rounds	N	Y	Y	Y	Y	Y
TENNESSEE						
Alexander	N	Y	N	Y	Y	N
Blackburn	N	N	N	N	N	Y
TEXAS						
Cornyn	N	Y	Y	Y	Y	Y
Cruz	N	N	N	N	N	Y
UTAH						
Lee	N	N	Y	N	N	Y
Romney	N	Y	Y	N	Y	Y
VERMONT						
Leahy	Y	Y	N	Y	Y	N
Sanders	?	?	?	?	?	?
VIRGINIA						
Warner	Y	Y	N	Y	Y	N
Kaine	Y	Y	N	Y	Y	N
WASHINGTON						
Murray	Y	Y	N	Y	Y	N
Cantwell	Y	Y	N	Y	Y	N
WEST VIRGINIA						
Manchin	Y	Y	N	Y	Y	N
Capito	N	Y	N	Y	Y	Y
WISCONSIN						
Johnson	N	Y	Y	Y	N	Y
Baldwin	Y	Y	N	Y	Y	N
WYOMING						
Enzi	N	Y	Y	Y	Y	Y
Barrasso	N	Y	Y	Y	Y	Y

KEY:	Republicans	Democrats	*Independents*

Y	Voted for (yea)	N	Voted against (nay)	P	Voted "present"
+	Announced for	–	Announced against	?	Did not vote or otherwise
#	Paired for	X	Paired against		make position known

343. Tapp Nomination - Cloture. Motion to invoke cloture (thus limiting debate) on the nomination of on the nomination of David Tapp of Kentucky to be a judge of the U.S. Court of Federal Claims. Motion agreed to 83-9: R 49-0; D 33-9; I 1-0. *Note: A majority of senators voting (47 in this case), a quorum being present, is required to invoke cloture on all nominations.* Nov. 05, 2019.

344. Tapp Nomination - Confirmation. Confirmation of President Trump's nomination of David Tapp of Kentucky to be a judge of the U.S. Court of Federal Claims. Confirmed 85-8: R 51-0; D 33-8; I 1-0. *Note: A "yea" was a vote in support of the president's position.* Nov. 05, 2019.

345. Hunsaker Nomination - Cloture. Motion to invoke cloture (thus limiting debate) on the nomination of Danielle Hunsaker of Oregon to be a U.S. circuit judge for the 9th Circuit. Motion agreed to 75-18: R 51-0; D 23-18; I 1-0. *Note: A majority of senators voting (47 in this case), a quorum being present, is required to invoke cloture on all nominations.* Nov. 05, 2019.

346. Rudofsky Nomination - Cloture. Motion to invoke cloture (thus limiting debate) on the nomination of Lee Rudofsky of Arkansas to be a U.S. district judge for the Eastern District of Arkansas. Motion agreed to 51-41: R 51-0; D 0-40; I 0-1. *Note: A majority of senators voting (47 in this case), a quorum being present, is required to invoke cloture on all nominations.* Nov. 06, 2019.

347. Wilson Nomination - Cloture. Motion to invoke cloture (thus limiting debate) on the nomination of Jennifer Wilson of Pennsylvania to be a U.S. district judge for the Middle District of Pennsylvania. Motion agreed to 89-3: R 51-0; D 37-3; I 1-0. *Note: A majority of senators voting (47 in this case), a quorum being present, is required to invoke cloture on all nominations.* Nov. 06, 2019.

348. Hunsaker Nomination - Confirmation. Confirmation of President Trump's nomination of Danielle Hunsaker of Oregon to be a U.S. circuit judge for the 9th Circuit. Confirmed 73-17: R 49-0; D 23-17; I 1-0. *Note: A "yea" was a vote in support of the president's position.* Nov. 06, 2019.

	343	344	345	346	347	348
ALABAMA						
Shelby	Y	Y	Y	Y	Y	Y
Jones	Y	Y	Y	N	Y	Y
ALASKA						
Murkowski	Y	Y	Y	Y	Y	Y
Sullivan	Y	Y	Y	Y	Y	Y
ARIZONA						
Sinema	Y	Y	Y	N	Y	Y
McSally	Y	Y	Y	Y	Y	Y
ARKANSAS						
Boozman	Y	Y	Y	Y	Y	Y
Cotton	Y	Y	Y	Y	Y	Y
CALIFORNIA						
Feinstein	Y	Y	Y	N	Y	Y
Harris	N	-	?	?	?	?
COLORADO						
Bennet	Y	Y	Y	?	?	?
Gardner	Y	Y	Y	Y	Y	Y
CONNECTICUT						
Blumenthal	Y	Y	N	N	Y	N
Murphy	Y	Y	Y	N	Y	Y
DELAWARE						
Carper	Y	Y	Y	N	Y	Y
Coons	Y	Y	Y	N	Y	Y
FLORIDA						
Rubio	Y	Y	Y	Y	Y	Y
Scott	Y	Y	Y	Y	Y	Y
GEORGIA						
Isakson	?	?	?	?	?	?
Perdue	Y	Y	Y	Y	Y	Y
HAWAII						
Schatz	N	N	N	N	Y	N
Hirono	N	N	N	N	N	N
IDAHO						
Crapo	Y	Y	Y	Y	Y	Y
Risch	?	Y	Y	Y	Y	Y
ILLINOIS						
Durbin	Y	Y	N	N	Y	N
Duckworth	Y	Y	N	N	Y	N
INDIANA						
Young	Y	Y	Y	Y	Y	Y
Braun	Y	Y	Y	Y	Y	Y
IOWA						
Grassley	Y	Y	Y	Y	Y	Y
Ernst	Y	Y	Y	Y	Y	Y
KANSAS						
Roberts	Y	Y	Y	Y	Y	Y
Moran	Y	Y	Y	Y	Y	Y
KENTUCKY						
McConnell	Y	Y	Y	Y	Y	Y
Paul	Y	Y	Y	Y	Y	Y
LOUISIANA						
Cassidy	Y	Y	Y	Y	Y	?
Kennedy	Y	Y	Y	Y	Y	?
MAINE						
Collins	Y	Y	Y	Y	Y	Y
King	Y	Y	Y	N	Y	Y
MARYLAND						
Cardin	Y	Y	N	N	Y	N
Van Hollen	Y	Y	Y	N	Y	Y
MASSACHUSETTS						
Warren	?	?	?	?	?	?
Markey	N	N	N	N	N	N
MICHIGAN						
Stabenow	N	N	N	N	Y	N
Peters	Y	Y	Y	N	Y	Y
MINNESOTA						
Klobuchar	?	?	?	?	?	?
Smith	Y	Y	Y	N	Y	Y
MISSISSIPPI						
Wicker	Y	Y	Y	Y	Y	Y
Hyde-Smith	Y	Y	Y	Y	Y	Y
MISSOURI						
Blunt	Y	Y	Y	Y	Y	Y
Hawley	Y	Y	Y	Y	Y	Y

	343	344	345	346	347	348
MONTANA						
Tester	Y	Y	N	N	Y	Y
Daines	Y	Y	Y	Y	Y	Y
NEBRASKA						
Fischer	Y	Y	Y	Y	Y	Y
Sasse	?	Y	Y	Y	Y	Y
NEVADA						
Cortez Masto	Y	Y	Y	N	Y	Y
Rosen	Y	Y	Y	N	Y	Y
NEW HAMPSHIRE						
Shaheen	Y	Y	Y	N	Y	Y
Hassan	Y	Y	Y	N	Y	Y
NEW JERSEY						
Menendez	N	N	N	N	Y	N
Booker	?	?	?	?	?	?
NEW MEXICO						
Udall	Y	Y	N	N	Y	N
Heinrich	Y	Y	N	N	Y	N
NEW YORK						
Schumer	N	N	N	N	Y	N
Gillibrand	N	N	N	N	N	N
NORTH CAROLINA						
Burr	?	?	?	?	?	?
Tillis	Y	Y	Y	Y	Y	Y
NORTH DAKOTA						
Hoeven	Y	Y	Y	Y	Y	Y
Cramer	Y	Y	Y	Y	Y	Y
OHIO						
Brown	Y	Y	N	N	Y	N
Portman	Y	Y	Y	Y	Y	Y
OKLAHOMA						
Inhofe	Y	Y	Y	Y	Y	Y
Lankford	Y	Y	Y	Y	Y	Y
OREGON						
Wyden	Y	Y	Y	N	Y	Y
Merkley	N	N	N	N	Y	N
PENNSYLVANIA						
Casey	Y	Y	Y	N	Y	Y
Toomey	Y	Y	Y	Y	Y	Y
RHODE ISLAND						
Reed	Y	Y	N	N	Y	N
Whitehouse	Y	Y	Y	N	Y	Y
SOUTH CAROLINA						
Graham	Y	Y	Y	Y	Y	Y
Scott	Y	Y	Y	Y	Y	Y
SOUTH DAKOTA						
Thune	Y	Y	Y	Y	Y	Y
Rounds	Y	Y	Y	Y	Y	Y
TENNESSEE						
Alexander	Y	Y	Y	Y	Y	Y
Blackburn	Y	Y	Y	Y	Y	Y
TEXAS						
Cornyn	Y	Y	Y	Y	Y	Y
Cruz	Y	Y	Y	Y	Y	Y
UTAH						
Lee	Y	Y	Y	Y	Y	Y
Romney	Y	Y	Y	Y	Y	Y
VERMONT						
Leahy	Y	Y	Y	N	Y	Y
Sanders	?	?	?	?	?	?
VIRGINIA						
Warner	Y	Y	Y	N	Y	Y
Kaine	Y	Y	Y	N	Y	Y
WASHINGTON						
Murray	Y	Y	N	N	Y	N
Cantwell	Y	Y	N	N	Y	N
WEST VIRGINIA						
Manchin	Y	Y	Y	N	Y	Y
Capito	Y	Y	Y	Y	Y	Y
WISCONSIN						
Johnson	Y	Y	Y	Y	Y	Y
Baldwin	Y	Y	Y	N	Y	Y
WYOMING						
Enzi	Y	Y	Y	Y	Y	Y
Barrasso	Y	Y	Y	Y	Y	Y

KEY: **Republicans**   Democrats   *Independents*

Y	Voted for (yea)	**N** Voted against (nay)	**P** Voted "present"
+	Announced for	**–** Announced against	**?** Did not vote or otherwise
#	Paired for	**X** Paired against	make position known

349. Nardini Nomination - Cloture. Motion to invoke cloture (thus limiting debate) on the nomination of William Nardini of Connecticut to be a U.S. circuit judge for the 2nd Circuit. Motion agreed to 87-3: R 49-0; D 37-3; I 1-0. *Note: A majority of senators voting (46 in this case), a quorum being present, is required to invoke cloture on all nominations.* Nov. 06, 2019.

350. Rudofsky Nomination - Confirmation. Confirmation of President Trump's nomination of Lee Rudofsky of Arkansas to be a U.S. district judge for the Eastern District of Arkansas. Confirmed 51-41: R 51-0; D 0-40; I 0-1. *Note: A "yea" was a vote in support of the president's position.* Nov. 07, 2019.

351. Wilson Nomination - Confirmation. Confirmation of President Trump's nomination of Jennifer Wilson of Pennsylvania to be a U.S. district judge for the Middle District of Pennsylvania. Confirmed 88-3: R 51-0; D 36-3; I 1-0. *Note: A "yea" was a vote in support of the president's position.* Nov. 07, 2019.

352. Nardini Nomination - Confirmation. Confirmation of President Trump's nomination of William Nardini of Connecticut to be a U.S. circuit judge for the 2nd Circuit. Confirmed 86-2: R 49-0; D 36-2; I 1-0. *Note: A "yea" was a vote in support of the president's position.* Nov. 07, 2019.

353. Wolf Nomination - Cloture. Motion to invoke cloture (thus limiting debate) on the nomination of Chad Wolf of Virginia to be Homeland Security Department undersecretary for strategy, policy, and plans. Motion agreed to 54-40: R 52-0; D 2-39; I 0-1. *Note: A majority of senators voting (48 in this case), a quorum being present, is required to invoke cloture on all nominations.* Nov. 12, 2019.

354. Wolf Nomination - Confirmation. Confirmation of President Trump's nomination of Chad Wolf of Virginia to be Homeland Security Department undersecretary for strategy, policy and plans. Confirmed 54-41: R 52-0; D 2-40; I 0-1. *Note: A "yea" was a vote in support of the president's position.* Nov. 13, 2019.

	349	350	351	352	353	354
ALABAMA						
Shelby	Y	Y	Y	Y	Y	Y
Jones	Y	N	Y	Y	N	N
ALASKA						
Murkowski	Y	Y	Y	Y	Y	Y
Sullivan	Y	Y	Y	Y	Y	Y
ARIZONA						
Sinema	Y	N	Y	Y	Y	Y
McSally	Y	Y	Y	Y	Y	Y
ARKANSAS						
Boozman	Y	Y	Y	Y	Y	Y
Cotton	Y	Y	Y	Y	Y	Y
CALIFORNIA						
Feinstein	Y	N	Y	Y	N	N
Harris	?	?	–	–	?	?
COLORADO						
Bennet	?	N	Y	Y	N	N
Gardner	Y	Y	Y	Y	Y	Y
CONNECTICUT						
Blumenthal	Y	N	Y	Y	N	N
Murphy	Y	N	Y	Y	N	N
DELAWARE						
Carper	Y	N	Y	Y	N	N
Coons	Y	N	Y	Y	N	N
FLORIDA						
Rubio	Y	Y	Y	Y	Y	Y
Scott	Y	Y	Y	Y	Y	Y
GEORGIA						
Isakson	?	?	?	?	Y	Y
Perdue	Y	?	?	?	Y	Y
HAWAII						
Schatz	Y	N	Y	Y	N	N
Hirono	N	N	N	Y	N	N
IDAHO						
Crapo	Y	Y	Y	Y	Y	Y
Risch	Y	Y	Y	Y	Y	Y
ILLINOIS						
Durbin	Y	N	Y	Y	N	N
Duckworth	Y	N	Y	Y	N	N
INDIANA						
Young	Y	Y	Y	Y	Y	Y
Braun	Y	Y	Y	+	Y	Y
IOWA						
Grassley	Y	Y	Y	Y	Y	Y
Ernst	Y	Y	Y	Y	Y	Y
KANSAS						
Roberts	Y	Y	Y	Y	Y	Y
Moran	Y	Y	Y	+	Y	Y
KENTUCKY						
McConnell	Y	Y	Y	Y	Y	Y
Paul	Y	Y	Y	Y	Y	Y
LOUISIANA						
Cassidy	?	Y	Y	Y	Y	Y
Kennedy	?	Y	Y	Y	Y	Y
MAINE						
Collins	Y	Y	Y	Y	Y	Y
King	Y	N	Y	Y	N	N
MARYLAND						
Cardin	Y	N	?	?	N	N
Van Hollen	Y	N	Y	Y	N	N
MASSACHUSETTS						
Warren	?	?	?	?	?	?
Markey	N	N	N	N	N	N
MICHIGAN						
Stabenow	Y	N	Y	Y	N	N
Peters	Y	N	Y	Y	N	N
MINNESOTA						
Klobuchar	?	?	?	?	N	N
Smith	Y	N	Y	Y	N	N
MISSISSIPPI						
Wicker	Y	Y	Y	Y	Y	Y
Hyde-Smith	Y	Y	Y	Y	Y	Y
MISSOURI						
Blunt	Y	Y	Y	Y	Y	Y
Hawley	Y	Y	Y	Y	Y	Y

	349	350	351	352	353	354
MONTANA						
Tester	Y	N	Y	Y	N	N
Daines	Y	Y	Y	Y	Y	Y
NEBRASKA						
Fischer	Y	Y	Y	Y	Y	Y
Sasse	Y	Y	Y	Y	Y	Y
NEVADA						
Cortez Masto	Y	N	Y	Y	N	N
Rosen	Y	N	Y	Y	N	N
NEW HAMPSHIRE						
Shaheen	Y	N	Y	Y	N	N
Hassan	Y	N	Y	Y	N	N
NEW JERSEY						
Menendez	Y	N	Y	?	N	N
Booker	?	?	?	?	?	?
NEW MEXICO						
Udall	Y	N	Y	Y	N	N
Heinrich	Y	N	Y	Y	N	N
NEW YORK						
Schumer	Y	N	Y	Y	N	N
Gillibrand	N	N	N	N	N	N
NORTH CAROLINA						
Burr	?	Y	Y	Y	Y	Y
Tillis	Y	Y	Y	Y	Y	Y
NORTH DAKOTA						
Hoeven	Y	Y	Y	Y	Y	Y
Cramer	Y	Y	Y	Y	Y	Y
OHIO						
Brown	Y	N	Y	Y	N	N
Portman	Y	Y	Y	Y	Y	Y
OKLAHOMA						
Inhofe	Y	Y	Y	Y	Y	Y
Lankford	Y	Y	Y	Y	Y	Y
OREGON						
Wyden	Y	?	?	?	N	N
Merkley	Y	N	Y	Y	N	N
PENNSYLVANIA						
Casey	Y	N	Y	Y	N	N
Toomey	Y	Y	Y	Y	Y	Y
RHODE ISLAND						
Reed	Y	N	Y	Y	–	N
Whitehouse	Y	N	Y	Y	N	N
SOUTH CAROLINA						
Graham	Y	Y	Y	Y	Y	Y
Scott	Y	Y	Y	Y	Y	Y
SOUTH DAKOTA						
Thune	Y	Y	Y	Y	Y	Y
Rounds	Y	Y	Y	Y	?	?
TENNESSEE						
Alexander	Y	Y	Y	Y	Y	Y
Blackburn	Y	Y	Y	Y	Y	Y
TEXAS						
Cornyn	Y	Y	Y	Y	Y	Y
Cruz	Y	Y	Y	Y	Y	Y
UTAH						
Lee	Y	Y	Y	Y	Y	Y
Romney	Y	Y	Y	Y	Y	Y
VERMONT						
Leahy	Y	N	Y	Y	N	N
Sanders	?	?	?	?	?	?
VIRGINIA						
Warner	Y	N	Y	Y	N	N
Kaine	Y	N	Y	Y	N	N
WASHINGTON						
Murray	Y	N	Y	Y	N	N
Cantwell	Y	N	Y	Y	N	N
WEST VIRGINIA						
Manchin	Y	N	Y	Y	Y	Y
Capito	Y	Y	Y	Y	Y	Y
WISCONSIN						
Johnson	Y	Y	Y	Y	Y	Y
Baldwin	Y	N	Y	Y	N	N
WYOMING						
Enzi	Y	Y	Y	Y	Y	Y
Barrasso	Y	Y	Y	Y	Y	Y

KEY:		Republicans		Democrats		*Independents*

Y	Voted for (yea)	N	Voted against (nay)	P	Voted "present"
+	Announced for	–	Announced against	?	Did not vote or otherwise
#	Paired for	X	Paired against		make position known

355. Menashi Nomination - Cloture. Motion to invoke cloture (thus limiting debate) on the nomination of Steven Menashi of New York to be a U.S. circuit judge for the 2nd Circuit. Motion agreed to 51-44: R 51-1; D 0-42; I 0-1. *Note: A majority of senators voting (48 in this case), a quorum being present, is required to invoke cloture on all nominations.* Nov. 13, 2019.

356. Menashi Nomination - Confirmation. Confirmation of President Trump's nomination of Steven Menashi of New York to be a U.S. circuit judge for the 2nd Circuit. Confirmed 51-41: R 51-1; D 0-39; I 0-1. *Note: A "yea" was a vote in support of the president's position.* Nov. 14, 2019.

357. Luck Nomination - Cloture. Motion to invoke cloture (thus limiting debate) on the nomination of Robert Luck of Florida to be a U.S. circuit judge for the 11th Circuit. Motion agreed to 61-30: R 51-0; D 10-29; I 0-1. *Note: A majority of senators voting (46 in this case), a quorum being present, is required to invoke cloture on all nominations.* Nov. 18, 2019.

358. Luck Nomination - Confirmation. Confirmation of President Trump's nomination of Robert Luck of Florida to be a U.S. circuit judge for the 11th Circuit. Confirmed 64-31: R 53-0; D 11-30; I 0-1. *Note: A "yea" was a vote in support of the president's position.* Nov. 19, 2019.

359. Lagoa Nomination - Cloture. Motion to invoke cloture (thus limiting debate) on the nomination of Barbara Lagoa of Florida to be a U.S. circuit judge for the 11th Circuit. Motion agreed to 80-15: R 53-0; D 26-15; I 1-0. *Note: A majority of senators voting (48 in this case), a quorum being present, is required to invoke cloture on all nominations.* Nov. 19, 2019.

360. Lagoa Nomination - Confirmation. Confirmation of President Trump's nomination of Barbara Lagoa of Florida to be a U.S. circuit judge for the 11th Circuit. Confirmed 80-15: R 53-0; D 26-15; I 1-0. *Note: A "yea" was a vote in support of the president's position.* Nov. 20, 2019.

	355	356	357	358	359	360
ALABAMA						
Shelby	Y	Y	Y	Y	Y	Y
Jones	N	?	Y	Y	Y	Y
ALASKA						
Murkowski	Y	Y	Y	Y	Y	Y
Sullivan	Y	Y	Y	Y	Y	Y
ARIZONA						
Sinema	N	N	Y	Y	Y	Y
McSally	Y	Y	Y	Y	Y	Y
ARKANSAS						
Boozman	Y	Y	Y	Y	Y	Y
Cotton	Y	Y	Y	Y	Y	Y
CALIFORNIA						
Feinstein	N	N	Y	Y	Y	Y
Harris	-	?	-	-	-	-
COLORADO						
Bennet	N	?	N	N	N	N
Gardner	Y	Y	Y	Y	Y	Y
CONNECTICUT						
Blumenthal	N	N	N	N	Y	Y
Murphy	N	N	?	Y	Y	Y
DELAWARE						
Carper	N	N	Y	Y	Y	Y
Coons	N	N	Y	Y	Y	Y
FLORIDA						
Rubio	Y	Y	Y	Y	Y	Y
Scott	Y	Y	Y	Y	Y	Y
GEORGIA						
Isakson	Y	Y	?	Y	Y	Y
Perdue	Y	Y	Y	Y	Y	Y
HAWAII						
Schatz	N	N	?	N	N	N
Hirono	N	N	N	N	N	N
IDAHO						
Crapo	Y	Y	Y	Y	Y	Y
Risch	Y	Y	Y	Y	Y	Y
ILLINOIS						
Durbin	N	N	N	N	Y	Y
Duckworth	N	N	N	N	Y	Y
INDIANA						
Young	Y	Y	Y	Y	Y	Y
Braun	Y	Y	Y	Y	Y	Y
IOWA						
Grassley	Y	Y	Y	Y	Y	Y
Ernst	Y	Y	Y	Y	Y	Y
KANSAS						
Roberts	Y	Y	?	Y	Y	Y
Moran	Y	Y	Y	Y	Y	Y
KENTUCKY						
McConnell	Y	Y	Y	Y	Y	Y
Paul	Y	Y	Y	Y	Y	Y
LOUISIANA						
Cassidy	Y	Y	Y	Y	Y	Y
Kennedy	Y	Y	Y	Y	Y	Y
MAINE						
Collins	N	N	Y	Y	Y	Y
King	N	N	N	N	Y	Y
MARYLAND						
Cardin	N	N	N	N	Y	Y
Van Hollen	N	N	N	N	N	N
MASSACHUSETTS						
Warren	?	?	?	?	?	?
Markey	N	N	N	N	N	N
MICHIGAN						
Stabenow	N	N	N	N	N	N
Peters	N	N	N	N	Y	Y
MINNESOTA						
Klobuchar	N	?	?	?	?	?
Smith	N	N	N	N	Y	Y
MISSISSIPPI						
Wicker	Y	Y	Y	Y	Y	Y
Hyde-Smith	Y	Y	Y	Y	Y	Y
MISSOURI						
Blunt	Y	Y	Y	Y	Y	Y
Hawley	Y	Y	Y	Y	Y	Y

	355	356	357	358	359	360
MONTANA						
Tester	N	N	N	N	Y	Y
Daines	Y	Y	Y	Y	Y	Y
NEBRASKA						
Fischer	Y	Y	Y	Y	Y	Y
Sasse	Y	Y	Y	Y	Y	Y
NEVADA						
Cortez Masto	N	N	N	N	N	N
Rosen	N	N	N	N	N	N
NEW HAMPSHIRE						
Shaheen	N	N	N	N	N	Y
Hassan	N	N	N	N	N	Y
NEW JERSEY						
Menendez	N	N	N	N	Y	Y
Booker	?	?	?	?	?	?
NEW MEXICO						
Udall	N	N	N	N	N	N
Heinrich	N	N	N	N	Y	Y
NEW YORK						
Schumer	N	N	N	N	N	N
Gillibrand	N	N	N	N	N	N
NORTH CAROLINA						
Burr	Y	Y	Y	Y	Y	Y
Tillis	Y	Y	Y	Y	Y	Y
NORTH DAKOTA						
Hoeven	Y	Y	Y	Y	Y	Y
Cramer	Y	Y	Y	Y	Y	Y
OHIO						
Brown	N	N	N	N	N	N
Portman	Y	Y	Y	Y	Y	Y
OKLAHOMA						
Inhofe	Y	Y	Y	Y	Y	Y
Lankford	Y	Y	Y	Y	Y	Y
OREGON						
Wyden	N	N	N	N	N	N
Merkley	N	N	N	N	N	N
PENNSYLVANIA						
Casey	N	N	N	N	Y	Y
Toomey	Y	Y	Y	Y	Y	Y
RHODE ISLAND						
Reed	N	N	Y	Y	Y	Y
Whitehouse	N	N	Y	Y	Y	Y
SOUTH CAROLINA						
Graham	Y	Y	Y	Y	Y	Y
Scott	Y	Y	Y	Y	Y	Y
SOUTH DAKOTA						
Thune	Y	Y	Y	Y	Y	Y
Rounds	?	?	Y	Y	Y	Y
TENNESSEE						
Alexander	Y	Y	Y	Y	Y	Y
Blackburn	Y	Y	Y	Y	Y	Y
TEXAS						
Cornyn	Y	Y	Y	Y	Y	Y
Cruz	Y	Y	Y	Y	Y	Y
UTAH						
Lee	Y	Y	Y	Y	Y	Y
Romney	Y	Y	Y	Y	Y	Y
VERMONT						
Leahy	N	N	Y	Y	Y	Y
Sanders	?	?	?	?	?	?
VIRGINIA						
Warner	N	N	N	N	Y	Y
Kaine	N	N	N	N	Y	Y
WASHINGTON						
Murray	N	N	N	N	N	N
Cantwell	N	N	N	N	N	N
WEST VIRGINIA						
Manchin	N	N	Y	Y	Y	Y
Capito	Y	Y	Y	Y	Y	Y
WISCONSIN						
Johnson	Y	Y	Y	Y	Y	Y
Baldwin	N	N	Y	Y	Y	Y
WYOMING						
Enzi	Y	Y	Y	Y	Y	Y
Barrasso	Y	Y	Y	Y	Y	Y

KEY:	**Republicans**	Democrats	*Independents*

Y	Voted for (yea)	N	Voted against (nay)	P	Voted "present"
+	Announced for	-	Announced against	?	Did not vote or otherwise
#	Paired for	X	Paired against		make position known

361. Zuckerman Nomination - Cloture. Motion to invoke cloture (thus limiting debate) on the nomination of Adrian Zuckerman of New Jersey to be ambassador to Romania. Motion agreed to 65-30: R 53-0; D 11-30; I 1-0. *Note: A majority of senators voting (48 in this case), a quorum being present, is required to invoke cloture on all nominations.* Nov. 20, 2019.

362. Zuckerman Nomination - Confirmation. Confirmation of President Trump's nomination of Adrian Zuckerman of New Jersey to be ambassador to Romania. Confirmed 65-30: R 53-0; D 11-30; I 1-0. *Note: A "yea" was a vote in suport of the president's position.* Nov. 20, 2019.

363. HR3055. Further Fiscal 2020 Short-Term Appropriations - Motion to Table. Shelby, R-Ala., motion to table (kill) the Paul, R-Ky., motion to concur in the House amendment to the Senate amendment to the Further Fiscal 2020 Short-Term Appropriations Act (HR 3055) with a further amendment that would provide funding for federal government operations and services through Dec. 20, 2019 at one percent less than fiscal 2019 levels, except for the Highway Trust Fund, the EPA Agency Infrastructure Assistance program, and raises for members of the Armed Services. It would require the Treasury Department to transfer 95 percent of the funds saved from the reduction to the Highway Trust Fund, and five percent to the EPA Agency Infrastructure Assistance program. Motion agreed to 73-20: R 31-20; D 41-0; I 1-0. Nov. 21, 2019.

364. HR3055. Further Fiscal 2020 Short-Term Appropriations - Cloture. McConnell, R-Ky., motion to invoke cloture (thus limiting debate) on the motion to concur in the House amendment to the Senate amendment to the Further Fiscal 2020 Short-Term Appropriations Act (HR 3055) that would provide funding for federal government operations and services through Dec. 20, 2019 at fiscal 2019 levels. Motion agreed to 75-19: R 33-19; D 41-0; I 1-0. *Note: Three-fifths of the total Senate (60) is required to invoke cloture.* Nov. 21, 2019.

365. HR3055. Further Fiscal 2020 Short-Term Appropriations - Motion to Concur. McConnell, R-Ky., motion to concur in the House amendment to the Senate amendment to the Further Fiscal 2020 Short-Term Appropriations Act (HR 3055) that would provide funding for federal government operations and services through Dec. 20, 2019, at fiscal 2019 levels. Among other provisions, the bill would extend through Dec. 20 authorizations for certain expiring programs and entities, including certain Medicaid and Medicare programs and other health-related HHS programs. It would increase or modify funding rates for certain activities, including to provide for a 3.1 percent pay increase for the members of the armed forces and to provide $7.3 billion for activities related to the 2020 decennial census. It would repeal a $7.6 billion rescission of federal highway funding set to take effect in July 2020; extend certain federal surveillance authorities under the Patriot Act and other existing law through March 15, 2020; and modify provisions related to the Justice Department fund for victims of state-sponsored terrorism, including to designate 50 percent of funds for victims of the Sept. 11 terrorist attacks. Motion agreed to 74-20: R 32-20; D 41-0; I 1-0. Nov. 21, 2019.

366. Brouillette Nomination - Cloture. Motion to invoke cloture (thus limiting debate) on the nomination of Dan R. Brouillettee of Texas to be secretary of Energy. Motion agreed to 74-18: R 50-0; D 23-18; I 1-0. *Note: A majority of senators voting (47 in this case), a quorum being present, is required to invoke cloture on all nominations.* Nov. 21, 2019.

	361	362	363	364	365	366
ALABAMA						
Shelby	Y	Y	Y	Y	Y	Y
Jones	Y	Y	Y	Y	Y	Y
ALASKA						
Murkowski	Y	Y	Y	Y	Y	Y
Sullivan	Y	Y	N	Y	Y	Y
ARIZONA						
Sinema	Y	Y	Y	Y	Y	Y
McSally	Y	Y	N	Y	Y	Y
ARKANSAS						
Boozman	Y	Y	Y	Y	Y	Y
Cotton	Y	Y	?	Y	Y	Y
CALIFORNIA						
Feinstein	N	N	Y	Y	Y	Y
Harris	?	?	?	?	?	?
COLORADO						
Bennet	N	N	Y	Y	Y	N
Gardner	Y	Y	Y	Y	Y	Y
CONNECTICUT						
Blumenthal	N	N	Y	Y	Y	N
Murphy	Y	Y	Y	Y	Y	Y
DELAWARE						
Carper	Y	Y	Y	Y	Y	Y
Coons	Y	Y	Y	Y	Y	Y
FLORIDA						
Rubio	Y	Y	Y	Y	Y	Y
Scott	Y	Y	Y	N	N	Y
GEORGIA						
Isakson	Y	Y	Y	Y	Y	?
Perdue	Y	Y	Y	N	N	Y
HAWAII						
Schatz	N	N	Y	Y	Y	N
Hirono	N	N	Y	Y	Y	N
IDAHO						
Crapo	Y	Y	N	Y	Y	Y
Risch	Y	Y	N	N	N	Y
ILLINOIS						
Durbin	N	N	Y	Y	Y	Y
Duckworth	N	N	Y	Y	Y	Y
INDIANA						
Young	Y	Y	Y	Y	Y	Y
Braun	Y	Y	N	N	N	Y
IOWA						
Grassley	Y	Y	Y	Y	Y	Y
Ernst	Y	Y	N	N	N	Y
KANSAS						
Roberts	Y	Y	Y	Y	Y	Y
Moran	Y	Y	Y	Y	Y	+
KENTUCKY						
McConnell	Y	Y	Y	Y	Y	Y
Paul	Y	Y	N	N	N	Y
LOUISIANA						
Cassidy	Y	Y	?	?	?	?
Kennedy	Y	Y	N	Y	Y	Y
MAINE						
Collins	Y	Y	Y	Y	Y	Y
King	Y	Y	Y	Y	Y	Y
MARYLAND						
Cardin	N	N	Y	Y	Y	Y
Van Hollen	N	N	Y	Y	Y	N
MASSACHUSETTS						
Warren	?	?	?	?	?	?
Markey	N	N	Y	Y	Y	N
MICHIGAN						
Stabenow	N	N	Y	Y	Y	Y
Peters	N	N	Y	Y	Y	Y
MINNESOTA						
Klobuchar	?	?	?	?	?	?
Smith	N	N	Y	Y	Y	Y
MISSISSIPPI						
Wicker	Y	Y	Y	Y	Y	Y
Hyde-Smith	Y	Y	Y	Y	Y	Y
MISSOURI						
Blunt	Y	Y	Y	Y	Y	Y
Hawley	Y	Y	Y	N	N	Y
MONTANA						
Tester	N	N	Y	Y	Y	Y
Daines	Y	Y	N	N	N	Y
NEBRASKA						
Fischer	Y	Y	N	N	N	Y
Sasse	Y	Y	N	N	N	Y
NEVADA						
Cortez Masto	N	N	Y	Y	Y	N
Rosen	Y	Y	Y	Y	Y	N
NEW HAMPSHIRE						
Shaheen	Y	Y	Y	Y	Y	Y
Hassan	Y	Y	Y	Y	Y	Y
NEW JERSEY						
Menendez	Y	Y	Y	Y	Y	N
Booker	?	?	?	?	?	?
NEW MEXICO						
Udall	N	N	Y	Y	Y	Y
Heinrich	N	N	Y	Y	Y	Y
NEW YORK						
Schumer	N	N	Y	Y	Y	N
Gillibrand	N	N	Y	Y	Y	N
NORTH CAROLINA						
Burr	Y	Y	Y	Y	Y	Y
Tillis	Y	Y	N	N	N	Y
NORTH DAKOTA						
Hoeven	Y	Y	Y	Y	Y	Y
Cramer	Y	Y	Y	Y	Y	Y
OHIO						
Brown	N	N	Y	Y	Y	N
Portman	Y	Y	Y	Y	Y	Y
OKLAHOMA						
Inhofe	Y	Y	Y	N	N	Y
Lankford	Y	Y	N	Y	Y	Y
OREGON						
Wyden	N	N	Y	Y	Y	N
Merkley	N	N	Y	Y	Y	N
PENNSYLVANIA						
Casey	N	N	Y	Y	Y	Y
Toomey	Y	Y	Y	Y	Y	Y
RHODE ISLAND						
Reed	N	N	Y	Y	Y	N
Whitehouse	N	N	Y	Y	Y	N
SOUTH CAROLINA						
Graham	Y	Y	Y	Y	Y	Y
Scott	Y	Y	N	Y	N	Y
SOUTH DAKOTA						
Thune	Y	Y	Y	Y	Y	Y
Rounds	Y	Y	Y	N	N	Y
TENNESSEE						
Alexander	Y	Y	Y	Y	Y	Y
Blackburn	Y	Y	N	N	N	Y
TEXAS						
Cornyn	Y	Y	N	Y	Y	Y
Cruz	Y	Y	N	N	N	Y
UTAH						
Lee	Y	Y	N	N	N	Y
Romney	Y	Y	N	N	N	Y
VERMONT						
Leahy	N	N	Y	Y	Y	N
Sanders	?	?	?	?	?	?
VIRGINIA						
Warner	Y	Y	Y	Y	Y	Y
Kaine	N	N	Y	Y	Y	Y
WASHINGTON						
Murray	N	N	Y	Y	Y	Y
Cantwell	N	N	Y	Y	Y	Y
WEST VIRGINIA						
Manchin	Y	Y	Y	Y	Y	Y
Capito	Y	Y	Y	Y	Y	Y
WISCONSIN						
Johnson	Y	Y	Y	Y	Y	Y
Baldwin	N	N	Y	Y	Y	N
WYOMING						
Enzi	Y	Y	Y	N	N	Y
Barrasso	Y	Y	N	Y	Y	Y

KEY: **Republicans**   Democrats   *Independents*

Y Voted for (yea)	**N** Voted against (nay)	**P** Voted "present"
+ Announced for	**−** Announced against	**?** Did not vote or otherwise
# Paired for	**X** Paired against	make position known

▌▌▌ SENATE VOTES

367. Brouillettee Nomination - Confirmation. Confirmation of President Trump's nomination of Dan R. Brouillettee of Texas to be secretary of Energy. Confirmed 70-15: R 47-0; D 22-15; I 1-0. *Note: A "yea" was a vote in support of the president's position.* Dec. 02, 2019.

368. Komitee Nomination - Cloture. Motion to invoke cloture (thus limiting debate) on the nomination of Eric Komitee of New York to be a U.S. district judge for the Eastern District of New York. Motion agreed to 81-5: R 48-0; D 32-5; I 1-0. *Note: A majority of senators voting (44 in this case), a quorum being present, is required to invoke cloture on all nominations.* Dec. 02, 2019.

369. Komitee Nomination - Confirmation. Confirmation of President Trump's nomination of Eric Komitee of New York to be a U.S. district judge for the Eastern District of New York. Confirmed 86-4: R 51-0; D 34-4; I 1-0. *Note: A "yea" was a vote in support of the president's position.* Dec. 03, 2019.

370. Sinatra Nomination - Cloture. Motion to invoke cloture (thus limiting debate) on the nomination of John L. Sinatra, Jr. of New York to be a U.S. district judge for the Western District of New York. Motion agreed to 76-16: R 52-0; D 23-16; I 1-0. *Note: A majority of senators voting (47 in this case), a quorum being present, is required to invoke cloture on all nominations.* Dec. 03, 2019.

371. Pitlyk Nomination - Cloture. Motion to invoke cloture (thus limiting debate) on the nomination of Sarah E. Pitlyk of Missouri to be a U.S. district judge for the Eastern District of Missouri. Motion agreed to 50-43: R 50-0; D 0-41; I 0-1. *Note: A majority of senators voting (47 in this case), a quorum being present, is required to invoke cloture on all nominations.* Dec. 03, 2019.

372. Cole Nomination - Cloture. Motion to invoke cloture (thus limiting debate) on the nomination of Douglas Russell Cole of Ohio to be a U.S. district judge for the Southern District of Ohio. Motion agreed to 62-29: R 49-0; D 12-29; I 1-0. *Note: A majority of senators voting (46 in this case), a quorum being present, is required to invoke cloture on all nominations.* Dec. 03, 2019.

	367	368	369	370	371	372
ALABAMA						
Shelby	Y	Y	Y	Y	Y	Y
Jones	?	?	Y	Y	N	Y
ALASKA						
Murkowski	Y	Y	Y	Y	-	?
Sullivan	Y	Y	Y	Y	Y	Y
ARIZONA						
Sinema	Y	Y	Y	Y	N	Y
McSally	Y	Y	Y	Y	Y	Y
ARKANSAS						
Boozman	Y	Y	Y	Y	Y	Y
Cotton	Y	Y	Y	Y	Y	Y
CALIFORNIA						
Feinstein	Y	Y	Y	Y	N	N
Harris	?	-	-	-	-	-
COLORADO						
Bennet	?	?	?	Y	N	N
Gardner	Y	Y	Y	Y	Y	Y
CONNECTICUT						
Blumenthal	N	Y	Y	N	N	N
Murphy	Y	Y	Y	Y	N	Y
DELAWARE						
Carper	Y	Y	Y	Y	N	Y
Coons	Y	Y	Y	Y	N	Y
FLORIDA						
Rubio	Y	Y	Y	Y	Y	Y
Scott	Y	Y	Y	Y	Y	Y
GEORGIA						
Isakson	Y	Y	Y	Y	Y	?
Perdue	Y	Y	Y	Y	Y	Y
HAWAII						
Schatz	N	Y	Y	N	N	N
Hirono	N	N	Y	N	N	N
IDAHO						
Crapo	Y	Y	Y	Y	Y	Y
Risch	Y	Y	Y	Y	Y	Y
ILLINOIS						
Durbin	Y	Y	Y	N	N	Y
Duckworth	Y	Y	Y	N	N	N
INDIANA						
Young	Y	Y	Y	Y	Y	Y
Braun	Y	Y	Y	Y	Y	Y
IOWA						
Grassley	Y	Y	Y	Y	Y	Y
Ernst	Y	Y	Y	Y	Y	Y
KANSAS						
Roberts	Y	Y	Y	Y	Y	Y
Moran	Y	Y	Y	Y	Y	Y
KENTUCKY						
McConnell	Y	Y	Y	Y	Y	Y
Paul	Y	Y	Y	Y	Y	Y
LOUISIANA						
Cassidy	Y	Y	Y	Y	Y	Y
Kennedy	Y	Y	Y	Y	Y	Y
MAINE						
Collins	Y	Y	Y	Y	N	Y
King	Y	Y	Y	Y	N	Y
MARYLAND						
Cardin	Y	Y	Y	Y	N	N
Van Hollen	N	Y	Y	N	N	N
MASSACHUSETTS						
Warren	?	?	?	?	?	?
Markey	N	N	N	N	N	N
MICHIGAN						
Stabenow	Y	Y	Y	Y	N	N
Peters	Y	Y	Y	Y	N	N
MINNESOTA						
Klobuchar	?	?	?	?	?	?
Smith	Y	Y	Y	N	N	N
MISSISSIPPI						
Wicker	Y	Y	Y	Y	Y	Y
Hyde-Smith	Y	Y	Y	Y	Y	Y
MISSOURI						
Blunt	?	?	Y	Y	Y	Y
Hawley	Y	Y	Y	Y	Y	Y

	367	368	369	370	371	372
MONTANA						
Tester	Y	Y	Y	Y	N	N
Daines	Y	Y	Y	Y	Y	Y
NEBRASKA						
Fischer	Y	Y	Y	Y	Y	Y
Sasse	Y	Y	Y	Y	Y	Y
NEVADA						
Cortez Masto	N	Y	Y	Y	N	N
Rosen	N	Y	Y	Y	N	N
NEW HAMPSHIRE						
Shaheen	Y	Y	Y	Y	N	N
Hassan	Y	Y	Y	Y	N	N
NEW JERSEY						
Menendez	N	Y	Y	N	N	N
Booker	?	?	?	?	?	?
NEW MEXICO						
Udall	Y	Y	Y	N	N	N
Heinrich	Y	N	N	N	N	N
NEW YORK						
Schumer	N	Y	Y	Y	N	N
Gillibrand	?	?	?	?	N	N
NORTH CAROLINA						
Burr	Y	Y	Y	Y	Y	Y
Tillis	Y	Y	Y	Y	Y	Y
NORTH DAKOTA						
Hoeven	Y	Y	Y	Y	Y	Y
Cramer	Y	Y	Y	Y	Y	Y
OHIO						
Brown	N	Y	Y	N	N	Y
Portman	?	?	Y	Y	Y	Y
OKLAHOMA						
Inhofe	Y	Y	Y	Y	Y	Y
Lankford	Y	Y	Y	Y	Y	Y
OREGON						
Wyden	N	Y	Y	N	N	N
Merkley	N	Y	Y	N	N	N
PENNSYLVANIA						
Casey	Y	Y	Y	Y	N	Y
Toomey	?	?	Y	Y	Y	Y
RHODE ISLAND						
Reed	N	Y	Y	Y	N	Y
Whitehouse	?	?	?	?	N	Y
SOUTH CAROLINA						
Graham	?	Y	Y	Y	Y	Y
Scott	?	?	?	Y	Y	Y
SOUTH DAKOTA						
Thune	Y	Y	Y	Y	Y	Y
Rounds	?	?	?	?	?	?
TENNESSEE						
Alexander	Y	Y	Y	Y	Y	Y
Blackburn	Y	Y	Y	Y	Y	Y
TEXAS						
Cornyn	Y	Y	Y	Y	Y	Y
Cruz	Y	Y	Y	Y	Y	Y
UTAH						
Lee	Y	Y	Y	Y	Y	Y
Romney	Y	Y	Y	Y	Y	Y
VERMONT						
Leahy	N	Y	Y	Y	N	Y
Sanders	?	?	?	?	?	?
VIRGINIA						
Warner	Y	Y	Y	Y	N	N
Kaine	Y	Y	Y	Y	N	N
WASHINGTON						
Murray	Y	N	N	N	N	N
Cantwell	Y	N	N	N	N	N
WEST VIRGINIA						
Manchin	Y	Y	Y	Y	Y	Y
Capito	Y	Y	Y	Y	Y	Y
WISCONSIN						
Johnson	Y	Y	Y	Y	Y	+
Baldwin	N	Y	Y	Y	N	N
WYOMING						
Enzi	Y	Y	Y	Y	Y	Y
Barrasso	Y	Y	Y	Y	Y	Y

KEY:	**Republicans**	Democrats	*Independents*
Y Voted for (yea)	N Voted against (nay)		P Voted "present"
+ Announced for	– Announced against		? Did not vote or otherwise
# Paired for	X Paired against		make position known

373. Huffaker Nomination - Cloture. Motion to invoke cloture (thus limiting debate) on the nomination of R. Austin Huffaker, Jr. of Alabama to be a U.S. district judge for the Middle District of Alabama. Motion agreed to 88-4: R 50-0; D 37-4; I 1-0. *Note: A majority of senators voting (47 in this case), a quorum being present, is required to invoke cloture on all nominations.* Dec. 03, 2019.

374. Barlow Nomination - Cloture. Motion to invoke cloture (thus limiting debate) on the nomination of David B. Barlow of Utah to be a U.S. district judge for the District of Utah. Motion agreed to 88-4: R 50-0; D 37-4; I 1-0. *Note: A majority of senators voting (47 in this case), a quorum being present, is required to invoke cloture on all nominations.* Dec. 03, 2019.

375. Myers Nomination - Cloture. Motion to invoke cloture (thus limiting debate) on the nomination of Richard Ernest Myers II of North Carolina to be a U.S. district judge for the Eastern District of North Carolina Motion agreed to 72-22: R 51-0; D 20-22; I 1-0. *Note: A majority of senators voting (48 in this case), a quorum being present, is required to invoke cloture on all nominations.* Dec. 04, 2019.

376. Lydon Nomination - Cloture. Motion to invoke cloture (thus limiting debate) on the nomination of Sherri A. Lydon of South Carolina to be a U.S. district judge for the District of South Carolina. Motion agreed to 79-14: R 50-0; D 28-14; I 1-0. *Note: A majority of senators voting (47 in this case), a quorum being present, is required to invoke cloture on all nominations.* Dec. 04, 2019.

377. Duncan Nomination - Cloture. Motion to invoke cloture (thus limiting debate) on the nomination of Robert M. Duncan of Kentucky to be a governor of the U.S. Postal Service. Motion agreed to 91-1: R 50-0; D 40-1; I 1-0. *Note: A majority of senators voting (47 in this case), a quorum being present, is required to invoke cloture on all nominations.* Dec. 04, 2019.

378. Sinatra Nomination - Confirmation. Confirmation of President Trump's nomination of John L. Sinatra, Jr. of New York to be a U.S. district judge for the Western District of New York. Confirmed 75-18: R 50-0; D 24-18; I 1-0. *Note: A "yea" was a vote in support of the president's position.* Dec. 04, 2019.

	373	374	375	376	377	378
ALABAMA						
Shelby	Y	Y	Y	Y	Y	Y
Jones	Y	Y	Y	Y	Y	Y
ALASKA						
Murkowski	?	?	?	?	?	?
Sullivan	Y	Y	Y	Y	Y	Y
ARIZONA						
Sinema	Y	Y	Y	Y	Y	Y
McSally	Y	Y	Y	Y	Y	Y
ARKANSAS						
Boozman	Y	Y	Y	Y	Y	Y
Cotton	Y	Y	Y	Y	Y	Y
CALIFORNIA						
Feinstein	Y	Y	Y	Y	Y	Y
Harris	-	-	-	-	-	-
COLORADO						
Bennet	Y	Y	N	N	Y	Y
Gardner	Y	Y	Y	Y	Y	Y
CONNECTICUT						
Blumenthal	Y	Y	N	N	Y	N
Murphy	Y	Y	Y	Y	Y	Y
DELAWARE						
Carper	Y	Y	Y	Y	Y	Y
Coons	Y	Y	Y	Y	Y	Y
FLORIDA						
Rubio	Y	Y	Y	Y	Y	Y
Scott	Y	Y	Y	Y	Y	Y
GEORGIA						
Isakson	?	?	Y	?	?	?
Perdue	Y	Y	Y	Y	Y	Y
HAWAII						
Schatz	Y	Y	N	N	Y	N
Hirono	N	N	N	N	N	N
IDAHO						
Crapo	Y	Y	Y	Y	Y	Y
Risch	Y	Y	Y	Y	Y	Y
ILLINOIS						
Durbin	Y	Y	Y	Y	Y	N
Duckworth	Y	Y	Y	Y	Y	N
INDIANA						
Young	Y	Y	Y	Y	Y	Y
Braun	Y	Y	Y	Y	Y	Y
IOWA						
Grassley	Y	Y	Y	Y	Y	Y
Ernst	Y	Y	Y	Y	Y	Y
KANSAS						
Roberts	Y	Y	Y	Y	Y	Y
Moran	Y	Y	Y	Y	Y	Y
KENTUCKY						
McConnell	Y	Y	Y	Y	Y	Y
Paul	Y	Y	Y	Y	Y	Y
LOUISIANA						
Cassidy	Y	Y	Y	Y	Y	Y
Kennedy	Y	Y	Y	Y	Y	Y
MAINE						
Collins	Y	Y	Y	Y	Y	Y
King	Y	Y	Y	Y	Y	Y
MARYLAND						
Cardin	Y	Y	Y	Y	Y	Y
Van Hollen	Y	Y	N	N	Y	N
MASSACHUSETTS						
Warren	?	?	?	?	?	?
Markey	N	N	N	N	Y	N
MICHIGAN						
Stabenow	Y	Y	N	Y	Y	Y
Peters	Y	Y	Y	Y	Y	Y
MINNESOTA						
Klobuchar	?	?	N	N	?	N
Smith	Y	Y	N	N	Y	N
MISSISSIPPI						
Wicker	Y	Y	Y	Y	Y	Y
Hyde-Smith	Y	Y	Y	Y	Y	Y
MISSOURI						
Blunt	Y	Y	Y	Y	Y	Y
Hawley	Y	Y	Y	Y	Y	Y

	373	374	375	376	377	378
MONTANA						
Tester	Y	Y	Y	Y	Y	Y
Daines	Y	Y	Y	Y	Y	Y
NEBRASKA						
Fischer	Y	Y	Y	Y	Y	Y
Sasse	Y	Y	Y	Y	Y	Y
NEVADA						
Cortez Masto	Y	Y	N	Y	Y	Y
Rosen	Y	Y	Y	Y	Y	Y
NEW HAMPSHIRE						
Shaheen	Y	Y	Y	Y	Y	Y
Hassan	Y	Y	Y	Y	Y	Y
NEW JERSEY						
Menendez	Y	Y	N	Y	Y	N
Booker	?	?	?	?	?	?
NEW MEXICO						
Udall	Y	Y	N	Y	Y	N
Heinrich	Y	Y	N	Y	Y	N
NEW YORK						
Schumer	Y	Y	N	N	Y	Y
Gillibrand	N	N	N	N	Y	N
NORTH CAROLINA						
Burr	Y	Y	Y	Y	Y	Y
Tillis	Y	Y	Y	Y	Y	Y
NORTH DAKOTA						
Hoeven	Y	Y	Y	Y	Y	Y
Cramer	Y	Y	Y	Y	Y	Y
OHIO						
Brown	Y	Y	N	N	Y	N
Portman	Y	Y	Y	Y	Y	Y
OKLAHOMA						
Inhofe	Y	Y	Y	Y	Y	Y
Lankford	Y	Y	Y	Y	Y	Y
OREGON						
Wyden	Y	Y	N	Y	Y	N
Merkley	N	N	N	N	Y	N
PENNSYLVANIA						
Casey	Y	Y	Y	Y	Y	Y
Toomey	Y	Y	Y	Y	Y	Y
RHODE ISLAND						
Reed	Y	Y	Y	Y	Y	Y
Whitehouse	Y	Y	N	Y	Y	Y
SOUTH CAROLINA						
Graham	Y	Y	Y	Y	Y	Y
Scott	Y	Y	Y	Y	Y	Y
SOUTH DAKOTA						
Thune	Y	Y	Y	Y	Y	Y
Rounds	?	?	?	?	?	?
TENNESSEE						
Alexander	Y	Y	Y	Y	Y	Y
Blackburn	Y	Y	Y	Y	Y	Y
TEXAS						
Cornyn	Y	Y	Y	Y	Y	Y
Cruz	Y	Y	Y	Y	Y	Y
UTAH						
Lee	Y	Y	Y	Y	Y	Y
Romney	Y	Y	Y	Y	Y	Y
VERMONT						
Leahy	Y	Y	Y	Y	Y	Y
Sanders	?	?	?	?	?	?
VIRGINIA						
Warner	Y	Y	Y	Y	Y	Y
Kaine	Y	Y	Y	Y	Y	Y
WASHINGTON						
Murray	Y	Y	N	N	Y	N
Cantwell	Y	Y	N	N	Y	N
WEST VIRGINIA						
Manchin	Y	Y	Y	Y	Y	Y
Capito	Y	Y	Y	Y	Y	Y
WISCONSIN						
Johnson	Y	Y	Y	Y	Y	Y
Baldwin	Y	Y	N	Y	Y	Y
WYOMING						
Enzi	Y	Y	Y	Y	Y	Y
Barrasso	Y	Y	Y	Y	Y	Y

KEY:	Republicans	Democrats	*Independents*

Y Voted for (yea)	**N** Voted against (nay)	**P** Voted "present"
+ Announced for	**−** Announced against	**?** Did not vote or otherwise make position known
# Paired for	**X** Paired against	

379. Pitlyk Nomination - Confirmation. Confirmation of President Trump's nomination of Sarah E. Pitlyk of Missouri to be a U.S. district judge for the Eastern District of Missouri. Confirmed 49-44: R 49-1; D 0-42; I 0-1. *Note: A "yea" was a vote in support of the president's position.* Dec. 04, 2019.

380. Cole Nomination - Confirmation. Confirmation of President Trump's nomination of Douglas Russell Cole of Ohio to be a U.S. district judge for the Southern District of Ohio. Confirmed 64-29: R 50-0; D 13-29; I 1-0. *Note: A "yea" was a vote in support of the president's position.* Dec. 04, 2019.

381. Huffaker Nomination - Confirmation. Confirmation of President Trump's nomination of R. Austin Huffaker, Jr. of Alabama to be a U.S. district judge for the Middle District of Alabama. Confirmed 89-4: R 50-0; D 38-4; I 1-0. *Note: A "yea" was a vote in support of the president's position.* Dec. 04, 2019.

382. Barlow Nomination - Confirmation. Confirmation of President Trump's nomination of David B. Barlow of Utah to be a U.S. district judge for the District of Utah. Confirmed 88-4: R 49-0; D 38-4; I 1-0. *Note: A "yea" was a vote in support of the president's position.* Dec. 04, 2019.

383. Myers Nomination - Confirmation. Confirmation of President Trump's nomination of Richard Ernest Myers II of North Carolina to be a U.S. district judge for the Eastern District of North Carolina. Confirmed 68-21: R 47-0; D 20-21; I 1-0. *Note: A "yea" was a vote in support of the president's position.* Dec. 05, 2019.

384. Lydon Nomination - Confirmation. Confirmation of President Trump's nomination of Sherri A. Lydon of South Carolina to be a U.S. district judge for the District of South Carolina. Confirmed 76-13: R 47-0; D 28-13; I 1-0. *Note: A "yea" was a vote in support of the president's position.* Dec. 05, 2019.

	379	380	381	382	383	384		379	380	381	382	383	384
ALABAMA							**MONTANA**						
Shelby	Y	Y	Y	Y	Y	Y	Tester	N	N	Y	Y	Y	Y
Jones	N	Y	Y	Y	Y	Y	Daines	Y	Y	Y	Y	Y	Y
ALASKA							**NEBRASKA**						
Murkowski	-	?	?	?	?	?	Fischer	Y	Y	Y	Y	Y	Y
Sullivan	Y	Y	Y	Y	Y	Y	Sasse	Y	Y	Y	Y	Y	Y
ARIZONA							**NEVADA**						
Sinema	N	Y	Y	Y	Y	Y	Cortez Masto	N	N	Y	Y	N	Y
McSally	Y	Y	Y	Y	Y	Y	Rosen	N	N	Y	Y	Y	Y
ARKANSAS							**NEW HAMPSHIRE**						
Boozman	Y	Y	Y	Y	Y	Y	Shaheen	N	N	Y	Y	Y	Y
Cotton	Y	Y	Y	Y	Y	Y	Hassan	N	Y	Y	Y	Y	Y
CALIFORNIA							**NEW JERSEY**						
Feinstein	N	N	Y	Y	Y	Y	Menendez	N	N	Y	Y	N	Y
Harris	-	-	-	-	-	-	Booker	?	?	?	?	?	?
COLORADO							**NEW MEXICO**						
Bennet	N	N	Y	Y	N	N	Udall	N	N	Y	Y	N	N
Gardner	Y	Y	Y	Y	Y	Y	Heinrich	N	N	Y	Y	N	Y
CONNECTICUT							**NEW YORK**						
Blumenthal	N	N	Y	Y	N	N	Schumer	N	N	Y	Y	N	N
Murphy	N	Y	Y	Y	Y	Y	Gillibrand	N	N	N	N	N	N
DELAWARE							**NORTH CAROLINA**						
Carper	N	Y	Y	Y	Y	Y	Burr	Y	Y	Y	Y	Y	Y
Coons	N	Y	Y	Y	Y	Y	Tillis	Y	Y	Y	?	Y	Y
FLORIDA							**NORTH DAKOTA**						
Rubio	Y	Y	Y	Y	Y	Y	Hoeven	Y	Y	Y	Y	Y	Y
Scott	Y	Y	Y	Y	Y	Y	Cramer	Y	Y	Y	Y	Y	Y
GEORGIA							**OHIO**						
Isakson	?	Y	Y	Y	?	?	Brown	N	N	Y	Y	N	N
Perdue	Y	Y	Y	Y	?	?	Portman	Y	Y	Y	Y	Y	Y
HAWAII							**OKLAHOMA**						
Schatz	N	N	Y	Y	N	N	Inhofe	Y	Y	Y	Y	Y	Y
Hirono	N	N	Y	Y	N	N	Lankford	Y	Y	Y	Y	Y	Y
IDAHO							**OREGON**						
Crapo	Y	Y	Y	Y	Y	Y	Wyden	N	N	Y	Y	N	Y
Risch	Y	Y	Y	Y	Y	Y	Merkley	N	N	N	N	N	N
ILLINOIS							**PENNSYLVANIA**						
Durbin	N	Y	Y	Y	Y	Y	Casey	N	Y	Y	Y	Y	Y
Duckworth	N	N	Y	Y	Y	Y	Toomey	Y	Y	Y	Y	Y	Y
INDIANA							**RHODE ISLAND**						
Young	Y	Y	Y	Y	Y	Y	Reed	N	Y	Y	Y	Y	Y
Braun	Y	Y	Y	Y	Y	Y	Whitehouse	N	Y	Y	Y	N	Y
IOWA							**SOUTH CAROLINA**						
Grassley	Y	Y	Y	Y	Y	Y	Graham	Y	Y	Y	Y	Y	Y
Ernst	Y	Y	Y	Y	Y	Y	Scott	Y	Y	Y	Y	Y	Y
KANSAS							**SOUTH DAKOTA**						
Roberts	Y	Y	Y	Y	Y	Y	Thune	Y	Y	Y	Y	Y	Y
Moran	Y	Y	Y	Y	+	?	Rounds	?	?	?	?	?	?
KENTUCKY							**TENNESSEE**						
McConnell	Y	Y	Y	Y	Y	Y	Alexander	Y	Y	Y	Y	Y	Y
Paul	Y	Y	Y	Y	?	?	Blackburn	Y	Y	Y	Y	Y	Y
LOUISIANA							**TEXAS**						
Cassidy	Y	Y	Y	Y	Y	Y	Cornyn	Y	Y	Y	Y	Y	Y
Kennedy	Y	Y	Y	Y	Y	Y	Cruz	Y	Y	Y	Y	Y	Y
MAINE							**UTAH**						
Collins	N	Y	Y	Y	Y	Y	Lee	Y	Y	Y	Y	Y	Y
King	N	Y	Y	Y	Y	Y	Romney	Y	Y	Y	Y	Y	Y
MARYLAND							**VERMONT**						
Cardin	N	N	Y	Y	Y	Y	Leahy	N	Y	Y	Y	Y	Y
Van Hollen	N	N	Y	Y	N	N	*Sanders*	?	?	?	?	?	?
MASSACHUSETTS							**VIRGINIA**						
Warren	?	?	?	?	?	?	Warner	N	N	Y	Y	Y	Y
Markey	N	N	N	N	N	N	Kaine	N	N	Y	Y	Y	Y
MICHIGAN							**WASHINGTON**						
Stabenow	N	N	Y	Y	N	N	Murray	N	N	Y	Y	N	N
Peters	N	N	Y	Y	Y	Y	Cantwell	N	N	Y	Y	N	N
MINNESOTA							**WEST VIRGINIA**						
Klobuchar	N	N	N	N	?	?	Manchin	N	Y	Y	Y	Y	Y
Smith	N	N	Y	Y	N	N	Capito	Y	Y	Y	Y	Y	Y
MISSISSIPPI							**WISCONSIN**						
Wicker	Y	Y	Y	Y	Y	Y	Johnson	Y	+	+	+	Y	Y
Hyde-Smith	Y	Y	Y	Y	Y	Y	Baldwin	N	N	Y	Y	N	Y
MISSOURI							**WYOMING**						
Blunt	Y	Y	Y	Y	Y	Y	Enzi	Y	Y	Y	Y	Y	Y
Hawley	Y	Y	Y	Y	Y	Y	Barrasso	Y	Y	Y	Y	Y	Y

KEY:	Republicans	Democrats	*Independents*
Y Voted for (yea)	**N** Voted against (nay)	**P** Voted "present"	
+ Announced for	**-** Announced against	**?** Did not vote or otherwise	
# Paired for	**X** Paired against	make position known	

385. Duncan Nomination - Confirmation. Confirmation of President Trump's nomination of Robert M. Duncan to be a governor of the U.S. Postal Service. Confirmed 89-0: R 47-0; D 41-0; I 1-0. *Note: A "yea" was a vote in support of the president's position. Dec. 05, 2019.*

386. Bumatay Nomination - Cloture. Motion to invoke cloture (thus limiting debate) on the nomination of Patrick J. Bumatay of California to be a U.S. circuit judge for the Ninth Circuit. Motion agreed to 47-41: R 47-0; D 0-40; I 0-1. *Note: A majority of senators voting (45 in this case), a quorum being present, is required to invoke cloture on all nominations. Dec. 09, 2019.*

387. Bumatay Nomination - Confirmation. Confirmation of President Trump's nomination of Patrick J. Bumatay of California to be a U.S. circuit judge for the Ninth Circuit. Confirmed 53-40: R 53-0; D 0-39; I 0-1. *Note: A "yea" was a vote in support of the president's position. Dec. 10, 2019.*

388. VanDyke Nomination - Cloture. Motion to invoke cloture (thus limiting debate) on the nomination of Lawrence VanDyke of Nevada to be a U.S. circuit judge for the Ninth Circuit. Motion agreed to 53-40: R 53-0; D 0-39; I 0-1. *Note: A majority of senators voting (47 in this case), a quorum being present, is required to invoke cloture on all nominations. Dec. 10, 2019.*

389. S2740. Over-the-Counter Drug Policies - Passage. Passage of the bill that would set rules, regulations, and fees on over-the-counter drugs. Among other provisions, the bill would regulate non-prescription drugs marketed without an approved drug application by testing their conformity to a tentative final monograph, which is a checklist the Food and Drug Administration uses to assist in designating non-prescription drugs as safe and effective. Passed 91-2: R 51-2; D 39-0; I 1-0. Dec. 10, 2019.

390. HR2333. Statistics on Suicide Prevention Coordinators - Passage. Passage of the bill that would require the Government Accountability Office to submit a report to Congress within one year of enactment assessing the responsibilities, workload, training, and vacancy rates of Veterans Affairs Department suicide prevention coordinators, including a determination of the extent of oversight of such coordinators and the extent to which their use and staffing varies between different VA facilities. Passed (thus cleared for the president) 95-0: R 52-0; D 42-0; I 1-0. Dec. 11, 2019.

	385	386	387	388	389	390
ALABAMA						
Shelby	Y	Y	Y	Y	Y	Y
Jones	Y	N	N	N	Y	Y
ALASKA						
Murkowski	?	Y	Y	Y	Y	Y
Sullivan	Y	Y	Y	Y	Y	Y
ARIZONA						
Sinema	Y	N	N	N	N	Y
McSally	Y	Y	Y	Y	Y	Y
ARKANSAS						
Boozman	Y	Y	Y	Y	Y	Y
Cotton	Y	Y	Y	Y	Y	Y
CALIFORNIA						
Feinstein	Y	N	N	N	Y	Y
Harris	?	-	?	?	?	Y
COLORADO						
Bennet	Y	?	?	?	?	?
Gardner	Y	Y	Y	Y	Y	Y
CONNECTICUT						
Blumenthal	Y	N	N	N	Y	Y
Murphy	Y	N	N	N	Y	Y
DELAWARE						
Carper	Y	N	N	N	Y	Y
Coons	Y	N	N	N	Y	Y
FLORIDA						
Rubio	Y	+	Y	Y	Y	Y
Scott	Y	Y	Y	Y	N	Y
GEORGIA						
Isakson	?	Y	Y	Y	Y	Y
Perdue	?	Y	Y	Y	Y	Y
HAWAII						
Schatz	Y	N	N	N	Y	Y
Hirono	Y	N	N	N	Y	Y
IDAHO						
Crapo	Y	Y	Y	Y	Y	Y
Risch	Y	?	Y	Y	Y	Y
ILLINOIS						
Durbin	Y	N	N	N	Y	Y
Duckworth	Y	N	N	N	Y	Y
INDIANA						
Young	Y	Y	Y	Y	Y	Y
Braun	Y	Y	Y	Y	Y	Y
IOWA						
Grassley	Y	Y	Y	Y	Y	Y
Ernst	Y	Y	Y	Y	Y	Y
KANSAS						
Roberts	Y	Y	Y	Y	Y	Y
Moran	+	Y	Y	Y	Y	Y
KENTUCKY						
McConnell	Y	Y	Y	Y	Y	Y
Paul	?	Y	Y	Y	Y	?
LOUISIANA						
Cassidy	Y	Y	Y	Y	Y	Y
Kennedy	Y	Y	Y	Y	Y	Y
MAINE						
Collins	Y	Y	Y	Y	Y	Y
King	Y	N	N	N	Y	Y
MARYLAND						
Cardin	Y	N	N	N	Y	Y
Van Hollen	Y	N	N	N	Y	Y
MASSACHUSETTS						
Warren	?	?	?	?	?	?
Markey	Y	N	N	N	Y	Y
MICHIGAN						
Stabenow	Y	N	N	N	Y	Y
Peters	Y	N	N	N	Y	Y
MINNESOTA						
Klobuchar	?	?	?	?	?	Y
Smith	Y	N	N	N	Y	Y
MISSISSIPPI						
Wicker	Y	Y	Y	Y	Y	Y
Hyde-Smith	Y	Y	Y	Y	Y	Y
MISSOURI						
Blunt	Y	Y	Y	Y	Y	Y
Hawley	Y	Y	Y	Y	Y	Y

	385	386	387	388	389	390
MONTANA						
Tester	Y	N	N	N	Y	Y
Daines	Y	Y	Y	Y	Y	Y
NEBRASKA						
Fischer	Y	Y	Y	Y	Y	Y
Sasse	Y	?	Y	Y	Y	Y
NEVADA						
Cortez Masto	Y	N	N	N	Y	Y
Rosen	Y	N	N	N	Y	Y
NEW HAMPSHIRE						
Shaheen	Y	N	N	N	Y	Y
Hassan	Y	N	N	N	Y	Y
NEW JERSEY						
Menendez	Y	N	N	N	Y	Y
Booker	?	?	?	?	?	?
NEW MEXICO						
Udall	Y	N	N	N	Y	Y
Heinrich	Y	N	N	N	Y	Y
NEW YORK						
Schumer	Y	N	N	N	Y	Y
Gillibrand	Y	N	N	N	Y	Y
NORTH CAROLINA						
Burr	Y	Y	Y	Y	N	Y
Tillis	Y	Y	Y	Y	Y	Y
NORTH DAKOTA						
Hoeven	Y	Y	Y	Y	Y	Y
Cramer	Y	Y	Y	Y	Y	Y
OHIO						
Brown	Y	N	N	N	Y	Y
Portman	Y	Y	Y	Y	Y	Y
OKLAHOMA						
Inhofe	Y	Y	Y	Y	Y	Y
Lankford	Y	Y	Y	Y	Y	Y
OREGON						
Wyden	Y	N	N	N	Y	Y
Merkley	Y	N	N	N	Y	Y
PENNSYLVANIA						
Casey	Y	N	N	N	Y	Y
Toomey	Y	Y	Y	Y	Y	Y
RHODE ISLAND						
Reed	Y	N	N	N	Y	Y
Whitehouse	Y	N	N	N	Y	Y
SOUTH CAROLINA						
Graham	Y	Y	Y	Y	Y	Y
Scott	Y	?	Y	Y	Y	Y
SOUTH DAKOTA						
Thune	Y	Y	Y	Y	Y	Y
Rounds	?	?	Y	Y	Y	Y
TENNESSEE						
Alexander	Y	+	Y	Y	Y	Y
Blackburn	Y	Y	Y	Y	Y	Y
TEXAS						
Cornyn	Y	Y	Y	Y	Y	Y
Cruz	Y	Y	Y	Y	Y	Y
UTAH						
Lee	Y	Y	Y	Y	Y	Y
Romney	Y	Y	Y	Y	Y	Y
VERMONT						
Leahy	Y	N	N	N	Y	Y
Sanders	?	?	?	?	?	?
VIRGINIA						
Warner	Y	N	?	?	?	Y
Kaine	Y	N	N	N	Y	Y
WASHINGTON						
Murray	Y	N	N	N	Y	Y
Cantwell	Y	N	N	N	Y	Y
WEST VIRGINIA						
Manchin	Y	N	N	N	Y	Y
Capito	Y	Y	Y	Y	Y	Y
WISCONSIN						
Johnson	Y	Y	Y	Y	Y	Y
Baldwin	Y	N	N	N	Y	Y
WYOMING						
Enzi	Y	Y	Y	Y	Y	Y
Barrasso	Y	Y	Y	Y	Y	Y

KEY: Republicans Democrats *Independents*

Y Voted for (yea)	N Voted against (nay)	P Voted "present"
+ Announced for	- Announced against	? Did not vote or otherwise make position known
# Paired for	X Paired against	

391. VanDyke Nomination - Confirmation. Confirmation of President Trump's nomination of Lawrence VanDyke of Nevada to be a U.S. circuit judge for the Ninth Circuit. Confirmed 51-44: R 51-1; D 0-42; I 0-1. *Note: A "yea" was a vote in support of the president's position.* Dec. 11, 2019.

392. Sullivan Nomination - Cloture. Motion to invoke cloture (thus limiting debate) on the nomination of John Joseph Sullivan of Maryland to be ambassador to Russia. Motion agreed to 69-25: R 51-0; D 17-25; I 1-0. *Note: A majority of senators voting (48 in this case), a quorum being present, is required to invoke cloture on all nominations.* Dec. 11, 2019.

393. Hahn Nomination - Cloture. Motion to invoke cloture (thus limiting debate) on the nomination of Stephen Hahn of Texas to be commissioner of Food and Drugs for the Department of Health and Human Services. Motion agreed to 74-19: R 50-0; D 23-19; I 1-0. *Note: A majority of senators voting (47 in this case), a quorum being present, is required to invoke cloture on all nominations.* Dec. 11, 2019.

394. Skipwith Nomination - Cloture. Motion to invoke cloture (thus limiting debate) on the nomination of Aurelia Skipwith of Indiana to be director of the U.S. Fish and Wildlife Service. Motion agreed to 53-41: R 50-0; D 3-40; I 0-1. *Note: A majority of senators voting (48 in this case), a quorum being present, is required to invoke cloture on all nominations.* Dec. 11, 2019.

395. Skipwith Nomination - Confirmation. Confirmation of President Trump's nomination of Aurelia Skipwith of Indiana to be director of the U.S. Fish and Wildlife Service. Confirmed 52-39: R 49-0; D 3-38; I 0-1. *Note: A "yea" was a vote in support of the president's position.* Dec. 12, 2019.

396. Sullivan Nomination - Confirmation. Confirmation of President Trump's nomination of John Joseph Sullivan of Maryland to be ambassador to Russia. Confirmed 70-22: R 50-0; D 19-22; I 1-0. *Note: A "yea" was a vote in support of the president's position.* Dec. 12, 2019.

	391	392	393	394	395	396
ALABAMA						
Shelby	Y	Y	Y	Y	?	Y
Jones	N	Y	Y	Y	Y	Y
ALASKA						
Murkowski	Y	Y	Y	Y	Y	Y
Sullivan	Y	Y	Y	Y	Y	Y
ARIZONA						
Sinema	N	Y	Y	Y	Y	Y
McSally	Y	Y	Y	Y	Y	Y
ARKANSAS						
Boozman	Y	Y	Y	Y	Y	Y
Cotton	Y	Y	Y	Y	Y	Y
CALIFORNIA						
Feinstein	N	Y	Y	N	N	Y
Harris	N	N	N	N	N	N
COLORADO						
Bennet	?	?	?	N	N	N
Gardner	Y	Y	Y	Y	Y	Y
CONNECTICUT						
Blumenthal	N	N	N	N	N	N
Murphy	N	Y	Y	N	N	Y
DELAWARE						
Carper	N	Y	Y	N	N	Y
Coons	N	Y	Y	N	N	Y
FLORIDA						
Rubio	Y	Y	Y	Y	Y	Y
Scott	Y	Y	Y	Y	Y	Y
GEORGIA						
Isakson	Y	Y	?	?	?	?
Perdue	Y	Y	Y	Y	Y	Y
HAWAII						
Schatz	N	N	N	N	N	N
Hirono	N	N	N	N	N	N
IDAHO						
Crapo	Y	Y	Y	Y	Y	Y
Risch	Y	Y	Y	Y	Y	Y
ILLINOIS						
Durbin	N	N	Y	N	N	Y
Duckworth	N	N	N	N	?	?
INDIANA						
Young	Y	Y	Y	Y	Y	Y
Braun	Y	Y	Y	Y	Y	Y
IOWA						
Grassley	Y	Y	Y	Y	Y	Y
Ernst	Y	Y	Y	Y	Y	Y
KANSAS						
Roberts	Y	Y	Y	Y	Y	Y
Moran	Y	Y	Y	Y	Y	Y
KENTUCKY						
McConnell	Y	Y	Y	Y	Y	Y
Paul	?	?	?	?	?	?
LOUISIANA						
Cassidy	Y	Y	Y	Y	Y	Y
Kennedy	Y	Y	Y	Y	Y	Y
MAINE						
Collins	N	Y	Y	Y	Y	Y
King	N	Y	Y	N	N	Y
MARYLAND						
Cardin	N	Y	Y	N	N	Y
Van Hollen	N	Y	Y	N	N	Y
MASSACHUSETTS						
Warren	?	?	?	?	?	?
Markey	N	N	N	N	N	N
MICHIGAN						
Stabenow	N	N	N	N	N	N
Peters	N	N	Y	N	N	N
MINNESOTA						
Klobuchar	N	N	N	N	?	?
Smith	N	N	N	N	N	N
MISSISSIPPI						
Wicker	Y	Y	Y	Y	Y	Y
Hyde-Smith	Y	Y	Y	Y	Y	Y
MISSOURI						
Blunt	Y	Y	Y	Y	Y	Y
Hawley	Y	Y	Y	Y	Y	Y

	391	392	393	394	395	396
MONTANA						
Tester	N	Y	Y	N	N	Y
Daines	Y	Y	Y	Y	Y	Y
NEBRASKA						
Fischer	Y	Y	Y	Y	Y	Y
Sasse	Y	Y	Y	Y	Y	Y
NEVADA						
Cortez Masto	N	Y	Y	N	N	Y
Rosen	N	Y	Y	N	N	Y
NEW HAMPSHIRE						
Shaheen	N	N	Y	N	N	Y
Hassan	N	Y	N	N	N	Y
NEW JERSEY						
Menendez	N	N	Y	N	N	N
Booker	?	?	?	?	-	?
NEW MEXICO						
Udall	N	N	N	N	N	Y
Heinrich	N	N	N	N	N	N
NEW YORK						
Schumer	N	N	N	N	N	N
Gillibrand	N	N	N	N	N	N
NORTH CAROLINA						
Burr	Y	?	?	?	?	?
Tillis	Y	Y	Y	Y	Y	Y
NORTH DAKOTA						
Hoeven	Y	Y	Y	Y	Y	Y
Cramer	Y	Y	Y	Y	Y	Y
OHIO						
Brown	N	N	Y	N	N	N
Portman	Y	Y	Y	Y	Y	Y
OKLAHOMA						
Inhofe	Y	Y	Y	Y	Y	Y
Lankford	Y	Y	Y	Y	Y	Y
OREGON						
Wyden	N	N	Y	N	N	N
Merkley	N	Y	N	N	N	Y
PENNSYLVANIA						
Casey	N	N	Y	N	N	N
Toomey	Y	Y	Y	Y	Y	Y
RHODE ISLAND						
Reed	N	N	N	N	N	N
Whitehouse	N	N	Y	N	N	N
SOUTH CAROLINA						
Graham	Y	Y	Y	Y	Y	Y
Scott	Y	Y	Y	Y	Y	Y
SOUTH DAKOTA						
Thune	Y	Y	Y	Y	Y	Y
Rounds	Y	Y	Y	Y	Y	Y
TENNESSEE						
Alexander	Y	Y	Y	Y	Y	Y
Blackburn	Y	Y	Y	Y	Y	Y
TEXAS						
Cornyn	Y	Y	Y	Y	Y	Y
Cruz	Y	Y	Y	Y	Y	Y
UTAH						
Lee	Y	Y	Y	Y	Y	Y
Romney	Y	Y	Y	Y	Y	Y
VERMONT						
Leahy	N	Y	N	N	N	Y
Sanders	?	?	?	?	?	?
VIRGINIA						
Warner	N	N	Y	N	N	N
Kaine	N	Y	Y	N	N	Y
WASHINGTON						
Murray	N	N	N	N	N	N
Cantwell	N	N	N	N	N	N
WEST VIRGINIA						
Manchin	N	Y	Y	Y	Y	Y
Capito	Y	Y	Y	Y	Y	Y
WISCONSIN						
Johnson	Y	Y	Y	Y	Y	Y
Baldwin	N	N	Y	N	N	Y
WYOMING						
Enzi	Y	Y	Y	Y	Y	Y
Barrasso	Y	Y	Y	Y	Y	Y

KEY:	Republicans	Democrats	*Independents*

Y	Voted for (yea)	N	Voted against (nay)	P	Voted "present"
+	Announced for	-	Announced against	?	Did not vote or otherwise
#	Paired for	X	Paired against		make position known

397. Hahn Nomination - Confirmation. Confirmation of President Trump's nomination of Stephen Hahn to be commissioner of Food and Drugs for the Department of Health and Human Services. Confirmed 72-18: R 49-0; D 23-17; I 0-1. *Note: A "yea" was a vote in support of the president's position.* Dec. 12, 2019.

398. S1790. Fiscal 2020 Defense Authorization - Cloture. McConnell, R-Ky., motion to invoke cloture (thus limiting debate) on the conference report for the fiscal 2020 National Defense Authorization Act that would authorize, in total, $738 billion in discretionary defense spending, including $256.7 billion for Defense Department operations and maintenance, including operations in Afghanistan and Syria, $143 billion for weapons and other procurement, and $188 billion for personnel-related expenses. Within the total, the bill would authorize $71.5 billion for overseas contingency operations not subject to discretionary spending caps. Motion agreed to 76-6: R 41-4; D 34-2; I 1-0. *Note: Three-fifths of the total Senate (60) is required to invoke cloture.* Dec. 16, 2019.

399. S1790. Fiscal 2020 Defense Authorization - Motion to Waive. Inhofe, R-Okla., motion to waive applicable sections of the 2016 Budget Resolution with respect to the conference report for the fiscal 2020 National Defense Authorization Act that would authorize, in total, $738 billion in discretionary defense spending, including $256.7 billion for Defense Department operations and maintenance, including operations in Afghanistan and Syria, $143 billion for weapons and other procurement, and $188 billion for personnel-related expenses. Within the total, the bill would authorize $71.5 billion for overseas contingency operations not subject to discretionary spending caps. Motion agreed to 82-12: R 43-9; D 38-3; I 1-0. *Note: Three-fifths of the total Senate (60) is required to waive the 2016 Budget Resolution.* Dec. 17, 2019.

400. S1790. Fiscal 2020 Defense Authorization - Conference Report. Adoption of the conference report to accompany the bill that would authorize, in total, $738 billion in discretionary defense spending, including $256.7 billion for Defense Department operations and maintenance, including operations in Afghanistan and Syria, $143 billion for weapons and other procurement, and $188 billion for personnel-related expenses. It would authorize the creation of a Space Force within the Air Force; authorize funds for the deployment of the low-yield, submarine-launched W76-2 nuclear; and prohibit the transfer of F-35 aircraft to Turkey unless the Turkish government certifies that it will not purchase S-400 air defense technology from Russia. It would require the Defense Department to submit a number of reports on the effects of climate change and develop a climate vulnerability and risk-assessment tool. It would prohibit the use of any funds authorized to withdraw the U.S. from NATO; prohibit the use of funds authorized to close the U.S. naval station in Guantanamo Bay, Cuba; and extend prohibitions on the transfer of detainees from Guantanamo Bay to certain other countries. Adopted (thus cleared for the president) 86-8: R 48-4; D 37-4; I 1-0. *Note: A "yea" was a vote in support of the president's position.* Dec. 17, 2019.

401. McFarland Nomination - Cloture. Motion to invoke cloture (thus limiting debate) on the nomination of Matthew Walden McFarland of Ohio to be a U.S. district judge for the Southern District of Ohio. Motion agreed to 55-38: R 51-0; D 4-37; I 0-1. *Note: A majority of senators voting (47 in this case), a quorum being present, is required to invoke cloture on all nominations.* Dec. 18, 2019.

402. McFarland Nomination - Confirmation. Confirmation of President Trump's nomination of Matthew Walden McFarland of Ohio to be a U.S. district judge for the Southern District of Ohio. Confirmed 56-38: R 52-0; D 4-37; I 0-1. *Note: A "yea" was a vote in support of the president's position.* Dec. 18, 2019.

Senator	397	398	399	400	401	402
ALABAMA						
Shelby	Y	Y	Y	Y	Y	Y
Jones	Y	Y	Y	Y	Y	Y
ALASKA						
Murkowski	Y	Y	Y	Y	Y	Y
Sullivan	Y	Y	Y	Y	Y	Y
ARIZONA						
Sinema	Y	Y	Y	Y	Y	Y
McSally	Y	Y	Y	Y	Y	Y
ARKANSAS						
Boozman	Y	Y	Y	Y	Y	Y
Cotton	Y	Y	Y	Y	Y	Y
CALIFORNIA						
Feinstein	Y	Y	Y	Y	N	N
Harris	?	?	?	?	-	-
COLORADO						
Bennet	Y	?	Y	Y	N	N
Gardner	Y	Y	Y	Y	Y	Y
CONNECTICUT						
Blumenthal	N	Y	Y	Y	N	N
Murphy	Y	Y	Y	Y	N	N
DELAWARE						
Carper	Y	N	Y	Y	N	N
Coons	Y	Y	Y	Y	N	N
FLORIDA						
Rubio	Y	Y	Y	Y	Y	Y
Scott	Y	Y	Y	Y	Y	Y
GEORGIA						
Isakson	?	?	?	?	?	?
Perdue	Y	?	Y	Y	Y	Y
HAWAII						
Schatz	N	Y	Y	Y	N	N
Hirono	N	Y	Y	Y	N	N
IDAHO						
Crapo	Y	Y	Y	Y	Y	Y
Risch	Y	Y	Y	Y	Y	Y
ILLINOIS						
Durbin	Y	Y	Y	Y	N	N
Duckworth	?	?	Y	Y	N	N
INDIANA						
Young	Y	Y	Y	Y	Y	Y
Braun	Y	N	N	N	Y	Y
IOWA						
Grassley	Y	Y	Y	Y	Y	Y
Ernst	Y	Y	Y	Y	Y	Y
KANSAS						
Roberts	Y	Y	Y	Y	Y	Y
Moran	?	Y	Y	Y	Y	Y
KENTUCKY						
McConnell	Y	Y	Y	Y	Y	Y
Paul	?	N	N	N	Y	Y
LOUISIANA						
Cassidy	Y	?	N	Y	Y	Y
Kennedy	Y	?	N	Y	Y	Y
MAINE						
Collins	Y	Y	Y	Y	Y	Y
King	N	Y	Y	Y	N	N
MARYLAND						
Cardin	Y	Y	Y	Y	N	N
Van Hollen	Y	Y	Y	Y	N	N
MASSACHUSETTS						
Warren	?	?	?	?	?	?
Markey	N	?	N	N	N	N
MICHIGAN						
Stabenow	N	Y	Y	Y	N	N
Peters	Y	Y	Y	Y	N	N
MINNESOTA						
Klobuchar	?	?	?	?	?	?
Smith	N	Y	Y	Y	N	N
MISSISSIPPI						
Wicker	Y	Y	Y	Y	Y	Y
Hyde-Smith	Y	Y	Y	Y	Y	Y
MISSOURI						
Blunt	Y	Y	Y	Y	Y	Y
Hawley	Y	Y	Y	Y	Y	Y
MONTANA						
Tester	Y	Y	Y	Y	N	N
Daines	Y	?	Y	Y	Y	Y
NEBRASKA						
Fischer	Y	Y	Y	Y	Y	Y
Sasse	Y	?	Y	Y	Y	Y
NEVADA						
Cortez Masto	Y	Y	Y	Y	N	N
Rosen	Y	Y	Y	Y	N	N
NEW HAMPSHIRE						
Shaheen	Y	Y	Y	Y	N	N
Hassan	N	Y	Y	Y	N	N
NEW JERSEY						
Menendez	Y	Y	Y	Y	N	N
Booker	?	?	?	?	?	?
NEW MEXICO						
Udall	N	Y	Y	Y	N	N
Heinrich	N	Y	Y	Y	N	N
NEW YORK						
Schumer	N	Y	Y	Y	N	N
Gillibrand	N	N	N	N	N	N
NORTH CAROLINA						
Burr	?	Y	Y	Y	?	Y
Tillis	Y	Y	Y	Y	Y	Y
NORTH DAKOTA						
Hoeven	Y	Y	Y	Y	Y	Y
Cramer	Y	Y	Y	Y	Y	Y
OHIO						
Brown	Y	Y	Y	Y	Y	Y
Portman	Y	Y	Y	Y	Y	Y
OKLAHOMA						
Inhofe	Y	Y	Y	Y	Y	Y
Lankford	Y	Y	Y	Y	Y	Y
OREGON						
Wyden	N	?	N	N	N	N
Merkley	N	?	Y	N	N	N
PENNSYLVANIA						
Casey	Y	Y	Y	Y	N	N
Toomey	Y	?	N	Y	N	Y
RHODE ISLAND						
Reed	N	Y	Y	Y	N	N
Whitehouse	Y	Y	Y	Y	N	N
SOUTH CAROLINA						
Graham	Y	?	Y	Y	Y	Y
Scott	Y	Y	Y	Y	Y	Y
SOUTH DAKOTA						
Thune	Y	Y	Y	Y	Y	Y
Rounds	Y	Y	Y	Y	Y	Y
TENNESSEE						
Alexander	Y	Y	Y	Y	Y	Y
Blackburn	Y	Y	Y	Y	Y	Y
TEXAS						
Cornyn	Y	Y	Y	Y	Y	Y
Cruz	Y	Y	Y	Y	Y	Y
UTAH						
Lee	Y	N	N	N	Y	Y
Romney	Y	Y	N	Y	Y	Y
VERMONT						
Leahy	N	Y	Y	Y	N	N
Sanders	?	?	?	?	?	?
VIRGINIA						
Warner	Y	Y	Y	Y	Y	N
Kaine	Y	Y	Y	Y	N	N
WASHINGTON						
Murray	N	Y	Y	Y	N	N
Cantwell	N	Y	Y	Y	N	N
WEST VIRGINIA						
Manchin	Y	Y	Y	Y	Y	Y
Capito	Y	Y	Y	Y	Y	Y
WISCONSIN						
Johnson	Y	Y	N	N	Y	Y
Baldwin	Y	Y	Y	Y	N	N
WYOMING						
Enzi	Y	N	N	N	Y	Y
Barrasso	Y	Y	Y	Y	Y	Y

KEY: Republicans • Democrats • *Independents*

Y Voted for (yea)	**N** Voted against (nay)	**P** Voted "present"	
+ Announced for	**-** Announced against	**?** Did not vote or otherwise	
# Paired for	**X** Paired against	make position known	

403. Singhal Nomination - Cloture. Motion to invoke cloture (thus limiting debate) on the nomination of Anuraag Singhal of Florida to be a U.S. district judge for the Southern District of Florida. Motion agreed to 76-18: R 52-0; D 23-18; I 1-0. *Note: A majority of senators voting (48 in this case), a quorum being present, is required to invoke cloture on all nominations.* Dec. 18, 2019.

404. Marston Nomination - Cloture. Motion to invoke cloture (thus limiting debate) on the nomination of Karen Spencer Marston of Pennsylvania to be a U.S. district judge for the Eastern District of Pennsylvania. Motion agreed to 85-7: R 51-0; D 33-7; I 1-0. *Note: A majority of senators voting (47 in this case), a quorum being present, is required to invoke cloture on all nominations.* Dec. 18, 2019.

405. Traynor Nomination - Cloture. Motion to invoke cloture (thus limiting debate) on the nomination of Daniel Mack Traynor of North Dakota to be a U.S. district judge for the District of North Dakota. Motion agreed to 51-42: R 51-0; D 0-41; I 0-1. *Note: A majority of senators voting (47 in this case), a quorum being present, is required to invoke cloture on all nominations.* Dec. 18, 2019.

406. Dishman Nomination - Cloture. Motion to invoke cloture (thus limiting debate) on the nomination of Jodi W. Dishman of Oklahoma to be a U.S. district judge for the Western District of Oklahoma. Motion agreed to 76-17: R 51-0; D 24-17; I 1-0. *Note: A majority of senators voting (47 in this case), a quorum being present, is required to invoke cloture on all nominations.* Dec. 18, 2019.

407. Gallagher Nomination - Cloture. Motion to invoke cloture (thus limiting debate) on the nomination of John M. Gallagher of Pennsylvania to be a U.S. district judge for the Eastern District of Pennsylvania. Motion agreed to 82-10: R 51-0; D 30-10; I 1-0. *Note: A majority of senators voting (47 in this case), a quorum being present, is required to invoke cloture on all nominations.* Dec. 18, 2019.

408. Jones Nomination - Cloture. Motion to invoke cloture (thus limiting debate) on the nomination of Bernard Maurice Jones II of Oklahoma to be a U.S. district judge for the Western District of Oklahoma. Motion agreed to 88-5: R 51-0; D 36-5; I 1-0. *Note: A majority of senators voting (47 in this case), a quorum being present, is required to invoke cloture on all nominations.* Dec. 18, 2019.

	403	404	405	406	407	408
ALABAMA						
Shelby	Y	Y	Y	Y	Y	Y
Jones	Y	Y	N	Y	Y	Y
ALASKA						
Murkowski	Y	Y	Y	Y	Y	Y
Sullivan	Y	Y	Y	Y	Y	Y
ARIZONA						
Sinema	Y	Y	N	Y	Y	Y
McSally	Y	Y	Y	Y	Y	Y
ARKANSAS						
Boozman	Y	Y	Y	Y	Y	Y
Cotton	Y	Y	Y	Y	Y	Y
CALIFORNIA						
Feinstein	Y	Y	N	Y	Y	Y
Harris	-	-	-	-	-	-
COLORADO						
Bennet	N	Y	N	Y	N	Y
Gardner	Y	Y	Y	Y	Y	Y
CONNECTICUT						
Blumenthal	Y	Y	N	N	Y	Y
Murphy	Y	Y	N	Y	Y	Y
DELAWARE						
Carper	Y	Y	N	Y	Y	Y
Coons	Y	Y	N	Y	Y	Y
FLORIDA						
Rubio	Y	Y	Y	Y	Y	Y
Scott	Y	Y	Y	Y	Y	Y
GEORGIA						
Isakson	?	?	?	?	?	?
Perdue	Y	Y	Y	Y	Y	Y
HAWAII						
Schatz	N	N	N	N	N	N
Hirono	N	N	N	N	N	N
IDAHO						
Crapo	Y	Y	Y	Y	Y	Y
Risch	Y	Y	Y	Y	Y	Y
ILLINOIS						
Durbin	Y	Y	N	Y	Y	Y
Duckworth	Y	?	N	Y	Y	Y
INDIANA						
Young	Y	Y	Y	Y	Y	Y
Braun	Y	Y	Y	Y	Y	Y
IOWA						
Grassley	Y	Y	Y	Y	Y	Y
Ernst	Y	Y	Y	Y	Y	Y
KANSAS						
Roberts	Y	Y	Y	Y	Y	Y
Moran	Y	Y	Y	Y	Y	Y
KENTUCKY						
McConnell	Y	Y	Y	Y	Y	Y
Paul	Y	?	?	?	?	?
LOUISIANA						
Cassidy	Y	Y	Y	Y	Y	Y
Kennedy	Y	Y	Y	Y	Y	Y
MAINE						
Collins	Y	Y	Y	Y	Y	Y
King	Y	Y	N	Y	Y	Y
MARYLAND						
Cardin	Y	Y	N	Y	Y	Y
Van Hollen	N	Y	N	N	Y	Y
MASSACHUSETTS						
Warren	?	?	?	?	?	?
Markey	N	N	N	N	N	N
MICHIGAN						
Stabenow	N	Y	N	N	?	Y
Peters	Y	Y	N	Y	Y	Y
MINNESOTA						
Klobuchar	?	?	?	?	?	?
Smith	N	Y	N	N	Y	Y
MISSISSIPPI						
Wicker	Y	Y	Y	Y	Y	Y
Hyde-Smith	Y	Y	Y	Y	Y	Y
MISSOURI						
Blunt	Y	Y	Y	Y	Y	Y
Hawley	Y	Y	Y	Y	Y	Y

	403	404	405	406	407	408
MONTANA						
Tester	Y	Y	N	Y	Y	Y
Daines	Y	Y	Y	Y	Y	Y
NEBRASKA						
Fischer	Y	Y	Y	Y	Y	Y
Sasse	Y	Y	Y	Y	Y	Y
NEVADA						
Cortez Masto	Y	Y	N	Y	Y	Y
Rosen	Y	Y	N	Y	Y	Y
NEW HAMPSHIRE						
Shaheen	Y	Y	N	Y	Y	Y
Hassan	Y	Y	N	Y	Y	Y
NEW JERSEY						
Menendez	Y	Y	N	N	Y	Y
Booker	?	?	?	?	?	?
NEW MEXICO						
Udall	N	Y	N	N	Y	Y
Heinrich	N	Y	N	N	Y	Y
NEW YORK						
Schumer	N	N	N	N	N	N
Gillibrand	N	N	N	N	N	N
NORTH CAROLINA						
Burr	Y	Y	Y	Y	Y	Y
Tillis	Y	Y	Y	Y	Y	Y
NORTH DAKOTA						
Hoeven	Y	Y	Y	Y	Y	Y
Cramer	Y	Y	Y	Y	Y	Y
OHIO						
Brown	N	Y	N	N	Y	Y
Portman	Y	Y	Y	Y	Y	Y
OKLAHOMA						
Inhofe	Y	Y	Y	Y	Y	Y
Lankford	Y	Y	Y	Y	Y	Y
OREGON						
Wyden	N	N	N	N	N	N
Merkley	N	N	N	N	N	Y
PENNSYLVANIA						
Casey	Y	Y	N	Y	Y	Y
Toomey	Y	Y	Y	Y	Y	Y
RHODE ISLAND						
Reed	Y	Y	N	Y	Y	Y
Whitehouse	N	Y	N	N	Y	Y
SOUTH CAROLINA						
Graham	Y	Y	Y	Y	Y	Y
Scott	Y	Y	Y	Y	Y	Y
SOUTH DAKOTA						
Thune	Y	Y	Y	Y	Y	Y
Rounds	Y	Y	Y	Y	Y	Y
TENNESSEE						
Alexander	Y	Y	Y	Y	Y	Y
Blackburn	Y	Y	Y	Y	Y	Y
TEXAS						
Cornyn	Y	Y	Y	Y	Y	Y
Cruz	Y	Y	Y	Y	Y	Y
UTAH						
Lee	Y	Y	Y	Y	Y	Y
Romney	Y	Y	Y	Y	Y	Y
VERMONT						
Leahy	Y	Y	N	Y	Y	Y
Sanders	?	?	?	?	?	?
VIRGINIA						
Warner	Y	Y	N	Y	Y	Y
Kaine	Y	Y	N	Y	Y	Y
WASHINGTON						
Murray	N	Y	N	N	N	Y
Cantwell	N	Y	N	N	N	Y
WEST VIRGINIA						
Manchin	Y	Y	N	Y	Y	Y
Capito	Y	Y	Y	Y	Y	Y
WISCONSIN						
Johnson	Y	Y	Y	Y	Y	Y
Baldwin	N	Y	N	N	Y	Y
WYOMING						
Enzi	Y	Y	Y	Y	Y	Y
Barrasso	Y	Y	Y	Y	Y	Y

KEY:	Republicans	Democrats	*Independents*
Y Voted for (yea)	N Voted against (nay)	P Voted "present"	
+ Announced for	– Announced against	? Did not vote or otherwise	
# Paired for	X Paired against	make position known	

409. Vyskocil Nomination - Cloture. Motion to invoke cloture (thus limiting debate) on the nomination of Mary Kay Vyskocil of New York to be a U.S. district judge for the Southern District of New York. Motion agreed to 89-4: R 51-0; D 37-4; I 1-0. *Note: A majority of senators voting (47 in this case), a quorum being present, is required to invoke cloture on all nominations.* Dec. 18, 2019.

410. Riggs Nomination - Cloture. Motion to invoke cloture (thus limiting debate) on the nomination of Kea Whetzal Riggs of New Mexico to be a U.S. district judge for the District of New Mexico. Motion agreed to 92-1: R 51-0; D 40-1; I 1-0. *Note: A majority of senators voting (47 in this case), a quorum being present, is required to invoke cloture on all nominations.* Dec. 18, 2019.

411. Brown Nomination - Cloture. Motion to invoke cloture (thus limiting debate) on the nomination of Gary Richard Brown of New York to be a U.S. district judge for the Eastern District of New York. Motion agreed to 91-2: R 50-1; D 40-1; I 1-0. *Note: A majority of senators voting (47 in this case), a quorum being present, is required to invoke cloture on all nominations.* Dec. 18, 2019.

412. Davis Nomination - Cloture. Motion to invoke cloture (thus limiting debate) on the nomination of Stephanie Dawkins Davis of Michigan to be a U.S. district judge for the Eastern District of Michigan. Motion agreed to 90-1: R 49-0; D 40-1; I 1-0. *Note: A majority of senators voting (47 in this case), a quorum being present, is required to invoke cloture on all nominations.* Dec. 18, 2019.

413. HR1865. Fiscal 2020 Further Consolidated Appropriations - Cloture. McConnell, R-Ky., motion to invoke cloture (thus limiting debate) on his motion to concur in the House amendment to the Senate amendment to the bill that would provide approximately $540 billion in discretionary funding for eight of the twelve fiscal 2020 appropriations bills: Labor-HHS-Education, Agriculture, Energy-Water, Interior-Environment, Legislative Branch, Military Construction-VA, State-Foreign Operations, and Transportation-HUD. It would also include a number of other legislative provisions related to taxes, health care programs, and various federal program extensions. Motion agreed to 71-21: R 32-19; D 38-2; I 1-0. *Note: Three-fifths of the total Senate (60) is required to invoke cloture.* Dec. 19, 2019.

414. HR1865. Fiscal 2020 Further Consolidated Appropriations - Motion to Waive. Shelby, R-Ala., motion to waive applicable sections of the fiscal 2016 Budget Resolution for the bill that would provide approximately $540 billion in discretionary funding for eight of the twelve fiscal 2020 appropriations bills: Labor-HHS-Education, Agriculture, Energy-Water, Interior-Environment, Legislative Branch, Military Construction-VA, State-Foreign Operations, and Transportation-HUD. It would also include a number of other legislative provisions related to taxes, health care programs, and various federal program extensions. Motion agreed to 64-30: R 26-26; D 37-4; I 1-0. *Note: Three-fifths of the total Senate (60) is required to waive the 2016 Budget Resolution.* Dec. 19, 2019.

	409	410	411	412	413	414
ALABAMA						
Shelby	Y	Y	Y	Y	Y	Y
Jones	Y	Y	Y	Y	Y	Y
ALASKA						
Murkowski	Y	Y	Y	Y	Y	Y
Sullivan	Y	Y	N	Y	Y	N
ARIZONA						
Sinema	Y	Y	Y	Y	Y	Y
McSally	Y	Y	Y	Y	Y	Y
ARKANSAS						
Boozman	Y	Y	Y	Y	Y	Y
Cotton	Y	Y	Y	Y	?	N
CALIFORNIA						
Feinstein	Y	Y	Y	Y	Y	Y
Harris	-	+	?	+	?	?
COLORADO						
Bennet	Y	Y	Y	Y	Y	Y
Gardner	Y	Y	Y	Y	Y	Y
CONNECTICUT						
Blumenthal	Y	Y	Y	Y	Y	Y
Murphy	Y	Y	Y	Y	Y	Y
DELAWARE						
Carper	Y	Y	Y	Y	N	N
Coons	Y	Y	Y	Y	Y	Y
FLORIDA						
Rubio	Y	Y	Y	Y	Y	Y
Scott	Y	Y	Y	Y	N	N
GEORGIA						
Isakson	?	?	?	?	?	?
Perdue	Y	Y	Y	Y	Y	N
HAWAII						
Schatz	Y	Y	Y	Y	Y	Y
Hirono	N	N	N	N	Y	Y
IDAHO						
Crapo	Y	Y	Y	Y	Y	Y
Risch	Y	Y	Y	Y	N	N
ILLINOIS						
Durbin	Y	Y	Y	Y	Y	Y
Duckworth	Y	Y	Y	Y	Y	Y
INDIANA						
Young	Y	Y	Y	Y	Y	Y
Braun	Y	Y	Y	Y	N	N
IOWA						
Grassley	Y	Y	Y	Y	Y	Y
Ernst	Y	Y	Y	Y	N	N
KANSAS						
Roberts	Y	Y	Y	Y	Y	Y
Moran	Y	Y	Y	Y	Y	Y
KENTUCKY						
McConnell	Y	Y	Y	Y	Y	Y
Paul	?	?	?	?	N	N
LOUISIANA						
Cassidy	Y	Y	Y	Y	N	N
Kennedy	Y	Y	Y	?	Y	N
MAINE						
Collins	Y	Y	Y	Y	Y	Y
King	Y	Y	Y	Y	Y	Y
MARYLAND						
Cardin	Y	Y	Y	Y	Y	Y
Van Hollen	Y	Y	Y	Y	Y	Y
MASSACHUSETTS						
Warren	?	?	?	?	?	?
Markey	N	Y	Y	Y	Y	Y
MICHIGAN						
Stabenow	Y	Y	Y	Y	Y	Y
Peters	Y	Y	Y	Y	Y	Y
MINNESOTA						
Klobuchar	?	?	?	?	?	?
Smith	Y	Y	Y	Y	Y	Y
MISSISSIPPI						
Wicker	Y	Y	Y	Y	Y	Y
Hyde-Smith	Y	Y	Y	Y	Y	Y
MISSOURI						
Blunt	Y	Y	Y	?	Y	Y
Hawley	Y	Y	Y	Y	N	N

	409	410	411	412	413	414
MONTANA						
Tester	Y	Y	Y	Y	Y	N
Daines	Y	Y	Y	Y	N	N
NEBRASKA						
Fischer	Y	Y	Y	Y	Y	N
Sasse	Y	Y	Y	Y	N	N
NEVADA						
Cortez Masto	Y	Y	Y	Y	Y	Y
Rosen	Y	Y	Y	Y	Y	Y
NEW HAMPSHIRE						
Shaheen	Y	Y	Y	Y	Y	Y
Hassan	Y	Y	Y	Y	Y	Y
NEW JERSEY						
Menendez	Y	Y	Y	Y	Y	Y
Booker	?	?	?	?	?	?
NEW MEXICO						
Udall	Y	Y	Y	Y	?	Y
Heinrich	N	Y	Y	Y	Y	Y
NEW YORK						
Schumer	Y	Y	Y	Y	Y	Y
Gillibrand	N	Y	Y	Y	N	N
NORTH CAROLINA						
Burr	Y	Y	Y	Y	Y	Y
Tillis	Y	Y	Y	Y	Y	Y
NORTH DAKOTA						
Hoeven	Y	Y	Y	Y	Y	Y
Cramer	Y	Y	Y	Y	Y	Y
OHIO						
Brown	Y	Y	Y	Y	Y	Y
Portman	Y	Y	Y	Y	Y	Y
OKLAHOMA						
Inhofe	Y	Y	Y	Y	N	N
Lankford	Y	Y	Y	Y	N	N
OREGON						
Wyden	Y	Y	Y	Y	Y	Y
Merkley	Y	Y	Y	Y	Y	Y
PENNSYLVANIA						
Casey	Y	Y	Y	Y	Y	Y
Toomey	Y	Y	Y	Y	N	N
RHODE ISLAND						
Reed	Y	Y	Y	Y	Y	Y
Whitehouse	Y	Y	Y	Y	Y	N
SOUTH CAROLINA						
Graham	Y	Y	Y	Y	Y	Y
Scott	Y	Y	Y	Y	N	N
SOUTH DAKOTA						
Thune	Y	Y	Y	Y	Y	Y
Rounds	Y	Y	Y	Y	Y	Y
TENNESSEE						
Alexander	Y	Y	Y	Y	Y	Y
Blackburn	Y	Y	Y	Y	N	N
TEXAS						
Cornyn	Y	Y	Y	Y	Y	N
Cruz	Y	Y	Y	Y	N	N
UTAH						
Lee	Y	Y	Y	Y	N	N
Romney	Y	Y	Y	Y	Y	N
VERMONT						
Leahy	Y	Y	Y	Y	Y	Y
Sanders	?	?	?	?	?	?
VIRGINIA						
Warner	Y	Y	Y	Y	Y	Y
Kaine	Y	Y	Y	Y	Y	Y
WASHINGTON						
Murray	Y	Y	Y	Y	Y	Y
Cantwell	Y	Y	Y	Y	Y	Y
WEST VIRGINIA						
Manchin	Y	Y	Y	Y	Y	Y
Capito	Y	Y	Y	Y	Y	Y
WISCONSIN						
Johnson	Y	Y	Y	Y	N	N
Baldwin	Y	Y	Y	Y	Y	Y
WYOMING						
Enzi	Y	Y	Y	Y	N	N
Barrasso	Y	Y	Y	Y	N	N

KEY:		Republicans	Democrats		*Independents*
Y	Voted for (yea)	N Voted against (nay)		P Voted "present"	
+	Announced for	− Announced against		? Did not vote or otherwise	
#	Paired for	X Paired against		make position known	

415. HR1865. Fiscal 2020 Further Consolidated Appropriations - Motion to Concur. McConnell, R-Ky., motion to concur in the House amendment to the Senate amendment to the bill that would provide approximately $540 billion in discretionary funding for eight of the twelve fiscal 2020 appropriations bills: Labor-HHS-Education, Agriculture, Energy-Water, Interior-Environment, Legislative Branch, Military Construction-VA, State-Foreign Operations, and Transportation-HUD. It would reauthorize and extend a number of programs and authorizations, including to reauthorize the Export-Import Bank for seven years, the Terrorism Risk Insurance program through fiscal 2027, and the National Flood Insurance program through fiscal 2020. It would extend the Temporary Assistance for Needy Families program through May 22, 2020, and it would reauthorize a number of visa programs and the E-Verify employment eligibility verification system through fiscal 2020. Motion agreed to 71-23: R 31-21; D 39-2; I 1-0. *Note: A "yea" was a vote in support of the president's position.* Dec. 19, 2019.

416. Singhal Nomination - Confirmation. Confirmation of President Trump's nomination of Anuraag Singhal of Florida to be a U.S. district judge for the Southern District of Florida. Confirmed 76-17: R 51-0; D 24-17; I 1-0. *Note: A "yea" was a vote in support of the president's position.* Dec. 19, 2019.

417. Marston Nomination - Confirmation. Confirmation of President Trump's nomination of Karen Spencer Marston of Pennsylvania to be a U.S. district judge for the Eastern District of Pennsylvania. Confirmed 87-6: R 51-0; D 35-6; I 1-0. *Note: A "yea" was a vote in support of the president's position.* Dec. 19, 2019.

418. Traynor Nomination - Confirmation. Confirmation of President Trump's nomination of Daniel Mack Traynor of North Dakota to be a U.S. district judge for the District of North Dakota. Confirmed 51-41: R 51-0; D 0-40; I 0-1. *Note: A "yea" was a vote in support of the president's position.* Dec. 19, 2019.

419. Dishman Nomination - Confirmation. Confirmation of President Trump's nomination of Jodi W. Dishman of Oklahoma to be a U.S. district judge for the Western District of Oklahoma. Confirmed 75-17: R 51-0; D 23-17; I 1-0. *Note: A "yea" was a vote in support of the president's position.* Dec. 19, 2019.

420. Gallagher Nomination - Confirmation. Confirmation of President Trump's nomination of John M. Gallagher of Pennsylvania to be a U.S. district judge for the Eastern District of Pennsylvania. Confirmed 83-9: R 51-0; D 31-9; I 1-0. *Note: A "yea" was a vote in support of the president's position.* Dec. 19, 2019.

	415	416	417	418	419	420
ALABAMA						
Shelby	Y	Y	Y	Y	Y	Y
Jones	Y	Y	Y	N	Y	Y
ALASKA						
Murkowski	Y	Y	Y	Y	Y	Y
Sullivan	Y	Y	Y	Y	Y	Y
ARIZONA						
Sinema	Y	Y	Y	N	Y	Y
McSally	Y	Y	Y	Y	Y	Y
ARKANSAS						
Boozman	Y	Y	Y	Y	Y	Y
Cotton	N	Y	Y	Y	Y	Y
CALIFORNIA						
Feinstein	Y	Y	Y	N	Y	Y
Harris	?	?	?	?	?	?
COLORADO						
Bennet	Y	N	Y	N	Y	N
Gardner	Y	Y	Y	Y	Y	Y
CONNECTICUT						
Blumenthal	Y	Y	Y	N	N	Y
Murphy	Y	Y	Y	N	Y	Y
DELAWARE						
Carper	N	Y	Y	N	Y	Y
Coons	Y	Y	Y	N	Y	Y
FLORIDA						
Rubio	Y	Y	Y	Y	Y	Y
Scott	N	Y	Y	Y	Y	Y
GEORGIA						
Isakson	?	?	?	?	?	?
Perdue	Y	Y	Y	Y	Y	Y
HAWAII						
Schatz	Y	N	Y	N	N	Y
Hirono	Y	N	N	N	N	Y
IDAHO						
Crapo	Y	Y	Y	Y	Y	Y
Risch	N	Y	Y	Y	Y	Y
ILLINOIS						
Durbin	Y	Y	Y	N	Y	Y
Duckworth	Y	Y	Y	N	Y	Y
INDIANA						
Young	Y	Y	Y	Y	Y	Y
Braun	N	Y	Y	Y	Y	Y
IOWA						
Grassley	Y	Y	Y	Y	Y	Y
Ernst	Y	Y	Y	Y	Y	Y
KANSAS						
Roberts	Y	?	Y	Y	Y	Y
Moran	Y	Y	Y	Y	Y	Y
KENTUCKY						
McConnell	Y	Y	Y	Y	Y	Y
Paul	N	Y	Y	Y	Y	Y
LOUISIANA						
Cassidy	N	Y	Y	Y	Y	Y
Kennedy	N	Y	Y	Y	Y	Y
MAINE						
Collins	Y	Y	Y	Y	Y	Y
King	Y	Y	Y	N	Y	Y
MARYLAND						
Cardin	Y	Y	Y	N	Y	Y
Van Hollen	Y	N	Y	N	N	Y
MASSACHUSETTS						
Warren	?	?	?	?	?	?
Markey	Y	N	N	N	N	N
MICHIGAN						
Stabenow	Y	N	Y	N	N	N
Peters	Y	Y	Y	N	Y	Y
MINNESOTA						
Klobuchar	?	?	?	?	?	?
Smith	Y	N	N	N	N	Y
MISSISSIPPI						
Wicker	Y	Y	Y	Y	Y	Y
Hyde-Smith	Y	Y	Y	Y	Y	Y
MISSOURI						
Blunt	Y	Y	Y	Y	Y	Y
Hawley	N	Y	Y	Y	Y	Y

	415	416	417	418	419	420
MONTANA						
Tester	Y	Y	Y	N	Y	Y
Daines	N	Y	Y	Y	Y	Y
NEBRASKA						
Fischer	Y	Y	Y	Y	Y	Y
Sasse	N	Y	Y	Y	Y	Y
NEVADA						
Cortez Masto	Y	Y	Y	N	Y	Y
Rosen	Y	Y	Y	N	Y	Y
NEW HAMPSHIRE						
Shaheen	Y	Y	Y	N	Y	Y
Hassan	Y	Y	Y	N	Y	Y
NEW JERSEY						
Menendez	Y	Y	Y	N	N	Y
Booker	?	?	?	?	?	?
NEW MEXICO						
Udall	Y	N	Y	N	N	Y
Heinrich	Y	N	Y	N	N	Y
NEW YORK						
Schumer	Y	N	N	N	N	N
Gillibrand	N	N	N	N	N	N
NORTH CAROLINA						
Burr	Y	Y	?	?	?	?
Tillis	Y	Y	Y	Y	Y	Y
NORTH DAKOTA						
Hoeven	Y	Y	Y	Y	Y	Y
Cramer	Y	Y	Y	Y	Y	Y
OHIO						
Brown	Y	Y	Y	N	Y	Y
Portman	Y	Y	Y	Y	Y	Y
OKLAHOMA						
Inhofe	N	Y	Y	Y	Y	Y
Lankford	N	Y	Y	Y	Y	Y
OREGON						
Wyden	Y	N	N	N	N	N
Merkley	Y	N	N	N	N	N
PENNSYLVANIA						
Casey	Y	Y	Y	N	Y	Y
Toomey	N	Y	Y	Y	Y	Y
RHODE ISLAND						
Reed	Y	Y	Y	N	Y	Y
Whitehouse	Y	N	Y	N	Y	Y
SOUTH CAROLINA						
Graham	Y	Y	Y	Y	Y	Y
Scott	N	Y	Y	Y	Y	Y
SOUTH DAKOTA						
Thune	Y	Y	Y	Y	Y	Y
Rounds	Y	Y	Y	Y	Y	Y
TENNESSEE						
Alexander	Y	Y	Y	Y	Y	Y
Blackburn	N	Y	Y	Y	Y	Y
TEXAS						
Cornyn	N	Y	Y	Y	Y	Y
Cruz	N	Y	Y	Y	Y	Y
UTAH						
Lee	N	Y	Y	Y	Y	Y
Romney	Y	Y	Y	Y	Y	Y
VERMONT						
Leahy	Y	Y	Y	N	Y	Y
Sanders	?	?	?	?	?	?
VIRGINIA						
Warner	Y	Y	Y	?	?	?
Kaine	Y	Y	Y	N	Y	Y
WASHINGTON						
Murray	Y	N	Y	N	N	N
Cantwell	Y	N	N	N	N	N
WEST VIRGINIA						
Manchin	Y	Y	Y	N	Y	Y
Capito	Y	Y	Y	Y	Y	Y
WISCONSIN						
Johnson	N	Y	Y	Y	Y	Y
Baldwin	Y	N	Y	N	N	Y
WYOMING						
Enzi	N	Y	Y	Y	Y	Y
Barrasso	N	Y	Y	Y	Y	Y

421. Jones Nomination - Confirmation. Confirmation of President Trump's nomination of Bernard Maurice Jones II of Oklahoma to be a U.S. district judge for the Western District of Oklahoma. Confirmed 91-3: R 52-0; D 38-3; I 1-0. *Note: A "yea" was a vote in support of the president's position.* Dec. 19, 2019.

422. Vyskocil Nomination - Confirmation. Confirmation of President Trump's nomination of Mary Kay Vyskocil of New York to be a U.S. district judge for the Southern District of New York. Confirmed 91-3: R 52-0; D 38-3; I 1-0. *Note: A "yea" was a vote in support of the president's position.* Dec. 19, 2019.

423. Riggs Nomination - Confirmation. Confirmation of President Trump's nomination of Kea Whetzal Riggs of New Mexico to be a U.S. district judge for the District of New Mexico. Confirmed 94-0: R 52-0; D 41-0; I 1-0. *Note: A "yea" was a vote in support of the president's position.* Dec. 19, 2019.

424. Colville Nomination - Confirmation. Confirmation of President Trump's nomination of Robert J. Colville of Pennsylvania to be a U.S. district judge for the Western District of Pennsylvania. Confirmed 66-27: R 24-27; D 41-0; I 1-0. *Note: A "yea" was a vote in support of the president's position.* Dec. 19, 2019.

425. Liman Nomination - Confirmation. Confirmation of President Trump's nomination of Lewis J. Liman of New York to be a U.S. district judge for the Southern District of New York. Confirmed 64-29: R 22-29; D 41-0; I 1-0. *Note: A "yea" was a vote in support of the president's position.* Dec. 19, 2019.

426. Biegun Nomination - Confirmation. Confirmation of President Trump's nomination of Stephen E. Biegun of Michigan to be Deputy Secretary of State. Confirmed 90-3: R 51-0; D 38-3; I 1-0. *Note: A "yea" was a vote in support of the president's position.* Dec. 19, 2019.

	421	422	423	424	425	426
ALABAMA						
Shelby	Y	Y	Y	Y	Y	Y
Jones	Y	Y	Y	Y	Y	Y
ALASKA						
Murkowski	Y	Y	Y	Y	Y	Y
Sullivan	Y	Y	Y	N	N	Y
ARIZONA						
Sinema	Y	Y	Y	Y	Y	Y
McSally	Y	Y	Y	Y	Y	Y
ARKANSAS						
Boozman	Y	Y	Y	N	N	Y
Cotton	Y	Y	Y	N	N	Y
CALIFORNIA						
Feinstein	Y	Y	Y	Y	Y	Y
Harris	?	?	?	?	?	?
COLORADO						
Bennet	Y	Y	Y	Y	Y	Y
Gardner	Y	Y	Y	N	N	Y
CONNECTICUT						
Blumenthal	Y	Y	Y	Y	Y	Y
Murphy	Y	Y	Y	Y	Y	Y
DELAWARE						
Carper	Y	Y	Y	Y	Y	Y
Coons	Y	Y	Y	Y	Y	Y
FLORIDA						
Rubio	Y	Y	Y	N	N	Y
Scott	Y	Y	Y	Y	Y	Y
GEORGIA						
Isakson	?	?	?	?	?	?
Perdue	Y	Y	Y	Y	Y	Y
HAWAII						
Schatz	Y	Y	Y	Y	Y	Y
Hirono	Y	Y	Y	Y	Y	N
IDAHO						
Crapo	Y	Y	Y	Y	N	Y
Risch	Y	Y	Y	N	N	Y
ILLINOIS						
Durbin	Y	Y	Y	Y	Y	Y
Duckworth	Y	Y	Y	Y	Y	Y
INDIANA						
Young	Y	Y	Y	Y	Y	Y
Braun	Y	Y	Y	N	N	Y
IOWA						
Grassley	Y	Y	Y	Y	Y	Y
Ernst	Y	Y	Y	N	N	Y
KANSAS						
Roberts	Y	Y	Y	Y	Y	Y
Moran	Y	Y	Y	Y	Y	Y
KENTUCKY						
McConnell	Y	Y	Y	Y	Y	Y
Paul	Y	Y	Y	?	?	?
LOUISIANA						
Cassidy	Y	Y	Y	Y	N	Y
Kennedy	Y	Y	Y	Y	N	Y
MAINE						
Collins	Y	Y	Y	Y	Y	Y
King	Y	Y	Y	Y	Y	Y
MARYLAND						
Cardin	Y	Y	Y	Y	Y	Y
Van Hollen	Y	Y	Y	Y	Y	Y
MASSACHUSETTS						
Warren	?	?	?	?	?	?
Markey	N	N	Y	Y	Y	N
MICHIGAN						
Stabenow	Y	Y	Y	Y	Y	Y
Peters	Y	Y	Y	Y	Y	Y
MINNESOTA						
Klobuchar	?	?	?	?	?	?
Smith	Y	Y	Y	Y	Y	Y
MISSISSIPPI						
Wicker	Y	Y	Y	Y	Y	Y
Hyde-Smith	Y	Y	Y	Y	Y	Y
MISSOURI						
Blunt	Y	Y	Y	Y	Y	Y
Hawley	Y	Y	Y	N	N	Y

	421	422	423	424	425	426
MONTANA						
Tester	Y	Y	Y	Y	Y	Y
Daines	Y	Y	Y	N	N	Y
NEBRASKA						
Fischer	Y	Y	Y	N	N	Y
Sasse	Y	Y	Y	N	N	Y
NEVADA						
Cortez Masto	Y	Y	Y	Y	Y	Y
Rosen	Y	Y	Y	Y	Y	Y
NEW HAMPSHIRE						
Shaheen	Y	Y	Y	Y	Y	Y
Hassan	Y	Y	Y	Y	Y	Y
NEW JERSEY						
Menendez	Y	Y	Y	Y	Y	Y
Booker	?	?	?	?	?	?
NEW MEXICO						
Udall	Y	Y	Y	Y	Y	Y
Heinrich	Y	N	Y	Y	Y	Y
NEW YORK						
Schumer	N	N	Y	Y	Y	Y
Gillibrand	N	N	Y	Y	Y	N
NORTH CAROLINA						
Burr	Y	Y	Y	Y	Y	Y
Tillis	Y	Y	Y	N	Y	Y
NORTH DAKOTA						
Hoeven	Y	Y	Y	N	N	Y
Cramer	Y	Y	Y	N	N	Y
OHIO						
Brown	Y	Y	Y	Y	Y	Y
Portman	Y	Y	Y	Y	Y	Y
OKLAHOMA						
Inhofe	Y	Y	Y	N	N	Y
Lankford	Y	Y	Y	N	N	Y
OREGON						
Wyden	Y	Y	Y	Y	Y	Y
Merkley	Y	Y	Y	Y	Y	Y
PENNSYLVANIA						
Casey	Y	Y	Y	Y	Y	Y
Toomey	Y	Y	Y	Y	Y	Y
RHODE ISLAND						
Reed	Y	Y	Y	Y	Y	Y
Whitehouse	Y	Y	Y	Y	Y	Y
SOUTH CAROLINA						
Graham	Y	Y	Y	Y	Y	Y
Scott	Y	Y	Y	N	N	Y
SOUTH DAKOTA						
Thune	Y	Y	Y	N	N	Y
Rounds	Y	Y	Y	N	N	Y
TENNESSEE						
Alexander	Y	Y	Y	Y	Y	Y
Blackburn	Y	Y	Y	N	N	Y
TEXAS						
Cornyn	Y	Y	Y	Y	Y	Y
Cruz	Y	Y	Y	N	N	Y
UTAH						
Lee	Y	Y	Y	N	N	Y
Romney	Y	Y	Y	N	N	Y
VERMONT						
Leahy	Y	Y	Y	Y	Y	Y
Sanders	?	?	?	?	?	?
VIRGINIA						
Warner	Y	Y	Y	Y	Y	Y
Kaine	Y	Y	Y	Y	Y	Y
WASHINGTON						
Murray	Y	Y	Y	Y	Y	Y
Cantwell	Y	Y	Y	Y	Y	Y
WEST VIRGINIA						
Manchin	Y	Y	Y	Y	Y	Y
Capito	Y	Y	Y	N	N	Y
WISCONSIN						
Johnson	Y	Y	Y	Y	N	Y
Baldwin	Y	Y	Y	Y	Y	Y
WYOMING						
Enzi	Y	Y	Y	N	N	Y
Barrasso	Y	Y	Y	N	N	Y

||| SENATE VOTES

427. HR1158. Fiscal 2020 Consolidated Appropriations - Cloture.
McConnell, R-Ky., motion to invoke cloture (thus limiting debate) on his motion to concur in the House amendment to the Senate amendment to the bill that would provide $860.3 billion in discretionary spending for four of the twelve fiscal 2020 appropriations bills: Defense, Homeland Security, Commerce-Justice-Science, and Financial Services. Motion agreed to 77-16: R 42-9; D 34-7; I 1-0. *Note: Three-fifths of the total Senate (60) is required to invoke cloture.* Dec. 19, 2019.

428. HR1158. Fiscal 2020 Consolidated Appropriations - Motion to Concur. McConnell, R-Ky., motion to concur in the House amendment to the Senate amendment to the bill that would provide $860.3 billion in discretionary spending for four of the twelve fiscal 2020 appropriations bills: Defense, Homeland Security, Commerce-Justice-Science, and Financial Services. It would provide a 3.1% pay increase for all members of the armed forces and for federal civilian employees. Motion agreed to 81-11: R 46-4; D 34-7; I 1-0. *Note: A "yea" was a vote in support of the president's position.* Dec. 19, 2019.

	427	428
ALABAMA		
Shelby	Y	Y
Jones	Y	Y
ALASKA		
Murkowski	Y	Y
Sullivan	Y	Y
ARIZONA		
Sinema	Y	Y
McSally	Y	Y
ARKANSAS		
Boozman	Y	Y
Cotton	Y	Y
CALIFORNIA		
Feinstein	Y	Y
Harris	?	?
COLORADO		
Bennet	Y	Y
Gardner	Y	Y
CONNECTICUT		
Blumenthal	Y	Y
Murphy	Y	Y
DELAWARE		
Carper	N	N
Coons	Y	Y
FLORIDA		
Rubio	Y	Y
Scott	Y	Y
GEORGIA		
Isakson	?	?
Perdue	Y	Y
HAWAII		
Schatz	Y	Y
Hirono	Y	Y
IDAHO		
Crapo	Y	Y
Risch	Y	Y
ILLINOIS		
Durbin	Y	Y
Duckworth	Y	Y
INDIANA		
Young	Y	Y
Braun	N	N
IOWA		
Grassley	Y	Y
Ernst	N	Y
KANSAS		
Roberts	Y	Y
Moran	Y	Y
KENTUCKY		
McConnell	Y	Y
Paul	?	?
LOUISIANA		
Cassidy	N	Y
Kennedy	Y	Y
MAINE		
Collins	Y	Y
King	Y	Y
MARYLAND		
Cardin	Y	Y
Van Hollen	N	N
MASSACHUSETTS		
Warren	?	?
Markey	N	N
MICHIGAN		
Stabenow	Y	Y
Peters	Y	Y
MINNESOTA		
Klobuchar	?	?
Smith	Y	Y
MISSISSIPPI		
Wicker	Y	Y
Hyde-Smith	Y	Y
MISSOURI		
Blunt	Y	Y
Hawley	N	N

	427	428
MONTANA		
Tester	Y	Y
Daines	Y	Y
NEBRASKA		
Fischer	Y	Y
Sasse	Y	Y
NEVADA		
Cortez Masto	Y	Y
Rosen	Y	Y
NEW HAMPSHIRE		
Shaheen	Y	Y
Hassan	Y	Y
NEW JERSEY		
Menendez	Y	Y
Booker	?	?
NEW MEXICO		
Udall	Y	Y
Heinrich	Y	Y
NEW YORK		
Schumer	N	N
Gillibrand	N	N
NORTH CAROLINA		
Burr	Y	?
Tillis	Y	Y
NORTH DAKOTA		
Hoeven	Y	Y
Cramer	Y	Y
OHIO		
Brown	Y	Y
Portman	Y	Y
OKLAHOMA		
Inhofe	Y	Y
Lankford	Y	Y
OREGON		
Wyden	N	N
Merkley	N	N
PENNSYLVANIA		
Casey	Y	Y
Toomey	N	Y
RHODE ISLAND		
Reed	Y	Y
Whitehouse	Y	Y
SOUTH CAROLINA		
Graham	Y	Y
Scott	Y	Y
SOUTH DAKOTA		
Thune	Y	Y
Rounds	Y	Y
TENNESSEE		
Alexander	Y	Y
Blackburn	N	Y
TEXAS		
Cornyn	Y	Y
Cruz	N	N
UTAH		
Lee	N	N
Romney	Y	Y
VERMONT		
Leahy	Y	Y
Sanders	?	?
VIRGINIA		
Warner	Y	Y
Kaine	Y	Y
WASHINGTON		
Murray	Y	Y
Cantwell	Y	Y
WEST VIRGINIA		
Manchin	Y	Y
Capito	Y	Y
WISCONSIN		
Johnson	N	Y
Baldwin	Y	Y
WYOMING		
Enzi	Y	Y
Barrasso	Y	Y

KEY: Republicans   Democrats   *Independents*

Y Voted for (yea)	**N** Voted against (nay)
+ Announced for	**–** Announced against
# Paired for	**X** Paired against

P Voted "present"
? Did not vote or otherwise make position known